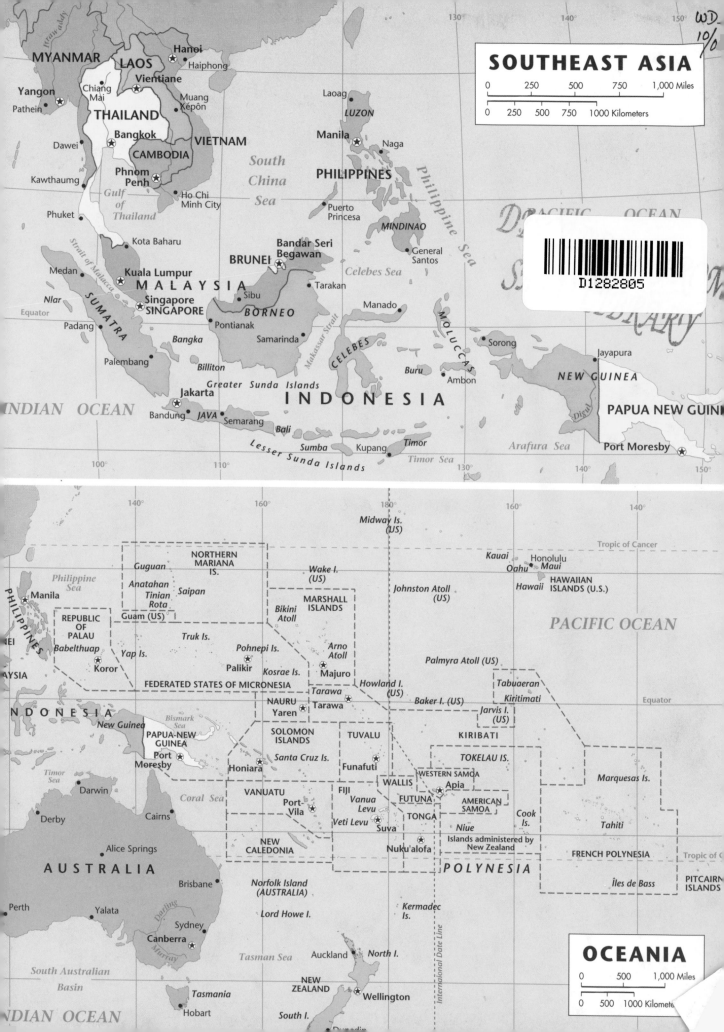

WORLDMARK ENCYCLOPEDIA OF THE NATIONS

Volume 4

ISSN 1531-1635

WORLDMARK
ENCYCLOPEDIA OF THE NATIONS

ASIA & OCEANIA

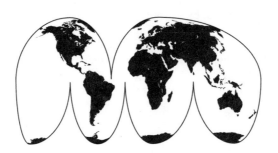

Formerly published by Worldmark Press, Ltd.

GALE GROUP

Detroit
New York
San Francisco
London
Boston
Woodbridge, CT

Gale Group Staff

Shelly Dickey, Project Editor
William H. Harmer, Contributing Editor
David Riddle, Jennifer M. York, Assistant Editors
Rita Runchock, Managing Editor

Mary Beth Trimper, Composition and Electronic Prepress Manager
Evi Seoud, Assistant Composition and Electronic Prepress Manager
NeKita McKee, Buyer

Kenn Zorn, Production Design Manager
Michael Logusz, Graphic Artist

ISBN 0-7876-0511-5 (set)
ISBN 0-7876-0512-3 (volume 1)
ISBN 0-7876-0513-1 (volume 2)
ISBN 0-7876-0514-X (volume 3)
ISBN 0-7876-0515-8 (volume 4)
ISBN 0-7876-0516-6 (volume 5)
ISBN 0-7876-4809-4 (volume 6)
ISSN 1531-1635

Printed in the United States of America

10 9 8 7 6 5 4 3 2 1

CONTENTS

For Conversion Tables, Abbreviations and Acronyms, Glossaries, World Tables, Notes to the Tenth Edition, and other supplementary materials, see Volume 1.

GUIDE TO COUNTRY ARTICLES

All information contained within a country article is uniformly keyed by means of small superior numerals to the left of the subject headings. A heading such as "Population," for example, carries the same key numeral (6) in every article. Thus, to find information about the population of Albania, consult the table of contents for the page number where the Albania article begins and look for section 6 thereunder. Introductory matter for each nation includes coat of arms, capital, flag (descriptions given from hoist to fly or from top to bottom), anthem, monetary unit, weights and measures, holidays, and time zone.

FLAG COLOR SYMBOLS

 Yellow   Red Green   Blue   Orange   Brown   White   Black

SECTION HEADINGS IN NUMERICAL ORDER

1 Location, size, and extent
2 Topography
3 Climate
4 Flora and fauna
5 Environment
6 Population
7 Migration
8 Ethnic groups
9 Languages
10 Religions
11 Transportation
12 History
13 Government
14 Political parties
15 Local government
16 Judicial system
17 Armed forces
18 International cooperation
19 Economy
20 Income
21 Labor
22 Agriculture
23 Animal husbandry
24 Fishing
25 Forestry
26 Mining

27 Energy and power
28 Industry
29 Science and technology
30 Domestic trade
31 Foreign trade
32 Balance of payments
33 Banking and securities
34 Insurance
35 Public finance
36 Taxation
37 Customs and duties
38 Foreign investment
39 Economic development
40 Social development
41 Health
42 Housing
43 Education
44 Libraries and museums
45 Media
46 Organizations
47 Tourism, travel, and recreation
48 Famous persons
49 Dependencies
50 Bibliography

SECTION HEADINGS IN ALPHABETICAL ORDER

Agriculture	22	Income	20
Animal husbandry	23	Industry	28
Armed forces	17	Insurance	34
Balance of payments	32	International cooperation	18
Banking and securities	33	Judical system	16
Bibliography	50	Labor	21
Climate	3	Languages	9
Customs and duties	37	Libraries and museums	44
Dependencies	49	Local government	15
Domestic trade	30	Location, size, and extent	1
Economic development	39	Media	45
Economy	19	Migration	7
Education	43	Mining	26
Energy and power	27	Organizations	46
Environment	5	Political parties	14
Ethnic groups	8	Population	6
Famous persons	48	Public finance	35
Fishing	24	Religions	10
Flora and fauna	4	Science and technology	29
Foreign investment	38	Social development	40
Foreign trade	31	Taxation	36
Forestry	25	Topography	2
Government	13	Tourism, travel, and recreation	47
Health	41	Transportation	11
History	12		
Housing	42		

FREQUENTLY USED ABBREVIATIONS AND ACRONYMS

ad—Anno Domini
am—before noon
b.—born
bc—Before Christ
c—Celsius
c.—circa (about)
cm—centimeter(s)
Co.—company
Corp.—corporation
cu ft—cubic foot, feet
cu m—cubic meter(s)
d.—died
e—east
e—evening
e.g.—exempli gratia (for example)
ed.—edition, editor
est.—estimated
et al.—et alii (and others)

etc.—et cetera (and so on)
f—Fahrenheit
fl.—flourished
FRG—Federal Republic of Germany
ft—foot, feet
ft³—cubic foot, feet
GATT—General Agreement on Tariffs and Trade
GDP—gross domestic products
gm—gram
GMT—Greenwich Mean Time
GNP—gross national product
GRT—gross registered tons
ha—hectares
i.e.—id est (that is)
in—inch(es)
kg—kilogram(s)
km—kilometer(s)

kw—kilowatt(s)
kwh—kilowatt-hour(s)
lb—pound(s)
m—meter(s); morning
m³—cubic meter(s)
mi—mile(s)
Mt.—mount
Mw—megawatt(s)
n—north
n.d.—no date
NA—not available
oz—ounce(s)

pm—after noon
r.—reigned
rev. ed.—revised edition
s—south
sq—square
St.—saint
UK—United Kingdom
UN—United Nations
US—United States
USSR—Union of Soviet Socialist Republics
w—west

A fiscal split year is indicated by a stroke (e.g. 1998/99).
For acronyms of UN agencies and their intergovernmental organizations, as well as other abbreviations used in text, see the United Nations volume.
A dollar sign ($) stands for US$ unless otherwise indicated.
Note that 1 billion = 1,000 million = 10^9.

AFGHANISTAN

Islamic Republic of Afghanistan
Jomhurriyati Afghanistan

CAPITAL: Kabul.

FLAG: The national flag has three equal horizontal stripes of green, white, and black. In the center is the national coat of arms.

ANTHEM: *Esllahte Arzi (Land Reform),* beginning "So long as there is the earth and the heavens."

MONETARY UNIT: The afghani (Af) is a paper currency of 100 puls. There are coins of 25 and 50 puls and 1, 2, and 5 áfghanis, and notes of 10, 20, 50, 100, 500, and 1,000 afghanis. Af1 = $0.00002 ($1 = Af42000.0) as of 31 March 2000.

WEIGHTS AND MEASURES: The metric system is the legal standard, although some local units are still in use.

HOLIDAYS: Now Rooz (New Year's Day), 21 March; May Day, 1 May; Independence Day, 18 August. Movable religious holidays include First Day of Ramadan, 'Id al-Fitr, 'Id al-'Adha', 'Ashura, and Milad an-Nabi. The Afghan calendar year begins on 21 March; the Afghan year 1376 began on 21 March 1997.

TIME: 4:30 PM = noon GMT.

¹LOCATION, SIZE, AND EXTENT

Afghanistan is a landlocked country in Central Asia with a long, narrow strip in the northeast (the Wakhan corridor). Afghanistan is slightly smaller than the state of Texas, with a total area of 647,500 sq km (250,001 sq mi), extending 1,240 km (770 mi) NE–SW and 560 km (350 mi) SE–NW. Afghanistan is bounded on the N by Turkenistan, Uzbekistan, and Tajikistan, on the extreme NE by China, on the E and S by Pakistan, and on the W by Iran, with a total boundary length of 5,529 km (3,436 mi). Afghanistan's capital city, Kabul, is located in the east central part of the country.

²TOPOGRAPHY

Although the average altitude of Afghanistan is about 1,200 m (4,000 ft), the Hindu Kush mountain range rises to more than 6,100 m (20,000 ft) in the northern corner of the Wakhan panhandle in the northeast and continues in a southwesterly direction for about 970 km (600 mi), dividing the northern provinces from the rest of the country. Central Afghanistan, a plateau with an average elevation of 1,800 m (6,000 ft), contains many small fertile valleys and provides excellent grazing for sheep, goats, and camels. To the north of the Hindu Kush and the central mountain range, the altitude drops to about 460 m (1,500 ft), permitting the growth of cotton, fruits, grains, ground nuts, and other crops. Southwestern Afghanistan is a desert, hot in summer and cold in winter. The four major river systems are the Amu Darya (Oxus) in the north, flowing into the Aral Sea; the Harirud and Morghab in the west; the Helmand in the southwest; and the Kabul in the east, flowing into the Indus. There are few lakes.

³CLIMATE

The ranges in altitude produce a climate with both temperate and semitropical characteristics, and the seasons are clearly marked throughout the country. Wide temperature variations are usual from season to season and from day to night. Summer temperatures in Kabul may range from 16°C (61°F) at sunrise to 38°C (100°F) by noon. The mean January temperature in Kabul is 0°C (32°F); the maximum summer temperature in Jalalabad is about 46°C (115°F). There is much sunshine, and the air is usually clear and dry. Rainfall averages about 25 to 30 cm (10 to 12 in); precipitation occurs in winter and spring, most of it in the form of snow. Wind velocity is high, especially in the west.

⁴FLORA AND FAUNA

There are over 3,000 plant species, including hundreds of varieties of trees, shrubs, vines, flowers, and fungi. The country is particularly rich in such medicinal plants as rue, wormwood, and asafetida; fruit and nut trees are found in many areas. Native fauna include the fox, lynx, wild dog, bear, mongoose, shrew, hedgehog, hyena, jerboa, hare, and wild varieties of cats, asses, mountain goats, and mountain sheep. Trout is the most common fish. There are more than 100 species of wildfowl and birds.

⁵ENVIRONMENT

Afghanistan's most significant ecological problems are deforestation, soil degradation, and overgrazing. Neglect, scorched earth tactics, and the damage caused by extensive bombardments have destroyed previously productive agricultural areas, and more are threatened by tons of unexploded ordnance. Afghanistan has responded to the fuel needs of its growing population by cutting down many of its already sparse forests. Consequently, by mid-1994, less than 3% of Afghanistan's land area was forest land. In 2000, melting snow and heavy rains, triggered floods in at least seven provinces, covering more than a quarter of Afghanistan and killing over 100 people.

By 1994, 13 species of mammals, 13 species of birds, and 4 plant species of were endangered. Endangered species in Afghanistan included the snow leopard, Bactrian red deer, Kabul markhor, Central Asian cobra, Siberian white crane and the hyena.

[6]POPULATION

Two decades of civil warfare make Afghanistan's population—never certain in any case—even more difficult to assess. As many as three million Afghans are estimated to have died, and an additional five million sought refuge in Pakistan, Iran, and elsewhere in the world during the worst of the fighting when thousands of Soviet troops were present. As of 2000, the population of Afghanistan was estimated at 26,668,251. An estimated 2.8% of the population is 65 years of age or older. The projected population for the year 2005 is 30,189,000 assuming a crude birthrate of 39 per 1,000 population and a death rate of 15, resulting in a natural rate of change of 2.5% for the period 2000–2005. The population rate of change between 1995 and 2000 was 5.3%.

Afghanistan's estimated overall population density (excluding nomads) was 35 per sq km (91 per sq mi) in 1995, but density on agricultural lands can reach as high as 1,630 per sq km (4,222 per sq mi). It was estimated that 22% of the population lived in urban areas in 2000. The capital city, Kabul, had a 2000 population of 2,029,000. Other cities, with their 1998 estimated populations, were Kandahār, 225,500; Herāt, 177,300; and Mazār-e Sharif, 130,600.

[7]MIGRATION

Following the Soviet intervention in Afghanistan in December 1979, a massive emigration of Afghans took place. According to the UNHCR, as of 1999, a total of 4.2 million Afghan refugees had returned home; however, 2.6 million refugees still remain outside the country. This is still the largest single refugee case load in the world for the 20th consecutive year. Most of these refugees are in Iran and Pakistan. There are also 56,000 Afghan refugees in CIS countries and 20,000 Afghan refugees in India. The northern part of Afghanistan was harboring about 18,000 refugees from Tajikstan in 1997.

A new wave of displacement occurred in September of 1996, with the fall of Kabul to the Taliban in Afghanistan's civil war. Between October of 1996 and May of 1997, 250,000 plus people were displaced within the country or became refugees in Pakistan. By March of 1997, 50,000 refugees had crossed into Pakistan. Between January and May of 1997, over 150,000 people fled the Shomali Valley, north of Kabul, into the capital. Another 47,000 people fled to the north of the country from the same region. By May 1 of 1997, around 40,000 people had fled the Badghis frontline for the Taliban-held western city of Herat.

Armed conflict over power between opposing political factions continued as of 1999. Late in 1997, the United Nations High Commissioner for Refugees (UNHCR) implemented a new strategy, known as targeted group repatriation, for individual families returning to Afghanistan. Refugee groups in Pakistan, who wanted to return but could not due to mines, destroyed houses, or lack of employment, were identified. Problems were evaluated, and UNHCR designed a reintegration assistance package for a particular group to help them return. By November 1998, a total of 28 convoys had repatriated 16,462 refugees from 16 different groups. However, a lack of staff and funding resulted in the program's suspension in late 1998.

[8]ETHNIC GROUPS

About the middle of the second millennium BC, Indo-Aryans began to move into and through the present area of Afghanistan. Much later came other tribal groups from Central Asia—Pactyes (from whom the present-day name "Pashtoons" derives), Sakas, Kushans, Hephthalites, and others—and a procession of Iranians and Greeks. In the 7th century AD, Arabs arrived from the south, spreading the new faith of Islam. In the same century, Turks moved in from the north, followed in the 13th century by Mongols, and, finally, in the 15th century by Turko-Mongols.

This multiplicity of movements made Afghanistan a loose conglomeration of racial and linguistic groups.

All citizens are called Afghans, but the Pashtoons (the name may also be written as "Pushtun" or "Pukhtun," and in Pakistan as "Pathan") are often referred to as the "true Afghans." Numbering about 38% of the population in 1999, they are known to have centered in the Sulaiman range to the east; it is only in recent centuries that they moved into eastern and southern Afghanistan, where they now predominate. They have long been divided into two major divisions, the Durranis and the Ghilzais, each with its own tribes and subtribes.

The Tajiks, of Iranian stock, comprise nearly 25% of the population and are mainly concentrated in the north and northeast. In the central ranges are found the Hazaras (about 19%), who are said to have descended from the Mongols. To the north of the Hindu Kush, Turkic and Turko-Mongol groups were in the majority until 1940. Each of these groups is related to groups north of the Amu Darya and within the former USSR; among them are the Uzbeks, who number about 6% of the population. Other groups include the Aimaks, Farsiwans (Persians) and Brahiu. In the northeast are the Kafirs, or infidels. After their conversion to Islam at the end of the 19th century, they were given the name of Nuristanis, or "people of the light."

[9]LANGUAGES

Both Pashtu (or Pushtu) and Dari (Afghan Persian) are the official languages of the country. Pashtu is spoken by about 35% of the population while approximately 50% speak Dari. Although Pashtu has a literature of its own, Dari, the language spoken in Kabul, has been the principal language of cultural expression, of the government, and of business. The Hazaras speak their own dialect of Dari. The Turkic languages, spoken by 11% of the population, include Uzbek and Turkmen, and the Nuristanis speak some seven different dialects belonging to the Dardic linguistic group. There are about 30 minor languages, primarily Balochi and Pashai, spoken by some 4% of the population. Balochi belongs to the same linguistic group, as do several languages spoken in the high Pamirs. Bilingualism is common.

[10]RELIGIONS

Almost all Afghans are Muslims. Approximately 84% are Sunnis; 15% are Shi'is; others comprise only 1%. The Pashtuns, most of the Tajiks, the Uzbeks, and the Turkmen are Sunnis, while the Hazaras are Shi'is. The country's small Hindu and Sikh population is estimated at less than 50,000. Before the 1978 Communist coup, Islam was the official religion of Afghanistan; in an effort to win over religious leaders, the Marxist regime set up a Department of Islamic Affairs in 1981 and began providing funds for new mosques and for the maintenance of old ones. Following the overthrow of the Communist regime, an Islamic State was again proclaimed.

In 1994 the Islamic militants who call themselves the Taliban—literally "the Seekers," a term used to describe religious students—began to impose their strict form of Islam observance in the areas that they control. The Taliban, composed mostly of Pashtoons, are puritanical zealots. Women have been ordered to dress in strict Islamic garb and are banned from working or from going out of their houses unless accompanied by a male relative. Some men have been forced to pray five times a day and grow full beards as a condition of employment in the government. As of mid-1999, the Taliban were in control of approximately 85% of the country. Also as of mid-1999, the Taliban claimed to be drafting a new constitution to ensure the rights of all Muslims and of religious minorities. However, custom and law require affiliation with some religion, and atheism is punishable by death. The small number of non-Muslim residents remaining in the country may practice their faith but are forbidden to proselytize.

LOCATION: 29°28' to 38°30' N; 60°30' to 74°53' E. **BOUNDARY LENGTHS:** China, 76 km (47 mi); Iran, 936 km (582 mi); Pakistan, 2,430 km (1,511 mi); Tajikistan, 1,206 km (750 mi); Turkmenistan, 744 km (463 mi); Uzbekistan, 137 km (85mi).

11 TRANSPORTATION

Many roads were built in the years prior to 1979 to connect the principal cities and to open up formerly isolated areas. As of 1996, Afghanistan had an estimated 21,000 km (13,000 mi) of roads, of which 2,793 km (1,736 mi) were paved. Roads connect Kabul with most provincial capitals and with Peshawar in Pakistan through the Khyber Pass. The road from Herat to Mashhad in Iran was completed in 1971. The Salang Tunnel through the Hindu Kush, completed with Soviet assistance in 1964, considerably shortened the travel time between Kabul and northern Afghanistan. The tunnel was modernized in the mid-1980s. However, in May 1997 the Tajik leader, Ahmad Shah Masud, blew up the southern entrance of the tunnel in an effort to trap the invading Taliban forces. The Kandahar-Torghundi

highway in the south was completed in 1965. In 1995 there were 34,000 passenger cars and 31,000 trucks and buses in use.

The Khyber Pass in Pakistan is the best known of the passes providing land access to Afghanistan. Transit arrangements with Iran provide an alternative route for its commercial traffic. However, the great bulk of the country's trade moves through the former USSR. The only railways in the country in 1996 were a 9.6-km (6-mi) spur from Kushka, Turkmenistan to Towrghondi, a 15 km (9.3 mi) line from Termez, Uzbekistan to the Kheyrabad transshipment point on the south bank of the Amu Darya, and a short span into Spin Baldak in the southeast. There are no navigable rivers except for the Amu Darya, on Turkmenistan's border, which can carry steamers up to about 500 tons. In 1998 the merchant marine had 1 container ship, weighing in at 11,982

GRT. Also in 1998, there were 44 airports, 11 of which had paved runways. During 1986, Afghanistan's domestic and international airlines were merged to form Bakhtar Afghan Airlines. Kabul and Kandahar have airports capable of receiving international flights. In 1997, 90,000 passengers were carried on scheduled domestic and international airline flights.

[12] HISTORY

Afghanistan has existed as a distinct polity for less than three centuries. Previously, the area was made up of various principalities, usually hostile to each other and occasionally ruled by one or another conqueror from Persia and the area to the west or from central Asia to the north, usually on his way to India. These included the Persian Darius I in the 6th century BC, and 300 years later, Alexander the Great. As the power of his Seleucid successors waned, an independent Greek kingdom of Bactria arose with its capital at Balkh west of Mazar-i-Sharif, but after about a century it fell to invading tribes (notably the Sakas, who gave their name to Sakastan, or Sistan). Toward the middle of the 3rd century BC, Buddhism spread to Afghanistan from India, and for centuries prior to the beginning of the 9th century AD, at least half the population of eastern Afghanistan was Buddhist.

Beginning in the 7th century, Muslim invaders brought Islam to the region, and it eventually became the dominant cultural influence. For almost 200 years, Ghazni was the capital of a powerful Islamic kingdom, the greatest of whose rulers, Mahmud of Ghazni (r.997–1030), conquered most of the area from the Caspian to the Ganges. The Ghaznavids were displaced by the Seljuk Turks, who mastered Persia and Anatolia (eastern Turkey), and by the Ghorids, who, rising from Ghor, southeast of Herat, established an empire stretching from Herat to Ajmir in India. They were displaced in turn by the Turko-Persian rulers of the Khiva oasis in Transoxiana, who, by 1217, had created a state that included the whole of Afghanistan until it disintegrated under attack by Genghis Khan in 1219. His grandson Timur, also called "Timur the Lame" or Tamerlane, occupied all of what is now Afghanistan from 1365 to 1384, establishing a court of intellectual and artistic brilliance at Herat. The Timurids came under challenge from the Uzbeks, who finally drove the them out of Herat in 1507. The great Babur, one of the Uzbek princes, occupied Kabul in 1504 and Delhi in 1526, establishing the Mughal Empire in which eastern Afghanistan was ruled from Delhi, Agra, Lahore, or Srinagar, while Herat and Sistan were governed as provinces of Persia.

In the 18th century, Persians under Nadir Shah conquered the area, and after his death in 1747, one of his military commanders, Ahmad Shah Abdali, was elected emir of Afghanistan. The formation of a unified Afghanistan under his emirate marks Afghanistan's beginning as a political entity. Among his descendants was Dost Muhammad who established himself in Kabul in 1826 and gained the emirate in 1835. Although the British defeated Dost in the first Afghan War (1838–42), they restored him to power, but his attempts and those of his successors to play off Czarist Russian interests against the British concerns about the security of their Indian Empire led to more conflict. In the second Afghan War (1877–79), the forces of Sher Ali, Dost's son, were defeated by the British, and his entire party, ousted. Abdur Rahman Khan, recognized as emir by the British in 1880, established a central administration, and supported the British interest in a neutral Afghanistan as a buffer against the expansion of Russian influence.

Intermittent fighting between the British and Pushtun tribes from eastern Afghanistan continued even after the establishment, in 1893, of a boundary (the Durand line) between Afghanistan and British India. An Anglo-Russian agreement concluded in 1907 guaranteed the independence of Afghanistan (and Tibet) under British influence, and Afghanistan remained neutral in both World Wars. Afghan forces under Amanullah Khan, who had become emir in 1919, briefly intruded across the Durand Line in 1919. At the end of brief fighting—the third Afghan War—the Treaty of Rawalpindi (1919) accorded the government of Afghanistan the freedom to conduct its own foreign affairs.

Internally, Amanullah's Westernization program was strongly opposed, forcing him to abdicate in 1929. After a brief civil war, a tribal assembly chose Muhammad Nadir Shah as king. In his brief four years in power, he restored peace while continuing Amanullah's modernization efforts at a more moderate pace. Assassinated in 1933, he was succeeded by his son, Muhammad Zahir Shah, who continued his modernization efforts, governing for 40 years, even though sharing effective power with his uncles and a first cousin, who served as his prime ministers.

In the 1960s, there was considerable tension between Pakistan and Afghanistan as a result of Afghanistan's effort to assert influence among, and ultimately responsibility for, Pushtu-speaking Pathan tribes living on both sides of the Durand Line under a policy calling for the establishment of an entity to be called "Pushtunistan." The border was closed several times during the following years, and relations with Pakistan remained generally poor until 1977.

In 1964, a new constitution was introduced, converting Afghanistan into a constitutional monarchy, and a year later the country's first general election was held. In July 1973, Muhammad Daoud Khan, the king's first cousin and brother-in-law, who had served as prime minister from 1953 until early 1963, seized power in a near-bloodless coup, establishing a republic and appointing himself president, and prime minister of the Republic of Afghanistan. He exiled Zahir Shah and his immediate family, abolished the monarchy, dissolved the legislature, and suspended the constitution. Daoud ruled as a dictator until 1977, when a republican constitution calling for a one-party state was adopted by the newly convened Loya Jirga (Grand National Assembly), which then elected Daoud president for a six-year term.

Afghanistan Under Communist Rule

On 27 April 1978, Daoud was deposed and executed in a bloody coup (the "Saur Revolution" because it took place during the Afghan month of Saur), and the Democratic Republic of Afghanistan emerged. Heading the new Revolutionary Council was Nur Muhammad Taraki, secretary-general of the communist People's Democratic Party of Afghanistan (PDPA), assisted by Babrak Karmal and Hafizullah Amin, both named deputy prime ministers. The former Soviet Union immediately established ties with the new regime, and in December 1978, the two nations concluded a treaty of friendship and cooperation. Soon after the coup, rural Afghan groups took up arms against the regime, which increasingly relied on Soviet arms for support against what came to be known as mujahidin, or holy warriors.

Meanwhile, the Khalq (masses) and Parcham (flag) factions of the PDPA, which had united for the April takeover, became embroiled in a bitter power struggle within the party and the government. In September 1979, Taraki was ousted and executed by Amin, who had beat out Karmal to become prime minister the previous March and who now assumed Taraki's posts as president and party leader. Amin was himself replaced on 27 December by Karmal, the Parcham faction leader. This last change was announced not by Radio Kabul but by Radio Moscow and was preceded by the airlift of 4,000 to 5,000 Soviet troops into Kabul on 25–26 December, purportedly at the request of an Afghan government whose president, Hafizullah Amin, was killed during the takeover.

The Soviet presence increased to about 85,000 troops in late January 1980, and by spring, the first clashes between Soviet troops and the mujahidin had occurred. Throughout the early and mid-1980s, the mujahidin resistance continue to build, aided by Afghan army deserters and arms from the United States, Pakistan, and the nations of the Islamic Conference Organization (ICO). Much of the countryside remained under mujahidin control as the insurgency waged on year by year, while in Kabul, Soviet advisers assumed control of most Afghan government agencies.

By late 1987, more than a million Afghans had lost their lives in the struggle, while the United Nations High Commission for Refugees (UNHCR) estimated that some 5 million others had sought refuge in Pakistan, Iran, and elsewhere. Soviet sources at the time acknowledged Soviet losses of between 12,000 and 30,000 dead and 76,000 wounded. Soviet troop strength in Afghanistan at the end of 1987 was about 120,000, while according to Western sources, Afghan resistance forces numbered nearly 130,000.

In early 1987, Babrak Karmal fled to Moscow after being replaced as the head of the PDPA in May 1986 by Najibullah, former head of the Afghan secret police. Najibullah offered the mujahidin a ceasefire and introduced a much publicized national reconciliation policy; he also released some political prisoners, offered to deal with the resistance leaders, and promised new land reform. The mujahidin rejected these overtures, declining to negotiate for anything short of Soviet withdrawal and Najibullah's removal.

International efforts to bring about a political solution to the war—including nearly unanimous General Assembly condemnations of the Soviet presence in Afghanistan—were pursued within the UN framework from 1982 onward. Among these efforts were "proximity talks" between Afghanistan and Pakistan conducted by a Special Representative of the UN Secretary General, Under Secretary-General Diego Cordovez. After a desultory beginning, these talks began to look promising in late 1987 and early 1988 when Soviet policymakers repeatedly stated, in a major policy shift, that the removal of Soviet troops from Afghanistan was not contingent on the creation of a transitional regime acceptable to the former USSR. On 14 April 1988, documents were signed and exchanged in which the USSR agreed to pull its troops out of Afghanistan within nine months, the US reserved the right to continue military aid to Afghan guerrillas as long as the USSR continued to aid the government in Kabul, and Pakistan and Afghanistan pledged not to interfere in each other's internal affairs.

The Russians completed the evacuation of their forces on schedule 15 February 1989, but in spite of continuing pressure by the well-armed mujahidin, the Najibullah government remained in power until April 1992, when Najibullah sought refuge at the UN office in Kabul as mujahidin forces closed in on the city.

Afghanistan After the Soviet Withdrawal

With the fall of the Najibullah government, the Seven-Party Alliance (SPA) of the Islamic groups based in Pakistan moved to consolidate its "victory" by announcing plans to set up an Interim Afghan Government (AIG) charged with preparing the way for elections. Meanwhile, they moved to assert their control of Afghanistan, but their efforts to establish the AIG in Kabul failed when within ten days of Najibullah's departure from office, well-armed forces of the Hizb-i-Islami and Jamiat-i-Islami—two of the seven SPA parties—clashed in fighting for the control of the capital. In July, Jamiat leader Burhanuddin Rabbani replaced Sibghatullah Mojaddedi as president of the AIG, as previously agreed by all the SPA parties but the Hizb-i-Islami.

Continued fighting between Jamiat and Hizb-i-Islami militias halted further progress, and Rabbani's forces, under Commander Ahmad Shah Masud, dug in to block those under the control of interim "Prime Minister" Gulbuddin Hekmatyar's Hizb-i-Islami and his ally, General Rashid Dostum (a former PDPA militia leader turned warlord from northern Afghanistan), from taking control of Kabul. In a 24-hour rocket exchange in August 1992 in Kabul, an estimated 3000 Afghans died, and before the end of the year, upwards of 700,000 Afghans had fled the city. Deep differences among the SPA/AIG leadership, embittered by decades of bad blood, ethnic distrust, and personal enmity, prevented any further progress toward creating a genuine interim government capable of honoring the 1992 SPA pledge to write a constitution, organize elections, and create a new Afghan polity. Despite UN attempts to broker a peace and bring the warring groups into a coalition government, Afghanistan remained at war.

Rise of the Taliban

By the summer of 1994 Rabbani and his defense minister, Ahmed Shuh Masud, were in control of the government in Kabul, but internal turmoil caused by the warring factions had brought the economy to a standstill. It was reported that on the road north of Kandahar a convoy owned by influential Pakistani businessmen was stopped by bandits demanding money. The businessmen appealed to the Pakistani government, which responded by encouraging Afghan students from the fundamentalist religious schools on the Pakistan-Afghan boarder to intervene. The students freed the convoy and went on to capture Kandahar, Afghanistan's second-largest city. Pakistan's leaders supported the Taliban with ammunition, fuel, and food. The students, ultra-fundamentalist Sunni Muslims who call themselves the Taliban (the Arabic word for religious students, literally "the Seekers") share Pashtun ancestry with their Pakistani neighbors to the south. Pashtuns make up about 43% of Afghanistan's population. The Taliban also found widespread support among Afghan Pashtuns hostile to local warlords and tired of war and economic instability. By late 1996, the Taliban had captured Kabul, the capital, and were in control of 21 of Afghanistan's 32 provinces. When Rabbani fled the capital, Pakistan and Saudi Arabia officially recognized the Taliban government in Kabul. In areas under Taliban control, order was restored, roads opened, and trade resumed. However, the Taliban's reactionary social practices, justified as being Islamic, do not appeal to Afghanistan's non-Pashtun minorities in the north and west of the country, nor to the educated population generally. The opposition, dominated by the Uzbek, Tajik, Hazara, and Turkoman ethnic groups, retreated to the northeastern provinces.

In May 1997 the Taliban entered Mazar-i-Sharif, Afghanistan's largest town north of the Hindu Kush and stronghold of Uzbek warlord Rashid Dostum. In the political intrigue that followed, Dostum was ousted by his second in command, Malik Pahlawan, who initially supported the Taliban. Dostum reportedly fled to Turkey. Once the Taliban were in the city, however, Pahlawan abruptly switched sides. In the subsequent fighting, the Taliban were forced to retreat with heavy casualties. The forces of Ahmad Shah Masud, Tajik warlord and former defense minister in ousted President Rabbani's government, were also instrumental in the defeat of the Taliban in Mazar. Masud controls the high passes of the Panjshir Valley in the east of the country. The opposition alliance is supported by Iran, Russia, and the Central Asian republics, who fear that the Taliban may destabilize the region.

By early 1998, the Taliban militia controlled about two-thirds of Afghanistan. Opposition forces under Ahmad Shah Masoud controlled the northeast of the country. Taliban forces mounted another offensive against their opponents in August-September 1998 and nearly sparked a war with neighboring Iran after a series of Shiite villages were pillaged and Iranian diplomats killed. Iran, which supplies Masoud's forces, countered by massing troops along its border with Afghanistan. Although the crisis subsided, tensions between the Taliban and Iran remained high.

Despite attempts to broker a peace settlement, fighting between the Taliban and opposition factions continued through 1999 and into the spring of 2000 with the Taliban now controlling 90% of the country. In March 1999, the warring factions agreed to enter a coalition government, but by July these UN-sponsored peace talks broke down and the Taliban renewed its offensive against opposition forces. The warfare led to yet more displacement among the civilian population.

[13]GOVERNMENT

Between 1964 and 1973, Afghanistan was a constitutional monarchy, for the first time in its history. The head of government was the prime minister, appointed by the king and responsible to the bicameral legislature. This system gave way to a more traditional authoritarian system on 17 July 1973, when Afghanistan became a republic, headed by Muhammad Daoud Khan, who became both president and prime minister. A new constitution in 1977 created a one-party state with a strong executive and a weak bicameral legislature. The communist PDPA abrogated this constitution after they seized power in April 1978.

Between 1978 and 1980, a communist-style 167-member Revolutionary Council exercised legislative powers. The chief of state (president) headed the presidium of that council, to which the 20-member cabinet was formally responsible. A provisional constitution, introduced in April 1980, guaranteed respect for Islam and national traditions, condemned colonialism, imperialism, Zionism, and fascism, and proclaimed the PDPA as "the guiding and mobilizing force of society and state." Seven years later, a new constitution providing for a very strong presidency was introduced as part of the PDPA's propaganda campaign of "national reconciliation." Najibullah remained as president until April 1992 when he sought refuge at the UN office in Kabul as mujahidin forces closed in on the city.

With the fall of the Najibullah government a Seven Party Alliance (SPA) of the Islamic groups announced plans to set up an Interim Afghan Government (AIG) charged with preparing the way for elections. However, Professor Burhanuddin Rabbani co-opted the process by forming a leadership council that elected him president. Subsequent fighting among warring factions plunged the country into anarchy and set the stage for the emergence of the ultra-conservative Islamic movement, Taliban, which ousted the Rabbani government and as of mid-2000 controlled all but the northern most provinces of the country. Consequently, no new constitution has been drafted since the end of the Najibullah government.

The Taliban, led by Mullah Mohammed Omar, formed a six-member ruling council in Kabul which ruled by edict. Ultimate authority for Taliban rule rested in the Taliban's inner Shura (Assembly), located in the southern city of Kandahar, and in Mullah Omar.

[14]POLITICAL PARTIES

Political parties have usually been illegal in Afghanistan, forcing most political activity—influenced by ideological, linguistic, and ethnic considerations—to operate underground or from abroad (or both). The 1964 constitution provided for the formation of political parties. However, since the framers of the constitution decided that political parties should be permitted only after the first elections, and since the Parliament never adopted a law governing the parties' operation, all candidates for the parliamentary elections of August and September 1965 stood as independents. Because a law on political parties was not on the books four years later, the 1969 elections were also contested on a non-party basis. Throughout the 1964–1973 period, however, the de facto existence of parties was widely recognized. Subsequently, the framers reversed their plan to allow political parties.

Under the 1977 constitution, only the National Revolutionary Party (NRP), the ruler's chosen instrument, was allowed.

The 1978 coup was engineered by the illegal People's Democratic Party of Afghanistan (PDPA) which had been founded in 1965. During its brief history, this Marxist party had been riven by a bloody struggle between its pro-Soviet Parcham (flag) faction and its larger Khalq (masses) faction. Babrak Karmal was the leader of the Parcham group, while the Khalq faction was headed until 1979 by Nur Muhammad Taraki and Hafizullah Amin. The factional struggle continued after the 1978 coup, prompting the Soviet intervention of 1979. Factional bloodletting continued thereafter also, with repeated purges and assassinations of Khalq adherents as well as bitter infighting within Parcham, this last leading to Babrak Karmal's replacement as PDPA secretary-general in May 1986 by Najibullah.

The Islamic resistance forces opposing the PDPA government and its Soviet backers in Afghanistan represent conservative, ethnically-based Islamic groups which themselves have had a long history of partisan infighting (and repression by successive Kabul governments). They came together in the early 1980s to fight the common enemy, the communist PDPA and the Soviet invaders and, in 1985, under pressure from Pakistan and the United States, they were loosely united into a Seven Party Alliance (SPA), headquartered in Peshawar, Pakistan. By 1987, commando groups affiliated with one or more of these seven parties controlled more than 80% of the land area of Afghanistan.

With arms flowing in from outside the country—a flow not halted until the end of 1991—the fighting continued, but with the final withdrawal of Soviet troops in February 1989, the SPA stepped up its military and political pressure on the communist PDPA government. However, President Najibullah proved to have more staying power than previously estimated, using Soviet arms supplies, which continued until the end of 1991 to buttress his position, while playing upon divisions among the resistance, embracing nationalism and renouncing communism, and even changing the name of the PDPA to the Wattan (Homeland) Party. It was only in April 1992, with the Soviet Union now history, his army defecting from beneath him, and the mujahidin closing on Kabul that he sought refuge at the UN office in the capital, leaving the city in the hands of the rival ethnic and regional mujahidin militias.

The leaders of the mujahidin groups agreed to establish a leadership council. This council quickly came under the control of Professor Burhanuddin Rabbani who was subsequently elected President by the council. Fighting broke out in August 1992 in Kabul between forces loyal to President Rabbani and rival factions. A new war for the control of Afghanistan had begun.

On September 26–27, 1996, the Pashtun-dominated ultra-conservative Islamic Taliban movement captured the capital of Kabul and expanded its control to over 90% of the country by mid-2000. The Taliban are led by Mullah Mohammed Omar. Ousted President Rabbani, a Tajik, and his defense minister Ahmad Shah Masud relocated to Takhar in the north. Rabbani claimed that he remained the head of the government. His delegation retained Afghanistan's UN seat after the General Assembly deferred a decision on Afghanistan's credentials. Meanwhile, the Taliban removed the ousted PDPA leader Najibullah from the UN office in Kabul, tortured and shot him, and hung his body prominently in the city. General Rashid Dostum, an ethnic Uzbek, controlled several north-central provinces until he was ousted on 25 May 1997 by his second in command Malik Pahlawan. Dostum reportedly fled to Turkey. The Shia Hazara community, led by Abdul Karim Khalily, retains control of a small portion of the center of the country.

[15]LOCAL GOVERNMENT

Afghanistan has traditionally been divided into 28 provinces governed by centrally appointed governors with considerable autonomy in local affairs. During the Soviet occupation and the development of country-wide resistance, local areas came increasingly under the control of mujahidin groups that were largely independent of any higher authority; local commanders, in some instances, asserted a measure of independence also from the mujahidin leadership in Pakistan, establishing their own systems of local government, collecting revenues, running educational and other facilities, and even engaging in local negotiations. Mujahidin groups retained links with the Peshawar parties to ensure access to weapons that were doled out to the parties by the government of Pakistan for distribution to fighters inside Afghanistan.

As of mid-2000, the ultra-conservative Taliban Islamic movement was in control of all but the northern most provinces of the country. In areas under their control, the Taliban set up a *shura* (assembly), made up of senior Taliban members and important tribal figures from the area. Each *shura* makes laws and collects taxes locally. The Taliban have set up a provisional government for the whole of Afghanistan, but it has yet to exercise central control over the local *shuras*.

[16]JUDICIAL SYSTEM

As of mid-2000 there was no rule of law or independent judiciary. In areas under Taliban control ad hoc rudimentary judicial systems have been established based on Taliban interpretation of Islamic law. Murderers are subjected to public executions and thieves have a limb or two (one hand, one foot) severed. Adulterers have been stoned to death in public. Taliban courts are said to have heard cases in sessions that lasted only a few minutes. Prison conditions are poor and prisoners are not given food. Normally, this is the responsibility of the prisoners' relatives who are allowed to visit to provide them with food once or twice a week. Those who have no relatives have to petition the local council or rely on other inmates.

In non-Taliban controlled areas, many municipal and provincial authorities rely on some form of Islamic law and traditional tribal codes of justice. The administration and implementation of justice could vary from area to area and depend on the whims of local commanders or other authorities, who could summarily execute, torture, and mete out punishments without reference to any other authority.

[17]ARMED FORCES

As of 2000, the Taliban controlled two-thirds of the country, with the remainder controlled by an alliance of government troops loyal to former president Berhannudin Rabbani. Taliban forces are estimated at 25,000. Weapons information dates back to 1992, at which time there were SU-17, MiG21, and Mi-8 combat aircraft in the country. The Taliban is believed to have about 26 combat aircraft; National Islamic Alliance (NIM) forces are believed to have 70. In 1998, defense spending was estimated at $250 million or 14.7% of GDP.

[18]INTERNATIONAL COOPERATION

Afghanistan has been a member of the UN since 19 November 1946 and is a member of ESCAP and all the nonregional specialized agencies except IMO and WIPO. Afghanistan also belongs to the Asian Development Bank and G-77. However, most of the world, as well as international organizations such as the UN continue to recognize the ousted government of Hekmatyar as the legitimate government of the country. Only Pakistan, Saudi Arabia, and the United Arab Emirates recognize the Taliban as the legitimate government of Afghanistan.

Since taking control, the Taliban movement has lost international support as it has tried to impose strict adherence to Islamic customs and has harshly punished and even executed transgressors. As a result, the UN and other aid organizations, including UNHCR, UNICEF, Save the Children, and Oxfam, have cut back or ceased operations in protest or for lack of available (female) staff.

[19]ECONOMY

Afghanistan's economy has been devastated by almost 20 years of war. Hampered by an unintegrated economy until relatively late in the post-World War II period, only in the 1950s did the building of new roads begin to link the country's commercial centers with the wool and fruit-producing areas. Largely agricultural and pastoral, Afghanistan depends on the cultivation of fruits and cotton, the production of wool and karakul skins, and traditional handicrafts like carpet weaving. Modern industry consisted of cotton and wool textiles, sugar refining, cement, fertilizers, and food processing. The country has valuable mineral resources, including large reserves of iron ore at Hajigak discovered before the war, but only coal, salt, lapis lazuli, barite, and chrome are being exploited. The discovery of large quantities of natural gas in the north, for which a pipeline to the former USSR was completed in 1967, increased the country's export earnings, at least until escalation of civil strife in the late 1970s and 1980s.

Since the outbreak of war in the late 1970s, economic data have been contradictory and of doubtful reliability. Journalists and other Westerners who have traveled inside Afghanistan have reported a steady erosion in the country's economic infrastructure overall, particularly in rural areas. In September 1987, the Afghan foreign minister asserted that 350 bridges and 258 factories had been destroyed since the fighting began in 1979. By the early 1990s, two-thirds of all paved roads were unusable, and the countryside appeared severely depopulated, with more than 25% of the population—twice the prewar level—residing in urban areas that until recently offered relatively more secure protection. With the escalation of open conflict, what little is left of the country's infrastructure is rapidly being destroyed. Lack of resources and the war have impeded reconstruction of irrigation systems, repair of market roads, and replanting of orchards. The presence of an estimated 10 million land mines has restricted areas for cultivation and slowed the return of refugees who are needed to rebuild the economy. Inflation, which topped 400% is 1996, has rendered the currency virtually wothless. More than half of the country is unemployed.

Agriculture, including high levels of opium poppy cultivation, remain the mainstay of the economy. In 1999, encouraged by good weather and high prices, poppy producers had increased the area under cultivation by 43 percent and harvested a bumper crop—a record 4,600 tons, compared with 2,100 tons the year before. Afghanistan has become the second largest opium producer in the world. The Taliban have been slow to stop the drug trafficking because there are no other jobs.

[20]INCOME

The US Central Intelligence Agency (CIA) reports that in 1998 Afghanistan's gross domestic product (GDP) was estimated at $20 billion. The per capita GDP was estimated at $800. The CIA defines GDP as the value of all final goods and services produced within a nation in a given year and computed on the basis of purchasing power parity (PPP) rather than value as measured on the basis of the rate of exchange. It was estimated that agriculture accounted for 53% of GDP, industry 28.5%, and services 18.5%.

[21]LABOR

Afghanistan's labor force was estimated at 5.6 million in 1976, 4 million in 1979, and 5 million in 1980, with about two-thirds engaged in agriculture and animal husbandry. As of 1990, 70% of the economically active population was engaged in agriculture, 19% in services, and the rest in other sectors. More recent estimates are not available. The textile industry is the largest employer of industrial labor; weaving of cloth and carpets is the most important home industry. In 1978, the government established the Central Council of Afghanistan Trade Unions in order to develop the trade union movement. In the mid-1980s, the council had some 285,000 members. As of 1999, the government did not appear to have the means to enforce worker rights, as there is no functioning constitution or legal framework that defines them. Little is known about labor laws and practices under Taliban rule.

[22]AGRICULTURE

About 12% of the land is arable. Of the country's total arable land area, only about 144,000 hectares (356,000 acres) was under cultivation with permanent crops in 1997. Normally, Afghanistan grew about 95% of its needs in wheat and rye, and more than met its needs in rice, potatoes, pulses, nuts, and seeds; it depended on imports only for some wheat, sugar, and edible fats and oils. Fruit, both fresh and preserved (with bread), is a staple food for many Afghans. Agricultural production, however, is a fraction of its potential. Agriculture and animal husbandry engaged 67.7% of the economically active population in 1998.

The variety of the country's crops corresponds to its topography. The areas around Kandahar, Herat, and the broad Kabul plain yield fruits of many kinds. The northern regions from Takhar to Badghis and Herat and Helmand provinces produce cotton. Corn is grown extensively in Paktia and Nangarhar provinces, and rice mainly in Kunduz, Baghlan, and Laghman provinces. Wheat is common to several regions. Estimated crop production in 1998 (in tons) included wheat, 2,834,000; fruits, 615,000; corn, 240,000; vegetables, 492,000; rice, 450,000; barley, 330,000; and seed cotton, 66,000.

Pistachios and almonds are grown, and substantial quantities are exported. An estimated 2,000 tons of pistachios and 9,000 tons of almonds were produced in 1998. Agricultural products accounted for about 58% of Afghanistan's exports in 1997, of which fruits and nuts were a large portion. In some regions, agricultural production had all but ceased due to destruction caused by the war and the migration of Afghans out of those areas. A law of May 1987 relaxed the restrictions on private landowning set in 1978: the limit of permitted individual holding was raised from 6 to 18 hectares (from 15 to 45 acres). Opium and hashish are also widely grown for the drug trade. In 1998, Afghanistan produced an estimated 1,350 tons of opium, or about 39% of the estimated worldwide production.

[23]ANIMAL HUSBANDRY

The availability of land suitable for grazing has made animal husbandry an important part of the economy. Natural pastures cover some 3 million hectares (7.4 million acres) but are being overgrazed. The northern regions around Mazar-i-Sharif and Maymanah are the home range for about 6 million karakul sheep. In 1998 there were an estimated 14.3 million sheep, and 2.2 million goats.

The output of livestock products in 1998, as projected by the FAO, included 300,000 tons of cows' milk, 201,000 tons of sheep's milk, 41,000 tons of goats' milk, 18,000 tons of eggs, 16,000 tons of wool (greasy basis), and 16,000 tons of sheep- and goatskins. Much of Afghanistan's livestock was removed from the country by early waves of refugees who fled to Pakistan

and Iran. Total meat output in 1998 was 231,000 tons, up from an average of 225,000 tons annually during 1989-91.

[24]FISHING

Some fishing takes place in the lakes and rivers, but fish does not constitute a significant part of the Afghan diet. The annual catch was about 1,250 tons in 1997.

[25]FORESTRY

Afghanistan's timber has been greatly depleted, and since the mid-1980s, only about 3% of the land area has been forested, mainly in the east. Significant stands of trees have been destroyed by the ravages of the war. Exploitation has been hampered by lack of power and access roads. In 1997, about 8,355,000 cu m of roundwood were produced.

[26]MINING

Afghanistan has valuable deposits of barite, beryl, chrome, coal, copper, iron, lapis lazuli, lead, mica, natural gas, petroleum, salt, silver, sulfur, and zinc. Reserves of high-grade iron ore, discovered years ago at the Hajigak hills in Bamyan Province, are estimated to total 2 billion tons.

On average, some 114,000 tons of coal were mined each year during 1978–84. Production in 1997 amounted to 185,000 tons. In 1997, Afghanistan produced 13,000 tons of salt, 3,000 tons of gypsum, 5,000 tons of copper, 2,000 tons of barite, and 116,000 tons of cement. Deposits of lapis lazuli in Badakhshan are mined in small quantities. Like other aspects of Afghanistan's economy, exploitation of natural resources has been disrupted by the civil war.

[27]ENERGY AND POWER

In 1998, production of electricity totaled 430 million kwh; total installed capacity was 312,000 kW. Three hydroelectric plants were opened between 1965 and 1970, at Jalalabad, Naghlu, and Mahi Par, near Kabul; another, at Kajaki, in the upper Helmand River Valley, was opened in the mid-1970s. Additional hydroelectric plants are at Sarobi, west of Kabul; Pol-e Khomri; and Kandahar.

Natural gas reserves were once estimated by the Soviets at 140 billion cu m. In 1991, a new gas field was discovered in Chekhcha, Jowzjan Province. Production started in 1967 with 342 million cu m but had risen to 2.6 billion cu m in 1995. Production occurs at Shiberghan and Sar-i-Pol and is used for fertilizer production and for generating electricity at Mazar-i-Sharif. Natural gas was the only economically significant export in 1995, going mainly to Uzbekistan via pipeline. As of 1997, natural gas production was 19 million cu ft. It was used domestically for urea production, power generation, and at a fertilizer plant. In August 1996, a multinational consortium agreed to construct a 1,430 km (890 mi) pipeline through Afghanistan to carry natural gas from Turkmenistan to Pakistan, at a cost of about $2 billion. Although Afghanistan's main rebel factions signed a pipeline safety agreement in September 1996, financing remains an issue because of high political risk and security concerns.

Two power facilities, financed with the help of Bulgaria, have helped ease power supply problems: a 400 kv substation in the Chaman-e Huzuri area of Kabul (at a cost of $3 million), and an 800 kW power station in Kabul which cost $1.4 million. Two more power stations, with a combined capacity of 600 kW, are planned to be built in Samandarah village, Charikar City. In 1991, a new 72-collector solar installation was completed in Kabul at a cost of $364 million. The installation heats 40,000 l (10,500 gal) of water to an average temperature of 60°c (140°F) around the clock.

28 INDUSTRY

As with other sectors of the economy, Afghanistan's already beleaguered industries have been devastated by civil strife that left most of the countries factories and even much of the cottage industry sector inoperative. Still in an early stage of growth before the outbreak of war, industry's development has been stunted since; those few industries that have continued production remain limited to processing of local materials. The principal modern industry is cotton textile production, with factories at Pol e Khomri, Golbahar, Begram, Balkh, and Jabal as Saraj, just north of Charikar. Important industries in 1999 included textiles, soap, furniture, shoes, fertilizer, cement, handwoven carpets, natural gas, oil, and copper. A large urea plant at Mazar-i-Sharif managed to stay in operation despite the war.

Carpet making is the most important handicraft industry, but it has suffered with the flight of rug makers. Production has fluctuated widely from year to year, increasing somewhat during the early 1990s with the establishment of selected "zones of tranquility" targeted for UN reconstruction assistance. Other handicrafts include feltmaking and the weaving of cotton, woolen, and silk cloth.

29 SCIENCE AND TECHNOLOGY

The Afghanistan Academy of Sciences, founded in 1979, is the principal scientific institution. Its Science Research Centre has 40 researchers and maintains a computer center, a botanical garden, plants museum, and institutes of botany, zoology, geology and chemistry, and seismology.

The Department of Geology and Mineral Survey within the Ministry of Mines and Industries conducts geological and mineralogical research, mapping, prospecting and exploration.

The Institute of Public Health, founded in 1962, conducts public health training and research and study of indigenous diseases, has a Government reference laboratory, and compiles statistical data.

Kabul University, founded in 1932, has faculties of Science, Pharmacy, Veterinary Medicine, and Geo-Sciences. Bayazid Roshan University of Nangarhar, founded in 1962, has faculties of Medicine and Engineering. The Institute of Agriculture, founded in 1924, offers courses in veterinary medicine. Kabul Polytechnic College, founded in 1951, offers post-graduate engineering courses.

30 DOMESTIC TRADE

Kabul, Kandahār, Mazār-e-Sharif, and Herāt are the principal commercial cities of eastern, southern, northern, and western Afghanistan, respectively. The first two are the main distribution centers for imports arriving from the direction of Pakistan; the latter two, for materials arriving from Iran and the former USSR. Hours of business vary. The destruction of paved roads has severely constrained normal domestic trade in most rural parts of the country. Heavy fighting in Kabul as completely destroyed the city's infrastructure.

31 FOREIGN TRADE

Although the Taliban had brought a repressive order to the 90% of the country under its rule, it remains unable to attract foreign investment as long as it is unable to gain international recognition or bring lasting peace to the country. Hyperinflation had increased the number of Afghanis (the country's currency) needed to equal one US dollar from 50 in the early 1990s to a virtually worthless 42,000 in 1999. In addition, various mujahidin groups and warlords have set up customs and tax collection posts on the main supply routes from Central Asia and Pakistan, further hampering trade. In wake of the country's economic and political disintegration, heroin has become its major export item.

The value of exports, including fruits and nuts, carpets, wool, cotton, hides and pelts, and gems totaled an estimated $80 million in 1996. Imports, including food, petroleum products, and most commodity items totaled an estimated $150 million.

Principal trading partners in 1998 (in millions of US dollars) were as follows:

COUNTRY	EXPORTS	IMPORTS	BALANCE
France	25	14	11
Pakistan	25	42	-17
United States	16	8	8
India	8	26	-18
United Kingdom	4	23	-19
Turkmenistan	3	26	-23
Japan	1	67	-66
China (inc. Hong Kong)	n.a.	34	
Kenya	n.a.	44	
Korea	n.a.	43	
Tajikistan	n.a.	24	

32 BALANCE OF PAYMENTS

Between 1951 and 1973, Afghanistan's year-end international reserves were never lower than $38 million or higher than $65 million. Development of the natural gas industry and favorable prices for some of the country's agricultural exports led to increases in international reserves, to $67.5 million in 1974 and to $115.4 million as of 31 December 1975. Exploitation of natural gas also freed Afghanistan from extreme dependence on petroleum imports and from the rapid increases in import costs that most countries experienced in 1973 and 1974. Increased trade with the former USSR and Eastern Europe in the late 1970s and 1980s resulted in a reduction of foreign exchange earnings, since trade surpluses are counted as a credit against future imports. Foreign exchange reserves declined from $411.1 million at the close of 1979 to $262 million as of 30 May 1987. The public foreign debt in early 1991 stood at $2.3 billion. Reliable statistics are not available for the ensuing years.

The US Central Intelligence Agency reports that in 1996 the purchasing power parity of Afghanistan's exports was $80 million while imports totaled $150 million resulting in a trade balance of -$70 million.

33 BANKING AND SECURITIES

The government central bank, the Bank of Afghanistan, founded in 1939 and with 65 branches throughout the country in 1996, issues bank notes, administers government loans, grants loans to municipalities and to other banks, and provides short-term loans.

All banks in Afghanistan were nationalized in 1975. In the early 1980s there were seven banks in the country, including the Agricultural Development Bank, the Export Promotion Bank, the Industrial Development Bank, and the Mortgage and Construction Bank. Foreign banks are not permitted in Afghanistan. Afghans may not own foreign securities. There is no organized domestic securities market.

34 INSURANCE

The fate of the Afghan National Insurance Co., which covered fire, transport, and accident insurance, is unknown as of 2000.

35 PUBLIC FINANCE

The fiscal year ends 21 September. Budget breakdowns have not been available since 1979/80, when revenues totaled Af15,788 million and expenditures Af16,782 million. As of mid-1997, there was no central authority recognized; governmental functions were sparse and split up between the contending political factions. No federal system of collecting and disbursing public finances is currently in place.

36TAXATION

In the early 1980s, direct taxes accounted for about 15% of government revenues. The share provided by indirect taxes declined from 42% to 30%, as revenues from natural gas and state enterprises played an increasing role in government finance. Tax collection, never an effective source of revenue in rural areas, has been essentially disabled by the disruption caused by fighting and mass flight.

37CUSTOMS AND DUTIES

Before the turmoil of the late 1970s, customs duties, levied as a source of revenue rather than as a protective measure, constituted more than one-fourth of total government revenue. As of 1993, both specific and ad valorem duties of 20–35% were levied on imports. Other costs included service and Red Crescent charges; monopoly and luxury taxes; authorization and privilege charges, and a commission-type duty.

38FOREIGN INVESTMENT

A 1967 law encouraged investment of private foreign capital in Afghanistan, but under the PDPA government, Western investment virtually ceased. Between 1979 and 1987, the former USSR provided technical and financial assistance on more than 200 projects, including various industrial plants, irrigation dams, agricultural stations, and a new terminal at the Kabul airport. Since 1990, reconstruction investments from Russia, Japan, and the US have been channeled through the United Nations.

The Taliban have called for Western support to help reconstruct Afghanistan, but Western donors—already reluctant to support UN programs in the country—are not responding. The UN called upon Western donors for $224 million in emergency contributions in 1995, but only received $53 million. Continued fighting in 2000 precluded little to no foreign investment, except from national gas agreements with Pakistan.

39ECONOMIC DEVELOPMENT

With international aid suspended, the infrastructure destroyed, and fighting ongoing, economic development was at a standstill in mid-2000. Despite unemployment figures hovering at 50%, the Taliban has done little to revive the economy except to turn a blind eye to opium production and drug trafficking.

40SOCIAL DEVELOPMENT

Social welfare in Afghanistan has traditionally relied on family and tribal organization. In the villages and small towns, a tax is levied on each man to benefit the poor. Disabled people are cared for in social welfare centers in the provincial capitals. Most other welfare activities are still unorganized and in private hands. In the early 1990s, a social insurance system provided old age, disability, and survivors' pensions, sickness and maternity benefits, and workers' compensation. The status of these programs under Taliban rule at the end of the decade was unknown.

Women have traditionally had few rights in Afghanistan, with their role limited largely to the home and the fields. Advances in women's rights were made from 1920 onward, and by the time of the communist coup, women attended school in large numbers, voted and held government jobs—including posts as cabinet ministers, and were active in the professions. The Communist regime also promoted women's rights, but the victory of the extremely conservative Taliban in 1996 has reversed this trend. Strict limits on the freedoms of women have been put in place. Women are now only allowed to appear in public if they are dressed in a chadri, a long black garment with a mesh veil covering the face, and only if accompanied by a male. The Taliban also banned girls from attending school, and have prohibited women from working outside the home. Certain restrictions on women were reportedly lifted in 1998. Women were allowed to work as doctors and nurses as long as they treated only women, and were able to attend medical schools. Widows with no means of support were allowed to seek employment.

The human rights record of the governing Taliban is poor. Taliban forces have been responsible for disappearances and political killings, including massacres and summary executions. In areas controlled by the Taliban, Islamic courts and religious police impose strict order based on conservative interpretations of Islamic law that mandate, among other measures, public execution for adultery and amputation for theft. Homes were burned and livestock destroyed in a military offensive in the summer of 1999 that resulted in the forcible relocation of many civilians. Basic freedoms of speech, assembly, religion, and association are abridged under Taliban rule. As of 1999, an estimated 260,000 persons had been forcibly displaced from their homes over a period of years.

41HEALTH

Starvation, disease, death, war, and migration had devastating effects on Afghanistan's health infrastructure in the 1990s. According to the World Health Organization, medication was scarce. Infectious diseases accounted for more than half of all hospital admissions (mostly malaria and typhoid) in 1994. Even before the war disrupted medical services, health conditions in Afghanistan were inadequate by western standards. There are modern pharmacies in Kabul and in provincial centers. A national medical school was established in 1931 and, in the following year, the first tuberculosis hospital was built. In 1990, for every 100,000 people, 278 were stricken with tuberculosis.

Efforts to take medical services to war-ravaged areas of Afghanistan and to areas left without public health programs due to the termination of services have been waged by volunteer medical programs from France, Sweden, the US, and other countries. In June 2000, the UN undertook a major effort to inoculate Afghani children against polio. Donkeys and bicycles were employed to transport thousands of volunteers in urban and rural areas. Both sides in the fighting agreed to a cease-fire to allow the immunization to take place.

In 1991, there were 2,233 doctors, 510 pharmacists, 267 dentists, 1,451 nurses, and 338 midwives. Between 1985-1995 only 29% of the population had access to health services. During those same years, few of the population had access to safe water (10%) and adequate sanitation (8%). For children under one the immunization rates are as follows: tuberculosis (44%), diphtheria, pertussus, and tetanus (18%), polio (18%), and measles (40%) between 1990–94.

In 1999, estimated life expectancy was 47.3 years—one of the lowest in the world—and infant mortality was estimated at 140 per 1,000 live births. The maternal mortality rate in 1992 was one of the highest in the Central Asia region with 1,700 maternal deaths per 100,000 live births. The death rate in 1999 was 17 per 1,000 people. From 1978 to 1991, there were over 1,500,000 war-related deaths. Cholera reached epidemic proportions with 19,903 cases reported in 1995.

42HOUSING

Houses in farming communities are built largely of mud brick and frequently grouped within a fortified enclosure, to provide protection from marauders. The roofs are flat, with a coating of mixed straw and mud rolled hard above a ceiling of horizontal poles, although in areas where timber is scarce, separate mud brick domes crown each room. Cement and other modern building materials are widely used in cities and towns. Every town has at least one wide thoroughfare, but other streets are narrow lanes between houses of mud brick, taller than those in the villages and featuring decorative wooden balconies. The war has severely damaged or destroyed countless houses. According to an official report, there were 200,000 dwellings in Kabul in the mid-1980s. The latest available figures for 1980–88 show a total housing stock of 3,500,000 with 4.4 people per dwelling.

43EDUCATION

Adult illiteracy for the year 2000 was estimated at 63.7% (males, 49.0%; females, 79.2%). Education is free at all levels. Primary education lasts for six years and is theoretically compulsory for 6 years. Secondary education lasts for another six years. Children are taught in their mother tongue, Dari (Persian) or Pashtu (Pashto), during the first three grades; the second official language is introduced in the fourth grade. Children are also taught Arabic so that they may be able to read the Koran (Qur'an). The school year extends from early March to early December. According to official reports, an estimated 1,312,197 pupils were enrolled in primary schools in 1995. UNESCO reports that in 1993 29% of the children in this age group (boys 42% and girls 14%) attended school. In 1995 secondary schools enrolled 512,851 students and employed approximately 18,000 teachers.

The University of Kabul, which is now coeducational, was founded in 1932. In 1962, a faculty of medicine was established at Jalalabad in Nangarhar Province; this faculty subsequently became the University of Nangarhar. By 1988 a total of 5 universities had been established in Afghanistan apart from 8 vocational colleges and 15 technical colleges. Teacher-training institutes have been established in the provinces of Balkh and Kandahar. In 1990 post-secondary institutions had 1,342 teaching staff and enrolled 24,333 students.

By mid-1980s, education of Afghan children in the Soviet Union and Eastern bloc countries was gaining popularity. After the collapse of communism in 1992 and the dissolution of the USSR, Afghan students were permitted by their government to continue their studies in Russia, Uzbekistan, Tajikistan, and Kazakhstan, under the terms of earlier agreements with the Soviet Union.

In 1997, the Taliban consolidated their hold on the capital city of Kabul, and set up a conservative Islamic regime. Most girls schools have been closed in Taliban-controlled areas, and it is expected that the access of female children to school will be further restricted.

44LIBRARIES AND MUSEUMS

For centuries, manuscript collections were in the hands of the rulers, local feudal lords, and renowned religious families. Printing came fairly late to Afghanistan, but with the shift from the handwritten manuscript to the printed book, various collections were formed. Kabul has a public library (1920) with 60,000 volumes, and the library of the University of Kabul has 250,000 volumes. There is a library at Kabul Polytechnic University with 6,000 volumes and a government library, at the ministry of education, also in Kabul, with 29,000 volumes.

Prior to the devastating civil war, the Kabul Museum (founded in 1922) possessed an unrivaled collection of stone heads, bas-reliefs, ivory plaques and statuettes, bronzes, mural paintings, and Buddhist material from excavations at Hadda, Bamian, Bagram, and other sites. It also contained an extensive collection of coins and a unique collection of Islamic bronzes, marble reliefs, Kusham art, and ceramics from Ghazni. In nearly a decade of warfare, however, the museum was plundered by the various armed bands, with much of its collection sold on the black market. Also in Kabul, is the Kabul University Science Museum, with an extensive zoological collection and a Pathology Museum. There are provincial museums at Bamyan, Ghazni, Herat, Mazar-i-Sharif, Maimana, and Kandahar. Major religious shrines have collections of valuable objects. Due to the chaotic political situation in the 1990s, it is impossible to determine the state of any of its collections.

45MEDIA

Limited service to principal cities and some smaller towns and villages is provided by the government-operated telegraph and telephone services. There are some 30,000 telephones currently in use. There is one public telephone in the capital city of Kabul. The phone system has access to 2 satellite earth stations, one of which is linked only to Iran. Most radio and television broadcasting originates in Kabul and is controlled by rival political factions. As of 1999, there were 6 AM and 1 FM radio station. In 1997 there was a television station in Mazar-e Sharif that reached four northern provinces, as well as a central government-operated station in Kabul and additional stations in the provinces, but it was not known if any of these stations were operative. The first television broadcast took place in 1978. As of 1997, there were 63 radios and 4 television sets per 1,000 population.

As with radio and television, Afghan newspapers and magazines are affiliated with different political factions. There are about 15 newspapers and 5 to 10 periodicals. The major newspapers, all headquartered in Kabul, (with estimated 1999 circulations) were *Anis* (25,000), published in Dari and Pashto; *Hewad* (12,200), and *New Kabul Times* (5,000), in English.

There have been reports of repressive activities on the part of political forces upon international journalists, ranging from mild intimidation to detention and physical assault. Particularly problematic have been attempts to interview female Afghans and female journalists attempting to work in Afghanistan. As of 1999, freedom of speech and the press were hampered by civil unrest and rivalry between competing factions.

46ORGANIZATIONS

Organizations to advance public aims and goals are of recent origin, and most are sponsored and directed by the government. The National Fatherland Front, consisting of tribal and political groups that support the government, was founded in June 1981 to bolster the PDPA regime.

An institute called the Pashto Tolanah promotes knowledge of Pashto literature, and the Historical Society (Anjuman-i-Tarikh) amasses information on Afghan history. The Women's Welfare Society carries on educational enterprises, provides training in handicrafts, and dispenses charitable aid, while the Maristun, a social service center, looks after children, men, and women and teaches them crafts and trades. The Red Crescent, the equivalent of the Red Cross, is active in every province. The Afghan Carpet Exporters' Guild, founded in 1987, promotes foreign trade of Afghan carpets and works for the improvement of the carpet industry.

47TOURISM, TRAVEL, AND RECREATION

The tourism industry, developed with government help in the early 1970s, has been negligible since 1979 due to internal political instability. A passport and visa are required for entrance into Afghanistan. In 1999, the UN estimated the daily cost of staying in Kabul at $70. Approximately 61% of these costs are estimated to be the price of a room in a guest house.

48FAMOUS AFGHANS

The most renowned ruler of medieval Afghanistan, Mahmud of Ghazni (971?–1030), was the Turkish creator of an empire stretching from Ray and Isfahan in Iran to Lahore in India (now in Pakistan) and from the Amu Darya (Oxus) River to the Arabian Sea. Zahir ud-Din Babur (1483–1530), a Timurid prince of Ferghana (now in the former USSR), established his base at

Kabul and from there waged campaigns leading to the expulsion of an Afghan ruling dynasty, the Lodis, from Delhi and the foundation of the Mughal Empire in India.

Many eminent figures of Arab and Persian intellectual history were born or spent their careers in what is now Afghanistan. Al-Biruni (973–1048), the great Arab encyclopedist, was born in Khiva but settled in Ghazni, where he died. Abdul Majid Majdud Sana'i (1070–1140), the first major Persian poet to employ verse for mystical and philosophical expression, was a native of Ghazni. Jalal ud-Din Rumi (1207–73), who stands at the summit of Persian poetry, was born in Balkh but migrated to Konya (Iconium) in Turkey. The last of the celebrated Persian classical poets, Abdur Rahman Jami (1414–92), was born in Khorasan but spent most of his life in Herat. So did Behzad (1450?–1520), the greatest master of Persian painting.

The founder of the state of Afghanistan was Ahmad Shah Abdali (1724–73), who changed his dynastic name to Durrani. He conquered Kashmir and Delhi and, with his capital at Kandahar, ruled over an empire that also stretched from the Amu Darya to the Arabian Sea. Dost Muhammad (1789–1863) was the founder of the Muhammadzai (Barakzai) dynasty. In a turbulent career, he both fought and made peace with the British in India, and unified the country. His grandson, Abdur Rahman Khan (1844–1901), established order after protracted civil strife. Amanullah Khan (1892–1960), who reigned from 1919 to 1929, tried social reforms aimed at Westernizing the country but was forced to abdicate. Muhammad Nadir Shah (d.1933), who was elected king by a tribal assembly in 1929, continued Amanullah's Westernization program. His son, Muhammad Zahir Shah (b.1914), was king until he was deposed by a coup in July 1973. Lieut. Gen. Sardar Muhammad Daoud Khan (1909–78), cousin and brother-in-law of King Zahir, was the leader of the coup and the founder and first president of the Republic of Afghanistan. Leaders in the violent years since the 1978 "Saur Revolution" have been Nur Muhammad Taraki (1917–79), founder of the PDPA; Hafizullah Amin (1929–79), Taraki's successor as president of the Revolutionary Council and secretary-general of the PDPA; Babrak Karmal (1929), leader of the pro-Soviet Parcham group of the PDPA and chief of state from December 1979 until May 1986; and Dr. Najibullah (1947–96), former head of the Afghan secret police who was brutally executed by the Taliban militia after they seized control of Kabul.

[49]DEPENDENCIES

Afghanistan has no territories or colonies.

[50]BIBLIOGRAPHY

Adamec, Ludwig W. *Dictionary of Afghan Wars, Revolutions, and Insurgencies.* Lanham, Md.: Scarecrow Press, 1996.

———. *Historical Dictionary of Afghanistan.* 2d ed. Lanham, Md.: Scarecrow Press, 1997.

Allchin, F. R., and N. Hammond (eds.). *The Archaeology of Afghanistan: From Earliest Times to the Timurid Period.* New York: Academic Press, 1978.

Bonner, Arthur. *Among the Afghans.* Durham, N.C.: Duke University Press, 1987.

Bradsher, Henry S. *Afghanistan and the Soviet Union.* Durham, N.C.: Duke University Press, 1985.

Clifford, Mary Louise. *The Land and People of Afghanistan.* New York: Lippincott, 1989.

Dupree, Louis. *Afghanistan.* Princeton, N.J.: Princeton University Press, 1973.

Emadi, Hafizullah. *State, Revolution, and Superpowers in Afghanistan.* New York: Praeger, 1990.

Grasselli, Gabriella. *British and American Responses to the Soviet Invasion of Afghanistan.* Aldershot, England: Dartmouth, 1996.

Giustozzi, Antonio. *War, Politics, and Society in Afghanistan, 1978–1992.* Washington, D.C.: Georgetown University Press, 2000.

Kakar, M. Hasan. *Afghanistan: The Soviet Invasion and the Afghan Response, 1979–1982.* Berkeley: University of California Press, 1995.

Magnus, Ralph H. *Afghanistan: Mullah, Marx, and Mujahid.* Boulder, Colo.: Westview Press, 1998.

Muhammad, Fayz. *Kabul under Siege: Fayz Muhammad's Account of the 1929 Uprising.* Princeton: Markus Wiener Publishers, 1999.

O'Balance, Edgar. *Afghan Wars, 1839–1992: What Britain Gave Up and the Soviet Union Lost.* New York: Barssey's, 1993.

Roy, Oliver. *Islam and Resistance in Afghanistan.* New York: Cambridge University Press, 1990.

Urban, Mark. *War in Afghanistan.* 2d ed. New York: St. Martin's Press, 1990.

AUSTRALIA

Commonwealth of Australia

CAPITAL: Canberra.

FLAG: The flag has three main features: the red, white, and blue Union Jack in the upper left quarter, indicating Australia's membership in the Commonwealth of Nations; the white five-star Southern Cross in the right half; and the white seven-pointed federal star below the Union Jack. The flag has a blue ground. Of the five stars of the Southern Cross, four have seven points and one has five points.

ANTHEM: *God Save the Queen* is reserved for regal and state occasions and whenever singing is appropriate; the national tune is *Advance Australia Fair.*

MONETARY UNIT: The Australian dollar (A$) is a paper currency of 100 cents. There are coins of 5, 10, 20, and 50 cents and 1 and 2 dollars, and notes of 5, 10, 20, 50 and 100 dollars. A$1 = US$0.62035 (US$1 = A$1.612) as of 31 March 2000.

WEIGHTS AND MEASURES: Metric weights and measures are used. The Australian proof gallon equals 1.37 US proof gallons.

HOLIDAYS: New Year's Day, 1 January; Australia Day, last Monday in January; Anzac Day, 25 April; Queen's Birthday, 2nd Monday in June; Christmas, 25 December; Boxing Day, 26 December. Numerous state holidays are also observed. Movable religious holidays include Good Friday, Easter Saturday, and Easter Monday.

TIME: Western Australia, 8 PM = noon GMT; South Australia and Northern Territory, 9:30 PM; Victoria, New South Wales, Queensland, and Tasmania, 10 PM. Summer time is one hour later in all states except Western Australia, Queensland, and the Northern Territory.

¹LOCATION, SIZE, AND EXTENT

Lying southeast of Asia, between the Pacific and Indian oceans, Australia, the world's smallest continent, is almost completely surrounded by ocean expanses. Australia is slightly smaller than the United States, with a total area of 7,686,850 sq km (2,967,909 sq mi). The five mainland states are New South Wales, 801,600 sq km (309,500 sq mi); Queensland, 1,727,200 sq km (666,900 sq mi); South Australia, 984,000 sq km (379,900 sq mi); Victoria, 227,600 sq km (87,900 sq mi); and Western Australia, 2,525,500 sq km (975,100 sq mi). The island state of Tasmania has an area of 67,800 sq km (26,200 sq mi); the Northern Territory, 1,346,200 sq km (519,800 sq mi); and the Australian Capital Territory, 2,400 sq km (900 sq mi). The country, including Tasmania, extends about 4,000 km (2,500 mi) E–W and 3,180 km (1,980 mi) N–S. Australia is bounded on the N by the Timor and Arafura seas, on the NE by the Coral Sea, on the E by the Pacific Ocean, on the SE by the Tasman Sea, and on the S and W by the Indian Ocean, with a total coastline of 25,760 km (16,007 mi). Neighboring areas include Irian Jaya (part of Indonesia) and Papua New Guinea to the north, New Zealand to the southeast, and Indonesia to the northwest.

Australia's capital city, Canberra, is located in the southeastern part of the country.

²TOPOGRAPHY

The continent of Australia is divided into four general topographic regions: (1) a low, sandy eastern coastal plain; (2) the eastern highlands, ranging from 300 to more than 2,100 m (1,000–7,000 ft) in altitude and extending from Cape York Peninsula in northern Queensland southward to Tasmania; (3) the central plains, consisting largely of a north-south series of drainage basins, including the Great Artesian Basin, which underlies about 1,751,480 sq km (676,250 sq mi) of territory and is the most extensive area of internal drainage in the world; and (4) the western plateau, covered with great deserts and "bigger plains" (regularly spaced sand ridges and rocky wastes), rising 300 to 600 m (1,000–2,000 ft) high and constituting most of the western half of the continent. Australian mountains have eroded over recent geological periods, and only about 5% of the continent is above 600 m (2,000 ft); the average elevation is less than 300 m (1,000 ft). The highest point is Mt. Kosciusko, 2,228 m (7,310 ft), in the Australian Alps of the southeastern corner of New South Wales; the lowest point is Lake Eyre in South Australia, 12 m (39 ft) below sea level. In 1983, grains of rock from Western Australia were dated at 4.1–4.2 billion years old, making them the oldest ever found on earth.

The most important river system, and the only one with a permanent, year-round flow, is formed by the Murray, Darling, and Murrumbidgee rivers in the southeast. The Murray River, Australia's largest, rises in the Australian Alps of New South Wales and flows some 2,600 km (1,600 mi) west and southwest to empty into the sea below Adelaide, South Australia. Several other rivers are important, but for the most part they carry great amounts of water in the wet season and are dry for the rest of the year. The largest lakes have no outlet and are usually dry. The coastline is smooth, with few bays or capes. The two largest sea inlets are the Gulf of Carpentaria in the north, between Arnhem Land and the Cape York Peninsula, and the Great Australian Bight in the south. The Great Barrier Reef, the longest coral reef in the world, extends for about 2,010 km (1,250 mi) off the east coast of Queensland.

³CLIMATE

Although it has a wide diversity of climatic conditions, Australia is generally warm and dry, with no extreme cold and little frost, its temperatures ranging from comfortably mild in the south to hot in the central interior and north. July mean temperatures average 9°C (48°F) in Melbourne in the southeast and 25°C (77°F) in Darwin in the north. January mean temperatures average 20°C (68°F) in Melbourne and 30°C (86°F) in Darwin. Summer readings often reach 38°C (100°F) or more in almost any area of the continent and may exceed 46°C (115°F) in interior regions. Winds are light to moderate, except along the coasts, where cyclones have occurred.

The continent is subject to great variations in rainfall, but except for a few areas rainfall is insufficient, and the rate of evaporation is high. Mean annual rainfall is 42 cm (17 in), much less than the world mean of 66 cm (26 in). About 40% of the continent is desert, and 40% is subhumid. Only about 20% has more than 76 cm (30 in) of rain annually, but these areas suffer from a long dry season, while others have too much rain. Only Tasmania, Victoria, and parts of New South Wales have enough rainfall all year round. Droughts and floods occur irregularly but frequently over large areas. On 25 December 1974, a cyclone and flood devastated most of Darwin; at least 49 people were killed, and some 20,000 were left homeless. Drought conditions became very severe in the early 1980s, leading to dust storms, fires, and multibillion-dollar crop losses. Again in 1994–95, a severe drought devastated eastern agricultural regions.

⁴FLORA AND FAUNA

Many distinctive forms of plant and animal life are found, especially in the coastal and tropical areas. There are some 500 species of eucalyptus and 600 species of acacia (wattle). Other outstanding trees are the baobab, blackwood, red cedar, coachwood, jarrah, Queensland maple, silky oak, and walnut. Native trees shed bark instead of leaves. Numerous types of wild flowers grow in the bush country, including boronia, Christmas bush, desert pea, flanner flower, Geraldton wax plant, kangaroo paw, pomaderris, and waratah. There are 470 varieties of orchids. About 400 kinds of mammals, 200 kinds of lizards, and 700 kinds of birds are indigenous. Apart from marsupials (bandicoots, kangaroos, koalas, opossums, Tasmanian devils, tree kangaroos, and wallabies), the most unusual animals are the dingo, echidna, flying fox (fruit bat), platypus, and wombat. Birds include the anhinga, bellbird, bowerbird, cassowary, emu, galah, kookaburra (laughing jackass), lyrebird, fairy penguin, rosella, and many types of cockatoos, parrots, hawks, and eagles.

Many species of trees, plants, and domestic animals have been imported, often thriving at the expense of indigenous types. Herds of wild buffalo, camels, donkeys, horses, and pigs, descendants of stock that strayed from herds imported by pioneers, roam the sparsely settled areas. The proliferation of rabbits resulted in a menace to sheep, and in 1907, a thousand-mile-long fence was built to keep rabbits out of Western Australia. Subsequently, a similar fence was erected in the east to prevent the incursion of dingos.

⁵ENVIRONMENT

The principal government institutions responsible for environmental matters are the Department of Home Affairs and Environment, the Australian Environment Council, and the Council of Nature Conservation Ministers. A national conservation strategy, developed by the states, the Northern Territory, and the federal government, in cooperation with the International Union for the Conservation of Nature and Natural Resources, the World Wildlife Fund, and the UNEP, became national policy in 1980.

The Environment Protection (Impact of Proposals) Act of 1974 establishes procedures for ensuring that environmental impact is considered in governmental decision making. The Whale Protection Act of 1981 prohibits killing, capturing, injuring, or interfering with a whale, dolphin, or porpoise within Australia's 200 mi economic zone or, beyond the zone, by Australian vessels and aircraft and their crews. The Environment Protection (Nuclear Codes) Act of 1978 mandates the development of uniform safety standards for uranium mining and milling and for the transport of radioactive materials. The Protection of the Sea (Discharge of Oil from Ships) Act of 1981 and the Protection of the Sea (Prevention of Pollution from Ships) Act of 1983 prevent or limit pollution from oil or noxious substances.

Water being a scarce resource in Australia, problems of water quality and availability are a constant concern. As of 1994, the country had only 82.3 cu mi of water supply, although safe drinking water was available to all urban and rural dwellers. A cause for concern has been the increased salinity in the Murray Valley, caused by diverting water inland from the coast for irrigation, as well as the rise in saline water tables in Western Australia, due to excessive land clearing for dry-land farming. Another significant environmental problem is inland damage due to soil erosion. The quality of the soil is also affected by salinization. As of 1993, Australia had 145 million ha of forest and woodland and had the third most extensive mangrove area in the world, covering over one million ha. In the mid-1990s Australia was among the top 20 world producers of carbon dioxide emissions from industry, which totaled 267.9 million tons per year, or 15.24 tons per capita.

During this period, 38 species of mammals, 39 species of birds, and 2,133 species of plants were threatened. Endangered or extinct species include the banded anteater, greater rabbit-eared bandicoot, Leadbeater's opossum, northern hairy-nosed wombat, woylie, bridled nail-tail wallaby, five species of turtle (western swamp, green sea, hawksbill, leatherback, and olive ridley), Tasmanian freshwater limpet, granulated Tasmanian snail, African wild ass, western ground parrot, paradise parakeet, helmeted honey eater, noisy scrub-bird, western rufous bristlebird, Lord Howe wood rail, Lord Howe currawong, small hemiphlebia damselfly, Otway stonefly, giant torrent midge, and Tasmanian torrent midge.

⁶POPULATION

Population growth in Australia between 1950 and 1986 averaged 1.45% annually; between 1987 and 1992, it was 1.51%. Annual growth from 1990–2000 was estimated at 1.1%. The actual population of Australia in 2000 was estimated at 18,950,108. An estimated 11.8% of the population is 65 years of age or older. The projected population for the year 2005 is 19,729,000 assuming a crude birthrate of 12 per 1,000 population and a death rate of 7, resulting in a natural rate of change of 0.01% for the period 2000–2005. The population rate of change between 1995 and 2000 was 1.1%.

One-third of Australia is virtually uninhabited; another third is sparsely populated. The population density in 1998 was 2 per sq km (5 per sq mi). Most of the people live in the southeast section and in other coastal areas. About 15% of the population is rural. It was estimated that 85% of the population lived in urban areas in 2000, slightly down from 86% in 1980. The national capital city, Canberra, located in the Australian Capital Territory, a specially designated area within New South Wales, had a 2000 population of 341,000. The 2000 population totals of the six state capitals were estimated as follows: Sydney, New South Wales, 3,665,000; Melbourne, Victoria, 3,094,000; Brisbane, Queensland, 1,450,000; Perth, Western Australia, 1,220,000; Adelaide, South Australia, 1,039,000; and Hobart,

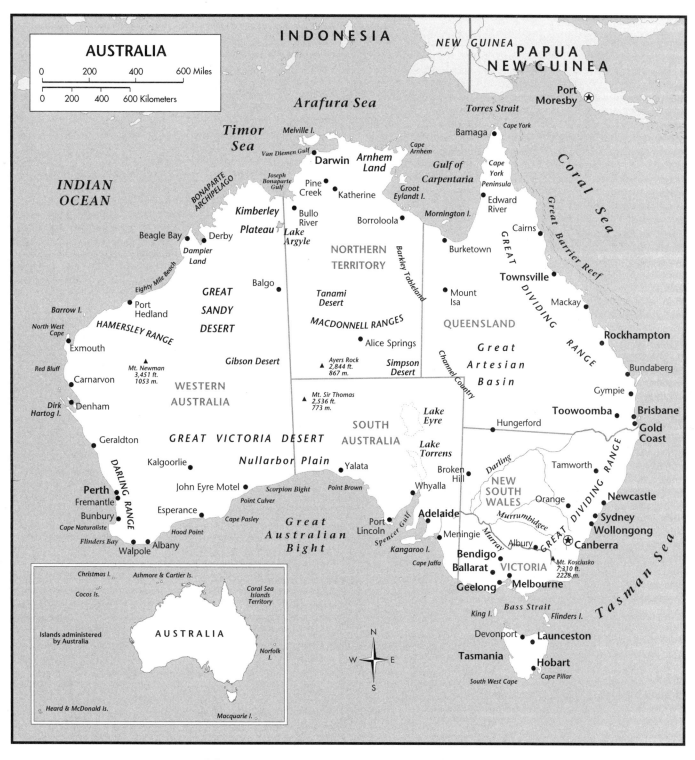

Tasmania, 183,838. Three other large cities are Newcastle, New South Wales, 433,000; Gold Coast, Queensland, 274,000; Wollongong, New South Wales, 240,000; and Geelong, Victoria, 153,000.

[7]MIGRATION

Since World War II, the government has promoted immigration of the maximum number of persons Australia can absorb without economic disequilibrium. In 1979, however, with the unemployment rate rising, the government tightened immigration requirements so that Australians would not lose jobs to the newcomers. Under the new system, assessments of applications are based on such factors as age, skills, and family ties, with priority given to reunion of families sponsored by Australian residents. In 1999, Australia was among the top three reset-tlement countries in the world, with an annual quota of 4,000 persons. This is in addition to a planned intake of 2,000 asylum-seekers on shore and 6,000 people who may be eligible for humanitarian, non-refugee visas. There is no limit to the number of refugees who may be recognized on shore.

Most of the 4.2 million immigrants to Australia between 1945 and 1985 were of working age, but although the government encouraged rural settlement, many immigrants had skills in short supply and preferred to work in the cities. The main countries of origin of such workers were the UK, Italy, and Greece. The number of permanent settlers arriving in 1991 was 116,650, up from a postwar low of 52,748 in 1975–76. The record high for new settlers was 185,099, in 1969–70. From World War II to 1991, over 460,000 refugees settled in Australia. These included more than 130,000 Indochinese. As of 1998, Australia had 61,800 refugees and 2,300 asylum-seekers.

8ETHNIC GROUPS

Most Australians are of British or Irish ancestry. In 1999, approximately 92% of the population was Caucasian. The Asian-born population tally stood at 7% while aboriginal and other groups comprised only 1% of the population.

After the coming of the Europeans, the aboriginal population declined drastically, from about 300,000–1,000,000 to some 60,000 by the early 1920s. By the 1950s, however, the decline was reversed. In the 1991 census 265,492 people identified themselves as being of aboriginal or Torres Strait Islander origin, or 1.5% of the population. (Of these, the latter numbered 26,902.) Many of them live in tribal conditions on government reservations in the north and northwest; some 39,918 were in the Northern Territory in the 1991 census and 41,792 in Western Australia. Queensland had 70,130, and New South Wales, 70,020. Their social organization is among the most complex known to anthropologists. They do not cultivate the soil but are nomadic hunters and food gatherers, without settled communities. Anthropologists believe the aboriginals, also known as Australoids, are relatively homogeneous, although they display a wide range of physical types. Their serological, or blood-group, pattern is unique, except for a faint affinity with the Paniyan of southern India and the Veddas of Sri Lanka. The aboriginals probably originated from a small isolated group subject to chance mutation but not to hybridization. There seems to be a sprinkling of Australoid groups in India, Sri Lanka, Sumatra, Timor, and New Guinea. In 1963, aboriginals were given full citizenship rights, although as a group they continued to suffer from discrimination and a lower living standard than European Australians generally.

Beginning in the 1960s, the government abandoned its previous policy of "assimilation" of the aboriginals, recognizing the uniqueness of aboriginal culture and the right of the aboriginals to determine their own patterns of development. From the passage of the Aboriginal Land Rights (Northern Territory) Act in 1976 to mid-1990, aboriginals in the Northern Territory were given ownership of about 34% of territorial lands (461,486 sq km or 178,180 sq mi). The South Australia state government and its aboriginals also signed a land-rights agreement, and similar legislation was developed in other states during the 1980s. In all, aboriginals held 647,772 sq km (250,104 sq mi) of land under freehold in mid-1989 and another 1871,801 sq km (70,193 sq mi) under leasehold. A reservation in Western Australia consisted of 202,223 sq km (78,078 sq mi). By the mid-1990s, however, more than two-thirds of the aboriginals had left rural lands to settle in urban areas.

9LANGUAGES

More than 99% of the population speaks English. There are no class variations of speech, and few if any local dialects.

Many languages or dialects are spoken by the aboriginal tribes, but phonetically they are markedly uniform. There is no written aboriginal language, but the markings on "letter sticks," sometimes carried by messengers from one tribe to another, are readily understood by tribal headmen. Aboriginal languages are in use in certain schools in the Northern Territories and, to a lesser extent, in schools of other states.

10RELIGIONS

Constitutionally, there can be no state religion or state aid to any religion; the exercise of any religion cannot be prohibited, and a religious test as qualification for public office is forbidden. However, in a 1998 report on freedom of religion in Australia by the federally funded but independent Human Rights and Equal Opportunity Commission (HREOC), the Commission stated that "despite the legal protections that apply in different jurisdictions, many Australians suffer discrimination on the basis of religious belief or non-belief, including members of both mainstream and non-mainstream religions and those of no religious persuasion." Many non-Christians have reportedly complained to the HREOC that the dominance of traditional Christianity in civic life has the ability to marginalize large numbers of citizens. As of 1999, 71% of citizens considered themselves Christians, including 27% Roman Catholic, 22% Anglican, and 22% other Christian denominations. About 17% of Australians consider themselves to have no religion, a 35% increase from 1991. Approximately 2% of Aborigines and 0.04% of all citizens practice traditional indigenous religions. Almost 72% of Aborigines practice some form of Christianity while 16% subscribe to no religion. The percentage of Aborigines who practice Christianity and who list no religion reflects almost exactly the percentages in the wider community.

11TRANSPORTATION

As of 1996, government-operated railways totaled about 38,563 km (23,961 mi). There are also some private railways, mainly for the iron ore industry in Western Australia. Australian railway systems do not interconnect well, and rail travel between principal cities involves changing trains. Modern equipment is gradually replacing older stock. As of August 1991, all interstate freight movements by rail were brought under the control of the National Rail Corporation (NRC).

Highways provide access to many districts not served by railroads. As of 1998 there were 913,000 km (567,338 mi) of roads, about 353,331 km (219,560 mi) of which were paved. Motor vehicles in 1995 totaled about 11,207,000, including 9,010,000 passenger cars and 2,197,000 commercial trucks, buses, and taxis.

Inland water transport is negligible, but ocean shipping is important for domestic and overseas transport. Most overseas trade is carried in non-Australian ships, while most coastwise vessels are of Australian registry. Although the fine natural harbors of Sydney and Hobart can readily accommodate ships of 11 m (36 ft) draft, many other harbors have been artificially developed. Other international shipping ports include Adelaide, Brisbane, Cairns, Darwin, Devonport, Fremantle, Geelong, Launceston, Mackay, Melbourne, and Townsville. All main ports have ample wharfage, modern cargo-handling equipment, and storage facilities. There are some 70 commercially significant ports. The nation's merchant marine in 1998 included 57 vessels of 1,000 GRT or over, with a combined GRT of 1,767,387.

Australia had 408 airports in 1998, 262 of which had paved runways. Principal airports include Adelaide, Brisbane, Cairns, Darwin, Melbourne International at Melbourne, Perth International at Perth, and Kingsford International at Sydney. In 1997, the government began privatizing many of the country's airports. The first round of such sales early in 1997 included the Melbourne, Brisbane, and Perth airports, which raised A$3.34

billion (US$2.5 billion)—far exceeding government projections. The main Sydney airport was explicitly excluded from the privatization plan. Domestic air services are operated primarily by the privately owned Ansett Airlines. The Australian overseas airline, Qantas, carries more than three million passengers per year to and from Australia, nearly 40% of the total carried by all airlines serving Australia. The airline was owned by the Commonwealth government until it was privatized in 1995. In 1997 Australian air carriers performed 75,873,000 passenger-km (47,147,482 passenger-mi) and 1,954,000 freight ton-km (1,214,216 freight

12HISTORY

Stone objects that were found in 1978 but are still only tentatively dated suggest that human beings may have inhabited what is now Australia as long as 100,000 years ago. The aboriginals migrated to Australia from Southeast Asia at least 40,000 years before the first Europeans arrived on the island continent. In 1999, scientists estimated a male skeleton found at Mungo Lake in 1974 to be between 56,000 and 68,000 years old. Covered in red ochre, this skeleton presents the first known use of pigments for religious or artistic purposes. Living as hunters and gatherers, roaming in separate family groups or bands, the aboriginals developed a rich, complex culture, with many languages. They numbered approximately 300,000 by the 18th century; however, with the onset of European settlement, conflict and disease reduced their numbers.

Although maps of the 16th century indicate European awareness of the location of Australia, the first recorded explorations of the continent by Europeans took place early in the 17th century, when Dutch, Portuguese, and Spanish explorers sailed along the coast and discovered what is now Tasmania. None took formal possession of the land, and not until 1770, when Capt. James Cook charted the east coast and claimed possession in the name of Great Britain, was any major exploration undertaken. Up to the early 19th century, the area was known as New Holland, New South Wales, or Botany Bay.

The first settlement—a British penal colony at Port Jackson (now Sydney) in 1788—was soon enlarged by additional shipments of prisoners, which continued through the mid 1800's, until approximately 161,000 convicts had been transported. With the increase of free settlers, the country developed, the interior was penetrated, and six colonies were created: New South Wales in 1786, Van Diemen's Land in 1825 (renamed Tasmania in 1856), Western Australia in 1829, South Australia in 1834, Victoria in 1851, and Queensland in 1859.

Sheep raising and wheat growing were introduced and soon became the backbone of the economy. The wool industry made rapid progress during the period of squatting migration, which began on a large scale about 1820. The grazers followed in the wake of explorers, reaching new pastures, or "runs," where they squatted and built their homes. Exports of wool increased from 111 kg (245 lb) in 1807 to 1.1 million kg (2.4 million lb) in 1831. With the increased flow of immigrants following the Ripon Land Regulations of 1831, the population grew from about 34,000 in 1820 to some 405,000 in 1850. The discovery of gold in Victoria (1851) attracted thousands, and in a few years the population had quadrupled. Under the stimulus of gold production, the first railway line—Melbourne to Port Melbourne—was completed in 1854. Representative government spread throughout the continent, and the colonies acquired their own parliaments.

Until the end of the 19th century, Australia's six self-governing colonies remained separate. However, the obvious advantages of common defense and irrigation led to the federation of the states into the Commonwealth of Australia in 1901. (The British Parliament had approved a constitution in the previous year.) The Northern Territory, which belonged to South Australia, became a separate part of the Commonwealth in 1911. In the same year,

territory was acquired from New South Wales for a new capital at Canberra, and in 1927, the Australian Parliament began meeting there. Liberal legislation provided for free and compulsory education, industrial conciliation and arbitration, the secret ballot, female suffrage, old age pensions, invalid pensions, and maternity allowances (all before World War I). Child subsidies and unemployment and disability benefits were introduced during World War II.

Australian forces fought along with the British in Europe during World War I. In World War II, the Australian forces supported the UK in the Middle East between 1940 and 1942, and played a major role in the Pacific theater after the Japanese attack on Pearl Harbor. After the war, a period of intense immigration began. The Labour government was voted out of office in 1949, beginning 23 years of continuous rule by a Liberal-Country Party (now known as the National Party) coalition. During that period, Australian foreign policy stressed collective security and support for the US presence in Asia. Australian troops served in Vietnam between 1965 and 1971.

When Labour returned to power in December 1972, it began the process of dissociating Australia from US and UK policies and strengthening ties with non-Communist Asian nations; in addition, it established diplomatic relations with the People's Republic of China. In 1975 a constitutional crisis resulted when Senate opposition successfully blocked the Labour Party's budgetary measures, thereby threatening the government with bankruptcy. The governor-general dismissed the Labour Prime Minister, Gough Whitlam, and called for new elections. The Liberal National Party coalition swept back into power, where it remained until 1983. The Australian Labour Party (ALP) returned to power in 1983, following a campaign in which such economic issues as unemployment and inflation predominated.

In 1993, the Mabo Ruling on Native Title recognized the land rights of the indigenous people (Aborigines) inhabiting Australia prior to the arrival of the Europeans. The Mabo Ruling did not void existing leases, but could allow the Aborigines to reclaim land when the leases granted by the national or state governments expired. The Mabo Ruling applied only to non-pastoral leases, but the Wik Judgment of 1996 extended the land rights of indigenous people to include their use of pastoral land for religious purposes.

In the March 1996 elections, the ALP was unseated by a coalition of the Liberal Party and the National Party, who chose Liberal MP John Howard to be Prime Minister. The newcomer Howard pledged to change the government, to make it more "rational." To that end, he cut ministries and cabinet posts, made budget cuts affecting higher education, Aborigine affairs, and jobs, and instituted an A$15 billion privatization program. Many government employees opposed these changes; violent demonstrations took place when the budget was made public. While the revised budget was less radical, social unrest continued through 1997–1998, and the October 1998 election found Howard's coalition party's majority greatly reduced, while the ALP gained in influence, winning 18 more seats than it did in the 1996 election.

In July 1998, after twice being rejected by the Senate, the government passed amendments to the 1993 Native Title Act. The amendments removed the time limit for lodging native claims, but weakened the right of Aboriginal groups to negotiate with non-Aboriginal leaseholders concerning land use.

In September 1999, Australian troops led the United Nations-sanctioned peacekeeping forces into East Timor, to protect civilians and control the militia violence following East Timor's referendum decision to seek full independence from Indonesia. Earlier that year, Indonesia cancelled its security treaty with Australia.

13 GOVERNMENT

The Commonwealth of Australia, an independent, self-governing nation within the Commonwealth of Nations, has a federal parliamentary government. The federation was formed on 1 January 1901 from six former British colonies, which thereupon became states. The constitution combines the traditions of British parliamentary practice with important elements of the US federal system. Powers of the federal government are enumerated and limited.

The government consists of the British sovereign, represented by a governor-general, and the Australian Parliament. Sir William Deane became the new Governor-General in February 1996, succeeding The Honorable William Hayden, who had held the post since 1986. Nominally, executive power is vested in the governor-general and an executive council, which gives legal form to cabinet decisions; in practice, however, it is normally exercised by a cabinet chosen and presided over by a prime minister, representing the political party or coalition with a majority in the House of Representatives. The number of cabinet ministers is variable.

Legislative power is vested in the Parliament, which is composed of a 76-member Senate, representing the states and territories, and a 148-member House of Representatives, representing electoral districts. Members must be Australian citizens of full age, possess electoral qualification, and have resided for three years in Australia. Twelve senators are elected by proportional representation from each state voting as a single electorate, and two senators each from the Northern Territory and Capital Territory. They are elected for six years, with half the members retiring at the end of every third year. House membership is not quite double that of the Senate, with a minimum of five representatives for each state. House members are elected according to population by preferential voting in specific electoral districts; they serve for three years, unless the House is dissolved sooner. There are two members from the Australian Capital Territory and one from the Northern Territory; they have been able to vote on all questions since 1968. Parliament must meet at least once a year. Taxation and appropriation measures must be introduced in the lower house; the Senate has the power to propose amendments, except to money bills, and to defeat any measure it may choose.

The parties in the House elect their leaders in caucus. The party or coalition with a majority of seats forms the government. The leader of the majority party becomes prime minister and selects his cabinet from members of his party who are members of Parliament, while the leader of the principal minority party becomes leader of the official opposition. The party in power holds office as long as it retains its majority or until the governor-general decides that new elections are necessary; he exercised this inherent constitutional power during the 1975 crisis when he dismissed Prime Minister Whitlam and called for new elections.

In the 1990's, the Labour Government, under the leadership of Prime Minister Paul Keating, proposed a referendum to change Australia to a republican form of government. The idea gained wide support. After the 1996 federal elections, the coalition majority decided to host a constitutional convention to decide the issue. The constitutional convention met in February 1998, and voted in favor of replacing the British monarch as the head of Australia's government (73 voted in favor, 57 against), and Australia becoming a republic by the year 2001 (89 voted in favor, 52 against). But in November 1999's popular referendum, the proposal to convert Australia to a republic failed to carry even a single state.

Suffrage is universal for all persons 18 years of age and older, subject to citizenship and certain residence requirements. Voting is compulsory in national and state parliamentary elections.

14 POLITICAL PARTIES

Since most Australians have been shaped by the same language and by a similar cultural and religious heritage, their internal differences are largely based on economic issues. Attachments to the UK are compounded of sentiment, tradition, and economic advantage. Australian nationalism has been associated more closely with the Australian Labour Party (ALP) than with its rivals, who tend to regard Australian interests as almost identical with those of the UK. Because of Australia's geographical position as a "European people on an Asian limb," the economic element in its nationalism has been mixed with the fear of external conquest or domination.

Except in 1929–31, when a Labour government was in office, interwar governments were dominated by non-Labour groupings. When war seemed certain in 1939, the government was resolutely imperial, considering Australia to be at war automatically when the UK went to war. The Labourites challenged this view. While they did not not oppose a declaration of war on Germany, they wanted the step to be taken so as to show Australia's independence.

Labour was in office from 1941 to 1949. The Liberal and Country Parties were in office as a coalition for a long period afterward, from 1949 to 1972, and again beginning in December 1975 (by that time, the Country Party had become the National Country Party, and it later became the National Party).

In the general elections of 13 December 1975, a caretaker government, formed the preceding month by the Liberal-National Country Party coalition after the dismissal of the Labour government of Prime Minister Gough Whitlam, obtained large majorities in both houses of the legislature. Although its majorities were eroded in the elections of December 1977 and October 1980, the coalition remained in power until March 1983, when Labour won 75 out of 147 seats in the House of Representatives. Robert Hawke, leader of the Labour Party, took office as Prime Minister; he was reelected in 1984, 1987, and 1990. Paul Keating replaced Hawke as Labour's leader, and as Prime Minister, in December 1991. This was the first time an Australian Prime Minister had been ousted by his own party. Keating led the ALP to an unprecedented fifth consecutive election victory in the 1993 general election, increasing both its percentage share of the vote and its number of seats in the legislature. In 1996, a Liberal-National Party coalition headed by John Howard ousted the ALP from the majority, with the Liberal-National coalition winning 94 seats compared to the ALP's 49 seats.

A direct descendant of the governments of the 1920s and 1930s, the Liberal-National coalition is principally linked with business (Liberal) and farming (National) and is officially anti-socialist. In economic and foreign affairs, its outlook is still involved with the Commonwealth of Nations, but it supports the UN, as well as the alliance with the US in the ANZUS pact. It is sympathetic toward the new Asian countries and values the link with these countries afforded by the Colombo Plan. The Labour Party is a trade-union party, officially socialist in policy and outlook. It initially maintained an isolationist posture, but since the early 1940s, its policy has been a mixture of nationalism and internationalism.

Smaller parties include the Democratic Labour Party, the Communist Party, the Australian Democrats Party, the Green Party, and the One Nation Party. Since its formation in 1997, the One Nation Party's platform has featured racial issues. In the 1998 Queensland state elections, it won 11 of 89 seats. In the federal elections of that same year, the One Nation Party called for an end to Asian immigration and a restriction to Aboriginal welfare programs, but failed to win any seats.

¹⁵LOCAL GOVERNMENT

Powers not specifically granted to the federal government in the constitution are reserved to the states, although some powers (such as health, labor, and social services) are held concurrently. Each state has an appointed governor who serves as the representative of the sovereign. Except for Queensland, which has a unicameral legislature, the parliament in each state is composed of two houses. The lower houses—the dominant legislative bodies—are popularly elected; the upper houses are elected by franchise limited to property holders and to those with certain academic or professional qualifications. The state prime minister achieves office and selects his cabinet in the same fashion as does the Commonwealth prime minister. The Northern Territory, which became self-governing in 1978, has a unicameral legislature.

Local communities (variously designated as boroughs, cities, district councils, municipalities, road districts, shires, and towns) have limited powers of government, but they are responsible for some health, sanitation, light, gas, and highway undertakings. Even the largest cities do not provide their own police protection, nor do they conduct or support education; these are state functions. Local aldermen or councilors ordinarily are elected on a property franchise, and mayors are elected annually or biennially by the aldermen from among their own number or by taxpayers. State departments of local government regulate the organization of local government. State governments directly control some large interior areas.

¹⁶JUDICIAL SYSTEM

The Constitution vests federal jurisdiction in a High Court of Australia which consists of a Chief Justice and six Associate Justices appointed by the General Governor. The High Court has the authority to conduct constitutional review of state and federal legislation and is the supreme authority on constitutional interpretation. The High Court also has original jurisdiction over interstate and international matters.

Until 1985, in certain cases involving state law, appeals from courts below the High Court could be taken to the Privy Council in the UK, the final court of the Commonwealth of Nations. Special cases may be referred to a 25-member federal court that deals with commercial law, copyright law, taxation, and trade practices. There is also a family court.

States and territories have their own court systems. Cases in the first instance are tried in local or circuit courts of general and petty sessions, magistrates' courts, children's courts, or higher state courts. Capital crimes are tried before state supreme courts.

The state and federal courts are fully independent. The High Court has recently ruled that indigent defendants have a right to counsel at state expense. Criminal defendants are presumed innocent, and a plethora of due process rights include the right to confront witnesses and the right to appeal.

The law provides for the right to a fair trial. In local courts, the magistrates sit alone. In the higher courts, trials are usually conducted by judge and jury. The law prohibits arbitrary interference with privacy, family, home, or correspondence.

¹⁷ARMED FORCES

The all-volunteer Australian armed forces numbered 55,200 in 2000. The army had an official strength of 25,200; the navy, 14,200; the air force, 15,800; and reserve forces, 27,730, for all three services. The active forces include 7,400 women. Military weapons systems included 71 Leopard 1A3 main battle tanks, 4 submarines, 3 destroyers, 8 frigates, 126 airforce combat aircraft, and 16 navy armed helicopters. One infantry company (reinforced) serves in Malaysia, another small task force in Papua New Guinea, and around 200 personnel on UN missions.

Australia's defense expenditure in 1997–98 was $6.9 billion, 1.9% of GNP.

¹⁸INTERNATIONAL COOPERATION

Australia is a charter member of the UN, to which it gained admission on 1 November 1945. It belongs to ESCAP and all the nonregional specialized agencies and is a signatory to the Law of the Sea and a member of the WTO. Australia also participates in the Commonwealth of Nations and ANZUS, as well as the Asian Development Bank, Colombo Plan, OECD, South Pacific Commission, South Pacific Forum, and other intergovernmental organizations.

¹⁹ECONOMY

Wool, food, and minerals provide raw materials for home processing industries and around two-thirds of foreign earnings. Australia grows all needed basic foodstuffs and has large surpluses for export. Australia is the world's largest wool-producing country, as well as one of the world's great wheat exporters, and also exports large quantities of meat and dairy products. The wool industry faces competition from synthetic fibers. The country is also a major world supplier of iron ore, bauxite, lead, zinc, and copper; coal, beach sand minerals, and nickel have become major industries as well. Since the 1960s manufactured goods have provided an ever-increasing share of the country's exports. Heavy-industry expansion has taken place at a rapid pace, with steel output more than quadrupling from 1960 to 1970; by the 1980s, however, Australian steel was facing stiff competition from abroad, and production was stagnating. The 1998 Asian financial crisis caused a distinct downturn in export revenues from heavy industry averaging -5%.

Australia's economy began to recover from a 1990 recession in mid-1991. Economic growth, supported by rising consumption and higher export demand, reached 4% in the fourth quarter of 1993. However, the unemployment rate of about 11% was near a postwar record. By 1995, unemployment had dropped to 8.5%; and had fallen to 7.5% by 1999. Growth, after hitting 5.4% in 1994, fell to a modest 3.1% in 1995, but rose to 4.7% in 1998. Growth was at 3.9% in 1999. Australia's economy as a whole weathered the Asian financial crisis of 1998 well, due to reforms that included a currency depreciation and the redirection of exports to non-Asian countries. Sixty percent of Australia's exports go to Asia, accounting for almost 10% of the GDP. Throughout the 1990s, growth averaged 3%.

²⁰INCOME

The US Central Intelligence Agency (CIA) reports that in 1998 Australia's gross domestic product (GDP) was estimated at $3.94 trillion. The per capita GDP was estimated at $21,200. The annual growth rate of GDP was estimated at 4.5%. The average inflation rate in 1998 was 1%. The CIA defines GDP as the value of all final goods and services produced within a nation in a given year and computed on the basis of purchasing power parity (PPP) rather than value as measured on the basis of the rate of exchange. It was estimated that agriculture accounted for 4% of GDP, industry 31%, and services 65%.

The World Bank reports that for the same period per capita private consumption (in PPP terms) was $14,890. Private consumption includes expenditures of individuals, households, and nongovernmental organizations. It was estimated that between 1990 and 1998 private consumption grew at an annual rate of 3.7%. Approximately 24% of household consumption was spent on food, 9% on fuel, 2% on health care, and 16% on education. The richest 10% of the population accounted for approximately 25% of household consumption and the poorest 10% approximately 2.0%.

21 LABOR

As of 1998, the Australian work force was 9,343,000 of whom 5.3 million were men. From 1966/67 to 1985/86, the work force grew faster than the population, primarily because of increasing participation by women and immigrants. During this period, the proportion of women in the labor force to the total adult female population increased from 31% to 46%. From 1989 to 1995, however, the population grew on average by 1.2% per year, while the labor force expanded by only 1.0% annually. In 1995, women made up 42.8% of the economically active population. Unemployment averaged 9.8% during 1994 and fell to 7.5% in 1999. The 1997 occupational pattern was as follows: services 73%, industry 22%, and agriculture 5%.

As in many other highly developed industrial nations, union membership has declined significantly: from around 53% of the work force in 1980 to 32% as of 1999. The drop has resulted in a consolidation of labor unions: there were 300 unions in 1989 but only 188 in 1993. The traditionally de facto right to strike was legalized in 1994.

Awards by federal and state industrial tribunals contain minimum or award rates of pay, extended to women in 1974. Although there is a standard minimum wage, 80% of workers have their pay determined by minimums that applied to their particular industry or profession. The standard workweek is under 40 hours, generally from Monday through Friday. Nearly all Australian workers receive four weeks of annual vacation, many at rates of pay 17.5% above regular pay.

22 AGRICULTURE

Australia is an important producer and exporter of agricultural products and a major world supplier of cereals, sugar, and fruit. Arable land in 1994 comprised about 53.1 million ha (131.2 million acres), representing about 6.9% of total land area. However, approximately 90% of the utilized land area is in its natural state or capable of only limited improvement and is used largely for rough grazing. Droughts, fires, and floods are common hazards. The area actively cultivated for crops is less than 3.6% of all utilized land. Lack of water is the principal limiting factor, but unsuitable soil and topography are also important determinants. As of 1997, some 2,700,000 ha (6,672,000 acres) of land were irrigated. Agriculture has declined from 20% of GDP in the 1950s to about 3% in 1998. Agricultural exports, which accounted for 60% of Australia's exports in the 1960s, now account for 29%. Total crop value in 1997/98 was at A$13,493 million, with New South Wales and Queensland accounting for half of the total value.

Grain crops have been cultivated since the first year of European settlement. In November 1790, plantings around Sydney of wheat, barley, and corn totaled 34 ha (84 acres). Today, winter cereals are cultivated in all states. Three cereals are often grown on one farm for grain, green fodder, and hay for livestock. Most wheat and barley and about half the oats are grown for grain. The estimated wheat area sown for grain decreased from 11,135,000 ha (27,515,000 acres) in 1986/87 to 10,439,000 ha (25,792,000 acres) in 1997/98. Production of wheat in 1997/98 was an estimated 19,224,000 tons. Western Australia and New South Wales are the chief wheat-producing states. In 1997/98, Australia produced 6,482,000 tons of barley, 1,634,000 tons of oats, and 1,324,000 tons of rice. In 1997/98, 272,000 tons of corn and 1,372,000 tons of potatoes were produced.

Sugarcane is grown along a 2,000 km (1,200 mi) stretch of coastal land in New South Wales and Queensland. About 95% of sugar production comes from Queensland. A normal crushing season is from June to December. The estimated 1997/98 harvest from 394,000 ha (974,000 acres), yielded about 36.8 million tons of sugar cane. The industry faces problems of excessive supply and price elasticity; sugar is sold primarily to Japan, the US, Canada, South Korea, Malaysia, China, and Singapore. In 1997/98, sugar exports were estimated to have amounted to $1.18 billion. Although tobacco growing is a relatively small industry, it is important in some areas. In 1997/98, some 4,000 ha (7,400 acres) were planted with tobacco, and about 8,000 tons were produced.

Cotton has been grown in the coastal river valleys of Queensland for more than a century but on a limited scale, and it has provided only a small percentage of Australia's lint requirements. In the 1980s, however, successful development of cotton-growing areas in New South Wales and Western Australia has resulted in spectacular production increases. In 1985/86, 685,000 tons of cotton were produced (almost triple the amount in 1979/80); in 1997/98, production amounted to 593,000 tons.

Australia's wide climate differences permit the cultivation of a range of fruits, from pineapples in the tropical zone to berry fruits in the cooler areas of temperate zones. In 1997/98, orchard fruit trees included orange, 7.8 million; apple, 9.7 million; pear, 1.5 million; and peach, 1 million. About 12.2 million ha (30.1 million acres) were cultivated for bananas and 4.8 million ha (11.9 million acres) for pineapples in 1997/98. Production of fruit in 1998 included (in thousands of tons): oranges, 369; bananas, 215; pineapples, 123; pears, 172; peaches, 96; tangerines, 74; lemons and limes, 39; apricots, 27; grapefruit, 22; mangoes, 35; and plums, 33. Australia's wine industry is also growing; viticulture engaged 99,000 ha (245,000 acres) and produced 1,112,000 tons of grapes for winemaking, drying, and other uses in 1997/98, valued at over A$1 billion.

23 ANIMAL HUSBANDRY

About 54% of Australia's land is used in stock raising. Animal husbandry is concentrated in the eastern highlands, but it spreads across the wide interior spaces and even to low-rainfall areas, in which up to 12 ha (30 acres) are required to support one sheep and from which cattle must be taken overland hundreds of miles to coastal meat-packing plants.

Sheep raising has been a mainstay of the economy since the 1820s, when mechanization of the British textile industry created a huge demand for wool. In 1850 there were 17.5 million sheep in Australia; by 1894, some 100 million; and in 1970, a record high of some 180 million. Sheep numbers fell to 120 million in 1994/95 (the lowest since 1953/54) due to severe drought. Australia's flocks, some 117.5 million in 1998, now constitute approximately 14% of the world's sheep but produce about 30% of the world's wool supply. Wool production, the largest in the world, was an estimated 655,000 tons in 1997/98, with a gross value of A$2.75 billion. About 95% is exported (mostly to China); nevertheless, wool, which represented 50% of Australia's merchandise exports (by value) in 1957/58, constituted only 6% by the mid-1990s. Since 1990, wool production has fallen by 35%, due in part to declining world demand. Australia produces about one-third of the world's wool, and accounts for 75% of the world's exports of wool apparel. During periods of great drought, such as the early 1980s, the number of sheep has diminished by 40 million or more. (A drop of 60 million occurred in the droughts of 1993/94.) In the better lands, however, animal husbandry ranks high on a world scale. Large, scientifically managed stations have produced some of the world's finest stock. Sheep of the Merino breed, noted for its heavy wool yield, make up about three-quarters of Australian flocks.

In 1998 there were an estimated 2.7 million hogs and 26.7 million head of cattle. In the same year, meat production totaled an estimated 3,517,000 tons. Of these, beef and veal constituted 1,955,000 tons; poultry, 573,000 tons; mutton and lamb,

615,000 tons; and ham, pork, and bacon, 343,000 tons. Butter production in 1998 (in factories) amounted to an estimated 161,000 tons; whole milk was estimated 9.7 million tons; and cheese (factory production) was about 295,000 tons. Milk production is expected to slow in 2000, when the government implements a dairy deregulation plan that will remove price supports. Egg production is around 190,000 tons per year, predominantly for domestic consumption. Australia produces some 25,000 to 30,000 tons of honey per year, half of which is exported. Beef exports in 1997 were $1.84 billion. Nearly 60% of total beef production is exported annually, most of it going to the US, South Korea, and Taiwan.

24FISHING

Fishing is relatively unimportant, even though the Australian Fishing Zone is the third largest in the world. Even with a low per capita fish consumption, Australia must import about half its normal requirements. Pearl and other shell fishing are relatively significant. The 1997 catch of fish, crustaceans, and mollusks totaled 235,624 tons, 98% from marine waters. Exports of fishery products in 1997 were valued at $949,213,000.

25FORESTRY

Forests and woodlands cover 145 million ha (358 million acres), or about 19% of the total land area; most timberland is neither exploited nor potentially exploitable. Native forests cover 43.2 million ha (106.7 million acres), of which 26.6% is state forest, 26.2% is privately owned, 24.5% is crown land, and 22.7% is in permanent national parks or reserves. About 60% of the state forest areas are available for sustainable logging; crown lands are mostly leased for cattle grazing with limited timber production. Native forests consist principally of hardwood and other fine cabinet and veneer timbers; eucalyptus dominates about 35 million ha (86.5 million acres). Limited softwood resources had become seriously depleted, but new plantations were established in the 1980s at a rate of 33,000 ha (81,500 acres) annually. Softwood plantations supply more than half the timber harvested annually. Plantation forests cover 1,118,823 ha (2,764,612 acres), of which 86% is coniferous. Although Australia is a net importer of forest products, the forest and wood products industries contribute 2% to GDP and employed about 62,000 in 1998.

Roundwood production in 1997 totaled about 23 million cu m, with exports of 8 million cu m. There was a 4% increase in roundwood production in 1997–98. Some 20.3 million metric tons of forest products were produced in 1997–98. Australia's leading forest products are softwood logs and chips. Whereas all of the softwood log production is consumed at home, all commercial woodchip production is exported. National parks and wildlife preserves occupy about 3.8 million ha (9.4 million acres), or 9% of the total forestlands. Extensive reforestation—62,000 ha (153,000 acres) annually during the 1980s—has been undertaken to combat soil erosion. Since hardwoods grow slowly, Australia will probably have to import a great deal of lumber in future years to meet its timber needs.

26MINING

More than 60 varieties of minerals and metals have been commercially produced in Australia, and successful exploration in the late 1960s led to a long-term mineral boom and a sharp increase in exports. Today Australia is the world's third-largest leading producer of minerals and metals. In 1997 the country was the world's leading producer of alumina, bauxite, chrysoprase, diamonds, ilmenite, monazite, opal, rutile, sapphire, and zircon, and the second-largest producer of mined zinc and lead. In addition, Australia is the third leading producer of iron ore and mined gold; fourth in cobalt and uranium; fifth in aluminum,

coal, copper, nickel, and silver. Australia is the world's leading exporter of alumina, coal, ilmenite, iron ore, refined lead, monazite, rutile, and zircon. Exports of mineral resources (including fuels) accounted for 60% of total exports in 1997/98. Australia exports about 70% of its coal production, accounting for about 35% of world coal trade. After coal, gold is the country's second-largest export earner. Gold production in 1997 reached a record 311 tons, increasing almost 8% over the previous year.

Australia possesses about 474,000 tons of recoverable uranium. Bauxite deposits in northern Queensland are among the world's largest, and bauxite deposits in the Northern Territory are also in production. The Argyle diamond mine, near the shores of Lake Argyle in Western Australia, began production in 1984; the largest diamond mine in the world, it can supply some 40 million carats a year; in 1994, about 5% of production was of gem quality, including a small number of very rare pink diamonds. Production of iron ore was 157,766 million tons in 1997. In the same year, reported production of alumina was 13.4 million tons; zinc, 1,035,000 tons; lead, 531,000 tons; copper, 560,000 tons; and nickel, 124,000 tons. Among mineral sands, 1994 production of ilmenite concentrates was 2,233,000 tons; zirconium concentrates, 424,000 tons; and rutile concentrates, 235,000 tons.

In 1997, the mining industry accounted for 6.5% of the Australian economy, or US$23.3 billion, with metallic minerals contributing an estimated 40% and industrial minerals 5%.

27ENERGY AND POWER

Between 1982/83 and 1993/94, energy consumption increased 36% for industrial, commercial, and residential use, according to the Australian Bureau of Statistics. Because of its relatively scant hydroelectric resources and only recently discovered oil, Australia has had to rely on coal-burning steam plants for about three-quarters of its public power requirements. The remainder has been supplied by hydroelectricity, gas turbines, and internal combustion generators. Net installed electrical capacity in 1998 was 38.5 million kW; power generation in 1998 totaled 186,387 million kWh.

Major electric power undertakings, originally privately owned and operated, were by 1952 under the control of state organizations. In the early 1990s however, many of the Australian state governments began privatizing sections of their energy utilities. Manufacturing has been developed most extensively in or near coal areas, and distribution of electricity to principal users is therefore relatively simple. All major cities except Perth use 240-volt, 50-cycle, three-phase alternating current; Perth has 250-volt, 40-cycle, single-phase alternating current.

The Snowy Mountains hydroelectric scheme in southeast New South Wales, Australia's most ambitious public works project, comprises seven power stations, a pumping station, 16 large and many smaller dams, and 145 km (90 mi) of tunnels and 80 km (50 mi) of aqueducts. It provides electricity to the Australian Capital Territory, New South Wales, and Victoria. The project took 25 years to complete and has a generating capacity of 3,740 MW (about 10% of Australia's total generating capacity). The Snowy Mountains scheme and other large power projects in New South Wales, Victoria, and Tasmania have greatly increased the nation's aggregate installed capacity. The only state with water resources sufficient for continuous operation of large hydro-electric power stations is Tasmania, which possesses about 50% of Australia's hydroelectric energy potential. Production and use of such power is on the increase throughout the country, however.

Since 1984, Australia has been the world's largest exporter of coal. In that time exports have doubled, reaching 162 million tons by 1997. Exports account for about 56% of total coal production. The major market is Japan, which imports about 50% of Australia's coal exports. Production in 1997 amounted to 293 million tons, of which around 80% was bituminous and 20% was lignite. New South Wales and Queensland account for more than 95% of Australia's black coal production and virtually all its exports; about 70% of annual coal production is exported. Australia has over 55 billion tons of recoverable reserves of bituminous coal, an amount that could satisfy production levels for about 260 years at current levels of demand. In early 1983, Alcoa Australia signed a contract with the Western Australian State Energy Commission, at an estimated cost of A$11.2 billion, for supplying natural gas from the Northwest Shelf (the North West Gas Shelf Project--NWGSP). In 1985, eight Japanese companies agreed to buy 5.84 million tons of liquefied natural gas a year from 1989 to 2009. Capacity increased in 1995 from the completion of additional offshore platform and onshore facilities. The $4 billion expansion of the North West Shelf LNG Project, slated for completion by 2003, will add seven million tons to LNG production. In early 1992, petroleum exploration began in the Timor Sea; the area had been off limits for over a decade in order to establish a zone of cooperation with Indonesia. Total gas reserves amounted to 20,100 billion cu m in 1996; production in 1998 was 30,575 million cu m. Oil production, which began in 1964, totaled 629,000 barrels per day in 1998; reserves in 1999 were estimated at 2.9 billion barrels, a figure nearly double that for 1996, thanks to a record amount of exploration activity and the resulting new discoveries. Commercially exploitable uranium reserves are estimated at 474,000 tons.

28INDUSTRY

In proportion to its total population, Australia is one of the world's most highly industrialized countries. The manufacturing sector has undergone significant expansion in recent years and turns out goods ranging from automobiles to chemicals and textiles. The leading industries are food processing, beverages, motor vehicles, metalworking, and paper and paper products. In 1995, manufacturing accounted for $48.8 billion, or about 15% of GDP. This figure had risen to 14% of GDP by 1998. Industry as a whole, which accounted for 31% of the GDP, grew by an annual average of 1.3% between 1987 and 1997. The Asian crisis caused metals and machinery and equipment sales to fall by about 5% in 1998; but the food and beverages, petrochemicals, and printing industries averaged growth of 6%.

Australia is self-sufficient in beverages, most foods, building materials, many common chemicals, some domestic electrical appliances, radios, plastics, textiles, and clothing; in addition, most of its needed communications equipment, farm machinery (except tractors), furniture, leather goods, and metal manufactures are domestically produced. Recent years have seen the rapid growth of high-tech industries including aircraft, communications and other electronic equipment, electrical appliances and machinery, pharmaceuticals, and scientific equipment, and the government has supported the growth of these new sectors. High-tech industry contributes a substantial amount to the economy, with an annual growth rate of 20% expected until 2010. Many manufacturing companies are closely connected—financially and technically—with manufacturers in the EU, the US, or Asia.

29SCIENCE AND TECHNOLOGY

Two organizations support most of Australian government research and development. The Commonwealth Scientific and Industrial Research Organization (CSIRO), headquartered in Melbourne and founded in 1926, is an independent government agency that supports research and development in all fields of the physical and biological sciences except defense science, nuclear energy, and clinical medicine. The Defense Science and Technology Organization (DSTO), headquartered in Canberra, supports military research and development by providing scientific and technological assistance to the Australian Defence Force and Department of Defence.

Several issues dominate current Australian science and technology policy: the concentration of research and development in national research centers; tensions among and between university researchers over allocation of research and development funding resources; effective communication between industry, government, and university researchers; the growing role which industry is playing in support of national research and development; and the role which Australia is playing in international science and technology collaboration. High-technology exports totaled $1.5 million in 1998.

Government funds about 55% of all research and development and industry about 40%. In 1996 there were 73 agricultural, medical, scientific, and technical professional associations and societies, the foremost of which is the Australian Academy of Science, founded in 1954 by royal charter. The Australian Academy of Technological Sciences and Engineering was founded in 1976. The Australian Science and Technology Council (ASTEC) provides an independent source of counsel for the Australian Prime Minister; its role was augmented in 1986 by the creation of a post for a Minister Assisting the Prime Minister with portfolio for science and technology.

In 1996, Australia had 36 universities offering courses in basic and applied science. In 1987–97, science and engineering students accounted for 24% of college and university enrollments. The Powerhouse Museum in Sydney, the largest museum complex in Australia, has 25 exhibitions in the areas of science, technology, social history, and decorative arts.

30DOMESTIC TRADE

There are many small specialty shops, but in the larger cities department stores sell all kinds of items. Supermarkets have been widely established, and telephone shopping and delivery services are becoming popular. Installment selling, called hire purchase, is used in the sale of many products. Reliable commercial credit agencies cover all the main cities and many smaller towns.

The usual business hours are from 9 AM to 5 PM, Monday–Friday, and from 9 AM to noon on Saturday.

Most advertising is done through the press, radio, and television. Principal advertising agencies are in Sydney and Melbourne.

31FOREIGN TRADE

Measured by foreign trade volume per capita, Australia is one of the great trading nations, and it continues to show a steady rise in trade volume. Throughout the 1970s, exports regularly exceeded imports. In the early 1980s, however, there was a deficit, which has continued into the 1990s.

Australia is mainly an exporter of primary products and an importer of manufactured and semifinished goods, although the export of manufactured goods increased by 10% per year during the 1990s. Exports of primary goods accounted for almost 60% of total exports in 1998. Transport or reexport trade is negligible. In recent years, Australia's foreign trade has tended to shift from European markets to developing Asian nations, which now account for nearly 60% of Australia's exports, compared with about 10% in 1975.

Australia's commodity exports are dominated by fossil, mineral, and plant fuels, including coal, lignite, and peat (11%). Wool may only amount to a small percentage of Australia's exports, but Australia supplies the world with almost half of its imported wool. Food products such as wheat, sugar, and meat exports tie with fuel exports as one of the top commodities leaving the country (11%). The top exports are as follows:

	% OF COUNTRY TOTAL	% OF WORLD TOTAL
Coal, lignite, and peat	11	29
Gold	7.7	18
Base metal ores	6.1	17
Meat	5.6	7.9
Wool	5.0	43
Iron ore	4.3	25
Aluminum	3.8	4.4
Wheat	3.1	9.8
Sugar	2.7	9.8

In 1997 Australia's imports were distributed among the following categories:

Consumer goods	18.7%
Food	4.4%
Fuels	6.1%
Industrial supplies	22.6%
Machinery	30.8%
Transportation	16.7%
Other	0.6%

Principal trading partners in 1998 (in millions of US dollars) were as follows:

COUNTRY	EXPORTS	IMPORTS	BALANCE
Japan	10,909	8,373	2,536
United States	5,292	13,639	-8,347
China (inc. Hong Kong)	4,592	4,399	193
Korea	3,852	2,619	1,233
New Zealand	3,524	2,404	1,120
United Kingdom	2,936	3,639	-703
Taiwan	2,673	1,846	827
Singapore	2,060	1,686	374
Indonesia	1,342	2,229	-887
Germany	873	3,652	-2,779

32BALANCE OF PAYMENTS

Australia's current account deficit reached a high of $20 billion in 1995; the figure was down to $18 billion in 1998, or 6% of GDP.

The US Central Intelligence Agency reports that in 1998 the purchasing power parity of Australia's exports was $56 billion while imports totaled $61 billion resulting in a trade balance of -$5 billion.

The International Monetary Fund (IMF) reports that in 1998 Australia had exports of goods totaling $55,839 million and imports totaling $61,232 million. The services credit totaled $16,163 million and debit $17,304 million. The following table summarizes Australia's balance of payments as reported by the IMF for 1998 in millions of US dollars.

Current Account		-17,512
Balance on goods	-5,393	
Balance on services	-1,141	
Balance on income	-10,918	
Current transfers	-61	
Capital Account		672
Financial Account		15,016
Direct investment abroad	-2,464	
Direct investment in Australia	6,255	
Portfolio investment assets	-1,775	
Portfolio investment liabilities	4,779	
Other investment assets	-371	
Other investment liabilities	8,592	
Net Errors and Omissions		-56
Reserves and Related Items		1,879

33BANKING AND SECURITIES

The Reserve Bank of Australia, the central bank, reconstituted in 1960, functions as a banker's bank and financial agent of the federal and some state governments, issuing notes, controlling interest and discount rates, mobilizing Australia's international reserves, and administering exchange controls and government loans. It was formerly connected with the Commonwealth Trading Bank—a general bank—the Commonwealth Savings Bank, and the Commonwealth Development Bank. The banking system has undergone progressive privatization and foreign investment since the deregulation of financial markets in the 1980s under the Wallis Inquiry into the Australian financial system of 1981. In 1996, the government privatized the Commonwealth Banks in the Reserve Bank Act, separating the Commonwealth Banks from the Reserve Bank. Rural credits, mortgage banking, and industrial financing are now administered wholly by private-owned banks. Fifty banks operate in Australia, 35 of which are foreign-owned; the largest banks include National Australia Bank, ANZ, Commonwealth Bank, and Westpac. The Australian Prudential Regulation Authority (APRA) regulates the banks and other financial institutions.

The Australian currency has floated freely since 1983, and was allowed to fall dramatically from 1984 to 1987. The Reserve Bank pointed to an expected upturn in economic activity in 1997 and anticipated a continuation of low inflation. It also indicated that firming economic growth, together with the uncertainties surrounding wage outcomes, made changes to monetary policy settings unlikely. Interest rate cuts were not on the bank's policy agenda, as it waited to see the impact of reductions made in late 1996. From 1996 to 2000, the Australian dollar fell by almost 30% against the US dollar; losing 12% in the first half of 2000 alone. The Reserve Bank increased interest rates a number of times in order to stave off inflation, but the introduction of the 10% GST in July threatened to raise inflation despite monetary policies.

The Australian stock market is where equity (shares), units in listed trusts, options, government bonds, and other fixed-interest securities are traded. It is operated on a national basis by the Australian Stock Exchange (ASX), which is responsible for the day-to-day running and surveillance of stock market trading. The ASX was established on 1 April 1987, with the passage of the Australian National Guarantee Fund Act through the Commonwealth Parliament. This Act converted the six former capital city Stock Exchanges into state subsidiaries of the ASX.

34INSURANCE

Australia has one of the most competitive insurance markets in the world, with a large number of insurers competing for a business from a small population base. Established in 1987, the Insurance and Superannuation Commission (ISC) was the ultimate regulatory authority for the insurance industry in Australia. It was replaced by the Australian Prudential Regulation Authority. Life insurance firms, through premiums on policies and interest earned on accumulated funds, account for substantial annual savings. The companies invest in government securities, in company securities (including shares and fixed-interest obligations), and in mortgage loans and loans against policies in force. Most loans (to individuals and building societies) are for housing.

Total assets of the 172 private general insurance companies at the end of 1998 amounted to approximately A$56.2 billion. Total assets of the public general life insurance industry for the same time was around A$25 billion, managed by 17 public insurers. Forty-three life insurance companies were managing A$175 billion in assets.

³⁵PUBLIC FINANCE

The fiscal year begins 1 July and ends 30 June. After World War II, the Commonwealth government assumed greater responsibility for maintaining full employment and a balanced economy, as well as for providing a wide range of social services. Social security and welfare payments are the largest category of government expenditure. The central government has financed almost all its defense and capital works programs from revenue and has made available to the states money raised by public loans for public works programs. Deficits are common. In the latter half of the 1980s, however, five consecutive years of significant surpluses occurred as a result of expenditure restraints. The late 1990s also saw consistent surpluses. In 2000, the government implemented a 10% goods and services tax (GST) on all items, while income tax and corporate tax rates were cut.

The US Central Intelligence Agency (CIA) estimates that in 1998 Australia's central government took in revenues of approximately $90.7 billion and had expenditures of $89 billion including capital expenditures of $11.6 billion. Overall, the government registered a surplus of approximately $1.7 billion.

The following table shows an itemized breakdown of government revenues and expenditures. The percentages were calculated from data reported by the International Monetary Fund. The dollar amounts (millions) are based on the CIA estimates provided above.

REVENUE AND GRANTS	100%	90,730
Tax revenue	92.2%	83,668
Non-tax revenue	6.3%	5,742
Capital revenue	1.5%	1,320
EXPENDITURES	100%	89,040
General public services	7.1%	6,283
Defense	7.0%	6,233
Public order and safety	0.9%	775
Education	7.6%	6,802
Health	14.8%	13,188
Social security	35.5%	31,577
Housing and community amenities	1.2%	1,083
Recreation, cultural, and religious affairs	1.0%	867
Economic affairs and services	6.1%	5,424
Other expenditures	12.8%	11,401
Interest payments	6.1%	5,407

³⁶TAXATION

The main taxes (personal and corporate income, payroll, and goods and services tax) are levied by the federal government, but the states and municipalities impose other levies. Federal rates are determined in legislation that is foreshadowed in the budget, presented each August; rates apply to the fiscal year beginning in July, except for company tax rates, which apply to the previous year's income.

In 2000, the Australian government conducted a complete tax system overhaul that implemented a 10% GST that replaced the sales tax, and reduced the income tax and corporate tax. The corporate tax rate was cut to 30% in 2001 for both public and private firms. Undistributed profits of private firms are taxed at a higher rate. Nonresident companies pay an additional tax of 5%. Both the federal government and states can levy land taxes, and states levy both stamp duties on various documents and payroll taxes. Excise taxes are levied on alcoholic beverages, tobacco products, luxury cars, coal, kerosene, liquefied petroleum gas, and indigenous crude oil.

Personal taxation is levied by the Commonwealth on a sharply progressive basis. The pay-as-you-earn system (called PAYE) is used. As of 2000, individual tax rates ranged from zero on income up to A$6,000 to 47% on income over A$60,001. Social security taxes are included as part of income taxes. Deductions are allowed for dependents, donations, medical expenses, and children's educational expenses, and for payment of life insurance or pension premiums. There is also a pensioner rebate that varies depending on income.

³⁷CUSTOMS AND DUTIES

Before the 1980s, federal policy was to use the tariff to protect local industries (especially the automobile industry), but in 1996 tariff rates were reduced to 5% or below. Textiles and clothes (25%), shoes (15%), and automobile products (15%) had higher duties in 2000. The GST of 10% applies for most imports and exports. Tariffs on industrial machinery and plant equipment ordinarily are low where they do not compete with Australian enterprise, and machinery and equipment required by new industries may be imported duty-free or at concessional rates.

As a contracting party to GATT, Australia consented to a number of tariff reductions after 1947. Under the South Pacific Regional Trade and Economic Cooperation Agreement (SPARTECA), which went into effect on 1 January 1981, Australia and New Zealand offered the other South Pacific Forum members duty-free or concessional access to their markets. The Australia New Zealand Closer Economic Relations Trade Agreement (ANZCERTA, abbreviated to CER) opened bilateral trade between the two countries in 1983. Australia is also a member of the Asia Pacific Economic Cooperation (APEC) forum.

The only free-trade zone is the Darwin Trade Development Zone (TDZ), located in the Northern Territory. There is a Manufacturing-in-Bond (MIB) site in Newcastle, and several others were on the way in 2000.

³⁸FOREIGN INVESTMENT

Foreign investment in Australia in 1997/98 reached a peak of nearly $22 billion. The US was the leading investor ($99 million), along with the UK ($99 million), and Japan ($39 million). In 1997/98, Australian direct investment abroad totaled $169 million, the majority going to the UK and the US ($28 and $57 million, respectively). The most recent focus of foreign investment has been the booming tourist industry, and commercial and residential property development. Hotels and resorts on the north New South Wales and Queensland coasts are attracting capital from abroad, as are large office block and hotel projects in the capital cities.

Australia prefers the inflow of long-term development capital to that of short-term speculative capital. It also welcomes the technical competence usually accompanying foreign investment. Investment incentives include tariff protection, and bounties for the manufacture of certain products. Total foreign ownership is permitted, but ownership in certain sectors is subject to restrictions.

³⁹ECONOMIC DEVELOPMENT

Commonwealth and state governments devoted special attention to the production and marketing of main primary products, and after 1920, legislation provided subsidies or other marketing aids to certain commodities. Federal and state aid was given to industries established in approved fields of manufacture during the 1970s. The Export Market Development Grant Acts of 1974 provided government assistance in the development of export markets. Recipients were eligible for up to 50% reimbursement for expenses incurred establishing foreign markets for domestic goods. In 1975, the government set up the Export Finance and Insurance Corp. (replacing the Export Payments Insurance Corp.) to provide Australian exporters with insurance and other financial services not readily available commercially.

The government endeavors to prevent undue fluctuation in the economy. Price controls were in effect during World War II and part of the postwar period and are now imposed on a few essential household items. As an alternative to price controls, the Commonwealth government, in mid-1975, introduced a policy of wage indexation, allowing wages to rise as fast as, but no faster than, consumer prices; major labor unions, however, opposed this restraint, which was ended in 1981. Monetary policy supported recovery from the 1980 recession by retaining a low inflation rate. After August 1993, the focus of fiscal policy shifted towards deficit reduction. In 2000, the new tax system aimed at increasing the government budget while stimulating economic growth in such sectors as tourism/services and high technology.

⁴⁰SOCIAL DEVELOPMENT

The Commonwealth Social Services Act of 1947, as amended in 1991, provides for invalid and old age pensions and a variety of other benefits. Disability pensions are payable to persons 16 years of age and older who have lived at least five years in Australia and have become totally incapacitated or permanently blind. Old age pensions are payable to men 65 years of age and over, and to women 61.5 years of age and over, who have lived in Australia continuously for at least 10 years at some stage in their lives. The continuous-residence requirement may be waived for those who have been residents for numerous shorter periods.

The family allowance legislation first passed in 1941 and updated in 1991 and every year since 1995 provides for weekly payments to children under 16 years of age. Widows' pensions are also provided. Employed persons are covered by workers' compensation, and unemployment assistance is provided for those aged 20 to 65. Youths aged between 16 and 20 are eligible for the youth training allowance, administered by the Department of Employment, Education and Training. Work-related sickness and maternity benefits are provided, as well as medical benefits for all residents.

The Sex Discrimination Act of 1984 bars discrimination on the basis of sex, marital status or pregnancy, and in 1992 the Parliament passed amendments that strengthened it significantly. The Office of the Status of Women was created to monitor the position of women in society. As of 1998, women held 56 of 223 parliamentary seats were held by women. Domestic violence remains a problem, particularly in aboriginal communities.

Discrimination on the basis of race, color, descent or national or ethnic origin was prohibited in the Racial Discrimination Act of 1975. Despite these measures, aboriginal Australians have poorer standards of living, are imprisoned more often, and die younger than white Australians. In 1998 the Australian government spent about $1.3 billion on a variety of social programs targeted at aboriginals.

⁴¹HEALTH

Australia is one of the healthiest countries in the world. The common cold and other respiratory infections are the most prevalent forms of illness; arteriosclerosis is the most common cause of death. Water in most cities is good and safe for household purposes, and garbage and trash are collected in cities and towns.

All levels of government are concerned with public health, with the municipalities functioning largely as agents for the administration of state policies. State health departments are responsible for infant welfare, school medical and dental services (provided free of charge), treatment and eradication of infectious and contagious diseases and tuberculosis, industrial hygiene programs, maintenance of food and drug standards, public and mental hospitals, and the regulation of private hospitals. The Commonwealth government makes grants for medical research, coordinates state health programs, and maintains specialist medical research institutions and laboratories.

Public sector funding accounts for over two-thirds of health care expenditure in Australia; of this, some is allocated via the central government and some via local authorities. Since the introduction of Medicare (the national health insurance program) in 1984, the share of funding provided by the federal government has risen. Under the Medicare system, all Australians have access to free care at public hospitals. The plan also meets three-fourths of the bill for private hospital treatment, while patients pay the remainder (and can take out private health insurance to cover this, although comprehensive private medical insurance was abolished in the 1984 act).

Since 1950, certain drugs have been provided free of charge when prescribed by a medical practitioner. All patients other than pensioners must pay a set amount for every prescription supplied under the scheme; the remainder is met by the government. For those not eligible for free public health care and who have basic medical insurance, the government pays 30% of the scheduled benefit fee for each medical service. Such insurance, including the government contribution, covers 85% of scheduled fees. The federal government provides grants to the states and aboriginal organizations for the development of special health services for aboriginals, who are often reluctant to use general community health services. As of 1992, aboriginals and Torres Strait Islanders had unacceptably low levels of health. They have access to the same health care system as any other Australian, but don't take full advantage of it. Unemployed persons, recent immigrants and refugees, and certain low-income persons are entitled to health care cards that entitle the bearer and dependents to free medical and hospital treatment.

Health services are efficient. Hospitals are generally modern and well equipped, but space often is at a premium. In 1994/95, there were more than 1,100 hospitals, excluding psychiatric hospitals and nursing homes. While most hospitals are public, there are approximately 350 private hospitals. From 1990 to 1997, there were 8.9 hospital beds per 1,000 people. Most private hospitals tend to be fairly small, and there are a large number of private hospitals run by religious groups. Hospital facilities are concentrated in the states of New South Wales and Queensland, which together account for about half the country's hospitals and hospital beds.

From 1990 to 1997, there were 2.2 doctors per 1,000 inhabitants. In the mid-1990s, there were more than 30,000 physicians, more than 6,000 dentists, and about 140,000 professionally registered nurses. Competent general physicians and specialists are available in most cities, and the Royal Flying Doctor Service provides medical care and treatment to people living in remote areas.

In 1999, the death rate was 6.9 per 1,000 population, and between 1985 and 1990, mortality per 100,000 people was due to the following: (1) communicable diseases, maternal/perinatal causes—31; (2) noncommunicable diseases—424; and (3) injuries—48. Infant mortality in 1999 was 5 per 1,000 live births. The under 5 mortality rate has steadily decreased from 24 in 1960 to 8 in 1994. Between 1980 and 1993, 67% of married women (ages 15-49) were using contraception. The 1999 birth rate was 13.2 per 1,000 inhabitants. The maternal mortality rate was 9 per 100,000 live births in 1990–97. The estimated life expectancy in 1999 was 80 years. Between 1990 and 1994, one-year-old children were immunized as follows: diphtheria, pertussis, and tetanus (95%); polio (72%); and measles (86%). In 1994, 1,020 people were diagnosed with tuberculosis. In 1997, the incidence of tuberculosis was 8 per 1,000 people.

Between 1986–94, 37% of the male and 30% of the female population were smokers.

The HIV-1 seroprevalence in 1990–97 was 0.1 per 100 adults. In 1996, Australia reported 6,442 new cases of AIDS. The year before only 110 were reported.

⁴²HOUSING

In the mid-1990s, there were 6,339,000 dwellings in Australia. Approximately 132,000 new houses and apartments were completed per year during this period, down from 134,000 in 1991. Central heating, formerly available only in the most modern and expensive homes and apartments, is now generally available in the coldest areas of the country. Most apartments and houses are equipped with hot-water service, refrigeration, and indoor bath and toilet facilities.

⁴³EDUCATION

Illiteracy is virtually nonexistent except among the aboriginals. Education is compulsory for children from the age of 6 to 15 (16 in Tasmania). Primary education generally begins at six years of age and lasts for seven years. Free education is provided in municipal kindergartens and in state primary, secondary, and technical schools. In 1997 primary schools enrolled 1,855,789 students in 8,123 schools, with 103,774 teachers. Secondary schools enrolled 2,367,692 students and employed approximately 104,000 teachers in the same year. Secondary usually lasts for six years, four years of lower secondary, followed by another two years of upper secondary. There are also state-regulated private schools, which are attended by approximately one-third of Australian children. Correspondence courses and educational broadcasts are given for children living in the remote "outback" areas and unable to attend school because of distance or physical handicap. One-teacher schools also satisfy these needs. Although most aboriginal and Torres Strait Islander students use the regular school system, there are special programs to help them continue on to higher education.

Although each state controls its own system, education is fairly uniform throughout Australia. The government expenditure on education in the latter part of the 1990s was approximately 13.5% of central government spending. Education is the joint responsibility of the federal government and each state government and territory. The federal government directly controls schools in the Northern Territory and in the Australian Capital Territory.

Australia has approximately 20 universities in addition to more than 200 technical institutes. There is a state university in each capital city and each provincial area; a national postgraduate research institute in Carberra and a university of technology in Sydney with a branch at Newcastle. There are also a number of privately funded higher-education institutions including theological and teacher training colleges. Adult education includes both vocational and non-vocational courses. Most universities offer education programs for interested persons. In 1997, there were a total of 1,041,648 students and 26,407 teachers in higher level educational institutes.

⁴⁴LIBRARIES AND MUSEUMS

The National Library of Australia traces its origins back to 1902, but it was not until 1960 that it was legislatively separated from the Commonwealth Parliamentary Library and made a distinct entity. The National Library is now housed in modern facilities in Canberra and has over 4.7 million volumes. Three other libraries in Australia of comparable size are the library of the University of Sydney (over three million volumes), founded in 1852; the State Library of New South Wales (over 1.9 million volumes), founded in 1826; and the State Library of Victoria (over 1.5 million), founded in 1854. The state capital cities have large noncirculating reference libraries, as well as municipal public circulating libraries. The university libraries in Brisbane, Adelaide, Canberra, and Melbourne all have sizable collections. Recent years have seen programs with increased cooperation between libraries, which has resulted in increased service. The Australian Institute of Aboriginal Studies in Acton has a specialized collection of

15,000 volumes, and dozens of museums and cultural centers house other specialized collections.

There are about 2,000 museums in Australia, of which over 200 are art museums. A national art collection has been assembled in the Australian National Gallery at Canberra, which was opened to the public in October 1982. The National Museum of Australia (founded 1980) in Canberra exhibits Australian history and social history. There are eight other major museums, two each in Sydney and Melbourne and one in each of the other state capitals. Of note in Melbourne are a Performing Arts Museum (1978); the Ancient Times House (1954); and the Jewish Museum of Australia. Sydney houses the Australian National Maritime Museum (1985), the Museum of Contemporary Art (1979) and the Nicholson Museum of Antiquities (1860). Some of the smaller cities also have museums. The National Gallery of Victoria in Melbourne has a fine collection of paintings and other artworks, and the South Australian Museum in Adelaide has excellent collections relating to Australian entomology, zoology, and ethnology. Botanical gardens are found in every capital city.

⁴⁵MEDIA

On 1 July 1975, responsibility for the nation's postal service was vested in the Australian Postal Commission, and for telecommunications in the Australian Telecommunications Commission; previously these functions had been administered by the Department of the Postmaster General. Local and long-distance telephone services are rated highly. As of 1995 there were 8,540,000 telephones, about one for every two Australians. Nearly 99% of the total service is automatic.

The government administers and supervises broadcasting through the Australian Broadcasting Commission, which operates a nationwide noncommercial radio and television service; the Australian Broadcasting Tribunal, which licenses and regulates commercial broadcasters; and the Special Broadcasting Service, which prepares and broadcasts multilingual radio and television programs. Federal government stations are financed from budget revenues, and the private commercial stations derive their income from business advertising. As of 1999 there were 262 AM and 345 FM radio stations and. 104 television stations. In 1997, there were 1,385 radios, 638 television sets, and 264 mobile phones in use per 1,000 population.

In general, news is presented straightforwardly, and political criticism is considered fair and responsible. The *Australian*, one of only two national newspapers, was established in 1964 and is published in all state capitals. It is independent and had an estimated daily circulation in 1999 of 153,000. The other national daily, the *Australian Financial Review,* had a Monday–Friday average circulation of 78,000 in the same year.

Other leading dailies and their estimated 1999 circulation figures are listed in the following table:

	ORIENTATION	CIRCULATION
Herald-Sun (Melbourne, m)	Conservative	600,000
Daily Telegraph-Mirror (NSW, m)	NA	442,980
Sydney Morning Herald (m)	Conservative	266,000

Major Sunday newspapers include the *Sun-Herald* (600,000) and the *Sunday Telegraph* (1,800,000) in Sydney, and the *Sunday Mail* in Brisbane (580,000).

The major news agency is the Australian Associated Press, founded in 1935; it has been associated with Reuters since 1946. Many international news services have bureaus in Sydney.

Though the Australian constitution does not have specific guarantees of freedom of expression, the High Court has, in two decisions, declared that freedom of political discourse is implied. The government is said to respect all such rights in practice.

In 1996, there were almost five million personal computers; in 1998, there were 400 Internet hosts per 1,000 population.

46ORGANIZATIONS

Chambers of commerce and chambers of manufacture are active throughout Australia, especially in the state capital cities; the Australian Chamber of Commerce (1091) coordinates their activities. The Australia Council (founded in 1943) encourages amateur activities in the arts and sponsors traveling exhibitions of ballet, music, and drama. There are associations or scholarly societies in the fields of architecture, art, international affairs, economics, political and social science, engineering, geography, history, law, literature, medicine, philosophy, and the natural sciences. Many publish scholarly journals. Theatrical, musical, and dance groups perform in the larger cities and towns. Skiing and tobogganing clubs function in the mountainous areas. Sydney, Melbourne, Hobart, and several other cities have large yacht clubs, and every state capital city has swimming and surfing clubs.

47TOURISM, TRAVEL, AND RECREATION

Among Australia's natural tourist attractions are the Great Barrier Reef, a mecca for scuba divers; the varied and unusual flora and fauna; and the sparsely inhabited outback regions, which in some areas may be toured by camel. Other attractions include Ballarat and other historic gold-rush towns near Melbourne; wineries, particularly in the Barossa Valley, 55 km (34 mi) northeast of Adelaide; Old Sydney Town, north of Sydney, a recreation of the Sydney Cove Settlement as it was in the early 19th century; and the arts festivals held in Perth every year and in Adelaide every two years, featuring foreign as well as Australian artists.

Among the sports that lure tourists are surfing, sailing, fishing, golf, tennis, cricket, and rugby. Melbourne is famous for its horse racing (Australia's most celebrated race is the Melbourne Cup) and for its 120,000-capacity cricket ground, reputedly the biggest in the world.

Except for nationals of New Zealand and certain other Commonwealth countries, visitors must have valid passports issued by an Australian or British consul or passport officer. They must also be in possession of sufficient funds to maintain themselves while in Australia and hold tickets for travel to a destination outside Australia. Immunizations are required only of tourists coming from an infected area.

In 1997, Australia attracted approximately 4,318,000 foreign visitors, of whom nearly two-thirds came from East Asia and the Pacific region. That year there were 177,587 hotel rooms with 515,757 beds and an occupancy rate of 62%. Tourist receipts that year totaled over US$9 billion. The government actively promotes tourism, and hopes to increase the number of foreign visitors in the year 2000, when the country is to host the Olympic Games. In 1999, the UN estimated the daily cost of staying in Melbourne at US$171, Sydney at US$171, and elsewhere at US$141.

48FAMOUS AUSTRALIANS

The most highly regarded contemporary Australian writer is Patrick White (1912–90), author of *The Eye of the Storm* and other works of fiction and winner of the 1973 Nobel Prize for literature. Other well-known novelists are Henry Handel Richardson (Henrietta Richardson Robertson, 1870–1946), Miles Franklin (1879–1954), Christina Stead (1902–83), and Thomas Michael Keneally (b.1935). Henry Lawson (1867–1922) was a leading short-story writer and creator of popular ballads. Germaine Greer (b.1939) is a writer on feminism. A prominent Australian-born publisher of newspapers and magazines, in the

UK and the US as well as Australia, is Keith Rupert Murdoch (b.1931).

Three renowned scholars of Australian origin are Sir Gilbert Murray, O.M. (1866–1957), classicist and translator of ancient Greek plays; Samuel Alexander, O.M. (1859–1938), influential scientific philosopher; and Eric Partridge (1894–1979), authority on English slang. An outstanding bacteriologist was Sir Frank Macfarlane Burnet, O.M. (1899–1985), director of the Melbourne Hospital and co-winner of the 1960 Nobel Prize for medicine. Elizabeth Kenny (1886–1952) made important contributions to the care and treatment of infantile paralysis victims. Sir John Carew Eccles (b.1903) shared the 1963 Nobel Prize for medicine for his work on ionic mechanisms of the nerve cell membrane. John Warcup Cornforth (b.1917) shared the 1975 Nobel Prize for chemistry for his work on organic molecules.

Among Australia's most prominent film directors are Fred Schepisi (b.1939), Bruce Beresford (b.1940), George Miller (b.1943), Peter Weir (b.1944), and Gillian Armstrong (b.1950); film stars have included Australian-born Errol Flynn (1909–50), Paul Hogan (b.1940), and US-born Mel Gibson (b.1956). Leading Australian-born figures of the theater include the actors Dame Judith Anderson (1898–1992) and Cyril Ritchard (1898–1977) and the ballet dancer, choreographer, and stage actor and director Sir Robert Murray Helpmann (1909–86). Musicians of Australian birth include the operatic singers Dame Nellie Melba (1861–1931), John Brownlee (1901–69), Marjorie Lawrence (1907–79), and Dame Joan Sutherland (b.1926) and the composers Percy Grainger (1882–1961), Arthur Benjamin (1893–1960), Peggy Glanville-Hicks (1912–1990), and Peter Joshua Sculthorpe (b.1929). Popular singers include Helen Reddy (b.1941) and Olivia Newton-John (b.UK, 1948). Alfred Hill (1870–1960) is regarded as the founder of the art of musical composition in Australia. Albert Namatjira (1902–59), an Aranda aboriginal, achieved renown as a painter, as has Sir Sidney Robert Nolan (b.1917). The aviator Sir Charles Edward Kingsford-Smith (1897–1935) pioneered flights across the Pacific Ocean. A popular figure of folklore was the outlaw Ned (Edward) Kelly (1855?–80).

In recent decades, the tennis world was dominated by such Australian players as Frank Sedgman (b.1927), Lewis Hoad (1934–94), Kenneth Rosewall (b.1934), Rod (George) Laver (b.1938), John David Newcombe (b.1944), and Evonne Goolagong Cawley (b.1951). Sir Donald George Bradman (b.1908) was one of the outstanding cricket players of modern times. Record-breaking long-distance runners include John Landy (b.1930) and Herb Elliott (b.1938). Jon Konrads (b.1942) and his sister Ilsa (b.1944) have held many world swimming records, as did Dawn Fraser (b.1937), the first woman to swim 100 meters in less than a minute, and Murray Rose (b.1939).

The principal modern Australian statesman is Sir Robert Gordon Menzies (1894–1978), who served as prime minister from 1939 to 1941 and again from 1949 to 1966. Subsequent prime ministers have included Edward Gough Whitlam (b.1916), who held office from 1972 to 1975; John Malcolm Fraser (b.1930), who succeeded Whitlam late in 1975; and Robert James Lee Hawke (b.1929), who served from 1983–91.

49DEPENDENCIES

Since 1936, Australia has claimed all territory in Antarctica (other than Adélie Land) situated south of 60°s and between 45° and 160°E, an area of some 6.1 million sq km (2.4 million sq mi), or nearly 40% of the continent. Three scientific and exploratory bases are now in operation: Mawson (established February 1954), Davis (established January 1957), and Casey (established February 1969).

Ashmore and Cartier Islands

The uninhabited, reef-surrounded Ashmore Islands, three in number, and Cartier Island, situated in the Indian Ocean about 480 km (300 mi) north of Broome, Western Australia, have been under Australian authority since May 1934. In July 1938, they were annexed as part of the Northern Territory.

Christmas Island

Situated at 10°30's and 105°40'E in the Indian Ocean, directly south of the western tip of Java, Christmas Island is 2,623 km (1,630 mi) northwest of Perth and has an area of about 135 sq km (52 sq mi). Until its annexation by the UK in 1888, following the discovery of phosphate rock, the island was uninhabited. The total estimated population in 1996 was 813, of whom 61% were Chinese and 25% were Malay. The only industry was phosphate extraction. The governments of Australia and New Zealand decided to close the mine in December 1987. Christmas Island was transferred from the UK to Australia on 1 October 1958. Abbott's booby is an endangered species on the island.

Cocos (Keeling) Islands

The Territory of Cocos (Keeling) Islands is a group of coral atolls consisting of 27 islands with a total land area of 14 sq km (5 sq mi) in the Indian Ocean, at 12°5's and 96°53'E, about 2,770 km (1,720 mi) northwest of Perth. The estimated population of the two inhabited islands was 609 in 1996. A British possession since 1857, the islands were transferred to Australia in 1955 and are administered by the minister for territories. In 1978, the Australian government bought out the remaining interests (except for personal residences) of the Clunies-Ross heirs on the islands. The climate is pleasant, with moderate rainfall. Principal crops are copra, coconut oil, and coconuts. The airport is a link in a fortnightly service between Australia and South Africa.

Coral Sea Islands

The Coral Sea Islands were declared a territory of Australia in legislation enacted during 1969 and amended slightly in 1973. Spread over a wide ocean area between 10° and 23°30's and 154° and 158°E, the tiny islands are administered by the minister for the Capital Territory and have no permanent inhabitants— although there is a manned meteorology station.

Territory of Heard and McDonald Islands

Heard Island, at 53°6's and 72°31'E, about 480 km (300 mi) southeast of the Kerguelen Islands and about 4,000 km (2,500 mi) southwest of Perth, is about 910 sq km (350 sq mi) in size. Bleak and mountainous, it is dominated by a dormant volcano, Big Ben, about 2,740 m (8,990 ft) high. There was a station at Atlas Cove from 1947 to 1955, but the island is now uninhabited and is visited occasionally by scientists. Just north is Shag Island, and 42 km (26 mi) to the west are the small, rocky McDonald Islands. The largest island of the group was visited for the first time, it is believed, on 27 January 1971, by members of the Australian National Antarctic Expedition. The territory was transferred from the UK to Australia at the end of 1947.

Macquarie Island

Macquarie Island, at 54°30's and 158°40'E, is about 1,600 km (1,000 mi) southeast of Hobart. The rocky, glacial island, 34 km (21 mi) long and about 3 to 5 km (2 to 3 mi) wide, is uninhabited except for a base maintained at the northern end since February 1948. Macquarie Island has been a dependency of Tasmania since the early 19th century. At the most southerly point, the island has what is believed to be the biggest penguin rookery in the world. Two small island groupings are off Macquarie Island: Bishop and Clerk, and Judge and Clerk.

Norfolk Island

Norfolk Island, with an area of 36 sq km (14 sq mi), is situated at 29°3's and 167°57'E, 1,676 km (1,041 mi) east-northeast of Sydney. Discovered in 1774 by Capt. James Cook, it was the site of a British penal colony during 1788–1814 and 1825–55. In 1856, it was settled by descendants of the *Bounty* mutineers. As of 1996, the estimated permanent population was 2,209. Transport is almost exclusively by motor vehicle. The soil is fertile and the climate conducive to the growing of fruits and bean seed, as well as the famed Norfolk Island pine. Tourism is also important. As of 1987, endangered species on Norfolk Island included the gray-headed blackbird, Norfolk Island parakeet, and white-breasted silver-eye.

[50]BIBLIOGRAPHY

Albinski, Henry S. *The Australian-American Security Relationship*. St. Lucia: University of Queensland Press, 1981.

A Life Together, a Life Apart: A History of Relations Between Europeans and Aborigines. Carlton, Vic., Australia: Melbourne University Press, 1994.

Altman, J. C., and J. P. Nieuwenhuysen. *The Economic Status of Australian Aborigines*. New York: Cambridge University Press, 1979.

Atkinson, Alan. *The Muddle-headed Republic*. New York: Oxford University Press, 1993.

Atlas of Australian Resources. Canberra: Department of National Development, 1953–date.

Australia in Pictures Publications Company. Minneapolis, Minn.: Lerner, 1993, 1990.

Australian Civilisation. New York: Oxford University Press, 1994.

Bassett, Jan. *The Oxford Illustrated Dictionary of Australian History*. New York: Oxford University Press, 1993.

Bell, Philip. *Implicated: the United States in Australia Bell*. Melbourne; New York: Oxford University Press, 1993.

Bell, Stephen. *Australian Manufacturing and the State: the Politics of Industry Policy in the Post-war Era*. New York: Cambridge University Press, 1993.

Berndt, Ronald Murray. *The Speaking Land: Myth and Story in Aboriginal Australia*. Rochester, VT: Inner Traditions International, 1994.

Blainey, Geoffrey. *The Tyranny of Distance: How Distance Shaped Australia's History*. Rev. ed. South Melbourne: Macmillan, 1982.

Blake, Barry. *Australian Aboriginal Languages: A General Introduction*. St. Lucia, Qld., Australia: University of Queensland Press, 1991.

Bolton, Geoffrey (gen. ed.) *The Oxford History of Australia*. New York: Oxford University Press, 1986–90.

Bottomley, Gill, and Marie M. de Lepervanche (eds.). *Ethnicity, Class, and Gender in Australia*. Sydney: Allen & Unwin, 1984.

Brugger, Bill, and Dean Jaensch. *Australian Politics: Theory and Practice*. Sydney: Allen & Unwin, 1985.

Cameron, Roderick. *Australia*. New York: Columbia University Press, 1971.

Castles, Francis G. *Australia Compared: People, Policies and Politics*. North Sydney, Australia: Allen & Unwin Pty Ltd, 1991.

Catley, Robert. Globalising Australian Capitalism. Cambridge, UK: Cambridge University Press, 1996.

Clark, C. M. H. *A Short History of Australia*. Rev. ed. Sydney: Mead & Beckett, 1983.

Cranston, Ross. *Law, Government and Public Policy*. New York: Oxford University Press, 1987.

Cribb, A. B. *Plant Life of the Great Barrier Reef and Adjacent Shores*. New York: University of Queensland Press, 1985.

Docherty, J. C. *Historical Dictionary of Australia*. Metuchen, N.J.: Scarecrow Press, 1992.

Dyster, B. *Australia in the International Economy: in the Twentieth Century*. New York: Cambridge University Press, 1990.

Gibson, Ross. *South of the West: Postcolonialism and the Narrative Construction of Australia*. Bloomington: Indiana University Press, 1992.

Goldberg, S.L. and F.B. Smith (eds.) *Australian Cultural History*. New York: Cambridge University Press, 1988.

Greenwood, Gordon (ed.). *Australia: A Social and Political History*. Sydney: Angus & Robertson, 1966.

Gunther, John. *John Gunther's Inside Australia*. New York: Harper & Row, 1972.

Hancick, Keith (ed.) *Australian Society*. New York: Cambridge University Press, 1989.

Heathcote, R. L. *Australia*. London: Longman, Scientific & Technical, 1994.

Hefford, Ron, *et al. An Introduction to the Australian Economy*. Brisbane: University of Queensland Press, 1980.

Jaensch, Dean. *The Australian Party System*. Sydney: Allen & Unwin, 1983.

Jones, Michael A. *The Australian Welfare State: Growth, Crisis, and Change*. Rev. ed. Sydney: Allen & Unwin, 1979.

Kasper, Wolfgang, et al. *Australia at the Crossroads*. New York Law & Business, Inc., 1980.

Kemp, David Alistair. *Foundations for Australian Political Analysis: Politics and Authority*. New York: Oxford University Press, 1988, 1989.

Kramer, Leonie, *et al.* (eds.). *The Oxford History of Australian Literature*. Melbourne: Oxford University Press, 1981.

Kurian, George Thomas. *Facts on File National Profiles. Australia and New Zealand*. New York: Facts on File Publications, 1990.

Lane, P. H. *The Australian Federal System*. 2d ed. Sydney: Law Book Co. of Australasia, 1979.

London, H. I. *Non-White Immigration and the "White Australia" Policy*. New York: New York University Press, 1970.

Lourandos, Harry. *Continent of Hunters-Gatherers: New Perspectives in Australian Prehistory*. Cambridge: Cambridge University Press, 1994.

Maddock, Rodney and Ian W. McLean (eds.) *The Australian Economy in the Long Run*. New York: Cambridge University Press, 1987.

Massola, Aldo. *The Aborigines of Southeastern Australia*. New York: Scribner, 1974.

McGregor, C. *The Australian People*. Sydney: Hodder & Stoughton, 1980.

Moore, Andrew. *The Right Road?: A History of Right-Wing Politics in Australia*. Melbourne: Oxford University Press, 1995.

Official Year Book of the Commonwealth of Australia. Canberra: Commonwealth Government Printer, 1908–to date.

Osborne, Charles (ed.). *Australia, New Zealand and the South Pacific: A Handbook*. New York: Praeger, 1970.

Parliamentary Handbook and Record of Elections. Canberra: Commonwealth Government Printer, 1915–to date.

Randall, John. *Fishes of the Great Barrier Reef and Coral Sea*. Honolulu: University of Hawaii Press, 1990.

Rickard, John. *Australia, A Cultural History*. London: Longman, 1996.

Robinson, K. W. *Australia, New Zealand and the Southwest Pacific*. London: University of London Press, 1960.

Sawer, Geoffrey. *Australian Government To-day*. Rev. ed. Melbourne: Melbourne University Press, 1978.

Shaw, John (ed.) *The Concise encyclopedia of Australia, Rev.* 2nd ed. Queensland: D. Bateman, 1989.

Sherington, Geoffrey. *Australia's Immigrants*. London: Allen & Unwin, 1981.

Solomon, D. H. *Australia's Government and Parliament*. 6th ed. Melbourne: Nelson, 1984.

Solomon, M. *The Geology and Origin of Australia's Mineral Deposits*. New York: Oxford University Press, 1994.

Spencer, Sir Baldwin, and Francis James Gillen. *The Arunta: A Study of a Stone Age People*. London: Macmillan, 1927.

Spencer, Sir Baldwin. *Wanderings in Wild Australia*. London: Macmillan, 1928.

The Australian Environment. Melbourne: Melbourne University Press, 1960.

Wannan, Bill. *The Australian: Yarns, Ballads, Legends and Traditions of the Australian People*. Melbourne: Australasian Book Society, 1954.

Ward, R. B. *The Australian Legend*. 2d ed. Melbourne: Oxford University Press, 1977.

Ward, R. B. *Concise History of Australia Drawings*. St Lucia, Qld.: University of Queensland Press, 1992.

Whitaker, Donald P. *Area Handbook for Australia*. Washington, D.C.: US Govt. Print. Off., 1974.

Who's Who in Australia. Melbourne: Colorgravure Publications, 1906–to date.

Wynes, William Anstey. *Legislative, Executive and Judicial Powers in Australia*. Sydney: Law Book Co. of Australasia, 1956.

AZERBAIJAN

Azerbaijani Republic
Azarbaijchan Respublikasy

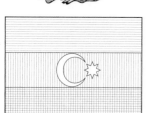

CAPITAL: Baku.

FLAG: Three equal horizontal bands of blue (top), red, and green; a crescent and eight-pointed star in white are centered in the red band.

ANTHEM: *Azerbaijan National Anthem,* composed by Uzeyir Hajibayov.

MONETARY UNIT: Manat, introduced in 1992, remains tied to the Russian ruble; exchange rates are widely fluctuating. As of 31 March 2000, manat1 = $0.00023 ($1 = manat4400.0).

WEIGHTS AND MEASURES: The metric system is in force.

HOLIDAYS: New Year's Day, 1 January; International Women's Day, 8 March; Novruz Bayrom (Holiday of Spring), 22 March; Day of the Republic, 28 May; Day of Armed Forces, 9 October; Day of State Sovereignty, 18 October; Day of National Revival, 17 November; Universal Azeri Solidarity Day, 31 December.

TIME: 4 PM = noon GMT.

¹LOCATION, SIZE, AND EXTENT

Azerbaijan is located in southeastern Europe, between Armenia and the Caspian Sea. Comparatively, Azerbaijan is slightly larger than the state of Maine with a total area of 86,600 sq km (33,436 sq mi). This area includes the Nakhichevan Autonomous Republic and the Nagorno-Karabakh Autonomous Oblast. Azerbaijan shares boundaries with Russia on the N, the Caspian Sea on the E, Iran on the S, Armenia on the W, and Georgia on the NW. Azerbaijan's boundary length totals 2,013 km (1,251 mi). Azerbaijan's capital city, Baku, is located on the Apsheron Peninsula that juts into the Caspian Sea.

²TOPOGRAPHY

The topography of Azerbaijan features the large, flat Kura-Aras Lowland (much of it below sea level) with the Great Caucasus Mountains to the north. The Karabakh Upland lies in the west. About 18% of Azerbaijan's land is arable with approximately 16% under irrigation.

³CLIMATE

The country's climate is subtropical in the eastern and central parts. In the mountainous regions the climate is alpine-like. The southeastern section of the country has a humid subtropical climate. The mean temperature in the capital, Baku, in July is 27.2°C (81°F). In January the mean temperature is 1.1°C (34°F). Rainfall varies according to the nine climate zones in the country.

⁴FLORA AND FAUNA

The country's flora and fauna is rich and varied. There are 16 nature reserves and more than 28 forest reserves and hunting farms.

⁵ENVIRONMENT

Azerbaijan's current environmental problems result in part from the effects of the economic priorities and practices of the former Soviet Union. General mismanagement of the country's resources has resulted in a serious threat to several areas of the environment. UN agencies report severe air and water pollution in Azerbaijan, which ranks among the 50 nations with the world's highest level of carbon dioxide emissions. In the mid-1990s, carbon dioxide emissions totaled 63.9 million metric tons per year, or 8.76 metric tons per capita. The combination of industrial, agricultural, and oil-drilling pollution has created an environmental crisis in the Caspian Sea. These sources of pollution have contaminated 100% of the coastal waters in some areas and 45.3% of Azerbaijan's rivers. The pollution of the land through the indiscriminate use of agricultural chemicals such as the pesticide DDT is also a serious problem. Azerbaijan's war with Armenia has hampered the government's ability to improve the situation. Due to the severity of pollution on all levels, the country's wildlife and vegetation are also seriously affected. From the mid-1980s to mid-1990s, the amount of forest and woodland declined by 12.5%. As of 1994, 14 species of mammals, 36 species of birds, 5 species of fish, 13 reptiles, and 40 species of insects were threatened with extinction.

⁶POPULATION

The population of Azerbaijan in 2000 was estimated at 7,955,772. Approximately 6.2% of the population is 65 years of age or older. The projected population for the year 2005 is 8,172,000, assuming a crude birthrate of 19 per 1,000 population and a death rate of 10, resulting in a natural rate of change of 1.0% for the period 2000–2005. The population rate of change between 1995 and 2000 was 0.8%. The population density in 1998 was 91 per sq km (236 per sq mi).

It was estimated that 57% of the population lived in urban areas in 2000, up from 53% in 1980. The capital city, Baku, had a 2000 population of 1,848,000. Gyanja (formerly Kirovabad) had a population of about 287,000 people, and Sumgait about 235,000.

⁷MIGRATION

As a result of the war with Armenia, which started in 1988, more than 1,000,000 people have been forced to leave the region. According to government estimates of Azerbaijan, there are 616,546 (8% of the total population) internally displaced persons as of 1999. Most of these persons were displaced between 1993 and 1994. Since May 1994, when the cease fire was enacted, only 60,000 persons have been able to return to their homes along the front line. Also as of 1999, Azerbaijan hosts 233,682 refugees. Most are Azeri refugees from Armenia. The Law on Citizenship allows for the automatic acquisition of Azerbaijani citizenship by refugees from Armenia. Also, there are some 48,000 Meshketians recently arrived from Central Asia. The Meshketians were originally deported from Georgia under the Stalin era.

Between 1989 and 1995, there was an emigration of Slavic peoples from Azerbaijan. These included 169,000 Russians, 15,000 Ukrainians, and 3,000 Belarusians as they emigrated back to their homelands. The net emigration rate for Azerbaijan as of mid-1996 was 5.8 migrants per 1,000 population.

8ETHNIC GROUPS

In 1998, 90% of the population was Azeri; about 3.2% were Dagestani peoples; 2.5% were Russian; another 2% were Armenian; and 2.3% were of other ethnic origins. Almost all Armenians live in the separatist Nagorno-Karabakh region.

9LANGUAGES

Azerbaijani (or Azeri) is a language related to Turkish and is also spoken in northwestern Iran. It is traditionally written in Arabic script. In 1995 approximately 89% of the population spoke Azeri; 3% spoke Russian; 2% spoke Armenian; and 6% other. In 1939, the Soviets introduced a Cyrillic alphabet, with eight special characters.

10RELIGIONS

For most of the 20th century, from 1920 to 1991, the Azerbaijan Soviet Socialist Republic observed the restrictions in religious belief and practice common throughout the former Soviet Union. According to statistics available after the declaration of independence of 30 August 1991, the population was 87% Muslim (70% of whom were Shi'is, and 17% were Sunnis). Because of the Persian influence on Azerbaijan, most Azerbaijanis are Shiites, even though all the other Turkic groups of the former Soviet Union are Sunni Muslims. In 1995, 93.4% of the population was Muslim; 2.5% was Russian Orthodox; 2.3% was Armenian Orthodox; other religions accounted for only 1.8%.

11TRANSPORTATION

Railroads in Azerbaijan (not including industrial lines) extend some 2,125 km (1,320 mi), with Baku as the hub. In 1998, the highway system totaled 57,770 km (35,898 mi), of which 54,188 km (33,672 mi) were paved. Azerbaijan's major port is at Baku. In 1998 the merchant marine had 57 ships (1,000 GRT or over), totaling 251,404 GRT. Ships from the Caspian fleet have called at some 125 ports in over 30 countries. In 1996 airports numbered 69, of which 29 had paved runways. There are flights from Baku's Bina Airport to more than 70 cities of the former Soviet Union. In 1997, 982,000 passengers were carried on scheduled domestic and international airline flights.

12HISTORY

The territory of present-day Azerbaijan has been continuously inhabited since the Paleolithic era. The first evidence of tribal alliances date to the first millenium BC, when such peoples as the Mannaians, the Medes, the Cadusiis, the Albanoi, and the Caspians appeared. In the 7th century BC, the state of Media appeared in what now is southern Azerbaijan, growing to cover large portions of the Near East. The Medians were displaced by the Persian dynasty of Achaemenids, who in turn were defeated by Alexander the Great. In the 4th century BC, another state arose which Greek sources called Atropatena, or "Land of the Fire Keepers"; it is this name, reflecting the predominance of Zoroas-

LOCATION: 40°30′N; 47°0′E BOUNDARY LENGTHS: Total boundary lengths, 2,013 km (1,251 mi); Armenia (west), 566 km (352 mi); Armenia (south), 221 km (137 mi); Georgia, 322 km (200 mi); Iran (south), 432 km (268 mi); Iran (southeast), 179 km (111 mi).

trianism, which may have given the present state its name. Around the beginning of the common era Atropatena was succeeded by a state called Albania, which the Romans attempted to conquer.

In the 3rd and 4th centuries AD, Azerbaijan existed with fluid boundaries between the Sassanid state in Persia and the Romans, whose battles inflicted great damage, leaving Azerbaijan open to raids by Turkic nomadic tribes from the north, including Khazars and Huns. Outside influence reappeared in the 7th and 8th centuries, when Arabs conquered much of Transcaucasia. As their influence receded, a number of small local states were established, the best known of which was the Shirvanshahs.

In the 11th century Azerbaijan was invaded by Oguz Turks, of the Seljuk dynasty. By the 13th century the gradual displacement of pre-Turkic local languages was complete, although many traces of non-Turkic predecessors remain in the Azerbaijani language. Persian, however, remained the language of art, science, and education.

In the 1230s Azerbaijan was conquered by Genghiz Khan, whose power remained in the Il-Khanid state, which at the end of the 14th century was displaced by the armies of Tamerlaine. In the 16th century, the Safawid state emerged, coming to control most of the land between the Syr Darya and the Euphrates, and reestablishing agriculture and commerce destroyed under the Mongols. In the 17th century, the Safawids became Persianized, which made present-day Azerbaijan decline in importance.

In the 18th century Azerbaijan became the intersection of the Turkish, Persian, and Russian empires, as well as the focus of British and French attempts to block Russian expansion. The northern part of the territory was incorporated into Russia in the first third of the 19th century, but the area did not become important until the 1880s, when the area's abundant oil gained commercial importance. The southern portion of what was originally Azerbaijan has remained in Iran, except for the period 1941–46, when it was occupied by Soviet troops.

When the 1917 Russian revolution came, Ottoman Turkish troops moved into Azerbaijan, and later British forces controlled the capital, Baku. The Azerbaijani Musavat, or Equality Party, established a government, declared Azerbaijan's independence, and received diplomatic recognition from several states. Azerbaijan was invaded by the Russian Bolsheviks' Red Army in April 1920, and Azerbaijan was declared a Soviet state. In 1922 it was made part of the Transcaucasian Federated Socialist Republic, along with Georgia and Armenia. That was dissolved in 1936, when the three states were each made into separate Soviet Socialist Republics.

In 1988, calls by ethnic Armenians living in Azerbaijan's Nagorno Karabakh (NK) region to be incorporated into the Armenian republic led to open conflict which lasted until 1994. This predominantly Armenian area had been unsuccessfully claimed by the Armenians in the 1920s, at the time of the creation of Soviet Azerbaijan. Inability to solve the NK conflict was one of the problems which ultimately brought down Mikhail Gorbachev and broke apart the USSR. Ethnic and civil violence in January 1990 prompted the occupation of Baku by Soviet armed forces and Moscow's replacement of Vezirov with Mutalibov as republic head. During this period of martial law, the legislature elected Mutalibov as president in May 1990. Independence was declared on 30 August 1991, and Mutalibov was reaffirmed as president in a popular, uncontested election in September 1991.

In December 1991, NK's Armenians held a referendum (boycotted by local Azerbaijanis) that approved NK's independence and elected a Supreme Soviet, which on 6 January 1992, declared NK's independence and futilely appealed for world recognition. Following a late February 1992 massacre of Azerbaijani civilians in the town of Khojaly in NK, Mutalibov was accused of failing to protect Azeri citizens and forced by the nationalist oppositionist Azerbaijani Popular Front (APF) and others to resign as president. His replacement, Legislative head Yakub Mamedov, was also forced to resign in May 1992, in the face of further Azerbaijani military defeats in NK. Mutalibov was then reinstated by loyalists in the Supreme Soviet, but he had to flee two days later, when the APF seized power. Former Soviet dissident and APF leader Abulfaz Elchibey, was elected president in a popular contest in June 1992.

The nationalist government took several moves to cut its ties to Russia, including demanding the withdrawal of Russian troops, refusing to participate as a member of the Commonwealth of Independent States, negotiating with Western firms to develop its oil resources, and improving relations with Turkey. However, military losses in NK increased. In 1993, Heydar Aliyev, who had been the Communist Party leader of the republic from 1971–85 but then was ousted and disgraced by Soviet leader Mikhail Gorbachev, began to press for Elchibey's dismissal.

An abortive attempt by the Elchibey government in June 1993 to disarm paramilitary forces in the town of Ganja precipitated the fall of the government and provided the opportunity for Aliyev to regain power. These forces were led by Suret Huseynov, formerly in charge of troops in NK, who had been fired by Elchibey. Huseynov's forces, supplied with Russian equipment, defeated an Azerbaijani Army attack and began to march on Baku. His government in chaos, Elchibey invited Aliyev to come to Baku, and on 15 June, he endorsed Aliyev's election by the legislature as its new speaker. El'chibey fled to NAR on 17 June. On 24 June 1993, a bare quorum of legislators met and formally stripped Elchibey of presidential powers, transferring them to Aliyev. Huseynov demanded and was given the post of Prime Minister.

On 3 October 1993, Aliyev was elected President with 98.8% of the vote. The referendum and election were viewed as not "free and fair" by many international observers because of suppression of APF and other opposition participation. In late September 1994, police and others in Baku launched a purported coup attempt. Aliyev darkly hinted at Russian involvement. After defeating the coup attempt, Aliyev also accused prime minister Huseynov of major involvement, and Huseynov fled the country. Other coup attempts were reported in 1995 and 1999. All of the alleged coup attempts triggered mass arrests of Aliyev's opponents.

On 11 October 1998, incumbent President Aliyev defeated five other candidates and was elected to a second five-year term, receiving over 76% of 4.3 million votes cast. The major "constructive opposition" candidate running was Etibar Mammadov of the NIP, who received 11.6% of the vote. Most international observers judged the vote not "free and fair," citing myriad irregularities, though also noting that the election marked some improvement in political pluralism.

The conflict with Armenian separatists over its Nagorno-Karabakh region continues to plague Azerbaijan. Azerbaijan asserts that NK forces occupy over 20% of Azerbaijan's territory both in and around NK. The conflict has resulted in about 15,000 casualties on both sides and over 840,000 Azerbaijani refugees and displaced persons (and over 300,000 Armenians). The Organization for Security and Cooperation In Europe (OSCE) began the "Minsk Group" peace talks in June 1992. A Russian-mediated cease-fire was agreed to in May 1994 and was formalized by an armistice signed by the ministers of defense of Armenia and Azerbaijan and the commander of the NK army on 27 July 1994 (and reaffirmed a month later). Moscow talks were held by the sides, with token representation by the OSCE, along with Minsk Group talks. With strong US backing, the OSCE at its Budapest meeting agreed in December 1994 to send OSCE peacekeepers to the region under UN aegis if a political settlement could be reached. Russia and the OSCE assented to merge their mediation efforts. France was nominated as a cochair in 1996. This elicited criticism from Azerbaijan that the French had appeared pro-Armenian, leading to the seating of US, French, and Russian cochairs. (Many Azerbaijanis also have voiced reservations about Russia's objectivity as a mediator, citing its defense ties to Armenia.) Direct Armenian-Azerbaijani contacts by the presidents and advisors have also occurred.

Prospects for a negotiated settlement remain elusive because the sides remain far apart on most substantive issues such as the placement and composition of a peacekeeping force and NK's ultimate political status. Personal meetings by the two presidents raised hopes that a statement of intention could be issued at the November 1999 OSCE Summit, but events such as resignations of some Azerbaijani officials apparently opposed to NK proposals, Aliyev's infirmity, and October 1999 assassinations in Armenia (apparently unrelated to the NK talks) appeared to set back progress.

13GOVERNMENT

Azerbaijan is a republic with a presidential form of government. Heydar Aliyev assumed presidential powers after the overthrow of his popularly-elected predecessor and was elected President in 1993. Aliyev and his supporters from his home region of Nakichevan and elsewhere dominate the government and the legislature.

The Azerbaijani constitution was approved by 91.9% of voters in a referendum held in November 1995. It establishes a strong presidency, sets up a new 125-member legislature (the Milli Mejlis), declares Azerbaijani the state language, proclaims freedom of religion and a secular state, stipulates ownership over part of the Caspian Sea, and gives NAR quasi-federal rights. The president appoints and removes cabinet ministers (the Milli Mejlis consents to his choice of Prime Minister), submits budgetary and other legislation that cannot be amended but only approved or rejected within 56 days, and appoints local officials. It is extremely difficult for the Milli Mejlis to impeach the president. According to the State Department, corruption is endemic in the government. It also reports that the judicial branch effectively functions as part of the executive branch and is corrupt and inefficient. In practice, the Milli Mejlis too exercises little legislative initiative, with most of its legislation and agenda dictated by the executive branch. The transition to democracy has been impeded by government efforts to hinder the opposition. In NK, political turmoil and war damage have slowed development, and ethnic Azerbaijans are prevented from returning to the region and surrounding areas by the lack of a peace settlement.

In the November 1995 election, 25 of the seats were allocated through a proportional party list vote and 100 through single-member district balloting. Eight parties were allowed to take part in the party list voting in the legislative elections, but only the APF was clearly an anti-Aliyev party. These were the New Azerbaijan (NAP), APF, Azerbaijan Democratic Independence (ADIP), National Independence (NIP), Azerbaijan Democratic Proprietors (ADPP), Motherland, Azerbaijan National Statehood (NSPA), and Alliance for Azerbaijan parties. Aliyev's NAP won most seats in the legislative races. The elections were marred by the harassment and exclusion of most opposition parties and candidates from participation and by rampant irregularities such as the open stuffing of ballot boxes, according to international observers. Some observers stressed that the elections marked some progress in holding a multi-party vote. Aliyev's NAP candidates ran unopposed in many electoral districts because of the exclusion of opposition candidates. Campaign advertising by most parties was severely restricted on state-owned television, while Aliyev received extensive positive coverage. New legislative elections are scheduled for late 2000.

14POLITICAL PARTIES

Nearly three dozen parties are registered, but some opposition parties have been arbitrarily refused registration. Some parties that are deemed explicitly ethnic or religiously based also have been refused registration. Six pro-Aliyev parties participated in the 1995 legislative party list vote, including New Azerbaijan (NAP; formed in November 1992), Azerbaijan Democratic Independence (ADIP; broke off from NIP in late 1993), Motherland (formed in 1990), and the Democratic Entrepreneurs' Party (formed in 1994). Only the NAP gained enough votes to win seats in the party list vote (though these other parties won seats in constituency balloting). Two centrist or opposition parties participated and won seats in the party-list voting: the APF (formed in 1988) and National Independence (NIP; broke off from APF in early 1992). Opposition parties excluded from the party list ballot included Musavat (formed in 1912). All parties are small; NAP is the largest with 100,000 members claimed. NAP, formed by Aliyev, encompasses many of his former ACP supporters. The

APF was at the forefront of the nationalist and anticommunist movement and its chair, Abulfaz Elchibey, was elected president in 1992. With Aliyev's return to power, APF members and officials have been arrested and harassed. NIP views itself as a moderate nationalist party in "constructive opposition" to Aliyev. Musavat has supported close ties with Turkey and has cooperated on some issues with the APF. The pro-Iranian Islamic Party was stripped of its registration in 1995. Preparing for the 1998 presidential race, in March 1998 46 pro-government political parties and groups formed the *Center for Democratic Elections* (CDE). Five prominent opposition political leaders and others formed the *Movement for Democratic Elections and Electoral Reform* (MDEER) in May 1998: Elchibey (the AFP), Isa Gambar (Musavat), Lala Shovkat Hijyeva (Azerbaijan Liberal Party or ALP), former speaker Rasul Guliyev, and Ilyas Ismayilov (Democratic Party of Azerbaijan). The Democratic Party finally achieved registration in early 2000, but co-leader Guliyev remained in forced exile.

15LOCAL GOVERNMENT

Soviet-era Azerbaijan was subdivided administratively into one autonomous republic, Nakhichevan, an area separated from the rest of Azerbaijan by a thin strip of Armenian territory, which had its own parliament of 110 members; and an autonomous region, Nagorno-Karabakh (NK). Azerbaijan dissolved NK's status as an autonomous region in November 1991 in an attempt to reassert central control. NK has claimed an independent existence since December 1991, and a swath of territory around it has been occupied by NK Armenian forces. Azerbaijan has 59 districts (*rayons*) and 11 cities, whose executive heads or mayors are appointed and dismissed by the president. Although the constitution called for the local election of legislative assemblies (councils) by the end of 1997, these elections did not take place until December 1999 (with runoffs in some municipalities in March 2000). In these races, nearly 2,700 municipal and district assemblies were formed. Some 36,000 candidates contested for 22,087 seats in these assemblies. Of these candidates, 18,000 were sponsored by 26 political parties, while others run as independents. The election was not viewed by many international monitors as "free and fair" because of government interference in the electoral process, including the stacking of territorial and precinct electoral commissions with members of the ruling party and other local government supporters, the harassment or disqualification of opposition candidates, and ballot box stuffing. Many of the local assemblies found it difficult to begin work because their roles were somewhat unclear and local executive heads, appointed by Aliyev, proved somewhat reluctant to share power.

16JUDICIAL SYSTEM

The old Soviet court system has been essentially retained, consisting of district courts and municipal courts of first instance and a Supreme Court which usually performs the function of appellate review. However, the Supreme Court also performs the function of court of first instance for some serious cases. District courts consist of one judge and two lay assessors and hear criminal, civil, and juvenile cases. Criminal defendants have the right to an attorney and to appointed counsel, the right to be present at trial, to confront witnesses, and to a public trial.

The 1995 Constitution provides for public trials in most cases, the presumption of innocence in criminal cases, and a defendant's right to legal counsel. Both defendants and prosecutors have the right of appeal. In practice, however, the courts are politically oriented, seeming to overlook the government's human rights violations. In July 1993, Aliyev ousted the Supreme Court chief justice because of alleged political loyalties to the opposition. The President directly appoints lower level judges. The President also appoints the Constitutional Court and Supreme Court Judges with confirmation by the legislature.

Prosecutors (procurators) are appointed by the President with confirmation by the legislature. The minister of Justice organizes prosecutors into offices at the district, municipal, and republic levels. The constitution provides equal status for prosecutors and defense attorneys before the courts, but in practice the arrest and investigatory powers of the prosecutors have dominant influence before the courts. Judges will often remand a case for further prosecutory investigation rather than render an innocent verdict. Investigations often rely on obtaining confessions rather than on gathering evidence.

According to the US State Department's *Report on Human Rights Practices for 1999* and human rights organizations, the Azerbaijan government's human rights record is poor, although some public policy debate is allowed and human rights organizations operate. The government restricts freedom of assembly, religion, and association. Numerous cases of arbitrary arrest, beatings (some resulting in deaths), unwarranted searches and seizures, and other human rights abuses were reported. Political oppositionists are harassed and arrested, and there are dozens of political prisoners in Azerbaijan, according to the US State Department. There is a moratorium on carrying out death sentences, but prisoners sentenced to death are subject to harsh treatment. The conflict between NK Armenians and Azerbaijan has contributed to widespread human rights violations by both sides. Some opposition newspapers are allowed to exist. In the run-up to the October 1998 presidential race, the Aliyev government ordered an end to censorship as a gesture to encourage opposition participation, but cracked down again after the election. Ethnic Lezgins and Talysh have complained of human rights abuses such as restricted educational opportunities in their native languages. Aliyev reported in November 1999 that US Congressional concerns about violations of religious freedom by officials had spurred him to order that "freedom of conscience is inviolable."

[17] ARMED FORCES

Azerbaijan has a total of 69,900 active personnel in its armed forces. Reserves include 575,000 members who have been in the military within the last 15 years. The navy numbers 2,200 and has one operable frigate and seven patrol craft. The army has approximately 55,600 personnel, and the Air Force has 8,100, with approximately 15 attack helicopters and 49 combat aircraft.

Azerbaijan also has an estimated 15,000 people serving in two separate paramilitary units. There is an ongoing conflict with an estimated 20,000–25,000 Armenian forces in the Nagorno-Karabakh region. The defense budget for 1999 was $121 million or 2.6% of GDP.

[18] INTERNATIONAL COOPERATION

Azerbaijan was admitted to the UN on 2 March 1992. The country is also a member of the Black Sea Cooperation Group (BSEC), USCE, EBRD, Economic Cooperation Organization (Turkey, Iran, Pakistan, Russia, the Central Asian states, and Afghanistan), IMF, Organization of the Islamic States, and UNCTAD. The country is also a member of the CIS and has observer status in the WTO. Several nations have recognized Azerbaijan's independence from the former Soviet Union and have established diplomatic ties. Foreign relations with Azerbaijan are dictated by the country's continued sovereignty over Nagorno-Karabakh, which would like to become part of Armenia. The US recognized Azerbaijan's sovereignty on 25 December 1991, but has not established diplomatic relations because of the situation with Nagorno-Karabakh.

[19] ECONOMY

Azerbaijan is one of the oldest oil-producing regions of the world. As a constituent republic of the USSR it was a leading supplier to the rest of the Union until the focus of Soviet oil development efforts shifted to the Ural mountains and western Siberia during the 1970s and 1980s. Remaining oil reserves are estimated to be about 3.6 to 12.5 billion barrels, and gas reserves about 11 trillion cu ft. In addition, the country is endowed with ample deposits of iron, aluminum, zinc, copper, arsenic, molybdenum, marble, and fire clay. Azerbaijan boasts a diversified industrial sector that accounts for approximately 18% of GDP and 15% of employment (including construction). Agriculture, which employs about 32% of the labor force and accounts for 22% of GDP (including forestry), also rests on a relatively diversified base, producing cotton, tobacco, grapes, and a variety of foodstuffs. The transport sector is well developed, integrating the country's various regions and facilitating both domestic and external trade.

Despite its economic potential, Azerbaijan has been slow in making the transition from a command to a market economy. Large state companies continue to dominate the economy and below-market price controls still cover many key commodities. The war with Armenia has also slowed economic growth by disrupting trade ties and draining government revenues. Trade has traditionally been with Russia and the former Soviet republics and the economy is still greatly affected by events in those countries. In 1994, Russia, citing its own conflict in Chechnya, closed all rail and road borders with Azerbaijan. Cut off from its major source of production inputs and main outlet for manufactured projects, Azerbaijan's industrial production fell by more than 20% in 1995. Recently, Azerbaijan has begun to shift trade to Iran and Turkey and away from Russian and Ukraine. Overall, it is estimated that from 1991 through 1995 the economy declined by about 60%. Oil investments in 1994, that came to fruition in the following years caused the GDP to grow by almost 6% in 1997, by 10% in 1998, and 7% in 1999. Foreign investment, the majority in hydrocarbons, accounted for approximately 20% of GDP in 1999. Localized fighting with Armenia broke out in the spring of 1997 and in the summer of 1999. Long term economic growth depends on diversifying export production and making progress on economic reforms.

[20] INCOME

The US Central Intelligence Agency (CIA) reports that in 1998 Azerbaijan's gross domestic product (GDP) was estimated at $12.9 billion. The per capita GDP was estimated at $1,640. The annual growth rate of GDP was estimated at 10%. The average inflation rate in 1998 was -7.6%. The CIA defines GDP as the value of all final goods and services produced within a nation in a given year and computed on the basis of purchasing power parity (PPP) rather than value as measured on the basis of the rate of exchange. It was estimated that agriculture accounted for 22% of GDP, industry 18%, and services 60%.

The World Bank reports that for the same period per capita private consumption (in PPP terms) was $1,675. Private consumption includes expenditures of individuals, households, and nongovernmental organizations. It was estimated that between 1990 and 1998 private consumption grew at an annual rate of 5.8%. Approximately 51% of household consumption was spent on food, 16% on fuel, 9% on health care, and 2% on education.

[21] LABOR

In 1998, there were 3,743,800 people in the Azerbaijani labor force. In 1997, agriculture accounted for 32% of employment; industry, 5%; and services 53%. As of 1998, unemployment stood at 1.1%.

As of 1999, labor unions still operated under the Soviet system. Strikes are legally permitted and increasing in frequency. Unions are free to form federations and participate in international bodies. However, most unions belong to the government-run Azerbaijani Labor Federation. Collective bargaining is at a rudimentary level; wages are still set by government ministries for organizations within the budget. The government runs the largest industrial and white-collar unions.

Although the minimum wage alone is far below the level needed to support a worker and family, the reliance on outside income sources and the structure of extended families generally ensure a decent living. In addition, most working Azeris earn in excess of the minimum wage. The legal workweek is 41 hours. There is a minimum working age of 16 with exceptions for children as young as 14 to work during vacations.

22AGRICULTURE

Some 22% of Azerbaijan's area was cultivated or considered arable in 1997. There are currently 59 agricultural regions in 10 geographic zones; the principal crops are grapes, cotton, and tobacco. Agriculture accounted for 22% of GDP in 1998.

Wheat production in Azerbaijan suffers from a number of problems common in the former Soviet Union, including inadequate production credit and lack of inputs. Most wheat is still produced on state farms, as privatization is only beginning. Production in 1998 amounted to 798,000 tons from 514,000 ha (1,270,000 acres). Cotton production amounted to 113,000 tons in 1998, from a harvested area of 155,000 ha (383,000 acres). Cotton production has been stagnant due to low producer prices, lack of incentives, and a shortage of both inputs and operating capital. Tobacco was grown on about 8,000 ha (19,800 acres) in 1998; production totaled 5,000 tons.

During the Soviet period, some 1,200 state and cooperative farms existed. Since independence, former state-owned farms have become more productive, and private fruit and vegetable farming is increasing. Of the total crop production of 1998, grapes totaled 144,000 tons; cotton (lint), 45,000 tons; fruits, 347,000 tons; vegetables, 769,000 tons; and grains, 1,009,000 tons.

Grapes were grown across 52,000 ha (128,500 acres) in 1998; wine production amounted to 65,000 tons that year. Azerbaijan has an expanding wine-producing industry whose wines have frequently won awards at international exhibitions.

23ANIMAL HUSBANDRY

Azerbaijan has some 2.2 million ha (5.4 million acres) of permanent pasture. The livestock population in 1998 included 13,000,000 chickens, 5,867,000 sheep, 1,843,000 cattle, 371,000 goats, 21,000 pigs, and 46,000 horses. Meat production in 1998 amounted to 95,000 tons, almost three-fourths of which was beef and mutton. In 1998, about 854,000 tons of cow's milk, 28,000 tons of eggs, 10,000 tons of greasy wool, and 1,000 tons of butter were produced.

24FISHING

The Caspian Sea is Azerbaijan's principal fishing resource. Commercial fishing traditionally centered on caviar and sturgeon. The total catch was 8,488 tons in 1997, primarily Azov sea sprat.

25FORESTRY

About 11% of the land area consisted of forests and woodlands in 1995. Soviet-era policies gave priority to high production and rapid growth at the expense of the environment. The State Committee for Ecology and Use of Natural Resources has recently introduced new regulations to protect forest resources.

26MINING

Besides its mineral fuel reserves of petroleum and natural gas along the Caspian Sea, Azerbaijan also has iron ore reserves near the disputed Nagorno-Karabakh region, as well as lead, zinc, and copper-molybdenum deposits in the Nakhichivan area. Other mineral commodities in Azerbaijan include alunite and bromine-iodine. Production of metallic and industrial minerals in 1996 included 200,000 tons of cement. In 1995, 26,100 tons of alumina were produced at the Gyandzha refinery, and 3,464 at the Sumgait smelter. Production totals for 1994 included alumina, 150,000; iron ore, 100,000; salt, 80,000; gypsum, 60,000; limestone, 50,000; and iodine, 30.

27ENERGY AND POWER

At the turn of this century, Azerbaijan accounted for half of the world's oil production. Oil wells have been operating in Baku since the 1840s. Almost all production now comes from offshore in the Caspian Sea. Azerbaijan was one of only four former Soviet republics (along with Russian, Kazakhstan and Turkmenistan) to be self-sufficient in petroleum. Proven oil reserves at the beginning of 1998 totaled between 3.6 and 12.5 billion barrels. Production in 1998 totaled 194,000 barrels per day.

The State Oil Company of Azerbaijan (SOCAR) has planned for joint development of the offshore fields (which are now largely untapped) and has entered into several agreements to build oil pipelines. For instance, a project with the Caspian Pipeline Consortium would carry oil from the Caspian Sea to the Russian Black Sea port of Novorossiysk. Another deal with Turkey will involve the construction of a pipeline to carry crude oil via Iran (bypassing Armenia) and connecting with the Iraq-Turkey pipeline which runs to the Mediterranean. In 1995 Azerbaijan had 17 offshore oil fields in production. Guneshli, about 60 mi off the Azeri coast, currently accounts for more than half the annual production.

Natural gas production has become more important in recent years, especially in Baku, where some of the oil wells have been exhausted. Estimated reserves amount to 11 trillion cu ft (310 billion cu m). Production of natural gas in 1995 totaled 210 billion cu ft (5.9 billion cu m). Ukraine and Iran are interested in running a natural gas pipeline through Azerbaijan en route to Eastern Europe.

Electricity production in 1998 totaled 16.5 billion kWh. Eight thermal plants supply more than 80% of capacity, and the rest comes from hydroelectric plants. The main power plants (both thermal) were near Ali-Bayramy (1100 MW) and Mingechaur (2100 MW). Installed capacity in 1998 was 5.1 million kW.

Petroleum and natural gas resources are the basis for an extensive system of refineries which produce gasoline, herbicides, fertilizers, kerosene, synthetic rubber, and plastics.

28INDUSTRY

The oil and gas industry has traditionally been pivotal to the economy; in 1891, Azerbaijan produced more than half of the world's total oil production. In 1999 oil production accounted for over 66% of total export earnings. Oil refining is concentrated in the Baku and New Baku Oil refineries, with a total capacity of 442,000 barrels per day, but the factories are only operating at 40% of their full potential. Petroleum production is situated in 40 deposits on land and 12 offshore deposits in the Caspian Sea. The offshore Gunashli petroleum mining operation supplies half of the country's petroleum. Specific outputs from the country's refineries include fuel oil, diesel oil, gasoline, kerosene, and other products. Failure to replace worn and outdated technology as well as falling demand from the rest of the former USSR has resulted in a steady decline in the production of oil products since the early 1980s; total output averaged 185,000 barrels per day in 1995, as compared with 285,000 barrels per day in 1987. Oil production is expected to peak between 1.5 and 2 million barrels per day between 2010 and 2015.

In line with the historic importance of the oil sector for the Azeri economy, the fabrication of equipment related to petroleum production is one of the country's major industries. As a source of 70% of the former Soviet Union's oilfield equipment, it also holds great importance for other oil-producing post-Soviet republics who will continue to depend on Azerbaijan as a source of affordable equipment for some time to come. Azerbaijan's petroleum equipment manufacturing industry comprises the second largest concentration of such industries in the world (behind that of the US). Like most other of the country's economic sectors, however, the industry is plagued by plant obsolescence; a significant portion of its own equipment needs is currently being supplied by Turkey in exchange for crude oil on a barter basis.

Other important industrial sectors in the Azeri economy include agro-based industry, light industry, finished metal goods, machine tools, chemicals and petrochemicals, and some electronics. As with fuel and oilfield equipment production, however, output in almost all of these sectors declined or stagnated in the 1990s due to the conflict with Armenia.

In aggregate terms, the real value of total industrial production in Azerbaijan dropped 21% in 1995, following already steep declines of 31% in 1992, 8% in 1991, and 17% in 1990. In the course of this decline, the structure of the industrial sector changed as well, with the fuel industry as well as metal processing and machinery replacing agro-based industry and light industry as the main sources of total industrial output in value terms (despite declining yields in volume terms in all sectors). This shift resulted mainly from the higher prices garnered for upstream products like fuel and processed metals, which were characterized by brighter prospects on the international market than most light and processed food industry goods in the wake of price liberalization.

In 1997 and 1998, the value of industrial production (namely oil) rose by 17% and almost 20% respectively, while the manufacturing sector lost 65% and 18% for those years.

29 SCIENCE AND TECHNOLOGY

The Azerbaijan Academy of Sciences in Baku has departments of physical engineering and mathematical sciences, chemistry, earth sciences, and biology; as of 1997, 19 science and technology-related research institutes were attached to it. The country has numerous other institutes conducting research in agriculture, medicine, and technology.

The Azerbaijan Technical University in Baku, founded in 1920, has faculties in automation and computing technology, electrical engineering, machine-building, automechanics, metallurgy, radio-engineering, robotics, and transport. Baku State University, founded in 1919, has faculties of mathematics, physics, chemistry, biology, geology, and geography. Azerbaijan also has five higher institutes offering courses in agriculture, medicine, petroleum engineering, engineering, and technology. In 1987–97, science and engineering students accounted for 37% of college and university enrollments. The Azerbaijan Scientific and Technical Library is located in Baku.

30 DOMESTIC TRADE

Despite the government's claims that it is moving towards a free market economy, government ownership is still common among large industries. Since independence, there has been an informal privatization of the trading sector as small shops have sprung up throughout Azerbaijan. Private traders now handle most retail sales. Private business people see trade as relatively low risk in an environment where private ownership rights do not exist. Business hours vary according to the owner's preference.

31 FOREIGN TRADE

Like other post-Soviet economies, Azerbaijan is highly trade-dependent; however, it is endowed with a more diversified export structure than many other former USSR countries, especially in neighboring Central Asia. While the centrally planned state ordering system is steadily losing its place as the basis for trade in the former Soviet Union, the Azeri Ministry of Foreign Economic Relations still controls the export of all products considered to be of strategic importance to the national economy.

Exports include oil and gas (66%), chemicals, oilfield equipment, textiles, and cotton. Imports include machinery and parts (50%), consumer goods, food, and textiles.

Principal trading partners in 1998 (in millions of US dollars) were as follows:

COUNTRY	EXPORTS	IMPORTS	BALANCE
Iran	190	49	141
Georgia	175	45	130
Russia	142	157	-15
Turkey	46	360	-314
Ukraine	25	99	-74
Italy	19	35	-16
Germany	12	120	-108
United Kingdom	12	103	-91
Kazakhstan	9	40	-31
United Arab Emirates	6	43	-37
United States	5	135	-130

32 BALANCE OF PAYMENTS

The war in and around Nagorno–Karabakh with Armenia has facilitated Azerbaijan's trade deterioration, which is further exacerbated by the collapse of the local currency. Reviving ruble-related trade links with Russia was a key reason for Azerbaijan's entry into the Commonwealth of Independent States in September 1992. In 1995 inflation fell and the currency was stable until it was devalued in 1999, causing inflation of 10% to 15%. The current account deficit was over one-third of GDP in 1998.

The US Central Intelligence Agency reports that in 1997 the purchasing power parity of Azerbaijan's exports was $781 million while imports totaled $794 million resulting in a trade balance of -$13 million.

The International Monetary Fund (IMF) reports that in 1998 Azerbaijan had exports of goods totaling $678 million and imports totaling $1,724 million. The services credit totaled $332 million and debit $701 million. The following table summarizes Azerbaijan's balance of payments as reported by the IMF for 1998 in millions of US dollars.

Current Account		-1,365
Balance on goods	-1,046	
Balance on services	-369	
Balance on income	-13	
Current transfers	64	
Capital Account		-1
Financial Account		1,326
Direct investment abroad	...	
Direct investment in Azerbaijan	1,023	
Portfolio investment assets	...	
Portfolio investment liabilities	...	
Other investment assets	22	
Other investment liabilities	280	
Net Errors and Omissions		-20
Reserves and Related Items		59

33 BANKING AND SECURITIES

The National Bank of Azerbaijan is the central bank of Azerbaijan. The central bank is charged with regulating the money supply, circulating currency, and regulating the commercial banks of the country. There are approximately 70 foreign and local banks in Azerbaijan. Of the four state-owned banks, only the International Bank of Azerbaijan (IBA) was solvent in 1999. The IBA was in the process of being privatized in that year. Major commercial banks include the Promtekhbank, Azakbank, Azerdemiryolbank, Bacobank, Gunay International Bank, Halgbank, ILKBANK, and the Universal Bank. Most businesses use the IBA, or the British Bank of the Middle East, Baku.

The central bank increased the minimum bank capital to $1.5 million in 1999, and expected to increase the figure to $3 million in 2001, effectively consolidating the sector.

There were plans for an Azerbaijani stock exchange in 1999, based on the Baku Interbank Currency Exchange that began operations in 1993.

34INSURANCE
As of 1995, at least 14 insurance companies were doing business in Azerbaijan.

35PUBLIC FINANCE
Since 1996, the Azerbaijani government has emphasized privatization as a means towards consolidation of the public debt and revitalization of the economy. Over 70% of all parastatals are set to be privatized; more than 20,600 companies were privatized during 1997 and 1998. Foreign investment was encouraged, especially in the oil sector, however the diversification needed for long-term growth is lacking.

The International Monetary Fund (IMF) estimates that in 1998 Azerbaijan's central government took in revenues of approximately $869 million and had expenditures of $992 million including capital expenditures of $188 million. Overall, the government registered a deficit of approximately $123 million. External debt totaled $593 million.

The following table shows an itemized breakdown of government revenues and expenditures in millions of US dollars. The percentages were calculated from data reported by the IMF.

REVENUE AND GRANTS	100%	869
Tax revenue	92.8%	806
Non-tax revenue	5.3%	46
Grants	1.9%	16
EXPENDITURES	100%	992
General public services	6.0%	59
Defense	11.1%	110
Public order and safety	11.3%	112
Education	3.2%	32
Health	0.8%	8
Social security	33.1%	329
Recreation, cultural, and religious affairs	1.3%	13
Economic affairs and services	8.5%	84
Other expenditures	24.4%	242
Interest payments	1.9%	19
Adjustments	-1.7%	-17

36TAXATION
Personal income is taxed at rates ranging from 12–40%, and the corporate tax rate of 32%. Also levied are a 20% VAT, an excise tax, and an employer payroll tax of 35%.

37CUSTOMS AND DUTIES
Tariffs are set at 15%, 5%, or 3%. Most goods carry the 15% import customs duty. Capital goods and some primary goods are exempt. There is also a 20% VAT on certain imports. A dividend withholding tax of 15% is applicable to monies sent abroad.

In 1992, Azerbaijan signed trade agreements with all the republics of the former USSR except Armenia and Russia. Azerbaijan joined the Commonwealth of Independent States in September 1993, it acceded to its economic union treaty the same year. Azerbaijan is a member of the Economic Cooperation Organization. In 1999, Azerbaijan entered into a Partnership and Cooperation Agreement with the European Union, and was seeking membership in the WTO.

38FOREIGN INVESTMENT
Foreign investment plays a major role in financing the development of much of Azerbaijan's industrial sector, especially the oil and gas-related industries. The 1992 Law on Foreign Investment provided many basic guarantees to foreign investors, including nondiscriminatory treatment, the repatriation of profits, guarantees against expropriation, and dispute settlement. The Privatization Law passed in 1995 allowed foreign investors to acquire shares in state companies and purchase real estate jointly. Starting in 1997, foreign tax privileges were revoked. As of 1999, foreign investors were required to obtain a license and pay a fee in order to open business in Azerbaijan.

Only about 100 joint venture projects were registered by mid-1992; these were dominated by Turkish firms and involved primarily trade and textiles. In the oil sector, preliminary agreements were signed with US, Scottish, British, and other foreign companies for the exploration and development of several major oil fields in the Caspian Sea. In 1992, Azerbaijan joined a consortium with Oman, Kazakhstan, and Russia aimed at constructing a pipeline through either Armenia, Iran and Turkey, or Georgia. Little action was taken on these agreements, due to heightened political tensions. The Azerbaijan International Operating Company (AIOC), led by BP Amaco, signed an $8 billion contract in 1994 to exploit oil reserves at Azeri, Chirag, and Guneshli. Foreign direct investment leapt from only $30 million in 1994 to an estimated $872 million in 1999 (or 20% of GDP), with approximately 80% of FDI concentrated in the hydrocarbons sector. Although the US government has banned public aid to Azerbaijan since 1992, US investors play a large role in exploiting Azerbaijani oil reserves.

39ECONOMIC DEVELOPMENT
Rapid development of the Azeri economy in the former USSR was based on the expansion of both its industrial sector, led by oil-related industries, and its agricultural sector, led by grape, tobacco, and cotton production. With grape and wine production weakened by the effects of Gorbachev's anti-alcoholism campaign in the 1980s, and much of the country's industrial sector afflicted by technological obsolescence, overall economic growth in the republic had already begun to decline by 1989, when NMP dropped 6%. Key strategies of the Azeri government to bring about economic revitalization have included both an economic restructuring program as well as efforts to expand its economic ties to countries beyond the former Soviet Union. To the latter end, Azerbaijan joined the Economic Cooperation Organization set up by Iran, Pakistan, and Turkey to promote trade among Muslim countries. It was also the first of the former Soviet republics to become a member of the Islamic Development Bank, which provides potential access to financing for programs related to agriculture, construction, training, and food aid.

The restructuring program in Azerbaijan has been similar to those of other countries in the former USSR. Its main points include stabilization measures (price liberalization, introduction of national currency, and establishment of an exchange rate stabilization fund); introduction of new legislation regarding privatization, foreign investment, and employment; fiscal and monetary reform (including introduction of a VAT and controls on government expenditures); civil service reform; and development of the banking sector. Four committees on antitrust, support for enterprises, state property, and land reform have been established to oversee the implementation of reform legislation. Privatization of the state enterprise sector is moving at a slow pace. Particular attention is being directed at modernizing those strategic sectors of the economy with the greatest potential for export growth, particularly the oil industry and, to a lesser extent, textile production; the role of foreign investment is seen as pivotal in these areas. The pursuit of development plans, however, remains hampered by ongoing political conflict in the country. The border between Azerbaijan and Armenia, still closed in 2000, limited the vital trade with Turkey. It was estimated that the money saved by transport costs if the border reopened would add $180 million to the GDP, not to mention the overall economic benefits of a lasting peace between the two countries.

40 SOCIAL DEVELOPMENT

The disintegration of the Soviet economy led to economic decline in Azerbaijan, with falling living standards and rising unemployment. The minimum wage was raised several times, but it still does not provide adequately for a worker and family. A decent living can only be assured by the "safety net" of the extended family structure. Health and safety standards are often ignored in the workplace.

Unemployment benefits were introduced in 1991. Contributions in the amount of 2% of payroll are made by employers. Unemployment benefits are paid for 26 weeks, with additional weeks provided for every year worked over 25 years. The maximum allowable time period to receive benefits is 52 weeks. The amount of benefits provided ranges from 55% to 75% of average earnings. Benefits are suspended if the applicant refuses two job offers. Old age and disability pension and survivor benefits are provided under a 1992 law amended in 1997. Workers' compensation provides both short-term disability benefits and pensions.

Women nominally enjoy the same legal status as men. Heydar Aliyer appointed several women to senior government positions. Women receive extensive opportunities for education, work, and political activity. However, social traditions of the Caucasus tend to keep them in a subordinate positions. During the last parliamentary elections, for example, it was noted that many men voted in the place of their wives. As of 1995, 15 of 125 parliamentary seats were held by women.

Ethnic tension and anti-Armenian sentiment is still strong. Many Armenians have either been expelled or emigrated. It is estimated that only 10,000–20,000 Armenians continue to reside in Azerbaijan. Other minorities, such as the Kurds and the Turks, also report problems of discrimination.

Azerbaijan's human rights record was poor. Excessive force was used by police, and the judicial system was inefficient and corrupt. Fifty political prisoners were held by the government in 1999, down from 75 in 1998.

41 HEALTH

As part of the former Soviet Union, Azerbaijan has had to develop and maintain its own health care system and standards. In 1992, there were 3.93 doctors and 10.2 hospital beds per 1,000 people. Total health expenditures for 1990 reached $785 million. In 1995, the total expenditure on health was 5% of the gross domestic product.

Azerbaijan's infant mortality rate for 1994 was 25 per 1,000 live births. In 1996, the country immunized one-year-old children against the following diseases: tuberculosis (90%); diphtheria, pertussis, and tetanus (95%); polio (97%); and measles (99%).

The overall death rate in 1999 was 10 per 1,000 inhabitants. Mortality from 1985 to 1990 was broken down as follows: communicable diseases, maternal/perinatal causes, 110 per 100,000 people; noncommunicable diseases, 595 per 100,000; and injuries, 46 per 100,00. In addition, thousands of lives were lost between 1989 and 1992 when the country was at war with Armenia. Few cases of AIDS have been reported in the last few years. In 1996, two cases were reported. Diptheria, tuberculosis, hepatitis A, and diarrheal and acute respiratory infections have been serious public health problems. There have also been outbreaks of anthrax, botulism, cholera, tetanus, and malaria. Measles and tuberculosis still remain in this country despite a high incidence of vaccination for one year old children. In 1995, the incidence of tuberculosis was 33 per 100,000 population.

42 HOUSING

At last estimate, Azerbaijan had 12.5 sq m of housing space per capita. Approximately 138,000 households (or 15.6%) were on waiting lists for housing in urban areas. Nearly 32% of all privately owned urban housing had running water, 6.7% had sewer lines, 5.7% had bathtubs, and 96.8% had gas.

43 EDUCATION

The educational system is extensive and illiteracy is practically unknown. In 1995, adult illiteracy rate was estimated at 0.4% (males, 0.3%; females, 0.5%). The usual language of instruction is Azerbaijani, although Russian, Armenian, and Georgian are also offered by some schools. In 1997 primary schools enrolled 719,013 students in 4,454 schools, with 35,514 teachers. In the same year, secondary schools enrolled 819,625 students taught by approximately 85,000 teachers.

Russian is more commonly used at higher level institutions, but this is slowly changing with a growing demand for the use of Azerbaijani. Education is free. In the latter half of the 1990s, approximately 18.8% of government expenditure was allocated to education.

Azerbaijan's most important institutes of higher learning are the Azerbaijan Polytechnic Institute, located in Baku, with seven departments and an enrollment of 12,000 students; and the State University, also located at Baku and founded in 1919. It has an enrollment of over 15,000 students in 11 departments. Other institutions include the Medical University, Technological University, the Economic Institute, and the Oil and Chemistry Academy. In total, 15,929 teachers were employed and 115,116 students were enrolled in institutions of higher learning in 1997.

Baku is sometimes referred to as an "oil academy" because of its ongoing research in the areas of turbine drilling, cementation of oil wells, and the development of synthetic rubber from natural gas.

44 LIBRARIES AND MUSEUMS

Azerbaijan has a National Library in Baku with 4.4 million volumes. There are 115 recognized museums in the country, 27 of which are art museums, and there are 20 theaters. The country also has 6,571 monuments and historic sights. The Ichari Shahar, or Old Town, in Baku has the Shirvanshah Palace, an architectural monument from the 15th and 16th centuries which has been restored and is now a museum. Other museums are the Museum of History of Azerbaijan (1920), which exhibits archeological, ethnographic, and other relics; the Rustam Mustfayev Azerbaijan State Arts Museum, displaying works of Azerbaijani, Russian and West European artists from the 15th–19th centuries along with the works of modern Azerbaijani artists; the State Museum of Azerbaijani Carpets and Folk and Applied Art; and the Nizami State Museum of Azerbaijani Literature, depicting the stages of literary development. The Gobustan Museum features prehistoric dwellings and cave paintings over 10,000 years old. Baku, the capital, remains an important cultural and intellectual center in Transcaucasia.

45 MEDIA

Azerbaijan is connected to other former Soviet republics by landline or microwave, and to other countries through Moscow. In 1998, there were 1.4 million telephones in use. Service is said to be of poor quality and inadequate. As of 1999, there were 10 AM and 17 FM stations and two television stations. Domestic and Russian television programs are received locally, while Iranian television is received from an Intelsat satellite through a receive-only earth station. In 1997, there were 20 radios, 211 television sets, and 5 mobile phones per 1,000 population.

In 1995 there were over 16 newspapers, most of them published in Azerbaijan. Those with the greatest circulation were *Khalg Gazeti* (50,000 circulation), *Azerbaijan* (70,000 circulation), and *Azadlig* (50,000 circulation). *Azerbaijan Ganjlari* (*Youth of Azerbaijan*) had a circulation of 161,000 in 1999. Over 100 periodicals are published, more than half in Azerbaijan.

The Constitution of Azerbaijan specifically outlaws press censorship; however, it is said that the government does not always respect freedom of the press in practice.

Online access is extremely limited, with less than one Internet host per 1,000 population in 1998.

⁴⁶ORGANIZATIONS

Important political associations in the Republic of Azerbaijan include the Helsinki Group, a human rights group, the National Democratic Movement, and Musavat (Equality). The Chamber of Commerce and Industry of the Republic of Azerbaijan promotes the country's goods and services in world markets.

⁴⁷TOURISM, TRAVEL, AND RECREATION

The capital city of Baku is one of the prime tourist destinations of the Caucasus region. Its Old Town, with the Shirvanshah palace dating back to the 15–16th centuries, is especially popular with sightseers. Other attractions include the Museum of History and the State Arts Museum, as well as museums of folk art and literature. Elsewhere in Azerbaijan, the Gobustan Museum displays prehistoric dwellings and cave paintings, and the village of Surakhani attracts visitors to the Atashgah Fire-Worshipper's Temple. Visitors are also welcome at the carpet-weaving factory in the village of Nardaran, the Wine-making State Farm in the Shamakhi area, the Fruit And Vegetable State Farm around the town of Guba, and the Mashtagha Subtropical Fruit State Farm. There were approximately 166,000 tourist arrivals in Azerbaijan in 1997.

In 1999 the UN estimated the cost of staying at the Hotel Hyatt in Baku at $286 per day. The cost of staying outside of Baku are estimated at $64.

⁴⁸FAMOUS AZERBAIJANIS

Heydar Aliyev has been acting president since June 1993. The poet Nizami Ganjavi (1141–1204) is celebrated for his *Khamsa*, a collection of five epic poems. Muhammed Fizuli (1438–1556) based his poems on traditional folktales, and his poetic versions provide the bases for many 20th century plays and operas. Satirical poet Sabir (1862–1911) was openly critical of the clergy at a time when their influence controlled much of society. Abul Hasan Bakhmanyar, an 11th century scientist, wrote respected books on mathematics and philosophy. Hasan Shirvani wrote a book on astronomy.

The composer Uzeyir Hajibeyov (1885–1948) wrote the first Azerbaijani opera, and also founded the Azerbaijani Symphonic Orchestra and composed Azerbaijan's National Anthem. Other famous composers from Azerbaijan include Gara Garayev (1918–82), Haji Khannmammadov (b.1918), Fikrat Amirov (1922–84), and Vasif Adigozal (b.1936). Vagif Mustafa Zadeh (1940–79) is considered the founder of the Azerbaijani music movement of the 1960s that mixed jazz with the traditional style known as *mugam*. His daughter, Aziza Mustafa Zadeh (b.1969), is a noted jazz pianist.

Prominent modern Azerbaijani scientists include Lofti Zadeh (b.1921), pioneer of the "fuzzy logic" concept, and Ali Javan (b. Iran, 1928), inventor of the gas laser.

⁴⁹DEPENDENCIES

Azerbaijan has no territories or colonies.

⁵⁰BIBLIOGRAPHY

Aganbegyan, Abel. *Perestrokda Revolution*. New York: Harper & Row, 1990.

Altstadt, Audrey L. *The Azerbaijani Turks: Power and Identity Under Russian Rule*. Stanford, Calif.: Hoover Institution Press, Stanford University, 1992.

Atabaki, Touraj. *Azerbaijan: Ethnicity and Autonomy in Twentieth-century Iran*. New York: British Academy Press, 1993.

Azerbaijan: From Crisis to Sustained Growth. Washington, D.C.: World Bank, 1993.

Edwards-Jones, Imogen. *The Taming of Eagles: Exploring the New Russia*. London: Weidenfeld & Nicolson, 1993.

Fawcett, Louise L'Estrange. *Iran and the Cold War: the Azerbaijan Crisis of 1946*. Cambridge, and New York: Cambridge University Press, 1992.

Federal Research Division, Library of Congress. *Armenia, Azerbaijan, and Georgia: Country Studies*. Washington, D.C.: Federal Research Division, Library of Congress, 1995.

International Monetary Fund. *Azerbaijan*. Washington, D.C.: International Monetary Fund, 1992.

Rost, Yuri. *Armenian Tragedy*. New York: St. Martin's, 1990.

Shoemaker, M. Wesley. *Russia, Eurasian States and Eastern Europe 1993*. Washington, D.C.: Stryker-Post, 1993.

Swietochowski, Tadeusz. *Russia and Azerbaijan: A Borderland in Transition*. New York: Columbia University Press, 1995.

Transcaucasia, Nationalism and Social Change: Essays in the History of Armenia, Azerbaijan, and Georgia. Ann Arbor: University of Michigan Press, 1996.

BAHRAIN

State of Bahrain
Dawlat al-Bahrayn

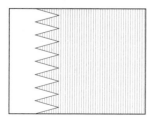

CAPITAL: Manama (Al-Manamah).

FLAG: Red with a white vertical stripe on the hoist, the edge between them being serrated.

ANTHEM: Music without words.

MONETARY UNIT: The Bahrain dinar (BD) is divided into 1,000 fils. There are coins of 5, 10, 25, 50, and 100 fils and notes of 500 fils and 1, 5, 10, and 20 dinars. BD1 = $2.6525 ($1 = BD0.377) as of 31 March 2000.

WEIGHTS AND MEASURES: The metric system is used; local measures are also used.

HOLIDAYS: New Year's Day, 1 January; National Day, 16 December. Movable Muslim religious holidays include Hijra (Muslim New Year), 'Ashura, Prophet's Birthday, 'Id al-Fitr, and 'Id al-'Adha'.

TIME: 3 PM = noon GMT.

¹LOCATION, SIZE, AND EXTENT

Situated in the western Persian Gulf, 29 km (18 mi) NW of Qatar, the State of Bahrain consists of a group of 33 islands (6 inhabited) with a total area of 620 sq km (239 sq mi), extending 48 km (30 mi) N–S and 19 km (12 mi) E–W. Comparatively, Bahrain occupies slightly less than 3.5 times the area of Washington, D.C. Bahrain, the main island, is linked by causeways and bridges to Muharraq and Sitra islands and to Sa'udi Arabia; other islands include the Hawar group, Nabih Salih, Umm an-Nasan, and Jidda. The total coastline is 161 km (100 mi). Bahrain's capital city, Manama, is located on the northeastern coast.

²TOPOGRAPHY

A narrow strip of land along the north coast of Bahrain is irrigated by natural springs and artesian wells. South of the cultivable area, the land is barren. The landscape consists of low rolling hills with numerous rocky cliffs and wadis. From the shoreline the surface rises gradually toward the center, where it drops into a basin surrounded by steep cliffs. Toward the center of the basin is Jabal ad-Dukhan, a rocky, steep-sided hill that rises 76 m (250 ft) above the surrounding plain and 137 m (450 ft) above sea level. Most of the lesser islands are flat and sandy, while Nabih Salih is covered with date groves.

³CLIMATE

Summers in Bahrain are hot and humid, and winters are relatively cool. Daily average temperatures in July range from a minimum of 29°C (84°F) to a maximum of 37°C (99°F); the January minimum is 14°C (57°F), the maximum 20°C (68°F). Rainfall averages less than 10 cm (4 in) annually and occurs mostly from December to March. Prevailing southeast winds occasionally raise dust storms.

⁴FLORA AND FAUNA

Outside the cultivated areas, numerous wild desert flowers appear, most noticeably after rain. Desert shrubs, grasses, and wild date palms are also found. Mammalian life is limited to the jerboa (desert rat), gazelle, mongoose, and hare; some 14 species of lizard and 4 types of land snake are also found. Bird life is especially varied. Larks, song thrushes, swallows, and terns are frequent visitors, and residents include the bulbul, hoopoe, parakeet, and warbler.

⁵ENVIRONMENT

Bahrain's principal environmental problems are scarcity of fresh water, desertification, and pollution from oil production. Population growth and industrial development have reduced the amount of agricultural land and lowered the water table, leaving aquifers vulnerable to saline contamination. In recent years, the government has attempted to limit extraction of groundwater (in part by expansion of seawater desalinization facilities) and to protect vegetation from further erosion. In 1994, 100% of Bahrain's urban dwellers and 57% of the rural population had pure water. Bahrain has developed its oil resources at the expense of its agricultural lands. As a result, lands that might otherwise be productive are gradually claimed by the expansion of the desert. Pollution from oil production was accelerated by the Persian Gulf War and the resulting damage to oil-producing facilities in the Gulf area, which threatened the purity of both coastal and ground water, damaging coastlines, coral reefs, and marine vegetation through oil spills and other discharges.

A wildlife sanctuary established in 1980 home to threatened Gulf species, including the Arabian oryx, gazelle, zebra, giraffe, Defassa waterbuck, addax, and lesser kudu. Bahrain has also established captive breeding centers for falcons and for the rare Houbara bustard. The goitered gazelle and the green sea turtle are considered endangered species.

⁶POPULATION

The population of Bahrain in 2000 was estimated at 641,539. An estimated 3.4% of the population is 65 years of age or older. The projected population for the year 2005 is 702,000, assuming a crude birthrate of 19 per 1,000 population and a death rate of 3, resulting in a natural rate of change of 1.6% for the period 2000–2005.

It was estimated that 92% of the population lived in urban areas in 2000. The capital city, Manama, had a 2000 population of 148,000; it is connected by causeway with the other major city, Al-Muharraq, population 75,906. Bahrain's next census is slated for 2001.

⁷MIGRATION

The proportion of aliens increased from 20% of the total population in 1975 to an estimated 33% (171,872) in 1990. Most of them are temporary workers from other Arab countries, Iran, Pakistan, India, and the Republic of Korea. Many skilled workers are Europeans. In mid-1996, the net immigration rate was 2.42 migrants per 1,000 population.

⁸ETHNIC GROUPS

In 1999, 63% of the population consisted of indigenous Bahrainis, the vast majority of whom were of northern Arab (Adnani) stock, infused with black racial traits. Asians accounted for 13% of the population; other Arab groups (principally Omanis) 10%; Iranians 8%; and other ethnic groups 6%.

⁹LANGUAGES

Arabic is the universal language; the Gulf dialect is spoken. English is widely understood, Farsi and Urdu less so.

¹⁰RELIGIONS

In 1999, an estimated 75% of indigenous Bahrainis were Shi'a Muslim and about 25% Sunni Muslim, the latter mostly in rural areas. Foreigners make up 35 to 40% of the total population; roughly half are non-Muslim. Christians and other non-Muslims, including Jews, Hindus, and Baha'is, are free to practice their religions, keep their own places of worship, and display the symbols for their religions. Islam, however, is the official religion.

¹¹TRANSPORTATION

The outline of the present road network was traced in the early 1930s, soon after the discovery of oil. The four main islands and all the towns and villages are linked by excellent roads. There were 3,103 km (1,928 mi) of roadways in 1997, of which 2,374 km (1,475 mi) were paved. A four-lane, 2.8-km (1.7-mi) causeway and bridge connect Manama with Al-Muharraq, and another bridge joins Sitra to the main island. A four-lane highway atop a 24-km (15-mi) causeway, linking Bahrain with the Sa'udi Arabian mainland via Umm an-Nasan, was completed in December 1986 and financed by Sa'udi Arabia.

Bahrain's port of Mina Sulman can accommodate 16 ocean-going vessels drawing up to 11 m (36 ft). In 1998, Bahrain had a merchant fleet of 8 ships of 1,000 GRT or over, totaling 228,273 GRT. Also in 1998, there were 3 airports, 2 of which had paved runways. The international airport near Al-Muharraq can handle large jet aircraft and serves more than two dozen international airlines. In 1997, the airport was in the midst of a major expansion. Gulf Air, headquartered in Bahrain and owned equally by the governments of Bahrain, Oman, Qatar, and the United Arab Emirates (UAE), flies to other Gulf countries, India, and Europe. In 1997, 1,165,000 passengers were carried on scheduled domestic and international flights.

¹²HISTORY

The history of Bahrain has been traced back 5,000 years to Sumerian times. Known as Dilmun, Bahrain was a thriving trade center around 2000 bc; the islands were visited by the ships of Alexander the Great in the 3d century bc. Bahrain accepted Islam in the 7th century ad, after which it was ruled alternately by its own princes and by the caliphs' governors. The Portuguese occupied Bahrain from 1522 to 1602. The present ruling family, the Khalifa, who are related to the Sabah family of Kuwait and the Sa'udi royal family, captured Bahrain in 1782. Following an initial contact in 1805, the ruler of Bahrain signed the first treaty with Britain in 1820. A binding treaty of protection, similar to those with other Persian Gulf principalities, was concluded in 1861 and revised in 1892 and 1951. After World War II, Britain maintained at Bahrain its headquarters for treaty affairs in the lower Gulf. Claims to Bahrain pressed by Iran were abandoned in 1971 after a UN mission ascertained that the Bahrainis wished to remain independent of that nation.

Between 1968 and 1971, Bahrain participated in discussions aimed at forming a federation of the nine sheikhdoms of the southern Gulf. On 14 August 1971, Sheikh 'Isa bin Salman al-Khalifa declared that, in view of the failure of the larger federation to materialize, Bahrain would declare its independence. Its treaties with the UK were replaced by a treaty of friendship and cooperation, and on 15 August, the country became the sovereign State of Bahrain. Bahrain promulgated its first constitution in 1973, which occasioned the convening of an elective National Assembly; the legislature was dissolved in August 1975 amid charges of Communist influence. The emir has continued to set state policy, and his brother, Crown Prince Hamad bin 'Isa al-Khalifa, has directed government administration. In 1993, Bahrain established an appointive Consultative Assembly (Majlis al-Shura).

Owing to its small size, Bahrain generally takes its lead in foreign affairs from its Arab neighbors on the Gulf. A founding member of the Gulf Cooperation Council, it shares with the other five members a concern with pressures from Iran and Iraq. During the Iran-Iraq War, Bahrain joined most other Arab states in supporting Iraq. Subsequently, it has carefully tried to foster better relations with Iran through trade. When Iraq invaded Kuwait, Bahrain stood with the allies, contributing military support and facilities to the defeat of Iraq.

Bahrain has long assisted the American naval presence in the Persian Gulf. In 1977, a formal agreement for home-porting US naval ships was replaced by arrangements to continue ship visits and other security cooperation. Since the Gulf War, this cooperation has expanded with arms sales, plans for joint exercises and US pre-positioning of military material for future contingencies. In 1991, the US signed an agreement giving the Department of Defense access to facilities on the island. The country is home to the US Navy's Fifth Fleet.

Since 1994, Bahrain, like several other traditional emirates of the Gulf, has experienced sometimes severe civil disturbances from a Shiite-led resistance opposed to the ruling family and supportive of establishing an Islamic democracy. In 1996, a band of 44 Bahraini Islamists were arrested for allegedly planning a coup to overthrow the ruling family. The emirate broke relations with Iran, which the former accused of fomenting its civil disturbances which between 1994 and 1996 had resulted in 25 deaths. In 1997, the US disclosed that it had uncovered a plot to attack its military forces stationed in the country.

On March 6, 1999, Sheikh 'Isa bin Salman al-Khalifa, who had ruled his country since its independence in 1971, died of a heart attack. He was succeeded on the throne by his son, Sheikh Hamad bin 'Isa al-Khalifa. Over the following year, there were signs that while the new ruler would continue his father's pro-Western foreign-policy orientation, domestically he would take a more liberal approach to government. In April, Sheikh Hamad released high-profile Shiite dissident, Sheik Abdul Amir al-Jamri, from jail together with hundreds of other political prisoners. Another broad pardon of dissidents took place in November. The following month, the sheikh announced that he would restore democratically elected municipal councils, which had been outlawed in the 1970s.

¹³GOVERNMENT

Under the constitution ratified in June 1973, Bahrain is a constitutional monarchy headed by an emir. Bahrain's emir from 1971 to 1999 was Sheikh 'Isa bin Salman al-Khalifa. He was succeeded by his son, Sheikh Hamad bin 'Isa al-Khalifa. A council of ministers, appointed by the emir, is presided over by the prime minister, who since 1973 has been Sheikh Khalifa bin Salman al-

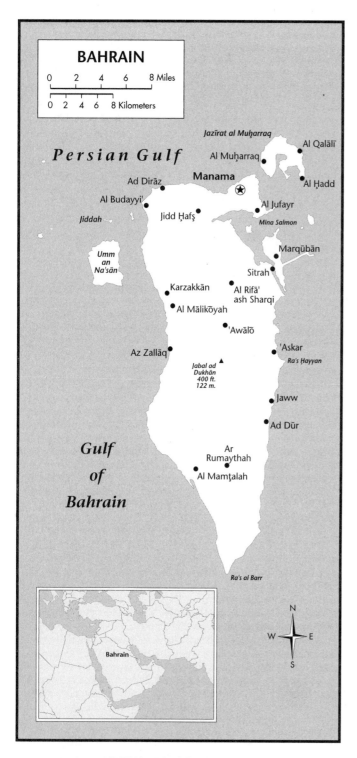

BAHRAIN

0   2   4   6   8 Miles

0   2   4   6   8 Kilometers

Persian Gulf

Jazīrat al Muḥarraq

Al Qalālī

Al Muḥarraq

Manama

Ad Dirāz

Al Ḥadd

Al Budayyi'

Al Jufayr

Jiddah

Jidd Ḥafṣ

Mina Salmon

Umm an Na'sān

Marqūbān

Sitrah

Karzakkān

Al Rifā' ash Sharqi

Al Mālikōyah

'Awālō

Az Zallāq

'Askar

Ra's Ḥayyan

Jabal ad Dukhān 400 ft. 122 m.

Jaww

Ad Dūr

Gulf of Bahrain

Ar Rumaythah

Al Mamṭalah

Ra's al Barr

N W E S

Bahrain

LOCATION: 25°47'10" to 26°17'3"N; 50°22'45" to 50°40'20"E.
TOTAL COASTLINE: 161 km (100 mi). **TERRITORIAL SEA LIMIT:** 3 mi.

Khalifa, a brother of the former emir. Members of the ruling family hold most of the important government posts, including the ministries of foreign affairs, defense, justice and interior. Although the constitution provides for a National Assembly composed of 30 elected members and 14 cabinet ministers, no National Assembly has been allowed to exist since 1975. The council of ministers exercises the legislative function. In 1993, the ruling family created the Consultative Council, a wholly appointed body that acts in concert with royal decrees. A new 40-member council was appointed in September 1996.

14 POLITICAL PARTIES

Political parties are illegal under the emirate. Several underground groups, including branches of Hizbollah and other pro-Iranian militant Islamic groups, have been active and are vigorously pursued by government security services. Anti-regime dissidents have frequently been jailed or exiled.

15 LOCAL GOVERNMENT

Bahrain's six major towns are administered by a single municipal council, whose members are appointed by the emir. At the end of 1999, Sheikh Hamad announced his intention of reinstating democratically elected municipal councils, which had been banned since the 1970s. In the five rural communities, administration continues to be conducted along traditional lines by village headmen (mukhtars).

16 JUDICIAL SYSTEM

The law of Bahrain represents a mixture of Islamic religious law (Shari'a) and government decrees dealing with criminal and commercial matters. The Al Khalifa family dominates the government and the judiciary. Professional judges serve on civil and criminal courts and on courts of appeal. In ordinary civil and criminal courts there are open trials, a right to counsel (including legal aid when determined to be necessary) and a right to appeal.

There are separate courts for members of the Sunni and Shiite sects. Religious courts handle divorces. While both women and men may initiate a divorce, religious courts have the discretion to refuse a woman's request. Military courts handle cases involving military personnel accused of violating the military code of justice. The Supreme Court of Appeals may sit as a security court. When so operating it conducts secret proceedings and is exempt form the usual procedures guaranteed by the penal code. Ordinary civil or criminal trial procedures provide for an open trial, right to appeal and right to council

Detentions without trial are permissible for up to 3 years under the 1974 State Security Act. Government interference in the judiciary was rampant in cases of anti-government activities that accompanied the civil unrest between 1994 and 1996. A special Security Court was established to handle anti-regime cases. International concern has been expressed over human rights violations in the handling of these cases.

17 ARMED FORCES

After an attempted coup in 1981, a bilateral defense agreement was signed with Sa'udi Arabia. Bahrain is a member of the Gulf Cooperation Council (GCC), which provided it and Oman $1.8 billion (1984–94) for defense modernization. The Bahrain army in 2000 had 8,500 officers and men in one combined arms brigade with US and UK weapons. The naval force had 1,000 men; the air force which numbers 1,500, flies 24 US F–5 or F–16 aircraft and 26 armed helicopters. The armed forces have doubled since the emergence of Iraq and Iran as threats, and Bahrain sent troops to Sa'udi Arabia in 1990–91. The total armed forces numbered 11,000 in 2000. Defense expenditures in 1998 were $298 million or 4.9% of GDP. The state police numbered 9,000.

18 INTERNATIONAL COOPERATION

Bahrain joined the UN on 21 September 1971 and is a member of ESCWA, all major regional organizations, and all the nonregional specialized agencies except IAEA, IDA, and IFAD. It also belongs to the Arab League and G-77, and is a signatory of the Law of the Sea and a member of the WTO. Bahrain was a founding member of the Gulf Cooperation Council, inaugurated in 1981.

[19]ECONOMY

For centuries, Bahrain depended almost exclusively on trade, pearl diving, and agriculture. The discovery of oil on 1 June 1932 came at a providential time, when the pearl trade was being drastically undercut by the development of cultured pearls. Although its economy has been based on oil for the last six decades, Bahrain's development has been tempered by relatively limited reserves. With present oil supplies limited to one diminishing oil field, the government has developed auxiliary sectors, such as petroleum refining and aluminum production, and increased natural gas production. Still, the oil industry accounted for 52% of export earnings and approximately 25% of GDP in 1998.

Significant progress has been made in enhancing Bahrain as an entrepôt (trade center) and as a service and commercial center for the Gulf region. Bahrain provides ample warehousing for goods in transit and drydock facilities for marine engine and ship repairs. Bahrain also acts as a major banking, telecommunications, and air transportation center. Bahrain made the move to diversify its economy—moving to rely on services to a higher degree—after the Lebanese civil war in the late 1970s and early 1980s essentially ended that country's status as a safe, regulation-free banking environment. The strategy has worked to a large extent. Since establishing itself as an off-shore banking center in 1975, the banking sector of the economy had assets of $100 billion and was growing at a rate of 10% to 15% in 1999. Services accounted for 53% of all economic activity in the nation.

The Bahrain economy slowed down considerably after 1993, grinding to a halt in 1994. Average annual growth averaged 4% between 1988 and 1998, buoyed by investment during the early 1990s. In recent years, Bahrain has experienced sluggish and even negative growth. GDP in 1998 contracted by 2%, due to low world oil prices and the Asian financial crisis.

[20]INCOME

The US Central Intelligence Agency (CIA) reports that in 1998 Bahrain's gross domestic product (GDP) was estimated at $8.2 billion. The per capita GDP was estimated at $13,100. The annual growth rate of GDP was estimated at -2%. The average inflation rate in 1998 was -0.2%. The CIA defines GDP as the value of all final goods and services produced within a nation in a given year and computed on the basis of purchasing power parity (PPP) rather than value as measured on the basis of the rate of exchange. It was estimated that agriculture accounted for 1% of GDP, industry 46%, and services 53%.

The World Bank reports that for the same period per capita private consumption (in PPP terms) was $3,930. Private consumption includes expenditures of individuals, households, and non-governmental organizations. Approximately 32% of household consumption was spent on food, 8% on fuel, 1% on health care, and 6% on education.

[21]LABOR

The Bahraini labor force in 1997 was estimated at 150,000, of whom some 44% were non-Bahrainis. Employment by sector was as follows: industry, commerce, and services, 79%, government, 20%, and agriculture, 1%. Bahrain boasts a high proportion of skilled workers, among both its foreign residents and the indigenous population, many of whom have benefited from local technical and vocational training programs. In recent years, the government has enacted regulations requiring the use of a certain percentage of Bahraini workers in private firms. In 1996, these requirements were codified in law. Every company must now have at least one Bahraini worker; firms employing more than 10 workers are required to increase their Bahraini workforce by 5% per year up to 50%; and all new enterprises

must be started with a 20% Bahraini workforce, to be increased by 5% per year.

Although the constitution permits workers to organize, there are no trade unions and the government openly discourages unionization. With this absence of legitimate trade unions, no collective bargaining entities or collective agreements exist. Workers may express grievances through joint labor-management committees (JLC's). JLC's are generally created at each major company and have an equal number of labor and management representation. As of 1998, there were a total of 19 ILC's.

Bahrain enacted a comprehensive labor law in 1958; it provides for an 8-hour day, 48-hour week, minimum wage plus overtime and severance pay, paid vacations, and sick and maternity leave. As of 1999, the minimum wage for public-sector wages were specified on a contract basis. All foreign workers must be sponsored by Bahrainis or Bahrain-based companies, which can revoke the residence permit of anyone under their sponsorship. Migrant workers from developing countries are often unwilling to report health and safety abuses for fear of forced repatriation. Nor do labor laws apply to foreign workers, who often work far in excess of official maximum hour laws. The minimum age for working is 14 years and until age 16, special work conditions and hour limits apply to workers. There is general compliance with this in the industrial sector, but there is rampant abuse outside it, especially in family-owned businesses.

[22]AGRICULTURE

Only 2.9% of the land is arable. Agriculture accounts for only about 1% of the GDP. Ninety farms and small holdings produce fruit and vegetables, as well as alfalfa for fodder. The date palm industry has declined sharply in recent years due to heavy demands on the limited water supply, and dates have become a luxury item. In 1998, 12,000 tons of vegetables and 21,000 tons of fruit crops were produced. The government's goal is for output to meet 16% of demand, compared with the current 6%.

[23]ANIMAL HUSBANDRY

Most domestic meat consumption is supplied through imports of live cattle, goats, and sheep. About 13,000 head of cattle, 17,000 sheep, and 16,000 goats were kept for milk and meat production in 1998. A thriving poultry industry provided 5,000 tons of meat and 3,000 tons of eggs in 1998. Dairy farming has recently been expanded, and a national dairy pasteurization plant has been established in order to centralize all milk processing and distribution. In 1998, milk production from 7,000 cows totaled 14,000 tons. An abattoir that opened in 1984 slaughters imported sheep and cattle.

[24]FISHING

Although the more than 300 species of fish found in Bahraini waters constitute an important food source for much of the population, local fishing and pearl diving have declined because of industrial pollution. The catch totaled 10,050 tons in 1997. The government operates a fleet of seven trawlers. By encouraging traditional angling, giving incentives to fishermen, improving fishing and freezing equipment, and establishing cooperatives, the government is attempting to increase the annual catch. There is a modern fishing harbor at Al-Muharraq which provides docking and landing facilities, storage areas, an ice plant, and a water supply.

[25]FORESTRY

There are no forests in Bahrain. In 1997, roundwood imports amounted to 11,000 cu m and sawn wood imports totaled 33,000 cu m. Bahrain's imports of forest products amounted to $33.9 million that year.

26 MINING

The mining industry consists almost entirely of oil and natural gas production. In 1997, Bahrain produced 14,124,000 barrels of crude oil. That year, 244 billion cu ft (6.9 billion cu m) of natural gas was produced. Cement production was estimated at 193,000 tons in 1997.

27 ENERGY AND POWER

The Arabian Peninsula's first oil well was drilled in Bahrain in 1932, and production began in 1934. From the 1930s to the mid-1970s, oil development was a monopoly of the Bahrain Petroleum Co. (BAPCO), which in 1936 came under the ownership of Caltex, a corporation registered in Canada and jointly owned by Texaco and Standard Oil of California. In 1975, the Bahrain government acquired a 60% holding in BAPCO, and it later formed the Bahrain National Oil Co. (BANOCO) to take over full ownership. In 1980, BANOCO announced its acquisition of a 60% interest in Bahrain's main refinery, which had been wholly owned by Caltex. In 1995, an estimated 90% of export revenues came from petroleum exports.

Total daily crude petroleum production, after reaching a peak in 1970, declined gradually. In 1998, total crude oil production was 38,000 barrels per day. Proven oil reserves in Bahrain were estimated at 210 million barrels by the Ministry of Oil and Industry in 1995. For 20 years, Bahrain had been sharing revenues from the Abu Sa'fa oil field; this small offshore field lies halfway within Sa'udi Arabian territorial waters, but its daily production is split between Bahrain and Sa'udi Arabia under an arrangement reached in 1972. From 1972 until the new agreement was reached in 1992, Bahrain's share was 70,000 barrels a day. In 1992, Bahrain's share was increased to 100,000 barrels a day. In 1996, the Sa'udi government ceded the remainder of its share of the field to Bahrain, increasing the government's revenue by about $200 million.

Bahrain's natural gas resources were estimated at 5.3 trillion cu ft (100 billion cu m) in early 1996, sufficient to last more than 22 years at 1995 extraction levels. Production of gas totaled 290 billion cu ft (6.7 billion cu m) in 1995, of which about 20% was associated with oil drilling, and 80% was produced directly from gas reserves.

The Directorate of Electricity operates plants at Manama, Sitra, and Rifaa. In 1998, Bahrain had a net installed power capacity of 1,100 Mw and total output of 4,777 million kwh, principally derived from a municipal power station at Jufair, from the Sitra power and water station, from two gas turbines at Al-Muharraq, and from the power station at East Rifaa, which was completed in 1985 and is the largest and most modern. BANOCO produces its own electricity from a 60 Mw plant.

In late 1996, resolution to the legal dispute between Bahrain and Qatar over the sovereignty of the possibly oil-rich Hawar Islands was still pending at the International Court of Justice at The Hague. The dispute nearly caused the two countries to go to war in April 1986.

28 INDUSTRY

Petroleum refining, begun modestly in 1942, was Bahrain's first modern industrial enterprise. By 1976, the oil refinery at Sitra had a daily output of 250,000 barrels, but its capacity has far outstripped the local supply of crude oil, and about 84% of the oil is pumped from Sa'udi Arabia by sea and land lines. The refinery is owned and operated by the Bahrain Petroleum Company (BAPCO), owned wholly by the government. Although modernization was delayed by the Gulf conflict, work began in 1992 to expand refining capacity to some 360,000 barrels per day. By 1995, however, this expansion was unrealized and the refinery had an average daily throughput of 251,300 barrels a day that year. In 1999, a seven-year $800 million modernization plan started upgrading the refinery. Output was recorded at 260,000 barrels per day in 1999.

A government-controlled aluminum industry, Aluminum Bahrain BSC (ALBA), was launched in 1971 with an original smelter capacity of 120,000 tons annually; the successful completion of a 1997 expansion project increased production to more than 500,000 metric tons in 1998. It is the world's second largest aluminum smelter, and is 77% owned by the government.

A gas liquefaction plant was opened by the Bahrain National Gas Co. (BANAGAS) in 1979. The Bahrain National Oil Company (BANACO) was planning to spend $60 million in 1999 on new gas projects. The Arab Shipbuilding and Repair Yard, a pan-Arab industrial venture undertaken by OAPEC, became operational in 1977. It is the Gulf's largest floating dock and repair facility, with expansion scheduled for 2000 involving up to $200 million.

29 SCIENCE AND TECHNOLOGY

The economy depends heavily on advanced petrochemical technologies, and many Bahrainis have had or are receiving technical training. The University of Bahrain, at Isa Town, has a college of engineering and science. The Arabian Gulf University, founded in 1980 by the seven Gulf states, has colleges of medicine and applied sciences. The Bahrain Society of Engineers and the Bahrain Computer Society, in Manama, and the Bahrain Medical Society in Adliya, are leading professional groups. The College of Health Sciences, founded in 1976, had 528 students in 1996. The Bahrain Centre for Studies and Research, founded in 1981, conducts scientific study and research.

30 DOMESTIC TRADE

Bahraini shops have become increasingly modernized and specialized. Business hours for most shops are from 8:30 AM to 12:30 and from 4 to 8 PM, Saturday through Thursday; government offices, banks, and some large companies are open in the mornings only. Of all the Gulf states, Bahrain offers the most scope for consumer advertising through its publications, cinemas, direct mail facilities, and radio and television stations.

31 FOREIGN TRADE

Refined petroleum products drive Bahrain's economy and export market (60%), which are processed from imported crude oil. Aluminum ranks as the country's second largest export commodity (24%), which is manufactured in government controlled enterprises. Other exports include industrial alcohol (2.7%), chemicals (1.9%) and pig iron (1.7%).

In 1996 Bahrain's imports were distributed among the following categories:

Consumer goods	9.9%
Food	10.2%
Fuels	41.0%
Industrial supplies	22.4%
Machinery	10.3%
Transportation	5.3%

Principal trading partners in 1998 (in millions of US dollars) were as follows:

COUNTRY	EXPORTS	IMPORTS	BALANCE
India	557	89	468
Saudi Arabia	292	203	89
Japan	225	324	-99
Korea	224	83	141
United States	154	293	-139
United Arab Emirates	138	95	43
United Kingdom	102	211	-109
France	76	101	-25
Italy	48	162	-114
Germany	41	161	-120

³²BALANCE OF PAYMENTS

Traditionally, Bahrain relied on a substantial influx of funds from Sa'udi Arabia, Kuwait, Abu Dhabi, and Iran to finance capital outlays. In recent years, however, increased income from tourism and financial services, have placed Bahrain in a favorable payments position.

The US Central Intelligence Agency reports that in 1997 the purchasing power parity of Bahrain's exports was $4.7 billion while imports totaled $4.4 billion resulting in a trade balance of $300 million.

The International Monetary Fund (IMF) reports that in 1998 Bahrain had exports of goods totaling $3,270 million and imports totaling $3,199 million. The services credit totaled $769 million and debit $740 million. The following table summarizes Bahrain's balance of payments as reported by the IMF for 1998 in millions of US dollars.

Current Account		-1,042
Balance on goods	71	
Balance on services	29	
Balance on income	-483	
Current transfers	-660	
Capital Account		100
Financial Account		127
Direct investment abroad	-181	
Direct investment in Bahrain	-2,136	
Portfolio investment assets	-1,221	
Portfolio investment liabilities	609	
Other investment assets	-14,636	
Other investment liabilities	17,692	
Net Errors and Omissions		799
Reserves and Related Items		17

³³BANKING AND SECURITIES

Bahrain is considered the pre-eminent fiancial services center in the Middle East. The Bahrain Monetary Agency (BMA), Bahrain's equivalent of a central bank, issues and redeems bank notes, regulates the value of the Bahrain dinar, supervises interest rates, and licenses and monitors the activities of money changers. One factor contributing to Bahrain's growth as a Middle Eastern financial services center is that unlike some of its larger, richer neighbors, there is no serious religious opposition to western banking practices—especially the accrual of interest—which some Islamic scholars consider to be contrary to Muslim teachings. There are, however, several large banks in Bahrain classified as Islamic; they don't pay or charge interest, don't finance or otherwise support "un-Islamic" enterprises, and make a conscious effort to invest in socially productive enterprises. Another important factor influencing the growth of the financial sector is the tax-free environment.

The value of assets and liabilities held by Bahrain's commercial banks rose by 43%, and offshore banking units (DBUs) rose by 20%; between 1991 and 1995. The consolidated assets and liabilities of commercial and offshore banks in Bahrain reached over $82 million in 1997. In 2000, Bahrain was home to 19 full commercial banks, 2 specialized banks, 47 offshore banks, 36 representative offices, 32 investment banks, 6 foreign exchange and money brokers, and 17 money-changing companies.

The Bahrain Stock Exchange (BSE) was planned in 1987 after the unofficial Kuwait Stock Exchange collapsed. The BSE has become an important Gulf center of share trading; volume or shares increased from its inception from 62 million in 1989 to almost 400 million in 1993. Beginning in 1995, the BSE listed foreign companies, bonds, and investment funds. Trading in foreign investment vehicles was made open to all Bahrainis, and resident and non-resident foreigners in late 1996. There were 34 funds and 41 companies listed on the BSE in 1999. The total value, volume, and number of transactions of shares traded in 1999 declined from 1998 by 23%, 13%, and 27% respectively.

The top three firms; Investcorp, the Bahrain Telecommunications Company (BATELCO), and the Arab Banking Corporation; account for over one-half of the exchange's total market capitalization of $7.3 billion in 1999.

³⁴INSURANCE

The total premiums underwritten in 1996 in Bahrain equaled approximately $100 million. Over 100 insurance companies were operating in Bahrain in 2000. The four major national companies are Al Ahlia Insurance, Bahrain Insurance, Bahrain & Kuwait Insurance, and National Insurance, comprising more than half of the market share.

³⁵PUBLIC FINANCE

The budget is presented biennually and regularly updated, and represents a large section of economic activity. More than half of government revenues come from oil production and refining. The public deficit is covered by internal borrowing, loans from Arab funds, and the IDB; although privatization has become increasingly important to controlling the budget.

The US Central Intelligence Agency (CIA) estimates that in 1999 Bahrain's central government took in revenues of approximately $1.5 billion and had expenditures of $1.9 billion including capital expenditures of $310 million. Overall, the government registered a deficit of approximately $400 million. External debt totalled $2 billion.

The following table shows an itemized breakdown of government revenues and expenditures. The percentages were calculated from data reported by the International Monetary Fund. The dollar amounts (millions) are based on the CIA estimates provided above.

REVENUE AND GRANTS	100%	1,500
Tax revenue	36.8%	552
Non-tax revenue	56.4%	846
Grants	6.8%	102

EXPENDITURES	100%	1,900
General public services	15.2%	288
Defense	17.3%	328
Public order and safety	14.7%	279
Education	13.2%	251
Health	9.0%	170
Social security	4.3%	82
Housing and community amenities	3.5%	67
Recreation, cultural, and religious affairs	1.8%	35
Economic affairs and services	17.3%	329
Interest payments	3.7%	71

³⁶TAXATION

The only taxes in Bahrain are an income tax on oil production and a municipal tax of 10% on residential rents; the rate is 7.5% on furnished rentals, office, and commercial rents. As an offshore tax haven, Bahrain allows foreign firms to remit accumulated profits and capital without taxation.

³⁷CUSTOMS AND DUTIES

Import licenses for items sold in Bahrain are issued only to local companies at least 51% Bahraini-owned. Principal prohibited items are arms, ammunition, liquor (except by authorized importers), and cultured pearls. Customs duties are 5% on foodstuffs, essential goods, and plant and equipment for use in local industry; 10% on non-essential goods; 20% on cars and boats; 70% on tobacco and cigarettes; and 125% on authorized imports of liquor. There is a tariff of 20% on corn and palm oil.

A free transit zone operates at the port of Mina Sulman. Free trade is available with Gulf Cooperation Council (GCC) countries if products have at least 40% local value-added content.

[38]FOREIGN INVESTMENT

While continuing to encourage foreign investment, the government has acquired majority holdings in most of the country's principal enterprises that were formerly foreign held. The government offers substantial incentives for companies wishing to establish plants in Bahrain. With the exception of petroluem royalties, Bahrain does not tax either corporate or individual earnings.

As of 1999, the Bahraini government had no vehicle for reporting statistics on foreign investment. Some of the larger foreign-owned or controlled companies in 1999 included the following: Aluminum Bahrain and the Gulf Petrochemical Industries Complex, both joint investments controlled by several Gulf states; the Arab Shipbuilding and Repair Yard, owned by several Gulf states; and the Bahrain Telecommunications Company, 20%-owned by Cable & Wireless. There were at least 90 US companies operating in Bahrain in 1999, including Kimberly-Clark, Coca-Cola, Shaw Industries, and DHL.

[39]ECONOMIC DEVELOPMENT

Since the late 1960s, the government has concentrated on policies and projects that will provide sufficient diversification in industrial, commercial, and financial activities to sustain growth in income, employment, and exports into the post-oil era. Despite diversification efforts, the oil and gas sectors remain the cornerstone of the economy.

[40]SOCIAL DEVELOPMENT

Impoverished families receive subsistence allowances from the Ministry of Labor and Social Affairs. Free child guidance clinics—the first in the Gulf—and expanded benefit and pension provisions for government employees were introduced in 1975. Since 1976, a social security fund has provided old age, disability, survivor, and accident insurance. Contributions amount to 5% of earnings by workers and 7% by employers. For accident insurance, the insured pays nothing and the employer contributes 3% of payroll. Work injury insurance exempts domestic servants, the self-employed and agricultural workers.

Islamic law, either Shi'a or Sunni, dictates the legal rights of Bahraini women. Women may initiate divorce proceedings, own and inherit property, and represent themselves in legal matters. However, men retain legal rights over children, even in case of divorce. Custody of young children is granted to women, but fathers automatically regain custody when the children reach the age of 9 (for daughters) and 7 (for sons). Women are allowed to work, drive cars, and wear Western-style clothing. Women make up over 20% of the labor force, and their employment is encouraged by the government, itself a leading employer of women. Bahrain's labor law does not recognize the concept of equal pay for equal work.

A small group of Shi'a originally of Iranian origin have been refused full citizenship under the Citizenship Act of 1963. These residents are second or third generation residents of Bahrain, but are unable to obtain a passport and are prohibited from owning land.

Bahrain's government regularly violates its citizens' human rights. However, the human rights situation improved somewhat with the installation of a new amir, who pardoned or released over 400 prisoners and initiated measures to improve conditions for the country's Shi'a Muslim minority. Nevertheless, long-standing human rights violations continued. In contrast to 1998, there were no extrajudicial killings, but there was a continuation of torture, arbitrary arrest, denial of the right to a fair trial, and restrictions on freedom of speech, press, assembly, association, and workers' rights.

[41]HEALTH

In 1960, Bahrain inaugurated a free national health service, available to both foreign and indigenous segments of the population through a system of primary care health centers and modern hospital facilities. Bahraini patients who require sophisticated surgery or treatment are sent abroad at government expense.

Medical services are provided by the government and a small private sector. Health care centers are accessible to the population free of charge. In 1990, there were 4 government-operated hospitals (including a psychiatric hospital and a geriatric hospital), 5 maternity hospitals, 19 health centers, 6 environment health centers, and 16 maternity and child welfare centers. In 1991, Bahrain had 668 physicians, 123 pharmacists, and 66 dentists. The effects of the Gulf War have endangered the health of many of Bahrain's people. Acute asthmatic attacks increased during the years after the war (1991–1993).

Infant mortality was 14.8 per 1,000 live births in 1999. The 1999 birth rate was 21.9 per 1,000 people, and the general mortality rate was 3.2 per 1,000 people. In 1994, 93% of the country's 1-year-old children were vaccinated against measles. In 1990, 100% of the population had access to health care services, and 93% had access to safe drinking water. Life expectancy in 1994 was 71 years. In Bahrain, there were 28 new cases of AIDS in 1996. Malaria was reported in 258 people and polio, measles, and neonatal tetanus were non-existent.

[42]HOUSING

There were 50,798 households at the 1981 census. Roughly 45% of all housing units were traditional dwellings with interior courtyards, 22% were flats, 17% were modern detached houses, 8% were villas, and 3% were collective compounds. Owners occupied 48% of all dwellings, 33% were rented, 9% were occupied rent free, and 7% were furnished by employers. About 69% were made of brick, 16% were stone, 8% were concrete, and 5% were prefabricated. 'Isa Town, the first low-cost government housing scheme, which was initiated in 1963 in barren desert between Manama and West Rifaa, had a population of 35,000 in 1984. Mamad Town was completed in 1984; in 1987, it had 12,000 residential units. A major program for low- and middle-income housing, costing $195 million, also was inaugurated with Sa'udi aid.

[43]EDUCATION

Bahrain introduced a free public education system to the Gulf region in 1919. The government aims to provide free educational opportunities for all children. Education was only recently made compulsory. In the latter part of the 1990s, approximately 12.0% of total government expenditure was allocated to education.

For the year 2000, adult illiteracy rates were estimated at 12.4% (males, 9.0%; females, 17.3%). Bahrain has the highest female literacy rate in the Arabian Gulf. The official language is Arabic, but English is widely spoken. School education is in three stages: primary lasts for six years, intermediate for three years, and secondary—general, industrial, or commercial—for three years. Primary and secondary curricula includes a 9-year course in Religious Study. Nearly 100% of school-aged children attend primary school, while 85% attend secondary school. In 1997 primary schools enrolled 72,876 students. Also in 1997 secondary schools enrolled 57,184 students, taught by approximately 3,200 teachers

Bahrain's principal unviversity is The University of Bahrain established in 1986 after a merger between the University College and Gulf Polytechnic. It is comprised of five colleges and an English language center: colleges of arts, sciences, engineering, education, and business administration. The Arabian Gulf University (founded in 1980) has faculties in science, engineering and medicine and is in fact a joint venture project among the six Gulf Cooperation Council members and Iraq. Each nation is allocated 10% of the seats (total 70%) and the remaining 30% are given to other countries. Also important is the Bahrain Training Institute, which currently has over 50% female students.

There are also 67 adult education centers in Bahrain, which have helped to reduce the illiteracy rate of the country. For promoting technical education, a "10,000 Training Plan" was launched in 1980. Nearly 6,500 students have participated in this program since its inception and scholarships are given to students to pursue higher studies at Bahrain or abroad. In 1994 all institutions of higher learning had 655 teachers and enrolled 7,147 students.

44LIBRARIES AND MUSEUMS

The Central Public Library in Isa Town has 124,000 volumes. The University of Bahrain in Manama (1978) holds 150,000 volumes. Bahrain National Museum in Manama holds archaeological and historical exhibits and is one of 12 museums in the nation.

45MEDIA

Modern telephone, cable, and telex systems are available; telephones numbered 124,400 in 1995. In that year there were 2 AM stations, 3 FM stations, and 4 broadcast television stations. The government operates a radio station and a color television station. In 1997 there were 499 radios and 420 television sets in use per 1,000 population.

Bahrain's first daily newspaper in Arabic, *Akhbar al-Khalij* (circulation 30,000 in 1999), began publication in 1976, and the first English daily, the *Gulf Daily News* (12,000), in 1991. *Al Ayam*, an Arabic daily founded in 1989, had a 199 circulation of 21,500.

Though the Bahraini Constitution has provisions for freedom of expression, press criticism of the ruling family or government policy is strictly prohibited.

The Internet was introduced in 1995, though a government controlled proxy restricts access to sites considered to be anti-government or anti-Islam. However, online access was still extremely limited as of 1998, with less than one Internet host per 1,000 population.

46ORGANIZATIONS

In addition to the Chamber of Commerce and Industry, there are numerous Bahraini and multinational groups, including the Bahrain Red Crescent Society, the Children's and Mothers' Welfare Society, and the Boy Scouts.

47TOURISM, TRAVEL, AND RECREATION

Bahrain has been the fastest growing destination in the Middle East since the early 1990s. In 1997, there were 1.8 million tourist arrivals, almost 80% from other Middle Eastern countries, and tourism receipts totaled $270 million. Tourist attractions include archeological sites, notably Qal-at Al-Bahrain (The Portuguese Fort), the National Museum, and the Heritage Center. Most visitors need a visa and valid passport.

The UN estimated the daily cost of staying in Bahrain at $194 in 1999. Room charges account for 58% of these costs.

48FAMOUS BAHRAINIS

Since 1961, the emir has been Sheikh 'Isa bin Salman al-Khalifa (b. 1933).

49DEPENDENCIES

Bahrain has no territories or colonies.

50BIBLIOGRAPHY

Al-Tajir, Mahdi Abdalla. *Bahrain, 1920–1945: Britain, the Shaikh, and the Administration.* London and New York: Croom Helm, 1987.

American University. *Area Handbook for the Persian Gulf States.* Washington, D.C.: Government Printing Office, 1984.

Fakhro, Munira A. (Munira Ahmed). *Women at Work in the Gulf: A Case Study of Bahrain Fakhro.* London and New York: Kegan Paul International, 1990.

Jenner, Michael. *Bahrain, Gulf Heritage in Transition.* New York: Longman, 1984.

Lawson, Fred Haley. *Bahrain: the Modernization of Autocracy.* Boulder, Colo.: Westview Press, 1989.

Nugent, Jeffrey B., and Theodore Thomas (eds.). *Bahrain and the Gulf: Past Perspectives and Alternate Futures.* New York: St. Martin's, 1985.

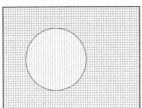

BANGLADESH

People's Republic of Bangladesh
Gana-Prajatantri Bangladesh

CAPITAL: Dhaka (formerly Dacca).

FLAG: The national flag is a red circle against a dark-green background.

ANTHEM: *Amar Sonar Bangla (My Golden Bengal).*

MONETARY UNIT: The taka (T) of 100 poisha is a paper currency set on a par with the Indian rupee. There are coins of 1, 2, 5, 10, 25, and 50 poisha, and notes of 1, 5, 10, 20, 50, and 100 taka. T1 = $0.01961 ($1 = T51.00) as of 31 March 2000.

WEIGHTS AND MEASURES: Bangladesh adopted the metric system as of 1 July 1982. Customary numerical units include the lakh (equal to 100,000) and the crore (equal to 10 million).

HOLIDAYS: New Year's Day, 1 January; National Mourning Day (Shaheel Day), 21 February; Independence Day, 26 March; May Day, 1 May; Victory Day, 16 December; Christmas, 25 December; Boxing Day, 26 December. Movable religious holidays include Good Friday, Jamat Wida, Shab-i-Bharat, 'Id al-Fitr, 'Id al-'Adha', and Durga Puja.

TIME: 6 PM = noon GMT.

¹LOCATION, SIZE, AND EXTENT

Situated in the northeastern corner of the South Asian subcontinent, Bangladesh, before it became an independent state, was the eastern province of Pakistan, known as East Bengal and, later, as East Pakistan. Bangladesh is slightly smaller than the state of Wisconsin with a total area of 144,000 sq km (55,599 sq mi), extending 767 km (477 mi) SSE–NNW and 429 km (267 mi) ENE–WSW. Bangladesh is bordered in the N, E, and W by India, on the SE by Burma, and on the S by the Bay of Bengal, with a total boundary length of 4,826 km (2,999 mi). A border demarcation agreement was signed with Burma in May 1979. Demarcation of the marine boundary with India remains unresolved. Bangladesh's capital city, Dhaka, is located near the center of the country.

²TOPOGRAPHY

Bangladesh is a tropical country, situated mainly on the deltas of large rivers flowing from the Himalayas. The Brahmaputra River, known locally as the Jamuna, unites with part of the Ganges to form the Padma, which, after its juncture with a third large river, the Meghna, flows into the Bay of Bengal. Offshoots of the Ganges-Padma, including the Burishwar, Garai, Kobadak, and Madhumati, also flow south to the Bay of Bengal. No part of the delta area is more than 150 m (500 ft) above sea level, and most of it is but a meter or two (a few feet) above sea level. Its soil consists mostly of fertile alluvium, which is intensively farmed; mineral deposits are negligible. During the rainy season floodwater covers most of the land surface, damaging crops and injuring the economy. The northwestern section of the country, drained by the Tista (Teesta) River, is somewhat higher and less flat, but the only really hilly regions are in the east, notably in the Chittagong Hill Tracts to the southeast and the Sylhet District to the northeast. Near the Burmese border, in the extreme southeast, is the Keokradang, which at 1,230 m (4,034 ft) is the highest peak in Bangladesh.

³CLIMATE

Bangladesh has a tropical monsoon climate. Annual rainfall is high, averaging from about 119 cm (47 in) up to 145 cm (57 in). There are three distinct seasons. The winter, which lasts from November through February, is cool and dry. The average January temperature for most of the country is about 7°C (45°F); total winter rainfall averages about 18 cm (7 in) in the east and less than 8 cm (3 in) in the northwest. Temperatures rise rapidly in early March, and during the summer season—March through May—average about 32°C (90°F). Rainfall also increases during this period. However, nearly 80% of the annual rainfall falls from June to October, when moisture-laden winds blow from the south and southeast. Temperatures drop somewhat, seldom exceeding 31°C (88°F), but humidity remains high. In April and May and from September through November, tropical cyclones, accompanied by high seas and heavy flooding, are common. There were cyclones in May 1963, May and December 1965, October 1966, and most notably during the night of 12–13 November 1970, when a storm and resultant flooding killed more than 200,000 persons. A cyclone on 30 April 1991 left over 131,000 people dead and nine million homeless. Monsoon floods in 1974, 1980, and 1983 also devastated the country and caused many deaths, and a cyclonic storm on 24–25 May 1985 took more than 11,000 lives. The monsoon in August and September 1988 left three-fourths of the country flooded, 1,300 persons dead, and over three million people homeless, with damage to the country's infrastructure estimated at $1 billion.

⁴FLORA AND FAUNA

Bangladesh has the plant and animal life typical of a tropical and riverine swamp. The landscape, which for most of the year is lush green, is dotted with palms and flowering trees. The large forest area of the Sunderbans in the southwest is the home of the endangered Bengal tiger; there are also cheetahs, leopards, crocodiles, elephants, spotted deer, monkeys, boars, bears, pheasants, and many varieties of birds and waterfowl.

[5]ENVIRONMENT

Overpopulation has severely strained Bangladesh's limited natural resources. Nearly all arable land is already cultivated, and forestland has been greatly reduced by agricultural expansion and by timber and firewood cutting. Between 1983 and 1993, forest and woodland declined by 12.5% to 1.9 million ha (4.7 million acres). Bangladesh's environmental problems have been complicated by natural disasters that add to the strain on an agricultural system which supports one of the world's most populous countries. Water supply is also a major problem because of population size, lack of purification procedures, and the spread of untreated contaminants into the usable water supply by flood waters. To ease these problems, the government has established drainage, irrigation, and flood protection systems, and has drilled thousands of tube wells to supply safe drinking water in villages. As of 1995, safe water was available to 100% of the urban and 89% of the rural population.

Despite passage of the Wildlife Preservation Act of 1973, wildlife continues to suffer from human encroachment. Only 0.7% of the country's total land area is protected. In the mid-1990s, 15 species of mammals, 27 species of birds and 33 plant species were considered endangered, including the Asian elephant, Bengal tiger, estuarine crocodile, gavial, and river terrapin. The Assam rabbit, Sumatran rhinoceros, Javan rhinoceros, and pygmy hog have become extinct.

[6]POPULATION

Bangladesh is one of the world's most densely populated nations, and controlling population growth is a major government priority. The annual population growth declined from 3.4% in 1975 to 2.2% in 1991 to an estimated 1.9% in 1996. The population of Bangladesh in 2000 was estimated at 129,146,695. An estimated 3.3% of the population is 65 years of age or older. The projected population for the year 2005 is 142,921,000, assuming a crude birthrate of 24 per 1,000 population and a death rate of 9, resulting in a natural rate of change of 1.5% for the period 2000–2005. The population rate of change between 1995 and 2000 was 1.6%. The population density in 1998 was 965 per sq km (2499 per sq mi), making Bangladesh one of the most densely populated countries on earth. The distribution is uneven, with extremely heavy concentrations in the districts of Dhaka and Comilla.

The population is heavily rural, with the great majority living in more than 85,000 villages. It was estimated that only 21% of the population lived in urban areas in 2000, up from 11% in 1980. The capital city, Dhaka, had a 2000 population of 10,979,000. Other large cities, with 2000 population totals, were Chittagong, 2,906,000, and Khulna, 1,229,000. Rajshahi, Barisal, Rangpur, and Jessore are also major cities. Bangladesh's next census is slated for 2001.

[7]MIGRATION

Since 1947 there has been a regular interchange of population between India and what is now Bangladesh, with Hindus migrating to India and Muslims emigrating from India. There was also substantial migration between Bangladesh (then East Pakistan) and West Pakistan until the 1971 war. Before and during the war, an estimated 8 to 10 million Bengalis fled to India; most of these refugees returned after the independence of Bangladesh was firmly established. Although more than 100,000 *Biharis* who had sided with Pakistan during the war later migrated to Pakistan, an estimated 238,000 Biharis were still living in 66 refugee camps in Bangladesh at the end of 1993, despite a repatriation agreement signed in 1992.

In 1993, repatriation began of an estimated 56,000 Chakma refugees from the Indian state of Tripura to the Chittagong Hill Tracts of Bangladesh. They had fled unrest in this area. As of May 1997, 47,000 Chakma refugees still live in northeastern India. In 1991–92 about 265,000 Rohingyas—Muslims from Myanmar—fled to Bangladesh to escape repression. Beginning in 1994, over 200,000 of these refugees have returned home to Myanmar (Burma). However, as of September 1999, around 22,000 Myanmar refugees still reside in southern Bangladesh in two camps. The repatriation process was suspended in 1997 but resumed in 1998. Nevertheless, the number of returns has been very limited (only 450 between 1998 and 1999) due to procedural difficulties. The UN has urged the governments of both Bangladesh and Myanmar to accelerate the process. Also, talks have been initiated regarding refugee self-reliance programs for those refugees who cannot or will not return. Reforestation and community support activities have been discussed has possible ways to lessen any adverse consequences of refugee presence. Bangladeshi authorities have not responded favorably to the proposed self-reliance programs for refugees, reiterating their position that all refugees must return to their homeland.

[8]ETHNIC GROUPS

Some 98% of the people are Bengalis (or Banglas). About 12 tribes inhabiting the Chittagong Hill Tracts, collectively totaling less than one million people, are ethnically distinct from the Bengalis; their facial features and language are closer to the Burmese. The government's policy of resettling Bengalis in the region, which is much less densely populated than Bangladesh as a whole, led to racial and religious disturbances and a small-scale tribal insurgency in the early 1980s. About 250,000 of the national population consists of Biharis, non-Bengali Muslims who migrated from India to what was then East Pakistan after the partition of the subcontinent in 1947. In the coastal areas of Bangladesh, Arab, Portuguese, and Dutch settlers have gradually come to adopt the Bengali life-style.

[9]LANGUAGES

Bengali (Bangla), part of the Indo-European language family, is the official language of Bangladesh and is spoken by about 98% of the population. The successful move to make Bengali coequal with Urdu as an official language was a hallmark of Bengali nationalism in the early 1950s. Non-Bengali migrants from India still speak Urdu (and Hindi) today, and this language is widely understood in urban areas. A few tribal groups, notably the tribal peoples of the Chittagong Hill Tracts, also speak distinct Tibeto-Burmese languages, akin to Burmese and Assamese. Among those speaking Bangla there are differences of dialect according to region. The people of Chittagong, Noakhali, and Sylhet are known for their distinctive dialects. Although today Bangla is the official language, English is also used for official and legal purposes and widely used in business.

[10]RELIGIONS

Nearly 88.3% of the people are believers in Islam (mostly Sunni), making Bangladesh one of the world's largest Muslim countries. Most of the remaining population, about 10.5%, is Hindu; the remaining 1.2% is Buddhist or Christian, the latter evenly divided between Roman Catholics and Protestants. Although Islam was established as the state religion in 1988, freedom of worship continues to be guaranteed under its constitution.

[11]TRANSPORTATION

The large number of rivers and the annual flooding hazard make it difficult to build and maintain adequate transportation facilities in Bangladesh. Railways and waterways are the chief means of transportation. The railways are managed by the government and reach most districts of the country. The Bangladesh Railway operated 2,745 km (1,706 mi) of track in 1998. The quality of service has declined because of the expense of importing new

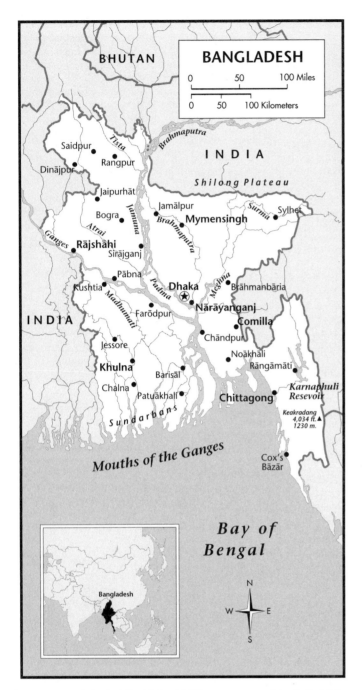

BANGLADESH

0	50	100 Miles
0	50	100 Kilometers

LOCATION: 20°34' to 26°38'N; 88°1' to 92°41'E. **BOUNDARY LENGTHS:** India, 2,583 km (1,605 mi); Myanmar, 197 km (122 mi); Bay of Bengal coastline, 574 km (357 mi). **TERRITORIAL SEA LIMIT:** 12 mi.

equipment. Enlarging and improving the railway system is also costly, partly because of the number of bridges needed.

The country has two deepwater ports: Chittagong, serving the eastern sector, and Chalna, serving the west. There are five main river ports—Dhaka, Nārāyanganj, Chandpur, Barisal, and Khulna—and more than 1,500 smaller ports. The inland water system has an estimated 5,150–8,046 km (3,200–5,000 mi) of navigable waterways, including 2,575–3,058 km (1,600–1,900 mi) of main cargo routes. The oceangoing merchant fleet in 1998 consisted of 40 ships of 1,000 GRT or over, with a combined capacity of 315,855 GRT.

Road connections are inadequate, but conditions have improved significantly in recent years. There were 204,022 km (126,779 mi) of roadways in 1998, of which 25,095 km (15,594 mi) were paved. A large part of the highway system becomes submerged in the rainy season; bridges, ferries, embankments, and dikes are therefore necessary to the inland transportation system. Because of the difficulties of land travel, the number of motor vehicles remains relatively small.

Bangladesh had 16 airports in 1998, 15 with paved runways. Zia International is the principal airport, located at Dhaka. Bangladesh Biman is the national airline. It has an extended network connecting major cities and operates international flights from Dhaka. In 1997, the airline carried 3,233,000 domestic and international passengers.

12HISTORY

In ancient times, the area now known as Bangladesh was the eastern portion of a huge river delta region called Bang, where the Ganges and Brahmaputra River systems empty into the Bay of Bengal and the Indian Ocean. The region became known as Bengal in more modern times, but recorded history of the region can be traced to the 4th century BC when it was home to an apparently flourishing riverain civilization. The oldest surviving remains of this civilization are the ruins of the city of Mahasthan, the ancient Pundranagar, which continued to flourish for more than 1500 years, even though the region was conquered by the Hindu Maurya empire that reached its height under Emperor Asoka around 207 BC. From this time onward, the history of Bengal was part of the wider historical experience of the Indian subcontinent, and during most of India's classical Hindu period— AD 320 to AD 1000—Bengal was a loosely incorporated outpost of empires centered in the Gangetic plain.

Islam came to South Asia in the years following AD 800 but did not reach Bengal until Muslim invaders from the west secured a foothold there around AD 1200. In the 13th and 14th centuries, after successive waves of Turkish, Persian, and Afghan invaders, Islam began to take a firm hold in the area now Bangladesh. The region was annexed by the Mughal Empire in 1576 under the Muslim Akbar and ruled by his successors into the 17th century. The fealty lesser Nawabs (or Nabobs) of the Bengal area paid to the Mughals ensured the political stability and economic prosperity of the region, which became known for its industries based on the weaving of silk and cotton cloth.

The arrival of the French and British East India Companies in the early 18th century coincided with Mughal decline, the death of Emperor Auranzeb, and an intense period of competition and conflict between Britain and France. By the middle of the 18th century, the British emerged supreme in what they created as the Bengal Presidency, establishing themselves in Calcutta and expanding with alacrity into all of what is now Bangladesh, as well as the Indian states of West Bengal, Bihar, Assam and Orissa. From Calcutta, British traders and administrators successfully played off rivalries among the satraps of the late Mughal empire to gain control of most of the subcontinent in the years between the Battle of Plassey in 1756 and the assumption of the company's domain by the British Crown in 1859. Calcutta remained the seat of British power in the subcontinent and the center of British control over the Indian Empire until 1931 when the capital was moved to the new city of New Delhi, adjacent to the traditional seat of Mughal power in old Delhi.

In general, Hindus in Bengal prospered under the British, apparently taking more easily to British ways and British law than the numerically dominant Muslims. The Muslim aristocracy of eastern Bengal—feudal barons under the Mughals—resisted British rule. By the turn of the 20th century, both communities had begun to develop a political-cum-cultural consciousness of their own in reaction to the Western culture brought by the

British. They took offense at British efforts to impose western educational systems on local universities, reducing their independence. Hindus were further enraged by the British decision in 1905, in an effort to improve administration and to placate Muslims, to divide the overly large Bengal Presidency in two, with the Muslim-dominant area of eastern Bengal and Assam to be a separate province. The 1905 partition was the first acknowledgment of a sense of separateness among Muslims by the British and foreshadowed events of 42 years later when Bengal was divided between Muslim-majority and Hindu-majority districts to create East Pakistan.

The 1905 action was strongly opposed by Bengali Hindus and resulted in increasing acts of violence. This lasted until it was undone six years later in favor of reuniting Bengal and instead separating out what would become the provinces of Orissa and Bihar. But the agitation provoked by the 1905 partition and the Hindu-Muslim enmities it left behind continued to provoke terrorist actions against British rule until headed off by the evolution of nonviolence as a mode of political struggle, as later enunciated in the cause of Indian self-rule by Mohandas (Mahatma) Gandhi of the Indian National Congress.

British reforms in 1909 and 1919 expanded local self-rule in their Indian domains, but the pace fell short of the pace of demands put forth by the rising tide of nationalists espoused by the Indian National Congress, which in 1929 committed itself to the goal of complete independence. As the struggle gained momentum, the majority Hindu and minority Muslim communities in India as a whole began to divide on the eventual "end game." While the majority Hindu community saw a single Indian polity committed to secularism and diversity as the goal of the independence movement, Muslims came to fear that their community would be a permanent electoral minority, an anxiety they saw borne out in the 1937 elections held under British auspices. To look after their unique cultural interests, they formed the All-India Muslim League, and under the Muslim League leadership, sentiment began to coalesce around the "two nation" theory propounded earlier by the poet Iqbal, a belief that South Asian Muslims and Hindus were and should be two separate nations, i.e. that Muslims required the creation of an independent nation of their own—Pakistan—in which they would predominate. In 1940, the Muslim League adopted this as its goal, under the leadership of Mohammad Ali Jinnah, a Mumbai (formerly Bombay) attorney who resisted all efforts at compromise through all the difficult days leading up to the grant of independence in 1947.

The new state of Pakistan, made up of Muslim-majority districts in both eastern and western reaches of formerly British India, was at best an unwieldy creation. It cut across long-established lines of trade and communication, divided families, provoked a mass movement of millions of refugees caught on the "wrong" side of the partition markers, and forced the creation of a new but divided polity. Pakistan consisted of two distinct territories, separated by 1600 km (1000 miles) of secular but predominantly Hindu India. West Pakistan, with a population of 34 million, consisted mainly of the former provinces of Baluchistan, Sindh, the Northwest Frontier, and (partially) Punjab (which, like Bengal, was also partitioned). East Pakistan, its 42 million people including nearly 9 million Hindus, encompassed the eastern half of Bengal province as shaped in 1912, plus the Sylhet District of Assam.

In language, culture, ethnic background, population density, political experience, and economic potential, East and West Pakistan were totally disparate—the main bonds being Islam and a fear of potential Indian (Hindu) revanchism. Pakistan's early years as a nation were dominated by unsuccessful attempts—punctuated by bouts of authoritarian rule—to create a national polity that would somehow bridge these differences. Larger in population and in economic importance than the west wing, the Bengali east wing chafed under national policies effectively dominated by the leadership residing in the west wing. When its influence was further reduced under repeated bouts of martial law and by the reconstruction of West Pakistan as a single province, demands for autonomy in the east began to mount. This insistent demand for autonomy in East Pakistan proved more than the fragile sense of Islamic nationhood could sustain.

Nationhood

After yet another round of martial law in Pakistan in the 1969, national elections were scheduled for 1970. But when the popular verdict in those elections—even in the national assembly—supported greater autonomy for East Pakistan than the West Pakistan-dominated national leadership was prepared to accord, the results were set aside.

Subsequent civil unrest escalated quickly to civil war in East Pakistan. Swamped with a million refugees from the fighting, India intervened militarily in December 1971, tipping the scales in favor of the rebels and facilitating the creation of Bangladesh in 1972. Sheikh Mujibur (Mujib) Rahman, leader of the Awami League and of the fight for autonomy, was released from prison in West Pakistan (which became the Islamic Republic of Pakistan) and became Prime Minister of the new nation of Bangladesh.

The 1971 civil war was a disaster for Bangladesh, undoing much of the limited progress East Pakistan had made in recovering from the socioeconomic disruption of the 1947 partition. The charismatic Mujib faced a task for which his administrative and political experience was lacking. He fought and won a massive victory at the polls in 1973, but two years later, he suspended the political process and took power into his own hands. Bangla opinion turned against Mujib, coalescing two main opposition groups that otherwise shared little in common besides their opposition to Mujib and to Indian influence: they were the ultra conservative Islamic groups, led by the Jamaat-i-Islami, and the radical left, led by Maoists, who opposed both Indian and Soviet influence.

On 15 August 1975, a group of young military officers seized power, killing Mujib and many of his family members and imposing martial law. A counter-coup three months later produced a new military government with Gen. Zia-ur Rahman at its head. In 1978, with limited political activity permitted, he was elected President and lifted martial law. In February 1979, he restored parliamentary government after elections gave his new party, the Bangladesh National Party (BNP) a two-thirds majority in the National Assembly.

Zia's assassination during an abortive military coup in May 1981 set back the progress he had made. He was succeeded in power by his vice president, Abdus Sattar, who was deposed the following March by his army chief, Gen. Hussain Mohammad Ershad. Declaring martial law, Ershad became Chief Martial Law Administrator (CMLA), suspended the 1972 constitution, and banned political parties.

Ershad gained support by cracking down on corruption and opening up the economy to foreign collaboration. In 1983, he assumed the presidency, and by January 1986, he had restored full political activity in which his own party, the Jatiya (People's) Party took a prominent part. He retired from the army and was elected president without opposition in October 1986, but in July 1987, mounting opposition to his often dictatorial rule among the united opposition parties led him again to declare a state of emergency, dissolve the assembly, and schedule new elections for March 1988. His Jatiyo Party triumphed in those elections, due mainly to the refusal of the opposition parties to participate. At the end of 1990, in the face of widespread demonstrations and some Hindu-Muslim violence, his opposition had grown so strong that Ershad was forced to resign the presidency, turning the government over to Supreme Court Chief Justice Shahabuddin Ahmed, the unanimous choice of the opposition parties.

An interim government scheduled elections for February 1991, and the result—in what has been described as the fairest polling ever held in the country—was the election of an assembly in which the BNP, now headed by Begum Khaleda Zia-ur Rahman, Zia's widow, held a plurality. However, the BNP lost popular support by March 1994, when opposition parties walked out of Parliament and boycotted the government, claiming the BNP had rigged a regional election. The main opposition groups—the Awami League, Jatiya Party, and the Jamaat-e-Islami—continued the protest for two years, boycotting February 1996 elections swept by the BNP. Amid further charges of vote-rigging, Khaleda Zia resigned, the BNP dissolved Parliament, and a caretaker government conducted new elections in June 1996. The Awami League, led by Sheikh Hasina Wajed, daughter of the Sheikh Mujid, gained control of Parliament in the elections, contested by all parties and monitored by international observers. Although initially dependent on the support of the Jatiya Party to form a government, by late September the Awami League held an absolute majority of seats in the legislature.

Prime Minister Sheik Hasina had no easier time ruling Bangladesh than her predecessor. Her government faced continuing protests, strikes, and often violent demonstrations organized by the BNP and other opposition parties. Targets for such actions included the government's historic agreement with India in December 1996 over sharing the waters of the River Ganges, higher taxes imposed by the government in July 1997, and problems of law and order in the country. During September 1997, Islamic militants took to the streets demanding the arrest and execution of controversial Bangladeshi author Taslima Nasreen. November 1998 saw a general strike organized by the BNP over alleged government repression and clashes between police and protesters over alleged electoral fraud. Tensions were heightened by the conviction and death sentences passed on several people involved in the assassination of Sheikh Hasina's father, Sheikh Mujib.

In August 1998, Bangladesh also saw some of the worst flooding in the country's history. Over 1,000 people died and flood waters covered some 60% of the country. Loss of crops raised the specter of widespread famine, and the total damage to the country's economy and infrastructure was estimated at over US $2 billion.

Among the AL government's achievements, however, were the Ganges water-sharing treaty, the December 1997 accord that ended the tribal insurgency in the Chittagong Hill Tracts (CHT) in southeastern Bangladesh, and a restructuring of local government to increase grassroots involvement in politics. On the international stage, Bangladesh was elected to serve a two-year term on the Security Council of the United Nations, effective 1 January 2000. Bill Clinton became the first US President to visit Bangladesh when he stopped there during his South Asia tour in March 2000. Although his visit did not resolve any of the pressing trade issues between the two countries, he arrived with a package of $97 billion in desperately-needed food aid for Bangladesh.

13 GOVERNMENT

Bangladesh inherited the provincial government under which first the Dominion, then Republic, of Pakistan was governed, a parliamentary system based on the Westminster model with a unicameral legislature. Following this model, the constitution of December 1972 established a unitary, democratic republic, with an indirectly-elected president as nominal head of state and a prime minister as head of government and chief executive. The prime minister and his government are responsible to a unicameral legislature—the National Assembly—elected no less frequently than every five years and composed of 330 members, including 30 in appointive seats reserved for women. The constitution incorporated four basic principles of state policy: nationalism, secularism, socialism, and democracy. With considerable controversy, because of its impact on the nearly 17% of the population which is non-Muslim, Islam replaced secularism as a state principle by constitutional amendment in 1977.

The constitution was amended in 1975, at the initiative of Prime Minister Mujibur Rahman, to abrogate most guarantees of civil liberties, to establish a one-party polity, and to make the presidency, rather than the prime ministership, the chief executive of the government. Mujib's assassination later that year, and the countercoup that occurred three months later resulted in a four-year suspension of the constitution by Bangladesh's martial law ruler, Gen. Zia-ur Rahman.

Rahman himself was assassinated in 1981, and in the turmoil that ensued, General H. M. Ershad seized power. Ershad declared himself president in 1982, and held office until 1990, when increasing antigovernment protests and violence resulted in his resignation. He was later jailed on corruption charges. The interim government then conducted what most observers regard as the most free and fair elections ever held in Bangladesh, in 1991.

Among her first acts as prime minister, Begum Khaleda Zia-ur Rahman, widow of General Rahman and the head of his Bangladesh Nationalist Party, reversed from her former position in favor of retaining a strong presidential system to restore the parliamentary system of 1972 and to return to the prime ministership the powers removed by Mujib in 1975. She led the campaign with strong Awami League support, which resulted in overwhelming parliamentary approval of a constitutional amendment. Kahleda Zia was forced to step down in March 1996, after two years of political turmoil following an opposition boycott of Parliament and elections. The opposition AL, which claimed the BNP had rigged two elections, was swept into power in the internationally monitored elections of June 1996. Wajed then formed a coalition majority in Parliament with the Jatiya Party. By September 1996, with several victories in by-elections, the Awami League controlled an absolute majority of seats in Parliament. The government was thus unaffected by the Jatiya Party's withdrawal from the coalition in March 1997. As of February 2000, the Awami League controlled 177 of Parliament's 300 seats. The BNP held 112 seats and the Jatiya Party 33. The next general election is scheduled for the year 2001.

14 POLITICAL PARTIES

From 1947 through the end of 1971, East Pakistan—now Bangladesh—was governed as a single province, one of the two wings of Pakistan. In all, there were more than 30 political parties operating in the east wing, most of the them small, fractious, and with few elected members. The major parties at that time operated on the all-Pakistan level as well, and included the moderate Pakistan Muslim League (PML), a national movement that became the party of independence and the ruling party of Pakistan; the moderate socialist Awami (Freedom) League (AL), a spin-off from the Muslim League and the advocate of Bengali autonomy, with the bulk of its support in the east wing; the ultra-conservative Islamic Jamaat-i-Islami (JI), grounded in Sunni Islamic orthodoxy (in Pakistan as in India) and initially opposed to the 1947 partition; and the leftist peasants and workers party, the Krishak Sramik Party (KSP) of Fazlul Haq. The Communist Party of Pakistan (CPP) was banned in 1952 and remained illegal until its east wing component became the Bangladesh Communist Party (BCP) after 1971.

The PML governed East Pakistan from 1947, but in elections in 1954, the Awami League and the Krishak Sramik, supported in a United Front by the Jamaat, ousted the Muslim League from office. After four years of political instability, however, the two parties were displaced by the central government under "Governor's Rule," and the emergency provisions of the 1935 Government of India Act, then Pakistan's constitution. When the East Pakistan government was restored in August 1955, the KSP ruled in its own right until displaced by an AL government headed by Maulana Bhashani in 1956. Loss of Hindu support in 1958 cost the AL its majority in 1958, but "Governor's Rule" was again imposed, the provision having been carried over into the 1956 Pakistan Constitution. Martial law was imposed in Pakistan in 1965 and in elections held thereafter, under a limited political franchise, the Muslim League, now a shadow of its former self and the vehicle for General Ayub Khan's entry into elective politics, came to power briefly. Imposition of martial law in 1969 suspended political activity again until the scheduling of elections in 1970 restored political activity.

By 1970, the moderate-to-left populist Pakistan People's Party (PPP) of Zulfikar Bhutto, and the Awami League of Sheikh Mujibur Rahman, now advocating far-reaching autonomy for East Bengal, had become the dominant political forces, respectively, in West and East Pakistan. Elections confirmed this position, with the AL winning 167 of East Pakistan's 169 seats in the National Assembly and absolute control in East Pakistan. The AL was the only constituent in the Bangla Government-in-Exile in 1971, with leftist parties in support and Islamic parties in opposition. After independence, the Islamic party leaders were jailed, their parties having been banned, and in 1973, Mujib's Awami League elected 293 members of the 300-elective seats in the Assembly.

In January 1975, with his power slipping, President Mujib amended the constitution to create a one-party state, renaming his party the Bangladesh Krishak Sramik Awami League (BKSAL). After the coup later in 1975, the BKSAL was disbanded and disappeared. When Zia-ur Rahman lifted the ban on political parties in 1978, his presidential bid was supported by a newly formed Nationalist Front, dominated by his Bangladesh National Party (BNP), which won 207 of the assembly's 300 elective seats. All political activity was banned anew in March 1982 when Gen. Ershad seized power, but as he settled into power, Ershad supported the formation of the Jatiya (People's) Party, which became his vehicle for ending martial law and transforming his regime into a parliamentary government. In elections marked by violence and discredited by extensive fraud, Ershad's Jatiya Party won more than 200 of the 300 elective seats at stake. The Awami League, now under the leadership of Mujib's daughter, Sheikh Hasina Wajid, took 76 seats as the leading opposition party. Begum Khaleda Zia's BNP, heading an alliance of seven parties, boycotted the elections and gained considerable respect by this action. The BNP, the AL, and all other parties boycotted Ershad's 1988 election as well, discrediting the result that gave the Jatiyo a two-thirds majority and fueling the fires of discontent that led to Ershad's resignation on 4 December 1990. Ershad was arrested on corruption charges eight days later by the interim government, convicted, and imprisoned on corruption charges.

A BNP plurality in the elections on 27 February 1991 enabled Begum Khaleda Zia to form a government with the support of 28 of the appointive members of the assembly and of the JI, which won 18 seats. The leader of the opposition is Sheikh Hasina Wajid of the Awami League (AL), which won 88 seats to claim the second ranking position in the assembly. However, Khaleda Zia resigned and Parliament was dissolved in March 1996 amid vote-rigging charges and a two-year government boycott by opposition parties. June 1996 elections brought Sheikh Hasina and the AL to a majority role in the new Parliament. The AL won 140 seats to the BNP's 116. New Prime Minister Hasina formed a cooperative government with the Jatiya Party, which won 32

seats. Although the Jatiya Party withdrew from the coalition in March 1997, the Awami League had by then acquired an absolute majority in the legislature and continued as the party in power.

Since 1997, the main opposition party, the BNP, has hindered the work of the Jatiya Sangsad (Parliament) by repeatedly boycotting its proceedings. One such boycott, over issues ranging from restoration of a floating footbridge to Ziaur Rahman's tomb to the dropping of criminal charges against BNP MPs, lasted for six months (August 1997–March 1998). Outside Parliament, the BNP continued to support public antigovernment demonstrations, and organized a three-day general strike (hartal) in November 1998 to protest alleged government repression. A month later, the opposition strengthened its position when the BNP and the Jamaat-e-Islami decided a month to accept Ershad and his Jatiya Party into the anti-Government movement. In the spring of 2000, a four-party alliance of opposition parties (BNP, Jatiya Party, Jamaat-e-Islami, and Islami Oikyo Jote) announced it was considering plans to form an electoral coalition to oppose the Awami League in the next general elections.

15 LOCAL GOVERNMENT

As a unitary state, the key administrative unit in Bangladesh is the region (also referred to popularly as the district), of which there are 21 in all. For administrative convenience, regions are grouped into (and report through) four divisions, under a senior civil servant with the title of division commander (formerly commissioner).

Regions or districts are under the charge of a senior civil servant with the title of deputy commissioner; they are appointed by the national government and are vested with broad powers to collect revenues and taxes, assist in development activities, and maintain law and order. As of 1985, regions or districts were subdivided into zilas; in urban areas, these were further broken down into municipalities, wards, mohallas, and thanas, while in rural areas, the breakdown was into upazilas (sub-districts), unions, mouzas, and villages.

In 1997, Bangladesh reorganized its local government structure in rural areas. New legislation created a four-tier local government system: gram (village), union (collection of villages), upazila (subdistrict), and zila (district) councils. The purpose of this reorganization was to democratize government at the grass roots level in a process that, in theory at least, is nonpartisan. Elections for union parishads (councils) held in December 1997 created widespread interest, with particularly high levels of participation from women, both as candidates as well as voters. Other legislation made the upazila level the most important tier in local government, giving the upazila council power to collect revenue, prepare its own budget and hire its own employees. The restructuring of local government in Bangladesh is an ongoing process aimed at increasing popular participation in the governmental process.

16 JUDICIAL SYSTEM

The judicial system, modeled after the British system, is similar to that of neighboring countries. Besides the 1972 constitution, the fundamental law of the land, there are codes of civil and criminal laws. The civil law incorporates certain Islamic and Hindu religious principles relating to marriage, inheritance, and other social matters.

The constitution provides for an impartial and independent judiciary. After the 1982 coup, the constitution was suspended, martial law courts were established throughout the country, and Lieut. Gen Ershad assumed the power to appoint judges. The constitution was reinstated in November 1986.

The judicial system consists of a Low Court and a Supreme Court, both of which hear civil and criminal cases. The Low

Court consists of administrative courts (magistrate courts) and session judges. The Supreme Court also has two divisions, a High Court which hears original cases and reviews decisions of the Low Court, and an Appellate Court which hears appeals from the High Court. The upper level courts have exercised independent judgment, recently ruling against the government on a number of occasions in criminal, civil and even political trials. The trials are public. There is a right to counsel and right to appeal. There is also a system of bail. An overwhelming backlog of cases remains the major problem of the court system.

The government, with the help of the World Bank, has undertaken an ambitious project to reform the judicial system. Changes include the creation of "Legal Aid Committees" to provide assistance to the poor, as well as the establishing of Metropolitan Courts of Sessions in Dhaka and Chittagong. A permanent Law Commission has been created to reform and update existing laws, and the government is committed to establishing a Human Rights Commission as well as an Office of the Ombudsman.

[17]ARMED FORCES

In 2000, Bangladesh had an army of 120,000 men, a navy of 10,500, and an air force of 6,500. Paramilitary forces of border guards, armed police, and security guards totaled 55,200. The military budget in 1996–97 was $559 million or 1.8% of GDP.

About 15,000 Bengali soldiers in the Pakistan army in 1971 defected to the liberation forces (Mukhti Bahini), and they formed the core of the Bangladesh army after independence. This force, armed mainly with Chinese weapons, is organized into one armored and 17 infantry brigades. The navy mans four Chinese frigates and 45 patrol and coastal craft. The air force flies 65 Chinese fighter-bombers of limited capability.

[18]INTERNATIONAL COOPERATION

Bangladesh joined the UN on 17 September 1974; it belongs to ESCAP and all the nonregional specialized agencies. A member of the Asian Development Bank, the Commonwealth of Nations, and G-77, Bangladesh participates in the nonaligned movement and in international Muslim organizations and conferences. The nation is a signatory to the Law of the Sea and a member of the WTO. In 1985, Bangladesh became one of seven constituent members of the SAARC, under which it is a signatory to the South Asia Preferential Trade Agreement. In 1977, Bangladesh signed an agreement with India on sharing water from the Ganges River.

Soon after independence, Bangladesh signed a friendship treaty with India, but the new leaders after the 1975 coup instituted a policy of equal cooperation with other neighboring countries. Pakistan recognized Bangladesh in February 1974, and the two have developed close relations, their past differences notwithstanding. Generally, Bangladesh follows a nonaligned foreign policy and in recent years has sought closer relations with other Islamic states, ASEAN, and China. Bangladesh also continues a healthy relationship with the US, with which it has bilateral trade agreements. In 1995, the country's trade exporters association signed an agreement with the United Nations Children's Fund and the International Labor Organization under which industry's rampant use of child labor would be eliminated.

[19]ECONOMY

Bangladesh is a poor country endowed with few natural resources and an economy dominated by subsistence agriculture. About 63% of the country's total land area is currently cropped, while almost 65% of the economically active population derive their livelihood from farming. The incidence of poverty is very high, with roughly one-half of the total population estimated to be earning less than enough to afford a daily diet considered minimally adequate by international standards. Nevertheless,

signs of modest improvement in the economy have been evident during the past decade, despite difficult weather and international market conditions. Agriculture still accounts for 30% of the GDP, although this proportion has dropped significantly from 50% in 1979/80, as industry's share has increased from 15.9% to 17% and that of services from 34.4% to 53%. GDP growth reached an annual average of 4.4% between 1987 and 1997, while growth reached 5.6% in 1998. This slowed to 5.2% in 1999 due to flooding.

Over the past several decades, Bangladesh has endured the ravages of the 1971 war with Pakistan, a severe famine in 1971, and a succession of weather-related disasters, the most recent of which included a devastating cyclone in April 1991 and widespread flooding in both 1998 and 1999. After the mid-1970s, financial stabilization measures, encouragement of private investment, and generally good weather contributed to an agricultural growth rate that exceeded the rate of population growth. However, real economic growth under the five-year plan that ended in mid-1985 averaged only slightly over 3% a year, well below the original target of 7.2%. A new 1985–90 five-year plan continued to emphasize agricultural production and envisaged a growth rate of 5.4% a year. Stabilization, export promotion, and flexible exchange rate management policies strengthened during the mid-1980s helped to decrease fiscal and external deficits, boost nontraditional exports, especially of garments, and reduce inflation to below double-digit figures by the end of the decade. Economic growth was, however, hampered by heavy flooding that occurred in 1987 and 1988, which resulted in negative to no real change in agricultural output for those years. Industrial growth, on the other hand, remained relatively strong, helping to sustain an average GDP growth of 3.7% for the 1985–90 period overall.

In 1990/91, the combined effects of the Gulf war, domestic political disturbances, and a devastating cyclone resulted in a drop in GDP growth rate from 6.6% in 1989/90 to only 3.4%. Pursuit of further stabilization and structural adjustment measures by the newly elected government in 1991 allowed Bangladesh to weather these crises, strengthen its revenue base, bring inflation to a record low of 1.4% in 1993, and maintain a good balance of payments position. However, political instability and a lack of continued economic reforms pushed inflation to 5.2% in 1995. Sluggish development investments, limited growth in value added by manufacturing, and bureaucratic inefficiency in aid disbursement and project realization persisted. Still, with the election of the Awami League government calming the political waters, growth rates and export and tax revenues rebounded in 1996. GDP grew 4.7% in 1996, while inflation fell to 5.04%. Though the indicators were promising as of 1997, the government's delay in instituting needed reforms threatened to slow economic advances. Inflation had risen to 7%, while GDP had slowed to 4%. The Awami League promoted the exploration, distribution and manufacture of oil and gas in Bangladesh in the late 1990s, but stalled on the details of contracts. The economy grew strongly during 1998, and flooding, instead of devastating the economy, brought in some much needed foreign aid.

[20]INCOME

The US Central Intelligence Agency (CIA) reports that in 1998 Bangladesh's gross domestic product (GDP) was estimated at $175.5 billion. The per capita GDP was estimated at $1,380. The annual growth rate of GDP was estimated at 4%. The average inflation rate in 1998 was 7%. The CIA defines GDP as the value of all final goods and services produced within a nation in a given year and computed on the basis of purchasing power parity (PPP) rather than value as measured on the basis of the rate of exchange. It was estimated that agriculture accounted for 30% of GDP, industry 17%, and services 53%.

The World Bank reports that for the same period per capita private consumption (in PPP terms) was $1,010. Private consumption includes expenditures of individuals, households, and nongovernmental organizations. It was estimated that between 1990 and 1998 private consumption grew at an annual rate of 3.7%. Approximately 49% of household consumption was spent on food, 18% on fuel, 8% on health care, and 9% on education. The richest 10% of the population accounted for approximately 29% of household consumption and the poorest 10% approximately 3.9%.

21LABOR

The civilian labor force in 1998 was estimated at approximately 64 million. In 1996 slightly under 10% of the civilian labor force was employed in the industrial sector. Official statistics are somewhat unreliable because of a large, informal, unreported market Average wages in 1999 ranged from $1.50 to $2.50 per day and were not sufficient to provide a decent standard of living for a family.

Although 1.8 million out of the five million workers in the formal sector of the economy were unionized, this represented only a small fraction of the economically active population, which is estimated at 58 million. There are industrial tribunals to settle labor disputes. The government can impose labor settlements through arbitration, as well as by declaring a strike illegal. In 1993, unemployment (1.7%) and underemployment (30%) continued to be high, and agricultural workers were not protected by disability compensation. Unions have become progressively more aggressive in asserting themselves, especially on the political scene. However, the minimum wage, which is set on an industry-by-industry basis, by a special wage commission, is often not observed in the private sector.

Children under the age of 14 are not allowed to work in factories but may work (under restricted hours) in other industries. However, such restrictions are rarely enforced and children work in every sector of the economy. In 1999, 6.3 million between the ages of 10 to 14 were reported to be working in the internal private sector.

22AGRICULTURE

Agriculture accounted for 30% of GDP and engaged 58% of the economically active population in 1998. Most of the farmers own no more than a few acres of land, and their holdings are badly fragmented. The land is fertile, but yields are low because of a lack of capital for input.

Rice dominates the production of about 60% of all cropped land in Bangladesh. Of the varieties grown, aman rice, which can be raised in inundated land and saline soil, occupies nearly 60% of the total land under rice. Aus rice, which cannot be grown in flooded fields, is raised mostly in higher areas of Bangladesh. Boro rice is grown in the winter, mainly in the swamps and marshy areas, but government-supported irrigation projects have encouraged its extension to other areas. To meet the challenge of the food shortages, the government of Bangladesh and international aid programs introduced a high-yielding variety of rice called IRRI with considerable success. Total rice production in 1998 was 28,293,000 tons. Before November 1992, the government artificially inflated rice prices by buying over one million tons per harvest. With subsidies gone, the subsequent fall in rice prices reflected an adjustment of the market after 20 years of prices propped up by government sales and purchases.

Jute is the main cash crop of Bangladesh, which produces about one-quarter of the total jute supply of the world. Grown in most parts of the country, jute is harvested from July to September. Its strong fibers are used to produce carpets, burlap bags, mats, upholstery, and other products. Jute is also used to manufacture textiles for clothes. The combined total export of jute and jute products represents about 13–15% of Bangladesh's annual export earnings. Although Bangladesh is the world leader in exports of jute, its prominence in the economy has slipped since the 1970s. The diminished role is due to mismanagement of the nationalized jute industry, labor strikes, and a drop in the worldwide use of jute for packing. In 1998, 1,088,000 tons of jute were produced (30% of world production).

Although tea is the second most important agricultural export, it accounted for only 1% of export earnings. Most tea plantations are in the Sylhet Region and the Chittagong Hill Tracts. Much of the tea is consumed domestically; total production in 1998 was 51,000 tons.

The agricultural economy, though disrupted by the 1971 war, largely recovered and grew by an average 2.7% annually during the 1980s and by an annual average of 2.2% during 1990–98. Agricultural exports accounted for 2.9% of total exports in 1997. Frequent monsoons and cyclones keep the economy vulnerable. Crop output (in tons) in 1998 included sugarcane, 7,379,000; wheat, 1,803,000; potatoes, 1,553,000; sweet potatoes, 398,000; tobacco, 37,000; and barley, 6,000. Fruit production in 1998 included 625,000 tons of bananas, 187,000 tons of mangoes, and 49,000 tons of pineapples. Coconut productions totaled 89,000 tons that year; pulses, 508,000 tons.

23ANIMAL HUSBANDRY

The livestock sector has made significant progress in the 1990s, rising from 1% of GDP in 1989 to 10% in 1996. Livestock provide most of Bangladesh's draft power, rural transportation, manure, and fuel, in addition to meat, milk, eggs, hides, and skins. Buffalo milk is an important item of consumption, especially in the form of clarified butterfat. Small dairy farms (with 5–20 crossbred cows) have been growing fast in recent years. Entrepreneurs are encouraged by high liquid milk prices as well as government incentives under which the farmers receive cash to purchase dairy cows. In 1996, there were an estimated 20,750 small dairies; total milk production in 1998 was 2.1 million tons. There were about 23.4 million head of cattle, 854,000 buffaloes, 33.5 million goats, 1,158,000 sheep and 153 million chickens in 1998.

Much of the cattle stock is smuggled from India because of the reduced local availability of cows and bulls, especially during the midyear Muslim holiday of Eid Ul Azha, when cattle are sacrificed throughout the country. The cattle brought in from India may account for up to 30% of beef production. The scarcity of cattle in recent years is the result of lack of vaccines and fodder, natural disasters, and an absence of farmer incentives.

24FISHING

Fish is a staple food of Bangladesh and the main source of protein. There are hundreds of varieties, including carp, salmon, pomfret, shrimp, catfish, and many local varieties. Dried fish is considered a delicacy in many parts of the country. About 1,342,730 tons of fish (74% from inland waters) were produced in 1997 (19th in the world). While much of the fish is consumed domestically, Bangladesh exports a sizable quantity of freshwater fish to India and other neighboring countries, and freshwater shrimp and lobster are exported to a number of countries. Exports of fish products in 1997 amounted to $291.6 million. It is also a major source of frogs' legs, which are "farmed" commercially. Fishermen's cooperatives foster the use of modern fish-catching trawlers in the Bay of Bengal, and the government has established a fisheries corporation to stimulate production of freshwater fish for export.

25FORESTRY

Bangladesh had an estimated 1,010,000 ha (2,496,000 acres) of forest in 1995, covering some 7.8% of land area. In recent years, the pressure of population has led to enormous deforestation. The government-controlled Forest Industries Development Corp. supervises the development and exploitation of forest resources. Roundwood production in 1997 came to 32,331,000 cu m. Over 98% of timber cut is used for firewood.

The main forest zone is the Sunderbans area in the southwest, consisting mostly of mangrove forests. Two principal species dominate the Sunderban forests: sundari trees, which grow about 15–18 m (50–60 ft) high and are of tough timber, and gewa trees, a softer wood used for making newsprint. Teak and bamboo are grown in the central forests.

26MINING

Aside from natural gas, Bangladesh has few mineral resources. The Bay of Bengal area is being explored for oil, and in some offshore areas, drilling is being conducted by international companies. Bangladesh has reserves of good quality coal in the northern districts, but extraction has been difficult since many deposits are located at a depth of more than 900 m (3,000 ft). Production estimates of mineral commodities in Bangladesh in 1997 included cement, 285,000 tons; marine salt, 350,000 tons; and limestone (mined in the Sylhet and Chittagong regions), 25,000 tons.

27ENERGY AND POWER

A substantial portion of Bangladesh's electrical supply is met by the country's only hydroelectric plant, at Kaptai, which has a capacity of 230 MW; the rest of the country's power is produced by burning coal, gas, and oil. Except for a few private installations on the tea plantations and a few other industries, the power and energy sector is controlled by a government-managed corporation. Total power production was 11,870 million kWh in 1998, of which less than 5% was hydroelectric. Installed capacity totaled 3,301,000 kW. As of 2000, only about 18% of the population has access to electricity.

In July 1997, Bangladesh contracted with four international power and refining companies for four new power plants with a combined capacity of 1,600 MW. The new plants were expected to double the country's electricity to 4,000 MW over five years. The power plants were part of investment proposals by German, UK, Swedish, and US firms in light of the discovery of new natural gas fields.

Reserves of natural gas in 13 fields were estimated at anywhere from 10 to 80 trillion cu ft in 2000; production totaled 6,647 million cu m in 1994 and 7,997 cu m in 1998. The government controls the gas industry but began accepting private exploration bids in 1991. In 1995, the World Bank was lending $120.8 million as part of a $171.7-million project to develop the natural gas sector. Also in 1995, the Iranian private sector, in a joint venture with the Bangladeshi government, planned to build an oil refinery. Chinese consultants confirmed the existence of 300 million tons of good quality coal at the Boropukuria coal field in northern Diajpur District during 1991.

28INDUSTRY

Although private investment in industry has been encouraged since the mid-1980s, until recently it remained closely regulated, and state-owned firms dominated production in many sectors, including the centrally important jute industry. Other industries include textile manufacturing, food processing, steel manufacturing, and fertilizer production. Lack of growth in manufacturing's share of total GDP during the 1980s reflected the constraints of a protectionist policy regime. In 1991, the government inaugurated an Industrial Policy, planning investment liberalization, the interim restructuring of several large parastatals, as well as the gradual privatization of public enterprises in all but the airways, railways, and mining sectors. However, a reluctance to privatize those sectors hampered economic growth. Although averaging 7% growth since the 1970s, 1999 industrial growth only reached 2.5% due to flood disruption. To promote development of export-oriented industries, two export processing zones were developed, one in the port city of Chittagong and one in Savar (30 km from Dhaka).

Recent discoveries of large natural gas reserves and plans for new power plants throughout the country are suspected to boost industrial growth in 2000 and beyond. However, transitional difficulties in the restructuring of important state enterprises resulted in some output decline in a few industries during the 1990s. The jute fiber processing industry, majority-owned by the government, lost $58 million in 1997 and $48 million in 1998 due to inefficiencies, lowering export earnings from the crop by at least one-third. The state chemicals industry also lost ground. Other state industries, including textile milling and steel, led manufacturing growth and a high industrial production growth rate of 8.1% in 1998. The state still owned 40% of industrial capacity in 1998.

29SCIENCE AND TECHNOLOGY

Bangladesh lacks the trained personnel necessary for intensive technological development. The Bangladesh University of Engineering and Technology (founded in 1962) does, however, train some technicians. Other institutions offering scientific and technical education include the Bangladesh Agricultural University in Mymensingh, the University of Chittagong, the University of Dhaka, Jahangirnagar University in Dhaka, Khulna University, and the University of Rajshahi. In 1987–97, there were only 52 scientists engaged in research and development per million people.

The Bangladesh Council for Scientific and Industrial Research and headquartered in Dhaka, operates seven research institutes, and the Bangladesh Atomic Energy commission, Founded in 1973, and also in Dhaka, operates two others. The Geological Society of Bangladesh, founded in 1972 at Dhaka, is a government organization under the Ministry of Energy and Natural resources. Leading professional groups are the Bangladesh Academy of Sciences, the Bangladesh Medical Association, and the Zoological Society of Bangladesh, all headquartered in Dhaka.

30DOMESTIC TRADE

Except for jute, tea, paper, garments, frozen shrimp, and a few other items, most of the commodities produced in Bangladesh are consumed inside the country. Normally, the farmers or fishermen sell to the wholesalers, and they in turn sell to distributors and retailers. Industrial commodities for domestic consumption are distributed through the same procedure. The middlemen in the distribution process have often benefited from excessive profits, creating hardships for farmers and consumers. To meet this situation, the government has introduced mechanisms by means of which farmers can sell directly to cooperative agencies acting on behalf of buyers. The government has also set up fair-price shops for consumers. Much domestic trade in rural areas is conducted in the marketplaces, where farmers sell directly to consumers.

Foreign products are imported by large commercial concerns located in the capital city of Dhaka or in the ports, and are then distributed through wholesalers and retailers. Normal business hours are between 9 AM and 5 PM, but most retail stores are open until 8 PM. Most establishments close on Fridays and on

Thursday afternoons and evenings. Limited advertising is done through the newspapers, movie houses, handbills, and television.

31 FOREIGN TRADE

Since independence, Bangladesh has had a strongly negative trade balance. Imports steadily ran more than double the value of exports between 1971 and 1991. With a surge in export growth since 1991, the trade deficit has improved; imports exceeded exports by about 56% in 1996, and by 62% in 1997 as opposed to more than 120% in 1989/90. As a result of successful export promotion measures undertaken by the government during the 1980s, exports of ready-made-garments and knitwear are now Bangladesh's leading earner of foreign exchange.

The garment and textile industry garners the highest percentage of Bangladesh's export commodities, including undergarments, women's and men's outerwear, leather, hats, and yarn (78%). At the mouth of the Ganges, shell fish are also harvested and exported (8.2%).

In 1996 Bangladesh's imports were distributed among the following categories:

Consumer goods	5.9%
Food	16.2%
Fuels	7.1%
Industrial supplies	52.7%
Machinery	11.8%
Transportation	6.0%
Other	0.3%

Principal trading partners in 1998 (in millions of US dollars) were as follows:

COUNTRY	EXPORTS	IMPORTS	BALANCE
United States	1,368	285	1,083
Germany	404	164	240
United Kingdom	347	314	33
France	254	75	179
Italy	232	52	180
Netherlands	189	55	134
China (inc. Hong Kong)	98	999	-901
Japan	64	456	-392
India	55	1,179	-1,124
Australia	16	197	-181

32 BALANCE OF PAYMENTS

The continuing trade deficit has been offset in small part by private transfers, mainly from earnings of workers in the Middle East, but large amounts of foreign aid and heavy short-term borrowing are needed to handle the balance-of-payments problem. In 1991/92, the infusion of $1.59 billion in foreign and transfers helped lessen a negative balance of payments. In 1995, the trade deficit widened and there was a stagnation in the growth of remittances from overseas workers. The rising trade deficit, coupled with a decline in international aid disbursements due to political turmoil, caused foreign exchange reserves to drop from a peak of $3.4 billion in April 1995 to $2.1 billion by the end of 1996, and $1.7 billion by 1999. The current account deficit improved from 5.1% of GDP to 2.7% of GDP in 1997, and 1.5% of GDP in 1998.

The US Central Intelligence Agency reports that in 1997 the purchasing power parity of Bangladesh's exports was $4.4 billion while imports totaled $7.1 billion resulting in a trade balance of -$2.7 billion.

The International Monetary Fund (IMF) reports that in 1998 Bangladesh had exports of goods totaling $5,141 million and imports totaling $6,862 million. The services credit totaled $724 million and debit $1,253 million. The following table summarizes Bangladesh's balance of payments as reported by the IMF for 1998 in millions of US dollars.

Current Account		-190
Balance on goods	-1,721	
Balance on services	-529	
Balance on income	-108	
Current transfers	2,168	
Capital Account		239
Financial Account		26
Direct investment abroad	26	
Direct investment in Bangladesh	308	
Portfolio investment assets	-	
Portfolio investment liabilities	1	
Other investment assets	-876	
Other investment liabilities	597	
Net Errors and Omissions		215
Reserves and Related Items		-290

33 BANKING AND SECURITIES

Central banking is conducted by the Bangladesh Bank, which has its head office in Dhaka. It is responsible for the circulation of money, supervision of commercial banks, and control of credit and foreign exchange. There are nine government-owned banks, 20 private banks, and 13 foreign bank branches operating in Bangladesh. The four major banks are all state-owned: Sonali Bank, Janata Bank, Agrani Bank, and Rupali Bank.

Trade on the Dhaka Stock Exchange (DSE) was dormant until 1993. The fourth quarter of 1996 was marked by feverish activity on the DSE, and on the smaller Chittagong Stock Exchange (CSE). In September, October, and the first two weeks of November, records were broken daily as share prices soared. Prices soon bore little relation to the current profitability or future prospects of the companies concerned. Up to 300,000 first-time buyers joined in the bonanza, driving the limited number of stocks traded—210—to a peak on 16 November, 1996, when the all-share index reached 3,627, up from around 1,000 in June. By 4 November, market capitalization had reached an unsustainable $6 billion, equivalent to some 20% of the country's GDP. The government began to cool down the market by selling off state-owned enterprises. In late December, the central bank announced that T2 billion ($47 million) would be available to the state-run Investment Corporation of Bangladesh to buy shares and give some support to the market, but the market crashed despite these preventative measures. In 1997, 37 stock brokers were charged with market manipulation in the DSE boom and crash of 1996. In 1998, market capitalization reached $1.4 billion, although very little foreign portfolio investment was recorded.

34 INSURANCE

The insurance business was nationalized in 1972, creating a government-controlled insurance corporation. The Ministry of Finance and Planning is the insurance regulatory body. Premiums are mainly in commercial or industrial fields. Life insurance is still limited to city dwellers and middle-class professionals.

35 PUBLIC FINANCE

The fiscal year runs from June to July. In 1993, Bangladesh successfully completed a three-year IMF structural adjustment program. This program resulted in a growth in money supply of 11% in 1993, 15% in 1994, and 16% in 1995. In addition, government spending was curbed by a decline in subsides to money-losing parastatals and the value added tax (VAT) continued to generate higher than predicted revenues for the government, with collections up 18% over 1994.

In 1996, the government reported that exports were up, the GDP grew by 4.4%, and that tax revenues climbed 9% to $3.06 billion. Encouraged by the good news, the government proposed a 1997 budget that would reduce domestic taxes, further cut import duties, and provide special incentives for foreign investors. The government stressed, however, a continuing need for foreign aid. International aid disbursements in 1996 totaled $1.45 billion, down from $1.74 in 1995. Almost half of government revenues come from foreign aid. In 1999, primarily because of flooding, foreign aid increased by 19% from $1.25 billion in 1998.

The US Central Intelligence Agency (CIA) estimates that in 1997 Bangladesh's central government took in revenues of approximately $3.8 billion and had expenditures of $50.5 billion. Overall, the government registered a deficit of approximately $46.7 billion. External debt totaled $16.7 billion.

36TAXATION
The principal direct taxes are personal income taxes and corporate income taxes (40–45%), and a VAT of 15% levied on all important consumer goods. Essential agricultural implements and irrigation pumps are excluded from certain taxes.

37CUSTOMS AND DUTIES
Bangladesh, with one of the most restrictive trade regimes in Asia, gets a major portion of its current revenue from import duties and excise taxes. In 1999 tariff reform was accelerated by the compression of customs duty rates into a range of 0–37.5%, ranging from raw materials to finished products. There is also a 15% VAT. Customs procedures are lengthy and burdensome, and Bangladesh's list of prohibited imports is lengthy.

There are three Export Processing Zones; one in Chittagong, one in Dakha, and one in Gazipur; three more are under construction in Comilla, Issardi, and Mongla. Bangladesh is a member of the South Asia Preferential Trade Agreement (SAPTA).

38FOREIGN INVESTMENT
Bangladesh nationalized most industries in 1972 and set up nine corporations to oversee them. Subsequently, the Bangladesh government relaxed its policy toward foreign investment and announced a program granting tax holidays to new foreign investors. In 1989 the Directorate of Industries was renamed the Board of Industries and delegated the task of providing various forms of assistance to new investors. More recently, government industrial policies have liberalized conditions for foreign investment much further—100% foreign equity is now allowed on investments anywhere in the country, not simply in export processing zones, and many regulations discriminating between foreign and domestic investors have been abolished. Reflecting the more favorable policy environment, foreign direct investment first flowed into the country in significant amounts, albeit still haltingly, in the late 1980s. As of 1999, the total estimated foreign investment in Bangladesh was $1.5 billion. The four largest investor nations were the US, Malaysia, Japan, and the UK. US investment was estimated to be $700 million in 1999, up from $25 million in 1997, due to massive investment in gas exploration and production, and power generation. Expanding the flow of foreign investment to the country is likely to hinge upon further proof of government commitment to facilitating private business activity.

39ECONOMIC DEVELOPMENT
The major objectives of planned development have been increased national income, rural development, self-sufficiency in food, and increased industrial production. However, progress in achieving development goals has been slow. Bangladesh's first five-year plan (1973–78) aimed to increase economic growth by 5.5% annually, but actual growth averaged only 4% per year. A special two-year plan (1978–80), stressing rural development,

also fell short of its projected growth target, as did the second five-year plan (1980–85), which targeted 7.2% annual growth. The third five-year plan (1985–90) had a 5.4% annual growth target though only 3.7% was actually achieved.

In 1991, a newly elected government instituted another economic initiation that included financial sector reform and liberalization measures to encourage investment, government revenue improvement efforts (realized largely through implementation of a value-added-tax), and tight monetary policy. Income transfer measures, Food-for-Work, and other programs were also implemented to help protect the poorest segments of the population from the transitional effects of structural reform. Political turmoil from 1994 to 1996 also scuttled economic advances. GDP growth slowed to 4.4% in 1994; exports, which grew 36% in 1994, increased by only 15% in 1995. However, 1996 elections brought renewed economic stability. Exports moderated at 14% growth in 1996, and GDP growth for 1996/97 was projected to be 5.5% as the economy rebounded. Floods during 1998 and 1999 caused a brief economic slowdown that was followed by huge growth in the gas production sector and electricity production.

40SOCIAL DEVELOPMENT
Promotion of social welfare was a declared objective of public policy under the constitution of December 1972, and a major government department—the Ministry of Social Welfare and Women's Affairs—is devoted to social welfare tasks. However, funding has been limited. There are also several hundred voluntary welfare organizations operating throughout the country.

A system of pensions exists for public employees only, and there is a limited work injury and unemployment insurance system. These programs are financed entirely by employer contributions and cover only small percentage of the population. Sickness and maternity benefits are also offered on a limited basis.

While women have and exercise full voting rights, they receive unequal treatment in many areas, including education, employment, and family matters such as divorce and inheritance. As of 1996, women held 30 of 330 parliamentary seats. While legislation has been passed in recent years to protect women, discrimination and spousal abuse continues to be a problem. The Cruelty to Women Law of 1983 and the Women Repression Law of 1995 have not been rigorously enforced. In 1998, police received 130 reports of women being disfigured by having acid flung at their faces—usually by rejected suitors.

Nongovernmental organizations have also reported that as of 1996, international trafficking in women and children persists. There is evidence that children are being sold to the Middle East, India, Pakistan, and Southeast Asia for their labor. The government is collaborating with nongovernmental organizations to put an end to this practice.

The use of child labor within Bangladesh is the result of widespread poverty and economic deprivation. Many young children are forced to work at a very young age in garment factories or other industries in order to contribute to family income. Some estimates place the number of child laborers as high as 10 million, including—according to a UNICEF report—some 10,000 child prostitutes.

Although the government is secular, discrimination against minority Hindus has led in recent years to violence and conflict. In 1995, however, there were no widespread cases of intercommunal violence.

The government's human rights record is poor, with many fundamental human rights restricted. Abuses include extrajudicial killings, torture, and violent suppression of demonstrators.

[41]HEALTH

Malaria, tuberculosis, and other serious diseases remain endemic, and public health problems are aggravated by widespread malnutrition and periodic natural disasters. In 1995, the prevalence of malnutrition in children under five years old was 84%. In 1993, access to health care decreased slightly from 1980 (74% of the population), but access to safe water (78%) and sanitation (35%) improved. Because the lack of Vitamin A plays a role in blindness and malnutrition, in 1993 the government of Bangladesh used a national system to distribute Vitamin A capsules to children (with about 25% having been served at that time).

In 1990, there were 8,566 doctors (15 per 1,000 people), 2,630 pharmacists, 523 dentists, and 5,074 nurses. In the mid-1990s, only 45% of the population had access to health services. There were 3,280 people per hospital bed. In 1995, there was one doctor for every 4,970 people. Approximately 74% had access to health care, and 83% had access to safe water.

Average life expectancy at birth in 1999 was 57 years. The government pays the majority of the vaccination costs, which has helped increase participation. In 1997, immunization for measles was 97% for children under one year of age. The rate for tuberculosis was 100%, diptheria, tetanus, and pertussis 98%, and polio 98%. The infant mortality rate was 82 per 1,000 live births in 1996. It was estimated that 40% of married women (ages 15–49) used contraception in 1991. Maternal deaths were 850 per 100,000 live births in 1990.

A new strain of cholera was reported late in 1992. Only seven new cases of AIDS were reported in 1995.

[42]HOUSING

Housing has long been a vital concern in Bangladesh. The government maintains an urban housing program but does not have any housing development program for villages. The House Building Finance Corp. lends money for private as well as public housing. Dhaka and Chittagong urban development is conducted under the guidance of town planning authorities, which develop land and allocate it for private dwelling and commercial purposes. At last estimate, 63% of all housing units were straw or bamboo, 20% were mud or unburnt brick, 12% were cement or wood roofed with iron sheets, and 5% were cement or brick.

[43]EDUCATION

For the year 2000, adult illiteracy rates were estimated at 59.2% (males, 48.3%; females, 70.5%). The government, as a matter of policy, is attempting to broaden the educational base to eradicate mass illiteracy. Education has now been made compulsory for five years, although rural girls are exempted from this law. Most educational institutions are supported by the government either fully or partially. The language of instruction is Bangla.

In the mid-1990s, the number of primary schools was estimated at 46,000 with 190,000 teachers and 12,000,000 students. At the secondary level, there were 131,000 teachers and 3,600,000 students. There are 7 universities, 10 medical colleges, and 10 teacher-training colleges. Research institutions include the Bangla Academy (which sponsors translations of scientific and literary works into Bangla), the Asiatic Society, and the National Institute of Public Administration's Institute of Law and International Affairs. In the mid-1990s, there were 23,000 teachers and 434,000 students in all higher level institutions.

According to recent statistics, approximately 70% of school age children attend primary school, while only 18% are enrolled in secondary school. In 1996, approximately 2.9% of the GDP was allocated to education.

[44]LIBRARIES AND MUSEUMS

The largest library in Bangladesh is the National library with one million volumes. The largest academic library is Dhaka University Library (1921; with 560,000 volumes). It houses the university's collection and that of the former Public Library of East Pakistan. Dhaka's Central Public Library (1958) has over one million volumes. The Bangla Academy maintains an excellent research collection, as does the Bangladesh Institute of Development studies in Dhaka (100,000 volumes).

The Dhaka Museum contains a variety of sculptures and paintings from the Buddhist, Hindu, and Muslim periods. Both it and the Balda Museum have outstanding collections of Bengali art and ancient artifacts. Also in Dhaka are a science and technology museum and the National Museum of Bangladesh. The Ram Mala Museum at Comilla houses 7th-century archaeological finds, and the museum in Rajshahi contains many artifacts from the ruins of an 8th-century Buddhist monastery excavated nearby, as well as significant relics from the Kushon, Gupta, Pala, and Sena periods of Bengali history. There is a gallery of contemporary paintings as well as an ethnological museum in Chittagong.

[45]MEDIA

There were 268,400 telephones in 1995. In that year, Bangladesh had 12 AM and 12 FM radio broadcasting stations and 11 television stations, which were accessible to about 90% of the population; color television was introduced in 1980. In 1997, there were 50 radios and 7 television sets per 1,000 population. All postal and telecommunications services are controlled by the government.

The major Bangla daily newspapers (with 1999 circulations), all in Dhaka, are *Ittefaq* (215,900), *Banglar Bani* (20,000), *Sangbad* (73,000), and *Dainik Bangla* (69,500); the largest English dailies, also in Dhaka, are the *Bangladesh Observer* (42,800) and *Bangladesh Times* (35,100).

The government is said, with some exceptions, to generally respect freedom of speech and press. On occasion, the government has censored criticism of Islam.

[46]ORGANIZATIONS

Various associations for the Muslim, Hindu, Christian, and Buddhist communities have long been active in organizing religious festivals and social activities. Every town also has several cultural groups. The Bangladesh Women's Association, the Boy Scouts, and the Girl Guides are active in social life. There are also many philanthropic organizations and workers' associations, along with several national athletic organizations.

[47]TOURISM, TRAVEL, AND RECREATION

At the end of the 1980s tourism declined due to political unrest. In 1997, 171,961 foreign visitors arrived, nearly half from South Asia. As of that year, there were 4,249 hotel rooms with 8,552 beds with a 44% occupancy rate. Tourism revenues totaled $59 million. The main tourist attractions include the old Mughal capital at Dhaka, nearby Sonargaon with its ancient architecture, the Buddhist cultural center of Mainamati, and the beach resort of Cox's Bazar.

In 1999, the UN estimated the daily cost of staying in Dhaka at $180, Sylhet at $40 and Rangpur at $40.

[48]FAMOUS BANGLADESHIS

Many Bengalis distinguished themselves in political life before the creation of Bangladesh. A. K. Fazlul Huq (d.1962), the former premier of Bengal Province, moved the Lahore Resolution of 1940, calling for an independent Pakistan, and dominated Bengali politics for half a century. H. S. Suhrawardy (1895–1964), another former premier of Bengal, served for a time as premier of Pakistan and was a mentor to the next generation of Bengali leaders. Sheikh Mujibur Rahman (1920–75), a leader of the Awami League, led the successful fight for the independence of East Pakistan and was the first premier of Bangladesh (1972–75). Maj. Gen. Zia-ur Rahman (1936–81) was military ruler of the country from 1976 until his assassination.

⁴⁹DEPENDENCIES

Bangladesh has no territories or colonies.

⁵⁰BIBLIOGRAPHY

Ahmed, Moudud. *Democracy and the Challenge of Development: A Study of Politics and Military Interventions in Bangladesh.* New Delhi: Vikas Publishing House, 1995.

Anwar, M. N. *Bangladesh and Neighbours.* Dhaka: Payra Prakashani, 1996.

Bangladesh: From Stabilization to Growth. Washington, D.C.: World Bank, 1995.

Baxter, Craig. *Bangladesh: From a Nation to a State.* Boulder, Colo.: Westview Press, 1997.

Baxter, Craig. *Historical Dictionary of Bangladesh.* Lanham, Md.: Scarecrow Press, 1996.

Bertocci, Peter J. *The Politics of Community and Culture in Bangladesh: Selected Essays.* Dhaka: Centre for Social Studies, 1996.

Chakrabarti, Dilip K. *Ancient Bangladesh, a Study of the Archaeological Sources.* Delhi; New York: Oxford University Press, 1992.

The Economy of Bangladesh: Problems and Prospects. Westport, Conn.: Praeger, 1996.

Heitzman, James, and Robert L. Worden, eds. *Bangladesh, a Country Study.* 2nd ed. Washington, D.C.: Library of Congress, U.S. Government Printing Office, 1989.

Johnson, B. L. *Bangladesh.* 2nd ed., rev. Totowa, N.J.: Barnes & Noble, 1982.

Khan, Azizur Rahman. *The Strategy of Development in Bangladesh and Mahabub Hossain.* New York: St. Martin's Press, 1990.

Sisson, Richard. *War and Secession: Pakistan, India, and the Creation of Bangladesh.* Berkeley: University of California Press, 1990.

Zaheer, Hasan. *The Separation of East Pakistan: the Rise and Realization of Bengali Muslim Nationalism.* Karachi; New York: Oxford University Press, 1994.

Ziring, Lawrence. *Bangladesh: from Mujib to Ershad: an Interpretive Study.* Karachi; New York: Oxford University Press, 1992.

BHUTAN

Kingdom of Bhutan

Druk-Yul

CAPITAL: Thimphu (Tashi Chho Dzong).

FLAG: The flag is divided diagonally into an orange-yellow field above and a crimson field below. In the center is a wingless white Chinese dragon.

ANTHEM: *Gyelpo Tenjur,* beginning "In the Thunder Dragon Kingdom, adorned with sandalwood."

MONETARY UNIT: The ngultrum (N) is a paper currency of 100 chetrum. There are coins of 5, 10, 25, and 50 chetrum and 1 ngultrum, and notes of 1, 5, 10, and 100 ngultrum. The ngultrum is at par with the Indian rupee (R), which also circulates freely. N1 = $0.0233 ($1 = N42.9083) as of 31 March 2000.

WEIGHTS AND MEASURES: The metric system is the legal standard, but some traditional units are still in common use.

HOLIDAYS: King's Birthday, 11–13 November; National Day, 17 December. Movable Buddhist holidays and festivals are observed.

TIME: 5:30 PM = noon GMT.

¹LOCATION, SIZE, AND EXTENT

Bhutan, a landlocked country in the Himalaya mountain range, has an area of 47,000 sq km (18,147 sq mi), extending 306 km (190 mi) E–W and 145 km (90 mi) N–S. Comparatively, the area occupied by Bhutan is slightly more than half the size of the state of Indiana. It is bordered on the E, S, and W by India and on the N and NW by China, with a total boundary length of 1,075 km (668 mi). The capital city of Bhutan, Thimphu, is located in the west central part of the country.

²TOPOGRAPHY

Bhutan is a mountainous country of extremely high altitudes and irregular, often precipitous terrain, which may vary in elevation by several thousand feet within a short distance. Elevation generally increases from south to north. The mountains are a series of parallel north-south ranges. The loftiest peaks, found in the Himalayan chain that stretches along the northern border, include Kula Kangri (7,554 m/24,783 ft) and Chomo Lhari (7,314 m/23,997 ft). Great spurs extend south from the main chain along the eastern and western borders. In the rest of the country are mainly ranges of steep hills separated by narrow valleys. Bhutan is drained by many rivers flowing south between these ranges and for the most part ultimately emptying into the Brahmaputra River in India. The Amo River drains the Chumbi Valley. The Wong, with its tributaries, drains the valleys of Paro Dzong and Thimphu; the Mo drains Punakha Valley. Several rivers of eastern Nepal flow into the Manas.

³CLIMATE

Because of the irregular terrain, the climate varies greatly from place to place. In the outer foothills adjoining the Indian plains, rainfall ranges from about 150 cm to 300 cm (60–120 in) a year; the jungles and forests are hot and steaming in the rainy season, while the higher hills are cold, wet, and misty. Violent Himalayan thunderstorms gave rise to Bhutan's Dzongkha name, Druk-Yul, which translates as "Land of the Thunder Dragon." Rainfall is moderate in the central belt of flat valleys (1,100–3,000 m/3,500–10,000 ft). The uplands and high valleys (above 3,700 m/12,000

ft) are relatively dry. There is less rainfall in eastern Bhutan. In general, the mountainous areas are cold most of the year. Temperatures average 4°C (39°F) in January and 17°C (63°F) in July.

⁴FLORA AND FAUNA

Dense jungle growth is characteristic at altitudes below 1,500 m (5,000 ft). Above that height the mountain slopes are covered with forest, including beech, ash, birch, maple, cypress, and yew. At 2,400–2,700 m (8,000–9,000 ft) are forests of oak and rhododendron. Above this level, firs and pines grow to the timber line. Primulas, poppies (including the rare blue variety), magnolias, and orchids abound.

The relative abundance of wild animals is attributed to the Buddhist reluctance to take life. In the lower parts of southern Bhutan, mammals include the cheetah, goral, sambar, bear, and rhinoceros; in the higher regions are snow deer, musk deer, and barking deer. Game birds include pheasants, partridges, pigeons, and quail.

⁵ENVIRONMENT

In 1994, the most significant environmental problems in Bhutan were soil erosion and water pollution. The erosion of the soil occurs because 50% of the land in Bhutan is situated on mountainous slopes which are subject to landslides during the monsoon season. Other contributing factors are overcutting of timber, road construction, and the building of irrigation channels. The nation has 22.8 cubic miles of water supply, but 25% of all city dwellers and 46% of people in rural areas do not have pure water.

The Manas Game Sanctuary is located along the banks of the Manas River in southeastern Bhutan. Altogether, 20% of Bhutan's total land areas was protected as of 1994. In the same year, there were 15 species of endangered mammals including the tiger, snow leopard, Asian elephant, and wild yak, and 10 bird species were threatened with extinction, as well as 15 threatened species of plants and one endangered reptile.

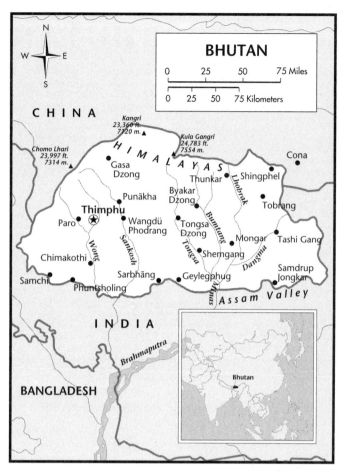

LOCATION: 26°42′ to 28°21′N; 88°45′ to 92°8′E. **BOUNDARY LENGTHS:** India, 607 km (377 mi); China, 412 km (256 mi).

⁶POPULATION

The population of Bhutan in 2000 was estimated at 1,996,221. An estimated 4.0% of the population is 65 years of age or older. The projected population for the year 2005 is 2,226,000, assuming a crude birthrate of 34 per 1,000 population and a death rate of 12, resulting in a natural rate of change of 2.1% for the period 2000–2005. The population rate of change between 1995 and 2000 was 2.8%.

Some 93% of the population was rural in 2000. The laboring population is not gathered into towns but lives in the countryside in the vicinity of fortresses called dzongs. A dzong, the official center of a region or district, often houses substantial numbers of Buddhist monks. Many place names incorporate the word dzong, which means "castle-monastery." It was estimated that only 7% of the population lived in urban areas in 2000. The capital city, Thimphu, had a 2000 population of 22,000, down from 27,000 in 1990. Phuntsholing had more than 10,000 people.

⁷MIGRATION

Bhutan opposes immigration and forbids the entry of new settlers from Nepal. Since 1959, when about 4,000 Tibetan refugees entered Bhutan, the border with Tibet has been closed to immigration. By 1980, most of the refugees had become citizens of Bhutan; the rest migrated to India. The border between Bhutan and India is open, and citizens of Bhutan are free to live and work in India. The net migration rate for 1999 was zero.

⁸ETHNIC GROUPS

Bhutanese are mainly of Tibetan stock, and are also known as Buotias; they account for approximately 50% of the population. The Ngalop (also called Bhobe) are people of Tibetan origin who live in northern and western Bhutan; the Sharchop inhabit the eastern regions and also have ethnic affinities with the people of China's Tibetan region. Aboriginal or indigenous tribal peoples live in villages scattered throughout Bhutan and account for approximately 15% of the population. The remaining peoples are Nepalese settlers (about 35% of the population), living mostly in the south. Some 85,000 were expelled to Nepal in 1992–93, and about 5,000–15,000 more moved to India.

⁹LANGUAGES

Four main languages are spoken in Bhutan. The official language is Dzongkha, a Tibetan dialect spoken mainly by Ngalop in the northern and western parts of the country. Bumthangkha, an aboriginal language, is spoken in central Bhutan, while Sharchopkha is spoken in eastern Bhutan. Both of these are used in primary schools in areas where their speakers predominate. The Nepalese largely retain their own language, Nepali.

¹⁰RELIGIONS

About 75% of the Bhutanese practice Buddhism, and about 25% practice Indian- and Nepalese-influenced Hinduism. While the law provides for religious freedom, the Drukpa sect of the Kagyupa School, a branch of Mahayana Buddhism, is the state religion, and the law prohibits religious conversions. The Drukpa (people of the dragon) subsect of the Kagyupa sect of Buddhism, introduced from Tibet in the 12th century, dominates the collective life of the Bhutanese through a large clerical body estimated at more than 6,000 lamas or monks, centered in 8 major monasteries (dzongs) and 200 smaller shrines (gompas) scattered throughout the land. This sect incorporates both the ideology of the classical Buddhist scriptures and the indigenous pre-Buddhist animistic beliefs called Bon.

¹¹TRANSPORTATION

Traditionally, Bhutan's communications have been mostly with Tibet, through several strategic mountain passes. Most travelers continue to journey on foot or mounted on hardy ponies bred to withstand great altitudes and steep slopes. Goods are transported by porters or on pack animals. Many of the rivers are still crossed by native cantilever bridges of excellent construction.

Prior to the 1961–66 development plan there were no surfaced roads in Bhutan. Since then, a network of roads and suspension bridges has been built by India. In 1998 there were about 3,285 km (2041 mi) of roads, including about 1,994 km (1,239 mi) of surfaced roads. Of the 186 suspension bridges projected in the 1981–87 economic plan, 102 were completed by 1985. There is bus service linking Paro Dzong and Tashi Gang Dzong with Indian border towns. In 1998 there were 2 airports, only 1 of which had a paved runway. The national air carrier, Druk Airlines, began operations in 1983 with regular flights between Calcutta and Paro Dzong, the site of Bhutan's main airfield. In 1997, 36,000 passengers were carried on scheduled domestic and international flights.

¹²HISTORY

Little is known of the history of Bhutan before the 17th century. Buddhism was originally introduced from India in the 8th century, although the Buddhism of today's Bhutan is very much Tibetan in character. The forebears of the Bhotes (or Bhotias) came from Tibet, probably in the 9th century, when Tibetans invaded the area and met little resistance from the indigenous Tephu tribe. In the middle of the fifteenth century, Shabdung Ngawang Nangyal, a Tibetan lama exercising temporal as well as spiritual power, united the country and built most of the fortified villages (dzongs). His successors in power established a dual system, separating the temporal ruler (Desi or deb raja) and the spiritual ruler (Je Khempo or dharma raja).

The first recorded contact with the West occurred in 1772, when the British East India Company repelled a Bhutanese invasion of the princely state of Cooch Behar in India; they concluded a peace treaty two years later. During the 18th century and most of the 19th, British efforts to open trade with Bhutan proved futile, with the Bhutanese frequently attacking the relatively level areas of Assam and Bengal along their southern border. In 1865, the British finally defeated the Bhutanese, and Bhutan formally accepted a British subsidy of r50,000 a year, which was dependent upon their keeping the peace.

With British approval, Ugyen Dorji Wangchuk became the first hereditary king in 1907, replacing the temporal ruler. In 1910, the Punakha Treaty was concluded between the British Indian Government and Bhutan, under which British India agreed explicitly not to interfere in Bhutanese internal affairs, while Bhutan accepted British "guidance" in handling external matters—a role independent India assumed after 1947. A formal Indo-Bhutanese accord concluded in 1949 reaffirmed and amplified the earlier Punakha Treaty. Besides increasing Bhutan's annual subsidy to r500,000 and returning to Bhutan 83 square kilometers (32 square miles) of territory around Dewangiri (wrested by the British in 1865), it made India responsible for Bhutan's defense and strategic communications, committing India to avoid interfering in Bhutan's affairs and affirming Bhutan's agreement to be "guided by the advice of" India in foreign affairs.

In 1959, China published maps of the Himalayan frontier with South Asia that showed as Chinese part of the territory claimed by Bhutan; Chinese representatives also asserted that Bhutan belonged to a greater Tibet. In response, Indian prime minister Jawaharlal Nehru warned that an attack on Bhutan would be deemed an act of war against India. Fighting between India and China in neighboring border regions in the fall of 1962 did not violate Bhutan's borders, although survivors from Indian army units decimated east of Bhutan straggled back to India through Bhutan.

In April 1964, the long-time prime minister, Jigme Dorji, was assassinated, revealing fissures among the ruling elite. The plotters who were caught were executed, including the deputy commander of the army; others fled to Nepal. In the 1960s, Bhutan's advance toward modernization and the end of its insularity were accelerated by economic plans prepared and underwritten by India.

Relations with Nepal have grown difficult in recent years, the result of violence and cross-border attacks in southern Bhutan from which thousands of ethnic Nepalese—both illegal immigrants and Bhutanese citizens—have migrated (or been forced to flee) in recent years. The king has used a mixture of firmness and conciliation in dealing with increasing violence by ethnic Nepalese who operate from Indian soil but with the tacit support of the Nepalese authorities, urging Bhutanese of Nepalese origin to remain in Bhutan. Meanwhile, his government has sought the cooperation of the governments of Nepal and India in dealing with this activity. In 1993, Bhutan and Nepal established a Joint Ministerial Committee to address the issue of ethnic Nepalese refugees.

Nepalese activism, spearheaded by the Bhutan People's Party based in Nepal, continued through the early 1990s. It resulted in violence from both sides, and brought charges of violations of human rights against Bhutan's security forces. In 1996, "peace marches" of refugees from Nepal into Bhutan were met by force, and the marchers deported by the Bhutanese police. The following year, the National Assembly adopted a resolution (later discarded) that prohibited family members of ethnic Nepalese

refugees from holding jobs in the government or armed forces. The government also began resettling Buddhist Bhutanese from other regions of the country on land vacated by the refugees. In 1998, Foreign Minister Jigme Thinley took office with a mandate to settle the refugee issue. Although Bhutan and Nepal agree in principal that the refugees be divided into four categories (1) bonafide Bhutanese; (2) Bhutanese emigres; (3) non-Bhutanese; and (4) Bhutanese who have committed crimes in Bhutan, the question of what to do with the more than 100,000 refugees living in camps in Nepal remains unresolved. Talks between Bhutan and Nepal are ongoing, the meetings being held in March 2000. In addition to the refugee problem, Bhutan faces unrest from "anti-nationals" in the southeastern region of the kingdom.

Reforms introduced by King Jigme Singye Wangchuck in June 1998 mark a milestone in Bhutan's political and constitutional history. Continuing his efforts toward modernization, the king issued a royal edict relinquishing some of the monarch's traditional prerogatives and giving a greater role in Bhutan's administration to elected government officials.

13 GOVERNMENT

Bhutan is a constitutional monarchy, ruled by a hereditary king, the "Druk Gyalpo," who governs with the aid of a Royal Cabinet and a National Assembly (the Tsongdu). In the past, the king appointed members to a Royal Advisory Council and to a Council of Ministers. Following the political reforms of 1998, however, these two councils were combined to form the cabinet. This body consists of six ministers elected by the National Assembly, six advisors also elected by the National Assembly, a member nominated by the king, and two representatives of the clergy.

The unicameral National Assembly (established in 1953), known as the Tsongdu, consists of 150 members. Of these, 35 are appointed by the king to represent government and other secular interests; 105 are elected to three-year terms by groups of village headmen, who are, in turn, elected by a one-family, one-vote system; and the remaining 10 are chosen by the lamas acting in concert. The Tsongdu meets twice a year at Thimphu, the capital (previously known as Punakha). Candidates file their own nominations. The assembly is charged with addressing the king on matters of national importance. It also enacts laws and approves senior government appointments. A simple majority is needed to pass a measure and is conducted by secret ballot. While the king may not veto legislation, he may return bills for further consideration; the king generally has enough influence to persuade the assembly to approve legislation he considers important or to withdraw proposals which he opposes. Since 1969, it has become a more active, independent influence on government policy through its power to overrule bills proposed by the king or his advisors.

During the 1960s, King Jigme Dorji Wangchuk (r.1952–72) was a prime mover behind political and administrative changes that took the country in the direction of constitutional monarchy. When Crown Prince Jigme Singye Wangchuk assumed the throne upon his father's death in July 1972 and was crowned in June 1974, he continued his father's policy of sharing authority with the Council of Ministers and the National Assembly. In 1998, the king announced ambitious political changes that moved Bhutan further down the road towards a true constitutional monarchy. He relinquished his role as Head of Government and assigned full executive powers to a cabinet consisting of ministers and advisors to be elected by the National Assembly (in reality, the National Assembly chooses from a list of nominees proposed by the king, who also retains authority relating to security issues). The Council of Ministers, a subgroup of the cabinet, elects one of its members on a rotational basis to serve a one-year term as chairman. It is this official who is the Head of Government. As part of his reforms, King Jigme Singye Wangchuk also introduced legislation by which any monarch would have to abdicate in favor of his hereditary successor if the National Assembly supported a vote of no-confidence against him by a two-thirds majority.

The government discourages political parties and none operate legally. Freedom of speech, the press, assembly, association and workers' rights are restricted by the government, and judicial processes are based on tradition rather than written criminal or civil procedure codes.

14POLITICAL PARTIES

Political parties are illegal in Bhutan. An opposition group known as the Bhutan State Congress (BSC) composed mainly of ethnic Nepalese has long maintained its headquarters in nearby India; other such groups, all very small and headquartered in either India or in Nepal, include the People's Forum for Democratic Rights and the Students' Union of Bhutan. A new, militant opposition group, operating under the banner of the Bhutan People's Party (BPP) and affiliated with the Bhutan National Democratic Party (BNDP) in Nepal, was founded in 1990 in Siliguri, India. It claims to represent the interests of thousands of ethnic Nepalese—both illegal immigrants and Bhutanese citizens—who have migrated (or been forced to flee) from farming areas of southern Bhutan in recent years. Allegedly supported by the Communist Parties of India (CPI) and Nepal (CPN), the BPP was responsible for demonstrations in September 1990 in Bhutan; it has charged the Bhutan government with human rights violations and "ethnic cleansing" in the area.

BPP tactics in 1991 and 1992 included hit-and-run terrorist raids into Bhutan, burning schools, census and land records, and health facilities and attacking ethnic Bhutanese (as well as loyal Nepalese) in national dress; BPP activists also organized camps for the tens of thousands of "refugees" said to be in southern Nepal. In 1992, Bhutan government policy toward the terrorist attacks stiffened, with arrests and long prison sentences meted out to captured BPP activists. While seeking the cooperation of the governments of India and Nepal to bring this problem under control in 1993, the Bhutan government also sought the help of state authorities in the Indian states of Assam and West Bengal in staunching cross-border violence by Bodo rebels and Assamese separatist groups.

15LOCAL GOVERNMENT

The country is divided into four regions—East, Central, West, and South—each administered by a governor appointed by the king. As of 1999 there were 18 districts (dzongkhas) under the supervision of district commissioners (dzongdas), who are appointed by the Royal Civil Service Commission and are responsible for law and order. Districts are further subdivided into blocks (gewog), of which there are 192 in the country. As part of the king's efforts to encourage decentralization in decision-making, the government began a program to establish Block Development Committees in the 192 Blocks in the country.

16JUDICIAL SYSTEM

The legal system is based on English common law and Indian law. Local headmen and magistrates (thrimpon) hear cases in the first instance. Appeals may be made to an eight-member High Court, established in 1968. From the High Court, a final appeal may be made to the King. Judges are appointed for life by the King. There is no written constitution. Criminal matters and most civil matters are resolved by application of the 17th century legal code as revised in 1965. Questions of family law are governed by traditional Buddhist or Hindu law. Minor offenses are adjudicated by village headmen. Criminal defendants have no right to court appointment of an attorney and no right to a jury trial. Under the

1979 Police Act, Police need a warrant to arrest a person and must bring the detainees before a court within 24 hours of arrest.

In keeping with the policies of modernization being pursued in Bhutan, the government formed a special committee in 1998 to review the country's laws and propose changes in the legal system. One of these changes saw the creation, in April 2000, of a Department of Legal Affairs to investigate and prosecute criminal and civil cases against civil servants. This may well turn out to be the forerunner of a fully-fledged Attorney-General's Office or a Department of Justice.

17ARMED FORCES

The army consists of about 4,000 lightly armed soldiers, trained by Indian officers, in the army and palace guard. There is also a royal police force and militia. India is responsible for Bhutan's defense.

18INTERNATIONAL COOPERATION

Bhutan joined the Colombo Plan organization in 1962 and became a UN member on 21 September 1971; it participates in ESCAP, FAO, IBRD, IDA, IFAD, IMF, UNESCO, UNIDO, UPU, and WHO. Bhutan also belongs to the Asian Development Bank and G-77 and is a signatory to the Law of the Sea. In addition, Bhutan is a member of the nonaligned movement and was a founding member of the South Asian Association for Regional Cooperation (SAARC). In 1978, its office in New Delhi was accorded the status of an embassy. Bhutan maintains full diplomatic relations with all of the South Asia countries, as well as several countries in the Middle East and Europe.

19ECONOMY

Isolated Bhutan has one of the smallest, and poorest, economies in the world. Much of the population functions outside the cash economy; 90% of the labor force lives by subsistence farming or herding. Agriculture and forestry together make up 40% of the country's GDP. Although the government relaxed its emphasis on maintaining food self-sufficiency during the 1980s, the country supplies most of its food needs through the production of grains, fruits, some meat, and yak butter. Services, with tourist-related business comprising a major share, account for a further 24% of GDP. By the mid-1970s, tourism had surpassed the sale of postage stamps as the chief source of Bhutan's limited foreign exchange revenue.

A series of five-year plans, initiated in 1961 and financed primarily by India, have begun to improve transportation, modernize agriculture, and develop hydroelectric power. Realization of several hydroelectric and industrial projects during the 1980s helped to increase industry's share of the GDP, and inflated overall GDP growth rates to 7.3% annually during 1985–90. A slowdown in government project investment in the early 1990s caused GDP growth stabilized at an average of around 3%, although an upturn in economic activity in 1995 brought the rate back up to 6%, and 7.3% in 1998. The overall GDP growth rate for 1988 to 1998 averaged an annual 6.1%. Bhutan's extensive forests, mineral resources, and swift-running rivers offer great potential for future development, although preservation of the country's environment continues to rank high among the government's priorities. Concern over the environment has also led the government to limit the number of tourists to about 4,000 per year and thereby constrain a key sector of the economy.

20INCOME

The US Central Intelligence Agency (CIA) reports that in 1998 Bhutan's gross domestic product (GDP) was estimated at $19 billion. The per capita GDP was estimated at $1,000. The annual growth rate of GDP was estimated at 6.5%. The average inflation rate in 1998 was 9.7%. The CIA defines GDP as the value of all final goods and services produced within a nation in a given year and computed on the basis of purchasing power parity (PPP) rather than value as measured on the basis of the rate of exchange. It was estimated that agriculture accounted for 38% of GDP, industry 38%, and services 24%.

[21]LABOR

About 95% of the economically active population consists of farmers and herdsmen. In 1996, there were 30 industrial plants which employed more than 50 people. There is a severe shortage of skilled labor. The salaried labor market is predominantly in the government service. Most of the industrial sector consists of home-based handicrafts and privately-owned small or medium-scale factories producing consumer goods.

As of 1999, Bhutan had a government set minimum wage which is approximately $1.50 per day. The government also mandates overtime pay for work in excess of 8 hours per day. Laborers are also entitled to 1 day's paid leave for every six work days, if the worker is retained on at least a monthly basis. There are no safety and health standards and no minimum work age. Trade unions are illegal, and workers do not have the right to strike.

[22]AGRICULTURE

Only about 3.4% of the land area, comprising 160,000 hectares (395,000 acres), was used for seasonal and permanent crop production in 1997. In 1998, agriculture contributed 40% to GDP, and engaged 94% of the economically active population. Nonetheless, Bhutan's near self-sufficiency in food permitted quantities of some crops to be exported to India, in exchange for cereals. Since there is little level space available for cultivation, fields are generally terraced. Stone aqueducts carry irrigation water. The low-lying areas raise a surplus of rice; in 1998, output of paddy rice was estimated at 50,000 tons. Other crops include wheat, maize, millet, buckwheat, barley, potatoes, sugarcane, cardamom, walnuts, and oranges. Part of the crop yield is used in making beer and chong, a potent liquor distilled from rice, barley, and millet. Paper is made from the daphne plant, which grows wild. Walnuts, citrus fruits, apples, and apricots are grown in government orchards.

Agricultural holdings are restricted to 12 hectares (30 acres) per family; almost all farm families own their own land. Since the mid-1960s, the government has established demonstration farms, distributed fruit plants, and implemented irrigation schemes. High-yielding varieties of rice, wheat, and corn seeds have been introduced. Under the 1987–92 economic plan, farming cooperatives were introduced and apiculture was promoted.

[23]ANIMAL HUSBANDRY

Yaks, cattle, and some sheep graze in the lowland forests and, during the summer, in the uplands and high valleys. In 1998 there were an estimated 435,000 head of cattle, 75,000 hogs, 59,000 sheep, and 42,000 goats. Draft animals that year included 30,000 horses, 18,000 donkeys, and 10,000 mules. Meat production in 1998 was estimated at 8,000 tons, 75% of it beef. Wool has been in short supply since its importation from Tibet was stopped by the government in 1960; sheep breeding is therefore encouraged. In 1995, 50 tons of greasy and 25 tons of scoured wool were produced.

[24]FISHING

The government has established a hatchery and started a program of stocking Bhutan's rivers and lakes with brown trout. Freshwater fish are found in most waterways. The total catch was 330 tons in 1997.

[25]FORESTRY

About 58.6% of Bhutan's land area was covered with forests in 1995. Although lack of transportation facilities has hampered forest development, timber has become a major export. Roundwood production in 1997 totaled 1,584,000 cu m, about 97% of which was used for fuel.

[26]MINING

For centuries, silver and iron have been mined in Bhutan for handicrafts. Deposits of beryl, copper, graphite, gypsum, lead, limestone, marble, mica, pyrite, quartzite, slate, talc, tin, tungsten, and zinc have also been found. In 1997 only coal and industrial minerals were produced. Dolomite has constituted an important export to India since 1960. A graphite-processing plant is established at Paro Dzong. Mineral production in 1997 included (in thousands of tons): limestone, 270,000; dolomite, 250,000; cement, 160,000; gypsum, 50,000; quartzite, 50,000; ferrosilicon, 13,000; and talc, 3,000. Marble and slate are quarried for use as a dimensional stone; marble production in 1995 totaled 4,000 square meters.

[27]ENERGY AND POWER

Over 95% of Bhutan's energy requirement is derived from firewood. Of commercial energy sources, petroleum accounts for 60% and coal for 30%, with electricity contributing only 10%. Electric power was introduced in Bhutan in 1962; by the mid-1980s, six hydroelectric and six diesel power stations were in operation. The 336-MW Chukha hydroelectric project, in south-western Bhutan, was completed in early 1987 and is connected to the Indian power grid; the project was funded by India, which is to receive all the electrical output not used by Bhutan. In 1998, Bhutan's net installed capacity was 371,000 kW; production totaled 1,788 million kwh, of which 99% was hydroelectric. Only about 13% of the electricity generated in 1994 was domestically consumed; the rest was exported to India. Bhutan suffers frequent power outages and shortages.

[28]INDUSTRY

Craft manufacture is the predominant industrial occupation, and homespun textiles—woven and embroidered cottons, wools, and silks—are the most important products. Other Bhutanese handicrafts include daphne paper; swords; wooden bowls; leather objects; copper, iron, brass, bronze, and silver work; wood carvings; and split-cane basketry. Completion of the 336-MW Chukha hydroelectric power plant has allowed the development of several modern industries as well. The country's first cement plant was completed by India in Penden, a border town, in 1982; the bulk of its output is exported to India. A second plant in Nanglam was established by the late 1980s, along with several manufacturing plants producing carbide, particle board and other products destined for the Indian market. A new cement plant was built at Nanglam in 1995 by a foreign investor from India. Industrial estates have been set up at Phuntsholing and Geylegphug, as well as a sawmill with a furniture-making unit at Thimphu. A large number of small, privately owned sawmills operate throughout the country. In April 1995, Bhutan Ferro Alloys Ltd. began commercial operations at a new ferrosilicon plant at Pasakha, near Phuntsholing in southeastern Bhutan. In 1988, the Bhutan Development Finance Corporation was established to promote small- and medium-scale industries in various sectors of the economy. Manufacturing, as a percentage of GDP, has risen from 3.2% in 1980 to 8.2% in 1990 to 12% in 1998. It is likely that liberalized trade policies recently adopted by the government will continue to stimulate growth among small as well as larger scale producers in the export-oriented sector.

29SCIENCE AND TECHNOLOGY

Royal Bhutan Polytechnic College, founded in 1974 in Deothang, offers courses in civil, mechanical and electrical engineering. The Royal Technical Institute in Phuntsholing offers courses in electronics, mechanics, and motor mechanics. Sherubtse Degree College, founded in 1983 in Tashigang, offers science courses.

30DOMESTIC TRADE

Retail sales are carried out mainly in small, local bazaars. Bartering is common at the local level, with grains, butter, and cloth being the principal commodities of exchange, although Indian and Bhutanese currencies are increasingly being employed. Indian traders sell imported articles and buy a number of handicraft items for export to India.

31FOREIGN TRADE

After the 1960 government ban on trade with Tibet, Bhutan's external sector became almost exclusively oriented towards trade with India. Over the last several years, however, exports to other countries have grown rapidly; third country trade now accounts for about 20% of the Bhutan's total. Major factors behind trade diversification include the recent depreciation of the Indian rupee to which the Bhutanese currency is closely linked as well as a 30% subsidy on third country exports introduced by the government in 1988 but is now being phased out.

Bhutan's principal exports include vegetables, dolomite, gypsum, timber, cement, coal, oranges, cardamom, some preserved food, handicraft items, yak tails for fly whisks, and yak hair. India accounts for over 94% of foreign trade, and 90% of the power generated by the Chukha hydroelectric plant is purchased by India. The chief imports from India are petroleum products (mainly kerosene), motor vehicles, cereals, and cotton textiles. In 1997, total exports were estimated at $99 million and imports at $131 million.

32BALANCE OF PAYMENTS

The principal sources of foreign exchange are tourism, sales of electricity, and Bhutanese stamps. Exports of apples and oranges give Bhutan a trade surplus in agricultural produce. Trade deficits are largely made up through grants and loans from the Indian government. Economic growth in 1999 helped maintain Bhutan's foreign reserves in a comfortable position.

The US Central Intelligence Agency reports that in 1997 the purchasing power parity of Bhutan's exports was $99 million while imports totaled $131 million resulting in a trade balance of -$32 million.

33BANKING AND SECURITIES

Bhutan's central bank is the Royal Monetary Authority, established in 1982 to manage currency and foreign exchange. Its agent, the Bank of Bhutan, founded in 1968, has its main office at Phuntsholing and 25 branches (as of 1993) throughout the country. Bank reserves in 1992 were $192.7 million. Securities are not traded.

34INSURANCE

The Royal Insurance Corporation of Bhutan, half state-owned, covers all classes of insurance. The use of insurance, however, is limited.

35PUBLIC FINANCE

The largest category of annual current expenditure is public works, which presumably includes the maintenance of monasteries. Most of the annual budget deficit is covered by grants from India and from the UN and other international agencies. Increased foreign aid and domestic revenues allowed the government to increase public expenditures.

The US Central Intelligence Agency (CIA) estimates that in 1998 Bhutan's central government took in revenues of approximately $146.5 million and had expenditures of $146.8 million including capital expenditures of $81.2 million. Overall, the government registered a deficit of approximately $.3 million. External debt totaled $120 million.

The following table shows an itemized breakdown of government revenues and expenditures. The percentages were calculated from data reported by the International Monetary Fund. The dollar amounts (millions) are based on the CIA estimates provided above.

REVENUE AND GRANTS	100%	146.5
Tax revenue	21.2%	31
Non-tax revenue	25.4%	37
Capital revenue	1.0%	2
Grants	52.3%	77
EXPENDITURES	100%	146.8
General public services	28.7%	42
Public order and safety	5.2%	8
Education	10.9%	16
Health	11.1%	16
Housing and community amenities	2.6%	4
Recreation, cultural, and religious affairs	1.6%	2
Economic affairs and services	38.1%	56
Other expenditures	0.0%	0
Interest payments	1.9%	3

36TAXATION

The principal sources of domestic funds are excise taxes, taxes on real estate income, and taxes on profits from public companies.

37CUSTOMS AND DUTIES

Under the Indo-Bhutanese Treaty of 1949, goods pass from one country to another without payment of customs duties.

38FOREIGN INVESTMENT

Foreign investment comes primarily from India.

39ECONOMIC DEVELOPMENT

Under Bhutan's first four development plans, considerable improvements were made in agriculture and irrigation, road transportation, forestry, and electric power generation. The plans were underwritten by India, which contributed more than $197 million over the 20-year period.

Under the fifth economic plan (1981–87), total investments were almost 31% financed by India and 30% provided by the UN and other foreign sources. This plan aimed to increase the GNP by 6–8% annually, with priority given to agriculture and animal husbandry (14% of the outlays) and public works (13%).

The sixth plan (1987–92) included among its goals encouragement of the private sector, revision of the tax system, greater decentralization to the district (dzongkha) level, and improvement of education and personnel training. The GDP was expected to grow by 6.9% annually, and priority was given to industry, trade, and commerce (20% of the outlays) and power (13%).

For 1992–97, the seventh plan reaffirmed basic goals of economic self-sufficiency, preserving national identity, and human resource development. In addition, the plan strengthened the government's emphasis on development of the private sector as well as its commitment to environmental preservation. Privatization of public sector manufacturing firms and other measures were planned to expand the role of private manufacturing and services firms, especially within export-oriented manufacturing and mining industries as well as the tourist sector. Specific environmental objectives included the promotion of sustainable agriculture through soil erosion control as well as the setting aside of 20% of the country's land area as nature reserves and other areas protected from commercial timber extraction. Ambitious targets were set for meeting all recurrent expenditures from domestic revenues by the end of the plan period. Successful achievement of this goal would minimize Bhutan's over-dependence on Indian financing for balancing its current fiscal debt. The expenditures required to meet other targets in the plan, however, made it difficult for progress to be achieved.

The eighth plan (1997 to 2002) supported expansion of the hydroelectric sector and educational development while protecting the natural environment.

40 SOCIAL DEVELOPMENT

There is no national social welfare system, although the government implemented a modest maternal and child welfare program in the early 1980s, including family planning. The sick, indigent, and aged are cared for within the traditional family structure.

Bhutan's culture does not isolate or disenfranchise women. Dowry is not practiced, and land is divided equally between sons and daughters. Girls receive nearly equal educational opportunities, and, while accorded a lower status than boys, they are cherished because they are the ones who care for parents in old age. Polygyny is legal, but only with the consent of the first wife. The National Women's Association of Bhutan was created by the National Assembly in 1981 to help improve the socioeconomic status of women. It is now an independent organization. A 1993 law clarified the definition of sexual assault and imposed harsher penalties on rapists, including sentences as long as 17 years and, in certain cases, life imprisonment.

A pattern of discrimination against the minority Hindus of Nepalese origin exists. Thousands of Nepalese were deported from Bhutan in the late 1980s, and many others fled to refugee camps in Nepal. The government launched an effort to promote the cultural assimilation of the remaining Nepalese. Nepali was no longer taught in schools, and national dress was required for official occasions. While this policy has lead to the cultural repression of Hindus, it has also contributed to a growing number of Nepalese obtaining employment in the public sector and in government. Repatriation of the exiled Nepalese remains an unresolved issue, one that the government formed in 1999 has promised to address.

Human rights are restricted by the government. Abuses include violence against Nepalese refugees and arbitrary arrest and detention.

41 HEALTH

Bhutan suffers from a shortage of medical personnel with only 65% of the population having access to any form of medical care. In 1990, there were 141 doctors (113,110 people per physician), 5 pharmacists, 9 dentists, 233 nurses, and 70 midwives.

The average life expectancy in 1999 was only 52.8 years (52.3 years for females and 53.2 years for males), and the overall death rate was 14.3 per 1,000 people. The infant mortality rate was 109 per 1,000 live births. In 1994, 38% of children under 5 were underweight. In 1993, it was estimated that 2% of married women (15–49 years) were using contraception. The fertility rate was reported as 5.2 in 1999.

Immunization rates between 1990 and 1992 for children up to one year old were: tuberculosis, 81%; diphtheria, pertussis, and tetanus, 79%; polio, 77%; and measles, 82%. Although smallpox has been wiped out, malaria, tuberculosis, and venereal disease remain widespread. Bhutanese refugees in the eastern Nepal region have high rates of measles, cholera, tuberculosis, malaria, diarrhea, beriberi, and scurvy. There were 25 new cases of cholera in this country in 1994.

42 HOUSING

Traditional houses are built of stone set in clay mixed with small stones and made into blocks or layers. Roofs are gently inclined and formed of pine shingles kept in place by heavy stones. As of 1990, 60% of urban and 30% of rural dwellers had access to a public water supply, while 80% of urban and 7% of rural dwellers had access to sanitation services.

43 EDUCATION

A modern educational system was introduced in Bhutan in the 1960s. Prior to that, education was provided only by monasteries. A growing number of children are attending school, but over 50% still do not attend. Bhutan's estimated rate of adult illiteracy for the year 2000 stood at 52.7% (males, 38.9%; females, 66.4%). The official language is Dzongkha (written in the Tibetan script). However, English is widely used. Education is not compulsory. The educational system consists of seven years of primary schooling followed by four years of secondary school. In 1994, primary schools enrolled 60,089 pupils. In the same year, secondary schools enrolled 7,299 students.

In 1991, Bhutan had 209 schools altogether, including 22 monastic schools; schools for Tibetan refugees, and 6 technical schools. There was at the highest level one junior college, two teacher training colleges, and one degree college which was affiliated to the university at Delhi in India. Many teachers from India are employed in Bhutan.

44 LIBRARIES AND MUSEUMS

The largest library in Bhutan is located in Konglung at Sherbutse College and holds 22,000 volumes. The National Institute of Education in Samtse, founded in 1968, holds 12,000 volumes, and the Royal Institute of Management in Thimphu holds 4,000 volumes.

The National Museum of Bhutan opened to the public in 1968 at Paro Dzong, in a seven-story 17th-century fortress, featuring religious art objects reflective of Bhutan's unique Northern Buddhist culture, as well as historical objects. Some monasteries have valuable collections of Buddhist manuscripts and art objects.

45 MEDIA

International postal service was inaugurated in 1963; there are direct postal, telex, and microwave links to India. In 1995, Bhutan had over 4,620 telephones. Telephone service is said to be very poor. There were 39 radio stations in 1988 for internal government communications, as well as shortwave programming by the Bhutan Broadcasting Service. As of 1998, there was 1 FM radio station. Bhutan did not have its own television station but received broadcasts from India and Bangladesh for government use. Since 1989, all television and satellite receiving dishes have been ordered dismounted, in accordance with a ban on private television reception. In 1997, the country had an estimated 11 radios per 1,000 population. A weekly government-subsidized newspaper, *Kuensel*, publishes simultaneous editions in Dzongkha, English, and Nepali, with a total circulation of about 10,500 as of 1999. Indian and other foreign publications are also available.

There are no legal provisions for the right of free expression in Bhutan; the government is said to restrict criticism of the King and government policies of the National Assembly.

46 ORGANIZATIONS

There are no commercial, scholarly, or professional organizations in the Western sense.

[47]TOURISM, TRAVEL, AND RECREATION

In 1974, Bhutan opened its door to tourists, but strict entry regulations, the remoteness of the country, and relatively limited transportation facilities have restricted the number of visitors. Income from tourism totaled approximately $6 million in 1997, and there were approximately 5,000 foreign visitors. Accounting for 22% of total arrivals, Japan represents the most important generating market to Bhutan. The US represented 17% of tourist arrivals that year. The beautiful Thimphu, Paro, and Punakha valleys, with their many monasteries, are accessible to tourists. Archery is the national sport.

In 1999, the UN estimated the cost of staying in Thimphu at $59. In rural areas, expenditures were estimated at $48 per day.

[48]FAMOUS BHUTANESE

Jigme Dorji Wangchuk (1928–72) instituted numerous social reforms during his reign as king of Bhutan. He was succeeded by his son Jigme Singye Wangchuk (b.1955).

[49]DEPENDENCIES

Bhutan has no territories or colonies.

[50]BIBLIOGRAPHY

Aris, Michael. *The Raven Crown: The Origins of Buddhist Monarchy in Bhutan*. London: Serindia, 1994.

Basu, Gautam Kumar. *Bhutan: The Political Economy of Development*. New Delhi: South Asian Publishers, 1996.

Bhutan: Aspects of Culture and Development. Gartmore, Scotland: Kiscadale, 1994.

Bhutan: Perspectives on Conflict and Dissent. Gartmore, Scotland: Kiscadale, 1994.

Das, B. S. (Brajbir Saran). *Mission to Bhutan: A Nation in Transition*. New Delhi: Vikas Pub. House, 1995.

Dhakal, D. N. S. *Bhutan: A Movement in Exile*. Jaipur: Nirala Publications, 1994.

Dogra, R. C. *Bhutan*. Oxford, England; Santa Barbara, Calif.: Clio Press, 1990.

Gibbons, Robert, and Bob Ashford. *Himalayan Kingdoms: Nepal, Sikkim, and Bhutan*. New York: Hippocrene, 1983.

Johnson, Gordon. *Cultural Atlas of India: India, Pakistan, Nepal, Bhutan, Bangladesh & Sri Lanka*. New York: Facts on File, 1996.

Kohli, Manorama, *From Dependency to Enterdependence: A Study of Indo-Bhutan Relations*. New Delhi: Vikas Pub. House, 1993.

Nepal and Bhutan: Country Studies Savada, 3rd ed. Washington, D.C.: Government Printing Office, 1993.

Pommaret-Imaeda, Françoise, and Yoshiro Imaeda. *Bhutan: A Kingdom in the Eastern Himalayas*. Translated by Ian Nobel. Boston: Shambhala, 1985.

Rose, Leo E. *The Politics of Bhutan*. Ithaca, N.Y.: Cornell University Press, 1977.

Singh, Amar Kaur Jasbir. *Himalayan Triangle: a Historical Survey of British India's Relations with Tibet, Sikkim and Bhutan 1765–1950*. London: British Library, 1988.

BRUNEI DARUSSALAM

Nation of Brunei, Abode of Peace

Negara Brunei Darussalam

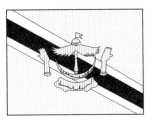

CAPITAL: Bandar Seri Begawan.

FLAG: On a yellow field extend two diagonal stripes of white and black, with the state emblem centered in red.

ANTHEM: National Anthem, beginning *Ya Allah lanjutkan usia* ("God bless His Highness with a long life").

MONETARY UNIT: The Brunei dollar (B$, or ringgit) of 100 cents is valued at par with, and is interchangeable with, the Singapore dollar. There are coins of 1, 5, 10, 20, and 50 cents, and notes of 1, 5, 10, 50, 100, 500, 1,000, and 10,000 Brunei dollars. B$1 = US$0.5848; (US$1 = B$1.710) as of 31 March 2000.

WEIGHTS AND MEASURES: Imperial weights and measures are in common use, as are certain local units, but a change to the metric system is slowly proceeding.

HOLIDAYS: New Year's Day, 1 January; National Day, 23 February; Anniversary of the Royal Brunei Armed Forces, 31 May; Sultan's Birthday, 15 July; Christmas Day, 25 December. Movable holidays include the Chinese New Year and various Muslim holy days.

TIME: 8 PM = noon GMT.

¹LOCATION, SIZE, AND EXTENT

Brunei occupies 5,770 sq km (2,228 sq mi) on the northwestern coast of the island of Borneo. Comparatively, the area occupied by Brunei is slightly larger than the state of Delaware. It comprises two small enclaves separated by the Limbang River Valley, a salient of the Malaysian State of Sarawak, which surrounds Brunei on the E, S, and W. Brunei's total boundary length is 542 km (337 mi).

Brunei's capital city, Bandar Seri Begawan, is located in the northern part of the country.

²TOPOGRAPHY

Brunei's western enclave contains most of the country's population, as well as the capital; the thinly populated eastern zone is mainly jungle. The land generally consists of primary and secondary tropical rain forest, with a narrow coastal strip on the western enclave. The eastern enclave is more hilly, rising to 1,850 m (6,070 ft) in the peak of Mt. Pagon in the extreme south.

³CLIMATE

The country has a tropical climate, with uniform temperatures ranging from 23° to 32°C (73–89°F). Humidity is high—about 80% all year round—and annual rainfall varies from about 275 cm (110 in) along the coast to more than 500 cm (200 in) in the interior. Rainfall is heaviest during the northeast monsoon season (landas), especially in November and December.

⁴FLORA AND FAUNA

The country is largely covered by mangrove and peat swamp, heath, montane vegetation, and dipterocarpaceous forest. The rain forest and swampland are inhabited by a plethora of small mammals, tropical birds, reptiles, and amphibians. Mammals include both wild and domesticated buffalo, honey bear, deer, and monkeys. Insects are abundant and sometimes harmful, in particular the malarial mosquito and biting midge.

⁵ENVIRONMENT

The nation has an extensive oil industry with reserves that are estimated to last 20 years. The forests, which account for 79% of Brunei's land area, are strictly protected by the government. Endangered species in 1987 included the estuarine crocodile. Brunei is a party to international agreements on ozone layer protection, endangered species, whaling, and ship pollution and has signed but not ratified the Law of the Sea.

⁶POPULATION

The population of Brunei Darussalam in 2000 was estimated at 330,689. An estimated 5.4% of the population is 65 years of age or older. The projected population for the year 2005 is 370,000, assuming a crude birthrate of 24 per 1,000 population and a death rate of 6, resulting in a natural rate of change of 1.8% for the period 2000–2005.

It was estimated that 72% of the population lived in urban areas in 2000. The capital city, Bandar Seri Begawan (formerly Brunei Town), had a 2000 population of 75,000. Other important towns are Seria, Kuala Belait, and Tutong. Brunei's next census is scheduled to take place in 2001.

⁷MIGRATION

There is little emigration except among the Chinese minority. The government is battling considerable illegal immigration, especially from Indonesia and Sarawak. In 1999, the net immigration rate was 4.35 migrants per 1,000 population.

⁸ETHNIC GROUPS

Malays formed 64% of the population in 1999. Minorities included an estimated 20% Chinese and 16% designated as other. There is a small Caucasian minority, chiefly of English, Dutch, American, and Australian stock.

total capacity of 348,476 GRT. The Brunei River, which flows by the capital, is a major thoroughfare.

There were only about 1,150 km (715 mi) of main roads at last estimate, of which 399 km (248 mi) were paved. Links between the capital and the other western towns are good. Road connections between Brunei and Sarawak are being built. Buses are inexpensive but unreliable; river taxis and cars are for hire. In 1995, the sultanate had 115,377 passenger cars and 13,019 commercial vehicles registered.

A 13-km (8-mi) railway is operated by the Brunei Shell Petroleum Co. In addition, there were 2 airports in 1998, only 1 of which had a paved runway. The national carrier, Royal Brunei Airlines, operates regular flights to Singapore, Hong Kong, Manila, Bangkok, Jakarta, Kuala Lumpur, and other cities. Some foreign airlines serve Brunei International Airport at Barakas, outside the capital.

12HISTORY

From the 14th to the 16th century, Brunei was the center of a powerful native sultanate occupying what is now Sabah and Sarawak and extending northward through the Philippines almost to Manila. By the 19th century, much of this empire had been whittled away by war, piracy, and the colonial expansion of European nations. In 1847, the sultan concluded a treaty with Great Britain for the suppression of piracy and furtherance of commercial relations. In 1888, Brunei became a British protectorate, and in 1906 a resident British commissioner was established. By a 1959 agreement (amended in 1971), Brunei was recognized as fully self-governing, with Britain retaining responsibility for defense and foreign affairs. Brunei's first elections, held in 1962, resulted in a victory for the Brunei People's Party, militant nationalists who denounced Brunei's entry into a proposed federation with Malaysia, which had attained independence in 1957. Prevented from taking office, the nationalists, with Indonesian backing, revolted against Sultan Omar Ali Saifuddin in December 1962; the revolt was quickly put down with British assistance, but the sultan decided against federation in any case. From that time on, the sultanate has ruled by decree under a national state of emergency. In 1967, Sultan Omar abdicated in favor of his son, Muda Hassanal Bolkiah. Sultan Omar, who after his abdication remained as defense minister and assumed the royal title of Seri Begawan, died in 1986.

During the 1970s, Brunei emerged as the richest state in Southeast Asia, profiting from its oil wealth and the steep increases in international oil prices. Much of this vast oil income has been expended by the state on modernization and social services. Brunei renegotiated its treaty with the UK in mid-1978 and, on 7 January 1979, concluded a new treaty providing for independence within five years.

On 1 January 1984, the country attained full independence and was also proclaimed a member of the British Commonwealth. On 7 January 1984 Brunei joined the Association of South-East Asian Nations (ASEAN) and joined the United Nations in the same year. Brunei is also a member of the Organization of Islamic Conference.

In 1985 a new political party was formed, the Brunei National Democratic Party (BNDP), comprised predominantly of businessmen loyal to the Sultan. However, government employees were forbidden by the Sultan to join. The Chinese community was also excluded from membership. In 1986 an offshoot of the BNDP was formed, the Brunei National United Party (BNUP), which emphasized greater cooperation with the government. The BNUP's membership was open to Muslims and non-Muslims, but still excluded Chinese. In 1986, Brunei was solicited by the US government to aid the Nicaraguan Contras, but the $10 million donation was credited to the wrong bank account and never

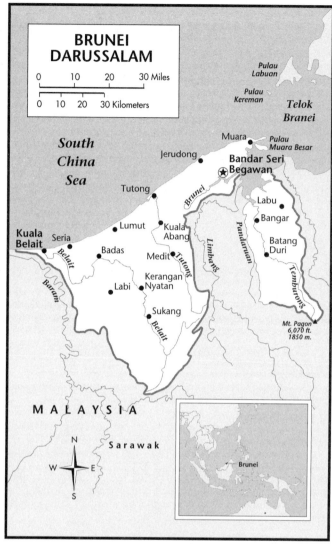

LOCATION: 4°2′ to 5°3′N; 114° to 115°22′E. **BOUNDARY LENGTHS:** Malaysia, 418 km (260 mi); South China Sea and Brunei Bay coastlines, 161 km (100 mi). **TERRITORIAL SEA LIMIT:** 12 mi.

9LANGUAGES

Malay is the official language. English is also widely spoken, as is Chinese. The principal Chinese dialect is Hokkien, with Hakka, Cantonese, and Mandarin dialects also in use. Many native dialects are spoken as well.

10RELIGIONS

Islam, the official religion, dominates everyday life. Religious practice is controlled by the influential Religious Affairs Department. According to unofficial estimates, 63% of the population is Muslim. Fourteen percent practice Buddhism. Another 8% of the people are Christian; the remaining 15% are comprised of tribal folk-religionists and other groups.

11TRANSPORTATION

Two seaports, at Muara and Kuala Belait, offer direct shipping services to Hong Kong, Singapore, and several other Asian ports. But wharf facilities at the deepwater port of Muara, though expanded to about 550 m (1,800 ft) in the mid-1980s, remain inadequate. In 1998, Brunei had 7 liquefied gas tankers with a reached its intended destination. The donation was eventually traced and returned to Brunei with interest.

In 1988 the top two leaders of the BNDP, President Haji Abdul latif bin Abdul Hamid, and Secretary-General, Haji Abdul Latif bin Chuchu, were arrested as they were about to fly to Australia. They were held under the Internal Security Act, which allows detention for up to two years without charges being filed, and were detained until 1990. In May of that year, Haji Abdul latif bin Abdul Hamid died. In 1990 the government released six other political prisoners who had been detained since 1962.

Increasing emphasis on Melayu Islam Beraja (MIB) as a state ideology has resulted in the affirmation of traditional values due to increasing concern about an affluent and worldly younger generation. In 1991 the import of alcohol and the public celebration of Christmas were banned. His Majesty Sultan Haji Hassanal Bolkiah Mu'izzaddin Waddaulah celebrated 25 years on the throne in October 1992. As of 1997 Fortune magazine's estimate of the Sultan's personal wealth, us$38 billion, indicates that he may be the richest man in the world. Brunei established diplomatic relations in 1993 with China, Vietnam and Laos.

In 1998 Brunei's economy was hit simultaneously by falling oil prices, regional currency depreciation stemming from the region's economic crisis, and the collapse of the multibillion-dollar Amedeo conglomerate run by the Sultan's brother, Prince Jefri Bolkiah, who was removed from his post as the country's finance minister. However, tensions persisted between the Sultan and his brother, who fled to London. Upon his return in early 2000, the government sued him and dozens of other persons for misuse of public funds. As the new century began, Brunei was looking for ways to diversify its heavily petroleum-dependent economy as its oil and gas reserves waned.

In August 1999, the Sultan met with Philippine president Joseph Estrada, with whom he discussed the establishment of a Philippines-Brunei Joint Commission for Bilateral Cooperation. In November 1999, Brunei and the five other members of the Association of Southeast Asian Nations (ASEAN), agreed informally to create a free-trade zone by eliminating duties on most goods traded in the region by 2010.

Brunei, along with the People's Republic of China, Vietnam, Malaysia, Taiwan, and the Philippines, is engaged in a regional dispute over claims to the Spratly Islands, situated in the South China Seas, which are strategically important and may have large oil reserves.

[13] GOVERNMENT

Brunei is an independent Islamic sultanate. The 1959 constitution (parts of which were suspended in 1962) confers supreme executive authority upon the sultan and provides for four Constitutional Councils: a Privy Council, Council of Ministers, Legislative Council, Religious Council, and Council of Succession to assist him. The members of these bodies are appointed by the sultan. The chief minister (mentri besar) is also appointed by the sultan and is responsible to him for the exercise of executive authority.

At his 1992 Silver Jubilee celebration the Sultan emphasized his commitment to preserving Brunei's political system based on the concept of Melayu Islam Beraja (MIB), or Malay Islam Monarchy, as the state ideology. MIB combines Islamic values and Malay culture within a monarchical political framework with the monarchy as defender of the faith.

[14] POLITICAL PARTIES

Parties were organized shortly after self-government was achieved in 1959. However, when the Brunei People's Party won 98% of the legislative seats in the country's only election, held in 1962, the sultan barred its candidates from office and outlawed all political parties under a continuing state of emergency. Political parties reemerged in the 1980s, but in 1988 they were banned and many of their leaders were arrested. At that time, the political parties were: the Brunei National Democratic Party (BNDP), founded in 1985, and the Brunei National United Party (BNUP), founded in 1986 by an offshoot of the BNDP. In contrast to the BNDP, membership in the BNUP was open not to Brunei Malays only, but to other indigenous people, whether Muslim or not. The Chinese were left with the option of forming their own party. (Under Brunei's restrictive naturalization policies only 6,000 Chinese had been granted citizenship.)

In 1995, the Brunei National United Party (PPKB), one of the initial parties that had been banned in 1962, formally requested authorization to hold a convention and elected Abdul Latif Chuchu, the former secretary-general of the BNDP, as its president. As of 1999, the party's application to resume active political activity was still pending.

[15] LOCAL GOVERNMENT

There are four administrative districts: Brunei-Muara, Kuala Belait, and Tutong in the western enclave, and Temburong in the east. Government is centrally controlled, but allowance is made for local tribal customs. District officers responsible to the ministers of home affairs administer each district. As part of the MIB ideology, village consultative councils have been introduced, making direct elections unnecessary. Instead, popularly elected headmen would function as mediators between the people and the central government. In June 1993 the Sultan stated "Brunei will strictly adhere to the MIB concept without resorting to fruitless political culture."

[16] JUDICIAL SYSTEM

There are five levels of courts with final recourse available through the Privy Council in London. Beginning with the courts of first instance, there are courts of Kathis which handle family matters such as marriage and divorce by applying Islamic law (Shari'a). Lower courts called sultan's courts, presided over by magistrates, hear other ordinary cases involving minor disputes. Such cases may be appealed to the High Court, a court of unlimited original jurisdiction in both civil and criminal matters. The High Court is presided over by a Chief Justice and justices appointed by the Sultan. Decisions of the High Court can be taken to the Court of Appeal, presided over by the President and two commissioners appointed by the Sultan. The Supreme Court consists of the High Court and the Court of Appeal.

In 1995, the right to appeal to the Privy Council in London was terminated in criminal cases. This final recourse remains available only for civil cases.

Certain provisions of the 1959 Constitution have been suspended under the State of Emergency since 1962.

[17] ARMED FORCES

The Royal Brunei Armed Forces in 2000 consisted of an army of 3,900 men and women, a navy of 700, and an air force of 400 for counterinsurgency air operations. Great Britain provides an active Gurkha infantry battalion with helicopter support, and Singapore a force of 500 instructors and advisers. Paramilitary forces include a Gurkha reserve unit of 2,000 men and 1,750 members of the Brunei Royal Police. Brunei spent $343 million for defense in 1997 or 6% of gross national product.

[18] INTERNATIONAL COOPERATION

Brunei was admitted to UN membership on 21 September 1984, and is a member of ICAO, IMF, IMO, ITU, UPU, WHO, WIPO, and WMO. It is also a member of the Commonwealth of Nations, ASEAN, and the Organization of the Islamic Conference, as well as a member of the WTO.

19 ECONOMY

Discovery of extensive petroleum and natural gas fields in the 1920s brought economic stability and modernization to Brunei. Today, the economy continues to depend almost entirely on oil and gas resources. This sector generates around half of GDP. Brunei's per capita GPD is one of the highest in Asia. Brunei's oil production peaked in 1979 at an estimated 240,000 to 261,000 barrels per day, but was deliberately cut back since then to preserve the country's oil reserves, which are conservatively estimated to last another 20–25 years. In 1999 average production was about 163,000 barrels a day. A 20-year contract to supply Japan with liquefied natural gas (LNG) was renewed for another 20 years by the newly established Brunei Oil and Gas Authority in April 1993. Meanwhile, attempts to diversify the economy pursuant to the national development plan were moving slowly. GDP declined in 1998 by one percent due to the Asian financial crisis and low oil prices.

20 INCOME

The US Central Intelligence Agency (CIA) reports that in 1998 Brunei Darussalam's gross domestic product (GDP) was estimated at $5.4 billion. The per capita GDP was estimated at $17,000. The annual growth rate of GDP was estimated at -1%. The average inflation rate in 1998 was 1.1%. The CIA defines GDP as the value of all final goods and services produced within a nation in a given year and computed on the basis of purchasing power parity (PPP) rather than value as measured on the basis of the rate of exchange. It was estimated that agriculture accounted for 5% of GDP, industry 46%, and services 49%.

21 LABOR

Most of the Ibans and Dusans have forsaken hunting and gathering for government housing and paddy fields, while the majority of Malays, in turn, have deserted farming for more lucrative jobs in government and the oil industry. Brunei's acute labor shortage has drawn temporary workers, many of them illegal immigrants, from neighboring countries. Some 40% of all workers are employed by the government; only about 3% of all workers are farmers or fishermen. The Trade Unions Act of 1962 permits the formation of trade unions in the sultanate, but prohibits affiliation with labor organizations outside Brunei. There are three registered trade unions, all in the oil sector, with a total membership amounting to less than 5% of the work force.

The workweek runs from Monday through Thursday with overtime pay for hours in excess of 48 hours. There are occupational health and safety standards which are enforced on a routine basis. There is no minimum wage.

22 AGRICULTURE

Temporary and permanent crops are actively cultivated on an estimated 7,000 hectares (17,300 acres), which represent 1.3% of total land area. Agriculture accounts for 3% of GDP and employs some 2% of the work force. Rice production is low (only about 1,000 tons per year), and Brunei imports more than 80% of its requirements. Urban migration and more profitable jobs in the oil industry have led to a shortage in farm labor. An agricultural training center, sponsored by Brunei Shell and the Department of Agriculture, was established in 1978 to encourage young people to return to the land. Crops for home consumption include bananas, sweet potatoes, cassava, coconuts, pineapples, and vegetables.

23 ANIMAL HUSBANDRY

Cattle, buffalo, hogs, goats, and fowl are raised. In 1978, McFarm (a Mitsubishi subsidiary) set up a cattle-breeding station in order to reduce meat imports. The government owns a cattle station in Australia that is larger in area than Brunei itself.

Livestock within Brunei in 1998 included an estimated 4,000 head of buffalo, 5,000 goats, 5,000 pigs, 2,000 head of cattle, and 3 million chickens. Meat production that year was estimated at 10,000 tons, with poultry meat accounting for 80% of the total. The government also encourages livestock production through the Mitsubishi Cattle Breeding Project.

24 FISHING

Traditional fishing has declined in recent years, with only 60% of home consumption provided by local fishermen. The Fisheries Department has supplied a small trawling fleet, and continuing efforts are being made to develop both freshwater and saltwater aquaculture. Fish hatcheries are in operation on a 6-hectare (15-acre) site near Muara. The annual fish harvest in 1997 totaled 4,677 tons, up from 4,517 tons in 1994.

25 FORESTRY

Forests and woodlands covered and estimated 82.4% of the land area in 1995. Forest reserves constitute about 41% of the land area. Exports of timber are restricted. There is a small sawmill and logging industry for local needs. In 1997, Brunei produced about 296,000 cu m of roundwood.

26 MINING

Brunei's mining industry was engaged only in the production and processing of crude oil and natural gas in 1997. Brunei's principal nonfuel mineral resource is its known reserves of silica sand of glassmaking quality.

27 ENERGY AND POWER

Commercial oil production, which began in 1929, dominates the economy. Production of crude oil in 1995 amounted to 8.6 million tons; output of natural gas was 10.3 billion cu m. In 1995, Brunei was the fifth-largest producer of liquefied natural gas (LNG) in the world. In 1991, Brunei's export earnings were estimated at $2.1 billion, of which about 47% was derived from LNG exports, 42% from exports of crude petroleum, and 6% from exports of refined petroleum products. Exploratory drilling for new reserves continues, and capital expenditure on petroleum development remains high. As of early 1996, proven reserves of oil totaled 200 million tons (1.3 billion barrels); at the current rate of extraction, known oil reserves will have been depleted by 2017. In 1988, a self-imposed conservation quota of 150,000 barrels of oil per day was set; in 1995, production amounted to 175,000 barrels per day. Electric power and natural gas supplies are readily available at low cost. Net installed capacity in 1998 was 406,000 kW, all of it in conventional thermal plants; production of electricity totaled 2,560 million kWh.

28 INDUSTRY

Industry is almost entirely dependent on oil and natural gas production. Brunei ranks 32nd in the world in oil production, but is the third-largest oil producer in Southeast Asia, after Indonesia and Malaysia. Revenues from the petroleum sector account for around 50% of GDP. At Lumut, Brunei has one of the world's largest liquefied natural gas plants, which is owned by Brunei Shell Petroleum (BSP), a joint venture owned in equal shares by the government and the Royal Dutch/Shell Group of companies. After the government, BSP and four sister companies constitute the largest employer in Brunei. Brunei is the fourth largest producer of LNG in the world.

Production of industrial goods in 1999 included 163,000 barrels of oil per day, and 150 trillion BTU of LNG. The small manufacturing sector includes production for the construction sector, sawmills and brick and tile factories. Government support of small-scale projects in food and beverage processing, textiles, furniture making and specialist optics has had limited results.

Small commercial enterprise is still carried on mainly by Chinese entrepreneurs. In 1976, the government set up the Economic Development Board to assist new industries by granting tax and import exemptions, and recent efforts are aimed at increasing the employment of the local Malay population in the private sector.

The industrial production growth rate was listed as 4% in 1997.

29SCIENCE AND TECHNOLOGY

Advanced science and technology have been imported in connection with development of the oil industry. Foreign technical expertise is employed in communications and other infrastructural programs. The Ministry of Industry and Primary Resources conducts agricultural research. The University of Brunei Darussalam, founded in 1985, has a faculty of science. The Technological Institute of Brunei, located in Bandar Seri Begawan, and the Jefri Bolkiah College of Engineering in Kuala Belait, offer engineering courses. Research and Development expenditures for 1999 were unavailable.

30DOMESTIC TRADE

Retail trade is largely in the hands of Chinese merchants. Since 1974, local cooperative societies have developed. As the result of heavy food subsidies and the increased availability of imported goods, Brunei has become a consumer society. Shops are generally open from 7:30 AM to 8 PM (some to 10 PM), seven days a week. Banking hours are 9 AM to 3 PM on weekdays, and 9 to 11 AM on Saturdays. Newspapers and television are the principal advertising media. The mainly English-language *Borneo Bulletin* is the only national newspaper that accepts advertising.

31FOREIGN TRADE

Crude oil, petroleum products, and natural gas constitute more than 99% of Brunei's export value. Most of Brunei's beef is supplied by a government-owned cattle ranch in Australia which is larger than Brunei itself.

Natural and manufactured gas exports are in the majority in Brunei-Darussalam (42%), along with crude petroleum, and refined petroleum products (45%). The country also exports gold, silver ware, and jewelry (7.2%).

In 1994 Brunei Darussalam's imports were distributed among the following categories:

Consumer goods	17.8%
Food	12.8%
Fuels	0.4%
Industrial supplies	32.7%
Machinery	21.4%
Transportation	14.6%
Other	0.3%

Principal trading partners in 1998 (in millions of US dollars) were as follows:

COUNTRY	EXPORTS	IMPORTS	BALANCE
Japan	934	103	831
Korea	309	20	289
United Kingdom	277	468	-191
United States	204	135	69
Singapore	159	677	-518
Thailand	21	56	-35
Indonesia	7	57	-50
Malaysia	3	256	-253
Germany	1	50	-49
France	n.a.	324	

32BALANCE OF PAYMENTS

Brunei's huge trade surpluses have enabled it to maintain an enviable payments position. Foreign exchange reserves stood at about US$20 billion in 1986, or more than US$87,000 per capita. In 1997, foreign reserves are estimated at $40 billion.

The US Central Intelligence Agency reports that in 1996 the purchasing power parity of Brunei Darussalam's exports was $2,620 million while imports totaled $2,650 million resulting in a trade balance of -$30 million.

33BANKING AND SECURITIES

The banking industry is controlled by the Association of Banks, in liaison with the government. In 1999 there were 9 banks operating in Brunei. Of these, 3 were locally incorporated and 6 were foreign, among them the Hongkong Bank, Malayan Banking Berhard, and Citibank. The International Bank of Brunei, in which the sultan has a 51% stake, is the larger of the local banks. The other, the National Bank of Brunei, was seized in 1986 by the government, which charged the majority shareholders with irregularities, and later closed in the early 1990s. Other banks are the Baiduri Bank, Sime Bank, the Development Bank of Brunei, the Overseas Union Bank, and the Standard Chartered Finance (Brunei) Berhad.

The managing director of the Brunei Investment Agency (BIA), Abdul Aziz Abdul Rahman, met France's Treasury director, Jean Lemierre, in mid-December, 1996 to discuss the possibility of opening a BIA office in Paris. BIA's French investments are currently managed from the agency's offices in London and Brussels. Approximately half of the country's revenue is now derived from the income from these investments.

The Brunei Investments and Commercial Bank, a subsidiary of the Brunei Investment Agency, acquired a 13.4% stake in the Australian Macquarie Bank in November 1996, making the BIA the single largest shareholder.

34INSURANCE

In 1995, there were 19 insurance companies doing business in Brunei.

35PUBLIC FINANCE

Brunei continues to maintain large surpluses in its annual budgets. The largest single items of expenditure were defense, education, and public works; taxes and royalties from the oil industry are by far the leading sources of government income.

The US Central Intelligence Agency (CIA) estimates that in 1995 Brunei Darussalam's central government took in revenues of approximately $2.5 billion and had expenditures of $2.6 billion including capital expenditures of $768 million. Overall, the government registered a deficit of approximately $100 million. Brunei had no external debt in 1995.

36TAXATION

Taxation on petroleum income is subject to special legal provisions, dating from 1963. At the present time individual income tax is waived, however, legislation for the collection of personal income tax does exist. Companies pay a 30% tax on earnings. There is a double-taxation agreement between Brunei and the UK. Exemption from taxes can be granted by the sultan in council to industries deemed essential for the country's development.

37CUSTOMS AND DUTIES

Brunei levies tariffs ranging from zero to 30% on selected items including perfume, and has a simple-column tariff structure. The country joined ASEAN in 1984 and has reduced trade barriers with member nations.

38FOREIGN INVESTMENT

In July 1983, the sultanate withdrew its investment portfolio of more than B$3 billion (about half of total investment) from agents of the British crown, who traditionally had handled investment banking for Brunei. The Brunei Investment Agency, established in 1983, manages a substantial portfolio of assets invested around the world in long-term securities. Reportedly, the interest earned on these investments is greater than the hydrocarbon revenues.

Brunei's investments abroad, believed to total between $40 billion and $50 billion in 1995, earn an estimated $2.5 billion a year, roughly equal to the country's entire oil and gas income.

39ECONOMIC DEVELOPMENT

The development plan for 1986–90 envisioned diversification of the economy in order to prepare for the time when oil and gas reserves would run out. Thus, it emphasized development of the agricultural sector to lessen the country's reliance on imported foods. Industrial development projects focused on light industries, but also included plants for the production of cement and precast concrete. Service industries were encouraged, especially banking and finance, in the hope of developing Brunei into an international financial center. The establishment of a development bank also ranked high on the government's agenda. The Sixth National Development Plan (1991–95) was created to stimulate growth of the private sector, and to promote human resources and industrial development. The largest budget allocation was for social services (29.3%), with equal percentages for public utilities and transport and communications (20% each), 10% allocated to trade and industry, and about 7% to security forces. The 1991–96 National Development Plan focused on economic diversification, as did the 1996 to 2000 plan. The two main traditional employers were the government, which absorbs about half the work force, and Brunei Shell Petroleum. Development efforts for a non-oil, non-state sector and the potential for increasing foreign investment are limited by the small domestic market, a shortage of skilled manpower, and relatively high labor and transport costs.

40SOCIAL DEVELOPMENT

Typical of the problems of managing the transition from traditional tribal life to a modern life-style is that of Kampong Ayer, a "water village" along the Brunei River in the center of the capital. The village survives despite the government's efforts to induce the residents to move ashore, in part because the villagers' homes are already equipped with television sets and other modern comforts. Citizens enjoy extensive state welfare services, including free education and health care, wedding and burial allowances, and subsidized food and housing. The state provides pensions for the old and disabled, and financial aid for the destitute. An underlying social change in recent years has been the increasing influence of Islam as a way of life; converts include Bruneians of all ethnic backgrounds, including an increasing number of Chinese.

Women are denied equal status with men in areas including divorce, inheritance, and child custody. Citizenship is passed on through males only and the children of Bruneian women who marry foreigners are not entitled to citizenship. It has been estimated that by 1995 this policy was responsible in part for the existence of a small class of stateless residents numbering 5,000 who were born and raised in Brunei, but are not entitled to full citizenship rights and privileges. Stateless residents are issued an International Certificate of Identity which functions as an international travel document. A law strengthening the rights of non-Muslim married women took effect in 1999, as did amendments to the Islamic Family Law also aimed at increasing women's rights.

Most Muslim women wear the head covering known as the tudong. Non-Muslim women are not pressured to follow this dress code.

The government restricts the freedoms of speech, assembly, association, and the press.

41HEALTH

The state provides free medical care, and remote regions are served by mobile clinics and a flying doctor service; there is also a school health service. As of 1996, there were 8 hospitals (4 of which are run by the government). Medical personnel in 1991 included 197 physicians, and, in 1989, 8 pharmacists and 30 dentists. The death rate went from 4.2 per 1,000 population in 1974 to 5.2 per 1,000 in 1999. In 1999, the infant mortality rate was 22.8 per 1,000 live births. Life expectancy in 1999 was estimated at 71.8 years. In 1990, 96% of the population had access to health care services, and 90% had access to safe drinking water. During 1994, 92% of the country's children were immunized against measles. Malaria has been eradicated from Brunei (although it remains a problem in adjacent Sarawak), and cholera is close to nonexistent. There is, however, still some risk of filariasis, tuberculosis, typhoid fever, and intestinal flu. In 1996, there were 6 new cases of AIDS reported.

42HOUSING

As of 1980, 36% of all houses had no electricity. Development plans for 1986–90 included a public housing program; government allocations for housing development totaled an estimated B$94 million in 1985. Most people who wish to leave their traditional homes have been able to find accommodations in housing units provided either by the government or by the oil companies.

43EDUCATION

The state provides free education from kindergarten up, including university training abroad. In 1996 there were 160 primary schools, with 432,941 pupils. Secondary schools had 30,470 students and 2,961 teachers in the same year. For the year 2000, adult illiteracy rates were estimated at 8.4% (males, 5.3%; females, 11.8%). Education is compulsory between the ages of 5 and 16. Six years of primary are followed by seven years of secondary education. The official policy is to promote bilingual education, Malay and English, in all government-supported schools.

Foreigners generally attend private mission schools, the International School, and the Chinese School. Brunei Shell also funds several schools, and there are numerous religious academies. There are two teacher-training colleges and five vocational technical schools, including an agricultural training center. Brunei also has a university, established in 1985, and institutes of education and technology. The University of Brunei Darussalam (founded in 1985) has faculties for education, arts and social sciences, science, and management and administration. In 1996, 1,270 students were enrolled in institutes of higher education. Many students, however, continue their education in foreign universities at government expense.

44LIBRARIES AND MUSEUMS

The Language and Literature Bureau Library (founded in 1961) serves as a reference and lending library in Bandar Seri Begawan and holds 311,300 volumes. The library at the University of Brunei Darussalam has 200,000 volumes, and the Brunei Technological Institute has 25,000. The library has a central facility, 4 branches, and 5 mobile units providing library services in remote areas. The Churchill Memorial Museum (founded 1971) illustrates the life of the famous statesman. Adjacent to the museum is the Sultan Hassanal Bolkiah Aquarium, one of the finest in Asia and the Constitutional History Gallery. Also notable are the Malay Technology Museum (founded 1988) and the Brunei Museum (founded 1970), the latter with archaeological and natural history collections. The Exhibition Gallery of the Islamic Center (1985) houses religious art and details the history of Islam in Brunei.

45 MEDIA

In 1997, there were 90,000 telephones in use. The government owned Radio Television Brunei broadcasts radio programs in English, Malay, and Chinese. As of 1999, there were 3 AM and 10 FM radio stations and 2 television stations. There is a 10-channel cable network widely available which includes CNN, BBC World News, and several entertainment channels. In 1997, there were 859 radios and 523 television sets per 1,000 population

The only commercial daily newspaper serving Brunei is the English *Borneo Bulletin,* with a circulation of 20,000 in 1999. The government publishes the Malay weekly *Peilta Brunei* (1999 circulation 45,00) and a monthly newsletter in English, *Brunei Darussalam* (12,000 in 1995). *The Straits Times of Singapore* circulates widely in Brunei, as do Chinese papers from Sarawak.

Though there is no law restriction freedom of speech or press, the government traditionally has arrested those attempting to propagate opinions of a political nature which are critical of the government or the Sultan. On occasion, the government has censored international newspapers and magazines by blacking out objectionable articles or photographs. Articles with a Christian theme are said to be invariably censored.

Though statistics are currently unavailable, reports show an increasing use of the Internet and satellite transmissions.

46 ORGANIZATIONS

The powerful Religious Affairs Department permeates daily life; its activities include sponsoring Islamic pilgrimages and establishing village mosque committees. Sports facilities tend to be privately maintained. There are four chambers of commerce in the country.

46 ORGANIZATIONS

The powerful Religious Affairs Department permeates daily life; its activities include sponsoring Islamic pilgrimages and establishing village mosque committees. Sports facilities tend to be privately maintained. There are four chambers of commerce in the country.

47 TOURISM, TRAVEL, AND RECREATION

There were approximately 837,000 visitor arrivals to Brunei in 1996. That year there were 1,170 hotel room with an occupancy rate of 67%, and more new hotels are under construction. Among Brunei's newest and most remarkable sights is the sultan's 1,788-room palace, built at a reported cost of us$300 million and topped by two golf-leaf domes. Native longhouses are also a tourist attraction but are hard to reach, and trips up the Brunei and Tutong rivers are interesting but not yet well organized. Every visitor must have a valid passport; visas are normally required, but there are exemptions based on nationality, and purpose and length of visit.

In 1999, the UN estimated that the cost of staying in Brunei was us$175 per day.

48 FAMOUS BRUNEIANS

Omar Ali Saifuddin (1916–86) was sultan from 1950 to 1967 and minister of defense from 1984 to 1986. His son, Muda Hassanal Bolkiah (Bolkiah Mu'izuddin Waddaulah, b.1946), one of the wealthiest men in the world, has been sultan since 1967.

49 DEPENDENCIES

Brunei has no territories or colonies.

50 BIBLIOGRAPHY

Braighlinn, G. *Ideological Innovation Under Monarchy: Aspects of Legitimation Activity in Contemporary Brunei.* Amsterdam: VU University Press, 1992.

Chalfont, Arthur Gwynne Jones, Baron. *By God's Will: A Portrait of the Sultan of Brunei.* 1st American ed. New York: Weidenfeld & Nicolson, 1989.

Cleary, Mark. *Oil, Economic Development, and Diversification of Brunei Darussalam.* New York: St. Martin's, 1994.

Crowther, Goeff et al. *Malaysia, Singapore and Brunei.* 4th ed. South Yarra, Australia: Lonely Planet, 1991.

Gunn, Geoffrey C. *Language, Power, and Ideology in Brunei Darussalam.* Athens, Ohio: Ohio University Center for International Studies, 1997.

Krausse, Sylvia C. Engelen. *Brunei.* Oxford; Santa Barbara, Calif.: Clio, 1988.

Major, John S. *The Land and People of Malaysia and Brunei.* New York, NY: HarperCollins, 1991.

Singh, Ranjit. *Brunei, 1839–1983: The Problems of Political Survival.* New York: Oxford University Press, 1984.

Saunders, Graham E. *A History of Brunei,* New York: Oxford University Press, 1994.

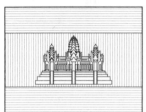

CAMBODIA

Cambodia

CAPITAL: Phnom Penh

NOTE: Cambodia (formerly known as Kampuchea and the Khmer Republic) was known as Cambodia until 1976 and again since 1989. As of 1994, there are two rival claimants for legitimate government authority. One of these, the People's Republic of Kampuchea (PRK), was established in January 1979 in the wake of a Vietnamese invasion; it maintained de facto control of the capital by means of an occupation force of Vietnamese troops. The other, Democratic Kampuchea (DK; Kampuchea Pracheathipateyy), is represented by a coalition government-in-exile, but with considerable following in the Cambodian countryside; it continues to hold Cambodia's seat in the UN.

FLAG: The flag has a red center field with a white silhouette of the temple complex at Angkor Wat. The center field is bordered top and bottom by blue bands.

MONETARY UNIT: Money was officially abolished in 1975, and for nearly five years the domestic economy operated almost exclusively on a system of barter and government rationing. In March 1980, the PRK reintroduced the riel (R) of 100 sen, equal in value to 1 kg (2.2 lb) of rice and with an approximate exchange value of R1 = $0.00026 ($1 = R3805.00) as of 31 March 2000.

WEIGHTS AND MEASURES: Both the metric system and traditional weights and measures are in general use.

HOLIDAYS: National Day, 9 January; New Year, April; Victory over American Imperialism Day, 17 April; Labor Day, 1 May; Day of Hatred, 20 May; Feast of the Ancestors, 22 September.

TIME: 7 PM = noon GMT.

¹LOCATION, SIZE, AND EXTENT

Situated in the southeast corner of Indochina, Cambodia has an area of 181,040 sq km (69,900 sq mi), extending 730 km (454 mi) NE-SW and 512 km (318 mi) SE-NW. It is bounded on the NE by Laos, on the E and SE by Viet-Nam, on the SW by the Gulf of Thailand, and on the W, NW, and N by Thailand, with a total boundary length of 3,015 km (1,873 mi). Comparatively, the area occupied by Cambodia is slightly smaller than the state of Oklahoma. In 1982, the PRK signed an agreement with Vietnam on their mutual maritime frontier. A treaty delineating the land border was signed in December 1985.

Cambodia's capital city, Phnom Penh, is located in the south-central part of the country.

²TOPOGRAPHY

Cambodia is a country of forested mountains and well-watered plains. The central part of the country forms a gigantic basin for the Tonle Sap, or Great Lake, and the Mekong River, which flows down from Laos to the southern border with Viet-Nam. Between the Tonle Sap and the Gulf of Thailand lie the Cardamom Mountains and the Elephant Range, which rise abruptly from the sea and from the eastern plains. In the north, the Dangrek Mountains, 320 km (200 mi) long and 300 to 750 m (1,000–2,500 ft) high, mark the Thailand frontier. The short coastline has an important natural harbor, Kompong Som Bay, where the port of Kompong Som (formerly Sihanoukville) is located.

The Mekong and the Tonle Sap dominate the life and economy of Cambodia. The Mekong overflows during the rainy season, deposits vast quantities of alluvial soil, and, backing toward the Tonle Sap, causes that lake to increase in size from about 260 sq km (100 sq mi) to almost 2,100 sq km (800 sq mi).

³CLIMATE

The climate is tropical, with a wet season from June through November and a dry season from December to June. Temperatures range from 20° to 36°C (68–97°F), and humidity is consistently high. The lowlands, which are inundated during the rainy season, receive about 200 cm (80 in) of rainfall annually, but there is less precipitation in the western and northern portions of the country.

⁴FLORA AND FAUNA

Cambodia, covered in its mountainous areas with dense virgin forests, has a wide variety of plant and animal life. There are palm, rubber, coconut, kapok, mango, banana, and orange trees, as well as the high sharp grass of the savannas. Birds, including cranes, pheasants, and wild ducks, and mammals such as elephants, wild oxen, panthers, and bears abound throughout the country. Fish, snakes, and insects also are present in abundance.

⁵ENVIRONMENT

Deforestation and the resulting soil erosion cause significant environmental problems in Cambodia. By 1985, logging activities, the clearing of the land for agricultural purposes, and the damage from the Vietnam war resulted in the destruction of 116 square miles of forest land. Between 1983 and 1993, the nation's forest and woodland were reduced by an additional 11.3% to 11.7 million ha. The nation has 21.1 cubic miles of water with 94% used for farming activity and 1% used for industrial purposes. Most rural dwellers do not have access to pure water. Cambodia's cities produce 0.2 million tons of solid waste per year. Three-fourths of Cambodia's wildlife areas have been lost through the destruction of its forests, and strip mining for gems in the western part of the country poses an additional threat to the nation's biodiversity and wildlife habitats. Natural fisheries have been endangered by the destruction of Cambodia's mangrove swamps. As of 1994, 21 of Cambodia's mammal species and 13 of its bird species were endangered and 11 of its plant species were also threatened. Endangered or extinct species in Cambodia include 3 species of gibbon (pileated, crowned, and caped), several species of wild dog and wild cat, leopard, tiger, Asian elephant, Sumatran rhinoceros, Thailand brow-antlered deer, kouprey, giant catfish, Indian python, Siamese crocodile, and estuarine crocodile.

⁶POPULATION

Estimates of Cambodia's population vary with the assessment of the impact of the 1970–75 war and the millions killed in its tumultuous aftermath. The population of Cambodia (Kampuchea) in 2000 was estimated at 11,918,865. An estimated 3.0% of the population is 65 years of age or older. The projected population for the year 2005 is 13,463,000, assuming a crude birthrate of 38 per 1,000 population and a death rate of 14, resulting in a natural rate of change of 2.4% for the period 2000–2005. The population rate of change between 1995 and 2000 was 2.2%. The population density in 1998 was 61 per sq km (158 per sq mi).

A great majority of the people live in rural areas, with 90% of the rural population living in the plains of the central third of the country. It was estimated that only 24% of the total population lived in urban areas in 2000, up from 12% in 1980.

At the war's end, in April 1975, the population of the capital, Phnom Penh, had swollen to nearly 3 million because of a mass influx of refugees. The new government immediately embarked on a forced evacuation of all urban areas, and by March 1976, only 100,000–200,000 were thought to remain in Phnom Penh. After the installation of the PRK in 1979, the population of Phnom Penh began to increase, and by 2000 was estimated at 429,000. Other cities include Batdambang, Kampong Cham, Kampot, Siemreab, Kampong Saom, and Kracheh.

⁷MIGRATION

The first migration of persons in independent Cambodia took place during the 1950s and 1960s, when ethnic Chinese were permitted to settle in the mountainous and wasteland areas and cultivate land that otherwise would have remained useless. After 1970, about 200,000 Vietnamese living in Cambodia were repatriated to the RVN, ostensibly as a security measure. With the insurgent victory in April 1975, most of the country's remaining Vietnamese were reported to have emigrated to Viet Nam. In addition, thousands of refugees, including many former officials and military personnel, fled across the Thai border or were evacuated by US aircraft.

The new government launched a sweeping nationwide resettlement program under which some 2.5–3 million persons were moved from Phnom Penh and other cities into the countryside, where they were organized into work brigades. The food shortage in rural areas was only slightly less critical than in the cities, and widespread starvation led to the deaths of probably over one million people during the transition. After the installation of the PRK in January 1979, continued fighting and political instability resulted in a new exodus of refugees. About 630,000 Cambodians left the country between 1979 and 1981, of which about 208,000 were able to resettle in other countries, including 136,000 in the US. Most of the rest remained in camps on the border with Thailand, but they were repatriated to Cambodia in May 1993.

Between 1979 and 1987 there was a new migration of ethnic Vietnamese into Cambodia. Official sources insisted that the total number was under 60,000, and was comprised, for the most part, of residents who had left in the early 1970s, but opposition groups contended that the number totaled over 500,000 and was intended to consolidate Vietnamese control over the country.

In 1997, the conflicts between government forces and the National Army of Democratic Kampuchea (a.k.a. Khmer Rouge) drove rural populations from their homes. In 1997 and 1998, UNHCR assisted up to 60,000 Cambodian refugees who had the fled fighting in Northwest Cambodia. Also in 1997, the UNHCR helped several thousand ethnic Vietnamese fisher families return to their Cambodian homes after having camped on the Vietnam border. Following the peace settlement between the government of Cambodia and resistance forces in December 1998, the repatriation of approximately 36,000 refugees remaining in camps in Thailand was rapidly implemented. By April 1999, all of the camps were closed, and by June 1999 some 47,000 refugees had returned home. The net migration rate for Cambodia in 1999 was zero.

⁸ETHNIC GROUPS

Over 90% of the entire population in 1999 were ethnic Khmers, descendants of the original population in the area. The largest minority groups were the Vietnamese, estimated at 5% of the population, and the Chinese, estimated at 1%. Groups designated as other comprised the remaining 4% of the population. National minorities are the Cham and a number of small tribal groups.

⁹LANGUAGES

Khmer, the national language, is spoken by most inhabitants. Unlike Thai or Vietnamese, Khmer is a non-tonal language; most words are monosyllabic. French, the second language, is often used in commercial and official circles. The Vietnamese and the Chinese use their own languages, as do other minorities.

¹⁰RELIGIONS

Although Theravada Buddhism is the religion of some 95% of the inhabitants (1999), and has been the state religion since 1989, animism is adhered to by most persons as well. The Chinese and most Vietnamese in Cambodia practice a traditional mixture of Mahayana Buddhism, Taoism, Confucianism, ancestor worship, and animism. Before 1975 there were some 100,000 Muslims (mostly Cham-Malays), 50,000 Roman Catholics (Europeans and Vietnamese), and a few Protestants. The mountain tribes are animists; in the post-World War II years, Christian missionaries made some converts among them.

The government that took power in 1975 virtually abolished Buddhism, defrocking some 70,000 monks and turning pagodas into warehouses. Islamic spokesmen have claimed that 90% of Cambodia Muslims were massacred after 1975. Of some 6,000 Roman Catholics left in Cambodia at the time of the revolution, only a few survived. All mosques and Catholic churches were razed. The PRK regime that came to power in 1979 permitted the return of religious practice, and hundreds of pagodas were reopened. In insurgent areas controlled by the Khmer Rouge, Buddhism was allowed after 1979, and in non-Communist resistance camps there reportedly was full freedom of religion.

As of 1999 the Constitution provides for freedom of religion, and the government reportedly respects this right in practice. The remaining 5% of the population that does not practice Buddhism is made up mostly of ethnic Cham Muslims, who are generally located in Phnom Penh and in rural fishing villages in Kompong Cham, Kompong Chhnang, and Kampot provinces.

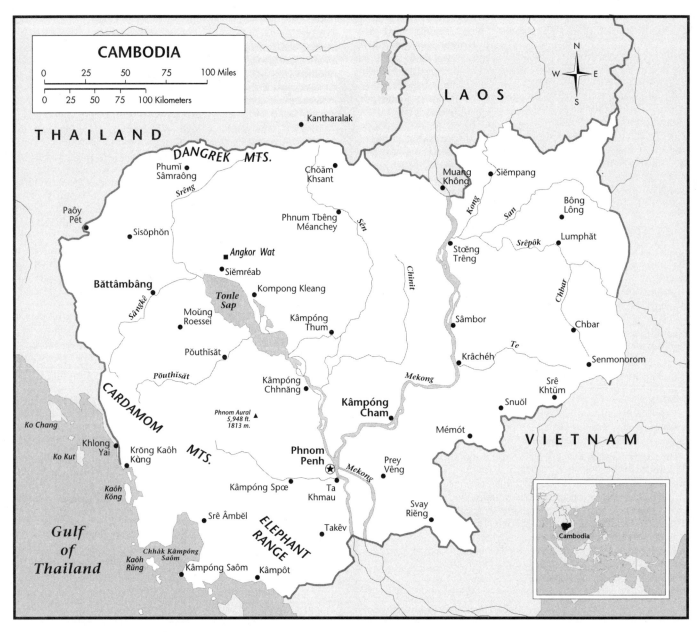

CAMBODIA

0 25 50 75 100 Miles

0 25 50 75 100 Kilometers

THAILAND

LAOS

DANGREK MTS.

Kantharalak

Phumĭ Sâmraŏng

Chŏăm Khsant

Muang Không

Siĕmpang

Paôy Pét

Srêng

Phnum Tbêng Méanchey

Sên

Kong

San

Bông Lông

Sisŏphŏn

Stœ̆ng Trêng

Srêpôk

Lumphăt

Angkor Wat

Siĕmréab

Băttâmbâng

Tonle Sap

Kompong Kleang

Chinit

Sâmbor

Chbar

Moŭng Roessei

Kâmpóng Thum

Sângkê

Te

Krâchéh

Chbar

Pŏuthĭsăt

Senmonorom

Pŏuthĭsăt

Kâmpóng Chhnăng

Mekong

Srê Khtŭm

CARDAMOM

Phnom Aural
5,948 ft.
1813 m.

Kâmpóng Cham

Snuŏl

Ko Chang

VIETNAM

Khlong Yai

Krŏng Kaôh Kŭng

MTS.

Phnom Penh

Mémót

Ko Kut

Mekong

Prey Vêng

Kaôh Kŏng

Kâmpóng Spœ

Ta Khmau

Cambodia

Gulf
of
Thailand

Srê Âmbĕl

ELEPHANT RANGE

Takêv

Svay Riĕng

Chhâk Kâmpóng Saôm

Kaôh Rŭng

Kâmpóng Saôm

Kâmpôt

LOCATION: 102°31′ to 108°E; 10° to 15°N. **BOUNDARY LENGTHS:** Laos, 541 km (336 mi); Viet-Nam, 982 km (610 mi); Gulf of Thailand, 389 km (242 mi); Thailand, 803 km (499 mi). **TERRITORIAL SEA LIMIT:** 12 mi.

¹¹TRANSPORTATION

Land transport facilities suffered wholesale destruction during the 1970–75 war. Cambodia's first railway, a 385-km (239-mi) single track from Phnom Penh to Paoy Pet, was badly damaged in the fighting; moreover, a just-completed 262-km (163-mi) line from Phnom Penh to Kampong Sam was also disabled. The line to Kampong Sam was restored in November 1979, and a Phnom Penh–Battambang railway was reopened in February 1980. Rail service has been periodically disrupted by guerrilla operations. In 1996 rail trackage totaled 603 km (375 mi).

All major cities and towns are connected with Phnom Penh by highway, and from there roads connect to Vietnam, Laos, and Thailand. The US-built 214-km (133-mi) Khmer-America Friendship Highway links Phnom Penh with Kampong Sam. As of 1997, Cambodia had an estimated 35,769 km (22,226 mi) of main roads, of which only 4,165 km (2,588 mi) were paved; most are in poor condition.

The Mekong is the most important inland waterway. Total length of navigable waterways is 3,700 km (2,300 mi) for craft drawing 0.6 meters, but only 282 km (175 mi) for craft with a draft of 1.8 meters. Until 1975, Saigon was the major transshipment point for outgoing and incoming Cambodian goods; the opening of the deepwater port of Kompong Som made Cambodia largely independent of Vietnam for oceangoing shipping. In 1998 Cambodia's merchant fleet totaled 141 ships (1,000 GRT or over) with a capacity of 598,867 GRT. The fleet includes ships of 8 countries under a flag of convenience registry.

Cambodia had 20 airports in 1998, 7 of which had paved runways. The main airport is at Phnom Penh; there are regular flights between Phnom Penh, Hanoi, Vientiane, and Ho Chi Minh City.

12HISTORY

Most Cambodians are descendants of the Khmers, who in the 6th century established the Indian-influenced Angkor Empire, and for the next 900 years ruled the area of present-day Cambodia. According to legend, the founder of the Khmer dynasty was Kampu Svayambhuva, from whose name "Kampuchea" derives. From the 10th to the 14th century, after years of military expansion, the Khmers reached their apogee. Their empire extended over most of Southeast Asia (from central Vietnam south-west into the Malay Peninsula, and from Thailand north to the border of Burma, now known as Myanmar). Angkor, the capital city, was a flourishing complex of great temples, palaces, and shrines. In the subsequent centuries, however, continuing attacks by the Thai (who captured Angkor in 1431) and the Vietnamese weakened the empire, and by the end of the 18th century much of Cambodia had become a Thai and Vietnamese condominium. In 1863, the king of Cambodia placed the country under French protection.The French, joining Cambodia to Laos and Vietnam to form French Indochina, ruled the protectorate until the end of World War II. Cambodian nationalism received its greatest impetus during the World War II period, while Japan controlled Indochina. King Norodom Sihanouk, who had ascended the throne in 1941 and had been held a virtual prisoner under the Japanese occupation, proclaimed Cambodia independent in 1945, but yielded before a temporary resumption of the French protectorate, enforced by Allied troops, which occupied Phnom Penh. Cambodia became a constitutional monarchy on 6 May 1947, and was granted nominal independence within the French Union on 9 November 1949. King Sihanouk, meanwhile, had assumed leadership of Cambodia's growing nationalist movement. On 17 October 1953, during the height of the Franco-Indochinese war, he was granted full military control of his country by France. Sihanouk, a skilled politician, abdicated in March 1955 in favor of his father and mother, King Suramarit and Queen Kossamak, and then emerged as prime minister with the unanimous support of the national legislature. King Suramarit died on 31 April 1960, but Prince Sihanouk, although retaining the title of chief of state, did not return to the throne. During the Franco-Indochinese war, Communist-controlled Viet-Minh troops from Vietnam operated in Cambodia (1954), and gave support to a small Khmer Communist movement.

The Geneva agreements of July 1954, which ended the Franco-Indochinese war, secured the withdrawal of French and Viet-Minh troops from Cambodia and the surrender of most of the Khmer rebels. During the next 15 years, Sihanouk sought to keep Cambodia neutral in the deepening Vietnam conflict. This proved increasingly difficult, however, as the National Liberation Front (also known as the Viet-Cong) used Cambodian border areas as bases from which to launch attacks on the Republic of Vietnam (RVN, or South Vietnam), and as the US in 1969 launched an undeclared air war against the guerrilla sanctuaries. On 18 March 1970, Marshal Lon Nol, prime minister and army chief, overthrew the chief of state, Prince Sihanouk, while the prince was on a visit to the USSR; the right-wing coup ended 1,168 years of rule by Khmer monarchs. Sihanouk thereupon took up residence in Beijing, where, on 5 May, he announced formation of the Royal Government of National Union of Kampuchea (GRUNK) under the political auspices of the National United Front of Kampuchea. In the interim, on 30 April, US President Richard M. Nixon announced an "incursion" into Cambodia of 30,000 US and 40,000 RVN troops, with the object of destroying their opponents' strongholds along the Vietnam border. The operation was terminated on 30 June with its military objectives apparently unfulfilled, and bombing of the region continued, to devastating effect on Cambodia's economy.

Formal diplomatic relations with the US, severed by Sihanouk in 1965, were resumed on 2 July 1970, and Sihanouk was condemned to death (in absentia) three days later. On 9 October, the Lon Nol government in Phnom Penh abolished the monarchy and changed Cambodia's name to the Khmer Republic. In elections held during June 1972, Lon Nol was elected president of the republic. Pressures from GRUNK insurgents continued to mount, especially following the conclusion of a cease-fire in Vietnam in January 1973 and the withdrawal of the last US troops from that country in March. US aid to the Lon Nol government had been substantial, totaling $1.18 billion in military supplies and $503 million in economic assistance for the whole of the 1970–75 period, but with most of the aid concentrated in the early years of direct involvement. With the reversal of US policy in Vietnam, however, support for the Khmer Republic began to taper off, and by the start of 1975, the Lon Nol government was plunged into a struggle for survival. In January, GRUNK military forces, generally referred to as the Khmer Rouge, launched a major offensive aimed at gaining control of the Mekong River and isolating Phnom Penh. Fierce and costly fighting ensued over the next three months, with the US undertaking a massive airlift to Phnom Penh in February to fend off starvation and military collapse. On 1 April, the strategic Mekong ferry crossing at Neak Luong fell to the insurgents, clearing the way to a direct, final assault on the capital. On that day, Lon Nol fled the country, to be followed by much of the ruling hierarchy. On 17 April, the Khmer Republic government officially capitulated to GRUNK forces, commanded by Khieu Samphan.

The GRUNK government reported in March 1976 that the war had resulted in 1 million casualties, including 800,000 killed. On 5 January 1976, the country was officially renamed Democratic Kampuchea (DK). On 20 March, the first general elections were held for a new 250-member People's Assembly. The Assembly on 14 April named Khieu Samphan chairman of the State Presidium, replacing Prince Sihanouk, who had returned to the country in September 1975, as head of state. Pol Pot was named prime minister. Even before these political reforms were undertaken, the GRUNK government had undertaken a massive—and perhaps unprecedented—reorganization of the country's economic and social life. As an initial step, the new government ordered the near-total evacuation of Phnom Penh, where food, shelter, and medical resources had been stretched to the limit by the press of some 2.5 million refugees. The country was thereupon plunged into almost complete isolation, even from its neighbors in Vientiane and Hanoi. Currency was abolished, social relations completely overhauled, religion almost eradicated, education suspended, and families divided. From 2 million to 3 million people may have died from starvation, exhaustion, disease, or massacre under the Pol Pot (Cambodian Communist leader Saloth Sar) regime.

Meanwhile, tensions with Vietnam (traditional enemy of Cambodia until 1976 and again after 1989) were growing, and there were border clashes during 1977 and 1978. In December 1978, Vietnam invaded Cambodia with a force of more than 100,000 troops; by January 1979, they had installed a pro-Vietnamese government, the People's Republic of Kampuchea (PRK), headed by Heng Samrin, a former division commander in the GRUNK army. The PRK had to contend with resistance from the very beginning, and the Khmer Rouge rebels, who had fled to the jungles in the west and south, continued to harass the government despite Vietnamese counteroffensives. In order to improve its international standing, the Khmer Rouge began in 1981 to pursue a united-front strategy; Pol Pot, branded with the 1975–79 atrocities, reportedly withdrew into the background, and Khieu Samphan, supposedly the most moderate of the Khmer Rouge leaders, emerged as chief spokesman. In 1982, the Khmer

Rouge formed the Coalition Government of Democratic Kampuchea (CGDK), with two non-communist factions led by Prince Sihanouk and a former politician, Son Sann. The fighting during 1982–83 reflected a pattern of PRK and Vietnamese dry-season offensives alternating with an upsurge of guerrilla operations during the wet season. Militarily, the PRK and Vietnam appeared firmly in control at the end of 1987; diplomatically, however, the PRK had won recognition only from Vietnam, the former USSR, and their allies, with most nations joining the US and China in giving qualified support to the CGDK. In March 1986, an eight-point plan to settle the Cambodian conflict was issued by the leaders of the coalition.

Progress towards a peaceful settlement had an uneven course in 1988. Prince Sihanouk resigned, retracted his resignation, and resigned again as president of the Democratic Kampuchean Government-in-exile. Informal meetings in Indonesia, one in July shunned by Prince Sihanouk and the other in October ignored by the Khmer Rouge, made no progress on peace plans. However, a subsequent announcement supported the creation of an international peacekeeping force. A conciliatory statement made in August of 1988 indicated the Khmer Rouge was ready to reduce its armed forces to the level of the other Cambodian factions. Vietnam announced the repatriation of 50,000 troops from Cambodia in 1988 and the complete withdrawal of troops by late 1989, or early 1990. In January of 1989 Heng Samrin pledged that, if a political settlement could be achieved, all Vietnamese troops would be repatriated by September. Further encouraging gestures were made by Vietnam, China and Thailand: Thai and Vietnamese officials met in Hanoi; Vietnamese and Chinese ministers met in Beijing; and, Thailand abandoned its policy of isolating the Heng Samrin government and invited talks with them. In 1989 Prince Sihanouk resumed leadership of the Democratic Kampuchean Government-in-exile, later resigning from leadership of the National Front for an Independent, Neutral, Peaceful and Co-operative Cambodia (FUNCINPEC). In protest of Thailand's contact with the Heng Samrin government, Sihanouk refused to attend a second "informal meeting" in Jakarta. This meeting still failed to resolve two outstanding major issues: the make-up of an international force to oversee troop withdrawals and the composition of an interim government before elections. As a further sign of its commitment to change, in April 1989 an extraordinary session of Cambodia's National Assembly ratified amendments to the Constitution: the name of the country was changed to the State of Cambodia (SOC), a new national flag, emblem and anthem were introduced; Buddhism was reinstated as the state religion; and the death penalty abolished. Hun Sen met in Bangkok with the Thai Prime Minister who appealed for a cease-fire among the four Cambodian factions [The government of the Kampuchean People's Revolutionary Party (KPRP) installed by the Vietnamese (the Heng Samrin government), and three antigovernment gropus that comprised the umbrella organization, the national Government of Cambodia (NGC): FUNCINPEC, the Khmer Rouge, and the Khmer People's National Liberation Front (KPNLF)]; the Khmer Rouge rejected this suggestion. In July 1989 Hun Sen and Prince Sihanouk met in Paris prior to the Paris International Conference on Cambodia (PICC). In September 1989 Vietnam completed the timely withdrawal of its forces from Cambodia. Throughout 1988 and 1989 the Khmer Rouge forces continued to make military gains in Cambodia. The UN adopted a resolution supporting the formation of an interim government which included the Khmer Rouge, although past atrocities of the Khmer Rouge were alluded to indirectly.

In January 1990 the UN Security Council approved an Australian peace initiative—UN monitored cease-fire, the temporary assumption of executive powers by the UN secretary-general, formation of a national supreme council, and the holding of internationally supervised elections. Prince Sihanouk resigned as Supreme Commander of the High Council of National Defense and leader of the resistance coalition, but retained his position as President of Democratic Kampuchea. In February 1990 the Government-in-exile of Democratic Kampuchea was formally renamed by Sihanouk as the National Government of Cambodia and restored the traditional flag and anthem. This change distanced the coalition from association with the Khmer Rouge's former regime, Democratic Kampuchea (DK). (The DK had been named the Khmer Rouge by Sihanouk.) In a third meeting held in Jakarta in February the four Cambodian factions as well as representatives of Vietnam, Laos, ASEAN, France, and Australia met and agreed to the main principles of the UN plan. Prince Sihanouk resumed the presidency of the resistance coalition in May and in June he and Hun Sen signed a conditional cease-fire in Bangkok. In June a meeting in Tokyo was attended by representatives of all four Cambodian factions including Hun Sen and Prince Sihanouk. The Khmer Rouge, however, refused to sign a cease-fire agreement and proposed that each faction should have equal representation on a supreme national council. Prince Sihanouk offered support for the Khmer Rouge proposal, despite his previous agreement with Hun Sen; the discussions collapsed. In June and July reformist political allies of Hun Sen were dismissed or arrested for alleged attempts to establish a new party. Supporters of conservative Chea Sim, Chairman of the National Assembly, replaced them. Also in July the US withdrew its support for the National Government of Cambodia's occupation of Cambodia's seat at the UN and indicated willingness to provide humanitarian assistance for the Phnom Penh regime. The UN Security Council in late August endorsed a plan for a comprehensive settlement in Cambodia: UN supervision of an interim government, military arrangements for the transitional period, free elections, and guarantees for the future neutrality of Cambodia. In addition, a special representative of the UN secretary-general would oversee the proposed United Nations Transitional Authority in Cambodia (UNTAC). The UN would also assume control of government ministries. Both China and the former USSR subsequently pledged to cease providing supplies of military equipment to their respective allies, the Khmer Rouge and the Phnom Penh regime. In reversals of previous policy the US announced it would hold talks with the Phnom Penh regime, and the USSR declared that it would hold talks with Prince Sihanouk. The four Cambodian factions accepted the UN proposals at an "informal meeting" in Jakarta in September 1990. In addition, they agreed to the formation of the Supreme National Council (SNC), with six representatives each from the National Government of Cambodia and Phnom Penh regime. The SNC was to occupy the Cambodian seat at the UN General Assembly. At its first meeting in September the SNC failed to elect a chairman. The Khmer Rouge heightened military action in the northern provinces. Even as the final draft of the peace plan was prepared by the UN Security Council the Phnom Penh regime continued to oppose the principal provisions of the plan. In December all 12 members of the SNC attended another meeting of the PICC and all factions endorsed most components of the UN plan.

The SOC replaced three of its six SNC members in February 1991. In May a temporary cease-fire was agreed upon by the four factions in order to facilitate discussions. In June the Khmer Rouge refused to discuss SNC leadership issues, requiring the Phnom Penh regime's prior acceptance of the full terms of the UN peace plan, and the Khmer Rouge refused to comply with a proposed extension of the temporary cease-fire. Prince Sihanouk became an ordinary member of the SNC chairing a meeting in Thailand where all four factions resolved several issues: implementation of an indefinite cease-fire, pledges not to receive further foreign military aid, approval of a flag and anthem for the

SNC, and establishment of Phnom Penh as the headquarters for the SNC. Prince Sihanouk was elected to the chairmanship of the SNC and resigned as leader of the resistance coalition and as President of the National Government of Cambodia. His replacement in both positions was Son Sann. >From August through October the SNC worked out the details of the armed forces reduction and election procedures. Elections would be held to establish a constituent assembly comprised of 120 seats, which would subsequently become a legislative assembly. The electoral system would be proportional representation based on the 21 provinces. The constituent assembly would be empowered to adopt a new constitution. In October the SOC released hundreds of political prisoners including associates of Hun Sen arrested in 1990 for starting a political party. The Kampuchean (or Khmer) People's Revolutionary Party (KPRP), the communist party aligned with the Vietnamese communist movement, changed its name to the Cambodian People's Party (CPP), removed the hammer and sickle from the party emblem, and replaced Heng Samrin as Chairman of the Central Committee with the conservative Chea Sim. Reformist Hun Sen was elected Vice-Chairman of the CPP.

On 23 October 1991 what was hoped to be an end to thirteen years of war in Cambodia was achieved with the signing of the Comprehensive Political Settlement for Cambodia by the four Cambodian factions and 19 participating countries. The agreement called for the creation of a United Nations Transitional Authority in Cambodia (UNTAC) to carry out the peace-keeping operations which included the demobilization of 70% of each faction's army and enforcement of a ceasefire; verifying the withdrawal of foreign forces; administering the country until an election in 1993 by taking over certain portfolios; assuring that human rights were maintained; and the repatriation of 600,000 refugees and internally displaced people. In November a threat to the tenuous peace process occurred when a mob attacked Khmer Rouge leaders Khieu Samphan and Son Sen in a Phnom Penh villa. The SNC government's response was slow, and it was alleged that Hun Sen sanctioned this incident and that Vietnamese officials were involved in it. In December violent student demonstrations protesting against high level corruption and in support of human rights were suppressed by the armed forces and in later demonstrations several protestors were killed. Several high level government officials were dismissed based on the corruption charges.

In January 1992 the four factions approved the formation of political associations and the promotion of freedom of expression. However, on 22 January Tea Bun Long, minister for religious affairs and an outspoken critique of corruption was killed, and on 28 January Oung Phan, organizer of a new political party emphasizing anti-corruption was shot, but survived. These and other arrests, threats, and disappearances were viewed as intimidation by the secret police geared at undermining the peace process and free elections, and served to intimidate government critics. Yasushi Akashi, the Japanese UN Under Secretary-General for Disarmament Affairs, was appointed as the UN Special Representative to Cambodia in charge of UNTAC. The UN Security Council authorized mine clearing operations, the dispatch of a 22,000 member peace keeping force to establish UNTAC, at an estimated cost of $2 billion.

In September 1991 approximately 5% of the Cambodian population was in refugee camps along the Thai-Cambodian border, 340,000 refugees in border area camps, and another 190,000 refugees within Cambodia. The plan was to move refugees to transit camps in Thailand, then on to six reception centers in Cambodia, and finally to villages. In October the Khmer Rouge began to forcibly repatriate tens of thousands of civilians in UN refugee camps to areas under its control in Cambodia. International reaction prevented the Khmer Rouge

from forcibly repatriating inhabitants of the Khmer Rouge controlled camp, Site 8, just one of the eight refugee camps. The UNTAC refugee repatriation program began in March, in spite of cease-fire violations between the Khmer Rouge and the State of Cambodia forces. Throughout 1992 the Khmer Rouge denied free access to the zones it controlled, refused to comply with the disarmament phase, violated the cease-fire agreement, played upon long-standing racial/ethnic tensions by contending that Vietnamese soldiers were concealed in Cambodia, complained that the UN peacekeepers were not impartial to them, failed to attend meetings, and demanded the dismantling of the Phnom Penh regime as a precondition for the implementation of the peace accords, amongst other demands.

In May 1992 the Khmer People's National Liberation Front (KPNLF), the political and military party formed by Son Sann for the purpose of resisting the Vietnamese, was transformed into a political party called the Buddhist Liberal Democracy Party (BLDP) and still headed by Son Sann. FUNCINPEC also became a party, headed by Prince Ranariddh. At a Ministerial Conference on the Rehabilitation and Reconstruction of Cambodia held in Tokyo in June, the application of economic sanctions against the Khmer Rouge was considered and 33 donor nations and 12 non-governmental organizations attending the conference pledged $880 million to finance the peace-keeping operation. In August Akashi, the head of UNTAC, approved elections, and the registration of parties began. He also affirmed that the elections would proceed without the participation of the Khmer Rouge if it continued to refuse to co-operate. The demands of the Khmer Rouge were impossible to meet and were viewed as efforts to gain territory in order to increase its representation in the proposed national assembly, perhaps with as much as 35% of the population (a tactic laid down by Pol Pot in a 1988 speech). In September the Khmer Rouge made two new demands, the resignation of Akashi and for a redrawn border between Cambodian and Vietnam. This latter demand referred to territory allegedly annexed by Vietnam which would make the elections incomplete if not returned to Cambodia. The Khmer Rouge protested an electoral law drafted by UNTAC which enfranchised citizens aged more than 18 years whose parents or grandparents were born in Cambodia, effectively permitting Vietnamese immigrants to take part in the election.

October 1992 UNTAC began voter registration. The Khmer Rouge boycotted voter registration and escalated destruction of bridges and roads, effectively cutting off its territory in the northeast from the rest of the country. The UN Security Council set a November deadline for the Khmer Rouge's compliance with the terms of the peace accord, but eventually extended the deadline to 31 January 1993 as the Khmer Rouge's last chance to participate in the elections. The Security Council also approved an embargo on supplies of petroleum products to the Khmer Rouge and a ban on timber exports (a principal source of income for the Khmer Rouge). The Khmer Rouge announced the formation of the Cambodian National Unity Party to contest the elections on the day the UN resolution was adopted. Ethnic and racial tensions were increasing as the Khmer Rouge incited and escalated actions against the Vietnamese based on deep rooted Cambodian sentiments towards the Vietnamese. In December the KPNLF joined the Khmer Rouge in the ethnic cleansing of the "Vietnamese germs." Six members of the UN peace-keeping forces were seized and held for a few days by the Khmer Rouge in December 1992.

In January Prince Sihanouk ceased cooperation with UNTAC and suggested that a presidential election be held prior to the legislative election, but in February he reversed his position. Voter registration was completed in February; registered voters numbered 4.5 million and 20 political parties were registered. The election was set for May 23–25, 1993. The CPP intimidated its political rivals with attacks and stopped the gradual expansion of the Khmer Rouge into Phnom Penh government territory. In a dry season offensive the SOC attacked 3 of 4 of the Khmer Rouge's most important zones. In early 1993 the Khmer Rouge refused to disarm and attacked UN offices, cars, helicopters, and personnel. In addition to the Khmer Rouge's accusations of collusion between UNTAC and the SOC, the presence of the UN forces was a source of growing tension and dissatisfaction in Cambodia. Inflation, official corruption, and crime were increasing and UNTAC's presence and policies were blamed. The Khmer Rouge issued their own currency, thus emphasizing steps toward further partition. In a secret speech a year earlier, (6 February 1992), Pol Pot had set out an incremental approach by which the Khmer Rouge could gain popular strength which he considered more important than land: develop local autonomy; set up a money economy with their own banks which would hold the surplus earnings of farmers (projected to be 30% of earnings); distribute land, sell land in order to support the army, and continue to fight the "yuon" (savage), or Vietnamese. As the Khmer Rouge again refused to disarm and take part in the elections, it appeared to follow this program as it also increased attacks on Vietnamese fishermen and their families, killing 34 and injuring 29 in March at the floating village of Chong Kneas. Furthermore, citing its allegations that UNTAC colluded with the Vietnamese aggressors and rubber stamped the Vietnamese occupation, the Khmer Rouge refused to cooperate with the peace process. The UN goal was to have all refugees back in Cambodia by mid-April for elections. By 19 March 330,000 refugees were repatriated. A cash inducement had been added as incentive ($50/adults and $25 for children), and this rapidly accelerated the process. Roughly 87% had taken the cash option, nearly one–third going to Phnom Penh; 80-85% of the returnees chose areas under Phnom Penh government (Hun Sen) control, (about 85% of the country's) territory; 10% chose areas controlled by the Khmer People's National Liberation Front; 2% chose zones controlled by forces loyal to Prince Sihanouk; and 1% chose Khmer Rouge areas. In April the Khmer Rouge closed its office in Phnom Penh and slipped out of the city; it pledged to prevent the planned elections. A Japanese UN worker was killed and eventually 30 of the 460 volunteers for the election work resigned. In May the Khmer Rouge mounted its boldest offensives yet with targets defined for maximum political impact including major cities; they took briefly the Siem Reap airport. Under these pressures UNTAC abandoned 400 of its 1800 polling places.

The election took place May 23–28, 1993; four million Cambodians or 85% of those registered voted. FUNCINPEC won the election with 45% of the vote, or 58 of 120 seats in the constituent assembly; the CPP took 38% of the votes, or 51 seats in the assembly; the BLDP had over 3% of the votes, which gave them 10 seats; and, MOULINAKA (Movement for the Liberation of Kampuchea, a pro-Sihanouk group formed in 1979 by Kong Sileah, considered an offshoot of FUNCINPEC) took one seat. The constituent assembly had three months within which to draft a constitution and form a new government. To the CPP its political defeat was an unacceptable surprise and it demanded a revote and threatened riots; the Khmer Rouge denounced the CPP for contesting the election. The CPP's 51 assemblymen were technocrats and education officials (people who never wielded power within the party); this supported the belief that the CPP paid only lip service to constitutional arrangements as it maintained its grip on power. The CPP's two leaders, hardliner Chea Sim and reformer Hun Sen, were foci of an internal struggle. In a move towards cooperation FUNCINPEC leader Prince Norodom Ranariddh and CPP Primer Minister Hun Sen served as co-chairmen of the government, and control of the major ministries was divided, with FUNCINPEC getting the finance and foreign affairs portfolios while the CPP retained the

Information Ministry;. The CPP had 200,000 armed forces and 40,000 national police; FUNCINPEC's armed forces numbered 5,000. In August for the first time the three government factions, royalist FUNCINPEC, former Phnom Penh ruling regime CPP, and the BLDP, agreed to joint military operations. The Khmer Rouge would not be allowed to enter the political mainstream until it agreed to unconditionally join the unified armed forces and open up areas under its control, estimated to be 20% of Cambodia.

Cambodia's new constitution was adopted on 21 September 1993. Prince Norodom Sihanouk was crowned king, resuming the title first bestowed on him in 1941. In an attempt to restore central control of the economy to the government on December 28 the National Assembly passed a national budget and financial laws. These new laws stripped individuals of the power to collect taxes independently and by law all revenue would be channeled to the national treasury. Minister of Economics and Finance Sam Rainsy set about to root out official corruption and centralize Cambodia's budget. The entrenched businesses protested, but Rainsy received the backing of Sihanouk and international lending institutions. The two co-prime ministers, First Premier Norodom Ranariddh and Second Premier Hun Sen, asked King Sihanouk for sanction to fire Rainsy, but instead received a statement praising Rainsy, who was becoming a popular hero. King Sihanouk also urged the government to grant total freedom to the domestic and foreign press.

In early 1994 while the new government sought to consolidate and to gain control of the economy, military activity continued between government forces and the Khmer Rouge. Cambodian currency, the riel, was stabilized and tax revenues increased. International donors pledged an extra $773 million in aid. Corruption and a free press were major issues. King Sihanouk was seriously ill with cancer. The government captured Pailin, official headquarters of the Khmer Rouge on 19 March, but the Khmer Rouge retook it one month later. The dry season campaign by the government against the Khmer Rouge was a failure. Both sides were scheduled to resume peace negotiations on May 2–7. The Khmer Rouge looked to its military successes as leverage for a power sharing compromise with the government; Sihanouk sought to make deals that gave the Khmer Rouge some key posts in return for laying down its arms and opening areas under its control. One year after the elections major problems were security, corruption, and the economy. Security issues included demobilized unpaid soldiers turning to banditry, new mines being laid, Westerners being kidnapped, villagers fleeing the fighting, and closed schools. It was unsafe to farm. Corruption included national assembly members keeping their seats while serving in other branches of government; parties swelling the number of senior officers and civil servants as they vied to match each other in number and in rank; and the National Assembly voting themselves a raise equal to 100 times that of a typical soldier. The economy was undermined by continuing military activity, and privatization was stalled by lack of capital and skilled workers, and political instability.

Within the SOC there was significant difference of opinion on how to deal with the Khmer Rouge. FUNCINPEC's Ranariddh counted on diplomacy to isolate the Khmer Rouge while using development aid and investment for poverty reduction and infra-structure improvement. On the other hand, many of his counter-parts in Hun Sen's CPP sought a military solution to the Khmer Rouge problem. There was consensus, however, that Cambodia should look to Malaysia's experience with the Malayan Communist Party, which consisted of marginalizing the Malaysian communists. UNTAC's failure to disarm the Khmer Rouge was a burden for the new government. The Khmer Rouge was emerging with its prestige enhanced, territory expanded, and weaponry intact. Cambodia had been critical of the role Thailand played in supporting the Khmer Rouge, and renewed its appeals to Thai neutrality. The Khmer Rouge presence benefited Thailand by aiding in securing its border, and with lucrative trade in gems, timber, and armaments. The Khmer Rouge radio station was located inside Thai territory.

On 3 July 1994 there was a coup attempt. Less than 300 troops were involved and it was directed against FUNCINPEC, and possibly Hun Sen as well, by hard line figures at the highest levels of the CPP attempting to take over the government. After the coup attempt the National Assembly voted to outlaw the Khmer Rouge and seize its assets, a move that was partly directed at Thailand. The Khmer Rouge's response was to announce the formation of a parallel government, with its headquarters in northern Cambodia and Khieu Samphan as president.

In July of 1994, it was estimated that 55,000 Cambodians were again fleeing Khmer Rouge attacks in the western provinces. For the first time since the 1970s, the US provided military aid to Cambodia. The need to remove the land mines infesting the fields of Cambodia became a high priority. Mines may have inflicted more wounds than any other weapon, and Cambodia has the world's highest percentage of physically disabled persons. As foreign advisors sought to strengthen the country's human rights laws, ethnic considerations were raised. Cambodia's constitution fails to guarantee basic rights for racial groups other than ethnic Cambodians. The definition of Cambodians does include ethnic minority Chams and Chinese, but excludes ethnic Vietnamese.

The Khmer Rouge began to weaken in 1995, with mass defections of guerrilla fighters. The government remained worried by the hard core of dedicated Khmer Rouge rebels and their leaders, who remained at large in northern and western strongholds, though. Tensions continued within the fragile coalition government, with the CPP fighting off royalist political movements wherever they cropped up. There were also factional disputes within each of the coalition parties. Sam Rainsy's role as an opponent of foreign aid to Cambodia's "undemocratic" government earned him the condemnation of FUNCINPEC and the CPP. The Khmer National Party, formed by Sam Rainsy, was officially unrecognized. Internal rivalries essentially disbanded the government's third partner, the Buddhist Liberal Democratic Party.

Marginalization of the Khmer Rouge continued in 1996, as the group split between the leadership of ailing Pol Pot and a breakaway faction headed by Ieng Sary. In late 1996, Ieng Sary received a royal pardon, and his force became the object of courtship by CPP and FUNCINPEC. The government parties sought the votes and arms of Ieng Sary's supporters, plotting against each other in the process. This jockeying for position, accompanied by political violence and rumors of coups, continued into 1997.

In February 1997, FUNCINPEC's Ranariddh began an alliance with Sam Rainsy in strong opposition to Hun Sen's CPP. Hun Sen announced in March that he would seek to amend the constitution to prevent members of the royal family from involvement in politics, a direct hit at Ranariddh, Prince Sihanouk's son. Hints of negotiations between Ranariddh and the Khmer Rouge fueled Hun Sen's fears about his government "partner." A demonstration on 30 March, by Sam Rainsy's supporters, was attacked with hand grenades, which killed several protesters and wounded scores. The violence and tensions came to a head on July 2, with open fighting between forces loyal to FUNCINPEC and CPP. A brief coup d'etat set up Hun Sen as the sole power in charge. Ranariddh fled Cambodia and Hun Sen's forces killed many of Ranariddh's party leaders and supporters in the days immediately following the coup.

Hun Sen moved to establish CPP legitimacy, with the party winning a flawed national election in July 1998 with 41.4% of the vote to FUNCINPEC's 31.7%. Ranariddh was able to return

as an opposition leader, and he, along with Sam Rainsy, whose party gained 14.3% of the vote, condemned the election as rigged. Foreign aid, suspended due to the coup, resumed. Throughout 1998, the Khmer Rouge continued to disintegrate, as Pol Pot, the architect of their genocidal regime died on 15 April, and other leaders surrendered or were captured.

With the entire top echelon of living Khmer Rouge leaders in custody, Cambodian government concerns from 1999 through early 2000 centered on how to bring them to justice. Hun Sen's preference was for a series of trials conducted within Cambodia's own legal system, while the UN, fearing mere "show trials," called for an international tribunal. Compromises involving foreign judges participating in the Cambodian trials were proposed.

Finally at peace for the first time in decades, Cambodia was accepted as the tenth member of the Association of Southeast Asian Nations (ASEAN) in May 1998. The country's troubles did not vanish with the end of the Khmer Rouge, and Cambodia must deal with underdevelopment, violent crime, corruption, environmental degradation, an out of control AIDS epidemic, and slow economic recovery, as the new century begins.

13 GOVERNMENT

Cambodia was a constitutional monarchy from 6 May 1947 until 9 October 1970, when Marshal Lon Nol formally established the Khmer Republic. On 30 April 1972, a new constitution was passed by a national referendum. It provided for a directly elected president and a bicameral legislature consisting of an elective 126-member National Assembly and 40-member Senate. Upon the surrender of the Lon Nol government to insurgent forces on 17 April 1975, rule by the Royal Government of National Union of Kampuchea (Gouvernement Royal de l'Union Nationale de Kampuchea—GRUNK) was installed in Phnom Penh, with Prince Norodom Sihanouk as titular head of state. A new constitution, effective 5 January 1976, provided for a unicameral, 250-member People's Assembly, elected for a five-year term by universal suffrage of citizens over age 18. The PRK government, installed in January 1979, enacted a new constitution in June 1981. Under this constitution, an elected National Assembly was the supreme organ of state power; it was headed by a 7-member Council of State, which the Assembly elected from among its own members.

On 23 October 1991 the UN peace accord was signed by Cambodia's four factions. From May 23–28, 1993 a six day election, the first multiparty election in more than 20 years, was held to determine the 120 members of the National Assembly. FUNCINPEC took 45.5% of the votes amounting to 58 seats in the assembly; the Cambodian People's Party (CPP), formerly the Kampuchean People's Revolutionary Party (KPRP), received 38.2% of the votes equaling 51 assembly seats; and Buddhist Liberal Democratic Party (BLDP) had 3% of the votes giving them 10 seats; and Moulinaka (Movement for the Liberation of Kampuchea, a pro-Sihanouk group formed in 1979 by Kong Sileah, considered an offshoot of FUNCINPEC) took one seat. This newly elected National Assembly was authorized to draft a constitution. In June 1993 FUNCINPEC and the Cambodian People's Party agreed to joint control of the defense and interior ministries, while FUNCINPEC controlled the foreign and finance ministries; Hun Sen and Prince Ranariddh served as co-chairmen of the interim government. The National Assembly ratified a new constitution on 21 September 1993. The monarchy was re-established and commitments to liberal democracy, the rule of law, and women's rights were included. Prince Norodom Sihanouk ratified the constitution and again became King of Cambodia. The government of the State of Cambodia was an extremely fragile coalition after the elections, with enormous rivalries between Hun Sen's CPP, and Ranariddh's FUNCINPEC, as well as opposition from Sam Rainsy's unrecognized Khmer Nation Party.

Much of the tension centered on attempts to win over factions of the Khmer Rouge, which were "coming out of the cold" en masse, their fighters and votes up for grabs by the rival political parties. In July 1997 Hun Sen's forces defeated FUNCINPEC in a brief but violent coup d'etat. July 1998's national election legitimized Hun Sen's CPP dominance of the nation, but FUNCINPEC won a high percentage of seats as well, and Ranariddh became Speaker of the National Assembly.

14 POLITICAL PARTIES

Under Sihanouk, the People's Social Community Party (Sang Kam) was the most important political group. In the 1955, 1958, 1962, and 1966 elections, with a platform of nonalignment, economic aid, and development, it captured all seats in the National Assembly. Exiled in Beijing following his overthrow by Lon Nol in March 1970, Sihanouk allied himself with Cambodia's leftist insurgents under a group called the National United Front of Kampuchea (Front National Uni de Kampuchea—FNUK). Under the Khmer Republic government headed by Lon Nol, five political groups came to the fore. The Socio-Democratic Party (SDP), Lon Nol's own group, was quickly established as the most powerful political organization. Centrist opposition groups included the Republican Party and the Democratic Party. In the presidential elections held in June 1972, Lon Nol, the SDP's candidate, won by a relatively narrow margin of 55%.

With the victory of their forces in April 1975, leaders of the pro-communist FNUK became the dominant political power in Kampuchea. The leading element in FNUK was the Khmer Communist Party (KCP), founded in 1951 and now dominated by radicals Pol Pot (previously known as Saloth Sar) and Khieu Samphan. Khieu Samphan was named prime minister of the new regime, while Pol Pot remained party head. During the next few years the Pol Pot faction systematically purged all suspected pro-Vietnamese members of the party organization. In late 1978, opposition elements, headed by Heng Samrin, formed the Kampuchean National United Front for National Salvation (KNUFNS) in an effort to overthrow the Pol Pot regime. Following a Vietnamese invasion in December, Heng Samrin became the head of the pro-Vietnamese PRK government installed in January 1979. In 1981, the KNUFNS was renamed the Kampuchean United Front for National Construction and Defense, the primary mass organization in the PRK. Popularly known as the Khmer Rouge, the movement allied during the 1980s with two non-Communist factions, the Sihanoukists and Son Sann's KPNLF.

The Coalition Government of Democratic Kampuchea (CGDK), the tripartite, anti-Vietnamese resistance group formed in June 1982, changed is name to the National Government of Cambodia (NGC) in 1990. Autonomous coalition members were the Sihanoukist FUNCINPEC, the KPNLF, and the Khmer Rouge. Prince Sihanouk's main political organization, formed in 1981, was known as the National United Front for an Independent, Neutral, Peaceful, and Cooperative Cambodia, or its French acronym, FUNCINPEC; he resigned as its head in 1989. In 1992 the Front was registered as a political party for the1993 elections and Prince Norodom Ranariddh was elected president.

In 1992 the Khmer People's National Liberation Front (KPNLF), headed by Son Sann, formed the Buddhist Liberal Democratic Party (BLDP), also headed by Son Sann. The military wing of the KPNLF was the KPNLAF, the Khmer People's National Liberation Army formed under Son Sann in 1979. Although it boycotted the elections and attempted to undermine the peace process, the Khmer Rouge had also formed a party to contest the elections, the Cambodian National Unity Party, headed by Kieu Samphan and Son Sen.

The Kampuchean People's Revolutionary Party (KPRP), the Communist Party originally installed by Vietnam in 1979 as the People's Republic of Kampuchea (PRK), was also known as the Heng Samrin Government in the late 1980s. In 1991 the KPRP dropped the word "Revolutionary" from the party name, becoming the Khmer People's Party or Cambodian People's Party (CPP). Hun Sen remained Chairman of the Council of Ministers of the government of the State of Cambodia a position he had held since 1985. At an extraordinary party congress, October 17–18 1991, Chea Sim was elected party president, replacing Heng Samrin, and Hun Sen was elected party vice-president; these events signaled a shift from hardline communist ideology to a reformist position prior to the UN-supervised elections. Chea Sim remained president of the national assembly.

In the coalition government following the 1993 election, Hun Sen was made Second Premier, and FUNCINPEC's Ranariddh became First Premier. Hun Sen was able to push Ranariddh out of that position with 1997's brutal coup d'etat, and the CPP won enough seats in the 1998 election to establish Hun Sen as sole prime minister.

Perennial opposition leader and anti-corruption crusader Sam Rainsy transformed his unrecognized Khmer Nation Party into the eponymous Sam Rainsy Party, which won significant Assembly seats in the 1998 election. Sam Rainsy has repeatedly stooped to race-baiting directed against Cambodia's Vietnamese population during his political career. At the same time, he is an eloquent spokesman for increased democratization and openness in Cambodia, and a persistent anti-authoritarian thorn in Hun Sen's side. In early 2000, Sam Rainsy brought the question of royal succession into the open, which seems to provokes Hun Sen's fear that his arch rival, Prince Ranariddh of FUNCINPEC could possibly follow his aged, ailing father, Prince Sihanouk, to the throne of Cambodia's constitutional monarchy.

15 LOCAL GOVERNMENT

Under the Lon Nol government, Cambodia was divided into 20 provinces (khet), 7 sub-provinces (anoukhet), 147 districts (srok), and more than 1,200 townships (sangkat or khum) and villages (phum). Under the Pol Pot regime, administration was essentially decentralized into several major regions. Regions were divided into 41 districts, and the population as a whole was organized in massive rural communes. Under the PRK regime, the pre-1975 system of administration has been restored. Based on the People's Republic of Kampuchea's new constitution of June 1981 Local Assemblies, popularly elected by the respective localities—province, district, sub-district, ward—were instituted with the number of representatives fixed by law, and People's Revolutionary Committee's chosen by the respective assemblies. In 1987 Cambodia was divided into 18 provinces, two special municipalities (krong), and Phnom Penh and Kampong Saom, which were under direct central government control. The provinces were subdivided into about 122 districts, 1,324 communes, and 9,386 villages. Municipalities were subdivided into wards (sangkat). The same system of assemblies and committees remains in place. The new constitution of the State of Cambodia was adopted on 21 September 1993. People's Committees established in all provinces, municipalities, districts, communes, and wards were responsible for local administration, public security, and local order. Within this system provincial officials and the governor effectively controlled the armed forces and security services, tax collection, civil service—and through them 80% of the Cambodian population. The country's provinces remained under the sway of the Cambodian People's Party (CPP) and responded to the old political loyalties rather than the central authority of the State of Cambodia. To alter this system the National Assembly passed laws to secure central control of the economy. Effective 1 January 1994 a national budget and financial laws were enacted to try to ensure that all revenues came totally and directly to the national treasury. Provincial corruption and lawlessness remain severe problems, as communications and infrastructure are extremely underdeveloped within Cambodia and smuggling is rife.

16 JUDICIAL SYSTEM

The 1993 constitution of the Kingdom of Cambodia provides due process protections such as presumption of innocence and also guarantees an independent judiciary. Efforts are still being made to train judicial personnel to implement these principles, and to ensure basic human rights for Cambodians.

Prior to 1989, the constitution of 1976 provided for a supreme judicial tribunal whose members were to be appointed by a People's Assembly. Because of the civil and military turmoil, however, this system was never fully implemented.

The judicial system which was outlined in the constitution of 1989 provided for provincial court judges named by state officials. In practice, the judiciary was controlled by the government.

The current legal system consists of lower courts, an appeals court and a Supreme Court. There is also a military court system. The 1993 Constitution provides for a Constitutional Council, and a Supreme Council of Magistrates which appoints and disciplines judges. With low revenues and high crime rates plaguing Cambodia, the justice system is burdened by substandard police procedures. Many serious crimes, notably political killings, go unsolved. Police corruption and abusive imprisonment conditions remain endemic.

17 ARMED FORCES

At the time of the Lon Nol coup in April 1970, the government's armed forces consisted of only 37,000 personnel. By September 1970, the army had been expanded to nearly 200,000. With the fall of the Lon Nol government in April 1975, the Khmer Republic's armed forces were disbanded. The GRUNK government's People's National Liberation Armed Forces of Kampuchea may have numbered 80,000 personnel in 1975.

As of mid-1986, the armed forces of the PRK were estimated at about 35,000 men. Khmer Rouge guerrillas reportedly numbered 40,000, and guerrillas loyal to Prince Sihanouk or the KPNLF totaled 25,000.

The restored Cambodian government has a regular army of 99,000, an air force of 2,000, and a navy of 3,000, armed with Russian and Chinese equipment, some left by the departed Vietnamese army. Provincial and village militia comprise 10 to 20 thousand members per village; not all are armed. The Khmer People's Liberation Front has an estimated one to two thousand members. Defense expenditures in 1998 were $85.3 million or 2.4% of GDP. The figures given for Cambodia many not be deemed reliable.

18 INTERNATIONAL COOPERATION

Cambodia has been a member of the UN since 14 December 1955 and participates in ESCAP and all the nonregional specialized agencies. Cambodia is also a member of the Asian Development Bank, FAO, IBRD, ILO, IMF, and G-77, and is an applicant to the WTO.

China is the major ally of Cambodia, although it also has observer status with the ASEAN alliance.

19 ECONOMY

Cambodia's economy has been based traditionally on agriculture. About 85% of the cultivated area is devoted to the production of rice, while rubber trees account for a major part of the remainder. Prior to the war years, Cambodia's rice crop was usually ample enough to permit exports. The Tonle Sap is one of the major fishing reservoirs in Asia, and its products have played a key role in the Cambodian economy and diet. Cattle breeding is another important source of income. During the 1970–75 period, Cambodia's economy came to rely critically on US assistance, as the expansion of the war caused widespread damage and limited economic activity. The Pol Pot regime which came to power in April 1975 was determined to emphasize the growth of agriculture and restore national self-sufficiency. The entire population was mobilized in a mass labor campaign to improve agricultural production through massive irrigation projects in the countryside. The cities were virtually emptied, and industrial production drastically declined. Private ownership of land was disallowed, and landholdings were transferred to the state or to state-organized cooperatives. All industrial enterprises were similarly transferred to state ownership. Sparse food supplies were distributed through a system of government food rationing and other forms of allotment. When the PRK government took over in 1979, it was faced with a major challenge in restoring the national economy. The first problem was to end the threat of famine. A massive international campaign to feed the population took place during 1979–82. In the meantime, similar efforts were undertaken to stimulate the industrial sector and expand exports in order to obtain needed foreign exchange. By the mid-1980s, the economy had essentially returned to the level of the pre-1975 period, although the regime was still vitally dependent on foreign aid, chiefly from Viet Nam and the former USSR. In July 1986, the PRK issued an emergency appeal to international organizations for rice. The World Food Program provided some food aid, but most international organizations adopted a wait-and-see posture.

Rule by the Khmer Rouge, 20 years of civil war, economic isolation, and a centrally planned economy imposed heavy burdens on Cambodia. Serious damage to basic infrastructure, industrial and agricultural production, and human resources required massive rehabilitation and reconstruction. Reliable sources note that the infrastructure was so severely degraded that it had only 40–50% of prewar capacity. Market-oriented reforms have been introduced which dismantle the centrally-planned economy. Since 1989 Cambodia passed legislation to restore the right to own and inherit property, freed prices, passed a liberal foreign investment code, began to privatize state assets, and property, decontrolled the official exchange rate, and liberalized foreign trade. Reforms generated increased agricultural production and foreign investment. Phnom Penh and other urban areas received the greatest benefit from this economic activity. In the 1990s Cambodia remained predominantly agricultural with more than 80% of workers employed in agriculture. Inflation rose steadily, the price of domestic commodities increased at least 140% in 1990, but by only 15% in 1998. In 1991 Cambodia halted the free trade of gold as part of an effort to stabilize the value of the currency, the riel. Triple-digit inflation made currency worthless in 1992 and it was pulled from circulation. In 1994 the riel was stabilized at 2,400-2,600 Riel to the $1. In 1991–1993, the transition period from a command to a market-driven system, the presence of 22,000 UN personnel aided the Cambodian economy, although the growth was mainly urban, barely affecting rural areas. Western consumer goods such as motor vehicles, tinned food, alcohol, and cigarettes, were readily available in Phnom Penh and other cities. In 1990 GDP was negative, increasing to 13.5% in 1991 and estimated of 6–8% in 1992. On 4 January 1992 President Bush announced the lifting of the US trade embargo against Cambodia shortly after the signing of the Paris Peace Agreement on Cambodia in 1991. One outcome of the May 1993 elections was a division of government portfolios between the winning party, FUNCINPEC, and the surprised runner-up, the Cambodian People's Party (CPP). FUNCINPEC took over the financial and economic portfolios.

An aggressive campaign was mounted to restructure tax, investment, banking and currency laws. As part of the battle against official corruption some contracts signed by the previous government were revised or abrogated. The International Monetary Fund promised to finance Cambodia's balance-of-payments needs for four years. The government moved to strengthen currency and provide new banking legislation. Effective 1 January 1994 were Cambodia's national budget and Financial Structure Laws aimed at establishing central control of the economy. Cambodian labor is inexpensive and unskilled, and labor is plentiful, however, there is a severe shortage of educated and trained personnel. In addition, economic recovery still must overcome debilitating corruption and mismanagement, and the widening gap between the urban rich and the rural poor. Realization to take advantage of Cambodia's tourism potential awaits the maintenance of a sustained peace, as does development of Cambodia's significant natural resources– timber, rubber, gems, and oil and natural gas.

In 1998, the GDP real growth rate was nil. The Asian financial crisis, drought, civil violence, and political squabbles all worked against the country; negating the advances of the early 1990s. However, acceptance to ASEAN signaled the beginning of a brighter era. Cambodia also remains a key transshipment country for Golden Triangle heroin en route to the West, and is emerging as a major money-laundering center. It is a large producer of cannabis, and is plagued by high-level narcotics-related corruption.

20INCOME

The US Central Intelligence Agency (CIA) reports that in 1998 Cambodia's gross domestic product (GDP) was estimated at $7.8 billion. The per capita GDP was estimated at $700. The annual growth rate of GDP was estimated at 0%. The average inflation rate in 1998 was 15%. The CIA defines GDP as the value of all final goods and services produced within a nation in a given year and computed on the basis of purchasing power parity (PPP) rather than value as measured on the basis of the rate of exchange. It was estimated that agriculture accounted for 51% of GDP, industry 15%, and services 34%.

Private consumption includes expenditures of individuals, households, and non-governmental organizations. The richest 10% of the population accounted for approximately 34% of household consumption and the poorest 10% approximately 2.9%.

21LABOR

In 1998, the economically active population was estimated at six million, of which 52% were female, due in large part to the holocaust of the Khmer Rouge. As before the war, the vast majority of Cambodia's population (about three quarters) engages in farming, forestry, or fishing. From 1990–1998, the labor force size grew by 3.1% per year. In August 1992, a new labor law was passed which allowed the right for workers to form unions, prohibited forced or compulsory labor, set a minimum wage, and set the legal working age at 16 (unless employment is within a family enterprise). This law was updated and reinforced by a 1997 law, but enforcement remains uneven. As of 1999, there were 77 unions, organized into four labor federations. There were 85 strikes in the first ten months of 1999. By necessity, however, many youths under 16 engage in street trading, construction, and light manufacturing.

A 48 hour work week and minimum safety and health standards are provided by law. However, these rules are not effectively enforced. Separate minimum wages are established for each sector of the economy and average wages are so low that second jobs and subsistence agriculture are usually necessary.

22AGRICULTURE

Because of the lack of natural resources and the primitive industrial base in Cambodia, agriculture is the key sector in the economy. Arable land amounted to 3,700,000 hectares (9,142,000 acres) in 1997, or 21% of the total land area. In 1998, agriculture accounted for 51% of GDP and engaged 70.8% of the economically active population.

Rice provides the staple diet and prior to 1970 was Cambodia's major export, along with rubber. Production peaked at 3,200,000 tons in 1968; it began falling because of the expansion of the war and by 1974 had declined to 635,000 tons, but had risen back to 2,155,000 tons in 1990. Production in 1998 totaled 3,515,000 tons from 1,961,000 ha (4,846,000 acres).

Upon coming to power in April 1975, the Pol Pot regime embarked on a major rice production program, but the highest output achieved was only 1,800,000 tons in 1976 and in 1977; civil war, holocaust, and the Vietnamese invasion lowered the rice harvest in 1979 to 1 million tons. During the 1980s, rice production gradually increased, from about 1,564,000 tons in 1980/81 to an estimated 1,680,000 tons in 1985/86. During the mid–1980s the Khmer Rouge government attempted to stimulate production by delaying its plans for collectivization of the countryside. In 1989, the new government returned agricultural land to the tiller, which significantly boosted food production.

Rubber has traditionally been the second most important agricultural crop. However, rubber plantings, which covered 48,000 hectares (119,000 acres) in 1969, were almost completely destroyed by the end of 1971. Production, up to 51,100 tons in 1969, declined to virtually nil in 1971, recovering to about 16,000 tons in 1974. The Pol Pot and Khmer Rouge governments continued efforts to revive the rubber industry, the latter with aid from the former USSR and GDR. Recovery has been uneven and slow, however, and reached 40,000 tons in 1998. Other crops, with 1998 production levels, are: coconuts (58,000 tons), corn (62,000 tons), soybeans (59,000 tons), sweet potatoes (26,000 tons), dry beans (14,000 tons), cassava (39,000 tons), tobacco (11,000 tons), and peanuts (6,000 tons).

23ANIMAL HUSBANDRY

Livestock, raised primarily by private households, traditionally supplied an important supplement to the Cambodian diet. The Pol Pot regime placed heavy stress on cattle and poultry breeding, but thousands died during the chaotic years of the late 1970s. Estimated livestock levels in 1998 were cattle, 2,900,000 (as compared with 700,000 in 1979), and pigs, 2,200,000 (as compared with 100,000 in 1979). Cambodia also had 837709,000 head of buffalo, 12 million chickens, and 4 million ducks in 1998. In 1998, Cambodia produced an estimated 165,000 tons of meat, with pork accounting for 53%; poultry, 14% beef, 25%; and other meats, 8%.

24FISHING

Production of freshwater fish, the main protein element in the Cambodia diet, traditionally ranked next to rice and rubber in the national economy. About half of Cambodia's freshwater catch came from the Tonle Sap. Offshore fishing grounds present a potential resource not yet fully exploited.

Marine fishing developed significantly developed during the 1980s; the saltwater catch totaled 3,015 tons in 1982 and 30,066 tons in 1997. In 1997, inland fishing amounted to 84,534 tons, up from 72,640 tons in 1994.

25FORESTRY

About 56% of the country was forested in 1995. Forestry has been limited because of transportation difficulties and damage from war. The main products of the forest industry are timber, resins, wood oil, fuel, and charcoal. Production of roundwood, averaging about 4 million cu m in the late 1960s, fell off sharply during the 1970–75 war, but increased to over 7.9 million cu m in 1997. Export of roundwood was 260,000 cu m in that year (down from 506,000 cu m in 1996). Fuel wood production was 6.9 million cu m in 1997.

26 MINING

Cambodia's known mineral resources are limited. Iron deposits and traces of gold, coal, copper, and manganese have been reported in the Kampong Thum area. Substantial deposits of bauxite, discovered in the early 1960s north of Battambang and southeast of Phnom Penh, have yet to be worked. Potter's clay is common, and deposits of phosphates, used for fertilizer, exist in southern Kampot province, as well as near Phnom Sampou. Precious gems are mined in Pallin, near the Thai border. High quality cornflower-blue sapphires have been the most valued gemstone produced to date, and high quality rubies also have been found. Reliable estimates of mineral output are unavailable except for salt production, which totaled 40,000 tons in 1997. It is unlikely that exploitation of the nation's limited mineral resources can be undertaken, however, unless landmine removal continues.

27 ENERGY AND POWER

Wood is the most widely used fuel for transportation, industrial, and domestic purposes. Most of the few existing electric power plants must use imported diesel oil and natural gas; there is no national electricity grid. Several new power-generating facilities were installed in the mid-1960s, but total capacity was reduced by about one-third in the course of the war, reaching 41,000 kW by 1973/74; in that period, production stood at 150 million kWh. Total generating capacity was 35,000 kW in 1998, and production was 210 million kWh. Electricity consumption was 195 million kwh in 1996. A 1,000 kW hydroelectric plant is under construction at O Chum with the assistance of Vietnam.

Offshore oil was reportedly discovered by a French firm in August 1974 in the vicinity of the Wai Islands. In 1995 a total of 17 foreign companies submitted bids to explore for oil and gas both onshore and offshore; the offshore areas are near Sihanoukville on the Gulf of Thailand.

28 INDUSTRY

Industrial activity has traditionally centered on the processing of agricultural and forestry products and on the small-scale manufacture of consumer goods. Rice milling has been the main food-processing industry. Industrial expansion came to a virtual halt in 1970 with the outbreak of war. A few sectors (such as textiles and beverages) enjoyed a short wartime boom due to military orders, but losses in territory and transport disruptions had caused a rapid decline in activity by 1973. The Pol Pot government placed all industries under state control in 1975. In the course of the next four years, some 100 industries were abolished or destroyed. When the PRK took over in 1979, industrial plants began to reopen. By late 1985 there were a reported 60 factories in the state sector producing household goods, textiles, soft drinks, pharmaceutical products, and other light consumer goods. Most plants operate below capacity because of poor management and shortages of electricity, raw materials, and spare parts. There is little information on the small Cambodian private sector. The overall value of local and handicrafts industries in 1984 was estimated at about 50% of the output value in state industry.

Efforts at recovery continued in the early 1990s, but were hampered by dilapidated equipment and shortages which continued to affect industrial production, principally textiles and rubber production. For instance, following the cutback of assistance from the former Soviet Union in 1990, Cambodia's primitive industrial sector suffered from raw material shortages; three of six government-owned textile mills shut down because of shortages of cotton. When major Soviet oil supplies were depleted local companies imported oil, but the cash-strapped state companies suffered electricity brownouts daily. Major industries include rice milling, fishing, wood and timber products, rubber (largely abandoned since 1975), cement, and gem mining. Cambodia has significant mineral deposits of gold, silver, iron, copper, marble, limestone and phosphate, and a gem industry. Construction in urban areas boomed with the signing of the Paris peace accords in 1991. After Cambodia opened oil fields to foreign investors in February 1991, sixteen companies expressed interest in oil exploration. In January 1994 it was reported that five oil companies were conducting offshore oil and gas exploration.

In 1996, clothing industry exports more than doubled. Some 36 factories employed around 20,000 people. The average annual industrial growth rate for 1988 through 1998 was 8.5%, however growth slumped in 1997 and 1998 alone due to the Asian financial crisis, civil violence, drought, and political disruptions. Lack of basic infrastructure and the flight of foreign capital since 1997 have halted most industrial growth.

29 SCIENCE AND TECHNOLOGY

Since 1979, foreign technicians have been helping to revive the economy. Aside from a School of Medicine and Pharmacy, there is virtually no opportunity within Cambodia to pursue scientific training or research. In 1987–97, science and engineering students accounted for 13% of college and university enrollments.

30 DOMESTIC TRADE

Phnom Penh has traditionally been Cambodia's principal commercial center. Formerly, most wholesale and retail business was in the hands of French, Chinese, and Vietnamese. In April 1975, all private shops in the country were closed, and virtually all domestic trade fell under the control of the state. Official currency was abolished in favor of barter. Following the installation of the PRK, currency was reestablished, and some private trade resumed, with official encouragement. Since 1983, private shops have resumed operation in Phnom Penh. In 1986, the government began collecting license fees, rents, and utility fees from private businesses and substantially increased their taxes. In the early 1990s the Heng Samrin government fell behind in its payments to government troops and bureaucrats, printing more money to meet these obligations. Without revenue this vicious cycle peaked in triple-digit inflation by 1992, when the currency was rendered worthless and pulled from circulation. Market prices rose as the currency value dropped meaning poorer Cambodians could not afford their staple food, rice. The United Nations Transitional Authority in Cambodia (UNTAC) introduced imported rice and sold it at a fixed price in an effort to halt the inflationary spiral. With the presence of the UN peacekeeping force, Phnom Penh and other urban areas experienced an economic boom. Consumer goods and products increased as did construction, and rents rose. Despite the economic benefits of the UN presence, political disruptions and violence in 1997 and 1998 reversed economic growth. In Cambodia depressed economic output is supplemented by goods smuggled in from Thailand and Singapore.

31FOREIGN TRADE

Cambodia has traditionally been an exporter of primary products and an importer of finished goods. The country's normal trade patterns virtually disintegrated during the war as exports declined, and Cambodia was largely sustained by US-subsidized imports. Under the Pol Pot regime, foreign trade virtually ceased. According to Western estimates, total trade (excluding trade with China) was $3 million in exports and $22 million in imports in 1977. With the installation of the PRK government, foreign trade began to rise in volume. The value of total exports rose from an estimated $3–4 million in 1982 to approximately $10 million in 1985; imports in that year came to about $120 million. Almost all foreign trade has been with the former USSR and its allies, and most imports are in the form of grants. In 1985 Cambodia imported R100.2 million of goods from the USSR, compared to R18.8 million in 1984. Cambodia exported R14.9 million worth to the USSR in 1985, up from R3.9 million in 1984. The main import categories are food, vehicles, fuels, and raw materials. Cereal imports dropped from 223,000 tons in 1974 to 60,000 tons in 1985. Foreign trade is legally restricted to licensed private-sector firms and government agencies, although there is considerable smuggling between Cambodia and Thailand. In 1985, Cambodia and Viet Nam signed an agreement to double their mutual trade in 1986.

In 1986 major export trading partners with Cambodia were Vietnam, the former USSR, Eastern Europe, Japan, and India. For imports major trading partners were the same countries. Soviet Union and CMEA assistance to Cambodia ceased in 1991. The US trade embargo against Cambodia was lifted in January 1992 by President Bush. As of 1992 Cambodian exports were mostly agricultural, comprised of timber mainly and rubber. Logging is a ready source of badly needed export revenues for both the government and the other political factions. The United Nations Development Program (UNDP) estimated that the forest cover had fallen to as little as 40% of the land area by 1992. Cambodia's own forestry department figured that in 1969 forests covered 73% of the country's land area. The UNDP concluded that deforestation was a major threat to Cambodia's development.

In 1996, a textiles factory opened. In 1997, major export commodities were timber, garments rubber, soybeans, and sesame. Major import commodities were cigarettes, gold, construction materials, petroleum products, machinery, and motor vehicles.

Principal trading partners in 1998 (in millions of US dollars) were as follows:

COUNTRY	EXPORTS	IMPORTS	BALANCE
United States	293	39	254
Singapore	133	96	37
Thailand	77	169	-92
Germany	72	11	61
China (inc. Hong Kong)	69	226	-157
Vietnam	42	91	-49
Taiwan	21	126	-105
France	12	41	-29
Japan	8	71	-63
Malaysia	6	47	-41
Korea	1	68	-67

32BALANCE OF PAYMENTS

Cambodia's balance-of-payments position showed a deficit every year during the period 1954–74. Payments transactions with other countries virtually ceased under the Pol Pot regime, when China conducted Kampuchea's external financial dealings. Since 1979, Kampuchea continued to run a substantial trade deficit, much of which had been financed by grant aid and credits extended by the former USSR and Vietnam. The country holds virtually no foreign exchange reserves.

The government had hoped to reduce the current account deficit to around 9% of GDP by the year 2000. To do this, Cambodia needed to reform its military and civil service. As of 1998, the current account balance was 7.4% of GDP.

The US Central Intelligence Agency reports that in 1997 the purchasing power parity of Cambodia's exports was $736 million while imports totaled $1.1 billion resulting in a trade balance of -$364 million.

The International Monetary Fund (IMF) reports that in 1998 Cambodia had exports of goods totaling $705 million and imports totaling $1,097 million. The services credit totaled $110 million and debit $189 million. The following table summarizes Cambodia's balance of payments as reported by the IMF for 1998 in millions of US dollars.

Current Account		-224
Balance on goods	-391	
Balance on services	-80	
Balance on income	-50	
Current transfers	297	
Capital Account		62
Financial Account		123
Direct investment abroad	...	
Direct investment in Cambodia (Kampuchea)		121
Portfolio investment assets	...	
Portfolio investment liabilities	...	
Other investment assets	-42	
Other investment liabilities	44	
Net Errors and Omissions		55
Reserves and Related Items		-16

33BANKING AND SECURITIES

All banking institutions were nationalized by the Sihanouk government on 1 July 1964. The National Bank of Cambodia, a semi-autonomous government agency functioning as the sole currency authority, was charged with central banking responsibilities, including the control of credit. The decision by then Premier Lon Nol to permit foreign banks to do business in the country in early 1970 was a factor leading to his break with Prince Sihanouk and to the latter's overthrow in March 1970.

In April 1975, the Pol Pot government assumed control of the National Bank, and virtually all banking operations in Kampuchea were liquidated. The PRK government reintroduced a money economy, and by 1983 the National Bank of Cambodia and a Foreign Trade Bank had been established. In 1991 the government created a state commercial bank to take over the commercial banking operations of the national bank. Banks in Cambodia include the Cambodian Commercial Bank, Cambodian Farmers Bank, and the Cambodian Public Bank. There were at least 30 commercial banks operating in 2000, without any notable problems. There is no securities trading in Cambodia.

The riel resumed its fall against the dollar in January and February of 1997 after briefly strengthening in December 1996. It fell by a total of 25% before 1998.

34INSURANCE

All insurance companies were "Cambodianized" in 1960; 16 companies were in operation prior to 1975. Under the Pol Pot government, normal insurance operations were suspended. No current information is available concerning insurance in the PRK.

35PUBLIC FINANCE

All government budgets of the two decades preceding 1975 were marked by an excess of expenditures over domestic revenues; foreign aid and treasury reserves made up the difference. There probably was no domestic public finance system during 1975–78; any public funds came from China. During the 1980s, public expenditures were financed by the former USSR, either directly or through Vietnam.

From 1989–91, the public deficit nearly tripled as a result of falling revenue collection. As assistance from the Soviet bloc ceased after 1990, monetary expansion soared to cover the deficit. By the middle of 1992, with hyperinflation imminent, the government began a series of stabilization efforts to halt the fiscal deterioration. With only limited international aid, however, public expenditures for the necessary reconstruction and development of Cambodia have been limited.

The US Central Intelligence Agency (CIA) estimates that in 1995 Cambodia's central government took in revenues of approximately $261 million and had expenditures of $496 million. Overall, the government registered a deficit of approximately $235 million. External debt totaled $2.2 billion.

[36]TAXATION

Until 1975, indirect taxes were the most profitable source of domestic revenue, especially such monopoly excises as the sales tax on salt. Other indirect taxes included those on alcohol, tobacco, sugar, radios, and livestock. Taxes ceased to exist with the abolition of currency during the Pol Pot regime and were replaced by payments in-kind. In 1984, the PRK introduced an agricultural tax to soak up profits earned by private farmers. The tax reportedly amounted to about 10% of total output. In 1986, taxes on private business were increased, which forced some shopkeepers out of business. In 2000, there was a general corporate tax of 9%, except for in the fields of resource exploitation.

[37]CUSTOMS AND DUTIES

Since the 1960s and early 1970s, Cambodia has operated under a two-column tariff with minimum and general rates. Minimum rates apply to GATT contracting parties and other countries that have special agreements with Cambodia. Goods of other countries were subject to the general rates. Import duties range from 5–10% on essential goods, to 15–25% on consumer goods, and 35–100% on luxury items. Most duties are assessed ad valorem on c.i.f. value, and there are excise taxes of 50% for tobacco and 30% for alcohol. Lower rates are assessed for imports on countries with diplomatic relations with Cambodia. The United States resumed diplomatic ties with Cambodia in September 1993. Cambodia joined ASEAN in 1998.

[38]FOREIGN INVESTMENT

There was little private foreign capital in pre-1975 Cambodia. French capital in rubber plantations represented more than half of the total investment. Foreign investment was prohibited under the Pol Pot regime and was not resumed under its successor, the People's Republic of Kampuchea (PRK). As part of Cambodia's economic reforms the July 1989 Foreign Investment Law and the regulations implementing the law contained in the May 1991 sub-decree on foreign investment created a favorable foreign investment climate in Cambodia. From 1989 to 1991 there were over 200 investment applications, 20 being granted and 70 given tentative approval. Foreign investors from Thailand, Singapore, Taiwan, Hong Kong, France, and the US accounted for over half these applications; overseas Khmers accounted for 30%, and 10% were from local investors. By 1993 it was reported that final contracts had been signed for 45 of these 200 applications. The value of these proposals is small, $1–5 million, and the proposals are concentrated in services, tourism, and textiles. The most visible projects are the 380-room Cambodiana Hotel in Phnom Penh, a satellite earth station project which provides international direct dial service, and a cellular telephone system in Phnom Penh. The primary hindrance to foreign investment is the lack of infrastructure—roads are in dismal condition, bandits roam, power outages are common, and phone service is inadequate.

The new foreign investment law was adopted by the National Assembly on 4 August 1994. It guarantees that investors shall be treated in a non-discriminatory manner, except for land ownership; that the government shall not undertake a nationalization policy which adversely affects private properties of investors; that the government shall not impose price controls on the products or services of an investor who has received prior approval from the government; and that the government shall permit investors to purchase foreign currencies through the banking system and to remit abroad those currencies as payments for imports, repayments on loans, payments of royalties and management fees, profit remittances, and repatriation of capital.

[39]ECONOMIC DEVELOPMENT

Until 1975, Cambodian governments sought aid from public and private foreign sources and attempted to improve the climate for private foreign capital investment, although the volume of investment was small. Both Sihanouk and Lon Nol also increased local control of economic activities within the country. Aliens were prohibited from engaging in 18 professions or occupations, including those of rice merchant and shipping agent. The Sihanouk government promoted economic development through two five-year plans designed to improve the nation's light industrial sector and its educational and technological infrastructure. Progress was mixed. Strained economic conditions were a factor leading to the overthrow of Sihanouk in 1970. The outbreak of war following his fall brought almost all major production to a halt. The economic objectives of the 1975–79 Pol Pot regime were centered almost entirely on agriculture and the improvement of the irrigation network. Self-sufficiency was stressed, and foreign aid was almost nil except for an estimated $1 billion from China. When the PRK government took over, it inherited a shattered economy and a depleted population. The 1986–90 five-year plan stressed growth in the agricultural sector, the restoration of light industry (which faces shortages of raw materials and electrical supply), gradual socialist transformation of ownership, dependence upon the former USSR and its allies for foreign assistance, and an increase of economic cooperation with its Indochinese neighbors. The PRK signed a number of aid, trade, and cooperation agreements with the former USSR and other Eastern European countries and was receiving substantial technological aid from neighboring Vietnam. Development assistance from the CMEA bloc totaled an estimated $700 million between 1980 and 1984. The PRK moved slowly on its plan to transform the Cambodian economy to full socialist ownership, in recognition of the relatively low socialist awareness of the population. A small private manufacturing and commercial sector was recognized by the constitution in 1981, and farmers were being introduced to collectivization through the formation of low-level "solidarity groups" which combined socialist and private ownership. PRK plans were to advance more rapidly toward socialist transformation during the 1990s. However, since the mid-1980s the emphasis has been placed on private sector economic activities. Newly introduced market-oriented reforms dismantled the old central planning regime. However, the structural underpinnings of a capitalist systems—the legal, financial, and institutional—exist only in rudimentary form. Many of Cambodia's nationalized industries were allowed to operate with limited autonomy from the state planning system, but the lack of capital and management expertise, as well as institutionalized corruption and bureaucratic red tape have mired this recovery process. In 1991 at the Tokyo Conference on the Rehabilitation and Reconstruction of Cambodia, $880 million in assistance was pledged to Cambodia by donor countries and multilateral institutions. An additional $80 million in aid was pledged by the Asian Development Bank, and the World Bank planned a $75-million assistance program. Under Sam Rainsy, Minister of Finance and Economy, the national assembly passed a budget and new Financial Structure Laws effective 1 January 1994. The government's aim was to establish central control of the economy and at the same time strike out at corrupt practices. About 48% of the budget was made up of international assistance; there was no land or income taxes with tax revenues providing only 6% of GDP, and customs duties provided 54% of total revenue. Estimates were made that underground trade was equal to official trade and thus a further drain on state revenue. The new law required that all state revenues "be sent to the national treasury totally, directly, and immediately." Development in Cambodia is inextricably linked to the government's ability to maintain peace.

40 SOCIAL DEVELOPMENT

The Sihanouk and Lon Nol governments enacted limited social legislation regulating hours of work, wages, and workers' compensation. During the Pol Pot period, the social fabric of the country was severely damaged. Although installation of the PRK government brought an end to the wide-ranging trauma of 1975–79, overall social conditions in Cambodia remain among the worst in southeast Asia. Political violence crested in the period before the UN-sponsored elections of May 1993 and then fell sharply. Unstable conditions have also limited improvement in the standard of living, still one of the lowest in the region.

Cambodia's 1993 constitution provides equal rights for women in areas including work and marriage. Women have property rights equal to those of men, and have equal access to education and certain jobs. However, traditional views of the roles of women act to prevent women from reaching senior posts in government and business. In 1999, women held a total of 17 out of 183 parliamentary seats.

In 1993, widespread racial violence led many ethnic Vietnamese to flee the country. Some of these refugees have now returned to Cambodia, but they continue to face considerable official and social discrimination. Further instances of ethnic violence against Vietnamese were reported in 1998 and 1999.

Cambodia's human rights record includes a number of abuses, including extrajudicial killings, and other uses of excessive force by security forces. However, in 1999 the government made it easier to arrest and prosecute members of the police and the military through the repeal of civil service legislation.

41 HEALTH

Life expectancy in Cambodia in 1999 was 48 years, and the infant mortality rate was 108 per 1,000 live births in the same year. The general mortality rate was 16 per 1,000 in 1999. Dysentery, malaria, tuberculosis (in 1996, 145 reported cases per 100,000 people), trachoma, and yaws are widespread. The 1970–75 war and the 1975–79 upheaval exacerbated many of these problems. Malnutrition became widespread among the millions driven to Phnom Penh in the wake of the fighting and who were driven out of that city when the Khmer Rouge took over. Tens of thousands died from food shortages, and medical facilities and supplies. In 1994 and 1995, only 13% of the population had access to safe water, compared to 36% in 1991, and a mere 14% had adequate sanitation in 1991. Prior to 1975 there were 3 hospitals, with 7,500 beds (about 1 bed for every 893 persons). During 1979–81, 7 large hospitals and 3 pharmaceutical factories opened. In 1990, there were 2.2 hospital beds per 1,000 people. In 1994, there was 1 doctor per 9,505 people. In Cambodia, the HIV seroprevalence rate in 1997 was 2.4 per 100 adults. Eighty-

six new cases of AIDS were reported in 1996. Eighty percent of the urban population and only 50% of the rural population had access to health services between 1985 and 1995. Forty percent of children under 5 were malnourished between 1990 and 1995. The maternal death rate was high; nearly 900 women died in childbirth or pregnancy per 100,000 live births. Cambodia's 1999 birth rate was 41 per 1,000 people. The 1997 immunization rates for children up to 1 year old were tuberculosis, 82%; diphtheria, pertussis, and tetanus, 70%; polio, 70%; and measles, 68%.

42 HOUSING

Cambodia's housing traditionally compared favorably with that of other countries in Southeast Asia. The most common type of dwelling consists of one or more rooms raised on mangrove piles some 3 m (10 ft) above the ground; it is generally crowded. Many houses in the cities are larger and of better quality.

Mass emigration from the cities during 1975–76 resulted in many dwellings being left vacant, in contrast to the dire overcrowding that occurred in the last years of the war. In the countryside, meanwhile, the waves of new migrants placed inordinate pressures on existing facilities, with much of the transplanted population forced to reside in improvised shelters. By the early 1980s, this pattern had been reversed somewhat, and Phnom Penh was once again experiencing population growth. According to the latest available information for 1980–88, total dwellings numbered 1,474,000 with five people per dwelling.

43 EDUCATION

Under the Pol Pot regime, education was virtually abolished, as all children were sent to work in the fields; education was limited to political instruction. Most of the educated class had been killed by 1979. According to PRK sources, only 50 of 725 university instructors and 307 of 2,300 secondary-school teachers survived the Pol Pot era.

Currently, the educational system is being rebuilt and is recovering. Adult illiteracy was estimated at 34.7% (males, 20.3%; females, 46.6%) in 1993. The number of teachers at the primary school level increased from 30,316 in 1980 to 43,282 in 1998, while the number of students increased from 1,328,053 to 2,011772. At the secondary level, there were 19,135 teachers and 191,135 students in 1998. A total of 8,901 students were enrolled in post-secondary education, with 1,001 teachers, in the same year.

All schooling is public, and six years of primary education (ages 6–12) is compulsory. Following this, children may go through six years of secondary education. Most students continue their higher education at foreign universities.

44 LIBRARIES AND MUSEUMS

Library facilities before the war were limited largely to the National Library (33,000 volumes, mostly French) in Phnom Penh. Also in the capital are the libraries of the University of Phnom-Penh (10,000 volumes) and Buddhist Institute (40,000 volumes). There were smaller libraries at the higher schools. The Khmer National Museum won repute as an excellent repository of national art. The École Française de l'Extrême-Orient, which previously had charge of all archaeological research in the country, also had its own research library in Phnom Penh.

Cambodia, in effect, is a museum of the cultural achievements of the Khmer Empire. Surviving stone monuments, steles, temples, and statuary attest to a formidable and unique artistic heritage. Particularly imposing are the world-famous temple of Angkor Wat and the Bayon of Angkor Thom. In the chaotic years of the 1980s and early 1990s, there were many press reports of pillaging of these historic sites. The PRK government established museums in what it portrayed as GRUNK death camps, with exhibits on atrocities committed during 1975–79. The National Museum of Phnom-Penh (1917) has an extensive collection of Khmer art from the 5th through 13th centuries.

45 MEDIA

As of 1995, the telephone service was said to be barely adequate for government needs and almost non-existent for the general public. In all, there were over 7,000 telephones in use. TV-Kampuchea began color transmission in 1986. As of 1999, there were 7 AM and 3 FM radio stations and 1 government-owned television station. In 1997 there were 127 radios, 124 television sets, and 3 mobile phones per 1,000 population.

There are three daily newspapers, *Rasmei Kampuchea* (1999 circulation 15,000), and *The Cambodia Daily* (2,000), and the *Phnom Penh Post*. There are over 50 newspapers in all, including weeklies, bi-weeklies, and monthlies, mostly in the Khmer language. The official news agency is the Agence Khmer de Presse (AKP). Most newspapers are nominally independent, but many receive funding from political parties and the government. English language weeklies were launched in July 1997.

The Constitution provides for freedom of speech and press, but the government is said to sometimes limit the press in practice. The intimidation of journalists is said to be declining. The government, political forces and the military dominate the broadcast media.

Online access is extremely limited, with less than 1 Internet host per 1,000 population in 1998.

46 ORGANIZATIONS

In 1975, cooperative organization became a central tenet of the GRUNK government's social and economic reorganization policy. By 1976, cooperative ownership had become a countrywide phenomenon, playing a major role in both agriculture and industry. Virtually all other social and commercial organizations, including chambers of commerce, were disbanded by mid-1975.

47 TOURISM, TRAVEL, AND RECREATION

Until the encroachments of war in the late 1960s, Angkor Wat and other remains of the ancient Khmer Empire were the major attractions for visitors to Cambodia. Under the Pol Pot regime, tourism was nonexistent, and it was not substantially revived under the PRK. However, since the 1992 UN peace plan, tourism has rebounded, spurred by the opening of hundreds of new facilities and scores of new diplomatic missions. In 1997, 218,843 tourists visited Cambodia, and tourist receipts totaled $143 million. There are two government-run tourist agencies and a number of new private tour groups. Dozens of hotels have opened in the capital, which only had 400 rooms in 1989. As of 1997 there were 6,385 hotel rooms with 10,845 beds and an occupancy rate of 30%.

In 1999, the UN estimated the cost of staying in Phnom-Penh at $87 to $156, depending upon the choice of hotel. Travel outside the capital is significantly less expensive, with estimates as low as $37 per day.

48 FAMOUS CAMBODIANS

Foremost among ancient heroes were Fan Shihman, greatest ruler of the Funan Empire (150–550), and Jayavarman II and Jayavarman VII, monarchs of the Khmer Empire who ruled between the 10th and 13th centuries. Prince Norodom Sihanouk (b.1922), who resigned the kingship and won Kampuchea's independence from France, is the best-known living Cambodian. In exile in China during 1970–75, he founded the GRUNK government, from which he resigned in April 1976. In July 1982, he became president of the CGDK. Khieu Samphan (b.1931), a former Marxist publisher and leader of the insurgency in Kampuchea, was named chairman of the State Presidium in the GRUNK government in April 1976, replacing Sihanouk as chief of state. The de facto head of the GRUNK regime during 1975–79 was Pol Pot, the nom de guerre of Saloth Sar (1925–98), who presided over the drastic restructuring of Kampuchean society that left as many as 2–3 million dead in its wake. Heng Samrin (b.1934) became president of the Council of State of the PRK in 1979. Photographer Dith Pran (b. 1943), whose ordeal with the Khmer Rouge was portrayed in the film *The Killing Fields*, helped chronicle the atrocities of the Pol Pot regime.

49 DEPENDENCIES

Cambodia has no territories or colonies.

50 BIBLIOGRAPHY

Cady, John Frank. *The Roots of French Imperialism in Eastern Asia.* Ithaca, N.Y.: Cornell University Press, 1954.

Carney, Timothy (ed.). *Communist Party Power in Kampuchea: Documents and Discussion.* Ithaca, N.Y.: Cornell University Press, 1977.

Chandler, David P. *The Land and People of Cambodia.* New York: HarperCollins, 1991.

———. *The Tragedy of Cambodian History: Politics, War, and Revolution since 1945.* New Haven: Yale University Press, 1991.

———. *A History of Cambodia.* 2d ed. Boulder, Colo.: Westview Press, 1992.

———. *Facing the Cambodian Past: Selected Essays 1971–1994.* Bangkok: Silkworm Books, 1996.

Cole, Allan Burnett (ed.). *Conflict in Indochina and International Repercussions: A Documentary History, 1945–1955.* Ithaca, N.Y.: Cornell University Press, 1956.

Ebihara, May M, Carol A. Mortland, and Judy Ledgerwood (eds.) *Cambodian Culture since 1975: Homeland and Exile.* Ithaca: Cornell University Press, 1994.

Frings, Viviane. *The Failure of Agricultural Collectivization in the People's Republic of Kampuchea, 1979–1089.* Clayton, Victoria, Australia: Centre of Southeast Asian Studies, Monash University, 1993.

———. *Allied and Equal: The Kampuchean People's Revolutionary Party's Historiography and its Relations with Vietnam (1979–1991).* Clayton, Australia: Centre of Southeast Asian Studies, Monash University, 1994.

Genocide and Democracy in Cambodia: New Haven, Conn.: Yale University Southeast Asia Studies, 1993.

Kiernan, Ben. *How Pol Pot Came to Power.* London: Verso, 1985.

Peou, Sorpong. *Cambodia After the Cold War: The Search for Security Continues.* Clayton, Vic.: Centre of Southeast Asian Studies, Monash University, 1995.

Peou, Sorpong. *Conflict Neutralization in the Cambodia War: From Battlefield to Ballot-box.* Kuala Lumpur: Oxford University Press, 1997.

Picq, Laurence. *Beyond the Horizon: Five Years with the Khmer Rouge.* New York: St. Martin's, 1989.

Pradhan, Bhagwan B. *Super Powers and Non-alignment in Third World Conflicts: A Study of Kampuchea.* New Delhi: Deep & Deep Publication, 1990.

Pradhan, Prakash C. *Foreign Policy of Kampuchea.* Atlantic Highlands, N.J.: Humanities, 1983.

Propaganda, Politics, and Violence in Cambodia: Democratic Transition under United Nations Peace-keeping. Armond, N.Y.: M. E. Sharpe, 1996.

Ross, Russell R. (ed.). *Cambodia: A Country Study.* 3rd ed. Washington, D.C.: Library of Congress, 1990.

Shawcross, William. *Sideshow: Kissinger, Nixon, and the Destruction of Cambodia.* New York: Simon & Schuster, 1987.

Sihanouk, Norodom. *War and Hope: The Case for Cambodia.* New York: Pantheon, 1980.

Sutter, Robert G. *The Cambodian Crisis and U.S. Policy Dilemmas.* Boulder, Colo.: Westview Press, 1991.

Wang, Chien-wei. *Managing Arms in Peace Processes. Cambodia.* New York: United Nations, 1996.

Welaratna, Usha. *Beyond the Killing Fields: Voices of Nine Cambodian Survivors in America.* Stanford, Calif.: Stanford University Press, 1993.

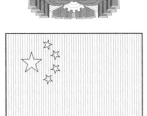

CHINA

People's Republic of China
Zhonghua Renmin Gongheguo

CAPITAL: Beijing (Peking).

FLAG: The flag is red with five gold stars in the upper left quadrant; one large star is near the hoist and four smaller ones are arranged in an arc to the right.

ANTHEM: *March of the Volunteers.*

MONETARY UNIT: The renminbi, or "people's money," denominated in yuan (Y), is equivalent to 10 jiao or 100 fen. There are coins of 1, 2, and 5 fen, 1, 2, and 5 jiao, and 1 yuan, and notes of 1, 2, and 5 fen, 1, 2, and 5 jiao, and 1, 2, 5, 10, 50, and 100 yuan. Y1 = $0.1210 ($1 = Y8.27) as of 31 March 2000.

WEIGHTS AND MEASURES: The metric system is the legal standard, but some Chinese units remain in common use.

HOLIDAYS: New Year's Day, 1 January; Spring Festival (Chinese New Year), from the 1st to the 3d day of the first moon of the lunar calendar, usually in February; International Women's Day, 8 March; May Day, 1 May; Army Day, 1 August; Teachers' Day, 9 September; and National Day, 1–2 October.

TIME: 8 pm = noon GMT.

¹LOCATION, SIZE, AND EXTENT

The People's Republic of China (PRC), the third-largest country in the world after the former USSR and Canada and the largest nation in Asia, claims an area of 9,596,960 sq km (3,705,406 sq mi), including Taiwan, which the PRC claims as a province; the major administrative divisions, excluding Taiwan and the offshore islands, cover 9,444,292 sq km (3,646,448 sq mi). Comparatively, the area occupied by China is slightly larger than the United States. The mainland has an extension of 4,845 km (3,011 mi) ENE–WSW and 3,350 km (2,082 mi) SSE–NNW. The mainland's 5,774 km (3,588 mi) coastline, extending from the mouth of the Yalu River in the northeast to the Gulf of Tonkin in the south, forms a great arc, with the Liaodong and Shandong peninsulas in the north protruding into the Yellow Sea and the Leizhou Peninsula in the south protruding into the South China Sea. China's territory includes several large islands, the most important of which is Hainan, off the south coast. Other islands include the reefs and islands of the South China Sea, extending as far as 4°N. These reefs and islands include Dongsha (Pratas), to which Taiwan has also laid claim. China's claims to the Xisha (Paracel) and Nansha (Spratly) archipelagoes are also in dispute. In 1986, the UK agreed to transfer Hong Kong to the PRC in 1997; in March 1987, the PRC and Portugal reached an agreement for the return of Macau to the PRC on 20 December 1999.

China is bordered on the N by Mongolia (Mongolian People's Republic–MPR) and the former USSR; on the NE by the Democratic People's Republic of Korea (DPRK); on the E by the Yellow and the East China seas; along the southern border are Hong Kong, Macau, the South China Sea, the Gulf of Tonkin, Vietnam, and Laos; on the SW by Burma, India, Bhutan, and Nepal; on the W by India, Jammu and Kashmir (disputed areas), Pakistan (west of the Karakoram Pass), and Afghanistan; and on the NW by the USSR. China's total boundary length is 36,644 km (22,769 mi). China's capital city, Beijing, is located in the northeastern part of the country.

²TOPOGRAPHY

China may be divided roughly into a lowland portion in the east, constituting about 20% of the total territory, and a larger section consisting of mountains and plateaus in the west. The principal lowlands are the Manchurian (Dongbei) Plain, drained by the Songhua (Sungari) River, a tributary of the Amur (Heilongjiang), and by the Liao River, which flows to the Yellow Sea; the North China Plain, traversed by the lower course of the Yellow (Huang he) River; the valley and delta of the Yangtze (Chang jiang) River; and the delta of the Pearl (Zhu) River surrounding Guangzhou (Canton). West of these lowlands, the country's topography rises to plateaus of 1,200–1,500 m (about 4,000–5,000 ft): the Shanxi and Shaanxi loess plateaus, in central China, and the Mongolian Plateau, in the north.

Beyond lie the high plateaus of Tibet, with an average elevation of 4,600 m (15,000 ft), and the great mountain ranges. The highest mountains are the Kunluns and the Himalayas. North of Tibet are two plateau basins of Central Asia, the Tarim and the Junggar, which are separated from each other by the Tian Mountains. The Chinese portion of the Tian range, which also extends into the former USSR, rises above 7,000 m (23,000 ft).

The great rivers of China flow eastward toward the Pacific. In the northeast, the Amur drains a great part of the Manchurian Basin as it winds along its 4,000 km (2,500 mi) course. Other northeastern rivers include the Liao, the Tumen, and the Yalu, the last two both rising in Mt. Paaktu, flowing respectively northeast and southwest, and forming the boundary between China and the DPRK. The main river of north China, and the second largest in the country, is the Yellow River. From Gansu it winds about 4,800 km (3,000 mi) eastward to Shandong Province, where it empties into Bo Hai (Gulf of Zhili, or Chihli). The valley of the Yellow River covers an area of 1,554,000 sq km (600,000 mi).

Central China is drained mainly by the Yangtze and its tributaries. The largest river in China, the Yangtze travels 6,300 km (3,915 mi) and drains 1,808,500 sq km (698,300 sq mi) of land. As China's only long river with no natural outlet, the Huai River, flowing between the Yangtze and the Yellow and roughly parallel to them, is subject to frequent flooding. To the southwest are the upper courses of the Mekong (Lancang) and Brahmaputra (Yarlung Zangbo) rivers.

Northern China is in a major earthquake zone; on 28 July 1976, a tremor measuring 8.2 on the Richter scale struck the city of Tangshan (145 km/90 mi east of Beijing), causing widespread devastation and the deaths of over 650,000 people.

³CLIMATE

Although most of China lies within the temperate zone, climate varies greatly with topography. Minimum winter temperatures range from –27°C (–17°F) in northern Manchuria to –1°C (30°F) in the North China Plain and southern Manchuria, 4°C (39°F) along the middle and lower valleys of the Yangtze, and 16°C (61°F) farther south. Although summer temperatures are more nearly uniform in southern and central China, with a July mean of about 27°C (81°F), northern China has a shorter hot period and the nights are much cooler.

Rain falls mostly in summer. Precipitation is heaviest in the south and southeast, with Guangzhou receiving more than 200 cm (80 in), and diminishes to about 60 cm (25 in) in north and northeast China, and to less than 10 cm (4 in) in the northwest. Approximately 31% of the total land area is classified as arid, 22% as semiarid, 15% as subhumid, and 32% as humid.

⁴FLORA AND FAUNA

Much of China's natural vegetation has been replaced or altered by thousands of years of human settlement, but isolated areas still support one of the world's richest and most varied collections of plants and animals. Nearly every major plant found in the tropical and temperate zones of the northern hemisphere can be found there. In all, more than 7,000 species of woody plants have been recorded, of which there are 2,800 timber trees and over 300 species of gymnosperms. The rare gingko tree, cathaya tree, and metasequoia, long extinct elsewhere, can still be found growing in China. Among flowering plants, 650 of the 800 known varieties of azalea occur in China, while 390 of the 450 known varieties of primrose and about 230 of the 400 known varieties of gentian are also found there. The tree peony, which originated in Shandong Province, appears in 400 varieties.

The richest and most extensive needle-leaf forests occur in the Greater Hinggan ling (Khingan) Mountains of the northeast, where stands of larch, Asian white birch, and Scotch pine flourish, and in the Lesser Hinggan ling (Khingan) Mountains, with stands of Korean pine and Dahurian larch. In the Sichuan (Szechuan) Basin, vegetation changes with altitude to embrace a variety of conifers at high levels, deciduous trees and cypresses at middle elevations, and bamboo in lower elevations. Farther south, in subtropical Fujian and Zhejiang provinces, broadleaf evergreen forests predominate. Forests give way to natural grasslands and scrub in drier western and northwestern areas, especially in the semiarid regions of Shanxi and Shaanxi, in the steppes of Inner Mongolia, and along the desert margins of the Tarim and Junggar basins.

China's most celebrated wild animal is the giant panda, a rare mammal now found in the wild only in remote areas of Sichuan, Gansu, and Shanxi provinces; as of 1994, just over 500 wild pandas were still in their natural state. Other fauna unique to China include the golden-haired monkey, found in remote parts of Shaanxi, Gansu, Sichuan, Guizhou, and Yunnan; the northeast China tiger, found in the Lesser Hinggan ling and Changbai mountains along the Korean border; the Chinese river dolphin and Chinese alligator, both found along the middle and lower Yangtze River; the rare David's deer and the white-lipped deer, the latter found mainly in Qinghai Province and Tibet; a rare kind of white bear found in Hubei Province; and the lancelet, an ancient species of fish representing a transitional stage between invertebrate and vertebrate development, now found only in Fujian Province. In addition, more than 1,000 species of birds have been recorded. Among the rarer kinds are the mandarin duck, the white-crowned long-tailed pheasant, golden pheasant, Derby's parakeet, yellow-backed sunbird, red-billed leiothrix, and red-crowned crane.

⁵ENVIRONMENT

It is estimated that China has lost one-fifth of its agricultural land since 1957 due to economic development and soil erosion. Since 1973, China has taken significant steps to rectify some of the environmental damage caused by rampant use of wood for fuel, uncontrolled industrial pollution, and extensive conversion of forests, pastures, and grasslands to grain production during the Cultural Revolution. Reforestation, including construction of shelter belts, has emphasized restoration of the erosion-prone loesslands in the middle reaches of the Yellow River. In 1979, the Standing Committee of the Fifth National People's Congress adopted an Environmental Protection Law and a Forestry Law. In 1989, China began a nationwide program called the Great Green Wall of China which began to accelerate the rate of reforestation. In 1994, China had 490,000 square miles of forest land.

Water supplies are limited—per capita consumption in China's cities is about 34 gallons a day, less than half that in many developing countries—and conservation, reclamation, and redistribution of water constitute major national priorities. Safe drinking water is unavailable to much of the population (as much as one-third, according to some estimates). By 1989, 436 of 532 rivers were polluted. In 1994, the World Health Organization reported that Chinese cities pollute water supplies more than those of any other country in the world. Legislation provides for the protection of aquatic resources, including water quality standards for farmland irrigation and fisheries. To alleviate water shortages in the heavily populated Beijing-Tranjin region, a massive water transfer project from the Yangtze River to the north by means of a dam, first proposed in the 1930s, has been seriously reconsidered in recent years. The project has aroused considerable controversy because hundreds of thousands of people would be uprooted, prime farmland flooded, many archaeological treasures submerged, and the ecology of the river area damaged.

The use of high-sulfur coal as a main energy source causes air pollution and contributes to acid rain. In the mid-1990s, China had the world's second highest level of industrial carbon dioxide emissions, totaling 2.67 billion metric tons per year, a per capita level of 2.27 metric tons per year. Investment in pollution-reducing technology is required of all industrial enterprises. Penalties are imposed for noncompliance, and incentives, in the form of tax reductions and higher allowable profits, are available for those enterprises that meet environmental standards. Beijing has implemented programs for controlling discharges of effluents, smoke and soot emissions, and noise pollution. Special success has been claimed for the recovery of oil from effluents of the Daqing oil field in Heilongjiang, refineries, and other oil-processing establishments; use of electrostatic precipitators and bag collectors by the cement and building industries; recovery of caustic soda and waste pulp from effluents of the pulp and paper industries; introduction of nonpolluting processes into the tanning and depilating of hides; use of nonmercuric batteries; recovery of fine ash from coal-burning power plants for use in the manufacture of bricks, tiles, cement, and road-surfacing materials; and development of new methodologies for recycling coal wastes and marine oil discharges.

To protect the nation's botanical and zoological resources, a program was adopted in 1980 to establish 300 new reserves, with a total area of 9.6 million ha (23.7 million acres). That goal was achieved by the end of 1985, one year ahead of schedule. The largest reserve, covering 800,000 ha (1,980,000 acres), is the Changbai Mountain Nature Reserve, in the northeast. Others

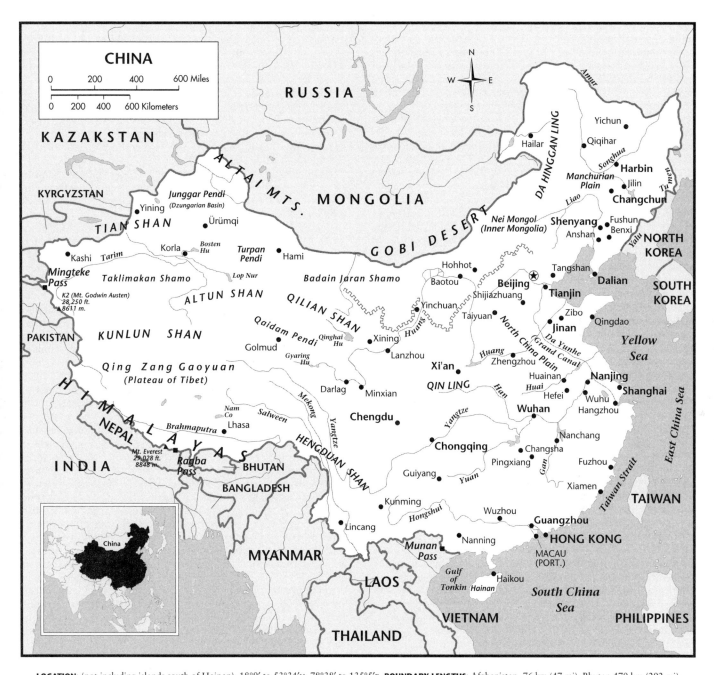

CHINA

0	200	400	600 Miles
0	200 400	600 Kilometers	

LOCATION: (not including islands south of Hainan): 18°9′ to 53°34′N; 78°38′ to 135°5′E. **BOUNDARY LENGTHS:** Afghanistan, 76 km (47 mi); Bhutan 470 km (292 mi); Myanmar 2,185 km (1,358 mi); India 3,380 km (2,100 mi); Kazakhstan 1,533 km (953 mi); North Korea 1,416 km (880 mi); Kyrgyzstan 858 km (533 mi); Laos, 423 km (263 mi); Mongolia 4,673 km (2,904 mi); Nepal, 1,236 km (768 mi); Pakistan, 523 km (325 mi); Russia (NE) 3,605 km (2,240 mi); Russia (NW) 40 km (25 mi); Tajikistan 414 km (257 mi); Vietnam, 1,281 km (796 mi); **TERRITORIAL SEA LIMIT:** 12 mi.

include the Wolong reserve in Sichuan Province, covering 200,000 ha (494,000 acres) and famous for its research on the giant panda; the Dinghu Mountain reserve in Guangdong Province, where a subtropical evergreen broadleaf monsoon forest that has remained virtually untouched for four centuries provides opportunities for ecological studies; and the Nangun River area in Yunnan Province, where the principal focus of protection is the tropical rain forest.

Endangered or extinct species in China include Elliot's pheasant, Cabot's tragopan, yarkand deer, Shansi sika deer, South China sika, North China sika, the Chinese alligator, the Amur leopard, Javan rhinoceros, Thailand brow-antlered deer, the white-lipped deer, Bactrian camel, the giant panda, and the Siberian white crane.

In total, 42 species of mammals out of 394 were endangered along with 86 species of birds and 343 plant species in the mid-1990s. Trade in endangered species has been reported.

⁶POPULATION

China is the most populous country in the world, accounting for 21% of the estimated world population. Until recently, it was also the only one to have attained the status of demographic billionaire; according to 2000 population statistics, India has also reached a one billion population. Government policy in the 1990s called for an extensive family planning program to limit population growth to no more than 1.7 billion by the year 2000. The population of China in 2000 was estimated at 1,256,167,701. However, the population estimates did not include Taiwan (23,325,000), or the territories of Hong Kong (7,438,000) and Macau (533,000) which recently reverted to Chinese control. An estimated 6.6% of the population is 65 years of age or older. The projected population for the year 2005 is 1,296,200,000, assuming a crude birthrate of 13 per 1,000 population and a death rate of 7, resulting in a natural rate of change of 0.6% for the period 2000–2005. The population rate of change between 1995 and 2000 was 0.9%. The population density in 1998 was 133 per sq km (344 per sq mi), but the distribution of the population throughout China is extremely uneven.

The overwhelming majority of the population is crowded onto 36% of the land, in eastern and southeastern China, while the remainder is thinly distributed throughout the west and north. In 1990 about 795 million Chinese lived in the 12 most densely populated provinces—Anhui, Guangdong, Guangxi, Hebei, Henan, Hubei, Hunan, Jiangsu, Liaoning, Shandong, Sichuan, and Zhejiang—and the three municipalities of Beijing, Shanghai, and Tianjin (Tientsin).

It was estimated that only 34% of the population lived in urban areas in 2000, up from 20% in 1980. The capital city, Beijing, had a 2000 population of 12,033,000. Government policy has sought to limit the growth of the large eastern cities, especially Beijing, Shanghai, and Tianjin, and to promote the growth of smaller cities away from the coast. In 1995, China had over 60 metropolitan areas with populations greater than 750,000. The largest urban centers in 2000 were Shanghai, 14,173,000; Beijing, 12,033,000; and Tianjin, 10,239,000. Other large metropolitan areas in 2000 included Shenyang, 5,681,000; Guangzhou, 5,162,000; Harbin, 5,475,000; Chengdu, 5,293,000; Wuhan, 4,750,000; Hangzhou, 6,389,000; Changchun, 5,566,000; Chongqing, 3,896,000; Jinan, 4,789,000; Qingdao, 4,376,000; Xi'an, 3,352,000; and Dalian, 3,153,000.

7 MIGRATION

The overseas migration of millions of Chinese reached its peak in the 1920s, when thousands of farmers and fishermen from the southeastern coastal provinces settled in other countries of Southeast Asia. Chinese constitute a majority in Singapore and Hong Kong, are an important ethnic group in Malaysia, and make up a significant minority in the Americas. In 1949, after the Communist victory, some two million civilians and 700,000 military personnel were evacuated to Taiwan.

Since in many places abroad the Chinese population has been growing at a rate faster than that of the local non-Chinese population, most countries have been trying to curtail the entrance of new Chinese immigrants. Emigration from China under the PRC government was once limited to refugees who reached Hong Kong, but is now denied only to a few political dissidents, if the state is reimbursed for postsecondary education costs. Immigration is for the most part limited to the return of overseas Chinese. At the end of 1999, the UNHCR reported 285,000 Vietnamese refugees in China, 91% of whom are of Chinese ancestry.

During the Cultural Revolution of the 1960s and 1970s, more than 60 million students, officials, peasant migrants, and unemployed were sent "down to the countryside" in a gigantic rustication movement. The goals of this program were to relocate industries and population away from vulnerable coastal areas, to provide human resources for agricultural production, to reclaim land in remote areas, to settle borderlands for economic and defense reasons, and, as has been the policy since the 1940s, to increase the proportion of Han Chinese in ethnic minority areas.

Another purpose of this migration policy was to relieve urban shortages of food, housing, and services, and to reduce future urban population growth by removing large numbers of those between 16 and 30 years of age. Most relocated youths eventually returned to the cities, however.

Efforts to stimulate "decentralized urbanization" have characterized government policy since the late 1970s. Decentralized urbanization and the related relocation of industries away from established centers has also been promoted as a way for China to absorb the increasing surplus labor of rural areas, estimated at 100 million for the year 2000.

As of 1997, there were 287,000 Indo-Chinese refugees, mostly living and working at government farms and factories in Southern China. Most of these refugees are from Vietnam, Laos, and Cambodia, as they expect to be granted Chinese citizenship and settle permanently. China also harbors a small number of refugees from Iran, Sri Lanka, Sudan, Somalia, Burundi, and Rwanda. Chinese authorities refuse to acknowledge the presence of refugees amongst the illegal North Korean (DPRK) population.

On 1 July 1997, the sovereignty of Hong Kong reverted back to China. As of 1999, 1,562 ex-CPA refugees and screened-out non-refugees still remained in the Hong Kong Special Administrative Region (SAR). In 1999, the net emigration rate for China was -0.41 migrants per 1,000 population.

8 ETHNIC GROUPS

According to the latest estimates, the largest ethnic group, accounting for 91.9% of the total population, is the Han. The Han form a majority in most of the settled east and south but remain a minority, despite continuing immigration in the west.

The remaining 8.1% of the population is comprised of minority groups. Because of their predominance in strategically sensitive border areas, they hold a political and economic importance disproportionate to their numbers. The largest minority, at last estimate was the Zhuang, a Buddhist people, related to the Thai, who are primarily concentrated in Guangxi, Yunnan, and Guangdong. Other large minorities were the Manchu, concentrated in Heilongjiang, Jilin, and Liaoning; the Hui, a Chinese-speaking Muslim people concentrated in Ningxia, Gansu, Henan, and Hebei; the Uygur, a Muslim Turkic people of Xinjiang; the Yi, formerly called Lolo, a Buddhist people related to the Tibetans and concentrated in Yunnan, Sichuan, and Guizhou; the Miao, in Guizhou, Hunan, Yunnan, and Guangxi; and the Tibetans, concentrated in Xizang (Tibet), Qinghai, and Sichuan. Other minority nationalities, with estimated populations of more than one million, included the Mongolians; Tujia; Buyi; Koreans; Dong; Yao; Bai; Hani; Li; and the Kazaks, concentrated in Xinjiang, Gansu, and Qinghai.

The ethnic minorities have been exempt from nationally imposed birth limits; the 1990 census recorded an increase in the minority population of 24.7 million, or 37.1%, since 1982, compared with an increase of 10.9% among the majority Han during the same period. Two or more children per minority couple are generally allowed instead of the one-child norm promoted among the Han.

9 LANGUAGES

Chinese, a branch of the Sino-Tibetan linguistic family, is a monosyllabic tone language written by means of characters representing complete words. The Chinese script is not phonetic and remains constant throughout China, but the spoken language has regional phonetic differences. Spoken Chinese falls into two major groups, separated roughly by a northeast-southwest line running from the mouth of the Yangtze River to the border of Vietnam. North and west of this line are the so-called Mandarin dialects, based on the Beijing dialect and known as *putonghua* ("common language"). The most important dialect south of the linguistic divide is that of Shanghai, the Wu dialect spoken in the Yangtze River Delta. Hakka and Hokkien are dialects of the southeastern coastal province. Cantonese, the Yue dialect spoken in southern China, is the language of the majority of Chinese emigrants. Others include the Minbei or Fuzhou dialect, the Xiang, and Gan dialects. Mandarin Chinese was adopted as the official language of China in 1955.

To communicate in written Chinese, thousands of Chinese characters must be memorized. Since the establishment of the PRC in 1949, reform of the written language has been a major priority. A simplified system of writing, reducing the number of strokes per character, has been adopted, and the language restructured so that anyone familiar with the basic 2,000–3,000 characters is functionally literate (defined as being able to read a newspaper).

A number of systems have been developed to transcribe Chinese characters into the Latin alphabet. The principal romanization scheme was the Wade-Giles system until 1979, when the PRC government adopted Pinyin, a system under development in China since the mid-1950s. Inside China, Pinyin is used in the schools to facilitate the learning of Chinese characters, in minority areas where other languages are spoken, and on commercial and street signs. Pinyin has replaced the Wade-Giles system in all of China's English-language publications and for the spelling of place names. In general, pronunciation of Pinyin follows standard American English, except that among initial sounds, the sound of *q* is like the sound of *ch* as in *chart,* the sound of *x* like the sound of *sh* as in *ship,* and the sound of *zh* like the sound of *j* as in *judge,* and among final sounds, the sound of *e* is like the sound of *oo* as in *look,* the sound of *eng* like the sound of *ung* as in *lung,* the sound of *ui* like the sound of *ay* as in *way,* and the sound of *uai* like the sound of *wi* as in *wide.*

Of the 55 recognized minority peoples in China, only Hui and Manchus use Chinese as an everyday language. More then 20 minority nationalities have their own forms of writing for their own languages. Minority languages are used in all state institutions in minority areas and in all newspapers and books published there.

10RELIGIONS

Three faiths—Confucianism, Buddhism, and Taoism—have long been established in China. The religious practice of the average Chinese traditionally has been an eclectic mixture of all three. Confucianism has no religious organization but consists of a code of ethics and philosophy; filial piety, benevolence, fidelity, and justice are among its principal virtues. Taoism, a native Chinese religion that evolved from a philosophy probably founded in the 6th century BC by Lao-tzu (Laozi), and Buddhism, imported from India during the Han dynasty, both have elaborate rituals. Tradition-minded Chinese base their philosophy of life on Confucianism, but such old habits of thought came under strong attack during the Cultural Revolution.

Suppression of religion and the introduction of programs of antireligious indoctrination began in 1949 and intensified, with the closure of temples, shrines, mosques, and churches, from the mid-1960s through the mid-1970s. Overt antireligious activity eased in 1976, and the government reactivated its Bureau of Religious Affairs. The Constitution of 1982 provides for freedom of belief and worship. According to 1997 estimates, Buddhists make up the largest body of organized religious believers, with more than 100 million followers, most of whom are from the dominant Han ethnic group.

Islam claims an estimated 18 million followers, or 2–3% of the population, nearly all are members of the ethnic minority nationalities; most belong to the Sunni branch, but the Tajiks are Shi'is. The tiny Jewish minority has virtually disappeared through emigration and assimilation. It is estimated that when the PRC was founded in 1949 there were up to three million Roman Catholics and 700,000 Protestants in China. As late as 1981, only small numbers of Christians were attending the approximately 80 Protestant and 40 Roman Catholic churches open in urban areas. By the mid-1990s, however, interest in religion was exploding and the number of Christians was increasing rapidly. Conservative estimates in 1998 put the number of Protestants at 10 to 15 million and Catholics at four million. The increase in the number of Christians has resulted in an increase in the demand for Bibles. In 1998 the government approved the printing of more than three million Bibles, and there are currently more than 18 million Bibles in print.

11TRANSPORTATION

Railways, roads, and inland waterways all play an important role in China's transportation system, which has undergone major growth since the 1940s. China's rail network forms the backbone of the transportation system. Chinese railways increased in length from 21,989 km (13,663 mi) in 1949 to 68,000 km (42,255 mi) in 1999, of which about 12,000 km (7,457 mi) were electrified. In the rush to expand rail facilities during the "Great Leap Forward," the Chinese laid rails totaling 3,500 km (2,175 mi) in 1958; some 4,600 km (2,900 mi) were added in 1959. The construction pace slowed somewhat in the 1960s, but many major projects were completed in the 1970s, including double-tracking of major lines in the east; the electrification of lines in the west, including the 671 km (417 mi) Baoji-Chengdu link; and the addition of several new trunklines and spurs, many providing service to the country's more remote areas. While the total rail network is more than twice what it was in 1949, the movement of freight is more than 25 times that of 1949. Increased freight volumes have been achieved by loading freight cars up to 20% over their rated capacity and by containerization. Shortages of freight and tank cars continue to delay deliveries of coal and other industrial raw materials to their destinations. In 1991, China invested $8 billion for infrastructure improvements, including the upgrade of 309 km (192 mi) of double-track railway and the electrification of 849 km (528 mi) of track.

Road transportation has become increasingly important. Motor roads grew from about 400,000 km (249,000 mi) in 1958 to 550,000 km (342,000 mi) in 1964 and to 1.21 million km (751,894 mi) by 1998. About 271,300 km (168,586 mi) were paved, including 24,474 km (15,208 mi) of motorways. Major roads completed in the 1970s included the 2,413 km (1,499 mi) Sichuan-Tibet Highway, the 2,100 km (1,305 mi) Qinghai-Tibet Highway, and the 1,455 km (904 mi) Xinjiang-Tibet Highway. Between 1981 and 1985, 50,000 km (31,000 mi) of highways and more than 15,000 bridges were built. By 1995, an estimated 4,179,000 passenger automobiles used the highway system, up from 50,000 in 1949. In addition, there were some 6,221,000 commercial vehicles operating in the same year. Bicycles are the chief mode of transport in large cities; in Beijing, there are an estimated seven million bicycles, accounting for 57% of the city's road traffic.

Navigable inland waterways reached a peak of 161,900 km (100,600 mi) in 1962 and decreased to 109,800 km (68,230 mi) in 1997. About 25% of the waterways are navigable by modern vessels; wooden junks are used on the remainder. The principal inland waterway is the Yangtze River; much work was done in the early 1980s to dredge and deepen the river, to improve navigational markers and channels, and to eliminate the treacherous rapids of the Three Gorges section east of Yibin. Steamboats can now travel inland throughout the year from Shanghai, at the river's mouth, upstream as far as Yibin; 10,000-ton ocean-going vessels can travel inland as far as Wuhan in the high-water season and Nanjing in the low-water season. Major ports on the river include Chongqing, the principal transportation hub for the southwest; Wuhan, its freight dominated by shipments of coal, iron, and steel; Wuhu, a rice-exporting center; Yuxikou, across the river from Wuhu and the chief outlet for the region's coal fields; Nanjing; and Shanghai. The Pearl River is navigable via a tributary as far as Nanning. The ancient Grand Canal, rendered impassable by deposits of silt for more than 100 years, has been dredged and rebuilt; it is navigable for about 1,100 km (680 mi) in season and 400 km (250 mi) year-round.

China's merchant fleet expanded from 402,000 GRT in 1960 to over 10,278,000 GRT in 1986, and to 16,828,349 GRT in 1998. China's 1,759 merchant ships of 1,000 GRT or over can accommodate most of the country's foreign trade; the balance is divided among ships leased from Hong Kong owners and from other foreign sources. The principal ports are Tianjin, the port for Beijing, which consists of the three harbors of Neigang, Tanggu, and Xingang; Shanghai, with docks along the Huangpu River channel; Lüda, the chief outlet for the northeast and the Daqing oil field; and Huangpu, the port for Guangzhou, on the right bank of the Pearl River. Other important ports include Qinhuangdao; Qingdao; Ningbo, the port for Hangzhou; Fuzhou; Xiamen; and Zhanjiang.

The Civil Aviation Administration of China (CAAC) operates all domestic and international air services. Operations have grown significantly with the purchase, since the 1970s, of jet aircraft from the US, UK, and other Western sources. In 1996 there were 206 airports, of which 192 had paved runways. Principal airports include Capital at Beijing, Shuangliu at Chengdu, Hongqiao at Shanghai, Baiyun at Guangzhou, Wujiaba at Kunming, and Gaoqi at Xiamen. From Beijing there are scheduled daily flights to Shanghai, Guangzhou, Kunming, Chengdu, Shenyang, Changchun, Changsha, Wuhan, Zengzhou, and Harbin. The total scheduled international and domestic service performed in 1997 included 72,964 million passenger-km (45,340 million passenger-mi) and 2,084 million freight ton-km (1,295 million freight ton-mi), as well as 52,277,000 passengers carried.

12HISTORY

Fossils attest to hominid habitation in China more than 500,000 years ago, and Paleolithic cultures appeared in the southwest by 30,000 BC. Neolithic peoples appeared before 7000 BC; by 3000 BC there were millet-growing settlements along the Yellow River. The original home of the Chinese (Han) people is probably the area of the Wei, Luo (Lo), and middle Yellow rivers. According to tradition, the Xia (Hsia) dynasty (c.2200–c.1766 BC) constituted the first Chinese state. Its successor, the Shang, or Yin, dynasty (c.1766–c.1122 BC), which ruled over the valley of the Yellow River, left written records cast in bronze or inscribed on tortoiseshell and bone. The Shang was probably conquered by the Western Zhou (Chou) dynasty (c.1122–771 BC), which ruled a prosperous feudal agricultural society. Fleeing foreign attack in 771 BC, the Western Zhou abandoned its capital near the site of Xi'an and established a new capital farther east at Luoyang (Loyang). The new state, known as the Eastern Zhou dynasty (771–256 BC), produced the great Chinese philosophers including Confucius (K'ung Fu-tzu or Kong Fuzi) and the semi-historical figure, Lao Tzu (Lao Zi). Between 475 and 221 BC, the Qin (Ch'in) dynasty (221–207 BC) gradually emerged from among warring, regional states to unify China. Shi Huangdi (Shih Huang Ti, r.221–210 BC), the first Qin emperor (the outer edges of whose tomb, opened in the 1970s, were discovered to contain stunningly lifelike terra-cotta armies), ended the feudal states and organized China into a system of prefectures and counties under central control. For defense against nomadic proto-Mongolian tribes, Shi Huangdi connected walls of the feudal states to form what was later to become known as the Great Wall. By this time,

the Yellow River had an irrigation system, and cultivation had begun in the Yangtze Valley; at the end of Shi Huangdi's reign, China probably had close to 40 million people. During the period of the Han dynasties (206 BC–AD 8, AD 25–220), China expanded westward, nomadic tribes from the Mongolian plateau were repelled, and contacts were made with Central Asia, the West, and even Rome. The Han saw the invention of paper. Under the later Han, Buddhism was introduced into China. After the Han period, the Three Kingdoms (Wei, Shu, and Wu) contended for power, and nomadic tribes from the north and west raided northern China. From the 4th century AD on, a series of northern dynasties was set up by the invaders, while several southern dynasties succeeded one another in the Yangtze Valley, with their capital at Nanjing (Nanking). Buddhism flourished during this period, and the arts and sciences were developed. The empire was reunited by the Sui (589–618) dynasty, which built the Grand Canal, linking the militarily strategic north with the economic wealth of the south and laying the basis for the Tang (T'ang, 618–907) dynasty.

Under the early Tang, especially under Emperor Taizong (T'ai-tsung, r.627–49), China became powerful. The bureaucratic system, begun by the Han, was further developed, including the regular use of an examination system to recruit officials on the basis of merit. Handicrafts and commerce flourished, a system of roads radiated from the capital (at the site of Xi'an), successful wars were fought in Central Asia, and China became the cultural and economic center of Asia. Poetry and painting flourished, particularly under Emperor Xuan-Zong (Hsüan-tsung, r.712–56). Civil wars and rebellion in the late Tang led to a period of partition under the Five Dynasties (r.907–60) which was followed by the Northern and Southern Song (Sung) dynasties (960–1127, 1127–1279), distinguished for literature, philosophy, the invention of movable type, the use of gunpowder in weapons, and the improvement of the magnetic compass. However, Mongol and Tatar tribes in the north forced the Song to abandon its capital at Kaifeng in 1126 and move it to Hangzhou (Hangchow). In 1279, Kublai Khan (r.1279–94) led the Mongols to bring all of China under their control and became the first ruler of the Mongols' Yuan dynasty (1279–1368). The Mongols encouraged commerce and increased the use of paper money. The Grand Canal was reconstructed, and a system of relay stations ensured safe travel. Many European missionaries and merchants, notably Marco Polo, came to the Mongol court.

After a long period of peasant rebellion, Mongol rule was succeeded by the native Chinese Ming dynasty (1368–1644). The famous Ming admiral, Zheng He (Cheng Ho, 1371–1433) led seven naval expeditions into the South China Sea and the Indian Ocean between 1405 and 1433, reaching as far as the east coast of Africa. The Portuguese reached China in 1516, the Spanish in 1557, the Dutch in 1606, and the English in 1637. The Ming dynasty was overthrown by the Manchus, invaders from the northeast, who established the last imperial dynasty, the Qing (Ch'ing or Manchu, 1644–1911). The first century and a half of Manchu rule was a period of stability and expansion of power, with outstanding reigns by Kang xi (K'ang-hsi, 1662–1722) and Qian long (Ch'ien-lung, 1736–96). Although the Manchus ruled as conquerors, they adopted indigenous Chinese culture, administrative machinery, and laws. Under Manchu rule, Chinese territories included Manchuria, Mongolia, Tibet, Taiwan, and the Central Asian regions of Turkestan. The population of over 300 million by 1750 grew to over 400 million a century later.

By the close of the 18th century, only one port, Guangzhou (Canton), was open to merchants from abroad, and trade was greatly restricted. Demands by the British for increased trade, coupled with Chinese prohibition of opium imports from British India, led to the Opium War (1839–42), which China lost. By the Treaty of Nanjing (1842), the ports of Guangzhou, Xiamen

(Amoy), Fuzhou (Foochow), Ningbo, and Shanghai were opened, and Hong Kong Island was ceded to Britain. The Taiping Rebellion (1850–64), nearly overthrew the Manchus and cost 30 million lives. A second war (1856–60) with Britain, joined by France, resulted in the opening of Tianjin (Tientsin) to foreign trade. The West's interest then turned from trade to territory. Russia acquired its Far Eastern territories from China in 1860. China's defeat in the Sino-French War (1884–85), in which it came to the defense of its tributary, Vietnam, resulted in the establishment of French Indo-China. In the First Sino-Japanese War (1894–95), Japan obtained Taiwan, the opening of additional ports, and the independence of Korea (which Japan subsequently annexed in 1910). This was a major turning point and led to the "scramble for concessions". In 1898, Britain leased Weihai in Shandong and the New Territories (for 99 years) of Hong Kong, Germany leased part of Shandong, Russia leased Port Arthur at the tip of Liaedong Peninsula, and France leased land around Guangzhou Bay in the south. The Boxer Rebellion, an uprising in 1899–1901 by a secret society seeking to expel all foreigners and supported by the Manchu court, was crushed by the intervention of British, French, German, American, Russian, and Japanese troops.

A revolution that finally overthrew Manchu rule began in 1911 in the context of a protest against a government scheme that would have handed Chinese-owned railways to foreign interests. City after city repudiated the Manchus, and in February 1912, the dowager empress, Ci Xi (Tz'u Hsi), signed an abdication document for the infant emperor, Puyi (P'u-yi). The Chinese republic, ruled briefly by Sun Zhongshan (Sun Yat-sen), followed by Yuan Shikai (Yüan Shih-kai), entered upon a period of internal strife. Following Yuan's death in 1916, the Beijing regime passed into the hands of warlords. The Beijing regime joined World War I on the Allied side in 1917. In 1919, the Versailles Peace Conference gave Germany's possessions in Shandong to Japan, sparking the May Fourth Movement as student protests grew into nationwide demonstrations supported by merchants and workers. This marked a new politicization of many social groups, especially those intellectuals who had been emphasizing iconoclastic cultural change.

Meanwhile, civil war grew more intense. In the south, at Guangzhou, the Nationalists (Guomindang, Kuomintang) led by Sun Zhongshan in alliance with the Communists (whose party was founded in Shanghai in 1921) and supported by Russia, built a strong, disciplined party. After Sun Zhongshan's death in 1925, his successor, Chiang Kai-shek (Jiang Jieshi), unified the country under Nationalist rule in 1928 with the capital in Nanjing. In 1927, the Nationalists began a bloody purge of the Communists, who sought refuge in southern Jiangxi Province. Their ranks severely depleted by Nationalist attacks, the Communists embarked on their arduous and now historic Long March during 1934–35. The Communists eventually reached Shaanxi Province in northwestern China, where, under the leadership of Mao Zedong (Tse-tung), they set up headquarters at Yan'an (Yenan). Japan, taking advantage of Chinese dissension, occupied Manchuria (Dongbei) in 1931.

Increasing Japanese pressure against northern China led, in July 1937, to the second Sino-Japanese war, which continued into World War II and saw Japanese forces occupy most of China's major economic areas. Nationalist China, established in the southwestern hinterland with its capital at Chongqing, resisted with US and UK aid, while the Communists fought the Japanese in the northwest. Japan evacuated China in 1945, and both Communist and Nationalist forces moved into liberated areas. The rift between the two factions erupted into civil war. Although supported by the US, whose mediation efforts had failed, the Nationalists steadily lost ground through 1948 and 1949, were expelled from the mainland by early 1950, and took refuge on Taiwan.

The People's Republic

The Communists, under the leadership of Mao, as chairman of the Chinese Communist Party (CCP), proclaimed the People's Republic of China (PRC) on 1 October 1949, with the capital at Beijing. A year later, China entered the Korean War (1950–53) on the side of the Democratic People's Republic of Korea (DPRK). In the fall of 1950, China entered Tibet, which had asserted its independence after the overthrow of the Manchu dynasty, despite formal claims to it by all subsequent Chinese governments. In 1959, the Dalai Lama fled to India during a Tibetan revolt against Chinese rule. Tibet became an autonomous region in 1965. The Nationalists held, in addition to Taiwan, islands in the Taiwan (Formosa) Strait: the Pescadores, Quemoy (near Xiamen), and the Matsu Islands (near Fuzhou).

In domestic affairs, a rapid program of industrialization and socialization up to 1957 was followed in 1958–59 by the Great Leap Forward, a crash program for drastic increases in output and the development of completely collectivized agricultural communes. The program ended in the "three bad years" of famine and economic crisis (1959–61), which produced 20 million deaths above the normal death rate, followed by a period of restoration and retrenchment in economics and politics. In the early 1960s, Chinese troops intermittently fought with Indian border patrols over conflicting territorial claims in Ladakh and the northeastern Indian state of Assam. Mediation attempts failed, but in 1963, the Chinese withdrew from the contested areas that they had occupied, and war prisoners were repatriated. Meanwhile, growing discord between China and the former Soviet Union had become more open, and in 1960, the USSR withdrew its scientific and technical advisers from China. Public polemics sharpened in intensity in the succeeding years, as the two powers competed for support in the world Communist movement.

After the Chinese economy had recovered in 1965, Mao again steered the country onto the revolutionary path, and gradually he built up momentum for the Great Proletarian Cultural Revolution, one of the most dramatic and convulsive periods in modern Chinese history. It continued until Mao's death in 1976, but the most tumultuous years were from 1966 to 1969, during which the cities witnessed a chaotic and violent pattern of factional fighting, accompanied by attacks on bureaucrats, intellectuals, scientists and technicians, and anyone known to have overseas connections.

Increasing confrontation between Mao and the party establishment, beginning in the fall of 1965, culminated in August 1966 with the CCP Central Committee's "16-Point Decision" endorsing Mao's Cultural Revolution policy of criticizing revisionism. In response to Mao's initiative, high levels of urban protest demonstrated widespread dissatisfaction with bureaucracies and privilege. In the latter half of 1966, the Red Guard movement of radical students attacked educational and state authorities and split into competing factions. Amid the rising conflict, the party institution collapsed in major cities. Liu Shaoqi, second to Mao in the political hierarchy and Chairperson of the People's Republic, was ousted from power as the chief target of the Cultural revolution. In 1968, Liu was formally dismissed from all positions and expelled from the party. He died at the end of 1969. From January 1967 through mid-1968, the discredited political establishment was replaced by Revolutionary Committees, comprised of the new radical organizations, the officials who remained in power, and representatives of the army. Finally, the army was told to restore order. In 1968 and 1969, students were sent out of the cities into the countryside. Colleges did not reopen until 1970. At the Ninth Party Congress in April

1969, the military's role was confirmed when Lin Biao, the Minister of Defense, was named Mao's successor.

Estimates place the number of dead as a direct result of the Cultural Revolution from 1966 to 1969 at 400,000. Much of the countryside, however, was unaffected and the economy, despite a setback in 1968, suffered little. The remaining years of the Cultural Revolution decade, up to 1976, were marked by a legacy of struggles over policies and over political succession to the aging Mao (83 at his death in 1976). In September 1971, Lin Biao died in a plane crash, allegedly while fleeing to the former USSR following an abortive coup. The decade from 1966 to 1976 left persistent factionalism in Chinese politics and a crisis of confidence, particularly among the young.

These years of domestic upheaval also brought profound changes in international alignments. In 1969, Chinese and Soviet forces clashed briefly along the Amur River frontier of eastern Heilongjiang Province. Throughout the late 1960s and early 1970s, China played a major role in supporting the Democratic Republic of Vietnam (North Vietnam) in the Vietnamese conflict. In November 1971, the PRC government replaced Taiwan's Nationalist government as China's representative at the UN and on the Security Council, following a General Assembly vote of 76–35, with 17 abstentions, on 25 October. Following two preliminary visits by US Secretary of State Henry Kissinger, President Richard M. Nixon journeyed to China on 21 February 1972 for an unprecedented state visit, and the two countries took major steps toward normalization of relations as the two nations sought common ground in their mutual distrust of Soviet intentions. In the period following the Nixon visit, US-China trade accelerated, cultural exchanges were arranged. In May 1973, the two countries established liaison offices in each other's capital and full diplomatic relations were established by 1979.

In 1975 at the Fourth National People's Congress, Zhou Enlai (Chou En-lai) announced a reordering of economic and social priorities to achieve the Four Modernizations (of agriculture, industry, national defense, and science and technology). Factional strife reminiscent of the late 1960s emerged between radical party elements led by Mao's wife, Jiang Qing (Chiang Ch'ing), and three associates (later collectively dubbed the Gang of Four), who opposed the modernization plans, and veteran party officials, such as Deng Xiaoping (previously associated with Liu Shaoqi and restored to power in 1973), who favored them. When Zhou died on 8 January 1976, the radicals moved to block the appointment of Deng (Zhou's heir apparent) as premier, with Mao resolving the impasse by appointing Hua Guofeng, a veteran party official and government administrator, as acting premier. Attacks on Deng continued until he was blamed for spontaneous disorders at a Beijing demonstration honoring Zhou on the Festival of the Dead, 5 April 1976 and, for the second time in his career, Deng was removed from all official positions.

After Mao

When Mao Zedong died on 9 September 1976, Hua Guofeng was quickly confirmed as party chairman and premier. A month later, the Gang of Four was arrested, and in early 1977, the banished Deng Xiaoping was again "reinstated." By 1978, Deng Xiaoping had consolidated his political dominance, and a new era of economic reforms began. The Third Party Plenum and the Fifth National People's Congress in 1978 adopted a new constitution and confirmed the goals of the Four Modernizations. Another new constitution in 1982 again confirmed policies of economic reform and emphasized legal procedure. The Cultural Revolution was officially condemned and Mao's historical role reevaluated. After a show trial from November 1980 to January 1981, the Gang of Four, together with Mao's former secretary and five others associated with Lin Biao, were convicted of crimes of the Cultural Revolution. Jiang Qing, whose death sentence was commuted to life imprisonment, committed suicide in 1991 after being diagnosed with cancer.

In 1980, Zhao Ziyang, a protégé of Deng Xiaoping, replaced Hua Guofeng as Premier, and Hu Yaobang, another Deng protégé, became General Secretary of the CCP while Hua resigned as party chairperson (a position which was abolished) in 1981. The 1980s saw a gradual process of economic reforms, beginning in the countryside with the introduction of the household responsibility system to replace collective farming. As the rural standard of living rose, reforms of the more complex urban economy began in the mid-1980s in an attempt to use the economic levers of the market instead of a command system of central planning to guide the economy. These included, with varying degrees of success, reforms of the rationing and price system, wage reforms, devolution of controls of state enterprises, legalization of private enterprises, creation of a labor market and stock markets, the writing of a code of civil law, and banking and tax reforms. At the same time, the Chinese pursued a policy of opening toward the outside world, establishing Special Economic Zones, and encouraging joint ventures and foreign investment.

In the 1980s and 1990s, China attempted to settle its relations with neighboring states. After a border clash with Vietnam in 1979, there were agreements with Great Britain in 1984 for the return of Macao, a Portuguese colony since the 16th century, in 1999. In May 1989, Soviet President Mikhail Gorbachev visited Beijing in the first Sino-Soviet summit since 1959. Top Vietnamese leaders came to China in 1991, normalizing relations between the two countries after a gap of 11 years. In the early 1990s, China and South Korea established regular relations.

Until 1989, economic reforms were accompanied by relatively greater openness in intellectual spheres. A series of social and political movements spanning the decade from 1979 to 1989 were critical of the reforms and reacted to their effects. In the Democracy Wall movement in Beijing in the winter of 1978–79, figures like Wei Jingsheng (imprisoned from 1979 to 1994 and subsequently reimprisoned) called for democracy as a necessary "fifth modernization". A student demonstration in Beijing in the fall of 1985 was followed in the winter of 1986–87 with a larger student movement with demonstrations of up to 50,000 in Shanghai, Beijing, and Nanjing, in support of greater democracy and freedom. In June 1987, blamed for allowing the demonstrations, Hu Yaobang was dismissed as party General Secretary, and several important intellectuals, including the astrophysicist Fang Lizhi and the journalist Liu Binyan, were expelled from the party. At the 15th Party congress of November 1987, many hard-line radicals failed to retain their positions, but Zhao Ziyang, who was confirmed as General Secretary to replace Hu, had to give up his position as Premier to Li Peng. By the end of 1988, economic problems, including inflation of up to 35% in major cities, led to major disagreements within the government, resulting in a slowdown of reforms. In December 1988, student disaffection and nationalism were expressed in a demonstration against African students in Nanjing.

On 15 April 1989, Hu Yaobang died of a heart attack. Students in Beijing, who had been planning to commemorate the 70th anniversary of the May Fourth Movement, responded with a demonstration, ostensibly in mourning for Hu, demanding a more democratic government and a freer press. Student marches continued and spread to other major cities. The urban population, unhappy with high inflation and the extent of corruption, largely supported the students and, by 17 May, Beijing demonstrations reached the size of one million people, including journalists, other salaried workers, private entrepreneurs and a tiny independent workers' organization, as well as students. On 19 May, martial law was imposed to no effect, and the government attempted to send troops to clear Beijing's Tiananmen Square, where demonstrators were camped, on 19–20

May and 3 June. Finally, in the early hours of 4 June 1989, armed troops, armored personnel carriers, and tanks, firing on demonstrators and bystanders, managed to reach the Square. Firing continued in the city for several days, and estimates of the total number killed range from 200 to 3,000. The events of 4 June sparked protests across the country, and thousands were arrested as the movement was suppressed. On 24 June, Zhao Ziyang was dismissed as General Secretary and Jiang Zemin, the mayor of Shanghai, was named in his place.

Parallel to but separate from the student movements were ongoing demonstrations by ethnic minorities. The most visible were those of the Tibetans, due to their international connections, but there have also been protests by other minorities, such as Muslims in Xinjiang province. Violent Tibetan demonstrations in the fall of 1987 and spring of 1988 were forcibly suppressed, and from March 1989 to April 1990, martial law was imposed in Lhasa, Tibet.

Following 4 June 1989, economic reforms were curtailed and some private enterprises closed down as the leadership launched an anticorruption drive. Ideological expression, higher education, and the news media were more tightly controlled in the ensuing years. The move toward a market-oriented economy began again, with increased speed, after Deng Xiaoping made a publicized visit in the spring of 1992 to the most developed areas in southern China. China's economy became one of the most rapidly growing in the world but continued to be plagued by inflation, corruption, and a growing disparity among the provinces. With a high rate of tax evasion, state revenues were shrinking and one-third went to subsidize state enterprises. Having been at the forefront of change in the early 1980s, peasants in the early 1990s were being left behind. In 1993 and 1994, there were peasant protests and riots over receiving IOUs for their produce and over local corruption. There were workers' disputes and strikes (250,000 between 1988 and 1993) in response to low pay and poor working conditions.

Labor unrest continued into 1997 as thousands of workers in several impoverished inland provinces rioted when promises of back pay went unfulfilled. A March 1997 labor protest involving 20,000 workers in Nanchong was the largest since the Communist revolution.

China's uneven economic development also led to the growth of a migrant worker class. By 1996, it was estimated that some 100 million peasants left their homes in northern and western provinces in search of menial work along the coast.

Unrest also flared anew in Tibet and other border provinces. A Muslim uprising in Xinjiang, near Kazakhstan, was met with force by the Chinese military in February 1997, leaving an estimated 100 ethnic Uygur and 25 Chinese dead. But the situation in Tibet posed the most difficulty for Beijing. China's efforts to control Tibet and dilute its culture led in 1995 to the indefinite detention of the six-year-old boy chosen by the exiled Dalai Lama as his reincarnation, or Panchen Lama. Beijing selected another six-year-old and forced Tibetan leaders to accept him.

In September 1997, the CCP's 15th National Congress elected a Central Committee which selected the 22-member Politburo. Jiang Zemin became the General Secretary of the party in addition to his title of President. Li Peng was appointed Prime Minister, and Zhu Rongji, Deputy Prime Minister. During this Congress, political power was consolidated in the triumvirate, with Jiang Zemin officially taking the deceased Deng Xiaoping's position.

As the government prepared for the 50th Anniversary of the proclamation of the People's Republic of China, it witnessed the return of Hong Kong (1 July 1997) and Macao (20 December 1999). Both former colonies were designated Special Administrative Regions (SAR) and Jiang stated that each SAR would continue to operate with considerable degree of economic autonomy.

Also in 1999, Chinese nationalism increased with the US bombings of the Chinese Embassy in Belgrade, Yugoslavia in May as an outpouring of government sanctioned anti-American demonstrations took place in Beijing. Despite rising nationalism, the political leadership felt threatened by a small but rapidly growing religious sect, the Falun Gong. On 22 July 1999, Chinese authorities banned the sect and arrested its leaders despite international human rights watch groups' criticism. The country celebrated its 50th anniversary on 1 October 1999 with a 500,000 person military parade showcasing its new technological achievements in armaments.

In March 2000, Zhu Rongji, the Deputy Prime Minister warned Taiwan and the United States that Taiwanese independence could lead to armed conflict. A Chinese newspaper also quoted a government white paper stating that war with the US is inevitable in the future and that if the US intervened on behalf of Taiwan, the Chinese may use nuclear weapons. Meanwhile, China began construction of military bases on the mainland across the Formosa Straits.

13 GOVERNMENT

On 4 December 1982, China adopted its fourth constitution since 1949, succeeding those of 1954, 1975, and 1978. In theory, the highest organ of state power is the National People's Congress (NPC), in which legislative power is vested. The constitution stipulates, however, that the Congress is to function under the direction of the Chinese Communist Party. The NPC meets annually for about two weeks to review major new policy directions, to adopt new laws, and to approve the national budget submitted to it by the State Council. Each congress consists of more than 3,000 deputies elected indirectly for a term of five years. The NPC elects a Standing Committee as its permanent working organ between sessions. The State Council, the executive organ of the NPC, consists of a Premier (the head of government), five vice-premiers, ministers, and heads of other major government agencies. The State Council issues administrative regulations and both formulates and executes the economic plan and the state budget. The 1982 constitution restored the largely ceremonial post of State Chairman, or President, a position abolished by Mao Zedong in 1968. The Eighth National People's Congress, in March 1993, elected Jiang Zemin as President and reelected Li Peng, first elected in 1988, to a second five-year term as Premier. Since the 1980s, the NPC has slowly increased its function as a locus for discussion of issues instead of merely being a rubber stamp. The 1992 debate on the Yangtze River (Chang jiang) dam project is an example of this.

The death of Communist Party patriarch Deng Xiaoping in February 1997 brought to a head the infighting between Jiang Zemin, Li Peng, and Vice-Premier Zhu Rongji. At the 15th Party Congress, Jiang was chosen to succeed Deng Xiaoping. The political leadership settled into one of shared leadership.

14 POLITICAL PARTIES

The Chinese Communist Party (CCP) has been the ruling political organization in China since 1949. Eight other minor parties have existed, since 1949, as members of a United Front, but their existence has been purely nominal. The party, with 50 million members (1990 estimate), plays a decisive role in formulating broad and detailed government policies and supervising their implementation at all levels of administration. Party supervision is maintained not only through placement of CCP members in key government posts, but also through specialized organs of the Central Committee of the CCP, which focus their attention on given subjects (e.g., propaganda or rural work). The CCP also forms branches within individual government units, as well as in factories, communes, schools, shops, neighborhoods, and military units.

Theoretically, the highest organ of party power is the National Party Congress, which usually meets once every five years. At each party congress a Central Committee is elected to oversee party affairs between sessions. The Central Committee (189 members elected in 1997) meets annually in plenary session to elect a Political Bureau, or Politburo (with 22 members as of 1997), and its Standing Committee, the party's most powerful organ (7 members in 1997). Directing day-to-day party affairs at the highest level is the Secretariat, headed by Jiang Zemin as General Secretary since June 1989. In 1982, the post of party Chairman, formerly the most powerful in the nation, was abolished; the title had been held by Mao Zedong until his death in 1976, by Hua Guofeng from 1976 until his ouster in 1981, and by Hu Yaobang thereafter.

Deng Xiaoping, China's acknowledged political leader since 1977, retired from the Central Committee in 1987, retired as chairperson of the party's Central Military Commission in 1989, and retired as Chairperson of the state's Central Military Commission, his last formal position, in 1990. A new CCP charter adopted at the 12th Communist Party Congress in September 1982 forbids "all forms of personality cult" and, in an implicit criticism of Mao, decrees that "no leaders are allowed to practice arbitrary individual rule or place themselves above the party organization." A major purge of party members in the early 1980s sought to exclude elements opposed to Deng's modernization policies. A re-registration program applicable to all party members, about half of whom were believed to have joined during the Cultural Revolution, was announced in 1983. The 13th Party Congress, convened in October 1987, affirmed Deng's reform policies and the drive for a younger leadership.

In the wake of the June Fourth massacre in 1989, Deng Xiaoping declared that Jiang Zemin, former mayor of Shanghai, should be the "core" of collective leadership after Deng's death. The Politburo announced prohibitions, largely ineffectual, against some forms of party privileges and nepotism, the corruption which had sparked the 1989 protests. The 14th Party Congress in October 1992 removed Yang Shangkun, State President (1988–1993), from the Politburo, weakening the power of his clique in the military. In 1993, the National People's Congress reelected Jiang Zemin, already party General Secretary, as Chairperson of the Central Military Commission and elected him as state President. This was the first time since the late 1970s that top, formal positions in the party, government, and military were concentrated in one leader's hands.

After the 15th Communist Party Congress, a highly publicized anticorruption drive resulted in the execution of several prominent cases. In addition, Jiang has begun to remove the Communist Party from state owned enterprises through an aggressive privatization strategy.

15 LOCAL GOVERNMENT

The People's Republic of China (PRC) consists of 22 provinces (*sheng*) (the PRC claims Taiwan as its 23rd province), five autonomous regions (*zizhiqu*), and four centrally administered municipalities (*zhixiashi*). Provinces and autonomous regions, in turn, are divided into "special districts," counties (*xian*), and cities (*shi*) under provincial jurisdiction, as well as into autonomous minor regions (*zhou*) and autonomous counties (*zizhixian*), where non-Han Chinese minority groups reside. Counties, autonomous counties, and autonomous zhou are divided into townships (*xiang*), autonomous townships (for small minority groups), towns, and rural communes. Hong Kong and Macao are designated as Special Administrative Regions (SAR).

From 1958 to 1982, local administrative authority formerly held by the xiang was transferred to the communes and their local people's councils. In 1988, Hainan Island, formerly part of Guangdong, was made China's newest province. The 1982 constitution returned local administrative control to the xiangs as the communes began to be disbanded. Local revolutionary committees, which replaced the local people's councils during the Cultural Revolution and under the 1975 constitution, were abolished in 1980. The restored local people's councils have the power to formulate local laws and regulations. The local people's governments are administrative organs of the state and report to the State Council.

In the 1980s an emphasis was placed on recruiting and promoting younger and better educated officials in local party and government posts. Many provinces along the coastal regions have adopted more decentralized forms of administration while interior provinces remain highly beholden to the central party. Local elections involving multiple candidates have taken place, especially in the more urbanized coastal areas.

16 JUDICIAL SYSTEM

China's legal system, instituted after the establishment of the PRC in 1949, is largely based on that of the former USSR. However, after 1957, Mao Zedong's government consistently circumvented the system in its campaign to purge the country of rightist elements and "counter-revolutionaries." The Ministry of Justice was closed down in 1959, not to reopen until 1979, and the excesses of the Cultural Revolution wrought havoc on legal institutions and procedures. Efforts to reestablish a credible legal system resumed in 1977 (when there were no lawyers in China), as party moderates came to power. These efforts were accelerated in the early 1980s as China sought to provide the legal protection required by foreign investors.

The highest judicial organ is the Supreme People's Court, which, with the Supreme People's Procuratorates, supervises the administration of justice in the basic people's courts and people's tribunals (courts of first instance), intermediate people's courts, and higher people's courts. The Judiciary is independent but subject to the Communist Party's policy guidance. The legal profession was still in an incipient stage of development in the mid-1980s. Over 25 law departments at universities and four special schools for training legal officials were in operation in 1987, when China had 26,000 lawyers. By 1993, there were 70,000 lawyers with plans to increase this number to 150,000.

A major anticrime campaign during the autumn of 1983 resulted in public executions at the rate of at least 200 a month; capital punishment may be meted out for 65 offenses, including embezzlement and theft. Under the Chinese criminal codes, as revised in 1979, local committees may sentence "hoodlums" to terms in labor camps of up to four years, in proceedings that grant the suspect no apparent opportunity for defense or appeal. Government records for 1990 indicated that nearly 870,000 persons were assigned to such camps during the 1980s. Since 1990, sentences to labor camps may be judicially challenged under the Administrative Procedures Law. In practice the review of such a sentence is rarely sought.

Due process rights are afforded in the 1982 Constitution, but they have limited practical import. The Criminal Procedural Law requires public trials, with an exception for cases involving state secrets, juveniles, or personal privacy. Cases are rapidly processed and conviction rates are about 99%. The 1976 Criminal Code contained 26 crimes punishable by death. A 1995 law raised this number to 65, including financial crimes such as passing fake negotiable notes and letters of credit, and illegal "pooling" of funds. Appeal is possible but with little chance of success. However in 1996, the National Peoples' Congress passed new legislation to reform criminal procedure and the legal profession. The new legislation recognized for the first time that lawyers represent their clients, not the state. Under the new system lawyers may establish private law firms. Defendants may also ask near relatives or guardians to provide additional defense.

Amendments to the criminal procedure became effective in January 1997. The amendments state that suspects may retain a lawyer after being first interrogated by an investigative organ. Attorneys may conduct limited investigation, call defense witnesses, and argue their client's cases in open court. According to the amendments defendants will enjoy a presumption of innocence.

Beginning in 1998, the government began a comprehensive "internal shake-up" of the judiciary, resulting in the punishment or dismissal of over 4,200 judicial branch employees. In January 1999, the former head of the Anticorruption Bureau of the Supreme People's Procuratorate was dismissed for corruption.

17ARMED FORCES

Under the 1982 constitution, the military was removed from the command of the chairman of the CCP and placed under the supervision of a separate Central Military Commission, headed by Deng Xiaoping. Military service is voluntary. In a major reorganization in October 1985, the country was divided into 7 military regions, 28 military districts (based in the provinces), and 3 garrison commands. All armed forces and services, including naval and air units, are under the command of the People's Liberation Army (PLA). Army personnel in 2000 numbered 2.48 million (1.27 million conscripts). In addition, there are over one million men and women in the militia reserves, who receive some training but are mostly unarmed. Most of the 100-plus-division army is prepared for territorial defense. Chinese ground combat weapons are locally produced from adaptations of Russian designs.

The Chinese navy in 2000 consisted of 230,000 personnel, including 5,000 marines, 26,000 naval air personnel, and 26,000 coastal defense forces, with 53 major combat ships, 71 submarines, and one nuclear-powered strategic missile submarine, armed with 12 missiles. The naval air force had 541 land-based combat aircraft. The air force in 2000 was estimated to have 420,000 personnel, with about 3,520 combat aircraft, mostly jet fighters but also including a bomber fleet.

China has developed a sizable tactical nuclear capacity. China's first nuclear test occurred on 16 October 1964 and consisted of a 20-kiloton bomb exploded at the test site. A series of 25 tests followed, including a 3-megaton hydrogen bomb test in the atmosphere in October 1970. A multistage intercontinental ballistic missile with a range of 7,000 km was tested in 1976, and missiles with ranges of up to 15,000 km reached maturity in the 1980s. In 2000 the Strategic Missile Forces (100,000 personnel) manned 15–20 ICMBs (2 with 15,000 km range) with single 3–5 megaton warheads and an estimated 66 IRBMs of 2,700 km range with 2 megaton warheads.

Chinese defense spending for 1998 was estimated at $11 billion or 1.5% of GDP. No Chinese forces are deployed in other countries except for UN and other peacekeeping teams.

18INTERNATIONAL COOPERATION

China has held a seat in the UN since 24 October 1945. After the Communist victory in 1949, UN representation was exercised by the Republic of China (ROC) government on Taiwan until November 1971, when the PRC replaced the ROC in the world organization and its member agencies. As of January 1988, the PRC belonged to ESCAP and all the nonregional specialized agencies. The PRC displaced the ROC in the IBRD and IMF in 1980. China is a signatory to the Law of the Sea and an applicant for membership in the WTO.

The US extended recognition to China on 15 December 1978 and resumed full diplomatic relations as of 1 January 1979. Continued US links with Taiwan in the 1980s, however, remained an irritant in US-PRC relations. The future of Hong Kong, for which part of the lease (the New Territories) expired in 1997, dominated UK-Chinese discussions, and in 1986, an agreement to give Hong Kong back to China in 1997 was formally signed. Relations with the USSR, severed during the Sino-Soviet split in the 1960s, improved somewhat in the 1980s but remained strained over China's support of anti-Soviet forces in Cambodia and Afghanistan. By the end of 1985, more than 130 nations had extended full diplomatic recognition to the PRC, with a parallel drop to about 10 in the number recognizing Taiwan's government. By the mid-1980s, the PRC had achieved normal relations with most of its Asian neighbors, including Japan, India, Pakistan, Malaysia, Thailand, and Singapore. Relations with Vietnam, Cambodia, and Laos (all allies of the former USSR) were tense after the late 1970s, but among non-Communist nations, only the Republic of Korea (ROK) appeared firmly resistant to rapprochement.

19ECONOMY

Traditional China was predominantly agricultural. Adhering to farming patterns developed over a score of centuries, China could sustain a harsh level of self-sufficiency, given surcease from natural calamities. For almost three decades prior to 1949, the incessant ravages of civil disorder, foreign (principally Japanese) invasion, and gross economic neglect virtually decimated China's frail abilities to sustain itself. The first task of the new PRC government thus was to restore the flow of natural resources to prewar levels. By the early 1950s, the government had succeeded in halting massive starvation. Almost all means of production and distribution were brought under state control, and vast parcels of land were redistributed to the peasantry. During 1953–57, China's first five-year plan stressed heavy industry. Economic development was aided by imports of machinery and other industrial equipment from the former USSR and East European countries. In return, China exported agricultural produce to them. A major geological prospecting drive resulted in the discovery of mineral deposits that provided a major thrust toward industrialization.

The Great Leap Forward of 1958–59 initially produced sharp gains in industry and agriculture, but the zeal for increased quotas quickly resulted in undue strain on resources and quality. The Great Leap was followed by "three bitter years" of economic crisis brought on by bad harvests and the economic dislocation of the previous period. By 1961, the GNP had fallen to an estimated $81 billion, roughly the level reached in 1955. By 1965, however, a readjustment of expectations, coupled with a careful program of industrial investment, helped the economy to recover. China's trade patterns, meanwhile, had shifted radically away from the USSR and toward Japan and Western Europe.

During the late 1960s, in the Cultural Revolution period, long-range central economic planning was abandoned in favor of policies promoting local self-reliance. Self-sufficiency in grain production was particularly stressed. The negative impact of this emphasis on agricultural development, together with the turmoil of the Cultural Revolution, resulted in a drop in industrial production of 10–20%, while agricultural output, aided by good weather, improved only marginally.

Centralized planning resumed in 1970 with Zhou Enlai's announcement of key goals for the fourth five-year plan (1971–75), including an increase in grain output. The fifth five-year plan (1976–80), disrupted during the political upheaval that followed the deaths of Mao and Zhou in 1976, was restructured in 1978 to embody the Four Modernizations, with the use of Western technology as necessary. At the same time, a 10-year plan (1975–85) calling for the traditional expansion of agriculture and heavy industry was revamped to emphasize the growth of light industries and the accelerated development of industrial raw materials. Trade with the US expanded after full diplomatic relations were restored in 1979, and four special economic zones were established as centers for foreign investment.

The sixth five-year plan (1981–85), adopted in 1982, reflected this new pragmatic approach to economic development by emphasizing agriculture, light industry, energy, and improved transportation facilities. During the 1980s, the Chinese economy underwent a major restructuring under the leadership of Zhao Ziyang. Rural reforms launched in 1979, which linked remuneration to output and centered on household responsibility, had a profound and beneficial impact on the rural economy, and output and income rose to record levels for rural residents. The commune system was disbanded in 1983–84 and replaced by a system of townships, and the household or family became the main unit of rural production. In the wake of the success of these rural reforms, the CCP Central Committee published "A Decision on the Reform of the Economic Structure" in October 1984, with the goal of totally overhauling the national economy and bringing urban industrial organization in line with rural practice. The main points of the decision were that all urban enterprises would be responsible for their own profits and losses, managers would have greater decision-making authority, and national and local governments would relinquish direct control over enterprises and assume a regulatory and supervisory position. Renumeration would be based on productivity, subsidies would be abolished, wages and prices would find their own level, and private and collective enterprises would be encouraged.

The seventh five-year plan (1986–90) made reform its paramount concern. The reforms put forth in 1984 and firmly anchored in the 1988 Enterprise Law proved remarkably successful, leading to much higher rates of industrial and general economic growth than previously expected. Real GNP grew by an average of 9.6% annually between 1979–1988, reaching 11% in 1988. By this time, however, indicators of a seriously overheated economy were also clearly emerging; inflation accelerated to 20.7% and shortages in raw material and energy supply as well as transportation capacity rapidly worsened. Growth fell to only 4% in 1989 before austerity measures initiated by the government brought inflation to below 10% and eventually restored growth to double digit levels.

Infrastructure development was given special priority in the China's eighth plan covering 1991–1995. During this period economic growth accelerated, averaging more than 10% annually, giving China one of the fastest growing economies in the world. With growth came rising inflation and infrastructural bottlenecks which highlighted the need for further improvements in macroeconomic management. The 1996–2000 economic plan, which called for economic growth of 9–10% through 2000, reaffirmed the importance of the private sector and opening the economy to the outside world. To attract and maintain foreign investors China needed to reform its legal and financial institutions. Despite the government's endorsement of market reforms, the plan continued to affirm the role of state-owned enterprises, which still accounted for more than one-third of total industrial output. In 1996, China committed two-thirds of fixed-asset investment to state-owned enterprises even though most were heavily in debt. By propping up the state sector China risked continuing budget deficits and the higher debt service that came with the borrowing necessary to pay for those expenditures.

Investment in the state sector accounted for nearly all of the new investment in 1998, in the form of a special infrastructure spending package forwarded by the government, supporting a GDP growth rate of 7% in 1999. Economic growth, which slowed during the late 1990s, was expected to rebound after China gained entrance to the WTO.

[20]INCOME

The US Central Intelligence Agency (CIA) reports that in 1998 China's gross domestic product (GDP) was estimated at $4,420 billion. The per capita GDP was estimated at $3,600. The annual growth rate of GDP was estimated at 7.8%. The average inflation rate in 1998 was -0.8%. The CIA defines GDP as the value of all final goods and services produced within a nation in a given year and computed on the basis of purchasing power parity (PPP) rather than value as measured on the basis of the rate of exchange. It was estimated that agriculture accounted for 19% of GDP, industry 49%, and services 32%.

Private consumption includes expenditures of individuals, households, and nongovernmental organizations. It was estimated that between 1990 and 1998 private consumption grew at an annual rate of 9.2%. The richest 10% of the population accounted for approximately 30% of household consumption and the poorest 10% approximately 2.4%.

[21]LABOR

In 1998, China's total civilian employment was estimated at 699,570,000. The civilian labor force was 743 million. About 45% of the labor force was female. In 1997, 54% of civilian employment was in agriculture, forestry, and fishing; 27% in industry; and 19% in services. Unemployment in urban areas was 3.1% in, 1998.

China's labor policies have vacillated since 1949 between "to each according to his need," operative during the Great Leap Forward and the Cultural Revolution, and "to each according to his work." The first gave rise to job security—known as the "iron rice bowl" in China—but was generally associated with falling output. In 1978, a new economic formula, known as the "responsibility system," called for agricultural and industrial workers to sign a contract to produce a fixed amount of goods but provided for disposal on the free market for goods produced in excess of contractual levels.

On 27 December 1966, forces within the Cultural Revolution dissolved the All-China Federation of Trade Unions (ACFTU), previously the only nationwide labor organization. Some of its functions were then carried on by "revolutionary" organizations set up in factories, and by workers' congresses and trade unions organized on municipal and provincial levels. Strikes and lockouts became widespread during the Cultural Revolution. Other labor problems encountered during this period were "economism" among workers (i.e., emphasis on wages, bonuses, awards, and benefits, and appropriating factory funds and facilities under various pretexts); breakdowns in labor discipline (referred to as "anarchy"); disorders from fights between rival workers' factions (called "factionalism"); and slowness in developing sensitivity to nonmaterial incentives, as required by the prevailing ideology. Signs of labor unrest stemming from low wages and many of these same issues reemerged during 1974, bringing on notable disruptions among railway workers; in 1975, labor clashes in Hangzhou led to the calling in of the military. In October 1976, the ACFTU was restored to power. A new constitution of trade unions was adopted in 1978 and subsequently revised in 1982 to permit workers the right to strike when conditions are hazardous; strikes for purely economic advantages are forbidden, however.

As of 1999, the Communist Party-Controlled ACFTU was the country's sole labor confederation. It had 16 industry-based and 31 province-based member unions, and 586,000 grassroots-level unions. Over 90% of the ACFTU's reported 103 million members worked in state-owned enterprises. Independent trade unions are illegal, although some allegedly exist in secrecy.

A new labor code enacted in 1995 gives workers the right to collective bargaining. However, union officials are proceeding cautiously on asserting such a right. Union officials working outside the official confines of the ACFTU have reported being harassed and detained by authorities. Any union activity outside of the ACFTU is deemed "illegal" by the authorities.

In 1992 the government made agreements to stop the use of forced labor (primarily in prisons) and allow foreign inspectors to monitor compliance. However, the government has hampered prison access by international monitors, and human rights groups report that the use of forced prison labor continues.

There is a minimum working age of 16 but compliance with this is irregular, especially in the burgeoning and unregulated private economy. The huge surplus of adult labor reduces the incentive to employ children. Children are most often found working on farms in poorer, isolated areas.

In 1999, the minimum wage varied, depending on the area of the country. It provides, at most, a basic amount for survival and most families benefit also from subsistence farming, government subsidies and employment in the informal sector.

22AGRICULTURE

With some 68% of the economically active population engaged in farming, agriculture forms the foundation of China's economy. Limitations in topography, soil, and climate, however, have restricted cultivation to only about 14.5% of the total land area. Despite recent advances—grain crops totaling an estimated 447.14 million tons were produced in 1998 (21.7% of the world's total)—the enormous pressures of feeding and clothing China's vast and growing population remain among the country's most compelling concerns. From 1980 to 1990, agricultural output grew at an average annual rate of 5.9%, above the population growth rate and the first sustained expansion of agriculture since 1966; output increased at an average annual rate of 4.9% from 1990 to 1998.

The PRC government expropriated large landholdings in a land reform carried out in 1951–52, redistributing the land among poor peasants. By the end of 1954, 11.5% of all peasant households had been collectivized; by 1955, 65%; and by 1965, 99%. The Chinese collective farms had virtually no mechanical equipment, but the peasants pooled their labor in various projects, such as water management, which were beyond the capacity of individual peasants. In 1958, the collective farms were merged into larger units as people's communes. The communes were concerned not only with agricultural output but also with subsidiary farm activities, such as light industry and handicrafts, usually produced for local consumption.

Far-reaching changes in the organization of communes took place during 1961–62. Formerly, the production brigade (the major division of a commune), of which there were about 719,438 in 1982, was regarded as the commune's "basic accounting unit." In 1962, however, the production team (the subdivision of a commune) became the commune's basic organizational element. The average production team consisted of 33 households and cultivated about 8 ha (20 acres). Production teams functioned almost autonomously, making basic decisions on production and distribution of income, while the commune mainly exercised the functions of a township government. Households, the final link in the system, were permitted the use of private plots, which made up about 5% of the arable land assigned to a team. In the early 1980s, these private holdings accounted for 19% of total agricultural output and the bulk of the country's production of vegetables, fruits, hogs, and poultry. Under the "responsibility system," which was introduced in 1978 and by 1983 was operating in 90% of rural China, all production in excess of assigned levels could be sold on the open market to yield a profit for individual production teams. In 1982, in addition to the rural communes, which provided most of China's agricultural output, there were 2,078 state farms working approximately 4.5% of all farmland. These farms, under the Ministry of State Farms and Reclamation, generally served as commodity production centers and as research units for the improvement of crop and livestock yields.

In 1983–84, a major reform of the agricultural system was launched. The 50,000 communes were disbanded and replaced by 92,000 townships, and the six million production brigades were broken up. Production decisions are now made by the household, which sets production targets in contracts with the government; households can sell their surpluses in the open market for cash. Crop diversification is encouraged. By the late 1980s, 60% of agricultural output was free of state controls, and most of China's peasants practiced the household responsibility system.

Grains are the chief crop, accounting for 70% of the total value of crop output and occupying 80% of all land under cultivation. Shandong, Jiangsu, and Henan together account for about 25% of the total crop value.

The main food crops are rice, wheat, and corn, followed by kaoliang (a type of sorghum), millet, potatoes, and soybeans. China is the world's leading producer of rice, with production increasing from 106.6 million tons in 1970 to an estimated 193 million tons (34% of the world's total) in 1998. Over 90% of all rice is produced in southern China, with two (and in the far south, three) crops being grown each year where irrigation facilities permit. Early rice is planted in April and harvested in July; single-crop rice is planted in May and harvested in September; and late double-cropped rice is planted in June and harvested in October. The total wheat crop in 1998 amounted to 110 million tons, more than double the 1970 output. Wheat is cultivated throughout the country, often as a dry-season crop in the rice-growing south, with specialized production centered in the Yangtze Valley and North China Plain. Output of other coarse grains, including corn in the southwest and drought-tolerant millet and kaoliang in northern and northeastern China, exceeded 144.4 million tons in 1998. Production of roots and tubers, including sweet potatoes grown as a second crop in areas south of the Yellow River and white potatoes in cooler areas north of the Great Wall, totaled 164.5 million tons in 1998.

Industrial crops occupy only 8–9% of the cultivated areas. Among the most important are cotton (the chief raw material for the important textile industry), various oil-bearing crops, sugar, tobacco, silk, tea, and rubber. Cotton output totaled four million tons in 1998, down from 5.6 million tons in 1991, with production concentrated along the middle and lower reaches of the Yangtze River and on the plains of the Yellow and Huai rivers. Oilseed output in 1998 was derived from a diverse assortment of widely grown industrial crops, including sunflower seeds (1,200,000 tons) and rapeseed (6,000,000 tons). Other oilseed products included 192,000 tons of castor beans, 390,000 tons of sesame seeds, and 420,000 tons of linseed in 1998. Sugar production reached 8.6 million tons in 1998, up from 1.8 million tons in 1974; an estimated 84% of all sugar is derived from sugarcane grown in the south, and the remaining 16% from sugar beets grown in the north and northeast. Production of tea, also an important traditional export, increased from 120,000 tons in 1956 to 648,000 tons in 1998 (22% of world production), with most of the tea grown in hilly regions of the south and southeast. Most tobacco is produced as a sideline by commune householders working private plots; output was 2.5 million tons in 1998. Most natural rubber is produced on specialized state farms; production totaled 450,000 tons in 1998.

The irrigated area is estimated to have increased from about 15.3 million ha (37.8 million acres) in 1950 to 51.8 million ha (128 million acres) in 1997, making China the world's leader in irrigated land. The expansion of fertilizer production is viewed as a key to major growth in the agricultural sector. Toward this end, China during 1972–74 contracted for the purchase of 13 large urea plants from Japan, the US, and Western Europe. China's use of chemical fertilizers increased from 184 kg per ha in 1984 to 261 kg per ha in 1993. Farm machinery in 1997 included 703,117 tractors and 114,000 combines.

[23]ANIMAL HUSBANDRY

Except in outlying areas, nearly all of China's arable land is devoted to crops. Most agricultural units, however, also support the raising of large quantities of hogs and poultry. Natural grasslands for the grazing of sheep and cattle occupy 3.53 million sq km (1.36 million sq mi), or 37% of China's total area; the four major pasture areas are Xinjiang, Gansu, Qinghai, and Inner Mongolia. In an effort to improve these pastures, 303 million ha (749 million acres) were planted with improved forage seed strains from 1976 to 1980. Nonetheless, animal husbandry continues to be the weak link in the agricultural economy.

China leads the world in swine production, the total number of hogs reaching about 400.3 million at the beginning of 1998 (55% of the world's total), as compared with 89.8 million in 1952. The provinces with the largest hog populations are Sichuan, Hunan, Henan, and Shandong. Pig raising, often pursued as a private sideline by peasants, is the fastest-growing sector of the livestock industry, and hogs and pork products are becoming valuable export earners.

The number of sheep expanded from 36.9 million in 1952 to nearly 118.1 million in 1998. Most sheep are raised by pastoral herders, mostly the ethnic minorities, in the semiarid lands of Xinjiang, Inner Mongolia, Gansu, and Sichuan (Szechuan). Goats, also raised primarily in semiarid areas but increasingly promoted throughout China as a profitable household sideline for milk and dairy production, increased in number from 24.9 million in 1952 to 137.7 million in 1998. Sheep and goats together numbered 269 million at the beginning of 1999. Provinces with the greatest numbers of sheep and goats include Shandong, Inner Mongolia, Xinjiang, and Itenan. In 1998 there were also 117 million head of cattle and buffalo, up from 66.6 million in 1965; 8.9 million horses (792,000 in 1965); and 350,000 camels (448,000). Chickens and ducks are raised throughout China on private plots and constitute, together with fish and pork, China's chief sources of dietary protein. The provinces with the largest cattle populations are Itenan, Shandong, Sichuan, and Guangxi. China produced 217,000 tons of honey in 1998, more than any other nation. China also led the world in silk production in 1998, at some 51,000 tons (59% of world production).

In 1998, China produced 55.1 million tons of meat, ranking first in the world with 26% of the total. Some 11.1 million tons consisted of poultry, second only to the US and accounting for 18% of world production. Pork production in 1998 amounted to 36.9 million tons (first in the world), equivalent to 44% of global production.

[24]FISHING

With a coastline of some 6,500 km (4,000 mi) adjoining a broad continental shelf, China has excellent coastal fisheries. A vast number of inland lakes and ponds, covering a total area of about 300,000 sq km (116,000 sq mi), are also used for fish culture, and a 30 km (19 mi) section of the Yangtze below Gezhouba Dam at Yichang is a designated sturgeon preserve. The principal marine fisheries are located on the coast of southern and southeastern China, in the provinces of Guangdong, Fujian, and Zhejiang. The total catch in 1997 was 39,936,927 tons, the highest in the world. Of that total, 14,253,256 tons came from inland waters and 25,683,401 tons from marine fishing. China typically accounts for about 10% of the world's catch, but per capita Chinese consumption of fish amounts to only 9.3 kg (20.5 lb) per year (live weight equivalent), one of the lowest amounts in Asia.

Exports of fisheries products in 1997 accounted for 5.7% of the commodity's world exports, and were valued at over $3 billion (second after Norway). Regulations for the protection of aquatic resources were enacted in 1979.

In 1997, Chinese aquacultural production was valued at $23.5 billion. The leading products are carp, kelp, oysters, and scallops.

[25]FORESTRY

Forest cover has grown from 8.6% of the land base in 1949 to over 14% in 1995. Mature stands are decreasing, however, while the share of plantation and commercial forests continues to rise in response to government policies. Most of the forests are in remote regions, however, and lack of transportation limits exploitation. China has three major forest areas: the northeast (Heilongjiang, Jilin, and Inner Mongolia); the southwest (Sichuan and Yunnan); and the southeast (Guangdong, Guangxi, Fujian, Jiangxi, and Hainan). In 1997, the Chinese government put the gross output of the forestry sector at Y81.8 billion, with Fujian, Zhejiang, Anhui, and Guangdong together accounting for 29% of the total value. Coniferous stands, which yield the most valuable commercial timber, are found mainly in the northeast and adjoining parts of Inner Mongolia. Deciduous trees are felled in Sichuan and Yunnan. Between 1990 and 1995, however, the northeast's share of production fell to from 38% to 30%, as production shifted from state-owned forests in the north to plantation forests in the south. While China is a major producer of softwood logs and lumber, virtually all of its production is domestically consumed. Paper production, which has benefited from the substitution of rice straw and other nonwood materials for wood pulp, nearly tripled during the 1980s. Special forestry products originating in southwestern China include tung oil, cassia oil, and aniseed oil. Wood imports can vary widely from year to year. China's imports of wood products amounted to $12.4 billion in 1997, while wood exports totaled $3.6 billion. Production, consumption, import, and export amounts for 1997 (in 1,000 cu m) are shown in the following table:

	PRODUCTION	CONSUMPTION	IMPORTS	EXPORTS
Roundwood	313,223	318,348	9,151	4,026
Sawnwood	27,410	29,998	3,816	1,228
Wood-based panels	14,540	19,147	6,504	1,897
Wood pulp	2,210	4,637	2,458	31
Paper and paperboard	31,863	38,977	10,463	3,350

Deforestation has been a persistent and serious problem in China, leading to massive erosion and desertification. The government has, from the start of its first five-year plan in 1953, given high priority to campaigns for afforestation. By 1980, 26 million ha (64 million acres) of new forests had been planted, and during the 1980s, afforestation proceeded at the rate of 4.55 million ha (11.24 million acres) per year. However, cutting of trees for fuel continued in rural areas, and many of the trees planted as part of afforestation efforts were lost because of neglect after planting. In its ninth five-year plan commencing in

January 1996, the Ministry of Forestry had the following goals: operating 10 major forest conservation projects by 2000; increasing the variety of wood species in state-owned forest plantations; developing the paper making industry; exploring and developing growing trees in marginal land (such as hilly, mountainous, or sandy terrain); and classifying forests as either industrial (for environmental protection) or economic (for commercial production).

²⁶MINING

Intensive geologic exploration has yielded greatly expanded mineral reserves. This increase in known subsurface resources is reflected in production rises for China's most important mineral products, including coal, petroleum, iron ore, copper, lead, zinc, tungsten, mercury, antimony, tin, and molybdenum.

Virtually all provinces contain coal deposits. Production rose from 66.5 million tons in 1952 to 1,090 million tons in 1991. In 1997, production was 1,356 million tons. The major coal-producing areas are Shanxi, Shandong, and Inner Mongolia. The top 10 producing coal mines in China had proven reserves in 1990 of 12,996 million tons.

Iron ore reserves were estimated at 55 billion tons, with the largest resources in Liaoning, Hebei, and Sichuan. Iron ore production increased from 17.7 million tons in 1957 to 245 million tons in 1997. The metal content of the ore is relatively low (less than 35% on the average) and requires concentration; nevertheless, quantities have been sufficient to supply the country's sizable steel industry. In 1998 the Chinese government announced plans to abandon production quotas, allowing steel producers to adjust their output to market demand. Virtually all iron mining is presently carried out north of the Yangtze River. China is the world's largest producer of tin (65,000 tons estimated in 1997), mined chiefly in Yunnan, and a major producer of tungsten (25,000 tons), mainly from Jiangxi, and antimony (102,000 tons), from Guangxi, Guizhou, and Hunan. Other metallic ores, with their 1997 production, were bauxite, 8,000,000 tons; copper, 414,000; lead, 650,000 tons; magnesium, 92,000 tons; and molybdenum, 32,700 tons. Industrial mineral production in 1997 included cement, 492.6 million tons; gypsum, 7.8 million tons, graphite, 190,000 tons; boron, 140,000 tons; asbestos, 245,000 tons; and bromine, 31,000 tons.

China is a world leader in the production of industrial minerals, metals, and fuels. In 1997 its exports of minerals and metals rose 25% in value from the previous year. It plans to increase the production of cement, copper, fertilizer, iron, lead, nickel, salt, soda ash, and zinc; but capital and technological constraints have caused the government to postpone plant construction and expansion. The interior has been opened for foreign exploration, and China is expected to retain its dominance in the world market for antimony, barite, fluorspar, magnesite, rare earths, and tungsten.

²⁷ENERGY AND POWER

China's petroleum resources are a key to its industrial development. Crude oil production increased from 102,000 barrels per day in 1960 to 3.2 million per day in 1998, when China had proven reserves of 24 billion barrels. The major producing centers are the Daqing field in Heilongjiang, which came into production in 1965 and accounts for nearly one-third of national production; the Shengli field, developed in 1965 and located on the Bo Hai coast, near the mouth of the Yellow River, and the Liaohe field, located in Liaoning. In addition to numerous other mainland finds, China has potential offshore reserves in the Bo Hai area and the South China Sea, especially in the vicinity of Hainan Island.

By the mid-1970s, China no longer had to rely on oil imports; petroleum exports had, in fact, emerged as a major source of foreign exchange earnings. More than 9,740 km (6,050 mi) of long-distance pipelines transport the oil from fields to refineries and other points of consumption and export. China, however, became a net importer of oil in 1996, because rapid increases in oil demand from high economic growth rates outpaced the slower increases in oil production.

After rising dramatically in the early 1980s, owing largely to the discovery and exploitation of vast deposits in Sichuan Province during the late 1950s and early 1960s, natural gas output has stagnated somewhat in the late 1980s, indicating only modest reserves. Proven reserves of natural gas in 1999 totaled 1.4 trillion cu m (48 trillion cu ft). By 1997, total national production had reached 21.2 billion cu m (750 billion cu ft). Some 10 billion cu m of gas production came from Sichuan, most of the remainder being oil-associated gas.

Although China's rivers provide a vast hydroelectric potential (an estimated 378 million kW), only a small part (9%) has been developed. As of 1991, 65 hydropower projects, with a total capacity of 16,000 MW, were under construction. However, in the late 1990s, after economic growth slowed due to the Asian economic crisis, the government declared a 2–3 year moratorium on construction of new power plants due to an oversupply problem. The main hydroelectric projects include Ertan in Sichuan Province, Yantan in Guangxsi Zhuang Autonomous Region, Manwan in Yunan Province, Geheyan in Hubei Province, Wuqiangxi in Hunan Province, Yamzho Yumco in Xizang Autonomous Region, and Lijia Xia in Qinghai Province. In April 1992, the government approved the construction of the largest hydropower project in China—the Three Gorges Project on the middle reaches of the Chang Jiang. Construction began in 1996; completion of the 26 hydropower generating units is targeted for 2009. The Three Gorges Project has a designed capacity of 17,680 MW and will require the relocation of millions of people just in Sichuan Province alone.

In 1998, China's net installed electrical generating capacity was 253.9 million kW, up from 115.5 million kW in 1988. The installed capacity of thermal power plants, fired by coal and oil, totaled 137 million kW in 1994, up from 82.7 million kW in 1988; the capacity of hydroelectric plants totaled 44.6 million kW in 1994 (32.7 million in 1988). Total output of electricity increased during the 1988–98 period from 545 billion to 1,098 billion kWh.

Traditionally, coal has been the major primary-energy source, with auxiliary biomass fuels provided by brushwood, rice husks, dung, and other noncommercial materials. The abundance of coal continues to provide cheap thermal power for electric plants. China was the world's largest coal producer in 1998, at 1,200 million tons. China was also the world's leading consumer of coal, at 1,530 million tons in 1997. Coal comes from over two dozen sites in the north, northeast, and southwest; Shanxi Province is the leading producer. Recoverable reserves as of 1999 were estimated at over 126.2 billion tons. As of 1996, China accounted for 11.1% of the world's proven reserves of coal. Large thermal power plants are situated in the northeast and along the east coast of China, where industry is concentrated, as well as in new inland industrial centers, such as Chongqing, Taiyuan, Xi'an, and Lanzhou. In 1995, coal accounted for 76.9% of primary energy consumption; oil, 18.9%; hydropower, 1.9%; natural gas, 1.9%; and nuclear power, 0.4%.

The 279 MW Qinshan nuclear power plant, near Shanghai, began commercial operation in 1994. That same year, two 944-MW reactors at the Guangdong facility at Daya Bay also started commercial service. In 1995, Chinese authorities approved the construction of four more reactors. Net capacity for China's three nuclear reactors was estimated at 2,167,000 kW in 1996. Nuclear generation is to play a secondary but important role, especially in areas that lack both hydropower potential and major coal resources.

China ranks as the world's second-largest consumer of energy (after the US). In 1995, China accounted for 10.2% of the world's primary energy consumption. The goals of China's ninth Five-Year Plan (1996–2000) included building power plants (primarily coal), strengthening oil and gas exploration and development, improving energy inefficiency, and developing rural energy (including small hydropower, solar, geothermal, and biogas).

28INDUSTRY

China has achieved a rapid increase in the gross value of industrial output (used before China switched to GNP accounting in 1986), which, according to official Chinese statistics, rose by 13.3% annually between 1950 and 1979. The greatest sustained surge in growth occurred during the first decade, with the rate averaging 22% annually during 1949–60. During 1961–74, the yearly growth rate fell to about 6%, partly as a result of the disruptions brought on by the collapse of the Great Leap Forward (which accompanied the withdrawal of Soviet technicians in mid-1960) and of work stoppages and transportation disruptions during the Cultural Revolution. Growth averaged 10% from 1970 to 1980 and 10.1% from 1979 to 1985. Major policy reforms of 1984 further accelerated the pace of industrial growth, which reached 20.8% by 1988. After a brief retrenchment period in 1989–90 as government policies prioritized inflation control over other concerns, expansion of the country's industrial sector resumed apace, exceeding 20% in 1992 and 18% in 1994. Industrial output was officially up 13.4% in 1995, with state enterprises contributing the majority.

While approximately 50% of total industrial output still derives from the state-owned factories, a notable feature of China's recent industrial history has been the dynamic growth of the collectively owned rural township and village enterprise as well as private and foreign joint-venture sectors. Also apparent has been the spatial unevenness of recent industrial development, with growth concentrated mainly in Shanghai, the traditional hub of China's industrial activity, and, increasingly, a number of new economic centers along the southern coast. The coastal provinces of Jiangsu, Guangdong, Shandong, Shanghai and Zhejiang provinces together account for close to 33% of the country's total industrial output and most of its merchandise exports. One key factor in this industrial geography has been the government's establishment of several Special Economic Zones in Guangdong, Fujian and Hainan provinces, and its designation of over 14 "open coastal cities" where foreign investment in export-oriented industries was actively encouraged during the 1980s.

Before the first five-year plan (1953–57), China had only one major steel center—Anshan, in the northeast—and several minor ones. All these produced 1.93 million tons of pig iron and 1.35 million tons of steel in 1952. By 1995, China was producing 92,970 million tons of crude steel and 101,700 million tons of pig iron. China had one trillion tons of confirmed coal reserves and an estimated five trillion tons of coal reserves and 48.7 billion tons of iron ore in 2000. Anshan continues to be the hub of the industry, but other huge steel complexes have been constructed at Baotou, Benxi (about 50 km/30 mi east of Anshan), Taiyuan, Wuhan, and Ma'anshan (near Nanjing).

China's cotton textile industry is the largest in the world, producing yarn, cloth, woolen piece goods, knitting wool, silk, jute bags, and synthetic fibers. Labor-intensive light industries played a prominent role in the industrial boom of the late 1980s and early 1990s, accounting for 49% of total industrial output, but heavy industry and high technology took over in the late 1990s. In addition to garments and textiles, output from light industry includes footwear, toys, food processing, and consumer electronics. Heavy industries include iron and steel, coal, machine building, armaments, petroleum, cement, chemical fertilizers, and autos. High technology industries produce high-speed computers, 600 types of semiconductors, specialized electronic measuring instruments, and telecommunications equipment.

Since 1961, industry has been providing agriculture with farm machines, chemical fertilizers, insecticides, means of transportation, power, building materials, and other essential commodities. Handicraft cooperatives also have been busy making hand-operated or animal-drawn implements. Production of a variety of industrial goods has expanded, increasingly in order to supply the country's own expanding industrial base. In addition to fertilizers, the chemicals industry produces calcium carbide, ethylene, and plastics. Since 1963, great emphasis has been placed on the manufacture of transportation equipment, and China now produces varied lines of passenger cars, trucks, buses, and bicycles. In 1995, output included 1,452,697 motor vehicles (more than double the 1991 figure). Output for 1997 was over 1.6 million units. The industry underwent a major overhaul in the late 1990s in order to stimulate efficiency and production.

29SCIENCE AND TECHNOLOGY

Modern China is the heir to a remarkably inventive civilization that pioneered in the development of the abacus (the first mechanical calculating device), paper (and paper money), printing by movable type, gunpowder, the magnetic compass, and the rocket. Contact with the West during the 19th century revealed how technologically backward China had become, and it is only in recent decades that the nation has begun to catch up.

China detonated its first fission device in 1964 and its first hydrogen bomb in 1967; the nation now possesses a variety of nuclear weapons mounted on missiles, bombers, submarines, and other delivery systems. Its first satellite was launched in 1970. By 1992, the PRC had launched an INTELSAT satellite on a Chinese launch vehicle. Other priorities have been the development of high-energy physics, laser research, powerful computer memory chips, color television broadcasting technology, and laser infrared devices, although the PRC still relies heavily on outside investment and technology transfer. Major advances have also been claimed in rice hybridization, insecticides, fertilizers, biogas digesters for rural electrification, and pollution control technology.

Two scientific exchange agreements between the US and China were signed in January 1984 during Premier Zhao Ziyang's visit to Washington, D.C. China has proposed to several Western nations that it provide long-term storage facilities in remote provinces for radioactive waste—a proposal that Western observers believed would provide China not only with hard currency but also with nuclear materials for possible reprocessing.

China's principal technological handicap is lack of skilled personnel. Only 1% of the PRC's 127 million 22-year-olds receive a university degree. However, 37% of all Chinese degrees are in engineering, the highest ratio in Asia. Part of China's response to this shortage has been to send tens of thousands of students overseas for advanced study, especially in the US. In 1987–97, science and engineering students accounted for 43% of college and university enrollments. China had 454 scientists and engineers and 200 technicians per million people engaged in research and development during the same period. Scientific research is coordinated by the prestigious Chinese Academy of Sciences, founded in 1949 and headquartered in Beijing. China in 1996 had 90 specialized learned societies in the fields of agriculture, medicine, science, and technology. Most are affiliated members of the China Association for Science and Technology, founded in 1958. International science and technology cooperation is also increasing. In 1998 high-technology exports were valued at $23.3 billion and accounted for 15% of manufactured exports. However, concerns over human rights issues has had the effect of cooling US-PRC science and technology exchanges. In 1996, China had 105 universities and colleges offering courses in basic and applied science.

30 DOMESTIC TRADE

Three types of retail trade outlets—the periodic market, the peddler, and the urban shop—constituted the basis of the traditional commercial structure. In the early 1950s, however, a number of state trading companies were established for dealing in commodities such as food grains, cotton, textiles, coal, building materials, metals, machinery, and medicines. These companies, under the control of the Ministry of Commerce, have established branch offices and retail stores throughout the country. In the 1960s, the establishment of state-owned department stores and cooperative retail outlets virtually replaced private trade. There was a resurgence of periodic open markets and private traders when domestic trading regulations were relaxed in 1978. In addition, the government has progressively loosened or eliminated many of its former price controls; an estimated 90% of all retail sales are no longer controlled.

The China Export Commodities Fair, usually held each spring and fall in Guangzhou, was for more than 20 years an important point of contact for Westerners doing business with China. Though still important as an initial introduction to the full range of China's potential suppliers, the decentralization of trading activities in recent years has greatly reduced the fair's role in mediating sustained contact between producers and buyers. Local foreign trade commissions in various industrial centers of the country have taken on a much more active role in organizing many of the services associated with the commodities fair, while any domestic enterprise with foreign trading rights may now participate directly in all events related to trade promotion. Guangzhou still hosts two annual trade fairs, though on a reduced scale. In the major cities, Friendship Stores and other restaurants, hotels, service bureaus and taxis cater exclusively to foreign visitors; payment is made in foreign exchange certificates. By the mid-1980s, international credit cards could be used to obtain cash advances in selected outlets and for direct purchases in Friendship Stores. Some Internet commerce took place in China after 1998.

31 FOREIGN TRADE

Though China has only recently become a major trading nation, its enormous trading potential is attracting great attention by both advanced and newly industrializing nations, shown by the world's interest in China's membership with the WTO. Trade has performed important functions within the economy, providing needed capital goods and modern technology to abet development, as well as primary commodities (such as grains) to supplement local supply in slack years. Foreign trade is under the direction of a single Ministry of Foreign Economic Relations and Trade, created in 1982 through the merger of the former ministries of Foreign Trade and Foreign Economic Relations with the Export-Import and Foreign Investment commissions. A major issue since the early 1980s, however, has been the decentralization of trade management and greater reliance on currency devaluation (major devaluations were implemented in 1989 and 1991) and market incentives rather than direct export and import controls to promote desired trade patterns. After the Asian financial crisis of 1998, officials were tempted to devalue the currency once more; instead the Ministry of Foreign Trade and Economics (MOFTEC) spent massive sums of money on state industry, while dismantling trade barriers in anticipation of WTO membership.

Prior to 1949, some three-fourths of China's exports were agricultural products. This proportion ebbed to a low of 13% during the agricultural crisis of 1961. Foodstuffs and other primary products including crude nonfood raw materials, minerals and fuels averaged about 43–50% of exports through 1985, after which the proportion declined steadily to reach only 6% in 1998, as manufactured exports expanded rapidly. Textiles (excluding garments) accounted for 10% of all exports in 1994 and clothing for about 19.7% (up from 7.5% in 1985). However, China's efforts to emulate the success of Japan, British Hong Kong, Taiwan, and the ROK in basing economic expansion on textile and clothing exports have encountered protectionist resistance from major potential markets in the US and EC.

The textile and clothing industry created the large majority of China's commodity exports in 1998. China's special administrative region of Hong Kong also produces clothes for a large percentage of its export market (31%), averaging 7% of the world's total clothes exports. The majority of Hong Kong's exports go to China. Other exports include electrical parts (12%), watches and clocks (5.3%), telecoms equipment (4.6%), and jewelry (3.0%). Hong Kong produces 9.4% of the world's exports in watches and clocks. China's top 10 exports (excluding Hong Kong) are as follows:

	% OF COUNTRY TOTAL	% OF WORLD TOTAL
Women's outerwear, nonknit	4.8	18
Footwear	4.4	18
Toys and sporting goods	4.1	19
Men's outerwear, not knit	3.9	20
Outerwear knit, nonelastic	2.9	13
Telecoms equipment	2.6	3.4
Cotton fabrics, woven	2.3	16
Headgear and nontextile clothing	2.0	24
Under garments, knitted	1.9	13
Travel goods and handbags	1.9	27

Food imports, which made up only about 2% of the import volume in the 1950s, averaged 20% of the total in 1973 and 1974 but, as total imports rose, fell to less than 4% by 1985 and remained at 2.4% in 1994 and 5% in 1998. In 1997 China's imports were distributed among the following categories:

Consumer goods	3.9%
Food	3.5%
Fuels	7.1%
Industrial supplies	48.2%
Machinery	32.0%
Transportation	4.6%
Other	0.8%

The direction of China's trade has followed three major patterns since the 1930s. Prior to World War II, Japan, Hong Kong, the US, and the UK together made up about three-fourths of the total trade volume. With the founding of the PRC in 1949, trade shifted in favor of the former USSR and Eastern Europe. During 1952–55, more than 50% of China's trade was with the former USSR; during 1956–60, the proportion averaged about 40%. As Sino-Soviet relations deteriorated during the 1960s, trade exchanges steadily declined, reaching a bare 1% of China's total volume in 1970 (3.6% in 1986). By the early 1980s, most of China's leading trade partners were industrialized non-Communist countries, and China's trade pattern overall reflected a high degree of multilateralism.

In recent years, as China has rapidly enlarged its role on the international market, the importance of Hong Kong as an entrepot and major source of revenue has increased. In 1992, Hong Kong accounted for close to 35% of China's total trade (up from about 21% in 1986). Hong Kong reverted to Chinese rule in 1998. During the 1990s, Japan ranked as the second largest trading partner, importing oil and other raw material and claiming 15% of China's total trade. The most dramatic change in the mid-1980s was the emergence of the US as China's third largest trading partner, and China's second largest trading partner in 1997.

Principal trading partners in 1998 (in millions of US dollars) were as follows:

COUNTRY	EXPORTS	IMPORTS	BALANCE
United States	38,001	16,290	21,711
Japan	29,718	28,307	1,411
Germany	7,350	6,998	352
Korea	6,266	15,021	-8,755
Netherlands	5,162	835	4,327
United Kingdom	4,633	1,953	2,680
Singapore	3,901	4,226	-325
Taiwan Province of China	3,866	16,694	-12,828
France	2,830	3,206	-376
Russia	1,833	3,627	-1,794

32 BALANCE OF PAYMENTS

Both foreign trade and international financing in China are state monopolies, with policies and transactions administered by the People's Bank of China (PBC). Among its various functions, the PBC sets exchange rates for foreign currencies. The PBC releases foreign exchange to the Bank of China, which plays a major payments role through its branches in Hong Kong, Singapore, and other overseas financial centers.

The government has, overall, maintained a record of financial stability, linked to a policy of stringent controls over its international transactions. Adhering generally to a principle of self-reliance, it has resorted to the use of commercial credit at certain junctures but until the 1970s avoided falling into long-term indebtedness as a means of financing major development goals. In the period 1958–60, the Great Leap Forward and the succeeding years of economic crisis caused a sharp deterioration in China's international payments position. In 1960, large negative clearing account balances with Communist countries (–$625 million) were even more than the foreign exchange reserves of $415 million. By the end of 1964, however, the negative balance with Socialist nations had been reduced to $55 million, and China's net international financial resources stood at a surplus of $345 million, owing to monetary gold holdings of $215 million and foreign exchange balances from trade with non-Communist countries amounting to $185 million. By 1965, the Chinese had completely cleared their long-term debt to the former USSR, and by 1968, China had redeemed all national bonds and was free of all long-term external and internal debts.

Publication of official balance-of-payments statistics was discontinued during the Cultural Revolution and not resumed until September 1985. According to Western analyses, the period 1978–81 saw a continuing surplus in current accounts, as rising levels of imports were generally matched or exceeded by increases in exports over the same period. In addition, transfers of an estimated $1.1 billion in 1978 and $1 billion in 1980, derived from increased earnings in tourism, shipping, and remittances from Hong Kong and other sources, resulted in overall current accounts surpluses of $900 million and $1.2 billion in 1978 and 1980, respectively.

China's drive to industrialize under the Four Modernizations policy resulted in an unprecedented deficit on capital accounts of $1.1 billion in 1978. The subsequent unilateral decisions to cancel $2.6 billion in contracts with Japan (1979) and $2 billion with Japan and Western nations (1981) were interpreted by some observers as an indication of acute cash-flow problems and a reordering of investment priorities at the highest levels.

The trade account was helped by the slow but steady devaluation that occurred after China went to a managed float

exchange rate system in January 1991. Tourism receipts and visitor figures also continued to grow, passing pre-Tiananmen levels. Foreign investment boomed in the 1990s, with a total of nearly $45 billion committed in 1998 alone. Approximately half of China's loans came from the Asian Development Bank, the World Bank, and Japan; external debt reached $159 billion in 1998.

A usually positive current account balance stockpiled China's reserves. In 1998, China had some $147 billion in official reserves, but state industries had accumulated a huge amount of what was called triangular debt with the state banks and other lending agencies. Government infrastructure and industrial projects received funding for goods that could not be sold domestically in 1999 due to lower demand, losing money for each party involved. In effect, external trade plays a secondary role in China's economy because of normally high, unsatisfied domestic demand. Agreements with the WTO threaten to increase China's dependence on foreign trade.

The US Central Intelligence Agency reports that in 1998 the purchasing power parity of China's exports was $183.8 billion while imports totaled $140,170 million resulting in a trade balance of $43,630 million.

The International Monetary Fund (IMF) reports that in 1998 China had exports of goods totaling $183,527 million and imports totaling $136,914 million. The services credit totaled $24,057 million and debit $28,980 million. The following table summarizes China's balance of payments as reported by the IMF for 1998 in millions of US dollars.

Current Account		29,325
Balance on goods	46,613	
Balance on services	-4,923	
Balance on income	-16,644	
Current transfers	4,279	
Capital Account		-47
Financial Account		-6,276
Direct investment abroad	-2,634	
Direct investment in China	43,751	
Portfolio investment assets	-3,830	
Portfolio investment liabilities	97	
Other investment assets	-35,040	
Other investment liabilities	-8,620	
Net Errors and Omissions		-16,754
Reserves and Related Items		-6,248

33 BANKING AND SECURITIES

Economic reforms under the Four Modernizations program adopted in 1978 brought major changes in China's highly centralized and tightly controlled banking system. In 1982, the People's Bank of China (PBOC) became the central bank and turned over its commercial operations to the new Industrial and Commercial Bank. The State Administration of Foreign Exchange (SAFE) helps set foreign exchange policy. Other specialized agencies include the People's Construction Bank, the Agricultural Bank of China, the Bank of China, the Bank of Communications, the China Development Bank, and the Export-Import Bank of China. The Construction Bank of China (CBC) makes payments for capital construction according to state plans and budgets. The Agricultural Bank of China finances agricultural expansion, grants rural loans, supervises agricultural credit cooperatives, and assists in the modernization of agriculture. The Bank of China (BOC) handles foreign exchange and international settlements for the PBC. It has branches throughout China as well as in Singapore, Hong Kong, Paris, London, Luxembourg, New York, and Tokyo. The BOC is charged with financing China's foreign trade and also acquiring and channeling into appropriate areas the foreign capital needed for imports of industrial equipment and other items for modernization.

The foreign-owned Standard Chartered Bank maintains long-established offices in China. Over 90 foreign banks, representing Japan, the US, France, Italy, Pakistan, and the UK, received permission to establish offices in Beijing in the early 1980s. In 1985, for the first time, foreign banks were allowed to do business in the four special economic zones (established to attract foreign investment) in foreign currency. In mid-1997, 10 foreign banks were given permission to operate outside of the special zones; and in 1996, foreign banks were given limited authority to do business in rembi (the local currency).

China enjoyed a fairly stable exchange rate in 1998 and foreign exchange reserves continued to grow, reading $147 billion by the end of 1998, from $73.5 billion at the end of 1995. Deflation occurred in 1999, at -1%.

In 1987, stock exchanges opened in Shanghai and several other cities, and several stock and bond issues were floated domestically. Securities exchanges are controlled by the PBC, and trading in securities is very limited. In 1997, China accelerated stock-market listings of about 50 large and medium-sized state-owned enterprises (SOEs) and considered raising the number of enterprises piloting group holding structures from 57 to 100. In November 1996, the Shanghai Stock Exchange President, Yang Xianghai, predicted that China's two exchanges (Shanghai and Shenzhen) would number in excess of 1,000 companies by 2000. At the time he was speaking, there were 472 companies listed on the stock exchanges. In 2000, China's stock market had a capitalization of $350 billion, Asia's second largest behind Tokyo. The stock exchange is split into two sections, the "A" share market and the "B" share market. Foreigners may only participate in the B-share market, denominated in foreign currencies and consisting predominantly of foreign private companies. The A-share market is reserved for domestic investors (who are not allowed to participate in the B-share market) and dominated by state enterprises.

34INSURANCE

The People's Insurance Co. of China, formed in 1949 under the supervision of the PBC, is authorized to handle all kinds of insurance, including the insurance of China's foreign trade and foreign insurance operations in China. In the mid-1990s, it controlled 95% of China's insurance industry, with 4,200 branches and a workforce of 110,000. Two additional state enterprises, the China Insurance Co. and the Tai Ping Insurance Co., are in operation, and several foreign insurance companies have established representative offices in Beijing. By October 1995, 77 insurance companies from over 10 nations had established 199 agencies in China. Demand for insurance projects is predicted to grow as economic reforms limit the social security benefits provided by state enterprises. Total life and nonlife insurance premiums were expected to reach $20 billion by the year 2000.

35PUBLIC FINANCE

The annual state budget is prepared by the Ministry of Finance and approved by the National People's Congress. A major reform in public finance, introduced in 1980, was a new system of allocating revenues and expenditures between local and national levels of government. Previous revenue-sharing procedures allowed the central government to fix maximum spending levels for each province, autonomous region, and centrally administered municipality. The new system fixed for a five-year period the proportion of local income to be paid to the central government and (except for emergency appropriations for floods and other such disasters) the level of subsidies to be provided by the central government, as well as the proportion of local income to be retained by local governments. Autonomous regions receive proportionately greater state subsidies than the provinces and

centrally administered municipalities, and they are entitled to keep all revenues from local industrial and commercial taxes.

During the 1990s, the Chinese consolidated budget deficit grew at a rapidly increasing rate. According to the IMF, the 1998 budget deficit amounted to 4% of GDP, due to rising expenditures and tax evasion. Deficits are largely financed by domestic debt issuance rather than by money creation. In 1999, the central government performed an audit of embezzlement, finding that some $2.4 billion in state funds had been diverted into private bank accounts, and that a total equaling one-fifth of the central government's tax revenues were misused. In all, the governments liabilities were equal to 100% of GDP in 2000, according to some sources. Annual tax revenues equal 13% of GDP, one-fifth of which goes annually to paying interest on government debts.

The International Monetary Fund (IMF) estimates that in 1997 China's central government took in revenues of approximately $59.5 billion and had expenditures of $72.6 billion. Overall, the government registered a deficit of approximately $13.1 billion. External debt totaled $156 billion.

The following table shows an itemized breakdown of government revenues and expenditures in million of US dollars. The percentages were calculated from data reported by IMF.

REVENUE AND GRANTS	100%	59,506
Tax revenue	85.4%	50,836
Non-tax revenue	2.3%	1,372
Capital revenue	<1%	5
Grants	12.3%	7,293
EXPENDITURES	100%	72,600
General public services	7.5%	5,457
Defense	13.6%	9,876
Public order and safety	2.6%	1,894
Education	2.0%	1,479
Health	0.2%	171
Social security	0.2%	115
Housing and community amenities	0.1%	83
Recreation, cultural, and religious affairs	0.4%	281
Economic affairs and services	17.0%	12,353
Other expenditures	56.3%	40,890

36TAXATION

An overhaul of China's tax system began in 1979 as part of the Four Modernizations program. The principal domestic levies, as in the past, were commercial and industrial taxes imposed on all enterprises, but, after 1979, taxes were due only on assigned production quotas. In 1993, the Consolidated Industrial and Commercial Tax was levied (usually at 5–10%) on agricultural and industrial production, commercial retailing, and service, transportation, and communication earnings.

On 1 January 1994, a new PRC Individual Income Tax law came into effect in China. The PRC introduced a new turnover tax system consisting of a VAT, business tax and consumption/excise tax, to replace the CICT. Under the new system the sale or importation of goods and services are subject to VAT at a standard rate of 17%. Other services and the transfer of real property and intangible assets are subject to a business tax with a rate ranging from 3% to 20%. Consumption/excise taxes were also introduced to tax 11 categories of goods, including cigarettes and alcoholic beverages.

Under a tax law that took effect on 1 July 1991, joint and foreign owned ventures pay a combined national and provincial tax levied at 33% of pre-tax income. A foreign-owned enterprise with income from sources in China but not established there pays a 20% withholding income tax, and royalties for certain types of technical knowledge are taxed at 10% of the revenue amount. Individuals are required to submit individual income tax returns to the Tax Bureau on a monthly basis. As of 1 January 1996, tax rates ranged from 5% to 45% for individual income tax.

³⁷CUSTOMS AND DUTIES

Although China is in the process of aligning its trade system with international standards, prohibitively high tariffs and quotas discourage many imports. It uses the Harmonized System for tariff classification. A minimum tariff rate is granted to countries that have special agreements with China, including the United States. Tariff rates range from 3–100% with the highest rates reserved for goods such as automobiles. Raw materials are exempt. As a step toward WTO compliance, in 1996 China reduced tariffs on more than 4,000 products by an average of 30%. In 2000, the US China Trade Relations Working Group successfully opened trade relations with China, with such agreements as: reducing the automobile tariff from a maximum of 100% to a maximum of 25%; a reduction in auto parts tariffs from 23.4% to 10%; and quota elimination by 2005. In addition, China agreed to a reduction in chemical tariffs from about 15% to 7%, and a reduction in textile tariffs from 25% to 12% by 2005 (but a quota safeguard would be available in the event that the industry failed). Steel tariffs were to be reduced from 10% to 6% by 2003. These reductions would be implemented on a sliding yearly basis. Most other tariffs were reduced by more than 50%, to an average of 9.4% by 2005 on industrial tariffs and an average of 17% on agricultural tariffs by 2004.

Official PRC policy is that direct trade with Taiwan is interregional, rather than international, since Taiwan is considered a province of China, and therefore no customs duties are levied. There are free-trade zones in Shanghai, Tianjin, Dalian, Haikov, the Hainan Island Special Economic Zone, and within the Shenzhen Special Economic Zone. Smuggling, reportedly well organized along the coasts of Guangdong, Fujian, and Zhejiang provinces and in the frontier regions of Tibet and Yunnan, is a major governmental concern.

³⁸FOREIGN INVESTMENT

China strongly emphasizes attracting foreign investment in projects that will enhance the nation's export capabilities. Beginning in the early 1970s, China contracted for the construction of a substantial number of complete plants, notably for iron and steel, automobile, and fertilizer manufacture and power generation, including nuclear power. Such agreements, often made with private firms from Japan, the FRG, Italy, France, the UK, and Canada, as well as with agencies of the Communist states, all called for direct purchase of materials and services, and residual ownership by foreigners or remittance of profits from production were expressly disallowed. In 1979, China established the Foreign Investment Control Commission to attract and coordinate the use of more foreign investment funds.

China attracts capital in four ways: (1) by soliciting loans and credits from foreign governments and international financial institutions; (2) by floating bonds and debentures on international capital markets; (3) by promoting direct foreign investment through joint ventures and other cooperative enterprises; and (4) by accumulating trade surpluses from export sales.

Under the Joint Ventures Law, enacted in 1979 and revised in 1982, direct nongovernmental investment by foreigners and remittance of profits overseas became possible for the first time since 1950. The development of joint ventures for the production of exports has been particularly stressed as a means of securing for China the foreign exchange needed to pay for purchases of advanced technology. Foreign investment in products for the domestic market, other than those needed for modernization, is discouraged. Under the Joint Ventures Law, the foreign company is expected to invest between 35% and 100% of all registered capital for an enterprise, but there must be some Chinese participation in the venture, including a Chinese chairman of the board of directors. Joint ventures are coordinated by the China International Trust and Investment Corp., established in 1979.

Most provinces, regions, and major municipalities have their own international and trust investment corporations, of which the one in Shanghai is the largest. Special corporations for the attraction of investment by overseas Chinese have been established in Fujian and Zhejiang provinces. The attraction of "spillover" investment from Hong Kong was a major factor in the establishment of the Shenzhen special economic zone (which includes the Shekou special industrial zone and the city of Shenzhen) in southern Guangdong Province in 1979. The other four special economic zones, also designed to attract foreign investment, are located at Zhuhai, near Macau; Shantou, along the east coast of Guangdong; Xiamen, across the Taiwan Strait from Taiwan and on Hainan island. Further foreign investment incentives were developed through the designation of open coastal cities, where investment terms similar to those of SEZ's are offered to foreign companies. By the end of 1992, there were 18 open cities in China, mainly along the southern coast but also along the North Korean, Russian and Mongolian borders.

By the end of 1999, actual foreign direct investment in China since 1979 amounted to $267 billion. Investment inflows contracted sharply in wake of the open political conflicts in 1989, but rebounded strongly in 1991 and 1992. By the end of 1995, over 258,000 foreign-invested enterprises had registered in China. In 1996 a World Bank study found that China attracted more than one-third of all investment in factories and other manufacturing plants in developing nations. As of 1999, China was the second largest recipient of foreign direct investment in the world. Foreign investment equaled $45.6 billion in 1997, as well as in 1998 (based on MOFTEC figures, which do not discriminate between mainland China and the administrative regions: it is estimated that 10% to 30% of FDI from Hong Kong actually comes from Chinese mainland companies looking for a tax break). Foreign invested firms numbered 300,000 and accounted for almost 50% of China's exports in 1999. In 2000, the services sector was opened up to foreign investment at a maximum percentage of 49% foreign ownership.

A breakdown foreign direct investment in China by country of origin for 1998 follows:

COUNTRY	% OF TOTAL
Hong Kong	40
US	8.6
Singapore	7.5
Japan	7.5
Taiwan	6.4
Korea	4.0
Germany	1.6

Until the early 1980s, the flow of Chinese funds abroad was confined to assistance to developing countries and to investment in Hong Kong real estate. In 1983, however, China began making direct investments overseas, in the US, Canada, the Solomon Islands, and Sri Lanka. China has been a significant supplier of development aid to other countries. Recipients of Chinese military and economic assistance have included the DPRK, Vietnam, Egypt, Pakistan, and Tanzania.

³⁹ECONOMIC DEVELOPMENT

A profound restructuring of China's economy began in 1949 following the founding of the PRC. Adhering to orthodox models borrowed wholesale from the former USSR, the PRC brought all major industrial, infrastructure, and financial enterprises directly under state ownership. Agriculture was collectivized. Management of the economy was closely controlled by central authorities, whose powers extended to the allocation of basic commodities and the basic division of resources into investment, consumption, and defense channels. Centralized planning for economic development was introduced in the form of five-year economic plans.

The first five-year plan (1953–57), belatedly announced in 1957, pursued rapid industrialization along Soviet lines, with a special emphasis on increases in steel and other heavy industries. The plan reportedly achieved its goals of a 5% gain in gross value of agricultural output and a 4% gain in grain production, and exceeded the 19% growth target in gross value of industrial output.

The second five-year plan (1958–62) was voided at its start by the social and economic upheavals of the Great Leap Forward. At the heart of the Great Leap was the establishment of the self-sufficient rural commune; decentralization of industry was stressed, and the rural unemployed put to work in "backyard steel furnaces" and other industrial enterprises of dubious efficiency. Incomes were determined by need, and coercion and revolutionary enthusiasm replaced profit as the motivation for work. Publication of economic data ceased at this time, but Western observers estimated a 1% decline in agriculture for the 1958–60 period, an increase in GNP of only 1%, and no more than a 6% increase in industrial output. After the bad harvests of 1960 and 1961, an "agriculture first" policy was adopted under which large areas of semiarid steppe and other marginal lands in the north and west were converted to agricultural use.

A third five-year plan (1966–70), formulated by governmental pragmatists and calling for rapid growth of all sectors, was aborted by the outbreak of the Cultural Revolution. In 1969, the government published a report calling for a more open approach to foreign assistance and trade. Domestically, it confirmed the use of the "mass line"—the system of calling upon workers and peasants to take responsibility and initiative, and to work without material incentives. It favored the simultaneous use of modern and traditional employment methods (the "walking on two legs" policy), and recommended expansion of industry through investment of profits derived from the sale of agricultural and light industrial products. At the heart of the 1969 policy was a reversion to the commune system of 1958—a program to make the countryside self-sufficient, with every commune not only growing its own food but also producing its own fertilizer and tools, generating its own electricity, and managing its own small handicrafts factories, health schemes, and primary schools. In contrast to the hastily organized communes of 1958–60, however, the new units frequently adhered to the traditional—and more manageable—structure of Chinese rural life.

Long-range economic planning resumed in 1970 with the announcement of a fourth five-year plan, for 1971–75. In late 1975, Premier Zhou Enlai proclaimed the plan successful. Agricultural output was reported to have grown by 51% during the 1964–74 period, while gross industrial output was said to have increased by 190%. Specifically, the following growth rates (1964–74) for mining and industry were reported: petroleum, 660%; coal, 92%; steel, 120%; cotton yarn, 86%; tractors, 540%; chemical fertilizers, 350%; and electric power, 200%.

A fifth five-year plan (1976–80), announced in 1975, gave priority to modernization of the economy and, for the first time, emphasized the development of light rather than heavy industry. Implementation of this new departure was, however, delayed by the deaths of Mao and Zhou in 1976 and did not occur until 1978, by which time the economic pragmatists, led by Deng Xiaoping, had emerged victorious from the subsequent political and ideological struggles.

The sixth five-year plan (1981–85), announced in November 1982, reemphasized China's commitment to the pragmatic line and to the Four Modernizations. Approximately $115 billion was allocated for capital construction, and another $65 billion for renovation of existing infrastructure. GNP increased by an annual average of 10%, industrial output by one of 12%, and agricultural output by one of 8.1%.

The seventh five-year plan (1986–90), announced in March 1986 and called by Deng Xiaoping "The New Long March," featured the following major goals: increasing industrial output 7.5% annually (to $357 billion), agricultural output 4% annually (to $95.4 billion), national income 6.7% annually (to $252.7 billion), and foreign trade 40% (to $83 billion); spending $54 billion on 925 major development projects in energy, raw materials, transportation, and postal and telecommunications; and investing $74.6 billion in technological transformation of state enterprises. Rural per capita income was to rise to $151 annually.

Concerns about the unevenness of China's economic development progress, both in geographic and sectoral terms, shaped the country's eighth five-year plan. To ameliorate potentially crippling bottlenecks in the supply of raw materials, energy, transportation, and communications capacity, the government prioritized the financing of infrastructure investments. Streamlining of inefficient state industrial enterprises was targeted as well, with the setting up of an unemployment security fund planned in order to assist laid-off workers make the transition to employment in non-state industry and the services sector. Direct foreign investment in industry, services as well as infrastructure (especially energy and communications development) were promoted. The plan also emphasized better distribution of the country's development momentum. Inland cities, especially along the Russian, Mongolian, and North Korean borders were targeted for development as export-oriented special economic zones in addition to coastal areas. Particular emphasis was given to developing major infrastructure projects to link Hong Kong, Macao and the Pearl River delta area of Guangdong province into an integrated economic area and major export base for the 21st century.

The Ninth Five-Year Plan (1996–2000) called for a shift from a centrally planned economy to a "socialist market economy." It also stressed resource allocation to achieve higher efficiency. The goals included continuing progress toward quadrupling the 1980 GNP by the year 2000 (a goal that had already been met by 1996) and doubling the 2000 GNP by the year 2010. To reach the 2010 goal, China needed to sustain annual GNP growth rates of 8%, but fell just short of the goal at an average growth rate of 7%. The plan also continued to support China's state-owned enterprises with the majority of national investment. Although inefficient and heavily in debt, they provided salaries and social services (including education and health) for over 100 million workers and their families. Nevertheless, the government enrolled 1,000 state-owned firms in a program designed to force them to become self-reliant in the marketplace. Cutting down on state enterprises was the plan after 2000, resulting in major job losses, the further privatization of the economy, and the liberalization of trade through the WTO.

40 SOCIAL DEVELOPMENT

Social welfare programs cover workers in state-operated enterprises and institutions, which include virtually all employees of government agencies, mining, manufacturing, industry, railroad, shipping, and construction units. Welfare in rural areas is administered by the state and collective farms, which provide clothing, shelter, and food for sick and disabled people and place the aged in homes. Recreational and cultural services are also supported through welfare payments.

Although wage scales in China remain low, the range of benefits has been expanding. According to the 1994 Labor Law, male workers and professional women are eligible to retire at age 60, female non-salaried workers at 55, and other women at age 50.

Workers may receive six months' sick leave at 60–100% of salary. For work-related total disability, workers are entitled to lifetime compensation of 75–90% of the standard wage. Maternity leave at full pay is provided for up to 90 days. In addition, numerous health, day-care, and educational benefits are provided free of charge. In urban areas, housing rentals rarely exceed 5% of the monthly wage.

The economic status of women, formerly considered little more than chattels for their husband's family, improved considerably after 1950, aided by the introduction of a work-point system of payment on the communes and by legislation guaranteeing equal pay for equal work. A campaign to increase literacy among women, formerly denied education, also opened doors to increased employment opportunities. The 1950 Marriage Law abolished arranged marriages, outlawed polygamy, and further protected women's rights by granting widows the right to remarry without the consent of the dead husband's family and guaranteeing to women as well as to men the right of divorce. Nonetheless, it is still usual for a woman to move in with her husband's family after marriage, and women continue to be significantly underrepresented at the higher levels of government and the CCP.

Despite constitutional provisions, women may face discrimination in the workplace. A 1995 survey found that 70% of persons fired during the restructuring of unprofitable state enterprises were women. In addition, some enterprises are reluctant to hire women because of the additional costs of maternity leave. In spite of the 1992 Law on the Protection of Women's Rights designed to provide improved access to education and property and inheritance rights, there is growing concern that the market reforms of the 1990s have led to a regression in the status of women in Chinese society. As of 1998, 650 of 2,979 parliamentary seats were held by women.

A serious human rights problem is female infanticide by families wishing for sons. The imbalance of sex ratios in the country has lead to a shortage of women of marriagable age, and a dramatic increase in the abduction of women for this purpose. The government continued to condemn and took steps to curb traditional abuse of women.

China's human rights record continued to draw international censure as of 1999. Ongoing human rights abuses include arbitrary and lengthy detention, forced confessions, torture and the mistreatment of prisoners. Repression of political dissent continues. The crackdown on the fledgling China Democracy Party, begun in 1998, intensified in 1999. In the same year, the Falun Gang spiritual movement was banned and thousands of its members were arrested. Some were confined in psychiatric hospitals. Prison conditions are poor and China does not allow any independent monitoring of its prisons. Widespread human rights abuses have also been reported in Chinese-occupied Tibet. The government does not tolerate any political dissent or pro-independence movements in Tibet.

41HEALTH

A revamping of China's health system is underway to manage serious diseases. The Ministry of Public Heath's ninth Five-Year Plan on the control of serious diseases outlined major reforms to be reached by the year 2000. Among these include strengthening epidemic-prevention management systems and facilities. National health practices, including the provision of both Western and traditional Chinese health services, are under the supervision of the Ministry of Health. The ministry has emphasized preventive medicine and general improvement of sanitary conditions. Since the early 1950s, mass campaigns have been mounted to deal with major public health problems. These have included nationwide cleanup campaigns and mass educational programs in the sanitary preparation of food, the treatment of drinking water,

personal hygiene, and waste disposal. The entire population was mobilized to eradicate the four pests—rats, sparrows, flies, and mosquitoes—with mixed results. Epidemic prevention centers were established to carry out massive immunizations, while parasitic diseases, affecting hundreds of millions in China, were also attacked. As a result, schistosomiasis, malaria, kala-azar, and hookworm are thought to have been largely brought under control. The country's 1991–1995 five-year plan was instituted to upgrade services yet again. Infectious diseases were to be 20% lower than in 1990; all provinces were to provide primary medical care to citizens; there were plans to add 450,000 hospital beds and 500,000 technical health workers; and the availability of health insurance was forecast to increase. From 1985 to 1992, 90% of inhabitants had access to health care services.

There were 62,000 hospitals at the end of 1990 (a rise of 3,000 over 1985), and total beds numbered 2.6 million (up by 370,000), a rate of 2.33 per 1,000. In 1990–97, this rate rose to 2.4, and there were 1.6 doctors per 1,000 population. During the Cultural Revolution, in an effort to even out the disparity between rural and urban health services, medical personnel from hospitals (as much as 30–50% of a hospital's medical staff) were included in groups of people sent down to the countryside, and the number of locally trained paramedical personnel, called barefoot doctors, expanded. An increasingly important medical factor since the Cultural Revolution, these young peasants or middle-school graduates have been trained on the job by township doctors or in two-month courses at township health clinics. Barefoot doctors and production teams and brigade health stations are still the major deliverers of health care in the countryside.

From 1989 to 1995, 83% of married women (ages 15 to 49) used contraception. The infant mortality rate was reduced from as high as 200 per 1,000 live births before 1949 to an estimated 43.3 per 1,000 in 1999. In the mid-1990s, China vaccinated a high percentage of its children up to one year of age: tuberculosis (94%); diphtheria, pertussis, and tetanus (93%); polio (94%); and measles (89%). Despite the high immunization rates, diseases still persist. China had the greatest number of tuberculosis of any UN member state. In 1994, 363,804 Chinese were infected. According to the World Health Organization, cholera was reported in 10,344 individuals. In China, which accounts for 20% of the world's tetanus cases; over 90,000 die from neonatal tetanus a year. In the mid-1990s, only 10% of pregnant women were immunized against tetanus.

Average life expectancy in 1999 was 69.9 years, up from an average of 45 years in 1950. From 1985 to 1990, major causes of death were recorded as: communicable diseases and maternal/perinatal causes (117 per 100,000); noncommunicable diseases (696 per 100,000); and injuries (88 per 100,000). In an effort to prevent the spread of AIDS, the government in 1987 required the testing of all foreigners for the HIV virus. HIV seroprevalence in 1997 was 0.1 per 100 adults. The number of AIDS cases reported in 1996 was only 117.

42HOUSING

China has an acute shortage of housing, attributable not only to the large annual increases in population (over 10 million a year) that must be accommodated but also to the long-standing policy of directing investment funds into heavy industry rather than into housing and other social amenities. According to official Chinese sources, some 25 million peasant families, or 14% of all rural households, built new homes or rebuilt their existing homes between 1978 and 1980. Extensive rebuilding was reported in Tangshan, which had been virtually leveled during the 1976 earthquake. By the end of 1980, 7.69 million sq m (82.77 million sq ft) of housing had been rebuilt in the city, and more than 500,000 families relocated there. In 1985, housing construction in rural areas, reflecting the impact of rural reforms and the increasing capital accumulation of the peasantry, exceeded 700 million sq m (7,535 million sq ft) of dwelling space; in cities and towns, the 1985 total was 187.5 million sq m (2,018 million sq ft), of which 35 million sq m (377 million sq ft) was in Beijing. Of the new urban housing, about 6.3 million sq m (67.8 million sq ft) came in the form of private homes. In the mid-1990s, the total number of housing units in China stood at 276,502,000. Approximately 400,000 new dwellings were completed per year and 90.6% of all homes had piped water.

43 EDUCATION

Prior to 1949, schools were available for less than 40% of school-age children; 85% of the people were illiterate. During 1949–59, school attendance increased nearly fourfold. In 1959, about 50 million children received preschool education; primary schooling was nearly universal, with some 92.6 million students (between 85% and 90% of all school-age children) in primary schools; 12 million were in secondary schools. By 1966, total school enrollment in China reached 116 million, with the average pupil receiving 5.5 years of formal schooling.

The Cultural Revolution affected education more than any other sector of society. Schools were shut down in mid-1966 to give the student Red Guards the opportunity to "make revolution" on and off campus. The Cultural Revolution touched off purges within the educational establishment. Upper- and middle-level bureaucrats throughout the system were removed from office, and virtually entire university faculties and staffs dispersed. Although many lower schools had begun to reopen during 1969, several universities remained closed through the early 1970s, as an estimated 10 million urban students were removed to the countryside to take part in labor campaigns. During this period and its aftermath, revolutionary ideology and local conditions became the principal determinants of curriculum. A nine-year program of compulsory education (compressed from 12 years) was established for youths 7–15 years of age.

Education was reoriented in 1978 under the Four Modernizations policy, which restored the pre-1966 emphasis on competitive examinations and the development of special schools for the most promising students. The most striking changes were effected at the junior and senior high school levels, in which students were again streamed, according to ability, into an estimated 5,000 high-quality, well-equipped schools; into lower-quality high schools; or into the technical and vocational schools, which were perceived as the least prestigious. In addition, 96 universities, 200 technical schools, and 7,000 primary schools were designated as "key" institutions. Universities were reopened, with a renewed emphasis given to science and technology. During the 1980s, having universal primary education instituted by 1990 became a main goal.

By 1998, there were 628,840 primary schools with 5,794,000 teachers and 139,954,000 students. Student-to-teacher ratio stood at 24 to 1. At the secondary level, there were 4,437,000 teachers and 718,883,000 students. For the year 2000, adult illiteracy rates (per UNESCO) were estimated at 15.0% (males, 7.7%; females, 22.6%).

In 1985 there were 1,016 colleges and universities in China. Among the largest and most prestigious institutions were Beijing University and Qinghua University, both in Beijing; Zhongshan University, in Guangzhou; Nanjing University and Nanjing Institute of Technology; Nankai University and Tianjin University, in Tianjin; and Fudan University, in Shanghai. Graduate education resumed in the late 1970s; the number of graduates increased from 147,111 in 1981 to 645,510 in 1991. By 1998, the number of students enrolled in post-secondary institutions totaled 6,075,215, with 516,400 teachers.

Tuition has traditionally been free in vocational secondary schools and in training schools for elementary teachers, as well as in colleges and universities; students in need of food, clothing, and textbooks receive state grants-in-aid. Primary and general secondary school students pay a nominal tuition fee. Part-time primary and secondary schools, evening universities, and correspondence schools exist for adult workers and peasants.

44 LIBRARIES AND MUSEUMS

The National Library in Beijing (founded in 1909) is the largest in China, with over 21 million volumes, including more than 200,000 rare ancient Chinese books and manuscripts. The Chinese Academy of Sciences Central Library, in Beijing, has a collection of 5.62 million volumes, with branches in Shanghai, Lanzhou, Wuhan, and Chengdu. The Capital Library in Beijing (2.7 million volumes) is the city's public library and operates lending, reference, and children's services. The Shoudou Library, also in Beijing, has 2.35 million volumes.

Small lending libraries and reading rooms can be found in factories, offices, and rural townships. The library of Beijing University, with over four million volumes, is the largest university library. Other important university collections are at Nanjing University in Nanjing (3.2 million volumes), Fudan University in Shanghai (3.6 million volumes), and Qinghua University in Beijing (2.5 million volumes). The Central Institute of Nationalities in Beijing—one of dozens of private institutions with libraries—has a collection of 800,000 volumes, including 160 foreign-language journals.

China has about 1,000 museums, most of them cultural museums. The Imperial Palace Museum in Beijing houses collections of art, sculpture, silk fabric, and furniture. The Museum of the Chinese Revolution, on Tiananmen Square, has exhibits of the revolutionary movement in China from the Opium War to the founding of the PRC. In Shanghai is the Museum of Art and History, with some of the country's outstanding archaeological and art collections. Many museums are memorials to Chinese artists and writers, and house collections of their work. China also has 500 historical sites with exhibitions. With the return of Hong Kong to China, the country gained the Hong Kong Museum of Art, the University Museum and Art Gallery, the Hong Kong Museum of History, and the Hong Kong Space Museum.

45 MEDIA

Postal service and telecommunications facilities fall under the authority of the Ministry of Posts and Telecommunications. The posts are responsible for the sale and distribution of newspapers and magazines, an important function in a country that relies heavily on these media for mass communication. Mail is delivered twice a day seven days a week. There were 53,600 post offices in 1990. In 1998, there were an estimated 105 million telephones, and more than 240,000 fax machines as of 1995.

Radio and Television

Television broadcasting began in 1958, and color transmissions in 1973. As of 1999 China had 569 AM radio broadcasting stations. In the same year, China Central Television operated 209 government-owned television stations, and there were also 31 provincial stations and almost 3,000 city stations. The most important station is Beijing's Central People's Broadcasting Station (CPBS); from there, programs are relayed by local stations. CPBS broadcasts daily on several channels using a variety of languages, including Mandarin (or standard Chinese), the Hokkien and Hakka dialects, Cantonese, Mongolian, Tibetan, Uygur, Kazakhi and Korean.

In 1997 there were 195 radios, 270 television sets, and 10 mobile phones per 1,000 population. Many of the TV sets are installed in public meeting places and in government and economic enterprises, although increasingly a television set has become a much-prized private acquisition. Since large segments of the rural population are as yet without radios and television sets, the government operates a massive wired broadcast network linked to over 100 million loudspeakers.

The Press

The press is closely controlled by the government, the CCP, or the various political and mass organizations associated with the CCP. Minority newspapers are published in Mongolian, Uygur, Tibetan, Korean, and other languages. The main news agencies are the official New China (Xinhua) News Agency; the China News Service, which supplies information to overseas Chinese newspapers and journals; and China Feature, which supplies articles to magazines and newspapers worldwide.

The Cultural Revolution caused substantial upheaval in the Chinese press establishment. Many publications closed down, and others underwent purges of editorial staffs. Publication of *Hongqi (Red Flag)*, the most authoritative of the CCP publications, resumed in 1968. The major newspapers, with their locations and circulations in 1999, are *Renmin Ribao (People's Daily;* Beijing, 3,000,000); *Jiefangjun Bao (Liberation Army Daily;* Beijing, 800,000), the army organ, which played a leading role in the Cultural Revolution; *Wenhui Bao (Wenhui Daily;* Shanghai, 1,700,000); *Jiefang Ribao (Liberation Daily;* Shanghai, 1,000,000); and *Beijing Ribao (Beijing Daily;* Beijing, 700,000). China's first English-language newspaper, the *China Daily,* founded in 1981, is published in Beijing and had a circulation of 150,000 in 1999. The most authoritative publication for foreigners is the multilingual weekly *Beijing Review,* which distributed in China and abroad, with a 1995 circulation of more than 100,000.

Though China's constitution states that freedom of speech and of the press are fundamental rights, in practice the Communist Party and the government control all print and electronic media, which are compelled to propagate the current ideological line. All media are under explicit, public orders to guide public opinion as directed by the authorities.

Despite controls, a rapidly growing number of Chinese have access to satellite television and the Internet. As of 1996, there were 2,659,450 personal computers. Online access is extremely limited, with less than one Internet host per 1,000 population in 1998.

46ORGANIZATIONS

Prior to 1966, the leading mass organizations, all closely tied to the regime, were the Communist Youth League, the Women's Federation, the Federation of Literary and Art Circles, the Federation of Scientific Societies, and the Federation of Industry and Commerce. These bodies were to some extent eclipsed by the Cultural Revolution, which spawned a host of new groups. After the Cultural Revolution passed its peak, many of the new organizations lost ground, while local Communist Youth League organizations, including the Young Pioneers, gained prestige. By the mid-1980s, the pre-Cultural Revolution groups were once again ascendant.

47TOURISM, TRAVEL, AND RECREATION

Chinese restrictions on tourism were eased to allow access by foreigners on group tours in 1976 and further relaxed in 1983, when the ban on individual travel was lifted. By 1985, 244 Chinese cities and scenic spots were open to foreign tourists, and a number of resorts specifically designed for foreigners were in operation. China was opened to tourists from Taiwan in 1987. All visitors to China must have visas. In 1998, 7,107,747 tourists arrived in China. Total receipts from tourism in 1997 were

estimated at $12 billion. That year there were 701,736 hotel rooms with 1,411,708 beds and a 54% occupancy rate.

Tourist Attractions

The most famous tourist attraction in China is the Great Wall, the construction of which began in the 3rd century BC as a barrier against northern invaders. Other leading tourist attractions include the Forbidden City, or Imperial Palace, in Beijing; the nearby tombs of the Ming emperors; historic Hangzhou, with its famous West Lake and gardens; busy Shanghai, with its well-stocked stores and superb cuisine; Xi'an, the site of monumental Qin dynasty excavations; and Guangzhou, the center of Cantonese cooking, with an extensive Cultural Park.

Sports

Sports activities in China are coordinated by the State Physical Culture and Sports Commission and the All-China Sports Federation. Active sports, represented by national associations, include gymnastics, diving, basketball, soccer, tennis, cycling, swimming, tennis, volleyball, weight lifting, and mountain climbing.

Distinctively Chinese pastimes include wushu, a set of ancient exercises known abroad as gonfu (kung fu), or the "martial arts"; taijiquan, or shadow boxing, developed in the 17th century; and liangong shibafa, modern therapeutic exercises for easing neck, shoulder, back, and leg ailments. Qigong (literally "breathing exercises") is also widely practiced both as a sport and as physical therapy. A popular traditional spectator sport is Chinese wrestling. Traditional pastimes for the national minorities are horse racing, show jumping, and archery among the Mongolians; the sheep chase (in which the winner successfully locates and defends possession of a slaughtered sheep) among Uygurs and Kazaks; and yak and horse racing among Tibetans.

The costs of traveling in China vary from city to city. In 1999 the UN estimated the daily cost of staying in Shanghai at $125, Beijing at $108, and Zhengzhor at $85.

48FAMOUS CHINESE

Confucius (K'ung Fu-tzu or Kong Fuzi, 551–479 BC) is generally regarded as the most important historical figure, as well as the greatest scholar, of ancient China. His philosophy and social ideas include observance of filial piety, the sanctity of the family, and social responsibility. Other early philosophers were Lao-tzu (Laozi; Li Erh, 604?–531 BC), the traditional founder of Taoism; Mencius (Meng-tzu or Mengzi, 385–289 BC), who stressed the essential goodness of human nature and the right of subjects to revolt against unjust rulers; and Mo Ti (Di, 465?–390? BC), who stressed the theme of universal love. Among the principal early poets was Chu (Chü) Yuan, (340–278 BC), whose *Li Sao,* a melancholy rhapsody, is among the world's great poems. Sima Qian (Ssu-ma Ch'ien, 145–87 BC) produced the monumental *Shiji (Shih-chi; Historical Records),* the first general history of China. Ban Gu (Pan Ku, AD 32–92) wrote *Qian Hanshu (Ch'ien-Han shu; History of the Former Han Dynasty),* a continuation of Sima Qian's work. Zhang (Chang) Heng (78–139), an astronomer, is credited with having invented the first seismograph. Zhang Zhongjing (Chang Chung-ching, 152–219) was a celebrated physician, and Zu Zhongzhi (Tsu Chung-chih, 429–500) calculated the figure 3.14159265 as the exact value for π. Three brilliant poets of the Tang dynasty were Li Bo (Po, 701–62), Du (Tu) Fu (712–70), and Bo Juyi (Po Chü-yi, 772–846). Li Shizhen (Shi-chen, 1518–93), an outstanding pharmacologist, wrote a monumental *Materia Medica.* Great authors of the Qing dynasty were Wu Jingzi (Ching-tzu, 1701–54), who wrote *Rulin Waishi (Ju-lin wai-shih; Unofficial History of the Scholars),* a superb satire on the civil service system, and Cao Xuequin (Ts'ao Hsüeh-ch'in, 1715?–63), who produced a remarkable novel, *Honglou meng (Hung-lou meng; The Dream of the Red Chamber).* Lu

Xun or Lu Hsun (Zhou Shuren or Chou Shu-jen, 1881–1936) is generally regarded as China's greatest writer of the modern period. Mao Dun (Shen Yanbing, 1896–1981) and Ba Jin (Li Feigan, b.1904) are leading novelists. Lin Yutang (Yu-t'ang, 1895–1976) popularized Chinese culture in the West.

Political Figures

Sun Yat-sen (Zhongshan or Chung-shan, 1866–1925) planned the revolution against the Manchus and became the first president (1911–12) of the republic. Mao Zedong (Tse-tung, 1893–1976), the foremost figure of postrevolutionary China, served as chairman of the Central Committee of the CCP from 1956 to 1976. Other prominent Chinese Communist leaders include Zhu De (Chu Teh, 1886–1976), who became commander in chief of the Red Army in 1931 and chairman of the Standing Committee of the NPC; Zhou Enlai (Chou En-lai, 1898–1976), first premier of China's State Council; Liu Shaoqi (Shao-ch'i, 1898–1969), who became China's head of state in 1959 and was purged during the Cultural Revolution but posthumously rehabilitated in 1985; and Lin Biao (Piao, 1908–71), who became deputy premier and minister of defense in 1959 and who, prior to his death and subsequent political vilification, had been certified as Mao's successor in the constitution drawn up in 1969. Women in the political hierarchy have included Song Qingling (Soong Ch'ing-ling, 1892–1981), Sun Zhongshan's wife, and Jiang Qing (Chiang Ch'ing, 1913–1991), Mao's fourth wife, who emerged as a radical leader during the Cultural Revolution. Jiang, with other prominent radicals, was purged in the wake of the ascension of Hua Guofeng (b.1920) as CCP chairman in 1976. Deng Xiaoping (1904–97), twice disgraced (1966–73 and 1976) by radical administrations, reemerged in 1977 to become China's most powerful political figure, albeit without major office, and a major figure in its modernization drive; he officially retired in 1987. A protégé, Hu Yaobang (1915–1989), was party secretary until his ouster in 1987. Another protégé, who emerged in 1987 as the likely preeminent Chinese leader of the future, although still currently in the political shadow of Deng, was Zhao Ziyang (b.1919), who became general secretary of the CCP in 1987; Li Peng (b.1928) was named premier in the same year.

49 DEPENDENCIES

Hong Kong

Hong Kong consists of 237 small islands off the southeast coast of the mainland of China and a small peninsula adjoining Guangdong Province on the mainland between 22°29′ and 22°37′N and 113°52′ and 114°30′E. With a total area, including recent reclamation, of 1,068 sq km (412 sq mi), it comprises the island of Hong Kong and adjacent islands, 79 sq km (30 sq mi); the Kowloon Peninsula, 11 sq km (4 sq mi); and the New Territories (a leased section of the Chinese mainland) and the remaining islands, 978 sq km (377 sq mi). Most of Hong Kong territory is rocky, hilly, and deeply eroded. The climate is subtropical, with hot and humid summers. Rainfall is heavy, and there are occasional typhoons.

Total population, which was under 600,000 in 1945, was approximately 7.4 million in 1999. Some 60% of Hong Kong's residents in 1996 were born there. The phenomenal increase since World War II resulted primarily from a large influx of mainland Chinese. During the late 1970s and early 1980s, hundreds of thousands of "boat people" arrived from Vietnam. Most have been resettled in other countries, and by mid-1987 only 8,500 remained in camps. In the summer of that year, however, Hong Kong faced another influx of Vietnamese, most of them ethnic Chinese. These people—more than 6,000 of them—had fled to China after the Vietnam war but found it difficult to assimilate there.

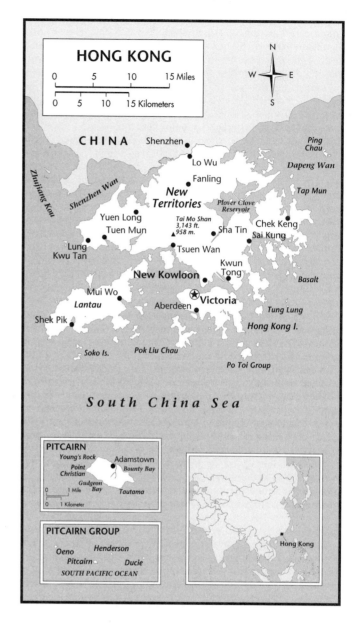

The overall population density in 1996 was 5,796 per sq km (14,500 per sq mi). About 98% of the inhabitants are Chinese, and about 95% of the people live in metropolitan areas. Chinese (Cantonese dialect) is the principal spoken language; both Chinese and English are official languages. Taoists, Confucianists, and Buddhists constitute a majority of the population. The Christian population (10%) is split about evenly between Roman Catholics and Protestants. There are also Muslim and Hindu communities (1%). The capital is Victoria, commonly known as Hong Kong.

Hong Kong has regular shipping, air, cable, and wireless services to every part of the world. Government-maintained roads span more than 1,450 km (901 mi). The mile-long Cross Harbour Road Tunnel connecting Hong Kong Island to Kowloon was opened in 1972, and the Lion Rock Tunnels link Kowloon with Sha Tin; the Aberdeen Tunnel beneath Hong Kong Island entered service in 1982. The government-owned Mass Transit Railway, a 38.6 km (24 mi) subway system, was begun in November 1975 and started operations in October 1979. The government also owns and operates a 56 km (35 mi) rail line, known as the Kowloon-Canton Railway. The railroad links up with the rail system of Guangdong Province and constitutes a major land-entry route to China; passenger service, suspended in 1949, was resumed in 1979. The Kowloon-Canton Railway operates a 34 km (21 mi) light rail system for the New Territories.

Hong Kong has one of the finest natural harbors. There are deepwater berths in Kowloon Peninsula and in Hong Kong; a container terminal at Kwaichung in Kowloon handles some 60% of Hong Kong's exports. An extensive ferry service connects Hong Kong's islands; hydrofoils provide service to Macau. The Hong Kong airport, Kai Tak, is the world's fourth largest in terms of passenger traffic; it can handle upwards of 27 million passengers a year. A new airport, Chep Lap Kok, a US$20 billion project that included bridges, highways, tunnels, and a high-speed railway, opened in 1998. The first phase of the airport project, the West Kowloon expressway connecting the airport to Hong Kong Island, opened in February 1997. In April that year, another link—the Tsing Ma Bridge, the longest suspension bridge for road and rail travel in the world—opened with lavish ceremonies. Three days later, a tunnel with capacity for 180,000 cars a day opened to provide another link between Hong Kong Island and the West Kowloon expressway.

A bleak fisherman's island for most of its early history, Hong Kong was occupied in 1841 by the British. Formal cession by China was made in 1842 by the Treaty of Nanking. The Kowloon Peninsula and adjacent islands were added in 1860, and in 1898, the New Territories were leased from China for 99 years. Hong Kong fell under Japanese occupation from 25 December 1941 to 30 August 1945. Negotiations between the UK and China culminated in an agreement on 26 September 1984 under which sovereignty over the entire colony would be transferred to China as of 1 July 1997. For a 50-year period, Hong Kong would be a Special Administrative Region and would retain its capitalist economy, its political rights, and its general way of life. A Basic Law, forming a constitution for this period, took effect in 1990.

In the interim, the colony was ruled by a UK-appointed governor, with an advisory Executive Council headed by the local commander of UK forces, and an appointed Legislative Council presided over by the governor. Chris Patten, appointed governor in 1992, held the post until the transfer of control to China 1 July 1997. The Urban Council of 30 members (15 elected and 15 appointed by the governor) dealt primarily with municipal affairs, and the government secretariat was responsible for the work of some 40 executive departments. The public sector's share of GDP decreased steadily after 1973. Under a 1981 defense agreement, about three-fourths of the cost of the maintenance of a garrison of 8,945 troops (including four Gurkha battalions) in Hong Kong was borne by the Hong Kong government. The currency unit is the Hong Kong dollar; exchange rates as of 1999 were HK$1 = US$7.736; US$1 = HK$0.1293).

Located at a major crossroads of world trade, Hong Kong has become a center of commerce, shipping, industry, and banking. Rapid industrialization, accelerated by the influx of new labor, skills, and capital, changed the pattern of the economy after World War II. While heavy industries, such as shipbuilding and ship repairing, iron, and steel, remain important, light industries—especially watches, clocks, toys, and electronics—have developed more rapidly in recent years. The service sector has also experienced growth; as of 1997, approximately 84% of Hong Kong's GDP derived from services. In 1998, the GDP stood at US$168.1 billion, with annual growth from 1989–97 averaging about 5% per year; in 1998, economic difficulties in Asia resulted in a 5% decline in GDP in Hong Kong.

Although less than 10% of the total land area is used for farming, agriculture has been expanding and has changed from subsistence rice farming to intensive vegetable cultivation. However, most of Hong Kong's agricultural produce still has to be imported. Hong Kong is among the top three export markets for US oranges, apples, grapes, tomatoes, celery, lettuce, pepper, and onions.

Electricity is supplied by two franchise companies. Water resources, for long a serious deficiency, have been increased by converting Plover Cove into a lake. About one-quarter of the water supply is purchased annually from China.

Imports in 1997 were valued at US$208.6 billion, and exports and reexports at US$188.1 billion. As the world's third-largest banking center, Hong Kong receives a continuous flow of outside capital. The Hong Kong Association of Banks was created in January 1981 to regulate charges and deposit interest rates and oversee banking standards. There is no central bank; currency is issued by two commercial banks. In addition to the licensed banks, many Chinese firms handle Chinese remittances from overseas. Hong Kong reportedly supplies about one-third of China's foreign exchange.

Hong Kong is self-supportive except for external defense. Revenues in 1998 were at US$30.1 billion, derived mainly from internal taxation and import duties. Government expenditures on social welfare programs amounted to US$26 billion in 1997/98. The income tax rate that year was 19%.

Tourism has become an important industry. About 25% of the tourist earnings came from the US, Canada, and Western Europe and another 25% from Japan.

Telephones numbered about 3.4 million in 1996. Broadcasting services are provided by a government station, Radio Television Hong Kong, and by commercial operators. Broadcasting services are in both Chinese and English. An estimated 90% of all households have one or more television sets. The Hong Kong press included 734 newspapers and periodicals. Almost all the newspapers are in Chinese; five are English-language dailies.

The infant mortality rate was 5.2 per 1,000 live births in 1999. The average life expectancy as of 1999 was 78.9 years. Despite law enforcement efforts, drug addiction afflicts an estimated 38,000 persons; more than 15,000 receive daily treatment through government-owned or aided health centers. In 1995, there were 4.7 hospital beds per 1,000 population, and the daily cost of a hospital bed in a public hospital was $60.

The Hong Kong Housing Authority plans, builds, and manages public housing developments. About 40% of the population lived in public and aided housing as of the late 1990s.

In September 1980, education until the age of 15 was made compulsory; six years of primary and three years of secondary schooling are provided by the government free of charge. Schools are of three types: Chinese, English, and Anglo-Chinese. Prevocational training was offered in more than a dozen government-run institutions. Student enrollment in primary and secondary school is about a quarter of the population. Higher education is provided primarily by the University of Hong Kong and the Chinese University of Hong Kong. Hong Kong Polytechnic and the City Polytechnic of Hong Kong also provides post-secondary education for the colony's residents. As of the late 1990s, approximately 15% of the population had received education beyond secondary school.

MACAU

Macau (Macao) is situated on the south coast of China, at the mouth of the Pearl (Zhu) River, almost directly opposite Hong Kong, which is about 65 km (40 mi) away. Located at 22°6' to 22°13'N and 113°33' to 113°37'E, Macau consists of a peninsula, about 5 km (3 mi) long and 1.6 km (1 mi) wide, and two small islands, Taipa and Coloane. The total area is about 16 sq km (6 sq mi), and the total coastline is 41 km (25 mi). The climate is subtropical, with high humidity from April to October, when Macau receives most of its rainfall. Daily maximum temperatures

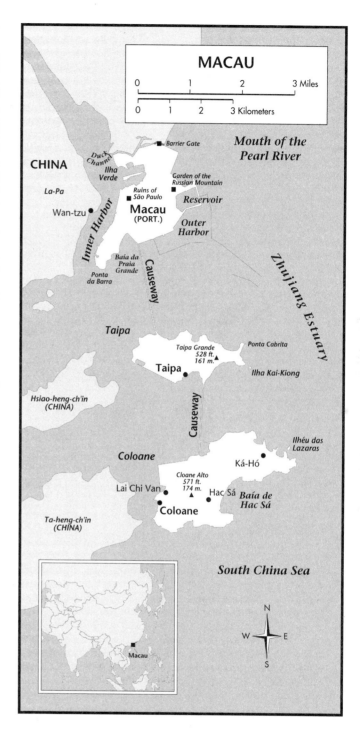

average 29°C (84°F) during the summer; normal daily temperatures are less than 20°C (68°F) during the winter months.

Macau's population was estimated at 533,000 in mid-2000, up from 496,837 in mid-1996. The population density of 29,866 per sq km (79,642 per sq mi) was among the highest in the world. Chinese, many of them refugees from the People's Republic of China (PRC) before Macau reverted to the PRC in 1999, constitute 97% of the total; the remaining 3% are Portuguese or of mixed Chinese-Portuguese ancestry. Large-scale movement of Chinese in and out of Macau has inevitably affected the economic and social life of the territory. The common language is Chinese, usually spoken in the Cantonese or Mandarin dialect. Portuguese is spoken by government officials, and some English, French, and Spanish are also understood. Buddhism and Roman Catholicism are the dominant religions.

In 1996 there were about 50 km (31 mi) of highways. A causeway links Taipa and Coloane islands, and a 2.7-km (1.7-mi) bridge connects Macau and Taipa. Macau's main asset is its harbor; ferries, hydrofoils, and jetfoils offer shuttle service between Macau and Hong Kong. In 1994, a 240-km (149-mi) road connecting Macau and Hong Kong opened, running through Guangdong Province in the PRC.

Macau is the oldest European settlement in the Far East. The first Portuguese attempts to establish relations with China were made in the early 16th century. In 1557, the Chinese authorities agreed to Portuguese settlement of Macau, with leaseholder rights. The Portuguese, however, treated Macau as their possession and established a municipal government in the form of a senate of the local inhabitants. Disputes concerning jurisdiction and administration developed. In 1833, Macau together with Timor became an overseas province of Portugal under the control of the governor-general of Goa, and in 1849, Portugal succeeded in having Macau declared a free port. On 26 March 1887, China confirmed perpetual occupation and governance of Macau and its dependencies by Portugal, but the question of the delimitation of the boundaries was left unsettled.

As the only neutral port on the South China Sea during World War II, Macau enjoyed a modicum of prosperity. In 1949, the government of the PRC renounced the "unequal treaty" granting Portuguese suzerainty over Macau. Civil disturbances in late 1966 between Macau police and Chinese leftist groups resulted in concessions to the territory's pro-China elements. The 1974 military coup in Portugal led to a constitutional change in Macau's status from a Portuguese province to a "special territory." In January 1976, Portugal's remaining few hundred troops were withdrawn from Macau. China and Portugal established diplomatic ties in 1980. In March 1987, the PRC and Portugal reached an agreement for the return of Macau to the PRC on 20 December 1999. The PRC has guaranteed not to interfere in Macau's capitalist economy and way of life for a period of 50 years.

Until December 1999, Macau was ruled by a governor appointed by Portugal, although it was empowered to make its own laws, appoint and control its own civil service, and contract directly for foreign loans.

Prior to and immediately following Macau's transfer to PRC control, the unit of currency was the Macau pataca (P) of 100 avos; Hong Kong dollars also circulated freely. There are coins of 10, 20, and 50 avos and 1 and 5 patacas, and notes of 5, 10, 50, 100, and 500 patacas. The pataca is linked to the Hong Kong dollar at the rate of HK$1=P1.03. Corporate taxes and import duties are important sources of revenue; major expenditures are for finance, security, education, and health and welfare. The territory has its own currency-issuing bank, 12 commercial banks, and 10 foreign banks.

Macau's economy is consumer-oriented. There is little agriculture, and the territory is heavily dependent on imports from China for food, fresh water, and electricity. Important economic sectors are commerce, tourism, gambling, fishing, and light industry. There are small- and medium-scale enterprises concerned especially with the finishing of imported semimanufactured goods, in particular the manufacture of clothing, ceramics, electronic equipment, toys, and fireworks, and the printing and dyeing of cloth and yarn.

Macau's historic role has been that of a gateway for southern China. It has close trade relations with neighboring Hong Kong, another free port. Gold trading, formerly a major facet in Macau's economy, virtually came to a halt in 1974–75 following Hong Kong's decision to lift its own restrictions on gold trading. The principal exports were textiles, clothing, toys, electronics, cement, fireworks, footwear, and machinery. Principal export partners are the US, 45%; EU, 24%; Hong Kong, 8%; and China, 6%. The principal imports for domestic use are raw materials, food, fuel, machinery, and lubricants. Total imports in 1997 were valued at just over $2 billion, of which China provided 29%; Hong Kong, 25%; EU, 12.4%; and Japan, 9%.

Government schools are operated mainly for the children of civil servants and wealthier families, while poor Chinese students are educated in schools supported by China. Macau's University of East Asia opened in 1981. The Medical and Health Department, although critically understaffed, operates a 400-bed hospital. The 800-bed Kiang Vu Hospital has a largely China-trained staff.

Macau has six postal stations, two telephone stations, and two telegraph stations. Macau has 4 AM and 3 FM stations and has access to satellite communications. A government and a private radio station each broadcast in Portuguese and Chinese; there are 11 newspapers, 6 in Chinese and 5 in Portuguese. Macau receives television broadcasts from Hong Kong.

With its picturesque seaport and varied gambling facilities, tourism provides about 25% of GDP, and the gambling industry accounts for about 40% of GDP. Travelers must have a valid passport and a visa, which is generally purchased at the point of disembarkation.

[50]BIBLIOGRAPHY

Bailey, Paul. *China in the Twentieth Century*. New York: B. Blackwell, 1988.

Bannister, Judith. *China's Changing Population*. Stanford, Calif.: Stanford University Press, 1987.

Bauer, E. E. *China Takes Off: Technology Transfer and Modernization*. Seattle: University of Washington Press, 1986.

Bernstein, Richard. *The Coming Conflict with China*. New York: A. A. Knopf, 1997.

Bianco, Lucien. *Origins of the Chinese Revolution, 1915–1949*. Stanford, Calif.: Stanford University Press, 1971.

China: from the Long March to Tiananmen Square. New York: H. Holt, 1990.

Clubb, O. Edmund. *Twentieth Century China*. 3d ed. New York: Columbia University Press, 1978.

Cotterell, Arthur. *China: a Cultural History*. New York: New American Library, 1988.

Creel, Herrlee Glessner. *Chinese Thought from Confucius to Mao Tse-tung*. Chicago: University of Chicago Press, 1953.

De Keijzer, Arne J. *China: Business Strategies for the '90s*. Berkeley, California: Pacific View Press, 1992.

Dryer, June Teufel. *China's Forty Millions: Minority Nationalities and National Integration in the People's Republic of China*. Cambridge, Mass.: Harvard University Press, 1976.

Ebrey, Patricia B. *The Cambridge Illustrated History of China*. New York: Cambridge University Press, 1996.

Evans, Harriet. *Women and Sexuality in China: Dominant Discourses of Female Sexuality and Gender Since 1949*. Cambridge, U.K.: Polity Press, 1997.

Evans, Richard. *Deng Xiaoping and the Making of Modern China*. New York: Viking, 1994.

Fairbank, John King. *The Great Chinese Revolution, 1800–1985*. New York: Harper & Row, 1986.

———. *China: a New History*. Cambridge, Mass.: Harvard University Press, 1992.

Feinstein, Steve. *China in Pictures*. Minneapolis: Lerner Publications Co., 1989.

Garside, Roger. *Coming Alive!: China After Mao*. New York: McGraw-Hill, 1981.

Goldman, Merle. *China's Intellectuals: Advice and Dissent*. Cambridge, Mass.: Harvard University Press, 1981.

Gray, Jack. *Rebellions and Revolutions: China from the 1800s to the 1980s*. New York: Oxford University Press, 1990.

Hamilton, Gary (ed.). *Cosmopolitan Capitalists: Hong Kong and the Chinese Diaspora at the End of the 20th Century*. Seattle: University of Washington Press, 1999.

Howard, Pat. *Breaking the Iron Rice Bowl: Prospects for Socialism in China's Countryside*. Armonk, N.Y.: M.E. Sharpe, 1988.

Howland, Douglas. *Borders of Chinese Civilization: Geography and History at Empire's End*. Durham, N.C.: Duke University Press, 1996.

Hsiung, James C., and Samuel S. Kim. *China in the Global Community*. New York: Praeger, 1980.

Hsu, Immanuel Chung-yueh. *The Rise of Modern China*. 5th ed. New York: Oxford University Press, 1995.

Hsu, Kai-yu. *Literature of the People's Republic of China*. Bloomington: Indiana University Press, 1980.

Hucker, Charles O. *China's Imperial Past: An Introduction to Chinese History and Culture*. Stanford, Calif.: Stanford University Press, 1975.

Kaplan, Fredric M. and Julian M. Sobin (ed.). *Encyclopedia of China Today*. 3rd ed., revised and expanded. New York: Eurasia, 1981.

Lardy, Nicholas R. *Agriculture in China's Modern Economic Development*. New York: Cambridge University Press, 1983.

———. *Foreign Trade and Economic Reform in China, 1978–1990*. Cambridge; New York: Cambridge University Press, 1992.

Leung, Edwin Pak-wah. *Historical Dictionary of Revolutionary China, 1839–1976*. New York: Greenwood Press, 1992.

Leys, Simon. *The Burning Forest: Essays on Chinese Culture and Politics*. New York: Holt, Rinehart & Winston, 1986.

Lin, Bih-jaw (ed.). *The Aftermath of the 1989 Tiananmen Crisis in Mainland China*. Boulder, Colo.: Westview Press, 1992.

Link, Perry, Richard Madsen, Paul G. Pickowicz (eds.) *Unofficial China: Popular Culture and Thought in the People's Republic*. Boulder, Colo.: Westview Press, 1989.

Mackerras, Colin. *China's Minorities: Integration and Modernization in the Twentieth Century*. New York: Oxford University Press, 1994.

———. *Dictionary of the Politics of the People's Republic of China*. London: Routledge, 1998.

McGivering, Jill. *Macao Remembers*. New York: Oxford University Press, 1999.

Meyer, David R. *Hong Kong as a Global Metropolis*. New York: Cambridge University Press, 2000.

Michael, Franz. *China Through the Ages: History of a Civilization*. Boulder, Colo.: Westview, 1986.

Milwertz, Cecilia N. *Accepting Population Control: Urban Chinese Women and the One-Child Family Policy*. Richmond, Surrey, UK: Curzon, 1997.

Nathan, Andrew J. *Chinese Democracy*. Berkeley: University of California Press, 1985.

Ogden, Suzanne. *China's Unresolved Issues: Politics, Development, and Culture*. Englewood Cliffs, N.J.: Prentice Hall, 1995.

Oi, Jean Chun. *State and Peasant in Contemporary China: the Political Economy of Village Government*. Berkeley: University of California Press, 1989.

Orleans, Leo A. (ed.). *Science in Contemporary China*. Stanford, Calif.: Stanford University Press, 1980.

Pepper, Suzanne. *China's Universities: Post-Mao Enrollment Policies and their Impact on the Structure of Secondary Education*. Ann Arbor, Mich.: Center for Chinese Studies, 1984.

Perkins, Dorothy. *Encyclopedia of China: The Essential Reference to China, Its History and Culture.* New York: Facts on File, 1999.

Perry, Elizabeth, and Christine Wong (eds.). *The Political Economy of Reform in Post-Mao China.* Cambridge, Mass.: Harvard University Press, 1985.

Rawski, Thomas G., and Lillian M. Li (eds.). *Chinese History in Economic Perspective.* Berkeley: University of California Press, 1992.

Rawski, Thomas G. *China's Transition to Industrialism.* Ann Arbor: University of Michigan Press, 1980.

Reynolds, Bruce L. (ed.). *Reform in China: Challenges and Choices.* Armonk, N.Y.: M.E. Sharpe, 1987.

Ross, Robert S. *Negotiating Cooperation: The United States and China, 1969–1989.* Stanford, Calif.: Stanford University Press, 1995.

Salisbury, Harrison E. *The Long March: The Untold Story.* New York: Harper & Row, 1985.

Scalapino, Robert, and George Yu. *Modern China and Its Revolutionary Process: Recurrent Challenges to the Traditional Order, 1850–1920.* Berkeley: University of California Press, 1985.

Schram, Stuart R. *The Thought of Mao Tse-Tung.* New York: Cambridge University Press, 1989.

Schrecker, John E. *The Chinese Revolution in Historical Perspective.* New York: Greenwood Press, 1991.

Snow, Edgar. *Red Star over China.* New York: Bantam, 1978 (orig. 1938).

Sullivan, Michael. *The Arts of China.* 3rd ed. Berkeley: University of California Press, 1984.

Terrill, Ross. *Mao: A Biography.* New York: Harper & Row, 1980. Updated, with a new introduction, N.Y.: Simon & Schuster, 1993.

Wakeman, Frederick, Jr. *The Great Enterprise: The Manchu Reconstruction of Imperial Order in 17th Century China.* Berkeley: University of California Press, 1985.

Wittwer, Sylvan. *Feeding a Billion: Frontiers of Chinese Agriculture.* East Lansing: Michigan State University Press, 1987.

Worden, Robert L., Andrea Matles Savada, and Ronald E. Dolan (eds.). *China, a Country Study.* 4th ed. Washington, D.C.: Library of Congress, 1988.

World Bank. *China: Long-Term Development: Issues and Options.* Baltimore: Johns Hopkins University Press, 1985.

Wortzel, Larry M. *Class in China: Stratification in a Classless Society.* Westport, Conn.: Greenwood, 1987.

CYPRUS*

Republic of Cyprus
Kypriaki Dimokratia

CAPITAL: Nicosia.

FLAG: The national flag consists of the map of Cyprus in gold set above two olive branches in green on a white field.

ANTHEM: *Ethnikos Hymnos (National Hymn),* beginning "Se gnorizo apo tin kopsi" ("I recognize you by the keenness of your spade").

MONETARY UNIT: The Cyprus pound (c£) is a paper currency of 100 cents. There are coins of 1, 2, 5, 10, 20, and 50 cents and 1 pound, and notes of 50 cents, and 1, 5, 10, and 20 pounds. c£1 = $1.6821 ($1 = c£0.5945) as of 31 March 2000. The Turkish lira (TL) of 100 kuruş is the currency in the Turkish Cypriot zone.

WEIGHTS AND MEASURES: The metric system is the legal standard. Imperial and local measures are also used.

HOLIDAYS: New Year's Day, 1 January; Epiphany, 6 January; Late President Makarios' Day, 19 January; Greek Independence Day, 25 March; Cyprus National Day, 1 April; Labor Day, 1 May; Cyprus Independence Day, 1 October; Greek Resistance Day, 28 October; Christmas, 25 December; Boxing Day, 26 December. Holidays observed by the Turkish Cypriot community include Founding of the Turkish Federated State of Cyprus, 13 February; Turkish National Sovereignty and Children's Day, 23 April; Turkish Youth and Sports Day, 19 May; Turkish Victory Day, 30 August; Turkish Independence Day, 29 October. Movable Christian religious holidays include Green Monday, Good Friday, Holy Saturday, and Easter Monday. Movable Muslim religious holidays are observed in the Turkish Cypriot zone.

TIME: 2 PM = noon GMT.

1 LOCATION, SIZE, AND EXTENT

Cyprus is the largest Mediterranean island after Sicily and Sardinia. Including small island outposts of Cape Andreas known as the Klidhes, its area is 9,250 sq km (3,571 sq mi). Comparatively, the area occupied by Cyprus is about three-fourths the size of the state of Connecticut. Since 1974, the northern third of the island, or 3,367 sq km (1,300 sq mi), has been under the de facto control of the Turkish Cypriot Federated State (proclaimed in 1975), which on 15 November 1983 proclaimed its independence as the Turkish Republic of Northern Cyprus; the southern two-thirds (5,884 sq km/2,272 sq mi) are controlled by the government of the Republic of Cyprus. A narrow zone called the "green line," patrolled by UN forces, separates the two regions and divides Nicosia, the national capital.

Cyprus is situated in the extreme northeast corner of the Mediterranean; it is 71 km (44 mi) s of Turkey, 105 km (65 mi) w of Syria, and some 800 km (500 mi) E of the Greek mainland. Cyprus extends 227 km (141 mi) ENE–WSW from Cape Andreas to Cape Drepanon and 97 km (60 mi) SSE–NNW. The average width is 56–72 km (35–45 mi); the narrow peninsula known as the Karpas, which is nowhere more than 16 km (10 mi) wide, extends 74 km (46 mi) northeastward to Cape Andreas. Cyprus has a total coastline of 648 km (403 mi).[1]

The capital city of Cyprus, Nicosia, is located in the north central part of the country.

2 TOPOGRAPHY

Two dissimilar mountain systems, flanking a central plain, occupy the greater part of the island. The Troodos Massif, in the southwest, attaining its highest point in Mt. Olympus (1,953 m/ 6,406 ft), sends out numerous spurs to the northwestern, northern, and southern coasts. In the north, a geologically older range, the Kyrenia Mountains, extend more than 160 km (100 mi) along the coast in a series of rocky peaks, capped often by medieval castles. Between these principal formations lies the Mesaoria, a low plain extending from Famagusta Bay on the east to Morphou Bay on the west. Once forested, this now treeless region, varying in width from 16 to 32 km (10–20 mi), contains the bulk of the island's cultivable and pastoral area. There are few lakes or rivers; rivers are little more than rocky channels that carry away torrents during the thaw of spring and early summer.

3 CLIMATE

Cyprus is for the most part dry, sunny, and healthful. The warm currents of the Mediterranean ensure mild winters but bring humidity to the coastal area in the summer, when the central plain is hot and dry. On the hills, daily sunshine is interrupted only occasionally by a wet period rarely lasting more than a week. The mean annual temperature is about 20°C (68°F). A cool, rainy season lasts from November to March. In winter, snow covers the higher peaks of the Troodos; elsewhere the temperature seldom falls below freezing, and conditions are mild and bracing. Rainfall is erratic and varies greatly in different parts of the island. The annual average precipitation ranges from below 30 cm (12 in) in the west-central lowlands to more than 114 cm (45 in) in the higher parts of the southern massif. The main

---

1. *Unless otherwise noted, all statistical data refers to that part of the island controlled by the government of the Republic of Cyprus, i.e., the Greek Cypriot zone.

agricultural areas receive rainfall of from 30 to 40 cm (12–16 in) annually. Earthquakes are not uncommon.

⁴FLORA AND FAUNA

Except for some small lowland areas in which eucalyptus has been planted, the forests are natural growths of great antiquity, from which the Phoenician shipbuilders drew much of their timber. Forests consist principally of Aleppo pine; other important conifers, locally dominant, are the stone pine, cedar (which is becoming rare), Mediterranean cypress, and juniper, the last growing chiefly on the lower slopes of the Kyrenia Mountains. Oriental plane and alder are plentiful in the valleys, while on the hills, Olympus dwarf oak mingles with pines of various species. Wild flowers grow in profusion, and herbs are numerous.

Cyprus has few wild animals, but birdlife is varied and includes partridge, quail, snipe, plover, and woodcock. Eagles are commonly seen in the mountains.

⁵ENVIRONMENT

Under the Town and Country Planning Law of 1972, the government has the power to issue "reservation orders" in order to protect historic buildings, trees, or other specific points. Other conservation laws seek to preserve forests, restrict the hunting of wildlife, and maintain environmental health. The most significant environmental problems in Cyprus are water pollution, erosion, and wildlife preservation. The purity of the water supply is threatened by industrial pollutants, pesticides used in agricultural areas, and the lack of adequate sewage treatment. Other water resource problems include uneven rainfall levels at different times of the year and the absence of natural reservoir catchments. Cyprus has 0.2 cu mi of water, of which 91% is used for farming activity. One hundred percent of Cyprus' urban and rural dwellers have access to safe water. Another environmental concern is erosion, especially erosion of Cyprus's coastline. In accordance with the Foreshore Protection Law, several coastal areas have been zoned to prevent undesirable development. The Ministry of Agriculture and Natural Resources has primary responsibility for environmental matters. The expansion of urban centers threatens the habitat of Cyrpus' wildlife. As of 1994, one mammal species, 17 types of birds and 43 plant species in a total of 2,000 are threatened with extinction. About 20 species of flora are protected. The Cyprus mouflon or wild sheep is protected in the Paphos Forest game reserve.

⁶POPULATION

The population of Cyprus (Greek and Turkish zones) in 2000 was estimated at 759,048. An estimated 11.5% of the population is 65 years of age or older. The projected population for the year 2005 is 817,000, assuming a crude birthrate of 14 per 1,000 population and a death rate of 7, resulting in a natural rate of change of 0.7% for the period 2000–2005.

It was estimated that 57% of the population lived in urban areas in 2000. At the beginning of 1995, the population distribution among the districts administered by the Cypriot government was as follows: Lefkosia, 40.6%; Lemesos, 28.9%; Larnaka, 16.7%; Pafos, 8.7%; and Ammochostos, 5.1%. Nicosia, the capital city, located near the center of the island in the Mesaoria plain, had a 2000 population of 178,000. Other chief towns—all seaports—are Limassol, Famagusta, Larnaca, Paphos, and Kyrenia. Cyprus' next census is scheduled to take place in April 2001.

⁷MIGRATION

Cyprus suffered massive population shifts following the Turkish military occupation of the northern third of the island in July 1974. Some 120,000 Greek Cypriots fled from the occupied area to the south, and about 60,000 Turkish Cypriots fled in the opposite direction. As of the 1989, some 611 Greek Cypriots lived in the north, mostly on the Karpas Peninsula, and about 100 Turkish Cypriots remained in the south.

In the 1990s, asylum seekers originated mainly from the Middle East and North Africa. Until 1998, a yearly average of 70 to 100 people applied for refugee status. This figure rose significantly in the second half of 1998 due to the arrival of approximately 150 asylum seekers who arrived in Cyprus by boat from Lebanon.

Some asylum seekers are detained as illegal entrants or overstayers. While acknowledging the difficulties in dealing with the increased number of asylum seekers, the UNHCR has encouraged the government to find alternatives to detention. The Republic of Cyprus allows recognized refugees to remain with work permits while waiting for resettlement to a third country; however resettlement is a lengthy process, and many refugees never obtain employment. Local integration is to be the preferred solution after adoption of the new refugee law, a work in progress as of 1999.

In 1999, the net immigration rate was 0.44 migrants per 1,000 population.

⁸ETHNIC GROUPS

Following the 16th-century Turkish conquest, Cyprus received a substantial permanent influx of Ottoman Turks. Many soldiers became owners of feudal estates, and there was immigration from Anatolia and Rumelia. There was virtually no intermarriage; each community preserved its own religion, language, dress, and other national characteristics, and major cities and towns had their Greek and Turkish quarters. The 1974 war had the effect of almost completely segregating the two communities.

Greek Cypriots outnumber Turks more than four to one. Estimates in 1999 put the proportion of Greek and Turkish Cypriots at 78% (99.5% of whom live in the Greek Cypriot area; 0.5% in the Turkish Cypriot area) and 18% (1.3% of whom live in the Greek Cypriot area; 98.7% in the Turkish Cypriot area) respectively. The remaining 4% of the population included Lebanese Maronites, Armenians, British, and others.

⁹LANGUAGES

After independence in 1960, Greek and Turkish became the official languages. Since 1974, Greek has been the language of the south and Turkish the language of the north. English is also used extensively.

¹⁰RELIGIONS

In 1999, 78% of the total population of Cyprus was Greek Orthodox, 18% Muslim, and 4% Maronite, Armenian Apostalic, and other persuasions. Religion holds a significantly more prominent place in Greek Cypriot society than in Turkish Cypriot society, with correspondingly greater cultural and political influence. Under the Cyprus ethnarch Archbishop Makarios III, who was president of Cyprus from 1960 until his death in 1977, the church was the chief instrument of Greek Cypriot nationalism. Makarios' successor as ethnarch, Archbishop Chrysostomos, elected for life, also has played an active role in Greek Cypriot political affairs.

The independence of the Church of Cyprus was recognized by the Council of Ephesus in AD 431 and confirmed by Emperor Zeno in 478. The Church of Cyprus is one of the oldest constituent bodies of the Holy Orthodox Eastern Church, being senior by centuries to the Orthodox Church of Greece, and junior only to the four original patriarchates of Constantinople, Alexandria, Antioch, and Jerusalem. Virtually all Turkish Cypriots are Sunni Muslims of the Hanafi sect.

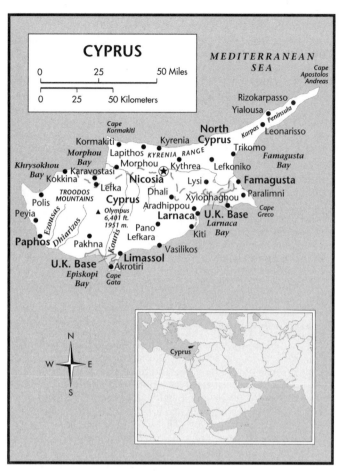

CYPRUS

0   25   50 Miles

0   25   50 Kilometers

MEDITERRANEAN
SEA

Cape
Apostolos
Andreas

Rizokarpasso
Yialousa
Karpas Peninsula
Cape
Kormakiti
North
Cyprus
Leonarisso
Kormakiti   Kyrenia
Morphou
Bay
Lapithos   KYRENIA RANGE   Trikomo
Khrysokhou
Bay   Morphou   Kythrea   Lefkoniko   Famagusta
Bay
Kokkina   Karavostasi
Nicosia   Lysi   Famagusta
Lefka   Cyprus   Dhali   Xylophaghou   Paralimni
TROODOS
Polis   MOUNTAINS   Aradhippou   Cape
Greco
Peyia   Olympus   Larnaca
6,401 ft.   Larnaca
1,951 m.   Pano   Bay
Paphos   Lefkara   Kiti
Pakhna   Vasilikos
Limassol
U.K. Base   Akrotiri
Episkopi   Cape
Bay   Gata

N
W   E
S

Cyprus

LOCATION: 34°33′ to 35°34′N; 32°16′ to 34°37′E.
TERRITORIAL SEA LIMIT: 12 mi.

11 TRANSPORTATION

Internal transport is exclusively by road. In 1996, there were 10,415 km (6,472 mi) of roads in the Greek area and 2,350 km (1,460 mi) of roads in the Turkish area. In the Turkish area, 1,370 km (851 mi) of the roads were paved, compared with 5,947 km (3,695 mi) in the Greek area. In addition to numerous taxicabs, the chief towns are served by private buses, whose services are regulated by the Road Motor Transport Board. In 1995 there were 219,700 licensed private motor cars and 103,800 commercial vehicles.

Although off the main world shipping routes, Cyprus is served by passenger and cargo shipping lines. Famagusta on the east coast was the main port, but it and the ports of Kyrenia and Karavostasi were closed to national shipping after the Turkish invasion in 1974. (The port of Famagusta was reopened by the Turkish Cypriots in 1978.) The Limassol and Larnaca ports have been modernized and are now considered good deepwater harbors. Other ports include Moni, Vasiliko-Ziyyi, and Paphos. In 1998, 1,469 ships totaling 23,362,067 GRT comprised the merchant fleet, one of the world's leaders in terms of deadweight tonnage, at 36,945,331. About two-thirds of the trade passed through Limassol. There are no inland waterways.

There were 15 airports in 1998, of which 12 had paved runways. The civil airport at Nicosia was used by many international airlines until the 1974 war, after which nearly all flights were diverted to the new international airport built at Larnaca. In 1983, a new international airport opened in Paphos. In 1997,

1,278,000 passengers were carried on scheduled domestic and international flights. Cyprus Airways has services to Middle Eastern countries, but there is no regular internal air service.

12 HISTORY

Numerous Stone Age settlements excavated in Cyprus indicate that as early as 4000 BC a distinctive civilization existed on the island. Living in circular huts, this Neolithic people produced decorated pottery of great individuality, and used vessels and tools ground from the close-grained rocks of the Troodos Mountains. Cyprus was famous in the ancient world for its copper, which, from about 2200 BC, was used throughout the Aegean in the making of bronze. The island is believed either to have derived its name from or to have given it to this mineral through the Greek word kypros—copper. Although celebrated also for its cult of Aphrodite, Cyprus was at first only a far outpost of the Hellenic world. Greek colonizers came there in sizable numbers in 1400 BC, and were followed soon afterward by Phoenician settlers. About 560 BC, Cyprus was conquered by Egypt. Coveted by each rising civilization, it was taken in turn by Persia, Alexander the Great, Egypt again, Rome, and the Byzantine Empire. Its Christian history began with the visits of Paul, accompanied first (as described in the Acts of the Apostles) by Barnabas, and later by the apostle Mark. For several centuries after AD 632, Cyprus underwent a series of Arab invasions. The island was wrested from its Byzantine ruler Isaac Comnenus in 1191 by Richard I (the Lion-Hearted) during the Third Crusade. Sold by the English king to the Knights Templar, it was transferred by that order to Guy de Lusignan, under whose dynasty the island experienced a brilliant period in its history, lasting some 300 years. Conquered in 1489 by Venice, Cyprus fell to the Turks in 1571.

The administration of Cyprus by the UK began in 1878 at a convention with Turkey initiated by the British prime minister, Benjamin Disraeli, at the Congress of Berlin. He sought to establish Cyprus as a defensive base against further Russian aggression in the Middle East. Upon the entry of Turkey into World War I, Cyprus was annexed to the British crown. It was declared a crown colony and placed under a governor in 1925.

For centuries, under Ottoman and British rule, Greek Cypriots had regarded Greece as their mother country and had sought union (enosis) with it as Greek nationals. In 1931, enosis agitation, long held in check, broke into violence. The Government House was burned amid widespread disturbances, and the British colonial administration applied severe repressive measures, including the deportation of clerical leaders. Agitation was dormant until the close of World War II, when it recommenced, and demands that the UK cede the island to Greece were renewed. The National Organization of Cypriot Fighters, led by Col. George Grivas, a retired Greek army officer, began a campaign of terrorism in 1955; upward of 2,000 casualties were recorded. The unity of NATO was endangered by the opposing positions taken on the Cyprus question by Greece and Turkey, but efforts by NATO members to mediate the dispute proved unsuccessful.

Against this background, the prime ministers of Greece and Turkey met in Zürich, Switzerland, early in 1959 in a further attempt to reach a settlement. Unexpectedly, the Greek Cypriots set aside their demands for enosis and accepted instead proposals for an independent republic, with representation of both the Greek and Turkish Cypriot communities guaranteed. A formula for the island's future, approved by the governments of the UK, Greece, and Turkey, also received the blessing of the Cyprus ethnarch, Archbishop Makarios III, who returned in triumph to the island from which he had been deported by the British government on charges of complicity with terrorism.

Besides determining Cyprus' legislative institutions, the Zürich settlement provided for a number of instruments defining the island's future international status. Enclaves on Cyprus were set aside for the continuation of British military installations in an effort to restore constitutional order. The UK, Greece, and Turkey, the guarantor powers, had the right to act together or singly to prevent either enosis or partition. In addition, provision was made for Greek, Turkish, and Cypriot forces to be stationed together at a tripartite headquarters. By 1 July 1960, agreement was reached on all outstanding differences, and independence was officially declared on 16 August.

From the outset, the two Cypriot communities differed on how the Zürich settlement would be implemented, and how much autonomy the Turkish minority would enjoy. In December 1963, Turkish Cypriots, protesting a proposed constitutional change that would have strengthened the political power of the Greek Cypriot majority, clashed with Greek Cypriots and police. When fighting continued, the Cyprus government appealed to the UN Security Council. On 4 March 1964, the Security Council voted to send in troops. Turkey and Cyprus agreed on 10 August to accept a UN Security Council call for a cease-fire, but on 22 December, fighting again erupted in Nicosia and spread to other parts of the island. The UN General Assembly passed a resolution in December 1965 calling on all states to "respect the sovereignty, unity, independence, and territorial integrity of the Republic of Cyprus, and to refrain from any intervention directed against it." The General Assembly requested the Security Council to continue UN mediation.

Violent clashes between Greek and Turkish Cypriots nearly precipitated war between Greece and Turkey in 1967, but the situation was stabilized by mutual reduction of their armed contingents on Cyprus. By January 1970, the UN peacekeeping force numbered some 3,500 troops; both Greek Cypriot National Guard and Turkish Cypriot militia also maintained sizable national guards of their own. Although talks continued between the two communities, no agreement was reached on the two basic points of dispute. Politically, the Turks wanted full autonomy, while the Greeks demanded continued unitary majority rule. Territorially, the Turks wanted Cyprus divided into Greek and Turkish-controlled zones, a position that was likewise at odds with the Greek Cypriot concept of a unitary state.

Meanwhile, tensions had developed between Makarios, who continued to oppose enosis, and the remnants of the military junta that had ruled Greece since 1967. On 2 July 1974, Makarios accused the Greek government of seeking his overthrow and called for the immediate withdrawal of 650 Greek officers in the Cypriot National Guard. Less than two weeks later, the National Guard toppled the Makarios government, forcing the Archbishop into exile and installing Nikos Sampson as president. To counter the threat of Greek control over Cyprus, Turkish Cypriot leaders asked Turkey to intervene militarily. Turkish troops landed on 20 July, but within two days the UN force had been augmented and a UN Security Council cease-fire resolution had taken effect. The coup failed, Sampson resigned on 23 July, and Glafkos Clerides became acting president in accordance with the Cyprus constitution. However, Turkey did not withdraw its forces, and while peace talks were conducted in Geneva, the Turkish military buildup continued. When talks broke down, a full-scale Turkish offensive began, and by mid-August, when a second cease-fire was accepted, Turkish forces controlled about 38% of the island. Makarios returned to Cyprus and resumed the presidency in December. On 13 February 1975, in an action considered illegal by the Cyprus government, the Turkish-held area proclaimed itself the Turkish Cypriot Federated State; Rauf Denktash, a former vice-president of Cyprus and the president of the interim Autonomous Turkish Cypriot Administration (formed after the 1967 crisis), became president. A

Security Council resolution on 12 March regretted the proclamation of the new state and called for the resumption of intercommunal talks. The government of the Republic of Cyprus continued to be recognized as the legally constituted authority by the UN and by all countries except Turkey, although its effective power extended only to the area under Greek Cypriot control.

After the de facto partition, Greek and Turkish Cypriot leaders met several times under UN auspices to explore a possible solution to the Cyprus problem. President Makarios conferred with Denktash in Nicosia early in 1977. When Makarios died of a heart attack on 3 August, Spyros Kyprianou became president, and he also held talks with Denktash in May 1979. Further negotiations between leaders of the two communities were held in August 1980, but again no agreement was reached. In February 1982, Greek Premier Andreas Papandreou visited Nicosia, where he pledged to argue the Greek Cypriot cause before the UN, the EC, and the Council of Europe; three months later, in May, the Turkish prime minister paid an official visit to northern Cyprus, drawing protests from the governments of both Greece and the Republic of Cyprus. On 15 November 1983, the Turkish sector proclaimed itself an independent state, the Turkish Republic of Northern Cyprus (TRNC). Denktash was named president, but only Turkey recognizes the TRNC. The UN, which condemned the TRNC's declaration of independence, tried repeatedly to end the partition between north and south, but all proposals were rejected by both parts. The major stumbling block was the south's demand that the estimated 25,000 Turkish troops in the north be withdrawn before negotiations began and the north's refusal to remove the troops before a final solution was reached. In February 1988, George Vassiliou was elected president of Cyprus, and he stated that he would call for reunification talks with the Turkish Cypriots.

Talks between him and Turkish Cypriot President Denktash, who was reelected in 1990, have taken place at intervals since 1988. In 1991, the UN Security Council called on both sides to complete an overall framework agreement. Despite speculation in 1994 that UN peacekeeping forces might be withdrawn if some progress was not registered, the mandate was renewed. In 1993 voting, Glafcos Clerides, a conservative, replaced right-wing George Vassiliou as president. Clerides won reelection to a second five-year term in 1998.

August of 1996 saw the most violent border clashes since the 1974 partition. In the space of one week, protestors broke through Greek-Cypriot security lines and clashed with Turkish-Cypriot and Turkish military forces in the buffer zone lying between the two divided parts of the island. Two Greek-Cypriots were killed and over 50 were injured by the Turkish military. The killing of the protestors, who were unarmed, brought general expressions of condemnation from the West but was supported by the Turkish government as acts of self-defense.

While they have not yet led to violence, there have been choleric clashes between Greek and Turkish Cypriot leaders over Cyprus' proposed entrance into the EU. The EU has invited Cyprus to be one of six nations to join the EU in the next round of the Union's enlargement. Having declared that it would prefer a united Cyprus to join, the EU has stipulated that if a settlement to the issue of unification is not reached before entry negotiations are scheduled to begin (probably in early to mid-1988), then the negotiations will be begun with the Greek-Cypriot Republic of Cyprus. Both the government of Turkey and Turkish-Cypriot leaders have vociferously denounced such a plan.

Further complicating the relationship between the Northern and Southern parts of the island was the proposed sale to the Republic of Cyprus by Russia of sophisticated antiaircraft missiles to be stationed at a newly-constructed Greek air force base in Paphos. The proposed sale brought threats of invasion from the Turkish government. In January 1999, Greek Cypriots reversed their decision to install the missiles in Cyprus and agreed to station them on the Greek island of Crete instead. Tensions were eased further by the resumption of proximity talks on the reunification of the island. Under this format, Clerides and Denktash met separately with UN Secretary General Kofi Annan in New York in December 1999 and in Geneva in January-February 2000. As of publication, a third round is expected to begin in Geneva in the summer of 2000. A chief stumbling block in the current round of discussions is the Turkish Cypriot demand that a reunified Cyprus be a confederation, while the Greek Cypriots favor a federation.

13 GOVERNMENT

The 1960 constitution of the Republic of Cyprus respects the two existing ethnic communities, Greek and Turkish, by providing specifically for representation from each community in the government. The president must be Greek and the vice-president Turkish. Under the constitution, these officers are elected for five years by universal suffrage by the Greek and Turkish communities, respectively; each has the right of veto over legislation and over certain decisions of the Council of Ministers, a body composed of seven Greek and three Turkish ministers, designated by the president and vice-president jointly. Legislative authority is vested in the 50-member House of Representatives, elected by the two chief communities in the proportion of 35 Greek and 15 Turkish. In January 1964, following the outbreak of fighting, Turkish representatives withdrew from the House, and temporary constitutional provisions for administering the country were put into effect.

Archbishop Makarios, who became president of Cyprus in 1960, was reelected in 1968 and 1973. Following his death in 1977, the leader of the House of Representatives, Spyros Kyprianou, became president; he was elected to two five-year terms in 1978 and 1983. (George Vassiliou, an independent, succeeded him in 1988 and Glafcos Clerides was elected in 1993.) Rauf Denktash was elected vice-president in 1973, but the post has remained effectively vacant since the 1974 war, in the absence of Turkish participation. Denktash has been president of the Turkish area since 1975.

On 13 February 1975, subsequent to the Turkish invasion of Cyprus, the Turkish Cypriot Federated State (TCFS) was proclaimed in the northern part of the island, and Denktash became its president. A draft constitution, approved by the state's Constituent Assembly on 25 April, was ratified by the Turkish Cypriot community in a referendum on 8 June. Establishment of the TCFS was described by Denktash as "not a unilateral declaration of independence" but a preparation for the establishment of a federal system. Denktash was elected president of the TCFS in 1976 and again in 1981; elections to a unicameral legislature of 40 seats were held those same years. On 15 November 1983, the TCFS proclaimed itself the Turkish Republic of Northern Cyprus (TRNC), separate and independent from the Republic of Cyprus. In June 1985, TRNC voters approved a new constitution that embodied most of the old constitution's articles. The new constitution, however, increased the size of the Legislative Assembly to 50 seats. In elections held in June 1985, Rauf Denktash won reelection to a five-year term as president with more than 70% of the vote. Dervis Eroglu was made prime minister. Denktash has since been reelected in 1990, 1995, and 2000.

14 POLITICAL PARTIES

The four principal political parties of the Greek community in 1996 were the center-right Democratic Party (*Demokratiko Komma*—DIKO), led by former president Spyros Kyprianou; the Progressive Party of the Working People (*Anorthotikon Komma Ergazomenou Laou*—AKEL), a pro-Communist group; the right-wing Democratic Rally (*Demokratikos Synagermos*—DISY); and the Socialist Party (*Eniea Demokratiki Enosi Kyprou*—EDEK). Party representation in the House and percentages of the popular vote won by the parties in the elections of May 1996 were DISY, 19 seats (34%); DIKO, 9 seats (16%); AKEL, 19 seats (33%); and EDEK, 5 seats (9%), and other parties, 4 seats (8%). The Orthodox Church of Cyprus also exercises substantial political influence.

The Turkish Republic of Northern Cyprus held elections for a 50-seat Legislative Assembly on 6 December 1993. The right-wing National Unity Party won 24 seats (40.3% of the vote); the Democratic Party, 13 seats (22.6%); the Communal Liberation Party, 7 seats (15.4%), and the Republican Turkish Party, 6 seats (13.4%); and. Other minor parties, won the remaining 8.3% of the popular vote.

15 LOCAL GOVERNMENT

Elected municipal corporations function in the chief towns and larger villages. The smaller villages are managed by commissions comprising a headman (*mukhtar*) and elders (*azas*). Voluntary district committees are responsible for activities outside the scope of the major government development projects. There were six administrative districts for the island: Famagusta, Kyrenia, Larnaca, Limassol, Nicosia, and Paphos.

The 1960 constitution provided for two communal chambers, these bodies having wide authority within the two main ethnic groups, including the power to draft laws, impose taxes, and determine all religious, educational, and cultural questions. The Greek Communal Chamber, however, was abolished in 1965, and its functions reverted to the Ministry of Education. The Turkish Communal Chamber embraces municipalities that are exclusively Turkish. Originally the duties of the Turkish Communal Chamber were to supervise Turkish cooperatives, sports organizations, and charitable institutions. But since the late 1960s, the Turkish communities have maintained strict administrative control of their own areas and have insisted on civil autonomy.

16 JUDICIAL SYSTEM

In the Greek Cypriot area, the Supreme Court is the final appellate court and has final authority in constitutional and administrative cases. It deals with appeals from assize and district courts, as well as from decisions by its own judges, acting singly in certain matters. There are six district courts and six assize courts, as well as seven Orthodox Church courts. The church courts have exclusive jurisdiction in matrimonial cases involving Greek Orthodox Church members. Appeals go from these courts to the appellate tribunal of the Church. The Supreme Council of Judicature appoints judges to the district and assize courts.

In the Turkish-held area, a Supreme Court acts as final appellate court, with powers similar to those of the Supreme Court in the Greek Cypriot area. In addition to district and assize courts, there are two Turkish communal courts as well as a communal appeals court.

The Cypriot legal system incorporates a number of elements of the British tradition including the presumption of innocence, due process protections, and the right to appeal. Both parts of Cyprus provide for fair public trials. Both in theory and in practice, the judiciary is independent of executive or military control.

17 ARMED FORCES

Under the Zürich agreement, Cyprus was to have an army of 2,000 men, of whom 60% were to be Greek and 40% Turkish. Subsequently, the government passed a military conscription law, enlisting men between the ages of 19 and 26 for 26 months of service. The Cypriot national guard, which is wholly Greek, comprised 10,000 personnel in 1999, backed by 88,000 reservists. A paramilitary force of 720 men provides police services. About 1,250 troops and advisors from Greece were stationed in the south in 1999.

The Turkish community has its own police force and army of some 4,500 regulars and 26,000 reserves. A sizable Turkish military presence on Cyprus (about 30,000 in a combined arms corps in 1999) has complemented these native forces since the 1974 intervention.

British forces, 3,200 ground troops and airmen in 1999, are stationed at two British bases, Akrotiri and Dhekelia. British economic aid, pledged in return for the bases, was suspended in 1965 following the outbreak of intercommunal conflict. The UN force (UNFICYP) is composed of three infantry battalions with a total of 1,228 troops.

The Cypriot government spent $405 million for defense in 1996 or 5.4% of gross domestic product.

18INTERNATIONAL COOPERATION

Cyprus was admitted to UN membership on 20 September 1960 and is a member of ECE and all the nonregional specialized agencies. Cyprus is also a member of the Commonwealth of Nations, Council of Europe, G-77, and the WTO, as well as a signatory to the Law of the Sea. A cooperation agreement between Cyprus and the EU became effective in June 1973, and an application for membership was pending as of 1999.

19ECONOMY

The 1974 coup and the Turkish armed intervention badly disrupted the economy. Physical destruction and the displacement of about a third of the population reduced the output of the manufacturing, agricultural, and service sectors. The lands occupied by Turkish forces accounted for about 70% of the country's prewar economic output. In general, the Greek Cypriot zone recovered much more quickly and successfully than the Turkish-held region, which was burdened with the weaknesses of Turkey's economy as well as its own. Scarcity of capital and skilled labor, the lack of trade and diplomatic ties to the outside world, and the consequent shortage of development aid have aggravated the problems of northern Cyprus. In the south, on the other hand, tourism has exceeded prewar levels, foreign assistance has been readily available, and the business community has benefited from the transfer to Cyprus of the Middle Eastern operations of multinational firms driven from Beirut by the Lebanese civil war.

The Republic of Cyprus has seen strong economic growth throughout the 1990s. In 1998, the economy grew by 5%. Inflation and unemployment continue to remain low. In 1998, they were 2.3% and 3.3% respectively.

In the North, however, the economy continued to grow slowly (0.5%) in 1995. The per capita GDP of the North is less than a third of the Republic of Cyprus. In 1998, unemployment stood at 6.4%, while inflation remained high at 87.5%.

20INCOME

The US Central Intelligence Agency (CIA) reports that in 1997 Cyprus's gross domestic product (GDP) was estimated at $10 billion. The per capita GDP was estimated at $13,000. The annual growth rate of GDP was estimated at 2.3%. The CIA defines GDP as the value of all final goods and services produced within a nation in a given year and computed on the basis of purchasing power parity (PPP) rather than value as measured on the basis of the rate of exchange.

CIA estimates differentiate between the Greek and Turkish zones on Cyprus. In the Greek zone, the inflation rate for consumer prices was 2.3% in 1998. Agriculture accounts for 4.4% of GDP, industry 22.4% and services 73.2%.

In the Turkish zone, the inflation rate was estimated at 87.5%. Agriculture accounts for 10% of GDP, industry 24.6%, and services 65.4%.

21LABOR

In 1996, according to provisional data, the economically active population totaled 299,700 in the Greek Cypriot area and 76,500 in the Turkish Cypriot area. Of total domestic employees in the Greek Cypriot area in 1995, 62% were employed in services, 25% in industry, and 13% in agriculture. In the Turkish Cypriot area, the breakdown was services 66%, industry 11%, and agriculture 23%.

Trade unions, legalized in 1937, represent employees in agriculture, forestry, fishing, mining, quarrying, building construction, utilities, governmental services, trade, and general labor. Registration of trade unions is compulsory, but membership in a union is not. Most labor disputes are resolved by government mediation. Workers of the Turkish community have their own labor organizations: the Turkish Cypriot Trade Union Federation and the Revolutionary Trade Unions Federation. More than 70% of the Greek Cypriot workforce belonged to a union in 1999. Approximately 50 to 60% of the Turkish Cypriot workforce is unionized.

The minimum working age in both communities is 16, with apprentice programs allowing 15 year olds to work in the Turkish Cypriot community.

There is a legislated minimum wage in the Greek Cypriot community; because of inflation this figure is adjusted twice yearly. In 1999 it was $470 per month. In the same year, the Turkish Cypriot minimum wage was $256 per month. These wages are insufficient to support a wage earner and family, but most workers earn significantly more than this.

22AGRICULTURE

Agricultural methods are adapted to the island's hot and dry summers and generally limited water supply. Spring and early summer growth is dependent on moisture stored in the soil from the winter rains, but summer cultivation is dependent on irrigation. About 15.7% of the total land area is arable.

Most farmers raise a variety of subsistence crops, ranging from grains and vegetables to fruits. Since 1960 there has been increased production of citrus fruits and potatoes. These two commodities, along with grapes, kiwi, and avocados are grown both for the domestic market and as exports to EU nations. Principal crops in 1998 (in tons) included barley, 136,000; potatoes, 136,000; grapes, 125,000; grapefruit, 48,000; oranges, 45,000; lemons, 20,000, and wheat, 12,000. Tomatoes, carrots, olives, and other fruits and vegetables are also grown. The areas that have been Turkish-held since 1974 include much of Cyprus' most fertile land; citrus fruits are a major export. Citrus production in 1998 reflected a decline since 1992 because of continued dry weather. Gross output of crop production in 1998 was valued at C£178 million.

The Agricultural Research Institute, through experiments with solar-heated greenhouses, soil fertility, and water usage optimization, and introduction of new varieties of grain, attempts to improve the efficiency of Cypriot agriculture. Unprocessed agricultural products account for 25% of exports.

23ANIMAL HUSBANDRY

Grazing land for livestock covered about 1,100 ha (2,700 acres) in 1998. Animal husbandry contributes about one-third of total agricultural production. Output of pork, poultry, and eggs meets domestic demand, but beef and mutton are imported. Sheep and goats, which feed upon rough grazing land unsuitable for cultivation, provide most of the milk products. In 1998, sheep numbered about 240,000, hogs 431,300, and goats 322,000.

Indigenous cattle, kept primarily as draft animals, are decreasing with the advance of farm mechanization. There is no indigenous breed of dairy cattle, but near main towns, dairy stock, mostly shorthorns, are kept under stall-fed conditions, and Friesian cattle have been imported from the Netherlands and the UK. Cattle numbered about 55,800 in 1998.

Livestock products in 1998 included 46,000 tons of pork, 34,000 tons of poultry meat, 134,000 tons of milk, and 9,000 tons of eggs. Gross output of livestock production was valued at C£138 million in 1998.

24FISHING

Year-round fishing is carried on mostly in coastal waters not more than 3.2 km (2 mi) from shore. The fish in Cyprus waters are small from the lack of nutrient salts, and the catches are meager. The 1997 catch was 3,358 tons. Fish exports in 1997 were valued at $2.9 million. There is no deep sea fishing. Sponges of good quality are taken, mostly by licensed fishermen from the Greek Dodecanese Islands. Cypriot aquaculture produced 769 tons of gilthead seabream in 1997.

25FORESTRY

About 175,400 ha (433,000 acres) are forested; 137,800 ha (340,500 acres) are reserves managed by the Forest Department, the remainder being natural growths of poor scrub used by village communities as fuel and as grazing grounds. Besides furnishing commercial timber, the forests provide protective cover for water catchment areas and prevent soil erosion. Their value is also scenic, numerous holiday resorts being situated in the forest reserves. Most numerous by far among forest trees is the Aleppo pine. The stone pine is found on the highest slopes of the Troodos Massif; the cedar, once a flourishing tree, has become a rarity. In the lowlands, eucalyptus and other exotic hardwoods have been introduced. Other important local species include cypress, plane, alder, and golden oak. The demand for timber during World War I resulted in some overcutting, and in 1956 large fires further reduced forests, particularly in Paphos, where 6 million cu ft of standing timber were destroyed. To offset these losses, all felling of fresh trees for timber was stopped and systematic reforestation begun. The timber cut decreased from 152,415 cu m in 1977 to 47,100 cu m in 1997. Most of Cyprus' timber requirements must be met by imports. Roundwood imports totaled 39,000 cu m in 1997.

26MINING

Mineral production reached a peak in 1960, when minerals formed 58% of total exports, but by 1997, they represented only 6% of exports; the decline was attributed to depletion of minerals and unfavorable marketing conditions abroad. The place of mining in the GDP similarly declined from 16.7% in 1952 to 0.3% by 1994. In recent years, production of Cyprus' historically important export minerals (such as asbestos, celestite, chromite, copper, and iron pyrite) has stopped. Cyprus is a significant source for the world's supply of umber and yellow ochre, which are used as pigments.

Ownership and control of minerals and quarry materials are vested in the government, which may grant prospecting permits, mining leases, and quarrying licenses. Royalties on extracted mineral commodities ranged from 1% to 5%.

Mining and quarrying production was valued at almost $100 million in 1996, with the cement industry accounting for about half that total. Production in 1996 included 1,000,000 tons of cement, 70,660 tons of bentonite, 6,000,000 tons of sand and gravel, 150,468 tons of crude gypsum, and 4,604 tons of umber. Other mine and quarry products included lime, marl, and marble.

27ENERGY AND POWER

The principal source of power is steam-generated electricity, which is distributed by the Electricity Authority of Cyprus (EAC) from three generating stations at Dhekelia and Momi. These plants in 1998 had an installed capacity of 699,000 kW. Total generation has risen from 12 million kWh in 1952 to 2,675 million kWh in 1998. Consumption of electricity was 2.2 billion kWh in 1996. The grid system includes all towns and most villages. The south provides the Turkish sector with all of its electricity, although the EAC is prevented from collecting revenue from the Turkish sector.

28INDUSTRY

Industries are numerous and small in scale, most of them employing fewer than 10 workers. Working owners make up a large part of the industrial labor force. Manufacturing, encouraged by income tax concessions and protected by import tariffs, primarily involves the processing of local products for both export and the home market, or the production of consumer items such as canned fruits and vegetables; wine, beer and soft drinks; confectionery products, dairy products, and other foods; footwear, hosiery, and other wearing apparel; quilts, pottery, and earthenware; plastic products; vegetable and essential oils; chemical products; and cigarettes and tobacco. Wines, leather handbags and luggage, canned fruits and vegetables, lithographed crown corks, and nails are made principally for export. Major plants include modern flour mills, tire-treading factories, knitting mills, preprocessing facilities, and a petroleum refinery. Furniture and carts are also manufactured. Nine industrial estates have been established.

29SCIENCE AND TECHNOLOGY

The Cyprus Research Center promotes research principally in the social sciences and in history, ethnography, and philology. In addition, Cyprus has three universities and several colleges offering degrees in basic and applied sciences. In the mid-1990s total expenditures for research and development amounted to 5.6 million Cyprus pounds per year; 165 technicians and 147 scientists and engineers were engaged in research and development.

30DOMESTIC TRADE

A flourishing cooperative movement provides facilities for marketing agricultural products. There are more than 500 Greek cooperative societies, with some 100,000 members. Many towns and villages have cooperative stores; the towns also have small independent shops, general stores, and bazaars.

Business hours are from 8 AM to 1 PM, and 2:30 to 5:30 PM in winter and from 7:30AM to 1 PM and 4 to 6:30 PM in the summer. Shops are open only in the morning on Wednesday and Saturday. Normal banking hours are from 8:30 AM to noon, Monday–Saturday. Advertising is mainly through newspapers and television; limited use is made of advertising agencies.

As a result of the island's division in 1974, there is no trade between the two communities across the UN buffer zone.

31FOREIGN TRADE

With limited natural resources, Cyprus is dependent on other countries for many of its needs. Other than some agricultural commodities, it has few surpluses, and the balance of trade has steadily grown more unfavorable.

The garment industry in Cyprus provides the export market with the largest portion of revenues (18%), while vegetable farming takes care of a similar proportion of exports (17%). Other exports include fruits and nuts (7.8%), medicinal and pharmaceutical products (7.5%), fruit (4.7%), and building compounds (4.2%).

Principal trading partners in 1998 (in millions of US dollars) were as follows:

COUNTRY	EXPORTS	IMPORTS	BALANCE
United Kingdom	162	416	-254
Russia	108	108	0
Greece	104	302	-198
Germany	35	314	-279
Israel	30	103	-73
United States	20	459	-439
France	13	184	-171
Italy	10	345	-335
Spain	7	134	-127
Japan	3	274	-271

In 1997 Cyprus's imports were distributed among the following categories:

Consumer goods	33.4%
Food	9.0%
Fuels	8.3%
Industrial supplies	22.6%
Machinery	12.7%
Transportation	8.9%
Other	5.1%

Lack of international recognition for the Turkish Cypriots severely hampers their foreign trade. Because of the Greek Cypriot economic boycott, all goods originating in northern Cyprus must transit through Turkey, thereby adding to shipping costs. Moreover, a 1994 ruling by the European Court of Justice declared that phyto-sanitary certificates issued by the "Turkish Republic of Northern Cyprus" were invalid due to the "illegality" of the entity.

32BALANCE OF PAYMENTS

Since Cyprus has persistently imported more than it exports, it consistently runs a trade imbalance which has grown steadily over the past two decades. Cyprus' trade deficit has been somewhat offset by tourist dollars, spending by foreign military forces, and remittances from workers abroad.

The US Central Intelligence Agency reports that in 1998 the purchasing power parity of Cyprus's exports was $1,270 million while imports totaled $4,120 million resulting in a trade balance of -$2,850 million.

The International Monetary Fund (IMF) reports that in 1998 Cyprus had exports of goods totaling $1,065 million and imports totaling $3,490 million. The services credit totaled $2,957 million and debit $1,138 million. The following table summarizes Cyprus's balance of payments as reported by the IMF for 1998 in millions of US dollars.

Current Account		-561
Balance on goods	-2,426	
Balance on services	1,819	
Balance on income	-67	
Current transfers	112	
Capital Account		...
Financial Account		572
Direct investment abroad	-79	
Direct investment (Greek and Turkish zones)		37
Portfolio investment assets	-106	
Portfolio investment liabilities	322	
Other investment assets	596	
Other investment liabilities	-197	
Net Errors and Omissions		-94
Reserves and Related Items		83

33BANKING AND SECURITIES

In 1963, the Ottoman Bank (since renamed the Central Bank of Cyprus) was designated as the government's banking and currency clearing agent. The Banking law of 1997 provided for a properly-funded deposit insurance scheme and regulation were before the Hose of Representatives in late 1999. In general, banking services compare with the level experienced in European countries and the United States. There are six domestic banks.

The Cyprus Stock Exchange, which opened in March 1996, ended 1996 with gains of just 0.2%, but experienced an extended bull run starting in late November of 1998. Since 1996, foreign investors are no longer required to obtain the Central Bank's permission to invest in the CSE, although there are limits on foreign participation. Legislation passed in 1999 prohibited insider trading and a new screen-based automated trading system helped enhance investor confidence. The CSE index reach 162.8 by June 1999, up from its initial starting point of 100 in 1996. Market capitalization is $5.4 billion.

34INSURANCE

Insurance companies, mostly British, make available life, fire, marine, accident, burglary, and other types of insurance. Auto collision insurance is compulsory. At the beginning of the 1990s, more than 50 insurance companies operated in Cyprus.

35PUBLIC FINANCE

The fiscal year follows the calendar year. Import duties and income tax are the principal sources of government revenue. The principal ordinary expenditures are education, defense, and police and fire services. Due to the introduction of a value-added tax and a more efficient tax collection system, Cyprus made steady progress in reducing its budget deficit in the early 1990s, which reached 1% of GDP in 1995. The deficit, however, due in part to a slowing economy, is now again on the increase.

Turkish Cypriots use the Turkish lira for currency, and the Turkish government reportedly provides a large part of the TRNC annual budget.

The International Monetary Fund (IMF) estimates that in 1997 Cyprus's central government took in revenues of approximately $710.9 million and had expenditures of $830.4 million including capital expenditures of $83.2 million. Overall, the government registered a deficit of approximately $120 million.

The following table shows an itemized breakdown of government revenues and expenditures in millions of US dollars. The percentages were calculated from data reported by the IMF.

REVENUE AND GRANTS	100%	710
Tax revenue	78.0%	554
Non-tax revenue	21.8%	155
Grants	0.1%	1
EXPENDITURES	100%	830
General public services	6.3%	53
Defense	3.8%	32
Public order and safety	5.6%	46
Education	11.9%	99
Health	6.3%	52
Social security	24.5%	203
Housing and community amenities	4.0%	34
Recreation, cultural, and religious affairs	1.7%	14
Economic affairs and services	12.9%	107
Other expenditures	0.6%	5
Interest payments	14.3%	119
Adjustments	7.9%	66

36TAXATION

Taxes on expenditure (customs, excise, etc.) and taxes on income are the main sources of government revenue. Income tax was introduced in 1941. Individuals whose taxable income does not exceed c£2,000 are exempt; for others, the tax ranges from 20% on taxable income of c£2,001–4,000 to 40% on income over c£8,000. A withholding system, applying to both salaried employees and wage earners, has been in operation since 1953. On 1 January 1991, a unified tax rate for public and private companies was introduced. A 20% tax is levied on the first c£100,000 and 25% on the excess. Other taxes include a 20% capital gains tax, a value-added tax introduced in 1992 at a current rate of 8%, and a defense contribution tax for the defense of Cyprus that is currently pending renewal. Cyprus is steadily conforming its tax code to that of the EU in anticipation of eventual membership.

37 CUSTOMS AND DUTIES
As of 1 January 1998, tariffs on many goods imported from the EU fell to zero as Cyprus adopted the EU's Common Customs Tariff on most products from third countries. In addition, Cyprus is a member of the World Trade Organization (WTO). The Republic of Cyprus also provides a 20% price preference on domestic goods and services for public tenders, although foreign pressure—the EU and WTO forbid such practices—may halt this practice. A 8% VAT (soon to increase to 10–15%) is also levied.

38 FOREIGN INVESTMENT
The majority of factories are owned by domestic companies but, in most of the major industrial concerns, there has been considerable British and Greek capital. The central government encourages foreign investment that results in the import of new technology or new production methods and improves the quality of the goods produced, especially for export. Any purchase of shares in a domestic company by nonresidents requires approval by the Central Bank of Cyprus. Specific investment incentives include full repatriation of profits and capital gains, accelerated depreciation, and reduced tax rates for public companies during their first seven years of operation; additional incentives are offered to companies using Cyprus as a base for overseas operations. By 1996, there were some 1,168 offshore companies operating out of Cyprus. In 1986, the government liberalized the investment code in order to encourage foreign investment. In 1996, the government further liberalized the investment code to allow foreign participation of up to 49% in Cypriot companies. Certain services are allowed 100% foreign participation. Since 1986, foreigners have invested about $300 million in Cyprus. An industrial estate near Larnaca functions as a duty-free zone, and a free-trade zone with warehousing facilities is planned for the Limassol area.

Because Turkish Cyprus is recognized as a sovereign nation by no other nation besides Turkey, it has attracted little foreign investment.

39 ECONOMIC DEVELOPMENT
The first development plan (1962–66), designed to broaden the base of the economy and to raise the standard of living, resulted in an average annual real growth rate of 5.4%. The second development plan (1967–71) called for an annual growth rate of 7% in the GDP; actual growth during this period was nearly 8% annually. The third development plan (1972–76) envisaged an annual economic growth rate of 7.2%, but a drought in 1973 and the war in 1974 badly disrupted development programs. Physical destruction, a massive refugee problem, and a collapse of production, services, and exports made it impossible for Cyprus to reach the targets.

Since 1975, multi-year emergency economic action plans inaugurated by the Republic of Cyprus have provided for increased employment, incentives to reactivate the economy, more capital investment, and measures to maintain economic stability. The 1994–98 Strategic Development Plan emphasized a free-market, private-sector economic approach with a target GDP growth of 4% annually. The plan called for a domestic savings rate of 22.3% of GDP; an increase of labor productivity of 2.8%

between 1994–96; an inflation rate of approximately 3%, and unemployment no greater than 2.8%. As of 1996, Cyprus has largely met these goals with the exception of less than target levels of savings and productivity.

While Cyprus used to receive substantial amounts of development aid, due in part to its own improving economy and a recession in the European donor countries, it now receives little direct financial assistance from other nations.

Since its military intervention in 1974, Turkey has provided substantial financial aid to the Turkish Cypriot area. In 1996, this assistance was estimated to be approximately one-third of the area's GDP, or approximately $175 million.

Membership in the European Union (EU) is a major goal of the Republic of Cyprus. As a result, Cyprus is harmonizing its laws in accordance with EU standards. At the December 1999 EU summit in Helsinki, Cyprus joined the list of candidates for entry. The Republic of Cyprus has also offered to allow a Turkish Cypriot delegation in its negotiating group. Turkish Cypriots, however, oppose Greek Cypriot entry into the EU prior to both a political settlement of the island's division and Turkish accession to the EU. Many observers believe it unlikely that the EU will allow the Republic of Cyprus to join prior to the island's reunification. Greece, however, has threatened to veto any EU expansion if Cyprus is denied entry, regardless of the political situation on the island.

40 SOCIAL DEVELOPMENT
A social insurance scheme that became effective in 1980 is compulsory for all employees and self-employed persons in the Greek Cypriot zone. It provides unemployment and sickness benefits; old age, widows', and orphans' pensions; maternity benefits; missing persons' allowances; injury and disablement benefits; and death and marriage grants. Benefits are financed through contributions of 6.3% of earnings, paid by employees (11% for self-employed), 6.3% of payroll, paid by employers, and of 4% of earnings, paid by the government on a maximum salary of c£364 per week (in 1999). There is a dual system of social insurance of cash benefits for sickness, and a national health insurance system.

Although women have the same legal status as men, women's groups maintain that the divorce law discriminates in favor of men. A 1989 law requiring equal pay for both sexes in private sector employment was satisfactorily implemented by October 1992. Legislation passed in 1998 now makes it possible for women to pass on their citizenship to their children if they marry a foreigner. A Turkish Cypriot law passed the same year strengthens the rights of married women. As of 1996, 4 of 56 parliamentary seats were held by women. Spousal abuse is a serious social problem, and legislation passed in 1994 was designed to make abuse easier to report and prosecute. Few cases, however, are tried in court.

Although human rights are generally respected, police brutality continues to be a problem. There are also reports of the mistreatment of domestic servants, usually of East or South Asian origin. Freedom of movement between the Greek and Turkish zones is restricted.

41 HEALTH
In 1999, the birth rate was 13.6 per 1,000 people. There were 1,199 doctors, 96 pharmacists, and 428 dentists in 1990. In the mid-1990s there were 400 inhabitants per doctor and there were 6 hospital beds per 1,000 people in the Republic. There are both public and private medical facilities, including about 50 rural health centers. The island has a low incidence of infectious diseases, but hydatid disease (echinococcosis) is endemic. Malaria has been eradicated, and thalassaemia, which affected 15% of the population in 1960, is now eliminated. In 1996, 50 new cases of

AIDS were reported. The fertility rate in 1999 was two children per mother. The infant mortality rate was estimated at 7.7 per 1,000 live births in 1999, and the average life expectancy was 77 years in 1999. The general mortality rate in 1999 was 7.4 per 1,000 inhabitants. In 1994, 83% of children were vaccinated against measles. In 1990, 95% of the population had access to health care services, and 100% had access to safe water.

42HOUSING

Village homes in Cyprus are generally constructed of stone, sundried mud bricks, and other locally available materials; in the more prosperous rural centers, there are houses of burnt brick or concrete. A growing population has resulted in a shortage of dwellings, especially in urban areas. This was further aggravated by the 1974 war, which resulted in the displacement of more than 200,000 people and the destruction of 36% of the housing stock. The government provided temporary accommodations for about 25,000 displaced people and embarked on a long-term plan to replace the lost housing units. Between 1974 and 1990, 50,227 families were housed in a total of 13,589 low-cost dwellings.

In 1982, the Cyprus Land Development Corporation was formed to address the housing needs of low- and middle-income families, including the replacement of old housing stock. By 1991, the corporation had disposed of 573 building plots and helped construct 391 housing units. Between 1975 and 1991, the private sector constructed 83,197 housing units. The total number of housing units grew from about 75,000 in 1976 to about 125,000 at last estimate.

43EDUCATION

Adult illiteracy rates for the year 2000 were estimated at 3.1% (males, 1.3%; females, 5.0%). In 1959, the Greek and Turkish communities were made responsible for their own school systems. Education is compulsory for nine years with children attending six years of primary school and six years of secondary. In 1997, there were 376 primary schools with 4,202 teachers and 64,761 students attending them. At the secondary level, there were 4,934 teachers and 61,266 students attending in that same year.

Cyprus has no college, so about 14,000 Cypriot students were studying abroad in 1983, including some 3,000 in the US. The Greek community made plans to open a university for both Greek and Turkish students. Unwilling to agree, the Turkish community instead upgraded the Higher Technological Institute, which is situated near Famagusta, to university level. It opened under the name of Eastern Mediterranean University in 1986. In 1997 the number of students enrolled in post-secondary institutions totaled 9,982, with 1,061 teachers.

44LIBRARIES AND MUSEUMS

Cyprus has numerous school, private, and public libraries. The Ministry of Education Library in Nicosia (85,000 volumes) serves as a central public library for the Republic of Cyprus. There are also municipal libraries in Famagusta, Limassol, Ktima, Larnaca, and Paphos, and bookmobile services in the Nicosia environs. Among the most important specialized libraries are those of the Cyprus Museum (15,000 volumes), the Phaneromeni Library of the Eastern Orthodox Church (33,000), and the Cyprus Turkish National Library (56,000), all in Nicosia. The University of Cyprus holds 150,000 volumes in Nicosia.

The Department of Antiquities is responsible for a wide, continuing program of research at Neolithic and classical sites; on behalf of ecclesiastical authorities, it conserves the cathedrals, mosques, monasteries, and other monuments, and over a period of many years has cooperated with numerous scientific expeditions. The entire range of archaeological discoveries from prehistoric to medieval times is displayed in the Cyprus Museum at Nicosia. In addition to the Cyprus Historical Museum and Archives and the Folk Art Museum in Nicosia, there are important collections in museums at Paphos, Larnaca, and Limassol. In all, there are about 20 museums in Cyprus, the majority being archaeological and historical. There are over 1,000 monuments and historic sites.

45MEDIA

The Cyprus Telecommunications Authority (CTA) operates the internal communications system. The telephone network is nearly wholly automatic, and the CTA connects Cyprus with more than 67 other countries; in 1980, its first telecommunications satellite, Makarios, was placed in earth orbit. In 1996, there were an estimated 367,000 telephones in use in the Greek Cypriot sector and 80,000 in the Turkish Cypriot area.

The Cyprus Broadcasting Corp. maintains regular service. Commercial spot announcements and a few sponsored programs are permitted on both radio and television. Radio programming in both AM and FM is transmitted by the CBC on two channels in Greek, Turkish, Arabic, and English. Private radio stations have been allowed since 1990, and there were 30 licenses issued by the end of 1992. The CBC has two channels, and licenses have been granted to four private stations (one of them cable) since April 1993. The main television transmitting station is located on Mt. Olympus. Since 1980, the television service has been linked via satellite with the Eurovision network for live transmission of major events in Europe. As of 1999, the Greek sector had 4 AM and 36 FM radio stations; the Turkish sector had 2 AM and 6 FM stations. In 1997, both sectors together had 830 radios and 241 television sets per 1,000 population.

Nicosia has traditionally been the publishing center for the island and the editorial headquarters of nearly all the daily newspapers and weeklies. There is no censorship in the south, and newspapers are outspoken on political matters. The following are the major daily newspapers (with estimated 1999 circulations):

	ORIENTATION	CIRCULATION
O Phileleftheros (Greek)	Independent moderate	27,000
Haravghi (Greek)	Communist	7,500
I Simerini (Greek)	Conservative	8,000
Apogevmatini (Greek	Independent moderate	10,000
Agon (Greek)	Independent right-wing	5,000
Halkin Sesi (Turkish)	Independent Turkish nationalist	5,000
Cyprus Mail (English	)Independent conservative	4,000

Freedom of speech and the press are mandated by law and are said to be in full support by the government. Private television and radio stations and university-run stations compete successfully with the government-controlled stations.

46ORGANIZATIONS

The government encourages cooperative societies in many ways, including exemption from certain forms of taxation. There are a great number of youth organizations, particularly athletic clubs. In 1962, the island's main commercial organizations, the Cyprus Chamber of Commerce, the Cyprus Federation of Trade and Industry, and the Union of Industrialists, combined to form the Cyprus Chamber of Commerce and Industry. There is also a Turkish Cypriot Chamber of Commerce in Nicosia.

47TOURISM, TRAVEL, AND RECREATION

Although Cyprus is located off the main routes of travel and has few luxury hotels, the island's salubrious climate, scenic beauties, extensive roads, and rich antiquarian sites have attracted numerous visitors. In 1997 there were 35,742 rooms with 83,288 beds available in hotels, primarily located in the larger towns on the coasts, with a 52% occupancy rate. Tourism generated $1.6

billion in earnings that year. During the 1997 tourist season, Cyprus attracted 2.08 million foreign visitors, of whom an estimated 90% came from Europe.

All visitors must have a valid passport. Tourists from certain countries, including the United States, Canada, and the UK, many stay for up to three months without a visa.

In 1999 the UN estimated the daily cost of staying in Cyprus as $106 per day.

48FAMOUS CYPRIOTS

Most widely known of Cypriots in the pre-Christian world was the philosopher Zeno (335?–263? BC), who expounded his philosophy of Stoicism chiefly in the marketplace of Athens.

Makarios III (1913–77), archbishop and ethnarch from 1950 and a leader in the struggle for independence, was elected the first president of Cyprus in December 1959, and reelected in 1968 and 1973. His successor as president, Spyros Kyprianou (b. 1932), also was twice elected to the office, in 1978 and 1983. Rauf Denktash (Denktaş; b. 1924), the leader of the Turkish Cypriot community, was elected vice-president of Cyprus in 1973, became president of the TCFS in 1975, and of the TRNC in 1983; he was reelected in 1985.

49DEPENDENCIES

Cyprus has no territories or colonies.

50BIBLIOGRAPHY

Bahcheli, Tozun. *Greek-Turkish Relations Since 1955*. Boulder, Colo.: Westview Press, 1990.

Bolukbasi, Suha. *The Superpowers and the Third World: Turkish-American Relations and Cyprus*. Charlottesville: The University of Virginia, 1988.

Crawshaw, Nancy. *The Cyprus Revolt: The Origins, Development, and Aftermath of an International Dispute*. Winchester, Mass.: Allen & Unwin, 1978.

Cyprus—A Long-Term Development Perspective. Washington, D.C.: The World Bank, 1987.

Cyprus in Pictures. Minneapolis: Lerner, 1992.

Denktash, Rauf. *The Cyprus Triangle*. Winchester, Mass.: Allen & Unwin, 1982.

Early Society in Cyprus. Edinburgh, Scotland: Edinburgh University Press in association with the National Museums of Scotland and the A. G. Leventis Foundation, 1989.

Foley, Charles, and W. I. Scobie. *The Struggle for Cyprus*. Stanford, Calif.: Hoover Institution Press, 1975.

Hart, Parker T. *Two NATO Allies at the Threshold of War: Cyprus, a Firsthand Account of Crisis Management, 1965–1968*. Durham, N.C.: Duke University Press, 1990.

Jennings, Ronald C. *Christians and Muslims in Ottoman Cyprus and the Mediterranean World, 1571–1640*. New York: New York University Press, 1993.

Kitromilides, Paschalis and Marios Evriviades. *Cyprus*. Santa Barbara, Calif.: ABC-Clio, 1982.

Knapp, Arthur Bernard. *Provenience Studies and Bronze Age Cyprus: Production, Exchange and Politico-economic Change*. Madison, Wis.: Prehistory Press, 1994.

Koumoulides, John T.A. (ed.). *Cyprus in Transition, 1960–1985*. London: Trigraph, 1986.

Necatigil, Zaim M. *The Cyprus Question and the Turkish Position in International Law*, 2nd ed. New York: Oxford University Press, 1993.

Polyviou, Polyvios G. *Cyprus: Conflict and Negotiation, 1960–1980*. New York: Holmes & Meier, 1981.

Salem, Norma (ed.). *Cyprus: a Regional Conflict and its Resolution*. New York: St. Martin's Press, 1992.

Solsten, Eric (ed.). *Cyprus, a Country Study*. 4th ed. Washington, D.C.: Government Printing Office, 1993.

Tatton-Brown, Veronica. *Ancient Cyprus*. Cambridge, Mass.: Harvard University Press, 1988.

EAST TIMOR

East Timor, originally a Portuguese colony that has endured a bloody struggle for independence from Indonesia through the turn of the millennium, survives within Timor, an island roughly the size of the Netherlands (32,000 square kilometers) that forms an arc between Asia and Australia and is situated within the Nusatengarra Archipelago. Opposite the well-traveled island of Bali, East Timor is one of over 13,500 islands that comprise Indonesia, and it is surrounded by the Indian Ocean at the south and the Pacific Ocean at the north. Its size rivals New Jersey or Israel, and its 19,000 kilometre territory extends beyond its mainland to include the enclave of Ocussi-Ambeno in West Timor, and the islands of Atauro in the north and Jaco in the east. The landscape offers a patchwork of rugged mountains, waterfalls, coastal lagoons, and diverse features that span variable vegetation, dry grasslands, savannah forests, gullies and patches of dense rainforests. Gunung Tata Mai Lau, a mountain that forms the highest point on East Timor, reaches some 2,900 meters just south of the capital city of Dili, and the Laclo river in the north stretches some 80 kilometers, forming the longest river.

Though "Timor" is the Malay word for "Orient," the estimated 850,000 people who populate East Timor's thirteen districts betray a long procession of migrations from the west, north and east. Incessant warfare and the consequent political and social upheaval that has ravaged the island since its decolonization from Portugal has shaped the population to be 20% Indonesian, 78% Timorese, and 2% Chinese. Historically, the ethnic population was largely defined by the Atoni and the more dominant Belu, the latter a blend of Malay, Melanesian and Austronesian peoples who were fluent in the Tetun language, still widely spoken to this day. In addition to Tetun, eleven other indigenous languages are spoken within East Timor, and can be categorized as either Austronesian or non-Austronesian; Tetun, Galoli, Mambai, Tokodede are classified as Austronesian languages, while Bunak, Kemak, Makassai, Dagada, Idate, Kairui, Nidiki, and Baikenu comprise the non-Austronesian tongues. Despite this linguistic mosaic, as of 11 February 2000, Portuguese was declared the country's official language to be used in areas of government, commerce, bureaucracy and education.

Since the mid-to-late 1500's, the island of Timor and its lush offering of sandalwood lured both Portuguese and Dutch explorers, who contested for the territory until an official territorial division was determined through the Sentenca Arbitral in April 1913. Unlike the Dutch, Portugal's sphere of influence was concentrated in the local leadership of the East Timorese "liurai rei": rulers, chieftains and bi-racial mestico families known as the "Black Portuguese" who were of Timorese and Portuguese parentage. While Portugal's colonial hold on East Timor failed to avail the local population to educational and general advancement opportunities, even leaving the island with barely thirty kilometers of paved asphalt road, its detachment enabled the East Timorese cultural identity to remain largely intact and unscathed by modernity. Still, in sharp contrast to Indonesia, the world's largest Islamic country, the current population of East Timor has abandoned its historic animist tribal religions and instead largely embraces Catholicism under the direction of Nobel Peace Prize winner Bishop Carlos Filipe Ximenes Belo, whose humanitarian efforts were jointly acknowledged along with pro-independence activist Jose Ramos-Horta in 1996.

Ironically, efforts to crush the East Timorese are not traced to the Portuguese, but to the Indonesian people and their brutal tactics for integration following Portugal's exodus from the island. When the "Carnation Revolution" of April 1974 prompted the demise of nearly fifty years of dictatorship in Portugal, the decolonization of East Timor, among Portugal's other colonies, seemed a favorable consequence. By the start of May 1974 three political parties surfaced within the island: the Apodeast Timori (Timorese Democratic People's Union), largely a device of the Indonesian government that advocated that East Timor be integrated into Indonesia; the UDT (Democratic Union of Timor), advocating a progressive process of autonomy under Portugal; and the ASDT (Timorese Social Democratic Association), which later became the left-wing independence movement Fretilin (Revolution Front for an Independent East Timor), advocating the island's total independence.

The subsequent union and mounting popularity of UDT and Fretilin by January 1975 proved threatening enough to the Indonesian government that President Suharto, whose integrationist stance was already endorsed by the United States, Australia, Japan and other nations, justified his military intervention in East Timor through the "Operasi Komodo". Authored by the president's intelligence-supremo Ali Moertopo (1924-84), Operasi Komodo essentially slandered Fretilin as being secretly Communist and served to splinter its alliance with the UDT by May. Consequently, on 6 June 1975, Indonesia already occupied the Oecussi-Ambeno enclave under the guise of restoring order in East Timor, which had not endured any form of foreign occupation with the exception of a brief but brutal occupation by the Japanese during World War II.

Despite Indonesian presence and pressure within East Timor, Fretilin still gained 55% of the popular vote on 29 July 1975. Thus again threatened, Indonesia manipulated the UDT to counter Portuguese authority and Fretilin's influence through a coup staged from 11 August 1975 through 24 September 1975. However, the coup failed against Fretilin, which instead gained control of the entire East Timorese territory and actually launched humanitarian advancements (in education, medical treatment, and local decision making) that had been historically denied to the islanders. Still, reports generated by the United States Central Intelligence Agency discerned Indonesian infiltration and fighting within East Timor and around its borders during mid September and through October 1975. When four foreign journalists who captured this violence were abruptly executed by Indonesian militia on 17 October 1975, tension between pro and anti-independence forces were heightened. On 28 November 1975, Fretilin's formal assertion of an independent state of East Timor was answered the very next day by Moertopo's "petition" for the integration of East Timor into

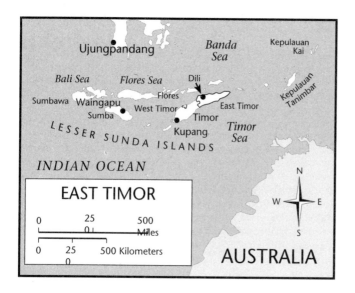

Indonesia through the "Balibo" Declaration, which UDT leaders were forced to sign.

On 7 December 1975, only one day after United States President and Secretary of State Gerald Ford and Henry Kissinger visited Jakarta, Indonesia deployed 10,000 troops - by sea, air, and land - into Dili after an already devastating naval and aerial bombardment led by General Benny Murdani. Within days of an invasion marked by public torture, rape, and the random killing of mass civilians, Portuguese Governor Mario Lemos Pires and his remaining administration made a covert and final exodus during the night to the Island of Atauro, marking the end of over 460 years of colonization, without decolonization achieved. On 17 July 1976, Indonesia claimed East Timor its 27th province despite condemnation from the United Nations, and it continued full scale attacks through March 1979 through weaponry largely supplied by the United States under the Carter administration. Within a year of the attack, an estimated 60,000 East Timorese had been killed, while tens of thousands sought refuge from the Armed Forces of the Republic of Indonesia (ABRI) in the rugged mountainous interior of East Timor, where Fretilin guerilla forces remained; others were forced into Indonesian resettlement camps, where disease, malnutrition, and death were rampant. The island was relegated to a "closed colony" status by the military from December 1975 through 1 January 1989.

As Indonesia continues to force ruthless integration tactics on the East Timorese despite the disapproval from the United Nations General Assembly and Security Council, some 250,000 have been killed since warfare seized the island during 1975. An estimated 100,000 East Timorese are believed to subsist in the squalid, disease-infested settlement camps that are found along the countryside of West Timor. Mass terror and killings have since been widespread, including 1,000 in Aitana in July 1981, 400 in Lacluta in September 1981, and, finally securing international attention, some 270 during the Santa Cruz massacre of 12 November 1991, in which peaceful mourners and demonstrators were killed by Indonesian troops' open fire in a cemetary in Dili. While Indonesia experienced a shift in leadership with the forced resignation of President Suharto in 1997 and rise to power of his vice president, B.J. Habibie, East Timor continues to endorse Fretilin leader Jose Alexandre "Xanana" Gusmao, currently the President of the National Council of Timorese Resistance (CNRT). Their continued resistance against military occupation and terror, coupled with heightened international scrutiny of the atrocities within the island, may have prompted Habibie in January 1999 to extend the East Timorese the option of autonomy under Indonesian rule, or outright independence. An overwhelming 99% of eligible voters were present during the 30 August 1999 referendum, which secured the vote for independence.

However, post-election violence and killings, which drove some 250,000 from East Timor following the election, were a dark reminder of East Timor's subjugation to the Indonesian military, which has long remained the source of ultimate government authority. The island still struggles with the absence of local police, any organized legal or judicial infrastructure, established courts and judges, and fully-equipped health care facilities, among a myriad of other necessary services. Sparse facilities include some 67 community health centers (31 lacking physicians), eight district hospitals, and one central hospital, Dili's Tokuboro hospital. The number of doctors in East Timor in 1999 totaled around 69, and virtually no surgeons or surgical equipment are present. Urban unemployment looms at a towering 80%, and despite the presence of rich off shore oil reserves, the December 1989 Timor Gap Treaty carved up the oil-rich seabed of the Timor Sea and its mining profits between Indonesia and Australia. Following a unanimous decision on 25 October 1999 by the United Nations Security Council, East Timor is currently governed by UNTAET (the United Nations' Transitional Administration in East Timor) and the National Consultative Council (originally formed by 15 East Timorese whose representation was recently increased to 33), with the mission to rebuild the island and establish a new government by the close of 2001. The initial UN mandate expires on 31 January 2001.

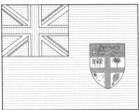

FIJI

Republic of Fiji

CAPITAL: Suva.

FLAG: The national flag of Fiji consists of the red, white, and blue Union Jack at the upper left quadrant of a light blue field, with the Fiji shield in the fly.

ANTHEM: God Bless Fiji.

MONETARY UNIT: The Fiji dollar (F$) of 100 cents is the national currency. There are coins of 1, 2, 5, 10, 20, and 50 cents, and notes of 1, 2, 5, 10, and 20 Fiji dollars. F$1 = US$0.49529 (US$1 = F$2.019) as of 31 March 2000.

WEIGHTS AND MEASURES: The metric system is official, but some British weights and measures are still in use.

HOLIDAYS: New Year's Day, 1 January; Constitution Day, 24 July; Independence Day, 10 October; Christmas Day, 25 December; Boxing Day, 26 December. Movable religious holidays include Good Friday, Easter Monday, Dewali, and Milad an-Nabi.

TIME: 12 midnight = noon GMT.

¹LOCATION, SIZE, AND EXTENT

Fiji, situated in the South Pacific about 4,450 km (2,765 mi) SW of Hawaii and 1,770 km (1,100 mi) N of New Zealand, comprises some 850 islands, of which only about 100 are inhabited. The island of Rotuma, added to Fiji in 1881, is geographically separate from the main archipelago and has an area of 44 sq km (17 sq mi). The total area (including Rotuma) is 18,270 sq km (7,054 sq mi). Comparatively, the area occupied by Fiji is slightly smaller than the state of New Jersey. Fiji (not including Rotuma) extends 595 km (370 mi) SE–NW and 454 km (282 mi) NE–SW. The largest islands are Viti Levu, with an area of 10,386 sq km (4,010 sq mi), and Vanua Levu, with 5,535 sq km (2,137 sq mi). Fiji's total coastline is 1,129 km (702 mi).

Fiji's capital city, Suva, is located on the island of Viti Levu.

²TOPOGRAPHY

The larger Fiji islands are volcanic, with rugged peaks, and flatland where rivers have built deltas. Coral reefs surround the islands. Viti Levu's highest point, Mt. Victoria, is 1,323 m (4,341 ft); 28 other peaks are over 910 m (3,000 ft). Its main river, the Rewa, is navigable by small boats for 113 km (70 mi).

³CLIMATE

Temperatures at sea level range from 16° to 32°C (61–90°F); easterly trade winds blow during the greater part of the year. Annual rainfall is well distributed and averages 312 cm (123 in) in Suva. At sea level on the leeward sides of the islands there are well-defined wet and dry seasons, with a mean annual average of 178 cm (70 in) of rain.

Cyclone Meli devastated part of Fiji on 27 March 1979, killing 52 persons and leaving thousands homeless. Nearly four years later, on 1 March 1983, Cyclone Oscar claimed several lives and caused extensive property damage.

⁴FLORA AND FAUNA

The larger islands have forests on the windward side and grassland on the leeward slopes. Mangroves and coconut planta-tions fringe the coasts. Among indigenous fauna are bats, rats, snakes, frogs, lizards, and many species of birds.

⁵ENVIRONMENT

The main challenges to the environment in Fiji are deforestation, soil erosion, and pollution. Over the last 20 years, 30% of Fiji's forests have been eliminated by commercial interests. The rainfall pattern, the location of agricultural areas, and inadequate agricultural methods contribute to the loss of valuable soils. Fiji is also concerned about rising sea levels attributed to global warming caused by the burning of fossil fuels in the industrial world.

The land and water supply are polluted by pesticides and chemicals used in the sugar and fish processing industries. The nation has 6.9 cu mi of water with 60% used for farming purposes and 20% used for industrial activity. The nation's cities produce 0.1 million tons of solid waste per year.

Fiji's natural environment is protected by the National Trust, which under the 1981–85 development plan began to establish national parks to conserve the island's unspoiled landscape, reefs, and waters, as well as indigenous flora and fauna. As of the mid-1990s, 1 species of mammal, 5 types of birds, 4 species of reptiles and 1 type of amphibian were considered endangered, as well as 25 of Fiji's 1,500 plant species. Threatened species include the Fiji banded iguana and crested iguana, the Fiji petrel, the insular flying-fox, and the Samoan flying-fox.

⁶POPULATION

The population of Fiji in 2000 was estimated at 823,376. An estimated 4.0% of the population is 65 years of age or older. The projected population for the year 2005 is 878,000, assuming a crude birthrate of 22 per 1,000 population and a death rate of 6, resulting in a natural rate of change of 1.6% for the period 2000–2005. The population rate of change between 1995 and 2000 was 1.6%.

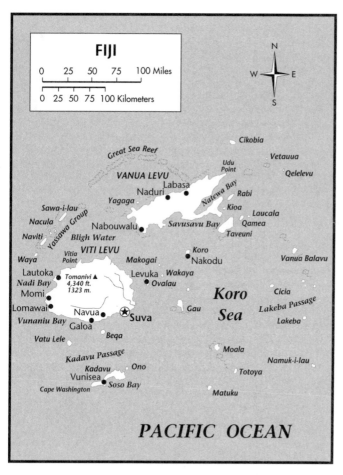

FIJI

| 0 | 25 | 50 | 75 | 100 Miles |
| 0 | 25 | 50 | 75 | 100 Kilometers |

LOCATION: 15°43′ to 21°2′s; 176°54′e to 178°28′w (not including Rotuma, which is at 12°30′s; 177°5′e). **TERRITORIAL SEA LIMIT:** 12 mi.

It was estimated that 42% of the population lived in urban areas in 2000. The capital city, Suva, had a 2000 population of 166,000.

7MIGRATION

In the late 19th and early 20th centuries, about 50,000 Indian laborers arrived in the islands to work on sugar plantations. Most recent immigrants come from neighboring islands. There has been steady internal migration from rural to urban areas. There was a substantial increase in emigration by Indians in the immediate aftermath of the coup of May 1987. There are no restrictions on emigration, as 40,000 have done so since 1987. Most of these emigrants were professionals or Indo-Fijians. In 1996, it was estimated that Indians emigrated at a rate of between 4,000 and 5,000 a year. In 1999 the net emigration rate was -3.78 migrants per 1,000 population.

8ETHNIC GROUPS

The indigenous Fijian population is predominantly Melanesian, with a Polynesian admixture. In 1998, the population was estimated to be 51% indigenous Fijian, 44% Indian, and 5% European, other Pacific Islanders, overseas Chinese, and other.

9LANGUAGES

English is the official language, but Fijian and Hindi are also used in Parliament. Fijian dialects belong to the Malayo-Polynesian language group; the Bau dialect is used throughout the archi-

pelago except on Rotuma, where Rotuman is spoken. Hindustani (a local dialect of Hindi) is the lingua franca of the Indians of Fiji.

10RELIGIONS

About 52% of Fijians are Christians, primarily Methodist (37%) and Roman Catholic (9%). Among Indian Fijians, 38% are Hindu, 8% Muslim, and 2% other. The newly amended constitution (1998) provides for freedom of religion, and the government reportedly respects this right in practice.

11TRANSPORTATION

During the late 1970s, Fiji completed a new highway between Suva and Nadi and constructed 885 km (550 mi) of rural roads. As of 1996, Fiji had 3,440 km (2,138 mi) of main roads, of which 1,692 km (1,051 mi) were paved. Registered automobiles numbered about 30,100 as of 1995, and commercial vehicles, 29,000. A private rail system of about 597 km (371 mi) serves most of the sugar-producing areas. Major ports are Suva, Lautoka, and Levuka. In 1998, Fiji had five merchant ships in service, with a capacity of 10,721 GRT. Inland waterways consist of 203 km (126 mi), of which 122 km (76 mi) are navigable by motorized craft and 200-ton barges. There were 24 airports in 1998, but only three had paved runways. An international airport at Nadi serves regularly scheduled flights to neighboring Pacific islands, Australia, and New Zealand, via Air Pacific. Fiji Air provides domestic and charter service. In 1997, 517,000 passengers were carried on scheduled domestic and international airline flights.

12HISTORY

Fiji was settled by voyagers from the east at least 2,500 years ago. Some of their descendants later moved on to settle the Polynesian islands to the west. The first known European contact came when the Dutch navigator Abel Tasman sighted the Fiji group in 1643. English Captain James Cook visited it in 1774, and Charles Wilkes headed a US expedition there for three months in 1840.

European sandalwood traders, army deserters, and shipwreck survivors also landed on the islands during the first half of the 19th century, a period in which the chiefs of Bau rose to a dominant position. Protestant missionaries from Tonga arrived in 1835, and French Catholic priests in 1844. After a few chiefs had been converted, more and more Fijians embraced Christianity, usually in the form of Wesleyan Methodism.

In the course of a civil war in the 1850s, Cakobau, the most powerful chief in Fiji, combined forces with the king of Tonga to become paramount chief of western Fiji. The growing presence of Europeans contributed to political and economic instability. In 1871, some 3000 Europeans supported Cakobau's claim to rule as king of all Fiji, but unrest continued. Cakobau's government appealed to Britain for assistance and, on 10 October 1874, Fijian chiefs signed a Deed of Cession making Fiji a British Crown Colony.

From 1879 to 1916, more than 60,000 indentured laborers from India arrived to work on European-owned sugar plantations, and by 1920 they had settled as free farmers. European settlers were granted elective representation in the Legislative Council in 1904, and Indians were admitted in 1929. Ethnic Fijian representation was based on traditional hierarchies until 1963, when the council was reconstituted; the franchise was extended to women, and direct election of Fijian members was provided for. In 1966, the council was enlarged and again reconstituted, and Fiji attained virtual internal self-government. On 10 October 1970, Fiji became a sovereign and independent state within the Commonwealth of Nations, with Kamisese K. T. Mara, head of the Alliance Party, as prime minister. He and his majority party won elections in 1972, 1977, and 1982, but lost the April 1987 elections to a coalition of the Indian-based

National Federation Party and the Labour Party. The new government was short-lived, however. Within a month, it was toppled by a military coup led by Lt. Col. Sitiveni Rabuka and aimed at restoring political leadership to ethnic Fijians. On 20 May thousands of rioting Fijians attacked Indians. Under a compromise reached the next day, the governor-general temporarily was to head the government, assisted by an 18-member advisory council, including the coup leader and former Prime Minister Mara. Elections were to be held within six months, and the council was to propose constitutional revisions that would safeguard the political dominance of indigenous Fijians.

On 25 September 1987, however, Rabuka led a second coup. He subsequently suspended the constitution, dissolved the parliament, and declared Fiji a republic. The governor-general, Ratu Sir Penaia Ganilau, was appointed president of the republic, and Mara was reappointed prime minister. Full civilian rule returned in January 1990 when Rabuka gave up his position as Minister of Home Affairs and returned to barracks as head of the armed forces.

The second coup in 1987 and the adoption of the 1990 Constitution, which favored ethnic Fijian control of the government, led to heavy Indian emigration, especially among those Indians with sufficient capital to move. This emigration caused serious economic difficulties for Fiji, but it also ensured that the native Fijian population became the majority. In May of 1992 the Soqosoqo ni Vakavulewa ni Taukei (SVT) or the Fijian Political Party, led by now Major-General Rabuka, won 30 of the 37 seats reserved for ethnic Fijians. Rabuka formed a coalition government with the General Voters Party (GVP) and with the informal support of the Fijian Labour Party (FLP), and became prime minister. After President Ganilau's death in December 1993, the Council of Chiefs elected Ratu Sir Kamisese Mara as the new president in January 1994. Rabuka's government fell in November 1993 when the legislature defeated the government's budget. New elections were held in February 1994. The SVT won 31 seats, and Rabuka was able to form a coalition government with the GVP. However, Rabuka's hold on power was tenuous as pressure mounted from within and outside the country for constitutional reform.

Beginning in 1995, a Constitutional Review Commission spent almost two years to develop a system that would avoid purely ethnic politics and, at the same time, take account of the concerns of the native Fijian community. Its recommendations were unanimously adopted by parliament in July 1997.

13 GOVERNMENT

Before December 1987, the head of state was the British monarch, as represented by a governor-general. The cabinet, responsible to the parliament of Fiji, consisted of a prime minister and ministers appointed by the governor-general on the former's advice. Parliament consisted of an elected House of Representatives and an appointive Senate. The electoral process was distinctive in establishing communal, or ethnic rolls, in which only members of a specified group might vote, versus national rolls in which anyone could vote. The Senate consisted of 22 members: eight nominated by the Council of Chiefs, a traditional body that had veto power over bills passed by the House involving native Fijians' customs or land rights; seven by the Prime Minister, six by the leader of the opposition; and one by the Rotuman Council.

The new post-coup constitution went into effect in July 1990. It established Fiji as a sovereign, democratic republic with a bicameral legislature. Fiji's president was to be appointed to a five-year term by the Great Council of Chiefs, which would also nominate 24 Fijians to the 34-member Senate. Nine seats were guaranteed to Indians and other races, and one to Rotuma. The Senate would have veto power over legislation affecting Fijians.

The 71-member House of Representatives was to be elected every five years by universal suffrage under the communal system. In addition to stipulating that the office of the Prime Minister must be held by an ethnic Fijian, the 1990 constitution also guaranteed a majority of seats to the Fijian community. This constitution prohibited cross-race voting; that is, Fijians could only vote for Fijians and Indians only for Indians. It provided for an independent judiciary.

The 1997 constitution specifies that the president, who is head of state, must always be a native Fijian. It also gives considerable recognition to the Great Council of Chiefs, which not only nominates and participates in electing the president, but maintains its responsibility for matters relating to native Fijians. Parliament consists of two houses. The Lower, where all legislation must originate, has 71 members. Of these, 46 are communal: 23 for Fijians, 19 for Indians, 3 for General Electors, and 1 for Rotumans. The remaining 25 are "open" seats contested on a common roll basis without any reference to ethnicity, either for the voters or for the candidates.

The president appoints as prime minister the member of parliament who commands majority support in the Lower House. The Constitution also provides for mandatory power sharing in cabinet. Any party holding more than eight Lower House seats is invited to join cabinet in proportion to the number of seats it holds. The Upper House consists of 32 appointed members: 14 nominated by the Great Council of Chiefs, 9 by the Prime Minister, 8 by the leader of the opposition, and 1 by the Council of Rotuma. Parliament serves for a maximum of four years after a general election though it can be dissolved by the president on the advice of the Prime Minister.

In the 1999 election, the first held under this constitution, the Fiji Labour Party won a stunning victory, gaining 37 seats and an absolute majority of the Lower House. Rabuka's SVT took only eight seats, and the once powerful NFP won no seats at all. Mahendra Chaudhry, leader of the FLP, became the first Indian prime minister of Fiji.

14 POLITICAL PARTIES

Fiji's political parties have been in a state of flux since the FLP's unexpected victory. FLP is a multiethnic party, though some see it as Indian-dominated. After SVT's disappointing showing, Sitiveni Rabuka resigned as leader, and this Fijian-based party is now headed by Ratu Inoke Kabuabola, leader of the opposition. The Fijian Association Party, also focused on ethnic interests, is led by a woman, Adi Kuini Speed, who serves as Deputy Prime Minister. It is not clear if the Indian-based National Federation Party will ever come back from its stunning defeat.

15 LOCAL GOVERNMENT

Local government is organized under provincial and urban councils. Fiji is divided into 14 provinces, each with its own council. Some members are appointed, but each council has an elected majority. The councils have powers to make bylaws and to draw up their own budgets, subject to central government approval. Suva has a city council, Lautoka a town council, and certain other urban areas are administered by township boards. A few members of urban councils are appointed, but most members are elected on a common roll of taxpayers and residents.

16 JUDICIAL SYSTEM

The 1990 constitution reorganized the judicial system, but it retains elements of the British system. The courts include the Magistrate Courts, a High Court, the Court of Appeals, and the Supreme Court. There are no special courts, and the military courts try only members of the armed forces.

The magistrate courts are courts of first instance which try most cases. The High Court hears more serious cases in first instance and hears appeals from decisions in the magistrate courts. The appellate courts, including the High Court, may engage in constitutional review. The High Court has jurisdiction to review violations of individual rights provided by the Constitution.

The 1990 Constitution makes the judiciary independent of the other branches of government. Due process rights are similar to those in English common law.

Dependents have the right to a public trial and to counsel. A public legal adviser assists indigent persons in family law cases. Detainees must be brought before a court within 24 to 48 hours. Incommunicado and arbitrary detention are illegal. The criminal law permits corporal punishment as a penalty for certain criminal acts, but this provision is seldom invoked.

[17]ARMED FORCES

Fiji's armed forces in 2000 consisted of 3,500 men, of whom 3,200 were in the army and 300 in the navy, which has nine patrol aircraft. Of Fiji's seven infantry battalions, two are deployed abroad in Egypt (MFO) and Lebanon (UNIFIL), and observers are stationed in Iraq and Papua New Guinea. Fiji spent $34 million in 1997, or 1.6% of GDP, on defense.

[18]INTERNATIONAL COOPERATION

Since joining the UN on 13 October 1970, Fiji has been a leading spokesman for Pacific island states and has contributed contingents to UN peacekeeping forces in Lebanon (1978) and the Sinai (1982). It belongs to ESCAP and all UN nonregional specialized agencies except IAEA. A member of the WTO, Fiji also is a member of the Asian Development Bank, G-77, and the South Pacific Commission and Forum. Its membership in the Commonwealth of Nations was said to have "lapsed," according to a meeting of Commonwealth heads of government held shortly after the September 1987 coup.

On 10 December 1982, Fiji became the first nation to ratify the Law of the Sea. Fiji's delegates had taken a prominent role in framing the document.

[19]ECONOMY

Agriculture, mining and fishing have dominated the economy in the past, but manufacturing and tourism are becoming progressively more important in Fiji. The first five years after independence (1970–75) were years of high growth for Fiji, when growth averaged 5.9%, driven by primary commodities. In the next five years, growth continued but at a slower rate—about 3.5% per year. In 1980–86, Fiji suffered the effects of high inflation, especially in energy prices. It also endured three recessions. In 1986, growth rebounded, with GDP increasing 8.1%. This was immediately stopped by the 1987 coup. Since then, real GDP has grown at an average of 2.5% a year. During and since independence (1971–96), Fijian GDP grew at an average annual rate of 3.3%. Fiji's pattern of growth, characterized by bursts of high growth followed by stagnation or reversal, is common for developing economies reliant on basic commodities. In 1997, economic growth fell by 1.6%, and was declined by 3.7% in 1998. The decline was blamed on the sizeable fall in sugarcane output, stunted by drought, cyclones, and strikes. In 2000, a coup caused neighboring countries to threaten trade sanctions. Despite political unrest, a 20% currency devaluation, tax reforms, and privatization improved the economy.

[20]INCOME

The US Central Intelligence Agency (CIA) reports that in 1998 Fiji's gross domestic product (GDP) was estimated at $5.4 billion. The per capita GDP was estimated at $6,700. The annual growth rate of GDP was estimated at 2.4%. The average inflation rate in 1998 was 2.9%. The CIA defines GDP as the value of all final goods and services produced within a nation in a given year and computed on the basis of purchasing power parity (PPP) rather than value as measured on the basis of the rate of exchange. It was estimated that agriculture accounted for 19% of GDP, industry 22%, and services 59%.

The World Bank reports that for the same period per capita private consumption (in PPP terms) was $3,040. Private consumption includes expenditures of individuals, households, and nongovernmental organizations. Approximately 35% of household consumption was spent on food, 19% on fuel, 2% on health care, and 13% on education.

[21]LABOR

In June 1995, the entire labor force in Fiji was 285,000, or 35.8% of the population. Many more Fijians engage in subsistence agriculture. Wages and conditions of employment are regulated by agreements between trade unions and employers. The normal workweek ranges from 40 to 48 hours but there is no statutory regulated workweek. All unions must be registered, but they are not controlled by the government. The only central labor organization is the Fiji Trade Union Congress (FTUC). Workers have the right to collective bargain and strike, although a union may not strike in connection with a union recognition dispute. There was sporadic labor unrest, including a one-day national strike in 1998, over layoffs, a wage freeze and other issues. About 55% of the paid workforce is unionized. The unemployment rate was about 5.4% in 1995.

[22]AGRICULTURE

In 1997, agriculture comprised about one-third of Fiji's export earnings. More than three-quarters of all households engage in agriculture, livestock production, forestry, or fishing. A total of 285,000 ha (704,000 acres), or over 15.6% of Fiji's area, was used for crop production in 1997. Sugarcane production was 3,300,000 tons in 1998. In 1997, sugar exports accounted for about 25% ($147.9 million) of total exports and 79% of agricultural exports. Fijians retain legal ownership of the lands, but Indians farm it and produce about 90% of Fiji's sugar. In 1995, the average sugarcane farm was 4 ha (9.9 acres), produced 183 tons of cane, and made f$9.810. Cane is processed into raw sugar and molasses by the Fiji Sugar Corporation, which is 68% owned by the government. The sugar industry is vital to the national economy; as such, the government plays a leading role in all aspects of its production and sale.

Production of copra and coconuts in 1998 was 11,000 tons and 220,000 tons, respectively; paddy rice output was 17,000 tons. Corn, tobacco, cocoa, ginger, pineapples, bananas, watermelons, and other fruits and vegetables are also grown.

[23]ANIMAL HUSBANDRY

Beef production was some 9,000 tons in 1998; pork, 4,000 tons; and goat meat, 1,000 tons. A breed of sheep highly adapted to the tropics was introduced in 1980. Fiji is self-sufficient in poultry (11,000 tons in 1998) and eggs (3,000 tons).

[24]FISHING

The fishing industry has expanded in recent years, and a new cannery has increased tuna exports. The fish catch in 1997 was estimated at 36,704 tons, over 25% of which was tuna. Barracuda, snapper, grouper, mackerel, and mullet are other principal species caught. In the early 1980s, several new fish farms began to produce carp, prawns, oysters, eels, and mussels. In 1997, prepared and preserved fish exports were valued at $35.5 million.

25FORESTRY

Some 45.7% of the land area is forested, and 253,000 ha (625,000 acres) are suitable for commercial use. Large-scale planting of pines under the 1986–90 development plan involved reforestation of 50,000 ha (120,000 acres). Output of logs in 1997 totaled 598,000 cu m. Exports of sawn timber and other wood products were valued at $25.1 million in 1997. The first exports of pine logs started in 1980.

26MINING

The mining sector of Fiji contributes 3% to the GDP, virtually all of it from gold, the most important mineral. Mined gold was Fiji's third-largest source of export income in 1997. In that year, gold and silver (2,500 kg) were the only minerals mined in Fiji. Ownership of minerals is vested in the state, which grants mining and prospecting rights. Production of gold has risen steadily since 1994, reaching 4,500 kg in 1997. Large copper deposits have been found on Viti Levu, and prospecting continues for oil, manganese, bauxite, phosphates, and other minerals. Cement production was 84,000 tons in 1997.

In addition to existing sites, 930 million tons of copper and gold reserves have been reported.

27ENERGY AND POWER

The Fiji Electricity Authority, set up in 1966, is responsible for the generation and distribution of electricity, which provides only about 10% of energy consumed. Sugar mills generate their own power, as do hotels and other establishments outside town limits. To lessen dependence on imported oil, the Monasavu hydro-electric project was completed in 1984, with a capacity of 80 MW. Net installed capacity in 1998 was 200 MW; output was 550 million kWh. In recent years, exploration for oil and natural gas has taken place, but has been unsuccessful. In December 1990, the government began creating a state-owned petroleum company, Finapeco, to act as the exclusive petroleum importer to Fiji. Finapeco is also a supplier of petroleum to smaller countries in the region (e.g., Kiribati, Tonga, and Tuvalu). Finapeco is most likely the first step toward creating a Fijian-based petroleum product industry, which might also include a refinery, shipping terminals, and tanker farms in the future.

28INDUSTRY

Fiji's industry is based primarily on processing of agricultural products, mainly sugarcane and coconut, and on mining and processing of gold and silver. Other major product groups are processed foods, and garments. Estimated industrial production in 1997 included 347,000 cubic tons of sugar and 150,300 oz of gold. The gold industry suffered due to low world market prices. Expensive power, lack of trained labor, and the limited local market have inhibited industrial production. The demand for labor increased by 2% following a 13% increase in 1989, when a tax-free factory scheme was introduced. Garment exports rose 31.2% in 1995, and employed 14,000 persons (almost exclusively women), representing more than half of total manufacturing employment. In 1996, there were at least 68 garment manufacturing factories located in tax-free zones, earning $141 million. In 1997, the manufacturing sector's growth rate as a whole fell by 3.4% due to low sugar production, but the apparel industry grew by 10%.

29SCIENCE AND TECHNOLOGY

The University of the South Pacific at Suva, founded in 1968, has schools of agriculture and pure and applied science. Other institutions of higher education are the Fiji College of Agriculture at Nausori, and the Fiji Institute of Technology and the Fiji School of Medicine, both at Suva. The major learned societies are the Fiji Society, concerned with subjects of historic and scientific interest to Fiji and other Pacific islands, and the Fiji Medical Association, both in Suva.

30DOMESTIC TRADE

Fiji has several large trading corporations and hundreds of small traders. The corporations own retail stores, interisland ships, plantations, hotels, travel services, copra-crushing mills, and breweries. Small enterprises range from a single tailor or shopkeeper to larger family businesses, most of which are operated by Indians or Chinese. Businesses are normally open from 8:00 AM to 1 PM and from 2 to 4:30 PM on weekdays, and from 8 or 8:30 AM to 1 PM on Saturdays.

31FOREIGN TRADE

Like most developing countries that export primarily basic commodities—which are subject to wide market price fluctuations and to which no value can be added—and import high-valued manufactured products, Fiji has traditionally run a merchandise trade deficit. The years of 1995 and 1996 saw unprecedented trade surpluses while the 1998 merchandise trade deficit was $263 million.

Sugar and honey dominate Fiji's export commodities, with over a third of export revenues tied to the sugar trade (35%). Clothing production accounts for the second level of export sales (21%). Other exports include gold (8.0%) and fish (7.7%). Most of Fiji's exports go to Australia, the UK, and New Zealand.

In the mid-1990s, Fiji's imports were distributed among the following categories:

Consumer goods	13.9%
Food	14.8%
Fuels	11.2%
Industrial supplies	28.1%
Machinery	12.3%
Transportation	18.6%
Other	1.1%

Principal trading partners in 1998 (in millions of US dollars) were as follows:

COUNTRY	EXPORTS	IMPORTS	BALANCE
Australia	212	359	-147
United States	102	38	64
United Kingdom	99	12	87
Japan	29	40	-11
New Zealand	27	121	-94
Korea	9	15	-6
China (inc. Hong Kong)	8	34	-26
Malaysia	8	19	-11
Singapore	1	53	-52
Thailand	n.a.	27	

32BALANCE OF PAYMENTS

Fiji has an annual trade deficit and an annual deficit on current accounts. Long-term capital inflows, both public and private, generally cover the deficits, however in 1991, the trade deficit was $37 million, down from $84 million in 1990. By 1992, the current account balance registered a surplus (as in 1989), due to increased earnings from exported sugar cane and growing tourism. The next year, however, deficits returned, but by 1996, the government was again posting a surplus. In 1997, Fiji just about broke even, but the 1998 figure reported a current account deficit equal to 2.5% of the GDP. A banking collapse due to mismanagement and corruption in the National Bank of Fiji severely damaged the financial account that year.

The US Central Intelligence Agency reports that in 1996 the purchasing power parity of Fiji's exports was $655 million while imports totaled $838 million resulting in a trade balance of -$183 million.

The International Monetary Fund (IMF) reports that in 1998 Fiji had exports of goods totaling $393 million and imports totaling $612 million. The services credit totaled $506 million and debit $341 million. The following table summarizes Fiji's balance of payments as reported by the IMF for 1998 in millions of US dollars.

Current Account		-55
Balance on goods	-218	
Balance on services	166	
Balance on income	-33	
Current transfers	31	
Capital Account		65
Financial Account		26
Direct investment abroad	-31	
Direct investment in Fiji	76	
Portfolio investment assets	...	
Portfolio investment liabilities	...	
Other investment assets	-70	
Other investment liabilities		51
Net Errors and Omissions		-32
Reserves and Related Items		-5

33BANKING AND SECURITIES

The Reserve Bank of Fiji is the central bank, (formerly the Central Monetary Authority), created in 1983 to replace the Currency Board; the Fiji Development Bank is the main development finance agency. Commercial banking facilities consist of the National Bank of Fiji (NBF) and branches of several foreign banks. As of 1997, there were six commercial banks in Fiji. The NBF enjoys the status of a commercial bank, but it does little business. The troubled NBF is undergoing a process of restructuring following revelations of a high level of non-performing loans. The government had to spend upwards of $105 million to keep the bank operating. Other banks include two Australian banks, one Indian bank, one Pakistani bank, and the Bank of Hawaii. The government-owned Fiji Development Bank provides financing for development projects.

Growth in money supply has fluctuated largely in response to trends in foreign trade, affecting the level of reserves. The government tends to follow a cautious monetary policy, which has concentrated on maintaining price stability and on managing high levels of liquidity in the commercial banking system resulting from low levels of private investment. Total assets of financial institutions in 1997 reached $2.3 billion. The government devalued the currency by 20% in January 1998 due to economic woes.

The Suva Stock Exchange operates in Suva, Fiji.

34INSURANCE

In 1986 there were 11 insurance companies, of which five were life insurance firms. Premiums were divided almost equally between life (49%) and non-life (51%) insurance. Third-party motor liability coverage is compulsory. Some of the companies listed as doing business in Fiji in 1995 were Dominion Insurance, Fiji Reinsurance Corp., Guardian Royal Exchange Assurance, National Insurance Co., the New India Assurance Co., Panpacific Insurance Com., and Queensland Insurance.

35PUBLIC FINANCE

From 1985–96, Fiji suffered a crisis in both private and public investment. Total investment—both public and private—stood at 21.3% of GDP in 1985 and had dropped to 15.8% in 1994. Investment in public enterprises rose for the same period, however, from 3.2% of GDP in 1985 to 6.5% in 1994. The fiscal position of the government also worsened after 1996 due to the collapse of the National Bank of Fiji. During that time, the public deficit increased to 6.5% of GDP, but fell to 2.4% of GDP in 1998. Foreign reserves rose to $280 million in 1996.

The US Central Intelligence Agency (CIA) estimates that in 1997 Fiji's central government took in revenues of approximately $541 million and had expenditures of $743 million including capital expenditures of $341 million. Overall, the government registered a deficit of approximately $202 million. External debt totaled $218 million.

The following table shows an itemized breakdown of government revenues and expenditures. The percentages were calculated from data reported by the International Monetary Fund. The dollar amounts (millions) are based on the CIA estimates provided above.

REVENUE AND GRANTS	100%	540,650
Tax revenue	85.2%	461
Non-tax revenue	13.0%	70
Capital revenue	0.8%	5
Grants	1.0%	5
EXPENDITURES	100%	742,650
General public services	26.0%	193
Defense	5.8%	43
Public order and safety	5.0%	37
Education	18.2%	135
Health	8.7%	64
Social security	4.1%	31
Housing and community amenities	2.9%	21
Recreation, cultural, and religious affairs	0.9%	6
Economic affairs and services	18.9%	140
Other expenditures	0.0%	0
Interest payments	9.5%	71

36TAXATION

Local councils levy taxes to meet their own expenses. National taxes include a nonresident dividend withholding tax (30%), an interest withholding tax (15%), and a dividend tax. For a resident with taxable income over F$15,000, normal tax is F$2,300 plus 35% of the excess. For a nonresident with taxable income over F$15,000, normal tax is F$3,925 plus 35% of the excess. The normal corporate tax rate in 1997 was 35% on chargeable resident income and 45% on profits of branches of foreign companies. Other taxes include a land sales tax, an excise tax, and a VAT of 10%.

37CUSTOMS AND DUTIES

About one-third of Fiji's revenues derive from customs duties. Tariffs range from 5% to 30% on most goods except motor vehicles, for which the tariff imposed is 80%. Duties are levied on the c.i.f. value of the goods. Excise tariffs are levied on cigarettes, tobacco, and liquor. The customs duty is charged at the low rates of 7.5% on most items and 5% on selected items.

There are several Tax-Free Zones in Fiji, and 133 Tax Free Factories as of 1996. TFZ's offer a 13 year tax holiday, duty exemptions on capital goods and raw materials, and free repatriation of profits.

38FOREIGN INVESTMENT

The development of existing industries has been made possible largely by foreign investment. Fiji continues to promote overseas capital investment through the Fiji Trade and Investment Board because it requires foreign goods and services to meet many of its needs, including domestic employment. Tax and tariff concessions are offered to approved new industries, and special incentives apply to fuel-efficient or export-oriented enterprises.

39ECONOMIC DEVELOPMENT

Under the development plan for 1986 to 1990, the government emphasized diversification of industries and expansion of tourism, and set the goal for real GDP growth at 5% annually. Four key areas that were supported for future economic growth were domestic and foreign development in the sugar sector; trade liberalization in major export markets; the resolution of industrial disputes; and the replacement of middle-level skills lost to emigration caused by political turmoil. During the 1990s, Fiji attempted to diversify its economy away from the sugarcane industry by focusing on the garment manufacturing and exporting trade. Bad weather conditions and political turmoil conspire to hinder economic development in the future.

40SOCIAL DEVELOPMENT

General welfare work includes relief of destitution, maintenance of homes for the aged, free medical and legal aid to the needy, child care, and social casework to deal with delinquency. Employed workers are eligible for retirement, disability, and survivor benefits, to which they contribute 7% of their wages, matched by their employers. A lump sum is payable to citizens moving out of the country, and to female employees after marriage. Employers also pay for workmen's compensation, covering both temporary and permanent disability benefits.

The constitution provides women with equal rights and includes affirmative action provisions for the disadvantaged. Amendments that took effect in 1998 address legal discrimination against women in the areas of spousal and offspring rights. Fijian women primarily fulfill traditional roles, although some do attain leadership roles in the public and private sectors. Garment workers, who are mainly female, are subject to a lower minimum wage than that stipulated for other workers. Women are underrepresented in government. In 1999, women held eight of 71 seats in parliament.

The government overtly promotes the rights of ethnic Fijians over that of other ethnic groups. Ethnic Fijians predominate in senior government positions and in the ownership of land. Although Indo-Fijians may be found in senior positions in the private sector, few are in government. Indo-Fijians are sometimes subject to discrimination. Human rights abuses are occasionally reported. However, Fiji's major human problem remains discrimination against ethnic minorities.

41HEALTH

Fiji's health standards are relatively high. In 1986, there were 385 doctors, 67 dentists, and 1,572 nurses. Medical facilities included three main hospitals and three specialized hospitals; a total of 27 hospitals had 1,743 beds. The principal health problem is influenza; venereal diseases have increased in recent years, and infantile diarrhea persists. The fertility rate was 2.7 in 1999. The infant mortality rate was estimated at 16.3 per 1,000 live births, and estimated average life expectancy was 66.6 years. The overall death rate in 1999 was 6.2 per 1,000 people, and the birth rate was 22.8 per 1,000 that same year. Between 1991 and 1994, 96% of children were immunized against measles. In 1996, seven AIDS cases were reported.

Cardiovascular disease and cancer have become the top two causes of death in hospitals during the last few years. The increasing mortality has been attributed to hypertension and diabetes mellitus. Diabetes, once relatively unknown in the Fijian community, increased tenfold among Fijian urban dwellers between 1967 and 1980. A cancer survey conducted in 1989 showed extremely high dietary intakes of fat, cholesterol, and energy.

42HOUSING

According to government estimates, Fiji requires more than 4,200 new houses each year to maintain adequate housing standards. The Fiji Housing Authority provides accommodations for urban workers and extends credit for houses it builds and sells. At last estimate, housing stock exceeded 126,000 units, of which 30% were made of corrugated iron or tin; 30% were concrete; more

than 25% were wood; and nearly 10% were bure. The water supply was mostly either individually piped (53%), communally piped (20%), or obtained from wells (13%). Roughly 32% of all dwellings had private flush toilets while 42% used latrines, and 49% had electricity.

43EDUCATION

Education is not compulsory but is free through the first eight years. During the mid-1990s, 99% of children ages 6–11 attended school. There are government schools as well as private schools operated by individual groups or by missions under government supervision. There were 4,644 teachers and 145,630 pupils in 693 primary schools. Secondary schools had 3,631 teachers and 66,890 students. Of these, 6,653 students were enrolled in technical and vocational schools. The University of the South Pacific, which opened in Suva in 1968, had more than 3,600 students in the mid-1990s. Its students are drawn from several Pacific island states. All third-level institutions and universities had approximately 8,000 students and a faculty staff nearing 300 personnel. Adult illiteracy rates for the year 2000 were estimated at 7.1% (males, 5.0%; females, 9.1%).

44LIBRARIES AND MUSEUMS

The Ministry of Education runs the Library Service of Fiji in Suva and provides public, special, and school services through 3 mobile libraries and 33 government libraries with a total collection of over 960,000 volumes. Suva maintains its own public library of 77,000 volumes, most of which is a children's collection. The library at the University of the South Pacific contains 680,000 volumes. There are several libraries associated with theological institutions and colonial cultural centers. The Fiji Museum, established at Suva in 1906, has a collection of Fijian artifacts and documents Fijian oral traditions.

45MEDIA

Suva and its surrounding area are served by an automatic telephone exchange that had 45,000 telephones in 1995. Fiji is a link in the world Commonwealth cable system and has radiotelephone circuits to other Pacific territories. The Fiji Broadcasting Commission offers programs in Fijian, English, and Hindustani over Radio Fiji on three channels. There are seven AM and one FM radio station. There is one television broadcast station, Fiji One TV, which is owned by private and government interests. In 1995, Fiji had 455,000 radios; in 1997, there were 14 television sets per 1,000 population. The two daily newspapers, both published at Suva, are the English-language *Fiji Times* (with an estimated circulation of 34,000 in 1997) and *Fiji Post* (9,000). The Fijian *Nai Lalakai* and the Hindi *Shanti Dut* (1995 circulations, respectively, 9,600 and 10,750) are two of the most widely read periodicals.

Freedom of speech and press are said to be generally respected by the government, and political figures and other citizens can speak out against the government freely.

46ORGANIZATIONS

A few organizations represent specialized cultural, commercial, or professional interests, among them the Chamber of Commerce in Suva. At last estimate, there were more than 1,200 registered cooperatives.

47TOURISM, TRAVEL, AND RECREATION

Tourism slowed following the 1987 coup but has since recovered. In 1997, there were approximately 359,000 tourist arrivals, nearly two-thirds from East Asia and the Pacific region. That year gross receipts from tourism amounted to US$297 million. There were 5,437 rooms in hotels and other establishments with 13,592 beds and a 55% occupancy rate in 1997.

Popular tourist attractions are the beach resorts and traditional Fijian villages. Visitors with valid passports are granted tourist visas renewable for up to six months. Spectator sports include soccer, cricket, rugby and basketball, and Fiji has excellent golf facilities.

In 1999 the UN estimated the cost of staying in Suva at us$100 and Nadi at us$90 per day. In other towns where commercial hotels exist, daily expenses were approximately us$67.

48FAMOUS FIJIANS

The best-known Fijians are Ratu Sir Lala Sukuna (d.1958), the first speaker of the Legislative Council in 1954; Ratu Sir George Cakobau (1911–89), the first Fijian to be governor-general; and Ratu Sir Kamisese K. T. Mara (b.1922), the prime minister since 1970 and president as of 1994.

49DEPENDENCIES

Fiji has no territories or colonies.

50BIBLIOGRAPHY

Bayliss-Smith, Tim. *Islands, Islanders, and the World: The Colonial and Post-colonial Experience of Eastern Fiji.* New York: Cambridge University Press, 1988.

Brown, Stanley. *Men from under the Sky: The Arrival of Westerners in Fiji.* Rutland, Vt.: Tuttle, 1973.

Fiji. Oxford, England: Clio, 1994.

Kaplan, Martha. *Neither Cargo Nor Cult: Ritual Politics and the Colonial Imagination in Fiji.* Durham: Duke University Press, 1995.

Kelly, John Dunham. *A Politics of Virtue: Hinduism, Sexuality, and Countercolonial Discourse in Fiji.* Chicago: University of Chicago Press, 1991.

Lal, Brij V. *Broken Waves: A History of the Fiji Islands in the Twentieth Century.* Honolulu: University of Hawaii Press, 1992.

Lawson, Stephanie. *Tradition Versus Democracy in the South Pacific: Fiji, Tonga, and Western Samoa.* Cambridge: Cambridge University Press, 1996.

Premdas, Ralph R. *Ethnic Conflict and Development: The Case of Fiji.* Aldershot, England: Avebury, 1995.

Roth, G. K. *Fijian Way of Life.* 2d ed. Melbourne: Oxford University Press, 1973.

Scarr, Deryck. *Fiji: Politics of Illusion, the Military Coups in Fiji Scarr.* Kensington, N.S.W., Australia: New South Wales University Press, 1988.

Siers, James. *Fiji: Celebration.* New York: St. Martin's, 1985.

FRENCH PACIFIC DEPENDENCIES

FRENCH POLYNESIA

The overseas territory of French Polynesia (Polynésie Française) in the South Pacific Ocean includes five island groups: (1) The Society Islands (Îles de la Société), discovered by the British in 1767 and named after the Royal Society, are the most important. They include Tahiti (at 17°40′s and about 149°20′w), the largest French Polynesian island, with an area of 1,042 sq km (402 sq mi); Moorea; and Raiatea. The French established a protectorate in 1844 and made the islands a colony in 1880. (2) The Marquesas Islands (Îles Marquises, between 8° and 11°s and 138° and 141°w), about 1,500 km (930 mi) NE of Tahiti, were discovered by Spaniards in 1595 and annexed by France in 1842. (3) The Tuamotu Islands, about 480 km (300 mi) s and sw of the Marquesas and consisting of 78 islands scattered over an area of 800 sq km (310 sq mi), were discovered by Spaniards in 1606 and annexed by France in 1881. (4) The Gambier Islands, SE of the Tuamotus, were discovered by the British in 1797 and annexed by France in 1881. Three of the islands, Mangareva, Taravai, and Akamaru, are inhabited. (5) The Tubuai or Austral Islands (Îles Australes), s of the Society Islands, were discovered in 1777 by James Cook and annexed by France in 1880. Clipperton Island (10°18′N and 109°12′w), an uninhabited atoll sw of Mexico and about 2,900 km (1,800 mi) w of Panama, was claimed by France in 1858 and given up by Mexico, which also had claimed it, in 1932. In 1979, it was placed under direct control of the French government. Total area of the territory is between 3,600 and 4,200 sq km (1,400 and 1,600 sq mi).

The estimated mid-1996 population was 224,911, of whom about 78% were Polynesian, 12% Chinese, and 10% European. About 55% of the population is Protestant and 30% is Roman Catholic; there are also small animist and Buddhist minorities. French is the official language; Tahitian (a Maori dialect) and English are also spoken. Marine life is abundant, both in the surrounding ocean and in rivers and streams; there are no indigenous mammals.

The territory is divided into five administrative areas (circonscriptions). A 48-member Territorial Assembly is elected every five years by universal suffrage. A Council of Ministers, headed by a president picked by the Assembly, chooses a vice-president and nine other ministers. The president assists the French-appointed high commissioner, who is the administrator for the whole territory of French Polynesia. The Economic and Social Committee, composed of representatives of industry and professional groups, is a consultative body. Two deputies and a senator represent the territory in the French parliament.

Tourism accounts for 20% of GDP; in 1991, 121,000 persons vacationed in the territory. Seven international airlines operate to and from French Polynesia. Tropical fruit, vanilla, coffee, and coconuts are the principal agricultural products. Fishing has intensified in recent years; the annual catch rose from 2,407 tons in 1991 to 8,571 in 1994. Phosphate deposits, mined on Makatea in the Tuamotu Islands, were exhausted by 1966. The Pacific Nuclear Test Center, constructed on the atoll of Mururoa in the 1960s, employed some 9,000 persons in 1986, including 5,000 military personnel. The Office for Overseas Scientific and Technical Research and the Oceanological Center of the Pacific (which experiments with shrimp and oyster breeding) also operate in the region. A space telecommunications station is based at Tahiti.

Currency is the Communauté Française de Pacifique franc, linked to the French franc at a rate of Fr1=CFP Fr18.18. Exports in 1994 totaled US$230 million (mostly cultured pearls and coconut products); imports, US$912 million.

There is 1 general hospital, 7 secondary hospitals, and 12 medical centers; the total number of hospital beds is 903. There are 161 public, 15 private primary schools, 4 public, 3 private secondary schools, and 18 colleges. Agricultural and technical schools offered postsecondary education.

French Polynesia in 1995 had 3 daily newspapers, 5 AM stations, 2 FM radio stations, and 6 TV stations.

FRENCH SOUTHERN AND ANTARCTIC TERRITORIES

The French Southern and Antarctic Territories (Terres Australes et Antarctiques Françaises), an overseas territory of France, have a total area of 7,781 sq km (3,004 sq mi), not including Adélie Land, and are administered by an appointed administrator and consultative council from Paris. Most of the population (145 in 1995) in the territories were researchers.

The Kerguélen Archipelago, situated at 48° to 50°s and 68° to 70°E, about 5,300 km (3,300 mi) SE of the cape of good hope, consists of one large and about 300 small islands with a total area of 7,215 sq km (2,786 sq mi). France maintains a captive register for French-owned merchant ships in the archipelago.

Crozet Archipelago, at 46°s and 50° to 52°E, consists of 5 main and 15 smaller uninhabited islands, with a total area of 505 sq km (195 sq mi).

St. Paul, at about 38°25′s and 77°32′E, is an uninhabited island with an area of about 7 sq km (2.7 sq mi). Some 80 km (50 mi) to the N, at about 37°50′s and with an area of about 54 sq km (21 sq mi), is Amsterdam Island.

Adélie Land (Terre Adélie), comprising some 432,000 sq km (167,000 sq mi) of Antarctica between 136° and 142°E, s of 67°s, was discovered in 1840 by Dumont d'Urville and claimed by him for France.

NEW CALEDONIA

New Caledonia (Nouvelle-Calédonie), a French overseas territory NE of Australia in the South Pacific Ocean, lies between 18° and 23°s and 162° and 169°E. the main island is about 400 km (250 mi) long and 50 km (30 mi) wide, with a surface area of 16,192 sq km (6,252 sq mi). mountainous and partly surrounded by coral reefs, the island is mostly forested or covered with low bush. with its dependencies and protectorates, it has an overall area of 18,576 sq km (7,172 sq mi). native fauna is sparse, but plant life is abundant; among the plants unique to the territory is niaouli, a tree of the eucalyptus family whose leaves are processed for the pharmaceutical industry.

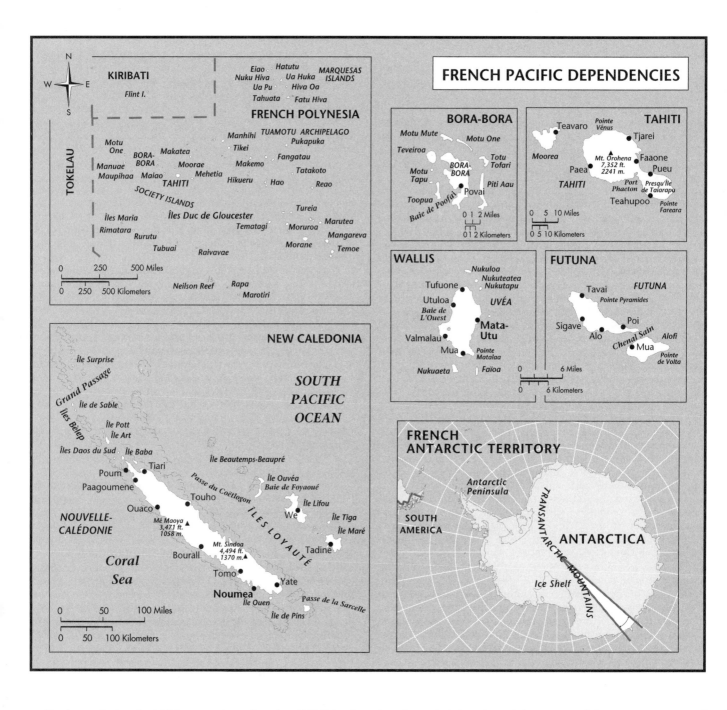

Total population in 1996 was estimated to be 187,784, of whom 42.5% were native Melanesians and 37% were Europeans. French and various Melanesian and other local languages are spoken. Roman Catholicism is the majority religion.

New Caledonia was discovered in 1768 by Louis Antoine de Bougainville and was named by James Cook, who landed there in 1774. Local chiefs recognized France's title in 1844, and New Caledonia became a French possession in 1853. In 1946, it became a French overseas territory, and in 1958, its Assembly voted to maintain that status. Under 1976, 1984, and 1985 laws, New Caledonia is administered by an appointed high commissioner, an executive council, and a 46-seat Territorial Congress, consisting of the complete membership of the four regional councils. New Caledonia has two representatives in the French National Assembly and one in the Senate. The territory is divided

into four administrative subdivisions, and there are 32 municipal communes.

The economy is based on agriculture and mining. Coffee, copra, potatoes, cassava, corn, wheat, and fruits are the main crops, but agricultural production does not meet the domestic demand. New Caledonia is the fourth largest producer of ferronickel in the world, after Canada, Indonesia, and Russia. Nickel mining and smelting accounted for an estimated 25% of GDP and 80% of export earnings in 1995. Coffee, copra, and chromium make up most of the other exports. Trade is mainly with France, Australia, Japan, and the US. In 1992, exports totaled US$477 million, imports totaled US$926 million.

WALLIS AND FUTUNA

Wallis Island and the Futuna, or Hoorn, Islands in the Southwest Pacific constitute a French overseas territory, with the capital at

Mata-Utu, on Wallis (also called Uvéa). Lying about 400 km (250 mi) w of Pago Pago, American Samoa, at 13°22′s and 176°12′w, Wallis, 154 sq km (59 sq mi) in area, is surrounded by a coral reef with a single channel. The Futuna Islands are about 190 km (120 mi) to the sw at 14°20′s and about 177°30′w. They comprise two volcanic islands, Futuna and Alofi, which, together with a group of small islands, have a total area of about 116 sq km (45 sq mi).

The Futuna group was discovered by Dutch sailors in 1616; Wallis (at first called Uvéa) was discovered by the English explorer Samuel Wallis in 1767. A French missionary established a Catholic mission on Wallis in 1837, and missions soon followed on the other islands. In 1842, the French established a protectorate, which was officially confirmed in 1887 for Wallis and in 1888 for Futuna. As of mid-1996, Wallis and Futuna had an estimated 14,659 inhabitants. Most of the population is Polynesian; only 2.5% are European. French and Uvean are the principal languages spoken; 99% of the population is Roman Catholic. A high administrator, representing the French government, is assisted by a Territorial Assembly. Principal commercial activities are the production of copra and fishing for trochus. The total fish catch in 1994 was 193 tons. The chief food crops are yams, taro, bananas, manioc, and arrowroot.

INDIA

Republic of India
Bharat Ganarajya

CAPITAL: New Delhi.

FLAG: The national flag, adopted in 1947, is a tricolor of deep saffron, white, and green horizontal stripes. In the center of the white stripe is a blue wheel representing the wheel (chakra) that appears on the abacus of Asoka's lion capital (c.250 BC) at Sarnath, Uttar Pradesh.

ANTHEM: *Jana gana mana (Thou Art the Ruler of the Minds of All People).* A national song of equal status is *Vande Mataram (I Bow to Thee, Mother).*

MONETARY UNIT: The rupee (R) is a paper currency of 100 paise. There are coins of 5, 10, 20, 25, and 50 paise, and 1, 2, and 5 rupees, and notes of 2, 5, 10, 20, 50, 100, and 500 rupees. R1 = 0.02299 ($1 = R43.50) as of 31 March 2000.

WEIGHTS AND MEASURES: Metric weights and measures, introduced in 1958, replaced the British and local systems. Indian numerical units still in use include the lakh (equal to 100,000) and the crore (equal to 10 million).

HOLIDAYS: Republic Day, 26 January; Independence Day, 15 August; Gandhi Jayanti, 2 October; and Christmas, 25 December. Annual events—some national, others purely local, and each associated with one or more religious communities—number in the hundreds. The more important include Shivarati in February; and Raksha Bandhan in August. Movable religious holidays include Holi, Ganesh Chaturthi, Durga Puja, Dussehra, 'Id al-Fitr, and Dewali.

TIME: 5:30 PM = noon GMT.

¹LOCATION, SIZE, AND EXTENT

The Republic of India, Asia's second-largest country after China, fills the major part of the South Asian subcontinent (which it shares with Pakistan, Nepal, Bhutan, and Bangladesh) and includes the Andaman and Nicobar Islands in the Bay of Bengal and Lakshadweep (formerly the Laccadive, Minicoy, and Amindivi Islands) in the Arabian Sea. According to 1986 figures, the total area is 3,287,590 sq km (1,269,345 sq mi), including 222,236 sq km (85,806 sq mi) belonging to Jammu and Kashmir; of this disputed region, 78,932 sq km (30,476 sq mi) are under the de facto control of Pakistan and 42,735 sq km (16,500 sq mi) are held by China. Comparatively, the area occupied by India is slightly more than one-third the size of the United States. China claims part of Arunachal Pradesh. Continental India extends 3,214 km (1,997 mi) N–S and 2,933 km (1,822 mi) E–W. India is bordered on the N by the disputed area of Jammu and Kashmir (west of the Karakoram Pass), China, Nepal, and Bhutan; on the E by Burma, Bangladesh, and the Bay of Bengal; on the S by the Indian Ocean; on the W by the Arabian Sea; and on the NW by Pakistan. The total boundary length is 21,103 km (13,113 mi).

India's capital city, New Delhi, is located in the northcentral part of the country.

²TOPOGRAPHY

Three major features fill the Indian landscape: (1) the Himalayas and associated ranges, a geologically young mountain belt, folded, faulted, and uplifted, that marks the nation's northern boundary and effectively seals India climatically from other Asian countries; (2) the Peninsula, a huge stable massif of ancient crystalline rock, severely weathered and eroded; and (3) the Ganges-Brahmaputra Lowland, a structural trough between the two rivers, now an alluvial plain carrying some of India's major rivers from the Peninsula and the Himalayas to the sea. These three features, plus a narrow coastal plain along the Arabian Sea and a wider one along the Bay of Bengal, effectively establish five major physical-economic zones in India.

Some of the world's highest peaks are found in the northern mountains: Kanchenjunga (8,598 m/28,208 ft), the third-highest mountain in the world, is on the border between Sikkim and Nepal; Nanda Devi (7,817 m/25,645 ft), Badrinath (7,138 m/23,420 ft), and Dunagiri (7,065 m/23,179 ft) are wholly in India; and Kamet (7,756 m/25,447 ft) is on the border between India and Tibet.

The Peninsula consists of an abrupt 2,400-km (1,500-mi) escarpment, the Western Ghats, facing the Arabian Sea; interior low, rolling hills seldom rising above 610 m (2,000 ft); an interior plateau, the Deccan, a vast lava bed; and peripheral hills on the north, east, and south, which rise to 2,440 m (8,000 ft) in the Nilgiris and Cardamoms of Kerala and Tamil Nadu. The Peninsula holds the bulk of India's mineral wealth, and many of its great rivers—the Narbada, Tapti, Mahanadi, Godavari, Krishna, and Kaveri—flow through it to the sea. The great trench between the Peninsula and the Himalayas is the largest alluvial plain on earth, covering 1,088,000 sq km (420,000 sq mi) and extending without noticeable interruption 3,200 km (2,000 mi) from the Indus Delta (in Pakistan) to the Ganges-Brahmaputra Delta (shared by India and Bangladesh), at an average width of about 320 km (200 mi). Along this plain flow the Ganges, Brahmaputra, Son, Jumna, Chambal, Gogra, and many other major rivers, which provide India with its richest agricultural land.

³CLIMATE

The lower east (Coromandel) and west (Malabar) coasts of the Peninsula and the Ganges Delta are humid tropical; most of the Peninsula and the Ganges-Brahmaputra Lowland are moist subtropical to temperate; and the semiarid steppe and dry desert of the far west are subtropical to temperate. The northern mountains display a zonal stratification from moist subtropical to dry arctic, depending on altitude.

Extremes of weather are even more pronounced than the wide variety of climatic types would indicate. Thus, villages in western Rajasthan, in the Thar (Great Indian) Desert, may experience less than 13 cm (5 in) of rainfall yearly, while 2,400 km (1,500 mi) eastward, in the Khasi Hills of Assam, Cherrapunji averages about 1,140 cm (450 in) yearly. Sections of the Malabar Coast and hill stations in the Himalayas regularly receive 250–760 cm (100–300 in) yearly; many areas of the heavily populated Ganges-Brahmaputra Lowland and the Peninsula receive under 100 cm (40 in). Winter snowfall is normal for the northern mountains and Kashmir Valley, but for most of India, scorching spring dust storms and severe hailstorms are more common. The northern half of the country is subject to frost from November through February, but by May a temperature as high as 49°C (120°F) in the shade may be recorded. The daily temperature range in humid, tropical Kerala often averages only 2–3°C (4–5°F), while in dry Rajasthan the range may be 33–39°C (60–70°F). High relative humidity is general from April through September. Extra-tropical cyclones (similar to hurricanes) often strike the coastal areas between April and June and between September and December.

The monsoon is the predominant feature of India's climate and helps to divide the year into four seasons: rainy, the southwest monsoon, June–September; moist, the retreating monsoon, October–November; dry cool, the northeast monsoon, December–March; hot, April–May. The southwest monsoon brings from the Indian Ocean the moisture on which Indian agriculture relies. Unfortunately, neither the exact times of its annual arrival and departure nor its duration and intensity can be predicted, and variations are great. In 1987, the failure of the southwest monsoon resulted in one of India's worst droughts of the century.

[4]FLORA AND FAUNA

Almost one-fourth of the land is forested. Valuable commercial forests, some of luxuriant tropical growth, are mainly restricted to the eastern Himalayas, the Western Ghats, and the Andaman Islands. Pine, oak, bamboo, juniper, deodar, and sal are important species of the Himalayas; sandalwood, teak, rosewood, mango, and Indian mahogany are found in the southern Peninsula. Some 15,000 varieties of midlatitude, subtropical, and tropical flowers abound in their appropriate climatic zones.

India has over 500 species of mammals, 2,100 species of birds, 30,000 species of insects, and a great diversity of fish and reptiles. Wild mammals, including deer, Indian bison, monkeys, and bears, live in the Himalayan foothills and the hilly section of Assam and the plateau. In the populated areas, many dogs, cows, and monkeys wander as wild or semiwild scavengers.

[5]ENVIRONMENT

Among India's most pressing environmental problems are land damage, water shortages, and air and water pollution. During 1985, deforestation, which, especially in the Himalaya watershed areas, aggravates the danger of flooding, averaged 1,471 sq km (568 sq mi) per year. India also lost 50% of its mangrove area between 1963 and 1977. Despite three decades of flood-control programs that had already cost an estimated $10 billion, floods in 1980 alone claimed nearly 2,000 lives, killed tens of thousands of cattle, and affected 55 million people on 11.3 million hectares (28 million acres) of land. As of the mid-1990s, 60% of the land where crops could be grown had been damaged by the grazing of the nation's 406 million head of livestock, deforestation, misuse of agricultural chemicals, and salinization.

Due to uncontrolled dumping of chemical and industrial waste, fertilizers and pesticides, 70% of the surface water in India is polluted. The nation has 443.9 cu mi of water, of which 93% is used for farming. Safe drinking water is available to 85% of urban and 79% of rural dwellers. Air pollution is most severe in urban centers, but even in rural areas, the burning of wood, charcoal, and dung for fuel, coupled with dust from wind erosion during the dry season, poses a significant problem. Industrial air pollution threatens some of India's architectural treasures, including the Taj Mahal in Agra, part of the exterior of which has been dulled and pitted by airborne acids. In what was probably the worst industrial disaster of all time, a noxious gas leak from a Union Carbide pesticide plant in Bhopal, the capital of Madhya Pradesh, killed more than 1,500 people and injured tens of thousands of others in December 1985. In 1992 India had the world's sixth-highest level of industrial carbon dioxide emissions, which totaled 769 million metric tons, a per capita level of 0.88 metric tons.

The environmental effects of intensive urbanization are evident in all the major cities, although Calcutta—once a symbol of urban blight—has been freed of cholera, and most of the city now has water purification and sewer services. Analogous improvements have been made in other leading cities under the Central Scheme for Environmental Improvement in Slum Areas, launched in 1972, which provided funds for sewers, community baths and latrines, road paving, and other services. However, as of the mid-1990s, only 21 of India's 3,245 cities had effective sewage treatment.

The National Committee on Environmental Planning and Coordination was established in 1972 to investigate and propose solutions to environmental problems resulting from continued population growth and consequent economic development; in 1980, the Department of the Environment was created. The sixth development plan (1979–84), which for the first time included a section on environmental planning and coordination, gave the Planning Commission veto power over development projects that might damage the environment; this policy was sustained in the seventh development plan (1985–90). The National Environmental Engineering Research Institute has field center areas throughout the country.

The Wildlife Act of 1972 prohibits killing of and commerce in threatened animals. In 1985 there were 20 national parks and more than 200 wildlife sanctuaries. As of the mid-1990s, 4.4% of India's total land area was protected. In addition to 39 mammals 72 birds are endangered as well as 1,336 plant species. Endangered or extinct species in India include the lion-tailed macaque, five species of langur, the Indus dolphin, wolf, Asiatic wild dog, Malabar large-spotted civet, clouded leopard, Asiatic lion, Indian tiger, leopard, snow leopard, cheetah, Asian elephant, dugong, wild Asian ass, great Indian rhinoceros, Sumatran rhinoceros, pygmy hog, swamp deer, Himalayan musk deer, Kashmir stag or hangul, Asiatic buffalo, gaur, wild yak, white-winged wood duck, four species of pheasant, the crimson tragopan, Siberian white crane, great Indian bustard, river terrapin, marsh and estuarine crocodiles, gavial, and Indian python. Although wardens are authorized to shoot poachers on game reserves, poaching continues, with the Indian rhinoceros (whose horn is renowned for its supposed aphrodisiac qualities) an especially valuable prize.

[6]POPULATION

India has attained the status of demographic billionaire, with a population count surpassed only by that of China. Moreover, the US Census Bureau expects India's population to surpass China's by 2035. The population of India in 2000 was estimated at 1,017,645,163. An estimated 4.7% of the population is 65 years of age or older. The projected population for the year 2005 is

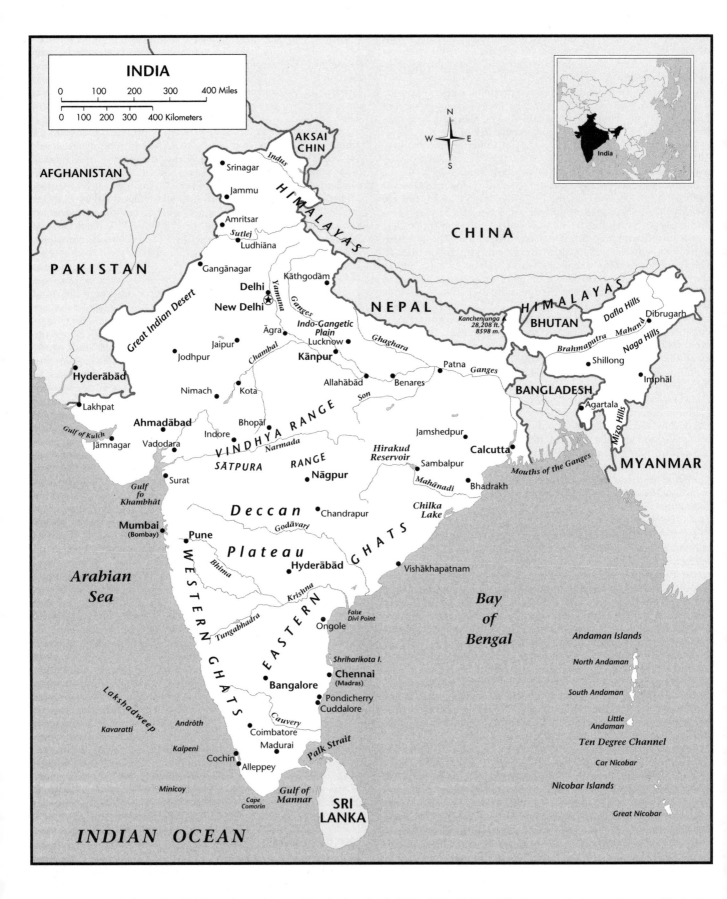

LOCATION: 8°4′ to 37°6′N; 68°7′ to 97°25′E. **BOUNDARY LENGTHS:** China (not including the 523-km/325-mi Pakistan-China boundary that is part of Jammu and Kashmir), 1,893 km (1,176 mi); Nepal, 1,508 km (937 mi); Bhutan, 573 km (356 mi); Myanmar, 1,403 km (872 mi); Bangladesh, 2,583 km (1,605 mi); total coastline, 5,110 km (3,175 mi); Pakistan, 2,028 km (1,260 mi). **TERRITORIAL SEA LIMIT:** 12 mi.

1,096,929,000, assuming a crude birthrate of 22 per 1,000 population and a death rate of 8, resulting in a natural rate of change of 1.5% for the period 2000–2005. The population rate of change between 1995 and 2000 was 1.6%. The population density in 1998 was 330 per sq km (855 per sq mi).

The key to India's rapid population growth since the 1920s has been a sharp decline in the death rate because of improvements in health care, nutrition, and sanitation. In 1921, when India's population stood at 251,321,213, the birthrate was 48.1 but the death rate was 47.2; by 1961, when the population reached 439,234,771, the birthrate was still high at 40.8, but the death rate had dropped by more than half to 22.8. A drop in the birthrate from 41.1 in 1971 to 30.2 in 1990–91, presumably attributable to an aggressive program of family planning, contraception, and sterilization, had little immediate impact on the compounded population growth rate, which averaged 2.1% in the 1980s and 1.9% in 1990–95. The government considers the rapid population growth a serious problem, particularly in relation to reducing poverty. The goal of the Indian government is to reach zero population growth by 2050 with a population of 1.3 billion.

The majority of the population inhabits rural areas, most living in some 555,315 villages with fewer than 10,000 residents each. In 2000, it was estimated that only 28% of the population lived in urban areas, up from 23% in 1980. The capital city, New Delhi, had a 2000 population of 9,948,000.

In 1995 there were 44 metropolitan areas with populations of 750,000 or more. Those containing more than 1.5 million inhabitants each in 2000 were Mumbai (formerly Bombay) (18,042,000), Calcutta (12,900,000), Delhi (11,680,000), Madras (6,639,000), Hyderabad (6,833,000), Bangalore (5,554,000), Ahmadabad (4,154,000), Pune (3,485,000), Kanpur (2,447,000), Lucknow (2,565,000), Surat 2,341,000), Nagpur (2,060.000), and Jaipur (2,143,000). India's next census is slated for March 2001.

7MIGRATION

The partitioning of the South Asian subcontinent to create India and Pakistan in 1947 produced one of the great mass migrations in human history, involving some 20 million people. Historically, major migratory movements have been to and from Sri Lanka, Malaysia, Burma, and Bangladesh. The influx of Muslim refugees (estimated at 280,000 in 1983) from Bangladesh to Assam state has sparked protests among Hindus since the late 1970s. Persons of Indian origin domiciled abroad (excluding Pakistan) reside mainly in Sri Lanka, Malaysia, Nepal, Burma, South Africa, Mauritius, Trinidad and Tobago, Guyana, Fiji, the US, and the UK. Indian minority groups in foreign countries generally do not become assimilated with the local population but live as separate groups, intermarry, and retain their own distinctive culture even after a residence of several generations.

There has been a steady migration within India from rural to urban areas. Linguistic differences limit the degree of interstate migration, as do efforts by some states to limit job opportunities for migrants and to give preference in public employment to longtime local residents.

As of 1999, there were around 66,000 Sri Lankan refugees located in 133 camps in the southern state of Tamil Nadu. An estimated 40,000 Sri Lankans live outside the camps. They began arriving in the early 1990s. Since 1992, 54,000 repatriated voluntarily. However, repatriation stopped in 1995 due to violence in Sri Lanka. Some 3,800 people arrived in 1998, and the arrivals continue. Indian authorities have not requested international assistance for Sri Lankan refugees, and the repatriation of Sri Lankans to their country is voluntary.

According to figures from 1999, there are also some 100,000 refugees from Tibet in India, and 47,000 Chakmas from Bangladesh living in northeast India. Some 2,400 Tibetans continue to arrive in India via Nepal each year. The official position of the Indian authorities is that Tibetans come to India on pilgrimage; no mention is made of returns. Also, the UNHCR has recognized around 20,000 refugees living around the Delhi area, mostly from Afghanistan. In 1999 the net immigration rate was -0.08 migrants per 1,000 population.

8ETHNIC GROUPS

India's ethnic history is extremely complex, and distinct racial divisions between peoples generally cannot be drawn clearly. However, Negroid, Australoid, Mongoloid, and Caucasoid stocks are discernible. The first three are represented mainly by tribal peoples in the southern hills, the plateau, Assam, the Himalayas, and the Andaman Islands. The main Caucasoid elements are the Mediterranean, including groups dominant in much of the north, and the Nordic or Indo-Aryan, a taller, fairer-skinned strain dominant in the northwest. The dark-complexioned Dravidians of the south have a mixture of Mediterranean and Australoid features. In 1999, 72% of the population was Indo-Aryan, 25% Dravidian, 3% Mongoloid and other.

9LANGUAGES

The 1961 census recorded 1,652 different languages and dialects in India; one state alone, Madhya Pradesh, had 377. There are officially 211 separate, distinct languages, of which Hindi, English, and 15 regional languages are officially recognized by the constitution. There are 24 languages that are each spoken by a million or more persons.

The most important speech group, culturally and numerically, is the Indo-Aryan branch of the Indo-European family, consisting of languages that are derived from Sanskrit. Hindi, spoken as the mother tongue by about 240 million people (30% of the total population) in 1999, is the principal language in this family. Urdu differs from Hindi in being written in the Arabic-Farsi script and containing a large mixture of Arabic and Farsi words. Western Hindi, Eastern Hindi, Bihari, and Pahari are recognized separate Hindi dialects. Other Indo-Aryan languages include Assamese, Bengali, Gujarati, Kashmiri, Marathi, Oriya, Punjabi, Rajasthani, and Sindhi. Languages of Dravidian stock are dominant in southern India and include Telugu, Tamil, Kannada, and Malayalam. A few tribal languages of eastern India, such as Ho and Santali, fit into the aboriginal Munda family, which predates the Dravidian family on the subcontinent. Smaller groups in Assam and the Himalayas speak languages of Mon-Khmer and Tibeto-Chinese origin.

English is spoken as the native tongue by an estimated 10–15 million Indians and is widely employed in government, education, science, communications, and industry; it is often a second or third language of the educated classes. Although Hindi in Devanagari script is the official language, English is also recognized for official purposes. According to government policy, Hindi is the national language; for that reason, Hindi instruction in non-Hindi areas is being rapidly increased, and large numbers of scientific and other modern words are being added to its vocabulary. However, there has been considerable resistance to the adoption of Hindi in the Dravidian-language areas of southern India, as well as in some of the Indo-Aryan-speaking areas, especially West Bengal.

The importance of regional languages was well demonstrated in 1956, when the states were reorganized along linguistic boundaries. Thus, multilingual Hyderabad state was abolished by giving its Marathi-speaking sections to Mumbai (formerly Bombay, now in Maharashtra), its Telugu sections to Andhra Pradesh, and its Kannada sections to Mysore (now Karnataka). The Malayalam-speaking areas of Madras were united with Travancore-Cochin to form a single Malayalam state, Kerala.

Madhya Bharat, Bhopal, and Vindhya Pradesh, three small Hindi-speaking states, were given to Madhya Pradesh, a large Hindi state, which, at the same time, lost its southern Marathi areas to Mumbai (formerly Bombay) state. Many other boundary changes occurred in this reorganization. Mumbai state originally was to have been divided into Gujarati and Marathi linguistic sections but remained as one state largely because of disagreement over which group was to receive the city of Mumbai (formerly Bombay). In 1960, however, it, too, was split into two states, Gujarat and Maharashtra, on the basis of linguistic boundaries. In 1966, the government of India accepted the demand of the Punjabi-speaking people, mainly Sikhs, to divide the bilingual state of Punjab into two unilingual areas, with the Hindi-speaking area to be known as Haryana and the Punjabi-speaking area to retain the name of Punjab.

India has almost as many forms of script as it has languages. Thus, all of the Dravidian and some of the Indo-Aryan languages have their own distinctive alphabets, which differ greatly in form and appearance. Some languages, such as Hindi, may be written in either of two different scripts. Konkani, a dialect of the west coast, is written in three different scripts in different geographic areas.

10RELIGIONS

India is the cradle of two of the world's great religions, Hinduism and Buddhism. The principal texts of Hinduism—the *Rig Veda* (Verses of Spiritual Knowledge), the *Upanishads* (Ways of Worship), and the *Bhagavad-Gita* (Song of the Lord)—were written between 1200 and 100 BC. The teachings of Buddha, who lived during the 6th–5th centuries BC, were first transmitted orally and then systematized for transmission throughout Asia. Jainism, a religion that developed contemporaneously with Buddhism, has largely been confined to India. The Sikh religion began in the 15th century as an attempt to reconcile Muslim and Hindu doctrine, but the Sikhs soon became a warrior sect bitterly opposed to Islam.

Freedom of worship is assured under the constitution. In 1999, an estimated 80% of the population adhered to Hinduism. Hindus have an absolute majority in all areas except Nagaland, Jammu and Kashmir, and the tribal areas of Assam. Sikhs (about 2% of the population) are concentrated in the state of Punjab, which since 1980 has been the site of violent acts by Sikh activists demanding greater autonomy from the Hindu-dominated central government. Other religious groups include Muslims (14% in 1999) and Christians (2.4%). The remaining religion followers consisted of Buddhists (0.7%), Jains (0.5%), and other groups (0.4%). Muslims comprise more than 10% of the population in Maharashtra, Bihar, Karnataka, and West Bengal, and more than 30% of the total population in Assam and Kerala. Christians form the majority in Nagaland and are a sizable minority in Kerala. The Jains are an important minority in Rajasthan and Gujarat, and the Parsees (Zoroastrians) in Maharashtra.

The caste system is a distinct feature of Hinduism, wherein every person either is born into one of four groups—Brahmans (priests and scholars), Kshatriyas (warriors and rulers), Vaisyas (shopkeepers, artisans, and farmers), and Sudras (farm laborers and menial workers)—or is casteless and thus untouchable (now known as Harijan, from the term used by Gandhi). Within the four major castes there are 2,500 to 3,000 subcastes based upon occupation, geographic location, and other factors. Although the constitution outlaws caste distinctions and discrimination, especially those applying to untouchability, progress in changing customs has been slow.

11TRANSPORTATION

The railway system is highly developed and is the major means of long-distance internal transport. In 1998, the railways spanned some 62,915 km (39,095 mi), forming the largest system in Asia and the fourth largest in the world. Also in 1998, a total of 12,307 km (7,648 mi) of track was electrified. Virtually all railways are state owned. The state-owned railways are the nation's largest public enterprise. In October 1984, India's first subway began operation in Calcutta over 3 km (1.9 mi) of track.

The national and state road network in 1996 was about 3,319,644 km (2,062,827 mi), of which 1,517,077 km (942,712 mi) were paved. In 1995, there were 6,550,000 motor vehicles, including 3,500,000 automobiles and 3,050,000 commercial vehicles.

India has about 16,180 km (10,054 mi) of inland waterways, with 3,631 km (2,256 mi) navigable by large vessels. Most important are the Ganges, Brahmaputra, Godavari, and Krishna rivers and the coastal plain canals of Kerala, Madras, Andhra Pradesh, and Orissa. Canals span some 4,300 km (2,700 mi), but only 331 km (206 mi) are used by motorized vessels.

In 1998, India's merchant fleet totaled 311 vessels, with a combined GRT of 6,627,497, sufficient to handle almost all of the country's coastal trade and much of its trade with adjacent countries; the rest of India's trade is handled by foreign ships. Eleven major ports handle the bulk of the import-export traffic; the leading ports are Mumbai (formerly Bombay) and Mormugao. There are 140 smaller ports along the Indian coastline.

In 1998, there were 341 airports, of which 230 had paved runways. International airports are at Mumbai, formerly Bombay (Santa Cruz), Calcutta (Dum Dum), Delhi (Indira Gandhi), Madras (Meenambakkam), and Trivandrum. The Indian Airlines Corp., a nationalized industry, operates all internal flights and services to neighboring countries with daily flights to 60 cities. Air-India, also government owned, operates long-distance services to foreign countries on five continents. A new national airline, Vayudoot, was established in 1981 to provide service to otherwise inaccessible areas in the northeast. Private airlines are growing in importance as well. In 1997, 16,040,000 passengers were carried on scheduled domestic and international airline flights.

12HISTORY

India is one of the oldest continuously inhabited regions in the world. In Harappa, an area in the Indus Valley (now in Pakistan), between 3000 and 2000 BC, scores of thriving municipalities developed a distinct urban culture. This riverain civilization disappeared around 1500–1200 BC, probably owing to the arrival of Aryan (Indo-European-speaking) invaders, who began pouring through Afghanistan onto the lush plains of northern India. There followed over a thousand years of instability, of petty states and larger kingdoms, as one invading group after another contended for power. During this period, Indian village and family patterns, along with Brahmanism—the ancient form of Hinduism—and its caste system, became well established. Among the distinguished oral literature surviving from this period are two anonymous Sanskrit epics, the *Ramayana* (traditionally attributed to the legendary poet Valmiki) and the *Mahabharata* (the longest poem in the world, containing over 100,000 verses, including the *Bhagavad-Gita*).

The South Asian subcontinent already had a population of about 30 million, of whom approximately 20 million lived in the Ganges Basin, when Alexander the Great invaded the Indus Valley in 326 BC. His successors were absorbed by the new Maurya dynasty (c.321–c.184 BC); under Chandragupta (r. c.321–c.297 BC), from his capital at Pataliputra (now Patna), the Mauryans subdued most of northern India and what is now Bangladesh. His successor, Asoka (r.273–232 BC), put all of India under unified control for the first time; an early convert to Buddhism, his regime remembered for its sectarian tolerance, as well as for remarkable administrative, legal, and cultural achievements. Many of the Buddhist monuments and elaborately carved cave temples found at Sarnath, Ajanta, Bodhgaya, and other places in India date from the reigns of Asoka and his Buddhist successors.

In the years following Asoka, India divided again into a patchwork of kingdoms, as other invaders arrived from central and western Asia. In the process, Hinduism prevailed over Buddhism, which found wide acceptance in Asian lands other than India, its birthplace. Although predated by other states of Brahmanic origin, true Hindu kingdoms first appeared in the Peninsula after the 4th century AD. The era of the Gupta dynasty rule (AD 320–c.535) was a golden age of art, literature, and science in India. And Hindu princes of the Rajput sub-caste, ruling in the north, reached their peak of power from AD 700 to 1000, although their descendants retained much of their influence well into British days.

In the 8th century, the first of several waves of Islamic invaders appeared at the traditional northwest portals; between the years 1000 and 1030, Mahmud of Ghazni made 17 forays into the subcontinent. The first Muslim sultan of Delhi was Kutb-ud-din (r. c.1195–1210), and Islam gradually spread eastward and southward, reaching its greatest territorial and cultural extent under the Mughal (or Mogul) dynasty. "Mughal" comes from the Farsi word for Mongol, and the Mughals were descendants of the great 14th-century Mongol conqueror Timur (also known as "Timur the Lame" or Tamerlane), a descendant in turn of Genghis Khan.

One of the Timurid princes, the great Babur (r.1526–30), captured Kabul in 1504 and defeated the Sultan of Delhi in 1526, becoming the first of the Mughals to proclaim himself emperor of India. It was not until 1560 that Akbar (r.1556–1605), Babur's grandson, extended the dynasty's authority over all of northern India, and it was Akbar who was the first of the Muslim emperors to attempt the establishment of a national state in alliance with Hindu rajahs (kings). Though illiterate, he was a great patron of art and literature. Among his successors were Shah Jahan and his son Aurangzeb, who left their imprint in massive palaces and mosques, superb fortresses (like the Lahore fort), dazzling mausoleums (like the Taj Mahal at Agra), elaborate formal gardens (like those in Srinagar), and the abandoned city of Fatehpur Sikri (37 km/23 mi w of Agra). Under Aurangzeb (r.1658–1707), who seized his father's throne, the Mughal Empire reached its greatest extent and then began its decline, largely the result of his repressive policies. The Hindu Marathas fought the Mughals and established their own empire in western India.

Vasco da Gama reached India's southwest coast by sea in 1498, and for a century the Portuguese had a monopoly over Indian sea. Although it continued to hold bits of Indian territory until 1961, Portugal lost its dominant position as early as 1612 when forces controlled by the British East India Company defeated the Portuguese and won concessions from the declining Mughals. The Company, which had been established in 1600, had permanent trading settlements in Madras, Mumbai (formerly Bombay), and Calcutta by 1690. Threatened by the French East India Company, which was founded in 1664, the two companies fought each other as part of their nations' struggle for supremacy in Europe and the western hemisphere in the 18th century. They both allied with rival Indian princes and recruited soldiers (sepoys) locally, but the French and their allies suffered disastrous defeats in 1756 and 1757, against the backdrop of the larger sweep of the Seven Years' War (1756–63), and by 1761, France was no longer a power in India. The architect of the British triumph, later known as the founder of British India, was Robert Clive, later Baron, who became governor of the Company's Bengal Presidency in 1764, to be followed by Warren Hastings

and Lord Cornwallis in the years before 1800. The Company's rule spread up the Gangetic plain to Oudh and Delhi, and eventually, to western India where the Maratha Confederacy, the alliance of independent Indian states that had succeeded the Mughal Empire there, was reduced to a group of relatively weak principalities owing fealty to the British in 1818.

The British Government took direct control of the Company's Indian domain during the Sepoy Mutiny (1857–59), a widespread rebellion by Indian soldiers in the company's service, and in 1859, Queen Victoria was proclaimed Empress of India. The succeeding decades were characterized by significant economic and political development, but also by a growing cultural and political gap between Indians and British. Indian troops were deployed elsewhere in the world by the Crown in defense of British interests but without any recourse of Indian views.

Nationalism and Independence

In this century, while the British moved gradually to expand local self-rule along federal lines, British power was increasingly challenged by the rise of indigenous movements advocating a faster pace. A modern Indian nationalism began to grow as a result of the influence of groups like the Arya Samaj, in the last century, of Western culture and education among the elite, and of the Indian National Congress (INC). Founded as an Anglophile debating society in 1885, the INC grew into a movement leading agitation for greater self-rule in the first 30 years of this century. Under the leadership of Mohandas Karamchand Gandhi (called the Mahatma, or Great Soul) and other nationalist leaders, such as Motilal and Jawaharlal Nehru, the INC began to attract mass support in the 1930s with the success of its noncooperation campaigns and its advocacy of education, cottage industries, self-help, an end to the caste system, and nonviolent struggle. But Muslims had also been politicized, beginning with the abortive partition of Bengal during the period 1905–12. And despite the INC leadership's commitment to secularism, as the movement evolved under Gandhi, its leadership style appeared—to Muslims—uniquely Hindu, leading Indian Muslims to look to the protection of their interests in the formation of their own organization, the All-India Muslim League (ML).

National and provincial elections in the mid-1930s persuaded many Muslims that the power the majority Hindu population could exercise at the ballot box, however secular the INC's outlook, could leave them as a permanent electoral minority in any single democratic polity that would follow British rule. Sentiment in the Muslim League began to coalesce around the "two nation" theory propounded by the poet Iqbal, who argued that Muslims and Hindus were separate nations and that Muslims required creation of an independent Islamic state for their protection and fulfillment. A prominent Mumbai (formerly Bombay) attorney, Muhammad Ali Jinnah, who came to be known as "Quaid-i-Azam" (Great Leader), led the fight for a separate Muslim state to be known as Pakistan, a goal formally endorsed by the ML in Lahore in 1940.

Mahatma Gandhi, meanwhile, had broadened his demand in 1929 from self-rule to independence in 1929; in the 1930s, his campaigns of nonviolent noncooperation and civil disobedience electrified the countryside. In 1942, with British fortunes at a new low and the Japanese successful everywhere in Asia, Gandhi rejected a British appeal to postpone further talks on Indian self-rule until the end of World War II. Declining to support the British (and Allied) war effort and demanding immediate British withdrawal from India, he launched a "Quit India" campaign. In retaliation, Gandhi and most of India's nationalist leaders were jailed.

The end of World War II and the British Labor Party's victory at the polls in 1945 led to renewed negotiations on independence between Britain and the Hindu and Muslim leaders. Jawaharlal

Nehru and the INC leadership pressed anew for a single, secular nation in which the rights of all would be guarded by constitutional guarantees and democratic practice. But Jinnah and the Muslim League persevered in their campaign for Pakistan. In mid-August 1947, with Hindu-Muslim tensions rising, British India was divided into the two self-governing dominions of India and Pakistan, the latter created by combining contiguous, Muslim-majority districts in British India, the former consisting of the remainder. Partition occasioned a mass movement of Hindus, Muslims, and Sikhs who found themselves on the "wrong" side of new international boundaries; as many as 20 million people moved, and up to three million of these were killed in bloodletting on both sides of the new international frontier. Gandhi, who opposed the partition and worked unceasingly for Hindu-Muslim amity, became himself a casualty of heightened communal feeling; he was assassinated by a Hindu extremist five months after Partition.

Among the unresolved legacies of Partition was that it did not address the more than 500 princely states with which the British Crown had treaty ties. Most princely rulers chose one or the other dominion on grounds of geography, but the state of Jammu and Kashmir, bordering both new nations, had a real option. A Muslim-majority state with a Hindu maharaja, Kashmir opted first for neither but then chose to join the Indian Union when invaded in 1948 by tribesmen from Pakistan. Quickly, Indian and Pakistani armed forces were engaged in fighting that cut to the heart of the "two-nation" theory and brought the dispute to the fledgling United Nations. A UN cease-fire in 1949 left the state divided, one-third with Pakistan and the rest, including the prized Vale of Kashmir, under Indian control. An agreement to hold an impartial plebiscite broke down when the antagonists could not agree on the terms under which it would be held. While Pakistan administers its portion of the former princely state as Azad ("free") Kashmir and as the Northern Areas, under a legal fiction that they are separate from Pakistan, the Indian portion is governed as Jammu and Kashmir, a state in the Indian Union. Periodic state-wide elections were held in Jammu and Kashmir through the 1980s, but no plebiscite has been held on the state's future.

The issue has since defied all efforts at solution, including two spasms of warfare in 1965 and 1971. In the late 1980s, India's cancellation of election results and dismissal of the state government led to the start of an armed insurrection by Muslim militants. Indian repression and Pakistan's tacit support of the militants have threatened to spark renewed warfare and keeps the issue festering.

India and China have been at odds about their Himalayan border since the Chinese occupation of Tibet in 1959, leading to clashes between Indian and Chinese troops at a number of locations along the disputed Himalayan border, including remote areas of Ladakh. In 1962, Chinese troops invaded—then withdrew from—Chinese claimed areas along the border, defeating India's under-equipped and badly led forces. The border dispute with China remains unresolved, although tensions have been eased by a standstill accord signed by the two countries in September 1993.

Nehru's Successors

After Nehru's death on 27 May 1964, his successor, Lal Bahadur Shastri, led India in dealing with an unprecedented round of Hindu-Muslim violence occasioned by the theft of a holy Islamic relic in Kashmir. In August and September 1965, his government successfully resisted a new effort by Pakistan to resolve the Kashmir dispute by force of arms. India was victorious on the battlefield, and an agreement both nations signed at Tashkent in January 1966, essentially restored the status quo ante. Shastri died of a heart attack at Tashkent, while at the height of his

power, and his successor, Indira Gandhi (Nehru's daughter), pledged to honor the accords. India again went to war with Pakistan in December 1971, this time to support East Pakistan in its civil war with West Pakistan; Indian forces tipped the balance in favor of the separatists and led to the creation of Bangladesh from the former East Pakistan; in Kashmir, there were minor territorial adjustments.

Domestically, Indira Gandhi consolidated her power, first dividing, then converting the ruling Congress Party to her own political instrument. The party lost its accustomed majority in parliament in the 1967 elections, but she continued to govern with the support of other parties and independents, winning again in 1972. In June 1975, after her conviction on minor election law violations in the 1972 polls, which required her to resign, she continued in power by proclaiming a state of emergency. By decree, she imposed press censorship, arrested opposition political leaders, and sponsored legislation that retroactively cleared her of the election law violations. These actions, although later upheld by the Supreme Court, resulted in widespread public disapproval.

Two years later, she held parliamentary elections in which she was defeated, forcing the CP into the parliamentary opposition for the first time. The state of emergency was lifted, and Morarji Desai, formerly Nehru's deputy prime minister and the compromise choice of the winning five-party Janata coalition, became prime minister. But Janata did not last. Formed solely to oppose Mrs. Gandhi, the Janata coalition had no unity or agreed program, and it soon collapsed. Mrs. Gandhi's newly reorganized Congress Party/I ("I" for Indira) courted Hindu votes to win a huge election victory in January 1980, and she regained office.

In February 1983, India was beset by communal violence, a residue of the police excesses during the alleged emergency. Hindu mobs in the state of Assam (where direct central government rule had been imposed after student-led protests toppled the government the year before) attacked Muslims from Bangladesh and West Bengal, killing at least 3,000 persons. In October, Sikh factionalism triggered by her partisan maneuvering led to widespread violence by Sikh separatist militants in Punjab and to the imposition of direct rule in that state. A year later, with the Sikh separatist violence unchecked, she became herself one of its victims—assassinated by Sikh members of her own guard.

Rajiv Gandhi immediately succeeded his mother as prime minister and, in parliamentary elections held in December 1984, led the CP/I to its largest victory. But during the next two years, Rajiv proved unequal to the task, and his popularity declined precipitously as the public reacted to government-imposed price increases in basic commodities, his inability to stem escalating sectarian violence, and charges of military kickbacks and other scandals. In October 1987, Rajiv Gandhi sent Indian troops to Sri Lanka to enforce an agreement he and the Sri Lankan president had signed in July, aimed at ending the conflict between the country's Sinhalese majority and Tamil minority.

After a rise in Indo-Pakistan tensions in 1986–87, Rajiv Gandhi and Prime Minister Benazir Bhutto of Pakistan signed a protocol in which both nations agreed not to attack the nuclear facilities of the other in 1988. And in September 1989, Rajiv agreed with Sri Lanka's request to pull his 100,000 troops out of their bloody standoff with Tamil separatists by the end of the year. In elections later that fall, his Congress/I Party won only a plurality of seats in the Lok Sabha, and he resigned. Vishwanath Pratap Singh, formerly Rajiv's rival in the CP and leader of the second largest party (Janata Dal) in the house, formed a government with the support of two other parliamentary groups. Despite an encouraging start, V.P. Singh's government lost first its momentum, then its ability to command a majority in the parliament. He resigned on losing a confidence vote 11 months later and was succeeded, with Congress/I support, by longtime

Janata and Congress leader Chandra Shekhar, who resigned after four months.

During the election campaign that followed in the spring of 1991, Rajiv Gandhi was assassinated by a disgruntled Sri Lankan Tamil while on the hustings in Tamil Nadu. Congress/I rallied around longtime party stalwart P.V. Narasimha Rao, a former minister under both Rajiv and Indira Gandhi, drawing on a sympathy vote, to finish close enough to a majority to form a minority government. As prime minister, Rao—who was also Congress Party president—dealt sensitively with widespread Hindu-Muslim violence focused on a dispute over the land on which "Babur's Mosque" sits at Ayodhya in the state of Uttar Pradesh. He and his finance minister were dynamic and innovative on economic reform, opening India to foreign investors and market economics, including rupee convertibility. And, despite frail health and advancing years, he brought new vigor to India's foreign policy in light of the end of the Cold War.

Rao lost his hold on power in 1996, however, after three cabinet members resigned amid charges of corruption and two elections weakened the Congress Party's rule. In May 1996, President Shankan Dayal Sharma appointed Hindu nationalist A. B. Vajpayee as Prime Minister, beginning a whirlwind of power struggles and political instability during which India changed governments four times in 11 months. Vajpayee's BJP government was short-lived, replaced in October by the H. D. Deve Gowda-led United Front, India's first coalition government. The Congress Party withdrew its support for Gowda in April 1997, and the UF selected I. K. Gujral, foreign minister in the outgoing government, to replace him. Gujral, a compromise choice between the United Front and Congress Party, survived in office only seven months. In November 1997, Congress again withdrew its support from the UF government. General elections were held in early 1998 and the BJP emerged as the largest single party in Parliament. A. B. Vajpayee, the BJP leader, was appointed prime minister and succeeded in forming a coalition government. This coalition collapsed in April 1999, but in elections held in September–October, the country returned Vajpayee to office at the head of the BJP-led National Democratic Alliance.

In May 1998, Vajpayee's government surprised the world by exploding several underground nuclear devices. Pakistan responded by holding its own nuclear tests later in the month. This was a cause of great concern in the international community: two countries, historical enemies whose armies faced each other in Kashmir, were now nuclear powers. The tests brought economic sanctions against both India and Pakistan from the US and other countries. Tension's eased somewhat in February 1999, however, when Vajpayee inaugurated the first ever bus service between India and Pakistan by traveling to Lahore to meet Pakistan's prime minister. This resulted in the Lahore Declaration (signed 21 February 1999), by which India and Pakistan pledged to resolve their differences peacefully and work for nuclear security. Nevertheless, both countries continued to test medium-range missiles capable of delivering nuclear warheads on targets throughout the region.

Significantly, the Lahore Declaration made no mention of Kashmir. This hit the international headlines in the summer of 1999 when Pakistani troops and armed Islamic militants infiltrated the Indian-held Kargil region of Kashmir, bringing India and Pakistan close to full-scale war. Pakistan eventually withdrew from Kargil, after heavy fighting and casualties on both sides. This ill-fated military adventure contributed to the military coup in Pakistan in October 1999. Border clashes between Indian and Pakistani troops along the Line of Control in Kashmir are commonplace. On 24 December 1999, Kashmiri militants hijacked an Indian Airlines plane flying between Nepal and Delhi to Afghanistan, an incident India blames on Pakistan. The Kashmir problem and India's relations with Pakistan remain foremost among Vaypajee's foreign policy concerns. The Indian prime minister gained some unexpected support when US President Bill Clinton, on his visit to South Asia in February 2000, made it evident he supported New Delhi's position on Kashmir. This was welcomed by India, which has seen the US as traditionally backing Pakistan on South Asian issues.

Vajpayee's NDA government faces a variety of pressing domestic issues, including unrest over soaring prices, persecution of Christians and other minorities (the Pope's November 1999 visit to India caused an outcry among Hindu extremists), communal violence, and terrorism in Kashmir. Natural disasters such as the cyclone that hit Orissa in October 1999 and the drought in Rajasthan during the early summer of 2000 have strained the central government's resources to the limit. Yet, for the first time in four years, a government in India appears to have been given a mandate to rule by the Indian people. Given the nature of coalition politics, there is no guarantee that the NDA government will complete a full five-year term in office. However, Vajpayee has at least been given a fighting chance to bring political stability and economic direction to India in the immediate future.

13GOVERNMENT

India is a sovereign socialist secular democratic republic. Its constitution, which became effective 26 January 1950, provides for a parliamentary form of government, at the center and in the states. The constitution also contains an extensive set of directive principles akin to the US Bill of Rights. Legislative acts and amendments have weakened some of those guarantees, while a number of decisions by the Supreme Court have left some weakened and others—like the commitment to secularism and to representative government—strengthened. Suffrage is universal at age 21.

The parliament, or legislative branch, consists of the president, the Council of States (Rajya Sabha), and the House of the People (Lok Sabha). The Rajya Sabha has a membership of 244, of whom 12 are appointed by the president and 232, indirectly elected by the state legislatures and by the union territories for six-year terms, with one-third chosen every two years. The Lok Sabha had 542 directly elected members (525 from the states, 17 from the union territories) and two members appointed by the president to represent the Anglo-Indian community. More than 22% of the seats are reserved for so-called "backward classes," that is, Schedule Castes (formerly "Untouchables") and Scheduled Tribes. The Lok Sabha has a maximum life of five years but can be dissolved earlier by the president; under the state of emergency proclaimed in June 1975, elections scheduled for early 1976 were postponed until 1977.

The president and vice president are elected for five-year terms by an electoral college made up of the members of both parliamentary houses and the legislative assemblies of the states. Legally, all executive authority, including supreme command of the armed forces, is vested in the president, as head of state, who, in turn, appoints a Council of Ministers headed by a prime minister. In fact, power is exercised by the prime minister who, as head of government, is chosen by legislators of the political party, or coalition of parties, that commands the confidence of the parliament. The prime minister forms—and the president then appoints—the Council of Ministers, consisting of cabinet ministers, ministers of state, and deputy ministers to formulate and execute the government program. The vice president serves as President of the Rajya Sabha and usually succeeds the president at the end of the latter's term.

Shankar Dayal Sharma became president in July 1992; K. R. Narayanan became vice president in August 1992. By tradition, the presidency and vice presidency trade off between northern and southerner, although a Muslim and a Sikh—nonregional identifications—have also held these positions. P. V. Narasimha Rao from Andhra Pradesh became the first southerner to hold the office of prime minister in June 1991.

Elections at the state level are no longer timed to coincide with national elections, and their schedule has become erratic, as state governments have been more or less stable. But state elections have come to influence national politics. Hindu party victories in 1995 assembly elections in what were Congress Party strongholds precipitated the CP's ouster from majority status in 1996 national elections.

Moderate Hindu party leader A. B. Vajpayee emerged from the May 1996 election as the new Prime Minister. Deve Gowda became Prime Minister in 1996 after Vajpayee's government was given a vote of no confidence. Gowda's United Front, with support of the Congress Party, formed the country's first coalition government. However, Gowda's leadership ended in April 1997 when he, too, lost a parliamentary vote of confidence. He was succeeded by his foreign minister, I. K. Gujral, a compromise candidate of the United Front and the Congress Party. Gujral himself was forced to resign in November 1997 when the Congress withdrew its support. As neither Congress nor the BJP were able to form a government, India's president, Kocheril Ramayan Narayanan, dissolved Parliament. (Narayanan himself made history when he was elected to office in July 1997, becoming the first President of India to come from the Dalit or "untouchable" community.) Following elections held in February–March 1998, A. B. Vajpayee of the BJP became prime minister at the head of a 14-party coalition government. Vajpayee remained in office for over a year, resigning in April 1999 when, after defections from the coalition, his government lost a vote of no confidence by one vote. In elections held in September–October 1999, however, Vajpayee was returned to office at the head of a BJP-led coalition called the National Democratic Alliance (NDA).

14 POLITICAL PARTIES

India began its independent existence with the Indian National Congress supreme at the center and in all state legislatures. In its various manifestations, it has controlled the government for most of the years since independence in 1947. Founded in 1885, the Indian National Congress, known after 1947 as the Congress Party (CP), was the most powerful mass movement fighting for independence in British India. It became the ruling party of a free India by reason of its national popularity and because most leaders of the independence movement were among its members, including Indian first prime minister, Jawaharlal Nehru. In its progression from independence movement to ruling party, the CP spawned many offshoots and continues to do so to this date, as often for personal reasons as for matters of party policy. The first to do so was the socialist wing that split off shortly after independence to form a party in its own right, dividing again several times thereafter.

Other major parties at the time of independence included the Communist Party of India (CPI), with its origins in the peasants and workers parties of the past, representing, like them, the communist left. The CPI began the independence period under a cloud because of its Moscow-directed cooperation with the British during World War II. On the right were parties like the Hindu Mahasabha (HMS), doomed to ignominy when one of its kind killed Mahatma Gandhi in 1948. Within the political system, the HMS, nonetheless, reflected a vital Hindu nationalist strain that has seen several party iterations in the years since and continues to be force in the Hindi-speaking belt of north India. Parties on the left, right, and center have continued to divide or split off over the years, and more recently, with the decline of the Congress Party as an All-India national party, there has been a rise in the number of single state linguistic, sectarian, and regional parties capable of governing only at the state level but available for coalition building at the center.

Over time, ideology, as traditionally defined, has come to mean less and less in Indian politics even though use of the word socialism is widespread. The Congress Party platform supports a secular democratic state with planned economic and social development. In November 1969, as Indira Gandhi consolidated her political position as prime minister, she and her supporters split the party. Her splinter group called itself the New Congress Party and advocated a stronger socialist line than the other CP group. In elections held in March 1971, the New Congress Party (which later resumed calling itself the Congress Party) won an overwhelming majority in the Lok Sabha. Prime Minister Gandhi's declaration of a state of emergency in 1975, followed by the arrest of thousands of her political foes, led several opposition parties of otherwise divergent viewpoints to form the Janata (People's) coalition, which, campaigning against her "dictatorship," scored a major election victory in March 1977. The Janata government began a judicial inquiry into Mrs. Gandhi's activities as prime minister (along with investigations of her son Sanjay and others), denied her a parliamentary seat that she had won in a by-election in late 1978 and briefly had her jailed.

Rather than disgracing the former prime minister, these measures revived her popular following as the Janata coalition leadership began to unravel. Mrs. Gandhi and her reorganized Congress/I Party—"I" for Indira—reemerged as the nation's dominant political force, winning a large majority of seats in elections to the Lok Sabha in January 1980. Congress–I subsequently won control of 17 of 22 state governments.

Janata reverted to its three principal constituents: the Lok Dal, with strong caste support in certain rural areas; the Bharatiya (Indian) Janata Party (BJP), a descendant of the Hindu nationalist Bharatiya Jana Sangh Party (and heir to the HMS tradition); and the rump Janata Dal (JD), Congress in all but name, reflecting various populist, socialist, business, personal, and regional interests. Other active parties include the traditional Congress/S—"S" for Socialist—Party; the once Maoist, now nationalist, Communist Party of India/Marxist (CPI/M), which has long controlled governments in the states of West Bengal and Kerala); the pro-Moscow Communist Party of India (CPI); Telugu Desam, an Andhra Pradesh-based party; the All-India Dravida Munetra Kazagham (AIDMK) of Tamil Nadu, the Akali Dal factions representing Sikhs; the All-India Muslim League (AIML); and other ethnically or regionally based parties and groups.

In the 1990s, three changes took place in the government. In elections in the fall of 1989, the Congress/I lost its majority, and although it remained the largest single party, Rajiv Gandhi resigned as prime minister. Vishwamath Pratap (V.P.) Singh, leader of the Janata Dal, formed a government and became prime minister, with the help of two other parliamentary groups in December 1989. Eleven months later, he lost a confidence vote and was replaced by Chandra Shekhar, a former Congress leader, who formed a government with Congress/I support, only to resign himself four months later. During the 1991 election campaign that followed, former prime minister Rajiv Gandhi was assassinated, but the Congress Party/I was swept back into power under P.V. Narasimha Rao, a former minister in both Gandhi governments and Rajiv Gandhi's successor as party leader. Rao became prime minister in June 1991.

The election results of June 1991, as modified by party shifts later that year, established the following party standings in the Lok Sabha: Congress (I), 245; the Bharatiya Janata Party (BJP), 119; the CPI/M, 35; the Janata Dal Party (JDP) of V. P. Singh, 31; the breakaway Janata Dal (JD) of Ajit Singh, 20; the CPI, 14; the Telegu Desam, 13, the AIDMK, 11; others 38 (including five parties with fewer than 5), and nine vacancies. Congress strength rose to 256 by July 1993 when Rao narrowly survived a confidence vote, but in December, Ajit Singh and nine JD members of parliament joined the Congress Party, giving Rao a slender majority of 266 members (with 16 other seats vacant). Flux continued in June 1994 when the former prime minister V. P. Singh and 13 others left the JDP and sought recognition from the Speaker of the House as a separate party.

The BJP rose to power as the country's most popular party in the 1996 elections, when it won 161 seats in the Lok Sabha and its leader, A. B. Vajpayee, was named prime minister. Meanwhile, Congress/I was in decline as the national party, winning only 30% of the vote as corruption charges rocked the party.

Vajpayee had difficulty holding his government together amid several corruption scandals, however. He was replaced in 1996 by Deve Gowda, leader of the dozen small factions which formed the 176-seat United Front in the Lok Sabha. Gowda lost a no-confidence vote in April 1997 and resigned. He was replaced by Foreign Minister I. K. Gujral.

Several scandals affecting major political figures erupted in the summer of 1997. In June, Laloo Prasad Yadav, president of the Janata Dal, was arrested on conspiracy charges in his home state of Bihar. Though he resigned from the Janata Dal, he subsequently formed the breakaway Rashtriya Janata Dal party. Former prime minister Narasimha Rao was charged with corruption and criminal conspiracy. Results of an investigation into the destruction of the mosque at Ayodhya in 1992 also resulted in criminal charges being brought against senior BJP figures such as L. K. Advani and the Shiv Sena's Bal Thackeray.

In May 1997, Rajiv Gandhi's widow, Sonja Maino, formally joined the Congress Party/I, a move many hoped would help restore the party's failing fortunes. Sitaram Kesri was reelected president of Congress/I in June. Within six months, Congress/I brought down the UF government after Gujral rejected its demand that the DMK, the Tamil Nadu-based party allegedly linked to Rajiv Gandhi's assassination, be expelled from the UF coalition. As neither Congress/I nor the BJP could form a coalition government, new elections were called for February–March 1998. Sonja Gandhi campaigned actively for Congress/I, but no party was able to gain an absolute majority in the elections. The BJP emerged as the largest party with 182 seats in the 545-seat Lok Sabha, followed by Congress/I with 142 seats. A. B. Vajpayee, parliamentary leader of the BJP, was appointed prime minister and asked to form a coalition government. He succeeded in putting together a fragile 14-party coalition that survived a vote of confidence on 28 March by 13 votes. This narrow parliamentary majority, however, clearly hampered Vajpayee's legislative program. In July, for example, the government was force to shelve a bill which would have reserved one-third of the seats in the Lok Sabha and state legislatures for women because of strong opposition from (mostly male) deputies.

Sonja Gandhi began to take a more active role in Congress politics in 1998, and shortly after the elections she was elected to the post of president of Congress/I. Towards the end of the year, Congress/I showed signs of recovery by regaining Delhi and Rajasthan, both traditional BJP strongholds, in regional elections. However, this did not carry over to the national elections resulting from the fall of Vajpayee's government in April 1999, following the AIDMK leaving the coalition. In the run up to the September–October 1999 elections, both Sonja Gandhi and her daughter actively campaigned for Congress. The party split, however, over the issue of whether a foreign-born individual (i.e. Sonja Gandhi) could become leader of the country. Gandhi resigned as president of Congress in May 1999, although the party refused to accept her resignation. Shortly afterwards, Congress/I expelled Sharad Pawar, P. A. Sangma, and Tariq Anwar, the chief opponents of Gandhi within the party.

Sonja Gandhi won a seat in Parliament in the October 1999 elections and was also elected the Congress/I parliamentary leader. The Gandhi name, however, did not halt the decline of Congress. The party won only 112 seats (compared to 142 in the 1998 elections) and with its allies controlled only 135 votes. The BJP claimed 182 seats, and once again A. B. Vajpayee was asked to form a government. He succeeded in putting together a coalition government, the National Democratic Alliance, that controlled 298 seats in the Lok Sabha. For the first time in four years, an Indian government—albeit a coalition government—appeared to have a decisive working majority in the legislature.

15 LOCAL GOVERNMENT

The Republic of India is a union of states. The specific powers and spheres of influence of these states are set forth in the constitution, with all residual or non-specified powers in the hands of the central government (the reverse of the US Constitution). The central government has the power to set state boundaries and to create and abolish states. The state governments are similar to the central government in form, with a chief minister and a cabinet responsible to the state legislature, which may be unicameral or bicameral. State governors, usually retired civil servants or politicians, are appointed by the president for a five-year term and act only on the advice of the state cabinet.

The constitution gives the president the power—on the advice of the prime minister—to dissolve a state legislature and dismiss a state government if no party commands the support of a majority or if the state's constitutional machinery is incapable of maintaining order. The Lok Sahba, which must approve each six-month extension of direct rule, acts as the state legislature during its imposition, governing through the governor. Termed as "President's Rule" in the constitution, this power derives from a provision for "Governor's Rule" in the Government of India Act of 1935 and survives in the Pakistan constitution of 1973 in that form. It was invoked for the first time in 1959 by Prime Minister Nehru, and on the advice of Indira Gandhi, who was then Congress Party president; in power herself, she invoked the power repeatedly, often for partisan political purposes and, especially in the early 1980s, in the wake of ethnic/communal violence in Punjab, Assam, and Jammu and Kashmir. Limitations on its partisan use were imposed in a Supreme Court decision in spring 1994.

Under the States Reorganization Act of 1956, there were 14 states and five union territories, organized, where appropriate, on linguistic grounds. Through a gradual process of reorganization and division, two former union territories have become states while new ones have been created (there are now seven), and the number of states has grown to 25.

Administratively, the states and union territories are divided into districts, under the control of senior civil servants who are responsible for collecting revenues, maintaining law and order, and setting development priorities. Districts are further divided into subdivisions, and subdivisions into taluks or tehsils. State government and lower levels of representative councils vary in organization and function, but all are based on universal adult suffrage. Large towns are each governed by a corporation headed by a mayor; health, safety, education, and the maintenance of normal city facilities are under its jurisdiction. Smaller towns have municipal boards and committees similar to the corporations but with more limited powers. District boards in rural areas provide for road construction and maintenance, education, and public health. The constitution provides for the organization of village councils (panchayats), and nearly all the villages have been so organized. The panchayats are elected from among the villagers by all the adult population and have administrative functions and a judicial wing that enables them to handle minor offenses.

In the mid-1990s, there were several campaigns to form new states in India, carving new borders along factional lines in existing states. A promise by former Prime Minister Deve Gowda to create a new state in Uttar Pradesh in 1996 renewed separatist sentiments in several other states.

The Hindu nationalist party (BJP) proposed five new states in 1996, hoping to control their assemblies rather than fight political foes in larger entities. Both proposals ignore potentially chaotic consequences in favor of political gain; existing state boundaries were drawn on language differences, while there appears to be no motive other than politics for the boundaries suggested by the new proposals. On its return to power in 1998, the BJP government succeeded in drafting bills that created three new states (Uttaranchal, Vanachal and Chhattisgarh), but put on hold its plans for making Delhi, presently a Union Territory, a state.

16 JUDICIAL SYSTEM

The laws and judicial system of British India were continued after independence with only slight modifications. The Supreme Court consists of a chief justice and up to 17 judges, appointed by the president, who hold office until age 65. The Court's duties include interpreting the constitution, handling all disputes between the central government and a state or between states themselves, and judging appeals from lower courts.

In 1986 there were 18 high courts, subordinate to but not under the control of the Supreme Court. Each state's judicial system is headed by a high court (two high courts have jurisdiction over more than one state), whose judges are appointed by the president and over whom state legislatures have no control. High court judges can serve up to the age of 62. Each state is divided into districts; within each district, a hierarchy of civil courts is responsible to the principal civil courts, presided over by a district judge. The 1973 Code of Criminal Procedure, effective 1 April 1974, provides for the appointment of separate sets of magistrates for the performance of executive and judicial functions within the criminal court system. Executive magistrates are responsible to the state government; judicial magistrates are under the control of the high court in each state.

Different personal law are administered through the single civil court system. Islamic law (Shari'a) governs many noncriminal matters involving Muslims, including family law, inheritance and divorce.

There are strong constitutional safeguards assuring the independence of the judiciary. In 1993–94, the Supreme Court rendered important judgements imposing limits on the use of the constitutional device known as "President's Rule" by the central government and reaffirming India's secular commitment.

In Kashmir the judicial system barely functions due to threats by militants against judges and witnesses.

India accepts the compulsory jurisdiction of the International Court of Justice with reservations.

17 ARMED FORCES

The Indian Armed Forces have a proud tradition, having provided one million soldies during World War I and two million in World War II battles in Asia, Africa, the Middle East, and Europe. The armed forces are entirely volunteer and consist of the regular army, navy, and air force; the territorial (reserve) army; and 13 different full-time or reserve special purpose paramilitary units for border, transportation, and internal defense. The home guard and provincial armed constabulary alone number over 800,000 while the Ministry of Home Affairs controls 165,300 riot police and 185,000 in the Border Security Force (BSF).

In 2000, armed forces personnel totaled 1,173,000. The army had 980,000 personnel, organized into three armored divisions,

one mechanized division, 18 infantry divisions, nine mountain divisions, five independent armored brigades, five independent infantry brigades, three independent artillery brigades, four air defense brigades, and three engineer brigades. Armaments included 3,414 main battle tanks and 90 light tanks. The navy (including the naval air force) had 53,000 personnel; naval vessels included 16 submarines, two aircraft carriers, seven destroyers, 13 frigates, five corvettes, 15 patrol boats, and 18 mine-warfare ships. The naval air force had 5,000 personnel, with 79 combat aircraft and 83 armed helicopters. The air force had 140,000 personnel and 774 combat aircraft; there were 38 fighter and ground attack squadrons, four reconnaissance squadrons, and 11 helicopter squadrons. There is a coast guard of over 5,500 personnel, with 14 aircraft and 36 patrol craft.

Budgeted defense expenditures in 1998–99 were $10 billion or 2.7% of gross domestic product. India has purchased submarines from Germany, Mirage jet fighters from France, and Jaguar jets from the UK. The US has not been a significant supplier of weapons to India since the 1965 war with Pakistan.

India provides personnel to three peacekeeping operations. Although India has exploded a nuclear device, it has no operational, deployed nuclear forces.

18 INTERNATIONAL COOPERATION

India is a member of the Commonwealth of Nations. Even before its independence in 1947, India became a charter member of the UN on 13 October 1945, and it belongs to ESCAP and all the nonregional specialized agencies. India also has joined the Asian Development Bank and G-77, and has signed the Law of the Sea.

India was a founder of the nonaligned movement and has pursued a formally neutralist foreign policy since independence. Relations between the US and India have ranged from correct to cordial; relations with China, hostile during the early 1960s, have been normalized since 1976. India's primary ally among the superpowers had been the former USSR, with which a 20-year treaty of peace, friendship, and cooperation was signed in 1971. Indian armed forces and political missions have assisted in implementing truce and cease-fire agreements in Korea, Vietnam, Laos, Cambodia, the Middle East, Congo (formerly Zaire), and Cyprus. India also negotiated a settlement in Sri Lanka's civil unrest in July 1987, sending in troops to enforce the agreement.

Since independence, India has fought three wars with neighboring Pakistan, in 1947–48, 1965, and 1971. Relations between the two countries improved in the early 1980s. On 10 March 1983, India and Pakistan signed a five-year agreement for improving economic and cultural ties, which was viewed as a major step in the normalization of their relations. Tension between India and Pakistan increased again in 1986–87, when both countries conducted military exercises near their common border in the sensitive Punjab region. Indo-Pakistan relations worsened again in 1990 and in the years immediately following as a consequence of Pakistan's support of Islamic insurgents in Indian Kashmir.

India became a founding member of the World Trade Organization on 1 January 1995.

19 ECONOMY

The Indian economy is the fifth largest in the world when measured by GDP purchasing power parity. Agriculture is the largest sector of the Indian economy. It provides the livelihood for 67% of the population and (with forestry and fishing included) contributes about one-quarter of the GDP. The country is rich in mineral, forest, and power resources, and its ample reserves of iron ore and coal provide a substantial base for heavy industry. Coal is the principal source for generating electric power although hydroelectric and nuclear installations supply a rising proportion of India's power needs. The government also promotes considerable expansion in oil exploration and production.

The Indian economy is a mixture of public and private enterprises. Under a planned development regime since independence, the public sector provided the impetus for industrialization and for absorption of sophisticated technology. Nevertheless, a large proportion of the total manufacturing output continued to be contributed by small, unorganized industries. In recent years, and especially so since 1991, the government has placed greater emphasis on private enterprise to stimulate growth and modernization. Reflecting this policy shift, public enterprises accounted for only about 7% of the country's GDP in 1999, down from 23% in the mid-1980s. In 1999, the government announced plans to disinvest in 247 companies owned by the central government by 74% except in the railway, defense, and nuclear energy sectors.

Following the proclamation of a state of emergency in June 1975, a 20-point economic reform program was announced. Price regulations were toughened, and a moratorium on rural debts was declared. A new campaign was mounted against tax evaders, currency speculators, smugglers, and hoarders. This program, which lapsed when Indira Gandhi was out of power (1977–80), was revised and incorporated into the sixth and seventh five-year plans (1980–85 and 1985–90). Recurring episodes of severe weather and fluctuating oil prices contributed to variable GDP growth performance during the 1980s; nevertheless, annual growth in the GDP during the latter half of the decade averaged 6.2%. This expansion was, however, accompanied by numerous indicators of underlying structural weaknesses in the economy: meager growth in formal sector employment, persistent inefficiency and limited technological improvement in the public sector, accelerating fiscal and balance of payment deficits, as well as double-digit inflation by 1990. Given these already unfavorable conditions, political volatility in the late 1980s and oil price shocks resulting from the Gulf War catalyzed an acute balance of payment crisis in early 1991.

Swift stabilization measures taken by the newly elected government proved highly successful. Foreign exchange reserves recovered to a comfortable margin (equal to five months of imports) by mid-1992 and inflation declined from 13.1% in 1991–92 to 8.6% in 1993–94. Further reforms initiated as part of a wider structural adjustment program were credited with keeping GDP growth at an average annual rate of about 6% between 1993 and 1996. In 1997, however, there were signs that new reforms were needed if the economy was to sustain its recovery. Exports were growing at an annual rate of only 1.2% while imports grew by 26%; industrial output was down due to a decline in consumer demand, competition from imports, and excess capacity; and lending by commercial banks was slowing. The budget for 1999–2000 focused on opening foreign trade and encouraging foreign investment. The growth in GDP slowed marginally in 1997 to 4.6%; but leapt to around 6% in 1998 and 1999, accompanied by a high inflation rate of 14% in 1998. Currency depreciation between April 1998 and March 1999 by almost 12% brought inflation down to about 6% in 1999. The 2000–2001 budget included a 30% increase on defense spending because of the conflict with Pakistan, increasing the public debt; and outlined limited cuts in government industries.

20INCOME

The US Central Intelligence Agency (CIA) reports that in 1998 India's gross domestic product (GDP) was estimated at $1,689 billion. The per capita GDP was estimated at $1,720. The annual growth rate of GDP was estimated at 5.4%. The average inflation rate in 1998 was 14%. The CIA defines GDP as the value of all final goods and services produced within a nation in a given year, and computed on the basis of purchasing power parity (PPP)

rather than value as measured on the basis of the rate of exchange. It was estimated that agriculture accounted for 25% of GDP, industry 30%, and services 45%.

Private consumption includes expenditures of individuals, households, and nongovernmental organizations. It was estimated that between 1990, and 1998 private consumption grew at an annual rate of 5.8%. The richest 10% of the population accounted for approximately 34% of household consumption and the poorest 10% approximately 3.5%.

21LABOR

In 1999, India's active labor force totaled 397.2 million. As of 1995, 67% were employed in agriculture, 13% in industry, and 20% in services. The labor force size grew by 2% annually during 1980–85, 2.1% per year during 1985–93, and 2.7% in 1990–98. The female labor force comprised 32% of the total in 1998.

Working hours are limited by law to 48 per week for adults, and factory employment of children under 14 years of age is prohibited, although estimates place the number of child laborers as of 1999 at anywhere between 11 to 55 million. Many of them work in the hand-knotted carpet industry. Bonded labor was abolished in 1976, but is still prevalent. Estimates of the number of bonded laborers range as high as 40 million. By law, earned income also includes a cost-of-living allowance and an annual bonus (applicable to factories and all other establishments with 20 employees). Employers and employees contribute to the Employees State Insurance Scheme.

In 1999, there were an estimated 13 to 15 million organized industrial workers, all belonging to the formal economy, which accounted for 30 million workers, or less than 10% of the total labor force. The leading trade union federations are the Indian National Trade Union Congress and the All-India Trade Union Congress. There were 601 strikes in the first nine months of 1999, involving 400,000 workers.

22AGRICULTURE

In 1997, of the total land area of 297 million hectares (734 million acres), the net sown area was 169 million hectares (420 million acres), or about 57%. The irrigated area totaled 57 million hectares (140.8 million acres) in 1997. At least 10 million hectares (24.7 million acres) were redistributed under land reform programs during 1951–79. Agriculture employs about 67% of India's population and contributes about 25% to GDP.

Agricultural production increased at an average annual rate of 2.9% during the 1970s, 3.1% during the 1980s, and 3.8% during 1990–98, mainly as the result of the "green revolution," which has made India basically self-sufficient in grain output through the use of improved hybrid seeds, irrigation, and fertilizers. Cereal production averaged over 104 million tons per year from 1979 to 1981; in 1998, production totaled 219.4 million tons. Rice leads all crops and, except in the northwest, is generally grown wherever the conditions are suitable. In 1998, 122.2 million tons of rice were produced on 43.5 million hectares (104.5 million acres). The combined acreage and production of other cereals, all to a large extent grown for human consumption, considerably exceed those of rice. These include jowar, a rich grain sorghum grown especially in the Deccan; wheat, grown in the northwest; and bajra, another grain sorghum grown in the drier areas of western India and the far south. A wheat crop of 66 million tons was harvested on 25.6 million hectares (63.2 million acres) in 1998. Vegetables, pulses, and oilseeds are the other main food crops. Oilseed production in 1998 included five million tons of cottonseed and 4.9 million tons of rapeseed.

Nonfood crops are mainly linseed, cotton, jute, and tobacco. The cotton crop in 1998–99 was 12.7 million bales (170 kg each) and was large enough to both supply the increasing demands of the domestic textile sector and provide export receipts. For centuries, India has been famous for its spices and today is one of the world's largest producers, consumers, and exporters of a wide range of spices. Of the 63 spices grown in the country, black pepper, cardamom, ginger, turmeric, and chilles are the most economically important. Since World War II, India has been the world's largest producer of black pepper (45,000 tons in 1998–99). Pepper production is concentrated in the southern states of Kerlala (65%), Karnataka (20%), and Tamil Nadu (15%).

India was the world's second-leading producer (after Brazil) of sugarcane in 1998, with an output of 265 million tons. Tea, coffee, and rubber plantations contribute significantly to the economy, although they occupy less than 1% of the agricultural land (in hill areas generally unsuited to Indian indigenous agriculture), and are the largest agricultural enterprises in India. Tea, the most important plantation crop, is a large foreign exchange earner, with an export value of $485 million in 1997, based on exports of 203,000 tons. Production in 1998 was 870,000 tons, the highest in the world. It is grown mostly in Assam and northern Bengal, but also in southern India. Coffee (228,000 tons in 1998) is produced in southern India, and rubber (542,000 tons in 1998) in Kerala. Leaf tobacco production totaled 635,000 tons in 1998.

Because of the ever-present danger of food shortages, the government tightly controls the grain trade, fixing minimum support and procurement prices and maintaining buffer stocks. The Food Corp. of India, a government enterprise, distributes 12 million tons of food grains annually and is increasing its storage capacity.

23 ANIMAL HUSBANDRY

The livestock population of India is huge and animals as a whole play an important role in the agricultural economy even though they often receive inadequate nourishment. Slaughter of cattle in India is prohibited in all but a few states since Hindus believe that cows and other animals may contain reincarnated human souls. The slaughter of buffaloes is not as offensive to the religious beliefs of Hindus, and buffaloes are slaughtered for meat.

In 1998 there were an estimated 194.6 million head of cattle, representing about 15% of the world's total and more than in any other country. There are eight breeds of buffalo, 26 cattle breeds, and numerous crossbreeds. The bovine inventory at the beginning of 1998 was estimated at 301.3 million, including 209.4 million cattle and 91.5 million buffalo. Other livestock in 1998 included 120.1 million goats, 56.5 million sheep, 16 million hogs, one million camels, one million asses, 949,000 horses, and 343 million chickens. Bullocks (steers) and water buffalo are important draft animals. Dairy farming has made India self-sufficient in butter and powdered milk. Dairying in India is undertaken on millions of small farms, where one to three milk animals are raised on less than a hectare (2.5 acres), and yields consist of two to three liters of milk daily. To improve milk production, a dairy development program was begun in 1978 to build up the milch herd to 150 million crossbred cows. Milk output in 1998 from 35 million dairy cows was estimated at 35.5 million tons, second in the world. Egg production in 1998 was 1,612,000 tons. The production of cattle and buffalo hides and goat- and sheep-skins is a major industry. About 44,000 tons of wool were produced in 1998. Silk production that year amounted to 16,000 tons, second highest after China. Animal dung is also used for fuel and fertilizer.

24 FISHING

Fishing is an important secondary source of income to some farmers and a primary occupation in small fishing villages. Almost three-fifths of the catch consists of sea fish. The bulk is marketed fresh; of the remainder, more than half is sun dried. Fish and fish products account for about 2.5–3% of the total

export value. Deep-sea fishing is not done on a large scale. Inland fishing is most developed in the deltaic channels of Bengal, an area where fish is an important ingredient of the diet. In recent years, the government has been encouraging ocean fishing through the establishment of processing plants and the introduction of deep-sea craft. Fishing harbors have been built along the coasts of the Bay of Bengal and the Arabian Sea. Under the fifth national plan (1974–79), fish farming was encouraged through the creation of Fish Farmers' Development Agencies. Fish production achieved a new high of about 3.7 million tons at the end of the seventh national plan (1986–91).

The total fish catch in 1997 was 5,473,059 tons (6th in the world), of which marine fish accounted for 3,022,369 tons and inland sources for 2,450,690 tons. Fish exports, still only a fraction of the potential, have shown a steady gain in recent years. In 1997, exports of fish products amounted to over $1.1 billion.

25 FORESTRY

The major forestlands lie in the foothills of the Himalayas, the hills of Assam state, the northern highlands of the Deccan, the Western Ghats, and the Andaman Islands. Other forestlands are generally scrub and poor secondary growth of restricted commercial potential. India's forests are mostly broad-leaved; the most important commercial species are sal (10.9% of forest trees), mixed conifers (8.1%), teak (6.8%), fir (3.2%), chir-pine (2.4%), and upland hardwood (2.4%). In 1995 there were 63,960,000 hectares (158,045,000 acres) of forestland, according to a satellite survey. About 40% of the forest area is highly degraded and devoid of wood producing trees.

India's forests have historically suffered tremendous pressure from its large human and animal populations as a source of fuel wood, fodder, and timber. In recent decades, harvesting and encroachment resulted in a 2.3% reduction of forest land each year. According to the government's national forest policy, 33% of the land area should be covered by forest, but actual forest coverage is just 19.5%. About 138,000 hectares (341,000 acres) were planted annually during the 1980s under afforestation programs. Most forests (98%) are owned by state governments and are reserved or protected for the maintenance of permanent timber and water supplies. The government has prohibited commercial harvesting of trees on public land, except for mature, fallen, or sick trees. In order to help meet the fuel needs of much of the population, harvesting dead and fallen branches is permitted is government forests, but this policy is widely violated. About 92% of the total timber cut in 1997 was burned as fuel.

The total timber cut in 1997 was 306.5 million cu m. Production that year included (in million of cubic meters): sawn wood, 17.7; paper and paperboard, 3; wood-based panels, 0.34; and wood pulp, 1.2. Other forestry products include bamboos, canes, fibers, flosses, gums and resins, medicinal herbs, tanning barks, and lac. Imports of forest products nearly totaled $762 million in 1997, and mainly consisted of newsprint ($288.8 million), printing and writing paper ($112.7 million), logs and wood products ($109.2 million), and recovered paper products ($41.5 million).

26 MINING

India is well endowed with industrial minerals. The minerals industry of India produces more than 80 mineral commodities in the form of ores, metals, industrial minerals, and mineral fuels and is among the world's leading producers of bauxite, iron ore, bituminous coal, and zinc. An estimated 4,400 mines operated in the country in 1997. In the same year, total mineral production was valued at $9.5 billion, or about 3.5% of GDP. Most mines are small surface operations using only handtool methods and having low output. There are also about 300 underground mines in the nonfuel sector, most of which are operated manually. Employment in the minerals industry was estimated at more than 1 million in 1997 (4.5% of the employed labor force), with the public sector employing 90% of the total. In 1993 a revision of the National Mineral Policy opened development of 13 minerals to private investment, both foreign and domestic.

Iron ore reserves, estimated at 11 billion tons of hematite ore containing at least 55% iron, are among the largest in the world. The best quality of mica comes from Bihar; India produced 2,000 tons of crude mica in 1997. Manganese deposits are estimated at 154 million tons. Bauxite deposits are estimated at 2.3 billion tons (around 10% of the world's total); India's output was 5,800,000 tons in 1997. There are extensive workable reserves of fluorite, chromite, ilmenite (for titanium), monazite (for thorium), beach sands, magnesite, beryllium, copper, and a variety of other industrial and agricultural minerals. However, India lacks substantial reserves of some nonferrous metals and special steel ingredients. The exploration and processing of chrome, copper, diamonds, gold, iron ore, lead, manganese, molybdenum, nickel, platinum-group metals, sulfur, tungsten, and zinc were exclusively controlled by the Indian government.

Principal iron ore output comes from the rich fields along the Bihar-Orissa border, which are close to all major existing iron and steel works. Smaller amounts are mined in the Bababudan Hills of Karnataka and elsewhere. Iron content in mined ore output totaled 42.9 million tons in 1997. Manganese is mined in Andhra Pradesh, Karnataka, the Nagpur section of Maharashtra, northward in Madhya Pradesh, along the Bihar-Orissa border adjoining the iron ore deposits, along the Maharashtra–Madhya Pradesh–Rajasthan border, and in central coastal Andhra Pradesh. Content of manganese in mined ore produced was 680,000 tons in 1997. Gold and silver come largely from the Kolar fields of southeastern Karnataka, where the gold mines have reached a depth of more than 3.2 km (2 mi) and contain reserves to produce about 55,000 kg of gold. Diamonds, emeralds, and fissionable materials also are mined. In 1997, 2,500 kg of gold and 20,000 carats of gem diamonds were produced.

Coal reserves, scattered through the central peninsula and the northeast, are estimated at 191,857 million tons (97% bituminous, 3% lignite). Coal is among India's most important natural resources and has been the basis of the power, railway, and steel industries. The largest reserves are in the states of West Bengal and Bihar in the northeast. Almost the entire coal industry was nationalized by the government in 1972 and 1973. Bituminous coal output was about 290 million tons in 1997.

Estimated mineral production in 1997 also included 40,000 tons of mined copper ore, 1,363,000 tons of chromite, 142,000 tons of zinc concentrates (zinc content), 2.5 million tons of gypsum, and 24,000 tons of secondary lead.

27ENERGY AND POWER

Petroleum reserves were estimated at 4.8 billion barrels in early 2000. From less than 100,000 tons in 1951, crude oil production rose to 37.1 million tons in 1995. Production was 661,000 barrels per day in 1998. Oil exploration and production are undertaken in joint ventures between government and private foreign companies. As of 1992, 2,800 wells were in operation. Oil accounts for roughly 30% of India's energy consumption. Extraction of natural gas increased from 920 million cu m in 1973 to 21,500 million cu m in 1998. Pipelines consisted of 3,497 km (2,173 mi) for crude oil, 1,703 km (1,058mi) for refined products, and 902 km (561 mi) for natural gas in 1991.

In 1996, India consumed 406.02 billion kWh of electricity, of which 1.675 billion kWh was imported. Total installed electric capacity, which was 18,500 MW in 1974, rose to 100,333 MW in 1998. Production was 446.1 billion kWh.

A 380-MW nuclear power station, India's first, was completed with US assistance in 1969 at Tarapur, near Mumbai (formerly Bombay). (The Tarapur plant has long been a center of controversy because of India's alleged failure to observe international safeguards to prevent the diversion of nuclear materials for military purposes.) Another nuclear station, in Rajasthan, began partial operations in the early 1970s, and two more plants were added by the end of the decade. In 1996, India had 10 operating reactors with a combined capacity of 1,695 MW, and four more under construction with a planned capacity of 808 MW. As of 1996, nuclear power accounted for less than 2% of India's total; conventional thermal plants produced about 80%, and hydroelectric facilities about 18%. In 1999, the 740 MW initial phase of the Dabhol LNG-fired power plant began operation.

Under the Commission on Additional Sources of Energy, within the Department of Science and Technology, research programs in biogas and biomass have been established. Demonstration projects in solar and wind energy were also undertaken in the early 1980s.

28INDUSTRY

Modern industry has advanced fairly rapidly since independence, and the industrial sector now contributes 26% of the GDP. Large modern steel mills and many fertilizer plants, heavy-machinery plants, oil refineries, and locomotive works have been constructed; the metallurgical, chemical, cement, and oil-refining industries have also expanded. Yet, though the total product is large, factories in these industries still absorb only a token fraction of the labor force. Nine states—Maharashtra, West Bengal, Tamil Nadu, Gujarat, Uttar Pradesh, Bihar, Andhra Pradesh, Karnataka, and Madhya Pradesh—together account for most of Indian industry.

Industrial production expanded at an average annual rate of 5–6% between 1970 and 1990. Forceful austerity and demand management measures taken to stabilize rapidly worsening macroeconomic imbalances in 1991–92 slowed growth in the industry sector to 0% for that year. This was followed by a modest rebound to 1.9% in 1992–93, though declining to an estimated 1.6% in 1993–94, due to lingering effects of the earlier stabilization measures as well as poorer than expected demand in key export markets. In 1995–96, the index of industrial production was up 11.7%, the highest in 25 years. Industrial growth is attributable to the strength of the manufacturing sector, which increased output by 13% in 1995–96. Industry grew by 5.9% in 1996–97 and by 3.9% in 1998. The average annual industrial growth rate between 1988 and 1998 was 6.4%.

Under the planned development regime of past decades, government directives channeled much of the country's resources into public enterprises. Private investment was closely regulated for all industries, discouraging investors from formal entry into the sector. However, industrial policy changes of recent years have modified this pattern. Since 1991 government licensing requirements have been abolished for all but distillation and brewing of alcoholic drinks, cigars and cigarettes, defense equipment, industrial explosives, hazardous chemicals, and drugs and pharmaceuticals. Other industries are still closed to most forms of private investment including: arms, ammunition and defense equipment, atomic energy, minerals used in atomic energy, railway transport, and coal and lignite. The oil industry was opened to joint foreign investment in 1997. The credit and capital markets have been greatly liberalized. Since 1992, all foreign companies have been on par with Indian companies in the area of foreign exchange solvency and on the stock market. With these reforms, private investment in industry is now proceeding at a steady if still modest pace, fostering increased competition in most mining and manufacturing sectors previously monopolized by parastatals.

Textile production dominates the industrial field, accounting for more than one-third of total export earnings in 1998–99. About 64.2 million workers throughout the country are engaged in textile production, looming cotton, wool, silk, and rayon. Powerlooms have accounted for an increasingly large share of production since the 1980s. Mill-based textile manufactures, stagnated over the last several decades, but changes in textile policy aimed at lifting government controls on the industry to promote modernization of the mill sector. Mumbai (formerly Bombay), Ahmadabad, and the provincial cities in southern India lead in cotton milling, which accounted for 65% of the raw material consumed by the textile industry in 1998–99. There were 1,782 cotton and man-made fiber mills in 1999, and only 192 of them were publicly owned. Total spindlage was 34 million in 1998–99, up from 11 million in 1951. Jute milling is localized at Calcutta, center of the jute agricultural area; India is the world's number one jute manufacturer. Wool, silk, coir, and a growing rayon textile industry are also important. Export-oriented garment production has expanded rapidly over the last several years. The export of textiles in 1998–99 was estimated at R52,720 billion, an increase of 14.4% from the previous year.

In 1998–99, seven integrated and 180 mini steel plants produced approximately 30 million tons of finished steel. The metallurgical sector also produced 640 million tons of aluminum products. Automobile production in has grown at a rate of over 20% since liberalization in 1993, but slowed to 19% in 1998–99. The production of computers and a wide range of consumer electronics (color televisions, VCRs, electronic watches and watches) has been boosted by the liberalization of technology and component imports. Production of computer software (for export) was valued at $2.65 billion in 1999. The information technology sector grew at an annual rate of over 50% during the late 1990s. The oil-refining industry yielded 345 million barrels of refined petroleum products in 1995. Nitrogen fertilizer production grew to 105 million tons, and cement production to 83 million tons, in 1998.

²⁹SCIENCE AND TECHNOLOGY

Total expenditures on research and development amounted to 41.9 billion rupees in 1987–97; India had an estimated 149,000 scientists and engineers and 108,000 technicians engaged in research and development that year. Allocations are divided among government and industry, with government providing the major share. There has been a marked growth in the training of engineers and technicians. In 1987–97, science and engineering students accounted for 25% of college and university enrollments. Among the technological higher schools are the Indian Institute of Science at Bangalore and the Indian Institutes of Technology at Mumbai (formerly Bombay), Delhi, Kanpur, Kharagpur, and Madras. In 1947, there were 620 colleges and universities; by 1996, that number was nearly 7,700. One of the primary science and technology issues facing India is a "brain drain." Over 13,000 Indian students annually seek science and engineering degrees in the United States. Such an exodus may greatly reduce the quality of science and engineering education in India.

There are more than 2,500 national research and development institutions connected with science and technology in India. Principal government agencies engaged in scientific research and technical development are the Ministry of Science and Technology, the Council of Scientific and Industrial Research, the Ministry of Atomic Energy, and the Ministry of Electronics. The Council for Scientific and Industrial Research (founded 1942) has 39 national laboratories under its umbrella. In March 1981, a cabinet committee, headed by the prime minister, was established to review science and technology programs and to decide future policy.

An importer of nuclear technology since the 1960s, India tested its own underground nuclear device for the first time in 1974 at Pokaran, in Rajasthan. In May 1996, India once again performed nuclear tests, dropping three bombs from 700-foot-deep shafts in the desert at Pokoran, with an impact of 80 kilotons. Pakistan responded later the same month with tests of its own. The first Indian-built nuclear power plant, with two 235-MW heavy-water reactors, began operating in July 1983, and an experimental fast-breeder reactor was under construction.

The country's largest scientific establishment is the Bhabha Atomic Research Center at Trombay, near Mumbai (formerly Bombay), which has four nuclear research reactors and trains 150 nuclear scientists each year. In the area of space technology, India's first communications satellite, *Aryabhata*, was launched into orbit by the former USSR on 19 April 1975, and two additional satellites were orbited by Soviet rockets in 1979 and 1981. The Indian Space Research Organization constructed and launched India's first satellite-launching vehicle, the SLV-3, from its Vikram Sarabhai Space Center at Sriharikota on 18 July 1980; the four-stage, solid-fuel rocket put a 35 kg (77 lb) Rohini satellite into near-earth orbit. Indian-built telecommunications satellites have been launched into orbit from Cape Canaveral, Florida, by the US National Aeronautics and Space Administration, by the European Space Agency, and from French Guiana. India has established a satellite-tracking station at Kavalur, in Tamil Nadu. In 1984, the first Indo-Soviet manned mission was completed successfully; in 1985, two Indians were selected for an Indo-US joint shuttle flight. An important international sciences program is the United States-India Fund (USIF), through which scientists and engineers participate in Indo-US joint research projects at 15 institutions in each country. Projects include earthquake, atmospheric, marine, energy, environment, medical, and life sciences.

Major learned societies in the country are the Indian Academy of Sciences (founded 1934 in Bangalore), the Indian National Science Academy (founded 1935 in New Delhi), and the National Academy of Sciences (founded 1930 in Allahabad).

³⁰DOMESTIC TRADE

Under a nationwide scheme launched in 1979 for the distribution of essential commodities, goods are procured by the central government and then supplied to citizens. Each state has its own consumer cooperative federation; all of these groups are under the aegis of the National Cooperative Consumers Federation with the Minister of Consumer Affairs and Public Distribution. By 2000, more than 26,000 cooperatives, and 681 wholesale stores shared in the distribution of sugar, edible oils, and grains in rural areas.

With the government's new emphasis on growth in private enterprise since the late 1980s, the expansion of privately-owned retail outlets have competed with the cooperative sector. Most private commercial enterprises are small establishments owned and operated by a single person or a single family; retail outlets are often highly specialized in product and usually very small in quarters and total stock. Often the Indian retail shop is large enough to hold only the proprietor and a small selection of stock; shutters fronting the store are opened to allow customers to negotiate from the street or sidewalk. Fixed prices are rare, and bargaining is the accepted means of purchase. In cities and larger towns, similar stores tend to agglomerate in specialized bazaar areas.

Distribution networks for consumer products can be complicated by truck size limitations, excise taxes, city taxes, regional marketing systems, and the sheer number of independent retailers. India's 300,000 wholesalers and 400,000 semi-wholesalers are therefore the most important link in the country's distribution system, supplying 80% of the stores.

Government and business hours are generally from 10 AM to 5 PM, Monday through Friday, with a lunch break from 1 to 2 PM. Larger shops in Delhi are open from 9:30 AM to 1:30 PM and from 3:30 to 7:30 PM. Normal banking hours are from 10 AM to 4 PM on weekdays and from 10 AM to 12 noon on Saturdays.

India's domestic trade is widely influenced by informal and unreported commerce and income, known as "black money."

³¹FOREIGN TRADE

Initially, India's foreign trade followed a pattern common to all underdeveloped countries: exporting raw materials and food in exchange for manufactured goods. The only difference in India's case was that it also exported processed textiles, yarn, and jute goods. Until the late 1980s, the government's strongly import substitution-oriented industrial policy limited the significance of exports for the Indian economy. The ratio of foreign trade to GDP increased from 11.6% in 1985–86 to 21% in 1998–99. With imports exceeding exports almost continuously in the 1970s and 1980s, the country registers a chronic trade deficit. Stabilization and structural adjustment measures taken in 1991, including a 50% currency devaluation, have improved the country's balance of trade position both by depressing imports and promoting expanded exports. Given the country's relatively well-developed manufacturing base, items like textile goods, gems and jewelry, engineering goods, chemicals, and leather manufactures now comprise the country's leading exported items, replacing jute, tea, and other food products that dominated its export base in the 1960s and early 1970s.

India's exports in 1998 were dominated by textiles, followed by agricultural products, gems and jewelry, and engineering goods. Important imports included petroleum and petroleum products, gold and precious stones, machinery, chemicals, and fertilizers.

Principal trading partners in 1998 (in millions of US dollars) were as follows:

COUNTRY	EXPORTS	IMPORTS	BALANCE
United States	7,682	3,968	3,714
China (inc. Hong Kong)	2,561	1,882	679
Germany	2,118	2,411	-293
United Kingdom	2,090	2,397	-307
Japan	1,888	2,659	-771
United Arab Emirates	1,626	1,801	-175
Belgium	1,223	2,827	-1,604
Saudi Arabia	697	2,572	-1,875
Singapore	553	2,496	-1,943
Malaysia	399	2,059	-1,660

³²BALANCE OF PAYMENTS

India has a chronic deficit on current accounts. What bridges the gap between payments and receipts is mainly external aid (especially nonproject assistance), tourism earnings, and remittances from Indians working abroad. Heavy imports of food grains and armament purchases caused a decline in India's foreign exchange reserves in the mid-1960s. An economic recovery from 1968–69, however, eased the problem, and by 30 September 1970, foreign exchange reserves amounted to $616 million, as compared with $383 million on 31 December 1965. Reserves declined to $566 million by the end of 1972 but increased to $841 million as of 31 December 1975, despite massive deficits on current accounts, attributable to the quadrupling of oil import prices during 1973–74. Foreign exchange reserves declined from $6,739 million at the end of 1979 to $3,476 million as of 30 November 1982 but subsequently rose to $5,924 million by March 1987. The Gulf War crisis worsened the ratio of current account deficit to GDP. Foreign exchange reserves plummeted because of export losses in Kuwait, Iraq, and other nations. Remittances from Indian workers fell, and sudden price increases

for oil imports caused an estimated loss to India of over $2.8 billion in earnings. By November 1993, however, India's foreign exchange reserves had risen to $8.1 billion, the highest level since 1951. A substantial reduction in the trade deficit, increased inflows from foreign institutional investors, a stable exchange rate, and improved remittances all contributed in the recovery of reserves. Although export growth remained strong. The current account deficit tripled from 1993–94 to 1995–96. The increase was attributed to a continuing surge in imports and higher debt service requirements. However, between 1995 to 1998 the current account deficit shrank to about 1% of GDP due to increased textile exports and a liberalizing trade regime. India's total external debt in 1998 was estimated at $93 billion.

The US Central Intelligence Agency reports that in 1998 the purchasing power parity of India's exports was $32,170 million while imports totaled $41,340 million resulting in a trade balance of -$9,170 million.

The International Monetary Fund (IMF) reports that in 1998 India had exports of goods totaling $34,076 million and imports totaling $44,828 million. The services credit totaled $11,691 million and debit $14,540 million. The following table summarizes India's balance of payments as reported by the IMF for 1998 in millions of US dollars.

Current Account		-6,903
Balance on goods	-10,752	
Balance on services	-2,849	
Balance on income	-3,637	
Current transfers	10,335	
Capital Account		...
Financial Account		8,584
Direct investment abroad	-48	
Direct investment in India	2,635	
Portfolio investment assets	...	
Portfolio investment liabilities	-601	
Other investment assets	-3,239	
Other investment liabilities	9,837	
Net Errors and Omissions		1,390
Reserves and Related Items		-3,071

³³BANKING AND SECURITIES

A well-established banking system exists in India. The Reserve Bank of India, founded in 1935 and nationalized in 1949, is the central banking and note-issuing authority. The Reserve Bank funds the Deposit Insurance and Credit Guarantee Corporation, which provides deposit insurance coverage to the banking sector. The largest public-sector bank is the State Bank of India, which, at the end of 1996, accounted for one-third of income. Banks operating in the public sector account for 80% of commercial banking, while private banks take 5% of the market and foreign banks account for the remainder. In 1997, 58% of commercial banks operated regionally, extending credit to small borrowers in rural areas. Scheduled banks maintain branches, mainly in the major commercial and industrial centers of Maharashtra, West Bengal, Uttar Pradesh, and Tamil Nadu states and the Delhi territory. Over 100 branches of Indian commercial banks operate overseas as well, primarily in the UK, US, Fiji, Mauritius, Hong Kong, and Singapore. As of March 1999, there were 45 foreign banks in India with 180 branches, as well as 26 foreign representative offices. Total deposits in commercial banks reached $171 billion in 1999.

The cost of borrowing remains very high, because of bad debts and non-performing assets. Most Indian banks lend approximately 30% to 40% of their capital to the government of India, and over 80% of investment is in government securities. In an attempt to regulate lending practices and interest rates, the government encouraged the formation of cooperative credit societies. Long-term credit is provided by the cooperative land development banks. Nonagricultural credit societies and employees' credit societies supply urban credit. A process of gradual liberalization is being applied to government institutions that supply most medium- and long-term credit. These term-lending institutions also control about 30% of all share capital and act as a channel for most foreign borrowing by the private sector. The main bodies are the Industrial Development Bank of India (IDBI), the Industrial Finance Corporation of India (IFCI), the Industrial Credit and Investment Corp. of India (ICIC), and the Export-Import Bank of India (Eximbank).

The main stock exchanges are located in Calcutta, Mumbai (formerly Bombay), and Madras, and there are secondary exchanges in Ahmadabad, Delhi, Kanpur, Nagpur, and other cities. The Securities and Exchange Board of India supplies regulation of the stock market. These regulations are not strict, and at times margin trading and other questionable practices have tended to produce wild speculation. Rules favor exchange members rather than public protection or benefit. Brokerage and jobbing are commonly combined. Of India's 21 stock exchanges, the Mumbai Stock Exchange (BSE) and National Stock Exchange (NSE) are the most important. There are more than 5,000 companies listed in Mumbai (formerly Bombay), the largest on the Indian market and on this criterion the largest outside New York. Total market capitalization on the NSE's 1,482 listed companies was R670,000 trillion as of March 1996, compared with 5,861 companies and R312,000 trillion on the BSE. Adding to its appeal, the NSE is perceived as more transparent, has faster trading cycles, more timely settlements, and is in the process of setting up a share depository. Major efforts have been made to strengthen the stock market institutionally and make it less like a casino.

In 1996–97 negative market sentiment, particularly among foreign institutional investors, took the overall price earnings ratio down from 19.6 in June 1996 to 11.3 in November. In the two years ending October 1996, all but 436 of the 2,531 most-traded shares lost over half their value; more than 1,000 lost over 80% of their value. The market continued to lose ground in 1997 and 1998 due to the Asian financial crisis. In 1999–2000, though, both the BSE and the NSE gained approximately 40% in market share value due to the growth in information technology (IT) stocks.

34INSURANCE

The life insurance business was formally nationalized on 1 September 1956 by the establishment of the Life Insurance Corp. of India (LIC), which absorbed the life insurance business of 245 Indian and foreign companies. LIC also transacts business in certain African and Asian countries where there are large Indian populations. The general insurance business was nationalized as of 1 January 1973, and all nationalized general insurance companies were merged into the General Insurance Corp. (GIC) of India.

In 1997, despite repeated promises to allow private insurers into the industry, an announcement on privatization in the financial services sector was postponed in the face of institutional resistance. The unions and left-wing parties led a struggle to stop an opening up of the insurance sector. They were alarmed by government plans to introduce legislation that would set up an independent Insurance Regulatory and Development Authority (IRA). Under the Insurance Regulatory and Development Authority Act of 1999, the IRA finally gained the power to issue licenses to private insurance companies in 2000, to Indians and foreigners.

35PUBLIC FINANCE

The government's financial year extends from 1 April to 31 March, and the budget is presented to the parliament on the last day of February. The executive branch has considerable control over public finance. Thus, while parliament can oversee and investigate public expenditures and may reduce the budget, it cannot expand the budget, and checks exist that prevent it from delaying passage.

Budgets in recent decades have reflected the needs of rapid economic development under rising expenditures of the five-year plans. Insufficient government receipts for financing this development have led to yearly deficits and a resulting increase of new tax measures and deficit financing. The Gulf crisis, increased interest payments, subsidies, and relief in 1991 caused the central government's fiscal deficit to reach 9% of GDP. It fell to 5.7% in 1992–93 but rose to 7.3% of GDP in 1993–94. Principal sources of government revenue are customs and excise duties and individual and corporate income taxes. Major items of expenditure are defense, grants to states and territories, interest payments on the national debt, and economic, social, and community services. High interest rates, 8% inflation, slow industrial growth, and weak foreign investment prompted the government to recommend dramatic new initiatives in the 1997–98 budget, including cuts in taxes and duties. The proposed budget projected a 15% increase in expenditures to $65 billion and a reduction in the deficit to 4.5% of GDP. While expenditures were cut, the budget deficit actually grew in 1997–98 to about 8.5% of the GDP due to currency devaluation and the Asian financial crisis. The budget for 2000 included a 30% increase on defense spending due to the Pakistani conflict.

Although applauded by the business community as market-friendly, some observers were chagrined by the 2000 budget's failure to squarely tackle infrastructure reforms. Most analysts agree that India spends too much on current expenditures and not enough on public investment. India suffers from inadequate roads and ports, a substandard educational system, and unreliable power supplies.

The US Central Intelligence Agency (CIA) estimates that in 1998 India's central government took in revenues of approximately $42.12 billion and had expenditures of $63.79 billion including capital expenditures of $13.8 billion. Overall, the government registered a deficit of approximately $21.67 billion. External debt totaled $98 billion.

The following table shows an itemized breakdown of government revenues and expenditures. The percentages were calculated from data reported by the International Monetary Fund. The dollar amounts (millions) are based on the CIA estimates provided above.

REVENUE AND GRANTS	100%	42,120
Tax revenue	71.8%	30,236
Non-tax revenue	25.0%	10,543
Capital revenue	2.7%	1,138
Grants	0.5%	204
EXPENDITURES	100%	63,790
General public services	7.2%	4,592
Defense	15.8%	10,055
Education	3.0%	1,898
Health	1.7%	1,069
Housing and community amenities	6.4%	4,081
Economic affairs and services	16.0%	10,178
Other expenditures	-50.0%	-31,913
Interest payments	50.0%	31,913
Adjustments	26.9%	17,138

36TAXATION

Taxes are levied by the central government, the state governments, and the various municipal governments. The sources of central government tax revenue are union excise duties, customs duties, corporate and personal income (nonagricultural) taxes, wealth taxes, and gift taxes. State government sources, in general order of importance, are land taxes, sales taxes, excise duties, and registration and stamp duties. The states also share in central government income tax revenues and union excise duties, and they receive all revenues from the wealth tax on agricultural property. Municipal governments levy land and other property taxes and license fees. Many also impose duties on goods entering the municipal limits. There is no uniformity in types or rates of state and municipal taxes.

The lowest level of income subject to taxation is R50,000 for individuals in 2000, which was more than halved in four years because the rate was above the income of most Indians, therefore the federal personal tax was paid by only a fraction of the total number of households. The rates ranged from 10% on the amount over R50,000; to R1,000 and 20% on the amount over R60,000; and R19,000 plus 30% on the amount over R150,000 (which was the previous limit for any form of taxation). There is also a surcharge ranging from 0% to 15% on personal income. The tax rate for domestic companies is 35%, plus a surcharge of 10%. There are also personal capital gains, wealth, and gift and inheritance taxes of 20%. Tariffs are the chief source of revenue for the central government, and excise tax can reach 40%; sales tax is the chief source of revenue for state governments.

37CUSTOMS AND DUTIES

The majority of imports and some exports are subject to tariffs. There are both revenue and protective tariffs, although the former are more important and have long been a major source of central government income. The Indian government has been steadily reducing tariff rates in order to increase trade and investment. A 30% tariff ceiling was set in the 1999–2000 budget. However, India's tariffs are still one of the highest in the world. To increase revenue, the government implemented a 10% customs duty on all commodity imports except crude oil and petroleum. Additional, special duties can more than double the barriers to importing a product, including textiles and apparel. Gold is taxed at an added rate of 9% at the state level, and an added 3% at the least at the local level. Indians spend more money on gold than anything but oil, at a rate of $7 billion in 2000. India intends to lift most import curbs by the year 2003.

38FOREIGN INVESTMENT

Until recently, foreign investment remained closely regulated. Rules and incentives directed the flow of foreign capital mainly toward consumer industries and light engineering, with major capital-intensive projects reserved for the public sector. Under the Foreign Exchange Regulation Act of 1973, which went into effect on 1 January 1974, all branches of foreign companies in which nonresident interest exceeded 40% were required to reapply for permission to carry on business; most companies had reduced their holdings to no more than 40% by 1 January 1976. Certain key export-oriented or technology-intensive industries were permitted to maintain up to 100% nonresident ownership. Tea plantations were also exempted from the 40% requirement. Although the government officially welcomed private foreign investment, collaboration and royalty arrangements were tightly controlled. Due to the restrictiveness of these policies, foreign investment remained remarkably low during the 1980s, ranging between $200 and $400 million a year.

Government reform measures after 1991 changed this picture dramatically. The amount of money invested in the country doubled annually from 1991 to 1995. Abolition of licensing requirements and other liberalization measures improved the conditions for private investment overall. Efforts to attract foreign investment got a further boost in the 1999–2000 budget which cut the top import-tariff rate from 50% to 30% and allowed foreign companies to own up to 51% of Indian companies in high priority industries, and 100% of other industries not reserved for the public sector, provided that foreign equity did not exceed $357 million in infrastructure projects. Foreign investment through the stock market is limited to 30% to 40%.

The United States is one of India's largest investors, accounting for about 12% of total foreign direct investment in 1998 ($493 million). Other major investors include Mauritius ($942 million), Germany ($142 million), the UK ($49 million), and Japan ($249 million). Foreign investment reached approximately $2.5 billion in 1998. From 1991 to 1996, the telecommunications industry attracted 30% of cumulative foreign investment even though investment was limited to 49% foreign involvement ($5.5 billion); followed by the fuel industry ($3.6 billion); the metallurgical industries ($1.3 billion); chemicals ($1.09 billion); the service sector ($975 million); transportation ($908 million); and electrical equipment ($846 million).

Indian investment abroad has been largely through export of machinery and equipment/technology. The total investment abroad was estimated at $659 million in 1995. Investment by Indian firms is concentrated in South East Asian countries lie Nepal, Bangladesh, Pakistan and Sri Lanka. Indian firms also have operations in the US and UK.

39ECONOMIC DEVELOPMENT

Under a series of five-year plans through 2000, the government became a participant in many industrial fields and increased its regulation of existing private commerce and industry. Long the owner-operator of most railway facilities, all radio broadcasting, post, and telegraph facilities, arms and ammunition factories, and river development programs, the government reserved for itself the right to nationalize any industries it deemed necessary. Yet the government's socialist approach was pragmatic, not doctrinaire; agriculture and large segments of trade, finance, and industry remained in private hands. Planning is supervised by an eight-member Planning Commission, established in 1950 and chaired by the prime minister.

India's first four five-year plans entailed a total public sector outlay of R314.1 billion. The first plan (1951–56) accorded top priority to agriculture, especially irrigation and power projects. The second plan (1956–61) was designed to implement the new industrial policy and to achieve a "socialist pattern of society." The plan stressed rapid industrialization, a 25% increase in national income (in fact, the achieved increase was only 20%), and reduction of inequalities in wealth and income. The focus of the third plan (1961–66) was industrialization, with 24.6% spent on transportation and communications and 20.1% on industry and minerals. Drought, inflation, and war with Pakistan made this plan a major disappointment; although considerable industrial diversification was achieved and national income rose, per capita income did not increase (because of population growth), and harvests were disastrously low. Because of the unsettled domestic situation, the fourth five-year plan did not take effect until 1969. The 1969–74 plan sought to control fluctuations in agricultural output and to promote equality and social justice. Agriculture and allied sectors received 16.9%, more than in any previous plan, while industry and minerals received 18.5%, transportation and communications 18.4%, and power development 17.8%, also more than in any previous plan.

The fifth plan (1974–79) aimed at the removal of poverty and the attainment of self-reliance. A total outlay of R393.2 billion was allocated (26% less than originally envisaged), and actual expenditures totaled R394.2 billion. Once again, the emphasis was on industry, with mining and manufacturing taking 22.5%, electric power 18.7%, transportation and communications 17.2%, and agriculture 12.1%. The fifth plan was cut short a year early, in 1978, and, with India enmeshed in recession and political turmoil, work began on the sixth development plan (1980–85). Its goal, like that of the fifth, was the removal of poverty, although the planners recognized that this gigantic task could not be accomplished within five years. The plan aimed to strengthen the agricultural and industrial infrastructure in order to accelerate the growth of investments and exports. Projected outlays totaled R975 billion, of which electric power received 27.1%, industry and mining 15.4%, transportation and communications 12.7%, and agriculture 12.2%. The main target was a GDP growth rate of 5.2% annually. The seventh development plan (1985–90) projected 5% overall GDP growth (which was largely achieved and even exceeded) based on increases of 4% and 8% in agricultural and industrial output, respectively. Outlays were to total R1,800 billion.

The eighth development plan (for 1992–97), drafted in response to the country's looming debt crisis in 1990–91, laid the groundwork for long-term structural adjustment. The plan's overall thrust was to stimulate industrial growth by the private sector, and thereby free government resources for greater investment in basic infrastructure and human resources development. In addition to liberalized conditions for private and foreign investment, the foreign exchange system was reformed, the currency devalued, the maximum tariff reduced from 350% to 85%, import barriers generally loosened, and those for key intermediate goods removed altogether. Reform of the tax system, reduction of subsidies, and restructuring of public enterprises were also targeted. While the eighth plan generally supported expansion of private enterprise, unlike structural adjustment programs in other developing countries, it did not stipulate a large-scale privatization of the public sector.

As the eighth plan came to an end in 1997 most analysts proclaimed it a success; economic growth averaged 6% a year, employment rose, poverty was reduced, exports increased, and inflation declined. Although impressed with India's economic performance since 1991, observers see a need for substantial further reform if growth is to be increased to 9% or 10% a year in the future. Areas for improvement include a reduction in the government's deficit, privatization of state owned enterprises, increased investment in infrastructure, a further reduction in tariffs, and increased fiscal responsibility.

The ninth development plan (1997–2002) focused on the redistribution of wealth and alleviation of poverty, the further privatization of the economy and attraction of foreign investment, and the reduction of the deficit. The proportion of the population living in poverty has remained at about one-third throughout a decade of relatively high growth. The government still owns the majority of industries in India, but hopes to reduce equity from 51% to 26%. Foreign investors, who fund India at the low rate of about $3 billion per year, have little incentive to pay into a state-controlled economy. The deficit continues to grow because the majority of government investment goes into funding the straining parastatals, instead of developing the capital market. An unsettled political climate also impedes economic development.

40SOCIAL DEVELOPMENT

India's governments have established an extensive social welfare system. Programs for children include supplementary nutrition for expectant mothers and for children under seven years of age, immunization and health programs, vacation camps for low-income families, and prevocational training for adolescents. There are also services for the blind, deaf, mentally retarded, and orthopedically handicapped. Programs for women include welfare grants, women's adult education, and working women's hostels. Special measures are aimed at rehabilitating juvenile delinquents, prostitutes, and convicts. Begging in public places is forbidden by law in most states and localities. Other social welfare programs cover displaced persons; family planning and maternity care; rural community development; emergency relief

programs for drought, flood, earthquake, and other disasters; untouchability (the Harijans); and underdeveloped tribal peoples.

There are welfare funds for providing medical, educational, and recreational facilities for workers in coal mines, mica mines, plantations, and certain government enterprises. A limited state health insurance scheme applies to workers in large factories, and many government employees and their families in Mumbai (formerly Bombay) and New Delhi are covered under a contributory health scheme. Other limited insurance extends to employees of factories, mines, and plantations. A provident paid for by both employers and employees provides old age and disability pensions and survivor benefits. Employers are required to pay 15 days' salary for every year of employment as severance pay.

During the administrations of Indira Gandhi legislation was passed in 1976 guaranteeing men and women equal pay for equal or similar work. Below the highest political levels, however, and especially in rural India, the position of women remains subordinate to that of men. Laws aimed at preventing employment discrimination, female bondage and prostitution, and the Sati (widow-burning), are not always enforced. Wife murder, usually referred to as "dowry deaths," still numbered 4,277 in 1994 according to government figures. In 1997, a high court ruling accepted spousal abuse alone as grounds for divorce for Christian women.

Not only does the male population exceed that of females, but India is also one of the few countries where men, on the average, live longer than women. To explain this anomaly, it has been suggested that daughters are more likely to be malnourished and to be provided with fewer health care services. Female infanticide and feticide is a growing problem is a society that values sons over daughters. Despite the Dowry Prohibition Act of 1961, the payment of dowries is a practice that remains widespread in all sectors of society. As of 1999, 68 of 763 parliamentary seats were held by women.

According to 1999 estimates, there are nearly 500,000 children living and working on the streets. Child prostitution is widespread. Despite its illegality, child marriages are still arranged in many parts of India.

Human rights abuses, including incommunicado detention, are particularly acute in Kashmir, where separatist violence has flared. Although constitutional and statutory safeguards were in place, serious abuses still occurred in 1999, including extrajudicial killings, abuse of detainees, and poor prison conditions.

41HEALTH

Great improvements have taken place in public health since independence, but the general health picture remains far from satisfactory. The government is paying increasing attention to integrated health, maternity, and child care in rural areas. An increasing number of community health workers and doctors are being sent to rural health centers. Primary health care is provided to the rural population through a network of over 150,000 primary health centers and sub-centers by trained midwives and health guides. In the mid-1990s, India had nearly 400,000 physicians and almost 700,000 hospital beds.

Public health care expenditures in 1995 were equal to 1% of GDP. Average life expectancy increased from 48 years in 1971 to 63 years in 1999. Infant mortality declined from 135 per 1,000 live births in the mid-1970s to 78.4 in the mid-1990s. The high mortality rate among infants and children is directly linked to size of family, which is being reduced through the small family norm (National Family Planning Program). The overall mortality rate in 1999 was nine per 1,000 people. The government's goal is to raise the life expectancy to 64 years.

The government of India took stringent measures to prevent plague following outbreaks during 1994. Mandatory screenings at airports and inspections of passengers were instituted. A short-term multi-drug therapy launched in India in 1995 led to a dramatic fall in the leprosy prevalence. The incidence of malaria was reduced by 98% between 1953 and 1965, but the number of reported cases increased from 14.8 million in 1966 to 64.7 million in 1976 because DDT-resistant strains of mosquitoes had developed. The incidence of malaria in 1995 was 295 cases per 100,000 population. The death toll from smallpox was reduced to zero by 1977 through a massive vaccination program, and plague has not been reported since 1967. Between 1948 and 1980, 254 million people were tested for tuberculosis, and 252 million received BCG, an anti-tuberculosis vaccine. In 1996, there were 137 reported cases of tuberculosis per 100,000 people. And in 1994, there was a serious outbreak of pneumonic plague in western India which spread to others parts of the country, killing thousands. Many diseases remain, especially deficiency diseases such as goiter, kwashiorkor, rickets, and beriberi. However, India's immunization rates for children up to one year old are high. Data from 1997 shows vaccinations against tuberculosis (96%); diphtheria, pertussis, and tetanus (90%); polio (91%); and measles (81%). There is also a national system to distribute Vitamin A capsules to children because a lack of this vitamin contributes to blindness and malnutrition. As of the mid-1990s, nearly 25% of the country's children had been reached. Hypertension is a major health problem in India. Between 3.5% and 6.5% of adults have high blood pressure.

The government's eighth 5-year plan from 1990 to 1995 included eradication of malaria and control of leprosy, tuberculosis, and cataracts. India also wants to achieve a goal of one hospital bed per 1,000 people. In the mid-1990s, there were nearly 40,000 hospitals and dispensaries. In addition, the rural population was served by more than 130,000 subcenters, over 20,350 primary health centers, and nearly 2,000 community health centers. There are also numerous herb compounders, along with thousands of registered practitioners following the Ayurvedic (ancient Hindu) and Unani systems.

India has modern medical colleges, dental colleges, colleges of nursing, and nursing schools. More than 100 colleges and schools teach the indigenous Ayurvedic and Unani systems of medicine, and 74 teach homeopathy. New drugs and pharmaceutical plants, some assisted by the UN and some established by European and American firms, manufacture antibiotics, vaccines, germicides, and fungicides. However, patent medicines and other reputed curatives of dubious value are still widely marketed; medical advisors of the indigenous systems and their curatives probably are more widely followed than Western doctors, drugs, and medical practices. UN data shows that India is currently the country with the most HIV-infected people. Some 4.1 million of India's one billion people had been infected with HIV as of 1997.

42 HOUSING

Progress has been made toward improving the generally primitive housing in which most Indians live. According to the 1971 census, the usable housing stock consisted of 82.5 million units, of which 66.4 million units were in rural areas and 16.1 million in urban areas. By the mid-1990s, the total housing stock exceeded 120,740,000. A number of subsidized, low-cost housing schemes have been launched by the government, but the goal of providing a house for every homeless family cannot be met because of the prohibitive cost. The sixth five-year plan envisaged an expenditure of R94 billion for rural housing and R35 billion for urban housing during 1980–85, including R11.9 billion to provide shelter for homeless people. The eighth five-year plan (1990–95) called for an investment of $40 billion in housing, with 90% of this sum earmarked for the private sector. The government's goal is to provide eight million new housing units between 1990 and 2000, two million to fill the existing backlog

and six million to meet the needs that will be created by population growth.

43 EDUCATION

According to 2000 UNESCO estimates, 44.2% of India's population was illiterate (males, 31.4%; females, 57.9%). This figure represents a slow decline from the 59.2% illiteracy rate reported in 1981. In 1986, the National Education Policy (NPE) was adopted in order to bring about major reforms in the system, primarily universalization of primary education. In 1988, a national literacy mission was launched, following which states like Kerala and Pondicherry achieved 100% literacy. In 1992, the second program of action on education was introduced to reaffirm the 1986 policy with plans to achieve total literacy and free education for all children up to grade eight by the year 2000.

Since 1947, public educational facilities have been expanded as rapidly as possible. The main goal has been primary education for children in the 6–11 age group. An emphasis on "basic education"—learning in the context of the physical and cultural environment, including domestic and commercial productive activities—has met with some success. In addition to expansion of primary education, there has been marked increase in educational facilities in secondary schools, colleges, universities, and technical institutes. An intensive development of adult education is under way in both urban and rural areas.

Free and compulsory elementary education is a directive principle of the constitution. In 1997, there were 598,354 primary level schools with 1,789,733 teachers and 110,390,406 pupils. There were a total of 68,872,393 pupils, with 2,738,205 teachers, in secondary schools in that same year.

India's system of higher education is still basically British in structure and approach. The University system is second only to that of the United States in size with 150 universities and over 5,000 colleges and higher level institutions. Educational standards are constantly improving and especially in the area of science and mathematics are as high as those found anywhere in the world. The older universities are in Calcutta, Mumbai (formerly Bombay), and Madras, all established in 1857; Allahabad, 1877; Banares Hindu (in Varanasi) and Mysore (now Karnataka), both in 1916; Hyderabad (Osmania University), in 1918; and Aligarh and Lucknow, both in 1921. Most universities have attached and affiliated undergraduate colleges, some of which are in distant towns. Christian missions in India have organized more than three dozen college-rank institutions and hundreds of primary, secondary, and vocational schools. In addition to universities there are some 3,500 arts and sciences colleges (excluding research institutes) and commercial colleges, as well as 1,500 other training schools and colleges. The autonomous University Grants Commission promotes university education and maintains standards in teaching and research. Many college students receive scholarships and stipends. In 1997, a total of 6,060,418 students were enrolled in institutions of higher learning.

44 LIBRARIES AND MUSEUMS

The National Library in Calcutta, with over 4.24 million volumes, is the largest in the country. Some of the other leading libraries are the Delhi Public Library in Delhi (1.3 million volumes), the Central Secretariat Library in New Delhi (700,000 volumes), and the libraries of some of the larger universities. The Khuda Baksh Oriental Library in Patna, with a collection of rare manuscripts in Arabic, Urdu, and Farsi, is one of ten libraries declared "institutions of national importance" by an act of parliament. The National Archives of India, in New Delhi, is the largest repository of documents in Asia, with 25 km (16 mi) of shelf space. There is an extensive public library system as well as cultural and religious institutions and libraries throughout the country.

Most of India's hundreds of museums specialize in one or several aspects of Indian or South Asian culture; these include 25 archaeological museums at ancient sites, such as Konarak, Amravati, and Sarnath. Some of the more important museums are the Indian Museum in Calcutta, the Prince of Wales Museum of Western India in Mumbai (formerly Bombay), and the National Museum and the National Gallery of Modern Art, both in New Delhi. There are also municipal museums throughout the country and dozens of museums and galleries devoted to prominent South Asian artists. There are science museums in Bhopal, Calcutta, Mumbai (formerly Bombay), and New Delhi, and Bhavongor houses the Gandhi Museum, one of several sites devoted to the history of the national hero. There also are thousands of architectural masterpieces of antiquity—the palaces, temples, mausoleums, fortresses, mosques, formal gardens, deserted cities, and rock-hewn monasteries—found in every section of the subcontinent.

Noted botanical gardens are located in Calcutta, Mumbai (formerly Bombay), Lucknow, Ootacamund, Bangalore, Madras, and Darjeeling, and well-stocked zoological gardens are found in Calcutta, Mumbai, Madras, Trivandrum, Hyderabad, Karnataka, and Jodhpur.

45 MEDIA

All postal and telegraph and most telephone services are owned and operated by the government. In 1994–95 there were 152,792 post offices in operation (88% in rural areas), the highest in the world. At the same time there were 44,054 telegraph offices. National telex service in English was inaugurated in 1963, and the first Devanagari script telex service began at New Delhi in 1969; there were 331 telex exchanges in 1990. International telephone services, both radio and cable, are available between India and all major countries of the world. In 1996, there were 12 million telephone lines.

All-India Radio (AIR), government-owned, operates short- and medium-wave transmission through 148 stations and broadcasts in all major languages and dialects for home consumption. AIR also operates external services in 24 foreign and 36 Indian languages. In 1959, India's first television station was inaugurated in Delhi, and color television broadcasting was inaugurated in 1982. By the end of 1985, the government's Doordarshan television network operated 22 broadcasting centers. As of 1999, there were, altogether, 153 AM and 92 FM radio stations and 562 television stations. The number of radios totaled about 105 and televisions 69 per 1,000 population in 1997. The School Television Section broadcasts regular in-school instruction programs on selected subjects. India has a thriving film industry, centered at Mumbai (formerly Bombay), Madras, Calcutta, and Bangalore. Indians are avid film-goers and users of videocassettes.

The first newspaper in India, an English-language weekly issued in Calcutta in 1780, was followed by English-language papers in other cities. The first Indian-language newspaper (in Hindi) appeared in Varanasi (Benares) in 1845. There are newspapers published in some 85 languages, led by Hindi, English, Bengali, Urdu, and Marathi. The majority of Indian newspapers are under individual ownership and have small circulations. About 30% are published in Delhi, Mumbai (formerly Bombay), Calcutta, and Madras.

There were 2,300 daily newspapers being published in 1995. The principal national English-language newspapers are the *Indian Express,* with editions published in Mumbai (formerly Bombay) and 10 other cities, and the *Times of India,* published in Ahmadabad, Mumbai, Delhi, and three other cities. The largest

Hindi daily is the *Navbharat Times,* published in Mumbai. Principal dailies (with estimated 1999 circulation) are as follows:

	LANGUAGE	CIRCULATION
MUMBAI (FORMERLY BOMBAY)		
Indian Express	English	576,200
Times of India	English	813,300
Navbharat Times	Hindi	450,000
Lokasatta	Marathi	258,000
Maharashtra Times	Marathi	163,600
CALCUTTA		
Ananda Bazar Patrika	Bengali	393,400
DELHI		
Hindustan Times	English	345,800
Hindustan	Hindi	141,813
MADRAS		
The Hindu	English	424,100
Daily Thanthi	Tamil	313,600

In 1976, the four leading Indian news agencies—the Press Trust of India (English), United News of India (English), Hindustan Samachar (Hindi), and Samachar Bharati (Hindi)—merged to form Samachar, which means "news" in Hindi. The merger followed the cancellation by AIR of subscriptions to all four services. Samachar was dissolved in 1978, and as of 1991 there were three separate agencies: Indian News and Features Alliance, Press Trust of India and United News of India.

Freedom of the press has been nominally ensured by liberal court interpretations of the constitution, but the government has long held the right to impose "reasonable restrictions" in the interest of "public order, state security, decency, and morality." The government's censorship of newspapers imposed in June 1975 was declared illegal by the courts, and press restrictions proclaimed by Indira Gandhi's government in 1976 were relaxed by the Janata government in 1977. The independent Press Council, which had been abolished in 1975, was restored in 1979 with the function of upholding freedom of the press. On a day-to-day basis, the press is essentially unfettered, and news magazines abound in addition to the newspapers.

As of 1996, there were 1,194,000 personal computers. Online access is extremely limited, with less than one Internet host per 1,000 population in 1998.

46 ORGANIZATIONS

Cultural activities, especially traditional arts and crafts, are promoted throughout India by the National Academy of Fine Arts; the National Academy of Music, Dance, and Drama; and the National Academy of Letters. Other state organizations for the furthering of cultural activities include the Ministry of Information and Broadcasting, the Indian Council for Cultural Relations, and the National Book Trust. There are a great many private cultural and institutional organizations based on religion and philosophy, language (including Sanskrit and Pali), drama, music and dancing, modern writing, the classics, and painting and sculpture. There are many political, commercial, industrial, and labor organizations, and rural cooperatives and recreational organizations are of some importance. Almost all commercial and industrial centers have chambers of commerce.

47 TOURISM, TRAVEL, AND RECREATION

The national Department of Tourism maintains tourist information offices at home and abroad. It has constructed many facilities for viewing wildlife in forest regions (by minibus, boat, or elephant) and operates tourist lodges in wildlife sanctuaries. All major cities have comfortable Western-style hotels that cater to tourists; in 1997 there were 64,573 hotel rooms with 129,146 beds and a 63% occupancy rate. That year tourist arrivals numbered 2,374,094, with Europe being the most important generating region of tourists to India. Tourist receipts totaled $3.2 billion. The principal tourist attractions are India's distinctive music, dance, theater, festivals, and cuisines; the great cities of Calcutta, Mumbai (formerly Bombay), and Madras; and such monuments as the Red Fort and Jama Masjid mosque in Delhi, the Taj Mahal at Agra, and the Amber Palace in Jaipur. Tourists and pilgrims also flock to the sacred Ganges River, the Ajanta temple caves, the temple at Bodhgaya where the Buddha is said to have achieved enlightenment, and many other ancient temples and tombs throughout the country. In general, all visitors must have a valid passport and an entry, transit, or tourist visa. Inoculation against cholera is recommended.

The big-game hunting for which India was once famous is now banned, but excellent fishing is available, and there are many golf courses. Cricket, field hockey, polo, football (soccer), volleyball, and basketball are all popular, as are pony-trekking in the hill stations and skiing in northern India.

In 1999 the UN estimated the cost of staying in New Delhi at $192 per day. Daily expenses were estimated at $145 in Calcutta, $170 in Madras, $191 in Mumbai (formerly Bombay), and $137 in Bangalore. Costs in smaller towns and villages were estimated at $88.

48FAMOUS INDIANS

Unquestionably, one of the greatest Indians was Siddartha Gautama (624–544 BC according to Sinhalese tradition; 563?–483? BC according to most modern scholars), later known as the Buddha ("the enlightened one"). Born in what is now Nepal, he spent much of his life in eastern Uttar Pradesh and Bihar, propounding the philosophical doctrines that were later to become Buddhism. Contemporary with the Buddha was Vardhamana (599?–527 BC), also known as Mahavira ("great hero"), a saintly thinker of Bihar from whose teachings evolved Jainism. A great many later religious and political leaders left their indelible mark on the Indian scene. Some of the noteworthy were Chandragupta (r.321?–297? BC), founder of the Maurya Dynasty; Asoka (r.273–232 BC), who made Buddhism the religion of his empire; Chandragupta II (r. AD 375?–413), whose era marked a high point of Hindu art and literature; Shivaji (1627?–80), a hero of much Hindu folklore; Nanak (1469–1539), whose teachings are the basis of Sikhism; and Govind Singh (1666–1708), the guru who gave Sikhism its definitive form. Akbar (1542–1605) greatly expanded the Mughal Empire, which reached its height under Shah Jahan (1592–1666), builder of the Taj Mahal, and his son, the fanatical emperor Aurangzeb (1618–1707).

One of the greatest scholars of ancient times was the Sanskrit grammarian Panini (5th?–4th? cents. BC), who wrote the first book on scientific linguistics. The Bengali educator and reformer Rammohan Roy (1772–1833) has been called "the father of modern India." Swami Vivekananda (1863–1902), founder of the nonsectarian Ramakrishna Mission and a great traveler both in India and abroad, did much to explain the Hindu philosophy to the world and to India as well. Sarvepalli Radhakrishnan (1888–1975), a leading 20th-century Hindu scholar and philosopher, also served as president of India from 1962 to 1967. Another revered religious philosopher was Meher Baba (1894–1969). The rising position of India in science and industry is well exemplified by Jamshedji Nusserwanji Tata (1822–1904), founder of the nation's first modern iron and steel works as well as many other key industries; the physicist Jagadis Chandra Bose (1858–1937), noted for his research in plant life; Srinivasa Ramanujan (1887–1919), an amazingly original, although largely self-taught, mathematician; Chandrasekhara Venkata Raman (1888–1970), who was awarded the 1930 Nobel Prize for research in physics; and

Vikram A. Sarabhai (1919–71), the founder of the Indian space program. Mother Teresa (Agnes Gonxha Bojaxhiu,1910–97, in what is now Yugoslavia) won the Nobel Peace Prize in 1979 for her 30 years of work among Calcutta's poor.

In modern times no Indian so completely captured the Indian masses and had such a deep spiritual effect on so many throughout the world as Mohandas Karamchand Gandhi (1869–1948). Reverently referred to by millions of Indians as the Mahatma ("the great-souled one"), Gandhi is considered the greatest Indian since the Buddha. His unifying ability and his unusual methods of nonviolent resistance contributed materially to the liberation of India in 1947. A leading disciple of the Mahatma, Vinayak ("Vinoba") Narahari Bhave (1895–1982), was an agrarian reformer who persuaded wealthy landowners to give about 600,000 hectares (1,500,000 acres) of tillable land to India's poor.

Gandhi's political heir, Jawaharlal Nehru (1889–1964), had a hold on the Indian people almost equal to that of the Mahatma. Affectionately known as Chacha (Uncle) Nehru, he steered India through its first 17 years of independence and played a key role in the independence struggle. Indira Gandhi (1917–84), the daughter of Nehru and prime minister from 1966 to 1977 and again from 1980 to 1984, continued her father's work in modernizing India and played an important role among the leaders of nonaligned nations. Her son Rajiv (1944–91) succeeded her as prime minister and, in the 1985 election, achieved for himself and his party the largest parliamentary victory since India became independent.

The greatest classical Sanskrit writer, and perhaps the greatest writer in Indian history, was the poet and playwright Kalidasa (fl. 5th cent. AD), whose best-known work is *Shakuntala*. In modern times, Rabindranath Tagore (1861–1941), the great Bengali humanist, profoundly influenced Indian thought in his many songs and poems. Tagore received the Nobel Prize in literature in 1913 and through his lifetime wrote more than 50 dramas and about 150 books of verse, fiction, and philosophy. Another Bengali writer highly esteemed was the novelist Bankim Chandra Chatterjee (1838–94). Tagore and Chatterjee are the authors, respectively, of India's national anthem and national song. The novel in English is a thriving genre; notable modern practitioners include Rasipuram Krishnaswamy Narayan (b.1906), Bhabani Bhattacharya (1906–88), and Raja Rao (b.1909) and Khushwant Singh. Influential poets of the last two centuries include the Bengalis Iswar Chandra Gupta (1812–59) and Sarojini Naidu (1879–1949), known as "the nightingale of India," a close associate of Gandhi and a political leader in her own right.

Modern interpreters of the rich Indian musical tradition include the composer and performer Ravi Shankar (b.1920) and the performer and educator Ali Akbar Khan (b.1922). Zubin Mehta (b.1936) is an orchestral conductor of international renown. Uday Shankar (1900?–1977), a dancer and scholar, did much to stimulate Western interest in Indian dance. Tanjore Balasaraswati (1919?–84) won renown as a classical dancer and teacher. Preeminent in the Indian cinema is the director Satyajit Ray (1921–1992).

49DEPENDENCIES

Andaman and Nicobar Islands

The Andaman and Nicobar Islands are two groups of islands in the Indian Ocean, extending approximately 970 km (600 mi) N–S and lying about 640 km (400 mi) W of both the Tenasserim coast of Burma and peninsular Thailand. Their total area is 8,293 sq km (3,202 sq mi); their population was estimated to exceed 188,000 in the mid-1990s. These islands together form a union territory with its capital at Port Blair. The legal system is under the jurisdiction of the high court of Calcutta.

The Andaman Islands extend more than 354 km (220 mi) between 10° and 14°N and 92°12′ and 94°17′E. Of the 204 islands in the group, the three largest are North, Middle, and South Andaman; since these are separated only by narrow inlets, they are often referred to together as Great Andaman. Little Andaman lies to the south.

The Nicobars extend south from the Andamans between 10° and 6°N and 92°43′ and 93°57′E. Of the 19 islands, Car Nicobar, 121 km (75 mi) S of Little Andaman, holds more than half the total population; the largest, Great Nicobar, 146 km (91 mi) NW of Sumatra, is sparsely populated.

The Andamans were occupied by the British in 1858, the Nicobars in 1869; sporadic settlements by British, Danish, and other groups were known previously. During World War II, the islands were occupied by Japanese forces. They became a union territory in 1956. That same year, the Andaman and Nicobar Islands (Protection of Aboriginal Tribes) Act came into force; this act, designed to protect the primitive tribes that live in the islands, prohibited outsiders from carrying on trade or industry in the islands without a special license. Six different tribes live in the Andaman and Nicobar Islands, the largest being the Nicobarese. There are lesser numbers of Andamanese, Onges, Jarawas, Sentinalese, and Shompens in the dependency. Access to tribal areas is prohibited.

Agriculture is the mainstay of the economy. The principal crops are rice and coconuts; some sugarcane, fruits, and vegetables are also grown. There is little industry other than a sawmill and plywood and match factories, but the government is making plans to promote tourism in the islands. These plans include the construction of a 1,000-bed hotel, a casino, and duty-free shopping facilities in Port Blair.

Lakshadweep

The union territory of Lakshadweep consists of the Laccadive, Minicoy, and Amindivi Islands, a scattered group of small coral atolls and reefs in the Arabian Sea between 10° and 13°N and 71°43′ and 73°43′E and about 320 km (200 mi) W of Kerala state. Their total area is about 32 sq km (12 sq mi). Minicoy, southernmost of the islands, is the largest.

In the mid-1990s, the population of Lakshadweep was estimated to exceed 40,000. The inhabitants of the Laccadives and Amindivis are Malayalam-speaking Muslims; those on Minicoy are also Muslim, but speak a language similar to Sinhalese. The islanders are skilled fishermen and trade their marine products and island-processed coir in the Malabar ports of Kerala. The main cottage industry is coir spinning. Politically, these islands were under the control of the state of Madras until 1956. The present territorial capital is at Kavaratti. Judicial affairs are under the jurisdiction of the high court of Kerala.

[50]BIBLIOGRAPHY

Abbas, K. A. *Indira Gandhi: The Last Post.* Columbia, Mo.: South Asia Books, 1986.

Allchin, Bridget and Raymond. *The Rise of Civilization in India and Pakistan.* Cambridge: Cambridge University Press, 1982.

Becker, Charles M. *Indian Urbanization and Economic Growth since 1960.* Baltimore: Johns Hopkins University Press, 1992.

Bhattacharyya, Narendra Nath. *Indian Religious Historiography.* New Delhi: Munshiram Manoharlal Publishers, 1996.

Bhattacharya, Sabyasachi (ed.). *The South Indian Economy: Agrarian Change, Industrial Structure, and State Policy, c. 1914–1947.* New York: Oxford University Press, 1991.

Brown, Judith M. *Modern India: The Origins of an Asian Democracy.* 2d ed. New York: Oxford University Press, 1994.

Cassels, Jamie. *The Uncertain Promise of Law: Lessons from Bhopal.* Toronto: University of Toronto Press, 1993.

Caste Today. Delhi: Oxford University Press, 1996.

Choudhury, R. A., Shama Gamkhar, and Aurobindo Ghose (eds.). *The Indian Economy and its Performance since Independence.* Delhi: Oxford University Press, 1990.

Contesting the Nation: Religion, Community, and the Politics of Democracy in India. Philadelphia: University of Pennsylvania Press, 1996.

Copley, A. R. H. *Gandhi: Against the Tide.* New York: Blackwell, 1987.

Dash, Narendra Kumar. *An Encyclopaedic Dictionary of Indian Culture.* Delhi: Agam Kala Prakashan, 1992.

Diwan, Paras. *Human Rights and the Law: Universal and Indian.* New Delhi: Deep and Deep, 1996.

Economic History of India. Mumbai (formerly Bombay): Shri Bhagavan Vedavyasa Itihasa Samshodhana Mandira (Bhishma), 1996.

Embree, Ainslie Thomas. *Imagining India: Essays on Indian History.* New York: Oxford University Press, 1989.

Encyclopaedia Indica: India, Pakistan, Bangladesh. New Delhi: Anmol Publication, 1996.

Encyclopaedia of India and Her States. New Delhi: Deep and Deep, 1996.

Gehlot, N. S. *Indian Government and Politics.* New Delhi: Rawat Publications, 1996.

Ghosh, Arun (ed.). *An Encyclopedia of Indian Archaeology.* New York: E. J. Brill, 1990.

——. *Indian Industrialization: Structure and Policy Issues.* New York: Oxford University Press, 1992.

Hazarika, Joysankar. *Geopolitics of North East India: A Strategical Study.* New Delhi: Gyan Publishing House, 1996.

Heehs, Peter. *The Bomb in Bengal: The Rise of Revolutionary Terrorism in India, 1900–1910.* Oxford: Oxford University Press, 1993.

Jalan, Bimal. *India's Economic Crisis: The Way Ahead.* New York: Oxford University Press, 1991.

——(ed.). *The New Cambridge History of India.* New York: Cambridge University Press, 1987–1993.

Lal, Deepak. *Cultural Stability and Economic Stagnation: India, c. 1500 BC–AD 1980.* Oxford: Clarendon Press; New York: Oxford University Press, 1988.

Mahmud, S. F. *A Concise History of Indo-Pakistan.* 2d ed. New York: Oxford University Press, 1988.

Mansingh, Surjit. *Historical Dictionary of India.* Lanham, Md.: Scarecrow Press, 1996.

Mathur, Krishan D. *Conduct of India's Foreign Policy.* New Delhi: South Asian Publishers, 1996.

Moorhouse, Geoffrey. *India Britannica.* New York: Harper & Row, 1983.

Palmer, Norman. *The United States and India: The Dimensions of Influence.* Westport, Conn.: Praeger, 1984.

Rothermund, Dietmar. *India.* New York: St. Martin's, 1982.

Shepperdson, M. J., and C. P. Simmons. *The Indian National Congress Party and the Political Economy of India, 1885–1985.* Brookfield, Vt.: Gower, 1987.

Studdert-Kennedy, Gerald. *British Christians, Indian Nationalists, and the Raj Studdert-Kennedy.* New York: Oxford University Press, 1991.

Tobias, Michael. *A Day in the Life of India.* San Francisco: Collins Publishers San Francisco, 1996.

Tomlinson, B. R. *The Economy of Modern India, 1860–1970.* New York: Cambridge University Press, 1993.

Vohra, Ranbir. *The Making of India: A Historical Survey.* Armonk, N.Y.: M. E. Sharp, 1997.

Wolpert, Stanley A. *India.* Berkeley: University of California Press, 1991.

——. *A New History of India.* 4th ed. New York: Oxford University Press, 1993.

INDONESIA

Republic of Indonesia
Republik Indonesia

CAPITAL: Jakarta.

FLAG: The national flag, adopted in 1949, consists of a red horizontal stripe above a white stripe.

ANTHEM: *Indonesia Raya (Great Indonesia).*

MONETARY UNIT: The rupiah (Rp) consists of 100 sen. There are coins of 1, 2, 5, 10, 25, 50, and 100 rupiahs, and notes of 100, 500, 1,000, 5,000, and 10,000 rupiahs. Rp1 = $0.00014 (or $1 = Rp7400.0) as of 31 March 2000.

WEIGHTS AND MEASURES: The metric system is standard.

HOLIDAYS: New Year's Day, 1 January; Independence Day, 17 August; Christmas, 25 December. Movable religious holidays include the Prophet's Birthday, Ascension of Muhammad, Good Friday, Ascension Day of Jesus Christ, the end of Ramadan, 'Id al-Fitr, 'Id al-'Adha', and the 1st of Muharram (Muslim New Year).

TIME: Western, 7 PM = noon GMT; Central, 8 PM = noon GMT; Eastern, 9 PM = noon GMT.

¹LOCATION, SIZE, AND EXTENT

The Republic of Indonesia consists of five large islands and 13,677 smaller islands (about 6,000 of which are inhabited) forming an arc between Asia and Australia. With a total area of 1,919,440 sq km (741,100 sq mi), Indonesia is the fourth-largest Asian country, after China, India, and Sa'udi Arabia. Comparatively, the area occupied by Indonesia is slightly less than three times the size of the state of Texas. It extends 5,271 km (3,275 mi) E–W and 2,210 km (1,373 mi) N–S. The five principal islands are Sumatra, 473,606 sq km (182,860 sq mi); Java, with an area of 132,600 sq km (51,200 sq mi); Borneo, of which the 72% belonging to Indonesia is known as Kalimantan, 539,460 sq km (208,286 sq mi); Sulawesi, formerly called Celebes, 189,216 sq km (73,056 sq mi); and Irian Jaya (West Irian), the western portion of the island of New Guinea, 421,981 sq km (162,927 sq mi). Indonesia claims East Timor (14,874 sq km/5,743 sq mi), a former Portuguese colony that was abandoned by Portugal in 1974 and declared an Indonesian province in 1976; as of 1994, the UN still declined to recognize the Indonesian claim. Indonesia has land boundaries with Malaysia (on Borneo) and Papua New Guinea (on New Guinea). It is bounded on the N by the South China Sea, on the N and E by the Pacific Ocean, and on the S and W by the Indian Ocean. Indonesia's total boundary length (including East Timor) is 57,318 km (35,616 mi).

Indonesia's capital city, Jakarta, is located on the island of Java.

²TOPOGRAPHY

The Indonesian archipelago consists of three main regions. One of the regions consists of Sumatra, Java, Kalimantan, and the islands that lie between them, which stand on the Sunda shelf, where the ocean depths are never more than 210 m (700 ft). Another region consists of Irian Jaya and the Aru Isles, which stand on the Sahul shelf, projecting northward from the north coast of Australia at similar depths. Between these two shelves is the remaining region, consisting of the Lesser Sunda Islands, the Maluku Islands (Moluccas), and Sulawesi, which are surrounded by seas with depths that reach 4,570 m (15,000 ft). The large islands have central mountain ranges rising from more or less extensive lowlands and coastal plains. Many inactive and scores of active volcanoes dot the islands, accounting for the predominantly rich volcanic soil that is carried down by the rivers to the plains and lowlands; there are 112 volcanoes, 15 of them active, on Java alone. Peaks rise to 3,650 m (12,000 ft) in Java and Sumatra. Java, Bali, and Lombok have extensive lowland plains and gently sloping cultivable mountainsides. Extensive swamp forests and not very fertile hill country are found in Kalimantan. Sumatra's eastern coastline is bordered by morasses, floodplains, and alluvial terraces suitable for cultivation farther inland. Mountainous areas predominate in Sulawesi.

³CLIMATE

Straddling the Equator, Indonesia has a tropical climate characterized by heavy rainfall, high humidity, high temperature, and low winds. The wet season is from November to March, the dry season from June to October. Rainfall in lowland areas averages 180–320 cm (70–125 in) annually, increasing with elevation to an average of 610 cm (240 in) in some mountain areas. In the lowlands of Sumatra and Kalimantan, the rainfall range is 305–370 cm (120–145 in); the amount diminishes southward, closer to the northwest Australian desert. Average humidity is 82%.

Altitude rather than season affects the temperature in Indonesia. At sea level, the mean annual temperature is about 25–27°C (77–81°F). There is slight daily variation in temperature, with the greatest variation at inland points and at higher levels. The mean annual temperature at Jakarta is 26°C (79°F); average annual rainfall is about 200 cm (80 in).

⁴FLORA AND FAUNA

The plant life of the archipelago reflects a mingling of Asiatic and Australian forms with endemic ones. Vegetation ranges from that of the tropical rain forest of the northern lowlands and the seasonal forests of the southern lowlands, through vegetation of the less luxuriant hill forests and mountain forests, to subalpine shrub vegetation. The bridge between Asia and Australia formed by the archipelago is reflected in the varieties of animal life. The fauna of Sumatra, Kalimantan, and Java is similar to that of Peninsular Malaysia, but each island has its peculiar types. The orangutan is found in Sumatra and Kalimantan but not in Java, the siamang only in Sumatra, the proboscis monkey only in Kalimantan, the elephant and tapir only in Sumatra, and the wild ox in Java and Kalimantan but not in Sumatra. In Sulawesi, the Maluku Islands, and Timor, Australian types begin to occur; the bandicoot, a marsupial, is found in Timor. All the islands, especially the Malukus, abound in great varieties of bird life, reptiles, and amphibians. The abundant marine life of Indonesia's extensive territorial waters includes a rich variety of corals.

5ENVIRONMENT

An extensive "regreening" and reforestation of barren land, initiated under the 1975–79 national economic development plan, was greatly expanded and integrated with flood control and irrigation programs under the national plans for 1979–84 and 1984–89. From the mid-1980s to the mid-1990s, Indonesia's forests and woodland areas increased by 1.4%. Indonesia also has the world's most extensive mangrove area, which covered over 4 million ha (9.9 million acres) in 1994. Flood-control programs involve river dredging, dike strengthening, construction of new dams, and sandbagging of river banks at critical points. The burning of oil and coal along with the abuse of fertilizers and pesticides results in significant damage to the environment. The nation used 3.1 million tons of fertilizer per year at last estimate. The nation's cities produce 12.9 million tons of solid waste per year. Indonesia has 607.1 cu mi of water with 76% used in farming activity and 11% used for industrial purposes. About 85% of all city dwellers and 79% of rural dwellers have access to pure drinking water. Legislation introduced in 1982 endorsed the establishment of penalties for environmental pollution.

Protection of indigenous wildlife is entrusted to the Directorate of Nature Conservation and Wildlife Management. In 1984/85, the government set up three new national parks, part of 19 included in the 1984–89 plan, and four new natural reserves. As of 1986 there were 146 parks and nature reserves, with more in the planning stage; the government's goal was to allocate 10% of the nation's land area to reserves. By the mid-1990s this goal had nearly been met—protected lands totaled 9.7% of Indonesia's total land area. Indonesia's coastal waters are among the world's richest in biodiversity of marine life. As of 1994, 49 of Indonesia's mammal species were endangered, and 135 bird species were threatened with extinction. Endangered or extinct species in Indonesia include the pig-tailed langur, Javan gibbon, orangutan, tiger, Asian elephant, Malayan tapir, Javan rhinoceros, Sumatran rhinoceros, Sumatran serow, Rothschild's starling, lowland anoa, mountain anoa, Siamese crocodile, false gavial, river terrapin, and four species of turtle (green sea, hawksbill, olive ridley, and leatherback).

6POPULATION

The population of Indonesia in 2000 was estimated at 219,266,557. An estimated 4.4% of the population is 65 years of age or older. The projected population for the year 2005 is 234,876,000, assuming a crude birthrate of 21 per 1,000 population and a death rate of 8, resulting in a natural rate of change of 1.3% for the period 2000–2005. The population rate of change between 1995 and 2000 was 1.5%. The population density in 1998 was 112 per sq km (290 per sq mi).

It was estimated that 40% of the population lived in urban areas in 2000, up from 22% in 1980. The capital city, Jakarta, had a 2000 population of 8,621,000. Other large cities, with 2000 population statistics, include Bandung, 3,420,000; Surabaya, 2,507,000; Medan, 1,910,000; Palembang, 1,429,000; Ujung Pandang, 1,064,000; and Semarang, 826,000.

7MIGRATION

Historically, there has been considerable migration from and to China. Following a decree banning foreigners from participating in retail trade in rural Indonesia, some 120,000 Chinese left Indonesia in 1960 and the first six months of 1961. After the attempted coup of 1965 and the resultant deterioration in relations with China, many more Chinese left Indonesia. Migration between the Netherlands and Indonesia has been greatly reduced since independence; nearly all the 250,000 Netherlands nationals in Indonesia in 1949 returned home.

Resettlement of people from crowded areas to the less populous outer islands is official government policy. The 1979–84 National Economic Plan had as a target the "transmigration" of 500,000 families from Java, Bali, and Madura to Sumatra, Kalimantan, Sulawesi, Maluku Province, and Irian Jaya. Participation was voluntary, and the actual number of families that resettled was about 366,000, containing about 1.5 million people. Since the annual population increase of Java is more than two million, the costly transmigration scheme did little to relieve that island's human congestion, but it had a considerable impact in developing sparsely settled areas. Each family was entitled to 2 ha (5 acres) and was provided with housing, food, seedlings, fertilizers, pesticides, and other supplies that it could use to become productive. Under the 1987–91 plan, 338,433 families were resettled.

First asylum was granted to over 145,000 Indochinese refugees between 1975 and 1993. Of these refugees, 121,708 were from Vietnam. Of the Vietnam asylum seekers, 112,000 had left for resettlement in the West by March of 1996. A total of 8,400 returned home voluntarily, and 4,300 remained on Galang Island. This remaining group of Vietnamese are also expected to return home. In 1999 the net migration rate for Indonesia was zero.

8ETHNIC GROUPS

The indigenous peoples, ethnologically referred to as Malays or Indonesians, also are found on the neighboring islands of the Philippines, in Peninsular Malaysia, and even as far away as Taiwan and Madagascar. Indonesians are characterized by smallness of stature, light to dark-brown pigmentation, thick, sleek black hair, broad formation of the head, a wide nose, and thick lips. The inhabitants of eastern Indonesia have Negroid features, the result of intermarriage with the Papuans of New Guinea.

The population is officially classified into four main ethnic groups: Melanesians, who constitute the majority; Proto-Austronesians, including the Wajaks and the Irianese on Irian Jaya; Polynesians, including the Ambonese on the Maluku Islands; and Micronesians, found on the tiny islets of Indonesia's eastern borders. The Melanesians are subdivided into the Acehnese of north Sumatra; the Bataks of northeastern Sumatra; the Minangkabaus of west Sumatra; the Sundanese of west Java; the Javanese in central and east Java; the Madurese on the island of Madura; the Balinese on Bali; the Sasaks on the island of Lombok; the Timorese on Timor; the Dayaks in Kalimantan; and the Minahasa, Torajas, Makassarese, and Buginese on Sulawesi. In 1999, 45% of the population was Javanese, 14% Sundanese, 7.5% Madurese, 7.5% coastal Malays, and 26% other.

Ethnic Chinese, the principal minority, were the target of riots in 1974 and 1980. Active mainly in business in the major cities, they are relatively prosperous and widely resented by ethnic Indonesians.

9LANGUAGES

Bahasa Indonesia, a product of the nationalist movement, is the official language, serving as a common vehicle of communication for the various language groups. Based primarily on Malay and

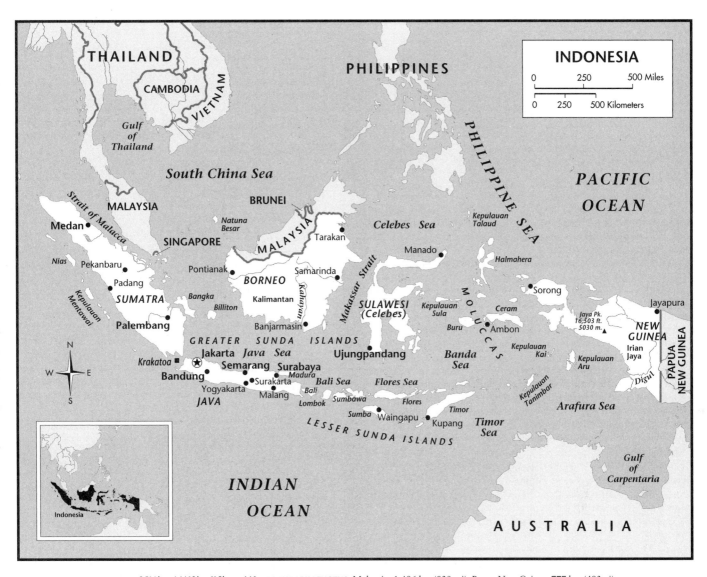

LOCATION: 95°1′ to 141°2′E; 6°5′N to 11°S. **BOUNDARY LENGTHS:** Malaysia, 1,496 km (930 mi); Papua New Guinea, 777 km (483mi); total coastline, 37,461 km (23,277 mi). **TERRITORIAL SEA LIMIT:** 12 mi.

similar to the official language of Malaysia, it also contains many words from other Indonesian languages and dialects, as well as from Dutch, English, Arabic, Sanskrit, and other languages. In 1973, Indonesia and Malaysia adopted similar systems of spelling. Outside of Jakarta, only 10–15% of the population speaks the language in the home, but more than half the population uses it as a secondary language. Use of some 669 local languages persists, including Sundanese, Malay, and the most widely used, Javanese. English and Dutch are widely used in industry and commerce.

10 RELIGIONS

An estimated 88% of the inhabitants are adherents of Islam; 5% are Protestants; 3% are Roman Catholics; 2% are Hindus; 1% are Buddhists or Confucianists; and 1% follow tribal and other religions (1998). Freedom of religion is guaranteed by the constitution for members of five out of six officially recognized religions. Restrictions on some unrecognized religions do exist; however, in 1998 the People's Consultative Assembly adopted a new Human Rights Charter, which provides for citizens' freedom to practice their religion without specifying any particular religions. The government actively supports Islamic religious schools and pays for a number of annual pilgrimages to Mecca. Hinduism was the religion of Java for several centuries, but when Islam swept over Indonesia in the 15th century, Hinduism retreated to Bali, and some three million Indonesians on Bali and elsewhere have remained Hindu in religion and culture. The religious faith of the Chinese in Indonesia may be characterized as Christian or Buddhist-Confucianist. The chief Christian communities are found on Ambon and adjacent islands, in northern Sulawesi, in north-central Sumatra, and on Timor and adjacent islands. In central Kalimantan and Irian Jaya, as well as a few other areas, substantial numbers of Indonesians follow animist tribal religions.

11 TRANSPORTATION

Indonesia is politically and economically dependent upon good communications and transportation among the islands. Transportation facilities suffered greatly from destruction and neglect during World War II and immediately thereafter. The revitalized and partially modernized system suffered an additional setback during 1957–58 as a result of the withdrawal of Dutch equipment and personnel.

Of the 342,700 km (121,954 mi) of roadways in 1997, 158,670 km (98,598 mi) were paved. Indonesia had 1,900,000 passenger cars and 1,850,000 commercial vehicles as of 1995. Railways connect the main cities in Java and parts of Sumatra. The state owns all of the 6,458 km (4,013 mi) of railroad track in service. Air-conditioned cars and express service have been introduced in parts of Java, but no new lines have been built in recent years.

About 21,579 km (13,409 mi) of inland waterways form the most important means of transportation in Kalimantan and in parts of Sumatra. The principal ports of international trade are Tanjungpriok (for Jakarta) and Tanjungperak (for Surabaya) in Java, and Belawan (near Medan) and Padang in Sumatra. Ports with less traffic but capable of handling sizable ships are Cirebon and Semarang in Java; Palembang in Sumatra; Banjarmasin, Balikpapan, and Pontianak in Kalimantan; Tanjungpinang in Bintan; and Ujung Padang in Sulawesi. In 1998, Indonesia's total fleet included 587 vessels of 1,000 gross tons or more, totaling 2,707,004 GRT. Regulations were imposed in 1982 requiring that all government imports and exports be shipped in Indonesian vessels, and port charges were substantially altered to benefit Indonesia's national carriers. In 1984, a policy of scrapping old vessels was implemented.

Indonesia had 443 airports in 1998, of which 125 had paved runways. The center of international air traffic is Jakarta's Sukarno-Hatta International Airport. Other principal airports include Halim Perdanak at Jakarta and Polonia at Medan. In 1997, 12,650,000 passengers were carried on scheduled domestic and international flights.

12HISTORY

Evidence for the ancient habitation of Indonesia was discovered by the Dutch paleontologist Eugène Dubois in 1891; these fossil remains of so-called Java man (Pithecanthropus erectus) date from the Pleistocene period, when Indonesia was linked with the Asian mainland. Indonesia's characteristic racial mixture resulted from at least two waves of invasions from South China by way of the Malay Peninsula and from intermarriage of these Indonesians with later immigrants, especially from India. The important population groups of today trace their descent from the immigrants of the second wave, which occurred around the 2nd or 3rd century BC. They subjugated and absorbed most of the other inhabitants. Indian influences permeated Java and Sumatra from the 1st to the 7th century AD. During this period and extending into the 15th century, local Buddhist and Hindu rulers established a number of powerful kingdoms. Among the most powerful of these was the Buddhist kingdom of Srivijaya, established on Sumatra in the 7th century; it prospered by gaining control of trade through the Strait of Malacca. To the east, in central Java, the Sailendra dynasty established its Buddhist kingdom in the 8th century. Relics of Sailendra rule include the great temple of Borobudur, Asia's largest Buddhist monument, with hundreds of bas-reliefs depicting the life of Buddha. Succeeding the Sailendra dynasty in 856 were followers of the Hindu god Shiva; these Shivaites built the great temple at Prambanan, east of Yogyakarta. Other Hindu kingdoms subsequently extended Indian influence eastward into east Java and Bali. The last of these was the Hindu kingdom of Majapahit, which was at the height of its power during the 13th century, when Marco Polo visited Java and northern Sumatra. When Majapahit collapsed around 1520, many of its leaders, according to tradition, fled to Bali, the only island in Indonesia that retains Hinduism as the chief religion. Even before Majapahit disintegrated, Muslim missionaries, probably Persian merchants, had begun to win much of the archipelago for Islam. About this time,

also, the first Europeans arrived, and the first Chinese settlements were made. The Portuguese captured Malacca (Melaka), on the west coast of the Malay Peninsula, in 1511 and established control over the archipelago.

Dutch ships visited Java in 1596. The Dutch came in increasing numbers and soon drove the Portuguese out of the archipelago (except for the eastern half of the island of Timor), beginning nearly 350 years of colonial rule. The States-General of the Dutch Republic in 1602 incorporated the East Indian spice traders as the United East India Company and granted it a monopoly on shipping and trade and the power to make alliances and contracts with the rulers of the East. By force and diplomacy, the company thus became the supreme ruler of what became known as the Dutch East Indies. However, maladministration and corruption weakened the company after its early years of prosperity, and the Dutch government nullified its charter in 1799 and took over its affairs in 1800. The British East India Company ruled the Indies during the Napoleonic wars, from 1811 to 1816. During this period, Sir Thomas Stamford Raffles became governor of Java. When Dutch rule was restored, the Netherlands government instituted the "culture system" on Java, under which the Javanese, instead of paying a certain proportion of their crops as tax, were required to put at the disposal of the government a share of their land and labor and to grow crops for export under government direction. From a fiscal point of view the system was very successful, yielding millions of guilders for the Netherlands treasury, but this "net profit" or "favorable balance" policy fell under increasing moral attack in the Netherlands and was brought to an end about 1877. Thereafter, private Dutch capital moved into the Indies, but the augmentation of Dutch prosperity at the expense of Indonesian living standards was increasingly resented. With the adoption of what colonial administrators called the "ethical policy" at the beginning of the 20th century, the first steps were taken to give Indonesians participation in government. A central representative body, the Volksraad, was instituted in 1918. At first it had only advisory powers, but in 1927 it was given colegislative powers. An Indonesian nationalist movement began to develop during those years and steadily gained strength. Although retarded in the 1930s by the world economic depression, which was strongly felt in Indonesia, the movement revived during the Japanese occupation (1942–45) in World War II. A nationalist group under the leadership of Sukarno and Mohammad Hatta proclaimed an independent republic on 17 August 1945, adopted a provisional constitution providing for a strong presidential form of government, formed a revolutionary government, and resisted Dutch reoccupation. After four years of intermittent negotiations, frequent hostilities and UN intervention, the Netherlands agreed to Indonesian demands.

On 27 December 1949, the Dutch recognized the independence of all the former Dutch East Indies except West New Guinea (Irian Jaya) as the Republic of the United States of Indonesia. A few months later, on 17 August 1950, the federal system was rejected and a unitary state, the Republic of Indonesia, was established under a new constitution. West New Guinea remained under Dutch control until October 1962, when the Netherlands transferred the territory to the United Nations Temporary Executive Administration (UNTEA). On 1 May 1963, Indonesia took complete possession of the disputed territory as the province of Irian Barat (West Irian); the province was renamed Irian Jaya in 1973. Indonesia, which aimed to acquire Sarawak and Sabah (which are on the island of Borneo with Kalimantan), opposed the formation of the Federation of Malaysia in September 1963 and announced a "crush Malaysia" policy. This policy was implemented by guerrilla raids into Malaysian territory that continued until August 1966, when a formal treaty was concluded between the two countries.

Sukarno became the first president of the new nation in 1949, and Hatta the vice-president. Internal difficulties, fostered by a multiplicity of political parties inherited from Dutch colonial days, soon developed, and regional rivalries also threatened the unity of the new nation. Then as now, Java had some two-thirds of the country's population, but the great sources of wealth were found on the other, much less densely settled islands. Those living in the so-called Outer Islands believed too much governmental revenue was being spent in Java and too little elsewhere. After Vice-President Hatta, a Sumatran, resigned in December 1956, many in the Outer Islands felt they had lost their chief and most effective spokesman in Jakarta. Territorial army commanders in Sumatra staged coups and defied the central government; other rebel movements developed in Sulawesi. The government took measures providing for greater fiscal and administrative decentralization, but discontent remained, and the rebellions were put down by force. Thereafter, Sukarno bypassed parliamentary procedures and pursued an increasingly authoritarian, anti-Western policy of "guided democracy." In 1959, he decreed a return to the 1945 constitution, providing for a centralized form of government, and consolidated his control.

Communist agitation within the country and secessionist uprisings in central and eastern Java came to a head in the 30th of September Movement under the direction of Lt. Col. Untung. Sukarno, whose foreign policy had turned increasingly toward the Communist Chinese, may have had advance knowledge of the Communist-led coup attempt on 30 September 1965, which was directed against Indonesia's top military men; the coup was crushed immediately by the army, however, and in the ensuing anti-Communist purges more than 100,000 persons (mostly Indonesian Chinese) lost their lives and another 700,000 were arrested. By mid-October, the army, under the command of Gen. Suharto, was in virtual control of the country. On 12 March 1966, following nearly three weeks of student riots, President Sukarno transferred to Suharto the authority to take, in the president's name, "all measures required for the safekeeping and stability of the government administration." In March 1967, the People's Consultative Assembly (*Majetis Permusyawaratan Rakyat*—MPR) voted unanimously to withdraw all Sukarno's governmental power and appointed Gen. Suharto acting president. One year later, it conferred full presidential powers on Suharto, and he was sworn in as president for a five-year term. The Congress also agreed to postpone the general elections due in 1968 until 1971. Sukarno died in June 1970. On 3 July 1971, national and regional elections were held for the majority of seats in all legislative bodies. The Joint Secretariat of Functional Groups (*Sekber Golongan Karya*—Golkar), a mass political front backed by Suharto, gained 60% of the popular vote and emerged in control of both the House of Representatives (DPR) and the MPR.

Suharto Gains Control

In March 1973, the MPR elected Suharto to a second five-year term. Thus Suharto, with key backing from the military, began a long period of dominance over Indonesian politics. Under Suharto's "New Order," Indonesia turned to the West and began following a conservative economic course stressing capital development and foreign investment. In foreign affairs, Suharto's government achieved vastly improved ties with the US, Japan, and Western Europe while maintaining links with the USSR.

On 7 December 1975, following Portugal's withdrawal from East Timor, a power struggle developed among various political groups, including the Revolutionary Front for an Independent East Timor (*Frente Revolucionário de Este Timor Independente*—Fretilin). The left-wing independence movement achieved military dominance forcing the Indonesian government to send troops into the former Portuguese colony and assume full control of the territory. On 17 July 1976, the Suharto government incorporated the territory as an Indonesian Province. This action was neither recognized by the UN, which called on Indonesia to withdraw and allow the Timorese the right to self-determination, nor accepted by Fretilin. Discontent with the Suharto regime mounted after the elections of 1977, in which Suharto's Golkar Party gained an overwhelming majority. The government acknowledged holding 31,000 political prisoners; according to Amnesty International, the total was closer to 100,000. Student riots and criticism of government repression resulted in further government measures: political activity was suspended, and leading newspapers were temporarily closed. Suharto was elected by the MPR to a third five-year term in 1978; during late 1977 and 1978, some 16,000 political prisoners were released, and the remainder of those detained in 1965 were released by the end of 1979. Golkar made further gains in the 1982 elections, and Suharto was elected for a fourth five-year term in March 1983.

To strengthen the government in the face of rising Muslim militancy, Suharto began to reestablish Sukarno as a national hero eight years after his death. Suharto called for greater loyalty by all political groups to the Pancasila ("five principles") framed by Sukarno in 1945. The credo encompassed belief in the one supreme being, humanitarianism, national unity, consensus democracy, and social justice. Muslim groups strongly objected to the new government program and organized demonstrations took place in 1984 and 1985. The war against Fretilin continued into the 1980s, with reports of massacres by government troops and severe economic hardship among the Timorese. Negotiations with Portugal, still considered responsible for decolonization by the UN, began in July 1983. In Irian Jaya, the Organization for a Free Papua (*Organisasi Papua Merdeka*—OPM), which desires unification with Papua New Guinea and has been active since the early 1960s, increased its militant activities in 1986. The Indonesian Army (ABRI) continued to play a dual military and socioeconomic function, and this role was supported by legislation in 1988. Golkar made further gains in the 1987 elections, and Suharto was again reelected for a fifth five-year term in March 1988. During disagreements over nomination procedures for the vice-presidency ABRI's influence was eroded.

Golkar sought to create national unity through its resettlement policies. From 1969–92, the Transmigration Program, a policy aimed redistributing population in Indonesia for political purposes and for demographic reasons resulted in almost 1,488,000 families moved from the Inner Islands to the Outer Islands. The Transmigration Program suffered from land disputes with local residents and environmental concerns over deforestation. The program alienated local populations and fueled ethnic conflict throughout the country. In Irian Jaya, the Free Papua Movement (OPM), attempted to sabotage the government's program that was turning the indigenous Melanesian majority into a minority. Indonesian troops attempting to capture Melanesian separatists would cross the border into Papua New Guinea. Indonesia and Papua New Guinea agreed to provide greater cooperation on security and trade issues and the leader of OPM, Melkianus Salossa was eventually arrested in Papua New Guinea and deported to Indonesia and sentenced to life in prison in 1991. In 1989, tension from land disputes in Java and the Outer Islands produced social unrest that resulted in clashes between villagers and the armed forces. In 1990 an armed rebellion in northern Sumatra at Aceh arose over hostility toward government exploitation of mineral resources and its transmigration program. The government squashed the rebellion with a massive display of force.

Political openness was increasingly espoused during 1990–91 by political and labor organizations. In 1990 a group of prominent Indonesians publicly demanded that Suharto retire from the presidency at the end of his current term; in 1991 labor unrest increased with a rash of strikes which the army was called in to quell. Government efforts to raise funds through a state lottery were opposed and finally forbidden on religious grounds when the country's highest Islamic authority declared the lottery "haram" or forbidden.

On 12 November 1991, during a funeral for a young Timorese killed in demonstrations against Indonesia's rule of East Timor, soldiers opened fire on the defenseless mourners provoking worldwide condemnation. Although the government took unprecedented steps to punish those involved, western governments threatened to suspend aid, and demands were made linking aid to human rights issues. The Netherlands' demand linking its aid to improvements in human rights was rejected when Suharto refused Dutch economic aid on 25 March 1992. In the aftermath of these events Suharto spoke at the Nonaligned Movement summit in Jakarta and to the UN General Assembly suggesting that developing nations needed to take a more prominent role in opposing North-South economic inequality. Suharto's challenge received a cool reception from Western nations, but it clearly signaled a reassessment of Indonesia's future international presence. In early December 1992 government forces captured Jose Alexandre (Xanana) Gusmao, leader of the Fretilin, who was hiding in Dili, in East Timor. On 21 May 1993 he was sentenced to life imprisonment. In late 1992, tensions between Muslims and Christians increased to the point of violence and vandalism of churches and mosques. Suharto requested that religious tolerance be practiced. By 1993 US policy toward Indonesia shifted toward criticism of Indonesia's rule in East Timor, and a threat to revoke trade privileges pursuant to Indonesia's treatment of the largest independent trade union, the SBSI (Indonesian Prosperous Labor Union). Adding further scrutiny to Indonesia's tarnished international image was a UN resolution on Indonesia's human rights violations placing the country on a rights "watch" list in 1993.

Although its total share of votes declined, Golkar won the 1992 elections, securing 282 of the 400 elective seats. In March 1993, Suharto was elected to a sixth term as president. Try Sutrisno, the commander in chief of ABRI, was chosen as vice president. Despite Golkar's victory, the country continued to experience economic and political difficulties. A major scandal occurred in March 1993 with the sale of $5 million in fake shares on the Jakarta Stock Exchange (JSE). In January 1994 President Suharto inaugurated 12 electric power plants with combined installed capacity of more than 2,000 MW. Violent labor unrest broke out in Medan in April 1994 with the mysterious death of a union activist. Ethnic Chinese, who are only about 3% of the population of Indonesia, were the target of demonstrators; one Chinese factory manager was killed. The success of the Chinese is widely envied and they are accused of exploiting the workers. On 21 June 1994 the government closed *Tempo* and two other publications by revoking publishing licenses. *Tempo* was accused of violating the journalistic code of ethics and pitting one person against another to the point where it affected national security based on its coverage of a controversial purchase of 39 warships from the former East German navy. Other publications were accused of more technical infractions including the failure to comply with registration procedures and publishing political and general news in spite of license restrictions limiting a popular tabloid's coverage to detective stories and crime stories.

Violent outbreaks, clashes, and riots increased in Indonesia from 1995–97. Riots between Catholics and Muslims broke out in East Timor in September 1995, leaving Dili's central marketplace in ashes. This was before Timor's Roman Catholic bishop, Carlos Filipe Ximenes Belo, and pro-independence advocate José Ramos-Horta shared the Nobel Peace Prize in 1996. Many incidents of rural unrest, including land disputes and ethnic strife, continued in 1995–96. The campaign for the 29 May 1997 elections was an unusually violent one, dubbed the "festival of democracy," as voters and demonstrators brought rocks, bricks, knives, machetes, and even snakes to the campaign. There was a ban on parades of trucks, cars, and motorcycles. This followed the uproar resulting from the ouster of Megawati Sukarnoputri as the Indonesian Democratic Party chairperson in June 1996. Her political involvement was seen as a rallying point for democratic change. Golkar took 74% of the vote in elections that were seen to be marked by fraud and over 200 people were killed during the campaign. The Muslim-oriented United Development Party (PPP) obtained 22%, and 3% went to the PDI.

In other violence, hundreds of lives were lost in a full-scale ethnic war in Kalimantan, as clashes between the Dayaks, the indigenous people of the area, and Muslim settlers from the island of Madora, broke out in December 1996. The fighting led to Malaysia closing part of its border with Indonesia in February 1997. In 1997, the country experienced the dual effect of increased ethnic conflict and economic decline. These twin forces were the harbinger for the decline of Golkar and the departure of Suharto from Indonesian politics. In the May 1997 legislative elections, Golkar managed to allegedly secure 74.3% of the popular vote, amid massive violence which killed over one-hundred political activists. Violence continued after the elections and was worsened by the Asian economic crisis. After severe devaluation of the rupiah in August and October of 1997, Suharto accepted an International Monetary Fund (IMF) loan package but failed to carry out IMF imposed conditions for economic reform. By December, news of Suharto's worsening physical health also cast doubt on his ability to see Indonesia through a worsening economic and political situation.

After Suharto won an unopposed presidential election in March 1998, student protests swept Jakarta and ethnic tensions also swelled as Chinese merchants were attacked. In East Timor, Jose Ramos Horta, the leader of FRETILIN, a revolutionary liberation organization, urged the government to agree to a cease-fire and cooperation with the UN to determine the ultimate governance structure for the country. In July 1998, B.J. Habibie's, the former Vice President, became president. Upon assuming the presidency, he adopted a conciliatory posture toward defusing the East Timor crisis by stating that East Timor may be given "special status" with increased autonomy within Indonesia. In August 1998, Portugal and Indonesia met to discuss the future of the province. After significant pressure from the United Nations, Australia, and Portugal, Habibie agreed on 27 January 1999 to hold a referendum for the province. Despite widespread violence instigated by the pro-Indonesia armed militia, 98% of voters cast their ballots on August 30, with 78.5% in favor of independence. This was followed by a rampage by pro-Indonesia forces who looted and burned the entire province creating a major humanitarian situation and refugee crisis. With the aid of Australian troops, the United Nations intervened with approximately 8,000 troops to restore order and establish humanitarian programs. Meanwhile, in Irian Jaya and Aceh, the military forces and the national police continued to commit extra-judicial killings in 2000.

B. J. Habibie's political fortunes waned in the aftermath of the UN sponsored referendum in East Timor. His state of the nation address to the People's Consultative Assembly in October did not allay the perception that he had not exercised the appropriate leadership in handling domestic and international matters. Pressure on Habibie mounted and he subsequently resigned as a result of a no confidence vote. In 20 October elections in the People's Consultative Assembly, Abdurrahman Wahid, the leader of the National Awakening Party and a Muslim cleric, secured 373 votes to Megawati Sukarnoputri 313 votes. Despite protest from her supporters, Megawati asked backers to refrain from violent protest. She became vice-president. Wahid worked to curb the influence of the military and promised major reforms in the government.

13GOVERNMENT

The provisional constitution of 17 August 1950 provided for a unitary republic. The president and vice-president, "elected in accordance with rules to be laid down by law," were to be inviolable, but cabinet ministers were jointly and individually responsible. The House of Representatives was to be a unicameral parliament. Its members were elected by a system of proportional representation for a four-year term, but it might be dissolved earlier by presidential decree. Sukarno and Hatta, the first president and vice-president, were elected by parliament; no term of office was stipulated by the constitution. In practice, the government was not truly parliamentary, since President Sukarno played a role far greater than is usual for the head of state in a parliamentary system. He was the great national revolutionary hero, and his popularity with the masses enabled him to exert great influence on government policy. Parliament was not strong enough to hold the president to the role prescribed by the constitution. In 1957, Sukarno adopted a more authoritarian policy of "guided democracy." He further strengthened his powers in 1959 by decreeing a return to the provisional 1945 constitution, which called for a strong president and stressed the philosophy of Pancasila as a national ideology. On 5 March 1960, Sukarno suspended parliament and began to rule by decree. In June, he appointed a new 283-member parliament drawn from 9 political parties and 14 "functional groups." In mid-August, Sukarno named another 326 legislators who, with the 283 members of parliament, were to constitute the Provisional People's Congress. This Congress was to meet at least once every five years and to be responsible for drawing up the outlines of national policy and electing the president and vice-president. In 1963, the Congress elected Sukarno president for life. Following the political upheavals of 1965–66, the army, led by Gen. Suharto, moved to establish a "New Order." In 1967, Sukarno formally relinquished power to Suharto, who had become Indonesia's effective ruler in March 1966. Suharto reorganized the cabinet, making all of its 12 ministers responsible to him. In February 1968, he dismissed 123 members of the People's Consultative Assembly (MPR), an outgrowth of the Provisional People's Congress, and replaced them with his own nominees. In June of that year, following his appointment to a five-year term as president, Suharto formed a new cabinet, with himself as prime minister and defense minister.

On 3 July 1971, general elections—the first since 1955—were held for portions of two reconstituted national bodies, a 460-seat House of Representatives (often shortened to DPR) and a 920-seat MPR. In 1987, the memberships were increased to 500 and 1,000, respectively. Under the new system, legislative responsibility is vested in the DPR, which consists of 400 elected members and 100 members appointed by the president from the military (Armed Forces of People's Republic of Indonesia, Angkatan Bersenjata Republik Indonesia or ABRI) and other groups. DPR members also sit as members of the MPR, forming one-half of the membership; two-thirds of the total membership consists of elected officials. As of 1992, 147 seats in the DPR were held by delegates elected by provincial-level legislative assemblies. The remainder of seats, 253 in 1992, were assigned on a provincial basis to representatives of the political parties, as determined in the 1987 DPR elections, depending on their respective membership in the DPR. In 1987 Golkar won 299 of the 400 elected DPR seats, the largest number of seats. (Golkar, or Golongan Karya, is the government formed de facto political parties organized around functioning groups in society.) As a result Gokar took a total of 540 seats in the MPR. Under the Suharto government, the MPR has acted as a consultative body, setting guidelines for national policy; its principal legislative task is to approve the Broad Outlines of State Policy. In March 1973, the MPR elected President Suharto to a second five-year term; he was reelected to a third term in 1978, a fourth in 1983, a fifth in 1988, a six in 1993, and a seventh in 1998. However, Suharto was forced to step down in July 1998 in favor of his Vice-President, B.J. Habibie. Habibie sought to decrease the role of the military in Indonesia politics and promised major political and economic reform. He too was forced to resign after the People's Consultative Assembly questioned his leadership. In a surprise move, the body chose Abdurrahman Wahid as president in October 1999. Wahid, a well respected Muslim cleric, promised democratization and an end to corruption.

14POLITICAL PARTIES

Until the autumn of 1955, when the first national elections were held, members of the House of Representatives were appointed by the president in consultation with party leaders. Of the 37,785,299 votes cast in the 1955 general election, six parties received more than one million votes each: the Indonesian Nationalist Party (Partai Nasional Indonesia—PNI), 22.3% of the total; the Council of Muslim Organizations (Masjumi), 20.9%; the Orthodox Muslim Scholars (Nahdlatul Ulama—NU), 18.4%; the Indonesian Communist Party (Partai Komunis Indonesia—PKI), 16.4%; the United Muslim Party, 2.9%; and the Christian Party, 2.6%. In all, 28 parties won representation in the 273-member Parliament. Almost all the political parties had socialist aims or tendencies. The PNI, many of whose prominent members were leaders in the prewar nationalist movement, represented a combination of nationalism and socialism. Government officials and employees had originally constituted its backbone, but subsequently it grew powerful among labor and farmer groups as well. The Masjumi was more evenly distributed throughout Indonesia than any other party. Although it contained a large percentage of the small middle class, its principles were markedly socialist, owing to the influence in the party of a religious socialist group. The NU, which broke away from the Masjumi largely because of differences in religious outlook, represented the orthodox but not strictly conservative views of the rural people and religious teachers. The Christian Party was founded by Protestants; a smaller Roman Catholic Party was also formed. On 17 August 1960, Sukarno ordered the dissolution of the Masjumi and socialist parties on the grounds of disloyalty. A month later, on 13 September, political action by all parties was barred.

Early in 1961, notice was given that all political parties were required to apply for permission to function. On 15 April, parties certified to continue in existence included the PKI, PNI, NU, Catholic, Islamic Association, Indonesian, Indonesian Protestant Christian, Indonesian Islam Sarekat, and the League for Upholding Indonesian Independence. The PKI, which at the height of its power in 1965 had an estimated three million members and was especially strong on Java, was banned by Gen. Suharto in March 1966, by which time more than 100,000 PKI members were estimated to have been killed in riots, assassinations, and purges; many more PKI members were arrested. Since then, the party has operated underground. The Masjumi dissolved in 1960. Under the Suharto government, political opposition in Indonesia has become increasingly quiescent. Prior to the 1971 elections, the government formed a mass organization, known as Golkar (Golongan Karya), as the political vanguard for its "New Order" program. Golkar drew upon elements outside traditional party ranks—the civil service, labor, youth, cooperatives, and other groups—and succeeded in effectively circumventing the parties' ability to play a national role. Prior to the 1971 voting, a government-appointed election committee screened all prospective candidates, eliminating 735 from the initial list of 3,840; only 11 of those eliminated were from Golkar. Candidates were forbidden to criticize the government or to discuss religious issues. In the elections, held on 3 July 1971, Golkar candidates received 63% of the vote, while winning 227 of the 351 contested seats in the House of Representatives. Besides Golkar—which is not formally considered a political party—nine parties took part in the elections, as compared with 28 in 1955. The Orthodox Muslim NU placed second in the balloting, with 58 seats; the moderate Indonesian Muslim Party (*Parmusi*), an offshoot of the banned Masjumi Party, won 24 seats; and the PNI, Sukarno's former base, won only 20 seats. Four smaller groups—the Muslim Political Federation, the Protestant Christian Party, the Catholic Party, and the Islamic Party—divided the remaining 22 seats. The government subsequently announced that 57 million persons, or over 95% of the electorate, had taken part in the voting. An act of 1975 provided for the fusion of the major political organizations into two parties—the United Development Party (*Partai Persuatan Pembangunan*—PPP) and the Indonesian Democratic Party (*Partai DemoKrasi Indonesia*—PDI)—and Golkar. The PPP, Golkar's chief opposition, is a fusion of the NU, Parmusi and other Muslim groups, while the PDI represents the merger of the PNI, the Christian Party, the Roman Catholic Party, and smaller groups. In the third general election, held on 2 May 1977, Golkar won 232 seats in the House of Representatives, against 99 seats for the PPP and 29 seats for the PDI. Golkar made further gains in the elections of 4 May 1982, winning 246 of the 364 contested seats, against 94 for the PPP and 24 for the PDI. Both opposition parties charged that the government had falsified the vote totals. Rioting marred the campaign period, and 35,000 army troops were stationed in Jakarta on election day. In the election of 23 April 1987, Golkar won 292 of the 400 elected seats (73.2%), against 64 for the PPP (16%), and 44 for the PDI (10.8%).

For the 1992 election the campaign rules banned automobile rallies and picture posters of political leaders; large outdoor rallies were discouraged, radio and televised appeals had to be approved in advance by the elections commission, and no campaigning took place in the five days before the elections. In 1992 there were 17 million first-time voters in a population of 108 million registered voters. More than 97 million Indonesians voted, 90% of the registered voters. Golkar won 68% of the popular vote, down by 5% from 1987. The PPP took 17% of the vote. The PDI (a democratic opposition party) took 15% of the vote compared to 10.9% in 1987. These results in terms of DPR seats were: Golkar took 281 DPR seats (down 18 seats from 1987); PPP took 63 seats (down 2 seats from 1987); and the PDI took 56 seats (an increase of 16 seats).

1997 was the most violent election campaign in recent years as the ruling Golkar party took 74% of the vote. The 29 May 1997 elections were marked by fraud. More than 200 people were killed in the campaign, which banned motorcades. The PPP took 22% of the vote, and the PDI, 3%. The departure of Suharto and Habibie from the political scene in 1999 is likely to usher in a period of political instability as the Golkar seeks new leadership to prevent its disintegration. The government will seek to modify the role of the military in People's Consultative Assembly.

15LOCAL GOVERNMENT

The structure and organization of local governments follow the pattern of national government. Indonesia is divided into 27 provinces (including East Timor). Three of the provinces are special territories, namely the Capital City of Jakarta, the Special Territory of Yogyakarta, and the Special Territory of Aceh. Each province is administered by a governor chosen by the central government from candidates proposed by the provincial assembly. Governors must be approved by the President. Provinces are divided into 241 districts (*kabupatens*), administered by Bupati appointed in the same manner as governors. Both

provincial and district governments are granted autonomy. As of 1993 there were also 56 municipalities (*kotamadyas*) headed by a mayor (*walikota*), 3,625 subdistricts (*kecamatan*) headed by a camat, and 67,033 villages. *Desa* are rural villages and *kelurahans* are urban villages. The head of a desa is elected by the villages community. The head of a kelurahan, a *lurah*, is a civil servant appointed by a camat on behalf of the governor. A unique feature of village life is the Village Council of Elders, composed of 9 to 15 prominent village leaders.

16JUDICIAL SYSTEM

Since 1951, the administration of justice has been unified. Government courts, each with a single judge, have jurisdiction in the first instance in civil and criminal cases. In December 1989, the Islamic Judicature Law gave wider powers to Shari'a courts. The new law gave Muslim courts jurisdiction over civil matters, including marriage. Muslims and non-Muslims can decide to appear before secular courts. The Supreme Court is the highest court in the country; its primary function is review of decisions by lower courts. The High Court hears appeals in civil cases and reviews criminal cases. Judges are appointed by the central government. In the villages, customary law (*adat*) procedures continue unchanged.

Islamic law (*Shari'a*) governs many noncriminal matters involving Muslims, including family law, inheritance and divorce; a civil code based on Roman law is applied to Europeans; a combination of Codes is applied to other groups such as ethnic Chinese and Indians. Since 1985, the Supreme Court since 1985 has the power to review ministerial decrees and regulations for legality and conformity to the constitution, but it has yet to use this power. The Supreme Court does not have the power to review the constitutionality of laws passed by the national assembly. Military and administrative courts also exist below the Supreme Court level. Codifying these disparate forms of law will require considerable work.

17ARMED FORCES

The Indonesian armed forces, established on 5 October 1945, consist of an army, a navy, and an air force, totaling 298,000 personnel in 2000. The army of 230,000, some of whom are engaged in nonmilitary tasks, is organized as a combined arms "Strategic reserve" of 30 battalions and 10 territorial commands that control 90 battalions (mostly infantry). It is manned through a two-year conscription law and armed with US and NATO equipment. There are five special forces battalions. The air force, with a total complement of 21,000, has 91 combat aircraft, largely of US origin. The navy, with 47,000 personnel (including naval aviators and marines), had two submarines, 17 frigates, and 58 large patrol craft. Naval forces include a naval air wing of aircraft and helos and a 12,000-member marine brigade. Paramilitary forces include a 194,000-man police force and three other armed security forces, including a trained People's Security force of 1.5 million.

Indonesia spent $959.7 million for defense in 1997–98 or 1% of GDP.

Indonesia has one infantry battalion in Cambodia (UNTAC). It faces three small guerrilla groups of 550 at home.

18INTERNATIONAL COOPERATION

Indonesia was admitted to UN membership on 28 September 1950 and is a member of ESCAP and all the nonregional specialized agencies. Following the seating of Malaysia in the Security Council, Indonesia withdrew from the UN on 7 January 1965; it resumed its seat on 28 September 1966. Indonesia is also a member of the Asian Development Bank, Colombo Plan, G-77, the WTO, International Tin Council, OPEC, and other intergovernmental organizations. Indonesia became one of the founding members of ASEAN in 1967. In March 1970, a treaty of friendship was signed between Indonesia and Malaysia; the treaty also established the boundary between the two countries in the Strait of Malacca. Indonesia is a signatory to GATT and the Law of the Sea.

19ECONOMY

In colonial times Indonesia depended upon the export of a relatively small range of primary commodities. In the 17th and 18th centuries, the basis of the export-oriented economy was spices. In the 19th century, it shifted to sugar and coffee; in the 20th century, production of oil, tin, timber, and rubber has become fundamental. Despite export gains, however, subsistence agriculture, with rice as the chief crop, remains the principal occupation of the vast majority of Indonesians, and standards of living are low. Indonesia's record of economic growth and diversification is among the most successful in the developing world; but the 1998 political unrest and drought that contributed to a recession hit the country hard, severely depressing the economy and halting economic growth.

Indonesia is exceptionally rich in coal, oil, and other industrial raw materials, but industrial development has lagged in relation to the size of the population and the national income. In part, this was a consequence of expropriation policies carried out by Sukarno and of chronic inefficiency and corruption among government officials. After the 1964–66 political crisis, the government of President Suharto took steps to stabilize the economy. Exporters were allowed to keep a larger proportion of their foreign exchange earnings. The government also imposed strict controls on imports, encouraged foreign investment, returned many nationalized assets, ended nonproductive projects, and reduced government control of the economy. The inflation rate, which had been 635% in 1966 and 120% in 1967, fell to 85% in 1968 and further declined to 10% in 1971. National economic planning was used to guide economic growth. Under the 1969–74 plan, the government successfully introduced fiscal and credit restraints, rescheduled internal debts, returned expropriated properties, liberalized foreign investment laws, and actively sought assistance from overseas. Economic growth was set back by the near-collapse of Pertamina, the giant government-backed oil conglomerate, in 1975 and the financing of its $10.5 billion debt, but accelerated as rising oil prices increased revenues in the late 1970s. The economy was again severely strained in the early 1980s as falling oil prices forced the government to cut back on its spending plans. Legislation requiring majority participation of ethnic Indonesians (*pribumi*) in all enterprises formed since 1974 has also slowed foreign investment. Indonesia's obligation to reduce production of oil, its chief export, in line with OPEC agreements, together with the decline in non-oil export earnings brought about by the worldwide recession, severely strained the government's resources. In an effort to meet the nation's developmental needs, Suharto was forced to make the unpopular move, long advocated by the IBRD and IMF, of ending subsidies on food and reducing subsidies on kerosene and other fuels. He also announced new trade policies to spur exports in an effort to reverse the nation's worsening economic condition.

In the 1980s policies were designed to reduce restrictions on imports and to encourage foreign investment. In areas of trade, debt, and currency management, Indonesia took a pro-active stance that was internationally acknowledged by increasing foreign investment and endorsement by multilateral organizations. Efforts focused on bureaucratic reform and efficiency, incentives to private investors, and diversification of sources of foreign exchange earnings resulted in steady growth in the manufacturing sector and in industrial exports. Specific structural reforms were deregulation of foreign investment allowing broader ownership rights in export oriented manufacturing

sectors; and streamlining of the investment process, including the adjustment of procedural requirements; progressive reduction in tariffs and non-tariff barriers; major banking deregulation that opened the banking sector to foreign investment; privatization of the Jakarta Stock Exchange; the elimination of major subsidies and supports; and increasing participation of the private sector. The basis of recent Indonesian development still consists of small-holders (0.5 ha on average) in a rural-based economy with pockets of industry and large-scale mining and forestry, and a sizeable range of state-owned enterprises.

From 1989 to 1993 real GDP growth averaged 6.7%. Through restrictive monetary policy and a conservative fiscal stance the inflation rate remained under 10%. Export performance was strong, although in 1994 nonoil export growth showed signs of slowing down. While overall investment levels were high, the value of foreign investment projects outside the oil and gas and financial sectors declined. The government continued deregulation in order to stimulate growth but barriers to investment remained, such as inefficient procedures, overlapping jurisdictions, corruption, and inadequacies in the legal system and infrastructure. Indonesia altered its development philosophy away from import-substitution and toward a market-oriented approach, but struggled and ultimately failed to keep the economy from devaluing in the late 1990s. GDP grew an annual average of 7% during most of the 1990s, but contracted by approximately 14% in 1998. Inflation grew to 78%, compared to 10% in 1997; and the banking system collapsed. Although the picture was looking fairly grim in 1998, it improved moderately in 1999, but faltered again in 2000 as guerila warfare broke out and civil unrest caused the currency to depreciate further.

20INCOME

The US Central Intelligence Agency (CIA) reports that in 1998 Indonesia's gross domestic product (GDP) was estimated at $602 billion. The per capita GDP was estimated at $2,830. The annual growth rate of GDP was estimated at 13.7%. The average inflation rate in 1998 was 77%. The CIA defines GDP as the value of all final goods and services produced within a nation in a given year and computed on the basis of purchasing power parity (PPP) rather than value as measured on the basis of the rate of exchange. It was estimated that agriculture accounted for 18.8% of GDP, industry 40.3%, and services 40.9%.

The World Bank reports that for the same period per capita private consumption (in PPP terms) was $1,700. Private consumption includes expenditures of individuals, households, and nongovernmental organizations. It was estimated that between 1990 and 1998 private consumption grew at an annual rate of 7.6%. Approximately 47% of household consumption was spent on food, 6% on fuel, 5% on health care, and 14% on education. The richest 10% of the population accounted for approximately 30% of household consumption and the poorest 10% approximately 3.6%.

21LABOR

In 1998, the total employment including armed forces was 87,672,400. In 1997, 41% were engaged in agriculture; 19% in industry, and 40% in services. Women made up about 40% of the work force in 1998.

Skilled workers and trained management personnel are few, and labor productivity is low. Unemployment was estimated at 5.5% in 1998, but actual unemployment likely is much higher, and about half of the work force is underemployed. Problems faced by the government in creating jobs include a rate of population growth in excess of economic growth; a preponderance of workers under 25 years of age with little working experience; the uneven distribution of labor, which makes for labor shortages in the resource-rich outer islands; and low levels of vocational training. Labor-intensive projects, including irrigation, terracing, and reforestation, are given high priority by the government; training centers instruct rural workers in the use of automotive and other equipment needed by an emerging industrial society. Some of the larger industrial enterprises offer training programs and courses.

Before 1965, the labor movement was linked with nationalist movements, and unions were regarded as important political and revolutionary groups. SOBSI, the largest federation, was Communist-oriented and wielded great influence, not only because its membership was large but also because Indonesians identified it with anticolonialism and the struggle for independence. Following the upheavals of 1965, SOBSI was banned. Unions were replaced by government-backed labor organizations that must belong to the All-Indonesian Labor Federation in order to receive official recognition. A 1963 presidential decree prohibiting strikes in vital industries was repealed. There was a rash of strike activity in Surabaya in 1999 fueled by rising inflation and including a two-week strike by 25,000 workers in February.

There is no national minimum wage. Wages are set by area wage councils who estimate the amount a worker needs to earn to provide for his or her basic needs. In 1999 the minimum wage in Jakarta was $33 per month. However, many employers do not pay this wage, and it was estimated that in 1999 between 30 and 60% of the population received minimum wage.

The 40-hour workweek and a basic 7-hour day are standard throughout Indonesia. Under the labor accident law of 1951, in enterprises in which there are hazardous risks, an employer is liable for medical care and full or partial wages for workers injured on the job, as well as for burial expenses and compensation to dependents in the event of work-related death. In January 1978, a Government Social Insurance Program (ASTEK) providing accident insurance, life insurance, and retirement benefits was imposed on all large companies (those with more than 10 employees as of 1991), although in practice foreign companies (those with more than 10 employees as of 1991) are excluded.

22AGRICULTURE

About 41% of Indonesian workers are engaged in agriculture, which accounts for 18.8% of GDP in 1998. Some 31 million ha (76.6 million acres) are under cultivation, with 35% to 40% of the cultivated land devoted to the production of export crops. Some 60% of the country's cultivated land is in Java.

There are three main types of farming: smallholder farming (mostly rice), smallholder cash cropping, and about 1,800 large foreign-owned or privately owned estates, the latter two producing export crops. Small-scale farming is usually carried out on modest plots—those in Java average about 0.8–1 ha (2–2.5 acres)—often without benefit of modern tools and methods, good seed, or fertilizer. Although rice, vegetables, and fruit constitute the bulk of the small farmer's crops, about 20% of output is in cash crops for export, the chief of which is rubber. Of the estate-grown crops, rubber, tobacco, sugar, palm oil, hard fiber, coffee, tea, cocoa, and cinchona are the most important. Dutch, UK, US, French, and Belgian capital financed estate agriculture in colonial times, with the Dutch share being the largest. Management of Dutch interests was taken over by the Indonesian government in December 1957; in 1964, the 104 UK-operated plantations were confiscated without any compensation, and Indonesian managers were appointed. The following year, the US-operated plantations were expropriated, and all foreign plantations were placed under the control and supervision of the Indonesian government. In 1967, some of the estates seized in 1965, including the US-leased rubber plantations, were returned, but the majority were retained by the government.

Because the population is rapidly increasing, the government seeks to achieve food self-sufficiency through expansion of arable acreage, improved farm techniques (especially the use of fertilizers and improved seeds), extension of irrigation facilities, and expanded training for farmers. Production of rice, the staple food, has been gradually increasing, and production comes close to meeting domestic requirements. This increase has resulted less from extension of cultivated area through the government's resettlement policy than from expanded use of irrigation, fertilizers, and pesticides and cultivation of high-yielding hybrid rice, especially insect-resistant hybrids. It also reflects the success of the government's "mass guidance" program, which provides technical assistance, easy credit terms, and marketing support through a system of village cooperatives. Additional support was provided by the National Logistics Board, which is responsible for price regulation and the national rice-rationing programs. Due to the rapid growth of the industrial sector, the agricultural contribution to GDP is expected to decline to 11.8% by 2003.

Rice is the primary staple crop; production in 1998 totaled 48,472,000 tons. Other staple crops in 1998 included cassava (14,728,000 tons), corn (10,059,000 tons), and sweet potato (1,928,000 tons). Sugar is the largest commercial crop, with production reaching 27,500,000 tons in 1998. About 1,564,000 tons of rubber were produced in 1998, as compared with about 648,400 in 1964. Faced with the prospect of declining yields, the government began an extensive replanting and rehabilitation program in 1981. In 1998, Indonesia was the world's third largest producer of coffee (after Brazil and Colombia); some 455,000 tons of coffee were grown that year, as compared with 188,900 tons in 1972 and an annual average of 120,400 tons during 1960–65. Indonesia is the world's second-largest producer of palm oil (after Malaysia); 5.9 million tons were produced in 1998. Tobacco (138,000 tons in 1998) and copra (1.1 million tons) are also important export crops.

23ANIMAL HUSBANDRY

In 1998, the livestock population was 12,239,000 head of cattle, 15,198,000 goats, 8,151,000 sheep, 10,069,00 hogs and 740,000 horses. There are also about 3,145,000 buffalo in the country. The production of meat (about 2,077,000 tons in 1998) and cows' milk (434,000 tons) is secondary to the raising of draft animals for agricultural purposes and transportation. The government has established cattle-breeding stations and artificial-insemination centers to improve the stock and has been carrying on research to improve pastures. Technical and other assistance is also offered to chicken and duck farmers in an effort to increase protein supplies. There were an estimated 889 million chickens and 20 million ducks in 1998, when some 429,000 tons of eggs were produced. Local demand for animal products is constrained by low purchasing power, but increases in consumer income will raise demand for animal protein. Meat exports (primarily frogs' legs, poultry cuts, and meat products) totaled $142.7 million in 1997.

24FISHING

As Indonesia is the world's largest archipelago (13,667 islands), fish is a readily-available source of animal protein for domestic consumption. In 1997, the total catch was 4,577,310 tons, ranking Indonesia eighth in the world. Fishing is more important than statistics indicate, because the catch of many part-time fishermen never enters trade channels. Commercial fishing is confined to a narrow band of inshore waters, especially off northern Java, but other fishing also takes place along the coast, as well as in the rivers, lakes, coastal swamps, artificial ponds, and flooded rice fields. The government has stocked the inland waters, encouraged cooperatives to provide credit facilities, introduced improved fishing methods, provided for the use of motorized fishing boats and improved tackle, and built or rehabilitated piers. Fish and fish product exports had a value of $1,620,628,000 in 1997.

25 FORESTRY

Forests represent a potentially vast source of wealth in Indonesia. Of the 109.8 million ha (271.3 million acres) of forests, nearly three-fourths are in Kalimantan and eastern Indonesia. The more accessible forest areas of Sumatra and Kalimantan furnish the commercially cut timber for domestic consumption and export. Indonesia has over 4,000 species of trees, including 120 types of hardwood suitable for commercial use. Timber estates produce fast growth species such as pine, eucalyptus, albizia, and acacia for the pulp and paper industry. Practically all forestlands belong to the state. In Java, excessive cutting has caused soil erosion, aggravated floods, created water shortages, and damaged some irrigation facilities. Replanting and rehabilitation of the Javanese forests and reforestation in the Outer Islands are promoted as part of the nation's "regreening program." Teak and other tropical hardwoods are the most valuable species, but there is hope of obtaining wood pulp from pine and bamboo and commercial timber from new plantings of fir and pine.

Indonesia is the largest producer of tropical hardwood plywood in the world. Export sales of processed wood in 1997 amounted to $5.1 billion, representing 9.5% of all Indonesian exports. Production of lumber in 1997 totaled 203 million cu m; plywood, 9.6 million cu m; and particleboard, 440,000 cu m. About two-thirds of the timber output is exported. French, Japanese, US, and Philippine interests have large investments in the timber industry. Indonesia is the world's second largest producer of tropical hardwood logs and lumber, after Malaysia. Due to a hardwood log export ban enacted in 1985 to protect rapidly diminishing forests, Indonesia has exported no logs since then. Prohibitive export taxes imposed in 1990 have all but eliminated tropical hardwood exports, in order to conserve declining forest resources for production and export of higher value items such as plywood.

26 MINING

In addition to oil, of which Indonesia is one of the world's leading suppliers, the economically important mineral industry produces large quantities of tin and bauxite. In 1997, Indonesia was a major world producer of copper, nickel, and tin and a leading Southeast Asian producer of cement, bauxite, and nitrogen fertilizer. Indonesia supplied 40% of the world's traded steam coal, 30% of its tin, 11% of its nickel, 6% of copper, and 5% of gold. The chief deposits of tin are in Bangka, Belitung, and Singkep, three islands off the east coast of Sumatra. The state-owned tin producer, P.T. Tambang Timah, was listed on the London and Jakarta Stock Exchanges, and the state-owned general mining company, P.T. Aneka Tambang, has also gone public on the Jakarta Stock Exchange. Indonesia has 10.5% of the known world tin reserves. A tin-smelting plant began operations in Bangka in 1964, and by 1977, it was able to smelt all domestically produced tin ore. Indonesia possesses large deposits of high-grade bauxite; production, 648,000 tons in 1964, rose to 1,406,000 tons in 1991 before falling to 1,100,000 tons in 1997. The bauxite is produced at five mining localities on Sumatra. The output is exported primarily to Japan; the rest to the US.

The railroads use much of the low-grade coal mined in Indonesia. Coal production was 56,000,000 tons in 1997. Most coal is produced on Sumatra, but in 1982, contracts were signed to develop the coal resources of Kalimantan. Iron ore is found in sizable quantities but is not commercially exploited except in central Java; nickel is produced on Sulawesi and in the Maluku islands, with some of the largest reserves in the world. Copper production began at Tembagapura on Irian Jaya in 1974 and amounted to 529,121 tons by 1997. There are fair to good reserves of manganese, small amounts of gold and silver, numerous minor metals in small quantities, iodine, diamonds, phosphates, and considerable supplies of limestone, asphalt, clay, and kaolin. The search for other minerals is being actively pursued.

27 ENERGY AND POWER

Indonesia ranked among the world's leading petroleum-producing countries in 1998, with an estimated output of 1,518,000 barrels of oil daily, up from the 1.33 million barrels produced in 1988. Known reserves in 2000 were put at five billion barrels, and since most of the potential sources have not been surveyed, resources may be much larger. Sumatra, the richest oil area, produces about 70% of Indonesian oil. Kalimantan is the second-leading producer; Java and Madura have a scattering of smaller producing wells. Lesser amounts are also produced in Irian Jaya.

Before 1965, nearly 90% of Indonesia's petroleum was extracted by foreign companies and slightly more than 10% by state-owned companies. In March 1965, the government took over all foreign-owned oil companies, at the same time offering to allow the companies to continue operations under Indonesian control and supervision. The petroleum law of 1960 provided for foreign private enterprise to develop oil and related resources subject to contract agreements on a production-share basis. A public-sector enterprise, Pertamina, was set up to represent the government in all matters relating to the petroleum industry, including the negotiation and conclusion of contracts with foreign companies for exploration and production. Contracts have been signed with Pertamina by UK, US, Japanese, Australian, and French concerns; more than 60% of all exports go to Japan. By the mid-1970s, Pertamina had assumed a dominant role in oil exploration and production and in such related fields as petrochemicals, fertilizers, and natural gas. In late 1974, Pertamina began to encounter serious financial difficulties and by 1975 was found to have debts of $10.5 billion. This led to charges of corruption and a severe curtailment of its autonomy; as a result, Bank Indonesia was made the direct recipient of the national share in Pertamina's oil-export earnings. During the 1980s, Pertamina spent $3 billion per year on high-risk oil development projects, which helped to maintain a 20-year reserve level of oil and a 40-year reserve level of natural gas. In May 1993, reserves estimated at 225 million barrels were discovered (the largest find in Asia in a decade) at the Widuri field.

Natural gas production increased rapidly in the 1970s and 1980s, with output totaling 63.4 billion cu m by 1998, as compared with 19.9 billion cu m in 1982. Part of production goes for industrial and domestic use, but large amounts are exported in the form of liquefied natural gas. Indonesia is the world's largest exporter of LNG; its major customers are Japan, the ROK, and Taiwan.

Power facilities are overtaxed, despite heavy government investment in electrical installations. Net installed capacity in 1998 was 19,890,000 kW, as compared with 10,830,000 kW in 1988. Production totaled 73,130 million kWh in 1998, up from 2,932 kWh in 1973. The nation's first geothermal electric power station was inaugurated in 1974 in West Java, and a 750-MW hydroelectric plant was completed there in 1985. In 1995, P. T. Perusahaan Listrik Negara (PLN), the state-owned electric company, projected that electricity demand will rise by 14% annually, with a generating capacity at 25,000–30,000 million kW needed by 2010.

28INDUSTRY

Industrial expansion is given a high priority in development plans. Labor-intensive industries are stressed, together with industries producing consumer items for domestic consumption and export and products accelerating agricultural development. A large integrated industrialization project on Batam Island in the Malacca Strait was designed to attract trade and industries away from crowded Singapore, 20 km (12.5 mi) away. The Batam industrial park is a 485 ha facility that began operation in 1991. Ownership is shared between a state-owned company from Singapore and two private Indonesian firms. Petroleum, wood, sugar, rubber, tea, coconuts, palm kernels, sisal, kapok, rice, and cassava are among Indonesia's primary products. Secondary industries produce consumer goods such as tires and tubes, rubber shoes, radios, batteries, soap, margarine, cigarettes, light bulbs, textiles, glass, paper, tractors, and trucks. Other industries established in recent decades include a modern steel plant at Cilegon (in northwest Java), plywood factories, cement works, spinning mills, knitting plants, iron works, copper and other foundries, a ceramics plant, a leather-goods plant, and a glass factory, as well as facilities for automobile assembly, shipbuilding, and the manufacture of petrochemicals and urea fertilizers.

Despite the new industries, overall industrial growth has been small since World War II with agriculture the dominant sector of the Indonesian economy. However, during the 1990s, manufacturing took over as the dominant sector, with the highest growth rate (10%). Coal production reached 70 million tons per year by 1999. Steel production increased, and Indonesia also produced large amounts of fertilizer, cement, paper, cloth, yarn, and plywood. The chemical industry experienced an annual growth rate of 13% prior to 1993; and after 1997, the depreciation of the currency encouraged chemical production for the export market. In the consumer goods manufacturing sector, activities are run primarily by private enterprise. All oil and natural gas processing have historically been controlled by government enterprises, as have been other major heavy industries, such as basic metals, cement, paper products, fertilizer, and transport equipment. After the recession in 1998, the government proposed liberalizing heavy industry. Of the 168 parastatals, 140 were scheduled for privatization.

During the 1990s, Indonesia's eight oil refineries, all owned by the state company Pertamina, produced about one million barrels of refined petroleum per day, contributing 9% of the GDP in 1999. In 1997, the fuel sector contributed about 20% to Indonesia's foreign exchange earnings and a waning amount of government tax revenues. Prior to 1997, these sectors accounted for nearly 80% of exports and 70% of government revenues. Natural gas production has steadily increased, and may take over from petroleum as a major source of export revenue. Natural gas proven reserves will last 40 years at current production rates, which reached 180,000 barrels per day in 1999.

In July 1992 non-tariff barriers were reduced and key industries were deregulated to allow free importation of essential manufacturing inputs. There is a shortage of skilled technical personnel to support high-tech industries; most technology has been imported through joint ventures. The agency for Strategic Industries (BPIS), a state-owned holding company including aircraft, telecommunications and high-technology industries, formed a joint venture with a major foreign multinational technology corporation to promote technology transfer to Indonesia. Most industrial enterprises were negatively affected by the 1998 recession, with an overall decline of at least 15%. The Indonesian Bank Restructuring Agency (IBRA) took over the majority of Indonesia's non-performing industrial assets in 2000 with plans to sell, including: cement factories, mining facilities, manufacturing plants, food processing firms, plywood production plants, vehicle assembly lines, chemical plants, property, and agribusinesses.

29SCIENCE AND TECHNOLOGY

Like many developing nations, Indonesia has a shortage of scientific personnel and engineers. The Indonesian Institute of Sciences, a government agency established in 1967, has centers for research and development in biology; oceanology; geotechnology; applied physics and applied chemistry; metallurgy; limnology; biotechnology; electricity and electrical engineering; information and computer sciences; telecommunication, strategic electronics, component and material sciences; and calibration, instrumentation, and metrology. The country has 45 other research institutes concerned with agriculture and veterinary science, medicine, the natural sciences, and technology. Courses in basic and applied sciences are offered at 53 state and private universities. At a more basic level, Agricultural Training Center programs provide workshops throughout Indonesia to acquaint rural workers with the use of plumbing and automotive equipment, small engines, electric tools, and chain saws, and to familiarize farmers with the use of modern hybrid seeds, pesticides, and fertilizers. In 1987–97, total expenditures for research and development amounted to 0.07% of GDP; 182 scientists and engineers per million population were engaged in research and development. During the same period, science and engineering students accounted for 39% of all college and university students. In 1998, high-tech exports were valued at $2.1 billion and accounted for 10% of manufactured exports.

30DOMESTIC TRADE

Jakarta, the capital and chief commercial city, is Indonesia's main distribution center. The principal business houses, shipping and transportation firms, and service agencies have their main offices there and branches in other cities. Since the end of World War II, the government has sought to channel trade and business activities into Indonesian hands by a policy of granting special privileges to Indonesian firms—including export license monopolies, sole agency rights, and exclusive licenses to import and sell specific goods—and of making government purchases through Indonesians. Indonesians have been moving into every sector of marketing operations, particularly in the import business. In an attempt to break the Chinese grip on the rural economy and develop indigenous trade, regulations were adopted late in 1959 barring alien traders from operating in rural areas after 1 January 1960 and calling for the evacuation of aliens from rural areas in western Java to larger cities; about 300,000 Chinese merchants were affected. Laws passed in 1974 required majority ethnic Indonesian participation in all economic ventures. In 1994, most requirements for domestic equity and joint ventures were removed.

Commercial business hours vary, but many are the same as those in government offices—usually 8 AM to 3 PM. Retail stores and some other businesses are open from 8 AM to 4 PM. Some shops are open from 9 AM to 8 PM. Offices and most businesses close at 11 AM on Fridays and 1 or 2 PM on Saturdays. Local banks transact business from 8 AM to 1 PM and 2 to 3 PM, Monday through Friday, and 8 to 11 AM on Saturdays. Newspapers, magazines, posters, and billboards are the most popular advertising media. English is widely used in business and government. There is little advertising by mail, and none at all on radio or television.

31 FOREIGN TRADE

Trade balances in the post World War II period have invariably been favorable. Trade liberalization began in 1982 as an effort to increase nonoil exports. By 1987, nonoil exports matched revenue from oil and gas exports for the first time. Imports, which are closely regulated in government efforts to restrain growth of merchandise imports, consist mainly of machinery and raw materials, indicating a reliance on imports to support industrialization. Discrepancies in trade figures are common and reflect widespread smuggling and corruption of customs and government officials. The late 1990s revealed shrinking exports of plywood, and slow growth in exports of garments and textiles. Emerging exports such as footwear and consumer electronics also showed weak growth. However, rising world prices for oil (except in 1997 and 1998), rubber, and other commodities kept these exports high. The surge in nonoil imports owes much to the demand for consumer goods. In 1998, Indonesia was the world's largest rice importer due to drought, and imported little else. Economic, political, and social crisis was accompanied by a small leap in exports due to currency depreciation, but earnings in the nonoil sector remained low nonetheless.

In the 1970s, Japan became Indonesia's dominant trade partner taking over 41% of Indonesia's exports (mainly petroleum) and supplying over 25% of its imports. Although Japan remains the dominant trade partner, other trade partners have become important to the economy including the US, Singapore, and China. Trade with the Netherlands, which was of primary importance in colonial times, has decreased since 1957. With the creation in 1992 of the ASEAN Free Trade Area (AFTA) intraregional trade has increased.

Indonesia puts out a large amount of crude petroleum (12%) and gas (9.0% of country exports, and 11% of world exports) into its commodities export market. Other exports include plywood (9.3%), shoes (4.5%), and natural rubber (3.8%), with substantial percentages of the world market in those categories (28%, 5.9%, and 26%, respectively).

In 1997 Indonesia's imports were distributed among the following categories:

Consumer goods	2.4%
Food	6.4%
Fuels	9.5%
Industrial supplies	38.8%
Machinery	33.1%
Transportation	9.6%
Other	0.2%

Principal trading partners in 1998 (in millions of US dollars) were as follows:

COUNTRY	EXPORTS	IMPORTS	BALANCE
Japan	9,600	4,729	4,871
United States	8,583	2,520	6,063
Singapore	5,865	3,743	2,122
China (inc. Hong Kong)	4,143	1,862	2,281
Korea	2,838	1,963	875
Australia	2,090	1,476	614
Germany	1,878	2,089	-211
Taiwan	1,845	1,154	691
Malaysia	1,443	1,110	333
United Kingdom	1,359	695	664

32 BALANCE OF PAYMENTS

Indonesia has had persistent balance-of-payments difficulties since independence. Typically, surpluses on merchandise trade have been achieved by restricting imports, but these surpluses have not provided sufficient exchange for debt repayments or for other invisibles, such as profit remittances on foreign investment and interest payments on government loans from abroad. Indonesia's payments position brightened considerably in the late 1970s as a result of a rapid increase in oil prices mandated by OPEC. However, expansion of the nonoil export industries failed to keep pace with burgeoning import requirements for some consumer goods and machinery, equipment, and spare parts for development programs. The current account deficit averaged -2% of GDP between 1992 and 1997, but accrued a surplus of over 4% of GDP in 1998 due to currency devaluation and a cut in imports of one-third.

The US Central Intelligence Agency reports that in 1998 the purchasing power parity of Indonesia's exports was $49 billion while imports totaled $24 billion resulting in a trade balance of $25 billion.

The International Monetary Fund (IMF) reports that in 1998 Indonesia had exports of goods totaling $50,371 million and imports totaling $31,942 million. The services credit totaled $4,479 million and debit $11,813 million. The following table summarizes Indonesia's balance of payments as reported by the IMF for 1998 in millions of US dollars.

Current Account		3,972
Balance on goods	18,429	
Balance on services	-7,334	
Balance on income	-8,212	
Current transfers	1,089	
Capital Account		...
Financial Account		-10,347
Direct investment abroad	-44	
Direct investment in Indonesia	-356	
Portfolio investment assets	...	
Portfolio investment liabilities	-2,002	
Other investment assets	...	
Other investment liabilities	-7,945	
Net Errors and Omissions		2,727
Reserves and Related Items		3,648

33 BANKING AND SECURITIES

The government's Bank Negara Indonesia (BNI) was established in 1953 as the successor to the Java Bank. In 1965, all state banks with the exception of State Trading Bank were incorporated into the BNI as separate units. In 1969, this policy was reversed, and the state banks were again reorganized as individual banks. In 1967, as part of the new regime's policy of encouraging foreign investment, foreign banks were permitted to operate in Indonesia, on condition that they invested at least $1 million, of which at least $500,000 had to be brought into the country. The law also provided that foreign banks were to appoint Indonesian banks as their correspondents for any dealings outside Jakarta. The Indonesian banking system transformed after 1980, through a process of gradual but steady reform, which culminated in the 1992 banking law. Joint-ventures were allowed with Indonesian partners. The partial liberalization of the banking industry had a dramatic impact. One result was a sharp deterioration of the banking system's asset quality. The precipitous growth in bank credits threatened to undermine economic stability by stimulating a sharp increase in import demand and inflationary pressures. Responding to this threat, the government initiated an abrupt tightening of monetary policy during the 1990s. From 1992 until 1997, the rupiah was managed in relation to the dollar, but in 1997, the currency was allowed to float because of Asian currency depreciation. Unfortunately, political and social unrest resulted in a highly volatile currency. The 1998 economic failure brought about a major restructuring of the banking system which was literally bankrupted. State-owned banks held $80 billion in corporate debts and more than two-thirds of their loans were non-performing in 1999. The Bank of Indonesia alone faced a deficit of over $4.1 billion in 2000.

Bank Indonesia, as the central bank, is responsible for the administration and regulation of the four state banks and other banking operations. Among the state banks, Bank Rakjat Indonesia specializes in credits to agricultural cooperative societies but also provides fishing and rural credit in general. Bank Tabungan Negara promotes savings among the general public. Bank Negara Indonesia (BNI) provides funding for industry. After the financial crash in 1999, four of the state banks were merged into the new Bank Mandiri; including the Bank Bumi Daya, Bank Dagang Negara, Bank Ekspor Impor, and BAPINDO. Bank Bumi Daya provided credits to estates and forestry operations; Bank Dagang Negara provided credits to the mining sector; and Bank Ekspor Impor Indonesia specialized in credits for the production, processing, and marketing of export products, and the Development Bank of Indonesia (Bank Pembangunan Indonesia—or BAPINDO) provided financial assistance to government enterprises and approved new industries. There were 128 private domestic commercial banks in 1998; 38 of them were liquidated in 1999, eight of them were taken over by the government, eight of them were able to function with government aid, and 71 private banks were able to continue without assistance. Two joint-venture banks closed, out of a total of 32 jointly-owned banks. Foreign investment in the banking system is now allowed up to 99%.

Indonesia's first stock exchange was established in December 1912 in Jakarta, although both this and two subsequent exchanges established in Surabaya and Semarang in 1925 were shut down during the Japanese occupation. An attempt to revive the capital markets in the early 1950s proved futile, and it was not until August 1977 that the Jakarta Stock Exchange (JSE) was successfully relaunched amid a comprehensive set of institutional reforms that resulted in the establishment of the Capital Market Executive Agency (Badan Pelaksana Pasar Modal—BAPEPAM) to manage the market, as well as a state-owned securities firm, Danareksa, to facilitate the flotation of shares. After sinking to 276 in the fall of 1998, the JSI rose from just below 500 in early 1999 to above 700 in mid-1999, but was back down to 508 in mid-2000.

34INSURANCE

The insurance and reinsurance industry is governed by an insurance law issued in February 1992 that allows foreign ownership of insurance companies; and is regulated by the Ministry of Finance. The growth of the industry over the past decade is reflected in an impressive increase in many of the industry's financial variables, including assets, gross premiums, and investments. Third party motor liability insurance is compulsory. A 1998 Financial Services Agreement with the WTO equalized capital requirements for both domestic and foreign insurance firms.

35PUBLIC FINANCE

Government expenditures (including capital expenditures) have outrun public income by a considerable margin each year since 1952, and this cash deficit has been met by foreign aid receipts. Since 1985, however, Indonesia has discouraged public sector and monetary growth, resulting in an overall budgetary surplus in 1991/92, despite a significant drop in oil revenues from falling prices. In 1998, the government deficit reached over 3% of GDP, partially because of subsidized rice imports and investment in the failing banking sector.

The US Central Intelligence Agency (CIA) estimates that in 1998 Indonesia's central government took in revenues of approximately $35 billion and had expenditures of $35 billion including capital expenditures of $12 billion. External debt totaled $145 billion.

The following table shows an itemized breakdown of government revenues and expenditures. The percentages were calculated from data reported by the International Monetary Fund. The dollar amounts (millions) are based on the CIA estimates provided above.

REVENUE AND GRANTS	100%	35,000
Tax revenue	93.1%	32,571
Non-tax revenue	6.9%	2,422
Capital revenue	0.0%	7
EXPENDITURES	100%	35,000
General public services	10.6%	3,723
Defense	5.3%	1,849
Public order and safety	1.8%	642
Education	6.9%	2,409
Health	2.3%	801
Social security	5.0%	1,754
Housing and community amenities	13.9%	4,854
Recreation, cultural, and religious affairs	2.0%	708
Economic affairs and services	12.7%	4,430
Other expenditures	24.9%	8,713
Interest payments	14.6%	5,117

36TAXATION

Taxes on oil companies are the largest single source of central government income. Under the general corporation rate, corporate income up to Rp25 million is taxed at 10%, income between Rp25 million and Rp50 million is taxed at 15%, and income exceeding Rp50 million is taxed at 30%. A 20% withholding tax is payable on branch profits after corporate tax. However, concessional rates are available for tax treaty countries. Special corporation taxes, with generous depreciation and other deductions from taxable income, cover petroleum, mining, shipping, airline, and insurance companies. Individual incomes are taxed at the same rate as those of corporations. An eight-year carried-forward loss for investment in eastern Indonesia is allowed. Indirect taxes include a VAT, which will replace the sales tax after 2000, and excise taxes on luxury goods.

37CUSTOMS AND DUTIES

Most tariffs are designed to stimulate exports and to protect infant domestic industries. However, the tariff system is burdensome and time-consuming, and evasion is widespread. Exempt from import duties are raw materials and manufactured items imported for use in government-backed or approved labor-intensive enterprises. Duties on imports from ASEAN member countries were lowered to 20% in 1978. Two years later, duties on 384 products—including cement, sarongs, engine pistons, cameras, and telecommunications equipment—were reduced or abandoned, regardless of origin. Many items may only be imported by government-approved importers, and there are quotas for certain nondurable goods. An import sales tax is imposed on imports at point of entry (except for those goods considered essential by the government) at rates of 5–30%. Duties usually range between 10–40%, except for inessential goods, which generally range between 0% and 170%. Distilled spirits are dutied at a rate of 170%, and vehicle taxes range from 5% for trucks up to 80% for some sedans. There is a free trade zone on Batam Island that is exempt from all import and export taxes, and a number of other EPZ's. A May 1995 tariff reform package hopes to reduce import duties and taxes to 10% by 2003.

38FOREIGN INVESTMENT

Foreign investments have played a key role in the Indonesian economy since the turn of the 20th century. The Dutch were for decades the principal foreign investors in Indonesia, involving themselves heavily in the production of sugar, cinchona, coffee, tobacco, rubber, and oil. UK investments were in oil, rubber, and manufacturing. Rubber estates, particularly those in northern Sumatra, were operated by Belgian, UK, Danish, French, Norwegian, Swiss, and US individuals and companies. In the dispute with the Netherlands over Irian Jaya, the Indonesian government took over Dutch enterprises in the country and seized Dutch assets. Although Indonesians recognized that foreign capital was needed to develop their economy, government policies were ambiguous and hesitant throughout the 1950s and early 1960s. The foreign investment law of 1958 attempted to provide certain guarantees to foreign investors and to establish safeguards for Indonesian interests. At the same time, the government guaranteed some foreign-owned industrial enterprises that they would not be expropriated by the state or nationalized for a maximum period of 20 or, in the case of large agricultural enterprises, 30 years. In November 1964, the government began to reverse this policy by nationalizing all British-owned commercial enterprises and placing them under direct Indonesian management and control. A decree of 25 February 1965 nationalized all US-owned rubber plantations in northern Sumatra, and another decree of 19 March placed three oil companies—two of them US companies—under the supervision and control of the government. Finally, on 24 April 1965, President Sukarno ordered the seizure of all remaining foreign property in Indonesia. This policy was again reversed after the ouster of Sukarno.

During 1967–70, the confiscated estates were gradually returned to their former owners (except in cases where the owner opted to accept compensation). The Foreign Capital Investment Law of 1967 governed foreign direct investment. The overall flow of private investments from overseas sources increased during the early 1970s, in response both to liberal terms offered under the Suharto government and to favorable world markets for Indonesian oil and other primary products. The annual flow of foreign investment funds approved by the government increased from $333 million in 1972 to $521 million in 1973 and to $1,050 million in 1974. Some 65 US firms invested more than $1 billion in petroleum enterprises during 1967–74, accounting for about 90% of the country's total production; in 1975 alone, an additional $1.2 billion was spent in the oil sector by US interests. During 1967–85, Japanese investments led all others in nonoil sectors, totaling $3.9 billion; US investors were second, supplying $1.4 billion. In all, between 1967 and 1980, a total of $8 billion was invested by foreign companies, of which $6.6 billion was in the petroleum sector. Between 1982 and 1985, direct foreign investment averaged $242.3 million annually. Since 1973, all foreign investment has been channeled through the Investment Coordinating Board (BKPM), and Indonesian partners were mandated for all foreign concerns established after 1974. Among the incentives for investment approved in 1986 were regulations allowing foreign investment in more industries (arms production is still prohibited) and granting foreign partners in joint ventures the right to distribute the products themselves. The Negative Investment List, 1989 and as amended in 2000, specifies the business areas that are closed to, or impose limitations on, foreign investors.

Between 1967 and 1992, more than 1,590 manufacturing projects involving $59 billion in foreign investment were approved by the BKPM. Japan was a major investor accounting for 21% of the total, along with Hong Kong (9%), and Taiwan (7%). Foreign investment in manufacturing in Indonesia has been facilitated by the rising cost of labor and inputs in other Asian countries, incentives offered by Indonesia, easing of restrictions, and the streamlining of investment procedures. In 1993 new regulations on the requirements for share ownership in companies invested with foreign capital amended the 1967

Foreign Capital Investment Law, as well as streamlining the investment approval process, and reducing import tariffs on various goods. A new deregulation package approved in June 1994 further increased incentives for foreign investment by allowing 5% to 51% foreign ownership in infrastructure (harbors, electricity, telecommunications, shipping airlines, railways, and water supply). New foreign investment approvals for 1992 to 1998 were estimated at a total of $160 billion. From 1967 to 1998, Japan received approval for investments in Indonesia totaling approximately $35 billion; the UK, $24 billion; Singapore, $18 billion; and Hong Kong, $14 billion. In 1998 and 1999, new regulations paved the way for increased foreign investment; including concessions to foreign interests in distribution and the financial sector, tax concessions, and simplification of the licensing process. Sectors that remain closed to foreign investment include freshwater fishing, forestry, public transport, broadcasting and film, and medical clinics. More than one-third of the investment since 1967 has been in the chemicals industry, followed by mining, and natural gas.

[39]ECONOMIC DEVELOPMENT

From the late 1960s through the mid-1980s, the Suharto government focused its efforts on financial stabilization, relying heavily on advice and assistance from multilateral aid donors. The results were mixed. The fiscal crisis threatened by the accumulated debts of the Sukarno years was averted through debt rescheduling and improved economic management; nevertheless, the depth of Indonesia's continuing reliance on foreign aid remained apparent through the mid-1980s. Efforts to develop capital-intensive import-substitution industries afforded only marginal benefits to the vast majority of Indonesians. Public expenditures on the first five-year plan (1956–60) included 25% for mining and manufacturing, 25% for transport and communications, 15% for power projects, and 35% for all other categories. A new eight-year development plan was launched in January 1961. Funds were allocated for key "A" projects; including 25% for transport and communications, 22% for industry, 13% for special projects including the military, 12% for clothing, and 11% for food. Eight "B" projects (petroleum, rubber, tin, and forestry) were to supply the financing for the "A" projects. Because of the lack of foreign financing, upon which most of the "B" projects depended, all "A" and some "B" projects were suspended in November 1964. For the period 1965–68, economic rehabilitation took precedence over development, and all official projects were evaluated on purely economic lines. A subsequent plan (1969–74) placed emphasis on the development of agriculture. Aid to industries was encouraged for activities that support agricultural development, such as the production of fertilizers, cement, agricultural equipment, and machinery for processing agricultural products. Assistance was also given to such import-substitution industries as textiles, paper, rubber tires, and housing materials. The 1975–79 plan represented a shift from stabilizing policies to stepped-up development. The plan placed considerable focus on the rural economy, stressing labor-intensive industries along with improved provision of housing and education. In the program to aid farmers in increasing their output and marketing their commodities, emphasis was placed on encouraging farmers' cooperatives and banks. Labor unions were encouraged to help improve the lot of plantation and industrial workers.

Efforts to restructure the economy in the 1980s resulted in an expansion of real GDP 6% annually on average. The 1979–84 development plan, called Repelita III, emphasized the "development trilogy" of economic growth, equity, and national stability. Top priorities were tourism and communication (15%), agriculture and irrigation (14%), mining and energy (13%), education (10%), and regional and local development (10%).

The 1984–89 five-year plan, called Repelita IV, emphasized industry (9.5% growth rate), agriculture (3%), petroleum and mining (2.5%), transportation and communications (5.2%), and construction (5%). However, low oil prices caused the government to reduce its goals and to promote private and foreign investment. Repelita V, 1989–94 emphasized industry (8.5% growth rate), agriculture (3.6%), petroleum and mining (4.2%), trade (6%), transportation and communications (6.4%), and construction (6%). The development of mining and energy were prioritized, as well as certain areas of manufacturing, forestry, agriculture, transportation, communications, and tourism. The Sixth Five-Year Development Plan (1994–99), Repelita VI, forecast an annual average GDP growth rate of 6.2%, and estimated that per capita income would reach $1000 by 1999. The plan focused on the privatization of a number of industries, and the gradual opening up of foreign investment. These goals were met by 1997, but the 1998 breakdown of the economy prompted international aid agencies to step in.

The most important economic development policy before privatization and liberalization was outlined in the 1988 Guidelines of State Policy. This document introduced Transmigration Development; a policy aimed at overcoming uneven population distribution in Indonesia. The policy had multiple objectives: to ease the burden of densely populated regions, to upgrade regional development, to expand job opportunities, to support national unity, and to strengthen national defense. Transmigration in densely populated areas such as Java, Bali and West Tenggara aimed to increase population productivity and decrease environmental hazards. Transmigration in sparsely populated regions such as Sumatra, Kalimantan, Sulawesi, Maluku, Irian Jaya, and East Timor, aimed to increase productivity of natural resources, as well as increase employment and job opportunities. Declining extent of land ownership by farmers was a major problem in both densely and sparsely populated areas. These activities are overseen by the Coordinating Body for the Implementation of Transmigration (BAKOPTRANS). Forestry statistics from 1985 showed that some 30 million ha of forest land in sparsely populated areas could be converted to agricultural uses. Agriculture was an important sector for development in the transmigration policy. As new areas opened more employment opportunities were predicted to be available. Productive land use included, fisheries, industry, services and industrial forest products. In Repelita V the transmigration target was to relocate 550,000 families into new settlement areas outside of Java and Bali. The third year of Repelita V (1991/92) targeted 70,000 families for transmigration, including 28,240 families of public transmigration and 41,760 families of self-initiated transmigration. In fact 64,211 families (91.7%) were resettled, consisting of 25,720 families of public transmigration and 38,491 families of self-initiated transmigration.

Major obstacles to the implementation of the policy continued to delay the preparation of the settlements in the destination areas and at the places of origin during assembly and departure of transmigrants. Agricultural lassitude was one indicator of the program's failure. In 1991/92 rice production was about the same as the previous year, but compared to the national production rate per hectare, production was considered low. The production rate of nuts, bean crops, and cassava declined during the same time periods, and while coconut plantations increased, coffee and clove estates decreased by about 30%. The increase of large and medium livestock was minor, while poultry numbers declined by 21%.

Bilateral and multinational assistance has played a major role in Indonesia's development. Before 1965, Indonesia received substantial aid from the USSR and other Communist states; such funding included some $750 million in economic credits and more than $1 billion in military aid. Since 1966, the foreign-aid pattern has turned dramatically toward the West. A group of nations (including the US, Netherlands, Japan, Belgium, France, FRG, Italy, UK, Switzerland, Canada, and New Zealand) and organizations (including the IBRD and Asian Development Bank) have joined to form the Inter-Governmental Group on Indonesia (IGGI) as a major funnel for aid. Total IGGI assistance was estimated at $2.5 billion for 1985/86. During the 1970s and early 1980s, the IMF took a central part in reorganizing Indonesia's financial structure and planning methods. At the Indonesian government's invitation, the IMF has also evaluated the country's economic programs for the purpose of advising donor nations. More recently, the IMF expanded its role by advising the government on planning and foreign-aid allocation. In November 1991, in reaction to the Indonesian army's shootings of demonstrators in Dili, East Timor; the Netherlands, Denmark, and Canada suspended aid to Indonesia. In a blanket refusal to link foreign assistance to human rights issues, the government announced it would decline all future aid from the Netherlands. The Government also requested that the IGGI be disbanded and replaced by the Consultative Group of Indonesia (CGI) formed by the World Bank and comprised of 18 donor countries (Australia, Austria, Belgium, Canada, Denmark, Finland, France, Germany, Italy, Japan, New Zealand, Norway, South Korea, Spain, Sweden, Switzerland, the UK, and the US) and 12 multilateral agencies. An IMF-funded program that began in 1997 offered a total of $12.5 billion to Indonesia over a period of three years to support the financial system and aid in the restructuring of the economy. The total international aid package was projected at a total of over $40 billion by 1999.

40 SOCIAL DEVELOPMENT

The constitution enjoins the government to protect the family and to provide for the needs of the "poor and the waifs," but implementation of these principles has proceeded slowly because of the cost and the lack of professional personnel to put into effect a broad welfare program. Various government departments are responsible for welfare activities: juvenile delinquents are under the care of the Ministry of Justice; child care and maternal health programs are part of the public health program; the Ministry of Labor has responsibility for enforcement of labor welfare legislation; and the Ministry of Social Affairs is concerned with narcotics traffic, exploitation of women and children, prostitution, and people unable to provide for themselves (particularly demobilized soldiers). There is nothing approximating a general public-assistance program in the Western sense, but the society is one in which family and clan relationships run strong. Some social security provisions exist. Firms with 10 or more employees or a payroll of one million rupiah or more a month paid 3.7% of their payroll (and employees paid 2% of earnings) for retirement, disability, and survivor benefits in 1999, and coverage was gradually being extended to smaller companies and casual workers. Employers pay 6% of payroll for married employees (3% for single employees) to provide sickness and maternity benefits, and both employers and employees fund a workers' compensation program. In addition, many orphanages, homes for the aged, youth activities, and private volunteer organizations meet special needs, in some cases receiving government subsidies.

Women are accorded the same legal rights as men and they enjoy a more favorable position in Indonesia than is customary in Muslim societies. This situation is largely the result of the work of Princess Raden Ajeng Kartini at the turn of the century in promoting the development of Javanese women. The movement for the emancipation of women preceded the nationalist movement by at least 10 years. Improvement of the status of women was specifically included in the guidelines for the 1979–

84 national economic plan. A Ministry of Women's Affairs was created to promote the economic and social welfare of women.

In spite of women's official equality, in practice they often find it hard to exercise their legal rights. Although they constitute roughly one quarter of the civil service, they occupy very few of its top posts. In 1999, only 40 of 500 members of parliament were women. In 1999 Megawati Sukarnoputri was elected the country's first female vice president.

The economic crisis of the late 1990s took a toll on the welfare of the nation's children; infant mortality nearly doubled between 1995 and 1998. As of 1999, UNICEF estimated that eight million pre-school-age children suffered from malnutrition.

Ethnic Chinese face considerable discrimination. There are restrictions on the rights of noncitizen Chinese to operate and own businesses. It is illegal to import Chinese language publications and the celebration of Chinese New Year is prohibited by law. The country's economic downturn led to a wave of attacks on Chinese-owned businesses in 1998.

Gross violations of human rights in the former Portuguese colony of East Timor continued in 1999, including violence by pro-integration militias following a referendum in which a majority of Timorese voted for autonomy. Over 250,000 civilians fled the region in September to escape a wave of violence in which hundreds died. With the liberalization of Indonesia's government, human rights abuses decreased overall, although serious problems remained.

41HEALTH

The Ministry of Health places emphasis on preventive work, while private initiative is encouraged in the curative field. Only 1% of the GDP goes to public health expenditures (1990–95). National health programs, of which family planning is an important part, stress the building of small and healthy families. Eradication of contagious diseases focuses on malaria, rabies, elephantiasis, tuberculosis, cholera, and leprosy. Filariasis in Indonesia is widely distributed. This tropical disease is endemic in remote rural areas. The World Health Organization reported cholera active in Indonesia. Malaria is also endemic to the country; in 1994 there were 140,559 cases of malaria. The incidence of the disease was 729 per 100,000 population in 1996. There were also 49,647 cases of tuberculosis; 12 in every 100,000 people were infected in 1996. Overcrowded cities, poor sanitation, impure water supplies, substandard urban housing, and dietary deficiencies are contributing factors to health problems. In 1994–95, only 63% of the population had access to safe water, and 55% had adequate sanitation.

Average life expectancy in 1999 was 63 years for men and women. The 1999 infant mortality rate was 57 per 1,000 live births, and the overall death rate was 8 per 1,000 in the same year. The maternal mortality rate was 205 deaths per 100,000 live births in 1994–95. Malnutrition was present in 39% of all children under 5 years from 1989–95. As of September 1995 WHO reported 130,988 deaths of children under 5 from diarrheal diseases. The estimated goiter rate was 27.7 per 100 school-age children in 1996.

Indonesia has received much help from the UN, particularly through WHO and UNICEF, in solving health problems. The Ministry of Health is seeking to build up a health service, starting at the village level with a hygiene officer, who is an official of the village, and working up through groups of villages, with more facilities and better trained personnel, to the regional doctor, who directs the curative and preventive work.

In 1990, there were 25,752 doctors, 98,842 nurses, and 6,689 midwives. In 1994, there was one doctor per 5,959 people. More than one-third of the country's doctors practice in Jakarta and other big cities. In 1990–95, 80% of the population had access to

health care services. Tobacco consumption has increased from 1.4 kg in 1984–86 to 1.6 kg a year per adult in 1995.

In 1991, Indonesia had 1,552 hospitals, with about 120,711 beds (one bed per 1,515 people in 1994). In addition, there were 5,656 public health centers. Expenditures by the government on health care facilities accounted for just 1% of total development expenditures in 1990–91.

Indonesia's 1999 birth rate was 23 per 1,000 people. About 48% of married women (ages 15 to 49) were using contraception in 1994. A total of 40% of all Indonesian children under 5 were underweight in the years 1990–95.

Immunization rates for 1997 for children up to one year of age were as follows: tuberculosis (100%); diphtheria, pertussis, and tetanus (91%); polio (90%); and measles (92%). In 1995 the government paid 100% of the entire vaccine bill.

The HIV-1 seroprevalence was 0.1 per 100 adults in 1997. In 1996, 95 new cases of AIDS were reported.

42HOUSING

Housing is an acute problem in both urban and rural areas. In the rural areas, housing falls below even the most modest standards. In the 1970s, about one-fifth of the country's housing consisted of one-room dwellings; in the countryside, most had no electricity. Overall, only 12% of all Indonesians had access to safe water in the early 1980s. Recent estimates indicate that 55% of all households received their drinking water from wells, 13% from springs, 13% from pipes, 9% from air pumps, and 6% from rivers. Lighting was provided to 45% of all households by kerosene lamps, 44% by electricity, and 11% by pressure lamp. Roughly 43% of dwellings had private toilet facilities.

Under the 1970–75 plan, the government left construction of housing to private initiative and restricted itself to activities designed to stimulate house construction, such as town planning and the provision of water supplies and sanitation. The 1975–79 and 1979–84 plans included government construction of housing. The 1984–89 plan had a target of 300,000 units, of which 140,000 were to be provided by the government and 160,000 by private sources. In 1990 alone, 210,000 new housing units were completed and the total number of dwellings stood at 44,855,000 in the mid-1990s.

43EDUCATION

Vigorous efforts have been made to advance education and reduce illiteracy. In 1971, overall literacy was estimated to be about 58%, ranging from 77% in the cities to only 52% in rural areas. By the year 2000, adult illiteracy rates were estimated at 13.0% (males, 8.1%; females, 17.9%). Under the constitution, education must be nondiscriminatory, and six years of primary education are free and compulsory. In practice, however, the supply of schools and teachers is inadequate to meet the needs of the fast-growing under-15 age group. In the mid-1990s, an estimated 97% of school-age children were enrolled in primary schools. In 1997, 29,236,283 students were enrolled in Indonesia's 173,893 primary schools, with 1,327,178 teachers. The student-to-teacher ratio stood at 22 to 1. Secondary schools employed 986,896 teachers and enrolled 14,209,974 students in that same year. Schools are coeducational, except for certain vocational and religious schools. Private (mostly Islamic religious) schools receive government subsidies if they maintain government standards. Bahasa Indonesia is the medium of instruction, but local dialects may be used until the third level.

The school system includes a six-year primary school, a three-year junior secondary school, a three-year senior secondary school, and higher education in universities, faculties, teacher-training colleges, and academies. Junior and senior technical schools have been brought into line with junior and senior secondary schools. Patterned after Dutch practices, Indonesia's educational system divides secondary-school students into groups according to curriculum. In the third year of the junior secondary school, the students are separated into an A curriculum (languages) and a B curriculum (mathematics). In senior secondary school, the students normally continue in their previous curriculum, but B-curriculum students may shift to an economics curriculum (C). Teacher-training schools range from the basic teacher-training program of four years (postprimary education) up through teachers' colleges, academies, faculties, and universities. Upon entering institutions of higher learning, students must enter the division for which their curriculum has prepared them; thus, A-curriculum students enter the language and philosophical faculties.

There are 51 universities, the largest of which are the University of Indonesia (in Jakarta) and the University of Gajah Mada (in Yogyakarta). Most of the universities are new, having been established since the mid-1950s. In all universities and third-level institutions, there were a total of 157,695 teachers and 2,303,469 students in 1996.

44LIBRARIES AND MUSEUMS

Indonesia's largest library was created in 1980 with the merger of four libraries into the Perbustakaan National Library of Indonesia, located in Jakarta, with a collection of over 870,000 volumes. This library includes the large National Museum collection, which was established in 1778. Another well-established library is the Bibliotheca Bogoriensis, also called the Central Library for Biological Sciences and Agriculture; founded in 1814 as a library associated with the botanical gardens in Bogor, on Java, it holds more than 400,000 volumes. Another national library is the National Scientific and Technical Documentation Center, founded in 1965 in Jakarta, with a collection of more than 150,000 volumes. The Library of the Indonesian Parliament, also in Jakarta, has 150,000 volumes. There is little coordination of public libraries, but there are state libraries and local reading rooms in almost every province. University libraries tend to be autonomous faculty or departmental libraries lacking central coordination. The University of Indonesia in Jakarta has just over 200,000 volumes and is the largest in the country.

The two outstanding museums in Indonesia are the National Museum in Jakarta, which is a general museum of Indonesian history and culture, and the Zoological Museum in Bogor, on Java. There is also a Bali Museum at Denpassar, and there are several regional historical museums throughout the provinces. Jakarta also houses a museum of crime, a large military museum, a museum chronicling the country's fight for independence, and several decorative arts museums.

45MEDIA

The government owns and operates postal services and telecommunications facilities through Perumtel, a state enterprise. In 1995 there were 2,520,700 telephones in Indonesia. As of 1999, there were 618 AM and 38 FM radio stations and 41 television stations (18 government-owned and 23 commercial). Programs originating in Jakarta are in Bahasa Indonesia; programs from regional stations are usually in local languages or dialects. The overseas service (Voice of Indonesia) broadcasts 11 hours daily in Arabic, Chinese, English, French, German, Japanese, Malay, and Thai. Television service was inaugurated in 1962. In 1995 there were three television networks, TV-Indonesia (TVRI), Rejawali Citra TV, and an educational network in Jakarta. In 1997 there were 155 radios, 134 television sets, and 5 mobile phones per 1,000 population. The Indonesian-owned telecommunications satellite Palapa B was launched in 1983.

Most newspapers are published in Bahasa Indonesia, with a small number appearing in local dialects, English, and Chinese. The leading dailies, with their estimated 1999 circulations, are as follows:

	LANGUAGE	CIRCULATION
JAKARTA		
Kompas	Bahasa Indonesia	550,000
Pos Kota	Bahasa Indonesia	500,000
Berita Buana	Bahasa Indonesia	150,000
Merdeka	Bahasa Indonesia	130,000
Indonesia Times	English	41,000
OTHER CITIES		
Pikiran Rakyat (Bandung)	Bahasa Indonesia	150,000
Suara Merdeka (Semarang)	Bahasa Indonesia	200,000
Surabaya Post (Surabaya)	Bahasa Indonesia	115,000
Analisa (Medan)	Bahasa Indonesia	80,000
Sinar Indonesia Baru (Medan)	Bahasa Indonesia	75,000

The constitution declares that everyone has the "right to freedom of opinion and expression." Journalistic activities of foreigners, however, are limited in accordance with the policy that "freedom of expression" does not permit interference in domestic affairs or dissemination of "foreign ideologies" detrimental to the Indonesian system of government. The government censors foreign films and publications, and Indonesian newspapers have been temporarily closed down for violating news guidelines. In 1982, a new press law established a Press Council of government officials, journalists, and scholars empowered to decide what news may be printed. The government began to issue and revoke "publishing licenses" in 1984 to control the media. In 1994 the licenses of three well-known news magazines were revoked.

As of 1996, there were over 700,000 personal computers. Online access is extremely limited, with less than one Internet host per 1,000 population in 1998.

46ORGANIZATIONS

The most successful cooperatives in Indonesia have been village unit cooperatives, designed to meet the small farmer's need for credit and aid in marketing cash crops. The cooperatives have also been instrumental in distributing improved rice, fertilizers, pesticides, and superior cattle breeds and in instructing farmers in their handling. Village unit cooperatives also exist for such cottage industries as batik (a method of hand-painting textiles), textiles, and garment production, which are important forms of employment in rural areas.

Among social welfare and women's organizations are the Indonesian Women's Congress, a federation founded in 1928; the National Council on Social Welfare; the Indonesian Planned Parenthood Association; the Council of Muslim Women's Organizations; GOPTKI, a federation of organizations that run kindergartens; and the Indonesian National Commission on the Status of Women.

Many trade and business promotional organizations are concerned with individual sectors of the business world—exporters' organizations, sugar traders' associations, and so on. An Indonesian chamber of commerce and industries has connections with leading business organizations in the country. UK, Chinese, Indian, and Pakistani business people have national associations.

47TOURISM, TRAVEL, AND RECREATION

An estimated 5,036,271 foreign tourists visited Indonesia in 1997, nearly three-fourths from East Asia and the Pacific region, including 25% from Singapore. Tourist receipts amounted to $5.4 billion. In 1997 there were 184,507 hotel rooms with an occupancy rate of 48%. Among the most popular tourist destinations are Bali, the restored Borobudur Buddhist temple in Java, and historic Yogyakarta. Cultural attractions include traditional Balinese dancing, the percussive sounds of the Indonesian orchestra (*gamelan*), the shadow puppet (*wayang kulit*) theater, and the famous Indonesian rijsttafel, a banquet of rice and savories. Tourism, as a means of affording wider employment, is strongly promoted by the government, which has supported the development of surfing, skindiving, and other marine sports in the reefs and tropical seas of the archipelago and the creation of resorts in Sumatra, Kalimantan, Nusa Tenggara, Maluku Province, and Irian Jaya. Gambling has been prohibited since 1981.

A valid passport and an entry visa are required of most foreigners entering Indonesia. Citizens of Israel and South America must obtain special travel affidavits from Indonesian officials in their own countries. For certain countries, including the US, a tourist visa does not need a visa for up to 60 days. For other countries, a tourist visa for visits up to 30 days is obtainable. Precautions against malaria, hepatitis, typhoid, and cholera are recommended.

The cost of traveling in Indonesia varies greatly from city to city. According to 1999 UN estimates, the daily cost of staying in Jakarta was approximately $142 per day. Expenses were an estimated $53 for Semarang, $59 for Surabaya, $73 for Puncak, and $173 for Mataram. Elsewhere the estimated daily cost was $40.

[48]FAMOUS INDONESIANS

Gajah Mada, prime minister under King Hayam Wuruk (r.1350–89), brought many of the islands under one rule, the Majapahit Empire. Princess Raden Ajeng Kartini (1879–1904), founder of a school for girls, led the movement for the emancipation of women. Her posthumously published letters, *Door duisternis tot licht*, occasioned considerable interest in the Western world. Many creative and performing artists have attained local prominence, but Indonesia's only internationally known artist is the painter Affandi (1910–90). Contemporary novelists of considerable local importance include Mochtar Lubis (b.1922). H. B. Jassin (b.1917) is an influential literary critic. Sukarno (1901–70), a founder and leader of the nationalist movement, is the best-known figure of modern Indonesia; Mohammad Hatta (1902–80), one of the architects of Indonesian independence, served as Sukarno's vice-president and concurrently as prime minister. President Suharto (b.1921), leader of Indonesia since Sukarno's overthrow, has dominated Indonesia's political and economic life since 1968. Adam Malik (1917–84) established an international reputation as a negotiator in restoring and improving relations with Malaysia, the Philippines, the US, the UK, and the UN; formerly a foreign minister (1966–77), he became vice-president (1978–83). Umar Wirahadikusumah (b.1924), a retired army general, became vice-president in 1983.

[49]DEPENDENCIES

Indonesia has no territories or colonies.

[50]BIBLIOGRAPHY

Anderson, Benedict R. O'G. *Language and Power: Exploring Political Cultures in Indonesia*. Ithaca, N.Y.: Cornell University Press, 1990.

——. *The Oil Boom and After: Indonesian Economic Policy and Performance in the Soeharto Era*. New York: Oxford University Press, 1992.

Bresnan, John. *Managing Indonesia: The Modern Political Economy*. New York: Columbia University Press, 1993.

Buchori, Moctar. *Sketches of Indonesian Society: A Look from Within*. Jakarta, Indonesia: IKIP-Muhammadiyah Jakarta Press, 1994.

Comparative History of India and Indonesia. New York: E.J. Brill, 1987.

Cribb, R. B. *Historical Dictionary of Indonesia*. Metuchen, N.J.: Scarecrow Press, 1992.

Crouch, Harold A. *The Army and Politics in Indonesia*. Revised edition. Ithaca, N.Y.: Cornell University Press, 1988.

Dahm, Bernhard. *Sukarno and the Struggle for Indonesian Independence*. Ithaca, N.Y.: Cornell University Press, 1969.

——. *History of Indonesia in the Twentieth Century*. New York: Praeger, 1971.

Detlor, Pamela. *Gender and Development across Cultures: Searching for a Common Ground in Indonesia*. Jakarta, Indonesia: University Consortium on the Environment, 1994.

Drake, Christine. *National Integration in Indonesia: Patterns and Policies*. Honolulu: University of Hawaii Press, 1989.

Dumargay, Jacques. *Cultural Sites of Malaysia, Singapore, and Indonesia*. New York: Oxford University Press, 1998.

Feith, Herbert, and Lance Castles (eds.). *Indonesian Political Thinking, 1945–1965*. Ithaca, N.Y.: Cornell University Press, 1970.

Frederick, William H. *Visions and Heat: the Making of the Indonesian Revolution*. Athens: Ohio University Press, 1989.

—— and Robert L. Worden (eds.). *Indonesia: A Country Study*. 5th ed. Washington, D.C.: Library of Congress, 1993.

Gardner, Paul F. *Shared Hopes, Separate Fears: Fifty Years of U.S.-Indonesian Relations*. Boulder, Colo.: Westview Press, 1997.

Hill, Hal. *The Indonesian Economy since 1966: Southeast Asia's Emerging Giant*. New York: Cambridge University Press, 1996.

——(ed.). *Unity and Diversity: Regional Economic Development in Indonesia since 1970*. New York: Oxford University Press, 1989.

Istiadah. *Muslim Women in Contemporary Indonesia: Investigating Paths to Resist the Patriarchal System*. Clayton, Victoria, Australia: The Centre of Southeast Asian Studies, Monash University, 1995.

Kayam, Umar. *Literature of Indonesia*. New York: Festival of Indonesia Foundation, 1991.

Lubis, Mochtar. *Indonesia: Land under the Rainbow*. New York: Oxford University Press, 1990.

MacIntyre, Andrew. *Business and Politics in Indonesia*. North Sydney, Australia: Asian Studies Association of Australia, 1991.

Marshall, P. J., et. al. *India and Indonesia during the Ancient Regime: Essays*. New York: E. J. Brill, 1989.

Neill, Wilfred T. *Twentieth-Century Indonesia*. New York: Columbia University Press, 1973.

Noer, Deliar. *The Modernist Muslim Movement in Indonesia, 1900–1942*. New York: Oxford University Press, 1973.

Palmier, Leslie (ed.). *Understanding Indonesia*. Brookfield, Vt.: Gower, 1985.

Reeve, David. *Golkar of Indonesia: An Alternative to the Party System*. New York: Oxford University Press, 1985.

Ricklefs, M. C. *A History of Modern Indonesia since c. 1300*. 2nd ed. Stanford, Calif.: Stanford University Press, 1993.

Rose, Mavis. *Indonesia Free: A Political Biography of Mohammad Hatta*. Ithaca, N.Y.: Cornell University, 1987.

Schiller, A. Arthur. *The Formation of Federal Indonesia, 1945–1949*. New York: Institute of Pacific Relations, 1955.

Stewart, Ian C. *Indonesians: Portraits from an Archipelago*. New York: Methuen, 1984.

Suryadinata, Leo. *Indonesia's Foreign Policy Under Suharto: Aspiring to International Leadership*. Singapore: Times Academic Press, 1996.

Wilhelm, Donald. *Emerging Indonesia*. New York: Barnes & Noble, 1980.

IRAN

Islamic Republic of Iran
Jomhuri-ye Eslami-ye Iran

CAPITAL: Tehran.

FLAG: The national flag is a tricolor of green, white, and red horizontal stripes, the top and bottom stripes having the Arabic inscription *Allah Akbar* ("God Is Great") written along the edge nearest the white stripe. In the center, in red, is the coat of arms, consisting of a stylized representation of the word *Allah*.

MONETARY UNIT: The rial (R) is a paper currency of 100 dinars. There are coins of 1, 5, 10, 20, and 50 rials, and notes of 100, 200, 500, 1,000, 2,000, 5,000, and 10,000 rials. R1 = $0.00057 ($1 = R1,755.0) as of 31 March 2000.

WEIGHTS AND MEASURES: The metric system is the legal standard, but local units are widely used.

HOLIDAYS: National Day, 11 February; Oil Nationalization Day, 20 March; No Ruz (New Year), 21–24 March; Islamic Republic Day, 1 April; 13th Day of No Ruz (Revolution Day), 2 April. Religious holidays (according to the lunar calendar) include Birthday of Imam Husayn; Birthday of the Twelfth Imam; Martyrdom of Imam 'Ali; Death of Imam Ja'afar Sadiq; 'Id al-Fitr; Birthday of Imam Reza; 'Id-i-Qurban; 'Id-i-Qadir; Shab-i-Miraj; Martyrdom of Imam Husayn; 40th Day after the Death of Imam Husayn; Birthday of the Prophet; Birthday of Imam 'Ali.

TIME: 3:30 PM = noon GMT.

¹LOCATION, SIZE, AND EXTENT

Situated in southwestern Asia, Iran covers an area of 1,648,000 sq km (636,296 sq mi) and extends about 2,250 km (1,400 mi) SE–NW and 1,400 km (870 mi) NE–SW. Comparatively, the area occupied by Iran is slightly larger than the state of Alaska. Iran is bounded on the N by Armenia, Azerbaijan, Turkmenistan, and the Caspian Sea, on the E by Afghanistan and Pakistan, on the S by the Gulf of Oman and the Persian Gulf, on the W by Iraq, and on the NW by Turkey, with a total boundary length of 7,880 km (4,896 mi). Iran's territory includes several islands in the Persian Gulf.

Iran's capital city, Tehran, is located in the northwestern part of the country.

²TOPOGRAPHY

Most of the land area consists of a plateau some 1,200 m (4,000 ft) above sea level and strewn with mountains. The Zagros and Elburz ranges stamp a "V" upon the plateau; the apex is in the northwest, and within the lower area between the arms are to be found salt flats and barren deserts. Most of the drainage is from these two great ranges into the interior deserts, with limited drainage into the Caspian Sea and the Persian Gulf. The ranges run in parallel files, enclosing long valleys that provide most of the agricultural land. Mt. Damavand, northeast of Tehran, rises to 5,671 m (18,606 ft), while the Caspian littoral is below sea level and has a semitropical climate. Only the Karun River, emptying into the Persian Gulf, is navigable for any distance, but the rivers that rush down from high altitudes offer fine sources of power.

Harbors of limited depth are found along the Persian Gulf, and the Caspian Sea has similar facilities for coastal fishing and trade. Iran is geologically unstable: an earthquake that struck eastern Iran, in Khorasan Province, on 16 September 1978, resulted in at least 25,000 deaths.

³CLIMATE

Iran has a continental type of climate, with cold winters and hot summers prevalent across the plateau. On the plateau, the annual rainfall does not exceed 30 cm (12 in), with the deserts and the Persian Gulf littoral receiving less than 13 cm (5 in). Snow falls heavily on the mountain peaks and is the principal source of water for irrigation in spring and early summer. The Caspian littoral is warm and humid throughout the year, and the annual rainfall is from about 100 to 150 cm (40–60 in). Clear days are the rule, for the skies are cloudless more than half the days of each year. The seasons change abruptly. By the Persian New Year, the first day of spring, orchards are in bloom and wild flowers abound. The Tehran temperature ranges from an average low of –3°C (27°F) to an average high of 7°C (45°F) in January, and from an average minimum of 22°C (72°F) to an average maximum of 37°C (99°F) in July.

⁴FLORA AND FAUNA

More than one-tenth of the country is forested. The most extensive growths are found on the mountain slopes rising from the Caspian Sea, with stands of oak, ash, elm, cypress, and other valuable trees. On the plateau proper, areas of scrub oak appear on the best-watered mountain slopes, and villagers cultivate orchards and grow the plane tree, poplar, willow, walnut, beech, maple, and mulberry. Wild plants and shrubs spring from the barren land in the spring and afford pasturage, but the summer sun burns them away. Bears in the mountains, wild sheep and goats, gazelles, wild asses, wild pigs, panthers, and foxes abound. Domestic animals include sheep, goats, cattle, horses, water buffalo, donkeys, and camels. The pheasant, partridge, stork, and falcon are native to Iran.

⁵ENVIRONMENT

Iran's high grasslands have been eroded for centuries by the encroachment of nomads who overgrazed their livestock. Desertification resulting from erosion, and deforestation of the high plateau pose additional dangers to Iran's environment. UN sources estimate that 1 to 1.5 million hectares per year become desert land. The basic law controlling the use of forests dates from 1943. In 1962, the forests and pastures in Iran were nationalized to check trespassing deforestation. In early 1983, blownout oil wells in the Persian Gulf war zone between Iran and Iraq caused a huge oil slick that threatened ocean and shore life along the southwestern Iranian coast. Air and water pollution have become significant problems in Iran in the aftermath of the 1991 Persian Gulf War. The water in the Gulf is polluted with oil and black rain, and the burning of Kuwaiti oil wells caused significant air pollution as well. Iran also has the 19th highest level of industrial carbon emissions in the world, with a 1992 total of 235 million metric tons, a per capita level of 3.81 metric tons. Iran has 28.2 cubic miles of water with 87% used for farming activity and 9% used for industrial purposes. Twenty-five percent of the rural people do not have pure water. Iran's cities produce 6.2 million tons of solid waste per year. Iran's Department of Environment was established under the Environment Protection and Enhancement Act of 1974; no information is available on implementing legislation.

Thirty of Iran's mammal species and 20 bird species are endangered. More than 300 plant species are also threatened. Endangered or extinct species in Iran include the Baluchistan bear, Asiatic cheetah, Persian fallow deer, Siberian white crane, hawksbill turtle, green turtle, Oxus cobra, Latifi's viper, dugong, and dolphins.

6POPULATION

The population of Iran in 2000 was estimated at 65,865,302. An estimated 4.5% of the population is 65 years of age or older. The projected population for the year 2005 is 80,139,000, assuming a crude birthrate of 25 per 1,000 population and a death rate of 5, resulting in a natural rate of change of 2.0% for the period 2000–2005. The population rate of change between 1995 and 2000 was 2.2%. The population density in 1998 was 38 per sq km (98 per sq mi).

It was estimated that 62% of the population lived in urban areas in 2000, up from 50% in 1980. The capital city, Tehran, had a 2000 population of 6,836,000. The populations of other major metropolitan areas in 2000 were Mashad, 2,378,000; Esfahan, 2,644,000; Tabriz, 1,624,000; Shiraz, 1,113,000; Ahvaz, 1,018,000; and Kermanshan, 949,000.

7MIGRATION

Traditionally, there has been little immigration to Iran, with the exception of Shi'i Muslims coming from Iraq. There has been some emigration to Europe and the US, particularly by Iranians who were studying overseas at the time of the revolution of 1979. About 100,000 Kurds were repatriated from Iran to Iraq during the mid-1970s after the suppression of a Kurdish rebellion in the latter country. Between 1980 and 1990, however, an increased number of Shi'i Muslims fled Iraq because of the Iran-Iraq and Gulf wars; at the end of 1992, 1,250,100 were refugees in Iran. Perhaps 2.8 million Afghan refugees moved to Iran after the Soviet invasion of Afghanistan in December 1979. About 200,000 returned in 1992, and about 2.1 million remained in mid 1993. At least 50,000 refugees from Azerbaijan had fled to Iran by late 1993 to escape Armenian occupation. In the fall of 1996, 65,000 Iraqi Kurds entered Iran due to fighting between two different groups of Iraqi Kurds.

According to 1999 statistics, Iran has the largest refugee population in the world, hosting some 2 million refugees. There are an estimated 1.4 million Afghan refugees, 580,000 Iraqis, and 40,000 refugees from Tajikistan, Bosnia, Eritrea, and Somalia. Only 5% of refugees live in 30 designated camps, while the rest have integrated themselves in cities and villages around the country. An increase in unemployment and faltering economic conditions have resulted in increased pressure for refugees to return to their homelands. However, due to current conditions in Iraq and Afghanistan, chances for significant repatriation remain poor. The Iranian government feels a heavy economic and social burden and believes the international community should share more responsibility for these refugees. As of 1999, the net emigration rate was -4.6 migrants per 1,000 population.

8ETHNIC GROUPS

Present-day Iranians, or Persians, are considered to be direct descendants of the Aryans who moved into the plateau in the second millennium BC. They speak Persian, or Farsi, and number more than half the total population. In the Zagros range and its extensions are to be found the Kurds, Lurs, Bakhtiari, Qashqa'i, and Qajars; the first three are said to be of stock similar to the Iranian element, and they speak languages that stem from ancient Indo-European languages. At various times after the 10th century AD, Turkish tribes settled in the region, and Turkish-speaking groups are still found in several parts of the country. One-eighth of the total population dwells in East and West Azerbaijan, and there are sizable groups of Azerbaijanis in major cities elsewhere, including Tehran. Arab groups arrived during and after the 7th century AD; their descendants live in the south and southwest and in scattered colonies elsewhere.

In general, non-Iranian elements are to be found along the perimeter of the country. Of these, certain nomadic groups move back and forth across the frontiers. Tribal groups have been a conspicuous element in Iran for many centuries, migrating vertically in spring and fall between high mountain valleys and hot, lowland plains. The important migratory groups include the Qashqa'i, Qajars, Bakhtiari, Balochi, and Turkmen. A large proportion of these people are now settled, however. The nomadic way of life is on the decline, and official policy has sought to resettle these groups on farmlands.

According to 1999 estimates, Persians account for 51% of the population, Azerbaijani 24%, Gilaki and Mazandarani 8%, Kurd 7%, Arab 3%, Lur 2%, Balochi 2%, and Turkmen 2%.

9LANGUAGES

Farsi, commonly called Persian in the West, is the official language of Iran; it is taught in all schools and was spoken by 80% of the population in 1995. An estimated 50–60% spoke it as their native language. An Indo-European language of the Indo-Iranian group, Farsi derives from ancient Persian, with an admixture of many Arabic words. Arabic characters and script are used in writing modern Persian. Dialects of Turkish, or Turki—especially Azeri, the language of the Azerbaijanis—are spoken throughout northwestern Iran, by the Qashqa'i tribe in the southwest, and in parts of the northeast by Turkmen tribes and others. The Lurs, Kurds, and Bakhtiari have languages and dialects of their own that descend from earlier Indo-European languages, and the Balochi language spoken in southeastern Iran also is of Indo-European origin. A small number of Brahui in the southeast speak a Dravidian language. According to 1999 estimates, 58% of the population speaks Persian or Persian dialects, 26% Turkic or Turkic dialects, 9% Kurdish, 2% Luri, 1% Balochi, 1% Arabic, 1% Turkish, and 2% other.

10RELIGIONS

As of 1999, 89% of the people were Shi'a Muslims, 10% Sunni Muslims, 1% Zoroastrian, Jewish, Christian, and Baha'i. Iran is the only Islamic country where Shi'a Muslims hold the reins of power. Shi'a Islam is the official religion of the country, and the president, prime minister, and cabinet ministers must be Muslims. The Christian population (about 333,000) includes Armenians

LOCATION: 25° to 40°N; 44° to 63°E. **BOUNDARY LENGTHS:** Afghanistan, 936 km (582 mi); Armenia 35 km (22 mi); Azerbaijan (N) 432 km (268 mi); Azerbaijan (NW) 179 km (111 mi); Caspian Sea coastline, 740 km (460 mi); Gulf of Oman and Persian Gulf coastlines, 2,440 km (1,516 mi); Iraq, 1,458 km (906 mi); Pakistan, 909 km (565 mi); Turkey, 499 km (310 mi); Turkmenistan 992 km (616 mi). **TERRITORIAL SEA LIMIT:** 12 mi.

and, in the northwest area, Nestorian Christians (Assyrians). Colonies of Parsis, or Zoroastrians, in Yazd, Kerman, and other large towns number about 30,000. The Baha'is number about 340,000; their faith, which sprang from the teachings of a 19th-century Muslim in Iran, has been denounced as heresy to Islam. The Baha'is have been severely persecuted by the Shi'a government since the 1979 revolution, and many of their religious leaders have been executed. The Jewish community, which numbered about 25,000 in 1984, had dwindled to no more than 14,000 by 1990 and may have declined still further since then under the impact of persecution.

¹¹TRANSPORTATION

Iran had 162,000 km (100,667 mi) of roads in 1996, of which 81,000 km (50,333 mi) were paved, including 470 km (292 mi)

of expressways. A1, a major paved highway, runs from Bazargan on the Turkish border to the border with Afghanistan. Another major highway, A2, runs from the Iraqi border to the Pakistani border. Much of the revolutionary government's road-building activity has centered on improving roads in rural areas. In 1995 there were over 1,557,000 passenger cars and 588,900 commercial vehicles.

The state-owned Iranian State Railway has 7,286 km (4,528 mi) of track. The main line runs south for 1,392 km (865 mi) from Bandar Turkoman on the Caspian Sea, through Tehran, to Bandar-e Khomeini on the Persian Gulf. Rail construction from Bafq to Sirjan has been completed and is operational.

Iran's main port at Khorramshahr on the Persian Gulf, as well as the port at Abadan, were largely destroyed in fighting during the 1980–88 war with Iraq. Other ports on the Gulf are Bandar-e

Khomeini, Bandar 'Abbas, and Bushehr. Both Bandar-e Khomeini and Bushehr were damaged because of the war. The government is continuing the previous regime's program to modernize the port at Bandar 'Abbas. On the Caspian Sea, there are the ports of Bandar Anzeli (formerly Bandar Pahlavi), and Naushahr. In addition, there are the oil shipment ports of Kharg Island (a principal target in the war with Iraq) and Abadan. The principal inland waterways are Lake Orumieh and the Karun River. In 1998, the Iranian merchant marine included 132 vessels of at least 1,000 GRT, with a total capacity of 3,238,293 GRT.

Iran had 288 airports in 1998, 110 of which had paved runways. Principal airports include Bandar 'Abbas, Mehrabad International at Tehran, and Shiraz International at Shiraz. The state-owned Iran Air maintains frequent service to 15 cities in Iran and is an international carrier. In 1997, 9,804,000 passengers were carried on scheduled domestic and international flights.

12 HISTORY

As early as 6000 BC, communities on the Iranian plateau were carrying on agriculture, raising domestic animals, and producing pottery and polished stone implements. Sites datable to later than 3000 BC are numerous and offer quantities of bronze instruments and painted pottery of the finest types. About 1500 BC, masses of Indo-Europeans, or Aryans, began to cross the plateau of Iran. The Iranian group included Medes, Persians, Parthians, Bactrians, and others. The Medes settled in western Iran (Media) about 900 BC and established their capital at Ecbatana (modern Hamadan); the Persians settled to the south of them (Parsis) around 700 BC. The Median king Cyaxares (625–585 BC), along with the Chaldeans, destroyed the power of neighboring Assyria. In the area of Parsis, the Achaemenid clan became overlords, and in 550 BC, their leader, Cyrus the Great, revolted against the Medes; forming a union of Medes and Persians, he then drove with armies both into Asia Minor and to the east of the Iranian plateau and established the Achaemenid Empire. Cambyses, Darius, Xerxes I, and Artaxerxes I were notable rulers of this line who penetrated Greece, Egypt, and beyond the Oxus. The Achaemenid power was centered at Susa and Persepolis; the ruined site of the latter is impressive even today. Zoroastrianism was the religion of the rulers.

In his eastward sweep (334–330 BC), Alexander the Great defeated vast Achaemenid forces and went on to capture Susa and to burn Persepolis. In the 3rd century BC, the Parthians moved into the area east of the Caspian and then into the Achaemenid Empire, establishing the new Parthian kingdom; later rulers moved west to come in contact with and then to fight the Roman Empire. The Parthians considered themselves spiritual heirs of the Achaemenids and adopted Zoroastrianism as the official religion. Weakened by long wars with Rome, the Parthians were followed by a local dynasty, the Sassanian, which arose in the area of Fars in southwestern Iran. Wars with Rome continued and were followed by a struggle with the Byzantine Empire. The Sassanian period (AD 226–641) was one of cultural consolidation and was marked by economic prosperity and by a series of enlightened rulers.

During the first half of the 7th century AD, Arab warriors burst out of the Arabian Peninsula to overwhelm the Sassanian Empire and to spread the teachings of the prophet Muhammad, embodied in Islam. By the opening of the ninth century, Islamic doctrine and precepts had spread over the plateau, and local dynasties faithful to the Muslim creed emerged. Early in the 11th century, the Turkish Ghaznavid dynasty held power from western Iran to the Indus River. Their greatest ruler was Mahmud of Ghazni, a renowned conqueror and a patron of the arts. The Ghaznavids were replaced by the Seljuks, descended from Turkish nomad warriors enlisted in their service.

The Seljuk kingdom had its capital at Ray, just south of Tehran, and stretched from the Bosporus to Chinese Turkestan. Of rude origins, such rulers as Tughril Beg, Alp Arslan, and Malik Shah did much to promote cultural pursuits and enhance the character of Persian civilization.

In 1219, Mongol hordes under Genghis Khan (Temujin) began to move into Iran; successive waves subdued and devastated the country. Hulagu, a grandson of Genghis, settled in Maragheh in Azerbaijan and as Il-khan, or chief of the tribe, gave this title to the Il-khanid dynasty. His successors, such as Ghazan Khan and Oljaitu, ruled from Tabriz and Sultaniya, and once again untutored invaders became converts to Islam and patrons of Persian science, learning, and arts. Rivalries within the military leadership brought about the breakdown of Il-khanid power in the second half of the 14th century.

In 1380, Timur ("Timur the Lame," or, in the west Tamerlane) began to move into the Iranian plateau from the east. Within a decade, the entire area was in his power, bringing a renaissance of culture at Herat (in modern Afghanistan) and other towns, but later rulers lacked the force and ability to hold the empire together. Early in the 16th century a number of smaller, local dynasties emerged throughout Iran. The most powerful was the Safavid dynasty, whose leaders, descendants of a spiritual head of the Shi'i sect, imposed this form of Islam on their subjects. The fourth and greatest of this line, Shah Abbas (r.1587–1628), moved the capital to Esfahan, where he had many splendid buildings constructed. The Safavid period, marked by the emergence of a truly native Iranian dynasty after the lapse of many centuries, was a period of military power and general prosperity. However, decline set in, and in 1722, Esfahan fell to invading forces from Afghanistan. Nadir Shah, an Afshar tribesman from the north, drove off the Afghans and in 1736 established the Afshar dynasty. By the end of the 18th century, Zand rulers, dominant in the south, were replaced by the Qajars, a Turkish tribe.

Qajar power began to fade at the turn of the 19th century. In the 1890s, Shia clerics led a national boycott that made the shah rescind a decree awarding a tobacco monopoly to a foreign agent. In 1906, a coalition of bazaar merchants, clerics, intellectuals, and tribal leaders forced the shah to accept a constitution. This liberal initiative was frustrated, however, by the power of the British and Russians, who controlled spheres of influence in the south and north of Iran.

After a period of chaos, the British arranged for a Persian Cossack officer, Reza Rhan, to come to power, first as minister of war in 1921, then prime minister, finally in 1925 as Reza Shah, the first sovereign of the Pahlavi dynasty. With ruthless authority, he sought to modernize Iran along the lines of Ataturk in Turkey. In 1941, suspecting him of pro-German sympathies, the British forced Reza Shah to abdicate in favor of his 21-year-old son, Muhammad Reza. British and Russian forces set up a supply line across Iran to the USSR. In April 1946, the British left, but the USSR refused to withdraw its forces. Under pressure from the UN and the US, Soviet troops eventually withdrew in December 1946.

Oil, the source of nearly all Iran's national wealth, quickly came to dominate postwar politics. Muhammad Mossadeq, who as leader of the National Front in the National Assembly (Majlis) led the fight in 1947 to deny the USSR oil concessions in northern Iran, became chairman of the oil committee of the Majlis. On 15 March 1951, the Majlis voted to nationalize the oil industry, which was dominated by the Anglo-Iranian Oil Co. (AIOC), a prewar concession to the UK. When the government of Prime Minister Hosein Ala took no immediate action against the AIOC, the Majlis demanded his resignation and the appointment of Mossadeq, who became prime minister in April. The AIOC was nationalized, but its output rapidly declined when the UK imposed an embargo on Iranian oil, as well as other economic sanctions. As Iran's economic situation worsened, Mossadeq sought to rally the people through fervent nationalistic appeals. An attempt by the shah to replace him failed in the summer of 1952, but by August 1953, Mossadeq had lost his parliamentary majority, but not his popular support. With the backing of a referendum, Mossadeq dissolved the Majlis and then refused to resign when the shah again tried to oust him. The shah fled Iran for four days but returned on 22 August, with backing from the military, the US, and the UK. A new conservative government issued an appeal for aid; in September, the US granted Iran $45 million. Mossadeq was convicted of treason in December.

After 1953, the shah began to consolidate his power. New arrangements between the National Iranian Oil Co. and a consortium of US, UK, and Dutch oil companies were negotiated during April–September 1954 and ratified by the Majlis in October. The left-wing Tudeh (Masses) Party, which had been banned in 1949 but had resurfaced during the Mossadeq regime, was suppressed after a Tudeh organization was exposed in the armed forces. In 1957, the government sponsored two new pseudo-parties, which contested parliamentary elections in 1960 and 1961. Meanwhile, Iran became affiliated with the Western alliance through the Baghdad Pact in 1955, later the Central Treaty Organization. (CENTO was dissolved after Iran pulled out in 1979.) Frontier demarcation agreements were signed with the USSR in April 1957.

US assistance and goodwill were plainly essential for the shah. In 1961, President John F. Kennedy urged him to undertake a more liberal program. Under the "white revolution" of 1962–63, the shah initiated land reform, electoral changes (including, for the first time, the right of women to hold and vote for public office), and broad economic development. Opposition to the reform program, the dictatorial regime, and the growing American influence was suppressed. Political dissent was not tolerated.

The shah's autocratic methods, his repressive use of the secret police (known as SAVAK), his program of rapid Westernization (at the expense of Islamic tradition), his emphasis on lavish display and costly arms imports, and his perceived tolerance of corruption and of US domination fed opposition in the late 1970s. The economic boom of the previous 15 years also came to an end. Islamic militants, radical students, and the middle class all joined in the revolt, until virtually the entire population turned against the shah. Following nine months of demonstrations and violent army reactions, martial law was declared in Iran's major cities in September 1978, but antigovernment strikes and massive marches could not be stopped. On 16 January 1979, the shah left Iran, appointing an old-line nationalist, Shahpur Bakhtiar, as prime minister. However, the leader of the Islamic opposition, Ayatollah Ruhollah Khomeini (the term ayatollah is the highest rank of the Shia clergy), who had spent 15 years in exile, first in Iraq and briefly in France, refused to deal with the Bakhtiar regime. Demonstrations continued, and on 1 February the ayatollah returned to a tumultuous welcome in Tehran. He quickly asserted control and appointed a provisional government, which took power after a military rebellion and the final collapse of the shah's regime on 11 February.

After a referendum, Khomeini on 1 April declared Iran an Islamic Republic. However, the provisional government, led by Medhi Bazargan and other liberal civilians, was unable to exercise control; revolutionary groups made indiscriminate arrests and summary executions of political opponents. Increasingly, radical clerics sought to take power for themselves. The crisis atmosphere was intensified by the seizure, on 4 November 1979, of 53 US hostages (50 of them in the US embassy compound in Tehran) by militant Iranian students who demanded the return of the shah from the US (where he was receiving medical treatment) to stand trial in Iran. Despite vigorous protests by the US government, which froze Iranian assets in the US, and by the UN over this violation of diplomatic immunity, the hostages were held for 444 days; in the intervening period, a US attempt to free the hostages by military force failed, and the shah died in Egypt on 27 July 1980. The crisis was finally resolved on 20 January 1981, in an agreement providing for release of the prisoners and the unfreezing of Iranian assets. A new constitution providing for an Islamic theocracy was ratified by popular referendum in December 1979. In presidential elections in January 1980, 'Abolhassan Bani-Sadr, a moderate, who supported the revolution, was elected president. Later elections to the Majlis resulted in victory for the hard-line clerical Islamic Republican Party (IRP).

In June 1981, President Bani-Sadr was ousted by Khomeini; later that month, a bomb explosion at IRP headquarters in Tehran killed Ayatollah Beheshti, who had been serving as chief justice, as well as 4 cabinet ministers, 20 paramilitary deputies, and dozens of others. Another bombing, on 30 August, killed the new president, Muhammad 'Ali Rajai, and his new prime minister, Muhammad Javad Bahonar. The bombings were ascribed by the government to leftist guerrillas. By 1982, at least 4,500 people had been killed in political violence, and some estimates placed the total much higher. In September 1982, Sadegh Ghotbzadeh, who had been foreign minister during the hostage crisis, was executed on charges of plotting to kill Khomeini and establish a secular government.

Iraq, meanwhile, had taken advantage of Iran's political chaos and economic disorder to revive a border dispute that had been settled in 1975 when Iranian and Iraqi representatives reached agreement on the demarcation of their frontiers and Iran ended its support for rebellious Kurds, who were then defeated by the Iraqi army. Full-scale war erupted in September 1980, when Iraq demanded sovereignty over the entire Shatt al-'Arab waterway. Iraqi forces invaded Khuzistan in the southwest, and captured the town of Khorramshahr and the oil refinery center of Abadan. The Iranian army, decimated by the revolution, was slow to mobilize, but by June 1982 it had driven Iraqi soldiers out of Abadan and Khorramshahr and from all undisputed Iranian territory. Iran then launched its own offensive, invading Iraq and thrusting toward Basra, but failed to make significant gains. At this point the land war became stalemated, with Iranian and Iraqi troops setting up an elaborate system of trenches. In 1983, Iraq broadened the war zone to include oil-tanker traffic in the northern Persian Gulf.

The Iraqis first attacked Iranian oil installations, disrupting, but not stopping, oil exports from the main oil terminal at Kharg Island. In mid-1983, Iraq took delivery of French jets bearing Exocet missiles. Iran responded that it would close the Strait of Hormuz if Iraq used the missiles. The US declared the strait a vital interest and said it would use military force to keep the strait open because of the large volume of oil that passed through it on the way to the West. During 1983, the Iraqis also began to attack civilian targets in Iran with long-range missiles. The attacks caused heavy casualties, and Iran responded by shelling Iraqi border cities. In 1984, Iran began to attack Arab shipping in the Persian Gulf.

Iranian forces staged a surprisingly effective attack on Iraqi forces in the Fao Peninsula in February 1986. The Iranians now controlled all of Iraq's border on the Persian Gulf and were in reach of the major Iraqi city of Basra. In April, Khomeini renewed his demands for an end to the war: Iraqi President Saddam Hussein must step down, and Iraq must admit responsibility and pay war reparations. Iran rejected all demands for a cease-fire and negotiations until its demands were met.

In November 1986, it was revealed that US National Security Adviser Robert McFarlane had secretly traveled to Iran to meet with government leaders. The US supplied Iran with an estimated $30 million in spare parts and antiaircraft missiles in hopes that Iran would exert pressure on terrorist groups in Lebanon to release American hostages. In the wake of this affair, Iran in 1987 attacked Kuwaiti oil tankers reregistered as American tankers and laid mines in the Persian Gulf to disrupt oil tanker shipping. The US responded by stationing a naval task force in the region and attacking Iranian patrol boats and oil-loading platforms and accidentally shot down a civilian passenger jet.

As the war continued to take a heavy toll in casualties and destruction and economic hardships persisted on the home front, the clerics maintained firm control through repression and Khomeini's charismatic hold over the people. In 1988, Iran finally yielded to terms for a cease-fire in the war. On 3 June 1989, a few months after calling for the death of novelist Salman Rushdie for blasphemy, Khomeini died of a heart attack. Over 3 million people attended his funeral. He was succeeded as the country's spiritual guide by President Ali Khamenei. On 28 July 1989, Speaker of the Parliament Ali Akbar Rafsanjani, a moderate, was elected president with 95% of the vote. Iran remained neutral during the Gulf War, receiving (and retaining) Iraqi planes that were flown across the border for safekeeping. Iran also accepted thousands of Kurdish refugees from Iraq to add to its heavy burden of Afghan refugees from the civil strife in that country. Inflation, shortages, and unemployment—the products of revolution, war, and mismanagement—continue to generate widespread popular discontent, fueled also by dissatisfaction with the closed and repressive political system.

President Rafsanjani was reelected by a significantly smaller margin in 1993 but continued to press for free-market economic reforms. Rising prices in the wake of decreased government economic subsidies led to civil unrest in 1994 and 1995. Clerical conservatives led by Khamenei continued to battle the political moderates for dominance in the 1996 parliamentary elections, without a decisive victory for either side. Then, in the presidential election of May 1997, a moderate cleric, Muhammed Khatami, who favored economic reform, a more conciliatory foreign-policy stance, and less rigid clerical control of the government, won over two-thirds of the vote. In spite of continued opposition by Islamic conservatives, Khatami established a more tolerant climate in the country and expanded civil liberties. His policies received a decisive endorsement by the Iranian electorate when a political coalition led by the reformist president won 141 out of 290 parliamentary seats in the February 2000 elections and 189 seats in the May runoff elections, despite the shutdown of over a dozen liberal newspapers by conservative elements in the government in the weeks preceding the May polling.

13GOVERNMENT

Before the 1979 revolution, Iran was an absolute monarchy, with the constitution of 1906 modified by a supplement of 1907 and amendments of 1925, 1949, and 1957. The shah was the chief of state, with sweeping powers. He commanded the armed forces, named the prime minister and all senior officials, and was empowered to dissolve either or both legislative houses. The legislative branch comprised the National Assembly (Majlis) and the Senate. Members of the Majlis were elected for four-year terms from 268 constituencies by adults 20 years of age and older. Half of the 60 senators were named by the shah, and half were elected. Members of the Majlis ostensibly represented all classes of the nation, while the somewhat more conservative Senate consisted of former cabinet ministers, former high officials, and retired generals.

The constitution of December 1979, which was approved in a public referendum and revised in 1989, established an Islamic republic in conformity with the principles of the Shi'i faith. Guidance of the republic is entrusted to the country's spiritual leader (faqih) or to a council of religious leaders. An appointed Council of Guardians consists of six religious leaders, who consider all legislation for conformity to Islamic principles, and six Muslim lawyers appointed by the Supreme Judicial Council, who rule on limited questions of constitutionality. In accordance with the constitution, an 86-member Assembly of Experts chooses the country's spiritual leader and may nullify laws that do not conform to Islamic tenets. In 1998, seats on the council (which have eight-year terms) were opened for the first time to nonclerics.

The executive branch consists of a president and Council of Ministers. The president is elected by popular vote to a four-year term and supervises government administration. Candidates for the presidency and parliament must have the approval of Iran's spiritual leaders. As of 2000, the Majlis consisted of 290 members elected directly to four-year terms. Suffrage is universal for those over age 15.

14POLITICAL PARTIES

During the reign of Reza Shah (1925–41), political parties were not permitted to function. After 1941, parties sprang up, but most of them were of an ephemeral nature. The Communist-oriented Tudeh (Masses) Party was better organized than the others and benefited from the services of devoted followers and foreign funds. In 1949, an unsuccessful attempt to assassinate the shah was traced to the Tudeh, and it was banned. It continued to work through front groups, and its views were reflected in some periodicals, but the organization was extinguished in the Shah's post-1953 crackdown.

In 1957, the government created facade political parties, the Nationalist (Mellioun) Party, headed by Manochehr Eqbal, then prime minister and the People's (Mardom) Party, headed by former prime minister Asadullah Alam (the "loyal opposition"). None of these parties ever attracted any popular following. In 1975, the shah ordered the formation of a single political organization, the Iran Resurgence (Rastakhiz) Party, into which were merged all existing legal parties. Three cardinal principles were cited for membership in the party: faith in Iran's constitution, loyalty to the monarchical regime, and fidelity to the "white revolution." This party, like others before it, lacked a popular base.

After the overthrow of the shah's regime in February 1979, new political parties were formed, the most powerful being the Islamic Republic Party (IRP), which took control of the Majlis. However, power was wielded primarily by the military, the president, the clerical elite, and the heads of the banyads, autonomous financial organizations which have considerable power and which were formed from the confiscated wealth of the former royal family and its cronies.

Today Iran's parliament, or Majlis, is made up of various groups representing a spectrum of views ranging from hard line radical Islam to moderates and liberals. Moderates generally hold less hostile views about the West while still believing in an Islamic republic. In 1997, a moderate politician, Mohammad Khatami, was elected president of Iran. The moderates scored a further triumph in the parliamentary elections of February and May 2000. A moderate reformist coalition headed by Khatami won 189 out of 290 seats in the Majlis, with radical Islamists winning 54, independents 42, and religious minority parties 5.

15LOCAL GOVERNMENT

Iran is divided into 26 ostans (provinces), each headed by a governor-general; the governor-general and district officials of each province are appointed by the central government. The ostans are subdivided into 195 sharestans (counties), which are in turn divided into 500 bakhsh (districts). Each bakhsh consists of two or more dehistans, which are composed of groups of villages or hamlets. Each of the 475 municipalities (shahrdarys) is headed by a mayor. Some sharestan officials are elected; others are appointed by Tehran.

16 JUDICIAL SYSTEM

The overthrow of the shah and the approval in 1980 of a constitution making Iran an Islamic state have radically changed Iran's judicial system. The 1980 constitution was revised in 1989.

In August 1982, the Supreme Court invalidated all previous laws that did not conform with the dictates of Islam, and all courts set up before the 1979 revolution were abolished in October 1982. An Islamic system of punishment, introduced in 1983, included flogging, stoning, and amputation for various crimes. There are two different court systems: civil courts and revolutionary courts.

The judicial system is under the authority of the religious leader (faqih). A Supreme Judicial Council responsible to the faqih oversees the Supreme Court, which has 16 branches. The Ministry of Justice oversees law courts in the provinces.

The revolutionary courts try cases involving political offenses, narcotics trafficking and "crimes against God." Although the constitution guarantees a fair trial, the revolutionary courts provide almost no procedural safeguards. The trials in revolutionary courts are rarely held in public and there is no guarantee of access to an attorney.

Elements of the prerevolutionary judicial system continue to be applied in common criminal and civil cases. In these cases the right to a public trial and the benefit of counsel are generally respected. In 1995 the Government began implementing a law authorizing judges to act as prosecutor and judge in the same case.

The Constitution states that "reputation, life, property, (and) dwelling(s)" are protected from trespass except as "provided by law." However, in practice, security forces do not respect these provisions.

17 ARMED FORCES

Two years' military service is compulsory for all males at age 18. The war with Iraq led to an almost fourfold increase in the size of the armed forces after 1980, but this force has demobilized. In 2000, the army had 350,000 soldiers (220,000 conscripts). Their equipment included 1,345 main battle tanks, 440 armored fighting vehicles, and about 1,300 multiple rocket launchers. The air force had 50,000 men and 304 combat aircraft. The navy of 20,600 men had 2 destroyers, 3 frigates, 5 submarines, and 64 smaller patrol and coastal combatants. The Revolutionary Guards unit (Pasdaran) has an estimated 100,000-man army and 20,000 sailors and marines. Complementing the Pasdaran are the baseej, or Popular Mobilization Army of mostly young peacetime volunteers devoted to an Islamic Iran. The baseej were the mainstay of Iran's human wave attacks, and membership has been estimated at 200,000. The official military budget in 1998–99 was $5.79 billion or 2.9% of gross domestic product.

18 INTERNATIONAL COOPERATION

Iran is a charter member of the UN, having joined on 24 October 1945, and belongs to ESCAP and all the nonregional specialized agencies except WIPO. Iran is also a member of G-77 and a signatory to the Law of the Sea. It is a founding member of OPEC and a leading supporter of higher petroleum prices. In 1979, Iran withdrew from CENTO, causing its demise.

Iran's revolutionary government has aligned itself with the radical Arab states of Libya and Syria, which were the only Arab countries to support Iran in its war with Iraq. Since before 1979, Iranian foreign policy has been to curtail superpower influence in the Persian Gulf area. It also encourages the Islamization of the governments throughout the Middle East, in such countries as Sudan, Algeria, Bahrain and Sau'di Arabia.

19 ECONOMY

A country with a substantial economic potential, Iran witnessed rapid economic growth during the reign of Shah Muhammad Reza Pahlavi. Development of its extensive agricultural, mineral, and power resources was financed through oil revenues. The traditional land tenure system, under which farmers were sharecroppers, was replaced through a land reform program inaugurated in 1962. In addition to carpets, Iran produced a variety of consumer goods and building materials. Oil, however, became the lifeblood of the economy. With the astonishing growth of its oil revenues, Iran became a major world economic power, whose investments helped several industrialized countries pay for their oil needs during the 1970s.

The economy changed drastically after 1979. The war with Iraq, which curtailed oil exports, coupled with the decrease in the price of oil, especially in 1986, sent oil revenues spiraling downward from $20.5 billion in 1979 to an estimated $5.3 billion in 1986. This forced annual GDP growth down from 15.2% in 1982 to 0.2% in 1984; GDP was estimated to have fallen by 8% in 1986. The war's drain on the state budget, the drop in oil prices, poor economic management, declining agricultural output, an estimated 1987 inflation rate of 30–50%, and large budget deficits combined to put enormous strains on the economy.

After Iran accepted a UN cease-fire resolution in 1988, it began reforming the economy with the implementation of the Islamic Republic's First Five-Year Social and Economic Development Plan for the years 1989-l994. The plan emphasized revitalizing market mechanisms, deregulating the economy, and rebuilding basic infrastructure. These reforms led to economic growth and lowered budget deficits. GDP grew an average 7% a year in real terms over 1989–92. The general government deficit was reduced from 9% of GDP in 1988 to an estimated 2% in 1992. The inflation rate decreased from 29% in 1988 to around 10% in 1990. Since then, however, inflation edged up to an estimated 20% in 1991 and 1992.

Other impacts of the first plan included a growth in agricultural production of 5.6%; industrial production of 15%; water, gas and electricity of 18.9%; and transport of 11.9%. In 1991, the government adapted a structural adjustment program similar in nature to the kind the IMF imposes on developing nations in exchange for aid. Iran, however, did not need any aid but rather imposed the adjustments on itself in an effort to liberalize its economy, making it more market-oriented while still retaining an authoritarian regime. The structural adjustments advocated by then-president Rafsanjani included privatizations of state-owned enterprises, deregulation, cutting government subsidies, and encouraging foreign investment. While marginally well-intentioned, the Rafsanjani reforms have led to little economic improvement. Privatization was especially ineffective. Political corruption and rampant croneyism led to many enterprises ending up in the hands of a small clique of well-connected elites. By 1997, 86% of Iran's GDP came from state-owned businesses. Deregulation has also hit considerable snags. In 1996 alone, more than 250 regulations on imports and exports were issued by 24 ministries—many of them repetitive or contradictory.

In April of 1995, the US imposed trade and investment sanctions against Iran, in reprisal for what the US believed was Iran's continued support of international terrorism. This move, unduplicated even by the US's strongest allies, has had some economic impact—most notably a precipitous drop in the value of the rial, which the government was forced to prop up.

In 1994 the Second Five Year Plan, running through 1999, was implemented. Its priorities were completion of infrastructure and development projects and an increase in social spending. By 1996, Iran's economy was growing rather steadily at about 4.2%. Inflation, however, continued to be a problem. In 1995 it was above 50% but by the next year it had been brought somewhat under control, having been cut nearly in half to 27%. In 1998, the inflation rate was reported at 24%, and the unemployment rate was at 30%. Annual GDP growth occurred at a rate of 4.7% between 1988 and 1998, but fell to 1.7% in 1998 alone, and was at 2.3% in 1999. The Third Five Year Plan, implemented from 2000 to 2005, was to privatize at least six major state-owned enterprises such as communications and tobacco, and at least 2,000 smaller state-owned firms.

20INCOME

The US Central Intelligence Agency (CIA) reports that in 1998 Iran's gross domestic product (GDP) was estimated at $340 billion. The per capita GDP was estimated at $5,000. The annual growth rate of GDP was estimated at -2.1%. The average inflation rate in 1998 was 24%. The CIA defines GDP as the value of all final goods and services produced within a nation in a given year and computed on the basis of purchasing power parity (PPP) rather than value as measured on the basis of the rate of exchange.

The World Bank reports that for the same period per capita private consumption (in PPP terms) was $3,290. Private consumption includes expenditures of individuals, households, and non-governmental organizations. It was estimated that between 1990 and 1998 private consumption grew at an annual rate of 2.9%. Approximately 20% of household consumption was spent on food, 32% on fuel, 12% on health care, and 8% on education.

21LABOR

The total labor force was estimated at around 19 million in 1998, up from 15.4 million in 1988. According to official figures, 30% of the employed work force was in agriculture, 25% was in manufacturing, mining, construction, and utilities, and 45% was in the service industry. However, experts believe that these distributions of the work force are misleading because they do not show the unemployment levels that exist within each area. Unemployment has become pervasive because of the economy's poor performance and the large numbers of young people who have recently entered the work force. As of 1998, it stood at over 30%.

Article 131 of the Labor Code grants workers and employees the right to form and join their own organizations. The government-controlled Workers' House, founded in 1982, is the only authorized national labor organization. The Workers' House in turn coordinates the activities of labor councils, which are organized in many enterprises.

Strikes are strongly discouraged by the government and strikes by government employees are illegal. Iranian labor law (which exempts agriculture, domestic service, family businesses, and some other small businesses) forbids employment of minors under 15 years. Women and minors are also prohibited from engaging in hard labor or night work. In 1997, the minimum wage was $2.80 per day.

22AGRICULTURE

Of Iran's total area, 11.1% is cultivated, 26.9% consists of permanent pastures, and 7% is forest and woodland. The remaining 55% consists of wasteland, lakes, mountains, desert, and urban areas. About one-third of the labor force is employed in agriculture. In 1997, the total land area under cultivation was estimated at 19.4 million hectares (47.9 million acres).

Progress in Iranian agriculture was greatly stimulated by the land reform of 1962–63, under which 4,025,680 farmers and their family members had taken title to their land by 1975, after the old land tenure system was abolished. However, with a rapidly increasing population and a sharply rising standard of living, Iran is no longer self-sufficient in its agricultural production, and food imports have risen steadily in recent years.

In 1998, Iranian agricultural production (in thousands of tons) included wheat, 12,000; sugar beets, 4,754; barley, 2,300; rice, 2,600; grapes, 1,200; apples, 2,200; oranges, 2,000; dates, 900; cotton, 141; tea, 69; and tobacco, 20. Almonds and pistachios are grown primarily for export. In 1998, Iran was the largest producer of pistachios in the world (130,000 tons, or 40% of global production), and the fourth largest producer of almonds (after the US, Spain and Italy), at 76,000 tons.

As of 1997, some 7.26 million hectares (17.94 million acres) were under irrigation. The fifth development plan (1973–78) envisaged an overall increase of 5.5% in agricultural production, but the revised plan raised the target to 8% annually, rescheduled allocations over six years instead of five, and slowed down the projects. Under the revolutionary government's first five-year plan (1983–88), agriculture was to receive 15.5% of total allocations, with food self-sufficiency the primary objective. However, because of the war with Iraq, planned expenditures were never attained. Moreover, food self-sufficiency remains only a goal: imports of agricultural products exceeded exports by nearly $2.2 billion in 1997.

23ANIMAL HUSBANDRY

Not only is animal husbandry the major occupation of nomadic and seminomadic tribes scattered over Iran, but each farming village also keeps flocks that graze on the less productive areas. In 1998 there were 53,000,000 sheep, 27,000,000 goats, 8,600,000 head of cattle, 465,000 water buffalo, 143,000 camels, and 230,000,000 chickens. Cattle are raised as draft animals and for milk and are not fattened for beef. Sheep produce many staple items: milk and butter, animal fat for cooking, meat, wool for carpet making, and skins and hides. Poor weather during the 1970s sharply reduced the domestic flocks, and Iran became an importer of wool. The output of animal products has not kept pace with population growth.

24FISHING

The Caspian Sea provides a seemingly inexhaustible source of sturgeon, salmon, and other species of fish, some of which spawn in the chilly streams that flow into this sea from the high Elburz Mountains. In 1997, the total fish catch was 380,200 tons. Caviar of unrivaled quality is produced by the Iranian Fisheries Co., formerly a joint Russo-Iranian venture but now wholly owned by the government of Iran. About 200,000 kg of caviar are sold per year, most of which is exported, providing a substantial share of the world's supply. Exports of fish products in 1997 amounted to nearly $75.5 million. The fishing grounds of the Persian Gulf were long neglected, but during the 1970s new fishing fleets and packing and conserving facilities were established. The Iran-Iraq war and consequent environmental damage retarded the development of fisheries in this region. Total marine catch has more than doubled from 1982–84 levels.

25FORESTRY

About 12.4 million hectares (30.6 million acres) were covered by forest in 1995/96, according to the Iranian government. An estimated 7.5 million cu m of roundwood were produced in 1995; about 34% was used for fuel. Along the northern slopes of the Elburz Mountains from near sea level to an altitude of about 2,100 m (7,000 ft) are dense stands of oak, ash, elm, beech, ironwood, cypress, walnut, and a number of other varieties. The high plateau forests of Fars, Kurdistan, Luristan, and Khorasan comprise sparse stands of scrub oak, ash, maple, cedar, wild almond, and pistachio. Date palms, acacias, and tamarisks grow in the Persian Gulf area. The deciduous forests on the Caspian littoral are among the best in the world. The timber industry is controlled by the government; its potential annual capacity is 3 million cu m. Imports of forest products totaled $245.1 million in 1997.

A forest ranger school was started in 1957 as an extension of the government's forest service. In 1963, a forestry college was established at Karaj, west of Tehran, to train forestry engineers.

26MINING

Iran possesses extensive and varied mineral resources. Major iron and copper ore deposits are found in Kerman Province. Iran also has deposits of antimony, chromite, lead, zinc, manganese, sulfur, salt, mica, silica, limestone, and granite. Iran is the third largest producer of gypsum, mainly from the mines in the Semnan region about 200 km (125 mi) east of Tehran. The increase of metal production was high on the agenda of the government for postwar reconstruction and economic expansion. In 1996, Iran had 1,785 mines, which produced 42 different minerals (excluding sand and gravel). The mining sector accounted for 24% of Iran's industrial output of $15.4 billion, and mineral and metal exports amounted to $645 million. The government continued its program to privatize the mining sector. Production of bauxite in 1997 was 100,000 tons; chromite, 64,000 tons; copper concentrate, 107,600 tons; lead, 15,700 tons; manganese, 25,000 tons; molybdenum, 560 tons; and zinc, 76,000 tons. Production of hard coal in 1997 was 1,500,000 metric tons; iron ore concentrate, 4,500,000 tons; sulfur, 840,000 tons; and unrefined salt, 450,000 tons. Mineral exports include chromite, refined sulfur, lead, zinc, copper, and decorative stone.

27ENERGY AND POWER

Iran's oil reserves, estimated at 89.7 billion barrels at the start of 2000, constituted 9% of the world's known reserves and were exceeded only by those of Sa'udi Arabia, Iraq, UAE, and Kuwait. Iran was the second-largest oil producer among OPEC countries in 1999.

The first oil concessions were granted by the Iranian (Persian) government in 1872 and 1901, and the first recorded crude oil production began in 1913. Production was carried on by the Anglo-Iranian Oil Co. until the petroleum industry was nationalized in 1951, when the country's oil resources were placed under the management of the National Iranian Oil Co. (NIOC). Late in 1954, the active oil properties and facilities were awarded to a consortium of eight foreign companies, later joined by nine others, with US, British, Dutch, and French interests represented. In 1956, the Iranian Oil Co., another government enterprise, brought in a huge gusher at Qom, south of Tehran. The following year, the legislature ratified an agreement with an Italian company covering an exploited area of Iran, and a joint Italo-Iranian company (SIRIP) was formed to explore and produce. The Pan American Oil Co. acquired concession rights in the Persian Gulf in 1958, joining with the NIOC in a new mixed company, IPAC. By 1962, both SIRIP and IPAC were producing from wells in the Persian Gulf. Additional fields were explored, and production grew rapidly.

During the early 1970s, tremendous changes took place in the Iranian oil industry. The 1954 oil participation agreement was terminated, and on 31 July 1973 a new agreement was signed which replaced the concessionary arrangements with a buyer-seller relationship, the major Western oil companies agreeing to purchase crude petroleum under long-term contracts with the NIOC, which was given full control over the industry. In 1980, the revolutionary government ended joint-venture operations with Western oil companies and regrouped them under the Iranian Offshore Oil Co. of the Islamic Republic.

Meanwhile, largely through the concerted action of OPEC, world oil prices rose rapidly; the posted price of Iranian light crude oil increased from $1.36 a barrel in 1970 to $37 in 1981 before declining to $12.75 a barrel in 1989. The Gulf War caused prices to jump to $23.65 a barrel in 1991; by 1993, a barrel went for $16.70. In order to stabilize the price of oil, OPEC imposed quotas on its members. Iran consistently criticized the quota system and asked for a larger quota. Despite an OPEC-imposed production ceiling for Iran of 3,359,000 barrels per day (a 9% reduction agreed to in February 1992), petroleum production reached 3,705,000 barrels per day in 1995. However, daily production fluctuated by as much as 350,000 barrels. In 1999, production was 3.5 million barrels per day. More than half of Iran's 40 producing fields contain over 1 billion barrels of oil. Most of the reserves are located in onshore fields in the Khuzestan region. The onshore Ahwaz, Marun, Gachsaran, Agha Jari, Bibi Hakimeh, and Pars fields alone account for half of annual oil production. In 1999 Iran announced its largest oil discovery in 30 years, at the Azadegan field in Khuzestan. Oil revenues rose from $5.1 billion in 1986 to an estimated $13.9 billion in 1999, when they accounted for about 90% of total export revenues.

In early 2000, Iran's natural gas reserves were estimated at 22.9 trillion cu m (812 trillion cu ft), or 15% of the world's total reserves. Only Russia possesses larger natural gas reserves. Iran's output declined from 19,869 million cu m in 1973 to 7,300 million cu m in 1982 before climbing back to 53,800 million cu m in 1998. About 27% of Iran's natural gas reserves were only discovered since 1992. Exploitation of natural gas is controlled by the National Iranian Gas Co. In the mid-1990s, Iran began developing extensive gas export plans. Inside Iran, a network of pipelines connects Tehran, Qazvin, Esfahan, Abadan, Shiraz, and Mashhad to Ahvaz and the gas fields. In 1995, Iran played an important role in regional talks concerning the construction of a 3,200 km (2,000 mi) pipeline that would carry gas from Turkmenistan to European markets via Iran, Turkey, and possibly Ukraine. Also in 1995, Iran and Pakistan signed an agreement to ship up to 450 million cu m per day via a 1,600 km (1,000 mi) overland pipeline to Pakistan.

Although Iran is one of the world's leading oil-producing countries, Iranian industry formerly depended on other energy sources, such as electricity, coal, and charcoal. Recently, however, oil and especially gas have been used increasingly in manufacturing. In 1998, hydroelectric power plants generated about 10% and conventional thermal facilities 90% of the total electricity production of 95.3 billion kWh. Iran plans to construct ten nuclear power plants by 2015 in order to provide about 20% of the country's power needs. As of 2000, there were five small nuclear reactors in operation.

28INDUSTRY

Principal industries are oil refining, petrochemicals, steel, and copper. In 1987, there were six primary refineries—at Abadan, Bakhtaran, Tehran, Shiraz, Esfahan, and Tabriz—with a potential capacity of 950,000 barrels per day. In late 1980, Iraqi bombing forced the closure of the Abadan refinery, which had a total capacity of 600,000 barrels per day and was one of the world's largest refineries. Several other refineries suffered lesser damage during the war. The Kharg Island oil terminal also was severely damaged by bombing in 1985. Construction by a Japanese consortium of a $4-billion petrochemical complex at Bandar-e Khomeini, near the Iraqi border, was halted by the war; by mid-1983, the installation, which was 85% complete, had already been attacked six times. In September 1984, the Japanese withdrew their technicians from the site because of renewed Iraqi bombing. Iran has taken on much of the financial responsibility for the plant, and the ending of all payments of Japanese credits and loans in February 1986 most likely meant that the plant would never be completed according to the original plans. After the ceasefire in 1988, Iran began to rebuild its damaged oil export facilities, concentrating mainly on the rehabilitation of Kharg Island. A 500,000-barrel reservoir terminal at Uhang Island was put into operation in March 1993. The oil complex on the southern island of Lavan was reopened after reconstruction at the end of April 1993. The Abadan refinery became again operational at 200,000 barrels per day in May 1993. Isfaran's oil production unit became operational in 1992/93, while the construction of a new refinery at Bandar Abbas was underway. Major refinery products are motor fuel, distillate fuel oil, and residual fuel oil. Oil refining manufacturers had a combined capacity of 1.47 million barrels per day in 2000.

The natural gas industry has boomed in Iran, with the third largest proven reserves in the world. In 1990, the site was appraised at one-eighth of its true size, which was discovered in 1996. In 1998, Iran produced 1.9 trillion cubic feet of natural gas.

The Abadan plant for the production of plastics, detergents, and caustic soda was completed in the 1960s. Since then, the petrochemical industry has expanded considerably. It has been the main element of the post-war industrialization program. The heavy metals industry began in 1972 with the start of steel production at Esfahan National Steel Mill in Esfahan. It was also given priority by the Rafsanjani government. Manufactured goods include diesel engines, motor vehicles, television sets, refrigerators, washing machines, and other consumer items.

The textile industry has prospered in recent years with increased production of cotton, woolen, and synthetic fabrics. The making of handwoven carpets is a traditional industry in Iran that flourishes despite acute competition from machine-made products. However, carpet exports declined throughout the war years. To promote self-sufficiency, Iran has encouraged development of the food-processing, shoemaking, paper and paper products, rubber, pharmaceutical, aircraft, and shipbuilding industries. Other industrial products include cement, nitrogenous fertilizer, phosphate fertilizers, and refined sugar.

Iran's industrialization program was set back by the political turmoil and labor disruptions of the late 1970s and by the revolutionary government's nationalization of industries in the summer of 1979, causing a flight of capital and trained managers. However, the sector recovered somewhat by 1983/84, when industrial production registered a 23% gain, according to the government.

A more recent development plan (1989/90–1993/94) has increased funding to develop heavy industry. A privatization decree in June 1991 led to the identification of 390 public manufacturing and trading firms for divestiture; of these, 185 were already been divested. Industrial production grew at a rate of 5.3% from 1988 to 1998, as opposed to a -3.4% rate during the 1970s. Market reforms were set to continue after 2000.

29SCIENCE AND TECHNOLOGY

The "white revolution" of the 1960s, which emphasized industrialization, involved the importation of petroleum technology and the training of Iranian technicians abroad, but it did not improve Iran's indigenous technology. The principal scientific institution in Tehran is the International Scientific Research Institute, founded in 1955. Specialized learning societies include the Iranian Mathematical Society and the Iranian Society of Microbiology, both headquartered in Tehran. Also in the city are the Animal Husbandry Research Institute and the Institut Pasteur. Iran has 37 universities offering degrees in basic and applied sciences. Following the removal of the Shah and the formation of an Islamic revolutionary government, Iran suffered a "brain drain" as foreign-trained scientists and engineers either fled the country or refused to return after their education. In 1987–97, science and engineering students accounted for 37% of college and university enrollments.

30DOMESTIC TRADE

In summer, offices open as early as 7 AM and close at about 1 PM; during the rest of the year the hours are 8 AM until 4 PM, with a rest period in the middle of the day. Since Friday is the official holiday, many establishments close early on Thursday afternoon. Outside the major cities, most goods are sold in small shops or open-air markets. Banking hours in summer are 7:30 AM to 1 PM and 5 to 7 PM, Saturday–Wednesday, and 7:30 to 11:30 AM on Thursday; winter opening times are 30 minutes to an hour later.

31FOREIGN TRADE

In 1998, major imports included machinery, military supplies, metal works, food, pharmaceuticals, technical services, and refined oil products.

Iran's most expensive export is crude petroleum, which accounts for the majority of it's commodity exports revenues (81%), and 7.8% of the world's total oil exports. Other exports include floor coverings (5.0%) and fruits and nuts (3.0%). Iran holds ten percent of the world's carpet exports.

Principal trading partners in 1998 (in millions of US dollars) were as follows:

COUNTRY	EXPORTS	IMPORTS	BALANCE
Japan	2,230	962	1,268
Italy	1,169	1,002	167
Korea	904	843	61
United Arab Emirates	760	551	209
France	661	697	-36
China (inc. Hong Kong)	539	743	-204
India	523	238	285
Germany	451	1,518	-1,067
Spain	435	352	83
Netherlands	424	285	139

32BALANCE OF PAYMENTS

Throughout the 1960s and 1970s, Iran had a favorable trade balance, but substantial imports of services resulted in an annual deficit on current accounts. Long-term capital inflows from private sources reached a peak in 1965; between 1968 and 1973, capital from foreign governments played a prime role in Iranian development. By 1974, with a net trade surplus of $17,718 million and a current accounts surplus of $10,893 million, Iran was one of the world's major exporters of capital. The current accounts balance remained in surplus annually until the massive economic and civic turbulence caused by the revolution of 1979 and the long, devastating war with Iraq (1980-88). By the time the war had ended, Iran's position as a net foreign creditor has been badly eroded due to a substantial drop in the world price for oil and a sharp increase in dependence on imports—largely machinery and basic commodities to rebuild infrastructure. By 1993, Iran owed foreign creditors nearly $30 billion. In following years, the government, still plagued by lessening oil revenues and a quota of production imposed on it by OPEC, was forced to reschedule the debt—with payments coming due in 1996, when foreign debt went down to approximately $22 billion.

The US Central Intelligence Agency reports that in 1998 the purchasing power parity of Iran's exports was $12.2 billion while imports totaled $13.8 billion resulting in a trade balance of -$1.6 billion. Total foreign debt equaled approximately $11 billion in 1999.

The International Monetary Fund (IMF) reports that in 1998 Iran had exports of goods totaling $12,982 million and imports totaling $13,608 million. The services credit totaled $1,315 million and debit $2,581 million. The following table summarizes

Iran's balance of payments as reported by the IMF for 1998 in millions of US dollars.

Current Account		-1,897
Balance on goods	-626	
Balance on services	-1,266	
Balance on income	-502	
Current transfers	497	
Capital Account		...
Financial Account		3,099
Direct investment abroad	...	
Direct investment in Iran	24	
Portfolio investment assets	...	
Portfolio investment liabilities	...	
Other investment assets	2,779	
Other investment liabilities	296	
Net Errors and Omissions		-2,771
Reserves and Related Items		1,569

33BANKING AND SECURITIES

The Iranian fiscal year begins on 21 March and runs through 20 March of the following calendar year. Before the modern era in Iranian banking, which dates to the opening of a branch of a British bank in 1888, credit was available only at high rates from noninstitutional lenders such as relatives, friends, wealthy landowners, and bazaar money lenders. As recently as 1988 these noninstitutional sources of credit were still available, particularly in the more isolated rural communities. The Central Bank of Iran—Bank Markazil—established by the Monetary and Banking Law of 1960, issues notes, controls foreign exchange, and supervises the banking sector.

The revolutionary government nationalized all commercial banks shortly after taking office in 1979 and announced that banking practices would be brought in line with Islamic principles, which include a ban on interest payments. By 1993 there were five Islamic banks, which had incorporated the previous banks. Instead of paying interest, the new banks give "guaranteed returns" or commissions on loans; the commissions, which equal 4% of the loan's total, were introduced in 1984, and were known as "profit sharing." In Islamic terms, this meant that profit (interest) was acceptable only if a lender's money was "not at risk."

In 1991 measures to promote competition between banks, and to loosen Bank Markazi's control in order to encourage savings within the official banking sector were introduced. In 1994 Bank Markazi introduced reforms allowing private banking operations to register officially and offer most services in competition with the public sector. However, the raft of new currency and export regulations that followed the collapse of the rial in April 1995 put the recently legalized private sector under huge pressure because, for many of the bazaar traders, currency dealings represented a significant share of their total business. There is a basic lack of confidence in the banking system. Many informal banking operations are run from the bazaars. In addition, Iranians who are able to do so operate bank accounts outside the country, importing funds as needed rather than using the domestic system.

Bank Melli, which has acted for the central bank, handles most Iranian banking operations outside the country. The requirements to abide by Islamic principles were never imposed on Bank Melli.

The Tehran Stock Exchange, locally known as the Bourse, was created in 1968. Three years later, the National Bank of Iran and the Industrial and Mining Development Bank of Iran joined with the US firm of Merrill Lynch, Pierce, Fenner & Smith to begin international brokerage activities in Iran. The exchange has stayed open since the revolution but did not play a significant role in the nation's business until the 1990s. Since 1989, the stock exchange has expanded continuously. A total of 220 companies were being traded, and the capitalization of the exchange was reported to be $18 billion, in 1996.

34INSURANCE

The insurance industry in Iran had barely started in 1960, and had a negligible role in the accumulation of funds to finance development, largely because insurance was not used by most of the population. On 25 June 1979, the revolutionary government announced the nationalization of all insurance companies. Under a 1971 Act of Parliament, all companies operating in Iran must cede 25% of total acquired non-life business, and 50% of life business, to Bimeh Markazi Iran, the Central Insurance Co. of Iran. It writes all classes of insurance and reinsurance.

35PUBLIC FINANCE

Iran's fiscal year coincides with its calendar year, beginning on 21 March. The budget is prepared by the Finance Ministry and submitted to Parliament. Trade reforms implemented since 1991 have boosted economic growth and reduced budget deficits. The general government deficit fell from 9% of GDP in 1988 to 2% in 1992, but was up to almost 7% again in 1998.

The US Central Intelligence Agency (CIA) estimates that in 1996 Iran's central government took in revenues of approximately $34.6 billion and had expenditures of $34.9 billion including capital expenditures of $11.8 billion. Overall, the government registered a deficit of approximately $300 million.

The following table shows an itemized breakdown of government revenues and expenditures. The percentages were calculated from data reported by the International Monetary Fund. The dollar amounts (millions) are based on the CIA estimates provided above.

REVENUE AND GRANTS	100%	34,600
Tax revenue	41.8%	14,461
Non-tax revenue	57.2%	19,784
Capital revenue	1.0%	355
EXPENDITURES	100%	34,900
General public services	3.8%	1,313
Defense	8.5%	2,968
Public order and safety	3.3%	1,159
Education	16.0%	5,582
Health	6.4%	2,243
Social security	13.6%	4,736
Housing and community amenities	5.6%	1,968
Recreation, cultural, and religious affairs	3.1%	1,095
Economic affairs and services	29.9%	10,423
Other expenditures	9.0%	3,150
Interest payments	0.8%	263

36TAXATION

Under tax laws written in May of 1992, individual income is taxed at rates varying from 12–54%. Capital gains and investment income are also taxable, and employees pay a 7% social security contribution. Corporate income, which is also taxed at between 12% and 54%, varies among corporations, partnerships, and branches of foreign corporations. The taxable income of a company is subject to a 10% company tax, and the balance is subject to the income tax rates above. Also levied are real estate taxes, municipal tax, and a 23% levy on expatriate salaries. A new value-added tax of 1% of a manufacturing company's sales can be collected. Another tax is a public education cost levy to be paid by manufacturing and service companies.

37CUSTOMS AND DUTIES

Most goods entering Iran are subject to customs duties, the majority of which are on the c.i.f. value. A number of government organizations and charitable institutions have been permitted to import their requirements free of duty. The government has been considering eliminating quantitative trade restrictions and reducing tariff levels, with a maximum rate of 30% for most goods.

38FOREIGN INVESTMENT

Until the early 1970s, Iran rarely participated in foreign businesses. The National Iranian Oil Company (NIOC) did invest in the construction of oil refineries in Madras, India, and other places, and it participated in several mixed ventures with foreign oil firms that held concessions for Iranian oil. But with the vast increase in oil revenues, Iran became one of the world's leading creditor nations; in 1974 alone, bilateral agreements worth hundreds of billions of rials were signed with France, West Germany, Italy, and the UK. In July 1974, Iran agreed to purchase a 25% interest in the German steel-making firm of Krupp Hüttenwerke, an investment believed to be the largest single stake purchased by any oil-producing nation in a major European firm up to that time. In 1975, Iran began negotiating investments through the UNDP in developing nations.

Prior to World War II, foreign companies had important investments in Iranian banks, insurance companies, transport, and the oil industry. In 1955, the legislature enacted a law providing for withdrawal of invested capital in the currency that was brought into Iran, for the export of annual profits, and for adequate compensation in the event of nationalization of the industry or business. In 1957, the US and Iran exchanged notes recognizing that the US would guarantee its private investments in Iran against loss through actions by Iran, and the following year the Majlis enacted a law protecting foreign capital investments. Foreign companies moved into Iran to exploit mineral resources, to establish banks in partnership with Iranian capital, to build factories, and to carry out segments of the shah's vast economic development program.

Since 1979, the instability of the revolutionary government and the catastrophic war with Iraq have had a chilling effect on western investment in Iran. As of 1995, the US has imposed investment restrictions on US firms, and, in general, Iran looks with official disfavor on reliance upon the west for investment. The economic reality, however, is that the country emerged from the war with Iraq in terrible economic shape. In 1995, desperate for western assistance in rebuilding its oil sector, Iran contracted with the French Oil Company, Total, to develop its Sirri oil field. It is the first instance of foreign investment in the vital petroleum sector since the 1979 revolution. In 1995, Iran had negative direct foreign investment of about $50 million, reflecting repatriation of profits greater than inflows of new investment. Foreign direct investment was almost non-existent in 1998.

39ECONOMIC DEVELOPMENT

Iran's first development plan (1949–56) foundered because of the lack of oil revenues during the nationalization dispute and also because the IBRD refused to lend the hoped-for one-third of the projected development expenditures. The second plan (1956–63) also ran into financial difficulties when the domestic budget consumed a larger proportion of the oil revenues than expected. An austerity program from 1960, however, facilitated economic recovery. The third plan (1963–68) was successful, and the period witnessed rapid economic growth. This plan placed emphasis not only on the building of an infrastructure but also on quick-payoff projects making use of local resources. The private sector exceeded the target planned for investment. Substantial foreign aid, varied in its sources, was also forthcoming, and foreign investment in Iran totaled more than $2.7 billion. The fourth plan (1968–73) was far more successful than the previous ones, with most of its objectives realized beyond expectation. The mean annual GNP growth was 11.2%, as compared with the projected

figure of 9%. Similarly, per capita GNP rose to about $560 ($300 had been the goal).

In its revised form, the fifth plan (1973–78) provided for infrastructural development and other expenditures. However, a lag in oil revenues led to rescheduling of the plan for six years instead of five and the postponement or slowdown of individual projects. Because of political opposition and social unrest during the last year of the shah's reign, the plan was abandoned in 1978. The Islamic government that came to power in 1979 cut economic development funds because of a shortage of revenues, but in 1983 it proposed its own five-year development plan for 1983–88, with allocations totaling $166 billion and emphasis given to agriculture and service industries. However, the government's cutbacks on oil production (and, consequently, of the oil revenues that were to finance the plan), coupled with the diversion of resources to the war with Iraq, made it impossible to fulfill the plan's goals. The plan was revised twice after its introduction; in January 1986 the Parliament approved the outline of the revised plan, details of which were not available. The original plan called for 15.5% of development funds to be spent on agriculture, 5.3% on oil, 52.2% on industry and mines, and 27% on services.

The five-year plan (1989/90–1993/94) authorized up to $27 billion in foreign borrowing. It aimed to increase productivity in key industrial and economic sectors and to promote the non-oil export sector. The 1994/95–1998/99 plan aimed at investing money in transport, particularly in the railroad system and in the construction of a public underground for Tehran. Other projects were aimed at revitalizing the petroleum sector and developing the natural gas sector.

40SOCIAL DEVELOPMENT

Traditionally, the family and the tribe were supplemented by Islamic waqf (obligatory charity) institutions for the care of the infirm and the indigent. Iran's monarchical system was slow to awaken to the responsibility of the state in this respect. In 1974, the Ministry of Social Welfare was created with the object of coordinating and harmonizing the programs of social insurance organizations (previously affiliated with the Ministry of Labor) with those of the Social Security Organization, the Ministry of Health, and other government agencies engaged in social welfare. Social welfare programs include workers' compensation, disability benefits, maternity allowances, retirement benefits, death benefits, and family and marriage allowances.

In 1999, these programs covered only employed persons in specific occupations and geographical areas. There were also special pension systems in force for public employees. Old-age benefits were a percentage of average earnings multiplied by the number of years of contributions. Survivor benefits were 50% of the descendant's pension.

The human rights abuses that characterized the shah's regime were, if anything, intensified after his overthrow. The government rejected the principle of the universality of human rights, and argued that Islamic rather than Western precepts should be used in determining the rights of citizens. The revolutionary government was accused of conducting arbitrary arrests and summary trials, of using torture in interrogating political prisoners, and of persecuting such religious minorities as Baha'is and Jews.

The imposition of Islamic fundamentalism brought with it censorship of all media and a revocation, in large part, of the emancipation of women achieved during the previous regime. Women face legal and informal discrimination. Wearing of the chador, the traditional cloak, was reimposed and vigorously enforced, together with gender separation in public places. Family and property laws favor men. Although women may participate in government, in 1995 they held only 9 of 270 seats in the unicameral legislature. No women are represented in the cabinet.

The Jewish, Christian, and Baha'is minorities face government discrimination in areas including education, employment, public accommodations.

Human rights abuses reported in 1999 include extrajudicial killings, the widespread use of torture, arbitrary arrest, and the denial of fair trials. The Iranian government also has engaged in the assassination of political opponents overseas. Iranian groups protesting human rights abuses have also been severely harassed by the government. In spite of the installation of more moderate leaders since the death of Ayatollah Khomeini, the Iranian government continues to restrict freedoms of speech, assembly, religion, association, and the press.

41HEALTH

In 1997, there were 55 reported cases of tuberculosis per 100,000 people; in fact, one quarter of visits to health centers have been attributed to respiratory disease. Health expenditure comprised 4.2% of the gross domestic product between 1990–97. Beginning in the 1960s, national campaigns against such major diseases as malaria and smallpox were undertaken. Other major health problems included high infant mortality, smallpox outbreaks, venereal disease, trachoma, typhoid fever, amoebic dysentery, malaria, tuberculosis, and the debilitating effects of smoking opium. The creation in 1964 of a health corps, consisting of physicians and high-school graduates who agreed to spend the period of their military service serving in semimobile medical units in rural areas, helped to reduce the death rate. Roving health corps teams, comprising a doctor, a dentist, a pathologist, and (when possible) a nurse, served the villages, offering medical services to 10,000–15,000 rural inhabitants annually. In 1999, the death rate was 5.4 per 1,000 population. The infant mortality rate was 29.7 per 1,000 live births.

The Islamic republic has continued to provide health care programs to rural areas. There was one doctor for 3,142 people in 1993 and 0.3 doctors per 1,000 people in 1990–97. In 1991, there were 4,847 dentists in Iran. Many physicians left the country after the 1979 revolution, and health conditions were reportedly deteriorating; however, by the mid-1980s, many doctors who had been in exile during the shah's reign had returned. As of 1990–97, Iran had 1.4 hospital beds per 1,000 people and total health care expenditures equaling 4.2% of GDP. Average life expectancy in 1999 was estimated at 69.8 years for both women and men. Between 1990–95, 84% of the population had access to safe drinking water, and 67% had adequate sanitation. Between 1989–95, 80% of the population had access to health care services. Some form of contraceptive was used by 65% of married women ages 15–49. Iran's birth rate in 1999 was 20.7 per 1,000 people. In 1994, children up to 1 year old were immunized against tuberculosis (100%); diphtheria, pertussis, and tetanus (95%); polio (95%); and measles (95%).

The prevalence of low birth weight babies has risen from 4% of all births in 1980 to 10% in 1993–96. From 1989–95, 16% of all children were malnourished. Cholera was reported in 2,177 individuals. Malaria cases are high; in 1993 there were 65,000 reported cases. AIDS was documented in only 7 cases.

42HOUSING

Rapid urbanization has made housing one of the country's most acute social problems. Although housing has always been given top priority in development plans, the gap between supply and demand for dwellings has grown increasingly wide. During the fourth plan (1968–73), nearly 300,000 housing units were built, but because some 120,000 new families were added to the urban population during that period, the average density rose from 7.7 to 8.5 persons per dwelling. During the same period, the national urban housing deficit rose from 721,000 to 1.1 million units. However, housing starts fell sharply after the 1979 revolution, as construction declined precipitously because of lack of funding (construction of all buildings dropped by 21% in 1981/82 and 24% in 1982/83). In 1986 (the latest year for which statistics are available), 43% of all housing units were constructed of brick with iron beams, 19% were adobe and wood, 16% were brick with wooden beams, 10% were adobe and mud, 5% were cement block, and 3% were iron with a cement skeleton. Electricity was available in 84% of all housing units, 95% had a water toilet, 75% had piped water, 54% had a kitchen, and 47% had a bath.

43EDUCATION

Literacy training has been a prime concern in Iran. For the year 2000, adult illiteracy rates were estimated at 23.1% (males, 16.3%; females, 30.0%). A literacy corps was established in 1963 to send educated conscripts to villages. During its first 10 years, the corps helped 2.2 million urban children and 600,000 adults become literate. In 1997, there were 9,238,393 pupils enrolled in 63,101 primary schools, with 298,755 teachers. The student-to-teacher ratio stood at 31 to one. In that same year, secondary schools had 8,776,792 students and 280,309 teachers.

Education is virtually free in Iran at all levels, from elementary school through university. At university level, however, every student is required to commit to serve the government for a number of years equivalent to those spent at the university. During the early 1970s, efforts were made to improve the educational system by updating school curricula, introducing modern textbooks, and training more efficient teachers.

The 1979 revolution continued the country's emphasis on education, but Khomeini's regime put its own stamp on the process. The most important change was the Islamization of the education system. All students were segregated by sex. In 1980, the Cultural Revolution Committee was formed to oversee the institution of Islamic values in education. An arm of the committee, the Center for Textbooks (composed mainly of clerics), produced 3,000 new college-level textbooks reflecting Islamic views by 1983. Teaching materials based on Islam were introduced into the primary grades within six months of the revolution.

The tradition of university education in Iran goes back to the early centuries of Islam. By the 20th century, however, the system had become antiquated and was remodeled along French lines. The country's 16 universities were closed after the 1979 revolution and were then reopened gradually between 1982 and 1983 under Islamic supervision.

While the universities were closed, the Cultural Revolution Committee investigated professors and teachers and dismissed those who were believers in Marxism, liberalism, and other "imperialistic" ideologies. The universities reopened with Islamic curriculums. In 1997, all higher level institutions had 40,477 teachers and enrolled 579,070 students. The University of Tehran (founded in 1934) has 10 faculties, including a department of Islamic theology. Other major universities are at Tabriz, Mashhad, Ahvaz, Shiraz, Esfahan, Kerman, Babol Sar, Rasht, and Orumiyeh. There are about 50 colleges and 40 technological institutes.

44LIBRARIES AND MUSEUMS

Public libraries and museums are fairly new in Iran. The National Library at Tehran has a good general collection of about 451,500 volumes as of 2000. The Library of Parliament, with 170,000 volumes, has an extensive collection of manuscripts and an unrivaled collection of documentary material in Farsi, including files of all important newspapers since the inception of the press in Iran. The Central Library of the University of Tehran holds some 700,000 volumes.

Tehran has the Archaeological Museum, overflowing with fabulous treasures from the long cultural and artistic history of Iran, and the Ethnological Museum. Iran's crown treasures—manuscripts, jeweled thrones, and a vast variety of other objects—may be seen at the Golestan Palace. Museums at Esfahan, Mashhad, Qom, and Shiraz feature antique carpets, painted pottery, illuminated manuscripts, and fine craftsmanship in wood and metal; most of these objects date from the 12th to the 18th centuries.

45MEDIA

Telegraph, telephone, and radio broadcasting services are state-owned. In 1997 there were 8,991,800 telephones in service. In 1996, 25 regional telecommunications authorities were formed to oversee paging services and cellular systems. Both radio and television were nationalized in 1980. Principal stations are located in Tehran, and other major stations broadcast from Ahvaz, Zahedan, Tabriz, Rasht, Kermanshah, and Bandar-e Lengeh. As of 1999 there were 72 AM and 6 FM radio stations and 28 television broadcast stations. Television of Iran, a privately owned station, began broadcasting in 1956 in Tehran and Abadan. The national radio organization and the government television network were merged in 1971 to form National Iranian Radio and Television (NIRT). After 1979, it became the Islamic Republic of Iran Broadcasting Company. In 1997, Iran had 237 radios, 148 television sets, and 4 mobile phones per 1,000 population.

Until 1979, the local press operated under a law enacted by Parliament in 1955. To obtain licenses, newspaper owners had to have a B.A. degree, good character, and funds adequate for publishing for a stated period. Suspension of publication, fines, and imprisonment resulted from such violations of the law as printing false news or attacks on the royal family, revealing military secrets, and printing material injurious to Islam. At the time of the Khomeini revolution, Iran had 39 daily newspapers with a total circulation of about 750,000. The constitution of 1979 strictly limited freedom of the press; a new press law required publications to be licensed, and their editors were subject to imprisonment for printing reports the religious authorities deemed insulting. Newspapers that had favored the shah were closed down, and others considered unsympathetic to the ruling IRP were banned. In 1985, Khomeini stated "constructive" press criticism of the government would be allowed, but the government severely restricted all media, punishing all instances of criticism against the government or of Islam by imprisonment and beatings. As of 1999, there were reports of continuing government infringement on freedom of the press. Among Iran's most widely read newspapers are *Ettela'at* (1999 circulation 500,000) and *Kayhan* (350,000). There are also several weeklies and special interest magazines. Most print media originate in Tehran.

Online access is extremely limited, with less than 1 Internet host per 1,000 population in 1998.

46ORGANIZATIONS

Long renowned for their individualism, Iranians now actively associate with modern public and private organizations. Under the shah, the government greatly encouraged the growth of the cooperative movement; the first Workers' Consumers Society was established in 1948. Many villages have founded producers' cooperatives with official advice and support, and consumers' cooperatives exist among governmental employees and members of the larger industrial and service organizations. Rural cooperative societies are wide spread.

Private charitable organizations date from as early as 1923, when the Iranian Red Lion and Sun Society (corresponding to the Red Cross) was established. Other charitable institutions include the Organization for Social Services and the Mother and Infant Protection Institute. The Society to Combat the Use of Opium has waged a campaign against use of the drug. The Boy Scout movement in Iran began before World War II. The Chamber of Commerce, Industries, and Mines has its headquarters in Tehran.

47TOURISM, TRAVEL, AND RECREATION

Tourism, which had been stagnant since the 1979 revolution, has begun to grow since the death of Ayatollah Khomeini and the government's attempts to establish closer ties with the West. In 1997, approximately 740,000 tourists visited Iran, over 50% from Europe. Tourism receipts totaled $327 million. That year there were 24,786 hotel rooms with 50,880 beds and occupancy rate of 53%.

Principal tourist attractions include historic and beautifully decorated mosques, mausoleums, and minarets. There are many sports and physical culture societies in Tehran and the provinces; emphasis is upon skiing and weight lifting.

According to 1999 UN estimates, the cost of staying in Iran was approximately $142 per day.

48FAMOUS IRANIANS

The long history of Iran has witnessed a brilliant galaxy of conquerors, wise rulers and statesmen, artists, poets, historians, and philosophers. In religion, there have been diverse figures. Zoroaster (Zarathushtra), who probably lived in the 6th century BC, founded the religion known as Zoroastrianism or Mazdaism, with Ahura-Mazda as the god of good. In the 3d century AD, Mani attempted a fusion of the tenets of Mazdaism, Judaism, and Christianity. The Bab (Sayyid 'Ali Muhammad of Shiraz, 1819–50) was the precursor of Baha'ism, founded by Baha' Allah (Mirza Husayn 'Ali Nuri, 1817–92).

Great Persian rulers of the pre-Christian era include Cyrus ("the Great"; Kurush, r.550–529 BC), Cambyses II (Kambuiya, r.529–522 BC), Darius I ("the Great"; Darayavaush, r.521–486 BC), Xerxes I ("the Great"; Khshayarsha, r.486–465 BC), and Artaxerxes I (Artakhshathra, r.464–424 BC). Shah 'Abbas (r.1587–1628) expanded Persian territory and conquered Baghdad. Prominent political figures of modern times are Reza Shah Pahlavi (1877–1944), who reigned from 1925 to his abdication in 1941; and his son, Muhammad Reza Pahlavi (1919–80), who was shah from 1941 until his abdication in 1979. Until his death in 1989, Iran was under the leadership of Ayatollah Ruhollah Khomeini (1900–89).

The great epic poet Firdawsi (Abdul Qasim Hassan ibn-i-Ishaq ibn-i Sharafshah, 940–1020), writing about AD 1000, produced the *Shahnama (Book of Kings),* dealing with four ancient dynasties and full of romantic and heroic tales that retain their popularity today. Omar Khayyam (d.1123?), astronomer and poet, is known in the Western world for his *Rubáiyât,* a collection of quatrains freely translated by Edward FitzGerald. Important figures of the Seljuk period (11th and 12th centuries) include Muhammad bin Muhammad al-Ghazali (1058–1111), philosopher and mystic theologian, who exerted an enormous influence upon all later speculative thought in Islam; Farid ad-Din 'Attar (Muhammad bin Ibrahim, 1119–1229?), one of the greatest of mystic poets; and Nizami (Nizam ad-Din Abu Muhammad, 1141–1202), noted for four romantic epic poems that were copied and recopied by hand and illuminated with splendid miniatures. In the 13th century, Jalal ad-Din Rumi (1207–73) compiled his celebrated long mystic poem, the *Mathnavi,* in rhyming couplets; and Sa'di (Muslih ud-Din, 1184?–1291), possibly the most renowned Iranian poet within or outside of Iran, composed his *Gulistan (Rose Garden)* and *Bustan (Orchard).* About a hundred years later, in 1389, another poet of Shiraz died, Hafiz (Shams ud-Din Muhammad); his collected works comprise nearly 700 poems, all of them ghazals or lyrical odes.

Poets of the modern period include Iraj Mirza (1880–1926), Mirzadeh Eshqi (d.1924), Parveen Ettasami (d.1941), and the poet laureate Behar (Malik ash-Shuara Bahar, d.1951). Preeminent among prose writers was Sadeq Hedayat (1903–51), author of the novel *Buf i kur* (The Blind Owl) and numerous other works, including films.

Miniature painting came to full flower in the second half of the 15th century. The greatest figure in this field was Bihzad, whose limited surviving work is highly prized. The School of Herat was composed of his followers.

⁴⁹DEPENDENCIES

Iran has no territories or colonies.

⁵⁰BIBLIOGRAPHY

Abdulghani, Jasim M. *Iraq and Iran: The Years of Crisis.* Baltimore: Johns Hopkins University Press, 1984.

Abrahamian, Ervand. *Iran Between Two Revolutions.* Princeton, N.J.: Princeton University Press, 1982.

Amanat, Abbas. *Pivot of the Universe: Nasir al-Din Shah Qajar and the Iranian Monarchy, 1831–1896.* Berkeley: University of California Press, 1997.

Amirahmadi, Hooshang. *Revolution and Economic Transition: The Iranian Experience.* Albany: State University of New York Press, 1990.

Amirahmadi, Hooshang, and Manoucher Parvin (eds.) *Post-revolutionary.* Boulder, Colo.: Westview Press, 1988.

Amuzegar, Jahangir. *Iran's Economy under the Islamic Republic.* London and New York: St. Martin's, 1993.

Arjomand, Said Amir. *The Turban for the Crown: The Islamic Revolution in Iran.* New York: Oxford University Press, 1988.

Authority and Political Culture in Shi'ism Arjomand. Albany: State University of New York Press, 1988.

Bakhash, Shaul. *The Reign of the Ayatollahs: Iran and the Islamic Revolution.* New York: Basic Books, 1984.

Benard, Cheryl, and Zalmay Khalilzad. *The Government of God: Iran's Islamic Republic.* New York: Columbia University Press, 1984.

Bina, Cyrus, and Hamid Zangeneh (eds.). *Modern Capitalism and Islamic Ideology in Iran Bina and Hamid Zangeneh.* New York: St. Martin's Press, 1992.

Bulloch, John. *The Gulf War: Its Origins, History and Consequences.* London: Methuen London, 1989.

Chehabi, H. E. *Iranian Politics and Religious Modernism: The Liberation Movement of Iran under the Shah and Khomeini.* Ithaca, N.Y.: Cornell University Press, 1990.

Chubin, Shahram. *Iran and Iraq at War.* Boulder, Colo.: Westview Press, 1988.

Daneshvar, Parviz. *Revolution in Iran.* New York: St. Martin's Press, 1996.

El-Azhary, M. S. *The Iran-Iraq War: Historical, Economic, and Political Analysis.* New York: St. Martin's Press, 1984.

Elm, Mostafa. *Oil, Power, and Principle: Iran's Oil Nationalization and its Aftermath.* Syracuse, N.Y.: Syracuse University Press, 1992.

Gasiorowski, Mark J. *US Foreign Policy and the Shah: Building a Client State in Iran.* Ithaca, N.Y.: Cornell University Press, 1991.

Ghirshman, Roman. *Iran from the Earliest Times to the Islamic Conquest.* Harmondsworth: Penguin, 1954.

Hiro, Dilip. *Iran Under the Ayatollahs.* 2d ed. New York: Routledge and Kegan Paul, 1987.

Hunter, Shireen. *Iran after Khomeini.* New York: Praeger, 1992.

Iran and the Arab World. New York: St. Martin's Press, 1993.

Iran in Pictures. Minneapolis: Lerner, 1988.

Iranian Perspectives on the Iran-Iraq War. Gainesville: University Press of Florida, 1997.

Kamrava, Mehran. *The Political History of Modern Iran: From Tribalism to Theocracy.* Westport, Conn.: Praeger, 1992.

Karshenas, Massoud. *Oil, State, and Industrialization in Iran.* New York: Cambridge University Press, 1990.

Kashani-Sabet, Firoozeh. *Frontier Fictions: Shaping the Iranian Nation, 1804–1946.* Princeton, N.J.: Princeton University Press, 1999.

Keddie, Nikki R. *Iran and the Muslim World: Resistance and Revolution.* Hampshire, England: Macmillan, 1995.

Keddie, Nikki R., and Eric Hooglund (eds.). *The Iranian Revolution and the Islamic Republic.* 2d ed. Syracuse, N.Y.: Syracuse University Press, 1986.

Limbert, John W. *Iran, at War with History.* Boulder, Colo.: Westview Press, 1987.

Lorentz, John H. *Historical Dictionary of Iran.* Lanham, Md.: Scarecrow Press, 1995.

Loveday, Helen. *Iran.* 2d ed. London: Hi Marketing, 1999.

Mackey, Sandra. *The Iranians: Persia, Islam and the Soul of a Nation.* New York: Dutton, 1996.

Metz, Helen Chapin (ed.). *Iran, a Country Study.* 4th ed. Washington, D.C.: Library of Congress, 1989.

Mofid, Kamran. *The Economic Consequences of the Gulf War.* New York: Routledge, 1990.

Mottahedeh, Roy P. *Mantle of the Prophet.* New York: Pantheon, 1986.

O'Ballance, Edgar. *Islamic Fundamentalist Terrorism, 1979–95: The Iranian Connection.* Washington Square, N.Y.: New York University Press, 1997.

Paidar, Parvin. *Women and the Political Process in Twentieth-Century Iran.* Cambridge, England: Cambridge University Press, 1995.

Ramazani, R. K. *Revolutionary Iran: Challenges and Responses in the Middle East.* Baltimore: Johns Hopkins University Press, 1987.

Sanchez, James. *Index to the Iran-Contra Hearings Summary Report.* Jefferson, N.C.: McFarland, 1988.

Simpson, John. *Lifting the Veil: Life in Revolutionary Iran.* London: Hodder & Stoughton, 1995.

Standish, John F. *Persia and the Gulf: Retrospect and Prospect.* New York: St. Martin's Press, 1998.

Stempel, John D. *Inside the Iranian Revolution.* Bloomington: Indiana University Press, 1981.

Wiesehofer, Josef. *Ancient Persia: From 550 BC to 650 AD.* New York: I. B. Tauris, 1996.

Wright, Robin B. *In the name of God: The Khomeini Decade.* New York: Simon and Schuster, 1989.

Zonis, Marvin. *Majestic Failure: The Fall of the Shah.* Chicago: University of Chicago Press, 1991.

IRAQ

Republic of Iraq
Al-Jumhuriyah al-'Iraqiyah

CAPITAL: Baghdad.

FLAG: The national flag is a tricolor of red, white, and black horizontal stripes, with three five-pointed stars in green in the center of the white stripe.

ANTHEM: *Al-Salaam al-Jumhuri (Salute of the Republic).*

MONETARY UNIT: The Iraqi dinar (ID) is a paper currency of 1,000 fils. There are coins of 1, 5, 10, 25, 50, 100, and 250 fils, and notes of 250 and 500 fils and 1, 5, 10, 50, 100, and 250 dinars. The dinar is extremely unstable. ID1 = $0.00080 ($1 = ID1250.13) as of 31 March 2000.

WEIGHTS AND MEASURES: The metric system is the legal standard, but weights and measures in general use vary, especially in domestic transactions. The unit of land is the dunam, which is equivalent to approximately 0.25 hectare (0.62 acre).

HOLIDAYS: New Year's Day, 1 January; Army Day, 6 January; 14th Ramadan Revolution Day, 8 February; Declaration of the Republic, 14 July; and Peaceful Revolution Day, 17 July. Muslim religious holidays include 'Id al-Fitr, 'Id al-'Adha', Milad an-Nabi, and Islamic New Year.

TIME: 3 PM = noon GMT.

¹LOCATION, SIZE, AND EXTENT

Present-day Iraq, comprising an area of 437,072 sq km (168,754 sq mi), corresponds roughly to the former Turkish provinces of Baghdad, Mosul (Al-Mawsil), and Basra (Al-Basrah). Comparatively, the area occupied by Iraq is slightly more than twice the size of the state of Idaho. It extends 984 km (611 mi) SSE–NNW and 730 km (454 mi) ENE–WSW. Iraq is bordered on the N by Turkey, on the E by Iran, on the SE by the Persian Gulf and Kuwait, on the S by Sa'udi Arabia, on the W by Jordan, and on the NW by Syria, with a total boundary length of 3,689 km (2,292 mi). The Neutral Zone, administered jointly by Iraq and Sa'udi Arabia, was to be divided according to an agreement of 2 July 1975, which was confirmed by an agreement signed on 26 December 1981 in Baghdad. This pact was described by the Sa'udi signatory as defining and fixing the common border and dividing the Neutral Zone, but as of early 1988, no details of the agreement had been filed with the UN. A long-standing border dispute with Iran, seemingly resolved in 1975, led to a full-scale war in the 1980s. In August 1990, Iraq reasserted its claim, dating from the days of the monarchy (abolished in 1958), to Kuwait, invading and occupying it. In January 1991, Iraq was defeated by the US and its allies in an air war and withdrew.

Iraq's capital city, Baghdad, is located in the east central part of the country.

²TOPOGRAPHY

Iraq is divided into three distinct zones: the desert in the west and southwest; the plains; and the highlands in the northeast, which rise to 3,000 m (10,000 ft) or more. The desert is an upland region with altitudes of 600 to 900 m (2,000–3,000 ft) between Damascus in Syria and Ar-Rutbah in Iraq, but declines gently toward the Euphrates (Al-Furat) River. The water supply comes from wells and wadis that at times carry torrential floods and that retain the winter rains.

Dominated by the river systems of the Tigris (Dijlah) and Euphrates, the plains area is composed of two regions divided by a ridge, some 75 m (250 ft) above the flood plain, between Ar-Ramadi and a point south of Baghdad that marks the prehistoric coastline of the Persian Gulf. The lower valley, built up by the silt the two rivers carry, consists of marshland, crisscrossed by drainage channels. At Qarmat 'Ali, just above Basra, the two rivers combine and form the Shatt al-'Arab, a broad waterway separating Iraq and Iran. The sources of the Euphrates and Tigris are in the Armenian Plateau. The Euphrates receives its main tributaries before entering Iraq, while the Tigris receives several streams on the eastern bank within the country.

³CLIMATE

Under the influence of the monsoons, Iraq in summer has a constant northwesterly wind (shamal), while in winter a strong southeasterly air current (sharqi) develops. The intensely hot and dry summers last from May to October, and during the hottest time of the day—often reaching 49°C (120°F) in the shade—people take refuge in underground shelters. Winters, lasting from December to March, are damp and comparatively cold, with temperatures averaging about 10°C (50°F). Spring and autumn are brief transition periods. Normally, no rain falls from the end of May to the end of September. With annual rainfall of less than 38 cm (15 in), agriculture is dependent on irrigation.

⁴FLORA AND FAUNA

In the lower regions of the Euphrates and Tigris and in the alluvial plains, papyrus, lotus, and tall reeds form a thick underbrush; willow, poplar, and alder trees abound. On the upper and middle Euphrates, the licorice bush yields a juice that is extracted for commercial purposes; another bush growing wild in the semiarid steppe or desert yields gum tragacanth for pharmaceutical use. In the higher Zagros Mountains grows the valonia oak, the bark of which is used for tanning leather. About 30 million date palms produce one of Iraq's most important exports.

Wild animals include the hyena, jackal, fox, gazelle, antelope, jerboa, mole, porcupine, desert hare, and bat. Beaver, wild ass, and ostrich are rare. Wild ducks, geese, and partridge are the game birds. Vultures, owls, and ravens live near the Euphrates. Falcons are trained for hunting.

5ENVIRONMENT

The major sources of environmental damage are effluents from oil refineries, factory and sewage discharges into rivers, fertilizer and chemical contamination of the soil, and industrial air pollution in urban areas. An estimated 1% of agricultural land is lost each year through soil erosion and salinization. The government has not developed a comprehensive environmental conservation policy, but it has initiated programs to prevent water pollution, to reclaim land by reducing soil salinity, and to protect wildlife by limiting hunting. As a result of damage from the 1991 Persian Gulf War, water pollution has increased. Purification systems for water and sewage are inadequate. Toxic chemicals from damaged oil facilities contribute to water pollution. Iraq has 8.2 cubic miles of water with 92% used in farming activity. Seventy percent of people living in rural areas and 50% of urban dwellers do not have pure water. Iraq ranks among the 50 nations with the world's highest levels of industrial carbon dioxide emissions. Its 1992 emissions totaled 64.5 million metric tons, a per capita level of 3.33 metric tons. The nation's cities produce 6 million tons of solid waste per year. The Supreme Council for the Human Environment is the principal environmental agency; its implementing body, the Directorate General for the Human Environment, was established in 1975 and is attached to the Ministry of Health. As of 1994, 9 of Iraq's mammal species and 17 of its bird species were endangered. One plant species was threatened with extinction. Endangered or extinct species include the northern bald Ibis, Persian fallow deer, Sa'udi Arabian dorcas gazelle, Asiatic cheetah, and Syrian wild ass.

6POPULATION

The population of Iraq in 2000 was estimated at 23,150,926. An estimated 3.0% of the population is 65 years of age or older. The projected population for the year 2005 is 29,366,000, assuming a crude birthrate of 38 per 1,000 population and a death rate of 5, resulting in a natural rate of change of 3.3% for the period 2000–2005. The population rate of change between 1995 and 2000 was 2.8%. The estimated average population density in 1996 was 49 per sq km (128 per sq mi).

It was estimated that 77% of the population lived in urban areas in 2000. The capital city, Baghdad, had a 2000 population of 4,336,000. Other major cities, with 2000 estimated metropolitan area populations, included Arbil, 2,368,000, and Mosul, 1,034,000.

7MIGRATION

Immigration into Iraq was limited until the beginning of the 1970s. However, the rise in oil prices and the increase of oil exports, as well as extensive public and private spending in the mid-1970s, created a market for foreign labor. The result was a stream of foreign (mainly Egyptian) workers whose number may have risen as high as 1,600,000 before the Gulf War. During the Iran–Iraq war, many Egyptians worked in the public sector, filling a gap left by civil servants, farmers, and other workers who were fighting at the front. A number of Iraqis from the south, mainly Basra and its environs, influenced by family ties and higher wages, migrated to Sa'udi Arabia and Kuwait. To weaken local support in the north for Kurdish rebels, the government forced tens of thousands of Kurds to resettle in the south; in September 1987, a Western diplomat in Baghdad claimed that at least 500 Kurdish villages had been razed and 100,000 to 500,000 Kurds relocated.

In 1991 some 1.5 million Iraqis fled the country for Turkey or Iran to escape Saddam Hussein's increasingly repressive rule, but fewer than 100,000 remained abroad. Most of the refugees were Kurds who later resettled in areas in Iraq not controlled by the government. In September and October of 1996, around 65,000 Iraqi Kurds fled to Iran due to internal fighting between the Iraqi Kurds.

As of September 1999, the UNHCR assisted 31,400 refugees in Iraq. Of these, 19,000 were Iranian Kurds, and 11,300 were Turkish Kurds. Another some 1,100 urban refugees of various nationalities live in Baghdad. In addition to these UNHCR-assisted refugees, Iraq hosts some 62,000 Palestinian refugees and an estimated 10,000 Iranians in the south of the country.

UNHCR also facilitates the voluntary return of Turkish Kurds from Iraq to Turkey. More than half of the Iranian Kurd refugees in Al-Tash have likewise expressed their desire to return to Iran.

In 1999 the net migration rate was zero migrants per 1,000 population.

8ETHNIC GROUPS

Arabs constitute about 75–80% of the total population. The Kurds, an Islamic non-Arab people, are the largest and most important minority group, constituting about 15–20%. A seminomadic pastoral people, the Kurds live in the northeastern Zagros Mountains, mostly in isolated villages in the mountain valleys near Turkey and Iran. Kurdish opposition to Iraqi political dominance has occasioned violent clashes with government forces. Other minorities (5%) include Turkomans, living in the northeast; Yazidis, mostly in the Sinjar Mountains; Assyrians, mainly in the cities and northeastern rural areas; and Armenians.

9LANGUAGES

Arabic is the national language and is the mother tongue of an estimated 79% of the population. Kurdish—the official language in Kurdish regions—or a dialect of it, is spoken by the Kurds and Yazidis. Aranaic, the ancient Syriac dialect, is retained by the Assyrians. Another Syriac dialect, Mandaean, is the liturgical language of the Sabaeans. The Turkomans speak a Turkic dialect. Armenian is also spoken.

10RELIGIONS

Islam is the national religion of Iraq, adhered to by some 97% of the population in 1999. About 60–65% of Muslims belong to the Shi'a sect and 32–37% to the Sunni sect. Traditionally, the Shi'a majority has been governed and generally oppressed by members of the Sunni minority, which since the late 1970s has become increasingly concerned about the export of Shi'a militancy from Iran. There are also some heterodox Muslim groups, such as the Yazidis, who consider Satan a fallen angel who will one day be reconciled with God. They propitiate him in their rites and regard the Old and New Testaments, as well as the Koran (Qur'an), as sacred.

In 1999, about 3% of the population were adherents to Christianity and other religions. More than 500,000 of the Christians were Roman Catholic, and nearly all the remainder belonged to various branches of Oriental Christianity. The Assyrians (who are not descended from the ancient Assyrians) are Nestorians. In the 19th century, under the influence of Roman Catholic missions, Christian Chaldaeans, originally also Nestorians, joined the Uniate churches, which are in communion with Rome; their patriarch has his seat in Mosul. The Sabaeans, or Mandaeans, are often called Christians of St. John, but their religious belief and their liturgy contain elements of many creeds, including some of pre-Christian Oriental origin. Since baptism is their main ritual, they always dwell near water and are concentrated on the river-banks south of Baghdad. Iraq's Jewish community, which had its

IRAQ

0   50   100 Miles

0   50   100 Kilometers

TURKEY

Hakkâri

Daryācheh-ye Orūmiyeh

Orūmiyeh

Zākhū

Dahūk

Az Zibār

Shanidar Cave

Qezel Owzan

Al Ḥasakah

Tall ʿAfar

Tigris

Al Mawṣil ■ *Calah*

Arbil

Gundah Zhur 11,838 ft. 3608 m.

Saqqez

Al Hadar

Zāb aṣ Ṣaḡōr

As Sulaymāniyah

Euphrates

Dayr az Zawr

Nuzi ■ **Kirkūk**

Sanandaj

M E S O P O T A M I A

Baʿiji

Tigris

Al ʿUẓaym

S Y R I A

Euphrates

ʿAnah

Buḥayrat al Qādisiyah

Tharthār Lake

Sāmarrāʾ

Khānaqin

Diyalá

Kermānshāh

Z A G R O S   M T S .

I R A N

Baqūbah

Mandali

Ar Ramādi

Habbāniyah Lake

Al Fallūjah

☆ **Baghdād**

• *Ctesiphon*

S Y R I A N

JORDAN

Trebil

Ar Ruṭbah

Razzaza Lake

Babylon

Al Kūt

Dijlah

Dēzfūl

Karbalā • Al Ḥillah

An Najaf

Ad Diwānifsyah

Al ʿAmārah

Kārūn

D E S E R T

Badanah

Ash Shaṭrah

Al Furāt

As Samāwah

An Nāṣiriyah

Ur ■

Shaṭṭ al ʿArab

Al Baṣrah

Az Zubayr

Ābādān

Sahara ʾal Hijarah

KUWAIT

Jūn al Kuwayt

☆ **Kuwait**

Persian Gulf

SAʿUDI ARABIA

Iraq

LOCATION: 29° to 37°30′N; 39° to 48°E. **BOUNDARY LENGTHS:** Turkey, 305 km (190 mi); Iran, 1,458 km (906 mi); Persian Gulf coastline, 19 km (12 mi); Kuwait, 254 km (158 mi); Saʿudi Arabia, 895 km (556 mi); Jordan, 147 km (91 mi); Syria, 603 km (375 mi). **TERRITORIAL SEA LIMIT:** 12 mi.

origins in Babylonian times and which produced outstanding scholars during the first millennium AD, dwindled from about 90,000 in 1948 to 200 in 1990, virtually all Iraqi Jewry having emigrated to Israel by the early 1950s.

¹¹TRANSPORTATION

Major cities, towns, and villages are connected by a modern network of highways and roads which have made old caravan routes extinct. The city of Baghdad has been reshaped by the development of expressways through the city and by passes built since the 1970s. By 1996, Iraq had 47,400 km (29,454 mi) of roads, of which 40,764 km (25,331 mi) were paved. There were some 672,000 cars and 368,000 commercial vehicles in use as of 1995.

Railroads are owned and operated by the Iraqi State Railways Administration. A standard-gauge railroad connects Iraq with Jordan and Syria, and nearly all the old meter-gauge line connecting Irbil in the north with Basra, by way of Kirkuk and Baghdad, has been replaced. In 1998 there were about 2,032 km (1,263 mi) of railway lines.

Iraq had 109 airports in 1998, of which 77 had paved runways. Baghdad, Basra, and Mosul have international airports. Iraq Airways is the state-owned carrier; in the 1980s, its international flights landed only at night because of the Iraqi-Iranian war. The war also virtually closed Iraq's main port of Basra and the new port of Umm Qasr on the Persian Gulf. Expansion of Iraq's merchant marine, which totaled 1,470,000 GRT in 1980, was halted by the war with Iran and again by the Persian Gulf War; by 1998, the merchant marine totaled only 30 ships with a total capacity of 456,845 GRT.

12 HISTORY

Some of the earliest known human settlements have been found in present-day Iraq. Habitations, shrines, implements, and pottery found on various sites can be dated as early as the 5th millennium BC. Some sites bear names that are familiar from the Bible, which describes the region of the Hiddekel (Tigris) and Euphrates rivers as the location of the Garden of Eden and the city of Ur as the birthplace of the patriarch Abraham. Scientific exploration and archaeological research have amplified the biblical accounts.

Recorded history in Mesopotamia (the ancient name of Iraq, particularly the area between the Tigris and Euphrates) begins with the Sumerians, who by the 4th millennium BC had established city-states. Records and accounts on clay tablets prove that they had a complex economic organization before 3200 BC. The reign of Sumer was challenged by King Sargon of Akkad (r.c.2350 BC); a Sumero-Akkadian culture continued in Erech (Tall al-Warka') and Ur (Tall al-Muqayyar) until it was superseded by the Amorites or Babylonians (about 1900 BC), with their capital at Babylon. The cultural height of Babylonian history is represented by Hammurabi (r.c.1792–c.1750 BC), who compiled a celebrated code of laws. After Babylon was destroyed by the Hittites about 1550 BC, the Hurrians established the Mitanni kingdom in the north for about 200 years, and the Kassites ruled for about 400 years in the south.

From Assur, their stronghold in the north, the Assyrians overran Mesopotamia about 1350 BC and established their capital at Nineveh (Ninawa). Assyrian supremacy was interrupted during the 11th and 10th centuries BC by the Aramaeans, whose language, Aramaic, became a common language in the eastern Mediterranean area in later times. Assyrian power was finally crushed by the Chaldeans or Neo-Babylonians, who, in alliance with the Medes in Persia, destroyed Nineveh in 612 BC. Nebuchadnezzar II (r.c.605–c.560 BC) rebuilt the city-state of Babylon, but it fell to the Persians, under Cyrus the Achaemenid dynasty, in 539 BC. Under his son Cambyses II, the Persian Empire extended from the Oxus (Amu Darya) River to the Mediterranean, with its center in Mesopotamia. Its might, in turn, was challenged by the Greeks. Led by the Macedonian conqueror Alexander the Great, they defeated the Persians by 327 BC and penetrated deep into Persian lands. The Seleucids, Alexander's successors in Syria, Mesopotamia, and Persia, built their capital, Seleucia, on the Tigris, just south of Baghdad. They had to yield power to the Parthians, who conquered Mesopotamia in 138 BC.

The Arabs conquered Iraq in AD 637. For a century, under the "Orthodox" and the Umayyad caliphs, Iraq remained a province of the Islamic Empire, but the 'Abbasids (750–1258) made it the focus of their power. In their new capital, Baghdad, their most illustrious member, Harun al-Rashid (ar-Rashid, r.786–809), became, through the Arabian Nights, a legend for all time. Under Harun and his son Al-Ma'mun, Baghdad was the center of brilliant intellectual and cultural life. Two centuries later, the Seljuk vizier Nizam al-Mulk established the famous Nizamiyah University, one of whose professors was the philosopher Al-Ghazali (Ghazel, d.1111). A Mongol invasion in the early 13th century ended Iraq's flourishing economy and culture. In 1258, Genghis Khan's grandson Hulagu sacked Baghdad and destroyed the canal system on which the productivity of the region had depended. Timur, also known as Timur Lenk ("Timur the Lame") or Tamerlane, conquered Baghdad and Iraq in 1393. Meanwhile, the Ottoman Turks had established themselves in Asia Minor and, by capturing Cairo (1517), their sultans claimed legitimate succession to the caliphate. In 1534, Süleyman the Magnificent conquered Baghdad and, except for a short period of Persian control in the 17th century, Iraq remained an Ottoman province until World War I.

Late in 1914, the Ottoman Empire sided with the Central Powers, and a British expeditionary force landed in Iraq and occupied Basra. The long campaign that followed ended in 1918, when the whole of Iraq fell under British military occupation. The collapse of the Ottoman Empire stimulated Iraqi hopes for freedom and independence, but in 1920, Iraq was declared a League of Nations mandate under UK administration. Riots and revolts led to the establishment of an Iraqi provisional government in October 1920. On 23 August 1921, Faisal I (Faysal), the son of Sharif Hussein (Husayn ibn-'Ali) of Mecca, became king of Iraq. In successive stages, the last of which was a treaty of preferential alliance with the UK (June 1930), Iraq gained independence in 1932 and was admitted to membership in the League of Nations.

Faisal died in 1933, and his son and successor, Ghazi, was killed in an accident in 1939. Until the accession to the throne of Faisal II, on attaining his majority in 1953, his uncle 'Abdul Ilah, Ghazi's cousin, acted as regent. On 14 July 1958, the army rebelled under the leadership of Gen. 'Abd al-Karim al-Qasim (Kassim). Faisal II, Crown Prince 'Abdul Ilah, and Prime Minister Nuri al-Sa'id (as-Sa'id) were killed. The monarchy was abolished, and a republic established. Iraq left the anti-communist Baghdad Pact, which the monarchy had joined in 1955. An agrarian reform law broke up the great landholdings of feudal leaders, and a new economic development program emphasized industrialization. In spite of some opposition from original supporters and political opponents, tribal uprisings, and several attempts at assassination, Qasim managed to remain the head of Iraq for four and a half years. On 9 February 1963, however, a military junta, led by Col. 'Abd as-Salam Muhammad 'Arif, overthrew his regime and executed Qasim.

The new regime followed a policy based on neutralism and aimed to cooperate with Syria and Egypt and to improve relations with Turkey and Iran. These policies were continued after 'Arif was killed in an airplane crash in 1966 and was succeeded by his brother, 'Abd ar-Rahman 'Arif. This regime, however, was overthrown in July 1968, when Gen. (later Marshal) Ahmad Hasan al-Bakr, heading a section of the Ba'th Party, staged a coup and established a new government with himself as president. In the 1970s, the Ba'th regime focused increasingly on economic problems, nationalizing the petroleum industry in 1972–73 and allocating large sums for capital development. Bakr resigned in July 1979 and was followed as president by his chosen successor, Saddam Hussein (Husayn) al-Takriti.

Since 1961, Iraq's Kurdish minority has frequently opposed with violence attempts by Baghdad to impose authority over its regions. In an attempt to cope with this opposition, the Bakr government passed a constitutional amendment in July 1970 granting limited political, economic, and cultural autonomy to the Kurdish regions. But in March 1974, Kurdish insurgents, known as the Pesh Merga, again mounted a revolt, with Iranian military support. The Iraqi army countered with a major offensive. On 6 March 1975, Iraq and Iran concluded an agreement by which Iran renounced support for the Kurds and Iraq agreed to share sovereignty over the Shatt al-'Arab estuary.

Tensions between Iraq and Iran rose after the Iranian revolution of 1979 and the accession to power of Saddam Hussein. In September 1980, Iraq sought to take advantage of the turmoil in Iran by suddenly canceling the 1975 agreement and mounting a full-scale invasion. Iraqi soldiers seized key points in the Khuzistan region of southwestern Iran, captured the major southern city of Khorramshahr, and besieged Abadan, destroying its large oil refinery. The Iraqi army then took up defensive positions, a tactic that gave the demoralized Iranian forces time to regroup and launch a slow but successful counterattack that retook Khuzistan by May 1982. Iraq then sought peace and in June withdrew from Iranian areas it had occupied. Iran's response was to launch major offensives aimed at the oil port of Basra. Entrenched in well-prepared positions on their own territory, Iraqi soldiers repelled the attacks, inflicting heavy losses, and the war ground to a stalemate, with tens of thousands of casualties on each side.

Attempts by the UN and by other Arab states to mediate the conflict were unsuccessful; in the latter stages of the war, Iraq accepted but Iran regularly rejected proposals for a compromise peace. Although most Arab states supported Iraq, and the Gulf oil states helped finance Iraqi military equipment, the war had a destabilizing effect both on the national economy and on the ruling Ba'th Party. France also aided Iraq with credits to buy advanced weapons (notably, Super Étendard fighters and Exocet missiles), and it provided the technology for Iraq to construct the Osirak nuclear reactor near Baghdad. (In June 1981, this installation was destroyed in a bombing raid by Israel, which claimed that the facility would be used to produce nuclear weapons, a charge Iraq denied.) Other Western countries provided supplies, financing, and intelligence to Iraq but denied the same to Iran.

In February 1986, the Iranians made their biggest gain in the war, crossing the Shatt al-'Arab and capturing Fao (Al-Faw) on the southernmost tip of land in Iraq. In early 1987, they seized several islands in the Shatt al-'Arab opposite Basra. The war soon spread to Persian Gulf shipping, as both sides attacked oil tankers and ships transporting oil, goods, and arms to the belligerents or their supporters.

The war ended on 20 August 1988 after Iran accepted a UN cease-fire proposal on 18 July. Having suffered enormous casualties and physical damage plus a massive debt burden, Baghdad began the postwar process of reconstruction. Before and after the war, there were scores to settle, primarily against the Kurds, some of whom had helped Iran and were the victims of Iraqi poison gas attacks. Many border villages were demolished and their Kurdish populations relocated.

When Iraq's wartime allies seemed unwilling to ease financial terms or keep oil prices high and questioned Iraq's rearmament efforts, Saddam Hussein turned bitterly against them. Kuwait was the principal target. After threats and troop movements, Iraq reasserted its claim (which dated from the days of the monarchy) to that country and on 2 August 1990, invaded and occupied it. Saddam Hussein was unflinching in the face of various peace proposals, economic sanctions, and the threatening buildup of coalition forces led by the US.

A devastating air war began on 17 January 1991 followed by ground attack on 24 February. Iraq was defeated, but not occupied. Despite vast destruction and several hundred thousand casualties, Saddam's regime remained firmly in control. It moved to crush uprisings from the Shia in the south and Kurds in the north. To protect those minorities, the US and its allies imposed no-fly zones that gave the Kurds virtually an independent state, but afforded much less defense for the rebellious Arabs in the south whose protecting marshes were being drained by Baghdad. There have been several clashes between allied and Iraq forces in both areas. On 17 March 1995, Iraqi forces arrested two Americans who wandered over the border while trying to visit friends nearby in Kuwait. The McDonnell Douglas Corp. employees, David Daliberti and Bill Barloon, said they got lost and crossed the border by accident.

Since the United States and Iraq have no diplomatic ties, America had to work through officials of the United Nations and Poland to petition for the men's release. The efforts went for naught, however, and on March 23, an Iraqi court sentenced the men to eight years in prison on charges of entering Iraq illegally. The Clinton Administration condemned the severity of the sentences. The United States said it would follow diplomatic channels in pressing for the men's release. It denied an allegation that they had entered Iraq as saboteurs or spies. The Polish diplomat representing the United States in Iraq was allowed weekly visits with the men to check on their welfare. The two Americans were released by Saddam in July 1995.

In 1996, in an effort to boost morale in Iraq and bolster its image abroad, Iraq conducted its first parliamentary elections since 1989. However, only candidates loyal to Saddam Hussein were allowed to run. A Government screening committee reviewed and approved all 689 candidates, who either belonged to Hussein's Ba'ath Party or were independence who supported the 1968 coup that brought the party to power.

The Iraqi economy continued to decline throughout the 1990s, with the continuation of the UN sanctions, imposed in 1990, which prohibited Iraq from selling oil on the global market in major transactions and froze Iraqi assets overseas. The deteriorating living conditions imposed on the Iraqi population prompted consideration of emergency measures. In 1996 talks were held between Iraq and the United Nations on a proposed "oil for food" humanitarian program that would permit Iraq to sell a limited quantity of oil in order to purchase food and basic supplies for Iraqi citizens. The United States and Britain wanted money earmarked for Iraq's Kurdish provinces funneled through the existing United Nations assistance program there. They also raised the issue of equity with respect to Iraq's existing rationing system. In December 1996, the UN agreed to allow Iraq to export $2 billion in oil to buy food and medical supplies. Iraq began receiving 400,000 tons of wheat in the spring of 1997.

Since the end of the Gulf War, Iraq had demonstrated cooperation with UNSCOM, the special UN commission charged with monitoring weapons of mass destruction. However, Saddam refused to dismantle his country's biological weapons and had stopped cooperating with UNSCOM by August 1997, leading to increasing tension and a US military buildup in the region by early 1998. However, personal intervention by UN Secretary General Kofi Annan helped diffuse the situation temporarily. However, renewed disagreements arose in the latter half of the year, ultimately leading to a December bombing campaign (Operation Desert Fox) by US and UK forces, with the goal of crippling Iraq's weapons capabilities. In late 1998 the US Congress also approved funding for Iraqi opposition groups, in hopes of toppling Saddam politically from within.

In 1999 the oil for food program was expanded to allow for the sale of $5.25 billion in oil by Iraq over a six-month period to buy good and medicine. As of 2000, most observers agreed that the decade-long UN sanctions, while impoverishing Iraq and threatening its population with a major humanitarian crisis, had failed in their goal of weakening Saddam's hold on power.

13 GOVERNMENT

The coup d'état of 14 July 1958 established an autocratic regime headed by the military. Until his execution in February 1963, 'Abd al-Karim al-Qasim ruled Iraq, with a Council of State and a cabinet. On 27 July 1958, a fortnight after taking over, Qasim's regime issued a provisional constitution, which has been repeatedly amended to accommodate changes in the status of the Kurdish regions. Since the 1968 coup, the Ba'th Party has ruled Iraq by means of the Revolutionary Command Council, "the supreme governing body of the state," which selects the president and a cabinet composed of military and civilian leaders. The president (Saddam Hussein since 1979) serves as chairman of the Revolutionary Command Council, which exercises both executive and legislative powers by decree. He is also prime minister, commander-in-chief of the armed forces, and secretary-general of the Ba'th Party. A National Assembly of 250 members that was elected by universal suffrage in 1980, 1984, 1989, and 1996 has little real power. Most senior officials are relatives or close associates of Saddam Hussein; nevertheless, their job security is not great.

The precarious nature of working in the regime of Saddam Hussein, even for relatives, was made evident in 1995 when two of his sons-in-law defected to Jordan along with President Hussein's daughters. The defection was widely reported in the international media and considered a great embarrassment to the regime as well as a strong indicator of how brutal and repressive its machinations were. After a promise of amnesty was delivered to the defectors by Iraq, the men returned and were executed shortly after crossing the border into Iraq.

14 POLITICAL PARTIES

Under the monarchy, Prime Minister Nuri as-Sa'id dominated Iraq with the support of the upper-middle and upper classes. Tribal, religious, and local loyalties took precedence over any sense of Iraqi nationalism. Faisal I considered the existence of parties desirable for the political development of Iraq. During the decade 1935–45, however, they were ineffective as political factors. In 1946, five new parties were founded, including one that was Socialist (Al-Hizb al-Watani al-Dimuqrati, or the National Democratic Party), one avowedly close to communism (Ash-Sha'b, or the People's Party), and one purely reformist (Al-Ittihad al-Watani, or the National Union Party).

The response to these parties alarmed the conservative politicians. The Palestine War (1948) provided the pretext for suppression of the Sha'b and Ittihad parties. Only the National Democratic Party functioned uninterruptedly; in 1950, with the lifting of martial law, the others resumed work. In 1949, Nuri as-Sa'id founded the Constitutional Union Party (Al-Ittihad ad-Dusturi), with a pro-Western, liberal reform program to attract both the old and the young generations. In opposition, Salih Jabr, a former partisan of Nuri's turned rival, founded the Nation's Socialist Party (Al-Ummah al-Ishtiraki), which advocated a democratic and nationalistic, pro-Western and pan-Arab policy. In 1954, however, Sa'id dissolved all parties, including his own Constitutional Union Party, on the ground that they had resorted to violence during the elections of that year.

After the coup of 1958, parties "voluntarily" discontinued their activities. In January 1960, Premier Qasim issued a new law allowing political parties to operate again. Meanwhile, the Ba'thists, who first gained strength in Syria in the 1950s as a pan-Arab movement with strong nationalist and socialist leanings, had attracted a following among elements of the Syrian military. In February 1963, Qasim was overthrown and executed by

officers affiliated with a conservative wing of Iraq's Ba'th movement. In November, a second coup was attempted by Ba'thist extremists from the left, who acted with complicity of the ruling Syrian wing of the party. With the 1968 coup, rightist elements of the Ba'th Party were installed in prominent positions by Gen. Bakr. Since then, the Ba'thists, organized as the Arab Ba'th Socialist Party, have been the ruling political group in Iraq. In the National Assembly elections of 1980, the Ba'thists won more than 75% of the seats at stake; in the 1984 elections, they won 73% of the seats. Elections were again held in March 1996, with only Ba'thists or independent supporters of Saddam Hussein allowed to run for seats in the Assembly. Altogether, 220 seats were contested by 689 candidates. As of 1999, most real party activity in Iraq involved the country's Kurdish minority, which had established a number of political groups, most of them in opposition to the central government.

In 1991, the regime issued a decree theoretically allowing the formation of other political parties, but which in fact prohibits parties not supportive of the regime. Under the 1991 edict, all political parties must be based in Baghdad and all are prohibited from having ethnic or religious affiliations.

Outside of Iraq, ethnic, religious and political opposition groups have come together to organize a common front against Saddam Hussein, but they have achieved very little. The Shia al Dawa Party was brutally suppressed by Saddam before the Iran-Iraq war; its remnants are now based in Tehran.

15 LOCAL GOVERNMENT

Iraq is divided into 18 provinces (three of which form an autonomous Kurdish region), each headed by an appointed governor. Provinces are subdivided into districts, each under a deputy governor; a district consists of counties, the smallest units, each under a director. Towns and cities are administered by municipal councils led by mayors. Baghdad's municipality, the "governorate of the capital," under its mayor, or "guardian of the capital," serves as a model municipality. A settlement reached with the Kurds in 1970 provided for Kurdish autonomy on the local level. In 1974, the provisional constitution was further amended to provide the Kurdistan region with an elected 80-member legislative council; elections were held in 1980 and 1986, but, in fact, the Iraqi army controlled Kurdistan until the imposition of a UN-approved protected zone in the north at the end of the Gulf War. In May 1992, Kurds held elections there for a new 100-member parliament for the quasi-independent region. This marked the only relatively free elections held in Iraq in several decades. The Kurdish parliament last met in 1995, discussing primarily the establishment of an independent state. New elections were planned for the latter part of 1999.

16 JUDICIAL SYSTEM

The court system is made up of two distinct branches: a security component and a more conventional court system to handle other charges. There is no independence in the operation of the judiciary; the President may override any court decision.

The security courts have jurisdiction in all cases involving espionage, treason, political dissent, smuggling and currency exchange violations, and drug trafficking. The ordinary civil courts have jurisdiction over civil, commercial, and criminal cases except for those that fall under the jurisdiction of the religious courts. Courts of general jurisdiction are established at governorate headquarters and in the principal districts.

Magistrates' courts try criminal cases in the first instance, but they cannot try cases involving punishment of more than seven years in prison. Such cases are tried in courts of sessions that are also appellate instances for magistrates' courts. Each judicial district has courts of sessions presided over by a bench of 3 judges. There are no jury trials. Special courts to try national security cases were set up in 1965; verdicts of these courts may be appealed to the military supreme court. In other cases, the highest court of appeal is the Court of Cassation in Baghdad, with civil and criminal divisions. It is composed of at least 15 judges, including a president and two vice-presidents.

For every court of First Instance, there is a Shari'a (Islamic) court that rules on questions involving religious matters and personal status. Trials are public and defendants are entitled to free counsel in the case of indigents. The government protects certain groups from prosecution. A 1992 decree grants immunity from prosecution to members of the Ba'ath Party. A 1990 decree grants immunity to men who kill their mothers, daughters, and other female family members who have committed "immoral deeds" such as adultery and fornication.

[17]ARMED FORCES

Vastly reduced from their size before the Gulf War of 1990–91, the Iraqi armed forces are estimated at 429,000 men. The army had a strength of 375,000 men (100,000 recalled reservists) and about 2,200 tanks; the navy had 2,000 men; and the air force had 35,000 men with perhaps 300 combat aircraft. The army includes 6 Republican Guard divisions. Paramilitary forces include an armed militia, al-Jaish al-Sha'bi, of 45,000–50,000 men and 20,000 frontier and security guards.

During 1981–90, Iraq purchased some $45 billion in arms from the USSR, France, and China. It was the world's principal arms importer for this period. Much of the money for these arms imports was provided by Sa'udi Arabia, Kuwait, and other Persian Gulf oil states. During the war with Iran, Iraq's defense budget averaged more than $13 billion a year. Since the Gulf War, arms imports have shrunk dramatically because of a UN embargo. The defense budget was estimated at $1.3 billion in 1998 or 6.8% of GDP.

[18]INTERNATIONAL COOPERATION

Iraq is a charter member of the UN, having joined on 21 December 1945, and participates in ESCWA and all the nonregional specialized agencies. A founding member of the Arab League, Iraq also participates in G-77 and OPEC, and has signed the Law of the Sea. Iraq has given both military and economic support to Arab parties in the conflict with Israel. The war with Iran preoccupied Iraq during the 1980s, and Iraq's relations with other countries in the Arab world has been varied. During the 1980s, Iraq maintained friendly relations with some Western countries, notably France, a major arms supplier to Iraq. In November 1984, diplomatic relations between Iraq and the US were renewed after a break of 17 years, but were broken off again when Iraq invaded Kuwait in August of 1990. The US and its allies launched an air war against Iraq after diplomatic efforts and economic sanctions failed to convince Iraq to leave Kuwait. Since then, Iraq's international standing has deteriorated badly and in 1997 the nation was still under an international trade embargo.

[19]ECONOMY

In response to the Iraqi invasion of Kuwait on 2 August 1990, the UN imposed comprehensive economic, financial, and military sanctions, placing the Iraqi economy under siege. Acting on its own, the US also froze all Iraqi assets in the US and barred all economic transactions between US citizens and Iraq. Many other countries imposed similar sanctions on top of the UN-imposed embargo. UN Security Council resolutions authorized the export of Iraqi crude oil worth up to $1.6 billion over a limited time to finance humanitarian imports for the Iraqi people. After the food embargo took effect, Iraq recognized the strategic importance of agriculture. Implementation of the UN's oil--for-food program in 1996 helped improve social conditions. The effect of war in Kuwait and continuing economic sanctions reduced real GDP by at least 75% in 1991, on the basis of an 85% decline in oil production, and the destruction of the industrial and service sectors of the economy. Estimates for 1993 indicated that unemployment hovered around 50% and that inflation was as high as 1000%. There is a flourishing black market that is responsible for an increasing share of domestic commerce. Per capita GDP was estimated at $2,400 in 1998, but the estimate is not to be considered reliable due to extreme economic disarray. The UN began to allow limited exports of oil during 1998. At an average volume of 1.9 million barrels per day in 1998, oil exports were about 75% of their pre-war level.

Agriculture, both commercial and subsistence, remains the principal occupation, involving somewhat less than one-third of the total population and contributing 5.1% to the GDP (1989). Industrial development was handicapped by the war with Iran, lack of raw materials other than oil, insufficient private capital for investment, traditional preference for investing in land, lack of credit for the small entrepreneur and investor, and lack of skilled labor. The greatest long-term obstacle to the development of a stable economy and general prosperity has been the traditional imbalance between a relatively small number of prosperous landholders and businessmen and the overwhelming majority of impoverished fellahin, with minute or no holdings of land, and small wage earners (government clerks or unskilled workers).

[20]INCOME

The US Central Intelligence Agency (CIA) reports that in 1998 Iraq's gross domestic product (GDP) was estimated at $52.3 billion. The per capita GDP was estimated at $2,400. The annual growth rate of GDP was estimated at 10%. The CIA defines GDP as the value of all final goods and services produced within a nation in a given year and computed on the basis of purchasing power parity (PPP) rather than value as measured on the basis of the rate of exchange.

[21]LABOR

The trade union organization law of 1987 established a centralized trade union structure of committees linked to trade unions, which in turn are part of provincial trade union federations under the control of the Iraqi General Federation of Trade Unions, and ultimately are controlled by the ruling Ba'th Party. Although workers are legally allowed to strike upon informing the Labor Ministry, no strike has been reported in over 20 years.

Child labor is strictly controlled and in many cases prohibited. The minimum working age is 14, although economic necessity and lack of government enforcement have increased the number of children of all ages that are employed. There is a 6-day, 48-hour work week, although this does not apply to agricultural workers. Historically, working women have been accepted in Iraq, but the number of women in the work force dramatically increased because of the prolonged war with Iran as well as the Persian Gulf War, as women replaced men in the labor market.

In many cases rural labor and farmers employed in government projects get reasonable salaries and good housing, but small, independent farmers receive fewer benefits. Since 1958, the Iraqi government has passed a number of agrarian reform laws. As a general rule, however, the quality of life differs greatly between rural areas and the cities, especially that in Baghdad. This differential has resulted in massive rural to urban migration.

[22]AGRICULTURE

The rich alluvial soil of the lowlands and an elaborate system of irrigation canals made Iraq a granary in ancient times and in the Middle Ages. After the irrigation works were destroyed in the

Mongol invasion, agriculture decayed. Today, about 13% of the land is considered arable.

Under various agrarian reform laws—including a 1970 law that limited permissible landholdings to 4–202 hectares (10–500 acres), depending on location, fertility, and available irrigation facilities—about 400,000 previously landless peasants have received land. Agrarian reform has been accompanied by irrigation and drainage works, and by the establishment of cooperative societies for the provision of implements and machinery, irrigation facilities, and other services.

Agricultural production in Iraq declined progressively because of the war with Iran and the Persian Gulf War. In 1992, wheat production was estimated at 600,000 tons compared with 965,000 tons in 1982, but by 1998 had climbed to 1,100,000 tons. The comparable figures for barley were 400,000, 902,000, and 800,000 tons; for cotton, 5,000, 8,000, and 9,000 tons. Dates, Iraq's most important agricultural export, increased from 374,000 tons in 1982 to an estimated 660,000 in 1998. Crops grown for domestic consumption include millet, lentils, beans, cucumbers, melons, figs, potatoes, corn, sugarcane, tobacco (a government monopoly), and mulberries.

Because of the international embargo placed on Iraq for its invasion of Kuwait, the government has attempted to establish firm control over the distribution of domestic agricultural production. Farmers, however, have been reluctant to adhere to directives requiring them to sell the entirety of their harvests to the state marketing boards set up after the war, since food fetches a considerably higher price on the black market than the state is able to pay. In the early years after the war, the government engaged in terror tactics to intimidate recalcitrant farmers. These essentially stopped by 1995, but the government continued to issue veiled threats to farmers through the media. Nonetheless, most Iraqis were forced to seek about 50% of their food needs on the black market.

23ANIMAL HUSBANDRY

Animal husbandry is widespread. Sheep raising is most important, with wool used domestically for weaving carpets and cloaks. In 1998, Iraq had an estimated 6.9 million sheep; 1.5 million goats; 1.3 million head of cattle, and numerous donkeys, camels, mules, buffaloes, and poultry. In 1998, of the 544,000 tons of milk produced by all livestock, 58% came from cows, 28% from sheep, 10% from goats, and 4% from buffaloes.

24FISHING

Centuries of overfishing without restocking reduced the formerly plentiful supply of river fish, but the fishing industry has rebounded since the early 1970s. The 1997 fish catch (including salmon and, especially in the Tigris, carp) was 34,702 tons. Since the war, and the closure of Iraq's ports because of fighting, the Iraqi fishing fleet has been dispersed around the world and does not operate in the Persian Gulf.

25FORESTRY

Forests of oak and Aleppo pine in the north cover less than 4% of Iraq's entire area and have been depleted by excessive cutting for fuel or by fires and overgrazing. Since 1954, indiscriminate cutting has been prohibited, and charcoal production from wood has ceased. The forestry research center at Irbil has established tree nurseries and conducted reforestation programs. Output of roundwood was estimated at 161,000 cu m in 1997.

26MINING

Iraq's mineral resources other than oil are limited. Exploitation is rendered uneconomical by inadequate transport facilities and lack of coal for processing the ores. Geological surveys have indicated usable deposits of iron ore, copper, gypsum, bitumen, dolomite, and marble; however, these resources have remained largely unexploited. Phosphate rock is produced from the Akashat open pit mine in the west. Sulfur is produced from underground deposits at Mishraq, on the west bank of the Tigris River about 50 km (30 mi) south of Mosul. Production of phosphate in 1996 was an estimated 300,000 tons; sulfur, 475,000 tons; salt, 250,000 tons. Damage to the minerals industry from the Persian Gulf War and the earlier 1980–88 war with Iran has been substantially repaired. Production of all mineral commodities fell since international trade was halted by the UN embargo.

27ENERGY AND POWER

Iraq has the second-largest petroleum reserves in the Middle East (after Sa'udi Arabia), with proved deposits estimated at 112.5 billion barrels in early 1999. Oil revenues help to balance the budget, stabilize the currency, establish a surplus balance of payments, and finance the development program. Because of the war with Iran and the Gulf War, however, crude oil production fell drastically, from 3,476,900 barrels per day in 1979 to 897,400 barrels daily in 1981 and from 2,897,000 barrels per day in 1989 to 305,000 barrels daily in 1991, following an embargo on Iraqi oil exports; in 1999 it was an estimated 2.6 million barrels per day. In January, 1992, the Al-Bakr oil export terminal, the only outlet to the sea, was reopened at half capacity; by August, the full capacity of 1.6 million barrels per day was restored, even though UN sanctions prohibited Iraq from exporting its oil. In 1998, construction was authorized for a 100,000 barrel per day pipeline to pump Iraqi crude oil to Jordan's Zarga refinery.

The most important fields are at Kirkuk, with lesser fields at Naft Khaneh, 'Ayn Zalah, and Butmah in the Mosul area, and at Az-Zubayr and Ar-Rumaylah near Basra. Oil for export was formerly piped to the Mediterranean through Syria and Lebanon, or to the Persian Gulf, but Syria closed the pipeline when Iraq invaded Iran, which Syria supported, and Iran closed Iraq's Gulf shipping. A new pipeline through Turkey transported more than half of Iraq's oil exports in the early 1980s; this was expanded by additions in 1985 and 1987, supplemented by a pipeline completed in 1985 running to Sa'udi Arabia's Red Sea port of Yanbu' al-Bahr; the pipeline was closed during the Persian Gulf War. UN sanctions on Iraqi crude oil exports resulted in a complete closure of the Kirkuk-Ceyhan pipeline since 1991. In April 1996, there were an estimated 6.7 million barrels of oil trapped in the pipeline, which needed extensive repairs. Small amounts of crude oil are trucked to Jordan and Turkey.

Oil concessions were granted in 1925, and the first production began two years later. The three major oil companies operating in Iraq in the early 1970s were the Iraq Co. for Oil Operations (ICOO), the Basrah Petroleum Co. (BPC), and the Iraq National Oil Co. (INOC). By 1975, as a result of nationalizations carried out since 1972, state-owned operations controlled 100% of national oil production. In 1998, Iraq produced 2.9 billion cu m of natural gas.

The development of both hydroelectric and thermal capacity proceeded rapidly during the 1970s. In Baghdad, electricity is supplied by the Baghdad Light and Power Co. This thermo-electric fuel-oil plant was installed by British-Belgian firms, but was later nationalized and supplemented by a second plant. Other cities generate power in small municipal power stations. Iraq's budding nuclear energy program was set back by the destruction of the Osirak nuclear reactor by Israeli bombers in June 1981. Total electricity production in 1998 was 28,400 million kWh. The country's generating capacity was about 4,480 MW in 1998. Iraq's power installations were repeated targets of Iranian air attacks in the 1980s, and were badly damaged during the conflict in the Persian Gulf in 1991.

In September 1991, the UN proposed a plan to allow Iraq to raise revenue for humanitarian purchases and war reparations by exporting limited quantities of oil. Iraq repeatedly rejected the plan claiming that it would violate sovereignty, but in January 1996 began negotiations with the UN on implementation of the plan. By May 1996, Iraq and the UN agreed on how to carry out UN Resolution 986, which allows Iraq to sell $1 billion worth of oil every 90 days for a 180-day trial period. Proceeds from the sales were to go into a UN-managed escrow account and be used to provide humanitarian assistance to Iraq under UN supervision. In 1998, the UN Security Council voted to raise Iraq's six-month export quota to $5.26 billion, in Resolution 1153.

28 INDUSTRY

Main industries are oil refining, food processing, textiles, leather goods, cement and other building materials, tobacco, paper, and sulfur extraction. Iraq has ten oil refineries, all managed by the government's Oil Refineries Administration. The Iraq-Iran and Gulf wars seriously affected Iraqi refining. Iraq has total refinery capacity of 350,000 barrels per day (the Iraqi government claims 700,000), with the largest refinery, Baiji North, rated at 150,000 barrels per day. The second largest refinery, at Salaheddin, has a capacity of 140,000 barrels per day. The bulk of Iraq's refinery capacity is concentrated in the Baiji complex

In 1964, the government took over all establishments producing asbestos, cement, cigarettes, textiles, paper, tanned leather, and flour. Public-sector industrial establishments include a sulfur plant at Kirkuk, a fertilizer plant at Basra, an antibiotics factory at Samarra', an agricultural implements factory at Iskandariyah, and an electrical equipment factory near Baghdad. In the 1970s, Iraq put strong emphasis on the development of heavy industry and diversification of its current industry, a policy aimed at decreasing dependence on oil. During the 1980s, the industrial sector showed a steady increase, reflecting the importance given to military industries during the Iran–Iraq war. By early 1992 it was officially claimed that industrial output had been restored to 60% of pre-Gulf War capacity. The UN oil-for-food program has allowed limited oil sales in 1999 and 2000, despite economic sanctions resulting from the Gulf War.

29 SCIENCE AND TECHNOLOGY

Iraq has imported Western technology for its petrochemical industry. The Scientific Research Council was established in 1963 and includes nine scientific research centers. The Nuclear Research Center (founded 1967) has conducted nuclear physics experiments and produced radioisotopes with equipment supplied by France. In 1982, the French government agreed to help rebuild the institute's Osirak reactor, knocked out by an Israeli air attack the previous year. Eight universities offer degrees in basic and applied sciences. In addition, the Ministry of Higher Education has 18 incorporated technical institutes. The Agriculture and Water Resources Research Center (founded 1980) and the Iraq Natural History Research Center and Museum (founded 1946) are both located in Baghdad. The Iraqi Medical Society (founded 1920) is headquartered there.

30 DOMESTIC TRADE

Modern shops and department stores are spreading throughout the country, replacing traditional bazaars. Baghdad, Mosul, and Basra, as well as other large and medium-size cities, all have modern supermarkets and branches of the official department store, "al-Makhazin al-Iraqiyyah."

Baghdad leads in wholesale trade and in the number of retail shops. Normal banking hours in summer are 8 AM to noon, Saturday–Wednesday, and 8 to 11 AM on Thursday; winter openings and closings are an hour later.

31 FOREIGN TRADE

Iraq's most valuable export is oil, which has historically accounted for almost all of its total export value. Rising oil prices during the 1970s created increases in export value. However, the drop in world oil prices and Iraq's exporting problems due to international sanctions essentially put an end to Iraqi oil exports. The UN imposed trade restrictions on non-oil exports in August 1990. Non-oil exports (often illegal) were estimated at $2 billion for the 12 months following the March 1991 cease-fire. Iraq was traditionally the world's largest exporter of dates, with its better varieties going to Western Europe, Australia, and North America.

Until 1994, the UN committee charged with supervising what little international trade Iraq is permitted to engage in —food and medicine, essentially—kept records on the amount of goods it approved for import in exchange for oil. In the first half of 1994, the committee recorded $2 billion in food imports, $175 million in medicine, and an additional $2 billion in "essential civilian needs," a term that in this case refers to agricultural machinery and seeds and goods for sanitation.

In 1995, the Iraqi government rationed its people only one half of the minimum daily requirement in calories. In 1997, the UN permitted Iraq to expand its oil sales to increase its purchasing power of food and other sources of humanitarian relief. In the spring of that year the country received 400,000 tons of wheat to help feed its suffering population, who had been living under strict food rations for four years. Limited exports were organized by the UN, and the oil-for-food program brought in revenues during 1999 equaling $5.3 billion.

In 1998, Iraq exported crude petroleum (80%), refined petroleum products (18%), and natural and manufactured gas (2.0%). Principal trading partners in 1998 (in millions of US dollars) were as follows:

COUNTRY	EXPORTS	IMPORTS	BALANCE
United States	1,237	117	1,120
France	671	281	390
Spain	452	16	436
Italy	366	42	324
Netherlands	297	11	286
Austria	122	11	111
Taiwan	108	n.a.	
Portugal	107	n.a.	
China (inc. Hong Kong)	54	115	-61
Australia	33	216	-183

32 BALANCE OF PAYMENTS

The US Central Intelligence Agency reports that in 1998 the purchasing power parity of Iraq's exports was $5 billion while imports totaled $3 billion resulting in a trade balance of $2 billion.

33 BANKING AND SECURITIES

When Iraq was part of the Ottoman Empire, a number of European currencies circulated alongside the Turkish pound. With the establishment of the British mandate after World War I, Iraq was incorporated into the Indian monetary system, which was operated by the British, and the rupee became the principal currency in circulation. In 1931, the Iraq Currency Board was established in London for note issue and maintenance of reserves for the new Iraqi dinar. The currency board pursued a conservative monetary policy, maintaining very high reserves behind the dinar. The dinar was further strengthened by its link to the British pound. In 1947 the government-owned National Bank of Iraq was founded, and in 1949 the London-based currency board was abolished as the new bank assumed responsibility for the issuing of notes and the maintenance of reserves.

In the 1940s, a series of government-owned banks was established: the Agricultural Bank and the Industrial Bank, the

Rafidayn Bank, the Real Estate Bank, the Mortgage Bank, and the Cooperative Bank. In 1956 the National Bank of Iraq became the Central Bank of Iraq. In 1964, banking was fully nationalized. The banking system comprises the Central Bank of Iraq, the Rafidain Bank, the main commercial bank, and three others: the Agricultural Cooperative Bank, the Industrial Bank, and the Real Estate Bank. In 1991 the government decided to end its monopoly on banking. Data on the financial situation in Iraq are not generally available as the main source of official statistics, the Central Bank of Iraq, has not released figures since 1977. However, data from external authorities are available. After 1991, six new banks were established—the Socialist Bank, Iraqi Commercial Bank, Baghdad Bank, Dijla Bank, Al-Itimad Bank, and the Private Bank—as a result of liberalizing legislation and the opportunity for large-scale profits from currency speculation.

The Central Bank is striving to maintain the value of the dinar against the dollar through strict monetary policies. Because of the devastated state of the economy, however, it has largely failed in this attempt. In 1994, the black market value of the dinar stood at 750 to the dollar; by 1995, it had fallen to 3,000.

Preference for investing savings in rural or urban real estate is common. Major private investments in industrial enterprises can be secured only by assurance of financial assistance from the government. The establishment of a stock exchange in Baghdad was delayed by practical considerations such as a lack of computers, but it was eventually inaugurated in March 1992. Trading has not been heavy, and no exact statistics are available.

34INSURANCE

The insurance industry was nationalized in 1964. The State Insurance Organization supervises and maintains three companies: the National Life Insurance Co., the Iraqi Life Insurance Co., and the Iraqi Reinsurance Co. Third-party motor vehicle liability insurance is compulsory.

35PUBLIC FINANCE

There are several budgets: the ordinary budget, under which the regular activities of the government are financed; separate budgets for the Iraqi State Railways, the Port of Basra Authority, the Al-Faw Dredging Scheme, and the tobacco monopoly; municipal budgets requiring government approval; and allocations for semi-independent government agencies. In addition, there is a separate development budget, as well as an undeclared budget for the military believed to have absorbed over half of state funds during the war with Iran. Since 1980, the decline in oil exports and huge war expenditures forced Iraq to borrow and to raise funds from abroad. Iraq's invasion of Kuwait in 1990, with the consequent infrastructural damage, UN sanctions, and oil embargo, have severely diminished revenues.

36TAXATION

Direct taxes are levied on income and on property. The rental value of dwellings, commercial buildings, and nonagricultural land is taxed, with a certain tax-free minimum. In 1939, graduated income tax rates were established on income from all sources except agriculture. Most agricultural income is not taxed.

Indirect taxation predominates. The land tax must be paid by all who farm government lands with or without a lease. Owners of freehold (lazimah) land pay no tax or rent. Much farm produce consumed on the farm or in the village is not taxed at all, but when marketed, farm products are taxed.

37CUSTOMS AND DUTIES

Since about 1950, tariffs have been used primarily to protect Iraqi industry or to stimulate industries that might eventually reduce the need for foreign imports. This tariff system levies duties on luxury items but has reduced rates on industrial equipment and on certain raw materials and foodstuffs. Iraq has a single-column tariff, with duties collected at Basra and Baghdad. In October 1992, Iraq banned the import of 157 "luxury items," including cheese, onions, shampoo, matches, shoes, and carpets. In 1989, Iraq joined the newly formed Arab Cooperation Council with Egypt, Jordan, and Yemen. The ACC's goals included formation of a common market and economic integration in other areas. The international embargo levied against the nation after it invaded Kuwait has essentially ended Iraq's participation in the ACC. Egypt, one of its partners in the Council, was a leader in the military coalition that liberated Kuwait.

38FOREIGN INVESTMENT

UN sanctions have effectively frozen all of Iraq's foreign transactions for the near future. In October 1992, the UN Security Council permitted these frozen assets, including Iraqi oil in storage in Turkey and Sa'udi Arabia, to be sold without the permission of the Iraqi government. About $1 billion of frozen assets were to pay for compensation to Kuwaiti victims of the invasion and to cover UN operations inside Iraq.

39ECONOMIC DEVELOPMENT

The government both controls and participates in petroleum, agriculture, commerce, banking, and industry. In the late 1960s, it made efforts to diversify Iraq's economic relations and to conserve foreign exchange. As an example, it was announced in 1970 that contracts for all planned projects would be awarded to companies willing to receive compensation in crude oil or petroleum products. The government also undertook to build an Iraqi tanker fleet to break the monopoly of foreign oil-transport companies.

Iraq has an estimated foreign debt of more than $87 billion. The imposition of sanctions against Iraq has destroyed all attempts to stabilize Iraq's payments. Iraq also faces reparation claims. Iran is separately pursuing its claim for massive separation payments arising from the 1980–88 war. Iraq is also obligated by UN resolutions to pay for various UN agency activities.

40SOCIAL DEVELOPMENT

A social security law passed in 1971 provides benefits or payments for disability, maternity, old age, unemployment, sickness, and funerals. This law applies to all establishments employing five or more people, and excludes agricultural employees, temporary employees, and domestic servants. This social insurance system is funded by employee contributions of 5% of their wages, and employer contributions of 12% of payroll. Oil companies are required to pay 25% of payroll. Men may retire at age 60 and women at 55 after they have worked for 20 years. Maternity benefits for employed women include 100% of salary for a period of at least 10 weeks. Extended maternity leave is granted in cases of complications.

The government claims to support equality for women, who make up about 20% of the work force. As of 1996, 16 of 250 parliamentary seats were held by women. Laws have been passed protecting women from sexual harassment, permitting them to join the police and armed forces, and equalizing their rights in divorce, land ownership, taxation, suffrage, and election to political office. Despite these government claims of legal equality, severe discrimination against women remains. Women are not allowed to travel abroad unaccompanied. In 1990, a decree was passed that provides immunity to men who kill female family members who have committed an "immoral" act.

Although Iraq's constitution guarantees individual rights, the government sharply limits political freedoms and tolerates little public expression of dissent. Suspected political offenders are subject to arbitrary arrest and imprisonment, and torture is common in such cases. Amputations of limbs and branding are used to punish those accused of serious crimes. In 1995, the death penalty was established for persons found to be in possession of stolen goods.

Gross human rights violations continue to be committed. Iraq's minority Kurd population faces serious forms of discrimination and human rights abuses. In 1988, the government's Anfal campaign against the Kurds led to an estimated 100,000 deaths. In response, an international coalition established a no-fly zone in the north of Iraq in 1991 to protect the Kurds. The Iraqi government continued to harass and threaten relief workers and UN personnel in the area. The Iraqi government has refused to cooperate with international human rights organizations or to allow the establishment of independent local ones. Human rights monitors are denied visas to enter the country and must base their reports on published material and interviews with emigres and political opposition groups.

41HEALTH

There are many well-trained Iraqi physicians; however, their effectiveness is limited by a lack of trained nursing and paramedical staff. Between 1985–95, 93% of the population had access to health care services. Private hospitals are allowed to operate in Baghdad and other major cities. Considerable effort has been made to expand medical facilities to small towns and more remote areas of the country, but these efforts have been hampered by a lack of transportation and a desire of medical personnel to live and work in Baghdad and the major cities. Between 1990–95, 44% had access to safe water, and 74% had access to sanitation. Dentists and other specialists are almost unknown in rural districts. Child nutrition has been negatively affected by the aftermath of the Gulf War and UN sanctions. In a study of Iraqi children shortly after the war, 24% were malnourished or classified as stunted, and 8% were in the wasted category. The UN Children's Fund has documented 4,500 children under 5 die every month from hunger and disease. UN officials also estimate that the international trade embargo and the relative indifference of the regime cause the premature deaths of 4,000 to 5,000 sick and old Iraqis each month.

In 1991, Iraq had 10,900 physicians, 13,206 nurses, 1,719 pharmacists, and 1,628 dentists. In 1990–97, there were 60 doctors per 10,000 people. During the same period, there were 1.7 hospital beds per 1,000 inhabitants. Iraq's 1999 birth rate was 38.8 per 1,000 people. Of married women (ages 15 to 49), 14% used contraception in 1989. Life expectancy in 1999 averaged 66.5 years. The fertility rate decreased from 7.2 in 1960 to 5.1 children in 1999 for each woman during childbearing years. In 1997, immunization rates for children up to one year old were: tuberculosis (90%); diphtheria, pertussis, and tetanus (92%); and measles (98%). In 1997, there were 160 reported cases of tuberculosis per 100,000 people. The infant mortality rate in 1999 was 62.4 per 1,000 live births, and the general mortality rate was 6.6 per 1,000 people.

Tobacco consumption remained static between 1984 and 1994, when 3.1 kg a year was consumed per adult.

42HOUSING

In the last 20 years, living conditions for the vast majority of the population have improved greatly. Electricity and running water are normal features of all Iraqi villages in rural areas. Mud huts in remote places are rapidly being replaced by brick dwellings. Major cities like Mosul, Basra, and especially Baghdad have most of the amenities of modern living. Traditionally, Iraqis have lived in single family dwellings, but in the last 15 years, the government has built a number of high-rise apartments, especially in Baghdad. It has done so to control urban sprawl and

to cut down on suburban service expenditures. According to the latest available information for 1980–88, total housing units numbered 2,478,000 with 6.5 people per dwelling.

43EDUCATION

Six years of compulsory primary education has been in effect since 1978. An estimated 42% of adults were illiterate in 1995 (males, 29.3%; females, 55.0%). In 1996, 2,903,923 students attended 8,145 primary schools, with 145,455 teachers. Student-to-teacher ratio stood at 20 to one. In that same year, 1,160,421 students attended secondary schools, with 62,296 teachers. Primary schools provide a six-year course, at the end of which the student must pass an examination to be admitted to secondary school. The curriculum is based on Western patterns but also includes religious teaching. The language of instruction is Arabic. Secondary schools have a three-year intermediate course, followed by a two-year course in preparation for entrance to college. A national examination must be passed at its end. Secondary education for girls dates from 1929. Traditional Quranic schools are nearly extinct.

Education at all levels from primary to higher education is free, and no private schools are permitted to operate. There are seven universities in Iraq, four of them in Baghdad. The University of Baghdad is the most important higher education institution in the country. Other universities include Mosul, al-Mustansiriya, Basra, and as-Sulaymaniyah. In addition to these universities, there are 19 technical institutes throughout Iraq. In 1988, all higher level institutions had 209,818 pupils and 11,072 instructors. Education in Iraq is under the control of the Ministry of Education and the Ministry of Higher Education and Research.

44LIBRARIES AND MUSEUMS

The National Library in Baghdad, founded in 1961, houses 417,000 volumes in 2000. Two noteworthy academic libraries are the Central Library of the University of Baghdad (545,000 volumes) and the Central Library of the University of Mosul (750,000 volumes). One of the country's outstanding libraries is the Iraqi Museum Library (founded 1934), with modern research facilities and more than 229,000 volumes, many of them rare editions. The Directorate of Antiquities in Baghdad houses a library of 38,000 volumes. There are public library branches in many provincial capitals.

With the exception of the National History Research Center and Museum and the National Museum of Modern Art, museums are under the control of the Department of the Directorate-General of Antiquities in Baghdad. Two of the most outstanding collections are at the Iraqi Museum in Baghdad, which contains antiquities dating from the early Stone Age, and the Mosul Museum. The Abbasid Palace Museum and the Museum of Arab Antiquities, both located in Baghdad, are housed in restored buildings from the 13th and 14th centuries, respectively. Because of the international isolation imposed on the country following the Persian Gulf War, it is assumed that many of these institutions have suffered, although the extent is not known.

45MEDIA

The government's Radio Baghdad transmits in Arabic from 39 transmitters, and also has English, Kurdish, and some other foreign-language broadcasts. As of 1999 there were 16 AM and 1 FM radio station and 13 government-operated television stations. In 1997, there were 228 radios and 83 television sets per 1,000 population.

All communications media are owned and controlled by the government, and criticism of government policies is not permitted. Newspapers that failed to observe strict government censorship have been suspended. The two leading Arabic newspapers in 1999 were Al-Thawra (circulation 250,000) and Al-Jumhuriyah (150,000); the only English-language daily was the state-sponsored Baghdad Observer (22,000).

46 ORGANIZATIONS

Chambers of commerce are active in Baghdad, Basra, and Mosul. Cooperatives, first established in 1944, have played an increasingly important social role, especially under the post-1968 Ba'th government. Youth organizations have been stressed by the current regime; there are many youth centers and sports clubs. The General Federation of Iraqi Youth and the General Federation of Iraqi Women are government-sponsored mass organizations. Red Crescent societies provide social services in many cities and towns.

47 TOURISM, TRAVEL, AND RECREATION

Tourism declined sharply during Iraq's occupation of Kuwait and the Gulf War. In 1998, 340,000 visitors arrived in Iraq, and tourist receipts totaled $13 million, down from $55 million in 1990. Many visitors from other Arab states are pilgrims to Islamic shrines. The other principal tourist attraction is visiting the varied archeological sites. Popular forms of recreation include tennis, cricket, swimming, and squash.

According to 1999 UN estimates, the cost of staying in Baghdad was approximately $100 per day. The cities of Dohok, Erbil, and Suleimaniyah required an estimated daily expenditure of $80.

48 FAMOUS IRAQIS

The most famous kings in ancient times were Sargon (Sharrukin) of Akkad (fl.c.2350 BC), Hammurabi of Babylon (r.1792?–1750? BC), and Nebuchadnezzar II (Nabu-kadurri-utsur, r.605?–560? BC) of Babylon.

Under the caliphs Harun al-Rashid (ar-Rashid ibn Muhammad al-Mahdi ibn al-Mansur al-'Abbasi, r.786–809) and al-Mamun (abu al-'Abbas 'Abdullah al-Mamun, r.813–33), Baghdad was the center of the Arab scholarship that translated and modified Greek philosophy. A leading figure in this movement was Hunain ibn Ishaq (d.873), called Johannitius by Western scholastics. His contemporary was the great Arab philosopher Yaqub al-Kindi, whose catholicity assimilated both Greek philosophy and Indian mathematics. The founder of one of the four orthodox schools of Islamic law, which claims the largest number of adherents in the Muslim world, Abu Hanifa (d.767) was also a native Iraqi. Another celebrated figure in theology, 'Abd al-Hasan al-Ash'ari (c.913), who combated the rationalist Mu'tazila school, also lived in Baghdad; his influence still prevails in Islam. Al-Ghazali (Ghazel, d.1111), though Persian by birth, taught at the Nizamiyah University in Baghdad; he is one of the best-known Islamic philosopher-theologians. Iraq also produced famous mystics like Hasan al-Basri (642–728) and 'Abd al-Qadir al-Jilani (1077–1166); the latter's followers are numerous among Asian Muslims, and his tomb in Baghdad draws many pilgrims. Modern Iraq has produced no artist or writer famous outside the Arabic-speaking world.

The best-known contemporary Iraqi political leader is Gen. Saddam Hussein (Husayn) al-Takriti (b. 1937), who has served as chairman of the Revolutionary Command Council and president of the country since 1979.

49 DEPENDENCIES

Iraq has no territories or colonies.

50 BIBLIOGRAPHY

Afary, Janet. *The Iranian Constitutional Revolution, 1906–1911: Grassroots Democracy, Social Democracy, & the Origins of Feminism*. New York: Columbia University Press, 1996.

Alnasrawi, Abbas. *The Economy of Iraq: Oil, Wars, Destruction of Development and Prospects, 1950–2010*. Westport, Conn.: Greenwood Press, 1994.

Arnove, Anthony. *Iraq under Siege: The Deadly Impact of Sanctions and War*. Cambridge, Mass.: South End Press, 2000.

Bulloch, John. *Saddam's War: The Origins of the Kuwait Conflict and the International Response*. Boston: Faber and Faber, 1991.

Cordesman, Anthony H. *Iraq: Sanctions and Beyond*. Boulder, Colo.: Westview Press, 1997.

Dalley, Stephanie. *The Legacy of Mesopotamia*. New York: Oxford University Press, 1998.

Gunter, Michael M. *The Kurds of Iraq: Tragedy and Hope*. New York: St. Martin's Press, 1992.

Haykal, Muhammad Hasanayn. *Illusions of Triumph: An Arab View of the Gulf War*. London: HarperCollins, 1992.

Khadduri, Majid. *War in the Gulf, 1990–91: The Iraq-Kuwait Conflict and Its Implications*. New York: Oxford University Press, 1997.

Martin, Vanessa. *Islam and Modernism: The Iranian Revolution of 1906*. Syracuse, N.Y.: Syracuse University Press, 1989.

Nakash, Yitzhak. *The Shiis of Iraq*. Princeton, N.J.: Princeton University Press, 1994.

Simons, G. L. *Iraq: From Sumer to Saddam*. New York: St. Martin's Press, 1994.

———. *The Scourging of Iraq: Sanctions, Law and Natural Justice*. Hampshire, Eng.: Macmillan, 1996

Tauber, Eliezer. *The Formation of Modern Syria and Iraq*. Portland, Ore.: Frank Cass, 1994.

White, Paul K. *Crises after the Storm: An Appraisal of U.S. Air Operations in Iraq since the Persian Gulf War*. Washington, D.C.: Washington Institute for Near East Policy, 1999.

ISRAEL

State of Israel
Arabic: *Dawlat Israel*
Hebrew: *Medinat Yisrael*

CAPITAL: Jerusalem (Yerushalayim, Al-Quds).

FLAG: The flag, which was adopted at the First Zionist Congress in Basel in 1897, consists of a blue six-pointed Shield of David (Magen David) centered between two blue horizontal stripes on a white field.

ANTHEM: *Hatikvah (The Hope).*

MONETARY UNIT: The new Israeli shekel (NIS), a paper currency of 100 new agorot, replaced the shekel (IS) at a rate of 1,000 to 1 in 1985; the shekel replaced the Israeli pound (IL) in 1980 at the rate of 10 pounds per shekel. There are coins of 5, 10, and 50 agora, 1 and 5 shekels and notes of 10, 50, 100, and 200 shekels. NIS1 = $0.24802 ($1 = NIS4.032) as of 31 March 2000.

WEIGHTS AND MEASURES: The metric system is the legal standard, but some local units are used, notably the dunam (equivalent to 1,000 sq m, or about 0.25 acre).

HOLIDAYS: Israel officially uses both the Gregorian and the complex Jewish lunisolar calendars, but the latter determines the occurrence of national holidays: Rosh Hashanah (New Year), September or October; Yom Kippur (Day of Atonement), September or October; Sukkot (Tabernacles), September or October; Simhat Torah (Rejoicing in the Law), September or October; Pesach (Passover), March or April; Independence Day, April or May; and Shavuot (Pentecost), May or June. All Jewish holidays, as well as the Jewish Sabbath (Friday/Saturday), begin just before sundown and end at nightfall 24 hours later. Muslim, Christian, and Druze holidays are observed by the respective minorities.

TIME: 2 PM = noon GMT.

¹LOCATION, SIZE, AND EXTENT

Situated in southwestern Asia along the eastern end of the Mediterranean Sea, Israel claims an area of 20,770 sq km (8,019 sq mi), extending about 320 km (200 mi) N–S and 110 km (70 mi) E–W; at its narrowest, just north of Tel Aviv–Yafo, it is 19 km (12 mi) across. This total includes the Golan Heights area (1,176 sq km/454 sq mi), captured from Syria during the Six-Day War in 1967 and annexed on 14 December 1981; the annexation (technically described as the extension of Israeli "law, jurisdiction, and administration" to the region) was condemned by Syria and by unanimous resolution of the UN Security Council. The Labor Government in 1984 indicated that some (possibly all) of the Golan could be returned to Syria in a peace agreement. Other territories captured in 1967 and classified as administered territories were the West Bank (Judea and Samaria), 5,878 sq km (2,270 sq mi), and the Gaza Strip, 362 sq km (140 sq mi). (The Gaza Strip and Jericho area were transferred in 1994 to Palestinian administration). East Jerusalem, captured in 1967, was annexed shortly thereafter. The Sinai (53,242 sq km/20,557 sq mi), also taken in 1967, was fully restored to Egypt in 1982.

Israel is bordered on the N by Lebanon, on the E by Syria and Jordan, on the S by the Gulf of Aqaba (Gulf of Elat), on the SW by Egypt, and on the W by the Mediterranean Sea. Comparatively, the area occupied by Israel is slightly larger than the state of New Jersey. The total boundary length was 1,279 km (795 mi) following the 1949 armistice and 1,102 km (684 mi) in 1988, including the administered areas.

Israel's capital city, Jerusalem, is located near the center of the country (including the West Bank).

²TOPOGRAPHY

The country is divided into three major longitudinal strips: the coastal plain, which follows the Mediterranean shoreline in a southward widening band; the hill region, embracing the hills of Galilee in the north, Samaria and Judea in the center, and the Negev in the south; and the Jordan Valley. Except for the Bay of Acre, the sandy coastline is not indented for its entire length. The hill region, averaging 610 m (2,000 ft) in elevation, reaches its highest point at Mt. Meron (1,208 m/3,963 ft). South of the Judean hills, the Negev desert, marked by cliffs and craters and covering about half the total area of Israel proper, extends down to the Gulf of Aqaba on the Red Sea. The Jordan River, forming the border between Israel (including the West Bank) and Jordan, links the only bodies of water in the country: the Sea of Galilee (Yam Kinneret) and the heavily saline Dead Sea (Yam ha-Melah), which, at 393 m (1,290 ft) below sea level, is the lowest point on the earth's surface.

³CLIMATE

Although climatic conditions are varied across the country, the climate is generally temperate. The coldest month is January; the hottest, August. In winter, snow occasionally falls in the hills, where January temperatures normally fluctuate between 4° and 10°C (40–50°F), and August temperatures between 18° and 29°C (65–85°F). On the coastal plain, sea breezes temper the weather all year round, temperature variations ranging from 8° to 18°C (47–65°F) in January and 21° to 29°C (70–85°F) in August. In the south, at Elat, January temperatures range between 10° and 21°C (50–70°F) and may reach 49°C (120°F) in August. The rainy season lasts from November until April, with rainfall averaging 108 cm (43 in) annually in the Upper Galilee and only 2 cm (0.8

in) at Elat, although dewfall gives the south another several inches of water every year.

⁴FLORA AND FAUNA

The Bible (Deuteronomy 8:8) describes the country as "a land of wheat and barley, of vines and fig trees and pomegranates, a land of olive trees and honey." The original forests, evergreen and maquis, have largely been destroyed, but some 200 million new trees have been planted during this century, in a major reforestation program. Vegetation cover is thin except in the coastal plain, where conditions are favorable to the cultivation of citrus fruit, and in the Jordan Valley, with its plantations of tropical fruit. Among surviving animals, jackals and hyenas remain fairly numerous, and there are wild boar in the Lake Hula region. With the growth of vegetation and water supplies, bird life and deer have increased.

⁵ENVIRONMENT

In the 1990s, water pollution and adequate water supply were major environmental issues in Israel. Industrial and agricultural chemicals threaten the nation's already depleted water supply. Israel has only 0.4 cu mi of water with 79% used for farming activity and 5% used for industrial purposes. Nearly 80% of the people living in rural areas have pure water. Air pollution from industrial sources, oil facilities, and vehicles is another significant environmental problem. In the mid-1990s Israel's industrial carbon dioxide emissions totaled 41.6 million metric tons per year, a per capita level of 8.10 metric tons per year.

Reforestation efforts, especially since 1948, have helped to conserve the country's water resources and prevent soil erosion. Israel has reclaimed much of the Negev for agricultural purposes by means of large irrigation projects, thereby stopping the desertification process that had been depleting the land for nearly 2,000 years. Principal environmental responsibility is vested in the Environmental Protection Service of the Ministry of the Interior.

In the mid-1990s, 8 mammal species and 15 bird species were endangered. Three species of plants were threatened with extinction. Endangered species included the northern bald ibis, South Arabian leopard, Sa'udi Arabian dorcas gazelle, three species of sea turtles, and Israel painted frog. The Mediterranean monk seal, cheetah, Barbary sheep, and Persian fallow deer became extinct in the 1980s.

⁶POPULATION

The population of Israel in 2000 was estimated at 5,851,913. The population of the West Bank was estimated at 1,661,749. An estimated 9.3% of the population is 65 years of age or older. The projected population for the year 2005 is 6,303,000, assuming a crude birthrate of 19 per 1,000 population and a death rate of 6, resulting in a natural rate of change of 1.3% for the period 2000–2005. The population rate of change between 1995 and 2000 was 1.9%. The population density in 1998 was 290 per sq km (751 per sq mi).

It was estimated that 91% of the population lived in urban areas in 2000, up from 89% in 1980. The capital city, Jerusalem, had a 2000 population of 600,000. Tel Aviv (now Tel Aviv–Yafo), had a metropolitan population of 2,170,000 in 2000. Other large cities are Haifa (Hefa), 249,800; Holon, 162,800; Bat Yam, 145,300; Petah Tiqwa, 150,800; Beersheba (Be'er Sheva'), 134,700; Rishon LeZiyyon, 150,400; and Netanya, 141,800. Besides the population of Israel (including East Jerusalem), 1,571,575 persons, as of 1996, lived on the West Bank (also called Judea and Samaria), and 963,000 in the Gaza Strip.

⁷MIGRATION

In 1948, 65% of Israel's Jewish population consisted of immigrants; many of these 463,000 immigrant Jews had fled from persecution in Russia and, especially during the Nazi period, Central and Eastern Europe. Israel's declaration of independence publicly opened the state "to the immigration of Jews from all countries of their dispersion," and the 1950 Law of Return granted every returning Jew the right to automatic citizenship. The Nationality Law specifies other ways—including birth, residence, and naturalization—that Israeli citizenship may be acquired. In the years 1948–92, Israel took in 2,242,500 Jewish immigrants; during 1948–51, the flow was at its heaviest, averaging 171,685 per year, about evenly divided between Eastern European Jews, who were war refugees, and Oriental Jews from ancient centers of the Arab world. In the years 1952–56, most immigrants came from French North Africa; in 1957–58 there was a renewed inflow from Eastern Europe. After a lull in 1959–60, the flow of immigrants was renewed, reaching substantial proportions by 1963, when 64,364 Jews arrived. Immigration fell to an annual average of 20,561 persons for 1965–68, rose to an average of 43,258 per year for 1969–74, then declined to an average of 24,965 for 1975–79. The number declined further to an average of 15,383 for 1980–89. As of March, 1995, around 525,000 immigrants had arrived in Israel since 1990. Most of these immigrants came from the former Soviet Union; this was the largest wave immigration since the independence of Israel. In May of 1991, 14,000 Ethiopian Jews immigrated due to Operation Solomon airlift. The proportion of Jewish immigrants from Europe and North America (as opposed to those from Asia and Africa) varied during the 1960s, but it rose from 40.4% in 1968 to 97.3% in 1990. (For this purpose the Asiatic republics of the USSR were counted as part of Europe). In 1984–85, some 10,000 Ethiopian Jews, victims of famine, were airlifted to Israel via Sudan. In 1992, the Jewish immigrant population was 39.4% of all Israeli Jews and 31.8% of all Israelis. A certain amount of emigration has always taken place, but the pace increased after 1975. In a typical year after 1980, about 10,000 Israelis were added to the number who had been away continuously for more than four years. From 1967 to 1992, Israel established 142 settlements in the occupied territories; about 130,000 Jews were living there by 1995.

Considerable Arab migration has also taken place, including an apparent wave of Arab immigration into Palestine between World War I and World War II. During the 1948 war there was a massive flight of an estimated 800,000 Palestinians. As of 1997 there were 3.2 million Palestinian refugees living in the West Bank, the Gaza Strip, Jordan, Syria, and Lebanon under the mandate of the Gaza-based United Nations Relief and Works Agency for Palestine Refugees in the Near East (UNRWA). In 1999, the net migration rate for Israel was 4.42 migrants per 1,000 population.

⁸ETHNIC GROUPS

Of the estimated population of 5,749,760 in 1999, 80.1% were Jewish (European/American-born 32.1%; Israeli-born 20.8%; African-born 14.6%; Asian-born 12.6%) and 19.9% were non-Jewish (mostly Arab).

The traditional division of the Jews into Ashkenazim (Central and East Europeans) and Sephardim (Iberian Jews and their descendants) is still given formal recognition in the choice of two chief rabbis, one for each community. A more meaningful division, however, would be that between Occidentals and Orientals (now also called Sephardim). Oriental Jews, who are in the majority, generally believe themselves to be educationally, economically, and socially disadvantaged by comparison with the Occidentals.

The minority non-Jewish population is overwhelmingly Arabic-speaking, but Israel's minorities are divided into a number of religious groups and include several small non-Arab national groups, such as Armenians and Circassians. The government of

Israel has declared its intention to strive for equality between the Arab and Jewish sectors of the population. Israel's Arab citizens do not share fully in rights granted to, and levies imposed on, Jewish citizens. The rights of citizenship do not extend to Arabs in the administered territories. The living standards of Arabs in Israel compare favorably with those of Arabs in non-oil-producing Arab countries, but they are considerably below those of the Jewish majority, especially the Ashkenazim. As a consequence of repeated wars between Israel and its Arab neighbors and the development of Palestinian Arab nationalism and terrorism, tensions between Jews and Arabs are a fact of Israeli daily life, especially in the West Bank and Gaza Strip.

⁹LANGUAGES

The official languages are Hebrew and Arabic, the former being dominant. Hebrew is the language of most of the Old Testament; modern Hebrew is the biblical language as modified by absorption of elements from all historical forms of Hebrew and by development over the years. Arabic is used by Arabs in parliamentary deliberations, in pleadings before the courts, and in dealings with governmental departments, and is the language of instruction in schools for Arab children. English is taught in all secondary schools and, along with Hebrew, is commonly used in foreign business correspondence and in advertising and labeling. Coins, postage stamps, and bank notes bear inscriptions in Hebrew, Arabic, and Latin characters.

¹⁰RELIGIONS

The land that is now Israel (which the Romans called Judea and then Palestine) is the cradle of two of the world's great religions, Judaism and Christianity. In the Hebrew Scriptures, Jewish history begins with Abraham's journey from Mesopotamia to Canaan, to which the descendants of Abraham would later return after their deliverance by Moses from bondage in Egypt. Jerusalem is the historical site of the First Temple, built by Solomon in the 10th century BC and destroyed by the Babylonians in 586 BC, and the Second Temple, built about 70 years later and sacked by the Romans in AD 70. Belief in the life, teachings, crucifixion, and resurrection of Jesus of Nazareth (who, according to the Christian Scriptures, actually preached in the Second Temple) is the basis of the Christian religion. Spread by the immediate followers of Jesus and others, Christianity developed within three centuries from a messianic Jewish sect to the established religion of the Roman Empire. Jerusalem is also holy to Islam: the Dome of the Rock marks the site where, in Muslim tradition, Mohammed rose into heaven.

Present-day Israel is the only country where Judaism is the majority religion, professed by 80.1% of the population; over one-fourth of all the world's Jews live there. Freedom of religion is guaranteed. The Ministry of Religious Affairs assists institutions of every affiliation and contributes to the preservation and repair of their holy shrines, which are protected by the government and made accessible to pilgrims. Supreme religious authority in the Jewish community is vested in the chief rabbinate, with Ashkenazim and Sephardim each having a chief rabbi.

Most Arabs are Sunni Muslims (14.6%). Christians (2.1%) are largely Greek Catholic or Greek Orthodox, but there are also Roman Catholics, Armenians, and Protestants. Other religions are claimed by the remaining 3.2% of the population. The Druzes, who split away from Islam in the 11th century, have the status of a separate religious community. The Baha'i world faith is centered in Haifa.

¹¹TRANSPORTATION

In 1997, there were an estimated 15,464 km (9,609 mi) of paved highways, including 56 km (35 mi) of expressways. With the

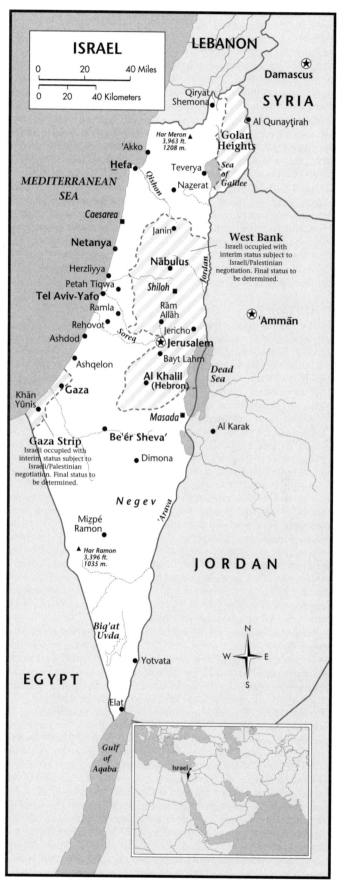

LOCATION: 29°29′ to 33°17′N; 34°16′ to 35°41′E.
TERRITORIAL SEA LIMIT: 6 mi.

building in 1957 of a highway extension from Beersheba to Elat, the Red Sea was linked to the Mediterranean. Trackage of the state-owned railway totaled 610 km (379 mi) in 1998. Railways, buses, and taxis formerly constituted the principal means of passenger transportation; however, private car ownership nearly tripled during the 1970s. In 1995 there were 1,394,323 motor vehicles, including 1,121,730 private cars and 272,600 trucks, taxis, and buses.

As of 1998, Israel had 23 merchant vessels, with a total capacity of 736,419 GRT. Haifa can berth large passenger liners and has a 10,000-ton floating dock, but Ashdod (south of Tel Aviv) has outstripped Haifa in cargo handled since the early 1980s. Elat is also a seaport.

Israel had 54 airports in 1998, 31 with paved runways. Israel Inland Airlines (Arkia) provides domestic service. Israel Airlines (El Al), which was founded shortly after Israel became a nation in 1948 and is almost entirely owned by the government, operates international flights from Ben-Gurion International airport near Tel Aviv. Another principal airport is J. Hozman at Eilat. In 1997 3,754,000 passengers were carried on scheduled domestic and international airline flights.

12HISTORY

Archaeologists have established that the world's earliest known city was Jericho, on the present-day West Bank, built about 7000 BC. The formative period of Israel began in approximately 1800 BC, when the Hebrews entered Canaan, and resumed in approximately 1200 BC, when the Israelite tribes returned to Canaan after a period of residence in Egypt. At various times, the people were led by patriarchs, judges, kings, prophets, and scribes, and the land was conquered by Assyrians, Babylonians (or Chaldeans), Persians, Greeks, and Romans. The ancient period neared its end in AD 70, when the Roman legions conquered Jerusalem after an unsuccessful revolt and destroyed the Temple, and it ended in AD 135, when the Roman Empire exiled most Jews after another unsuccessful revolt, led by Simon Bar-Kokhba, and renamed the region Syria Palaestina, which eventually became Palestine. During the next two millennia there were successive waves of foreign conquerors—Byzantines, Persians, Arabs, Crusaders, Mongols, Turks, and Britons. Most Jews remained in dispersion, where many nourished messianic hopes for an eventual return to Zion; however, Jews in varying numbers continued to live in Palestine through the years. It is estimated that by 1900, only about 78,000 Jews were living in Palestine (less than 1% of the world Jewish population), compared with some 650,000 non-Jews, mostly Arabs.

Modern Zionism, the movement for the reestablishment of a Jewish nation, dates from the late 19th century, with small-scale settlements by Russian and Romanian Jews on lands purchased by funds from Western European and US donors. The movement received impetus from the founding of the World Zionist Organization in Basel, Switzerland, in 1897, under the leadership of Theodor Herzl. Zionist hopes for a Jewish national homeland in Palestine were greatly bolstered when the British government pledged its support for this goal in 1917, in the Balfour Declaration, which was subsequently incorporated into the mandate over Palestine (originally including Transjordan) awarded to the UK by the League of Nations in 1922. Under the mandate, the Jewish community grew from 85,000 to 650,000, largely through immigration, on lands purchased from Arab owners. This growth was attended by rising hostility from the Arab community, which felt its majority status threatened by the Jewish influx. In 1939, shortly before the outbreak of World War II, the British mandatory authorities issued a White Paper that decreed severe restrictions on Jewish immigration and a virtual freezing of land purchase and settlement. Armed Jewish resistance to this policy, as well as growing international backing for the establishment of

a Jewish state as a haven for the survivors of the Nazi Holocaust, finally persuaded the British government to relinquish the mandate.

On 29 November 1947, the UN General Assembly adopted a plan for the partition of Palestine into two economically united but politically sovereign states, one Jewish and the other Arab, with Jerusalem as an international city. The Arabs of Palestine, aided by brethren across the frontiers, at once rose up in arms to thwart partition. The Jews accepted the plan; on 14 May 1948, the last day of the mandate, they proclaimed the formation of the State of Israel. The next day, the Arab League states—Egypt, Iraq, Jordan, Lebanon, Sa'udi Arabia, and Syria—launched a concerted armed attack. There followed a mass flight of hundreds of tens of thousands of Palestinian Arabs abroad. The war left Israel in possession of a much larger territory than that awarded the Jews under the UN partition plan; the planned Arab state failed to materialize, as Jordan annexed the West Bank. Meanwhile, the Palestinian refugees were resettled in camps on both banks of the Jordan River, in the Gaza Strip (then under Egyptian administration), in southern Lebanon, and in Syria.

Armistice agreements concluded in 1949 failed to provide the contemplated transition to peace, and sporadic Arab incursions along the borders were answered by Israeli reprisals. Tensions were exacerbated by Arab economic boycotts and by Egypt's nationalization of the Suez Canal on 26 July 1956. On 29 October 1956, Israel (with British and French support) invaded Egypt and soon gained control of the Gaza Strip and the Sinai Peninsula. Fighting ended on 4 November; Israel, under US pressure, withdrew from the occupied areas in March 1957 and recognized borders consistent with its military position at the end of the 1948 war. A UN Emergency Force (UNEF) patrolled the armistice line.

Violations by both sides of the armistice lines persisted, and in May 1967, Egypt, fearing an Israeli attack on Syria, moved armaments and troops into the Sinai, ordering withdrawal of UNEF personnel from the armistice line, and closed the Strait of Tiran to Israeli shipping. On 5 June, Israel attacked Egypt and its allies, Syria and Jordan. By 11 June, Israel had scored a decisive victory in the conflict, since termed the Six-Day War, and had taken control of the Sinai Peninsula, the Gaza Strip, the Golan Heights, and the West Bank (including Jordanian-ruled East Jerusalem). The Security Council on 22 November unanimously adopted UK-sponsored Resolution 242, calling for establishment of a just and lasting peace in the Middle East, withdrawal of Israeli armed forces from territories occupied during the war, and acknowledgment of the "sovereignty, territorial integrity, and political independence of every State in the area and their right to live in peace within secure and recognized boundaries free from threats or acts of force." Israel indicated that return of the captured territories would have to be part of a general settlement guaranteeing peace; in 1967, the Israeli government began Jewish settlement in these areas; due in good part to the later encouragement of the Likud governments, by 1997 there were some 160,000 settlers in the occupied territories.

Serious shooting incidents between Egypt and Israel resumed in June 1969, following Egypt's declaration of a war of attrition against Israel. In response to a US peace initiative, a cease-fire took effect in August 1970, but tensions continued, and Palestinian Arab guerrillas mounted an international campaign of terrorism, highlighted in September 1972 by the kidnap and murder of Israeli athletes at the Olympic Games in Munich.

On 6 October 1973, during Yom Kippur, Egypt and Syria simultaneously attacked Israeli-held territory in the Sinai Peninsula and the Golan Heights. The Arabs won initial victories, but by 24 October, when a UN cease-fire took effect, the Israelis had crossed the Suez Canal and were 101 km (63 mi) from Cairo and about 27 km (17 mi) from Damascus. Under the impetus of the "shuttle diplomacy" exercised by US Secretary of State Henry Kissinger, formal first-stage disengagement agreements were signed with Egypt on 18 January 1974 and with Syria on 31 May 1974. On 4 September 1975, a second-stage disengagement pact was signed in Geneva, under which Israel relinquished some territory in the Sinai (including two oil fields) in return for Egyptian declarations of peaceful intent, free passage of nonmilitary cargoes to and from Israel through the Suez Canal, and the stationing of US civilians to monitor an early-warning system.

The 30-year cycle of Egyptian-Israeli hostilities was broken in November 1977, when Egyptian President Anwar al-Sadat (as-Sadat) paid a visit to Jerusalem on 19–21 November 1977, during which, in an address to parliament, he affirmed Israel's right to exist as a nation, thereby laying the basis for a negotiated peace. In September 1978, at a summit conference mediated by US President Jimmy Carter at Camp David, Md., Israeli Prime Minister Menachem Begin and Sadat agreed on the general framework for a peace treaty which, after further negotiations, they signed in Washington, D.C. on 26 March 1979. The treaty provided for the withdrawal of Israeli forces from the Sinai over a three-year period and for further negotiations concerning autonomy and future status of Arab residents of the West Bank and the Gaza Strip, territories still under Israeli occupation. Israel withdrew from the Sinai oil fields within a year, and from the remainder of Sinai by 25 April 1982. However, the two countries failed to reach agreement on Palestinian autonomy in the West Bank and Gaza, and Israel continued to establish Jewish settlements in the West Bank despite Egyptian protests.

Israel's relations remained tense with other Arab countries, which ostracized Egypt for signing the peace accord. In March 1978, Israel (which had long been supporting Lebanese Christian militias against the Palestine Liberation Organization—PLO—and its Muslim backers) sent troops into southern Lebanon to destroy PLO bases in retaliation for a Palestinian terrorist attack; Israel withdrew under US pressure. In April 1981, Israeli and Syrian forces directly confronted each other in Lebanon; Israeli jet aircraft shot down two Syrian helicopters in Lebanese territory, and Syria responded by deploying Soviet-made antiaircraft missiles in the Bekaa (Biqa') Valley, which Syria had been occupying since 1976. On 7 June 1981, Israeli warplanes struck at and disabled an Iraqi nuclear reactor under construction near Baghdad; the Israeli government claimed that the reactor could be employed to produce nuclear bombs for use against Israel.

Hostilities between Israel and the PLO and Syria reached a climax in early June 1982, when Israel launched a full-scale invasion of southern Lebanon, citing continued PLO shelling of the north and terrorist acts elsewhere. An estimated 90,000 troops rapidly destroyed PLO bases within a 40 km (25 mi) zone north of the Israeli border, captured the coastal towns of Tyre (Sur) and Sidon (Sayda), and then moved on to bomb and encircle Beirut by 14 June, trapping the main force of PLO fighters in the Lebanese capital and causing massive casualties and destruction. Meanwhile, Israeli warplanes destroyed Syria's Soviet-built missile batteries in the Bekaa Valley—the announced objective of the invasion. A negotiated cease-fire was arranged by US envoy Philip Habib on 25 June, and more than 14,000 Palestinian and Syrian fighters were allowed to evacuate Beirut in late August. A multinational peacekeeping force of British, French, Italian, and US military personnel was stationed in the Beirut area.

Within Israel, the Lebanese war was divisive, and there were protest rallies against the Begin government. The protests increased when, after Israeli troops moved into West Beirut in the wake of the assassination of Lebanese President Bashir Gemayel, Christian militiamen were allowed to "mop up" remaining resistance in the Palestinian camps. The ensuing massacres, for which an Israeli government investigating commission determined that some of Israel's civilian and military leaders were indirectly responsible, led to the resignation of Ariel Sharon as defense minister. Subsequent Israeli attempts to extricate its occupying forces from Lebanon by negotiating an agreement for the withdrawal of all foreign forces were rejected by Syria. In September, Israel pulled back its forces from the Shuf Mountains, east of Beirut, to south of the Litani River. In 1985, withdrawal from southern Lebanon took place in stages over six months, punctuated by terrorist acts of Shi'i Muslim militants against departing Israeli troops, resulting in retaliatory arrests and detention of hundreds of Lebanese. Negotiations over a Trans World Airlines (TWA) jetliner hijacked en route from Athens to Rome by Shi'i militants in June 1985 led to gradual release by Israel of its Shi'i prisoners. In 1986, troubles continued despite the occupation of a swath of southern Lebanon, which Israel continued to term a "security zone", as Shi'i militants and infiltrating Palestinian guerrillas continued to launch attacks. The war was a drain on the economy, already suffering from hyperinflation and huge foreign-exchange deficits. Prime Minister Begin resigned because of failing health in the autumn of 1983 and was replaced by Yitzhak Shamir, who, after inconclusive elections in 1984, was replaced on a rotational basis by Labor Party leader Shimon Peres. In 1986, a ground-breaking summit meeting took place when Prime Minister Peres traveled to Morocco for two days of secret talks with King Hassan II. In that year, Israel also improved relations with Egypt when Prime Minister Peres conferred with Egypt's President Hosni Mubarek in the first meeting of the two nations since 1981. Shamir replaced Peres as prime minister in October 1986. Elections were again held with equally inconclusive results in November 1988, leading to a coalition government of the Labor and Likub parties. Four years later, Labor edged Likud in elections and was able to form a government supported by left-wing and religious parties. Yitzhak Rabin became Prime Minister with Shimon Peres as Foreign Minister; both were committed to reaching peace agreements with Arab antagonists.

In December 1987, unarmed Palestinians in Gaza began what became a multi-year series of stone-throwing riots against Israeli troops in the occupied territories. In this uprising (or *intifada* in Arabic), well over 1,000 Palestinians were killed and—by Palestinians—several hundred Israelis and Palestinian collaborators. Israeli use of lethal force, curfews, deportations, destruction of houses, and ten thousand detentions failed to stop the demonstrations while producing criticism abroad and anxiety at home. Waves of Jewish immigrants from the collapsing Soviet Union further provoked Palestinians.

During the Gulf War of 1991, Israel was hit by Iraqi missile attacks, demonstrating for some the state's vulnerability and need to move toward peace with the Arabs. Prime Minister Shamir, who opposed the return of occupied territory, reluctantly accepted a US and Russian invitation to direct peace talks in Madrid in October 1991. These and subsequent negotiations produced few results until, under a Labor Government, Israeli and Palestinian representatives met secretly in Oslo to work out a peace agreement involving mutual recognition and transfer of authority in Gaza and Jericho to interim Palestinian rule with the final status of a Palestinian entity to be resolved in five years. The agreement was signed at the White House in Washington on 13 September 1993. Promises of international aid for the new Palestinian units poured in but the agreement was opposed by extremists on both sides and further set back by a massacre of 30 Moslems at prayer in the Hebron mosque on 25 February 1994 by a militant Israeli settler. Finally, delayed by several months, the withdrawal of Israeli forces from certain sectors and establishment of Palestinian self-rule took place on 18 May 1994. By 1997, six West Bank cities had been turned over to the Palestinian Authority. Israel has balked at turning over control of Hebron even though it agreed to do so.

In November 1995, the greatest setback to the peace process occurred when a militant Israeli assassinated Prime Minister Yitzhak Rabin in retaliation for slowing Jewish settlement in the occupied territories and for his generally dovish policy toward the PLO. The nation then entered into a tumultuous period as Shimon Peres, Rabin's co-Prime Minister, took control of the government. Peres was not as popular as Rabin had been and in response to civil protest he called for early elections, which were held in May 1996. For the first time in these elections, Israelis were given the opportunity to directly elect their Prime Minister, and Peres and Likud-lead Benjamin Netanyahu fought a bitter campaign, focusing mainly on the status of the occupied territories and the threat of terrorism from radical Palestinians. The prime minister race was very close and some news reports early on suggested, based on exit polling, that Peres had won. By morning of the next day, however, Netanyahu had emerged as Israel's first directly-elected Prime Minister and Likud emerged with a slight majority (in coalition with a range of right wing parties) in the Knesset. Netanyahu immediately took a tough stance on the occupied territories, increasing the construction of Jewish settlements and enraging the Palestinians and the international community.

As expected, progress in the Middle East peace process slowed under Netanyahu. Hostilities between Palestinians and Israeli soldiers in the fall of 1996, following the opening of a tunnel in the Old City of Jerusalem, were the worst to occur since the days of the Intifada. In 1997 and 1998 peace talks stalled over the terms of Israeli withdrawal from the West Bank. A new agreement, the Wye Memorandum, was reached at an October 1998 meeting in the US between Netanyahu, Yassir Arafat, and President Bill Clinton. It set up a timetable for Israeli withdrawal from the West Bank. However, Netanyahu faced stiff opposition to the plan at home, and by the end of 1998, his governing coalition had collapsed, and implementation of the Wye plan was suspended until a new government could be formed following national elections the following May.

Labor candidate Ehud Barak triumphed in the May 1999 elections and formed a coalition government in July. In September, Barak and Arafat signed an agreement reviving the Wye accord, and in December peace talks between Israel and Syria—broken off in 1996—were resumed. By the end of 1999, Barak had also pledged the withdrawal of Israeli forces from south Lebanon as of July 2000.

13GOVERNMENT

Israel is a democratic republic, with no written constitution. Legislative power is vested in the unicameral Knesset (parliament), whose 120 members are elected for four-year terms by universal secret vote of all citizens 18 years of age and over, under a system of proportional representation. New elections may be called ahead of schedule, and must be held when the government loses the confidence of a majority of parliament.

The head of state is the president, elected by the Knesset for a five-year term. The president performs largely ceremonial duties and traditionally chose the Prime Minister from the ruling political party. In 1996, however, a new law went into effect whereby the Prime Minister is directly elected by the people. In May of that year, Benjamin Netanyahu became Israel's first directly elected prime minister. Three years later he was succeeded in that post by Ehud Barak. The cabinet, headed by the prime minister, is collectively responsible to the Knesset, whose confidence it must enjoy.

14POLITICAL PARTIES

Israel's multi-party system reflects the diverse origins of the people and their long practice of party politics in Zionist organizations. The first five Knessets were controlled by coalitions led by the Mapai (Israel Workers Party), under Israel's first prime minister (1949–63), David Ben-Gurion, and then under Levi Eshkol (1963–69). The Mapai formed the nucleus of the present Israel Labor Party, a socialist party, which in coalition with other groups controlled Israel's governments under prime ministers Golda Meir (1969–74) and Yitzhak Rabin (1974–77 and 1992-95).

In September 1973, four right-wing nationalist parties combined to form the Likud, which thus became the major opposition bloc in the Knesset. Unlike the Israel Labor Party, the core of support of which lies with the Ashkenazim and older Israelis generally, the Likud has drawn much of its strength from Oriental Jewry, as well as from among the young and the less well-educated. Besides the State List and the Free Center, the Likud consists of the Herut (Freedom) Movement, founded in 1948 to support territorial integrity within Israel's biblical boundaries and a greater economic role for private enterprise, and the Liberal Party, formed in 1961 to support private enterprise, a liberal welfare state, and electoral reform. The Likud originally advocated retention of all territories captured in the 1967 war, as a safeguard to national security. It won 39 seats in the 1973 elections and then became the largest party in the Knesset by winning 43 seats in the May 1977 elections, to 32 seats for the Israel Labor Party–United Workers (Mapam) alignment. Likud leader Menachem Begin became prime minister of a coalition government formed by Likud with the National Religious Party and the ultraorthodox Agudat Israel.

In elections on 30 June 1981, Likud again won a plurality, by taking 37.1% of the popular vote and 48 seats in the Knesset, compared with the Labor coalition's 36.6% and 47 seats. Begin succeeded in forming a new government with the support of smaller parties. The elections of July 1984 again left both Labor (with 44 seats) and Likud (with 41) short of a Knesset majority; under a power-sharing agreement, each party held an equal number of cabinet positions in a unity government, and each party leader served as premier for 25 months. Labor's Shimon Peres became prime minister in 1984, handing over the office to Likud's Yitzhak Shamir in late 1986. Elections in 1988 produced a similar power-sharing arrangement. In 1989, rotation was ended as Likud and Labor joined in a coalition. After a vote of no-confidence, Likud formed a coalition of religious and right-wing parties which held power for two years until 1992. Elections in June gave Labor 44 seats (32 for Likud) and enabled it to form a coalition with Meretz (a grouping of three left-wing parties) and Shas (a religious party) and the support of two Arab parties.

In 1995, Prime Minister Yitzhak Rabin was assassinated by an extremist Jew. Shimon Peres became Prime Minister and called for early elections, which were held in May 1996. The main issue of the election was Israel's response to terrorist attacks and the disposition of the occupied territories. Labor favored continued and increased negotiations with the PLO and the Palestinian Authority (PA), while Likud favored a tougher stance, increased settlement on occupied lands, and a rethinking of the Oslo accords—at the very least a slowing of the process of land-turnover. The elections were extremely close with the Likud-Geshe-Tsamet coalition winning a slim majority, or 62 seats. In a separate election, Benjamin Netanyahu was elected Prime Minister, the first such election in Israeli history after the passage of a 1996 law.

After Netanyahu's governing coalition collapsed at the end of 1998, new elections were called for May of 1999. In the election for a new prime minister, Ehud Barak, heading a Labor-led center-left coalition (One Israel), defeated Netanyahu 56% to 44%. In the legislative elections, Barak's One Israel/Israeli Labor Party coalition won a plurality of 26 seats, followed by 19 for the Likud. Overall, the distribution of seats in the Knesset after the election was as follows: Right-wing parties held 23 seats (Likud 19, National Unity 4); center-left parties held 38 (One Israel 26, Center Party 6, Shinui 6); left-wing parties held 22 (One Nation 2, Meretz 10, Hadash 3, United Arab List 5, Balad 2); religious parties accounted for 27 seats (Shas 17, National Religious Party 5, United Torah Judaism 5); and Russian immigrant and nonaligned parties held 10 (Israel Ba-Aliya 6, Israel Beiteinu 4).

15 LOCAL GOVERNMENT

Israel is divided into six administrative districts: Jerusalem, Tel Aviv, Haifa, Northern (Tiberias), Central (Ramle), and Southern (Beersheba). The occupied Golan Heights is a subdistrict of the Northern District. Each district is governed by a commissioner appointed by the central government. At the local level, government is by elected regional and local councils, which govern according to bylaws approved by the Ministry of the Interior. Local officials are elected for four-year terms. Until 1994, Israel governed all of the occupied territories through the Civil Administration, which is responsible to the Ministry of Defense. Palestinian towns have Israeli-appointed mayors. Israeli settlers in the territories are subject to Israeli law. In 1994, Israel withdrew its forces from Gaza and Jericho in favor of an interim Palestinian self-governing authority.

16 JUDICIAL SYSTEM

The law of Israel contains some features of Ottoman law, English common law, and other foreign law, but it is shaped largely by the provisions of the Knesset. Judges are appointed by the president on recommendation of independent committees. There are 29 magistrates' courts, which deal with most cases in the first instance, petty property claims, and lesser criminal charges. Five district courts, serving mainly as courts of appeal, have jurisdiction over all other actions except marriage and divorce cases, which are adjudicated, along with other personal and religious matters, in the religious courts of the Jewish (rabbinical), Muslim (Shari'ah), Druze, and Christian communities. Aside from its function as the court of last appeal, the 11-member Supreme Court also hears cases in the first instance brought by citizens against arbitrary government actions. There is no jury system. Capital punishment applies only for crimes of wartime treason or for collaboration with the Nazis, and has been employed only once in Israel's modern history, in the case of Adolf Eichmann, who was executed in 1962. In the administered territories, security cases are tried in military courts; verdicts may not be appealed, and the rules of habeas corpus do not apply. There are also labor relations and administrative courts.

There is no constitution, but a series of "basic laws" provide for fundamental rights. The judiciary is independent. The trials are fair and public. Legislation enacted in 1997 limits detention without charge to 24 hours. Defendants have the right to be presumed innocent, and to writs of habeas corpus and other procedural safeguards.

17 ARMED FORCES

The defense forces of Israel began with the voluntary defense forces (principally the Haganah) created by the Jewish community in Palestine during the British mandate. Today Jewish and Druze men between the ages of 18 and 26 are conscripted for 36 and 24 months, respectively. Drafted Jewish women are trained for noncombat duties. Christians and Muslims may serve on a voluntary basis, but Muslims are rarely allowed to bear arms. All men and unmarried women serve in the reserves until the ages of 54 and 24, respectively. Men receive annual combat training until age 45.

In 2000, the Israeli army had 130,000 active duty soldiers (85,000 conscripts) and could mobilize as many as 530,000 more soldiers, about half as combat-ready units. There were three armored divisions, four mechanized infantry brigades, and one artillery brigade in the standing force. Armaments included 3,800 main battle tanks and 5,500 armored vehicles. The navy had 6,500 regulars, 2,500 conscripts, and 11,500 reservists; vessels included 4 submarines, 14 missile-equipped fast patrol boats, and 36 patrol craft. The air force had 37,000 regulars, 20,000 conscripts, and 57,000 reserves. There were 459 functional combat aircraft, with 250 aircraft in reserve, and 133 armed helicopters. The reserve force (425,000) can be effectively mobilized in 48–72 hours. There are 6,000 paramilitary border police.

The Ministry of Defense's expenditure was $8.7 billion in 1999 or 9.5% of gross domestic product, but this sum excludes reserve pay and some other expenses. Israeli arms purchases are principally from the US. In recent years, Israel has itself become an important exporter of arms to Latin American, South Korea, Africa, and other countries.

Israel may have as many as 100 nuclear warheads, deliverable by Jericho I (500 km) or Jericho II (1,500 km) missiles.

18 INTERNATIONAL COOPERATION

Israel was admitted as the 59th UN member on 11 May 1949 and subsequently joined all the nonregional specialized agencies. It is also a permanent observer with the OAS and a member of the WTO. During the 1970s and early 1980s, Arab governments sought through the "oil weapon" to isolate Israel diplomatically and economically, but Israel's 1979 peace treaty with Egypt helped ease some of the pressure. The US is Israel's major political, economic, and military ally. A number of African countries reestablished diplomatic relations with Israel in the 1980s; these ties had been broken in 1973, following the Arab-Israeli war. After signing peace accords with the Palestinians in 1993 and 1994, Israel opened liaison and trade missions in certain Arab countries, including Qatar and Omon, bringing to six the number of Arab nations with which Israel conducts trade. Israel also signed a peace agreement with Jordan in 1994, and the two nations exchanged ambassadors in 1995.

19 ECONOMY

Since independence, Israel's economy has been faced with serious problems. The government makes large outlays for social welfare purposes, but is obliged to divert a considerable portion of its income to defense. In addition, traditional Middle Eastern sources of supply (e.g., of oil and wheat) and nearby markets for goods and services have been closed off. Israel must export on a large scale to maintain its relatively high standard of living; hence, it remains dependent on a continuing flow of investment capital and of private and public assistance from abroad.

The economy is a mixture of private, state, and cooperative ownership and holdings of the labor movement. In the first 35 years of Israel's existence, the number of industrial enterprises more than doubled; more than 700 agricultural settlements were established; and there were notable advances in housing, transportation, and exploitation of natural resources. From 1975 to 1980, GNP grew at an annual rate of 3.1% (at constant prices). Between 1980 and 1985, real GNP growth was 10%. Since 1990, the Israeli economy has experienced strong sustained growth, averaging about 6% a year between 1990–1996. In large part this is due to steps the government has taken—in housing construction, infrastructure expansion, and capital investment—in response to the huge influx of Russian immigrants which began in 1990. (The country has had to absorb more than half a million new immigrants.) Most of these immigrants have been relatively well-educated, adding to Israel's already considerable base of technologically-aware workforce and population. As such, sectors of importance to future economic growth are medical equipment, computer hardware and software, and telecommunications. By the mid-1990s, however, the immigrant influx ground to a near halt and the government introduced fiscal belt-tightening economic growth. Economic growth declined to an average of 2% in 1997–98.

The surging economic performance of the early and mid-1990s can also be attributed to the series of agreements it entered into with the PLO, granting the organization a limited sovereignty over small parcels of land in the occupied territories. The move brought an end to the embargo some Arab countries have maintained against Israel for decades and the opening of new markets, especially in Asia. From 1992–95, Israeli exports to Asia grew by 86% and now account for 20% of Israel's total exports. Tourism has also benefited from the peace accords and international investment, once nearly impossible to attract, has increased significantly. As of mid-2000, it was unclear what effects the unclear future of Israel-PLO relations would have on this scenario.

Following the election of a conservative Likud-led government in 1996, the Israeli government embarked upon a privatization program, symbolized by the 1997 divestment of Bank Hapoalim, the country's largest bank. Privatization continued in 1998 and 1999. The election of a Labor-led coalition in 1999, has not resulted in a reversal of the privatization initiatives.

Inflation, a chronic problem, worsened drastically in the early 1980s: the consumer price index (1976 = 100) rose from 134.6 in 1977 to 834.9 in 1980; the new index (1980 = 100) stood at 477.7 at the end of 1982, 5,560 in 1984, and 22,498 in 1985. Israel's 1982 invasion of Lebanon, which cost an estimated $2 billion, contributed to the inflationary increase of 131% in 1982. By early 1983, Israel's 130% rate of consumer price inflation was exceeded only by Argentina's. However, in 1985 and 1986, through a new austerity program that included strict wage and price controls as well as an 18.8% devaluation of the shekel, Israel's economy seemed to stabilize, and the triple-digit inflation had receded to 20.8% in 1989 and had been reduced to 5.4% in 1998.

The administered territories have expanded Israel's economic base, but living standards in these areas are much lower than in Israel proper. The territories' GNP in 1996 was $3.9 billion, or $1,400 per capita. Unemployment in the territories is a chronic problem and in 1996 stood at 30% in the West Bank and 40% in Gaza. Since the signing of an Interim Agreement in September 1995 between Israel and the PLO on the autonomous administration of small areas of the occupied territories, the economic prospects of these generally blighted areas has increased somewhat. International donors have pledged more than $2.4 billion over the years 1994–99, much of which is expected to be used in infrastructure development.

20 INCOME

The US Central Intelligence Agency (CIA) reports that in 1998 Israel's gross domestic product (GDP) was estimated at $101.9 billion. The per capita GDP was estimated at $18,100. The annual growth rate of GDP was estimated at 1.9%. The average inflation rate in 1998 was 5.4%. The CIA defines GDP as the value of all final goods and services produced within a nation in a given year and computed on the basis of purchasing power parity (PPP) rather than value as measured on the basis of the rate of exchange. It was estimated that agriculture accounted for 2% of GDP, industry 17%, and services 81%.

The World Bank reports that for the same period per capita private consumption (in PPP terms) was $10,850. Private consumption includes expenditures of individuals, households, and nongovernmental organizations. It was estimated that between 1990 and 1998 private consumption grew at an annual rate of 6.5%. Approximately 23% of household consumption was spent on food, 11% on fuel, 2% on health care, and 6% on education. The richest 10% of the population accounted for approximately 27% of household consumption and the poorest 10% approximately 2.8%.

21 LABOR

In 1997 there were 2,076,600 employed civilians in Israel, of whom approximately 31.2% were employed in public services; 20.2% in manufacturing; 12.8% in commerce; 13.1% in finance and business services; 6.2% in transportation and communications; 2.6% in agriculture; and the remainder in other sectors. The unemployment rate in 1998 was 8.6%.

The majority of Israeli workers, including those in agriculture, are union members belonging to the General Federation of Labor (Histadrut, founded by Jewish farm workers in 1920), which has a membership of 650,000 (including self-employed, professionals, housewives, and young people). Histadrut also has an industrial corporation (Koor), which owns and operates many large factories, and a contracting corporation (Solel Boneh). Additionally, it manages an agricultural marketing society (Tnuva), a cooperative wholesale corporation (Hamashbir Hamerkazi), and a workers' bank. Nonresidents, including Palestinians from the West Bank and Gaza, who work in Israel are not permitted to join Histadrut; however, nonresident Palestinian workers are entitled to the same protection of Histardut work contracts and grievance procedures. Palestinians in the occupied territories are allowed to organize their own unions and have the right to strike. Membership in Histadrut has fallen, since it is no longer necessary to belong to Histadrut to subscribe to its health plan. The right to strike is exercised; 15 days notice must be provided to the employer.

Wages and working conditions in the private sector are regulated by collective agreements between Histadrut and the Israel Manufacturers' Association. The law provides for a maximum 8-hour day and 47-hour week, establishes a compulsory weekly rest period of 36 hours, and lays down minimum rates for overtime. The private sector set a maximum workweek of 45 hours in 1988, and the public sector established a 5-day, 42½ hour workweek in 1989. This continues to be the present practice. At the end of 1999, the minimum wage was roughly $700 per month. There are about 200,000 foreign workers in Israel, and their role has been the subject of heated public debate in recent years.

22 AGRICULTURE

Between 1948 and 1997, the cultivated area was expanded from 165,000 to 437,000 ha (from 408,000 to 1,075,000 acres). Principal crops and 1998 production totals (in tons) were wheat, 116,000; cotton, 54,000; peanuts, 23,000; sunflowers, 20,000; and canning peas, 7,000.

Owing to the uniquely favorable soil and climatic conditions, Israel's citrus fruit has qualities of flavor and appearance commanding high prices on the world market. Total citrus production in 1998 was 845,000 tons, with grapefruit accounting for 43%. Exports of citrus in 1997 generated $74.8 million. Other fruits, and their 1998 production amounts (in thousands of tons) included: apples, 111; bananas, 112; avocados, 80; table grapes, 90; peaches, 48; olives, 19; plums, 18; pears, 20; and mangoes, 18.

The main forms of agricultural settlement are the kibbutz, moshav, moshav shitufi, and moshava (pl. moshavot). In the kibbutz all property is owned jointly by the settlement on land leased from the Jewish National Fund, and work assignments, services, and social activities are determined by elected officers. Although predominantly agricultural, many kibbutzim have taken on a variety of industries, including food processing and the production of building materials. Devoted entirely to agriculture, the moshavim (workers' smallholder cooperatives) market produce and own heavy equipment, but their land is divided into separate units and worked by the members individually. This form of settlement has had special appeal to new immigrants. The moshavim shitufiyim are 47 collective villages that are similar in economic organization to the kibbutzim but whose living arrangements are more like those of the moshav. The moshavot are rural colonies, based on private enterprise. They were the principal form of 19th century settlement, and many have grown into urban communities.

New immigrants settling on the land are given wide-ranging assistance. The Jewish Agency, the executive arm of the World Zionist Organization, absorbs many of the initial costs; agricultural credits are extended on a preferential basis, and equipment, seeds, livestock, and work animals are supplied at low cost.

Israeli agriculture emphasizes maximum utilization of irrigation and the use of modern techniques to increase yields. A national irrigation system distributed water to 199,000 ha (491,700 acres) in 1997, down from 219,000 ha (541,100 acres) in 1986 but still far exceeding the 30,000 ha (74,000 acres) served in 1948. Water is transported via pipeline from the Sea of Galilee to the northern Negev. More than 90% of Israel's subterranean water supply is being exploited. Agriculture accounted for 63% of Israel's water consumption in 1995.

23 ANIMAL HUSBANDRY

There is little natural pasturage in most areas, and livestock is fed mainly on imported feeds and farm-grown forage. Domestic beef production only satisfies between 33% and 40% of demand. Livestock farmers are aided by subsidies. There are 2,500 sheep and goat farms raising 420,000 head, 42% by the Bedu population, 36% by the Jewish sector, and 22% by the Arab and Druze populations. In 1998 there were 22,000,000 chickens, 4,000,000 turkeys, 370,000 head of cattle, 168,000 pigs, 11,000 equines, and 5,000 camels. About 93,000 tons of eggs, 253,000 tons of poultry meat, and 39,000 tons of beef were produced in 1998. That year, milk and honey production were 1,120,000 and 3,000 tons, respectively.

24 FISHING

Jewish settlers introduced the breeding of fish (mostly carp) into Palestine. The total fish catch was 23,274 tons in 1997. In addition to carp, important freshwater fish include catfish, barbel, and trout. The marine catch consists mainly of gray and red mullet, rainbow trout, grouper, sardines, and bogue.

25 FORESTRY

Natural forests and woodlands cover about 102,000 ha (252,000 acres), mostly in the north. About 180 million trees were planted between 1902 and 1986. Roundwood production in 1997 was 124,000 cu m. Forestry production in 1997 included 109,000 cu m of plywood and 58,000 cu m of particleboard, and 275,000 cu m of paper and paperboard.

26 MINING

Although Israel is not richly endowed with mineral resources, the Dead Sea is one of the world's richest sources of potassium chloride (potash), magnesium bromide, and other salts; more than 1% of the world's refractory-grade magnesia comes from the Dead Sea. The Negev Desert contains deposits of phosphate, copper (low grade), glass sand, ceramic clays, gypsum, and granite. Most of the phosphate deposits, located in the northeastern Negev, are at best medium grade; they are extracted by open-pit mining. As of 1996, Israel was the world's second-largest producer of bromine; it held sixth place in the production of potash and seventh in production of phosphate rock. The government is the principal owner of most mineral-related industries. Privately held industries include the diamond cutting and polishing industry, and cement and potassium nitrate manufac-

turing. Israel does not mine diamonds but cuts and polishes imported rough diamonds and gemstones.

Israel's mineral production in 1996 (in thousands of tons) included phosphate rock, 3,800; potash, 1,300; clays, 88.5; and glass sand, 175. The production of mineral products for the domestic building sector, especially cement, clay, crushed stone, and sand, increased in the early 1990s due to a surge in new home construction. Mineral exports, however, have stagnated due to low demand.

27 ENERGY AND POWER

Israel's energy sector is largely nationalized and state-regulated, ostensibly for national security reasons. Israeli production of crude petroleum fell sharply after the return to Egypt in 1980 of the Sinai oil fields that Israel had held since the 1967 war. In 1999, Israel produced less than 500 barrels per day of crude petroleum, compared with 1,000 barrels per day in 1986; consumption of crude oil amounted to 235,000 barrels per day in 1998. Oil has been produced in the Negev since 1955, and prospecting there continues.

Nearly all electricity is supplied by the government-owned Israel Electric Corp., which uses imported oil and coal. Electricity is generated principally by thermal power stations. Generating capacity has quadrupled since 1970, reaching 9,500 MW by 1998 (70% coal-fired, 25% oil-fired, 5% gas fired); total production in 1998 amounted to some 35 billion kWh. In November 1993, the Israeli government announced that Israel and Egypt would construct a natural gas pipeline to Israel to annually supply 3.9 million cu m of Egyptian natural gas by 1999. Progress on this plan stalled in 1996, but as of 1999 the governments of the two countries were discussing the sale of natural gas to Israel via a "peace pipeline" across the Sinai desert.

28 INDUSTRY

More than half of the industrial establishments are in the Tel Aviv–Yafo area, but a great deal of heavy industry is concentrated around Haifa. Most plants are privately owned. State enterprises are mainly devoted to exploitation of natural resources in the Negev; some other enterprises are controlled by the Histadrut. Israel is research and development-oriented. Currently, some 150 foreign companies are involved in high-technology projects in Israel in such fields as aviation, communications, computer-aided design and manufacturing (CAD/CAM), medical electronics, fine chemicals, pharmaceuticals, solar energy, and sophisticated irrigation.

Major expansion has taken place in textiles, machinery and transport equipment, metallurgy, mineral processing, electrical products, precision instruments, and chemicals. However, industry remains handicapped by reliance on imported raw materials, relatively high wage costs, low productivity, and inflation. Incentive schemes and productivity councils, representing workers and management, have been set up in an attempt to increase work output. Whereas in the past Israel's industry concentrated on consumer goods, by the 1980s it was stressing the manufacture of capital goods. The following illustrates Israel's industrial production in various sectors for 1995.

Natural Gas	21,300	cu m
Quartersand	222,300	tons
Potash	2,214,000	tons
Phosphate	2,642,000	tons
Milk and Pasteurized Beverages	271,000,000	liters
Cigarettes	4,933	tons
Plywood	31,393	cu m
Writing and Printing Paper	59,747	tons
Caustic Soda	44,361,000	tons
Paints	57,650,000	tons
Cement	6,204,000	tons

29SCIENCE AND TECHNOLOGY

Israel manufactures and exports an expanding array of high-technology goods, especially for military purposes. In 1987–97, Israel spent 2.4% of GNP on research and development in science, engineering, agriculture, and medicine. National and local governments and industry shared equally in the funding. A privatization program, begun by the government, has resulted in the creation of many science and technology parks and high technology towns, like Migdal He'Emck. Israel has an advanced nuclear research program, and it is widely believed that Israel has the capacity to make nuclear weapons.

Among scientific research institutes are seven institutes administered by the Agricultural Research Organization; the Rogoff–Wellcome Medical Research Institute; institutes for petroleum research, geological mapping, and oceanographic and limnological research directed by the Earth Sciences Research Administration; institutes of ceramic and silicate, fiber, metals, plastics, wine, and rubber research directed by the Office of the Chief Scientist, Ministry of Industry and Trade; the Institutes of Applied Research at the Ben-Gurion University of the Negev; the Israel Institute for Biological Research; the Israel Institute for Psychobiology; the National Research Laboratory; and the Soreg and Negev nuclear research centers attached to the Israel Atomic Energy Commission. The country has eight universities and colleges offering courses in basic and applied sciences; among them are the Weizmann Institute in Rehovot and the Technion–Israel Institute of Technology in Haifa. In 1987–97, science and engineering students accounted for 49% of all college and university students.

Immigration into Israel may be its best science and technology policy. Some consider this a "brain drain" in reverse, and that it will help Israeli high technology competitiveness in the future. In 1998, high technology exports were valued at $4.2 million and accounted for 20% of all manufactured exports.

30DOMESTIC TRADE

Banks, commercial institutions, and the Histadrut have their headquarters in Tel Aviv–Yafo, the business capital. Supermarkets and department stores are on the increase; installment sales are widespread. Packaged goods are becoming more common, but many sales are still made from bulk. Cooperative societies market the agricultural produce of their affiliated settlements and farms. Tnuva, the Histadrut agricultural marketing society, sells most of Israel's farm products. Advertising media include newspapers, periodicals, posters, billboards, radio broadcasts, and motion picture theaters.

Saturday closing is the custom for all shops, offices, banks, public institutions, and transport services, except in the Arab areas. Shopping and office hours are Sunday to Thursday, 8 AM to 1 PM and 4 to 7 PM. On Fridays and days preceding holidays, shops shut down about 2 PM, offices at 1 PM. Banks are open 8:30 AM to 12:30 PM and 4 to 5:30 PM; they close at noon on Fridays and days before holidays and have no afternoon hours on Wednesdays.

31FOREIGN TRADE

Israel is a relatively small country with limited natural resources and an affluent, bourgeois citizenry; as such, it is highly dependent on international trade, both to supply its industry with natural resources, and to purchase its value-added products. In 1995, foreign trade amounted to 80.4% of GDP. Exports that year totaled $17.9 billion, up 11% from the previous year. Imports, meanwhile, also grew to $28 billion. The vast majority (93%) of Israeli exports are manufactured goods and their primary destinations are the US and the EU—accounting for 62% of Israel's exports. By sector, Israeli export growth was greatest in 1994 in machinery and electronics (+14%), chemicals (+11%),

rubber and plastics (+17%), and mining and quarrying (+16%). Imports are primarily industrial resources (68%)—other large sectors are investment goods (19% and consumer products (13%).

Cut diamonds top the list of Israel's export commodities (30%), reflecting 15% of the world's total diamond exports. Machinery and equipment, including telecoms equipment (6.4%), printing presses (2.5%), and other manufactured items (10%) are important exports.

In 1997 Israel's imports were distributed among the following categories:

Consumer goods	11.1%
Food	6.1%
Fuels	7.8%
Industrial supplies	41.1%
Machinery	23.0%
Transportation	10.4%
Other	0.4%

Principal trading partners in 1998 (in millions of US dollars) were as follows:

COUNTRY	EXPORTS	IMPORTS	BALANCE
United States	8,254	5,386	2,868
United Kingdom	1,323	2,062	-739
Netherlands	1,116	1,142	-26
Germany	1,111	2,418	-1,307
Belgium	1,097	2,847	-1,750
China (inc. Hong Kong)	927	822	105
Italy	737	1,828	-1,091
France	667	1,126	-459
Switzerland	379	1,500	-1,121
Turkey	287	443	-156

32BALANCE OF PAYMENTS

Israel's foreign trade has consistently shown an adverse balance, owing mainly to the rapid rise in population and the expansion of the industrialized economy, requiring heavy imports of machinery and raw materials. The imbalance on current accounts has been offset to a large extent by the inflow of funds from abroad. Deficits are often offset by massive US aid and American Jewish philanthropy. Even with these funds, however, Israel has in recent years been running increasingly larger deficits, reaching 4.7% of GDP in 1995. Financing this deficit is easier on Israel than on many nations primarily because of its relationship with the US. In 1992, the US guaranteed loans of $10 billion over five years.

The International Monetary Fund (IMF) reports that in 1998 Israel had exports of goods totaling $22,972 million and imports totaling $26,197 million. The services credit totaled $9,049 million and debit $9,825 million. The following table summarizes Israel's balance of payments as reported by the IMF for 1998 in millions of US dollars.

Current Account		-668
Balance on goods	-3,225	
Balance on services	-776	
Balance on income	-2,809	
Current transfers	6,143	
Capital Account		1,765
Financial Account		87
Direct investment abroad	-830	
Direct investment in Israel	1,850	
Portfolio investment assets	-24	
Portfolio investment liabilities	506	
Other investment assets	-2,900	
Other investment liabilities	1,485	
Net Errors and Omissions		-735
Reserves and Related Items		-449

33 BANKING AND SECURITIES

The Bank of Israel, with headquarters in Jerusalem, began operations as the central state bank in December 1954. Foreign currency reserves stood at $11.8 billion in November 1996, due to an adoption of a restrictive monetary policy. Banking assets at year-end 1995 were NIS217,091 million. The bank issues currency, accepts deposits from banking institutions in Israel, extends temporary advances to the government, acts as the government's sole banking and fiscal agent, and manages the public debt. Among the largest commercial banks are the Bank Leumi, the Israel Discount Bank, and the Histadrut-controlled Bank Hapoalim. There were 24 licensed commercial banks in 1997; one investment bank; and nine mortgage banks. There are also numerous credit cooperatives and other financial institutions. Among the subsidiaries of commercial banks are mortgage banks (some of which were also directly established by the government). The largest of these specialized institutions, the Tefahot Israel Mortgage Bank, provides many loans to home builders.

Industrial development banks specialize in financing new manufacturing enterprises. The Industrial Bank of Israel, formed in 1957 by major commercial banks, the government, the Manufacturers' Association, and foreign investors, has received aid from the IBRD and has played a major role in the industrial development of the Negev area. The government-owned Bank of Agriculture is the largest lending institution in that sector. The Post Office Bank is concerned mainly with clearing operations, savings, sale of savings certificates, and postal orders.

The structure of the banking industry is based on the central European model of "universal banking," whereby the banks operate as retail, wholesale, and investment banks, as well as being active in all main areas of capital market activity, brokerage, underwriting, and mutual and provident fund management. However, the banks are barred from insurance operations, other than as owners of insurance agents, and have only recently been allowed to enter the pension market.

In the financial sector, the banks have benefited from a very slow program of financial deregulation and the absence of foreign competition; the only foreign bank licensed to operate in Israel, the Polish PKO Bank, is more of a historical curiosity than a serious commercial consideration. However, as deregulation has progressed, the prospect of foreign ownership, in part or whole, of Israeli banks, has become more real.

The Bank of Israel's power to fix the liquidity ratio that banks must maintain against deposits has been an important instrument in governing both volume and types of loans. Legal interest rate ceilings formerly were 10% on loans to industry and agriculture and 11% for commercial loans, but in the early 1980s, rampant inflation caused the large commercial banks to raise the interest rate to 136%.

Growing activity on the Israeli securities market made it necessary to convert the rather loosely organized Tel Aviv Securities Clearing House into the formally constituted Tel Aviv Stock Exchange (TASE) in 1953. A further expansion took place in 1955, when debentures linked either to the US dollar or to the cost-of-living index—with special tax privileges—made their first appearance on the market. The market is largely devoted to loans of public and semipublic bodies, with provident funds and banks acquiring most of the securities placed. There is only one quotation daily for each security.

By 1983 the price of bank shares was steadily becoming more detached from their true value. When it became obvious in 1983 that the government would have to devalue its currency, many people began to liquidate their holdings of shekel-denominated assets in favor of foreign currency. The assets most widely held and most easily liquidated were bank shares. The selling wave began in the summer of 1983 and peaked in October, forcing the government to intervene. The closing of the TASE, on 6 October 1983, became known as the "economic day of atonement" and represented the end of the speculators' paradise created and supported by leading Israeli banks.

By the mid-1990s, as Israel moved to liberalize its economy, the banking sector underwent significant reconstruction which continues as of mid-2000. In two sell-offs in 1997 and 1998, the government divested itself of a majority of Bank Hapoalim. It also sold sizeable shares of United Mizrahi Bank, Israeli Discount Bank, and Bank Leumi. In addition to bank privatization, the Israeli government moved to reduce capital markets regulations.

Occupied Territories

In 1994 the Palestinian Authority (PA) began to take over the management of an economy with a limited capacity to support its expanding population. The PA has acted within the constraints of the economic protocol to revive the financial sector. The reconstruction effort requires the creation of financial markets and institutions that perform the key functions of supplying liquidity, encouraging savings and investments, and facilitating the management of risk.

In expectation of a boom in the financial sector, a number of Jordanian and Palestinian banks opened, or reopened, branches in the West Bank and Gaza. By 1996, 42 branches of 10 banks were operating. The banks have mainly limited themselves to establishing checking accounts and accepting deposits, specifically non-interest bearing accounts. Despite their success in attracting deposits from Palestinians, the banks have maintained a limited role in lending; at the end of March 1995, total outstanding loans by the banks accounted for only 30% of total assets and 35% of total customer deposits. The reluctance to invest locally stems from doubts over the political environment and it is widely believed that banks are investing abroad, particularly in Central Bank of Jordan treasury bills.

A key factor in the success of the banks will be the supervisory activities of the Palestinian Monetary Authority (PMA), set up as a result of the Paris protocol. The PMA has most of the functions of a central bank. It is empowered to act as the PA's adviser and sole financial agent; to hold its foreign currency reserves; to regulate foreign-exchange dealers; and to supervise the banking sector, as the self-rule areas come under PA jurisdiction. However, in the absence of a Palestinian currency, the PMA's ability to be a lender of last resort is questionable. In 1996 the reality was that the PMA had no influence over the areas still under Israeli control and lacked a proper regulatory framework. Yet, since 1995, all money-changers have been required to put up capital of between $200,000 to $1 million, to pay permit and other fees, and to deposit 30% of their capital with the PMA.

At the end of 1996, plans for a Middle Eastern Development bank, supported by Jordan, Egypt, Israel, and the PA, were close to collapse, just a few weeks after the bank's official registration at the UN. This was the verdict following the US Congress's refusal to include provision for financing for the bank in an appropriations bill.

The Arab Palestine Investment Bank (APIB), scheduled to open in early 1997, held its first annual general meeting in Ramallah on 15 September 1996 and its first board meeting in Amman the next day. The bank, with paid-up capital of some $15 million, has four principal shareholders, Jordan's Arab Bank (55%), the International Finance Corp. (25%), the German Investment and Development Co. (15%), and the Palestinian private-sector Enterprise Investment Co. (5%). Total deposits of the Palestinian banking system expanded by over 125% during the year ended June 1996, reaching $2.06 trillion. However, it is estimated that over half the local deposits are invested abroad, while only $300 million have been loaned internally to the Palestinians.

³⁴INSURANCE

The State Insurance Controller's Office may grant or withhold insurance licenses and determine the valuation of assets, the form of balance sheets, computations of reserves, and investment composition. Automobile liability insurance is compulsory. War-damage insurance is compulsory on buildings and also on some personal property.

The insurance sector is dominated by a few large firms, of which Migdal and Clal Insurance are the most prominent. However, the easy, cartel-like conditions that have characterized the sector for many years are beginning to crumble and new direct insurance companies are gaining market share. In 1997 the US-based AIG group is due to enter the fray, via a direct insurance joint venture with an Israeli communications company, Aurec, and this will signal the opening up of the industry to much greater competition from both domestic and foreign entities.

³⁵PUBLIC FINANCE

The following table shows actual government revenues and expenditures for Israel in 1998. For comparison purposes, the figures also have been converted to millions of US dollars using exchange rates based on monthly averages for 1998.

The US Central Intelligence Agency (CIA) estimates that in 1998 Israel's central government took in revenues of approximately $55 billion and had expenditures of $58 billion including capital expenditures of $2.9 billion. Overall, the government registered a deficit of approximately $3 billion.

The following table shows an itemized breakdown of government revenues and expenditures. The percentages were calculated from data reported by the International Monetary Fund. The dollar amounts (millions) are based on the CIA estimates provided above.

REVENUE AND GRANTS	100%	55,000
Tax revenue	78.7%	43,264
Non-tax revenue	14.0%	7,699
Grants	7.3%	4,037
EXPENDITURES	100%	58,000
General public services	2.2%	1,264
Defense	17.8%	10,316
Public order and safety	3.1%	1,810
Education	13.4%	7,776
Health	13.9%	8,038
Social security	25.2%	14,634
Housing and community amenities	3.3%	1,928
Recreation, cultural, and religious affairs	0.9%	514
Economic affairs and services	6.1%	3,526
Other expenditures	1.2%	693
Interest payments	12.6%	7,291
Adjustments	0.4%	209

³⁶TAXATION

Israel's population is heavily taxed. There are personal income taxes on gross income from employment, trade, business, dividends, and other sources, with limited deductions. Rates range from 15–50%, with the highest rate for amounts over NIS172,800 per year. Special tax concessions are granted to residents in border settlements, new settlements, and the Negev. Taxes of salaried persons are deducted at the source; self-employed persons make advance payments in 10 installments, subject to assessment. Also levied are a value-added tax (VAT) of 17%, a purchase tax, various land taxes, and a national health insurance premium tax on a rising scale to 4.8%.

Municipalities and local and regional councils levy several taxes. There is an annual business tax on every enterprise, based on net worth, annual sales volume, number of employees, and other factors. General rates, a real estate tax (commonly based on

the number of rooms and the location of the building), and water rates are paid by the tenants or occupants rather than the owners.

³⁷CUSTOMS AND DUTIES

Israel has a single-column import tariff based on the Brussels nomenclature classification. Ad valorem rates predominate, although specific and compound rates are also used. Most basic food commodities, raw materials, and machinery for agricultural or industrial purposes are exempt from customs duties. The highest rates are applied to nonessential foodstuffs, luxury items, and manufactured goods that are of a type produced in Israel.

A free-trade agreement between Israel and the then-EC (today, the EU) took effect on 1 July 1975. Under this agreement, EC tariffs on Israel's industrial exports were immediately reduced by 60% and were subsequently eliminated. Preferential treatment has also been extended to Israel's agricultural exports. In return, Israel has granted concessions to the EC/EU on many categories of industrial and agricultural imports, and agreed to gradually abolish its customs duties on imports from the EC by 1989.

Israel also belongs to the World Trade Organization (WTO) and operates its trade regime according to WTO guidelines. Most significantly, the WTO calls on the elimination of non-tariff barriers. Israel also signed a free trade agreement with the United States in 1985, which called for the elimination of all remaining duties on US-made products by 1 January 1995. However, Israel and the United States differ on the interpretation of the treaty and it has yet to be fully implemented.

³⁸FOREIGN INVESTMENT

Apart from reparations, capital imports mainly consist of long-term loans and grants designed for investment by the government or the Jewish Agency.

A 1951 law was designed to encourage foreign investment in those industries and services most urgently required to reduce Israel's dependence on imports and to increase its export potential. Applying mainly to investments in industry and agriculture, the law offers such inducements as relief from property taxes during the first five years, special allowances for depreciation, exemption from customs and purchase tax on essential materials, and reductions in income tax rates. In a further effort to attract foreign investment, the government approved the "Nissim Plan" in 1990. This plan gives the investor the option of state loan guarantees for up to two-thirds of a project or the bundle of benefits offered under the "Encouragement of Capital Investments Law." A 1985 US–Israeli Free Trade Area (FTA) agreement reduces tariffs and most non-tariffs barriers for US firms. Israel also has an FTA agreement with the EU under which tariffs on industrial products and certain agricultural products fell to zero on 1 January 1989. In 1995, the most current year for which statistics are available, Israel attracted $2.5 billion in foreign investment. This figure came on the heels of several years of economic growth and fiscal austerity.

³⁹ECONOMIC DEVELOPMENT

Economic policy is dictated by goals of national security, full utilization of resources, integration of immigrants, and institution of a broad welfare program. The urgency of these goals imposes responsibilities on the government for planning, financing, and directly participating in productive activities. And, in fact, government infrastructure development since 1990 has played a large part in Israel's powerful economic performance in recent years. Major government projects include an expansion of the Ben-Gurion Airport, a subway for Tel-Aviv, a tunnel through Mt. Carmel, and a major new North-South highway.

In the years immediately following independence, the government influenced the setting in which private capital functions, through differential taxation, import and export licensing, subsidies, and high protective tariffs. The 1962 revaluation of the Israeli pound was accompanied by a new economic policy aimed at reduction of protective tariffs, continued support of development, planning and implementation of long-range development, and maximization of efficiency. Subsequently, the government has periodically decreed further monetary devaluations, new taxes, and other austerity measures designed to curb consumption and stimulate exports. By the mid-1990s, the Israeli government was actively engaged in an economic liberalization program that is a stark contrast from the largely state regulated economy of Israel's first few decades.

40SOCIAL DEVELOPMENT

Aside from supervising a wide network of public and private social welfare agencies, the Ministry of Labor and Social Welfare maintains special enterprises employing blind and handicapped people, operates institutions for mentally and physically handicapped children, and administers a nationwide preventive service for problem children and youth.

Special legislation has established the legal right to assistance of persons incapacitated for work, of survivors of those who died in state service, and under certain conditions, of persons whose claims antedated their immigration to Israel. Pensions have thus been paid to persons disabled while fighting with the Allied forces in World War II and to those invalided as a result of Nazi persecution.

Israel has a universal social insurance system that covers all residents aged 18 and over. Benefits include old age pensions, disability, medical care and monthly allowances for large families. Employee-based programs include maternity benefits, worker's compensation for injuries, and unemployment benefits. These programs are funded by contributions by employees, employers and the government. Pensions are set at a rate of 16% of average wage; 24% including income supplement. The National Insurance Institute is directly under the minister of labor and is governed by a 42-member council representing government, labor, and employers.

The Jewish Agency is primarily responsible for the initial phases of reception and absorption of immigrants. Hadassah provides vocational guidance and training to youth, and the Women's International Zionist Organization is active in family and child welfare. Mo'etzet Hapo'alot (Women's Workers Council), a Histadrut affiliate, is active in this area, along with Youth Aliyah, which operates a system of children's villages.

A series of laws have been enacted to protect women's rights including the Equal Rights for Women Law (1951) and the Employment of Women Law (1954), which requires equal pay for equal work. Legislation mandating affirmative action in the civil service and in government-owned companies was passed in 1995. Legislation has also been passed to protect women outside of the workplace. In 1991, the Domestic Violence Law strengthened the ability of the courts to protect women from abusive husbands. In 1993, common law spouses were permitted to take their partners' family names, and a new law barred discrimination in unemployment compensation for elderly female citizens. However, discrimination against women persists in many family and divorce matters. The courts that deal with these cases are bound by religious laws that generally favor men. A 1995 law gave rabbinical courts the power of imposing expanded civil sanctions on husbands in cases where the wife has ample grounds for divorce but cannot obtain one. As of 1999, 15 of 20 seats in the Knesset were held by women.

The subject of human rights in Israel and the administered territories has aroused much controversy, with international organizations citing police harassment of Arabs, especially on the West Bank and the Gaza Strip, and Israeli government officials pointing to the Arab terrorist threat. Within Israel, freedom of political expression is fully protected, and all shades of opinion are expressed; such guarantees do not extend to the administered territories, however, and the press, including foreign correspondents, is also monitored and censored for security reasons. Israeli Arabs face discrimination in employment, housing and education.

The use of limited physical force during interrogations has been legal, but a high court ruling in 1999 banned a variety of specific abuses, including sleep deprivation and violent shaking. Administrative detention without trial remains legal, but its use declined in 1999. Prison conditions for Palestinians have improved but still do not meet all international standards.

Palestinians do not have the full legal protections set out in Israeli law. Even when in Israel, they are subject to military law.

41HEALTH

The Ministry of Health supervises all health matters and functions directly in the field of medical care. The Israeli government allocates 4.1% of the GDP for health expenditures (1991). The Arab Department of the Ministry of Health recruits public health personnel from among the Arab population, and its mobile clinics extend medical aid to Bedouin tribes in the Negev. In 1999, the infant mortality rate was 8 per 1,000 live births. Life expectancy was 78.6 years for both men and women. The fertility rate has decreased steadily over the years from 3.9 in 1960 to 2.7 children in 1999 for each woman during childbearing years. In 1990–97, there were 3.8 doctors per 1,000 people. The Ministry of Health also operates infant welfare clinics, nursing schools, and laboratories. The largest medical organization in the country, the Workers' Sick Fund (Kupat Holim), the health insurance association of Histadrut, administers hospitals, clinics, convalescent homes, and mother-and-child welfare stations. In 1990–97, there were 6 hospital beds per 1,000 people.

The infant mortality rate was 7.8 per 1,000 live births in 1999. The maternal death rate is the lowest in the Middle East and North Africa. In 1990–97, 7 maternal deaths per 100,000 live births were documented. In 1999, Israel's birth rate was 19.8 per 1,000 people. Between 1990–94, immunization rates for children up to one year old were: diphtheria, pertussis, and tetanus (92%); polio (93%); and measles (95%). The overall death rate in 1999 was 6.2 per 1,000 people.

The HIV-1 seroprevalence was 0.1 per 100 adults in 1997. There were 0.6 AIDS cases per 100,000 people in 1994.

Tobacco consumption has decreased from 2.6 to 2.4 kg a year per adult in 1995. Between 1986 and 1994, 38% of men and 25% of women were smokers.

42HOUSING

Israel suffered from a severe housing shortage at its creation. Despite an extensive national building program and the initial allocation of some abandoned Arab dwellings to newcomers, in early 1958, nearly 100,000 immigrants were still housed in transit camps. By the mid-1960s, however, the extreme housing shortage had been overcome, and newcomers were immediately moved into permanent residences. From 1960 to 1985, a total of 943,350 housing units were constructed. In 1986, 94% of all housing units had piped water, 58.2% had flush toilets, and 99% had electric lighting. Between 1989 and 1991, a surge of immigration from the former Soviet Union and Ethiopia resulted in a dramatic increase in housing demand, and housing starts increased 28% in 1991 compared to 1990. By the mid-1990s, the immigration rate had dropped to 70,000 per year, generating a demand for 20,000 new apartments per year, which, added to the regular demand of 20,000, places the total demand at 40,000 annually. During the same period, the total number of dwellings in Israel was 1,488,000.

43 EDUCATION

Education is compulsory for 11 years and free for all children between 5 and 15 years of age. Primary education is for six years followed by three years of lower secondary and three more years of upper secondary education. A state education law of 1953 put an end to the separate elementary school systems affiliated to labor and religious groupings and established a unified state-administered system, within which provision was made for state religious schools. Four types of schools exist: public religious (Jewish) and public secular schools (the largest group); schools of the orthodox Agudat Israel (which operated outside the public school system but were assisted with government funds); public schools for Arabs; and private schools, mainly operated by Catholic and Protestant organizations. The language of instruction in Jewish schools is Hebrew; in Arab schools it is Arabic. Arabic is taught as an optional language in Jewish schools, while Hebrew is taught in Arab schools from the fourth grade.

In 1996, primary schools had a total of 631,916 students. Secondary level schools had 541,737 students and approximately 54,000 teachers in the same year.

Israel has eight institutions of higher learning. The two most outstanding are the Hebrew University (founded in 1918) in Jerusalem and the Israel Institute of Technology (Technion, founded in 1912) in Haifa, both of which receive government subsidies of about 50% of their total budgets; the remaining funds are largely collected abroad. The Tel Aviv University was formed in 1956. Other institutions include the Bar-Ilan University in Ramat-Gan, opened in 1955 under religious auspices; the Weizmann Institute of Science at Rehovot, notable for its research into specific technical, industrial, and scientific problems; Haifa University; and Ben-Gurion University of the Negev in Beersheba. An Open University, promoting adult education largely through home study, was established and patterned on the British model. In 1996, universities and equivalent institutions enrolled 198,766 students. Adult illiteracy rates for the year 2000 were estimated at 3.9% (males, 2.1%; females, 5.7%).

44 LIBRARIES AND MUSEUMS

Israel's largest library, founded in 1924, is the privately endowed Jewish National and University Library at the Hebrew University in Jerusalem, with 2.5 million volumes. Important collections are housed in the Central Zionist Archives and the Central Archives for the History of the Jewish People, both also in Jerusalem. There are more than 950 other libraries, and the Ministry of Education and Culture has provided basic libraries to hundreds of rural settlements. The Ben Gurion University of the Negev (1966) holds 260,000 volumes and the Hebrew University of Jerusalem holds 2.5 million volumes. Tel Aviv University holds 850,000 volumes, including a Holocaust Studies collection.

The country's most important museum is the Israel Museum, opened in 1965 in Jerusalem. Included in the museum are the Bezalel Art Museum, with its large collection of Jewish folk art; a Jewish antiquities exhibit; the Billy Rose Art Garden of modern sculpture; the Samuel Bronfman Biblical and Archaeological Museum; and the Shrine of the Book, containing the Dead Sea Scrolls and other valuable manuscripts. The Rockefeller Archaeological Museum (formerly the Palestine Museum), built in 1938, contains a rich collection of archaeological material illustrating the prehistory and early history of Palestine and Transjordan. The Tel Aviv Museum of Art, founded in 1926, has more than 30,000 paintings, drawings, and sculptures. Among Israel's newer cultural institutions are the Museum of the Diaspora in Tel Aviv–Yafo, founded in 1978; the Bible Lands Museum in Jerusalem, founded in 1992; the Museum of Israeli Art in Ramat Gan, founded in 1987; and the Tower of David Museum of the History of Jerusalem at the Jaffa Gate in Jerusalem, founded in 1989.

45 MEDIA

The state owns and operates the major telephone communications services, although radio and television are increasingly privately owned. The state radio stations include the government's Israel Broadcasting Authority (Shidurei Israel), the army's Defense Forces Waves (Galei Zahal), and the Jewish Agency's Zion's Voice to the Diaspora (Kol Zion la-Gola), aimed mostly at Jewish communities in Europe and the US. The purchase of color television sets has become widespread since taxes on imported receivers were cut and the government stopped filtering out the color from imported television programs. In 1996, there were 2.6 million telephones. The following year there were 530 radios, 321 television sets, and 283 mobile phone in use per 1,000 population. As of 1999 there were 9 AM and 45 FM radio stations and 24 TV stations.

All newspapers are privately owned and managed. Most newspapers have 4–16 pages, but there are weekly supplements on subjects such as politics, economics, and the arts. The largest national daily Hebrew newspapers (with their average 1999 circulations) are *Yediot Achronot* (390,000), *Ma'ariv* (250,000), *Hadashot* (55,000), and *Ha'aretz* (73,000), all published in Tel Aviv. The English-language *Jerusalem Post* (30,000) is published in Jerusalem.

Although there is no political censorship within Israel, restrictions are placed on coverage of national security matters. Individuals, organizations, the press, and the electronic media freely debate public issues and often criticize public policy and government officials.

As of 1996, there were more than half a million personal computers; in 1998 there were 147 Internet hosts per 1,000 population.

46 ORGANIZATIONS

The World Zionist Organization (WZO) was founded by Theodor Herzl in 1897 for the purpose of creating "for the Jewish people a home in Palestine, secured by public law." The organization is composed of various international groupings represented in its supreme organ, the World Zionist Congress. The Jewish Agency, originally founded under the League of Nations mandate to promote Jewish interests in Palestine, comprises the executive arm of the WZO; since 1948, it has been responsible for the organization, training, and transportation to Israel of all Jews who wish to settle there. The United Israel Appeal (Keren Hayesod) is the financial instrument of the Jewish Agency; it recruits donations from world Jewry. The Jewish National Fund (Keren Kayemet le'Israel) is devoted to land acquisition, soil reclamation, and afforestation. Hadassah, the Women's Zionist Organization of America, is also active in Israel; it sponsors the Hadassah Medical Organization, which provides hospital and medical training facilities.

The main labor organization is the General Federation of Labor (Histadrut), a large economic complex whose interests include some of the largest factories in the country, an agricultural marketing society (Tnuva), a cooperative wholesale association (Hamashbir Hamerkazi), and a workers' bank. An important youth organization is Youth Aliyah, founded in 1934, which has helped to rehabilitate and educate children from all countries of the world. First aid services in Israel are organized by the Red Shield of David (Magen David Adom), which cooperates with the International Red Cross.

There are numerous cultural, religious, business, and other societies and organizations.

47 TOURISM, TRAVEL, AND RECREATION

A valid passport is required for tourists, with visas issued at time of entry. In 1997, approximately 2,010,000 tourists visited Israel, over 50% from European countries. As of 1997, there were

39,335 rooms in hotels and other establishments with 85,598 beds and a 54% occupancy rate. Tourist receipts totaled $2.7 billion. The Tourist Industry Development Corporation fosters tourism by granting loans for hotel expansion and improvement.

Principal tourist attractions are the many holy and historic places which include sites sacred to three religions: Judaism, Islam, and Christianity. In particular, the Old City of Jerusalem contains the Western ("Wailing") Wall, the Dome of the Rock, and the Church of the Holy Sepulchre; nearby are the Mount of Olives and Garden of Gethsemane. Another holy place is Bethlehem, the birthplace of both King David and Jesus. Also of great interest are the ruins of Jericho, the world's oldest city; the caves of Qumran, near the Dead Sea; and the rock fortress of Masada, on the edge of the Dead Sea Valley and the Judean Desert. Tourists are also drawn to Israel's rich variety of natural scenery, ranging from hills and greenery in the north to rugged deserts in the south, and including the Dead Sea, the lowest spot on Earth. The most popular team sports are football (soccer) and basketball; popular recreations include swimming, sailing, and fishing.

According to 1999 UN estimates, the average daily cost of staying in Tel Aviv was $287. Estimated daily expenses in Jerusalem were $228 per day.

⁴⁸FAMOUS ISRAELITES AND ISRAELIS

The State of Israel traces its ancestry to the settlement of the Hebrews in Canaan under Abraham (b.Babylonia, fl.18th cent. BC), the return of the Israelite tribes to Canaan under Moses (b. Egypt, fl.13th cent. BC) and Joshua (b.Egypt, fl.13th cent. BC), and the ancient kingdom of Israel, which was united by David (r.1000?–960? BC) and became a major Near Eastern power under Solomon (r.960?–922 BC). A prophetic tradition that includes such commanding figures as Isaiah (fl.8th cent. BC), Jeremiah (650?–585? BC), and Ezekiel (fl.6th cent. BC) spans the period of conquest by Assyria and Babylonia; the scribe Ezra (b.Babylonia, fl.5th cent. BC) and the governor Nehemiah (b.Babylonia, fl.5th cent. BC) spurred the reconstruction of the Judean state under Persian hegemony. Judas (Judah) Maccabaeus ("the Hammerer"; fl.165–160 BC) was the most prominent member of a family who instituted a period of political and religious independence from Greek rule. During the period of Roman rule, important roles in Jewish life and learning were played by the sages Hillel (b. Babylonia, fl.30 BC–AD 9), Johannan ben Zakkai (fl.1st cent.), Akiba ben Joseph (50?–135?), and Judah ha-Nasi (135?–220), the compiler of the Mishnah, a Jewish law code; by the military commander and historian Flavius Josephus (Joseph ben Mattathias, AD 37–100?); and Simon Bar-Kokhba (bar Kosiba, d.135), leader of an unsuccessful revolt against Roman rule. Unquestionably, the most famous Jew born in Roman Judea was Jesus (Jeshua) of Nazareth (4? BC–AD 29?), the Christ, or Messiah ("anointed one"), of Christian belief. Peter (Simon, d.AD 67?) was the first leader of the Christian Church and, in Roman Catholic tradition, the first pope. Paul (Saul, b.Asia Minor, d.AD 67?) was principally responsible for spreading Christianity and making it a religion distinct from Judaism.

The emergence of Israel as a modern Jewish state is attributed in large part to Chaim Weizmann (b. Russia, 1874–1952), the leader of the Zionist movement for 25 years, as well as a distinguished chemist who discovered methods for synthesizing acetone and rubber. Theodor Herzl (b. Budapest, 1860–1904), the founder of political Zionism, is buried in Jerusalem. Achad Ha'am (Asher Hirsch Ginsberg; b. Russia, 1856–1927) was an influential Zionist and social critic. Vladimir Jabotinsky (1880–1940) was a dedicated advocate of Jewish self-defense, both in his native Russia and in Palestine. David Ben-Gurion (Gruen; b. Poland, 1886–1973), also a leading Zionist and an eloquent

spokesman on labor and national affairs, served as Israel's first prime minister. Golda Meir (Meyerson; b. Russia, 1898–1978), like Ben-Gurion a former secretary-general of Histadrut, became well known as Israel's prime minister from 1970 to 1974. Other prominent contemporary figures include Pinhas Sapir (b. Poland, 1907–75), labor leader and minister of finance; Abba Eban (Aubrey Eban; b. South Africa, 1915), former foreign affairs minister and representative to the UN; and Moshe Dayan (1915–81), military leader and cabinet minister. Menachem Begin (b. Russia, 1913–92), the former leader of guerrilla operations against the British, was prime minister from 1977 to 1983 and received the Nobel Peace Prize in 1978. He was succeeded by Yitzhak Shamir (b. Poland, 1915) in 1983, who gave way to Shimon Peres (b. Poland, 1923) in 1984. Shamir succeeded Peres in 1986. Yitzhak Rabin (1922–1995) was instrumental in the peace accords with the PLO signed in 1993 in Washington.

Israel's foremost philosopher was Martin Buber (b. Vienna, 1878–1965), author of *I and Thou*. Outstanding scholars include the literary historian Joseph Klausner (1874–1958); the Bible researcher Yehezkel (Ezekiel) Kaufmann (b. Ukraine, 1889–1963); the philologists Eliezer Ben-Yehuda (b. Lithuania, 1858–1922) and Naphtali Hertz Tur-Sinai (Torczyner; b. Poland, 1886–1973); the archaeologist Eliezer Sukenik (1889–1953); and the Kabbalah authority Gershom Gerhard Scholem (b. Germany, 1897–1982).

The foremost poets are Haim Nahman Bialik (b. Russia, 1873–1934), Saul Tchernichowsky (b. Russia, 1875–1943), Uri Zvi Greenberg (b. Galicia, 1896–1981), Avraham Shlonsky (b. Russia, 1900–1973), Nathan Alterman (b. Warsaw, 1910–70), Yehuda Amichai (b. Germany, 1924), and Natan Zach (b. Berlin, 1930); and the leading novelists are Shmuel Yosef Halevi Agnon (b. Galicia, 1888–1970), a Nobel Prize winner in 1966, and Hayim Hazaz (b. Russia, 1898–1973). Painters of note include Reuven Rubin (b. Romania, 1893–1975) and Mane Katz (b. Russia, 1894–1962). Paul Ben-Haim (Frankenburger; b. Munich, 1897–1984) and Ödön Partos (b. Budapest, 1907–77) are well-known composers. Famous musicians include Daniel Barenboim (b. Argentina, 1942), Itzhak Perlman (b. 1945), and Pinchas Zukerman (b. 1948).

Significant contributions in other fields have been made by mathematician Abraham Halevi Fraenkel (b. Munich, 1891–1965); botanist Hugo Boyko (b. Vienna, 1892–1970); zoologist Shimon (Fritz) Bodenheimer (b. Cologne, 1897–1959); parasitologist Saul Aaron Adler (b. Russia, 1895–1966); physicist Giulio Raccah (b. Florence, 1909–65); rheologist Markus Reiner (b. Czernowitz, 1886–1976); gynecologist Bernard Zondek (b. Germany, 1891–1966); and psychoanalyst Heinrich Winnik (b. Austria-Hungary, 1902–82).

⁴⁹DEPENDENCIES

Beginning at the end of the 1967 war and until recently, Israel administered the West Bank and the Gaza Strip. The Golan Heights, captured from Syria during the same war, was annexed in 1981; the Sinai Peninsula, taken from Egypt, was restored to Egyptian sovereignty in 1983, in accordance with a 1979 peace treaty. In 1994 Israel returned small pockets of some of the land captured in the war, to be administered, in a less than totally sovereign fashion, by the Palestinian Authority. The move was in accord with a peace agreement it signed with the PLO (Palestine Liberation Organization).

⁵⁰BIBLIOGRAPHY

Aronson, Shlomo. *The Politics and Strategy of Nuclear Weapons in the Middle East.* Albany: State University of New York Press, 1992.

Bailey, Sydney Dawson. *Four Arab-Israeli Wars and the Peace Process.* New York: St. Martin's Press, 1990.

Begin, Menachem. *The Revolt*. New York: Nash, 1977.

Beilin, Yossi. *Israel: A Concise Political History*. New York: St. Martin's, 1993.

Bickerton, Ian J. and Carla L. Klausner. *A Concise History of the Arab-Israeli Conflict*. Englewood Cliffs, N.J.: Prentice Hall, 1991.

Bright, John. *A History of Israel*. 3d ed. Philadelphia: Westminster, 1981.

Cohen, Michael Joseph. *Truman and Israel*. Berkeley: University of California Press, 1990.

Cohen, Mitchell. *Zion and State: Nation, Class, and the Shaping of Modern Israel*. New York: B. Blackwell, 1987.

Danzger, Murray Herbert. *Returning to Tradition: The Contemporary Revival of Orthodox Judaism*. New Haven: Yale University Press, 1989.

Eban, Abba. *My Country: The Story of Modern Israel*. New York: Random House, 1972.

Encyclopedia Judaica. 16 vols. Jerusalem: Keter, 1972.

Feinstein, Steve. *Israel in Pictures*. Minneapolis: Lerner, 1988.

Friedlander, Dov, and Calvin Goldscheider. *The Population of Israel: Growth, Policy, and Implications*. New York: Columbia University Press, 1979.

Garfinkle, Adam M. *Politics and Society in Modern Israel: Myths and Realities*. Armonk, N.Y.: M. E. Sharpe, 1997.

Gil, Moshe. *A History of Palestine, 634–1099*. New York: Cambridge University Press, 1992.

Gilbert, Martin. *Jewish History Atlas*. rev. ed. New York: Macmillan, 1976.

Hart, Alan. *Arafat, a Political Biography*. Bloomington: Indiana University Press, 1989.

Kass, Ilana. *Arab and Israeli Terrorism: The Causes and Effects of Political Violence, 1936–1993*. Jefferson, N.C.: McFarland & Co., 1997.

———. *The Deadly Embrace: The Impact of Israeli and Palestinian Rejectionism on the Peace Process*. Fairfax, Va.: National Institute for Public Policy, 1997.

Korn, David A. *Stalemate: The War of Attrition and Great Power Diplomacy in the Middle East, 1967–1970*. Boulder, Colo.: Westview Press, 1992.

Kretzmer, David. *The Legal Status of the Arabs in Israel*. Boulder, Colo.: Westview Press, 1990.

Mahler, Gergory S. (ed.). *Israel after Begin*. Albany: State University of New York Press, 1990.

Meir, Golda. *My Life*. New York: Putnam, 1975.

Metz, Helen Chapin (ed.). *Israel, a Country Study*. 3rd ed. Washington, D.C.: Library of Congress, 1990.

Morris, Benny. *Israel's Border Wars, 1949–1956*. New York: Oxford University Press, 1993.

———. *The Birth of the Palestinian Refugee Problem, 1947–1949*. New York: Cambridge University Press, 1987.

Rabinovich, Itamar. *The Road Not Taken: Early Arab-Israeli Negotiations*. New York: Oxford University Press, 1991.

Razin, Assaf. *The Economy of Modern Israel: Malaise and Promise and Efraim Sadka*. Chicago: University of Chicago Press, 1993.

Reich, Bernard and Gershon R. Kieval. *Israel: Land of Tradition and Conflict*. 2d ed. Boulder, Colo.: Westview Press, 1993.

———. *Historical Dictionary of Israel*. Metuchen, N.J.: Scarecrow Press, 1992.

Rubin, Barry M. *Revolution Until Victory?: The Politics and History of the PLO*. Cambridge, Mass.: Harvard University Press, 1994.

Sachar, Howard Morley. *A History of Israel: From the Rise of Zionism to Our Time*. 2d ed. New York: Knopf, 1996.

Safran, Nadav. *Israel: The Embattled Ally*. Cambridge, Mass.: Belknap Press/Harvard University Press, 1978.

Sharkansky, Ira. *Ancient and Modern Israel: An Exploration of Political Parallels*. Albany: State University of New York Press, 1991.

Silberstein, Laurence J. *New Perspectives on Israeli History: The Early Years of the State*. New York: New York University Press, 1991.

Slater, Robert. *Rabin of Israel*. New York: St. Martin's Press, 1993.

———. *Warrior Statesman: The Life of Moshe Dayan*. New York: St. Martin's Press, 1991.

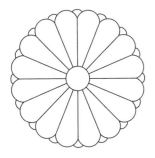

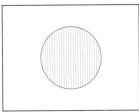

JAPAN

Nippon

CAPITAL: Tokyo.

FLAG: The Sun-flag (Hi-no-Maru) consists of a red circle on a white background.

ANTHEM: (de facto) *Kimigayo (The Reign of Our Emperor),* with words dating back to the 9th century.

MONETARY UNIT: The yen (¥) of 100 sen is issued in coins of 1, 5, 10, 50, 100, and 500 yen, and notes of 500, 1,000, 5,000, and 10,000 yen. ¥ = 0.00899 ($1 = ¥111.2) as of 31 March 2000.

WEIGHTS AND MEASURES: The metric system is the legal standard.

HOLIDAYS: New Year's Day, 1 January; Adults' Day, 15 January; Commemoration of the Founding of the Nation, 11 February; Vernal Equinox Day, 20 or 21 March; Greenery Day, 29 April; Constitution Day, 3 May; Children's Day, 5 May; Respect for the Aged Day, 15 September; Autumnal Equinox Day, 23 or 24 September; Health-Sports Day, 10 October; Culture Day, 3 November; Labor-Thanksgiving Day, 23 November; Emperor's Birthday, 23 December.

TIME: 9 PM = noon GMT.

¹LOCATION, SIZE, AND EXTENT

Situated off the eastern edge of the Asian continent, the Japanese archipelago is bounded on the N by the Sea of Okhotsk, on the E and S by the Pacific Ocean, on the SW by the East China Sea, and on the W by the Sea of Japan. The total area of Japan is 377,835 sq km (145,883 sq mi). Comparatively, the area occupied by Japan is slightly smaller than the state of California. It extends 3,008 km (1,869 mi) NE–SW and 1,645 km (1,022 mi) SE–NW and has a total coastline of 29,751 km (18,486 mi).

The five districts are Honshu, 231,058 sq km (89,212 sq mi); Hokkaido, 83,519 sq km (32,247 sq mi); Kyushu, 42,145 sq km (16,272 sq mi); Shikoku, 18,805 sq km (7,261 sq mi); and Okinawa, 2,254 sq km (870 sq mi). Each of the five districts consists of a main island of the same name and hundreds of surrounding islands.

Of the thousands of lesser islands, four are of significance: Tsushima, 698 sq km (269 sq mi), in the straits between Korea and Japan; Amami Oshima, 709 sq km (274 sq mi), of the northern Ryukyu Islands at the southern end of the Japanese archipelago; Sado Island, 857 sq km (331 sq mi), in the Sea of Japan off central Honshu; and Awaji Island, 593 sq km (229 sq mi), lying between Shikoku and Honshu. Two groups of islands returned to Japan by the US in 1968 are located some 1,300 km (800 mi) due east of the Ryukyus: the Ogasawara (Bonin) Islands, about 885 km (550 mi) south of Tokyo, and the Kazan (Volcano) Islands, directly south of the Ogasawara group.

Japan's principal island is Honshu, on which are located the capital city of Tokyo, the principal cities and plains, and the major industrial areas. This island is divided into five regions: Tohoku, from north of Kanto to Tsugaru Strait; Kanto, embracing seven prefectures in the Tokyo-Yokohama region; the Chubu, or central, region, from west of Tokyo to the Nagoya area; Kinki, including the important cities of Kyoto, Osaka, Kobe, and Nara; and Chugoku, a narrow peninsula thrusting westward from Kinki between the Sea of Japan and the Inland Sea, which lies between southern Honshu and the island of Shikoku.

The Japanese government maintains that the Habomai island group and Shikotan, lying just off Hokkaido and constituting fringe areas of the Kurils, belong to Japan and should be returned to Japanese administration. These islands and the Kuril Islands are currently occupied by the USSR, whose claims are not formally recognized by Japan.

Japan's capital city, Tokyo, is located on the east coast of the island of Honshu.

²TOPOGRAPHY

The Japanese islands are the upper portions of vast mountains belonging to what is sometimes called the Circum-Pacific Ring of Fire, which stretches from Southeast Asia to the Aleutian Islands. Mountains cover over 71% of the land's surface. Landforms are steep and rugged, indicating that, geologically speaking, Japan is still a young area. Through the central part of Honshu, running in a north–south direction, are the two principal mountain ranges: the Hida (or Japan Alps) and the Akaishi mountains. There are 25 mountains with peaks of over 3,000 m (9,800 ft). The highest is the beautiful Mt. Fuji (Fuji-san), at 3,776 m (12,388 ft). Japan has 196 volcanoes (including the dormant Mt. Fuji), of which 67 remain active. Earthquakes occur continually, with an average of 1,500 minor shocks per year. One of the world's greatest recorded natural disasters was the Kanto earthquake of 1923, when the Tokyo-Yokohama area was devastated and upward of 99,000 persons died.

The plains of Japan are few and small and cover only about 29% of the total land area. Most plains are located along the seacoast and are composed of alluvial lowlands, diluvial uplands, and low hills. The largest is the Kanto Plain (Tokyo Bay region), about 6,500 sq km (2,500 sq mi). Others include the Kinai Plain (Osaka-Kyoto), Nobi (Nagoya), Echigo (north-central Honshu), and Sendai (northeastern Honshu). There are four small plains in Hokkaido. The population is heavily concentrated in these limited flat areas.

Rivers tend to be short and swift. The longest is the Shinano (367 km/228 mi) in north-central Honshu, flowing into the Sea of Japan. The largest lake is Lake Biwa, near Kyoto, with an area of 672 sq km (259 sq mi). Lake Kussharo, in the Akan National Park of Hokkaido, is considered the clearest lake in the world, having a transparency of 41 m (135 ft). Good harbors are limited because in most areas the land rises steeply out of the sea. Yokohama, Nagoya, and Kobe are Japan's most prominent harbors.

The Ryukyu Islands, among which Okinawa predominates, are the peaks of submerged mountain ranges. They are generally hilly or mountainous, with small alluvial plains.

³CLIMATE

Japan is located at the northeastern edge of the Asian monsoon climate belt, which brings much rain to the country. The weather is under the dual influence of the Siberian weather system and the patterns of the southern Pacific; it is affected by the Japan Current (Kuroshio), a warm stream that flows from the southern Pacific along much of Japan's Pacific coast, producing a milder and more temperate climate than is found at comparable latitudes elsewhere. Northern Japan is affected by the Kuril Current (Oyashio), a cold stream flowing along the eastern coasts of Hokkaido and northern Honshu. The junction of the two currents is a bountiful fishing area. The Tsushima Current, an offshoot of the Japan Current, transports warm water northward into the Sea of Japan.

Throughout the year, there is fairly high humidity, with average rainfall ranging by area from 100 cm to over 300 cm (40–120 in). Autumn weather is usually clear and bright. Winters tend to be warmer than in similar latitudes except in the north and west, where snowfalls are frequent and heavy. Spring is usually pleasant, and the summer hot and humid. There is a rainy season that moves from south to north during June and July.

Average temperature ranges from 17°C (63°F) in the southern portions to 9°C (48°F) in the extreme north. Hokkaido has long and severe winters with extensive snow, while the remainder of the country enjoys milder weather down to the southern regions, which are almost subtropical. The Ryukyus, although located in the temperate zone, are warmed by the Japan Current, giving them a subtropical climate. The typhoon season runs from May through October, and each year several storms usually sweep through the islands, often accompanied by high winds and heavy rains.

⁴FLORA AND FAUNA

Hokkaido flora is characterized by montane conifers (fir, spruce, and larch) at high elevations and mixed northern hardwoods (oak, maple, linden, birch, ash, elm, and walnut) at lower altitudes. The ground flora includes plants common to Eurasia and North America. Honshu supports a panoply of temperate flora. Common conifers are cypress, umbrella pine, hemlock, yew, and white pine. On the lowlands, there are live oak and camphor trees and a great mixture of bamboo with the hardwoods. Black pine and red pine form the typical growth on the sandy lowlands and coastal areas. Shikoku and Kyushu are noted for their evergreen vegetation. Sugarcane and citrus fruits are found throughout the limited lowland areas, with broadleaf trees in the lower elevations and a mixture of evergreen and deciduous trees higher up. Throughout these islands are luxuriant growths of bamboo.

About 140 species of fauna have been identified. The only indigenous primate is the Japanese macaque, a small monkey found in the north. There are 32 carnivores, including the brown bear, ermine, mink, raccoon dog, fox, wolf, walrus, and seal. There are 450 species of birds and 30 species of reptiles. Japan's waters abound with crabs and shrimp; great migrations of fish are brought in by the Japan and Kuril currents. There are large numbers and varieties of insects. The Japanese beetle is not very destructive in its homeland because of its many natural enemies.

⁵ENVIRONMENT

Rapid industrialization has imposed severe pressures on the environment. Japan's Basic Law for Environmental Pollution Control was enacted in 1967, and the Environment Agency was established four years later.

Air pollution is a serious environmental problem in Japan, particularly in urban centers. Toxic pollutants from power plant emissions have led to the appearance of acid rain throughout the country. In the mid-1990s, Japan had the world's fourth highest level of industrial carbon dioxide emissions, which totaled 1.09 billion metric tons per year, a per capita level of 8.79 metric tons per year. Air quality is regulated under the Air Pollution Control Law of 1968; by 1984, compensation had been provided to 91,118 air-pollution victims suffering from bronchitis, bronchial asthma, and related conditions. However, the "polluter pays" principle was significantly weakened in 1987 as a result of years of business opposition. Nationwide smog alerts, issued when oxidant density levels reach or exceed 0.12 parts per million, peaked at 328 in 1973 but had declined to 85 (85% of which took place in the Tokyo and Osaka areas) by 1986, following imposition of stringent automobile emissions standards.

Water pollution is another area of concern in Japan. The nation has 131.3 cu mi of water with 49.5% used in farming activity and 33.4% used for industrial purposes. Increase in acid levels due to industrial pollutants has affected lakes, rivers, and the waters surrounding Japan. Other sources of pollution include DDT, BMC, and mercury. Environmental damage by industrial effluents has slowed since the promulgation of the Water Pollution Control Law of 1971, but there is still widespread pollution of lakes and rivers from household sources, especially by untreated sewage and phosphate-rich detergents. Factory noise levels are regulated under a 1968 law. Airplanes may not take off or land after 10 PM, and the Shinkansen trains must reduce speed while traveling through large cities and their suburbs.

Most of the nation's forests, which play a critical role in retarding runoff and soil erosion in the many mountainous areas, are protected under the Nature Conservation Law of 1972, and large areas have been reforested. Parks and wildlife are covered by the National Parks Law of 1967. In 1994 7.3% of Japan's total land areas was protected. Japan, one of the world's chief whaling nations, vigorously opposed the 1982 resolution of the IWC calling for a phaseout of commercial whaling by 1986/87. However, since most of its trading partners, including the US, supported the measure and threatened retaliatory measures if whaling continued, Japan finally agreed to comply with the ban.

Of Japan's mammal species, 5 are endangered, as are 31 bird species, and 41 plants. As of the mid-1990s, endangered species in Japan included the Ryukyu sika, Ryukyu rabbit, Iriomote cat, Southern Ryukyu robin, Okinawa woodpecker, Oriental white stork, short-tailed albatross, Japanese sea lion, green sea turtle, and tailless blue butterfly.

⁶POPULATION

The population of Japan in 2000 was estimated at 126,434,470. An estimated 15.5% of the population is 65 years of age or older. The projected population for the year 2005 is 127,338,000, assuming a crude birthrate of 10 per 1,000 population and a death rate of 9, resulting in a natural rate of change of 0.01% for the period 2000–2005. Japan is the only Asian country thus far with a birthrate that has declined to the level of industrial areas in other parts of the world. The estimated 10 births per 1,000 population in 2000 compares with about 343 births per 1,000 population in 1947. The steep drop since 1950 has been attributed to legalization of abortion, increased availability of contraceptives, and the desire to raise living standards. The population rate of change between 1995 and 2000 was 0.2%.

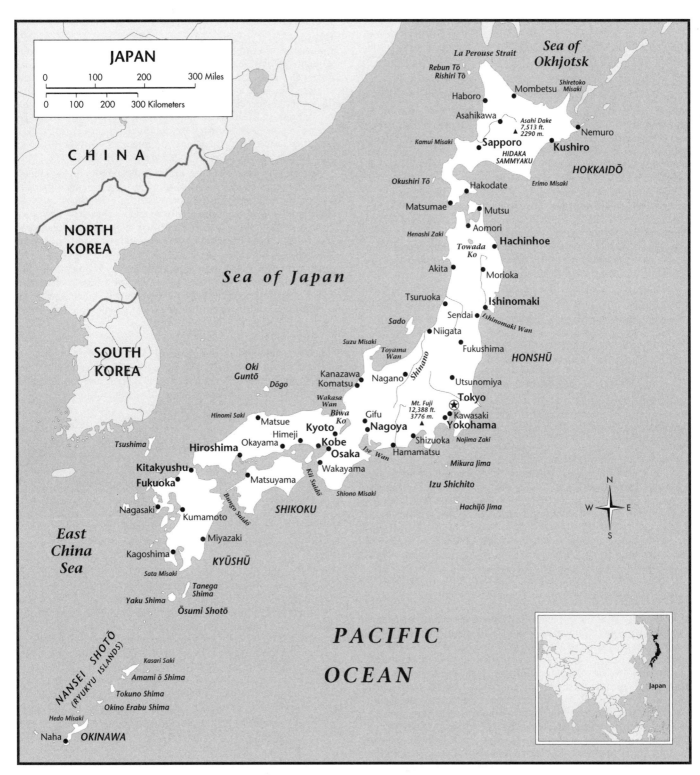

JAPAN

| 0 | 100 | 200 | 300 Miles |
| 0 | 100 | 200 | 300 Kilometers |

CHINA

NORTH KOREA

SOUTH KOREA

Sea of Japan

East China Sea

NANSEI SHOTŌ (RYUKYU ISLANDS)

Kasari Saki

Amami ō Shima

Tokuno Shima

Okino Erabu Shima

Hedo Misaki

Naha **OKINAWA**

La Perouse Strait

Sea of Okhjotsk

Rebun Tō
Rishiri Tō

Shiretoko Misaki

Mombetsu

Haboro

Asahikawa

Asahi Dake
7,513 ft.
2290 m.

Nemuro

Kamui Misaki

Sapporo **Kushiro**

HIDAKA SAMMYAKU

HOKKAIDŌ

Okushiri Tō

Hakodate

Erimo Misaki

Matsumae

Mutsu

Henashi Zaki

Aomori

Hachinhoe

Towada Ko

Akita

Morioka

Tsuruoka

Ishinomaki

Sendai *Ishinomaki Wan*

Sado

Niigata

Fukushima

HONSHŪ

Suzu Misaki

Toyama Wan

Kanazawa

Komatsu

Nagano

Shinano

Utsunomiya

Oki Guntō

Dōgo

Wakasa Wan

Biwa Ko

Gifu

Mt. Fuji
12,388 ft.
3776 m.

Tokyo

Kawasaki

Yokohama

Hinomi Saki

Matsue

Kyoto

Nagoya

Ise Wan

Shizuoka

Nojima Zaki

Himeji

Kobe

Hamamatsu

Hiroshima

Okayama

Osaka

Mikura Jima

Wakayama

Kii Suidō

Izu Shichito

Tsushima

Matsuyama

Shiono Misaki

Hachijō Jima

Kitakyushu

Fukuoka

Bungo Suidō

SHIKOKU

Nagasaki

Kumamoto

East China Sea

Miyazaki

Kagoshima

Sata Misaki

KYŪSHŪ

Tanega Shima

Yaku Shima

Ōsumi Shotō

PACIFIC OCEAN

N
W   E
S

Japan

LOCATION: 122°56′ to 153°59′E; 20°25′ to 45°33′N. TERRITORIAL SEA LIMIT: 12 mi.

The population density in 1998 was 335 per sq km (868 per sq mi).

In terms of density, Japan ranks among the world leaders, with 318 persons per sq km (823 per sq mi). In terms of density per unit of cultivated land, Japan has about 23 persons per ha (9.5 per acre). The major concentrations are found in Honshu, where four out of five Japanese live; the least densely populated major

island is Hokkaido, with less than 5% of the total population.

It was estimated that 79% of the population lived in urban areas in 2000, up from 76% in 1980. Since the 1965 census, however, the net population flow into the center cities has decreased, while the flow into the surrounding suburban areas has increased. The capital city, Tokyo, had a 2000 population of 26,959,000. The urban agglomeration centered on Tokyo had an estimated population of about 28,025,000 in 2000. Other major metropolitan areas, with 2000 populations counts, include Osaka, 10,609,000; Nagoya, 3,377,000; Sapporo, 1,827,000; Kyoto, 1,703,000; Kitakyushu, 2,898,467; Hiroshima, 912,677; and Sendai, 821,000.

7MIGRATION

Japanese nationals living in other countries totaled more than 600,000 in the 1990s, including some 250,000 in the US and over 100,000 in Brazil. More than one million Japanese have emigrated since 1880; about 70% of them arrived on the US mainland and in Hawaii during the decades prior to World War II. Emigration continued after the war, encouraged by government policy as a way of relieving population pressure. By the mid-1960s, emigration had considerably decreased, as economic opportunities and living standards in Japan improved. Since the early 1970s, however, the number of emigrants has again risen sharply, reaching 82,619 in 1992 (compared to 12,445 in 1975 and 34,492 in 1985).

Immigration to Japan is generally small-scale, although in recent years the illegal entry of workers from neighboring countries has come to be regarded as a problem. Since 1975 10,000 Indo-Chinese refugees have settled in Japan. In the mid-1990s there were 1,300,000 registered aliens, of which 690,000 were Koreans. The number of illegal aliens may be even higher. Some 150,000 Chinese constituted the second-largest group. Nearly 42,000 foreigners entered as permanent residents per year. Because citizenship is based on nationality of parent rather than place of birth, registered aliens may have spent their entire lives in Japan. In 1999 the net emigration rate was 0.34 migrants per 1,000 population.

Internal migration, providing a steady exodus of people from farm and mountain communities to the cities and suburbs, has been accelerating since 1952. Most such migrants flocked to the three major population centers—the Tokyo, Osaka, and Nagoya metropolitan areas. As pollution and congestion in these areas increased, the government instituted programs to decentralize industry by directing new growth to smaller cities of the north and west, and also began efforts to improve rural living conditions and employment opportunities.

8ETHNIC GROUPS

In 1999, 99.4% of the population was Japanese while only 0.6% belonged to other ethnic groups (mostly Korean). Although it is known that the Japanese are descended from many varied peoples of Asia, there is no agreement as to origins or specific ethnic strains. In physical characteristics, the Japanese belong to the Mongoloid group, with faint admixtures of Malayan and Caucasoid strains. Waves of migration from the continental hinterland reached Japan during the end of the Paleolithic period, blending into a complicated and diverse ethnic, linguistic, and cultural system. It is believed that the Japanese have their roots in the Old Stone Age race of at least 30,000 BC. A major migration appears to have taken place in the second and third centuries AD, and by the fourth century this group, called the Yamato clan, had established a monarchy in the present Nara prefecture. Other ethnic strains may have come from Indonesia and China in the south, Korea in the west, and Siberia and Alaska in the north.

The one remaining distinct ethnic group in Japan is the Ainu. These people, living on the northern island of Hokkaido, are physically distinct from the contemporary Japanese, having Nordic-like features, including more pervasive facial and body hair. There is no agreement as to their origins; their current population is less than 20,000.

9LANGUAGES

Japanese is the official language. Most linguists agree that Japanese is in a language class by itself, although there is some inconclusive evidence that traces it to the Malayo-Polynesian language family. In vocabulary, Japanese is rich in words denoting abstract ideas, natural phenomena, human emotions, ethics, and aesthetics, but poor in words for technical and scientific expression. For these latter purposes, foreign words are directly imported and written in a phonetic system (katakana). A distinct characteristic is the use of honorifics to show proper respect to the listener and his social status.

Written Japanese owes its origin almost entirely to Chinese forms. Having no indigenous script, the Japanese since the fifth century have used Chinese characters, giving them both an approximate Chinese pronunciation and a Japanese pronunciation. In addition, the Japanese invented phonetic symbols (kana) in the ninth century to represent grammatical devices unknown to the Chinese.

Attempts have been made to reduce the complexity of the written language by limiting the number of Chinese characters used. The government has published a list of 1,850 characters for use in official communications. Newspapers adhere to this list.

10RELIGIONS

The principal religions in Japan are Shintoism and Buddhism, observed by 84% of the population. Religious identities are not mutually exclusive, and many Japanese maintain affiliations with both a Buddhist temple and a Shinto shrine.

Shinto, originally concerned with the worship of spirits of nature, grew under the influence of Chinese Confucianism to include worship of family and imperial ancestors, and thus provided the foundation of Japanese social structure. Shinto became an instrument of nationalism after 1868, as the government officially sponsored and subsidized it, requiring that it be taught in the schools and that all Japanese belong to a state Shinto shrine. After World War II, Shinto was abolished as a state religion, and the emperor issued an imperial rescript denying divine origin. Today, Shinto exists as a private religious organization and was observed by some 44.7% of the population in 1998.

Buddhism, considered by some the most important religion in Japan, was observed by approximately 49.2% of citizens in 1998. Introduced through China and Korea around AD 552, Buddhism spread rapidly throughout Japan and has had considerable influence on the nation's arts and its social institutions. There are 13 sects (shu) and 56 denominations, the principal shu being Tendai, Shingon, Jodo, Zen, Soto, Obaku, and Nichiren. Japanese Buddhism was founded on the Mahayana school, which emphasizes the attainment of Buddhahood, whereas the Hinayana Buddhism of India emphasizes obedience to commandments and personal perfection. The great temples and gardens of Japan, the famous Japanese tea ceremony (chanoyu), and Japanese flower-arranging arts (ikebana) owe their development to the influence of Buddhism.

Religions designated as other are practiced by about 16% of the population (including 0.7% practicing Christianity). Christianity, introduced to Japan by the Jesuit St. Francis Xavier in 1549, was first encouraged by feudal lords but then banned in 1613, often under penalty of death. After that time, a unique sect known as "hidden Christians" developed, with no tradition of churches or public displays of faith and a syncretic doctrine that incorporated local ideas and history. The prohibition against Christianity was in force until 1873, following the reopening of Japan to international relations in 1854. Following World War II, when the emperor lost his claim to divinity, some Japanese gave up Shinto and converted to Christianity or Judaism.

After World War II, a considerable number of new religious groups sprouted up. One of these, the Soka-Gakkai, a Buddhist offshoot, controlled a political party (Komeito), the third-strongest political group in Japan, until politics and religion were officially separated in 1970. In addition to the established and new religions, Confucianism, an ethical system originating in China, has strongly influenced Japanese society since the earliest periods, providing underpinnings for some characteristically Japanese attitudes.

11 TRANSPORTATION

Despite its rugged terrain, Japan has a highly developed transportation system. At last estimate, Japan had 23,671 km (14,709 mi) of railways, of which about 90% is 1.067 m narrow gauge. The government-owned Japan National Railways (JNR) was privatized in April 1987 and divided into six railway companies; feeding into these six lines were 144 other private railroads. Like their counterparts elsewhere, Japan's rail lines face increasing competition from automotive, sea, and air transport, as well as rising operating costs. High-speed lines, however, have been successful in partially meeting these problems; the most famous of these is the Shinkansen, which opened to traffic in October 1964 between Tokyo and Osaka and was extended in March 1975 to Fukuoka in northern Kyushu; in 1984, the Shinkansen superexpress trains covered the 1,069 km (664 mi) between Tokyo and Fukuoka in less than seven hours, with maximum speeds of 210 km/hr (130 mph). In 1982, the first section of the northern Shinkansen line, between Tokyo and Omiya, began operations. This line was extended in 1983 to Niigata and to Morioka, in northern Honshu. By far the longest railway tunnel in the world, the 54.2 km (33.7 mi) Seikan tube linking Honshu with Hokkaido, was opened in 1983 and completed in 1985; the tunnel, lying beneath the Tsugaru Strait, cost well over $2 billion. A bridge linking Honshu and Shikoku was recently opened. Subway lines serve nine cities—Tokyo, Osaka, Nagoya, Kobe, Yokohama, Sapporo, Kyoto, Fukuoka, and Sendai. There are 410 km (255 mi) of track, with 196 km (122 mi) in Tokyo's 11 lines. Since 1964, downtown Tokyo has also been linked with that city's Haneda Airport by a monorail transport system, and several other monorails have been put into operation. In addition, a 7 km (4.3 mi) monorail serves the city of Yokohama.

Roads have become the most important means of domestic transport. Motor vehicles in 1995 numbered 44,680,000 passenger cars and 22,173,000 commercial vehicles, up from 25,848,000 and 8,306,000, respectively, in 1985. To speed traffic flow, a total of 6,070 km (3,772 mi) of expressways were open to traffic in 1996. There were about 1.16 million km (720,824 mi) of roadways, of which about 859,560 km (534,131 mi) were paved.

Japan is one of the world's great maritime nations. The chief ports are Yokohama (for Tokyo), Nagoya, and Kobe. In 1998, Japan's merchant fleet included 713 ships, totaling 13,753,027 gross tons. Since 1959, Japan has emerged as the world's leading shipbuilder, but output declined in the late 1970s and 1980s in the face of a worldwide recession and increased competition from the Republic of Korea (ROK).

Japan had 170 airports in 1998, of which 140 had paved runways. Principal domestic airports include Haneda in Tokyo, Itami in Osaka, Itazuke in Fukuoka, and Chitose on Hokkaido. Principal international facilities include Kansai International at Osaka and New Tokyo International at Tokyo. Japan Air Lines (JAL), the nation's major domestic and international airline, began operations in 1952 and inaugurated international flights in 1954. All Nippon Airways, established in 1957, began as a domestic system serving smaller areas of the country and acting as a feeder line to JAL but now serves overseas routes; it began to carry freight in 1987. In 1997, Japan's airlines performed 151,048 million passenger-km (93,861 million passenger-mi) in domestic and international traffic, and 7,505 million freight ton-km (4,664 million freight ton-mi). In the same year, 94,998,000 passengers were carried on scheduled domestic and international airline flights.

From 1991–2000, the government planned to spend $8 trillion on infrastructure improvements, especially for the expansion of airports, bridges, roads, ports, heliports, and marinas.

12 HISTORY

Recent archaeological discoveries revealed the existence of paleolithic humans in Japan when the islands were connected to the Asian continental landmass. Little is known about the origins of the earliest Japanese beyond the fact that they migrated from the continent. The first distinctive Neolithic culture, the Jōmon, existed in Japan from 11,000 BC to 300 BC. The Jōmon was displaced by the Yayoi culture, which introduced new agricultural and metallurgical skills from the continent. Tradition places the beginning of the Japanese nation in 660 BC with the ascendance to the throne of the legendary Emperor Jimmu. It is generally agreed, however, that as the Yayoi developed, the Yamato clan attained hegemony over southern Japan during the first three or four centuries of the Christian era and established the imperial family line. Earlier contacts with Korea were expanded in the fifth century to mainland China, and the great period of cultural borrowing began: industrial arts were imported; Chinese script was introduced (thereby permitting the study of medical texts), the Chinese calendar and Buddhism also arrived from China. Japanese leaders adapted the Chinese governmental organization but based power upon hereditary position rather than merit. The first imperial capital was established at Nara in 710. In 794, the imperial capital was moved to Heian (Kyoto), where it remained until 1868, when Tokyo became the nation's capital.

Chinese influence waned as native institutions took on peculiarly Japanese forms. Outside court circles, local clans gained strength, giving rise to military clan influence over a weakening imperial system. The Minamoto clan gained national hegemony as it defeated the rival Taira clan in 1185, and its leader, the newly appointed Yoritomo, established a military form of government at Kamakura in 1192, a feudal system that lasted for nearly 700 years. Under the shogunate system, all political power was in the hands of the dominant military clan, with the emperors ruling in name only. The Kamakura period was followed by the Ashikaga shogunate (1336–1600) which saw economic growth and the development of a more complex feudalism. For over 100 years, until the end of the 16th century, continuous civil war among rival feudal lords (*daimyo*) ensued. During this time, the first contact with the Western world took place with the arrival in 1543 of Portuguese traders, and with that, the first guns were imported. Six years later, St. Francis Xavier arrived, introducing Christianity to Japan.

By 1590, the country was pacified and unified by Toyotomi Hideyoshi, a peasant who had risen to a top military position. Hideyoshi also invaded Korea unsuccessfully, in 1592–93 and in 1598, dying during the second invasion. Ieyasu Tokugawa consolidated Hideyoshi's program of centralization. Appointed shogun in 1603, Tokugawa established the Tokugawa shogunate, which was to rule Japan until the imperial restoration in 1868. Tokugawa made Edo (modern Tokyo) the capital, closed Japan to foreigners except Chinese and Dutch traders (who were restricted to Nagasaki) and occasional Korean diplomats, and banned Christianity. For the next 250 years, Japan enjoyed stability and a flowering of indigenous culture, although from the end of the 18th century onward, Japan came under increasing pressure from Western nations to end its isolationist policy.

The arrival of Commodore Matthew C. Perry from the US in 1853—with his famous "black ships"—started a process that soon ended Japanese feudalism. The following year, Perry obtained a treaty of peace and friendship between the US and Japan, and similar pacts were signed with Russia, Britain, and the Netherlands based on the principle of extraterritoriality. A decade of turmoil and confusion followed over the question of opening Japan to foreigners. A coalition of southern clans led by ambitious young samurai of the Satsuma and Choshu clans forced the abdication of the Tokugawa shogun and reestablished the emperor as head of the nation. In 1868, Emperor Mutsuhito took over full sovereignty. This Meiji Restoration, as it is known, signaled the entry of Japan into the modern era.

Intensive modernization and industrialization commenced under the leadership of the restoration leaders. A modern navy and army with universal military conscription and a modern civil service based on merit formed the foundation of the new nation-state. The government undertook the establishment of industry, by importing technological assistance. In 1889, a new constitution established a bicameral legislature (*Diet*) with a civil cabinet headed by a Prime Minister responsible to the emperor.

By the end of the 19th century, irreconcilable territorial ambitions brought Japan into open conflict with its much larger western neighbors. The Sino-Japanese War (1894–95) was fought over the question of control of Korea, and the Russo-Japanese War (1904–05) over the question of Russian expansion in Manchuria and influence in Korean affairs. Japan emerged victorious in both conflicts, its victory over the Russians marking the first triumph of an Asian country over a Western power in modern times. Japan received the territories of Taiwan and the southern half of Sakhalin Island, as well as certain railway rights and concessions in Manchuria and recognition of paramount influence in Korea. The latter became a Japanese protectorate in 1905 and was annexed by Japan in 1910.

During the Taisho era (1912–26), Japan participated in a limited way in World War I, in accordance with the Anglo-Japanese Alliance of 1902. Japan was one of the Big Five powers at the Versailles Peace Conference and in 1922 was recognized as the world's third-leading naval power at the Washington Naval Conference. The domestic economy developed rapidly, and Japan was transformed from an agricultural to an industrial nation. Economic power tended to be held by the industrial combines (*zaibatsu*), controlled by descendants of those families that had instituted the modernization of the country decades earlier. In 1925, universal manhood suffrage was enacted, and political leaders found it necessary to take into consideration the growing influence of parties.

In 1926, Emperor Hirohito ascended the throne beginning the Showa era. By the 1930s, democratic institutions atrophied and the military-industrial complex became dominant. With severe social distress caused by the great depression, an ultranationalist ideology emerged, particularly among young army officers. Acting independently of the central government, the military launched an invasion of Manchuria in 1931, eventually establishing the puppet state of Manchukuo. In 1932, a patriotic society assassinated the prime minister, bringing an end to cabinets formed by the majority party in the Diet. Japan withdrew from the League of Nations (which had protested the Manchurian takeover) in 1933, started a full-scale invasion of China (the Second Sino-Japanese War, 1937–45), and signed the Anti-Comintern pact with Germany in 1936 and a triple alliance with Germany and Italy in 1940. The military leadership, viewing the former USSR and the US as chief barriers to Japanese expansion, negotiated a nonaggression pact with the USSR in April 1941, thus setting the stage for the attack on Pearl Harbor and other Pacific targets on 7 December of that year. Thereafter, Japanese military actions took place in the context of World War II.

With its capture of the Philippines on 2 January 1942, Japan gained control of most of East Asia, including major portions of China, Indochina, and the southwest Pacific. Japanese forces, however, could not resist the continued mobilization of the US military. A series of costly naval campaigns—including battles at Midway, Guadalcanal, and Leyte Gulf—brought an end to Japanese domination in the Pacific. By 1945, the Philippines had been recaptured, and the stage was set for a direct assault on Japan. After the US troops captured Okinawa in a blood battle, President Harry S. Truman argued that a full invasion of Japan would prove too costly and decided on aerial attacks to force Japan into surrendering. After four months of intense bombardment with conventional weapons, the US dropped an atomic bomb on Hiroshima on 6 August 1945 and a second bomb on Nagasaki on 9 August. An estimated 340,000 persons died from the two attacks and the subsequent effects of radiation.

On 14 August, Japan accepted the Potsdam Declaration for unconditional surrender with formal surrender documents signed aboard the USS Missouri on 2 September. The subsequent occupation (1945–52), under the direction of Gen. Douglas MacArthur, Supreme Commander for the Allied Powers, began a series of ambitious reforms. Political reforms included the adoption of a parliamentary system of government based on democratic principles and universal suffrage, a symbolic role for the emperor as titular head of state, the establishment of an independent trade union, and the disarmament of the military. Economic reforms consisted of land reform, the dissolution of the zaibatsu, and economic and political rights for women. A new constitution was promulgated on 3 November 1946 and put into force on 3 May 1947.

The Postwar Period

Heavy economic aid from the US and a procurement boom produced by the Korean War, coupled with a conservative fiscal and monetary policy allowed the Japanese to rebuild their country. The Japanese economy rapidly recovered, and the standard of living quickly surpassed the prewar level by a substantial margin. The state of war between the Western powers and Japan was formally ended by the San Francisco Peace Treaty, signed in September 1951 by 56 nations. The allied occupation ended officially when the treaty went into effect in April 1952. Japan renounced claims to many of its former overseas territories, including such major areas as Taiwan and Korea. The Amami island group, comprising the northern portion of the Ryukyu Islands, nearest to Kyushu Island, was returned to direct Japanese control by the US in December 1953; the remainder of the group, including Okinawa, was returned to full Japanese sovereignty in May 1972. The Ogasawara (Bonin) Islands and Kazan (Volcano) Islands were returned to Japanese sovereignty in June 1968. The former USSR never signed the San Francisco Peace Treaty, and Japan and Russia continue to dispute sovereignty over the Kurile Islands, to the northeast of Hokkaido, the USSR occupied in 1945. In 1956, Japan and the former USSR agreed to establish diplomatic relations.

In 1956 Japan was elected to UN membership. A revision of the 1952 defense treaty with the US, under which a limited number of troops were to remain in Japan for defense purposes, was signed amid growing controversy in 1960. On 22 June 1965, Japan signed a treaty with South Korea normalizing relations between the two countries. The US-Japanese Security Treaty was renewed in 1970, despite vigorous protest by the opposition parties and militant student organizations. In 1972, Japan moved to establish full diplomatic relations with the People's Republic of China. Formal diplomatic links with the Nationalist Chinese government on Taiwan were terminated by this move, but Japan's economic and cultural links with Taiwan nonetheless have survived virtually intact.

While Japan defined its new role in East Asian affairs, its remarkable economic expansion raised it to the level of a major trading power. Based on strong government support of export industries, political stability under the LDP, and public policy guidance from a powerful bureaucracy, Japan experienced a dramatic rise from the ruins of World War II. From 1955 to 1965, Japan experienced a nominal growth rate of 10–20% annually and real growth rates (adjusted for inflation) of 5–12%. In 1968, it surpassed the Federal Republic of Germany (FRG) to stand second after the US among non-Communist nations in total value of GNP. The oil crisis of 1973—a combination of shortages and rising prices—revealed the crack in Japan's economic armor, the lack of domestic petroleum resources. A second oil crisis during the late 1970s, was met by a reappraisal of Japan's dependence on foreign fuels and the institution of long-range programs for energy conservation and diversification.

The yen declined in value in the early 1980s, causing Japanese exports to become cheaper in overseas markets and leading to huge trade surpluses with the US and other leading trading partners, who began to demand that Japan voluntarily limit certain exports and remove the barriers to Japan's domestic market. During 1985–87, the yen appreciated in value against the dollar and, by 1994, the dollar had hit a post-World War II low, but Japan continued to register substantial trade surpluses.

Political stability, maintained since the 1950s by the majority Liberal-Democratic Party (LDP), began to unravel in the 1970s, following the retirement from politics of Prime Minister Eisaku Sato in 1972. Sato's successor, Kakuei Tanaka, was forced to resign in December 1974 amid charges using his office for personal gain in the Lockheed Corporation bribery scandal. Takeo Miki succeeded Tanaka and Takeo Fukuda became prime minister when Miki resigned in December 1976. Fukuda was defeated in intraparty elections by Masayoshi Ohira in 1978. When Ohira died in June 1980, he was succeeded by Zenko Suzuki. Suzuki stepped down as prime minister in November 1982 and was replaced by controversial and outspoken Yasuhiro Nakasone. Noboru Takeshita became prime minister in November 1987.

Policy regarding military force has been a major political issue in the postwar years. According to Article Nine of the 1947 constitution, Japan renounced the belligerency of the state but soon developed a Self-Defense Force with US encouragement. In 1986, breaking a long-standing policy, the government increased military spending to over 1% of the GNP. The Diet (parliament) approved a bill allowing the deployment of troops abroad for international peacekeeping in 1992 (with the United Nations in Cambodia).

Emperor Hirohito died of cancer on 7 January 1989, at the age of 87. He was succeeded by the Crown Prince Akihito, who was enthroned as the Heisei emperor in a formal ceremony in November 1990. The sense of entering a new era brought increased controversy over the assessment of Japan's role in the earlier part of the century, particularly during World War II. Some denied that Japan had committed atrocities during the war and there were attempts to further soften the wording of school textbooks. In March 1989, Prime Minister Takeshita apologized to North Korea (DPRK) for the suffering Japan caused over the 36 years of occupation of Korea (1910–45) and Emperor Akihito expressed similar regrets to President Roh Tae Woo of South Korea (ROK) in May 1990. In the same month, the government removed the requirement for fingerprinting of people of Korean descent living in Japan. In 1992, Prime Minister Miyazawa apologized for the forced prostitution of Korean, Chinese, and Japanese women in Japanese military brothels during World War II.

The 1980s ended with a major scandal involving illegal stock trading and influence peddling by the Recruit Cosmos Company.

Between the summer of 1988 and the closing of the case in May 1989, the scandal led to the implication and resignations of prominent business people and politicians in top government positions, among them the finance minister Kiichi Miyazawa, and the former prime minister, Yashuhiro Nakasone. Scandals continued into the 1990s with stock rebates for politicians in 1991 and then in 1992, contributions to politicians from a trucking company linked to organized crime became public knowledge.

The economy entered a period major stagnation and distress in the early 1990s. In 1990, the stock market declined more than 25% from January to April. Then, during the spring of 1992, the stock index fell rapidly again, until by the summer, the index was at its lowest point in six years at 62% below the record high of 1989. By the end of 1993, Japan was in the midst of its worst economic downturn in at least 20 years.

Against the background of scandals and an economic recession, the political landscape began a major change. Taking responsibility for political problems caused by the Recruit scandal, Noboru Takeshita resigned as prime minister in April 1989, to be succeeded in May by Sosuke Uno, who abruptly resigned when a sex scandal became public amidst the LDP loss of its majority in the upper house of the Diet. The next prime minister, Toshiki Kaifu, served his term from August 1989 to October 1991, but the LDP did not support him for a second term. Instead, Kiichi Miyazawa became prime minister in November 1991. When the lower house gave Miyazawa a vote of no confidence in June 1993 for abandoning electoral reform bills, Miyazawa dissolved the lower house and called for elections.

The dissolution of the House of Representatives and the ensuing election on 18 July 1993 marked a major turning point for Japanese politics as the LDP lost its political dominance as new parties formed. One new party, the Japan New Party (JNP), was formed by Morihiro Hosokawa, a former LDP member, in May 1992. On 21 June 1993, 10 more members of the LDP, led by Masayoshi Takemura, left to form the Sakigake (Harbinger Party) and another 44 LDP members quit two days later to create the Shinseito (Renewal Party) with Tsutomu Hata as its head. By 28 June, one-fifth (57 members) of the LDP bloc of the dissolved lower house left the party.

In the election for the 511 seats of the House of Representatives on 18 July 1993, the LDP, for the first time since its own formation in 1955, failed to secure the 256 seats needed for a majority. Without a majority, the LDP was unable to form a government and the new prime minister, Morihiro Hosokawa (JNP), was chosen on 29 July 1993, by a seven-party coalition of LDP defectors, Socialists, and conservatives. Hosokawa, too, was tainted by questions regarding personal finances and stepped down as prime minister to be replaced by Tsutomu Hata (Shinseito) in April 1994. Just as Hata took office, the Socialist Party left the governing coalition, leaving the prime minister as the head of a minority government for the first time in four decades. Hata soon resigned and, in a surprise move, the LDP and the Socialist Party, traditionally opponents, allied to form a new coalition, which also included the Sakigake. The coalition selected as prime minister Tomiichi Murayama, the head of the Socialist Party and the first Socialist prime minister since 1948. Within the coalition, the LDP was the dominant factor, but the decades of LDP rule appeared to be over and the nature of the LDP itself changed.

In June 1994, Tomiichi Murayama, a socialist, became prime minister in a coalition consisting of the LDP, the Social Democratic Party of Japan (SDPJ), and Sakigake. In an unprecedented move, Murayama recognized the legal right for the existence of the Japanese Self-Defense force, much to the disapproval of left leaning party members. The tumultuous reign of Murayama which included the Kobe earthquake and political scandals which led to the resignation of the Justice Minister and the director of the Management and Coordination Agency. Elections in October 1996 resulted in a victory for the LDP, but the party still failed to obtain a majority of seats, only capturing 239 of 500. The Sakigake and Democratic Party of Japan agreed to support Prime Minister Ryutaro Hashimoto. In July 1998, Hashimoto resigned after a poor performance of the LDP in the House of Councilors election and was replaced by Keizo Obuchi. During the Obuchi regime, the Japanese economy showed signs of recovering with major fiscal stimuli including a massive public works program. The LDP also orchestrated and implemented a plan to bail out failed and ailing banks with taxpayers funds. In April 1999, Obuchi entered into a coma and was replaced by Yoshiro Mori who called summarily for elections.

13 GOVERNMENT

Japan follows the parliamentary system in accordance with the constitution of 1947. The most significant change from the previous constitution of 1889 was the transfer of sovereign power from the emperor to the people. The emperor is now defined as "the symbol of the state and of the unity of the people." The constitution provides for the supremacy of the National Diet as the legislative branch of the government, upholds the separation of legislative, executive, and judicial powers, and guarantees civil liberties.

The executive branch is headed by a prime minister selected from the Diet by its membership. The cabinet consists of the prime minister and 19 state ministers (as of January 1999), each heading a government ministry or agency. At least half the ministers must be selected from the Diet, to which the cabinet is collectively responsible. Upon a vote of no confidence by the House of Representatives, the cabinet must resign en masse.

The National Diet is bicameral. The House of Representatives (the lower house) has a membership of 500, with terms of office for four years, except that all terms end upon dissolution of the House. From 1947 through 1993, Representatives were elected from 130 "medium" (multiple-member) constituencies, apportioned on the basis of population. The House of Councilors (the upper house) has 252 members, 100 of whom are elected from a national constituency on the basis of proportional representation, the remainder from 47 prefectural constituencies. The term of office is six years, with one-half elected every three years. The lower house holds primary power. In case of disagreement between the two houses, or if the upper house fails to take action within 60 days of receipt of legislation from the lower house, a bill becomes law if passed again by a two-thirds majority of the lower house.

Suffrage is universal, the voting age being 20 years, with a three-month residence requirement. The 1947 constitution granted suffrage to women. In January 1994, the Diet passed an electoral reform bill. In addition to new laws on campaign financing, the legislation abolished the multiple-member districts and replaced them with 300 single-member districts and 200 multimember districts. The 1996 elections resulted in the weakening minor parties, in particular the SDPJ and Sakigake. Elections for the House of Representatives were announced for the summer of 2000.

14 POLITICAL PARTIES

The Liberal-Democratic Party (LDP) represents a wide spectrum of Japanese society, but most especially the conservative elements. Formed in 1955 by the merger of the two leading conservative parties, this party held the reins of government since its formation until July 1993.

The Japan Socialist Party (JSP), Japan's principal opposition party, draws its support mainly from the working class, but it suffers from personality as well as ideological problems within its ranks. The JSP split into right and left wings over the ratification of the US-Japan Security Treaty of 1952. In October 1955, however, the two factions reunited, preceding the unification of the conservative parties and actually forcing the conservative groups into a unified front, thus creating a formal two-party system in Japan.

Beginning in the late 1960s, a shift took place toward a multiple-party system, with the gradual increase of opposition parties other than the JSP. The Democratic Socialist Party (DSP) represented moderate elements of the working class. The Komeito (Clean Government Party), professing middle-of-the-road politics, was the political wing of the Soka-Gakkai, a Buddhist sect. The Japanese Communist Party, founded as an underground group in 1922 and legalized after World War II, experienced major shifts in platform. The party has traditionally sided with China in the Sino-Soviet ideological dispute, although in recent years the Japanese Communists have eschewed close identification with either side, focusing instead on social conditions at home.

The LDP continued to hold its majority in both houses until 1993. Traditionally, the LDP has functioned as a coalition of several factions, each tightly organized and bound by personal loyalty to a factional leader. In the mid-1970s, policy differences among the factions and their leaders became acute, with the resignation under pressure of Prime Minister Tanaka in December 1974.

In the summer of 1993, after five years of scandals involving corruption, sex, organized crime, and in the midst of economic recession, the old political order disintegrated as dozens of younger LDP members defected to form new parties. Chief among these was the Japan New Party (JNP), formed in May 1992, and the Sakigake (Harbinger Party) and the Shinseito (Renewal Party), both formed in June 1993. A watershed election in July 1993 for the House of Representatives, the lower house of the parliament, resulted in the loss by the LDP, for the first time since 1955, of its majority. Of the 511 seats, the LDP won 223 seats (as compared with 275 in the 1990 election), the JSP won 70 seats (a loss of half of its previous seats), the Komeito won 51 seats, the Shinseito took 55 seats, the JNP 35 seats, and the Sakigake 13. A seven-party coalition, including new parties of LDP defectors, the JSP, and other conservative parties, formed the new cabinet, which governed for a year until the prime minister (Morihiro Hosokawa, JNP) resigned over a financial scandal. The coalition formed a new government, led by Tsutomu Hata of the Shinseito, in April 1993. However, the JSP, finding itself maneuvered out of any voice in the coalition, broke away and Hata, then with a minority in the House of Representatives, resigned after one month in office.

The next government was formed by a new, unorthodox coalition of the traditional opponents, the LDP and the JSP, as well as the Sakigake. Tomiichi Murayama, head of the JSP, was chosen prime minister in June 1994, the first Socialist to head a government since 1948, although the LDP appeared to be dominant in the coalition. This unusual partnership caused strains, leading to further defections, within the LDP and within the JSP. The Shinseito emerged as a serious focus of opposition, standing for an internationally more active Japan, including use of the military overseas, for a revision of the constitution, and for removing protective regulations to open the domestic economy to competition. The left wing of the JSP, unhappy with the alliance with the LDP, held that the Self-Defense Forces were unconstitutional, and that the North Korean government (DPRK) was the legitimate government of all of Korea, and advocated abolition of the security treaty with the United States.

The last parliamentary election took place on 20 October 1996. It combined the 300 single seat constituencies with the proportional representation for the remaining 200 seats. After the dissolution of Shinshinto, a highly fractionalized party system emerged. Going into the 200 election, the LDP had 266 seats, with the largest opponents being the Democratic Party of Japan (DPJ) with 94 seats, the Komeito with 52, the Liberal Party with 39, and the Communists with 23. The LDP worked closely with the Komei party and the Liberal Party, effectively making the DPJ the only significant opposition.

15LOCAL GOVERNMENT

Local government throughout Japan was strengthened by the Local Autonomy Law of 1947. Administratively, Japan is divided into 47 prefectures. Within these prefectures there are 652 cities, 2,002 towns, and 596 villages. The local chief executives, mayors, and village heads, together with prefectural assembly members, are directly elected. The city of Tokyo comprises 23 wards.

Local public bodies have the right to administer their own affairs as well as to enact their own regulations within the law. The National Diet cannot enact legislation for a specific public entity without the consent of the voters of that district. Local governments control school affairs, levy taxes, and carry out administrative functions in the fields of land preservation and development, pollution control, disaster prevention, public health, and social welfare. The Japanese government is seeking to decentralize power away from Tokyo by allowing prefectures to exercise greater fiscal and budgetary autonomy.

16JUDICIAL SYSTEM

The 1947 constitution provides for the complete independence of the judiciary. All judicial power is vested in the courts. The system consists of the Supreme Court, eight regional higher courts, district courts in each of the prefectures, and a number of summary courts. In addition, there are family courts, on the same level as the district courts, to adjudicate family conflicts and complaints such as partitions of estates, marriage annulments, and juvenile protection cases.

The Supreme Court consists of a chief justice and 14 other justices. The chief justice is appointed by the emperor on designation by the cabinet; the other justices, by cabinet appointment. All appointments are subject to popular review at the first general election following appointment and every 10 years thereafter in public referendum. Judges of the lesser courts also are appointed by the cabinet from lists of persons nominated by the Supreme Court. Their term of office is limited to 10 years, with the privilege of reappointment.

The Supreme Court is the court of last resort for determining the constitutionality of any law, order, regulation, or official act that is challenged during the regular hearing of a lawsuit. Abstract questioning of a law is prohibited and thus there is no judicial review. The Constitution affords criminal defendants a right to a speedy and public trial by an impartial tribunal. There is no right to a trial by jury. The constitution requires a judicial warrant issued by a judge for each search or seizure. Japan accepts compulsory jurisdiction of the International Court of Justice with reservation.

17ARMED FORCES

The reestablishment of Japanese defense forces has been a subject of heated debate in the period since World War II. Article 9 of the constitution renounces war as a sovereign right and the maintenance of "land, sea and air forces, as well as other war potential." During the Korean War, Gen. MacArthur recommended the establishment of a national police reserve. Following the signing of the San Francisco Peace Treaty, the reserve force was reorganized into a National Safety Agency (1 August 1952). Laws establishing a Defense Agency and a Self-Defense Force became effective on 1 July 1954, both under firm civilian control.

The strength of Japan's armed forces in 2000 was 236,300. The Ground Self-Defense Force had 145,900 personnel, organized into one armored and 11 infantry divisions, with independent infantry, airborne, artillery, training, engineer, and helicopter brigades; there were also 49,900 men in reserve components. The Maritime Self-Defense Force, consisting of 43,800 personnel, had 55 surface combatants, 16 combat submarines, and an air arm of about 90 combat aircraft and 90 armed helicopters. Air Self-Defense Force personnel numbered 45,200; combat aircraft totaled 330, including US-supplied jet fighters and air defense missiles. Many units in the armed forces are understrength because military service is voluntary and arduous. As a result of the war-renunciation clause of the constitution, Japan has armed itself with weapons for strategic defense. It has no long-range bombers or missiles, and its aircraft and naval vessels are deployed for air defense and antisubmarine warfare. These platforms could use deep strike missiles if required.

Although Japan's defense budgets—about $42.9 billion in 1998–99—rank high by world standards, they are modest in relation to gross domestic product (about 1%). In fact, Japan relies for its military security on US conventional and nuclear forces, and the US has repeatedly urged Japan to shoulder more of its own conventional defense burden. The US maintains extensive military facilities and 40,000 US troops in Japan. Japan is unlikely to reduce its defense budget due in part to China increasing theirs.

18INTERNATIONAL COOPERATION

Japan was admitted to UN membership on 18 December 1956, and it holds membership in ESCAP and all the nonregional specialized agencies. It is a member of the WTO and signatory to the Law of the Sea, participates in the Colombo Plan, and has permanent observer status with the OAS. In 1963, Japan became a member of IMF and the OECD. It is also a charter member of the Asian Development Bank, which came into operation in 1966; Japan furnished $200 million, a share equal to that of the US. Japan has been actively developing peaceful uses for nuclear energy, and in 1970 it signed the Geneva Protocol, which prohibits the use of poisonous and bacteriological weapons. In June 1976, Japan—the only nation to have suffered a nuclear attack—became the 96th signatory to the international Nuclear Nonproliferation Treaty.

Japan has been extending technical and financial aid to many countries, and in 1974 it established the Japan International Cooperation Agency to provide technical assistance to developing nations. Japan also was instrumental in establishing the Asian Productivity Organization, the objective of which is to organize national productivity movements in various Asian countries into a more effective movement on a regional scale. Japan has entered into cultural agreements with many European and Asian nations and maintains an educational exchange program with the US. Through the Japan Overseas Cooperation Volunteers, Japan sends youths to work in developing countries.

19ECONOMY

Japan's economy is the most advanced in Asia and the second largest in the world, behind that of the US; the size and wealth of its economic enterprises rival those of any nation. Estimates placed total GDP in 1998 at $2.903 trillion (purchasing power parity), according to the US Central Intelligence Agency. Japan was the first Asian country to develop a large urban middle-class industrial society. It was also the first Asian country where a sharp reduction in birthrate set the stage for notable further increases in per capita income.

Since 1952, the number of farmers has fallen sharply, while expansion has been concentrated in industry and trade. Domestic raw materials are far too limited to provide for the nation's needs, and imports are relied on for all the raw cotton, raw wool, bauxite, and crude rubber used, as well as for all oil supplies and varying proportions of other materials. To pay for these materials and for food and other import needs, Japan exports mainly manufactured products. Up until the mid-1980s, economic development depended on continued expansion in exports. With the steady appreciation of the yen in real terms since 1985, however, the country's economic structure has undergone some adjustment. Facilitated by growing wage rates, favorable credit conditions, cuts in personal and corporate income tax rates and other stimulative measures by the government, domestic demand as well as direct foreign investment have played an increasingly important role as a source of growth in recent years.

After two decades of rapid expansion following World War II, the Japanese economy, beginning with the world oil crisis in late 1973, suffered an extremely long and intense recession, one that weakened the world economy as well. In 1974, for the first time since World War II, the GNP fell (by 1.8%). The recession was cushioned, however, by the nation's ability to improve its trade balance (by $11 billion) by increasing exports while reducing imports. The recovery of the mid-1970s was slowed by a second oil crisis, and although the Japanese economy continued to outperform those of most other industrial countries, growth in GNP slowed to an estimated 4.1% yearly in real terms for 1979–82, compared with 8.9% for 1969–72. Meanwhile, the continued stimulation of exports, especially of automobiles and video equipment, combined with Japan's restrictive tariffs and other barriers against imports, led to increasingly strident criticism of the nation's trade practices in the US and Western Europe. As early as 1971, Japan agreed to limit textile exports to the US, and in the 1980s it also imposed limits on exports of steel, automobiles, and television sets. Similar limits were adopted for exports to Canada, France (where criticism focused on videocassette recorders), and the FRG. Nevertheless, Japan's trade surpluses with the US and other countries continued to swell through the mid-1980s, helped by a number of factors, most notably the misalignment of major currencies, particularly between the dollar and the yen.

During the late 1980s, a 70% appreciation of the yen's value against the US dollar helped narrow Japan's trade surplus by 19% for two consecutive years in 1988/89 and 1989/90. This was accompanied by low rates of unemployment as well as strong growth in consumer spending and private investment, in turn contributing to a healthy 5% annual growth rate in the GNP between 1987 and 1990. During the past several years, however, the trend has slowed considerably. The country's trade surplus rebounded to record high levels in 1993, while domestic demand has slackened and real GNP growth fell to 1.5% in 1992, its lowest level since the mid-1950s (aside from an episode of negative growth during the oil crisis-related recession of 1974). The recent downturn notwithstanding, it is likely that the country's educated and well-paid labor force, high rates of household savings and capital investment, and well managed government apparatus will facilitate a healthy pace of economic development in the long term.

In order to secure a stable and growing economy, there are reforms that have been proposed and are now in the process of being implemented. A major one is deregulation, which is being done selectively rather than across the board. The primary goal of deregulation is to increase competition. One consequence is that job security (which has been a staple in Japan) may diminish in less profitable companies.

Reform is more likely to succeed because it is not a political issue. There is a wide consensus for reform. As the economy has been stagnant by Japanese standards, reform is seen as the most viable way to achieve the rate of growth that occurred during the 1960s, 1970s, and 1980s. By early 1999, however, the government's spending program was bearing some fruit as the economy began to register some growth.

Finally, Japan's economy is not a planned economy, but in the past it has been a regulated one—and many argue that indeed it has been overregulated. Given the rate of growth in East Asia, it would appear that Japan has little choice except to institute reforms or be left behind.

[20]INCOME

The US Central Intelligence Agency (CIA) reports that in 1998 Japan's gross domestic product (GDP) was estimated at $2.9 trillion. The per capita GDP was estimated at $23,100. The annual growth rate of GDP was estimated at -2.6%. The average inflation rate in 1998 was 0.9%. The CIA defines GDP as the value of all final goods and services produced within a nation in a given year and computed on the basis of purchasing power parity (PPP) rather than value as measured on the basis of the rate of exchange. It was estimated that agriculture accounted for 2% of GDP, industry 38%, and services 60%.

The World Bank reports that for the same period per capita private consumption (in PPP terms) was $13,570. Private consumption includes expenditures of individuals, households, and nongovernmental organizations. It was estimated that between 1990 and 1998 private consumption grew at an annual rate of 1.9%. Approximately 12% of household consumption was spent on food, 7% on fuel, 2% on health care, and 22% on education. The richest 10% of the population accounted for approximately 22% of household consumption and the poorest 10% approximately 4.8%.

[21]LABOR

The labor force in 1998 comprised 67,930,000 persons. The distribution of employed workers was as follows: commerce, 22.8%; manufacturing, 21.2%; business, 9.1%; construction, 10.2%; agriculture, forestry, fishing, aquaculture, 5.3%; transportation and communications, 6.2%; and the remainder other sectors. Females comprised 41% of the work force in 1998. The number of unemployed reached 2,769,000, or 4.1% of the work force, in 1998, low by the standards of most industrial countries but high for Japan. Employers tend toward traditional paternalistic, often authoritarian, control over their workers, but in turn most regular workers have traditionally enjoyed permanent status.

Union membership was always less than half a million before World War II, but jumped to 6.2 million in 1955, 12.6 million in 1994, and 12 million by 1999. However, the rate of union membership has been decreasing in the past three decades, with 22% of all eligible workers unionized in 1999, compared to 39% in 1955. Union strength is greatest in local government employees, automobile workers, and electrical machinery workers. Most members are organized in units called enterprise unions, which comprise the employees of a single firm. Virtually all organized workers are affiliated with national organizations, of which the largest is the Japanese Trade Union Confederation (Shin-Rengo), established in 1987 following the dissolution of the Japanese Confederation of Labor (Domei), and incorporating the General Council of Trade Unions (Soyho) as of 1989. The Shin-Rengo was comprised of about 13,000 unions and had 7,600,000 members as of 1999. As of 1998, the minimum wage ranged from $34 to $50 per day, and labor legislation mandated a standard work week of 40 hours.

[22]AGRICULTURE

Crop production is vital to Japan despite limited arable land (11.7% of the total area) and the highest degree of industrialization in Asia. Steep land (more than 20°) has been terraced for rice and other crops, carrying cultivation in tiny patches far up mountainsides. With the aid of a temperate climate, adequate rainfall, soil fertility built up and maintained over centuries, and such a large farm population that the average farm has an area of only 1.2 ha (3 acres), Japan has been able to develop intensive cultivation. Agriculture exists in every part of Japan, but is especially important on the northern island of Hokkaido, which accounts for 10% of national production. Since World War II, modern methods, including commercial fertilizers, insecticides, hybrid seeds, and machinery, have been used so effectively that harvests increased substantially through the 1970s. Japan is the second-largest agricultural product importer in the world (after the US), with total agricultural product imports of $38.2 billion in 1997.

Almost all soybeans and feedstuffs and most of the nation's wheat are imported. In 1998, Japan produced 11.2 million tons of rice, the chief crop. In that year, rice accounted for about 94% of all cereal production. About 51% of all arable land is devoted to rice cultivation. Overproduction of rice, as a result of overplanting and a shift to other foods by the Japanese people, led the government in 1987 to adopt a policy of decreasing rice planting and increasing the acreage of other farm products. For many years the government restricted imports of cheaper foreign rice, but in 1995 the rice market was opened to imports, as the government implemented the Uruguay Round agreement on agriculture. Other important crops and their annual production in 1998 (in thousands of tons) include potatoes, 3,400; sugar beets, 3,685; mandarin oranges, 1,553; cabbage, 2,700; wheat, 570; barley, 193; soybeans, 145; tobacco, 68; and tea, 91.

As a result of the US-occupation land reform, which began in late 1946, nearly two-thirds of all farmland was purchased by the Japanese government at low prewar prices and resold to cultivators on easy terms. By the 1980s, nearly all farms were owner-operated, as compared with 23% before reform. A more telling trend in recent years has been the sharp growth in part-time farm households. Farmers are aging, and 77% of farm income is derived from other sources, such as industrial jobs. Although agriculture accounts for only 2% of GDP, about 10% of the population lives on farms. Despite increasing urbanization, 59% of all farms still cultivated less than 1 ha (2.7 acres) in 1999. As a result, Japanese agriculture intensively utilizes both labor and machinery for production. In 1995, Japan had 153,900 tractors, 85,700 rice-planting machines, and 66,800 combines.

23ANIMAL HUSBANDRY

Livestock production has been the fastest-growing sector in Japanese agriculture, with meat production increasing from 1.7 million tons in 1970 to three million tons in 1998. In 1997, Japan imported $7.6 billion in beef, pork, and poultry meat. In 1998 there were 9,800,000 hogs, 4,700,000 head of beef cattle, and 306 million chickens. That year, pork production reached 1,225,000 tons (up from 147,318 tons in 1960); beef, 527,000 tons (142,450 tons in 1960); milk, 8,595,000 tons (1,886,997 tons in 1960); and eggs, 2,580,000 tons. Japan is the single largest recipient of US agricultural exports; 36% of Japan's meat imports in 1995 came from the US.

24FISHING

Japan is one of the world's foremost fishing nations, accounting on average for about 8% of the world's catch. In 1997, the total catch was 7,363,775 tons, ranking third in the world. The waters off Japan include cold and warm currents in which fish abound. In 1990, there were 416,000 registered fishing boats which sailed both on nearby waters and in other fishing grounds in the Pacific Ocean, the South China Sea, and the Indian and Atlantic oceans. In 1989, per capita daily consumption of fish and shellfish was about 198 gm, one of the world's highest such averages. Annual per capita fish and shellfish consumption from 1988 to 1990

averaged 72 kg (158.7 lb). In 1997, despite domestic fish production, about $15.5 billion in fish and shellfish was imported in order to satisfy domestic demand.

Whales have been prized in Japan as a source of both food and a variety of byproducts, and Japanese whalers caught 2,769 whales in 1986. Japan ended commercial whaling in 1987, following the imposition of a worldwide ban on the hunting of endangered species of whales by the International Whaling Commission, but announced that it would catch 875 whales for "research" purposes. The 1991 Japanese whale catch of over 20,000 toothed whales of various species included 327 minke, 54 beaked, 355 pilot, and 1 humpback.

Competition for overseas fishing privileges has at various times brought Japan into conflict with Canada over salmon, with the former USSR over fishing in the Sea of Okhotsk and other Soviet waters (between 1905 and 1945 Japan had special treaty privileges in these waters), with the ROK and China over their limitations on Japanese fishing operations, with Australia over pearl fishing in the Arafura Sea, with Indonesia over fishing in what Indonesia regards as inland waters, and with the US, especially over fishing in north Pacific and Alaskan waters. Japan has been adversely affected by the adoption of the 200 mi fishing zone by the US and more than 80 other world nations. Fishing in waters claimed by the US (where about 70% of the Japanese catch originates) or by many other nations now requires payment of fees and special intergovernmental or private agreements.

Fish culture in freshwater pools, as well as in rice paddies, has long been practiced in Japan. Aquaculture provides an additional 1.5 million tons of fish annually. The leading species cultivated in 1997 were laver (nori), yesso scallops, Pacific cupped oysters, and Japanese amberjack. That year, aquacultural production was valued at $4.7 billion. Seaweed culture provides winter season activity for many fishermen. Pearl culture has for more than half a century been the foundation of a valuable export industry.

25FORESTRY

Forests cover nearly 67% of the total land area of Japan and in 1995 supplied about half the domestic demand for lumber and wood pulp. Of 25.1 million ha (62 million acres) of forest, the Japanese government owns 30.3%, which it maintains under strict regulations limiting overcutting. On private forest lands, cutting is less controlled. About 6.6 million ha (16.3 million acres) are reforested with trees less than 20 years old. Forest management and erosion control are urgent necessities in a land where gradients are very steep and flooding is frequent. Japan was the world's third leading producer of paper and paperboard in 1997 (after the US and China), at over 31 million tons.

About 40% of the forest area consists of plantations. The Japanese cedar (sugi), which grows in most of Japan, is the most exploited species, followed by Japanese cypress (hinoki) and Japanese red pine (akamatsu). These three species grow on 10 million ha (24.7 million acres) of plantation forest and were first planted in the 1950s and 1960s. In 1997, roundwood production totaled 22.5 million cu m, as compared with 49.1 million cu m in 1965. Domestic roundwood production met 45% of Japan's total wood fiber demand that year; the rest was supplied by imports. Total demand of wood products in 1995 consisted of lumber, 72%; plywood, 14%; wood chips, 10%; pulp, 3%; and others, 1%. In 1998, Japan's 12,810 saw mills processed 28 million tons of logs (48% domestic).

During the 1980s and 1990s, Japan became more reliant on imported wood to satisfy domestic demand. In 1995, Japan imported $19.4 billion in forest products, second only to the US. Japan is the world's dominant importer of softwood and tropical hardwood logs, and has become one of the largest importers of softwood lumber, which is mainly used for housing construction.

26MINING

Japan is not rich in minerals, and mining is a relatively insignificant economic activity, accounting for only 0.19% of GDP in 1997. However, mineral processing accounted for over 5% of GDP and played a key role in supplying raw material for the manufacturing sector. In 1997 Japan was the world's leading producer of selenium metal and electrolytic manganese dioxide; the second leading producer of cement, iodine, cadmium metal, pig iron, and crude steel; and the third-largest producer of copper metal, diatomite, limestone, nickel metal, and zinc metal.

Since the beginning of the 20th century, Japan has been compelled to import nearly all of its petroleum, iron ore, copper, aluminum, and nickel. Coal is the most important mineral product, accounting for slightly more than half of all mineral production by value. Like most other mineral production in Japan, coal production has been undergoing steady decline, falling from 38 million tons in 1970 to 4.3 million tons in 1997 (the lowest level since 1902). About 40% is produced on Hokkaido, and most of the remainder on Kyushu. The following figures give production in thousands of tons in 1997: iron ore, 4; metallic zinc, 71.6; lead, 5.2; and copper, 0.9. Mine output of gold and silver in 1997 amounted to 8,384 kg and 87,180 kg, respectively.

27ENERGY AND POWER

Japan is the fourth-largest energy consumer in the world. Japan's primary 1998 energy needs were supplied by oil (56%), coal (14%), natural gas (12%), nuclear power (14%), hydroelectricity (3.8%), and other sources. For many years, Japan has been second only to the US in oil consumption, using 5.5 million barrels of oil a day in 1998. In 1998, Japan imported some 5.4 million barrels of oil per day, primarily from the UAE, Saudi Arabia, and Indonesia; 140 million tons of coal, mostly from Australia and Canada; and 62.8 million cu m of natural gas, primarily from Indonesia. In 1998, more than 80% of Japan's energy needs were met by imports, the highest such percentage among industrial nations.

Japan produces less than 1% of its annual petroleum and natural gas requirements; exploration for petroleum continues in the East China Sea and the Sea of Japan. Japan also produced 4.8 million tons of coal in 1997; imports that year totaled 140.3 million tons, more than any other nation by a wide margin. To meet the growing requirements for steam coal by power plants, Japanese trading companies and energy firms are seeking long-term supply contracts with Australia, China, Colombia, New Zealand, South Africa, and the US.

Japan had an output of 995.9 billion kWh of electricity in 1998. Electricity is provided by several private companies, with the public Electric Power Development Co. and the Japan Atomic Power Co. playing supplementary roles in distribution. As of 1998, total electricity generating capacity stood at 219 million kW. Nuclear power plants accounted for roughly 20% of the total; thermal (oil, natural gas, coal) plants, 69%; hydroelectric plants, 10%; with the remainder from other plants (geothermal and other renewable resources). Japan ranks third, behind the US and France, in nuclear power production and plans to increase the percentage of nuclear-generated electricity to 42% by 2010 in spite of growing public opposition fueled by a series of accidents at nuclear power plants. As of 1998, Japan had 51 reactors in operation, with a total capacity of 43 GW million kW. These included the world's first Advanced Boiling Water Reactor, which came on line in 1997. Japan's amount of electricity consumed from nuclear plants increased by 73% between 1986 and 1995.

28INDUSTRY

Manufacturing has been a key element in Japan's economic expansion during three periods of phenomenal growth. First, during the 50-year rise of Japan from a feudal society in 1868 to a major world power in 1918, output in manufacturing rose more rapidly than that of other sectors. Second, during the 1930s, when Japan recovered from the world depression earlier and faster than any other country and embarked on an aggressive course in Asia, manufacturing, especially heavy industries, again had the highest rate of growth. Third, in the remarkable recovery since World War II, manufacturing, which had suffered severely during the latter stages of the war, was again a leader, although commerce and finance expanded even more rapidly.

Japanese industry is characterized by a complex system of exclusive buyer-supplier networks and alliances, commonly maintained by companies belonging to the same business grouping, or *keiretsu*. Such a system utilizes a web of vertical, horizontal, and even diagonal integration within the framework of a few large conglomerations. Keiretsu firms inhibit the foreign acquisition of Japanese firms through non-transparent accounting and financial practices, cross-holding of shares among keiretsu member firms (even between competitors), and by keeping a low proportion of publicly traded stock relative to total capital.

During the 1970s and early 1980s, the rate of Japan's industrial growth surpassed that of any other non-Communist industrialized country. Of the 26 largest industrial companies in the world in the mid-1980s—those with sales of $20 billion or more—four were Japanese: Toyota Motor, Matsushita Electric, Hitachi, and Nissan Motor. In addition to spectacular expansion in the volume of output, Japanese industry has also achieved impressive diversity, with maximal application of efficiency standards and technological input. As of 1997, industry accounted for about 38% of GDP and 33% of the total labor force.

A brief recession forced production cutbacks in 1965; longer and deeper recessions, related to rising world oil costs and diminished supplies, slowed Japan's economy in 1973–75 and again in 1978–80. At the same time, wage rates rose substantially, thereby reducing Japan's competitive advantage vis-á-vis other industrialized nations and prompting a major government effort to promote high-technology industries capable of making the most efficient use of the high educational level and technical competence of the Japanese labor force. Japan's industrial strategy, which involves close cooperation between business, government, and labor, is coordinated by the Ministry of International Trade and Industry (MITI). Particular emphasis has been given by MITI and other government agencies to encouraging and assisting research and development of new products and technologies.

Facing increasingly stiff competition from overseas trading partners in the 1980s, Japanese firms responded with several strategies, including product diversification, increased investment in overseas plants, as well as a greater focus on production for the domestic market. Despite declining profits with the economic downturn of the early 1990s, Japanese companies continued to make large investments in new plants and equipment; in 1992, these outlays amounted to over 20% of the GDP, well outstripping the level of private investment in the US.

Manufacture of electrical machinery ranks first in value added, accounting for about 18% of the total in 1991. Nonelectrical machinery ranks second, accounting for 12% of total manufacturing value added, followed by transportation equipment (10% of MVA) and chemicals (9% of MVA). The electronics industry grew with extraordinary rapidity in the 1980s and now leads the world. Radio and television sets and household appliances have been exported in large quantities since World War II; in addition to generators, motors, transformers, and other heavy equipment, the industry now produces automatic devices, electronic computers, videocassette recorders, tape recorders, calculators, and communications and broadcasting equipment. Major electronic products in 1991 included 4.5 million facsimile machines; 18.2 million telephones; 3.0 million computers; 28 billion transistors; and 17.7 billion semiconductor integrated circuits. Also produced that year were 11.2 million radios, 15.6 million television sets, and 30.7 million videocassette recorders. Other manufactures in 1991 included 389.8 million watches, 17.7 million 35-mm still cameras, and 4.3 million microwave ovens. Japan plays an increasingly important role in the computer industry. The production value of Japanese personal and general purpose computers totaled ¥2.4 trillion in 1991. By 1987, Japan was fiercely competing with the US in developing high-tech products, such as superconducting materials.

Japan is the world's leading shipbuilder; more than half the ships built are exported, including some of the world's largest oil tankers. Rapid increases in shipbuilding capacity by Brazil and the ROK reduced demand for Japanese-built ships from a peak of 38 million gross tons of new orders in 1973 to 7.0 million gross tons in 1991. The decline prompted direct government intervention in the ailing industry and the closing of close to 37% of dockyard facilities in 1980.

Passenger car production expanded rapidly in the 1970s, as Japan moved to fill rising demand for fuel-efficient cars in the US and Europe. In the early 1980s, Japan emerged as the world's leading automobile producer, topping the US for the first time in the history of the industry. Dominant industry giants are Nissan and Toyota which together produced about three-fifths of all passenger cars in the mid-1980s. In 1995, a total of 10,195,536 passenger cars, trucks, and buses were manufactured (down from a high of 13,486,796 in 1990). Restrictions imposed on Japanese automobile exports have promoted a marked increase in Japanese investment in automobile manufacturing facilities (engine manufacture, assembly as well as research and development) in the US, Western Europe, and other overseas markets. In recent years, Japanese manufactures have also sustained growth through greater focus on producing for the booming domestic motor vehicle market, currently the second largest in the world. Japan's superior technology in the design of bicycles, motorcycles, buses, and high-speed trains has been another major factor in the growth of the transport industry.

The chemical and petrochemicals industry has been another of the economy's key growth sectors since the late 1960s, in part due to rising domestic demand. Products include industrial chemicals such as sulfuric acid, caustic soda and fertilizers, as well as plastics, dyestuffs, paints, and other items for domestic use. Polyethylene production increased by 10–15% annually during the late 1980s; output in 1991 was 2,982,000 tons. Japan must import much of the iron ore and coking coal used in its steel industry, which ranked second only to the former USSR's in the mid-1980s. Output of crude steel peaked at 119.3 million tons in 1973 but declined to 101.6 million tons in 1995.

Textiles and apparel, Japan's main exports during the years immediately following World War II, have steadily declined in importance and accounted for only 2.5% of total value added in 1991 (as compared with 3.5% in 1985). Output of cotton and woolen fabrics, yarns, and rayon and acetate remains substantially below 1965 levels. The Japanese textile industry has been especially hard hit by rising wage rates and competition from developing nations, especially the other industrializing countries of East Asia.

Japan's semiconductor business has grown in size and profit due to the trade pact between Japan and the US. While some argue that this pact had a negative effect on Japan's domestic chip market, it now appears, that these chip companies have become more efficient and therefore more profitable. Both the US and Japan have become so intertwined in the semiconductor area that neither could afford to terminate the relationship.

During the severe recession of the 1990s, Japan's industrial production rate declined by 6.9% in 1998. Japan's major industries continue to be steel production, heavy electrical equipment, automobiles and parts, telecommunication equipment, chemical, ship building, and processed foods. Their fishing industry is still the largest and most productive in the world.

Finally, Japan has surpassed the US as the largest manufacturer of automobiles.

29 SCIENCE AND TECHNOLOGY

The Japanese rank second only to the United States in spending on scientific research and technology development. However, in Japan, 80% of all research and development is carried out by industry, in contrast to the United States, where industry undertakes about half of all research and development (the US government supports the rest). This is important because industry is more likely to support the type of research that will result in new technologies and products. For many people, this breakdown of research and development funding explains why Japan has become such an economic powerhouse: much more of the total research and development budget is focused on near-term and commercial science and technology. Some of the more successful applications of the fruits of Japanese research and development include high-speed trains, robotics, semiconductor chips, telecommunications, cancer research, and environmental technologies.

In 1987–97, science and engineering students accounted for 21% of college and university enrollments. Nearly 5,000 scientists and engineers per million population worked in research and development in 1987–97. Despite Japan's economic downturn in the 1990s, it is likely that investments in both equipment and personnel will grow. In 1998, high-tech exports were valued at $94.8 billion and accounted for 26% of manufactured exports.

In terms of the Japanese government's role in national science and technology, three ministries are important. The Ministry of Education, or Monbusho, provides most of the support and funding for scientific education and training at the university level in Japan. In the 1990s, Monbusho led a national effort to improve science and technology education at universities, particularly in "basic" research (areas where research does not necessarily have to pay off in commercial products). Another organization, the Science and Technology Agency (STA) promotes science and technology policies, and acts as the Prime Minister's leading policy and budgetary agency. It performs this function through annual "white papers" which describe the current state—and future goals—of Japanese science and technology. The Ministry of International Trade and Industry (MITI) is probably the ministry best known by Americans. MITI promotes and protects Japanese industry by sending them signals and giving guidance to those firms which undertake research and development. MITI has been instrumental in providing close government-industry cooperation in many high technology fields, including computers, electronics, and biotechnology.

Regional research institutions such as Tskuba Science City and Kansai Science Park also play a role in fostering Japanese research and development. Their growth since the 1970s has begun to shift some of the focus and power of the national government and industry in Tokyo to the regional prefectures. International cooperation with the United States in areas like global warming and space launches may create new opportunities for greater scientific research at local, regional, and national levels in Japan.

Japan has numerous universities and colleges that offer courses in basic and applied sciences. The country's National Science Museum, founded in 1877, is located in Tokyo. The University of Tokyo has botanical gardens that were established in 1684.

30DOMESTIC TRADE

Marketing services and channels are complex and varied. In 1991, 11,710,000 persons were engaged in domestic, wholesale, and retail trade. The number of wholesale and retail stores was 2,067,000; of these, 72% were small stores with fewer than four employees. Street hawkers and peddlers provide certain foods and small consumer items; street stalls offer food, clothing, and household and other goods. Specialty shops exist in great profusion, and about 100 associations of such shops represent common interests. Japan's first department store was opened in 1910. In 1957 there were 170 department stores; by 1991, the figure had risen to 2,004, accounting for 14% of total retail sales. There are chain stores owned and operated by a single management, and there are voluntary chains of independent stores operating in association. Japan also has numerous cooperatives, principally consumer, agricultural, and fishing. A key characteristic of the country's distribution system has been the long term and carefully cultivated nature of the supplier and wholesaler or retail store relationship, necessitating considerable commitment of time and outreach effort by foreign companies wishing to enter the Japanese market. Recent revisions in the Large Scale Retail Store Law has loosened government regulation of the distribution system, allowing the establishment of large discounters and mega-stores such as Toys-R-Us, which are likely to offer growing competition to smaller retailers in the future.

In retail trade, cash transactions have been traditional, but various forms of installment selling are increasingly being used, especially in the sale of durable goods. The use of charge accounts is growing rapidly. Promotion by displays, advertising, and other methods used in Western countries is growing rapidly in Japan. Advertising appears in the daily press, in the numerous weekly and monthly magazines, and in special publications of many kinds. Radio and television also carry extensive advertising, excepting those channels run by the government's Japan Broadcasting Corporation. Normal shop hours are 10 AM to 8 PM, seven days a week, although department stores shut their doors at 7 PM and are closed one day a week; government offices are open 9 AM to 5 PM, Monday through Friday, and from 9 to 12:30 on the first and third Saturday of every month only. Banks are open from 9 AM to 3 PM Monday through Friday, and are closed on Saturdays and Sundays.

In some ways, Japan's method of conducting retail business is beginning to resemble that of the US. One way to accomplish a more consumer-friendly market is to bring mega-malls to Japan. This will include not only retail stores, but also restaurants and entertainment. Sufficient parking has generally been regarded as a problem in the past but that, too, is being addressed. The malls will be a joint venture between American developers and MGS Japan. There are currently six sites being considered and the first is scheduled to open in 1998. There is a 10-year goal to open 10 mega malls. Although Japan already has a number of shopping malls, the ones being proposed will be far larger. The purpose is to provide the Japanese consumer with more choices and lower prices.

31FOREIGN TRADE

Foreign trade remains essential to the Japanese economy. Imports consist mostly of fuel, foodstuffs, industrial raw materials, and industrial machinery. Exports are varied, but manufactures now account for nearly all of the total. Cars represent a leading export product, with the US, Canada, Australia, Germany and the UK the main markets. The export of office machinery, scientific and optical equipment is also important. South Korea, China, and Taiwan are among the main buyers of Japan's iron and steel, while plastic materials and fertilizers are shipped primarily to South Korea and the Southeast Asian countries, and woven fabrics are supplied to China, the US, Hong Kong, and Saudi

Arabia. Only a small fraction of Japan's total exports (around 0.5%) consists of food items, mainly fish.

In light of growing overseas concern about Japan's continuing large trade surplus, the US and Japanese governments collaborated on the Structural Impediments Initiative of 1989. Steps taken in wake of the Initiative's 1990 report have included a variety of import and direct foreign investment promotion measures, including deregulation, accelerated government spending on public infrastructure, and support services for foreign businesses.

Manufactured products make up most of Japan's commodity exports, and 20% of the world's total manufactured exports. The automobile is the country's most important industry (19%), along with computers and electronic equipment (12%). Japan also makes 32% of the world's exported ships. The top 10 exports are:

	% OF COUNTRY TOTAL	% OF WORLD TOTAL
Automobiles	10.0	20
Transistors, valves, etc	8.4	24
Car parts	4.5	17
Telecommunications equipment	4.4	18
computers	3.9	15
Office machine parts	3.8	19
Electrical machinery	3.2	19
Engines	3.0	24
Ships and boats	2.7	32
Switchgear	2.5	18

In 1997 Japan's imports were distributed among the following categories:

Consumer goods	16.1%
Food	12.4%
Fuels	18.4%
Industrial supplies	26.5%
Machinery	20.0%
Transportation	5.2%
Other	1.4%

Principal trading partners in 1998 (in millions of US dollars) were as follows:

COUNTRY	EXPORTS	IMPORTS	BALANCE
United States	119,717	67,518	52,199
China	42,636	38,811	3,825
Taiwan	25,601	10,225	15,376
Germany	19,090	10,686	8,404
Korea	15,400	12,142	3,258
Singapore	14,780	4,717	10,063
United Kingdom	14,626	5,847	8,779
Thailand	9,352	8,165	1,187
Malaysia	9,330	8,684	646
Indonesia	4,299	10,824	-6,525

32BALANCE OF PAYMENTS

Beginning in 1981, surpluses in Japan's current accounts increased rapidly, reaching $49 billion in 1985 and $86 billion in 1986, the latter being 18 times the level of 1981. These huge surpluses resulted largely from the high value of the dollar relative to the yen; price declines of primary goods, such as petroleum, also enhanced Japan's favorable trade position. Japan's mounting surpluses and the rising deficits of the US forced the US and other leading industrial nations to attempt to realign their currencies, especially the dollar and the yen, in September 1985. Within two years the yen rose 70% against the dollar. The yen's appreciation increased the competitiveness of American products and contributed to the reduction of Japan's external imbalances through 1990, when the current account surplus fell by 37.4%, due to higher expenses for imported oil and rising expenditures by Japanese traveling abroad. Whereas long-term capital outflows exceeded Japan's current account surplus from 1984 through 1990, by 1991 the outflow shifted predominantly to short-term capital, and overseas direct investment slowed.

The US Central Intelligence Agency reports that in 1998 the purchasing power parity of Japan's exports was $440 billion while imports totaled $319 billion resulting in a trade balance of $121 billion.

The International Monetary Fund (IMF) reports that in 1998 Japan had exports of goods totaling $374 billion and imports totaling $252 billion. The services credit totaled $62 billion and debit $112 billion. The following table summarizes Japan's balance of payments as reported by the IMF for 1998 in billions of US dollars.

Current Account		121
Balance on goods	122	
Balance on services	-49	
Balance on income	57	
Current transfers	-9	
Capital Account		-14
Financial Account		-117
Direct investment abroad	-25	
Direct investment in Japan	3	
Portfolio investment assets	-114	
Portfolio investment liabilities	74	
Other investment assets	38	
Other investment liabilities	-93	
Net Errors and Omissions		4
Reserves and Related Items		6

³³BANKING AND SECURITIES

Japan's highly sophisticated banking system continues to play a dominant role in financing the country's and the world's economic development. In the mid-1980s, while the US was becoming a debtor nation, Japan became the world's largest creditor. Banks provide not only short-term but also long-term credit, which often in effect becomes fixed capital in industry. In terms of sheer size, Japanese banks occupy some of the top spots in world-wide bank ratings.

The controlling national monetary institutions are the Bank of Japan (founded in 1882) and the Ministry of Finance. The Bank of Japan, as central bank, has power over note issue and audits financial institutions to provide guidance for improving banking and management practices. Ceilings for interest rates are set by the bank, while actual rates, commissions, and discounts are arranged by unofficial agreements among bankers and other financial institutions, including the National Bankers' Association. A new banking law, replacing the National Banking Law of 1928, was adopted in 1982. Its objectives were to increase competition in the financial world by enabling banks to sell bonds and by authorizing both banks and securities firms to sell commercial paper and certificates of deposit.

Eleven important city banks, with branches throughout the country, account for about two-thirds of all commercial bank assets, the rest accruing to 131 regional banks, 7 trust banks, and 83 foreign banks. In addition, 112 foreign banks have representative offices in Japan. Of special interest are the postal savings facilities, which are used by many Japanese families and have assumed many of the aspects of a huge state-owned banking business.

The Foreign Exchange Law was changed to totally liberalize cross-border transactions in 1998. Important foreign exchange banks include the city banks, long-term credit banks, trust banks, major local banks, major mutual loan and savings banks, and the Japanese branches of foreign banks. Such governmental financial institutions as the Japan Export-Import Bank, the Central Bank for Commercial and Industrial Associations, and the Central Bank for Agriculture and Forestry also participate in foreign exchange markets.

The rapid expansion of bank lending and the importance of land and stocks as assets in Japan's financial sector have exposed its financial institutions to the risks stemming from falling asset prices. Thus one of the root problems of Japan's difficulty in returning to a trend rate of GDP growth lies in the fragility of the financial sector. Banks and other financial institutions have been rocked by the huge sums of non-performing debt, stemming from an earlier lending spree based on inflated land values as collateral. In the aftermath of the collapse of the "bubble economy," many of the generous loans extended, especially to land and property developers, cannot be repaid or even serviced. Japan's 21 major banks, including the 11 city banks, wrote off about ¥11 trillion ($102 billion) of bad debts at the end of March 1996.

The bad debt held by the seven failed "jusen" (housing loan companies established by banks and agricultural financiers), which were liquidated partly at public expense, led to huge secondary losses in other areas of the financial sector. The liquidated *jusen* moved their assets to the newly established Housing Loan Administration Corp., which had the responsibility, from the beginning of its operations in October 1996, of recovering loans from the seven companies. This was unlikely, however, since not only would many property companies go bankrupt, but also much of the bad debt was extended illegally or to companies associated with *yakuza* (gangsters). Consequently, several *jusen* executives were arrested in 1996 on charges of alleged aggravated breach of trust.

The most dramatic merger was that between the Bank of Tokyo and Mitsubishi Bank in April 1996. This "mega-merger" created the world's largest bank, which became highly competitive in global financial markets. In 1999, three Japanese banks: Dai-Ichi Kangyo Bank, Fuji Bank, and IBI, announced a merger worth more than $1.3 trillion, surpassing all other large financial institutions. The other premier Japanese banks in 1999 were Sumitomo Bank, Sanwa Bank, and Sakura Bank.

Major securities exchanges are in Tokyo, Hiroshima, Fukuoka, Nagoya, and Osaka; small regional exchanges are in Kyoto, Niigata, and Sapporo. Although prior to World War II most stocks were held by large business firms (zaibatsu), stocks are now available for public subscription. The Tokyo Stock Exchange, the largest in the world, is the most important in Japan.

In the late 1980s, there were three categories of securities companies in Japan, the first consisting of the "Big Four" securities houses (among the six largest such firms in the world): Nomura, Daiwa, Nikko, and Yamaichi. The Big Four played a key role in international financial transactions and were members of the New York Stock Exchange. Nomura was the world's largest single securities firm; its net capital, in excess of US$10 billion in 1986, exceeded that of Merrill Lynch, Salomon Brothers, and Shearson Lehman combined. In 1986 Nomura became the first Japanese member of the London Stock Exchange. Nomura and Daiwa were primary dealers in the US Treasury bond market. The second tier of securities firms were affiliates of the Big Four, while some were affiliated with banks. In 1986, 83 of the smaller firms were members of the Tokyo Securities and Stock Exchange. Japan's securities firms derived most of their incomes from brokerage fees, equity and bond trading, underwriting, and dealing. Other services included the administration of trusts. In the late 1980s a number of foreign securities firms, including Salomon Brothers and Merrill Lynch, became players in Japan's financial world.

The Tokyo Securities and Stock Exchange became the largest in the world in 1988, in terms of combined market value of outstanding shares and capitalization, while the Ósaka Stock Exchange ranked third after those of Tokyo and New York.

34 INSURANCE

After 56 years, the Japanese Insurance Business Law was revised in 1997. The purpose of the newly revised law is competition, to protect policy holders, and to promote greater management efficiency. The law allowed, for the first time, cross entries of life and non-life companies into each other's sector through the establishment of subsidiary companies. In response to this development, 6 life and 11 non-life companies have set up subsidiaries. Firms may not engage in life and non-life insurance at the same time. In 1987 there were 47 Japanese insurance firms (24 life and 23 non-life) and 41 foreign companies transacting insurance business. Premiums totaled $241 billion, or 9.07% of the GDP. Per capita premiums totaled $678.6 for life and $989.6 for non-life insurance. Both joint-stock and mutual companies are permitted.

Life insurance is by far the most extensive of all classes of insurance; premium income is more than three times that of all non-life premium income. In 1997, life premium income totaled ¥477 billion, the world's largest by far. Japan is now the world's largest holder of life and health insurance. More than 90% of the population owned life insurance at the end of the 1980s, and the amount held per person was at least 50% greater than in the US. Many Japanese used insurance companies as savings vehicles. Nippon Life Insurance Co., the world's largest insurance firm, was reportedly the biggest single holder of US Treasury securities in 1989.

In the non-life field, automobile insurance is the largest sector. (Automobile liability insurance is compulsory.) Personal accident insurance was next in importance, followed by fire, marine cargo, and marine hull insurance.

In the mid-1990s the combined Japanese life and non-life insurance market had the world's largest share with 30.8% of the world total premium amounting to $606 billion. The life insurance market was 42.6% of the world market, and the non-life market with 15.2% with the premium of $129 billion was the second largest in the world after the US where the premium was $342.8 billion. Until October 1996 the Japanese non-life market consisted of 23 domestic companies, but has reached 29 in 1997. On the life sector, the number has increased to 36.

35 PUBLIC FINANCE

Plans for the national budget usually begin in August, when various agencies submit their budget requests to the Ministry of Finance. On the basis of such requests, the ministry, other government agencies, and the ruling party start negotiations. The government budget plan usually is approved by the Diet without difficulty, and the budget goes into effect in April. Deficits, financed by public bond sales, have steadily increased in size since the 1973 oil crisis. As a result, the ratio of gross debt to GNP has risen from 8% in 1970 to 60% by 1987. By 1990, debt servicing was absorbing over 20% of budgeted expenditures.

Since 1982, Japan has pursued tight fiscal policies and has attempted to constrain government debt. In June 1987, however, as a response to appeals from other nations to reduce international imbalances, Japan initiated a $35 billion public works spending package, followed up by $10 billion in tax cuts. In recent years, however, fiscal stimulus policies have contributed to an increasing budget deficit. Japan's government deficit was 3% of GDP in 1994 and reached 4.3% of GDP in 1995, due to ongoing high levels of public sector borrowing. The government's focus on fiscal policy to compensate for a tight monetary policy has restricted spending on infrastructure.

The US Central Intelligence Agency (CIA) estimates that in 1999 Japan's central government took in revenues of approxi-
mately $407 billion and had expenditures of $711 billion including capital expenditures of $86 billion. Overall, the government registered a deficit of approximately $304 billion.

The following table shows an itemized breakdown of government revenues and expenditures. The percentages were calculated from data reported by the International Monetary Fund. The dollar amounts (millions) are based on the CIA estimates provided above.

REVENUE AND GRANTS	100%	407,000
Tax revenue	81.1%	330,155
Non-tax revenue	14.9%	60,752
Capital revenue	0.6%	2,319
Grants	3.4%	13,774
EXPENDITURES	100%	711,000
General public services	2.4%	16,990
Defense	4.1%	29,196
Public order and safety	1.2%	8,798
Education	6.0%	42,854
Health	1.6%	11,367
Social security	36.8%	261,641
Housing and community amenities	13.8%	97,825
Recreation, cultural, and religious affairs	0.1%	1,003
Economic affairs and services	3.3%	23,762
Other expenditures	30.6%	217,563

36 TAXATION

After World War II, Japan adopted a tax system relying mainly on direct taxes, like those in the US and the UK. The most important of these are the income tax and corporation tax.

The National Tax Administration Agency, a branch of the Ministry of Finance, administers income and corporation tax laws. In addition, the Tax System Council files recommendations for revision of the system every three years. Individuals are subject to a national income tax as well as local (prefectural and municipal) residence and business taxes. In 1996, income tax rates ranged from 10% on taxable income of ¥3.3 million or less to 50% on income over ¥30 million. Combined local taxes are applied at the rates of 5% to 15%. In 1993, the national corporate income tax rate was 37.5%, with a local inhabitants tax of 17.3% to 20.7% and a local enterprise tax of 6% to 13.2%. These rates are exclusive of temporary surtaxes and a capital gains tax.

Additional national taxes include customs duties; a 5% value-added tax; a stamp tax; inheritance and gift taxes; a monopoly profits tax; a sugar excise tax; taxes on liquor, gasoline, and other commodities; and travel, admissions, and local road taxes.

37 CUSTOMS AND DUTIES

The Japanese tariff system is administered by the Customs Bureau of the Ministry of Finance. Under pressure from trading partners alarmed over their trade deficits with Japan, the government in 1979 agreed to implement over an eight-year period (subsequently accelerated) a series of tariff cuts and associated market-opening measures known as the Tokyo Round Mutual Tariff Reductions. The Tokyo Round lowered the effective overall tariff rate from 3.7% to 3%, one of the world's lowest, with nearly half of all imports entering without levy. As of 1997, the tariff was 2%. However, import duties remain relatively high for certain agricultural and manufactured goods. In 1987, tariffs were removed from tobacco and liquor (except beer and sake), and the rates on aluminum products were lowered. Quantity quotas and tariff quotas are still applied to some goods. There is a free-trade zone at Naha, on Okinawa; no free-trade zones function on the main islands.

38FOREIGN INVESTMENT

Cumulative foreign investment in Japan (since 1950) totaled $37,918 million as of 1995, of which US firms held 41%; Netherlands, 9%; Switzerland, 6%; Germany, 5%; Canada, 4%; UK, 4%; and others, 31%. In 1995/96, most foreign direct investment in Japan was directed towards the manufacturing sector (40%, half of it in machinery), followed by services (31%), retail and wholesale trade (22%), and finance and insurance (4%). Annual new investment into Japan rose from $2.78 billion in 1989/90 to $7.08 billion in 1995/96; average annual new investment between 1989/90 and 1995/96 was $4.19 billion. Due to continued recession, new foreign direct investment slumped to $5.53 billion in 1997, the last year for which statistics are available.

Japanese investments abroad have expanded steadily since the 1970s, the result both of liberalization on the outflow of capital and of the prosperity of the Japanese economy. It has also been due in part to increased investment in the US and EU as a conciliatory move to lessen the trade gap between Japan and the two industrial regions. Net annual direct investment outflows remained near $5 billion in the late 1970s but climbed steadily between 1985 and 1991 when they reached $48 billion, declining somewhat to $30.7 billion in 1992. Overseas direct investments made by Japan totaled $41 billion in 1993/94 and $51.4 billion in 1994/95. In 1996, Japan reportedly invested $50 billion overseas and attracted only about $7 billion in inward direct investment. Of the total Japanese overseas investment of ¥5,409.4 billion outstanding in 1995/96, ¥2,478.9 billion was invested in the US (up from ¥1,852.5 billion in 1993/94), ¥387.3 billion in the UK, ¥282.8 billion in China, ¥272 in Indonesia, ¥167.5 billion in Hong Kong, ¥158.1 billion in Thailand, ¥125.6 billion in Singapore, ¥123.8 billion in the Netherlands, ¥117.3 billion in the Cayman Islands, and ¥113.7 billion in Panama. In 1995/96, some 48% of Japanese investment was in North America (up from 32% in 1985), 24% in Asia, 9% in Latin America and the Caribbean, 15% in Europe, 2% in Oceania, and the remainder in Africa and the Middle East. About 42% of the investment total in 1995/96 was in manufacturing: electronics accounted for 14%; transportation equipment, 8%; metals, 5%; chemicals, 4%; machinery, 3%; and other manufacturing, 8%. Non-manufacturing sectors (58% of total investment) included: finance and insurance, 16%; real estate, 13%; commerce and trade, 10%; services, 8%; transportation, 4%; mining, 3%; and other sectors, 4%.

Foreign investment in Japan is far less than in other G-7 countries. One reason for this is that in the past, the Japanese government discouraged foreign investment. A second but perhaps more significant reason is the high cost of doing business in Japan, which, in turn, reduces profits. Some of the barriers are now less significant with the signing of the US-Japan Investment Accord signed in July 1995.

There is still a marked imbalance in Japan's investment in other countries compared to other countries investing in Japan, i.e., the former is far greater than the latter. As an example, in terms of million of dollars invested by Japan in 1994 and 1995 Japan invested $17,331 million in the US in 1994 and $22,649 million in 1995. During those same two years, the US invested $1,915 million and $1,837 million, respectively, in Japan. During those same two years, Germany invested $502 million and $174 million in Japan, respectively, while Japan invested $727 million and $550 million, respectively, in Germany. In 1996 Japan's ratio of inward to outward foreign direct investment flows was 1:9.77.

Finally, if one examines Asia, South Korea invested $71 million and $68 million in Japan during 1996 and 1997, respectively, while Japan invested $415 million and $443 million in South Korea during those same years. The imbalance between China and Japan is even greater. During 1994 and 1995, China invested $19 million in Japan, while Japan invested slightly over $7,000 million in China.

One should not conclude that barriers account for this imbalance. As the world's second largest economy, a disparity of income would likely play a significant role as would Japan's limited natural resources.

39ECONOMIC DEVELOPMENT

Japan's phenomenal economic growth since the 1950s has been based on an efficient blend of two economic tendencies. First is government activism in national planning and implementation, with guidance of the largely free economy via sophisticated and powerful monetary and fiscal policies. Second is the distinctively Japanese way of coupling largely private ownership of assets with conservative, public-spirited management. Especially significant is the role of the Ministry of International Trade and Industry (MITI), which coordinates national industrial policies consistent with economic and social growth. In a unique government-industry collaboration sometimes referred to overseas as "Japan, Inc.," MITI selects and nurtures industries targeted as important to Japan's future economic growth. Industries so targeted have included chemicals, iron and steel, shipbuilding, and transistor radios in the 1960s; automobiles and electronics in the 1970s; and computers, computer chips, and other high-technology industries for the 1980s. In addition to stimulating new industries, MITI also smoothes the way for plant closings and worker retraining in industries targeted for de-emphasis, such as textiles in the 1970s and the ailing coal-mining and shipbuilding industries in the 1980s. Most recently, MITI has also assumed an active role in lessening Japan's positive trade imbalances through a variety of import promotion measures, in collaboration with both domestic companies and foreign firms. Close ties between government and industry are illustrated by the ministries' issuance of informal "administrative guidance" to Japanese companies, the frequent placement of retired bureaucrats in Japanese companies and trade associations, and the delegation of quasi-regulatory authority to trade associations (which are often allowed to devise and regulate their own insider rules).

The objectives of maintaining rapid GNP growth, controlling inflation, and developing Japan's social and industrial infrastructure have been the concern of the Economic Planning Agency, which produced the successful Ikeda plan (to double the national income between 1961 and 1970) and releases projections of key indicators at frequent intervals. In the main, the Ikeda plan consisted of a series of projections of growth in a free market economy, with the basic assumption—the continued growth of Japan's overseas trade—largely outside of government control. During the plan's 10-year span, an annual growth of 11% in GNP was realized, as against the forecast rate of 7.2%. An economic and social development plan (1967–75) accomplished a GNP growth rate of 10.6%, as against 8.2% projected.

A second economic and social plan (1970–75) projected a continued annual growth rate of 10.6%. The 1973 world oil crisis and its aftermath severely shook Japan's trade-dependent economy, however; in 1974, the GNP actually shrank by 1.8%, the first and only such negative growth in three decades. In 1975, the cabinet approved a new economic and social plan for 1979–85 calling for an average annual growth rate of 5.7%. However, the impact of the second oil crisis in 1978 necessitated downward revisions of projected growth targets. Plans to stimulate the economy by increasing public-works spending and cutting taxes were approved in October 1983 and in May 1987. Also enacted in 1989 was a Value-Added-Tax to strengthen the government's revenue base while allowing reductions in personal and corporate income tax.

In 1988, a five-year plan was adopted to sustain real GNP growth at 3.8% per year, maintain low unemployment (2.5% per year), contain inflation, reduce the country's trade surplus, and improve the quality of life through a shorter work week and stabilized property prices. Many these objectives were achieved or surpassed in the closing years of the decade. After 1992, however, the economy's downturn was likened by some analysts to the 1974 recession in its severity and length. Economic indicators included steep declines and sluggish recovery in the stock market index since 1989, falling real estate prices, as well as a shrunken rate of GNP growth, despite surging exports. To prompt a recovery, the Ministry of Finance approved large stimulus packages for 1992 and 1993, totaling $85.6 billion and $119 billion in expenditures, respectively. Under the Structural Impediments Initiative, the government sought to sustain growth while also reducing the country's external trade imbalances. Among the main steps taken under the Initiative was a 10-year program targeting the expenditure of up to $8 trillion for the construction or renovation of airports, bridges, roads, ports, telecommunications systems, resorts, retirement communities, medical facilities, and other forms of public infrastructure development. Real growth during the 1990s hovered around 1% a year. The reasons for this are not as clear as in the 1970s when oil interruptions slowed the pace of development. Since Japanese wages have been rising, wage pressures are creating a higher cost for business, which would tend to make Japan less competitive in a world that is becoming increasingly more competitive. The Asian Tigers such as Singapore, Taiwan, or Hong Kong, have seen their economies grow at a much higher rate than Japan and China's economic growth rate of 10% a year during the 1990s. In 1999, Japan began a tentative recovery from its longest and most severe recession since the end of World War II.

Japan's financial assistance to developing countries and international agencies has grown significantly in recent years, making it one of the world's leading donor countries and its largest net creditor. The government has committed itself to large increases in official development assistance to developing countries and multilateral agencies since the late 1980s. In 1991, ODA totaled $11.0 million, as compared with $3,797 million in 1985. Private outflows in 1991 totaled $11.1 million, as compared with $8,022 million in 1985. ODA projects in the construction sector totaled $9 billion in 1997. Among the top recipients of bilateral ODA from Japan were Indonesia, China, the Philippines, Thailand, Bangladesh, and Malaysia. Japan's increasing financial assistance to developing countries like China and Indonesia is an indication that the Japanese government is willing to sacrifice short term gain for longer term prosperity and stability. In essence, Japan is helping to create viable trading partners; and since Japan is a trading state, this strategy will enhance Japan's economic development over the long term.

40 SOCIAL DEVELOPMENT

Living standards reflect Japan's rapid economic development since the mid-1960s. Greatly contributing to the social stability of the nation is the strong sense of family solidarity among the Japanese; virtually every home has its butsudan, or altar of the ancestors, and most elderly people are cared for in the homes of their grown children. A further source of social stability has been Japan's employment system, noted for its "lifetime employment" of workers from the time they enter the company after completing their education to the time they retire. Traditionally, layoffs and dismissals of employees were rare, even during times of recession. With Japan's economic downturn of the early 1990s, however, companies were forced to downsize. By 1997 the nation's unemployment rate had climbed to a record 3.5%, and number of middle-aged workers who had expected to remain with the same firm until retirement found themselves job hunting.

The present social insurance system, considerably expanded in the 1970s, includes national health insurance, welfare annuity insurance, maternity coverage, unemployment insurance, workers' accident compensation insurance, seamen's insurance, a national government employees' mutual aid association, and day workers' health insurance. It also provides pension plans designed to maintain living standards for the elderly, based on years of employment, and for families of deceased workers. Per capita expenditure on social security programs remains low, however, in relation to expenditure in many other industrial nations.

Nearly the entire population receives benefits in one form or another from the health insurance system. Health insurance is compulsory for those employed at enterprises with five or more workers, and premiums are shared equally by the insured and their employers. Those not covered at work are insured through the National Health Insurance program. Other sickness and health insurance is in force among farmers, fishermen, and their dependents. Unemployment coverage is obligatory for all enterprises regardless of size; workers' compensation must also be provided by employers.

The Daily Life Security Law (1946) laid the groundwork for an ever-growing livelihood assistance (welfare) program. Out of this have come laws pertaining to child welfare, physically handicapped persons' welfare, social welfare service, welfare fund loans to mothers and children, aid to the war-wounded and ill, and aid to families of deceased soldiers. The system provides direct aid for livelihood; education; housing; medical, maternity, and occupational disability; and funerals. More than a thousand welfare offices throughout the nation are staffed by full-time, salaried welfare secretaries and assisted by voluntary help. Institutions have been established to care for the aged, those on relief, and those needing rehabilitation. Numerous private organizations assist government agencies.

In 1985, a two-tiered pension system was mandated by law. The first tier consists of "national pension insurance" paid to all residents at a flat rate; the second tier consists of employment or earnings-related coverage. There are special pension programs for public employees, private school teachers and employees, and employees of agricultural, forestry, and fishery cooperatives.

Social and economic change is evident in the fact that women made up 40% of Japan's employed workers in 1999. An increasing number of women pursue permanent careers, although very few have attained management positions. According to 1999 statistics, 9.3% of management positions are filled by women. The average wage of women was only 63% of that earned by men in 1997. As of 1998, 68 of 752 parliamentary seats were held by women. The Equal Employment Opportunity Law, passed in May 1987, encourages employers to avoid discriminating against women, but does not establish penalties for noncompliance. Discrimination against ethnic Koreans and other non-Japanese minorities also continues.

A serious social problem facing children in Japan is the increasing incidence of "ijime" or severe bullying at school. At least 11 children are known to have committed suicide in 1994 as a result of bullying. The Office of Ombudsman for Children's Rights is attempting to address this problem. Violence against teachers is also a growing problem.

Human rights are generally respected by the government, but there have been some reports of abuse of detainees and prisoners.

41 HEALTH

The Ministry of Health and Welfare has become the central administrative agency responsible for maintaining and promoting public health, welfare, and sanitation. All hospitals and clinics are subject to government control with respect to their standards and spheres of responsibility. In 1990–97, there were 16 hospital beds and 1.8 doctors per 1,000 people. Every practitioner in the field of medicine or dentistry must receive a license from the Ministry of Health and Welfare. In addition, the ministry recognizes and authorizes certain quasi-medical practices, including massage, acupuncture, moxa-cautery, and judo-orthopedics, all based upon traditional Japanese health professions.

Expanded examination and treatment have brought about a dramatic decrease in the death rate from tuberculosis, the major cause of death in the 1940s. At the same time, death rates from cancer and heart disease have risen considerably and now rank among the leading causes of death, trailing cerebrovascular diseases. In 1990, the number of cancer patients increased 60% (to 810,000) from 1985. Japanese medical researchers have been working on research for a new cure for breast cancer.

Infant mortality dropped to 4 per 1,000 live births in 1999, in contrast with the 1930 rate of 124. The overall mortality rate was 8.1 per 1,000 people in 1999. Only 3% of children under 5 during 1989–95 were malnourished. The total fertility rate was 1.5 in 1999. Average life expectancy was 80.1 years in 1999, among the highest rates in the world. The likelihood of death by heart disease after 65 was 213 for a man and 264 for a woman per 1,000 people (1990–1993). There were nearly 300,000 deaths per year in the mid-1990s strictly from cardiovascular diseases.

Immunization rates for children up to one year old in 1997 included diphtheria, pertussis, and tetanus (100%) and measles (94%).

A large portion of the male population smokes. Between 1986 and 1994, 66% of men and 14% of women smoked. In 1995 it was estimated that tobacco would cause 12% of all deaths (17% males and 5% females), numbers that are still increasing among males and, on current smoking trends, will eventually also increase in females.

42HOUSING

A severe housing shortage plagued Japan after World War II. It is estimated that in 1947, two years after the war's end, the housing deficit amounted to more than four million units. A construction program resulted in 9.7 million new units by the end of 1965. The following year, the government undertook a five-year plan for the construction of 7.6 million houses by mid-1971; the plan was designed to fulfill the goal of "one house for each family."

Housing construction peaked at 1.9 million units in 1973; despite efforts to promote construction as a means of stimulating the domestic economy, construction lagged in later years, falling to between 1.1 million and 1.5 million units in the 1980s. The decline reflects not so much a saturation of demand—many Japanese regard their housing as inadequate—as a rapid rise in land and construction costs, especially in the Tokyo, Nagoya, and Osaka metropolitan areas, which has put new housing out of the reach of potential buyers.

In the mid-1990s, the average salaried worker in Tokyo could only afford a house 40 km outside the Tokyo metropolitan area. Condominiums and prefabricated homes provided much of the nation's new housing in the 1980s. In fiscal 1987, low interest rates pushed new housing starts to 1.729 million units; they declined in 1988 to 1.6 million, and fell to 1.343 million in 1991 with the start of the recession. There were a total of 47,607,000 housing units in 1992.

43EDUCATION

Japan's entire educational system was reorganized along US lines after World War II, adhering to a 6-3-3-4 plan (6 years of primary school, 3 years of lower secondary school, 3 years of upper secondary school—full-time, part-time or correspondence—and 4 years of college). Education is compulsory and provided free of charge for the first 9 years, from age 6 through 14. Coeducation

has become an accepted principle. Virtually the entire adult population is literate.

Entrance into high schools, the stage following the compulsory level, is by examination only, and most of these schools charge tuition. Would-be national and local public university students must pass entrance examinations in Japanese, English, mathematics, science, and social studies. There are three types of institutions for higher education—universities, junior colleges and technical colleges, all of which receive prefectural and national support or annual subsidies. There are 95 national universities, with each prefectural capital having one school; the remainder are in the principal cities. The largest religious bodies, both Christian and Buddhist, maintain important universities and other educational institutions. There are many special schools for the handicapped.

Enrollment at the compulsory elementary and junior high school levels is very high, approaching 100%. Approximately 29.1% of students continued on to university level education in 1990.

In 1998, 7,855,387 students were enrolled in 24,376 elementary schools, with 420,901 teachers. In 1995, 9,878,568 students were enrolled in secondary schools, with 702,575 teachers. In 1995, there were a total of 401,509 teaching faculty and 3,917,709 students enrolled in all higher educational institutions.

Educational activities for adults and youths are organized both by government and private bodies. There is a board of education in each of the 47 prefectures and 3,000 municipalities and these serve as the local education authority. The central education authority is the Ministry of Education, which provides guidance and financial assistance to the local bodies. In 1996, approximately 3.6% of the Gross Domestic Product was allocated to education.

44LIBRARIES AND MUSEUMS

In 1948, the National Diet Library Law established the National Diet Library to provide reference service to the Diet, other libraries, and the general public. In 1949, this library absorbed the Ueno Library (the former national library) as one of its branches. The National Diet Library acts as a legal depository for Japanese publications and is also a depository library for the UN. There are over 6.6 million volumes in the library's collection. Keio University and the University of Tokyo (both located in Tokyo) both have libraries with holdings of over one million volumes.

Public libraries are beginning to find their place in Japanese life. Prior to the enactment of the Library Law of 1950, 70% of those who utilized libraries were students and scholars. Today, libraries are information centers, and increasing numbers of citizens are patronizing them.

Except in large cities, typical Japanese museums take the form of the treasure halls of shrines or temples, botanical gardens, and aquariums. Important museums include the National Science Museum, Museum of Contemporary Art, Calligraphy Museum, and the Tokyo Metropolitan Art Museum, all located in Tokyo. Also in Tokyo are the Baseball Hall of Fame and Museum, a criminal museum, and a clock museum. Osaka houses a museum of natural history and the National Museum of Ethnography. Yokohama is home to an equine museum and Kanazawa Bunko, a general museum dating back to 1275 and featuring Zen Buddhist documents.

45MEDIA

Telephone and telegraph services are offered by Nippon Telephone and Telegraph, which was privatized in 1986, and by Japan Telecom and other companies that entered the market after Nippon Telegraph and Telephone's monopoly ended in 1985. In

1995, Japan had 58,830,000 telephones. Telex, fax, and international telegram services are provided by Kokusai Denshin–Denwa (KDD).

A semigovernmental enterprise, the Japan Broadcasting Corp. (Nihon Hoso Kyokai—NHK), plays a large role in Japan's radio and television communications. Many commercial stations are connected with large newspaper companies. Started in 1935, Radio Japan is also beamed by NHK throughout the world. NHK initiated television broadcasting in 1953. As of 1999 there were 318 AM and 58 FM radio stations, and 7,549 television stations. Color television broadcasting began in 1960; multiplex broadcasting, for stereophonic or multiple-language programming, was made available in Tokyo and other metropolitan areas in 1978.

The Japanese press is among the world's largest in terms of newspaper circulation and is also a leader in ratio of copies to population.

The leading Japanese dailies, with their 1999 circulations, are as follows:

CIRCULATION

	MORNING	EVENING
TOKYO		
Yomiuri Shimbun	10,220,000	4,312,000
Asahi Shimbun	8,362,000	4,239,000
Mainichi Shimbun	1,616,300	723,500
Nihon Keizai Shimbun	1,770,800	953,000
Tokyo Shimbun	679,400	382,700
Sankei Shimbun	1,962,000	928,700
OSAKA		
Yomiuri Shimbun	2,559,200	1,426,000
Asahi Shimbun	2,333,500	1,387,800
Mainichi Shimbun	1,431,200	920,300
Sankei Shimbun	1,158,500	654,600
OTHER CITIES		
Chunichi Shimbun (Nagoya)	3,075,300	1,247,800
Kyoto Shimbun (Kyoto	503,100	336,300

There are two domestic news agencies: the Kyodo News Service, with 50 domestic bureaus and with foreign bureaus in every major overseas news center; and the Jiji Press, serving commercial and government circles.

The constitution of Japan provides for free speech and a free press, and the government is said to respect these rights in practice. The Japanese press enjoys the reputation of having the most vigorous and outspoken in the world. It operates under the constitutional provision of absolute prohibition of censorship.

As of 1996, there were more than 19 million personal computers; in 1998 there were 107 Internet hosts in Japan per 1,000 population.

46ORGANIZATIONS

There are an enormous number of organizations in Japan, including such standard bodies as the Japan Red Cross, Japan Chamber of Commerce (with regional and local branches), General Council of Trade Unions, Congress of Labor Unions, Federation of Employers Associations, Rotary Club, Japan Medical Association, Japan Actors' Society, Motion Picture Association of Japan, Japan Athletic Federation, All-Japan Boy Scouts League and Girl Scouts League, Japan YMCA and YWCA, and Japan Youth Association.

The Institute of Art Research and the National Institute of Japanese Literature are important in the cultural field. The Society for International Cultural Relations, established in 1934, is active in the publishing field and in cultural exchange.

47TOURISM, TRAVEL, AND RECREATION

Tourism in Japan is regarded as a major industry, since many foreign visitors as well as the Japanese themselves tour the country extensively. In 1997, Japan had an estimated 4.22 million foreign visitors. Tourist expenditures for that year totaled approximately $4.3 billion. Japan's 1,567,678 hotel rooms had a 70% rate of occupancy in 1997.

Japan's chief sightseeing attractions are in the ancient former capital of Kyoto: Nijo Castle, Heian Shrine, the 13th-century Sanjusangendo temple and the Kinkaku-ji (Temple of the Golden Pavilion), the Ryoan-ji (Temple of the Peaceful Dragon), famed for its garden of stones and raked sand, and numerous other ancient Buddhist temples and Shinto shrines. Nearby sights in the vicinity of Nara include the Great Buddha, a huge bronze statue originally cast in the eighth century; the Kofuku-ji pagoda; and Horyu-ji, the seventh century temple from which Buddhism spread throughout Japan. There are few historic sites in the capital—Tokyo was devastated by an earthquake in 1923 and virtually destroyed in World War II—but nearby attractions include Mt. Fuji and the hot springs of Fuji-Hakkone-Izu National Park; Nikko National Park, site of the Toshogu Shrine, where the first Tokugawa shogun is entombed; and the summer and winter sports facilities in the mountains of central Japan—the so-called Japan Alps. The Hiroshima Peace Park and Peace Memorial Museum commemorate the destruction of the city by an atomic bomb in 1945.

Baseball is Japan's national pastime; there are two professional leagues, each with six teams. Sumo, a Japanese form of wrestling, is also popular, with tournaments held six times a year. Golf, an expensive sport because of the lack of open space, is used mainly as a means of entertaining business clients. Other pastimes include judo, karate, table tennis, fishing, and volleyball. Gardening is the most popular hobby among men and women alike.

The costs of traveling in Japan, among the highest in the world, were reduced slightly when a 3% tourism tax, in effect since 1960, was abolished on 1 April 2000. According to 1999 UN estimates, daily expenses in Hakore were approximately $369 per day, $263 in Furano, $329 in Tokyo, $285 in Okinawa, $245 in Kanazawa, and $180 in Shizuoka City.

48FAMOUS JAPANESE

Murasaki Shikibu (late 10th–early 11th cent.) was the author of The Tale of Genji, probably the best-known Japanese literary classic in English since it was first translated in the 1920s. Zeami (Motokiyo, 1363–1443) was an actor who established Noh theater and wrote a number of plays that have been part of the Noh repertoire ever since. Monzaemon Chikamatsu (1653–1724) wrote plays for the Bunraku theater, many of which later became part of the repertoire of Kabuki. Basho (Matsuo Munefusa, 1644–94) perfected the writing of the poetic form now known as haiku. In this genre, three other poets are also known: Buson Yosa (1716–83), Issa Kobayashi (1763–1827), and the modern reformer Shiki Masaoka (1867–1902). Ryunosuke Akutagawa (1892–1927) is best known for his story "Rashomon." Prominent modern novelists include Jun'ichiro Tanizaki (1886–1965); Yasunari Kawabata (1899–1972), winner of the 1968 Nobel Prize for literature; Kobo Abe (1924–93); and Yukio Mishima (1925–70). A leading modern writer and Zen Buddhist scholar was Daisetz Teitaro Suzuki (1870–1966).

In art, Sesshu (1420–1506) was the most famous landscape artist of his day. Ogata Korin (1658–1716) was a master painter of plants, animals, and people. The leader of the naturalist school was Maruyama Okyo (1733–95). The best-known painters and wood-block artists of the "ukiyo-e" style were Kitagawa Utamaro (1754–1806), Katsushika Hokusai (1760–1849), Saito Sharaku (fl.1794–95), and Ando Hiroshige (1797–1858). Four

20th-century Japanese architects whose work has had a marked influence on international style are Mayekawa Kunio (1905–86), Hideo Kosaka (b.1912), Kenzo Tange (b.1913), and Yoshinobu Ahihara (b.1918).

Noted Japanese film directors include Kenjii Mizoguchi (1898–1956), Yasujiro Ozu (1903–63), and Akira Kurosawa (1910–92). Toshiro Mifune (b.1920) is the best-known film star abroad. Contemporary composers include Toshiro Mayuzumi (b.1929) and Toru Takemitsu (1930–96). Seiji Ozawa (b.1935) is a conductor of world renown. The leading home-run hitter in baseball history is Sadaharu Oh (b.1940), manager of the Yomiuri Giants, who retired as a player for the same team in 1980 after hitting 868 home runs.

Hideyo Noguchi (1876–1928), noted bacteriologist, is credited with the discovery of the cause of yellow fever and is famed for his studies on viruses, snake poisons, and toxins. Hideki Yukawa (1907–81), Japan's most noted physicist, received the 1949 Nobel Prize for research on the meson. In 1965, Shinichiro Tomonaga (1906–79), a professor at Tokyo University of Education, became one of the year's three recipients of the Nobel Prize for physics for work in the field of quantum electrodynamics. Leon Esaki (b.1925) won the Nobel Prize for physics in 1973; Kenichi Fukui (b.1918) shared the 1981 chemistry award; and Susumu Tonegawa (b.1939) won the 1987 medicine award.

Hirohito (1901–89) became emperor of Japan in 1926. His eldest son, Akihito (b.1933), succeeded him in 1990. The leading statesman after World War II was Eisaku Sato (1901–75), prime minister from 1964 to 1972 and winner of the Nobel Peace Prize in 1974.

⁴⁹DEPENDENCIES

Japan has no territories or colonies.

⁵⁰BIBLIOGRAPHY

Beasley, W. G. (William G.). *Japanese Imperialism, 1894–1945.* New York: Oxford University Press, 1987.

Boger, Karl. *Postwar Industrial Policy in Japan: An Annotated Bibliography.* Metuchen, N.J.: Scarecrow Press, 1988.

Bowring, Richard, and Peter Kornicki (eds.). *The Cambridge Encyclopedia of Japan.* New York: Cambridge University Press, 1993.

Burks, Ardath W. *Japan: A Postindustrial Power,* 3rd ed. Boulder, Colo.: Westview Press, 1991.

Contemporary Japan and Popular Culture. Honolulu: University of Hawaii Press, 1996.

Cortazzi, Hugh. *Modern Japan: A Concise Survey.* New York: St. Martin', 1993.

Currents in Japanese Culture: Translations and Transformations. New York: Columbia University Press, 1997.

Dolan, Ronald E., and Robert L. (eds.). *Japan, a Country Study,* 5th ed. Washington, D.C.: Library of Congress, 1992.

Encarnation, Dennis J. *Rivals Beyond Trade: America Versus Japan in Global Competition.* Ithaca: Cornell University Press, 1992.

Fukutake, Tadashi. *The Japanese Social Structure: Its Evolution in the Modern Century.* 2d ed. Tokyo: University of Tokyo Press, 1989.

Hane, Mikiso. *Modern Japan: A Historical Survey.* 2d ed. Boulder, Colo.: Westview Press, 1992.

Japanese Studies from Pre-History to 1990: A Bibliographical Guide. New York: St. Martin's, 1992.

Kodansha Encyclopedia of Japan. 9 vols. New York: Kodansha, 1983.

Koike, Kazuo. *The Economics of Work in Japan.* Tokyo: LTCB International Library Foundation, 1995.

Lu, David John. *Japan: A Documentary History.* Armonk, N.Y.: M. E. Sharpe, 1997.

Mason, T. David, and Abdul M. Turay (eds.). *US-Japan Trade Friction: Its Impact on Security Cooperation in the Pacific Basin.* New York: St. Martin's, 1991.

Masumi, Junnosuke. *Contemporary Politics in Japan.* Berkeley: University of California Press, 1995.

Mouer, Ross E. *Images of Japanese Society: A Study in the Social Construction of Reality.* New York: Kegan Paul International, 1990.

Packard, Jerrold M. *Sons of Heaven: A Portrait of the Japanese Monarchy.* New York: Scribner, 1987.

Perkins, Dorothy. *Encyclopedia of Japan: Japanese History and Culture, from Abacus to Zori.* New York: Facts on File, 1991.

Reischauer, Edwin O. *Japan: The Story of a Nation.* 4th ed. New York: Knopf, 1989.

Richardson, Bradley M. *Japanese Democracy: Power, Coordination, and Performance.* New Haven, Conn.: Yale University Press, 1997.

Rowland, Diana. *Japanese Business Etiquette: A Practical Guide to Success with the Japanese.* 2d ed. New York: Warner Books, 1993.

Sansom, Sir George Bailey. *A History of Japan.* 3 vols. Stanford, Calif.: Stanford University Press, 1958–63.

Shulman, Frank Joseph. *Japan.* Santa Barbara, Calif.: Clio Press, 1989.

Stevenson, Michael I. *Education in Japan: A Bibliography of Materials in English since 1973.* Monticello, Ill.: Vance Bibliographies, 1987.

Thomas, J. E. *Modern Japan: A Social History Since 1868.* New York: Longman, 1996.

The Political Economy of Japan. Stanford, Calif.: Stanford University Press, 1987.

Tsuru, Shigeto. *The Economic Development of Modern Japan.* Brookfield, Vt.: E. Elgar, 1995.

———. *Japan's Capitalism: Creative Defeat and Beyond.* New York: Cambridge University Press, 1993.

Waswo, Ann. *Modern Japanese Society, 1868–1994.* Oxford: Oxford University Press, 1996.

Woronoff, Jon. *The Japanese Economic Crisis.* New York: St. Martin's Press, 1993.

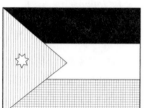

JORDAN

The Hashemite Kingdom of Jordan

Al-Mamlaka al-Urdunniyya al-Hashimiyya

CAPITAL: 'Amman.

FLAG: The national flag is a tricolor of black, white, and green horizontal stripes with a seven-pointed white star on a red triangle at the hoist.

ANTHEM: *As-Salam al-Maliki (Long Live the King).*

MONETARY UNIT: The Jordanian dinar (JD) is a paper currency of 1,000 fils. There are coins of 1, 5, 10, 20, 25, 50, 100, and 250 fils and notes of ½, 1, 5, 10, and 20 dinars. JD1 = $1.4122 ($1 = JD0.7081) as of 31 March 2000.

WEIGHTS AND MEASURES: The metric system is the legal standard, but some local and Syrian units are still widely used, especially in the villages.

HOLIDAYS: Arbor Day, 15 January; Independence Day, 25 May; Accession of King Hussein, 11 August; King Hussein's Birthday, 14 November. Muslim religious holidays include the 1st of Muharram (Islamic New Year), 'Id al-Fitr, 'Id al-'Adha', and Milad an-Nabi. Christmas and Easter are observed by sizable Christian minorities.

TIME: 2 PM = noon GMT.

¹LOCATION, SIZE, AND EXTENT

Situated in southwest Asia, Jordan has an area of 83,335 sq km (32,175 sq mi). (Until 1967, Jordan's land area also included the West Bank, which, as of 1994, is part of the area including the Gaza Strip and Golan Heights now to be under Palestine home rule.) Jordan extends 562 km (349 mi) NE–SW and 349 km (217 mi) SE–NW. Comparatively, the area occupied by Jordan is slightly smaller than the state of Indiana. It is bounded on the N by Syria, on the NE by Iraq, on the E and S by Sa'udi Arabia, on the SW by the Gulf of Aqaba, and on the W by Israel, with a total boundary length of 1,804 km (1,121 mi) following the 1949 armistice with Israel and of 1,645 km (1,022 mi) following the 1967 cease-fire.

Jordan's capital city, 'Amman, is located in the northwestern part of the country.

²TOPOGRAPHY

The Jordan Valley has a maximum depression of 392 m (1,286 ft) below sea level at the Dead Sea; south of the Dead Sea the depression, called Wadi'Araba, slowly rises to reach sea level about halfway to the Gulf of Aqaba. To the east of the Jordan River, the Transjordanian plateaus have an average altitude of 910 m (3,000 ft), with hills rising to more than 1,650 m (5,400 ft) in the south. Farther eastward, the highlands slope down gently toward the desert, which constitutes 88% of the East Bank. The Jordan River enters the country from Israel to the north and flows into the Dead Sea; its main tributary is the Yarmuk, which near its juncture forms the border between Jordan and Syria. The Dead Sea, 89 km (55 mi) long and about 16 km (10 mi) wide, is the lowest point on the earth's surface, at 397 m (1,302 ft) below the level of the Mediterranean; the Dead Sea itself has a maximum depth of 792 m (2,598 ft) below sea level. The Dead Sea has a mineral content of about 30%.

³CLIMATE

The Jordan Valley has little rainfall, intense summer heat, and mild, pleasant winters. The hill country of the East Bank—ancient Moab, Edom, and Gilead—has a modified Mediterranean climate, with less rainfall and hot, dry summers. The desert regions are subject to great extremes of temperature and receive rainfall of less than 20 cm (8 in) annually, while the rest of the country has an average rainfall of up to 58 cm (23 in) a year. Temperatures at 'Amman range from about –4°C (25°F) in winter to more than 38°C (100°F) in summer.

⁴FLORA AND FAUNA

Plants and animals are those common to the eastern Mediterranean and the Syrian Desert. The vegetation ranges from semitropical flora in the Jordan Valley and other regions to shrubs and drought-resistant bushes in the desert. Less than 1% of the land is forested. The wild fauna includes the jackal, hyena, fox, wildcat, gazelle, ibex, antelope, and rabbit; the vulture, sand grouse, skylark, partridge, quail, woodcock, and goldfinch; and the viper, diced water snake, and Syrian black snake.

⁵ENVIRONMENT

Jordan's principal environmental problems are insufficient water resources, soil erosion caused by overgrazing of goats and sheep, and deforestation. Water pollution is an important issue in Jordan. Jordan has 0.2 cubic miles of water with 65% used for farming activity and 6% used for industrial purposes. One-hundred percent of all city dwellers and 97% of rural people have pure water. It is expected that the rate of population growth, amounting to 4–7 million by the year 2000, will place more demands on an already inadequate water supply. Current sources of pollution are sewage, herbicides, and pesticides. Jordan's cities produce 1.2 million tons of solid waste per year. Jordan's wildlife was reduced drastically by livestock overgrazing and uncontrolled hunting between 1930 and 1960; larger wild animals, such as the Arabian oryx, onager, and Asiatic lion, have completely disappeared. Under a law of 1973, the government has prohibited unlicensed hunting of birds or wild animals and unlicensed sport fishing, as well as the cutting of trees, shrubs, and plants. As of 1994, 3.3% of Jordan's total land area was protected. In the same year, five of Jordan's mammal species and 11 bird species were endangered. Seven-hundred and fifty-two plant species were also endangered. Endangered or extinct species in Jordan include the South Arabian leopard and the goitered gazelle.

6 POPULATION

The UN estimated the 1996 population at 4,139,458 under Jordanian administration and 1,571,575 in the West Bank. However, the US Census Bureau estimated those same two 1996 figures at 4,212,000 and 1,717,000 respectively. The population of Jordan in 2000 was estimated at 4,700,843. An estimated 2.8% of the population is 65 years of age or older. The projected population for the year 2005 is 5,403,000, assuming a crude birthrate of 29 per 1,000 population and a death rate of 4, resulting in a natural rate of change of 2.6% for the period 2000–2005. The population rate of change between 1995 and 2000 was 3.3%. The population density in 1998 was 51 per sq km (132 per sq mi).

It was estimated that 74% of the population lived in urban areas in 2000, up from 60% in 1980. More than 20% lived in small villages; the remainder was nomadic or seminomadic. Over 80% of the East Bank population is concentrated in the northwestern 10% of area. The capital city, Amman, had a 2000 population of 1,183,000. Az-Zarqa' had an estimated population of about 359,000; and Irbid, 216,000. Jordan's next census is slated for 2004.

The West Bank, held by Israel since 1967, contains Arab Jerusalem (Al-Quds), Nabulus, Hebron (Al-Khalil), Jericho (Ar-Riha), and Bethlehem. In June 1996, 1,358,706 Palestinian refugees registered with the UNRWA were living on the East Bank, about 258,000 of them in the 10 refugee centers. Another 532,438 were on the West Bank.

7 MIGRATION

About one-half or more of the population consists of refugees from territory that became Israel. There is also considerable native-born migration by nomadic groups across the Syrian, Iraqi, and Sa'udi Arabian borders. Many Jordanians live abroad, attracted by job opportunities in the oil-rich Arab states. About 300,000 Jordanians returned from the Persian Gulf states after the 1991 war, mainly from Kuwait, and about 120,000 Iraqis fled to Jordan in 1991. By the end of 1993, no more than 30,000 of the latter remained in Jordan.

In 1999 the net emigration rate was zero migrants per 1,000 population. As of September 1999, there were some 900 urban refugees from Iraq, Sudan, Somalia, Syria, Libya, and Yugoslavia registered with the UNHCR office in Jordan. Also in 1999, Jordan was also host to some 1,263,000 Palestinians who fell under the mandate of UNRWA. Continuing instability in the region has resulted in an increase in the number of asylum seekers. Since the government of Jordan does not allow refugees to remain in the country on a long-term basis, all recognized refugees must be resettled in third countries.

8 ETHNIC GROUPS

Ethnically, the Jordanians represent a mixed stock. Most of the population is Arab (approximately 98% in 1999), but, except for the Bedouin nomads and seminomads of the desert and steppe areas, this element is overlain by the numerous peoples that have been present in Jordan for millennia, including Greek, Egyptian, Persian, European, and Negroid strains. The Palestinian Arabs

now resident in Jordan tend to be sedentary and urban. Perhaps 1% of the population is Armenian, and another 1% is Circassian. There are also small Kurd, Druze, and Chechen minorities.

9 LANGUAGES

Arabic is the official language of the country and is spoken even by the ethnic minorities who maintain their own languages in their everyday lives. The spoken Arabic of the country is essentially a vernacular of literary Arabic; it is common to neighboring countries as well but is quite different from the spoken language in Egypt. There also are differences between the languages of the towns and of the countryside, and between those of the East and West banks. English is widely understood by the upper and middle classes.

10 RELIGIONS

Islam is the state religion, although all are guaranteed religious freedom. Most Jordanians (about 96%) are Sunni Muslims (1997 est.). Christians constitute about 4% of the population and live mainly in 'Amman or the Jordan Valley; most are Greek Orthodox or Roman Catholic, and all are Arabic-speaking. Of the racial minorities, the Turkomans and Circassians are Sunni Muslims, but the Druzes are a heterodox Muslim sect. The Baha'is are mainly of Persian stock. A tiny community of Samaritans maintains the faith of its ancestors, a heterodox form of the ancient Jewish religion.

11 TRANSPORTATION

Jordan's transportation facilities are underdeveloped, but improvements have been made in recent years. The third development plan (1986–90) allotted JD445 million for transportation. A good road network links the principal towns and connects with Syria, Iraq, and Sa'udi Arabia. In 1998 all of Jordan's estimated 8,000 km (4,971 mi) of road was paved. Passenger automobiles numbered 167,800; trucks, buses, and other commercial vehicles totaled 82,500 in 1995.

The rail system, some 677 km (421 mi) of narrow-gauge single track, is a section of the old Hijaz railway (Damascus to Medina) for Muslim pilgrims. It runs from the Syrian border through 'Amman to Ma'an, where it connects with a spur line to the port of Al-'Aqabah. Reconstruction of the section from Ma'an to Medina in Sa'udi Arabia, which had been destroyed in World War I, was undertaken in the early 1970s as a joint venture by Jordan, Sa'udi Arabia, and Syria.

Al-'Aqabah, Jordan's only outlet to the sea, is situated at the head of the Gulf of Aqaba, an arm of the Red Sea. The port was initially developed after the 1948 Arab-Israeli war, which cut off Arab Palestine and Transjordan from Mediterranean ports; substantial development did not begin until the 1960s. The port has been enlarged for general use, including terminals for loading potash and fertilizers. In 1998 Jordan had 7 merchant ships, totaling 42,746 GRT.

Jordan had 17 airports in 1998, 14 of which were paved. The major airport is the Queen Alia International Airport, about 30 km (19 mi) south of Amman, which was opened in the early 1980s. The government-owned Alia–Royal Jordanian Airline operates domestic and international flights. In 1997, 1,353,000 passengers were carried on scheduled domestic and international flights.

12 HISTORY

As part of the Fertile Crescent connecting Africa and Asia, the area now known as Jordan has long been a major transit zone and often an object of contention among rival powers. It has a relatively well known prehistory and history. Neolithic remains from about 7000 BC have been found in Jericho, the oldest known city in the world. City-states were well developed in the

JORDAN

0 25 50 Miles

0 25 50 Kilometers

LOCATION: (1949): 29°17′ to 33°20′N; 34°53′ to 39°12′E. **BOUNDARY LENGTHS:** Syria, 356 km (221 mi). Iraq, 146 km (91 mi). Saʻudi Arabia, 744 km (462 mi). Gulf of Aqaba, 27 km (17 mi). Israel: 1949 armistice line, 531 km (330 mi); 1967 cease-fire line, 480 km (298 mi). **TERRITORIAL SEA LIMIT:** 3 mi.

Bronze Age (c.3200–2100 BC). In the 16th century BC, the Egyptians first conquered Palestine, and in the 13th century BC, Semitic-speaking peoples established kingdoms on both banks of the Jordan. In the 10th century BC, the western part of the area of Jordan (on both banks of the Jordan River) formed part of the domain of the Hebrew kings David and Solomon, while subsequently the West Bank became part of the Kingdom of Judah. A succession of outside conquerors held sway in the area until, in the 4th century BC, Palestine and Syria were conquered by Alexander the Great, beginning about 1,000 years of intermittent European rule. After the death of Alexander, the whole area was disputed among the Seleucids of Syria, the Ptolemies of Egypt, and native dynasties, such as the Hasmoneans (Maccabees); in

the 1st century BC, it came under the domination of Rome. In Hellenistic and Roman times, a flourishing civilization developed on the East Bank; meanwhile, in southern Jordan, the Nabataean kingdom, a native Arab state in alliance with Rome, developed a distinctive culture, blending Arab and Greco-Roman elements, and built its capital at Petra, a city whose structures hewn from red sandstone cliffs survive today. With the annexation of Nabataea by Trajan in the 2d century AD, Palestine and areas east of the Jordan came under direct Roman rule. Christianity spread rapidly in Jordan and for 300 years was the dominant religion.

The Byzantine phase of Jordan's history, from the establishment of Constantinople as the capital of the empire to the Arab conquest, was one of gradual decline. When the Muslim invaders appeared, little resistance was offered, and in 636, Arab rule was firmly established. Soon thereafter, the area became thoroughly Arabized and Islamized, remaining so to this day despite a century-long domination by the Crusaders (12th century). Under the Ottoman Turks (1517–1917), the lands east of the Jordan were part of the Damascus vilayet (an administrative division of the empire), while the West Bank formed part of the sanjak (a further subdivision) of Jerusalem within the vilayet of Beirut.

During World War I, Sharif Hussein ibn-'Ali (Husayn bin 'Ali), the Hashemite (or Hashimite) ruler of Mecca and the Hijaz, aided and incited by the UK (which somewhat hazily promised him an independent Arab state), touched off an Arab revolt against the Turks. After the defeat of the Turks, Palestine and Transjordan were placed under British mandate; in 1921, Hussein's son 'Abdallah was installed by the British as emir of Transjordan. In 1923, the independence of Transjordan was proclaimed under British supervision, which was partially relaxed by a 1928 treaty, and in 1939, a local cabinet government (Council of Ministers) was formed. In 1946, Transjordan attained full independence, and on 25 May, 'Abdallah was proclaimed king of the Hashemite Kingdom of Transjordan. After the Arab-Israeli war of 1948, King 'Abdallah annexed a butterfly-shaped area of Palestine bordering the Jordan (thereafter called the West Bank), which was controlled by his army and which he contended was included in the area that had been promised to Sharif Hussein. On 24 April 1950, after general elections had been held in the East and West banks, an act of union joined Jordanian-occupied Palestine and the Kingdom of Transjordan to form the Hashemite Kingdom of Jordan. This action was condemned by some Arab states as evidence of inordinate Hashemite ambitions. Meanwhile, Jordan, since the 1948 war, had absorbed about 500,000 of some 1,000,000 Palestinian Arab refugees, mostly sheltered in UN-administered camps, and another 500,000 nonrefugee Palestinians. Despite what was now a Palestinian majority, power remained with the Jordanian elite loyal to the throne. On 20 July 1951, 'Abdallah was assassinated in Jerusalem by a Palestinian Arab, and his eldest son, Talal, was proclaimed king. Because of mental illness, however, King Talal was declared unfit to rule, and succession passed to his son Hussein I (Husayn ibn-Talal), who, after a brief period of regency until he reached 18 years of age, was formally enthroned on 2 May 1953.

Between the accession of King Hussein and the war with Israel in 1967, Jordan was beset not only with problems of economic development, internal security, and Arab-Israeli tensions but also with difficulties stemming from its relations with the Western powers and the Arab world. Following the overthrow of Egypt's King Faruk in July 1952, the Arab countries were strongly influenced by "Arab socialism" and aspirations to Arab unity (both for its own sake and as a precondition for defeating Israel). Early in Hussein's reign, extreme nationalists stepped up their attempts to weaken the regime and its ties with the UK. Notwithstanding the opposition of most Arabs, including many Jordanians, Jordan maintained a close association with the UK in an effort to preserve the kingdom as a separate, sovereign entity. However, the invasion of Egypt by Israel in October 1956, and the subsequent Anglo-French intervention at Suez, made it politically impossible to maintain cordial relations with the UK. Negotiations were begun to end the treaty with Britain, and thus the large military subsidies for which it provided; the end of the treaty also meant the end of British bases and of British troops in Jordan. The Jordanian army remained loyal, and the king's position was bolstered when the US and Sa'udi Arabia indicated their intention to preserve Jordan against any attempt by Syria to occupy the country. After the formation of the United Arab Republic by Egypt and Syria and the assassination of his cousin, King Faisal II

(Faysal) of Iraq, in a July 1958 coup, Hussein turned again to the West for support, and British troops were flown to Jordan from Cyprus.

When the crisis was over, a period of relative calm ensued. Hussein, while retaining Jordan's Western ties, gradually steadied his relations with other Arab states (except Syria), established relations with the USSR, and initiated several important economic development measures. But even in years of comparative peace, relations with Israel remained the focus of Jordanian and Arab attention. Terrorist raids launched from within Jordan drew strong Israeli reprisals, and the activities of the Palestine Liberation Organization (PLO) often impinged on Jordanian sovereignty, leading Hussein in July 1966, and again in early 1967, to suspend support for the PLO, thus drawing Arab enmity upon himself. On 5 June 1967, an outbreak of hostilities occurred between Israel and the combined forces of Jordan, Syria, and Egypt. These hostilities lasted only six days, during which Israel occupied the Golan Heights in Syria, Egypt's Sinai Peninsula, and the Jordanian West Bank, including all of Jerusalem. Jordan suffered heavy casualties, and a large-scale exodus of Palestinians (over 300,000) across the Jordan River to the East Bank swelled Jordan's refugee population (700,000 in 1966), adding to the war's severe economic disruption.

After Hussein's acceptance of a cease-fire with Israel in August 1970, he tried to suppress various Palestinian guerrilla organizations whose operations had brought retaliation upon Jordan. The imposition of military rule in September led to a 10-day civil war between the army and the Palestinian forces (supported briefly by Syria which was blocked by Israel), ended by the mediation of other Arab governments. Subsequently, however, Hussein launched an offensive against Palestinian guerrillas in Jordan, driving them out in July 1971. In the following September, Premier Wasfi al-Tal was assassinated by guerrilla commandos, and coup attempts, in which Libya was said to have been involved, were thwarted in November 1972 and February 1973.

Jordan did not open a third front against Israel in the October 1973 war but sent an armored brigade of about 2,500 men to assist Syria. After the war, relations between Jordan and Syria improved. Hussein reluctantly endorsed the resolution passed by Arab nations on 28 October 1974 in Rabat, Morocco, recognizing the PLO as "sole legitimate representative of the Palestinian people on any liberated Palestinian territory," including, implicitly, the Israeli-held West Bank. After the Egyptian-Israeli Peace Treaty of 1979, Jordan joined other Arab states in trying to isolate Egypt diplomatically, and Hussein refused to join further Egyptian-Israeli talks on the future of the West Bank.

After the Israeli invasion of Lebanon in 1982 and the resulting expulsion of Palestinian guerrillas, Jordan began to coordinate peace initiatives with the PLO. These efforts culminated in a February 1985 accord between Jordan and the PLO, in which both parties agreed to work together toward "a peaceful and just settlement to the Palestinian question." In February 1986, however, Hussein announced that Jordan was unable to continue to coordinate politically with the PLO, which scrapped the agreement in April 1987. The following year the King renounced Jordan's claim to the West Bank and subsequently patched up relations with the PLO, Syria, and Egypt. In 1990, owing largely to popular support for Saddam Hussein, Jordan was critical of coalition efforts to use force to expel Iraqi forces from Kuwait. Relations with the US and the Gulf states were impaired; Jordan lost its subsidies from the latter while having to support hundreds of thousands of refugees from the war and the aftermath. Jordan's willingness to participate in peace talks with Israel in late 1991 helped repair relations with Western countries. In June 1994, Jordan and Israel began meetings to work out practical steps on water, borders, and energy which would lead to normal relations. And, later that year, Jordan and Israel signed a peace treaty, ending the state of war that had existed between the two neighbors for decades. Relations with the major players in the Gulf War also improved in the years after the war. In 1996, Jordan and Sa'udi Arabia, the UAE and Kuwait were well on the way toward establishing normal relations.

Internally in the 1980s, Hussein followed policies of gradual political liberalization which were given new impetus by serious rioting over high prices in 1989. In that year, for the first time since 1956, Jordan held relatively free parliamentary elections in which Islamists gained more than one-third of the 80 seats. Martial law was ended in 1991 and new parliamentary elections were held in 1993. The King's supporters won 54 seats with the Moslem Brotherhood and its allies taking 18 places, the largest bloc of any party. However, the 1997 elections were boycotted by a number of opposition groups, who complained of unfair election laws, and the new upper house of parliament appointed by King Hussein did not include any members of Islamist groups.

In 1998 Hussein underwent treatment for cancer in the US and delegated some of his powers to his brother, crown prince Hassan, who was next in the line of succession to the throne. The following winter, however, Hussein named his son Abdallah heir apparent. On 8 February 1999 King Hussein died, ending a 46-year reign; his funeral was attended by dignitaries from countries throughout the world. King Abdallah II pledged his support for the Middle East peace process, a more open government, and economic reforms requested by the IMF. However, there was widespread uncertainty about how the untested 34-year-old heir would meet the challenges thrust upon him.

His first year in power reassured many observers, both at home and abroad. Domestically, he pushed through a series of trade bills that helped pave the way of the country's admission to the WTO, which came in December 1999, and declared his intention of implementing wide-ranging administrative and educational reforms. On the international front, Abdallah played a role in the resumption of talks between Israel and Syria and also took a firm stance against the presence of Islamic extremists in his own country, driving the radical Hamas organization out of Jordan.

13GOVERNMENT

Jordan is a constitutional monarchy based on the constitution of 8 January 1952. The king has wide powers over all branches of government. The constitution vests legislative power in the bicameral National Assembly, composed of a 40-member Senate and a 80-member lower house, the Chamber of Deputies. Senators are appointed by the king for renewable eight-year terms; the Chamber of Deputies is elected by secret ballot for a four-year term, but the king may dissolve the chamber and order new elections. There is universal suffrage at age 18, women having received the right to vote in April 1973; general elections were held in 1989, 1993, and 1997. In February 1999, King Abdallah II succeeded to the throne following the death of his father, King Hussein.

The National Assembly is convened and may be prorogued by the king, who also has veto power over legislation. The executive power of the king is administered by a cabinet, or Council of Ministers. The king appoints the prime minister, who then selects the other ministers, subject to royal approval. The ministers need not be members of the Chamber of Deputies. In the prolonged emergency created by the wars with Israel and by internal disorders, especially since 1968, King Hussein exercised nearly absolute power. The National Assembly, adjourned by the king in 1974, met briefly in 1976 to amend the constitution; parliamentary elections were postponed indefinitely because of the West Bank situation, and the Assembly was then dissolved. In 1978, King Hussein established the National Consultative

Council of 60 appointed members. The National Assembly was reconvened in 1984, as King Hussein sought to strengthen his hand in future maneuvering on the Palestinian problem. Political parties were legalized in 1992. The freely elected parliaments of 1989 and 1993 have played an increasingly active and independent role in governance, with open debate and criticism of government personalities and policies. However, new press restrictions were imposed by 1997, and a majority of opposition groups boycotted the elections that year.

14POLITICAL PARTIES

Political parties were abolished on 25 April 1957, following an alleged attempted coup by pan-Arab militants. In the elections of 1962, 1963, and 1967, candidates qualified in a screening procedure by the Interior Ministry ran for office, in effect, as independents. The Jordanian National Union, formed in September 1971 as the official political organization of Jordan and renamed the Arab National Union in March 1972, became inactive by the mid-1970s. In 1990, the election law was amended to ban bloc voting or by party lists, substituting instead a "one person, one vote" system. In 1992, political parties were again permitted and 22 were authorized to take part in elections. The principal opposition group has been the Islamic Action Front, the political arm of the Moslem Brotherhood.

In the parliamentary elections of 8 November 1993, 22 political parties fielded candidates, representing a wide range of political views. Seats were widely dispersed among a range of largely centrist parties supportive of King Hussein's IMF-modeled reforms and his pro-Western stance. The largest bloc of seats, however, was won by the Islamic Action Front, an arm of the Muslim Brotherhood. In 1997, nine pro-government parties, hoping to gain leverage against the large Islamist bloc in upcoming elections, banded together to form the National Constitutional Party. However, the grouping won only a total of three seats, and the Islamic opposition boycotted the elections altogether. Only six parties fielded candidates. Independent pro-government candidates representing local tribal interests won 62 out of the 80 contested seats; 10 seats were won by nationalist and leftist candidates; and 8 by independent Islamists.

15LOCAL GOVERNMENT

Eastern Jordan is divided into 12 governorates—Ajlun, Aqabah, 'Amman, Irbid, Balga, Jarash, Karak, Ma'an, Madaba, Zarqa', Mafraq, and Tafilah,—each under a governor appointed by the king on the recommendation of the interior minister. The towns and larger villages are administered by elected municipal councils; mayors and council presidents are appointed by the Council of Ministers. Smaller villages are headed by a headman (mukhtar), who in most cases is elected informally.

16JUDICIAL SYSTEM

There are six jurisdictions in the judiciary: four levels of civil and criminal jurisdiction, religious jurisdiction, and tribal courts. The New Civil Code of 1977 regulates civil legal procedures. The Supreme Court, acting as a court of cassation, deals with appeals from lower courts. In some instances, as in actions against the government, it sits as a High Court of Justice. The courts of appeal hear appeals from all lower courts. Courts of first instance hear major civil and criminal cases. Magistrates' courts deal with cases not coming within the jurisdiction of courts of first instance. Religious courts have jurisdiction in matters concerning personal status (marriage, divorce, wills and testaments, orphans, etc.), where the laws of the different religious sects vary. The Shari'ah courts deal with the Muslim community, following the procedure laid down by the Ottoman Law of 1913. The Council of Religious Communities has jurisdiction over analogous cases among non-Muslims. Tribal courts, which have jurisdiction in most matters concerning tribe members, are losing their importance as more people take their cases to the government courts instead.

In 1991, the State Security Court, which hears security cases in panels of at least three judges, replaced the Martial Law Court. Under 1993 amendments to the state security court law, all security court decisions may be appealed to the Court of Cassation on issues of law and weight of evidence. Prior to 1993, the Court of Cassation reviewed only cases involving death or imprisonment for over 10 years, and review was limited to errors of law.

The judiciary is independent from executive pressure. The Constitution prohibits arbitrary interference with privacy, family, and home. Police must obtain a judicial warrant before conducting searches.

17 ARMED FORCES

In 2000, the Jordanian army had some 90,000 men. The air force had 13,500 men, 93 combat aircraft, and 16 armed helicopters. The navy had only about 480 men and 3 patrol craft. Reserve manpower was estimated at 35,000. Defense expenditures for 1997 (excluding foreign military assistance) were $608.9 million or 7.8% of gross domestic product. Jordan has peacekeepers stationed in Croatia, Georgia, and Tajikistan.

18 INTERNATIONAL COOPERATION

Jordan became a member of the UN on 14 December 1955 and belongs to ESCWA and all the nonregional specialized agencies. It is one of the founding members of the Arab League and also participates in G-77. Jordan has greatly benefited from the work of UNICEF and of UNRWA, which helps the Palestinian refugees. Jordan does not adhere to the Law of the Sea. In 1995 Jordan announced its intention to join the WTO; its application was still pending as of 1999. Jordan and Israel signed a peace treaty in 1994 and exchanged ambassadors the following year.

19 ECONOMY

Jordan's economy has been profoundly affected by the Arab-Israeli conflict. The incorporation of the West Bank after the war of 1948 and the first exodus of Palestinians from the territory that became Israel tripled the population, causing grave economic and social problems. The loss of the West Bank in 1967 resulted not only in a second exodus of Palestinians but also in the loss of most of Jordan's richest agricultural land and a decline in the growing tourist industry. The 1970–71 civil war and the October 1973 war also brought setbacks to development plans. The steadying influence has been foreign funds. An estimated 80% of annual national income in the early 1980s came from direct grants from and exports to oil-rich Arab countries and from remittances by Jordanians working there. Also important to the economy has been Western economic aid, notably from the US, the UK, and Germany. The economy expanded rapidly during 1975–80, growing in real terms by an average of 9% a year, but the growth rate slowed to 5% in 1985, primarily from reductions in aid from other Arab states because of their declining oil receipts. The onset of the recession in Jordan in the mid-1980s followed by the economic collapse of 1988–89 and the Gulf conflict in 1990 left the country with an unemployment rate of approximately 30–35%, high inflation, and about 25–30% of the population living below the poverty line. When in 1989 Jordan was unable to service its external debt due to 100 repayment commitments, the Jordanian government concluded an agreement with the IMF to reduce the budget deficit from 24% of GDP in 1988 to 10% of GDP by 1993, and to improve the current account balance from a deficit equivalent to 6% of GDP

in 1988 to a balanced position in 1993. Export earnings were slated to grow from a projected $1.1 billion in 1989 to $1.7 billion in 1993. The rate of inflation was expected to drop from 14% in 1989 to 7% in 1993. However the effects of the Gulf crisis undermined the IMF readjustment package.

In 1995 the government announced an IMF-modeled structural adjustment program for 1996-98. In that year, GDP expanded by 6.4% and expectations were 1996 would see a similar rate. These quite favorable economic statistics stem in large part from Jordan's liberalization reforms, commitment to international investment and the signing of trade and transportation protocols with Israel. Also, in January 1996, the Parliament implemented legislation allowing foreigners to invest in the country's stock market and put in motion a trade harmonization package with other Arab states; most significantly, Sa'udi Arabia.

Growth sectors of importance in 1999 included tourism (although projections in this sector have been impacted by increased hostility between the newly-elected right wing Israeli regime and the Palestinian Authority), the phosphate and potash industries, telecommunications (aided by 1996's Telecommunicators Law permitting private investment in this sector), and computer and information technology development.

In line with IMF-directed austerity measures, Jordan began a series of privitization initiatives in the mid-1990s. According to its plan, the government planned to reduce its holdings from 62% of total economic resources in 1984 to 55% in 1998. The Planning Ministr was charged with selling government interests. Primary sell-off targets in 1997 included the Jordan Electricity Authority, Telecommunications Corporation, and Royal Jordanian Airlines. The government set certain targets, which are as follows: 6.5% real GDP growth, increased foreign exchange reserves by $500 million, reduced customs ceilings to 50%, and an investment rate equal to 34% of GDP.

The international economic embargo against Iraq during the Gulf War meant that Jordan lost a lucrative export and re-export market. The loss of Iraq as the main source of the kingdom's oil supplies resulted in Jordan having to pay the market price for oil imports from Syria and Yemen. The balance of annual aid transfers, some $200 billion, promised by the Arab oil states in 1990, failed to take into consideration the influx of some 230,000 Jordanian nationals from Kuwait that resulted from the Iraqi invasion. They imposed a strain on government services, and added to the pool of unemployment.

GDP growth averaged 4.5% between 1988 and 1998, although it took a downswing in 1998 alone with a rate of 2.2% and reached only 1.4% in 1999. A new agreement with the IMF in 1999 was meant to provide loans for the following three years, offsetting stagnant growth.

20 INCOME

The US Central Intelligence Agency (CIA) reports that in 1998 Jordan's gross domestic product (GDP) was estimated at $15.5 billion. The per capita GDP was estimated at $3,500. The annual growth rate of GDP was estimated at 2.2%. The average inflation rate in 1998 was 4%. The CIA defines GDP as the value of all final goods and services produced within a nation in a given year and computed on the basis of purchasing power parity (PPP) rather than value as measured on the basis of the rate of exchange. It was estimated that agriculture accounted for 6% of GDP, industry 30%, and services 64%.

The World Bank reports that for the same period per capita private consumption (in PPP terms) was $2,830. Private consumption includes expenditures of individuals, households, and non-governmental organizations. It was estimated that between 1990 and 1998 private consumption grew at an annual rate of 4.4%. Approximately 32% of household consumption was spent on food, 17% on fuel, 5% on health care, and 8% on education. The richest 10% of the population accounted for approximately 30% of household consumption and the poorest 10% approximately 3.3%.

21 LABOR

Jordan's labor shortage of the early 1980s changed to a serious labor surplus a decade later because of a high population growth rate (at 3.8% one of the highest in the world) combined with an influx of expatriate Jordanians from the Persian Gulf strained by the tight labor market. Ironically, in the 1980s, the government offered incentives to professionals to come to or to remain in Jordan, and integrated more women into the labor force. In 1991, with an unemployment rate of 18.9%, the government reduced the number of foreign workers and increased funding for job retraining programs accessible to Jordanian workers. It also secured job set-asides for Jordanian workers in Libya, Oman, and Yemen. In 1998, Jordan had a fairly well educated labor force of about one million. In recent years, the government has instituted measures to restrict the employment of foreigners. The Ministry of Labor must approve all such hirings.

The General Federation of Jordanian Trade Unions, formed in 1954, was comprised of 17 trade unions in 1999. Unions are allowed to collectively bargain but they are not allowed to strike or demonstrate without a permit. Labor disputes are mediated by the Ministry of Labor. About 30% of the labor force is unionized. The minimum working age is 16 and this is effectively enforced by the Ministry of Labor except for children working in family businesses or on family farms.

The government set a national minimum wage of $114 per month in 1999 for all sectors except agriculture and domestic labor.

In 1995, Jordan passed a new labor law to bring the country into compliance with international and Arab labor agreements. The law, which came into effect in June 1996, allows employers to fire employees in the event they are forced to undergo re-organization and to reduce the wages—or fire—any employee for any reason. The law also expands worker compensation rules, provides for mandatory unpaid maternity leave, with mandatory full pay in the ten weeks before and after delivery, and establishes a scheme for providing vacation days.

22 AGRICULTURE

Agriculture still plays a role in the economy, although 40% of the usable land consists of the West Bank, lost to Jordan since 1967. As of 1997, only 4.4% of all land in Jordan was utilized for crop sown feed production. Rain-fed lands make up 75% of the arable land, while the remaining 25% is partially or entirely irrigated and lies mostly in the Jordan Valley and highlands. While the system of small owner-operated farms, peculiar to Jordan among the Arab countries and originating in the Land Settlement Law of 1933, limits the number of large landowners and share tenancy, the minuscule holdings have inhibited development. Agriculture accounted for 3% of GDP in 1998.

Production of principal field crops in 1998 included wheat, 55,000 tons; barley, 45,000 tons; tobacco, 2,000 tons; and lentils, 2,000 tons. Prominent vegetables and fruits produced in 1998 included tomatoes, 640,900 tons; eggplant, 70,000 tons; cucumbers, 125,000 tons; and cauliflowers and cabbages, 29,000 tons. Some 16 million fruit trees that year produced 148,000 tons of citrus, 75,000 tons of olives, 73,000 tons of bananas, and 70,000 tons of grapes. The output of fruits and vegetables has been encouraging, in part because of increased use of fertilizers, herbicides, and plastic greenhouses by the nation's farmers in the Jordan Valley.

Irrigation schemes and soil and water conservation programs have received emphasis in Jordan's economic development. The 77-km (48-mi) East Ghor Canal, substantially completed in 1966 and reconstructed in the early 1970s after heavy war damage, siphons water from the Yarmuk River and provides irrigation for about 13,000 hectares (32,000 acres). Water conservation in other areas has been undertaken with the rehabilitation of old water systems and the digging of wells. As of 1997, an estimated 75,000 hectares (185,000 acres) were irrigated.

The cooperative movement has made progress in the agricultural sector; the Central Cooperative Union, established in 1959, provides seasonal loans and advice to local cooperatives. The Agricultural Credit Corporation, founded in 1960, provides low-cost loans to finance agricultural investments.

23 ANIMAL HUSBANDRY

Raising livestock for both meat and dairy products is an important part of Jordanian agriculture. Animal husbandry is usually on a small scale and is often of the nomadic or semino-madic type indigenous to the area. The large nomadic tribes take their camels into the desert every winter, returning nearer to the cultivated area in summer. The camels provide transportation, food (milk and meat), shelter, and clothing (hair); the sale of surplus camels is a source of cash. Sheep and goat nomads make similar use of their animals. Imported milk and meat are sold at subsidized prices.

Animal products account for about one-third of agricultural output. Sheep and goats account for 90% of the livestock, and are raised for both meat and milk. The Awasi is the major breed of sheep used, and the goat is the Baladi. In 1998, the Department of Animal Health and Production at the Ministry of Agriculture put the number of sheep at 1,581,131, goats at 631,408, and cattle at 56,820 head. Jordan had an estimated 23,000,000 chickens in 1998; poultry meat production was 95,000 tons that year. Meat production from cattle and sheep reached 16,000 tons in 1998. Production of fresh milk from cattle and sheep was 135,000 tons in 1998. Jordan produces about 31% of its needs in red meat and 50% of milk.

24 FISHING

Fishing is unimportant as a source of food. The rivers are relatively poor in fish; there are no fish in the Dead Sea, and the short Gulf of Aqaba shoreline has only recently been developed for fishing. The total fish catch was only 552 tons in 1997.

25 FORESTRY

Jordan formerly supported fairly widespread forests of oak and Aleppo pine in the uplands of southern Jordan, both west and east of the Jordan River, but forestland now covers less than 1% of the total area. Scrub forests and maquis growths are the most common; the olive, characteristic of the Mediterranean basin, is widely cultivated. The important forests are around 'Ajlun in the north and near Ma'an. By 1976, some 3,800 hectares (9,400 acres) had been newly planted as part of a government afforestation program. From 1976 to 1991, an additional 10,000 hectares (24,700 acres) also was reforested. Roundwood production was 11,000 tons in 1997. Imports of forestry products totaled $119 million in 1997.

26 MINING

Jordan's mineral resources consist chiefly of phosphate, potash, and limited manganese, copper, kaolin, and gypsum deposits. In 1996, Jordan was the sixth-largest producer of phosphate rock and the seventh-largest producer of potash. Phosphate deposits at Ruseifa, Wadi Al Abyad, Ash Shidiya, and Al-Hasa, are estimated at about 1 billion tons. Phosphate rock production in 1996 was

5,355,000 tons. The Jordan Natural Resources Authority has estimated Jordanian phosphate rock reserves at 1 billion tons. Development of potash was advanced by the completion in 1982 of the Arab Potash Co. plant near the Dead Sea, with a current annual productive capacity of 1.4 million tons. Production was a reported record 1,800,000 tons in 1996. The World Bank has estimated that of the dissolved solids contained in the Dead Sea, 33 billion tons were sodium chloride and magnesium chloride and about 2 billion tons were potassium chloride. Copper deposits between the Dead Sea and the Gulf of Aqaba remained undeveloped. Other potential for progress lies in the availability of bromine, dolomite, gypsum, glass sands, iron, lead, oil shale, tin, travertine, and tripoli.

27 ENERGY AND POWER

Jordan does not have petroleum deposits. Before the Gulf War, its imports of oil from Sa'udi Arabia via the Trans-Arabian pipeline (Tapline) and its refinery at Az-Zarqa', with an annual productive capacity of 22 million barrels, supplied virtually all the country's energy needs. Sa'udi Arabia stopped supplying Jordan via the Tapline during the Gulf War to protest Jordan's tacit support of Iraq during the war. Since the UN embargo, however, Jordan has become the sole legal recipient of Iraqi oil exports, which typically are imported by tanker truck. As of 1999, Jordanian officials were discussing the possibility of reducing this dependence by importing oil from Sa'udi Arabia or Kuwait. Crude oil imports in 1998 averaged 98,000 barrels per day. Large deposits of oil shale have been found, and exploratory drilling for oil and gas has begun in the eastern desert.

Over 99% of electric power was thermal as of 2000, with hydroelectric power accounting for less than half of 1%. The government electrification plan calls for establishment of a national grid, linking the major cities. A project linking the Jordanian and Egyptian power grids via an underwater cable from Aqaba to Talra was inaugurated in 1999. As of 1998, net installed electrical capacity was 1,260 MW, and electricity generated totaled 6,080 million kWh.

28 INDUSTRY

With government encouragement, industry plays an increasingly important part in Jordan's economy. In 1990, the manufacturing sector contributed 15% to GDP at factor cost. Manufacturing output fell by 2.9% in 1991 due to the adverse impact of the Gulf War. In 1992, the sector grew by 6.2%. In 1998, industry as a whole accounted for 26% of GDP, while manufacturing contributed 14%. The sector grew at an annual rate averaging 6.7% between 1988 and 1998. Most industrial income comes from four industries: cement, oil refining, phosphates, and potash. Cement production has been rising since the 1980s. Output of the oil refinery at Az-Zarqa' rose to 90,400 barrels per day in 1999. Phosphate production has been declining since the 1980s. Jordan's Dead Sea potash extraction plant began posting a profit in 1989. The plant has an estimated 1.4 million tons capacity.

29 SCIENCE AND TECHNOLOGY

Expenditures for research and development in 1987–97 totaled 0.26% of GNP. A dozen institutes offer scientific training. The Islamic Academy of Sciences, founded in 1986, is an international organization that promotes science, technology, and development in the Islamic and developing worlds. The Jordan Research Council, founded in 1964, coordinates scientific research in the country. The Royal Scientific Society, founded in 1970, is an independent industrial research and development center. All three institutions are in 'Amman. In 1996 Jordan had 13 universities and colleges offering courses in basic and applied science. In 1987–97, science and engineering students accounted for 26% of college and university enrollments.

30 DOMESTIC TRADE

Lack of proper storage facilities, inadequate transportation service, and a lack of quality controls and product grading are chronic handicaps to Jordanian trade. However, these deficiencies have been alleviated, directly and indirectly, under progressive development plans. Traditional Arab forms of trade remain in evidence, particularly in villages, and farm products generally pass through a long chain of middlemen before reaching the consumer. In 'Amman, however, Westernized modes of distribution have developed, and there are supermarkets and department stores as well as small shops. Business hours are from 8 AM to 1 PM and from 3:30 to 6:30 PM, six days a week. Shops close either on Friday for Muslims or on Sunday for Christians. Banks stay open from 8:30 AM to 12:30 PM and from 3:30 to 5:30 PM, Saturday through Thursday.

31 FOREIGN TRADE

About a quarter of Jordan's commodity exports are fertilizers (35%), amounting to almost a quarter of the world's total exports of crude fertilizers (23%). Other exports include processed animal and vegetable oils (12%), medicinal and pharmaceutical products (10%), vegetables (5.4%), and building materials (3.8%).

In 1995 Jordan's imports were distributed among the following categories:

Consumer goods	9.7%
Food	17.2%
Fuels	13.0%
Industrial supplies	33.4%
Machinery	14.0%
Transportation	12.1%
Other	0.6%

Principal trading partners in 1998 (in millions of US dollars) were as follows:

COUNTRY	EXPORTS	IMPORTS	BALANCE
Saudi Arabia	225	148	77
Japan	58	212	-154
United Kingdom	41	227	-186
China (inc. Hong Kong)	23	183	-160
Italy	22	226	-204
Korea	18	158	-140
United States	16	388	-372
Germany	15	350	-335
Turkey	7	156	-149
France	3	164	-161

32 BALANCE OF PAYMENTS

Jordan's chronically adverse trade balance has long been offset by payments from foreign governments and agencies, especially from Jordan's oil-rich Arab allies, and by remittances from Jordanians working abroad, chiefly in Sa'udi Arabia. During the Gulf War, expatriate remittances and aid from Arab countries dropped sharply, causing the improvement of the trade deficit to halt. This trend continued into the mid-1990s despite an increasing surplus in the services sector.

The US Central Intelligence Agency reports that in 1997 the purchasing power parity of Jordan's exports was $1.5 billion while imports totaled $3.9 billion resulting in a trade balance of -$2.4 billion.

The International Monetary Fund (IMF) reports that in 1998 Jordan had exports of goods totaling $1,802 million and imports totaling $3,404 million. The services credit totaled $1,825 million and debit $1,784 million. The following table summarizes Jordan's balance of payments as reported by the IMF for 1998 in millions of US dollars.

Current Account		14
Balance on goods	-1,602	
Balance on services	41	
Balance on income	-138	
Current transfers	1,712	
Capital Account		81
Financial Account		-177
Direct investment abroad	...	
Direct investment in Jordan	310	
Portfolio investment assets	...	
Portfolio investment liabilities	...	
Other investment assets	-80	
Other investment liabilities	-407	
Net Errors and Omissions		-454
Reserves and Related Items		536

33BANKING AND SECURITIES

The Central Bank of Jordan, founded in 1964 with a capital of JD2 million and reorganized in 1971, is in charge of note issue, foreign exchange control, and supervision of commercial banks, in cooperation with the Economic Security Council. In 1995, the Central Bank established the dinar as a fully convertible currency for non-capital remittances. In November of that year the bank announced a fixed dollar-dinar rate for current payments. Because of Jordan's IMF-led structural adjustments and trade and investment liberalizations, it became the first Arab country to receive credit ratings from both Standard and Poor and Moody's.

The banking system includes, besides the Central Bank, thirteen commercial banks (five of which are branches of foreign banks), five investment banks, two Islamic banks, one Industrial Development Bank, and several other institutions. Commercial banks have a tradition of being both small, with a low capital base, and highly conservative. The Arab Bank, by far the largest "high street" bank, and the Housing Bank are the largest banks in Jordan. Jordanian banks have acted rapidly to fill the banking void in the Occupied Territories, since the agreement between the PLO and Israel transferred administrative authority to the Palestinians. State banks include the Arab Bank, The Bank of Jordan, Cairo Amman Bank, Jordan-Kuwait Bank, and the Jordan National Bank. Commercial banks included those of Jordan, other Arab countries, the UK, and the US. Foreign commercial banks in Jordan include the British Bank of the Middle East, Citibank (US), the Arab Land Bank, and the Arab Banking Corporation (Jordan). The late 1970s and 1980s saw an expansion of niche institutions, such as four investment banks, six specialized credit institutions (three of which are under public ownership), four non-banking financial institutions, and one Islamic bank. Unfortunately, many of these have been either too small to have had a strong impact on the provision of credit, or have replicated the approach of the commercial banks. Since 1992, moneychangers have been able to operate legally, having been closed down in February 1989, but their area of operation has been heavily circumscribed.

Loans are extended by the Jordan Industrial Bank, Agricultural Credit Corp., Jordan Co-operative Organization, and other credit institutions.

The Amman Financial Market (AFM) has been in existence since the late 1970s. Like most of the equity markets in the Middle East, the AFM is small and lacking in the dynamism that has seen markets in Latin America and Asia take off over the past ten years. A total of 115 companies were listed in 1997, making the AFM second in the Arab world only to Egypt, which quoted some 700 stocks. The capitalization of the AFM stood at around $5 billion, putting it level with Bahrain, but ahead of Oman and Tunisia. In 1996, the government instituted a law allowing foreigners to invest in the AFM. In 1999, the Amman Stock Exchange was established as a privately managed institution. There were 149 listed public-shareholding companies at that time, with a market capitalization of approximately $6 billion.

34INSURANCE

The Al Ahlia Insurance Co. and the Jordan Insurance Co. offer commercial insurance. Several US and British insurance companies have branches or agents in Jordan. A new Insurance Law in 1998 brought about stricter regulation of the industry.

35PUBLIC FINANCE

Jordan has had to rely on foreign assistance for support of its budget, which has increased rapidly since the 1967 war. During the late 1980s, Jordan incurred large fiscal deficits, which led to a heavy burden of external debt. Efforts at cutting public expenditures reduced the budget deficit from 21% of GDP in 1989 to 18% in 1991. The Persian Gulf war, however, forced Jordan to delay the IMF deficit reduction program begun in 1989. In 1992, expenditures exceeded revenues by $600 million. By 1993, the current account deficit stood at 11.4% of GDP, far higher than IMF targets. By 1994, the government's austerity measures reduced this figure to 6.7%, and in 1995 it had come into line with targets at 3.7% of GDP. The current account had a surplus of .4% of GDP in 1997, and was balanced in 1998.

The US Central Intelligence Agency (CIA) estimates that in 1999 Jordan's central government took in revenues of approximately $2.8 billion and had expenditures of $3 billion including capital expenditures of $672 million. Overall, the government registered a deficit of approximately $200 million. External debt totaled $8.5 billion.

The following table shows an itemized breakdown of government revenues and expenditures. The percentages were calculated from data reported by the International Monetary Fund. The dollar amounts (millions) are based on the CIA estimates provided above.

REVENUE AND GRANTS	100%	2,800
Tax revenue	64.5%	1,806
Non-tax revenue	21.9%	614
Capital revenue	0.1%	2
Grants	13.5%	378
EXPENDITURES	100%	3,000
General public services	6.1%	184
Defense	17.9%	537
Public order and safety	8.3%	248
Education	14.6%	437
Health	10.2%	307
Social security	17.8%	533
Housing and community amenities	2.0%	61
Recreation, cultural, and religious affairs	2.1%	63
Economic affairs and services	8.7%	261
Other expenditures	0.3%	10
Interest payments	11.9%	358

36TAXATION

Corporations are taxed at a rate of 15% (35% for those involved in banking and finance). The personal income tax rate is 5% to 30%, less deductions and exemptions. There are no capital gains or net worth taxes on individuals, and social security taxes are paid jointly by employers and employees. Sales taxes range from 0% to 20%, with a 10% services tax. There is an added social service tax of 10% on income.

37CUSTOMS AND DUTIES

Customs and excise duties provide a large portion of all tax revenues. All imports and exports are subject to licenses. Import duties are levied by c.i.f. value, with a 0% to 40% rate. Jordan grants preferential treatment to imports from Arab League countries, under bilateral trade agreements that exempt certain items from duty and under multilateral trade and transit agreements with Arab League countries.

38 FOREIGN INVESTMENT

In the past there was little foreign investment in Jordan apart from the oil pipelines, but since the early 1970s, the government has offered liberal tax inducements, including a six-year corporate tax holiday established in 'Amman and a tax holiday of up to 10 years outside the capital, to encourage foreign investors; 100% foreign ownership of local enterprises is permitted in some cases. In 1980, the government formed the Jordanian Industrial Estates Corp., near 'Amman, to attract new industries to planned industrial complexes; investors were granted two-year income tax exemptions. Jordan also has established four free-trade zones, at Al-'Aqabah, Az-Zarqa', and the Queen Alia International Airport and along the Syrian frontier, near the Jordan-Syria rail link.

In 1995, Jordan hosted an international conference on investment in the Kingdom as part of its recent opening to international investment. It also announced intentions to begin selling off government shares in major enterprises, including telecommunications and the Royal Jordanian Airlines. In 1997, the country had $1.2 billion in foreign exchange reserves.

39 ECONOMIC DEVELOPMENT

Before the upheavals caused by the war of 1967, the government had begun to design its first comprehensive development plans. The Jordan Development Board, established in 1952, adopted a five-year program for 1961–65 and a seven-year program for 1964–70, which was interrupted by war. In 1971, a newly created National Planning Council, with wide responsibility for national planning, prepared the 1973–75 plan for the East Bank, with a planned total outlay of JD179 million. The main objectives were to reduce the trade deficit, increase the GNP, expand employment, and reduce dependence on foreign aid. At least 60% of the planned projects were completed, and a new five-year plan was instituted on 1 January 1976.

The 1976–80 plan entailed outlays of JD844 million (at 1975 constant prices) and achieved an annual GDP growth rate of 9.6%, below the goal of 11.9% Notable development projects included port expansion at al-'Aqabah and construction of Queen Alia International Airport. The 1981–85 development plan allocated funds totaling JD3,300 million and projected an economic growth rate of 10.4% annually (17% for industry and mining, 7% for agriculture). The plan envisaged completion of large potash and fertilizer installations, as well as the first stage of construction of the 150 m (492 ft) Maqarin Dam project on the Yarmuk River, which would store water for irrigation. This project also was to extend the East Ghor Canal 14 km (9 mi) from Karama to the Dead Sea. The Maqarin Dam project was shelved indefinitely, however.

The 1986–90 development plan allocated JD3,115.5 million, to be shared between the public sector (52%) and the private and mixed sector (48%). The goals of the plan were the following: realization of a 5.1% annual growth rate in the GDP; creation of 97,000 new employment opportunities; a decrease in imports and an increase in exports to achieve a more favorable balance of trade; expansion of investment opportunities to attract more Arab and foreign capital; development of technological expertise and qualified personnel; attainment of a balanced distribution of economic gains nationally through regional development; and expansion and upgrading of health, education, housing, and other social services.

Between 1953 and 1986, Jordan received development assistance from the IBRD and other international agencies, other Arab countries, the UK, Germany, and the US. The US provided nearly

$1.7 billion in nonmilitary assistance and more than $1.4 billion in military aid. Aid from Arab oil-producing countries totaled $322 million in 1984. The April 1989 riots in Jordan led to a new surge of aid transfers. Arab grants to Jordan in 1989 fell between $360 million and $430 million. Political dissatisfaction in Kuwait and Saudi Arabia at Jordan's policy during the Gulf crisis resulted, however, in the Gulf states denying further direct grant assistance.

In 1988, Jordan began working with the IMF on restructuring its economy. These plans were thrown into considerable disarray by political events in the Gulf (most notably Jordan's ill-conceived support of Iraq in the face of global opposition to that country's 1990 invasion of Kuwait), but new agreements were concluded in 1991, as Jordan began to institute democratic reforms. Foremost in the IMF plan are reductions in government spending, taming of inflation, increasing foreign exchange, and decreasing government ownership of economic enterprises. In the economic plan of 1996–98, Jordan is expected to decrease its ownership of enterprises from 1994's level of 64% to 55% by 1998.

40 SOCIAL DEVELOPMENT

The social insurance system provides old-age, disability, and survivor benefits, as well as workers' compensation. Public employees and workers over the age of 16 working in private companies with 5 or more employees are covered. In 1999, workers contributed 5% of their wages, employers paid 8% of payroll, and the government covered any deficit. The retirement age is 60 for men and 55 for women if coverage requirements are met. A funeral grant of 150 dinars is also provided.

The UNRWA conducts an extensive welfare program for Palestinian refugees. Many Christian sects maintain hospitals, orphanages, and schools, financed mainly from foreign sources.

Women's rights are often dictated by Islam. Under Shari'a law, men may obtain a divorce more easily than women, a female heir's inheritance is half that of a male, and in court, a woman's testimony has only half the value of a man's. Married women are required by law to obtain their husband's permission to apply for a passport. As of 1997, 3 of 120 parliamentary seats were held by women. The Criminal Code provides for lenient sentences for men accused of murdering wives they believed to be adulterous in order to "cleanse the honor" of their families. This defense is not available to women.

The rights of children are generally well respected in Jordan. The government makes an effort to enforce child labor laws.

Palestinian refugees arriving after 1967 are not entitled to citizenship. Bedouins are entitled to full citizenship, but nonetheless experience professional and social discrimination. Six seats in the Chamber of Deputies are set aside for Bedouin representatives. Human rights violations by the government included police brutality, arbitrary arrest and detention, and there were also allegations of torture. A 1998 law placed restrictions on freedom of the press, but they were partially reduced the following year.

41 HEALTH

In 1994, Jordan had 1 hospital bed per 613 people. In 1995, Jordan had 6,839 physicians, 3,118 pharmacists, 2,015 dentists, and 4,304 nurses. The UNRWA maintains its own hospitals and maternity centers. A medical faculty was added at the University of Jordan in 1972.

Medical services are concentrated in the main towns, but in recent decades the government has attempted to bring at least a minimum of modern medical care to rural areas. Village clinics are staffed by trained nurses, with regular visits by government physicians. As modern medicine has spread to the more remote areas, traditional methods have been dying out. The Ministry of

Health, created in 1950, in cooperation with UNICEF, WHO, and the UNRWA, has greatly reduced the incidence of malaria and tuberculosis. In 1996, there were only 8 reported cases of tuberculosis per 100,000 people. Trachoma, hepatitis, typhoid fever, intestinal parasites, acute skin inflammations, and other endemic conditions remain common, however. In 1990–95, 89% of the population had access to safe water, and 95% of the population had adequate sanitation. Total health care expenditures for 1995 were $347 million. Public expenditures on health in 1994 were 4% of the gross domestic product.

In 1999, average life expectancy was 73 years. In 1999, the crude birth rate was 34 per 1,000 people. About 35% of married women (ages 15 to 49) used contraception in 1994.

The infant mortality rate was 33 per 1,000 live births in 1999, and the general mortality rate was 4 per 1,000 people.

The under-5 mortality has been reduced dramatically from 149 in 1960 to 33 in 1999 for every 1,000 live births. Immunization rates for children up to one year old between 1990–94 were tuberculosis (93%); diphtheria, pertussis, and tetanus (87%); polio (94%); and measles (69%). Only four cases of polio were reported in 1994. None were seen in 1996. From 1989 to 1995, 17% of all children under 5 were malnourished.

The HIV-1 seroprevalence rate was 0.0 per 100 adults in 1997.

42 HOUSING

A general housing shortage in the mid-1960s was aggravated by the influx of West Bank refugees after the 1967 war, and Jordan still lacked adequate housing in the early 1980s. During 1981–86, some 42,300 new residential building permits were issued. According to the latest available information for 1980–88, the total number of dwellings was 660,000 with 4.1 people per dwelling.

43 EDUCATION

Jordan has made great strides in reducing illiteracy, the rate of which has declined from 68% 1961 to 13.5% in 1995. Adult illiteracy rates for the year 2000 were estimated at 10.2% (males, 5.1%; females, 15.6%). Education is compulsory between the ages of 6–15. Ten years are devoted to primary education, followed by two years at the secondary stage. In 1998, Jordan had 2,623 primary schools with 45,367 teachers and 1,121,866 pupils. Secondary schools had a total of 155,008 pupils, with 9,300 teachers, in the same year. The United National Relief and Works Agency (UNRWA) operates 208 schools in refugee camps.

Jordan has five universities: the University of Jordan (founded in 1962), at 'Amman; Yarmuk University at Irbid; Mut'ah University, in Karak governorate in southern Jordan; the University of Jordan for Science and Technology; and the Zaqa University established in 1993. In addition there are 53 community colleges; two of these are UNRWA schools on the East Bank for Palestinian students. In 1997, 112,959 students were enrolled at all higher level institutions while higher education teaching staff numbered 5,275.

44 LIBRARIES AND MUSEUMS

The library at the University of Jordan has 560,000 volumes. In 1977, the department of Libraries, Documentation, and Archives was founded to establish the national library, which had 70,000 volumes in 2000. The Scientific and Technical Information Center in Amma holds 47,000 volumes. The University of Jordan for Women, founded in 1991, holds 17,000 volumes. More than half of Jordan's museums are archaeological and historical. Amman has four major museums: the Jordan Archaeological Museum, the Folklore Museum, the Popular Life Museum, and the Mosaic Gallery.

45 MEDIA

Public communications and broadcasting facilities are government controlled. Telephone and telegraph facilities were introduced soon after World War II. Telephone service, at first rudimentary, was expanded in the 1950s; in 1998 Jordan had 425,000 telephones, mostly in 'Amman and the larger towns. In the same year, there were two cellular telephone providers with approximately 8,000 subscribers and four Internet service providers with some 8,000 subscribers.

Radio Jordan transmits AM and FM broadcasts in English, and the government-owned television station broadcasts programs in English, Arabic, French, and Hebrew on two channels. As of 1999, there were 6 AM and 7 FM radio stations and 8 television stations. In 1997 there were 287 radios, 43 television sets, and 2 mobile phones per 1,000 population.

Jordan's three major daily newspapers (with 1999 estimated daily circulations) are Al-Dustur ("Constitution") (90,000), Al-Rai ("Opinion") (90,000), Al Aswaq (10,000), and Jordan Times (12,000). All except the English-language Jordan Times are in Arabic, and all are published in 'Amman and are owned and operated by the private sector. Al-Rai is a government-controlled paper, founded after the 1970–71 civil war; Al-Dustur is 25% government owned. There are also weeklies and less frequent publications published in Arabic in 'Amman. One weekly, The Star, is published in English. The press code, enacted in 1955, requires all newspapers to be licensed and prohibits the publishing of certain information, mainly relating to Jordan's national security, unless taken directly from material released by the government.

The constitution provides for freedom of speech and the press; however, in practice there are some significant restrictions on these rights. Private citizens can be prosecuted for slandering the Royal Family, and the Press and Publication Law of 1993 restricts the media coverage of 10 subjects, including the military, the royal family, and economic policy.

As of 1996, there were over 40,000 personal computers; in 1998 there were less than one Internet host per 1,000 population.

46 ORGANIZATIONS

Religious organizations still are of major importance, and membership in the hamula, the kinship group or lineage comprising several related families, also is of great significance as a framework for social organization. Literary and theatrical clubs have become popular, especially since World War II, but political organizations died out after the 1957 ban on political parties. There are chambers of commerce in 'Amman and other large towns.

47 TOURISM, TRAVEL, AND RECREATION

Tourism has recovered from the decline caused by the Gulf War; 1,256,428 tourists arrived in Jordan in 1998. Of these arrivals, more than 50% were from Saudi Arabia. Tourism receipts totaled $810 million that year. There were 12,109 rooms in hotels and other establishments with 23,777 beds and a 44% occupancy rate in 1997.

The East Bank is an area of immense historical interest, with some 800 archaeological sites, including 224 in the Jordan Valley. Jordan's notable tourist attractions include the Greco-Roman remains at Jerash (ancient Garasi), which was one of the major cities of the Decapolis (the capital, 'Amman, was another, under the name of Philadelphia) and is one of the best-preserved cities of its time in the Middle East. Petra (Batra), the ancient capital of Nabataea in southern Jordan, carved out of the red rock by the Nabataeans, is probably the East Bank's most famous historical site. Natural attractions include the Jordan Valley and the Dead Sea, which—at 392 m below sea level—is the lowest spot on Earth.

Eastern Jordan has modern hotel facilities in 'Amman and Al-'Aqabah, and there are government-built rest houses at some of the remote points of interest. Tourists are permitted to bring in unlimited foreign currency. Passport and visa are required for entry except for nationals of certain Middle Eastern countries.

The beaches on the Gulf of Aqaba offer holiday relaxation for Jordanians, as well as tourists. Sports facilities include swimming pools, tennis and squash courts, and bowling alleys.

In 1999, the UN estimated the cost of staying in Amman at $143 per day. Daily costs elsewhere were about $134.

48FAMOUS JORDANIANS

The founder of Jordan's Hashemite dynasty—the term stems from the Hashemite (or Hashimite) branch of the tribe of the Prophet Muhammad—was Hussein ibn-'Ali (Husayn bin 'Ali, 1856–1931), sharif of Mecca and king of the Hijaz.

As a separate Arab country, Jordan has had a relatively short history, during which only two men have become internationally known. The first of these was the founder of the kingdom, 'Abdallah ibn-Husayn (1882–1951). Although he was born in Hijaz and was a son of the sharif of Mecca, he made 'Amman his headquarters. He was recognized as emir in 1921 and king in 1946. The second was his grandson, King Hussein I (Husayn ibn-Talal, 1935–99), ruled from 1953 until his death. In June 1978, 16 months after the death by helicopter crash of Queen Alia (1948–77), Hussein married his fourth wife, the Queen Noor al-Hussein (Elizabeth Halaby, b. US, 1951).

49DEPENDENCIES

Jordan has no territories or colonies.

50BIBLIOGRAPHY

Al Madfai, Madiha Rashid. *Jordan, the United States, and the Middle East Peace Process, 1974–1991*. Cambridge: Cambridge University Press, 1993.

Badran, Adman, and Bichara Khader. *The Economic Development of Jordan*. Wolfeboro, N.H.: Longwood, 1986.

Brand, Laurie A. *Jordan's Inter-Arab Relations: The Political Economy of Alliance Making*. New York: Columbia University Press, 1994.

Garrard, Andrew N. and Hans Georg Gebel (eds.). *The Prehistory of Jordan: The State of Research in 1986*. Oxford, Eng.: B.A.R., 1988.

Hussein, King, of Jordan. *My War with Israel*. New York: Morrow, 1969.

Jordan in Pictures. Minneapolis: Lerner, 1988.

Jordan in the Middle East: The Making of a Pivotal State, 1948–1988. Ilford, England: Frank Cass, 1994.

Lavy, Victor. *Foreign Aid and Economic Development in the Middle East: Egypt, Syria, and Jordan*. New York: Praeger, 1991.

Lawrence, T. E. *The Seven Pillars of Wisdom*. New York: Penguin, 1976 (orig. 1926).

Layne, Linda L. *Home and Homeland: The Dialogics of Tribal and National Identities in Jordan*. Princeton, N.J.: Princeton University Press, 1994.

Lewis, Norman N. *Nomads and Settlers in Syria and Jordan, 1800–1980*. New York: Cambridge University Press, 1987.

Lunt, James D. *Hussein of Jordan: A Political Biography*. London: Macmillan, 1989.

Marashdeh, Omar. *The Jordanian Economy*. Amman, Jordan: Al-Jawal Corporation, 1995.

Metz, Helen Chapin (ed.). *Jordan, A Country Study*. 4th ed. Washington, D.C.: Library of Congress, 1991.

Mutawi, Samir A. *Jordan in the 1967 War*. New York: Cambridge University Press, 1987.

Pappe, Ilan. *Britain and the Arab-Israeli Conflict, 1948–51*. New York: St. Martin's, 1988.

Pundik, Ron. *The Struggle for Sovereignty: Relations Between Great Britain and Jordan, 1946–1951*. Cambridge, Mass: B. Blackwell, 1994.

Rollin, Sue. *Jordan*. 2d ed. New York: W.W. Norton, 1998.

Salibi, Kamal S. *The Modern History of Jordan*. New York: I.B. Tauris, 1993.

Satloff, Robert B. *From Abdullah to Hussein: Jordan in Transition*. New York: Oxford University Press, 1994.

Seccombe, Ian J. *Jordan*. Santa Barbara, Calif.: ABC-Clio, 1984.

Wilson, Rodney (ed.). *Politics and the Economy in Jordan*. New York: Routledge, 1991.

KAZAKHSTAN

Republic of Kazakhstan
Kazakstan Respublikasy

CAPITAL: Almaty (Alma Ata).

FLAG: Light blue with a yellow sun and soaring eagle in the center and a yellow vertical ornamentation in the hoist.

ANTHEM: National Anthem of Kazakhstan.

MONETARY UNIT: The tenge (T), issued in 15 November 1993, is the national currency. There is a coin, the tyin. One hundred tyin equal one tenge. As of 31 March 2000 T1=$0.00713 ($1=T140.25), but exchange rates fluctuate widely.

WEIGHTS AND MEASURES: The metric system is in force.

HOLIDAYS: New Year, 31 December–1 January; International Women's Day, 8 March; Nauryz (Kazak New Year), 28 March; Solidarity Day, 1 May; Victory Day, 9 May; Independence Day, 25 October.

TIME: 5 PM = noon GMT.

¹LOCATION, SIZE, AND EXTENT

Kazakhstan is located in southern Asia between Russia and Uzbekistan, bordering on the Caspian Sea and the Aral Sea, with a total area of 2,717,300 sq km (1,049,155 sq mi). Kazakhstan shares boundaries with Russia on the N and W, China on the E, Kyrgyzstan, Uzbekistan, and Turkmenistan on the S, and the Caspian Sea on the W. Kazakhstan's boundary length totals 12,012 km (7,464 mi). Its capital city, Almaty (Alma-Ata) is located in the southeastern part of the country. The process is underway to shift the capital to Aqmola, in the north central part of the state.

²TOPOGRAPHY

The topography of Kazakhstan is varied, as it extends from the Volga River to the Altai Mountains, and from plains in western Siberia to central Asian oasis and desert. About 13% of Kazakhstan's land is arable with less than 1% under irrigation.

³CLIMATE

The country has an arid continental climate. In the capital the mean temperature in July is 27°C (81°F). In January, the mean temperature is −5°C (23°F). Rainfall averages between 25 cm (9.8 in) and 38 cm (15 in). Because of the wide ranges in elevation in the country, there are wide variations in temperature and rainfall.

⁴FLORA AND FAUNA

The sparse plant covering in the desert consists of saltworts, wormwoods, alhagi, and a haloxylon typical of the southern desert. Animals include the antelope, sand cat, and jerboa.

⁵ENVIRONMENT

Kazakhstan faces several important environmental issues. As the site of the former Soviet Union's nuclear testing programs, areas of the nation have been exposed to high levels of nuclear radiation, and there is significant radioactive pollution. The nation also has 30 uranium mines, which add to the problem of uncontrolled release of radioactivity. Kazakhstan has sought international support to convince China to stop testing atomic bombs near its territory, because of the dangerous fallout.

Mismanagement of irrigation projects has caused the level of the Aral Sea to drop by 13 m, decreasing its size by 50%. The change in size has changed the climate in the area and revealed 3 million hectares of land that are now subject to erosion.

Air pollution in Kazakhstan is another significant environmental problem. Acid rain damages the environment within the country and also affects neighboring countries. In 1992 Kazakhstan had the world's 14th highest level of industrial carbon dioxide emissions, which totaled 297.9 million metric tons, a per capita level of 17.48 metric tons. Pollution from industrial and agricultural sources has also damaged the nation's water supply. UN sources report that, in some cases, contamination of rivers by industrial metals is 160 to 800 times beyond acceptable levels. Pollution of the Caspian Sea is also a problem.

Kazakhstan's wildlife is in danger of extinction due to the overall level of pollution. According to current estimates, some areas of the nation will not be able to sustain any form of wildlife by the year 2015. In the areas where pollution is the most severe, 11 species of mammals and 19 species of birds and insects are already extinct. Threatened species include the argali, great bustard, snow leopard, and tiger.

⁶POPULATION

The population of Kazakhstan in 2000 was estimated at 16,816,150. An estimated 7.1% of the population is 65 years of age or older. The projected population for the year 2005 is 16,904,000, assuming a crude birthrate of 18 per 1,000 population and a death rate of 11, resulting in a natural rate of change of 0.8% for the period 2000–2005. The population rate of change between 1995 and 2000 was 0.1%. The population density in 1998 was 6 per sq km (16 per sq mi).

It was estimated that 62% of the population lived in urban areas in 2000, up from 54% in 1980. The capital city, Alma-Ata, and the surrounding metropolitan area had a 2000 population of 1,309,000. Other major metropolitan areas, with estimated population counts, include Karaganda, 596,000; Chimkent, 404,000; Pavlodar, 349,000; Semipalatinsk, 342,000; and Ust-Kamenogorsk, 334,000.

⁷MIGRATION

Kazakhs abroad (in China, Mongolia, and other newly independent republics of the former USSR) are encouraged to return. Those who fled in Stalin's time automatically received citizenship; others must apply.

In 1996, there was an organized return of 70,000 Kazakhs from Mongolia, Iran, and Turkey. During 1991–95, 82,000 Ukrainians and 16,000 Belarussians repatriated. Between 1991–96, 614,000 Russians repatriated and 70,000 Kazakhs had repatriated from CIS countries. During 1992–96, 480,000 ethnic Germans had returned to Germany. These Germans were forcibly deported to Central Asia during World War II as from the Volga region.

As of 1996, 42,000 Kazakhs had been displaced internally or had left for other CIS countries as a result of the ecological problems of the Aral Sea, which had lost three-fourths its volume of water. There were also 160,000 displaced persons as a result of Semipalatinsk, an above-ground nuclear testing site in northern Kazakhstan. Since 1991, 45,000 Kazakhs were displaced internally, and 116,000 had left for other CIS countries.

As of September 1999, there were an estimated 35,000 refugees and asylum seekers in Kazakhstan. Of these, there were some 25,000 returnees of ethnic Kazakh origin, 6,000 Tajiks, 3,000 Afghans, Chechens, Georgians, and Armenians, as well as individual cases from China, African and other countries. The majority of the refugee population is located in the former capital Almaty and the southern part of the country. In 1999 the net migration rate was -7.73 migrants per 1,000 population.

⁸ETHNIC GROUPS

Kazakhs constituted 46% of the population in 1996 and Russians, 34.7%. The remaining population consists of Ukrainians (4.9%), Germans (3.1%), Uzbeks (2.3%), Tatars (1.9%), and other groups collectively constituting 7.1%.

⁹LANGUAGES

The constitution declares Kazak to be the state language and requires the president to be a Kazak speaker. Kazak is a Turkic language written in Cyrillic script with many special letters (but in Roman script in China since 1960). Modern Kazak utilizes many words of foreign origin from Russian, Arabic, Persian, Mongol, Chinese, Tatar, and Uzbek. Not even half of all Kazakhs can speak the language effectively (only about 40%). Almost everyone can speak Russian (66%), which has special status as the "language of interethnic communication."

¹⁰RELIGIONS

The Kazakhs, a distinct ethnic group originating with Turkic and Mongol settlers who arrived there in late antiquity (first century BC) are the dominant element in the population and are primarily Sunni Muslims of the Hanafi persuasion (approximately 47%). Islam had been adopted by the Kazakhs as early as 1043, but many of its popular religious practices did not become common until the late 18th century.

The rest of the population is composed of Russian Orthodox (44%), Protestants (2%), and others (7%).

¹¹TRANSPORTATION

About 14,400 km (8,948 mi) of railroad tracks traverse Kazakhstan, all 1.52-m-gauge. Highways totaled 141,000 km (87,617 mi) in 1997, of which 104,200 km (64,750 mi) were paved. In 1994, General Motors Corp. signed an agreement to distribute North American-built vehicles in Kazakhstan. The primary port is Guryev, on the Caspian Sea. There are 3,900 km (2,423 mi) of inland waterways on the Syrdariya and Ertis rivers. Much of the infrastructure connects Kazakhstan with Russia rather than points within Kazakhstan. In 1997 there were 10 airports, 9 of which had paved runways. In the same year, 568,000 passengers were carried on scheduled domestic and international flights.

¹²HISTORY

There is evidence of human habitation in present-day Kazakhstan from the earliest Stone Age, more than 300,000 years ago. The steppe characteristics of most of the region are best suited for nomadic pastoralism, which an ever-shifting pattern of peoples have pursued in this territory. Achaemenid documents give the name Sacae to the first such group to be historically recorded. In the 3rd and 2nd centuries BC they were displaced by the Usun in the east, the Kangiui in the south central region, and the Alani in the west.

The first well-established state was that of the Turkic Kaganate, in the 6th century AD, replaced in the early 8th century by the Turgesh state. In 766, the Karluks established dominance in what now is eastern Kazakhstan. Some of the southern portions of the region fell under Arab influence in the 8th–9th centuries, and Islam was introduced. Western Kazakhstan was under Oghuz control in 9th to the 11th centuries; at roughly the same time the Kimak and Kipchak tribes, of Turkic origin, controlled the east. The large central desert of Kazakhstan is still called "Dashti-Kipchak," or the Kipchak Steppe.

The Karluk state was destroyed by invading Iagmas in the late 9th and early 10th centuries. They formed the Karakhanid state, which controlled extensive lands into what is now China. The Karakhanids were in a constant state of war with the Seljuks, to the south, and control of parts of what is now Kazakhstan passed back and forth between them. The Karakhanids collapsed in the 1130s when they were invaded by Khitans, who established the Karakitai state. In the mid-12th century, Khwarazm split off from the weakening Karakitais, but the bulk of the state survived until the invasion of Genghiz Khan, 1219–1221.

Kazakhstan was part of Batu's Golden Horde, which in the 14th century broke up into the White Horde and Mogulistan. By the early 15th century, the White Horde had split into several large khanates, including the Nogai Horde and the Uzbek Khanate.

The present-day Kazakhs formed in the mid-15th century when clan leaders Janibek and Girei broke away from Abul Khair, leader of the Uzbeks, to seek their own territory in Semirechie, between the Chu and Talas rivers. First to unite the Kazakhs into one people was Khan Kasym (1511–23). When the Nogai Horde and Siberian Khanates broke up in the mid 16th century, tribes from both joined the Kazakhs. The clans separated into three Hordes: the Great Horde, which controlled Semirechie; the Middle Horde, which had central Kazakhstan, and the Lesser Horde, which had western Kazakhstan.

Russian traders and soldiers began to appear on the northwestern edge of Kazakh territory in the 17th century, when Cossacks founded the forts which became the cities of Uralsk and Gurev. The Kazakh khanate was in disarray at the time, badly pressed by Kalmyk invaders who had begun to move in from the east. Pushed west in what the Kazakhs call their "Great Retreat," the Kazakh position deteriorated until, in 1726, Lesser Horde khan Abul'khair requested Russian assistance. From that point on the Lesser Horde was under Russian control. The Middle Horde was conquered by 1798. The Great Horde remained independent until the 1820s, when pressure from both the Kokand Khanate and Russia forced them to choose what they regarded as the lesser of evils, the Russians.

There was, however, considerable resistance, led by Khan Kenen (Kenisary Kasimov), of the Middle Horde, whose followers fought the Russians 1836–47. Khan Kene is now regarded as a Kazakh national hero. Russian attempts to quell this resistance led to establishment of a number of forts and

LOCATION: 48°N; 60°E. BOUNDARY LENGTHS: Total boundary lengths, 12,012 km (7,464 mi); Russia, 6,846 km (4,254 mi); China, 1,533 km (954 mi); Kyrgyzstan, 1,051 km (653 mi); Uzbekistan, 2,203 km (1,369 mi); Turkmenistan, 379 km (236 mi).

settlements in Kazakh territory, which made Kazakh nomadism impossible and destroyed the Kazakh economy.

In 1863, Russia promulgated a policy in the Gorchakov Circular which asserted the right to annex "troublesome" border areas. It was on this basis that Russian troops began the conquest of Central Asia. Most of Kazakhstan was made part of the Steppe district of the Russian empire; the rest was in Turkestan.

Beginning in the 1890s Russian settlers were aggressively moved into fertile lands in northern and eastern Kazakhstan, further displacing the nomadic Kazakhs. Between 1906 and 1912 more than a half-million Russian farms were started as part of the Stolypin reforms. By the time of the 1916 uprising the Kazakhs were broken and starving. Despite a strong effort against the Russians, they were savagely repressed.

At the time of the revolution a group of secular nationalists called the Alash Orda attempted to create a Kazakh government, but it lasted less than two years (1918–20) before surrendering to the Bolsheviks.

The Kazakh Autonomous Soviet Socialist Republic was declared in 1920 and elevated to full republic status in 1936. In the period 1929–34, when Stalin was abolishing private agriculture and establishing huge collective farms, Kazakhstan suffered repeated famines which killed at least 1.5 million Kazakhs, as well as destroying 80% of the republic's livestock.

In World War II much Russian industry was evacuated to Kazakhstan; this was followed in 1953–65 by the so-called Virgin Lands campaign, which converted huge tracts of Kazakh grazing land to wheat and other cereal production. This campaign brought thousands more Russians and other non-Kazakhs to Kazakhstan; as a result Kazakhstan became the only Soviet republic in which the eponymous people were not a majority of the population. Because Russians and other Europeans nearly equal the number of Kazakhs in the republic, virtually every public act requires a delicate balancing of differing interests.

On 16 December 1986, Mikhail Gorbachev replaced Kazakhstan's longtime leader Dinmukhamed Kunayev, a Kazakh, with a Russian from outside the republic. This set off three days of rioting, the first public nationalist protest in the Soviet Union. In June 1989, more civil disturbances hastened the appointment of Nursultan Nazarbayev as republic leader. A metallurgist and a Kazakh, Nazarbayev became prominent in the last Soviet years as a spokesman both for greater republic sovereignty and for the formation of a confederation of former Soviet republics. He was elected president by the Kazakhstan parliament in 1990, which was reaffirmed by public vote in an uncontested election in December 1991. Not a party to the dissolution of the Soviet Union announced in early December 1991, Nazarbayev prevailed in arguments that Kazakhstan and other Central Asian states must join the new Commonwealth of Independent States. Kazakhstan was the only Soviet republic to declare independence after dissolution of the Soviet Union, on 16 December 1991.

Nazarbayev arranged a call by an extra-constitutional quasi-legislative 327-member People's Assembly composed of various cultural and ethnic leaders for an April 29, 1995 referendum on extending his rule until the year 2000. The extension was approved by over 93% of voters.In October 1998, the Kazakh legislature approved constitutional amendments that enabled Nazarbayev to call for an early presidential race for January 10, 1999. The U.S. State Department in November 1998 criticized a decision of the Kazakh Central Electoral Commission (CEC) and the Supreme Court that major opposition figure Akezhen Kazhegeldin was ineligible to run in the presidential race because of his participation in an "unauthorized" democracy meeting. Three candidates were registered besides Nazarbayev, but only one ran as a true opposition candidate. Onerous registration requirements included a $30,000 deposit (forfeited by the losers) and 170,000 signatures gathered in at least eleven of sixteen regions. Nazarbayev's candidacy was extensively covered by state-owned media. The Kazakh Central Electoral Commission reported that Nazarbayev had won with 79.8% of about seven million votes cast. The Organization for Security and Cooperation in Europe (OSCE) sent only token monitors, and declared on January 11, 1999, that "the electoral process ... was far removed" from OSCE standards which Kazakhstan had pledged to follow. At his January 20 inauguration, Nazarbayev pledged to work to create a "democratic society with a market economy," to raise the standard of living, and to uphold existing foreign and ethnic policies.

Nazarbayev has stated that the geographic location of Kazakhstan and its ethnic makeup dictate its "multipolar orientation toward both West and East." He has pursued close ties with Turkey, trade ties with Iran, and better relations with China, which many Kazakhs have traditionally viewed with concern as a security threat. Kazakhstan has extensive trade ties with China's Xinjiang Province, where many ethnic Kazakhs and Uighurs reside.

While seeking to protect Kazakh independence, Nazarbayev has also pursued close relations with Russia and other Commonwealth of Independent States (CIS) members for economic and security reasons. During Nazarbayev's July 1998 visit to Moscow, he and Yeltsin signed a Declaration of Eternal Friendship and Alliance Cooperation in which both sides pledged to assist each other in the case of threats against each other, including by providing military support. In early 1999, Kazakhstan reaffirmed a CIS collective security agreement pledging the parties to provide military assistance in case of aggression against any one of them. In 1995, Kazakhstan joined the customs union formed by Russia and Belarus, which was reaffirmed in an accord on "deeper integration" signed in 1996 (Kyrgyzstan also signed and Tajikistan joined in 1998). Nazarbayev has been highly critical of the feeble union. Another customs union, formed in 1994 between Kazakhstan, Kyrgyzstan, and Uzbekistan (joined by

Tajikistan in 1998), has been set back by the repercussions of the 1998 Russian and Asian financial crises.

Kazakhstan is the most economically developed of the former Soviet Central Asian republics. Kazakhstan's economic prospects are promising because of its vast energy and mineral resources, low foreign debts, and well-trained work force. There is more Western private investment in Kazakhstan than elsewhere in Central Asia, because of Kazakhstan's oil resources and efforts to attract investment. Second to Russia, Kazakhstan has the largest oil and gas reserves of the Caspian Sea regional states, holding promise of large export revenues. Russia's pipelines are currently the major means for exporting Kazakh oil, though a Caspian Pipeline Consortium (CPC; formed by Russian, U.S., other Western, and Omani partners) is building a 930-mile oil pipeline from Kazakhstan to Russia's Black Sea port of Novorossiisk. It is planned for completion in 2002 and slated to eventually carry up to one million barrels per day. Kazakhstan has also been involved in an oil swap arrangement with Iran, whereby Kazakhstan sends oil by tanker to northern Iran, and Iran in exchange exports some oil from its Persian Gulf ports. On November 18, 1999, Azerbaijan, Georgia, Turkey, and Kazakhstan signed the "Istanbul Protocol" on constructing a trans-Caucasus oil pipeline from Azerbaijan to Turkey (expected to be completed in 2004 with a capacity of one million barrels per day), boosting chances for international financing for this route.

¹³GOVERNMENT

In March 1995, the Kazakh Constitutional Court ruled that the March 1994 legislative election was invalid because it violated the principle of "one person, one vote." Constituencies had not been drawn up representing approximately equal populations, and confused voting procedures resulted in electors voting for several candidates, it declared. On March 11, Nazarbayev announced that the decision was in accordance with the constitution and dissolved the legislature. Some of the dismissed deputies tried to set up an alternative parliament, but the rebel movement soon fell apart. Nazarbayev announced that he would rule by decree pending new elections and called for a new constitution to be drafted, using France's parliamentary system as a model. On 30 August 1995, a referendum on a new constitution that widened presidential powers was passed with 89% of the vote. According to the U.S. State Department, proposals by democracy and human rights advocates during the discussion phase were not incorporated into the final constitutional draft submitted to the referendum, and the turnout and results were "exaggerated."

Compared to an earlier 1993 constitution, the 1995 constitution increases the president's powers and reduces those of the legislature, and places less emphasis on protecting human rights. As fleshed out by a presidential edict, the legislature does not control the budget or its agenda, cannot initiate changes to the Constitution, or exercise oversight over the executive branch. The president's nominees for premier and state bank head are ratified by the Majlis, but he appoints the rest of the cabinet. If the legislature fails within 30 days to pass an "urgent" bill brought by the President, he may issue it by decree. About 10% or less of bills are initiated by deputies, but they debate and have forced minor changes in bills initiated by the Presidency. While the President has broad powers to dissolve the legislature, it may only remove him for disability or high treason.

In October 1998, without any public debate, the legislature quickly rubber-stamped nineteen constitutional amendments and announced an early presidential election. The changes included increasing the presidential term from five to seven years, lifting the 65-year age limit on governmental service, creating party list representation in the Majlis, extending the term of office from four to five years for the lower legislative chamber (the Majlis) and from four to six years for the upper legislative chamber (the Senate).

Kazakhstan held September 17, 1999 indirect elections by regional legislatures of 32 members of a 39-seat upper legislative chamber, the Senate (on November 29, 1999, the remaining seven Senators were constitutionally appointed by Nazarbayev). The Organization for Security and Cooperation in Europe (OSCE) reported that Kazakh Central Electoral Commission (CEC) officials had improperly blocked some monitoring, and cited reports that other officials had threatened local legislators not to vote for oppositionists.

Elections to Kazakhstan's lower legislative chamber, the Majlis, took place on October 10, 1999, with 595 candidates and nine parties competing for 77 seats. Ten seats were reserved for a party list vote. Runoffs on October 24 were required for over two-thirds of constituency seats where no one candidate received over 50%. Ten seats were elected by party lists based on the percentage of votes parties received nationally (with a minimum vote threshold for representation of 7%), and the other 67 by single constituency voting. The Kazakh Communist Party (KPK), Otan, the Civic Party, and the Agrarian Party won seats under party list voting. No candidate nominated by a non-communist opposition party gained a party list or single constituency seat. About one-half of the winning deputies ran as independents, though many of them were former government officials who were presumably pro-government. OSCE monitors concluded that the race was "a tentative step" in democratization, but decried interference in the race by officials, biased local electoral commissions, manipulation of results, unfair campaign practices by pro-government parties, and harassment of opposition candidates. Members of the KPK, Republican Party, and Azamat joined in a "Forum of Democratic Forces" that on October 27 stated that the Senate and Majlis elections were rigged by the government and were invalid.

14 POLITICAL PARTIES

The constitution permits the formation of registered political parties, but in practice it is difficult to get the necessary legal permissions. Most parties are small, ephemeral, based on personalities, and lack detailed programs. Nine parties and groups participated in the party list part of the October 1999 lower-chamber legislative races, and four passed a 7% vote hurdle to win seats (the Republican People's Party withdrew from the party list vote after its leader, Akezhen Kazhegeldin, was not registered as a candidate). The nine were Otan (Fatherland), Azamat (Citizen), Alash (Patriot), the People's Congress, the Civic Party, the Communist Party, the Agrarian Party, the Labor Party, and the Revival Party. The pro-government Otan party bloc won the most seats in the party vote. Others included the Civic Party, Agrarian Party, and the Communist Party (KPK). Otan was formed in early 1999 from several prominent pro-Nazarbayev parties. The Civic Party, formed in 1998, represents state-industrial interests and hails Nazarbayev as its "spiritual father." Azamat was formed in 1999. Deputy Chair of the party Petr Svoik has called it the "constructive opposition." The Kazakh Communist Party (KPK), reregistered in July 1994, has advocated some economic re-centralization and anti-Western policies. The People's Congress, or Social-Democratic Party, has both Kazakh and Russian members and is headed by the Kazakh poet Olzhas Suleymenov. Originally pro-Nazarbayev, the party became increasingly critical of the government after 1993. The nationalist Alash Party has refused to register because of legal requirements that it submit personal information about members to the government. Members of unregistered parties may run for elected office as individuals, but not as party members.

In Uralsk (Western Kazakhstan) and Petropavlovsk (Northern Kazakhstan) there are Cossack obshchinas, or communities, agitating for autonomous status. Denied registry by Kazakhstan, many are active in Cossack obshchinas across the border in Russia, where Cossacks have the right to maintain military organizations and carry weapons.

15 LOCAL GOVERNMENT

Kazakhstan is divided into 14 oblasts (provinces); the city of Almaty has special administrative status equivalent to that of oblasts. The 14 oblasts are in turn divided into rayons (districts). Each oblast, rayon, and even settlement has its own elective assembly, charged with drawing up a budget and supervising local taxation. Cities have local assemblies as well; if large enough, cities are also divided into rayons, each with its own assembly. These assemblies are also elected for five-year terms. The number of oblasts was reduced from nineteen to fourteen in 1997 under the government's consolidation program.

The oblast and rayon assemblies do not choose the local executives. According to the 1995 constitution, the local executives, known as glavs or akims, are appointed by the president, upon recommendation by the prime minister. The akims serve at the pleasure of the president, and he has the power to annul their decisions. The akim appoints the members of his staff, who become the local department heads. There is some discussion of shifting to local election of the regional akims.

16 JUDICIAL SYSTEM

A new constitution was adopted by referendum in 1995, placing the judiciary under the control of the president and the executive branch. There are local and oblast (regional) level courts, and a national-level Supreme Court and Constitutional Council. A special arbitration court hears disputes between state enterprises. There is also a military court system. Local level courts serve as courts of first instance for less serious crimes such as theft and vandalism. Oblast level courts hear more serious criminal cases and also hear cases in rural areas where no local courts have been established. A judgment by a local court may be appealed to the oblast level. The Supreme Court hears appeals from the oblast courts. The constitution establishes a seven member Constitutional Council to determine the constitutionality of laws adopted by the legislature. It also rules on challenges to elections and referendums and interprets the constitution. The president appoints three of its members, including the chair.

Under constitutional amendments of 1998, the president appoints a chairperson of a Supreme Judicial Council, which nominates judges for the Supreme Court. The Council consists of the chairperson of the Constitutional Council, the chairperson of the Supreme Court, the Prosecutor General, the Minister of Justice, senators, judges, and other persons appointed by the president. The president recommends and the senate (upper legislative chamber) approves these nominees for the Supreme Court. Oblast judges (nominated by the Supreme Judicial Council) are appointed by the president. Lower level judges are appointed by the president from a list presented by the Ministry of Justice. The Ministry receives the list from a Qualification Collegium of Justice, composed of deputies from the Majlis (lower legislative chamber), judges, prosecutors, and others appointed by the president). Under legislation approved in 1996, judges serve for life.

The constitution calls for public trials where the defendant has the right to be present, the right to counsel, and the right to call witnesses. There is the presumption of innocence of the accused, and the defendant has the right of appeal. In practice, trials of political oppositionists have been closed, and there is widespread corruption among poorly paid judicial personnel. A new criminal code that took effect in 1998 increases penalties for some crimes but also removed some types of Soviet-era crimes such as parasitism.

Nazarbayev has stated that "the path from totalitarianism to democracy lies through enlightened authoritarianism" but has nonetheless allowed some degree of pluralism. The U.S. State Department concluded in its *Country Reports on Human Rights Practices for 1999* that the Kazakh government respected the human rights of its citizens in some areas, but serious problems remained in others. The government infringed on citizens' right to change their government, most recently in the flawed preparations for the January 1999 presidential election. Members of the security forces often beat or otherwise abuse detainees, and there were allegations of arbitrary arrest and detention of political opponents. The government infringed on citizens' rights to privacy by conducting unlawful monitoring of correspondence and searches of premises. The government increasingly moved against independent media, closing several opposition newspapers or forcing them to sell to pro-government interests. Academic freedom and freedom of religion are circumscribed, according to the State Department. Criminal cases were brought against foreign Muslim missionaries perceived to be teaching fundamentalism, and some evangelical Protestants have alleged government hostility toward proselytizing. The government abets or tolerates discrimination against ethnic Russians and women.

[17]ARMED FORCES

The total armed forces of Kazakhstan are estimated at 65,800, of which approximately 46,800 are estimated to be in the army. The army has 630 T-72 battle tanks plus an additional 300 being stored. There is no navy, and the air force is estimated at 19,000 personnel. There are 131 combat aircraft. There is a paramilitary consisting of 2,000 republican guards, an estimated 20,000 internal security troops, and an estimated 12,000 border guards.

The defense budget in 1998 was $232.4 million or 1% of GDP.

[18]INTERNATIONAL COOPERATION

Kazakhstan was admitted to the UN on 2 March 1992. It is a member of the OSCE, EBRD, ECO, ESCAP, IMF, UNCTAD, and the World Bank. It is applying for membership in other international organizations, including the WTO, and is a member of the CIS. It has established especially good relations with neighboring Central Asian states and China.

[19]ECONOMY

The Kazakhstan economy is extremely well-endowed with large tracts of arable land and rich reserves of coal, oil, and rare metals. Animal herding was the mainstay of the nomadic Kazak population before their incorporation into the Soviet Union; wool production remains an important agricultural product today, along with grains and meat.

Like other countries of the former USSR, Kazakhstan faced serious economic dislocation after 1991, resulting from the disruption of trade with other post-Soviet republics, an end to the flow of official revenues from the Soviet central government, the decline in state production orders, and the need for sudden currency adjustments. Estimated GDP fell by 8.5% in 1991, 14% in 1992, 15.3% in 1993, and 25% in 1994. Overall output is estimated to have shrunk by one-third between 1990–93. In 1996, however, GDP grew by 1.1%, and increased by 1.7% in 1997. Inflation reached a staggering 2,000% in 1993, but declined to 35% in 1994 and to just 7% by 1998. GDP declined by 2.5% in 1998 due to low oil prices and the financial crisis in Russia.

The current crisis notwithstanding, given its rich resource endowments, the potential for strong growth in the near future is more apparent in Kazakhstan than many other Central Asian republics. Legislation adopted since 1992 has promoted the rapid transfer of small shops and services to the private sector, the spread of private ownership in housing, and the inflow of large foreign investments. In 1996, Kazakhstan signed the Caspian Pipeline Consortium agreement to build a pipeline from the western Tengiz oil field to the Black Sea, promising further development of the oil sector.

[20]INCOME

The US Central Intelligence Agency (CIA) reports that in 1998 Kazakhstan's gross domestic product (GDP) was estimated at $52.9 billion. The per capita GDP was estimated at $3,100. The annual growth rate of GDP was estimated at -2.5%. The average inflation rate in 1998 was 10%. The CIA defines GDP as the value of all final goods and services produced within a nation in a given year and computed on the basis of purchasing power parity (PPP) rather than value as measured on the basis of the rate of exchange. It was estimated that agriculture accounted for 11.5% of GDP, industry 32.6%, and services 55.9%.

The World Bank reports that for the same period per capita private consumption (in PPP terms) was $3,500. Private consumption includes expenditures of individuals, households, and nongovernmental organizations. Approximately 37% of household consumption was spent on food, 20% on fuel, 9% on health care, and 6% on education. The richest 10% of the population accounted for approximately 26% of household consumption and the poorest 10% approximately 2.7%.

[21]LABOR

The labor force consists of some 7.8 million persons. The service sector engaged an estimated 23%; agriculture, 19%; manufacturing and mining, 21%; construction, 12%; transportation and communications, 11%; trade, 8%; and utilities, 4%; with finance, public administration, and defense accounting for the remaining 2%. The labor force grew about 0.8% annually from 1985 to 1991 and fell by 0.3% from 1990 to 1998. The mining and quarrying industry is a significant provider of employment opportunity.

All workers are entitled to join or form unions of their choosing. Union registration generally is a lengthy and difficult process. The Confederation of Free Trade Unions had about 250,000 members in 1999. Some workers who have joined independent unions are subjected to various forms of harassment, indicating hostility by local authorities and state-sponsored trade unions. An agreement signed by labor, management, and the government in December, 1996, may ameliorate the antiunion activity of which both the government and management have been accused.

The minimum age for employment is 16, and there is no minimum wage that covers all employment sectors. The legal maximum workweek is 48 hours, although most enterprises maintain a 40-hour work week. As of 1997, the government once again sets a minimum wage, in 1998 it was about $20 per month.

[22]AGRICULTURE

In 1997, Kazakhstan had an estimated 30,135,000 ha (74,464,000 acres) of arable land, representing 11.3% of the total land area. Most cropland is found in the northern steppes, where the failed Virgin and Idle Land Project of the 1950s occurred. Small-scale privatization resulted in the formation of 31,055 private farms by 1995, up from 3,333 in 1991. The average peasant farm size in 1995 was 428 ha (1,058 acres).

Between 1990 and 1998, annual agricultural output fell an average of 6.9%.

Kazakhstan is the only former Soviet republic that exports grain. Wheat accounted for 30% of all sown acreage in 1998. Wheat production declined from 18,285,000 tons in 1992 to 4,746,000 tons in 1998. Similarly, barley production fell from 8,511,000 tons to 1,003,000 tons during that time. Rice is produced in irrigated stretches along the Syrdar'ya near Qyzlorda and around Taldyqorghan in the east. Production amounted to 236,000 tons in 1998.

Potatoes, fruits, and vegetables are other significant food crops. Less than 2% of agricultural land is used to cultivate commercial crops such as cotton, sugar beets, sunflowers, and flax.

During the Soviet period, groundwater resources and chemical fertilizers were overused, resulting in depleted soils, decreasing yields, and environmental pollution.

[23]ANIMAL HUSBANDRY

About 70% of Kazakhstan's total land area is permanent pastureland. In 1995, the livestock population included 17 million chickens, 8.9 million sheep, 860,000 pigs, 1.1 million horses, and about 0.7 million goats. Total meat production in 1998 amounted to 1,646,000 tons, of which 55% was beef, 18% mutton and lamb, 11% pork, 3% chicken, and 13% other meat.

Wool is an important animal product; in 1998, 24,000 tons of greasy wool and 15,000 tons of scoured wool were produced. That year, fresh cow milk production totaled 3,355,000 tons, and 70,000 tons of hen eggs were laid.

[24]FISHING

Fisheries are concentrated around the Caspian Sea, and are of some importance to the local economy. The total catch in 1997 was 41,367 tons, all from inland fishing. Freshwater bream and Azov sea sprat were the principal species.

[25]FORESTRY

Only 3.9% of Kazakhstan is covered by forests and woodlands; forestry is of little commercial importance. Imports of forestry products amounted to nearly $48.4 million in 1997.

[26]MINING

The eastern region of Kazakhstan is rich in many metallic minerals, including: alumina, arsenic, bauxite, beryllium, bismuth, cadmium, chrome, copper, gold, iron ore, lead-zinc, manganese, molybdenum, rhenium, silver, titanium, and tungsten. Output of metals in 1996 included (in tons): iron ore, 14,500,000; chromite, 1,190,000; copper, 270,000; zinc, 170,000; lead, 67,000; silver, 480; cadmium, 1,200; molybdenum, 400; tin, 400; tungsten, 222; bismuth, 84.5; and gold, 12,000 kg. Production of tin was reported at 100 tons in 1995.

Copper mining, which had declined between 1991 and 1995, began to recover after foreign companies acquired management rights to the nation's copper producers, most notably the Zhezqazghan complex, which also includes concentration, smelting, and refining facilities. Chromium is also an important mineral commodity; Kazakhstan had supplied more than 95% of chromite production for the former USSR through the Donskoy mining and beneficiation complex at Khromtau. Iron ore found near Rudnyy in the north supplies the iron and steel plants in the Russian Urals region as well as plants at Karaganda and Temirtau. Asbestos, barite, and phosphate are also mined.

Kazakhstan's plan to develop its metal industries, begun in 1994, continued through 1996. The plan called for developing reserves of bauxite, copper, iron, lead and zinc, and titanium raw materials, to be partly financed through foreign investment and combined government ownership, privatization, and foreign management as a preparatory step to privatization. The list of enterprises to be privatized included various copper, manganese, gold, and lead-zinc mining and metallurgical complexes. Kazakhstan's major mining and metals industries were to be transferred to the trust management of foreign firms for a limited number of years.

[27]ENERGY AND POWER

Kazakhstan is richly endowed with energy reserves and is the second-largest oil producer among the former Soviet republics. Oil is the most promising energy source destined for exploitation in the post-Soviet era. Whereas current oil sources are located along the northeastern shore of the Caspian Sea near Aqtau, the enormous Tengiz oil field lies further north along the coast. Kazakhstan's total proven oil reserves in 1998 stood between 10 and 17 billion barrels.

In May 1992, Chevron entered into a joint venture agreement with Kazakhstan to develop the Tengiz oil field which is estimated to contain 6–9 billion barrels of recoverable crude oil reserves. By April 1993, a 40-year agreement was signed, creating the Tengizchevroil joint venture. In early 1995, however, Chevron announced cutbacks in the joint venture due to lack of progress in development. Production has been constrained by the lack of an export outlet and by Russian complaints of mercaptans (corrosive foul-smelling compounds of carbon, hydrogen, and sulfur) in the oil. Russian restrictions on oil exports from Kazakhstan have led to doubts regarding the billions of dollars in foreign investment around the Caspian Sea and raised suspicions among Western companies about Russia's motives. In May 1996, the Mobil Corp. announced the acquisition of a 25% interest in the Tengiz oilfield. Mobil agreed to pay $1.1 billion and also obtained the option to acquire another production or exploration interest in Kazakhstan. In 1996, Kazakhstan and Oman agreed to build a major oil pipeline to connect the Tengiz oilfield to a Russian port on the Black Sea. As of 1999, the 900-mile, $2.3 billion oil pipeline was under construction, with completion slated for 2001. Production of oil in 1997 totaled 573,000 barrels per day, up from 570,000 barrels per day in 1991.

Some natural gas is also produced as a derivative from oil fields on the shores of the Caspian Sea. Production of natural gas in 1997 totaled 6.2 billion cu m. Hard coal is mined from the Qaranghandy and Ekibastuz basins. Total coal production in 1997 was 80 million tons.

Several hydroelectric projects also operate. The Qapshaghay Dam on the Ile River, north of Almaty, and the Shardara Dam, on the Syrdar'ya in the extreme south, produce electricity for various industries. In 1998, Kazakhstan's total installed electrical capacity was 19,055,000 kW, and production amounted to 49,299 million kWh.

[28]INDUSTRY

Overwhelmingly dominated by state-owned enterprises under the centrally planned economy of the former USSR, Kazakhstan's industrial sector is slowly being privatized and reoriented toward market-driven production. Through a combination of auctions, investment coupons issued to the public, and case-by-case deliberation (particularly for large enterprises), government plans mandated the privatization of almost all industrial enterprises by 2000. However, the process of structural adjustment in Kazakhstan's industrial sector has been fraught with difficulty. Industrial production declined by 13.8% in 1992, followed by drops of 14.8% in 1993 and 28.5% in 1994. By 1995, however, the trend appeared to slow as industrial production fell by only 7.9% from the previous year, and rose by 4.7% in 1997. The share of industrial production fell from 25.9% of GDP in 1994 to 21.8% of GDP in 1995, but had risen to 28% by 1998. To stimulate recovery, foreign investment and joint ventures are being encouraged particularly in agro-processing, nonferrous metals, and light industry, as well as oil, gas, and energy. New joint ventures with foreign investors thus far involve photocopier, window frame, and mining, agricultural, and oilfield equipment manufactures. Among the largest enterprise sales has been the 1993 purchase of the Almaty Tobacco Factory by the Philip Morris Corporation, which invested $350 million through 1998.

Reflecting Kazakhstan's resource-based economy, agro-processing and metallurgy and mining are important components of industrial production. Output from the metal processing and mining sector in 1999 included crude steel, pig iron, refined copper, and refined lead. Over half a million barrels per day of oil is produced in Kazakhstan.

Textiles and leather manufacturing is relatively well-developed in Kazakhstan thanks to inputs of wool and other material from the country's own livestock sector as well as cotton imports from other areas of the former USSR. Specific manufactured products include knitted wear, fabrics (wool, cotton and silk), and shoes. Other goods produced by light industry enterprises include tape recorders, radios, electric irons, and washing machines. Reflecting Kazakhstan's specialized role as a supplier of specific industrial goods within the former USSR, machine-building is also among the largest of Kazakhstan's industries accounting for a large amount of total industrial output and much of the total manufacturing value. Production includes bulldozers, excavators, and metal-cutting equipment. Other significant manufactures are construction materials, sawn wood, paper, and chemicals, including mineral fertilizers, sulfuric acid, caustic soda, and synthetic plastics.

29SCIENCE AND TECHNOLOGY

The Kazakhstan Academy of Sciences, founded in 1946 in Almaty, has departments of physical and mathematical sciences, earth sciences, chemical-technological sciences, and biological sciences. Kazakhstan in 1996 had 47 research institutes concerned with agriculture and veterinary science, medicine, natural sciences, and technology. There is a botanical garden in Almaty. Scientific training is available at two universities and 25 higher educational institutes. In 1987–97, science and engineering students accounted for 20% of college and university enrollments.

30DOMESTIC TRADE

The wholesale and retail sector, previously dominated by state-controlled distribution channels, has seen the dynamic growth of independent small shops and traders. Price controls have been lifted for 90% of consumer and 80% of wholesale prices, although basic goods and services such as bread, flour, baby food, medicines, fodder, housing rents, utilities, and public transportation have been excluded from liberalization.

31FOREIGN TRADE

In 1990, about 89% of Kazakhstan's exports and 88% of its imports represented trade with other former Soviet republics (at foreign trade prices). A serious disruption in the country's trading patterns occurred as the input procurement system within the Soviet centrally planned economy disintegrated, the use of hard currency and world market-determined transaction prices was adopted by former USSR republics, and export demand from Eastern European countries shrank in the early 1990s. To facilitate adjustment to these hard new realities, the government decreed key trade liberalization measures in early 1992, ending export license requirements. With liberalization, exports and imports increased substantially through the 1990s.

Exports are dominated by petroleum products, followed by nonferrous and ferrous metals—a pattern likely to continue for some time to come. Kazakhstan's largest imports were machinery and oil and gas products.

Principal trading partners in 1998 (in millions of US dollars) were as follows:

COUNTRY	EXPORTS	IMPORTS	BALANCE
Russia	1,700	2,045	-345
China (inc. Hong Kong)	392	228	164
Germany	326	455	-129
Ukraine	314	99	215
Italy	243	538	-295
Turkey	231	236	-5
United States	162	113	49
Uzbekistan	149	66	83
Japan	109	51	58
United Kingdom	61	175	-114

32BALANCE OF PAYMENTS

The US Central Intelligence Agency reports that in 1998 the purchasing power parity of Kazakhstan's exports was $6.3 billion while imports totaled $7.4 billion resulting in a trade balance of -$1.1 billion.

The International Monetary Fund (IMF) reports that in 1998 Kazakhstan had exports of goods totaling $5,839 million and imports totaling $6,589 million. The services credit totaled $897 million and debit $1,128 million. The following table summarizes Kazakhstan's balance of payments as reported by the IMF for 1998 in millions of US dollars.

Current Account		-1,201
Balance on goods	-750	
Balance on services	-231	
Balance on income	-299	
Current transfers	78	
Capital Account		-369
Financial Account		2,241
Direct investment abroad	-8	
Direct investment in Kazakhstan	1,158	
Portfolio investment assets	-5	
Portfolio investment liabilities	66	
Other investment assets	-179	
Other investment liabilities	1,210	
Net Errors and Omissions		-1,114
Reserves and Related Items		443

33BANKING AND SECURITIES

In December 1990, the Alma-Ata branch of Gosbank (the former Soviet State Bank) was made into the Independent Kazak (National Bank of Kazakhstan–NBK). In the next year the existence of private and public financial institutions were legalized. In 1993, the parliament approved a new banking law that separated the National Bank of Kazakhstan from the government, and gave the central bank the power to conduct monetary and credit policies and regulate the commercial banking sector. Before November 1993, monetary and credit policy was under the control of two central banks, the Russian Central Bank (RCB), which also acted as the ruble zone's central bank, and the NBK. Until November 1993, the currency unit in the country was the ruble. On 15 November 1993, Kazakhstan established its own currency, the tenge.

In 1995 the NBK continued the tight monetary stance it adopted in 1994, although the government was known to have been unhappy about this. The NBK has become increasingly sophisticated in its monetary operations, and now has a repo and a Lombard facility. The NBK's ability to react rapidly to sterilize hot money inflows was demonstrated in the summer of 1995. Large short-term capital inflows helped prop up the tenge but also threatened to expand the money supply. The NBK issued short-term notes and cut credit to commercial banks in a successful move to mop up excess liquidity.

The reform of the banking sector is set up according to a two-tier system, with the central bank and specialized, sector-oriented banks: Sherbank (now Narodny Bank) for savings, Kazakhstan Bank for industry and agriculture, Turan Bank for the construction sector, Kredsotsbank for housing and municipal services, and Agroprombank for agriculture. New private banks were opened, and the specialization requirement was relaxed. As a result, the number of banks in Kazakhstan grew rapidly and the monopoly position of the few state-owned banks was ended. There were 210 banks in Kazakhstan in mid-1993. After the tight monetary policy took hold in 1994, 55 banks were closed in 1995 and by the end of the first quarter of 1996 there were only 123 banks left. In 1995 the state disposed of holdings in 52 banks. Privatization revenue from bank sales in 1995 was a mere $6.4 million. In 1999, there were 71 commercial banks, including one state bank (3% of total financial sector assets), one intergovernmental bank, 23 banks with foreign participation, and 13 foreign representative offices.

The NBK admits that corporate governance and management in banks is weak: Kazakhstan's banks tend to be very small, concentrated in Almaty, and more interested in dealing in treasury bills than in providing long-term credits to lenders. There is as yet, also, no deposit insurance scheme in operation. Supervision and credit risk evaluation by the country's commercial banks is weak. Organized crime is also a problem for many banks, with security therefore assuming a considerable cost.

The Kazakhstan Stock Exchange and the Central Asian Stock Exchange both operate in Kazakhstan.

34INSURANCE

Approximately 73 insurance companies were registered in 1999.

35PUBLIC FINANCE

The US Central Intelligence Agency (CIA) estimates that in 1998 Kazakhstan's central government took in revenues of approximately $2.9 billion and had expenditures of $4.2 billion including capital expenditures of $383 million. Overall, the government registered a deficit of approximately $1.3 billion. External debt totaled $5,715 million.

The following table shows an itemized breakdown of government revenues and expenditures. The percentages were calculated from data reported by the International Monetary Fund. The dollar amounts (millions) are based on the CIA estimates provided above.

REVENUE AND GRANTS	100%	2,900
Tax revenue	68.3%	1,982
Non-tax revenue	2.1%	61
Capital revenue	25.1%	728
Grants	4.5%	129
EXPENDITURES	100%	4,200
General public services	7.9%	330
Defense	5.1%	215
Public order and safety	7.3%	308
Education	4.8%	201
Health	7.7%	325
Social security	38.1%	1,601
Recreation, cultural, and religious affairs	2.0%	86
Economic affairs and services	10.0%	421
Other expenditures	12.7%	533
Interest payments	4.3%	181

36TAXATION

Individual income is taxable at between 5% and 40%, and 1% of salaries is deducted for social security. The corporate tax rate is 30% for corporations. There was also a profits tax ranging from 10% for agricultural business to 70% for the entertainment and gaming industries. There is a VAT of 28% on most goods.

37CUSTOMS AND DUTIES

In Kazakhstan, licenses are required to import certain products and the importation of others is prohibited. An import tariff schedule eliminated duties for most consumer goods in April 1994. Most export tariffs were reduced that same year. However, tariffs have increased on certain products, including alcoholic beverages, leather, and carpets. Kazakhstan, Kyrgyzstan, and Uzbekistan have formed an Economic Union. In May 1992, the Republic of Kazakhstan and the US signed a most-favored nation agreement for reciprocal tariff treatment.

38FOREIGN INVESTMENT

In early 1991, the government adopted a new foreign investment code, allowing investment by foreign companies in any economic activity except the manufacture of military goods. The law specifies provisions for duty-free imports as well as tax breaks for firms with foreign investment, especially those involved in producing consumer goods, agricultural goods, and electronic and medical equipment. The code also established a number of free economic areas where imports of intermediate products and exports of finished goods are allowed without customs duties. Further revisions in legislation are now being formulated in order to provide stronger guarantees and greater clarity on investment requirements and credit facilities open to foreign investors. In 1996, net foreign direct investment was estimated at $1.22 billion, and was estimated at $1.3 billion in 1997. In 1999, FDI equaled $1.2 billion.

In 1999 extensive projects involving US and EU corporations (including Chevron, Mobil, Agip, Elf-Aquitaine, and British Gas) were arranged to expand the exploitation of the country's immense oil and gas deposits and develop its energy sector. The expansion of gold production in partnership with foreign concerns is also being promoted as a means of quickly boosting the inflow of foreign exchange. The Philip Morris Co. planned to build a new cigarette manufacturing plant in the Almaty region, investing about $300 million over five years. RJR Nabisco planned to invest more than $100 million in a venture making consumer products and cigarettes. Kazakhstan has also attracted significant private foreign investment, most notably for the development of the Tengiz and Korolev oil fields, which are estimated to require $1.5 billion of development capital over the next several years. Infrastructure projects in electricity generation and transportation are needed in order to serve a growing influx of industries.

39ECONOMIC DEVELOPMENT

Under the economic development regime of the USSR, the republic underwent rapid development of its agricultural as well as industrial sectors. Vast tracts of land were brought into cultivation with the expansion of irrigation under the USSR's "Virgin Lands" program, while within the industrial sector, development of its metallurgical, mining, and machinery industries were prioritized. Growth in these various economic sectors was fueled by a high labor force participation rate in the local population, especially among women, as well as the import of some skilled labor from Russia. Although achieving impressive expansion of production capacity in the span of just a few decades, by the 1980s growing problems of inefficiency and inadequate technological development in the overwhelmingly dominant state sector resulted in a flagging rate of output growth overall.

The region's industrial and agricultural development had, moreover, come at some high environmental costs. The structure of Kazakhstan's transportation and energy sectors today clearly highlight the overall orientation of the economic base fostered under the Soviet regime; railroads and paved roads are clustered mainly in the north and the south, serving more to link Kazakhstan with Russia, Uzbekistan, and Kyrgyzstan rather than to integrate the republic itself. Similarly, electricity transmission networks facilitate the exchange of energy with different republics in the former USSR rather than between different parts of Kazakhstan.

Since sovereignty was declared in 1990, Kazakhstan has embarked on a process of economic restructuring, aimed at establishing a market economy. Gradual privatization of most state enterprises has been the focal point of the restructuring program and the centralized state ordering system was abolished in 1992.

In addition to price liberalization, government decrees since 1991 have mandated the gradual elimination of various subsidies to industry and other sectors, further reductions in state expenditures, and the development of a social safety net to assist households at high poverty risk. The government is also placing great emphasis on realizing the infusion of foreign capital both to the oil and gas industry as well as various other industrial subsectors, such as agro-processing, light industry and ferrous metals. In February 1994, the government released 38 state-owned businesses for privatization and foreign investment. In June 1994, Unilever agreed to pay $60 million to buy two state-owned margarine factories. In 1997, South Korea's Daewoo Corp. bid $1.37 billion for a 40% share in Kazaktelecom, the state-owned national telecommunications company. In 1999, advances in the natural gas and oil industries produced favorable results on the Kazakhstan economy. Extensive foreign investment is shaping the economic development of the country, taking it from a dilapidated heavy-industrial complex to a productive market for two-way trade.

40SOCIAL DEVELOPMENT

Social security programs were first introduced in 1956, and were revised in 1991 and 1996 following independence. All employed persons, including noncitizens, qualify for old age, disability, and survivorship pensions. Employers contribute 30% of payroll, while employees contribute 1% of earnings. Residents of ecological disaster areas are entitled to early retirement. Workers' compensation is offered under a dual social insurance and universal system. The economic and financial crisis in the mid to late 1990s, however, has meant that the government is often unable to pay pensions or other forms of benefits owed to citizens.

Women have equal rights under the law. They generally have access to higher education but are still channeled into mostly low-level, low-paid jobs. In 1999, only 5 women were voted into the 39-member Senate, while 8 were elected to the 77-member Majilis. There are about 30 women's rights organizations, including the Union of Women of Kazakhstan, the Union of Women Entrepreneurs, the League of Muslim Women, and the Union of Feminists. There are also mothers' groups organized around specific issues. Most women's groups work to obtain support for families and increase women's participation in public life.

The government has signed the UN Convention in children's rights. The constitution provides for the upkeep and education of orphans, although limited financial resources result in many children receiving inadequate education and medical care.

Ethnic tensions between Kazakhs and Russians continue to exist. Ethnic Kazakhs receive preferential treatment in housing, education, and employment. Although the Russian language still predominates, the 1995 Constitution specifies that Kazak is the official state language. The government is responsible for numerous violations of democratic freedoms and human rights. Prisoners are beaten and tortured, and killings are committed by security forces. A top political opposition leader was jailed for a year for insulting the president, then barred from running for parliament because he had served time in prison.

41HEALTH

The average life expectancy in 1999 was 63.4 years. The total fertility rate was 2.1 children per woman during her childbearing years, and the infant mortality rate was 59 per 1,000 live births. For every 100,000 live births 53 women died during pregnancy or in childbirth in 1990–97. More than half of married women 15–49 used some form of contraceptive in 1995 (59%). The overall death rate in 1999 was 10.3 per 1,000 inhabitants. Major causes of death per 100,000 people in 1990 were communicable diseases and maternal/perinatal causes, 86; noncommunicable diseases, 700; and injuries, 103. There were 77 reported cases of tuberculosis per 100,000 people in 1990. In 1990–94, immunization rates for children up to one year old were tuberculosis, 87%; diphtheria, pertussis, and tetanus, 80%; polio, 75%; and measles, 72%. In 1990–97, Kazakhstan had 3.6 doctors and 10.3 hospital beds per 1,000 inhabitants. Total health care expenditures in 1990 were $2.6 million. A small portion of Kazakhstan's gross domestic product (3.3%) went to health expenditures. A majority (67%) of children under 5 suffer from some form of anemia (1995). The HIV-1 seroprevalence was 0.0 per 100 adults in 1997. By 1996 there were 5 AIDS cases reported.

42HOUSING

In 1989, 23.3% of all privately owned urban housing had running water, 13.6% had sewer lines, 23.3% had central heating, and 0.9% had hot water. In 1990, Kazakhstan had 14.2 sq m of housing space per capita and, as of 1 January 1991, 520,000 households (or 18.8%) were on waiting lists for housing in urban areas.

43EDUCATION

In 1995, the adult illiteracy rate was estimated at 0.4% (males, 0.3%; females, 0.5%). Both at the primary and secondary level, education is free and state funded. Although Russian is the most commonly taught language, Kazak, which is the official state language, is now gaining popularity and is being extended to all areas. A small percentage are also taught Uzbek, Uighur, and Tajik.

In 1997 there were 1,342,035 primary school students. Secondary schools enrolled 1,921,302 students and employed approximately 178,900 teachers in the same year. There are 55 institutions of higher education are three universities. Third level educational institutes had a total of 260,043 pupils in 1996. The University of Kazak Al-Farabi State University was founded in 1934 and offers history, philosophy, economics, sociology, journalism, mathematics, physics, chemistry, biology, and geography. The Karaganda State University was founded in 1972 and teaches philosophy, economics, law, history, mathematics, physics, chemistry, and biology. The Technical University at Karaganda Metallurgical Combine was founded in 1964 and has faculties of metallurgy, mechanics and technology, and chemical technology.

44LIBRARIES AND MUSEUMS

Three outstanding libraries are the State Public Library of Kazakhstan in Almaty (5.1 million volumes), the Scientific and Technical Library of Kazakhstan also in Almaty (22.3 million volumes), and the Central Library of the Kazak Academy of Science (6 million volumes). The Al-Farabi Kazak State University Library in Almaty has 1.5 million volumes. Kazakhstan has an extensive public library system, with 8,770 branches holding more than 100 million volumes as of 1993.

Kazakhstan has over 100 museums. The Central State Museum of Kazakhstan in Almaty features 90,000 exhibits exploring the history and physical conditions of the region. The A. Kasteyer Kazak State Art Museum (formerly the Kazak T.G. Shevchenko State Art Gallery) in Almaty primarily contains works of Russian and Kazak artists from the 15th to 20th centuries. There are regional and general interest museums throughout the country.

⁴⁵MEDIA

As of 1997, there were two million phones. Kazakhstan is connected to the other former Soviet republics by land line or microwave and to other countries through Moscow. Kazak Radio broadcasts in Kazak, Russian, Uighur, German, and Korean. Kazak Television, established in 1959, broadcasts in the same languages except for Korean. As of 1999, there were 20 television broadcast stations, of which eight are government owned. In 1997, there were 384 radios, 234 television sets, and one mobile phone per 1,000 population.

Leading newspapers in 1999 included Kazakhstanskaya Pravda, circulation 170,000, and there were four dailies. They are as follows, with 1999 circulations: *Egemen Kazakhstan* (80,500); *Express K* (45,000); *Karavan-Blits* (60,000); and *Kazakhstan Pravda* (45,800).

The constitution and 1991 Press Law provide for a free press, although in practice the media is said to perform self-censorship in key subject areas, especially criticism of the president and other government officials.

As of 1996, there were more than 560 Internet hosts in Kazakhstan.

⁴⁶ORGANIZATIONS

The two major economic organizations in Kazakhstan are the Chamber of Commerce and Industry of Kazakhstan and the Union of Cooperative Entrepreneurs.

⁴⁷TOURISM, TRAVEL, AND RECREATION

Kazakhstan is open to both business travelers and tourists. Visas are required by all visitors and are obtainable upon arrival or through embassies abroad and companies that sell package tours of Central Asia. The principal accommodations are hotels that formerly belonged to the Soviet Intourist system. However, foreign chains are currently developing a number of projects in Central Asia.

Kazakhstan offers a wide variety of natural landscapes to the hardier traveler, ranging from forests and mountain ranges to the vast steppes where Kazak nomads live in tents called yurts and race thoroughbred horses and camels. The capital, Almaty (Kazak for "mountain of apples"), has no historic attractions but is an attractive city where tree-lined streets, parks, fountains, and canals give it a European flavor. In the winter, ice skating is popular on its waterways. Air service to Kazakhstan is good, with direct flights to Alma-Ata from Ankara, Frankfurt, Hamburg, and other cities, as well as frequent daily flights from Moscow.

According to 1999 UN estimates, the daily estimated cost of staying in Alma Ata was $141–220, depending on the choice of hotel. Elsewhere in the country, travel expenses averaged $33 per day.

⁴⁸FAMOUS KAZAKHS

Nursultan A. Nazarbayev (b.1940) has been president of Kazakhstan since his election in December 1991. Sergey Tereshchenko and Akezhan Kazhegeldin have each served as prime minister since independence in 1991. Abay Ibragin Kunanbayev (1845-1904) is internationally known as a 19th century humanist and poet, and is considered the founder of modern Kazak literature. Contemporary writer Mukhtar Awezov wrote *Abay*, a novel about steppe life that was translated into English. The novelist Kaltay Muhamedjanov is from Kazakhstan.

⁴⁹DEPENDENCIES

Kazakhstan has no territories or colonies.

⁵⁰BIBLIOGRAPHY

Edwards-Jones, Imogen. *The Taming of Eagles: Exploring the New Russia*. London: Weidenfeld & Nicolson, 1993.

Kazakhstan. Minneapolis: Lerner, 1993.

Kazakhstan. Washington, D.C.: International Monetary Fund, 1992.

World Bank. *Kazakhstan: The Transition to a Market Economy*. Washington, D.C.: World Bank, 1993.

KIRIBATI

Republic of Kiribati

CAPITAL: Tarawa.

FLAG: Above a blue and white heraldic representation of Pacific waters, a golden sun rises against a red background, with a golden frigate bird at the top.

ANTHEM: *Teiraki kain Kiribati (Stand Kiribati).*

MONETARY UNIT: The Australian dollar is the national currency. A$1 = US$0.62035 (US$1 = A$1.612) as of 31 March 2000.

WEIGHTS AND MEASURES: Kiribati is in transition from imperial to metric standards.

HOLIDAYS: New Year's Day, 1 January; Independence Day, 12 July; Youth Day, 4 August; Christmas Day, 25 December; Boxing Day, 26 December. Movable holidays include Good Friday, Easter Monday, Queen's Birthday (June), Bank Holiday (August), and Prince of Wales's Birthday (November).

TIME: Midnight = noon GMT.

¹LOCATION, SIZE, AND EXTENT

Kiribati (pronounced "Kiribass") consists of 33 islands in the central Pacific, situated around the point where the International Date Line intersects the Equator. Scattered over more than 5 million sq km (2 million sq mi) of ocean are the 17 islands of the Gilberts group (including Banaba, formerly Ocean Island); the 8 Line Islands (including Christmas Island); and the 8 Phoenix Islands. The distance between Christmas Island in the E and Banaba in the W is more than 3,200 km (2,000 mi). Kiribati's total land area is 717 sq km (277 sq mi), and its total coastline is 1,143 km (710 mi). Comparatively, the area occupied by Kiribati is slightly more than four times the size of Washington, D.C.

Kiribati's capital city, Tarawa, is located on the island of Tarawa.

²TOPOGRAPHY

With the exception of Banaba, an upthrust coral formation that reaches a high point of 265 m (868 ft), the islands are coral atolls built on a submerged volcanic chain and seldom rise more than 4 m (13 ft) above sea level. Christmas Island is the largest atoll in the world, with an area of 481 sq km (186 sq mi). In most of the atolls the reef encloses a lagoon, on the eastern side of which is a narrow stretch of land varying in length from about 45 m (150 ft) to 80 km (50 mi).

³CLIMATE

Tempered by prevailing easterly trade winds, the islands have a maritime equatorial climate, with high humidity during the November–April rainy season. Although the islands lie outside the tropical hurricane belt, there are occasional gales and even tornadoes. Rainfall varies from an average of 102 cm (40 in) near the Equator to 305 cm (120 in) in the extreme north and south. Severe droughts can also occur. On average, there is less than 1% variation between the cool and hot months, but daily temperatures range from 25°C (77°F) to 32°C (90°F), with an annual mean temperature of 27°C (81°F).

⁴FLORA AND FAUNA

The extreme poverty of the soil and the variability of the rainfall make cultivation of most crops impossible. Only babai (a kind of taro root), coconut palms, and pandanus trees grow easily on most islands. Pigs and poultry were probably introduced by Europeans. Sea life abounds.

⁵ENVIRONMENT

According the United Nations Report for Pacific Island Developing Countries (1992), the most significant environmental problems facing the nations in this area of the world are global warming and the rise of sea levels. Variations in the level of the sea may damage forests and agricultural areas and contaminate fresh water supplies with salt water. A rise in sea level by even two feet (60 cm) would leave Kiribati uninhabitable; in 1996, such a rise was forecast as a possibility by 2100. Kiribati, along with the other nations in the area, is vulnerable to earthquakes and volcanic activity. The nation also has inadequate facilities for handling solid waste, which has been a major environmental concern since 1992, particularly in the larger population centers. The environment in Kiribati has also been adversely affected by metals and chemicals from mining activities, and agricultural chemicals have polluted coastal waters. Phosphate mining was especially devastating, rendering the island of Banaba almost uninhabitable. The Banabans, who were forced to move to the Fijian island of Rabi, sued the owners of the mines and have won special compensation. A fund was also set up to compensate the people of Kiribati. Called the Phosphate Revenue Equalization Fund (PREF), in 1996 it amounted to A$200 million. The lagoon of the south Tarawa atoll has been heavily polluted by solid waste disposal. Like other Pacific islands, Kiribati is sensitive to the dangers of pollution and radiation from weapons tests and nuclear waste disposal. The UN Report describes the wildlife in these areas as "among the most critically threatened in the world." Endangered or extinct species include the green sea turtle and mukojima bonin honeyeater.

Kiribati is a party to the Biodiversity, Endangered Species, Marine Dumping, and the Ozone Layer Protection international agreements.

⁶POPULATION

The population of Kiribati in 2000 was estimated at 87,025. An estimated 3.7% of the population is 65 years of age or older. The

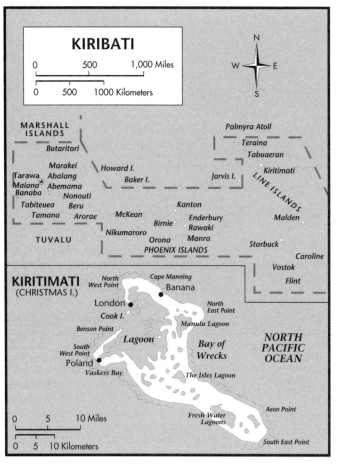

LOCATION: 4°N to 3°S; 168° to 176°E. **TOTAL COASTLINE:** 1,143 km (710 mi). **TERRITORIAL SEA LIMIT:** 12 mi.

projected population for the year 2005 is 92,000, assuming a crude birthrate of 24 per 1,000 population and a death rate of 7, resulting in a natural rate of change of 1.7% for the period 2000–2005. The estimated population density in 1996 was 113 per sq km (292 per sq mi).

The population is unevenly distributed. Tarawa, the capital, had a 2000 population estimated at 28,000, or 40% of the total, while some islands of the Phoenix and Line groups were uninhabited. It was estimated that 37% of the population lived in urban areas in 2000.

7MIGRATION

For the islanders, migration has been a perennial form of escape from drought and starvation. In the 19th century, recruiting ships forcibly took Gilbert Islanders for plantation work in Hawaii, Australia, Fiji, and Peru; some voluntarily reenlisted after the great drought of 1870. Although the majority eventually returned home, it is reckoned that between 1860 and 1890 some 10,000 islanders of a total population of 30,000 were overseas. In the 20th century, Fiji and the Solomon Islands continued to be popular places for Gilbert Islanders in search of work. Internal migration was mainly to Banaba Island for work in the phosphate industry until 1979, and since then to Nauru or to copra plantations in the Line Islands. During 1988–93, 4,700 people were resettled on Teraira and Tabuaeran atolls of the Line Islands because of overcrowding on the main island group. In 1999 the net migration rate was -0.77 migrants per 1,000 population.

8ETHNIC GROUPS

About 99% of the people are Gilbertese of Micronesian extraction. Polynesians (mainly from Tuvalu) make up 0.5% of the total; Europeans and people of mixed races, 0.6%.

9LANGUAGES

The principal languages spoken are Gilbertese and English. The official language is English, but it is seldom used on the outer islands. Gilbertese is an Austronesian language related to many other Pacific tongues.

10RELIGIONS

Virtually the entire population is Christian, comprised of some 53% Roman Catholics, 41% Protestant (Congregational). Religious minorities make up the remaining 6%, including the Seventh-Day Adventists, the Church of God, Assemblies of God, Mormons, and Baha'is. Christian missionaries first arrived in 1857, when Dr. Hiram Bingham, of the American Board of Foreign Missionaries, began to spread Protestantism in the northern Gilberts with the help of Hawaiian pastors. In 1888, Catholicism was introduced to the islands by the Sacred Heart Mission. The American Board withdrew from the territory in 1917 and was succeeded by the London Missionary Society, which had placed Samoan pastors on the islands as early as 1870. The Kiribati Protestant Church identifies itself as Congregational.

11TRANSPORTATION

The remoteness of the scattered islands has severely hampered transport and communications. There are only about 670 km (416 mi) of roads, mostly on Tarawa. The Nippon Causeway, completed in 1987 with Japanese assistance, has replaced ferry service between Betio and Bariki. A series of similar causeways links north and south Tarawa. In 1995, there were about 2,000 vehicles in Kiribati, almost three-quarters of which were motorcycles.

There is no rail, river, or lake transport, although canoes travel freely on the lagoons. The main ports are Betio islet, near Tarawa, and on Tabuaeran and Christmas islands. Betio is equipped for handling containers, and Banaba has a cantilever for phosphate loading. In 1998 Kiribati had 1 passenger-cargo ship at 1,291 GRT. A number of shipping lines call at the islands, and government boats provide interisland service. There were 21 airports in 1998, 4 with paved runways. All the major islands have airstrips; the airports on Christmas Island and at Bonriki (Tarawa) are used for scheduled overseas flights. Air Tungaru, the national airline, operates regularly scheduled flights to Honolulu and Tuvalu. In 1997 28,000 passengers were carried on scheduled domestic and international flights.

12HISTORY

The main wave of Micronesian settlement is thought to have come from Samoa in the 13th century, but Gilbertese tradition suggests that the Samoans were not the first settlers. European discovery dates from 1537, when Christmas Island was sighted by Spanish explorers. The English sea captain James Cook encountered the islands in 1777, and commercial activities in the region began early in the 19th century. The Gilbert Islands were a favorite whaling ground, and deserting crews began to settle in the islands in the 1830s. Trading ships were calling there regularly by the 1850s, and a flourishing copra and coconut trade was established by the 1860s, as well as an illicit human traffic. The Office of British High Commissioner to the Western Pacific was created in 1877 to help suppress abuses by recruiting ships seeking Labour for overseas service. In 1888, Christmas, Fanning (now Tabuaeran), and Washington (now Teraina) islands were annexed by the British, and Phoenix Island was placed under their protection. A declaration of a British protectorate over the

Gilbert and Ellice groups followed in 1892. A handful of administrators established local native governments, and a period of stability ensued.

Ocean Island was annexed by Britain in 1900, following Sir Albert Ellis's discovery of its valuable phosphate deposits. The Gilbert and Ellice groups (including Ocean, Fanning, and Washington islands) were declared a British colony in 1916. British control was extended to Christmas Island in 1919 and to the uninhabited Phoenix group in 1937, but after the US laid claim to Canton and Enderbury, a joint British-American administration over these islands was established. During World War II, the Gilberts were occupied by Japanese forces until 1943, when the invaders were driven out by US forces, after heavy casualties on both sides. Ocean Island was liberated by the Australians in 1945.

In a 1974 referendum, the Ellice Islands voted for separation, subsequently becoming the independent nation of Tuvalu. Internal self-government for the Gilberts was established as of 1 January 1977, and the islands became the independent Republic of Kiribati on 12 July 1979. In September, the new nation signed a treaty of friendship with the US (ratified by the US Senate in 1983), by which the US relinquished its claims to the Line and Phoenix groups (including Canton, Enderbury, and Malden).

Ieremia Tabai, chief minister at the time of independence, became president of the new republic in 1979 and was reelected in May 1982 and February 1983. Although the constitution limits a president to three terms, Tabai argued that he had not completed three full terms and was reelected in May 1987. In 1991, Tabai stepped down and was replaced by Teatao Teannaki, head of the National Progressive Party. Teannaki served until 1994, when Teburoro Tito, head of the nation's first real political party, the Maneaban Te Mauri Party (MTM), was elected. The MTM won 19 of 39 seats in the House.

A special problem was posed by the Banabans, who were resettled in 1946 on Rabi (Fiji)—bought for them by means of phosphate royalties—so that strip mining on their native island could continue unimpeded. In 1975, the Banabans sued, petitioning the British courts for damages. After a lengthy legal battle, representatives of the Banabans (most of whom still reside on Rabi) agreed in 1981 to the creation of a trust fund of nearly a\$15 million for Banaban development. Recognition of Banaban minority rights is enshrined in Kiribati's constitution. Kiribati established diplomatic relations with the former Soviet Union in 1979 and with the People's Republic of China in 1980.

Kiribati opposes French nuclear testing in the Pacific and signed the 1985 Raratonga Agreement declaring the South Pacific a nuclear-weapons-free zone. In 1985, Kiribati signed a one-year fishing agreement with the former USSR that aroused controversy at home and abroad. The agreement was not renewed after talks for its renegotiation broke off in September 1986.

Kiribati began resettling more than 4,700 people on outlying atolls in August 1988 in an attempt to relieve overcrowded conditions on the Tarawa atolls. In September 1988 Kiribati ratified the South Pacific Regional Fisheries Treaty, which permits US tuna ships to operate within its 200-mile exclusive zone. In early 1992 the Parliament of Kiribati instructed the government (against its wishes) to seek compensation from the US for damage done to the country during the Pacific War, 1941–45.

In 1994 the government of Kiribati underwent a constitutional crisis when President Teatao Teannaki was forced to resign following a no-confidence vote by the opposition in parliament, who had charged him with misusing travel funds. As specified in the constitution, executive authority was then transferred to a Council of State until new parliamentary and presidential elections could be held, but one member of the council refused to resign when his term expired and had to be forcibly removed, prompting calls for constitutional reform to prevent a similar

situation from occurring in the future. Teburoro Tito was elected president in September, and elected to a second term in November 1998.

Together with Nauru and Tonga, Kiribati was admitted to the United Nations in 1999. In March of that year, the government declared a state of emergency as water shortages reached crisis levels due to an extended drought and pollution of the available water supply. Long-term elevation of the surrounding sea level due to global greenhouse emissions remains a serious concern for Kiribati, which reportedly has already lost two uninhabited islands and been forced to move segments of its population inland, away from coastal regions.

[13]GOVERNMENT

Under the independence constitution of 1979, Kiribati is a democratic republic within the Commonwealth of Nations. It has a unicameral legislature, the House of Assembly (Maneaba ni Maungatabu), the members of which are elected every four years. The number of elected representatives was increased from 35 to 39 in 1987. One appointed seat is reserved for a representative of the Banaban community. The president (*beretitenti*), who is both head of state and head of government, is elected directly by popular vote, from among members of the Assembly, to a term of up to four years; candidates are selected by the House from among its own members. When the president no longer enjoys the confidence of the legislature, the House is dissolved and new parliamentary and presidential elections are held, with a Council of State (consisting of the head of the Civil Service Commission, the chief justice, and the speaker of the House) governing in the interim. The cabinet consists of the president, vice-president, attorney general, and up to eight other ministers.

Teatao Teannaki, head of the National Progressive Party, was elected the nation's second president in July 1991. He was obliged to resign following a no-confidence vote in 1994, and Teburoro Tito, head of the Maneaban Te Mauri Party (MTM), was elected president. Tito was reelected in 1998.

[14]POLITICAL PARTIES

Kiribati had no formally constituted political parties until 1985, when opponents of the Soviet fishing agreement founded the Christian Democratic party, headed by Dr. Harry Tong. The Christian Democrats, now known as the Maurin te Maneaba party, led by President Teburoro Tito, won 14 seats in the September 1998 parliamentary elections, and the principal opposition party, Boutokaan te Koaua, won 11; 14 seats were won by independents.

Other parties that have been formed since 1991 include the Liberal Party, led by Tewareka Tentoa; the Maneaba Party, led by Roniti Teiwaki; the New Movement Party; and the Health Peace and Honour Party.

[15]LOCAL GOVERNMENT

There are fully elective local councils on all the islands, in accordance with a local government ordinance of 1966. For administrative purposes the islands are divided into six districts: Tarawa (including the Phoenix group); North, South, and Central Gilberts; Banaba; and the Line Islands. This structure has been further divided into 21 island councils, one for each of the inhabited islands. The geographic dispersion of the islands leaves considerable freedom for the districts; their councils have wide taxing powers, including land taxes, and draw up their own estimates of revenues and expenditures.

[16]JUDICIAL SYSTEM

The 1979 constitution provides for a High Court, with a chief justice and other judges, to act as the supreme court and court of appeal. Island courts were established in 1965 to deal with civil and criminal offenses. Native land courts have jurisdiction over property claims. High court and court of appeal judges are appointed by the president.

The judiciary is independent and free from government influence. Civil rights and civil liberties are guaranteed in the Constitution and respected in practice. Procedural due process safeguards are based on English common law. The trials are fair and public. The law prohibits the arbitrary interference with privacy, family, home and correspondence. The government authorities respect these provisions.

17ARMED FORCES

Legislation providing for the establishment of a defense force of 170 men was repealed in 1978. There is a small police force. Australia and New Zealand provide defense assistance.

18INTERNATIONAL COOPERATION

Kiribati participates in many Commonwealth activities and hosted the South Pacific Forum in 1981. Kiribati was admitted to the UN on 14 September 1999. It is also an associate member of ESCAP and a member of ICAO, IBRD, IMF, ICFTU, IDA, IFC, IFRCS, IMF, INTELSAT, INTERPOL, ITU, SPC, SPF, UNESCO, UPU, and WHO. Kiribati participates in the Asian Development Bank and G-77 and is an applicant to the WTO.

19ECONOMY

Kiribati's economy was supported by revenues from phosphate mining on Banaba until the deposits were exhausted in 1979. Since then, the nation has relied on fishing, subsistence agriculture, and exports of copra. In the 1990s, GDP growth averaged 2.4%. Still, the nation relies heavily on international assistance and such aid, primarily from Japan and the UK, accounts for 25–50% of GDP. Inflation in 1998 was -.60% and unemployment was officially 2%. Underemployment was estimated by the government to be about 70%.

20INCOME

The US Central Intelligence Agency (CIA) reports that in 1996 Kiribati's gross domestic product (GDP) was estimated at $62 million. The per capita GDP was estimated at $800. The annual growth rate of GDP was estimated at 1.9%. The average inflation rate in 1996 was 4.2%. The CIA defines GDP as the value of all final goods and services produced within a nation in a given year and computed on the basis of purchasing power parity (PPP) rather than value as measured on the basis of the rate of exchange. It was estimated that agriculture accounted for 14% of GDP, industry 7%, and services 79%.

21LABOR

Most of the population engages in subsistence agriculture or copra production, including the copra plantations on the Line Islands. As of 1996, about 90% of the labor force was engaged in agriculture or fishing. Overseas workers remitted most of their wages to Kiribati.

In urban areas there is a small but strong trade union movement. Affiliates of the Kiribati Trades Union Congress (KTUC), founded in 1982 with Australian assistance, include the Fishermen's Union, the Cooperative Workers' Union, the Seamen's Union, the Teacher's Union, and the Public Employees' Association; in 1999, the KTUC had about 2,500 members.

There is no statutory minimum wage; however, the government sets wage levels in the large public sector, which is the major employer in the cash economy.

Children may not work under the age of 14. This is effectively enforced by the government in the modern, industrial sector of the economy, but many children do perform light labor in the traditional fishing economy.

22AGRICULTURE

Agriculture is limited chiefly to coconut and pandanus production. About 37,000 ha (91,400 acres) of land is considered arable, representing 5.1% of the total land area. Overseas technical aid has allowed some islands to cultivate bananas and papaws for the Tarawa market. An estimated 12,000 tons of copra, 80,000 tons of coconuts, and 5,000 tons of bananas were produced in 1998. Agricultural trade in 1997 consisted of $8.7 million in exports and $19.2 million in imports. Agriculture contributed 23% to GDP in 1994.

23ANIMAL HUSBANDRY

There were 10,000 pigs in Kiribati in 1998; annual pork production is about 1,000 tons. The Agricultural Division has introduced improved breeds of livestock.

24FISHING

Sea fishing is excellent, particularly for skipjack tuna around the Phoenix Islands. Kiribati has one of the world's longest maritime zones, covering approximately 3 million sq km. Commercial fishing has expanded dramatically since 1979 as the result of projects funded by Japan, the UK, and the EU. The total sea catch in 1997 was 24,930 tons. Kiribati also receives revenue from the sales of licenses permitting foreign vessels to fish its offshore waters. Seaweed is also exported. In 1992, the country earned us $5.7 million in fishing fees from the US alone.

25FORESTRY

There is little useful timber on the islands. Imports of forest products totaled $769,000 in 1995.

26MINING

There has been no mining in Kiribati since the closing in 1979 of the Banaba phosphate industry. In its last year of operation, 445,700 tons of phosphates worth A$18 million were exported.

27ENERGY AND POWER

The government maintains electricity generating plants on Tarawa and Christmas Island, and there are private generators on Banaba and several other islands. In 1998, electric power generating capacity was 2,000 kW; production of electricity totaled 7 million kWh that year.

28INDUSTRY

Several small industries have been established, including a soft-drink plant, a biscuit factory, boat-building shops, construction companies, furniture plants, repair garages, bakeries, and laundries. The government also promotes local handicrafts. A pilot project on Kiritimati for producing solar-evaporated salt began operations in 1985. In 1988, manufacturing accounted for only 1.8% of GDP. By 1996, this figure had risen to 7%.

29SCIENCE AND TECHNOLOGY

The Foundation for the Peoples of the South Pacific, founded in 1982 and located at Bairiki, Tarawa, provides technical assistance for agriculture and nutrition programs.

30DOMESTIC TRADE

The village economy is on a subsistence and barter basis. Retail sales are handled by cooperative societies, which distribute the bulk of consumer goods and perform all merchandising functions not dealt with by the government. Although private trade is growing, cooperatives are preferred as a matter of public policy because they are closer to the local tradition than are individual enterprises.

31 FOREIGN TRADE

The loss of the phosphate industry, copra price fluctuations, and the islands' remoteness have hindered overseas trade, but an upward trend in foreign trade was perceptible in the 1980s. Copra—the only commodity exported by Kiribati—accounted for 62% of total domestic exports in 1996. Fish and seaweed are also exported, accounting for 15% and 16% of total exports, respectively. Kiribati's main export partners are the US, Australia, and New Zealand. Australia provides 46% of imports; Japan, 18%; Fiji, 17%; New Zealand, 6%; and the US, 4%.

In 1995 Kiribati's imports were distributed among the following categories:

Consumer goods	15.3%
Food	35.2%
Fuels	10.0%
Industrial supplies	22.8%
Machinery	9.3%
Transportation	6.2%
Other	1.3%

32 BALANCE OF PAYMENTS

Continued deficits in the trade balance are often met by grants from the UK to the government's current and capital accounts. Foreign aid, in fact, accounts for between 25–50% of GDP.

The US Central Intelligence Agency reports that in 1996 the purchasing power parity of Kiribati's exports was $6.7 million while imports totaled $37.4 million resulting in a trade balance of -$30.7 million.

The International Monetary Fund (IMF) reports that in 1994 Kiribati had exports of goods totaling $6 million and imports totaling $27 million. The services credit totaled $18 million and debit $17 million. The following table summarizes Kiribati's balance of payments for 1994 in millions of US dollars.

Current Account		1
Balance on goods	-21	
Balance on services	...	
Balance on income	15	
Current transfers	7	
Capital Account		3
Financial Account		-5
Direct investment abroad	-	
Direct investment in Kiribati	...	
Portfolio investment assets	-7	
Portfolio investment liabilities	...	
Other investment assets	...	
Other investment liabilities	1	
Net Errors and Omissions		-5
Reserves and Related Items		6

33 BANKING AND SECURITIES

The Bank of Kiribati in Tarawa is jointly owned by the Westpac Banking Corp. (Australia) and the government of Kiribati (49%). The Kiribati Development Bank, opened in 1987, was to take over the assets of the National Loans Board when it became fully operational.

34 INSURANCE

Individual coverage is available in Tarawa through private and government agencies.

35 PUBLIC FINANCE

Local revenues are derived mainly from import duties, fishing fees, and investment income from the phosphate fund. The country has been running a capital account deficit since independence. Overall, budgetary deficits have appeared in recent years, growing substantially in the 1990s.

The US Central Intelligence Agency (CIA) estimates that in 1996 Kiribati's central government took in revenues of approxi-

mately $33.3 million and had expenditures of $47.7 million. Overall, the government registered a deficit of approximately $14.4 million.

36 TAXATION

The main source of tax revenue, the phosphate industry, ended in 1979. Other taxes have brought meager returns, except for a copra export tax, with producers protected by a government stabilization fund. An income tax, introduced in 1975, is levied on a sliding scale. Companies pay a flat rate on all chargeable income. Island councils levy local rates; a landowners' tax is based on land area and fertility.

37 CUSTOMS AND DUTIES

Since a single line tariff was introduced on 1 January 1975, trade preferences are no longer granted to imports from Commonwealth countries. Tariffs, applying mostly to private imports, are imposed as a service of revenue at rates up to 75%. Most duties are levied ad valorem, with specific duties on alcoholic beverages, tobacco, certain chemicals, petroleum, cinematographic film, and some other goods. Goods from all sources are subject to an additional freight levy charge.

38 FOREIGN INVESTMENT

There is little private investment, although in the 1990s, the government enacted various incentives to attract foreign capitol, including tax holidays.

39 ECONOMIC DEVELOPMENT

The economic development plans for 1979–82 and 1983–86 were financed chiefly by the UK and supplemented by Australia, New Zealand, and Japan, with loans from the Asian Development Bank and EC. Canada, the Federal Republic of Germany, and the Republic of Korea also have started small aid programs. The plan stressed infrastructure development, support for fisheries, and rural health programs. The goal of the 1987–91 plan was economic self-reliance through gradual and sustainable development, with particular emphasis on the subsistence life-style of the outer islands. The UN Development Program is implementing an economic development plan for the northern Line Islands focusing on infrastructure, agriculture, and tourism.

40 SOCIAL DEVELOPMENT

A provident fund system provides old age, disability, and survivor benefits in the form of lump sum payments only, with the worker contributing 5% of earnings and the employer paying an equal percentage of payroll. Retirement is allowed at ages 45–50 and benefits are paid as a lump sum. Workers' compensation is compulsory for employed persons earning A$4,000 a year (as of 1999) or less. The cost is covered by the employer.

Migration and missionaries have proved to be the principal agents of social change. Mission lands are still used for social welfare purposes. The majority of the population still clings to traditional village life and the extended family system, which renders state welfare largely unnecessary. Problems exist mainly in the rapidly urbanized south Tarawa area, where some juvenile delinquency has developed. Women's clubs, organized by the women's section of the Ministry of Welfare, have raised funds for local projects. Rural training centers have also been established.

Women are accorded the same legal rights as men, but have traditionally been relegated to a subordinate role in society. However, they are gradually breaking out of their traditional role and entering both skilled and unskilled occupations. There have also been signs of affirmative action in government hiring and promotions. As of 1998, 2 of 42 parliamentary seats were held by women. Violence against women is uncommon.

There were no reports of human rights abuses or of the systematic discrimination of minorities. Corporal punishment remains legal for some crimes.

41HEALTH

The population of Kiribati had increased access to safe water (99%) and sanitation (100%) in 1993. Tuberculosis remains the most serious public health problem (about 200 cases per 100,000 people in 1990); other endemic diseases are leprosy, filariasis, and dysentery. There was a cholera outbreak in 1977, after which projects to construct water and sewage pipes were speeded up. Vitamin A deficiency, frequently causing night blindness and xerophthalmia, is a common occurrence among children in Kiribati. The prevalence of xerophthalmia was almost 15% in children in 1994. All health services are free. A nurses' training school is maintained at the 160-bed Central Hospital in Tarawa. There are four medical districts, each with its own medical officer and staff. Each inhabited island has a dispensary, and there is a medical radio network linking all the islands. In 1990, there were 14 doctors and 116 nurses. In 1992, there were 0.31 doctors per 1,000 people, with a nurse to doctor ratio of 3.0. In 1990, there were 1.8 hospital beds per 1,000 inhabitants.

Infant mortality was estimated at 48 per 1,000 live births in 1999, and average life expectancy was 62.9 years. The immunization rates for a child under one were as follows in 1995: diphtheria, tetanus, and whooping cough (60%); polio (100%); measles (100%); and tuberculosis (60%). The general mortality rate in 1999 was estimated at 7.5 per 1,000 people. The total fertility rate was 3 in 1999.

42HOUSING

Most Kiribatians live in small villages of from 10 to 150 houses and construct their own dwellings from local materials. The use of more permanent building materials, such as concrete with corrugated aluminum roofing, is becoming common in urban areas. Loans to prospective homeowners are provided by the National Loans Board. Dwellings range from traditional houses with thatched roofs to nontraditional houses with metal roofs.

43EDUCATION

The government has gradually taken over control of primary education from the missions. Education has been made compulsory by the government for children between the ages of 6 and 15 years. They go through seven years of primary education and five years of secondary education. In 1997, there were 17,594 students attending 86 primary schools, with 727 teachers. Student-to-teacher ratio stood at 24 to one. In secondary schools, there were 215 staff and 4,403 students in that same year. Secondary school pupils take the New Zealand school certificate. The estimated adult literacy rate is 93%.

Higher education courses are available at the Kiribati Extension Centre of the University of the South Pacific (Fiji) in Tarawa. Other post-secondary education is provided by scholarships for study abroad. The Tarawa Technical Institute offers instruction in technical and vocational skills. The Marine Training Centre offers 18-month instruction in deck, engine room, and catering work on foreign shipping lines; there are approximately 200 students enrolled in these programs.

44LIBRARIES AND MUSEUMS

The National Library and Archives in Tarawa has a collection of 50,000 volumes, including those in small units throughout the islands. The University of the South Pacific has a campus in Tarawa with a small library of 5,700 volumes. Items are being stored in the National Archives in anticipation of the formation of the national museum which is to be in Tarawa.

45MEDIA

Radio Kiribati, operated by the Broadcasting and Publications Authority, transmits daily in I-Kiribati and English and broadcasts a few imported Australian programs. The authority also publishes a fortnightly bilingual newspaper, *Te Uekera*. There is no commercial press; all publications are government- or church-sponsored. The Information Department at Tarawa publishes *Atoll Pioneer*, a weekly newspaper. *Te Itoi ni Kiribati*, a weekly newsletter, is published by the Roman Catholic Church. *Te Kaotan te Ota* is a newspaper published monthly by Protestant Church. Kiribati is on the Peacesat network, which provides educational transmissions from Suva. A satellite link with Australia was established in 1985. There were an estimated 1,400 telephones in use in 1991 on South Tarawa and Betio, and a direct link service for seven other islands. In 1990 there were four cinemas. As of 1999 there was one AM radio station and one television station. In 1997, there were 172 radios per 1,000 population.

Although the one radio station and *Te Uekera* are government owned, they offer a variety of views; the constitution provides for legally guaranteed freedom of speech and press.

46ORGANIZATIONS

The most important organization is the *mronron* (a word meaning "sharing"), a cooperative society based on kinship or locality.

47TOURISM, TRAVEL, AND RECREATION

Tourism is undeveloped because of a lack of regular transport. There is a visitors' bureau at Tarawa, and there are hotels in Betio and on Abemama and Christmas islands. The bureau makes available fishing, swimming, and boating facilities on Tarawa and arranges trips by sea or air to other islands.

Modern forms of recreation are developing, especially soccer. Traditional dancing and singing styles have survived. In 1997, 5,825 tourists arrived in Kiribati, a 71% increase over the prior year. More than 1,000 tourists were from the US. That year there were 211 rooms in hotels and other establishments, with 322 beds. Tourist receipts totaled $900,000 in 1996.

In 1999 the UN estimated the cost of staying in Christmas Island at $150 per day. Staying in the outer islands was significantly less expensive, requiring an estimated $29 in daily expenses.

48FAMOUS KIRIBATIANS

Ieremia Tabai (b.1950) was president from independence until 1991.

49DEPENDENCIES

Kiribati has no territories or colonies.

50BIBLIOGRAPHY

American University. *Oceania: A Regional Study*. Washington, D.C.: Government Printing Office, 1984.

Geddes, W. H., et al. *Atoll Economy: Social Change in Kiribati and Tuvalu*. Canberra: Australian National University Press, 1982.

Graham, Michael B. *Mantle of Heroism: Tarawa and the Struggle for the Gilberts, November 1943*. Novato, Calif.: Presidio, 1993.

Grimble, Arthur Francis. *Migrations, Myth, and Magic from the Gilbert Islands*. London: Toutledge & K. Paul, 1972.

———. *Return to the Islands: Life and Legend in the Gilberts*. New York: Morrow, 1957.

Wilson, Craig. *Kiribati: State of the Environment Report, 1994*. Apia, Western Samoa: South Pacific Regional Environment Programme, 1994.

KOREA, DEMOCRATIC PEOPLE'S REPUBLIC OF (DPRK)

Democratic People's Republic of Korea
Choson Minjujuui Inmin Konghwa-guk

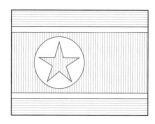

CAPITAL: P'yongyang.

FLAG: A wide horizontal red stripe is bordered on top and bottom by narrow blue stripes, separated from the red by thin white stripes. The left half of the red stripe contains a red five-pointed star on a circular white field.

ANTHEM: *The Song of General Kim Il-sung.*

MONETARY UNIT: The won (w) of 100 ch'on (or jeon) is the national currency. There are coins of 1, 5, 10, and 50 ch'on, and 1 won, and notes of 1, 5, 10, 50, and 100 won. w1 = $0.4545 (or $1 = w2.20) as of 31 March 2000.

WEIGHTS AND MEASURES: The metric system and native Korean units of measurement are used.

HOLIDAYS: New Year's Day, 1 January; Kim Jong Il's Birthday, 16 February; International Women's Day, 8 March; Kim Il-sung's Birthday, 15 April; May Day, 1 May; Liberation Day, 15 August; National Foundation Day, 9 September; Founding of the Korean Workers' Party, 10 October; Anniversary of the Constitution, 27 December.

TIME: 9 PM = noon GMT.

¹LOCATION, SIZE, AND EXTENT

The Democratic People's Republic of Korea (DPRK), often called North Korea, occupies the northern 55% of the Korean Peninsula in East Asia. It has an area of 120,540 sq km (46,541 sq mi), extending 719 km (447 mi) NNE–SSW and 371 km (231 mi) ESE–WNW. Comparatively, the area occupied by DPRK is slightly smaller than the state of Mississippi. It is bordered on the N by China, on the NE by the Russia, on the E by the Sea of Japan (including East Korea Bay), known in Korea as the East Sea, on the S by the Republic of Korea (ROK), and on the S and W by the Yellow Sea and Korea Bay, with a total boundary length of 2,309 km (1,435 mi). A demilitarized zone (DMZ), 4,000 m (13,100 ft) wide, covering 1,262 sq km (487 sq mi), and located north and south of the 38th parallel, separates the DPRK from the ROK, which occupies the southern part of the Korean Peninsula.

The DPRK's capital city, P'yongyang, is located in the southwestern part of the country.

²TOPOGRAPHY

The DPRK is mostly mountainous. Mt. Paektu (2,744 m/9,003 ft), an extinct volcano with a scenic crater lake, is the highest point; it is located on the border with China and forms part of the Mach'ol Range. Other peaks of note include Mt. Kwanmo (2,541 m/8,337 ft), in the Hamgyong Range; Mt. Myohyang (1,909 m/6,263 ft), in the Myohyang Range, north of P'yongyang; and Mt. Kumgang ("Diamond Mountain," 1,638 m/5,374 ft), in the Taebaek Range in the southeast. Only about 20% of the country consists of lowlands and plains, but it is in these areas that the population is concentrated. The principal lowlands are the Unjon, P'yongyang, Chaeryong, Anju, and Yonbaek plains, extending from north to south along the west coast; and the

Susong, Yongchon, Kilchu, Hamhung, and Yonghung plains, along the eastern shore.

The principal rivers are the Tumen (521 km/324 mi) and Yalu (790 km/491 mi) along the northern border of the peninsula, both of which rise in Mt. Paektu, and the Taedong (397 km/247 mi), which flows past P'yongyang. The Imjin (254 km/158 mi) rises in the DPRK near the 38th parallel in the west and crosses into the ROK before entering the Yellow Sea. Yellow Sea tides on the west coast rise to over 9 m (30 ft) in some places; Sea of Japan tides on the east rise to only about 1 m (3 ft).

³CLIMATE

The climatic range is greater than the limited size of the peninsula would suggest. The average January temperature is –17°C (1°F) at Chunggang on the north-central border and –8°C (18°F) at P'yongyang. In the hottest part of the summer, however, the variation is not nearly so marked, average temperatures ranging from 24°C (75°F) in P'yongyang to 21°C (70°F) along the relatively cool northeast coast. Spring and fall are unusually pleasant, but winters are colder than average for the latitude, and summers are hot and humid. Precipitation is around 50 cm (20 in) along the upper reaches of the Tumen, but more than half of the peninsula receives 75–100 cm (30–40 in) per year. Nearly all the rainfall occurs in the April–September period, especially during the rainy season, from late June to early August. Typhoons occur occasionally in the early fall. Days without frost number about 180 in the northern part of the peninsula and increase toward the south.

⁴FLORA AND FAUNA

Cold temperate vegetation, including firs, spruces, and other needled evergreens, predominate in mountainous areas of the

DPRK, with alpine varieties flourishing at the higher altitudes. The hilly terrain of Mt. Paektu is believed to be the peninsula's last remaining habitat for Siberian tigers and is also, along with other alpine areas, the home of bears, wild boar, deer, snow leopards, and lynx. Common at lower elevations are the roe deer, Amur goral, wolf, water shrew, and muskrat. Birds seen in the DPRK include the black Manchurian ring-necked pheasant, black grouse, and three-toed woodpecker; the hawk owl, lesser-spotted woodpecker, and willow tit are indigenous to Mt. Paektu.

[5]ENVIRONMENT

The Democratic People's Republic of Korea has environmental problems in the area of water pollution from agricultural and industrial sources. The nation has 16.1 cubic miles of water with 73% used for farming activity and 16% used for industrial purposes. Korea's cities produce 2.6 million tons of solid waste per year. Of Korea's total land area, 20% can be used for agricultural purposes. In 1992 the DPRK was among the 20 countries with the world's highest levels of industrial carbon dioxide emissions, which totaled 253.7 million metric tons, a per capita level of 11.21 metric tons. The Korean government has established 220 facilities to regulate environmental conditions, industrial areas, protected land, and water reserves. The government has also created the Law of Environmental Protection. In 1994, 5 of Korea's mammal species and 25 of its bird species were endangered. As of 1994, endangered species in the DPRK included the tiger (particularly the Siberian tiger), Amur leopard, Japanese sea lion, Oriental white stork, Japanese crested ibis, and Tristram's woodpecker.

[6]POPULATION

The population of the Democratic People's Republic of Korea (DPRK) in 2000 was estimated at 21,687,550, less than half of the estimated population of the ROK, but more than double the post-Korean War low of 8,491,000 in 1953. An estimated 4.8% of the population is 65 years of age or older. The projected population for the year 2005 is 23,348,000, assuming a crude birthrate of 13 per 1,000 population and a death rate of 7, resulting in a natural rate of change of 0.6% for the period 2000–2005. The population rate of change between 1995 and 2000 was 1.6%.

The population density varies greatly from region to region, with an average of 198 per sq km (514 per sq mi) in 1996. It was estimated that 63% of the population lived in urban areas in 2000 (as compared with 45% in 1965). The capital city, P'yongyang, had a 2000 population of 2,484,000 and a 2000 metropolitan population of 2,726,000. Other large cities include Hamhung, with 670,000 inhabitants; Ch'ongjin, 530,000; Kaesong, 310,000; and Sinuiju, 330,000.

[7]MIGRATION

During the generation of Japanese occupation (1910–45), some 3 million Koreans, mainly from the northern provinces, emigrated to Manchuria and parts of China, 700,000 to Siberia, some 3 million to Japan, and about 7,000 to the US (mostly to Hawaii). From the end of World War II in 1945 through 1950, at least 1.2 million Koreans crossed the 38th parallel into the ROK, refugees either from Communism or from the Korean War. Repatriation of overseas Koreans is actively encouraged in an attempt to ameliorate the nation's chronic labor shortages. Between 1945 and 1950, an estimated 300,000 Koreans were repatriated from Manchuria and Siberia; over 93,000 out of about 600,000 Koreans in Japan were repatriated to the DPRK between December 1959 and the end of 1974. The General Association of Korean Residents in Japan actively promotes the DPRK cause, and the P'yongyang government subsidizes some Korean schools on Japanese soil. Some 250,000 people of Korean origin in Japan

have links to the DPRK, providing $600–$1,800 million in annual remittances to relatives. Under a 1986 treaty with China, North Koreans apprehended as illegal immigrants in China are quickly returned to the DPRK and executed. Between 1992 and 1996, about 1,000 North Koreans fled to China, where refugees can avoid detection within large ethnic-Korean communities. Both China and South Korea have begun to construct refugee camps in anticipation of a mass exodus of the population should the North Korean government collapse. In 1999, the net migration rate was zero migrants per 1,000 population.

[8]ETHNIC GROUPS

The Koreans are believed to be descended primarily from Tungusic peoples of the Mongoloid race, who originated in the cold northern regions of Central Asia. There is scant evidence of non-Mongoloid admixture. There is a small Chinese community and a few ethnic Japanese; however, the DPRK has no sizable ethnic minority.

[9]LANGUAGES

The Korean language is usually acknowledged to be a member of the Altaic family and is clearly related to other agglutinative tongues like Turkish, Mongolian, and Japanese. Linguistic unification of the Korean Peninsula apparently followed political unification in the 7th century AD, and today the dialect differences are comparatively slight.

Korean is written with a largely phonetic alphabet called Han'gul. Created in 1443 under the great King Sejong, the Korean alphabet originally consisted of 14 consonants and 10 vowels; since then, 5 consonants and 11 vowels have been added. Han'gul letters are combined into syllables by clustering, in imitation of Chinese characters. Before the invention of Han'gul, Koreans wrote in Chinese, which continued to be both the official language and the language of most literature until the beginning of the 20th century. With the beginning of the Japanese colonial administration in 1910, Japanese became the official language, and the use of Korean was restricted.

Since 1949, the DPRK has used only Han'gul (calling it Choson Muntcha) for writing. North Korean linguists have studied Han'gul extensively, publishing comprehensive dictionaries in 1963 and 1969. In 1964, Kim Il-sung called for purification of Korean by replacing borrowings from English and Japanese with native Korean or familiar Chinese terms. The traditional honorifics of polite language remain in use, though in simplified forms, and have been sanctioned by the government.

Some Chinese (Mandarin dialect) and Russian are spoken in border areas.

[10]RELIGIONS

The constitution provides for "freedom of religious belief," but in practice the government discourages all organized religious activity except that which serves the interests of the State. Real religious freedom does not exist. The constitution also states that "no one can use religion as a means to drag in foreign powers" or to disrupt the social order.

According to current estimates a majority of the population professes no religion or are avowed atheists. Indigenous shamanism, notable for its emphasis on exorcising evil spirits, is practiced by an estimated 16% of the population, mostly in rural areas. Followers of Ch'ondogyo (Religion of the Heavenly Way), an eclectic indigenous sect incorporating both Christian and Buddhist elements, originating in 1860, account for about another 14%; its organization went underground following the arrest of 10,000 Ch'ondogyo members in 1948. Almost 2% of the population continues to practice Buddhism despite the conversion of many Buddhist temples to secular uses. Up to the mid-1940s, P'yongyang was an important center of Korean

Christianity. Most of the nation's Christians, predominantly Protestants, fled to the ROK to escape persecution between 1945 and 1953. Christians now make up less than 1% of the population.

11 TRANSPORTATION

The rail network, which has been rebuilt and extended following its almost complete destruction during the Korean War, is the principal means of transportation, carrying nearly all of the nation's freight and most of its passenger traffic. In 1996, railways in use comprised 5,000 km (3,107 mi) of track. The principal lines run along the west coast from P'yongyang to Sinuiju and across the peninsula from P'yongyang to Wonsan, Hamhung, and Ch'ongjin. A northern line, completed in the early 1980s, links P'yongyang to Hyesan and Musan. The major trunk routes are electrified. A subway system opened in P'yongyang in 1973 and was expanded under the 1978–84 development plan. There are also train services to Moscow and Beijing.

Road transportation is of secondary importance. In 1998, highways totaled an estimated 31,200 km (19,388 mi), of which only 1,997 km (1,241 mi) were paved. The exceptions are a superhighway connecting P'yongyang with Kaesong and two multi-lane highways, which link the national capital with the ports of Wonsan and Namp'o.

Most of the nation's 2,253 km (1,400 mi) of navigable waterways are suitable for small craft only. Rivers utilized for freight transportation are the Yalu, Taedong, and Chaeryong. The principal ports are Namp'o on the west coast, and Ch'ongjin and Hungnam on the east coast. In 1998, there were 110 ships in the merchant fleet, with a total capacity of 691,802 GRT. Also in 1998, there were 49 airports, of which 22 had paved runways. Limited air services connect P'yongyang with other cities within the DPRK and in China and the former USSR. In 1997 280,000 passengers were carried on scheduled domestic and international flights.

12 HISTORY

The history of the Korean people begins with the migration into the Korean Peninsula of Tungusic tribes from northern China and Manchuria about 3,000 BC. The archaeological evidence indicates that these tribes possessed a Neolithic culture and that it was not until about the 8th century BC that the art of metal-working came to Korea from China. The recorded history of Korea begins around 194 BC, when the ancient kingdom of Choson ("Land of Morning Calm") in northwestern Korea was seized by Wiman, a military figure from China of either Chinese or Korean origin. He usurped the throne from a king who, according to legend, was a descendant of Kija, a historical Chinese nobleman who emigrated from China at the end of the Shang dynasty (c.1122 BC). A popular Korean legend of much later origin asserts that Kija was preceded in his rule over the Korean Peninsula by a dynasty started in 2333 BC by the semidivine figure Tan-gun, an offspring of the son of the divine creator and a "bear woman" (possibly a woman from a bear-totem tribe). Both Tan-gun and Kija are still widely revered.

The primitive state controlled by Wiman's successors fell victim to expanding Chinese power in 108 BC, and there followed more than four centuries of Chinese colonial rule. During this period, the advanced Chinese culture slowly spread into nearly every corner of Korea, giving impetus to the coalescence of the loosely knit Korean tribes into statelike formations. By AD 313, when the Chinese power was destroyed, three Korean kingdoms had emerged: Paekche, in the southwest; Silla, in the southeast; and Koguryo, in the northwest. The three kingdoms had advanced cultures for the time, each compiling a written history during the 4th–6th centuries. During the same period, Buddhism was introduced into Korea, from which it was later taken to

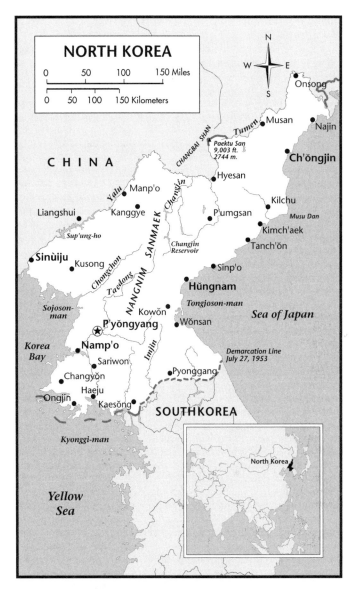

LOCATION: 37°38′ to 43°1′N; 124°13′ to 130°39′E. **BOUNDARY LENGTHS:** China, 1,025 km (637 mi); USSR, 16 km (10 mi); ROK, 240 km (149 mi); total coastline, 1,028 km (639 mi). **TERRITORIAL SEA LIMIT:** 12 mi.

Japan. Ultimately, the Silla kingdom crushed the other two and united all but the northernmost portion of the peninsula, ushering in the age of the Silla Unification (668–900). After rebellions broke out, Korea again suffered threefold division, until reunification was achieved in 936 under the leadership of Wang Kon, who had proclaimed a new dynasty in the kingdom of Koryo (founded in 918), which derived its name from Koguryo; the name Korea is derived from Koryo.

Chinese influence on political and social institutions and on Korean thought went on at an accelerated pace during the Koryo period, and there were some notable cultural achievements, including the traditional invention of the use of movable metal type in printing in the early 12th century. Beginning in 1231, however, the Mongols invaded Koryo, devastating the land and, from 1259 on, making puppets of the Korean kings. Following a revolt against the Mongol Empire in 1356 and a subsequent period of disorder, Gen. Yi Song-gye assumed the throne as King T'aejo in 1392, adopting the name Choson for Korea, moving the capital from Kaesong (the capital of Koryo since 918) to Seoul, and ushering in the long-lived Yi (or Li) Dynasty (1392–1910).

The first hundred years of Yi rule witnessed truly brilliant cultural achievements, especially during the reign of King Sejong (1418–50). The world's first authenticated casting of movable metal type was made in 1403. The Korean alphabet, Han'gul, was developed. A rain gauge was invented and put into use throughout the peninsula. A spate of basic texts—including histories, geographies, administrative codes, and works on music—were compiled and issued under state auspices. Scholars competed for government posts through the civil service examination system. By about 1500, however, factionalism divided the kingdom, and the Yi rulers were ill-prepared to meet foreign invasion. In 1592, in the course of an attempt to conquer China, the Japanese, under Hideyoshi Toyotomi, invaded Korea and were repulsed by an allied Chinese army and the Korean navy under Yi Sun-sin; in 1597 there was another invasion, which ended with Hideyoshi's death in 1598. After being invaded by the Manchus in 1636, Korea became a vassal state, eventually falling under the official but loose control of the Qing (Ch'ing), or Manchu, dynasty in China. During the 18th century, two energetic kings, Yongjo (r.1724–76) and Chongjo (r.1776–1800), were able to arrest somewhat the process of dynastic decline. The intellectual and cultural revival that they engendered, known as the Practical Learning Movement (Sirhak), was short-lived, however, and the Yi kingdom's bitterest century followed.

The first six decades of the 19th century were marked by a succession of natural disasters, by mounting peasant unrest and insurrection, and by administrative relapse into hopeless corruption and inefficiency. Eventually a Korean figure came forward to attempt to rescue the dynasty from impending collapse. This was Yi Ha-leng, known as the Taewon'gun (Prince Regent), who was the father of the king, Kojong, and held the actual power during the decade 1864–73. While his domestic reforms were generally enlightened and beneficial, he adopted an isolationist policy, including persecutions of the growing Roman Catholic community in Korea. Such a policy was doomed to failure. Soon after the Taewon'gun's downfall, the Kanghwa Treaty of 1876 with Japan opened Korea by force both to Japan and to the clamoring Western nations. During the last quarter of the 19th century, Korea was the prize in a complex rivalry for mastery of the peninsula among Japan, China, Western imperialist powers, and domestic political forces. During 1894–95, Japan seized upon the pretext of peasant uprisings in Korea's southern provinces (the Tonghak Rebellion, led by followers of what later came to be called the Ch'ondogyo religion) to destroy waning Chinese power in Korea in the First Sino-Japanese War. A decade later, Japan turned back the Russian bid for supremacy in the Russo-Japanese War (1904–5). In 1910, with the tacit approval of the US and the European powers, the Yi Dynasty came to an end with the formal annexation of Korea by Japan.

For 35 years, Korea (renamed Choson) remained under the Japanese yoke, until liberated by US and Soviet troops at the end of World War II. Although Japanese colonial rule brought to Korea considerable economic development along modern Western lines, the benefits went primarily to the Japanese, and the process was accompanied by ever harsher political and cultural oppression. The Korean people staged a nationwide passive resistance movement beginning on 1 March 1919 (the Samil or "March 1" Movement), only to have it swiftly and brutally crushed by their Japanese overlords. In the 1920s and 1930s, nationalist and Communist movements developed both within Korea and among Korean exiles in the former USSR, Manchuria (which was occupied by Japan in 1931), and the rest of China. After the onset of the Second Sino-Japanese War in 1937, the Japanese aimed to eradicate Korean national identity; even the use of the Korean language was banned.

The Democratic People's Republic

After Japan accepted the Potsdam Declaration for unconditional surrender on 14 August 1945, the 38th parallel was chosen, as a result of US initiative, as a line of demarcation between Soviet occupation forces (who had entered the north on 8 August) and US occupation forces (who were introduced on 8 September). While the Americans set up a full military government allied with conservative Korean political forces, the Soviets allied their government with leftist and Communist Korean forces led by Kim Il-sung, who had been an anti-Japanese guerrilla leader in Manchuria. After a joint commission set up by the US and the USSR failed to agree on plans for the reunification of Korea, the problem was placed on the UN agenda in September 1947. In accordance with a UN resolution, elections were held on 10 May 1948 in South Korea alone; North Korea did not recognize UN competency to sponsor the elections. The newly elected National Assembly formulated a democratic constitution and chose Syngman Rhee, who had been the leader of an independence movement in exile, to be the first president of the Republic of Korea, proclaimed on 15 August 1948. On 9 September, the Democratic People's Republic of Korea was established in the north, with Kim Il-sung at the helm. Like its southern counterpart, the DPRK claimed to be the legitimate government of all Korea. In December, however, the ROK was acknowledged by the UN General Assembly as the only government in Korea to have been formed according to the original UN mandate. The next year and a half brought sporadic border clashes between the two Koreas, coupled with increasing guerrilla activity in the south.

On 25 June 1950, the People's Army of the DPRK struck across the 38th parallel at dawn in a move to unify the peninsula under Communist control. The DPRK forces advanced rapidly; Seoul, the ROK capital, fell within three days, and the destruction of the ROK seemed imminent. At US urging, the UN Security Council branded the DPRK an aggressor and called for the withdrawal of the attacking forces. President Harry S. Truman ordered US air and naval forces into battle on 27 June and ground forces three days later. A multinational UN Command was then created to join with and lead the South Koreans. An amphibious landing at Inch'on (15 September) in the ROK under Gen. Douglas MacArthur brought about the complete disintegration of the DPRK's military position.

MacArthur then made a fateful decision to drive into the north. As the UN forces approached the Yalu River, China warned that it would not tolerate a unification of the peninsula under US/UN auspices. After several weeks of threats and feints, "volunteers" from the Chinese People's Liberation Army entered the fighting en masse, forcing MacArthur into a costly, pell-mell retreat back down the peninsula. The battle line stabilized nearly along the 38th parallel, where it remained for two years. On 27 July 1953, an armistice agreement finally was signed by the North Korean People's Army, the Chinese volunteers, and the UN Command at P'anmunjom in the DPRK, ending a conflict that cost the lives of an estimated 415,000 South Koreans, 23,300 Americans (combat dead), and 3,100 UN allies; casualties among Communist forces are officially estimated by the DPRK at 50,000 but may have been as high as 2 million. A military demarcation line, which neither side regarded as a permanent border, was established, surrounded by the DMZ. After the armistice agreement, all but a token force of UN Command troops withdrew, except those of the US, which in 1954 guaranteed the security of the ROK under a mutual defense treaty. A postwar international conference held in 1954 to resolve the problem of Korea's political division was unable to find a satisfactory formula for reunification. Meanwhile, the DPRK, with the aid of China and the former USSR, began to restore its war-damaged economy. A series of purges consolidated political power in the hands of Kim Il-sung and his supporters. By the end of the 1950s, Kim had emerged as the unchallenged leader of the DPRK and the focus of a personality cult that developed around him and his family.

In 1972, the government replaced the original 1948 constitution with a new document (which would be further revised in 1992), and reunification talks, stalled since 1954, resumed under Red Cross auspices, though without lasting effect. Throughout the 1970s and 1980s, as part of its "cold war" with the ROK, the DPRK extended its diplomatic relations to over 100 countries. The ROK continued to charge the DPRK with attempts at sabotage and subversion, including infiltration by tunnels under the DMZ. In the 1980s, Korea's basic divisions remained unresolved. Since 1980, President Kim has proposed that both the North and South be reunited as a confederal state, with each part retaining regional autonomy and its own ideological and social system, but the ROK has rejected the concept; the DPRK likewise has rejected the ROK's repeated proposals for the resumption of North-South talks on reunification unless the US is a third party in the negotiations, but neither the ROK nor the US has accepted that condition. Kim was unanimously reelected president in May 1990, and his son, Kim Jong-il (1942–), groomed since the 1960s as his designated successor, appeared to be running the nation's day-to-day affairs, though without benefit of any formal administrative post. Indications of an improvement in relations between the North and South included material relief provided by the DPRK to the ROK after a flood in 1984, talks under Red Cross auspices that led to a brief reunion of separated families in 1985, economic discussions, and interparliamentary contacts. The DPRK did not participate in the 1988 summer Olympic Games, officially hosted by the ROK, since it was not named as cohost.

During the 1990s, the DPRK was less able to rely on its allies, the large communist states of the former USSR and China. In 1990, the USSR and the ROK opened formal diplomatic relations and, by the 1990s, the collapse of the Soviet Union cut off an important source of economic and political support for the DPRK. After a break of twelve years since the DPRK sided with the former USSR in the Sino-Soviet clash of 1969, China and the DPRK had reestablished ties in 1982. Yet in 1990, China and the ROK began to encourage mutual trade and in 1992 established formal diplomatic relations. Beginning in 1993, China demanded that all its exports to the DPRK be paid for with cash instead of through barter. The DPRK found itself increasingly isolated and in severe economic difficulty. Reunification talks, and the DPRK's relations with the US, took on added urgency as the DPRK sought international recognition and economic aid.

In the first half of the 1990s, the DPRK's foreign relations revolved around issues of joint US-ROK military exercises and of nuclear capabilities. Repeatedly, since 1986, the DPRK canceled negotiations with the ROK during the annual "Team Spirit" exercises of US and ROK militaries. In 1991, the US withdrew its nuclear weapons from the ROK and the two Koreas signed a bilateral agreement to create a nuclear weapons-free peninsula. Yet it was suspected that the DPRK was developing the capability to reprocess nuclear fuels and build nuclear weapons. (Both the ROK and Japan had stockpiles of plutonium.) Conflicts over the access of an International Atomic Energy Agency inspection team, which the DPRK allowed into North Korea in May 1994, to a reprocessing plant led to new tensions. These tensions were defused with an agreement for high-level talks between the US and the DPRK, previously refused by the US, to be held on 8 July 1994, followed on 25 July by a summit in P'yongyang between the presidents of the two Koreas, the first such summit since Korea was divided in 1945.

On 8 July 1994, just as the US-DPRK talks were beginning, President Kim Il-sung died, and the talks were suspended. Kim Jong-il replaced his father as leader of the country, without assuming Kim Il-sung's previous titles of state president and general secretary of the Korean Workers Party. The official mourning period for Kim Il-sung was extended to three years.

On 10 September 1995 Russia advised the DPRK that it would not extend the 1961 treaty on friendship, cooperation and mutual assistance. The DPRK closed the Neutral Nations Supervisory Committee offices in the northern half of the joint security area at Panmunjim in an effort to dismantle the Military Armistice Agreement in May of 1994, following the expulsion of the Czech and Polish representatives and the withdrawal of China, one of the three original signatures to the agreement. This post-Cold War framework was designed to pressure the US into guaranteeing the DPRK's survival by means of a bilateral peace treaty. Marshall O Jen U, the armed forces supreme commander and the second in the hierarchy behind Kim Il-sung died 25 February 1995. He had been a prominent symbol of military acceptance of the younger Kim.

After he had served as North Korea's de facto leader for four years without formally being named as president, Kim Jong-il's position was made official. On September 5, 1998, the Supreme People's Assembly paid tribute to his father, Kim Il-sung, by permanently abolishing the post of president, which left Kim Jong-il, in his capacity as Chairman of the National Defense Commission, the nation's top political official. At the same session, the assembly approved a number of other changes to the nation's constitution.

Tensions over North Korea's nuclear capabilities were revived when it reportedly fired a three-stage ballistic missile into the Pacific; claims that the vehicle was a satellite launcher were initially greeted by skepticism on the part of the US and Japan, over which it had been fired.

Widespread flooding, due in part to North Korea's efforts to expand the land under collectivization by massive deforestation, has led to a national famine. Relief efforts have not been able to raise nearly enough food to feed North Korea's starving population. The policies of North Korea's government have led to reticence on the part of those nations that normally would have contributed to the UN-sponsored World Food Program (WPF). Nevertheless, in 1998 the WPF mounted the largest aid effort on record in an attempt to save millions of North Koreans from starvation. That year the DPRK accepted nearly $1 billion in food aid. Famine conditions continued through 1999 and into 2000, with the WPF issuing renewed calls for assistance from the international community.

As part of an effort to bring North Korea out of its self-imposed isolation, its government renewed the diplomatic initiative toward the South that had been interrupted by the death of Kim Il-sung in 1994. In the spring of 2000 a North-South summit meeting was scheduled for June 12–14 of that year.

[13]GOVERNMENT

In theory, the highest organ of state power is the unicameral Supreme People's Assembly (SPA), with 687 members in 1999. In practice, however, governmental control rests with the leadership of the Korean Workers' (Communist) Party and the military. SPA members are elected every four years and meet for only a few days each year to ratify decisions made by other governmental and party organs. As part of a series of constitutional changes made by the SPA in its 1998 session, a Presidium was created to operate as the top governmental body between sessions of the SPA, performing functions that formerly belonged to a 19-member Standing Committee and the 24-member Central People's Committee.

Under the constitution (first adopted in 1948, completely revised in 1972, revisions in 1992), the SPA also elected the president of the DPRK; however, as of 1998, following the death of Kim Il-sung four years earlier, the post of president was abolished. In addition, the responsibilities of the cabinet (formerly called the Administrative Council) were expanded.

The state ideology is self-reliance (Chuch'e or Juch'e), the Korean version of Marxism-Leninism that was formulated in 1930 and adopted by the party in 1955. Under the new constitution (which created the post of president), Kim Il-sung, who had previously held state power as premier (1948–72), was elected to the presidency in 1972 and reelected in 1977, 1982, 1986, and 1990. Kim Il-sung died 8 July 1994. Kim Jong-il assumed his father's responsibilities and was formally acknowledged as the nation's leader at the 1998 session of the SPA. Hong Song Nam has been Premier since September 1998.

Suffrage extends to all men and women 17 years of age or older. Elections are on a single slate of Communist-approved candidates, on a yes or no basis. Following elections, it is usually asserted that nearly all those eligible voted and that their votes were unanimous in favor of the candidates.

14POLITICAL PARTIES

The Korean Workers' (Communist) Party, the ruling party of the DPRK, was formed on 10 October 1945 through a merger of the Communist Party and the New Democratic Party. By the mid-1980s, party membership was estimated to have risen to over 3 million, or about 16% of the population, the largest percentage of any Communist country. The principal party organ is the National Party Congress. The Congress adopts the party program and approves the political line set by its Central People's Committee. The party constitution states that a congress is to be convened every four years; however, as of 1999, no party congress had convened since 1980.

To guide the party between sessions of the National Party Congress, the Congress elects a Central People's Committee and a Central Auditing Commission, which looks after the party's financial affairs. The Central People's Committee (with 171 regular and 141 alternate members as of 1998) elects the 10 members of the Politburo or Political Bureau. At the top of the party hierarchy is the Presidium of the Politburo, of which the only remaining member is Kim Jong-il. The other members either died or were dismissed, and a new Politburo could not be appointed because the party congress has not met. In October 1997, Kim Jong-il was also named to succeed his father as general secretary of the party.

A "united front" policy confers nominal status on two ostensibly non-Communist political parties: the Korean Social Democratic Party, founded in 1945 and known as the Korean Democratic Party until 1981, and the Friends Party, founded in 1946 for adherents of the Ch'ondogyo faith.

15LOCAL GOVERNMENT

Of Korea's 13 historic provinces (do), 6 were wholly or partly within the DPRK after 1945. The Communist regime subsequently established 2 new provinces and divided another into two sections, thus raising the number of provinces to 9: North P'yongan, South P'yongan, Chagang, North Hwanghae, South Hwanghae, Kangwon, North Hamgyong, South Hamgyong, and Yanggang. In addition there are 3 provincial-level cities (jikhalsi) under the central government (P'yongyang, the capital, and Kaesong and Namp'o). The provinces were in turn divided into 20 cities (si) and 152 counties (kun, or gun) in the mid-1980s.

There are people's assemblies and people's committees at all levels of administration. Members of the people's assemblies are elected for four-year terms at the provincial level and for two-year terms at the county, township, and village levels. The assemblies supervise public, economic, and cultural activities. They also elect and recall people's committees, which are the permanent executive and administrative organs of the state at the local level.

16JUDICIAL SYSTEM

The DPRK's judicial system consists of the Central Court, formerly called the Supreme Court; the courts of provinces, cities, and counties; and special courts (courts-martial and transport courts). Most cases are tried in the first instance by people's courts at the city or county level. Provincial courts try important cases and examine appeals from lower court judgments. Members of the Central Court are named by the Standing Committee of the SPA to four-year terms concurrent with those of the SPA; lower courts are appointed by the people's assemblies at the corresponding level. A prosecutor-general, who is also appointed by the SPA, is the country's chief law-enforcement officer. He appoints prosecutors at the provincial, city, and county levels. Paralleling the court system is the Central Procurator's Office, a supervisory and investigative body.

Judges at the city and county levels serve two-year terms and are usually Korea Workers' Party members. Prosecution of alleged crimes against the state is conducted outside the judicial system and in secret. Reports from the DPRK in the mid 1990s were that up to 150,000 political prisoners and family members were being detained in DPRK security camps in remote areas.

The Constitution declares that courts shall be independent and that judicial proceedings must be conducted according to elaborate procedural regulations. In practice, however, the principles of procedural due process as guaranteed by Western democratic systems are not respected.

The Constitution provides for the protection of the inviolability of person and residence, and the privacy of correspondence. However in practice these protections are not always afforded.

17ARMED FORCES

The DPRK has one of the world's largest and best-equipped armed forces. Out of an estimated total of 1,082,000 personnel on active duty in 2000, 950,000 were in the army, 46,000 in the navy, and 86,000 in the air force (with 593 combat aircraft). An additional 4.7 million were in the reserves, and there was a civilian militia of 3.5 million. North Korea provides advisors to 12 African countries. The Ministry of Public Security controls 189,000 internal security forces. All males between the ages of 17 and 28 are required to serve 5–8 years in the army, 5–10 years in the navy or 3–4 years in the air force. Defense expenditures in 1997 totaled an estimated $5 to 7 billion or 25% to 33% of GDP. In the 1980s, the DPRK emerged as an important supplier of weapons and military training to the third world, but its foreign sales sunk from $130 million (1986) to $30 million (1991). The most worrisome developments are the DPRK's growing capacity to produce weapons-grade nuclear material, improvement of its No-dong missile to reach regional targets beyond Korea, and its failure to submit to legal INEA inspections.

Because of the secrecy inherent in the DPRK, reliability of the figures provided is uncertain, as is information on the combat readiness of its forces.

18INTERNATIONAL COOPERATION

During the mid-1970s, the DPRK came out of its relative isolation to pursue a vigorous international diplomacy. By 1986, it had diplomatic relations with 103 countries, including 67 that also had relations with the ROK. Although not a member of the UN, the DPRK maintains an observer group at UN headquarters and is a member of several nonregional specialized agencies, including FAO, ICAO, ITU, UNESCO, UNIDO, UPU, WHO, WIPO, and WMO. The nation has signed the Law of the Sea and has been particularly active in third-world diplomacy; in August 1975, the DPRK entered the League of Non-Aligned Nations, and it has since joined G-77. In addition, the DPRK pursues a variety of exchanges with China and East European nations. The DPRK retains treaties of friendship, cooperation, and mutual defense concluded with China and the republics of the former USSR in 1961. In 1986, a 20-year treaty of friendship and cooperation with Mongolia was signed. The DPRK was the only Asian Communist country to remain neutral in the Sino-Soviet dispute.

19ECONOMY

By the end of the 1960s, the government's pursuit of a self-reliant economic policy had succeeded in transforming the DPRK into one of the most strictly regulated economies in the world. The Korean War devastated much of the DPRK's economy, but growth after postwar reconstruction was rapid. The Communist regime has used its rich mineral resources to promote industry, especially heavy industry. By 1965, industry accounted for 78% of the total output, and agriculture 22%; the two sectors had thus precisely reversed the proportions reported in 1946. A generally accepted figure put annual industrial growth during 1956–63 at about 25%. Since 1965, greater emphasis has been placed on agriculture and light industry, the latter stress owing to increasing demands for consumer goods. The industrial growth rate slowed in the late 1960s to around 14% and averaged about 16% during the 1970s. Efforts to accelerate the growth rate during the mid-1970s, requiring substantial imports of heavy industrial equipment from Japan and Western Europe, led to a payments crisis, and the DPRK was repeatedly compelled to reschedule its foreign debt.

Reliable data on recent economic developments in the DPRK are scant; however, available indicators suggest that since the early 1990s, the country has suffered serious economic dislocation. In particular, declining oil imports from Russia resulting from the latter country's insistence on hard currency transactions constrained production in many key sectors of the economy. Between 1984 and 1988, economic growth averaged 2–3% per year, but output fell by 4–5% annually between 1989 and 1995. The ROK's Bank of Korea estimated that the economy declined by 1.7% in 1994. Total economic output has fallen by at least half since 1991. From 1994 to 1998, famine and disease killed hundreds of thousands of North Koreans, perhaps up to two million. Economic aid from the US, Russia, and international donors has alleviated the situation, which is still quite dire.

A State Planning Committee coordinates the economy, with corresponding committees at city, county, and province levels. Local and regional planning committees have been given greater latitude in planning since 1964. During 1981, management responsibilities were reportedly reassigned from central government ministries to new provincial economic guidance committees, which were controlled by provincial officials of the Korean Workers' Party. In order to foster some decentralization of the economic environment, since the mid-1980s various economic ministries have been consolidated into a smaller number of commissions and greater autonomy reportedly allowed in the management of state enterprises. Thus far, however, these measures have resulted in little further change in the overall structure of the North Korean economy.

The US agreed in 2000 to lift some of the economic sanctions implemented against North Korea since 1950, in order to aid the starving population.

20INCOME

The US Central Intelligence Agency (CIA) reports that in 1998 North Korea's gross domestic product (GDP) was estimated at $21.8 billion. The per capita GDP was estimated at $1,000. The annual growth rate of GDP was estimated at -5%. The CIA defines GDP as the value of all final goods and services produced within a nation in a given year and computed on the basis of purchasing power parity (PPP) rather than value as measured on the basis of the rate of exchange. It was estimated that agriculture accounted for 25% of GDP, industry 60%, and services 15%.

21LABOR

Although figures on occupational distribution have not been published since 1963, it is known that the DPRK faces a chronic labor shortage. The civilian labor force is estimated at more than 6.1 million, about 38% of whom are engaged in agriculture, forestry, and fishing. Women are believed to constitute about 46% of the labor force. Girls are prepared for entering the labor force as early as nursery school. School children are occasionally assigned to factories or farms for short periods to help meet production goals.

There are no free trade unions in North Korea, instead there is one labor organization controlled by the government, the General Federation of Trade Unions of Korea, of which virtually all industrial and office workers are members. There is no minimum wage; salaries in joint venture and foreign-owned businesses were $110 per month in 1999. Under a 1996 law, foreign enterprises are not permitted to directly recruit and hire DPRK citizens. The average salary in the public sector is not known. Labor conditions are governed by a national labor law of 1978. The eight-hour workday is standard but most laborers work 12-16 hours daily during production campaigns. Office and shop workers spend Fridays in public works and urban maintenance projects. In addition, some work time is spent on mandatory study of the writings of Kim Il-Sung and Kim Jong-Il.

22AGRICULTURE

About 2 million hectares (4.9 million acres), or 16% of all land, can be classified as arable. Most of the agricultural land is concentrated in the west-coast provinces of North and South P'yongan and North and South Hwanghae. Irrigation, land reclamation, and flood-control projects have been carried out, especially in rice-growing areas; about one-half of the arable land is irrigated.

Rice is the principal crop, occupying 30% of all farmland in 1998. Total rice production was put at 2,063,000 tons in 1998, compared to 5.6 million tons in 1985. Improved rice yields have been achieved through the use of "miracle" rice strains, intensive application of fertilizer, and mechanization. In 1994 there were some 75,000 tractors in use, or about 1 for every 27 hectares (67 acres) of cultivated land. Double-cropping of rice is not possible because of the climate, but double-cropping of other grains has been maximized through the use of cold-bed seeding and new seed varieties, so that an estimated half of all cultivated land yields two harvests. The leading grains after rice are corn, wheat, millet, and barley. Other important crops include soybeans, potatoes, sweet potatoes, pulses, oats, sorghum, rye, tobacco, and cotton. The DPRK long claimed to be self-sufficient in grain products, with total production (including rice) increasing from 7 million tons in 1974 to 13.6 million tons in 1985, but falling to 5.2 million tons in 1995. Heavy rains in 1995 caused severe flooding in the DPRK, affecting over 5.2 million people and damaging crop production. In April 1996 the government appealed to the UN for food aid. Since 1996, there have been reports of widespread food shortages and famine in the DPRK.

The country's farms were collectivized after the Korean War. The movement began late in 1953, and the process was completed by August 1958, when all of the DPRK's 1,055,000 farm families had become members of over 16,000 cooperatives. In order to establish larger and more efficient operating units, the cooperatives were merged in the autumn of 1958 into approximately 3,800 units with about 300 families each. Produce is delivered to the government, which controls distribution through state stores. Most farm workers retain small private plots (less than 100 sq m/1,100 sq ft) and can sell produce from them to the state or in peasant markets.

23ANIMAL HUSBANDRY

Since the 1950s, a major effort has been made to increase corn and fodder supplies, to improve breeding practices, and to raise sharply the numbers of livestock in all categories. In 1995, livestock totals were estimated as follows: cattle, 1,500,000 head; hogs, 1,600,000; sheep, 1,000,000; goats, 150,000; and horses, 40,000. Livestock raising is generally associated with the state farms. Meat produced in 1998 totaled 114,000 tons; milk, 80,000; and eggs, 75,000. The DPRK was the world's fourth leading producer of silk in 1998 (after China, India, and Turkmenistan), at 4,000 tons.

24FISHING

The catch from the sea and from freshwater aquaculture includes mackerel, anchovy, tuna, mullet, rainbow trout, squid, kelp, sea urchin eggs, pollack eggs, and shrimp. The FAO estimated production for 1997 was 725,783 tons. About 97% of fishing activity is marine, concentrated in the Sea of Japan. Much of the annual catch is now used for export.

The fishing industry is entirely socialized, with some 230 maritime cooperatives and more than 30 state-run fishery stations. The main fishing ports are on the east coast.

25FORESTRY

Forests and woodland comprised about 6,170,000 hectares (15,246,000 acres) in 1995. There are rich stands of coniferous forests in the northern provinces. Predominant trees include oak, alder, larch, pine, spruce, and fir. Timber production was estimated at 4.8 million cu m in 1997, an increase of more than 400,000 cu m over the 1980 figure. About 88% of the timber cut was used for fuel. Sawn wood production in 1997 was 280,000 cu m; wood pulp, 56,000 tons; and paper and paperboard, 80,000 tons. The Ministry of Forestry, created in 1980, was expected to spur development of forest industries.

26MINING

Coal deposits include adequate supplies of anthracite and lignite, but bituminous coal must be imported for use as coke in the steel industry. Anthracite is mined chiefly along the middle course of the Taedong River (South P'yongan Province) and lignite in the Tumen River basin (North Hamgyong Province). The government reported a total coal production in 1997 of 90 million tons, with anthracite accounting for 78%. Iron ore production was 10 million tons in 1997. High-grade iron ore deposits lie off the coast of Unryl county in South Hwanghae Province. Other mineral output that year included gold (5,000 kg), magnesite (1,600,000 tons), tungsten (900 tons), phosphate rock (520,000 tons), sulfur (260,000 tons), zinc (210,000 tons), lead (75,000 tons), silver (50 kg), and copper (15,000 tons). Mineral trade between the DPRK and the Republic of Korea has been increasing, with the DPRK exporting coal, gold, steel, and zinc to the south. Its total exports to the south in 1997—including gold and other minerals as well as other commodities—totaled $190 million.

27ENERGY AND POWER

Coal, oil, and natural gas provided 35% of the DPRK's electricity generation in 1997. Hydroelectricity accounted for the remainder. Coal is by far the most important component of energy production. The major coal-producing center is in South Pyongan Province, where the Anju, Sunchon, Tokchon, Pukchang, and Kaechon coal-producing complexes are located. In 1997, coal accounted for more than 80% of primary energy consumption and hydropower about 12%. Estimated coal production in 1997

was 68 million tons, and domestic consumption was 70 million tons that year. Installed electric capacity was 9.5 million kW as of 1998; production of electricity that year totaled 31.9 billion kWh, up from 9.1 billion kWh in 1960 but down from 51.9 billion kWh in 1991. In 1998, engineers and technical advisers from the US assisted with the installation of windmills in coastal villages in the Pyongyang region.

In 1986, the former USSR agreed to the construction of a nuclear power plant with an expected capacity of 1.8 million kW. In the same year, a hydroelectric power station at Taipingwan, jointly built by China and the DPRK, began operations. In February 1994, North Korea agreed to UN-supported demands that it open part of its nuclear program to international inspections. The International Atomic Energy Agency (IAEA) began inspections of North Korean nuclear facilities in March 1991 (almost one year after North Korea withdrew from the nuclear Non-Proliferation Treaty), in order to determine whether or not North Korea was reprocessing spent nuclear reactor fuel, which could be used to make a nuclear weapon. During 1995 the IAEA was still trying to verify the status of the nuclear material, as the DPRK had agreed to some safeguard measures but declined to accept others. As of 2000, nuclear energy in North Korea continues to arouse security concerns as it involves graphite technology that can be applied to the construction of nuclear weapons.

28INDUSTRY

Under Japanese rule, northern Korea was regarded mainly as a supplier of war materials, while manufacturing and processing branches were neglected. The Communist regime, however, emphasized the development of manufacturing. By 1963, the metal-fabricating, textile, and food-processing industries accounted for 33%, 18.6%, and 13.7% of industrial output, respectively. By the late 1980s, heavy industry (including metal fabricating and textile production) accounted for 50% of total industrial production. Private enterprise in industry declined from 27.6% of total output in 1946 to only 2% in 1956, and the private sector was said to have disappeared by 1959. About 90% of all industry is state-owned, and 10% is owned by cooperatives.

Under the 1978–84 economic plan, industrial output was scheduled to grow at an average annual rate of 12.2%; however, Western estimates put actual growth at less than 10%. An annual growth of 10% was targeted under the 1987–93 plan. The economic readjustment plan for 1994–96 put an emphasis on agricultural and light industrial production. However, in 1995 economic deterioration caused manufacturing to decline further; the government's budgetary process broke down, and allocations to industry became inconsistent. The ROK government makes statistical estimates for the DPRK, which does not release reliable economic data. The ROK government estimated that in 1995, manufacturing output in the DPRK dropped by 5.3%, following declines of 3.8% in 1994, 1.9% in 1993, and 17.8% in 1992. In 1995, manufacturing accounted for an estimated 26.9% of GDP; heavy industry, 20.5%; and light industry, 6.4%. Manufacturing output declined through the late 1990s as well.

Rough production estimates are available for a few key industries only. These include the iron and steel manufactures, which reportedly amounted to 6.6 million tons of pig and conversion pig iron and 8.1 million tons of steel (including rolled steel) in 1995. Major iron and steel works are located at Ch'ongjin, Kimch'aek, Kangso, Namp'o, and Kaesong. Industrial plants produce sophisticated machinery, including generators, bulldozers, high-speed engines, and diesel locomotives. Other plants produce cement (17 million tons in 1995), refined lead (80,000 tons), and zinc (200,000 tons), metal cutting lathes, tractors, and trucks. The chemical industry produced an estimated 1.2 million tons of chemical fertilizers and 56,000 tons of synthetic fibers in 1994. The petrochemical industry is centered in the Hungnam area. Oil refining capacity was recorded at approximately 71,000 barrels per day in 2000. Textiles production increased rapidly in the 1970s; North Korea now also produces clothing, jackets, and shoes.

29 SCIENCE AND TECHNOLOGY

The Fifth Party Congress in 1970 called for the education of 1 million new technicians and specialists to aid economic modernization and development. By the mid-1990s, the government claimed that there were agricultural specialists on most rural cooperatives, although severe economic deprivation has curtailed DPRK agricultural output. Throughout this period, Russian and Chinese technicians helped train DPRK workers, and the DPRK actively sought to acquire advanced foreign technology through the importation of entire petrochemical and other manufacturing plants from Japan, France, Sweden, and other developed nations. In the 1990s, its nuclear energy program—with both peaceful and military applications—gained international attention.

The principal scientific and technical institutions are the Academy of Sciences (founded 1952), the Academy of Agricultural Science (founded 1948), the Academy of Fisheries (founded 1969), the Academy of Forestry (founded 1948), the Academy of Medical Sciences, the Academy of Light Industry Science (founded 1954), and the Academy of Railway Sciences. All of these academies are located in Pyongyang, and each has numerous attached research institutes.

By 1994, Kim Il-sung University in Pyongyang (founded 1946) included faculties of computer science, chemistry, biology, atomic energy, geology, mathematics, and physics. Also in Pyongyang are the Kim Chaek University of Technology, the Pyongyang University of Agriculture, and the Pyongyang University of Medicine.

30 DOMESTIC TRADE

Wholesale and retail trade is almost entirely in state and cooperative hands. In 1946, private trade accounted for 96.5% of total business volume. By 1960, private merchants had been entirely eliminated, and 78.8% of trade was conducted by the state, 20.4% by cooperatives, and 0.8% by farmers' markets. In 2000, 90% of the economy was in the State's hands.

Wholesale distribution is administered by the state ministries and enterprises, under the general jurisdiction of the Ministry of Material Supply. Most retail shops are run by the People's Service Committee, established in 1972. There are several state-run department stores in P'yongyang, and there is at least one in each provincial capital. All-purpose stores, cooperatives, factory outlets, and special stores for the military and for railroad workers also play an important part in retailing. Normal business hours are from 9 AM to 12 noon and 1 to 6 PM, Monday–Friday. Saturday is a "study" day.

With the decay of the formal economy, black market activity has rapidly grown throughout the country during the mid-1990s. The underground economy has begun to replace formal domestic trade throughout much of North Korea.

31 FOREIGN TRADE

The DPRK's principal exports include rice, pig iron, rolled steel, cement, machinery of various types, chemicals, magnesite, textiles, armaments, and gold. Imports include petroleum, coking coal, wheat, cotton, and machinery. A steep drop in the DPRK's trade earnings in the early 1990s was primarily a result of a policy shift by Russia and the CIS countries requiring trade to be denominated in hard currency at world prices, ending a previous goods exchange arrangement much more favorable to the North Korean situation. No published trade figures are available from the North Korean government at present.

With the change in Russian-North Korean trade relations, China took the lead as the DPRK's largest trading partner in 1992, followed by Japan and Russia. Inter-Korean trade expanded particularly rapidly after 1988. By 1992, South Korea became the DPRK's fourth largest trading partner, behind China, Japan, and Russia. Total trade between the two countries was reported to have reached $199 million, 90% of which consisting of exports from North to South. However, after tensions flared in the late 1990s, inter-Korean trade slowed.

As the North Korean economy has deteriorated, smuggling activity across the Chinese border has increased. An estimated 100,000 people are involved in illegal trade across the border, which may be worth as much as $30 to $300 million per year.

Principal trading partners in 1998 (in millions of US dollars) were as follows:

COUNTRY	EXPORTS	IMPORTS	BALANCE
Japan	197	193	4
China (inc. Hong Kong)	83	425	-342
Bangladesh	52	1	51
Saudi Arabia	44	3	41
Brazil	43	72	-29
Lebanon	36	n.a.	
India	32	41	-9
Germany	27	27	0
Ireland	11	119	-108
Russia	8	54	-46

32 BALANCE OF PAYMENTS

During the late 1970s, the DPRK enjoyed consistent trade surpluses, due in part to increasing shipments of agricultural products, gold and silver, and armaments in exchange for hard currencies. Despite the improving trade picture, the DPRK had still not emerged from the shadow of foreign debt left over from the mid-1970s. Declining prices for precious metals in the early 1980s made it difficult for the nation to meet its debt obligations, even after repeated rescheduling. In 1987, a new rescheduling agreement was worked out, after Western banks threatened to freeze the DPRK's bank assets if it failed to service bank loans. External debt was estimated at $12 billion in 1996.

The US Central Intelligence Agency reports that in 1997 the purchasing power parity of North Korea's exports was $743 million while imports totaled $1,830 million resulting in a trade balance of -$1,087 million.

The International Monetary Fund (IMF) reports that in 1998 the DPRK had exports of goods totaling $132,122 million and imports totaling $90,495 million. The services credit totaled $24,580 million and debit $23,951 million. The following table summarizes North Korea's balance of payments as reported by the IMF for 1998 in millions of US dollars.

Current Account		40,552
Balance on goods	41,627	
Balance on services	629	
Balance on income	-5,055	
Current transfers	3,353	
Capital Account		171
Financial Account		-8,438
Direct investment abroad	-4,799	
Direct investment in Korea	5,415	
Portfolio investment assets	-1,587	
Portfolio investment liabilities	-292	
Other investment assets	6,693	
Other investment liabilities	-13,868	
Net Errors and Omissions		-6,355
Reserves and Related Items		-25,930

33 BANKING AND SECURITIES

The Central Bank, established in 1946, is the sole recipient of national revenues and the repository for all precious metals. It supplies basic operating funds to various sectors of the economy and is subordinate to the Ministry of Finance. The Central Bank is also an administrative organ that executes the fiscal policies of the State Planning Commission. It supervises the Foreign Trade Bank, established in 1959, and the Industrial Bank, established in 1964. The latter provides loans and credits to farm and fishing cooperatives and has an extensive system of branches which help to manage the financial operations of all cooperatives.

The Kumgang Bank is a specialized bank that handles transactions of foreign trade organizations dealing with exports and imports of machinery, metals, mineral products, and chemical products. The Daesong Bank handles transactions of the Daesong Trading Co. and other trading organizations. There were also three joint venture banks, as of 1994. As of 1997, the Central Bank had a network of 227 local branches. Another state bank is the Changgwang Credit Bank, founded in 1983. Two reportedly unpopular changes of currency in recent years suggest that some citizens are inclined to hoard rather than bank such savings as they make on their meagre incomes. A consortium of 60 Western banks, including Russia, filed suit in 1996 in a US district court against the DPRK's Foreign Trade Bank for a total of $1.4 billion in principal and accumulated interest.

There are savings facilities at all post offices, in industrial enterprises, and in the "trust" sections in the agricultural cooperatives. Through the latter, large farm and fishing cooperatives perform local banking functions, especially the raising and allocation of capital for local needs.

There are no securities exchanges in the DPRK.

34INSURANCE

The State Insurance Bureau and the Korea Foreign Insurance Company carry fire and natural disaster insurance and, as appropriate, livestock, marine, and passenger insurance on a compulsory basis. Individuals may take out various types of property, life, and travel insurance, all provided by the government.

35PUBLIC FINANCE

The annual state budget, the leading element of the command economy, is approved at regular sessions of the SPA. In April 1995, the government failed to announce its 1995/96 budget at the annual meeting of the Supreme People's Assembly, which exacerbated the economic stagnation. Foreign aid, important after the Korean War, has not appeared as budgetary income since 1961.

The US Central Intelligence Agency (CIA) estimates that in 1992 North Korea's central government took in revenues of approximately $19.3 billion and had expenditures of $19.3 billion. Total external debt is estimated to exceed $12 billion, 75% owed to OECD countries.

36TAXATION

All direct taxes were abolished in 1974; the DPRK thus became the first country in the world to abolish income taxes collected from its citizens. The government collects a percentage (turnover tax) on all transactions between producers and state marketing agencies. Fees are charged to farmers for seeds, fertilizer, irrigation water, and equipment, and consumers pay a tax for the use of water and certain other household amenities.

All foreign-invested enterprises are subject to income, property, turnover, and local taxes. Resident aliens in the DPRK must pay personal income taxes; the rate varies from 4% to a top rate of 20%.

37CUSTOMS AND DUTIES

No information is available.

38FOREIGN INVESTMENT

In 1984, the Joint Venture Act permitted direct foreign investment for the first time. Relations have been established with Western companies in the areas of hotel construction, hydroelectricity, nonferrous metals, light industry, and services.

In 1991 plans were initiated for a multinational special economic zone in the Tumen River estuary region, involving investments from China and Russia as well as North Korea. The Rajin-Sonbong Free Economic and Trade Zone restricts foreign trade to this remote northeastern area of the DPRK. New laws on foreign investment were passed in 1992, allowing 100% foreign ownership as well as loosened government control over employee layoffs. The foreign investment laws detail three distinct types of enterprises: contractual joint ventures, equity joint ventures, and "foreign enterprises." Most trade with the ROK is conducted through contractual joint ventures. The Daewoo Corp. has the ROK's only equity joint venture in the DPRK (capitalized at a reported $10 million), producing textiles and clothing for export in Namp'o. Applications for investment by foreign companies remain very limited; most of the modest foreign investments which have been made in the country derive from Japan-based Korean investors.

39ECONOMIC DEVELOPMENT

The economy is operated on a planned basis, with priority given to the development of industry, particularly heavy industry. Planning began in 1947, when the economy operated first under two consecutive one-year plans (1947 and 1948), followed by a two-year plan (1949–50), which was interrupted by the Korean War in June 1950. After the war, economic reconstruction followed the terms of a three-year plan (1954–56) and a five-year plan (1957–61). The industrial goals of the five-year plan were fulfilled in just half the allotted time, so 1960 was set aside as a year of adjustment. An ambitious seven-year plan was then launched in 1961, with the general objectives of a 220% increase in industrial output and a 150% rise in grain production. This plan had to be extended until 1970, however, before its targets were fulfilled. In 1975, the DPRK announced completion of its six-year plan (1971–76) one year ahead of schedule, although certain outputs fell somewhat short of projected levels. Industrial growth slowed in 1976. A second seven-year plan (1978–84) called for a 12% annual industrial growth rate. Although the government claimed that its goals had been met or exceeded, neither the actual results nor a new plan was announced during the following two years. The third seven-year plan (1987–93) had as its general aims increases of 90% in industrial output, 40% in agricultural production, and 70% in national income. Unofficial economic indicators of recent years suggest that actual performance has fallen far short of these targets (in some cases by as much as 50%) and that a drop in overall industrial output has occurred since the late 1980s. Statements released by the Korean Workers' Party Central Committee in late 1993 confirmed the overall failure of the last seven-year plan and announced a two-to-three year period of economic adjustment during which investments in agriculture, light industry and foreign trade would be prioritized.

In the past, the DPRK's principal economic benefactors were the USSR and China. However, following a developing rapprochement between the former USSR and South Korea in 1990, with the latter now offering badly needed economic aid to the Soviet government, Soviet assistance to the North was curtailed in 1991. Credits extended by Japan reached $350 million by 1978; recent requests for more assistance from Japan have as yet not been filled, pending resolution of the current nuclear dispute and questions over the closed nature of the DPRK economy. For the 1983–86 period, the UNDP allocated $18.4 million, the largest such program since Korea was divided. Net concessional flows from UN organizations totaled $5 million in 1994, including $2.9 million from the UNDP. Official development assistance given to the DPRK in 1994 totaled $6 million. Widespread famine and disease costing hundreds of thousands of lives brought in much needed relief from the US, China, nongovernmental organizations, and other countries.

40 SOCIAL DEVELOPMENT

All citizens are entitled to medical care, disability benefits, and retirement allowances provided by the state. About 1% of workers' salaries is deducted for programs allowing paid vacations and paid maternity leaves, with the state making up the rest of the cost. The state runs about 400 rest centers and resorts providing free vacations to workers. Retirement pensions are roughly one-half of the annual average wage; those who continue working after retirement age receive both their salary and their pension.

The 1992 constitution guarantees equal rights for women. The state provides nurseries and day-care centers, and large families are encouraged. Like men, women are obligated by law to work, although few occupy high official positions. Women with large families are entitled to shorter work hours. Female workers are legally guaranteed five weeks of maternity leave. In 1997 a UNICEF official reported that some 800,000 north Korean children were suffering from malnutrition and about 80,000 were in danger of dying from hunger and disease.

The government rejects international human rights standards, and human rights organizations are not permitted to operate. Dissent is not tolerated, and capital punishment is meted out for a wide variety of offenses, including attempted defection.

The government classifies all citizens into three groups: core, wavering and hostile. These security ratings reflect the perceived degree of loyalty exhibited by citizens. These ratings may be taken into account in the allocation of housing, employment, medical and other benefits. All citizens are subjected to extensive indoctrination. Listening to foreign broadcasts or possession of banned reading materials are punishable by death. Travel within the country is also strictly controlled. Travel passes must be requested for intervillage travel.

41 HEALTH

The Ministry of Public Health is responsible for all national health services, including disease prevention and sanitation. All of the population had access to health care in 1993. In 1992, immunization rates for children up to one year old were as follows: tuberculosis, 100%; diphtheria, pertussis, and tetanus, 99%; polio, 100%; and measles, 99%. Polio has been nearly eradicated; in 1995 there were only 7 cases. In 1990–94, there were 2.72 doctors and 13.5 hospital beds per 1,000 people. Western medicine is used alongside traditional Eastern medicine (tonguihak). In 1997, there were 178 cases of tuberculosis per 100,000 people. Cancer is now the leading cause of death, followed by heart disease and hypertension.

The total fertility rate has decreased from 5.8 in 1960 to 2.3 children per woman in her childbearing years, as of 1999. Average life expectancy in 1999 was 70.1 years for both men and women. The infant mortality rate was 25.5 per 1,000 in 1999, and the general mortality rate was 6.9 per 1,000 people.

42 HOUSING

A serious housing shortage was produced by the government's early stress on industrial rather than residential construction. The housing deficit was aggravated by the Korean War, which demolished about one-third of the country's housing. Since then, residential housing has received serious attention. About 886,000 new units were completed under the 1971–76 economic plan. Construction levels of 200,000–300,000 units a year were targeted for 1978–84, and 150,000–200,000 units a year were projected for 1987–93. Available figures for 1980–88 show a total housing stock of 4,566,000 with 4.5 people per dwelling.

The government reported that the catastrophic floods in August 1995 caused 500,000 residents to become homeless.

43 EDUCATION

Both primary and secondary education are free and compulsory for ten years, beginning at age 5. Children ages 1–5 are cared for in nursery schools, followed by one year of kindergarten, four years of primary school, and six years of secondary school. The adult literacy rate was reported to be 99% in 1991. In 1987, there were an estimated 4,813 primary institutions with 1,543,000 students enrolled. An additional 2,468,000 students were enrolled in general secondary schools. In the 1990s, school curricula was balanced between academic and political subject matter. According to South Korean scholar Park Youngsoon, such subjects as Korean language, mathematics, and physical education did account for most instructional time in the classroom; however, more than 8% of instructional time was spent on the "Great Kim Il Sung" and "Communist Morality."

Kim Il-sung University (founded in 1946) in P'yongyang is the only university, with about 16,000 full-time and part-time students and about 3,000 faculty, including teachers and research staff, as of the early 1990s. Admission to the university is by intensely competitive examination. Other institutions of higher learning include the Kimch'aek Polytechnic Institute, P'yongyang Agricultural College, and P'yongyang Medical School. In 1987 there were 220,000 students attending two- or three-year higher specialized schools and 301,000 students attending four- to six-year colleges and university courses. A system of adult schools, correspondence courses, and workplace schools makes higher education widely available.

44 LIBRARIES AND MUSEUMS

The DPRK has more than 200 public libraries, the largest being the Grand People's Study House in P'yongyang, with 20 million volumes. In addition, there are research libraries at the academies of sciences and social sciences and at Kim Il-sung University.

Museums include the Central Historical Museum, the Memorial Museum of the War of Liberation, the Korean Art Gallery, the Ethnographic Museum, and the Korean Revolutionary Museum, all in P'yongyang. There is a large museum at Mangyongdae, Kim Il-sung's birthplace, near the capital.

45 MEDIA

Postal, telephone, and telegraph services are operated by the government. Telephones are believed to be used primarily for government business. The central broadcasting station in P'yongyang has a 1,500-kW transmitter. Broadcasts reach to every corner of the country through a system of more than one million loudspeakers, as well as through private radios. In addition, news is broadcast to other countries in English, Russian, French, and Spanish. There are two radio networks (Korean Central Radio and Radio P'yongyang) and two television networks, (Korean Central TV and Mansudae TV). In total there are 27 AM radio stations, 14 FM stations, and 38 TV stations. In 1999 there were 147 radios per 1,000 population.

All newspapers and periodicals in the DPRK are published by government, party, or front organizations; each edition is subjected to prepublication review and censorship. There were, as of 1999, four daily newspapers in publication. The leading national newspapers and their publishers are: *Rodong Sinmun* (Central Committee of the Korean Workers' Party) (circulation 1,500,000); *Minju Choson* (Presidium of the Supreme People's Assembly and the cabinet) (circulation 200,000); *Joson Immingun*; and *Radong Changuyon*. Each province has a newspaper, and other mass organizations have their own organs. A state news service, the Korean Central News Agency, is the sole organ for the gathering and dissemination of news.

Though there are articles of the constitution that provide for freedom of speech and the press, in practice the government prohibits the exercise of these rights, controlling all information. The receiving of foreign broadcasts is illegal, as is any criticism of the government in any media.

At present, there is no information regarding the use of computers or the Internet in DPRK.

[46]ORGANIZATIONS

Mass organizations established for specialized political, economic, or cultural purposes include the powerful Democratic Front for the Reunification of the Fatherland, commonly known as the Fatherland Front. Among its constituent members are the Socialist Working Youth League, under the direct guidance of the Korean Workers' Party Central People's Committee; the Young Pioneer Corps, open to children aged 9–15; and the Korean Democratic Women's League. Also important are the Korean Red Cross Society and the Korean Agricultural Workers' Union.

[47]TOURISM, TRAVEL, AND RECREATION

Most sightseeing takes place in the capital city of P'yongyang. Travel outside P'yongyang is closed to individual tourists but available to groups. Nampe, the port city for P'yongyang, has a beach resort area. The two most outstanding tourist sites outside the capital are the Kumgang (Diamond) Mountains in the southwest and Packdu Mountain on the Chinese border. All visitors need visas secured in advance from DPRK diplomatic representatives. Increasingly anxious to obtain foreign exchange, the government has invited touring delegations from numerous nations, especially developing nations. All tourism from the US, Israel, the ROK, and South Africa, is banned without invitation.

According to the UN, the daily cost of travel in DPRK in 1999 was $179 in Pyongyang and $104 elsewhere.

Wrestling, tug-of-war, chess (with pieces different from the European form), and kite fighting are traditional sports.

[48]FAMOUS KOREANS

Among the many historical figures of united Korea are Ulchi Mundok, a Koguryo general of the early 7th century AD; Kim Yosin (595–673), a warrior and folk hero in Silla's struggle to unify the peninsula; Wang Kon (877–943), the founder and first ruler of the Koryo Dynasty; Yun Kwan (d.1111), a Koryo general who repulsed Chinese invaders; Kim Pu-sik (1075–1151), a scholar-official who wrote the great *History of the Three Kingdoms;* Yi Song-gye (1335–1408), a general and founder of the Yi (or Li) Dynasty; King Sejong (1397–1450), who called for the invention of Han'gul and was Korea's greatest monarch; Yi Hwang (1501–70) and Yi I (1536–84), Neo-Confucianist philosophers and officials; Yi Sun-sin (1545–98), an admiral who invented the "turtleboat," the first ironclad ship, and defeated the Japanese in every naval engagement of the Hideyoshi invasions, dying in the climactic battle; Chong Yag-yong (1762–1836), a pragmatic scholar-official and prolific writer; and Yi Ha-ung (1820–98), known as the Taewon'gun (Prince Regent), the regent for his son, Kojong, and the central political figure of the late 19th century.

The preeminent political figure of the DPRK is Kim Il-sung (1912–94), the leader of the nation from 1948 until his death. Other influential figures have included Kim Il (1910–84), a prominent officeholder since 1954; Kim Jong-il (b. 1941), the son of Kim Il-sung, who succeeded him; Nam Il (1914–76), a chief of staff who became well known as an armistice negotiator at P'anmunjom (1951–53), and Marshal O Jin U (1918–95), head of the army from 1976 until 1993.

[49]DEPENDENCIES

The DPRK has no territories or colonies.

[50]BIBLIOGRAPHY

Attar, Chand. *Nuclear Asia and Security: A Study in North Korean Perspective.* Delhi, India: Independent Publishing Company, 1993.

Choi, Sung-Chul, ed. *Human Rights in North Korea.* Seoul: Center for the Advancement of North Korean Human Rights, 1995.

Chun Sin-yong (ed.). *Korean Society.* Seoul: International Cultural Foundation, 1976.

Cumings, Bruce. *The Origins of the Korean War.* Princeton, N.J.: Princeton University Press, 1981.

Eberstadt, Nick. *The Population of North Korea.* Berkeley: University of California, 1992.

Eckert, Carter J. *Korea, Old and New: A History.* Cambridge, Mass.: Harvard University Press, 1990.

Foot, Rosemary. *The Wrong War: American Policy and the Dimensions of the Korean Conflict, 1950–53.* Ithaca, N.Y.: Cornell University Press, 1985.

Gills, Barry K. *Korea Versus Korea: A Case of Contested Legitimacy.* New York: Routledge, Inc., 1996.

Grayson, James Huntley. *Korea: A Religious History.* New York: Oxford University Press, 1989.

Hoare, James. *Korea: An Introduction.* New York: Kegan Paul International, 1988.

Howe, Russell Warren. *The Koreans: Passion and Grace.* San Diego: Harcourt Brace Jovanovich, 1988.

Hwang, Eui-Gak. *The Korean Economies: A Comparison of North and South.* New York: Oxford University Press, 1993.

Kihl, Young W. *Politics and Policies in Divided Korea: Regimes in Contest.* Boulder, Colo.: Westview Press, 1984.

Koh, Byung Chul. *The Foreign Policy Systems of North and South Korea.* Berkeley: University of California Press, 1984.

Lee, Chong-sik. *Korean Workers' Party: A Short History.* Stanford, Calif.: Hoover Institution Press, 1978.

Lone, Stewart. *Korea since 1850.* Melbourne, Australia: Longman Cheshire; New York: St. Martin's, 1993.

Macdonald, Donald Stone. *The Koreans: Contemporary Politics and Society.* Boulder, Colo.: Westview Press, 1990.

McNamara, Dennis L. *The Colonial Origins of Korean Enterprise, 1910–1945.* New York: Cambridge University Press, 1990.

Merrill, John. *Korea: The Peninsular Origins of the War.* Newark: University of Delaware Press, 1989.

Myers, Brian. *Han Sthorya and North Korean Literature: The Failure of Socialist Realism in DPRK.* Ithaca, N.Y.: East Asia Program, Cornell University, 1994.

Oliver, Robert Tarbell. *A History of the Korean People in Modern Times: 1800 to the Present.* Newark: Univ. of Delaware Press; London: Associated University Presses, 1993.

Olsen, Edward A. *US Policy and the two Koreas.* Boulder, Colo.: Westview Press, 1988.

Palais, James B. *Politics and Policy in Traditional Korea.* Cambridge: Harvard University Press, 1991.

Smith, Hazel, ed., et al. *North Korea in the New World Order.* Nw York: St. Martin's Press, 1996.

Soh, Chung-Hee. *Women in Korean Politics.* 2d ed. Boulder, Colo.: Westview Press, 1993.

Song, Pyong-nak. *The Rise of the Korean Economy.* Hong Kong; New York: Oxford University Press, 1990.

Suh, Dae-Sook. *Kim Il Sung: The North Korean Leader.* New York: Columbia University Press, 1988.

Tennant, Roger. *A History of Korea.* London: Kegan Paul International, 1996.

KOREA, REPUBLIC OF (ROK)

Republic of Korea

Taehan Min-guk

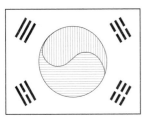

CAPITAL: Seoul.

FLAG: The flag, called the T'aegukki, shows, on a white field, a central circle divided into two parts, red on top and deep blue below, in the shape of Chinese yin and yang symbols. Broken and unbroken black bars in each of the four corners are variously arranged in sets of three, representing divination diagrams.

ANTHEM: *Aegukka (The Song of Patriotism),* officially adopted on 15 August 1948.

MONETARY UNIT: The won (w) is the national currency. There are notes of 500, 1,000, 5,000, and 10,000 won. w1 = $0.00088 ($1 = w1131.0) as of 31 March 2000.

WEIGHTS AND MEASURES: Both the metric system and ancient Korean units of measurement are used.

HOLIDAYS: New Year's Days, 1–3 January; Independence Movement Day, 1 March; Labor Day, 10 March; Arbor Day, 5 April; Children's Day, 5 May; Buddha's Birthday, 24 May; Memorial Day, 6 June; Constitution Day, 17 July; Independence Day, 15 August; Armed Forces Day, 1 October; National Foundation Day, 3 October; Han'gul (Korean Alphabet) Day, 9 October; Christmas, 25 December.

TIME: 9 PM = noon GMT.

¹LOCATION, SIZE, AND EXTENT

Occupying the southern 45% of the Korean Peninsula in East Asia, the Republic of Korea (ROK), also known as South Korea, has an area of 98,480 sq km (38,023 sq mi), extending 642 km (399 mi) NNE–SSW and 436 km (271 mi) ESE–WNW. Comparatively, the area occupied by South Korea is slightly larger than the state of Indiana. Bounded on the N by the Democratic People's Republic of Korea (DPRK), on the E by the Sea of Japan (known in Korea as the East Sea), on the S by the Korea Strait, and on the W by the Yellow Sea, the ROK has a total boundary length of 2,651 km (1,647 mi). A demilitarized zone (DMZ), 4,000 m (13,100 ft) wide, covering 1,262 sq km (487 sq mi) and located north and south of the 38th parallel, separates the ROK from the DPRK, which comprises the northern part of the Korean Peninsula.

Although the ROK's general (facing) coastline is estimated at 1,318 km (819 mi), a measurement taking account of its manifold indentations would be closer to 6,200 km (3,850 mi). Over 3,000 islands, most of them off the southern and western coasts and belonging to the ROK, add another 8,600 km (5,350 mi) of coastline.

The ROK's capital city, Seoul, is located in the northwestern part of the country.

²TOPOGRAPHY

Elevations in the southern part of the Korean Peninsula are generally lower than those in the north. Only about 30% of the ROK consists of lowlands and plains. The principal lowlands, all bordering the Yellow Sea along the west coast, include the Han River Plain, near Seoul; the Pyongtaek and Honam plains, south of the capital; and the Yongsan Plain in the southwest. Mt. Halla (1,950 m/6,398 ft), on volcanic Cheju Island, is the nation's highest point, while Mt. Chiri, or Chii (1,915 m/6,283 ft), is the highest point on the mainland.

Principal rivers of the ROK include the Han (514 km/319 mi), with Seoul near its mouth; the Kum (401 km/249 mi) and Yongsan (116 km/72 mi), which water the fertile plains areas of the southwest; and the Somjin (212 km/132 mi), in the south. The longest river in the ROK is the Naktong (521 km/324 mi), which waters the southeast. Yellow Sea tides on the west coast rise to over 9 m (30 ft) in some places, while Japan Sea tides on the east coast rise only about 1 m (3 ft).

³CLIMATE

The average January temperature ranges from –5°C (23°F) at Seoul to –2°C (28°F) at Pusan and 4°C (39°F) on Cheju Island. In the hottest part of the summer, however, the regional variation in temperature is not nearly so marked, with average temperatures ranging from 25°C to 27°C (77–81°F) in most lowland areas. Most of the nation receives between 75 and 100 cm (30 and 40 in) of rain a year, but more than 130 cm (50 in) of precipitation falls in the southeast. Nearly all the rainfall occurs in the April–September period, especially during the rainy season, late June to early August. From one to three mild typhoons normally strike the south in the early fall, with a severe one occurring every two or three years. Days free of frost number about 240 in the southern regions.

⁴FLORA AND FAUNA

The Korean Peninsula is rich in varieties of plant life typical of temperate regions. More than 3,000 species, some 500 of them unique to Korea, have been noted by botanists. Warm temperate vegetation, including camellias and other broad-leaved evergreens, predominate in the south and on Cheju Island. Zoologists have identified more than 130 freshwater fishes, 371 birds, 78 mammals, and 39 reptiles and amphibians on the peninsula. Bear, wild boar, deer, and lynx still are found in the highlands, but the shrinking of the forested area has reduced the animal population in recent years. Migratory water fowl, cranes, herons, and other birds are visible on the plains. Noxious insects and household pests infest the warmer regions, and aquatic life is generally infected with parasites.

⁵ENVIRONMENT

Efforts to control the detrimental effects of rapid industrialization, urbanization, and population growth focus on the Office of Environment, established in 1980 to control air, water, and land pollution and manage solid wastes. The Environmental Preservation Law, revised in 1979, covers air, water, and noise pollution, soil preservation, and disposal of solid wastes.

The nation has 15.1 cu mi of water with 75% used for agriculture and 14% used for industrial purposes. The purity of the nation's water is threatened by agricultural chemicals. In 1990, the nation dumped 10 million tons of sewage and 7 million tons of industrial chemicals into its water sources. Air pollution, associated mainly with the use of coal briquettes for home heating and the increase in automobile traffic, is also severe, with smog a common problem in Seoul. In the mid-1990s, South Korea had among the world's highest level of industrial carbon dioxide emissions, which totaled 289.8 million metric tons per year, a per capita level of 6.56 metric tons per year.

The Naktong River delta, a marshland where thousands of birds spend the winter, is threatened by environmental pollution and by plans to dam the mouth of the river. The beginning of construction of the Kumgangsan hydroelectric dam by the DPRK near the DMZ in 1986 was protested by the ROK on the grounds that the central Korean Peninsula could be flooded. In response, the ROK began construction of its own Peace Dam near the DMZ in 1987.

Although 28 species of birds and 8 species of mammals— chipmunk, wild boar, squirrel, raccoon dog, badger, hare, river deer, and roe deer—are still classified as game species, hunting was banned by the government from August 1972 through December 1981, except in such game preserves as that of Cheju Island. In the mid-1990s, 6 of Korea's mammal species and 22 bird species were endangered, as were 33 plant species. Endangered species in the ROK include the Amur leopard, Japanese sea lion, Oriental white stork, Japanese crested ibis, and Tristram's woodpecker.

[6]POPULATION

The population of the Republic of Korea (ROK) in 2000 was estimated at 47,350,529, more than twice the estimated population of the DPRK. An estimated 6.0% of the population is 65 years of age or older. The projected population for the year 2005 is 49,490,000, assuming a crude birthrate of 14 per 1,000 population and a death rate of 6 resulting in a natural rate of change of 0.8% for the period 2000–2005. The population rate of change between 1995 and 2000 was 0.9%. The population density in 1998 was 470 per sq km (1217 per sq mi).

It was estimated that 86% of the population lived in urban areas in 2000, up from 57% in 1980. The capital city, Seoul, and its surrounding metropolitan area had a 2000 population of 12,215,000. The 2000 populations of other large urban areas were Pusan, 4,239,000; Taegu, 2,559,000; Inch'on, 2,837,000; Kwangju, 1,665,000; Taejon, 1,431,000; Pun'chon, 1,264,000; Suwon, 1,268,000; and Ulsan, 967,000.

[7]MIGRATION

During the Japanese occupation (1910–45), some three million Koreans emigrated to Manchuria and other parts of China, 700,000 to Siberia, approximately three million to Japan, and about 7,000 to the US (mostly to Hawaii). The great majority of those who went to Japan were from the populous southern provinces, and large numbers (1.5–2 million) of them returned home following the end of hostilities in 1945. In addition, from 1945 through 1949, at least 1.2 million Koreans crossed the 38th parallel into the ROK, refugees from Communism or from the Korean War. Under the Emigration Law of 1962, the ROK government encouraged emigration to South America (especially Brazil), the Federal Republic of Germany (FRG), the Middle East, and elsewhere. Most of the emigrants are workers who remit earnings back home. A total of 409,922 Koreans emigrated

during the 1962–80 period; emigration peaked at 48,270 in 1976 but had declined to 27,163 in 1990. In addition, Koreans have emigrated permanently to the US in large numbers since 1971; the population in the US of Korean origin was 798,849 as of 1990 (72.7% foreign-born). In all, more than two million South Koreans were living abroad in 1988. Migration within South Korea, mainly from the rural areas to the cities, remains substantial, despite government efforts to improve village living conditions.

As of March 1997, the 1,400 boat people that were granted temporary refugee status were resettled to third countries. In 1999, the net migration rate was -0.3 per 1,000 population.

[8]ETHNIC GROUPS

The Koreans are believed to be descended primarily from Tungusic peoples of the Mongoloid race, who originated in the cold northern regions of Central Asia. There is scant evidence of non-Mongoloid admixture. There are about 20,000 Chinese; however, the ROK has no sizable ethnic minority.

[9]LANGUAGES

The Korean language is usually held to be a member of the Altaic family; there are only slight differences between the various dialects. Korean is written in a largely phonetic alphabet called Han'gul, created in 1443. The Korean alphabet originally consisted of 14 consonants and 10 vowels; since then, 5 consonants and 11 vowels have been added. Han'gul letters are combined into syllables by clustering, in imitation of Chinese characters. ROK governments have launched several "language beautification" drives designed to purge Korean of borrowings from Japanese and other languages, but more than half of the vocabulary consists of words derived from Chinese.

English is widely taught in junior high and high school.

[10]RELIGIONS

Most South Koreans are quite eclectic in their religious beliefs, the majority subscribing to varying mixtures of Taoism, Confucianism, Buddhism, Christianity, Ch'ondogyo (Religion of the Heavenly Way, an indigenous sect originating in 1860), and local animism. Shamanism, especially its aspect of exorcism of evil spirits, survives in some rural areas of the ROK. Geomancy is also used in matters such as the selection of auspicious building and tomb sites.

In 1999, 49% of the population practiced Christianity (including 8,760,336 Protestants and 2,950,730 Roman Catholics), 47% Buddhism, 3% Confucianism, and 1% folk religion (shamanism), Ch'ondogyo (Religion of the Heavenly Way), and other. Other religions with significant popular followings included Taejongyo, based on the worship of a trinity of ancient deities, and Soka Gakkai, a Buddhist sect of Japanese origin. There were also practicing Muslims, members of the Unification Church, Mormons, and Jehovah's Witnesses.

The constitution provides for freedom of religion, and the government reportedly respects this right in practice. There is no state religion, and the government does not subsidize or favor a particular religion.

[11]TRANSPORTATION

The bulk of ROK railroads, totaling 6,240 km (3,878 mi) of track in 1998, are government owned. The Seoul subway system opened in 1991. Construction of Pusan's first subway line was completed in 1985.

The ROK had 63,500 km (39,459 mi) of roadway in 1998, of which 16,700 km (10,377 mi) were paved, including 1,720 km (1,069 mi) of expressways. There were 6,006,000 passenger automobiles, and 2,462,000 commercial vehicles in 1995. Bus transportation networks of varying quality serve most of the rural towns.

Maritime shipping expanded rapidly during the 1970s. By 1998, the ROK had a merchant fleet of 442 vessels, accounting for a total of 5,212,089 GRT. Pusan is the chief port; other major ports include Inch'on (the port for Seoul), Kunsan, and Mokp'o.

There were 103 airports in 1998, 68 of which had paved runways. Major airports include Cheju International at Cheju, Kimhae International at Pusan, and Kimpo International at Seoul. Civil aviation in the ROK in 1997 amounted to 59,372 million passenger-km (36,894 million passenger-mi) and 7,889 million freight ton-km (4,902 million freight ton-mi) of service. Also in 1997, 35,506,000 passengers were carried on scheduled domestic and international flights. Korean Air Lines (KAL), privately owned since 1969, grew rapidly during the 1970s and now ranks as a major world carrier. On the morning of 1 September 1983, a KAL jetliner en route from New York to Seoul via Anchorage, Alaska, strayed over airspace of the former USSR and was shot down by Soviet interceptors, reportedly because they thought it was a military aircraft engaged in espionage; all 269 persons on board were killed, and worldwide protest followed. In November 1983, 115 people were killed when a bomb was apparently detonated aboard a KAL jet en route to Seoul.

12HISTORY

[For Korean history before 1948, see Korea, Democratic People's Republic of.]

The Republic of Korea, headed by President Syngman Rhee (Rhee Syngman), was proclaimed on 15 August 1948 in the southern portion of the Korean Peninsula, which had been under US military administration since 8 September 1945. Like the Democratic People's Republic of Korea (DPRK), established in the north on 9 September 1948 with Soviet backing, the ROK claimed to be the legitimate government of all Korea. The ROK was recognized as the legitimate government by the UN General Assembly.

At dawn on 25 June 1950, following a year and a half of sporadic fighting, the well-equipped People's Army of the DPRK struck south across the 38th parallel. Proclaiming that the war was for national liberation and unification of the peninsula, the DPRK forces advanced rapidly; Seoul fell within three days, and the destruction of the ROK seemed imminent. At US urging, the UN Security Council (with the Soviet delegate absent) branded the DPRK an aggressor and called for the withdrawal of the attacking forces. On 27 June, US President Harry S. Truman ordered US air and naval units into combat, and three days later, US ground forces were sent into battle. The UK took similar action, and a multinational UN Command was created to join with and lead the ROK in its struggle against the invasion. Meanwhile, DPRK troops had pushed into the southeast corner of the peninsula. At that juncture, however, UN lines held firm, and an amphibious landing at Inch'on (15 September 1950) in the ROK under Gen. Douglas MacArthur brought about the complete disintegration of the DPRK army.

MacArthur, commanding the UN forces, made a fateful decision to drive northward. As the UN forces approached the Yalu River, however, China warned that it would not tolerate a unification of the peninsula under US/UN auspices. After several weeks of threats and feints, "volunteers" from the Chinese People's Liberation Army entered the fighting en masse, forcing MacArthur into a costly, pell-mell retreat back down the peninsula. Seoul was lost again (4 January 1951) and then regained before the battle line became stabilized very nearly along the 38th parallel. There it remained for two weary years, with bitter fighting but little change, while a cease-fire agreement was negotiated.

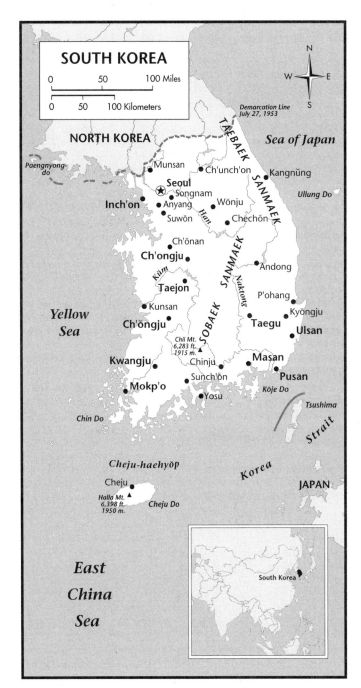

LOCATION: 33°7′ to 38°38′N; 124°36′ to 130°56′E. **BOUNDARY LENGTHS:** DPRK, 240 km (149 mi); total coastline, 1,318 km (819 mi). **TERRITORIAL SEA LIMIT:** 12 mi.

On 27 July 1953, an armistice agreement finally was signed at P'anmunjom in the DPRK. The Korean War was ended, but it had brought incalculable destruction and human suffering to all of Korea (some 1,300,000 military casualties, including 415,000 combat deaths, for the ROK alone), and it left the peninsula still more implacably divided. A military demarcation line, which neither side regarded as a permanent border, was established, surrounded by the DMZ. An international conference envisioned in the armistice agreement was not held until mid-1954. This conference and subsequent efforts failed to reach an agreement on unification of the north and south, and the armistice agreement, supervised by a token UN Command in Seoul and by the Military Armistice Commission and the Neutral Nations Supervisory Commission, both in P'anmunjom, remains in effect.

In 1954, the US and ROK signed a mutual defense treaty, under which US troops remained in the country. Financial assistance throughout the 1950s was provided by the US, averaging $270 million annually between 1953 and 1958, and by other nations under UN auspices. Syngman Rhee ran the government until 1960, when his authoritarian rule provoked the "April Revolution," the culmination of a series of increasingly violent student demonstrations that finally brought about his ouster. The Second Korean Republic, which followed Rhee, adopted a parliamentary system to replace the previous presidential system. The new government, however, was short-lived. Premier Chang Myon and his supporters were ousted after only 10 months by a military coup in May 1961, headed by Maj.-Gen. Park Chung-hee. The military junta dissolved the National Assembly, placed the nation under martial law, established the Korean Central Intelligence Agency (KCIA) as a means of detecting and suppressing potential enemies, and ruled by decree until late 1963 through the Supreme Council for National Reconstruction. Gen. Park created a well-organized political party—the Democratic-Republican Party (DRP)—designed to serve as a vehicle for the transition from military to civilian rule, and in October 1963, under a new constitution, he easily won election as president of the Third Republic.

During the summer of 1965, riots erupted all over the ROK in protest against the ROK-Japan Normalization Treaty, which established diplomatic relations and replaced Korean war-reparation claims with Japanese promises to extend economic aid. The riots were met with harsh countermeasures, including another period of martial law and widespread arrests of demonstrators. Further demonstrations erupted in 1966, when the ROK's decision to send 45,000 combat troops to Vietnam became known. Park was elected to a second term in May 1967, defeating his chief opponent, Yun Po-sun, and the DRP won a large majority in the National Assembly. In 1969, Park pushed through the National Assembly a constitutional amendment permitting him to run for a third term. He defeated Kim Dae Jung, leader of the opposition New Democratic Party (NDP), in the elections of April 1971, but Kim's NDP made significant gains in the National Assembly elections that May.

Student demonstrations against the government in the fall of 1971 prompted Park to declare a state of national emergency on 6 December. Three weeks later, in a predawn session held without the knowledge of the opposition, the Assembly granted Park extraordinary governmental powers. These failed to quell mounting opposition and unrest, and in October 1972 martial law was declared. A new constitution, promulgated at the end of the month and ratified by national referendum in November 1972, vastly increased the powers of the presidency in economic as well as political affairs. Under this new document, which inaugurated the Fourth Republic, Park was elected for a six-year term that December, with a decisive legislative majority for his DRP. Soon the economy began to expand at a rapid rate. But Park's regime became increasingly repressive. Typical of its heavy-handed rule was the abduction by KCIA agents of Kim Dae Jung from a Japanese hotel room back to Seoul, an incident that provoked considerable friction between Japanese and Korean officials. On 15 August 1974, a Korean gunman carrying a Japanese passport and sympathetic to the DPRK attempted to assassinate the president but killed Park's wife instead. Park responded by drafting a series of emergency measures; the harshest of these, Emergency Measure No. 9, issued in May 1975, provided for the arrest of anyone criticizing the constitution and banned all political activities by students.

Park was reelected for another six-year term in July 1978, but the NDP, now led by Kim Young Sam, made major gains in the National Assembly. In October 1979, Kim was expelled from the legislature after calling for governmental reform. Riots protesting Kim's ouster were reported in several major cities. On 26 October 1979, in what may have been an attempted coup, Park was assassinated by KCIA Director Kim Jae-gyu, who was later executed. Martial law was again imposed, and a period of relative calm followed as some of the more restrictive emergency decrees were lifted by Park's constitutional successor, the prime minister, Choi Kyu-hah, who promised a new constitution and presidential elections.

The Chun and Roh Regimes

In December 1979, Maj. Gen. Chun Doo Hwan led a coup in which he and his military colleagues removed the army chief of staff and took effective control of the government. Demonstrations, led by university students, spread through the spring of 1980 and, by mid-May, the government once more declared martial law (in effect until January 1981), banned demonstrations, and arrested political leaders. In the city of Kwangju, more than 200 civilians were killed in what became known as the Kwangju massacre. Choi Kyu-hah was pressured to resign and Chun Doo Hwan, now retired from the military, was named president in September 1980. Chun Doo Hwan came to power under a new constitution inaugurating the Fifth Republic. A total of 567 political leaders, including Kim Dae Jung and Kim Young Sam, were banned from political activity. Kim Dae Jung, arrested several times after his 1973 kidnapping, was originally sentenced to death but allowed to go to the United States in 1982. All existing political parties were dissolved, and all political activity banned until three months before the 1981 elections.

Twelve new parties (reduced to eight) were formed to enter the 1981 elections, in which Chun Doo Hwan was elected to a seven-year presidential term by a new electoral college and his Democratic Justice Party (DJP) secured a majority in the reconstituted National Assembly. Despite harsh controls, opposition to Chun continued. In 1982, 1,200 political prisoners were released, and in early 1983, the ban on political activity was lifted for 250 of the banned politicians. On 9 October 1983, Chun escaped an apparent assassination attempt in Rangoon, Burma, when an explosion took the lives of 17 in his entourage, including 4 ROK cabinet ministers. Chun subsequently blamed the DPRK for the bombing. In 1984, under increasing pressure for political reforms prior to the 1985 parliamentary elections, the government lifted its ban on all but 15 of the 567 politicians banned in 1980. In 1985, the ban was lifted on 14 of the remaining 15. Kim Dae Jung was allowed to return from exile in the United States in 1984 but rearrested. He remained banned from all political activity because of his conviction for sedition in 1980.

Opposition groups quickly formed the New Korea Democratic Party (NKDP) to challenge the DJP in the 1985 election; the new party became a strong minority voice in the National Assembly. The issue of constitutional reforms, particularly changes in the way in which presidents are elected and the way in which "bonus" seats in the legislature are distributed, became prominent, especially after Chun reaffirmed a commitment to step down in February 1988 and, in April 1986, dropped his long-standing opposition to any constitutional changes prior to that date. Demonstrations against Chun continued and became violent at Inch'on in May 1986 and at Konkuk University that fall. Opposition groups began collecting signatures on a petition demanding direct (instead of indirect, as at present) election of the president. In April 1987, as demonstrations became increasingly violent, Chun banned all further discussion of constitutional reform until after the 1988 Olympic Games in Seoul. The ban, which could have guaranteed the election of a handpicked DJP successor, set off violent antigovernment demonstrations throughout the nation. In June 1987, the DJP nominated its chairman, Roh Tae Woo, a former general and a close friend of Chun, as its candidate for his successor. When Roh accepted opposition demands for political reforms, Chun announced in July that the upcoming election would be held by direct popular vote. On 8 July, 100,000 people demonstrated in Seoul in the largest protest since 1960 and, on the same day, the government restored political rights to 2,000 people, including the longtime opposition leader, Kim Dae Jung.

In the elections, held on 16 December 1987, Roh Tae Woo, as the DJP candidate, won a plurality of 37%, defeating the two major opposition candidates, Kim Young Sam and Kim Dae Jung, who had been unable to agree on a single opposition candidacy and split 55% of the total vote. Two minor candidates divided the remainder. A reported 89% of all eligible voters participated. The two leading opposition candidates charged massive fraud, and a series of demonstrations were held to protest the results. However, no evidence of extensive fraud was produced, and the demonstrations did not attract wide support. Roh Tae Woo was inaugurated as president in February 1988 when Chun Doo Hwan's term expired.

In the elections for the National Assembly, held on 26 April 1988, President Roh Tae Woo's party, the DJP, won only 34% of the vote. This gave the DJP 125 seats in the assembly, while Kim Dae Jung's Peace and Democracy Party (PDP) gained 70 seats, Kim Young Sam's Reunification Democratic Party (RDP) won 59 seats, 35 seats went to the new Democratic Republican Party (NDRP), and 10 to independent candidates. Thus, for the first time in 36 years, the government did not have a controlling vote in the National Assembly, which quickly challenged President Roh's choice for head of the Supreme Court and by year's end forced the president to work with the assembly to pass the budget.

In the fall of 1988, the National Assembly audited the government and held public hearings into former President Chun's abuses of power. In November, Chun apologized to the nation in a televised address, gave his personal wealth to the nation, and retired into a Buddhist temple. Following the revision of the constitution in 1987, South Koreans enjoyed greater freedoms of expression and assembly and freedom of the press and, in 1988, several hundred political dissidents were released from prison.

Unrest among students, workers, and farmers continued, however, and beginning in April 1989, the government repressed opposition. In October 1989, the government acknowledged making 1,315 political arrests so far that year. The National Assembly became less of a check on President Roh after two opposition parties (RDP, NDRP), including that of Kim Young Sam, merged with Roh's DJP, forming a new majority party, the Democratic Liberal Party (DLP) in January 1990. Kim Dae Jung was then left as the leader of the main opposition party (PDP).

There were continuing demonstrations into 1990 and 1991, calling for the resignation of President Roh and the withdrawal of United States troops. In May 1990, 50,000 demonstrators in Kwangju commemorated the tenth anniversary of the massacre, resulting in clashes with police which lasted several days. The US agreed to withdraw its nuclear weapons from the ROK in November 1991. And, on the last day of the year, the ROK and the DPRK signed an agreement to ban nuclear weapons from the entire peninsula.

In the presidential election on 19 December 1992, Kim Young Sam, now leader of the majority DLP, won with 41.9% of the vote, while Kim Dae Jung (DP) took 33.8%. Inaugurated in February 1993, Kim Young Sam began a new era as the first president in 30 years who was a civilian, without a power base in the military. President Kim granted amnesty to 41,000 prisoners and instituted a series of purges of high-ranking military officials, including four generals who had roles in the 1979 coup. Among political and economic reforms was a broad anticorruption campaign, resulting in arrests, dismissals, or reprimands for several thousands of government officials and business people. In

March 1994, a former official of the National Security Planning Agency made public President Roh Tae Woo's authorization of a covert program to develop nuclear weapons at the Daeduk Science Town through 1991.

South and North Korea continue to have a rocky relationship. In April of 1996, North Korean troops on three successive days violated the 1954 armistice which had ended the Korean War by entering Panmunjom. The soldiers, who were apparently conducting training exercises, withdrew after a few hours on all three occasions. In September of the same year, a small North Korean submarine was grounded off the Eastern coast of South Korea and 26 crew members fled into the interior of South Korea. The ship appeared to be carrying a team of North Korean spies who intended to infiltrate into South Korea to carry out what remain unknown missions against South Korean targets. Twenty-four of the crewmen were killed, one escaped and one remains at large. In a surprise unusual move, the North Korean government apologized in February of 1997 for the incursion.

Meanwhile recent domestic events inside South Korea have been equally tumultuous. In August of 1996, former President Chun Doo Hwan and his successor, Roh Tae Woo were tried and found guilty of treason and mutiny for the 1980 coup that brought them to power, and the subsequent Kwangju massacre, in which troops killed at least 154 pro-democracy demonstrators. The court gave Mr. Chun a death sentence (extremely rare in Korea) and sentenced Mr. Roh to 22½ years in prison. An appellate court later reduced Mr. Chun's sentence to life imprisonment and Mr. Roh's sentence to 17 years. When Kim Dae Jung was inaugurated as president in 1998, both leaders were released from prison under Kim's grant of amnesty.

On 11 April 1996, legislative elections took place amid allegation of corruption that reached to the inner circle of President Kim Young Sam and his New Korea Party. During the pre-election campaigning, Kim promised to launch an anti-corruption effort if his party gained power; in a major upset, the NKP catured 139 of the 299 seats, while the main opposition party (National Congress for New Politics—NCNP) or Kim Dae Jong won only 79 seats. Kim Dae Jung lost his own seat in the legislature. Several important New Korea Party officials and even Kim Young Sam's son, were implicated on charges of taking or giving millions of dollars in bribes to arrange loans to Hanbo Steel Industry Co., which eventually went bankrupt under $6 billion of debt. Some of those officials were indicted in February of 1997 but Mr. Kim's son, Kim Hyun-chul, was cleared. However, in May of the same year Kim Hyun-chul was arrested on bribery and tax-evasion charges unrelated to the Hanbo scandal.

By 1997, many of the large *chaebols* (business conglomerates) reported serious problems with debt. A portion of Kia Group, a major manufacturer of automobiles, was nationalized to prevent bankruptcy. Increased domestic economic instability coupled with economic crisis sweeping through Asia, led to a severe decline in the value of the currency. The ensuing financial panic coincided with presidential elections on 18 December 1997, the month that negotiations with the International Monetary Fund (IMF) began. In the election Kim Dae Jung narrowly defeated the ruling party's candidate Lee Hoe Chang by 40.3% to 38.7%. A third candidate Yi In Che garnered 19.2% of the votes, effectively splitting the pro-government vote. Kim Dae Jung pledged to adhere to IMF conditionality and reform government-business relations in South Korea by increasing transparency. In 1998 and 1999, the government reduced the role of government intervention in the domestic economy despite numerous strikes by workers protesting layoffs.

By mid-2000, Kim Dae Jung managed to steer Korea's economy out of the worst of the crisis. The economy started to grow in 1999 and economic estimates suggested that economic growth would top 10% for 2000. In April 2000, the legislative elections improved the position of Kim's party, renamed the New Millenium Party (NMP) to 115 seats. However, the Grand National Party (GNP), successor to the NKP obtained 133 seats and the United Liberal Democrats, allied to the GNP won 17. Thus, Kim's objective to continue economic reform has become imperiled.

In June 2000, Kim Dae Jung traveled to Pyongyan, the capital of the Democratic People's Republic of Korea (North Korea) for an historic meeting with his counterpart, Kim Jong Il. The two agreed to pursue further cooperation in the future.

13GOVERNMENT

The Republic of Korea's (ROK) first constitution was adopted on 17 July 1948. Through repeated revisions, power remained concentrated in the hands of the president until the most recent revision, adopted by 93.1% of the vote in a popular referendum on 28 October 1987. Under the new constitution, which took effect in February 1988, the president is elected by direct popular vote, rather than indirectly as before, for a single term of five years. There are also a prime minister and two deputy prime ministers, who head the State Council (the cabinet). Kim Young Sam was elected president on 18 December 1992 for a five-year term beginning on 25 February 1993.

The ROK legislature is the unicameral National Assembly (Kuk Hoe). It has 299 seats; 253 are filled by direct election, while the remaining 46 are filled proportionally. During the first four decades of the ROK, the National Assembly had little authority. The 1987 constitution strengthened the National Assembly, giving it power to audit government activities and removing the president's power to dissolve the Assembly. Suffrage is universal at age 20.

In the elections of 1997, Kim Dae Jung and the National Congress for New Politics won a narrow victory with 40.3% of the vote.

14POLITICAL PARTIES

From 1948 to 1988, politics in the Republic of Korea were dominated by the executive arm of the government with military backing. Despite this, there were active opposition parties and, with the implementation of the revised 1987 constitution, political parties have had a greater governmental role. In the presidential election of December 1987, the governing Democratic Justice Party (DJP), with Roh Tae Woo as its candidate, won 37% of the vote; the Reunification Democratic Party (RDP), with Kim Young Sam, won 28%; the Peace and Democracy Party (PDP), with Kim Dae Jung, won 27%; and the New Democratic-Republic Party (NDRP), with Kim Jong Pil, won 10%. In a crucial election for the National Assembly in April 1988, the DJP gained only 34% of the popular vote, allowing the opposition parties to control the assembly. This was the first time since 1952 that the government party did not have a majority in and, hence control of, the National Assembly.

In a surprise move in January 1990, the DJP merged with two of the opposition parties, the RDP and the NDRP, to form a new majority party, the Democratic Liberal Party (DLP). In July of that year, two opposition parties, the PDP and the Democratic Party (DP) merged, retaining the name DP. In September 1991, the DP agreed to merge with another opposition party, the New Democratic Party (NDP), then led by the veteran oppositionist, Kim Dae Jung, forming a new DP.

The National Assembly election on 24 March 1992 saw 38.5% of the vote going to the DLP; 29.2% to the DP; 17.3% to the Unification National Party, which later changed its name to the United People's Party(UPP); and 15% to other parties. The actual distribution of seats in the National Assembly shifts as members frequently switch among parties. In the presidential election on 18 December 1992, 41.5% of the vote went to Kim Young Sam of the DLP; 33.8% to Kim Dae Jung of the DP;

16.3% to Chung Ju Yung of the UPP; and 8% to candidates of various smaller parties.

Following the 1992 elections, Korea's largest political parties began a period of reorganization. The DLP transformed into the New Korea Party (NKP) while Kim Dae Jung formed a new opposition party, the National Congress for New Politics (NCNP). In the National Assembly election on 11 April 1996, the NKP won 139 seats; the NCNP, 79 seats; the ULD, 50 seats; and the DP, 15 seats. The remaining 16 seats were won by independents. The surprise of the election was the success of the ULD, a conservative party led by former premier Kim Jong Pil.

In the presidential election of 18 December 1997, Kim Dae Jung won 40.3% and Yi Hoe Chang of the Grand National Party (GNP) won 38.7%. In January 2000, Kim reorganized his cabinet; his party, the National Congress for New Politics, assumed a new name: New Millennium Party (NMP).

The 13 April 2000 election involved Kim Dae-Jung's New Millennium Party, which captured 115; the former governing party—Grand National Party (formerly the New Korea Party) obtained 133 seats; and a minor party, the United Democratic Liberal Party captured 17 seats.

15LOCAL GOVERNMENT

The Republic of Korea (ROK) is divided into nine provinces (do), Cheju, North Cholla, South Cholla, North Ch'ungch'ong, South Ch'ungch'ong, Kangwan, Kyonggi, North Kyongsang, and South Kyongsang. There are six provincial-level cities (jikhalsi) directly under the central government: Seoul, the capital; Inch'on; Kwangju; Pusan, Taegu; and Taejon. Provinces are divided into cities (si), counties (kun or gun), townships (myon), and villages (i or ri). Between 1961 and March 1990, there were no local elections.

16JUDICIAL SYSTEM

The highest judicial court is the Supreme Court, under which are three intermediate appellate courts, located in Seoul, Taegu, and Kwangju. Lower tribunals include district and family courts. Since 1988 constitutional challenges go to the Constitutional Court.

The President, with the consent of the National Assembly, appoints the Chief Justice, the other justices of the Supreme Court to six-year terms, and the Constitutional Court. The Chief Justice in consultation with the other justices of the Court, appoints lower court justices.

The Constitution provides for a presumption of innocence, protection from self-incrimination, the rights to a speedy trial, protection from double jeopardy and other procedural due process safeguards.

The Constitution provides for an independent judiciary. There are no jury trials. The legal system combines some elements of European civil law systems, Anglo-American law, and classical Chinese philosophies.

17ARMED FORCES

The ROK has one of the world's largest and best-equipped armed forces, but it faces an even more impressive foe. Defense spending was $9.9 billion in 1998–99 or 3.2% of GDP. Of a total of 672,000 personnel on active duty, 560,000 were in the army, 60,000 in the navy and marines, and 52,000 in the air force (with 488 combat aircraft). An additional 4.5 million were in the reserves. Paramilitary forces included 3.5 million in the Civilian Defense Corps and its student branches. Military service is compulsory for all males at age 19 and ranges from 26 to 30 months. Veterans retain reserve status until age 33.

South Korea's defense industry is capable of producing medium and short-range missiles and other sophisticated armaments, but it also uses US and European armaments and equipment. The country imported arms worth $4.9 billion during the 1980s, of which 95% came from the US. Arms exports were valued at $29,570 million during the same period. In the mid-1990s, the US had 35,500 troops stationed in the ROK under the terms of the 1954 Korea-US Mutual Defense Treaty. Since 1978, these troops have been integrated with Korean forces under the Korea-US Combined Force Command, headquartered in Seoul.

[18]INTERNATIONAL COOPERATION

ROK is a member of the UN and participates in ESCAP and all the nonregional specialized agencies. The UN Commission on the Unification and Rehabilitation of Korea was dissolved in 1973, but the UN Command originating from the Korean War continues to supervise implementation of the 1953 armistice agreement.

The ROK pursues a vigorous international diplomacy, and in recent years has modified both its militant anti-Communist stance and its close alliance with the US. By 1986, the ROK was recognized by 122 nations, 67 of which also had diplomatic relations with the DPRK. The ROK participates in the Asian Development Bank and G-77, is a permanent observer with the OAS, and is a signatory to the Law of the Sea and a member of the WTO.

[19]ECONOMY

Under a centralized planning system initiated in 1962, the ROK was one of the fastest growing developing countries in the postwar period, shifting from an agrarian to an industrial economy in the course of only a few decades. By 1998 industry contributed 43% of the GDP, compared with 16.2% in 1965, while agriculture, forestry and fishing accounted for 6%, down from 46.5%. Much of this industrialization has been fueled by the government's stimulation of heavy industry, notably steel, construction, shipbuilding and technologically advanced goods such as electronics. To finance industrial expansion the ROK borrowed heavily up until the mid-1980s. By the end of 1986 its foreign debt equalled about 52% of GNP, making the country one of the world's four most deeply indebted developing economies. Steady current account surpluses scored during much of the 1980s allowed the ROK to reduce this figure, but total foreign debts still reached about 50% of GDP in 1998. Total foreign debt was $149 billion, while net foreign debt was only $19.6 billion, due to Korea's sizeable overseas assets.

The annual rate of GDP growth declined from an average of 9.6% between 1985–90 to 9.0% in 1990 and 8.4% in 1991, as a result of slow export growth due to rising labor costs and steady appreciation of the won against the US dollar. However, Korea's economy started to grow once again at the phenomenal rate that it saw in the 1970s and 1980s in the later 1990s. The economy grew by 9.1% in 1995, 9.1% in 1996, and 5% in 1997. Thanks in part to the thriving economy, the growth rate of the country's imports surged ahead of exports, with domestic demand replacing the external sector as the primary growth factor. In 1990 the country ran a trade deficit for the first time since 1986. By 1997, this gap had increased dramatically to a deficit of over $6 billion. That year, due to a loss of international confidence in the region, the ROK currency lost over 50% of its value against the dollar. A $58 billion IMF aid package included structural reforms to begin the liberalization of the economy. The ROK's GDP declined by 5.8% in 1998, in the worst economic performance since the Korean War. In 1998, due to a 35% drop in imports caused by the depreciated currency, the ROK recorded a $40 billion trade surplus. The economy was expected to improve by approximately 5% in 1999, and over 7% in 2000.

[20]INCOME

The US Central Intelligence Agency (CIA) reports that in 1998 South Korea's gross domestic product (GDP) was estimated at $585 billion. The per capita GDP was estimated at $12,600. The annual growth rate of GDP was estimated at -6.8%. The average inflation rate in 1998 was 7.5%. The CIA defines GDP as the value of all final goods and services produced within a nation in a given year and computed on the basis of purchasing power parity (PPP) rather than value as measured on the basis of the rate of exchange. It was estimated that agriculture accounted for 6% of GDP, industry 43%, and services 51%.

The World Bank reports that for the same period per capita private consumption (in PPP terms) was $6,695. Private consumption includes expenditures of individuals, households, and nongovernmental organizations. Approximately 18% of household consumption was spent on food, 7% on fuel, 5% on health care, and 14% on education. The richest 10% of the population accounted for approximately 24% of household consumption and the poorest 10% approximately 2.9%.

[21]LABOR

The civilian labor force (over age 15) averaged 21,390,000 in 1998. Of the total of 19,926,000 employed in 1997, 11% were engaged in agriculture, forestry, and fishing; 31.3% in manufacturing; and 57.7% in other occupations, mostly in the service sector. The unemployment rate in 1998 averaged 6.8%. The drop in employment between the summer peak and the winter off-season annually exceeds one million, virtually all of it in the agricultural sector.

Before 1987, the labor movement was heavily controlled by the government, but since 1991, democratic reform has brought some changes. A 1997 law authorized the formation of competing unions within a single work place beginning in 2002. In 1998, the government authorized the establishment of work place agencies by white collar public employees. In 1999, about 12% of the work force (excluding farmers and soldiers), belonged to 5,560 registered local unions. In 1999, there were about 129 strikes. In 1998, the minimum wage was raised to $1.17 per hour.

[22]AGRICULTURE

Some 20% of the ROK's land area is arable, with about 70% of it sown in grain, rice being the chief crop. In 1965, agriculture (including forestry and fishing) contributed nearly 50% to GNP, but by 1998 only accounted for 6%. Double-cropping is common in the southern provinces. Rice production in 1998 was 7,312,000 tons. Barley production in 1998 stood at 410,000 tons; potatoes, 638,000 tons; and soybeans, 156,000 tons. Despite increased yields due to mechanization, the use of hybrid seeds, and increased employment of fertilizers, the ROK runs a net deficit in food grains every year. In 1995, imports of cereals, mostly from the US, amounted to $1,858 million, consisting almost entirely of wheat and corn. Virtual self-sufficiency has been attained in rice production, but at a cost of nearly $2 billion per year in direct producer subsidies.

Hemp, hops, and tobacco are the leading industrial crops. The ROK was the world's leading producer of chestnuts in 1998. The orchards in the Taegu area are renowned for their apples, the prime fruit crop; output in 1998 was 652,000 tons. Pears, peaches, persimmons, and melons also are grown in abundance. About two-thirds of vegetable production is made up of the mu (a large white radish) and Chinese cabbage, the main ingredients of the year-round staple kimchi, or "Korean pickle."

Until the Korean War, tenant farming was widespread in the ROK. The Land Reform Act of June 1949, interrupted by the war, was implemented in 1953; it limited arable land ownership to 3 ha (7.4 acres) per household, with all lands in excess of this limit to be purchased by the government for distribution among farmers who had little or no land. By the late 1980s, farms averaged 0.5–1 ha (1.2–2.5 acres). The New Village (Saemaul) Movement, initiated in 1972, plays a major role in raising productivity and modernizing villages and farming practices.

23ANIMAL HUSBANDRY

The raising of livestock, traditionally a supplementary occupation among ROK farmers, expanded rapidly during the 1970s and 1980s. In 1998, 3,279,000 head of cattle were raised (as well as 300,000 dairy cattle); pigs totaled 6,700,000, and chickens, 88 million. Production in 1998 included (in thousands of tons): beef, 318; pork, 975; chicken, 378; eggs, 465; milk, 1,900; butter, 5.4. The silkworm industry has declined radically since the mid-1970s. Although the dairy industry has been protected by import restrictions, an incremental lifting of such trade constraints is underway, which will eventually include livestock imports.

24FISHING

Korean waters comprise some of the best fishing grounds in the world. The Sea of Japan off the east coast provides deep-sea fishing with an average water depth of 1,700 m (5,600 ft). Warm and cold water alternate each season; the area is known for its Alaskan pollack, cod, squid, king crab, hairing crab, turban shell, and abalone. Off the west coast, the Yellow Sea has an average depth of 44 m (144 ft); major species include corker, hairtail, mackerel, surf clam, large clam abalone, lobster, Japanese paste shrimp, and blue crab. Off the south coast, the warm Pacific Ocean currents move towards the northeast, bringing diverse species such as anchovy, mackerel, oyster, mussels, shellfish, octopus, beka squid, laver, and sea mustard.

Industrialization and urbanization have led to a dramatic reduction in the number of families directly involved with fishing; from 1980 to 1995, the number of fishing families declined from 157,000 to 104,000. The fishing fleet consisted of 77,931 vessels in 1995, of which 616 were deep-sea vessels. That year, fisheries contributed w2.5 trillion, or 0.7%, to GNP.

According to the FAO, the total catch in 1997 was 3,267,551 tons. Mackerel and anchovies account for about half the coastal fish landings; oysters are the principal aquacultural species; Alaskan pollack and tuna provide 80% of the deep-sea fish catch. Korean fishing bases have been established in Western Samoa and Las Palmas, and cuttlefish caught in waters off the Falkland Islands are now available. Since the declaration of 200 mi economic sea zones by many nations in the 1970s, the ROK negotiated fishing agreements with several coastal nations to secure fishing rights in their waters. Seaweed is another important aquacultural product, with 650,000 tons harvested in 1995.

The ROK exports seafood to about 65 countries throughout the world. Fisheries exports typically include tuna, shellfish, frozen/canned products, and seaweed. Japan is the largest destination for exports, annually accounting for about 75% of ROK seafood exports by value. In 1997, fisheries exports were valued at $1,376,465,000. Fresh, chilled, and frozen fish accounted for 45% of the value; crustaceans and mollusks, 26%; canned fish, 18%; and other products, 1%. The rate of fish consumption in the ROK was 32.6 kg (71.9 lb) per person in 1995. Although domestic consumption is still largely tied to local production, the ROK imported $1,017,949,000 of fish products in 1997. Major suppliers were Russia, the US, China, Argentina, Chile, New Zealand, and Japan.

25FORESTRY

Forests covered 7,626,000 ha (18,843,000 acres) in 1995, or about 77.2% of the ROK's total area, but wood supplies are grossly inadequate to meet the needs of the fast-growing plywood and paper industries. Most of the original forests were destroyed during the Korean War and have been transformed into pine forests under a massive government reforestation program. Conifers now account for 45% of the forest; broad-leaved species (such as oak), 28%; and mixed forests, 27%. About 21% of all forested land is nationally owned and is the focus of extensive reforestation efforts. The government is supporting local efforts to invest in forest development projects abroad. According to the

FAO, estimated production of roundwood in 1997 was 1,461,000 cu m; sawnwood, 4,759,000 cu m; and plywood, 1,014,000 cu m. Softwoods (mostly red pine and larch) accounted for about 80% of the production; hardwoods (mainly oak), 20%. Because of low quality, domestic roundwood is mainly used for chopsticks, crates, match wood, and wood chips. Whereas plywood and wood pulp were once traditional export items, the role of forestry products in generating export earnings is now shrinking. The ROK is now a significant importer of forest products. Imports of forest products amounted to nearly $3.8 billion in 1997 (primarily from Indonesia, Malaysia, and the US). Imports have been boosted by a growing demand for single and multifamily wood frame houses.

26MINING

The ROK's limited supplies of iron ore, coal, copper, lead, and zinc must be supplemented by imports. Two-way trade with North Korea continued to grow; in 1997 imports of gold, other minerals, and other commodities totaled $190 million. Among mineral ores (metal content) produced in 1997, iron totaled 166,000 tons; zinc, 8,992 tons; lead, 3,632 tons; and refined primary copper, 265,426 tons. In addition, the ROK produced 14,872 kg of gold and 267,911 kg of silver metal.

27ENERGY AND POWER

Coal is the chief fuel mined, with recoverable reserves estimated at 90 million tons and production totaling 4.8 million tons in 1998. Most of the coal is low-quality anthracite, used mainly for home cooking and heating; imports of higher-grade coal (44.4 million tons in 1994) are required for industry.

In 1998, crude oil provided 54.6% of all primary energy consumed, up from 9.4% in 1962, and coal, 21%. Nuclear energy, natural gas, and hydroelectricity provided the rest. Oil consumption totals two million barrels per day, all of it imported. In 1996, nuclear power was generated by 11 reactors at four plants (Kori, Ulchin, Wolsong, and Yonggwang). Since the 1960s, the ROK's oil sector has been heavily regulated as a means of providing manufacturers with inexpensive energy. Prices are controlled and market entry is restricted. In 1997, the ROK began to loosen controls over oil pricing, importing, and the export of refined petroleum products. Plans for the future call for a de-emphasis on oil and promotion of atomic energy, coal, and hydroelectricity as energy sources, together with importation of liquefied natural gas from Indonesia and crude oil from the US.

In 1998, the ROK had an installed electrical generating capacity of 43.7 million kW, up from 9.8 million kW in 1981, of which about 8% was from hydroelectric plants and 25% from nuclear plants. The output of electricity in 1998 totaled 221.3 billion kWh. Industry accounts for about two-thirds of the electricity consumed. Electricity use has been growing at 1.5 times the rate of economic growth in recent years.

28INDUSTRY

Up until the 1960s, manufacturing was chiefly confined to production for domestic consumption, and a substantial proportion of the output was produced by handicraft methods in homes and small factories. While textiles, apparel and footwear were the first modern industries to be developed, heavy industry has grown rapidly over the last four decades, promoted by a series of development plans. In the 1980s, the manufacture of metals, machinery, electronic and other equipment overtook textile production as the country's leading industries in terms of value, employment and export earnings. During the past decade, increasing domestic production costs has encouraged the relocation of production plants in some industries—particularly textiles and footwear but more recently also consumer electronics—to overseas locations in Southeast Asia, Eastern Europe, China, Mexico, and Turkey. The ROK now ranks as a major Asian producer of electronics, automobiles, chemicals, ships, steel, textiles, clothing, shoes, and processed food. In 1999, industrial production grew by almost 25% from 1998. The biggest growth in the first half of 2000 was in heavy industries, including the automobile, semiconductors, and machinery sectors.

Manufacturing in the ROK is dominated by a few dozen vertically-integrated industrial conglomerates, known as *chaebol*, which have privileged access to financing and set the standards for contracting and procurement throughout the country. In 1995, the 30 largest chaebol accounted for 16.2% of GNP (up from 13.5% in 1992), according to the Korea Economic Research Institute. In 1999, the debts of the four biggest chaebol stood at approximately $140 billion. Unfortunately, many of the country's chaebol have racked up huge debts in order to finance industrial expansion, some more than five times their annual intake. Asset sell-offs by the four biggest chaebols, including Hyundai, Samsung, LG, and SK amounted to $15 billion in 1999.

Joint venture production with major US and Japanese car companies, growing domestic demand, and successful penetration of overseas markets by Korean-owned corporations has fuelled steady growth in automobile output. The production of passenger cars more than doubled from 1990 to 1995. Total vehicle production in 1995 was 2,526,400, or 5% of world output. Vehicle production in 1998 was about two billion, or eighth of all OECD countries. South Korea's automotive industry is dominated by Hyundai, which accounted for 48% of all passenger cars, trucks, and buses domestically produced in 1995. Kia accounted for 25% of production that year; Daewoo, 18%; and others, 9%. In 1999, ROK president Kim Dae Jung accused Hyundai of failing to restructure and refinance more than $46 billion in debts. The biggest chaebol; Hyundai's bankruptcy had the potential to cause crisis in the ROK economy. In June of 2000, creditors called for the company's breakup. Kia was also bankrupted by 1999.

Production of electronics has shifted from assembly of imported parts to the manufacture of competitive high-technology products, such as office automation systems, for both the international and domestic markets. Daewoo Electronics (the second largest chaebol, with substantial debts), LG and Samsung Electronics dominate in the production of consumer electronics; the televisions, videocassette recorders, stereos, refrigerators, washing machines, and microwave ovens produced by these companies are sold across the world. Daewoo Electronics also operates 36 overseas factories and planned to capture 10% of the world's market in consumer electronics by 2000. Samsung Electronics was the world's largest producer of computer memory chips in 1996.

In 1998, the ROK was the second largest world producer of new ships, with an annual production capacity of about seven million GRT. P'ohang Iron and Steel Co. (POSCO) produces about half of the nation's total steel output of approximately 40 million tons.

29 SCIENCE AND TECHNOLOGY

The ROK has often been compared to its powerful neighbor, Japan, but is said to be about 10 years behind that nation in scientific and technological innovation. However, in areas such as semiconductor memory chips, cars, and steel, Korean industries provide innovation equal to that in the US and Japan. In 1998, high technology exports were valued at $30.5 billion and accounted for 27% of all manufactured exports.

Two organizations provide most of the main support for Korean science and technology. The Korean Institute of Science and Technology (KIST) was started in 1965 with the help of the United States. The Korean Advanced Institute of Science and Technology (KIST), the leading university in scientific research.

KAIST attracts researchers from all over the world, and is considered one of the top universities in the world for electrical and molecular engineering and computer science. In 1987–97, science and engineering students accounted for 32% of college and university enrollments.

30 DOMESTIC TRADE

The small family outlet, traditional in Korea, is giving way to chain stores and supermarkets. Large, modern department stores now operate in Seoul, Pusan and other major urban centers, although some trade in rural areas is still carried on by itinerant peddlers, mobile sidewalk stands, and periodic market fairs. Black markets offering all manner of foreign goods are much in use; haggling over prices is common. Seoul is the nation's wholesaling center. Most private offices are open from 8:30 AM to 6:00 PM weekdays and from 9:00 AM to 12:00 PM on Saturdays. Korean government offices keep similar hours, except for a 5:00 PM closing from November through February. Banking hours are 9:30 AM to 4:30 PM, Monday through Friday and 9:30 AM to 1:30 PM Saturdays.

31 FOREIGN TRADE

The most important commodity exports of the Republic of Korea are electrical equipment (25%). The Republic of Korea also exports a large amount of woven fabrics and ships. The top six exports are:

	% OF COUNTRY TOTAL	% OF WORLD TOTAL
Transistors, valves	14	11
Woven fabrics	5.6	20
Ships	4.7	15
Electrical machinery	4.0	6.4
Telecoms equipment	3.6	3.9
Automatic data processing equipment	3.0	3.0

Oil and related products, chemicals, and raw materials are major imports, as most raw inputs for the country's industrial sector are imported. A lack of small companies and technological research compels the ROK to import components and production machines for the cars, videocassette recorders, computer chips, and ships that it manufactures. In 1996 South Korea's imports were distributed among the following categories:

Consumer goods	5.6%
Food	4.1%
Fuels	16.7%
Industrial supplies	32.7%
Machinery	34.6%
Transportation	6.0%
Other	0.3%

The US, China and Japan have continued to be the ROK's chief trading partners, although potential new markets in Eastern Europe and the rest of Asia are being explored. Saudi Arabia and Indonesia have been major providers of oil and liquefied natural gas. Australia is a leading supplier of iron ore, coal, and grains. Principal trading partners in 1998 (in millions of US dollars) were as follows:

COUNTRY	EXPORTS	IMPORTS	BALANCE
United States	22,987	20,423	2,564
China (inc. Hong Kong)	21,205	7,024	14,181
Japan	12,238	16,840	-4,602
Switzerland	4,832	1,523	3,309
United Kingdom	4,179	1,763	2,416
Singapore	4,065	1,713	2,352
Germany	4,009	3,345	664
Malaysia	3,602	2,211	1,391
Australia	2,791	4,615	-1,824
Saudi Arabia	1,324	4,384	-3,060

[32] BALANCE OF PAYMENTS

Robust export performance turned the ROK's overall balance of payments deficit into a $1.7 billion surplus in 1986, which grew to $12.1 billion in 1988. Since then, the balance of payments surplus has declined; in 1990, the balance of payments had a deficit of $274 million because of declining exports, rising imports, and a current account deficit. Over the long term, growth in exports will depend on industry's efforts to regain competitiveness lost through wage increases, labor unrest, and exchange rate changes. The deficit grew to over 4% of GDP in 1996, before subsiding in 1997 due to a shrinking currency base.

The US Central Intelligence Agency reports that in 1998 the purchasing power parity of South Korea's exports was $133 billion while imports totaled $94 billion resulting in a trade balance of $39 billion. The value of exports for 1999 brought in a surplus of $24 billion.

[33] BANKING AND SECURITIES

In 2000, finance, insurance, real estate, and business services accounted for over half of GDP. The Bank of Korea serves as the central bank, the bank of issue, and the depository for government funds. It was established in 12 June 1950. The banking system is regulated by the Financial Supervisory Service. Other banking services are provided by the state-run Korea Development Bank, the Export-Import Bank of Korea, and 9 state-run specialized banks. Commercial banking operations in 1999 were handled by 11 nationwide commercial banks, 10 provincial banks, and 42 foreign banks. Total assets of Korea's commercial banks at the end of 1998 were $300 billion.

By 1986, as part of the government's economic stabilization program initiated in 1980, all of the five commercial banks previously under government control were denationalized. In 1993, the Korean government began a five-year financial sector reform program, including the deregulation of interest rates, and liberalization of foreign exchange. During the financial crisis of late 1997 and 1998, non-performing loan levels skyrocketed. The credit hunger of South Korean corporations can be explained in part by the failure of the stock exchange to generate the equity capital they needed. On 25 June 1998, the Korean government ordered the takeover of five failing banks, and seven other banks were put on a warning list. Of the seven; five merged, and two continued operations. Banks directly effected by these measures included Shinhan Bank, the Housing and Commercial Bank, Kookmin Bank, KorAm Bank, Hana Bank, and Hanvit Bank, among others. In 1998, efforts continued to stabilize the banking sector by increasing the capital adequacy ratio to 8%, and the government encouraged lending to small and medium-sized companies as opposed to the large conglomorate chaebols.

The Korean Stock Exchange, a share-issuing private corporation, functions as the country's only stock exchange. Clearly, all was not well with the stock market in 1996, when the stock price index late in was lower than that of 1988, although the economy had virtually doubled in size in real terms over the same period. Direct access by foreigners to the stock market has been allowed since 1992; Seoul implemented unrestricted foreign access in 1998. Stock issues raised $32 billion in 1999, as opposed to $11 billion in 1997. International links were being forged in 2000, and the KOSDAQ was to begin stock transactions for small- and medium-sized firms.

[34] INSURANCE

The insurance industry is poorly developed. In 1985/86, there were 6 life and 14 non-life insurance companies in operation. Per capita life insurance premiums totaled 8.3% of the GDP and nonlife totaled 1.9% in 1989. In 1992, w587,598 billion of life insurance was in force.

[35] PUBLIC FINANCE

The US Central Intelligence Agency (CIA) estimates that in 1997 South Korea's central government took in revenues of approximately $100.4 billion and had expenditures of $100.5 billion including capital expenditures of $18 billion. Overall, the government registered a deficit of approximately $100 million. External debt totaled $154 billion.

The following table shows an itemized breakdown of government revenues and expenditures. The percentages were calculated from data reported by the International Monetary Fund. The dollar amounts (millions) are based on the CIA estimates provided above.

REVENUE AND GRANTS	100%	100,400
EXPENDITURES	100%	100,500
General public services	5.1%	5,085
Defense	16.7%	16,741
Public order and safety	6.1%	6,092
Education	20.5%	20,612
Health	0.8%	784
Social security	10.8%	10,847
Housing and community amenities	2.3%	2,267
Recreation, cultural, and religious affairs	0.9%	856
Economic affairs and services	23.7%	23,796
Other expenditures	10.5%	10,549
Interest payments	2.9%	2,872

[36] TAXATION

The principal sources of tax revenue are customs duties, corporate taxes, a defense tax surcharge imposed on corporations, a VAT of 10%, personal income taxes, and various excise taxes. As of 2000, the rates for corporate taxation ranged from 16% on taxable income up to w100 million to 28% on income over w100 million. In addition, there is a resident tax surcharge of 10% and a special agriculture and fishery tax imposed on corporations having taxable income over w500 million. There is a 24.2% withholding tax on interest. The capital gains tax is set at three rates of 20%, 30%, and 40%. Tax relief for up to five years, with a 50% exemption in the ensuing two years, is offered to new industries and corporations that are foreign exchange earners. Those in electronics receive seven years of exemption, and three years at 50%. The personal income tax is graduated from 10% to 45%.

[37] CUSTOMS AND DUTIES

In January 1999, Korea had an average tariff of 7.9%. However, tariffs remain high on a number of agricultural and fishery products, at 30% to 100%. Korea plans to further reduce tariffs in the future. Other import taxes include a VAT of 10% and excise taxes ranging from 15% to 100%. The special excise tax on consumer electronic goods and automobiles was cut by 30% in 1998. There were 57 items subject to quotas, and 29 items subject to excise tariffs in 1999. The Information Technology Agreement (ITA) dropped most IT tariffs by 2000, with the remainder to be phased out by 2004.

[38] FOREIGN INVESTMENT

The Foreign Investment Promotion Act (FIPA) and related regulations have governed foreign investment in ROK since 1998. Japanese share of foreign investments fell from about 50% in 1987 to 5.7% in 1998, as Japanese investors have been increasingly attracted to new centers of economic growth in Southeast Asia. While foreign investment is prohibited or restricted in 21 industries, including seven which are entirely closed to foreign investment, most manufacturing activities are open. Seeking to facilitate further technology transfer, the government offers particular incentives to foreign companies in 533 categories of high technology industries. Two free export zones geared towards highly technical business activities have been established at Masan (near Pusan) and Iri (near Kunsan) to provide additional incentives for investment in favored industries. There were also completed in 1996 two industrial parks, in Chonan and Kwangju. The parks are for the exclusive use of Korean firms with heavy foreign investment. Net foreign direct investment flow to the ROK was negative in 1996 (–$1.1 billion), as compared to a high of $720 million in 1988, reflecting the trend towards growing overseas investment by private investors in the country. In 1998, new foreign investment totaled $8.9 billion; $3 billion of which came from the US, and $3 billion from the EU. The largest receptors of investment funds were the electronics and woods and paper products manufacturing sectors, accounting for one-third of all investment. Foreign investment was expected to double in 1999, due to the FIPA and increased stability in the region.

39ECONOMIC DEVELOPMENT

The ROK has a market economy in which both private enterprise and foreign investors play an important role. Overall economic development is guided, however, by the Economic Planning Board and, since 1962, by a series of five-year plans. A Seventh Five-Year Economic and Social Development Plan for 1992–96 aimed at establishing the ROK as an advanced industrialized economy by the year 2000. More specific goals included improving social and economic equity, continued liberalization, improving industrial and export competitiveness, as well as strengthening the role of the private sector while government intervention in economic management, especially in the financial sector, is reduced. The Plan targeted an annual GDP growth rate of 7% and a decline of consumer price inflation to 3%. While inflation hovered over the projection that the Plan proposed, GDP growth kept pace with the Plan's goal until 1997, when the financial crisis effectively shrank the economy. The IMF, World Bank, and Asia Development Bank lent $58 billion in aid following the crisis, including structural adjustments meant to stimulate foreign investment and the liberalization of the economy. GDP growth in 2000 was forecast for over 7%.

40SOCIAL DEVELOPMENT

Few countries have faced health and social welfare problems as acute as those caused in the ROK by the devastation of the Korean War. The war left a residue of 348,000 war widows, most of them with dependent children, and 100,000 war orphans. Some 595,260 homes were destroyed, 5,000 villages wiped out, and many large cities badly damaged. Military relief payments consist mainly of financial support to veterans and their families.

Plans to establish a national welfare pension plan were approved in 1973 but never implemented; however, the government passed legislation in 1988 that included old age, disability, and survivors' pensions, and extended these benefits to farmers, fishermen and the rural self-employed in 1995. In 1999, workers and employers contributed 4.5% of earnings and payroll, respectively. Medical benefits are provided to all permanent residents under 1963 and 1997 laws, and workers' compensation is extended to employees of firms with five or more workers.

Conservative Confucian tradition encourages married women to remain at home. Few women hold political office, and as of 1996 only 12 females held seats in the 299-member parliament. The wage of the average female worker is roughly half of that earned by a male counterpart.

The amended family law that took effect in 1991 recognizes women as heads of households and strengthens their property rights. However, divorce remains socially unacceptable in most sectors of Korean society, and this leads many women to remain in abusive marriages. A new sexual harassment law went into effect in 1999.

Korean citizenship is determined exclusively by genealogy, and as a result, many Chinese born and raised in Korea are deprived of citizenship rights. Human rights are generally respected by the government. Some abuses have been reported involving detainees, but these are declining.

41HEALTH

Health care has improved substantially and is directly related to improvement of diet, the rise in living standards, and the development of health and medical programs. Since the late 1970s, medical security, in the form of medical insurance and medical aid, has been expanded to cover a substantial portion of the population. The national medical insurance system was expanded in 1989, covering 94% of the population. In 1985–1995, 100% of the population had access to health care services. About 4% of the gross domestic product went to health expenditures in 1990–1997.

In the mid-1990s, there were 236 general hospitals, 351 hospitals, 6 dental hospitals, 12,629 clinics, 6,708 dental clinics, 269 maternity clinics, 53 herb doctor hospitals, and 4,062 herb doctor clinics. In 1990–97, there were 4.4 hospital beds and 1.2 physicians per 1,000 people. Safe water is accessible to over 90% of the population.

The fertility rate in 1999 was 1.8 children per woman surviving her child-bearing years. In 1993–96, 4% of all births were low birth weight. About 79% of married women (aged 15-49) used contraception in the years 1989–1995. Tobacco consumption has risen substantially from 2.7 kg to 3.2 kg a year per adult in 1995. There were three AIDS cases in 1996. In 1994 there were 68,907 deaths related to cardiovascular disease and 14,730 deaths caused by traffic motor vehicle accidents. In 1990-1994, immunization rates for children up to one year of age were tuberculosis, 72%; diphtheria, pertussis, and tetanus, 74%; polio, 79%; and measles, 93%. The 1999 infant mortality rate was 7.6 per 1,000 live births, and the general mortality rate was 5.7 per 1,000 inhabitants. In 1997, there were about 142 reported cases of tuberculosis per 100,000 people. Life expectancy was 74.3 years in 1999.

42HOUSING

After the liberation in 1945, southern Korea faced a housing shortage greatly compounded by high population growth rates. A housing shortage continues to plague the nation, especially in Seoul, Pusan, and other large cities, where shantytowns house many recent rural arrivals. The 1985 census counted 9,588,723 households but only 6,274,462 housing units, for a deficit of 3,314,261. A total of 1,460,000 units were built under the 1981–86 economic plan. In 1988, the government inaugurated a plan to build two million new housing units in four years and exceeded its goal, reaching a total of 2,717,000 units by 1992. As of that year, the per capita housing space was 9.6 sq m (103 sq ft). The government, through the Korean Housing Corporation, plans to construct 500,000 to 600,000 housing units per year from 1993 to 1998, increasing the rate of home ownership to 90%. The program will continue to focus on small housing units. Through government efforts, the supply of piped water is projected to rise from 80% of dwellings in 1991 to 90% in 2001. The per capita water supply is slated to rise from 376 liters in 1991 to 440 liters in 2001.

43EDUCATION

The Education Law of 1949 provided for a centralized system under the control of the Ministry of Education and made the six-year elementary schools free and compulsory for children between 6 and 12 years of age. Secondary education begins at 12 years of age and lasts for up to six years which are divided into two cycles of three years each. Children attend middle school for three years, and subsequently attend either general academic high school or vocational high school for the remaining three years. Nearly 95% of children in this age group were enrolled in the secondary schools in 1995. In 1998 there were 3,794,447 students in 5,721 primary schools, with 122,743 teachers. Student-to-teacher ratio stood at 31 to 1. In 1997, secondary schools enrolled 4,662,492 students and employed 192,947 teachers. Also in 1997, all post-secondary institutions had a combined enrollment of 2,541,659 students and 114,231 teachers.

The leading government university is Seoul National University. The principal private institutions, all of them in Seoul, are Korea, Sung Kyun Kwan, Yonsei, Hanyang, Chungang, and Ewha universities; the last named is one of the largest women's universities in the world. The country had a total of 121 colleges and universities in 1996, along with 335 graduate schools with a combined 1,556,949 students enrolled. For the year 2000, UNESCO estimated the rate of adult illiteracy at 2.2% (males, 0.8%; females, 3.6%). In the latter half of the 1990s, the government allocated approximately 17.5% of its total expenditure to education.

44 LIBRARIES AND MUSEUMS
In the mid-1990s, the Central National Library, founded in 1923, had approximately 2,900,000 volumes. Most other sizable libraries in the ROK are found at universities. The largest academic collection is at the Seoul National University Library, (1.9 million volumes).

The National Museum, with centers in Seoul, Kyongju, Kwangju, Puyo, Chinju, Chunju, Chongju, and Kongju contains art objects reflecting more than 5,000 years of cultural history, including statuary pieces, ceramics, and painting. A major private museum is the Ho-Am Art Museum in Seoul. The National Museum of Modern Art in Seoul presents many special exhibits as well a permanent collection. The National Science Museum of Korea, completed in 1990 in Daejon, is one of the country's most recent cultural sites. The ROK also possesses collections of early printing, dynastic histories, and art in its palaces and Buddhist temples, and in university, college, and public libraries.

45 MEDIA
In 1995, the number of telephone lines totaled 17,647,000. As of 1999, there were 79 AM radio stations, 46 FM stations, and 121 television broadcast stations. Television broadcasting began in 1956; in 1992 there were 57 commercial television stations, plus a US Armed Forces–Korea network broadcasting in English. In 1997, Koreans owned 1,037 radios, 341 television sets, and 150 mobile phones per 1,000 population.

Most of the leading newspapers are published in Seoul. The leading Korean-language newspapers, with their estimated daily circulations (in 1999), include *Joong-ang Ilbo*, 1,550,000; *Hankook Ilbo*, 1,150,000; *Dong-A Ilbo*, 2,150,000; *Seoul Shinmun*, 900,000; *Choson Ilbo*, 2,225,000; and *Kyung-hyang Shinmun*, 1,470,000.

Though most radio and television stations and newspapers are state-supported, the government is said to have abandoned direct control over the news media, though some journalists report aggressive government lobbying to soften criticism, using the latent threat of KX investigations against media companies.

As of 1996, there were 5.3 million personal computers; in 1998 there were 38 Internet hosts per 1,000 population.

46 ORGANIZATIONS
Clan and county associations are a conspicuous aspect of Korean social life. A traditional type of organization with a primarily economic function is the kye, a mutual loan association formed to provide funds for a specific and typically short-term purpose, such as to defray the expenses of a wedding or funeral. The National Agricultural Cooperative Federation comprises millions of farmers who work in cooperatives. There are also hundreds of religious, political, cultural, labor, business, and sports associations.

47 TOURISM, TRAVEL, AND RECREATION
The tourist industry has grown rapidly, with 4,250,216 foreign visitors in 1998, a 9% increase over the previous year. The number of hotel rooms totaled 67,466 in 1997, with 134,932 beds and a 63% occupancy rate. Tourist receipts reached $5 billion that year. Major tourist attractions are Seoul, the former royal capital of the Yi (or Li) Dynasty, and Kyongju, with its treasures from the ancient kingdom of Silla.

Soccer and baseball are the most popular modern sports. Traditional sports for men are wrestling, archery, kite fighting, and t'aekwondo (a martial art). Popular games include paduk, the Korean name for Japan's board game go; changgi, or Korean chess, with pieces different from the European form; and yut, or Korean dice, played with four wooden sticks.

In 1999, the UN estimated the cost of staying in Seoul at $266 per day; expenses in Daejon were estimated at $187.

48 FAMOUS KOREANS (ROK)
The dominant political figures of the contemporary period in the ROK have been Syngman Rhee (1875–1965), president from 1948 to 1960, and Park Chung-hee (1917–79), president from 1963 until his assassination in 1979. Chun Doo Hwan (Chon Du-hwan, b.1931) became president in 1981. Other well-known modern figures include Kim Chong-p'il (b.1926), prime minister 1971–75; Bishop Daniel Chi (Chi Hak-sun, b.1921); and Kim Dae Jung (Kim Tae-jung, b.1925) and Kim Young Sam (Kim Yong-sam, b.1927), prominent opposition leaders during the 1970s and 1980s. The Rev. Sun Myung Moon (Mun Son-myong, b.1920), a controversial evangelist and founder of the Tong-il (Unification) Church, and Kyung Wha Chung (Chung Kyung-wha, b.1943), a violinist, are both internationally well known.

49 DEPENDENCIES
The ROK has no territories or colonies.

50 BIBLIOGRAPHY
Grayson, James Huntley. *Korea: A Religious History*. New York: Oxford University Press, 1989.

Hoare, James. *Korea: An Introduction*. New York: Kegan Paul International, 1988.

Howe, Russell Warren. *The Koreans: Passion and Grace*. San Diego: Harcourt Brace Jovanovich, 1988.

Hwang, Eui-Gak. *The Korean Economies: A Comparison of North and South*. New York: Oxford University Press, 1993.

Lone, Stewart. *Korea Since 1850*. New York: St. Martin's Press, 1993.

Macdonald, Donald Stone. *The Koreans: Contemporary Politics and Society*. Boulder, Colo.: Westview Press, 1990.

McNamara, Dennis L. *The Colonial Origins of Korean Enterprise, 1910–1945*. Cambridge [England]; New York: Cambridge University Press, 1990.

Nahm, Andrew C. *Historical Dictionary of the Republic of Korea*. Metuchen, N.J.: Scarecrow Press, 1993.

Oliver, Robert Tarbell. *A History of the Korean People in Modern Times: 1800 to the Present*. Newark: University of Delaware Press, 1993.

Olsen, Edward A. *US Policy and the Two Koreas*. Boulder, Colo.: Westview Press, 1988.

Sanford, Dan C. *South Korea and the Socialist Countries: The Politics of Trade*. New York: St. Martin's Press, 1990.

Sohn, Hak-Kyu. *Authoritarianism and Opposition in South Korea*. London; New York: Routledge, 1989.

Song, Pyong-nak. *The Rise of the Korean Economy*. Hong Kong; New York: Oxford University Press, 1990.

KUWAIT

State of Kuwait
Dawlat al-Kuwayt

CAPITAL: Kuwait (Al-Kuwayt).

FLAG: The flag adopted in 1961 is a rectangle, twice as long as it is high, divided equally into green, white, and red horizontal stripes, with a black trapezoid whose longer base is against the staff and is equal to the breadth of the flag, and whose shorter base is equal to the breadth of the white stripe.

ANTHEM: National Anthem, melody only; no words.

MONETARY UNIT: The Kuwaiti dinar (KD) has 1,000 fils. There are coins of 1, 5, 10, 20, 50, and 100 fils, and notes of 250 and 500 fils and of 1, 5, 10, and 20 Kuwaiti dinars. KD1 = $3.2648 ($1 = KD0.306) as of 31 March 2000.

WEIGHTS AND MEASURES: The metric system is the legal standard, but imperial weights and measures also are in use, and some US measures are recognized.

HOLIDAYS: New Year's Day, 1 January; Emir's Accession Day, 25 February. Movable religious holidays include Muslim New Year (1st of Muharram); Laylat al-Miraj; Milad an-Nabi; 'Id al-Fitr; and 'Id al-'Adha'.

TIME: 3 PM = noon GMT.

¹LOCATION, SIZE, AND EXTENT

Kuwait is situated at the western head of the Persian (or Arabian) Gulf. Its undemarcated borders preclude any definite figure for its area, which is estimated at about 17,820 sq km (6,880 sq mi). Comparatively, the area occupied by Kuwait is slightly smaller than the state of New Jersey. Kuwait extends 205 km (127 mi) SE–NW and 176 km (109 mi) NE–SW. Islands that form part of Kuwait include Faylakah (an archaeological site that is the only inhabited island), Bubiyan, Maskan, 'Auha, Al-Warbah, Al-Kubr, Umm al-Maradim, Umm al-Nami, and Qaruh. Bounded on the E by the Persian Gulf, on the S and W by Sa'udi Arabia, and on the NW and N by Iraq, Kuwait has a total boundary length of 963 km (598 mi).

Kuwait's boundary with Sa'udi Arabia was settled by a treaty in 1922 that established a Neutral Zone, an area of approximately 6,500 sq km (2,500 sq mi) in which each country was to have an undemarcated half interest. In 1965, the two countries signed an agreement formally dividing the Neutral Zone and establishing a new international boundary; the agreements were ratified in 1969.

Kuwait's boundary with Iraq remains unsettled. Following Kuwait's declaration of independence in June 1961, the emir requested UK assistance to ward off an Iraqi invasion; the British forces were later replaced by troops from Arab League states. The UN upheld Kuwait's sovereignty, and in October 1963, Iraq formally recognized Kuwait's independence. In March 1973 there were armed clashes on the Iraq-Kuwait border, but a settlement was announced in June 1975; negotiations to demarcate the border have continued intermittently. Again in August 1990, Iraq invaded Kuwait, asserting their right to reclaim it as their territory. US-led international forces responded with a massive air attack in January 1991, and Iraq was defeated. Some Iraqi officials continued to assert their claim to Kuwait, and relations between the two countries remained tense. On 27 May 1993, the UN Security Council reaffirmed the established border between the two nations.

Kuwait's capital, Kuwait city, is located on the Persian Gulf coast.

²TOPOGRAPHY

Kuwait consists almost entirely of flat rolling desert and mud flats. There is a 120-m (400-ft) ridge at Mina' al-Ahmadi and a 275-m (900-ft) prominence in the southwest corner. There are no streams.

³CLIMATE

During the summer, which lasts roughly from May to October, the air generally is dry, but southeasterly winds often raise daytime humidity to 90% for a few weeks in August or September. Between November and April, the climate is pleasant, with cool nights and warm sunny days. In December and January, night temperatures occasionally touch the freezing point. Summer temperatures range from 29°C (84°F) in the morning to more than 49°C (120°F) in the shade at noon. Frost, almost unknown on the coast, is common in the interior. Annual rainfall, which averages less than 10 cm (4 in), comes in the form of showers or storms between October and April. Cloudbursts have amounted to as much as 6.4 cm (2.5 in) of rain in one day, and can heavily damage roads and houses. The prevailing northwest wind (shamal) is a cooling breeze in summer.

⁴FLORA AND FAUNA

Plants and animals are those common to the arid parts of Arabia. There is little vegetation except camel thorn in the desert and some shrubs along the coastal strip. Between October and March, however, when at intervals sufficient rain falls, the desert is transformed: grass and foliage are plentiful, flowers and plants appear in great variety, and in the spring truffles and mushrooms can be found. The fox and jackal have decreased in numbers; other mammals found in Kuwait include gerbils, jerboas, and desert hares. Reptile species include various lizards, geckos, and snakes. Fish are plentiful. Among the species of migratory birds are

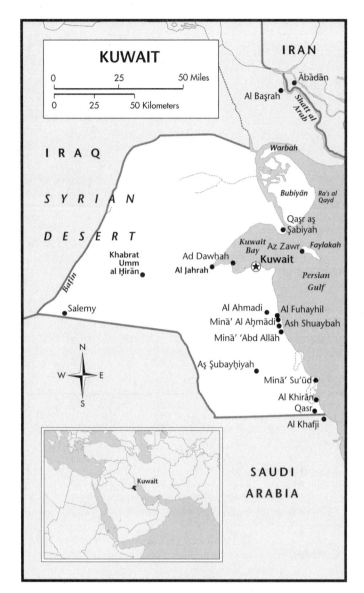

KUWAIT

| 0 | 25 | 50 Miles |
| 0 | 25 | 50 Kilometers |

IRAN
Ābādān
Al Baṣrah
Shatt al Arab

I R A Q

S Y R I A N

D E S E R T

Warbah

Bubiyān   Ra's al Qayd

Qaṣr aṣ Ṣabiyah
Kuwait Bay   Az Zawr   Faylakah
Ad Dawḥah   ⊛ Kuwait
Khabrat Umm al Ḥirān
Al Jahrah
Persian Gulf

Salemy
Baṭin

Al Ahmadi   Al Fuhayhil
Minā' Al Aḥmādi   Ash Shuaybah
Minā' 'Abd Allāh

N
W   E
S

Aṣ Ṣubayḥiyah
Minā' Su'ūd
Al Khirān
Qaṣr
Al Khafji

SAUDI
ARABIA

Kuwait

LOCATION: 28°32' to 30°6'N; 46°33' to 48°27'E. **BOUNDARY LENGTHS:** Persian Gulf shoreline, 212 km (132 mi); Sa'udi Arabia, 163 km (101 mi); Iraq, 257 km (160 mi). **TERRITORIAL SEA LIMIT:** 12 mi.

swallows, wagtails, chiffchaff, skylarks, wrens, eagles, cormorants, hoopoes, and terns.

[5] ENVIRONMENT

The Persian Gulf War of 1991 and its aftermath caused severe environmental problems for Kuwait, releasing large quantities of oil into the environment and threatening the water supply. Kuwait has no renewable water resources and must rely on wells and desalination of sea water. The nation has some of the largest and most advanced desalination plants in the world, which provides much of its water. Kuwait's cities produce 0.9 million tons of solid waste per year. In 1994, five of Kuwait's mammal species and seven of its bird species were endangered. One plant species was also endangered.

[6] POPULATION

The Kuwaiti population declined on average by 6.5% per year during 1990-95, due in part to the Iraqi invasion and Gulf War of 1990-91. According to the 1995 census, Kuwait had a total population of 1,575,983, of which only 655,820 were Kuwaiti citizens. However, by 2000, the Kuwaiti population rose to an estimated 2,067,728. An estimated 1.8% of the population is 65 years of age or older. The projected population for the year 2005 is 2,437,000, assuming a crude birthrate of 19 per 1,000 population and a death rate of 3, resulting in a natural rate of change of 1.6% for the period 2000–2005. The population rate of change between 1995 and 2000 was 3.0%. The population density in 1998 was 105 per sq km (272 per sq mi).

It was estimated that 98% of the population lived in urban areas in 2000, up from 90% in 1980. The capital city, Kuwait, and its surrounding metropolitan area had a 2000 population of 1,187,000.

[7] MIGRATION

With the discovery of oil and the consequent rise in living standards, Kuwait acquired a large immigrant population, attracted by jobs, free education for their children, and free medical care. The number of foreign residents more than doubled during the 1970s, and in 1994 they accounted for an estimated 56.4% of the population. After the Persian Gulf war, Kuwait deported tens of thousands of foreign workers from countries whose leaders had backed Iraq in the conflict. Of the estimated 400,000 Palestinians living in Kuwait before the 1990–91 Gulf War, reportedly only about one-sixth were allowed to remain. Only about 120,000 of the 220,000 prewar Bedouins (mostly nomads from Syria, Jordan, and Iraq) were allowed to stay. These stateless Arabs had remained in Kuwait under Iraqi occupation and were suspected of collaboration. Most other foreign workers were able to return to their home countries. By 1996, however, Egyptians, Pakistanis, Filipinos and others had filled the void that the previous foreign workers left behind.

In 1999, the total estimated number of persons of concern to UNHCR in Kuwait was 25,000, including some 15,000 Iraqis, 8,000 Palestinians from Gaza holding Egyptian Travel Documents (ETDs), and 2,000 Somalis. There were also an estimated 117,000 Bedouins awaiting a resolution to their legal status. The citizenship law requires Arabs to have 8 years of continuous residence before applying for Kuwaiti citizenship; others need 15 years. In 1999, the net migration rate was 20.65 migrants per 1,000 population.

[8] ETHNIC GROUPS

Ethnic Kuwaitis are mostly descendants of the tribes of Najd (central Arabia) but some descend from Iraqi Arabs. Still others are of Iranian origin. The number of non-Kuwaitis are divided roughly in half between Arabs and non-Arabs such as Iranians, Indians, Pakistanis, and Filipinos. In 1999, 45% of the population was Kuwaiti, 35% other Arab, 9% South Asian, 4% Iranian, and 7% other.

[9] LANGUAGES

Arabic is the official language. The Arabic spoken in Kuwait is closer to classical Arabic than to the colloquial Arabic spoken in many other parts of the Middle East. English is used generally by business people, employees of oil companies, foreign residents, and students, and it is the second language taught in the schools.

[10] RELIGIONS

Muslims comprise about 85% of the population (Sunni 45%, Shi'a 40%). Other religious groups are present, primarily among foreign worker groups, and these include Christians (mostly Roman Catholics and Anglicans), Hindus, Parsis, and others. Islam is the official religion of the state.

11 TRANSPORTATION

Kuwait has a modern network of roads, with all-weather highways running north to Iraq and south to Sa'udi Arabia. Roadways extended 4,450 km (2,777 mi) in 1996, including 3,587 km (2,229 mi) of paved roads. In 1995 there were some 545,000 passenger cars, and 155,000 commercial taxis, trucks, and buses in use. Land transport accounts for a significant share of Kuwait's imports and exports. There are no railways.

Kuwait has five ports, including a cargo port at Ash-Shuwaykh, on Kuwayt Bay, and an oil port at Mina' al-Ahmadi that is equipped with a huge pier at which eight large tankers can be loaded simultaneously. In 1998, Kuwait had 49 merchant ships in service with a capacity of 2,509,061 GRT. Kuwait has regular calls from ocean shipping, and local sailing craft carry goods between Kuwait and the neighboring sheikhdoms, Iraq, and Sa'udi Arabia. Sea transport accounts for most of Kuwait's foreign trade.

In 1998 there were 8 airports, 4 of which had paved runways. The principal airport is located at the city of Kuwait. Air transportation is highly advanced, with Kuwait Airways providing service to and from the major Middle Eastern and European cities. In 1997 the airline carried 2,114,000 passengers on domestic and international flights.

12 HISTORY

The historical records of the Arab coast of the Persian Gulf are meager. Archaeological discoveries on Faylakah Island reveal an ancient civilization about 2800 BC that had trade links with the Sumerians. By the 6th century BC, this part of the Gulf was a principal supply route for trade with India. There is evidence of early migrations to the East African coast by the seafaring inhabitants. The historical turning point for the entire Arabian Peninsula was the conversion of the people to Islam in the 7th century AD, during the lifetime of Muhammad.

Kuwait's recent history starts in 1716, when several clans of the tribe of Aniza migrated from the interior of the Arabian Desert to a tiny Gulf coastal locality, later to be called Kuwait (a diminutive of the word kut, meaning "fort"). In 1756, the settled tribesmen rallied around the As-Sabah family and chose as their ruler Sheikh Sabah 'Abd ar-Rahim, founder of the present ruling dynasty. During the latter part of the century, raids by land and by sea resulted in the decline of Kuwait, but after the British suppression of piracy in the region, trading and shipbuilding prospered.

During the period in which Sheikh 'Abdallah as-Sabah ruled Kuwait (1866–92), a dynastic battle raged in Arabia between the rival houses of Ar-Rashid and As-Sa'ud. The Ottoman Turks, supporting Ibn Rashid, sought to extend their control over the coastal area to the south of Kuwait. Fearing that his territory would be lost to the Turks which considered it part of their province of Basra, Sheikh Mubarak as-Sabah (r.1896–1915) asked to be taken under British protection. The British were concerned not only because of the Turkish claims but also because the Russians were seeking to set up a coaling station in Kuwait, and both the Germans and the Turks had planned to make it a terminus of the Berlin–Baghdad railroad. In 1899, Sheikh Mubarak agreed not to alienate any of his territory or to receive representatives of any foreign power without British consent. In return, the British offered their services as well as an annual subsidy to support the sheikh and his heirs.

On 19 June 1961, the protective treaty relations with the UK were terminated by mutual consent, and Kuwait declared itself fully sovereign and independent. By this time, the sheikhdom had already become a major oil producer and had acquired a controlling interest in the petroleum industry. Iraq refused to recognize Kuwait's independence, asserting it had inherited the Ottoman claim to the territory. Baghdad's threat of an invasion was foiled by the dispatch of British troops and later the support for Kuwait of the Arab League. Iraq then appeared to acquiesce in Kuwait's sovereignty, although border issues were never definitely resolved. During the next two decades, Kuwait succeeded in establishing an open and prosperous economy, based in large part on foreign, especially Palestinian and Egyptian, labor.

During the Iran-Iraq War, Kuwait, albeit technically neutral, rendered important assistance to Baghdad, including the transshipment of goods and the provision of over $6 billion in loans. As a response, members of Kuwait's large Shi'a minority and other radical dissidents waged a war of terrorism against the government. Throughout the 1980s, there were bombings, assassination attempts, hijackings, and sabotage against oil facilities.

In 1987, Iranian attacks on Persian Gulf shipping led Kuwait to request US protection for its supertankers. Washington agreed and when a "reflagged" Kuwaiti vessel was attacked, American forces retaliated against an Iranian offshore oil rig.

With the end of the war, Iraq-Kuwait relations were stable until 1990 when Saddam Hussein accused his neighbor of waging economic warfare against Iraq by illegally drilling oil from the shared Rumailia field, overproducing oil to drive down prices and unfairly demanding repayment of wartime loans. Tensions could not be defused by negotiations or mediation and on 2 August 1990, Iraqi forces invaded Kuwait, asserting that they were rightfully reclaiming their territory. Kuwaiti defense forces offered little resistance and most senior officials fled the country.

The US led an international coalition of Arab and other nations to demand the withdrawal of Iraqi forces. After a lengthy buildup of forces, Iraq was assaulted by massive air and land forces; after six weeks, its defenses collapsed and Kuwait was liberated in February 1991. Kuwait's leaders returned to find a disgruntled population that resented their abandonment and demanded greater political participation. Enormous physical damage had been inflicted on the country, including over 700 oil well fires that did serious ecological damage before being extinguished after almost nine months' effort.

The regime, and many Kuwaitis turned, harshly against those suspected of collaboration with Iraq. As a consequence, much of the large Palestinian community was ejected from the country.

Relations with Iraq naturally remained tense, with some Baghdad officials continuing to assert their claim to Kuwait. On 27 May 1993, the UN Security Council reaffirmed the decision of a Boundary Demarcation Commission establishing the border between the two nations. Kuwait's vulnerability to possible attack from Iraq or Iran drew the nation closer to the US, which has been willing to offer enhanced security collaboration.

In October 1994, Iraq began moving 60,000 troops to within 32 km (20 mi) of the Kuwaiti border. The UN Security Council voted unanimously to condemn Iraq's actions, and the US, UK, and other countries came to Kuwait's assistance. Kuwait agreed to allow the US to station a squadron of 24 warplanes there as part of a broad effort to curb Iraqi military power. The plan kept reserves of American warplanes and a division's worth of tanks and armor stationed in the region. On 10 November 1994 Iraq agreed to recognize the independence and current borders of Kuwait, a major step apparently aimed at allowing at least some UN sanctions against Iraq to be lifted. However, in August 1995, Iraqi troop movements along the Kuwaiti border caused alarm again, and the US began sending ships carrying equipment and supplies to the Persian Gulf. In April 1996, an international military exercise (involving forces of the US, UK, Russia, China, Italy, and other Arab nations) was held in Kuwait. The UN also renewed its multinational force of border observers in April 1996 to oversee the 14-km (9-mi) demilitarized zone that separates Kuwait from Iraq.

Although some of its neighbors in the Persian Gulf began to pursue a rapprochement with Iraq over the following years, Kuwait maintained its vigilance against the regime of Saddam Hussein. Early in 1998 it granted expanded staging areas to the US in anticipation of possible military action in response to Iraq's failure to cooperate with UN weapons inspections. At the end of 1998 it supported NATO air strikes against Iraq over the same issue. In January 1999, Kuwait placed its military on full alert in response to renewed threats from Iraq. As of 2000, a special UN commission had awarded $15.7 billion in reparations for damages suffered in Iraq's 1990 invasion of Kuwait.

In May 1999, the emir of Kuwait dissolved the National Assembly in the wake of a long-standing political deadlock between government and opposition forces. However, the opposition gained even more ground in national elections held in July, with both Islamists and liberals gaining addition seats. Among the matters awaiting parliamentary consideration was a controversial decree by the emir that would allow women to vote and run for office by the next election, scheduled for 2003.

13GOVERNMENT

According to the constitution of 16 November 1962, Kuwait is an independent sovereign Arab state, under a constitutional monarch. Executive power is vested in the emir, who exercises it through a Council of Ministers. Succession is restricted to descendants of Mubarak as-Sabah; an heir apparent must be appointed within one year of the accession of a new ruler. The emir appoints a prime minister after traditional consultations and appoints ministers on the prime minister's recommendation. Emir Sabah as-Salim as-Sabah died in December 1977 after a reign of 12 years and was succeeded by Emir Jabir al-Ahmad al-Jabir as-Sabah. The as-Sabah family, advised by wealthy merchants and other community leaders, dominates the government.

The National Assembly (Majlis) consists of 50 elected representatives and 25 appointed members. Elections are held every four years among adult literate males who resided in Kuwait before 1920 and their descendants; candidates must be Kuwaiti males at least 21 years of age. As a result, the electorate only accounts for about 10% of Kuwait's total population. In 1996, naturalized citizens who did not meet the pre-1920 qualification but had been naturalized for 30 years became eligible to vote. The assembly may be dissolved at any time by the emir. It was dissolved in 1976, as part of a political crackdown that followed the government's announced support of Syrian intervention in Lebanon. Elections were held in February 1981 and a new assembly was convened after elections in 1985; it was dissolved once again in 1986 as a result of national tensions over the Iran-Iraq war. It remained suspended until elections in October 1992. In 1993, the new Assembly actively produced new legislation, including a national budget. The emir suspended the Assembly once again in 1999, but new elections were held within two months.

14POLITICAL PARTIES

Political parties are prohibited, but opposition groups are active in the nation's political life. Several political groups act as de facto parties: Bedouins, merchants, Sunni and Shi'ite activists, and secular leftists and nationalists. Political opinions are freely expressed in informal gatherings in the homes of government officials and leading citizens.

Pro-government forces gained ground over Muslim fundamentalist candidates in the elections of 8 October 1996. Following the 1999 elections, the Assembly was split almost evenly between pro-government, liberal, and Islamic members. Pro-government forces held 13 seats, with the rest held by Islamic and liberal parties, and unaffiliated independents.

15LOCAL GOVERNMENT

There are five governorates (Ahmadi, Al Jahrah, Al Kuwayt, Hawalli, and Al Farwaniyah), but political authority is highly centralized in the capital.

16JUDICIAL SYSTEM

The system of Muslim law (the Shari'ah) was augmented by 1959 legislation that established courts of law, regulated the judicial system, and adopted modern legal codes. A tribunal of first instance has jurisdiction over matters involving personal status, civil and commercial cases, and criminal cases, except those of a religious nature. The Court of Appeals, the highest in the land, is divided into two chambers, one with jurisdiction over appeals involving personal status and civil cases, the other over appeals involving commercial and criminal cases. State security court decisions may be appealed to the court of Cassation. Ordinary criminal cases may be appealed to the High Court of Appeals. A military court handles offenses committed by members of the security forces. Religious courts, Sunni and Shi'a, decide family law matters, but there is also a separate domestic court for non-Muslims. There is no Shi'a appellate court. Shi'a cases are adjudicated by Sunni court of appeals on appeal.

While the 1962 constitution guarantees an independent judiciary, the executive branch retains control over its administration and budget. The Emir, after recommendation of the Justice Ministry, appoints judges in the regular courts. Kuwaiti nationals receive lifetime appointments; non-Kuwaiti judges receive renewable terms of one to three years.

The constitution gives the authority to pardon and commute sentences to Emir. The Special State Security Court was abolished in 1995.

17ARMED FORCES

Kuwait's rebuilt armed forces totaled 15,300 volunteers in 2000. The army had 11,000 men equipped with 150 main battle tanks and another 218 on order; the air force had 2,500 men and 76 combat aircraft; and the navy, 1,800 men, and 5 patrol craft. There is a 5,000-member National Guard. UN observers and advisors number 149. The US provides an air defense training battery. Estimated defense expenditures in 1998–99 were $2.7 billion or 7.9% of GDP.

18INTERNATIONAL COOPERATION

Kuwait was admitted to UN membership on 14 May 1963 and is a member of ESCWA and all the nonregional specialized agencies except WIPO. It belongs to the Arab League, G-77, OPEC, and OAPEC; in 1981, it was a leader in forming the GCC with Sa'udi Arabia and four other Gulf states. Kuwait is a signatory of the Law of the Sea and a member of the WTO.

19ECONOMY

The discovery of oil in 1934 transformed the economy. Kuwait's enormous oil reserve of 94 billion barrels and huge quantities of natural gas have provided the base for an economic presence of worldwide significance. The Kuwaiti standard of living was among the highest in the Middle East and in the world by the early 1980s. Oil wealth has stimulated trade, fishery development, and service industries. The government has used its oil revenues to build ports, roads, an international airport, a seawater distillation plant, and modern government and office buildings. The public has also been served by the large-scale construction of public works, free public services, and highly subsidized public utilities, transforming Kuwait into a fully developed welfare state. Prudent management of budgetary allocations and development priorities, as well as substantial interest from overseas investment, helped cushion the adverse impact of the collapse of the Souk al-Manakh—an unregulated curbside securities market—in 1982, the collapse in world oil prices during the mid-1980s, and the 1980–88 Iran-Iraq war. In addition, acquisition in Western Europe of 5,000 retail outlets (marketed under the name "Q-8") and expansion into the manufacture and sale of refined oil products bolster the Kuwaiti economy.

Oil extraction and processing accounts for about 50% of GDP, 90% of export earnings, and 75% of government revenues. Kuwait's economy suffered enormously from the effects of the Gulf War and the Iraqi occupation, which ended in February 1991 with the destruction of much of Kuwait's oil production capacity and other economic infrastructure. The damage inflicted on the economy was estimated at $20 billion. Real growth in the GDP was estimated at 22.4% in 1993, 1.1% in 1994, and 3% in 1995. Economic improvement from 1994 to 1997 was largely from growth in the industrial and financial sectors. The "Difficult Debts Law," which aided investors with losses incurred during the Iraqi invasion and an informal stock crash in the early 1980's significantly improved investor confidence. Reversing this trend, the economy shrank in 1998 by 5% due to a large decline in world oil prices. GDP in that same year declined by 16%. The government expected a continuing budget deficit in following years.

20INCOME

The US Central Intelligence Agency (CIA) reports that in 1998 Kuwait's gross domestic product (GDP) was estimated at $43.7 billion. The per capita GDP was estimated at $22,700. The annual growth rate of GDP was estimated at -5%. The CIA defines GDP as the value of all final goods and services produced within a nation in a given year and computed on the basis of purchasing power parity (PPP) rather than value as measured on the basis of the rate of exchange. It was estimated that agriculture accounted for 0% of GDP, industry 55%, and services 45%.

Private consumption includes expenditures of individuals, households, and nongovernmental organizations. It was estimated that between 1990 and 1998 private consumption grew at an annual rate of 5.7%.

21LABOR

In 1996, the civilian labor force amounted to 1,140,000 and the government continued its postwar policy of reducing the number of expatriate workers, but with limited success. At the end of 1992, about 437,000 non-Kuwaitis were working in the private sector, and approximately 50,000 in the government sector. Also, over 100,000 non-Kuwaitis work as domestic servants. The private sector expatriate work force includes Egyptians, Indians, and other groups.

Approximately 50,000 workers belonged to one of the fourteen unions in 1999. Twelve of these unions belonged to the Kuwait Trade Union Federation, the only trade federation allowed by law. The government performs a pervasive supervisory role of all unions, both subsidizing union expenses and carefully monitoring union activities. The right to strike is severely limited, and strikes rarely occur.

About 10% of union members are foreign workers, but foreign workers must be in Kuwait for five years before they join a union and then may not vote in elections or hold official positions.

The Ministry of Social Affairs and Labor controls manpower allocation, employment of foreign workers, vocational training, enforcement of labor regulations, and industrial relations. The General Confederation of Kuwaiti Workers is sponsored by the government. In general, all workers are entitled to a 48-hour workweek, compensation for overtime, sick leave, termination pay, and access to arbitration for settlement of disputes. However, many laborers from developing countries are willing to tolerate poor or unhealthy working conditions in order to earn a wage significantly higher than in their own countries.

The minimum working age is 18, although children who are at least 16 may work limited hours in nonhazardous occupations. Foreign workers must be at least 18 to work in Kuwait. In 1999, the public sector minimum wage was about $742 per month for citizens and $296 per month for noncitizens.

22AGRICULTURE

Only 0.3% of the total land area is utilized for the cultivation of crops; permanent pasture land amounts to 7.7% of total land area. Despite the absence of rivers and streams, and the paucity of rain, the development of agriculture has been actively pursued. The government apportions arable land at nominal prices on a long-term basis among farmers to stimulate production of vegetables and other crops. It also provides farmers with long-term loans and low-cost irrigation. The state has supplied extension services and demonstration centers for new farming techniques in the attempt to increase agricultural production. Nevertheless, farming contributed less than 1% of the non-oil GDP before the Gulf War. Agricultural output in 1998 included 118,000 tons of vegetables and melons, and 8,000 tons of fruit.

23ANIMAL HUSBANDRY

When the desert is green (from the middle of March to the end of April), about one-fourth of Kuwait's meat supply is provided locally. The 1998 livestock population included: cattle, 22,000; sheep, 445,000; goats, 125,000); and chickens, 26,000,000. Kuwait's poultry production has recovered from damages inflicted during the 1990 invasion. Production in 1998 was estimated at 33,000 tons, exceeding the previous high of 21,000 tons in 1989. A small number of Bedouins raise camels, goats, and sheep for meat and milk.

24FISHING

Small boats catch enough fish to satisfy local demand. Species caught include sardines, mackerel, tuna, shark (for the fins exported to China), barracuda, and mullet. Crabs, crayfish, and oysters are plentiful, and undik and zubaidi (butterfish) are both tasty and very popular. Shrimp are produced for a growing export market. The fish catch in 1997 totaled 7,980 tons, down from 8,466 in 1993 but up from the low of 2,034 in 1991, the year of the Iraqi invasion.

25FORESTRY

There are no natural forests in Kuwait. The government's afforestation projects cover an area of about 2,000 hectares (4,900 acres). Imports of forest products totaled $94 million in 1997.

26MINING

Aside from petroleum and natural gas, the only minerals and mineral products are cement and fertilizer. The production plants of both the cement and fertilizer industries were damaged by retreating Iraqi troops during the Gulf War. Cement production rose from 98,000 tons in 1991 to 500,000 tons in 1996; ammonia production (nitrogen content) was 325,000 tons, and urea production was 400,000 tons.

27ENERGY AND POWER

The Persian Gulf is geologically unique: sedimentary deposits are combined with large, relatively unbroken folding that results in underground oil reservoirs 16 to 240 km (10–150 mi) long, containing billions of barrels of oil. Kuwait's known petroleum deposits outrank those of any other country except Sa'udi Arabia and Iraq. With proved reserves of about 96.5 billion barrels (13.3 billion tons) in early 2000, Kuwait possesses 9.5% of the known global resources of petroleum.

Since its liberation from Iraqi occupation in February 1991, Kuwait has focused on the quick rebuilding of its pre-invasion oil-based economy. During the occupation, oil production totally ceased following Iraqi sabotage and the havoc of Operation Desert Storm (the name of the allied military operation to free Kuwait). Iraqi troops had blown up 752 wells; 603 were ablaze while another 44 were gushing oil, creating oil lakes throughout the country. By November 1991, the fires were extinguished and the wells were under control, but the sabotage resulted in the loss of 1.1 billion barrels of oil. Crude oil production resumed in June 1991, exports in August 1991. The US firm, Bechtel Corp., was hired to oversee the reconstruction of Kuwait's oil, gas, and petrochemical facilities. Losses during the invasion had cost Kuwait $120 million per day. By 1994, Kuwait's oil industry was back to full strength, producing a total of 2.0 million barrels a day, a rate last reached in 1989. Kuwait plans to expand production and to win new markets in Asia, Europe and the US. Kuwait's growth strategy has been influenced by the Gulf War.

In 1998, Kuwait had a crude oil output averaging 2,000,000 barrels per day. The cost of production is perhaps the lowest in the world because Kuwait's vast pools of oil lie fairly close to the surface and conveniently near tidewater; the oil rises to the surface under its own pressure and, owing to a natural gradient, flows downhill to dockside without pumping. Reserves of natural gas in early 1999 were estimated at 1.5 trillion cu m (52.7 trillion cu ft); 9.3 billion cu m (170 billion cu ft) of natural gas were produced in 1997.

Oil was first discovered in commercial quantities in 1936, but only small amounts were produced before the end of World War II. In 1960, the Kuwait National Petroleum Co. (KNPC) was organized (60% government owned and 40% privately owned) to participate in all phases of the oil industry from prospecting to final sales. KNPC has a monopoly on all petroleum sold domestically and, since 1968, has operated a refinery complex at Sha'iba.

The Kuwait Oil Co. (KOC), originally owned in equal shares by British Petroleum Co. (BP) and Gulf Oil Corp., discovered commercial oil fields at Burgan, Magwa, Mina' al-Ahmadi, and Minagish in southern Kuwait, and at Rawdhatain, Sabriya, and Al-Bahrah in the north. Commercial production began in 1946, and from 1951 on, a 50–50 profit-sharing plan governed the split of revenue between the company and the emir. KOC's concession (which was to run to the year 2026) had covered all of Kuwait and its territorial waters, but in May 1962, it relinquished nearly half its area to the state. The Arabian Oil Co., owned by Japanese industrial interests, operates in the offshore region of the partitioned zone which is jointly administered by both Sa'udi Arabia and Kuwait. A London-based subsidiary, Kuwait Petroleum International (KPI), was organized in 1983 to manage newly acquired distribution outlets, mainly in Europe. As of 1996, Kuwait was privatizing many of its state-owned companies, upon the recommendation of the World Bank. Privatization moves include the 1995 sale of nearly $1 billion in assets of the Kuwait Investment Authority. In March 1996 the Kuwait National Petroleum Company announced it would sell off 80% of its retail assets. In 1998, the government approved the merger of Kuwait National Petroleum and Kuwait Oil Company, which would consolidate the state's production and refinery operations as part of a continuing effort to streamline the industry.

The Kuwait government owns and controls all oil production within its boundaries through the Kuwait Petroleum Corp., the KNPC's parent company, and it has a 30% share in offshore operations in the partitioned zone. Kuwait's policy with regard to oil before the Iraqi invasion was to conserve its reserves as much as possible, primarily to stabilize prices. This policy, however, failed to prevent falling prices in the 1980s, and petroleum export revenues declined from $19.5 billion in 1980 to $6.3 billion in 1986. In 1995, oil exports brought in 89% of foreign revenues, or $11.2 billion.

All electric power is produced thermally from oil or natural gas. Installed capacity has grown dramatically during the past two decades and reached 6.9 million kW in 1998. Electric power production increased from 2,661 million kWh in 1970 to 20,610 million kWh in 1990 before falling to only 9,100 million kWh in 1991, due to the Iraqi invasion. In 1998, electricity generation totaled 26,995 million kWh. Most of the country is provided with electrical service; electric refrigeration and air conditioning are widely available. An extensive diesel power generating system serves outlying villages.

28 INDUSTRY

Although oil extraction continues to be the economic mainstay, Kuwait has diversified its industry. Small-scale manufacturing plants produce ammonia, fertilizer, paper products, processed foods, and other consumer goods. In 1999, Kuwait's refineries produced 2 million barrels per day of refined petroleum products; major refinery products were fuel oil, gas oil, naphtha, kerosene, and diesel fuel. Industrial products include desalinated water, chemical detergents, chlorine, caustic soda, urea, concrete pipes, soap, flour, cleansers, asbestos, and bricks. The construction industry is highly developed.

Manufacturing all but stopped during the Iraqi invasion due to shortages of inputs and looting of equipment. After liberation the sector was hard-hit by the departure of Palestinian skilled labor. Low international oil prices have cut down on the value of industrial exports.

29 SCIENCE AND TECHNOLOGY

High technology in Kuwait has been largely confined to the oil industry and has been imported, along with the scientists and technicians needed to install and operate oil refineries and related facilities.

The Kuwait Institute for Scientific Research, founded in 1967 at Safat, promotes and conducts scientific research in the fields of food resources, water resources, oil sector support, and environmental studies. The Agriculture Affairs and Fish Resources Authority has an experimental research station in Safat.

Kuwait University, founded in 1962 at Safat, has colleges of science, medicine, engineering and petroleum, medicine, and allied health sciences and nursing. The College of Technological Studies, in Shuwaikh, was founded in 1976. The Telecommunications and Navigation Institute, at Safat, was founded in 1966. In 1987–97, science and engineering students accounted for 29% of college and university enrollments.

30 DOMESTIC TRADE

Until the early 1960s, the traditional small shop or market stall dominated retail trade. In recent decades, however, modern business centers with hundreds of new shops and offices have opened, and some smaller villages have developed retail stores with impressive stocks of foreign goods. The city of Kuwait is the distribution center for the emirate and serves the transit trade of nearby states.

Usual business hours in summer (May to October) are from 6 AM to noon and from 4 to 6 PM; during the rest of the year, from 7 AM to noon and from 3 to 6 PM. Stores are closed Fridays.

31 FOREIGN TRADE

Kuwait had maintained a boycott of imports from Israel. However, after liberation, Kuwait relaxed regulations relating to this, so that Israeli companies previously subject to boycott were permitted to do business in Kuwait. Kuwait also announced a trade embargo against the countries which it regarded as having supported Iraq during the occupation—Jordan, Yemen, Tunisia, Sudan, Algeria, and Mauritania. Major export partners in 1997 were Japan (24%), India (16%), the US (13%), South Korea (11%), and Singapore (8%). Imports came primarily from the US (22%), Japan (15%), the UK (13%), Germany (8%), and Italy (6%).

The export of crude petroleum sustains Kuwait, accounting for the vast majority of commodity exports (94%), and 6.0% of the world market. Other exports include fertilizers (1.1%) and aircraft (.49%).

In 1996 Kuwait's imports were distributed among the following categories:

Consumer goods	19.8%
Food	14.2%
Fuels	0.4%
Industrial supplies	24.5%
Machinery	24.8%
Transportation	16.2%
Other	0.1%

32 BALANCE OF PAYMENTS

Kuwait enjoys a highly favorable payments position because of its huge trade surpluses. The Kuwaiti dinar is completely covered by the country's reserve fund, 50% of which must be in gold.

The US Central Intelligence Agency reports that in 1997 the purchasing power parity of Kuwait's exports was $14.3 billion while imports totaled $7.8 billion resulting in a trade balance of $6.5 billion.

The International Monetary Fund (IMF) reports that in 1998 Kuwait had exports of goods totaling $9,614 million and imports totaling $7,714 million. The services credit totaled $1,762 million and debit $5,483 million. The following table summarizes Kuwait's balance of payments as reported by the IMF for 1998 in millions of US dollars.

Current Account		2,527
Balance on goods	1,900	
Balance on services	-3,721	
Balance on income	5,867	
Current transfers	-1,520	
Capital Account		79
Financial Account		-2,920
Direct investment abroad	1,867	
Direct investment in Kuwait	59	
Portfolio investment assets	-4,768	
Portfolio investment liabilities	...	
Other investment assets	646	
Other investment liabilities	-725	
Net Errors and Omissions		571
Reserves and Related Items		-256

33 BANKING AND SECURITIES

The Central Bank of Kuwait, established in 1969, formulates and implements the nation's monetary policy, regulates the currency, and controls the banking system. There are seven commercial banks with 96 branches in Kuwait, of which one is a single-branch operation belonging to a joint-venture bank (the Bank of Bahrain and Kuwait). Apart from this special case, foreign banks are not permitted to operate within Kuwait or to own shares in Kuwaiti-banks. Kuwaiti bank shares are typically closely held, either by the government and its agencies or by the merchant families who founded them. The preeminent bank is the National

Bank of Kuwait, which at the end of 1999 accounted for one-third of all Kuwaiti bank branch assets.

The Central Bank of Kuwait only took on a serious regulatory role in 1984, after a debt crisis engulfed commercial banks, all of which had exposure to the collapsed informal stock market. However, the Central Bank's powers are limited, and, although it considers some of the banks to be too weak to be competitive, it has so far been unable to force mergers.

There are three specialized banks, one of which, Kuwait Finance House, operates as a commercial bank restricted to Islamic financial transactions. The other two, Industrial Bank of Kuwait and Kuwait Real Estate Bank, were created to provide long-term credit at a time when the supply of fresh capital from the public sector was not constrained. In the more austere environment since the war, they function like a US investment bank. The idea of establishing more Islamic banks has been welcomed.

Kuwait's official securities exchange, the Kuwait Stock Exchange (KSE), first introduced in 1962, was founded in 1977, and handles only government bonds and securities of Kuwaiti companies. An unofficial and unregulated securities exchange, the Souk al-Manakh, listing the stocks of 45 Gulf companies outside Kuwait and considered highly speculative, collapsed suddenly in August 1982. At the time of the crash, some 6,000 investors and $94 billion in postdated checks drawn in anticipation of future stock price increases were said to be involved. In order to limit the effect of the collapse on the Kuwaiti economy, the government created a special rescue fund to pay compensation to small investors for validated claims. All trading operations of the KSE were suspended on the Iraqi invasion of Kuwait on 2 August 1990. The KSE recommenced trading on 28 September 1992. On the exchange, 1995 was a banner year. The combined effect of rapidly expanding credit and privatization resulted in a 36% increase in the stock price index and a 226% increase in trading volume. At the end of 1995, 51 companies were listed with a total capitalization of KD3.33 billion ($11.2 billion). Only Gulf Cooperation Council (GCC) citizens are permitted to buy shares in Kuwaiti companies.

34 INSURANCE

The insurance sector is closed to foreign institutions. As of 1997, it was dominated by three companies: Al Awhile, Warble, and Kuwait Insurance Co. Marine, fire, accident, and life insurance policies constitute the bulk of all policies issued. Third-party liability insurance for motor vehicles is compulsory.

35 PUBLIC FINANCE

Much of the recent improvement in public finances is the result of higher oil prices and production, rather than government reforms. In 1994, the Kuwaiti government began to consider various austerity measures, which became a source of debate in parliament. Several plans in discussion call for reductions in government subsidies and welfare benefits, increases in taxes, privatization of state-owned businesses, and banking sector reforms. Subsidies are one of the most contentious and politicized austerity measures; in 1995, the Ministry of Finance stated that the country annually spends $1.8 billion on utility subsidies and free health care. The Kuwaiti cabinet passed a reform package in 1999, including a reduction in subsidies and increasing taxes on luxury goods.

The US Central Intelligence Agency (CIA) estimates that in 1998 Kuwait's central government took in revenues of approximately $8.1 billion and had expenditures of $14.5 billion including capital expenditures of $154.5 million. Overall, the government registered a deficit of approximately $6.4 billion.

The following table shows an itemized breakdown of government revenues and expenditures. The percentages were calculated from data reported by the International Monetary Fund. The dollar amounts (millions) are based on the CIA estimates provided above.

REVENUE AND GRANTS	100%	8,100
EXPENDITURES	100%	14,500
General public services	9.6%	1,397
Defense	20.3%	2,938
Public order and safety	9.7%	1,401
Education	11.9%	1,731
Health	7.4%	1,074
Social security	18.6%	2,698
Housing and community amenities	3.3%	483
Recreation, cultural, and religious affairs	3.6%	517
Economic affairs and services	10.9%	1,583
Other expenditures	4.7%	678

36 TAXATION

Income from oil concessions is based on royalties, generally at the rate of 50% or higher. Individual or local company incomes are tax exempt. Profits of foreign corporations are taxed at rates ranging from 5-55% of the total Kuwait-source profit. The only other tax is a 5% levy on a shareholding company's profit payable to the Kuwait Foundation for Scientific Research. Kuwaiti citizens are exempt from paying taxes. The government passed a law to introduce limited taxation in 2000, in the form of sales taxes.

37 CUSTOMS AND DUTIES

Customs duties are generally 4% ad valorem, but some goods are admitted duty-free and the tariff on cigarettes was raised to 70% as of July 1997. Imports of liquor are prohibited by law. Protective tariffs may be levied at up to 25%.

38 FOREIGN INVESTMENT

Through tax concessions, Kuwait welcomes foreign investment in heavy and light industries. While foreign investment is not permitted in certain sectors such as banking or insurance, it is restricted to less than 49% of ownership shares in permitted areas. A sizable proportion of public and private savings in Kuwait is held in the form of foreign assets. In July 1995, the Union Carbide Corp. and Kuwait's Petrochemical Industries Co. began construction of a $2 billion petrochemical plant, the biggest joint venture involving a foreign company in Kuwait. Foreign investment totaled $110 million in 1995. Kuwait's foreign portfolio investments are estimated at up to $45 billion. Major foreign investors in Kuwait in 1998 included Japan's Arabian Oil Company, and the US-owned Texaco.

39 ECONOMIC DEVELOPMENT

Since the mid-1970s, Kuwait has restrained its spending on economic development and has fostered a policy of controlled growth. From 1977 to 1982, allocations for development projects remained steady at $1.7–2.5 billion annually, of which 76% was spent on public works, electric power plants, and desalination and irrigation projects. Development plans for the 1980s, stressing industrial diversification, included the expansion of local oil refineries and major projects in petrochemicals, electricity, water supply, highway construction, and telecommunications. Overseas, refining and marketing operations were stepped up.

Post-war economic planning was hampered by the expulsion of the mainly Palestinian middle-ranking civil servants in various government departments. The Industrial Bank of Kuwait has played a major role in the industrial redevelopment of the emirate following the war. In 1994, the World Bank urged Kuwait to begin privatization (including the oil industry). The Kuwait Investment Authority sold nearly $1 billion of its foreign assets in 1995. In March 1996, Kuwait National Petroleum Co. announced that it would sell off one-third of its 90 gasoline stations as a preliminary move in divesting 80% of its retail assets.

In December 1961, Kuwait established the Kuwait Fund for Arab Economic Development, patterned after Western and international lending agencies, to issue loans at low rates of interest for Arab economic development. By the end of 1985, Kuwait had extended loans to developing countries amounting to $4.3 billion. The Kuwait-based Arab Fund for Economic and Social Development also has contributed to various development institutions. However, in 1990 the AFESD transferred its operations to Bahrain. Since Iraq's invasion most of Kuwait's aid commitments have taken the form of government-to-government agreements.

40 SOCIAL DEVELOPMENT

Kuwait has a widespread system of social welfare on a paternalistic basis, financed by government oil revenues. It offers welfare services for the poor, provides free medical service and education to all Kuwaiti citizens, and spends heavily for waterworks, public gardens, and other public facilities. Social insurance legislation enacted in 1976 provides for old age, disability, and survivor pensions, for which the worker pays 5% of earnings and the employer pays 10% of payroll. In 1999, retirement benefits ranged from 65% to 95% of earnings, depending upon the length of employment. Large subsidies for electricity, gasoline, and rice hold prices below market rates but contribute to the government's annual deficit. Kuwait in 1982 became the first Gulf state to legalize abortion, on limited health grounds.

Women are denied equal rights and legal protection under Kuwaiti law, and their testimony in a court of law is not considered to be equal to that of men. Women must first obtain their husband's permission before applying for a passport. Kuwaiti women married to foreign men suffer legal discrimination and are not entitled to government housing subsidies. Women (including foreign women) who wear Western clothing are often subject to sexual harassment. The Kuwaiti government has set up a telephone counseling hot line for battered wives and other women suffering from male violence. The Islamic Affairs Ministry started the service in November 1995 in cooperation with independent counselors for women suffering verbal, physical, sexual, or mental abuse.

Bedouin minorities face considerable legal discrimination. They are not entitled to citizenship, and are unable to work or enroll their children in schools. In addition, the abuse of foreign domestic servants is a serious and ongoing social problem.

Female political parties are banned, and women are not allowed to vote or seek national elective office. In two separate votes in late 1999 the parliament defeated initiatives that would have given women these political rights. In 1999 the government introduced a program to naturalize 4,000 of the more than 100,000 stateless persons in the country and grant permanent residency to the rest.

41 HEALTH

Kuwait has a highly advanced public health service which is extended to all Kuwait residents, citizens and noncitizens alike. In 1993, 100% of the population had access to health care services. Between 1990 and 1995, 7.0% of GDP went to health expenditures. The incidence of typhoid fever and most infectious diseases is comparatively low; however, influenza is common, and measles has resulted in a high fatality rate among children up to age 5. Between 1990 and 1994, immunization rates for children up to one year of age were as follows: tuberculosis, 93%; diphtheria, pertussis, and tetanus, 98%; polio, 98%; and measles, 97%. Common diseases were malaria (1,379 new cases in 1993) and measles (432 new cases in the same year). In 1999, 100% of the urban population had access to safe water, and 100% of the urban population had adequate sanitation. In 1994, there were 16 public hospitals and sanatoriums (with 4,271 beds) and 70 clinics and other health centers. Medical personnel included 2,717 doctors and 399 dentists in 1994. Life expectancy in 1999 was 77.1 years. In 1999, infant mortality was estimated at 10.3 per 1,000 live births. The birth rate was 20.5 per 1,000 people according to 1999 statistics. The total fertility rate was 3.3 children per woman during childbearing years. The general mortality rate in 1999 was 2.3 per 1,000 people; in 1990 and 1991, there were approximately 200,000 deaths attributed to the war between Kuwait and Iraq.

42HOUSING

For centuries, housing in Kuwait consisted of small cottages, mud huts, and a few larger dwellings built of coral and plastered with cement and limestone. Improved housing for the general population has been a main government objective. The National Housing Authority built about 50,000 dwelling units in 1977–85. Between 1989 and 1994, 25,213 applications were presented for the housing distribution program. According to the 1995 census, there were 255,477 households in Kuwait. The total number of dwellings that year was 251,682, of which 234,153 were private and 17,529 were collective dwellings. Including vacant dwellings and those under construction, the total number was 287,574 in 1995. About 50% of all housing units were apartments, 19% were villas, 15% were traditional dwellings, 10% were annexes, and 4% were shacks and other marginal dwellings.

43EDUCATION

Kuwait offers its citizens free education, including free food, clothing, books, stationery, and transportation, from kindergarten through the fourth year of college. Most expatriates are not eligible for free education and must register their children at a private school. The Ministry of Education sets tuition levels for private schools. In 1998, 142,308 students were enrolled in 286 primary schools, with 10,798 teachers. Student-to-teacher ratio stood at 13 to one. In the same year, secondary schools had 224,293 students and 21,187 teachers. Schools below university level are segregated by sex.

Kuwait University was opened in 1966 with 866 students and in 1995 had a student enrollment of 12,712 and a graduating class of 1,880. Kuwaiti nationals composed 92% of the student body. Kuwaiti students who complete their secondary-school science courses in the upper 80% of their class and arts courses in the upper 70% are eligible to study abroad at government expense. Universities and equivalent institutions had a total of 29,509 students and 1,691 teachers in 1997. For the year 2000, adult illiteracy rates were estimated at 17.7% (males, 15.7%; females, 15.7%).

The government has adopted a program to wipe out illiteracy by opening adult education centers. The estimated rate of illiteracy in 1995 was 21.4% (males: 17.8%, females: 25.1%).

44LIBRARIES AND MUSEUMS

The Kuwait Central Library has over 150,000 volumes, 90% of them in Arabic; it has established 22 branches throughout the country. The Kuwait University library system has over 238,000 volumes. Other schools and the oil companies maintain special libraries. In 2000, Kuwait had 5 museums. The Kuwait Museum displays ancient Kuwaiti artifacts (recovered from excavations on Faylakah Island), as well as exhibits concerning local plant, bird, and animal life. The Educational Science in Safat Museum was established in 1972 and features sections on natural history, space, oil, health, and meteorology.

45MEDIA

The government administers telephone, television, radio, postal, and telegraph services. By 1994 damage to the telecommunications infrastructure from the Gulf War had been repaired and operations returned to normal. In 1998, 408,000 telephones were operated from a fully automatic exchange; a cellular telephone system also operates throughout Kuwait and had about 150,000 subscribers in 1996. Kuwait Television is government-controlled and has offered color broadcasts since 1974; it broadcasts over three channels. Radio Kuwait produces programs in English, Urdu, Persian, and Arabic. There are three AM radio stations and 13 television stations. In 1997, there were 688 radios, 491 television sets, and 116 mobile phones in use per 1,000 population.

As of 1999, Kuwait had approximately seven daily newspapers. Major Arabic dailies (with estimated 1999 circulations), include *Al-Seyassa* (264,100), *Al-Qabas* (115,900), *Al-Rai al-'Amm* (84,700), and *Al-Anbaa* (121,000). English-language dailies include the *Arab Times* (70,000) and *Kuwait Times* (35,000). The popular monthly magazine *Al-'Arabi* (350,000 in 1995), similar to the *Reader's Digest,* is widely read in Kuwait.

The constitution provides for freedom of speech and the press, and with a few exceptions, citizens are said to freely criticize the government in all media. The government ended pre-publication censorship in 1992. The government does not censor foreign journalists and allows them open access to the country.

As of 1996, there were over 93,000 personal computers; in 1998 there were about 30 Internet hosts in Kuwait per 1,000 population.

46ORGANIZATIONS

The Ministry of Social Affairs and Labor encourages and supports cultural and recreational organizations and sponsors theatrical activities for youth. Boy Scouts are active, and cultural and recreational centers encourage hobbies and sports. There is a chamber of commerce and industry in the capital.

47TOURISM, TRAVEL, AND RECREATION

Except for nationals of the other Gulf states, visitors must obtain visas in advance from Kuwaiti embassies or consulates. By the second anniversary of the Iraqi invasion, many of the physical scars of war and occupation had already been erased, and the government was well on its way to restoring the country's extensive prewar accommodations and amenities, although hotel prices have risen steeply since the war. In 1997, there were 2,823 hotel rooms with a total of 3,331 beds. That year there were approximately 79,000 tourist arrivals in Kuwait and receipts reached $188 million.

In 1999 the UN estimated the daily cost of staying in any area of Kuwait at $211 per day.

48FAMOUS KUWAITIS

During the reign of Emir Sir 'Abdallah as-Salim as-Sabah (1870–1965), Kuwait attained a prominent position among the great oil-producing nations of the world, and the state adopted a social welfare program founded on a unique patriarchal system; the emir was revered as a man of simplicity, devotion, and deep concern for his people. His successors as emir have been Sabah as-Salim as-Sabah (1913–77), from 1965 to 1977; and Jabir al-Ahmad al-Jabir as-Sabah (b. 1928), since 1977.

49DEPENDENCIES

Kuwait has no territories or colonies.

50BIBLIOGRAPHY

Al-Moosa, Abdulrasool, and Keith McLachlan. *Immigrant Labour in Kuwait*. Dover, N.H.: Longwood, 1985.

Assiri, Abdul-Reda. *Kuwait's Foreign Policy: City-state in World Politics*. Boulder, Colo.: Westview Press, 1990.

Cordesman, Anthony H. *Kuwait: Recovery and Security After the Gulf War*. Boulder, Colo.: Westview Press, 1997.

Crystal, Jill. *Kuwait: The Transformation of an Oil State*. Boulder, Colo.: Westview Press, 1992.

Crystal, Jill. *Oil and Politics in the Gulf: Rulers and Merchants in Kuwait and Qatar*. New York: Cambridge University Press, 1990.

Finnie, David H. *Shifting Lines in the Sand: Kuwait's Elusive Frontier with Iraq*. Cambridge, Mass.: Harvard University Press, 1992.

Ismael, J. S. *Kuwait: Social Change in Historical Perspective*. Syracuse, N.Y.: Syracuse University Press, 1982.

Khadduri, Majid. War in the Gulf, 1990-91: The Iraq-Kuwait Conflict and its Implications. New York: Oxford University Press, 1997.

Sapsted, David. *Modern Kuwait*. London: Macmillan, 1980.

Slot, B. *The Origins of Kuwait*. New York: E.J. Brill, 1991.

KYRGYZSTAN

Kyrgyz Republic
Kyrgyzstan Respublikasy

CAPITAL: Bishkek.

FLAG: Red field with a yellow sun in the center; in the center of the sun is a red ring crossed by two sets of three lines, a stylized representation of the arched opening in a Kyrgyz yurt.

ANTHEM: *Kyrgyz National Anthem.*

MONETARY UNIT: The som, established in May 1993, is the national currency. Som1=$0.02134 ($1 = som46.85) as of 31 March 2000.

WEIGHTS AND MEASURES: The metric system is in force.

HOLIDAYS: Constitution Day, 5 May; Independence Day, 31 August; National Day, 2 December.

TIME: 5 PM = noon GMT.

¹LOCATION, SIZE, AND EXTENT

Kyrgyzstan is located in southern Asia, between China and Kazakhstan. Comparatively, it is slightly smaller than the state of South Dakota with a total area of 198,500 sq km (76,641 sq mi). Kyrgyzstan shares boundaries with Kazakhstan on the N, China on the E, Tajikistan on the S, Uzbekistan on the W. The country's boundary length totals 3,878 km (2,410 mi), and its capital city, Bishkek is located in the north central part of the country.

²TOPOGRAPHY

The topography of Kyrgyzstan features the peaks of Tien Shan, which rise to 7,000 m (23,000 ft), and associated valleys and basins which encompass the entire nation. About 90% of Kyrgyzstan has an elevation exceeding 1,500 m (4,900 ft). Slightly over 5% of Kyrgyzstan's land is under irrigation.

³CLIMATE

The country's climate is continental to polar in the Tien Shan Mountains. In the Fergana Valley the average temperature in July is 28°C (82°F). In January, the mean temperature is –21°C (–5°F). The climate is temperate in the foothill regions of the north.

⁴FLORA AND FAUNA

The country's flora and fauna is similar to Tajikistan, with wildflowers in the valleys of the mountains, and yak and snow leopards in the mountains.

⁵ENVIRONMENT

Among Kyrgyzstan's most significant environmental issues are water pollution and soil salinity resulting from improper irrigation methods. The pollution of the nation's water causes health problems for 25% of its people, many of whom draw water directly from contaminated wells and streams. Eighty percent of the nation's rural dwellers do not have a publicly regulated water supply. As of 1994, 1.4% of Kyrgyzstan total land area was protected. In the same year, four mammal species and five species of birds were threatened, as well as one plant species. Threatened animal species include the great bustard, snow leopard, and tiger.

⁶POPULATION

The population of Kyrgyzstan in 2000 was estimated at 4,584,341. An estimated 5.8% of the population is 65 years of age or older. The projected population for the year 2005 is 4,829,000, assuming a crude birthrate of 22 per 1,000 population and a death rate of 9, resulting in a natural rate of change of 1.3% for the period 2000–2005. The population rate of change between 1995 and 2000 was 0.4%. The population density in 1998 was 24 per sq km (62 per sq mi).

It was estimated that 40% of the population lived in urban areas in 2000, up from 38% in 1980. The capital city, Bishkek (formerly Fronze), had a 2000 population of 662,000.

⁷MIGRATION

As of September 1999, the total number of refugees is estimated between 40,000 and 50,000 registered and unregistered (1% of the total population). There are about 13,000 officially registered refugees, mainly from Tajikistan, and about 700 from Afghanistan. The great majority of Tajik refugees are of ethnic Kyrgyz origin and desire to stay in Kyrgyzstan permanently. The government is working with UNHCR to implement an integration package to assist Tajik refugees in their transition to Kyrgyz citizenship. Between 1989-95, 296,000 Russians, 39,000 Ukrainians, and 3,000 Belarussians all departed from Kyrgyzstan. Also, 46,000 Germans (formerly deported under Stalin during World War II from Soviet and Volga regions) returned to Germany. Currently there are 17,000 ecologically displaced Kazakhs in Kyrgyzstan. In 1999, the net migration rate was -6.28 migrants per 1,000 population.

⁸ETHNIC GROUPS

Kyrgyz constituted 52.4% of the population in 1999. Russians accounted for 18%, Uzbeks for 12.9%, Ukrainians 2.5%, Germans 2.4%, and others 11.8%. About 420,000 ethnic Kyrgyz reside elsewhere in the former Soviet Union and 170,000 in China. Kyrgyz speak a Turkic language and most are Sunni Muslims. There are major ethnic and clan-based cleavages, including north-south clan and regional tensions that threaten fragmentation. According to some reports, 10% or more of Russians left Kyrgyzstan during 1991 because of ethnic tensions. Ethnic Germans, deported to Kyrgyzstan by Stalin during World War II, are also leaving Kyrgyzstan. In June 1990, in the Osh

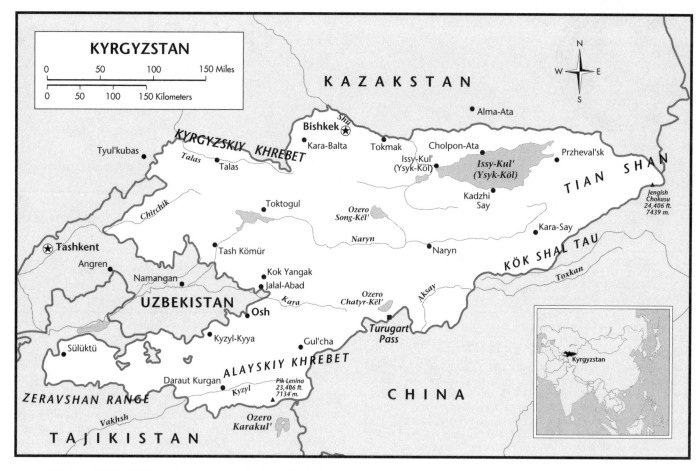

LOCATION: 41°30′N; 75°0′E. **BOUNDARY LENGTHS:** Total boundary lenths, 3,878 km (2, 410 mi); China, 858 km (533.2 mi); Kazakhstan, 1,051 km (653 mi); Tajikistan, 870 km (541 mi); Uzbekistan, 1,099 km (683 mi).

region on the eastern edge of the fertile Fergana Valley, a major ethnic conflict broke out between Kyrgyz and Uzbek inhabitants over land distribution. Approximately 250 people died in what has been termed "the most explosive region of Central Asia," because of its mixed population of Uzbeks and Kyrgyz, poverty, and high unemployment. Periodic clashes also occur between Kyrgyz and Tajiks along the border with Tajikistan over water resources. Beefed-up Kyrgyz security forces were placed in Osh and Alais regions in early 1993 to prevent spillover from fighting going on between Tajik ex-communists and oppositionists in the mountains of northern Tajikistan and to halt the inflow of Tajik refugees.

9LANGUAGES

A Turkic tongue, Kyrgyz is the official language. Until 1926, the Kyrgyz and Kazakh languages were not officially recognized as two distinct languages. Kyrgyz orthography was formally organized in 1923 and was modeled after the northern dialects using Arabic script. Afterwards, Roman letters were used until 1940, when the Cyrillic alphabet was mandated by the Soviet government, with three special additional characters. Since independence, there has been discussion about switching back to the Roman alphabet.

Although the Kyrgyz language is the traditional language, most of Kyrgyzstan's population also speaks Russian, the language of business and commerce. In March 1996, the Kyrgyzstani legislature amended the constitution to make Russian an official language, along with Kyrgyz, in territories and work places where Russian-speaking citizens predominate.

10RELIGIONS

Some 75% of the population is Muslim, mostly Sunni of the Hanafi persuasion. Approximately 20% is Russian Orthodox, and 5% practice various other religions. Although it is not known how many Roman Catholics live in Kyrgyzstan, diplomatic relations with the Vatican were opened in 1992.

11TRANSPORTATION

As of 1995, a single east-west rail line of 370 km (230 mi) went from Issyk-kul' across the Chuskaya region into Kazakhstan. There were some 18,500 km (11,496 mi) of highways, of which 16,854 km (10,473 mi) were paved in 1996. Irregular service with public transportation occurs frequently. As a landlocked nation, water transportation is of minor importance, although inland travel is possible on several east-west rivers. Kyrgyzstan has 54 airports and airfields, of which 14 have paved runways. The principal airport is Manas, located at Bishkek. In 1997, 423,000 passengers were carried on scheduled domestic and international airline flights.

12HISTORY

The area of present-day Kyrgyzstan contains evidence of human habitation from the time of the Lower Paleolithic on, approximately 300,000 years ago. Archeologists suggest that two types of economies developed in the territory—farming and pastoral nomadism. By the 7th century BC nomadism had become predominant, and the area was controlled by various tribal alliances. In the north the Saki (7th–3rd centuries BC) were succeeded by the Usuni (2nd century BC–5th century AD); in the south the Parkan state (2nd–1st centuries BC) was replaced by the Kushani kingdom (1st–4th century AD). The ethnic identity of those peoples is the subject of much debate, but they were not Turkic. From the 6th century on, various Turkic tribes began to push westward, eventually settling most of Central Asia, including Kyrgyzstan. Much of present Kyrgyzstan was united by the 7th century as part of the West Turkic Kaganate, and replaced in the 8th century by the Turgash, who in turn were conquered by the Karluk, who originated in the Altai region further north.

When the present-day Kyrgyz first came to this territory is the subject of much debate. References to tribes of that name living in the Altai occur in the 10th century, but another people with the same name who lived along the Enisei River are first mentioned in records from 2nd century BC. The Enisei Kyrgyz formed the Kyrgyz Kaganate in about AD 650, which survived until defeat by Genghiz Khan in 1209. Kyrgyz tradition prefers to see its origin in that state, but ethnographers and archeologists view the claim with considerable skepticism.

Evidence suggests instead that the present-day Kyrgyz are an amalgamation of various peoples, as existing tribes incorporated themselves into fresh waves of conquerors. The territory was part of the Karakhanid state from about 950–1150, during which the urban population was actively involved in trade and manufacturing along the Silk Road. Conversion to Islam also began in this period.

Genghiz Khan's Mongols conquered the area in the 13th century, destroying most of the Karakhanid culture and introducing large numbers of new peoples into the area, of Turkic, Mongol, and Tibetan stock. The resulting mix of tribes was almost certainly the basis for the present-day Kyrgyz people, who retain much of the memory of those origins in the orally preserved genealogies of their 40 clans and tribes. The present Kyrgyzstan flag includes the depiction of a sun with one ray for each tribe. The Kyrgyz follow Mongol practice of dividing their people into left (*ong*) and right (*sol*) "wings," said to reflect either the deployment of troops in military formation, or the tribe's original place of habitation. There is also a third group, the ichkilik, that seems to include parts of the Kyrgyz identity.

From the 15th century until the 17th century the Kyrgyz tribes were part of the larger delineation of Central Asian history, which distinguished agricultural sedents from pastoral nomads. The appearance of the same tribal names among Kazakhs, Kyrgyz, and Uzbeks suggests how the people of this territory formed a series of tribal alliances, rather than a true state.

In the 18th century the Kyrgyz began to come under pressure from Mongol tribes farther east. This prompted some of the northern tribes to send delegations to the Russians, who had pushed into Siberia in the 17th century, and who were beginning to take what is now northern Kazakhstan under its control. The Russians made no distinction between the Kazakhs and Kyrgyz, calling both Kyrgyz. The southern Kyrgyz, however, were conquered by the Kokand Khanate, established in the late 18th century, separating them from the northern Kyrgyz. This split between south and north continues to the present day in Kyrgyz life.

Russian expansion into what it called the Steppe included Kyrgyzstan. Most of northern Kyrgyzstan was incorporated into the empire by 1863; the south followed in 1876, when Russia destroyed the Kokand Khanate. Administratively, present-day Kyrgyzstan was split among four guberniias. Beginning in the 1890s Russia settled Russian and other European farmers into the fertile river valleys of the north, forcing Kyrgyz nomads higher into the mountains.

By 1916, Russia's policies of livestock requisition and land use had left the Kyrgyz badly impoverished. When Russia attempted to issue a draft call-up for Central Asian males, including the Kyrgyz, widespread fighting broke out all across the territory. The uprisings were suppressed, with great loss of life; population in the northern part dropped as much as 40%. Since independence in 1991, the state has commemorated the 1916 uprising as a genocide.

Hostility to the tsars meant that there was some support for the Bolsheviks, at least until it became clear that Lenin was not going to encourage the development of national states. Resistance to the Russians continued sporadically until the mid-1920s, in what Russian historians have labeled the Basmachi Rebellion.

As Bolshevik power was consolidated, Kyrgyzstan was first made an autonomous oblast (political unit) of the Russian Federation in 1924; it was upgraded in 1926 to an autonomous republic, but still within Russia. (At that time Russia was one of the Soviet Republics.) Kyrgyzstan did not become a full Soviet Republic until 1936.

The republic was regarded as one of the least developed of the Soviet states, politically and economically. Thus, it came as a great surprise when, on 28 October 1990, Kyrgyzstan became the first Soviet republic to select its own leader. The Kyrgyzstan legislature refused to ratify Communist Party leader Masaliyev's bid to become the republic's president, and elected instead Askar Akayev, president of the republic's Academy of Science. Akayev and his supporters began asserting Kyrgyz nationalism and wresting political and economic control over the republic from the Soviet Communist Party. These efforts were briefly interrupted by an attempted coup in Moscow by Communist Party hard-liners in August 1991. Akayev bravely condemned the coup and, after it fizzled, on 30 August 1991 he severed ties with the Communist Party and Kyrgyzstan declared its independence. On 12 October 1991, Akayev's presidency was confirmed by direct popular election.

A constitution was adopted on 5 May 1993. An economic and political crisis led to the resignation of the first government in December 1993, but Akayev's presidency was reaffirmed by a popular referendum of support conducted on 30 January 1994. Over 95% of registered voters participated in the referendum; 97% of those who voted supported President Akayev.

In September 1995, Akayev's supporters submitted a petition signed by 1.2 million (52% of the voting age population) urging the legislature to approve a referendum extending Akayev's term to the year 2001. After contentious debate, the legislature rejected holding a referendum, and Akayev instead announced that a presidential election would be held on December 24, 1995. Thirteen candidates were registered, but ten were disqualified, leaving Akayev, Masaliyev, and former speaker Medetken Sherimkulov. Akayev won reelection to a five year term, receiving 72% of about 1.9 million votes in a race deemed generally "free and fair" by international observers, though questions were raised about the disqualifications. In July 1998, Akayev hailed a Constitutional Court decision permitting him to run for a third term in the year 2000.

Severely shaking Kyrgyzstan's stability, several hundred Islamic extremists and other guerrillas entered Kyrgyzstan from Tajikistan in July-August 1999. The guerrillas seized hostages, including four Japanese geologists, and several Kyrgyz villages, stating that they would cease hostilities if Kyrgyzstan provided a safe haven for refugees and would release hostages if Uzbekistan released jailed extremists. The guerrillas were rumored to be seeking to create an Islamic state in south Kyrgyzstan as a springboard for a jihad in Uzbekistan. A Kyrgyz Security Council member in October 1999 alleged that the guerrillas were trying to seize the major drug trafficking route in southern Kyrgyzstan. Kyrgyzstan called out reservists and admitted that its military was unprepared for combat. Kyrgyzstan received air support from Uzbekistan and Kazakhstan, but protested Uzbek bombing of a Kyrgyz village. The Kyrgyz defense minister on October 18, 1999, announced success in forcing virtually all guerrillas back into Tajikistan.

13GOVERNMENT

When Kyrgyzstan was still a Soviet republic, the legislature elected Askar Akayev president. Under his leadership, Kyrgyzstan declared independence and drafted a new constitution, ratified 5 May 1993. This constitution established a democratic presidential system with separation of powers and expansive human rights guarantees. In early September 1994, Akayev's supporters in the legislature–a slim majority of 168 out of 323 sitting deputies, most of whom were local administrators–boycotted the last session of the legislature before the expiration of its mandate in February 1995. This boycott prevented formation of a quorum, causing the dissolution of the legislature. Oppositionists alleged that the timing of the dissolution was aimed to squelch a legislative investigation into corruption in the government, and to open the way for Akayev to create a more malleable legislature. Akayev took over legislative powers, and decreed that legislative elections would be held by the end of the year. He also decreed that a referendum would be held in October 1995 to approve amendments to the constitution, including provisions revamping the legislative system to weaken it relative to the presidency. He argued that legislative and other provisions of the May 1993 constitution were too "idealistic" since the "people are not prepared for democracy," and a "transitional period" was needed. Although the amendment process, like the dissolution of the legislature, contravened the constitution, the referendum questions were approved by over 80% of the voters.

Akayev spearheaded a referendum on 10 February 1996, to further alter the constitution. The amendments specify that Kyrgyzstan, or the Kyrgyz Republic, will be a secular, unitary state. It creates three branches of government: executive, legislative, and judicial. The Jogorku Kenesh, (parliament or Supreme Council), which has legislative responsibilities. The Jogorku Kenesh is made up of two houses—the 35-member Legislative Assembly and the 70-member Assembly of People's Representatives. The Legislative Assembly is responsible for day-to-day operations of the legislature, such as interpreting laws and ratifying international treaties. The Legislative Assembly also has the power to impeach the president. The Assembly of the People's Representatives meets periodically during the year to consider budget, tax, and appointment issues.

Under the 1996 amendments, the president was given expanded powers to veto legislation, dissolve the legislature, and appoint all ministers (except the prime minister) without legislative confirmation, while making legislative impeachment more difficult. The legislature confirms the prime minister and high judges.

The executive branch is comprised of the cabinet of ministers, or ministries, appointed by the president and approved by the parliament. The head of the cabinet is the prime minister, also appointed by the president and confirmed by the parliament.

The president is to be elected once every five years, for no more than two terms, from among those citizens who are between 35 and 65 years of age, who have lived at least 15 years in the republic, and who are fluent in the state language, which is Kyrgyz.

There is no vice-president. The usual functions of vice-president, including the duty to replace the president in case of death or incapacity, are borne by the speaker of the parliament, who is elected from among the membership of the parliament.

Judges are chosen by the president, subject to parliamentary affirmation. Potential judges must be citizens between 35 and 65 years who have legal training and legal experience of at least ten years. The length of their service is unlimited, but can be terminated by the parliament.

In theory, the constitution provides a number of basic guarantees of human freedom, including freedom of religion, of the press and other forms of media, of movement about the republic and place of dwelling, of association, and unarmed assembly. It guarantees the privacy of post and other forms of communication, and guarantees private property. In terms of social benefits, the constitution guarantees pensions, unemployment compensation, legal representation, medical treatment, and free basic education.

Despite restrictions on its powers, in 1997–98, the legislature showed increasing signs of independence from executive power. Moving to further weaken it, Akayev spearheaded another referendum on 17 October 1998, to amend the constitution. Approved by 91.14% of voters, the amendments sharply restricted the legislature's influence over bills involving the budget or other expenditures, limited a legislator's immunity from removal and prosecution, increased the size of the Legislative Assembly to 60, and decreased the size of the Assembly of People's Representatives to 45. It also provided for private land ownership and upheld freedom of the press. The legislature has acted in subordination to the executive branch, but has at times asserted itself by overriding presidential vetoes. In November 1999, the Assembly of People's Representatives rejected the government's budget for 2000, calling for added social and defense spending.

Kyrgyzstan's 20 February 2000 legislative election (with a runoff on March 12) reflected the erosion of Kyrgyzstan's earlier signal progress in Central Asian democratization, according to the U.S. State Department. Under new laws, fifteen seats in the upper chamber were set aside for party list voting. The Central Electoral Commission ruled that sixteen parties out of 27 legally registered were disqualified from fielding party list candidates, though it urged that such candidates could instead seek single-member seats. The major opposition Democratic Movement of Kyrgyzstan-Dignity Party bloc was initially registered but then decertified. The Organization for Security and Cooperation in Europe (OSCE) on February 8 criticized the de-certification as a narrow interpretation of the law and as restricting popular choice in the election. In all, 545 candidates were finally permitted to run for 105 seats. Six parties received over 5% of the vote, giving them seats: the Party of Communists (5 seats), Union of Democratic Forces (4), Democratic Party of Women (2), Party of Veterans (2), My Country (1), and Ata-Meken (1). Only Ata-Meken and the Communist Party are clear opposition parties. Only three constituency races were decided in the first round. In the second round on March 12, 84 members were elected in a confusing vote. Prominent opposition politician Daniyar Usenov was disqualified after the first round, although he actually had won, according to the OSCE. Similarly, opposition Dignity Party head Feliks Kulov received more votes than his opponents in the first round, but was heavily defeated in the second through apparent legerdemain, according to the OSCE. After the second round, the opposition Democratic Movement, Dignity Party, and the People's Party protested the results.

About 120 OSCE observers and 2,000 local observers monitored the election. In the first round, OSCE monitors pointed to problems such as the disqualification of prominent opposition parties and the pro-government composition of electoral boards, and in the second round criticized continued government harassment of opposition candidates, politically motivated court decisions disqualifying some opposition candidates, and irregularities in vote-counting. U.S. State Department spokesman James Foley on March 14 stressed that "the United States is disappointed in the conduct of the 2000 parliamentary election in Kyrgyzstan," which "amounted to a clear setback for the democratic process." On March 23, he criticized Kyrgyz authorities for forcibly suppressing a peaceable demonstration and for arresting Kulov the day before on vague charges of committing crimes several years ago.

14POLITICAL PARTIES

There is no formal ruling party. Over two dozen parties are legally registered, though all are small and some are inactive. Fewer than one-half of legislators claim party affiliation. Pro-Akayev parties include the Birimdik (Unity) Party (9,500 members), and the Adilet (Justice) Party (40,000 members; formed by writer Chingiz Aitmatov in October 1999). The main "constructive opposition" party is the People's Party (35,000 members). Among other parties, the Party of Communists (PCK; headed by Masaliyev; 25,000 members) calls for reunification with Russia. The Erkin (Free) Kyrgyzstan Progressive Democratic Party (12,000 members) calls for elevating the rights of ethnic Kyrgyz. Democratic Movement, (15,000 members) calls for democratic socialism. Erkin Kyrgyzstan, Asaba, the Social Democratic Party, Unity, Democratic Movement, My Country, and others decided in July 1999 to form a bloc to contest the legislative elections. The Dignity Party (11,000 members), headed by Felix Kulov (former vice president, security minister, and Bishkek mayor) was formed in August 1999. The electoral code forbade parties from taking part in the February 2000 legislative races unless they were more than one year old, eliminating eight new parties. The Central Electoral Commission in late 1999 also declared the People's, Citizens of Bishkek, Labor-Popular, and the People of Manas Parties disqualified on technicalities from taking part in the race. Religious parties are banned. Regional interests are important in the political process. The Kyrgyz leadership reportedly favors interests of the Chu region.

15LOCAL GOVERNMENT

The republic is divided into six administrative regions, plus the capital city of Bishkek. In addition, there are 43 rayons, or districts. Each oblast and rayon has a local administration consisting of a governor, and a local assembly. According to a presidential decree of March 1996, regional governors are appointed by the president to four year terms, and are responsible for making sure that the local executive and legislative branches cooperate in carrying out state decisions, for upholding law and order, for ensuring citizens' rights and freedoms, for obtaining funds to maintain local government and public property, for adhering to state budget strictures, for ensuring that taxes are collected, for making sure that local pensions and state wages are paid, and for generally ensuring the local welfare. Although in theory answering to the president, in practice some of the governors have become powerful spokesmen for regional interests, and run their districts with considerable autonomy. In October 1999, the first elections of municipal, rayon (district) and oblast (region) assemblies or keneshs took place. A new electoral law called for the candidate who gained a simple majority of votes to be declared the winner, introduced multi-seat constituencies, and dictated that only a Kyrgyz citizen who has lived in a constituency for no less than two years could become an assembly deputy.

16JUDICIAL SYSTEM

The 1993 constitution declares the independence of the judiciary from the other branches of government. Thus far, however, the courts remain under the supervision of the Ministry of Justice and continue to operate mostly under Soviet-era laws and procedures. Some judicial reforms are being introduced, such as a separate judicial budget and more judicial training. There are three levels of criminal courts: local courts, which handle petty crimes; provincial courts, which consider most categories of crime, and the appellate Supreme Court. Traditional elders' courts may also handle petty crimes in rural areas. Defendants in elders' courts may appeal to the local administrative court.

A state prosecutor, or procurator, remains responsible for criminal arrests, investigations, and presentations before a panel consisting of a judge and two people's assessors (pensioners or members of labor collectives). Since 1990 there has been a right to have legal counsel in criminal cases. In 1996, the Constitutional Court ruled that only the defense has the right of appeal. Counteracting these restrictions on prosecutorial power, the law continues to allow judges to remand a case to the procurator for further investigation, rather than to declare the defendant guilty or innocent.

Judges hold varying terms of office. Constitutional Court judges are appointed to fifteen-year terms, Supreme Court judges to ten-year terms, and first-term local court judges to three-year terms by recommendation of the president and confirmation by the Jogorku Kenesh (legislature). The 1993 constitution instituted a Western concept of judicial review by a Constitutional Court which did not exist under the former Soviet regime. Formed in 1993, the Constitutional Court reviews legislation and administrative acts for consistency with the constitution. It also considers cases on appeal involving individual rights and liberties of citizens. Constitutional Court decisions are final. There is also a Higher Court of Arbitration, and a system of lower courts for economic cases.

Compared to other Central Asian states, many observers stress, Kyrgyzstan has a less objectionable human rights record. According to the State Department's *Country Reports on Human Rights Practices for 1999*, the Kyrgyz government generally respected the human rights of its citizens, but there were problems with freedom of speech and the press, due process for the accused, religious freedom, ethnic discrimination, and electoral irregularities. There are cases of police brutality and arbitrary arrest. Citizens have only a limited ability to peaceably change their government. Elections and referenda have involved "irregular" procedures. There are independent newspapers, magazines, and radio stations, and some independent television broadcasts, though the government can influence the media through subsidies. The constitutional referendum of October 1998 aimed to make libel a noncriminal offense, though reporters continue to face civil prosecution for supposedly maligning the "honor and dignity" of public officials.

17ARMED FORCES

Active armed forces are estimated at 9,200 personnel, with 57,000 reserves. The army has 6,800 personnel and is equipped with 210 main battle tanks. An air force of 2,400 relies on aircraft and helicopters left at the former Soviet Air Force training school. There is also a paramilitary force of 3,000. Defense expenditures were estimated at $10.8 million in 1996 or 1% of GDP.

18INTERNATIONAL COOPERATION

Kyrgyzstan was admitted to the UN on 2 March 1992. The country is a member of the CIS, EBRD, ECE, ECO, IFC, IMF, UNCTAD, UNESCO, WTO, and the World Bank. As a member of the CIS, Kyrgyzstan has formal diplomatic relations with all the republics of the former Soviet Union.

The US and the EU nations, along with many others, have diplomatic relations with the country. Kyrgyzstan has especially good relations with Germany, neighboring Central Asian states, and China.

[19] ECONOMY

Kyrgyzstan is among the poorest of the post-Soviet countries. Although coal, gold, mercury, and uranium deposits are considerable, the country boasts few of the oil and gas reserves that promise a badly needed economic windfall to other Central Asian republics.

Under the presidency of Askar Akayev, the process for economic restructuring toward a free market orientation outpaced that of most other post-Soviet republics, yet the transition has been an extremely difficult one. Dissolution of the state ordering system in Kyrgyzstan and its reduction in other post-Soviet republics have disrupted the traditional supply channels and effective markets for the country's industries, severely affecting overall economic performance. As of 1995, 59.5% of enterprises had been privatized or converted to joint stock companies; privatized firms accounted for more than half the GDP that year. Some 50% of industrial firms, 75% of agriculture, and 90% of retail trade were privatized by 1995. By 1999, most of the state-owned enterprises had been sold. The Kyrgyz government instituted tight monetary and fiscal policies in 1994 that reduced inflation from 23% per month in 1993 to 5.4% in 1994 and further, to 2.3% in 1995. Inflation was up again to 18% in 1998. GDP grew by an average annual rate of 7% from 1987 to 1998, with a 1998 growth rate of 1.8%.

A reform of the government structure in early 1992 consolidated 41 ministries into 13 ministries and 7 commissions. As part of this change, the Ministry of Economy and Finance was established to assume the fiscal and economic planning duties previously carried out separately by the Ministry of Finance and the State Planning Committee. In May 1993, Kyrgyzstan was the first country of the CIS countries to announce the introduction of its own currency, the som. Although taken in order to stabilize the national economy in face of continuing turmoil in the ruble zone, this step posed a large setback to previous negotiations for a single monetary union with other post-Soviet republics. The som has been remarkably stable since 1994, and is considered the most stable currency in central Asia, although the government still faces excessive debt.

[20] INCOME

The US Central Intelligence Agency (CIA) reports that in 1998 Kyrgyzstan's gross domestic product (GDP) was estimated at $9.8 billion. The per capita GDP was estimated at $2,200. The annual growth rate of GDP was estimated at 1.8%. The average inflation rate in 1998 was 18%. The CIA defines GDP as the value of all final goods and services produced within a nation in a given year and computed on the basis of purchasing power parity (PPP) rather than value as measured on the basis of the rate of exchange. It was estimated that agriculture accounted for 47% of GDP, industry 12%, and services 41%.

The World Bank reports that for the same period per capita private consumption (in PPP terms) was $1,715. Private consumption includes expenditures of individuals, households, and nongovernmental organizations. Approximately 33% of household consumption was spent on food, 11% on fuel, 3% on health care, and 22% on education. The richest 10% of the population accounted for approximately 32% of household consumption and the poorest 10% approximately 2.7%.

[21] LABOR

In 1998, the labor force included an estimated two million persons. As of 1995, agriculture engaged 23%; industry (including mining), 9%; personal services, 35%; trade, 7%; transportation and communication, 5%, finance and business services, 1%; and other sectors, 10%.

In February 1992, a comprehensive law was passed protecting the rights of all workers to form and belong to unions. The Feder-

ation of Independent Trade Unions of Kyrgyzstan (FITUK), successor to the former Soviet-era official unions, remains the single trade union umbrella organization. Nineteen of the 20 union organizations in Kyrgyzstan are affiliated with FITUK. The exception is the union of entrepreneurs and cooperative members, which essentially is an association of over 80,000 self-employed persons.

Strikes are legally permitted. Collective bargaining was legally recognized as a right in April 1992. The standard workweek is 41 hours, and safety and health regulations in factories are often left unenforced. The government now generally allows employers to set their own wages provided they exceed a legal minimum.

[22] AGRICULTURE

In 1997, Kyrgyzstan's crop-producing land amounted to 1,425,000 ha (3,521,000 acres), or 7.4% of the total land area. About 50% of this area is used to cultivate fodder crops, 42% for winter wheat and barley, 5% for commercial crops (cotton, sugar beets, mulberry trees for silkworms, and tobacco), with the remaining 3% used for growing potatoes and other vegetables. Cultivation occurs primarily in the Shu, Talas, and Fergana valleys. About 46% of GDP was derived form agriculture in 1998. Since independence, about 75% of state farms have been privatized.

Wheat is Kyrgyzstan's main grain crop. Total wheat production was estimated by the government at 1,203,000 tons in 1998, with individual farmers accounting for 56% of production; state farms, 38%; and private households, 6%. Production of barley in 1998 was officially estimated at 161,700 tons; corn, 227,800 tons; and rice, 11,100 tons.

Tobacco is an important cash crop in Kyrgyzstan. The areas around Osh and Jalalabad in the Fergana Valley and the Talas oblast to the north of Osh are the three major tobacco growing regions. The government estimated total production at 28,100 tons in 1998.

[23] ANIMAL HUSBANDRY

About 44% of the total land area is considered permanent pastureland. Because of the rugged topography, pasture-based stock breeding is the agricultural mainstay.

Livestock in 19989 included 2,000,000 chickens, 3,350,000 sheep, 1,286,000 dairy and beef cattle, 320,000 horses, 168,000 goats, and 185,000 pigs. Yaks are also bred. Meat production in 1998 totaled 189,000 tons; cow's milk, 947,000 tons; wool (greasy), 13,000 tons; and eggs, 9,000 tons.

[24] FISHING

The Naryn River is the primary site of fishing activity; but fishing is of little commercial significance. The Yssk Kol Lake is slightly saline and not conducive to the development of fresh water species fishing. The total catch in 1997 was 300 tons, including 140 tons of carp.

[25] FORESTRY

Forests and woodlands account for about 3.8% of the total land area. With 85% of the country covered by high-altitude mountain ranges, and coupled with an underdeveloped transportation system, the forestry sector is not commercially significant. Imports of forest products totaled $12.2 million in 1997.

[26] MINING

Southwestern Kyrgyzstan contains most of the nation's mineral wealth, which includes antimony (often found with lead-zinc) and mercury (often found with fluorspar). Principal deposits of these minerals are found in the Kadamzhay and Khaydarkan regions, in the Alay foothills on the southern margin of the Fergana Valley. The Khaydarkan mercury plant was the largest in the former Soviet Union. Antimony produced at Kadamzhay is one of Kyrgyzstan's important exports because it is suitable for technical purposes requiring high purity antimony. Uranium, from the center of the country, is processed in the Shu Valley. The mountains also contain deposits of gold, mercury, tungsten, molybdenum, rare earth metals, indium, sulfur, tin, and arsenic. Gold is mined in the Issyk-Kul' region. A rich deposit of tin, a regionally scarce mineral commodity, is being developed in the eastern mountains. Mine output of antimony in 1996 was 1,400 tons; mercury, 500 tons; fluorspar concentrate, 2,500 tons; and gold, 5,000 kg.

The principal organization in mining and metallurgical production is the state-owned Kyrgyzaltyn. Beginning in 1995, the government developed a plan to begin privatizing its mineral enterprises (except for gold mining), with the goal of converting these enterprises into joint stock companies.

27 ENERGY AND POWER

Unlike its Central Asian neighbors, Kyrgyzstan has insignificant reserves of petroleum and natural gas. Kyrgyzstan's principal energy resources are its deposits of coal; subbituminous coal deposits are found on the southern fringe of the Fergana Valley (at Suluktu and Kyzl-Kyya), while hard coal comes from the west and northwest fringes of the valley (at Tash-Komur, Jalal-Abad, and Osh) and in the Tien Shan foothills east of Ysyk Kol Lake. In 1998 coal production amounted to 0.5 million tons.

In 1998, 89% of Kyrgyzstan's generated electricity came from hydropower. Several large hydroelectric projects are spread along the Naryn River and its headwater tributaries, and a series of dams, built on irrigation canals, produce power for the manufacturing sector around Bishkek. The two major electric power plants are a 1,200-MW facility at Toktogul and a 760-MW generator at Bishkek. In 1998, electrical production totaled 12,200 million kWh, of which 75% was used for domestic consumption and 25% was exported (mainly to Uzbekistan). Total installed capacity was 19 billion kW.

Production of oil and natural gas in small quantities comes from fields at the northeastern edge of the Fergana Valley; in 1998, Kyrgyzstan produced about 2,000 barrels per day of oil. Kyrgyz natural gas satisfies less than 2% of domestic demand. In 1998, Kyrgyzstan imported 1.9 billion cu m of natural gas, more than half of it from Uzbekistan. A crude oil refinery was built in Dzhalal-ahad in 1997 by a Kyrgyz-Canadian joint venture. It produces heavy fuel oil, diesel fuel, and gasoline.

28 INDUSTRY

During the Soviet era, industry in Kyrgyzstan was totally dependent on the other republics for raw materials and other resources. Between 1985 and 1989, industrial output increased at a rate of over 5% annually. With the disruption of traditional supply and export arrangements within the former USSR, however, industrial output declined by 1% in 1990 and dropped by over 23% in 1992. Industrial production decreased by 24% in 1994 and by another 12.5% in 1995. By mid-1995, production began to recover and in 1997, Kyrgyzstan reported an industrial growth rate of 7%, one of 14% for 1998. The high growth rate in 1998 was associated with a steep rise in gold production. Nearly all of Kyrgyzstan's industrial output derives from the capital of Bishkek and surrounding areas. Mechanical and electrical engineering (vehicle assembly, washing machines, electrical appliances, electronics), light industry (mainly textiles and wool processing), and food processing make up close to 75% of the country's industrial production and 80% of its industrial exports. Other important industries include chemicals, leather goods such as shoes, and construction materials (primarily cement).

The government passed the "Privatization and Denationalization Act" in December 1991, authorizing the transfer of all small, medium, and large-scale industrial enterprises to the private sector. The Concept Law on Privatization passed in 1994 was designed to correct early problems with the transition. By 1995, about 600 enterprises had been sold, with 250 fully privatized. The transition is also expected to involve the conversion of defense industries to civilian use under private ownership. One important conversion thus far involves the participation of a South Korean firm in establishing electronics manufacture at a plant previously geared toward military-related production. The government is encouraging the purchase of substantial shares of individual enterprises by worker collectives, although more widespread and non-collective ownership is also being promoted. By 1999, much of the government's stock had been sold.

29 SCIENCE AND TECHNOLOGY

The Kyrgyz Academy of Sciences, founded in 1954 at Bishkek, has departments of physical engineering, mathematics, mining geological sciences, chemical-technological, medical-technological, agricultural, and biological sciences. Attached to the academy are 24 specialized learned societies and research institutes concerned with agriculture, medicine, natural sciences, and technology. Kyrgyz State University has faculties of geography, physics, mathematics, information science and applied mathematics, biology, and chemistry. Agricultural and medical institutes and a technical university are located in Bishkek. In 1987–97, science and engineering students accounted for 14% of college and university enrollments. The city also has a botanical garden and a scientific and technical library.

30 DOMESTIC TRADE

As in other post-Soviet republics, structural reform appears to be proceeding most rapidly in the domestic retail sector. Small shops and traders predominate among the country's private retailing entities. However, expansion in the number of private wholesale distributors has been much less marked, placing small retailers in a disadvantaged position compared with large-scale and potentially monopolistic producers within the country's industrial sector.

Most businesses open around 8 AM and close at about 5 PM, with lunch taken sometime between noon and 2 PM. Retail shops are usually open from 7 AM to 8 PM, with an afternoon lunch period. Department stores, book stores, and other shops usually open according to state institution hours. Bazaars are open from 6 AM until 7 or 8 PM.

31 FOREIGN TRADE

Since 1992, Kyrgyzstan's trade balance has been negative, continuing the structural deficit caused by the costs of oil and gas, pharmaceuticals, and agricultural resources formerly supplied through internal trade with other Soviet republics. The countries of the former USSR still represent the major export markets, but 25% of total exports are typically sent to countries outside the former USSR.

Kyrgyzstan exports metals, including gold, mercury, iron, steel and uranium (15%), hydropower (7.8%), cotton (6.8%), wool (6.6%), alcohols (4.5%), tobacco (4.1%), animal hides and furs (4.0%), and sugar (3.6%).

In 1996 Kyrgyzstan's imports were distributed among the following categories:

Consumer goods	5.6%
Food	20.3%
Fuels	28.4%
Industrial supplies	18.7%
Machinery	20.6%
Transportation	6.2%

Principal trading partners in 1998 (in millions of US dollars) were as follows:

COUNTRY	EXPORTS	IMPORTS	BALANCE
Germany	197	53	144
Kazakhstan	86	75	11
Russia	84	204	-120
Uzbekistan	39	122	-83
China (inc. Hong Kong)	16	45	-29
United States	8	41	-33
Belarus	8	10	-2
Turkey	7	37	-30
Italy	3	27	-24
Korea	n.a.	26	

32 BALANCE OF PAYMENTS

Kyrgyzstan maintains a trade deficit, derived mostly from dependence on imports from other former Soviet republics; from 1989 to 1998, the trade deficit annually averaged about 14% of GDP. Foreign exchange reserves are minimal.

The US Central Intelligence Agency reports that in 1998 the purchasing power parity of Kyrgyzstan's exports was $630 million while imports totaled $670 million resulting in a trade balance of -$40 million.

The International Monetary Fund (IMF) reports that in 1998 Kyrgyzstan had exports of goods totaling $535 million and imports totaling $756 million. The services credit totaled $63 million and debit $180 million. The following table summarizes Kyrgyzstan's balance of payments as reported by the IMF for 1998 in millions of US dollars.

Current Account		-371
Balance on goods	-221	
Balance on services	-118	
Balance on income	-81	
Current transfers	49	
Capital Account		-8
Financial Account		292
Direct investment abroad	-1	
Direct investment in Kyrgyzstan	109	
Portfolio investment assets	30	
Portfolio investment liabilities	-4	
Other investment assets	-99	
Other investment liabilities	256	
Net Errors and Omissions		63
Reserves and Related Items		24

33 BANKING AND SECURITIES

The central bank of Kyrgyzstan is the National Bank of the Kyrgyz Republic. It heads all 18 banks in the system, the savings bank, three former specialized state banks that have been converted into joint-stock commercial banks, two foreign joint-venture banks, and commercial banks. The specialized banks still dominate the allocation of credit and the taking of deposits, although some smaller banks are starting to challenge the major banks. However, many of the country's commercial banks have only one office. The larger banks have large bad loan portfolios; Promstroybank (Construction Bank) had 80% of its loans overdue at the end of 1994. Bank failures and bank consolidation were common during the late 1990s.

The NBK, formerly the local branch of Gosbank (the State Bank of the former Soviet Union), began to operate independently in December 1991 and is intended to perform all the functions of a central bank. The government has stuck with a tight monetary policy. The currency unit was initially the ruble following independence; however, with IMF support, the government introduced a new currency, the som, in May 1993 in order to stabilize the economy, avoid the inflation of the ruble, and attract foreign investment.

The country has a small stock exchange, opened in May 1995. As of January 1996, 298 companies issued securities, with 7 trading on the stock exchange.

34 INSURANCE

No recent information is available.

35 PUBLIC FINANCE

During the early 1990s, economic output declined, while inflation escalated. As a result, the proportion of public revenues in GDP plummeted. Transfers from the former Soviet Union amounting to over 11% of GDP largely created an overall budget surplus equivalent to 4.1% of GDP in 1991. In 1992, parliament agreed to a further tightening of fiscal policy (including decreased expenditures and the elimination of transfers to inefficient state enterprises) due to the virtual termination of in-flowing subsidies caused by the demise of the Soviet Union. The som, currency introduced by the government in May 1993, has proven fairly stable, and monthly inflation has slowed from 40% to about 10%.

The US Central Intelligence Agency (CIA) estimates that in 1996 Kyrgyzstan's central government took in revenues of approximately $225 million and had expenditures of $308 million including capital expenditures of $11 million. Overall, the government registered a deficit of approximately $83 million. External debt totaled $1.57 billion.

The following table shows an itemized breakdown of government revenues and expenditures. The percentages were calculated from data reported by the International Monetary Fund. The dollar amounts (millions) are based on the CIA estimates provided above.

REVENUE AND GRANTS	100%	225
Tax revenue	77.4%	174
Non-tax revenue	18.1%	41
Capital revenue	1.4%	3
Grants	3.1%	7

EXPENDITURES	100%	308
General public services	13.5%	41
Defense	6.5%	20
Public order and safety	5.6%	17
Education	22.3%	69
Health	12.8%	39
Social security	13.0%	40
Housing and community amenities	5.0%	15
Recreation, cultural, and religious affairs	2.5%	8
Economic affairs and services	11.2%	35
Other expenditures	7.6%	23

36 TAXATION

The personal income tax varies up to a maximum rate of 40%; the corporate rate ranges from 15–55% with a standard rate of 35%. Also levied are a 20% value-added tax; a withholding tax ranging from zero to 5%; and a social security contribution of 37% by employers and 1% by employees.

37 CUSTOMS AND DUTIES

Imports are subject to customs duties at an average rate of 10%. The rate is higher for certain products, including beer (15%), tobacco (20%), and alcoholic beverages (30%). Imported raw materials and imports from the former USSR are exempt. Kyrgyzstan, Kazakhstan, and Uzbekistan have formed an economic union. Kyrgyzstan and the US signed a most-favored nation agreement in 1992. Although Kyrgyzstan levies excise and VAT, these are not applied to imports.

38FOREIGN INVESTMENT

In June 1991, the Kyrgyzstan parliament passed the Foreign Investment Law guiding the establishment of local enterprises with foreign shareholding as well as 100% foreign ownership. The law secures the right to repatriation of profits and allows foreign investment in all sectors of the economy except military production and certain forms of ownership in agriculture. Foreign buyers may acquire small enterprises being transferred from the state to the private sector directly on the open market; foreign participation in auctions or other forms of bidding for medium and large-scale enterprises requires special government permission. At present the government is attempting to attract overseas investors, particularly to the minerals, electronics, and agro-processing sectors of the economy. In 1995, the Foreign Investment Law was amended to expand foreign investment opportunities, to clarify investors' rights, and to remove or extend some time limits on certain aspects of foreign investment. Direct foreign investment that year amounted to about $800 million, and was rising at a slow but steady rate. Investments from Canada represented 45% of the total; these were concentrated primarily in gold mining (the largest single project being the $375 million development of the Kumtor gold field). Investments from Turkey comprised about 20% of the total; those from the US, 12%; and China, 10%. In 1998, foreign direct investment totaled $102 million, up from $83 million in 1997.

39ECONOMIC DEVELOPMENT

Under the Soviet system, economic planning efforts in Kyrgyzstan focused on increasing agricultural production (particularly in the meat and dairy subsectors during the 1980s) and specialized development of industrial sectors in line with the wider Soviet economy. Transfer payments from the central government as well as capital inflows into state enterprises covered the republic's modest balance of trade deficit with its Soviet trading partners and countries beyond. With this support, GDP growth was sustained at moderately high levels in the late 1980s, averaging 5.1% in 1985–89.

Kyrgyzstan declared its independence in 1991. Since then, the Kyrgyzstan government faced the task of sustaining a viable national economy despite the sudden cessation of transfers from the central government, the country's critical dependence on oil and gas imports, and its landlocked geographic position that has hampered development of trading ties outside the economically troubled former Soviet Union. Reforms have aimed at making the transition to a market-oriented economy.

Kyrgyzstan experienced declines in gross domestic product (GDP) from 1991–94. Both per capita income and overall output fell to well below the 1990 level. Agricultural output fell by an estimated 20%, and industrial output, by 42%. By 1996, however, Kyrgyzstan had begun to show progress, especially when compared to the other former Soviet republics, in the areas of privatizing state enterprises, ending the state ordering system, lifting price controls, and converting military enterprises to civilian uses. Prime Minister Apas Jumagulov reported in 1995 that the economic crises had eased, and the rates of decline were slowing.

A value-added tax was introduced in 1992 to help strengthen the government revenue base. Expected state revenues however, have fallen short of expectation due to steeply declining consumption and collection difficulties within the new tax system. With seriously declining revenues since 1991, the government's ability to make new development investments in either the productive sectors or physical and social infrastructure has been severely constrained. Capital expenditures as a percentage of total budgetary expenditures declined from 15% in 1990 to only 7% in 1992. Because of its commitment to democracy, Kyrgyzstan has received favorable treatment from international economic aid agencies. In 1992, the government signed a formal agreement with Russia transferring its share of the former Soviet Union's external debt to the latter in return for relinquishing most claims to the financial and other assets of the former USSR.

In May 1996, President Akayev negotiated an aid package from the Asian Development Bank that included $60 million in loans to finance privatization of agriculture and to renovate power and heating facilities in Bishkek. In support of the government's efforts to evolve the country's agriculture from large communes to private farms, the Asian Development Bank also offered loans to small farmers. In July 1996, the International Finance Corporation promised $40 million to finance a project to mine for gold near Issy-Kul', a large lake in the northeast. In November 1996, the World Bank moved to support programs to reform the Kyrgyzstan banking system and to modernize the electric power generating system.

40SOCIAL DEVELOPMENT

After independence, a social security law was introduced in 1990, and amended in 1992 and 1994. All employed persons and members of cooperatives and collective farms are eligible for old age, disability and survivor's pensions. Contributions of 2.5% of earnings from employees, and 34% of payroll by employers finance the program. A universal medical care system exists from all residents. Maternity benefits for employed women include 100% of pay for 126 days of leave. Workers' compensation, unemployment benefits, and family allowances are also provided. Severe economic difficulties, however, have meant that the government is often unable to pay pensions.

Women have equal status under the law and are well represented in the work force in urban areas. However, they appear to be disproportionately affected by growing unemployment. A women's congress in Bishkek convenes periodically to consider women's issues. The government is developing a comprehensive program on the rights and welfare of youth.

In 1993, parliament narrowly rejected a law to legalize polygamy, a Muslim custom practiced in Kyrgyzstan. Polygyny (one man having multiple wives) is more common, and a husband must financially provide each wife with her own separate household. In order for a woman to have multiple husbands (polyandry), she must have substantial wealth or influence. In 1997 a crisis center and hotline were opened in Narym for women affected by violence.

Non-Kyrgyz complain of discrimination in housing and employment. A 1996 decree designed to prevent the further emigration of ethnic Russians gave the Russian language official status. This decree also provides for Russian representation in local and national government.

Police brutality has been reported, as well as arbitrary arrest and detention. The government violates basic civil rights, including the freedoms of speech, assembly, association, and the press.

41HEALTH

In 1990–97, the country had three physicians and 8.8 hospital beds per 1,000 inhabitants.

The infant mortality rate in 1999 was 75.9 per 1,000 live births, and the maternal mortality rate was 32 per 100,000 live births during 1990–97. The overall mortality rate in 1999 was 8.7 per 1,000 people, and major causes of death in 1990 (per 100,000 people) were communicable diseases and maternal/perinatal causes, 124; noncommunicable diseases, 651; and injuries, 95. Between 1990 and 1994, immunization rates for children up to one year old were tuberculosis, 97%; diphtheria, pertussis, and tetanus, 82%; polio, 84%; and measles, 88%. Total health care expenditures in 1990 were $517 million. In

1999, the life expectancy was 63.6 years for both men and women. About 5% of Kyrgyzstan's gross national product went to health expenditures in 1991.

Tuberculosis incidence and mortality rates are rising steeply, reflecting economic hardship and the deterioration of the health infrastructure. In 1997, there were 99 cases of tuberculosis per 1,000 population. Controlled for 30 years, diphtheria has reemerged since the breakup of the Soviet Union. In 1994, there were 489 new cases of diphtheria. Nearly 50% of these cases occurred in persons 15 or under.

The cancer mortality rates in Kyrgyzstan were higher than the medium human development countries during 1990–1993.

42HOUSING

During the Soviet era, there was a severe lack of urban housing in Kyrgyzstan. In 1989, 42.7% of all privately owned urban housing had running water, 32.4% had sewer lines, 14% had central heating, and 1.4% had hot water. In 1990, Kyrgyzstan had 12.1 sq m of housing space per capita and, as of 1 January 1991, 85,000 households (or 18.6%) were on waiting lists for housing in urban areas.

43EDUCATION

The adult illiteracy rate in 1995 was estimated at 0.4% (males, 0.3%; females, 0.5%). The educational system was not developed until after the 1920s when the country came under Soviet control. In 1996, 473,077 students were enrolled in 1,885 primary schools, with 24,086 teachers. In the same year, secondary schools had 530,854 students and 42,286 teachers. Also in 1996, there were 49,744 students enrolled and 3,691 teaching staff employed at institutions of higher learning, including the State University of Kyrgyzstan.

44LIBRARIES AND MUSEUMS

Important libraries in Kyrgyzstan include the State Public Library of Kyrgyzstan, with over 3.6 million volumes, and the Scientific Technical Library of Kyrgyzstan, with over 5.8 million volumes. The Kyrgyzstan State University library contains over 930,000 volumes, the Kyrgyzstan Agricultural Institute holds 600,000, and the Kyrgyzstan Technical University holds 766,000 volumes.

The State Historical Museum of Kyrgyzstan has 20,000 items on display depicting the history of Kyrgyzstan. The Kyrgyzstan Museum of Fine Arts collects primarily modern work. There are several regional museums exhibiting primarily archaeological findings.

45MEDIA

Telephone links to other former Soviet republics are via land line or microwave, and to other countries through Moscow. The telephone network is underdeveloped, with some 100,000 residents waiting for telephone lines. In 1996 there were an estimated 356,000 telephones in use. Dom Radio in Bishkek broadcasts in Kyrgyz, German, Dungan, and Russian. In 1997 there were 115 radio sets and 44 television sets in use per 1,000 population. Television programming is provided through Orbita and INTELSAT.

In 1999 there were two daily newspapers. They were *Vecherny Bishkek* (in Russian, with a circulation of 51,500) and *Slovo Kyrgyzstan* (also in Russian, 111,000). *Kyrgyz Tuusu* was published five times per week.

On 2 July 1992 the government passed a law on the press and mass media which supports freedom of the press but also provides guidelines proscribing publication of certain information. The law supports the right of journalists to work, obtain information, and publish without prior restraint. The law prohibits publication of state secrets, material which advocates the overthrow of, or changes to, the existing constitutional order in Kyrgyzstan or elsewhere, It also prohibits publication of material that advocates war, violence, or intolerance toward ethnic or religious groups. Desecration of national norms, ethics, and symbols like the national seal, anthem, or flag is prohibited. Publication of pornography is prohibited, as is propagation of untrue information.

The press is free to publish material without prior government approval or restraint, although some infringement of press freedoms was reported as of 1999.

Online access is extremely limited, with less than one Internet host per 1,000 population in 1998.

46ORGANIZATIONS

Important economic organizations in Kyrgyzstan include the Chamber of Commerce and Industry, and the Kyrgyzstan Federation of Trade Unions. Active political organizations include the Committee for the Defense of Human Rights, Slavic Fund, Free Kyrgyzstan, Agigat, and Ashar. The Kyrgyz Bar Association was formed in August 1995.

47TOURISM, TRAVEL, AND RECREATION

Osh, Kyrgyzstan's second-largest city, is considered a holy city by Muslim pilgrims who visit it annually to pray at its Islamic shrines. The capital city of Bishkek is surrounded by some of the highest mountain ranges in the world. Bishkek is known for its large public parks and gardens, shady avenues, and botanical gardens. Equestrian sports are very popular in Kyrgyzstan.

Visas are required for entry to Kyrgyzstan and are obtainable upon arrival or through Kyrgyz embassies abroad and tour companies. The principal accommodations are hotels that formerly belonged to the Soviet Intourist system. However, foreign chains are currently developing a number of projects in Central Asia. In 1995 there were 12,000 visitor arrivals, and tourism receipts totaled $7 million by 1997.

According to 1999 UN estimates, the daily cost of staying in Bishkek is approximately $159 per day. Elsewhere the daily cost averages $77.

48FAMOUS KYRGYZSTANIS

Askar A. Akayev was elected president of the republic of Kyrgyzstan, in October 1990, prior to the republic declaring its independence. Chingiz Aitmatov (b.1928), winner of two Lenin Prizes for literature, is a native Kyrgyzstani.

49DEPENDENCIES

Kyrgyzstan has no territories or colonies.

50BIBLIOGRAPHY

Foreign Investment and Privatisation in Kyrgyzstan. London: Clifford Chance, 1993.

Kolsto, Pal. *Russians in the Former Soviet Republics*. Bloomington: Indiana University Press, 1995.

Kyrgyzstan. Washington, D.C.: Central Intelligence Agency, 1996.

Kyrghyzstan. Washington, D.C.: International Monetary Fund, 1992.

Kyrgyzstan: The Transition to a Market Economy. Washington, D.C.: World Bank, 1993.

Pisarskoi, E. G. *Architecture of the Soviet Kirghizia*. Moskow: Stroiizdat, 1986.

Rasputin, Valentin G. *Siberia, Siberia*. Evanston, Ill.: Northwestern University Press, 1996.

The History of Siberia: From Russian Conquest to Revolution. New York: Routledge, 1991.

LAO PEOPLES' DEMOCRATIC REPUBLIC (LAOS)

Lao People's Democratic Republic

Sathalanalat Paxathipatai Paxaxon Lao

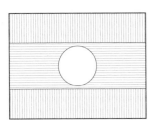

CAPITAL: Vientiane (Viangchan).

FLAG: The national flag, officially adopted in 1975, is the former flag of the Pathet Lao, consisting of three horizontal stripes of red, dark blue, and red, with a white disk, representing the full moon, at the center.

ANTHEM: *Pheng Sat Lao (Hymn of the Lao People).*

MONETARY UNIT: The new kip (NK) is a paper currency of 100 at, or cents. There are notes of 10, 20, 50, 200, and 500 new kip. NK1 = $0.0001 ($1 = NK7503) as of 31 March 2000.

WEIGHTS AND MEASURES: The metric system is the legal standard, but older local units are also used.

HOLIDAYS: Anniversary of the Founding of the Lao People's Democratic Republic, 2 December. To maintain production, the government generally reschedules on weekends such traditional festivals as the Lao New Year (April); Boun Bang-fai (Rocket Festival), the celebration of the birth, enlightenment, and death of the Buddha (May); Boun Khao Watsa, the beginning of a period of fasting and meditation lasting through the rainy season (July); Boun Ok Watsa (Water Holiday), a celebration of the end of the period of fasting and meditation (October); and That Luang, a pagoda pilgrimage holiday (November).

TIME: 7 PM = noon GMT.

¹LOCATION, SIZE, AND EXTENT

Laos is a landlocked country on the Indochinese Peninsula near the eastern extremity of mainland Southeast Asia. Laos occupies an area of 236,800 sq km (91,429 sq mi), extending 1,162 km (722 mi) SSE–NNW and 478 km (297 mi) ENE–WSW. Comparatively, the area occupied by Laos is slightly larger than the state of Utah. It is bordered on the N by China, on the E and SE by Vietnam, on the S by Cambodia, on the W by Thailand, and on the NW by Myanmar, with a total boundary length of 5,083 km (3,158 mi).

The capital of Laos, Vientiane, is located along the country's western boundary.

²TOPOGRAPHY

The terrain is rugged and mountainous, especially in the north and in the Annam Cordillera, along the border with Vietnam. The mountains reach heights of more than 2,700 m (8,860 ft), with Pou Bia, the highest point in Laos, rising to 2,817 m (9,242 ft) in the north-central part of the country. Only three passes cross the mountains to link Laos with Vietnam. The Tran Ninh Plateau, in the northeast, rises to between 1,020 m and 1,370 m (3,350–4,500 ft), and the fertile Bolovens Plateau, in the south, reaches a height of about 1,070 m (3,500 ft). Broad alluvial plains, where much of the rice crop is grown, are found only in the south and west along the Mekong River and its tributaries. Of these, the Vientiane plain is the most extensive.

Except for a relatively small area east of the main divide, Laos is drained by the Mekong and its tributaries. The Mekong flows in a broad valley along the border with Thailand and through Laos for 1,805 km (1,122 mi). In its low-water phase, it is almost dry, but it rises more than 6 m (20 ft) during the monsoon period. The river is wide, but except for a navigable stretch between Vientiane and Savannakhét, rapids are numerous. Below Savan-

nakhét and at the extreme south there are large rapids and waterfalls. Floods are common in the rainy season.

³CLIMATE

Laos has a tropical monsoon climate with two main seasons, rainy and dry, each of five months' duration. From May through September, rainfall averages 28 to 30 cm (11–12 in) a month, but from November through March the monthly average is only about 1.3 cm (0.5 in). Humidity is high throughout the year, even during the season of drought. Average daily temperatures in Vientiane range from 14° to 28°C (57–82°F) in January, the coolest month, and from 23° to 34°C (73–93°F) in April, the hottest.

⁴FLORA AND FAUNA

Nearly two-thirds of Laos is covered by forest or thick jungle. The forests of southernmost Laos are an extension of the Kampuchean type of vegetation, while the highland forests of the north, consisting of prairies interspersed with thickets, resemble central Vietnam. Bamboo, lianas, rattan, and palms are found throughout Laos.

Roaming the forests are panthers and a dwindling number of tigers, elephants, and leopards. The elephant, until 1975 depicted on the national flag as the traditional symbol of Lao royalty, has been used throughout history as a beast of burden. A local breed of water buffalo also is universally used as a draft animal. Reptiles include cobras, geckos, kraits, and Siamese crocodiles. There are many varieties of birds, fish, and insects.

⁵ENVIRONMENT

Soil erosion, deforestation, and flood control are the principal environmental concerns in Laos, there being only minimal industrial development. The government seeks to control erosion by discouraging the traditional slash-and-burn agriculture practiced by many mountain tribes, and by resettling the tribes in permanent villages. Reforestation projects have been promoted by the government as a means of increasing lumber exports and of restoring valuable hardwoods to logged-out forest areas. Each person was required to plant five trees in the course of the 1981–85 economic plan. In 1986, the government prohibited the cutting of 15 different varieties of trees. At that time, forests were reportedly being consumed at a rate of 300,000 hectares (741,000 acres) per year. Between 1983 and 1993, Laos suffered a further decline of 11.3% in its forest and woodland area. Laos has 64.8 cubic miles of water with 82% used in farming activity and 10% used for industrial purposes. Forty-one percent of the rural population and sixty percent of city dwellers do not have pure drinking water. The nation's water supply has begun to decrease due to a combination of factors, among them the loss of forest land, uncontrolled agricultural practices, flooding and drought. Pollution from fires, dust, and cars is also becoming a national problem.

In 1994, 23 of Laos' mammal species and 18% of bird species were threatened. Three of the nation's plant species were endangered. Endangered or extinct species in Laos included the douc langur, three species of gibbon (pileated, crowned, and capped), tiger, Asian elephant, Sumatran rhinoceros, Javan rhinoceros, Thailand brow-antlered deer, kouprey, and Siamese crocodile.

⁶POPULATION

The first national census was taken, with the assistance of the UNFPA, in 1985, when the population was 3,584,803, up 21% from 1970 estimates. The population of Laos in 2000 was estimated at 5,556,821. An estimated 3.6% of the population is 65 years of age or older. The projected population for the year 2005 is 6,338,000, assuming a crude birthrate of 36 per 1,000 population and a death rate of 10, resulting in a natural rate of change of 2.5% for the period 2000–2005. The population rate of change between 1995 and 2000 was 3.1%.

The population density in 1998 was a sparse 22 per sq km (57 per sq mi), but the population is unevenly spread, with the greatest concentration in the Mekong Valley. More than 70% of the population is rural, living in some 9,000 villages. It was estimated that only 24% of the population lived in urban areas in 2000, up from 13% in 1980. The capital city, Vientiane, had a 2000 population of 534,000. Other large towns, all on or near the Mekong and its tributaries, are Savannakhét, Pakxé, Luang-phrabang (the former royal capital), Xaignabouri, and Ban Houayxay.

⁷MIGRATION

There has been only limited population movement into Laos in modern times. During the late 1960s and early 1970s, under pressure of combat operations, Black Tai tribesmen moved southward into the Mekong Valley. Between 1975–90, over 360,000 Laotians fled to Thailand and China. The majority resettled and were given new lives in Western nations. To date, more than 27,000 Laotians have repatriated. In 1996, some 6,000 Laotian refugees remained in Thailand, and several hundred remained on collective farms in China. As of 1999, about 1,100 of the small number of refugees still remaining in Ban Napho camp in Thailand were determined not to have valid refugee claims. The two governments agreed that they should return to Laos, with UNHCR assistance; however, only a few families and individuals have volunteered to do so thus far. In the mid-1990s, as Laos opened up to international investment and development, Vietnamese workers began migrating to Laos—although in relatively small numbers—to work in the construction industry, primarily. The net migration rate for 1999 was zero migrants per 1,000 population.

⁸ETHNIC GROUPS

There are officially 68 ethnic groups in Laos. About 68% of all Laotians are Lao-lum, or lowland Lao, a people related to the people of Thailand; thought to have migrated to Laos from southwestern China in the 8th century, the Lao-lum are concentrated in the lowlands along the Mekong. On the hillsides live the Lao-theung, or slope dwellers, a diverse group dominated by the Lao-tai (with various subgroups, including the Black Tai), who are ethnically related to the Lao-lum. They account for 22% of the population. At higher altitudes are the Lao-soung, or mountain dwellers, a diverse group of ethnic minorities of mainly Malayo-Polynesian or proto-Malay backgrounds. They constitute 9% of the population. Important among the Lao-soung, and more prosperous than most Lao because of the opium poppies they grow, are the Hmong (Meo), a people of Tibeto-Burman origin who supported the American presence until 1975 and, because of their continuing insurgency, became the targets of harassment by government and Vietnamese troops. Other important upland tribes, all with customs and religions considerably different from those of the lowland Lao, are the Ho, Kha, Kho, and Yao (Mien). Ethnic Vietnamese and Chinese account for 1% of the population.

⁹LANGUAGES

Lao, the official language and the language of the ethnic Lao, is closely related to the language of Thailand. It is monosyllabic and tonal and contains words borrowed from Sanskrit, Pali, and Farsi. Pali, a Sanskritic language, is used among the Buddhist priesthood.

Other groups speak the Tibeto–Burman, Non-Khmer, or Miao–Yao languages. French, formerly the principal language of government and higher education, has been largely replaced by Lao. English and various ethnic languages are also spoken.

¹⁰RELIGIONS

Religious activity was discouraged by the state from 1976 to 1979, but freedom of religion has been legally guaranteed since the constitution of 1991. Almost 60% of all Laotians, including nearly all the Lao-lum, are adherents of Hinayana Buddhism, a large part of whose daily life is shaped by its rituals and precepts. Buddhist temples, found in every village, town, and city, serve as intellectual as well as religious centers. Vientiane and Luang-prabang have been called cities of thousands of temples. More than 70 pagodas were built in Vientiane alone in the 16th century, including the famous Wat Phra Keo and That Luang. Despite the major role that Buddhism, its temples, and its priests have played in Laotian life, the average lowland Lao regulates a large part of daily activities in accordance with animistic concepts. Certain spirits (phi) are believed to have great power over human destiny and to be present throughout the material world, as well as within nonmaterial realms. Thus, each of the four universal elements (earth, sky, fire, and water) has its special phi; every road, stream, village, house, and person has a particular phi; forests and jungles are inhabited by phi. Evil phi can cause disease and must be propitiated by sacrifices.

Approximately 40% of the population practice animism and other religions. About 34% of Laotians, including the upland tribes, are almost exclusively animists, although influenced by Buddhism to some extent. Christian missionaries have been active in Laos, but less than 2% of all Laotians profess the religion.

¹¹TRANSPORTATION

Lack of adequate transportation facilities continues to be a major deterrent to economic progress. Of the approximately 21,716 km (13,494 mi) of roads, only about 9,674 km (6,011 mi) were paved in 1998; many are impassable in the rainy season. Only a single major road connects the northern and southern regions.

Most of the roads were damaged by US bombing in the Vietnam war, but the main links with Vietnam (notably Highway 9, from Savannakhét to the Vietnamese port of Da Nang, and Highways 7 and 13, from Vientiane and Savannakhét to the Vietnamese port of Vinh and Ho Chi Minh City, respectively) are being rebuilt with Vietnamese aid. Under the 1981–85 economic plan, 844 km (524 mi) of roads were built or improved. The 1986–90 plan projected an additional 1,500 km (932 mi), 50% of which was to be asphalted. There are no railroads in Laos, although in 1994, the government entered into an agreement with a Thai company to build a railroad from Nong Khai in Thailand to Vientiane.

In 1998 there were 52 airports, only 9 of which had paved runways. Vientiane has the only international airport. Major cities in Laos are connected by air services operated by state-run Lao Aviation, founded with Soviet aid in 1976. In 1995, the government signed an agreement with China's Yunnan Airlines forming a joint venture projected to increase Yunnan's holdings of Lao Aviation to 60% while the former pays off the latter's debt. In 1997 125,000 passengers were carried on scheduled domestic and international airline flights.

Landlocked, Laos' only water-transport link with the outside world is via the Mekong River, which forms a large part of the border with Thailand and flows through Cambodia and Vietnam into the South China Sea. The Mekong is navigable for small transport craft and, with its tributaries in Laos, forms a 4,587-km (2,850-mi) inland waterway system, although rapids make necessary the transshipment of cargo. To lessen dependence on Thailand, Laos in 1977 signed an agreement with Vietnam whereby the Vietnamese port of Da Nang would replace Bangkok as the chief outlet for Laos. In 1998 Laos had 1 merchant vessel, a cargo ship at 2,370 GRT.

¹²HISTORY

Although archaeological evidence indicates that settlers along the Mekong had learned agriculture, metallurgy, and pottery making by 3000 BC, little is known about the early history of the land that today bears the name of Laos. The lowland Lao are believed to be the descendants of Thai tribes that were pushed southward in the 8th century. According to tradition, the kingdom called Lan Xang ("a million elephants") was established in 756 by King Thao Khoun Lo. In 1353, it was reunified by Fa-Ngoum, who had been raised at the court of Angkor in Kampuchea and returned with a force of Khmer troops. He is also credited with the introduction of Hinayana Buddhism into Laos. Lan Xang waged intermittent wars with the Khmers, Burmese, Vietnamese, and Thai and developed an effective administrative system, an elaborate military organization, and an active commerce with neighboring countries. In 1707, internal dissensions brought about a split of Lan Xang into two kingdoms, Luangphrabang in the north (present-day upper Laos) and Vientiane in the south (lower Laos). Strong neighboring states took advantage of this split to invade the region. Vientiane was overrun and annexed by Siam (Thailand) in 1828, while Luangprabang became a vassal of both the Chinese and the Vietnamese. In 1893, France, which had already established a protectorate over what is now central and northern Vietnam, extended its control to both Vientiane and Luangphrabang, and Laos was ruled by France as part of Indochina. Although French control over Luangphrabang took the nominal form of a protectorate, the French colonial administration directly ruled the rest of Laos, legal justification being ultimately provided in the Lao-French convention of 1917.

During World War II, Laos was occupied by Japan. After the Japanese proclaimed on 10 March 1945 that "the colonial status of Indochina has ended," the king of Luangphrabang, Sisavang Vong, was compelled to issue a declaration of independence. The nationalist Free Lao (Lao Issarak) movement deposed the

LOCATION: 100° to 107°E; 13°40′ to 22°40′N. **BOUNDARY LENGTHS:** China, 425 km (264 mi); Vietnam, 1,555 km (966 mi); Cambodia, 541 km (336 mi); Thailand, 1,754 km (1,090 mi); Myanmar, 238 km (148 mi). **TERRITORIAL SEA LIMIT:** 12 mi.

monarch soon after, but French forces reoccupied Laos, and on 27 August 1946, France concluded an agreement establishing him as king of Laos and reimposing French domination over the country. In May 1947, the king established a constitution providing for a democratic government. On 19 July 1949, Laos nominally became an independent sovereign state within the French Union. Additional conventions transferring full sovereignty to Laos were signed on 6 February 1950 and on 22 October 1953. All special economic ties with France and the other Indochinese states were abolished by the Paris pacts of 29 December 1954. In the meantime, Vietnamese Communist (Viet-Minh) forces had invaded Laos in the spring of 1953. A Laotian Communist movement, the Pathet Lao (Lao State), created on 13 August 1950 and led by Prince Souphanouvong, collaborated with the Viet-Minh during its Laotian offensive. Under the Geneva cease-fire of 21 July 1954, all Viet-Minh and most French troops were to withdraw, and the Pathet Lao was to pull back to two northern provinces, pending reunification talks with the national government under the leadership of Souvanna Phouma (Souphanouvong's half-brother). The negotiations were completed on 2 November 1957, and the Pathet Lao transformed itself into a legal political party called the National Political Front (Neo Lao Hak Xat). However, a political swing to the right that led to the ouster of Souvanna Phouma as prime minister, coupled with the refusal of the Pathet Lao forces to integrate into the Royal Lao Army, led to a renewal of fighting in May 1959.

A bloodless right-wing coup in January 1960 was answered in August by a coup led by paratroops, under the command of Capt. Kong Le; in the ensuing turmoil, Souvanna Phouma returned to power. After a three-day artillery battle that destroyed much of Vientiane, right-wing military elements under Gen. Phoumi Nosavan and Prince Boun Oum occupied the capital on 11 December. A new right-wing government under Prince Boun Oum was established, but further military reverses, despite a heavy influx of US aid and advisers, caused the government to ask for a cease-fire in May 1961. An international conference assembled in Geneva to guarantee the cease-fire. All three Laotian political factions agreed on 11 June 1962 to accept a coalition government, with Souvanna Phouma as prime minister. On 23 July, the powers assembled at Geneva signed an agreement on the independence and neutrality of Laos, which provided for the evacuation of all foreign forces by 7 October. The US announced full compliance, under supervision of the International Control Commission (ICC), set up in 1954. Communist forces were not withdrawn. Fighting resumed in the spring of 1963, and Laos was steadily drawn into the role of a main theater in the escalating Vietnam war. The Laotian segment of the so-called Ho Chi Minh trail emerged as a vital route for troops and supplies moving south from the Democratic Republic of Vietnam (DRV), also known as North Vietnam, and was the target for heavy and persistent US bombing raids. While the Vientiane government was heavily bolstered by US military and economic support, the Pathet Lao received key support from the DRV, which was reported to have 20,000 troops stationed in Laos by 1974. Efforts to negotiate a settlement in Laos resumed with US backing in 1971, but a settlement was not concluded until February 1973, a month after a Vietnam peace agreement was signed in Paris. On 5 April 1974, a new coalition government was set up, with equal representation for Pathet Lao and non-Communist elements. Souvanna Phouma, 73 years old and in failing health, stayed on as prime minister, while Prince Souphanouvong was brought closer to the center of political authority as head of the newly created Joint National Political Council.

The Pathet Lao had by this time asserted its control over three-fourths of the national territory. Following the fall of the US-backed regimes in Vietnam and Cambodia in April 1975, the Laotian Communists embarked on a campaign to achieve complete military and political supremacy in Laos. On 23 August, Vientiane was declared "liberated" by the Pathet Lao, whose effective control of Laos was thereby secured. On 2 December 1975, the Lao People's Democratic Republic (LPDR) was established, with Prince Souphanouvong as president and Kaysone Phomvihan as prime minister. King Savang Vatthana abdicated his throne, ending the monarchy that had survived in Laos for 622 years. Elections for a new National Assembly were called for April 1976; however, voting was put off indefinitely, amid reports of civil unrest and sabotage. A Supreme People's Council was convened, meanwhile, with Prince Souphanouvong as chairman, and was charged with the task of drafting a new constitution.

During the late 1970s, the Communists moved to consolidate their control and socialize the economy. Private trade was banned, factories were nationalized, and forcible collectivization of agriculture was initiated. "Reeducation" camps for an estimated 40,000 former royalists and military leaders were established in remote areas; as of 1986, the government maintained that almost all the inmates had been released, but Amnesty International claimed that about 5,000 remained. A 25-year friendship treaty with Vietnam, signed in July 1977, led to closer relations with that country (already signaled by the

continued presence in Laos of Vietnamese troops) and with the former USSR, and also to the subsequent dismissal from Laos of all Chinese technicians and advisers. China, for its part, began to give support and training to several small antigovernment guerrilla groups. With the economy in 1979 near collapse, in part because of severe drought in 1977 and flooding in 1978, the Laotian government slowed the process of socialization and announced a return to private enterprise and a readiness to accept aid from the non-Communist world. Throughout the 1980s armed opposition to the Government persisted, particularly from the Hmong hill tribe rebels. At the Fourth Party Congress of the Lao People's Revolutionary Party (LPRP), in December 1986, a "new economic management mechanism" (NEM) was set up, aiming at granting increased autonomy in the management of formerly state-run enterprises to the private sector.

In 1988 the Lao national legislature, the Supreme People's Assembly (SPA), adopted new election laws and the first elections since the formation of the LPDR in 1975 were held. Local and provincial elections were held in 1988, and on 27 March 1989 national elections took place for an enlarged Supreme People's Assembly. In March 1991 the Fifth Party Congress of the LPRP changed Kaysone Phomvihan's title from Prime Minister to President, elected a new 11-member politburo, pledged to continue economic reforms in line with free-market principles while denying the need for political pluralism, and changed the national motto by substituting the words "democracy and prosperity" for "socialism." The newly elected SPA drafted a constitution adopted on 14 August 1991. The constitution provided for a national assembly functioning on principles of "democratic centralism," established the LPRP as the political system's "leading organ," created a presidency with executive powers, and mandated a market-oriented economy with rights of private ownership.

President Kaysone Phomvihan, longtime LPRP leader, died on 21 November 1992. A special session of parliament on 24 November 1992 elected hard-line Communist Nouhak Phoumsavan as the next president. Gen. Khamtai Suphandon, who had been prime minister since 15 August 1991, remained in that post. National Assembly elections were held in December 1992. One day before these elections, three former officials who called for a multiparty democracy and had been detained in 1990 were sentenced to 14 years imprisonment. The National Assembly convened in February 1993 and approved government reorganization designed to improve public administration. On 9 January 1995, longtime leader Prince Souphanouvong died, unofficially marking an end to Laos' long dalliance with hard-line Marxism. Although the NEM had initiated an opening up to international investment and improved relations with the rest of the world, there remained elements of the old guard in positions of power. With the death of Souphanouvong, the only old-time hard-line Marxist still in power as of 1996 was the country's president, Nouhak Phoumsavan. Khamtay Siphandone, prime minister and party chief, was more powerful than Nouhak and is largely credited with exerting a moderating influence on the hard-liner. Nonetheless, there remains a strongly conservative mindset among the politboro members that still pulls the government back from economic flexibility or any hint of political liberalization.

Laos has actively improved its already "special relations" with Vietnam and Cambodia, while always seeking to improve relations with Thailand, the People's Republic of China (PRC), and the US. Periodic meetings are held to promote the cooperative development of the Mekong River region by Laos, Thailand, Vietnam, and Cambodia. Laos and the People's Republic of China restored full diplomatic relations in 1989 and are now full-fledged trading partners. Mutual suspicions, characterizing the relationship between Laos and Thailand, improved with agreements to withdraw troops and resolve border disputes, and agreements between the United Nations High Commissioner for Refugees (UNHCR) to repatriate or resettle nearly 60,000 Lao refugees in Thailand. Laos has cooperated with the US in recovering the remains of US soldiers missing in action in Laos since the Vietnam War and in efforts to suppress drug-trafficking. The US Department of State objects to Laos' restrictions on free speech, freedom of assembly and religious freedom. US Assistant Secretary of State Stanley Roth commented in March 2000 that Laos is unlikely to gain Most Favored Nation trading status unless it accounts for the fate of two naturalized US citizens, Hmong activists who disappeared in Laos during 1999.

13GOVERNMENT

Under the constitution of 1947 (as subsequently amended), Laos was a parliamentary democracy with a king as the nominal chief executive. The monarch was assisted by a prime minister (or president of the Council of Ministers), who was the executive and legislative leader in fact. The prime minister and cabinet were responsible to the National Assembly, the main repository of legislative authority, whose 59 members were elected every five years by universal adult suffrage. With the establishment of the Lao People's Democratic Republic in December 1975, governmental authority passed to a national congress made up of 264 delegates elected by newly appointed local authorities. The congress in turn appointed a 45-member Supreme People's Council to draw up a new constitution. Pending the completion of this task effective power rested with Kaysone Phomvihan, a longtime Pathet Lao leader who headed the government as chairman of the Council of Ministers and was also secretary-general of the Lao People's Revolutionary (Communist) Party.

Prince Souphanouvong, the head of state and president of the Supreme People's Council since 1975, left office in October 1986 because of poor health. He was replaced first by Phoumi Vongvichit, a former vice-chairman of the Council of Ministers, and later by Sisomphon Lovansay, a former vice-president of the Supreme People's Council. The Lao national legislature, the Supreme People's Assembly (SPA), adopted new election laws in 1988, and the first national elections under the current government took place in March 1989 (local elections were held in 1988). Kaysone Phomvihan was elected President and Khamtai Siphandone was named Prime Minister. The newly elected SPA set out to draft a constitution, which was finished in mid-1990, and adopted on 14 August 1991 by the SPA. The executive branch consists of the president, prime minister and two deputy prime ministers, and the Council of Ministers (cabinet) which are appointed by the president with the approval of the National Assembly. The legislative branch is the National Assembly which is elected by universal suffrage for a period of five years. The judicial branch is the Supreme People's Court Leaders. The constitution calls for a strong legislature elected by secret ballot, but most political power continues to rest with the party-dominated council of ministers, who are very aligned much aligned with the military.

14POLITICAL PARTIES

Elections to the National Assembly were first held in 1947. In the elections of 4 May 1958, the Pathet Lao's newly organized National Political Front (Neo Lao Hak Xat) won 9 of the 21 seats in contention; 4 were won by the Santiphab faction, a neutralist group allied with them, and 8 were obtained by the Nationalist and Independent parties. After the elections, the Nationalists and Independents combined to establish a new political party, the Rally of the Lao People (Lao Luam Lao), which held 36 of the 59 Assembly seats. The remaining 23 seats were divided among the National Political Front (9), the Santiphab grouping (7), the Democrats (3), the National Union (2), and unaffiliated deputies (2). The leaders of the Rally, upon formation of that party, announced its purpose to be the defense of Laos against "an extremist ideology contrary to the customs and traditions of the Lao country" and the establishment of true unity and independence of the nation against "subversion from within and without." The Front then and later called for a reduction in the size of the armed forces and of US military aid. In December 1959, because of emergency conditions, election of new Assembly deputies was postponed until April 1960. When the balloting was finally held, the opposition Committee for the Defense of the National Interests won a landslide victory. The Committee leader, Phoumi Nosavan, then formed a new political party, the Social Democrats (Paxa Sangkhom).

In August 1960, a coup led by Kong Le brought down the government. After a period of struggle, Souvanna Phouma, who had earlier established the Neutralist Party (Lao Pen Kang) in order to build a broader popular following, became prime minister on 11 June 1962. In his 19-man cabinet, 4 posts were held by right-wing politicians, 11 by Neutralists, and 4 others by Pathet Lao adherents. The National Assembly came to the end of its five-year term in 1965. Political instability prevented the holding of national elections, and a provisional assembly was convened to amend the constitution so as to provide a means for maintaining the legislature. The result was a general election held on 18 July, with the franchise limited to civil servants, teachers, merchants, and village headmen. The new National Assembly was convened on 16 August, with the Neutralists retaining 13 seats, the Social Democrats 11, the Rally 8, and various independents 27. The endorsement gained in the limited polling of 1965 was not sufficient to sustain Prime Minister Souvanna Phouma for long, and new voting—the first real and effective election in a decade—took place on 1 January 1967. About 60% of 800,000 eligible voters went to the polls in 1967, despite the Pathet Lao charge that the balloting was illegal. Souvanna Phouma's United Front took 32 of 59 seats in the National Assembly voting.

In the last years of the constitutional monarchy, the gulf between the Pathet Lao and the enclave of rightists and neutralists that held governmental power widened appreciably. The pressures of war—both the civil strife within Laos and the larger conflict pressed by the external forces of the US and the DRV—had thwarted the effectiveness of normal political processes. General elections held on 2 January 1972 were confined to government-controlled areas, with representatives for the Pathet Lao provinces elected by refugees from those regions. Despite the narrow range of political choices available to voters, only 20 of the 60 National Assembly deputies were reelected, reflecting a growing uneasiness both with the war and with the increasing evidence of corrupt practices among government officials. Despite right-wing pressures from within the National Assembly, Souvanna Phouma—whose neutralist policy was favored by both the US and the DRV—retained the position of prime minister. The withdrawal of US military support for the Thieu regime in the Republic of Vietnam (South Vietnam) was followed, in April 1974, by the creation of a new coalition in Vientiane that gave equal political footing to the Pathet Lao. The National Assembly, which had become little more than a forum for disputes among right-wing factions, was dissolved by King Savang Vatthana on 13 April 1975, an act that signaled the end of domestic political opposition to the inexorable progress of the Pathet Lao.

The formation of the Lao People's Democratic Republic in December 1975 effectively established the Communist Lao People's Revolutionary Party (LPRP) (Phak Pasason Pativat Lao), the political incarnation of the Pathet Lao movement, as the sole political force in Laos. Kaysone Phomvihan, general secretary of the LPRP, was named head of government, and Prince Souphanouvong head of state. The LPRP plays the leading role in the

Lao Front for National Reconstruction, which sought to promote socialism and national solidarity. The Third Party Congress of the PPPL, and the first since the party assumed control, was held in Vientiane in April 1982. The congress, whose 228 delegates represented a party membership of 35,000, elected an enlarged Central Committee with 49 full and 6 alternate members. The Central Committee reelected Kaysone as general secretary. The Fourth Party Congress, held in Vientiane in December 1986, established the "new economic management mechanism."

In 1988 the Supreme People's Assembly (SPA) adopted new elections laws and elections were held the next year—the first since 1975. In 1991, the Fifth Party Congress changed Prime Minister Phomvihan's title to president, a post he held until his death one year later. Elevated to the post of prime minister was Khamtai Suphandon, a generally pro-free market antidemocratic pragmatist of the Singaporean variety. Suphandon had for a time studied Marxism in Hanoi, but in his position as prime minister is considered essentially a transitional figure between the old guard and a new generation of leaders. After Phomvihan's death in 1992, a special session of the SPA elected and old-guard communist, Nouhak Phoumsavan, to the presidency.

Elections for the SPA were again held in 1992 but they were marred by the sentencing of three pro-democracy activists to 14 years in prison on the day before balloting. By 1996, Laos' leadership was made up primarily of party functionaries, regardless of the makeup of the SPA. Prime Minister Suphandon held considerable power as did Deputy Prime Minister Khamphoui Keoboualapha, who also serves as the administrator of the State Committee for Planning and Cooperation (CPC), considered by many analysts to be a government within a government.

A 1998 election retrenched the hard-liners, as "technocrats" vanished from the pre-approved slate, replaced with old style LPRP functionaries. This was viewed as a reaction to the social tensions (such as crime and corruption) arising with economic openness, as well as an attempt to reestablish centralized control over provincial matters.

Several governments-in-exile have been set up by former ministers of pre-1975 regimes, and overseas Hmongs and other dissidents have formed opposition organizations. A young pretender to the throne, Prince Soulivong Savang, has rallied support in exile. Some Hmong groups and others continue a low-level insurgency in rural Laos. Underground antigovernment sentiment may be on the rise among the urban intellectuals.

At the beginning of the new century, parties other than the LPRP continue to be proscribed. A glimpse of popular discontent emerged with reports of an October 1999 demonstration in Vientiane, led by students and professors calling for democracy and human rights. The protest was quickly suppressed, and Khamtay's government disavowed all knowledge of its occurrence.

15 LOCAL GOVERNMENT

Laos consists of 16 provinces (khoueng) and the municipality of Vientiane. The provinces are subdivided into districts (muong), townships (tasseng), and villages (ban). The president appoints provincial governors and mayors of municipalities. The prime minister appoints deputy provincial governors and deputy mayors and district chiefs. Since 1975, local administration has been restructured, with elected people's committees in the villages functioning as basic units. Both suffrage and candidacy are open to citizens 18 and over. Village heads administer at the village level. Lack of control over local party members in the rural areas appears to be a source of worry for the politburo, with its implications of corruption and even potential unrest.

16 JUDICIAL SYSTEM

The 1991 Constitution provides for freedom of speech, assembly, and religion, although, in practice, organized political speech and activities are severely restricted. The reality of religious freedom is equally illusory, with imprisonment of Christian activists in recent years. The Constitution contains provisions designed to guarantee the independence of judges and prosecutors, but in practice the courts appear to be subject to influence of other government agencies. Provincial courts are at the next level as appellate courts. There is also a Central Supreme Court in Vientiane. In 1993 the government began publishing an official gazette in which all laws and regulations are disseminated. A bar association was formed in 1996 to strengthen the legal profession and individual rights to counsel. Rising crime rates place a burden on Laos' under-funded and understaffed legal system.

17 ARMED FORCES

In 2000 the armed forces in Laos numbered 29,100, with 18 months of military service compulsory for all males. A total of 25,000 Laotians served in the army. The navy, equipped with 16 patrol craft and boats, enlisted 600. The air force, with 3,500 men, was equipped with antiaircraft missiles and 26 combat aircraft. Village self-defense forces number 100,000. Weapons are a mix of American and Russian arms. The armed forces face about 2,000 rebels from the United Lao National Liberation Front (ULNLF). Defense expenditures in 1996–97 were $77.4 million or 4.2% of GDP. The military is also funded from private enterprises it runs, most significantly, the Bolisat Phatthana Khet Phoudi Import Export Co., better known as the BPKP, which has earned $105 million from a variety of enterprises from handicrafts to tourism since it was formed in 1984.

18 INTERNATIONAL COOPERATION

Laos, a UN member since 14 December 1955, belongs to ESCAP and all the nonregional specialized agencies except IAEA and IMO. The nation participates in the Asian Development Bank and G-77, is a signatory to the Law of the Sea, and has observer status with the WTO. Since 1961, it has been a member of the nonaligned movement. Laos's main diplomatic, economic, and military allies have been Vietnam and the former USSR. In 1977, Laos signed a 20-year treaty of cooperation with Vietnam. A four-year agreement with Vietnam and Cambodia that pledged cooperation in regulating forestry, processing agricultural goods, producing consumer goods, and increasing trade was signed in 1986. In 1997, Laos joined ASEAN.

19 ECONOMY

One of the world's poorest and least-developed nations, Laos is overwhelmingly agricultural, with some 80% of the population engaged in farming. Because industrialization is minimal, Laos imports nearly all the manufactured products it requires. Distribution of imports is limited almost entirely to Vientiane and a few other towns, and even there consumption is low. The hostilities of the 1960s and 1970s badly disrupted the economy, forcing the country to depend on imports from Thailand to supplement its daily rice requirements. With the curtailment of hostilities in 1975, the development of a unified political structure offered an immediate advantage. The government began in late 1975 to pursue in earnest a variety of projects to repair and improve the infrastructure and make use of the country's ample mineral, lumber, and hydroelectric resources. During 1978–80, the government gave priority to postwar reconstruction, collectivization of agriculture, and improvements in rice production. The first five-year plan (1981–85) had among its goals achievement of self-sufficiency in food and a doubling of industrial activity by

1985. The second five-year plan (1986–90) had similar overall objectives, but the specific strategies were designed to increase savings and reduce waste. Progress was hindered by shortages of capital and skilled workers, inefficient management, and inadequate equipment and spare parts. The third five-year plan (1991–95) continued to emphasize infrastructure improvement, promote export growth, and encourage import-substitution industries in order to redress the balance-of-payments deficit.

By 1997, Laos had made modest improvements. In international investment, it had opened up its economy considerably. More than $5 billion in foreign investment had been made by more than 500 investors, mainly from other ASEAN countries (Laos joined the regional group in 1977). The government had also made considerable progress in the construction of a modern road network linking Laos to China and Vietnam. The country also announced plans for a second bridge into Thailand and the construction of its first railroad, linking Vientiane with Nong Khai in Thailand.

Despite these improvements, however, the domestic numbers continued to disappoint in 1998. Inflation stood at 112% as the kip continued to slip in value against the Thai baht—the most commonly used foreign currency in the country. The inflation and currency devaluation were widely regarded to be the result of continued poor management and a misguided attempt to stem budget deficits by simply printing more notes. The Asian financial crisis also contributed to the poor state of affairs. Although GDP grew at a rate of 4.9% between 1988 and 1998; droughts, floods, and pests plague the country. The 1997–98 budget deficit was in deficit by 4.5% of the GDP. Problems collecting taxes from the largely impoverished populace have also contributed to the problem, resulting in the need for large amounts of aid.

20 INCOME

The US Central Intelligence Agency (CIA) reports that in 1998 Laos's gross domestic product (GDP) was estimated at $6.6 billion. The per capita GDP was estimated at $1,260. The annual growth rate of GDP was estimated at 4%. The average inflation rate in 1998 was 112%. The CIA defines GDP as the value of all final goods and services produced within a nation in a given year and computed on the basis of purchasing power parity (PPP) rather than value as measured on the basis of the rate of exchange. It was estimated that agriculture accounted for 51% of GDP, industry 21%, and services 28%.

Private consumption includes expenditures of individuals, households, and nongovernmental organizations. It was estimated that between 1990 and 1998 private consumption grew at an annual rate of -4.2%. The richest 10% of the population accounted for approximately 26% of household consumption and the poorest 10% approximately 4.2%.

21 LABOR

The estimated labor force is about 1.5 million. In the absence of additional data, it is estimated that 85% are subsistence farmers, with most of the remainder in the public sector as of 1996. Since late 1975, labor has been organized into a single Federation of Lao Trade Unions (FLTU). In November 1990, the government permitted the formation of labor unions in private enterprises as long as they conform to the policies of the FLTU. In 1999, most of the 78,000 members of the FLTU were in the public sector.

There is no right to organize, strike, or bargain collectively. Labor disputes have so far been infrequent and the desperate economic situation means that workers have little bargaining power.

Children under the age of 15 are forbidden by law from working, but many children work for their families in farms or in shops.

The daily minimum wage was $1.09 in 1996.

22 AGRICULTURE

In 1997, Laos' sown-field area was estimated at 852,000 hectares (2,105,000 acres), or less than 4% of the country's total area. Agriculture accounts for 53% of production and as much as 77% of employment. The main crop is rice, almost entirely of the glutinous variety. Except in northern Laos, where some farmers grow dry rice in forest clearings or on hillsides, most Lao are wet-rice farmers. The total area of rice plantings in 1998 was estimated at 618,000 hectares (1,527,000 acres), up from 554,000 hectares (1,369,000 acres) in 1996. Yields, which are relatively low, could be raised substantially through wider use of irrigation and fertilizers. Production, which averaged 609,000 tons annually during 1961–65, rose to 1,675,000 tons in 1998. Less important crops include corn (favored by some upland tribes and stressed by the government as a means of increasing livestock production), manioc, peanuts, and soybeans. The main commercial crops, emphasized by the government as part of its export drive, are coffee, cotton, and tobacco. Also grown are cardamom, tea, ramie, hemp, sugar, bananas, and pineapples. In 1997, the trade surplus for agricultural products was nearly $27 million. The mountain peoples have been known to grow large quantities of opium poppies, sold to dealers in the plains.

23 ANIMAL HUSBANDRY

Cattle raising is important, especially in the southern plains and in the valleys of the Noy, Banghiang, and Don rivers. Much of the livestock population was killed in the final stages of the civil war that ended in 1975. As of 1998, livestock included an estimated 1,112,000 head of cattle, 1,093,000 buffalo, 1,468,000 hogs, and 13,000,000 chickens. Livestock products in 1998 included 41,000 tons of buffalo meat, 31,000 tons of pork, 15,000 tons of beef and veal, 11,000 tons of poultry, and 8,000 tons of eggs.

24 FISHING

Edible fish, found in the Mekong and other rivers, constitutes the main source of protein in the Laotian diet. The prize catch is the pa beuk, weighing 205 kg (450 lb) or more. Despite the abundance of fish and their important contribution to the Laotian subsistence economy, there has been no systematic commercial fishery development. The total catch in 1997 was 40,000 tons.

25 FORESTRY

Timber is a major resource and one of Laos' most valuable exports. About 54% of the total area is forested, and about half of the forested area is commercially exploitable. The principal timber-producing areas are around Champasak, Savannakhét, Khammouan, and Vientiane. Muang Paklay, in western Laos, is noted for its teak. Exploitation is easiest in areas near the Mekong River, which facilitates transportation. Elephants and oxen are used in most forestry operations. Aside from timber, firewood, and charcoal, forestry products include benzoin and benzoin bark, bamboo, copra, kapok, palm oil, rattan, various resins, and sticklac. Production of roundwood totaled an estimated 5.5 million cu m in 1997; over 80% of the annual output is burned as fuel. Sawn wood output in 1997 was about 560,000 cu m; wood-based panels, 125,000 cu m.

26 MINING

Although much of the country remains unprospected, the nature of the terrain has led to ardent speculation about the nation's mineral resources. Laos is fairly rich in gold, gypsum, iron ore, limestone, potash, precious stones, and tin. Currently, only gypsum, salt, and tin are mined. Other mineral resources known to exist in Laos are magnesium, antimony, copper, lead, manganese, pyrites, and sulfur.

Tin production totaled 618 tons of tin concentrate in 1997, down from 906 tons in 1996. Important iron deposits, with reserves of 68% ore estimated at 11 billion tons, have been discovered on the Plain of Jars near Xiangkhoang. A substantial deposit of low-grade anthracite coal has been found at Saravan. Sapphire production went from 4,006 carats in 1996 to 9,229 carats in 1997. Tungsten and copper deposits and gold-bearing alluvials produce a limited income for the local population but have not been exploited by modern industrial methods.

27 ENERGY AND POWER

In 1998, Laos had a net installed electrical generating capacity of 256,000 kW, up from 225,000 kW in 1988. Production of electricity in 1998 totaled 1,340 million kWh (up from 532 million in 1988), of which 99% was hydropower and the remainder from conventional thermal sources. The nation has an estimated hydroelectric potential of 12,500,000 kW, most of which is undeveloped. The largest power project is the Nam Ngum Dam, located on the Mekong 72 km (45 mi) from Vientiane. Construction began in 1969, with the first stage completed in 1971 and the second stage in 1978. Annual output at Nam Ngum is around 900 million kWh, with about 90% of the electricity produced being supplied to Thailand. In 1994, Laos exported 71% of its electrical production. An additional 3,000 kW of capacity comes from several smaller hydroelectric facilities, and about 14,000 kW is provided by diesel-powered generators throughout Laos.

28 INDUSTRY

Industrial development is rudimentary. There are some small mining operations, charcoal ovens, a cement plant, a few brick works, carpenter shops, a tobacco factory, rice mills, some furniture factories, and more than two dozen sawmills. Industrialization plans center on cotton spinning, brewing, coffee and tea processing, and plywood milling. New resource developments, including the Nam Ngum hydroelectric project and the Vientiane sylvite field, have aided industrial growth. Handicrafts account for an important part of the income of many Laotians. Some villages or areas specialize in certain types of products: silk fabrics, baskets, lacquerware, and gold and silver jewelry and ornaments. Bricks, pottery, iron products, and distilled beverages are made in individual villages. Manufacturing is largely confined to the processing of agricultural and forestry products. In 1994, major industries in Laos included garments, 10.45 million pieces; fabrics, 350,000 m; beer, 92,000 hectoliters; detergent powder, 703 tons; timber, 595,000 cu m; plywood, 1.8 million sheets.

In 1998 the incipient industrial sector contributed to 21% of GDP. Industrial activity in 1998 was based predominantly on hydroelectric production accounting for more than 15% of GDP. Based on its water resources the potential for electricity generation has led to Laos' being dubbed the "battery" of Southeast Asia. Environmental degradation from mining and illegal logging has already impacted decisions to construct dams for hydropower. Hydrocarbon exploration undertaken in Laos by three western oil companies has not yet led to commercially exploitable discoveries.

29 SCIENCE AND TECHNOLOGY

Like many developing nations, Laos depends primarily on external expertise in science and technology. Sisavangvong University, founded in 1958 at Vientiane, has faculties of agriculture, forestry, and irrigation, and of medicine, a technical college, and a polytechnic. Regional technical colleges are located in Luang Pradang, Savannakét, and Champasak. In 1987–97, science and engineering students accounted for 20% of college and university enrollments.

30 DOMESTIC TRADE

Before the Pathet Lao came to power, there was a growing market in Laos for capital and consumer goods. Vientiane was the wholesale distributing point for much of the country. In late 1975, private trade was banned and many small traders and businessmen—including Chinese, Japanese, Pakistani, Thai, and Vietnamese—fled the country. The new government subsequently made it clear that the trend toward consumerism would be reversed in favor of a production-oriented society. The Pathet Lao entered directly into the distribution and sale of essential commodities, such as rice and sugar, and prices were brought under control. In 1979, however, the ban on private trade was lifted, and consumer items, which had all but disappeared from circulation, were once again available. In the countryside, barter replaces money as the principal method of exchange. Markets are held at regular intervals, generally one day a week, at central villages or smaller towns. Once or twice a year, lowland farmers barter cloth and handicraft products with the mountain peoples for cereals, deer and rhinoceros horns, and ivory. Certain items recognized as media of exchange include tea, opium, tobacco, salt, silver, and gold.

The New Economic Mechanism (NEM), a set of economic reforms instituted in 1986 across all sectors of the economy, has begun to demonstrate results in establishing a market-based economy. The government freed the market price of rice and other food staples in 1986, increasing agricultural output despite severe climatic conditions. Later reforms—floating the national currency, the kip, and freeing interest rates—stimulated a market-based economy and controlled inflation. Major land reforms in 1988 included the freedom to sell products at market-determined prices. Growth from these stimuli is demonstrated by the doubling of private shops in Vientiane and abundant fairly-priced goods in the markets. The usual hours of business are from 8 AM until sunset. Banking hours are 8 to 10:30 AM and 2 to 3:30 PM, Monday–Friday.

31 FOREIGN TRADE

The political reorganization of 1975 brought changes in Laos' foreign trade pattern, because regional alignments were shifting and because the aid needed to finance the nation's imports was no longer available from the US. In the 1980s, much of the nation's trade was subsidized by the former USSR. The export of electricity, the sale of overflight rights to foreign airlines, wood products, green coffee, and tin are sources of foreign earnings. In 1991 Laos' largest export earner, logging, was banned pending steps to prevent further destruction of the forests. There are 11 million ha of mature forests in Laos, and about 4.4 million are considered commercially exploitable. The ban on log exports was modified to allow the export of already cut logs and logs from stipulated cutting areas. Foreign aid grants exceeded export earnings in 1991. In that year export revenue decreased by 22%, compared with 1990, owing to the reduction of timber exports and a decline (caused by drought) in the production of electricity for export. At the same time the cost of imports increased by 62%, owing to the newly adopted free trade measures, which ended restrictions on imported goods.

In 1998, major exports included wood products, garments and textiles, electricity (60%), coffee, and tin. Agriculture as a whole contributes about 40% of export earnings. Major imports include machinery and equipment, vehicles, and fuel.

Principal trading partners in 1998 (in millions of US dollars) were as follows:

COUNTRY	EXPORTS	IMPORTS	BALANCE
Japan	398	21	377
Thailand	29	411	-382
France	23	6	17
Germany	21	15	6
United States	20	4	16
Belgium	13	2	11
United Kingdom	8	3	5
China (inc. Hong Kong)	7	29	-22
Singapore	1	22	-21
Vietnam	n.a.	29	

³²BALANCE OF PAYMENTS

Laos has experienced severe trade deficits since independence. From 1963 through mid-1975, substantial deficit financing was provided through the Foreign Exchange Operations Fund (FEOF), an agency backed largely by the US but also receiving funds from Japan, France, the UK, and Australia. In June 1975, the flight of gold and hard currencies from the country forced the government to ban exports of gold and silver bullion. A devaluation of the kip had the effect of further inflating its price, with the black market exchange rate soaring. In the 1980s, financing came mainly from the former USSR, with smaller amounts from multilateral agencies. Since the collapse of communism in Europe, Laos has lost this vital means of support. Even with its recent attraction of international investment ($5 billion from 1988–94), it still relies heavily on aid. Primary sources are Scandinavia, the US, and Japan. In 1995, the IMF announced a $17 million loan to the country, its second in a series of structural adjustment loans. Laos received a total of $290 million in economic aid in 1998.

The US Central Intelligence Agency reports that in 1998 the purchasing power parity of Laos's exports was $330 million while imports totaled $630 million resulting in a trade balance of -$300 million.

The International Monetary Fund (IMF) reports that in 1998 Laos had exports of goods totaling $342 million and imports totaling $507 million. The services credit totaled $145 million and debit $96 million. The following table summarizes Laos's balance of payments as reported by the IMF for 1998 in millions of US dollars.

Current Account		-150
Balance on goods	-165	
Balance on services	50	
Balance on income	-35	
Current transfers	...	
Capital Account		43
Financial Account		-43
Direct investment abroad	...	
Direct investment in Laos	...	
Portfolio investment assets	...	
Portfolio investment liabilities	...	
Other investment assets	-23	
Other investment liabilities	-21	
Net Errors and Omissions		-104
Reserves and Related Items		254

³³BANKING AND SECURITIES

The central bank, the Bank of the Laotian People's Democratic Republic, regulates a rapidly expanding sector comprising 13 national and foreign-owned banks under the terms of the Commercial Bank and Financial Institutions Act of January 1992. Most of the wholly foreign-owned banks are Thai (such as the Thai Military Bank and Siam Commercial) and many of the joint-venture banks are backed by Thai financiers (such as the Joint Development Bank). The central bank continues to receive technical assistance from multilateral lending agencies, and is gradually strengthening the prodential framework. The banks are now believed to be more efficient. The largest commercial bank, established in 1953, is the Bank of Indochina.

The large-scale flight of foreign currency that accompanied the Pathet Lao's ascendancy to power led the new government to shut down Vientiane's banks in September 1975. Officials subsequently announced the expropriation of most private accounts, claiming they were the property of former rightists and "traitors."

Banking reforms of the 1988–89 period opened Laos to foreign banks. Banks in Laos include: Banque Pour le Commerce Exterieur Lao, Joint Development Bank, Nakhonelouang Bank, and the Vientiane Commercial Bank.

All banks now provide basic business services and offer a range of deposit and credit facilities. Interest rates are increasingly responsive to market conditions but tend to remain close to rates set by the central bank. Public confidence in the banking system as measured by the level of domestic capital mobilization is still low. Until 1988 the wholly state-controlled system serviced the needs of the command economy, offering uncompetitive rates of interest to savers or producers in need of regular credit. Most families continued to save by investing in gold and jewelry. The system suffered severe liquidity problems in 1990–91 when the "privatization" of former state-owned enterprises was at its peak: old debts were not repaid and new capital arriving as a result of the opening of the economy to foreign investors was coming in too slowly. Laos was badly hit in 1997 by the Asian financial crisis, leading to further liquidity problems in 1998.

³⁴INSURANCE

There are no private insurance firms.

³⁵PUBLIC FINANCE

The civil war rendered normal budgetary procedures impossible, the budget being covered largely by US aid and monetary inflation. Deficit financing continued in the 1970s and 1980s, covered mostly by foreign aid from communist nations. With the collapse of this support, however, Laos has increasingly looked to foreign investment capital and Western lending agencies for financial support. Beginning in 1994, the IMF initiated an annual program of loans to assist the country with a structural adjustment program. It lent Laos $17 million in 1995. Still, 31% of the 1995 budget was international aid.

The US Central Intelligence Agency (CIA) estimates that in 1996 Laos's central government took in revenues of approximately $230.2 million and had expenditures of $365.9 million including capital expenditures of $317 million. Overall, the government registered a deficit of approximately $135.7 million. External debt totaled $2.4 billion.

³⁶TAXATION

In 1977, the government introduced a progressive agricultural tax on production. The tax revenues were to be used to develop forestry and mining without the need for outside aid, but the tax had the unwanted side effect of discouraging production by some of the largest landowners and slowing the achievement of self-sufficiency in food. The 1992–93 budget included a new profits tax and a law requiring foreign firms engaged in construction projects to pay taxes. The agricultural tax was replaced by a land tax, and consumption taxes were raised on fuel oil, liquor, beer, and tobacco. The 1989 economic reforms included a new flat tax rate of 20% on profits for foreign-owned companies.

37CUSTOMS AND DUTIES

Import duties are determined on a specific and an ad valorem basis and range from 2–80%, mostly not exceeding 25%. Compensatory duties are imposed on imports of commodities in competition with local goods. A general internal tax is collected on the c.i.f.-plus-duties value of most imports. Certain commodities—including radios, alcoholic beverages, tobacco, and sugar—are subject to special excise taxes. A duty-free unloading zone for Laotian imports is located in the Vietnamese port of Da Nang.

38FOREIGN INVESTMENT

Before 1975, Laotian foreign economic relations were conducted under the FEOF and the US Commodity Import Program, under which dollar exchange was provided; Laos in turn allocated dollars to local importers, who then made kip payments to the government for the purchase of foreign goods. There was little direct foreign investment, however. From 1975 until the mid-1980s, all foreign capital has come in the form of development assistance.

Reforms, as part of the New Economic Mechanism (NEM) initiated in 1986, included the introduction of a the Laos Foreign Investment Code and Decree in 1989. The Foreign Investment Management Committee (FIMC) has the power to interpret the Code and to authorize and approve investment. The Code and Decree focus on three types of transactions: contractual business, joint ventures, and wholly foreign-owned enterprises. Investment is now allowed in the areas of agriculture, forestry, industry, communications, transport, service, and tourism, for projects using the indigenous raw materials and natural resources of Laos. The Decree details the permitted sectors of foreign investment and outlines restrictions and prohibitions. For instance, environmentally damaging investment, investors with overwhelming debt, long-term projects making great use of imported materials, and enterprises that would compete with local entrepreneurs are prohibited and/or discouraged. Hindrances to foreign investment are poor legal and physical infrastructure and a lack of skilled labor and capital. Additional disadvantages in the landlocked country are high transportation costs and limited domestic and foreign markets. In 1994 a new foreign investment law streamlined regulations and tax structures and included a flat corporate tax rate of 20%.

Between 1988–94, foreign investment increased considerably as the NEM took full force. By 1996, total foreign investment in the country since 1988 was more than $5 billion, more than three-quarters of which was in hydroelectricity production. The nation became a member of ASEAN in 1997, which increased investment as Laos was forced to lower trade, immigration, and other barriers to member countries. Japan was the largest bilateral aid donor in 1999.

The following shows the countries with the highest amount of investment in Laos, from 1988 through 30 June 1996 (in thousands of US dollars):

	NUMBER OF PROJECTS	CAPITAL
Thailand	233	2,377,017
US	40	1,736,926
South Korea	16	592,126
France	68	317,606
Australia	42	303,465
Malaysia	11	188,731

39ECONOMIC DEVELOPMENT

The National Plan and Foreign Aid Council was established in June 1956 to prepare a general plan for the development of Laos and to set up a series of five-year plans. In view of its limited capital resources, the government sought increased private foreign investment, continued US governmental economic assistance, and help from international monetary bodies and the Colombo Plan organization. An economic plan drafted by the Laotian government in 1962 was never fully implemented, however, owing to internal instability. Little of the infrastructure for public works, industry, and mining that was abandoned in 1961 has been resumed. Although a major goal of the 1969–74 economic and social development plan, completion of the Nam Ngum Dam, was fulfilled, a host of other targets had to be abandoned because of disruption stemming from the war. Following the Pathet Lao takeover in 1975, efforts were made to restructure the Laotian economy along socialist lines. By 1979, with the economy reduced to a virtual standstill because of poor harvests, rapid inflation, and the absence of any private incentive, the government abandoned centralized planning as the sole route to economic development. Instead, a centrally coordinated amalgam of state-run enterprises, cooperatives, and private ventures was pursued. Laos' first five-year plan (1981–85) envisioned increases of 65–68% in the gross social product, 23–24% in agricultural production, and 100–120% in industrial production, as well as completion of repairs on major highways and waterways. These goals were not met because of managerial inefficiency and waste. The second five-year plan (1986–90) emphasized exportation of food products, strengthening of economic management, rehabilitation of routes to seaports and rural feeder roads, reform of general education and training, and development of small- and medium-scale projects.

US aid to Laos began in 1955 and continued until the US pullout in 1975. During this period, the Laotian economy became almost totally dependent on US aid, which amounted to over $900 million in nonmilitary loans and grants and $1.6 billion in military assistance. After the Pathet Lao took power, China supplied much of the needed assistance between 1975 and 1979. Since 1979, Laos has received direct aid mainly from the former USSR, Vietnam, and their allies. Aid from Council for Mutual Economic Assistance (CMEA) countries totaled $90 million in 1985. Among non-Communist nations, Japan, Australia, Sweden, and the Netherlands have also furnished assistance. In 1985, the US ban on aid to Laos was lifted, largely because of Laotian cooperation in accounting for US military personnel missing in action in Laos during the Vietnam war. Aid from international agencies totaled $183.1 million between 1946 and 1986. In the 1990s the US suspended aid and preferential treatment based on Laos' failure to assist the suppression of drug traffic, but reversed this decision following renewed cooperation by Laos.

The New Economic Mechanism (NEM) approved in 1986 (based on *chin tanakan may*, "new thinking,") introduced free enterprise initiatives including decentralized decision making, deregulation of pricing and financial systems, and promotion of domestic and international trade and foreign investment. Reforms have been introduced in phases. In 1988 land use reforms and market determined prices were introduced. In 1989 the tax system was modified, the Foreign Investment Code and Decree was implemented, the banking system was restructured, and the privatization of state economic enterprises commenced. Creation of a national taxation system and a customs administration are aimed at increasing government revenue. The Ministry of Industry and Primary Resources, the Economic Planning Unit, which monitors existing and new businesses, and the Economic Development Board (EDB), which assists in the establishment of new industries, facilitate foreign investment in most sectors of the economy. Incentives offered to encourage the development of industrial and commercial enterprises include allowing 100% foreign ownership.

The third Five Year Plan (1991–95) continued previous policies of infrastructure improvement, export growth, and import substitution. Four sectors are considered as areas of future income for Laos: mining and energy; agriculture and forestry; tourism; and service, as a way-station and service center between

China, Vietnam, and Cambodia. Laos has untapped mineral resources and proven reserves of gold, gemstones and iron ore. Pulp and paper tree plantations would be substituted for the export of timber and agricultural products to serve the Thai market. Based on Thailand's experience, the government recognizes that mass tourism involves environmental degradation, yet the opening of the Mittaphap (Friendship) Bridge over the Mekong between Laos and Thailand (1994) is an opportunity for both trade and tourism which is readily exploited. (A second bridge was approved in 1996.) In 1993 three western oil companies, Enterprise Oil and Monument Oil, both from the UK, and Hunt Oil of Dallas, engaged in exploration for oil and gas in Laos. The potential for finding hydrocarbons in Laos is largely unknown and exploration risks are considerable, including inadequate geological maps, unexploded ordnance, tough terrain, encounters with the remnants of the anticommunist insurgency movement, tropical and dietary illness, and the expense of drilling and pipeline construction for transport to the Vietnamese coast. Two major hydroelectric projects, the Nam Thuen Dam on a tributary of the Mekong in Khammouan province, and the Xeset dam in southern Laos produce electricity sold to Thailand.

At the sixth party congress, held in March 1996, Laotian officials debated the country's slow pace of opening up to the international investment community. By that year, the country had allowed more than 500 foreign investors, in a variety of sectors, to either establish or buy (in whole or in part) Laotian businesses. The majority of $5 billion (75%) was invested in hydroelectric power. Problems associated with the 1997 Asian financial crisis were minor setbacks on Laos' economic development, but climactic challenges continue to haunt the country.

40 SOCIAL DEVELOPMENT

By almost any measure, Laos is one of the world's most impoverished nations. Food intake does not meet basic requirements; there are virtually no sanitary facilities; and contamination of drinking water is widespread. Almost no families own cars, and bicycles and radios are considered luxuries. In general, the lowland Lao have the highest living standards, with lower standards prevailing among the upland tribes.

Although the Constitution establishes equal rights for women, they have traditionally been subservient to men and have generally been discouraged from obtaining an education. However, the government claims that it has encouraged women to assume a larger role in national life, and girls are increasingly attending school. It has been reported that in urban areas, working women have higher incomes than their male counterparts. The Family Code provides women with equal inheritance and marriage rights. In 1997–99 the government implemented new programs to raise the participation of women in the political system. As of 1997, 21 of 99 parliamentary seats were held by women.

Minority highland tribes have limited ability to influence government decisions. The highland Hmong tribe, furthermore, reports instances of discrimination and harassment, including at least one disappearance of a prominent Hmong activist in 1993. The 1990 Law on Nationality, which took effect in 1994, grants greater citizenship rights to the Chinese and Vietnamese minorities.

In spite of the adoption of a Constitution in 1991 and National Assembly elections in 1993 and 1997, human rights abuses remain. Overt political dissent is not tolerated, and detention without due process is not uncommon. Prison conditions are harsh, and the government suppresses the freedoms of speech, assembly, and association and restricts freedom of religion.

41 HEALTH

The use of Western medicine has improved health generally and reduced the incidence of malaria and smallpox specifically, but a high infant mortality and a variety of health problems remain. Most urban areas, including Vientiane, lack pure water and sanitary disposal systems. In 1995, only 51% of the population had access to safe water, and merely 32% had adequate sanitation. In parts of Laos, malaria—the most serious health threat—is known to affect the majority of children. In 1995 there were 1,365 new cases of cholera. Other health problems are acute upper respiratory infections (including pneumonia and influenza), diarrhea and dysentery, parasites, yaws, skin ailments, various childhood diseases, hepatitis, venereal disease, and tuberculosis. Common diseases in recent years have been malaria (41,787 cases in 1993); measles (3,174 cases in 1995); and leprosy (967 cases in 1995). In 1997, there were 167 reported cases of tuberculosis per 100,000 inhabitants. In the mid-1990s, a UNICEF survey found iodine deficiencies and goiter to be common problems in rural areas of Laos. Programs to increase iodine levels via salt intake were being instituted. An estimated 25% of school-age children were reported to have goiter. Children up to 1 year of age were vaccinated in 1990–94 against tuberculosis (69%); diphtheria, pertussis, and tetanus (48%); polio (57%); and measles (73%). The prevalence of underweight children in 1995 was 44%, greater than the average of developing countries in South East Asia.

Average life expectancy in 1999 was estimated at 54.2 years for men and women; infant mortality in 1999 was estimated at 89.3 per 1,000 live births. The total fertility rate has remained nearly constant over the last years. The fertility rate in 1999 was 5.5 children per woman during her childbearing years. The overall mortality rate in 1999 was 12.6 per 1,000 people; the maternal mortality rate in 1991–93 was 300 per 100,000 live births.

In 1990–97, there were 0.2 doctors and 2.6 hospital beds per 1,000 people. In 1990–97, total health care expenditures were 2.6% of GDP.

42 HOUSING

The typical house is rectangular, built entirely of wooden planks and bamboo, with a thatched roof, and is raised off the ground on wooden pilings 1–2 m (3–6 ft) high. There is a critical housing shortage in the towns, and many dwellings are substandard. As of 1990, 47% of urban and 25% of rural dwellers had access to a public water supply, while 30% of urban and 8% of rural dwellers had access to sanitation services.

43 EDUCATION

Education in Laos is compulsory for five years of primary education. In 1997, there were 7,896 primary schools with 25,831 teachers and 786,335 students. Student-to-teacher ratio stood at 30 to one. In 1996, secondary schools had 11,269 teachers and 169,691 students. Attendance at Laotian primary and secondary schools increased from 300,000 in 1972 to 600,000 in 1979.

In 1997 there were 1,369 teaching faculty and 12,732 students enrolled at all higher level institutions. Sisavongvong University at Vientiane includes a school of education, a school of law and administration, a school of medicine, a school of vocational training, a school of agriculture, and a school of public works. There were also regional technical colleges and 63 teacher training colleges as of 1985. For the year 2000, adult illiteracy rates were estimated at 38.2% (males, 26.4%; females, 49.5%).

44 LIBRARIES AND MUSEUMS

The National Library (Vientiane), with 265,000 volumes in French, Lao, and English, is the nation's largest library. In addition, a Buddhist institute owns a number of classical manuscripts. Many excellent traditional works of art and architecture may be seen in Vientiane and Luangphrabang. Of particular interest in the latter city is the former royal palace and the Prabang (Golden Buddha), which was brought to Laos from Cambodia in the days of Fa-Ngoum. Also in Vientiane are the National Museum and the Museum of Religious Art.

45MEDIA

All communications, including the radio network, are operated by the government. Regular radio broadcasts were begun from Vientiane in 1968 and are now carried by Lao National Radio. Most broadcasts are in Lao, but government news broadcasts are also in English, French, and other languages. Domestic television service from Lao National TV began in 1983; in addition, programs are available by satellite from the former USSR, and it is possible to pick up Thai broadcasts. As of 1999 there were nine AM and 4 FM radio stations and four television stations. There were 139 radios, four television sets, and one mobile phone per 1,000 population as of 1998, as well as an estimated 28,000 telephones. (An additional 48,000 telephone lines were expected to be added by 2001.) Beginning in 1992 telephone owners were able to direct dial internationally, and private facsimile machines were permitted.

The press is government-controlled. The sole news agency is the Laos News Agency; the only foreign news bureaus are those of the former USSR and Vietnam. As of 1999, there were three daily newspapers. The principal Vientiane newspapers are *Paxaxon* (*The People*), with a 1999 circulation of 28,000; *Vientiane Mai* (*New Vientiane*), with a circulation of 4,700; and *Khao San Pathet Lao* (*Laos Newsletter*), with a circulation of 1,200.

Although there are constitutional provisions for freedom of speech and the press, the government is said to exert broad control over the exercise of these rights. All domestically produced newspapers, radio, and television are controlled by the Ministry of Information, which reacts harshly to expressions of political dissent.

As of 1999, establishment of Laos's first Internet host was pending.

46ORGANIZATIONS

Before 1975 there were chambers of commerce in Vientiane and Pakxé. Boy Scout and Girl Scout organizations had long been active. Since 1975, the Lao People's Revolutionary Party and its allied social and political groups in the Lao Front for National Reconstruction have dominated Laotian life. The cooperative movement has been intensively developed. There is also a Lao Unified Buddhists' Association.

47TOURISM, TRAVEL, AND RECREATION

The Pathet Lao government has had little interest in tourism, and foreigners are rarely granted permits to travel outside Vientiane. Although individual tourist visas are difficult to obtain, the government's official tourist organization, Inter-Lao Tourisme, has been issuing growing numbers of visas to tour groups. The main tourist destinations are Vientiane, with its Buddhist pagodas, and the city of Luangphrabang at the junction of the

Nam Khan and Mekong Rivers in the North. In 1998 Laos recorded 500,200 tourist arrivals, and receipts from tourism reached $73 million in 1997. That year there were 4,108 rooms in hotels and guest houses with a total of 7,116 beds.

According to 1999 UN estimates, the cost of staying in Vientiane was $50–$80 per day. Estimated costs in small towns were as low as $21 per day.

48FAMOUS LAOTIANS

One of the most cherished figures in Laotian history is Fa-Ngoum, who unified Lan Xang in the 14th century. Another dynastic personage still revered is the monarch Sethathirat, in whose reign (1534–71) the famous That Luang shrine was built. Chao Anou (r.1805–28) is remembered for having fought a war to recover Laotian independence from the Siamese (Thais) and for having restored Vientiane to a glory it had not known since the 16th century. Important 20th-century figures include Souvanna Phouma (1901–84), former prime minister; Prince Souphanouvong (1902–95), a half-brother of Souvanna Phouma, leader of the Pathet Lao and president of Laos from 1975 to 1986; and Kaysone Phomvihan (1920–1992), former chairman of the Council of Ministers.

49DEPENDENCIES

Laos has no territories or colonies.

50BIBLIOGRAPHY

Brown, MacAlister, and Joseph J. Zasloff. *Apprentice Revolutionaries: The Communist Movements in Laos, 1930–1985.* Stanford, Calif.: Stanford University Hoover Press, 1986.

Buckley, Michael. *Vietnam, Cambodia, and Laos Handbook.* Chico, Calif.: Moon Publications, 1996.

Castle, Timothy N. *At War in the Shadow of Vietnam: U.S. Military Aid to the Royal Lao Government, 1955–1975.* New York: Columbia University Press, 1993.

Chan, Sucheng. *Hmong Means Free: Life in Laos and America.* Philadelphia: Temple University Press, 1994.

Cordell, Helen. *Laos.* Santa Barbara, Calif.: Clio, 1991.

Evans, Grant. *Lao Peasants under Socialism.* New Haven: Yale University Press, 1990.

Hamilton-Merritt, Jane. *Tragic Mountains: The Hmong, the Americans, and the Secret Wars for Laos, 1942–1992.* Bloomington: Indiana University Press, 1993.

Ivarsson, Soren. *The Quest for Balance in a Changing Laos: A Political Analysis.* Copenhagen: NIAS Books, 1995.

Laos' Dilemmas and Options: The Challenge of Economic Transition in the 1990s. New York: St. Martin's Press, 1997.

Stuart-Fox, Martin. *Buddhist Kingdom, Marxist State: The Making of Modern Laos.* Bangkok: White Lotus, 1996.

———. *Contemporary Laos: Studies in the Politics and Society of the Lao People's Democratic Republic.* New York: St. Martin's Press, 1982.

———. *Historical Dictionary of Laos.* Metuchen, N.J.: Scarecrow Press, 1992.

Zasloff, Joseph J. *The Pathet Lao: Leadership and Organization.* Lexington, Mass.: Heath, 1973.

Zasloff, Joseph J., and Leonard Unger (eds.). *Laos: Beyond the Revolution.* New York: St. Martin's Press, 1991.

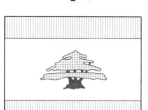

LEBANON

Republic of Lebanon

Al-Jumhuriyah al-Lubnaniyah

CAPITAL: Beirut (Bayrut).

FLAG: The national flag, introduced in 1943, consists of two horizontal red stripes separated by a white stripe which is twice as wide; at the center, in green and brown, is a cedar tree.

ANTHEM: *Kulluna lil watan lil'ula lil'alam (All of Us for the Country, Glory, Flag).*

MONETARY UNIT: The Lebanese pound, or livre libanaise (LL), is a paper currency of 100 piasters. There are coins of 1, 2½, 5, 10, 25, and 50 piasters and 1 Lebanese pound, and notes of 1, 5, 10, 25, 50, 100, 250, 1,000 and 10,000 Lebanese pounds. LL1 = $0.00066 ($1 = LL1505.0) as of 31 March 2000.

WEIGHTS AND MEASURES: The metric system is the legal standard, but traditional weights and measures are still used.

HOLIDAYS: New Year's Day, 1 January; Arab League Day, 22 March; Independence Day, 22 November; Evacuation Day, 31 December. Christian religious holidays include Feast of St. Maron, 9 February; Good Friday; Easter Monday; Ascension; Assumption, 15 August; All Saints' Day, 1 November; and Christmas, 25 December. Muslim religious holidays include 'Id al-Fitr, 'Id al-'Adha', and Milad an-Nabi.

TIME: 2 PM = noon GMT.

¹LOCATION, SIZE, AND EXTENT

Situated on the eastern coast of the Mediterranean Sea, Lebanon has an area of 10,400 sq km (4,015 sq mi), extending 217 km (135 mi) NE–SW and 56 km (35 mi) SE–NW. It is bordered on the N and E by Syria, on the S by Israel, and on the W by the Mediterranean Sea, with a total boundary length of 679 km (422 mi). Comparatively, the area occupied by Lebanon is about three-fourths the size of the state of Connecticut.

The Lebanon of today is the Greater Lebanon (Grand Liban) created by France in September 1920, which includes the traditional area of Mount Lebanon—the hinterland of the coastal strip from Sidon (Sayda) to Tripoli (Tarabulus)—some coastal cities and districts such as Beirut and Tripoli, and the Bekaa (Biqa') Valley in the east. As of January 1988, more than two-thirds of the territory was under foreign military occupation. Syrian forces have held northern Lebanon and the Bekaa Valley since 1976; West Beirut and the Beirut-Sidon coastal strip fell into their hands in February 1987. In southern Lebanon, Israeli troops in conjunction with the South Lebanese Army, a local militia, control a 1,000-sq-km (400-sq-mi) strip along the Israeli border.

Lebanon's capital city, Beirut, is located on the Mediterranean coast.

²TOPOGRAPHY

The Mount Lebanon area is rugged; there is a rise from sea level to a parallel mountain range of about 2,000–3,000 m (6,600–9,800 ft) in less than 40 km (25 mi), and heavy downpour of winter rains has formed many deep clefts and valleys in the soft rock. The terrain has profoundly affected the country's history in that virtually the whole landscape is a series of superb natural fortresses from which guerrilla activities can render the maintenance of control by a centralized government an intermittent and costly affair. East of the Mount Lebanon Range is the Bekaa Valley, an extremely fertile flatland about 16 km (10 mi) wide and 129 km (80 mi) long from north to south. At the eastern flank of the Bekaa rise the Anti-Lebanon Range and the Hermon extension, in which stands Mount Hermon straddling the border

with Syria. Lebanon contains few rivers, and its harbors are mostly shallow and small. Abundant springs, found to a height of 1,500 m (4,900 ft) on the western slopes of the Lebanon Mountains, provide water for cultivation up to this height.

³CLIMATE

Lebanon's extraordinarily varied climate is due mainly to the wide range of elevation and the westerly winds that make the Mediterranean coast much wetter than the eastern hills, mountainsides, and valleys. Within a 16-km (10-mi) radius of many villages, apples, olives, and bananas are grown; within 45 minutes' drive in winter, spring, and fall, both skiing and swimming are possible. Rainfall is abundant by Middle Eastern standards, with about 90 cm (35 in) yearly along the coast, about 125 cm (50 in) on the western slopes of the mountains, and less than 38 cm (15 in) in the Bekaa. About 80% of the rain falls from November to March, mostly in December, January, and February. Summer is a dry season, but it is humid along the coast. The average annual temperature in Beirut is 21°C (70°F), with a range from 13°C (55°F) in winter to 28°C (82°F) in summer.

⁴FLORA AND FAUNA

Lebanon is rich in flora, with approximately 2,500 species. Olive and fig trees and grapevines are abundant on lower ground, while cedar, maple, juniper, fir, cypress, valonia oak, and Aleppo pine trees occupy higher altitudes. Vegetation types range from subtropical and desert to alpine. Although hunting has killed off most wild mammals, jackals are still found in the wilder rural regions, and gazelles and rabbits are numerous in the south. Many varieties of rodents, including mice, squirrels, and gerbils, and many types of reptiles, including lizards and snakes (some of them poisonous), may be found. Thrushes, nightingales, and other songbirds are native to Lebanon; there are also partridges, pigeons, vultures, and eagles.

[5]ENVIRONMENT

Lebanon's forests and water supplies suffered significant damage in the 1975–76 war and subsequent fighting. Rapid urbanization has also left its mark on the environment. Coastal waters show the effects of untreated sewage disposal, particularly near Beirut, and of tanker oil discharges and oil spills. The water pollution problem in Lebanon is in part due to the lack of an internal system to consistently regulate water purification. The nation has 1.2 cubic miles of water with 85% used for farming activity and 4% used for industrial purposes. Lebanon's cities produce 0.5 million tons of solid waste per year. Air pollution is a serious problem in Beirut because of vehicular exhaust and the burning of industrial wastes. In 1992, industrial carbon dioxide emissions totaled 11 million metric tons, a per capita level of 3.88 metric tons. Control efforts have been nonexistent or ineffective because of political fragmentation and recurrent warfare since 1975. The effects of war and the growth of the nation's cities have combined to threaten animal and plant life in Lebanon. In 1986, the National Preservation Park of Bte'nayel was created in the region of Byblos to preserve wooded areas and wildlife. Four of the nation's mammal species and 14 of its bird species are endangered. Five of its plant species are also threatened with extinction. The Arabian gazelle and Anatolian leopard are extinct.

[6]POPULATION

The fragile political balance between the many ethnic and religious groups prevented a census from being conducted from 1932 until 1995 (although in 1970 a sample survey was taken), when the results were used to reapportion government offices. In 1995, the official population figure was 3,111,828, excluding Palestinians. By 2000, the population of Lebanon was estimated at 3,619,971. An estimated 5.6% of the population is 65 years of age or older. The projected population for the year 2005 is 3,904,000, assuming a crude birthrate of 20 per 1,000 population and a death rate of 6, resulting in a natural rate of change of 1.4% for the period 2000–2005. The population rate of change between 1995 and 2000 was 1.8%. The population density in 1998 was 412 per sq km (1067 per sq mi).

It was estimated that 90% of the population lived in urban areas in 2000, up from 74% in 1980. The capital city, Beirut, and its surrounding metropolitan area had a 2000 population of 2,058,000. Tripoli had approximately 160,000 inhabitants.

[7]MIGRATION

The economic roots of emigration may be traced to the increase of crop specialization during the 19th century and to the subsequent setbacks of the silk market toward the end of the century. Political incentives also existed, and many Lebanese left their country for Egypt (then under British rule) or the Americas at the turn of the century. After the mid-1960s, skilled Lebanese were attracted by economic opportunities in the Persian Gulf countries. Large numbers fled abroad, many of them to France, Syria. Jordan, Egypt, and the Gulf countries, during the civil war in 1975–76. In 1986, the Lebanese World Cultural Union estimated that some 13,300,000 persons of Lebanese extraction were living abroad, the largest numbers in Brazil, the US, and Argentina.

Since the outbreak of war in 1975, internal migration has largely followed the pattern of hostilities, peaking in 1975/76 and again after the Israeli invasion of 1982. In 1993, the number of refugees in various parts of the country was estimated at over 600,000. As of April 1998, the UNHCR was helping to assist 3,191 refugees in Lebanon, including 1,990 Iraqis, 550 Afghans, 284 Sudanese, 152 Somalis, and 250 refugees from various other countries. Also in 1998, there were more than 350,000 Palestinian refugees who had asylum in Lebanon, where they were assisted by UNRWA. In 1999, the net migration rate was zero per 1,000 population.

[8]ETHNIC GROUPS

Ethnic mixtures dating back to various periods of immigration and invasion are represented, as are peoples of almost all Middle Eastern countries. A confusing factor is the religious basis of ethnic differentiation. Thus, while most Lebanese are Arabs, they are divided into Muslims and Christians, each in turn subdivided into a number of faiths or sects, most of them formed by historical development into separate ethnic groups. The Muslims are divided into Sunnis and Shi'is. The Druzes, whose religion derives from Islam, are a significant minority. The Christians are divided mainly among Maronites, Greek Orthodox, and Greek Catholics. All the major groups have their own political organizations, paramilitary units, and territorial strongholds. Other ethnic groups include Armenians (most of them Armenian Orthodox, with some Armenian Catholics) and small numbers of Jews, Syrians, Kurds, and others. The number of Palestinians is estimated at 450,000–500,000. In addition there are about 180,000 stateless undocumented persons. Some of these are inhabitants of disputed border areas. As of 1999, population statistics stood at 95% Arab, 4% Armenian, and 1% other.

[9]LANGUAGES

Arabic is the official language and is spoken throughout the country. Much of the population is bilingual, with French as the main second language. There are also significant numbers of English, Armenian, and Turkish speakers. The distinctive Lebanese Arabic dialect contains various relics of pre-Arabic languages and also shows considerable European influence in vocabulary.

[10]RELIGIONS

Religious communities in the Ottoman Empire were largely autonomous in matters of personal status law and were at times treated as corporations for tax and public security matters. Membership in a millet, as these groups were called in Ottoman law, gave the individual citizenship, and this position, although somewhat modified, has given Lebanese politics its confessional nature. Religion is closely connected with civic affairs, and the size and competing influence of the various religious groups are matters of overriding political importance. The imbalance of power between Christians and Muslims, aggravated by the presence of large numbers of Palestinians, was a major factor contributing to the bitter civil war in 1975–76. As of 1999, 70% of the population practiced Islam (5 legally recognized groups—Alawite or Nusayri, Druze, Isma'ilite, Shi'a, and Sunni). Christians made up 30% of the population (11 legally recognized groups—4 Orthodox Christian, 6 Catholic, and 1 Protestant). The number practicing Judaism was negligible. Muslims have come to outnumber Christians as the result of long-term demographic trends and population displacements during and after the civil war.

Under an unwritten agreement made at the time of the National Covenant of 1943, the president of Lebanon must be a Maronite Christian and the prime minister a Sunni Muslim, with a ratio of six Christians to every five Muslims in the legislature. But this arrangement has subsequently ceased to reflect the strength of competing religious groups in the population and is widely criticized.

[11]TRANSPORTATION

As of 1998, Lebanon had an estimated 6,270 km (3,896 mi) of paved roads. Construction of new roads have been frequently delayed by recurrent hostilities. Many roads were badly in need of repair; since 1982, fully one-third of the country's roads have been rehabilitated. Some new mileage has also been added.

The 222 km (138 mi) state-owned railway consists of a 1.435-m-gauge line running parallel to the coastal area where civil hostilities kept the railway virtually inoperable in 1991.

Beirut, a major Mediterranean port, was closed during the 1975–76 war and intermittently thereafter, reopening by March 1991. When Beirut port was closed, Sidon became the principal port for Muslims and Juniyah for Christians. Other ports include Tripoli and Tyre. As of 1998, Lebanon had a merchant fleet of 64 ships with a capacity of 267,562 GRT.

There were nine airports in 1998, seven with paved runways. Beirut International, Lebanon's principal airport, remained generally open until bombing during the Israeli invasion forced its closure in June–October 1982. It had handled 1,660,000 passengers in 1980; by 1985, the number was down to 599,000. Lebanon's two airlines, Middle East Airlines (MEA) and Trans-Mediterranean Airways (TMA), suffered heavy losses during the 1975–76 war and the Israeli invasion. In 1997, 857,000 passengers were carried on scheduled domestic and international flights.

¹²HISTORY

The geographical features of Lebanon have had a major effect on its history. Its mountains enabled the minority communities to survive the despotisms that submerged the surrounding areas. The sea provided trade routes in ancient times for exports from Lebanese cedar and spruce forests, and for commerce in copper and iron during the time of the Ptolemies and the Romans. Both Lebanon and Syria were historically associated from early times as part of Phoenicia (c.1600–c.800 BC), and both were later swept up into the Roman Empire. In the 7th century AD, the Arabs conquered part of Lebanon. Maronite Christians had long been established there; Islam gradually spread by conversion and migration, although the country remained predominantly Christian. In the 11th century, the Druzes established themselves in the south of the Mount Lebanon area as well as in Syria. Parts of Lebanon fell temporarily to the Crusaders; invasions by Mongols and others followed, and trade declined until the reunification of the Middle East under the Ottoman Empire.

For the most part, Ottoman officials of the surrounding areas left the Mount Lebanon districts to their own emirs and sheikhs. Fakhr ad-Din (1586–1635) of the Ma'an family set out to create an autonomous Lebanon, opened the country to Western Europe through commercial and military pacts, and encouraged Christian missionary activity. In 1697, the Shihab family acquired dominance, and from 1788 to 1840, except for a few intervals, Mount Lebanon was ruled by Bashir II of the Shihab family, who extended his power and was partly successful in building a strong state. The Egyptian occupation of Syria (1832–40) opened the Levant to large-scale European penetration and tied Lebanese affairs to international politics. It also heightened the antipathy between Christians and Druzes, with the occupiers from time to time using armed groups of one against the other. The British invasion of 1840–41 served to deliver Lebanon from Egyptian rule and forced Bashir II into exile, but it also involved France and the UK in the problem of finding a modus vivendi for the religious factions. A partition of government did not work. Economic discontent was inflamed by religious antagonisms, and the Druzes, feeling their power dwindling, organized a major onslaught against the Christians in 1860. When the latter, fearing annihilation, requested European intervention, major powers sent fleets into Syrian waters and the French sent an army into Mount Lebanon. Under European pressure, the Ottoman government agreed to the establishment of an international commission to set up a new, pro-Christian government; an autonomous province of Mount Lebanon was created in 1864, with a Christian governor

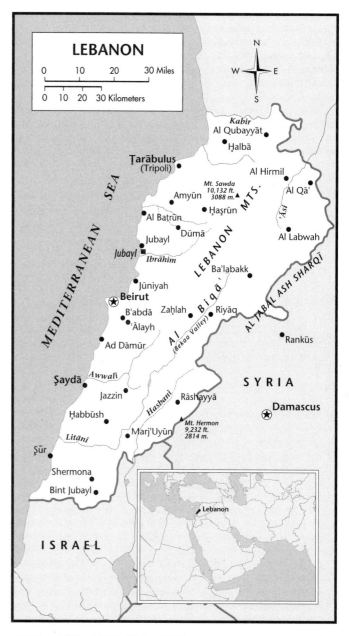

LOCATION: 35°6′ to 36°36′E; 33°4′ to 34°41′N. **BOUNDARY LENGTHS:** Syria, 359 km (223 mi); Israel, 102 km (63 mi); Mediterranean coastline, 195 km (121 mi). **TERRITORIAL SEA LIMIT:** 12 mi.

who, though the servant of the Ottoman state, relied upon European backing in disputes with his sovereign.

The entry of the Ottoman Empire into World War I led to an Allied blockade, widespread hunger, and the destruction of Lebanese prosperity. An Anglo-French force took the country in 1918, and in 1920, an Allied conference gave France a mandate over Syria, in which Mount Lebanon was included. The French separated from Syria the area they called Greater Lebanon (Grand Liban), which was four times as large as the traditional Mount Lebanon and included a Muslim population almost as large as the Christian. The mandate years were a time of material growth and little political development.

Lebanon came under Vichy control in 1940, but in 1941, Lebanon and Syria were taken by a combined Anglo–Free French force. The Free French proclaimed Lebanese independence in

November 1941, but when a strongly nationalistic government was created in 1943, the French intervened and arrested the new president, Bishara al-Khuri. An insurrection followed, prompting UK intervention and the restoration of the government. In 1945 agreement was achieved for the withdrawal of both UK and French forces, and in 1946 Lebanon assumed complete independence.

The 1950s and 1960s were generally characterized by economic and political stability. Beginning in 1952, Lebanon received increased US aid and also benefited from an influx of Western commercial personnel and from growing oil royalties. It also seemed the calmest center of the Middle East, taking little part in the Arab-Israeli war of 1948 and no action in the wars of 1967 and 1973. In 1958, however, a reported attempt by President Camille Chamoun (Sha'mun) to seek a second term precipitated a civil war, and in July the US sent forces to help quell the insurrection; this move was in keeping with the Eisenhower Doctrine, which pledged US military and economic aid to any country requesting it in order to counter a Communist threat. The crisis was settled when Gen. Fu'ad Shihab (Chehab), who was supported by both government and opposition groups, was elected president in July. By October US forces were withdrawn, and public security was reestablished.

In the late 1960s and early 1970s Lebanon's economy was disrupted by conflict in the Middle East, vividly brought home by the presence, near the border with Israel, of thousands of well-armed Palestinian guerrillas, many of whom had come from Jordan following the "Black September" fighting there in 1970–71. Serious clashes between them and the Lebanese army occurred in 1969. Fearing civil war, the government that year signed the so-called Cairo Accord with the Palestinian Liberation Organization (PLO), which virtually made it a state within the state. The PLO gained the right to establish military bases and launch cross-border raids into Israel. This inevitably led to Israeli reprisals, and PLO interference in Lebanese affairs accelerated a slide toward anarchy. In April and May 1974, a series of Palestinian attacks on Lebanese villages killed scores of persons and injured hundreds. Government efforts to deal with the problem were denounced as insufficient by Christian rightists, while Muslim leftists defended the Palestinians, and both factions formed private militias.

During the early months of 1975, sporadic violence between the two factions gradually erupted into a full-scale civil war that pitted Maronite Christians against Muslims and against other Christian sects, and rightist militants against Palestinian guerrillas and other leftist Arab forces. At least 100,000 people on all sides were killed and some 600,000 persons displaced during the eighteen months of fighting. In April 1976 Syrian forces entered Lebanon, in an apparent effort to prevent an all-out victory by left-wing Muslims and Palestinians; by the fall, some 20,000 Syrian troops controlled the Bekaa Valley. A cease-fire arranged through the mediation of Sa'udi Arabia and other Arab countries enabled a peacekeeping force (including Syrian troops) to separate the combatants and end the war in October. The conflict not only devastated Lebanon economically, but so weakened the central government that effective power lay with the Syrians, the Palestinians, and some thirty sectarian militias. In general, the Christian Phalangists held sway over east-central Lebanon; fighters loyal to Major Sa'ad Haddad, a right-wing Lebanese army officer, controlled the southern border area, in a security zone set up by Israel; and the PLO, other Muslim leftists, and Syrian forces occupied northern and eastern Lebanon.

Intermittent fighting between the armed factions continued, and raids by Palestinian guerrillas based in southern Lebanon drew Israel into the conflict. In March 1978 the Israeli army invaded southern Lebanon, destroyed PLO bases, and then withdrew when the UN Interim Force in Lebanon (UNIFIL) was established to keep the peace. Continuing PLO rocket attacks on northern Israel and Syria's installation of antiaircraft missiles in the Bekaa Valley prompted Israel to launch a full-scale invasion of Lebanon in June 1982. Israeli forces quickly destroyed PLO bases in the south and in Tyre and Sidon, penetrated to the outskirts of Beirut, and disabled the Syrian missile bases. Several cease-fires arranged by US envoy Philip Habib broke down, but following a two-month Israeli siege of West Beirut, where the Palestinians were encamped, a truce was agreed to by Israel, the PLO, and Syria; by 1 September, more than 14,000 Palestinian and Syrian fighters had been evacuated. The Lebanese estimated their war casualties at more than 19,000 dead and 30,000 wounded (figures disputed by Israel). A multinational peacekeeping force, comprising British, French, and Italian soldiers and US marines, was stationed in the Beirut area in early September.

Despite the truce, the violence continued. On 14 September Bashir Gemayel, a Phalangist leader who in August had been elected president by the Lebanese parliament, was assassinated. Almost immediately, Israeli troops moved into West Beirut to wipe out pockets of Palestinian resistance causing tens of thousands of casualties. Phalangist forces were allowed into the Sabra and Shatila refugee camps, and at least 600 Palestinians, many of them civilians, were massacred; a subsequent Israeli government inquiry was critical of senior officials for indirect responsibility for the killings. In 1983 Israeli and Syrian troops still occupied large portions of Lebanon, and they became targets of attack by Muslim and Druze forces. In May 1983 Lebanon, Israel, and the US signed an agreement by which Lebanon and Israel agreed to end their state of war. Israel agreed to withdraw all its forces, and both countries agreed to establish a security zone in southern Lebanon patrolled by Lebanese forces and joint Israeli-Lebanese teams. However, Syria opposed it and the agreement, never implemented, was repudiated by Lebanon in 1984.

The American embassy in Beirut was bombed in April 1983, and US marines were harassed by sniper fire. On 23 October, 241 of them were killed by a truck-bomb explosion in their barracks at Beirut airport; on the same day, a similar bombing caused at least fifty-eight deaths at a French paratroop barracks. Shortly before, Lebanon and Syria had agreed to a cease-fire pending a reconciliation conference, which began in Switzerland in November, with all major Lebanese political factions participating. Meanwhile, fighting broke out between a radical Syrian-supported PLO faction and guerrillas loyal to Yasser Arafat, chairman of the organization; defeated at Tripoli, Arafat withdrew from Lebanon in December.

As 1984 began, the position of the government headed by Amin Gemayel, who had been elected president to succeed his brother, was deteriorating. In February the US, UK, and Italy pulled their ground troops and nonessential personnel out of the Beirut area. In March, the Lebanese reconciliation conference dissolved without reaching substantial agreement. The following month a "national unity" government was formed, bringing together the leaders of all the major warring factions. But it almost never met and could not pacify the country; intermittent clashes between factions continued. Israel's withdrawal of its troops from Lebanon (except the south) in early 1985 left in its wake renewed fighting for the evacuated territory. In December a Syrian-sponsored cease-fire agreement that included constitutional reforms was signed by the Druze, Amal (Shi'i), and Christian factions, but its terms were never implemented. The general lawlessness encouraged terrorist groups of all kinds to promote their own ends by assassinations, kidnappings, and bombings. Among the most feared was the Hezbollah, or Party of God, which was aligned with fundamentalist Iranian Revolutionary Guards.

In 1985–86 there was sporadic fierce fighting between Palestinian and Shi'i Amal militia. Syria pushed for political reform and, when opposed by Gemayel and militant Christians, influenced Muslim ministers not to deal with the President, thus paralyzing the government. With the economy in serious decline, Prime Minister Rashid Karami was assassinated to be succeeded by Salim al-Huss. The badly divided factions could not agree on a successor to Gemayel when his term expired in September 1988. Christian Army Commander Michel Aoun asserted himself as prime minister, giving Lebanon two governments, a Muslim one in West Beirut and a Christian one in East Beirut. Aoun was opposed by the Syrians and Muslims and by rival Christian factions.

In January 1989 the Arab League appointed a committee on Lebanon which eventually, in September, arranged for a seven-point cease-fire and convened a meeting of Lebanese parliamentarians in Taif, Sa'udi Arabia. The Taif Accord that resulted in November led to the election of Elias Hrawi, a Maronite Christian, as president. He named al-Huss prime minister. When forces of General Aoun (who was technically deposed by Hrawi) attacked Christian and Syrian positions, they retaliated in strength and finally obliged him to take exile in France in 1991.

In 1991–92 the government gradually began to reassert its authority. Militias, except notably Hezbollah and the Israeli-backed army of South Lebanon, were dissolved in May 1991. Palestinian militants were repressed in Sidon in July. In May 1992 the last western hostages were released after years of confinement. Lebanon joined the Israeli-Arab peace talks in Madrid in October 1991. Internally, the poor economy aggravated political instability, but parliamentary elections, the first in twenty years, were scheduled for 1992. Poor preparations, widespread irregularities, and Christian abstention produced results that did not prepare Lebanon for an assured future. Yet, the appointment of Prime Minister Rafiq al-Hariri in November 1992 promised a serious effort at reconstruction.

Al-Hariri, a self-made billionaire who made his fortune in Sa'udi Arabia, was perceived by many to be a savior of sorts for the war-torn country. He had a long history of philanthropic giving, donating large sums to rebuild Beirut, for instance. As Prime Minister, he has been frequently accused of corruption and of making sure government rebuilding efforts were directed toward companies under his control. Still most Lebanese approved of his efforts to stabilize the country and unite its many long-warring factions. In 1996, al-Hariri was reelected Prime Minister in a unanimous vote of Parliament.

In 1996 Lebanon was still subject to political violence, especially in the Israeli occupied south, where that year 255 people were killed (twenty-seven Israeli soldiers) in violence. Fifty-four of the dead were members of Hezbollah, and nineteen were militiamen in the Israeli-controlled South Lebanon Army (SLA). The violence continued into 1997.

The President Ilyas Hrawi had been elected to the six-year post in 1989. In 1995 when his term was set to expire in accordance with the constitution, Parliament extended his term for an additional three years. Hrawi proved to be a weak leader and his standing with the Maronites was low. Emile Lahoud, of a prominent Maronite family, had been promoted to major-general in 1985, and general and army commander in 1989. In 1998 his name surfaced as a potential successor to Hrawi. In October 1998 the Assembly introduced a unparalleled amendment to the constitutional clause requiring senior public officials to leave office before running for president. Within two days Lahoud was elected president of the National Assembly. Lahoud was sworn in on 24 November 1998 as Lebanon's eleventh president. On 4 December 1998 Salim al-Huss began his fifth term as prime minister after Hariri's sudden resignation.

In early 1999 fighting in southern Lebanon escalated as the Hezbollah staged attacks on Israeli forces and the Israeli-backed SLA. Israel retaliated on Hezbollah strongholds, and by February expanded air strikes beyond the "security zone" to southern and northern Lebanon. The Huss government's fiscal austerity aimed at reducing the deficit, which had grown to 15% of Gross Domestic Product, met with resistance from the trade unions. On 24 June 1999 Israel destroyed bridges and power stations with its heaviest air raids in three years. In July 1999 the UN Security Council renewed for six months the mandate for UNIFIL, the UN Interim Force in Lebanon, and restated its support of the territorial integrity and sovereignty of Lebanon.

At the end of 1999 in anticipation of elections in August 2000, the government passed a law creating fourteen constituencies of suspiciously varying sizes based on rewarding or punishing political foes or friends. A bill to curb the media, limiting all elections news, advertisements, and coverage to the state-run Tele-Liban and Radio Liban, and limiting campaign spending was also drafted. On 24 May 2000 Israel made a quick withdrawal from southern Lebanon. With the Israeli withdrawal the SLA disintegrated. The exact border between Lebanon and Israel remained unsettled as they disputed ownership of the Shabaa Farms. The Lebanese government sent police and intelligence officers to the newly liberated area, but refused to deploy troops until their was evidence of stability or a comprehensive peace treaty with Israel.

13 GOVERNMENT

As defined by the constitution of 1926 and subsequent amendments, Lebanon is an independent republic. Executive power is vested in a president (elected by the legislature for six years) and a prime minister and cabinet, chosen by the president but responsible to the legislature. Under an agreement dating back to the French mandate, the president must be a Maronite Christian, the prime minister a Sunni Muslim, and the president of the National Assembly a Shi'i Muslim. Decisions by the president must be countersigned by the prime minister and concerned minister(s) after approval by the National Assembly. Legislative power is exercised by a 128-member National Assembly (formerly the Chamber of Deputies), elected for a four-year term by universal adult suffrage (compulsory for males of twenty-one or over, permitted for women over twenty-one with elementary education). The electoral reform law of 1960 determined the denominational composition of the legislature as follows: thirty Maronites; twenty Sunni, nineteen Shi'i; eleven Greek Orthodox; six Greek Catholics; six Druzes; four Armenian Orthodox; one Armenian Catholic; one Protestant; and one Others. Deputies were elected to the legislature in 1972, but elections scheduled for 1976 were postponed because of the war, and the legislature has extended its term every two years until 1992. The Taif Accord of 1989 set the Christian-Muslim balance in parliament at fifty-fifty, but the failure of Christians to participate in the elections of 1992 and 1996 gave Muslim groups the largest number of seats in the Chamber. There has been no official census in the country since 1932, but most observers believe Muslims now form the majority with the Shi'i as the largest single group.

14 POLITICAL PARTIES

Political life in Lebanon is affected by the diversity of religious sects and the religious basis of social organization. The mainly Christian groups, especially the Maronites, favor an independent course for Lebanon, stressing its ties to Europe and opposing the appeals of Islam and pan-Arabism. The Muslim groups favor closer ties with Arab states and are opposed to confessionalism (political division along religious lines). Principal political groups, with mainly Christian membership, are the National Liberal

Party and the Phalangist Party. There are various parties of the left, including the Progressive Socialist Party (of mostly Druze membership), the Ba'th Party, and the Lebanese Communist Party. The various Palestinian groups, allied under the umbrella of the Palestine Liberation Organization, played an important role in the political life of Lebanon from the late 1960s until Israel's invasion drove them from the country in the 1980s. Amal, a conservative grouping, and Hezbollah, more militant, represent the Shi'i community. The former gained eighteen seats and the latter twelve seats in the elections of 1992. The Christian community, which was supposed to have half the seats, largely boycotted the elections and, as a result, won only fifty-nine seats.

There are currently at least eighteen religious-based political parties in Lebanon. In 1996, parliamentary elections were again held, and again certain Christian sects called for a boycott. Still, turnout was much higher than in the 1992 elections, reflecting the country's increasing political stability (turnout was about 45%). International observers found the elections substantially fair, but noted some irregularities, including Syrian interference, vote buying and ballot stuffing. The government itself acknowledges these shortcoming and has instituted some reforms.

The 1996 elections took place in five stages between August and September. The balloting gave a strong majority to a coalition of pro-Syrian parties, notably the Hezbollah-Amal coalition. There were forty-nine newcomers elected—three of whom were female—and nineteen seats are being contested on charges of voter fraud. Following the election, Prime Minister al-Hariri stepped down, as is tradition, so that President Hrawi and the new parliament could chose a new Prime Minister. In late October, the Parliament, with presidential backing, nominated al-Hariri for his second term, as was expected. The vote in Parliament was 121-0 with four abstentions.

Al-Hariri, a billionaire, is one of the richest men in the world: in 1996 there were three billionaires and thirty-five millionaires in Parliament. Asked by Lahoud to be prime minister in 1998, Hariri resigned office.

Palestinian refugees have no right to vote, despite numbering over 300,000 in 1996.

15LOCAL GOVERNMENT

Lebanon is divided into the five provinces (*muhafazat*) of Beirut, North Lebanon, South Lebanon, Bekaa, and Mount Lebanon, each with its district administration. The muhafazat are subdivided into districts (*aqdiya*), municipalities, and villages. Provincial governors and district chiefs are appointed by presidential decree. In most villages, councils of village elders or heads of families or clans still play a considerable role.

Municipal elections had not been held since 1963, despite widespread civil desire for such elections. In 1995, Parliament passed a law extending the term of municipal officers until 31 December 1996, after which elections were slated to be held.

16JUDICIAL SYSTEM

Ultimate supervisory power rests with the minister of justice, who appoints the magistrates. Courts of first instance, of which there are fifty-six, are presided over by a single judge and deal with both civil and criminal cases. Appeals may be taken to eleven courts of appeal, each made up of three judges. Of the four courts of cassation, three hear civil cases and one hears criminal cases. A six-person Council of State handles administrative cases. Religious courts—Islamic, Christian, and Jewish—deal with marriages, deaths, inheritances, and other matters of personal status in their respective faiths. There is also a separate military court system dealing with cases involving military personnel and military related issues.

The law provides for the right to a fair public trial and an independent and impartial judiciary. In practice, politically influential elements succeed in intervening to obtain desired results.

Matters of state security are dealt with by a five-member Judicial Council. The Judicial Council is a permanent tribunal, and the cabinet, on the recommendation of the Ministry of Justice, decides whether to bring a case before the Judicial Council.

In the refugee camps, the Palestinian elements implement an autonomous system of justice in which rival factions try opponents without any semblance of due process. Hezbollah applies Islamic law in the area under its control.

17ARMED FORCES

The conflict of 1975–90 split the regular Lebanese army along Christian-Muslim lines. The force was later reformed, first by the US, then by Syria. In 2000, it numbered 65,000 men. There was a navy of 1,200 and an air force of 1,700 personnel, neither well-armed.

Much of the sectarian militia has disbanded, and the Moslem Hezbollah (3,000 active) is the only significant communal army remaining. The South Lebanese Army, mostly Christian, numbers 2,500 and receives Israeli support for its border patrol duties. The government's defense budget was $445 million in 1997 or 5% of gross domestic product. Also stationed in Lebanon are 4,496 UNIFIL (UN peacekeeping) troops, 150 Iranian Revolutionary Guard Troops, and 22,000 Syrian troops stationed in Beirut.

18INTERNATIONAL COOPERATION

Lebanon has been a charter member of the UN since 24 October 1945 and belongs to ESCWA and all the nonregional specialized agencies. It is the host to UNRWA and UNIFIL and is one of the founding members of the Arab League. Lebanon also is a member of G-77, and a signatory of the Law of the Sea.

19ECONOMY

Lebanon is traditionally a trading country, with a relatively large agricultural sector and small but well-developed industry. Until the civil war, it had always figured prominently as a center of tourist trade. The 1975–76 war caused an estimated $5 billion in property damage and reduced economic activities to about 50% of the prewar level. The cost of reconstruction after the Israeli-Palestinian-Syrian war of 1982 was estimated at $12–15 billion. Lebanon has been able to survive economically because of remittances from abroad by Lebanese workers and companies, external aid by the US, France, Germany, and Arab countries, and foreign subsidies to various political groups. A residual effect of the 1982 war was political uncertainty, which poisoned the economic climate in the following years. In 1984 and after, there was a pronounced deterioration in the economy. In 1987 inflation peaked at 487%. After the 1989 Taif Accord for National Reconciliation ended hostilities, the economy began to recover. Economic activity surged in 1991, and in 1993 the Hariri Government was able to stabilize the economy, and launch a program to reconstruct the economy's infrastructure. Real GDP grew 4.2% in 1992, after growing by about 40% in 1991. Since 1988, the economy has continued to post growth rates averaging 7.5%, although a rising budget deficit threatens to hamper economic reforms. Israel's Operation Grapes of Wrath in April 1996 cut economic development short, but in the same year, the stock market had reopened, and investment had made significant returns. In 1997, unemployment remained high at about 18% although inflation had been reduced to around 5% by 1998. GDP grew by 3% in 1998. The absence of a government department of statistics (it was closed because of the war) makes all figures questionable.

²⁰INCOME

The US Central Intelligence Agency (CIA) reports that in 1998 Lebanon's gross domestic product (GDP) was estimated at $15.8 billion. The per capita GDP was estimated at $4,500. The annual growth rate of GDP was estimated at 3%. The average inflation rate in 1998 was 5%. The CIA defines GDP as the value of all final goods and services produced within a nation in a given year and computed on the basis of purchasing power parity (PPP) rather than value as measured on the basis of the rate of exchange. It was estimated that agriculture accounted for 4% of GDP, industry 23%, and services 73%.

The World Bank reports that for the same period per capita private consumption (in PPP terms) was $6,135. Private consumption includes expenditures of individuals, households, and nongovernmental organizations. It was estimated that between 1990 and 1998 private consumption grew at an annual rate of 7.2%. Approximately 31% of household consumption was spent on food, 10% on fuel, 7% on health care, and 9% on education.

²¹LABOR

The labor force in 1998, having been drastically reduced by the wages of war—death, injury, and emigration—was estimated to number about a million people, up from 452,900 in 1985. During the civil war, it was estimated that 50% of industrial workers, 30% of construction workers, and 25% of workers in service industries fled the country. In all, an estimated 600,000-900,000 persons fled the country during the 1975-76 civil strife. Some returned, but continued instability has resulted in more emigration; many work in Persian Gulf area nations. Both the consequent labor shortage and loss of jobs due to war damage has contributed to serious labor unrest and frequent strikes. Labor productivity is low compared with the US and Western Europe, but higher than in many developing countries. In 1992, unemployment averaged 35%.

There are some 160 labor unions and organizations enrolling about 42% of the workforce as of 1999. The General Confederation of Workers is composed of 22 unions with about 200,000 members as of 1999. Organized labor has grown slowly, partly because of the small number of industrial workers, but also because of the availability of a large pool of unemployed. Agricultural and most trade workers are not organized. Palestinians in Lebanon are free to organize their own unions, but few do so because of their restrictions on the right to work in the country. While Lebanese workers have the right to strike, there are limitations on public demonstrations which somewhat undermine this right. Lebanese workers have the right to organize and bargain collectively and this is the standard practice in employment situations.

Workers as young as 8 may legally work with restrictions as to working hours and conditions. However, in reality, age limitations are not effectively enforced. In 1999, a monthly minimum wage of $200 was in effect.

²²AGRICULTURE

In 1998, 4.3% of the working population was engaged in agricultural activity, and agriculture accounted for about 13% of GDP. Less than 30% of Lebanon's land is arable, and expansion of cultivated areas is limited by the arid and rugged nature of the land.

Agricultural production was severely disrupted by the 1975-76 war, and production of citrus fruits, the main crop, was reduced to low levels in the fertile Bekaa Valley by Israeli-Syrian fighting during 1982. Principal crops and estimated 1998 production (in thousand tons) were sugar beets, 300; potatoes, 264; oranges, 155; apples, 119; lemons and limes, 111; bananas, 110; olives, 100; grapefruit, 55; and wheat, 59. In 1998, Lebanon exported 116,129 tons of vegetables and 169,540 tons of fruits, primarily to Sa'udi Arabia, Kuwait, and the UAE. Two profitable, albeit illegal, crops produced are opium poppy (for heroin) and cannabis (for hashish). A joint Lebanese-Syrian 1994 eradication effort practically wiped out the opium crop and reduced the cannabis crop by 50%.

²³ANIMAL HUSBANDRY

Much of Lebanon's livestock was lost during the protracted hostilities since the 1975–76 war and the Israeli invasion in 1982. In 1998 there were an estimated 450,000 goats, 350,000 sheep, 80,000 head of cattle, and 30,000,000 poultry. As Lebanon's own meat and milk production is below consumption needs, animal and milk products are imported.

²⁴FISHING

The fishing industry has not progressed significantly, despite a government-sponsored effort to reduce fish imports and provide employment in the canned-fish industry. The catch in 1997 was 3,955 tons.

²⁵FORESTRY

Forests comprised about 52,000 hectares (128,500 acres), or nearly 5.1% of the total area, in 1995. Most of the forests are in the central part of the country, with pine and oak predominant. Few of the ancient cedars have survived; small cedar forests have been planted at high altitudes. Roundwood production in 1997 was 538,000 cu m.

²⁶MINING

Mining activity is limited to the production of salt and the quarrying of raw materials for the construction industry, particularly limestone and silica for cement manufacture. In 1996, cement production amounted to 4 million tons; gypsum, 3,000 tons; lime, 30,000 tons; and salt, 3,000 tons.

²⁷ENERGY AND POWER

Political instability and conflict curtailed petroleum exploration in the 1970s and 1980s. In early 1991 natural gas discoveries near El-Marq encouraged further exploration.

In 1993, Kuwait promised to supply 25,000 barrels of crude oil per day to Lebanon at a reduced price for one year. The Islamic Development Bank approved a soft loan of $40 million to cover part of Lebanon's petroleum debt to Kuwait. The Tripoli refinery only satisfies about 15% of domestic demand; imports from Syria, Romania, Bulgaria, Greece, and Italy meet the remaining demand for petroleum products.

Italian, French, and Korean firms have been contracted to rehabilitate power stations, install transmission networks, and distribute electricity outside greater Beirut. Another project involves the construction of two new 415-MW power stations. Lebanon's largest hydroelectric plants are on the Litani River. In 1998, net installed electrical capacity was about 1,220,000 kW and production totaled 9,700 million kWh.

²⁸INDUSTRY

The 16-year civil war that ended in 1991 caused tremendous damage to the industrial sector. By 1993, it was estimated that the Lebanese industry suffered losses of $1.5 billion. Inadequate infrastructure and shortage of skilled labor are major obstacles in the process of rehabilitation. By 1995, the industrial sector was showing signs of improvement. Industrial exports in the first quarter of 1995 were up 76% (to $79.5 million) compared with the same period in 1994. Industry accounted for an estimated 28% of GDP in 1995. Major industrial products are clothing, metal, food, marble and sanitary equipment, cement, jewelry, furniture, paper, beverages, and plastic. Iron and steel production totaled 80,000 tons in 1995. Industrial production grew at a rate of 3.8% in 1997 and 2.8% in 1998.

Lebanon's two main oil refineries have suspended operations since 1992.

29SCIENCE AND TECHNOLOGY

Lebanon's advanced technology is limited to oil refining, the facilities for which were installed by international oil companies. The National Council for Scientific Research, established in Beirut in 1962, draws up national science policies and fosters research in fundamental and applied research. The council operates a marine research center at Al-Batrun. Seven colleges and universities in Beirut offer degrees in basic and applied sciences. In 1987–97, science and engineering students accounted for 30% of college and university enrollments.

30DOMESTIC TRADE

Trade is by far the most important sector of the Lebanese economy. Before the 1975–91 civil war, Beirut was an important commercial center of the Middle East. During the first year of civil violence alone, 3,600 commercial establishments were destroyed, burned, or looted. Reconstruction and returning confidence have improved commercial activities since 1995.

The main trading activity is related to the importation of goods and their distribution in the local market. Distribution is generally handled by traders who acquire sole right of import and sale of specific trademarks, and although competition is keen, the markup tends to be high. Distribution of local products is more widely spread among traders. The smallness and competitiveness of the market have discouraged the development of wholesale houses but have fostered the growth of small shops dealing directly with local and foreign suppliers.

There is no single price level for the same item; the actual price charged generally depends on the short-term condition of the market and on the result of bargaining. Retail credit is common, and advertising has developed rapidly in motion picture theaters and the press.

Government offices and the larger banks are generally open from 8 or 8:30 AM to 2 PM (to 1 PM in summer), and commercial offices from 8 or 8:30 AM to 1 PM (to 1 or 2 PM in summer) and from 3 to 6 or 7 PM, but shops stay open long hours.

31FOREIGN TRADE

Foreign trade has been important in the economic life of Lebanon as a source of both income and employment. Some 40% of total exports are actually reexports, principally machinery, metal products, foods, wood products, textiles, and chemicals.

The most expensive products that Lebanon exports are gold, silverware, jewelry, and precious stones (21%). Other exports include fruits, nuts and vegetables (10.5%), scrap metal (7.2%), and printed matter (4.5%). Major imports include food (29%), machinery and transport equipment (28%), consumer goods (18%), and chemicals (9%).

Principal trading partners in 1998 (in millions of US dollars) were as follows:

COUNTRY	EXPORTS	IMPORTS	BALANCE
France	63	688	-625
United States	47	660	-613
Syria	47	259	-212
Switzerland	24	447	-423
Germany	23	613	-590
United Kingdom	21	319	-298
Turkey	20	179	-159
Italy	19	813	-794
Japan	4	295	-291
China (inc. Hong Kong)	2	279	-277

32BALANCE OF PAYMENTS

Lebanon has maintained a favorable balance of payments, with rising trade deficits more than offset by net earnings from services, transfers of foreign capital, and remittances from Lebanese workers abroad. Although the trade deficit increased substantially between 1977 and 1984, a balance of payments deficit was recorded only for the last two years of the period. By 1985, a surplus of $249 million was again achieved, with a modest trade recovery following in 1986–87. Hostilities in the industrial and prosperous areas of Lebanon in 1989–90 triggered a substantial outflow of capital and a deficit in the balance of payments. Order was restored in 1991 and a resumption of capital inflows averted larger deficits in the following years. In 1995, net capital inflows offset a large trade deficit to produce a $256 million surplus in the balance of payments. A large portion of the trade imbalance consists of imports of machinery which should ultimately increase productivity.

The US Central Intelligence Agency reports that in 1997 the purchasing power parity of Lebanon's exports was $711 million while imports totaled $7.5 billion resulting in a trade balance of -$6,789 million.

33BANKING AND SECURITIES

The Bank of Lebanon, established on 1 April 1964, is now the sole bank of issue. Its powers to regulate and control commercial banks and other institutions and to implement monetary policy were expanded by amendments to the Code of Money and Credit promulgated in October 1973. To encourage the movement and deposit of foreign capital in Lebanon, a bank secrecy law of 1956 forbids banks to disclose details of a client's business even to judicial authorities. There are no restrictions on currency conversions and transfers, and no foreign exchange controls effect trading.

In the late 1990s, the banking sector was undergoing s period of expansion and consolidation with a number of banks listed on the Beirut Stock Exchange. In 1998, over 70 banks were operating in Lebanon with total assets of around $31 billion.

The Beirut Stock Exchange was officially opened in 1952 as a center in which the few available company shares could be traded. The exchange closed during the civil war but reopened in 1979; however, there was little trading in stock during 1980–81. In 1982, Beirut was chosen as the headquarters of the Arab Stock Exchange Union, reflecting Lebanon's continuing importance as financial center of the Middle East.

In September 1995, the Beirut Stock Exchange reopened after a 12-year closure. Trading began in January 1996, but with just three companies listed, all of them producers of cement or construction material. A fourth company joined in mid-1996. A secondary market was opened to trade shares in the private property company, Solidere. Solidere is developing the destroyed business heart of Beirut. With the secondary market considerably more successful than the stock exchange, plans to list Solidere on the latter have, for the moment, been shelved. In 1997, however, Solidere moved its shares from the secondary market to the Beirut Stock Exchange. An important reason for the move was a plant to cross-list Solidere shares on the Kuwait Stock Exchange. Kuwait said it would do so only if shares were traded on the official bourse rather than on the secondary market. The Lebanese Stock Exchange authority signed an agreement to cross-list shares not only with Kuwait but also with Egypt from early in 1997. Solidere has a 115 million–125 million GDR (global depository receipt) to be listed on the London Stock Exchange.

In 1998, the stock market remained sluggish, with only four commercial banks and six companies, including Solidere, listed. Market capitalization was at around $2.4 billion.

34INSURANCE

Activities of insurance companies are regulated by the National Insurance Council. All insurance companies must deposit a specific amount of money or real investments in an approved bank and must retain in Lebanon reserves commensurate with their volume of business. There are at least 85 insurance companies operating in Lebanon.

35PUBLIC FINANCE

The annual budget of the central government must be approved by the National Assembly. The Lebanese government annually faces the formidable problem of financing a massive deficit resulting from heavy financial obligations and huge shortfalls in revenues. To reduce the deficit, the government has tried to increase revenues by raising taxes and tightening the budget. The government relies heavily on grants and loans from multilateral agencies, Arab governments, and the French to cover the deficit.

The US Central Intelligence Agency (CIA) estimates that in 1998 Lebanon's central government took in revenues of approximately $4.9 billion and had expenditures of $7.9 billion including capital expenditures of $1.05 billion. Overall, the government registered a deficit of approximately $3 billion. External debt totaled $5.96 billion.

The following table shows an itemized breakdown of government revenues and expenditures. The percentages were calculated from data reported by the International Monetary Fund. The dollar amounts (millions) are based on the CIA estimates provided above.

REVENUE AND GRANTS	100%	4,900
Tax revenue	74.6%	3,658
Non-tax revenue	25.4%	1,242
EXPENDITURES	100%	7,900
General public services	13.3%	1,051
Defense	9.7%	763
Public order and safety	3.8%	300
Education	8.3%	655
Health	2.6%	208
Social security	6.4%	505
Housing and community amenities	2.1%	164
Recreation, cultural, and religious affairs	0.8%	62
Economic affairs and services	12.4%	976
Other expenditures	0.7%	57
Interest payments	40.0%	3,158

36TAXATION

A graduated tax is imposed on individual salaries, real profits, and real estate income. Corporations and joint stock companies generally are taxed on net real profits derived in Lebanon at a flat rate of 10%, and 5% on dividends. Also levied are inheritance and gift taxes, social security payroll taxes, flat and graduated property taxes, and a stamp duty.

37CUSTOMS AND DUTIES

Restrictions on some imports and exports were imposed in 1977, and licenses are needed for certain import items. Import duties ranging from 10–75% are levied on most goods. There is a stamp tax and surcharge on a number of luxury items, including cars, jewelry, garments, and alcoholic beverages.

Preferential duties are applicable to imports from Arab countries and from EC countries. A free zone in Beirut is widely used as a point of entrepôt trade.

38FOREIGN INVESTMENT

Lebanon's liberal investment policies are designed to attract foreign direct investment to foster economic recovery and rebuild its war damaged infrastructure. Some analysts estimated that the rebuilding costs would exceed $18 billion with construction accounting for a large part of foreign investment. As of 1997, French, Italian, German, British, Korean, and Finnish companies were the predominant investors in Lebanon. Their presence is most strongly felt in the fields of electricity, water, and telecommunications. In addition to limiting the maximum income tax rate to 10% for foreign investors, the movement of funds in and out of Lebanon is free from taxes, fees, or restrictions. Lebanon also has bilateral trade investment agreements with China and a number of European, East European, and Arab countries.

To conserve cash, the government uses "build, operate, transfer" (BOT) agreements to finance major projects. These agreements require the contractor to use its own funds to finance the project. Upon completion, the company operates the business until it has recouped its investment and made a pre-agreed upon profit. At that point, the project to transferred to the state.

39ECONOMIC DEVELOPMENT

Since World War II, Lebanon has followed free-enterprise and free-trade policies. The country's favorable geographical position as a transit point and the traditional importance of the trading and banking sectors of the economy helped make Lebanon prosperous by the early 1970s. Lebanon became a center of trade, finance, and tourism by means of a stable currency backed largely with gold, by a conservative fiscal policy, by various incentives for foreign investors, and by minimization of banking regulations.

Lebanon's development went awry in the mid-1970s, as factional conflict, always present in Lebanese society, erupted into open warfare. The loss to the economy was enormous, particularly in Beirut. The reconstruction plan submitted in 1979 by the Council for Development and Reconstruction (CDR) envisaged total expenditures of LL22 billion for rebuilding, including LL10 billion in the public sector and LL12 billion in the private sector. The cost of new housing and repair of damaged homes was estimated at LL4.5 billion, and of major road construction at LL1.5 billion. Redevelopment of the port of Beirut and reconstruction of Beirut airport were begun under the program.

In November 1979, Sa'udi Arabia and six other oil-producing Arab countries promised to contribute $2 billion for Lebanon's reconstruction effort over a five-year period, but only $381 million had been provided by October 1987. (After Israel invaded Lebanon in June 1982, the Arab countries decided to withhold future funds until Israeli forces had withdrawn completely.)

Under the leadership of Prime Minister Rafiq al–Hariri, Lebanon embarked on the Horizon 2000 program in 1993. Areas of major activity targeted by the plan are the rehabilitation of telecommunications, electricity grids, highways, sewage, waste management, water networks, renovation of the Beirut International Airport, harbor, education, and housing. The plan also calls for investment in commercial facilities that will reestablish Beirut as an international business center in competition with Hong Kong and Singapore. Although in 1997 the government reset the target date to 2007, the plan had been scheduled for completion by 2000. The total cost is estimated at over $18 billion.

40SOCIAL DEVELOPMENT

A government social security plan is intended to provide sickness and maternity insurance, accident and disability insurance, family allowances, and end-of-service indemnity payments. The employer contributes 8.5% of payroll, while the employee and government make no contribution. The system provides lump sum payments only for retirement, disability, and survivor benefits. Foreigners employed in Lebanon are entitled to benefits if similar rights are available for Lebanese in their home countries. Family allowances are provided for households with children and nonworking wives. Voluntary social work societies also conduct relief and welfare activities.

Careers in government, the professions, and, less commonly, business are open to women. However, in some segments of society, social pressure prevents them from taking full advantage of employment opportunities. As of 1996, 3 of 128 parliamentary seats were held by women. Until 1994, women needed their husband's permission in order to open a business or engage in trade. Lebanese citizenship is passed on only by fathers to their children. The children of Lebanese women married to foreigners are unable to secure citizenship. Many of the religious laws governing family and personal status discriminate against women. Despite these circumstances, there are a growing number of women in business and in government. In the 1992 elections, three women were elected to Parliament.

Child labor is widespread, especially in rural areas. Education was not compulsory as of 1999.

Since 1991, Palestinians have been entitled to work permits, but in practice many face employment discrimination. An estimated 370,000 Palestinian refugees live in Lebanon with limited access to employment, health care, and education.

Human rights abuses reported in 1999 included arbitrary arrest and detention and the use of excessive force and torture. Prison conditions are substandard and include severe overcrowding. Human rights organizations are allowed to operate freely.

41HEALTH

In 1990–97, there were 1.9 physicians and 3.1 hospital beds per 1,000 population. The Lebanese Ministry of Health's review of hospital use identified the major health problems as follows: hypertension, diabetes, and asthma, in addition to eye and ear diseases, cardiac conditions, and dermatological problems. In 1999, the birth rate was 22.5 per 1,000 people. About 55% of married women (ages 15 to 49) used contraception in 1995. Life expectancy in 1999 was 70.9 years, and the infant mortality rate was 30.5 per 1,000 live births. The fertility rate was 2.3 births per childbearing woman. The maternal mortality rate in 1990–97 was 300 per 100,000 live births. The general mortality rate in 1999 was 6.5 per 1,000 inhabitants. Between 1982 and 1990, there were approximately 144,000 war-related deaths due to the Israeli invasion. In 1994, 100% of the population had access to safe water, and 95% had access to health care services. In 1997, immunization rates for children up to one year old included diphtheria, pertussis, and tetanus (92%) and measles (89%).

The major causes of death between 1987–1991 were violence and acts of war. War has had a significant impact on the development of many Lebanese children. Many children suffer from post traumatic stress disorders. Vitamin deficiencies are also a problem since 25.7% of all school age children have goiter (1996).

The HIV-1 seroprevalence in 1997 was 0.1 per 100 adults. In 1996, there were 91 cases. Malaria, polio, and neonatal tetanus were rare. Tuberculosis was seen in 940 cases during 1994.

42HOUSING

Despite substantial construction activity since World War II and a boom in construction during the 1960s, which increased the number of housing units to 484,000 in 1970, there was a housing shortage, especially of low-cost residential units, in the early 1970s. The situation was aggravated by the civil war and subsequent factional strife in which half of the country's real estate was severely damaged or destroyed. Under the CDR 1983–91 plan, nearly 30% of total expenditures were allocated to build new dwellings and to restore war-damaged houses. According to the latest available information for 1980-88, total housing units

numbered 820,000 with 3.3 people per dwelling. Housing needs until the year 2000 have been estimated at 400,000 units.

43EDUCATION

Lebanon's illiteracy rate is relatively low for the Middle East. For the year 2000, adult illiteracy rates were estimated at 13.9% (males, 7.7%; females, 19.6%). Free primary education was introduced in 1960, but about two-thirds of all students attend private schools. In 1997 there were 382,309 pupils in 2,160 primary schools. In the same year, there were 347,850 secondary school students. In 1996, the total enrollment for all higher level institutions was 81,588 students with 10,444 instructors. Leading universities include the American University in Beirut; St. Joseph University; the Lebanese (State) University; the University of the Holy Spirit; and the Arab University of Beirut.

44LIBRARIES AND MUSEUMS

Lebanon has about a dozen sizable libraries with specialized collections of books, manuscripts, and documents. Most libraries are in Beirut, but there are also collections at Sidon and Harissa. The National Library of Lebanon, founded in 1921, had more than 100,000 volumes when it was destroyed at the beginning of the war in 1975. By 1995, it had restored most of that collection. The Arab University Library has 200,000 volumes, but the largest library is that of the American University in Beirut, with 461,000 volumes. St. Joseph University has several specialized libraries, including the Bibliothèque Orientale, with 174,000 volumes. The library of the St. John Monastery in Khonchara, founded in 1696, contains the first known printing press in the Middle East. The Université Saint-Esprit de Koslik in Jounieh has the largest provincial collection with 200,000 volumes.

The National Museum of Lebanon (1920), in Beirut, has a collection of historical documents and many notable antiquities, including the sarcophagus of King Ahiram (13th century BC), with the first known alphabetical inscriptions. The American University Museum also has an extensive collection of ancient artifacts. Beirut also houses the Museum of Fine Arts and the Museum of Lebanese Prehistory of St. Joseph University. There is a small Khalil Gibran museum in Bghori.

45MEDIA

Before the civil war, Beirut was an international communications center with an earth satellite station and two oceanic cables linking it to Marseille and Alexandria. As of 1999, the rebuilding of Lebanon's telecommunications system was well under way. Government-controlled Radio Lebanon broadcasts in Arabic, and Tele-Liban broadcasts on three channels in Arabic, French, and English. Some 350,000 telephones were estimated to be in use as of 1995. In 1997, there were 892 radios, 354 television sets, and 135 mobile phones per 1,000 population.

Historically, Lebanon has had the freest press in the Arab world, and even during the civil war some 25 newspapers and magazines were published without restriction. Newspapers freely criticize the government but refrain from criticizing political groups that have the power to retaliate forcibly. As of 1999, the largest Arabic dailies included *Al-Amal* (circulation 35,000), *Al-Anwar* (58,700), *Al Hayat* (31,000), *Al-Liwaa* (79,000), *An-Nahar* (circulation 65,000), *As-Safir* (34,500), and *Al-Sharq* (36,000). Also influential are the French-language papers *L'Orient–Le Jour* (18,400) and *Le Réveil* (10,000).

Though the constitution provides for freedom of the press, the government uses several means short of censorship to control freedom of expression. The Surete Generale is authorized to approve all foreign materials, including magazines, plays, books, and films. The law prohibits attacks on the dignity of the head of state or foreign leaders, prosecuting through a special Publications Court. A 1991 security agreement between Lebanon and

Syria effectively prohibits the publication of any material deemed harmful to either state.

As of 1996, there were more than 36,000 personal computers; Online access is extremely limited, with fewer than five Internet hosts per 1,000 population.

46ORGANIZATIONS

There are chambers of commerce and industry in Beirut, Tripoli, Sidon, and Zahlah, and a Rotary Club in Beirut. Lebanon has an Automobile and Touring Club, a French Chamber of Commerce, an Association of Lebanese Industries, and several voluntary social welfare agencies.

47TOURISM, TRAVEL, AND RECREATION

Before the civil war, Lebanon's antiquities—notably at Sidon, Tyre, Byblos, and Ba'albek—combined with a pleasant climate and scenery to attract many tourists (more than 2 million in 1974), especially from other Arab countries. During the war, however, fighting and bombing destroyed or heavily damaged major hotels in Beirut and reduced the number of tourists to practically zero. Tourists who are not Arab nationals need visas to enter Lebanon. In 1998, Lebanon had 632,217 tourist arrivals, a 32% increase over the previous year. Hotel rooms numbered 9,681 in 1997, with 14,858 beds and an occupancy rate of 32%. That year tourist receipts totaled $1 billion.

In 1999 the UN estimated the cost of staying in Beirut at $149 per day. Elsewhere in Lebanon the daily cost averages $93.

48FAMOUS LEBANESE

Khalil Gibran (Jibran, 1883–1931), a native of Lebanon, achieved international renown through his paintings and literary works. He is best known for his long poem *The Prophet*. Charles Habib Malik (1906–87), for many years Lebanon's leading diplomat, was president of the 13th UN General Assembly in 1958/59.

49DEPENDENCIES

Lebanon has no territories or colonies.

50BIBLIOGRAPHY

Abraham, Antoine J. *The Lebanon War*. Westport, Conn.:Praiger, 1996.

AbuKhalil, As'ad. *Historical Dictionary of Lebanon*. Lanham, Md.: Scarecrow, 1998.

Akarli, Engin Deniz. *The Long Peace: Ottoman Lebanon, 1861–1920*. Berkeley: University of California Press, 1993.

Bleaney, C. H. *Lebanon*. Santa Barbara, Calif.: Clio Press, 1991.

Bustros, Gabriel M. *Who's Who in Lebanon: 1990–1991*. 11th ed. Beirut: Publitec, 1990.

Collelo, Thomas. *Lebanon, a Country Study*. 3rd ed. Washington, D.C.: Library of Congress, 1989.

Cooke, Miriam. *War's Other Voices: Women Writers on the Lebanese Civil War*. New York: Cambridge University Press, 1988.

Deeb, Marius. *The Lebanese Civil War*. New York: Praeger, 1980.

Eshel, Isaac. *Lebanon in Pictures*. Minneapolis: Lerner, 1988.

Friedman, Thomas L. *From Beirut to Jerusalem*. New York: Farrar, Straus, Giroux, 1989.

Gabriel, Philip L. *In the Ashes: The Story of Lebanon*. Ardmore, Pa.: Whitmore, 1978.

Gordon, David C. *The Republic of Lebanon: A Nation in Jeopardy*. Boulder, Colo.: Westview, 1983.

Harik, Ilya F. *Politics and Change in a Traditional Society: Lebanon 1711–1845*. Princeton, N.J.: Princeton University Press, 1967.

Harris, William W. *Faces of Lebanon: Sects, Wars, and Global Extensions*. Princeton, N.J.:Markus Wiener Publishers, 1997.

Hiro, Dilip. *Lebanon: Fire and Embers: A History of the Lebanese Civil War*. New York: St. Martin's, 1993.

Khalaf, Samir. *Lebanon's Predicament*. New York: Columbia University Press, 1987.

Khalidi, Walid. *Conflict and Violence in Lebanon: Confrontation in the Middle East*. Cambridge, Mass.: Harvard University Press, 1979.

Labaki, Georges T. *The Lebanon Crisis (1975–1985): A Bibliography*. College Park, Md.: Center for International Development and Conflict Management, 1987.

Makdisi, Samir A. *Financial Policy and Economic Growth: The Lebanese Experience*. New York: Columbia University Press, 1979.

Meo, Leila T. *Lebanon, Improbable Nation*. Bloomington: Indiana University Press, 1965.

Norton, Augustus Richard. *Amal and the Shia: Struggle for the Soul of Lebanon*. Austin: University of Texas Press, 1987.

Picard, Elizabeth. *Lebanon, A Shattered Country: Myths and Realities of the Wars in Lebanon*. New York: Holmes & Meier, 1996.

Rabinovich, Itamar. *The War for Lebanon 1970–1985*. Ithaca, N.Y.: Cornell University Press, 1985.

Rubin, Barry M. *The May 1983 Agreement over Lebanon Blum*. Washington, D.C.: The Johns Hopkins University, 1987.

Salibi, Kamal S. *A House of Many Mansions: The History of Lebanon Reconsidered*. Berkeley: University of California Press, 1988.

Sirriyeh, Hussein. *Lebanon, Dimensions of Conflict*. London: Brassey's for the International Institute for Strategic Studies, 1989.

Toward a Viable Lebanon. Washington, D.C.: Center for Contemporary Arab Studies, Georgetown University, 1988.

Vocke, Harold. *The Lebanese Civil War*. New York: St. Martin's, 1978.

Winslow, Charles. *Lebanon: War and Politics in a Fragmented Society*. New York: Routledge, 1996.

MALAYSIA

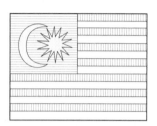

CAPITAL: Kuala Lumpur.

FLAG: The national flag consists of 14 alternating horizontal stripes, of which 7 are red and 7 white; a gold 14-pointed star and crescent appear on a blue field in the upper left corner.

ANTHEM: *Negara Ku (My Country).*

MONETARY UNIT: The Malaysian ringgit (M$), or dollar, is divided into 100 sen, or cents. There are coins of 1, 5, 10, 20, and 50 sens and 1 ringgit, and notes of 1, 5, 10, 20, 100, 500, and 1,000 ringgits. M$1 = US$0.2632 (US$1 = M$3.799) as of 31 March 2000.

WEIGHTS AND MEASURES: The metric system became the legal standard in 1982, but some British weights and measures and local units are also in use.

HOLIDAYS: National Day, 31 August; Christmas, 25 December. Movable holidays include Vesak Day, Birthday of His Majesty the Yang di-Pertuan Agong, Hari Raya Puasa, Hari Raya Haji, the 1st of Muharram (Muslim New Year), Milad an-Nabi, Dewali, Thaipusam, and the Chinese New Year. Individual states celebrate the birthdays of their rulers and other holidays observed by indigenous ethnic groups.

TIME: 7 PM = noon GMT.

¹LOCATION, SIZE, AND EXTENT

Situated in Southeast Asia, Malaysia, with an area of 329,750 sq km (127,581 sq mi), consists of two noncontiguous areas: Peninsular Malaysia (formerly West Malaysia), on the Asian mainland, and the states of Sarawak and Sabah, known together as East Malaysia, on the island of Borneo. Comparatively, the area occupied by Malaysia is slightly larger than the state of New Mexico. Peninsular Malaysia, protruding southward from the mainland of Asia, comprises an area of 131,587 sq km (50,806 sq mi), extending 748 km (465 mi) SSE–NNW and 322 km (200 mi) ENE–WSW. It is bordered on the N by Thailand, on the E by the South China Sea, on the S by the Strait of Johore, and on the W by the Strait of Malacca and the Andaman Sea, with a total boundary length of 2,068 km (1,285 mi). Sarawak, covering an area of 124,449 sq km (48,050 sq mi), on the northwest coast of Borneo, extends 679 km (422 mi) NNE–SSW and 254 km (158 mi) ESE–WNW. It is bounded by Brunei on the N, Sabah on the NE, Indonesia on the E and S, and the South China Sea on the W. Sarawak's total boundary length is 2,621 km (1,629 mi). Situated at the northern end of Borneo, Sabah has an area of 74,398 sq km (28,725 sq mi), with a length of 412 km (256 mi) E–W and a width of 328 km (204 mi) N–S. To the N is the Balabac Strait, to the NE the Sulu Sea, to the SE the Celebes Sea, to the S Indonesia, to the SW Sarawak, and to the W the South China Sea, with a total boundary length of 2,008 km (1,248 mi). The total boundary length of Malaysia is 7,344 km (4,563 mi).

Malaysia claims several atolls of the Spratly Island group in the South China Sea. The claim, in a region where oil is suspected, is disputed by China, the Philippines, Taiwan, and Vietnam. Malaysia's capital city, Kuala Lumpur, is located in the western part of Peninsular Malaysia.

²TOPOGRAPHY

Four-fifths of Peninsular Malaysia is covered by rain forest, jungle, and swamp. The northern regions are divided by a series of mountain ranges that rise abruptly from the wide, flat coastal plains. The highest peaks, Gunong Tahan (2,190 m/7,185 ft) and Gunong Korbu (2,183 m/7,162 ft), are in the north central region. The main watershed follows a mountain range about 80 km (50 mi) inland, roughly parallel to the west coast. The rivers flowing to the east, south, and west of this range are swift and have cut some deep gorges, but on reaching the coastal plains they become sluggish. The western coastal plain contains most of the country's population and the main seaports, George Town (on the offshore Pulau Pinang) and Kelang (formerly Port Swettenham). The eastern coastal plain is mostly jungle and lightly settled. It is subject to heavy storms from the South China Sea and lacks natural harbors.

Sarawak consists of an alluvial and swampy coastal plain, an area of rolling country interspersed with mountain ranges, and a mountainous interior. Rain forests cover the greater part of Sarawak. Many of the rivers are navigable. Sabah is split in two by the Crocker Mountains, which extend north and south some 48 km (30 mi) inland from the west coast, rising to over 4,100 m (13,450 ft) at Mt. Kinabalu, the highest point in Malaysia. Most of the interior is covered with tropical forest, while the western coastal area consists of alluvial flats making up the main rubber and rice land.

³CLIMATE

The climate of Peninsular Malaysia is equatorial, characterized by fairly high but uniform temperatures (ranging from 23° to 31°C/73° to 88°F throughout the year), high humidity, and copious rainfall (averaging about 250 cm/100 in annually). There are seasonal variations in rainfall, with the heaviest rains from October to December or January; except for a few mountain areas, the most abundant rainfall is in the eastern coastal region, where it averages over 300 cm (120 in) per year. Elsewhere the annual average is 200–300 cm (80–120 in), the northwestern and southwestern regions having the least rainfall. The nights are usually cool because of the nearby seas. The climate of East Malaysia is relatively cool for an area so near the equator.

⁴FLORA AND FAUNA

About 70% of Malaysia consists of tropical rain forest. In Peninsular Malaysia, camphor, ebony, sandalwood, teak, and many varieties of palm trees abound. Jungle fauna includes seladang (Malayan bison), deer, wild pigs, tree shrews, honey bears, forest cats, civets, monkeys, crocodiles, huge lizards, and snakes. The seladang weighs about a ton and is the largest wild ox in the world. An immense variety of insects, particularly butterflies, and some 575 species of birds are found.

On Sabah and Sarawak, lowland forests contain some 400 species of tall dipterocarps (hardwoods) and semihardwoods; fig trees abound, attracting small mammals and birds; and groves are formed by the extensive aerial roots of warangen (a sacred tree to indigenous peoples). As altitude increases, herbaceous plants—buttercups, violets, and valerian—become more numerous, until moss-covered evergreen forests are reached from 1,520 to 1,830 m (5,000–6,000 ft). Large butterflies, brilliantly colored birds of paradise, and a great wealth of other insect and bird species inhabit the two states.

⁵ENVIRONMENT

The Environmental Quality Act of 1974 and other environmental laws are administered by the Division of Environment of the Ministry of Science, Technology, and Environment. Discharge of untreated sewage has contaminated the nation's water; the most heavily polluted areas are along the west coast. Malaysia's water pollution problem also extends to its rivers, of which 40% are polluted. The nation has 109.4 cu mi of water with 47% used for farming and 30% used for industrial activity. Of the people in rural areas, 34% do not have pure water. Malaysia's cities produce 1.5 million tons of solid waste per year. Clean-air legislation limiting industrial and automobile emissions, was adopted in 1978. However, air pollution from both of these sources is still a problem. In the mid-1990s, Malaysia ranked among 50 nations with the world's highest industrial carbon dioxide emissions, which totaled 70.5 million metric tons per year, a per capital level of 3.74 metric tons per year. Discharge of oil by vessels in Malaysian waters is prohibited. Of Malaysia's total land area, 59% is tropical rainforest. Malaysia has the world's fifth most extensive mangrove area, which total over a half a million ha (over 1.2 million acres). The country's forests are threatened by commercial interests.

In the mid-1990s, 23 of the nation's mammal species and 35 bird species were endangered. Endangered or extinct species in Malaysia include the orangutan, tiger, Asian elephant, Malayan tapir, Sumatran rhinoceros, Singapore roundleaf horseshoe bat, four species of turtle (green sea, hawksbill, olive ridley, and leatherback), and two species of crocodile (false gavial and Siamese).

⁶POPULATION

The population of Malaysia in 2000 was estimated at 21,820,143. An estimated 3.9% of the population is 65 years of age or older. The projected population for the year 2005 is 24,087,000, assuming a crude birthrate of 24 per 1,000 population and a death rate of 5, resulting in a natural rate of change of 1.9% for the period 2000–2005. The population rate of change between 1995 and 2000 was 2.0%. The population density in 1998 was 68 per sq km (176 per sq mi).

It was estimated that 57% of the population lived in urban areas in 2000, up from 42% in 1980. The capital city, Kuala Lumpur, and its surrounding metropolitan area had a 2000 population of 1,378,000. Malaysia's next census is slated to take place in 2001.

⁷MIGRATION

Not until British economic enterprise first attracted foreign labor after 1800 did large-scale Chinese, Indian, and Malaysian migration (nonnative Indonesians and Borneans) take place. The early migrants were transients: in 1921, only 20.3% of the Chinese and 11.9% of the Indians were Malayan-born. However, migration data for subsequent years show a general tendency toward permanent settlement by these nonindigenous portions of the population. The percentages of the total Chinese population reporting Peninsular Malaysia as their birthplace were 29.1%, 62.5%, and 74.4% for the years 1931, 1947, and 1957, respectively; the percentages of Indians reporting their birthplace as Peninsular Malaysia were 21.1%, 51.4%, and 64.6% for the same respective years. By 1953, the Malays were a minority in their own territory. The government enacted legislation restricting further immigration, and by 1968 the Malays formed slightly more than 50% of the population. Regulations which took effect in 1968 concerning passports and border crossings between Malaysia and Indonesia and between Malaysia and the Philippines were also intended to restrict immigration. By 1970, more than four-fifths of the Chinese and Indians were born in Peninsular Malaysia. Between 1975 and 1996, Malaysia hosted more than 250,000 Indo-Chinese refugees and permitted the local integration of some 45,000 Filipino refugees in Sabah. Between 1975 and 1989, more than 250,000 Vietnamese refugees found asylum in Malaysia; the vast majority subsequently migrated to other countries. Some 3,797 Vietnamese refugees still remain in Malaysia, but are to return home according to government authorities. The legal position of the 5,000 or so Muslims from Myanmar, who possess no documentation as citizens of Myanmar, had not been addressed by the government as of September 1999. The net migration rate in 1999 was zero; however, this figure does not reflect the number of illegal immigrants, including large numbers from Indonesia and smaller numbers from the Philippines, Bangladesh, Myanmar (Burma), China, and India.

⁸ETHNIC GROUPS

The population of Malaysia consists of three main ethnic groups—Malays, Chinese, and peoples of the South Asian subcontinent. Malays and other indigenous groups are known as Bumiputras ("sons of the soil"). Estimates for 1999 reported the following distribution: Malays and other indigenous groups (Bumiputras), 58%; Chinese, 26%; persons of Indian descent, 7%; and other groups, 9%. Malays predominate in the rural areas, while the Chinese are concentrated in urban and mining areas, where they control much of the nation's wealth; enmity between the two communities has occasionally erupted into violence. The non-Malay indigenous groups on the peninsula are collectively called the Orang Asli (aborigines) and number about 50,000.

Non-Malay indigenous tribes constitute about half of Sarawak's residents; the largest indigenous group consists of the Sea Dayaks, or Ibans, followed by the Land Dayaks, or Bidayuh. The majority of Sabah's population consists of indigenous peoples, principally Kadazans, Bajaus, and Muruts. The balance is dominated by Chinese.

⁹LANGUAGES

Bahasa Malaysia, or Malay, is the national language and the lingua franca of all Malaysia. The traditional Bahasa Malaysia script is Jawi, which derives from Arabic script, but Rumi, based on the Roman alphabet, is officially used in government, education, and business. English is widely employed in government and commerce and is a compulsory subject in all schools. Chinese (notably the Mandarin, Cantonese, Hokkien, Hakka, Hainan, and Foochow dialects), Tamil, Telugu, Malalalam, Punjabi, and Thai are spoken. In addition, in East Malaysia several indigenous languages are spoken, the largest of

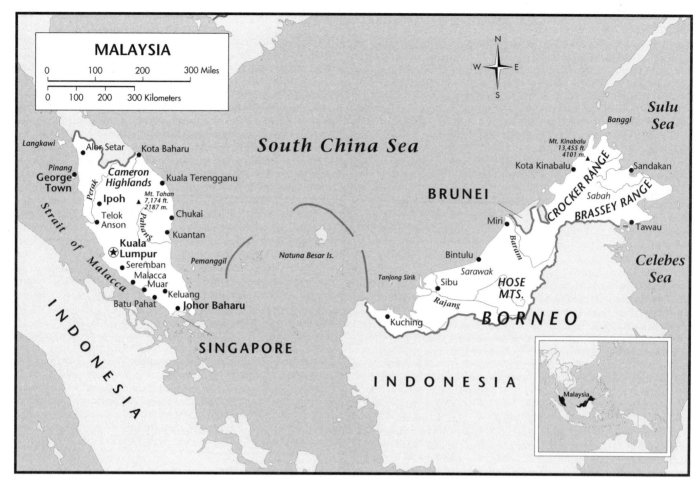

LOCATION: Peninsular Malaysia: 1°17′ to 6°43′N; 99°38′ to 104°39′E. Sarawak: 0°52′ to 4°59′N; 109°38′ to 155°43′E. Sabah: 4°6′ to 7°22′N; 115°7′ to 119°17′E
BOUNDARY LENGTHS: Peninsular Malaysia: Thailand, 506 km (316 mi); coastline, 2,068 km (1,292 mi). East Malaysia: Brunei, 381 km (238 mi); Indonesia, 1,728 km
(1,080 mi); coastline, 2,607 km (1,629 mi). Total boundary length (land and coastline): 7,290 km (4,555 mi). **TERRITORIAL SEA LIMIT:** 12 mi.

which are Iban and Kadazan. Most Malaysians are bilingual or multilingual.

¹⁰RELIGIONS

Islam is the official religion, and about 53% of all Malaysians are Muslims. The head of state, the *yang di-pertuan agong,* is also the national leader of the Islamic faith. The constitution, however, guarantees freedom to profess, practice, and propagate other religions. Religious lines generally follow ethnic lines. Almost all Malays are Muslims; most Indians are Hindus, with a substantial minority of Muslims, Sikhs, and Parsees; and most Chinese are Confucian-Buddhists, with a minority Muslim representation. Christianity has won some adherents among the Chinese and Indians. The indigenous peoples of Sabah and Sarawak are still largely animist, although many have become Christian. Shamanism is also practiced on East Malaysia.

¹¹TRANSPORTATION

In 1996, the highway system of Malaysia consisted of 94,500 km (58,722 mi) of roads, of which 70,970 km (44,101 mi) were paved, including 580 km (360 mi) of expressways. The major highways on Peninsular Malaysia run north–south along the east and west coasts; east–west links connect George Town and Kota Baharu in the north and Kuala Lumpur and Kuantan farther south. As of 1991, (according to the Malaysian Highway Authority) the East-West Highway (Federal Route 2) crossing

Peninsular Malaysia, as well as the Klang Valley Expressway connecting Kuala Lumpur to Port Klang were completed. The 924 km (574 mi) North-South Highway along the west coast of Peninsular Malaysia connects Thailand and Singapore. In 1995, registered vehicles included 2,550,000 automobiles and 35,000 commercial vehicles.

The national Malayan Railway Administration operates some 1,798 km (1,117 mi) of Peninsular Malaysia, which provides links to Thailand, Singapore, and eastern parts of the peninsula. Sabah State Railways provides diesel service along the west coast and in the interior for 136 km (85 mi). There are no railroads in Sarawak.

The three leading ports, all located on the busy Strait of Malacca, are Kelang (the port for Kuala Lumpur), Johor Baharu, and George Town. Kuching is the main port for Sarawak, and Kota Kinabalu the main port for Sabah. The Malaysian merchant fleet in 1998 consisted of 378 ships with a combined capacity of 5,059,272 GRT.

Also in 1998, there were 115 airports, 32 of which had paved runways. Most international flights enter or leave Malaysia through Kuala Lumpur International Airport. Other principal airports include Kota Kinabalu, Kuching, and Penang. The Malaysian Airline System (MAS) provides domestic service to most major cities of the peninsula and to Sarawak and Sabah. In 1997, 15,592,000 passengers were carried on scheduled domestic and international flights.

¹²HISTORY

The ancestors of the Malays came down from South China and settled in the Malay Peninsula about 2000 BC. Sri Vijaya, a strong Indo-Malay empire with headquarters at Palembang in southern Sumatra, rose about AD 600 and came to dominate both sides of the Strait of Malacca, levying tribute and tolls on the ships faring between China and India. In the 14th century, however, Sri Vijaya fell, and Malaysia became part of the Majapahit Empire centered in Java. About 1400, a fugitive ruler from Temasik (now Singapore) founded a principality at Malacca (now Melaka) and embraced Islam. It was at Malacca that the West obtained its first foothold on the peninsula. At the height of glory and power, the Malacca principality fell to Portugal in 1511. In their turn, the Portuguese were driven out by the Dutch in 1641. The British East India Company laid the groundwork for British control of Malaya in 1786 by leasing from the sultan of Kedah the island of Pinang, off the west coast of Malaya, about 800 km (500 mi) north of Singapore. Fourteen years later, it obtained from him a small area on the mainland opposite Pinang. In 1819, Sir Thomas Stamford Raffles obtained permission to establish a settlement at Singapore; in 1824, by agreement and financial settlement, the island was ceded to the British East India Company. In the following year, the Dutch settlement at Malacca was ceded to Great Britain. Pinang, Singapore, and Malacca were combined under British rule in 1829 to form the Straits Settlements. The states of Perak and Selangor in 1874 secured treaties of protection from the British. Similar treaties were subsequently made with the sultans of Negri Sembilan (1874–89) and Pahang (1888). In 1895, these four states became a federation (the Federated Malay States), with a British resident-general and a system of centralized government. In 1909, under the Bangkok Treaty, Siam (now Thailand) ceded to British control the four northern states of Kelantan, Trengganu, Perlis, and Kedah. These four, together with Johor, which in 1914 was made a British protectorate, became known as the Unfederated Malay States. Separate British control was extended to Sabah, then known as North Borneo, in 1882. Six years later, North Borneo and Sarawak each became separate British protectorates. Tin mining and rubber grew rapidly under British rule, and large numbers of Chinese and Indian laborers were imported, respectively, for these industries.

Japanese forces invaded Malaya and the Borneo territories in December 1941 and occupied them throughout World War II. Within a year after the Japanese surrender in September 1945, the British formed the Malayan Union, consisting of the nine peninsular states, together with Pinang and Malacca; also in 1946, Singapore and the two Borneo protectorates became separate British crown colonies. The Malayan Union was succeeded by the Federation of Malaya on 1 February 1948. Over the next decade, the British weathered a Communist insurgency, as Malaya progressed toward self-government. On 31 August 1957, the Federation of Malaya became an independent member of the Commonwealth of Nations. On 1 August 1962, Great Britain and Malaya agreed in principle on the formation of the new state of Malaysia—a political merger of Singapore and the British Borneo territories (Sarawak, Brunei, and North Borneo) with the Federation. On 1 September 1962, by a 70% plurality, Singapore voted in a referendum for incorporation in the proposed Malaysia, but an abortive revolt staged by Brunei's ultranationalist Brunei People's Party in December 1962 eliminated the sultanate from the proposed merger. On 16 September 1963, the Federation of Malaya, the State of Singapore, and the newly independent British colonies of Sarawak and Sabah merged to form the Federation of Malaysia ("Federation" was subsequently dropped from the official name). On 7 August 1965, Singapore seceded from the Federation and established an independent republic. From the outset, Indonesia's President Sukarno attempted by economic and military means to take over the young nation as part of Indonesia; cordial relations between the two countries were not established until after Sukarno's ouster in 1966. Internal disorders stemming from hostilities between Chinese and Malay communities in Kuala Lumpur disrupted the 1969 national elections and prompted the declaration of a state of emergency lasting from mid-1969 to February 1971. Successive governments managed to sustain political stability until 1987, when racial tensions between Chinese and Malay increased over a government plan to assign non-Mandarin-speaking administrators to Chinese-language schools.

In October 1987 the Malaysian government, under provisions of the Internal Security Act (ISA) which allows detention without trial on grounds of national security, arrested 79 political and civil leaders and closed four newspapers in an effort to stifle dissent. The government called its actions necessary to prevent racial violence, but many prominent Malaysians, including Tunku Abdul Rahman, the country's first prime minister, condemned the actions. At the same time the government clamped down on all news sources disseminating what the government considered false news, and new legislation denied licensing to news sources not conforming to Malaysian values. In 1981 Dato' Hussein bin Onn was succeeded as prime minister by Sato' Sei Dr. Mahathir Mohamad, whose leadership came under criticism from within the UMNO and other political parties as racial tensions increased. Part of the challenge to Dr. Mahathir's party leadership came in the form of a legal suit claiming that some of the delegates to the UMNO elections of 1987 had not been legally registered, therefore, the election should be declared null and void. The High Court ruled that due to the irregularities UMNO was an unlawful society and that in effect the election was invalid. Dr. Mahathir held that the ruling did not affect the legal status of the government; he was supported by the ruling Head of State, Tunku Mahmood Iskandar. In 1988 Dr. Mahathir formed a New UMNO, Umno Baru, and declared that party members would have to reregister to join. (Umno Baru was thereafter referred to as UMNO.) Under provisions of the ISA four people linked to the Parti Bersatu Sabah (PBS) were detained over alleged involvement in a secessionist plot in Sabah in June 1990. In July 1990 elections the PBS won 36 of 48 seats in the Sabah State Legislative Assembly. Prior to the general election of 1990 the PBS aligned itself with the opposition, which had formed an informal electoral alliance, Gagasan Rakyat (People's Might). The National Front (BN) won 127 of the 180 seats, thus maintaining control of the House of Representatives with the two-thirds majority necessary to amend the Constitution. The opposition increased its seats from 37 to 53. In 1992 the People's Might registered as a political organization and Razaleigh was elected Chairman.

In 1990 the restructuring of the portfolio of the Ministry of Trade and Industry was rationalized into two new Ministries, the Ministry of International Trade and Industry (MITI) and the Ministry of Domestic Trade and Consumer Affairs (MDTCA). In an action that was widely regarded as politically motivated, Datuk Seri Joseph Pairin Kitingan, Chief Minister of Sabah and President of the PBS, was arrested in January 1991 and charged with corruption, then released on bail. After subsequent meetings with Dr. Mahathir it was announced that the PBS state Government had proposed power sharing with United Sabah National Organization (USNO). The head of USNO, Tun Mustapha Harun, resigned from USNO and joined UMNO. This switch necessitated a by-election and in May 1991 UMNO took its first seat in Sabah. The rise of Dayak nationalism in Sarawak was considered as less of a threat after the 1991 state elections. The Sarawak Native People's Party (PBDS, Parti Bansa Dayak Sarawak) retained only 7 of the 15 seats it had won in the 1987 election. A High Court ruling in 1991 upheld a ruling by the

Ministry of Home Affairs banning the public sale of party newspapers. Speculation was that by targeting limited media outlets the government was muzzling the opposition press.

In 1991 UMNO raised the issue of the alleged abuse of privilege by Malaysia's nine hereditary rulers. A resolution tabled in 1990 had demanded the rulers be restrained from interfering in politics. In November 1992 the issue of the constitutional status of the Sultans again arose when it was proposed that the rulers' immunity from prosecution be removed. The cases in point were the recent alleged assault on a hockey coach by the Sultan of Johore, and the 1981 incident in which the Sultan of Johore (before he became Sultan) was convicted of homicide but pardoned by his father the pervious Sultan. In January 1993 these proposed amendments to the Constitution were passed. Immediately after passage of the bill royal privileges other than those sanctioned and allocations not expressly provided in the constitution were withdrawn. The nine hereditary rulers first rejected the constitutional changes; however, they agreed to a compromise formula on the bill that effectively removed the blanket legal immunity granted to them. The compromise upheld the constitutional stipulation of royal assent for laws affecting the monarchy. Criticism arose over Dr. Mahathir's handling of this situation as it emphasized the antipathy between his authoritarian style and the "Malay way." These constitutional changes also highlighted Dr. Mahathir's previous moves to strengthen executive power at cost of the judiciary, to consolidate UMNO's control of the legislature, and to control the press. On 17 January 1994 Sabah's Chief Minister, Datuk Joseph Pairin Kitingan, was found guilty of corruption. The fine imposed on him fell short of the minimum required to disqualify him from office. Although PBS won the Sabah polls in February 1994, Pairin resigned as the PBS's leading members joined the National Front, and the Sabah wing of UMNO (with 18 of 48 seats) was about to be installed. In August 1994 the government moved to ban the radical Islamic sect, Al-Arqam.

Between 1978 and 1989 Malaysia provided asylum to about 230,000 Vietnamese refugees as they awaited resettlement in the West. In March 1989 Malaysia responded to the continuing influx of refugees and the Western nations' slow efforts to place them with a plan to screen refugees in order to separate economic migrants from political refugees. This policy was confirmed by the United Nations. In its biggest victory ever, the ruling National Front captured 162 parliamentary seats out of a possible 192 in the general election held 25 April 1995. The coalition won 64% of the popular vote and easily retained its two-thirds parliamentary majority.

The Asian economic crisis of 1997 affected both the economy and the political landscape in Malaysia. By the beginning of 1998, the Malaysian economy had undergone its first downturn in 13 years, and tensions over the handling of the crisis erupted between Prime Minister Mahathir, an economic isolationist, and his deputy, Anwar Ibrahim, who favored open-market policies. In September 1998, Mahathir removed Anwar from his cabinet and party posts and imposed currency controls. When Anwar publicly protested these moves and attempted to rally opposition to his former mentor's policies, he was arrested and later tried for corruption and sexual misconduct. In 1999 Anwar was sentenced to six years in prison, and his wife launched a new political party to contest the upcoming national elections.

The economy began to recover by the end of 1998, and the government officially announced that the recession into which it had been plunged was over by August 1999. Responding to an April 2000 deadline for national elections, Mahathir called a snap election in November 1999. Although the arrest of Anwar and his treatment while in custody ignited widespread criticism of Mahathir and his government, the UMNO-led coalition maintained its two-thirds majority in parliament and Mahathir

remained in power. However, electoral gains by the Islamist party PAS suggested a significant challenge to the popularity of the government and made PAS the country's largest opposition party.

13GOVERNMENT

Malaysia is a constitutional monarchy consisting of 13 states, 9 of which were formerly sultanates under British protection and 4 of which (Melaka, Pulau Pinang, Sarawak, and Sabah) were former British settlements ruled by appointed governors.

The constitution, promulgated on 31 August 1957 and subsequently amended, derives from the former Federation of Malaya, with provisions for the special interests of Sabah and Sarawak. It provides for the election of a head of state, the *yang di-pertuan agong,* or paramount ruler, for a single term of five years by the Conference of Rulers. The constitution also provides for a deputy head of state, chosen in the same manner and for the same term.

The Conference of Rulers consists of the nine hereditary sultans. Its consent must be obtained for any law that alters state boundaries; affects the rulers' privileges, honors, or dignities; or extends any religious acts, observances, or ceremonies to the country as a whole. The conference must also be consulted on proposed changes of administrative policy affecting the special position of the Malays or the vital interests of other communities.

The yang di-pertuan agong, who must be one of the hereditary sultans, is commander-in-chief of the armed forces and has the power to designate judges for the Federal Court and the High Courts on the advice of the prime minister, whom he appoints. Until January 1984, the paramount ruler had the right to veto legislation by withholding his assent; this right was lost in a constitutional compromise that gave the paramount ruler the right to delay new laws for up to 60 days but also stipulated that, if passed by a two-thirds majority, a bill may become law after six months without his signature.

The yang di-pertuan agong from 1979 to 1984 was Ahmad Shah al-Musta'in Billah Ibni al-Marhum, the sultan of Pahang. The leading candidate to succeed him was Idris al-Mutawakil Allahi Shah Ibni al-Marhum, the sultan of Perak, but when Idris died of a heart attack on 31 January 1984, the Conference of Rulers selected Mahmud Iskandar Ibni al-Marhum Sultan Ismail. As crown prince of Johor he had been convicted of homicide in a shooting incident in 1977 but had been pardoned by his father and became sultan in 1981. In 1989 the Sultan of Perak, Azlan Muhibuddin Shah, became the yang di-pertuan agong. He was succeeded in 1994 by Tuanku Ja'afar ibni Al-Marhum Tuanku Abdul Rahman, who was in turn succeeded in 1999 by Salehuddin Abdul Aziz Shah ibni Al-Marhum Hismuddin Alam Shah.

Executive power rests with the cabinet, chosen by the prime minister, who is the leader of the majority party or coalition of the House of Representatives (*Dewan Rakyat*), the lower house of Parliament. The 192 members of the House of Representatives must be at least 21 years old; they are elected by universal adult suffrage (at age 20). Their term is five years unless the House is dissolved earlier. The 70-member Senate (*Dewan Negara*) consists of 26 elected members (two from each state); 4 members (two from each territory) appointed by the paramount ruler to represent the Federal Territories of Kuala Lumpur and the island of Labaun; and 40 members appointed by the paramount ruler on the basis of distinguished public service or their eligibility to represent the ethnic minorities. Senators must be at least 30 years old; they hold office for six-year terms.

14POLITICAL PARTIES

Before World War II, there was limited political activity in Malaya, but the Japanese occupation and its aftermath brought a new political awareness. Postwar political parties sought independence, and although the Malays feared domination by the populous minorities, particularly the economically stronger Chinese, the United Malays National Organization (UMNO), the leading Malay party, and the Malaysian Chinese Association (MCA) formed the Alliance Party in 1952. This party was later joined by the Malaysian Indian Congress (MIC) and became the nation's dominant political party. The Malayan Communist Party, a powerful and well-organized group after the war, penetrated and dominated the trade unions. In 1948, after the Communists had resorted to arms, they were outlawed.

In the elections of April 1964, the Alliance Party won a majority of 89 of the 154 House seats. The third general election since independence was held in Peninsular Malaysia on 10 May 1969; in the balloting, the Alliance Party suffered a setback, winning only 66 seats. The election was followed by communal rioting, mainly between Malays and Chinese, resulting in much loss of life and damage to property. The government suspended Parliament and declared a state of emergency; elections in Sarawak and Sabah were postponed until July 1970. By the time Parliament was reconvened on 22 February 1971, the Alliance had achieved a two-thirds majority (required for the passage of constitutional amendments) with the addition of 10 unopposed seats from Sabah and through a coalition with the Sarawak United People's Party, which controlled 12 seats.

The elections for state assemblies also resulted in a setback for the Alliance Party, which before the elections had controlled 10 of the 13 state assemblies, but after the elections only 7. In September 1970, Tunku Abdul Rahman retired as prime minister and was replaced by the deputy prime minister, Tun Abdul Razak. In 1973, the Alliance Party formed a broader coalition consisting of the UMNO, MCA, MIC, and eight minority parties. Known as the National Front and led by the UMNO, the ruling coalition was returned to power in the 1974, 1978, 1982, and 1986 elections with overwhelming majorities (148 of 177 seats in 1986). The principal opposition parties, which win few seats owing to a legislative apportionment scheme that heavily favors Malay voters, are the Chinese-based Democratic Action Party (DAP), founded in 1966, and the Pan-Malayan Islamic Party, dedicated to establishing an Islamic state.

In July 1981, Datuk Seri Mahathir bin Mohamad replaced Datuk Hussein bin Onn as prime minister. As of 1986, the National Front also had majorities in 11 of 13 state legislatures; the state assembly of Sabah, the lone exception, was under the control of the Sabah People's Union (Berjaya). In the 1986 elections, Chinese voters moved away from the MCA and toward the DAP. In April 1987, Mahathir narrowly overcame a challenge to his leadership of the UMNO.

As of 1999 there were more than 30 registered parties. The governing coalition is the Barisan Nasional (National Front), led by the United Malays National Organization (UMNO) and comprising 13 other parties, most ethnically based. Major opposition groups are the Muslim Unity Movement (APU), dominated by the Parti Se-Islam Malaysia (PAS), the Democratic Action Party (DAP), which is predominantly Chinese and socialist, the Parti Bersatu Sabah (PBS), and the newly formed National Justice Party formed by Wan Azizah Wan Ismail, the wife of jailed government official Anwar Ibrahim.

In the election held 28 and 29 November 1999, the 193 seats of the lower house were distributed as follows: National Front (148 seats), DAP (10), PBS (3), and PAS (27), and Parti Keadilan Nasional (5).

15LOCAL GOVERNMENT

Of the 11 Peninsular Malaysian states, nine are headed by sultans, who act as titular rulers and as leaders of the Islamic faith in their respective states. The other two Peninsular states, Pinang and Melaka, are headed by federally appointed governors. State governments are parliamentary in form and share legislative powers with the federal parliament. Effective executive authority in each state is vested in a chief minister, selected by the majority party in the state legislature. The legislative assembly, composed of elected members, legislates in conformity with Malaysian and state constitutions, subject to the sultan's assent. In Peninsular Malaysia the states are divided into districts, each of which consists of 5 to 10 subdistricts, called *mukims* (derah in Kelantan). Each mukim is responsible for varying numbers of *kampongs* (villages or compounds). The mukim may include villages or consist of large, sparsely populated tracts of land. Each one is headed by a *penghulu* (penggawa in Kelantan), a part-time official locally elected for five years, who serves as the principal liaison between the district and the village. The village elects a chief (*ketua*).

Upon incorporation into the Federation of Malaysia in 1963, both Sabah and Sarawak adopted separate constitutions for their local self-government; each is headed by a chief minister, appointed by the majority party of the elective legislature. In Sarawak, divisions and districts are the main subdivisions; in Sabah their counterparts are residencies and districts. The district officer is the most important link between the governing and the governed. His responsibilities are administrative, fiscal and judicial. Kuala Lumpur, the national capital and former capital of Selangor State, was constituted as a separate federal territory, under the national government, on 1 February 1974. The mayor is appointed by the paramount ruler on the advice of the prime minister.

16JUDICIAL SYSTEM

Malaysia has a unified judicial system, and all courts take cognizance of both federal and state laws. The legal system is founded on British common law. Most cases come before magistrates and sessions courts. Religious courts decide questions of Islamic law and custom. The Federal Court, the highest court in Malaysia, reviews decisions referred from the High Court of Peninsular Malaysia, the High Court of Sabah and Sarawak, and subordinate courts. The Federal Court, of which the yang di-pertuan agong is lord president, has original jurisdiction in disputes among states or between a state and the federal government. Administrative detention is permitted in security cases, in which certain other guarantees of due process are reportedly suspended.

The judiciary has traditionally functioned with a high degree of independence. Most civil and criminal cases are fair and open. The accused must be brought before a judge within 24 hours of arrest. Defendants have the right to counsel and to bail. Strict rules of evidence apply in court and appeal is available to higher courts. Criminal defendants may also appeal for clemency to the King or to the local state ruler. Severe penalties, including the death penalty, are imposed for drug-related offenses.

High courts have jurisdiction over all serious criminal cases and most civil cases. The sessions courts hear the cases involving landlord-tenant disputes and car accidents. Magistrates' courts hear criminal cases in which the maximum sentence does not exceed 12 months. The Court of Appeals has jurisdiction over high court and sessions court decisions.

17ARMED FORCES

In 2000, the all-volunteer active armed forces numbered 105,000. The total strength of the army was 80,000, including infantry and armored battalions, artillery regiments, and supporting air defense, signal, engineer, special forces, and administrative units. Contingents of the Malaysian army patrol the Malaysia-Thailand border against Communist guerrillas and provide two UN observer teams. The navy had 12,500 personnel, 4 frigates, 6 missile-equipped fast-attack craft, and 27 large patrol craft. The air force had 12,500 personnel and 87 combat aircraft. Paramilitary forces numbered 20,100, and the People's Volunteer Corps had 240,000. There are 40,600 reserves. Malaysian arms and equipment are a mixture of domestic, UK, and US material. Australia provides a small training mission. Expenditures on defense amounted to $2.1 billion (1998) or 2.1% of the gross domestic product.

[18]INTERNATIONAL COOPERATION

Malaysia is a member of the UN, having joined on 17 September 1957, and participates in ESCAP and all the nonregional specialized agencies. It also belongs to the Asian Development Bank, ASEAN, the Commonwealth of Nations, and G-77. Malaysia is a signatory of the Law of the Sea and a member of the WTO.

Before the 1970s, Malaysia pursued a pro-Western policy, but it later promoted the neutralization of Southeast Asia while establishing ties with China, the Democratic People's Republic of Korea, and Cuba and strengthening relations with the former USSR and other East European states. Links with its traditional allies, including the US, remained strong in the course of this transition. Relations with the UK were strained in the early 1980s, after the British imposed surcharges on foreign students attending universities in the UK and issued new regulations reducing opportunities for foreign takeovers of British-owned companies. Malaysia agreed to drop its "buy British last" campaign in 1983 after the UK expanded scholarship opportunities for Malaysian students. In 1986 there was some friction with Singapore because of its improved relations with Israel. Malaysia shares the anti-Zionist ideology of the Arab League countries.

[19]ECONOMY

Malaysia was one of the most prosperous nations in Southeast Asia before 1998, with the small mood swings inherent in an export-oriented economy. Until the 1970s, Malaysia's economy was based chiefly on its plantation and mining activities, with rubber and tin the principal exports. Since then, however, Malaysia has added palm oil, tropical hardwoods, petroleum, natural gas, and manufactured items, especially semiconductors, to its export list. This diversification greatly reduced the nation's dependence on overseas commodity markets. By 1980, rubber accounted for about 7.5% of the value of all exports, down from 30% in the 1970s, and tin for about 4.3%, down from about 20% in the 1970s. The worldwide recession in 1981–82 hurt the Malaysian economy. Prices of Malaysia's traditional commodity exports were depressed, growth slowed, and investment fell. Government efforts to stimulate the economy through spending on heavy industry and infrastructure projects financed by borrowing pushed foreign debt from $4 billion in 1980 to $15 billion in 1984. In 1985, the GDP in current prices was estimated at $31 billion, up from $25 billion in 1981. Real growth rates were estimated at 6.9% in 1981, 7.6% in 1984, and −1.0% in 1985. In 1985–86 Malaysia's long period of high growth abruptly halted as oil and palm oil prices were halved. Recovery began in late 1986 and 1987; growth was spurred by foreign demand for exports. Growth rates continued on the average in the 8-9% range from 1987–92. During most of the 1990s, the economy grew by an average of just under 9%. However, in 1998, the economy slipped by at least 7% due to the Asian financial crisis.

In 1990, Malaysia was the world's largest producer of natural rubber accounting for one-quarter of world production, however, by 1993 production was overtaken by both Thailand and Indonesia. During the late 1990s, production of synthetic rubbers antiquated the natural rubber industry. In 1990 Malaysia was the world's largest exporter of tropical hardwood, the world's fourth largest producer of cocoa, and the source of 60% of the world's palm oil (1990). By 1996, Malaysia exported over half of the world's fixed vegetable oils, bringing in approximately 5.8% of the GDP. The manufacturing sector made up 69% of exports in 1993; and 86% of exports for 1998, accounting for about one-third of the GDP; including semiconductors and electronics. Malaysia remains a major producer of commodities including rubber, tin, palm oil, tropical hardwoods, cocoa and pepper. It also produces and exports oil, petroleum products and liquefied natural gas, amounting to 5% of total exports in 1998.

The government or government-owned entities dominate a number of sectors (plantations, telecommunications, and banking). Since 1986 the government has moved toward corporatization and the eventual privatization of telecommunications, ports, highways, and electricity production and distribution. The estimated unemployment rate for 1996 was 2.6%. Malaysia's labor force is educated and disciplined but the labor market is tight. Pressure is being exerted on wages and imported contract labor is used to relieve this shortage. The estimated inflation rate based on consumer prices for 1998 was 5.3%. Sarawak's basic economy is subsistence agriculture, supplemented by petroleum production and refining, the collection of forest produce, fishing, and the cultivation of cash crops, primarily rubber, timber and pepper. Sabah's economy rests primarily on logging and petroleum production.

[20]INCOME

The US Central Intelligence Agency (CIA) reports that in 1998 Malaysia's gross domestic product (GDP) was estimated at $215 billion. The per capita GDP was estimated at $10,300. The annual growth rate of GDP was estimated at -7%. The average inflation rate in 1998 was 5.3%. The CIA defines GDP as the value of all final goods and services produced within a nation in a given year and computed on the basis of purchasing power parity (PPP) rather than value as measured on the basis of the rate of exchange. It was estimated that agriculture accounted for 13% of GDP, industry 46%, and services 41%.

Private consumption includes expenditures of individuals, households, and nongovernmental organizations. It was estimated that between 1990 and 1998 private consumption grew at an annual rate of 5.0%. The richest 10% of the population accounted for approximately 38% of household consumption and the poorest 10% approximately 1.8%.

[21]LABOR

In 1998, Malaysia's total civilian employment was estimated at 8,883,600. Of these, approximately 17% were in agriculture; 34% in industry; and the remaining 59% in services. Unemployment in 1997 was 2–3%. Malays constitute the bulk of the agriculturalists, cultivating most of the rice paddies or working on self-owned smallholdings in rubber. The Chinese, Indians, and Pakistanis live mainly in urban areas and are active in trade, manufacturing, and other nonagricultural pursuits.

Plantation workers and mining employees make up the two largest unions. Altogether there are 544 trade unions. About 11% of the work force was unionized in 1999. The trade union movement is generally organized along ethnic lines. Indians have tended to dominate the central labor organization, the Malaysian Trade Unions Congress. Negotiations between unions and employers are voluntary; strikes are permitted, but not if the dispute has already been referred to an industrial court for settlement.

Commerce and industry operate on a 48-hour week, although actual weekly hours tend to be closer to 44. Protective labor legislation in Malaysia is more extensive than in most Asian countries. Employment and labor legislation enacted in 1955 ensures fair contracts and safe working conditions; regulating the employment of children (the adult working age is 14) and women; and establishing rest days, as well as housing and medical care. The Employees' Social Security Act of 1969 comprises an Employment Injury Insurance Scheme and an Invalidity Pension Scheme. Coverage extends mostly to urban industrial workers and was expanded in March 1974 to include Sabah and Sarawak.

There is no national minimum wage, but a minimum wage does exist on a sector or region basis.

Occupational safely and health provisions are set by law and are erratically enforced. The provisions are most exactly enforced in the formal economic sector and are least enforced on plantations and construction sites where immigrant workers are employed. Since 1996, the government has taken steps to correct this imbalance.

22AGRICULTURE

Agriculture is no longer the most important sector of the Malaysian economy, contributing 13% of GDP (down from 38% in 1960) and occupying about 17% of the employed work force in 1998. Nevertheless, agriculture still accounted for 9% of export earnings in 1997. Diversification—including development of such newer crops as oil palm, cocoa, and pineapples—is promoted by the government. Much of Sabah and Sarawak is covered with dense jungle and is not conducive to farming. Peninsular Malaysia, however, is predominantly an agricultural region. Cultivation is carried out on the coastal plains, river valleys, and foothills.

Domestic rice furnishes Peninsular Malaysia with about 80% of its requirements; most of the rice supply for Sabah and Sarawak, however, must be imported. Milled rice production for 1998 totaled 940,000 tons, of which about 70% came from Peninsular Malaysia. Rubber production totaled 1,082,000 tons in 1998. The government, through the Rubber Research Institute of Malaysia, has concentrated on improving production, but many estates have switched to production of the more profitable oil palm. Although Malaysia produced 16% of the world's rubber in 1998, and typically accounts for over one-third of the world's rubber exports, rubber is no longer the country's primary source of export income. Competition from Thailand and Indonesia has recently diminished the Malaysian market share for rubber.

Production of palm oil and palm kernel oil totaled 11,100,000 tons in 1998, more than any other country in the world. More than 90% of all rubber and palm oil is produced in Peninsular Malaysia. Black and white peppers are grown on Sarawak; 15,400 tons of black pepper and 5,800 tons of white pepper were produced in 1998/99. Output of lesser agricultural products in 1998 included copra, 50,000 tons; coconuts, 967,000 tons; cocoa, 118,000 tons; and pineapple, 163,000 tons.

23ANIMAL HUSBANDRY

Peninsular Malaysia is free of most of the infectious and contagious diseases that plague livestock in the tropical zone, but the livestock industry is of minor importance. The livestock population in 1998 included 3,400,000 hogs, 725,000 head of cattle, 320,000 goats, 255,000 sheep, and 150,000 buffalo. The swamp buffalo and indigenous breeds of cattle are used mainly as draft animals. Production of meat in 1998 included (in tons): poultry, 685,000; pork, 241,000; beef (cattle), 19,000; beef (buffalo), 8,000; and mutton (goat), 1,000. Malaysia is self-sufficient in pork and poultry production and also exports to other countries in the region, particularly Singapore and Japan. Sarawak's poultry sector is growing by 7% annually in response to increased demand from neighboring Kalimantan, Indonesia, where during certain festive months there is a poultry shortage. Hog raising and export are handled mainly by non-Muslim Chinese. The government prohibits the importation of chicken and chicken parts in order to protect domestic producers. Milk production was 33,000 tons in 1998.

24FISHING

Fishing is being developed both as a means of reducing unemployment and as a primary source of protein in the country's diet. The total catch in 1997 was 1,280,372 tons, as compared with 296,300 tons in 1966; the increase has been largely the result of expanded and improved marketing facilities. Exports of fisheries products were valued at $337 million 1997, with imports of $347 million that year. A government training program in navigation and engine care is also accelerating the use of powered boats. Freshwater fishing, which accounts for 2% of the total catch, occurs in paddy fields or irrigation ditches and is integrated with rice farming and hog production.

25FORESTRY

Malaysia produced an estimated 46 million cu m of roundwood from a forest area of 15.4 million ha (38.2 million acres) in 1997. About 31.8% of the forest area is located in Peninsular Malaysia, 22.5% in Sabah, and 45.7% in Sarawak.

After 40 years of large scale conversion of lowland forest areas into agricultural plantations, the pace of new land development declined in the mid-1990s. Reduced land availability and a growing need to preserve remaining forests have resulted in a 60% reduction from the government's 1991–95 plan in the total acreage of land scheduled for development. Under the government's Seventh Malaysia Plan (1996–2000), log output is estimated to drop to 27 million cu m by 2000.

Exports of timber products in 1997 amounted to $4 billion, or 7% of total exports. Exports of tropical hardwoods in 1997 included (in thousands of cubic meters): logs, 6,994; lumber, 3,109; veneer, 747; and plywood, 3,285. Malaysia is the world's leader in production of veneer sheets, accounting for 28% of global production in 1997. In keeping with the National Forestry Policy of 1978, exports of sawlogs are being progressively reduced in favor of domestic development of veneer, plywood, furniture, and other wood-using industries. Many states ban the export of logs. Only Sarawak exports tropical hardwood logs, but its state government has also placed further restrictions on exporting logs in order to encourage expansion of value-added activities.

26MINING

Malaysia was the second-largest producer of refined tin in 1997. Production and employment in the tin sector, however, have declined significantly in recent decades. In 1997, Malaysia mined and processed some 5,065 tons of tin metal and concentrates, down from the 1985 total of 36,900 tons. The number of working mines also declined, from about 1,000 in 1974 to 84 at the end of 1995. Continued low prices and sluggish world demand for the metal are the main reasons for the slump.

Iron ore production increased markedly after World War II under the stimulus of Japanese demand, but production subsequently dwindled from a peak of 3,899,000 tons in 1965 to 181,600 tons in 1985 and 269,000 tons in 1997. The output of bauxite, all of which is exported, decreased from 703,561 tons in 1975 to 279,000 tons in 1997. Output of copper, of which there are large reserves on Sabah, increased from 21,190 tons in 1975 to 131,832 tons in 1985, before dropping to 18,555 tons in 1997. Silver production amounted to 9,647 kg in 1997, nearly all of it from Sabah. Other minerals extracted include gold, columbite, monazite, tungsten, manganese, kaolin, and ilmenite. Malaysia is a net exporter of all its coal, copper concentrate, ilmenite, rare earths, and zircon concentrate, and most of its smelted tin. Mining contributed 6.8% to Malaysia's GDP in 1997. Major export earnings of nonfuel minerals in 1997 included refined tin, $176 million; copper concentrates, $45 million; and other minerals, including ilmenite, kaolin, bauxite, clays, iron ore, monazite, silica, zircon concentrate, and mica, $28 million.

Subsoil resources are public property of the states, which grant prospecting licenses and mining leases. Royalties on coal and gold accrue to the states, and export duties are levied on other minerals by the government, which returns part to the states.

27ENERGY AND POWER

Malaysia's net installed electrical generating capacity in 1998 stood at 13,541 MW. Electrical energy production increased from 1,622 million kWh in 1963 to 4,971 million kWh in 1974 and 57,435 million kWh in 1998. In 1996, 16% of electrical production was hydrogenerated, and over 83% was of thermal origin. The National Electricity Board, a state-owned corporation, supplies the greater part of the nation's power.

Crude oil, developed in the 1970s, is now the chief mineral produced, with reserves estimated at 4.3 billion barrels in early 1996. In 1998, output averaged 733,000 barrels per day. Oil production occurs offshore and mostly near peninsular Malaysia. Of new and increasing importance are large offshore natural gas deposits, with reserves estimated at more than 1.9 trillion cu m. Production in 1998 totaled 38 billion cu m. The principal gas fields are the Trengganu, off the east coast of Peninsular Malaysia, and the Central Luconia, Bintulu, and Labuan fields, located off the coasts of Sabah and Sarawak. In 1998, net exports totaled over 300,000 barrels per day. Production of oil and natural gas is controlled by the National Petroleum Co. (PETRONAS).

Since reserves of oil are limited and local coal is of an inferior grade, the government has greatly expanded efforts to harness the country's hydroelectric potential and natural gas as alternative energy sources. In 1994, the government approved the construction of the 2,400 MW Bakun hydroelectric project in Sarawak. However, in 1996 Kuala Lumpur's High Court ruled the project was invalid because it failed to comply with the country's environmental laws. Construction continues temporarily, pending the outcome of the appeal.

28INDUSTRY

Early industrialization efforts centered on the establishment of import-substitution industries and resulted in construction of sugar refineries and motor vehicle assembly plants. Industrialization accelerated after the mid-1960s under the provisions of the Investment Incentives Act and the formation of the Malaysian Industrial Development Authority (MIDA). Special incentives were offered for industries that were labor intensive or export oriented or that utilized domestic rubber, wood, and other raw materials. In the mid-1980s the Malaysian economy changed from a commodity-based to a manufacturing-based economy. In 1986, the leading manufacturing industries included rubber processing, the manufacture of tires and other rubber products, palm oil processing, tin smelting, and the manufacture of chemicals, plywood, furniture, and steel. Other industries were textiles, food processing, and the manufacture of electronic and electrical components. Industrial products in 1985 included 3,128,000 tons of cement, 13,839 tons of cigarettes, 70,147 passenger cars, 568,387 television sets, 3,600,000 tires, and 180,746 m of cotton fabric. Most early industries were controlled by ethnic Chinese and foreigners, but current policies call for greater participation by ethnic Malays.

In 1998 the manufacturing sector accounted for one-third of GDP and 86% of exports. The leading manufacturing industries included rubber processing, palm oil processing, light manufacturing, electronics, tin smelting, and timber processing. Industrial products in 1990 included 5,881,000 metric tons of cement,

17,331 metric tons of cigarettes, and an estimated 6,094,000 metric tons of crude palm oil.

Oil refineries in Malaysia have a capacity of 524,400 barrels per day, and oil production reaches 810,000 barrels per day. Singapore, Japan, Thailand and South Korea are the major customers for Malaysian crude oil. Malaysia's oil fields are split between the South China Sea off Borneo and those off Peninsular Malaysia. All exploration is conducted under production-sharing contracts between PETRONAS, the national oil company, and foreign companies. In 1999, foreign oil companies involved in the production of oil and gas in Malaysia included Exxon, Shell, Sonoco, Statoil, Union Carbide, Amerada, and Lundin. Gas reserves were being developed to fuel power stations and to supply industries in Peninsular Malaysia and Singapore. In 1998, Malaysia exported 18% of the world's LNG.

A top industrial priority in 2000 is the development of the "multimedia super corridor" (MSC), an area Malaysia hopes will become its version of California's Silicon Valley. It is composed of a number of projects: the completion of the tallest building in the world, the 1,483-ft Petronas Twin Towers; the building of an $8 billion capital city to be called Putrajaya and of an information-technology center called Cyberjaya; the construction of a $3.6 billion international airport; and the installation of a fiber-optic telecommunications system linking them all.

29SCIENCE AND TECHNOLOGY

Training in science, technology, and related subjects was promoted at all levels during the 1970s and 1980s. Enrollment at technical and vocational secondary schools rose from 4,510 in 1970 to 20,720 in 1985. The National University of Malaysia at Selangor, the University of Malaya at Kuala Lumpur, the University of Agriculture at Selangor Darul Ehsan, the University of Science at Penang, the Technological University at Johor Bahru, Kolej, Damansaura Utama College at Selangor, Politeknik Kuching at Surawak, and Tunku Abdul Rahman College at Kuala Lumpur offer degrees in basic and applied sciences. In 1987–97, science and engineering students accounted for 54% of college and university enrollments. National science policy is administered by the Ministry of Science, Technology, and Environment. The Ministry of Agriculture undertakes all aspects of research for improvement of crops. The Institute of Medical Research is a branch of the Ministry of Health.

At Kuala Lumpur are located the Forest Research Institute Malaysia (FIRM), the Freshwater Fish Research Center, the Malaysian Agricultural Research and Development Institute (MARDI), the Malaysian Institute of Microelectronic Systems (MIMOS), and the Rubber Research Institute of Malaysia.

In 1987–97, total expenditures on research and development amounted to 0.24% of GNP. During the same period, 93 scientists and engineers per million population were engaged in research and development. In 1998, high-tech exports were valued at $31.4 billion and accounted for 54% of manufactured exports.

30DOMESTIC TRADE

Imported goods are channeled into the Malaysian market through local branches of large European mercantile firms; by local importers with buying agents abroad; through branch offices and representatives of foreign manufacturers; by local Chinese, Indian, and Arab merchants who import directly; and by commission agents. Chinese merchants occupy an important place in the marketing structure and control a large share of the direct import trade. For warehousing of imported goods, the facilities of the port of Singapore are used, while rubber for export is warehoused mainly on plantations.

The usual business hours are from 8:00 AM to 4:15 PM, Monday–Friday including an hour long lunch break, with generally a half-day on Saturday. In Kelantan, Terengganu, Johor, Perlis, and Kedah states, Thursday is a half-day and (in keeping with Islamic practice) Friday is the day of rest. English is widely used in commerce and industry.

Newspaper and motion picture advertising is directed toward the higher-income consumer, while radio advertising, outdoor displays, and screen slides are used for the lower-income consumer, who is less likely to be literate. A code of practice and ethics governing advertising is in force. There are about 80 English, Malay, Chinese, and Tamil daily and weekly newspapers. Radio and television broadcasts are in Malay, Chinese, Tamil, and English. Trade fairs are supervised by the Ministry of Trade and Industry.

31 FOREIGN TRADE

During the 1970s, petroleum and manufactures displaced rubber and tin as Malaysia's leading exports. Malaysia now exports almost half of the world's fixed vegetable oil, and one-fifth of the world's radio broadcast receivers, but it's largest export revenues come from sales of transistors and valves. The top nine exports are:

	% OF COUNTRY TOTAL	% OF WORLD TOTAL
Transistors and valves	17	7.7
Office machines	6.3	5.0
Telecoms equipment	5.3	3.4
Fixed vegetable oil	5.2	48
Radio broadcast receivers	4.8	19
Crude petroleum	3.9	1.4
Sound recorders	3.8	13
Television receivers	3.0	9.2
Shaped wood	2.8	7.3

In 1996 Malaysia's imports were distributed among the following categories:

Consumer goods	4.7%
Food	4.3%
Fuels	2.7%
Industrial supplies	24.8%
Machinery	52.9%
Transportation	8.1%
Other	2.5%

Exports went primarily to the US (22%), Singapore (17%), and Japan (11%). Imports came primarily from the US (20%), Japan (20%), and Singapore (14%). Principal trading partners in 1998 (in millions of US dollars) were as follows:

COUNTRY	EXPORTS	IMPORTS	BALANCE
United States	15,885	11,444	4,441
Singapore	12,444	7,902	4,542
Japan	7,716	11,470	-3,754
China (inc. Hong Kong)	5,404	3,367	2,037
Netherlands	3,443	511	2,932
Taiwan	3,018	2,975	43
United Kingdom	2,637	1,293	1,344
Thailand	2,317	2,259	58
Germany	2,210	2,294	-84
Korea	1,672	3,359	-1,687

32 BALANCE OF PAYMENTS

Malaysia sustained a favorable trade balance throughout the 1960s and 1970s, recording its first trade deficits in 1981 and 1982, as world prices for tin, crude oil, rubber, and palm oil, the major exports, weakened simultaneously. Malaysia's balance of payments, like that of many other producers of primary products, was adversely affected in 1981–82 by the prolonged recession in the world's industrial nations. From 1983 to 1986, however, Malaysia registered trade surpluses. The substantial rise in imports in 1988 resulted in the trade surplus declining by 42%.

In recent years, a significant growth in exports and a decrease in imports have led to trade surpluses, along with a fairly large services deficit.

The US Central Intelligence Agency reports that in 1998 the purchasing power parity of Malaysia's exports was $74.3 billion while imports totaled $59.3 billion resulting in a trade balance of $15 billion.

The International Monetary Fund (IMF) reports that in 1997 Malaysia had exports of goods totaling $77,881 million and imports totaling -$74,005 million. The services credit totaled $15,016 million and debit $17,516 million. The following table summarizes Malaysia's balance of payments for 1997 in millions of US dollars.

Current Account		-4,792
Balance on goods	3,876	
Balance on services	-2,500	
Balance on income	-5,073	
Current transfers	-1,094	
Capital Account		-239
Financial Account		2,742
Direct investment abroad	...	
Direct investment in Malaysia	5,106	
Portfolio investment assets	...	
Portfolio investment liabilities	-248	
Other investment assets	-989	
Other investment liabilities	-1,126	
Net Errors and Omissions		-1,571
Reserves and Related Items		3,859

33 BANKING AND SECURITIES

In 1958, the Bank Negara Tanah Melayu (renamed the Bank Negara Malaysia in 1963) was created as the central banking institution. Bank Negara requires banks to maintain a minimum risk-weighted capital ration (RWCR) of 8%. At the end of 1997, Malaysia had 35 licensed commercial banks with 1714 branches, 25 finance companies, 12 merchant banks, and 7 discount houses. A total of 36 foreign banks have offices in Malaysia, but their banking privileges are restricted. Specialized credit institutions include the Federal Land Development Authority (FELDA), the Agricultural Bank of Malaysia (Bank Pertanian Malaysia), and Bank Rakyat, serving rural credit cooperative societies. International trade is financed mainly by the commercial banks. Total banking system assets were $279 billion in 1997. There were 51 offshore banks operating on the island of Lauban in 1997, and a total of more than 1600 companies in operation.

Malaysia offers Islamic banking, which is based on the concept of profit sharing as opposed to the use of interest in the conventional banking system. One such Islamic bank is Bank Islam Malaysia Berhad. The central bank has embarked on a plan to develop Malaysia as a regional Islamic financial center. Toward this end, the central bank formed a consultative committee on Islamic banking in January 1996 to serve as a think-tank group to develop strategies and proposals to map out the future direction of Islamic banking. Although Islamic operations are still only a small proportion of total business, Malaysia has achieved more than most other Islamic countries in this respect, and its developments are regarded as models by them.

The principal market for securities is the Kuala Lumpur Stock Exchange (KLSE), which separated from the joint Stock Exchange of Malaysia and Singapore in 1973. A second, smaller exchange has operated since 1970 to serve indigenous Malay interests. In October 1991 the Kuala Lumpur Stock Exchange completely severed its links with the Singapore Stock Exchange. As of 31 December 1995, the KLSE was capitalized at approximately M$565.6 billion. Foreign investors are permitted to buy and sell on the stock market, subject only to compliance with regulatory requirements. In June 1995, a wide range of measures liberalizing the Malaysian capital market were introduced. These included the lowering of commission rates on the KLSE, the easing of controls on loans secured against shares and less stringent conditions for overseas fund managers. Overseas funds can now set up 100% subsidiaries for conducting non-Malaysian business, and rules on work permits for expatriate staff have been relaxed. By the end of 1997, the Kuala Lumpur Stock Exchange Composite Index (KLCI) capitalization had declined 53% from its high that year of 1271.57. The KLCI hit a low of 262.70 in September 1998.

34INSURANCE

The law requires insurance firms to maintain a minimum of 80% of their assets in authorized Malaysian holdings, including (by an amendment passed in 1978) 24% in government securities. Third-party motor liability insurance is compulsory.

35PUBLIC FINANCE

The US Central Intelligence Agency (CIA) estimates that in 1996 Malaysia's central government took in revenues of approximately $22.6 billion and had expenditures of $22 billion including capital expenditures of $5.3 billion. Overall, the government registered a surplus of approximately $600 million. External debt totaled $39.8 billion in 1998.

The following table shows an itemized breakdown of government revenues and expenditures. The percentages were calculated from data reported by the International Monetary Fund. The dollar amounts (millions) are based on the CIA estimates provided above.

REVENUE AND GRANTS	100%	22,600
Tax revenue	81.9%	18,501
Non-tax revenue	17.9%	4,050
Capital revenue	0.2%	42
EXPENDITURES	100%	22,000
General public services	11.0%	2,422
Defense	11.1%	2,452
Public order and safety	5.3%	1,164
Education	22.8%	5,017
Health	6.3%	1,377
Social security	7.2%	1,584
Housing and community amenities	7.3%	1,608
Economic affairs and services	21.6%	4,757
Other expenditures	11.5%	2,522
Interest payments	12.0%	2,635
Adjustments	-16.1%	-3,537

In 1998, Malaysia's central government took in revenues equaling approximately 20% of GDP, with an overall deficit of 1.8% of GDP.

36TAXATION

Income tax is levied on all individual and corporate income accrued in Malaysia during the previous year. As of 2000, income of resident individuals is taxed at rates ranging from 2% to 29%. Resident and nonresident companies are charged a flat rate of 28%. A 38% income tax is levied on petroleum corporations.

Incentives are available for pioneer industries and for certain capital investments. Capital gains taxes are levied on real estate. Indirect taxes include a general 10% sales tax (5% for more essential items, and 15% for liquor and cigarettes), and a services tax.

37CUSTOMS AND DUTIES

Import tariffs on textiles and other items already produced in Malaysia are applied in order to protect domestic industries. Rates vary from 0% to 300%, and imports are also subject to a 10% sales tax and excise taxes. However, the average duty rate is less than 8.1%. Imported luxury goods have the highest rates.

Items imported for industrial development, including machinery and raw materials imported for processing and reexport, are usually duty-free. Exports are generally free of control, except that licenses and export duties apply to exports of petroleum (25%), rubber, tin, palm oil, timber, and pepper.

As a member of the ASEAN free trade area, Malaysia is a part of the Common Effective Preferential Tariff Scheme (CEPT), which aims to liberalize trade in the region. By 2003, all tariffs on manufactured goods between member countries will be reduced to 0% to 5%, including Singapore, Brunei, Thailand, Philippines, and Indonesia. Vietnam, Lao PDR, Myanmar, and Cambodia are scheduled to join the CEPT by 2008. Malaysia has bilateral trade agreements with 59 countries as well. There are several Free Zones (FZ's) and a Free Port at Port Klang.

38FOREIGN INVESTMENT

The government encourages foreign investors with a tax holiday of up to 10 years for investments in new industries and assurance of convertibility and repatriation of capital and profits. In 1975, the Industrial Coordination Act established new equity participation guidelines that required a substantial majority of Malaysian ownership of new import-substitution industries catering to the domestic market and using local technology; 70% Malaysian ownership was stipulated for export industries. Export industries using imported raw materials could be as much as 100% foreign owned. Some of these regulations were eased under the Fifth Malaysia Plan (1986–90). The Promotion of Investment Act of 1986 allowed 100% foreign ownership if a company exported at least 50% of its product and did not compete with local industry, or if it exported at least 80% of its product regardless of competition. In 1998, 100% foreign ownership was granted to projects exporting at least 80% of output, 79% foreign ownership for exports of at least 51% of output, up to 50% foreign ownership for exporting at least 20% of output, and a maximum foreign ownership of 30% for projects exporting less than 20%; regardless of the origin of raw materials.

In October 1990 the government established the Federal Territory of Labuan as an International Offshore Financial Center (IOFC) to provide offshore banking and insurance, trust fund management, offshore investment holding and licensing companies, and other offshore activities carried out by multinational companies. Free Zones (FZs) are specially designated geographic areas which create "climates of opportunity" for industry and trade. Areas specifically designed for manufacturing businesses producing or assembling products primarily for export are known as Free Trade Zones (FTZs) or Free Industrial Zones (FIZs). In Malaysia FIZ facilities provide export-oriented industries with minimum customs controls and formalities when importing raw materials, parts, machinery, and equipment. FIZs have been established in Bayan Lepas, Bukit Baru, Mukim Damansara, Mukim Pringgit, Mukim Plentong, Prai, Tanjong Kling, Telok Panglima Garang, Ulu Kinta, and Ulu Klang in the states of Johor, Melaka, Perak, Penang, and Selangor.

There are specially designated FCZs for businesses engaged in commercial activities including trading, breaking bulk, grading, repacking, relabeling, and transit. Within an FCZ goods are allowed to be imported without being subject to customs procedures, provided the goods are ultimately exported after processing. Two FCZs have been established for trading purposes in Bukit Kayu Hitam, Kedah and Pengkalan Kubor, Kelantan. A third in Mukim of Plentong, Johor, has been established for commercial activities other than trading.

Assets attracting foreign investors to Malaysia are location, cultural ties with Singapore and Taiwan and its economic and political stability, competent labor force, and good infrastructure. Liberalized tax and regulatory treatment attracted total foreign direct investment in 1997 of $4 billion. The largest investment sources are the US, Japan, Germany Taiwan, Singapore, and Korea. The US has emerged as an important investment source in recent years, with manufacturing investments in 1998 totaling $1.7 billion. Most foreign investment is concentrated in the production of electronic components, consumer electronics, and electrical goods (dominated by US and Japanese firms), petroleum production and distribution, textiles, vehicle assembly, steel, cement, rubber products, and electrical machinery.

In 1996 the government announced a list of 31 major infrastructure projects to be built between 1995 and 2020 at a cost of M$163 billion. The Second Industrial Master Plan (1996 to 2005) determined strategic projects for investment. These have drawn a huge influx of foreign investment. They include the Bukun hydroelectric dam in Sarawak, Southeast Asia's largest; the Petronas Twin Towers, the world's tallest; one of the region's most modern airports; and Putrajaya, a new capital city. The Multimedia Super Corridor (MSC) is being developed by the government to attract high technology companies to Malaysia.

39ECONOMIC DEVELOPMENT

The government remains generally committed to a policy of free enterprise, although it owns and operates the railway and the majority of the communications systems and has become increasingly involved in certain key industries. In 1970, a government holding company, Perbadanan Nasional (PERNAS), was created to encourage Malay-controlled businesses; in 1975, the government attempted, through PERNAS, to strengthen Malaysian interests in the tin-mining sector. Also in 1975, the government established the National Oil Co. (PETRONAS), with the overall aim of acquiring majority control of the country's petroleum operations. The Industrial Coordination Act of 1975 attempted to accelerate indigenous Malay participation in the economy by setting limits on foreign participation in the processing, domestic distribution, and export of local raw materials. In 1971, the New Economic Policy (NEP) was adopted, with the aim of channeling a greater share of future economic growth into Malay hands. It specifically called for raising the level of corporate ownership by Malays to 30% by 1990, reducing corporate ownership by other Malaysians (i.e., Chinese and Indians) to 40%, and restricting foreigners to ownership of no more than 30%. Short-term investment strategies are set forth in a series of economic plans. The Fourth Malaysia Plan (1981–85) proposed a level of development spending of M$42.8 billion and called for acceleration of the NEP goals for Bumiputra economic participation. Major industrial and infrastructural development projects included a M$900-million bridge between Pulau Pinang and the mainland and a M$600-million automobile-manufacturing plant, both of which opened in 1985. Recent economic planning has stressed a "look East" policy, with Malaysia attempting to emulate the economic successes of Japan and the Republic of Korea by importing technology from those countries. In response to deteriorating prices for oil and other exports, the Fifth Malaysia Plan (1986–90) has moved away from the goals of the NEP, aiming instead at promoting foreign investment, particularly in export industries.

The year 1990 marked the culmination of several economic development plans: the Fifth Malaysia Plan (FMP) 1986–90; the conclusion of the First Outline Perspective Plan (OPP1) 1971–1990; and the completion of the New Economic Policy (NEP) 1971–1990. The FMP emphasized industrialization. Specific targets were formulated to ensure that the distribution of ownership and participation in the commercial and industrial sector would be characterized by ethnic group participation, 30% bumiputra—Malays and other indigenous peoples of Malaysia, 40% other Malaysians (Chinese and Indian descent), and 30% foreign. The government provided funds to purchase foreign-owned shareholding on behalf of the Bumiputra population, increasing their equity to 20% by 1990. These policies are part of the new National Development Policy, although specific targets and time tables have been dropped. A post-1990 NEP defined Malaysian economic strategy for full development by 2020. Three 10-year Outline Perspective Plans which included a New Development Plan and six five-year plans made up the NEP. A Second Outline Perspective Plan (OPP2) 1991–2000 aimed to sustain growth momentum and to achieve a more balanced development of the economy. The Sixth Malaysia Plan called for an average annual growth rate of 7.5%, and expenditures on infrastructure were included to ensure prospects for further development. Development trends are toward privatization, encouraging the spread of industry throughout the country, increasing manufacturing in the free trade zones, and providing financing for industry through the establishment of specialized financing institutions.

A five-year development plan announced by Dr. Mahathir on 6 May 1996 forecasted average growth of 8% per year from 1996 to 2000. But it also tackled issues that bothered skeptics of the Malaysian economy: low rises in productivity, a skills shortage, and a gaping current-account deficit. In 1997 and 1998, these issues, along with a global financial crisis based in Asia caused the downturn that skeptics expected. Prospects for continuation of the Second Industrial Master Plan for 1996 through 2005 seemed grim, although the economy began to rebound in 1999. Massive capital and infrastructure projects have attracted foreign investment and international respect.

40SOCIAL DEVELOPMENT

Public financial assistance should be considered within the framework of Malaysian society, with its highly developed sense of family and clan responsibility. The government has generally encouraged volunteer social welfare activities and has subsidized programs of private groups. The Department of Social Welfare, under the Ministry of Welfare Services, administers and coordinates social assistance programs. The government's program of public assistance takes the form of cash, commodities, and institutional care. Children's services, begun in 1952, provide casework services and administer children's homes. A probation service provides care and assistance for juvenile delinquents and dependents, and a handicapped persons' service aids the deaf, mute, and blind. In addition, care is provided for the aged and chronically ill.

Since 1951, a provident fund has provided lump-sum benefits for old age, disability, and death. As of 1999, pensions were funded by 11% contributions of earnings by workers, and 12% of payroll by employers. The retirement age is 55. In 1969, legislation was enacted to provide injury insurance and disability pensions to low-income workers.

In recent years, the government has taken active measures to improve the rights and standing of women. In 1989, the Islamic Family Law was revised to strengthen the inheritance rights of Muslim women and to increase their access to divorce. In 1994, the government passed a domestic violence bill that allows the courts to protect victims of spousal abuse. However, this law falls short of making domestic violence a criminal act that may be tried under the existing law regarding assault and battery. A 1996 law added further measures to control domestic violence, but women's rights groups still claimed that further protection under the law was needed for victims of spousal abuse. Most Muslim women play subordinate roles in public and private life in spite of their growing legal rights. As of 1999, 38 of 262 parliamentary seats were held by women. In family and religious matters, Muslim women are subject to Islamic law, which allows polygyny. Custom favors men in matters of inheritance. Some Malays practice a modified form of female genital mutilation.

Women were expected to make up 52% of the nation's total labor force by the end of 2000, but, except in teaching and nursing, they are underrepresented in professional occupations. In 1999 women held about 40% of all civil service positions.

Human rights abuses reported in 1999 included arbitrary arrest and detention, torture, and other types of prisoner abuse. Caning is still used for some crimes.

41HEALTH

Malaysia enjoys a comparatively high standard of health, the consequence of long-established health and medical services. The country has improved its health care and social conditions, and is considering a national health insurance plan. There are three main hospitals in Malaysia, all located in the capital, Kuala Lumpur: Subang Jaya Hospital, General Hospital, and Penang Adventist Hospital. In 1990–97, hospital beds totaled 2 per 1,000 people. As of 1990–97, total health care expenditures were 2.9% of GDP. Approximately 80% of the population had access to health care in 1993.

Malaysia's 1999 birth rate was 26 per 1,000 people. In 1990–95, 51% of married women (ages 15 to 49) used contraception. Life expectancy has risen over the last decade and was 70.7 years in 1999.

Under the tuberculosis control campaign, begun in 1961, the number of annual deaths from tuberculosis declined to 971 in 1970 and 672 in 1983. In 1997, there were only 112 reported cases of tuberculosis per 100,000 people. As a result of the yaws elimination campaign, begun in 1954, the disease was virtually eliminated in the late 1960s. A malaria eradication program, begun in 1967, resulted in a drop in the number of hospital admissions for malaria from 25,400 in 1970 to 8,274 in 1984. Malaria remains a common disease in Malaysia. At least 39,890 cases of malaria were reported in 1993. In 1994–95, 90% of the population had access to safe water, and 94% had adequate sanitation. In 1989–95, 23% of children under five years of age were still considered malnourished. Immunization rates from 1990–94 for children up to one year old were quite high: tuberculosis (99%); diphtheria, pertussis, and tetanus (90%); polio (90%); and measles (81%).

Tobacco use has increased since the mid-1980s. As of 1995, each adult smoked an average of 1.9 kg of tobacco per year. Between 1970 and 1989, cardiovascular disease death rates more than doubled. Among the main ethnic groups in Malaysia, Malaysians of Indian origin have the highest mortality rates compared to the Chinese and Malay. Similar trends exist for diabetes mortality.

Infant mortality in 1999 was 21.7 per 1,000 live births, and the general mortality rate was 5.3 per 1,000 people. The maternal mortality rate from 1990–97 was 34 per 100,000 live births. The total fertility rate has dropped from 4.2 in 1980 to 3.4 in 1999.

The HIV-1 seroprevalence rate in 1997 was 6 adults per 100 infected with HIV-1.

42HOUSING

A total of 744,000 new housing units were built during 1970–80, and an estimated 923,300 units—43% public and 57% private—were planned under the 1981–85 development plan. About 92% of all housing units were detached houses, 7% were apartments, and 1% were single rooms.

The need for urban housing is acute: an estimated 24% of Kuala Lumpur's population consists of recently arrived squatters living in overcrowded shantytowns with few urban amenities. A government plan for low-cost housing was expected to provide 80,000 units per year from 1986 to 1988. In the mid-1990s, the total number of housing units was 3,403,000.

43EDUCATION

Six years of free primary education is followed by three years of comprehensive general and prevocational education. Two further years of education at the postcomprehensive level, in either a vocational or an academic program, is offered. A two-year preuniversity course prepares students for admission to the universities. Malay is the medium of instruction in primary and secondary schools, with English as a compulsory second language. Muslim religious instruction is compulsory for all Muslim children while private Christian schools offer religious training to their students. For the year 2000, an estimated 12.5% of the adult population (males, 8.5%; females, 16.4%) was illiterate.

In 1997, primary schools enrolled 2,840,667 pupils, instructed by 148,000 teachers. Student-to-teacher ratio stood at 19 to 1. In secondary schools, there were 1,889,592 pupils, instructed by 102,139 teachers, in 1998. In 1996, 210,724 students were enrolled and 14,960 teaching faculty were employed in institutions of higher education, which include the Universiti Kebangsaan Malaysia (the National University of Malaysia), the University of Malaya, and the Technological University of Malaysia, all in or near Kuala Lumpur, and the University of Science Malaysia (formerly the University of Pinang). The MARA Institute of Technology is the largest post-secondary institute in the country.

44LIBRARIES AND MUSEUMS

The National Library of Malaysia, with more than 700,000 volumes, was established in 1971 and has been charged with wide responsibilities under the National Library Act. Both the National Library and the National Archives are in Kuala Lumpur. The National University of Malaysia (Universiti Kebangsaan Malaysia) in Bargi has 678,500 volumes. Other important libraries are those at the universities; the Sabah (380,000) and Sarawak (500,000) state libraries; Tun Abdul Razak Library at the MARA Institute of Technology (273,000); and the library of the Rubber Research Institute of Malaysia (120,000). The largest public libraries are in Denang, Malacca, and Selangor.

The National Museum of Malaysia in Kuala Lumpur, constructed on the site of the former Selangor Museum (destroyed in World War II), houses extensive collections of Malayan archaeology, ethnography, and zoology. The Perak Museum in Taiping, founded in 1883, has a varied collection exhibiting antiquities, ethnographic, and zoological materials. Also in Kuala Lumpur are the Museum of Asian Art (1974), the Postal Museum, the Air Force Museum, and the National Art Gallery (1958). Sabah and Sarawak maintain anthropological and archaeological collections pertinent to East Malaysia. There is an Aboriginal People's Museum in Gombak.

45MEDIA

The government owns and operates a well-developed and well-equipped telecommunications system. In 1995, Malaysia had over 2.5 million telephones, including private wire and public coin stations. Automatic dialing for the majority of exchanges is provided by a VHF radio circuit. Telegraph and radiotelephone connections link Peninsular Malaysia with most foreign countries.

Radio-Television Malaysia (RTM) operates radio and television stations in Kuala Lumpur, Sabah, and Kuching, and there is a commercial station, Sistem TV-3 Berhad, in Kuala Lumpur as well. Broadcasts are in English, Malay, five Chinese dialects, Tamil, and numerous local languages and dialects. As of 1999 Malaysia had 28 AM and 3 FM radio stations and 27 television stations. In 1997, there were 432 radios, 166 televisions, and 133 mobile phones per 1,000 population. Color television transmission began in 1978.

Malaysia generally has enjoyed a large measure of press freedom. In October 1987, however, the government closed four newspapers in an effort to end criticism of its policies. While the press is normally moderate and objective, it treads carefully when dealing with Malaysia's plural ethnic and cultural foundations. There are about 80 English, Malay, Chinese, and Tamil daily and weekly newspapers. The Malay-language press is the largest segment, followed by English, Chinese, Tamil, Punjabi, and Kadazan. The leading Kuala Lumpur dailies (with their 1999 circulations) are as follows:

	LANGUAGE	CIRCULATION
Utusan Malaysia	Malay (Rumi)	240,000
Berita Harian	Malay	350,000
New Straits Times	English	178,500
China Press		133,000
Malaysian Nanban		192,800
Nanyang Siang Pau		180,000

Though the Constitution provides for freedom of speech and a free press, in practice the government is said to restrict the flow of information deemed "sensitive" including issues regarding citizenship of non-Malays and the special position of Malays in society. The media generally practices self censorship, providing laudatory, noncritical coverage of government activities.

By 1996, there were 780,000 personal computers; in 1998 there were 18 Internet hosts in Malaysia per 1,000 population.

46ORGANIZATIONS
The Malaysian government promotes thrift, credit, processing, marketing, farming, consumer, and housing cooperatives. The cooperative movement was introduced in Malaya in 1922. The Chinese are organized along clan, common dialect, or occupational lines into rural credit associations. These local associations set up and maintain schools, build temples, and provide burial, relief, and employment services. In the larger cities, chambers of commerce, organized along ethnic lines, promote the economic welfare of the group represented.

47TOURISM, TRAVEL, AND RECREATION
In 1999 Malaysia had 98,440 hotel rooms with an occupancy rate of 58%. Most large hotels are in the major cities of Kuala Lumpur and George Town. The best-known hill resort areas are Cameron Highlands, Raub, and Pinang Hill. Island resorts off the coast of the peninsula are Langkawi and Pangkor. Tourists numbered 6,210,921 in 1997. Passports are required of all entrants, although Malaysia has visa abolition agreements with all Commonwealth countries, the US, and other countries. Yellow fever inoculations are necessary for those arriving from infected areas.

Horse racing, soccer, rugby, cricket, and sepak raga (a form of badminton) are popular spectator sports. Kite fighting and top spinning are traditional pastimes for children and adults, and silat (a Malay martial art) is popular in rural areas.

The estimated cost of staying in Kuala Lumpur, according to 1999 UN estimates, was $105 per day. Daily expenses in Peninsular Malaysia are estimated at $74.

48FAMOUS MALAYSIANS
Among the foremost Malaysian leaders of the past was Sultan Mahmud, 16th-century ruler of Malacca. A great figure in Malay culture was 'Abdallah bin 'Abd al-Kabir (surnamed Munshi', 1796–1854), sometimes called the greatest innovator in Malay letters. The best-known figure in the political life of modern Malaysia is Tunku Abdul Rahman Putra bin Abdul Hamid Halimshah (b.1903), first prime minister of the Federation of Malaysia. Other political leaders are Tun Abdul Razak (1922–76), the nation's second prime minister (1970–76); Datuk Seri Mahathir bin Mohamed (b.1925), prime minister since 1981; Dato Onn bin Ja'afar (1895–1962), a founder of the United Malays National Organization; and Sir Cheng-lock Tan (1883–1960), leader of the Malaysian Chinese Association.

49DEPENDENCIES
Malaysia has no territories or colonies.

50BIBLIOGRAPHY
ABECOR. *Malaysia and Brunei Darussalam*. London: Barclays Bank, 1993.

Ahmad, Zakaria Haji (ed.). *Government and Politics of Malaysia*. New York: Oxford University Press, 1987.

American University. *Malaysia: A Country Study*. Washington, D.C.: Government Printing Office, 1985.

Andaya, Leonard and Barbara W. *A History of Malaysia*. New York: St. Martin's, 1982.

Bedlington, Stanley S. *Malaysia and Singapore: The Building of New States*. Ithaca, N.Y.: Cornell University Press, 1978.

Bowie, Alasdair. *Crossing the Industrial Divide: State, Society, and the Politics of Economic Transformation in Malaysia*. New York: Columbia University Press, 1991.

Clutterbuck, Richard. *Conflict and Violence in Singapore and Malaysia, 1945–1983*. Boulder, Colo.: Westview, 1984.

Crouch, Harold A. Government and Society in Malaysia. Ithaca, N.Y.: Cornell University Press, 1996.

Dumargay, Jacques. *Cultural Sites of Malaysia, Singapore, and Indonesia*. New York: Oxford University Press, 1998.

Fisk, E. K., and H. Osman-Rani (eds.). *The Political Economy of Malaysia*. New York: Oxford University Press, 1982.

Gomez, Edmund T. *Malaysia's Political Economy: Politics, Patronage, and Profits*. 2d ed. New York: Cambridge University Press, 1999.

Jaaffar, Johan. *History of Modern Malay Literature*. Kuala Lumpur, Malaysia: Desan Bahasa dan Pustaka, Ministry of Education Malaysia, 1992.

Kaur, Amarjit. *Historical Dictionary of Malaysia*. Metuchen, N.J.: Scarecrow Press, 1993.

Kaur, Amarjit and Ian Metcalfe (eds.) *The Shaping of Malaysia*. New York: St. Martin's Press, 1999.

Leete, Richard. *Malaysia's Demographic Transition: Rapid Development, Culture, and Politics*. New York: Oxford University Press, 1996.

Lucas, Robert E. B. *Restructuring the Malaysian Economy Development and Human Resources*. New York: St. Martin's Press, 1999.

Mackie, J. A. C. *Konfrontasi: The Indonesia–Malaysia Dispute, 1963–1966*. New York: Oxford University Press, 1974.

Mohamed Ariff. *The Malaysian Economy: Pacific Connections*. New York: Oxford University Press, 1991.

Munro-Kua, Anne. *Authoritarian Populism in Malaysia*. New York: St. Martin's Press, 1996.

Nonini, Donald Macon. *British Colonial Rule and the Resistance of the Malay Peasantry, 1900–1957*. New Haven, Conn.: Yale University Southeast Asia Studies, 1992.

Ongkill, James. *Nation Building in Malaysia, 1946 to 1974*. New York: Oxford University Press, 1985.

Peletz, Michael G. *Reason and Passion: Representation of Gender in a Malay Society*. Berkeley, Calif.: University of California Press, 1996.

Runciman, Steven. *The White Rajahs: A History of Sarawak from 1841 to 1946*. Kuala Lumpur, Malaysia: S. Abdul Majed & Co., 1992.

Ryan, N. J. *The Making of Malaysia and Singapore: A History from Earliest Times to 1966*. 4th ed. New York: Oxford University Press, 1969.

Saw, Swee-Hock. *The Population of Peninsular Malaysia.* Singapore: Singapore University Press, 1988.

Spruit, Ruud. *The Land of the Sultans: An Illustrated History of Malaysia.* Amsterdam: Pepin Press, 1995.

Stubbs, Richard. *Hearts and Minds in Guerrilla Warfare: The Malayan Emergency, 1948–1960.* New York: Oxford University Press, 1989.

U.S. Department of Commerce, *Survey of Current Business* (August 1991): Vol. 71, No. 8.

Von Vorys, K. *Democracy without Consensus.* Princeton, N.J.: Princeton University Press, 1975.

Winstedt, Sir Richard Olof. *Malaya and Its History.* 7th ed. London: Hutchinson, 1966.

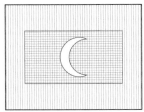

MALDIVES

Republic of Maldives

CAPITAL: Malé.

FLAG: The national flag consists of a white crescent at the center of a green field which, in turn, is at the center of a red field.

MONETARY UNIT: The Maldivian rupee, or rufiyaa (MR), is a paper currency of 100 laris. There are notes of 1/2, 1, 2, 5, 10, 50, and 100 rufiyaa. The dollar circulates freely and is the only currency accepted at some resorts. MR1 = $0.08575 ($1 = MR11.661) as of 31 March 2000.

WEIGHTS AND MEASURES: The metric system has been adopted, but some local units remain in use.

HOLIDAYS: National Day, 7 January; Independence Day, 26 July; Republic Day, 11 November; Fishermen's Day, 10 December. 'Id al-Fitr, 'Id al-'Adha', and Milad an-Nabi are some of the Muslim religious holidays observed.

TIME: 5 PM = noon GMT.

¹LOCATION, SIZE, AND EXTENT

The smallest country in Asia, the Republic of Maldives consists of an archipelago of nearly 1,200 coral islands and sand banks in the Indian Ocean, some 200 of which are inhabited. The chain of islands sits astride the equator, south of India and west of Sri Lanka, extending 820 km (510 mi) but occupying an area of just 300 sq km (116 sq mi). The area occupied by Maldives is slightly more than 1.5 times the size of Washington, D.C. Grouped in 26 atolls, with a total coastline of 644 km (400 mi), the northernmost atoll lies some 110 km (70 mi) south of India's Minicoy Atoll, about 480 km (300 mi) southeast of India's Cape Comorin, and 649 km (400 mi) west of Sri Lanka.

Maldives' capital, Malé, is situated on a 2.5 sq km (1 sq mi) island, the largest in the entire chain, in the Malé Atoll.

²TOPOGRAPHY

The islands vary from tiny banks to real islets. Some of the islands are in process of formation and are constantly increasing in size; others are gradually washing away. The islands are level and extremely low-lying, with elevations rarely exceeding 1.8 m (6 ft) above sea level. Many contain freshwater lagoons.

³CLIMATE

The Maldives' equatorial climate is generally hot and humid, with a mean temperature of about 27°C (81°F). The weather during the northeast monsoon (November–March) is mild and pleasant; the southwest monsoon (June–August) is violent and very rainy. The northern atolls are subject to more violent storms than those in the south. Annual rainfall in the south averages about 380 cm (150 in); in the north, 250 cm (100 in).

⁴FLORA AND FAUNA

The islands are covered with a dense scrub. The northern and southern islands are more fertile than those in the central group, and the eastern islands generally are more fertile than the western. Coconut, breadfruit, plantain, papaya, mango, and banyan trees flourish. Shrubs and flowers are widespread. Rats, rabbits, and flying foxes are the only indigenous mammals. Birds include ducks, bitterns, crows, curlews, snipes, and various sea birds. Small scorpions, beetles, and land crabs are common.

Inland lagoons and coastal reefs contain tropical ocean fish, crustaceans, and turtles; the surrounding waters contain sharks, swordfish, and porpoises.

⁵ENVIRONMENT

Environmental issues in the Maldives include dwindling freshwater supply and inadequate sewage treatment. Recent estimates indicate that the nation's water supply may be exhausted in the near future, and population increases have created a sanitation problem that threatens the waters surrounding this island nation. Another significant environmental problem is a rise in sea levels due to global warming. The islands are particularly susceptible to flooding. Environmental preservation is complicated by the unique problems of a nation consisting of 1,200 islands spread over 510 miles of the Indian Ocean. Preservation of the desert island ecology, protection of marine life and coral reefs, and coconut tree rehabilitation are additional environmental goals.

⁶POPULATION

The population of Maldives in 2000 was estimated at 310,425. An estimated 3.2% of the population is 65 years of age or older. The projected population for the year 2005 is 364,000, assuming a crude birthrate of 35 per 1,000 population and a death rate of 4, resulting in a natural rate of change of 3.1% for the period 2000–2005.

It was estimated that 28% of the population lived in urban areas in 2000. Malé, the capital and sole urban settlement, had a 2000 population of 68,000, concentrated on an island of only about 1.9 sq km (0.75 sq mi).

⁷MIGRATION

Interisland migration is limited to settlement in Malé; between 1967 and 2000, population in the capital rose from one-tenth to nearly one-quarter of the national total. In 1999, the net migration rate was zero.

⁸ETHNIC GROUPS

The original inhabitants of the Maldives are thought to have been of south Indian and Arab origin. The people of the northern atolls have to some extent intermarried with peoples from

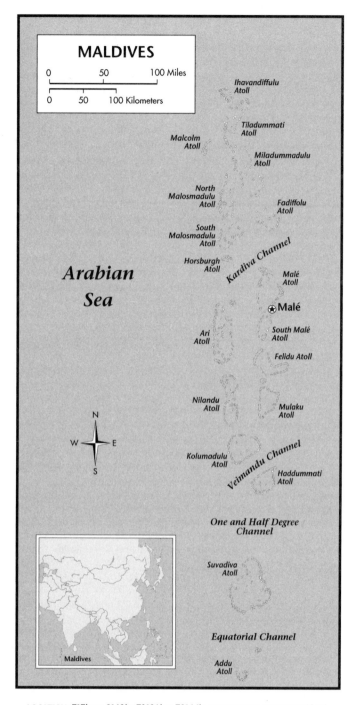

MALDIVES

0   50   100 Miles

0   50   100 Kilometers

Ihavandiffulu Atoll

Tiladummati Atoll

Malcolm Atoll

Miladummadulu Atoll

North Malosmadulu Atoll

Fadiffolu Atoll

South Malosmadulu Atoll

Horsburgh Atoll

Kardiva Channel

Arabian Sea

Malé Atoll

⊛ **Malé**

Ari Atoll

South Malé Atoll

Felidu Atoll

Nilandu Atoll

Mulaku Atoll

N
W   E
S

Kolumadulu Atoll

Veimandu Channel

Haddummati Atoll

One and Half Degree Channel

Suvadiva Atoll

Equatorial Channel

Maldives

Addu Atoll

LOCATION: 7°7′N to 0°43′s; 72°31′ to 73°46′E. **TERRITORIAL SEA LIMIT:** 12 mi.

western India, Arabia, and North Africa. Inhabitants of the southern islands show stronger physical affinities with the Sinhalese of Sri Lanka. Black African slaves imported from Zanzibar and Arabia have intermarried with the Maldivians, and there are also some Caucasian and Malayan elements.

⁹LANGUAGES

The Maldivian language, called Divehi, is similar to the old Sinhala (Elu) of Ceylon. It has contributed the word *atoll* to international terminology. In recent years, the language has been influenced by Arabic and Urdu. Thaana, developed during the 17th century, is the corresponding script, written from right to left.

English is spoken by most government officials, but only by a small number of the Maldivian population.

¹⁰RELIGIONS

There is evidence that the early Maldivians were Buddhists. Their conversion to Islam dates from 1153. With few exceptions, the people are Sunni Muslims, and both land ownership and citizenship are limited to adherents to this faith. The government's Department of Religious Affairs regulates matters pertaining to religion.

¹¹TRANSPORTATION

Malé, the capital, and some other islands have fairly good streets. Most people travel by bicycle or on foot. Interatoll transportation still depends mostly on local sailing boats, called *batheli* and *odi*. Although some mechanized boats carry cargo and, occasionally, passengers between Malé and other atolls, interisland transport is mainly by means of *dhonis* (small boats). Oceangoing shipping has been increasing. As of 1998, the Maldives had a fleet of 21 vessels, totaling 75,585 GRT, serving worldwide destinations, all controlled by Maldives Shipping Ltd., a public enterprise. Also in 1998, the Maldives had 5 airports, 2 of which had paved runways. Hulule, Malé's international airport, two km (one mi) away over water from the capital, was completed in 1966. Built with assistance by Sri Lanka under the Colombo Plan, it consists of two islands that were joined together to create a runway. It is served by Singapore Airlines, Air Lanka, various European tourist carriers, and Indian Airlines, the last also operating as Air Maldive on certain flights. In 1997, 189,000 passengers were carried on scheduled domestic and international airline flights.

¹²HISTORY

The first inhabitants of the Maldives were probably Dravidian speakers from south India, who were followed by Indo-European speaking Sinhalese from Ceylon in the 4th and 5th centuries BC. The island chain first become known in the West through the writings of Ptolemy, during the 2nd century AD. The island chain may have been ruled in ancient times by the Chinese; later, its rulers paid an annual tribute to principalities of western India. Maldivians were converted to Sunni Islam from Buddhism by Arab traders from east Africa and the Middle East in the middle of the 12th century, and from 1153, an unbroken line of 92 sultans served as local rulers for 800 years until 1953. In 1343, Ibn Battutah, the Arab traveler and historian, visited the islands and served for a time as a qadi.

After their discovery by the Portuguese traveler Dom Lourenço de Alameida in 1507, the Maldives were occupied by the Portuguese and forced to pay a tribute to Goa, the center of Portugal's South Asian holdings. But the Portuguese were driven out in 1573 by Muhammad Thakurufaani al-Azam, who, after becoming sultan, introduced a monetary system, a new script, and a standing militia. In the 17th century, the Dutch, who controlled neighboring Ceylon (now Sri Lanka), concluded a treaty with the sultanate which thereafter paid tribute to the rulers of Ceylon and claimed their protection.

The British completed their occupation of Ceylon in 1815, and British responsibility for the protection of the Maldives was formally recorded in 1887. By terms of the compact, the sultan recognized the suzerainty of the British sovereign and disclaimed all rights or intention to enter into any treaty or negotiations with any foreign state except through the (British) ruler of Ceylon. When Ceylon became independent in 1948, a new agreement was signed with the British government, providing for the Maldives to remain under the protection of the British crown, for external affairs to be conducted by or in accordance with the advice of the British government, for Britain to refrain from interfering in the internal affairs of the islands, and for the sultan to afford such facilities for British forces as were necessary for the defense of the islands or the Commonwealth. No tribute was to be paid by Maldives. New agreements reaffirming these provisions were signed in 1953, 1956, and 1960.

The sultanate, dominated by the Didi family since 1759, was abolished in 1953, and the Maldives was declared a republic. The first president, Amin Didi, ordered the emancipation of women and other reforms that were resented by more conservative elements among the people, and nine months later he was overthrown. His cousins Muhammad Farid Didi and Ibrahim 'Ali Didi became co-presidents in September 1953, and a month later the National Assembly voted to restore the sultanate. The new sultan, Muhammad Didi, was installed at Malé on 7 March 1954, and Ibrahim 'Ali Didi, the prime minister, formed a new government.

The government's agreement in 1956 to permit Britain to maintain an air base on Gan Island in the southern Maldives produced a public reaction so strong that Prime Minister Ibrahim was forced to resign in December 1957. Ibrahim Nasir, who succeeded him, asserted that the British base would violate Maldivian neutrality, but when his government sent a representative to Gan to tell the islanders to stop working for the British, the islanders attacked him.

Early in 1959, the people of Addu Atoll, in which Gan Island is located, declared their independence. At the same time, a rebellion broke out in the three southernmost atolls (including Addu). The rebel headmen declared the formation of the United Suvadiva Republic (with a population of 20,000) and demanded recognition from London. The British refused to comply, but the Nasir government made public its suspicions that the coup had been engineered by the British. In the event, government forces crushed the rebels in two of the atolls but made no attempt to interfere on Gan or any of the other seven main islands in the Addu group. By March 1960, the Suvadiva Republic was declared dissolved, and a committee ruling under the sovereign control of the sultan was set up, including among its members 'Abdallah Afif, leader of the rebellion.

In February 1960, the Maldivian government made a free gift to the British government of the use of Gan Island and other facilities in Addu Atoll for 30 years, and a fresh agreement was drawn up between the governments. In return, the British agreed to assist in bringing about a reconciliation between the Maldivian government and the disaffected inhabitants of the southern islands. But by 1962, resentment had grown against the British owing to their lack of progress in implementing the agreement; in late 1962 a Royal Navy frigate was sent to the capital island of Malé to protect British citizens. 'Abdallah Afif was evacuated by the British to the Seychelles.

The Sultanate of the Maldive Islands achieved complete independence on 26 July 1965, with the British continuing to retain use of the facilities on Gan in return for the payment of $2,380,000, most to be spent over a period of years for economic development. In March 1968, a referendum resulted in an 81% vote to abolish the sultanate and to reestablish a republic. A new republican constitution came into force on 11 November 1968, establishing the Republic of Maldives, and Nasir—then prime minister—became president.

With the British secure in their control of facilities they share with the United States outside the Maldives in Diego Garcia, 650 km (400 mi) east of Gan, Britain vacated the Gan air base on 31 December 1975, and the UK-Maldivian accord was formally terminated the following year.

Nasir declined renomination and was succeeded as president on 11 November 1978 by Maumoon Abdul Gayoom, who was chosen by the Citizens' Majlis (parliament) in June and was confirmed in a popular referendum by a majority of 90% on 28 July. Reelected president by the Majlis in August 1983, Gayoom won confirmation in a national referendum on 30 September with a majority of 95.6%. Gayoom was reelected to a third term in August 1988. He successfully resisted a brief attempt to overthrow him by Sri Lankan Tamil mercenaries in November 1988 with the help of an Indian military contingent flown to the Maldives at his request. In addition to the presidency, Gayoom is also Minister of Defense and Minister for National Security.

Gayoom was reelected for a fourth term as president in August 1993 and confirmed by popular referendum in September. He was elected to a fifth term, unopposed, in 1998. Gayoom's only principal rival for the presidency came in the 1993 election when his brother-in-law Ilyas Ibrahim ran against him. Ibrahim subsequently was tried in absentia for violation of the constitution, found guilty of treason, and sentenced to more than 15 years banishment from the islands.

13 GOVERNMENT

Under the 1968 constitution, the Citizens' Majlis (parliament) nominates a single candidate for the presidency, who is confirmed in office thereafter by popular referendum. The president heads the executive branch and appoints the cabinet and is constitutionally permitted to have as many vice-presidents as he desires. Presidential elections must be held by October 2003.

The unicameral Majlis is a body of 48 members, 40 of whom are directly elected (2 from each of the 19 inhabited atolls and 2 from the capital island of Malé) by universal suffrage of citizens over 21. Eight members are appointed by the president. The Majlis drafts legislation that becomes law after ratification by the president. The Majlis also nominates the president by secret ballot. The candidate is then approved by referendum of the population.

Elections to the Majlis are held individually and do not necessarily coincide with its sessions. Elections were held in December 1994 and December 1999.

14 POLITICAL PARTIES

There are no organized political parties. While not banned, they are officially discouraged. Candidates for office stand for election as independents and campaign on their family and personal stature.

15 LOCAL GOVERNMENT

The Maldives is divided administratively into 19 districts, each a discrete atoll headed by a government-appointed verin, or chief, who functions in the manner of a District Officer. On each inhabited island a khatib, or headman, also appointed by the government, supervises and carries out the orders of the government under the supervision of the atoll chief.

16 JUDICIAL SYSTEM

Justice is meted out according to traditional Islamic law (Shari'ah) by the High Court and lower courts appointed for that purpose by the president and functioning under the Ministry of Justice. Civil law is also applied but remains subordinate to Shari'ah.

On the capital island, Malé, there is a High Court and four lower courts. The High Court hears a range of cases as a court of first instance and also serves as a court of appeal. The four lower courts each deal with a specific area such as theft, property or family law issues. The 1995 presidential decree gives power to a five-member advisory council appointed by the president to review the High Court's decisions.

On the other islands, there is one all-purpose lower court in which cases are often adjudicated by traditional legal practitioners. Complex cases are referred to the appropriate specialized court in Malé. There are 204 general courts on the islands.

In criminal cases there is no jury trial. The accused may call witness and may be assisted by a lawyer. There are, however, few professionally trained lawyers in Maldives, and the court does not provide a lawyer to an indigent defendant. The judiciary is subject to executive influence. The president may grant pardons and amnesties.

17ARMED FORCES

The armed forces of the Maldives consist of a paramilitary national security service and militia of a few hundred. Armed boats patrol the territorial waters to protect the local fishing industry.

18INTERNATIONAL COOPERATION

The Maldives, which joined the UN on 21 September 1965, is a member of ESCAP and all the nonregional specialized agencies except IAEA, ILO, and WIPO. Special membership status in the Commonwealth of Nations was granted 9 July 1982. Maldives is member of the WTO, participates in G-77, and is a signatory to the Law of the Sea.

An active member of the nonaligned movement, Maldives has led efforts to declare an Indian Ocean Peace Zone, free of nuclear arms. In October 1977, the government rebuffed an offer from the former USSR to lease Gan as a base for its fishing fleet for $1 million annually. The Maldives participates in the Islamic Conference and has been a recipient of Arab financial and technical aid.

19ECONOMY

The Maldives is among the least developed countries in the world, yet economic progress has been steady. In 1989, the government lifted import quotas and liberalized some sectors of trade. Since the early 1990s, the country's GDP has grown at an estimated 6–7% per year; the real growth rate of GDP was estimated to be 5.8% in 1998. Fishing, tourism, and shipping are the mainstays of the economy. The tourism industry has become particularly important, accounting for about 18% of GDP in 1997 and over 60% of the country's foreign exchange earnings. The government is seeking to continue diversifying the economy through further promotion of tourism, processing industries, and garment production. Over 90% of government revenues comes from tourism. Besides tourism, GDP is comprised of distribution, 20%; construction, 11%; fisheries, 10%; agriculture, 7%; transportation, 7%; services, 6%; and manufacturing and electricity, 6%.

20INCOME

The US Central Intelligence Agency (CIA) reports that in 1998 Maldives' gross domestic product (GDP) was estimated at $500 million. The per capita GDP was estimated at $1,840. The annual growth rate of GDP was estimated at 5.8%. The average inflation rate in 1998 was 8.2%. The CIA defines GDP as the value of all final goods and services produced within a nation in a given year and computed on the basis of purchasing power parity (PPP) rather than value as measured on the basis of the rate of exchange. It was estimated that agriculture accounted for 22% of GDP, industry 15%, and services 63%.

21LABOR

There were approximately 64,000 members of the Maldives workforce in 1999, one-third of whom were foreign workers. About 20% of the workforce in 1999 was employed in fishing; 15% in industry; 10% in tourism, and 55% in other sectors.

Union organization is not prohibited but the government does not recognize union organization or striking as a right.

The minimum working age is 14 (16 for government work) and there were no reports of children working in the formal economic sector in 1999.

There are no specific statutory provisions regarding working hours, the workweek length, or overtime pay. Administrative orders from the president's office have set a seven-hour workday and a five-day workweek.

There is no national minimum wage, but wage floors exist for certain kinds of work. Although no statutory provisions are in place, employers offer competitive pay and working conditions.

22AGRICULTURE

Only 10% of the land is estimated to be cultivable. Millet, corn, pumpkins, sweet potatoes, pineapples, sugarcane, almonds, and many kinds of tropical vegetables and fruits are successfully grown, largely in homestead gardens. Coconut palms provide copra and coir, the most important exports after fish. Virtually all rice, a staple food for the population, must be imported. Breadfruit, mangoes, papayas, limes, bananas, pumpkins, watermelon, taro, and chili peppers are also valuable crops. As of 1998, small amounts of corn, millet, and sorghum were cultivated. Production in 1998 included 13,000 tons of coconuts and 2,000 tons of copra.

23ANIMAL HUSBANDRY

Fodder is insufficient for more than a few head of cattle, but there are many goats and chickens.

24FISHING

Fishing is the chief industry (accounting for 11% of GDP), with the main catch being skipjack and yellowfin tuna. About half the annual harvest is frozen, canned, or dried and exported to Thailand, Europe, and Sri Lanka. The Maldivian fisheries sector underwent a major transformation during the 1980s and became increasingly productive through modernization of catch collection and processing methods. Expansion of the canning industry and investment in fisheries diversification is ongoing. The fish catch in 1997 totaled 107,676 tons; exports of fish were valued at $56.3 million that year. Annual per capita consumption of fish and shellfish in the mid-1990s averaged 175.5 kg/386.9 lb (live-weight equivalent), greater than that of any other nation. Shell gathering is a relatively important activity in the Maldives, with large quantities of cowries exported for use as ornaments. Several rare shell species are also collected.

25FORESTRY

There are no forests as such. Coconut wood, however, is used in the building of boats and the construction of houses. Imports of forest products amounted to $4.2 million in 1997.

26MINING

There are no known mineral resources.

27ENERGY AND POWER

The power plant in Malé, with a capacity of 25,000 kW, provided 85 million kWh of electricity for the island in 1998. More than half of this amount was distributed to residences, and one-quarter to government buildings. A smaller plant on Hulule supplies power for the airstrip on that island. About 55% of total energy consumption comes from wood. Nearly all of the inhabited islands of the Maldives (194 out of 199) have access to electricity.

28INDUSTRY

The manufacturing sector is small and limited by the shortage of domestic labor. After the fish industry, important traditional industries in the Maldives include the manufacture of coir, a rope made from dried coconut fibers, and lacemaking (handmade pillow lace), introduced by the Dutch in the 17th century. Maldivian lacquerwork and finely woven mats are famous for their quality and design. Coconuts, copra, shells, tortoiseshell, bone dust, red stone, ambergris, and handicrafts are also produced locally as well as exported. A fish-canning plant and several apparel factories built during the past decade have given a large boost to export-oriented manufactures. In the late 1990s, the tourism industry was being vigorously developed.

29 SCIENCE AND TECHNOLOGY

Mechanized fishing operations have been the focus of research and development efforts since the 1980s, with the help of UNDP.

30 DOMESTIC TRADE

Malé Island is the chief commercial center. Sri Lankan and Indian merchants in Malé act as their own importers, exporters, and wholesalers. The importing of rice and exporting of ambergris are government monopolies. Most shops are open from 8 AM to 1:30 PM and from 2:30 to 5 PM, Sunday through Thursday. Banks and government offices are open from 9 AM to 1 PM on the same days.

31 FOREIGN TRADE

In 1989, the government initiated an economic reform program that lifted import quotas and opened exports of some commodities to the private sector (until then, exports had been entirely controlled by a state trading organization). In 1997, exports consisted mainly of fish products, but also included garment manufactures; apparel and clothing accessories have become important export goods. Also exported are coconuts, copra, coir, cowrie shells, and some local handicraft products. Rice, wheat flour, and salt are imported, as are tobacco, beverages, manufactured goods, and petroleum products.

Leading trade partners of the late 1990s are listed in the accompanying table. In the late 1970s, Mauritius, Japan, and Pakistan comprised almost 90% of the country's export market. The majority of Maldives' commodity exports are fish (64%) and garments (27%).

Principal trading partners in 1998 (in millions of US dollars) were as follows:

COUNTRY	EXPORTS	IMPORTS	BALANCE
United States	33	5	28
United Kingdom	17	8	9
Sri Lanka	16	31	-15
Japan	9	10	-1
Thailand	8	10	-2
Singapore	4	117	-113
Germany	4	11	-7
Qatar	n.a.	95	
Malaysia	n.a.	30	
United Arab Emirates	n.a.	25	

32 BALANCE OF PAYMENTS

Balance of payments deficits during the first half of the 1980s were caused largely by the international shipping recession, the collapse of world tuna prices, and a brief downturn in tourism caused by the violence in nearby Sri Lanka.

The US Central Intelligence Agency reports that in 1996 the purchasing power parity of Maldives' exports was $59 million while imports totaled $302 million resulting in a trade balance of -$243 million.

The International Monetary Fund (IMF) reports that in 1998 Maldives had exports of goods totaling $98 million and imports totaling $312 million. The services credit totaled $329 million and debit $99 million. The following table summarizes Maldives'

balance of payments as reported by the IMF for 1998 in millions of US dollars.

Current Account		-23
Balance on goods	-214	
Balance on services	231	
Balance on income	-28	
Current transfers	-12	
Capital Account		...
Financial Account		61
Direct investment abroad	...	
Direct investment in Maldives	12	
Portfolio investment assets	...	
Portfolio investment liabilities	...	
Other investment assets	31	
Other investment liabilities	18	
Net Errors and Omissions		-17
Reserves and Related Items		-20

33 BANKING AND SECURITIES

The Maldives Monetary Authority, established 1 July 1981, issues currency, advises the government on banking and monetary matters, supervises commercial banks, and manages exchange rates and exchange assets. Other banking services are provided by the Bank of Maldives (created in 1982) and commercial banks with headquarters in India, Pakistan, and Sri Lanka. There is no securities exchange.

34 INSURANCE

No recent information is available.

35 PUBLIC FINANCE

Public enterprises, including the State Trading Organization, the state shipping line, and public utilities, account for nearly half of government revenues; customs and tourist receipts make up most of the rest.

The US Central Intelligence Agency estimates that, in 1995, government revenues totaled approximately $88 million and expenditures $141 million. External debt was estimated at $179 million in 1996.

The International Monetary Fund estimates that in 1998 Maldives' central government took in revenues of approximately $166 million and had expenditures of $184 million including capital expenditures of $76 million. Overall, the government registered a deficit of approximately $18 million. External debt totaled $187 million.

The following table shows an itemized breakdown of government revenues and expenditures. The percentages were calculated from data reported by the International Monetary Fund. The dollar amounts (millions) are based on the CIA estimates provided above.

REVENUE AND GRANTS	100%	166
Tax revenue	45.9%	76
Non-tax revenue	45.8%	76
Capital revenue	0.1%	0.16
Grants	8.2%	14
EXPENDITURES	100%	184
General public services	21.3%	39
Defense	11.7%	21
Public order and safety	2.7%	5
Education	14.6%	27
Health	11.3%	21
Social security	2.8%	5
Housing and community amenities	5.3%	10
Economic affairs and services	25.5%	47
Interest payments	4.8%	9

36TAXATION

Aside from customs duties, taxes on tourism constitute the main source of tax revenue accounting for 29% of government tax revenue in 1998. There is no income tax. License fees are charged for boats and motor vehicles. Uninhabited islands are leased for farming to individuals, who pay annual dues to the government; over 90% of these absentee landlords reside in Malé.

37CUSTOMS AND DUTIES

Customs duties are a primary source of government revenues and vary from 5–20% on essentials to 35–200% on luxury goods. Staple commodities (rice, wheat, flour, and sugar) and specified medicines and textbooks are duty-free. Import duties comprised 63% of government tax revenue in 1997. Duties on consumer goods were reduced in May 1988.

38FOREIGN INVESTMENT

Assistance has been received from IBRD, WHO, UNDP, UNICEF, the EU, the Colombo Plan, CARE, and other international agencies, mostly in the form of grants and low-interest loans. Liberalized foreign investment policies have been adopted in recent years in order to attract needed development capital, especially for hotel and resort construction and other businesses related to the tourism industry.

39ECONOMIC DEVELOPMENT

The government has implemented a series of development programs to improve and expand fishing and related industries, textile manufacturing, food processing, tourism, communications, and health and education services. Effective 1 July 1997, the Companies Act governed the formation, registration, and management of companies doing business in Maldives. Part of the economic thrust has been to lessen the reliance on fishing and to diversify the economy. In 1986, Malé's new commercial harbor was opened, considerably speeding up cargo handling from 200–300 tons to 1,500 tons a day.

Malé's international airport was upgraded in the late 1980s, comprising a critical factor in the growth of the country's tourism sector. Given the growing wealth in the country in recent years, in 2000 the government was considering bolstering government development revenues by instituting a personal income tax, though concerns remain that enforcement may prove difficult. Continued expansion of tourism has been particularly targeted in government development plans for the immediate future, along with facilitating a spread of economic activity to outlying island groups. Water taxis and scheduled sea vessel and light aircraft transportation services were developing in the late 1990s for this purpose.

40SOCIAL DEVELOPMENT

The government has focused its spending on social services and preventive health services. There is no organized social welfare system. Assistance is traditionally provided through the extended family. Employees are entitled to medical and maternity leave.

In spite of traditional Islamic restrictions on the role of women, they have increased their participation in public life. Under the terms of the 1997 constitution, men and women are considered equal before the law. Women generally receive pay equal to men in similar positions. A Department of Women's Affairs and a National Women's Council protect women in traditional roles and help them enter nontraditional occupations. Approximately 10% of uniformed military personnel were women in 1995. However, Islamic law discriminates against women in matters of divorce and inheritance. Women are less able to initiate and obtain a divorce. Few women choose to participate in politics, largely because of tradition and custom. In 1999, only three women held seats in the 48-member parliament.

Although children's rights are explicit in law and provisions are in place to protect children from abuse, education is not compulsory. Female children are much more likely to be withdrawn from school than boys.

Human rights violations by the government include arbitrary arrest and detention and infringement of the freedoms of assembly, association, the press, and religion.

41HEALTH

In 1993, the Maldives had 15 physicians and 6 midwives. There is a relatively modern 86-bed hospital in Malé, backed by a 12-bed regional hospital and medical rescue services in the outlying atolls and the new Indira Gandhi Memorial Hospital (200 beds). In 1999 the fertility rate was 5.7. Between 1976–1994, 30% of children under 5 were underweight. The under 5 mortality rate has improved greatly during the last decades. The rate was 78 in 1994 but 258 in 1960. Life expectancy was 68.3 years in 1999, and the infant mortality rate was 38 per 1,000 live births. In 1994, 96% of the country's children had been vaccinated against measles. In 1996, 5 AIDS cases were reported; in 1994, 249 tuberculosis cases; and in 1993, 29 malaria cases. Between 1994-1995, 88% of the population had access to safe water; 40% had access to adequate sanitation. Malaria and diarrheal diseases have been drastically reduced. Water-borne disease epidemics have occurred, often caused by contamination of wells. Safe water is available to urban dwellers. Four desalination plants were completed by 1988, and a nationwide project is providing sewage systems to the atolls.

42HOUSING

Some of the houses on Malé are built in imitation of those in Colombo. Most, however, have coral or coconut-wood walls; the roofs are tiled or made of corrugated galvanized iron. The poorer houses are walled from the street with mats, called *cadjan*, or palm leaves. Almost all housing units are permanent dwellings, with just over 1% mobile homes or collective housing. In 1999, the government announced a ban on coral mining for construction to encourage use of other materials.

43EDUCATION

For 2000, adult illiteracy rates were estimated at 3.7% (males, 3.7%; females, 3.6%). Primary level education is for five years and secondary education is in two stages: five years at the lower level and two years at the higher level. Education is not compulsory. There are three streams of Maldivian education: traditional religious schools (makhtabs), which teach the Koran (Qur'an), basic arithmetic, and the ability to read and write Divehi; modern Divehi-language primary schools; and modern English-language schools. Primary and secondary schooling is based on the British educational system. Distance educational courses and educational programs on the radio are also provided.

In 1998 there were 48,895 students enrolled in 228 primary schools, with 1,992 teachers. Student-to-teacher ratio stood at 25 to one. In the same year, secondary schools had a total of 36,905 students. Maldivians must go abroad for higher education. In the 1990s, the government began making large investments in secondary, vocational, and post-secondary education. Currently the Science Education Centre in Malé provides pre-University courses, and the Centre may evolve into a university.

44LIBRARIES AND MUSEUMS

A National Library founded in 1945 contains 14,000 volumes and serves as a public library facility. A National Museum was founded in 1952 in Malé to conserve and display historical items.

45MEDIA

Interatoll communication is through a network of high-frequency transceivers; within atolls, communication between islands and with boats is by walkie-talkie. A satellite earth station was installed in 1977 to facilitate external communications. The Voice of Maldives has been transmitting radio broadcasts since 1962 in Divehi and English. Television Maldives is the country's only TV station. As of 1999 there were two AM and one FM radio stations and one television station. In 1997, there were 91 radio receivers and 23 television sets per 1,000 population; in addition, at least 10,000 telephones were in operation; telecommunication services were planned to be available on all populated islands by 2000. There are two daily newspapers, *Aafathis* (1995 circulation 2,000) and *Haveeru* (1999 circulation 4,500).

The Penal Code prohibits speech against Islam or the government, though it is said that journalists are more self-confident than in the past and that self-censorship has abated. There are legal prohibitions on the import of foreign publications.

46ORGANIZATIONS

Several sport clubs and a Muslim religious organization operate in Malé.

47TOURISM, TRAVEL, AND RECREATION

Tourism is the principal industry and leading foreign exchange earner. It has developed rapidly with government support, climbing from 9,000 visitors in 1975 to 196,112 in 1991 and 395,725 in 1998. Income from tourism reached $292 million that year. There were 7,063 hotel rooms in 1997 with 14,125 beds and an occupancy rate of 77%. Natural attractions are crystal-clear lagoons and white beaches that are ideal for swimming, fishing, and both snorkeling and scuba diving. Modern, one- and two-story tourist facilities have been built on various otherwise uninhabited islands, mainly in the Malé atoll but also in neighboring atolls. Developed with European, Sri Lankan, and Indian assistance and part ownership, such resorts are confined to these individual islands, thus allowing the conservative Islamic government to profit from the presence of foreign tourists while shielding its citizens from the presence and consumption of alcoholic beverages and other un-Islamic holiday practices of these tourists. Maldivian resort workers maintain their homes and families on other islands, and non-Maldivians—often Sri Lankans—are hired to serve the alcohol. Passports are required of all visitors, as are yellow fever inoculation certificates for those arriving from infected areas.

In 1999 the UN estimated the cost of staying in Malé at $102 per day, with costs elsewhere as low as $28.

48FAMOUS MALDIVIANS

Ibn Battutah (Muhammad bin 'Abdallah bin Battutah, b.Tangier, 1304–77), the remarkable Arab traveler and geographer, lived in the Maldives for several years, served as a quadi there, and married the daughter of a Maldivian vizier. Sultan Iskandar Ibrahim I, who reigned for nearly 40 years during the 17th century, had the Hukuru Miskit (the principal mosque on Malé Island) built in 1674. Modern-day leaders include Amir Ibrahim Nasir (b.1926) and Maumoon Abdul Gayoom (b.1937).

49DEPENDENCIES

Maldives has no territories or colonies.

50BIBLIOGRAPHY

Cambridge Encyclopedia of India, Pakistan, Bangladesh, Sri Lanka, Nepal, Bhutan, and the Maldives, The. Cambridge, England: Cambridge University Press, 1989.

Chawla, Subash. *The New Maldives.* Colombo, Sri Lanka: Diana Agencies, 1986.

Haq, Khadija. *Crisis of Government in South Asia.* New York: Mahbub ul Haq Foundation, 1999.

Heyerdahl, Thor. *The Maldive Mystery.* Bethesda, Md.: Adler & Adler, 1986.

The Maldives: An Introductory Economic Report. IBRD. Washington, D.C., 1980.

Maloney, Clarence. *The People of the Maldive Islands.* Columbia, Mo.: South Asia Books, 1981.

Phadnis, Urmila. *Maldives, Winds of Change in an Atoll State.* New Delhi: South Asian Publishers, 1985.

Reynolds, C. H. B. *Maldives.* Santa Barbara, CA: Clio Press, 1993.

Status of Women: Maldives. Bangkok: Unesco Principal Regional Office for Asia and the Pacific, 1989.

Stoddard, Theodore L. *Area Handbook for the Indian Ocean Territories.* Washington: Government Printing Office, 1971.

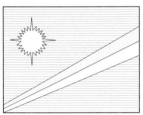

MARSHALL ISLANDS

Republic of the Marshall Islands

CAPITAL: Majuro, Majuro Atoll.

FLAG: The flag, adopted in 1979, is blue, with two diagonal strips of orange over white; in the canton is a white star with 4 large rays and 20 shorter ones.

ANTHEM: *Ij iokwe lok aelon eo ao ijo iaar lotak ie (I Love My Island, Where I Was Born).*

MONETARY UNIT: The US dollar is the official medium of exchange.

WEIGHTS AND MEASURES: British units are used, as modified by US usage.

HOLIDAYS: The government has not legislated official holidays.

TIME: 11 PM = noon GMT.

¹LOCATION, SIZE, AND EXTENT

The Marshall Islands is located in the central Pacific Ocean, just north of the Equator. Isolated from major population centers, Majuro, the capital, lies 3,438 km (2,136 mi) w of Honolulu, 3,701 km (2,300 mi) SE of Tokyo, and 3,241 km (2,014 mi) SE of Saipan, the former trust territory capital. The country consists of 29 atolls and 5 islands extending over a sea area exceeding 1,942,500 sq km (750,000 sq mi), but a land area of only about 181 sq km (70 sq mi).

Comparatively, the area occupied by the Marshall Islands is slightly larger than Washington, D.C. The atolls and islands form two almost parallel chainlike formations: the Ratak ("Sunrise"), or Eastern, group and the Ralik ("Sunset"), or Western, group. The largest atolls in the Ratak group are Mili, Majuro, Maloelap, Wotje, Likiep, and Bikini; in the Ralik group, Jaluit, Kwajalein, Wotho, and Enewetak. The Marshall Islands have a coastline of 370.4 km (230 mi).

The capital city of the Marshall Islands, Majuro, is located on the island of Majuro. Majuro Atoll is 3440 km (2,136 mi) from Honolulu, 3,700 km (2,300 mi) from Tokyo, and 3245 km (2,016 mi) from Saipan.

²TOPOGRAPHY

The majority of islands are in typical atoll formations, consisting of low-lying narrow strips of land enclosing a lagoon. Soils are porous, sandy, and of low fertility. There are five islands and 29 atolls scattered over 1.94 million sq km (750,000 sq mi) of the central Pacific Ocean. Kwajalein Atoll in the Ralik, or Western, atoll is the largest atoll in the world.

³CLIMATE

The maritime tropical climate is hot and humid, with little seasonal temperature change. Diurnal variations generally range between 21° and 34°c (70° and 93°F). Trade winds from the northeast cool the high temperatures from December through March.

Rainfall averages about 30–38 cm (12–15 in) per month, with October and November the wettest and December to April the driest. Average rainfall increases from the north to the south; the northern atolls average 178 cm (70 in) annually, compared with 432 cm (170 in) in the southern atolls.

⁴FLORA AND FAUNA

The flora and fauna of the atolls are limited in number and variety. The flora consists of species resilient to porous soils, salt spray, and relatively strong wind force. The dominant tree species include coconut palms, pandanus, breadfruit, and citrus trees. Fauna include rodents and indigenous strains of pig.

⁵ENVIRONMENT

Among the Marshall Islands' more significant environmental problems are water pollution due to lack of adequate sanitation facilities, inadequate supplies of drinking water, and the rise of sea levels due to global warming. Any rise in the sea level is a constant and serious threat to an island nation whose land mass is 2–3 meters (6–10 ft) above sea level.

The Marshall Islands Environmental Protection Agency, established in 1984, is concerned with programs for water quality standards, solid waste disposal, earthworks, and use of pesticides. The environments of the Bikini, Enewetak, Rongelap, and Utirik atolls were contaminated by nuclear testing. Nuclear tests were carried out in the region from 1946 to 1958. The long-term environmental effects on these atolls and their populations remained undetermined.

⁶POPULATION

The population of Marshall Islands in 2000 was estimated at 68,088. An estimated 3.6% of the population is 65 years of age or older. The projected population for the year 2005 is 83,000 assuming a crude birthrate of 45 per 1,000 population and a death rate of 6 resulting in a natural rate of change of 3.9% for the period 2000–2005.

It was estimated that 72% of the population lived in urban areas in 2000. About 60% of the total population resided on two atolls, Majuro and Ebeye. Of the 34 atolls and major islands, 24 are inhabited. The capital city, Majuro, had a 2000 population of 28,000.

⁷MIGRATION

Population has been steadily migrating from the outer atolls to the urban concentrations on Majuro and Ebeye. As a result, outer atolls have been left with unbalanced population structures of children, females, and the aged.

Provisions under the Compact of Free Association with the US permit unrestricted entry into the US and allow high-school graduates to join the US armed forces. In 1999, the net migration rate was zero.

8ETHNIC GROUPS

The Marshallese people are Micronesians, who are physically similar to the Polynesian peoples. The largest non-Marshallese ethnic group is from Kosrae in the Federated States of Micronesia. There are also small numbers of Americans and Filipinos.

9LANGUAGES

English is universally spoken and is the official language. Two major Marshallese dialects are also spoken. Marshallese is a Malayo-Polynesian language and the common source of each of the atolls' dialects. Both English and Marshallese are used in official communications and in commerce. Japanese is also spoken.

10RELIGIONS

The people are almost entirely Christian, primarily Protestant, as a result of the arrival of American and Hawaiian Protestant missionaries in the 1860s. The United Church of Christ is the principal denomination, representing some 90% of the population. The United Church of Christ is the successor of the Congregationalists from New England and Hawaii who converted the islanders in the latter half of the 19th century. Other religious denominations represented include Roman Catholics, Assemblies of God, Seventh Day Adventists, Baptists, Baha'i, Mormons, and Jehovah's Witnesses.

11TRANSPORTATION

There are 56 km (35 mi) of paved road on the Majuro atoll and 3.7 km (2.3 mi) on the Kwajalein atoll. On the outer islands, roads consist primarily of cleared paths and roads surfaced with stone, coral, or laterite. There are few motor vehicles.

The many scattered atolls separated by long distances make sea and air transportation essential. Domestic sea transportation is provided by interisland ships, which service each of the outer islands about once every three months. Two commercial dock facilities in Majuro and one in Ebeye furnish port facilities for international shipping. In 1998, the merchant fleet consisted of 131 ships with a capacity totaling 6,572,915 GRT.

Also in 1998, the Marshall Islands had 16 airports, only 4 of which had paved runways. Majuro International Airport, completed in 1974, accommodates aircraft up to Boeing 707 size. The government-owned Airline of the Marshall Islands (AMI), established in 1980, provides service to all outer islands with airstrips. International airline connections are provided to Tarawa in Kiribati, Funafuti in Tuvalu, and Nadi in Fiji. Air Micronesia/Continental Airlines links Majuro with major foreign destinations, including Hawaii, Guam, Manila, and Tokyo. In 1997, 33,000 passengers were carried on domestic and international airline flights.

12HISTORY

Sighting of the islands was first recorded by the Spanish navigator Alvaro de Saavedra in 1529. The British captain John Marshall, after whom the islands are named, explored them in 1788. Throughout the late 1800s and early 1900s, foreign powers ruled the islands for such advantages as trade, religious propagation, exploitation of resources, strategic considerations, and maintenance of sea routes. Spain claimed the islands in 1874, but sold them to Germany in 1899. At the outbreak of World War I, Japanese naval squadrons took possession of the Marshalls and began formal administration under a League of Nations mandate in 1920.

In World War II, after bitter fighting between US and Japanese forces that included battles for Kwajalein and Eniwetok (now Enewetak), the islands came under US control. In 1947, the Marshalls became a district of a UN trusteeship, called the Trust Territory of the Pacific Islands, which was administered by the US.

The US used Bikini and Enewetak atolls as nuclear testing sites from 1946 to 1958, exploding 66 atomic and nuclear tests during this period. The nuclear testing program resulted in the displacement of the indigenous people due to radiation contamination. The people of Bikini and Enewetak, along with those exposed to radioactive fallout in the 1954 Bravo Blast fought for compensation from the US, which in February 1990 agreed to pay $45 million to the victims of the nuclear testing program. Fifty years after testing began, Bikini Island has begun to attract a few tourists and scientific surveys have declared the island habitable again, although there is still a danger in eating too many of the local coconuts. Despite the scientific assurances, the US government has yet to issue a statement saying that the island is safe to inhabit. Because of the US promise to care for the Islanders until they can return to their home, Bikinians have made President Clinton their king and expect him to look after his people. In October 1999, the US, through the Majuro-based Nuclear Claims Tribunal, paid nearly another $2.3 million toward the $45 million originally promised in 1990, bringing the amount paid toward the total so far to $39.4 million.

The Marshallese people adopted a constitution in 1978, under which the Marshalls were designated the Republic of the Marshall Islands. In 1979, the constitution went into effect and the republic became a self-governing territory. Amata Kabua was elected the Republic's first president. In 1983, a Compact of Free Association with the US, providing for full self-government except for defense, was approved by plebiscite. In January 1986, the compact was ratified by the US, and on 21 October 1986 it went into effect. The UN Security Council voted in December 1990 to terminate the Marshall Islands' status as a UN Trust Territory. The Republic became an independent state and joined the UN in September 1991. The Compact of Free Association with the US is due to expire in 2001. Alan Stayman, the new US negotiator for the Compacts of Free Association, expected immigration policy to be a major issue when the US and the Marshall Islands began negotiating the terms of a new compact at the end of 1999.

In late 1999 and early 2000, two major political changes took place. For the first time, an opposition party, the newly formed United Democratic Party (UDP), gained a majority in parliament in the November 1999 elections. Then, in January 2000, Kessai Note, the Speaker of the Nitijela, was elected to the presidency, becoming the first president of the Marshall Islands who is a commoner (not a traditional chief).

Also in the late-1990s, global warming and the possibility of rising sea levels have raised concern over the long-term prospects for the islands in the middle of the Pacific Ocean. The Marshall Islands, along with Kiribati and Tuvalu, rise only a few feet above sea level. The Intergovernmental Panel on Climate Change has suggested that the sea could rise 18 inches by 2100, but that figure could be much lower or higher.

13GOVERNMENT

The Marshall Islands is an independent republic. The constitution effective on 1 May 1979 incorporates a blend of the British and American constitutional concepts. It provides for three main branches of government: the legislature, the executive, and the judiciary.

Legislative power is vested in the Parliament, known as the Nitijela, which consists of 33 members elected from 24 electoral districts, each corresponding roughly to an atoll. The Council of

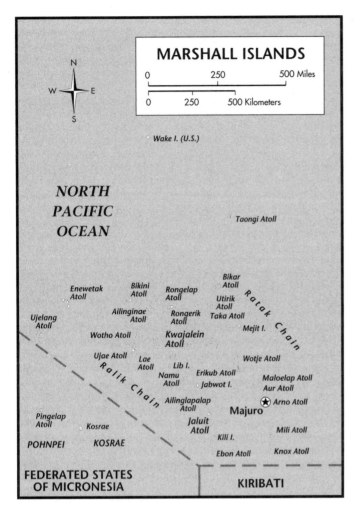

MARSHALL ISLANDS

NORTH
PACIFIC
OCEAN

Wake I. (U.S.)

Taongi Atoll

Bikar Atoll

Enewetak Atoll
Bikini Atoll
Rongelap Atoll
Utirik Atoll
Ailinginae Atoll
Rongerik Atoll
Taka Atoll
Ujelang Atoll
Wotho Atoll
Kwajalein Atoll
Mejit I.
Ratak Chain

Ujae Atoll
Lae Atoll
Lib I.
Wotje Atoll
Namu Atoll
Erikub Atoll
Jabwot I.
Maloelap Atoll
Aur Atoll
Ralik Chain
Ailinglapalap Atoll
Arno Atoll
Majuro

Pingelap Atoll
Kosrae
Jaluit Atoll
Mili Atoll
Kili I.
POHNPEI   KOSRAE
Ebon Atoll   Knox Atoll

FEDERATED STATES OF MICRONESIA

KIRIBATI

LOCATION: 4° to 14°N; 160° to 173°E.

Iroij (Chiefs) has 12 members, whose main functions are to request reconsideration by the Nitijela of any bill affecting customary law, traditional practice, or land tenure, and to express on opinion to the cabinet on any matter of national concern.

Executive power is vested in the cabinet, headed by the president, who is also head of state. The president, a member of the Nitijela, is elected by a majority of that assembly. The constitution requires the president to nominate not more than 10 or fewer than 6 members of the Nitijela as ministers. All citizens who have attained the age of 18 are eligible to vote.

After the US trusteeship administration of the Marshall Islands came to an end on 21 October 1986, the governments of the US and the Marshall Islands entered into a Compact of Free Association which provides defense, economic, technical, trade, and other benefits to the Marshall Islands for an initial period of 15 years set to expire in 2001. In late 1999 representatives from the US and Marshall Islands began negotiations to extend the terms of the compact.

14POLITICAL PARTIES

There are two political parties on the islands. The Our Island's Party of former President Amata Kabua has been in power since 1979. Kabua, the nation's only president since nationhood, was re-elected to a fifth term in 1995. When President Kabua died on

12 December 1996, the government named Kunio Lemari, Minister of Transport and Communications, as Acting President. New presidential elections, held on 14 January 1997, were won by Amata Kabua's cousin Imata Kabua. The president serves a four-year term. The Ralik Ratak Democratic Party, founded by Tony DeBrum in June 1991 and currently led by Ramsey Reimers, acts as the opposition to the Kabua Government.

15LOCAL GOVERNMENT

There are 24 local governments for the inhabited atolls and islands. Typically, each is headed by a mayor, and consists of an elected council, appointed local officials, and a local police force.

16JUDICIAL SYSTEM

The judiciary consists of the Supreme Court, the High Court, the District Court, and 22 community courts. The Supreme Court has final appellate jurisdiction. The High Court has trial jurisdiction over almost all cases and appellate jurisdiction over all types of cases tried in subordinate courts. The District Court has limited civil and criminal jurisdiction nationwide.

Community courts in local government areas adjudicate civil and criminal cases within their communities. In 1984, a Traditional Rights Court was established to determine questions relating to titles or land rights and other legal interests involving customary law and traditional practice.

The constitution provides for an independent judiciary. The constitution also provides for the right to a fair trial. It prohibits the arbitrary interference with privacy, family, home, or correspondence. Government authorities respect these provisions in practice.

17ARMED FORCES

There are no armed forces. Under the Compact of Free Association, the US provides defense for a minimum 15-year period and operation of the Kwajalein Missile Range for 30 years.

18INTERNATIONAL COOPERATION

Until 21 October 1986, the Marshall Islands was administered by the US under a UN Trusteeship Agreement. The Marshall Islands was admitted to the UN on 17 September 1991, and participates in agencies including UNCTAD, UNESCO, and WHO. In 1986, it became an associate member of ESCAP. The government continues to support and participate in the activities of regional bodies and has full membership in the SPC. The Marshall Islands has no diplomatic missions overseas, although an office of a resident representative to the US was established in 1986.

In 1996 the Marshall Islands joined with 38 other nations to form the Alliance of Small Island States. The Alliance, concerned with global warming and rising sea levels, wants the industrialize nations to reduce greenhouse gas emissions by 20% by 2005.

19ECONOMY

The economy consists of a monetary sector and a nonmonetary subsistence sector. The monetary sector is localized in Majuro and Ebeye and is sustained largely by expenditures of the government and Kwajalein Missile Range employees. Copra (dried coconut meat) production provides a source of cash income for outer-atoll families engaged in subsistence activities. The labor force was estimated (the most recent survey taken in 1988) at just over 11,000, with 69% employed in the services sector and 21% in agriculture and fishing. Of those engaged in agriculture and fishing, the main activities are copra (dried coconut meat) production, and the cultivation of breadfruit, taro, and pandanus. The tourism industry is in its infancy although efforts are being made to capitalize on the Island's beaches WWII relics. Radioactive fallout deters visitors.

The islands have few natural resources, and imports far exceed exports. The Marshall Island's closest major trading partner is Hawaii, located 2,100 miles to the northeast. The US government provides grants of $65 million annually under the Compact of Free Association, which amounts to 70% of GDP. These funds are given in exchange for furnishing military facilities. Radioactive testing was done on the inhabitants during the 1950s, affecting at least half of the population. Negotiations to extend terms of the agreement under which the US provides aid to Marshall Islands were initiated in 1999.

20INCOME

The US Central Intelligence Agency (CIA) reports that in 1998 the Marshall Islands's gross domestic product (GDP) was estimated at $91 million. The per capita GDP was estimated at $1,450. The annual growth rate of GDP was estimated at -5%. The average inflation rate in 1998 was 7%. The CIA defines GDP as the value of all final goods and services produced within a nation in a given year and computed on the basis of purchasing power parity (PPP) rather than value as measured on the basis of the rate of exchange. It was estimated that agriculture accounted for 15% of GDP, industry 13%, and services 72%.

21LABOR

There is a considerable shifting of labor between the monetary and subsistence sectors of the economy, depending on opportunities for wage employment. As of 1992, over 50% of the population was under the age of 15, creating an acute labor shortage of trained and skilled workers. The labor force was 11,488 in 1988. Over 21% of employment is in agriculture, fishing and mining; 11% in construction, 14% in trade, 30% in personal services, 9% in manufacturing, 8% in business services and finance, and 7% in other sectors. The vast majority of monetary-sector employment is found in Majuro, Ebeye, and Kwajalein.

The government is the largest source of employment, followed by the service and construction sectors. Unemployment was 16% in 1991; there is a high and rising number of unemployed youth.

There are no labor unions. A minimum wage of $2 per hour (as of 1999) set by the government can be waived by new businesses or by employers who are training Marshallese employees. In order to create local jobs, the government is considering the creation of a duty-free transshipment zone.

There is no statutory provision permitting strikes by workers nor is there a right to collectively bargain or organize. In practice, wages are usually set by market factors in accordance with the minimum wage regulation.

There is no prohibition against child labor but the law requires compulsory education until the age of 14. In practice this requirement is not effectively enforced and many children work, especially in the fishing industry.

22AGRICULTURE

The traditional interplanting of root crops and other vegetables with coconuts, which maintained self-sufficiency in food and provided the Marshallese with dietetic variety before modern times, is still widely practiced as a subsistence activity. Dried coconut meat, known as copra, is produced on almost all islands and atolls; some 6,500 ha (16,000 acres) of coconut palm were productive. Taro, breadfruit, and pandanus are also grown.

23ANIMAL HUSBANDRY

Livestock on the islands consists of pigs and poultry. Most families raise pigs for subsistence and for family and community feasts. In 1981, pigs were imported from New Zealand to improve the strains of the local breed.

24FISHING

While subsistence fishing for inshore species is carried out from all atolls, there is little domestic commercial fishing in the nation's 1,942,500 sq km (750,000 sq mi) of sea. The total catch in 1997 amounted to 515 tons. Principal marine resources include tuna, prawns, shrimp, seaweed, sponges, black pearls, giant clams, trochus, and green mussels. Colorful baby giant clams for ornamental aquariums are grown for export to the US.

A fisheries base with a freezer plant (200 tons capacity) and a chilling plant (50 tons capacity) was constructed in Majuro with Japanese government assistance. In 1986, the Marshall Islands Maritime Authority (MIMA) was reestablished to organize all marine resource activities, including protection, management, and development, under one agency. During the mid-1990s, about 10,500 foreign fishing vessels annually operated in the Marshall Islands' waters, about three-fourths of them Japanese.

25FORESTRY

Some 8,900 ha (22,000 acres) are planted with coconut palm. Replanting has been undertaken on Arno, Lae, Maloelap, Rongelap, Ujae, Wotho, and Wotje. Pine species are under experimentation in a windbreak tree project on Ebeye. In 1984, a sawmill was purchased for processing coconut trunks and other tree species as lumber. In 1997, forest product imports totaled $1.9 million.

26MINING

There is no mining of mineral resources. However, preliminary surveys have revealed the presence of phosphate and manganese nodules in the seabed within the territorial waters. Lagoon dredging of sand and coral for construction purposes is undertaken in Majuro and Ebeye.

27ENERGY AND POWER

The Marshall Islands is dependent on imported fossil fuels for electric-power generation. In 1995, mineral fuels and lubricants accounted for about 25% of its merchandise import expenditures. The urban centers of Majuro and Ebeye have major generating facilities. The Majuro power plant, commissioned in 1982, has an installed power capacity of 14,000 kW. A new power plant was commissioned in Ebeye in 1987, with a capacity of 5,200 kW of electricity. The low power requirements in the outer islands are met by solar-powered systems. In 1988, fuel imports amounted to $3.6 million, or 10% of total imports.

28INDUSTRY

The economy's small manufacturing sector, localized largely in Majuro, accounts for less than 4% of the gross revenues generated in the private sector. The largest industrial operation is a copra-processing mill under a government and private-sector joint enterprise. (Copra is dried coconut meat.) The rest of the manufacturing sector consists of small-scale and domestic operations, such as coin making, furniture making, handicrafts, and boat making. A small fish-drying plant, preparing smoke-dried tuna for exportation to Japan, began operation after 1985. In 1986, a government-owned dairy factory was established in Majuro, producing liquid milk, ice cream, and yogurt from imported milk powder and butterfat. In 1987, a small tuna cannery began production in Majuro. As of 2000, a small but promising tourism industry was under development.

29SCIENCE AND TECHNOLOGY

While there are no institutions involved in scientific research or training, the College of Micronesia nursing facility and science center, located in the Majuro Hospital, provides instruction in nursing technology and science.

³⁰DOMESTIC TRADE

Domestic trade accounts for the majority of the total gross trade revenue from urban private enterprises. Trade is concentrated in Majuro and Ebeye and consists mainly of imported goods, although increasing amounts of locally produced vegetables and fish are being marketed.

³¹FOREIGN TRADE

Heavy and increasing trade deficits result from limited exports and dependency on imports for consumer and capital goods. Over 90% of the value of exports is accounted for by fish, coconut oil, and copra cake (made of dried coconut meat). The US, Japan, and Australia are the main export partners, while those three nations and New Zealand are the main sources of imports. The major imports are foodstuffs, machinery and equipment, fuels, beverages, and tobacco.

³²BALANCE OF PAYMENTS

The economy suffers from a long-standing imbalance of trade, with imports far exceeding exports. A comprehensive record of international transactions in the form of standardized balance-of-payments accounts was not maintained during the trusteeship period (prior to 1986). The chronic trade deficit is offset by official unrequited transfers, predominantly from the US.

The US Central Intelligence Agency reports that in 1996 the purchasing power parity of the Marshall Islands's exports was $17.5 million while imports totaled $71.8 million resulting in a trade balance of -$54.3 million.

³³BANKING AND SECURITIES

Financial services are provided by three commercial banks: the Bank of Guam, and the Bank of Marshalls, located in Majuro, and the Bank of Hawaii, located in Ebeye. The Marshall Islands Development Loan Office in Majuro was established as an independent government corporation in 1982. There were four credit unions, operated by over 2,000 members. The Marshall Islands has no stock issues or securities trading.

³⁴INSURANCE

Two foreign insurance companies, located in Majuro, provide coverage. A US insurance company provides loan protection policies to credit unions.

³⁵PUBLIC FINANCE

Government revenues are derived from domestic sources and US grants. Domestic revenues are from taxes and nontax sources (fishing rights, philatelic sales, and user charges). The leading areas of expenditure include health services, education, public works, and transportation and communication. The US Central Intelligence Agency (CIA) estimates that in the 1995–96 fiscal year the Marshall Islands's central government took in revenues of approximately $80.1 million and had expenditures of $77.4 million including capital expenditures of $19.5 million. Overall, the government registered a surplus of approximately $2.7 million.

³⁶TAXATION

Income tax is applied to wages and salaries at graduated rates. Business tax is applied to gross revenues of service-related enterprises generated anywhere in the Marshall Islands, the Federated States of Micronesia, and Palau, except on Kwajalein. A sales tax is applied only in Kwajalein. There is also a fuel tax.

³⁷CUSTOMS AND DUTIES

Import taxes are generally ad valorem; duties range from 5% to 75%. The average rate is 10%. Specific duties apply to cigarettes, soft drinks, beer, spirits, wine, gasoline, and other gases and fuels.

³⁸FOREIGN INVESTMENT

The government favors joint ventures with foreign private investors. Foreigners may lease but not own land. The US department of defense operates a missile testing range on behalf of the strategic defense command in Kwajalein.

³⁹ECONOMIC DEVELOPMENT

The first five-year national development plan (1985–89), which was rephased to 1986/87–1990/91 to meet the requirements of the Compact of Free Association with the US, constituted the first phase of a 15-year development program. The plan focused on economic development, with emphasis on private-sector expansion, personnel development and employment creation, regional development, population planning and social development, and cultural and environmental preservation. Total funding requirements for implementation of the plan were $201 million, compared with identified funding sources of $155 million.

Financial aid from the United States totals over US$65 million per year under the terms of the Compact of Free Association, due to expire in 2001. Tourism was under development in the late 1990s with the opening of a first-calls resort hotel, the first in the Marshall Islands.

⁴⁰SOCIAL DEVELOPMENT

Private-sector provision of community and social services is mainly through the Marshalls Community Action Agency, a nonprofit organization. Among government agencies, the Ministry of Social Services is involved in five major areas: housing, women's and youth development, feeding programs, aging, and other community development welfare programs. Funding of these services is provided almost entirely by the US. A social security system provides old age, disability, and survivor benefits, paid for by employers and employees. As of 1999, this program was funded by 5% contributions from both employers and employees. Retirement is set at age 55.

The Marshallese society retains a traditional matrilineal structure. Each person belongs to the bwij, or clan, of his or her mother, and has the right to use the land and other property of the bwij. The head of the bwif is called an alap. The alap is the spokesperson between the clan members and the members of the iroij, or royal clan. Inheritance of traditional rank and of property is matrilineal, and women occupy important positions within the traditional social system. However, within the economic system, many hold low-paid dead-end jobs, and as of 1999, only one of 33 parliamentary seats were held by women. No overt instances of sex discrimination have been reported.

The government is committed to protecting and promoting the rights of children. Current laws on child abuse are vague and difficult to implement, and are presently being reevaluated by the Attorney General's Office.

The government fully respects the human rights of its citizens. No human rights organizations exist, but there are no legal restrictions against their formation.

⁴¹HEALTH

Infant mortality was 43.4 per 1,000 live births in 1999, a sharp increase from the 1980s. The birth rate in 1999 was 45, and the overall mortality rate was 6.7 per 1,000 population. Life expectancy was 64.8 years. The under-five mortality rate was 92 in 1994. Immunization rates were as follows in 1994: diphtheria, tetanus, and pertussis (67%); measles (59%); polio (62%); and tuberculosis (96%). The prevalence of anemia in children under 5 years of age was 43% in 1990. No polio, measles, or neonatal tetanus cases were reported in 1994. Alcoholism and drug abuse are common, and there is a relatively high incidence of sexually transmitted diseases. There were two new cases of AIDS reported in 1996.

There are two hospitals: the Armer Ishoda Hospital in Majuro, with an 81-bed capacity, and a recently renovated hospital in Ebeye. Both hospitals provide dental services. In 1991, there were 20 doctors, 130 nurses, and 4 midwives.

Rudimentary health care on the outer atolls is provided through 69 dispensaries, staffed by health assistants. Emergency cases are sent to the Majuro or Ebeye hospital and, when necessary, to hospitals in Honolulu. Dental services to the outer atolls are provided by periodic visits by dental teams from Majuro and Ebeye.

Once the site for nuclear testing, the Marshall Islands government once again considered testing on the uninhabitable islands of Bikini and Enewetak. As of 1996, radioactive dose assessments have been commissioned by the Republic of the Marshall Islands to measure radioactivity.

[42]HOUSING

Houses in the urban centers are simple wooden or cement-block structures, with corrugated iron roofs; because of the limited land availability, houses are heavily crowded. In the outer atolls houses are constructed of local materials, with thatched sloping roofs and sides of plaited palm fronds.

The Ministry of Social Services provides housing grants, principally to low-income families, through a low-cost housing program and a grant-in-aid program. Government housing is administered by the Public Service Commission.

In 1988 (the latest year for which statistics were available), there were 4,943 dwellings on the Marshall Islands, of which 43% received their water supply from rain catchment, while 30% had piped indoor water. About 44% had flush toilets, 56% had electricity, and 48% used kerosene for cooking.

[43]EDUCATION

The Ministry of Education provides for public education at the elementary, secondary, and higher education levels. Public elementary schools provide eight years of compulsory education to students ages 6–14. A high school entrance examination is given to all eighth graders in order to determine the 300 or so students who will be admitted into the two public high schools each year. During the 1994–95 school year, a combined total of 15,755 students were enrolled in the Marshall Islands' 115 public and non-public primary and secondary schools. Fifty-one percent of all students were male, and 49% were female. The public schools employed a total of 512 teachers while non-public institutions employed 297 teachers. For students who are admitted to high school, a comprehensive four-year program of secondary education provides instruction in general studies, college preparatory courses, and vocational training.

Higher education is provided through formal programs of teacher training and the provision of grants for university training abroad. In 1986, approximately 160 students received financial assistance for foreign training. The Majuro campus of the College of Micronesia opened its School of Nursing and Science Center in 1986. In 1991, the Marshall Islands campus separated from the College of Micronesia system and became accredited by the Accrediting Commission for Community and Junior Colleges of the Western Association for Schools and Colleges (WASC). On 1 April 1993, the College of the Marshall Islands was established as an independent institution with its own Board of Regents. In 1994–95, approximately 1,149 students were enrolled at the college, with 42 teaching staff members.

[44]LIBRARIES AND MUSEUMS

In Majuro, the Alele Museum, which also houses a library, was completed in 1973. Alele Museum showcases both the traditional and colonial history of the Marshalls. The library houses historical documents and photographs from the trust territory archives. More than 2,000 glass-plate negatives taken between 1890 and 1930 are on loan to the museum. Alele's newest attraction is the elaborate shell collection from Mili Atoll.

[45]MEDIA

The inter-island communications network consists of shortwave outer-island radio stations, which link all major islands and atolls. The island of Ebeye is linked to Majuro by radio and also by satellite. There are three broadcast stations. The government radio station, which has advertising, relays world news from Voice of America and Radio Australia. As of 1999, there was 1 AM and 2 private-sector FM stations, and 3 television stations. In 1997 there were an estimated 2,000 telephones on all islands.

There are no daily newspapers. A weekly newspaper, *The Marshall Islands Journal* (1999 circulation 3,700), is published in Majuro in English and Marshallese. *The Marshall Island Gazette*, established in 1982, is a free four-page government newsletter, printed in English.

The constitution provides for free expression, and the government is said to respect these provisions in practice.

[46]ORGANIZATIONS

Marshallese society is matrilineal and organized on the basis of the clan *(bwij)*. The head of the clan *(alap)* serves as spokesman between clan members and members of the royal clan.

At the community level there are youth organizations, including Boy Scouts and Girl Scouts, women's organizations, and various religiously affiliated social organizations. A national women's organization began in 1986. A number of consumers' cooperatives are in operation.

[47]TOURISM, TRAVEL, AND RECREATION

Tourist attractions include the sandy beaches on the atolls, protected lagoons, underwater coral reefs, and abundant marine life, including large gamefish. The outer atolls of Mili, Maloelap, Wotje, and Jaluit offer many Japanese and American relics from World War II. However, tourism remains undeveloped, and the outer atolls do not have any accommodations for visitors. In 1997 there were 6,400 tourist arrivals, and tourism receipts totaled $3 million. That year there were 300 hotel rooms with a total of 658 beds.

In 1999 the UN estimated the cost of staying in Majuro at $154 and Ebeye at $109 per day.

[48]FAMOUS MARSHALLESE

Amata Kabua (1928–96), president from 1979 until his death, was founder and leader of the Political Movement for the Marshall Islands Separation from Micronesia in 1972. He previously served as a member of the Congress of Micronesia and guided his country to self-governing status under the US-administered UN trusteeship. He was a graduate of the Mauna Olu college in Hawaii and taught secondary school before starting his political career.

[49]DEPENDENCIES

The Marshall Islands have no territories or colonies.

[50]BIBLIOGRAPHY

Bank of Hawaii, Economics Dept. *Pacific Islands Economic Trends*. Honolulu: Bank of Hawaii, 1992.

Compacts of Free Association with the Marshall Islands, Federated States of Micronesia, and Palau. Washington, D.C.: U.S. Government Printing Office, Congressional Sales Office, 1998.

Dibblin, Jane. *Day of Two Suns: US Nuclear Testing and the Pacific Islanders*. New York: New Amsterdam, 1990.

Hezel, Francis X. *Strangers in Their Own Land: A Century of Colonial Rule in the Caroline and Marshall Islands*. Honolulu: Center for Pacific Island Studies, 1995

Republic of the Marshall Islands First Five Year Development Plan 1985–1989. Majuro: Office of Planning and Statistics, 1984.

Spennemann, Dirk H. R. *Ennaanin Etto: A Collection of Essays on the Marshallese Past*. Majuro Atoll: Republic of the Marshall Islands Historic Preservation Office, 1993.

Trust Territory of the Pacific Islands, 1986. Washington, D.C.: US Department of State, 1986.

Weisgall, Jonathan M. *Operation Crossroads: The Atomic Tests at Bikini Atoll*. Annapolis, Md.: Naval Institute Press, 1994.

FEDERATED STATES
of MICRONESIA

Federated States of Micronesia

CAPITAL: Palikir, Pohnpei Island.

FLAG: Adopted in 1978, the flag is light blue, bearing four five-pointed stars arranged in a diamond in the center.

ANTHEM: As of January 1988, the government had not yet adopted an anthem.

MONETARY UNIT: The US dollar is the official medium of exchange.

WEIGHTS AND MEASURES: British units are used, as modified by US usage.

HOLIDAYS: New Year's Day, 1 January; Federated States of Micronesia Day, 10 May; Independence Day, 3 November; Christmas Day, 25 December.

TIME: In Pohnpei and Kosrae, 10 PM = noon GMT; in Yap and Truk, 9 PM = noon GMT.

¹LOCATION, SIZE, AND EXTENT

The Federated States of Micronesia (FSM) is located in the western Pacific Ocean within the Carolinian archipelago. The four states consist of 607 islands with a total area of 7,866 sq km (3,037 sq mi), comprising 702 sq km (271 sq mi) of land, and 7,164 sq km (2,766 sq mi) of lagoons. Comparatively, the area occupied by the Federated States of Micronesia is slightly less than four times the size of Washington, D.C. Kosrae, the smallest and easternmost state, consists of five closely situated islands. Pohnpei consists of the single large island of Pohnpei and 25 smaller islands within a barrier reef, in addition to 137 outer islands, of which the major atolls are Mokil, Pingelap, Kapingamarangi, Nukuoro, and Ngatik. Truk includes the large Truk lagoon, enclosing 98 islands, and major outer island groups, including the Mortlocks, Halls, Western, and Namwunweito islands. Yap, the westernmost state, consists of 4 large islands and 7 smaller islands surrounded by barrier reefs, in addition to 134 outer islands, of which the largest groups are Ulithi and Woleai. The cumulative coastline distance is 6,112 km (3,798 mi).

The capital city of the Federated States of Micronesia, Kolonia, is located on the island of Pohnpei.

²TOPOGRAPHY

The 607 islands constituting the four states include large, mountainous islands of volcanic origin and coral atolls. Kosrae is largely mountainous, with two peaks, Fenkol (634 m/2,080 ft) and Matanti (583 m/1,913 ft). Pohnpei contains a large volcanic island, with the highest elevation that of Mt. Totolom (791 m/2,595 ft). Truk contains 14 islands that are mountainous and of volcanic origin. Yap contains four large high islands, with the peak elevation that of Mt. Tabiwol (178 m/584 ft). The outer islands of all states are mostly coral atolls.

³CLIMATE

The climate is maritime tropical, with little seasonal or diurnal variation in temperature, which averages 27°C (80°F). The islands are subject to typhoons. The short and torrential nature of the rainfall, which decreases from east to west, results in an annual average of 508 cm (200 in) in Pohnpei and 305 cm (120 in) in Yap.

⁴FLORA AND FAUNA

There is moderately heavy tropical vegetation, with tree species including tropical hardwoods on the slopes of the higher volcanic islands and coconut palms on the coral atolls. The only native land mammal is the tropical bat. A rich marine fauna inhabits the open sea, reefs, lagoons, and shore areas.

⁵ENVIRONMENT

Solid waste disposal in urban areas is a continuing problem, and the land is threatened by toxic pollutants from mining operations. Micronesia's water supply is also threatened by industrial and agricultural pollutants. Population increases in urban areas, untreated sewage, and contaminants from industrialized countries in the region add to the problem of water pollution.

United Nations research shows that global warming and the rise of sea levels are a threat to Micronesia's forests, agricultural areas, and fresh-water supply. Pollution from industrial and agricultural sources also threatens the nation's mangrove areas. The fish population is endangered by waterborne toxins and explosives used in commercial fishing. The country also has a problem with the degeneration of its reefs due to tourism. In 1984, the government established an FSM Environmental Protection Board.

Threatened species include the chuuk flying-fox, the chuuk monarch, and the Mortlock Islands flying-fox.

⁶POPULATION

The population of the Federated States of Micronesia in 2000 was estimated at 133,144. The majority of the population live in the coastal areas of the high islands, leaving the mountainous interiors largely uninhabited.

It was estimated that 30% of the population lived in urban areas in 2000. The capital city is Palikir. Population estimates for other large urban areas include 7,200 in Kosrae, 33,100 in Pohnpei, 53,700 in Truk, and 13,900 in Yap.

⁷MIGRATION

No significant permanent emigration has occurred; most emigration has been undertaken temporarily for higher education. In 1999, the net migration rate was 11.65 migrants per 1,000 population.

8ETHNIC GROUPS

The islanders are classified as Micronesians of Malayo-Mongoloid origins. The people of the Nukuoro and Kapingamarangi atolls in southwestern Pohnpei are of Polynesian descent. In total, there are nine ethnic Micronesian and Polynesian groups.

9LANGUAGES

English is the official language and is taught in the schools. The indigenous languages are of the Malayo-Polynesian family. Yapese, Ulithian, Woleaian, Trukese, Pohnpeian, and Kosraean are classed as Malaysian. Kapingamarangi and Nukuoro, spoken on two isolated atolls of the same names in Pohnpei, are Polynesian languages.

10RELIGIONS

Roman Catholicism and Protestantism have been widely accepted throughout the country following their introduction by missionaries in the 1880s. Protestantism is predominant in Kosrae. In 1999, Roman Catholics comprised 50% of the population; Protestants 47%; other and none 3%. Other churches represented include Assembly of God, Seventh-day Adventist, and United Church of Christ.

11TRANSPORTATION

There are approximately 240 km (149 mi) of roadways on the major islands, of which 42 km (26 mi) are paved. Over 90% of all vehicles are located on the main islands of Pohnpei, Moen (in Truk), Kosrae, and Yap. The state of Yap provides public bus transportation, primarily used by students. International shipping services are provided by 8 companies, some of them Japanese. There are commercial harbor facilities at Kolonia, Moen, Okat, and Colonia. The Federated States of Micronesia have no merchant marine, but inter-island shipping service is provided by 6 government-owned vessels. In 1998, there were 6 airports, 5 of which had paved runways. International and interstate scheduled airline services are provided by Continental/Air Micronesia, Air Nauru, and Pacific Missionary Aviation.

12HISTORY

The Carolinian archipelago was sighted by European navigators in the 16th century. In 1686 the Spanish captain Francisco Lezcano named Yap Island "La Carolina" after King Charles II of Spain; the name was later generalized to the islands as a whole. Until the end of the 19th century, the islands were under Spanish colonial administration. In 1899 following the Spanish-American War, Spain sold the islands to Germany. Japanese administration commenced at the end of World War I, and in 1947, following World War II, the four states of the FSM came under US administration as part of the UN Trust Territory of the Pacific Islands. Beginning in the 1960s, the people of Micronesia began making clear their desire for political independence. The US, ever interested in maintaining good relations with the strategically significant Pacific islands, gave in to such demands and helped Micronesia to form a consultative body called the Congress of Micronesia in 1967. The congress declared the area sovereign in 1970. The history of the FSM as a political entity began on 12 July 1978, when a constitution drafted by a popularly elected constitutional convention was adopted; it went into effect on 10 May 1979. The government of the FSM and the government of the US executed a Compact of Free Association in October 1982; in November 1986, that compact went into effect. The UN Security Council voted in December 1990 to terminate the FSM's status as a UN Trust Territory. A new capital was built about 10

km southwest of Kolonia in the Palikir Valley; it has served the FSM since 1990.

The FSM became an independent state and joined the UN in September 1991. John R. Haglelgam of Yap was elected FSM's president in 1987. In May 1991 Bailey Olter of Pohnpei defeated Haglelgam and was elected president. On 11 May 1995 Bailey Olter was reelected to a second term as president and Jacob Nena was reelected to a second terms as vice-president. On 18 July 1996 Olter suffered a stroke and underwent treatment in Texas. Nena served as acting president while Olter was incapacitated. When Olter was unable to resume his duties, Nena became the FSM's fourth president on 8 May 1997. In a new election Leo A. Falcam, of Pohnpei, was elected vice-president. In the May 1999 elections Falcam was elected president and Redley Killion, of Chuuk, was elected vice president.

The Compact of Free Association between the FSM and the United States was due to expire in 2001. Prior to beginning negotiations and before any other assistance was considered, the US requested a full accounting of the approximately $3 billion in US funding provided to FSM since 1986. During further discussions of the Compact in 2000 the US suggested that restrictions on Micronesian immigration may be tied to future funding.

13GOVERNMENT

The national executive branch includes the president and vice-president, elected by the Congress from its membership, who serve a four-year term and may not be from the same state. The principal officers of the executive branch are appointed by the president, with the advice and consent of Congress. The judiciary consists of a Supreme Court that applies criminal and civil laws and procedures closely paralleling those of the US. The legislature consists of a unicameral Congress of fourteen senators. Of the senators, four are elected at large on the basis of state equality and ten on the basis of population apportionment, with five from Truk, three from Pohnpei, and one each from Yap and Kosrae. The four at-large senators serve four-year terms and the remaining senators serve two-year terms. Congressional elections were held in four states (Chuuk, Kosrae, Pohnpei, and Yap) to fill 14 seats in March 1999.

14POLITICAL PARTIES

There are no formal political parties.

15LOCAL GOVERNMENT

The state executive branch consists of state governors and lieutenant-governors, popularly elected for four-year terms. The state legislative branch consists of members popularly elected on the basis of proportional representation, numbering twenty in Pohnpei, thirty in Truk, thirteen in Kosrae, and nine in Yap. Municipalities are districts composed of a number of small communities (sections), some of which may be located in different islands.

Municipal government is considered by many to be the most important level of government in Micronesia. The leaders of local bodies are generally tribal chiefs, who are considered to be more important figures than nationally elected politicians by a sizable body of Micronesians. The Council of Chiefs can veto any legislation it considers detrimental to traditional ways.

16JUDICIAL SYSTEM

The national judiciary consists of a Supreme Court, headed by a chief justice, and such subordinate courts as are established by statute. Justices are appointed by the president, with the advice and consent of Congress, and serve for life. The Supreme Court has both trial and appellate divisions. It may review cases heard in state or local courts if they require interpretation of the Consti-

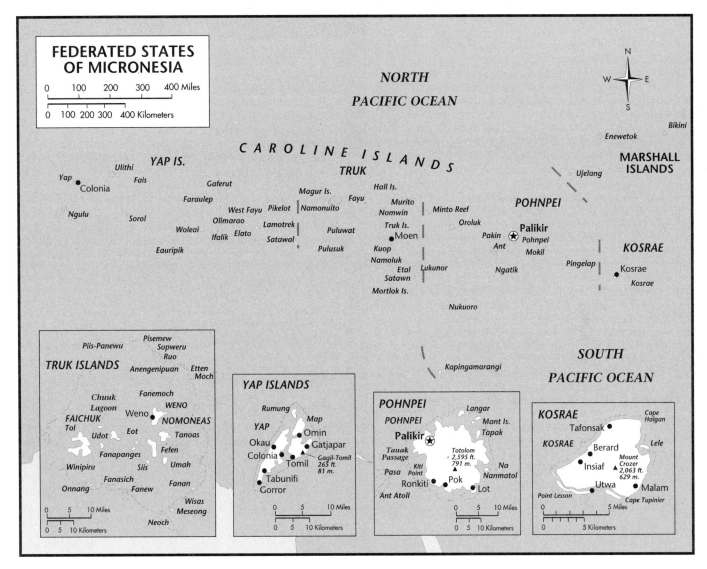

FEDERATED STATES OF MICRONESIA

LOCATION: 0° to 14°N; 135° to 166° E.

tution, national law, or treaties, and it may hear appeals from the highest state court where permitted by a state's constitution.

State and municipal court systems have been established in each of the states. State courts have jurisdiction over all matters not within the exclusive jurisdiction of the national courts. Municipal courts have jurisdiction over civil and criminal matters arising within their municipalities.

The Micronesian Constitution and judicial system are modeled after those of the United States. The civil and criminal laws also parallel those of the United States.

The Constitution provides for an independent judiciary and the government respects this provision in practice.

[17]ARMED FORCES

The FSM maintains no armed forces. External security is the responsibility of the US.

[18]INTERNATIONAL COOPERATION

The FSM participates in such regional organizations as the South Pacific Commission (SPC), and South Pacific Forum. In 1986, the FSM became an associate member of ESCAP. It also participates in the activities of other UN agencies, including IMF, UNCTAD,

and WHO. In 1999, FSM signed the constitution of the United Nations Educational, Scientific and Cultural Organization (UNESCO) to become the 188th member of that agency. The government maintains overseas offices in Washington, D.C., Tokyo, Honolulu, and Guam.

[19]ECONOMY

The gross domestic product (GDP) in 1994 was $205 million—about $100 million of which was grant aid. Per-capita GDP that year was $1,700. It is estimated that after US-led grants end in 2002, per-capita GDP could drop to below $500.

In 1993, the US, whose aid constitutes a large share of GDP, enlisted the Asian Development Bank in a plan to devise and implement an economic development scheme for the country. In 1995, an economic summit was convened to discuss some solutions. Privatization was high on the list of recommendations and Yap has already initiated a plan to reduce government employment by 37%. The ADB-led summit also recommended resources be spent in the development of fisheries and tourism, two sectors with substantial potential. In recent years, licensing fees paid by foreign fisherman for tuna fishing in Micronesia's

Exclusive Economic Zone have provided between $18–24 million annually.

Other than US payments, the Micronesian economy is markedly underdeveloped. A clothing plant in Yap employs 500 workers in the country's largest private-sector industrial enterprise. The subsistence economy is thought to generate about 25% of GDP, but statistics from the government are incomplete and unreliable.

The Second National Development Plan, for the years 1992–96, featured as its primary objective decreasing dependence on aid and, at the same time, making better use of its aid. Little has been done, however. In 1999 FSM created a trust fund,

[20]INCOME

The US Central Intelligence Agency (CIA) reports that in 1996 Micronesia's gross domestic product (GDP) was estimated at $220 million. The per capita GDP was estimated at $1,760. The annual growth rate of GDP was estimated at 1%. The average inflation rate in 1996 was 3.9%. The CIA defines GDP as the value of all final goods and services produced within a nation in a given year and computed on the basis of purchasing power parity (PPP) rather than value as measured on the basis of the rate of exchange.

[21]LABOR

The national labor force was estimated at about 23,190 in 1994, with 4,216, or 18% unemployed. Agriculture, forestry, and fishing employed 1,718 (7.4%) and manufacturing 656 (2.8%), and other sectors accounted for the rest. While unemployment remains high, the economy faces shortages of skilled personnel since over 50% of the population is under 16 years of age. In 1984, a training and trade-testing program was established by the ILO in cooperation with the government. While labor laws are applied mostly without variance in all four states, the minimum wage varies from state to state. Minimums for government-employed workers in 1999 ranged from $0.80 per hour for Yap to $2.00 per hour in Pohnpei. Only Pohnpei had a minimum wage for private sector workers. In 1999, it stood at $1.35 an hour.

There is no minimum working age for children and many children assist their families in subsistence farming activities.

[22]AGRICULTURE

Agricultural production has traditionally been for subsistence and is based on a system of shifting cultivation in the high islands. Staple crops include taros, sweet potatoes, bananas, cassavas, and breadfruit. Yams are grown on Pohnpei, Kosrae, Yap, and Fais islands. Other vegetables, such as cucumbers, eggplant, head cabbage, Chinese cabbage, bell peppers, green onions, and tomatoes, are also produced. Other fruits include mangoes, papayas, pandanus, pineapples, lemons, and limes, with oranges and tangerines also produced on Kosrae. The ubiquitous coconut palm is used for a wide range of subsistence purposes, and copra is the main cash crop and the nation's leading export. Crop production in 1998 included (in thousands of tons): coconuts, 140; copra, 18; cassava, 12; and bananas, 2. Black and white peppers were introduced to Micronesia in 1938, but pepper growing only began in Pohnpei (the FSM's most important pepper-producing island) in 1960. Rich volcanic soil and heavy rainfall make gourmet Pohnpei peppers highly regarded.

[23]ANIMAL HUSBANDRY

Livestock in 1998 included some 14,000 head of cattle, 32,000 pigs, and 4,000 goats. Pigs, traditionally kept by many households for ceremonial purposes, are being upgraded through the introduction of improved strains, two pig farms operate on Pohnpei. The largest cattle herd is on Pohnpei Island. Eggs are produced commercially, and limited success has been achieved by commercial poultry chicken projects in the states of Pohnpei and Chuuk. Chickens are kept by many households. Goat projects are also operating in Kosrae and Chuuk. A few head of water buffalo are privately raised on Pohnpei and on Pata in Chuuk. In the mid-1990s, the government started encouraging domestic feed production in order to decrease the reliance on imported feed meal.

[24]FISHING

Inshore marine resources of the reefs and lagoons are harvested mainly for subsistence. The FSM's exclusive economic zone covers some 2.6 million sq. km (1 million sq. mi) of ocean which contain the world's most productive tuna fishing grounds. Although the FSM now has sole ownership of tuna stocks capable of a sustained yield of well over 100,000 tons per year, there is virtually no national participation in its exploitation. The total catch in 1997 was 9,588 tons, including 5,518 tons of skipjack tuna, 2,338 tons of yellowfin tuna, and 222 tons of bigeye tuna. The tuna catch is valued at about $200 million annually. The Micronesian Maritime Authority and the National Fisheries Corporation assist in the development and promotion of Commercial fisheries. Pohnpei and Kosroe have embarked on the construction of cold storage and tuna processing plants, and the Yap Fishing Corporation began upgrading its fleet. Total fisheries exports were valued at $413,000 in 1997.

[25]FORESTRY

The nation has abundant forestry resources, particularly on the high islands, consisting of approximately 45,200 ha (112,000 acres) of woodland, with some 26,700 ha (66,000 acres) suitable for harvesting. Two privately owned commercial sawmills are operated on Pohnpei; one in Kitti logging mangrove cedar, and one in Kolonia utilizing upland timber. Exploitation of the nation's forestry resources is limited, and virtually all lumber used in construction is imported ($2.1 million in 1997). Mangrove timber is used for handicrafts and furniture making.

[26]MINING

There are deposits of phosphates on Fais Island in Yap and bauxite in Pohnpei, Truk, and Yap, but there is no commercial exploitation. Clays, coral, sand, rock aggregate, and quarry stone works supply construction materials.

[27]ENERGY AND POWER

The nation is dependent on imported petroleum, which supplies about 80% of the total energy requirements. Fuel wood for household use provides most of the remainder. Diesel fuel, which accounts for over two-thirds of petroleum imports, is used primarily for electrical generation and ship services. Electricity is generated by government power stations located in each state center. About one-half of the electricity produced is used by the government. Small quantities of electricity are produced in outer island communities. In early 1993, the state governments of Yap and Kosrae placed priority on the expansion and upgrading of utilities to encourage economic growth.

[28]INDUSTRY

Manufacturing activity is nearly non-existent and accounts for only a fraction of a percent of GDP. Cottage industries involving handicrafts and small-scale processing are carried out in all states and constitute an important source of income for those not integrated into the monetary economy. In Truk, a small industries center, a garment factory, a coconut-processing plant, a boat-building plant, and a breadfruit flour plant are in operation; in Pohnpei, a coconut processing and soap and oil plant, a feedmill, an ice production plant, a brick-manufacturing plant; in Yap, a cottage industries program; and in Kosrae, a small industries center and a wood-processing plant. In late 1999, a tuna processing plant opened in Majuro.

29SCIENCE AND TECHNOLOGY

There are no institutions for advanced instruction or research and development in science and technology.

30DOMESTIC TRADE

Domestic commercial activity is dominated by wholesale and retail trade, which is highly localized in the four state centers of Kolonia, Tofol, Moen, and Colonia.

31FOREIGN TRADE

The FSM sustains a severe trade deficit. Exports include agricultural products (black pepper, tropical fruits and vegetables, coconuts, cassava, sweet potatoes), pigs, and chickens. Copra, formerly the country's largest export crop, suffered a severe decline in the late 1990s. Major export partners are Japan, the US, and Guam; major import partners are the US, Japan, and Australia.

32BALANCE OF PAYMENTS

Foreign receipts are predominantly grants and rental payments from the US and aid from other sources. Economic aid totaled $77.4 million in 1995. The US Central Intelligence Agency reports that in 1996 the purchasing power parity of Micronesia's exports was $73 million while imports totaled $168 million resulting in a trade deficit of $95 million.

33BANKING AND SECURITIES

Commercial banking operations are regulated by the FSM Banking Board. There are two foreign commercial banks: the Bank of Hawaii, with branches in Pohnpei, Yap and Kosrae; and the Bank of Guam, with branches in Pohnpei and Truk. The FSM Development Bank commenced operations in 1982. It provides loans for projects that meet criteria based on the government's development priorities and is authorized to provide loan guarantees to other financial institutions in the FSM. The FSM Employees Credit Union was chartered in 1986. Tradable securities are not issued by the FSM government, state governments, or enterprises residing in the FSM. The currency is the US dollar.

In 1996, national and state governments considered measures designed to cope with the winding down of US funding under the Compact of Free Association (payments scheduled to end in 2001). The restructuring of national government is now underway, with the aim of reducing the number of employees and departments. The government is also seeking to improve basic infrastructure through private-sector investment; infrastructure improvements should in turn encourage growth of the private sector. In 1999, the FSM Trust Fund was established to foster financial independence.

34INSURANCE

The Public Service System administers life insurance and worker's compensation programs. In 1984, a government-employee group health insurance program was instituted, and in 1987, a retirement pension program—for both state and national government employees—was initiated.

35PUBLIC FINANCE

The state and national governments had a series of surpluses in the late 1980s, followed by years of deficits in the early 1990s. Government revenues remained nearly constant during the 1990s, while spending was unrestrained. By the late 1990s, the deficits had come under control.

The US Central Intelligence Agency (CIA) estimates that in 1996 Micronesia's central government took in revenues of approximately $58 million and had expenditures of $52 million including capital expenditures of $4.7 million. Overall, the government registered a surplus of approximately $6 million.

36TAXATION

National taxes on wages and salaries are levied, as well as a business gross receipts tax. The states are constitutionally limited in the types of taxes they may impose; they may levy sales taxes on alcoholic beverages, soft drinks, and cigarettes. The municipal governments usually levy head taxes and boat license and business license fees.

An important tax revenue service is from the sale of tuna fishing rights, which rose from $12.7 million in 1990 to $18.2 million in 1994. In 1999, FSM, Palau, and the Republic of Marshall Islands agreed to cooperate in policing illegal fishing in the region.

37CUSTOMS AND DUTIES

As of 1988, specific duties were levied on cigarettes, beer and malt beverages, wine, distilled alcohol, and gasoline and diesel fuel. Ad valorem duties were levied as follows: tobacco, 50%; perfumes, cosmetics, and toiletries, 25%; soft drinks, 2% per 12 fl oz; foodstuffs for human consumption, 1%; and all other products, 3%. Micronesia's import taxes are among the lowest in the Pacific.

38FOREIGN INVESTMENT

There is little foreign private investment. The Foreign Investment Act of 1997 was enacted to prohibit foreign investment in specific business activities, namely arms manufacture, minting of coins or printing of currency notes, and nuclear power or radioactivity-related businesses. The Act also restricts investment by foreigners in banking, telecommunications, fishing, air transport, and shipping.

39ECONOMIC DEVELOPMENT

The first National Development Plan (1985–89) was the initial stage of the government's 15-year program designed to achieve national self-sufficiency. Funds accruing under the Compact of Free Association were required for implementing the plan, and rephasing of the plan was necessary. A multi-million dollar US-implemented capital improvement plan was scheduled for completion in 2001. It included new airports, docks, water and sewage systems, paved roads, and hospitals. Under the terms of the Compact, the US provided $1.3 billion from 1986–2001 in grant aid.

A Second National Development Plan covering the years 1992–96 sought to diversify Micronesia's economy; mainly to wean it from dependence on Compact funds. Little was accomplished. In late 1999, representatives of the US and FSM began negotiations aimed at renewing some provisions of the Compact of Free Association.

40SOCIAL DEVELOPMENT

The extended family and clan system, headed by traditional leaders or chiefs, is retained in varying degrees, especially in the outer islands. Rapid Westernization has resulted in an increasing incidence of juvenile delinquency, drug and alcohol abuse, and crime. A wide range of national and state social programs are ameliorating these trends. A social insurance system, first instituted in 1967 and updated in 1983 and 1996, includes old age, disability, and survivor benefits. Employees contribute 5% of their earnings; employers make a 5% payroll contribution. The basic retirement pension benefit in 1999 was 16.5% of the first $10,000 and marginal rates beyond that level. Survivor payments totaled 60% of the descendant's pension. A UNFPA family health and planning program was instituted in 1986.

In spite of Constitutional safeguards, sex discrimination and violence against women are serious problems. Women's roles within the family remain essentially the traditional ones. Women, however, face no discrimination in education. There are currently a higher percentage of graduates who are female at all educational levels. In 1992, a National Women's Advisory Council was formed to promote and protect the rights of women. As of 1999, 8 of 71 parliamentary seats were held by women.

Minorities generally do not face discrimination or prejudice. Non-citizens, however, are prohibited from owning land. Human rights are generally respected.

41HEALTH

The infant mortality rate in 1999 was 33.9 per 1,000 live births, and the life expectancy was 68.5 years. In the same year, the general mortality rate was 6 deaths per 1,000 population, and the fertility rate was 3.9 children per woman. The annual population growth rate was 2.8% in 1990–95. The maternal mortality rate was 121 per 100,000 live births in 1991–93. All of Micronesia had access to safe water and sanitation in 1993. Immunization rates for Micronesian children under one year of age were as follows: measles (80%); tuberculosis (50%); polio (77%); and diphtheria, tetanus, and pertussis (78%) in 1994.

Although polio has been eradicated, there have been cases of tuberculosis (173 in 1994) and measles (905 in 1994). Anemia was seen in 33% of children under the age of five in 1993.

There are hospitals in each state center, with approximately 500 beds. In 1986, a community health center was established in Pohnpei, and in 1987, a medical school was started. In the outer islands, primary medical services are provided through dispensaries staffed by health assistants. In 1982, a superdispensary was initiated in the Lower Mortlock Islands to serve 3,769 people scattered on seven atolls. Tertiary medical treatment is provided through patient referral to hospitals in Guam and Hawaii.

42HOUSING

In 1980 (the latest year for which statistics are available), the total housing consisted of 11,562 units, of which 47% were in Truk, 32% in Pohnpei, 16% in Yap, and 5% in Kosrae. The average occupancy was seven persons per house. There has been a marked movement away from traditional construction materials toward imported lumber, plywood, and corrugated metal roofing.

43EDUCATION

The state governments are responsible for the provision of education. Elementary education is compulsory up to the eighth grade or until age 15. In 1986 there were 142 primary schools, 9 of them private, with 968 teachers and 23,636 pupils. Secondary education was provided through 5 public high schools, 1 in each state center and one in Falalop on the Ulithi atoll, serving Yap's outer islands, and through 5 private secondary schools, 2 in Truk and 3 in Pohnpei. The only postsecondary institution is the College of Micronesia (COM) in Pohnpei. However, in 1999 COM was in the process of opening a new campus built with US assistance, the beneficiary of Land Grant status through the US Department of Agriculture. FSM students are eligible for postsecondary education grants from the US government and attend institutions mainly in Guam, Hawaii, and the US mainland. Vocational education is provided by the Pohnpei Agriculture and Trade School and the Micronesian Occupational College in Palau.

A 1994 census poll reported that 22.8% of the FSM population had no schooling; 30.3% had some elementary schooling; 15.1% had some high school education; 13.6% had a high school diploma; 7.5% had some college; 6.1% had an Associate degree; 3.1% had a Bachelor's degree; and 1.6% had engaged in graduate study.

44LIBRARIES AND MUSEUMS

Most library materials are contained in the educational institutions; there are no public libraries. The library of the Congress of the Federated States of Micronesia holds 10,000 book volumes. The Community College of Micronesia is the depository for documents from the trust territory government's archives in Saipan. There is a small museum in Kolonia, Pohnpei. The Nan Madol archaeological site was designated a historical landmark in 1986.

45MEDIA

In 1983, the FSM Telecommunications Corp. provided interstate telecommunications via its satellite ground station in each state center and international connections through the Pohnpei and Truk stations. An interstate and international telex service has been available through the Pohnpei station since 1984. Telecommunications services to all inhabited outer islands are provided by radio links with the Pohnpei, Truk, and Yap stations. In 1995 there were 6,100 telephones.

There are no private newspapers. Newsletters are published by the national government, *The National Union* (twice monthly), and the four state governments, *Mogethin* (Yap), *Uss Me Auus*, (Truk), *Pohnpei Reports*, and *Kosrae State Newsletters*.

There is a state-owned radio station in each state capital that broadcasts in English and local languages; there are also private radio stations in Pohnpei and Truk. Yap has a government-owned television station, and Pohnpei has a private television station. As of 1999, there were a total of 1 FM and 5 AM radio stations, 2 television stations, and 1 shortwave station. In 1997, there were 127 radios and 10 television sets per 1,000 population.

The Constitution provides for free speech and a free press, and the government is said to respect these rights in practice.

46ORGANIZATIONS

There are Community Action Agencies in Yap, Truk, and Pohnpei, which organize youth clubs and community self-help projects. Private institutions, most of them church-affiliated, play an active role in youth and community development. Many municipalities sponsor local women's organizations and community centers.

47TOURISM, TRAVEL, AND RECREATION

Tourist facilities have been developed in each state but are limited. Tourist attractions include the spectacular beauty of the high islands; the rich marine environment; World War II artifacts, including sunken Japanese ships in the Truk lagoon; and remains of an ancient culture on Yap Island, including stone platforms and large circular stones used as money.

The cost of staying in Truk, according to 1999 UN estimates, was $124 per day. Hotel costs accounted for 67% of daily expenditure. Daily expenses were estimated at $146 in Yap and $131 in Ponape. As of 1991, the country offered a total of only 290 rooms for tourists.

48FAMOUS MICRONESIANS

John Haglelgam, a former senator in the Congress, was elected president of the FSM from 1987 to 1991. In 2000, FSM's first 5-story building (and first building with an elevator) opened; it was named for Raymond Setik (d.1997), a successful businessman and one of the first members of the legislator in 1979.

[49]DEPENDENCIES

The FSM has no territories or colonies.

[50]BIBLIOGRAPHY

Karolle, Bruce G. *Atlas of Micronesia.* 2d ed. Honolulu, Hawaii: Bess Press, 1993.

Kluge, P. F. *The Edge of Paradise: America in Micronesia.* New York: Random House, 1991.

Peattie, Mark R. *Nanyo: The Rise and Fall of the Japanese in Micronesia, 1885–1945.* Honolulu: University of Hawaii Press, 1988.

Poyer, Lin. *The Ngatik Massacre: History and Identity on a Micronesian Atoll.* Washington, D.C.: Smithsonian Institution Press, 1993.

Wuerch, Wiliam L. *Historical Dictionary of Guam and Micronesia.* Metuchen, N.J.: Scarecrow Press, 1994.

MONGOLIA

Mongolia
Mongol Uls

CAPITAL: Ulaanbaatar.

FLAG: The national flag, adopted in 1946, contains a light blue vertical stripe between two red stripes; in gold, on the stripe nearest the hoist, is a five-pointed star surmounting the soyombo, Mongolia's independence emblem.

ANTHEM: *Bügd Nayramdah mongol ard ulsyn töriin duulal (State Anthem of the Mongolian People's Republic).*

MONETARY UNIT: The tugrik (T) of 100 mongos is the national currency. There are coins of 1, 2, 5, 10, 15, 20, and 50 mongos and notes of 1, 3, 5, 10, 20, 25, 50, and 100 tugriks. T1 = $0.00093 ($1 = T1077.24) as of 31 March 2000.

WEIGHTS AND MEASURES: The metric system is the legal standard.

HOLIDAYS: New Year's Day, 1 January; Women's Day, 8 March; Popular Revolution Day, 11 July. Movable holidays include Mongol New Year's Day, in February or March.

TIME: 8 PM = noon GMT.

¹LOCATION, SIZE, AND EXTENT

Situated in east-central Asia, Mongolia has an area of 1,565,000 sq km (604,250 sq mi), extending 2,368 km (1,471 mi) E–W and 1,260 km (783 mi) N–S. Comparatively, the area occupied by Mongolia is slightly larger than the state of Alaska. The largest landlocked country in the world, Mongolia is bordered on the N by Russia and on the E, S, and W by China, with a total boundary length of 8,114 km (5,042 mi).

²TOPOGRAPHY

Mongolia is essentially a vast plateau with an average elevation of 1,580 m (5,184 ft). Mongolia comprises a mountainous section in the extreme west, where the peak of the Khuiten (formerly Mönh Hayrhan) of the Mongolian Altay Mountains rises to a height of 4,374 m (14,350 ft). Other mountain ranges are the Hentiyn, along the Soviet border, and the Hangayn, in west-central Mongolia. The southern part of the country is occupied by the Gobi, a rocky desert with a thin veneer of shifting sand. Explorations have uncovered large reservoirs of water 2–3 m (7–10 ft) beneath the desert surface.

³CLIMATE

Mongolia has an arid continental climate with a wide seasonal range of temperature and low precipitation. In winter, it is the site of the great Siberian high, which governs the climate of a large part of Asia and gives Mongolia average January temperatures of –22° to –18°C (–8° to 0°F) and dry, virtually snowless winters. In summer, remnants of the southeasterly monsoon bring most of the year's precipitation. Annual precipitation ranges from 25 to 38 cm (10 to 15 in) in mountain areas to less than 13 cm (5 in) in the Gobi.

⁴FLORA AND FAUNA

Mongolia is divided into several natural regions, each with its characteristic plant and animal life. These regions are the mountain forests near the Soviet Siberian border; the mountain steppe and hilly forest farther south, followed by the lowland steppe grasslands; the semidesert; and finally the true desert. Larch and Siberian stone pine are characteristic trees of the northern forests, which are inhabited by bear, Manchurian red deer, snow panther, wild boar, and elk. The saiga antelope and the wild horse are typical steppe dwellers.

⁵ENVIRONMENT

Environmental problems facing Mongolia include desertification, inadequate water supply, and air and water pollution. The presence of the Gobi Desert in the southeastern part of the country and mountains in the northwest provide natural limits to the amount of agricultural land. Areas affected by deforestation and excessive grazing are eventually overtaken by the desert.

Water pollution is a particularly significant problem in Mongolia because the water supply is so limited. The country has only 5.9 cubic miles of water, 62% of which is used for farming. In 1995, 42% of the people living in rural areas did not have access to pure water.

The country's air pollution problems are due to increased industrial activity within the country, including the burning of soft coal, and airborne industrial pollution from the former Soviet Union and the People's Republic of China. The heavy concentration of factories in Ulaanbaatar has polluted the environment in that area.

Przewalski's horse, the Bactrian camel, the snow leopard, and the saiga are among 8 mammals and 11 birds which are considered endangered.

After a winter of little snow, wildfires spread across northern Mongolia from March until June of 1996. The fires were the most extensive since records were first compiled in 1978, resulting in 26 deaths and nearly 800 people injured or rendered shelterless. An estimated 20% of Mongolia's coniferous forest was damaged in the blaze.

6POPULATION

The population of Mongolia in 2000 was estimated at 2,654,572. An estimated 3.9% of the population is 65 years of age or older. The projected population for the year 2005 is 2,834,000, assuming a crude birthrate of 20 per 1,000 population and a death rate of 7, resulting in a natural rate of change of 1.2% for the period 2000–2005. The population rate of change between 1995 and 2000 was 2.1%. The population density in 1998 was 2 per sq km (5 per sq mi).

It was estimated that 64% of the population lived in urban areas in 2000, up from 52% in 1980. The capital city, Ulaanbaatar, had a 2000 population of 666,000. Darhan has a population of 90,000; Erdenet, 58,200.

7MIGRATION

Few Mongolian nationals live outside the country, but 3.4 million persons of Mongolian extraction lived in the Inner Mongolia province of China. About 500,000 live in Russia—in the Buryat and Kalmyk republics. Between 1955 and 1962, some 20,000 Chinese laborers entered Mongolia to work on construction projects, but in 1964 Mongolia expelled about 2,000 Chinese nationals who had refused to take part in an agricultural resettlement program, and another 1,700 in 1983. In addition, Mongolia expelled 7,000 ethnic Chinese between 1983 and 1993. Since the independence of Kazakhstan, many Kazakhs have emigrated.

Nomadic herders account for nearly half of Mongolia's population. Mongolia is one of the only developing countries where internal migration to rural areas exceeds migration to cities. The number of families formally registered as nomadic herders grew from an estimated 74,000 in 1990 to 170,000 in 1995.

8ETHNIC GROUPS

In 1999, 90% of the population consisted of Mongols, approximately three-quarters of them Khalkha. The Kazakhs are the leading minority group, making up about 4%. Peoples of Soviet and Chinese origin are also present in substantial numbers (2% each); other varied ethnic groups make up the remaining 2%.

9LANGUAGES

Khalkha Mongolian, the official language, is spoken by about 90% of the population. It is one of a large dialect group in the Mongolic branch of the Altaic language family. Early in the 13th century, the Mongols adopted an alphabet written in vertical columns from the Turkic Uighurs, and they retained that script until modern times. The literary language differed increasingly from the living spoken language, and in 1941 the Mongolian government decided to introduce a new phonetic alphabet that would accurately reflect modern spoken Mongolian. The new alphabet consisted of the Cyrillic letters used in Russian, except for two special characters needed to render the Mongolian vowels represented as ö and ü in Western European languages. After a period of preparation (1941–45), the new alphabet was introduced in 1946 in all publications and in 1950 in all business transactions, but, following independence, the traditional script was due to be restored in 1994. The differences between the Khalkha language spoken in Mongolia, the Buryat language spoken in the Buryat Republic of the Russian Federation, the Chahar and Ordos languages of China's Inner Mongolian Autonomous Region, and other Mongolian dialects are comparatively small and chiefly phonetic. A characteristic phonetic feature of Mongolian is the law of vowel harmony, which requires that a word contain either the so-called back vowels, represented as a, o, and u in Western European languages, or the so-called front vowels, represented as e(ā), ö, and ü, but not an association of the two types of vowels. Turkic, Russian, and Chinese are also spoken.

10RELIGIONS

About two-thirds of the people do not profess any religion or are avowed atheists. Of the remainder, most practice Tibetan Buddhism; about 4% are Muslim. Before the government's campaign against religion in the 1930s, there were about 700 monasteries, with about 100,000 lamas (theoretically celibate), in Mongolia. During 1936–39, the Communist regime closed virtually all monasteries, confiscated their livestock and landholdings, tried the higher lamas for counterrevolutionary activities, and induced thousands of lower lamas to adopt a secular mode of life. In the mid-1980s, only about 100 lamas remained. The new constitution of 1992 established freedom of religion for all. Mahayana Buddhism, the primary religious following before the suppression of religion in the 1930s is making a surprising resurgence. Former monasteries are being restored, and there is a seminary at Gandantegchinlen Hiyd. In 1992, Roman Catholic missionaries were also encouraged to come to Mongolia to continue the presence they had initiated earlier in the century.

11TRANSPORTATION

The Trans-Mongolian Railway, about 1,496 km (930 mi) in length, connects Mongolia with both China and Russia. Ulaanbaatar has been connected to the Trans-Siberian Railway via Bayantümen since 1939 and via Sühbaatar since 1950, and to the Chinese Railways via Dzamïn üüd since the end of 1955. Choybalsan is also connected to the Trans-Siberian system via Ereenstav. Ulaanbaatar Railways has been linked to Nalayh since 1938 and to Darhan and Tamsagbulag since 1964. The Sharïn Gol Open-Pit Coal Mining Industry was connected to the Darhan industrial center during the third five-year plan (1961–65) by a 60-km (37-mi) rail line. A 200-km (124-mi) railroad line connects Erdenet, a copper-molybdenum mining and industrial center near the Russian border, with the Trans-Mongolian Railway. The total length of railroads at last estimate was 1,928 km (1,198 mi).

Mongolia had about 46,470 km (28,876 mi) of roadways in 1997, of which 3,730 km (2,318 mi) were paved. Freight and passenger traffic are carried on the Selenge River and across Hövsgöl Lake.

There were 34 airports in 1998, of which 8 had paved runways. Mongolia's first air service began operating between Ulaanbaatar and Verkhneudinsk in eastern Siberia in 1926. Miat-Air Mongol is the principal airline. In 1997, 240,000 passengers were carried on scheduled domestic and international airline flights.

12HISTORY

Archaeological investigations show that the land now known as Mongolia has been inhabited since the Lower Paleolithic period, more than 130,000 years ago. By about 1000 BC, animal husbandry of the nomadic type had developed, and by the 3d century BC, a clan style of organization based on horsemanship had emerged. The Huns, a Turkic-speaking people, driven westward during the Han dynasty in China (206 BC–AD 220), created a nomadic empire in central Asia that extended into Europe, beginning about ad 370. It reached almost to Rome under the leadership of Attila (r.433?–453) and declined after his death. Mongolia first played an important part in world history in ad 1206, when the Mongol tribes united under the leadership of the conqueror Temujin, or Genghis Khan. The Mongols set up their capital at Karakorum and established a vast empire extending from the northern Siberian forest to Tibet and from the Caspian Sea to the Pacific. After the death of Genghis in 1227, his empire was divided among his sons into Mongol states, or

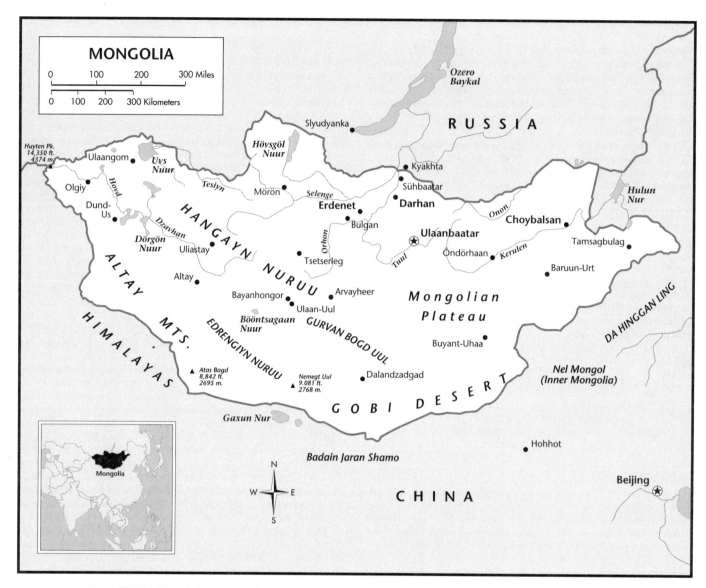

MONGOLIA

Huyten Pk.
14,350 ft.
4374 m.

Ulaangom

Olgiy

Dund-
Us

Slyudyanka

Hövsgöl Nuur

Uvs Nuur

Hovd

Tesiyn

Mörön

Selenge

Dzavhan

H A N G A Y N   N U R U U

Uliastay

Dörgön Nuur

Altay

Bayanhongor

Orhon

Tsetserleg

Erdenet

Bulgan

Arvayheer

Ulaan-Uul

Bööntsagaan Nuur

A L T A Y   M T S.

H I M A L A Y A S

E D R E N G I Y N   N U R U U

G U R V A N   B O G D   U U L

▲ Atas Bagd
8,842 ft.
2695 m.

▲ Nemegt Uul
9,081 ft.
2768 m.

Gaxun Nur

G O B I   D E S E R T

Badain Jaran Shamo

O z e r o
B a y k a l

R U S S I A

Kyakhta

Sühbaatar

Darhan

Onon

Choybalsan

Tamsagbulag

Baruun-Urt

⚝ **Ulaanbaatar**

Öndörhaan

Kerulen

Tuul

Hulun Nur

Mongolian Plateau

Buyant-Uhaa

Dalandzadgad

*Nel Mongol
(Inner Mongolia)*

D A   H I N G G A N   L I N G

Hohhot

Beijing ⚝

C H I N A

Mongolia

LOCATION: 87°47′ to 119°54′E 41°31′ to 52°16′N. **BOUNDARY LENGTHS:** Russian Federation, 3,441 km (2,138 mi); China, 4,673 km (2,904 mi).

khanates: the Great Khanate of East Asia, which included the Yüan dynasty of China, and reached its peak under Kublai Khan (r.1260–94), who established his capital at Cambaluc (now Beijing); the Khanate of Chaghadai (Djakhatai) in Turkestan; the Hulagid Khanate, founded by Hulagu Khan in Persia; and the Golden Horde in southern Russia, founded by Batu Khan, who invaded Poland and Hungary in 1240. Having crossed the Danube River, Batu withdrew in 1241. The Mongols' century of dominance in Asia allowed for great trade and cultural interchange but also led to the spread of the bubonic plague to Europe.

During the 14th century, the great Mongol states disintegrated. The Yüan dynasty in China collapsed in 1368, to be replaced by the Ming dynasty; the western part of the Turkestan Khanate was incorporated into the empire of Timur in 1390; Hulagu's Persian empire disintegrated after 1335; and the Golden Horde was attacked and shaken by the forces of Prince Dmitry Donskoy in Russia in 1380 but ruled South Russia into the 15th century. In 1369, at the age of 33, Timur, also called Timur Lenk ("Timur the Lame") or Tamerlane, proclaimed himself ruler of all

the land lying between the Tien Shan and the Hindu Kush mountain ranges. The Mongols retired to their original steppe homelands, splitting into three major groups: the northern Khalkha Mongols, north of the Gobi Desert; the southern Chahar Mongols, south of the Gobi; and the western Oirat Mongols. Babur, a descendant of Timur, founded the Mughal (or Mogul) Empire (so called from the Farsi word for "Mongol") in India in 1526; it lasted until the 18th century. Buddhism, which had been introduced by Tibetan monks in the 15th century, became widespread in the 16th and 17th centuries.

A cleavage developed between the northern (outer) Mongols and the southern (inner) Mongols, who had been more closely associated with Mongol rule in China. In the course of conquering China, the Manchus subdued the southern Mongols in 1636, placing them under the eventual rule of China's Qing (Ch'ing) or Manchu dynasty (1644–1911). The northern Mongols, who had been fighting with western Mongols for supremacy, sought Manchu aid against their foes and accepted Manchu suzerainty in 1691. Finally, the Manchus destroyed the western Mongols as a historical force in 1758. The Russian-

Chinese border treaties of Nerchinsk (1689) and Kyakhta (1727) confirmed Chinese rule over both the southern and northern Mongols but assigned the Buryats to Russia.

Following the overthrow of the Manchu dynasty by the Chinese revolution in 1911, northern Mongol princes proclaimed an autonomous Outer Mongolia under the rule of Bogdo Khan, the Living Buddha (Jebtsun Damba Khutukhtu) of Urga, an earlier name of Ulaanbaatar. A treaty with the tsar's government pledged Russian assistance for the autonomous state. After the Bolshevik Revolution, the Chinese exploited Russia's weakness, reoccupying Outer Mongolia in 1919 and ending its autonomy. In early 1921, the Chinese were driven out by Russian counterrevolutionary forces under Baron von Ungern-Sternberg. He, in turn, was overcome in July 1921 by the Mongol revolutionary leaders Sukhe Baatar and Khorloin Choybalsan, assisted by the Soviet Red Army. Under Soviet influence, a nominally independent state, headed by the Living Buddha, was proclaimed on 11 July 1921 and lasted as a constitutional monarchy until his death in 1924.

The Mongolian People's Republic (MPR), the second Communist country in world history, was proclaimed on 26 November 1924. With the support of the former USSR, Communist rule was gradually consolidated. Large landholdings of feudal lords were confiscated, starting in 1929, and those of monasteries in 1938. A 10-year mutual assistance treaty, signed in 1936 and renewed for another 10 years in 1946, formalized the close relations between the former USSR and the MPR. In the summer of 1939, with Soviet support, the Mongolians fought invading Japanese along the border with Manchuria, ending with a solid defeat for the Japanese in September. After a virtually unanimous plebiscite by the Mongolians in favor of independence, the Nationalist government of the Republic of China formally recognized the MPR in 1945 (it withdrew its recognition in 1953) and the Nationalists on Taiwan still claim Mongolia as part of China. On 14 February 1950, the People's Republic of China and the former USSR signed a treaty that guaranteed the MPR's independence. In October 1961, the MPR became a member of the United Nations. Conflicting boundary claims between the MPR and China were settled by treaty on 26 December 1962, and on 30 June 1964 the MPR and the former USSR signed a 20-year treaty of friendship, cooperation, and mutual assistance. In June 1987, the MPR and the United States established diplomatic relations. With the growth of cities around the mining industry, Mongolian society shifted from being 78% rural in 1956 to being 58% urban in 1989.

With their close ties with the former USSR, Mongolians were well aware of Soviet policies of glasnost (openness) and perestroika (restructuring) and of the democratic movements in Eastern Europe after the mid-1980s. The MPR initiated its own policy of "openness" (il tod) and began economic reforms to serve as transitional steps away from a centrally planned, collective economy and toward a market economy. Following the first popular demonstrations calling for faster reforms, in Ulaanbaatar in December 1989, the ruling Mongolian People's Revolutionary Party (MPRP) opted for political as well as economic reforms. The MPRP's leadership resigned in March 1990 and in May the constitution (of 1960) was amended to allow for new, multiparty elections, which took place in July. The MPRP won a majority (85% of the seats) in the legislature, the People's Great Hural (PGH), which took office in September. The PGH elected as President a member of the MPRP, Punsalmaagiyn Ochirbat, but invited the opposition parties to join in forming the new government.

During 1991, the new government discussed Mongolia's economic and political transformation. It issued vouchers to all citizens for the purchase of state property as a step toward priva-

tization. Economic reform was made more difficult by the economic collapse of the former Soviet Union. In 1991, Russia insisted on trade based on cash rather than barter and dramatically cut aid. By 1992, Mongolia faced severe energy shortages. In 1991, the PGH also discussed the writing of a new constitution, which took effect in February of the next year. Based on that constitution, elections in June 1992 created a new legislature (with a MPRP majority), the State Great Hural (SGH) and, in June 1993, President Ochirbat was reelected (but with the support of a coalition of new parties, not the MPRP) in the first direct presidential elections. By September 1992, some 67,000 former Soviet troops (in Mongolia since 1966 when Sino-Soviet tensions increased) completed a process of withdrawal begun in 1990.

In the 1996 parliamentary elections, discontent, especially among the young, led to the defeat of the MPRP. The leaders of the winning Democratic Union Coalition (DUC), mostly political novices, promised to intensify market reforms. The election results marked the first smooth transfer of power in Mongolia's modern history and one of the most peaceful among all the former communist nations. In the following years, however, the stability and effectiveness of Mongolia's democratic government were hobbled by disunity within the majority DUC and by the political stalemate between the DUC and the ex-communists of the opposition MPRP. In late 1996 and early 1997, the MPRP prevailed in local elections, and its candidate, Natsagiyn Bagabandi, was elected president. After the resignation of two prime ministers, the nation was left with an interim government in the second half of 1998, as Bagabandi rejected multiple DU nominees for the post.

In October 1998 the country was shaken by the murder of Sanjaasurengiyn Zorig, a pro-democracy leader and government minister who had been tapped to be the next DUC nominee for prime minister. By August 1999, yet another DUC government had fallen, and Rinchinnyamiin Amarjargal, the 38-year-old former foreign minister, became Mongolia's third prime minister in 15 months. Major government initiatives resisted by the opposition included a proposed merger between the ailing government-owned Renovation Bank and a private bank, and plans for the privatization of Erdenet, the state-owned copper mine.

[13] GOVERNMENT

A new constitution went into effect 12 February 1992, replacing the 1960 constitution and completing Mongolia's transition from a single-party state to a multiparty, parliamentary form of government. At that time, the country's name was officially changed from "Mongolian People's Republic" to "Mongolia." Suffrage is universal at age 18. The unicameral legislature, the State Great Hural (SGH), has 76 members, who are elected by district to four-year terms. The SGH meets twice each year. It can enact and amend laws, set domestic and foreign policy, ratify international agreements, and declare a state of emergency.

A president, the head of state and commander-in-chief of the armed forces, is selected by direct, popular vote for a four-year term, with a limit of two terms. The president nominates the prime minister and can call for the dissolution of the government, initiate and veto legislation (subject to override by two-thirds vote of the SGH), and issue decrees which take effect with the signature of the prime minister.

A prime minister, the head of government, is nominated by the president and confirmed by the SGH to a four-year term. The prime minister selects a cabinet which must be confirmed by the SGH. The government dissolves when the prime minister resigns, when half the cabinet resigns simultaneously, or upon a vote for dissolution by the SGH.

[14]POLITICAL PARTIES

The Mongolian People's Revolutionary Party (MPRP), which had been the single ruling party since 1924, legalized opposition parties in 1990. In addition to the MPRP, major parties include the Democratic Union Coalition (DUC), which includes the Mongolian National Democratic Party (MNDP), the Mongolian Social Democratic Party (MSDP), the Green Party (NYAM), and the Mongolian Democratic Party of Believers (MDPB); Mongolian Conservative Party (MCP); Democratic Power Coalition, which includes Mongolian Democratic Renaissance Party (MDRP) and Mongolian People's Party (MPP); Mongolian National Solidarity Party (MNSP); Bourgeois Party/Capitalist Party; United Heritage Party (UHP), which includes the United Party of Herdsman and Farmers, Independence Party; Traditional United Conservative Party, and Mongolian United Private Property Owners Party; and the Mongolian Workers Party.

In the first election for the State Great Hural (SGH) 28 June 1992, the MPRP won 56.9% of the vote and 71 of 76 seats in the SGH. In the first direct presidential election, 6 June 1993, President Punsalmaagiyn Ochirbat (first elected president 3 September 1990) was reelected with 58% of the vote. A former member of the MPRP, Ochirbat defeated that party's candidate, running as head of a coalition of the SDP and MNDP.

In the elections of 30 June 1996, the Democratic Union Coalition (which included the MNDP, the MSDP, and two smaller parties) defeated the MPRP, winning 50 of 76 seats (an increase of 44 seats). The MPRP won 25 seats, and the remaining seat went to the MCP. The DUC campaign platform included the Mongolia's Contract With Voters, which promised to cut government spending, reduce welfare, and reorganize the transformation of the government. In 2000 parliamentary elections, MRPR candidates won 72 or the 76 seats, with DUC candidates winning 3, and a nonpartisan candidate winning 1.

[15]LOCAL GOVERNMENT

Mongolia administratively consists of 21 provinces (aymag), divided into 334 counties (soums) and lesser administrative units called baghs, as well as one autonomous city, Ulaanbaatar, which is divided into districts and horoos. Each level of local administration has its own legislative body, or hural. These hurals nominate the provincial governors, who are then appointed by the prime minister.

[16]JUDICIAL SYSTEM

Prior to the 1992 Constitution, justice was administered through a Supreme Court elected by the People's Great Hural; province and city courts, elected by the corresponding assemblies of people's deputies; and lower courts. Under the 1993 Constitution the 9-member Supreme Court remains the highest judicial body with a Constitutional Court vested with sole authority for constitutional review. While these two courts are now functioning, the new Constitution introduces a number of other structural changes in the court system await enactment of implementing legislation. In the interim, the existing three-level court system remains in operation. The local courts (people's courts) handle most routine civil and criminal cases. Provincial courts hear more serious cases and review local court decisions. The Supreme Court hears appeals from the local and provincial courts. The old specialized military justice and railway courts have been abolished. All courts are now organized under a single unified national system.

The General Council of Court nominates and the president appoints the lower and the Supreme Court judges.

The new Constitution provides for a completely independent judiciary. It also promises procedural due process rights to a fair trial, legal assistance, right to appeal, and access to requests for pardons, among others.

[17]ARMED FORCES

The Mongolian People's Army is under the jurisdiction of the Ministry of Defense. Two years of service is compulsory for all males. In 2000, the armed forces totaled 9,100 active personnel. The army had 7,500 (4,000 conscripts) and a reserve strength of 140,000. The air force had 800 personnel and was equipped with 9 combat aircraft and 12 armed helicopters. Virtually all military equipment is of Soviet origin. Paramilitary forces consisting of about 7,200 frontier guards and security police are under the jurisdiction of the Ministry of Public Security. Mongolia spent an estimated $20.3 million for defense in 1997 or 2% of GDP.

[18]INTERNATIONAL COOPERATION

Admitted to the UN on 27 October 1961, Mongolia participates in ESCAP, FAO, IAEA, ILO, ITU, UNESCO, UNIDO, UPU, WHO, WIPO, and WMO. It is a signatory to the Law of the Sea treaty, and a member of the WTO.

The principal ally of Mongolia was the former USSR, which provided substantial economic and military assistance over the years. In 1986, the MPR made efforts toward normalizing relations with China, which had become strained after the expulsion of Chinese laborers in 1983, by establishing the first five-year trade agreement between the two countries, restoring air service and improving rail service between them, and exchanging consular delegations for the first time.

[19]ECONOMY

After 70 years as a centrally planned economy, Mongolia has undergone a difficult transition towards a free market system since 1990. With the help of active government promotion, the country's industrial sector grew steadily for several decades, expanding from 7% of the national income in 1940 to 35% by 1997, as agriculture's share of total production declined from 79% to 31%. Despite these changes, animal husbandry has remained a dominant sector of the economy, with live animals and animal products accounting for a major share of current exports, and livestock providing much of the raw material processed in the country's industrial sector. Total Soviet assistance at the height of Soviet support amounted to 30% of GDP. A number of factors, including the sudden cessation of economic aid from the former Soviet Union and allied countries, the disruption of trade with traditional trading partners, as well as a severe winter in 1990/91, caused a steep decline in the country's economic activity in the early 1990s. The annual growth rate of the GDP dropped steeply from 8.3% in 1986 to −9.1% in 1991, −9.5% in 1992, and −3% in 1993.

Despite these difficulties, the government continued its economic transformation program involving the privatization of most previously state-owned enterprises and other policy reforms. In 1994, GDP grew by 2.3%, followed by further increases of 6.3% in 1995, 2.6% in 1996, 4% in 1997, and 3.5% in 1998. Although the economy has grown steadily since 1994, the economic well-being of most people is still in decline. Inflation reached a peak of over 325% in 1992, accelerating faster than wages, but dropping to about 4% in 1995. Development of the country's rich oil and mineral resources continues to be a high priority, and negotiations for the exploitation of oil, gold and rare earth elements with foreign companies are being actively pursued.

[20]INCOME

The US Central Intelligence Agency (CIA) reports that in 1998 Mongolia's gross domestic product (GDP) was estimated at $5.8

billion. The per capita GDP was estimated at $2,250. The annual growth rate of GDP was estimated at 3.5%. The average inflation rate in 1998 was 6%. The CIA defines GDP as the value of all final goods and services produced within a nation in a given year and computed on the basis of purchasing power parity (PPP) rather than value as measured on the basis of the rate of exchange. It was estimated that agriculture accounted for 31% of GDP, industry 35%, and services 34%.

The World Bank reports that for the same period per capita private consumption (in PPP terms) was $1,085. Private consumption includes expenditures of individuals, households, and non-governmental organizations. Approximately 56% of household consumption was spent on food, 9% on fuel, 8% on health care, and 14% on education. The richest 10% of the population accounted for approximately 25% of household consumption and the poorest 10% approximately 2.9%.

21 LABOR

In 1998, the total workforce was estimated at 840,877. About half of the population engages in animal husbandry as nomadic herders. In 1998, there were 48,307 unemployed persons, up from 45,100 in 1995 but an improvement over the 74,900 in 1993. Unemployment officially stood at 5.7%, but was actually much higher, with about one-quarter of the unemployed residing in the Ulaanbaatar aymag. About 47% of the labor force is female. A shortage of skilled labor had required the procurement of a large supplementary work force from the former USSR and Eastern Europe.

The right to organize trade unions and professional organizations is granted by the 1990 Constitution. Nonessential workers have a right to strike. About 75% of the entire work force is unionized in Mongolia. In 1990, the Association of Free Trade Unions (AFTU) which includes about 70 unions, was chartered. In 1999, there were 430,000 unionized workers, amounting to less than 50% of the work force. According to the labor code, the working week is fixed at 40 hours, and for those under 18, at 36 hours. Children as young as 14 or 15 may work with parental permission. In reality, regulations regarding child labor are not effectively enforced.

The minimum wage varied by region from $13 to $17 per month in 1999, although most workers earn in excess of this amount.

22 AGRICULTURE

As of 1997, cropland amounted to 1,320,000 hectares (3,262,000 acres), up from only 1,160,000 hectares (2,866,000 acres) in 1979; the cultivated area represents only 1% of potentially arable land. The high altitude, temperature extremes, long winters, and low precipitation provide limited potential for agricultural development. Crop production accounts for 3% of all employment.

Shortages of fuels and parts for agricultural equipment caused crop production to decline by 70% during the 1990s. Principal crops produced in 1998 (in 1,000 tons) included: wheat, 192; barley, 2; potatoes, 65; and vegetables, 25. Trade in agricultural products in 1997 consisted of $66.3 million in imports and $62.1 in exports.

23 ANIMAL HUSBANDRY

Animal husbandry is the backbone of Mongolia's economy, employing some 160,100 persons. After Mongolia became the world's second communist country in 1924, many nomads settled down to raise livestock on state-owned collectives. Pastures constitute about 75% of the national territory. In 1998 there were 14,166,000 sheep, 10,265,000 goats, 3,613,000 cattle, 2,900,000 horses, 350,000 camels, and some 21,000 hogs. The goat population increased by over one million in 1994/95, due to a boom in the cashmere industry. The meat produced in 1998 was 240,000 tons. Because of the harsh climate, Mongolians consume much fat and meat during winter, and dairy products in the summer.

Mongols claim that the Mongolian thoroughbred is the progenitor of many breeds of race horses worldwide; furthermore, its stamina and speed over long distances surpass Arabic and Akhaltec racers. The Mongolian Horse Association was founded in February 1989 in Zunmod to increase the population and preserve traditional horse-breeding techniques, which were largely being forgotten over the past three decades.

Hunting remains an important commercial activity, with furs and skins the chief products. In 1998, production of skins and hides was estimated at 25,000 tons from sheepskins and 21,000 tons from cattle hides.

24 FISHING

Fishing is not a significant industry in Mongolia. The total catch in 1997 was 181 tons.

25 FORESTRY

Forests cover about 9% of the total territory of Mongolia, mainly in the area around Hövsgöl Lake. It is estimated that the country's total timber resources represent at least 1.25 billion cu m. Birch, cedar, larch, and fir trees predominate. In 1997, the timber cut was 884,000 cu m, with 43% burned as fuel. The lumber industry yielded 200,000 cu m of sawn wood that year.

26 MINING

Mongolia has many exploitable mineral resources; geological surveys over the past 25 years have uncovered deposits of some 80 minerals. The minerals sector accounted for 58% of export earnings in 1997. It contributed 16.8% of GDP and 33% of state budget revenues. Coal, copper and fluorospar are heavily mined, while clay, gold, gypsum, limestone, molybdenum, salt, sand and gravel, silver, precious stones, tin, tungsten, and uranium are mined by smaller operations. Most mining operations are in the northcentral and eastern regions. In 1997, Mongolia was the world's third-largest fluorospar producer and was among the top three producers of copper and molybdenum in Asia and the Pacific. Output in 1997 included (in tons): fluorospar, 250,000; copper, 125,300; gypsum, 58,000; molybdenum, 1,992; tungsten, 100; tin, 50; uranium, 100, and gold, 8 (8,000 kg). The Erdenet copper-molybdenum mine, completed in 1981, was developed by the state in cooperation with the former USSR; it is now 51% owned by the Mongolian government and 49% by the government of Russia. In 1997 privatization of the mining sector continued as several small coal and gold mining companies were partially privatized. In the same year, the government modified Mongolia's mining laws to increase to 40% the total percentage of land open to exploration, change policies regarding exploration licenses, and grant tax incentives to promote mining.

27 ENERGY AND POWER

In 1998, the installed capacity of the electric power stations in Mongolia amounted to 901,000 kW. About half the population is served with electricity. Three major power plants are in Ulaanbaatar, one is in Darhan, and smaller facilities are in Sühbaatar and Choybalsan. In 1998, the output was 2,660 million kWh. Electric power outages in rural areas can last for months. Declining diesel imports since August 1990 have significantly reduced harvests and internal distribution of food. Mongolia had been reliant on the former USSR to meet its refined petroleum requirements. Coal production in 1995 dropped to a nine-year low (4,871,000 tons) because of the continued shortage of spare parts for mining equipment. The Baga Nuur and Shariyn Gol mines were the two major coal mines in 1995. Mongol Gazry Tos, a state-owned petroleum company, is exploring for new oil wells in the Dzuunbayan oil field near Saynshand in Dornogovi Aimag. Oil sands in the Tamstag Basin were determined to be commercially viable in 1995. Shortages of gasoline are common in the countryside, due to the declining deliveries from Russia.

28 INDUSTRY

Small-scale processing of livestock and agricultural products has historically been a mainstay of Mongolia's industrial sector. With the establishment of the Erdenet copper plant in the late 1970s, metal processing also became an important part of the economy. In 1996, industrial output was estimated at т239.3 billion, with production of metals accounting for 32.6%; energy production, 19.1%; processed foods, 15.8%; wool and woolen apparel, 11.5%; mineral fuels, 6.8%; chemicals, 6.7%; and other items, 7.5%. Much of the country's industrial activity is concentrated in four centers: Ulaanbaatar, Erdenet, Darhan, and Choybalsan. Industry employed approximately 74,100 persons in 1996.

Industrial production in Mongolia included about 40 different commodities. In the late 1990s, the production of food, leather, shoes, glass, and garments were on the decline, while production of copper and molybdenum concentrates, coal mining, and the food and beverage industries were increasing.

Mongolia's industrial development has been severely affected by dwindling imports of fuel, spare parts, and equipment formerly obtained from the former USSR and allied trading partners. As a result, total output from the industrial sector generally declined in the early 1990s, falling by 2.5% in 1996; by 1997, the industrial sector had begun to recover, with growth estimated that year at 4.5%.

29 SCIENCE AND TECHNOLOGY

The Academy of Sciences, in Ulaanbaatar, was founded in 1921 and reorganized in 1961. It includes departments of agriculture, chemistry and biology, geography and geology, medicine, and technology; and numerous research institutes concerning agriculture, fisheries and veterinary science, medicine, natural sciences, and technology. The Natural History Museum in Ulaanbaatar features Gobi Desert dinosaur eggs and skeletons. The National University of Mongolia, founded in 1942 at Ulaanbaatar, has faculties of mathematics, natural sciences, physics, and biology, and undertakes research with the State Construction Research Institute in pursuit of knowledge related to nuclear physics, biophysics, mineral resources, energy, and communications. The Mongolian Technical University, founded in 1969 at Ulaanbaatar, has schools of power engineering, mechanical engineering, civil engineering, and geology and mining engineering. In 1987–97, science and engineering students accounted for 24% of college and university enrollments.

30 DOMESTIC TRADE

Prior to economic reforms of the early 1990s, consumer goods produced at Ulaanbaatar or imported from abroad were distributed by state marketing agencies to retail outlets in local administrative centers. Prices for all items except consumer services and some luxury goods were set by the government. With steady price liberalization undertaken since 1990, prices are now closely regulated for only a few staples, such as fuel, rice, and flour. Because the rapid dismantling of the government's centrally planned distribution system proceeded without an effective alternative yet in place, severe supply shortages have been experienced especially in the country's urban centers. To reduce these shortages, a system of public markets has been developed where supplies in excess of targeted deliveries can be sold freely. Commodity exchanges, however, still retain some of the charac-

teristics of a centrally planned economy. Bartering is still common among Mongolia's nomadic population.

31 FOREIGN TRADE

Minerals, mainly copper concentrates and molybdenum, were Mongolia's largest exports. In 1998, exports totaled $316.8 million. The second most important export category includes wool, hides, and skins, followed by consumer goods, mainly manufactured garments. The liberalization and expansion of free trade zones have promoted the export of manufactured goods such as spun wool and cashmere, carpets, leather goods, green tea, canned meat, and light consumer goods. In 1999, imports amounted to $472.4 million. Imports included machinery and equipment, fuels, rice, wheat flour, industrial consumer goods, chemicals, building materials, sugar, and tea.

Although Mongolia continues to depend on the republics of the former USSR (especially Russia) as its dominant trading partners, the country's trading profile has changed greatly since the mid-1980s. In 1985, communist countries, excluding China and North Korea, accounted for 95.5% of Mongolia's exports and 98.1% of its imports. In 1997 Mongolia joined the World Trade Organization. By 1998 Russia accounted for only 12.1% of exports, while their share of imports fell to 30.6%.

Principal trading partners in 1998 (in millions of US dollars) were as follows:

COUNTRY	EXPORTS	IMPORTS	BALANCE
China (inc. Hong Kong)	95	63	32
Switzerland	68	1	67
Russia	38	145	-107
Korea	31	36	-5
United States	26	33	-7
Japan	12	55	-43
Germany	2	24	-22
Singapore	1	16	-15
Austria	n.a.	16	
France	n.a.	21	

32 BALANCE OF PAYMENTS

Mongolia consistently imports more than it exports. The sudden discontinuance of grants and debt cancellations by the former Soviet Union devastated the balance of payments position.

The US Central Intelligence Agency reports that in 1998 the purchasing power parity of Mongolia's exports was $316.8 million while imports totaled $472.4 million resulting in a trade deficit of $155.6 million.

The International Monetary Fund (IMF) reports that in 1998 Mongolia had exports of goods totaling $462 million and imports totaling $524 million. The services credit totaled $78 million and debit $147 million. The following table summarizes Mongolia's balance of payments as reported by the IMF for 1998 in millions of US dollars.

Current Account		-129
Balance on goods	-62	
Balance on services	-69	
Balance on income	...	
Current transfers	2	
Capital Account		...
Financial Account		126
Direct investment abroad	...	
Direct investment in Mongolia	19	
Portfolio investment assets	...	
Portfolio investment liabilities	...	
Other investment assets	-55	
Other investment liabilities	162	
Net Errors and Omissions		-50
Reserves and Related Items		53

33 BANKING AND SECURITIES

Before 1924, Mongolia lacked its own banks and currency. Mongolians bartered, using such commodities as livestock, tea, and salt for exchange, or such foreign currencies as the US dollar, the Russian ruble, the British pound, and the Chinese Mexican dollar in commerce. Chinese and Russian banks offered credit, as did monasteries and private moneylenders. The government began to transform this chaotic monetary situation with a series of reforms, starting with the establishment of Mongolbank, or the Mongolian Trade-Industrial Bank, in June 1924. Mongolbank was founded as a Mongolian-Soviet joint-stock company. In February 1925, the tugrik was made the official national currency, and it was slowly introduced into circulation over the next three years. In April 1928, all other currencies were withdrawn from circulation. In 1929, the government drove private moneylenders out of business by establishing a monopoly on foreign trade and outlawing private lending.

In April 1954, the Soviet Union handed over its shares in Mongolbank, which was renamed the State Bank of the Mongolian People's Republic.

The State Bank of Mongolia remains the official bank of Mongolia but recent economic reforms have allowed the formation of a commercial banking sector. The economic reforms were brought about by the collapse of the Soviet Union in the early 1990s.

Mongolia has a two-tier banking system where control of the money supply is invested in the central bank. The Bank of Mongolia has established lending rules the commercial banks must follow. Also, reserve requirements are set by the national bank. In 1991, commercial functions were separated from the Mongol Bank, and two commercial banks were created; by the late 1990s there were 18. On advice from the Asian Development Bank, the government closed a number of banks in 1999 and 2000, leaving 12 in operation in an effort to restructure the two-tier system. In 2000, the World Bank gave Mongolia a loan earmarked for restructuring of its financial systems.

The Mongolian Securities Exchange opened in August 1995. About 60,000 individuals have opened accounts on the stock market. By 1996, more than 7.8 million shares from 400 companies had been traded and 28,000 contracts concluded; average daily trade volume is 60,000–80,000 shares.

34 INSURANCE

In the 1980s, insurance was offered by the State Directorate for Insurance, or Mongoldaatgal, which was under the control of the Ministry of Finance. The government was planning to introduce health insurance in 1993 as a cooperative effort between individuals, government agencies, and the private sector.

35 PUBLIC FINANCE

The annual budget is submitted to the People's Great Hural for approval. The US Central Intelligence Agency (CIA) estimates that in 1998 Mongolia's central government took in revenues of approximately $260 million and had expenditures of $330 million including capital expenditures of $32.9 million. Overall, the government registered a deficit of approximately $70 million. External debt totaled $739 million.

The following table shows an itemized breakdown of government revenues and expenditures. The percentages were calculated from data reported by the International Monetary Fund. The dollar amounts (millions) are based on the CIA estimates provided above.

REVENUE AND GRANTS	100%	260
Tax revenue	61.4%	160
Non-tax revenue	27.6%	72
Capital revenue	6.5%	17
Grants	4.5%	12

EXPENDITURES	100%	330
General public services	8.6%	28
Defense	8.3%	27
Public order and safety	3.7%	12
Education	8.0%	26
Health	2.1%	7
Social security	25.3%	83
Housing and community amenities	0.7%	2
Recreation, cultural, and religious affairs	3.4%	11
Economic affairs and services	11.8%	39
Other expenditures	22.5%	74
Interest payments	5.5%	18

36 TAXATION

The turnover tax, accounting in 1986 for 66.3% of all state revenues, is an indirect sales tax levied at the production stage on all manufactured commodities. Personal taxes consist of income taxes, paid by salaried industrial workers and office employees, and livestock taxes on private herders, based on the number of livestock owned. In 1993, there was a ceiling of 40% on taxes levied on enterprises with foreign capital.

37 CUSTOMS AND DUTIES

In May 1997, Mongolia abolished all tariffs, becoming the first country in the world to levy no taxes at all on trade. Customs duties had been insignificant, yielding less than 1% of total state revenues.

38 FOREIGN INVESTMENT

Prior to 1990, no private investments were possible in Mongolia; much of the country's investment capital was derived from government loans and grants provided by the former USSR and allied countries. New government policy and laws since the late 1980s, including the Foreign Investment Law of 1990, provide the legal basis and incentive for foreign investments. Thus far, however, private foreign capital remains a small source of investment in the country, due in part to contradictions between newly passed laws for foreign and private investment that have yet to be resolved. Mongolia's lack of infrastructure is also an impediment to foreign investment. The primary countries with investments in Mongolia are ROK, Russia, and China. In 1995, the government reported that foreign investments authorized that year totaled $42.8 million from 29 different countries. Leading investors that year included Sumitomo Corp. and KDD (Japan), Telecom (ROK), and Nescor (US). As of 1996, Soco International (US) had invested $17 million exploring the Tamsag Basin oil field.

39 ECONOMIC DEVELOPMENT

In the past, Mongolia operated on the basis of a planned economy, with five-year plans implemented from 1947 until 1990, with assistance from the former USSR and China. In 1990, with the establishment of a new consensus government, there followed a three-year plan that aimed for achieving greater efficiency in the allocation of resources and a diversified economic base by undertaking a sustained transition to a free market economy. The change was a fundamental shift, as the government relinquished its role as the primary factor in the economy and began limiting itself to policies supporting a market-oriented economy. Main components of the government's program have included privatization of state enterprises, price liberalization, changes in national law, as well as drafting an action plan for environmental protection. Current plans specify development of the country's energy and mining sectors, and further action in environmental protection as well as continued reforms in a number of areas including fiscal management, land tenure, and social benefit entitlements.

In 1996, the initial phase of privatization of state property was completed. According to the government, 100% of small- and medium-sized enterprises were privatized as well as 97% of the country's livestock. In 1994, the private sector accounted for 60% of GDP, and over 10,000 private businesses have been created since 1991. At the end of 1995, however, the government still held shares in more than 200 companies. The next phase of privatization utilized securities market activities to replace the transitional voucher program.

40 SOCIAL DEVELOPMENT

The social insurance program provides for free medical services, benefits for temporary disability, and pensions for permanent disability and old age. Pensioners, who numbered some 220,000 in 1996, collected about T5,000 to T7,000 per month (around $10 to $12).

Women have equal rights and freedoms under Mongolian law, with the exception of a law barring them from hazardous work. In 1999 women accounted for approximately half of the work force. Women receive equal pay for equal work, and many hold mid-level government and professional jobs. As of 1996, there were 6 women in the 76-member parliament.

Although the government generally respects the human rights of its citizens, there were reports in 1999 of the mistreatment of detainees and prisoners. Human rights organizations operate openly in Mongolia.

41 HEALTH

Health care is administered under state auspices, and all medical and hospital services are free. The government gives special priority to increasing the number of physicians and other health personnel and expanding facilities in rural areas. Each province has at least two hospitals, and each agricultural cooperative and state farm has a medical station. In 1990–97, there were 2.7 physicians and 11.5 hospital beds per 1,000 population. During 1990–95 most Mongolians had access to health services (95%), adequate sanitation (74%), and safe water (80%). Health expenditures were 4.7% of the GDP in 1990–97.

Average life expectancy in 1999 was an estimated 61.8 years (45 years in 1950). Pulmonary and bronchial infections, including tuberculosis and brucellosis, are widespread but are being brought under control through the use of ayrag, an indigenous drink brewed from horse's milk and possessing demonstrated healing qualities. Cholera, smallpox, typhus, and other epidemic diseases have been virtually eliminated. In 1990–94, immunization rates for children up to one year of age were as follows: tuberculosis, 90%; diphtheria, pertussis, and tetanus, 78%; polio, 87%; and measles, 80%.

The general mortality rate in 1999 was 7.9 per 1,000 people, and the infant mortality rate was 64.6 per 1,000 live births. The under-5 mortality rate has decreased from 112 in 1980 to 76 in 1994. At least 30.4% of children in 1996 had goiter. About 12% of children under 5 years of age were malnourished between 1990–95, and 5% of births were of low birth weight in 1990. Maternal mortality in 1990–97 was 65 per 100,000 live births. The total fertility rate decreased steadily from 5.4 in 1980 to 2.6 in 1999.

There were 205 tuberculosis cases per 100,000 population in 1997. The adult HIV-1 seroprevalence was 0.0 in 1997. No data on new AIDS cases was available in 1996.

42 HOUSING

Although there are many stone and wood buildings in Ulaanbaatar and some of the larger provincial centers, the standard housing of the nomadic herders, as well as of many city dwellers, is the yurt, a light, movable, dome-shaped tent consisting of skin or felt covering stretched over a lattice frame. However, more permanent housing facilities have been appearing in rural areas throughout the country. Large apartment-house complexes with stores, services, and cultural facilities are being built in Ulaanbaatar, as well as in various other cities and towns.

43 EDUCATION

Eight years of schooling is compulsory, starting at age eight, and free of charge under a new education law. Since the 1950s, the MPR has claimed that the entire adult population is literate; in 1995, however, UNESCO estimated the illiteracy rate at 10.9% for males and 21.9% for females. For the year 2000, adult illiteracy rates were estimated at 0.7% (males, 0.8%; females, 0.7%). In 1997, there were 7,587 teachers and 234,193 pupils in primary schools. Student-to-teacher ratio stood at 31 to one. In the same year, secondary schools had 13,171 teachers and 195,408 pupils. Attendance at vocational schools has declined sharply in recent years, from 23,236 in 1985 to 7,480 in 1994. More than 70% of students from rural areas reside in dormitories adjoining the schools. The Mongolian State University, in Ulaanbaatar, was founded in 1942 and includes faculties in the social sciences, trade, and philology, as well as in science and technology. In 1998 all institutions of higher learning had a combined enrollment of 50,961, with 3,331 teachers.

The 1991 Education Law introduced a number of changes in the system. The traditional Mongolian script was to be introduced from the first grade, and teaching of English in all schools was made compulsory. While higher and professional education is not free, tuition fees are subsidized by the government for poor students. Non-formal education offered by private institutions was also given due importance and recognition.

Primary school enrollment has been in decline for a number of years. By 1994, average national enrollment in primary schools was 78%, although in rural areas this is likely to be substantially lower. Many children in rural areas are withdrawn from school in order to work at home. An absence of heat in many rural schools is also a problem which may contribute to poor enrollment levels.

44 LIBRARIES AND MUSEUMS

The Mongolian State University has a library of 350,000 volumes. The State Public Library, which is under the jurisdiction of the Academy of Sciences, contains 4 million volumes in Mongolian, Chinese, English, French, German, Manchu, Russian, Tibetan, and other languages. It also has a collection of valuable Buddhist manuscripts, including a 335-volume Buddhist encyclopedia. In 1991, the country opened a college of business and commerce, which houses a library of 21,000 volumes. Also that year, it opened the College of Economics with 40,000 volumes. The State Central Museum, containing art treasures and antiquities, the Museum of National History, the Ulaanbaatar Museum (a public affairs museum), the Fine Arts Museum, and the Museum of Religion, all in Ulaanbaatar, are under the jurisdiction of the Academy of Sciences. Also in the capital are the Mongolian Art Gallery, opened in 1989, and the Palace Museum, in the home of Bodg Geegen, former head of state and leader of the Buddhist Church of Mongolia.

45 MEDIA

In 1995, 89,000 telephones were in use. Radio broadcasting began in the MPR in 1934. Radio Ulaanbaatar broadcasts programs in Mongolian, Russian, Chinese, English, French, and Kazakh. Mongel Telev 12, which transmits locally produced programs, and a satellite station are also located in Ulaanbaatar. In 1999 there were a total of 12 AM and 1 FM radio stations, and 1 television station. In 1997 there were 139 radios, 63 television sets, and 1 mobile phone per 1,000 population.

The newspapers of the MPR (together with the organizations that publish them) include *Unen* (Central Committee of the

MPRP, 1999 circulation 170,000); *Ardyn Erh* (Mongolian Great Hural and Cabinet, circulation 77,500); *Novosti Mongoliy* (the Mongolian News Agency); *Hodolmor,* the organ of the trade unions; *Dzaluuchuudyn Unen* (Central Committee of the Mongolian Revolutionary Youth League); *Shine Hodoo* (Ministry of Agriculture and the Supreme Council of the Federation of Agricultural Cooperatives); *Utga Dzohiol Urlag* (the Union of Mongolian Writers and the Ministry of Culture); and *Ulaan Od* (Ministry of Defense and the Ministry of Public Security). Also published are 41 periodicals, including *Namyn Am'dral,* a journal of the Central Committee of the MPRP, and *Shinjleh Uhaan Am'dral,* a bimonthly publication of the Mongolian Academy of Sciences.

The constitution provides for freedom of expression, including free speech and a free press, and the government is said to respect these rights in practice.

As of 1996, there were some 470 personal computers. Online access is extremely limited, with less than one Internet host per 1,000 population in 1998.

46 ORGANIZATIONS

Mongolia's mass organizations, all of which work closely with the MPRP, include the Mongolian Revolutionary Youth League (founded in 1922), Mongolian Pioneers' Organization, Committee of Mongolian Women (founded in 1933), and Mongolian-Soviet Friendship Society (founded in 1947). Professional and cultural organizations include the Union of Mongolian Artists, Union of Mongolian Composers, Mongolian Association for Lawyers, Union of Mongolian Journalists, Union of Mongolian Students, Union of Mongolian Writers, and Union of Mongolian Philatelists. Other organizations are the Mongolian Committee for Afro-Asian Solidarity, Mongolian Union for Peace and Friendship Organizations, and Mongolian Committee for the Defense of Peace.

47 TOURISM, TRAVEL, AND RECREATION

In 1998, approximately 135,621 travelers visited the MPR from abroad. Despite the birth of multiparty democracy in the 1990s, Mongolia has not encouraged tourism. Tourist facilities are in short supply, and prices are high.

Points of interest include the Gandan Lamasery in Ulaanbaatar and the ruined city of Karakorum, once the capital of the Mongol Empire. Mongolia offers abundant and varied scenery, including forests, steppes, lakes, and deserts, and a wide variety of wildlife. Traditional sports in Mongolia include wrestling, archery, and horse racing.

The estimated cost of staying in Ulaanbaatar, according to the UN, was $121 per day in 1999. In small towns and villages, daily expenses were an estimated $32 per day.

48 FAMOUS MONGOLIANS

A long line of Mongol khans have left their mark on history ever since Temujin, or Genghis Khan (1162–1227), set up the first Mongol empire in 1206. Outstanding among them were Kublai Khan (1216–94), a grandson of Genghis, who conquered most of China; Hulagu Khan (1217–60), a brother of Kublai, who conquered Persia and Syria; Batu Khan (d.1255), Kublai's cousin, who overran Russia, Poland, and Hungary; Timur, also known as Timur Lenk ("Timur the Lame") or Tamerlane (1336?–1405), a descendant of Genghis, who extended his military power for short periods into southern Russia, India, and the Levant; and Babur (Zahir ad-Din Muhammad, 1483–1530), a descendant of Timur, who established an empire in India.

In recent times, two national leaders were Sukhe Baatar (1894–1923) and Khorloin Choybalsan (1895–1952). Yumjaagiin Tsedenbal (b.1916), intermittently general secretary of the Central Committee of the MPRP since 1940, became

chairman of the Council of Ministers in 1952, was elected chairman of the Presidium of the People's Great Hural in 1974, and was named the MPRP general secretary in 1981. Jambyn Batmunkh (b.1926) became chairman of the Council of Ministers in 1974 and was elected chairman of the Presidium and general secretary of the MPRP in 1984.

The founder of modern Mongolian literature is D. Natsagdorj (1906–37). Tsendyn Damdinsuren (b.1908) is one of the most important writers. Leading playwrights are Ch. Oydov (1917–63) and E. Oyuun (b.1918). Other prominent writers are B. Rindhen (1905–78), D. Namdag (b.1911), U. Ulambayar (b.1911), and Ch. Lodoydamba (1917–70). B. Damdinsuren (b.1919) and L. Murdorzh are noted composers. Jugderdemidiyn Gurragcha (b.1947) became the first Mongolian in space in 1981, when he was carried into orbit aboard the former USSR's *Soyuz 39*.

49 DEPENDENCIES

The MPR has no territories or colonies.

50 BIBLIOGRAPHY

Avery, Martha. *Women of Mongolia.* Boulder, Colo.: Asian Art & Archaeology, 1996; distributed in the U.S. by University of Washington Press.

Bawden, Charles R. *The Modern History of Mongolia.* 2d ed. New York: Kegan Paul International, 1989.

Brown, William A., and Urgunge Onon. *History of the Mongolian People's Republic.* Cambridge, Mass.: Harvard University Press, 1976.

Cultural Policy in the Mongolian People's Republic. New York: Unipub, 1982.

Goldstein, Melvyn C. *The Changing World of Mongolia's Nomads.* Berkeley: University of California Press, 1994.

Information Mongolia: The Comprehensive Reference Source of the People's Republic of Mongolia (MPR). New York: Pergamon, 1990.

Jagchid, Sechin, and Paul Hyer. *Mongolia's Culture and Society.* Boulder, Colo.: Westview, 1979.

——. *Essays in Mongolian Studies.* Provo, Utah: Brigham Young University, 1988.

Kotkin, Stephen and Bruce A. Elleman (ed.). *Mongolia in the Twentieth Century: Landlocked Cosmopolitan.* Armonk, N.Y.: M.E. Sharpe, 1999.

Lai, Chuen-yan David. *Land of Genghis Khan: The Rise and Fall of Nation-States in China's Northern Frontiers.* Victoria, B.C.: Dept. of Geography, University of Victoria, 1995.

Major, John S. *The Land and People of Mongolia.* New York: Lippincott, 1990.

Mongolia in Transition. Surrey, England: Curzon, 1996.

Moses, Larry, and Stephen A. Halkovic, Jr. *Introduction to Mongolian History and Culture.* Bloomington: Indiana University Research Institute, 1985.

Nordby, Judith. *Mongolia.* Santa Barbara, Calif.: Clio, 1993.

Onon, Urgungge. *Asia's First Modern Revolution: Mongolia Proclaims Its Independence in 1911.* New York: E.J. Brill, 1989.

Poverty and the Transition to a Market Economy in Mongolia. New York: St. Martin's, 1995.

Sanders, Alan J. K. *Historical Dictionary of Mongolia.* Lanham, Md.: Scarecrow, 1996.

Soucek, Svatopluk. *A History of Inner Asia.* New York: Cambridge University Press, 2000.

Worden, Robert L. *Mongolia: A Country Study.* Washington, D.C.: Library of Congress, 1990.

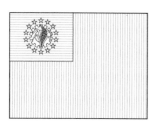

MYANMAR

Union of Myanmar

Pyidaungzu Myanma Naingngandaw

CAPITAL: Yangon (formerly Rangoon).

FLAG: The national flag is red with a blue canton, within which 14 white stars encircle a rice stalk and an industrial wheel.

ANTHEM: *Kaba Makye (Our Free Homeland).*

MONETARY UNIT: The kyat (K) is a paper currency of 100 pyas. There are coins of 1, 5, 10, 25, and 50 pyas and 1 kyat, and notes of 1, 5, 10, 25, and 100 kyats. K1 = $0.2992 ($1 = K3.3423) as of 31 March 2000.

WEIGHTS AND MEASURES: Both British and metric weights and measures are in general use, but local units are also employed.

HOLIDAYS: Independence Day, 4 January; Union Day, 12 February; Peasants' Day, 2 March; Defense Services Day, 27 March; Burmese New Year, 17 April; World Workers' Day, 1 May; Martyrs' Day, 19 July; Christmas, 25 December. Movable religious holidays include Full Moon of Tabaung, February or March; Thingyan (Water Festival), April; Full Moon of Kason, April or May; Waso (Beginning of Buddhist Lent), June or July; Thadingyut (End of Buddhist Lent), October; and Tazaungdaing, November.

TIME: 6:30 PM = noon GMT.

¹LOCATION, SIZE, AND EXTENT

Situated in Southeast Asia, Myanmar has an area of 678,500 sq km (261,970 sq mi), extending 1,931 km (1,200 mi) N–S and 925 km (575 mi) E–W. Comparatively, the area occupied by Myanmar is slightly smaller than the state of Texas. It is bounded on the N and E by China, on the E by Laos, on the SE by Thailand, on the S by the Andaman Sea, and on the W by the Bay of Bengal, Bangladesh, and India, with a total boundary length of 7,806 km (4,850 mi).

Myanmar's capital city, Yangon (formerly Rangoon), is located in the southern part of the country.

²TOPOGRAPHY

Myanmar is divided into four topographic regions: (1) a mountainous area in the north and west, ranging from about 1,830 to 6,100 m (6,000–20,000 ft) in altitude, and including the Arakan coastal strip between the Arakan Yoma mountain range and the Bay of Bengal; (2) the Shan Highlands in the east, a deeply dissected plateau averaging 910 m (2,990 ft) in height and extending southward into the Tenasserim Yoma, a narrow strip of land that projects some 800 km (500 mi) along the Malay Peninsula, in the southeast; (3) central Myanmar, a principal area of cultivation, bounded by the Salween River (2,419 km/1,503 mi) in the east and the Irrawaddy River (2,016 km/1,253 mi) and its tributary, the Chindwin, in the west; and (4) the fertile delta and lower valley regions of the Irrawaddy and Sittang rivers in the south, covering an area of about 25,900 sq km (10,000 sq mi) and forming one of the world's great rice granaries. Good harbors are located along the coastline.

³CLIMATE

Myanmar has a largely tropical climate with three seasons: the monsoon or rainy season, from June to mid-October; the hot season, generally from April through May and from October through November, immediately preceding and following the wet season; and the cool season, from December to March. Rainfall during the monsoon season totals more than 500 cm (200 in) in upper Myanmar and over 250 cm (100 in) in lower Myanmar and Yangon (formerly Rangoon). Central Burma, called the dry zone, and Mandalay, the chief city in the area, each receive about 76 cm (30 in). The mean annual temperature is 27°C (81°F); average daily temperatures in Yangon (Rangoon) range from 18° to 32°C (64–90°F) in January, during the cool season, and from 24° to 36°C (75–97°F) in April, during the hot season. The climate in upper Myanmar, particularly at altitudes ranging from about 300 to 1,220 m (1,000–4,000 ft), is the most temperate throughout the year, while lower Myanmar, especially in the delta and coastal regions, is the most humid.

⁴FLORA AND FAUNA

Myanmar has a wide variety of plant and animal life. Teak, representing about 25% of the total forested area, thrives mainly in the mountainous regions; evergreen, bamboo, and palm in the freshwater delta swamps and along the coastlands; mangrove in the salty coastal marshes; mixed temperate forests and rolling grasslands in the Shan Highlands; and scrub vegetation in the dry central area. There are about 12 species of monkeys, as well as tigers, leopards, elephants, and half-wild pariah dogs. Fish abound along the coastline, in the tidal waters of the delta, and in the rivers and streams.

⁵ENVIRONMENT

In Myanmar the principal environmental threat comes from cyclones and flooding during the monsoon season, and regular earthquakes. Deforestation for farming or illegal economic gain is the most persistent ecological effect of human encroachment. In 1985, 405 square miles were lost through deforestation. By 1994, two-thirds of Myanmar's tropical forests had been eliminated. However, the nation still had the world's eighth largest mangrove area, totaling approximately half a million hectares. Little information is available about the long-term effects of industrialization on the natural environment, although evidence of industrial pollutants has been found in the air, water, soil, and food. Myanmar has 259.6 cubic miles of water. About 64% of city dwellers and 41% of the rural population do not have pure water. Inadequate sanitation and water treatment are leading contributors to disease. Environmental concerns have been given low priority by the government.

Endangered or extinct species in Myanmar include the tiger, Asian elephant, Malayan tapir, Sumatran rhinoceros, Fea's muntjac, river terrapin, estuarine crocodile, and four species of turtle (green sea, hawksbill, olive ridley, and leatherback). The Javan rhinoceros is extinct. Out of a total of 300 species of mammals, 23 are endangered; of 1,000 bird species, 42 are endangered, and 10 reptiles in 360 indigenous species are threatened along with 2 types of freshwater fish. Myanmar also has 23 threatened species of plants in a total of 7,000. Threatened species include the banteng, gaur, and sun bear.

6POPULATION

The population of Myanmar (Burma) in 2000 was estimated at 48,852,098. An estimated 4.5% of the population is 65 years of age or older. The projected population for the year 2005 is 52,698,000, assuming a crude birthrate of 26 per 1,000 population and a death rate of 11, resulting in a natural rate of change of 1.5% for the period 2000–2005. The population rate of change between 1995 and 2000 was 1.8%. The population density in 1998 was 68 per sq km (176 per sq mi).

It was estimated that 28% of the population lived in urban areas in 2000, up from 24% in 1980. The capital city, Yangon (formerly Rangoon), and its surrounding metropolitan area had a 2000 population of 4,458,000. Other principal cities are Mandalay, 532,985; Pathein (formerly Bassein), 144,092; Bago (formerly Pegu), 150,447; and Mawlamyine (formerly Moulmein), 219,991.

7MIGRATION

Indians were the most significant Asian minority in Myanmar until World War II, when hundreds of thousands fled the Japanese invasion; although many returned after the war, the Indian minority never regained its prewar proportions, because after independence in 1948 the government of Myanmar instituted rigid restrictions on Indian migration. The Indian population was substantially reduced between April 1963 and June 1965, when 100,000 were repatriated as part of a program to increase the wealth and holdings of Myanmar nationals. (Indians had dominated Myanmar's commerce.) The government has sought to curtail both immigration and emigration, although as many as 500,000 persons may have left Myanmar during 1962–71. About 187,000 Muslims who fled to Bangladesh in 1978 were repatriated with the help of UN agencies by the end of 1981; they had left Myanmar because of alleged atrocities by its soldiers in Arakan State. They lost their citizenship in 1982.

About 500,000 poor urban residents were forcibly relocated to rural areas between 1989 and 1992. Rural residents are also subject to forced resettlement in connection with counterinsurgency operations.

In 1992, 250,000 Muslim refugees from Myanmar's Northern Rakhine state began arriving in Bangladesh claiming human rights abuses in Myanmar. As of October 1996, around 50,000 of these refugees from were still living in South Bangladesh in five refugee camps. Between 1994 and 1997, some 230,000 of these refugees returned home to Northern Rakhine state. The repatriation resumed in November 1998, following meetings between the UNHCR and Myanmar authorities, but returns were limited to some 450 people due to procedural problems. UNHCR has appealed to the governments of Myanmar and Bangladesh to accelerate the repatriation process.

8ETHNIC GROUPS

The Burmans, ethnically related to the Tibetans, constituted about 68% of Myanmar's total population in 1999. In remote times, the Burmans, migrants from the hills east of Tibet, descended the Irrawaddy Valley and intermarried with the previously settled Mon and Pyu peoples. Since then, however, many other migrant peoples from the northeast and northwest have settled in Myanmar: the Shans, Karens, Kachins, Kayahs, and Chins are among the more numerous. Although much ethnic fusion has taken place among these peoples and the Burmans, most of the later migrant groups remain distinct cultural entities, and have sought to preserve their autonomy, sometimes by violent means. As of 1999, Shans made up about 9% of the population, Karens 7%, Rakhine 4%, Chinese 3%, Mon 2%, Indian 2%, and other 5%.

9LANGUAGES

Burmese, the official language, is spoken by at least 80% of the population. Pronunciation varies greatly from area to area. Although Burmese is monosyllabic and tonal like other Tibeto-Chinese languages, its alphabet of 10 vowels and 32 consonants is derived from the Pahlavi script of South India; loan words from other languages are common. Burmese is the language of government, but the ethnic minorities have their own languages; according to the 1974 constitution, "if necessary the language of the national race concerned may be used."

10RELIGIONS

The constitution guarantees freedom of religion. As of 1999, an estimated 89% of the people were Hinayana or Theravada Buddhists. Under the government of U Nu (overthrown in 1962), Buddhism was the state religion, but there is no longer any link between church and state. Many Buddhists, including most of the people of the hill areas, are also animists, believing in powerful spirits called nats.

The Chinese in Myanmar practice a traditional mixture of Mahayana Buddhism, Taoism, Confucianism, and ancestor worship; the Indians are Hindus; the Pakistanis are Muslims; and most of the Europeans are Christians. Although Christian missionaries had some success with peoples of the hill areas—the Karens, Kayahs, Kachins, and Chins—conversion among the Burmans and the Shans was negligible. In addition to the Buddhist population, 4% are Christian (3% Baptist, 1% Roman Catholic); 4% are Muslim; 1% subscribe to animist beliefs; and 2% are other.

11TRANSPORTATION

Because of Myanmar's near encirclement by mountain ranges, international land transportation is virtually nonexistent. Historically, Myanmar has been dependent on sea and river transport externally and internally, supplemented in modern times by the airplane. The Myanmar Road, connecting Lashio with Kunming in southern China, and the Ledo Road between Myitkyina and Ledo in Assam, northeastern India, are the only land ties between Myanmar and adjacent nations. There were an estimated 28,200 km (17,523 mi) of roads in 1996, but only 3,440 km (2,138 mi) were paved. In 1995, Myanmar had about 44,000 passenger cars and 42,000 commercial vehicles.

Myanmar's railway system, a government monopoly, operates 3,740 km (2,324 mi) of track, all of which is meter-gauge. The main lines are from Yangon (Rangoon) to Prome (259 km/161 mi) and from Yangon to Mandalay (621 km/386 mi) and then to Myitkyina (1,164 km/723 mi from the capital).

MYANMAR

Scale: 0 100 200 300 400 Miles
0 100 200 300 400 Kilometers

Hkakabo Razi
19,294 ft.
5881 m.

INDIA

CHINA

KUMON RANGE

Chindwin

Putao

BANGLADESH • Silchar

Tamu

Bhamo

Myitkyinā

Gengma

Chin Hills

Irrawaddy

Lashio

Monywa   Shwebo

Mandalay

Salween

Meiktila

Kēng Tung

Taunggyi

Mekong

Akyab

ARAKAN YOMA

Irrawaddy

Fang

Ramree I.

Cheduba I.

Toungoo

Prome

Sittang

THAILAND

Henzada

Bago

Bay
of
Bengal

Pathein   Yangon

Mawlamyine

Gulf
of
Martaban

Ye

Mouths of the
Irrawaddy

Preparis I.

Little   Great
Coco I. Coco I.

Andaman
Sea

Dawei

Tavoy Point

Mergui

MERGUI
ARCHIPELAGO

Gulf
of
Thailand

Zadetki Kyun   Kawthaumg

Myanmar (inset locator map)

LOCATION: 92°10′ to 101°11′E; 9°35′ to 28°28′N. **BOUNDARY LENGTHS:** China, 2,185 km (1,358 mi); Laos, 238 km (148 mi); Thailand, 1,799 km (1,118 mi); total coastline, 2,276 km (1,414 mi); Bangladesh, 233 km (145 mi); India, 1,403 km (872 mi). **TERRITORIAL SEA LIMIT:** 12 mi.

Inland waterways, including some 12,800 km (7,954 mi) of navigable passages (25% of which are navigable by commercial vessels), are the key to internal transportation, partly compen-

sating for limited railroad and highway development. Some 500,000 small river craft ply the Irrawaddy (navigable for about 640 km/400 mi), the Salween, the Sittang, and numerous tributaries. The Irrawaddy Delta, the focus of most water transportation, has some 2,700 km (1,700 mi) of rivers and streams, providing a seaboard for all types of craft. The state merchant fleet totaled 41 ships in 1998, with a combined GRT of 464,478.

Ocean shipping, the traditional means of external transport, is controlled by the government, which operates coastal and ocean-going freight-passenger lines. Yangon, on the Rangoon River about 34 km (21 mi) inland from the Andaman Sea, is the chief port for ocean shipping, handling the majority of the country's seaborne trade; it is also the principal terminus for the highways, railroad, inland waterways, and airways. Other ports include Sittwe (Akyab), serving western Myanmar; Pathein (Bassein), serving the delta area; and Mawlamgine (Moulmein), Dawei (Tavoy), and Mergui, which handle mineral and timber exports of the Tenasserim region.

As of 1998 there were 80 airports, 11 with paved runways. Mingaladon, outside of Yangon, is the principal airport. In 1997, 334,000 passengers were carried on scheduled domestic and international airline flights.

12 HISTORY

The founding of a kingdom at Pagan in 1044 by Anawrahta marks the beginning of the history of Myanmar (Burma) as a distinct political entity. The kingdom survived until 1287, when it was destroyed by the armies of Kublai Khan, and the next five centuries were marked by disunity. In 1754, Alaungpaya defeated the Shan kingdom in northern Myanmar and the Mon kingdom in southern Myanmar and founded the last ruling dynasty, which was in power until the British came in the early 19th century. The British conquest of the land then known as Burma spanned 62 years: the first Anglo-Burmese War took place during 1824–26, when the British East India Company, acting for the crown, took possession of the Arakan and Tenasserim coastal regions. In 1852, at the end of the second war, the British acquired the remainder of lower Burma; and on 1 January 1886, following Burma's defeat in the third war, total annexation of Burma was proclaimed. Incorporated into the British Indian Empire, Burma was administered as a province of India until 1937, when it became a separate colony. At this time, Burma was permitted some steps toward self- government; however, the British governor retained authority over foreign affairs, defense, currency, and the administration of frontier peoples. From 1886 to 1948, many Burmese agitated and fought continually for independence. The nationalists who finally gained independence for Burma were a group of socialist-minded intellectuals, called the Thakins, from the University of Rangoon. They included Aung San, one of the founders of modern Burma; U Nu, independent Burma's first premier; Shu Maung, also known as Ne Win, later U Nu's chief of staff; and Than Tun, a leader of a Communist revolt (1948–50) against the independent government. At the start of World War II, these anti-British nationalists collaborated with the Japanese, and with the aid of the Burma Independence Army, led by Aung San, the capitol, Rangoon (now Yangon) fell to Japan on 8 March 1943. They were soon disappointed with the Japanese occupation, however, and the Burma Independence Army was converted into an anti-Japanese guerrilla force called the Anti-Fascist People's Freedom League, which later assisted the British liberation of Burma. Many of the ethnic nationalities of the frontier regions, such as the Karens and Kachins, had remained loyal to the British, as valued fighters for the Allies. After the war, Aung San negotiated with frontier ethnic leaders, signing the Panglong Agreement on 12 February 1947 with them, as a pledge of autonomy and other rights.

Having assumed leadership of the nationalist movement following the 19 July, 1947 assassination of Aung San and six of his associates, U Nu signed an agreement with British Prime Minister Clement Attlee covering economic and defense relationships between the two countries. On 4 January 1948, the sovereign Union of Burma came into being outside the Commonwealth of Nations. After severe setbacks in 1948–49, the U Nu government was able to control a Communist insurgency and consolidate its own power, and in 1951 the nation held its first parliamentary elections. The decade of the 1950s also brought the implementation of an ambitious land reform program and an attempt to forge a neutralist foreign policy, in the face of sporadic Communist resistance and an intermittent border dispute with China. U Nu appointed Gen. Ne Win to head an interim "caretaker government" during a period of instability from 1958 to 1960's national election (which U Nu's party won.) Ne Win returned to power with a coup d'etat on 2 March 1962. The U Nu government was overthrown, and a military regime headed by a Revolutionary Council and led by Ne Win assumed control. Student protests following the 1962 coup, and again in 1974, were crushed by the army with many civilian casualties. Most major political figures in the democratic governments of the years 1948–62 were arrested but were released in 1966–68, including U Nu. Ne Win rejected a return to a multiparty parliamentary system and proclaimed the Socialist Republic of Burma on 3 January 1974. Under a new constitution, Ne Win became president, and the government continued to be dominated by the military. Ne Win retired as president in November 1981, with Gen. San Yu succeeding him in office; but Ne Win retained his dominance, as chairman of the country's only legal political organization, the Burma Socialist Program Party (BSPP). Insurgency by the underground Communist Party of Burma (CPB) and numerous ethnic armies had begun just after World War II and continued throughout Ne Win's time in power. The general sought to unify the country by giving it a Burmese-ethnic majority identity, and to defeat insurgency with the "four cuts policy" of taking civilian support away from the rebels. Instead, the tactics of his armed forces in ethnic regions drove more and more inhabitants into rebellion.

Despite President San Yu's reelection in 1985 to a four-year term and his appointment as vice-chairman of the BSPP, Ne Win continued to dominate the political scene and to make all major and many minor government policy decisions. One such decision, to withdraw large currency notes from circulation in September 1987, threw the economy and the country into turmoil. The move, possibly aimed against black marketeers who had accumulated large sums of money, made 80% of the country's currency valueless, touching off student-led demonstrations. Citing his personal responsibility for dire economic conditions, Ne Win resigned as BSPP party chairman in July 1988. A protégé of Ne Win, Sein Lwin, was made BSPP chairman and president of the country. Sein Lwin's appointment triggered nationwide revolts. A broad spectrum of the population joined in, marching in the streets and going on general strikes throughout Burma. The army opened fire on unarmed protesters, killing thousands, particularly during the first week of August. Sein Lwin resigned on 12 August and Dr. Maung Maung, a civilian lawyer and journalist, was appointed his successor on 19 August. Although Maung Maung proposed multiparty elections and decreed that government employees could not be members of any political party, his refusal to step down provoked further protests. On 18 September 1988 the army abolished the BSPP, took over the government and imposed military rule under the State Law and Order Restoration Council (SLORC) headed by the army Chief of Staff, General Saw Maung. He also named himself prime minister and retained the portfolios of the Defense Ministry and Ministry of Foreign Affairs. Several days of violence occurred countrywide with

thousands of civilians, including children, students, and monks, killed by the armed forces. In announcing the takeover, General Saw Maung stated that the military rule would be temporary and that multiparty elections would be held once law and order were reestablished. In February 1989 Japan was the first nation to officially recognize SLORC as the legitimate government. Elections were set for 27 May 1990. On 18 June 1989 the Saw Maung regime renamed Burma "Myanmar Naing Ngan," a formal historical Burmese name for the country. It is colloquially known as "Myanmar," while democracy advocates and the US government continue to use the name "Burma."

With the elections called, political parties formed. First to organize was U Nu's League for Democracy and Peace, later known as the League for Democracy. The BSPP was reformed as the pre-regime National Union Party (NUP). U Nu had declared an interim government on 9 September 1988, but he garnered little support with his surprise move. In 1988 Aung San Suu Kyi, daughter of assassinated legendary hero General Aung San, had returned to Myanmar to visit her ailing mother. In the midst of the chaos of this period of demonstrations and protests Aung San Suu Kyi rose to prominence delivering speeches and establishing a coalition party opposing the military regime. On 24 September 1988 Suu Kyi with U Tin Oo and Aung Gyi formed the National League for Democracy (NLD). In early 1989 Aung Gyi formed his own organization, the Union Nationals Democracy Party (UNDP). In speeches and interviews Suu Kyi challenged Ne Win's record, characterizing it as one of economic and sociopolitical degeneration. She also protested SLORC's repressive laws and actions. Aung San Suu Kyi was placed under house arrest in Yangon (Rangoon) by Ne Win on 20 July 1989.

The top contenders in the elections were the NUP, the NLD, the UNDP, and the League for Democracy. The NUP was the party favored by the SLORC; and other parties had immense difficulty in campaigning and obtaining publicity. Six other parties figured prominently: the Coalition League for Democratic Multi-Party Unity; the Democracy Party; the Union of Burma Main AFPFL Party led by the children of former Premier U Ba Swe; the Democratic National Front for National Reconstruction, a former leftist NUF group; the Graduates and Old Students Democratic Association; and the Original Anti-Fascist People's Freedom League. A total of 93 parties fielded 2,209 candidates who, along with 87 independent candidates, contested 485 seats out of a total of 492 constituencies designated for holding elections. Seven constituencies that were excluded from the election represented mostly the ethnic minority states of insurgency. Over 100 candidates each were fielded by only five parties: The National League for Democracy (NLD), 447 candidates; the National Unity Party backed by SLORC, 413 candidates; the League for Democracy and Peace (LDP), 309 candidates (another source indicates 325 candidates); the Union Nationals Democracy Party (UNDP), 247 candidates (another source indicates 270 candidates), and the Democracy Party, 105 candidates. Despite its leader, Aung San Suu Kyi's incommunicado house arrest, the NLD won the 27 May 1990 general elections by a landslide (392 candidates elected out of its field of 447, or 87.7% of the votes). The NUP took 2.4% of the votes for 10 seats out of 413 fielded. The UNDP, with 0.4% of the vote, took 1 seat in Shan State out of the 247 (270) fielded. The Democracy Party with 0.95% of the vote took 1 seat out of 105 fielded. Of the candidates fielded by the LDP none won a seat. On 18 June 1989 Saw Maung indicated that the transfer of power to the winner of the election would not occur until a new constitution was drafted, one which met with SLORC's approval. However, on 13 July the powerful junta member Lt.-General Khin Nyunt denied the initial promise of an immediate transfer of power made by General Saw Maung. SLORC's further response was to alter the purpose of the newly elected assembly from its original function as a legislative body, to that of a constituent assembly formed to draft the new constitution. SLORC would not transfer power until the resulting draft constitution had been approved both by a referendum and by SLORC.

1990–Present

In September 1990 SLORC revealed its intention to remain in power for a further five to ten years. After his mental collapse in December 1991, Senior General Saw Maung resigned due to ill health on 23 April 1992. On the same day he was replaced as Chairman of SLORC by General Than Shwe who was also named (and remains) Chief of State and Head of the Government. First Secretary is Lt.-General Khin Nyunt and Second Secretary is Lt.-General Tin Oo. Accompanying these leadership changes SLORC initially indicated that an effort was being made to appease criticism of its methods as hundreds of political prisoners were released. Aung San Suu Kyi's family was allowed to visit her. Two martial law decrees imposed in July 1989 also were lifted in September 1992, and a constitutional convention was promised. In early 1993 a National Convention of 700 mostly hand-picked members met to draft a new constitution. Meeting with resistance and presented with a proposal by Yo E La of the Lahu National Development Party suggesting a return to the basic principles of Myanmar's pre-1962 constitution, a bicameral parliament and the granting of basic freedoms, the convention was adjourned until 7 June 1993. Another impasse occurred with further resistance to certain clauses in the new constitution that the ruling military wanted implemented; the National Convention was adjourned until January 1994. On 18 January 1994 the convention met again to approve six objectives and 104 basic principles which would entrench and perpetuate the power of the military.

The plight of Aung San Suu Kyi garnered the attention of human rights groups internationally. In March 1991, the Geneva UN Human Rights Commission passed a resolution to condemn and monitor the human rights abuses of SLORC, and in subsequent years Special Rapporteurs have been appointed to investigate Myanmar's human rights situation. In 1991 Aung San Suu Kyi was awarded the 1990 Sakharov Prize for Freedom of Thought by the European Parliament, the 1990 Thorolf Rafto Human Rights Prize by Norway, and on 10 December 1991 Aung San Suu Kyi's son, Alexander, accepted the 1991 Nobel Peace Prize on her behalf. In December 1993 the UN General Assembly unanimously rebuked the military rulers of Myanmar for their refusal to hand over power to the Parliament democratically elected in May 1990, and called for the release of political prisoners, including Aung San Suu Kyi, in her fifth year of house arrest. Eight fellow Nobel prize-winners met in Thailand in February 1993 to speak on behalf of Aung San Suu Kyi, but were denied visas to visit Myanmar. US Congressman William Richardson visited with Aung San Suu Kyi, who was still under house arrest in Yangon, on 14–15 February 1994, her first non-family visit in four-and-a-half years. Richardson also met with Lieutenant-General Khin Nyunt of the State Law and Order Restoration Council (SLORC).

Another dissenting voice in Myanmar, that of 74-year-old Aung Gyi, founder of the UNDP, was silenced when on 27 April 1993 he was sentenced to a six-month prison term. He had written a series of letters to Ne Win (much as he had paved the way for the pro-democracy movement in 1987–88 with a similar series of letters), and criticized the military regime in interviews with foreign journalists, but was convicted for failing to pay for eggs ordered as supplies for his tea and pastry shops. A type of human rights violation in Myanmar which drew international attention was forced labor, which the government used on tourist projects such as the reconstruction of the palace in Mandalay. Of Mandalay's 500,000 residents each family had to contribute at least three days of free labor each month. The work lasted from dawn until evening and was so strenuous that it took several days to recover from it. Prison inmates were required to work every day. Many military families could be exempted, as could any family that agreed to pay a monthly fine of about US$6, about a week's wages for some families. Forced labor was also used on a vast scale throughout Myanmar, on many building projects including roads and railroads, as well as for carrying supplies and munitions for the SLORC troops in insurgent areas. According to the testimony of escapees, the labor was accompanied by beatings, rape, execution of the ill or slow, and use of civilians as human shields and human mine-detectors. Muslim refugees who fled Myanmar said that Muslims had to pay two to three times as much as others to retain their rice ration card as a fine to escape labor. The SLORC commonly used euphemisms such as "merit-making" or "self reliance" in reference to the forced labor. Asia Watch also reported in 1994 that the government turned a "blind eye" to traffic in women and girls from Myanmar to Thailand for forced-prostitution." Corrupt officials on both sides of the border were involved. It was estimated that there were about 20,000 women from Myanmar in Thai brothels, where they were at severe risk of HIV/AIDS infection.

A casualty of the China-Myanmar border agreement of 1988 was the Communist Party of Burma (CPB) which collapsed with the withdrawal of Chinese support and the mutiny of its Wa troops in 1989. The CPB split into four different ethnic armies. SLORC's main objective was to neutralize the border rebel minorities and to prevent urban dissidents from getting access to arms and ammunition. SLORC's strategy was to divide and rule. Karen National Union President Bo Mya held that guerilla armies should hold joint talks with the government and not negotiate separately. The junta, however, would only negotiate separate agreements or treaties with individual rebel groups. To achieve its objectives SLORC introduced its Border Areas Development Program into ex-CPB areas. Infrastructure improvements of US$11.1 million in roads, bridges, schools, and hospitals were pledged in the state-run media. Necessities such as diesel, petrol, kerosene and rice were distributed. The Wa were the first to negotiate with the junta. In 1989 they were promised development assistance, were allowed to retain their arms, maintain control of their areas, and to engage in any kind of business. In exchange they promised not to attack government forces and to sever their ties with the other dissident groups and students. Throughout the 1990s the cease-fired Wa complained from time to time that little of the promised aid had been delivered, and that their demand to create a separate state was never discussed. The next deal was made with the 2,000-member Shan State Army (SSA), one of the Shan rebel factions, on 2 September 1989. The SSA was followed in December 1990 by a breakaway faction of the Kachin Independence Army (KIA). On 23 April 1991 the 600-member Palaung State Liberation Army made a truce with SLORC. The 500-member Pa-O National Army rebel group also signed a peace treaty with the military regime. Accusations were leveled that the smaller forces were pushed into signing accords by the unremitting abuse of their ethnic civilians by SLORC troops. The Tatmadaw, the SLORC's armed force, had increased its own troop strength from approximately 190,000 to well over 300,000 since the suppression of 1988's pro-democracy uprising.

The Karenni rebels, angry over SLORC logging encroachments in their territory, reversed their ceasefire, in September 1992. The government launched a major counter attack on the Karenni that spilled over the Thai border. Since 1984 the rebel Karen National Union (KNU) had its camps near the Thai border; and tens of thousands of Karen civilians fled from SLORC attacks and forced labor, to the Thai side. Manerplaw was the KNU headquarters and also the seat of the National Coalition Government of the Union of Burma (NCGUB), set up by fugitive members of National League for Democracy and other pro-democracy Members of Parliament elected in the thwarted 1990 polls.

Far to the north, the Kachins who had been in rebellion since 1961, had been the largest military group in a coalition of anti-SLORC ethnic forces. On 24 February 1994 the Kachin Independence Organization (KIO) signed a peace treaty with SLORC. They agreed to a ceasefire in exchange for permission to participate in commerce. Conflict between the SLORC and Shan groups continued. The Mong Tai Army (MTA) of the notorious "opium warlord" Khun Sa fought the Tatmadaw in the mid-1990s, then made a surprise surrender. He was able to spend his "retirement" living in comfort in Yangon (Rangoon). Like another rehabilitated drug lord, Lo Hsing Han, he has engaged in various legitimate business ventures, giving rise to charges of large-scale narcotics money laundering involvement on the part of the junta. Cease-fired Wa officers, from Myanmar's primary opium/heroin production region, are also said to have legitimate business access in Yangon and Mandalay. Some factions of the SSA refused to sign truces with SLORC, and joined in shifting alliances with anti-cease-fire factions of the MTA, continuing to battle the Tatmadaw. In response to Shan and Karenni defiance of the cease-fire policy, the SLORC engaged in enormous forced village relocations in those regions.

Ethnic peoples of western Burma also suffered. The Muslim residents of Arakan, called the Rohingyas, became refugees en masse in the early 1990s. Previously in 1978 the Burmese government had denied them citizenship and launched Operation Naga Min (Dragon King) forcing over 200,000 Rohingyas to seek refuge in Bangladesh. This pattern was repeated in 1991-92. The Rohingyas whose history in the area went as far back as the 9–15th centuries when Moorish, Arab, and Persian traders arrived and married local women and settled in the area, were displaced from their land and homes. As many as 300,000 Rohingyas fled to Bangladesh when they were forced from their land, their belongings were confiscated and women were raped by government troops. Some co-religionists made statements of protest, but ASEAN offered a policy of "constructive engagement" thus resisting pressures by the US and EC to adopt a stand on human rights abuses. According to this regional attitude, taking a stand would amount to interference in the internal affairs of a neighboring country. The countries of the region for the most part entered into "constructive engagement" with SLORC, gaining trade and investment opportunities, thus altering the status of the Myanmar exiles and refugees within their borders.

The international community has continued to debate the most effective approach for dealing with Myanmar. Up to and following Myanmar's acceptance into ASEAN in July 1997, ASEAN countries and Japan have argued that "engaging" Myanmar is more productive than "isolating" it. This approach gained them controversial timber concessions, energy projects, and some tourism plus manufacturing opportunities. It did not inspire liberalization by the junta. The US and EU have imposed limited economic sanctions, but allowed their petroleum corporations to remain in Myanmar as major investors. Proposals by groups of nations to offer Myanmar's generals economic rewards for steps toward liberalization have been rejected by the junta as "bribery." Aung San Suu Kyi's NLD continues to call for strong economic sanctions as the best way to pressure the junta to the negotiation table, and to deprive the Tatmadaw of the weapons it buys with hard currency (mainly from China and Singapore.) The NLD has called for a tourism boycott and for withdrawal of foreign corporations until democracy arrives.

SLORC released Aung San Suu Kyi from house arrest on 10 July 1995. Her freedom was short-lived, however. After large crowds of people began gathering in front of her house for weekly speeches, she was forbidden to address such gatherings. In November 1995, the NLD withdrew from the National Convention which was to formulate a SLORC-approved constitution, in protest of undemocratic policies; in turn SLORC permanently barred the NLD from participation and eventually the Convention meetings were suspended. Suu Kyi announced in May 1996 the NLD's plan to draft its version of the constitution, one that would oust the junta and implement new economic policies for the country.

SLORC curtailed Suu Kyi's attempts at movement outside of Yangon, which she protested with car sit-ins in 1998. NLD members have been detained by the hundreds, and many publicly renounced their membership. The Union Solidarity Defense Association (USDA) was formed by SLORC as a "mass organization" modeled after Sukarno's Golkar in Indonesia. It staged rallies denouncing the NLD, and Suu Kyi was physically threatened by some of its members. A steady campaign of insults against Suu Kyi was featured in the state-run press. In 1999, Suu Kyi's terminally ill British husband, Michael Aris, was denied a visa to see her one last time. The junta stated that she was free to leave Myanmar, but the implication was that she would not be permitted back. Student demonstrations took place in 1996, and institutions of higher learning were closed down by SLORC. Most universities and colleges have remained shut down the majority of the time since 1988. Attempts by student activists to mark the tenth anniversary of the "four eights" (8-8-88) democracy uprising, and another auspicious date, 9-9-99, were quickly surpressed. Long jail sentences have been handed down for even mild forms of public protest, and human rights groups report that torture of student dissidents is routine in Myanmar's prisons. Min Ko Naing, an important leader of the 1988 demonstrations, remains in prison. Leo Nichols, an honorary consul for European nations, died in a Myanmar prison, where he was held for unauthorized possession of a fax machine. As the junta attempts to control information, Internet access is extremely limited and unauthorized possession of a modem can earn a 17 year prison sentence.

Using a Buddhist breakaway Karen faction, the Democratic Karen Buddhist Army (DKBA), against the Christian-led KNU, the Tatmadaw was able to over-run Manerplaw and destroy most of the Karen rebel bases in 1995. Tatmadaw and DKBA troops entered Thailand in late January 1997 and attacked Karen refugee camps. A highly controversial natural gas pipeline across the region of southern Burma called the Tenasserim apparently inspired SLORC military campaigns against Mon and Karen rebels in that area. The Mon rebels signed a ceasefire agreement, but numerous Tatmadaw battalions were brought in to protect the pipeline project from Karen sabotage. The multinational petroleum companies involved, Total of France and Unocal from the US, were accused by human rights and environmental groups of complicity in human rights violations, including forced labor and forced relocation, committed by the SLORC's security forces. Victims of such abuses sued Unocal in a ground-breaking US court case. The pipeline began bringing natural gas from Myanmar's Andaman Sea to an electrical generating plant on the Thai side of the border in 1999. Outside economic pressure built up during the 1990s, in the form of consumer boycotts of companies doing business in Myanmar, limited US economic sanctions, and "selective purchasing" laws by cities. Massachusetts' "Burma selective purchasing law" was brought to the Supreme Court in 2000. By that year, foreign investment in Myanmar had decreased markedly, due to sanctions pressures, the Asian economic crisis, and concerns about corruption in the SPDC-controlled economy. In June 1999, the International Labor Organization of the UN essentially expelled Myanmar from its ranks, following a detailed investigation of forced labor under the SPDC. In early 2000, the World Bank issued a report highly critical of Myanmar's economic and political climate. The World Bank and International Monetary Fund have been barred from lending to Myanmar.

The Myanmar government has also come under considerable international criticism for its complicity in the country's massive drug trade. Myanmar is one of the world's largest producers of opium and heroin. Since 1990, the country has also become one of the largest manufacturers of illicit methamphetamine. Thai officials voiced dismay over the flood of "speed" pills into Thailand from Myanmar (particularly the Wa region, where a cease-fire is in effect) and the seeming callousness of the Myanmar government regarding the drug trade. Myanmar is the main source of heroin in China, where addiction grew seven-fold from 1989 to 1997. A 1999 Interpol conference on narcotic suppression, held in Yangon, was boycotted by the US and other governments as a protest against the junta's apparent profiting from drug trafficking.

With burgeoning drug production in the north of Myanmar has also come a raging HIV/AIDS epidemic. International health organizations estimated the number of Burmese infected in the north alone at 350,000–400,000 in 1996. The HIV/AIDS virus has spread unchecked in Myanmar through the use of contaminated needles by drug addicts, by unsafe medical practices, and by infected Burmese women returning from forced prostitution in Thailand. AIDS education, prevention, and care programs have been a low priority in Myanmar.

13 GOVERNMENT

The Socialist Republic of the Union of Burma was announced on 3 January 1974, after a new basic law had been approved by plebiscite. Under the 1974 constitution (which was suspended in September 1988), the leading organ of state power was the 489-member unicameral People's Assembly (Pyithu Hluttaw). The head of state was the chairman of the Council of State (29 members in 1986), which was elected by the People's Assembly and theoretically responsible to it. The prime minister headed the Council of Ministers (24 members in 1986) and also served on the Council of State. Other main governmental organs were the Council of People's Justices (9 members), the Council of People's Attorneys (6), the Council of People's Inspectors (6), and the people's councils at the level of the state (or division), township, and ward or village tract. Nationwide legislative elections were held in 1974, 1978, 1981, and 1985; in each election, voters either accepted or rejected candidates from a single slate presented by the ruling BSPP. Suffrage is universal at age 18, although the military has taken measures to discourage voter registration. A military coup in September 1988 brought the State Law and Order Restoration Council (SLORC) to power. SLORC abolished the previous government and placed the country under martial law. In June 1989 the official title of the country was changed to Myanmar Naing Ngan. The SLORC junta supervised and coordinated the work of the central and local organs of state power. It renamed itself the State Peace and Development Council in November 1997.

In the multi-party election held 27 May 1990, Aung San Suu Kyi's National League for Democracy (NLD) received 87.7% of the total vote and took 392 of its 447 contested seats, and the National Unity Party (NUP), the former BSPP re-registered as a new party, took only 10 seats with 2.4% of the votes.

SLORC refused to hand over power to the NLD, instead voiding the election and insisting that a new constitution need be drafted and approved by referendum, and by SLORC, prior to the transfer of power. Senior General Saw Maung resigned due to ill health on 23 April 1992 and General Than Shwe replaced him on the same day as Chairman of SLORC and as Chief of State and Head of the Government. First Secretary is Lt.-General Khin Nyunt and Second Secretary is General Tin Oo. Army chief

General Maung Aye is another highly influential junta member. Some observers have noted possible tensions among the top generals, especially between Khin Nyunt and Maung Aye. Both can be described as anti-democratic, but the "pragmatist" Khin Nyunt seems to prefer to pacify the border regions with negotiated cease-fires, while "hard-liner" Maung Aye seems inclined to launch military offensives in the remaining rebel frontier areas.

14 POLITICAL PARTIES

Between 1948 and 1962, Burma's parties were mostly socialist in economic orientation. The most important of these was the Anti-Fascist People's Freedom League (AFPFL), which gained independence for the country and which included within its ranks the distinct Burma Socialist Program Party. The AFPFL governed the country from 1948. In 1958, tensions within the government, and insurgency in the countryside, prompted Prime Minister U Nu to temporarily hand over power to a "caretaker" government headed by Gen. Ne Win. When U Nu's new Union Party won a landslide victory in 1960 elections, Ne Win relinquished power to him. Then on 2 March 1962, Ne Win staged a coup d'etat and began his long rule with the one-party (Burma Socialist Program Party) state.

Other parties before 1962 included two Communist movements, the "White Flags" and the "Red Flags," both of which took up arms early after independence and were later defeated by the government (the White Flags, however, were not completely eradicated until 1975). An above-ground Communist Party existed after 1949 and became the nucleus of the National United Front (NUF) in 1952. Both the Communists and the NUF, like all other parties except the ruling military-dominated Burma Socialist Program Party (BSPP), were banned in 1974. The well-armed Communist Party of Burma (CPB) insurgents based themselves primarily in northeast Burma, along the China border. Chinese support for the Communist party of Burma (CPB) continued well after support for the Communist parties of Malaysia and Thailand was withdrawn, but from the mid-1980s aid did not compare with a decade earlier. In 1989 the CPB was overthrown by its troops, many of whom regrouped as the United Wa State Army, which soon signed a cease-fire deal with SLORC.

Burmese independence leader Gen. Aung San had negotiate the Panglong Agreement with representatives of frontier ethnic groups in 1947, but issues of autonomy and federalism have never been resolved. Numerous ethnic parties with armed wings were formed in the mid- to late-twentieth century, including the Karen National Union, Kachin Independence Organization, New Mon State Party, Karenni National Progressive Party, Shan State Progress Party, Arakan Liberation Party, and Chin National Front. Umbrella groups of the ethnic insurgents were established, notably the National Democratic Front, followed by the Democratic Alliance of Burma. In the 1990s, many ethnic organizations signed cease-fire agreements with the SLORC. A continuous demand of the opposition is "tri-partite negotiations" between the SLORC/SPDC junta, Aung San Suu Kyi's National League for Democracy, and representatives of the ethnic groups. Most of the ethnic leaders favor a federal union of Burma based on ethnic regions.

The democracy uprising of 1988 ended with the 18 September coup which installed the military officers of the State Law and Order Restoration Council (SLORC). The Burma Socialist Program Party was formally abolished, and all governing authority was concentrated in the hands of the military. The earliest formation of the State Law and Order Restoration Council (SLORC) was made up of seventeen active military commanders of the Defense Services. On 18 September 1988 it was renamed the Organization for Building Law and Order in the State (OBLOS) and two more members were added. On 20

September 1988 the final version of the SLORC government was formed by maintaining the 19 members and adding two non-members to the Cabinet, increasing the number of Cabinet ministers from seven to nine. On 24 September 1988 the BSPP was reborn as the National Unity Party (NUP), inheriting the buildings and machinery of the old BSPP. Allied to the NUP were satellite parties, the former supporters of the BSPP.

On 24 September 1988 the National League for Democracy (NLD), a coalition party, was formed in opposition to the military regime. Leaders Aung San Suu Kyi, and Aung Gyi soon parted ways over the later's accusations of communist infiltration of the NLD. On 28 August 1988 U Nu at age 83, with his followers from the older generation formed the League for Democracy and Peace (LDP), later known as the League for Democracy. The NLD won the 27 May 1990 elections by a landslide, electing 392 candidates; the NUP took 10 seats; the UNDP and the Democracy Party took 1 seat each; and the LDP did not win any seats. In April/May 1991 the Election Commission dropped the names of the NLD's General Secretary Aung San Suu Kyi and President, U Tin Oo from a roster of NLD leaders, as well as the names of all other Central Executive Committee members who were jailed. NLD leader Aung San Suu Kyi was placed under house arrest from 20 July 1989 to 10 July 1995. NLD members have been detained and imprisoned in ever-increasing numbers, and many have been pressured to renounce their membership at public rallies of the junta-sponsored Union Solidarity Defense Association (USDA) a mass organization formed in September 1993 to support the ruling military.

Dr. Sein Win of the Party for National Democracy, winner of a seat in Pegu District, and seven NLD members legitimately elected to parliament but not recognized by SLORC, fled to border areas and formed a parallel government, the National Coalition Government Union of Burma (NCGUB). Sein Win was named prime minister of the NCGUB, which is now headquartered in Washington, D.C., where it serves as a diplomatic vehicle for the international exiled Burmese democracy movement.

On 29 January 1992 SLORC appointed additional ministers, mostly serving or ex-military, to the original nine-member cabinet, and three new military commanders were added to the original nineteen-member SLORC. Senior General Saw Maung resigned due to ill health on 23 April 1992. He was replaced as Chairman of SLORC by General Than Shwe on 23 April 1992. Than Shwe was named Chief of State and Head of the Government. First Secretary is Major-General Khin Nyunt and Second Secretary is Major-General Tin Oo. The SLORC changed its name to State Peace and Development Council (SPDC) in November 1997. The National Convention, aimed at drafting a new constitution has been suspended, and the NLD withdrew from the process in protest at its being used to legitimize the junta. Other parties have objected to the National Convention's insensitivity to ethnic rights issues.

15LOCAL GOVERNMENT

Myanmar is a unitary nation, ruled by a military junta, comprising seven states and seven divisions. The main distinction between the two kinds of units, which are functionally the same, is that the states represent an area where a national ethnic minority is the local majority, while the divisions have no such communal basis. The states are Arakan (Rakhine), Chin, Kachin, Karen (Kayin), Kayah, Mon, and Shan. The divisions are Irrawaddy, Magwe, Mandalay, Bago (Pegu), Sagaing, Yangon (Rangoon), and Tenasserim. States and divisions are segmented into 317 townships. Village tracts consist of villages, and towns are divided into wards. Law and Order Restoration Councils (LORCs) serve as local administration, although regional army commanders control the actual decision making process. A LORC was formed for each State, Division, Township Sector and Ward/ Village Sector. Military campaigns of forced village relocations, especially in the Shan and Karenni states and Tenasserim Division, have changed the rural map of Myanmar and placed much of the agricultural population under direct army control. In some frontier areas where cease-fire groups (such as the UWSA or KIO) still hold significant territory, administration is by the former insurgent leadership.

16JUDICIAL SYSTEM

The British-style judicial organs with which Burma began its independence, including a Supreme Court, were disbanded by Ne Win's Revolutionary Council. The 1974 constitution, suspended since 1988, provided for a Council of People's Justices, state and divisional judges' committees, and township, ward, and village tract judges' committees. The Council of People's Justices was elected by the National Assembly from among its own members; nominations were made by the Council of State, which coordinated relations between central and local levels of government. Military tribunals which enforced orders issued by the State Law and Order Restoration Council (SLORC) were abolished in 1992. Ordinary courts now handle such cases, with heavy military influence. The Supreme Court appoints judges after approval of the SPDC. The SPDC has used laws such as the Emergency Provisions Act and the Unlawful Associations Act to crack down on dissent. Human rights organizations such as Amnesty International, and the United Nations, have criticized the SPDC for unfair trials and arbitrary imprisonment, as well as use of torture and summary execution.

17ARMED FORCES

The armed forces play the major role in Myanmar's politics and administration; senior members of the government are officers who govern under martial law.

Myanmar's armed forces totaled an estimated 429,000 in 2000; military service for men and women is compulsory. The army, with 325,000 personnel, is organized in infantry battalions chiefly for internal security duties, mainly against the various insurgent groups that have challenged successive governments almost from the start of independence. The navy has 10,000 members, and the air force 9,000. The navy's responsibilities relate primarily to antismuggling and other coastal patrol duties; its ships include 29 gunboats and 31 river patrol craft. The air force is also concerned mainly with internal security; it has 83 combat aircraft, 14 transports, and 29 armed helicopters. The armed forces use European and Chinese weapons, including 100 main battle tanks of several makes. Paramilitary forces total 85,250. Military expenditures were $3.9 billion in 1997–98 or 2.1% of GDP. Various rebel groups are estimated at perhaps 15,000 and operate inside and outside of northern Myanmar.

18INTERNATIONAL COOPERATION

Myanmar was admitted to UN membership on 19 April 1948; it is a member of ESCAP and all the nonregional specialized agencies except WIPO. Regional bodies to which Myanmar belongs include the Asian Development Bank and the Colombo Plan; it also is a member of G-77, a member of the WTO, and a signatory to the Law of the Sea. Myanmar's foreign policy is neutralist, and the country belongs to no alliances.

19ECONOMY

Myanmar has an agricultural economy. As of 1999 nearly 75% of the economy was in the private sector comprised chiefly of agriculture (including fish and forestry), which is almost entirely private, contributing nearly 60% of GDP and employing close to 63% of the work force. Myanmar is self-sufficient in food. Principal crops are paddy rice, corn, oilseed, sugarcane, and pulses. Traditionally rice was the major product and the major foreign exchange earner, accounting for about 70% of the country's cultivated land. In 1996, rice exports quadrupled to $197 million, and accounted for 22% of merchandise exports. The Asian financial crisis hit Myanmar hard, reducing rice exports by about one-third. The major recipients of Myanmar's rice are Indonesia and China. Myanmar also has the world's largest stand of hardwood trees.

Industries include agricultural processing, textiles and footwear, wood and wood products, petroleum refining, mining production (mainly copper, tin, tungsten, and iron), construction materials, pharmaceuticals, and fertilizer. In 1998, industrial production accounted for 11% of GDP. In the past Myanmar was a net petroleum exporter, but production decreased steadily. Both oil and gas exploration is on-going with the participation of foreign companies, and in 1997/98 the energy sector grew by 37.7% (from virtual non-existence) due to investment in the Yadana natural gas pipeline to Thailand, which came on-line in 1998. In addition, Myanmar's significant mineral resources have not been fully developed due to out-dated equipment and poor management.

Infrastructure is a major impediment to economic growth. Water treatment and distribution, sewage disposal, and irrigation systems, as well as, power transmission and distribution, require up-grading. Industry faces chronic shortages of electricity. Roads are poor and many are not passable during parts of the year. Telephone facilities are lacking; in 1993 there were only 100,000 telephone lines for the entire country. Presently a telecommunications modernization program includes the installation of a cellular telephone system in Yangon. The financial sector suffers from excessive bureaucratic red tape and footdragging by state economic enterprises fearing competition. The government drafted new laws on a central banking and financial institutions as steps toward improvement in the financial sector.

The government reported that the economy grew by 6% in 1995 and 6.8% in 1996. Growth was estimated by the US State Department at 1.1% for 1998. However, it is difficult to assess the true economic situation due to the existence of an enormous and all-pervasive informal market. Much of Myanmar's economic activity is illicit, notably the smuggling of drugs. Myanmar, which forms part of the "Golden Triangle" (along with Laos and Thailand), is the world's largest supplier of illegal opiates. The government's efforts to control poppy production and drug traffic to China and Hong Kong were ineffective. Due to Myanmar's inability to stop the flow of drugs from its sector of the Golden Triangle, in February 1989 the US removed Myanmar from a list of countries eligible to receive aid for combating the drug trade. By 1995 Myanmar's opium production was estimated at 2,340 metric tons (the source for over 60% of US heroin imports). Large quantities of smuggled consumer goods are sold in Myanma cities, where the black market thrives.

The military regime, SLORC, which took over Myanmar in 1988, proclaimed a market oriented economic policy and invited foreign investment. A 1992 United Nations Development Programme report noted that Myanmar after a few years of recovery from the economic and political upheaval of 1988 was again slipping into recession and hyperinflation. Myanmar's main donors suspended aid. The country has not fully serviced its foreign debt since 1988. Two trends have been apparent in the government's economic policies: the capture of revenues from short term, quick turnover sources such as hardwoods, prospecting rights, and taxes on profits from illegal sources; and spending patterns which emphasize defense spending and acquisition of armaments. Myanmar receives no aid from US or EC programs and aid from Japan is run at a maintenance level. The International Monetary Fund (IMF), the World Bank, and the Asian Development Bank (ADB) extend no credit to Myanmar.

20 INCOME

The US Central Intelligence Agency (CIA) reports that in 1998 Myanmar's gross domestic product (GDP) was estimated at $56.1 billion. The per capita GDP was estimated at $1,200. The annual growth rate of GDP was estimated at 1.1%. The average inflation rate in 1998 was 26%. The CIA defines GDP as the value of all final goods and services produced within a nation in a given year and computed on the basis of purchasing power parity (PPP) rather than value as measured on the basis of the rate of exchange. It was estimated that agriculture accounted for 59% of GDP, industry 11%, and services 30%.

Private consumption includes expenditures of individuals, households, and non-governmental organizations. It was estimated that between 1990 and 1998 private consumption grew at an annual rate of 3.9%.

21 LABOR

In 1998, about two-thirds of Myanmar's civilian wage labor force, estimated at 24 million, was engaged in agriculture, primarily rice cultivation. Roughly 12% were employed in industry, and the remainder in services.

No trade union or independent labor movement activity has occurred since 1988, when the government banned the workers' and peasants' organizations of the previous government, thereby eliminating any right to bargain collectively. Forced labor is frequently used by the military for building projects. Prison labor is also extensively used, especially in stone quarrying projects. Wage levels continue to be low and have been eroded by inflation.

There were some 535,290 officially unemployed in 1997, although the actual amount is likely to be much higher.

While the official minimum working age is 13, the presence of child labor is conspicuous in both rural and urban areas. Most children must work to help support their families and only about 40% of children complete 5 years at primary schooling.

Only government workers and employees of a few traditional industries are covered by minimum wage laws, which set a monthly wage of $2 per month (as of 1999), not including additional allowances and subsidies.

22 AGRICULTURE

Myanmar is one of the few developing nations that is a net exporter of food, which accounted for 39% of its foreign exchange earnings in 1997. About 15% of the land is under cultivation. Agriculture generated 70% of employment and 53% of the recorded GDP in 1998.

Rice, by far the most important agricultural product, in 1995 covered about 5.4 million hectares (13.3 million acres) of land in the fertile Irrawaddy delta region, the lower valleys of the Sittang and Salween rivers, and along the Arakan and Tenasserim coasts. Prior to World War II, Myanmar was the world's leading exporter of rice; annual production ranged between 13 million and 14 million tons, of which about 3 million tons were exported. However, the war caused extensive damage to the economy, and Myanmar did not achieve prewar levels of rice acreage and output until 1964. Rice production totaled 16,651,000 tons in 1998. Farmers have been instructed by the government to double-crop wet season paddy and triple-crop in areas with year-round access to water. In some areas near the sea, multiple cropping brings saltwater intrusion, high flood risks, and seasonal pest problems. New high-yield varieties of rice have contributed to the increases in recent years, along with the completion of new irrigation systems and flood-control dams in the Irrawaddy delta during the early 1980s.

Other crops in 1998, grown mainly in central Myanmar and the state of Shan, included 5,213,000 tons of sugarcane, 540,000 tons of groundnuts, 308,000 tons of corn, and 296,000 tons of sesame. The use of high-yield varieties of seeds helped to more than triple the output of wheat, corn, and sunflower seeds and to double cotton production during 1976–86. Tobacco and jute are also produced, and rubber is grown on small plantations in the Tenasserim and Irrawaddy delta regions. Myanmar is the world's largest producer of opium and heroin. In 1998, opium poppy production was estimated at 1,750 tons.

The total amount of land under cultivation declined in the 1970s, but the amount of paddy land increased. The Mu Valley irrigation project, implemented in north-central Myanmar with UNDP aid in the 1970s, irrigated 1.7 million hectares (4.2 million acres) of farmland. With the completion of the Nawin Dam in 1982, about 40,000 hectares (99,000 acres) of new irrigated land in the Prome region, north of Yangon (Rangoon), were added to the cultivated area. With IBRD and Asian Development Bank aid, new rice storage facilities, a system of drainage canals in the heavy-rainfall paddy land of lower Myanmar, and gravity irrigation systems in dry zones were constructed.

23 ANIMAL HUSBANDRY

Despite Buddhist prohibitions against any kind of animal slaughter, the Myanma eat beef and other meats. Zebu cattle and water buffalo are mainly raised as draft animals; the output of such hides was 25,000 tons in 1998. Dairy farming is confined to the Shan and Kachin states; hogs and poultry are found in virtually every village.

In 1998, Myanmar had an estimated 10,493,000 head of cattle, 3,501,000 hogs, 2,337,000 water buffalo, 1,319,000 goats, 369,000 sheep, and 23,000,000 chickens, and 5,000,000 ducks. Meat production was 388,000 tons; milk from cattle, 581,000 tons (82% cow, 18% buffalo); eggs, 54,000 tons.

24 FISHING

Fishing is the most significant nonagricultural pursuit in Myanmar. Fish, which supply the main protein element in the Myanma diet, generally are dried and salted before marketing or consumed fresh or as fish paste. Roho labeo and various carp are the main species caught. Aquacultural production in 1997 was valued at $865.3 million. Traditionally, the Myanma preferred fish from fresh or brackish water; but saltwater fishing in the shallow waters of the Bay of Bengal, Andaman Sea, and Gulf of Martaban has increased in recent years. To encourage a larger saltwater catch, the government embarked on expanded deep-sea fishing operations and erected a cold storage plant, a fish cannery, and a fish oil and meal factory. The total fish catch in 1997 was 917,666 tons (73% saltwater, 27% freshwater), up from 686,515 tons in 1986. Exports of fish products were valued at $109.3 million in 1997.

25 FORESTRY

Forests and woodland cover nearly half the country. Myanmar has a major share of the world's teak reserves, which constitute about one-third of the forested area. As the world's leading exporter of teak, Myanmar supplies about 75% of the world market. The lumbering of teak, a 10-year process from the first girdling of the tree to its arrival at the sawmill, was disrupted by World War II; production rebounded to about 136,000 tons in 1986. Increased output of teak in the 1980s was attributable to completion of four modern timber-extraction projects. Roundwood production in 1997 totaled 23,445,000 cu m. Other forest products include lac, catechu resin, and bamboo.

All foreign timber concessions have been nationalized, and all forests are government-owned; the State Timber Board (STB) lumbers, mills, and markets forest products. The export of forest products decreased in value from $294.1 million in 1993 to $162 million in 1997.

26 MINING

The government controls all mineral exploration, extraction, regulation, and planning through the two departments and six enterprises of the Ministry of Mines. In 1997, mining contributed about 1.7% to GDP and 5% to export earnings. Metallic ores are mined in small amounts; production in 1997 included (in tons): copper (6,000), lead (2,800), zinc (400), tin (400), and tungsten (280). Industrial mineral production in 1997 included (in tons): barite (22,000), fire clay (2,600), dolomite (5,000), limestone (3,500,000), and gypsum (39,000). Lead, zinc, silver, copper, nickel, and cobalt are produced at the Baldwin mine in Namtu. Jade, rubies, sapphires, and gold are also extracted, and deposits of iron ore, antimony, and coal have been found. Production of jade and refined silver totaled 1.4 million kg and 2,000 kg, respectively.

27 ENERGY AND POWER

Myanmar's petroleum industry was completely nationalized in 1963–64, and the Petroleum and Mineral Development Corp. was formed by the amalgamation of the Mineral Resources Development Corp., the Mines and Explosives Department, and the Burma Geological Development Corp. Petroleum and natural gas deposits were found in 1963 in the Irrawaddy basin and delta. Myanmar has been self-sufficient in oil since 1977; petroleum reserves were estimated at 51.3 million barrels in 1991. Most natural gas comes from the field at Prome. Exploitation of the natural gas discovery in the Gulf of Martaban, Natmi, and Payagon will significantly raise Myanmar's energy reserves. Oil production was estimated at 11,000 barrels per day in 1998. In 1995, natural gas production totaled 51,044 million cu ft (1,446 million cu m). Pipelines in Myanmar include 1,343 km (835 mi) for crude petroleum and 330 km (205 mi) for natural gas, although some of these lines are believed to be in disrepair. Coal resources in Myanmar are of relatively low thermal value. The two principal mines are an underground mine south of Kalewa and an opencast mine at Namma, south of Lashio. About 32,191 tons of coal came from the two mines in 1995.

Production of electricity totaled 4,310 million kWh in 1998, of which thermal plants provided about 60% and hydroelectric power roughly 39%. Electric power capacity rose to 1,393 MW in 1998, but power supply remained inadequate to meet the country's needs and shortages were on the rise across the country.

28 INDUSTRY

Industry is geared largely to the processing of agricultural, mineral, and forest products. More than half of Myanmar industrial production is accounted for by the public sector. Principal industrial products are cement, steel, bricks and tiles, fertilizers, and processed foods. Consumer goods which were imported before 1962 and are now manufactured domestically include blankets, paper, glass products, bicycles, and water pumps. Other major consumer manufactures are aluminum ware, jute and cotton cloth, pharmaceuticals, beverages, matches, and cigarettes. There is also a growing segment engaged in the assembly of television sets and motor vehicles. The main industrial area is Bago (formerly Pegu). Some manufacturing industries are privately owned and operated under government supervision.

Industrial production grew by 9.2% in fiscal year 1995–96, and represented about 11% of the gross domestic product in 1997. In 1995, production of pig iron totaled 1,500 tons; crude steel, 25,000 tons; and refined tin, 190 tons. The petroleum and petrochemical sector in Myanmar is entirely state-owned (excluding indigenous fuels such as charcoal). In 1995, local refineries produced 5.3 million barrels of refined petroleum products. A natural gas pipeline connecting to Thailand was scheduled to begin operations in late 1998, but there were significant delays in Thailand.

29SCIENCE AND TECHNOLOGY

Scientific research is conducted by the private Burma Research Society, founded in 1910, and by the government's Central Research Organization, consisting of various departments of the state ministries. Four institutes conduct research in applied sciences, medicine, and atomic energy. In addition, the Department of Land Management Studies Research of the Institute of Economics investigates problems posed by modernization techniques and industrial development. The Universities of Mandalay, Mawlamyine, and Yangon offer degrees in basic sciences. In 1987–97, science and engineering students accounted for 56% of college and university enrollments.

30DOMESTIC TRADE

In 1964, the Ne Win government nationalized all wholesale businesses and the large private and cooperative shops; small retail shops, hotels, restaurants, and village cooperatives were exempted. The People's Stores Corp., established in 1964, was initially responsible for the importation and distribution of essential foreign goods, the distribution of consumer goods produced in Myanmar, and the sale of domestic products in foreign markets. The corporation was administered by a council headed by the Ministry of Supplies and Cooperatives. In 1970, the "people's stores," most of which had been unsuccessful, were replaced by consumer cooperatives. Beginning in 1966, the government set all commodity prices and controlled distribution systems; in September 1987, the Burmese people were told that they could buy, sell, and store rice and other grains free of government restrictions. As of 1997, these liberalization measures have been most effective in the agricultural sector, although overall, the military still controls the lion's share of the economy.

Although significant marketing is done at Bago (Pegu), Mandalay, Mawlamyine (Moulmein), Pathein (Bassein), Henzada, Akyab (Sittwe), and Dawei (Tavoy), Yangon (Rangoon) is Myanmar's most important business center. Myanmar's domestic economy is paralleled by a huge black market economy that coexists with the official one; the underground economy may be at least as large as the legal economy. A factor in the decline of Myanmar's domestic production is dependence on border trade, which undermines Myanmar's manufacturing sector with cheap foreign consumer goods. Normal business hours are 9:30 AM to 1 PM and 1:30 to 4 PM, Monday–Friday, and 9:30 AM to 12:30 PM on Saturday; small private shops keep longer hours than government offices and enterprises. Banks are usually open 10 AM to 2 PM, Monday–Friday, and 10 AM to noon on Saturday.

31FOREIGN TRADE

It is estimated than from 1992 to 1995 the legal merchandise trade deficit (excluding military imports) grew from $412 million to $737 million. All financial estimates are suspect because of the exclusion of a large extralegal sector and substantial military imports, neither of which are included in official figures. The value of opiate exports alone may now be roughly comparable to all legal merchandise and service exports receipts. Border areas not under the control of the government also engage in unreported exports of timber, rice, jade, gems, minerals, and rare animals.

The US Central Intelligence Agency reports that in 1997 the purchasing power parity of Myanmar's exports was $940 million while imports totaled $2.2 billion resulting in a trade deficit of $1.26 billion.

The International Monetary Fund (IMF) reports that in 1998 Myanmar had exports of goods totaling $1.171 billion and imports totaling $2.455 billion. The services credit totaled $543

million and debit $445 million. The following table summarizes Myanmar's balance of payments as reported by the IMF for 1998 in millions of US dollars.

Current Account		-454
Balance on goods	-1,284	
Balance on services	99	
Balance on income	-29	
Current transfers	760	
Capital Account		...
Financial Account		536
Direct investment abroad	...	
Direct investment in Myanmar (Burma)	315	
Portfolio investment assets	...	
Portfolio investment liabilities	...	
Other investment assets	...	
Other investment liabilities		221
Net Errors and Omissions		-22
Reserves and Related Items		-60

33BANKING AND SECURITIES

Effective 23 February 1963, all 24 commercial banks in Myanmar—10 foreign and 14 indigenously owned—were nationalized and amalgamated into 4 state banks. In addition to the Central Bank of Myanmar, Union of Burma Bank, which serves as a central bank, the other state banks were the State Agricultural Bank, the State Commercial Bank, and the Industrial Bank. After subsequent reorganizations of the banking system, these became the Myanma Investment and Commercial Bank, Myanma Economic Bank, and the Myanma Foreign Trade Bank. Agricultural credit is provided by a separate Myanmar Agricultural and Rural Development Bank. Public savings increased sharply in 1977 after the banks raised interest rates. Efforts to attract the considerable liquidity in the hands of the public into the banking sector, and thence into investment, have not had much success.

By the end of 1994, licenses to open representative offices had been issued to 19 banks from overseas—six from Thailand, five from Singapore, three from Malaysia, and one each from France, Indonesia, Cambodia, Hong Kong, and Bangladesh. Since 1994 four private domestic banks have been permitted to conduct foreign exchange transactions for the first time. Various types of foreign exchange licenses have been issued recently to the private sector by the Central Bank. It issued seven authorized dealer licenses, three money changer licenses, 396 acceptor and holder licenses, and 66 FEC changer licenses in August 1994. Despite the liberalization of its economy, the country still lacks a capital market. By1997, there were around 43 foreign banks with representative offices in Myanmar.

34INSURANCE

All 78 foreign insurance companies registered in Myanmar were nationalized on 1 March 1963. All forms of insurance, including life, fire, marine, automobile, workers' compensation, personal accident, and burglary, are handled by the Myanma Insurance Corp. Life insurance coverage is compulsory for government employees.

35PUBLIC FINANCE

The government presents its budget in March for the 1 April–31 March fiscal year. The public sector budget typically shows an overall deficit.

The US Central Intelligence Agency (CIA) estimates that in 1997 Myanmar's central government took in revenues of approximately $7.9 billion and had expenditures of $12.2 billion including capital expenditures of $5.7 billion. Overall, the government registered a deficit of approximately $4.3 billion.

The following table shows an itemized breakdown of government revenues and expenditures. The percentages were calculated from data reported by the International Monetary

Fund. The dollar amounts (millions) are based on the CIA estimates provided above.

REVENUE AND GRANTS	100%	7,900
Tax revenue	56.0%	4,425
Non-tax revenue	41.3%	3,264
Capital revenue	0.9%	72
Grants	1.8%	139
EXPENDITURES	100%	12,200
General public services	8.9%	1,085
Defense	30.6%	3,735
Public order and safety	0.0%	0
Education	9.4%	1,141
Health	3.5%	428
Social security	2.3%	279
Housing and community amenities	0.4%	45
Recreation, cultural, and religious affairs	2.3%	280
Economic affairs and services	34.9%	4,261
Other expenditures	7.7%	945

36TAXATION

Residents pay a progressive individual income tax of 3–30%. The corporate tax rate is 30% with a 10% capital gains tax (40% for non-residents). Indirect taxes include a commercial tax on sales and services, as well as social security taxes, customs duties, royalties on natural resources, stamp tax, and property tax.

37CUSTOMS AND DUTIES

Duties are primarily intended to raise revenue, although their financial importance is limited by the fact that the government itself—through its Myanma Export-Import Corp.—is by far the country's predominant importer. Import licenses are required for shipment of almost anything into the country. Customs tariffs range from 0% to 500%. Until Myanmar joined ASEAN in July 1997, customs tariffs ranged from zero to 500%; in 1997, a new tariff schedule went into effect ranging from zero to15% for most industrial inputs to a maximum of 40% for cars and luxury items. In spring 1998 a 10% service fee (reduced to 8% by September) on all border-trade exports was enacted.

38FOREIGN INVESTMENT

Foreign investment in Myanmar was heavy before World War II, but in the postwar period, and particularly after independence, a government policy of economic nationalism (and later socialism) strongly discouraged private foreign investment. After the nationalization of industry in 1963–64, private foreign investment in Myanmar was eliminated entirely. In 1976, the government indicated a willingness to establish "mutually beneficial economic cooperation" with foreign enterprises having the technology that Myanmar needed. The scope of state capitalism was expanded when the Saw Maung regime legalized internal and external trade without giving up control of major industries. Foreign investment in Myanmar has been permitted only since 1988 under the Union of Myanmar Foreign Investment Law, and the level and variety of investment is limited. Sectors eligible for foreign investment include manufacturing, oil and gas exploration and development, mining (except gold and precious stones), jewelry production, and agriculture. The Foreign Investment Commission (FIC) screens foreign investment proposals for export generation potential, technology transfer, and the size of the investment. Various investment incentives are provided, such as exemption from income tax, and relief or exemption from customs duties. Bureaucratic procedures and a antiquated and inadequate infrastructure hamper foreign and local investments alike. Foreign entities cannot own land in Myanmar. The government's maintenance of an official exchange rate for the domestic currency, the kyat, which is overvalued by some 60 times its unofficial value, is the major obstacle to foreign investment.

Foreign investors also fear being criticized by the west for investing in a country with a long record of human rights violations. In 1997, Myanmar was admitted to the Association of Southeast Asian Nations (ASEAN), a step that might have relieved some of the international pressure against doing business in the country; however, in May of that year, the US government enacted restriction against new investment in Myanmar by US companies or citizens.

39ECONOMIC DEVELOPMENT

The major aim of Myanmar's government has been to rehabilitate, modernize, and diversify an economy that was extensively disrupted by World War II and that failed to develop from the 1940s through the 1960s. To this end, all foreign companies, all banks, the entire transport system, all foreign and much domestic trade, and all the main branches of industry have been nationalized. Some nationalized industries initially showed declines in output, while others were hard pressed to hold their own. By 1974, the government had no choice but to modify some of its more rigidly Socialist economic policies. Economic development proceeded slowly under the four-year plan for 1974–78 and the 1978–82 development program, which was allocated 60% more funding than its predecessor and which achieved an annual growth rate exceeding 6%. The four-year plan for 1982–86, costing an estimated $5 billion, set an average annual growth target of 6.2%. The plan stressed infrastructural development, with particular emphasis on agriculture, construction, and energy production. The four-year plan for 1986–90 encouraged foreign investment. Since 1990, private investment has been encouraged as the government attempts to revitalize the economy. However, economic development has been limited by the government's failure to implement basic structural reforms. Such needed reforms include dismantling unproductive state-owned enterprises, establishing an independent state bank, making available private sector credit, controlling government spending, and adjusting the official exchange rate. Basic infrastructure, transportation, telecommunications, and energy are inadequate.

40SOCIAL DEVELOPMENT

Although considerable advances have been made in health services, Myanmar's goal of establishing a welfare state has been limited by lack of public funds. In 1956, the government inaugurated a social security program that compensates workers for wage losses arising from sickness, injury, and maternity leave, provides free medical care, and establishes survivors' benefits. The program is funded by contributions from employers, employees, and the government. As yet, Myanmar does not have unemployment insurance, but public employees are entitled to old age pensions.

Women have a high status in Myanmar's society and economic life. They may retain their maiden name after marriage, may obtain divorces without undue difficulty, and enjoy equal property and inheritance rights with men. Spousal abuse is infrequent. Traditional views of women, however, often prevent them from entering male dominated occupations, and they do not always receive equal pay for equal work.

Myanmar's military regime continues to systematically engage in human rights abuses. Prison conditions are poor and mistreatment of prisoners is widespread. There was a slight improvement after the International Red Cross gained access to prisons in 1999 for the first time in four years. Arrests are often made arbitrarily and many detainees are held incommunicado. As of 1999, the government continued to detain over 55 persons elected to parliament as opposition candidates in 1990, thus preventing parliament from convening. Hundreds of other supporters of the National League for Democracy were detained as well, and its general secretary, Aung San Suu Kyi, remained under house arrest. In all, there were over 1,300 political prisoners at the end of 1999.

Many ethnic minorities are denied full citizenship. Those of Muslim, Indian and Chinese descent, for example, are not free to travel domestically and are barred from certain university programs. The ethnic Chinese face discrimination and harassment by officials.

41HEALTH

Until the 1980s and 1990s, few people in rural areas had the benefit of modern medicine. To correct this deficiency, the country's health services were reorganized by sending more doctors to rural areas and increasing the number of rural health centers. Doctors in private practice were inducted for two years of national service.

The progress of the health services in the 1980s is reflected in the reduction of the physician/population ratio from 1 per 15,560 in 1960 to 1 per 3,578 by 1986. To staff the new hospitals and dispensaries, medical schools have been expanded, nurse and midwife training courses increased, an institute of paramedical science established, and a new college of dentistry opened.

A team of nutritionists conducts research on the nation's diet and disseminates its findings and recommendations through the press, radio, and demonstrations in offices and factories. One result of these efforts has been that the average height and weight of Myanmar's populace have increased.

Smallpox and plague have been virtually eliminated as health hazards, and programs are under way to eradicate malaria and tuberculosis. However, gastrointestinal diseases such as typhoid, dysentery, and cholera remain prevalent. One of the problems yet to be overcome is the lack of potable water for residents; in 1990, only 31% had access to safe water. Another serious health problem is drug addiction, exacerbated by the easy availability and low cost of opium. Under a drug abuse control program financed by the US and the UN, a new 300-bed hospital for addicts opened in 1982 at Thayetmyo, along the Irrawaddy in central Myanmar; smaller facilities have been established in two dozen other towns.

The infant mortality rate dropped from 129.9 deaths per 1,000 live births in 1960 to about 76 in 1999, while average life expectancy rose to 54.7 years. Between 1990 and 1995, the population had access to health services (60%), adequate sanitation (36%), and safe water (38%).

During 1987–1990 immunization was estimated to have saved 60,000 young children and averted 2.4 incidences of vaccine-preventable diseases. Between 1990-1994 the immunizations for children under 1 were as follows: tuberculosis (83%); diphtheria, pertussis and tetanus (77%); and polio (77%). The level of measles immunization rose by more than 50 percentage points between 1988 and 1994. By 1997, 88% of children were immunized for measles.

The total fertility rate decreased from 5.1 in 1990 to 3.6 in 1999. The maternal mortality rate was 580 per 100,000 live births in 1990–97. Between 1990-1995, 31% of children under 5 were malnourished.

There were 1,093 new cases of AIDS in 1996; that year, international health organizations estimated the number of Myanma infected in the north alone to be 350,000–400,000.

42HOUSING

Prewar housing in Myanmar compared favorably with that in other Southeast Asian nations, but housing conditions have deteriorated. Only about one-third of the population has access to safe water. Urban dwellings are overcrowded and often unsafe. In the same year, 54% of all housing units were built of wood and bamboo, 26% were thatch and bamboo, 15% were wooden, 2% were made from pucca, and 1% from semi-pucca.

43EDUCATION

Education is free, although informal fees were increasingly imposed in the late 1990s. Primary education is compulsory for five years, although observers estimate that between two-thirds and three-fourths of students drop out before completing five years. Generally, Burmese is the language of instruction, and English is taught in the secondary schools; as of 1982, however, English became the medium of instruction in the universities.

The system of education initiated by the Ne Win government in 1964 equates learning with livelihood. At that time, the government announced its intention of opening at least one agrarian high school and one technical high school in each district. By 1967 there were six agricultural high schools, seven industrial trade schools, and one technical high school in the country, and the government had taken over about 880 private schools. In 1996, Myanmar had 35,752 primary schools with 5,413,752 students. In the same year, secondary schools had approximately 107,000 teachers and 1,923,323 students. Primary education lasts for five years followed by four years of secondary education at the first stage and two years at the second stage. Postsecondary institutions, including 18 teacher-training colleges, 6 agricultural institutes, 8 technical institutes, and 35 universities and colleges, had a total enrollment of 245,317 students with 5,730 teaching staff in 1996.

The Mass Education Council has attempted to increase literacy through special programs. The 2000 adult illiteracy rate was estimated at 15.3% (males, 11.0%; females, 19.4%), although international observers question this figure, estimating illiteracy to be much higher since up to 40% of children in rural areas do not enroll in school and those who do drop out early.

44LIBRARIES AND MUSEUMS

The National Library in Yangon (Rangoon), founded in 1952, contains 155,000 volumes. Other large libraries are the Arts and Science University Library in Mandalay, with 175,000 volumes, and the University of Yangon with 350,000 volumes. There are also several small college libraries, as well as state libraries and museums at Pathein (Bassein), Kyaukpyu, Mandalay, and Mawlamyine (Moulmein). The National Museum of Art and Archaeology in Yangon was founded in 1952 and includes among its collection a replica of King Mindon's Mandalay Palace. The National Museum of Mandalay (1905) is housed in the Glass Palace and features historical relics of Burmese culture. Sometimes called the "land of golden pagodas," Myanmar also has thousands of Buddhist temples, many of which have been repaired and restored.

45MEDIA

The director-general of posts and telegraphs controls the telephone, telegraph, radio, and postal communications systems. In 1995 there were an estimated 131,000 telephones in use; internal communication is mainly by wireless. A satellite communications station that began operating in 1979 links Myanmar with more than 100 countries. The government provides the only radio and television transmissions through Voice of Myanmar and TV–Myanmar (which broadcasts in color). As of 1999, there were 2 AM and 3 FM radio stations and 2 television stations. In 1997, there were 89 radios and 7 TV sets per 1,000 population.

Chinese- and Indian-language newspapers are not allowed by the government, but two daily papers are still published in English. Leading newspapers in 1999 included *Kyemon* (1999 circulation, 100,000), *Myanma Alin* (400,000), and *The New Light of Myanmar* (14,000). There are some privately published magazines, but none has a high circulation or major influence.

The government professes to uphold freedom of the press, but there are no privately owned newspapers, and the print media are government-controlled. In 1963, the government established its own press agency, the News Agency of Burma, with a monopoly on internal news distribution.

46ORGANIZATIONS

Although Myanmar has most common types of educational, religious, cultural, and social organizations, those associated with capitalist economic activity have all but disappeared. The Rotary Clubs were forced by the government to disband in late 1975, as were numerous other Western-style organizations before them. In 1988/89 there were 20,594 cooperative and producers' societies, as well as substantial numbers of consumer cooperatives.

47TOURISM, TRAVEL, AND RECREATION

With the inception of military rule in 1988, tourism declined sharply but has risen again since 1990. From 1988 to 1995, the number of hotels increased from 19 to 256. There were a total of 13,338 hotel rooms with 20,007 beds and an occupancy rate of 26% in 1997. In 1998, there were 195,500 tourist arrivals. Principal attractions include the palaces and Buddhist temples and shrines in the two largest cities and in the ancient city of Pagan. A visitor to Myanmar must have a passport, visa, and certificate of yellow fever inoculation if arriving from an infected area.

In 1999, the UN estimated the cost of staying in Yangon at $140 per day, elsewhere daily costs were $43.

48FAMOUS MYANMA

Anawrahta, who founded the early Burmese kingdom of Pagan in 1044 and established Hinayana Buddhism as the official religion, is a great figure in Burmese history, as are the Toungoo warrior-king Bayinnaung (r.1551–81) and Alaungpaya (r.1752–60), who established the dynasty that ruled Myanmar until 1886. Great writers of the Burmese past include Bhikkhu Ratthasara, author of the poem *Hatthipala Pyo,* on the life of Gautama Buddha; Nawedegyi and Natshinnaung, poets of the Toungoo dynasties; and Binnyadala, who wrote of the long struggles of the Burmese king of Ava. In more recent times, U Ba Nyan and U Ba Zaw, well-known painters of the 1920s, introduced Western-style art into Myanmar; both died in the 1940s.

U Nu (Thakin Nu, 1907-1995) was independent Myanmar's first premier (1948–62) and shares fame as founder of modern Myanmar with Aung San (1916–47), called the Father of the Burmese Revolution. Ne Win (Maung Shu Maung, b.1911) became premier in March 1962 and was president from 1974 to 1981. U Thant (1909–74) served as UN secretary-general from 1961 through 1971. Human rights activist Aung San Suu Kyi (b.1946) was awarded the 1990 Sakharov Prize for Freedom of Thought by the European Parliament, the 1990 Thorolf Rafto Human Rights Prize by Norway, and the 1991 Nobel Peace Prize.

49DEPENDENCIES

Myanmar has no territories or colonies.

50BIBLIOGRAPHY

American University. *Burma: A Country Study.* Washington, D.C.: Government Printing Office, 1983.

Aung-Thwin, Michael. *Pagan: The Origins of Modern Burma.* Athens: Ohio University Press, 1985.

Becka, Jan. *Historical Dictionary of Myanmar.* Metuchen, N.J.: Scarecrow, 1995.

Cady, John Frank. *The United States and Burma.* Cambridge, Mass.: Harvard University Press, 1976.

Harvey, Godfrey Eric. *History of Burma.* New York: Octagon, 1967.

Herbert, Patricia M. *Burma.* Santa Barbara, Calif.: Clio Press, 1991.

Lehman, F. K. (ed.). *Military Rule in Burma since 1962.* Singapore: Maruzen Asia, 1981.

Maung, Mya. *The Burma Road to Poverty.* New York: Praeger, 1991.

Nash, Manning. *The Golden Road to Modernity.* Chicago: University of Chicago Press, 1973.

Nu, U. *Burma under the Japanese.* New York: St. Martin's, 1954.

———. *Saturday's Son.* New Haven, Conn.: Yale University Press, 1975.

Saito, Teruko and Lee Kin Kiong. *Burmese Economy.* Singapore: Institute of Southeast Asian Studies, 1999.

Silverstein, Josef. *Burmese Politics: The Dilemma of National Unity.* New Brunswick, N.J.: Rutgers University Press, 1980.

———. *The Political Legacy of Aung San.* Ithaca, N.Y.: Cornell University, 1993.

Steinberg, David J. *Burma's Road toward Development: Growth and Ideology under Military Rule.* Boulder, Colo.: Westview, 1981.

———. *The Future of Burma: Crisis and Choice in Myanmar.* New York: Asia Society, 1990.

Taylor, Robert (ed.). *Marxism and Resistance in Burma, 1942–1945.* Athens: Ohio University Press, 1984.

———. *The State in Burma.* London: Hurst, 1987.

Than Tun. *Essays on the History and Buddhism of Burma.* Whiting Bay, Isle of Arran, Scotland: Kiscadale Publications, 1988.

Win Pe. *Dos & Don'ts in Myanmar.* 1st ed. Bangkok, Thailand: Book Promotion and Service Ltd., 1996.

NAURU

Republic of Nauru

CAPITAL: There is no formal capital. The seat of government is in the district of Yaren.

FLAG: The flag has a blue background divided horizontally by a narrow gold band, symbolizing the equator. Below the band is a white 12-pointed star, representing the island's 12 traditional tribes.

ANTHEM: *Nauru Ubwema* (*Nauru, Our Homeland*).

MONETARY UNIT: The Australian dollar (A$) of 100 cents is the legal currency. A$1 = US$0.6203 (US$1 = A$1.612) as of 31 March 2000.

WEIGHTS AND MEASURES: Imperial weights and measures are used.

HOLIDAYS: New Year's Day, 1 January; Independence Day, 31 January; Angam Day, 26 October (a celebration of the day on which the population of Nauru reached the pre-World War II level); Christmas Day, 25 December; and Boxing Day, 26 December.

TIME: 11:30 PM = noon GMT.

¹LOCATION, SIZE, AND EXTENT

Situated in the western Pacific, Nauru is one of the world's smallest independent nations, with an area of 21.0 sq km (8.1 sq mi), extending 5.6 km (3.5 mi) NNE–SSW and 4 km (2.5 mi) ESE–WNW. Comparatively, the area occupied by Nauru is about one-tenth the size of Washington, D.C. It lies between two island groups, the Solomons and the Gilberts, 53 km (33 mi) S of the Equator and 3,930 km (2,442 mi) NNE of Sydney; its nearest neighbor is Banaba (formerly Ocean Island, now part of Kiribati), situated 305 km (190 mi) to the E. Nauru has a coastline of 30 km (18.6 mi).

²TOPOGRAPHY

Nauru, one of the largest phosphate-rock islands in the Pacific, is oval-shaped and fringed by a wide coral reef. It has no natural harbor or anchorage. A relatively fertile belt varying in width from 150 to 300 m (490–980 ft) encircles the island. From this belt a coral cliff rises to a central plateau about 60 m (200 ft) above sea level. Buada Lagoon, a permanent, often brackish lake, covers some 120 ha (300 acres) in the southeastern end of the plateau. Apart from some brackish ponds and an underground lake, the nation's water supply is provided by rainfall.

³CLIMATE

Nauru has a dry season, marked by easterly trade winds, and a wet season with westerly monsoons extending from November to February. The average annual rainfall is about 45 cm (18 in), but the amount varies greatly from year to year, and long droughts have been a recurrent problem. Temperatures remain steady, between 24° and 33°C (75–91°F) the year round, and relative humidity is also constant at about 80%.

⁴FLORA AND FAUNA

The plateau area contains large phosphate deposits that almost completely inhibit any natural growth useful for subsistence or commerce. Large areas of scrub and creeper, with occasional coconut and tamanu trees, grow in this region. On the coastal belt, coconut palms and pandanus (a type of screw pine) thrive. Some hibiscus, frangipani, and other tropical flowers grow, but they do not abound here as on other Pacific islands. Bird life is not plentiful, although noddies, terns, and frigate birds frequent the island. There are no indigenous land animals; however, hogs and poultry were introduced many years ago. Fish life is abundant in the seas encircling Nauru, and good catches of tuna and bonito are taken.

⁵ENVIRONMENT

Nauru's phosphate mining industry has done significant damage to the land. In 1987, the Nauruan government began to investigate the nation's mining operations with the goal of developing a plan to regenerate the land and replace lost vegetation. Land in the coastal region, however, has not been affected by the development of the country's mining industry. Vegetation in the coastal areas, such as pandanus and coconut palms, is plentiful. Nauru has limited freshwater resources. Its residents collect rainwater in rooftop storage tanks. Periodic droughts pose an additional hazard to the environment.

Nauru is also affected by the global warming trend which has caused sea levels to rise, placing low-laying areas at risk from tidal surges and flooding.

⁶POPULATION

The population of Nauru in 2000 was estimated at 10,704. Most Nauruans live around the coastal fringes, in their traditional districts. About half the population consists of immigrant contract laborers, technicians, and teachers. Most Chinese, as well as immigrants from Kiribati and Tuvalu, are settled in communities near the phosphate works. The estimated population density in 1996 was 489 per sq km (1,267 per sq mi).

It was estimated that 100% of the population lived in urban areas in 2000. The Yaren District, which functions as the capital city, had a 2000 population of 10,000.

⁷MIGRATION

Immigration to Nauru is strictly controlled by the government. Nauruans are free to travel abroad.

In 1999 the net migration rate was zero migrants per 1,000 population.

⁸ETHNIC GROUPS

The Nauruan people are the only indigenous ethnic group on the island. They are of mixed Micronesian, Melanesian, and Polynesian origin and resemble the last strain most closely. Nauruans are traditionally divided into 12 clans or tribes in which descent is matrilineal, although kinship and inheritance rules have some patrilineal features. The 12 clans are Eamwit, Eamwidumwit, Deboe, Eoaru, Emea, Eano, Emangum, Ranibok, Eamwidara, Iruwa, Irutsi (extinct), and Iwi (extinct). Admixtures of Caucasian and Negroid lineage in the 19th century and frequent intermarriage with other Pacific islanders have changed the present-day features of Nauruans from those of their forebears.

The Caucasians on the island are almost all Australians and New Zealanders employed in administrative or teaching posts or in the phosphate industry. The Chinese and immigrants from Kiribati and Tuvalu originally came to the island as laborers in the phosphate industry, some being accompanied by their families. Filipino contract workers are also present but are not permitted to bring their families.

As of 1999, 58% of the population was Nauruan, 26% other Pacific Islander, 8% Chinese, and 8% European.

⁹LANGUAGES

Nauruan, which is distinct from all other Pacific tongues, is the official language. However, English is still commonly used in the schools, in government, and in business transactions. Most Nauruans are bilingual but use Nauruan in everyday life.

¹⁰RELIGIONS

The Nauruans have accepted Christianity since the end of the 19th century. In 1999, two-thirds of the population was Protestant, and one-third was Roman Catholic.

¹¹TRANSPORTATION

Transport to and from Nauru has traditionally been by ships calling at the island to unload freight and pick up phosphates for delivery to Australia, New Zealand, and other countries. There is no merchant marine, but the public Nauru Pacific Line has a fleet of six ships. In 1998, there was one airport with a paved runway. The government-owned Air Nauru flies regular air services to the Pacific islands, Taiwan, the Philippines, Hong Kong, Japan, Australia, and New Zealand. In 1997 it carried 137,000 passengers on scheduled flights.

The road system extended for a total of 30 km (19 mi) in 1996, of which 24 km (15 mi) were paved. Apart from a 3.9-km (2.4-mi) railway (used to carry phosphates), a school bus service, and fewer than 2,000 registered motor vehicles, there is no local transport.

¹²HISTORY

The original settlers are thought to have been castaways who drifted to Nauru from another Pacific island. The first recorded discovery of Nauru by a Westerner was made by Captain John Fearn of the whaling ship Hunter in November 1798. He named the island Pleasant Island. From the 1830s to the 1880s, the Nauruans had a succession of visitors—runaway convicts, deserters from whaling ships, and other men who can be classed as beachcombers. The beachcombers provided the Nauruans with their first real contact with Western civilization and introduced them to firearms and alcohol. They acted as a buffer between two cultures but were often a bad influence on the Nauruans. Several times beachcombers and Nauruans attempted to cut off and capture visiting ships, so that eventually Nauru came to be avoided as a watering place by ships whaling in the area. The advent of firearms also disturbed the balance of power between the tribes on the island; sporadic tribal warfare culminated in a

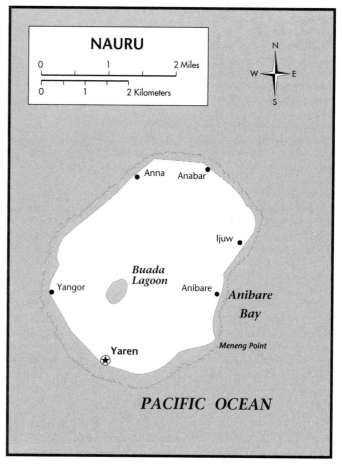

LOCATION: 0°32′s and 166°56′ᴇ. **TERRITORIAL SEA LIMIT:** 12 mi.

10-year civil war from 1878 to 1888 that reduced the native population to less than 1,000.

The British and German imperial governments agreed to the partition of the Western Pacific in 1886. Their purely arbitrary line of demarcation left Nauru in the German sphere of influence quite accidentally. It was not until 1888, on the petition of the beachcombers-turned-traders, that the German government annexed Nauru as a protectorate and disarmed the people. Christian missionaries arrived in 1899 and had a greater impact on the Nauruan culture than did the German administration.

In 1901, Sir Albert Ellis, a New Zealand geologist, discovered that there were large deposits of phosphate on both Nauru and Banaba (then called Ocean Island). Phosphate mining on Nauru began in 1907, after the German government had granted a concession to the British-owned Pacific Phosphate Co. Laborers from the German Caroline Islands were hired because the Nauruans had no interest in working in the mines.

Nauru was occupied by the Australian Expeditionary Force in 1914, and phosphate continued to be shipped all through World War I. In 1919, Nauru was made a League of Nations mandate of the British Empire, and the governments of Australia, New Zealand, and the UK agreed to administer the island jointly through an administrator to be appointed by Australia. At the same time the three governments obtained the mandate, they jointly purchased the Pacific Phosphate Co.'s rights to Nauruan phosphate for ᴜᴋ£3.5 million and began to work the deposits through a three-man board called the British Phosphate Commissioners (BPC).

The phosphate industry expanded greatly in the years between the wars. Australian and New Zealand farmers enjoyed substantial savings, for Nauru phosphate was sold at a much lower price than phosphate from other countries. As for the Nauruans, with their small royalty of eightpence a ton in 1939, they opted out of the industry completely and turned to their own culture for sustenance.

War came to Nauru in December 1940, when the island was shelled by a roving German raider, and four phosphate ships were sunk. Nauru was flattened by Japanese bombings beginning in December 1941, and all its industrial plant and housing facilities were destroyed. The Japanese occupied the island from August 1942 until the end of the war three years later. They deported 1,200 Nauruans to build an airstrip on Truk, a small atoll about 1,600 km (1,000 mi) northwest of Nauru, and many died there. Australian forces reoccupied Nauru in September 1945, and the surviving Truk Nauruans, who had been reduced in number to only 737, were repatriated in January 1946. Nauru's population thus fell from 1,848 in 1940 to 1,369 in 1946.

The three mandatory governments placed the mandate of Nauru before the UN. On 1 November 1947, the UN approved an agreement by which the island became a trust territory administered jointly by Australia, New Zealand, and the UK, who were to share the task of developing self-government on the island. The Nauruans had a Council of Chiefs to represent them since 1927, but this body had advisory powers only. Dissatisfied Nauruans made a number of complaints to the administering authority and to the UN Trusteeship Council, with the result that a Nauruan local government council was established by the election of nine council members in December 1951. Since control of the council was exercised by the administrator, however, the Nauruans continued to press for further political power. They asked for positions of importance in the administration and an increase in royalty payments, and expressed concern about the future of the island because the increased rate of phosphate exportation would, it was feared, exhaust the deposits by the end of the century. By constant negotiations, the Nauruans forced the BPC to pay royalties on a rights rather than needs basis, and with the establishment of a world price in 1964, phosphate royalties were raised. The Nauruans achieved control of the industry in 1967 by purchasing the plant and machinery owned by the BPC, and in 1970 they took over the industry completely.

Meanwhile, in 1964, Australia had attempted to resettle the Nauruans on Curtis Island, off the coast of Queensland. The Nauruans, although in principle not averse to resettlement, refused it because of political considerations. They wanted to own their island and to maintain their identity by political independence. Australia would not agree to this, and the plan collapsed. This failure reinforced the Nauruans' desire for political independence. With the support of the Trusteeship Council, they established an elected Legislative Council in 1966. Although Australia wished to maintain control of defense and external affairs, the Nauruans insisted on complete self-determination. Thus, on 31 January 1968, the 22nd anniversary of the return of the Nauruan survivors from Truk, Nauru became the smallest independent republic in the world. Since that time, Nauru has pursued a policy of isolation and nonalignment, although it does have a role in Commonwealth affairs. In October 1982, Queen Elizabeth II visited the island, the first British monarch to do so. Nauru established diplomatic ties with the former Soviet Union in 1988. Nauru filed a claim in 1989 for compensation from Australia at the International Court of Justice for the loss of nearly all its topsoil from phosphate mining during the League of Nations mandate and the UN trusteeship. In July 1992 Nauru hosted the 24th South Pacific Forum heads of government meeting, which focused on environmental issues, including opposition to nuclear testing in the area. Nauru's first

president Hammer DeRoburt died on 15 July 1992 in Melbourne, Australia. Australia agreed to pay A$2.5 million for 20 years, and New Zealand and the UK additionally agreed to pay a settlement of $12 million each in August 1993 to settle the loss of topsoil case.

Nauru's government announced plans to rehabilitate the island at the 1994 Small Island States Conference on Sustainable Development.

Incumbent president Bernard Dowiyogo lost his 1995 bid for reelection to Lagumot Harris in 22 November 1995. However, a series of no-confidence votes over the succeeding years brought several changes in what has come to be called a "revolving door" presidency. Most recently, Dowiyogo was returned to office for the third time in five years, following an election in April 2000.

Nauru became a member of the Commonwealth of Nations in May 1999 and joined the United Nations in September of the same year.

13GOVERNMENT

The constitution of the Republic of Nauru, adopted at the time of independence and subsequently amended, provides that the republic shall have a parliamentary type of government. It contains provisions for the protection of fundamental rights and freedoms—a subject of particular importance because many of the inhabitants are short-term migrants ineligible for citizenship (defined in the constitution as being restricted to those of Nauruan or of Nauruan and Pacific islander parentage). Legislative power is vested in the Parliament, composed of 18 members elected for a three-year term by Nauruan citizens who have attained the age of 20 years. Seven of the eight constituencies (representing 10 out of 14 districts) return two members each, and the constituency of Ubenide (representing 4 districts) returns four members. The first woman was elected in 1986.

Executive power is exercised by the president, who also fulfills the residual duties of head of state; he is elected by Parliament and is assisted by a cabinet, which he appoints. Hammer DeRoburt became president at independence in 1968 and was reelected in 1971 and 1973. He was defeated for reelection after the legislative voting in 1976, and Bernard Dowiyogo was chosen to succeed him as president. After DeRoburt's supporters forced Dowiyogo's resignation in 1978, DeRoburt again became president. He was reelected in 1980 and in 1983; after the 1983 victory, he persuaded his opponent Dowiyogo to become a cabinet member. In 1986, DeRoburt resigned in protest over opposition to his budget and was replaced by Kennan Adeang; however, DeRoburt's supporters quickly forced Adeang to resign, and DeRoburt was elected again. Because he did not have a clear majority, he called for a new election in 1987 and was reelected decisively. A vote of no confidence forced DeRoburt to resign in August 1989. He was replaced by Kenas Aroi, who then resigned in December 1989 for reasons of ill-health. The December 1989 general election resulted in Bernard Dowiyogo's election to the Presidency. He was reelected President for a second three year term in November 1992, but lost his 1995 bid for reelection to Lagumot Harris. However, a series of no-confidence votes brought seven changes in the presidency over the next five years. The election of April 2000 returned Dowiyago to office for the third time since his loss to Harris in 1995.

14POLITICAL PARTIES

After DeRoburt's reelection in 1987, Kennan Adeang formed the Democratic Party of Nauru, which aimed to curb the power of the presidency. Eight members of Parliament joined the party. The only political party in Nauru, it did not play an important part in the electoral process and was no longer in existence by 1995. As of 1999, however, a new Democratic Party had been formed by supporters of Bernard Dowiyogo.

15 LOCAL GOVERNMENT

The Nauru Island Council (NIC) is elected from the same constituencies as is the Parliament, except that seven of the eight constituencies return one member, and the constituency of Ubenide returns two members, making nine in all. The council elects a chairman, treasurer, and secretary. It holds its sessions in the Domaneab, a Nauruan meetinghouse. It acts as the local government and is responsible for public services. Many members of Parliament also serve as councilors.

Besides fulfilling the traditional functions of local government, the Nauru Local Government Council manages the Nauru Corporation, the Nauru Pacific Line, and is responsible for overseas investments.

16 JUDICIAL SYSTEM

The constitution provides for a Supreme Court, with a chief justice presiding. Cases are also heard in the District Court or Family Court. The Supreme Court, which has original and appellate jurisdiction, is the supreme authority on the interpretation of the constitution. Cases may be appealed further to the High Court of Australia.

The judiciary is independent of the executive. The Constitution guarantees protection of fundamental human rights which in practice are generally respected.

Many cases never reach the formal legal system. Most of the conflicts are resolved by the traditional reconciliation process.

17 ARMED FORCES

Nauru has no armed forces. Although there is no formal agreement, Australia ensures its defense.

18 INTERNATIONAL COOPERATION

Nauru was admitted to the UN on 14 September 1999 and participates in ESCAP, ICAO, ITU, and UPU. The nation belongs to the South Pacific Commission and South Pacific Forum and is a special member of the Commonwealth of Nations, taking part in some Commonwealth functions but not represented at heads-of-government conferences. Nauru has signed the Law of the Sea.

19 ECONOMY

The economy of Nauru has long been dependent on phosphates. Estimates are that the deposits will be exhausted soon after 2000. In anticipation of this event, substantial amounts of phosphate income are invested in trust funds to help cushion the transition. By 1987, an estimated $450 million had been set aside to support the country after the phosphates run out. However, dividends from the trusts have declined sharply since 1990 and the government has been borrowing from the trusts to finance fiscal deficits. In addition, a 1994 audit of the trust revealed that about $8.5 million had been lost due to bad investments and corruption. By 1996 deficit spending had caused the country to default on servicing its external debt and was also creating problems in meeting the government payroll. A strict government austerity program reduced government spending 38% in 1998–99.

The government has attempted to use the now-dwindling revenue from phosphates to diversify the island's economy, mainly through overseas investment and the development of a national airline and shipping line. Aside from phosphates, Nauru has few domestic resources, and many food products and virtually all consumer manufactures are imported. The government subsidizes imports so that food and other necessities are available at nominal cost. Nauru's economy is currently very weak and increasingly dependent on Australia. Offshore financial operations were begun in 1993, but the economy suffered in that year due to a major financial scandal.

20 INCOME

The US Central Intelligence Agency (CIA) reports that in 1993 Nauru's gross domestic product (GDP) was estimated at $100 million. The per capita GDP was estimated at $10,000. The average inflation rate in 1993 was -3.6%. The CIA defines GDP as the value of all final goods and services produced within a nation in a given year and computed on the basis of purchasing power parity (PPP) rather than value as measured on the basis of the rate of exchange.

21 LABOR

In the mid-1980s, about 1,200 workers were employed in the state-owned phosphate industry; about 1,000 others were employed by the government and the Nauru Cooperative Society. As of the early 1990s, about half of the over 9,000 inhabitants relied on the phosphate industry for their means of support. Only about 1% of employment is in the private sector. As of 1992, there were some 3,000 guest workers in Nauru, mostly from Vanuatu or Kiribati. There were no trade unions as of 1999. The annual minimum wage in the public sector is $6,562.

22 AGRICULTURE

Since the cultivated area is limited to about 200–240 ha (500–600 acres), there is little commercial agriculture. The main crop is coconuts; in 1998, production amounted to 2,000 tons. Some vegetables are grown, mainly by the Chinese population.

23 ANIMAL HUSBANDRY

Pigs and chickens roam uncontrolled on the island; hence, there is no organized production. In 1998, there were an estimated 3,000 pigs.

24 FISHING

There is as yet no organized fishing industry on Nauru, although the government plans to develop fishing facilities. The Nauru Fishing Corp., formed in 1979, is owned by the Local Government Council. Fish are plentiful and consumption is high, since almost all meat has to be imported from Australia. The total catch in 1997 was 400 tons.

25 FORESTRY

There are no forests on Nauru. All building timber has to be imported; forest product imports amounted to $205,000 in 1995.

26 MINING

Nauru's only natural resource is high-grade phosphate rock, which is exported to New Zealand, Australia, the Philippines, and South Korea. The government-owned Nauru Phosphate Corp. is the country's primary producer, employer, and exporter. Extraction is done mainly by mechanical shovels from between the coral pinnacles. Phosphate rock is trucked to a central storage pile and transported to storage hoppers by rail. After being crushed and dried, the rock is placed on conveyor belts to pass to the arm of two cantilevers, each about 60 m (200 ft) long, that project out over the reef to waiting ships. As of 1990, the cumulative total of mined phosphate was over 61 million tons. Production in 1994 was 613,000 tons. Phosphate rock reserves are expected to be depleted by the early 2000s.

In 1994, New Zealand and the UK agreed to help Australia pay its $73 million compensation package to Nauru for environmental damage caused by the mining of the island's phosphate deposits. Australia and Nauru also signed an agreement in 1994 to begin a rehabilitation and development program for the mined-out phosphate lands in Nauru.

27ENERGY AND POWER

Power requirements on the island are met by a diesel oil generator to which nearly all buildings are connected. In 1998, net installed electrical power capacity was 10,000 kW; production was 30 million kWh. Imports of refined petroleum products amounted to 950 barrels per day in 1994.

28INDUSTRY

The phosphate industry is the only industry on the island. It is under the control of the Nauru Phosphate Corp., a statutory corporation that is responsible to the president of the republic in his capacity as minister for island development and industry. About 75% of the profit from phosphate sales is invested in long-term trust funds that have been established to take care of the Nauruans after phosphate deposits are depleted, estimated to be in 2000 or 2001.

29SCIENCE AND TECHNOLOGY

Nauru has little advanced technology, and Nauruans must travel abroad, usually to Australia, for scientific training.

30DOMESTIC TRADE

The Nauru Cooperative Society conducts most of the nation's retail trade. The island is completely dependent on imported goods; foodstuffs come mainly from Australia.

31FOREIGN TRADE

Nauru's only export is phosphate rock, with most going to Australia and New Zealand. The value of exports fluctuates as world phosphate prices rise or decline. Imports consist mostly of machinery and construction materials for the phosphate industry and food, water, fuel, and other necessities. About half of the imports come from Australia, and almost all the rest from New Zealand, the UK, and Japan. Virtually all manufactured goods must be imported.

32BALANCE OF PAYMENTS

Nauru has a strongly favorable balance of trade, and investments abroad are substantial.

The US Central Intelligence Agency reports that in 1991 the purchasing power parity of Nauru's exports was $25.3 million while imports totaled $21.1 million resulting in a trade balance of $4.2 million.

33BANKING AND SECURITIES

The government-owned Bank of Nauru was founded in 1976. The Commonwealth Savings Bank of Australia and the Bank of New South Wales have branches in Nauru. The only commercial bank in the country is the Jefferson Bank and Trust Co. (1980). Most of the income from phosphates is invested in long-term funds overseas. There is no stock exchange.

34INSURANCE

The Nauru Insurance Corp., founded in 1974, is the only licensed insurer and reinsurer on the island. It underwrites all classes of insurance, including aviation and marine.

35PUBLIC FINANCE

Administrative costs in Nauru are met from the proceeds of phosphate sales, which are in decline as reserves approach exhaustion. In 1993, the governments of Nauru and Australia reached a US$73 million out-of-court settlement as restitution for Nauruan lands ruined by Australian phosphate mining. This payment assisted the government (which relies almost entirely on phosphate receipts for revenue) in facilitating economic diversification. The fiscal year extends from 1 July to 30 June. The US Central Intelligence Agency (CIA) estimates that in 1996 Nauru's

central government took in revenues of approximately $23.4 million and had expenditures of $64.8 million. Overall, the government registered a deficit of approximately $41.4 million.

36TAXATION

There is no income or other tax in Nauru, although Parliament has power to impose taxes.

37CUSTOMS AND DUTIES

Duties are payable only on imported cigarettes, tobacco, and alcoholic beverages.

38FOREIGN INVESTMENT

Apart from the investment in the phosphate industry, now owned by the government of Nauru, there has been little investment on the island. The government of Nauru has large investments overseas in long-term funds financed from phosphate royalties. Nauru also has invested in commercial property development, notably a 53-story office building in Melbourne, Australia.

Plans were approved in 1985 to build an industrial, commercial, and residential complex in Honolulu and, with the help of Japanese companies, a 19-story, 450-room hotel on Guam.

Nauru received US$6.7 million from the Japanese government to build the new Anibare Community Boat Harbor at Yaren, scheduled to open in the spring of 2000.

39ECONOMIC DEVELOPMENT

Government policy is to exploit the phosphate deposits to the fullest extent for the highest returns. The government has diversified into aviation and shipping and plans to develop fishing and tourism. It acquired the Grand Pacific Hotel on the Fijian Island of Suva and, in 1993, undertook a F$18 million renovation of the facility. In 1993, Australia agreed to provide US$73 million in compensation for pre-independence mining of phosphate to aid in restoring the extensive areas damaged by it.

In December 1998 Nauru won approval for a $5 million loan from the Asian Development Bank to aid in implementing structural reforms, including privatization.

40SOCIAL DEVELOPMENT

Medical, dental, and hospital treatment and education are free. Other benefits—old age and disability pensions, widows' and sickness benefits, and child endowment—are administered by the Local Government Council.

The Constitution guarantees women equal rights with men, although traditional social values still discourage many from pursuing careers. In particular, women face great social pressure to marry and raise families because Nauru's population was decimated in World War II due to massive removals by the Japanese. Women's educational and employment opportunities are severely limited by these traditional views on the roles of women, and there have been reports of educational scholarships being suspended for young women contemplating marriage.

Human rights are generally well respected, and as of 1999, there were no human rights organizations in existence in Nauru.

41HEALTH

Tuberculosis, leprosy, diabetes, and vitamin deficiencies have been the main health problems, partly due to the switch to a Westernized diet. A national foot care education program was launched in 1992 to decrease the number of diabetic amputations. With modern facilities and treatments, many of these diseases have been brought under control. Cardiovascular disease has also been a major cause of illness and death.

There are two modern hospitals. One hospital serves phosphate industry employees; the other provides free medical treatment for the rest of the population. Patients who need specialized care are flown to Australia. In 1990, the infant mortality rate was estimated at 25 per 1,000 live births. The life expectancy in 1993 was 68 years. The infant mortality rate was 40.6 per 1,000 live births in 1995.

The immunization rates for children under one year old in 1990 were as follows: diphtheria, tetanus, and pertussis (74%); polio (74%); measles (74%); and tuberculosis (93%).

Both polio and AIDS were absent from Nauru in 1995. Tuberculosis was reported in only 4 cases during 1994.

42HOUSING

Ownership of houses built for Nauruans under a housing scheme is vested in the Local Government Council, but some Nauruan homes are privately owned. Nearly all houses have electricity, and newer homes have a greater number of amenities.

43EDUCATION

Attendance at school is compulsory for Nauruan children from 6 to 16 years old. Two types of schools are available, both coeducational: those run by the government and those conducted by the Roman Catholic Church. Education is provided free by the government. Education on Nauru is up to intermediate standard; higher education overseas, mainly in Australia, is assisted by the government in the form of competitive scholarships. There is also a university extension center affiliated with the University of the South Pacific. In 1985 there were 1,451 students in seven government primary schools, with 71 teachers. Student-to-teacher ratio stood at 20 to one. In the same year, 482 students were enrolled in secondary schools, with 40 teachers.

44LIBRARIES AND MUSEUMS

Nauru has one small lending library but no museums. There is a university library with 1,000 volumes.

45MEDIA

Communication with the outside world is maintained by a ground satellite station established in 1975, providing 24-hour telephone, telegraph, and telex services worldwide. A small telephone exchange, handling 2,000 telephones in 1989, provides on-island communication. A satellite earth station was commissioned in 1990. Government-owned Radio Nauru broadcasts in English and Nauruan. Though there is no local news reporting; the station rebroadcasts new services from Radio Australia and the BBC. As of 1997 there was one television station in operation. In the same year, there were 374 radios in use per 1,000 population.

Most newspapers are imported. There are two regular publications: the private fortnightly newspaper, the *Central Star News*; and the government *Gazette*.

The constitution provides for free expression, and the government is said to support this in practice.

46ORGANIZATIONS

The Boy Scouts, Girl Guides, and similar organizations function on the island. One community group and several Nauruan district organizations are also active.

47TOURISM, TRAVEL, AND RECREATION

With its sandy beach, coral reef, tropical climate, and sea breezes, Nauru has the potential for the development of tourism. Visas are required for entry, but inoculations are not mandatory.

In 1999 the UN estimated that daily expenses required by travelers in Nauru was US$83 per day. Hotel costs account for 52% of this expenditure.

48FAMOUS NAURUANS

The best-known Nauruan is its first president, Hammer DeRoburt (1923–92), who led the Nauruan people to political independence; he was president from 1968 to 1976 and again from 1978 until his death in 1992 (except for a brief period in 1986).

49DEPENDENCIES

Nauru has no territories or colonies.

50BIBLIOGRAPHY

American University. *Area Handbook for Oceania*. Washington, D.C.: Government Printing Office, 1984.

Baker, Mark. "The Dying Island." Melbourne: *Saturday Extra*, February 28, 1987.

Carter, John (ed.). *Pacific Islands Year Book*. (15th ed.) Sydney: Pacific Publications, 1984.

Oliver, Douglas. *The Pacific Islands*. Garden City, NY: Doubleday, 1951.

Osborne, Charles, ed. *Australia, New Zealand and the South Pacific: A Handbook*. New York: Praeger, 1970.

Petit-Skinner, Solange. *The Nauruans*. San Francisco: Macduff Press, 1981.

Pollock, Nancy J. *Nauru Bibliography*. Wellington, N.Z.: Dept. of Anthropology, Victoria University of Wellington, 1994.

Skinner, Carlton. *Actualities in the Pacific: Micronesia: Nauru, the Remarkable Community*. Santa Cruz: Center for South Pacific Studies, University of California, 1977.

Trumbull, Robert. "World's Richest Little Isle." *New York Times Magazine*, March 7, 1982.

Viviane, Nancy. *Nauru: Phosphate and Political Progress*. Canberra: Australian National University Press, 1970.

Weeramantry, C. G. *Nauru: Environmental Damage under International Trusteeship*. New York: Oxford University Press, 1992.

Williams, Maslyn. *Three Islands*. Melbourne: British Phosphate Commissioners, 1971.

——— and Barrie Macdonald. *The Phosphateers*. Melbourne: Melbourne University Press, 1985.

NEPAL

Kingdom of Nepal

Nepal Adhirajya

CAPITAL: Kāthmāndu.

FLAG: The national flag consists of two red adjoining triangles, outlined in blue and merging at the center; the points are at the fly. On the upper triangle, in white, is a symbolic representation of the moon; on the lower triangle, that of the sun.

ANTHEM: The national anthem begins "May His Majesty, solemn and supremely valiant, be prosperous forever."

MONETARY UNIT: The Nepalese rupee (NR) is a paper currency of 100 paisa. There are coins of 1, 2, 5, 10, 20, 25, and 50 paisa and 1, 2, 5, 10, 20, 25, 50, and 100 rupees, and notes of 1, 2, 5, 10, 20, 50, 100, 500, and 1,000 Nepalese rupees. NR1 = $0.01456 ($1 = NR68.70) as of 31 March 2000.

WEIGHTS AND MEASURES: The metric system is in use, but some traditional Indian standards are also employed.

HOLIDAYS: National Unity Day, 11 January; Martyrs' Day, 30 January; Rashtriya Prajatantra Divas—National Democracy Day, 18 February; Nepalese Women's Day, 8 March; Navabarsha—Nepalese New Year's Day, mid-April; UN Day, 24 October; Queen Aishworya's Birthday, 7 November; Constitution Day, 9 November; National Day (King Birendra's Birthday), 28 December. Hindu and Buddhist religious holidays are based on the lunisolar calendar. Saturday is the general day of rest.

TIME: 5:45 PM = noon GMT.

¹LOCATION, SIZE, AND EXTENT

A comparatively narrow strip of territory dividing India from China, landlocked Nepal has an area of about 140,800 sq km (54,363 sq mi), extending 885 km (550 mi) SE–NW and 201 km (125 mi) NE–SW. Comparatively, the area occupied by Nepal is slightly larger than the state of Arkansas. In its length lie some 800 km (500 mi) of the Himalayan mountain chain. Nepal is bounded on the N by China and on the E, S, and W by India, with a total boundary length of 2,926 km (1,818 mi). Nepal's capital city, Kāthmāndu, is located in the central part of the country.

²TOPOGRAPHY

Nepal is made up of three strikingly contrasted areas. Southern Nepal has much of the character of the great plains of India, from which it extends. Known as the Terai, this region comprises both cultivable land and dense jungle, the latter being for the most part a game preserve inhabited by the wild elephant, tiger, and other typically South Asian fauna. Besides being a hunting ground, the forests are worked for their valuable timber. The Terai contains about one-third of Nepal's population and makes up about one-fourth of the total area. The second and by far the largest part of Nepal is formed by the Mahabharat, Churia, and Himalayan mountain ranges, extending from east to west. Their altitude increases toward the north, culminating on the Tibetan border in Mt. Everest (Sagarmatha in Nepali), standing amid other noble peaks. Three principal rivers originate from glaciers and snow-fed lakes, break southward through deep Himalayan gorges, and enter, respectively, the Karnali, Gandak, and Kosi basins. Flowing toward India, they become tributaries (as are all Nepal's rivers) of the Ganges system. The third area is a high central region, some 890 km (344 sq mi) in extent between the main Himalayan and Mahabharat ranges; this region is known as the Kāthmāndu

Valley, or the Valley of Nepal. Overlooked by mountains, the valley, with its fertile soil and temperate climate, supports a thriving agriculture. Here Kāthmāndu, the capital, is situated, with the foothill towns of Bhaktapur and Patan nearby. This is the only region of Nepal that has any considerable population density.

Eight of the world's highest mountains are situated in the Himalaya range on the Tibetan border. Triangulated in 1850, Mt. Everest was officially given the status of the world's highest peak in 1859. The summit (29,028 ft; 8,848 m) was reached for the first time on 29 May 1953 by Sir Edmund Hillary, a New Zealander, and Tenzing Norgay, a Sherpa guide.

³CLIMATE

Below the Kāthmāndu Valley and throughout the Terai, the climate is subtropical and, in the swamps and forests, extremely humid. The valley itself enjoys the temperate conditions generally found between altitudes of 1,200 and 3,400 m (4,000–11,000 ft). At 1,300 m (4,300 ft) above sea level, the elevation of Kāthmāndu, the rainy season lasts from June to October; 80% of annual precipitation falls during this monsoon season. Colder weather follows, lasting until the middle of March, when the warm season begins. The warm season increases in intensity until broken by the rains, which account for precipitation of about 150 cm (60 in) annually. Temperatures in Kāthmāndu in January range from an average minimum of 2°C (36°F) to an average maximum of 18°C (64°F); the July range is 20–29°C (68–84°F). Northward of the Kāthmāndu Valley, a subalpine zone continues to altitudes of about 4,300 m (14,000 ft); above that elevation, the country is covered with snow during the long winter, and extreme cold is experienced in the upper Himalayas.

[4]FLORA AND FAUNA

The wide range of climate accounts for correspondingly marked contrasts in flora and fauna between different regions of the country. In the south, the sal (the wood of which is used for railroad ties), sisu, and other subtropical trees are abundant in forests; in the extreme north, junipers are seen even at the altitude of the glacial moraines. Many kinds of conifers also exist in the alpine zone, along with the yew, various hollies, birch, dwarf rhododendrons, and other alpine flora. At temperate altitudes are found the oak and maple.

Dominant in the Langtang Valley are the chir pine, willow, alder, and evergreen oak. Blue pine and silver fir are frequent in the subalpine zone, which also supports tree rhododendrons—magnificent plants often reaching a growth of 12 m (40 ft). Ground orchids, lilies, yellow and blue poppies, and crimson anemones are prevalent in central Nepal. The profusion of wild flowers extends to very high altitudes; at 5,200 m (17,000 ft), several varieties of primula, pink and white cotoneaster, and white erica have been gathered, along with many kinds of alpine mosses and ferns.

The tiger, hyena, and jackal still exist in southern Nepal, although in decreasing numbers. Rhesus monkeys and a variety of other small jungle mammals and rodents are common. At middle altitudes are found the black bear, several species of cats, squirrel, hare, deer, and antelope. Higher in the mountains, wild sheep and goats, marmots, and a species of tailless mouse-hare are numerous. Small black spiders were found at 6,900 m (22,500 ft) on rocky ledges traversed by the Mt. Everest expedition of 1953. Birds of Nepal include the green finch, dove, woodpecker, nuthatch, warbler, flycatcher, bulbul, and other familiar species. At about 2,700 m (9,000 ft) are found the hill partridge, pheasant, yellow-backed sunbird, minivet, and many of the flowerpeckers; the redstart, pipit, wagtail, snow pigeon, snowcock, and golden eagle thrive in both the alpine and subalpine zones.

[5]ENVIRONMENT

Nepal's environment has suffered the effects of agricultural encroachment, deforestation and consequent soil erosion, and contamination of the water supply. Between the mid-1960s and the late 1970s, forestland declined from 30% to 22% of the total area, mainly because of the felling of timber for firewood, which supplies over 90% of Nepal's fuel requirements. Moreover, it is estimated that erosion causes the loss of about 240 million cu m of topsoil each year. All of Nepal's forests were nationalized in 1957, but reforestation efforts have been minimal. A forest conservation program, begun in 1980, includes the establishment of village tree nurseries, free distribution of seedlings, and provision of wood-burning stoves of increased efficiency. By 1985, however, deforestation averaged 324 sq mi per year, while reforestation was only 4,000 hectares (9,900 acres) per year. An additional 4.4% of forest and woodland were lost between 1983 and1993. The FAO estimates that at the present rate of depletion, the forests will be virtually wiped out by 2015.

Air and water pollution are significant environmental problems in Nepal. According to United Nations sources, the nation produces 18,000 tons of carbon monoxide and 3,300 tons of hydrocarbons per year. Roughly one-third of the nation's city inhabitants and two-thirds of all rural dwellers do not have pure water, and the use of contaminated drinking water creates a health hazard. Untreated sewage is a major pollution factor: the nation's cities produce 0.4 million tons of solid waste per year.

In 1994, 22 of Nepal's mammal species and 20 of its bird species were endangered, as well as 33 plant species. Species classified as endangered in Nepal include the snow leopard, tiger, Asian elephant, pygmy hog, great Indian rhinoceros, Assam rabbit, swamp deer, wild yak, chir pheasant, and gavial.

[6]POPULATION

The population of Nepal in 2000 was estimated at 24,920,211. An estimated 3.6% of the population is 65 years of age or older. The projected population for the year 2005 is 28,173,000, assuming a crude birthrate of 33 per 1,000 population and a death rate of 9 resulting in a natural rate of change of 2.4% for the period 2000–2005. The population rate of change between 1995 and 2000 was 2.5%. The population density in 1998 was 160 per sq km (414 per sq mi).

Population distribution is uneven, with about 45% of all Nepalese concentrated in the hilly central region, 47% in the fertile Terai plain, and only 8% in the mountains. The government seeks to reduce the population growth rate through social, cultural, economic, and educational reforms, as well as child health and family planning programs. It was estimated that only 12% of the population lived in urban areas in 2000, down from 14% in 1995. The capital city, Kathmandu, had a 2000 population of 533,000. Biratnāgar (130,129) and Patan (117,203) are the other chief towns. Nepal's next census was scheduled to take place in 2001.

[7]MIGRATION

Nearly 20,000 Tibetans arrived in Nepal between the Chinese annexation of Tibet in 1959 and 1989.

Hundreds of thousands of Nepalese were believed to be working in India in the 1980s, and over 100,000 Indians were working in Nepal, particularly in the garment industry and on the building of highways.

An influx of Bhutanese refugees into Nepal began in late 1991 and peaked in 1992; the flow of new arrivals has slowed since 1997. As of May 1997, there were 91,000 refugees and asylum seekers from southern Bhutan. As of September 1999, there were 96,000 Bhutanese in seven refugee camps in eastern Nepal. In 1999, the net migration rate was zero.

[8]ETHNIC GROUPS

Nepal consists of two primary ethnic elements: Mongoloids, who migrated to Nepal by way of Tibet, Sikkim, Assam, and northern Bengal; and Indo-Aryans, who came from the Indian plains and from the sub-Himalayan hill areas to the west of Nepal. There are also small remnants of Dravidian tribes. Bhotes, of Tibetan origin, are the principal occupants of northern Nepal. In the central valley, Newars and Murmis predominate, the former being responsible for most of the agriculture and trade. Less numerous groups include Gurungs and Magars in west-central Nepal and Kirantis and Rai in the east. Sherpas, a Himalayan people, have become well known as guides for mountain-climbing expeditions.

[9]LANGUAGES

Nepali is the official language, although some 20 different languages divided into numerous dialects are spoken. Nepali is the mother tongue of about 58% of the population and is the language for most intertribal communication; it is used in government publications and has been the language of most of the written literature since the Gurkha unification of Nepal. More than 11% of the people speak Maithili as their first language, 7.6% Bhojpuri, 4% Tharu, and about 3% Newari and Tamang each. Except in primary schools, where children are taught in their own language, Nepali is the medium of instruction. English is taught as a second language in secondary schools and colleges and is widely understood in business and government circles.

[10]RELIGIONS

Although the royal family is Hindu—as is, nominally, about 90% of the population—Hinduism and Buddhism, the latter practiced

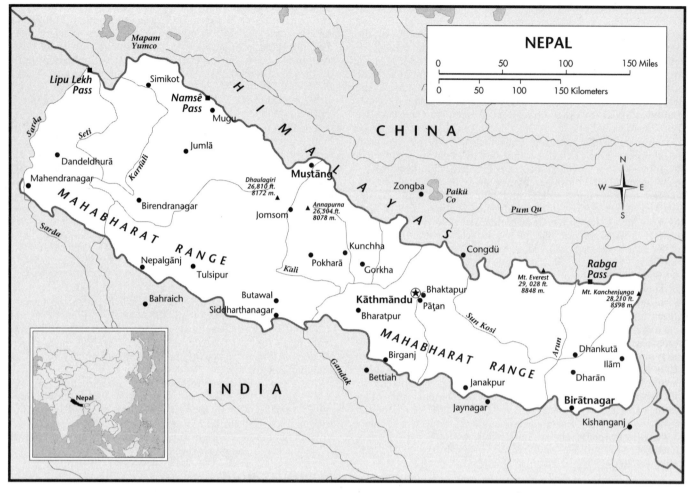

See continental map: **LOCATION:** 26°20′ to 30°16′N; 80°15′ to 88°15′E. **BOUNDARY LENGTHS:** China, 1,078 km (670 mi); India, 1,593 km (990 mi).

by about 5% of the population, exist side by side in Nepal and to some extent are intermingled. The importance of both in the national life is everywhere manifest; more than 2,700 temples and shrines have been counted in the Kāthmāndu Valley alone, while innumerable others are scattered along trails and roads extending to the most distant mountain passes. Bodhnath and Shambunath are famous Buddhist temples. The ancient temple of Chandra-higiri is dedicated to both religions. The Baghmati River, flowing through central Nepal, is considered sacred and is visited by pilgrims, as are certain mountains and lakes. Muslims constitute about 3% of the population. Minorities, including Christians, Baha'is, and Jains, constitute the remaining 2% of the population. The constitution forbids proselytizing.

11TRANSPORTATION

Nepal's ratios of road mileage to area and to population are among the lowest in the world, and the principal means of land transport is by porters with pack animals. The main highways are the 190-km (118-mi) road that penetrates the Kāthmāndu Valley, connecting it with the Indian border; the 87-km (54-mi) road between Kāthmāndu and Kodari on the Tibetan (Chinese) border, which was severely damaged by flooding in late 1982 and was later rebuilt with Chinese assistance; the 862-km (536-mi) east–west Mahendra Highway; and the 200-km (124-mi) Kāthmāndu-Pokhara highway, which is being extended to Surkhet. In all, Nepal had 7,700 km (4,785 mi) of roadway in 1996, of which 3,196 km (1,986 mi) were paved.

Nepal had a total of 101 km (63 mi) of railways in 1998. A narrow gauge railway, opened in 1927, runs from Jayanagar, in India, to Janakpur, a distance of 52 km (32 mi), of which 10 km (6 mi), running from Raxaul, India, to the frontier town of Birganj, is government owned. An electrically driven ropeway, inaugurated in 1925 and improved with US aid in 1962, carries 25 tons an hour a distance of 43 km (27 mi), to a height of nearly 1,400 m (4,500 ft) from Hetaura to Kāthmāndu.

Much of Nepal is easily accessible only by air. In 1998 there were 45 airports, of which 5 had permanently surfaced runways. The leading air terminal is Tribhuwan airport at Kāthmāndu, which can handle medium-sized jets. Domestic flights are operated by the Royal Nepal Airlines Corp., which also schedules flights to Great Britain, Germany, India and eight other Asian countries. In 1997, 755,000 passengers were carried on scheduled domestic and international airline flights.

12HISTORY

Fact, myth, and legend are intertwined in Nepal's historical literature, which, in the Vamshavali, traces the origins of the country in the distant past when Nepal was allegedly founded by Ne-Muni and derived its name from this source. A reliable chronology can be established only after the conquest of Nepal by Harisinha-deva, rajah of Simraun in about 1324. Under the Malla dynasty, Nepal was administered in four separate states: Banepa, Bhadgaon (now Bhaktapur), Kantipur (modern Kathmandu), and Lalitpur (now Pātan).

Prithwi Narayan Shah, the ruler of Gorkha, a small principality west of Kathmandu, established the modern kingdom of Nepal in 1768 by incorporating the Kathmandu Valley into his domain and unifying with it many small independent principalities and states. Under his descendants, most of the present boundaries of Nepal were established and Hinduism was introduced from India as the official religion.

Nepal came in contact with the influence of larger powers outside South Asia in the late 18th century as a consequence of the British East India Company's conquest of India to its south and a trade dispute with Tibet that led to a Nepalese confrontation with China. Peace was imposed by China in 1792, after Chinese forces had invaded, then withdrawn from Nepal. In the same year, a commercial treaty was ratified between Britain and Nepal. Relations with British in India remained peaceful until 1814 when a border dispute led to inconclusive hostilities between Nepal and the British East India Company. When the fighting ended two years later, Nepal's independence was preserved in an agreement in which Nepal yielded a large piece of territory to the Company on its southern border and agreed to the establishment of a permanent British resident at Kathmandu.

The 1816 agreement (reaffirmed by a formal treaty of friendship between Nepal and Great Britain in 1923) also laid the groundwork for more than a century and a half of amicable relations between Britain and Nepal. Included under the agreement was Nepalese approval for British recruitment of Nepalese Gurkha mercenaries for the British-officered Indian army. During the Indian Mutiny of 1857, Nepal's Rana prime minister sent some 12,000 additional Nepalese troops in support of British garrisons; he also offered troops to US President Abraham Lincoln in 1866 during the US civil war. Over the years, the Gurkha regiments serving in the British Indian army (and after 1947 under both Indian and British flags) won renown for their bravery, skill, and endurance—in Afghanistan in 1879 and Tibet in 1904, in Europe, Asian, and Africa in the 20th century's two world wars, in the UN action in the Belgian Congo in the 1960s, in India's conflicts with China and Pakistan, and in 1982, in Britain's conflict with Argentina over the Falkland Islands.

In 1846, Shumshere Jung Bahadur (Rana) became Nepal's de facto ruler, banishing the king and ruling as regent for the king's minor heir. The prime ministership became a hereditary office in his Rana family, not unlike the Tokugawa Shogunate in Japan, ruling successively until 1951. Following the end of World War II, the termination of British rule on the South Asian subcontinent in 1947 caused deep stirrings of change in Nepal. Resentment grew against the autocratic despotism of the Ranas, who—as regents— had kept successive monarchs virtual prisoners. A political reform movement, begun in 1946 with the founding of the Nepali Congress Party on the model of the Indian Congress Party, won the support of King Tribhuvana Bir Bikram Shah, but in a power struggle in 1950, the king was forced to flee from the Ranas to India. With Indian support, insurgents began operations against the Rana government until, with the mediation of Indian Prime Minister Nehru, a political compromise was reached that returned the king to Kathmandu and ended a century of hereditary Rana family rule. By late 1951 a new government took office, headed by Matrika Prasad Koirala, with his brother, a co-founder of the Nepali Congress Party (NC).

Political life in Nepal in the years since the restoration of the monarchy in 1951 has been dominated by the struggle between the monarchy and the country's political elements to define the terms under which they will co-exist and bring the country into the modern world. Six different cabinets, each lacking popular support and riddled with dissension, held office in rapid succession between 1951 and 1957, and in 1957-58, King Mahendra Bir Bikram Shah, who had succeeded to the throne upon the death of his father in 1955, ruled directly for a period of months. In April 1959, he promulgated a democratic constitution, providing for a constitutional monarchy, two houses of parliament, and a cabinet and prime minister responsible to the lower house, in the Westminster model. Bisweswar Prasad (B.P.) Koirala of the NC assumed office on 24 July 1959 as first prime minister under this constitution.

Less than 18 months later, on 15 December 1960, the king suspended the constitution, dissolved parliament, dismissed the cabinet, and again established his own government, this time with an appointed council of ministers. He ruled directly until April 1962 when he promulgated a new constitution establishing an indirect, non-party system of rule through a tiered system of panchayats (council) culminating in a National Panchayat. Five years later, after growing agitations and hit-and-run attacks by NC elements based in India, the king—again under Indian pressure—promulgated a series of amendments introducing gradual liberalization.

In January 1972, Mahendra died suddenly and was succeeded by his 27-year-old son, Birendra Bir Bikram Shah Dev. The young monarch, who had attended Harvard University in the United States, was committed to maintaining the authority of the monarchy while keeping Nepal on the course of gradual political and social reform set by his father. Student demonstrations in early 1979 led him to call for a national referendum on whether to continue the panchayat system or create a more conventional multi-party system. With the king promising further liberalization, the existing panchayat system was endorsed by 55% of the voters in May 1980, and later that year, the king's subsequent constitutional amendments established direct elections and permitted the Panchayat, not the king, to choose the prime minister. The king's failure to lift the ban on political parties led party members—ineffectively—to boycott the elections of 1981 in which Surya Bahadur Thapa, a former civil servant who had become prime minister in 1979, was reaffirmed in June 1981 and continued in office until 1983 when he was replaced by Lokendra Bahadur Chand following the government's loss of its majority on an opposition "no confidence" motion.

In non-party elections to the National Panchayat in May 1986, again in the face of a major party boycott, a majority of the incumbents were defeated, and Marich Man Singh Shrestha became prime minister. Most new members were opponents of the panchayat system, foreshadowing a new struggle between the king and his legislators. By early 1990, the NC and the United Leftist Front (ULF), a Communist alliance of seven parties, again went to the streets, organizing agitations that forced the king to make further constitutional changes in April; included were an end to the ban on political parties and their activities. The king dissolved the National Panchayat and appointed NC president Krishna Prasad Bhattarai interim prime minister, who was assisted by a cabinet made up of members of the NC, the ULF, independents, and royal appointees. A Constitutional Reforms Commission produced a new constitution in November 1990 that ended the panchayat era and restored multi-party democracy in a constitutional monarchy. In May 1991, the first openly partisan elections in 32 years were held, resulting in an NC majority in the new House of Representatives which chose Girija Prasad Koirala as prime minister.

Nepal has had ten prime ministers in the ten years since a multi-party democracy was established in 1990. The latest government, which took office in March 2000, is led by Giriraj Prasad (G. P.) Koirala. A Nepali Congress party veteran, the 75 year-old Koirala holds the office of prime minister for the 4th time in his career. Koirala engineered the downfall of his predecessor, the NC's K. P. Bhattarai, by splitting his own party. Similar tactics by Koirala in 1994 had resulted in the formation of a short-lived minority Communist government by the UML (Unified Marxist-Leninist) Party.

The personal ambitions of its political leaders rather than policy differences seems to drive politics in Nepal, and virtually all post-1991 governments have followed the same domestic agenda. The only significant exception to this politics as usual mindset is the problem posed by the "people's war" launched by several Maoist organizations in the central-western hill districts of Nepal in 1996. With its aims being the removal of both the monarchy and the multi-party political system, this movement continues, in early 2000, to stage deadly attacks on police and civilian targets. This, along with the dismal performance of the economy in recent years, remains the main items concerns of the government's domestic policies.

In the area of foreign policy, Nepal has remained generally nonaligned, maintaining friendly relations with China and with India, despite efforts to minimize traditional Indian influence and the occasional clash of policies on matters of relating to trade. In 1961, Nepal signed an agreement with China (which had earlier absorbed Tibet) defining the boundary between the two countries along the traditional watershed. Nepal was uninvolved in the 1962 hostilities between India and China on portions of the border to the east and west of Nepal. One result of this conflict however, was India's occupation of Kalapani, a border region of northwestern Nepal which, as of May 2000, was still a matter of dispute with India. In January 1999, however, Nepal and India renewed their bilateral Transit Treaty which governs commerce across the Indo-Nepalese border and provides Nepal access to the port facilities of Calcutta. Nepal also has pursued friendly relations with the great powers and has been the recipient of economic aid from India, the US, the former USSR, and the World Bank.

13GOVERNMENT

The 1990 constitution, Nepal's third (with variations) since 1951, established a constitutional monarchy in which the legislature consists of the king and two houses of parliament, the lower house called the House of Representatives and the upper house, the National Council. The House of Representatives has 205 members elected to terms of five years; at least 5% of the contestants from every party must be women. The National Council has 60 members, 35 of whom—including 3 women—are elected by the House of Representatives. Suffrage is universal at 18 years of age.

The National Council is a permanent body, retiring one-third of its members every two years in elections that take place in May of even-numbered years. The king appoints 10 of the 60 members in the National Council.

Nepal's Supreme Court Chief Justice is appointed by the King on recommendation of the Constitutional Council. The Supreme Court has recently ruled that the Parliament may not be dissolved if a new government can be formed by members of an existing house.

For development purposes, the country is also divided into 5 development regions by geography, i.e. Eastern, Central, Western, Mid-Western, and Far-Western, each of which serve also as a parliamentary constituency, electing three members of the lower house. In 1992, the government undertook a reform of the civil service, lowering the age of retirement from 60 to 58, committing itself to reducing its overall size by 25% by 1993, and engaging in wholesale dismissals of those with 20 or more years of service.

The King is Birendra Bir Bikram Shah Dev, the descendent of an unbroken Rajput line going back to more than 200 years. Prime Minister Girija Prasad Koirala was sworn into office by King Birendra on 20 March 2000.

14POLITICAL PARTIES

The 1962 constitution originally prohibited the formation of political parties and associations, even though political groups continued to exist and operate underground, at times on a quasi-legal basis. Parties were legalized in 1990 and now operate freely in Nepal's multi-party constitutional monarchy. The main party through Nepal's modern history—providing nearly all of the country's prime ministers even when the ban on parties prohibited party activity—is the Nepali Congress Party (NC). Inspired by the socialist wing of the Indian National Congress and founded by the Koirala brothers, M.P. and B.P., in 1946, the party led Nepal's first democratic government in 1959. Most of its leaders were imprisoned during the 1960s, but with Indian help, the party operated from India, mounting hit-and-run attacks and maintaining an underground presence in Nepal.

The NC leadership led the opposition to King Mahendra's tiered panchayat system of indirect government. Although NC leaders called for a boycott of the May 1986 elections to the National Panchayat, 1,547 candidates ran for office, and only 40 of the previously elected members retained their seats. After these elections, a Democratic Panchayat Forum (DPF) was formed by NC members to mobilize voters on a non-party basis to counter the influence in local elections of the Communist Party of Nepal (CPN), whose members had won 16 seats in the National Panchayat.

The communist movement in Nepal has been severely fragmented for years by personal and ideological schisms, some of them occasioned by splits and the loss of orthodoxy in the communist movement worldwide in the 1960s and 1980s. Operating for electoral and agitational purposes in the 1980s as the United Leftist Front (ULF), the Communist Party (CPN) and its several communist allies have since split, fragmenting the movement into a number of splinter parties but leaving the CPN, now reassembled as the United Marxist-Leninists (UML) as the leading opposition party in the parliament. The UML returned 68 members to parliament in the 1999 elections.

In 2000, the prime minister was Girija Prasad Koirala, whose Nepali Congress party controlled 110 seats in the 205-member lower house of the parliament.

15LOCAL GOVERNMENT

For centuries, the heads of petty principalities within Nepal exercised local judicial, police, and other powers. Under the panchayat reforms introduced in 1962, the country was divided into 14 zones, which in turn were divided into 75 districts. The zones were directly administered by commissioners appointed by the central government, and the zonal panchayats were executive bodies elected from the 11-member panchayats at the district level, the members of which were in turn selected from village and town panchayats. Each of the 3,600 villages with populations of more than 2,000 and each of the 33 towns with populations over 10,000 also had an 11-member panchayat, as well as its own local assembly.

The country remains divided into 14 zones (headed by appointed commissioners) and 75 districts (under the charge of district officers responsible for law and order, collecting revenues, and setting development priorities); municipal councils and district development committees are directly elected.

16JUDICIAL SYSTEM

Each district has a court of first instance, civil and criminal, as well as a court of appeals and 14 zonal courts. There are five regional courts—at Kathmandu, Dhankuta, Pokhara, Surkhet, and Dipayal—to which further appeals may be taken. At the apex is the Supreme Court in Kathmandu, which is empowered to issue writs of habeas corpus and decide on the constitutionality of laws. The Court is composed of a chief justice, assisted usually by six other judges, with seven additional judges in reserve; all are appointed by the king. The Supreme Court is the court of last resort, but the King may grant pardons and suspend, commute or remit sentences of any court. There are separate military courts which generally deal only with military personnel. In 1992, the Supreme Court ruled that civilians may not be tried in the military courts.

The 1990 Constitution declared the independence of the judiciary. The Supreme Court has exercised considerable independence in practice, declaring provisions of the Citizenship Act of 1991 and parts of the Labor Act of 1992 unconstitutional. In 1995 the Constitutional Court also ruled that the dissolution of the Parliament at the request of a former primer minister was unconstitutional.

The 1990 Constitution affords a number of procedural safeguards for criminal defendants including the right to counsel and protection from double jeopardy and from retroactive application of laws.

There is no jury system. Special tribunals hear cases involving terrorism or treason under the Treason Act.

17ARMED FORCES

Nepal maintains a 46,000-member army which is adequate to its main role of backing civil authority within the country and providing occasional contingents for international peacekeeping units, like UNIFIL in Lebanon in the 1980s and the UNEF in Sinai in the 1970s. The force is predominantly made up of hardy hill people, generally known as gurkhas, who account for most of the regulars organized in 7 infantry brigades, 44 independent infantry companies, and several independent brigades. They also predominate in the police force of 40,000. The army maintains 14 air transports and helicopters. In 1996–97, Nepal spent $44 million on defense or about 1% of gross domestic product.

Under separate treaty arrangements going back to 1816, gurkhas of the same mountain stock (especially Magars, Gurungs, Rais, and Limpus) are recruited in Nepal by Great Britain and, since 1947, by the Republic of India. Under British and Indian flags, and with arms, training, and officers provided by their foreign recruiters, gurkhas are among the world's most renowned fighting men with extensive service in all parts of the globe in both world wars and several UN actions of this century.

18INTERNATIONAL COOPERATION

Nepal was admitted to UN membership on 14 December 1955 and is a member of ESCAP and all the UN nonregional specialized agencies except IAEA. It also belongs to the Asian Development Bank and G-77, is a signatory to the Law of the Sea, and has applied for membership in the WTO. Nepal joined the Colombo Plan group in 1952. In 1985, Nepal joined with six other Asian nations to form the South Asian Association for Regional Cooperation (SAARC); the secretariat is in Kāthmāndu.

19ECONOMY

Despite social and economic reforms begun in the 1950s, Nepal's per capita income was only $1,100 (PPP) in 1998, and general living standards are low. The economy is based on subsistence agriculture, which engages about 80% of the labor force but is inefficiently organized and limited by a shortage of arable land in relation to population. Eight development plans, extending from 1955 to 1992, have slowly built up the nation's infrastructure. Nevertheless, the industrial sector is still small and dominated by traditional handicrafts, spinning and weaving, and similar occupations. Growth in medium-scale and cottage industry-based production of carpets and garments for export, expanding tourism, and some government-promoted development of heavy industry sustained an average GDP growth rate of over 5% from 1980–88. In 1989/90, Nepal weathered a major trade and transit dispute with India, maintaining a GDP growth rate of 2%, despite the potentially debilitating tariffs suddenly placed on trade with its largest import supplier and external market.

Nepal's economic potential is by no means insignificant. Kāthmāndu Valley and the Terai zone are fertile areas; there is great forest wealth, including valuable medicinal plants such as pyrethrum, belladonna, and ipecac; deposits of several minerals are known to exist; and swift Himalayan rivers offer great possibilities for hydroelectric development.

The principal challenge for the Nepalese is to provide for a rising and unequally distributed population and to achieve material progress without irrevocably depleting the environmental resource base. Structural adjustment measures initiated in 1989 have reduced the regulation of industry and imports, and are supported by similar liberalization in India, to which Nepal's economy is closely tied. However, aggregate economic growth remained sluggish during the early 1990s. GDP growth declined from 4.6% in 1990/91 to only 2.1% in 1991/92, due in large part to declining agricultural output following poor weather. GDP growth averaged an annual rate of 5% between 1988 and 1998. International actors fund more than 60% of Nepal's development budget and account for more than 28% of total budgetary expenditures. In 1995 Nepal joined the South Asian Association for Regional Cooperation (SAARC) in the South Asian Preferential Trade Area, scheduling a free trade area by 2001.

20INCOME

The US Central Intelligence Agency (CIA) reports that in 1998 Nepal's gross domestic product (GDP) was estimated at $26.2 billion. The per capita GDP was estimated at $1,100. The annual growth rate of GDP was estimated at 4.9%. The average inflation rate in 1998 was 7.8%. The CIA defines GDP as the value of all final goods and services produced within a nation in a given year and computed on the basis of purchasing power parity (PPP) rather than value as measured on the basis of the rate of exchange. It was estimated that agriculture accounted for 41% of GDP, industry 22%, and services 37%.

The World Bank reports that for the same period per capita private consumption (in PPP terms) was $695. Private consumption includes expenditures of individuals, households, and non-governmental organizations. It was estimated that between 1990 and 1998 private consumption grew at an annual rate of 4.4%. Approximately 44% of household consumption was spent on food, 7% on fuel, 5% on health care, and 14% on education. The richest 10% of the population accounted for approximately 30% of household consumption and the poorest 10% approximately 3.2%.

21LABOR

As of 1995, about 80% of the population were subsistence farmers while handicrafts, porterage, trade, military service, industry, and government work engaged the remainder. As of 1998, the labor force was estimated to number about 11 million. Most agriculturists are peasant farmers, and there are many wage laborers, but only in the peak seasons. Among some tribes, women do most of the farm work, while in others, especially among strict Hindus, they do no farming at all. Many occupations are effectively restricted to certain castes, although the practice has been declared illegal.

Unions are allowed to organize and strike. The right of a union to strike is limited to nonessential services. About 20% of the workforce is covered by collective bargaining agreements.

Minimum wage rates and working conditions in the small industrial sector are set by the Nepal Factories and Factory Workers' Act of 1959, as amended. In 1997, the minimum wage was $22 per month for unskilled, $23 for semiskilled, and $25 for skilled workers in the organized industrial sector. Wages can be as low as 50% of the minimum in the informal economy and the agricultural sector. The 1990 Constitution grants the freedom to form and join unions and associations, and permits strikes except against public utilities.

22AGRICULTURE

In 1998, agriculture provided about 40% of GDP. Only about 19% of the land can actually be cultivated. Regional imbalance and lack of integration also hamper Nepal's agriculture. Although the country produces an overall exportable surplus of food grains, some areas of the country, particularly Kāthmāndu Valley and the hill areas, have a food deficit. Lack of transportation and storage facilities prevents the movement of food grains from the Terai to the hills, with the result that Nepal both exports and imports the same food items.

Agriculture has been hampered by the lack of irrigated land, by the small size of farms (an average of 4 hectares/10 acres), and by inefficient farming methods. Some of the arable land is still held free of taxation by a few large landowners and farmed by tenants, whose productivity is low. The government has officially abolished tax-free estates (birta), eliminated the feudal form of land tenure (jagira), set a limit on landholdings, and redistributed the extra land to farm tenants. Its economic plans also include the use of fertilizers, insecticides, improved seeds, and better implements; the extension of irrigation; and the construction of transportation and storage facilities.

Rice, Nepal's most important cereal, is grown on more than half the cultivated land, mainly in the Terai but also on every available piece of ground in the Kāthmāndu Valley during the monsoon season. In 1998, rice production totaled 3,641,000 tons. Production of maize, grown on the carefully terraced hillsides, was 1,476,000 tons in 1998; land under cultivation with maize was 25% of the area allotted to food grains. The output of wheat in 1998 was 1,030,000 tons; millet, 288,000 tons; and barley, 39,000 tons. Cash crops (with 1998 output) included sugarcane, 1,763,000 tons; potatoes, 972,000 tons; linseed, 25,000 tons; jute, 14,000 tons; and tobacco, 4,000 tons. Sugarcane, jute, and tobacco are the major raw materials for Nepal's own industries. Potatoes are grown in Ilam and fruit mainly in Dharan, Dhankuta, and Pokhara. Tea is also grown in Ilam and elsewhere. In 1997, exports of agricultural products totaled $67.6 million, while agricultural imports amounted to $194.4 million.

23ANIMAL HUSBANDRY

Livestock, adapted to many uses, forms an essential part of the economy. Livestock accounts for about 30% of gross agricultural output. In farm work, bullocks and asses are largely used. Herds of yaks, cows, and their hybrids, zobos, are grazed in the central valley and to some extent along the borders of the foothill jungles. A few hogs usually are kept on the larger farms. Sheep and goats are used for food and also as pack animals, particularly in the distribution of salt over the trade routes; the sheep also supply a valuable type of wool.

In 1998, Nepal had an estimated 7,025,000 head of cattle, 3,400,000 water buffalo, 870,000 sheep, 6,000,000 goats, and 725,000 hogs. Modern poultry farms are operated principally by the Newaris, who carry on most of the agriculture in the Kāthmāndu Valley. There were about 16 million chickens in 1998, when 12,000 tons of poultry meat were produced. Traditionally, butter and cheese are among the leading exports of Nepal. Livestock products in 1998 included an estimated 729,000 tons of buffalo milk, 319,000 tons of cow's milk, 21,000 tons of butter and ghee, and 1,000 tons of wool (greasy basis).

24FISHING

The commercial fish catch amounted to 23,206 tons in 1997 (up from 9,443 tons in 1986). In the Terai are many small fish ponds and several government fish farms. Common fish species are carp, gar, and murrel.

25FORESTRY

In 1995, forests covered an estimated 33.7% of Nepal's total land area. Timber cutting has been contracted out to private firms. About 97% of the 21.4 million cu m of roundwood cut in 1997 was for fuel.

In 1961, the government established a department of medicinal plants to encourage Nepal's commercially important herb exports. There are regional herbal farms at Kāthmāndu and Nepalgānj. There is also a royal research laboratory for drug analysis.

26MINING

Although mining in Nepal is an ancient occupation, the country's mineral resources have been little exploited. Mining and quarrying account for about 0.5% of GDP. Exports of mineral commodities are estimated to account for about 8% of Nepal's export earnings. There are known deposits of iron, copper, zinc, lignite, graphite, cobalt, mica, limestone, marble, talc, quartz, ceramic clays, and slate. A lead and zinc deposit near Lari supposedly has reserves of 2 million tons. Development plans include the encouragement of small-scale mining and provide for continuing mineral surveys. The Department of Mines and Geology, under the Ministry of Industry at Kāthmāndu, is the government agency responsible for implementing Nepal's mineral policy and carrying out prospecting and development. Copper mining activity has increased in recent years; production in 1997 amounted to 20 tons, up from 6 tons in 1987. Mineral production in 1997 included (in tons) limestone, 368,666; marble slaps, 769,400 (sq m); and cement, 360,000.

27ENERGY AND POWER

Although Nepal's hydroelectric potential is great and development has been rapid in recent years, the kingdom still lacks an adequate power supply with only 9% of the population having access to electricity in 1996. In 1998, total installed capacity was 292,000 kW; production (not including losses) was 1,170 million kWh, more than 95% of which was hydropower. The remainder was either imported from India or produced by diesel generators. India has joined with Nepal in the construction of hydroelectric and irrigation projects on the Kosi and Gandak rivers. China has helped build a 10-MW plant on the Kosi as well. India has also constructed a 14-MW hydroelectric station at Devighat, in central Nepal. A 60-MW hydroelectric project on the Kulekhani, funded by the IBRD, Kuwait, and Japan, has been completed. It is estimated that only about 1% of Nepal's hydroelectric potential had been activated as of 1999. There is an integrated grid system in central Nepal. In 1996 the World Bank cancelled financing for a proposed $760 million, 200 MW Arun III hydroelectric power project. However, as of late 1996, the Asian Development Bank was moving ahead on a 144 MW facility to be based on the Kaligandhaki river in central Nepal. As of 2000, other hydroelectric projects under way included the 750-MW West Seti project. Exploration for oil and natural gas deposits began in the mid-1980s. An exploration concession won by Texana Resources in 1998 will be the first such venture in almost a decade.

28INDUSTRY

Until the 1980s, modern industry was almost nonexistent; only 0.66% of Nepal's GDP was derived from industry in 1964/65. Since then, industrial development has been given emphasis in economic planning. Manufacturing as a percent of total GDP at current factor cost rose from 4.2% in 1980 to 6.1% in 1990 to 9.2% in 1995. Industrial output grew by an estimated 14.7% in 1994/95.

Aside from small-scale food processing (rice, wheat and oil mills), light industry, largely concentrated in southeastern Nepal, includes the production of jute goods, refined sugar, cigarettes, matches, spun cotton and synthetic fabrics, wool, footwear, tanned leather, and tea. The carpet, garment and spinning industries are the three largest industrial employers, followed by structural clay products, sugar and jute processing. Sugar production was 49,227 tons in 1995, jute goods, 20,1870 tons; and soap, 23,477 tons. That year, 14.7 million m of synthetic textiles and 5.06 million m of cotton textiles were produced. Industrial production from agricultural inputs included 20,800 tons of vegetable ghee, 16.76 million l of beer and liquor, 9 billion cigarettes, and 2,351 tons of tea.

Heavy industry includes a steel-rolling mill, established in 1965, which uses imported materials to produce stainless steel. During the 1980s, the government gave priority to industries such as lumber, plywood, paper, cement, and bricks and tiles, which make use of domestic raw materials and reduce the need for imports. Production by heavy industries in 1995 included 326,839 tons of cement and 95,118 tons of steel rods.

[29]SCIENCE AND TECHNOLOGY

The only advanced technology is that brought in under the various foreign aid programs. Foreign technicians provide training in cottage industries, and local workers are trained at the Cottage Industry Center in Kāthmāndu. In 1982, the Royal Nepal Academy of Science and Technology was established at Kathmandu to aid in socioeconomic development. The National Council for Science and Technology aims to formulate science and technology policy, promote scientific and technological research, coordinate research among ministries and Mehendra Sanskrit University, and disseminate information to the public. Tribhuvan University has faculties of science and technology, medicine, agriculture and animal science, engineering, and forestry. In 1987–97, science and engineering students accounted for 13% of college and university enrollments.

[30]DOMESTIC TRADE

For many Nepalese, local trade is a part-time activity, limited to such products as cigarettes, salt, kerosene, and cloth. Marketing centers are along the main trails and are supplemented by small local markets. Poor communications facilities make extensive domestic trade impractical.

Most shops are open from 10 AM to 8 PM, and government offices and banks from 10 AM to 5 PM. Saturdays are holidays.

[31]FOREIGN TRADE

Traditionally, Nepal's foreign trade was limited to Tibet and India. After 1956, Nepalese trading agencies were confined in Tibet to Xigaze, Gyirong, and Nyalam, with Lhasa, Xigaze, Gyangze, and Yadong specified as markets for trade. In 1980, however, Nepal and China agreed to open 21 new trade routes across the Tibetan frontier. Treaty arrangements with China strictly regulate the passage of both traders and pilgrims in either direction across the border. Up until 1989, treaty agreements between India and Nepal allowed for unrestricted commerce across 21 customs posts along the border, and duty-free transit of Nepalese goods intended for third countries through India. India remitted levies on most goods intended for Nepal, subject to the possibility of export controls being tightened by the Nepalese government to prevent such imports from leaking back into India for sale at lower than market rates. In 1989, a breakdown in the treaty renewal negotiations resulted in retaliatory actions and the replacement of previous arrangements with far less favorable relations for both sides. India's share of Nepali exports plummeted from 38% in 1986/87 to 9% in 1989/90. India's share of the country's imports declined by about one-half to

25%. Despite the sudden shock sustained by the Nepali economy overall, the signing of a new interim agreement in 1990 prevented a prolonged crisis, helping to fuel a robust recovery in export growth as exports increased by 28% in 1990/91 over 1989/90, and again by 35% in 1991/92.

Carpets and garments accounted for 85% of foreign exchange earnings in 1993/94, far surpassing timber, rice, and jute; major imports are machinery, transport equipment, textiles, chemicals, fertilizers, metal manufactures, and petroleum products.

As the export of manufactured goods has expanded since the mid-1980s Nepal has diversified its trading partners somewhat. Nepal's main export commodities in 1995 were carpets (51%) and clothes (37%). Other exports include leather (2.1%), oil seeds (0.8%), and jute goods (0.7%).

In 1995 Nepal's imports were distributed among the following categories:

Consumer goods	8.7%
Food	15.0%
Fuels	19.5%
Industrial supplies	30.8%
Machinery	12.8%
Transportation	5.1%

Principal trading partners in 1998 (in millions of US dollars) were as follows:

COUNTRY	EXPORTS	IMPORTS	BALANCE
India	146	440	-294
United States	115	22	93
Germany	110	24	86
Switzerland	4	30	-26
Japan	3	44	-41
Singapore	1	204	-203
Saudi Arabia	n.a.	31	
United Arab Emirates	n.a.	70	
Thailand	n.a.	28	
China (inc. Hong Kong)	n.a.	117	

[32]BALANCE OF PAYMENTS

Despite large annual trade deficits, Nepal usually maintains a fairly consistent surplus in its balance of payments. Unrecorded, informal exports to India lessen the significance of the trade deficit. Increasingly, tourism has become a significant source of revenue, and air service to Kathmandu was expanded in 1998. Foreign aid remains a significant revenue source, also.

The US Central Intelligence Agency reports that in 1997 the purchasing power parity of Nepal's exports was $394 million while imports totaled $1.7 billion resulting in a trade deficit of $1,306 million.

The International Monetary Fund (IMF) reports that in 1998 Nepal had exports of goods totaling $486 million and imports totaling $1,238 million. The services credit totaled $565 million and debit $196 million. The following table summarizes Nepal's balance of payments as reported by the IMF for 1998 in millions of US dollars.

Current Account		-63
Balance on goods	-753	
Balance on services	369	
Balance on income	19	
Current transfers	302	
Capital Account		...
Financial Account		213
Direct investment abroad	...	
Direct investment in Nepal	12	
Other investment assets	91	
Other investment liabilities		110
Net Errors and Omissions		130
Reserves and Related Items		-280

33BANKING AND SECURITIES

Nepal's first commercial bank, the Nepal Bank Ltd., was established in 1937. The government owned 51% of the shares in the bank and controlled its operations to a large extent. Nepal Bank Ltd. was headquartered in Kathmandu, and had branches in other parts of the country.

Nepal's domestic banking system consists of the Nepal Rastra (National) Bank (NRB), the central bank, with its commercial subsidiary, the Rastriya Banijya (National Commercial) Bank; the Nepal Bank, three commercial banks; and state-owned banks for industrial and agricultural development- the Nepal Industrial Development Corp. (NIDC) and the Agricultural Development Bank of Nepal (ADBN). In 1984, Nabil, or Nepal Arab Bank, a joint venture with the UAE, was established. The French Indosuez Bank followed in 1986. The Rastra Bank was inaugurated by King Mahendra in 1956 as the central banking institution, with a capital of NR10 million. Besides regulating the national currency, it issues notes of various denominations and assists in preparation of the government budget. The Rastra Bank may advance loans to industry if both the government and the bank consider the loan sound.

In May 1996, net foreign assets of government monetary authorities totaled $621.3 million. In 1994, the money supply, as measured by M2, totaled NR72,696 billion. A vast expansion of paper currency resulted from the progressive monetization of the Nepalese economy and from the decree making Nepalese currency the only legal tender, thus abolishing the old dual currency system under which both Indian and Nepalese rupees circulated freely. In May 1986, the 30-year direct link between the Nepalese and Indian rupees was ended. Since then, the Nepalese rupee has floated against a group of international currencies, including the Indian rupee.

Since 1984, the government has allowed foreign banks to open offices in Nepal. Citibank opened an office in November 1984 to deal with foreign currency loans and short-term and trade finance, and to provide electronic banking facilities. Brindlays has set up a joint venture with Nepal Bank. The Bank of Dubai has set up the Nepal Arab Bank with the aim of channelling funds from Arab countries for industry, agriculture, and trade.

In the last few years several new banks have received permission from the government to operate on a joint-venture basis and there has been rapid development of the financial sector as a result of the liberal economic policies adopted by the government. There has been a continuous increase in the number and size of banks, financial companies, and insurance companies. In 1999 the government announced plans to allow foreign branch banks to be licensed in Nepal and to develop legislature to allow offshore banking to operate in the country.

The Nepal Bank of Ceylon, the biggest bank opened in the private sector through joint investments, was inaugurated at Siddharthanaga on 14 October 1996. In mid-December 1996, General Finance Ltd. went public by issuing 8,000 shares at NRs100 each.

The Nepal Rastra Bank directed all commercial banks to raise their capital to a minimum of NRs500 million by July 2001.

The Securities Exchange Center (SEC) was set up in 1981 under the control of the NRB and the NIDC, as a first step to setting up an organized stock exchange.

A stock exchange was established in 1984 in Kāthmāndu. Since 1964, the government has issued several series of 6% and 7% development bonds. On 4 January 1997, the Nepal Stock Exchange (NSE) suspended the share transactions of 23 companies for four months. The move was made after the companies failed to pay their annual fees to the NSE. This is the latest in a series of problems besetting the bourse. Only 11 out of the 90 listed companies published notices for annual general meetings for 1996–97. In 1995–96, only three companies submitted income and expenditure accounts to the exchange.

34INSURANCE

The National Insurance Corp. is Nepal's sole insurer.

35PUBLIC FINANCE

For many years, government revenue was derived chiefly from privately owned land (amounting to about 30% of the country's area), customs duties, and forest and mining royalties. In 1955, however, because of increasing costs of development projects and administration, the government discarded the practice of adjusting the budgetary deficit by drawing on reserves and adopted a policy of raising additional revenue through taxation. Subsequently, a progressive income tax was introduced. Budget deficits grew steadily during the 1970s and 1980s, but were offset by foreign grants, domestic loans, foreign exchange borrowings, and transfers.

The US Central Intelligence Agency (CIA) estimates that in 1998 Nepal's central government took in revenues of approximately $560 million and had expenditures of $857 million. Overall, the government registered a deficit of approximately $297 million. External debt totaled $2.68 billion.

The following table shows an itemized breakdown of government revenues and expenditures. The percentages were calculated from data reported by the International Monetary Fund. The dollar amounts (millions) are based on the CIA estimates provided above.

REVENUE AND GRANTS	100%	560
Tax revenue	70.9%	397
Non-tax revenue	14.4%	81
Capital revenue	0.2%	1
Grants	14.5%	81
EXPENDITURES	100%	857
General public services	3.7%	32
Defense	4.5%	38
Public order and safety	4.3%	37
Education	13.6%	116
Health	6.5%	55
Social security	2.1%	18
Housing and community amenities	4.7%	40
Economic affairs and services	33.7%	289
Other expenditures	26.9%	231

36TAXATION

The principal sources of public revenues are customs tariffs, sales tax, and excise duties. A progressive income tax is levied, as well as a tax on income from industrial undertakings. Rent-free land is taxed on a modest scale. Registration taxes are levied on houses and land. In 1997 a new value-added tax was introduced to replace sales and excise taxes.

37CUSTOMS AND DUTIES

Exports and imports are subject to tariffs and surcharges, which combine to form the second most important source of revenue. Much potential revenue is lost, however, because of the open borders and untrained customs officers at the customs checkpoints. Indian imports receive preferential tariff treatment. In 1986, the government began to auction licenses for importing luxury goods. Critics of this policy complained that it led to increased smuggling and placed an economic burden on the Nepalese by raising the rates on such goods from 25% to 81%. Duties are on an ad valorem basis. In 1997 a value-added tax replaced sales and excise taxes on imports.

38 FOREIGN INVESTMENT

Foreign investment remains low and overwhelmingly dominated by Indian investors benefiting from the preferential trade regime. On 4 December 1996, Nepal and India signed a trade treaty that lifted all customs duties on Nepalese industrial products. Liberalization measures undertaken with structural reform, including a review of the Industrial Policy Act, are expected to attract more foreign investment in the future. Since 1994, however, a remote location, child-labor concerns, a communist government, an inadequate infrastructure, and a susceptibility to natural disaster have limited foreign investment. Investment that does come into the country tends to be limited to tourism and power production.

39 ECONOMIC DEVELOPMENT

Planned economic development began in 1953 with construction of roads and airfields and of irrigation projects to bring more acreage under cultivation. In 1956, these projects were integrated into a five-year plan (1956–61) to assist existing industries, revive and expand cottage industries, encourage private investment, and foster technological training. After a plan for three years (1962–65), declared successful by the government, had run its course, a new plan (1965–70) was drawn up. This five-year program, which aimed at a 19% increase in national income, was the first to be framed within the context of the panchayat system, which was to serve as an important medium of project administration. The fourth (1970–75) and fifth (1975–80) plans continued to emphasize infrastructural development, primarily in transportation, communications, electricity, irrigation, and personnel. The sixth development plan (1980–85) allocated nearly one-third of its total expenditure to agriculture and irrigation. However, money targeted for development projects was used for other purposes.

The objectives of the seventh plan (1986–90) were to increase production, create opportunities for employment, and fulfill basic needs. Of the total expenditure, 65% was to be used for investment, allocated as follows: agriculture, irrigation, and forestry, 30.6%; industry, mining, and electricity, 26%; transportation and communications, 17.7%; social services, 25.2%; and other sectors, 0.5%. Foreign aid was expected to fund about 70% of these projects.

The newly elected government in 1991 initiated a series of reforms affecting virtually all sectors of the economy. To streamline government investments in economic development, a list of priority development projects was drafted and public enterprises were transferred to private ownership, freeing government revenues for social sector projects, improved drinking water, and rural infrastructure development.

Nepal's ninth five-year economic plan, introduced in July 1997, emphasized agriculture, liberal economic policies, and hydropower projects.

40 SOCIAL DEVELOPMENT

The government maintains a countrywide village development service, which endeavors to meet the villagers' needs for food, clothing, shelter, health services, and education. Village development workers demonstrate improved methods of sanitation and health and teach the villagers to read and write. The Employee Provident Fund administers a program of old age, disability, and death benefits for government and corporate employees, funded by contributions from both employers and employees. Pensions are provided as a lump sum equal to contributions plus interest. Miners and employees of factories with 10 or more workers are protected by a workers' compensation program run by the Labor Department.

Women are subject to gender discrimination, especially in traditional rural areas. The present constitution has strengthened provisions protecting women, including equal pay for equal work, but few women work in the money economy. Women's inheritance and marriage rights have been strengthened in recent years. Discrimination against foreign spouses of Nepalese women was barred by a 1994 law. In 1998 legislation was introduced that would allow unmarried daughters to inherit parental property. As of 1999, 17 of 265 parliamentary seats were held by women.

The abduction of young girls to be taken to India to work as prostitutes is a serious problem. Human rights groups also claim that in Kathmandu, most prostitutes are under the age of 16.

Members of lower castes suffer from widespread discrimination and many are in positions of bonded labor. Senior positions in politics and the civil service are dominated by urban-oriented castes, such as the Brahmin and Chhetri.

41 HEALTH

Although protected by mountain barriers, Nepal is in frequent danger from epidemics, notably cholera. Japanese encephalitis is endemic in the Terai plain and inner Terai zone. Common afflictions are black fever (kala-azar), amoebic dysentery, eye diseases, typhoid, and venereal diseases. Malnutrition, contaminated water, and inadequate sanitation cause widespread health problems. Improved health programs in rural areas have helped control malaria, leprosy, and tuberculosis. In 1996, 61% of urban dwellers and 59% of rural dwellers had access to safe water. In 1997, immunization rates for children up to one year old were as follows: tuberculosis (96%); diphtheria, pertussis, and tetanus (78%); polio (78%); and measles (85%).

Nepal has a large number of drug addicts. Stringent amendments to the Narcotic Drug Control Act were adopted in 1986 in response to pressure from the US and UK.

The birth rate in 1999 was 35 per 1,000 people. Birth control was used by 21.8% of married women in 1991. The general mortality rate in 1999 was 10 per 1,000 people, and the average life expectancy was 58 years. Malnutrition is a common problem. Over half of all children under 5 were underweight in 1996. During the years 1989–1995 at least 70% of children under 5 were malnourished.

In 1994, there was 1 hospital bed per 4,281 inhabitants. Medical personnel in 1990 included 1,124 physicians, 19 pharmacists (in urban areas), 24 dentists (in urban areas), 601 nurses, and 2,380 midwives. In 1993, the population per physician was 16,634, and per nursing professional was 2,257. Most of the medical personnel work in the Kāthmāndu Valley, and health services elsewhere are in short supply. Traditional medicine and faith healing are still used frequently, especially in the hill districts. Public health care expenditures in 1995 were 1% of GDP.

The HIV-1 sero prevalence was 0.2 per 100 adults in 1997. There were only 48 AIDS cases reported in 1995.

42 HOUSING

In the Kāthmāndu Valley, village houses are made of stone or mud bricks, with thatched roofs and raised eaves. Elsewhere, houses are often made of bamboo and reeds. Most houses have two stories, but some contain only two rooms, a sleeping room and a room for cooking. The well-constructed houses of the Sherpas are generally built of stone and timber, roofed with wooden slats. About four out of five urban dwellings in Nepal are owner occupied. The latest available figures for 1980–88 show a total housing stock of 3.1 million units with 5.6 people per dwelling.

43 EDUCATION

The proportion of illiterate persons is declining and was estimated in 2000 at 58.6% of adults (males, 40.9%; females, 76.2%). After free primary education was introduced in 1975, school enrollment for children ages 6–11 increased from about one-fourth of the total to over one-half by the mid-1980s. By 1996, there were 22,218 primary schools with 3,447,607 pupils and 89,378 teachers. Secondary students numbered 1,121,335 and were instructed by 36,127 teachers in 1996.

Traditional schools (pathshalas) provide a classical education emphasizing languages. Gompas along the northern border train boys and men to become Buddhist religious leaders. English schools are modeled after those in India. Under a 1954 plan, a national school system with a single curriculum has been replacing the traditional schools, although English schools have increased.

In 1996, 105,694 students were enrolled in all higher level institutions.

44LIBRARIES AND MUSEUMS

The National Library in Lalitpur has 45,000 volumes. The Bir Library, founded in the 14th century, contains 15,000 manuscripts. Other important collections are maintained by the library of Tribhuvan University (163,000 volumes) and the Singh Darbar, Nepal-Bharat (41,000), and the British Council libraries, all in Kāthmāndu. The National Museum (1928) and the Natural History Museum (1975) are both in Kathmandu, along with a postage museum and the King Tribhuvan Memorial Museum. There is a Museum of Excavated Archeological Antiquities in Lalitpur and a woodworking museum housed in the Palace of Fifty-Five Windows in Bhaktapur.

45MEDIA

Postal, telephone, and telegraph services are operated by the government. Telephone service connects Kathmandu with Birganj on the Indian frontier, and another line links the capital with foothill towns in the eastern Terai. The telecommunications network includes a 5,000-telephone automatic exchange of over 90 radio relay stations, and an earth satellite station established with help from the UK in 1982. In 1996 there were an estimated 115,911 telephones in use, up from 18,000 in 1985 with the completion of a $56-million IDA project to consolidate the Nepal Telecommunications Corp. Radio Nepal, a commercial, semi-governmental network, broadcasts in Nepali and English on both short and medium wavelengths. Television was introduced into the Kathmandu Valley in 1986, and the Nepalese Television Corporation broadcasts about 23 hours a week. As of 1999 there were 88 AM radio stations, 1 FM station, and 6 television stations. In 1997, there were 37 radios and 4 television sets per 1,000 population.

Dailies, weeklies, and monthlies in Nepali, Newari, Hindi, and English are published mainly in Kathmandu. The largest daily newspapers (with 1999 circulations) are the *Nepali Gorkhapatra* (50,000), the *Nepali Hindi Daily* (50,000), *Samaya* (18,000), and the English-language *Rising Nepal* (12,000).

Though the constitution specifies that the government may not censor expression, including that of the press, the press is licensed by the government, and licenses have been suspended and individuals arrested for criticism of the monarchy or support of a political party.

Online access is extremely limited, with less than 1 Internet host per 1,000 population in 1998.

46ORGANIZATIONS

The leading commercial organization is the Nepal Chamber of Commerce. Professional organizations include the Nepal Medical Association and the Nepal Drivers' Association. Social organizations include the Nepal Women's Organization, the Nepal Youth Organization, the Nepal Peasants' Organization, the Nepal Children's Organization, and an organization for ex-servicemen.

47TOURISM, TRAVEL, AND RECREATION

In 1951, the government of Nepal reversed its long-standing policy and began to encourage visitors; before then, mountaineering expeditions had been permitted into the country only under severe official scrutiny and restraining regulations. For the first time in 1956, tourism was officially included among the country's major potential assets. There were approximately 422,000 foreign tourists by 1997, and receipts from tourism totaled $116 million. There were 13,084 hotel rooms with 25,638 beds and an occupancy rate of 50% in 1996.

For mountain trekkers, travel agencies in Kāthmāndu provide transportation to mountain sites, as well as Sherpa guides and porters. Tents, sleeping bags, and other mountain-climbing gear are available in Kāthmāndu. Travel is difficult; roads are generally poor.

In 1999 the UN estimated the cost of staying in Kathmandu at $124. Travel elsewhere in the country is significantly less expensive.

48FAMOUS NEPALESE

Buddhism, one of the world's great religions, is based on the teachings of Siddhartha Gautama, who became known as the Buddha ("Enlightened One"). He was born (traditionally about 624 BC but according to most modern scholars about 563 BC) in Lumbini, near Kapilavastu in the Terai, then part of India, and died at Kushinagara (traditionally about 544 BC but according to the modern view about 483 BC).

Amar Singh Thapa, Nepalese military leader of the 19th century and rival of Gen. David Ochterlony in the war between British India and Nepal, is a national hero. The two best-known Rana prime ministers were Sir Jung Bahadur Rana (1817–77) and Sir Chandra Shamsher Jang Rana (1863–1929). The most highly regarded writers are Bhanubhakta, a great poet of the 19th century, and the dramatist Bala Krishna Sama (Shamsher, b.1903).

King Mahendra Bir Bikram-Shah (1920–72), who introduced the partyless political system, based on the Nepalese tradition of the village panchayat (council), was succeeded on the throne by his son, King Birendra Bir Bikram Shah Dev (b.1945), who democratized the panchayat system. Well-known political leaders include the brothers Matrika Prasad Koirala (b.1912), head of the Nepali Congress Party and the first post-Rana prime minister of Nepal (1951–52 and 1953–55), and Bisweswar Prasad Koirala (1915–82), head of the Nepali Congress Party and the first elected prime minister of Nepal (1959–60).

World renown was gained for Nepal by a Sherpa porter and mountaineer, Tenzing Norgay (Namgyal Wangdi, 1914–86), who, with Sir Edmund Hillary, a New Zealander, ascended to the summit of Mt. Everest in 1953.

49DEPENDENCIES

Nepal has no territories or colonies.

50BIBLIOGRAPHY

Dastider, Mollica. *Religious Minorities in Nepal: An Analysis of the State of Buddhists and Muslims in the Himalayan Kingdom.* New Delhi, India: Nirala Publication, 1995.

Fisher, James F. *Sherpas: Reflections on Change in Himalayan Nepal.* Berkeley: University of California Press, 1990.

Gellner, David N., et al. (eds.) *Nationalism and Ethnicity in a Hindu Kingdom: The Politics of Culture in Contemporary Nepal.* Amsterdam, The Netherlands: Harwood, 1997.

Landon, Perceval. *Nepal.* New Delhi: Asian Educational Services, 1993.

Maskey, Govinda. *Social Life in Nepal: From Tradition to Modernity (1901–1925).* New Delhi, India: Anmol Publications, 1996.

Pradhan, Kumar. *The Gorkha Conquests: The Process and Consequences of the Unification of Nepal, with Particular Reference to Eastern Nepal*. Calcutta: Oxford University Press, 1991.

Savada, Andrea Matles (ed.). *Nepal and Bhutan: Country Studies*. 3rd ed. Washington, D.C.: Library of Congress, 1993.

Sever, Adrian. *Aspects of Modern Nepalese History*. New Delhi, India: Vikas Publishing House, 1996.

Shaha, Rishikesh. *Modern Nepal: A Political History, 1769–1955*. Riverdale, Md.: Riverdale Co., 1990.

Shrestha, Nanda R. *In the Name of Development: A Reflection on Nepal*. Lanham, Md.: University Press of America, 1997.

Shrivastava, L.P.S. *Nepal at the Crossroads*. New Delhi, India: Allied Publishers, 1996.

Thapa, Asoke K. *Bramu: A People in Transistion*. Kathmandu, Nepal: Walden Book House, 1996.

Thapa, N. B. and D. P. *Geography of Nepal*. Columbia, Mo.: South Asia Books, 1981.

Watkins, Joanne C. *Spirited Women: Gender, Religion, and Cultural Identity in the Nepal Himalaya*. New York: Columbia University Press, 1996.

Whelpton, John. *Nepal*. Santa Barbara, Calif.: Clio, 1990.

Zivetz, Laurie. *Private Enterprise and the State in Modern Nepal*. Oxford: Oxford University Press, 1992.

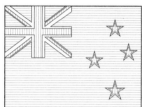

NEW ZEALAND

CAPITAL: Wellington.

FLAG: The flag has two main features: the red, white, and blue Union Jack in the upper left quarter and the four-star Southern Cross in the right half. On the blue state flag the stars are red outlined in white; on the red national flag, used by individuals or commercial institutions at sea, the stars are white.

ANTHEM: *God Save the Queen* and *God Defend New Zealand* have, since 1977, enjoyed equal status.

MONETARY UNIT: The New Zealand dollar (NZ$) is a paper currency of 100 cents; it replaced the New Zealand pound on 10 July 1967. There are coins of 5, 10, 20, and 50 cents and 1 and 2 dollars, and notes of 5, 10, 20, 50, and 100 dollars. NZ$1 = US$0.4941 (US$1 = NZ$2.024) as of 31 March 2000.

WEIGHTS AND MEASURES: Metric weights and measures are used.

HOLIDAYS: New Year's Day, 1 January; Waitangi Day, 6 February; Anzac Day, 25 April; Queen's Birthday, 1st Monday in June; Labor Day, 4th Monday in October; Christmas Day, 25 December; Boxing Day, 26 December. Movable holidays are Good Friday and Easter Monday. Each province has a holiday on its own anniversary day.

TIME: 12 midnight = noon GMT.

¹LOCATION, SIZE, AND EXTENT

Situated in the southwest Pacific Ocean, New Zealand proper, with a total area of 268,680 sq km (103,738 sq mi), consists of the North Island, covering 114,669 sq km (44,274 sq mi) including small islands nearby; the South Island, 149,883 sq km (57,870 sq mi); Stewart Island, 1,746 sq km (674 sq mi); and various minor, outlying islands. Comparatively, the area occupied by New Zealand is about the size of the state of Colorado. The Chatham Islands, lying 850 km (528 mi) E of Lyttelton, on South Island, have a land area of 963 sq km (372 sq mi). Other outlying islands have a combined area of 778 sq km (about 300 sq mi). New Zealand extends 1,600 km (994 mi) NNE–SSW and 450 km (280 mi) ESE–WNW. It has a total coastline of 15,134 km (9,404 mi).

New Zealand's capital city, Wellington, is located on the southern tip of North Island.

²TOPOGRAPHY

Less than one-fourth of the land surface of New Zealand lies below the 200-m (650-ft) contour. The mountain ranges in the North Island do not exceed 1,800 m (6,000 ft) in height, with the exception of the volcanic peaks of Egmont, or Taranaki (2,518 m/ 8,261 ft), Ruapehu (2,797 m/9,176 ft), Ngauruhoe (2,290 m/ 7,513 ft), and Tongariro (1,968 m/6,457 ft), the last three of which are still active. This volcanic system gives rise to many hot springs and geysers.

The South Island is significantly more mountainous than the North Island, but is without recent volcanic activity. The Southern Alps, running almost the entire length of the South Island from north to south, contain 19 peaks of 3,000 m (9,800 ft) or above, of which the highest is Mt. Cook or Aorangi, 3,764 m (12,349 ft). There are also several glaciers in the Southern Alps, the largest being the Tasman Glacier, 29 km (18 mi) long and 1 km (0.6 mi) wide. The rivers are mostly swift-flowing and shallow, few of them navigable. There are many lakes, those in the South Island being particularly noted for their magnificent mountain scenery.

³CLIMATE

New Zealand has a temperate, moist ocean climate without marked seasonal variations in temperature or rainfall. The prevailing winds are westerly, with a concentration of strong winds in the Cook Strait area. The generally mountainous nature of the country, however, causes considerable variation in rainfall (e.g., between the eastern and western sides of the Southern Alps), and, by preventing stratification of air into layers of different density, results in an absence of extensive cloud sheets and a consequent high percentage of sunshine. Mean annual temperatures at sea level range from about 15°C (59°F) in the northern part of the North Island to 12°C (54°F) in the southern part of the South Island. Mean annual rainfall ranges from around 300 cm (120 in) near Dunedin to more than 800 cm (315 in) in the Southern Alps.

⁴FLORA AND FAUNA

Like other regions separated from the rest of the world for a long period, New Zealand has developed a distinct flora. About 75% of the native flora is unique, and it includes some of the world's oldest plant forms. However, the flowering plants, conifers, ferns, lycopods, and other vascular tracheophytes that constitute much of the land vegetation do show affinities with plants of the Malayan region, supporting the theory of an ancient land bridge between the two regions. More than 250 species are common to both Australia and New Zealand. The Antarctic element, comprising more than 70 species related to forms in the flora of South America and the Southern Ocean islands, is of great interest to botanists. The kauri pine, now found only in parts of the North Island, for more than a century has been world famous for its timber. The rimu and the totara also are timber trees. Other handsome trees include the pohutukawa and other species of rata and kowhai. New Zealand flax, formerly of great importance in the Maori economy, is found in swampy places. Undergrowth in the damp forests consists largely of ferns, of which there are 145 species; they clothe most of the tree trunks and branches, and tree ferns form part of the foliage. Tussock grass occurs on all mountains above the scrub line and over large areas in the South Island.

Apart from seals and two species of bats, New Zealand has no indigenous land mammals. Some of the land mammals introduced to New Zealand have become pests, such as the rabbit, the deer, the pig (now wild), and the North American opossum. Sea mammals include whales and dolphins.

There is a great diversity of birds, some 250 species in all. Among the flightless birds the most interesting is the kiwi, New Zealand's national symbol and the only known bird with nostrils at the tip of the bill instead of at the base. Other characteristic birds are the kea, a bird of prey, and the tui, a beautiful songbird. All but one of the genera of penguins are represented in New Zealand. Several species of birds, the most famous being the Pacific godwit, migrate from breeding grounds in the Arctic Circle to spend spring and summer in New Zealand. There are many flightless insects and a diversity of small life forms.

5ENVIRONMENT

Because of its relatively small population, New Zealand's natural resources have so far suffered less from the pressures of development than have those of many other industrialized nations. Air pollution from cars and other vehicles is an environmental concern in New Zealand. The use of fossil fuels contributes to the problem. New Zealand's concern about the effects of air pollution on the atmosphere is, in part, due to the fact that the nation is among the world leaders in incidence of skin cancer. In 1992, New Zealand produced 26,179,000 million metric tons of carbon dioxide emissions from industrial sources, a per capita level of 7.58 metric tons. Water pollution is also a problem due to industrial pollutants and sewage. The nation has 95.3 cu mi of water, of which 44% is used for farming activity and 10% for industrial purposes. The nation's cities produce 2.3 million tons of solid waste per year. Another environmental issue in New Zealand is the development of its resources—forests, gas and coal fields, farmlands—without serious cost to natural beauty and ecological balance. Two-thirds of the nation's forests have been eliminated. Principal governmental agencies with environmental responsibilities are the Commission for the Environment (established in 1972), an investigatory and advisory agency that audits environmental impact reports; the Environmental Council (1970), an advisory body that publishes information on environmental issues; and the Nature Conservation Council (1962), an advisory body that may inquire into the environmental effects of proposed public or private works projects and is free to make its reports and recommendations public.

In 1994, 1 of New Zealand's mammal species and 26 types of birds were endangered, as well as 232 plant species. Native species have been seriously endangered by species introduced from outside the country. Endangered or extinct animal species in New Zealand include the takahe, two species of petrel (black and New Zealand Cook's), the black stilt, orange-fronted parakeet, kakapo, and Codfish Island fernbird. Extinct are the bush wren, South Island kokako, and New Zealand grayling. Endangered species on the Chatham Islands were the Chatham Island petrel, magenta petrel, Chatham Island oystercatcher, New Zealand plover, Chatham Island pigeon, Forbes's parakeet, and Chatham Island black robin.

6POPULATION

The population of New Zealand in 2000 was estimated at 3,697,850. An estimated 11.3% of the population is 65 years of age or older. The projected population for the year 2005 is 3,868,000, assuming a crude birthrate of 13 per 1,000 population and a death rate of 8, resulting in a natural rate of change of 0.6% for the period 2000–2005. The population rate of change between 1995 and 2000 was 1.1%. The population density in 1998 was 14 per sq km (36 per sq mi), with nearly 75% of the population living on the North Island.

It was estimated that 87% of the population lived in urban areas in 2000, up from 83% in 1980. The two largest of the urban areas are Auckland (1,014,000 in 2000), and Wellington, the capital (326,000). Other large cities include Christchurch (307,179), Dunedin (109,503), Hamilton (148,625), Palmerston North (70,951), and Tauranga (70,803).

7MIGRATION

Between 1946 and 1975, New Zealand experienced a net gain from migration of 312,588; from 1975 to 1990, however, there was a net outflow of 110,877. Under new immigration policy guidelines issued by the government in May 1974, immigrants are selected according to specific criteria, such as job skills, health, character, age, and family size. The same restrictions now apply to British subjects as to others who wish to take up permanent residence. Citizens of Fiji, Tonga, and Western Samoa may be admitted under special work permits for up to 11 months. About 7,000 Indochinese refugees settled in New Zealand between 1975 and 1990. The number of asylum applications increased from 712 in 1995 to 1,964 in 1998. New Zealand is one of only ten countries in the world with an established resettlement program, with an annual quota of 750 as of 1999.

Australia is the preferred destination for New Zealanders departing permanently or long term. In 1999, the net migration rate was 3.01 migrants per 1,000 population.

8ETHNIC GROUPS

About 74.5% of the population is classified as New Zealand European; 9.7% Maori; 4.6% are considered other European; 3.8% Pacific Islander; and 7.4% Asian and others. The most significant minority group, the indigenous Maori people, is a Polynesian group with a distinctive culture and a well-ordered social system.

Although the Treaty of Waitangi (1840) guaranteed to the Maori people all the rights and privileges of British subjects and full and undisturbed possession of their lands, these guarantees were often overlooked. As a result of war and disease, the Maori population declined to fewer than 42,000 by 1896. At the turn of the century, however, a group calling itself the Young Maori Party began to devote itself to the promotion of Maori welfare and status. In the 20th century, and especially after World War II, a more enlightened government policy prevailed.

In the early 1990s there were 321,396 Maoris or part-Maoris (those reporting a Maori ancestry of 50% or more). In all, there were 511,947 people with Maori ancestry, representing 14.9% of the census population. About 90% live on North Island. Although Maori acquisition and development of land have been promoted, there is not enough land to afford a livelihood to more than about 25% of the Maori population. Thus, many Maoris leave their tribal villages to seek job opportunities in the towns and cities. By 1981, four-fifths of all Maoris lived in urban areas.

During recent years, increasing numbers of migrants from New Zealand's former colonies and from other Pacific islands have come to New Zealand. Many of these, especially the Cook Islanders, are Polynesians having ethnic and linguistic ties with the Maoris.

9LANGUAGES

English is the universal language, although Maori, a language of the Polynesian group, still is spoken among the Maori population and is taught in Maori schools. It is the first language of about 50,000 Maori New Zealanders and became an official language in 1987, with the right of use in courts of law and before a number of tribunals. There are Maori-language preschools, immersion primary schools, and many radio stations.

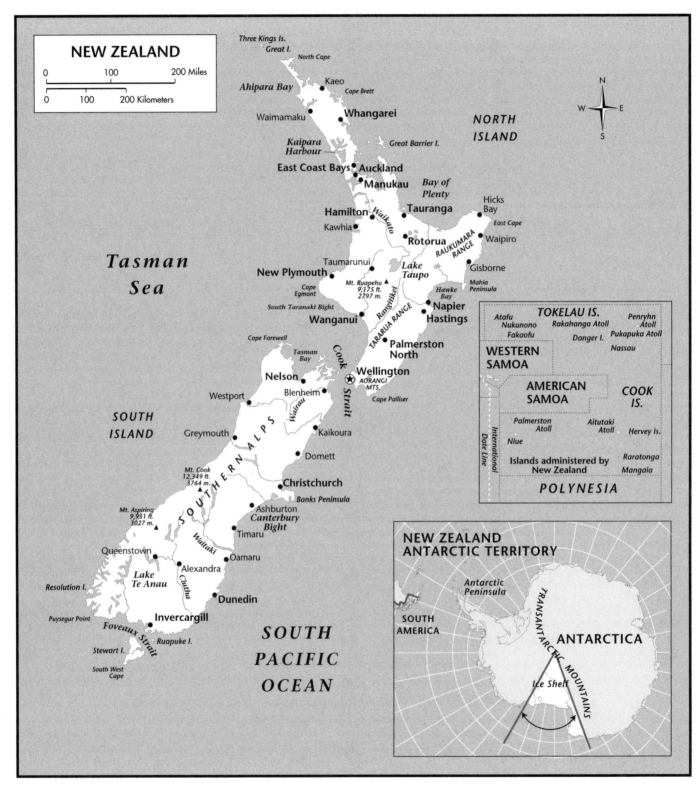

NEW ZEALAND

0   100   200 Miles

0   100   200 Kilometers

Three Kings Is.
Great I.
North Cape
Ahipara Bay   Kaeo
Cape Brett
Waimamaku   **Whangarei**
NORTH ISLAND
Kaipara Harbour
Great Barrier I.
East Coast Bays   **Auckland**
Manukau   *Bay of Plenty*
Hicks Bay
Hamilton   **Tauranga**
Waikato   East Cape
Kawhia   **Rotorua**   Waipiro
RAUKUMARA RANGE
Taumarunui   *Lake Taupo*   Gisborne
New Plymouth   *Mahia Peninsula*
Cape Egmont   Mt. Ruapehu   *Hawke Bay*
9,175 ft.
2797 m.   **Napier**
South Taranaki Bight   **Hastings**
Wanganui
Rangitikei
TARARUA RANGE   **Palmerston North**

Tasman Sea

Cape Farewell   Cook Strait
Tasman Bay   **Wellington**
Nelson   *AORANGI MTS.*
Westport   Blenheim   *Cape Palliser*
Wairau
SOUTH ISLAND
Greymouth   Kaikoura
SOUTHERN ALPS   Domett
Mt. Cook
12,349 ft.
3764 m.   **Christchurch**
Banks Peninsula
Ashburton
Mt. Aspiring   *Canterbury Bight*
9,931 ft.
3027 m.   *Waitaki*   Timaru
Queenstown   Oamaru
Lake Te Anau   Alexandra
Clutha
Resolution I.   **Dunedin**
Puysegur Point
Invercargill
Foveaux Strait
Stewart I.   *Ruapuke I.*
South West Cape

Tasman Sea

SOUTH PACIFIC OCEAN

TOKELAU IS.
Atafu   Penryhn
Nukunono   Rakahanga Atoll   Atoll
Fakaofu   Pukapuka Atoll
Danger I.
WESTERN SAMOA   Nassau

AMERICAN SAMOA   *COOK IS.*

Palmerston   Aitutaki
Atoll   Atoll   *Hervey Is.*
Niue
Raratonga
Islands administered by New Zealand   Mangaia

International Date Line

POLYNESIA

NEW ZEALAND ANTARCTIC TERRITORY

Antarctic Peninsula
SOUTH AMERICA
TRANSANTARCTIC MOUNTAINS
ANTARCTICA
Ice Shelf

LOCATION: 33° to 53°s; 162°E to 173°w. **TERRITORIAL SEA LIMIT:** 12 mi.

¹⁰RELIGIONS

New Zealand has no state church. Anglicans make up 24% of the population; Presbyterians 18%; Roman Catholics 15%; Methodists 5%; Baptists 2%; other Protestants 3%; and unspecified or none 33%. There are also two Christian sects (Ratana and Ringatu) that are indigenous to New Zealand, a small Hindu community, and a small Jewish community.

¹¹TRANSPORTATION

The mountainous nature of New Zealand has made the development of rail and road communications difficult and expensive, particularly on the South Island. In 1998, 3,973 km (2,469 mi) of state-owned railways were operative. New Zealand has electrified some 519 km (323 mi) of its rail lines in order to reduce dependence on imported fuel.

Capital investment in roads exceeds that for all other forms of transport service. Total length of maintained roadways as of 1996 was 92,200 km (52,293 mi), of which 53,568 km (33,287 mi) were paved, including 144 km (89 mi) of expressways. As of 1995, registered motor vehicles included 1,658,000 passenger cars and 352,600 commercial vehicles.

With a registered merchant marine of only 14 ships, totaling 138,687 gross tons in 1998, New Zealand is largely dependent on the shipping of other nations for its overseas trade. In 1974, a government-owned firm, the Shipping Corp. of New Zealand, was set up to operate shipping services; its trade name, the New Zealand Line, was adopted in 1985. Auckland and Wellington, the two main ports, have good natural harbors with deepwater facilities and modern port equipment. Other ports capable of efficiently handling overseas shipping are Whangarei, Tauranga, Lyttelton (serving Christchurch), Bluff, Napier, Nelson, Dunedin, and Timaru.

New Zealand had 111 airports in 1998, 44 with paved runways. Thirteen are major air facilities, of which those at Auckland, Christchurch, and Wellington are international airports. The government-owned Air New Zealand Ltd. operates air services throughout the Pacific region to Australia, Singapore, Hong Kong, Tokyo, Honolulu, and Los Angeles, among other destinations. In 1997, 9,435,000 passengers were carried on scheduled domestic and international flights.

12HISTORY

New Zealand's first people were the Maoris. Owing to the absence of written records, it is impossible to give any accurate date for their arrival, but according to Maori oral traditions, they migrated from other Pacific islands to New Zealand several centuries before any Europeans came, with the chief Maori migration taking place about 1350. It seems likely, however, that the Maoris arrived from Southeast Asia as early as the end of the 10th century. The first European to discover New Zealand was Abel Tasman, a navigator of the Dutch East India Company, who sighted the west coast of the South Island in 1642. He did not land, because of the hostility of the Maori inhabitants. No other Europeans are known to have visited New Zealand after Tasman until Captain James Cook of the British Royal Navy made his four voyages in 1769, 1773, 1774, and 1777. In this period, he circumnavigated both islands and mapped the coastline.

In the 1790s, small European whaling settlements sprang up around the coast. The first mission station was set up in the Bay of Islands in 1814 by Samuel Marsden, chaplain to the governor of New South Wales. In 1840, the Maori chieftains entered into a compact, the Treaty of Waitangi, whereby they ceded sovereignty to Queen Victoria while retaining territorial rights. In the same year, the New Zealand Company made the first organized British attempt at colonization. The first group of British migrants arrived at Port Nicholson and founded the city of Wellington. The New Zealand Company made further settlements in the South Island: in Nelson in 1842, in Dunedin in 1848 (with the cooperation of the Presbyterian Church of Scotland), and in Canterbury in 1850 (with the cooperation of the Church of England). After the Maori Wars (1860-70), which resulted largely from discontent with the official land policy, the colony of New Zealand rapidly increased in wealth and population. Discovery of gold in 1861 resulted in a large influx of settlers. The introduction of refrigerated shipping in 1882 enabled New Zealand to become one of the world's greatest exporters of dairy produce and meat. The depression of the early 1930s revealed to New Zealand the extent of its dependence on this export trade and led to the establishment of more local light industry.

The British Parliament granted representative institutions to the colony in 1852. In 1907, New Zealand was made a dominion, and in 1947 the New Zealand government formally claimed the complete autonomy that was available to self-governing members of the British Commonwealth under the Statute of Westminster, enacted by the British Parliament in 1931.

New Zealand entered World Wars I and II on the side of the UK; New Zealand troops served in Europe in both wars and in the Pacific in World War II. After World War II, New Zealand and US foreign policies were increasingly intertwined. New Zealand signed the ANZUS Pact in 1951 and was a founding member of the Southeast Asia Treaty Organization (SEATO) in 1954. New Zealand troops fought with UN forces in the Korean conflict and with US forces in South Vietnam. The involvement in Vietnam touched off a national debate on foreign policy, however, and all New Zealand troops were withdrawn from Vietnam by the end of 1971. New Zealand's military participation in SEATO was later terminated.

In 1984, a Labour government led by Prime Minister David Lange took office under a pledge to ban nuclear-armed vessels from New Zealand harbors; a US request for a port visit by one of its warships was denied because of uncertainty as to whether the ship carried nuclear weapons. The continuing ban put a strain on New Zealand's relations within ANZUS, and in 1986 the US suspended its military obligations to New Zealand under that defense agreement, also banning high-level contacts with the New Zealand government. The US ended its ban on high-level contacts in March 1990; however, New Zealand's official stance against nuclear presence in its territory remained strong.

In the late 1990's, New Zealand's environmental concerns extended beyond nuclear issues. In 1999, when pirates decimated the population of Patagonian toothfish in the Southern Ocean off Antarctica, threatening not only fish, but also the sea birds that fed upon them, New Zealand responded to the threat to the fragile ecosystem by sending a patrol frigate to the area.

Extensive Maori land claims (to all the country's coastline, 70% of the land, and half of the fishing rights) led, in December 1989, to the formation of a new Cabinet committee designed to develop a government policy towards these claims. The committee, including former Prime Minister Lange, aimed to work with the 17-member Waitangi Tribunal, established in 1975 to consider complaints from Maoris.

The 1993 general election resulted in the governing National Party (NP) winning a bare majority of 50 seats to the Labour Party's 45. In 1996 the NP formed a coalition government with the New Zealand First Party. The coalition was led by James Bolger, who in 1994 lobbied to convert New Zealand into a republic—a move that was met by NP resistance and public apathy. This was the first election under New Zealand's 1993 referendum on proportional representation. It issued in Bolger's third term as Prime Minister. Winston Peters, a fierce critic of Bolger, became the country's deputy Prime Minister and treasurer—a new post responsible for New Zealand's budget. Peters brought the First Party into the coalition over the Labour Party, which won 37 of the 120 seats in the 1996 election. In 1996 the government settled a nz$170 million agreement with the Waikato Tainui tribe in the North Island for its wrongful confiscation of lands during the 1860s. The Queen signed the legislation, which also contained an apology.

The National Party – First Party coalition government remained in power until 1999, when the Labour Party won 49 seats and again became the majority government. The Labour Party formed a government in coalition with the progressive Alliance Party, with Helen Clark as Prime Minister. In 1999 tension arose between the Maori and white New Zealanders, centering on the growing Maori claims to the natural resources of the country. The Clark administration expressed its commitment to goals aimed at benefiting all New Zealanders, and closing the economic gap between the Maori and the rest of the population. The Labour – Alliance coalition also built alliances with other non-nuclear states and worked to strengthen the Nuclear Free Zone in the South Pacific.

13 GOVERNMENT

New Zealand is an independent member of the Commonwealth of Nations. Like the UK, it is a constitutional monarchy, the head of state being the representative of the crown, the governor-general, who is appointed for a five-year term.

The government is democratic and modeled on that of the UK. The single-chamber legislature, the House of Representatives, has 120 members (1999), elected by universal adult suffrage for a term of three years. Adult male suffrage dates from 1879; adult women received the right to vote in 1893. The voting age was lowered to 18 in November 1974. Since 1867, the House has included representatives of the Maoris, and in 1985, the Most Reverend Paul Reeves, Anglican archbishop of New Zealand, became the first person of Maori descent to be appointed governor-general. As of 1999, five seats in the 120-member Parliament were reserved for its native Maori minority population. Persons of at least half-Maori ancestry may register in either a Maori electoral district or a European district. Members are elected by simple majority. Although both the 1996 and 1999 elections resulted in coalition governments (National Party and New Zealand First, 1996; Labour Party and Alliance, 1999), a two-party system usually operates. The party with a majority of members elected to the House of Representatives forms the government; the other party becomes the Opposition.

On his appointment, the Prime Minister, leader of the governing party, chooses some 20 other ministers to form the cabinet. Each minister usually controls several government departments, for which he is responsible to the House of Representatives. Although the cabinet is the de facto governing body, it has no legal status. Members of the cabinet and the governor-general form the Executive Council, the highest executive body.

An act of 1962 established the post of ombudsman, whose principal function is to inquire into complaints from the public relating to administrative decisions of government departments and related organizations. In 1975, provision was made for the appointment of additional ombudsmen under the chief ombudsman.

In a September 1992 referendum, nearly 85% of voters rejected the established electoral system of simple plurality (first-past-the-post) in favor of a system based upon a mixed member proportional system, as used in Germany. Final approval came in a second referendum held as part of the 1993 general election, and the proportional voting system was introduced during the 1996 elections. Under New Zealand's proportional representation system each voter casts two votes, one for a candidate and one for a political party. Each party is awarded seats according to its share of the overall vote, with a minimum set at 5%.

14 POLITICAL PARTIES

Although the New Zealand legislature began to function in 1854 under an act of 1852, it was not until near the end of the century that political parties with a national outlook began to form. This development was hastened by abolition of the provincial parliaments in 1876.

From 1890 to 1912, the Liberal Party was in power. It drew its strength from small farmers and from the rapidly increasing working class in the towns. It enacted advanced legislation on minimum wages, working conditions, and old age pensions, and established the world's first compulsory system of state arbitration. A Reform Party government replaced the Liberal government in 1912; the main items in the Reform platform were the "freehold" for certain types of farmers (i.e., the right to purchase on favorable terms the land they leased from the crown) and the eradication of patronage in the public service. During part of World War I, there was a coalition of Reform and Liberal parties. The Labour Party was formed in 1916 when several rival Labour groups finally came together. This party derived partly from old Liberal tradition, but its platform on socialization and social welfare was more radical.

The Reform Party continued in office until 1928 and was then succeeded by the United Party, a revival of the old Liberal Party. In 1931, these two parties came together, governing as a coalition until 1935. In that year, after a severe economic depression, a Labour government came to power. Labour remained the government until 1949, although for periods during World War II a coalition war cabinet and later a war administration were created, in addition to the Labour cabinet. During its term of office, Labour inaugurated an extensive system of social security and a limited degree of nationalization.

After their defeat in 1935, the old coalition parties joined to form the National Party. Coming to power in 1949, this party held office until 1957, when it was replaced by Labour. The National Party returned to power in the 1960 election, and maintained its majority in the elections of 1963, 1966, and 1969. A Labour government was elected in 1972, but in 1975 the National Party reversed the tide, winning 55 seats and 47.4% of the total vote; a National Party cabinet was formed, with Robert Muldoon as Prime Minister. Led by Muldoon, the National Party was returned again in the 1978 and 1981 elections, but by much lower margins.

On 14 July 1984, the National Party was defeated at the polls, winning only 37 seats (36% of the vote), to 56 seats (43%) for Labour. The Social Credit Political League won 2 seats (8%), and the New Zealand Party, a conservative group formed in 1983, won most of the remaining popular vote, but no seats. David Lange formed a Labour government and was reelected in August 1987, when Labour won 56 seats and 47.6% of the vote, and the National Party won 41 seats and 45% of the vote. No other parties won seats.

David Lange resigned as Prime Minister on 7 August 1989 after Roger Douglas, a political foe in the Labour Party, was reelected to the Cabinet. Labour's MPs selected Geoffrey Palmer as Prime Minister and party leader. Palmer resigned as Prime Minister in September 1990 and was replaced by Michael Moore, also of the Labour Party. In October 1990 the National Party, led by Jim Bolger, won a general election victory. Bolger's government instituted major cuts in New Zealand's welfare programs. The National Party won reelection in the November 1993 general election, capturing 50 of 99 seats. The Labour Party won 45, and both the New Zealand First Party, led by Winston Peters, and The Alliance, led by Jim Anderton, won 2 seats. In December 1993 Helen Clark replaced Michael Moore as leader of the Labour Party, becoming the first woman to lead a major party in New Zealand.

The 1996 elections were the first under proportional representation. James Bolger was elected as Prime Minister for a third term, to lead a coalition government formed by the National Party and the First Party. The National Party won 44 seats; Labour, 37; New Zealand First Party, 17; Alliance Party, 8; and the United Party, 1.

In the November 1999 elections, the balance of power once again shifted, with the New Zealand National Party losing 5 seats and capturing only 30.5% of the total vote, while the New Zealand Labor Party gained 12 seats and took 38.7% of the vote, thus becoming the majority party. Under Prime Minister Helen Clark, a coalition government was formed between the Labour Party and the Alliance Party, which consisted of 5 small parties:

the New Labor Party, the Democratic Party, the New Zealand Liberal Party, the Green Party, and Mana Motihake.

While the Liberal and Reform Parties, and in more recent times, the Labour and National Parties, have played the major roles in New Zealand's government, many other political groups have existed over the years, with varying agendas and membership. In 1999, those with enough support to win parliamentary seats included ACT New Zealand (libertarian), the New Zealand First Party (nationalistic), the Green Party of Aotearoa (ecologist), and the United New Zealand Party (liberal).

15LOCAL GOVERNMENT

The Local Government Act (1974), with subsequent modifications, substantially changed the structure of local government in New Zealand. The previous system was based on territorial local authorities: boroughs, which served concentrated populations of at least 1,500; counties, which were predominantly rural; and town districts, an intermediate form. In addition, there were special-purpose authorities to administer harbors, hospitals, electricity and water distribution, and other public services. The 1974 legislation added two tiers to this structure. Regional bodies—including united councils, which are appointed by the constituent territorial authorities in a region, and regional councils, which are directly elected—are charged with two mandatory functions, regional planning and self-defense, and may undertake other regional functions. Moreover, within territorial local authorities, communities may be established. Each community may have either a district community council (if the population is 1,500 or more), which exercises nearly all the powers of its parent territorial authority, or a community council, to which the parent authority may delegate powers. The purpose of these community bodies is to increase residents' participation in local government. The Local Government Act also introduced a new form of territorial local authority, the district council, established to serve areas of mixed rural and urban character.

The Local Government Commission was charged with the task of constituting the regional bodies, of which there were 22 (2 regional councils and 20 united councils) by 1983. As of 1996 there were also 93 county councils, 9 district councils, and 3 town districts. By 1999, a new administrative structure was instituted that divided local government into 17 regions that were subdivided into 57 districts and 16 cities. Most units of local government are elected at three-year intervals. In boroughs the mayor is elected directly by the voters, while the council itself elects the chairman of a county council.

16JUDICIAL SYSTEM

In most civil and criminal cases heard first in district courts (known until 1980 as magistrates' courts), there is the right of appeal to the High Court (formerly Supreme Court), which is usually the court of first hearing for cases where a major crime or an important civil action is involved. Family courts were established in 1980 to hear cases involving domestic issues. The highest court, the Court of Appeal, exercises an appellate jurisdiction only. Its decisions are final unless leave is granted to appeal to the Privy Council in London. There are also several special courts, such as the Arbitration Court, the Maori Land Court, and the Children and Young Persons Court. The judicial system is based on British common law. The judiciary is independent and impartial. The judicial system provides citizens with a fair and efficient judicial process.

The law prohibits arbitrary interference with privacy, family, home, or correspondence and the authorities respect these provisions in practice.

17ARMED FORCES

Service in the New Zealand regular armed forces is voluntary, but some white males (18–21) may be required to have military training for service in the territorial force (3,890).

In 2000, the army had a full-time regular force of 4,400 and 1,500 reserves; the navy had 2,080 regulars (350 women) and 850 reserves; and the air force had 3,050 regulars (500 women) and 1,050 reserves. Army forces include two infantry battalions, one artillery regiment, one engineer regiment, and two special forces squadrons. The navy has 4 small surface combatants and 4 ASW helos, and the air force 42 combat aircraft. Weapons are US and European. New Zealand forces participate in peacekeeping and other UN missions in 11 countries. The defense budget in 1997–98 was $562 million or 1% of GDP.

18INTERNATIONAL COOPERATION

A charter member of the UN, New Zealand joined the world organization on 24 October 1945. It participates in ESCAP and all the nonregional specialized agencies. In addition, New Zealand belongs to the Asian Development Bank, Colombo Plan, Commonwealth of Nations, OECD, South Pacific Commission, and South Pacific Forum, among other intergovernmental organizations. A member of the WTO and signatory to the Law of the Sea and the South Pacific Regional Trade and Cooperation Agreement, New Zealand also forms part of the ANZUS alliance with Australia and the US; in 1986, however, following New Zealand's decision to ban US nuclear-armed or nuclear-powered ships from its ports, the US renounced its ANZUS treaty commitments to New Zealand.

19ECONOMY

New Zealand's economy has traditionally been based on pastoral farming. The last decades, however, have seen the beginnings of heavy industry, and there has been a large expansion in light industries such as plastics, textiles, and footwear, mostly to supply the home market. In recent years there has been a trend toward the development of resource-based industries, and the forest industry has greatly expanded. Pulp, log, and paper products are now a major earner of overseas exchange. As of 1995, 10% of the work force was employed in agriculture, hunting, forestry, and fishing; 25% in industry; and 65% in services. In 1995, agricultural production amounted to approximately 7% of GDP, industry 26%, and services 67%.

For financing imports both of raw materials and of a high proportion of manufactured goods, New Zealand has traditionally relied on the receipts from the export of its restricted range of primary products (mainly wool, meat, and dairy products). This dependence on the income from so few commodities makes the economy vulnerable to fluctuations in their world prices, and sharp drops in these prices, as have occurred periodically, inevitably result in the restriction of imports or a substantial trade deficit. Other important industries in 1999 were the manufacture of machinery and transportation equipment, banking and insurance, and eco-tourism.

The economy has been subjected to two major crises in 20 years: first, the loss of a large part of the British market for New Zealand's agricultural products when the UK joined the EC in 1973, and, secondly, the curtailment of overspending by the government in the early 1980's, which enforced a 10-year economic program. The program has been very successful, transforming New Zealand from among the most heavily protected and regulated economies to one of the most market-oriented and open in the world. By 1999, New Zealand had posted growth rates averaging 2.5% between 1988 and 1998, surpluses in the government's budget after 1996, and a per capita GDP in line with those of the big European economies.

[20]INCOME

The US Central Intelligence Agency (CIA) reports that in 1998 New Zealand's gross domestic product (GDP) was estimated at $61.1 billion. The per capita GDP was estimated at $17,000. The annual growth rate of GDP was estimated at -0.2%. The average inflation rate in 1998 was 1.1%. The CIA defines GDP as the value of all final goods and services produced within a nation in a given year and computed on the basis of purchasing power parity (PPP) rather than value as measured on the basis of the rate of exchange. It was estimated that agriculture accounted for 9% of GDP, industry 25%, and services 66%.

The World Bank reports that for the same period per capita private consumption (in PPP terms) was $10,915. Private consumption includes expenditures of individuals, households, and non-governmental organizations. It was estimated that between 1990 and 1998 private consumption grew at an annual rate of 3.1%. Approximately 21% of household consumption was spent on food, 12% on fuel, 3% on health care, and 2% on education. The richest 10% of the population accounted for approximately 30% of household consumption and the poorest 10% approximately 0.3%.

[21]LABOR

In 1998, total civilian employment amounted to 1,725,000, including 147,000 in agriculture, 289,700 in manufacturing, and 370,000 in wholesale or retail trade. Before 1978, New Zealand had maintained virtually full employment, but the oil crisis had a major impact, and from 1978 unemployment climbed from about 3% to 10.6% in 1991. After peaking in 1991–92, unemployment was reduced to 6.3% in 1995 as a result of a sustained economic recovery, but had risen to 7.5% by 1998.

Compulsory unionization during the 1936–61 period resulted in the creation of many small unions; the law was modified in 1962, and abolished in 1991 with the Employment Contracts Act, which radically deregulated the labor market and put the employer-employee relationship on a civil contract basis. In 1987, the private sector Federation of Labor and the public sector Combined State Unions merged to form the New Zealand Council of Trade Unions (NZCTU). A smaller federation, the New Zealand Trade Union Federation, was formed in 1993.

The Industrial Relations Act of 1973 restructured New Zealand's industrial legislation and institutions, setting up three bodies to aid in the settlement of disputes: the Industrial Mediation Service, the Industrial Conciliation Service, and the Industrial Commission. The Commission is involved only if conciliation fails, and its arbitration is binding. The 1973 act also provides for the right to strike, although there are restrictions once a dispute is before conciliation. Higher unemployment and lower welfare benefits created a decreased willingness for workers to strike. In 1984, there were 364 work stoppages; by 1990 that number had fallen to 137, and in 1999 to 35. Legislation enacted in 1991 prohibits strikes designed to force an employer to become a party to a multicompany contract.

In 1999, the minimum wage rate was $3.50 per hour. These wage rates are set lower than the standard rate for unskilled labor. By law, employees in most occupations have a 40-hour workweek, 8 hours a day, 5 days a week. Excess hours are generally paid at overtime rates. Legislation or industrial contracts secure sick leave, paid holidays, and accident compensation for all workers. The safety, health and welfare benefits, holiday provisions, hours of work, and overtime of all workers are closely regulated.

[22]AGRICULTURE

Over 14% of the total land area of New Zealand is devoted to agriculture. Capital investment in land improvement and mechanization has contributed greatly to the steady growth in agricul-

tural production without an increase in the farm labor force. About 76,000 tractors and 3,100 combines were in use in 1997. Agriculture contributes about 7% to GDP.

Cereal cultivation, more than 90% of which takes place on the South Island plains and downlands, fluctuates in terms of both acreage and size of crop. In 1998, areas harvested to wheat totaled an estimated 51,000 ha (126,000 acres), with a yield of 265,000 tons; 12,000 ha (29,000 acres) yielded 49,000 tons of oats; and 73,000 ha (180,000 acres) yielded 340,000 tons of barley.

New Zealand is largely self-sufficient in horticultural products and exports some of these, such as apples and honey. In 1998, 970,000 tons of fresh fruit, (excluding melons) were produced. The kiwi, a fruit that has become popular in the US, Japan, and elsewhere, represented 90% of horticultural exports. In 1985, New Zealand accounted for more than half the world's supply of kiwi fruit. Since the mid-1980s, New Zealand has lost some of its market share in the production of kiwi, as other countries began or expanded their own domestic kiwi production—by the late 1990s, New Zealand accounted for one-third of world kiwi supply. Due to unfavorable weather, kiwi production in 1999 was estimated at 221,000 tons, down 10% from 1998. In 1998, New Zealand produced 501,000 tons of apples, 52,000 tons of peas, and 176,000 tons of corn. About 70% of apple exports is derived from the Braeburn, Gala, and Royal Gala varieties developed in New Zealand. The New Zealand Apple and Pear Marketing Board handled exports of 250,200 tons of apples and pears from the country's 1,500 growers in 1998, valued at nz$535.3 million.

The Department of Agriculture and the Department of Scientific and Industrial Research provide farmers and horticulturalists with advice and encouragement on new farming methods, elimination of plant diseases, and improvement of unproductive land. Government subsidies have assisted in improving and bringing under cultivation marginal and hitherto unused scrub land. However, since the mid-1980s there has been a shift in government policy, and many subsidies to agriculture have been removed or phased out.

[23]ANIMAL HUSBANDRY

Relatively warm temperatures, combined with ample rainfall, make New Zealand one of the world's richest pastoral areas. In 1996, pastures occupied 13.7 million ha (33.9 million acres), or 51% of the total land area. Even in the south, where winters may be quite severe, animals need not be housed. In 1998, there were 46.2 million sheep, 8.8 million head of cattle (including 4.4 million head of dairy cattle), and about 340,000 pigs. Dairying and beef production are concentrated in the North Island, and sheep farming is more evenly distributed between the North and South islands. The natural tussock land in the mountainous areas of the South Island and the surface-sown grassland in the less steep parts of the North Island are used to raise sheep for wool. The extensive use of aircraft for the spread of top dressing has greatly improved hill pasture, most of which is not readily accessible to normal top dressing with fertilizers. Some 24,000 farms stock mainly sheep, occupying over 11 million ha (27.1 million acres), with an average flock of 1,800 head. Although fine-woolen Merino sheep have grazed in New Zealand since the 1830s, most of the clip nowadays comes from Romney sheep, whose coarser, thicker wool is ideal for carpet-making and knitting yarns.

Products of animal origin account for more than half the total value of New Zealand's exports, with meat industry products accounting for about 18% of exports. New Zealand is the world's largest exporter of mutton and lamb, second largest exporter of wool, and a leading exporter of cheese. The wool clip, which, having increased steadily since 1948, had fallen during the early 1970s, later rose to 380,700 tons in 1980/81; in 1998,

254,000 tons were produced. Exports of wool were valued at nz$25.8 million in 1997/98. Beef and veal production in that year reached 570,000 tons; and mutton, 547,000 tons. New Zealand accounts for over 50% of the world's mutton exports. Other livestock products in 1997/98 included (in thousands of tons): whole milk powder, 356; butter, 271; cheese, 266; non-fat dry milk, 170; and casein, 104.

With many more cows than people to milk them, New Zealand pioneered and relies on mechanical milking. In 1997, New Zealand had 20,000 milking machines. Whole milk is pumped through coolers to vats where it is transferred to tanker trucks. In 1998, 11,288,000 tons of fresh milk was produced. Milkfat production averages about 330,000 tons annually, of which 13% is consumed as milk or fed to stock. The balance is used for dairy products.

Although wild goats and deer were once regarded as vermin, over the last decade, the profitability of venison and mohair exports led to the domestication of both animals. About 1.2 million deer and 227,000 goats are being farmed. Alpacas, llamas, and water buffalo have recently been imported to improve the breeding potential as well as wool and meat production.

[24] FISHING

Although many kinds of edible fish are readily obtainable in New Zealand waters, the fishing and fish-processing industry has remained relatively small. Since the 1960s, however, the government has taken a number of measures to expand the industry and increase fishery exports. In 1978, the government began implementing a 322-km (200-mi) exclusive economic zone. During the next four years, it approved nearly 40 joint ventures with foreign companies in order to exploit the zone, which, with an area of about 1.3 million sq mi (nautical), is one of the world's largest. These waters support over 1,000 species of fish, about 100 of which have commercial significance. The volume of fish landed in New Zealand increased from 6,488 tons in 1936 to 669,352 tons in 1997. New Zealand's domestic vessels account for about 60% of the catch. With the rapid growth of fishing in the 1980s, about 75% of the catch is exported (with a value of $830.5 million in 1997), mostly to the US, Japan, and Australia. The principal finfish species caught included blue grenadier, mackerel, whiting, snoek, and orange roughy. In addition, New Zealand fishermen in 1997 landed 65,000 tons of New Zealand mussels and 3,400 tons of cupped oysters. The most valuable part of the catch is made of orange roughy, hoki, squid, and rock lobster. Oyster and mussel aquaculture are well established; scallop, salmon, and abalone farming are developing. In 1997, greenshell mussels and salmon exports totaled nz$84.5 million and nz$31.5 million, respectively; Australia, Japan, and the US were the major markets.

[25] FORESTRY

At the time Europeans began coming to New Zealand, about 70% of the land was forest. The major indigenous tree species are beech, kauri, rimu, taraire, and tawa. This proportion has been reduced by settlement, farming, and exploitation to about 29%. Much of the remaining natural forest is reserved in national parks, or as protection forest on mountain land. About 5% of New Zealand is covered by planted forests, which provides a large and sustainable volume of wood. The Ministry of Agriculture and Forestry (MAF) estimated the planted forest area at 1.7 million ha (4.2 million acres) in 1998.

For wood production, New Zealand relies heavily on its planted forests of quick-growing exotic species, mainly radiata pine, which can be harvested every 25–30 years. These provide over 90% of the wood for production of sawn timber, wood panel products, pulp, paper, and paperboard. Due to these replanting efforts and privatization of forest lands, exports of softwood logs have skyrocketed since the early 1980s. Exports of forestry products in 1998 amounted to nz$2,242 million, according to the MAF. Most of New Zealand's softwood logs and lumber go to Australia, the ROK, and Japan. Forestry accounts for about 13% of export earnings. Imports of forest products consist mostly of specialty papers.

The MAF put roundwood production in 1998 at an estimated 16,425,000 cu m. Logs for export and sawlog production that year were estimated at 5.3 million and 5.8 million cu m, respectively. Plywood production for 1998 was estimated at 189,447 cu m.

The Forestry Corporation (FC) was established as a state-owned enterprise in April 1991. The FC manages 188,000 ha (465,000 acres) of forest in the Bay of Plenty on North Island. The FC consists of three principal forests: Rotoehu Forest, Whakarewarewa Forest, and the Kaingaroa Forest in the Rotorua district that covers 149,735 ha (370,001 acres) and is claimed to be the largest planted forest in the world. In 1996, the government sold FC for nz$2 billion to a joint venture consortium, which planned to invest nz$260 million over the next several years.

[26] MINING

Many different minerals are found in New Zealand, but few have been extensively exploited. In 1997, the mineral industry constituted about 7% of the GDP, of which 4% was provided by the mineral processing sector.

The mineral industry in New Zealand began with the discovery of gold on the Coromandel Peninsula, North Island in 1852. Gold deposits were discovered on the South Island in 1861. Production for 1997 was estimated at 11,500 kg. Silver production was reported at 30,000 kg that year.

The existence of large quantities of iron-bearing sands has been known for more than a century, especially along the west coast beaches of North Island. However, the steelmaking industry was not able to successfully exploit the iron-sands until the late 1960s. An estimated 2.3 million tons of iron-sand was extracted in 1997. Concentrates of titaniferous magnetite are produced for export to Japan from the iron-sand deposits. Uranium-bearing minerals have been located on the South Island. Output of building materials in 1997 included 5,300,000 tons of sand and gravel for building aggregate, and 500,000 tons of limestone for roads.

[27] ENERGY AND POWER

New Zealand's per capita consumption of electricity is among the highest in the world. A network of transmission lines links all major power stations, bringing electricity to 99% of the population. Of the 35,789 million kwh generated for public supply in 1998, roughly 75% was produced from hydroelectric resources, 20% from conventional thermal plants, and 6% from geothermal steam. Future hydroelectric potential is limited, however, and thermal power based primarily on coal and natural gas is becoming increasingly important. Net installed generating capacity was 7,794,000 kw in 1998. Hydroelectricity's net installed capacity from 30 stations was 5,059,000 kw in 1994. The geothermal power station at Wairakei has been operating since 1958, while a second at Ohaaki was commissioned in 1989.

New Zealand now meets some 75% of its total energy requirements from indigenous resources, the balance coming from imports of crude oil and refined petroleum products. In 1995, petroleum accounted for 43% of New Zealand's primary energy consumption; natural gas, 30%; coal, 17%; and hydroelectricity, 10%. The Kapuni natural gas field, discovered in 1959, began production in 1970; the Maui offshore natural gas and condensate field, one of the largest in the world, began production in 1979. Oil and gas exploration and development of indigenous resources continue to be stressed, in efforts to reduce dependence on imports. Crude oil and natural gas liquid production levels in 1998 were 47,000 barrels per day and 4.8 million cu m, respectively. Proven reserves of natural gas total 100 billion cu m; oil reserves, 200 million barrels. Coal mining began in the 1850s; over the last 40 years, coal's contribution to the energy supply has fallen from 50% to about 11%. Within the next ten years, however, coal mining will likely increase to meet increased demands for electricity and steel production. Coal reserves are estimated at 129 million tons, of which 85% is located in the untapped lignite fields in Southland.

28 INDUSTRY

Industrial production has increased rapidly since the end of World War II, stimulated by intermittent import controls that often enabled domestic industry to increase output without competition. A most significant feature of New Zealand industry in recent decades has been the establishment of heavy industry with Commonwealth and US capital. Plants include metal and petroleum processing, motor vehicle assembly, textiles and footwear, and a wide range of consumer appliances. The New Zealand Steel company manufactures billet slabs and ingots using domestically produced iron sands; Pacific Steel, which processes scrap metal, uses billets from New Zealand Steel. In 1995, crude steel production totaled 800,000 tons. The Tiwai Point aluminum smelter, operated by an Australian-Japanese consortium, has an annual capacity of 244,000 tons. New Zealand's aluminum smelter production amounted to 280,296 tons in 1995. The small but growing electronics industry produces consumer goods as well as commercial products, such as digital gasoline pumps. Wool-based industries have traditionally been an important part of the economy, notably wool milling, the oldest sector of the textile industry. Other significant industrial areas include a diverse food-processing sector, tanneries, sheet glass, rubber, and plastics.

Progressive withdrawal of government support beginning in 1985 led manufacturing to decline from 1987–89 due to a more competitive environment. However, after cutting overcapacity, many firms increased productivity and were ultimately in a stronger financial position. Industrial output has recovered since 1990. Manufacturing's contribution to GDP (at current prices) rose by 2.3% annually between 1988 and 1998.

29 SCIENCE AND TECHNOLOGY

Most scientific research in New Zealand is funded by the government, principally by the Department of Scientific and Industrial Research (DSIR) and the Ministry of Agriculture and Fisheries. The Cawthron Institute at Nelson, established in 1919, conducts research in chemistry, biology, and environmental and marine studies. New Zealand has 20 other institutes conducting research in agriculture, veterinary science, medicine, and general sciences and 17 universities and technical institutes offering degrees in basic and applied sciences. In 1987–97, science and engineering students accounted for 20% of college and university enrollments. Among New Zealand's 42 scientific and technical learned societies, the most prominent is the Royal Society of New Zealand, founded in 1867.

In 1987–97, research and development expenditures totaled 1.04% of GNP; 1,663 scientists and engineers and 809 technicians per million people were engaged in research and development.

30 DOMESTIC TRADE

Many smaller retailers are being supplanted by small supermarkets and shopping centers; others have converted to self-service operations. There is very little retail mail-order trade.

Automobiles and large appliances are increasingly being sold on the installment (hire-purchase) plan. General and trade papers, regional publications, and television and radio are used extensively as advertising media.

Business hours vary, especially since the introduction of staggered work hours, known as glide time. Offices open as early as 7:30 AM and remain open until about 6 PM. Stores may be open at any time between 7 AM and 9 PM, Monday through Saturday. Saturday trading is becoming more prevalent at popular beach resorts near the larger urban areas. Sunday trading is confined to "dairy shops," permitted by law to sell a restricted range of foodstuffs. All offices and banks are closed on Saturdays, Sundays, and statutory holidays.

31 FOREIGN TRADE

New Zealand's trade per capita and as a percentage of GNP is among the highest in the world. In 1974/75, more than 70% of export receipts derived from meat, dairy products, and wool; but this figure was down to 56% by 1984/85 and was only 32% in 1994/95, as manufactured goods and forest products have taken an increasing share of the total. Imports consist mainly of manufactured goods, petroleum and petroleum products, and raw materials for industry. Foreign trade more than doubled in value between 1976 and 1981 and again from 1981 to 1985. Between 1992/93 and 1995/96, the value of trade increased by nearly 16%.

New Zealand produces a large amount of food, including meat, dairy products, fruits and nuts, and fish. Other important exports include wool, aluminum, wood, and starch. The top ten exports are as follows:

	% OF COUNTRY TOTAL	% OF WORLD TOTAL
Meat	14	4.6
Milk and cream	6.9	7.0
Wool	6.0	14
Fruit and nuts	4.2	2.1
Butter	3.9	14
Aluminum	3.7	1.1
Fish	3.6	2.3
Wood rough, squared	3.4	4.6
Starch	3.1	5.5
Cheese and curd	3.0	3.6

In 1996 New Zealand's imports were distributed among the following categories:

Consumer goods	18.3%
Food	6.9%
Fuels	6.1%
Industrial supplies	26.6%
Machinery	24.6%
Transportation	17.2%
Other	0.2%

Principal trading partners in 1998 (in millions of US dollars) were as follows:

COUNTRY	EXPORTS	IMPORTS	BALANCE
Australia	2,395	2,744	-349
Japan	1,528	1,428	100
United States	1,488	2,389	-901
United Kingdom	671	638	33
China (inc. Hong Kong)	640	718	-78
Korea	356	243	113
Germany	315	587	-272
Taiwan	262	293	-31
Italy	223	284	-61
Malaysia	205	295	-90

32BALANCE OF PAYMENTS

Since New Zealand's foreign trade depends on agricultural and livestock products, and since prices for these commodities are volatile, New Zealand's balance of payments may swing sharply from one year to the next. Generally, deficits outweighed surpluses during the 1950s and 1960s. Consistent surpluses were recorded between 1969 and 1973, when international reserves nearly quadrupled. However, a poor trade performance in 1974, largely attributable to increased oil import costs, contributed to a large current accounts deficit. Since then, New Zealand has continued to register payments deficits, which have been partially offset by compensatory financing, including overseas loans.

The US Central Intelligence Agency reports that in 1998 the purchasing power parity of New Zealand's exports was $12.9 billion while imports totaled $13 billion resulting in a trade balance of -$100 million.

The International Monetary Fund (IMF) reports that in 1997 New Zealand had exports of goods totaling $14,123 million and imports totaling $13,248 million. The services credit totaled $4,230 million and debit $5,031 million. The following table summarizes New Zealand's balance of payments for 1997 in millions of US dollars.

Current Account		-4,750
Balance on goods	875	
Balance on services	-801	
Balance on income	-5,148	
Current transfers	323	
Capital Account		236
Financial Account		3,337
Direct investment abroad	77	
Direct investment in New Zealand	2,657	
Portfolio investment assets	-1,631	
Portfolio investment liabilities	-638	
Other investment assets	1,175	
Other investment liabilities		1,697
Net Errors and Omissions		-265
Reserves and Related Items		1,442

33BANKING AND SECURITIES

The Reserve Bank of New Zealand, established in 1933, exercises control over monetary circulation and credit. It is the bank of issue, handles all central government banking transactions, manages the public debt, and administers exchange control regulations. The Reserve Bank of New Zealand Amendment Act (1973) empowers the Bank to regulate credit from all sources and requires it to make loans (as the minister of finance may determine) in order to ensure continued full employment.

New Zealand's financial services sector is dominated by the commercial banks, leaving only a minor role for non-bank finance companies and savings institutions. In part this reflects the impact of deregulation since the mid-1980s. Before 1984, the financial sector was highly segmented with tight government controls on what different institutions could offer. (For example, only trading banks could offer checking accounts to clients.) The easing of regulations means that there are now only two formal categories of financial institution: registered banks and other financial institutions. However, both can offer a wide range of financial and banking services.

To be defined as a bank, a financial institution must register with the central Reserve Bank and meet a range of eligibility criteria, such as minimum capital adequacy, experience in the financial intermediation industry, and a commitment to stability of the financial system. The number of registered banks peaked at 24 in 1994, and in mid-1996 there were 16.

A number of bank mergers has increased the concentration of total banking assets in foreign ownership. Over 95% of total banking assets are foreign-owned, compared with 65% in 1990. The New Zealand banking industry is increasingly influenced by developments in Australia, since Australian banking groups control over two-thirds of banking assets in New Zealand; this share is unlikely to increase further, with the announcement in April 1996 of a conditional buy-out by Westpac Banking Corp. of Trust Bank, New Zealand's last domestically owned bank with a national branch network. The Post Office Savings Bank (established in 1865) has about 1,270 offices and agencies throughout New Zealand.

New Zealand is advantageously placed, since its trading day opens before the US market closes and before the Asian and Australian markets open. The main functions of the New Zealand Stock Exchange (NZSE) are to provide an orderly market for the trading and transfer of securities, to protect investors' interests, and to ensure that the market is fully informed. As of 1992, there were 38 corporate and partnership members of the NZSE.

The Stock Exchange Association of New Zealand, the forerunner to the NZSE, was founded in 1915. The stock exchanges in Auckland, Wellington, Christchurch, Dunedin, and Invercargill are members of the New Zealand Stock Exchange (NZSE), with headquarters in Wellington. Official listing is granted to companies that comply with the Exchange's requirements. These do not impose qualifications as to share capital but do provide that the company must be of sufficient magnitude and its shareholding sufficiently well distributed to ensure a free market for its shares. Subject to the recommendation and approval of the stock exchange nearest to the registered offices, companies may secure unofficial listing for their shares. All transactions in shares quoted in the unofficial list are subject to special brokerage rates.

34INSURANCE

The government provides insurance through the Government Life Insurance Office and the State Insurance Office, which undertakes accident, fire, and marine insurance.

New Zealand has one of the world's highest ratios of value of life insurance policies to national income. Life insurance offices mobilize long-term household savings in conjunction with the provision of life insurance coverage, and are also closely associated with the management of pension and superannuation funds. The long-term contractual nature of household-sector savings through life insurance offices gives them the capacity to acquire long-term government and corporate debt instruments and to take equity positions in commercial property and company shares as well as provide mortgage financing to policy holders. General insurance companies have substantial funds available for investment to cover claims outstanding and unexpired risks. These funds are available on a short-term basis and are invested mainly in marketable securities and liquid assets.

Like its Australian counterpart, the New Zealand insurance market is on of the most competitive in the world, with some 50 general insurers and the same number of life insurers. The top five general insurers accounted for more than 70% of the total premiums written in 1997; the same pattern exists for life business.

35PUBLIC FINANCE

In 1994, in response to a decade of economic reforms that have opened the economy to foreign investment and triggered strong economic growth, the budget produced a surplus for the first time in 50 years. In 1995, public debt service dropped to 1.9% of GDP and 12% of expenditures. External debt accounted for 23% of total government debt. Interest on external debt equaled 3.5% of exports of goods and services plus investment income. The surpluses continued in 1996, but showed signs of weakness in 1997 as forecasts of slower economic growth and uncertainty over the intentions of the newly elected government prompted a drop in business confidence. Nevertheless, in June of 1997, the new government proposed a three-year program of increased spending on social programs and postponed a round of promised tax cuts.

The US Central Intelligence Agency (CIA) estimates that in 1998 New Zealand's central government took in revenues of approximately $24.9 billion and had expenditures of $23.7 billion including capital expenditures of $1.36 billion. Overall, the government registered a surplus of approximately $1.2 billion.

The following table shows an itemized breakdown of government revenues and expenditures. The percentages were calculated from data reported by the International Monetary Fund. The dollar amounts (millions) are based on the CIA estimates provided above.

REVENUE AND GRANTS	100%	24,900
Tax revenue	93.6%	23,314
Non-tax revenue	6.1%	1,511
Capital revenue	0.3%	75
EXPENDITURES	100%	23,700
General public services	4.5%	1,078
Defense	3.3%	776
Public order and safety	4.5%	1,076
Education	16.2%	3,835
Health	16.4%	3,893
Social security	39.1%	9,259
Housing and community amenities	0.1%	21
Recreation, cultural, and religious affairs	0.9%	223
Economic affairs and services	6.7%	1,580
Other expenditures	1.1%	252
Interest payments	7.2%	1,708

36TAXATION

Earnings are taxed in one combined general income and social security tax, which for wage and salary earners is deducted by the employer on a pay-as-you-earn basis (called PAYE), with annual adjustments. The rates are 24% on income up to NZ$30,875, and 33% on additional income. The system of special tax rebates (credits) includes a standard rebate for the taxpayer and other rebates for dependent relatives, housekeeping or child-care expenses, and tuition. There are also deductions for certain dividend and interest income, life insurance premiums, and contributions to retirement funds. The income tax rate for corporations, including subsidiaries of overseas corporations, was 33%, applied to net income after certain deductions. There are tax incentives for exporters. On 1 October 1986, a 10% value-added tax on goods and services (GST) was introduced, replacing the previous sales tax except in a few instances. As of 1996, this tax was 12.5%. Excise taxes are imposed on motor vehicles, gasoline, tobacco products, and alcoholic beverages.

Local authorities are largely dependent on property taxes. There are three main systems of rating: (1) capital (land improvements) value; (2) annual value; (3) unimproved value. The actual amount of the rate is fixed by each local authority.

37CUSTOMS AND DUTIES

Customs taxation is based principally on an ad valorem scale, but specific duties are applied to some goods. Rates of duty payable depend on the country of origin. With the exception of some automotive products, preferential rate scales for the UK were phased out by 1 July 1977, as a result of that nation's entry into the EC. In 1978, preferential rates for Commonwealth countries were also discontinued. Two years earlier, New Zealand had introduced a revised Generalized System of Preferences favoring the developing countries. Tariffs range from 0% to 30%. New Zealand hopes to reduce all tariffs to 0%–15% after the year 2000.

38FOREIGN INVESTMENT

Investment in New Zealand's economy by overseas companies through New Zealand subsidiaries has increased steadily, with the largest contribution from Australian sources, which have outstripped UK sources in recent years. Total overseas investment reached $11 billion at the end of 1991. Of this total, $1.9 billion was from the UK, $4.8 billion from Australia, $2.8 billion from the US, and $950 million from Japan.

39ECONOMIC DEVELOPMENT

Economic policy is established and directed by the government through taxation, Reserve Bank interest rates, price and monopoly controls, and import and export licensing. Import controls, introduced early in 1958, were further tightened in 1961 and 1973 to correct deficits in the balance of payments. Since then, the government has gradually liberalized import controls; in 1981, about 79% of private imports to New Zealand were exempt from licensing. An industrial restructuring program, begun in the mid-1970s, focuses on certain industries (e.g., textiles, footwear, automobiles, and electronics) whose domestic prices are much higher than those of foreign substitutes, with the aim of reducing the protection granted such products.

To help maintain economic stability, the government assists, and in some cases controls, various economic enterprises (agricultural distribution and marketing, commercial banking, and some insurance). In June 1982, in an effort to reduce inflation, the government announced a freeze on wages, prices, rents, and dividends. The freeze was lifted in March 1984, temporarily reimposed by a new Labour government, then terminated late in 1984. Its termination, combined with a devaluation of the dollar, led to a resumption of high inflation. The government implemented severe monetary policies to reduce inflation in order to enhance a market- and export-led recovery from the October 1987 financial markets crash. The cost was a large increase in unemployment (from 7% to 10.4% of the labor force), but by 1991 inflation had been practically eliminated (2.2% for the year ending September 1991).

Since 1977, the New Zealand Planning Council has been charged with advising the government on economic, social, and cultural planning and in the coordination of planning. Working independently of the Planning Council, the Economic Monitoring Group, established in 1978, produces reports on economic trends.

In 1984/85, New Zealand contributed a total of NZ$61.4 million in technical and capital assistance and direct aid or loans to developing nations. An additional NZ$12.5 million was given in multilateral aid through the UN, the South Pacific Commission, ADB, and other organizations. The major recipients of development assistance are the nations of the South Pacific, who receive about 70% of New Zealand's bilateral aid and about 62% of its total overseas aid.

40SOCIAL DEVELOPMENT

The Social Security Act of 1964 consolidated and advanced existing social legislation. By a system of monetary benefits on a compulsory contributory basis and a system of medical and hospital benefits, all persons in New Zealand are now protected economically in the event of sickness, unemployment, and widowhood, and when they age. The former separate social security tax was combined, as of 1 April 1969, with the graduated general income tax applicable to all wage earners. Monetary benefits under the Social Security Act are paid for retirement, unemployment, sickness, and emergencies; and to widows, orphans, families, invalids, and miners. National superannuation (retirement) benefits replaced separate retirement and old age benefits in 1977. In 1999, retirement was set at age 64, but was subject to a progressive increase to age 65 by the year

2001. Benefits are funded by ordinary government revenues and provide a percentage of the average weekly wage after tax. Benefits are taxable, but are not subject to an income test. Medical benefits include medical, hospital, and pharmaceutical payments.

A revised accident compensation plan enacted in 1998 provides for dual universal and compulsory insurance systems. The plan is financed by insurance premiums paid by employers and the self- employed and by a contribution from general revenue. Compensation for temporary disability is 80% of average earnings.

New Zealand law penalizes spousal rape, and there is effective coordination between police and agencies providing support services for rape victims. A 1996 law broadened the definition of domestic violence to include various kinds of psychological abuse. New Zealand was the first country to grant full suffrage to women, and it celebrated the 100th anniversary of that event in 1993 with conferences and other activities. In 1999, 35 of the 120 members of Parliament were women.

41 HEALTH

New Zealand's health care system has been undergoing a restructuring since the mid-1980s. Area health boards, formed to combine primary and hospital care facilities for each region under a single administrative unit, were established in 1985. In 1991, the government announced plans to expand health care resources for those in financial need. The number of purchases of private health insurance has risen steadily and, by 1991, covered about half the population. At that time, there were six main companies in the private health insurance market.

During the years 1990–97, 7.6% of the gross domestic product went to health expenditures.

In 1990–97, there were 2.1 doctors per 1,000 people. Most physicians practice under the National Health Service, established by the Social Security Act of 1938, but private practice outside the scheme is permitted.

For over 50 years, comprehensive health services, most of them supported by the State, have been available to all New Zealanders. About 80% of all health care costs are met by the public sector. There are about 1,000 voluntary health service groups, often state subsidized. Treatment at public hospitals is free for people ordinarily resident in New Zealand. In private hospitals, medical care is subsidized; a full range of maternity services is paid for by the Department of Health. The Health Service provides hospital treatment, maternity services from a general practitioner, most prescribed drugs, laboratory diagnostic services, dental care, routine immunizations for children under 16, and some health appliances free of charge. Partial benefits are paid for private hospitalization, X-ray services, physiotherapy, and hearing aids. Care is free for infants and preschool children. Most children are immunized free by their family doctors, but the Department of Health also has immunization clinics. In 1994, children up to one year old were vaccinated against tuberculosis (20%); diphtheria, pertussis, and tetanus (84%); polio (84%); measles (87%); and hepatitis B (81%).

In 1990–97, there were 7.3 hospital beds per 1,000 inhabitants. Public hospitals are managed under the supervision of the Minister of Health by local hospital boards, whose members are elected; all costs are borne by the state. Private hospital costs are partly paid for by the state; additional fees may be claimed from patients. Voluntary welfare organizations make valuable contributions to public health and are assisted by grants from public funds. Total health care expenditures in 1990 were $3,150 million. The government of New Zealand paid for 90% of health bills in 1991.

New Zealand's birth rate was 14.4 per 1,000 inhabitants in 1999. About 70% of married women (ages 15 to 49) were using contraceptives in 1990–95. The total fertility rate was 1.8 children per woman living throughout her childbearing years. Infant mortality in 1999 was 6.2 per 1,000 live births for the total population. The overall death rate in 1999 was 7.5 per 1,000 inhabitants. Life expectancy at birth was 77.8 years in 1999. The principal causes of death are heart disease, cancer, and cerebrovascular diseases. There were about 5 reported cases of tuberculosis per 100,000 people in 1997. Alcoholism is a significant public health problem in New Zealand. Estimates of the number of chronic alcoholics range upward from 53,000, and another 250,000 New Zealanders may be classified as excessive drinkers. Tobacco consumption in New Zealand has decreased from 2.3 kg a year per adult in 1984–86 to 2.0 kg in 1995. The heart disease mortality rate for those over 65 years old is higher than the average for countries defined as high human development by the World Bank. There were 1.2 AIDS cases per 100,000 people in 1994. In 1996 there were 523 new cases reported. New Zealand has adopted needle exchange programs to reduce HIV spread among IV users.

42 HOUSING

The number of houses and apartments built in New Zealand fell steadily from 1974/75, when 34,000 new houses and flats were built, to 1981, when only 14,300 were constructed; since then, numbers have generally risen, reaching 18,000 in 1992, when New Zealand's housing stock totaled 1,220,000. More than half the total housing stock has been constructed since 1957. In recent decades, the government has introduced measures designed to assist the financing of housing by contractors and private owners. These include increases in the maximum housing loans advanced by the State Advances Corporation, low-interest loans for families with low incomes, and the establishment of a home savings scheme through the Post Office Savings Bank. Since 1937, the government Housing Corp. has built houses and flats for rental, with preference given to low-income families; by March 1985, 90,469 of these had been completed. Since 1951, the government has generously subsidized local authorities to provide pensioners' housing.

The average weekly expense for rent and home ownership in 1995/96 was about NZ$127. The average bank loan to homeowners was about two-thirds to three-fourths of the sale price. Most families own their own homes. The average private dwelling has three bedrooms, a living room, dining room, kitchen, laundry, bathroom, toilet, and garage. Most units are built of wood and have sheet-iron or tiled roofs.

43 EDUCATION

Education in New Zealand is compulsory for 10 years for children between ages 6 and 16, although most children attend school from the age of 5. The adult literacy rate is 99%. Public primary and secondary schools are administered by district education boards (or boards of governors) and school committees (the latter elected by householders), under the authority of the Department of Education. Kindergartens are run either by private persons or by voluntary organizations with partial state subsidies. Primary education is given at primary and intermediate schools (the latter giving the last two years of primary education), and postprimary education at secondary schools, technical high schools, or consolidated schools for pupils who live in rural areas. Evening classes are given by technical and secondary schools, and adult education classes are offered by the universities. Most state schools are coeducational, but some private schools not. New Zealand has 2,300 state primary schools and 60 privately owned schools. At the secondary level, there are 315 state-run schools and 15 private schools.

In 1997, 357,569 students attended 2,296 primary schools, with 19,523 teachers. Student-to-teacher ratio stood at 18 to one. In the same year, secondary schools had 433,347 students and 28,548 teachers. Attendance at vocational schools has grown tremendously in recent years, from a total enrollment of 3,071 in 1980 to 63,658 in 1994. For children in isolated areas, there is a public Correspondence School. In some regions there are special state primary and secondary schools for Maori children, but most Maori children attend public schools. Private primary and secondary schools are operated by individuals and religious bodies. Since 1975, under new legislation, many private schools have been voluntarily integrated into the public system.

There are six universities, all operating under the aegis of the University Grants Committee and the Universities Entrance Board: the University of Auckland, University of Waikato (at Hamilton), Massey University (at Palmerston North), Victoria University of Wellington, University of Canterbury (at Christchurch), and University of Otago (at Dunedin). All universities offer courses in the arts, social sciences, commerce, and science. An agricultural institution, Lincoln College, is associated with the University of Canterbury. Law is offered at Auckland, Waikato, Victoria, Canterbury, and Otago, and medicine at Auckland and Otago. The Central Institute of Technology, near Wellington, is the leading institution in a network of 24 polytechnic institutions. There are evening classes for adults interested in continuing their education at secondary schools, institutes and community centers. University tuition fees are low, and financial assistance is given to applicants who have passed special qualifying examinations. A total of 169,656 students were enrolled in tertiary institutions in 1997, with 10,833 teaching faculty.

44 LIBRARIES AND MUSEUMS

The National Library of New Zealand was founded in 1966 by the amalgamation of three state libraries and service divisions. It contains 5.2 million volumes, not including material in certain special collections. Its Extension Division provides services to public and school libraries throughout the country, and the Library School offers courses for the training and certification of librarians. The two largest libraries are at the University of Auckland (1.6 million volumes) and the University of Otago (571,000). The largest public libraries are in Auckland, Christchurch, Dunedin, and Wellington.

Outstanding art galleries and museums are the Auckland City Art Gallery (European and New Zealand paintings); the Canterbury Museum, Christchurch (ornithology, anthropology, and history); the Dunedin Public Art Gallery (paintings, period furniture, and china); the Otago Museum, Dunedin (ethnography, classical antiquities, ceramics); and the National Museum, Wellington (botany, ethnology, history). The nation's largest collection of Maori and Polynesian artifacts is found in the War Memorial Museum in Auckland. The Auckland Museum, founded in 1852, also has a fine collection of Maori artifacts. There is also a Museum of Puppets in Auckland and a Melanesian Mission House highlighting the Christian conversion of the indigenous peoples. There are hundreds of other historical and anthropological museums and sites throughout the country.

45 MEDIA

The government is in the process of privatizing and deregulating the telecommunications sector. In 1990, Telecom Corp., which runs the country's telephone services, was sold to a consortium led by American Information Technologies Corp. and Bell Atlantic. The number of telephones as of 1995 was at least 1.7 million.

After undergoing decentralization in the early 1970s, the national broadcasting system was again reorganized in the latter half of the decade, and united under one central board, the

Broadcasting Corp. of New Zealand. Under its authority are the Radio New Zealand network, a unified television service operating the two formerly competing national networks, TV1 and TV2, and one privately owned channel. As of 1999 there were 64 AM and 4 FM radio stations and 41 television broadcast stations. Color television was introduced in October 1973, and most households now have color sets. In 1997, there were 1,027 radios, 501 television sets, and 149 mobile phones per 1,000 population.

The Taranaki Herald, founded in 1852, is New Zealand's oldest surviving newspaper. The largest daily newspapers and their estimated 1999 circulation figures are:

New Zealand Herald (m)	Auckland	250,000
The Press (m)	Christchurch	102,000
The Dominion (m)	Wellington	64,200

The law provides for freedom of expression including free speech and a free press. Aside from the usual British legal limit for libel, the press enjoys complete editorial freedom.

As of 1996, there were 786,353 personal computers; in 1998 there were 468 Internet hosts per 1,000 population.

46 ORGANIZATIONS

Almost all aspects of New Zealand life have their appropriate organizations. A few of the more important ones are the Federated Farmers of New Zealand, the New Zealand Fruitgrowers' Association, the New Zealand Employers' Federation, the Chamber of Commerce (represented in almost every large town), the Returned Servicemen's Association, the New Zealand Federation of Labour, the Plunket Society (which deals with child welfare), the Royal Society of New Zealand, "Heritage" (devoted to the assistance of children deprived of one parent), the New Zealand Red Cross Society, the New Zealand Press Association, the New Zealand Institute of Public Administration, and the New Zealand Public Service Association. Important cultural organizations are the New Zealand Symphony Orchestra, the New Zealand Opera Company, the New Zealand Ballet, the Queen Elizabeth II Arts Council, and the New Zealand Music Federation.

47 TOURISM, TRAVEL, AND RECREATION

New Zealand draws many thousands of tourists to its shores because of the beauty, diversity, and compactness of its natural attractions and its varied sporting facilities. There are 10 national parks and 3 maritime parks. Of these, Fiordland is the largest, with some portions still unexplored. Urewera, noted for its forests and bird life, is the park in which early Maori culture is most strongly preserved; Tongariro includes two active volcanoes and is an important ski resort; and Mount Cook National Park includes Tasman Glacier, the largest glacier outside the polar regions. New Zealand has numerous thermal spas, particularly in the Rotorua area, which also offers Maori villages where traditional arts and crafts may be observed. The Waitomo Cave, on the North Island, is lit by millions of glowworms and may be toured all year. Lake Taupo and its streams form one of the world's richest trout fishing areas; Christchurch is home to one of the world's finest botanical gardens. Skiing is available on both the North and South Islands, and good deep-sea fishing along the North Island coast. New Zealand has first-class golf courses. Spectator sports include horse racing, soccer, cricket, and rugby.

All overseas visitors (except Australian nationals) need passports valid for at least six months beyond their intended stay in New Zealand. No visas are required for persons who are traveling on valid British passports; for citizens of Belgium, Canada, Denmark, Finland, France, Germany, Ireland, Liechtenstein, Luxembourg, Monaco, the Netherlands, Norway, Sweden, or Switzerland; or for US or Japanese nationals not planning to stay in New Zealand more than 30 days. There are no vaccination requirements.

Tourism slowed from 1989 to 1991 due to the strengthening of the New Zealand dollar, rising costs, and international developments, including the 1991 Persian Gulf War. Since that time it has grown steadily. In 1998, there were 1,484,512 visitor arrivals, 501,892 from Australia, 162,343 from the United States, 155,291 from the United Kingdom, and 152,977 from Japan. Tourism receipts totaled US$2.1 billion in 1997. That year there were 22,837 hotel rooms with a 50% occupancy rate. The average daily cost of staying in New Zealand, according to the 1999 UN estimate, was US$152 per day.

48FAMOUS NEW ZEALANDERS

Among New Zealand's best-known statesmen are Sir George Grey (1812–98), governor and later prime minister; Richard John Seddon (1845–1906), prime minister responsible for much social legislation; William Ferguson Massey (1856–1925); and Peter Fraser (1884–1950), World War II prime minister. Robert David Muldoon (1921–92) was prime minister from 1975 to 1984, when David Lange (b.1942) became the youngest man to hold that office in the 20th century. Sir John Salmond (1862–1924) was an eminent jurist. William Pember Reeves (1857–1932), outstanding journalist, politician, and political economist, was the director of the London School of Economics. Frances Hodgkins (1869–1947) was a highly regarded painter. Katherine Mansfield (Kathleen Beauchamp Murry, 1888–1923), author of many evocative stories, was a master of the short-story form. Other well-known authors include Sylvia Ashton-Warner (1908–84) and Maurice Shadbolt (b.1932). Two outstanding leaders of the Maori people were Sir Apirana Ngata (1874–1950) and Sir Peter Buck (1880–1951). Sir Truby King (1858–1938) pioneered in the field of child care.

Lord Ernest Rutherford (1871–1937), pioneer in atomic research and 1908 Nobel Prize winner for chemistry, was born in New Zealand. Other scientists include Sir Harold Gillies (1882–1960) and Sir Archibald McIndoe (1900–62), whose plastic surgery methods did much to rehabilitate war victims; Sir Brian G. Barratt-Boyes (b.1924), a researcher in cardiac-thoracic surgery; and Albert W. Liley (b.1929), a researcher in perinatal psychology. Prominent in the arts have been ballet dancers Alexander Grant (b.1925) and Rowena Jackson (b.1926); the singer and actor Inia Watene Te Wiata (1915–71); and the soprano Kiri Te Kanawa (b.1944). Sir Edmund Percival Hillary (b.1919) was the conqueror of Mt. Everest. The celebrated political cartoonist David Low (1891–1963) was born in New Zealand.

49DEPENDENCIES

Cook Islands

Part of New Zealand since 1901, the Cook Islands became internally self-governing on 4 August 1965. The Cook Islands Constitution Act of 1964 established the island group as wholly self-ruling but possessed of common citizenship with New Zealand as well as of a common head of state (the Queen). New Zealand exercises certain responsibilities for the defense and external affairs of the islands, in consultation with the Cook Islands government. Full independence from New Zealand is planned for 2007.

A parliamentary type of government, like New Zealand's, characterizes the new political relationship, with a cabinet composed of a prime minister and six other ministers. The 24-member Legislative Assembly—to which the prime minister and other cabinet members are responsible—is elected by the adult population of the islands every four years and can void the applicability of New Zealand laws to the territory under its juris-

diction. The constitution of the autonomous islands also allows a declaration of independence, if ever this should be the wish of the political leadership. The office of New Zealand high commissioner was abolished in 1975 and replaced by the office of Queen's representative. Cook Islands products continue to enter New Zealand freely, and the level of subsidies to the islands from the New Zealand government has persisted.

The Cook Islands, 15 islands lying between 8° and 23°s and 156° and 167°w, more than 3,220 km (2,000 mi) northeast of New Zealand, were discovered by James Cook in 1773. They became a British protectorate in 1888 and were annexed to New Zealand in 1901. They consist of the Southern Group, 8 islands the largest of which are Rarotonga (6,666 ha/16,472 acres) and Mangaia (5,191 ha/12,827 acres), and the Northern Group, 7 islands varying in size from Penrhyn (984 ha/2,432 acres) to Nassau (121 ha/299 acres). The total area is 241 sq km (93 sq mi). The northern islands are low-lying coral atolls, while the southern islands, including Rarotonga, the administrative seat, are elevated and fertile, and have the greater population. Except for Rarotonga, the islands suffer from lack of streams and wells, and water must be conserved. The islands lie within the hurricane area and sometimes experience destructive storms.

The population (estimated in 1993 at 18,903) is Polynesian and close in language and tradition to the New Zealand Maori. They are converts to Christianity. The islands are visited by government and freight vessels, and interisland shipping services are provided by commercially owned boats. An international airport opened for full services in 1973. Each inhabited island has a radio station.

The economy is based on agriculture, with the main exports being citrus fruits and juices, tomatoes, bananas, and pineapples. Other exports are copra, pearl shell, and clothing. The total fish catch was 950 tons in 1994, and fisheries exports were valued at $385,000 that year. In 1988, exports amounted to US$4.0 million. The main imports are foodstuffs, piece goods, oils, gasoline, tobacco, vehicles and parts, timber, and cement. In 1988, imports amounted to US$39.7 million.

Revenue for public finances is derived mainly from import duties and income tax. The 1990–91 budget envisioned expenditures of US$34.5 million. The New Zealand government provided grants and subsidies for capital development in health, education, other social services, economic development, and other purposes, covering one-third of the budget.

Free compulsory education is provided by the government at primary and secondary levels for all children between the ages of 6 and 15. All Cook Islanders receive free medical and surgical treatment, and schoolchildren receive free dental care.

Niue

An isolated coral island, Niue is 966 km (600 mi) northwest of the southern Cook Islands, and located at 19°02's and 169°52'w. Nieue became a British protectorate in 1900 and was annexed to New Zealand in 1901. Although Niue forms part of the Cook Islands, because of its remoteness and cultural and linguistic differences it has been separately administered. Niue has an area of 258 sq km (100 sq mi). Its population (of Polynesian stock) was 1,997 in 1993, down from a peak of 5,194 in 1966, and is continuing to decline, principally because of emigration to New Zealand, where Niueans outnumber those remaining on the island by two to one.

Niue became self-governing on 19 October 1974, in free association with New Zealand. Under the constitution, the former leader of government became the premier. An assembly of 20 members is elected by universal suffrage; 14 members represent village constituencies, and 6 are elected at large. The constitution provides for New Zealand to exercise various responsibilities for the external affairs and defense of Niue and to furnish economic and administrative assistance.

Niue's soil, although fertile, is not plentiful; arable land is confined to small pockets of soil among the coral rocks, making agriculture difficult. Since there are no running streams, the island is dependent on rainwater. The economy is based mainly on agriculture. Passionfruit products, coconut cream, lime juice and lime oil, and honey are exported, along with leather footballs and handicrafts. There are 124 km (77 mi) of all-weather roads. A steamship company maintains monthly service to New Zealand. A telephone system connects the villages, and an airport became fully operational in 1971.

Budget deficits are met by the New Zealand government, which also makes grants for capital development. Between 1970 and 1989 Western (non-US) and ODA and OOF bilateral commitments total US$62. Health services and education are free. Education is compulsory for children 5 to 14 years of age.

Tokelau Islands

The Tokelau Islands, situated between 8° and 10°s and 171° and 173°w, about 483 km (300 mi) north of Western Samoa, consist of three atolls, Fakaofo, Nukunonu, and Atafu. Total area is about 10 sq km (4 sq mi). Each atoll has a lagoon encircled by a number of reef-bound islets varying in length from about 90 m to 6.4 km (100 yards to 4 mi), in width from 90 m to 360 m (100–400 yards), and extending more than 3 m (10 ft) above sea level. All villages are on the leeward side, close to passages through the reefs. Lying in the hurricane belt, the islands have a mean annual rainfall of 305 cm (120 in). The inhabitants, of Polynesian origin, are British subjects and New Zealand citizens. Total population in 1992 was estimated at 1,760. Formerly part of the Gilbert and Ellice Islands group, the Tokelaus were transferred to New Zealand at the beginning of 1949. There is no resident European staff; executive functions are carried out on each atoll by appointed Tokelau mayors, magistrates, clerks, and other officials. An administrative officer based in Western Samoa coordinates administrative services for the islands. Samoan is the official language.

Subsistence farming and the production of copra for export are the main occupations. The total fish catch was 190 tons in 1994. Visits are made regularly by New Zealand Air Force planes, and a chartered vessel makes regular trading visits. Sources of revenue are an export duty on copra, customs dues, postage stamps, and trading profits.

Government expenditure is devoted mainly to agriculture, the provision of social services, and administrative costs. Annual deficits are met by New Zealand government subsidies. New Zealand's budgetary aid for 1991/1992 totaled US$2.4 million. Nutrition and health are reasonably good.

Ross Dependency

The Ross Dependency (between 160°E and 150°w and south of 60°s) is a section of the Antarctic continent that was brought under the jurisdiction of New Zealand in 1923. Its area is estimated at 414,400 sq km (160,000 sq mi). It is almost entirely covered by ice and is largely uninhabited. New Zealand activities in the dependency are coordinated and supervised by the Ross Dependency Research Committee (a government agency) and implemented by the Antarctic division of the Department of Scientific and Industrial Research. Exploitation of the region, apart from scientific expeditions, has been confined to whaling. A joint US-New Zealand scientific station established at Cape Hallett in 1957 for participation in the International Geophysical Year continues to operate for purposes of scientific research.

50 BIBLIOGRAPHY

Alley, Roderick (ed.). *New Zealand and the Pacific.* Boulder, Colo.: Westview, 1984.

Belich, James. *Making Peoples: A History of the New Zealanders, From Polynesian Settlement to the End of the Nineteenth Century.* Honolulu: University of Hawaii Press, 1996.

Bloomfield, G. T. *New Zealand: A Handbook of Historical Studies.* Boston: G. K. Hall, 1984.

Camilleri, Joseph A. *The Australia, New Zealand, US Alliance: Regional Security in the Nuclear Age.* Boulder, Colo.: Westview Press, 1987.

Chatham Islands: Heritage and Conservation. Christchurch, New Zealand: Canterbury University Press, 1996.

Gupta, S. M. *The Indian Origin of New Zealand's Maori.* New Delhi, India: Hindu World Publications, 1995.

Hawke, G. R. *The Making of New Zealand.* Cambridge: Cambridge University Press, 1985.

Hoadley, Steve. *The New Zealand Foreign Affairs Handbook.* Auckland: Oxford University Press, 1989.

Ip, Manying. *Dragons on the Long White Cloud: The Making of Chinese New Zealanders.* North Shore City, New Zealand: Tandem Press, 1996.

Jackson, William Keith. *Historical Dictionary of New Zealand.* Lanham, Md.: Scarecrow Press, 1996.

Johnston, Carol Morton. *The Farthest Corner: New Zealand, a Twice Discovered Land.* Honolulu, Hawaii: University of Hawaii Press, 1988.

Lealand, Geoffrey. *A Foreign Egg in Our Nest?: American Popular Culture in New Zealand.* Wellington: Victoria University Press, 1988.

Levine, Stephen. *The New Zealand Political System.* Auckland: Allen & Unwin, 1979.

Maori Art and Culture. Edited by D. C. Starzecka. London: British Museum Press, 1996.

Mascarenhas, R. C. *Government and the Economy in Australia and New Zealand: The Politics of Economic Policy Making.* San Francisco: Austin & Winfield, 1996.

McKinnon, Malcolm. *Independence and Foreign Policy: New Zealand in the World since 1935.* Auckland: Oxford University Press, 1993.

McLauchlan, Gordon (ed.). *The Illustrated Encyclopedia of New Zealand.* Auckland: D. Bateman, 1992.

Metge, Joan. *The Maoris of New Zealand.* London: Routledge & Kegan Paul, 1976.

Miller, Harold Gladstone. *New Zealand.* Westport, Conn.: Greenwood, 1983.

Mulgan, R. G. *Democracy and Power in New Zealand: A Study of New Zealand Politics.* 2d ed. New York: Oxford University Press, 1989.

Nga patai: Racism and Ethnic Relations in Aotearoa/New Zealand. Edited by Paul Spoonley, David Pearson, and Cluny Macpherson. Palmerston North, New Zealand: Dunmore Press, 1996.

Oddie, Graham, and Roy W. Perrett (eds.). *Justice, Ethics, and New Zealand Society.* New York: Oxford University Press, 1992.

Rice, Geoffrey W. (ed.) *The Oxford History of New Zealand.* 2nd ed. Auckland; New York: Oxford University Press, 1992.

Sharp, A. *Justice and the Maori: Maori Claims in New Zealand Political Argument in the 1980s.* New York: Oxford University Press, 1990.

The Oxford Illustrated History of New Zealand. New York: Oxford University Press, 1990.

OMAN

Sultanate of Oman
Saltanat 'Uman

CAPITAL: Muscat (Masqat).

FLAG: The flag is red with a broad stripe of white at the upper fly and green at the lower fly; in the canton, white crossed swords overlay a ceremonial dagger.

ANTHEM: *Nashid as-Salaam as-Sutani (Sultan's National Anthem).*

MONETARY UNIT: The Omani rial (RO), established in November 1972, is a paper currency of 1,000 baizas. There are coins of 2, 5, 10, 25, 50, 100, 250, and 500 baizas, and notes of 100, 250, and 500 baizas (the last two being replaced by coins) and 1, 5, 10, 20, and 50 rials. RO1 = $2.5974 ($1 = RO0.3850) as of 31 March 2000.

WEIGHTS AND MEASURES: The metric system was adopted on 15 November 1974; the imperial and local system are also used.

HOLIDAYS: Accession of the Sultan, 23 July; National Day, 18 November; Sultan's Birthday, 19 November. Movable Muslim religious holidays include 'Id al-Fitr, 'Id al-'Adha', and Milad an-Nabi.

TIME: 4 PM = noon GMT. Solar time is also observed.

¹LOCATION, SIZE, AND EXTENT

The Sultanate of Oman is the second-largest country after Sa'udi Arabia on the Arabian Peninsula, with an area officially estimated at 212,460 sq km (82,031 sq mi). Comparatively, the area occupied by Oman is slightly smaller than the state of Kansas. Oman's territory includes the tip of the strategically important Ra's Musandam, which juts into the Strait of Hormuz. Oman's part of the peninsula is separated from the rest of the country by the territory of the United Arab Emirates (UAE). Oman proper extends 972 km (604 mi) NE–SW and 513 km (319 mi) SE–NW. It is bordered on the N by the Strait of Hormuz, on the NE by the Gulf of Oman, on the E and S by the Arabian Sea, on the SW by the People's Democratic Republic of Yemen (PDRY), on the W by the Ar-Rub' al-Khali (Empty Quarter) and Sa'udi Arabia, and on the NW by the UAE. The total estimated boundary length is 3,466 km (2,154 mi).

²TOPOGRAPHY

Physically, Oman, except for the Dhofar (Zufar) region, consists of three divisions: a coastal plain, a mountain range, and a plateau. The coastal plain varies in width from 16 km (10 mi) to practically nothing near Muscat, where the hills descend abruptly to the sea. The mountain range reaches its greatest height in the Jabal al-Akhdar, about 3,075 m (10,090 ft). The plateau has an average height of about 300 m (1,000 ft) and is mostly stony and waterless, extending to the sands of the Ar-Rub' al-Khali. The coastline southward to Dhofar is barren and forbidding. From Salalah, a semicircular fertile plain extends to the foot of a steep line of hills, some 1,500 m (4,920 ft) high, and forms the edge of a stony plateau also extending to the sands of the Empty Quarter.

³CLIMATE

Annual rainfall in Muscat averages 10 cm (4 in), falling mostly in January. Dhofar is subject to the southwest monsoon, and rainfall up to 64 cm (25 in) has been recorded in the rainy season from late June to October. While the mountain areas receive more plentiful rainfall, some parts of the coast, particularly near the

island of Masirah, sometimes receive no rain at all within the course of a year. The climate generally is very hot, with temperatures reaching 54°C (129°F) in the hot season, from May to October.

⁴FLORA AND FAUNA

Desert shrub and desert grass, common to southern Arabia, are found. Vegetation is sparse in the interior plateau, which is largely gravel desert. The greater rainfall in Dhofar and the mountains makes the growth there more luxuriant. Coconut palms grow plentifully in Dhofar, and frankincense grows in the hills. Oleander and varieties of acacia abound.

Indigenous mammals include the cheetah, hyena, fox, wolf, and hare. Birds include the Arabian see-see partridge, redleg chukor partridge, and Muscat bee eater.

⁵ENVIRONMENT

Maintaining an adequate supply of water for agricultural and domestic use is Oman's most pressing environmental problem. The nation has only 0.5 cubic miles of water. Ninety-four percent is used in farming and 3% for industrial activity. Half of all rural dwellers do not have pure drinking water. Both drought and limited rainfall contribute to shortages in the nation's water supply. The nation's soil has shown increased levels of salinity. Pollution of beaches and other coastal areas by oil tanker traffic through the Strait of Hormuz and Gulf of Oman is also a persistent problem. In 1994, the nation had six endangered species of mammals and one endangered type of bird. Two plant species are threatened with extinction. Decrees have been passed to protect endangered species, which include the South Arabian leopard, Arabian oryx, mountain gazelle, goitered gazelle, Arabian tahr, green sea turtle, hawksbill turtle, and olive turtle.

⁶POPULATION

The population of Oman in 2000 was estimated at 2,532,556. An estimated 2.6% of the population is 65 years of age or older. The projected population for the year 2005 is 3,000,000, assuming a

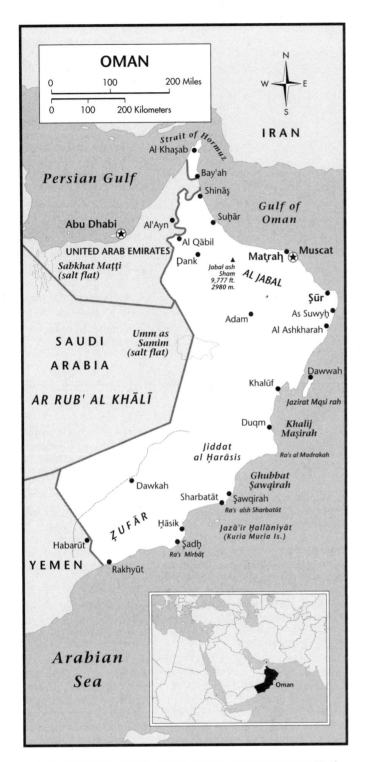

OMAN

IRAN

Persian Gulf

Strait of Hormuz

Al Khaşab

Bay'ah

Shināş

Abu Dhabi   Al'Ayn   Suḥār

Gulf of Oman

UNITED ARAB EMIRATES

Al Qābil

Ḏank

Jabal ash Sham 9,777 ft. 2980 m.   Maṭraḥ   Muscat

Sabkhat Maţţi (salt flat)

AL JABAL

Şūr

Adam   As Suwyḥ

Al Ashkharah

SAUDI ARABIA

Umm as Samim (salt flat)

AR RUB' AL KHĀLĪ

Khalūf   Dawwah

Jazirat Mqsi rah

Duqm   *Khalij Maşirah*

Jiddat al Ḥarāsis   Ra's al Madrakah

Ghubbat Şawqirah

Dawkah

Sharbatāt   Şawqirah

Ra's alsh Sharbatāt

ŻUFĀR   Ḥāsik   *Jazā'ir Ḥallāniyāt (Kuria Muria Is.)*

Habarūt   Şadḥ

Ra's Mirbāţ

YEMEN   Rakhyūt

Arabian Sea

Oman

LOCATION: 51°50′ to 59°40′E; 16°40′ to 26°20′N. **BOUNDARY LENGTHS:** Total coastline, 2,092 km (1,301 mi); Yemen, 288 km (179 mi); Sa'udi Arabia, 676 km (420 mi); UAE, 410 km (255 mi). **TERRITORIAL SEA LIMIT:** 12 mi.

crude birthrate of 37 per 1,000 population and a death rate of 4, resulting in a natural rate of change of 3.3% for the period 2000–2005. The population rate of change between 1995 and 2000 was 4.2%.

It was estimated that 84% of the population lived in urban areas in 2000. The greatest concentrations are around Muscat and on the Batinah coast; together, they have more than half the population. Salalah is the principal town of the south. The capital

city, Muscat, had a 2000 population of 635,000. Oman's next census is slated for 2003.

7MIGRATION

There is frequent movement of workers between Oman and neighboring states. As of December 1994, there were 455,000 guest workers, principally from Southeast Asia, Egypt, Jordan, and the Philippines. In 1999 the net migration rate was 0.84 migrants per 1,000 population.

8ETHNIC GROUPS

The indigenous population is predominantly Arab except on the Batinah coast, where there is significant Baluchi, Iranian, and African representation, and in Muscat and Matrah, where there are Khojas and other Indians, Baluchis, and Pakistanis. Tribal groups are estimated to number over 200.

9LANGUAGES

The official language is Arabic. Urdu, Baluchi, and several Indian dialects are also spoken, especially in the cities of Muscat and Matrah. English is taught as a second language.

10RELIGIONS

The state religion is Islam. Three-quarters of the population belongs to the Ibadhi sect. Tribes in the north are mainly Sunni Muslims of the Hanbali, Shafai, and Wahhabi rites. A minority of the population is Shi'a Muslim. There is a small community of Indian Hindu citizens, and there is reportedly a very small number of Christians. Non-Muslims, the majority of whom are non-citizen immigrant workers from South Asia, are free to worship at churches and temples, some of which are built on land donated by the Sultan.

11TRANSPORTATION

As of 1996 there were 32,800 km (20,382 mi) of roadways, of which only 9,840 km (6,115 mi) were paved, including 550 km (342 mi) of expressways. A major 800-km (500-mi) highway links Nazwa in the north to Thamarit and Salalah in the Dhofar region. A main coastal road has been laid from Muscat to Suhar, a distance of 240 km (150 mi), and the road from Muscat to Buraymi on the UAE border has been completed. In 1995, passenger car registrations totaled 166,300,000 and commercial vehicle registrations totaled 83,800.

In 1998 there were 143 airports, only 6 of which had paved runways. Seeb International airport, 30 km (19 mi) northwest of Muscat, is served by numerous international carriers, including Gulf Air, in which Oman holds a 20% interest. A second modern airport, at Salalah in the south, serves domestic flights. In 1997, 1,678,000 passengers were carried on scheduled international and domestic airline flights.

Mina's Qabus, near Muscat, is the main port in the north, serving international and regional shipping. Mina's Raysut, adjacent to Salalah, is the main port for the south. All Omani crude oil is exported from Mina's al-Fahl, west of Matrah. In 1998, Oman had 3 merchant vessels totaling 16,306 GRT.

12HISTORY

Oman's history can be traced to very early times. In Genesis 10:26–30, the descendants of Joktan are said to have migrated as far as Sephar (now Dhofar). The area was already a commercial and seafaring center in Sumerian times, and Phoenicians probably visited the coastal region. Other groups that probably came to the area in ancient times include the Baida and Ariba, Semitic tribes from northern Arabia, now extinct; the first Himyar dynasty from Yemen, which fell to the Persians in the time of Cyrus, about 550 BC; ancient Greek navigators; and the Parthians (174–136 BC).

The entire population was converted to Islam during the lifetime of Muhammad, but Oman soon became—and remains today— the center of the Ibadhi sect, which maintained that any pious Muslim could become caliph or imam and that the imam should be elected. Omani tribes have elected their imams since the second half of the 8th century.

The first prolonged contact with Europe came in 1507–08, when the Portuguese overran Muscat. They maintained control until they were driven out with Persian aid in 1649. During the next 75 years, Oman conquered Mombasa, Mogadishu, the island of Zanzibar, and the Portuguese possessions in East Africa. Later it held parts of what are now Iran and Pakistan.

The first sultanate was established in Muscat about 1775. In 1798, Britain concluded its first treaty with Muscat. Sa'id bin Sultan (r.1804–56) became dependent on British support, and after his death his sons quarreled over his succession (the basic Ibadhi tenet having been rejected). Thus weakened by political division, Muscat lost control of the interior. In 1920, the Treaty of Seeb was signed between the sultan of Muscat and the imam of Oman, acknowledging the autonomy of the imamate of Oman under the sovereignty of the Sultan. From 1920 to 1954 there was comparative peace. On the death of the imam in 1954, Sultan Sa'id bin Taymur moved to succeed him.

That year, Sa'id concluded a new agreement with Petroleum Development (Oman) Ltd., a British-managed oil company that had the oil concession for Oman. By this agreement, the company maintained a small army, the Muscat and Oman Field Force (MOFF), raised and led by the British. In early 1955, it subdued the area up to and including the town of 'Ibri. When British troops took Buraymi, MOFF occupied the rest of Oman and expelled the rebellious new imam. By 1959 when the last of the insurgents supporting the imam were defeated, the sultan voided the office and declared the Treaty of Seeb terminated. The imam, exiled in Sa'udi Arabia, tried in vain to muster Arab support for his return.

Under the terms of the Anglo-French Declaration of 10 March 1962, the sultanate of Muscat was proclaimed an independent and sovereign state. Certain Arab states charged, however, that the UK was maintaining a colonial presence in the former imamate of Oman. In 1965 and repeatedly thereafter, the UN called unsuccessfully for the elimination of the British presence. Oman joined the UN late in 1971.

Meanwhile, as early as 1964, a tribal rebellion had been brewing in the Dhofar region. The rebel tribes, organized as the Dhofar Liberation Front and aided by South Yemen, later joined forces with the Marxist Popular Front for the Liberation of Oman and the Arab Gulf. The insurgency was suppressed in 1975 with direct military assistance from Jordan and Iran. A treaty with Yemen defining the border was ratified in 1992.

Qabus bin Sa'id ousted his father, Sa'id bin Taymur, on 23 July 1970 and has ruled as sultan since that time. He immediately changed the name of the country from Muscat and Oman to the Sultanate of Oman and has presided over an extensive modernization program, easing his father's harsh restrictions and opening the country to the outside world, while preserving political and military ties with the British. Oman has been a proponent of cooperation among the Gulf states. A member of the GCC, it has also sought to keep good relations with Iran. Because Oman dominates the Strait of Hormuz, which links the Gulf of Oman with the Persian Gulf, its strategic importance drew it and the US closer together with the start of the Iran–Iraq war in 1979. Under the terms of a pact signed in 1980, US military personnel and ships have been given access to Omani military and naval bases and are permitted to preposition military material for use in contingencies.

Oman pursues a moderate, independent foreign policy. Unlike most Arab states, it supported the Camp David accords and did not break relations with Egypt following its peace treaty with Israel. Similarly, during the Gulf War, Oman sent forces to Sa'udi Arabia and granted strategic facilities to the US, but did not sever diplomatic relations with Iraq during the conflict.

In 1994 reports began appearing of arrests of critics of the Omani government. It was estimated that nearly 500 such critics with points of view ranging from the Arab nationalist Ba'th movement to Islamists supporting the Sunni Muslim Brotherhood were detained by the Omani government.

Through 1995 Oman was considered as having "graduated" from the ranks of under-developed nations needing World Bank loans. Its ambitious economic goals include a 10-year plan for cultivating tourism and plans to improve its infrastructure, including water desalinization. However, in 1998, the economy was adversely affected when the price of oil dropped below $10 per barrel, a 25-year low. Oman agreed with the Organization of Oil Exporting Countries (OPEC), of which Oman is not a member, to reduce global oil production by 2.1 million barrels of crude per day until April 2000 in the hope of raising oil prices to $18 per barrel. In October 1999, the Omani oil minister recommended extending oil production cuts beyond the date originally proposed. Meanwhile, Oman has sought to diversify its economic base and ease its dependence on oil. A gas liquefaction plant at Sur was slated for completion in 2000.

As of 1999, Oman held to a middle-of-the-road stance of conciliation and compromise in Middle Eastern politics. In January 1999, Oman's foreign minister met with his counterparts from Egypt, Sa'udi Arabia, Syria, and Yemen at a closed meeting in Cairo to forge a position on the question of Iraq. Also in 1999, Oman's sultan, Qabus bin Sa'id, signed an agreement with the president of the United Arab Emirates defining the borders between Oman and the emirate of Abu Dhabi.

13 GOVERNMENT

Oman's sultan is an absolute monarch. The sultanate has no constitution, legislature, or suffrage. In 1970, Sultan Qabus appointed a cabinet of ministers responsible for various government departments and functions.

A State Consultative Council, established in 1981, consisted of 55 appointed representatives of government, the private sector, and regional interests.

This body was replaced in 1991 by a Majlis Ash-Shura, a 59-seat Consultative Council, which was seen as a first step toward popular participation in government. The Sultan expanded the membership to 80 seats after the country's first national census in 1993.

The Council has no formal legislative powers but may question government ministers, and recommend changes to new laws on economic and social policy. These recommendations have led to amendments to proposed decrees.

On 6 November 1996 the Sultan decreed the country's first "basic law" which provides for citizens' basic rights in writing and a body known as the Majlis Oman (Council of Oman) which includes a new Council of State (Majlis Al-Dawla) and the current Consultative Council.

14 POLITICAL PARTIES

There are no legal political parties nor, at present, any active opposition movement. As more and more young Omanis return from education abroad, it seems likely that the traditional, tribal-based political system will have to be adjusted.

15 LOCAL GOVERNMENT

The nation is divided into three governates (Muscat, Musandam, Dhofar) and 41 wilayats (districts), governed by walis, who are responsible to the Ministry of the Interior. The Governorate of the Capital is responsible for the administration of Muscat.

[16]JUDICIAL SYSTEM

Shari'ah courts based on Islamic law administer justice, with the Chief Court at Muscat. Qadis, or religious judges, appointed by the sultan, function within each wilayat. Appeals from the Chief Court are made to the sultan, who exercises powers of clemency. The Shari'ah courts, adhering to Islamic law, equate the testimony of one man with that of two women. The magistrate court, a criminal court, adjudicates violations of the criminal code. There is also a security court, rarely used, which handles internal security cases. A commercial dispute may be resolved at the Authority for Settlement of Commercial Disputes. A rent dispute committee hears landlord-tenant disputes.

In 1996, a basic law providing for citizens' basic rights was promulgated by the Sultan. The basic law affirms the independence of the judiciary. There are no jury trials.

[17]ARMED FORCES

Oman's armed forces, including foreign personnel and British advisors numbered 43,500 in 2000. The army had 25,000 personnel, the air force 4,100, and the navy 4,200. Another 4,000 men (Jebalis, or mountain dwellers) are organized into paid Home Guard units (Firqats) in their tribal areas. The elite Royal Household brigade, naval unit, and air unit number 6,500, including 2 special forces regiments. All military service is voluntary. In 1998 Oman spent $1.7 billion on defense or 11% of gross domestic product.

[18]INTERNATIONAL COOPERATION

On 7 October 1971, Oman gained membership in the UN; the nation belongs to ESCWA and all the nonregional specialized agencies except IAEA. Oman also participates in G-77, GCC, and the Arab League, as well as the Islamic Conference.

[19]ECONOMY

Oman's location at the entrance to the Persian Gulf for centuries made it an entrepôt for trade, including a substantial traffic in arms and slaves. Its prosperity declined in the 19th century, when, as a result of Western dominance in Asia, traditional trade patterns and communications routes were radically changed. Oman's economy then became predominantly dependent on agriculture and fishing.

The situation changed with the discovery of oil in 1964. Production began in August 1967, and by the mid-1970s most of the economy revolved around oil. The hydrocarbons sector accounted for 75% export earnings and government revenues, and 40% of GDP in 1999. Despite diversification efforts, petroleum's share of GDP rose from 37% in 1994 to 38.2% in 1995. Oman's proven oil reserves exceed 5.3 billion barrels. Based on current oil production of about 890,000 to 910,000 barrels per day, oil reserves should last some 20 to 25 years. In recent years, the production of natural gas has become a significant factor of the economy. Gas reserves increased from 9.8 trillion cubic feet in 1990 to 27.5 trillion cubic feet at the end of 1995 to 28.4 trillion cubic feet in 1999 and are further increasing. A project was launched to build an underwater gas pipeline to Korea, India, and Japan for the export of gas, which was scheduled for completion in 2000. GDP grew annually at an average rate of 6.3% between 1988 and 1998.

[20]INCOME

The US Central Intelligence Agency (CIA) reports that in 1998 Oman's gross domestic product (GDP) was estimated at $18.6 billion. The per capita GDP was estimated at $7,900. The annual growth rate of GDP was estimated at -8.5%. The average inflation rate in 1998 was -2.9%. The CIA defines GDP as the value of all final goods and services produced within a nation in a given year and computed on the basis of purchasing power parity

(PPP) rather than value as measured on the basis of the rate of exchange. It was estimated that agriculture accounted for 2% of GDP, industry 50%, and services 48%.

The World Bank reports that for the same period per capita private consumption (in PPP terms) was $6,750. Private consumption includes expenditures of individuals, households, and non-governmental organizations. Approximately 22% of household consumption was spent on food, 25% on fuel, 13% on health care, and 21% on education.

[21]LABOR

The estimated Omani work force was about a million in 1997. A large proportion of the population were still engaged in subsistence agriculture or fishing. The skilled local labor force is small, and many of the larger industries depend on foreign workers from India, Pakistan, the Philippines, Bangladesh, and Sri Lanka—foreign laborers constituted over 80% of the modern-sector workforce in 1996.

Omani law does not address the right of union formation. Any employee, though, may file a grievance with the Labor Welfare Board. Lower-paid workers, such as clerks, mechanics, and salesmen, use the board frequently.

The minimum working age is 13 but this provision is not enforced against the employment of children in family businesses or on family farms.

The minimum wage for nonprofessional workers was $260 per month in 1999. However, many classes of workers (domestic servants, farmers, government employees) are not required to receive the minimum wage and the government is not consistent in its enforcement of the minimum wage law.

The private sector workweek is 40 to 45 hours long, while government officials have a 35 hour workweek.

[22]AGRICULTURE

Agriculture contributes only about 3% to GDP, but engages 38% of the economically active population, mostly at a subsistence level. The potential for expanding agriculture in Oman is good. Land use is determined primarily by the availability of water. There is extensive cultivation along the Batinah and Shumailiyah coasts; in the interior, however, cultivation is confined to areas near wadis, where water is taken off by a system of water channels (fallaj). The total area under cultivation is estimated to be about 63,000 hectares (155,600 acres).

The principal agricultural product is the date, at 135,000 tons in 1998. On the Baunah coast, groves containing some 10 million date palm trees form a strip 240 km (150 mi) long and 40 km (25 mi) wide. Fruits grown in Dhofar include bananas, mangoes, and coconuts. Citrus fruits (notably limes), nuts, melons, bananas, coconuts, alfalfa, and tobacco are also grown. Tomatoes, cabbages, eggplant, okra, and cucumbers are important winter crops. Frankincense is traditionally produced from about 8,000 trees growing wild in Dhofar. Along the Batinah coast, a wide variety of produce is grown, including fruits, wheat, rice, and durra. Agricultural exports were valued at $269.8 million in 1997, while agricultural imports amounted to $862.4 million that year.

[23]ANIMAL HUSBANDRY

Goats, sheep, donkeys, and camels are widely raised. In 1998 there were 725,000 goats, 155,000 sheep, 146,000 head of cattle, 95,000 camels, and 27,000 donkeys. There is a relatively large-scale cattle-raising industry in Dhofar. Total meat production in 1998 was 27,000 tons. Oman estimates that it is 53% self-sufficient in milk production, 46% in beef, 44% in eggs, and 23% in milk. The camels of Oman are famous for their fine riding qualities.

24FISHING

The waters of the Gulf of Oman are rich in sardines, mackerel, shrimp, lobsters, crayfish, tuna, barracudas, groupers, and sharks. The annual catch in 1997 was 117,049 tons, mainly sardines. Fishing employs about 26,000 persons. Recent investment in onshore processing and refrigeration plants, harbors, and repair yards has facilitated commercial fishing development. Exports of fish products amounted to $67.6 million in 1997. The government subsidizes the cost of boats and engines to promote employment in fishing. Fish stocks and breeding patterns are studied at a research center south of Muscat. In 1996, three new fishing harbors were opened (at Bukha in Musandam, Quriyat, and Shinas), at a combined cost of r 10.3 million and with a capacity for about 1,000 small boats.

25FORESTRY

Forest coverage is less than 5%. The use of wood as the sole fuel and overgrazing by goats have depleted the forests of Oman, but the interior of the country is fairly well wooded. Oman imported $14.3 million in forest products during 1997.

26MINING

Large copper deposits have been discovered northwest of Muscat; the Sohar mining and smelting complex was built by the government-owned Oman Mining Co. in the early 1980s. As of 1991, the Sahar copper deposits were nearly exhausted; however, other deposits were discovered at Hajl al-Safi and at Raka in Ibri. More than half of Oman's copper production was taken from the Lasail Mine, with much of the remaining output from the Aarja surface mine. The Ministry of Petroleum and Minerals has reported proven copper reserves at 8 tons and proven chromite ore reserves at 1.6 tons. Oman also has large deposits of limestone, gypsum, asbestos, and marble, along with chromite and manganese. Output of chromite in 1996 was 15,252 tons; sulfur, 30,000 tons; sand and gravel, 9.6 million tons; gold, 576 kg; silver, 97 kg; and marble, 150,000 tons.

27ENERGY AND POWER

Oil, discovered in 1964 in western Oman, has transformed the nation's economic life. As of 1998, oil export revenues totaled $5.2 billion and accounted for 80% of all export revenues. When production began in 1967, several foreign interests combined to form a majority backing in Petroleum Development Oman (PDO). In July 1974, foreign participation dropped to 40%, with the remaining 60% held by the government. PDO was the lone oil producer in the country until the Elf-Sumitomo-Wintershall group was granted a concession in 1980. Oman is unlike the other Middle Eastern oil producers, because its oil was discovered decades after most of its neighbors, and its oil fields are generally smaller, less productive, and more costly to maintain. Also, Oman is not a member of OPEC, but a leader in IPEC, the main independent petroleum exporter's organization. In 1998, however, Oman cooperated with OPEC in reducing its oil production to help stabilize world oil prices.

Output of oil in 1998 averaged 906,000 barrels per day. Petroleum reserves were estimated at 5.3 billion barrels in early 1999, enough to last until around 2020 at the current rate of production. Proved reserves of natural gas were estimated to be 28.4 trillion cu ft (804 million cu m) at that time (over 100 years' supply at current production levels), and it is anticipated that Oman will increasingly replace oil with gas as fuel. Although Oman currently does not export natural gas, it is currently constructing a $2.5 billion, 6.6-million-ton per year LNG plant at Qalhut. Government plans call for gas to contribute 15% of GDP by 2002.

With limited oil reserves, Oman is currently trying to reduce its reliance on oil as the chief source of revenue. Oman is trying to establish itself as a consultant to other independent oil and natural gas producing nations, like Kazakhstan and India.

In 1998, net installed electric capacity was 2,037,000 kW and production totaled 7,360 million kWh.

28INDUSTRY

Besides oil, industry in Oman still consists largely of small-scale food-processing enterprises. Many new industries were set up in the 1980s, including a cement plant with an annual capacity of 609,000 tons. In 1995, Oman's cement production totaled 1.4 million tons. The majority of these manufacture non-metallic mineral products followed by wood and wood products, and fabricated metal products. The Rusail industrial estate had 81 working factories by 1996, with 15 more under construction. Another four such industrial sites are planned in Salalah, Sohar, Sur, and Nizwa.

29SCIENCE AND TECHNOLOGY

Most research conducted in Oman has been done at the behest of the government; agriculture, minerals, water resources, and marine sciences have drawn the most attention. Sultan Qaboos University, founded in 1985, has colleges of science, medicine, engineering, and agriculture. In 1987–97, science and engineering students accounted for 13% of college and university enrollments. The Institute of Health Sciences, under the Ministry of Health, was founded in 1982. Muscat Technical Industrial College, founded in 1984, has departments of computing and mathematics, laboratory science, and electrical, construction, and mechanical engineering. The Oman Natural History Museum, founded in 1983, includes the national herbarium and the national shell collection. All of these organizations are located in Muscat.

30DOMESTIC TRADE

In Muscat and Matrah, much of the business is carried on by long-established and settled Khoja and Hindu merchants. Normal business hours are 8:30 AM to 1:30 PM and 4 to 7 PM, Saturday–Wednesday; banking hours are generally 8 AM to noon, though some banks reopen from 4 to 6 PM. Banks and businesses close at 11:30 AM on Thursday and remain closed Friday. Business hours are reduced during the Ramadan fast.

31FOREIGN TRADE

Since 1967, oil has been the chief export. In 1999 Oman's major export commodities were crude petroleum (77%) and motor vehicles and parts (8.6%). Other exports included tobacco (2.0%), copper (1.1%), and fresh fish (0.9%). In 1996 Oman's imports were distributed among the following categories: consumer goods, 16.7%; food, 14.0%; fuels, 1.1%; industrial supplies, 21.1%; machinery, 18.5%; transportation, 23.4%, and other, 5.3%.

Principal trading partners in 1998 (in millions of US dollars) were as follows:

COUNTRY	EXPORTS	IMPORTS	BALANCE
Japan	1,009	868	141
Korea	694	78	616
Thailand	1,009	31	978
China (inc. Hong Kong)	662	71	591
Philippines	154	2	152
United States	209	333	-124
Singapore	120	64	56
United Kingdom	138	519	-381
Germany	11	282	-271
United Arab Emirates	1	1,093	-1,092

32BALANCE OF PAYMENTS

Oman's balance of payments account is dominated by crude oil export earnings, consumer and capital goods and services, imports payments, and by large outgoing remittances by foreign workers.

The US Central Intelligence Agency reports that in 1997 the purchasing power parity of Oman's exports was $7.6 billion while imports totaled $4 billion resulting in a trade balance of $3.6 billion.

The International Monetary Fund (IMF) reports that in 1997 Oman had exports of goods totaling $7,631 million and imports totaling $4,649 million. The services credit totaled $18 million and debit $1,166 million. The following table summarizes Oman's balance of payments for 1997 in millions of US dollars.

Current Account		-57
Balance on goods	2,982	
Balance on services	-1,148	
Balance on income	-460	
Current transfers	-1,431	
Capital Account		...
Financial Account		553
Direct investment abroad	...	
Direct investment in Oman	49	
Portfolio investment assets	...	
Portfolio investment liabilities	...	
Other investment assets	-39	
Other investment liabilities		544
Net Errors and Omissions		34
Reserves and Related Items		-531

33BANKING AND SECURITIES

The Central Bank of Oman, set up in April 1975, has powers to regulate credit and is authorized to make temporary advances to the government.

Banks in Oman are generally in good financial shape because of close regulation by the Central Bank of Oman. All commercial banks in the sultanate instructed to raise their paid-up capital to RO10 million for local banks and RO3 million for foreign banks. The Central Bank of Oman advised all banks which were unable to comply with these new requirements to merge with other commercial banks. The Central Bank has been encouraging banks to merge in order to cut down on the oversupply of banking services. Banks are required to maintain a 12% level of capital adequacy and restrict consumer lending to 30% of the loan portfolio. In 1999, there were 16 local and foreign commercial banks and four specialized banks. The largest local bank is the National Bank of Oman followed by Oman International Bank, Bank Muscat, Commercial Bank of Oman, Oman Arab Bank, and Bank Dhofar Al Omani Al Fransi.

The British Bank of the MIddle East (BBME) was the first foreign bank to establish itself in Oman in 1948. Today, foreign banks, in descending order of local branch asset size, include British Bank, Standard Chartered Bank, The British Bank, Bank of Baroda, Bank Saderate Iran, Bank Melli Iran, Banque Banorabe, National Bank of Abu Dhabi, and Citibank. The banking sector has been under pressure to increase its proportion of Omani staff to 90%, but the deadline for such a move has been progressively delayed. Because of the proliferation of branches concentrated in coastal areas, commercial banks now have to open two branches in the interior for every branch opened along the coast.

An Omani stock market, the Muscat Securities Market (MSM), was officially established in 1988, but trading did not begin until the following year. By 1999 there were 131 companies listed on the exchange with a combined capitalization of $4.4 billion. The MSM has now established a link with the Bahrain Stock Exchange (BSE) where shares can be cross-listed. A similar agreement with Kuwait is expected. The MSM Index showed a 52.5% loss in 1998 after posting a spectacular 141% gain the year before. The drop-off has been attributed to speculation, over-valued offerings, the impact of the Asian financial crises, and the drop in oil prices.

34INSURANCE

As of 1997, one national insurance firm, the Oman National Insurance Co. (SAOG), and around 17 foreign-owned firms were operating in Oman. Gross premiums for the Oman National Insurance Co. in 1995 were RO5.75 million.

35PUBLIC FINANCE

Although Oman is a relatively small oil producer, oil revenues support 69% of government expenditures. Higher oil prices in 1997 and a 5% cut in capital spending produced a budget deficit of only $47 million, a substantial improvement over 1996. With the fall in oil prices in 1998, however, the government's budget fell deeply into deficit, and had to be financed by loans and by drawing down the State General Reserve Fund. In anticipation of still further drops in the price of oil, the government increased a number of taxes and imposed spending cuts of between 5 and 10% on most government ministries. Still, the US Central Intelligence Agency (CIA) estimates that in 1999 Oman's central government took in revenues of approximately $4 billion and had expenditures of $5.6 billion including capital expenditures of $2.2 million. Overall, the government registered a deficit of approximately $1.6 billion, or about 11% of GDP. Total external debt is estimated to exceed $3 billion.

The following table shows an itemized breakdown of government revenues and expenditures. The percentages were calculated from data reported by the International Monetary Fund. The dollar amounts (millions) are based on the CIA estimates provided above.

REVENUE AND GRANTS	100%	4,000
Tax revenue	25.6%	1,025
Non-tax revenue	72.9%	2,917
Capital revenue	0.8%	33
Grants	0.6%	25
EXPENDITURES	100%	5,600
General public services	9.7%	544
Defense	32.4%	1,816
Public order and safety	6.0%	337
Education	15.6%	872
Health	7.2%	404
Social security	5.0%	278
Housing and community amenities	6.1%	342
Recreation, cultural, and religious affairs	2.0%	110
Economic affairs and services	10.4%	584
Interest payments	5.6%	313

36TAXATION

Introduced in 1971, a corporate income tax on commercial enterprises other than individual traders remains the only tax in the country. Rates range from 5% to 50%. Legislation in 1981 reduced the maximum tax rate to 15% for companies in which Omanis hold at least a 51% equity, and to 20% for companies in which the Omani equity is between 35% and 50%. Companies engaged in agriculture, fishing and any other essential activity deemed by the government are exempt from income taxes. Oman has a comprehensive double taxation treaty with France.

37CUSTOMS AND DUTIES

General import duties are 5% ad valorem on the c.i.f. value of the good. There are a number of exempt goods, including many imports from GCC member states. Protective tariffs are levied seasonally on a number of fruits and vegetables.

38 FOREIGN INVESTMENT

The principal foreign investment is in the oil sector. Foreign private investment is officially encouraged in certain areas—such as industry, agriculture, and fishing—through an initial five-year tax exemption, which may be renewed for another five years. Foreign participation in a local company cannot exceed 65% (this also applies to the sharing of profits). Companies holding commercial agencies must also have at least 51% Omani participation. In 1999, the largest foreign investor was Royal Dutch Shell Oil, which holds a 34% of the shares of the state oil company, Petroleum Development Oman, and 30% of Oman Liquid Natural Gas. Other investors in the oil industry include Occidental Petroleum, Hapex, Amoco, and Elf Aquitaine.

39 ECONOMIC DEVELOPMENT

Oman's economic policy operates under five-year development plans. Oman's second five-year plan (1981–85) suffered to some extent from the impact of declining oil prices in the early 1980s. The objectives of the third development plan (1986–90) were to encourage the private sector to play a larger role in the economy and to expand such areas as agriculture, fishing, manufacturing, and mining. The fourth five-year development plan (1991–1995), aimed to achieve average annual GDP growth rates of just over 6% and the diversification of the sources of national income in order to reduce the dependence on the oil sector. The declared aim of the fifth five-year plan (1996–2000) was to achieve a balance budget. To meet this goal the government plans to increase non-oil revenues, reduce public spending, enhance privatization of the economy, and encourage foreign investment. The largest project in the plan is a $2.4 billion liquefied natural gas project in Sur. Deliveries to Korea, India, and Japan were expected to begin in mid-2000. An emphasis on income diversification has opened the country to foreign participation in the form of joint ventures.

40 SOCIAL DEVELOPMENT

Oman maintains a social security system that provides old-age pensions, disability and survivorship benefits to employed citizens ages 15–59. This program is funded by 5% contributions from employees and the government, and 8% contribution by employers. Retirement is set at age 60 for men and age 55 for women. Work injury legislation was introduced in 1977, and provides disability and medical benefits for injured workers.

Oman does not have a written constitution or anti-discrimination laws. Islamic precepts result in de facto discrimination against women in a number of areas, such as inheritance. Traditional views on the subordinate role of women in society lead most women to work exclusively inside the home. Land grants and housing loans are rarely given to females. Some progress is being made, however, and women have begun to enter professional areas such as medicine and communications in greater numbers. In 1999, about 30% of all civil servants were women. The government has also made efforts to increase educational opportunities for women. Women comprise roughly half of the 5,000 students at Sultan Qaboos University, and 50% of the total student body in the public school system. In addition, government scholarships for study abroad, formerly granted almost exclusively to men, were divided evenly between men and women in 1999.

Ethnic tensions exist in Oman, and the Shihuh tribe in the province of Musadam complain about police harassment. There have been periodic episodes of violence between Shihuh and security forces.

The 1996 Basic Charter guaranteed fundamental human rights, but as of 1999 the government had yet to pass the laws needed to implement it. Human rights abuses in 1995 included arbitrary arrest, prolonged detention and the mistreatment of prisoners. Human rights organizations are prohibited by law from operating in Oman, and international monitors are unable to inspect prisons.

41 HEALTH

In 1990–97, there were 0.9 doctors per 1,000 population. Around 12% of children under 5 were underweight in 1993, and goiter was prevalent in 10% of school-age children.

Average life expectancy in 1999 was 71.3 years. Infant mortality was 24.7 per 1,000 live births, and the general mortality rate was 4.3 per 1,000 in 1990-1995. The birth rate was 38 per 1,000 people. About 16% of married women (ages 15 to 49) were using contraception in 1989–90. The fertility rate, 6.1 children per Omanian woman living through her childbearing years, is one of the highest in the Middle East and North Africa.

In 1994-95, 89% of the population had access to safe water, and 56% had adequate sanitation. In 1993, 89% of the population had access to health care services. In 1995, children up to one year old were vaccinated against tuberculosis (96%); diphtheria, pertussis, and tetanus (99%); polio (99%); measles (98%); and hepatitis B (99%).

There were only 59 AIDS cases in 1996. The HIV-1 seroprevalence rate was 0.1 per 100 adults in 1997.

42 HOUSING

In May 1973, Sultan Qabus approved the Law of People's Housing to make housing loans to needy Omanis. By 1985, 5,300 low-income units had been built. In 1989, 34% of all housing units were traditional Arabic houses, 30% were flats, and 27% were villas. Owners occupied 70% of all dwellings, 20% were rented, and 9% were provided by employers.

43 EDUCATION

Pre-university education in Oman has three stages: primary, preparatory, and secondary. Six years of primary schooling are followed by preparatory school. Academic results of the preparatory exams determine the type of secondary education the student will receive.

The adult illiteracy rate was estimated at 28.1% for the year 2000 (males, 19.6%; females, 38.3%). In 1998, there were 411 primary schools with 313,516 students and 12,052 teachers. Student-to-teacher ratio stood at 26 to one. In secondary schools in 1998, there were 12,436 teachers and 217,246 students. In 1993, there were 252 Literacy Centers and 176 Adult education centers. Three teachers' colleges were functioning as of 1986. The Institute of Agriculture at Nazwa became a full college by 1985. Sultan Qaboos University opened in 1986. In 1998, all higher level institutions had 1,307 teachers and 16,032 students.

44 LIBRARIES AND MUSEUMS

The library at Sultan Qaboos University has 102,300 volumes, and the Muscat Technical and Industrial College has 10,000 volumes. A British Council Library of almost 8,000 volumes was founded in 1973 in Matrah. The Ministry of National Heritage and Culture administers the National Museum of Ruwi, the Qurm Museum, and the Oman Natural History Museum, which includes the National Herbarium of Oman and the National Shell Collection.

45 MEDIA

Postal, telephone, and telex systems are supervised by the Ministry of Posts, Telegraphs, and Telephones. By the end of 1991, the entire country was connected to a 79,000-line telephone network. As of 1995, there were 150,000 main telephone lines. Oman now has international direct dialing to most major countries. Radio and television facilities are government owned; color television was introduced in 1974. As of 1999 there were 2 AM and 4 FM radio stations and 13 television broadcast stations. In 1997 there were 582 radios, 602 television sets, and 25 mobile phones in use per 1,000 population.

Newspapers and journals in Arabic include the daily *Al-Wattan* (1999 circulation, 32,500) and *Oman* (21,500) and weekly periodicals such as *Al-Aquida* and *Al-Usra*. Two English-language newspapers are also published.

A 1984 Press and Publication Law authorizes the state to censor domestic and imported foreign publications. Journalists are said to practice self-censorship to avoid harassment. Criticism of the sultan is explicitly illegal.

[46]ORGANIZATIONS

There is a Chamber of Commerce and Industry in Muscat. Among the social and cultural organizations are the Oman Women's Association, the Oman Cultural Club (for university graduates), and the Omani Historical Association (open to non-Omanis).

[47]TOURISM, TRAVEL, AND RECREATION

Oman is cautiously developing tourism, which was discouraged by previous rulers. All travelers except citizens of other Gulf states, must obtain a visa and a No Objection Certificate. Most large hotels have clubs that offer various recreational activities; water sports are popular, but spear fishing has been prohibited as a conservation measure. In 1998, 612,000 foreign tourists visited Oman, spending an estimated $112 million. There were 3,065 hotel rooms with 4,460 beds and a 49% occupancy rate in 1996.

According to 1999 UN estimates, the cost of staying in Muscat was $151 per day, and $156 per day in Salalah.

[48]FAMOUS OMANIS

Oman's great Islamic religious leader, whose followers are called Ibadhis, was 'Abdallah bin Ibad (fl.8th century); many of his teachings are still followed in Oman. Ahmad ibn Sa'id (r.1741–83), founder of the present dynasty, freed Muscat from Persian rule. Sultan Qabus bin Sa'id (b.1940) has ruled Oman since his removal of Sa'id bin Taymur (1910–72), his father, in 1970.

[49]DEPENDENCIES

Oman has no territories or colonies.

[50]BIBLIOGRAPHY

Allen, Calvin H. *Oman: the Modernization of the Sultanate.* Boulder, Colo.: Westview; London: Croom Helm, 1987.

American University. *Persian Gulf States: Country Studies.* Washington, D.C.: Government Printing Office, 1984.

Casey-Vine, Paula. (ed.) *Oman in History.* London: Immel Publishers, 1995.

Chatty, Dawn. *Mobile Pastoralists: Development Planning and Social Change in Oman.* New York: Columbia University Press, 1996.

Clements, Frank. *Oman.* (rev. ed.) Santa Barbara, Calif.: Clio, 1994.

———. *Oman: The Reborn Land.* New York: Longman, 1980.

Oman and the United Arab Emirates. London: Lonely Planet, 2000.

Pridham, B.R. (ed.). *Oman: Economic, Social, and Strategic Developments.* Wolfeboro, N.H.: Croom Helm, 1987.

Skeet, Ian. *Oman: Politics and Development.* New York: St. Martin's, 1992.

Stannard, Dorothy. (ed.) *Oman and the United Arab Emirates.* Singapore: APA Publications, 1998.

Townsend, John. *Oman: The Making of the Modern State.* London: Croom Helm, 1977.

Wilkinson, John Craven. *The Imamate Tradition of Oman.* New York: Cambridge University Press, 1987.

PAKISTAN

Islamic Republic of Pakistan
Islami Jamhooria Pakistan

CAPITAL: Islāmābād.

FLAG: The national flag is dark green, with a white vertical stripe at the hoist and a white crescent and five-pointed star in the center.

ANTHEM: The opening lines of the national anthem, sung in Urdu, are "Blessed be the sacred land, Happy be the bounteous realm, Symbol of high resolve, land of Pakistan, Blessed be thou citadel of faith."

MONETARY UNIT: The rupee (R) is a paper currency of 100 paisa. There are coins of 1, 2, 5, 10, 25, and 50 paisa and of 1 rupee, and notes of 1, 2, 5, 10, 50, 100, 500, and 1,000 rupees. R1 = $0.01948 ($1 = R51.33) as of 31 March 2000.

WEIGHTS AND MEASURES: The metric system was introduced in 1966 and made mandatory as of 1 January 1979.

HOLIDAYS: Pakistan Day, 23 March; May Day, 1 May; Independence Day, 14 August; Defense of Pakistan Day, 6 September; Anniversary of Death of the Quaid-e-Azam, Mohammad Ali Jinnah, 11 September; Christmas and Birthday of the Quaid-e-Azam, 25 December. Religious holidays include 'Id al-Fitr, Id al-'Adha', 1st of Muharram, and Milad an-Nabi.

TIME: 5 PM = noon GMT.

¹LOCATION, SIZE, AND EXTENT

Situated in southern Asia, Pakistan has an area of 803,940 sq km (310,403 sq mi), extending 1,875 km (1,165 mi) NE–SW from the ranges of the Hindu Kush and the Himalaya to the Arabian Sea and 1,006 km (625 mi) SE–NW. Comparatively, the area occupied by Pakistan is slightly less than twice the size of the state of California. The enclave of Junagadh, claimed by Pakistan, and Jammu and Kashmir, divided between Pakistan and India by the 1971 "line of control," are not included in the area. Pakistan is bordered on the NE by China, on the E by Jammu and Kashmir to the Karakoram Pass, on the E and SE by India, on the S by the Arabian Sea, on the SW by Iran, and on the W and NW by Afghanistan. The total boundary length is 7,790 km (4,840 mi). Pakistan's capital city, Islāmābād, is located in the northern part of the country.

²TOPOGRAPHY

More than two-thirds of Pakistan is arid or semiarid. The west is dominated by the Baluchistan plateau, consisting of arid plains and ridges. Rivers, streams, and lakes exist only seasonally. The arid south ends at the rugged Makran coast and rises to the east into a series of rock-strewn ranges, the Kirthar, and to the north, the Sulaiman, which extends to the Indus plains. A semiwatered plateau surrounds Rawalpindi, bounded to the south by the salt range. Southward, the extensive Punjab plains support about 60% of the country's population.

In the northern areas of Pakistan, the forest-clad hills give way to lofty ranges, including 60 peaks over 6,700 m (22,000 ft) high. K-2 (Godwin Austen), at 8,611 m (28,250 ft), is the second-highest mountain in the world.

The principal ranges, trending NW–SE, include several Himalayan ranges—notably the Pir Panjal and Zaskar—leading into the Karakoram Mountains. The Indus is the principal river of Pakistan. Its major tributaries are the Jhelum, Chenab, Ravi, and Sutlej.

³CLIMATE

Pakistan's climate is dry and hot near the coast, becoming progressively cooler toward the northeastern uplands. The winter season is generally cold and dry. The hot season begins in April, and by the end of June the temperature may reach 49°C (120°F). Between July and September, the monsoon provides an average rainfall of about 38 cm (15 in) in the river basins and up to about 150 cm (60 in) in the northern areas. Rainfall can vary radically from year to year, and successive patterns of flooding and drought are not uncommon.

⁴FLORA AND FAUNA

The mangrove forests of the coastal region give way to the mulberry, acacia, and date palms of the sparsely vegetated south; the foothills support phulai, kao, chinar, and wild olive, and the northern forests have stands of oak, chestnut, walnut, pine, ash, spruce, yew, and fir. Above 3,000 m (10,000 ft), birch, dwarf willow, and juniper are also found.

Pakistan's wide range of animal life includes the Siberian ibex, wild sheep, buffalo, bear, wolf, jackal, fox, wildcat, musk cat, hyena, porcupine, gazelle, peacock, python, and boar.

⁵ENVIRONMENT

Relatively high population growth contributed to the depletion of forestland from 9.8% of Pakistan's total area in 1947 to 4.5% by 1986, despite the forest conservation measures mandated by the Forest Act of 1927. Pakistan lost 14.5% of its remaining forest and woodland between 1983 and 1993. Deforestation has contributed to increased soil erosion, declining soil fertility, and severe flooding.

Primary responsibility for environmental matters belongs to the Environmental and Urban Affairs Division of the Ministry for Housing and Works. Laws to set air and water quality standards and regulate coastal zones to prevent pollution were under consideration in the 1980s. In the mid-1990s, Pakistan was among the 50 nations with the world's highest levels of industrial carbon dioxide emissions, which totaled 71.9 million metric tons per year, a per capita level of 0.59 metric tons per year. The nation's water supply is at risk due to untreated sewage along with agricultural and industrial pollutants. Some 23% of the people living in cities and 48% of rural dwellers do not have pure drinking water. It is estimated that 80% of the nation's diseases are related to impure water.

In the mid-1990s, 15 mammal species were endangered, as well as 25 bird species and 14 plant species. Endangered or extinct species include the Indus dolphin, Baluchistan bear, tiger, Pakistan sand cat, snow leopard, Indian wild ass, green sea turtle, olive ridley turtle, gavial, Central Asian cobra, Kabul markhor, chi pheasant, western tragopan, great Indian bustard, and Siberian white crane. Hunting or capturing wild animals was banned in 1981.

6POPULATION

The population of Pakistan in 2000 was estimated at 141,145,344. An estimated 3.1% of the population is 65 years of age or older. The projected population for the year 2005 is 156,136,000, assuming a crude birthrate of 29 per 1,000 population and a death rate of 9, resulting in a natural rate of change of 2.0% for the period 2000–2005. The population rate of change between 1995 and 2000 was 2.7%. The population density in 1998 was 171 per sq km (443 per sq mi).

It was estimated that 37% of the population lived in urban areas in 2000, up from 28% in 1980. The capital city, Islāmābād, and its surrounding metropolitan area had a 2000 population of 1,066,000. The following metropolitan areas had more than 750,000 inhabitants, according to 2000 estimates: Karāchi (the former national capital), 11,774,000; Lahore, 6,030,000; Faisalābād (formerly Lyallpur), 2,228,000; Peshāwar, 2,094,000; Gujrānwāla, 2,048,000; Rāwalpindi, 1,529,000; and Multān, 1,498,000.

7MIGRATION

Some 6,000,000 Muslims migrated to Pakistan from India at the time of independence in 1947, and Muslims have continued to arrive from India in much lesser numbers since then. The Soviet military intervention in Afghanistan in December 1979 led to an influx of Afghan refugees.

After the Taliban captured Kabul on 27 September 1996, there was a new outflow of Afghan refugees to Pakistan. By March of 1997, around 50,000 new Afghan refugees entered the country. As of September 1999, there were still around 1.2 million Afghan refugees living in refugee villages in Pakistan. An unknown number of unregistered Afghans were living in the main Pakistani cities of Rawalpindi, Lahore, and Karāchi. Pakistan also hosts 2,600 non-Afghan refugees, including Iraqis, Iranians, and Somalis. In 1999, the net migration rate was -1.3 migrants per 1,000 population.

8ETHNIC GROUPS

The majority of the population is Punjabi (an estimated two-thirds). Other major ethnic groups include the Sindhi, Pathan, Baloch, and Muhajirs (immigrants from India and their descendants). The Rajputs and the Jats are the most numerous of the Punjabi castes. In the area of the delta and the lower course of the Indus River are Sindhi peasant tribesmen. In the north and northwest are the hardy, warlike nomadic and seminomadic Pathans. The Balochi live in the vast western section of Pakistan and are divided into 12 major tribes, some of them purportedly of Dravidian origin. Native speakers of Urdu, the Muhajirs are refugees, or descendants of refugees, from pre-partition India. They are well represented in the cities.

9LANGUAGES

Punjabi is spoken by 48% of the population; Sindhi by 12%; Siraiki (a Punjabi variant) by 10%; Pashtu by 8%; Urdu by 8%; Balochi by 3%; Hindko by 2%; Brahui by 1%; English, Burushaski, and other by 8%. During the Mughal (or Mogul) period, a fusion of local dialects and Persian produced Urdu, a "language of the camp" (zaban-i-urdu). Although regional languages and dialects persist, Urdu is the official language of Pakistan; while it is spoken by only a minority, it is understood everywhere except in the rural or mountainous areas on the western frontier. English also claims official status and is the lingua franca of Pakistani elite and most government ministries.

10RELIGIONS

Pakistan is an Islamic state. In 1999, some 97% of the population was Muslim (Sunni 77%, Shi'a 20%), giving Pakistan one of the largest Islamic communities in the world. While most Muslims are of the Sunni and Shi'a sects, there are a few members of the Isma'ili sect concentrated at Karāchi. Ahmadis, who consider themselves Muslims but are not accepted as orthodox by other Muslim groups and were officially declared non-Muslims by the government in 1974, numbered perhaps 2,500,000 by 1985. Christians, Hindus, and others constituted an estimated 3% of the population in 1999. About 5,000 Parsis, believers in Zoroastrianism, live in Karāchi.

11TRANSPORTATION

Railways are a major carrier of passenger and freight traffic. In 1996, Pakistan Railways operated 8,163 route km (5,072 mi) of track.

Also in 1996, Pakistan's road system totaled 224,774 km (139,675 mi) of roads, of which 128,121 km (79,614 mi) were paved. Road traffic drives on the left. The 800 km (500 mi) Karakoram highway, built jointly by Pakistan and China to connect Islāmābād with western China, was opened in 1979. There were 770,000 passenger cars and 275,000 commercial vehicles in use in 1995. The road network carries 85% of all goods and passengers moving within the country. The harbor of Karāchi, which provides Pakistan with its major port, covers an area of 6.5 sq km (2.5 sq mi) and handles over 10.5 million tons annually. Port Qasim, 22 km (14 mi) south of Karāchi, was developed during the 1970s to help handle the increased shipping traffic. As of 1998, Pakistan's merchant marine operated 23 oceangoing vessels, totaling 384,304 GRT.

Pakistan had 116 airports in 1998, of which 80 had paved runways. Karāchi Airport is the main international terminus. The government-run Pakistan International Airlines (PIA) maintains all domestic services as well as flights to Europe, the US, and the Far East. In 1997, 5,883,000 passengers were carried in scheduled domestic and international flights.

12HISTORY

The ruins of ancient civilizations at Mohenjodaro and at Harappa in the southern Indus Valley testify to the existence of an advanced urban civilization that flourished in what is now Pakistan in the second half of the third millennium BC during the same period as the major riverain civilizations in Mesopotamia and Persia. Although overwhelmed from 1500 BC onward by large migrations of nomadic Indo-European-speaking Aryans from the Caucasus region, vestiges of this civilization continue to exist in the traditional Indic culture that evolved from interaction of the Aryans and successive invaders in the years following. Among the latter were Persians in 500 BC, Greeks under Alexander the Great in 326 BC, and—after AD 800—Arabs, Afghans, Turks, Persians, Mongols (Mughals), and Europeans, the last of whom first arrived, uniquely, by sea beginning in AD 1601.

PAKISTAN

0 50 100 150 200 250 Miles

0 50 100 150 200 250 Kilometers

TURKMENISTAN

UZBEKISTAN TAJIKISTAN TAJIKISTAN CHINA

HINDU KUSH KARAKORAM RANGE

K2 (Mt. Godwin Austen)
28,250 ft.
8611 m.

Kunar Gilgit

Chitrāl *Indus*

AFGHANISTAN

Kabul ✪

Khyber Pass Mardān

Peshāwar Islāmābād ✪

Rāwalpindi

Khowst

Jhelum Gujrāt Siālkot

Dera Ismāil Khān Gujrānwāla

Sargodha

Lahore Amristar

Darakht-e Yaḥyá Faisalābād Kasūr

Zhob *Rāvi* Okāra

Zhob SULAIMĀN RANGE Multān

Khojak Pass ■

Quetta Dera Ghāzi Khān *Sutlej*

Mastung Bahāwalpur

Saindak *Chaghai Hills* Sibi Ahmadpur East INDIA

Hāmūn-i-Lori

Hāmūn-i-Māshkel

Khuzdār Sukkur

IRAN Panjgur Khairpur Thar Desert

CENTRAL MAKRĀN RANGE *Kech* *Nal* KIRTHAR RANGE Great Indian Desert

MAKRĀN COAST RANGE Bela *Nāra Canal* *Indus*

Gwādar Pasni *Sonmiāni Bay* Hyderābād

Karāchi Jhudo Mithi

Arabian Sea

Mouths of the Indus

Pakistan

LOCATION: 23°41′ to 37°5′N; 60°52′ to 77°49′E. **BOUNDARY LENGTHS:** China, 523 km (325 mi), including boundary of Jammu and Kashmir to the Karakoram Pass; India, 2,028 km (1,260 mi); Arabian Sea coastline, 814 km (506 mi); Iran, 830 km (516 mi); Afghanistan, 2,466 km (1,532 mi). **TERRITORIAL SEA LIMIT:** 12 mi.

Islam, the dominant cultural influence in Pakistan, arrived with Arab traders in the 8th century AD. Successive overland waves of Muslims followed, culminating in the ascendancy of the Mughals in most of the subcontinent. Led initially by Babur, a grandson of Genghis Khan, the Mughal empire flourished in the 16th and 17th centuries and remained in nominal control until well after the British East India Company came to dominate the region in the early 18th century. Effective British governance of the areas that now make up Pakistan was not consolidated until well into the second half of the 19th century.

In 1909 and 1919, while the British moved gradually and successfully to expand local self-rule, British power was increas-

ingly challenged by the rise of indigenous mass movements advocating a faster pace. The Indian National Congress, founded in 1885 as little more than an Anglophile society, began to attract wide support in this century—especially after 1920—with its advocacy of nonviolent struggle. But because its leadership style appeared to many Muslims to be uniquely Hindu, Muslims formed the All-India Muslim League to look after their interests. National and provincial elections held under the Government of India Act of 1935 confirmed many Muslims in this view by showing the power the majority Hindu population could wield at the ballot box.

Sentiment among Muslims began to coalesce around the "two-nation" theory propounded by the poet Iqbal, which declared that Muslims and Hindus were separate nations and that Muslims required creation of an independent Islamic state for their protection and fulfillment. A prominent Bombay (now Mumbai) attorney, Muhammad Ali Jinnah, who came to be known "Quaid-i-Azam" (Great Leader), led the fight—formally endorsed by the Muslim League at Lahore in 1940—for a separate Muslim state to be known as Pakistan.

Despite arrests and setbacks during the Second World War, Jinnah's quest succeeded on 14 August 1947 when British India was divided into the two self-governing dominions of India and Pakistan, the latter created by combining contiguous, Muslim-majority districts in British India, the former consisting of the remainder. Partition occasioned a mass movement of Hindus, Muslims, and Sikhs who found themselves on the "wrong" side of new international boundaries; more than 20 million people moved, and up to three million of these were killed.

The new Pakistan was a state divided into two wings, East Pakistan (with 42 million people crowded mainly into what had been the eastern half of Bengal province) and West Pakistan (with 34 million in a much larger territory that included the provinces of Baluchistan, Sind, the Northwest Frontier, and western Punjab). In between, the wings were separated by 1600 km (1000 miles) of an independent, mainly Hindu, India professing secularism for its large Muslim, Christian, and Sikh minorities.

From the capital in Karāchi, in West Pakistan, the leaders of the new state labored mightily to overcome the economic dislocations of Partition, which cut across all previous former economic linkages, while attempting to establish a viable parliamentary government with broad acceptance in both wings. Jinnah's death in 1948 and the assassination in 1951 of Liaquat Ali Khan, its first prime minister, were major setbacks, and political stability proved elusive, with frequent recourse to proclamations of martial law and states of emergency in the years following 1954.

Complicating their task were the security concerns that Pakistan's new leaders had regarding India in the aftermath of the bitterness of partition and the dispute over Jammu and Kashmir. In the early 1950s, they sought security in relationships external to the subcontinent, with the Islamic world and with the United States, joining in such American-sponsored alliances as the Baghdad Pact (later—without Baghdad—the Central Treaty Organization or CENTO) and the Southeast Asia Treaty Organization (SEATO). They received extensive American economic and security assistance.

In the years leading up to 1971, the domestic political process in Pakistan was dominated by efforts to bridge the profound political and ethnic gap that—more than geography—separated the east and west wings despite their anxiety about India and shared commitment to Islam. Economically more important, the Bengali east wing, governed as a single province, chafed under national policies laid down in a west wing dominated by Punjabis and recent refugees from northern and western India. Seeking greater autonomy, voters in East Pakistan voted the Muslim League (ML) out of office as early as 1954, resulting in a period of direct rule from Karāchi.

In 1958, the Army chief, Gen. Muhammad Ayub Khan, seized control of Pakistan, imposing martial law and banning all political activity for several years. Ayub later dissolved provincial boundaries in the west wing, converting it to "one unit," to balance East Pakistan. Each "unit" had a single provincial government and equal strength in an indirectly elected national legislature; the effect was to deny East Pakistan its population advantage, as well as its ability, as the largest province, to play provincial politics in the west wing.

Ayub's efforts failed to establish stability or satisfy the demands for restoration of parliamentary democracy. Weakened by his abortive military adventure against India in September 1965 and amid rising political strife in both wings in 1968, Ayub was eventually forced from office. Gen. Muhammad Yayha Khan, also opposed to greater autonomy for the east wing, assumed the presidency in 1969. Again martial law was imposed and political activity, suspended.

Yahya's attempt to restore popular government in the general elections of 1970 failed when the popular verdict supported those calling for greater autonomy for East Pakistan, even in the national assembly. The results were set aside, and civil unrest in the east wing rapidly spread to become civil war. India, with more than a million refugees pouring into its West Bengal state, joined in the conflict in support of the rebellion in November 1971, tipping the balance in Bengali favor and facilitating the creation of Bangladesh from the ruins in early 1972.

Bhutto and his successors

The defeat led to the resignation on 20 December 1971 of Yahya Khan and brought to the presidency Zulfikar Ali Bhutto, whose populist Pakistan Peoples Party (PPP) had won a majority of seats in the west wing. A longtime minister under Ayub Khan, the experienced Bhutto quickly charted an independent course for West Pakistan, which became the Islamic Republic of Pakistan. He distanced Pakistan from former close ties with the United States and the west, seeking security from India by a much more active role in the Third World and especially in the growing international Islamic movement fueled by petrodollars.

His political base broadened by his promises of "clothing, food, and housing" to the rural and urban poor, Bhutto launched limited land reform, nationalized banks and industries, and obtained support among all parties for a new constitution promulgated in 1973, restoring a strong prime ministership, which position he then stepped down to fill. In the years following, Bhutto grew more powerful, more capricious, and autocratic. His regime became increasingly dependent on harassment and imprisonment of foes and his popular support seriously eroded by the time he called for elections in March 1977. His PPP had lost many of its supporters, and he came to rely increasingly on discredited former PML members for support.

At the polls, the PPP was opposed by the Pakistan National Alliance (PNA), a nine-party coalition of all other major parties including the Jamaat-i-Islami (JI) on the Islamic right, the National Democratic Party on the secular left, the Pakistan Muslim League (PML/Pagaro) in the center, Asghar Khan's Tehrik Istiqlal (TI) on the secular right, and others. Although the results gave the PPP a two-thirds majority in parliament, allegations of widespread fraud and rigging undercut its credibility. PNA leaders demanded new elections, and Bhutto's exercise of emergency powers to arrest them led to widespread civil strife. On 5 July 1977, the army intervened, with the support of the civil and uniformed services and tacit acceptance of the PNA leaders. In ousting Bhutto, army chief Gen. Muhammad Zia-ul-Haq partially suspended the 1973 constitution, imposed martial law, and assumed the post of Chief Martial Law Administrator (CMLA). As calm returned to Pakistan, Zia promised elections for October 1977, but for the first of many times to come, he reversed himself before the event, arguing that he needed more time to set matters aright. And as the months passed, he began to assume more of the trappings of power, creating a cabinet-like Council of Advisers of made up of serving military officers and senior civil servants, chief among whom was longtime Defense Secretary, Ghulam Ishaq Khan, who became Finance Advisor and Zia's strong right arm.

In mid-1978, Zia brought Bhutto to trial for conspiracy to murder a political rival in which the rival's father was killed. He also expanded his "cabinet" with the addition of several PNA leaders as advisors, and, when the incumbent resigned, he assumed the added responsibilities (and title) of president. He allowed a return of limited political activity but put off elections scheduled for fall when he was unable to get agreement among the PNA parties on ground rules that would keep the PPP from returning to power.

Bhutto's conspiracy conviction was upheld by the Supreme Court in March 1979, and he was hanged on 4 April. In the fall, and with the PNA now in disarray, Zia again scheduled, then postponed elections and restricted political activity. But he did hold "non-party" polling for district and municipal councils, only to find at year's end confirmation of his concerns about PPP strength when PPP members, identifying themselves as "Friends of the People," showed continuing appeal among the electorate.

Opposition to martial law began slowly to coalesce in 1980 when most of the PNA leadership joined with PPP leaders Ghulam Mustafa Jatoi and Nusrat Bhutto, Zulfikar's widow, to form the Movement for the Restoration of Democracy (MRD) and to demand Zia's resignation and the restoration of the 1973 constitution. But Zia, benefiting from excellent monsoons and from Ishaq Khan's sound economic policies, proceeded by a series measures to expand the role of Islamic values and institutions in society. The public mood stayed quiescent, encouraged by Zia's regular reminders of the turmoil his predecessors had created.

Meanwhile, in neighboring Afghanistan, following a communist coup in 1978 and a Soviet invasion in 1979, Zia assumed a strong anticommunist leadership role, rallying the Islamic world and the UN. He resurrected close ties with the United States to enhance Pakistan's security and in the 1980s signed $3.2 and $4.02 billion economic and security assistance agreements with the US. He also improved relations—normally parlous—with India with normalization in trade, transport, and other non-sensitive areas. Nonetheless, Pakistan's anxiety about the much more powerful India on its borders remained high in the absence of a solution of the dispute with India over the status of the former princely state of Jammu and Kashmir.

The Kashmir dispute cuts to the heart of the "two-nation" theory and as such is part of the unresolved legacy of the 1947 partition of British India which did not address the future of the over 500 princely states with which the British Crown had treaty ties. Most chose one or the other dominion on grounds of geography, but Kashmir bordered both new nations and thus had a real option. A Muslim-majority state, with a Hindu ruler, Kashmir opted first for neither but then chose to join the Indian Union when invaded by tribesmen from Pakistan. Open warfare ensued in Kashmir between Indian and Pakistani troops in 1948–49 and brought the dispute to the fledgling United Nations.

A UN cease-fire left a third of Kashmir under Pakistani control and the remainder, including the Vale of Kashmir, under Indian control. A 1949 agreement to hold an impartial plebiscite broke down when the protagonists could not agree on the conditions under which it would be held. Pakistan today administers its part—Azad (free) Kashmir—legally separate from the rest of Pakistan; Indian Kashmir is a state in the Indian Union, which has held stateside elections but no plebiscite.

The Kashmir issue has defied all efforts at resolution, including two additional spasms of warfare in 1965 and 1971, and subsequent Indo-Pakistan summits at Tashkent (1966) and Simla (1972). In the late 1980s, India's cancellation of election results and the dismissal of the state government led to the beginning of an armed insurrection against Indian rule by Kashmiri Muslim militants. Indian repression and Pakistan's support of the militants has threatened to spark new Indo-Pakistan conflict and keeps the issue festering.

In Pakistan in 1984, President Zia held a referendum on his Islamization policies in December and promised that he would serve a specified term of five years as president if the voters endorsed his policies. The MRD opposed him but did not prevent what Zia claimed was a 63% turnout, with 90% in his favor. On the strength of this disputed showing, Zia announced national and provincial elections, on a non-party basis, for February 1985. The MRD again boycotted, but the JI and part of the Pakistan Muslim League (PML) supported Zia. Deemed reasonably fair by most observers, the elections gave him a majority in the reconstituted National Assembly and left the opposition in further disarray.

Ten months later, on 30 December 1985, Zia ended martial law, as well as the state of emergency he had inherited from Zulfikar Bhutto, turning over day-to-day administration to the PML's Mohammad Khan Junejo, whom he had appointed prime minister in March. He also restored the 1973 constitution but not before amending it to strengthen presidential powers vis-a-vis the prime minister. As the Eighth Amendment to the constitution, these changes were approved by the National Assembly in October 1985. They remain a contentious issue today, having subsequently played a key role in institutional tension between incumbents of the presidency and the prime ministership. In the first such instance, frictions developed slowly through 1987, but on 29 May 1988, Zia suddenly fired Junejo, alleging corruption and a lack of support for his policies on Islamization and on Afghanistan. He called for new elections in November, and in June he proclaimed the Shari'a (Islamic law) supreme in Pakistan.

However, Zia was among 18 officials (including the American Ambassador) killed in the crash of a Pakistan Air Force plane two months later, leading to the succession to power of the Chairman of the Senate, Ghulam Ishaq Khan. As acting president, Ghulam Ishaq scheduled elections for November 1988 in which the PPP emerged with a strong plurality in the National Assembly. Benazir Bhutto, Zulfikar's daughter, who had returned from exile abroad in April 1986, became prime minister with a thin majority made up of her party members and independents. With her support Pakistan's electoral college chose Ghulam Ishaq President of Pakistan in his own right on 12 December 1988.

On 20 August 1990, with Bhutto and Ghulam Ishaq in a growing constitutional struggle over their respective powers, the president, with the support of the army chief, used his Eighth Amendment powers to oust her, alleging corruption, illegal acts, and nepotism. Declaring a state of emergency, he dissolved the National Assembly, named Ghulam Mustafa Jatoi (then leader of the opposition) prime minister, and called for new elections on 24 October. The Punjab High Court upheld the constitutionality of his actions, and on 24 October, the voters gave a near-majority to the Islamic Jamhoori Ittehad (IJI), a multi-party coalition resting mainly on a partnership of the PML and the JI. Mian Muhammad Nawaz Sharif, PML leader and former Chief Minister of Punjab, became prime minister on 6 November and quickly ended the state of emergency.

During late 1992 and early 1993, the president and the new prime minister moved toward a new confrontation over the exercise of their respective powers. Challenged by Nawaz Sharif on the president's choice of a new army chief, Ghulam Ishaq again used his Eighth Amendment powers to dismiss the government and dissolve the Assembly on 18 April, alleging mismanagement and corruption. But public reaction to the president's actions was strong, and on 26 May, a Supreme Court ruling restored Nawaz Sharif to power, creating a period of constitutional gridlock until 18 July when the army chief brokered a deal in which both Ghulam Ishaq and Nawaz Sharif left office. Sharif resigned and was replaced by Ishaq Khan as interim prime minister by Moeen Qureshi, a former World Bank

Vice President; the president was then replaced by Wasim Sajjad, Chairman of the Senate.

Under Qureshi, Pakistan entered a period of fast-paced nonpartisan rule and reform in which widespread corruption was exposed, corrupt officials dismissed, and political reforms undertaken. In his actions, Qureshi was strengthened by public support and his disavowal of interest in remaining in power. He held elections as promised on 19 October, and the PPP, leading a coalition called the People's Democratic Alliance (PDA), was returned to power, with Benazir Bhutto again Prime Minister, this time with a thin majority. On 13 November, with her support, longtime PPP stalwart Farooq Leghari was elected president. Three years later in 1996, Leghari dismissed Bhutto and her cabinet and dissolved the National Assembly. Bhutto challenged her dismissal and the dissolution of the National Assembly in the Supreme Court. In a 6–1 ruling, the Court upheld the President's actions and found her ousted government corrupt.

Nawaz Sharif won the general election held in February 1997 with one of the largest democratic mandates in Pakistan's history. He immediately set about consolidating his hold on power by repealing major elements of the 1985 Eight Constitutional Amendment. This transferred sweeping executive powers from the president to the prime minister. Within the next few months Nawaz Sharif dismissed his Chief of Naval Staff, arrested and imprisoned Benazir Bhutto's husband for ordering the killing of a political opponent, and froze the Bhutto family's assets. In March 1998, a warrant was issued for the arrest of Benazir Bhutto (who was abroad at the time) on charges of misuse of power during her tenure as prime minister.

The early months of 1998 were marked by increasing civil disorder in Pakistan, with sectarian killings, terrorist bombings, and violent demonstrations against a controversial Islamic blasphemy law. In January 1999, Nawaz Sharif himself escaped an apparent assassination attempt when a bomb exploded near his residence in the Punjab.

Despite increasing political opposition and a deteriorating economic situation, Nawaz Sharif's popularity received a temporary boost when Pakistan successfully tested five nuclear devices on 28 May and 30 May 1998. This was in response to India's nuclear tests earlier in the month and raised international concerns over a potential nuclear confrontation between Pakistan and India. Tensions eased when Nawaz Sharif and India's prime minister, Atal Behari Vajpayee, signed the historic "Lahore Declaration" on 21 February 1999, committing their countries to a peaceful solution of their problems.

In May 1999, however, several hundred Pakistani troops and Islamic militants infiltrated the Indian-held Kargil region of Kashmir. Two months of intense fighting brought Pakistan and India to the brink of all-out war. Under intense diplomatic pressure from the US, but against the wishes of Pakistan's military, Nawaz Sharif ordered a withdrawal from Kargil in July 1999. This unpopular decision, plus the widely held view that Sharif' was preparing to impose one-man dictatorial rule in the name of Islam, contributed to the prime minister's eventual downfall.

Distrustful of his Army Chief of Staff, General Pervez Musharraf, Nawaz Sharif dismissed Musharraf on 12 October 1999 while he was in the air returning from a visit to Sri Lanka. However, when the general's plane was denied permission to land at Karáchi Airport, army troops loyal to Musharraf seized the airport, arrested Sharif, and returned Pakistan to military rule for the fourth time in the country's short history.

General Musharraf did not impose full martial law. Instead, he declared a state of emergency, suspended the constitution and assumed power as Chief Executive. Many Pakistanis welcomed the military takeover as a change from the corruption and abuses of Nawaz Sharif's rule. Musharraf introduced modest economic reforms (mostly in the area of revenue collection), restricted the activities of Islamic extremists, and instituted policies to curb lawlessness and sectarian violence. On 23 March 2000, Musharraf announced local elections to be held over a period of seven months between December 2000–July 2001. Significantly, however, no mention was made of national elections or a return to civilian rule. Moreover, the independence of the judiciary was seriously compromised in January 2000, when Musharraf required all judges to take an oath of loyalty to his regime. Nawaz Sharif was tried and found guilty of hijacking and terrorism for trying to prevent Musharraf's plane, a commercial flight with civilians on board, from landing at Karáchi in October 1999. Sharif was sentenced on 16 April 2000 to life in prison.

As of April 2000, no timetable for a return to civilian government had been set and Pakistan remained under military rule.

13 GOVERNMENT

Pakistan came into being as a self-governing dominion in the British Commonwealth in 1947 and declared itself a republic in 1956. Under a constitution framed by Zulfikar Bhutto and effective as of 14 August 1973, it is federal in nature, and Westminster-style cabinet systems operate at the federal and provincial levels. All powers not otherwise specified are reserved for the federal government, which is armed also with extensive emergency powers in the event of a breakdown in constitutional government.

Pakistan is governed under the constitution of 14 August 1973 (as amended) which declared Islam the state religion and provided for a president as a nominal head of state and a prime minister as executive head of government. The president and prime minister were chosen by members of parliament, and the prime minister was responsible to that body, which was elected under universal suffrage at 18 (since changed to 21) years of age. In 1973, the parliament consisted of a National Assembly of 200 elected members plus 10 seats reserved (until 1982) for women and 6 for tribal areas, these reserved seats filled by vote of the elected members. A Senate of 63 members included 14 legislators from each of the four provincial legislatures, plus 5 seats reserved for tribal areas and 2 for the federal capital area.

This constitution was suspended in part by the martial law administration that seized power in 1977; army chief Gen. Zia-ul Haq retained his military position while exercising executive powers as Chief Martial Law Administrator (CMLA). He took on the position of president in 1978 when the incumbent stepped down, In an interim document of 24 March 1981, Zia revived much of the 1973 constitution, although its Fundamental Principles and its electoral provisions remained suspended until martial law was lifted in 1985. The CMLA was initially assisted by an appointive council of advisors, then by an advisory Federal Council (Majlis-e-Shoora) of 277 appointed members that was formed in 1982 to assist and advise the martial law government.

The 1973 constitution was fully restored with the lifting of martial law in December 1985, although amended in a number of ways. It redressed—in favor of the presidency—the balance of powers between the positions of prime minister and president, who also remained commander-in-chief of the armed forces. It established term limits of five years for the incumbents, and provided that their successors in 1990 would be elected, the president by an electoral college composed of members of the National Assembly, the Senate, and the provincial assemblies, and the prime minister, by the National Assembly.

The National Assembly now has 217 members (including 10 reserved for non-Muslims) elected for five-year terms, plus 20 seats to be filled by vote of the elected members for women and others deserving of representation. The Senate has 84 members elected for six-year terms by the provincial assemblies and tribal councils, plus three seats reserved for the federal capital area.

In May 1994, after what appeared to be an encouraging start, Benazir Bhutto's government again appeared haunted by ineffectiveness when she failed to get her candidate elected president of the senate—effectively vice president. Instead, she was forced to acquiesce in the reelection, one more time, of the PML's Wasim Sajjad.

Bhutto was ousted in 1996 after President Leghari's charges that her government was corrupt, a move that was supported by a 6–1 Supreme Court ruling. Nawaz Sharif was elected in February 1997 and immediately instituted sweeping changes affecting the government, military, and economy. On 1 April 1997, both houses of the parliament voted unanimously to repeal the Eighth Constitutional Amendment. The measure, introduced by Sharif, curtailed the president's power to dismiss elected governments and placed the appointment of provincial governors and the chiefs of the armed services in the hands of the prime minister. Sharif reduced the influence of the military in government by dissolving the Council for Defence and National Security. The prime minister also announced he was intending to place plans for introducing "Islamic government" to Pakistan before the legislature in March 2000.

President Leghari stepped down from office in December 1997, and Nawaz Sharif's strengthened his hold on the government when his nominee for president, Mohammad Rafiq Tarar, was elected by a record margin on 31 December 1997.

Sharif's government was overthrown on 12 October 1999, in a military coup staged by the Army Chief, General Pervez Musharraf, who suspended the Constitution and assumed the title Chief Executive. He governs with the aid of a largely nominal National Security Council. General Musharraf's stated aim was to restore "true democracy," order, and stability to Pakistan. Although Musharraf announced plans for local elections to be held from December 2000 to July 2001, no mention was made of a timetable for return to democratic government.

14POLITICAL PARTIES

Political parties have existed in Pakistan during all of its turbulent political history but have been regulated by legislation to ensure that they support the concept of Pakistan—a vestige of an early effort to repress the activities of the National Democratic Party (NDP) and the Jamaat-i-Islami (JI), which had opposed Partition in 1947. Parties have been frequently banned or restricted by the government, beginning with the 1952 ban on—and suppression of—the Communist Party of Pakistan (CPP). In most instances, banning of political activity has simply limited overt, outdoor rallies and demonstrations, while banning of parties has left the parties essentially intact, merely forcing them underground, as in the most recent ban in 1979.

In February 1981, leaders of nine political parties opposing the martial law regime, and led by the Pakistan Peoples Party (PPP), formed the Movement for the Restoration of Democracy (MRD) and by declaration called for an immediate end to martial law and restoration of the parliamentary system of 1973. Following the end of martial law in 1985, political parties were legalized, although regulated by the Political Parties Act that required all parties to register to be eligible for election. The elections that followed President Zia's sacking of Prime Minister Junejo in 1986, coupled with national elections called after Zia's subsequent death in an airplane crash in 1988, have resulted in a rebirth of full and open political activity.

The populist Pakistan Peoples Party (PPP) led by Benazir Bhutto, daughter of the late Prime Minister Zulfikar Bhutto, won a plurality in the National Assembly and formed a government with the support of appointed members and independents. The opposition coalesced around other parties, especially the Pakistan Muslim League (PML), and the Jamaat-i-Islami (JI), as well as disaffected PPP members who had been displaced when Benazir Bhutto claimed the party leadership on her return from exile overseas in 1986. One of these, Ghulam Mustafa Jatoi, joined with Nawaz Sharif, the PML chief minister of Punjab, to become leader of the opposition in the Assembly. In 1990, Jatoi became interim prime minister when Benazir Bhutto was dismissed by the president.

In the elections of fall 1990, Nawaz Sharif emerged as prime minister and leader of the Islamic Jamhoori Ittehad (IJI), a multiparty coalition based on Sharif's PML and the JI. But in elections in the fall of 1993, following the resignations of both the president and the prime minister, Bhutto's PPP, the lead party in the PDA, commanded a thin majority in the National Assembly, guaranteeing her return to power. The IJI came in a close second even though and the Islamic parties suffered severe reverses nationally.

In the 1990s, party politics in Pakistan became increasingly regional, and party lines relatively porous, with much shifting of supporters into and out of the PPP and the PML. Each of these parties drew nearly 40% of the popular vote, and they have emerged as the only parties with national scope; both improved their positions in provincial assemblies.

In 1994, the PPP government depended on the support of former PML members and nonelected assembly members, plus leaders like Jatoi, a charter PPP member who had been in and out of the party in recent years. Similarly, during its period in power from 1990 to 1993, the PML formed a government only with the support of other parties, most of which have strength only in regional terms, mainly the JI, the Jamhoori Watan Party (JWP), the Jamiat Ulema-i-Pakistan (JUP), and the Jamiat-ul-Ulema-Islam (JUI). And both the PPP and the PML have competed successfully in forming governments in provincial assemblies only when they have recruited (or neutralized) strong regional parties, like the Awami National Party (ANP) in the Northwest Frontier Province (NWFP) and the Muhajir Quami Movement (MQM) in Sindh.

The two main political parties are Sharif's Muslim League and Bhutto's Pakistan Peoples Party, with the Muslim League winning a resounding victory in the last national elections held in February 1997. In 1996, noted Pakistan cricketer Imran Khan founded the Pakistan Tahreek-e-Insaf (PTI) or "Movement for Justice," a new political party dedicated to creating an "egalitarian, modern Islamic state" in Pakistan. With a party constitution adopted only in January 1999 and seemingly dependent on Khan's personal appeal and fame, the PTI has yet to prove itself in national elections.

Unlike in the past, political parties have not been banned under General Musharraf's military government, but they have been sidelined from the political process. With the suspension of the national and provincial legislatures, political parties have no role in the governing of Pakistan. The local elections to be held beginning December 2000 are to be fought on a non-party basis.

15LOCAL GOVERNMENT

Pakistan is divided into four provinces, each with deep historic roots and both linguistic and cultural associations, since 1972. Outside the provinces, there are 11 federally administered tribal areas and the Federal Capital of Islāmābād. In addition, provincial governments directly administer 11 tribal areas within their territories.

The provinces, in order of population size, are Punjab (with its capital at Lahore), Sindh (Karāchi), Northwest Frontier Province (Peshawar), and Baluchistan (Quetta), the largest in area. Under the 1973 constitution, provinces have popularly elected provincial assemblies, a governor appointed by the president, and a chief minister in whom executive power is vested. The governor acts on the advice of a chief minister who is elected from the party commanding the support of the assembly.

The senior administrative officer of each province is the chief secretary. Each province is divided administratively into divisions headed by commissioners who, like the chief secretary and the secretaries of provincial ministries, are senior members of the Pakistan Civil Service (CSP). Divisions are further subdivided into districts headed (depending on local usage) by deputy commissioners, district officers, or collectors, also members of the CSP, who manage development funds, collect the revenues, supervise the police, adjudicate disputes, administer justice, and interface with the elected councils at the local level which have limited taxing authority, decide on priorities for local development programs, and try certain local legal cases.

The Pakistan-controlled third of the original state of Jammu and Kashmir is divided into two areas. The southern portion, referred to as Azad Kashmir, is administered from Muzaffarabad by an appointed president and council of ministers. The larger portion to the north is known as the Northern Areas and is administered by a Commissioner and an elected council.

The normal structures of local government have been modified under the military regime of General Pervez Musharraf. With the provincial legislatures suspended, provincial governors report directly to the Chief Executive.

16JUDICIAL SYSTEM

Pakistan's judicial system stems directly from the system that was used in British India. The Supreme Court has original, appellate, and advisory jurisdictions. The president of Pakistan appoints the justices. Each province has a high court, the judges of which are also named by the president. Below the high courts are district and session courts, and below these are subordinate courts and village courts on the civil side and magistrates on the criminal side. There are no jury trials in Pakistan.

The British tradition of an independent judiciary has been undermined in Pakistan by developments over the last 50 years. In May 1991, for example, the National Assembly adopted legislation which incorporated the Islamic legal code, the Shari'a into Pakistan's legal system. A Federal Shari'at Court has the power to nullify any law it finds repugnant to Islam.

Courts in Pakistan are also subject to pressure from the executive branch, in part because of presidential power over transfer and tenure of High Court justices and lower court judges. Judges in the special courts are retired jurists hired on renewable contracts so that their decisions may be influenced by a desire for contract renewal. Nonetheless, the provincial High Courts and the Supreme Court have exercised some degree of independence in handing down a number of cases against the government. In 1996 the Supreme Court issued orders curtailing the powers of the executive to appoint and transfer high courts' judges.

Again, in late 1997, the issue of the appointment of judges to the Supreme Court led to deteriorating relations between Prime Minister Nawaz Sharif and the Chief Justice of the Supreme Court, Sajjad Ali Shah. In November, the Supreme Court brought charges of contempt against Nawaz Sharif, but the Chief Justice was forced out of office before a verdict could be handed down (a guilty verdict would have disqualified Sharif from office).

The position of the judiciary in Pakistan has also been affected by periods of military rule in the country. When General Zia al-Huq imposed martial law in 1977, military courts were given jurisdiction over trial and punishment of civilians found guilty of violating martial law regulations. The verdicts could not be appealed to a higher civilian court. Moreover, a provision of the 1973 constitution that judges could be removed only by the Supreme Judicial Council, consisting of the chief justice and two

ranking judges from the Supreme Court and the high courts, was revoked by the military government in June 1979. Under the 1981 interim constitution, a new oath was imposed on all Supreme Court, high court, and Shari'at Court judges, and all laws promulgated by the martial law regime were exempted from judicial review. The Supreme Court chief justice and several other judges were replaced after refusing to take the oath. Although the military courts were abolished in December 1985, their decisions still cannot be appealed to civilian courts.

Similarly, in January 2000, Musharraf required all judges to take an oath of loyalty to his regime. The Supreme Court Chief Justice, Saiduzzaman Siddiqui, and five colleagues refused and were dismissed. This was just a week before the Court was due to hear the first of several cases challenging the legality of the new government. Legal experts argue this action has done irreparable harm to Pakistan's judiciary; with all sitting judges having accepted the military regime, there is no independent judiciary to protect the constitution.

17ARMED FORCES

In 2000, Pakistan's armed forces totaled 587,000. Its army of 520,000 men, comprised 2 armored division, 19 infantry divisions, and 40 brigades of specialized troops and supporting arms. The navy, (22,000) had 10 submarines, 8 frigates, and 10 patrol and coastal combatants with a small naval air arm. The air force, with a total strength of 45,000 men, had 389 combat aircraft. Paramilitary forces, including the Pakistan rangers, the frontier corps, a maritime security agency, a national guard and local defense units, totaled 247,000. Military service is voluntary. Defense expenditures in 1998–99 were $2.48 billion or 4.4% of gross domestic product.

18INTERNATIONAL COOPERATION

Pakistan became a member of the UN on 30 September 1947 and is a member of its specialized agencies, including ESCAP.

As an Islamic state, Pakistan is an active member of the Organization of the Islamic Conference (OIC) and participates in various Muslim Afro-Asian organizations. Pakistan also belongs to the Asian Development Bank, the Colombo Plan, G-77, and the WTO and has signed the Law of the Sea. Following the establishment of Bangladesh, Pakistan withdrew from the Commonwealth of Nations in 1972.

In 1960, Pakistan and India signed an Indus water basin treaty opening the way to the peaceful use and development of water resources. Pakistan, Turkey, and Iran established a tripartite arrangement, called Regional Cooperation for Development (RCD), in 1964. In 1985, Pakistan and six other South Asian countries, including India and Bangladesh, formed the South Asian Association for Regional Cooperation (SAARC).

19ECONOMY

Despite steady expansion of the industrial sector during the 1990s, Pakistan's economy remains dominated by agriculture. In 1998, agriculture engaged 47% of the labor force, and accounted for 24% of the GDP as well as close to 70% of export revenues, including agriculture-based manufactures. Exports of primary agricultural products are concentrated in cotton and rice. At $448 in 1998, per capita income has improved marginally since the 1980s, when per capita income averaged $400. One-fourth of the land is farmed or used for grazing, and much of this is planted to food crops for domestic consumption. Pakistan is generally poor in natural resources, although extensive reserves of natural gas and petroleum are being exploited. Iron ore, chromite, and low-quality coal are mined.

When the country was created in 1947, there were no industries, and few banks, or mercantile firms. Since that time, industrial production has risen significantly. In 1998, industry accounted for about 26% of the GDP, compared with only 7% in 1950. Thanks in part to significant expansion of power facilities, largely in the Indus basin, the pace of economic development was particularly rapid during the 1980s. For most of the decade, the annual GDP growth rate averaged 6.5%, reflecting an expansion of over 4% annually in the agricultural sector and over 7% in value added in the industrial sector.

This strong performance not withstanding, a growing debt-servicing burden, large government expenditures on public enterprises, low tax revenues, high levels of defense spending, and a rapid rise in imports with burgeoning domestic demand contributed to serious fiscal and current account deficits during the late 1980s. In response, in 1988 the government initiated a major structural reform program with World Bank and IMF support.

The government pursued policies aimed at private sector-led development, macro economic stability, and structural reforms. Overall growth indicators remained promising with the reform measures, as GDP increased by 5.5% in 1990/91 and 7.8% in 1991/92, and export growth averaged a robust 14% between 1989 and 1992. These improvements notwithstanding, reform efforts secured less than expected reductions in the country's balance of payment deficits, due in part to deteriorating terms of trade in the wake of rising oil prices during the 1991 Gulf War. Severe floods in the Sindh and Punjab provinces in late 1992 and a contraction in international commodity markets weakened Pakistan's export sector during 1992/93, further exacerbating the country's trade and current account deficits and helping to reduce GDP growth to only 3% in 1993. In March of 1994 the government received IMF approval of a three-year Enhanced Structural Adjustment Facility (ESAF) to support reforms. The IMF wanted austerity measures aimed at reducing the government deficit to 4% of GDP, a reduction in the maximum tariff rate from 70% to 45%, increased privatization of large state-owned enterprises, and a tax on agricultural income. However, the government's failure to follow the IMF recommendations and liberalize the economy caused the IMF to suspend the $1.5 billion loan in mid-1995. The suspension of the loan worried investors and damaged Pakistan's debt ratings. The trade deficit grew, foreign exchange reserves dwindled, and inflation remained high. After the government recommitted itself to reform, the IMF approved a new $600 million standby arrangement in September. Still, by 1996 the economy was in its worst recession in 25 years. Tax receipts were falling well below their targets and export earnings had declined, leaving the government with a deepening foreign-exchange crises as reserves fell to only $500 million by the end of the year. By mid-1997, the government owed $1.6 billion in interest on $30 billion owed to foreign creditors, putting the country perilously close to default. Growth in GDP was only 1.2% in 1997, down from 6.1% in 1996. Growth rebounded at 5.4% in 1998. The national debt matched the country's annual GDP of $70 billion in 2000.

20INCOME

The US Central Intelligence Agency (CIA) reports that in 1998 Pakistan's gross domestic product (GDP) was estimated at $270 billion. The per capita GDP was estimated at $2,000. The annual growth rate of GDP was estimated at 5%. The average inflation rate in 1998 was 7.8%. The CIA defines GDP as the value of all final goods and services produced within a nation in a given year and computed on the basis of purchasing power parity (PPP) rather than value as measured on the basis of the rate of exchange. It was estimated that agriculture accounted for 24.2% of GDP, industry 26.4%, and services 49.4%.

The World Bank reports that for the same period per capita private consumption (in PPP terms) was $1,180. Private consumption includes expenditures of individuals, households, and nongovernmental organizations. It was estimated that between 1990 and 1998 private consumption grew at an annual rate of 5.2%. Approximately 45% of household consumption was spent on food, 19% on fuel, 6% on health care, and 5% on education. The richest 10% of the population accounted for approximately 28% of household consumption and the poorest 10% approximately 4.1%.

21LABOR

In 1998, the total labor force was estimated at 33,191,000 compared with 20,500,000 in 1975. The low proportion of the population included in the labor force (about 27%) is in part attributable to the limited participation of women. In 1995, agriculture accounted for 47% of the total work force, and industry for 19%. Some 70% of rural residents engage in agricultural pursuits. Unemployment and underemployment are major problems; while unemployment was officially 6.1% in 1997, underemployment has frequently gone as high as 25%. The Ministry of Labor operates employment exchanges.

There are sizable numbers of Pakistani workers in the Middle East and European countries, most of them from the poor regions of Pakistan's NWFP. There are also several million refugees from Afghanistan who have become part of the Pakistan labor force in those regions and in Karāchi.

The trade union movement is of recent origin. The principal federations include the National Labor Federation and the All Pakistan National Federation of Trade Unions. Labor-management differences are handled by the central conciliation machinery, established under the provisions of the Industrial Disputes Act of 1947. Benefits such as bonuses, paid holidays, and job security regulations are set forth in the basic West Pakistan Industrial and Commercial Employment Ordinance of 1968. The practice of child labor is widespread. According to a government survey, three or four million children between the ages of five and 14 worked as of 1996. However, informal estimates have placed this figure as high as 8 to 10 million. There may also be some 20 million bonded laborers in Pakistan. Bonded labor is particularly common among the persecuted Christian minority. Children are often kidnapped to serve as forced labor.

22AGRICULTURE

Agriculture engaged 47% of the economically active population in 1998. Agricultural production increased by an annual average of 4.5% during 1990–98, accounting for 24% of GDP in 1998. The development of a huge irrigation network covering two-thirds of the total cultivated area—together with massive land reclamation projects—has made possible the farming of vast tracts of previously barren and unusable land. The Indus Valley of Punjab is Pakistan's agricultural heartland. There are two principal growing seasons: the kharif season starts between April and June and ends between October and December, while the rabi season starts between October and December and ends during April or May. Grains constitute the most important food crops, with wheat, rice, corn, and citrus the major products. Cotton, the most important cash crop, generates more foreign trade income than any other export item. Cotton production suffered in the late 1990s from leaf curl virus. In 1998/99, production totaled 8.8 million bales, down 4.3% from 1997/98. Rice, sugarcane, tobacco, rapeseed, and mustard are also large export earners. Rice covers 10.5% of all cropland—exports of 1.293 million tons in 1998/99 were valued at $383.2 million.

Improved government policies over the past decade have made Pakistan a net exporter of guar products, tobacco, cotton, and rice. Other major agricultural exports include molasses, fruits and vegetables, guar and guar products, and tobacco. Principal crops with estimated 1998/99 output (in thousands of tons) were wheat, 18,054; sugarcane, 55,191; and rice, 4,674. Production of sunflower seed amounted to 299 tons in 1998/99. Other crops include millet, barley, sesame, flax, groundnuts, mangoes, citrus fruits, and vegetables. Opium poppies are grown in the North-West Frontier Province (with an estimated 65 tons produced in 1998), despite sporadic government efforts to stamp out the opium and heroin trade, which grew rapidly during the 1980s.

Farming production remains limited by primitive methods, and mechanization is uncommon. The introduction of improved wheat and rice varieties has met with some success, although the greatest impact on agriculture has derived from the Indus basin irrigation schemes, which by the 1970s had provided Pakistan with the largest irrigated network in the world. The availability of water has made possible increased use of chemical fertilizers, with the most intensive consumption occurring in cotton production. The government has instituted soil conservation, farm mechanization, land reclamation, and plant protection programs.

To increase smallholders' equity and provide further incentives for agricultural improvement, the government decreed in 1959 that the maximum holding for any person should be 200 ha (500 acres) of irrigated land or 400 ha (1,000 acres) unirrigated. Land in excess of these amounts was acquired by the government and paid for in interest-bearing 30-year bonds. In March 1972, the maximum permissible size of a holding, measured in terms of production index units, was reduced by two-thirds, with the government empowered to confiscate without payment all excess land for free redistribution to landless peasants and small tenants. To help the new landowners, the government provided loans for purchase of seed, feed, and bullocks. In accordance with a statement of national agricultural policy issued in 1980, the Agricultural Price Commission was established to provide incentives to Pakistani farmers through higher prices for farm products.

23ANIMAL HUSBANDRY

Some 30 to 35 million people are engaged in the livestock industry. Camels are used for transport throughout the more barren south and west, and bullocks and donkeys elsewhere. Sheep range widely over the grazing lands of middle and northern Pakistan; the bulk of their wool is exported. Among local breeds of cattle, the Red Sindhi, the Tharparker, the Sahiwal are renowned for milk, and the Bhagnari and Dhanni for draft purposes. The production of powdered milk, cheese, butter, and ice cream is carried out by several large dairy plants. From 1984 to 1990, milk production increased by 41%, and meat production rose 48%. Even so, domestic milk production still falls short of demand. Poultry production has recently became prominent, especially through scientific research in breeding, feeding, and disease control. With the assistance of the Asian Development Bank, several livestock development projects are currently underway.

In 1998/99 there were 22 million buffaloes, 21.6 million head of cattle, 45.8 million goats, and 23.9 million sheep. Commercial poultry numbered 170.1 million broilers and 10.36 million layers that year. There were also an additional 108 million poultry kept by people in rural areas. Modern poultry production in Pakistan is constrained by high mortality and incidence of disease in chicks and an inefficient marketing system. The livestock industry contributed 37% to the total value of agricultural output in 1998/99, and 9% to GDP. Production estimates for 1998/99 included (in tons): beef, 963,000; mutton, 633,000; poultry, 297,000; wool, 38,700; and milk, 24,876,000. In an effort to increase domestic milk production, the government has initiated a comprehensive livestock development program with $55 million in assistance from the Asian Development Bank. The government has also broadened extension and artificial breeding

services, taken measures to improve slaughterhouses, and introduced high-yield fodder varieties. Cattle dung is an important cooking fuel and fertilizer.

24FISHING

With a coastline of 814 km (506 mi), Pakistan is rich in fishery resources that remain to be fully developed. Almost the entire population of the coastal areas of Sindh and Balochistan depends on fisheries for its livelihood. During 1998/99, fisheries engaged 404,500 persons, of which 113,850 were in the marine sector and 290,600 were involved with inland fishing. The fish catch in 1998/99 was 616,500 tons, 70% of it landed off coastal waters. Species include salmon, mullet, pomfret, mackerel, shrimp, and local varieties. About 10% of the annual catch is exported. Export earnings from fish products amounted to $89.8 million in 1998/99.

To exploit potential fishery resources, the government has undertaken such projects as construction of a modern harbor for fishing vessels at Karāchi, procurement of diesel-powered vessels, establishment of cold storage and marketing facilities, export of frozen shrimp, and encouragement of cooperative fish-marketing societies. An aquaculture project financed by the Asian Development Bank and the EU aimed to increase the annual fish catch and to promote prawn farming.

25FORESTRY

Of Pakistan's depleted forest resources, amounting to about 2.3% of the total area, only about 1,748,000 ha (4,319,500 acres) are classified as commercial or productive forests. Privately-owned forests cover some 3,783,000 ha (9,348,000 acres), located primarily in the North Western Frontier Province (NWFP) and Punjab. Hill forests predominate in the north and northwest temperate and subtropical regions. Fir, spruce, deodar, bluepine, chirpine, Chalghoza, and juniper, as well as broad-leaved species like oak, maple, walnut, poplar, and chestnut are found in the hill forests. These forests are the main source for constructional timber and supply great quantities of fuelwood, while providing groundcover to the fragile mountain ecosystems (thereby lessening floods and droughts in the plains). Forests in the foothills consist of broadleaved evergreens, with main species of olive and phulai. Irrigated plantation forests grow such species as sheesham, mulberry, bakain, and semal, mostly for timber, furniture, and sporting goods production.

About 500,000 cu m of timber is produced annually by state forests, which are under the authority of the Pakistan Forest Institute. In its 1999–2004 five-year plan, the government plans to implement 151 reforestation projects, and a cost of r1.6 billion. The total timber cut in 1997 was 30,908,000 cu m, with 93% consumed as fuelwood. Since forest resources are limited, Pakistan must import wood and wood products in increasing volumes to satisfy rising demand. In 1997, forest product imports totaled $138.1 million.

26MINING

The prospecting and exploitation of mineral resources are subject to government planning and regulation. The Mineral Development Corp. and the Resource Development Corp. (RDC), both established in 1974, direct development of the mining sector and manage government-owned mining enterprises.

Except for petroleum and natural gas, mineral reserves are meager and of poor quality. Local coal is of inferior grade, and the demand requires massive imports; coal production stood at three million tons in 1995. Chromite is one of the few valuable minerals available; chromium content in mined ore rose from 1,090 tons in 1988 to 10,380 tons in 1991. After dropping as low as 2,810 in the succeeding years, production reached a record high of 13,500 in 1997. Small quantities of antimony, fire clays, iron ore, uranium, gold, and silver are also produced. The Mineral Development Corp. operates three coal mines in Baluchistan, and one each in Punjab and Sind.

27ENERGY AND POWER

In early 2000 Pakistan had crude oil reserves estimated at 208 million barrels (chiefly at the Meyal oil field, near Rawalpindi) and large natural gas reserves of 611 billion cu m (mainly at Sui, Baluchistan). In the early and mid-1980s, accelerated exploitation of these resources reduced the nation's oil imports and improved its trade balance. Crude oil production peaked in 1991 at 62,000 barrels per day.

Oil, about two-thirds of which is imported, satisfies about 43.5% of primary energy needs, natural gas (38.3%), coal (5.1%), while the remainder is met by hydroelectricity and nuclear power. Energy production in 1998 included petroleum, 55,000 barrels per day; natural gas, 19,817 million cu m; and coal, 3.5 million tons. Electricity generation in 1998 totaled 59,262 million kWh. Installed electrical generating capacity that year was 12,969,000 kW, of which 30% came from thermal plants, 40% from hydroelectric sources, and about 25% from natural gas.

Two factors have contributed to the growth of the electric power sector: the initial harnessing of the vast hydroelectric potential of the Indus basin (estimated at 25,000 MW) and the increased availability of natural gas as a fuel for thermal generators. About 42% of Pakistan's electrical output in 1996 came from hydroelectric sources. The Tarbela Dam, the world's largest earth- and rock-filled dam, completed in 1976 at a cost of $1.1 billion, generates 2.1 million kW of hydroelectric power. Pakistan's nuclear plant at Karāchi has a single 137-MW reactor that began commercial operation in 1972. As of early 1996, a 300-MW installation at Chashma was under construction.

Despite increases in installed generating capacity, Pakistan faces chronic electricity shortages due to rapid demand growth, high system losses, power theft, and seasonal reductions in the availability of hydropower. Rotating power outages are common and many villages are not yet electrified. As of 2000, less than half of Pakistan's population was connected to the nation's power grid. Pakistan's eighth Five Year Plan (1993–98) allocated $10.5 billion for electric power projects, including private sector projects.

28INDUSTRY

Since 1947, the government has given the highest priority to development of the industrial sector. Manufacturing grew by 5.8% between 1988 and 1998, and increased by 7.9% in 1998 after growth slowed to only 1.3% in 1997. Industry employs about 19% of the work force and accounts for about 26.4% of GDP.

During the 1960s and 1970s, light industry expanded rapidly—especially textiles, sugar refining, fertilizers, and other manufactures derived from local raw materials. Large government investments in the 1970s established the country's first large-scale ship-building and steel milling operations; the production of chemical fertilizers was also given special government support. The Pakistan Industrial Development Corp., established in the early 1980s with IDA credit, developed industrial estates for small- and medium-scale industries, assisting their occupants in obtaining credit, raw materials, technical and managerial assistance, access to production facilities, as well as marketing support. Despite steady overall industrial growth during the 1980s, the sector remains concentrated in cotton processing, textiles, food processing and petroleum refining.

The 1973 nationalization program, which placed 10 basic industries wholly within the public sector, was reversed in 1991 with the enactment of an ambitious privatization program. In 1992, the government began auctioning off majority control in nearly all public sector industrial enterprises, including those manufacturing chemicals, fertilizers, engineering products, petroleum products, cement, automobiles, and other industrial products requiring a high level of capital investment, to private investors. In 1995, however, the speed of privatization began to slow as the sale of some large state-owned units were stalled and postponed. In 1998, the Production Wing of the Ministry of Industries and Production held eight public industries employing some 46,000 workers, including Pakistan Steel, the State Cement Corporation (PACO), Federal Chemical and Ceramics Corporation (FCCC), State Petroleum Refining & Petrochemical Corporation (PERAC), State Engineering Corporation (SEC), and the Pakistan Industrial Development Corporation (PIDC).

Cotton textile production is the most important of Pakistan's industries, accounting for about 18% of large-scale industrial employment, and 60% of total exports. Pakistan has become self-sufficient in cotton fabrics and exports substantial quantities. Factories also produce synthetic fabrics, worsted yarn and jute textiles. Jute textile output amounted to over 68,600 tons in 1998/99. The textile industry as a whole employs about 40% of the industrial work force.

Other important industries include food processing, chemicals manufacture, and the iron and steel industries. In 1998/99, output of pig iron was 1.1 million tons; crude steel, 409,000 tons; cement, 8,586,000 tons; and soda ash, 177,593 tons. Industrial output from other major industries also includes refined sugar, vegetable ghee, urea, rubber tubes, electric motors and sewing machines.

29SCIENCE AND TECHNOLOGY

Pakistan has made notable advances in nuclear technology since the 1980s, when its Atomic Energy Commission (AEC) developed a nuclear plant for electric power generation and research programs. The AEC's three nuclear centers for agricultural research have employed nuclear techniques to improve crop varieties. Six nuclear medical centers provide diagnosis and treatment of patients with radioisotopes produced from Pakistan's own uranium resources. In May 1998, Pakistan conducted nuclear weapons tests in the desert of the Chagai Hills in response to Indian testing earlier that month. Five nuclear bombs were fired on 28 May and a sixth on 30 May.

The Karāchi Export Processing Zone (EPZ), established in 1980, has attracted foreign capital investment in advanced technologies. Another EPZ has been proposed for Lahore. EPZ now include those for computer assembly and parts manufacture, television assembly, other electrical and electronic products, and engineering.

Scientific learned societies include the Pakistan Academy of Science, founded in 1953 at Islāmābād, the Pakistan Association for the Advancement of Science (founded in 1947 at Lahore) and the Scientific Society of Pakistan (founded in 1954 at Karāchi). The Pakistan Council for Science and Technology is the chief government advisory body. The Pakistan Council of Scientific and Industrial Research and the Pakistan Medical Research Council (both in Karāchi), and the Pakistan Agricultural Research Council (in Islāmābād) promote research in their respective fields. In 1987–97, research and development expenditures totaled 0.92% of GNP; 72 scientists and engineers and 13 technicians per million people were engaged in research and development in Pakistan in the 1990s. Pakistan in 1996 had 28 universities and colleges offering courses in basic and applied sciences. In 1987–97, science and engineering students accounted for 32% of college and university enrollments.

30DOMESTIC TRADE

The government supervises the supply and pricing of essential commodities, including fruits, vegetables, livestock, and dairy products, and has established several cooperative marketing and distribution organizations. Foreign goods are brought in by large importing concerns, centered at Karāchi, and distributed to retailers through many intermediaries. There are several produce exchanges at Karāchi, and the trade organizations are represented by the Federation of Chambers of Commerce and Industry. Steps have been taken to improve marketing and distribution facilities throughout the country.

Banks are customarily open from 9 AM to 1 PM. Private businesses and multinationals usually operate from 9 AM to 5 PM during weekdays. Advertising remains small in scope, in part because of the high rate of illiteracy. Outlets include television, newspapers, posters, handbills, and color slides shown in the motion-picture houses.

31FOREIGN TRADE

Pakistan has suffered a weak trade position since the early 1970s, as the cost of oil imports have risen while prices for the country's main exports have declined on the international market. Exports fell 11% in 1998, and imports dropped 8.9%. Pakistan's commerce ministry estimates that up to $1.5 billion of unregistered trade annually occurs, mostly from smuggled imports.

The important commodity exports for Pakistan are cotton, textiles, and clothes. Other major exports include rice and leather. The following chart shows the top 10 exports.

	% OF COUNTRY TOTAL	% OF WORLD TOTAL
Textile yarn	20	5.0
Cotton fabrics	13	5.4
Textile articles	8.7	5.8
Woven man-made fiber fabric	7.5	1.9
Rice	5.2	6.0
Headgear	5.0	3.4
Knitted undergarments	4.4	1.7
Leather	3.3	1.9
Men's outerwear, not knit	3.0	0.9
Toys and sporting goods	2.5	0.7

In 1997 Pakistan's imports were distributed among the following categories:

Consumer goods	3.1%
Food	18.6%
Fuels	19.8%
Industrial supplies	30.4%
Machinery	21.8%
Transportation	5.7%
Other	0.5%

Smuggled goods (tea, soap, domestic appliances, batteries, tires, bicycles, and televisions) enter the country primarily from Afghanistan.

During the 1980s, the UK, traditionally Pakistan's most important trading partner, slipped behind the US, Japan, and Germany. Principal trading partners in 1998 (in millions of US dollars) were as follows:

COUNTRY	EXPORTS	IMPORTS	BALANCE
United States	1,821	914	907
China (inc. Hong Kong)	751	478	273
United Kingdom	567	415	152
Germany	550	421	129
United Arab Emirates	424	582	-158
Japan	289	749	-460
France	261	186	75
Saudi Arabia	204	594	-390
Korea	140	378	-238
Kuwait	35	474	-439

32BALANCE OF PAYMENTS

Pakistan's payments problems have been chronic since the 1970s, with the cost of oil imports primarily responsible for the trade imbalance. The growth of exports and of remittances from Pakistanis working abroad (mostly in the Middle East) helped Pakistan to keep the payments deficit in check. Since the oil sector boom began subsiding in the early 1980s, however, remittances have been declining. Remittances from overseas workers peaked at $2.9 billion in 1982/83, then dropped to $1.4 billion by 1997/98. This trend especially accelerated during the Gulf War, when nearly 80,000 Pakistanis in Kuwait and Iraq lost their jobs. Only about 25% of these jobs had been regained a year after the end of the conflict. Increased imports and softer demand for Pakistan's textiles and apparel in major markets also caused the current account deficit to further increase.

The balance of payments position weakened in 1995/96 as imports grew by 16% and exports by only 6%. The Rupee was devalued by 11% during 1995 and 1996 to encourage exports. Nevertheless, foreign reserves fell to around $800 million by mid-1997. By 2000, foreign debt equaled 100% of GDP.

The US Central Intelligence Agency reports that in 1998 the purchasing power parity of Pakistan's exports was $8.5 billion while imports totaled $10.1 billion resulting in a trade balance of -$1.6 billion.

The International Monetary Fund (IMF) reports that in 1997 Pakistan had exports of goods totaling $8,503 million and imports totaling $10,946 million. The services credit totaled $1,678 million and debit $2,707 million. The following table summarizes Pakistan's balance of payments for 1997 in millions of US dollars.

Current Account		-1,792
Balance on goods	-2,443	
Balance on services	-1,029	
Balance on income	-2,291	
Current transfers	3,970	
Capital Account		...
Financial Account		2,345
Direct investment abroad	25	
Direct investment in Pakistan	729	
Portfolio investment assets	...	
Portfolio investment liabilities	420	
Other investment assets	-40	
Other investment liabilities		1,212
Net Errors and Omissions		-6
Reserves and Related Items		-547

33BANKING AND SECURITIES

The central banking institution is the State Bank of Pakistan (SBP), established in 1948 at Karāchi and with branches in the larger cities. The government holds 51% of the bank's paid-up capital; 49% is held by corporations, societies, and individuals. The State Bank has exclusive responsibility for the issuance of currency; it is the financial agent of the central and provincial governments, and is responsible for the flotation and management of the public debt. As of 2000, there were 45 commercial banks and 36 non-banking financial institutions (NBFI's) in Pakistan. Of the commercial banks, four were nationalized, 17 private, 20 foreign, and four specialized banks. Citibank is the largest foreign bank operating in Pakistan. NBFI's included 10 development financial institutions, 16 investment banks, four housing finance companies, two venture capital companies, and four discount houses. Consumer banking in Pakistan is largely undeveloped; commercial banks lend predominantly to corporations. There is a minimum capital level of 8% on all risk assets. The total volume of default loans from all financial institutions in 1998 was $2.8 billion.

The nation's largest commercial banks were nationalized in 1974 and regrouped under five state banking institutions: the

National Bank of Pakistan, Habib Bank, United Bank, Muslim Commercial Bank, and Allied Bank of Pakistan. The government-controlled banking system thus comprised all but a few of the nation's banks and accounted for a large share of total bank deposits and outstanding domestic credit. In 1981, in accordance with the Islamic condemnation of usury, virtually all banks opened special accounts for depositors who preferred, in lieu of interest, to share in the profits or losses from investments made with their money. In 1985, all savings accounts stopped yielding interest and converted to sharing in profit and loss. Pakistan instituted banking reforms in 1991. The Muslim Commercial Bank and the Allied Bank of Pakistan Ltd. reverted to private ownership shortly thereafter. In 1991 banking licenses were granted to private commercial banks that wanted to establish foreign bank branches in the country. Major weaknesses persist and are particularly marked in the case of the four remaining government-run commercial banks, which account for the bulk of deposits and advances. The government announced plans to privatize Habib Bank in 1998.

The portfolios of the state-owned development finance institutions, which provide the bulk of long-term lending to industry and agriculture, likewise tend to be of poor quality. Their lending is less diversified and more risky than that of commercial banks, while their costs are higher and margins lower. The state provides credit through the Agricultural Development Bank of Pakistan and the House Building Finance Corp. Industrial loans are made available through the Pakistan Industrial Credit and Investment Corp. (established in 1957), the Industrial Development Bank of Pakistan (1961), and the National Development Finance Corp. (1973).

There are stock exchanges at Lahore, Karāchi, and Islāmābād, with Karāchi accounting for a major share of the business. In the nine months to end-March 1996, there were 33 new listings on the Karāchi Stock Exchange, the largest of the country's three bourses, bringing the total to 780 in 1998.

34INSURANCE

Pakistan's life insurance sector, nationalized in 1972, operated under the aegis of the State Life Insurance Corp. and Postal Life Insurance until 1992, when the government opened it to private sector participation. Foreign companies are no longer barred from the life insurance business, but they are restricted to minority ownership. Private companies function in non-life insurance areas, but the government insurance business is controlled by the National Insurance Corp. One of the state's first steps was to standardize and reduce premium rates and to encourage coverage among a wider segment of the population.

35PUBLIC FINANCE

The fiscal year extends from 1 July to 30 June. The federal government frames two separate budgets: revenue (current account) and capital. Deficits have appeared since 1971/72, a combined result of the loss of revenues from East Pakistan, stepped-up defense expenditures, lax expenditure controls, and a low and inelastic tax base. Current expenditures (debt service, defense, administration) now consume over 70% of the budget; development needs (education, health, energy, and rural development) receive the remainder. Tax revenues have not kept pace with expenditure growth due to widespread evasion, corruption among tax officials, overreliance on foreign trade taxes, and a tax exemption for agricultural income, which comprises 24% of GDP.

The US Central Intelligence Agency estimates that, in 1995, government revenues totaled approximately $11.9 billion and expenditures $12.4 billion. The budget deficit was hovering at about 6.2% of GDP in 1995 and 1996 and was projected to reach almost 7% in 1997. Interest payments on the accumulated

debt threatened to bankrupt the government by mid-1997. As a condition for a $1.6 billion loan from the IMF and World Bank, the government agreed to reduce the deficit to 4% of GDP. To do so, the government is attempting to raise revenues by expanding the tax base beyond the 1% of Pakistanis who currently pay income tax. Other proposals included a reduction in government payrolls, improved tax administration, and an end to the tax exemption for agricultural income. The IMF approved an Enhanced Structural Adjustment Facility in January 1999, when Pakistan was almost halfway through the three-year Structural Adjustment Program worth $1.6 billion. In April 2000, the IMF discovered that the former Prime Minister Nawaz Sharif had purposely minimized reports of the government's budget deficit, by about 1%, in order to keep the extra $2 billion in funds. Despite the dismal financial situation, the government has yet to reduce defense spending which accounts for almost 25% of the budget.

The International Monetary Fund estimates that in 1999 Pakistan's central government took in revenues of approximately $11.25 billion and had expenditures of $13.8 billion including capital expenditures of $1.43 billion. Overall, the government registered a deficit of approximately $2.55 billion. External debt totaled $29.6 billion.

The following table shows an itemized breakdown of government revenues and expenditures in millions of US dollars. The percentages were calculated from data reported by the International Monetary Fund.

REVENUE AND GRANTS	100%	11,250
Tax revenue	75.3%	8,466
Non-tax revenue	23.8%	2,682
Grants	0.9%	102
EXPENDITURES	100%	13,800

36TAXATION

Pakistan lives predominantly by foreign trade, and its import tariffs and export tariffs are essentially revenue-producing. The national government does not levy income tax on agricultural income; only about 1% of the population pays income taxes. Rates are progressive, rising from 5% in the lowest category to 35% in the highest, with a net wealth tax of up to 2.5%. The basic corporate tax is 43%. This rate is higher for banks (58%) and lower for certain other public companies (33%). A value-added tax of 15% is levied on the value of goods. Shopkeepers went on strike in May of 2000 after hearing news that the sales tax would actually be enforced.

Established proportions of the various taxes levied by the federal government are distributed to the provincial governments. In addition, the provinces collect, for their exclusive use, taxes on land revenue, immovable property, vehicles, professions and services, and mineral rights, as well as excise taxes. Municipalities and other local governments also levy taxes.

37CUSTOMS AND DUTIES

Pakistan's customs tariff brings in the largest single share of national revenue. Most dutiable items are subject to ad valorem duties that range from 0% to 35%. There is, in many cases, a 15% sales tax on imported goods (Food, raw materials, and capital goods are exempt from this tax). Alcohol is levied at a rate up to 65%, but can be as high as 225%. These rates were substantially lowered in the late 1990s from an average high of 30% in the early 1990s.

Tariffs are levied on major items of export, but these rates are subject to change as measures are taken to encourage or discourage the export of raw materials. Exports of certain foods, used copper and brass utensils, and some hides and skins are banned. Trade with Israel, South Africa, and Taiwan is prohibited.

38 FOREIGN INVESTMENT

Foreign aid and investment have played a critical role in Pakistan's economic development since the first years of independence. Since 1954, the government has tried to attract foreign investment to maintain economic development, provide specialized technical knowledge, and bring in much-needed foreign exchange. Incentives for private investment include guarantees for the repatriation of capital invested in approved industries, facilities for remittance of profits, and guarantees for equitable compensation in the event of nationalization of an industry. In addition, special tax concessions available to certain local industries are also available to foreign investors. Since the late 1980s, a series of regulatory reforms related to exchange controls, repatriation of profits, credit for foreign-owned firms, issuing of equity shares, foreign currency accounts, and transactions on the stock exchange have significantly reduced the restrictions on general foreign investor activity in the wider Pakistani economy. Despite the reforms, foreign direct investment totaled only $548 million in 1996/97 down from $1.1 billion in 1995/96. The decline was in response to a foreign exchange crises which has diminished investor confidence. Investors are also put off by Pakistan's reputation as the second most corrupt nation on earth; Nigeria ranked first. Another drop in FDI occurred in 1998/99, in part due to the war hysteria resulting from nuclear threats between Pakistan and India. The total for 1998/99 was $327 million, including $135 million from US sources, $77 million from the UK, and $51 million from Japan.

39 ECONOMIC DEVELOPMENT

After the founding of the Pakistani state in 1947, the government's economic policy concentrated attention on developing an economic infrastructure, achieving self-sufficiency in food, and developing export industries. A major new land reform program introduced in March 1972 had resulted by March 1975 in the confiscation (for eventual redistribution) of 45.3% of all privately cultivated farmland. By November 1973, the government had nationalized industries in 10 major categories of production. In a third major step, most of the commercial banks were nationalized on 1 January 1974, resulting in control of more than 90% of all banking business by the State Bank and the five newly created units.

By the late 1970s, however, Pakistan's martial law government, claiming the nationalization program had stifled production and discouraged private investment, moved to restore private sector confidence by fostering economic stability and by redressing the balance-of-payments deficit, which was causing large overseas debt obligations. A new five-year plan (1978–83), Pakistan's fifth, reserved 48% of industrial investment for the private sector and set goals for an annual economic growth rate of 7.2%, a 4.2% rise in per capita income, and increases of 6% in agricultural output and 10% in industrial production. The plan was allocated a budget of $21 billion, of which 25% was to come from external sources. Indications were that the agricultural sector would meet its target, but that rising oil costs and the burden of providing for the Afghan refugees had impeded progress in other sectors.

The sixth five-year plan (1983–88), with a proposed outlay of R210 billion, envisioned further investments in water and power development, deregulation to increase private sector activity, and a new emphasis on provision of social services and infrastructural improvements for rural areas. Prime Minister Junejo announced a program for 1986–90, with an outlay of R70 billion, focusing on rural development, particularly in the areas of education, village electrification, potable water supply, roads, health care, and employment.

By the late 1980s, a number of structural factors resulted in increasingly critical fiscal and balance of payment deficits. With less than 30% of the budget devoted to infrastructural development and other needs in health and education, the prognosis for long-term social and economic development remained poor. In response, a medium-term structural reform program was developed under the government of Prime Minister Benazir Bhutto for implementation in 1989–91. Aimed at correcting fiscal and external imbalances, the program targeted a reform of the tax collection system, tighter government spending controls and monetary management, the privatization of state-owned industrial enterprises, banks and utilities, the phasing out of state monopolies in the transportation, insurance, telecommunications and energy sectors, and liberalization of investment and foreign exchange regulations. Implementation of the ambitious program proceeded under the government of Nawaz Sharif who assumed the prime minister's office in 1991. Results were somewhat uneven, with little effective improvements scored in the country's tax system or its fiscal and balance of payments deficits. While the rapid change of government in 1993 and ongoing political tensions dampened private investment, officials assured that structural reform and privatization would continue.

Fiscal indecision and post-nuclear test economic sanctions dried up foreign investments while budget and trade deficits soared in 1999. The US lifted some sanctions, clearing the way for the IMF to negotiate a bailout package of $1.5 billion with Pakistan. Key demands included cuts in government budget deficits, further privatization, and improved tax collections. With little concessions made for these demands, Pakistan has been increasingly alienated from the World Bank and the IMF.

Since the early 1950s through 1993, Pakistan is estimated to have received about $37 billion in aid disbursements, including both long-term and medium-term loans and grants, making it one of the largest recipients in the developing world. For the Indus Valley project, Pakistan received funding of more than $1.3 billion from the IBRD, IDA, ADB, US, UK, and other countries. In addition to US aid (a six-year commitment of $4.02 billion made in 1988 with $2.1 billion disbursed by 1990), Pakistan has also received aid from Iran and the Arab states. New economic aid from the US was halted in 1990, under the terms of a Congressional amendment requiring certification of Pakistan's status as a nuclear weapons-free country. These sanctions were alleviated in 1996 by the Brown Amendment, but the nuclear tests of 1998 caused further economic sanctions that were only partially lifted by 2000.

40 SOCIAL DEVELOPMENT

Although traditionally described by its leaders and politicians as an Islamic social welfare state, Pakistan has been slow in taking over major responsibility for such welfare problems as unemployment, sickness, handicaps, and old age. Until the 1970s, the full scope of social welfare programs remained to be implemented. Some modest improvements were effected by setting up service units in rural communities, instituting pilot projects to overcome extreme poverty, opening centers for vocational training of the handicapped, and providing instruction in local welfare in the schools. The initial social security legislation passed in 1972 was never implemented. The current social security scheme, enacted in 1976, covers employees of firms with 10 or more workers. Family and self-employed labor is excluded, and there are separate systems for the armed forces, police, and other public employees. Social security coverage includes old age, disability, and survivor benefits, as well as sickness and maternity payments, workers' compensation, and unemployment benefits. This program is funded by 5% contributions from employers and any necessary subsidies from the government. The Worker's Compensation Act is supplemented by a Social Insurance Law and provides disability and worker's injury benefits to workers earning 3,000 rupees or less a month.

An Islamization program to promote social welfare in accordance with Islamic precepts was introduced in 1977 under martial law. Islamic welfare taxes, the zakat and ushr, were levied to redistribute wealth. The ushr tax on landowners took effect in 1983. Islamic beliefs are inculcated in the public schools and disseminated widely by the mass media. Laws against drinking alcoholic beverages, adultery, and bearing false witness have been strictly enforced.

The government's 1991 Shari'a Bill, aimed at bringing Pakistani society more fully into conformity with Islamic tenets, included provisions to protect women's constitutional and property rights. Despite these provisions, women face serious social and legal discrimination. In a court of law, the testimony of women is not permitted in serious cases which may result in harsh corporal punishment (lashing, stoning, amputation). In cases dealing with financial matters, the testimony of two women must be introduced as evidence. The Hadood Ordinances, introduced in 1979, engrained Islamic precepts into the Penal Code. Women who have been raped may be subject to charges of adultery under these provisions. The incidence of rape is high in Pakistan, and most women are afraid to file charges. The country's first crisis center for women opened in 1997 in Islāmābād, under the auspices of the Ministry of Women's Development. The same year, the National Assembly passed a law mandating a death sentence for gang rape. Most women are unaware of their legal rights concerning inheritance, and in following with Muslim custom, widows give up their share of the joint assets. Women's rights were further weakened in 1992, when the Supreme Court decided that men may divorce their wives without any legal or written notification.

The use of child labor in Pakistan is widespread. Children not only work in the agricultural sector, but are also engaged in low-paying work in carpet weaving centers. Bonded child labor, in which the employer makes a payment to the child's parent and keeps the child to work off the long-term debt, has been made illegal but still may affect hundreds of thousands, if not millions, of children.

Human rights violations in 1999 included arbitrary arrest, prolonged detention, and torture. Pakistan's human rights situation declined with the coup, led by General Musharraf, that ousted the Sharif government.

41HEALTH

Health facilities in Pakistan are inadequate, mainly due to a lack of resources and a high population growth rate. In 1993, 85% of the population had access to health care. Total health care expenditures in 1990 were $1,394 million. Public health care expenditures in 1995 equaled 1% of GDP.

The country needs food availability, a proper water supply, and adequate sanitation. Its goal, under the direction of the Federal Ministry of Health, is to be able to provide health care services to every Pakistani by the year 2000. Pakistan is the first country to nearly completely eradicate dracunculiasis, having reported fewer than 100 cases in 1995. Pakistan is also working towards universal immunization, disease prevention, health promotion, and curative and rehabilitative services, and, as of 1990, there were several programs underway to improve health care coverage and control tuberculosis, leprosy, and cancer. One such program is a Child Survival/Primary Health Care program to reduce mortality, malnutrition, and deaths due to diarrheal diseases. In 1989–95, 40% of children under five years old were considered malnourished. The goiter rate was high in 1996; 40 of every 100 school children were affected by goiter. In 1997, 90%

of children up to one year of age were immunized against tuberculosis; 74% against diphtheria, pertussis, and tetanus; 74% against polio; and 74% against measles. In 1996, there were three reported cases of tuberculosis per 100,000 people and 80 cases of malaria per 100,000.

In 1991–92, there were 60,250 physicians, 2,410 dentists, and 33,740 nurses, and 20,000 registered homeopathic medical practitioners. Many medical students have been sent abroad under an advanced medical training program. Special attention has been given to the training of nurses, and several training centers are in operation. However, medical personnel ratios, though much improved, remain inadequate: one doctor per 1,923 persons and one nurse per 1,769 in 1993. In 1993, there was one hospital bed per 1,455 inhabitants. There were 302 health centers with 2,462 beds serving the rural population. In 1991, centers for the disabled included 11 physical therapy centers, 12 mental retardation centers, 11 centers for the visually impaired, and 12 centers for the hearing impaired.

Malaria, tuberculosis, intestinal diseases, venereal diseases, and skin diseases remain Pakistan's main public health problems. Common diseases were diarrheal diseases (157,660 deaths in 1995); leprosy (6,104 cases in 1994); malaria (92,634 cases in 1993); and tuberculosis (11,020 cases in 1993). Drug addiction, especially among university students, is an increasing concern, and government detoxification centers have helped many addicts recover. In 1999, the infant mortality rate was 92 per 1,000 live births. Major causes of infant mortality are immunizable diseases, diarrhea, malnutrition, and poor environmental sanitation. Safe water was accessible to 74%, and adequate sanitation was accessible to 47% of the Pakistani population in 1990–95. The overall mortality rate was 10 per 1,000 people in 1999. The leading causes of death were diarrhea, pneumonia, tuberculosis, cardiovascular diseases, and cancer. Average life expectancy in 1999 was estimated at 59 years.

The HIV seroprevalence per 100 adults was 0.1 in 1997. In 1995, 55 AIDS cases were reported.

42HOUSING

The rapid increase in urbanization, coupled with the rising population, has added to the housing shortage in urban areas. About 25% of the people in large cities live in katchi abadis (shantytowns). The Public Works Department has built more than 8,000 units in Islāmābād, Lahore, Peshāwar, and Quetta at a cost of R1,588 million. Under the 1986–90 program, the residents in the katchi abadis were to be given proprietary rights. In 1987, the National Housing Authority was created to coordinate the upgrading of the existing katchi abadis and prevent the growth of new ones. As of 1991, 171 abadis had been renovated at a cost of R454 million, and 522 more were under development. Overall, 53% of Pakistanis have adequate sanitation facilities.

43EDUCATION

The education system is poor, notwithstanding a massive educational reform announced in 1972 and aimed at providing free and universal education through the 10th year of formal schooling for both boys (by 1983) and girls (by 1987). In addition, the study of Islam was to be compulsory at all levels. For the year 2000, adult illiteracy rates were estimated at 56.7% (males, 42.4%; females, 72.2%). As an initial step, private educational institutions at all levels were nationalized. Additional steps included a reform of the curriculum away from general education and in favor of agricultural and technical subjects, equality of access to formal schooling for low-income groups and females, financial aid programs for poor students, and broad expansion and improvement of higher-level facilities. Curriculum bureaus were set up at federal and provincial levels, and the National Council of Education was established to formulate and evaluate educational development policy.

As of the mid-1990s, there were 15,532,000 pupils attending primary schools, 31% of which were female. In that same year, 5,022,416 students attended secondary schools. Girls attend separate schools at both primary and secondary levels.

In the same period, 1,656,815 students were enrolled at institutions of higher learning. Arts and sciences colleges are affiliated with the universities of the Punjab (at Lahore, established 1882), Sind (at Hyderabad, 1947; at Karāchi, 1951), Peshawar (1950), Baluchistan (1970), and Multan (1975). An agricultural university was established in 1961 at Lyallpur (now Faisalabad). Two engineering and technological universities have been founded at Lahore (1961) and Islāmābād (1966). Research institutions include the Institute of Islamic Studies at Lahore, the Iqbal Academy at Lahore, and the Pakistan Institute of International Affairs at Karāchi. In 1995, there were a total of 29 universities, seven of which are privately operated. Urdu and English are the languages of instruction.

Many adult literacy centers, including women's literacy centers, have been established in recent years, the majority in Sind. In addition, the People's Open University was established at Islāmābād (1974) to provide mass adult education via correspondence and the communications media.

44LIBRARIES AND MUSEUMS

The National Library of Pakistan in Islāmābād holds 116,000 volumes. The largest university library in Pakistan is that of the Punjab University at Lahore, with a collection of about 395,000 volumes, including some 20,000 manuscripts. Sizable collections are also found at the University of Karāchi (100,000 volumes) and the University of Sind (244,000 volumes). Other important libraries are the Punjab Public Library in Lahore (233,000 volumes), the Liaquat Memorial Library (147,000 volumes), the Central Secretariat Library (110,000 volumes), and the National Archives (35,000 volumes), all in Karāchi. The International Islamic University in Islāmābād holds 100,000 volumes.

The National Museum of Pakistan (Karāchi) contains prehistoric material from the Indus Valley civilization, Buddhist statues and carvings, and material from the Islamic centuries, including the renowned Mughal period. The Peshawar Museum has a splendid collection of Buddhist sculpture of the Gandhara style. The Lahore Museum has an outstanding collection of Greco-Buddhist sculpture. Fine mosques, shrines, and mausoleums of the Islamic centuries are scattered throughout the country. Among the best of the surviving gardens of the Mughal period are those at Lahore, including the Shalimar gardens. There is a museum dedicated to the work of Shakir Ali in Lahore and the Pakistan Army Museum is in Rawalpindi.

45MEDIA

Postal, telegraph, and telephone services are owned and operated by the state. As of 1999, telecommunications services were not readily available to most of the urban population. In 1998, the number of telephones in use totaled 2.8 million. Automatic telephone service has been installed in most cities and large towns. Radiotelephone and radiotelegraph services are available within the country and to foreign countries.

Through Azad Kashmir Radio and the Pakistan Broadcasting Corporation, the government operates 18 shortwave radio stations. Karāchi is the broadcasting center, and there are important transmitters at Hyderabad, Quetta, Lahore, Rawalpindi, Peshawar, Multan, Bahawalpur, and Islāmābād. Government-run Pakistan-TV broadcasts at least 10 hours a day through 28 transmitters. In total, as of 1999, there were 26 AM, 3 FM, and 22 television stations in use. In 1997 the country had radios, 65 television receivers, and one mobile phone per 1,000

population. Pakistan's Indian Ocean INTELSAT communications stations began service in 1971 near Karāchi.

Daily newspapers–most of them with very small circulations— are published in Urdu, English, and a few other languages. English-language newspapers are read by less than 1% of the population but are very influential, especially *Dawn* (1999 estimated circulation, 70,000), published in Karāchi, and *Pakistan Times* (75,000), published in Lahore and Rawalpindi. Leading Urdu-language dailies (with 1999 circulations) are *Jang* (820,000) and *Hurriyet* (600,000), both in Karāchi, and *Nawa-e-Waqt* (573,900), in Lahore.

While freedom of the press has always been provided for constitutionally, censorship was imposed on the press by the martial law governments. Between 1979 and 1982, local censors reviewed items prior to publication, and some books and periodicals were confiscated. Even after the lifting of censorship, the government continued to influence press coverage by controlling the availability of newsprint, which must be imported, and the placement of government advertising, which is a source of newspapers' revenue. There are no longer restrictions on the importation of newsprint. There is a constitutional prohibition on the ridicule of Islam, the armed forces, or the judiciary.

As of 1996, there were about 164,000 personal computers. Online access is extremely limited, with less than one Internet host per 1,000 population in 1998.

46ORGANIZATIONS

Most major cities contain chambers of commerce, and there are numerous employers' associations, such as the All-Pakistan Textile Mills Association, the Pakistan Carpet Manufacturers' and Exporters' Association, and the Pakistan Shipowners' Association. The Islamic community is represented by several flourishing organizations, and other religious communities, such as the Zoroastrians, have their own groups.

47TOURISM, TRAVEL, AND RECREATION

The government actively promotes tourism to boost its foreign-exchange earnings. Pakistan Tours, a government subsidiary, provides daily tours of Karachi, Rawalpindi, and other main cities. In Karāchi are the National Museum and the Mausoleum of the Quaid-e-Azam. In Lahore, the "city of gardens" and Pakistan's foremost cultural and educational center, remnants of the Mughal Empire are resplendently preserved. Islāmābād, the wholly planned capital, offers notable examples of architecture in the modern style. Popular recreations include mountain climbing in the Himalaya foothills, sailing, and deep-sea fishing off the Arabian Sea coast. Hockey and cricket are the leading sports, but golf is also popular, with courses in Lahore, Rawalpindi, Islāmābād and other cities.

Most visitors to Pakistan are required to have a visa and a valid passport. Tourists planning to stay more than 30 days must register with the government. Road permits are available for land crossings into India at Wagah (between Lahore and Amritsar in India). There are no health restrictions on visitors entering Pakistan except in regard to cholera and yellow fever immunizations for those who have been in infected areas. In 1997, 374,800 tourists visited the country, and receipts were valued at $117 million. That year there were 32,021 hotel rooms and 48,032 beds with a 47% occupancy rate.

The UN estimated the cost of staying in Islāmābād in 1999 at $78 to $134 per day, depending on the choice of hotel. Estimated daily expenses in Karāchi were $97 per day.

48FAMOUS PAKISTANIS

Several figures of monumental stature are associated with the creation and establishment of Pakistan. The poet and philosopher of a revitalized Islam, Mohammad Iqbal (1873–1938), who wrote in Urdu, Farsi, and English, first called for the establishment of a Muslim state on the subcontinent in a statement made in 1930. Mohammad Ali Jinnah (1876–1948), the Quaid-e-Azam, or "Great Leader," rallied the Muslims to this cause and became the first governor-general of the Commonwealth of Pakistan. His "right hand," Liaquat Ali Khan (1896–1951), was the first prime minister of the nation until his assassination. Chaudhury Mohammad Ali (1905–80), a former prime minister, played a key role in the organization of the new government in 1947. Field Marshal Mohammad Ayub Khan (1908–74) served as commander-in-chief of the Pakistani army, as minister of defense in 1954–55, and as president of Pakistan from October 1958 to March 1969. Sir Mohammad Zafrulla Khan (1893–1985), a distinguished jurist, was several times minister of foreign affairs and later a member of the World Court at The Hague; in 1962, he served as president of the 17th UN General Assembly. Zulfikar Ali Bhutto (1928–79), who rose to prominence as founder and leader of the socialist-leaning Pakistan People's Party, was prime minister during 1973–77 and guided the country's political and economic transformation following the loss of East Pakistan. After Bhutto's execution in 1979, his elder daughter, Benazir (b.1953), became titular head of the Pakistan People's Party. Gen. Mohammad Zia-ul-Haq (1924–1987) came to power in 1977 and assumed the presidency in 1978. The Pakistani-born scientist Abdus Salam (1926–96) shared the 1979 Nobel Prize for Physics for his work in electromagnetism and the interaction of elementary particles.

In literature, the paramount position is still held by the great Urdu writers who lived before the establishment of Pakistan. Ghalib (1796–1869) and Iqbal are recognized as the two greatest Urdu poets. Contemporary writers who have won fame include the Urdu poet Faiz Ahmad Faiz (1911–84), imbued with a strongly socialist spirit, and the Urdu short story writer Saadat Hasan Manto (1912–55). Foremost among Pakistan's artists is Abdur Rahman Chughtai (1899–1975).

[49]DEPENDENCIES

Pakistan has no territories or colonies.

[50]BIBLIOGRAPHY

Ahmed, Akbar S. (ed.). *Pakistan: the Social Sciences' Perspective.* Karāchi: Oxford University Press, 1990.

Ali, Akhtar. *The Political Economy of Pakistan: An Agenda for Reforms.* Karāchi, Pakistan: Royal Book Co., 1996.

American University. *Pakistan: A Country Study.* Washington, D.C.: Government Printing Office, 1984.

Burki, Shahid Javed. *Historical Dictionary of Pakistan.* Metuchen, N.J.: Scarecrow Press, 1991.

Chopra, Pran. *India, Pakistan, and the Kashmir Tangle.* New Delhi: Indus, 1994.

Contemporary Issues in Pakistan Studies. Edited by Saeed Shafqat. Lahore: Gautam Publishers, 1995.

Donnan, Hastings and Pnina Werbner (eds.). *Economy and Culture in Pakistan: Migrants and Cities in a Muslim Society.* New York: St. Martin's Press, 1991.

Encyclopaedia Indica: India, Pakistan, Bangladesh. Edited by S. S. Shashi. New Delhi: Anmol Publications, 1996.

Hasan, Mushirul (ed.). *India's Partition: Process, Strategy and Mobilization.* Delhi: Oxford University Press, 1993.

Khan, Riaz M. *Untying the Afghan Knot: Negotiating Soviet Withdrawal.* Durham, N.C.: Duke University Press, 1991.

Korson, J. Henry (ed.). *Contemporary Problems of Pakistan.* Boulder, Colo.: Westview Press, 1993.

Mahmud, S. F. *A Concise History of Indo-Pakistan.* 2d ed. New York: Oxford University Press, 1988.

Malik, Iftikhar H. *State and Civil Society in Pakistan: Politics of Authority, Ideology, and Ethnicity.* Houndmills, U.K.: Macmillan, 1997.

Noman, Omar. *Pakistan: A Political and Economic History since 1947.* New York: Kegan Paul International, 1990.

Pakistan: A Country Study. Washington, D.C.: Government Printing Office, 1995.

Pakistan-American Relations: The Recent Past. Edited by M. Raziullah Azmi. Karāchi, Pakistan: Royal Book Co., 1994.

Political System in Pakistan. Edited by Verinder Grover and Ranjana Arora. New Delhi: Deep and Deep, 1995.

Qasir, Nadeem. *Pakistan Studies: an Investigation into the Political Economy, 1948–1988.* Oxford: Oxford University Press, 1991.

Raza, M. Hanif. *Portrait of Pakistan.* Lahore, Pakistan: Ferozsons, 1994.

Saeed, Khawaja Amjad. *Economy of Pakistan.* Lahore, Pakistan: S. A. Salam Publications, 1995.

Shebab, Rafi Ullah. *The Political History of Pakistan.* Lahore, Pakistan: Dost Associates, 1995.

Taylor, David D. *Pakistan.* Santa Barbara, Calif.: Clio Press, 1990.

Weinbaum, Marvin G. *Pakistan and Afghanistan: Resistance and Reconstruction.* Boulder, Colo.: Westview Press, 1994.

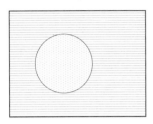

PALAU

Republic of Palau
Belau

CAPITAL: Koror, Koror Island.

FLAG: The flag, adopted 1 January 1981, is light blue, with a yellow disc set slightly off center toward the hoist.

ANTHEM: *Belau er Kid.*

MONETARY UNIT: The US dollar is the official medium of exchange.

WEIGHTS AND MEASURES: British units are used, as modified by US usage.

HOLIDAYS: New Year's Day, 1 January; Youth Day, 15 March; Senior Citizens Day, 5 May; Constitution Day, 9 July; Labor Day, 1st Monday in September; United Nations Day, 24 October; Thanksgiving Day, 4th Thursday in November; Christmas, 25 December.

TIME: 8 PM = noon GMT.

¹LOCATION, SIZE, AND EXTENT

Palau (also known as Belau) is located in the western extremities of the Pacific Ocean. It consists of the Palau group of islands, in the western Caroline Islands, and four remote islands to the sw. Palau is isolated from larger land masses, with Papua New Guinea/Irian Jaya (Indonesia) 660 km (410 mi) to the s, the Philippines 885 km (550 mi) to the w, and Japan 3,042 km (1,890 mi) to the N. Yap Island in the Federated States of Micronesia lies 579 km (360 mi) to the NE. The country consists of more than 200 islands, with a total land area of 441 sq km (170.4 sq mi). Babeldaob is the largest island, with an area of 397 sq km (153.2 sq mi); Koror Island, containing the capital, has an area of 18 sq km (7.1 sq mi). The islands of Peleliu and Angaur are about 50 km (30 mi) s of Koror. Sonsorol and Hatohobei, the two smallest island states, lie 560–640 km (350–400 mi) sw of Koror. Kayangel is a coral atoll 45 km (28 mi) N of Babeldaob.

²TOPOGRAPHY

The islands include four types of topographical formation: volcanic, high limestone, low platform, and coral atoll. The Palau barrier reef encircles the Palau group, except Angaur Island and the Kayangel atoll. The reef encloses a lagoon (1,267 sq km/489 sq mi) on the western side, containing a large number of small elevated limestone islets known as the Rock Islands. Babeldaob and Koror, with peak elevations of 217 m (713 ft) and 628 m (2,061 ft), respectively, contain elevated limestone and volcanic formations. Arakabesan, Malakal, and several small northern islands are volcanic formations. Peleliu and Angaur are low-platform reef islands.

³CLIMATE

Located near the Equator, Palau's climate is maritime tropical, characterized by little seasonal and diurnal variation. The annual mean temperature is 28°C (82°F) in the coolest months. There is high precipitation throughout the year and a relatively high humidity of 82%. Heavy rainfall occurs from May to January. The short torrential nature of the rainfall produces up to 381 cm (150 in) of precipitation annually. Typhoons and tropical storms occur from July through November.

⁴FLORA AND FAUNA

Plant life, abundant throughout most of the islands, includes mangrove swamps, savanna land, and rain forest in upland areas. Food crops, such as taros, cassavas, sweet potatoes, coconuts, bananas, papayas, and citrus fruits, are mostly wild. Marine life is also abundant, with more than 1,500 species of tropical fish and 700 species of coral and anemones in the lagoons and reefs. Fauna includes the sea turtle, which is consumed as a delicacy, and the dugong, or sea cow, a marine mammal that is close to extinction.

⁵ENVIRONMENT

While much of Palau's fragile natural environment remains free of environmental degradation, there are several areas of concern, including illegal fishing with the use of dynamite, inadequate facilities for disposal of solid waste in Koror, and extensive sand and coral dredging in the Palau lagoon. Like the other Pacific island nations, a major environmental problem is global warming and the related rising of sea level. Water coverage of low-lying areas is a threat to coastal vegetation, agriculture, and the purity of the nation's water supply. Palau also has a problem with inadequate water supply and limited agricultural areas to support the size of the population. The nation is also vulnerable to earthquakes, volcanic activity, and tropical storms. Sewage treatment is a problem, along with the handling of toxic waste from fertilizers and biocides.

⁶POPULATION

As a result of a family planning program, Palau's crude birthrate declined from 31 per 1,000 population in 1974 to 17.4 in 1988. In 1996, there were 22 births and 7 deaths per 1,000 population, for a natural rate increase of 1.5%. Population increased at an estimated annual rate of 1.7% during the 1990s. By 2000, the population of Palau was estimated at 18,827. Koror and Airai were the most populous states, together containing over 77% of the total population.

It was estimated that 73% of the population lived in urban areas in 2000. The capital city, Koror, had a 2000 population of 12,000.

[7]MIGRATION

In 1999, persons not Palau-born accounted for nearly 30% of the total population. Most were born in the Philippines, China, and Bangladesh; there were also significant numbers from the Federated States of Micronesia, the US, and Japan. Most were workers, whose numbers have been rapidly increasing; in 1999, foreigners made up 46% of the total work force. The vast majority of these foreigners were located in Koror. About one-fifth of all Palauans live abroad, many on Guam. In 1999, the net migration rate was 5.63 migrants per 1,000 population.

[8]ETHNIC GROUPS

Palauans are a composite of Polynesian, Malayan, and Melanesian races. At last estimate, the largest non-Palauan ethnic groups included Filipinos (9.8%), other Micronesians (1.8%), Chinese (1.3%), and people of European descent (0.8%).

[9]LANGUAGES

English is the official language in all of Palau's 16 states. However, Palauan, a Malayo-Polynesian language related to Indonesian, is the most commonly spoken language. It was the language spoken at home by 81% of the people five years of age or over in 1990, in contrast to 3% who spoke only English at home. Palauan is used, in addition to English, as an official language in 13 states. Sonsorolese is official in the state of Sonsoral; Anguar and Japanese in the state of Anguar; and Tobi in the state of Tobi.

[10]RELIGIONS

Most Palauans are Christians (Roman Catholics, Seventh-Day Adventists, Jehovah's Witnesses, the Assembly of God, the Liebenzell Mission, and Latter-Day Saints). One-third of the population observes the Modekngei religion, which is indigenous to Palau.

[11]TRANSPORTATION

The nation's roads at last estimate totaled 61 km (37.9 mi), of which 36 km (22 mi) were paved. Asphalt roads are found only in Koror, Airai, and Melekeok. A two-lane concrete bridge, constructed in 1976, links Koror with Airai. The Koror state government provides a public bus service. Palau's deepwater harbor at Malakal in Koror offers international port facilities. Heavy reliance is placed on small private watercraft throughout the country.

As of 1998, there was 1 airport, the international airport located in Airai, 10 km (6 mi) from Koror. Three airlines provide international service: Air Micronesia/Continental, Air Nauru, and South Pacific Island Airways. There are 3 domestic airlines: Palau Paradise Air, Aero Belau, and Freedom Air.

[12]HISTORY

As part of the Carolinian archipelago, the islands were sighted by European navigators as early as the 16th century. In 1686, the Spanish explorer Francisco Lezcano named Yap Island (now in the Federated States of Micronesia) "La Carolina" after King Charles II of Spain. The name was later generalized to include all the islands. Spanish sovereignty was established in 1885. In 1899, after Spain's defeat in the Spanish-American War of 1898, Palau, with the rest of the Carolines, was sold to Germany. At the outbreak of World War I in 1914, the islands were taken by the Japanese. As a member of the League of Nations, Japan was given a mandate over Palau in 1920, and Koror was developed as an administrative center of Japanese possessions in the north Pacific.

In 1947, following occupation by US forces in World War II, Palau became part of the UN Trust Territory of the Pacific Islands, which was administered by the US. After the adoption of a constitution in 1980, Palau became a self-governing republic in 1981. Since 1982, the republic has been involved in negotiating a Compact of Free Association (CPA) with the US. Negotiations were stalled because the 1980 constitution prohibits any placement of nuclear weapons, and the US has wanted to use the islands as a military site. In June 1985, President Haruo Remeliik was assassinated; Vice-President Alfonso Oiterang served as acting president until August 1985, when he was defeated in an election by Lazarus E. Salii. President Salii committed suicide in August 1988. Kuniwo Nakamura was elected President in November 1992. On 1 October 1994 Palau became an independent nation in free association with the US; under the CPA the US is responsible for Palau's defense. In 1995, Palau entered into diplomatic talks with the US, Japan, and Taiwan. In February 1999, Palau opened an embassy in Tokyo, Japan.

Under the 1994 CPA, Compact funds were allocated to finance the building of roads and infrastructure on Babeldaob, across from the capital Koror, in order to attract people and economic activity. As of 1999, despite President Nakamura's support, Paramount Chief Ibedul Yutaka Gibbons of Koror, the most powerful traditional leader in Palau, opposed the Compact and its channeling of resources away from Koror and to Babeldaob, arguing the Compact will erode Palau's autonomy and threaten traditional values.

In March 1999, a strong movement emerged in the Palau Congress to change the existing bicameral congress (House of Representatives and Senate) to a unicameral form of government to reduce the cost of government. The proposal was to be put to the people in a vote, possibly in November 2000.

In July 1999, Palau hosted the First Micronesian Traditional Leaders' Conference. In October 1999, Palau hosted the 30th South Pacific Forum with more than 300 foreign delegates, observers, and media members. The Forum considered issues on climate and sea level change, regional security and law enforcement, fisheries, and the United Nations Special Session on Small Island Developing States. Trade ministers of the South Pacific Forum endorsed the proposal for a Pacific Free Trade Area (FTA) that would create a regional market of six million people. The FTA allows goods produced in the fourteen island countries to be traded freely.

[13]GOVERNMENT

The government comprises three branches: the executive, the legislative, and the judicial. The executive branch is headed by the president, who is elected by popular vote for not more than two terms of four years each. The president is assisted by a cabinet of ministers, one of whom is the vice president and is also elected by popular vote. A council of chiefs, based on Palau's clan system, advises the president on traditional and customary matters.

The legislative branch, known as the Olbiil Era Kelulau, or National Congress, is a bicameral form of legislature, comprising 14 senators and 16 delegates. The senators, elected for four-year terms, are apportioned throughout Palau on the basis of population and traditional regional political groupings. The delegates are elected from each of the 16 states and have the same four-year term as the senators.

In November 1992 Kuniwo Nakamura was elected Palau's new President, with 50.7% of the vote. Palau's Vice President, Tommy E. Remengesau, Jr. was also elected at that time.

[14]POLITICAL PARTIES

Palau has one political party, the Palau Nationalist Party, currently led by Polycarp Basilius.

[15]LOCAL GOVERNMENT

Each of Palau's 16 states has a government headed by a governor, who is popularly elected, in most cases, for a four-year term. The

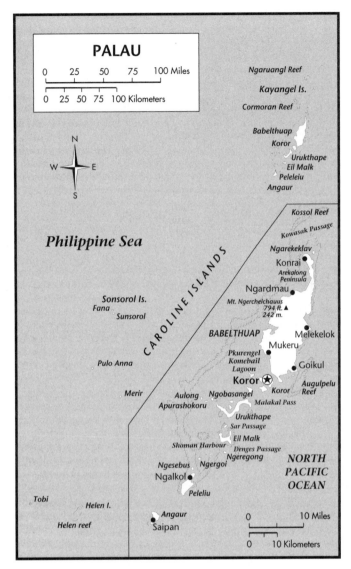

LOCATION: 131° to 135°E; 3° to 8°N.

members of the state legislatures are popularly elected for a four-year term, although in a few states, the term of office is limited to two years. The states are empowered to make their own laws, which must not be in conflict with the national constitution or any existing laws.

16JUDICIAL SYSTEM

The Supreme Court is the highest court in the land. Other courts include the National Court, which, although constitutionally mandated, was not operational as of 1987, and the lower court system, consisting of the Court of Common Pleas. In October, 1990 US Interior Secretary Manuel Lujan issued an order granting the Interior Department in Washington the power to veto laws and reverse decisions by Palau's courts. This reassertion of legal authority by the United States was partially in response to the decade of unsuccessful negotiations concerning a plan for eventual self-government.

The Constitution provides for an independent judiciary and the government respects this provision in practice. Palau has an independent prosecutor and an independent public defender system.

17ARMED FORCES

The US is responsible for defense. Palau has no armed forces and does not have US armed forces within its borders except for a small contingent of US Navy Seabees who undertake civil action projects.

18INTERNATIONAL COOPERATION

Palau is a member of the UN and participates in the World Bank, ICAO, IMF, UNCTAD, and WHO. Palau is a full member of the SPC and other regional agencies and an associate member of ESCAP. The government maintains liaison offices in Guam, Hawaii, and Washington, D.C.

19ECONOMY

The economy has a narrow production base as a result of limited natural resources and few skilled personnel. The services sector consists largely of government administration and trade. Large gaps exist between government revenues and expenditures and between imports and exports. These gaps are financed largely by grant assistance from the US. Unemployment is a major problem. Recently, expansion of air travel in the Pacific has fueled growth of the tourist sector. Tourist arrivals were up 56% in 1996. Hotel accommodations are expected to double and a new airport was under construction. The Asian financial crisis was expected to negatively effect the burgeoning tourist sector.

20INCOME

The US Central Intelligence Agency (CIA) reports that in 1997 Palau's gross domestic product (GDP) was estimated at $160 million. The per capita GDP was estimated at $8,800. The annual growth rate of GDP was estimated at 10%. The CIA defines GDP as the value of all final goods and services produced within a nation in a given year and computed on the basis of purchasing power parity (PPP) rather than value as measured on the basis of the rate of exchange.

21LABOR

The economically active population was 8,347 persons in 1995, of whom 588 (7%) were unemployed. The service sector employed 75.7% of the population, construction 15%, and mining 9.3%.

There are no specific provisions granting the right to strike or organize unions, but the issue has never come up and there were no organized trade unions.

There is no minimum age for employment, but children do not typically work except to help out in small scale family enterprises such as fishing or agriculture. Education is compulsory until age 14, and this is enforced by the government.

Palau's first minimum wage law, passed in 1998, set a rate of $2.50 per hour.

22AGRICULTURE

Agricultural production belongs almost entirely to the nonmonetary, or subsistence, sector. Most households outside Koror are fully or partially engaged in subsistence agriculture. Staple subsistence crops include taros, cassavas, sweet potatoes, bananas, and papayas. Commercial produce is marketed mainly in Koror, consisting mostly of copra and coconut oil, vegetables, and a wide variety of tropical fruits.

23ANIMAL HUSBANDRY

Livestock is limited to pigs, chickens, ducks, cattle, and goats. Pigs and chickens are raised by most households. Several small commercial egg-producing operations supply eggs to the Koror market. The Livestock Branch of the Division of Agriculture maintains breeding herds of pigs, cattle, and goats.

²⁴FISHING

Palau's marine resources are rich and diverse. Subsistence fishing within the reef is a major activity and dominates market production. The total catch was 1,550 tons in 1997. Deep-sea fishing for pelagic species resulted in a tuna catch of 93 tons in 1997. Seasonal trochus harvesting for shell button manufacture is an important source of income for most fishermen. Other marine resources include pearls, shrimp, ornamental fish, seaweed (agar agar), and mollusks. Palau is known for having some of the best diving, snorkeling, and sport fishing areas in the world.

²⁵FORESTRY

Forestry resources consist of coastal mangrove, coconut and pandanus palms, and rain forest species in upland areas. Palau is heavily dependent on imported forestry products, including furniture and lumber for house construction. The government's forestry station at Nekken on Babeldaob Island, of which more than half of the 1,257 ha (3,105 acres) consists of natural forest, provides primarily mahogany seedlings to farmers. Palau imported $1.1 million in forest products during 1997.

²⁶MINING

Crystalline calcite from glistening limestone caves was first quarried as long as 1,500–2,000 years ago. The doughnut-shaped finished carved products would be transported by canoe some 250 miles to Yap (now part of the Federated States of Micronesia), and used as currency.

The Koror state government engages in commercial production of dredged coral from the Palau lagoon, with a production capacity of 800 cu m per day. Other states are also involved in coral dredging. A private company supplies aggregates for concrete from crushed basalt rock and beach sand.

²⁷ENERGY AND POWER

The economy is almost totally dependent on imported petroleum for energy. Electricity is supplied from the Malakal power plant, located in the state of Koror, with an installed capacity of approximately 8,000 kW. There are state-owned power plants with capacities ranging from 30 kW to 120 kW in Peleliu, Angur, Ngiwal, Ngeremlengui, Airai, Ngaraard, and Ngerchelong.

²⁸INDUSTRY

Manufacturing plays a limited role in the economy. A copra-processing plant is located in Malakal. Concrete blocks are manufactured, utilizing imported cement, and there is a small-scale sawmill industry.

²⁹SCIENCE AND TECHNOLOGY

Palau's Micronesian Mariculture Demonstration Center, established in 1973, promotes the cultivation of commercially valuable and ecologically threatened marine species. The center attracts visiting marine scientists; its giant clam hatchery was the first and remains the largest of its kind.

³⁰DOMESTIC TRADE

Domestic trade is centered in Koror. Private-sector activities in tourism, restaurants and hotels, small workshops, banking, wholesale and retail outlets, transportation, and freight handling are located in Koror and, to a limited extent, the adjacent state of Airai.

³¹FOREIGN TRADE

The economy sustains a large trade deficit. Food, beverages, and tobacco account for 28% of imports; manufactured goods, 26%; machinery and transportation equipment, 23%; mineral fuel and lubricants, 9%; and other imports, 14%. The country's low volume and limited range of exports include trochus shell, 37.3%; fresh, frozen, and smoked fish, 31.6%; wooden handicrafts, 29.8%; and other exports, 1.3%. The US and Japan are Palau's predominant trading partners.

³²BALANCE OF PAYMENTS

Standardized balance-of-payments accounts have not yet been prepared by the government. The chronic trade deficit is largely offset by US grant assistance.

The US Central Intelligence Agency reports that in 1996 the purchasing power parity of Palau's exports was $14.3 million while imports totaled $72.4 million resulting in a trade balance of -$58.1 million.

³³BANKING AND SECURITIES

In 1993, there were five commercial banks. Two are branches of foreign banks, the Bank of Hawaii and the Bank of Guam; the other, a local bank which started in 1985, is the Bank of Palau.

³⁴INSURANCE

Social security and pension fund contributions are made by the government on behalf of its employees.

³⁵PUBLIC FINANCE

The US Central Intelligence Agency (CIA) estimates that in 1997 Palau's central government took in revenues of approximately $52.9 million and had expenditures of $59.9 million. Overall, the government registered a deficit of approximately $7 million. Total external debt is estimated to exceed $100 million.

³⁶TAXATION

Graduated income taxes are levied on wages and salaries. Business gross revenue tax is imposed at a flat rate minus employees' remuneration. There is also a profits tax on financial institutions.

³⁷CUSTOMS AND DUTIES

There are no import duties on raw materials if they are processed for sale outside Palau. There is also an import duty rebate offered by Palau as an investment incentive.

³⁸FOREIGN INVESTMENT

There is a Foreign Investment Board for processing applications from foreign investors; the Division of International Trade of the Bureau of Foreign Affairs is responsible for establishing contacts with foreign companies to promote Palau's trade interests.

³⁹ECONOMIC DEVELOPMENT

The government's first 5-year national development plan (1987–91) was the first phase of its 15-year development program. The plan focuses on the development of a private-sector production-based economy, efficient public-sector management, development of natural resources to earn foreign exchange, personnel development, regional development, and environmental preservation.

Long term prospects for the tourist sector have brightened because of the expansion of are travel in the Pacific and the rising prosperity of leading East Asian countries.

⁴⁰SOCIAL DEVELOPMENT

Social organization is based on the maternal kin group, or clan. Villages ideally consist of ten clans, with the leader of the highest ranking clan serving as village chief. Rapid socioeconomic change has given rise to a range of social problems for communities and social groups, particularly youth. Most social development activities in the areas of health and education are funded by US government programs.

A system of old age, disability and survivor's pensions was first introduced in 1967. This program covers all gainfully employed persons, and provides old age pensions after the age of 60. It is financed by 4% of employee earnings, matched by an equal contribution from employers.

In the traditional social structure, rank and inheritance matrilineal. Women are accorded considerable respect within the clan system. In urban areas, women face minimal sex linked discrimination in employment.

Foreigners residing in Palau are barred from owning land or obtaining citizenship. Some foreigners complain of discrimination in access to housing, education and employment.

Human rights are well respected in Palau, and nongovernmental organizations operate without government interference.

41 HEALTH

Hospital services are provided by the MacDonald Memorial Hospital in Koror, which has 60 beds. Medical services in Koror are also provided by the Belau Medical Clinic and the Seventh-Day Adventist Eye Clinic.

In 1999, Palau's birth rate was 21.5 per 1,000 population, and its death rate was 7.7. Life expectancy averaged 67.8 years, and the fertility rate was 2.6 children per woman. The infant mortality rate was 18.5 per 1,000 births.

Immunization rates for children under one were as follows in 1995: diphtheria, pertussis and tetanus (100%); polio (100%); measles (100%); and hepatitis B (100%). No measles or polio were reported in 1995.

Only 1 case of AIDS was reported in 1996.

42 HOUSING

There were 2,501 occupied houses in 1986, of which 72% were located in Koror and the adjacent state of Airai. Most house walls are constructed from metal sheets, wood, or concrete blocks, and roofs are of corrugated material. About 80% of all houses have water and electricity. The majority of homeowners finance their house construction under the traditional "ocheraol" system, whereby clan members contribute to construction costs.

43 EDUCATION

Elementary education is free and compulsory for all Palauan children ages 6–14. In 1990, there were 369 students in private schools and 1,756 in public schools. The Palau High School in Koror, the only public high school, enrolls 64% of the total secondary-school enrollment. In 1990, 445 secondary students attended private schools, and 165 were in public schools. Postsecondary education is provided by the College of Micronesia's Micronesian Occupational College (MOC) in Koror. The adult literacy rate is 98%.

44 LIBRARIES AND MUSEUMS

There is a small public library in Koror, with a collection comprising about 5,000 books. The Belau National Museum, established in 1973, is also located in Koror.

45 MEDIA

The Palau National Communications Corp., established in 1982, provides domestic and international telephone connections, radio broadcasting, telex and telegram communications, and navigational and weather services. A radio station in Koror broadcasts to listeners in the outer islands. Television is limited to one channel in the Koror area, provided by a local private company. As of 1997, there were 478 radios and 85 television sets in use per 1,000 population.

There are no daily papers. Two popular periodicals are *Palau Gazette* (monthly, 1995 circulation 3,000), and *Tia Belau* (weekly, 5,000).

The constitution provides for free speech and a free press, and the government respects these rights in practice.

46 ORGANIZATIONS

The clan system forms the basic unit of social organization. Youth, women's, and community development organizations provide economic self-help, community involvement and leadership training, skills training, and sports and recreation.

47 TOURISM, TRAVEL, AND RECREATION

Palau's scenic areas include the Rock Islands, a large number of small, mushroom-shaped islands that are unique in the region. The marine environment is rich in live coral formations and tropical fish, making the country a prime destination for snorkeling and scuba diving. Many tourists visit the World War II battlefields, war memorials, and shrines. The recent growth in the Pacific economies together with expansion of air travel has led to the recent growth in tourism. In 1994 Palau had 40,548 tourist arrivals in 1994, 52,000 in 1995, and 74,000 in 1997. There has been an increase in the number and variety of hotel rooms. According to 1999 UN estimates, the daily cost of staying in Koror was $144. Staying elsewhere in Palau was estimated as low as $25 each day.

48 FAMOUS PALAUANS

Lazarus E. Salii (1937–1988) became the third president of Palau in September 1985.

49 DEPENDENCIES

Palau has no territories or colonies.

50 BIBLIOGRAPHY

Hijikata, Hisakatsu. *Society and Life in Palau*. Tokyo: Sasakawa Peace Foundation, 1993.

Leibowitz, Arnold H. *Embattled Island: Palau's Struggle for Independence*. Westport, Conn.: Praeger, 1996.

Parmentier, Richard J. *The Sacred Remains: Myth, History, and Polity in Belau*. Chicago: University of Chicago Press, 1987.

Roff, Sue Rabbitt. *Overreaching in Paradise: United States Policy in Palau Since 1945*. Juneau, Alaska: Denali Press, 1991.

Trust Territory of the Pacific Islands, 1986, 39th Annual Report to the United Nations. Washington, D.C.: Department of State, 1986.

PAPUA NEW GUINEA

Independent State of Papua New Guinea

CAPITAL: Port Moresby.

FLAG: The flag is a rectangle, divided diagonally. The upper segment is scarlet with a yellow bird of paradise imposed; the lower segment is black with five white stars representing the Southern Cross.

ANTHEM: O, Arise All You Sons.

MONETARY UNIT: The kina (K) of 100 toea is linked with the Australian dollar. There are coins of 1, 2, 5, 10, 20, and 50 toea and 1 kina, and notes of 2, 5, 10, 20, and 50 kina. K1=us$0.31496 (us$1=K 3.1750) as of 31 March 2000.

WEIGHTS AND MEASURES: The metric system is the legal standard.

HOLIDAYS: New Year's Day, 1 January; Queen's Birthday, 1st Monday in June; Remembrance Day, 23 July; Independence Day, 16 September; Christmas, 25 December; Boxing Day, 26 December. Movable religious holidays include Good Friday and Easter Monday.

TIME: 10 PM=noon GMT.

¹LOCATION, SIZE, AND EXTENT

Situated to the north of Australia, Papua New Guinea has a total land area of 461,690 sq km (178,259 sq mi), including the large islands of New Britain, New Ireland, and Bougainville and hundreds of smaller islands. Comparatively, the area occupied by PNG is slightly larger than the state of California. The country extends 2,082 km (1,294 mi) NNE–SSW and 1,156 km (718 mi) ESE–WNW. Mainland Papua New Guinea shares the island of New Guinea, the second-largest island in the world, with Irian Jaya, a province of Indonesia. To the N is the US Trust Territory of the Pacific Islands; to the E, the Solomon Islands; to the W, Irian Jaya; and about 160 km (100 mi) to the S, the nearest neighbor, Australia. Papua New Guinea has a total boundary length of 5,972 km (3,711 mi).

PNG's capital city, Port Moresby, is located on the country's southern coast.

²TOPOGRAPHY

Papua New Guinea is situated between the stable continental mass of Australia and the deep ocean basin of the Pacific. The largest section is the eastern half of the island of New Guinea, which is dominated by a massive central cordillera, or system of mountain ranges, extending from Indonesia's Irian Jaya to East Cape in Papua New Guinea at the termination of the Owen Stanley Range, and including the nation's highest peak, Mt. Wilhelm (4,705 m/15,436 ft). A second mountain chain fringes the north coast and runs parallel to the central cordillera. Active and recently active volcanoes are prominent features of New Guinea landscapes; there are no glaciers or snowfields. In the lowlands are many swamps and floodplains. Important rivers are the Sepik, flowing about 1,130 km (700 mi) to the north coast, and the Fly, which is navigable for 800 km (500 mi) in the southwest.

The smaller islands of Papua New Guinea are also areas of extreme topographic contrast and generally feature mountain ranges rising directly from the sea or from narrow coastal plains. Volcanic landforms dominate the northern part of New Britain and Bougainville, and some of the smaller islands are extremely volcanic. The Bougainville–New Ireland area comprises Bougainville and Buka islands, the Gazelle Peninsula of New Britain, New Ireland, New Hanover, the St. Matthias group, and the Admiralty Islands.

³CLIMATE

The climate of Papua New Guinea is chiefly influenced by altitude and by the monsoons. The northwest or wet monsoon prevails from December to March, and the southeast or dry trade winds from May to October. Annual rainfall varies widely with the monsoon pattern, ranging from as little as 100 cm (40 in) at Port Moresby to as much as 750 cm (300 in) in other coastal regions. Most of the lowland and island areas have daily mean temperatures of about 27°C (81°F), while in the highlands temperatures may fall to 4°C (39°F) at night and rise to 32°C (90°F) in the daytime. Relative humidity is uniformly high in the lowlands at about 80%.

⁴FLORA AND FAUNA

The flora of Papua New Guinea is rich and varied, with habitats ranging from tidal swamps at sea level to alpine conditions. In low-lying coastal areas, various species of mangroves form the main vegetation, together with the beautiful casuarina, sago, and palm. Most of the country is covered by tropical and savanna rain forest, in which valuable trees such as kwila and cedar are found. Orchids, lilies, ferns, and creepers abound in the rain forests. There are large stands of pine at elevations of 910 to 1,220 m (3,000–4,000 ft). At the highest altitudes, mosses, lichens, and other alpine flora prevail.

Papua New Guinea supports a great diversity of bird life. About 850 species have been recognized, as compared with about 650 known in Australia and 500 in North America. Papua New Guinea is the major center for a number of bird families, particularly the bird of paradise, bower bird, cassowary, kingfisher, and parrot. There are about 200 species of mammals, many nocturnal, of which rodent and marsupial orders predominate. Butterflies of Papua New Guinea are world famous for their size and vivid coloring.

[5]ENVIRONMENT

Papua New Guinea's environmental concern includes pollution, global warming, and the loss of the nation's forests. Coastal waters are polluted with sewage and residue from oil spills. The nation has 192.2 cu mi of water, of which 49% is used to support farming and 22% for industrial activity. Some 16% of the nation's city dwellers and 83% of the rural population do not have pure water. Another significant source of pollution is open-pit mining. The country's cities produce 0.1 million tons of solid waste per year. Global warming and the resulting rise in sea level are a threat to Papua New Guinea's coastal vegetation and water supply. The Department of Physical Planning and Environment is responsible for integrating environmental planning and conserving natural resources. In 1994, 5 of the nation's mammal species and 25 of its bird species were endangered, as well as 88 types of plants. Endangered or extinct species in Papua New Guinea include four species of turtle (green sea, hawksbill, olive ridley, and leatherback) and Queen Alexandra's birdwing butterfly.

[6]POPULATION

The population of Papua New Guinea in 2000 was estimated at 4,811,939. An estimated 3.0% of the population is 65 years of age or older. The projected population for the year 2005 is 5,363,000, assuming a crude birthrate of 29 per 1,000 population and a death rate of 8, resulting in a natural rate of change of 2.1% for the period 2000–2005. The population rate of change between 1995 and 2000 was 2.2%. The population density in 1998 was 10 per sq km (26 per sq mi).

It was estimated that 17% of the population lived in urban areas in 2000, up from 13% in 1980. The major areas of population are in the highlands and eastern coastal areas of the island of New Guinea. The capital city, Port Moresby, had a 2000 population of 247,000. Other large cities include Lae, 80,665; Goroka, 17,855; Madang, 27,057; Wewak, 23,224; and Rabaul, on New Britain, 17,855.

[7]MIGRATION

The numbers of emigrants and immigrants have been roughly equal in recent years. In 1982–86, an average of 4,079 residents left the country each year, while 5,109 persons entered intending residency. Many more came as refugees from Irian Jaya. In 1993, some 3,750 such immigrants were living in a camp in Western Province, while another 6,000 or so had land or kinship ties with Papuan New Guineans and were living near the border. The emigration in earlier years of nonindigenous residents may have been influenced by constitutional provisions that restricted eligibility for naturalization to those with eight years' residency, but limited their tax and business rights to the same status as those of aliens. Many rural dwellers migrated to Port Moresby and other urban centers during the 1970s and 1980s. In 1999, the net migration rate was zero.

[8]ETHNIC GROUPS

Papua New Guinea has more than 1,000 different ethnic groups. Indigenous Papua New Guineans vary considerably in ethnic origins, physical appearance, and spoken languages. The indigenous people are Melanesians. They are usually classified by language group, with Papuans representing the descendants of the original Australoid migration and Austronesian speakers descended from later migrants. The former are generally found in the highlands and the latter in coastal areas and on the islands other than New Guinea. Other groups with significant populations include Negritos, Micronesians, and Polynesians.

[9]LANGUAGES

Under the Australian administration of the former Territory of Papua and New Guinea, English became the official language; however, it is only spoken by 1–2% of the population. More widely spoken, there are now two other official languages: Pidgin, a Melanesian lingua franca with roots primarily in English and German, and Hiri Motu, another lingua franca of Papuan derivation. In all, there are more than 700 indigenous languages, most of them spoken by a few hundred to a few thousand people.

[10]RELIGIONS

Indigenous religions, varying widely in ritual and belief, remain important in tribal societies in Papua New Guinea. However, most of the population is nominally Christian. Of these, 22% are Roman Catholics; 16% are Lutheran; another 8% are Presbyterian/Methodist/London Missionary Society; 5% are Anglican; 4% Evangelical Alliance; and 1% Seventh-Day Adventist. Other Protestant sects account for 10% of the population, and indigenous beliefs for 34%. Baha'ism is the only other nonindigenous faith that has gained a foothold.

[11]TRANSPORTATION

Transportation is a major problem in Papua New Guinea because of the difficult terrain. Major population centers are linked chiefly by air and sea, although road construction has increased to supplement these expensive means of transport. Of some 19,600 km (12,179 mi) of roads in 1996, only 686 km (426 mi) were paved. In 1995 there were 55,000 motor vehicles, of which about one-third were cars and station wagons and the rest commercial vehicles. Papua New Guinea has no railroads.

The government operates a fleet of coastal work boats, none more than 9 m (30 ft) long. The principal harbors are Madang, Port Moresby, Lae, and Rabaul. There are international shipping services by refrigerated container ships, other cargo vessels, and some passenger service to Australia, Southeast Asian and Pacific island countries, the US west coast, and Europe. The main shipping lines are government owned. In 1998, the merchant fleet was comprised of 20 ships with a total of 35,400 GRT.

Papua New Guinea had 492 airports in 1998, of which 19 were principal airports with paved runways. Papua New Guinea's national air carrier, Air Niugini, established in 1973, has undertaken most of the services previously provided by Australian lines. In 1997, 1,114,000 passengers were carried on scheduled domestic and international flights.

[12]HISTORY

Papua New Guinea appears to have been settled by 14,000 BC, with migrations first of hunters and later of agriculturists probably coming from the Asian mainland by way of Indonesia. Early communities had little contact with each other because of rough terrain and so maintained their autonomy, as well as their distinct languages and customs.

New Guinea was first sighted by Spanish and Portuguese sailors in the early 16th century and was known prophetically as Isla del Oro (Island of Gold). The western part of the island was claimed by Spain in 1545 and named New Guinea for a fancied resemblance of the people to those on the West African coast. ("Papua" is a Malay word for the typically frizzled quality of Melanesian hair.) Traders began to appear in the islands in the 1850s, and the Germans sought coconut oil available in northern New Guinea about that time. The Dutch and the British had earlier agreed on a division of their interests in the island, and from 1828, the Dutch began to colonize the western portion.

Although the British flag was hoisted on various parts of eastern New Guinea, the British government did not ratify annexation. Some Australian colonists were eager to see New Guinea

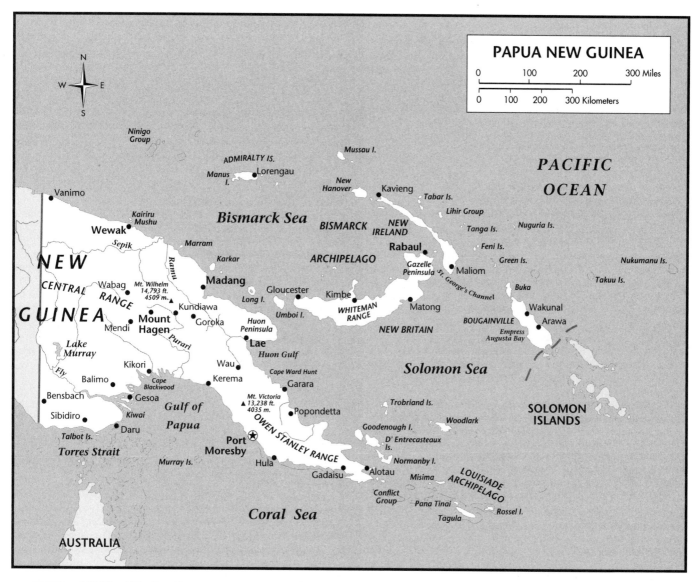

LOCATION: 140°51′ to 160°E; 0° to 12°S. **BOUNDARY LENGTHS:** Total coastline, 3,795 km (2,358 mi); Indonesia, 777 km (483 mi). **TERRITORIAL SEA LIMIT:** 12 mi.

become a British possession, for trade, labor, gold mining, and missionary reasons. However, it was not until 1884, after an abortive Australian annexation attempt and under fear of German ambitions in the area, that Britain established a protectorate over the southern coast of New Guinea and adjacent islands. The Germans followed by laying claim to three different parts of northern New Guinea. British and German spheres of influence were delineated by the Anglo-German Agreement of 1885. Germany took control of the northeastern portion of the island, as well as New Britain, New Ireland, and Bougainville, while Britain took possession of the southern portion and the adjacent islands.

British New Guinea passed to Australian control in 1902 and was renamed the Territory of Papua in 1906. German New Guinea remained intact until the outbreak of war in 1914, when Australian forces seized it. Although the territories retained their separate identities and status, they were administered jointly by Australia from headquarters at Port Moresby. In 1921, the former German New Guinea was placed under a League of Nations mandate administered by Australia; in 1947, it became the Trust Territory of New Guinea, still administered by Australia

but now subject to the surveillance of the UN Trusteeship Council.

Both territories were merged into the Territory of Papua and New Guinea in 1949. A Legislative Council, established in 1953, was replaced by the House of Assembly in 1964. Eight years later, the territory was renamed Papua New Guinea, and on 1 December 1973, it was granted self-government. Separatist movements in Papua in 1973 and secessionist activities on the island of Bougainville in 1975 flared briefly and then subsided, though debates over citizenship and land-reform provisions were vigorous until the passage of a constitution in 1975. Papua New Guinea achieved complete independence on 16 September 1975, with Michael Somare as Prime Minister of a coalition government.

Somare was voted out of office in 1980 but reelected in 1982; subsequently, he put through a constitutional change giving the central government increased authority over the provincial governments. Soon after, he suspended three provincial administrations for financial mismanagement. Somare also had to contend with social unrest, which culminated in June 1985 in a state of emergency after a prolonged wave of violent crime in Port

Moresby. At the same time, his Pangu Pati was split by his deputy, Paias Wingti, who then founded a new party, the People's Democratic Movement (PDM). In November 1985, Somare was again voted out of office on a no confidence motion, and Wingti formed a cabinet. Though unrest continued, with serious riots in the Highlands in 1986, elections in mid-1987 returned Wingti to office at the head of a shaky five-party coalition.

Wingti's government was defeated in a no confidence vote in July 1988; a coalition government led by Rabbie Namaliu replaced the PDM government. A secessionist crisis on Bougainville dominated domestic politics during 1990–91. The Bougainville Revolutionary Army (BRA) declared the island of Bougainville to be independent from Papua New Guinea in May 1990, and in response government forces landed on the north of Bougainville in April 1991. Namaliu adjourned parliament early in 1991 to avoid a vote of no confidence over the Bougainville crisis. Paias Wingti, the leader of the People's Democratic Movement (PDM), was reelected Prime Minister in July 1992 as the leader of a new coalition government with the support of the People's Progress Party, and the League for National Advancement.

During 1993 the Government continued to extend its control over Bougainville, partly because of popular revulsion against human rights violations by members of the BRA. In September 1994, rebel troops withdrew to the surrounding hills of the Bougainville copper mine allowing government forces to reclaim it. In 1995, the Prime Minister halted cease-fire talks. The eight-year-old secessionist movement continues in 1997, as does the Port Moresby crime wave.

In 1997, reformist premier Bill Skate, governor of Port Moresby, was elected by members of PNG's 109-seat parliament defeating Michael Somare who was also defeated for the post of parliamentary speaker by John Pundari who is a member of Pangu. Skate represents Julius Chan who lost his seat in the elections but who supported Skate's selection as premier. Chan had hired a group of mercenaries to put down the rebellion in Bougainville, angering Brig. Gen. Jerry Sinigirok. Chan dismissed Sinigirok; a decision that led to rioting by 2,000 Sinigirok loyalists. Ultimately Chan made the decision to step aside pending a judicial inquiry into the hiring of mercenaries. Chan had been elected Prime Minister on 30 August 1994.

Resolution to the Bougainville problem remained elusive until the government of Bill Skate reached a truce with the rebels in 1998. In April 1998, a permanent cease-fire agreement was signed and the reconstruction of war-torn Bougainville commenced. In 1999, the rebels leaders and the PNG government signed an agreement known as the Matakana and Okataina Understanding which established an agreement to continue discussions about the island's political future. In 1998 and 1999, Bill Skate came under criticism for alleged bribery charges.

Throughout the 1990s, crime increased in PNG, especially in the capital of Port Moresby, leading to a dusk-to-dawn curfew and a ban on the sale of alcohol in 1997. In July 1999, Bill Skate resigned as Prime Minister as allegations regarding the misappropriation of development funds arose. On July 14, 1999, the national assembly chose Sir Mekere Morauta as Prime Minister in a 99 to 5 vote. Morauta sought to restore damaged relations with PR China, which was angered by the Skate government's decision to accept normal relations with Taiwan in return for economic assistance.

13GOVERNMENT

Papua New Guinea is an independent, parliamentary democracy in the Commonwealth of Nations, with a governor-general representing the British crown.

Under the 1975 constitution, legislative power is vested in the National Parliament (formerly the House of Assembly) of 109 members, including 20 representing provincial electorates and 89 from open electorates, serving a term of up to five years. Suffrage is universal and voting compulsory for adults at age 18. The government is formed by the party or coalition of parties, that has a majority in the National Parliament, and executive power is undertaken by the National Executive Council, selected from the government parties and chaired by the prime minister.

The government has constitutional authority over the Defense Force, the Royal Papua New Guinea Constabulary, and intelligence organizations.

14POLITICAL PARTIES

Political parties in PNG lack ideological conviction and rely almost exclusively on patronage politics, personalism, and regional bases. Several parties have emerged in Papua New Guinean politics. In the House of Assembly elected in 1973, the Pangu Pati, headed by Michael Somare, formed a coalition government with the People's Progress Party, and Somare became Prime Minister. Opposition parties at the time were the United Party, which maintains a strong following in the Highlands, and the Papua Besena Party, which stands for the secession of Papua from Papua New Guinea and has had fluctuating support even on its home ground.

Generally, party allegiances have been fluid, with regional and tribal politics impacting greatly on political events. No fewer than eight parties have been founded since 1978. One of them, the People's Democratic Movement, formed in 1985 by dissident members of the Pangu Pati, won 18 seats in the 1987 elections, while the Pangu Pati captured 25. Parties that participated in the 1997 elections were the Pangu Pati, People's National Congress, the People's Progress Party, and the People's Democratic Movement. In April 1998, Skate announced the formation of a new political alliance; the Papua New Guinea First Party led by his People's National Congress Party.

15LOCAL GOVERNMENT

Papua New Guinea is divided into 20 provinces, including the National Capital District. Each province has its own government, headed by a premier. In addition, there are more than 160 locally elected government councils. Bougainville presently exercises significant autonomy in its administrative affairs.

16JUDICIAL SYSTEM

The legal system is based on English common law. The Supreme Court is the nation's highest judicial authority and final court of appeal. Other courts are the National Court; district courts, which deal with summary and non-indictable offenses; and local courts, established to deal with minor offenses, including matters regulated by local customs.

The Papua New Guinea government has undertaken a process of legal reform under which village courts have been established to conserve and reactivate traditional legal methods. Special tribunals deal with land titles and with cases involving minors. An Ombudsman Commission has been established to investigate and refer to the public prosecutor cases involving abuse of official authority.

The Constitution declares the judiciary independent of executive, political, or military authority. It also provides a number of procedural due process protections including the right to legal counsel for criminal defendants. The Chief Justice of the Supreme Court is appointed by the governor-general upon selected by the National Executive Council in consultation with the Minister for Justice. The Judicial and Legal Services Commission appoint other judges.

17ARMED FORCES

The main armed force is the Papua New Guinea Defense Force, which in 2000 had an estimated total of 4,300 personnel. The army of 3,800 consisted of two infantry battalions and one engineering battalion. Maritime forces (400) were equipped with seven patrol and coastal craft and two amphibious craft. The air force (100) had no armed aircraft. Australia provides a 38-member training unit. Defense costs $41.5 million a year (1998) or 1% of gross domestic product. The Bougainville peace monitoring group includes some 300 troops from Australia, New Zealand, Fiji, Tonga, and Vanuatu.

18INTERNATIONAL COOPERATION

Papua New Guinea became a member of the UN on 10 October 1975 and participates in ESCAP and all the UN nonregional specialized agencies. It also belongs to the Asian Development Bank, Commonwealth of Nations, G-77, South Pacific Forum, and South Pacific Commission. Papua New Guinea has signed the Lomé Convention, the Law of the Sea, and the Antarctic Treaty, and it has observer status at ASEAN. It also formally acceded to the WTO in June 1996.

19ECONOMY

Economic activity is concentrated in two sectors, agriculture and mining. The subsistence sector, which occupies more than two-thirds of the working population, produces livestock, fruit, and vegetables for local consumption; agricultural products for export include copra, palm oil, coffee, cocoa, and tea. Rubber production has declined in recent years, and in the mid-1980s, coffee crops were threatened by the spread of coffee rust fungus through Western Highlands Province. New mining operations have compensated for the 1989 closure of the Bougainville mine, which had been a chief foreign exchange earner since the early 1970s. Currently, the main gold and silver mines are located at Ok Tedi in the Star Mountains, on Misima Island, and at Porgera. Oil and natural gas have been discovered in Southern Highlands Province. Forestry and fishing hold increasing importance.

Economic growth, which averaged 3.7% in the late 1980s, rose to 9% in 1991, 11.8% in 1992, and 16.6% in 1993. The growth was driven by a mineral and petroleum boom centered in the Highlands region. Growth slowed to 3% in 1994, 2.9% in 1995, and 1.6% in 1996 and 1997 due to an anticipated drop in production from Papua New Guinea's aging mines and oil fields, and a 1997 drought that cut the coffee crop in half. To halt the economic decline, the government awarded a lease to private developers for the $800 million Lihir gold project. In addition, construction projects involving airports, highways, disaster rehabilitation, development of the Gobe oil field, and a petroleum refinery are planned or being implemented. These projects, together with the onset of new production at the mine, generated a slightly improved GDP growth rate of 1.6% in 1998. The economy did not reach the expected 4.5% increase in part because of the Asian financial crisis, and recurring drought.

20INCOME

The US Central Intelligence Agency (CIA) reports that in 1998 Papua New Guinea's gross domestic product (GDP) was estimated at $11.1 billion. The per capita GDP was estimated at $2,400. The annual growth rate of GDP was estimated at 1.6%. The average inflation rate in 1998 was 12%. The CIA defines GDP as the value of all final goods and services produced within a nation in a given year and computed on the basis of purchasing power parity (PPP) rather than value as measured on the basis of the rate of exchange. It was estimated that agriculture accounted for 28.2% of GDP, industry 34.5%, and services 37.3%.

Private consumption includes expenditures of individuals, households, and non-governmental organizations. It was estimated that between 1990 and 1998 private consumption grew at an annual rate of 3.5%. The richest 10% of the population accounted for approximately 41% of household consumption and the poorest 10% approximately 1.7%.

21LABOR

Although most of the adult population engages in productive activity, only some 250,000 persons were wage earners in 1999. While official information is incomplete, government indices show that employment in the country has not kept pace with the increase in population. An overwhelming majority of indigenous wage earners are male, and significantly more of them work in rural areas than in urban areas. Wage and salary earners are concentrated in agriculture, including fishing and forestry; commerce; and government and public authority employment. Legislation covers working conditions and wages, and provides for collective bargaining. The minimum weekly wage in urban areas was $9.87 as of 1999. The Papua New Guinea Trade Union Congress is the main union federation. About one-half of the wage earners were unionized, and there were about 50 trade unions. Unions have the right to organize and bargain collectively but the government may cancel wage agreements if they are deemed to be against "public policy." The status of the right to strike is unclear and there have been virtually no strikes in recent years.

The minimum working age is 18, although children may be employed in family-related work as young as 11. However, few children work in any capacity.

The law provides for minimum occupational health and safety standards; however, due to a shortage of inspectors, workplaces are not inspected regularly but only when a union or worker requests it.

22AGRICULTURE

Agriculture in Papua New Guinea is divided into a large subsistence sector and a smaller monetary sector for export. Agriculture's importance has steadily declined since 1985, when it made up 33.8% of GDP—in 1998, agriculture only contributed about 24% to GDP. About 85% of the population engages in subsistence agriculture. Subsistence crops include yams, taro, and other staple vegetables. Cash crops are increasing in rural areas, stimulated by government-financed development programs. Production by small farmers of coffee, copra, cocoa, tea, rubber, and oil palm is important for export, although production on plantations, which are usually foreign owned, is also significant. Such plantations are gradually being sold back to nationals. Exports of cocoa, coffee, palm oil, and copra are expected to increase over the next few years. Principal crops and 1998 output (in tons) included sweet potatoes, 250,000; sugar cane, 400,000; copra, 140,000; coffee, 66,000; cocoa, 25,000; and rubber, 7,000. Papua New Guinea grows very little rice, the staple food for many of its inhabitants. A single Australian company imports over 150,000 tons per year to satisfy demand.

23ANIMAL HUSBANDRY

Livestock in 1998 included an estimated 1,500,000 hogs, 6,000 sheep, and 4 million chickens. That same year there were 86,000 head of cattle, and production was being encouraged with the aim of achieving self-sufficiency in meat supplies. Local poultry and beef production is sufficient to almost meet domestic demand. Beef imports are subject to quota controls. The farming of crocodiles, whose hides are exported, has also been expanded.

[24]FISHING

In many coastal parts of Papua New Guinea, fishing is of great economic importance. The government is involved in the development of fishing through supply of freezers and of transport and research facilities. The total catch in 1997 was 45,347 tons, 30% from inland fishing. Fish exports in 1997 were valued at $12.2 million.

[25]FORESTRY

Forests and woodlands covered about 81.6% of the land area in 1995. Exploitable forests account for roughly 40% of the total land area and include a great variety of hardwood and softwood species. The total roundwood production in 1997 was 8,772,000 cu m, as compared with about 7,058,000 cu m in 1981. About 63% of all the timber cut in 1997 was used for fuel; production of sawn timber was estimated at 218,000 cu m. Plywood, hardwoods, and logs are regularly exported to Japan, New Zealand, Australia, and Europe.

[26]MINING

In 1888, gold was discovered on Misima Island, marking the start of the history of mining on Papua New Guinea. Prior to World War II, gold mining contributed 75% of Papua New Guinea's export earnings. This proportion declined greatly in subsequent years, but gold exports still accounted for 40% of the total export value in 1995. Gold production in 1997 was estimated at 49,900 kg.

In 1971/72, the Bougainville copper mine, one of the richest in the world, began to export copper ores and concentrates, which amounted to almost 220,000 tons in 1988 and accounting for 44% of all of Papua New Guinea's exports in the years it was operational. The mine closed in 1989 because of civil unrest caused by Bougainville Revolutionary Army militants. Nine years of civil unrest were temporarily halted by an interim cease fire in 1997, with the prospect of peace talks in 1998 leading to a final resolution of the conflict. All copper production now comes from the Ok Tedi mine in the Star Mountains near the Indonesian border. In 1997, production amounted to 111,200 tons. In the same year, production of silver totaled 49,500 kg.

Mineral exploration is being expanded. Bauxite is known to exist on Manus Island, in the Admiralty Islands, and on New Ireland Island. Additionally, lead, manganese, molybdenum, zinc, limestone, and phosphate guano and rock deposits are present. Major deposits of chromite, cobalt, and nickel are believed to be recoverable at a site on the Ramu River northeast of Ok Tedi. Reserves on Lihir Island in New Ireland Province have been estimated to contain some 613 tons of recoverable gold, and deposits at Porgera, near Ok Tedi, are considered to hold another 470 tons.

[27]ENERGY AND POWER

As of 1998, Papua New Guinea had a net installed electrical capacity of 490 MW; electricity generated was 1,740 million kWh. Of the total production in 1996, about 29% came from hydroelectric facilities and 70% from thermal plants. Several new hydro projects are at different stages of study and planning.

Exploration for oil and gas has been conducted in the Gulf of Papua, on the Turama River, and off Bougainville. The Kutubu oil project (the nation's first oil production project) in the Southern Highlands began exporting in June 1992. In 1998, Kutubu produced 79,000 barrels of oil per day; proved reserves were estimated at 100 million tons (400 million barrels) at the beginning of 1996.

[28]INDUSTRY

The industrial sector, constrained by the small domestic market and the population's low purchasing power, is largely undeveloped. Industries are concentrated in industrial metals, timber processing, machinery, food, drinks, and tobacco. Manufacturing accounts for about 9% of GDP.

Handicraft and cottage industries have expanded. A government-sponsored program assists Papua New Guineans in setting up businesses and purchases equity in existing firms. It has also encouraged small-scale import-substitution operations.

[29]SCIENCE AND TECHNOLOGY

The Papua New Guinea Scientific Society, founded in 1949 at Boroko, promotes the sciences, exchanges scientific information, preserves scientific collections, and establishes museums. The University of Papua New Guinea, founded in 1965 at Waigani, and the Papua New Guinea University of Technology, founded in 1965 at Lae, provide scientific and technical training. The Lowlands Agricultural Experiment Station, founded in 1928, is in Kerevat. The Papua New Guinea Institute of Medical Research was founded in 1968. In 1987–97, science and engineering students accounted for 10% of college enrollments.

[30]DOMESTIC TRADE

Trade in rural areas is mostly informal, and cash is used in transactions. The local market, particularly in fruit and vegetables, is an important feature of economic and social life. Domestic trade in urban centers is dominated by large Australian-owned stores with multiple outlets. Domestic trade is hampered by street gangs that terrorize local and foreign residents. Port Moresby, where almost 90% of the young men are unemployed, has seen an epidemic of assaults, burglaries, carjackings, and gang rapes.

Most stores are open weekdays from 8 AM to 5 PM and until noon on Saturdays; banks are open from 9 AM to 2 PM Monday to Thursday and from 9 AM to 5 PM on Fridays. Most businesses and government offices do not open on the weekends.

[31]FOREIGN TRADE

In 1997, Papua New Guinea's exports totaled $2.2 billion and imports totaled $1.7 billion. Imports amounted to $1.8 billion in 1996, increasing from $1.4 billion in 1995. Exports for 1996 were $2.4 billion. Consumer goods accounted for 29.4% of imports; machinery, 18.9%; industrial supplies, 18.5%; transportation equipment, 14%; food and beverages, 10.6%; and other imports, 8.6%. Of its natural resources, Papua New Guinea exports a majority of crude petroleum (26%), rough wood (20%), and copper ore (20%). Other exports include gold (18%), coffee (5.2%), palm oil (4.3%), and cocoa (1.7%). Papua New Guinea exports 5.7% of the world's logs.

Through most of the period when Papua New Guinea was a territory administered by Australia, the two were also major trading partners. In the 1970s, Papua New Guinea's trade with other countries, especially Japan and Germany, increased. Principal trading partners in 1998 (in millions of US dollars) were as follows:

COUNTRY	EXPORTS	IMPORTS	BALANCE
Australia	442	641	-199
Japan	291	97	194
Germany	166	23	143
United States	124	65	59
Korea	106	23	83
United Kingdom	81	11	70
China (inc. Hong Kong)	45	37	8
Singapore	26	120	-94
New Zealand	16	51	-35
Malaysia	15	31	-16

[32]BALANCE OF PAYMENTS

Papua New Guinea relies heavily on imported goods and services, both for consumption and as inputs for its exports. The country registered deficits on current accounts during the early 1980s, after recording annual surpluses in the late 1970s. In the late 1980s, mine closings, civil unrest, and sustained deterioration in prices for the country's principal agricultural exports severely tested the economy and led to a program of structural adjustment supported by the World Bank and IMF. When the economy rebounded in the early 1990s, however, the government lost interest in the reforms and instituted expansionist fiscal policies that led to a decline in international reserves. To restore foreign exchange levels, the government devalued the currency. When that failed to solve the problem, the government let the kina float, resulting in a depreciation of about 28% by 1996.

In 1995, Papua New Guinea reached an agreement with the World Bank and IMF on a series of economic reforms. The subsequent receipt of approximately $200 million in loans in August 1995 substantially bolstered foreign reserves.

The US Central Intelligence Agency reports that in 1997 the purchasing power parity of Papua New Guinea's exports was $2.2 billion while imports totaled $1.5 billion resulting in a trade balance of $700 million.

The International Monetary Fund (IMF) reports that in 1998 Papua New Guinea had exports of goods totaling $1,773 million and imports totaling $1,078 million. The services credit totaled $318 million and debit $794 million. The following table summarizes Papua New Guinea's balance of payments as reported by the IMF for 1998 in millions of US dollars.

Current Account		-29
Balance on goods	695	
Balance on services	-476	
Balance on income	-259	
Current transfers	11	
Capital Account		...
Financial Account		-180
Direct investment abroad	...	
Direct investment in Papua New Guinea	110	
Portfolio investment assets	-1,080	
Portfolio investment liabilities	1,167	
Other investment assets	-55	
Other investment liabilities		-321
Net Errors and Omissions		-13
Reserves and Related Items		221

33BANKING AND SECURITIES

The Bank of Papua New Guinea, the country's central bank, was established in 1973, and the currency, the kina, was first issued in April 1975. The kina is backed by a standby arrangement with Australia, and the value of the kina is tied to the Australian dollar. The money supply, as measured by M3, was ₭2,312.6 million at the end of 1996.

The Papua New Guinea Banking Corp. was set up in 1973 to take over the savings and trading business of the former Australian-government-owned bank operating in Papua New Guinea. It competes with seven other private commercial banks, three of which are subsidiaries of Australian banks. Liquidity increased over the first six months of 1996, with total liquid assets held by the commercial banks standing at ₭999.3 million at the end of June 1996.

There is no securities exchange in Papua New Guinea.

34INSURANCE

In 1997, there were at least 11 insurance companies operating in Papua New Guinea.

35PUBLIC FINANCE

The US Central Intelligence Agency (CIA) estimates that in 1997 Papua New Guinea's central government took in revenues of approximately $1.5 billion and had expenditures of $1.35 billion.

Overall, the government registered a surplus of approximately $150 million. External debt totaled $2.35 billion.

The following table shows an itemized breakdown of government revenues and expenditures. The percentages were calculated from data reported by the International Monetary Fund. The dollar amounts (millions) are based on the CIA estimates provided above.

REVENUE AND GRANTS	100%	1,500
Tax revenue	75.0%	1,124
Non-tax revenue	12.3%	185
Capital revenue	0.1%	1
Grants	12.7%	190
EXPENDITURES	100%	1,350
General public services	5.4%	73
Defense	3.3%	45
Public order and safety	6.3%	85
Education	17.6%	238
Health	8.9%	120
Social security	0.7%	9
Housing and community amenities	3.5%	48
Recreation, cultural, and religious affairs	1.4%	19
Economic affairs and services	25.8%	349
Other expenditures	18.0%	242
Interest payments	9.1%	123

36TAXATION

Company incomes are taxed at a rate of 25% to 50%. Additional profits tax is calculated on the net profits of mining and petroleum companies at a rate of 35% to 50%. In addition, progressive tax rates are applied to individuals' wages and salaries, with taxes automatically withheld from paychecks. Tax rates range from 10% to 35%. Land and property taxes, estate and death taxes, gift taxes, stamp taxes, excise taxes, and sales taxes are also imposed.

37CUSTOMS AND DUTIES

A general levy of 7.5% is charged on all imports, except on supplies for the government, the missions, and the Bougainville copper project. Tariff rates range from 0% to 55%—zero percent for essential items, 11% for basic goods, 33% for intermediate goods, and 55% for luxury goods. An export tax is levied on numerous items, such as agricultural products, logs, and minerals.

38FOREIGN INVESTMENT

The bulk of foreign investment is in the mining and petroleum sector. Statistic on foreign equity holdings for 1995 show that Australia was the largest investor with ₭1,446 million, followed by the UK with ₭160 million and the US with ₭91 million. Overall, foreign equity holdings fell from 55% of GDP in 1990 to 33% in 1994, primarily due to the completion of major mining and petroleum projects. In 1995, developers RTZ and Niugini Mining were awarded a lease for the $800 million Lihir gold project raising foreign equity holdings to 37% of GDP.

The Investment Promotion Authority (IPA), established in 1992, facilitates and certifies foreign investment. Corruption, civil unrest, and bureaucratic delays, however, frustrate the process. A number of free trade zones are in the early stages of development.

39ECONOMIC DEVELOPMENT

The fundamental purposes of Papua New Guinea's economic strategy have been distilled into the nation's eight aims: a rapid increase in the proportion of the economy under the control of Papua New Guineans; a more equal distribution of economic benefits; decentralization of economic activity; an emphasis on small-scale artisan, service, and business activity; a more self-reliant economy; an increasing capacity for meeting government spending from locally raised revenue; a rapid increase in the equal and active participation of women in the economy; and governmental control and involvement in those sectors where control is necessary to achieve the desired kind of development.

⁴⁰SOCIAL DEVELOPMENT

A social security system, called the National Provident Fund, was formed in 1981 and covers persons employed by firms with 25 or more workers, providing old age, disability, and survivor benefits. In 1999, this program was financed by 5% contribution of earnings from employees, and 7% of payroll from employers. Retirement is set at age 55, or at any age with 15 years of contributions. Benefits are provided as a lump sum, and include total contributions plus interest. Workers' compensation is provided by employers through direct provision of benefits or insurance premiums. Rural communities traditionally assume communal obligations to those in need.

Despite a Constitution guaranteeing them equal rights, women remain second-class citizens due to traditional patterns of discrimination. Village courts tend to enforce these patterns, and intertribal warfare often involves attacks on women. Polygamy is common, and the tradition of paying a bride-price persists. Violence against women is widespread, and few victims press charges. The government is working to improve the status of women, and has instituted an Office of Women's Affairs. As of 1997, 2 of 109 parliamentary seats were held by women.

In 1999, human rights violations included excessive use of police force, poor prison conditions, and limits on freedom of assembly.

⁴¹HEALTH

Government policy is to distribute health services widely and to provide comprehensive medical care, both preventive and curative. In 1990–97, there were 4 hospital beds per 1,000 people. Medical personnel in 1990 included 301 doctors and 2,447 nurses. In the same year, the population per physician was 12,870, and the population per nursing professional was 1,180. In 1990–97, there were 0.1 doctors per 1,000 people. In the years 1985–1995, 96% of the population had access to health care services. Adequate sanitation and safe water are available to 22% and 28% of the population respectively.

The main health problems are malaria, tuberculosis, leprosy, and venereal disease. Significant malnutrition occurs in some areas, and pneumonia and related respiratory infections are major risks. In 1997, there were about 250 reported cases of tuberculosis per 100,000 inhabitants. There were 797 malaria, 5,335 tuberculosis, and 6,821 measles cases in 1994. The increased incidence of malaria has been linked to importation from neighboring islands. Immunization rates for children up to one year old were fairly high in 1994: tuberculosis (91%); diphtheria, pertussis, and tetanus (66%); polio (66%); and measles (39%). While undernutrition remains the main nutritional problem, dramatic changes have occurred in some groups with exposure to more Westernized diets. Diabetes in the highland populations is low but has been documented to be as high as 16% in major cities of Papua New Guinea.

The country's birth rate in 1999 was 32 per 1,000 people. In 1994, only 4% of married women (ages 15 to 49) were using contraception.

The infant mortality rate decreased from 110 deaths per 1,000 live births in 1974 to 56 in 1999. In 1993–96, 23% of all births were low birth weight babies. The general mortality rate was 9.5 per 1,000 people in 1999, and the maternal mortality rate was 370 per 100,000 live births in 1990–97. Life expectancy was still only 58.5 years in 1999. Total health care expenditures in 1990 were $142 million.

The HIV seroprevalence rate was 0.2 per 100 adults in 1994. Only 158 AIDS cases were reported in 1996. Papua New Guinea had the highest per capita HIV prevalence in the North and South Pacific regions.

Coronary heart disease, previously rare or nonexistent, has played a larger role in past years. Total cholesterol values are higher in urban coastal and periurban subjects than in rural locations.

⁴²HOUSING

Traditional housing in rural areas appears to be adequate, but in urban areas there are acute shortages because of migration. In most urban areas, squatter settlements have been established. New housing (923 dwellings in 1984) has fallen far short of meeting the demand, especially for medium- and low-cost units. As of 1988, the housing stock totaled 555,000, and the number of people per dwelling averaged 5.8.

⁴³EDUCATION

Education in Papua New Guinea is not compulsory, and in the mid-1980s only one-third of the population was literate. The present government aims at upgrading and improving the system and quality of education. Children attend state-run community schools for primary education and provincial and national high schools for secondary education. After grade 6, they are tested and screened for continuing their studies in provincial high school. After grade 10, students have to qualify through an examination to enter one of the four national senior high schools, where they attend grades 11 and 12. After grade 10, students may enter one of the many technical or vocational schools which train them in various careers and skills, depending on their interests.

The adult illiteracy rate for the year 2000 was estimated at 24.0%, (males, 16.3%; females, 32.3%). In 1995, 2,790 primary schools had 13,457 teachers and a total enrollment of 516,797 students. Also in 1995, secondary schools had approximately 3,400 teachers and enrolled 78,759 students.

In addition to the National Government System, there is an international School System which ends at high school. Fees are considerably higher than the government run schools, and the curriculum is based on the British system. There are also privately run preschools and primary schools.

The University of Papua New Guinea in Port Moresby offers degrees in law, science, medicine and arts. The University of Technology in Lae offers degrees in technical subjects such as engineering, business, architecture, and forestry. The Pacific Adventist College, a privately run university outside Port Moresby, offers courses in education, business, accounting, secretarial studies, and theology. In 1995, there were a total of 13,663 students enrolled at institutions of higher education. Approximately 32% of these students were female.

⁴⁴LIBRARIES AND MUSEUMS

The largest libraries are at the University of Papua New Guinea (440,000 volumes) and at the Papua New Guinea University of Technology (125,000). Local libraries are well established in urban centers. The National Library Service in Boroko has 85,000 volumes. The Papua New Guinea Institute of Public Administration in Boroko holds 90,000 volumes. The Papua New Guinea National Museum and Art Gallery, in Boroko, has a good collection of art and general ethnography. The museum is implementing the National Cultural Property Act to protect the country's cultural heritage and to further establish appropriate museums. In 1981 the country opened the Madang Museum, Culture and Tourism Center in Yomba. The J.K. MacCarthy Museum, an ethnological collection, is located in Goroka.

⁴⁵MEDIA

Telephone, telegraph, and telex services are available; there were 39,300 telephones in 1995. A coastal radio service provides communications between land-based stations and ships at sea. The National Broadcasting Commission operates three radio networks and one national television station. It broadcasts in English, Pidgin, Hiri Motu, and a dozen other vernaculars. As of 1999 there were 31 AM and 2 FM radio stations and 3 television stations. In 1997 there were 91 radios, 24 television sets, and 1 mobile phone per 1,000 population.

The Papua New Guinea Post-Courier is published daily in English with a 1999 circulation of about 33,900. *The National,* another daily, is published on Boroko and had a 1999 circulation of 20,000. Other local news sheets are published, many in Pidgin. *Niugini Nius,* also in Boroko, is published Tuesday–Friday (circulation 31,000) and also has a weekend edition (16,000).

The constitution provides for free speech and free media, and the government is said to generally respect these rights in practice.

⁴⁶ORGANIZATIONS

Chambers of commerce and industry, service clubs, farmers' associations, and various trade unions form the nucleus of formal organizations in Papua New Guinea. Various youth and church groups also operate.

⁴⁷TOURISM, TRAVEL, AND RECREATION

In 1997, 66,102 tourists visited Papua New Guinea, over half from Australia. There were 2,640 rooms in hotels and other establishments in 1995, with 5,280 beds and an occupancy rate of 54%. Tourism receipts totaled $60 million that year.

Water sports, golf, tennis, and rock climbing are popular pastimes. Tourists must have a valid passport, obtain an entry visa to Papua New Guinea, and hold an onward ticket; malaria suppressants are advisable, although Port Moresby is considered a low-risk area.

According to 1999 UN estimates, the cost of staying in Port Moresby was $113 per day. Outside the capital, travel was less expensive. Daily expenses were estimated at $83 in Madang, $63 in Vanimo, and $102 in Minj. In smaller towns where commercial hotels exist, estimated daily expenses dropped to $35 per day.

⁴⁸FAMOUS PAPUA NEW GUINEANS

The best known Papua New Guineans are Michael Thomas Somare (b.1936), chief minister during colonial rule and the nation's first prime minister; Sir Albert Maori Kiki (1931–93),

author of *Kiki: Ten Thousands Years in a Lifetime;* and Vincent Eri, author of *The Crocodile.*

⁴⁹DEPENDENCIES

Papua New Guinea has no territories or colonies.

⁵⁰BIBLIOGRAPHY

Ballard, J. A. (ed.). *Policy Making in a New State: Papua New Guinea 1972–77.* Brisbane: University of Queensland Press, 1981.

Bulbeck, Chilla. *Australian Women in Papua New Guinea: Colonial Passages, 1920–1960.* New York: Cambridge University Press, 1992.

Feil, D. K. *The Evolution of Highland Papua New Guinea Societies.* New York: Cambridge University Press, 1987.

Fitzpatrick, Peter. *Law and State in Papua New Guinea.* New York: Academic Press, 1981.

Gillison, Gillian. *Between Culture and Fantasy: A New Guinea Highlands Mythology.* Chicago: University of Chicago Press, 1993.

Griffin, James. *Papua New Guinea: A Political History.* Portsmouth, N.H.: Heinemann, 1980.

Leahy, Michael J., 1901–1979. *Explorations into Highland New Guinea, 1930–1935.* Tuscaloosa: University of Alabama Press, 1991.

Lepowsky, Maria Alexandra. *Fruit of the Motherland: Gender in an Egalitarian Society.* New York: Columbia University Press, 1993.

May, Ronald James. *The Changing Role of the Military in Papua New Guinea.* Canberra, Australia: Strategic and Defence Studies Centre, Research School of Pacific Studies, Australian National University, 1993.

McConnell, Fraiser. *Papua New Guinea.* Santa Barbara, Calif.: Clio Press, 1988.

Mead, Margaret. *Growing Up in New Guinea.* Middlesex: Penguin, 1973 (orig. 1930).

Meigs, Anna S. *Food, Sex and Pollution: A New Guinea Religion.* New Brunswick, N.J.: Rutgers University Press, 1984.

Siers, James. *Papua New Guinea.* New York: St. Martin's, 1984.

Strathern, A. *A Line of Power.* New York: Methuen, 1984.

Turner, Ann. *Historical Dictionary of Papua New Guinea.* Metuchen, N.J.: Scarecrow, 1994.

Waiko, John. *A Short History of Papua New Guinea.* New York: Oxford University Press, 1993.

Wanek, Alexander. *The State and Its Enemies in Papua New Guinea.* Richmond, Surrey, U.K.: Curzon, 1996.

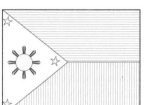

PHILIPPINES

Republic of the Philippines
Republika ng Pilipinas

CAPITAL: Manila.

FLAG: The national flag consists of a white equilateral triangle at the hoist, with a blue stripe extending from its upper side and a red stripe extending from its lower side. Inside each angle of the triangle is a yellow five-pointed star, and in its center is a yellow sun with eight rays.

ANTHEM: *Bayang Magiliw (Nation Beloved)*.

MONETARY UNIT: The peso (P) is divided into 100 centavos. There are coins of 1, 5, 10, 25, and 50 centavos and 1, and 2 pesos, and notes of 5, 10, 20, 50, 100, and 500 pesos. P1 = $0.02441 ($1 = P40.97) as of 31 March 2000.

WEIGHTS AND MEASURES: The metric system is the legal standard, but some local measures are also used.

HOLIDAYS: New Year's Day, 1 January; Freedom Day, 25 February; Labor Day, 1 May; Heroes' Day, 6 May; Independence Day (from Spain), 12 June; Thanksgiving, 21 September; All Saints' Day, 1 November; Bonifacio Day, 30 November; Christmas, 25 December; Rizal Day, 30 December; Last Day of the Year, 31 December. Movable religious holidays include Holy Thursday and Good Friday.

TIME: 8 PM = noon GMT.

¹LOCATION, SIZE, AND EXTENT

The Republic of the Philippines consists of an archipelago of 7,107 islands situated SE of mainland Asia and separated from it by the South China Sea. The total land area is approximately 300,000 sq km (115,831 sq mi), 67% of which is contained within the two largest islands: Luzon, 105,708 sq km (40,814 sq mi) and Mindanao, 95,586 sq km (36,906 sq mi). Other large islands include Samar, 13,079 sq km (5,050 sq mi); Negros, 12,704 sq km (4,905 sq mi); Palawan, 11,784 sq km (4,550 sq mi); Panay, 11,515 sq km (4,446 sq mi); Mindoro, 9,736 sq km (3,759 sq mi); Leyte, 7,213 sq km (2,785 sq mi); Cebu, 4,411 sq km (1,703 sq mi); Bohol, 3,864 sq km (1,492 sq mi); and Masbate, 3,269 sq km (1,262 sq mi). Comparatively, the area occupied by the Philippines is slightly larger than the state of Arizona. The Philippines' length is 1,851 km (1,150 mi) SSE-NNW, and its width is 1,062 km (660 mi) ENE-WSW.

The Philippines is separated from Taiwan on the N by the Bashi Channel (forming part of the Luzon Strait) and from Sabah, Malaysia (northern Borneo), on the SW by the Balabac Strait (off Palawan) and the Sibutu Passage (off the Sulu Archipelago). Bordering seas include the Philippine Sea and the Pacific Ocean on the E, the Celebes Sea on the S, the Sulu Sea on the SW, and the South China Sea on the W. The Philippines has a total coastline of 36,289 km (22,549 mi).

The Philippines claims the Spratly Islands, in the South China Sea, as do China, Malaysia, Taiwan, and Vietnam. About 1,000 Philippine marines were stationed in the Spratlys in 1983. The Philippines also has a claim on Sabah, dating back to 1670.

The Philippines' capital city, Manila, is located on the island of Luzon.

²TOPOGRAPHY

The topography is extremely varied, with volcanic mountain masses forming the cores of most of the larger islands. The range culminates in Mt. Pulog (elevation 2,928 m/9,606 ft) in northern Luzon and in Mt. Apo, the highest point in the Philippines (elevation 2,954 m/9,692 ft), in Mindanao. A number of volcanoes are active, and the islands have been subject to destructive earthquakes. Lowlands are generally narrow coastal strips except for larger plains in Luzon (Cagayan Valley and Central Plains), Mindanao (Cotabato and Davao-Agusan valleys), and others in Negros and Panay. Rivers are short and generally seasonal in flow. Important ones are the Cagayan, Agno, Abra, Bicol, and Pampanga in Luzon and the Cotabato and Agusan in Mindanao. Flooding is a frequent hazard. The shores of many of the islands are embayed (Manila Bay is one of the finest harbors in East Asia); however, several islands lack adequate harbors and require offshore lightering for sea transport. The only two inland water bodies of significant size are Laguna de Bay in Luzon and Lake Sultan Alonto in Mindanao.

³CLIMATE

The Philippine Islands, in general, have a maritime tropical climate and, except in the higher mountains, temperatures remain warm, the annual average ranging from about 26° to 28°C (79 to 82°F) throughout the archipelago. Daily average temperatures in Manila range from a minimum of 21°C (70°F) to a maximum of 30°C (86°F) in January and from 24°C (75°F) to 33°C (91°F) in June. Annual normal relative humidity averages 80%. Rainfall and seasonality differ markedly throughout the islands, owing to varying exposures to the two major wind belts, northeast trades or monsoon (winter) and southwest monsoon (summer). Generally, the east coasts receive heavy winter maximum rainfall (about 200–300 cm/80–120 in), the west coasts heavy summer maximum (200–360 cm/80–140 in); intermediate and southern locales receive lesser amounts more equally distributed (100–200 cm/40–80 in). Violent tropical storms (baguios), or typhoons, are frequent. Typhoons hit the Philippines 2-3 September 1984. Thirteen hundred people were killed during Typhoon Ike. On 5 November 1991 a typhoon hit central Philippines, killing 3,000 people. The average annual rainfall in the Philippines exceeds 250 cm (100 in).

⁴FLORA AND FAUNA

The Philippines supports a rich and varied flora with close botanical connections to Indonesia and mainland Southeast Asia. Forests cover almost one-half of the land area and are typically tropical, mixed in composition, with the dominant family, Dipterocarpaceae, representing 75% of the stands. The forest also has vines, epiphytes, and climbers. Open grasslands, ranging up to 2.4 m (8 ft) in height, occupy one-fourth of the land area; they are man-made, the aftermath of the slash-and-burn agricultural system, and most contain tropical savanna grasses that are nonnutritious and difficult to eradicate. The diverse flora includes 8,500 species of flowering plants, 1,000 kinds of ferns, and 800 species of orchids.

Common mammals include the wild hog, deer, wild carabao, monkey, civet cat, and various rodents. There are about 500 species of birds, among the more numerous being the megapodes (turkeylike wildfowl), button quail, jungle fowl, peacock pheasant, dove, pigeon, parrot, and hornbill. Reptilian life is represented by 100 species; there are crocodiles, and the larger snakes include the python and several varieties of cobra.

⁵ENVIRONMENT

Primary responsibility for environmental protection rests with the National Pollution Control Commission (NPCC), under whose jurisdiction the National Environmental Protection Council (NEPC) serves to develop national environmental policies and the Environmental Center of the Philippines implements such policies at the regional and local levels. Uncontrolled deforestation in watershed areas, with consequent soil erosion and silting of dams and rivers, constitutes a major environmental problem, together with rising levels of air and water pollution in Manila and other urban areas. The NPCC has established standards limiting automobile emissions but has lagged in regulating industrial air and water pollution. In the mid-1990s, industrial carbon dioxide emissions totaled 49.7 million metric tons per year, a per capita level of 0.77 metric tons per year. The nation's cities create 5.4 million tons of solid waste per year, and 38 of the country's rivers contain high levels of toxic contaminants. The nation has 77.5 cu mi of water, with 61% is used to support farming and 21% is used for industrial activity. About 23% of the nation's rural dwellers do not have pure water, compared with 93% of city dwellers. Pollution has also damaged the coastal mangrove swamps, which serve as important fish breeding grounds. Between the 1920s and 1990s, the Philippines lost 70% of its mangrove area. About 50% of its coral reefs are rated dead or dying as a result of pollution and dynamiting by fishermen. The nation is also vulnerable to typhoons, earthquakes, floods, and volcanic activity.

In the mid-1990s, 12 of the nation's mammal species and 39 bird species were endangered, and 159 plant species were threatened with extinction. Endangered or extinct species in the Philippines include the monkey-eating eagle, Philippine tarsier, tamarau, four species of turtle (green sea, hawksbill, olive ridley, and leatherback), Philippines crocodile, sinarapan, and two species of butterfly.

⁶POPULATION

The population of Philippines in 2000 was estimated at 80,961,430. An estimated 3.5% of the population is 65 years of age or older. The projected population for the year 2005 is 89,056,000, assuming a crude birthrate of 25 per 1,000 population and a death rate of 6, resulting in a natural rate of change of 1.9% for the period 2000–2005. The population rate of change between 1995 and 2000 was 2.0%. The population density in 1998 was 252 per sq km (653 per sq mi).

The population is unevenly distributed, being most densely concentrated in Luzon and the Visayan Sea islands. It was estimated that 59% of the population lived in urban areas in 2000, up from 37% in 1980. The capital city, Manila, and its surrounding metropolitan area had a 2000 population of 10,818,000. Created in 1975, metropolitan Manila includes four cities—Manila proper, Quezon City, Caloocan City, and Pasay City—and 13 surrounding municipalities. Other major cities (with 2000 populations) include Davao (1,196,000), Cebu (610,417), Zamboanga (442,345), Bacolod (364,180), Cagayan de Oro (339,598), and Iloilo (309,505).

⁷MIGRATION

The rapid growth of the Philippine population has led to considerable internal migration. On Luzon, frontierlike settlements have pushed into the more remote areas. Mindoro and Palawan islands also have attracted numerous settlers, and hundreds of thousands of land-hungry Filipinos have relocated to less densely populated Mindanao. There also has been a massive movement to metropolitan Manila, especially from central Luzon. Emigration abroad is substantial. In 1989 it came to 55,703. Emigration to the US particularly has been considerable: as of the 1990 US census, 1,406,770 Americans (chiefly in California and Hawaii) claimed Filipino ancestry. To reduce domestic unemployment, over 500,000 Philippine citizens were working abroad in the late 1980s and early 1990s, mainly in the Middle East, but also in Hong Kong and Singapore.

As of 1998, there were still 1,589 asylum-seekers from Vietnam in a Palawan camp, who were refused refugee status but allowed to stay pending a repatriation solution. Distinctions between Indochinese and other nationalities have been dropped, and all are now referred to as urban refugees. As of 1999, the Philippines hosted 306 urban refugees and their dependents. More than half of these were from the Middle East, including 33 Iranians, 24 Iraqis, 19 Palestinians, and 21 Somalis. Many refugees became legal exiles while studying in the Philippines following political or military upheavals in their homelands; a majority have since married Filipino nationals. In 1999, the net migration rate was -1.03 migrants per 1,000 population.

⁸ETHNIC GROUPS

Filipinos of Malay (Malayan and Indonesian) stock constitute about 91.5% of the total population. They are divided into nine main ethnic groups: the Tagalog, Ilocanos, Pampanguenos, Pangasinans, and Bicolanos, all concentrated in Luzon; the Cebuanos, Boholanos, and Ilongos of the Visayas; and the Waray-Waray of the Visayas, Leyte, and Samar. The Chinese minority totaled about 1.5% of the population in 1999. In addition, 10 Muslim groups, mainly of Mindanao and the Sulu Archipelago, comprised about 4% of the population. Numerous smaller ethnic groups inhabit the interior of the islands, including the Igorot of Luzon and the Bukidnon, Manobo, and Tiruray of Mindanao. These other groups accounted for the remaining 3% of the population in 1999.

⁹LANGUAGES

There are two official languages: Pilipino (based on Tagalog), the national language adopted in 1946 and understood by a majority of Filipinos; and English, which is also widely spoken and understood. Spanish, introduced in the 16th century and an official language until 1973, is now spoken by only a small minority of the population. More than 80 indigenous languages and dialects (basically of Malay-Indonesian origin) are spoken. Besides Tagalog, which is spoken around Manila, the principal languages include Cebuano (spoken in the Visayas), Ilocano (spoken in northern Luzon), and Panay-Hiligaynon. The teaching of Pilipino is mandatory in public and private primary schools, and its use is encouraged by the government.

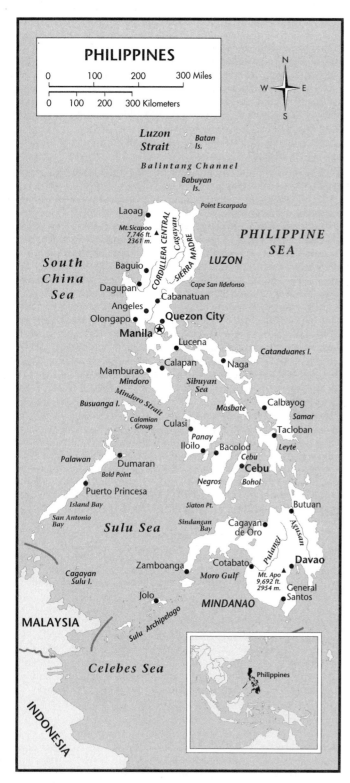

PHILIPPINES

| 0 | 100 | 200 | 300 Miles |
| 0 | 100 | 200 | 300 Kilometers |

Luzon Strait

Batan Is.

Balintang Channel

Babuyan Is.

Point Escarpada

Laoag

PHILIPPINE SEA

Mt.Sicapoo 7,746 ft. 2361 m.

LUZON

South China Sea

Baguio

Dagupan

Angeles

Olongapo

Manila

Quezon City

Cabanatuan

Cape San Ildefonso

Lucena

Calapan

Naga

Catanduanes I.

Mamburao

Mindoro

Sibuyan Sea

Busuanga I.

Mindoro Strait

Masbate

Calbayog

Calamian Group

Culasi

Panay

Samar

Tacloban

Iloilo

Bacolod

Leyte

Palawan

Dumaran

Cebu

Cebu

Bold Point

Negros

Bohol

Puerto Princesa

Siaton Pt.

Butuan

Island Bay

San Antonio Bay

Sindangan Bay

Cagayan de Oro

Agusan

Pulangi

Sulu Sea

Zamboanga

Cotabato

Moro Gulf

Davao

Cagayan Sulu I.

Mt. Apo 9,692 ft. 2954 m.

General Santos

Jolo

MINDANAO

MALAYSIA

Sulu Archipelago

Celebes Sea

INDONESIA

Philippines

LOCATION: 4°23′ to 21°25′N; 116° to 127°E. **TERRITORIAL SEA LIMIT:** 12 mi.

10 RELIGIONS

The Philippines is the only predominantly Christian country in Asia. Most of the population (about 83%) belongs to the Roman Catholic Church. Various Protestant churches represent about 9%. Among Christian and Protestant groups, there are numerous denominations. In addition, there are two churches established by

Filipino religious leaders, the Independent Church of the Philippines or Aglipayan, and the Iglesia ni Cristo (Church of Christ). Muslims (representing about 5%), commonly called Moros by non-Muslims, are concentrated in Mindanao and the Sulus. Buddhists, Baha'is, Chinese folk religionists, and tribal religionists, mainly in the more inaccessible mountainous areas of Luzon and Mindanao, constitute the remaining 3%. There are also small communities of Hindus and Jews. Freedom of religion is guaranteed by the constitution. In an effort to reduce tensions between Christians and Muslims in the southern islands and to answer Muslim autonomist demands, the government established an Office of Muslim Affairs in 1981 and allocated funds for Islamic legal training and for Muslim schools and cultural centers. Part of its role as of 1999 involved coordinating the travel of pilgrims to Mecca, Saudi Arabia, and coordinating diplomatic ties with countries that have contributed to Mindanao's economic development and to the "peace process" with insurgent groups.

11 TRANSPORTATION

The total length of roadways in 1997 was 161,313 km (100,240 mi), of which only 290 km (180 mi) were paved. Luzon contains about one-half of the total road system, and the Visayas about one-third. There were 572,700 passenger cars (including jeepneys, or minibuses) in 1995, nearly half of them registered in Manila; there were also 207,300 commercial vehicles. In 1996, there were 897 km (557 mi) of common-carrier railroad track on Luzon and Panay, which only plays a minor role in transportation.

Water transportation is of paramount importance for inter-island and intraisland transportation. A small offshore fleet registered under the Philippine flag is engaged in international commerce, but most ocean freight is carried to and from the Philippines by ships of foreign registry. In 1998, the merchant fleet numbered 513 ships, totaling 6,544,029 GRT. Manila is the busiest Philippine port in international shipping, followed by Cebu and Iloilo. Other ports and harbors include Batangas, Cagayan de Oro, Davao, Guimaras Island, Iligan, Jolo, Legaspi, Masao, Puerto Princesa, San Fernando, Subic Bay, and Zamboanga.

In 1998 there were 260 airports, of which 75 had paved runways. Ninoy Aquino International Airport, formerly Manila International Airport, is the principal international air terminal. Five other airports serve international flights as well. Philippine Air Lines (PAL), the national airline, provides domestic and international flights. Under the Aquino government there were plans to sell PAL stock to the private sector. In 1997, 7,475,000 passengers were carried on scheduled domestic and international airline flights.

12 HISTORY

Evidence of human habitation dates back some 250,000 years. In more recent times, experts believe that the Negritos, who crossed then existing land bridges from Borneo and Sumatra some 30,000 years ago, settled the Philippine Islands. Successive waves of Malays, who arrived from the south, at first by land and later on boats called barangays, a name also applied to their communities came t outnumbered the Negritos. By the 14th century, Arab traders made contact with the southern islands and introduced Islam to the local populace. Commercial and political ties also linked various enclaves in the archipelago with Indonesia, Southeast Asia, India, China, and Japan. Ferdinand Magellan, a Portuguese-born navigator sailing for Spain, made the European discovery of the Philippines on 15 March 1521 and landed on Cebu on 7 April, claiming the islands for Spain, but the Filipino chieftain Lapulapu killed Magellan in battle. The Spanish later named the islands in honor of King Philip II, and an invasion under Miguel Lopez de Legaspi began in 1565. The almost complete conversion of the natives to Christianity facilitated the Spanish conquest; by 1571, it was concluded, except for the Moro lands (Moro is the Spanish word for Moor). The Spanish gave this name to Muslim Filipinos, mostly inhabitants of southern and eastern Mindanao, the Sulu Archipelago, and Palawan. The Spanish administered the Philippines, as a province of New Spain, from Mexico. Trade became a monopoly of the Spanish government; galleons shipped Oriental goods to Manila, from there to Acapulco in Mexico, and from there to the mother country.

Although Spain governed the islands until the end of the 19th century, its rule was constantly threatened by the Portuguese, the Dutch, the English (who captured Manila in 1762, occupying it for the next two years), the Chinese, and the Filipinos themselves. After the 1820s, which brought the successful revolts of the Spanish colonies in the Americas, Filipinos openly agitated against the government trade monopoly, the exactions of the clergy, and the imposition of forced labor. This agitation brought a relaxation of government controls: the colonial government opened ports to world shipping, and the production of such typical Philippine exports as sugar, coconuts, and hemp began. Filipino aspirations for independence, suppressed by conservative Spanish rule, climaxed in the unsuccessful rebellion of 1896–98. Jose Rizal, the most revered Filipino patriot, was executed, but Gen. Emilio Aguinaldo and his forces continued the war. During the Spanish-American War (1898), Aguinaldo declared independence from Spain on 12 June. When the war ended, the US acquired the Philippines from Spain for $20,000,000. US rule replaced that of the Spanish, but Philippine nationalists continued to fight for independence. In 1899, Gen. Aguinaldo became president of the revolutionary First Philippine Republic and continued guerrilla resistance in the mountains of northern Luzon until his capture in 1901, when he swore allegiance to the US. Over the long term, the effect of US administration was to make the Philippines an appendage of the US economy, as a supplier of raw materials to and a buyer of finished goods from the American mainland. Politically, US governance of the Philippines was a divisive issue among Americans, and the degree of US control varied with the party in power and the US perception of its own security and economic interests in the Pacific. In the face of continued nationalist agitation for independence, the US Congress passed a series of bills that ensured a degree of Philippine autonomy. The Tydings-McDuffie Independence Law of 1934 instituted commonwealth government and further stipulated complete independence in 1944. In 1935, under a new constitution, Manuel Luis Quezon y Molina became the first elected president of the Commonwealth of the Philippines.

On 8 December 1941, Japan invaded the Philippines, which then became the focal point of the most bitter and decisive battles fought in the Pacific during World War II. By May 1942, the Japanese had achieved full possession of the islands. US forces, led by Gen. Douglas MacArthur, recaptured the Philippines in early 1945, following the Battle of Leyte Gulf, the largest naval engagement in history. In September 1945, Japan surrendered. On 4 July 1946, Manuel A. Roxas y Acuna became the first president of the new Republic of the Philippines. Both casualties and war damage wreaked on the Philippines were extensive, and rehabilitation was the major problem of the new state. Communist guerrillas, called Hukbalahaps, threatened the republic. Land reforms and military action by Ramon Magsaysay, the minister of national defense countered the Huks revolutionary demands. Magsaysay was elected to the presidency in 1953 but died in an airplane crash in 1957. Carlos P. Garcia succeeded Magsaysay and then won election to the office in 1958. Diosdado Macapagal became president in November 1961. He was succeeded by Ferdinand Edralin Marcos succeeded

Macapagal following the 1965 elections. Marcos was reelected in 1969 with a record majority of 62%. The Marcos government brutally suppressed renewed Hukbalahap insurgency, but armed opposition by Muslim elements, organized as the Moro National Liberation Front (MNLF), the Maoist-oriented New People's Army (NPA), and by other groups gathered force in the early 1970s.

Unable under the 1935 constitution to run for a third term in 1973, President Marcos, on 23 September 1972, placed the entire country under martial law, charging that the nation was threatened by a "full-scale armed insurrection and rebellion." Marcos arrested many of his more vehement political opponents, some of whom remained in detention for several years. In January 1973, the Marcos administration introduced a new constitution, but many of its provisions remained in abeyance until 17 January 1981, when Marcos finally lifted martial law. During the intervening period, Marcos consolidated his control of the government through purges of opponents, promotion of favorites, and delegation of leadership of several key programs—including the governorship of metropolitan Manila and the Ministry of Human Settlements—to his wife, Imelda Romualdez Marcos. Although Marcos made headway against the southern guerrillas, his human-rights abuses cost him the support of the powerful Roman Catholic Church, led by Jaime Cardinal Sin. Elections were held in April 1978 for an interim National Assembly to serve as the legislature until 1984, but local elections held in 1980 were widely boycotted. Pope John Paul II came to Manila in February 1981, and even though martial law was no longer in effect, he protested the violation of basic human rights. In June 1981, Marcos won reelection for a new six-year term as president under an amended constitution preserving most of the powers he had exercised under martial rule. New threats to the stability of the regime came in 1983 with the rising foreign debt, a stagnant economy, and the public uproar over the assassination on 21 August of Benigno S. Aquino, Jr. Aquino, a longtime critic of Marcos, was shot at the Manila airport as he returned from self-exile to lead the opposition in the 1984 legislative elections. The gunman was immediately killed, and 26 others suspected of conspiracy in the assassination were acquitted in December 1985 for lack of evidence. Public sympathy gave opposition parties 59 out of 183 elective seats in 1984.

In 1985, political pressures forced Marcos to call for an election in February 1986 in view of a widespread loss of confidence in the government. The Commission on Elections and the National Assembly, controlled by his own political party, proclaimed Marcos the winner. His opponent, Maria Corazon Cojuangco Aquino, the widow of Benigno S. Aquino, claimed victory, however, and charged the ruling party with massive election fraud. The National Movement for Free Elections, the US, and other international observers supported Aquino's charge, the Bishops' Conference. Accordingly, other countries withheld recognition of Marcos. On 21 February 1986, a military revolt grew into a popular rebellion, urged on by Jaime Cardinal Sin. US President Reagan gave Marcos only an offer of asylum, which Reagan guaranteed only if Marcos left the Philippines without resistance. Marcos went into exile in Hawaii.

After Marcos

On 25 February 1986, Corazon Aquino assumed the presidency. Her government restored civil liberties, released political prisoners, and offered the NPA a six-month cease-fire, with negotiations on grievances, in exchange for giving up violence. Because Aquino came to power through the forced departure of an officially proclaimed president, the legality of her regime was suspect. Consequently, she operated under a transitional "freedom constitution" until 11 February 1987, when the electorate ratified a new constitution. On 11 May 1987 the first free elections in nearly two decades were held under the new constitution. More than 83% of eligible voters cast their ballots, 84 candidates ran for the 24 senate seats, and 1,899 candidates ran for the 200 house seats. There were 63 election-related killings. Old-line political families still controlled the system, as 169 House members out of the 200 elected either belonged to or were related to these families.

On 20 December 1987 one of the worst disasters in maritime history occurred when an overcrowded passenger ship collided with an oil tanker off Mindoro Island and at least 1,500 people perished. This delayed local elections until 18 January 1988. Nationwide 150,000 candidates ran for 16,000 positions as governor, vice governor, provincial board member, mayor, vice mayor, and town council member. In 1988 election-related violence killed more than 100 people. Members of the pro-government parties, a faction of the PDP-Laban and Lakas ng Bansa, formed a new organization, Laban ng Demokratikong Pilipino (LDP) in June 1988. In March 1989 the thrice-postponed election for barangay officials was held, electing some 42,000 barangay captains. In August 1989 President Aquino signed a law giving limited autonomy to provinces where most Philippine Muslims lived: Mindinao, Palawan, Sulu, and Tawi-Tawi islands.

There were five coup attempts between the time Aquino took office and the end of 1987. This continuing succession of coup plots culminated in a large, bloody, well-financed attempt in December 1989. Led by Colonel Gregorio Honasan (who participated in the 1987 coup attempt, and was a close associate of Enrile) and involving more than 3,000 troops that targeted several bases, US air support helped to quelled this attempt. The Senate granted Aquino emergency powers for six months. President Aquino's administration lost international credibility with the appeal for US military support to quell the coup attempt. The authorities made arrests, but the Supreme Court ruled that Senator Juan Ponce Enrile could not be charged with murder, nullifying a criminal case against him. He was charged in a lower court with rebellion. In September 1990, 16 military members were convicted of the assassination of Senator Benigno Aquino in 1983 and sentenced to life in prison.

Former President Ferdinand Marcos had appealed to Aquino to allow him to attend the funeral of his mother, as he had appealed several times to visit his mother while she was ill; Aquino denied each request. The Philippine government had traced at least $5 billion in deposits to Swiss bank accounts made by Marcos. Marcos attempted to negotiate his return to the Philippines, promising his support for Aquino and the return of $5 billion to the Philippines. Aquino also rejected his wife Imelda's plea for her husband's return. The Philippine government filed an antigraft civil suit for $22.6 billion against Marcos in 1987. Marcos and his wife, Imelda, were indicted in the US, charged with the illegal transfer of $100 million in October 1988. On 28 September 1989 former President Ferdinand Marcos died in Honolulu. Aquino refused to allow his burial in the Philippines.

Under pressure from Communist rebels Aquino removed the US military bases from the Philippines in 1989. Three US servicemen were murdered outside Clark Air Force Base and the Communists took responsibility for the murders. A Communist guerrilla who admitted participating in the 21 April 1989 assassination of US Army Colonel James Row was arrested. In September 1989 US Vice President Dan Quayle met with Aquino to discuss the renewal of the lease on US military bases. Prior to his arrival two American civilians working on the bases were killed, the government attributed these deaths to Communist guerrillas. The Communists continued to threaten US servicemen and local politicians. Anti-American demonstrations at Clark Air Base and in Manila led to clashes with the police and to injuries. The Communists continued their threats and two more US servicemen were killed near the Clark Air Base. In June of 1990 the Peace Corps removed 261 volunteers from the Philippines after Communist threats against them. In September 1990 Aquino said it was time to consider an "orderly withdrawal" of US forces from the Philippines.

Within a year the Philippines was pummeled with three major natural disasters. In July 1990 an earthquake measuring 7.7 on the Richter scale struck. The epicenter was 55 mi north of Manila and more than 1,600 people were killed. A super-typhoon devastated the central Visayas in November 1990. An even more destructive natural disaster occurred on 12 June 1991 when Mount Pinatubo in Zambales province, a volcano dormant for more than 500 years, violently erupted, causing the abandonment of Clark Air Base in Angeles City; 20,000 US military, their dependents, and civilian employees evacuated to the US from Clark and the Subic Bay Naval Station.

The Philippine-American Cooperation Talks (PACT) reached agreement on military base and non-base issues, but Philippine Senate refused to ratify the proposed treaty. On 6 January 1992 the Philippines government served notice of the termination of the US stay at Subic Naval Base in Zambales. After almost a century of US military presence, on 30 September 1992 the US handed over Subic Naval Base to the Philippines. The Philippine government turned it into a free port, headed until 1998 by Dick Gordon.

Amnesty International (AI), the human rights organization, published a report in 1992 critical of the Aquino administration's assent to human rights violations perpetrated by the military; AI alleged that 550 extra judicial killings occurred during 1988–91. The military refuted the AI report citing its oversight of rebel activities.

In March 1991 President Aquino stated that Imelda Marcos could return to the Philippines, but that she faced charges that her husband stole $10 billion during his 20 years as president. Mrs. Marcos returned in November, after five years in Hawaii, to face civil and criminal charges, including tax fraud. In January 1992 Imelda Marcos announced that she would run for election in 1992; in the same month she was arrested, and then released, for failing to post bail on charges that she unlawfully maintained accounts in Switzerland. In September 1993 the government permitted the embalmed body of Ferdinand Marcos to return to the Philippines for burial near his home in northern Luzon. On 24 September 1993 Imelda Marcos was found guilty of participating in a deal that was "disadvantageous to the government" under the Anti-Graft and Corruption Practices Act. She faced a maximum prison sentence of 24 years, but she remained free on bail while her appeal was considered.

In national and local elections held 11 May 1992. Fidel V. Ramos and Joseph E. Estrada were elected president and vice president, respectively. On 30 June 1992 Fidel Ramos succeeded Corazon Aquino as president of the Philippines with a plurality of 23.6%. Nearly 85% of eligible voters turned out to elect 17,205 officials at national, regional, and local levels. The election was relatively peaceful with only 52 election-related deaths reported. Rules required voters to write the names of the candidate they wanted for office. This, combined with the number of candidates, meant it was several weeks before the votes were completely tallied. Ramos, a Methodist and the Philippine's first non-Catholic president, considered the country's population growth rate as an obstacle to development. A rally of 300,000 Catholics led by Cardinal Sin took place in Manila in 1993 to protest the Ramos administration's birth control policies and the public health promotion of prophylactics to limit the spread of AIDS.

Domestic insurgency by the Muslim population continued throughout the 1980s. By the 1990s, however, internal divisions among the Muslims, reduced external support, military pressure, and government accommodations, including the creation of the Autonomous Region in Muslim Mindanao in 1990 had greatly reduced the threat. In January 1994 the government signed a cease-fire agreement with the Moro National Liberation Front, ending 20 years of guerrilla war. Splinter groups among the Muslin population continue, however, to cause difficulties for both the MNLF and the government.

The last remaining communist insurgency in Asia was reduced temporarily by the Ramos government's peaceful signal, the 1992 Anti-Subversion Law, and the 1993 split in the ranks of the NPA that created a lull until issues related to the weakened leadership are resolved. The NPA returned to violent opposition sporadically throughout the 1990s, especially by the Revolutionary Proletarian Army, an offshoot of the NPA. The NPA significantly increased its use of children as armed combatants and noncombatants during this same time.

In January 1994 the Congress pass a law passed restoring the death penalty for 13 crimes including treason, murder, kidnapping and corruption. Police reform was a particular goal of the legislation. This legislation was partly in response to a series of abductions of wealthy ethnic Chinese Filipinos abducted for ransom, in which the Philippine National Police were found to be involved. The result, however, was that in February of 1999, the Philippines carried out its first execution in 23 years when Leo Echegaray, 38, a house painter convicted of raping his 10-year-old stepdaughter.

Conflicting claims to the Spratly Islands in the South China Sea are a source of tension between the Philippines and the People's Republic of China. In 1989 Chinese and Philippine warships exchanged gunfire in the vicinity of the Spratly Islands. The incident was resolved by diplomatic means. In June 1994 China protested an oil exploration permit granted to Vaalco Energy of the US, and to Alcorn Petroleum and Minerals, its Philippine subsidiary. The Philippine response was to refer to a principle of "common exploration" and development of the Spratlys. China had employed this same principle when the Philippines had protested China's granting the US permission to explore in the Spratlys in 1993. China, Vietnam, Taiwan, the Philippines, Malaysia, and Brunei all lay claim to all, or a portion, of the Spratly Islands. In June 1994 a 5-day conference on East Timor held in Manila ended with an agreement to establish a coalition for East Timor in the Philippines and proposed a peace plan based on the gradual withdrawal of Indonesian troops. But turmoil in the Spratlys did not end. In 1995, China briefly occupied Mischief Reef in a part of the islands claimed by the Philippines. In spring of 1997, Chinese warships were seen near Philippine-occupied islands in the chain. The two countries have also traded occupation of Scarborough Shoal, heightening tensions and prompting Manila to seek renewed American military presence. In May 1999 the Philippine Senate ratified a new Visiting Forces Agreement with the United States, despite claims by opponents that the VFA would the US military the opportunity to bring nuclear weapons, without declaration, into the Philippines, violating the Philippine constitution.

The issue of Filipino women forced to work abroad, long a controversy in the country's large impoverished class, came to a head in 1995. In March, Filipina domestic worker Flor Contemplacion was executed in Singapore for the murder of a maid and a child. Outraged Filipinos claimed the girl was framed; they filled the streets of Manila in protest. The crisis, the product of unemployment and underemployment forcing families to export their children to low-wage overseas jobs, culminated in Mr. Ramos's sacking of two cabinet ministers.

In January 1996, Philippines police uncovered and thwarted a plot by Islamic extremists to assassinate Pope John Paul II during his visit to Manila that month.

Muslim rebels in Mindanao continued their insurgencies against the government, raiding the trading town of Ipil in April 1996. The terrorists killed 57 people and burned the town's business district. The rebels also took part in the resurgence of kidnappings and bank robberies in Manila and Mindanao. More than 100 kidnappings were reported in 1996, many in which police officers were also suspected. A peace agreement between the Philippine government and the Muslim group was signed on 2 September 1996, that ended the 24-year-old war in Mindanao. The agreement was signed by the government chief negotiator Manuel Yan, Nur Misuari, Indonesian Foreign Minister Ali Alatas, and Secretary General Hamid Algabid of the Organization of Islamic Conference(OIC). Later, Misuari ran for and won the governorship of the Autonomous Region for Muslim Mindanao (ARM) in the 9 September 1996, elections.

The Philippine economy suffered a harsh blow in 1995 when a typhoon ravaged the rice harvest, trebling the destruction of the rice acreage lost to the Mount Pinatubo eruption. But the economy rebounded in late 1995 and through 1996, buoyed by the government's massive infrastructure improvements and plans to develop former US military bases Subic Bay and Clark Air Force Base as tourist attractions and economic zones.

President Ramos introduced the Philippines 2000 movement, which was both a strategy and a movement; he called it the Filipino people's vision of development by the year 2000. As envisioned, the Philippines by the year 2000 would have a decent minimum of food, clothing, shelter, and dignity. The major goal of Philippines 2000 was to make the Philippines the next investment, trade, and tourism center in Asia and the Pacific. The Ramos administration achieved several of its economic goals but few of the social changes envisioned.

On 30 June 1998 the newly elected President, Joseph Ejercito Estrada, took office. The new Vice President was Gloria Macapagal-Arroyo.

[13]GOVERNMENT

Under the constitution of 11 February 1987 the Philippines is a democratic republican state. Executive power is vested in a president elected by popular vote for a six-year term, with no eligibility for reelection. The president is assisted by a vice-president, elected for a six-year term, with eligibility for one immediate reelection, and a cabinet, which can include the vice-president. Legislative power rests with a bicameral legislature. Congress consists of a Senate, with 24 members elected for six-year terms (limited to two consecutive terms). Senators are chosen at large. Senators must be native-born Filipinos and at least 35 years old. A House of Representatives is elected from single-member districts for three-year terms (limited to three consecutive terms). Districts are reapportioned within three years of each census. In 1998, 221 members were elected. Up to 50 more may be appointed by the president from "party lists" and "sectoral lists." Representatives must be native-born Filipinos and at least 25 years of age. Presidential and legislative elections are next scheduled for 11 May 2004.

[14]POLITICAL PARTIES

The first Philippine political party, established in 1900, was the Federal Party, which advocated peace and eventual statehood. Later, the Nationalist Party (NP) and the Democratic Party were established. They did not produce an actual two-party system, since the Nationalists retained exclusive control and the Democrats functioned as a "loyal opposition." However, following Japanese occupation and the granting of independence, an effective two-party system developed between the Liberal Party (LP) and the NP. The Progressive Party, formed in 1957 by adherents of Ramon Magsaysay, polled more than one million votes in the presidential election of 1958. In the elections of

November 1965, Senator Ferdinand Marcos, the NP candidate, received 55% of the vote. In the 1969 election, he was elected to an unprecedented second term. All political activity was banned in 1972, following the imposition of martial law, and was not allowed to resume until a few months before the April 1978 elections for an interim National Assembly. The Marcos government's New Society Movement (Kilusan Bagong Lipunan-KBL) won that election and the 1980 and 1982 balloting for local officials, amid charges of electoral fraud and attempts by opposition groups to boycott the voting. The principal opposition party was the People's Power Movement-Fight (Lakas Ng Bayan-Laban), led by Benigno S. Aquino, Jr., until his assassination in 1983. This party joined with 11 other opposition parties in 1982 to form a coalition known as the United Nationalist Democratic Organization (UNIDO). Following Aquino's murder, some 50 opposition groups, including the members of the UNIDO coalition, agreed to coordinate their anti-Marcos efforts. This coalition of opposition parties enabled Corazon Aquino to campaign against Marcos in 1986. In September 1986 the revolutionary left formed a legal political party to contest congressional elections. The Partido ng Bayan (Party of the Nation) allied with other left-leaning groups in an Alliance for New Politics. This unsuccessful attempt for electoral representation resulted in a return to guerrilla warfare on the part of the Communists.

After assuming the presidency, Aquino formally organized the People's Power Movement (Lakas Ng Bayan), the successor to her late husband's party. In the congressional elections of May 1987, Aquino's popularity gave her party a sweep in the polls, making it the major party in the country. Marcos's KBL was reduced to a minor party. Some of its members formed their own splinter groups, such as the Grand Alliance for Democracy (GAD), a coalition of parties seeking distance from Marcos. Others revived the LP and the NP, seeking renewed leadership. The left-wing People's Party (Partido Ng Bayan), which supports the political objectives of the NPA, was a minor party in the elections. In May 1989 Juan Ponce Enrile reestablished the Nacionalista Party. A new opposition party, the Filipino Party (Partido Pilipino), organized in 1991 as a vehicle for Aquino's estranged cousin Eduardo "Danding" Cojuangco's presidential campaign. He ran third in the election, taking 18.1% of the vote, behind Miriam Defensor Santiago with 19.8% of the vote. On 30 June 1992 Fidel Ramos succeeded Corazon Aquino as president of the Philippines with a plurality of 23.6%. In September 1992 Ramos signed the Anti-Subversion Law signaling a peaceful resolution to more than 20 years of Communist insurgency, with the repeal of the antisubversion legislation in place since 1957. On 26 August 1994 Ramos announced a new political coalition that would produce the most powerful political group in the Philippines. Ramos' Lakas-National Union of Christian Democrats (Lakas/NUCD) teamed with the Democratic Filipino Struggle (Laban ng Demokratikong Pilipino, Laban). Following the 1995 elections, the LDP controlled the Senate with 14 of the 24 members. The elections in 1998 changed the political landscape once more. In the Senate the newly created Laban Ng Masang Pilipino, led by presidential candidate, Joseph Estradad, captured 12 seats to the Lakas 5, PRP 2, LP 1, independents 3. The LAMP party also dominated the House of Representatives with 135 seats to the Lakas 37, LP 13, Aksyon Demokatiko 1, and 35 independents.

Political parties and their leaders in 1999 were: Laban Nb Masang Pilipino or LAMP—Struggle of the Filipino Masses—(Joeseph Estradad, titular head; Eduardo "Danding" Cojuango, chairman, Edgardo Angara, party president); Lakas (Raul Manglapus, chairman, Gloria Macapagal-Arroyo, secretary general, Jose De Venecia, party president); Liberal Party or LP (Raul Daza, president, Jovito Salonga, chairman, Florencio Abad, secretary general); People's Reform Marty or PRP (Miriam

Defensor-Santiago); Aksyon Demokatiko or Democratic Action (Raul Roco).

Parties organized in opposition to the Government are: Mindanao Independence Movement, Reuben Canoy; Moro Islamic Liberation Front (MILF), is based mainly in Lanao del Sur (receives support from Egypt), Hashim Salamat; Bangsa Moro National Liberation Front (BMNLF), supported by Saudi Arabia, Dimas Pundato; National Democratic Front, is a left-wing alliance of 14 groups, spokesperson Saturnino Ocampo; Communist Party of the Philippines (CPP), Jose Maria Sison; New People's Army (NPA), the military wing of the CPP, Romulo Kintanar.

15 LOCAL GOVERNMENT

Under the constitutions of 1935, 1973, and 1987, the country has been divided into provinces, municipalities, and chartered cities, each enjoying a certain degree of local autonomy. Each of the 72 provinces and subprovinces elects a governor, a vice-governor, and two provincial board members for terms of six years. There are 61 chartered cities headed by a mayor and a vice-mayor. Chartered cities stand on their own, are not part of a province, do not elect provincial officials, and are not subject to provincial taxation, but have the power to levy their own taxes. Municipalities, of which each province is composed, are public corporations governed by municipal law. There are approximately 1,500 municipalities, and within each municipality are communities (barangays), each with a citizens' assembly. There are about 42,000 barangays. Metropolitan Manila is a separate political unit, created in 1975, with Imelda Romualdez Marcos as the first governor. The 1987 constitution provides for special forms of government in the autonomous regions created in the Cordilleras in Luzon and the Muslim areas of Mindanao. Any region can become autonomous by a referendum. The Local Government Code of 1991 provided for a more responsive and accountable local-government structure. Local governments are to be given more powers, authority, responsibilities and resources through a system of decentralization.

16 JUDICIAL SYSTEM

Under the 1973 constitution, the Supreme Court, composed of a chief justice and 14 associate justices, was the highest judicial body of the state, with supervisory authority over the lower courts. The entire court system was revamped in 1981, with the creation of new regional courts of trials and of appeals. Justices at all levels were appointed by the president. Philippine courts functioned without juries. Delays in criminal cases were common, and detention periods in national security cases were long. Security cases arising during the period of martial law (1972–81) were tried in military courts. The 1987 constitution restored the system to what it had been in 1973. Despite the reinstitution of many procedural safeguards and guarantees, the slow pace of justice continues to be a major problem.

The Constitution calls for an independent judiciary and defendants in criminal cases are afforded the right to counsel. The legal system is based on both civil and common law. It is especially influenced by Spanish and Anglo-American laws. The Philippines accepts the compulsory jurisdiction of the International Court of Justice.

An informal local system for arbitrating or mediating certain problems operates outside the formal court system. There is no jury system. Defendants enjoy a presumption of innocence and have the right to confront witnesses, to present evidence and to appeal.

17 ARMED FORCES

The all-volunteer active armed forces numbered 110,000 in 2000, and reserves 131,000. The army, with 73,000 personnel, included

8 infantry divisions and 5 engineer battalions. The navy had a total of 20,500 personnel (including 8,500 marines), with one frigate, and 67 patrol and coastal combatants. The air force had a strength of 16,500, with 42 combat aircraft and 97 armed helicopters. The Coast Guard had 3,500 personnel. The Philippine national police totaled 40,500, and the Citizen Armed Forces had 40,500 personnel. Defense expenditures in 1998 were $995 million or 1.5% of gross domestic product.

The US has abandoned Clark Air Base and Subic Naval Base, southwest of Manila because of volcano damage and excessive rent charges. The government has a cease-fire agreement with the Bangsa Moro Army. Active rebel groups include the New People's Army (8,000), the Moro Islamic Liberation Front (8,000), the Moro Islamic Reformist Group (900), and the Abu Sayaf Group (500).

18 INTERNATIONAL COOPERATION

The Philippines is a charter member of the UN, having joined on 24 October 1945, and belongs to ESCAP and all the nonregional specialized agencies. It participates in the International Sugar Agreement and the International Wheat Agreement. The Philippines is a member of ASEAN and led in the formation of the Asian Development Bank, which opened its headquarters in Manila in 1966. The International Rice Research Institute and the Southeast Asia Research Center for Agriculture are both located in Los Banos, south of Manila. The Philippines is also a member of G-77 and the WTO and a signatory to the Law of the Sea.

19 ECONOMY

The Philippines is primarily an agricultural nation, raising crops for subsistence and export. About 40% of the total labor force is engaged in agriculture, fisheries, and forestry. Manufacturing, which has expanded and diversified since political independence, depends on imported raw materials and cannot supply internal needs. Production of electronics and telecommunications has expanded rapidly, accounting for at least 75% of export revenues in 1999. The Philippines has great potential as a tourist destination. However, since the early 1990s the tourist industry has been affected by political difficulties, natural disasters, and high fuel costs. The economy is heavily dependent on foreign trade. Traditionally, exports of primary products have failed to balance imports, leading the government to restrict imports. Structural change accelerated in the 1970s, as the contribution of industry (including construction) to GDP rose from 29.5% in 1970 to 36.5% by 1980, primarily as a result of export-oriented industrialization promoted by the Marcos government. The Aquino assassination in August 1983 had immediate economic consequences for the Marcos government. Hundreds of millions of dollars in private capital fled the Philippines, leaving the country with insufficient foreign exchange reserves to meet its payments obligations. The government turned to the IMF and its creditor banks for assistance in rescheduling the nation's foreign debt. In addition, imports and exports were tightly controlled, and an austerity program was set up during 1984–85.

The government of Corazon Aquino launched a privatization program in December 1986 with the establishment of the Assets Privatization Trust (APT). Aquino's agrarian reform program, the Comprehensive Agrarian Reform Programme, was only partially accomplished by the end of her term. The monopolies established under the Marcos administration in coconuts, sugar, meat, grains, and fertilizer were dismantled. The copra export ban was lifted, and all export taxes were abolished; in addition, the government allowed free access to lower-cost or higher-quality imports in order to improve the cost-competitiveness of domestic producers. Many difficulties remained, however. The prices of commodity exports, such as sugar, copper, and coconut products, were still

weak, while demand for nontraditional manufactured products, such as clothing and electronic components, failed to rise. Despite the structural reforms and an initial recovery between 1986 and 1989, sustainable growth eluded the Philippines.

Stagnant economic growth plagues the Philippines; inadequate infrastructure and prolonged drought curtail industrial and agricultural expansion. Widespread unemployment and underemployment characterize the Philippine labor market. High rates of labor migration abroad provide some relief and accounts for a substantial portion of the country's foreign exchange earnings. Since 1990 the most visible constraint on the economy has been the shortage of electric power. In Manila, the industrial hub, power outages lasted from four to six hours per day. Consumer protection was provided by the Price Act of 1992 through the stabilization of the price of basic necessities and prime commodities and by measures against undue price increases during emergency situations. In 1993 the inflation rate continued to decline and the return to economic growth was expected to accelerate through 1994. Further positive signs for sustained growth were the following government actions: opening the telecommunications market, liberalizing the foreign exchange market, an increase in the supply and reliability of electric power, and provision of a better investment climate. The country's program with the IMF expired in April 1993, and the necessity for new arrangements delayed pending agreement on growth plans. In turn, absence of new IMF arrangements delayed plans for a fifth Paris Club Debt rescheduling accord. Between 1993 and 1999, the Philippine government liberalized telecommunications, deregulated transportation, privatized water, and resolved the power crisis.

Real GDP growth averaged 3% from 1988 to 1998, but contracted in 1998 by 0.50% during the Asian financial crisis. A tentative growth rate of 1.8% to 2.5% was forecast for 1999. A strong year in exports during 1999, and lower import levels due to a weak Peso caused a dramatic decrease in the balance of payments deficit. Semiconductors, microelectronics, and computer peripherals accounted for most of the export growth.

20 INCOME

The US Central Intelligence Agency (CIA) reports that in 1998 the Philippines's gross domestic product (GDP) was estimated at $270 billion. The per capita GDP was estimated at $3,500. The annual growth rate of GDP was estimated at -0.5%. The average inflation rate in 1998 was 9.7%. The CIA defines GDP as the value of all final goods and services produced within a nation in a given year and computed on the basis of purchasing power parity (PPP) rather than value as measured on the basis of the rate of exchange. It was estimated that agriculture accounted for 20% of GDP, industry 32%, and services 48%.

The World Bank reports that for the same period per capita private consumption (in PPP terms) was $2,525. Private consumption includes expenditures of individuals, households, and nongovernmental organizations. It was estimated that between 1990 and 1998 private consumption grew at an annual rate of 3.7%. Approximately 37% of household consumption was spent on food, 11% on fuel, 1% on health care, and 14% on education. The richest 10% of the population accounted for approximately 37% of household consumption and the poorest 10% approximately 2.3%.

21 LABOR

The Philippines had an employed labor force estimated at 29.5 million in 1999. In 1997, 40% were engaged in agriculture, forestry, and fishing (compared with 58% in 1968), 17% worked in industry, and 43% in the service sector. Unemployment fluctuates seasonally. In 1998, the unemployment rate was estimated at 9.6% overall, with a much higher rate in metropolitan Manila, where manufacturing is concentrated.

In May 1974, the government passed a new labor code that restructured the trade union movement on a one-industry, one-union basis. Most of the more than 3,700 trade unions are small; industrial unions have been united in the Philippines Trade Union Congress, and agricultural workers in the Federation of Free Farmers. Strikes are prohibited in such essential services as transportation, communications, and health care. In 1999, about 12% of the labor force was unionized, although only 2% were covered by collective bargaining agreements. While the right to strike and bargain are recognized by law, numerous instances of intimidation of union officials have been reported. At times, local law enforcement officials have cooperated with foreign corporations to trump up criminal charges against union organizers.

In 1996, the average legal daily minimum wage for an eight-hour day was $5.63 for nonagricultural workers in metropolitan Manila. The minimum in the autonomous region in Muslim Mindanao (and the lowest in the country) was about $2.95 per day. Perhaps as many as one-fifth of businesses in the Philippines do not pay the minimum wage.

Overseas employment is a very important part of the Philippines' income.

The minimum working age is 15, although children even younger may work under the supervision of a parent or guardian. In practice, many children work in the informal economy, although serious efforts are being made by the government to reduce the number of children who are working.

22AGRICULTURE

About one-third of the total land area is classified as arable. Three-fourths of the cultivated area is devoted to subsistence crops and one-fourth to commercial crops, mainly for export. Farms tend to be small, and many areas are double-cropped. Soils are generally fertile, but 30% of the agricultural land is suffering erosion.

In 1973, the Marcos government began a land-reform program that undertook to transfer landowners to about half of the country's 900,000 tenant farmers. By February 1986, over one-half of the area—about 600,000 ha (1,482,600 acres)—had not been distributed. The Aquino administration proposed a program in two stages: the first, covering 1.5 million ha (3.7 million acres) in 1987–89, involved previously undistributed land and other land held by the state; the second, covering 3.9 million ha (9.6 million acres) in 1990–92, involved land cultivating sugar, coconuts, and fruits. A more detailed 1990–1995 plan sought to increase productivity of small farms, maintain self-sufficiency in rice and corn production, and to increase the agricultural sector's role in the trade balance.

Roughly half the cultivated land is devoted to the two principal subsistence crops, palay (unhusked rice) and corn. Production of palay was 8,555,000 tons in 1998; long-term production has increased, mainly through the use of high-yielding hybrid seeds under a government development program begun in 1973. The Philippines attained self-sufficiency in rice in 1974 and became a net exporter of rice for the first time in 1977. A similar development plan was aimed at raising yields of corn, which is the chief food crop in areas unsuitable for rice-growing and is increasingly important as feed for use in the developing livestock and poultry industries. The Philippines has been self-sufficient in corn for human consumption since the late 1970s, but since production of animal feed lags behind the demand, imports are still necessary. Corn output in 1998 was 3,823,000 tons. Lesser crops include peanut, mango, cassava, camote, tomato, garlic, onion, cabbage, eggplant, calamansi, rubber, and cotton.

Commercial agriculture, dominated by large plantations, centers on coconuts and copra, sugarcane, tobacco, bananas, and pineapples. Coconuts are the most important export crop, accounting for 22% of world production; in 1998, 10,493,000 tons were produced. Copra production, in which the Philippines leads the world, rose from 1,470,000 tons in 1965 to an estimated 2,015,000 tons in 1998. As oil milling capacity rose, the domestic market for copra expanded, accounting for almost all of the output and leaving only marginal amounts for exportation. The government put a ban on copra exports in March 1983, but it was lifted in March 1986. Sugarcane production provided the country's single largest export item until 1978, when output and prices fell. Production was 27 million tons in 1998 (compared with an annual average of 31.5 million tons during 1979–81). Pineapple production rose to 1,495,000 tons in 1998; production of coffee was 121,000 tons, and 3,550,000 tons of bananas were produced that year. Other important cash crops in 1998 included mangos, 950,000 tons; tobacco, 103,000 tons; and rubber, 211,000 tons.

23ANIMAL HUSBANDRY

Animal husbandry never has been important, meat consumption being very low. The carabao, or water buffalo, are the principal draft animals, particularly in the rice paddies; hogs are the chief meat animals (except in Muslim sections). The Philippines is self-sufficient in pork and poultry, but imports of beef and dairy products are still necessary. In 1998 there were 10.2 million hogs, 6.5 million goats, 3 million buffaloes, 2.4 million head of cattle, and 137 million chickens. Meat production in 1998 included (in thousands of tons): pork, 1,100; chicken, 525; beef from cattle, 125; beef from carabao, 134; and goat, 81. Dairy production totaled 20,000 tons from cows and 18,000 tons from carabao in 1998; hen eggs, 44,000 tons; and duck eggs, 60,000 tons. The livestock and poultry sectors each contribute about 13% to the total value of agricultural production. In 1997, exports of livestock, meat, and skins were valued at $1.7 million; and dairy products and eggs, $853,000.

24FISHING

Fish is the primary source of protein in the Filipino diet. Some 2,000 species abound in Philippine waters. Despite more than a doubling in output since the 1960s, the fishing industry remains relatively undeveloped, and large quantities of fish are imported. In 1996 the Bureau of Fisheries and Aquatic Resources (BFAR) cited the continued environmental degradation of Philippine waters as a major constraint on fish production. In 1997, the total domestic fish catch was 2,757,165 tons (12th in the world), of which 15% came from inland waters. Imports of fish products in 1997 totaled 135,303 tons.

Six species are most important, according to BFAR, because each has yielded 100,000 tons per year or more since the mid-1980s. These species are: sardines, roundscad, frigate tuna, anchovies, milkfish, and tilapia. Indian mackerel, skipjack and yellowfin tuna, sea bass, red snapper, mullet, kawakawa, squid, and prawn are also plentiful. Principal commercial fishing grounds are off Palawan, north of Panay and Negros, and to the south and west of Mindanao. Subsistence fishing is conducted throughout the archipelago. Fish ponds, chiefly for cultivation of bangos or milkfish, are principally in the swampy coastal areas of western Panay and around Manila Bay. Aquacultural production in 1997 was valued a $953.3 million. Pearl shells (including cultured pearls), sponges, sea cucumbers (trepang), shark fins, and sea turtles are exported.

25FORESTRY

Forests are an important economic resource in the Philippines. As of 1995, remaining forests occupy 6,766,000 ha (16,719,000 acres), equivalent to 22.7% of the total Philippine land area. Major commercial forest reserves are located in Mindanao,

Luzon, Samar, Negros, and Palawan. Areas devoted to industrial tree plantations in 1995 were estimated at 531,294 ha (1,312,827 acres). Some 65,233 ha (161,191 acres) were reforested in 1995, 67% by the private sector.

Roundwood production in 1997 was estimated at 41.5 million cu m. Production of lumber in 1997 was estimated at 258,000 cu m; wood pulp, 122,000 cu m; and plywood, 367,000 cu m. In the early 1980s, the Philippines was a significant exporter of tropical hardwood logs and lumber, but production fell by over 50% over the decade, leaving the country a net importer of tropical hardwood logs by 1990. The trade deficit for forest products was $590.6 million in 1997.

Among other forest products are bamboo, rattan, resins, tannin, and firewood.

26MINING

The mining and quarrying sector continued to decline in importance, accounting for only 1.2% of GDP in 1997 and engaging 1.5% of the labor force. Copper and gold are the principal commodities, but production has been hampered for the past two decades due to natural disasters (volcanic activity, severe flooding, and drought), political instability and declining foreign investment, low international prices, and an inadequate mining law. Mining for metals accounts for about 75% of the industry's production and nearly all of its export earnings. The Philippine Mining Act of 1995 was designed to help the domestic mining industry regain its competitiveness by allowing companies (contractors) to obtain an exploration permit for a specific area for up to four years. Upon finding a viable deposit, the code provides four basic types of production agreements (production sharing, co-production, joint-venture, or financial/technical assistance) with a duration of up to 50 years. A serious accident in March 1996 involving spilled mine tailings from a copper mine on Marinduque led the government to freeze almost all applications for exploration licenses by foreign companies until early 1997.

Copper (46,959 tons produced in 1997, from northern Luzon, Cebu, Negros, Marinduque, and Mindanao) is the leading mineral, followed by gold (33,800 kg in 1997 from northern Luzon, Mindanao, and Masbate Island), and nickel (15,000 tons of metal content in 1997 from Palawan Island and Surigao del Norte). The Philippines reportedly has the world's largest source of refractory chromite (from Masinloc) and produces sizable quantities of metallurgic chromite (from western Luzon); chromite ore production in 1997 totaled 87,500 tons. Silver, lead, and zinc also are produced for export. Clays, limestone, pyrites, guano, silica sands, and salt are produced for local consumption. Coal deposits are found in Antique Province, Cebu, and Mindanao; production rose from 331,000 tons in 1981 to 1,800,000 tons in 1997.

27ENERGY AND POWER

Net installed electrical capacity as of 1998 amounted to 11,755,000 kW, of which geothermal energy contributed about 24% and oil-fired plants 47%. Total electrical output in 1998 was 39,623 million kWh. As of 1996, 62% of production was conventional thermal, 20% was hydropower, and the remainder was geothermal. Large hydroelectric plants have been installed on the Agno and Angat rivers on Luzon and at María Cristina Falls on the Agusan River in Mindanao.

Brownouts and power outages in 1992 and 1993 were estimated to have cost the Philippine economy several billion dollars per year. The Power Development Program (PDP) calls for capacity additions of 13 million kW during 1996–2005, at an estimated cost of $1.2–$1.4 billion per year. Geothermal energy is produced on Luzon, Leyte, and Negros. Several nuclear power plants have been initiated, but they were all abandoned because

of ceilings on foreign borrowing and, in the case of the completed plant at Bataan, the location of the site near a seismic fault line.

Commercial oil deposits were found in 1978, with production beginning the following year. The largest oil production field is located at West Linapacan. Domestic production increased from 1.4 million barrels in 1981 to 3.3 million barrels in 1982 but decreased to less than 0.5 million barrels in 1994. In October 1996, exploration began in the potentially oil-rich Cotabato Basin of the southern Philippines. The Philippine government has developed an alternative energy program, including, for example, the use of "alcogas" (gasohol) and "cocodiesel" (coconut oil in diesel fuels). With the recent discovery of oil off the shores of Palawan, more drilling and deep-sea exploration is expected. In 1995, oil production amounted to about 4,000 barrels per day.

In 1998, as a step toward removal from IMF supervision, the Philippines deregulated its oil industry, removing price controls, instituting a uniform tariff duty, and eliminating inventory requirements. However, due in part to the Asian economic crisis, the three established oil companies still controlled over 90% of the market in early 1999.

28INDUSTRY

Industry is concentrated in the Manila area. The leading manufactured goods are textiles, pharmaceuticals, chemicals, wood, food, electronics, petroleum, and fish. There was growth in the number of plants that assemble imported components into finished products (such as transistors, radios, televisions, refrigerators, and stoves) during the 1970s, as there was in the production of intermediate goods (such as chemicals, textiles, timber products, structural steel, and cement).

The industrialization strategy proposed by the government in 1981 stressed development of exports and the accelerated implementation of 11 major industrial projects—a copper smelter, a phosphatic fertilizer plant, an aluminum smelter, a diesel-engine manufacturing plant, an expansion of the cement industry, a "cocochemical" complex (based on coconuts), an integrated pulp and paper mill, a petrochemical complex, heavy engineering industries, an integrated steel mill, and the production of "alcogas." The copper smelter, the phosphatic fertilizer plant, and the "cocochemical" complex went into operation in 1985.

By the 1990s manufacturing production was geographically concentrated in the Metro Manila area (50%) and the adjoining regions of Southern Tagalog and Central Luzon (20%). Most industrial output is concentrated in a few large firms. Although small and medium-sized businesses accounted for 80% of manufacturing employment, they accounted for only 25% of the value added in manufacturing. In 1993, food products accounted for 22% of industrial output; petroleum and coal, 12%; chemicals, 11%; electrical machinery, 11%; beverages, 8%; transport equipment, 6%; basic metals, 5%; and footwear, 5%.

Exports from the electronics industry surpassed those of food products and textiles in the late 1990s. In 1999, the Philippines continued its shift from an economy earlier based on agricultural produce and sweatshop factory output to an economy anchored by the assembly of computer chips and other electronic goods, many of them computer peripherals. Fifty chip assemblers and computer component makers have contributed $6.6 billion to the country since 1994. Intel has a $550 million Pentium assembly and testing center in the country. Philips Semiconductors inaugurated a $300 million facility in 1999. Other technology companies with major investments include Acer, Toshiba, Hitachi, Fujitsu, Cypress Semiconductor, and Amkor Technology. In a World Bank study published in 1999, the Philippines was credited with one of the world's most technologically advanced export structures.

²⁹SCIENCE AND TECHNOLOGY

Leadership in formulating and implementing national science policy is exercised by the Department of Science and Technology. Special training in science is offered by the Philippine Science High School, whose graduates are eligible for further training through the department's scholarship program. The International Rice Research Institute in Los Banos, founded by the Rockefeller and Ford foundations and US AID in 1960, conducts training programs in the cultivation, fertilization, and irrigation of hybrid rice seeds. The Southeast Asian Regional Center for Graduate Study and Research in Agriculture maintains genotype and information banks for agricultural research.

The Philippine Nuclear Research Institute, founded in 1958, is located in Quezon City. The French Institute of Scientific Research for Development and Cooperation has an institute in Manila conducting research in molecular biology. In 1996, the Philippines had 68 universities and colleges offering courses on basic and applied sciences. In 1987–97, science and engineering students accounted for 14% of college and university enrollments. In the same period, research and development expenditures amounted to 0.22% of GNP; 157 scientists and engineers and 22 technicians per million people were engaged in research and development. In 1998, high-tech exports were valued at $18.9 billion and accounted for 71% of manufactured exports.

³⁰DOMESTIC TRADE

The archipelagic structure of Philippine marketing requires the establishment of regional centers and adds considerably to distribution costs, alien domination of much of marketing, direct government participation, and the proliferation of small firms. Warehousing facilities are available at most ports. Small stores typify retail trade. Manila has major shopping centers and malls. Generally, sales are for cash or on open account. Retailing is conducted on a high markup, low-turnover basis. A law provides for price-tagging on retail items.

Shops are usually open from 10 AM to noon and from 2 to 7:30 PM, Monday through Saturday; banking hours are weekdays from 9 AM to 3 PM. Office hours, and hours for the Philippine government are generally from 10 AM to 5 PM. Staggered hours, with up to three shifts, are common in the metropolitan Manila area. English is the general language of commercial correspondence. Most advertising is local; the chief media are newspapers, radio, television, posters, billboards, and sound trucks.

³¹FOREIGN TRADE

Export growth averaged 18.5% per year during 1992–96, but imports increased at an annual average rate of 22% during that same period. The nation's trade balance has not shown a surplus since 1973, chiefly because of the rise in mineral fuel imports.

The Philippines' traditional exports were primary commodities and raw materials. In 1995, the government estimated that such exports (mainly coconut products and oil, mineral products, and fruits and vegetables) accounted for 10.2% of total exports. In the mid-1990s, exports of electric machinery (mostly microcircuits, diodes, and transistors) accounted for 13% of total exports, and garments contributed 6.9% to the total value of exports. In 1996, the Philippines exported a majority of electronics and telecommunications equipment, including transistors and valves (8.5%), telecoms equipment (3.1%), and electronic distributing equipment (3.1%). Other exports included vegetable oil (4.3%), copper (2.4%), fruits and nuts (2.4%), and garments (2.2%). The Philippines account for 8.9% of the world's soft vegetable oil exports. In 1998, electronics and computer products accounted for at least two-thirds of all exports.

In 1996 the Philippines's imports were distributed among the following categories:

Consumer goods	4.6%
Food	6.9%
Fuels	9.2%
Industrial supplies	28.2%
Machinery	41.4%
Transportation	9.7%
Other	0.1%

The US and Japan continue to be the Philippines' primary trading partners. Principal trading partners in 1998 (in millions of US dollars) were as follows:

COUNTRY	EXPORTS	IMPORTS	BALANCE
United States	10,145	6,887	3,258
Japan	4,234	6,371	-2,137
Netherlands	2,319	236	2,083
Singapore	1,832	1,824	8
United Kingdom	1,757	347	1,410
Taiwan	1,757	1,493	264
China (inc. Hong Kong)	1,670	1,686	-16
Malaysia	1,142	980	162
Germany	1,035	883	152
Thailand	634	848	-214

³²BALANCE OF PAYMENTS

Since World War II, the Philippines has experienced frequent trade deficits, aggravated by inflationary pressures. Deficits have been counterbalanced by US government expenditures, transfer of payments from abroad, official loans (US Export-Import Bank, IBRD, and private US banks), net inflow of private investment, tourist receipts, remittances from Filipino workers overseas, and contributions from the IMF.

In 1996, trade liberalization policies helped to push imports up by 22% while exports rose by only 18%. The result was a widening trade deficit that amounted to 13% of GDP. Foreign investment in the stock market and remittances from overseas workers helped to offset the deficit and avert a balance-of-payments crisis. In 1998, the Philippines recorded a trade surplus at about 2% of GNP in the current account due to high electronics exports and low imports due to the devaluation of the Peso. This was the first surplus in 12 years, with a positive outlook for 1999.

The US Central Intelligence Agency reports that in 1998 the purchasing power parity of the Philippines's exports was $25 billion while imports totaled $29 billion resulting in a trade balance of -$4 billion.

The International Monetary Fund (IMF) reports that in 1998 the Philippines had exports of goods totaling $29,496 million and imports totaling $29,524 million. The services credit totaled $7,477 million and debit $10,107 million. The following table summarizes the Philippines's balance of payments as reported by the IMF for 1998 in millions of US dollars.

Current Account		1,287
Balance on goods	-28	
Balance on services	-2,630	
Balance on income	3,510	
Current transfers	435	
Capital Account		...
Financial Account		959
Direct investment abroad	-160	
Direct investment in Philippines	1,713	
Portfolio investment assets	-604	
Portfolio investment liabilities	-276	
Other investment assets	430	
Other investment liabilities		-144
Net Errors and Omissions		-967
Reserves and Related Items		-1,279

[33]BANKING AND SECURITIES

The Philippine banking structure consists of the government-owned Central Bank of the Philippines (created in 1949), which acts as the government's fiscal agent and administers the monetary and banking system; and some 53 commercial banks, of which 17 are foreign-majority-owned. Other institutions include more than 100 thrift banks, over 800 rural banks, 38 private development banks, 7 savings banks, and 10 investment houses, and two specialized government banks. The largest commercial bank, the Philippine National Bank (PNB), is a government institution with over 194 local offices and 12 overseas branches. It supplies about half the commercial credit, basically as agricultural loans. The government operates about 1,145 postal savings banks and the Development Bank of the Philippines, the Land Bank of the Philippines, and the Philippine Amanah Bank (for Mindanao). There are also 15 offshore banking units in the country, and 26 foreign bank representative offices. Total assets reached approximately $65 billion in April 1999, 39% of which belonged to the five largest banks.

Philippine stock exchanges are self-governing, although the Philippine Securities and Exchange Commission, established in 1936, has supervisory power over registrants. The country's two stock exchanges, Manila and Makati (both in the capital), were formally merged in the Philippines Stock Exchange in March 1993. A computer link-up was effected a year later, although the two retained separate trading floors until November 1995. Only 220 companies were listed as of 1998. But the process of privatization is expected to push up listings, while domestic participation in the equity market is being specifically promoted by new regulations requiring that all initial public offerings reserve a 10% tranche for small investors. Before the Asian crisis, market capitalization of publicly listed companies had grown to $89 billion, or six times the amount of 1992. But in 1998, only 10 of the largest companies accounted for more than half of trading volume. In 2000, a financial scandal in which the SEC failed to regulate the market properly drove the stock market down by a quarter and destroyed investor confidence.

[34]INSURANCE

The Government Service Insurance System (GIS), a government organization set up in 1936, provides life, permanent disability, accident, old age pension, and burial insurance and salary and real estate loan benefits. Compulsory third-party motor liability insurance went into effect on 1 January 1976.

Private insurance companies consist of life and nonlife insurance companies that provide coverage against theft, fire, marine loss, accident, embezzlement, third-party liability, and other risks. Life insurance funds come from premium contributions of individuals insured through long-term contracts; nonlife insurance funds come mostly from businesses. These funds are in turn placed in long-term securities, such as stocks, bonds, real estate, mortgage policy, and other loans.

[35]PUBLIC FINANCE

The principal sources of revenue are income taxes, taxes on sales and business operations, and excise duties. Infrastructural improvements, defense expenditures, and debt service continue to lead among the categories of outlays.

The government's commitment to fiscal balance resulted in a budget surplus for the first time in two decades in 1994. The surplus was achieved by higher taxes, privatization receipts, and expenditure cuts. The budget again showed a surplus in 1995 when government revenues totaled approximately $14.1 billion and expenditures $13.6 billion. External debt totaled $41 billion, approximately 33% of which was financed abroad. In 1996, 31% of government revenues was spent on social services, 26.5%

on economic services, 9% on defense, 17% on general public service, 0.5% on net lending, and 16% on interest payments.

The US Central Intelligence Agency (CIA) estimates that in 1998 the Philippines's central government took in revenues of approximately $14.5 billion and had expenditures of $12.6 billion including capital expenditures of $1.84 billion. Overall, the government registered a surplus of approximately $1.9 billion. External debt totaled $47.8 billion.

The following table shows an itemized breakdown of government revenues and expenditures. The percentages were calculated from data reported by the International Monetary Fund. The dollar amounts (millions) are based on the CIA estimates provided above.

REVENUE AND GRANTS	100%	14,500
Tax revenue	87.4%	12,666
Non-tax revenue	10.3%	1,491
Capital revenue	2.0%	290
Grants	0.4%	53
EXPENDITURES	100%	12,600
General public services	9.7%	1,226
Defense	7.9%	999
Public order and safety	7.3%	921
Education	20.3%	2,555
Health	3.2%	402
Social security	2.5%	314
Housing and community amenities	0.5%	68
Recreation, cultural, and religious affairs	0.7%	92
Economic affairs and services	22.1%	2,783
Other expenditures	6.9%	866
Interest payments	16.6%	2,089
Adjustments	2.2%	283

[36]TAXATION

The individual income tax consists of taxes on compensation income (from employment), business income, and passive income (interests, dividends, royalties, and prizes). Compensation income tax rates vary from 1% to 35% and business rates vary from 3% to 30%. Income subject to final tax is usually on passive income at a maximum rate of 30%. Corporate taxes are at a uniform rate of 32% for 2000. For resident foreign corporations, after-tax profits remitted abroad are subject to a 15% tax, except for corporations registered with the Export Processing Zone Authority. New and necessary industries, including those authorized as investment priorities, may be wholly tax-exempt, subject to reduced taxation, or granted tax holidays. There is a VAT of 10%.

Excise taxes are imposed on selected commodities such as alcoholic beverages, tobacco products, and petroleum products. In addition, the government levies a variety of other taxes, including mining and petroleum taxes, stamp taxes, residence taxes, estate and gift taxes, a head tax on immigrants above a certain age and staying beyond a certain period, and a capital gains tax. Some cities, such as Manila, levy their own wholesale and retail sales taxes.

[37]CUSTOMS AND DUTIES

Imported goods are subject to ad valorem duties averaging 10% in 1999. A reduced rate of 3% applies to certain goods, while a higher rate of up to 80% for automobiles, locally manufactured items, and certain agricultural goods is imposed. Under the Aquino administration, import taxes were cut on 437 items; in addition, export duties, previously applied to shipments of mineral, vegetable, and animal products, including wood, were eliminated. Average 2000 tariff rates were: agriculture 17%, textiles 12%, metals 8%, machinery 7%, chemicals 4%, and minerals 3%. The government developed a plan in 1996 to lower tariffs to no more than 3% on raw materials, and 10% on finished products by January 2003, and a uniform 5% tariff rate by January 2004.

38 FOREIGN INVESTMENT

Investments have been concentrated in trade, utilities, mining, petroleum refining, and export-oriented agriculture, with accelerating interest in labor-intensive textiles, footwear, electronics, and other nontraditional export industries. Investment is affected by import controls, exchange controls, and equity controls that favor Filipino participation in foreign ventures. The Omnibus Investments Code of 1987 generally limited foreign equity ownership to 40%, but allowed 100% foreign ownership in a "pioneer" priority industry identified in the annual Investment Priorities Plan (IPP). Special encouragement is given to pioneer manufacturing endeavors, export-oriented and labor-intensive industries, projects outside metropolitan Manila, and to joint ventures with a minimum of 60% Filipino capitalization. Attempts to liberalize the economy of the Philippines are fighting three centuries of entrenched interests. Filipino political science research points out the influence and effects of Spanish colonialism which delivered the control of politics and economics into the hands of a small number of families. In support of nationalism these families legislated against foreign competition in the 1950s. The Foreign Investment Act of 1991 (FIA) liberalizes the investment climate of the Philippines. The FIA permits 100% foreign ownership, without prior BOI approval, of companies engaged in any activity not included in the foreign investment negative list. The foreign investment negative list is comprised of three categories where foreign investment is fully or partially restricted by the constitution or by specific laws. In all three categories foreign ownership is restricted to between zero and 40%. Restriction on setting up export processing zones has also been considerably relaxed. Since 1948 foreign banks have not been allowed to open branches; four existing banks were allowed to continue. Under a 1994 law, foreign banks were allowed to enter the Philippines.

Cumulative foreign equity investments since 1973 in millions of US dollars as of 1998 were as follows:

	US$(000)	(%)
Total	9,305	100.0
United States	2,722	29.3
Japan	2,157	23.2
Netherlands	931	10.0
Hong Kong	727	7.8
United Kingdom	465	5.0
British Virgin Islands	383	4.1
Singapore	322	3.5
Germany	215	2.3
Taiwan	168	1.8
South Korea	142	1.5
Switzerland	129	1.4
Australia	115	1.2

39 ECONOMIC DEVELOPMENT

Beginning in 1972, the main tenets of the Marcos government's economic policies, as articulated through the National Economic Development Authority, included substantial development of infrastructure, particularly through the use of labor-intensive rather than capital-intensive (i.e., mechanized) methods, and a shift in export emphasis from raw materials to finished and semifinished commodities. The policies of the Aquino administration have stressed labor-intensive, small and medium-scale agricultural projects and extensive land reform. In addition, wealth believed to have been amassed by President Marcos was actively being pursued all over the world. Long-range planning has followed a series of economic plans, most of them covering five-year periods. The development program for 1967–70 aimed to increase the growth rate of per capita income from the 0.9%

level in 1961–65 to 2.4%; to increase national income by 5.7% per year during the plan period, and to reduce the unemployment rate from 13% (1965) to 7.2% (1970). The government invested $3.5 billion in integrating the traditional and modern sectors of the economy. Marcos's first long-range plan following the 1972 declaration of martial law was a four-year (1974–77) infrastructure development program calling for 35% to be expended on transportation, 33% on energy and power, 20% on water resources, 10% on education, health, and welfare, and 2% on telecommunications. A 1974–78 plan, announced in late 1975, envisioned energy as the major focus of the new plan, with 34% of expenditures, followed by transportation, 30%; water resources, 23%; social programs, 7%; and other sectors, 6%. The goals of the 1978–82 plan included an 8% annual growth in GNP, rural development, tax incentives for export-oriented industries, continued self-sufficiency in grain crops despite rapid population growth, and accelerated development of highways, irrigation, and other infrastructure. The 1983–87 plan called for an annual expansion of 6.2% in GNP, improvement of the rural economy and living standards, and amelioration of hunger.

Under the Aquino administration the goals of the 1987–92 plan were self-sufficiency in food production, decentralization of power and decision making, job creation, and rural development. Economic performance for real growth fell far short of plan targets by 25% or more. Structural changes to provide a better investment climate were carried out. The Foreign Investment Act of 1991 liberalized the environment for foreign investment. An Executive Order issued in July 1991 reduced the number of tariff levels over five years and reduced the maximum duty rate from 50% to 30%. Quantitative restrictions were removed from all but a few products. The foreign exchange market was fully deregulated in 1992.

A new six-year medium-term development plan for 1993–98 was presented by the government in May 1993. The plan stressed people empowerment and international competitiveness within the framework of sustainable development. To do this, the government planned to disperse industries to regions outside the metropolitan Manila area. The plan also called for technological upgrading of production sectors, poverty alleviation, and human/social development. Over the six year period, agriculture's share of GDP was expected to decline from 23% to 19% of GDP while industry's share was to increase from 34% to 39%. The Medium-Term Philippine Development Plan (MTPDP) for 1999 through 2004 focused on rural development, especially on the modernization of the agricultural sector. The MTPDP targeted agricultural growth from 2.6% to 3.4% during the plan's time-frame, as well as growth in the industrial and service sectors. The Philippines finished three years of IMF supervision in March 1998, only to be hit by the Asian financial crisis. Financial assistance continued in 1998 and 1999 through the Asian Development Bank, World Bank, and Japan's Overseas Economic Cooperation Development Fund.

40 SOCIAL DEVELOPMENT

The government social program includes the purchase and subdivision of big estates for resale on installment plans, the settlement of landless families in new areas, building of rural roads, schools, and medical clinics, and the distribution of relief supplies to the needy. Other programs directly geared to social change fall under the Ministry of Human Settlements and Community Development. Among these are nutrition programs for infants, the Bagong Lipunan Improvement of Sites and Services (BLISS) program for depressed areas, and the Livelihood Improvement Program (Kilusang Kabuhayan at Kaunlaran—KKK) designed to channel economic growth into projects—notably in agriculture, fishing, and cottage and light industries—capable of enhancing self-sufficiency at the village level.

The Social Security System (SSS) covers both temporary and permanent employees, including domestic workers. Membership for employers is compulsory. Benefits include compensation for confinement due to injury or illness, pensions for temporary incapacity, indemnities to families in case of death, old age pensions, and benefits to widows and orphans. Charges to cover the system are paid jointly by employers and employees. These contributions vary according to 23 wage classes, but in 1999 averaged 3.3% from employees and 5.07% from employers. A medical care plan for employees provides hospital, surgical, medicinal, and medical-expense benefits to members and their dependents, as well as paid maternity leave.

A handful of women enjoy high prestige and visibility, but most women occupy traditional social roles and occupations. Women on average earn about half as much as men. Most, but not all, of the legal rights enjoyed by men are extended to women. A proposed law that would make rape a public crime, rather than a private offense, failed to pass through the legislature. Restrictions on property ownership were removed by a 1992 law. In the past, however, antidiscrimination laws have not always been implemented. Women also remain underrepresented in politics. As of 1998, 27 of the 217 members of the House and 4 of 23 Senators were female.

The government has enacted various measures in recent years to safeguard the rights of children. In 1995, the Intercountry Adoption Act was strengthened to prevent the sale and trafficking of children. Child prostitution, while illegal, is widespread and has contributed to the growing sex-tourism industry. A new family court system introduced in 1998 strengthened safeguards against the sale of children.

Some human rights violations remained in 1999, including arbitrary arrest and detention, torture, and disappearances.

[41]HEALTH

In the mid-1990s, there were 1,663 hospitals, 562 of which were operated by the government and 1,101 in the private sector. Government-financed child health malnutrition and early education programs are already well-established in the Philippines. These programs suffer from chronic underfunding in terms of inadequate equipment, numbers of field-level staff, and other operating expenses. Government hospitals had 46,388 beds, and private hospitals had 35,309. In addition, there were 2,299 rural health units.

In the same period, there were 31,375 physicians, 1,523 dentists, 10,117 nurses, and 12,408 midwives. There were 0.12 doctors per 1,000 people in 1992, with a nurse to doctor ratio of 3.1. The 1993 population per hospital bed was 934.

Pulmonary infections (tuberculosis, pneumonia, bronchitis) are prevalent. Malnutrition remains a health problem, despite government assistance in the form of Nutripaks, consisting of indigenous foods such as mung beans and powdered shrimp, made available for infants, children, and pregnant women. In 1989–95, 30% of children under five years old were considered malnourished. Protein malnutrition, anemia, and vitamin A and iodine deficiencies are commonly found in children. The goiter rate was 6.9 per 100. Heart disease is the third most common cause of death in the Philippines.

During the 1980s, a nationwide primary health care program was implemented. As a result, community involvement in health services increased; the prevalence of communicable diseases decreased; and the nutritional state of the population improved. Obesity and hypertension are more common in the cities. In 1996, 91% of the urban population and 81% of the rural population had access to safe water. Children up to one year of age were immunized in 1995 against tuberculosis (91%); diphtheria, pertussis, and tetanus (85%); polio (86%); and measles (96%).

The infant mortality rate declined from 78.4 per 1,000 live births in 1972 to 34 in 1999. The general mortality rate in 1999 was 6 per 1,000 people, and maternal mortality was 172 per 100,000 live births in 1997. Average life expectancy was 67 years in 1999.

The birth rate was 28 per 1,000 people in 1999, and 40% of married women (ages 15 to 49) were using contraception in 1995. Health care expenditures were $883 million per year in the early 1990s; public health expenditures were 1% of GDP.

The HIV-1 seroprevalence rate was 0.1 per 100 adults in 1997. There were 249 cases of AIDS in 1996. Tuberculosis incidence was high. In the mid-1990s, 180,444 tuberculosis cases were reported per year. Incidence of TB was 395 per 100,000 population in 1996. In 1995, there were 525 cases of malaria per 100,000 population.

[42]HOUSING

According to recent estimates, 93% of all housing units were detached houses, 4% were apartments, 2% were duplexes, and 1% were improvised housing. Owners occupied 80% of all dwellings, 12% were rented, and 7% were occupied rent free. In 1981, government officials placed the need for new housing at over 1.1 million units. Tens of thousands of barrios are scattered throughout the Philippines, each consisting of a double row of small cottages strung out along a single road. Each cottage is generally built on stilts and has a thatched roof, veranda, and small yard. Construction is largely undertaken by the private sector, with the support of government agencies. The Ministry of Human Settlements (MHS), created in 1978, sets housing programs in motion. Its first major program was the Bagong Lipunon Improvement of Sites and Services (BLISS), which undertook 445 projects involving 6,712 units housing 40,272 people. As with many programs begun during the Marcos administration, the projects became ridden with scandal. More creditable was the Pag-IBIG fund, which was set up to promote savings for housing and provide easy-term housing loans, with contributions from individuals, banks, industries, and the government. By the end of 1985, P98 million in loans had been provided to 171,585 members. In 1985, membership contributions totaled P1.34 billion, and 1,451 housing loans were approved. The Aquino administration offered tax exemptions to domestic corporations and partnerships with at least 300 employees that invest funds in housing. From 1984–87, an annual average of about 103,150 units were built by the private sector with minimal assistance from the government. The total number of dwellings in the mid-1990s was 10,550,000.

[43]EDUCATION

Education is free and compulsory in the primary schools and is coeducational. In 1987, a bill to provide free public secondary education for all students was due for approval in Congress. English is the main medium of instruction, although Pilipino or the local vernacular is used for instruction in the lower primary grades. For the year 2000, adult illiteracy rates stood at 4.6% (males, 4.5%; females, 4.8%).

In 1998, 38,631 primary schools had an enrollment of 12,159,495 students, and secondary schools had 4,979,795 students. The University of the Philippines, in Quezon City, with branches in major islands, is the leading institution of higher learning. In addition, there are some 50 other universities, including the University of Santo Tomás, founded in 1611 and run by the Dominican friars. In 1996, post-secondary institutions had a total enrollment of 2,017,972 students. Approximately 15.7% of central government expenditure was allocated to education in the latter part of the 1990s.

44 LIBRARIES AND MUSEUMS

The National Library in Manila has an estimated 1.2 million volumes. The Filipiniana and Asia Division contains over 100,000 Filipiniana books. Large libraries are in the universities, notably the University of the Philippines (748,700 volumes), the University of Santo Tomás (822,000), the University of the East (177,900), and the University of San Carlos. The International Rice Research Institute in Manila holds 160,000 volumes.

The National Museum in Manila collects and exhibits materials and conducts research in anthropology, ethnography, archaeology, botany, geology, history, and maps. The University of Santo Tomás Museum contains an art gallery and archaeology and anthropology collections. Three relatively new museums in Manila exhibit primarily art: Lopez Memorial Museum (1960) exhibits Filipino painters; Metropolitan Museum (1976) exhibits a variety of art forms; and the Philippines Presidential Museum (1986) exhibits fine and decorative arts. The Ateneo Art Museum in Quezon City features post-World War II Philippine paintings, and there is a Mabini Shrine in Tonauan, featuring relics of Apolinaria Mabina, a leader of Philippine independence.

45 MEDIA

There are four nationwide telephone networks, including the Philippine Long Distance Telephone Company, run mainly by the private sector, with services concentrated in urban areas. Overseas communications operate via satellites and undersea cables. In 1997 there were 1.9 million telephones. A 20-year national telecommunications development plan has been designed to modernize and improve the services in the country by the year 2000. Radio and television are operated by both government agencies and private concerns. Radio transmitting stations numbered 316 (261 AM and 55 FM) in 1999, and there were 5 major television networks and 37 broadcasting stations. In 1997, there were 159 radios, 109 television sets, and 18 mobile phones per 1,000 population.

In 1995 there were some 43 daily newspapers, as compared with six during the Marcos era. The following are among the leading dailies published in metropolitan Manila (with estimated 1999 circulations):

	LANGUAGE	CIRCULATION
People's Journal	English/Pilipino	382,200
Manila Times	English	150,000
Manila Bulletin	English	300,000
Philippine Daily Inquirer	English	250,000
Balita	Pilipino	181,400

Under martial law, censorship of the press, radio, and television was imposed by the Marcos government. Many reporters, editors, and publishers were arrested during this period. Censorship was revoked under the Aquino administration. However, there are reports of threats, assaults, and killings of journalists who report on illegal activities such as gambling, logging, prostitution, and the drug trade among powerful individuals or groups, especially outside Manila.

As of 1996, there were more than 75,000 personal computers. Online access is extremely limited, with about one Internet host per 1,000 population in 1998.

46 ORGANIZATIONS

Between 1939 and 1949, some 1,370 cooperative associations with 260,134 members were organized. In general, however, consumer cooperatives were ineffectual before 1952. In that year, the first effective cooperative movement, the Agricultural Credit Cooperative Finance Administration, was established with an authorized capital of ₱100 million; its general aims were to promote organization of small farmers, assist in obtaining credit, establish orderly and systematic marketing, and upgrade agriculture. However, because of graft and corruption within the agency and other parts of the cooperative movement, the cooperative associations slowly died out.

The Philippine Chamber of Commerce and Industry has branches in metropolitan Manila and other important cities, and there are associations of producers and industrial firms in many areas. The Philippine Academy is the oldest and best-known scholarly organization. There are many associations of persons active in such fields as agriculture, architecture, art, biology, chemistry, economics, library service, literature, engineering, medicine, nutrition, veterinary service, and the press.

47 TOURISM, TRAVEL, AND RECREATION

The increase in tourism that followed the ouster of Ferdinand Marcos was dampened by the national disasters of the early 1990's. The tourism industry had since rebounded. In 1998, 2,149,357 tourists arrived in the Philippines. Over 50% of tourists arrived from East Asia and the Pacific, and Americans accounted for close to 25%. Revenues from tourism totaled $1.9 billion.

In 1997, there were 29,661 hotel rooms with 59,322 beds and a 69% occupancy rate. Manila remains the chief tourist attraction. Other points of interest are the 2,000-year-old rice terraces north of Baguio; Vigan, the old Spanish capital; Cebu, the oldest city; numerous beaches and mountain wilderness areas; and homes formerly owned by the Marcoses. Each tourist must have a valid passport and an onward or return ticket; no visa is required for a stay of less than 21 days.

According to 1999 UN estimates, the cost of staying in Manila is $160 per day. Travel expenses are estimated at $85 for Cebu City and $56 for Bacolod City.

Basketball is the national sport, followed in popularity by baseball and soccer. Jai-alai is popular in Manila and Cebu. Cockfighting is legal and often televised.

48 FAMOUS FILIPINOS

Filipinos have made their most important marks in the political arena. Foremost are José Rizal (1861–96), a distinguished novelist, poet, physician, linguist, statesman, and national hero; Andrés Bonifacio (1863–97), the leader of the secret Katipunan movement against Spain; and Emilio Aguinaldo y Famy (1869–1964), the commander of the revolutionary forces and president of the revolutionary First Philippine Republic (1899). Notable Filipinos of this century include Manuel Luis Quezon y Molina (1878–1944), the first Commonwealth president; Ramón Magsaysay (1907–57), a distinguished leader in the struggle with the Hukbalahaps; and Carlos Peña Rómulo (1899–1985), a Pulitzer Prize-winning author and diplomat and the president of the fourth UN General Assembly. Ferdinand Edralin Marcos (1917–89), who won distinction as a guerrilla fighter during the Japanese occupation, was the dominant political figure in the Philippines from his first election to the presidency in November 1965 to his ouster in February 1986. His wife, Imelda Romualdez Marcos (b.1930), emerged as a powerful force within her husband's government during the 1970s. Leading critics of the Marcos government during the late 1970s and early 1980s were Benigno S. Aquino, Jr. (1933–83) and Jaime Sin (b.1928), who became the archbishop of Manila in 1974 and a cardinal in 1976. Maria Corazon Cojuangco Aquino (b.1933), the widow of Benigno, opposed Marcos for the presidency in February 1986 and took office when he went into exile in the same month.

Lorenzo Ruiz (fl.17th cent.) was canonized, along with 15 companion martyrs, as the first Filipino saint. Fernando M. Guerrero (1873–1929) was the greatest Philippine poet in Spanish. Two painters of note were Juan Luna y Novicio (1857–99) and Félix Resurrección Hidalgo y Padilla (1853–1913). Contemporary writers who have won recognition include Claro

M. Recto (1890–1960), José García Villa (1914–97), and Carlos Bulosan (1914–56). José A. Estella (1870–1945) is the best-known Filipino composer. Filipino prizefighters have included two world champions, Pancho Villa (Francisco Guilledo, 1901–25) and Ceferino García (1910–81).

⁴⁹DEPENDENCIES

The Philippines has no territories or colonies.

⁵⁰BIBLIOGRAPHY

Brands, H. W. *Bound to Empire: The United States and the Philippines.* New York: Oxford University Press, 1992.

Bresnan, John (ed.). *Crisis in the Philippines: The Marcos Era and Beyond.* Princeton, N.J.: Princeton University Press, 1986.

Carlson, Sevinc, and Robert A. Kilmarx (eds.). *U.S.–Philippines Economic Relations.* Washington, D.C.: Georgetown University Center for Strategic and International Studies, 1971.

Davis, Leonard. *The Philippines: People, Poverty, and Politics.* New York: St. Martin's, 1987.

Dolan, Ronald E. (ed.). *Philippines: A Country Study.* 4th ed. Washington, D.C.: Library of Congress, 1993.

Doronila, Amando. *The State, Economic Transformation, and Political Change in the Philippines, 1946–1972.* New York: Oxford University Press, 1992.

Karnow, Stanley. *In our Image: America's Empire in the Philippines.* New York: Random House, 1989.

Kessler, Richard J. *Rebellion and Repression in the Philippines.* New Haven: Yale University Press, 1989.

Marcos, Ferdinand. *The Democratic Revolution in the Philippines.* 3d ed. Manila: Marcos Foundation, 1974.

Miller, Stuart Creighton. *"Benevolent Assimilation": The American Conquest of the Philippines, 1899–1903.* New Haven, Conn.: Yale University Press, 1982.

O'Brien, Niall. *Revolution from the Heart.* New York: Oxford University Press, 1987.

Patanñe, E. P. *The Philippines in the 6th to 16th Centuries.* Quezon City, Philippines: LSA, 1996.

Pedrosa, Carmen Navarro. *Imelda Marcos.* New York: St. Martin's, 1987.

The Revolution Falters: The Left in Philippines Politics after 1986. Edited by Patricio N. Abinales. Ithaca, N.Y.: Southeast Asia Program, Cornell University, 1996.

Richardson, Jim. *Philippines.* Santa Barbara, Calif.: Clio, 1989.

Rodriguez, Socorro M. *Philippine Science and Technology: Economic, Political and Social Events Shaping Their Development.* Quezon City, Philippines: Giraffe Books, 1996.

Steinberg, David Joel. *The Philippines, a Singular and a Plural Place.* 3rd ed. Boulder, Colo.: Westview, 1994.

Thompson, W. Scott. *The Philippines in Crisis: Development and Security in the Aquino Era 1986–92.* New York: St. Martin's, 1992.

Women's Role in Philippine History: Selected Essays. 2d ed. Quezon City, Philippines: University of Philippines, Center for Women's Studies, 1996.

Wurfel, David. *Filipino Politics: Development and Decay.* Ithaca: Cornell University Press, 1988.

The University of the Philippines Cultural Dictionary for Filipinos. Edited by Thelma B. Kintanar. Quezon City, Philippines: University of Philippines Press and Anvil Publishing, 1996.

Vos, Rob. *The Philippine Economy: East Asia's Stray Cat?: Structure, Finance, and Adjustment.* New York: St. Martin's, 1996.

QATAR

State of Qatar
Dawlat Qatar

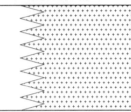

CAPITAL: Doha (Ad-Dawhah).

FLAG: Maroon with white serrated border at the hoist.

ANTHEM: *Qatar National Anthem.*

MONETARY UNIT: The Qatar riyal (QR) of 100 dirhams was introduced on 13 May 1973. There are coins of 1, 5, 10, 25, and 50 dirhams, and notes of 1, 5, 10, 50, 100, and 500 riyals. QR1 = $0.27480 ($1 = QR3.639) as of 31 March 2000.

WEIGHTS AND MEASURES: The metric system is the legal standard, although some British measures are still in use.

HOLIDAYS: Emir's Succession Day, 22 February; Independence Day, 3 September. Muslim religious holidays include 'Id al-Fitr, 'Id al-'Adha', and Milad an-Nabi.

TIME: 3 PM = noon GMT.

1LOCATION, SIZE, AND EXTENT
Comprising an area of 11,000 sq km (4,247 sq mi), the State of Qatar consists of a peninsula projecting northward into the Persian Gulf, extending about 160 km (100 mi) N-S and 90 km (55 mi) E-W. Comparatively, the area occupied by Qatar is slightly smaller than the state of Connecticut. It is bordered on the S by the United Arab Emirates (UAE) and Sa'udi Arabia and has a total boundary length of 623 km (387 mi). In the late 1970s, Sa'udi Arabia and the UAE reportedly reached a border agreement making Sa'udi Arabia Qatar's only land neighbor, but as of 1987, no documentation had been filed with the UN. Qatar also includes a number of islands, of which the most important is Halul. Qatar's boundary disputes with Bahrain disrupted relations between the two countries in the mid-1980s. In 1991, they agreed to refer their dispute over the Hawar Islands to the International Court of Justice at The Hague. In 1992, there was a minor clash between Qatari and Sa'udi troops over a disputed border. That quarrel was resolved with a boundary agreement signed in Cairo in December 1992.

Qatar's capital city, Doha, is located on the Persian Gulf coast.

2TOPOGRAPHY
The terrain is generally flat and sandy, rising gradually from the east to a central limestone plateau. About 56 km (35 mi) long, the Dukhan anticline rises from the west coast as a chain of hills of up to 100 m (325 ft) in height. Some low cliffs mark the northern end of the east coast. The presence of extensive salt flats at the base of the peninsula supports the theory that Qatar was once an island.

3CLIMATE
Qatar's summer, from May to October, is extremely hot. Mean temperatures in June are 42°C (108°F), dropping to 15°C (59°F) in winter. Humidity is high along the coast. Rainfall is minimal.

4FLORA AND FAUNA
Vegetation is generally sparse and typical of Gulf desert regions. The gazelle, once common in Qatar, is now rarely seen. Jerboas (desert rats) and an occasional fox are found. Birds include flamingo, cormorant, osprey, kestrel, plover, lark, and other migrants. Reptiles include monitors, other lizards, and land snakes. Life in the seas around Qatar is considerable and varied, including prawn, king mackerel, shark, grouper, and swordfish.

5ENVIRONMENT
Environmental responsibility is vested in the Ministry of Industry and Agriculture. An Environmental Protection Committee was created in 1984 to monitor environmental problems. Conservation of oil supplies, preservation of the natural wildlife heritage, and increasing the water supply through desalination are high on Qatar's environmental priority list. Air, water, and land pollution are also significant environmental issues in Qatar. In addition to smog and acid rain, the nation has been affected by the air pollution generated during the Persian Gulf War. Pollution from the oil industry poses a threat to the nation's water. The nation's soils have been damaged by pesticides and fertilizers, and its agricultural land is in danger of desertification. Endangered or extinct species include the hawksbill and green sea turtles, and protection has been afforded to a group of rare white oryx.

6POPULATION
The population of Qatar in 2000 was estimated at 749,542. About half the total population consists of foreign workers and their dependents. An estimated 3.4% of the population is 65 years of age or older. The projected population for the year 2005 is 874,000, assuming a crude birthrate of 17 per 1,000 population and a death rate of 4, resulting in a natural rate of change of 1.3% for the period 2000–2005. Average density in 1996 was 49.8 per sq km (129 per sq mi).

It was estimated that 93% of the population lived in urban areas in 2000. The capital city, Doha, on the eastern coast had a 2000 population of 355,000. Two other major towns have grown up around the oil industry: Dukhan, on the west coast, and the port of Umm Sa'id, south of Doha.

7MIGRATION
In 1993, the number of immigrant workers was about 85,000, including Pakistanis, Indians, and Iranians. In 1999 the net migration rate was 23.03 migrants per 1,000 population.

8 ETHNIC GROUPS

In 1999, Gulf and Palestinian Arabs constituted 40% of the population, Pakistanis 18%, Indians 18%, Iranians 10%, and others 14%. The indigenous population (about 100,000) descends from Bedouin tribes which migrated to Qatar during the 1700s.

9 LANGUAGES

Arabic is the national language, but English is widely spoken, and Farsi is used by smaller groups in Doha.

10 RELIGIONS

Islam is the official religion of Qatar and is practiced by the great majority (95%) of the people. The Qataris are mainly Sunni of the Wahhabi sect. There are also small populations of Christians, Hindus, and Bahais.

11 TRANSPORTATION

The modern road system dates from 1967. As of 1995 there were an estimated 1,230 km (764 mi) of highways, of which 1,107 km (688 mi) were paved. Qatar has overland truck routes from Europe through Sa'udi Arabia via the Trans-Arabian Highway and road links with the UAE and Oman. In 1995, there were 95,000 passenger cars and 83,600 commercial vehicles registered. In 1998 there were 4 airports, 2 with paved runways. Doha International Airport is served by more than a dozen international airlines. In 1997 1,165,000 passengers were carried on scheduled domestic and international flights. Qatar maintains modern deepwater ports at Doha and Umm Sa'id, where a tanker terminal is located. Qatar's National Navigation and Transport Co. enjoys a monopoly on arriving shipments. In 1998, the merchant fleet consisted of 22 vessels with 713,014 GRT.

12 HISTORY

Archaeological evidence shows that human habitation existed in Qatar for many centuries prior to the modern age; however, little is known of Qatar's history until the 18th century. The al-Thani family, forebears of the present rulers, arrived in Qatar then from what is now Sa'udi Arabia. During the same century, the al-Khalifah family, who currently rule Bahrain, arrived from Kuwait.

In 1868, Britain intervened on behalf of the Qatari nobles and negotiated the Perpetual Maritime Truce, signed by Muhammad bin Thani, an accord that terminated the Bahraini claim to Qatar in exchange for a tribute payment. In 1872, however, Qatar fell under Ottoman occupation, and Jasim bin Muhammad bin Thani became Turkish deputy-governor of Qatar. Turkish dominion prevailed until the outbreak of World War I and the subsequent withdrawal of the Turks from the Arabian Peninsula. Qatar thereupon established its independence and, in 1916, Sheikh 'Abdallah bin Jasim al-Thani signed a treaty with the UK granting British protection in exchange for a central role for the UK in Qatar's foreign affairs. A 1934 treaty further strengthened this relationship. Commercial quantities of high-quality oil were discovered at Dukhan in 1940, but full-scale exploitation did not begin until 1949.

In 1960, Sheikh Ahmad bin 'Ali al-Thani succeeded his father, who had become too old to rule effectively. Social and economic development during the subsequent decade was disappointing, especially in view of the increasing availability of oil revenues. In January 1968, the UK announced its intention to withdraw its forces from the Persian Gulf States by the end of 1971. Discussions took place among the Trucial States, Bahrain, and Qatar, with a view to forming a federation. The Trucial States formed the UAE, but Qatar could not agree to the terms of the union. On 3 September 1971, the independent State of Qatar was declared. A new treaty of friendship and cooperation was signed with the UK, and Qatar was soon admitted to membership in the Arab League and the UN.

On 22 February 1972, Sheikh Khalifa bin Hamad al-Thani, the deputy emir and prime minister, seized power in a peaceful coup, deposing his cousin, Sheikh Ahmad. Since his accession, Sheikh Khalifa pursued a vigorous program of economic and social reforms, including the transfer of royal income to the state. On 31 May 1977, Sheikh Khalifa appointed Sheikh Hamad bin Khalifa al-Thani, his son, as heir apparent and minister of defense.

In 1981, Qatar, along with the other Persian Gulf states of Bahrain, Kuwait, Oman, Sa'udi Arabia, and the UAE, established the Gulf Cooperation Council (GCC). The GCC attempted to mediate the war between Iran and Iraq, which had erupted in September 1980, but at the same time gave support to Iraq. Qatar's boundary disputes with Bahrain disrupted relations between the two countries in the mid-1980s. In 1991, they agreed to refer their dispute over the Hawar Islands to the International Court of Justice at The Hague. In 1992, there was a minor clash between Qatari and Sa'udi troops over a disputed border. That quarrel was resolved with a boundary agreement signed in Cairo in December 1992.

Qatari forces, although small in size, are active in the collective defense of the GCC and played a helpful role on the allied side in the Gulf War against Iraq.

In 1995, Sheikh Hamad seized power from his father amid a turbulent and secretive attempted coup in February of that year by unknown forces. Sheikh Khalifa, the aging ruler, had spent much of his time before being ousted sailing the Mediterranean on the royal yacht. Also a problem was the aging emir's eccentric method of funding the government, which was to siphon off half of the revenue generated from the country's oil into his personal bank accounts, and pay for government services from those funds. In the late 1980s and early 1990s, the emir felt less inclined to withdraw money than to deposit, and the resulting revenue drain was crippling the economy. When Sheikh Hamad took control of the government, while his father was away on business, the now former emir froze his personal bank accounts, which held, essentially, Qatar's treasury. Estimates of Sheikh Khalifa's personal accounts range from $4–$30 billion.

In 1996, the former emir set up a government in exile in the UAE. The hostile transfer of power has led to friction among the normally contention-free members of the GCC. Also that year, Sheikh Hamad issued writs demanding that his father turn over control of his assets to the state. Initially, the emir had resigned himself to the loss of revenue, but severe budget constraints caused him to cut government spending and, in order to develop the huge off-shore natural gas reserves the country will rely on in the future, huge infrastructure expenses needed to be made.

In 1999, the former emir still claimed to be the legitimate ruler of Qatar, and his allies within the ruling elite were still a source of problems for Sheikh Hamad. However, Sheikh Hamad has continued to rule and implement change in spite of outside threats.

In 1999, Qatar supported the Organization of Oil Exporting Countries (OPEC) efforts to increase oil prices by cutting back crude oil production from March 1999 to April 2000. Qatar was also practicing fiscal discipline and creating low-cost efficiencies. The government was developing a tariff structure with a monthly ceiling on water and electricity services, previously free of charge. In addition, plans were in the works to implement a foreign investment code in agriculture, industry, tourism, and education ventures.

Perhaps most striking, Sheikh Hamad was encouraging political openness. In 1999, women voted and ran for office in municipal elections for the first time. A constitutional committee was charged with drawing up a permanent constitution under which Qatar would have an elected parliament. Political openness was even extended to the media as Qatar's satellite news channel, Al Jareeza, broke a previous taboo with an open discussion and criticism of the state funding of the ruling family.

13GOVERNMENT

Qatar is a monarchy ruled by an emir. In 1970, in anticipation of independence, Qatar promulgated a Basic Law, including a bill of rights, that provides for a 9-member executive Council of Ministers (cabinet) and a 30-member legislative Advisory Council, whose members serve three-year terms. The Council of Ministers, appointed by the emir and led by a prime minister (the head of government), formulates public policy and directs the ministries. Sheikh Khalifa served as acting prime minister from the time of the 1972 coup until ousted by his son in 1995. Since then, Sheikh Khalifa has formed a government in exile in the UAE. The ruling ath Thani family continues to hold a majority of cabinet positions and most of the key posts.

14POLITICAL PARTIES

There are no organized political parties. Security measures against dissidents are firm and efficient. There is no serious opposition movement. Citizens with grievances may appeal directly to the emir.

15LOCAL GOVERNMENT

Municipal councils have been established in Doha, Khor, Ash-Shamal, and several other towns. The councils manage their own planning and development programs, but they remain directly accountable to the Ministry of Municipal Affairs.

16JUDICIAL SYSTEM

The legal system is based on the Shari'ah (canonical Muslim law). The Basic Law of 1970, however, provided for the creation of an independent judiciary, including the Court of Appeal, which has final jurisdiction in civil and criminal matters; the Higher Criminal Court, which judges major criminal cases; the Lower Criminal Court; the Civil Court; and the Labor Court, which judges claims involving employees and their employers. The Shari'ah Court has jurisdiction in family and criminal cases, and may also assume jurisdiction in commercial or civil cases if requested by a Muslim litigant. Non-Muslims may not bring suits as plaintiffs in the Shari'ah Court. As a result, non-Muslim residents have difficulty obtaining full legal recourse in disputes with Qatari nationals.

The losing party in all types of courts may submit their cases to an appeals court. In cases tried by the Shari'ah Court, however, it is possible that the same judge will hear both the original case and the appeal.

The judiciary is attached to three different ministries. The civil courts are subordinate to the Justice Ministry. Whereas Shari'ah courts fall under the Ministry of Islamic Affairs, the prosecutors fall under the Ministry of the Interior.

17 ARMED FORCES

The Qatar security force consists of 8,500 army, 1,800 naval, and 1,500 air force personnel. Military equipment includes 18 combat aircraft, 18 armed helicopters, and 7 missile-equipped coastal patrol boats; most of the weaponry has been purchased from France. Defense spending was $940 million in 1998–99 or 9.6% of GDP.

18INTERNATIONAL COOPERATION

Following independence, Qatar joined both the UN (21 September 1971) and the Arab League. Qatar participates in ESCWA and all the nonregional specialized agencies except IDA and IFC; it is also a member of the WTO. Qatar belongs to OPEC and OAPEC, as well as to G-77 and the GCC.

19ECONOMY

Until recent decades, the Qatar peninsula was an undeveloped, impoverished area, with a scant living provided by the traditional occupations of pearl diving, fishing, and nomadic herding. In 1940, a major oil discovery was made at Dukhan and, in the ensuing decades, oil has been the dominant factor in the Qatari economy. Oil revenues have provided Qataris with per capita incomes comparable those of the industrialized nations of the West. In 1996, oil revenues accounted for more than 30% of GDP, 70% of export earnings, and 66% of government revenues.

The discovery of a vast field of natural gas unassociated with Qatar's oil fields promises to add a new dimension to the economy. In 1987, work on the first phase of the North Gas Field project Phase I, with a production capacity of 800 million cubic feet per day, began and was inaugurated in 1991. While Phase I production is meant for domestic consumption, the Phase II development envisages the production of at least an additional 800 million cubic feet per day for export to Japan as liquefied natural gas. The first shipments to Japan began in January 1997. The project was heavily financed by Japanese banks under terms that will limit Qatar's revenues for the next decade. Qatar has 300 trillion cubic feet of proven natural gas reserves; third in the world behind Russia and Iran. Production of natural gas reached 690 billion cubic feet in 1998.

Other economic activities remain limited. Agriculture has received considerable attention in recent years, but most food is still imported. The state encourages free enterprise, provided it does not conflict with the public interest. Real property, however, may be acquired only by Qatari nationals.

The economy performed sluggishly during the first half of the 1990s but recovered somewhat in 1995 because of a surge in international oil prices and slightly higher rates of oil production. It is estimated that GDP grew by 1.9% in 1995. The government which took over after the coup of 1995 implemented economic reforms that updated the financial sector. In 1998, a temporary drop in international oil prices brought GDP down by 3%. The government expected no growth in 1999 and a further decline for at least three years beyond 2000.

20INCOME

The US Central Intelligence Agency (CIA) reports that in 1998 Qatar's gross domestic product (GDP) was estimated at $12 billion. The per capita GDP was estimated at $17,100. The annual growth rate of GDP was estimated at -3%. The CIA defines GDP as the value of all final goods and services produced within a nation in a given year and computed on the basis of purchasing power parity (PPP) rather than value as measured on the basis of the rate of exchange. It was estimated that agriculture accounted for 1% of GDP, industry 49%, and services 50%.

The World Bank reports that for the same period per capita private consumption (in PPP terms) was $7,310. Private consumption includes expenditures of individuals, households, and non-governmental organizations. Approximately 22% of household consumption was spent on food, 11% on fuel, 5% on health care, and 13% on education.

21LABOR

About 70% of the economically active population is engaged in industry (largely oil-related), commerce, and services. Of the remainder, about 10% work in the agricultural sector and 20% in government. The work force totaled 280,122, or 53.7% of the population, in 1998. No labor may be recruited without the approval of the Department of Labor, and vacancies must be offered first to Qataris, second to Arabs, and only then to foreigners, who comprised 85% of the work force in 1992. Working conditions are governed by the labor laws of 1972, which provide for a 48-hour workweek, (36 hours during the weeks of Ramadan) annual leave, severance notice, and holiday and sickness allowances. Trade unions are prohibited, and strikes are permitted only after the case has been presented to the Labor Conciliation Board and an agreement cannot be reached. Government employees, security forces employees, domestic workers, and members of an employer's family are not permitted to strike, nor are workers in public health or security if such a strike would harm the public or lead to property damage.

The standard work week is 48 hours. Children as young as 15 may work (with parental permission) and many young non-Qataris work in family businesses. However, youths of any nationality do not frequently work in Qatar. While the 1962 labor law gives the Amir the authority to set a minimum wage, he has not chosen to do so.

22AGRICULTURE

Agriculture is constrained by lack of adequate fertile soil, rainfall, and underground water sources; the aquifers which supply the crops are expected to soon run dry. Recently, treated waste water has been used for irrigation. In 1997, only 1.5% (17,000 hectares/42,000 acres) of the total land area was under cultivation. In 1998, 15,000 tons of dates were produced, mostly for local consumption. Rice is also grown for the domestic market.

23ANIMAL HUSBANDRY

According to 1998 estimates, Qatar had 200,000 sheep, 172,000 goats, 47,000 camels, 14,000 head of cattle, and 4 million chickens. Output in 1998 included about 14,000 tons of mutton and 4,000 tons of poultry. Dairy and poultry production meets about 25% of domestic needs. Public, private, and foreign financing have all been used recently to establish or expand dairy and poultry farming.

24FISHING

The Qatar National Fishing Co., formed as a Qatar-UK partnership in 1966, was wholly taken over by Qatar in 1980 and has its own shrimp fishing fleet and processing facilities. Fish and shellfish production in 1997 totaled 5,034 tons (down from 8,136 tons in 1991).

Pearl fishing, once important in Qatar, has virtually disappeared. The principal fishing facilities at Doha and Al Khor have been improved. Overfishing and pollution have adversely affected catches, and there is further concern that oil pollution from the Gulf War may worsen conditions even further.

25FORESTRY

There are no forests in Qatar. Imports of forestry products totaled $16.5 million in 1997.

26MINING

Aside from petroleum and natural gas, Qatar has few exploitable minerals. In 1996, estimated production of cement was 500,000 tons; limestone, 900,000 tons; and sulfur, 61,000 tons.

27ENERGY AND POWER

Qatar's substantial oil reserves, estimated at 3.7 billion barrels in early 1999, dominate the country's economy. For reasons of financial stability and resource conservation, the decision was made in the mid-1970s to limit oil production to no more than 500,000 barrels a day. Production has fluctuated but gradually risen from 310,000 barrels per day in 1983 to 485,000 in 1992. Production in 1998 amounted to 782,000 barrels per day. Offshore production accounts for about 40% of the total, mainly from three fields about 50 miles from the coast. Petroleum

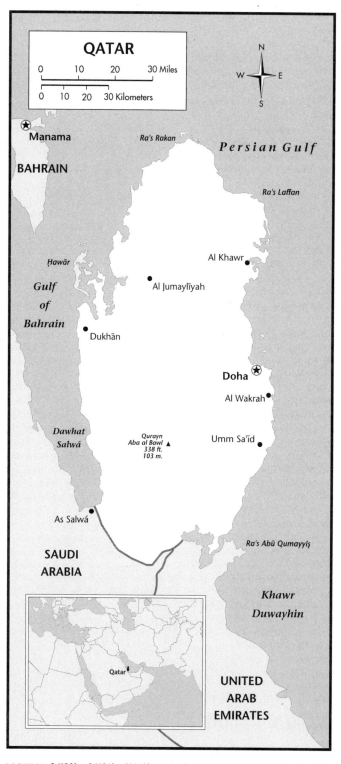

LOCATION: 26°23′ to 24°31′N; 50°43′ to 51°41′E. **BOUNDARY LENGTHS:** Persian Gulf coastline, 378 km (235 mi); UAE, 45 km (28 mi); Sa'udi Arabia, 67 km (42 mi). **TERRITORIAL SEA LIMIT:** 3 mi.

extraction and refining accounts for 50% of GDP; oil revenues for 1995 totaled $2.2 billion.

Total control over oil production and marketing was assumed by the government in early 1977. The Qatar General Petroleum Corp. (QGPC) controls all oil and gas extraction and refining and also acts as an umbrella organization for a number of joint ventures. Qatar's gas reserves, the world's third largest, are estimated at 300 trillion cu ft (8.5 trillion cu m), representing around 5% of the world's known reserves; output was about 630 billion cu ft (17.8 billion cu m) in 1997. Nearly all of Qatar's natural gas reserves are in the North Dome Field, considered to be the largest natural gas field (unassociated with oil) in the world.

Qatar's electrical capacity was 1,445 MW in 1998, as compared with 70 MW in 1970. Power production in 1998 reached 6.7 billion kWh. There are three main electrical power stations, at Ra's Abu Aboud, Al-'Arish, and Ra's Abu Fantas.

28INDUSTRY

Industry in Qatar is restricted by the small size of the population and the paucity of resources other than petroleum and natural gas. Qatar has nevertheless launched an ambitious industrialization plan aimed at diversifying the sources of national income and creating an economy which is not totally dependent on oil revenues. State enterprises include the Qatar Iron and Steel Co. (70% government-owned), which produced 614,000 tons of crude steel in 1995; the Qatar Fertilizer Co. (70% government-owned), responsible for 653,900 tons of ammonia and 886,000 tons of urea in 1995; the Qatar National Cement Co., with an output of 580,000 tons of cement in 1995; and the Qatar Petrochemical Company (80% government-owned), which produces ethylene, polyethylene, and sulfur. It is estimated that industry accounted for almost 7.5% of GDP in 1997 which represented an increase of 0.24% over 1996.

29SCIENCE AND TECHNOLOGY

The Scientific and Applied Research Center, within the University of Qatar at Doha, coordinates the nation's technological development and seeks to develop ways to utilize the country's natural resources. A soil research station is located at Rodet al-Farassa. The Qatar National Museum, founded at Doha in 1975, has an aquarium and botanical garden, and exhibits dealing with geology, botany, and zoology. In 1986, total expenditures on research and development amounted to 6.7 million riyals; 61 technicians and 229 scientists and engineers were engaged in research and development.

30DOMESTIC TRADE

As elsewhere in the Gulf, wholesale and retail operations in Qatar are frequently combined in the same enterprise. Local laws require that commercial agents be of Qatari nationality.

Normal business hours are from 7:30 AM to 12 noon and from 3:30 to 6 PM. Government offices are open from 8 AM to 12:30 PM, and banks from 8 to 12:30 AM. Private sector business hours are usually 8 AM to 12:30 PM and 3 PM to 6:30 PM, Saturday through Thursday. Consumer advertising can be displayed in motion picture theaters, in the press, and on billboards. Radio and television services do not accept advertising.

31FOREIGN TRADE

Qatar's most important commodity exports are crude petroleum (69%), refined petroleum products (6.0%), and natural and manufactured gas (5.2%). Other exports include manufactured fertilizers (3.8%) and steel (3.7%).

In general, imports are distributed among the following categories:

Consumer goods	18%
Food	4%
Fuels	0.6%
Industrial supplies	30%
Machinery	21%
Transportation	17%
Other	0.1%

Principal trading partners in 1998 (in millions of US dollars) were as follows:

COUNTRY	EXPORTS	IMPORTS	BALANCE
Japan	2,532	590	1,942
Korea	481	83	398
Singapore	431	45	386
United States	216	390	-174
Thailand	200	19	181
United Arab Emirates	114	164	-50
Saudi Arabia	72	189	-117
United Kingdom	45	533	-488
Germany	6	247	-241
France	5	428	-423

32BALANCE OF PAYMENTS

In recent years, Qatar has had a persistent trade surplus, while maintaining an overall balance of payments deficit. The gap in the balance of payments is largely due to massive imports in services and person transfers, and somewhat to outflowing capital transfers.

The Qatar Central Bank reports that in 1998 there was a surplus in the balance of goods of $358 million, a substantial decline from the surplus of $897 million posted in 1997. The central bank's numbers are based on an exchange rate of QR3.64 per $1. The decline was the result of a reduced rate of exports and an increased rate of imports. Although oil exports grew in volume, lower prices for oil resulted in less revenue. More than offsetting the surplus on goods, the balance on services posted a record deficit of $2.4 billion. Capital and private transfers, as represented in state borrowings from foreign sources and official and private investments in foreign markets recorded a surplus of $1.34 billion, a 13% increase over 1997. Overall, the 1998 balance of payments registered a deficit of $736 million in 1998. This deficit is largely due to increased borrowing necessary to expand the country's liquefied natural gas (LNG) industry. It is estimated that these deficits will continue for the next several years until revenues from LNG exports from the North Field begin to impact the economy.

33BANKING AND SECURITIES

Qatar's monetary and banking system is headed by the Qatar Central Bank (QCB). The Bank supervises all banks and money exchange companies in Qatar. In 1993, the QCB was established to assume the functions of the Qatar Monetary Agency. The bank was set up in part to make it independent of the Ministry of Finance and Petroleum. The QCB is responsibly for assuring that all banks operating in Qatar comply with international standards and auditing procedures. Total assets of all banks operating in Qatar was estimated at $10.6 billion in 1997. As of 1999, there were 14 banks operating in Qatar: seven national, two Arab, and six foreign. There were also 10 money exchange companies. The Qatar National Bank is the largest with total assets exceeding $5 billion.

There is no stock exchange. Shares in Qatari public companies are traded through banks.

34INSURANCE

In 1999 there were the eleven insurance companies represented in Qatar, seven of which were foreign owned. The Qatar National Insurance Co. has the largest market share and manages the government's insurance business.

35PUBLIC FINANCE

Revenues from oil and gas constitute about 90% of total government income. From 1986 to 1990, the government ran a deficit due to the drop in oil revenues from fallen prices. These deficits often have resulted in the procrastination of payments by the government, which creates a financial difficulty for many private companies. The US Central Intelligence Agency (CIA) estimates that in 1999 Qatar's central government took in revenues of approximately $3.4 billion and had expenditures of $4.3 billion including capital expenditures of $700 million. Overall, the government registered a deficit of approximately $900 million.

36TAXATION

The only tax levied om Qatar (besides customs duties) is a income and profits tax on corporations. The corporate income tax rate ranges from 5% to a maximum of 35% of net profits. There is no other personal or corporate tax liability in Qatar for either foreigners or nationals.

37CUSTOMS AND DUTIES

Import licenses are not required except for liquor (consumption of which is limited to non-Muslims). Customs duties are 4% on all commodities except for alcoholic beverages (50%), tobacco and cigarettes (50%), and records and phonographs (15%). A 20% tariff is imposed on cement, steel bars, and other products that compete with goods produced in Qatar. The importing of pork and any goods from Israel or South Africa is forbidden.

38FOREIGN INVESTMENT

The Qatar government encourages overseas investment in Qatar conditioned on a majority Qatari interest. For example, the Qatar Petrochemical Company is jointly owned by the government of Qatar (80%), the French company Cdf Chimie Atochem (10%), and the Italian company Enichem (10%). Qatar Liquefied Gas Company, which began production in 1996, is a venture between the state-owned Qatar General Petroleum Corporation (QGPC) with 65% and four other foreign firms including the US firm Mobil Oil with a 10% stake. In 1992 the firm signed a sales and purchase Agreement with the Chubu Electric Power Company in Japan for the sale of 4mmtpa of liquefied natural gas per year for a period of 25 years. Another US company, Phillips Corporation signed an agreement with QGPC in May 1977 for establishing a new $750 million petrochemical complex at Umm Said Industrial Area.

Until the mid 1990s, Japanese and European firms were the leading international suppliers to the following industrial sectors: power generation, water desalination, telecommunications, motor vehicles, heavy machinery, and petroleum equipment. Since then, however, the market share of US companies has risen to over 14%.

39ECONOMIC DEVELOPMENT

Qatar follows a policy of diversifying and extending its industrial and commercial activities to reduce the current dependence on oil. Infrastructure, heavy and light industry, agriculture, and fishing have all been development targets. The Industrial Development Committee encourages investment and supervises industrial growth. The government also uses surplus oil revenues on the international money market to protect the purchasing power of those revenues. Qatar is currently preparing to launch some major/minor projects worth about $7 billion: LNG plant expansion of the present fertilizer and petrochemical plants, aluminum smelter, Al-Wusail power/water desalination plant, new Doha international airport, and upgrading and expansion of the offshore oil fields.

Qatar has extended economic assistance to other Arab states, to other developing nations, and to Palestinian organizations.

40SOCIAL DEVELOPMENT

Public health services and education are provided free by the state through the Ministry of Labor and Social Affairs, which also provides help to orphans, widows, and other Qatari nationals in need of assistance.

Both law and Islamic customs closely restrict the activities of Qatari women, who are largely limited to roles within the home. Women are not allowed to obtain a driver's license without the permission of her husband. Shari'ah law governs inheritance and child custody matters and favors men. However, growing numbers of woman are receiving government scholarships to study abroad, and some women work in education, medicine, and the media.

Non-Muslims and Shi'a Muslims experience discrimination in employment and education. They are also unable to bring suits as plaintiffs in Shari'ah courts.

Recent democratic reforms have allowed both men and women to vote and to run for seats on the Central Municipal Council. A constitutional committee convened in 1999 to draft a permanent constitution that would allow for parliamentary elections. Corporal punishment is allowed by law, although amputation is not. In 1995, an American received 90 lashes for alleged homosexual activities.

41HEALTH

Free public health services are extended to all residents of Qatar, regardless of nationality. The Ministry of Health has tried with some success to keep pace with an expanding population. The birth rate in 1999 was 22.2 per 1,000 people, and the fertility rate was 2.6 children per woman living throughout her child-bearing years.

As of 1985 there were 3 hospitals, with a total of 885 beds, and 20 health centers. In 1990 there were 2.9 hospital beds per 1,000 inhabitants. In 1992 there were 1.04 doctors per 1,000 people, with a nurse to doctor ratio of 1.5.

Life expectancy in 1999 was 75.7 years. That same year, infant mortality was 6.9 per 1,000 live births. The overall death rate was 4.6 per 1,000 in 1999.

In 1991–93, 100% of the population had access to safe water, and 100% of the population had access to health care services. The immunization rates for a child under one were as follows in 1994: diphtheria, pertussis, and tetanus (91%); polio (91%); measles (86%); and tuberculosis (94%). Hepatitis vaccination was prevalent (90%) in the same year. In 1993, there were 310 malaria cases. In 1995, no polio or tetanus was reported.

42HOUSING

A "popular housing" scheme provides dwellings through interest-free loans and installment repayments on easy terms. Occupants are required to pay only 60% of the cost of their houses during a period of 20–35 years. To qualify for ownership, an applicant must be a married Qatari national with a limited income, between the ages of 20 and 50 years, and unable to build a house on his own. Qataris facing extreme hardship can receive a free house. In 1991–93, 100% of the population had access to safe water.

43EDUCATION

Adult illiteracy in the year 2000 was estimated at 18.7% (males, 19.5%; females, 16.8%) and continues to decline. Education is compulsory and free for all residents 6–16 years of age; a 100% attendance rate for primary levels is the immediate target. As of 1996, there were 174 schools with 5,864 teachers and 53,631 pupils at the primary level. Student-to-teacher ratio stood at 9 to one. Secondary level schools had approximately 4,000 teachers and 38,594 pupils in the same year. All children receive free books, meals, transport, clothing, and boarding facilities if required. Scholarships for higher education abroad are given to all who qualify.

The leading higher educational institution is the University of Qatar, founded at Doha in 1973. In addition to faculties of education, science, humanities, social sciences, Islamic studies, and engineering, the university comprised a Language Teaching Institute (founded in 1972) and a Regional Training Center, established in 1979 with UNDP technical assistance. Enrollment in all higher level institutions in 1997 was 8,475 pupils, with 643 teaching staff.

44LIBRARIES AND MUSEUMS

The Qatar National Library in Doha (founded in 1962) has 244,000 volumes. The University of Qatar library has 335,000 volumes. The British Council maintains a collection of 10,000 volumes. The Qatar National Museum in Doha has five major sections: the old Amiri Palace (11 buildings), and a new palace, aquarium, lagoon, and botanical gardens.

45MEDIA

Qatar enjoys excellent external telephone, telex, and cable facilities. Direct-dial telephone service is available for most parts of Europe, the Middle East, and the US. A second earth satellite station was completed in 1985, and domestic service and capacity are undergoing constant expansion. Radio transmissions include 12 hours per day of English-language service. A French-language service was instituted in 1985. As of 1999 there were 2 AM and 3 FM radio stations and 2 television stations, transmitting mostly in Arabic. There were an estimated 111,200 telephones in 1995, up from 29,000 in 1982. In 1997 there were 268 radios and 273 television sets per 1,000 population.

In 1999, there were four daily newspapers. Commercial publications available in Qatar (with 1999 circulation figures) include the daily newspapers *Al-'Arab* (25,000), *Ar-Rayah* (25,000), *Al-Sharq* (40,000), *Al-Usbun* (15,000), and *Gulf Times* (15,000); and the political weeklies (with 1995 circulations) *Al-Orouba* (50,000) and *Al-Ahad* (11,000).

The official censorship of the print media was lifted in 1995. Since then, it is said that the print media have been free of government interference. The censorship function continues for movies, videos, and radio and television programming. Also many foreign publications are banned, or have significant portions blacked out.

46ORGANIZATIONS

The Qatar Chamber of Commerce was founded in Doha in 1963. In 1993, there were numerous family, social, and sporting clubs, including the Beacon Club and the Doha Sailing Association.

47TOURISM, TRAVEL, AND RECREATION

International tourists in Qatar numbered 435,000 in 1997, a 33% increase over the previous year. There have been more international conferences and visa restrictions have been relaxed. Qatar Airways increased routes, and a direct flight to London has been implemented. Most of the tourist arrivals are from Europe. Hotels rooms numbered 1,998 with 2,710 beds and a 78% occupancy rate.

In 1999, the UN estimated the cost of staying in Qatar at $143 per day.

48FAMOUS QATARIS

Sheikh Khalifa bin Hamad al-Thani (b.1932) was emir of Qatar from 1972 to 1995. The heir-apparent Sheikh Hamad bin Khalifa al-Thani (b.1948) became emir in June 1995 following a bloodless coup that ousted his father.

49DEPENDENCIES

The State of Qatar has no territories or colonies.

50BIBLIOGRAPHY

Abu Saud, Abeer. *Qatari Women, Past and Present*. New York: Longman, 1984.

American University. *Area Handbook for the Persian Gulf States*. Washington, D.C.: Government Printing Office, 1984.

Anscombe, Frederick F. *The Ottoman Gulf: The Creation of Kuwait, Saudi Arabia, and Qatar*. New York: Columbia University Press, 1997.

Anthony, John Duke. *Arab States of the Lower Gulf*. Washington, D.C.: Middle East Institute, 1975.

Cordesman, Anthony H. *Bahrain, Oman, Qatar, and the UAE: Challenges of Security*. Boulder, Colo.: Westview, 1997.

Crystal, Jill. *Oil and Politics in the Gulf: Rulers and Merchants in Kuwait and Qatar*. New York: Cambridge University Press, 1990.

El Mallakh, Ragaei. *Qatar, Energy & Development*. Dover, N.H.: Croom Helm, 1985.

Graham, Helga. *Arabian Time Machine*. London: Heinemann, 1978.

Kelly, John B. *Britain and the Persian Gulf, 1795–1880*. Oxford: Oxford University Press, 1968.

Long, David. *The Persian Gulf*. Rev. ed. Boulder, Colo.: Westview, 1978.

Nafi, Zuhair Ahmed. *Economic and Social Development in Qatar*. Dover, NH: F. Pinter, 1983.

Unwin, P. T. (ed.). *Qatar*. World Bibliographic Series. Santa Barbara, Calif.: ABC-Clio, 1982.

Zahlan, Rosemarie Said. *The Creation of Qatar*. London: Croom Helm, 1979.

SAMOA

Independent State of Samoa

Malo Sa'oloto Tuto'atasi o Samoa i Sisifo

CAPITAL: Apia.

FLAG: The upper left quarter of the flag is blue and bears five white, five-rayed stars representing the Southern Cross; the remainder of the flag is red.

ANTHEM: *The Flag of Freedom.*

MONETARY UNIT: The Samoan tala (WS$) is a paper currency of 100 sene. There are coins of 1, 2, 5, 10, 20, and 50 sene and 1 tala, and notes of 2, 5, 10, 20, and 100 talas. WS$1 = US$0.3247 (US$1 = WS$3.080) as of 31 March 2000.

WEIGHTS AND MEASURES: British weights and measures are used.

HOLIDAYS: New Year's, 1–2 January; Anzac Day, 25 April; Independence Holidays (first three workdays of June); Labor Day, 7 August; Arbor Day, 3 November; National Women's Day, 24 November; Christmas Day, 25 December; Boxing Day, 26 December. Movable religious holidays are Good Friday, Easter, Easter Monday, and Whitmonday.

TIME: 1 AM = noon GMT.

¹LOCATION, SIZE, AND EXTENT

Samoa consists of the islands of Savai'i and Upolu and several smaller islands, of which only Manono and Apolima are inhabited. The group, situated almost centrally both in the Pacific Ocean and among the South Sea islands, has a total land area of 2,860 sq km (1,104 sq mi), extending 150 km (93 mi) ESE–WNW and 39 km (24 mi) NNE–SSW. Savai'i and Upolu, separated by the Apolima Strait at a distance of nearly 18 km (11 mi), have a combined coastline of 403 km (250 mi). Comparatively, the area occupied by Samoa is slightly smaller than the state of Rhode Island.

²TOPOGRAPHY

The islands are volcanic, with coral reefs surrounding most of them. Rugged ranges rise to 1,100 m (3,608 ft) on Upolu and 1,857 m (6,094 ft) on Savai'i. Apolima is a volcanic crater whose wall is pierced by a passage that connects its harbor with the sea. Manono, about 70 m (230 ft) high, consists chiefly of coral sand. The islands are in an area of active volcanism. Severe eruptions occurred in Savai'i during 1905–11.

³CLIMATE

The climate is tropical, but because of the oceanic surroundings, temperature ranges are not considerable. The hottest month is December, and the coldest is July; the mean daily temperature is about 27°C (81°F). The year is divided into a dry season (May to October) and a wet season (November to April). Rainfall averages 287 cm (113 in) annually, and the average yearly relative humidity is 83%. Although the islands lie outside the normal track of hurricanes, severe storms occurred in 1889, 1966, and 1968. Trade winds from the southeast are fairly constant throughout the dry season.

⁴FLORA AND FAUNA

Lush vegetation covers much of the land. Along the coast there are mangrove forests, pandanus, Barringtonia, hibiscus, and strand vegetation, commonly found throughout the Pacific. The adjacent lowland forest, which originally stretched inland over the lower slopes of the mountains, has been cut down extensively on Upolu and in more limited areas on Savai'i. Inland and at higher elevations, the rain forests contain trees and lianas of many genera and species. The higher elevations of Savai'i contain moss forest and mountain scrub.

Fifty species of birds are found; 16 of these are seabirds, many of which visit Samoa only during the breeding season. Sixteen of the 34 species of land birds are indigenous. Among the latter are small doves, parrots, pigeons, and wild ducks. The most interesting bird, scientifically, is the tooth-billed pigeon (*Didunculus strigirostris Peale*), which some ornithologists regard as the connecting link between bird life of the present and the tooth-billed birds of zoological antiquity.

The only indigenous mammals in Samoa are the rat (*Mus exulans Peale*) and the flying fox (*Pteropus samoensis Peale*). Numerous species of birds and mammals, chiefly domesticated, have been introduced by the Samoans and Europeans. Two species of snakes, several different lizards, and the gecko are found. Insect life includes many species of moths, beetles, spiders, and ants. The mosquito (*Stegomyia pseudoscutellaris*) is a carrier of human filaria.

⁵ENVIRONMENT

Samoa's environmental problems include soil erosion, damage to the nation's forests, and the need for protection of its wildlife. According to United Nation's sources, the forests are eliminated at a rate of 4–8,000 ha per year due to the expansion of farming activity. The lack of adequate sewage disposal facilities, as well as siltation and industrial by-products, threaten the nation's marine habitat's. Samoa's water supply is too small to support its current population. Threatened species include the insular flying fox and Samoan flying fox.

⁶POPULATION

The population of Samoa in 2000 was estimated at 235,302. An estimated 4.5% of the population is 65 years of age or older. The

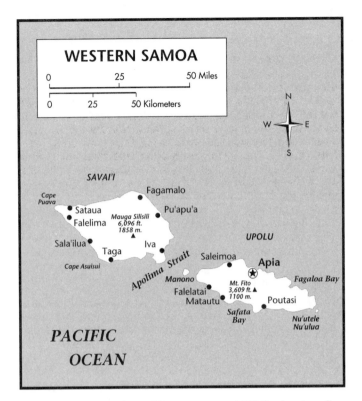

WESTERN SAMOA

SAVAI'I

Cape Puava
Sataua
Falelima
Mauga Silisili
6,096 ft.
1858 m.
Sala'ilua
Taga
Iva
Cape Asuisui
Apolima Strait

Fagamalo
Pu'apu'a

UPOLU
Saleimoa
Apia
Manono
Fagaloa Bay
Falelatai
Mt. Fito
3,609 ft.
1100 m.
Matautu
Poutasi
Safata Bay
Nu'utele
Nu'ulua

PACIFIC OCEAN

LOCATION: 13° to 15°s; 171° to 173°w. **BOUNDARY LENGTHS:** Savai<ayni coastline, 188 km (117 mi); Upolu coastline, 183 km (114 mi). **TERRITORIAL SEA LIMIT:** 12 mi.

projected population for the year 2005 is 262,000, assuming a crude birthrate of 25 per 1,000 population and a death rate of 5, resulting in a natural rate of change of 2.0% for the period 2000–2005. The population density in 1996 was 75 per sq km (195 per sq mi).

It was estimated that 22% of the population lived in urban areas in 2000. Apia, the capital city and only major town, had a 2000 population of 33,000.

7MIGRATION

Under German colonial rule, many Chinese laborers were imported to work on plantations. More recently, there has generally been a net annual loss of population through migration. Emigration (estimated at 5,278 in 1988) consists mainly of students going to New Zealand to continue their education, and Samoans seeking work there. In addition, several thousand Samoans live in American Samoa and other parts of the US. The total abroad in these countries and Australia was estimated at 76,200 in 1989.

The migration rate in 1999 was -0.39 migrants per 1,000 population.

8ETHNIC GROUPS

Samoans comprise 92.6% of the total population. The Samoans are the second-largest branch of the Polynesians, a people occupying the scattered islands of the Pacific from Hawaii to New Zealand and from eastern Fiji to Easter Island. Most of the remaining Samoans are of mixed Samoan and European or Asian descent. Euronesians (persons of European and Polynesian descent) make up 7% of the total, and Europeans constitute 0.4%.

For many years, all inhabitants of Samoa were accorded a domestic status as Samoan or European. Residents are now officially classed as either citizens or foreigners. Among Samoan citizens, however, the distinction between persons of Samoan or European status is still recognized. Most Samoans live in foreshore villages, while non-Samoans predominate in Apia and its environs.

9LANGUAGES

Samoan is the universal language, but both Samoan and English are official. Some Chinese is also spoken. Most of the part-Samoans and many others speak English, and it is taught in the schools.

10RELIGIONS

Over 99% of Samoans profess some form of Christianity, and religious observance is strong among all groups. The Congregational Christian Church of Western Samoa, a successor to the London Missionary Society, is self-supporting and is the largest religious body in the country, comprising about 43% of the population in 1999. The Roman Catholic (21%) and Methodist churches (17%) also had large followings in 1999. The Mormon (10%) and Seventh-Day Adventist (about 3%) churches, the Baha'is, Muslims, and a number of other denominations have smaller congregations located in various parts of the country.

11TRANSPORTATION

The road system in 1996 totaled 790 km (491 mi), of which 322 km (200 mi) were paved; most are on the northern coast of Upolu. Buses and taxis provide public transport. In 1995 there were 1,068 passenger cars and 1,169 commercial vehicles.

Diesel-powered launches carry passengers and freight around the islands, and small motor vessels maintain services between Apia and Pago Pago in American Samoa. Fortnightly cargo and passenger connections are maintained with New Zealand, and scheduled transpacific services connect Samoa with Australian, Japanese, UK, and North American ports. Apia is the principal port; Asau, on Savai'i, was opened as a second deep-sea port in 1972.

As of 1998, there were 3 airports, only 1 of which had a paved runway. Faleolo Airport, 35 km (22 mi) west of Apia, is the principal air terminal. Polynesian Airlines provides daily air connections with Pago Pago and regularly scheduled flights to other Pacific destinations; through Pago Pago there are connecting flights to New Zealand, Australia, and the US. Air Samoa and Samoa Aviation provide internal air services between Upolu and Savai'i, and Hawaiian Airlines provides direct service between Honolulu and Faleolo and commuter service between Faleolo and Pago Pago. In 1997, 75,000 passengers were carried on scheduled domestic and international flights.

12HISTORY

Archaeological evidence on Upolu indicates that Samoa was colonized by maritime traders of the Lapita culture at least as early as the 1st millennium BC. From the mid-13th century AD, genealogies, important titles, traditions, and legends give considerable information on the main political events. The first Europeans to sight the islands were the Dutch explorer Jacob Roggeveen in 1722 and the French navigator Louis de Bougainville in 1768. But the world knew little about Samoa until after the arrival of the missionary John Williams in 1830 and the establishment of the London Missionary Society.

Williams' arrival coincided with the victory of one group of chiefs over another, ending a series of violent internecine wars. Runaway sailors and other Europeans had already settled among the Samoans and had assisted the chiefs in their campaigns. Whalers also visited the islands, and from time to time the warships of great powers visited Apia to oversee the activities of whaling crews and settlers. Naval officers and missionaries both began to consult with the dominant group of chiefs as if it represented a national government and to treat its leader as a king. In time, semiofficial representatives of Great Britain and the US were stationed in Apia. Between 1847 and 1861, the US appointed a commercial agent, and Britain and the city of Hamburg appointed consuls.

Factional rivalries took a new turn as British, US, and German consular agents, aided sometimes by their countries' warships, aligned themselves with various paramount chiefs. Intrigues among the chiefs and jealousies among the representatives of the great powers culminated in civil war in 1889. In the Berlin Treaty, which followed, Britain, the US, and Germany set up a neutral and independent government under King Malietoa Laupepea, and their consuls were authorized to constitute Apia as a separate municipality. The death of King Malietoa in 1898 led to a dispute over the succession, and the three powers intervened once again. In 1899, they abolished the kingship, and in 1900, they signed a series of conventions that made Samoa a German protectorate. The German administration continued to experience difficulties, leading to the exile of several Samoan leaders and the suspension of others from office. With the outbreak of World War I in 1914, New Zealand military forces occupied Samoa, and from 1919 to 1946, New Zealand administered the islands as a mandate of the League of Nations.

In 1927, local opposition to the New Zealand administration among both the Samoan and the European communities resulted in the formation of a nationalistic organization known as the Mau, which embarked on a program of civil disobedience. Its members withdrew from political life, from schools, and from all contact with the government. The protests lasted in one form or another until 1936, when the leaders of the Mau reached an agreement with the administration and reentered the political life of the territory.

In 1946, a trusteeship agreement was approved by the UN General Assembly, and New Zealand formally committed itself to promote the development of Samoa toward ultimate self-government. The passage of the Samoa Amendment Act of 1947 and a series of further amendments governed Samoa's subsequent evolution toward independence. An Executive Council was reconstituted in 1957, and the New Zealand high commissioner withdrew from the Legislative Assembly, which thenceforth was presided over by an elected speaker. In 1959, an executive cabinet was introduced, and in 1960, the constitution of the Independent State of Samoa was adopted. This was followed by a plebiscite under UN supervision in 1961 in which an overwhelming majority of voters approved the adoption of the constitution and supported independence.

On 1 January 1962, Samoa became an independent nation under the name of Western Samoa. Tupua Tamasese Meaoli and Malietoa Tanumafili II became joint heads of state. When the former died on 5 April 1963, the latter became the sole head of state. Fiame Faumuina Mataafa was independent Western Samoa's first prime minister (1962–70) and served again in that post from 1973 until his death in 1975.

During the late 1970s and early 1980s, Western Samoa suffered from a worsening economy and growing political and social unrest. A divisive public-sector strike from 6 April to 2 July 1981 cut many essential services to a critical level. The leadership of Tupuola Taisi Efi, who later became head of the Christian Democratic Party and was prime minister from 1976, was successfully challenged by the Human Rights Protection Party (HRPP), which won the February 1982 general election. Judicial rulings subsequently nullified some of the election results, and Tupuola returned to power from September to December. On 30 December 1982, however, a second HRPP government was formed, with Tofilau Eti as prime minister. Controversy erupted in 1982 over the signing by the HRPP government in August of a protocol with New Zealand that reduced substantially the right

of Western Samoans to New Zealand citizenship. Tofilau resigned in December 1985, and Va'ai Kolone became prime minister in January 1986 as head of a new coalition government comprised of 15 CDP members and 12 former HRPP members. Tupuola was named deputy prime minister of the new government. In April 1988, Tofilau Eti was again appointed prime minister and approved by the legislative assembly.

In 1991, Western Samoa held its first elections under an arrangement of universal suffrage that was instituted after a national referendum passed in 1990. In that election, the HRPP won 28 of 47 seats and Tofilau once again became prime minister. In elections held 26 April 1996, Tofilau Eti retained his post as prime minister.

In July 1997, the country officially changed its name from Western Samoa to Samoa following a June affirmative vote by the legislative assembly. Tofilau Eti resigned due to poor health in November 1998 and died in March 1999 at the age of 74. He was succeeded by deputy prime minister, Tuila'epa Sailelel Malielegaoi

13GOVERNMENT

Executive power is vested in the head of state. Although Malietoa Tanumafili II, head of state in 1962, had lifetime tenure, the constitution took effect 1 January that year, it provides for his successors to be elected for a term of five years by the Fono, or Legislative Assembly. The powers and functions of the head of state are far-reaching. All legislation must have his assent before it becomes law. He also has power to grant pardons and reprieves and to suspend or commute any sentence by any court. Executive authority is administered by a cabinet consisting of a prime minister and eight other ministers appointed by him. The head of state and the cabinet members comprise the Executive Council.

The parliament consists of the head of state and the Fono, which comprises 1 elected member from each of 45 Samoan constituencies and 2 members elected by persons whose names appear on the individual voters' roll. The election of the 45 Samoan members is by universal adult suffrage, but candidates for office are confined to some 20,000 matai, or chiefs. Citizens of non-Samoan origin who qualify for registration on the individual voters' roll elect the two other members by universal suffrage.

14POLITICAL PARTIES

Technically, candidates for public office campaign as individuals, but political parties are becoming increasingly important. The Human Rights Protection Party (HRPP) was founded in 1979 as an opposition party to the government of Prime Minister Tupuola Efi. Tupuola's followers, although not yet formally organized, had, in effect, constituted the ruling party. Following the elections of 27 February 1982, the HRPP was able to command 23 votes in the Fono, as compared with 22 for Tupuola's party. The HRPP leader, Va'ai Kolone, was chosen as prime minister, but in September the Supreme Court, upholding charges of electoral fraud, voided the election of two HRPP candidates, including the prime minister himself. Tupuola was then named prime minister, but by-election victories soon restored the HRPP majority in the Fono, and in December his government fell. On 30 December 1982, Tofilau Eti, the new HRPP leader, was chosen prime minister. He remained prime minister following the February 1985 elections, in which the HRPP captured 31 of the 47 seats, but resigned that December after his budget failed to win approval and the head of state refused to call new elections. In January 1986, a new coalition government led by Va'ai Kolone was formed.

Tofilau Eti, leader of the HRPP, was reelected Prime Minister in April 1988 as the result of a contested election that was settled by a judge flown in from New Zealand. A gradual deterioration in the bilateral relationship between Samoa and New Zealand continued with a dispute concerning the special immigration quota applied to Samoans. In October 1990 a referendum on the issue of universal suffrage narrowly passed. A proposal to establish an upper legislative chamber composed of traditional chiefs failed. In a general election held in April 1991 the ruling HRPP won 28 of 47 seats in the Fono, and Tofilau was reelected prime minister. Among the new ministers appointed was Fiame Naomi, the first female Cabinet member, as Minister of Education, Youth, Sports and Culture, and Labour. Polling was again held 26 April 1996, and Tofilau Eti remained prime minister.

15 LOCAL GOVERNMENT

With the exception of the Apia area, local government is carried out by the village fono, or council of matai and orators, and where and when necessary, through meetings of matai and orators of a district. The main administrative link between the central government and the outside districts is provided by the part-time officials in each village who act as government agents in such matters as the registration of vital statistics; local inspectors represent the various government departments.

16 JUDICIAL SYSTEM

Court procedure is patterned after practices in British courts. Samoan custom is taken into consideration in certain cases. English is the official language of the court, but Samoan is also used. The Supreme Court has full civil and criminal jurisdiction for the administration of justice in Samoa. It is under the jurisdiction of the chief judge, who is appointed by the head of state, acting on the advice of the prime minister. The Court of Appeal consists of three judges who may be judges of the Supreme Court or other persons with appropriate qualifications.

Magistrates' courts are subordinate courts with varying degrees of authority. The highest, presided over by the senior magistrate, may hear criminal cases involving imprisonment of up to three years or cases involving only fines. The Land and Titles Court has jurisdiction in disputes over Samoan land and succession to Samoan titles. Samoan assessors and associate judges possessing a good knowledge of Samoan custom must be present at all sittings of the court. Lawyers are not permitted to appear in the Land and Titles Court; each party appoints its own leader, usually a chief or an orator. Court decisions are based largely on Samoan custom.

Some civil and criminal matters are handled by village "fonos" (traditional courts) which apply a considerably different procedure than that used in the official western-style courts. The Village Fono Law of 1990 affords legal status to the decision of the village fono and allows appeal from fono decisions to the Lands and Titles Court and to the Supreme Court.

17 ARMED FORCES

Samoa has no armed forces, and relies on its police force for internal security. The government foresees no military development because of financial considerations and the absence of threats from abroad. There are informal defense ties with New Zealand under the terms of the 1962 Treaty of Friendship.

18 INTERNATIONAL COOPERATION

Samoa became a member of the UN on 15 December 1976 and belongs to ESCAP, FAO, IBRD, IDA, IFAD, IFC, IMF, UNESCO, and WHO. The nation also participates in the Asian Development Bank, Commonwealth of Nations, G-77, South Pacific Commission, and South Pacific Forum, and is a signatory of the Law of the Sea. An Inter-Samoa Consultative Committee, made up of representatives from Samoa and American Samoa, holds meetings alternately in both countries to discuss matters of mutual interest. By treaty, New Zealand is the exclusive representative of Samoa in the conduct of its foreign affairs outside the Pacific region.

19 ECONOMY

The economy is based largely on agriculture, which, including fisheries, provides 50% of the GDP and employees two-thirds of the work force, mostly in subsistence farming of food crops. In addition to agricultural exports, tourist revenues and remittances from overseas workers are also important sources of foreign exchange. Economic performance has suffered since 1990 due to the devastation to crops, tourism, and infrastructure caused by cyclones Ofa and Val. In 1993/94 a fungal disease reduced taro production by 97%, threatening the island's basic food crop and causing negative growth in the economy. Samoa has the highest unemployment rate and the lowest wages in Oceania.

20 INCOME

The US Central Intelligence Agency (CIA) reports that in 1997 Samoa's gross domestic product (GDP) was estimated at $470 million. The per capita GDP was estimated at $2,100. The annual growth rate of GDP was estimated at 3.4%. The average inflation rate in 1997 was 2.2%. The CIA defines GDP as the value of all final goods and services produced within a nation in a given year and computed on the basis of purchasing power parity (PPP) rather than value as measured on the basis of the rate of exchange. It was estimated that agriculture accounted for 40% of GDP, industry 25%, and services 35%.

21 LABOR

Cash crops are raised as supplements to subsistence crops. No Samoan is entirely dependent on wages for sustenance; all share in the products of their family lands and can always return to them. The government and WSTEC were by far the next-largest sources of employment, followed by construction, tourism, transportation and communications, and services.

There are only two trade unions in the country, representing workers at the three major banks and the country's only factory. Although small, a trade union movement has been established. Public employees are represented by the Public Service Association. Labor is generally restricted to a 40-hour week. Payment is in cash, and in many cases rations are also supplied to workers either as part of their wages or in addition to them. In most cases, living quarters are provided for plantation workers.

Over the years, thousands of skilled and semiskilled Samoans have left the islands, mainly drawn away by better economic opportunities in New Zealand, Australia, and the United States. Agriculture, forestry and fishing account for 65% of wage employment; services account for 30% and industry for 5%.

The minimum hourly wage was $0.47 in 1999. Samoan labor law also provides for rudimentary safety and health standards, but these standards are not effectively enforced.

Children may not work before the age of 15, but the law does not apply to service rendered to the matai, who sometimes require children to work on village farms. Moreover, increasing numbers of children work as street vendors in Apia.

22 AGRICULTURE

Tropical agriculture occupies 43% of the land area, employs about 60% of the labor force, and makes up about 50% of GDP. Most Samoans grow food crops for home consumption and cash crops for export. Village agriculture, in which the family is the productive unit, involves the largest areas of land, occupies the preponderance of the labor force, and produces the major portion of food and cash crops. Coconut products, cocoa, taro, and bananas are produced for export, and bananas, taro, and ta'amu are grown for local sale. Village plantings are invariably mixed, containing some or all of the following crops: coconuts, cocoa, bananas, taro, ta'amu, breadfruit, sugarcane, yams, manioc, and various fruits. Plantation agriculture has been controlled mainly by non-indigenous residents.

Exports of unprocessed copra have been largely replaced by coconut oil, coconut cream, and copra cake. Due to a decline in world prices, coconut production fell to 95,000 tons in 1992. In 1998, coconut production was estimated at 130,000 tons. Taro (coco yam) production in 1998 amounted to 37,000 tons. Taro production dropped 97% in 1993/94 due to leaf blight, and the government is working on methods to control the disease. Exports of cocoa have fallen in recent years, thereby discouraging production. Since 1991, no production over 1,000 tons has been reported. Banana exports fluctuate greatly from year to year. Exports of agricultural products in 1997 amounted to $8.1 million, while agricultural imports totaled $28.9 million that year.

23 ANIMAL HUSBANDRY

Pigs and cattle form the bulk of the livestock. In 1998, pigs, which are common in the villages, were estimated to number 179,000 and cattle 26,000. A small number of cattle are kept for milk; the remainder are raised for beef. Nearly one-half of the cattle population is owned by WSTEC, the most progressive cattle breeder. Other livestock in 1998 included an estimated 7,000 donkeys and 3,000 horses. Meat production in 1998 was 5,000 tons, 80% of it pork.

24 FISHING

The government has sought to expand the fishing industry, but most fishing is still conducted along the reefs and coasts; deep-sea fishing, save for bonito and shark, is not developed. A $3-million fish market and wharf, built with Japanese aid, was completed in Apia in 1982. The local fish catch, however, steadily fell from 4,020 tons in 1982 to 565 tons in 1991; by 1997 the catch rebounded to 4,590 tons, with tuna comprising about 30%.

25 FORESTRY

The nation's forest area is estimated at 136,000 ha (336,000 acres). Reforestation projects are concentrated on Savai'i, which accounts for 80% of the nation's forest area. A large-scale timber-milling enterprise, established on Savai'i in 1970, began to produce kiln-dried sawn timber and veneer sheets for export. Roundwood production in 1997 was 131,000 cu m, with 53% used as fuel wood. Timber imports were estimated at $741,000 in 1997.

26 MINING

No minerals of commercial value are known to exist in Samoa.

27 ENERGY AND POWER

Samoa has depended heavily on imported energy, but hydroelectric power, first available in 1985, accounted for nearly 40% of electrical generation in 1996. Net electricity generating capacity in 1998 was 19,000 kw, and production totaled 65 million kwh.

28 INDUSTRY

The government has encouraged industrial growth, and manufacturing, geared mainly to processing primary products, is increasing steadily. Industries include food- and timber-processing facilities, a brewery, cigarette and match factories, and small individual enterprises for processing coffee and for manufacturing curios, soap, carbonated drinks, light metal products, garments, footwear, and other consumer products. A coconut oil mill, an additional coconut cream factory, a veneer mill, and a meat cannery began operations in the 1980s. In 1991, the Japanese Yazaki Samsa Company began manufacturing automotive seat belts. The firm also produces electrical wiring systems.

29 SCIENCE AND TECHNOLOGY

New Zealand provides extensive scientific and technical aid to Samoa. Other donors include Japan, the Federal Republic of Germany (FRG), Australia, the US, the UK, and the UNDP. UNESCO has an integrated field office in Apia to promote science in the Pacific States. The National University of Samoa, founded in 1988 at Apia, has a faculty of science. The University of the South Pacific, founded in 1977 at Apia, has a school of agriculture.

30 DOMESTIC TRADE

Apia, the capital, is the center of commercial life. Many firms act as agents for shipping and airlines and for overseas commercial organizations generally. Outside Apia, trading stations, linked with the capital by launch and road transport, collect produce and distribute consumer goods. Several major firms operate about 200 stations in the outer districts and secure a large share of the total commercial business. There are also a number of smaller firms and independent traders. In Apia, various firms and small shops sell imported commodities and domestic products. Office hours are from 8 AM to noon and resume from 1 PM to 4:30 PM.

31 FOREIGN TRADE

The fact that Samoa has a limited number of exports—principally agricultural and timber products—renders its economy extremely vulnerable to weather conditions and market fluctuations. Imports consist chiefly of food, fuels and chemicals, machinery, transportation equipment, and other manufactured articles. The principal exports coconut oil and cream, taro, and automotive seat belts. Also exported are coconuts, copra, cocoa, timber, and clothing. Foodstuffs and industrial supplies account for about 50% of the country's annual imports.

Samoa exports primarily to New Zealand, Australia, American Samoa, Fiji, and Germany. Imports originate mainly from New Zealand, Australia, Fiji, and the US. Principal trading partners in 1998 (in millions of US dollars) were as follows:

COUNTRY	EXPORTS	IMPORTS	BALANCE
Australia	36	24	12
United States	19	11	8
Germany	3	2	1
New Zealand	2	33	-31
Japan	n.a.	17	
Fiji	n.a.	25	
Czech Republic	n.a.	17	

32 BALANCE OF PAYMENTS

In the early 1970s, Samoa's heavy trade deficits were largely offset by tourist revenues, remittances from Samoans working abroad, and long-term investment capital. By the early 1980s, however, rising import costs and declining export earnings led to a critical balance-of-payments situation. By 1992, the external account deficit (excluding grants) had increased to about 28% of GDP.

The US Central Intelligence Agency reports that in 1997 the purchasing power parity of Samoa's exports was $14.6 million while imports totaled $99.7 million resulting in a trade balance of -$85.1 million.

The International Monetary Fund (IMF) reports that in 1998 Samoa had exports of goods totaling $20 million and imports totaling $97 million. The services credit totaled $62 million and debit $29 million. The following table summarizes Samoa's balance of payments as reported by the IMF for 1998 in millions of US dollars.

Current Account		20
Balance on goods	-76	
Balance on services	33	
Balance on income	4	
Current transfers	59	
Capital Account		...
Financial Account		-5
Direct investment abroad	...	
Direct investment in Samoa	...	
Portfolio investment assets	...	
Portfolio investment liabilities	...	
Other investment assets	...	
Other investment liabilities		-5
Net Errors and Omissions		-10
Reserves and Related Items		-5

33BANKING AND SECURITIES

Legislation in 1974 set up the Monetary Board to act as the central bank. The activities of the Monetary Board were taken over in May 1984 by the new Central Bank of Samoa. An Australian bank, ANZ, acquired the government's 25% stake in the Bank of Western Samoa (BWS), becoming its outright owner. The BWS is the largest bank in the country, with assets of about A$16 million (US$13 million). The government has also sold its Post Office Savings Bank (POSB) to a consortium of local businesses. The bank, to be renamed the National Bank of Samoa, is the country's first locally owned commercial bank. The other banks are Pacific Commercial Bank (owned by Westpac, the Bank of Hawaii, and local shareholders) and the Development Bank of Western Samoa.

Parliament passed legislation in early 1988 to allow the setting up of an offshore banking center. More the 1,000 companies have registered in Apia under the new tax haven legislation, contributing substantially to the national budget.

34INSURANCE

There is a private life insurance company in Apia, National Pacific Insurance Ltd., managed by the National Insurance Co. of New Zealand.

35PUBLIC FINANCE

Samoa's financial year ends on 31 December. Government budgets have commonly shown deficits in recent years. The US Central Intelligence Agency (CIA) estimates that in 1997 Samoa's central government took in revenues of approximately $52 million and had expenditures of $99 million including capital expenditures of $37 million. Overall, the government registered a deficit of approximately $47 million. External debt totaled $188 million.

36TAXATION

Individuals and companies are liable for the payment of income tax. The basic nonresident corporate tax rate is 48%, and the resident corporate tax rate is 39%; rates for both domestic and foreign insurance companies are lower. Personal income tax rates range from 5% to 50%. There are also gift, inheritance, and stamp taxes.

37CUSTOMS AND DUTIES

Customs duties provide almost half of current government revenue and are levied on all imports except those specifically exempted. Preferential rates for imports from Commonwealth countries were abolished in 1975.

38FOREIGN INVESTMENT

The government actively promotes the establishment of industries financed by overseas companies. These include milling and logging operations by a US company on Savai'i and by a joint Japanese-Samoan enterprise on Upolu, and a US hotel resort center near Apia.

39ECONOMIC DEVELOPMENT

The government has consistently stressed diversification of agriculture. It has also sought through a series of plans to promote growth in manufacturing, forestry, fishing, hydroelectric power, and tourism which received a boost when the Falento Airport got a new terminal and runway extension in 1985. In 1989, an offshore banking center was launched. New Zealand, Australia, the US, the Asian Development Bank, and the EC are major sources of development aid, and recently, Japan and the FRG have provided technical and financial aid. Assistance from the UN family of organizations totaled US$2.6 million in 1991. The country's fifth development plan (1985–87) called for an investment of WS$146.9 million, WS$114.2 million of it from external sources. Investment increased significantly in 1990 and 1992, mainly due to increased public capital expenditure. External aid has been a major source of public investment financing, providing approximately 68% of capital expenditure in 1991 and 47% in 1992.

40SOCIAL DEVELOPMENT

A social security system was established in 1972 under the Western Samoan National Provident Fund. It provides for employee retirement pensions, disability benefits, and death benefits. Employees contribute 5% of their earnings, and this amount is matched by their employers. Retirement is allowed at age 55. Workers' compensation is funded by employers and is compulsory. This program covers reasonable medical expenses, and is paid for entirely by employer contributions. In addition, a tax on motor fuel is used to finance benefits for victims of motor vehicle accidents.

In Samoan society, obligations to the aiga, or extended family, are often given precedence over individual rights. While there is some discrimination against women, they can play an important role in the traditional social structure, especially female matai, or heads of families. Domestic abuse is common and considered culturally acceptable, except in the most extreme cases. Universal suffrage was enacted in 1990, and the following year a Women's Affairs Ministry was established. In 1996, four females held positions in the 49-member parliament.

Human rights are generally well respected in Samoa.

41HEALTH

The Department of Health oversees health care on the islands. The country is divided into 14 health districts, each under a medical officer. In 1990, there were 50 physicians in the country.

District nurses are stationed at strategic points throughout the islands. Child health clinics, and particularly clinics for young children and infants, are a regular feature of their work. In 1991, 91% of children were vaccinated against measles. A mobile dental clinic operates in the villages, while all schools in Apia are visited at regular intervals by a team of dental practitioners.

Diabetic retinopathy and albuminous are common in Polynesian Samoans. The increase in diabetes in recent decades is linked the Westernization of the Samoan diet.

The life expectancy was 69.8 years in 1999. During the same year, the infant mortality rate was 30.5 per 1,000 births. The birth rate was much higher than the death rate (28.8 vs. 5.4 per 1,000 people).

The immunization rates for children under age one in 1995 were as follows: diphtheria, pertussis, and tetanus (95%); polio

(95%); measles (98%); and tuberculosis (98%). In 1994, there were 18 reported cases of tuberculosis.

In 1994, nearly 53% of men and 18.6% of women were smokers. Only 4 AIDS cases were reported in 1995.

42HOUSING

Most Samoans live in villages in traditional Samoan houses called fales. A fale is usually round or oval, with pebble floors and a thatch roof. It has no walls, being supported on the sides by posts. Coconut-leaf blinds can be lowered to exclude wind and rain. In areas more affected by contact with Europeans, the fale may have a concrete floor, corrugated iron roof, and lattice-work walls. Another fused Samoan-European type, much used by chiefs and pastors, is an oblong concrete house with some walls, often with separate rooms in each corner; like the fale it is open at the sides. Fales are grouped around an open area in the center of the village and have separate cookhouses behind them.

43EDUCATION

The adult literacy rate is estimated to be over 97%. Formal education is provided by the Department of Education and five religious missions. Government and mission schools have a uniform syllabus and common examinations. The government school system is the more comprehensive, with almost all its teachers holding Samoan teachers' certificates. Village schools provide four years of primary schooling. District schools draw the brighter pupils from village schools and educate them through the upper primary level. In the Apia area, urban schools provide a lower- through upper-primary curriculum. A major educational goal has been to make Samoans bilingual, with English as their second tongue. In the senior classes of the primary schools, all instruction is in English. In 1989 there were 37,883 primary school pupils. As of 1996, 85% of all school-aged children attended primary school.

The government maintains secondary schools, in which the medium of instruction is English. Samoa College is patterned after a New Zealand secondary school; each year, 100 pupils from government and mission schools are selected for admission by competitive examination. Vaipouli High School, in Savai'i, provides a general secondary curriculum, and Avele College, in Apia, offers training in modern agricultural methods. In addition, the University of the South Pacific School of Agriculture maintains a campus at Alafua, on the outskirts of Apia. The medium of instruction in mission secondary schools is English, with curriculum and textbooks similar to those used in New Zealand.

Samoa was one of the founders of the regional University of the South Pacific. The National University, which was established in 1984, was upgraded and provided with a new campus in 1997. Other tertiary institutions include the College of Tropical Agriculture and a Trades Training College.

44LIBRARIES AND MUSEUMS

The Nelson Memorial Public Library in Apia has 80,000 volumes. The library of the University of the South Pacific has around 15,000 volumes, and the Legislative Assembly has a library with 6,000 volumes. A bookmobile service operates on Upolu and Savai'i. The National Museum and Culture Center in Apia, established in 1984, includes a local museum, library, and theater and offers crafts workshops. Vailima is home to the Robert Louis Stevenson Museum.

45MEDIA

In 1995 there were 8,000 telephones in use; internal and overseas wireless telegraph services are available. The government-controlled Samoan Broadcasting Service, in Apia, transmits radio programs on two stations in Samoan and English and provides direct broadcasts from the Fono. As of 1999 there was 1 FM radio station and there were 6 television stations. In 1997 there were 323 radios and 25 television sets in use per 1,000 population. There is no domestic television service, but broadcasts may be received from American Samoa.

There are several bilingual weeklies, including the Samoa Weekly (1995 circulation, 4,500), Samoa Observer (3,500), and South Sea Star (2,000). There is one daily, Samoan Times, with a 1995 circulation of 5,000.

The constitution provides for free speech and a free press, and the government is said to respect these provisions in practice.

46ORGANIZATIONS

Among the numerous clubs, societies, and organizations in Samoa are the Chamber of Commerce, Red Cross, Catholic Club, Returned Servicemen's Association, Mothers' Club, Calliope Lodge of Freemasons, Federation of Women's Committees, and the South-East Asia and Pan-Pacific Women's Association.

47TOURISM, TRAVEL, AND RECREATION

Until 1965, official policy in Samoa was opposed to tourism, but during 1966–67 there was a complete reversal of policy. The government hired international tourist consultants to advise it on long-term means of developing a tourist industry. Samoa joined the Pacific Area Travel Association, extended tax holidays and import-duty concessions to hotel building, and appropriated money for the building of new hotels.

The major tourist attractions are the beaches and traditional villages. In Apia is Vailima, the residence of the head of state and once the home of Robert Louis Stevenson; Stevenson's grave is nearby. Pastimes include swimming, water skiing, and fishing. Soccer and cricket are popular local sports. In 1997, there were 68,000 tourist arrivals, and tourism expenditures totaled $39million. That year there were 747 hotel rooms with 1,614 beds. The estimated cost of staying in Apia was $114 per day, according to 1999 UN estimates.

48FAMOUS SAMOANS

The Scottish author Robert Louis Stevenson (1850–94) lived principally on Upolu from 1889 until his death. Samoans famous since independence include Malietoa Tanumafili II (b.1913), who was named head of state in 1962, and Fiame Faumuina Mataafa (d.1975), who served as prime minister from 1962 to 1970 and again from 1973 until his death. Tupuola Taisi Efi (b.1938), was prime minister from 1976 to 1982. Tofilau Eti (b. American Samoa, 1925?) was prime minister from December 1982 to December 1985, when he resigned and was succeeded by Va'ai Kolone.

49DEPENDENCIES

Samoa has no territories or colonies.

50BIBLIOGRAPHY

Freeman, Derek. *Margaret Mead and Samoa: The Making and Unmaking of an Anthropological Myth.* Cambridge, Mass.: Harvard University Press, 1983.

Gilson, R. P. *Samoa 1830 to 1900: The Politics of a Multi-Cultural Community.* New York: Oxford University Press, 1970.

Henderson, Faye. *Western Samoa, A Country Profile.* 2d ed. Washington, D.C.: Library of Congress, 1980.

Lockwood, Brian. *Samoan Village Economy.* New York: Oxford University Press, 1971.

Mead, Margaret. *Coming of Age in Samoa.* London: Penguin, 1961 (orig. 1928).

SA'UDI ARABIA

Kingdom of Sa'udi Arabia

Al-Mamlakah al-'Arabiyah as-Sa'udiyah

CAPITAL: Riyadh (Ar-Riyad).

FLAG: The national flag bears in white on a green field the inscription, in Arabic, "There is no god but Allah, and Muhammad is the messenger of Allah." There is a long white sword beneath the inscription; the sword handle is toward the fly.

ANTHEM: The National Anthem is a short instrumental selection.

MONETARY UNIT: The Sa'udi riyal (SR) is divided into 20 qursh (piasters), in turn divided into 5 halalah. There are coins of 1, 5, 10, 25, 50, and 100 halalah and notes of 1, 5, 10, 50, 100, and 500 riyals. SR1 = $0.267 ($1 = SR3.75) as of 31 March 2000.

WEIGHTS AND MEASURES: The metric system has been officially adopted.

HOLIDAYS: Muslim religious holidays include 1st of Muharram (Muslim New Year), 'Id al-Fitr, and 'Id al-'Adha'.

TIME: 3 PM = noon GMT.

¹LOCATION, SIZE, AND EXTENT

Sa'udi Arabia constitutes about four-fifths of the Arabian Peninsula in Southwest Asia. Although Sa'udi Arabia is known to be the third-largest country in Asia, after China and India, its precise area is difficult to specify because several of its borders are incompletely demarcated. According to the UN, the nation has an area of 1,960,582 sq km (756,985 sq mi); it extends 2,295 km (1,426 mi) ESE–WNW and 1,423 km (884 mi) NNE–SSW. Comparatively, the area occupied by Sa'udi Arabia is slightly less than one-fourth the size of the US. Sa'udi Arabia is bounded on the N by Jordan and Iraq, on the NE by Kuwait, on the E by the Persian Gulf, Qatar, and the United Arab Emirates (UAE), on the SE by Oman, on the S and SW by Yemen and on the W by the Red Sea and the Gulf of Aqaba, with a total estimated boundary length of 7,055 km (4,384 mi).

An agreement was reached in 1965 whereby the Neutral Zone separating Sa'udi Arabia from Kuwait was divided administratively between the two countries. A dispute between Sa'udi Arabia and the newly formed UAE over control of the Buraymi oasis was settled in 1974, when they reached an accord fixing their common border. An agreement dividing the Neutral Zone between Sa'udi Arabia and Iraq was reportedly reached in 1975 and confirmed in 1981, but as of early 1988, no details of the agreement had been filed with the UN. In the Ar-Rub' al-Khali ("Empty Quarter") of the southeast, Sa'udi Arabia's borders with Oman and the PDRY are not yet fully defined.

Sa'udi Arabia's capital city, Riyadh, is located in the east central part of the country.

²TOPOGRAPHY

A narrow plain, the Tihamat ash-Sham, parallels the Red Sea coast, as do, farther north, the Hijaz Mountains (with elevations of 910–2,740 m/3,000–9,000 ft), which rise sharply from the sea. The highest mountains (over 2,740 m/9,000 ft) are in 'Asir in the south. 'Asir is a region extending about 370 km (230 mi) along the Red Sea and perhaps 290–320 km (180–200 mi) inland. East of the Hijaz, the slope is more gentle, and the mountains give way to the central uplands (Najd), a large plateau ranging in elevation

from about 1,520 m (5,000 ft) in the west to about 610 m (2,000 ft) in the east. The Dahna, a desert with an average width of 56 km (35 mi) and an average altitude of 460 m (1,500 ft), separates Najd from the low plateau (Hasa) to the east (average width, 160 km/100 mi; average altitude, 240 m/800 ft). This, in turn, gives way to the low-lying Gulf region.

At least one-third of the total area is sandy desert. The largest of the deserts is the famed Ar-Rub' al-Khali in the south, with an area of roughly 647,500 sq km (250,000 sq mi). An-Nafud, its northern counterpart, has an area of about 57,000 sq km (22,000 sq mi). There are no lakes, and except for artesian wells in the eastern oases, there is no perennially flowing water.

³CLIMATE

The climate is generally very dry and very hot; dust storms and sandstorms are frequent. Day and night temperatures vary greatly. From May to September, the hottest period, daytime temperatures reach 54°C (129°F) in the interior and are among the highest recorded anywhere in the world. Temperatures are slightly lower along the coasts, but humidity reaches 90%, especially in the east, which is noted for heavy fogs. From October through April, the climate is more moderate, with evening temperatures between 16° and 21°C (61° and 70°F). Average annual rainfall is 9 cm (3.5 in), with most rain falling from November to May. Between 25 and 50 cm (10 and 20 in) of rain falls in the mountainous 'Asir area, where there is a summer monsoon.

⁴FLORA AND FAUNA

Vegetation is sparse, owing to aridity and soil salinity. The date palm, mangrove, tamarisk, and acacia are prevalent. Wild mammals include the oryx, jerboa, fox, lynx, wildcat, monkey, panther, and jackal. The favorite game bird is the bustard. The camel and Arab stallion are renowned, as is the white donkey of Al-Ahsa. Fish abound in the coastal waters, and insects, scorpions, lizards, and snakes are numerous.

5ENVIRONMENT

The Sa'udi government has traditionally not given priority to environmental protection, but in recent years it has become concerned about the continuing encroachment of sand dunes on agricultural land, the preservation and development of water resources, and pollution and sanitation problems. Legislation enacted in May 1978 forbids the felling of trees and regulates the protection of forestland. Sa'udi Arabia's natural environment was threatened by the Persian Gulf War. The dumping of up to six million barrels of oil in the surrounding waters and the destruction of Kuwait's oil wells by fire polluted the nation's air and water. Sa'udi Arabia has 0.5 cubic miles of water with 47% used for farming and 8% used for industrial purposes. Twenty-six percent of the nation's rural dwellers do not have pure water. At current rates of consumption, the nation's water supply may be exhausted in 10–20 years. Sa'udi Arabia's cities produce 4.8 million tons of solid waste per year. Sa'udi Arabia has signed the 1954 Convention for the Prevention of Pollution of the Sea by Oil. Under the 1976–80 and 1980–85 development plans, new desalination facilities were built, and urban sewage, waste, and storm drainage facilities were constructed.

The Directorate General for Environmental Protection is responsible for environmental protection measures and preservation of natural resources. In the late 1970s, the 'Asir Kingdom Park, in the southwest, was created to preserve the landforms, flora, and fauna of the 'Asir region, which forms part of the Great Rift Valley. As of 1994, 2.9% of Sa'udi Arabia's total land area was protected. In the same year, nine of the nation's mammal species and 12 types of birds were endangered. Two type of plants were threatened with extinction. Endangered or extinct species in Sa'udi Arabia include the Asiatic cheetah (possibly extinct), South Arabian leopard, two species of gazelle (Sa'udi Arabian dorcas and goitered), northern bald ibis, and two species of turtle (green sea and hawksbill).

6POPULATION

The population of Saudi Arabia in 2000 was estimated at 22,245,751. An estimated 2.8% of the population is 65 years of age or older. The projected population for the year 2005 is 26,336,000, assuming a crude birthrate of 37 per 1,000 population and a death rate of 4, resulting in a natural rate of change of 3.3% for the period 2000–2005. The population rate of change between 1995 and 2000 was 3.4%. The population density in 1998 was 10 per sq km (26 per sq mi).

Urbanization has proceeded swiftly. It was estimated that 86% of the population lived in urban areas in 2000, up from 66% in 1980. The capital city, Riyadh, and its surrounding metropolitan area had a 2000 population of 3,328,000. Estimates of the population in other major metropolitan areas in 2000 were: Jiddah, the principal port, 1,812,000; and Mecca (Makkah), containing Islam's holiest shrine, 920,000. Other major cities include At-Ta'if, 204,857; Medina (Al-Madinah), the second-holiest city of Islam, 500,000; Ad-Dammam, 127,884; and Al-Hufuf, 101,271. Saudi Arabia's next census is slated for 2002.

7MIGRATION

Emigration is limited. Immigration of professionals, technicians, and others from the surrounding Arab states and growing numbers from outside the region has been spurred by the development of the oil industry and by the lack of adequately trained and educated Sa'udi personnel. Palestinian Arabs, displaced by the establishment of the state of Israel, are the chief immigrant group. In the early 1990s there were significant numbers of expatriate workers from the US, European countries, Turkey, Jordan, Syria, Jordan, Kuwait, Yemen, the Republic of Korea (ROK), Pakistan, India, Sri Lanka, and the Philippines. In 1990 when Iraq invaded Kuwait, Sa'udi Arabia reacted by expelling workers from Jordan, Yemen, and Palestinians, for their countries' support of Iraq. The foreign population was 4,624,459 in 1992 (27% of the total population). After the Gulf War, 93,000 Iraqis were granted temporary asylum. Since then, 60,000 Iraqis were returned under the POW exchange. In April 1997, 20,800 had resettled in 33 different countries, 3,010 had voluntarily repatriated, and 9,000 were still in camps in Sa'udi Arabia. By September 1999, 5,390 Iraqi and 158 Afghan refugees were living in the Rafha Camp administered by the government. Another 266 refugees were of concern to the UNHCR, including Sudanese, Somalis, and Ethiopians, who were living in various parts of the country. In 1999, the net migration rate was 1.4 migrants per 1,000 population.

8ETHNIC GROUPS

The great majority (90%) of the Sa'udis have a common Arabian ancestry, and the population is homogeneous in religion and language. Divisions are based mainly on tribal affiliation or descent, the primary distinction being between groups with a tradition of being sedentary agriculturalists or traders, and the Bedouins, who have a tradition of nomadic pastoralism. The two groups traditionally have been antagonistic. There has been some loosening of tribal ties, however, caused by rapid economic development. Afro-Asians account for the remaining 10% of the population. Admixtures of Turks, Iranians, Indonesians, Pakistanis, Indians, various African groups, and other non-Arab Muslim peoples appear in the Hijaz, mostly descendants of pilgrims to Mecca.

9LANGUAGES

Arabic, the native language of the indigenous population, is a Semitic language related to Hebrew and Aramaic. Local variations in pronunciation do not prevent oral communication between people from opposite sections of the Arabian Peninsula. The language is written in a cursive script from right to left. The 28 letters of the alphabet have initial, medial, and terminal forms; short vowels are seldom indicated. Most business people and merchants in oil-producing areas and commercial centers understand English. Government correspondence must be written in Arabic.

10RELIGIONS

About 85% of the people of Sa'udi Arabia are Sunni Muslims. The dominant form of Islam is Wahhabism, a fundamentalist Muslim reform movement first preached by the 18th-century religious leader Muhammad bin 'Abd al-Wahhab. Most other Sa'udis up to 15% are Shi'i Muslims. The holy city of Mecca is the center of Islam and the site of the sacred Ka'bah sanctuary, toward which all Muslims face at prayer. A pilgrimage to Mecca is one of the five basic obligations of Islam and is incumbent on every Muslim who is physically and financially able to perform it.

There are several thousand foreign Christian employees—Arab, US, and European. Jews have not been allowed to enter the country since the establishment of the state of Israel in 1948 except under special circumstances.

11TRANSPORTATION

Until recent decades, the camel was the chief means of transportation in Sa'udi Arabia, but enormous strides have been made since the early 1970s. By 1996 there were 162,000 km (100,667 mi) of highways, of which 69,174 km (42,985 mi) were paved. Modern roads link Jiddah, Mecca, Medina, At-Ta'if, and Riyadh; a new highway connects Sa'udi Arabia with Jordan, and a causeway completed in 1986 offers a direct connection with Bahrain. In 1995, passenger car registrations totaled 1.7 million and there were 1.1 million commercial vehicles. The Sa'udi Government Railroad, which operates between Ad-Dammam

LOCATION: 16°23′ to 32°14′N; 34°30′ to 56°22′W. **BOUNDARY LENGTHS:** Jordan, 744 km (462 mi); Iraq, 895 km (556 mi); Kuwait, 163 km (101 mi); Persian Gulf coastline, 549 km (341 mi); Qatar, 67 km (42 mi); UAE, 586 km (364 mi); Oman, 676 km (420 mi); Yemen 1,458 km (906 mi); Red Sea and Gulf of Aqaba coastlines, 1,889 km (1,174 mi). **TERRITORIAL SEA LIMIT:** 12 mi.

and Riyadh over a length of 575 km (357 mi), was built by the Arabian American Oil Co. (ARAMCO) during the 1950s. Railroad lines totaled 1,390 km (864 mi) of standard-gauge track at last estimate.

In 1998 there were 205 airports, 70 with paved runways. Major airports include Dhahran International at Dhahran, King Abdul Aziz at Jeddah, and King Khaled International at Riyadh. The government-owned Sa'udi Arabian Airlines (Saudia) operates regular domestic and foreign flights to major cities. In 1997, 11,738,000 passengers were carried on scheduled domestic and international flights.

Jiddah, on the Red Sea, is the chief port of entry for Muslim pilgrims going to Mecca; other ports include Ad-Dammam, Yanbu' al-Bahr, Jizan, and Jubail (Al-Jubayl). In 1998 there were 73 ships with a capacity of 1,124,110 GRT in the merchant fleet. The traditional dhow is still used for coastal trade.

12 HISTORY

For several thousand years, Arabia has been inhabited by nomadic Semitic tribes. Towns were established at various oases and along caravan routes. During the seventh century ad followers of Muhammad expanded beyond the Mecca-Medina region and within a century conquered most of the Mediterranean region between Persia in the east and Spain in the west. Although Arabs were dominant in many parts of the Muslim world and there was a great medieval flowering of Arab civilization, the Peninsula itself (except for the holy cities of Mecca and Medina) declined in importance and remained virtually isolated for almost a thousand years. Throughout this period, Arabia was barely more than a province of successive Islamic caliphates that established their capitals in Damascus, Baghdad, Cairo, and Constantinople (now Istanbul).

The foundations of the kingdom of Sa'udi Arabia were laid in the 18th century by the fusion of the military power of the Sa'ud family and Wahhabism, an Islamic puritan doctrine preached by Muhammad bin 'Abd al-Wahhab. Muhammad ibn-Sa'ud (r.1744–65) and his son 'Abd al-'Aziz (r.1765–1803) gave the religious reformer refuge at Ad-Dar'iyah, in central Arabia, and together they embarked on a program of religious reform and territorial expansion. By 1801, Najd and Al-Ahsa were occupied. 'Abd al-'Aziz's son and successor, Sa'ud (r.1803–14), brought the Hijaz under Sa'udi control and took the holy city of Mecca. The Ottoman Turks called on their governor of Egypt, Muhammad 'Ali, to put down the Sa'udis. A long struggle (1811–18) finally resulted in Sa'udi defeat. During that time, Sa'ud died, and his son 'Abdallah (r.1814–18) was captured and beheaded.

When international conditions forced Muhammad 'Ali to withdraw his occupation forces in 1840, the Sa'udis embarked upon a policy of reconquest. Under Faisal (Faysal, r.1843–67), Wahhabi control was reasserted over Najd, Al-Ahsa, and Oman, with Riyadh as the new capital. (Hijaz remained under the control of the sharifs of Mecca until 1925.) After Faisal's death, conflict between his sons led to a decline in the family's fortunes. Taking advantage of these quarrels, the Ibn-Rashids, a former Sa'udi vassal family, gained control of Najd and conquered Riyadh. The Sa'udi family fled to Kuwait in 1891.

In January 1902, 'Abd al-'Aziz, a grandson of Faisal, who was to gain fame under the name Ibn-Sa'ud, succeeded in driving the Ibn-Rashid garrison out of Riyadh. At a decisive battle in 1906, the Rashidi power was broken. In 1913, the Sa'udis again brought Al-Ahsa under their control, and in December 1915, Ibn-Sa'ud signed a treaty with the British that placed Sa'udi foreign relations under British control in return for a sizable subsidy.

Warfare broke out again in Arabia in 1919, when Hussein ibn-'Ali (Husayn ibn-'Ali), the sharif of Mecca, who had become an independent king, attacked the Sa'udis. Hussein was defeated, and Ibn-Sa'ud annexed 'Asir. In 1921, he finally rid Arabia of the Rashids, and by 1923, he had consolidated his kingdom by occupying the districts west and north of Ha'il. Hussein of Mecca provoked another conflict with Ibn-Sa'ud in March 1924 by proclaiming himself caliph. War broke out, and the Sa'udis captured At-Ta'if, Mecca, and Medina (December 1925). 'Ali ibn-Hussein ('Ali ibn-Husayn), who had replaced his father as king of Hijaz, then abdicated, and in November 1925, Ibn-Sa'ud entered Jiddah. This increase in Ibn-Sa'ud's territory was acknowledged by the British in a treaty of 20 May 1927 that annulled the 1915 agreement and recognized his independence. On 22 September 1932, the various parts of the realm were amalgamated into the Kingdom of Sa'udi Arabia, with much the same boundaries as exist today.

With the discovery of oil in the 1930s, the history of Sa'udi Arabia was irrevocably altered. Reserves have proved vast—about one-fourth of the world's total—and production, begun in earnest after World War II, has provided a huge income, much of

it expended on infrastructure and social services. Sa'udi Arabia's petroleum-derived wealth has considerably enhanced the country's influence in world economic and political forums. Following the 1967 Arab-Israeli war, the Sa'udi government undertook a vast aid program in support of Egypt, Syria and Jordan. Sa'udi Arabia joined the 1973 Arab boycott against the US and the Netherlands and, as a key member of OPEC, lent its support to the huge rise in oil prices during the 1970s. This move had stunning consequences for the world economy and also caused a dramatic upsurge in Sa'udi Arabia's wealth and power. Since the 1980s, the government has regulated its petroleum production to stabilize the international oil market and has used its influence as the most powerful moderate member of OPEC to restrain the more radical members.

Political life in Sa'udi Arabia has remained basically stable in recent decades, despite several abrupt changes of leadership. In November 1964, Crown Prince Faisal (Faysal ibn 'Abd al-'Aziz as-Sa'ud), a son of Ibn-Sa'ud, became king and prime minister following the forced abdication of his brother King Sa'ud. His first act as prime minister was to announce a sweeping reorganization of the government, and his major social reform was the abolition of slavery. In March 1975, King Faisal was assassinated by a nephew in an apparently isolated act of revenge. Faisal was succeeded by Crown Prince Khaled (Khalid ibn-'Abd al-'Aziz as-Sa'ud), who embarked on an expanded development program. King Khaled died of a heart attack in June 1982, and his half-brother, Crown Prince Fahd ibn-'Abd al-'Aziz as-Sa'ud, ascended the throne. King Fahd has encouraged continuing modernization while seeking to preserve the nation's social stability and Islamic heritage. As the custodian of the holy Moslem shrines at Mecca and Medina, the monarchy has been deeply embarrassed by several incidents in recent years; e.g., seizure of the Grand Mosque in Mecca by about 500 Islamic militants in 1979, which led to the deaths of more than 160; a riot by Iranian pilgrims during the 1987 pilgrimage, which cost 400 lives; and the suffocation of over 1,400 pilgrims in a tunnel at the Grand Mosque in 1990. Misfortune continued in 1994, when a stampede in Mecca killed 270 pilgrims rushing toward a cavern for a symbolic stoning ritual, and in 1997, when as many as 300 pilgrims were killed in a fire at a campsite outside the holy city.

Sa'udi Arabia's wealth and selective generosity has given it great political influence throughout the world and especially in the Middle East. It suspended aid to Egypt after that country's peace talks with Israel at Camp David, Md., but renewed relations in 1987. It made substantial funds secretly available to US President Ronald Reagan's administration for combating Marxist regimes in Central America. The kingdom played a key role in creating the GCC and in working for an end to the civil strife in Lebanon. It actively supported Iraq during the war with Iran and tried, in vain, to prevent the conflict with Kuwait.

When Iraq invaded Kuwait in 1990, Sa'udi Arabia, fearing Iraqi aggression, radically altered its traditional policy to permit the stationing of foreign troops on its soil. (The government was criticized by senior Saudi religious scholars for taking this step.) Riyadh made substantial contributions of arms, oil, and funds to the allied victory. It also expelled workers from Jordan, Yemen, and members of the PLO for giving support to Iraq in the period after the invasion.

Sa'udi Arabia and the US consult closely on political, economic, commercial, and security matters. The US, with the UK, is a major supplier of arms and offers training and other support to the kingdom's defenses. These supports grew more visible following the Gulf War and continued Iraqi intransigence in the face of increased US and international pressure to disarm. The increased US military presence in Sa'udi Arabia in 1993–94 caused considerable irritation among conservative elements of Saudi society who felt that the US military presence was blasphemous to Islam. In 1995, seven people, including five Americans, were killed by terrorist attack on a Saudi National Guard Training Center in Riyadh. In June 1996, a car bomb detonated in front of a housing complex for US military personnel killed 19 US servicemen, causing considerable uproar in the US and leading military planners to relocate US military bases to remote desert areas.

By the end of the 1990s, the Islamist backlash that followed Saudi-US cooperation in the Gulf War had been contained through the (mostly) temporary detention of hundreds of Islamic radicals and the long-term detention of their most prominent leaders. Between 1997 and 1999, the reins of government had largely passed to Crown Prince Abdullah, the half-brother of the ailing King Fahd, who was believed to have suffered a stroke in 1995 and whose two-month stay in Spain in the summer of 1999 raised renewed speculations about his health. At the turn of the 21st century, much of the Saudis' attention was focused on unaccustomed economic pressures resulting from a 40% drop in oil prices in 1998. With almost half its GDP coming from oil, the country's budget deficit had soared as export revenues plummeted. Prince Abdullah was instrumental in pushing through the production cutbacks agreed to by the OPEC countries in March 1999.

13GOVERNMENT

Sa'udi Arabia is a religiously based monarchy in which the sovereign's dominant powers are regulated according to Muslim law (Shari'ah), tribal law, and custom.

There is no written constitution; laws must be compatible with Islamic law. In a decree of March 1992, the King was granted exclusive power to name the crown prince, his successor. The Council of Ministers, first set up in 1953, is appointed by the king to advise on policy, originate legislation, and supervise the growing bureaucracy. The post of prime minister has been reserved for the king, and the crown prince has been appointed first deputy prime minister. Most other important posts in the cabinet are reserved for members of the royal family.

In 1992, King Fahd announced the creation of the Majlis al Shura, an advisory body that would provide a forum for public debate. The King appointed 60 male citizens not belonging to the royal family to four-year terms on this body, which held its first meeting on 29 December 1992. In 1997, King Fahd increased the size of the Majlis to 90 members.

14POLITICAL PARTIES

Although there are no political parties in Sa'udi Arabia, various groups do function as blocs, contending for influence. Important among these groups are the conservative 'ulama (religious scholars) and the members of the royal family. Other alliances—by merchants, businessmen, professionals, and leading families—are concerned with economic matters. There is also a small but growing, middle class that seems to want greater political participation and a less restrictive social environment. Each group brings its weight to bear on the policymaking bodies of the government and the king, whose leadership is upheld so long as he adheres to Islamic law, tradition, and the collective decisions of the 'ulama. In opposition to the royal family are small, strictly outlawed groups of pro-democracy activists and extremist Islamists, who have engaged in terrorist attacks, principally against signs of Western influence. Identified groups connected with Islamists include the Committee for the Defense of Legitimate Rights, The Reform Movement, and the Islamic Awakening.

15LOCAL GOVERNMENT

The kingdom is divided into 13 emirates, each headed by a crown-appointed governor, often a prince or other member of the royal household or from an allied family. The provinces are subdivided into 103 governorates. Tribal and village leaders (sheikhs) report directly to provincial governors, giving the central government some control over outlying regions. Provincial governors, in turn, report to the Minister of the Interior. Each sheikh traditionally rules in consultation with a council. A large segment of the population remains tribally organized: tribes, headed by paramount sheikhs, are divided into subtribes, headed by local sheikhs. Decisions are made by tribal sheikhs, emirs, or other chiefs and their councils (majlis).

16JUDICIAL SYSTEM

The king acts as the highest court of appeal and has the power of pardon; access to the king and the right to petition him are well-established traditions. The judiciary consists of lower courts that handle misdemeanors and minor civil cases; high courts of Islamic law (Shari'ah), and courts of appeal. Islamic law of the Hanbali school prevails in Sa'udi Arabia, but justice is also based on tribal and customary law. Capital and corporal punishment are permitted; an 11-member Supreme Council of Justice reviews all sentences of execution, cutting, or stoning. A separate military justice system exercises jurisdiction over uniformed personnel and civilian government authorities.

There is no written constitution. The Justice Ministry is responsible for appointment and promotion of judges. Judges may be removed only by the Supreme Council of Justice or by royal decree. Although independence of the judiciary is guaranteed by law, courts are subject to the influence of royal family members. At the provincial level, governors also reportedly exercise influence over local judges.

Shari'a courts have no jurisdiction over common criminal cases and civil suits regarding marriage, divorce, child custody, and inheritance. While summary courts try cases involving small penalties, more serious crimes go to the general courts. Appeals from both courts are heard by the appeals courts in Mecca and Riyadh. There is also a Court of Cassation, as well as administrative tribunals that deal with the proceedings involving claims against the government and enforcement of foreign judgments.

The military tribunals have jurisdiction over military personnel and civil servants charged with violation of military regulations.

17ARMED FORCES

Sa'udi Arabia's armed forces totaled 105,500 personnel in 2000, having doubled in size at the time of the Gulf War. The army had 70,000 personnel, 1,055 main battle tanks, 570 armored fighting vehicles, and 33 batteries of surface-to-air missiles, manned by 4,000 special air defense troops. The navy's strength was about 13,500 personnel (3,000 marines), and equipment included 8 frigates and 26 other combatants. The air force had 18,000 personnel and manned 432 combat aircraft. The national guard, numbering 77,000, is used chiefly for internal security and is an elite strategic reserve loyal to the Royal family. Sa'udi Arabia also had a 10,000-member frontier force, a 4,500-member coast guard, a helicopter-equipped counterterrorist unit, and 7,000 foreign military personnel under contract from members of the GCC. The armed forces are equipped with the most advanced weaponry, including 5 Airborne Warning and Control Systems (AWACS) aircraft, which were sold to Sa'udi Arabia by the US in 1981, over Israel's strenuous objections, as part of an $8.5 billion arms deal. In 1997 Sa'udi Arabia spent $18.1 billion (12% of gross domestic product) on its own forces. The US maintains air defense missiles and interceptors on a rotational basis.

18INTERNATIONAL COOPERATION

Sa'udi Arabia is a charter member of the UN, having joined on 24 October 1945, and participates in ESCWA and all the nonregional specialized agencies. It is a founding member of the Arab League and of OPEC (as well as OAPEC), belongs to G-77 and GCC, and has permanent observer status with the OAS. It is also signatory to the Law of the Sea and has applied for membership in the WTO. Although supporting the Palestinian cause and the Arab League's boycott of Israel, the Sa'udi government in 1981 proposed that the Arab nations show willingness to extend diplomatic recognition to Israel in return for its withdrawal from lands occupied in the 1967 war (including the West Bank and East Jerusalem). Relations with Iran have long been tense and have worsened since that nation's Islamic revolution in 1979. In 1987, Iranian pilgrims rioted in Mecca in an attempt to destabilize the royal family. Although Sa'udi Arabia was not a combatant in the Iran-Iraq war, it actively supported Iraq against Iran.

[19]ECONOMY

The economy is heavily dependent on oil production, which provided over 90% of export value and 75% of government revenues in 1999. The country has the largest reserves of petroleum in the world (26% of the proved total). Rapidly increasing oil income during the 1970s was used to increase disposable income, economic development, and defense expenditures. However, the contribution of the oil sector to GDP has fluctuated. Because of the diversification effort during the second and third development plans and the precipitous decline of oil prices, the contribution of the oil sector (crude oil and refined products) to GDP declined from 70% in 1980 to 40% in 1999.

The government has tried to diversify the economy by development of industries utilizing petroleum, including steel and petrochemical manufacture, in the massive Jubail and Yanbu' al-Bahr industrial complexes, which were largely completed by 1989. The economy is generally open to private investors, but there is a large government sector and the government plays a significant role in influencing resource allocation within the economy. It was estimated that in 1999, the private sector accounted for 35% of GDP. The government is considering privatizing the national airline, petrochemical industries, the telecommunication sector, and electricity companies to foster diversification, but no firm plans have emerged. The government encourages growth in agriculture as a means to reduce Sa'udi Arabia's net reliance on food imports, but dramatic reductions in farm subsidies resulted in a continuing decline in agricultural output in 1999.

Real growth of the GDP averaged about 2.6% between 1988 and 1998. The economy shrank by 11% in 1998 due to low world oil prices, but posted a 1% gain in 1999 and is expected to go higher in 2000 due to a significant rebound in oil prices.

[20]INCOME

The US Central Intelligence Agency (CIA) reports that in 1998 Saudi Arabia's gross domestic product (GDP) was estimated at $186 billion. The per capita GDP was estimated at $9,000, substantially done from its all time high of $15,700 in 1980. The annual growth rate of GDP was estimated at -10.8%. The average inflation rate in 1998 was 1.4%. The CIA defines GDP as the value of all final goods and services produced within a nation in a given year and computed on the basis of purchasing power parity (PPP) rather than value as measured on the basis of the rate of exchange. It was estimated that agriculture accounted for 6% of GDP, industry 53%, and services 41%.

[21]LABOR

The concept of a hired labor force came to Sa'udi Arabia with the arrival of ARAMCO and other industrial ventures connected with the exploitation of oil. By 1991, about 3 million foreigners worked in Sa'udi Arabia, mostly in the oil and construction sector. The total labor force in 1998 stood at 7 million, with 40%

in government, 25% in industry and oil, 30% in services, and 5% in agriculture.

Labor unions are illegal and collective bargaining is forbidden as well. Workers have few protections against employers. This is especially true of foreign workers who are often forced to work long hours and beyond the term specified by their contracts. Foreign workers have little redress against Sa'udi employers, since the labor system usually sides with the latter and employers can delay cases until the workers have to return home. Sa'udi employers routinely prevent workers from obtaining exit visas. Traditional values, embodied in government decrees, continue to hinder the entry of women into the industrial work force.

A 1969 royal decree instituted a series of social insurance provisions that provide compensation for work-related disability, old age, and death. An 8-hour day and 48-hour week are the norms. Labor regulations require protection from hazard and disease for employees (except farmers, herdsmen, domestic servants, and family-operated business employees). Labor outdoors is prohibited when the temperature exceeds 122°F. Foreign workers report that these regulations are seldom enforced. With the consent of parents, children may work as young as 13 and children rarely work in Sa'udi Arabia outside of family businesses. There is no minimum wage.

[22]AGRICULTURE

Agriculture engaged 5% of the economically active population in 1998 and accounted for about 9% of GDP. Only about 1.1% of Sa'udi Arabia's land area is cultivated, although 40% is suitable for grazing. Small owner-operated farms characterize Sa'udi Arabia's land-tenure system. About 96% of the farm area is owned, and only 4% rented. Less than 3% of the agricultural holdings are of 8 hectares (20 acres) or more, and 45% are 0.4 hectare (1 acre) or less in size. About two-thirds of the cropped land is used for cereals and the remainder for vegetables and fruit. Although Sa'udi Arabia has more than 18 million date palms and provides about 12% of the world's supply of dates (an estimated 600,000 tons in 1998), the growing of dates has declined in recent decades in favor of wheat, corn, sorghum, tomatoes, onions, grapes, and a variety of other fruits and vegetables. Nevertheless, dates remain the only major staple food crop with production sufficient to meet local demand. Sa'udi Arabia is 85% self-sufficient for vegetables and 66% for fruit. Wheat output increased from an estimated 150,000 tons in the late 1970s to 1,700,000 tons in 1985, and the government claimed that it met total domestic demand by 1986/87. Production of wheat totaled 1,800,000 tons in 1998; government subsidies have led to a recurring overproduction of wheat. In 1989, the government attempted to discourage production by cutting price supports, but production is still several times higher than domestic demand. Barley production amounted to 400,000 tons in 1998.

Aquifers supply 80% of agriculture's water requirements, but are not renewable. Agricultural irrigation accounts for 90% of total water needs, with wheat production alone using about one-third of the country's annual water supply.

[23]ANIMAL HUSBANDRY

As of 1998, Sa'udi Arabia had an estimated 8,042,000 sheep, 4,390,000 goats, 422,000 camels, 200,000 head of cattle, 97,000 donkeys, and 3,000 horses. As imports of animal foodstuffs have increased and as greater varieties of agricultural products have been produced locally, camels have declined steadily in importance as a source of food. Arabia has long been famed for its horses, but the importance of the Arabian horse as an export item is now virtually nil. Donkeys and mules are still valued as pack animals, and the white donkeys of Al-Ahsa are well known. Sheep are found in all parts of Sa'udi Arabia where pasturage is available; they are raised for milk, as well as for meat and wool or hair. Goats are kept for milk; their hair is used in rugs and tents, and the skins serve as water bags. Traditional farmers account for 80% of the kingdom's sheep production. Overall sheep production is expected to significantly increase in the next few years as a result of expansion by existing farms and establishment of new sheep breeding and fattening projects. About 7 million head of live sheep are imported every year. The import level is expected to remain about the same in upcoming years, partly as a result of the increasing number of pilgrims who come to Mecca for the Hajj. Beef has not been a significant part of the Saudi diet and most beef and veal is consumed by expatriates, as traditional Saudis prefer camel meat. The concern over BSE (the so-called "Mad Cow" disease) in 1996 led the government to ban beef imports from Ireland, the UK, France, Switzerland, and Portugal.

The output of poultry and eggs doubled during 1975–80, and in 1998, Sa'udi Arabia had an estimated 95 million poultry. Sa'udi Arabia is self-sufficient in milk production—in 1998, 458,00 tons were produced. There is no hog raising, and importation of pork products is banned as contrary to Islamic law.

24FISHING

Fishing provides employment and self-sufficiency to some communities on both Sa'udi coasts, although cash earnings are negligible. With rare exceptions, traditional fishing techniques are used. One of the few growth areas in this sector has been the export of Gulf shrimp. The fish catch was estimated at 54,085 tons in 1997.

25FORESTRY

The only forest growth is found in the mountainous area that extends from southern Hijaz to 'Asir, accounting for no more than 0.6% of the total area. The principal varieties—acacia, date, juniper, wild olive, sidr, tamarind, and tamarisk—are generally not useful for timber, but some wood from date palms is used for construction. The trade deficit in forestry products was $686.3 million in 1997.

26MINING

Although the mining sector continued to be dominated by oil, Sa'udi Arabia has diversified by expanding its gold production in recent years, as well as production of cement, fertilizer, petrochemicals, and steel. Mining operations continued at the ancient gold and silver mine of Mahd adh-Dhahab (literally, "cradle of gold"), which is located southeast of Medina and probably dates from the time of King Solomon (10th century BC). In 1991, a surface mine northwest of Riyadh, Sukhaybirat, was opened. Substantial national reserves of gold, iron ore (up to 4 million tons), silver, copper, zinc, lead, pyrites, phosphate, magnesite, barite, marble, and gypsum have been suspected, and an intensive search is still being carried on by Sa'udi and foreign companies. About 3,000 showings for at least 50 metallic and nonmetallic minerals have been located. Production of metal concentrate and bullion in 1996 included copper, 834 tons; gold, 8,302 kg (crude bullion); and silver, 16,608 kg. A modern mining code encourages foreign participation, although majority holdings by national interests have increasingly been stressed. All minerals, including the vast petroleum and natural gas reserves, are owned by the government.

27ENERGY AND POWER

Oil was first discovered in Sa'udi Arabia in 1938, and exploitation of the world's largest oil field, Ghawar (west of Al-Hufuf), began 10 years later. By 1975, Sa'udi Arabia had become the world's third-leading producer (after the US and USSR) and largest exporter of crude oil. With the continued developed of Sa'udi Arabia's production capabilities and the dissolution of the Soviet Union in December 1991, Sa'udi Arabia became the world's largest oil producer. Most oil exports are transported by tanker from the Persian Gulf port of Jubail, and the rest moves by pipeline to the Red Sea port of Yanbu' al-Bahr. In 1999, oil exports contributed $35 billion and accounted for about 80% of the total export revenue. Proven reserves of crude oil, found along the Gulf in a quadrangular area northeast of Riyadh, were estimated at 263.5 billion barrels, or about 25% of the world's known deposits, in early 2000. ARAMCO, a US-controlled firm that held the original oil concession, divested 60% of its interests to the Sa'udi government in 1974 and the remainder in 1980, but continued to produce 96% of Sa'udi oil under a management contract with the Sa'udi government.

After the Iranian revolution of 1979 and the outbreak of war between Iran and Iraq in 1980, the Sa'udi government made up for the diminished oil exports of both countries by increasing its average oil output to a record 9.9 million barrels per day in 1980. Production remained high at 9.8 million barrels a day in 1981 but was cut to 6.5 million barrels daily in 1982. Because of the continued oversupply of oil, Sa'udi Arabia cut its production from 1983 to 1985, when it averaged about 3.3 million barrels per day. In 1986, in an attempt to increase its market share, Sa'udi Arabia temporarily abandoned its role as OPEC's swing producer and flooded the market, producing about 5 million barrels a day, forcing the price to less than $10 per barrel. Since 1987, when production amounted to 4.2 million barrels per day, Sa'udi Arabia has dramatically intensified production, especially since the end of the Persian Gulf War. In 1998, an estimated 8.5 million barrels of oil (7.8 million, crude oil) were produced per day.

In recent years, Sa'udi Arabia had been receiving oil by pipeline from Iraq to Yanbu' al-Bahr. The IPSA 1 pipeline, carrying 500,000 barrels per day, began operations in 1985. Sa'udi Arabia is also planning a network of pipelines that will connect the smaller fields with the larger pipeline running from Hawtah (south of Riyadh) to the East-West Pipeline, the capacity of which will be expanded from 3.2 to 4.7 million barrels per day.

Natural gas production was 46,700 million cu m (1,650 billion cu ft) in 1998. Reserves of natural gas were estimated at 5.8 trillion cu m (204.5 trillion cu ft) in 2000, and ranked as the world's fifth largest.

Sa'udi Arabia has limited waterpower resources, and oil-powered diesel engines generate most of its electric power. Electrical service, which reached 2.2 million people in 1975, was extended to 4.2 million in 1979 and, by 1990, reached 92% of the population. Total installed generating capacity was 21,000 MW at the beginning of 1998. Production in 1998 amounted to 110.1 billion kWh. As of 2000, demand for power was growing about 5% annually. Solar energy is becoming increasingly important as an alternative to diesel power, particularly for use in the desalination of seawater.

28INDUSTRY

Although the Sa'udi economy has been virtually synonymous with crude oil, the country is attempting to diversify its manufacturing. Industrial products include cement, steel, glass, metal manufactures, automotive parts, and building materials, along with petroleum refinery products and petrochemicals (primarily methanol, ethylene, and polypropylene).

Industries producing consumer goods for the local market rely for the most part on imported raw materials. The most notable growth has occurred in food processing and includes meat-packing plants, flour mills, ice cream, yogurt, other dairy processing plants, and vegetable canneries. Other companies produce canvas cloth, surgical supplies, paper products, plastic pipes, electric appliances, paints, detergents, and pharmaceuticals.

²⁹SCIENCE AND TECHNOLOGY

The government encourages importation of high technology, especially in the oil industry, but its own commitment to national technological development has been limited. The Industrial Studies and Development Center is located in Riyadh, and the King Fahad University of Petroleum and Minerals, founded in 1963, is in Dhahran. Other institutions offering courses in basic and applied sciences include King Abdulaziz University, founded in 1967 at Jeddah; King Faisal University, founded in 1975 at Dammam and Al-Hassa; King Saud University, founded in 1957 at Riyadh; and Yanbu Industrial College, founded in 1989 at Yanbu al-Sinaiyeh. In 1987–97, science and engineering students accounted for 17% of college and university enrollments. The King Abdul Aziz City for Science and Technology was founded in 1977 at Riyadh to formulate the national policy for science and technology development, and to draw up the strategy and plans for its implementation.

³⁰DOMESTIC TRADE

Barter is the traditional means by which nomads and farmers have obtained each other's products, and weekly markets are held in villages and small towns. However, the economy is being progressively monetized, and is now completely so in the towns and cities. Newspapers, magazines, and billboards are the principal means of advertising.

Normal business hours vary in different provinces but are usually from 7:30 AM to 1:30 PM and 2:30 to 8 PM, Saturday through Wednesday. The normal workday is eight hours; during the month of Ramadan, however, the workday is limited to six hours. Banks are generally open from 8:30 AM to 12 noon and 5 to 7 PM, Saturday through Wednesday, and 8:30 to 11:30 AM, Thursday. Friday is the day of rest in Sa'udi Arabia.

³¹FOREIGN TRADE

Saudi Arabia's commodity exports are dominated by crude petroleum (75%), which account for 18% of the world's total crude oil exports. Refined petroleum products are the second largest export (14%), accounting for 7.5% of the world's total. Other exports include polymers (2.5%), and industrial alcohols (1.9%), accounting for 6.7% of the world's industrial alcohol exports.

In 1996 Saudi Arabia's imports were distributed among the following categories:

Consumer goods	17.0%
Food	15.8%
Fuels	0.2%
Industrial supplies	27.8%
Machinery	20.1%
Transportation	17.4%
Other	1.7%

Principal trading partners in 1998 (in millions of US dollars) were as follows:

COUNTRY	EXPORTS	IMPORTS	BALANCE
Japan	6,524	4,392	2,132
United States	6,517	11,577	-5,060
Korea	3,986	1,456	2,530
Singapore	2,982	420	2,562
India	2,338	767	1,571
France	1,622	1,570	52
Netherlands	1,538	691	847
United Kingdom	1,345	4,896	-3,551
Italy	1,259	1,814	-555
Germany	527	2,652	-2,125

³²BALANCE OF PAYMENTS

In 1998 foreign worker remittances, approximately $16 billion per year, continued to drain the current account. The Interna-tional Monetary Fund (IMF) reports that in 1998 Saudi Arabia had exports of goods totaling $39,772 million and imports totaling $27,535 million. The services credit totaled $4,421 million and debit $17,098 million. Exports of goods fell 16% as a result of a drop in the price of oil, while imports remained essentially unchanged. The following table summarizes Saudi Arabia's balance of payments as reported by the IMF for 1998 in millions of US dollars.

Current Account		-12,880
Balance on goods	12,237	
Balance on services	-12,677	
Balance on income	2,642	
Current transfers	-15,081	
Capital Account		...
Financial Account		12,983
Direct investment abroad	...	
Direct investment in Saudi Arabia	4,646	
Portfolio investment assets	7,763	
Portfolio investment liabilities	...	
Other investment assets	1,356	
Other investment liabilities		-782
Net Errors and Omissions		...
Reserves and Related Items		-104

³³BANKING AND SECURITIES

Until the mid-20th century, Sa'udi Arabia had no formal money and banking system. To the degree that money was used, Sa'udis primarily used coins having a metallic content equal to their value (full-bodied coins) for storing value and limited exchange transactions in urban areas. For centuries, foreign coins had served the local inhabitants' monetary needs. Development of banking was inhibited by the Quranic injunction against interest. A few banking functions existed, such as money changers (largely for pilgrims visiting Mecca), who had informal connections with international currency markets. A foreign bank was established in Jiddah in 1926, but its importance was minor. Foreign and domestic banks were formed as oil revenues began to increase. Their business consisted mostly of making short-term loans to finance imports, commercial trading, and businesses catering to pilgrims. Although lending at interest is prohibited by Islamic law, banking has flourished in Sa'udi Arabia as a conduit for the investment of oil money. The Sa'udi Arabian Monetary Agency (SAMA) was established by royal decree in 1952 to maintain the internal and external value of currency. The agency issues notes and coins with 100% cover in gold and convertible foreign exchange and regulates all banks and exchange dealers.

In 1999 there were 11 commercial banking houses, the largest of which was The National Commercial Bank. Cumulatively, the total size of the bank's balance sheets stood at about $110 billion, with net foreign assets of over $11 billion at year-end 1998. Eight of the eleven are joint venture banks. The major foreign partners include Citibank, Arab Bank Ltd., Banque Indosuez, HSBC Holdings, and ABN Amro.

There is a stock exchange in Sa'udi Arabia, created in 1990 as an over-the-counter market in which the commercial banks buy and sell shares by means of an electronic trading system. Although this system has facilitated easy access to transacting, the market remains relatively illiquid because of the small numbers of issuers and the narrow investor base. There are 74 companies listed on the exchange. The value of traded shares was $13.7 billion in 1998, a turnover ratio of almost 27%. Total market capitalization was just over $42 billion. The new IFCG Sa'udi Index closed done 26.8% in 1998, its first year of existence, but rebounded in 1999 on news of an increase in oil prices. The market is closed to direct foreign investment, but foreigners can buy and trade shares of Sa'udi companies within a closed-end fund listed in the United Kingdom.

34 INSURANCE

There were at least 70 insurance firms operating in Sa'udi Arabia in 1998 offering all categories and classes on insurance. The National Company for Cooperative Insurance, founded by royal decree in 1985 and owned by three government agencies, had share capital of SR250 million. In all insurance premiums amounted to over $760 million. Premiums covering oil facilities, major projects, marine and aviation represent over 44% of total premium, motor insurance accounts for 23%, medical 18%, and fire 14%. Insurance organizations in Sa'udi Arabia are regulated by the Ministry of Commerce. Insurance companies operating in the country adhere to the tenets of Islam.

35 PUBLIC FINANCE

Public expenditures typically have acted as the vanguard for economic growth and development since the early 1970s. Deficits have been common since 1983, as oil revenues have declined. Oil revenues typically account for over 70% of government revenues. Deep budget cuts over the past years; higher charges on energy, electricity, water, telephone, worker and visa fees; and reduced subsidies on fuels, utilities, and airline fares; have combined to reduce the deficit, but the government's goal of a balanced budget in 2000 will be hard to achieve. To finance the deficit, the government borrows from domestic financial markets. By 1998, the ratio of accumulated public debt to GDP exceeded 100%.

The US Central Intelligence Agency (CIA) estimates that in 1999 Saudi Arabia's central government took in revenues of approximately $32.3 billion and had expenditures of $44 billion. Overall, the government registered a deficit of approximately $11.7 billion. It is estimated that government salaries and debt service exceed three-fourths of expenditures. Without increases in domestic taxes, government finances remain largely at the mercy of world oil prices.

36 TAXATION

The taxing authority in Sa'udi Arabia is the Department of Zakat and Income Tax. During the early 1970s, a progressive income tax was levied on all personal income of foreign residents in excess of SR6,000, at the rate of 5–30%; there was also a progressive tax of 25–45% on the profits of foreign companies. These taxes were abolished in 1975; in January 1988, an attempt was made to revive them, but it was rescinded almost immediately after widespread complaint. However, foreign companies that have not obtained exemption under the Foreign Investment Code and foreigners who are self-employed professionals or general partners in Sa'udi partnerships are subject to these taxes.

Corporate taxes range from 25-45% of net income. The zakat is an Islamic tax derived from the Shari'ah and applied directly to the income and property of Sa'udis (and resident Gulf state nationals); half of the zakat rate of 2.5% is paid to the government, and the other half is distributed by citizens to the poor. The income of members of the royal family is tax-exempt.

37 CUSTOMS AND DUTIES

Sa'udi Arabia has increasingly used the tariff to protect local industries. The general tariff rate is 12%; new Sa'udi industries are protected by a 20% tariff rate. Importation of liquor, firearms, ammunition, and narcotics, and certain other items is strictly forbidden, as are all imports from Israel and South Africa. No import taxes are levied beyond import tariffs.

38 FOREIGN INVESTMENT

A small group of upper-class Sa'udis have traditionally held substantial investments overseas. These Sa'udis hold large demand deposits in US and Western European banks and considerable investments in commercial ventures, especially real estate, in Egypt and other Middle Eastern countries. Since the early 1970s, the Sa'udi government has vastly increased its overseas investments in the US, Western Europe, and Japan.

The Sa'udi government generally encourages foreign direct investment, especially in the case of joint ventures with Sa'udi partners. The foreign capital investment code specifies that foreign investments: (1) must be a "development project," (2) must generate technology transfer, and (3) a Sa'udi partner should own a minimum of 25% equity in the project. However, in 1999, the government began revising its laws on foreign investment in an effort to attract more overseas capital and to lure back the large private Sa'udi capital that is invested abroad. Principal foreign investors include the US (41% of the total), Japan, the UK, Switzerland, France, and Germany.

39 ECONOMIC DEVELOPMENT

Sa'udi Arabia's first two development plans (1971–75 and 1976–80) stressed improvement of the country's economic infrastructure by expanding the highway system, port capacity, electric power output, water supply, and irrigated land. The third plan (1981–85), continuing the Sa'udi program of modernization without Westernization, aimed at diversifying and expanding the productive economic sectors of industry, mining, and agriculture. The government's long-term goal was to reduce the nation's dependence on oil exports and foreign labor. Expenditures for the 1981–85 plan were initially estimated (at current prices) at $235.8 billion, compared with $140 billion for the 1975–80 plan. At the end of the third development plan, most of the infrastructure had been put in place. The fourth development plan (1985–90) emphasized consolidation of the gains of the previous 15 years and rational planning of economic activity. From the plan's emphasis on cost reduction and improvement of economic performance, it was clear that it had been drawn up under the assumption that the days of huge surpluses in the oil sector were over. Planned expenditures for the fourth plan were reduced several times. The fifth plan (1990–95) followed the goals of the fourth plan closely. Stressing economic diversification, this plan supported industry, agriculture, finance, and business services. An important goal of the sixth plan (1995–2000) was to reduce water consumption by 2% annually over the plan's period.

By the late 1990s, low oil prices had substantially reduced the GDP. Low revenues from oil and a rapidly expanding population put pressure on the government to put more emphasis on private sector expansion. Accordingly, the government began the process of privatizing government-owned entities in the telecommunications, transportation, and power generation sectors. However, there is concern that the growth in private sector jobs will not keep pace with the more quickly expanding population.

40 SOCIAL DEVELOPMENT

Social welfare in Sa'udi Arabia is traditionally provided through the family or tribe. Those with no family or tribal ties have recourse to the traditional Islamic religious foundations or may request government relief, which is supported by the collection of the zakat. Social insurance provides health care, disability, death, old age pension, and survivor benefits for workers and their families. Retirement is allowed at age 60, and benefits are provided at 2% of average monthly earnings times time the number of years worked. This system is funded by 5% payroll deductions from workers, and 8% of payroll contributions from employers. The government provides an annual subsidy to the program. This program is compulsory for employees of firms with 10 or more workers, and is voluntary for smaller enterprises. A 1969 law requires employers to provide 100% of wages for a month of sick leave, and 75% of wages for two additional months.

The customs and regulations governing the behavior of women are strict even by the standards of the Islamic world.

Despite the shortage of Sa'udi labor, the government is unsympathetic to the participation of women in the workplace; in 1999, only 5% of the labor force was female. Extreme modesty of dress is required. Women wear the abaya, a long black garment, and they must also cover their face and head. Women are not permitted to drive motor vehicles. Women must enter public buses through a rear door, and sit in a segregated area. Women may not travel without the written permission of a male member of her family. This provision also applies to travel within the country.

Segregation also occurs in the workplace, where women may only contact clients by telephone or fax. The Ministry of Commerce will not issue business licenses for women in fields that might require them to be in regular contact with government officials or male clients.

The government does not recognize international standards on human rights. Rights of privacy, freedom of speech, the press, assembly, association, religion, and movement are not respected. Security forces commit human rights abuses with the acquiescence of the government, even though they are nominally illegal. Corporal punishment, including amputation of limbs, beheading, and stoning, are used. In 1995, executions were carried out for crimes including alcohol trafficking, armed robbery, adultery and the practice of witchcraft. Most of those executed were foreigners.

41HEALTH

The country has made important advances, after a slow start, in the provision of health care services. From 1990 through 1995, the government budgeted SR63.9 billion for health and social services (of a total budget of SR497.6 billion). Targets included improved immunization coverage and achieving better regional coverage of health care provision (which remains inadequate). The government wanted to have 1 doctor per 500 people, as well as 150 new health centers. Development of the private sector (and links between public and private) is to be encouraged; it also plans to have a local manufacturer of pharmaceuticals and medical equipment and supplies. In 1990–97, hospital beds per 1,000 people equaled 2.5. Health personnel in 1990 included 21,110 physicians (about 1.82 per 1,000), 1,967 dentists, and 48,066 nurses (about 3.8 per 1,000). In 1991, there were 1,811 pharmacists. It is the government's intention to provide integrated health services free of charge, or at a nominal fee, to all citizens. The public health care system is supplemented by a small but generally excellent private health sector. Despite these advances, Sa'udi Arabia still suffers from severe health problems. A major cause of disease is malnutrition, leading to widespread scurvy, rickets, night blindness, and anemia, as well as low resistance to tuberculosis. In 1993 there were 18,380 cases of malaria. Immunization rates for 1995 for children up to one year old were tuberculosis (93%); diphtheria, pertussis, and tetanus (97%); polio (97%); and measles (94%). Dysentery attacks all ages and classes, and trachoma is common. A government campaign was successful in eradicating malaria; typhoid is endemic, but acquired immunity prevents serious outbreaks of this disease. The HIV-1 seroprevalence rate in 1997 was 0.0 per 100 adults. There were 171 cases of AIDS reported in 1996. Sewage disposal and other health and sanitation facilities have been improved, but much still needs to be done. In 1995, 95% of the population had access to safe water, and 86% had adequate sanitation.

In 1960, life expectancy at birth was 43 years, but it averaged 70.5 years in 1999. During the same time period, infant mortality fell from 185 to 38.8 per 1,000 live births. The infant mortality rate stands considerably above those of middle-income countries. This fact may reflect the high infant death rate among the Bedouin, which has been estimated to account for about one-third of all infant deaths. The maternal mortality rate was 18 per 100,000 live births in 1990–97, and the general mortality rate was 4.9 per 1,000 people in 1999. The country's 1999 birth rate was 37.4 per 1,000 inhabitants. Birth control was used by 13.6% of married women in 1989–90. In 1992, 97% of the population had access to health care services. Total health care expenditures in 1990 were $4,784 million. During the years 1990–97, 8% of the gross domestic product went to health expenditures.

42HOUSING

The continuing influx of rural people to towns and cities, coupled with the rise in levels of expectation among the urban population, has created a serious housing problem; improvement in urban housing is one of Sa'udi Arabia's foremost economic needs. Some 506,800 dwelling units were built during 1974–85, 389,000 by the private sector, with the help of the Real Estate Development Fund, and 117,800 by the Deputy Ministry of Housing and other government agencies. In 1984, 78,884 building permits were issued, 84% of these for concrete dwellings and 8% for housing units of blocks and bricks. In the oil districts, ARAMCO, through loans and other assistance, has encouraged construction of private homes and has built accommodations for its unmarried Sa'udi staff members.

43EDUCATION

Until the mid-1950s, Sa'udi Arabia's educational system was primarily oriented toward religious schooling that stressed knowledge of the Qur'an (Koran) and Hadith (sayings of Muhammed and his companions). Except for basic arithmetic, reading, and writing, secular subjects were not taught in the schools. There was a highly developed oral culture, however.

Nearly all of the students were boys; education of girls was virtually nonexistent and took place in the home, if at all. Of those attending public schools, 96.2% were boys. The General Presidency for Girls' Education administers girls' schools and colleges. The first school for girls was built in 1964, and now girls' schools exist around the country. By the mid-1980s, about 43% of students were female.

As of 1985, attendance in primary school was required by law. Education is free at all levels, including college and postgraduate study. The literacy rate in the 1960s was 3%. By 1995, it was 62.8%. However, literacy among women remains significantly lower than that of men. For the year 2000, adult illiteracy rates were estimated at 23.0% (males, 15.9%; females, 32.8%).

By 1997 there were 11,506 primary schools, with 2,256,185 pupils and 175,458 teachers. Student-to-teacher ratio stood at 13 to one. Secondary schools had a total enrollment of 1,542,989 students and 119,881 teachers in the same year. Higher education was pursued in seven universities and 83 colleges. The principal universities are King Sa'ud University (formerly Riyadh University), founded in 1957, and King 'Abd al-'Aziz University of Jiddah, founded in 1967. All higher level institutions had 273,992 pupils and 15,868 teachers in 1997.

44LIBRARIES AND MUSEUMS

The National Library, founded in Riyadh in 1968, has 321,300 volumes. The largest library system is that of King Sa'ud University established in 1957, with 14 branches and a collection of more than 1.7 million volumes; the library at King 'Abd al-'Aziz University has 435,000 volumes. The library of the University of Petroleum and Minerals in Dhahran, with almost 335,000 volumes, is the nation's largest specialized collection. The largest public library, at Riyadh, contains 275,000 volumes.

There are 10,150 documented monuments and about a dozen museums in Saudi Arabia. The National Museum, originally opened at Riyadh in 1978, focuses on archaeology and ethnography. Major renovations were completed in 1999. Many of the other historic and cultural sites are religious in nature and the high figures for attendance reflect the huge numbers of Muslim pilgrims who visit the kingdom each year. Riyadh is also home to a local museum, an archaeological museum at King Sand University, and a geological museum.

45MEDIA

Postal, telephone, cable, and wireless services are regulated by the Ministry of Communications. Sa'udi Arabia is directly connected by radiotelephone with the US, other Arab countries, and Western Europe, and automatic internal lines connect most of the major cities. The telephone system was greatly expanded in the late 1970s, and in 1995 some 1.6 million telephones were in use. Broadcasting emanates from the government-owned Sa'udi Arabian Broadcasting Service, Saudi ARAMCO FM stations, Saudi-Arabian TV, and an ARAMCO channel in Dhahran. The number of radios per 1,000 population was estimated at 319, the number of television sets at 260, and the number of mobile phones at 17 in 1997.

The first newspaper in what is now Sa'udi Arabia was *Al-Qiblah,* the official publication of King Hussein of Hijaz, founded in 1915. With the end of the short-lived Hijaz kingdom in 1925, a Sa'udi-sponsored paper, called *Umm al-Qura* (The Mother of Towns, Mecca), was established. Newspapers are privately owned; criticism of the fundamental principles of Islam and of basic national institutions, including the royal family, is not permitted. The largest Arabic daily papers (with 1999 circulations) are *Al-Asharq Al-Awsat* (224,900); *Al-Jazirah* (90,000); *Okaz* (147,000), and *Al-Riyadh* (150,000). Leading English-language dailies are the *Arab News* (110,000) and *Saudi Gazette* (22,000).

The government is said to severely limit freedom of speech and the press, punishing any criticism of Islam, the ruling family, or the government with detention and arrest.

As of 1996, there were 438,000 personal computers. Online access is extremely limited, with less than 1 Internet host per 1,000 population in 1998

46ORGANIZATIONS

Sa'udi social tradition, which emphasizes the exclusiveness of family, clan, and tribe, militates against the formation of other social organizations. The absence of political and economic organizations also is a result of the prevalence of tradition. There are chambers of commerce in Ad-Dammam, Jiddah, Mecca, Medina, and Riyadh.

47TOURISM, TRAVEL, AND RECREATION

Sa'udi Arabia is one of the hardest places in the world to visit. Tourist visas are not issued, and foreign visitors must show letters of invitation from Sa'udi employers or sponsors to enter the country. Every year, however, there is a great influx of pilgrims to Mecca and Medina, cities that non-Muslims are forbidden to enter. In 1998 the number of pilgrims totaled over two million. Tourist arrivals totaled 3,700,00 that year, with receipts of $1.5 million. Evidence of a previous or planned trip to Israel is grounds for denial of admission to Sa'udi Arabia.

Traditional sports include hunting with salukis, falconry, and horse and camel racing. Modern sports facilities include the Riyadh Stadium, complete with Olympic-standard running tracks and soccer fields.

In 1999, the UN estimated the cost of staying in Riyadh at $184 per day. Daily expenses for travel in other areas of the country varied, ranging from $184 in Al-Khobar to $74 in smaller towns.

48FAMOUS SA'UDIS

Although Sa'udi Arabia has a relatively short history as a nation-state, it is heir to an Islamic civilization that developed from the teachings of Muhammad (570–632), born of the tribe of Quraysh in Mecca. The branch of Islam which claims most contemporary Sa'udis is that preached by Muhammad bin 'Abd al-Wahhab (1703?–91), a fundamentalist reformer.

The Sa'udi who has gained greatest renown outside the modern kingdom of Sa'udi Arabia is 'Abd al-'Aziz ibn 'Abd ar-Rahman al-Faysal as-Sa'ud, better known as Ibn-Sa'ud (1880–1953), the father of his country. Forced into exile with his family at a young age, he reconquered his patrimony and left behind him the state of Sa'udi Arabia.

In 1964, Faisal (Faysal ibn-'Abd al-'Aziz as-Sa'ud, 1906–75) was proclaimed king. In his role as prime minister, Faisal instituted many economic and social reforms, including the abolition of slavery. Upon his assassination in March 1975, he was succeeded as king and prime minister by Khaled (Khalid ibn-'Abd al-'Aziz, 1913–82). Together with Crown Prince Fahd ibn-'Abd al-'Aziz (b.1920), King Khaled broadened the country's development policies.

After Khaled's death, Fahd became king; he has pursued the same cautious program of modernization as his two predecessors. Ahmad Zaki Yamani (b.1930), a former minister of petroleum and mineral resources, gained an international reputation as a spokesman for the oil-exporting countries.

49DEPENDENCIES

Sa'udi Arabia has no territories or colonies.

50BIBLIOGRAPHY

Abir, Mordechai. *Sa'udi Arabia: Government, Society, and the Gulf Crisis.* New York: Routledge, 1993.

Al Munajjed, Mona. *Women in Saudi Arabia Today.* Houndmills, U.K.: Macmillan, 1997.

Anscombe, Frederick F. *The Ottoman Gulf: The Creation of Kuwait, Saudi Arabia, and Qatar.* New York: Columbia University Press, 1997.

Bahgat, Gawdat. *The Gulf Monarchies: New Economic and Political Realities.* London: Research Institute for the Study of Conflict and Terrorism, 1997.

Beling, Willard A. (ed.). *King Faisal and the Modernization of Sa'udi Arabia.* Boulder, Colo.: Westview, 1980.

Dukheil, Abdulaziz M. *The Banking System and its Performance in Saudi Arabia.* London: Saqi Books, 1995.

Farsy, Fouad. *Modernity and Tradition: The Saudi Equation.* New York: Kegan Paul International, 1990.

Gause, F. Gregory. *Saudi-Yemeni Relations: Domestic Structures and Foreign Influence.* New York: Columbia University Press, 1990.

Harrison, Martin. *Saudi Arabia's Foreign Policy: Relations with the Superpowers.* Durham: Centre for Middle Eastern and Islamic Studies, University of Durham Press, 1995.

Holden, David, and Richard Johns. *The House of Saud.* New York: Holt, Rinehart & Winston, 1981.

Katz, Mark N. *Russia and Arabia: Soviet Foreign Policy Toward the Arabian Peninsula.* Baltimore, Md.: Johns Hopkins University Press, 1986.

The Kingdom of Saudi Arabia. 9th ed. London: Stacey International, 1993.

Kostiner, Joseph. *The Making of Sa'udi Arabia, 1916–1936: from Chieftancy to Monarchical State.* New York: Oxford University Press, 1993.

Long, David E. *The Kingdom of Saudi Arabia*. Gainesville: University Press of Florida, 1997.

Looney, Robert E. *Economic Development in Sa'udi Arabia: Consequences of the Oil Price Decline*. Greenwich, Conn.: JAI Press, 1990.

Munro, Alan. *An Arabian Affair: The Gulf War from Saudi Arabia*. London: Brassey's, 1996.

Peterson, John. *Historical Dictionary of Saudi Arabia*. Metuchen, N.J.: Scarecrow Press, 1993.

Saudi Arabian Cultural Mission to the United States. *Saudi Arabia: A Kingdom in Transition*. Beltsville, Md.: Amana Publications, 1993.

Vasil'ev, Aleksei M. *The History of Saudi Arabia*. London: Saqi Books, 1998.

SINGAPORE

Republic of Singapore

CAPITAL: Singapore.

FLAG: The flag consists of a red stripe at the top and a white stripe on the bottom. On the red stripe, at the hoist, are a white crescent opening to the fly and five white stars.

ANTHEM: *Long Live Singapore.*

MONETARY UNIT: The Singapore dollar (s$) of 100 cents is a freely convertible currency. There are coins of 1, 5, 10, 20, and 50 cents and 1 dollar and notes of 2, 5, 10, 20, 50, 100, 500, 1,000, and 10,000 dollars. s$1 = us$0.58411 (us$1 = s$1.712) as of 31 March 2000.

WEIGHTS AND MEASURES: The metric system is in force, but some local measures are used.

HOLIDAYS: Major Western, Chinese, Malay, and Muslim holidays are celebrated, some of which fall on annually variable dates because of the calendars used. Major holidays include New Year's Day, 1 January; Chinese New Year; Good Friday; Vesak Day (Buddhist festival); Labor Day, 1 May; Hari Raya Puasa (Muslim festival); National Day, 9 August; Hari Raya Haji (Malay Muslim festival); Dewali; Christmas, 25 December.

TIME: 8 PM = noon GMT.

¹LOCATION, SIZE, AND EXTENT

The Republic of Singapore, the second smallest country in Asia, consists of Singapore Island and several smaller adjacent islets. Situated in the Indian Ocean off the southern tip of the Malay Peninsula, Singapore has an area of 632.6 sq km (244.2 sq mi), of which Singapore Island comprises 570.4 sq km (220.2 sq mi) and the islets 50.1 sq km (19.3 sq mi). Comparatively, the area occupied by Singapore is slightly less than 3.5 times the size of Washington, D.C. Singapore Island extends 41.8 km (26 mi) ENE–WSW and 22.5 km (14 mi) SSE–NNW and has a coastline of 193 km (120 mi), including about 84 km (52 mi) along the water channel between the island and the Malay Peninsula. Singapore is connected to the nearby western portion of Malaysia by a causeway 1,056 m (3,465 ft) in length across the narrow Johore Strait. Singapore's position at the eastern end of the Strait of Malacca, which separates western Malaysia and the Indonesian island of Sumatra, has given it economic and strategic importance out of proportion to its small size. Singapore's capital city, Singapore, is located on the country's southern coast.

²TOPOGRAPHY

Singapore Island is mostly low-lying, green, undulating country with a small range of hills at the center. The highest point of the island is Bukit Timah (177 m/581 ft). There are sections of rain forest in the center and large mangrove swamps along the coast, which has many inlets, particularly in the north and west. Singapore's harbor is wide, deep, and well protected.

³CLIMATE

The climate is tropical, with heavy rainfall and high humidity. The range of temperature is slight; the average annual maximum is 31°C (88°F), and the average minimum 24°C (75°F). The annual rainfall of 237 cm (93 in) is distributed fairly evenly throughout the year, ranging from 39 cm (15 in) in December to 28 cm (11 in) in May. It rains about one day in two.

⁴FLORA AND FAUNA

Singapore Island is in the main denuded, the dense tropical forest that originally covered it being mostly cleared. There is some rain forest in the central area of the island, however, as well as extensive mangrove swamps along the coast. Urban development has limited animal life.

⁵ENVIRONMENT

Environmental responsibility for Singapore is vested in the Ministry of the Environment and its Anti-Pollution Unit. Air quality is protected by the Clean Air Act, as adopted in 1971 and amended in 1975 and 1980, and by the Clean Air (Standards) Regulations of 1975. Regulations limiting the lead content of gasoline were imposed in 1981, and emissions standards for motor vehicles were tightened in 1986. Air pollution from transportation vehicles is a problem in the nation's growing urban areas. In 1992, Singapore was among 50 nations with the world's highest levels of industrial carbon dioxide emissions, which totaled 49.8 million metric tons, a per capita level of 17.99 metric tons. Water quality is regulated through the Water Pollution Control and Drainage Act of 1975 and the Trade Effluent Regulations of 1976. Singapore does not have enough water to support the needs of its people. In total, the nation has 0.1 cubic miles of water. Four percent is used for farming and 51% for industrial purposes. Pollution from the nation's oil industry is also a significant problem, and its cities produce 0.9 million tons of solid waste per year. Waste water is treated and recycled to conserve water supplies. Altogether, Singapore has lost 20 to 30% of its original mangrove area.

In 1994, 19 plant species were considered to be in danger of extinction. Endangered or extinct species in Singapore include the Ridley's leaf-nosed bat and the Singapore roundleaf horseshoe bat.

⁶POPULATION

The population of Singapore in 2000 was estimated at 3,571,710. An estimated 6.5% of the population is 65 years of age or older.

The projected population for the year 2005 is 3,751,000, assuming a crude birthrate of 11 per 1,000 population and a death rate of 5, resulting in a natural rate of change of 0.6% for the period 2000–2005. The population rate of change between 1995 and 2000 was 1.5%. The population density in 1998 was 5186 per sq km (13432 per sq mi).

Singapore is virtually a city-state, and the entire population (100%) is considered urban. The capital city, Singapore, and its surrounding metropolitan area had a 2000 population of 3,587,000.

7MIGRATION

Singapore had only a few Malay fishermen as inhabitants at the time of its founding as a British trading post in 1819. It was subsequently, and quite rapidly, populated by immigrant peoples, primarily Chinese but also Malays (from Sumatra as well as adjacent Malaya) and Indians (who took advantage of common British governance to migrate to Singapore in search of better employment). Thus immigration, rather than natural increase, was the major factor in Singapore's fast population growth through the mid-20th century.

In November 1965, following separation from Malaysia, Singapore's newly independent government introduced measures to restrict the flow of Malaysians entering the country in search of work. These immigrants, who averaged 10,000 a year up to 1964, had to establish residence for several years to qualify for citizenship. In addition, all noncitizens were required to apply for a work permit or employment pass. Immigration is now generally restricted to those with capital or with special skills. In 1999, the net migration rate was 2.83 migrants per 1,000 population.

8ETHNIC GROUPS

The people of Singapore are predominantly of Chinese origin. Of an estimated 1999 population of 3,531,600, about 76.4% were ethnic Chinese (most of them, however, born in Singapore or in neighboring Malaysia). Some 14.9% were Malays; 6.4% were Indians (including Pakistanis, Bangladeshis, and Sri Lankans); and 2.3% were of other varied ethnic origins.

9LANGUAGES

There are four official languages: Chinese (Mandarin dialect), Malay, English, and Tamil. English is the principal medium of government and is widely used in commerce. By 1987, under a government mandate, English was made the primary language of the school system. Malay is the national language.

10RELIGIONS

There is complete separation of state and religion in Singapore. Freedom of religion is both constitutionally guaranteed and honored in practice. The Chinese (about 54%) for the most part adhere in varying degrees to Buddhism, Taoism, and Confucianism. Malays and persons with origins in the Pakistani and Bangladeshi portions of the Indian subcontinent—approximately 15%—are almost exclusively Muslims. The Christian population was estimated in 1999 at 13%. Most of the Indian minority (3%) are Hindus. There are also small Sikh, Jewish, Zoroastrian, and Jain communities.

11TRANSPORTATION

Singapore's history is partly the history of the island-country's important regional role as a transportation link between East and West and between the mainland and insular portions of Southeast Asia. As long ago as 1822—only three years after the establishment of a British colonial presence on the island—1,575 ships called at the new port of Singapore from nearby islands, Europe, India, and China. With a natural deepwater harbor that is open the year round, Singapore now ranks as the largest container port

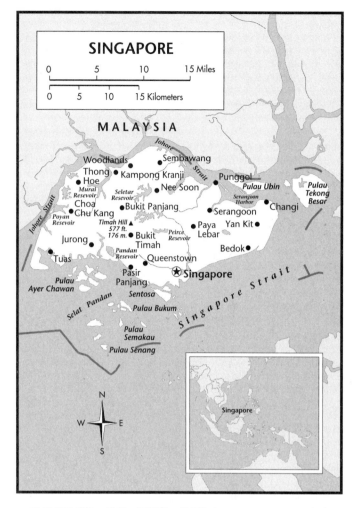

LOCATION: 1°9′ to 1°29′N; 103°38′ to 104°6′E. **TERRITORIAL SEA LIMIT:** 3 mi.

in the world, with anchorage facilities that can accommodate supertankers. Ships of some 600 shipping lines, flying the flags of nearly all the maritime nations of the world, regularly call at Singapore. In 1998, Singapore's merchant fleet was comprised of 875 ships, totaling 19,734,146 GRT.

Commercial air service was inaugurated in Singapore in 1930. In 1998 there were 9 airports, all of which had paved runways. The two principal air facilities are Changi International and Seletar Airport. Singapore's own flag carrier is Singapore Airlines. In 1997, 12,981,000 passengers were carried on scheduled domestic and international flights.

There were 3,017 km (1,875 mi) of roadways in 1997, of which 2,936 km (1,824 mi) were paved, including 148 km (92 mi) of expressways. In 1995, there were 460,862 motor vehicles, of which 324,000 were automobiles. Singapore's sole rail facility is a 38.6-km (24-mi) section of the Malayan Railways, which links Singapore to Kuala Lumpur. There is also a 67-km (42-mi) mass transit system with 42 stations.

12HISTORY

Some historians believe a town was founded on the Singapore Island as early as the 7th century, while other sources claim that "Singapura" (Lion City) was established by an Indian prince in 1299. Historians believe that during the 13th and 14th centuries, a thriving trading center existed until it was devastated by a Javanese attack in 1377. Singapore, however, was virtually uninhabited when Sir Stamford Raffles, in 1819, established a trading station of the British East India Company on the island. In 1824, the island was ceded outright to the company by the Sultan of Johore, the Malay state at the extreme southern end of the Peninsula. In 1826 it was incorporated with Malacca (Melaka, Malaysia) and Penang (Pinang, Malaysia) to form the Straits Settlements, a British Crown Colony until World War II. The trading center grew into the city of Singapore and attracted large numbers of Chinese, many whom became merchants.

With its excellent harbor, Singapore also became a flourishing commercial center and the leading seaport of Southeast Asia, handling the vast export trade in tin and rubber from British-ruled Malaya. In 1938, the British completed construction of a large naval base on the island, which the Japanese captured in February 1942 during World War II, following a land-based attack from the Malay Peninsula to the north.

Recaptured by the UK in 1945, Singapore was detached from the Straits Settlements to become a separate crown colony in 1946. Under a new constitution, on 3 June 1959, Singapore became a self-governing state, and on 16 September 1963, it joined the new Federation of Malaysia (formed by bringing together the previously independent Malaya and Singapore and the formerly British-ruled northern Borneo territories of Sarawak and Sabah). However, Singapore, with its predominantly urban Chinese population and highly commercial economy, began to find itself at odds with the Malay-dominated central government of Malaysia. Frictions mounted, and on 9 August 1965, Singapore separated from Malaysia to become wholly independent as the Republic of Singapore. Harry Lee Kuan Yew, a major figure in the move toward independence, served as the country's Prime Minister from 1959 until 1990. Singapore, Indonesia, Malaysia, the Philippines, and Thailand formed the Association of South-East Asian Nations (ASEAN) in 1967.

The People's Action Party (PAP) founded in 1954 has been the dominant political party winning every general election since 1959. The PAP's popular support rested on law and order policies buttressed by economic growth and improved standards of living. Although the PAP regularly carried 60–75% of the popular vote, it managed to capture virtually all seats repeatedly in the National Assembly. The PAP won all parliamentary seats in the general elections from 1968 to 1980. In the 1981 by-election J. B. Jeyaretnam, secretary-general of the Workers' Party, won a seat; he maintained it in the 1984 general election. Chiam See Tong, leader of the Singapore Democratic Party (SDP), won another seat for the opposition in the same election. (See Political Parties and Government) In March 1985 the third state President, Devan Nair, former trade unionist and member of the Singapore's "old guard," resigned from office under allegations related to alcoholism. The new President, Wee Kim Wee, took office in August. In May and June 1987 the Government detained 22 persons under the Internal Security Act (ISA) for alleged involvement in a "Marxist conspiracy." These detentions triggered international protests by those critical of the government's abuse of human rights, including detention without trial and allegations of torture. Most of the alleged conspirators were released by December, but eight were rearrested in April 1988 after issuing a joint press statement regarding the circumstances of their detention. Two of the eight remained in custody until June 1990.

The September 1988 general election took place under an altered electoral system that increased the total seats from 79 to 81. The new constituencies consisted of 42 single-member districts and the reorganization of the other 39 seats into 13 group representation constituencies (GRCs). Teams of three representatives for each party contested the GRCs; at least one of which must be from an ethnic minority, i.e., non-Chinese. Ostensibly these changes were to ensure minority participation, but at the same time small and/or resource poor opposition parties were handicapped by a requirement to field three candidates.

In November 1992 the media announced that Deputy Prime Minister, Lee Hsien Loong (son of Lee Kuan Yew) and Ong Teng Cheong were diagnosed with cancer. (The former was pronounced fully cured in 1994, but has been little seen in political circles.) On 28 November 1990 Lee Kuan Yew, Prime Minister of Singapore for over thirty-one years, transferred power to Goh Chok Tong, the former first deputy Prime Minister. Lee remained in the cabinet as senior minister to the prime minister's office and retained the position of secretary-general of the PAP. Singapore's first direct presidential elections were held on 28 August 1993 with Ong Teng Cheong becoming the first elected president.

An incident that garnered worldwide attention was the Singapore Government's arrest in October 1993 of nine foreign youths charged with vandalism involving the spray painting of some 70 cars. Michael Fay, an 18-year-old American student and the oldest in the group, was suspected to be the leader. Under police interrogation Fay admitted his guilt, pleaded guilty in court to two counts of vandalism and one count of receiving stolen property. In March 1994 Fay was sentenced to four months in prison, a fine of US$2,230 and six strokes of the cane. On 7 March 1994 President Clinton urged Singapore to reconsider the flogging of Fay amid a failed appeal. A plea to the Singaporean president for clemency was rejected, but as a "goodwill gesture towards President Clinton," the sentence of caning was reduced from six strokes to four. The sentence was carried out on 5 May 1994.

In 1994, Singapore made international news when the government sued the *International Herald Tribune* for libel over an editorial the paper published suggesting that Prime Minister Goh was simply a figurehead and that ultimate power rested, as it always had, with Senior Minister and former Prime Minister Lee. The Singapore High Court, in a move that halted critical comments from the press, ruled in favor of the government and ordered the Herald Tribune to pay $667,000 in damages to Goh, Lee, and Deputy Prime Minister Lee. In 1995, the government again was criticized in the international press, this time in the New York Times, in which columnist William Safire called the country a dictatorship. Singaporean leaders took center stage in the international arena and proclaimed their right to reject Western values. They claimed that Asian values eschewed individual liberty taking precedence over social stability and that these values promoted an increasingly wealthy, clean, and hospitable city-state devoid of social pathologies that plague both the West and other large Asian cities. The subsequent sentencing, on December 1, 1995 of Nick Leeson, an investment banker who single-handedly destroyed Barings through speculative investments in the Japanese stock market, seemed to confirm the bankruptcy of individual greed.

Parliamentary elections were held in 1997 and, unsurprisingly, the PAP retained its vast majority—opposition parties won only 2 of 83 seats. One seat, that won by Tang Liang Hong, remained vacant in 1997 as Tang fled the country fearing government persecution—including lawsuits, freezing of bank accounts, and restrictions on travel—began in earnest after his election. Tang's victory was seen as especially threatening to the rigid regime of the PAP because during the campaign Tang suggested that the English-speaking section of the ruling class monopolized power and that the Chinese needed to assert more control. These statements branded Tang as a Chinese chauvinist, an inflammatory label in the ethnically divided country.

In February 2000, Finance Minister Richard Hu rescinded some tax cuts introduced previously but also announced positive economic growth of 4.5% to 6.5% for calendar year 2000. Coming after two years of budgetary uncertainty related to the

Asian Economic Crisis, the government also announced a budget surplus.

¹³GOVERNMENT

The constitution of the Republic of Singapore, as amended in 1965, provides for a unicameral parliamentary form of government, with a president who, prior to 1991, served as titular head of state. Singapore practices universal suffrage, and voting has been compulsory for all citizens over 21 since 1959.

In 1993 the unicameral legislature consisted of an 81 elected-member parliament and six nominated members (NMPs) appointed by the president. The maximum term for parliamentary sessions is five years, although elections may be called at any time within that period. A general election is held within three months of dissolution. The number of parliamentary seats has increased with each general election, since the general election seating Singapore's First Parliament, 58 seats (1968), 60 seats (1972), 69 seats (1976), 75 seats (1980), 79 seats (1984), and 81 seats (1988).

Until the 1988 election, all constituencies were single-member constituencies. In 1988, sixty of the original 81 constituencies (out of the increased number for 1988, i.e., from 79 in 1984 to 81 in 1988) were reorganized into 13 group representation constituencies (GRCs). In each GRC teams of three candidates must be fielded, one of who must be from a minority community, i.e., of an ethnic minority group, Malay, Indian, or an Other (all persons other than Chinese, Malay, or Indian). A 1984 constitutional amendment allowed for the presence of at least three opposition representatives as non-constituency (nominated) Members of Parliament (NMPs), and in 1990 a law increasing their number was passed. Accordingly, up to six NMPs can be appointed from among opposition candidates who were unsuccessful in an election; these NMPs are given limited voting rights.

In the 1991 General Election, 60 members were elected from the 15 four-member GRCs, 21 from single-member constituencies, and the President appointed 6 Nominated Members of Parliament. Changes to the electoral procedures included the increase to a minimum of four candidates to contest a GRC and the maintenance of minority qualification for the one person representing the minority community.

The prime minister, who commands the confidence of a majority of Parliament, acts as effective head of government. The prime minister appoints a cabinet that, in 1993, consisted of a senior minister, two deputy prime ministers, and 11 other ministers. Prior to 29 November 1991 the president of the republic was elected by Parliament to a four-year term. Since 1991, under an amendment to the constitution passed by Parliament, the president is no longer elected by Parliament but by the electorate, and has custodial powers over the country's reserves, as well as a major role in deciding key appointments to the judiciary, civil service and statutory boards. The president is elected for a term of six years. The first direct presidential elections were held on 28 August 1993, electing Ong Teng Cheong, who was subsequently reelected in 1999 with a vote of 59% to 41% in the country's first popular presidential election.

Several constitutional reforms were enacted in 1996 and 1997. In 1996, Parliament enacted governmental reforms limiting the power of the president, curtailing his veto power—only granted in 1991. Under the new rules, Parliament can call a referendum if the president vetoes constitutional changes or other measures. In 1997, the number of nominated members of parliament increased from six to nine. However, the government also moved to tighten control over the political process in 1999 with the PAP filing a petition to close the Workers Party for failure to pay damages and costs associated with a defamation case. Earlier in 1998, the government banned all political parties from producing videos and appearing on television to discuss politics.

¹⁴POLITICAL PARTIES

Singapore in the late 1980s was effectively a single-party state. The ruling People's Action Party (PAP) of former Prime Minister Lee Kuan Yew has dominated the country since 1959. In 1961, the radical wing of the PAP split from Lee's majority faction to form a new party, the Socialist Front (SF), also known as the Barisan Socialis. In 1966, 11 SF members resigned their seats in Parliament, and 2 others joined the underground opposition to the Lee government, leaving the PAP as the sole party represented in Parliament. In the general elections of 1972, 1976, and 1980, the PAP won all seats in Parliament, but carried a declining percentage of the total votes; 65 seats (84.4%); 69 seats (72.4%); and 75 seats (75.5%)[Far Eastern Economic Review (FEER) 77.7%], respectively. The Workers' Party (WP), the strongest opposition party, won its first parliamentary seat in a 1981 by-election; under its leader, Joshua B. Jeyaretnam, the WP has been critical of undemocratic practices within the PAP government. In the 1984 general elections, the PAP won 77 of the 79 seats, even though it captured only 62.9% of the popular vote, compared with 75.5% in 1980.

In the 1984, 1988, and 1991 general elections opposition parties gained small ground, and the PAP continued to garner a declining percentage of the total votes: 77 seats (62.9%) PAP [FEER 64.8%], 1 seat Workers Party (WP), 1 seat Singapore Democratic Party (SDP); 80 seats (61.7%) PAP [FEER 63.2%], 1 seat SDP; 77 (61%) PAP [FEER 61%], 1 seat WP, 3 seats SDP, respectively. In the 1991 elections Chiam See Tong was again the winner for the SDP, along with Ling How Doong and Cheo Chai Chen. The Workers' Party MP was Low Thai Khiang.

The two other seats went to J. B. Jeyaretnam (WP) and to Chiam See Tong of the Singapore Democratic Party (SDP), the two main opposition parties that are tolerated but subject to almost continual harassment by the government. For instance, in 1984, Jeyaretnam was accused of making false statements involving irregularities in the collection of WP's funds; he was acquitted of two of three charges and fined. In 1986 the government appealed the case and the higher court set aside the initial judgment; Jeyaretnam was again fined and jailed for one month, enough to disqualify him from parliament and ban him from contesting elections for five years. On the basis of his criminal convictions he was disbarred and denied a pardon. He was refused permission to appeal against the conviction and sentence that resulted in his disqualification as an MP. But on appeal to the Privy Council against the decision to disbar him, he was vindicated and allowed to practice law again. In October 1991 Jeyaretnam avoided bankruptcy by paying legal costs in a defamation suit he lost, filed by Lee Kuan Yew over remarks made by Jeyaretnam in a 1988 election rally. On 10 November 1991, the ban on Jeyaretnam standing election expired. By avoiding bankruptcy he would be able to contest the by-elections that Prime Minister Goh promised to hold in the next 12–18 months. However, the WP failed to field the four required candidates for a GRC.

Then, in March 1993 Dr. Chee Soon Juan, an opposition politician from the SDP who ran against Prime Minister Goh Chok Tong in the 1992 by-election, was expelled from his post as lecturer in the Department of Social Work and Psychology at the National University of Singapore (NUS) based on claims of "dishonest conduct" for using us$138 out of his research grant to courier his wife's doctoral thesis to a US university. In the end, Dr. Chee ended up losing his case to be reinstated.

The main opposition parties are the SDP and the WP. Smaller minority parties are the United People's Front, which is also critical of antidemocratic aspects of the government rule and is pro-Malaysian; the Singapore Malays' National Organization; and the Singapore Solidarity Party, formed in 1986 by three former leaders of the SDP. There were 22 registered political parties at the beginning of 1993: Singapore Chinese Party; Persatuan Melayu Singapura; Partai Rakyat, Singapore State Division; Angkatan Islam; The Workers' Party; Pertubohan Kebangsaan Melayu Singapura; People's Action Party (PAP); United People's Party; Barisan Socialis (BS), Socialist Front (SF); Parti Kesatuan Ra'ayat (United Democratic Party); Singapore Indian Congress; Alliance Party Singapura; United National Front; National Party of Singapore; The People's Front; Justice Party, Singapore; Democratic Progressive Party; People's Republican Party; United People's Front; Singapore Democratic Party (SDP); National Solidarity Party (NSP); Singapore National Front. The Malay Communist Party and the underground Malayan National Liberation Front are illegal.

In 1997, Parliamentary elections were again held and, again, the PAP maintained its virtual monopoly of seats. Of 83 seats up for election, the long-ruling party captured 81 with 47 unopposed. The two opposition leaders Jeyaretnam and Tang Liang Hong, both with the WP won seats. After the election, in a move that has been commonplace in Singapore, leaders of the PAP, including Prime Minister Goh and Senior Minister (and longtime leader) Lee sued Tang for defamation. Tang promptly fled the country, saying he feared for his safety as the government froze his assets and imposed travel restrictions on his family. In the elections, the SDP lost all three seats it had won in the 1991 round.

15 LOCAL GOVERNMENT

Singapore, veritably a city-state, has no local government divisions. When the People's Action Party (PAP) came to power in 1959, the post-colonial City Council was abolished. The former city council and rural board were integrated into departments of the central government. The Town Councils Act enacted in June 1988 reintroduced a local organizational structure. Town councils were formed to take over the management and maintenance of the common properties of housing estates within towns. As of 1 March 1991, 27 town councils had been formed. After the general elections of August 1991, five town councils were dissolved and three new town councils were established, bringing the number of town councils to 25. Suggestions have been introduced to create the position of mayor for each council.

16 JUDICIAL SYSTEM

Singapore's legal system is based on British common law. The judiciary includes the Supreme Court as well as district, magistrate's, and special courts. Minor cases are heard in the country's ten magistrate's courts and in district courts (two civil and four criminal), each presided over by a district judge. The Supreme Court is headed by a chief justice and is divided into the High Court, the Court of Appeal, and the Court of Criminal Appeal. The High Court has unlimited original jurisdiction in both criminal and civil cases but ordinarily chooses to exercise such jurisdictional authority only in major cases. In its appellate jurisdiction, the High Court hears criminal and civil appeals from the magistrates' and district courts. Appeal in a civil case heard by the High Court in its original jurisdiction is to the Court of Appeal, and in a criminal case, to the Court of Criminal Appeal.

In 1993 the former Court of Appeal (for civil cases) and the Court of Criminal Appeal were combined to form a single Court of Appeal. This reform was part of an overall plan to the eventual elimination of referrals to the Privy Council in London. All appeals to the Privy Council in London were eliminated in 1994.

The President appoints judges of the Supreme Court to renewable two-year terms on the recommendation of the Prime Minister after consultation with the Chief Justice. A Legal Service Commission supervises and assigns the placement of the subordinate court judges and magistrates who have the status of civil servants; however, the President appoints subordinate courts judges on the recommendation of the chief justice. While the constitution provides for an independent judiciary and the judicial system provides a fair and efficient judicial process, the Internal Security Act allows the government to arrest, detain, and prosecute those who are deemed to threaten national security. Defendants have the right to be present at the trials, to have an attorney, and to confront witnesses against them.

17 ARMED FORCES

Singapore has made major efforts since 1965 to develop its own armed forces. Compulsory national service has been in effect since 1967. Male citizens are called up for 24–30 months' full-time military service at age 18. The active forces number 73,000 (39,800 conscripts) in 2000.

Singapore's armed forces are small, but they are well trained and equipped, and their reserve strength (275,000 in 2000) is substantial. The army has an estimated 50,000 personnel, including 3 combined arms divisions; the navy has 9,500 personnel and a fleet of 24 ships, including 6 corvettes and 18 missile craft. The air force was established in 1969. Paramilitary forces numbering an estimated 108,000 included a police force and a civil defense force of 120,000. The 1998–99 defense budget was $4.2 billion or approximately 5.1% of gross domestic product.

18 INTERNATIONAL COOPERATION

Singapore follows a policy of cooperation with international bodies and the community of nations. Having joined the UN on 21 September 1965, Singapore participates in ESCAP and all the nonregional specialized agencies except FAO, IDA, IFAD, UNESCO, and UNIDO. It is a participant in the Asian Development Bank, the Colombo Plan, the Commonwealth of Nations, and G-77 and has joined the WTO and signed the Law of the Sea. Probably its most important international association is its membership—along with Indonesia, Malaysia, Thailand, the Philippines, and Brunei—in ASEAN. Singapore has played a leading part in this important regional grouping, which has sought to maximize economic cooperation among its member states, to regularize political consultation on the part of the constituent governments, and to limit foreign political and military interference in the area.

19 ECONOMY

Historically, Singapore's economy was based primarily on its role as an entrepôt for neighboring countries due to its strategic geographic location. It did not have minerals or other primary products of its own to export, but it served a major economic function by processing and transshipping the goods of nearby lands. Its most significant natural resource is a deep water harbor. As a result of these circumstances, Singapore became highly active in shipbuilding and repair, tin smelting, and rubber and copra milling. Until about 1960, however, its economy was frequently shaken by major fluctuations in its export earnings (particularly from rubber and tin) as a consequence of often adverse commodity and price trends. Since the early 1960s, Singapore has attempted to break away from this economic pattern. Its government embarked on an ambitious and largely successful program of promoting industrial investment (both from abroad and locally), developing industrial estates, and providing industrial financing and technical services.

By the early 1980s, Singapore had built a much stronger and diversified economy, which gave it an economic importance in Southeast Asia out of proportion to its small size. Government plans during the first half of the 1980s called for realigning industrial activities from traditional labor-intensive, low-wage activities to capital-intensive, high-wage and high-technology activities, notably the electronic industries and oil refining. In

1985, however, Singapore's economy declined for the first time in 20 years. One of the reasons for the decline was high wages, which made Singaporean products less competitive on the world market. Other reasons for the economic downturn included a slumping demand for oil and electronic products and the economic woes of Malaysia, Indonesia, and other important trading partners.

By the late 1980s, Singapore had begun to further diversify its economy, making it capable of providing manufacturing, financial, and communications facilities for multinational firms. In the late 1980s one of the fastest growing sectors of Singapore's economy was international banking and finance, accounting for some 25% of GDP. It ranked behind Tokyo and Hong Kong amongst financial service centers in the Southeast Asia region. In 1989 earnings from manufacturing accounted for 30% of GDP.

In the 1990s productivity increased as did labor costs. Export growth in high-technology manufactured goods signaled Singapore's success in shifting to higher value-added production. The electronics industry accounted for the largest share of value-added in manufacturing. Manufacturing was dominated by the production of computer peripherals and oil processing. Between 1992 and 1995, property prices doubled and residential property prices peaked in 1996, after which they fell by over 40% in 1998. Prices improved somewhat in 1999. The main constraints on Singapore's economic performance are labor shortages, rising labor costs, and the erosion of productivity. The Government encourages local companies to invest in the region in order to internationalize the economy. The *World Competitiveness Report* ranked Singapore as the most competitive country in 1999.

Rapid expansion in regional economies and growth in key export markets has helped Singapore's GDP to grow by 8.8% in 1995, a slight drop from the 10% growth rates posted in 1993 and 1994. Growth in 1996 was expected to cool to 7%. Inflation has remained low with consumer prices increasing only 1.3% during 1996. In 1998, industrial restructuring moved fixed asset-intensive production industries out of the country, and drew higher-end manufacturing and service operations into Singapore. The Asian financial crisis caused GDP growth to fall to only 0.30% in 1998, as opposed to an average annual growth rate of 9% during the previous decade. GDP growth for 1999 was predicted at a rate of 5%.

20 INCOME

The US Central Intelligence Agency (CIA) reports that in 1998 Singapore's gross domestic product (GDP) was estimated at $91.7 billion. The per capita GDP was estimated at $21,828. The annual growth rate of GDP was estimated at 0.30%. The average inflation rate in 1998 was -0.3%. The CIA defines GDP as the value of all final goods and services produced within a nation in a given year and computed on the basis of purchasing power parity (PPP) rather than value as measured on the basis of the rate of exchange. It was estimated that agriculture accounted for 0% of GDP, industry 28%, and services 72%.

The World Bank reports that for the same period per capita private consumption (in PPP terms) was $10,385. Private consumption includes expenditures of individuals, households, and nongovernmental organizations. It was estimated that between 1990 and 1998 private consumption grew at an annual rate of 6.6%. Approximately 15% of household consumption was spent on food, 5% on fuel, 3% on health care, and 14% on education.

21 LABOR

In 1999, Singapore's employed work force totaled 1.9 million. Of this number, 30% were employed in industry and 70% in the service sector. About 24% of the work force consists of some 500,000 foreign workers. The unemployment rate was 1.9% in mid-1991, 2.7% in 1995, and 3.2% in 1998. Continued growth of the work force from the mid-1960s through the 1980s was largely the result of the government's successful industrialization program.

There is no minimum wage legislation. The standard legal work week is 44 hours, with one day off each week. An annual bonus equal to at least one month's salary is customarily paid. The Industrial Relations Act of 1968 controls relations between management (public and private) and labor.

In 1999, there were 82 registered trade unions in Singapore, with some 260,000 members. All but nine were affiliated with Singapore's National Trade Unions Congress (which represents, as a result, about 99% of the country's organized workers). The government generally asserts a strong influence over trade policies.

Minors as young as 12 may work with the permission of the Commissioner of Labor but there are few applications for such permission and one has never been granted. In practice, the minimum working age is 14 and violations of this regulation are very rare. The government has set minimum workplace health and safety regulations which are effectively enforced. There is no minimum wage.

22 AGRICULTURE

Urbanization and industrialization have taken ever larger amounts of land away from agricultural activity in post-World War II Singapore. Many of the rubber and coconut plantations that dominated Singapore's landscape before the war have disappeared altogether. Housing for a growing population—and factories for its employment—stand where rubber and coconut trees used to grow. Nonetheless, agriculture remains part of Singapore's total economic activity. Growing methods on the island are the most intensive in all of Southeast Asia.

About 1.6% of the land area is used for farming, and vegetables remain a significant source of income. Remarkably, through the decades of the 1960s and 1970s and into the 1980s, Singapore was able to increase its primary produce annually through intensification. In 1998, production of fresh vegetables totaled 5,000 tons, resulting in a decreased need to rely on foreign produce imports. Singapore's trade deficit in agricultural products was us$1.16 billion in 1997. Orchids are grown for export.

23 ANIMAL HUSBANDRY

Singapore has been self-sufficient (or nearly so) in the production of pork, poultry, and eggs since 1964, a notable achievement considering the modest amount of land available and the demands of growing urbanization and industrialization. Hog and poultry farming together constitute Singapore's largest primary products industry. However, hog farming is being phased out because of environmental pollution; domestic pork requirements are increasingly being met by imports. In 1998, the livestock population included 2 million chickens and 190,000 pigs. That year also, about 16,000 tons of eggs were produced.

The Pig and Poultry Research and Training Institute and Lim Chu Kang Veterinary Experimental Station conduct research on feeding, housing, breeding, management, and disease control.

24 FISHING

Local fishermen operate chiefly in inshore waters, but some venture into the South China Sea and the Indian Ocean. Traditional fishing methods are in use along coastal waters, but there is a trend toward mechanization in both offshore and deep-sea fishing. In 1997, Singapore's fishermen caught 13,338 tons of fish.

All fresh fish are auctioned at the Jurong Central Fish Market and at the Punggol Fishing Port and Wholesale Fish Market. The

Jurong facility provides modern shore-support assistance and processing plants. Aquaculture concentrates on the breeding of grouper, sea bass, mussels, and prawns; a marine fish-farming scheme to encourage aquaculture in designated coastal waters was implemented in 1981; by the end of 1985, 60 marine fish farms were in operation. In 1997, Singapore contributed 4.8% to the world's total exports of fish products, valued at us$494.2 million.

25 FORESTRY

In 1995, about 6.6% of Singapore's land area was classified as forest. There is little productive forestry left on the island, but Singapore continues to have a fairly sizable sawmilling industry, processing timber imported largely from Malaysia (with some additional imports from Indonesia). Both Malaysia and Indonesia are expanding their processing capacities, however, and the industry is declining in Singapore in the face of the government's policy shift to high-technology industries. Roundwood production in 1997 was 210,000 cu m, with imports of 133,000 cu m. In 1997, imports of forestry products totaled us$1,097.9 million while exports amounted to us$600.6 million.

26 MINING

There is no mining in Singapore.

27 ENERGY AND POWER

Net installed electrical capacity in 1998 was 5.8 million kW; all power was generated thermally, largely from imported mineral fuels. Electricity generated in 1998 totaled 26.5 billion kWh, more than six times the 1974 total of 3.9 billion kWh. To meet increasing demand for electricity, a new power station was built on the island of Pulau Seraya off the southwest coast of Singapore. The first stage of this station became operational in 1987. As of 2000, the electric power sector was undergoing reorganization; two subsidiaries of state-owned Singapore Power were scheduled to be divested in 2001. Singapore, a major petroleum-refining center, produced gasoline in 1994 at a rate of 100,490 barrels per day; distillate fuel oil, 372,200; residual fuel oil, 288,120; jet fuel, 147,740; and kerosene, 19,060. The total refinery capacity of 1.2 million barrels per day in 1998 ranked Singapore among the top producers in the Far East, alongside Japan, China, and South Korea. In the same year, the refinery sector accounted for 10.7% of total manufacturing.

28 INDUSTRY

Singapore's major industries were once rubber milling and tin smelting. The modern industrialization of Singapore began in 1961 with the creation of the Economic Development Board to formulate and implement an ambitious manufacturing scheme. Most of the first factories set up under this program were of an import-substitute nature requiring tariff protection, but many such protective tariffs were subsequently withdrawn. Large-scale foreign manufacturing operations in Singapore commenced in 1967 with the establishment of plants by several major multinational electronics corporations. The Jurong Town Corporation was established under the Jurong Town Corporation Act of 1968 to develop and manage industrial estates and sites in Singapore. The emphasis was on upgrading facilities to attract high-technology and skill-intensive industries. The manufacturing sector grew by an average annual rate of about 20% during the 1962–74 period, and it registered an average annual increase of over 10% from 1975 to 1981.

Industry's share of the GDP rose from 12% in 1960 to 29% in 1981. Such dramatic achievements were in large measure made possible by the existence in Singapore even before the 1960s of one of the most developed economic infrastructures in Southeast Asia, as well as by government efforts to provide a skilled, disci-plined, and highly motivated work force. Labor-intensive operations are encouraged to move offshore by the government, and service and high-technology industries are encouraged. Major industries are electronics, financial services, oil drilling equipment, petroleum refining, rubber processing and rubber products, processed food and beverages, ship repair, and biotechnology. In 1998, industry accounted for 35% of GDP.

In the first half of 1999, manufacture of electronic products and components grew by almost 17%; pharmaceuticals production expanded by almost 30%; and petroleum refining and petroleum products contracted due to oversupply. Manufacturing accounted for 22% of GDP in 1998.

Electronics have recently become the most important sector of manufacturing. Singapore is the world's leading supplier of computer disk drives; telecommunications and other computer equipment is also manufactured. Electronics contribute at least 10% to GDP and 61% to exports.

Financial and business services add 29% to GDP. Both sectors experienced declining growth rates in 1998, and non-performing loans were expected to continue the downward trend in 1999, but strong activity on the stock market and a return of investor confidence were expected in 2000.

Petroleum refining is a well-established industry in Singapore. After Rotterdam and Houston, Singapore is the world's third largest refining center. Production capacity from five refineries (capable of processing 40 different types of crude oil) exceeds one million barrels per day. A major petrochemical complex is planned to be built on a site created by joining five offshore islands through reclamation.

Government-Linked Companies (GLCs) include Singapore Airlines, Neptune Orient Lines, Development Bank of Singapore, Singapore Technologies, Keppel Corporation, Sembawang Corp., Chartered Semiconductor Manufacturing, Singapore Telecom Petrochemical Corp. of Singapore, and Singapore Refining Corp. These companies account for more than 60% of the country's GDP; they are majority-government-owned, but operate commercially (unlike traditional parastatals).

29 SCIENCE AND TECHNOLOGY

The Science Council, established in 1967, advises the Minister for Trade and Industry on scientific and technological matters relating to research and development and to the training and utilization of manpower. The Singapore National Academy of Science promotes the advancement of science and technology, and the Singapore Association for the Advancement of Science, founded in 1976, disseminates science and technology. Other major scientific and technical learned societies and research facilities include an academy of medicine, an institute of physics, an institute of technical education, botanical gardens, a mathematical society, and a medical association. Scientific education is stressed at the university level and supported by training programs for more than 20,000 students (1990) in the nation's technical and vocational institutes. Special centers have been established for research on cancer, human reproduction, viruses, and immunology. Two new research institutions were established in 1985: the Institute of Systems Science, which does research in the area of information technology, and the Institute of Molecular and Cell Biology, a center for biotechnological research. The Singapore Science Park, located near the National University of Singapore, was developed in 1987. In 1993, the National Computer Board announced an effort to create an "intelligent island" through an information infrastructure linking all of Singapore. In the 1987–97, Singapore had 2,318 scientists and engineers and 301 technicians per million population engaged in research and development. In 1998, high-technology exports were valued at $54.8 million and accounted for 59% of manufactured exports.

In 1991, the government announced a s$250 million spending program to create science and high technology parks. Expenditures for research and development totaled 1.13% of GNP in 1987–97 and were funded by both the private sector and government incentives.

Courses in basic and applied sciences are offered at Nanyang Technical University (founded 1981), the National University of Singapore (founded in 1980 by merger), Ngee Ann Polytechnic (founded 1963), Singapore Polytechnic (founded 1954), and Temasek Polytechnic (founded 1990).

30 DOMESTIC TRADE

Marketing has always been an activity in which Singapore's Chinese, Indian and Arab merchants have played a major role, and their participation has increased in recent years as local branches of European firms have become less important. Warehousing, packaging, freight forwarding, and related services are of a high standard. Usual business hours are 8:30 AM to 5:30 PM, with many businesses closed from 1 to 2 PM. Most major enterprises and foreign firms operate Monday through Friday and are open a half day on Saturday. A number of Chinese and Indian businesses maintain longer hours, with some open seven days a week. Bank hours are 9:30 AM to 3 PM Monday through Friday, and Saturday from 9:30 AM to 11:30 AM. Government offices are open from 8 AM to 5 PM Monday through Friday, and 8 AM to 1 PM on Saturday. Retail stores are open from 10 AM to 7:00 PM Monday through Saturday, with most shops also open on Sunday.

A wide range of consumer goods, such as luxury, electronic, handicraft, and food items, are available in Singapore from international department stores, brand name specialty stores, local department store chains, and neighborhood shops and markets. Singapore has four official languages, Malay, Chinese (Mandarin), Tamil, and English. English is the language of administration and the predominant language of commerce; the local version of Singapore English, i.e., Singlish, predominates in less formal settings. Advertising is done by radio and television, outdoor displays, slides in motion picture theaters, and newspapers. There are several advertising agencies. Consumers are highly brand-conscious, and advertising concentrates considerably on product trademarks. The retail sector is well developed; different retail chains compete for market niches.

31 FOREIGN TRADE

Since World War II, Singapore has changed from an entrepôt center for the incoming and outgoing traffic of its neighbors in Southeast Asia to an exporting country in its own right. The leading exports of the mid-1960s—rubber, coffee, pepper, and palm oil—were replaced in the early 1980s by a variety of capital-intensive manufactures. Except for an occasional slowing, annual levels of trade regularly record double-digit expansion. During the late 1990s, expansion in the high-end manufacturing and services sectors began replacing capital-intensive production.

Most of the advanced electronics that Singapore exports also take up a substantial percentage of the world export market. The following chart shows the top nine exports:

	% OF COUNTRY TOTAL	% OF WORLD TOTAL
Automatic data processing equipment	16	15
Transistors and valves	14	10
Refined petroleum products	7.7	9.7
Office machines	7.6	9.8
Telecoms equipment	6.0	6.3
Sound recorders	2.1	12
Switchgears	2.1	3.9
Electrical machinery	2.1	3.2
Radio broadcast receivers	2.1	13

In 1997 Singapore's imports were distributed among the following categories:

Consumer goods	12.0%
Food	3.3%
Fuels	9.5%
Industrial supplies	17.3%
Machinery	49.8%
Transportation	7.0%
Other	1.0%

Singapore's main trading partners are the ASEAN group—principally Malaysia—the US, Malaysia, China and Hong Kong, and Japan. Principal trading partners in 1998 (in millions of US dollars) were as follows:

COUNTRY	EXPORTS	IMPORTS	BALANCE
United States	21,856	18,783	3,073
Malaysia	16,726	15,691	1,035
China (inc. Hong Kong)	13,285	7,696	5,589
Japan	7,226	17,010	-9,784
Taiwan	4,739	3,893	846
Thailand	4,206	4,849	-643
United Kingdom	3,727	2,771	956
Germany	3,326	3,495	-169
Korea	2,566	3,041	-475
France	2,255	2,924	-669

32 BALANCE OF PAYMENTS

The traditional current account surplus is largely due to demand for non-oil exports (especially electronics) from the US, Japan, and regional countries with electronics production facilities. The account also benefits from high net investment income receipts. Total official reserves are estimated to be equal to 8.8 months of imports. A sharp contraction of imports in 1998 due to the financial crisis caused a high current account surplus, while the devalued currency caused an even larger outflow of cash from the financial accounts. The balance was expected to recover its equilibrium in 1999.

The US Central Intelligence Agency reports that in 1998 the purchasing power parity of Singapore's exports was $128 billion while imports totaled $133.9 billion resulting in a trade balance of -$5.9 billion.

The International Monetary Fund (IMF) reports that in 1998 Singapore had exports of goods totaling $110,379 million and imports totaling $95,702 million. The services credit totaled $18,327 million and debit $17,997 million. The following table summarizes Singapore's balance of payments as reported by the IMF for 1998 in millions of US dollars.

Current Account		17,614
Balance on goods	14,677	
Balance on services	330	
Balance on income	3,784	
Current transfers	-1,178	
Capital Account		-226
Financial Account		-17,641
Direct investment abroad	-3,108	
Direct investment in Singapore	7,218	
Portfolio investment assets	-8,741	
Portfolio investment liabilities	1,258	
Other investment assets	1,595	
Other investment liabilities		-15,863
Net Errors and Omissions		3,218
Reserves and Related Items		-2,965

33 BANKING AND SECURITIES

Singapore was founded as a trading outpost by Raffles of the East India Co. in 1819. The country's rigid development was closely linked to the government's efficient financial management. Conservative fiscal and monetary policies generated high savings, which, along with high levels of foreign investment, allowed growth without the accumulation of external debt. The banking system was open to foreign banks in the late 1960s. In 1988, Singapore had foreign reserves worth about $533 billion, which, per capita, put it ahead of Switzerland, Saudi Arabia, and Taiwan. Many sources of finance are available to organizations doing business in Singapore. The Monetary Authority of Singapore (MAS) requires banks to observe its policy of discouraging the internalization of the Singapore dollar. The MAS performs the functions of a central bank, except for the issuing of currency. The Board of Commissioners of Currency deals with currency issues. The MAS seeks to strike a balance between supervision on the one hand, and development of the financial markets on the other.

As of 1999, Singapore had more than 700 financial institutions, including approximately 230 commercial and merchant banks, 142 of them commercial banks. Some 9 of the 31 banks with full banking licenses were locally incorporated; the remainder were branches of various overseas banks. Since 1971, the government has sought to attract representation by a variety of foreign banks in terms of countries and geographical regions. Most of the new foreign banks allowed into Singapore have been offshore banks that have concentrated on foreign-exchange transactions. The Post Office Savings Bank (POSBank) is the national savings bank (est. 1877). Thirteen commercial banks have restricted licenses, and 98 banks operate offshore. Singapore's four largest banks: DBS Bank, United Overseas Bank (UOB), OCBC Bank, and Overseas Union Bank Ltd. (OUB) had a 90% jump in profits in 1999 over 1998, recovering from the financial crisis quickly.

Singapore has not encouraged the freewheeling financial services culture of Hong Kong; nor has it resorted to a *divigiste* approach, as in South Korea or Taiwan. Until quite recently, Singapore has tried to enjoy the best of both worlds. This is now starting to change, as Singapore's own major banks, long regarded as complacent due to their domestic oligopoly, are beginning to venture overseas.

Over 350 companies are listed on the Stock Exchange of Singapore. In October 1992, the Kuala Lumpur Stock Exchange severed all links with the Singapore Stock Exchange. All the Singapore stocks moved to the Singapore exchange and the Malaysian companies moved to the Kuala Lumpur Stock Exchange. As of mid-1999, the SES had a total market capitalization of $130 billion.

The Singapore International Monetary Exchange (SIMEX) opened in 1984. SIMEX traded, as of the end of 1985, futures contracts in gold, Eurodollar time deposit interest rates, and US/ Deutschemark and US/yen currency exchanges. Trading in Japanese stock index and sterling futures began in 1986. In 1989, SIMEX also became Asia's first energy market with the introduction of the High-Sulphur Fuel Oil futures, the world's most active contract of its kind. In 1999, SIMEX achieved its second highest annual volume of 25.8 million contracts. It was voted International Exchange of the Year in 1989, 1992, 1993, and 1998.

34INSURANCE

Most insurance firms are branches or agencies of UK (or other Commonwealth), European, and US companies, although local participation in insurance—particularly business insurance—is increasing. Marine and warehouse insurance constitutes most of the business insurance, but almost all types of commercial insurance are available.

The regulatory authority is the Insurance Commissioner of the Monetary Authority of Singapore. In 1998, total insurance premiums amounted to s7.8 billion. As of 30th June 1999, there were a total of 160 registered insurers. Singapore hopes to become the premier insurance hub in Asia by 2003.

35PUBLIC FINANCE

Budget surpluses have been registered since 1987. In 1996, government revenues totaled approximately $17.3 billion and expenditures $12.9 billion, including capital expenditures of US$4.5 billion. External debt totaled US$3.2 million.

The US Central Intelligence Agency (CIA) estimates that in 1998 Singapore's central government took in revenues of approximately $16.3 billion and had expenditures of $13.6 billion. Overall, the government registered a surplus of approximately $2.7 billion.

The following table shows an itemized breakdown of government revenues and expenditures. The percentages were calculated from data reported by the International Monetary Fund. The dollar amounts (millions) are based on the CIA estimates provided above.

REVENUE AND GRANTS	100%	16,300
Tax revenue	42.3%	6,892
Non-tax revenue	21.9%	3,577
Capital revenue	35.8%	5,832
EXPENDITURES	100%	13,600
General public services	8.3%	1,123
Defense	28.9%	3,930
Public order and safety	5.1%	689
Education	18.8%	2,560
Health	6.7%	914
Social security	1.8%	243
Housing and community amenities	5.2%	714
Recreation, cultural, and religious affairs	0.1%	10
Economic affairs and services	17.2%	2,335
Interest payments	4.2%	568

36TAXATION

Individual and commercial incomes are taxed whether derived in Singapore or from outside sources. Types of direct taxation include income, property, estate duty, and payroll taxes; the Inland Revenue Department is responsible for the assessment and collection of all such levies. Tax rates for individuals in the 2000 year of assessment ranged from 2%–28%. An across the board one-off rebate of 5% was granted in 2000. Companies are charged at a fixed rate of 25.5% on taxable income. Industrial establishments, companies, and various other businesses are eligible to deduct from their gross profits varying and usually generous depreciation allowances for building, plants, and machinery. There are tax holidays of 5 to 10 years for investing in robotics and other approved "pioneer" industries; other tax incentives for investing in export industries and for expansion of established enterprises; and special incentives for research and development companies to locate in Singapore. Other taxes include a goods and services tax (GST) at a rate of 3% and a stamp tax. The general property tax is 12% annually.

37CUSTOMS AND DUTIES

Prior to the 1960s, Singapore was essentially a free port, with import duties levied only on alcoholic beverages, tobacco and tobacco products, petroleum products, and certain soaps. In 1959, however, a law was passed empowering the government to levy import duties on other products to protect local industries. In the 1960s, many new tariffs were established with the primary aim of helping to support development of local manufacturing firms. In the early 1970s, many items were withdrawn from the tariff list, and by 1982 there were only 176 items on the list, compared with 349 in 1972. In 1985, excise duties on sugar and sugar substitutes and import and excise duties on fuel oil were lifted. By 1993, there were almost no import tariffs except for duties on alcoholic beverages, tobacco products, petroleum products, and a few other items. Duties ranged from 5–45%. There are no export duties. As of 1997, the average tariff in Singapore was below 1%, as more than 96% of goods entered duty-free. In 2000, duties were levied on tobacco products, alcoholic beverages, gasoline, automobiles (31%), and motor-cycles (12%).

Singapore has six free-trade zones, five for seaborne cargo (in the five gateways of the port) and one for air cargo. The GST (Goods and Service Tax) of 3%, which is levied on all imports, is not levied on goods stored in the free-trade zones.

38 FOREIGN INVESTMENT

Legislation to attract new foreign investments, the Economic Incentives Act, was passed in 1967; it granted exemption from taxation for a five-year period to investors for export development and provided inducements and guarantees with respect to repatriation of profits and capital. Overseas offices to promote such foreign investment were set up in New York, Chicago, San Francisco, London, Paris, Frankfurt, Zürich, Tokyo, Hong Kong, Stockholm, and Melbourne. The Capital Participation Scheme, adopted in 1973, permitted high-technology industries to set up branches in Singapore with 50% equity participation by the government. With changes in Singapore's industrial development, there have also been alterations in incentives. In the early 1980s, the main criteria for granting tax incentives were capital investment ratios (including training costs) per worker, value added per worker, and the ratio of technical personnel and skilled workers to the total work force. Major investment activity focused on petroleum refining, general manufacturing, electronics, and hotel construction, as well as on traditional endeavors.

Since the mid-1980s the government's incentive policies have broadened to include Singapore's development as a total international business center, an international air-sea cargo center, a location for the regional operational headquarters of multinational corporations, and a major exporter of services. Investment in the manufacturing sector is encouraged in areas of medium-range or higher technology, or the design and production of higher value-added products. Singapore does not require that foreign investors take on private sector or government joint venture partners.

In 1998, foreign companies invested $3.1 billion in Singapore's manufacturing sector, declining from $4 billion in 1997. US companies accounted for 44% of the total, bringing US investment to $1.4 billion. Overall, foreign firms account for about one-quarter of cumulative gross fixed assets in the manufacturing sector. Other major investors include Japan, the UK, and Germany.

39 ECONOMIC DEVELOPMENT

Technological change and political considerations in the post-World War II period—not least of all the nationalism that accompanied the quest for independence among the region's European colonies—have combined to alter dramatically the economic self-perception and public policies of this diminutive island-state. By the late 1950s, it was obvious that prospects for economic growth would be severely limited if Singapore remained bound by its old economic role as entrepôt. The decision to industrialize—and to do so rapidly—was deliberate policy. Initial emphasis in the government's economic development program was upon employment. The increasing trend toward economic self-sufficiency in neighboring Indonesia and Malaysia—and the steady retreat of the UK from defense responsibilities in the region as a whole (centered on its large Singapore naval and air facilities)—

prompted the government to focus completely on finding alternative employment for the island's highly skilled and disciplined workforce. By the end of the 1960s, this problem was effectively solved, with Singapore boasting one of the lowest unemployment rates in all of Asia.

Emphasis in the mid-1970s was on labor skills and technology, especially as these were identified with such modern industries as machine tools, petrochemicals, electronics, and other precision work. A high level of participation by private foreign capital provided an important cornerstone to this development. In 1979, the government abandoned its earlier policy of stimulating low-wage industries and adopted a policy of encouraging capital-intensive and technologically sophisticated industries. Especially targeted for investment promotion in the 1980s were computers, computer peripherals, electronic medical instruments, automotive components, specialty chemicals and pharmaceuticals, and optical and photocopying equipment. Following the recession of 1985–86, the government concentrated on developing new markets and on turning Singapore into a manufacturing, financial, and communications center for multinational corporations.

In the 1990s the economic development strategy emphasized both the manufacturing and service sectors. The Economic Development Board (EDB), formed in 1961, has guided Singapore's industrialization. Early emphasis was placed on promoting investment in manufacturing. The Strategic Economic Plan (SEP) announced in 1991 focused on education and human resources to enhance export competitiveness. Emphasis on developing the service sector has been supported and enhanced by the Operational Headquarters (OHQ) program, encouraging companies to use Singapore as regional headquarters or as a central distribution center. The Creative Business Program promotes investment in the film, media, and publishing, arts and entertainment, textile, fashion and design sectors. Currently the EDB works toward Singapore's vision of its future as a developed country through the promotion of business. Singapore's globalization strategy hinges on making a transformation from a production-driven economy to an innovation-driven one. Other key elements of this strategy are the reversal of downward trends in productivity, and sustaining foreign investment in Singapore's capital investment. Singapore initiated the formation of a growth-triangle, linking Johor, Malaysia, Singapore and Indonesia's Riau province focusing on Batam Island. Singapore benefits by tapping a supply of low-wage workers and offshore land to sustain its more labor-intensive industries.

The Asian financial crisis was only a temporary setback for the healthy economy of Singapore. Roadblocks to further economic development include rising labor costs; which have threatened investment in Singapore's industrial sector, causing the government to implement strategies to cut costs and increase productivity. The rise of Singapore's currency has also prompted the dispersion of new industrial enterprises from the country, which the government has answered by promoting the development of high-capital industries.

40 SOCIAL DEVELOPMENT

Government-provided social welfare services are directed by the Ministry of Community Development, which is often assisted by various voluntary organizations, most of them affiliated with the Singapore Council of Social Service. Besides institutionalized care, the Ministry of Community Development administers foster and homemaker service schemes for needy young persons. In January 1986, the government operated 88 child care centers and three welfare homes for aged and destitute persons. Social welfare assistance is also provided by mutual-benefit organizations and voluntary services.

All employers and employees earning more than s$50 per month must contribute to the Central Provident Fund, a public pension and retirement program which provides lump-sum benefits for old age, disability, death, sickness, and maternity. Retirement is at age 55. Employee contributions range from 3% to 20%; employers pay 10% of monthly earnings. If employees earn less that S$200 per month, they are exempt from contribution requirements. Employers fund workers' compensation benefits for job-related injuries. In addition, employers are required to provide 14 days of paid sick leave, and 8 weeks of paid maternity leave to their employees.

Women's legal rights are equal to those of men in most areas, including civil liberties, employment, business, and education. Women comprise 42% of the labor force and are well represented in the professions. Despite the legal principle of equal pay for equal work, women earn approximately 75% of the average male salary. This is due in part to the fact that most women work in the lower paying administrative jobs. Women also have a limited ability to transmit their citizenship to their children if they live overseas. In addition, the health benefits of female civil servants do not cover their spouses, as is the case for male employees. In 1999, however, women won the right to sponsor foreign-born husbands for citizenship. Four of 93 parliamentarians were female in 1997.

Prison conditions are considered to be good, but there are reports of the mistreatment of detainees. Caning is a common form of punishment for many different offenses. Cases of police abuse are generally investigated by the government and reported in the media. Freedom of assembly and association are restricted.

41 HEALTH

Singapore's population enjoys one of the highest health levels in all of Southeast Asia. This achievement is largely attributed to good housing, sanitation, and water supply, as well as the best hospitals and other medical facilities in the region. Fully 100% of the population had access to safe drinking water, and 99% had adequate sanitation in 1994–95. Nutritional standards are among the highest in Asia. In 1984, Singapore initiated a Medisave scheme, a compulsory savings plan for medical expenses. About half the population pays hospital bills through this plan, although as of 1990 the plan did not cover outpatient expenses. Singapore is financing medical care with a combination of personal contribution and government assistance. Workers must contribute 3–4% of their earnings to a medical savings account to be used for medical expenses. The contribution of workers is matched by employers. In 1990, there were 19 hospitals, 5 of which were administered by the government, and 5 were "government restructured" (as of 1989, given a large degree of administrative autonomy). The remaining nine hospitals were privately run. The main multidisciplinary hospitals are Alexandra Hospital, Changi Hospital, Tan Tock Hospital (all government run); and National University Hospital, Singapore General Hospital, and Toa Payoh Hospital (all government restructured). In 1990–97, there were 3.6 hospital beds in Singapore per 1,000 people. In 1991, there were 3,779 doctors, 600 dentists, and 10,240 nurses; in addition, there were almost 600 pharmacists (80% of whom operated privately).

In 1990–97, the number of physicians per 1,000 population was 1.4. The fertility rate in 1999 was 1.5 children per woman during her childbearing years. The 1999 birth rate was 13.4 per 1,000 people, and an estimated 74% of married women (ages 15 to 49) used contraception in 1993. Life expectancy in 1999 was 78.8 years, and infant mortality was 3.8 per 1,000 live births. In the same year, 100% of the population had access to health care services. According to a national health survey by the Ministry of Health, high cholesterol had fallen from 27% in 1984 to 19% in 1992; hypertension levels were also down from 15.3% to 13.6%

in the same period. There were 5,457 deaths due to cardiovascular disease in 1995. More men than women smoked in Singapore in 1995 (31.9% vs. 21.7%). However, smoking had increased among 18–19 year olds, from 12% in 1984 to 15.2% in 1992; for 20–39 year olds, the increase was 15.8% to 19.4%. The occurrence of diabetes increased from 4.7% in 1984 to 8.6% in 1992 among people 18–69 years; cancer increased as well. Fourteen percent of Singaporeans exercise regularly. The general mortality rate in 1999 was 4.7 per 1,000 inhabitants. Leading causes of death per 100,000 people in 1990 were communicable diseases and maternal/perinatal causes, 114; noncommunicable diseases, 498; and injuries, 39. There were 48 cases of tuberculosis per 100,000 people reported in 1997. In 1995, vaccination rates for children up to one year old were as follows: tuberculosis (97%); diphtheria, pertussis, and tetanus (95%); polio (93%); measles (88%); and hepatitis B (91%). Overall health care expenditures for 1990–97 were 3.3% of GDP.

The HIV-1 seroprevalence rate was 0.2 per 100 adults in 1997. In 1996, there were 179 AIDS cases. The slow growth of the HIV epidemic in Singapore may be attributed to general awareness and programs promoting condom use at STD clinics.

42 HOUSING

Sustained rapid population growth in the years preceding and following World War II provided Singapore with an acute housing shortage. In 1947, a housing committee determined that, with a squatter problem worsening each year, 250,000 persons required immediate housing, while another 250,000 people would need new housing by the late 1950s. In 1960, the Housing and Development Board was established by the new PAP government. During its first five-year building program (1960–65), the board spent s$230 million to construct 53,000 dwelling units for more than 250,000 people. It was in this period that Queens Town, Singapore's first satellite community, was developed; by the mid-1970s, Queens Town had a total of 27,000 living units in seven neighborhood complexes, housing upward of 150,000 people.

In the second five-year building program (1966–70), 67,000 additional units, accommodating 350,000 persons and costing s$305 million, were built. About 113,000 more units were erected by the board in the third building program (1971–75), and over 130,000 in the fourth building program (1976–80). Another 100,000 units were constructed in the fifth building program (1981–85), and 160,000 were planned for the sixth building program (1986–90). In 1985, as a result of these government-sponsored efforts, 2,148,720 persons—or 84% of the total population of Singapore—lived in 551,767 apartments under the management of the Housing and Development Board. Some 397,180 units had been sold to the public. In 1990, 84% of all housing units were apartments, 7% were bungalows and terrace houses, 5% were condominiums, and 1% were dwellings with attap or zinc roofs. The total number of housing units in 1992 was 758,000.

43 EDUCATION

For the year 2000, adult illiteracy was estimated at 7.6% (males, 3.6%; females, 11.5%). All children who are citizens are entitled to free primary education. Primary schooling is available in all four official languages. Under the education system implemented in stages after 1980, the first three years of primary schooling emphasize the learning of English and any other official language, after which students are streamed, on the basis of performance, into an additional three or five years of primary school. Upon completion of primary school, they can join the Vocational and Industrial Training Board for vocational training, or if they qualify, they can take four or five years of secondary schooling leading to two-year courses in junior colleges or three-year courses in school centers at the preuniversity level.

In 1996, there were 269,668 students 198 primary schools, with 10,618 teachers. Student-to-teacher ratio stood at 25 to one. Also in 1996, secondary schools had 207,719 students and 10,354 teachers. Fifteen vocational institutes offered training courses in the metal, woodworking, electrical, electronic, and building trades.

The National University of Singapore was established on August 8, 1980, through the merger of the University of Singapore and Nanyang University. In addition, there are the Singapore Technical Institute, Ngee Ann Polytechnic, Singapore Polytechnic, and Nanyang Technological Institute. In 1996, all institutions of higher education had 6,689 teaching staff and enrolled a total of 92,140 students.

44 LIBRARIES AND MUSEUMS

The National Library of Singapore (founded in 1844 and known, until 1960, as Raffles National Library) contains almost 2.9 million volumes, including books in the four official languages. The National Library houses the government archives and serves as a repository for official publications printed in Singapore since 1946. The library has nine full-time branches, and a mobile library service for rural portions of the island. The National University of Singapore Library contains over 2 million volumes, including extensive medical and science/technology collections. (The National University of Singapore was formed in 1980 with the merger of the former University of Singapore and Nanyang University.) Singapore Polytechnic holds 202,000 volumes, and the Institute of Southeast Asian Studies holds 139,000.

The National Museum (formerly Raffles Museum), established in 1849, has collections of natural history, ethnology, and archaeology. Since 1965, it has also specialized in the art, culture, and way of life of Singapore's multiracial communities. The National Art Gallery, established in 1976, features works by the peoples of Southeast Asia, and is a part of the National Museum. The Art Museum and Exhibition Gallery of the National University of Singapore includes in its collections Asian art objects and contemporary Singaporean and Malaysian painting and textiles. The new Singapore Art Museum opened in 1996 with a permanent collection of more than 3,000 contemporary paintings and sculptures from Southeast Asian artists. The Lee Kong Chian Art Museum, the Centre of Fine Arts, and Singapore Science Center are also found in the city-state.

45 MEDIA

Postal, telephone, and telegraph services in Singapore are among the most efficient in Southeast Asia. National and international telecommunications services are administered by the Telecommunication Authority of Singapore. Service is available on a 24-hour basis for worldwide telegraph, telephone, and telex communication. There were 1.4 million telephones in 1997.

Broadcasting services are operated by the Singapore Broadcasting Corporation, created in 1980; Radio Singapore, inaugurated in 1963, which broadcasts in Chinese, Malay, English, and Tamil; and Television Singapore. As of 1999, there were 13 AM and 4 FM radio stations and 4 television stations. In 1997, Singapore had 739 radios, 354 television sets, and 273 mobile phones per 1,000 population.

There are English, Chinese, Malay, Tamil and Malayalan daily newspapers. Foreign publications reporting on Southeast Asian political and social affairs must obtain an annual permit to distribute more than 300 copies of each edition in Singapore. Singapore has 10 daily newspapers, with at least one printed in each of the four official languages. The oldest and most widely circulated daily is the English-language *Straits Times,* founded in 1845.

In 1999 Singapore's largest newspapers, with their estimated daily circulations, were as follows:

	LANGUAGE	CIRCULATION
Straits Times (m)	English	313,000
Lian He Zao Bao (m)	Chinese	205,000
Lian He Wan Bao (e)	Chinese	85,000
Shin Min Daily News (e)	Chinese	102,000
Berita Harian (m)	Malay	44,700
Business Times (m)	English	23,000
Tamil Murasu (m)	Tamil	8,500

Although freedom of the press is guaranteed by law, the International Press Institute has on various occasions cited Singapore for interference with press freedom. Magazines, motion pictures, and plays are censored for sexual content and presentation of ethnically sensitive matters. In August 1986, parliament passed a bill enabling the government to restrict sales and distribution of foreign publications "engaging in domestic politics." Two months later, the government announced that the distribution of *Time* magazine would be reduced because the magazine had refused to print the entire text of a letter from a government official. In 1987, similar distribution restrictions were placed on the *Asian Wall Street Journal.*

As of 1996, there were 486,340 personal computers; there were 188 Internet hosts per 1,000 population in 1998.

46 ORGANIZATIONS

Singapore has a wide variety of organizations, some private in their origin and direction and others essentially government controlled. There are service clubs belonging to international associations; YMCAs and YWCAs; Chinese, Indian, and Malay chambers of commerce; and a multicommunal Singapore chamber of commerce. In addition to such largely private organizations, the government established in 1960 the People's Association, to organize and promote mass participation in social, cultural, educational, and recreational activities. In Singapore, there is a comprehensive network of 133 community centers throughout the country set up by the People's Association. Management, women's, youth, and senior-citizen subcommittees exist as active units of the association.

47 TOURISM, TRAVEL, AND RECREATION

Tourists wishing to enter or visit Singapore must have a valid passport or other internationally recognized travel document. Visas are required by nationals of Afghanistan, India, Cambodia, Laos, China, Russia, Viet Nam, and holders of Palestinian refugee papers and Hong Kong certificates of identity. Vaccinations are required against yellow fever for travelers from an infected country.

In 1997, 7,197,963 tourists visited Singapore, mostly from East Asia and the Pacific. That year Singapore earned US$6.8 billion from tourism. There were a total of 33,199 hotel beds, filled to 80% of capacity.

Shopping, with bargaining the usual practice, is a major tourist attraction. Points of interest include the Van Kleef Aquarium at Fort Canning Park, the Singapore Zoological and Botanical Gardens, and the resort island of Sentosa. Singapore has a number of other attractions, including an amusement park at Haw Pav Village, site of historic Chinese statues, and the restoration of the Alkaff Mansion.

Singapore has many sports clubs and associations, notably in the areas of badminton (in which Singaporeans have distinguished themselves internationally), basketball, boxing, cricket, cycling, golf, hockey, horse racing, motoring, polo, swimming, tennis, and yachting.

According to 1999 UN estimates, the cost of staying in Singapore was approximately US$207 per day.

⁴⁸FAMOUS SINGAPOREANS

Sir Thomas Stamford Bingley Raffles (1781–1826) played the major role in the establishment of a British presence on Singapore Island in 1819; he introduced policies that greatly enhanced Singapore's wealth, and he suppressed the slave trade. Raffles also distinguished himself as a collector of historical and scientific information. The English writer and educator Cyril Northcote Parkinson (1909–93), formerly a professor at the University of Singapore, became internationally known as the originator of Parkinson's Law. Singapore's dominant contemporary figure is Lee Kuan Yew (b.1923), prime minister of the Republic of Singapore from 1965 to 1990.

⁴⁹DEPENDENCIES

Singapore has no territories or colonies.

⁵⁰BIBLIOGRAPHY

Barr, Michael D. *Lee Kuan Yew, the Beliefs Behind the Man.* Washington, D.C.: Georgetown University Press, 2000.

Bedlington, Stanley S. *Malaysia and Singapore: The Building of New States.* Ithaca, N.Y.: Cornell University Press, 1978.

Chan, Heng Chee. *The Dynamics of One Party Dominance: The PAP at the Grass Roots.* Singapore: University of Singapore Press, 1976.

Chew, Ernest and Edwin Chew (eds.). *A History of Singapore.* New York: Oxford University Press, 1991.

Chiu, Stephen Wing-kai. *City States in the Global Economy: Industrial Restructuring in Hong Kong and Singapore.* Boulder, Colo.: Westview Press, 1997.

Chua, Beng Huat. *Communitarian Ideology and Democracy in Singapore.* London: Routledge, 1995.

———. *Culture, Multiracialism and National Identity in Singapore.* Singapore: Dept. of Sociology, National University of Singapore, 1995.

Darusman, Suryono. *Singapore and the Indonesian Revolution, 1945–50 of Suryono Darusman.* Singapore: Institute of Southeast Asian Studies, 1992.

Dumargay, Jacques. *Cultural Sites of Malaysia, Singapore, and Indonesia.* New York: Oxford University Press, 1998.

Fletcher, Nancy McHenry. *The Separation of Singapore from Malaysia.* Ithaca, N.Y.: Southeast Asia Program, Cornell University, 1969.

Flower, Raymond. *Raffles: The Story of Singapore.* Singapore: Eastern Universities Press, 1984.

Haas, Michael. *The Singapore Puzzle.* Westport, Conn.: Praeger, 1999.

Hassan, Riaz (ed.). *Singapore: Society in Transition.* Kuala Lumpur: Oxford University Press, 1976.

Jayapal, Maya. *Old Singapore.* New York: Oxford University Press, 1992.

Kennedy, Joseph. *When Singapore Fell: Evacuations and Escapes, 1941–42.* New York: St. Martin's, 1989.

Lee, W. O. *Social Change and Educational Problems in Japan, Singapore, and Hong Kong.* New York: St. Martin's, 1991.

LePoer, Barbara Leitch (ed.). *Singapore: A Country Study.* 2d ed. Washington, D.C.: Library of Congress, 1991.

Lingle, Christopher. *Singapore's Authoritarian Capitalism: Asian Values, Free Market Illusions, and Political Dependency.* Fairfax, Va.: Locke Institute, 1996.

Makepeace, Walter (ed.). *One Hundred Years of Singapore.* New York: Oxford University Press, 1986.

Managing Political Change in Singapore: The Elected Presidency. Edited by Kevin Tan and Peng Er Lam. London: Routledge, 1997.

Minchin, James. *No Man is an Island: A Portrait of Singapore's Lee Kuan Yew.* 2d ed. Sydney: Allen & Unwin, 1990.

Mulliner, K. *Historical Dictionary of Singapore.* Metuchen, N.J.: Scarecrow Press, 1991.

Murray, Geoffrey. *Singapore: The Global City-State.* Kent, U.K.: China Library, 1996.

Peebles, Gavin. *The Singapore Economy.* Cheltenham, U.K.: Edward Elgar, 1996.

Quah, Jon S., *et al.* (eds.). *Government and Politics of Singapore.* New York: Oxford University Press, 1985.

Quah, Stella R. *Singapore.* Oxford: Clio, 1988.

Rahim, Lily Z. *The Singapore Dilemma: the Political and Educational Marginality of the Malay Community.* New York: Oxford University Press, 1998.

Regnier, Philippe. *Singapore: City-state in South-East Asia.* Honolulu: University of Hawaii Press, 1991.

Tamney, Joseph B. *The Struggle Over Singapore's Soul: Western Modernization and Asian Culture.* Berlin: W. de Gruyter, 1996.

Trocki, Carl A. *Opium and Empire: Chinese Society in Colonial Singapore, 1800–1910.* Ithaca, N.Y.: Cornell University Press, 1990.

Turnbull, C. M. *A History of Singapore, 1819–1988.* 2d ed. New York: Oxford University Press, 1989.

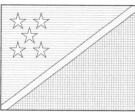

SOLOMON ISLANDS

CAPITAL: Honiara.

FLAG: The flag consists of two triangles, the upper one blue, the lower one green, separated by a diagonal gold stripe; on the blue triangle are five white five-pointed stars.

ANTHEM: *God Save the Queen.*

MONETARY UNIT: The Solomon Islands dollar (si$), a paper currency of 100 cents, was introduced in 1977, replacing the Australian dollar, and became the sole legal tender in 1978. There are coins of 1, 2, 5, 10, 20, and 50 cents and 1 dollar, and notes of 2, 5, 10, 20, and 50 dollars. si$1 = us$0.2002 (us$1 = si$4.995) as of 31 March 2000.

WEIGHTS AND MEASURES: The metric system is in force.

HOLIDAYS: New Year's Day, 1 January; Queen's Birthday, June; Independence Day, 7 July; Christmas, 25 December; Boxing Day, 26 December. Movable religious holidays include Good Friday, Easter Monday, and Whitmonday.

TIME: 11 PM = noon GMT.

¹LOCATION, SIZE, AND EXTENT

The Solomon Islands consists of a chain of six large and numerous small islands situated in the South Pacific, some 1,900 km (1,200 mi) NE of Australia and about 485 km (300 mi) E of Papua New Guinea. Extending 1,688 km (1,049 mi) ESE–WNW and 468 km (291 mi) NNE–SSW, the Solomon Islands has an area of 28,450 sq km (10,985 sq mi). Comparatively, the area occupied by the Solomon Islands is slightly larger than the state of Maryland. The largest island is Guadalcanal, covering 5,302 sq km (2,047 sq mi); other major islands are Makira (formerly Malaita), San Cristobal, Vella Lavella, Choiseul, Rennell, New Georgia, and the Santa Cruz group. The total coastline of the Solomon Islands is 5,313 km (3,301 mi).

The capital city of the Solomon Islands, Honiara, is located on the island of Guadalcanal.

²TOPOGRAPHY

The topography varies from the volcanic peaks of Guadalcanal to low-lying coral atolls. Densely forested mountain ranges are intersected by precipitous, narrow valleys. The highest peak is Mt. Popomanasiu, at 2,447 m (8,127 ft), on Guadalcanal, an island that also contains the country's most extensive alluvial grass plains. Rivers are narrow and impassable except by canoe. Extensive coral reefs and lagoons surround the island coasts.

³CLIMATE

The climate is tropical. From December to March, northwest equatorial winds bring hot weather and heavy rainfall; from April to November, the islands are cooled by drier southeast trade winds. Damaging cyclones occasionally strike during the rainy season. The annual mean temperature is 27°C (81°F); annual rainfall averages 305 cm (120 in), and humidity is about 80%.

⁴FLORA AND FAUNA

Dense rain forest covers about 90% of the islands, with extensive mangrove swamps and coconut palms along the coasts. The islands abound in small reptiles (over 70 species), birds (150 species), and mammals, as well as insect life. There are over 230 varieties of orchids and other tropical flowers.

⁵ENVIRONMENT

Most of the coral reefs surrounding the islands are dead or dying. As an island nation, the Solomon Islands are concerned with the effects of global warming and rising sea levels. Deforestation is another significant environmental problem. United Nations sources estimate that the nation's forests will be exhausted in 10–15 years. The related problem of soil erosion threatens the country's agricultural productivity. The nation has 10.7 cu mi of water, of which 40% is used for farming and 20% for industrial activity. Some 42% of the nation's rural people and 18% of city dwellers do not have pure water. Sources of pollution include sewage, pesticides, and mining by-products. Two mammal species and 20 bird species were endangered, as well as 28 types of plants. Endangered or extinct species include the gizo white-eye and the hawksbill, green sea, and leatherback turtles.

⁶POPULATION

The population of Solomon Islands in 2000 was estimated at 470,000. An estimated 3.3% of the population is 65 years of age or older. The projected population for the year 2005 is 545,000, assuming a crude birthrate of 31 per 1,000 population and a death rate of 4, resulting in a natural rate of change of 2.8% for the period 2000–2005. The population rate of change between 1995 and 2000 was 3.2%.

The estimated overall population density in 1996 was only 15 per sq km (39 per sq mi), but there are significant variations from island to island; moreover, most mountainous and heavily wooded areas are inaccessible (except to tribal groups of the interior), and most of the population is concentrated in the coastal regions. It was estimated that 20% of the population lived in urban areas in 2000. The most populous islands are Malaita and Guadalcanal. Honiara, on Guadalcanal, is the largest town and chief port. Also the capital city, Honiara had a 2000 population of 53,000.

7MIGRATION

Since 1955, immigrants from the Gilbert Islands (now Kiribati) have settled in underpopulated areas. Movements from the countryside to Honiara and north Guadalcanal have created problems of overcrowding. The resentment engendered by those who moved from the heavily populated island of Malaita to Guadalcanal resulted in violence in 1999. The net migration rate for 1999 was zero.

8ETHNIC GROUPS

In 1999, Melanesians constituted 93% of the total population. Also enumerated were Polynesians at 4%, Micronesians at 1%, Europeans at 0.8%, Chinese at 0.3%, and others accounting for 0.4%. Melanesians live mainly on the larger islands; Polynesians tend to inhabit the smaller islands and atolls.

9LANGUAGES

English is the official language but is only spoken by approximately 1–2% of the population. Melanesian pidgin is the lingua franca. Some 120 indigenous languages and dialects are spoken, each within a very restricted geographical area. Melanesian languages are spoken by about 85% of the population, Papuan languages by 9%, and Polynesian languages by 4%.

10RELIGIONS

Christianity, introduced by missionaries, is the principal organized religion. As of 1999, 34% of the islanders were Anglicans; 19% were Roman Catholics; 17% were Baptists; 11% were United (Methodist/Presbyterian); 10% were Seventh-Day Adventist; 5% were other Protestant; and 4% adhered to traditional indigenous religions. There is also a small Baha'i community.

11TRANSPORTATION

In 1996 there were an estimated 1,360 km (845 mi) of roads in the Solomons, of which only 34 km (21 mi) were paved. Of the 1,326 km (824 mi) of unpaved roads, about 800 km (497 mi) belong to private plantations. Shipping services link the Solomons with other Pacific islands, Australia, Japan, and Europe. Honiara is the principal port, followed by Ringi Cove. A fleet of government vessels provides interisland connections and handles about one-third of total tonnage carried. There were 33 airports in 1998, only 2 of which had paved runways. Henderson's Field, on the northern coast of Guadalcanal, is the site of Honiara's civil airport. Solomon Airlines provides regular flights between islands and to nearby Papua New Guinea and Vanuatu. In 1997, Solomon Airlines carried 94,000 passengers on domestic and international flights.

12HISTORY

The islands now known as the Solomons are thought to have been inhabited originally by Melanesians, whose language has affinities with Malay but whose precise origin has not been determined. The first European contact with the Solomons, in 1567, was the sighting of Santa Isabel Island by the Spanish explorer Alvaro de Mendaña; the following year, Mendaña and another Spaniard, Pedro de Queirós, explored some of the islands. Mendaña named the islands Islas de Salomon, thinking that the gold source for King Solomon's riches was located there.

European contact with the Solomons was cut off for nearly two centuries until they were visited by the English navigator Philip Carteret in 1767. Following Carteret's visit, the British navy began to make periodic calls at the islands. During the period 1845–93, the Solomons were frequently visited by missionaries and traders. Indigenous peoples were also subjected to exploitation by "blackbirders," who impressed their captives into forced labor, often on colonial sugar plantations in Fiji, Hawaii, Tahiti, or Queensland. The brutality of the kidnappers provoked reprisals by the islanders, resulting in mass slayings of both Europeans and local peoples.

In 1893, the British government stepped in and established a protectorate over certain islands in the southern Solomons, including Guadalcanal, Malaita (now Makira), San Cristobal, and the New Georgia group. The remainder of the Solomons had by this time fallen under German dominion; some of these, including Choiseul and Santa Isabel, were transferred by treaty to the UK in 1900. The British Solomon Islands Protectorate, as the entire group came to be known, initially was under the jurisdiction of the Office of the British High Commissioner for the Western Pacific.

During World War II, the Solomons provided the theater for some of the most bitter fighting of the Pacific war after Japanese troops invaded and occupied Guadalcanal in 1942. A Japanese airfield on the island's northern coast—later known as Henderson's Field—was captured by US marines on 7 August 1942, the opening foray in the Battle of Guadalcanal, which cost the lives of about 1,500 US soldiers and 20,000 Japanese. Guadalcanal was evacuated by Japan in February 1943, although Japanese forces remained elsewhere in the Solomons until 1945. Widespread destruction and loss of life were visited on the local peoples during the war, and the legacy of social dislocation gave impetus to the development of a pro-independence nationalist movement in Malaita known as the Marching Rule.

In 1953, local advisory councils were set up in Malaita, eventually spreading to other islands of the protectorate. In 1960, the territorial government appointed executive and legislative councils, which were granted their first elected minority in 1964. A new constitution promulgated in April 1970 provided for replacement of the two councils by a unitary Governing Council, the majority of whose members were to be elected. During May and June, the Solomon Islands' first general election was held, with voters selecting 17 of the council's 26 members. On 21 August 1974, a new constitution introduced a ministerial system of government headed by a Council of Ministers. A Legislative Assembly subsequently chose Solomon Mamaloni as the Solomons' first chief minister. In May 1975, a delegation from the Solomon Islands, led by Mamaloni, met with UK officials in London and set up a timetable for internal self-government and for full independence. On 22 June 1975, the territory's name was officially changed from the British Solomon Islands Protectorate to the Solomon Islands.

The islands achieved internal self-government in 1976 and became an independent member of the Commonwealth of Nations on 7 July 1978. Peter Kenilorea was prime minister until his coalition government collapsed in August 1981, after which Mamaloni returned to power. In October 1984, Sir Peter Kenilorea (as he had become) was reelected prime minister, but he resigned in November 1986, following allegations of mismanagement of funds; Ezekiel Alebua, deputy prime minister, succeeded him. In the general elections of February 1989 the People's Alliance Party (PAP), led by Solomon Mamaloni, defeated the Alebua government. Mamaloni became the new prime minister in March 1989. Mamaloni resigned as PAP leader in October 1990 and formed a coalition government with several members of the opposition. Francis Billy Hilly, an independent supported by members of the National Coalition Partners (a loose six-party coalition), became the Solomon Islands' new prime minister in June 1993. Hilly worked with the Melanesian Spearhead Conference to ease tension between the Solomon

Islands and Papua New Guinea. In 1994, Parliament voted to replace Hilly with Mamaloni, leader of the Group for National Unity and Reconciliation (GNUR), the largest political party in Parliament.

In the 1997 National Parliament elections, GNUR retained its majority, and Bartholomew Ulufa'ala was elected prime minister. He pledged to resolve the Solomons financial crisis by improving revenue collections and downsizing government ministries. He also grappled with the problem of finding a resolution to the ethnic conflict in Guadalcanal which dominated all other domestic political issues since late 1998. By 1999, Ulufa'ala reported increased support from the Guadalcanal members of parliament, and noted signs that social unrest was abating in Guadalcanal.

¹³GOVERNMENT

Under the independence constitution of 1978, the Solomon Islands is a parliamentary democracy with a ministerial system and a unicameral National Parliament, consisting of 47 (38 until the 1993 election) members elected to four-year terms; suffrage is universal for citizens over the age of 18. The prime minister, who must command a parliamentary majority, selects the 14-member cabinet. The head of state is the British monarch, represented by the governor-general. Governor-general since 1994, Sir Moses Pitakaka, was replaced in May 1999 by Anglican priest Father John Lapli, who was elected by the National Parliament over six other candidates, including Pitakaka. There is a constitutionally provided Ombudsman to provide protection against improper administrative treatment.

¹⁴POLITICAL PARTIES

The members of the first Parliament formed after independence in 1978 had no party affiliations. However, political parties emerged shortly before the elections of August 1980, in which the Solomon Islands United Party, headed by Peter Kenilorea, won 14 seats; the People's Alliance Party (PAP), led by Solomon Mamaloni, received 8 seats; the National Democratic Party (NDP), 2 seats; and independents, 14 seats.

In the August 1997 elections. the Group for National Unity and Reconciliation (GNUR) retained its 21 seats, the PAP won 7 seats; the National Action Party (NAPSI), 5; Labour (SILP), 4; United Party (UP), 4; and independents, 6, and other parties, 3. The next parliamentary elections were scheduled for August 2001.

¹⁵LOCAL GOVERNMENT

The islands are divided into eight administrative districts, of which seven are provinces with elected assemblies; the eighth is the town of Honiara, governed by an elected council. In outlying areas, village headmen exercise administrative responsibilities.

¹⁶JUDICIAL SYSTEM

The judicial system is based on a blend of British and traditional systems and consists of the High Court, magistrate's courts, and local courts. Appeals from magistrate's courts go to the High Court; customary land appeals courts hear appeals from the local courts.

Defendants in criminal cases are entitled to counsel and to the writ of habeas corpus. Violations of civil liberties are punishable by fines and jail sentences. An ombudsman with the power of subpoena can investigate complaints of violations of civil liberties. The traditional culture, in addition to legal provisions, provides strong protection against arbitrary interference with privacy, home, family, and correspondence.

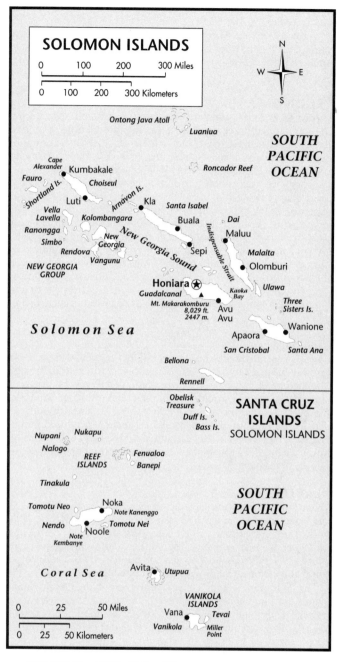

LOCATION: 5° to 12°30's; 155° to 170°E. **TERRITORIAL SEA LIMIT:** 12 mi.

¹⁷ARMED FORCES

The Solomon Islands has no military forces. There is a reconnaissance and surveillance force and a police force deployed among 19 stations in 5 police districts.

¹⁸INTERNATIONAL COOPERATION

The Solomon Islands joined the UN on 19 September 1978 and belongs to ESCAP, IBRD, IDA, IFAD, IFC, ILO, IMF, UPU, and WHO. It participates in the Asian Development Bank, Commonwealth of Nations, G-77, and South Pacific Commission and Forum. The nation is a member of the WTO and a signatory of the Law of the Sea. In December 1997, Solomon Islands achieved full membership in UNESCO. The Solomon Islands has resident diplomatic representation only at the UN; the UN ambassador is also accredited to the US. The minister for foreign affairs serves as a roving envoy. The UK, Australia, New Zealand, Japan, China, and Papua New Guinea maintain diplomatic missions in Honiara; US interests are handled by its ambassador to Papua New Guinea.

19ECONOMY

At least 80% of the population is tied to subsistence agriculture. The capital sector is dependent on the production of copra, timber, and fish for export, but outputs of other cash commodities—particularly cocoa, spices, and palm oil—have grown in recent years. The development of large-scale lumbering operations has increased timber production considerably, and concern about the preservation of forest resources led to government restriction of log exports in 1993. In the late 1990s, the economic downturn in Asia led to the collapse of the export market for logs—primarily Japan and South Korea. In late 1997, the government devalued the currency to encourage development of other export products and to discourage the growth of imports. The economy declined by 10% in 1998, and the government initiated cutbacks in government agencies. The islands are rich in undeveloped mineral resources such as lead, zinc, nickel, and gold.

20INCOME

The US Central Intelligence Agency (CIA) reports that in 1998 the Solomon Islands's gross domestic product (GDP) was estimated at $1.150 billion. The per capita GDP was estimated at $2,600. The annual growth rate of GDP was estimated at -10%. The average inflation rate in 1998 was 9.7%. The CIA defines GDP as the value of all final goods and services produced within a nation in a given year and computed on the basis of purchasing power parity (PPP) rather than value as measured on the basis of the rate of exchange.

21LABOR

About 90% of Solomon Islanders engage in subsistence farming. The wage labor force in 1992 totaled 26,842. As of 1993, 28% worked in agriculture; 14% had jobs in industry; and the remainder were in services. The country suffers from an acute shortage of skilled workers, and an estimated 80% of professional and technical employees are recruited from overseas.

The Solomon Islands' largest trade union is the Solomon Islands National Union of Workers. Unions are free to organize and strike, although unions seldom strike. About 60% to 70% of wage earners were unionized as of 1999. Most employed persons have a standard workday of between 5 and 6 hours, six days a week, with overtime bringing the average workweek to 45 hours. Government regulations require employers to provide housing for workers whose jobs do not permit them to travel to and from home each day. The law requires provision of medical attention in the case of illness; the payment of wages during sickness is customary rather than mandatory.

The minimum working age is 12, or 15 years old for work in factories or on ships. In practice, given low wages and high unemployment, there is little reason to hire children. The minimum wage was $0.31 per hour in 1999.

22AGRICULTURE

About 2% of the total land area is utilized for temporary or permanent crops. Agriculture accounts for about 31% of GDP. Copra is typically the dominant export and the economic lifeline of the Solomons; world copra prices strongly affect the economy, so that a decline in copra prices in 1985 inaugurated an economic slump, exacerbated by the effects of Cyclone Namu. In 1992,

production of copra increased by over 30% from 1991, for a total of 38,500 tons. The rebound in 1992 came from a near doubling of world prices and better coordination of domestic shipping. Copra production in 1998 was estimated at 66,000 tons. About 75% of the copra is produced by small holders, principally on Guadalcanal, Choiseul, the Russell Islands, San Cristobal, Santa Isabel, and Vella Lavella. Development plans called for crop diversification and the construction of a copra mill on the islands. The overseas marketing of copra is a monopoly of the government's Solomon Islands Copra Board. Other agricultural products in 1998 included cocoa, 4,000 tons; palm oil, 29,000 tons; and palm kernels, 7,000 tons. In 1997, the trade surplus in agricultural products was $6.6 million. Exports of palm, copra, and cocoa typically account for over 20% of total exports.

The major food crops are coconuts, yams, taro, sweet potatoes, cassava, and green vegetables. The government has encouraged the cultivation of rice, rotated with soybeans, in the Guadalcanal plains; however, cyclone losses resulted in increased dependence on imported rice.

23ANIMAL HUSBANDRY

Cattle were traditionally kept on coconut plantations as a means of controlling the growth of grass, and many large copra plantations raised cattle for slaughter. There were 10,000 head of cattle and 57,000 pigs on the islands in 1998. Over 40% of the cattle are raised by small holders. The government's Livestock Development Authority (LDA) maintains about 3,200 head on Guadalcanal and Western Province. The LDA is now mostly a producer of trader pigs and poultry, raising 25,000 chicks and 120 piglets per month for sale. Production of pork has doubled since the early 1980s, yet still has not kept up with domestic demand. About 3,000 tons of meat were produced in 1998.

24FISHING

Fish are an essential part of the local diet, and fishing has become an important commercial activity. In 1991, the total catch reached a record high of 69,292 tons; the total catch in 1997 was 53,765 tons. In 1997, the annual catch of skipjack tuna declined was 30,291 tons. Exports of fish products in 1997 were valued at nearly $38.8 million. Aquacultural production in 1997 consisted of 11 tons of giant prawns.

25FORESTRY

Forests cover about 85.4% of the total area, with about 2,389,000 ha (5,903,000 acres) of timber stands providing an estimated timber yield in 1997 of 872,000 cu m, of which about 700,000 cu m was exported as logs. Exports of forest products were valued at $131.8 million in 1997, 97% of it from logs. Important forest timbers are kuari, balsa, teak, Honduras and African mahoganies, Queensland maple, silky oak, and black bean. Several hundred chainsaw operators and about 40 portable sawmills produce over one-fifth of all sawn timber. Logging at current rates (15–16,000 ha/37–39,000 acres per year) exceeds the estimated maximum sustainable annual cut by three times, which means that logging at current rates will presumably exhaust commercially loggable forests in less than ten years. Forest preservation and management legislation has been proposed, but as of 2000, there was no long-term viable silvicultural plan in place.

26MINING

Although the archipelago was named in the 16th century for the fabled gold mines of King Solomon and has long-term mining potential, there have been insufficient high-quality mineral deposits to justify extensive mining investment. The Gold Ridge mine at Mavu on Guadalcanal is expected, however, to effect a significant increase in export earnings, possibly raising the mining sector's contribution to the GDP from 1% to 15%. Deposits of bauxite, nickel, copper, chromite, and manganese ores have also been found. Mineral production in 1997 consisted solely of clay, crusted stone, and construction sand and gravel, all in small quantities.

27ENERGY AND POWER

Most electric power is supplied by the government-controlled Solomon Islands Electricity Authority, although some private undertakings produce their own electricity. The Solomon Islands relies primarily on hydroelectric energy for power generation. Electric generating capacity was 12,000 kW in 1998, and electrical output was 30 million kWh. Honiara accounts for 90% of electricity consumption.

The Komarindi hydropower project, planned to produce up to 8,000 kW of power on the upper Lungga River, advanced from engineering design to provisional funding in 1992. The total cost for the project is estimated at $31 million, funded primarily by grant aid from Norway, the EC, and the ADB.

Oil and natural gas exploration continues, especially in Iron Bottom Sound, north of Guadalcanal. The government regulates petroleum exploration and production. In 1996, mineral fuels accounted for 11.3% of the total value of imports.

28INDUSTRY

Industrial activity in the Solomons is rudimentary, lacking in both the capital and the skilled labor necessary for significant development. The leading industries are fish processing and timber milling; soaps are made from palm oil and coconut oil. Small firms produce a limited array of goods for the local market: biscuits, tobacco products, rattan furniture, baskets and mats, concrete blocks, boats, and fiberglass products.

29SCIENCE AND TECHNOLOGY

The Solomon Islands College of Higher Education has schools of nursing, natural resources, marine and fisheries studies, and industrial development.

30DOMESTIC TRADE

Honiara is the commercial center. Most commercial enterprises have been controlled by Chinese or Europeans; a large segment of the population still relies on bartering. Normal banking hours are 9 to 11:30 AM and 1:30 to 3 PM, Monday–Thursday, and 9 AM to 3 PM on Friday. Normal office hours are 8 AM to 12 PM and 1 PM to 4:30 PM, Monday through Friday.

31FOREIGN TRADE

Overseas trade volume expanded rapidly in the mid-1990s, but the economic woes in Asia in the late 1990s caused the export market to contract significantly. The distribution of the Solomon Islands' trade continues to be limited by the huge distances to potential export markets. The Solomon Islands' major exports are timber (68%) and fish (14%). Other exports include palm oil (6.5%), oil seeds (4.3%), and cocoa (1.7%).

In 1996 the Solomon Islands's imports were distributed among the following categories:

Consumer goods	13.4%
Food	13.7%
Fuels	24.7%
Industrial supplies	20.1%
Machinery	13.2%
Transportation	12.8%
Other	2.1%

Principal trading partners in 1998 (in millions of US dollars) were as follows:

COUNTRY	EXPORTS	IMPORTS	BALANCE
Japan	55	9	46
Thailand	39	3	36
United Kingdom	13	2	11
Philippines	11	2	9
Korea	10	9	1
Germany	9	1	8
Singapore	6	12	-6
China (inc. Hong Kong)	6	5	1
Australia	4	60	-56
New Zealand	1	7	

32BALANCE OF PAYMENTS

In 1992, export earnings were exceptionally high, due to a massive income windfall from the steep rise in the volume of log exports at a time when prices in Asian markets were being driven up by a supply shortage. By the late 1990s, the market for logs had collapsed, causing strain to the Solomon Islands balance of payments.

The US Central Intelligence Agency reports that in 1996 the purchasing power parity of the Solomon Islands's exports was $184 million while imports totaled $151 million resulting in a trade balance of $33 million.

The International Monetary Fund (IMF) reports that in 1998 the Solomon Islands had exports of goods totaling $142 million and imports totaling $160 million. The services credit totaled $55 million and debit $55 million. The following table summarizes the Solomon Islands' balance of payments as reported by the IMF for 1998 in millions of US dollars.

Current Account		8
Balance on goods	-18	
Balance on services	1	
Balance on income	-8	
Current transfers	34	
Capital Account		7
Financial Account		17
Direct investment abroad	...	
Direct investment in Solomon Islands	9	
Portfolio investment assets	...	
Portfolio investment liabilities	...	
Other investment assets	...	
Other investment liabilities		8
Net Errors and Omissions		-14
Reserves and Related Items		-17

33BANKING AND SECURITIES

The Solomon Islands Monetary Authority became the Central Bank of the Solomon Islands (CBSI) in January 1983. Three commercial banks also operate on the islands: The Australia and New Zealand Banking Group, Westpac (which took over the Hong Kong and Shanghai Banking Corp.'s local operations in mid-1988), and the National Bank of Solomon Island (NBSI). Only the NBSI has branches outside the capital. Most villages rely on credit unions. The government's 49% shareholding in the NBSI was sold to the National Provident Fund as a part of a privatization program in 1992. The remaining 51% is held by the Commonwealth Banking Corp. of Australia (CBC).

The government participates in private investment projects through a holding company, the Investment Corp. of Solomon Islands (ICSI), the successor to the Government Shareholding Agency. It holds the government's equity in other financial institutions, notably the Development Bank of Solomon Islands (DBSI), as well as in many other companies, some of which are foreign-controlled. The government, via the ICSI, uses locally borrowed funds and foreign aid to assist industry. The government also guarantees commercial bank loans to companies in which the ICSI has an equity holding.

Money supply, as measured by M2, totaled sɪ$312.58 at the end of 1994. There is no securities market.

34INSURANCE

Insurance is sold through representatives of foreign firms. In 1997, GRE Insurance, the National Insurance Co. of New Zealand, QBE Insurance, and Zurich Australian Insurance were operating in the Solomon Islands.

35PUBLIC FINANCE

In 1997, the US Central Intelligence Agency (CIA) estimated that the government had revenues of $147 million and expenditures of $168 million. The budget continued to show a deficit in excess of $20 million despite government attempts in the late 1990s to restrain spending. External debt totaled $153 million.

36TAXATION

Individual incomes are taxed on a graduated scale ranging for single taxpayers from 14% on the first sɪ$2,100 of taxable income to 42% on taxable income exceeding sɪ$14,700. Companies incorporated in the Solomon Islands are taxed at a fixed rate of 35%; a rate of 50% applies to those incorporated elsewhere. A value-added tax on telephone services, restaurant food, and overseas travel tickets went into effect in August 1990. Employers contribute 7.5% of employee wages for social security; employees contribute 5% minimum. On 1 July 1990, a resident withholding tax went into effect for royalties, fishing operations, sales of copra and cocoa, and certain other sources of income.

37CUSTOMS AND DUTIES

All products imported into the Solomons are subject to customs duties, and a 20% surcharge is levied on all ad valorem goods. Specific duties apply to alcoholic beverages, tobacco, rice and sugar. Concessionary rates have been granted to imports of industrial machinery and equipment, raw materials, chemicals, and building materials. Licenses are required for the importation of firearms, ammunition, animals, seeds, soil, and plant material.

38FOREIGN INVESTMENT

The government encourages direct foreign investment through tax concessions, remission of customs duties, and other forms of assistance. Foreigners may repatriate profits (after taxes) and, under most conditions, capital investments. A primary role in the development of resources is reserved to the government. In 1990, Lever Brothers opened a coconut oil plant at Yandina.

39ECONOMIC DEVELOPMENT

The government has attempted to diversify agricultural production in order to make the economy less vulnerable to world price fluctuations of such key cash crops as copra. Important development projects during the 1980s included new sawmills, a fish cannery, a spice industry, and the Lungga hydroelectric plant. Fisheries receive significant portions of development funds. A rubber industry is being developed, and plans are under way to export the indigenous ngali nut as an upscale confectionery product under the name "Solomons nut." In 1991, plans were announced for a sɪ$60 million hydroelectric plant on Guadalcanal, financed by the Asian Development Bank.

Foreign assistance plays an essential role in the nation's development strategy, with Australia and Japan the largest donors. In 1996, the Solomon Islands received us$46.4 million in aid. Aid is also received from the IBRD, ADB, and EC.

40SOCIAL DEVELOPMENT

A National Provident Fund covering certain categories of wage workers provides old age, disability, and survivor benefits in lump-sum payments. This program is financed from worker and employer contributions. Employers cover the cost of workers' compensation. The 1981 Employment Act mandates that employers pay dismissal indemnity of 2 weeks' wages for each year of employment. The bulk of organized welfare services are provided by church missions. In small villages and outlying areas, assistance is traditionally provided through the extended family.

Although women are accorded equal rights by law, their role is limited by customary family roles in most Solomon Islands societies. Only one member of the 49-seat parliament in 1997 was female. Due to cultural barriers, a majority of women are illiterate, which contributes to a general shortage of employment opportunities for women.

The government generally respects the human rights of its citizens. In 1999, however, a state of emergency was declared during four months of 1999 in response to ethnic violence on Guadalcanal that resulted in several deaths and the flight of 23,000 persons from the island.

41HEALTH

Poor standards of general hygiene and inadequate sanitation continue to make malaria and tuberculosis endemic. Adequate sanitation was available to 60% of the entire Solomon Islands population in 1989–90. Infant mortality was estimated at 23 deaths per 1,000 live births in 1999; average life expectancy was 72 years for both men and women. The birth rate per 1,000 people was 35.9, and the death rate was 4.1.

The immunization rates for children under one year were as follows in 1995: diphtheria, pertussis, and tetanus (69%); polio (68%); measles (68%); and tuberculosis (77%). The overwhelmingly prevalent disease reported was malaria. Reports documented 153,359 cases in 1992. The incidence per 1,000 people was 437.6 in 1991.

Many of the five island nations in the South Pacific have insufficient vitamin A levels. The incidence of xerophthalmia, defined as the presence of night blindness, or corneal ulceration was present in 1.55% of all children in the Solomon Islands.

In 1999, 15 new cases of leprosy were reported by the World Health Organization. WHO is advocating multidrug therapy and screening of people in high risk areas to counter the spread of the disease, believed to have been eradicated.

42HOUSING

The government has built low-cost housing projects in Honiara to help ease congestion. Outside Honiara, housing is primitive, with overcrowding a problem even in the smaller villages. As of 1990, 82% of urban and 58% of rural dwellers had access to a public water supply, while 73% of the urban population had access to sanitation services.

43EDUCATION

About 60% of the adult population is estimated to be literate. Education is not compulsory, and many schools charge fees. In 1976, the government began substantial aid to primary as well as secondary schools. Christian missions (mainly Anglican), supported by government grants, continue to provide some primary schooling. In 1994 there were 60,493 students and 2,514 teachers at the primary school level. Student-to-teacher ratio stood at 24 to one. Secondary schools (general) had 7,811 pupils and approximately 400 teachers in 1994. Higher education is provided by the Solomon Islands Teachers College (Honiara), the Honiara Technical Institute, and the University of the South Pacific Solomon Islands Center, also in Honiara.

44LIBRARIES AND MUSEUMS

The National Library (founded in 1974) in Honiara has two branches and a collection of over 100,000 volumes. The library at the Solomon Islands Centre of the University of the South Pacific holds 9,000 volumes. The Solomon Islands National Museum and Cultural Center began collecting in the 1950s and opened a permanent site in 1969. The Center promotes and provides research into all aspects of Solomons culture.

45MEDIA

The main post office is at Honiara. As of 1995, there were some 6,000 main telephone lines on the islands; a radiotelephone service provides overseas links. A government-owned radio service has 5 transmitters. As of 1999 there were 4 AM radio stations, 2 FM stations, no television stations, and one daily newspapers. There were 80 radios and 4 televisions per 1,000 population in 1997. Periodicals include the *Solomon Voice* (weekly, 1995 circulation 2,500), *Solomon Star* (biweekly 1995 circulation 6,000; began daily publication in January 1999), and the *Solomon Nius* (monthly, 2,000). The government is said to generally respect constitutional provisions for freedom of speech and of the press.

46ORGANIZATIONS

Cooperative societies are important in rural areas for the distribution of locally produced goods. In 1986 there were 156 cooperatives. Honiara has a chamber of commerce.

47TOURISM, TRAVEL, AND RECREATION

Tourism, although encouraged by the government's Tourist Authority, is not seen as a major growth area, owing to lack of investment. In 1997, approximately 16,000 tourists visited the Solomon Islands, the vast majority arriving from East Asia and the Pacific. Tourism receipts totaled US$7 million. There were 511 rooms in hotels and other establishments, with 1,190 beds in 1993. A passport and an onward ticket are required for entry.

The cost of staying in Honiara, according to 1999 UN estimates, ranges from US$87. Travel expenses in Gizo are estimated at US$103, and in Auki at US$61.

Popular pastimes include rugby football, soccer, basketball, and water sports.

48FAMOUS SOLOMON ISLANDERS

Sir Peter Kenilorea (b.1943), Solomon Mamaloni (b.1943), and Ezekiel Alebua (b.1947) were the Solomons' political and government leaders from independence to the 1990s.

49DEPENDENCIES

The Solomon Islands have no territories or colonies.

50BIBLIOGRAPHY

Bennett, Judith A. *Wealth of the Solomons: A History of a Pacific Archipelago.* Honolulu: University of Hawaii Press, 1986.

Burt, Ben. *Tradition and Christianity: The Colonial Transformation of a Solomon Islands Society.* New York: Harwood Academic Publishers, 1994.

Feinberg, Richard. *Polynesian Seafaring and Navigation: Ocean Travel in Anutan Culture and Society.* Kent, Ohio: Kent State University Press, 1988.

House, William J. *Population Growth and Sustainable Development: The Case of the Solomon Islands.* Suva, Fiji: UNFPA/CST, 1995.

Keesing, Roger M. *Custom and Confrontation: The Kwaio Struggle for Cultural Autonomy.* Chicago: University of Chicago Press, 1992.

Oliver, D. L. *A Solomon Island Society.* Cambridge, Mass.: Harvard University Press, 1955.

Scott, Jonathan (ed.). *The Solomon Islands Project: A Long-term Study of Health, Human Biology, and Culture Change.* New York: Oxford University Press, 1987.

Trumbull, Robert. *Tin Roofs and Palm Trees: A Report on the New South Seas.* Seattle: University of Washington Press, 1978.

White, Geoffrey M. *Identity through History: Living Stories in a Solomon Islands Society.* New York: Cambridge University Press, 1991.

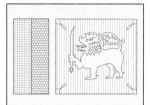

SRI LANKA

Democratic Socialist Republic of Sri Lanka

Sri Lanka Prajathanthrika Samajavadi Janarajaya

CAPITAL: Colombo.

FLAG: The national flag contains, at the hoist, vertical stripes of green and saffron and, to the right, a maroon rectangle with yellow bo leaves in the corners and a yellow lion symbol in the center. The entire flag is bordered in yellow, and a yellow narrow vertical area separates the saffron stripe from the dark maroon rectangle.

ANTHEM: *Sri Lanka Matha (Mother Sri Lanka).*

MONETARY UNIT: The Sri Lanka rupee (R) of 100 cents is a paper currency with one official rate. There are coins of 1, 2, 5, 10, 25, and 50 cents and 1 and 2 rupees, and notes of 10, 20, 50, 100, 500, and 1,000 rupees. R1 = $0.01363 ($1 = R73.350) as of 31 March 2000.

WEIGHTS AND MEASURES: The metric system is the national standard, but British weights and measures and some local units are also used.

HOLIDAYS: Independence Commemoration Day, 4 February; May Day, 1 May; National Heroes Day, 22 May; Bank Holiday, 30 June; Christmas Day, 25 December; Bank Holiday, 31 December. Movable holidays include Maha Sivarathri Day, Milad-an-Nabi, Good Friday, 'Id al-Fitr, Dewali, and 'Id al-'Adha'; in addition, the day of the rise of the full moon of every month of the Buddhist calendar, called a Poya day, is a public holiday.

TIME: 5:30 PM = noon GMT.

¹LOCATION, SIZE, AND EXTENT

Sri Lanka (formerly Ceylon) is an island in the Indian Ocean situated s and slightly E of the southernmost point of India, separated from that country by the 23 km- (14 mi-) wide Palk Strait. Including 958 sq km (370 sq mi) of inland water, Sri Lanka has a total area of 65,610 sq km (25,332 sq mi), extending 435 km (270 mi) N–s and 225 km (140 mi) E–w. Sri Lanka's total coastline is 1,340 km (833 mi). Comparatively, the area occupied by Sri Lanka is slightly larger than the state of West Virginia. Sri Lanka's capital city, Colombo, is located on the Gulf of Mannar coast.

²TOPOGRAPHY

The south-central part of Sri Lanka is a rough plateau cut by a range of mountains whose highest peak is Pidurutalagala, 2,524 m (8,281 ft). Narrow coastal plains skirt the mountainous section on the east, south, and west, but in the north the extensive coastal plain fans out, reaching from the eastern to the western shores of the island. Five-sixths of the land is less than 300 m (1,000 ft) in elevation. Numerous rivers and streams flow seaward in all directions from the central mountain area; the longest river, flowing northeastward, is the Mahaweli Ganga (335 km/208 mi).

³CLIMATE

The climate, although tropical and monsoonal, varies from warm in the coastal plains and lowlands to temperate in the hill and mountain regions. The lowlands in the northeast receive an average rainfall of about 130 cm (50 in), and the hill country in the southwest has an average of 510 cm (200 in), most of the rain coming during the monsoon season. Elsewhere, average rainfall varies from 63 cm (25 in) to 190 cm (75 in). Located only 879 km (546 mi) north of the equator, Sri Lanka has neither summer nor winter but only rainy and dry seasons. Average temperature is 27°C (80°F).

⁴FLORA AND FAUNA

Most plants and animals are those common to southern India, but there are additional varieties. The plant life ranges from that of the equatorial rain forest to that of the dry zone and the more temperate climate of the highlands. Tree ferns, bamboo, palm, satinwood, ebony, and jak trees abound. The wide range of mammals, birds, and reptiles once found in Sri Lanka has been reduced by the conversion of forests into rice fields, but water buffalo, deer, bear, elephants, monkeys, and leopards are among the larger animals still present. The Ceylon elk (sambhur) and the polonga snake are unique to Sri Lanka. Birds are numerous, many varieties from colder countries wintering on the island. Sri Lanka has well-organized game and bird sanctuaries. Insects abound, and numerous fish are found in the shallow offshore waters.

⁵ENVIRONMENT

Sri Lanka's principal environmental problem has been rapid deforestation, leading to soil erosion, destruction of wildlife habitats, and reduction of water flow. In 1985, the total amount of land affected by deforestation was 224 sq mi. The government began a reforestation program in 1970, and since 1977, it has banned the export of timber and the felling of forests at elevations over 1,500 m (5,000 ft) and the export of timber. Nevertheless, between 1981 and 1985, some 58,000 hectares (143,000 acres) of forestland were lost each year, and the nation lost an additional 21.4% of its forest and woodland between 1983 and 1993. The nation's water has been polluted by industrial, agricultural, and mining by-products along with untreated sewage. As a result, 13% of the nation's city dwellers and 53% of the people living in rural areas do not have pure water. Air pollution from industry and transportation vehicles is another significant environmental concern. The main environmental agency is the Central Environmental Authority within the Ministry of Industry and Scientific Affairs. Although legislation to protect flora and fauna and to conserve forests has been enacted, there has been inadequate enforcement of the laws, and the nation's wildlife population has been reduced by poaching.

Wildlife has been protected since 1937; by 1994, protected areas covered about 12% of the country's total land area. As of 1994, seven of Sri Lanka's mammal species and eight of its bird species were endangered. Endangered or extinct species include the Asian elephant, green labeo, spotted loach, and four species of turtle (green sea, hawksbill, olive ridley, and leatherback). In addition, 220 types of plants are threatened with extinction.

6POPULATION

The population of Sri Lanka in 2000 was estimated at 19,355,053. An estimated 6.2% of the population is 65 years of age or older. The projected population for the year 2005 is 20,418,000, assuming a crude birthrate of 17 per 1,000 population (down from 28.4 per 1,000 population in 1980) and a death rate of 6, resulting in a natural rate of change of 1.1% for the period 2000–2005. The population rate of change between 1995 and 2000 was 1.0%. The population density in 1998 was 290 per sq km (751 per sq mi), one of the highest among nonindustrial countries. About 50% of the population is concentrated in the southwestern quarter of the island.

It was estimated that 24% of the population lived in urban areas in 2000, up from 22% in 1980. Colombo, the commercial capital and chief city, had a 2000 population of 645,000. Other urban centers are Dehiwala-Mt. Lavinia, 96,000; Moratuwa, 70,000; Jaffna, 129,000; Kotic, 109,000; and Kandy, 104,000. Sri Lanka's next census is scheduled to take place in March 2001.

7MIGRATION

Under an agreement signed in 1964, India pledged to repatriate 525,000 of the 975,000 persons of Indian origin (Tamils) then on the island, while Ceylon agreed to absorb 300,000 and grant them Ceylonese citizenship. Of the remaining 150,000, 75,000 were repatriated by a separate agreement concluded in 1974, and an equal number became citizens of Sri Lanka.

In recent years, many Sri Lankan workers have migrated to work in Middle Eastern countries. Others—over 200,000 in all—have emigrated to Western Europe, Australia, and North America, in part as a result of the Tamil insurgency.

Due to the military activities in 1995 and 1996, an estimated 650,000 people have been internally displaced. As of May 1997, India's Tamil Nadu state had around 56,000 refugees from Sri Lanka with another 36,000 throughout India. Repatriation to Sri Lanka has ceased since the military conflicts started again in 1995. Over 54,000 refugees have returned from southern India since 1992. In 1999, the net migration rate was -1.13 migrants per 1,000 population.

8ETHNIC GROUPS

According to official 1999 data, the Sinhalese constitute the largest population group, making up 74% of the total population. Sri Lankan Tamils (descendants of medieval invaders from India) total 18%; Sri Lankan Moors 7%; Burghers (descended from the Dutch), Malays (mostly of Arab extraction), and Veddas account for 1%. The Veddas are a small aboriginal tribe located in the most inaccessible forest regions of southeastern Sri Lanka.

9LANGUAGES

English was the official language under the British and remained so until 1956, when Sinhala became the nation's one official language. This measure was bitterly opposed by the Tamil minority. Riots, disorders, and dissension grew, leading to a Tamil civil disobedience campaign and a temporary state of emergency. The 1978 constitution recognized Sinhala as the official language but also recognized Tamil as a national language. Sinhala is a member of the Indo-Aryan subgroup of the Indo-European language family, related to Pali. Tamil is a Dravidian language spoken in northern and eastern Sri Lanka and in southern India. It became an official language in December 1988. In 1999, Sinhala was spoken by approximately 74% of the population; Tamil was spoken by 18%. English is also commonly used in government and is spoken by about 10% of the population.

10RELIGIONS

Of the total population, Buddhists constitute nearly 70% and are almost without exception ethnic Sinhalese; Hindus amount to 15% of the total population and are almost exclusively ethnic Tamils; Muslims account for 8% (and may or may not be Tamil speakers) and include the Moor and Malay communities; and Christians, accounting for 8%, are to be found in the Sinhalese, Burgher/Eurasian, and Sri Lankan Tamil communities (not to be confused with the so-called Indian Tamils, who were imported as plantation workers in the last century and are exclusively Hindu). A majority of Christians are Roman Catholic, with Anglicans and Baptists also significant, the latter the result of American missionary activity in the north in the 19th century. The religious atmosphere is traditionally tolerant, and the issues involved in the Tamil insurgency are communal and ethnic rather than religious in origin. The 1978 constitution established Sri Lanka as a secular state and guarantees freedom of religion, while stipulating that Buddhism enjoys the foremost place in the republic.

11TRANSPORTATION

In 1996, the country had an estimated 99,200 km (61,643 mi) of roadways, of which 39,680 km (24,657 mi) were paved. Registered motor vehicles numbered 441,000 in 1995, including 210,000 passenger cars and 231,000 commercial vehicles.

At last estimate, there were 1,501 km (933 mi) railroad track, state-owned and state operated.

Colombo, one of the great commercial seaports of Asia, formerly was an open roadstead, but the construction of breakwaters has made it one of the world's greatest artificial harbors. In 1998, the merchant fleet consisted of 22 ships with a capacity of 178,867 GRT. Ports of the open roadstead type are Trincomalee, Galle, Batticaloa, Kankesanturai, Kayts, and Jaffna. A car ferry service links Mannar Island with the Indian mainland.

Sri Lanka had 13 airports in 1998, 12 of which had permanent runways. The principal international airport is Katunayaka, 39 km (24 mi) north of Colombo. Air Lanka (formerly Air Ceylon), the national airline company, serves international routes only. Upali Travels, a private carrier, provides domestic service. In 1997, 1,232,000 passengers were carried on scheduled domestic and international flights.

12HISTORY

The earliest Indo-European speaking settlers in present-day Sri Lanka, the Sinhalese, came late in the 6th century BC, probably from northern India. Later arrivals from India brought Buddhism beginning about 240 BC, and at such cities as Anuradhapura and Polonnaruwa, the Sinhalese developed a great civilization, much of which was later destroyed by civil wars and by the incursions of Hindu Dravidian-speakers from across the Palk Strait, who established a Tamil kingdom in the northern part of the island.

Netherlands fell under French control. After a brief period as part of the British East India Company's Indian domain, Ceylon was designated a crown colony in 1802, and by 1815, the entire island was united under British rule. The British introduced coffee, tea, coconut, and rubber plantations, and efficient and enlightened administration.

With the development of a nationalist movement across the Palk Strait in India in the 20th century, nationalists in Ceylon also pressured for greater self-rule, leading to further democratic political reforms in constitutions enacted in 1910, 1920, 1924, 1931, and 1947; included in the 1931 enactment was limited self-rule under universal suffrage. In 1948, with little actual struggle, and a year after Indian independence, Ceylon became a self-governing dominion within the British Commonwealth.

The period from 1948 through 1970 saw the evolution of Ceylon's multiparty parliamentary system in which orderly and constitutional elections and changes of government took place. Beginning in 1970, executive power began to be highly centralized under Prime Minister Sirimavo Bandaranaike, who from 1971–77 ruled with the use of unpopular emergency powers in support of her socialist, pro-Sinhalese policies. She introduced a new constitution in 1972, converting the dominion of Ceylon to the republic of Sri Lanka, reaffirming a parliamentary system under a weak, ceremonial presidency, and making the protection of Buddhism a constitutional principle.

The Sri Lanka Freedom Party (SLFP) defeat in the July 1977 elections brought Junius Richard Jayewardene of the more moderate United National Party (UNP) to power. He became Sri Lanka's first elected executive president in February 1978, under a constitutional amendment of fall 1977 establishing a presidential form of government. Seven months later, a new, more liberal constitution came into effect, rejecting many of the authoritarian features of the 1972 constitution, introducing proportional representation, and defining the presidential executive system. As his prime minister, he chose Ranadive Premadasa, a long-time follower with lower caste support. In October 1982, Jayewardene was popularly elected to a new six-year term, and two months later, in a successful effort to avoid general elections, the life of the sitting parliament was extended through July 1989 by means of a constitutional amendment endorsed by popular referendum.

Since 1978, rising tensions and violence between the majority (mostly Buddhist) Sinhalese and minority (mostly Hindu) Sri Lankan Tamil communities that have long shared the island have dominated political life. Going back to 1956, when the Sinhalese-dominated government had declared Sinhala the official language and replaced English with separate language tracks in education for Sinhala and Tamil speakers, a chasm had been developing between the communities. In the late 1970s, moderate Sri Lankan Tamils looked to the leadership in the Tamil United Liberation Front (TULF) and to negotiations with the new UNP government in 1978 to pursue changes aimed at protecting their cultural heritage by giving greater control to elected officials at the local level in Sri Lankan Tamil majority areas of the island.

By the early 1980s, their efforts had failed. Participation in Parliament as a responsible opposition had brought no changes, despite government promises; and many rounds of talks with Jayawardene and the majority Sinhalese community had netted no progress in redressing Tamil grievances. Violence was on the rise, and a spasm of communal bloodletting in summer 1983 had left hundreds, if not thousands, dead in Colombo and elsewhere. By 1984–85, Sri Lankan Tamil leadership had fallen into the hands of extremists advocating violence, dooming to failure before it began the government's eleventh-hour convening of an All-Party conference in 1984 to seek a political solution to the ethnic conflict.

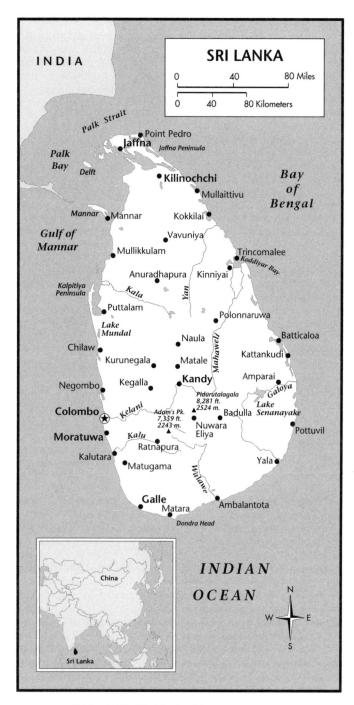

LOCATION: 5°55′ to 9°50′N; 79°42′ to 81°53′E. **TERRITORIAL SEA LIMIT:** 12 mi.

The Portuguese East India Company brought the first European rulers in the early 16th century, and in time, the Portuguese conquered the entire island with the exception of the Sinhalese kingdom in Kandy in the central plateau. By the middle of the 17th century, the Portuguese were driven out of Sri Lanka (and southern India) by the Dutch East India Company, which governed for more than 100 years, introduced plantation agriculture, developed trade, and left a legacy that includes Roman-Dutch law. But they too found themselves displaced.

Having won their struggle with France for mastery in India (and in North America), the British laid claim to Sri Lanka, which they called Ceylon, at the end of the 18th century after the

Fighting between the Sinhalese-dominated army and well-armed Sri Lankan Tamil separatists escalated in 1986 and 1987, with no solution in sight. It should be noted that the insurgency is limited to the larger group of Sri Lankan Tamils; the so-called Indian Tamils who were imported in the last century and continue to work the plantations in the highlands at the center of the island, and whose partial repatriation to India has been at times a subject for separate negotiations with India, have played no role in the insurgency.

In the spring of 1987, the government began a military offensive against Tamil forces in the Jaffna Peninsula in the Northern Province. India, sensitive to its own large Tamil population just across the strait, served as a base for rebels. Earlier, the Indian government had attempted to negotiate a settlement between the Sri Lankan government and the rebels, but in 1987 India reacted to the offensive by airlifting food and supplies to the rebels, creating considerable tension between the two countries. On 29 July, Jayewardene and Prime Minister Rajiv Gandhi of India signed an agreement by which the Sri Lankan government reluctantly accepted the need for devolution of power to the provinces, agreed that Tamil would have official status, and conceded that a semiautonomous administrative unit would be created for the Tamils in the Northern and Eastern provinces, subject to a vote by the Eastern Province on joining such a unit. An Indian peacekeeping force which grew eventually to more than 100,000 troops was sent to Sri Lanka to implement the agreement and enforce a cease-fire. But it was already too late. In the fall of 1987, Tamil separatists—notably and most prominently, the extremist Liberation Tigers of Tamil Ealam (LTTE)—resumed their attacks, killing about 300 people. When they refused the protection of the Indian Peacekeeping Force (IPKF), the IPKF launched an offensive against the rebel stronghold in Jaffna. Fighting continued, inconclusively, between the IPKF and (mainly) the LTTE for 18 months thereafter, with heavy casualties on both sides.

Meanwhile, through 1988 and 1989, the government was under attack from the militant Sinhalese nationalist political party, Janatha Vimukhti Peramuna (JVP), which sought its overthrow for agreeing to the presence of Indian forces in Sri Lanka. The rebellion was put down firmly and brutally by President Premadasa, who succeeded Jayewardene in 1988 in a close race against Sirimavo Bandaranaike.

In 1990, V. P. Singh, who had replaced Rajiv Gandhi as Indian Prime Minister, agreed to Sri Lanka's request that India pull its forces out of the country; the Indian effort to crush the rebellion had failed at the cost of an estimated 1,200 Indian lives alone. With the JVP opposition eliminated and the Indians gone, Premadasa turned his attention to the possibility of expanding the new situation, including a de facto cease-fire with LTTE, into a negotiated settlement. But a new spasm of LTTE violence in the eastern province led him to order an all-out army and air force campaign against the north in the second half of 1990, and guerrilla warfare resumed. Through 1991 and 1992, Premadasa's government continued to pursue the possibility of a negotiated settlement with the LTTE, denying it sought a military solution. But the LTTE's Velupillai Prabhakaran, dominating the separatist side, rejected most government terms.

Under President Wijetunga, who replaced Premadasa when the latter was assassinated by Tamil rebels on May Day 1993, the warfare, and the search for a solution, continued inconclusively, with frequently announced cease-fires and resumptions. The death toll and the cost, reportedly $1 million per day, continued to mount.

Chandrika Bandaranaike Kumaratunga, 49-year-old daughter of former prime minister Sirimavo Bandaranaike and widow of a Communist Party leader assassinated nearly a decade earlier, became prime minister when her seven-party alliance of leftist parties won a plurality in snap elections to parliament in August 1994. With President Wijetunga's approval, she made resolution of the conflict her first priority on taking office by arranging for the economic blockade of the insurgent-held Jaffna peninsula to be partially lifted and offering to restore electric power to the area. She also offered unconditional talks for a resolution of the dispute, actions welcomed by the LTTE's Prabhakaran, who responded by releasing ten police constables held prisoner by the LTTE since mid-1990. Talks were scheduled for mid-October 1994 and the situation calmed for a time. The optimism that characterized the political situation in Sri Lanka at the beginning of 1995 quickly vanished as the nation lapsed again into a savage civil war. Hostilities between the Sri Lankan government and ethnic separatist Tamil rebels came to a temporary end on January 3, 1995, when the parties announced a cease-fire. The war that raged for twelve years and killed over 34,000 people halted abruptly with government promises of negotiations and an $816 million aid package for the northern portion of the island.

The peace was shattered, however, after only three months. The LTTE had given the government an April 19 deadline to make additional concessions. When their demands were not met, rebels attacked and badly damaged two government gunboats, killing eleven sailors and wounding twenty-two. Before the end of May the Tamil Tigers had attacked an army base, ambushed two government military patrols, and shot down two troop transport planes, killing more than 350 government fighters. In response, on May 22 Sri Lankan President Chandrika Bandaranaike Kumaratunga pronounced the peace talks dead and vowed to crush the Tamil rebels.

Full scale war continued through the summer of 1995 as the government went on the offensive. Incensed by a series of June terrorist attacks against targets in Hikkadawa and Colombo, President Kumaratunga asked the Indian government for assistance in setting up a naval blockade of the Tamil stronghold of Jaffna on the island's north coast. The Sri Lankan army then attacked rebel positions on the Jaffna peninsula, announcing on July 15 that the operation had left 300 Tamil troops dead in six days of fierce fighting. The government capped the offensive by unveiling in early August a plan to end the civil war by sharing power with eight new states, one of which would be reserved for the minority Tamils.

Rebel leader Vellupillai Prabhakaran rejected the proposal out of hand and ordered that the Tamil terror campaign continue. On August 7 a bomb destroyed a government building in Colombo, killing twenty-four and wounding fifty. At the end of the month rebels hijacked a ferry carrying 136 passengers and sank two government gunboats. During the first week of October, the Tamil Tigers blew up the house of Douglas Devananda, a Sri Lankan legislator and severe critic of the militant separatist group. Less than two weeks later rebels attacked three villages on the northeastern portion of the island, killing over 100 civilians.

Deaths of non-military personnel strengthened the government's resolve to end the fighting quickly. By the beginning of November the Sri Lankan army had marched to within three miles of Tamil headquarters at Jaffna, displacing at least a half million civilians in the process. After days of savage combat, government forces captured the rebel political capital, and sealed off the area, trapping over 2,000 guerrillas. At the end of November, Sri Lanka authorities offered to work out a political settlement with the separatists, but the Tamil fighters announced that they would resume talks only if government troops left Jaffna. Fighting continued, culminating in a January 31 rebel attack on the financial district in Colombo which killed more than 90 and wounded 1,400. By the end of 1996 the death count for almost 15 years of civil war had surpassed 50,000.

By late spring 1996 government forces again appeared to have the upper hand. Pushing further into rebel territory, Sri Lankan army officials claimed in mid-May to have control of the northern Jaffna peninsula. On May 30, the government chief general offered amnesty to 20,000 deserters and announced plans to recruit 10,000 additional soldiers to end the civil war once and for all. Still, the war went on through the end of 1996 with no cease-fire in sight.

A strong showing in local elections in March 1997 was seen by the government as a mandate to continue with its plans for offering the Tamils limited autonomy. Despite opposition from the UNP, the government presented its proposals to Parliament in October. However, a series of bombing incidents diminished the prospects for peace. In mid-October a truck bomb exploded near a Colombo hotel, with foreign tourists apparently deliberately targeted by the LTTE. In late January 1998, following a suicide bombing in Kandy at the "Temple of the Tooth," Sri Lanka's most sacred Buddhist shrine, the government formally outlawed the LTTE. This, in effect, indicated that the government had put peace negotiations on hold and was leaning towards a military solution.

Following a spate of bombings and the assassinations of moderate Tamil leaders in Jaffna, the government declared a national state of emergency in August 1998. Its war against the LTTE, however, has fared badly. In December 1998, the army abandoned its costly campaign to capture the main northern highway to Jaffna. Disaster struck in November 1999 when, in one week, Tamil guerrillas regained nearly all the territory lost during the previous two years. LTTE successes have continued, with the capture of Elephant Pass in April 2000 trapping some 35,000 government troops on the Jaffna peninsula.

Citing the failure of Parliament to accept her plan for regional autonomy for the Tamil areas in October 1999, President Kumaratunga decided to hold presidential elections 10 months ahead of schedule. Surviving an assassination attempt a few days before polling in December, Kumaratunga was returned to office for a second term as President. Six years after she was first elected with a mandate to bring about an end to the civil war, Kumaratunga finds herself in an unenviable position. The government and the opposition cannot agree on a common policy for negotiations with the Tamils, the army is on the defensive, and it is unlikely that the LTTE is willing to accept anything short of a separate Tamil state on the island. Meanwhile, the carnage and bloodshed of a bitter 17-year civil war continues. As of June 2000, embattled government troops in the north are fighting back after their setbacks of recent months, while on June 7, 2000 a suspected Tamil suicide bomber in Colombo killed Sri Lanka's minister for industrial development, C. V. Goonaratne, and some 20 others in Colombo.

13GOVERNMENT

The constitution of September 1978 established the Democratic Socialist Republic of Sri Lanka as a free, sovereign, independent state based on universal suffrage at 18 years of age. The president of the republic is directly elected for a six-year term and serves as head of state and as executive head of government, appointing and heading the cabinet of ministers whom he chooses and who are (or must quickly become) members of parliament. A prime minister, similarly selected, serves mainly as parliamentary leader.

Legislation approved by parliament cannot be vetoed by the president, and the president may be removed by parliament upon a two-thirds majority vote, following a finding by the Supreme Court of incapacity, treason, corruption, or intentional constitutional violation. The constitution can be amended by two-thirds' majority vote in the parliament, subject to ratification (for certain provisions) by popular referendum. The constitution provides that popular referenda also may be held on issues of national importance, but the normal business of legislation is in the hands of a unicameral parliament consisting first of 168—now 225—

members elected for six-year terms under a proportional representation system. The sitting parliament elected in July 1977 took the unusual step of extending its own life for another six years by a national referendum in 1982, thus avoiding elections in which the competition for places on the ballot might have weakened the UNP's constitution-amending 2/3 majority.

In June 1994, the Wijetunga government scheduled "snap" elections for parliament on 16 August 1994, six months earlier than would have been required; elections to the presidency followed parliamentary polling. Paced by the electoral appeal of SLFP deputy leader Chandrika Bandaranaike Kumaratunga, the People's Alliance of seven leftist parties won a clear plurality in the elections, ousting the UNP after 17 years in power. To the 91 parliamentary seats the Alliance won directly were added an additional 14 under the proportional system, and with the further support of 9 members of the Sri Lanka Muslim Congress, the new Peoples' Alliance government was able to command a majority of 114 seats in the 225-member house and to elect Kumaratunga as leader of the house, facilitating her prompt appointment as prime minister—an office previously held by both her ailing 80-year old mother and her late father, S.W.R.D. Bandaranaike.

Because the presidential system incorporated in the 1978 constitution vests the substantial powers of head of state and head of government in the hands of the president, Kumaratunga's capacity for independent action remained limited. As prime minister, she was actually little more than leader of the house but in the November 1994 presidential elections, Kumaratunga, who is the daughter and the widow of prominent Sri Lankan politicians (both of whom were assassinated) was elected president by a sizeable majority. After assuming office, she appointed her mother, Sirimavo Bandaranaike, prime minister. Since the election, she has made her primary issue a negotiated peace with the Tamil separatists. Kumaratunga's repeated offers of a limited sovereignty within a greater Sri Lankan state have been spurned by the Tamils. Attempts to subdue the Tamils by military force have also failed, with the Sri Lankan army suffering serious reversals in November 1999. Despite this, in December 1999 Kumaratunga won a second six-year term in office as Sri Lanka's president.

14POLITICAL PARTIES

Political life in Sri Lanka is open and vigorous, with a wide range of views represented among the political parties, many of which have their roots deep in the pre-independence era. In the time since independence, considerations of religion, language, and culture have largely displaced ideology as the issues around which multi-ethnic Sri Lanka's political life evolves. In the last decade, ethnic struggle—and violence—between the government, dominated by majority Sinhalese, and militant minority Tamil separatists has dominated the political process.

The United National Party (UNP) was the main party of the independence movement, and its widely respected leader, D. S. Senanayake, as head of a coalition of which the UNP was the chief unit, became Ceylon's first prime minister after independence. He won a major victory in 1952 and continued in power until he died in 1956. The divided opposition failed to agree on a leader until 1951, when Solomon Bandaranaike left the UNP to form the Sri Lanka Freedom Party (SLFP). Over the years, the SLFP became the island's other major political party, advocating—like the UNP—a non-aligned foreign policy, with the UNP friendlier to the West, the SFLP, to the former Eastern bloc. Both find their support from within the majority Sinhalese community, and like most other parties, both are led mostly by high caste Sinhalese.

Shortly before the 1956 elections, Bandaranaike formed the People's United Front (Mahajana Eksath Peramuna—MEP), composed of his own SLFP, the Trotskyite Lanka Sama Samaja

(LSSP), and a group of independents. The MEP called for the extension of state control, termination of British base rights, nationalization of tea and rubber plantations, and a foreign policy of strict nonalignment. In the elections, the MEP won 51 seats, and Bandaranaike became prime minister, holding power until September 1959 when he was assassinated by a Buddhist monk.

In elections March 1960, the UNP won 50 of the 151 seats at stake, the SLFP, 46 seats, and other parties, the remaining 55. UNP leader Dudley Senanayake failed to muster a majority, and new elections were called for July. In this second round of polling, the UNP won a majority of the popular vote but only 30 seats. The SLFP, led by its slain leader's widow, Sirimavo Bandaranaike, won 75, and with her supporters on the left, she was able to form a government, becoming the first woman in the world to hold office as prime minister. She committed her government to pursuing continuation of her husband's agenda, including nationalization of enterprises.

In the 15 years that followed, the UNP and the SLFP alternated in power for periods no longer than seven years. In 1965, Dudley Senanayake became prime minister after the UNP won 66 of the 151 legislative seats, but the SLFP's Sirimavo Bandaranaike was returned to power in the 1970 elections as the head of a coalition that included the Trotskyite LSSP and the pro-Soviet Ceylon Communist Party (CCP). In response to an insurrection fomented in 1971 by the Janatha Vimukhti Peramuna (JVP), a militant Sinhalese party in the south, Bandaranaike imposed a state of emergency on the island that lasted for 6 years. She pushed through a new constitution in 1972.

By 1977, Banderanaike's public image had declined. No longer supported by her former coalition partners, she was humiliated at the polls by J. R. Jayewardene's UNP which was returned to power with 51% of the popular vote and 142 of (the then) 168 seats in parliament. The moderate Tamil United Liberation Front (TULF), which had swept Tamil areas of the north and east, became the major opposition party in parliament with 16 seats and the SLFP representation in the house fell to a bare eight seats.

Jayewardene's sweeping victory enabled him to fulfill the UNP's campaign pledge to introduce a French-style presidential system of government. Forsaking the now-eclipsed office of prime minister, he set out as president to use his new powers to open the economy and to make a new effort to reconcile with the increasingly disaffected Tamil minority. In the local elections and parliamentary by-elections of May 1983, the UNP strengthened its commanding position by gaining control of a majority of municipal and urban councils and winning 14 of 18 parliamentary seats contested.

The CCP and two other leftist groups, the People's Liberation Front and the New Socialist Party, were banned in 1983 on charges of playing a role in the ethnic riots which swept the island in July; leaders of the Communist Party were subsequently arrested. In August 1983, TULF members of parliament, after several fruitless years of negotiations with Jayewardene aimed at devolving power to local levels, were confronted with a constitutional amendment aimed at them by the UNP's two-thirds majority that required all MP's to pledge their allegiance to a unitary state. They abandoned parliament, and by now most have been killed, as the leadership of the Tamil movement fell into the hands of those advocating violence and complete independence as the only sure ways to protect Tamil ethnicity. The TULF was decimated in parliamentary elections in February 1989, which saw the emergence of several small Tamil parties with reputed ties to the rebels.

In presidential elections held in December 1988, Prime Minister Premadasa beat the SLFP's Sirimavo Bandaranaike in a close race marred by ethnic violence. He was sworn in as Jayewardene's successor on 2 January 1989. In February, he led the UNP to a strong victory in parliamentary polling, capturing 125 of the 225 seats under a new proportional voting system; he then named Dingiri Wijetunga as prime minister. These elections also saw the debut of the United Socialist Alliance (USA), a new political grouping set up in 1987 and composed of the SLFP's former coalition partners on the far left, including the CCP, the LSSP, and the Sri Lanka Mahajana Party (SLMP); the USA took 4 seats, while the SLFP won 67.

In the summer of 1991, Premadasa beat back a sudden challenge to his position by leading members of his party in parliament, suspending the parliament for a month to delay debate on a motion they had filed to impeach him for abuse of his authority. But in a rising tide of violence and assassinations of governmental officials across the island, President Premadasa himself became a victim of a Tamil bomber on 1 May 1993. The Parliament unanimously elected Prime Minister Wijetunga as his successor on 7 May 1993.

A "snap" election called six months early by President Wijetunga as part of his campaign for re-election himself in November 1994 backfired on 16 August 1994 when the voters rejected the UNP by a small margin. In its place, they elected to office a seven-party, leftist coalition—now dubbed the People's Alliance—led by the SLFP's Sirimavo Bandaranaike and Chandrika Bandaranaike Kumaratunga—mother and daughter, 80 and 49 years of age, respectively. More vigorous but less experienced, the younger Kumaratunga promptly became prime minister.

The results of the elections, by seats won, were as follows: People's Alliance, 105; United National Party, 94; Eelam People's Democratic Party, 9; Sri Lanka Muslim Congress, 7; Tamil United Liberation Front, 5; People's Liberation Organization of Tamil Eelam, 3; Sri Lankan Progressive Front, 1; and the Upcountry People's Front, 1.

In November 1994, presidential elections were held. UNP leader Gamini Dissanayake fell victim to the island's endemic violence and his widow Srima Dissanayake was appointed to run against the younger Kumaratunga. While the latter's political party won only a slim plurality and had to govern by coalition, in the presidential race she won a commanding majority (63%–36%) and, upon becoming president, appointed her mother prime minister.

Kumaratunga won election on the promise of ending the civil war, but so far she has failed to do so. Her offers of limited regional autonomy for Tamils within the Sri Lankan state have been turned down by the LTTE leader, Velupillai Prabakaran (most of the moderate Tamil leaders have been assassinated). Her attempts at a military solution have also been unsuccessful. Citing Parliament's rejection of her proposals for strengthening the prime minister's powers and for granting regional autonomy to the Tamils, Kumaratunga called for presidential elections ahead of schedule in December 1999. The race between the president and her UNP rival, Ranil Wickremesinghe, was close. However, three days before polling, Kumaratunga was injured in an assassination attempt, bringing out a sympathy vote. She was returned to office with 51.1% of the votes compared to her opponent's 42.7%. It remains to be seen how this vote will be reflected in the general elections which were scheduled for August 2000.

15 LOCAL GOVERNMENT

Although Sri Lanka is a unitary state, it is nonetheless divided into nine provinces whose borders follow historic and traditional lines. The key administrative unit has traditionally been the district, into which the provinces are further divided. A total of 24 districts under the control of senior civil servants who are District Officers responsible to the government in Colombo for ensuring justice, maintaining law and order, collecting revenues, and allocating development funds. There is, in addition a system of district ministers that was created after 1978 to assist the District Officers and to provide a political input at the district level. Appointed by the President, District Ministers are members of parliament but from a constituency other than one in the district for whom they bear district responsibility. Not full members of the cabinet, they nonetheless sit with the President in the Council of Ministers and otherwise enjoy ministerial perquisites.

Districts are also served in rural areas by popularly elected District Councils which have limited powers but which assist the District Officer and the District Minister in assessing public views and mood and in setting development priorities. Municipal and urban councils perform a similar function in urban areas.

In conformity with Indo-Lankan agreement in 1987 to devolve power to the provinces, the Parliament voted to establish, at the provincial level, elected councils headed by chief ministers. In presence of the IPKF in 1988, elections were held to these Provincial Councils (PC), and the UNP took control of 7 in non-Tamil areas; the ERPLF, a new, anti-LTTE Tamil party supported at the time by the IPKF, took control of the two in the Tamil north and east. While unsettled conditions have slowed progress on devolution, elections to the seven PC's in non-Tamil areas in 1993 reportedly produced more mixed results, with gains and losses for all parties, including the UNP, the SLFP, and the ERPLF. Although the PA was successful in gaining control of provincial councils in elections held in 1997 and 1999, its share of the popular vote show it running neck and neck with the opposition. For example, in elections held in April 1999 in non-Tamil areas, the PA gained control of all the provincial councils contested, but only achieved 43% of the votes compared to the UNP's 41%.

16 JUDICIAL SYSTEM

Civil law is based on Roman-Dutch law introduced during the period of Dutch rule, but in the area around Kandy, an indigenous type of law prevails. Criminal law is British. Tamils and Muslims have their own laws governing property disposition and certain observances. Sri Lanka's judicial system includes district courts, magistrates' courts, courts of request (restricted to civil cases), and rural courts.

In criminal cases, the Supreme Court (composed of a chief justice and from 6 to 10 associate justices, all appointed by the president) has appellate jurisdiction. Under the 1978 constitution, the other high-level courts are the Court of Appeal, High Court, and courts of first instance. The president also appoints judges to the Court of Appeals and the High Court. A judicial service commission appoints transfers and dismisses lower court judges. Sinhala is the official language of the courts.

The Constitution declares the independence of the judiciary and the courts appear to be independent in practice.

Defendants are guaranteed a number of procedural due process protections but trials under the Emergency Regulations (ER) and the Prevention of Terrorism Act (PTA) lack significant procedural safeguards.

17 ARMED FORCES

Budgeted defense expenditures have increased dramatically since 1984 as a consequence of the Sri Lankan Tamil insurgency in the northern half of the island. In 1998, they amounted to $719 million (4.2% of gross domestic product). Between 1983 and 1995 the army expanded from less than 15,000 to 90–95,000. In 2000, the navy had 10,000 personnel in uniform (with another 1,000 reserves). The air force (10,000) had 22 combat aircraft and 15 armed helicopters. Although it is primarily involved in combating the insurgency, the military's traditional duties also include backing up civilian authority, curbing illegal immigration, and providing air surveys and search and rescue services. The

armed forces, traditionally lightly armed, have been re-equipped with US and European weaponry purchased abroad.

Sri Lanka has a police force of 70,100, backed up by a national guard of 15,000 and a home guard of 15,200—also the product of expansion in the since 1985.

18 INTERNATIONAL COOPERATION

The government of Sri Lanka is opposed to all military defense alliances but actively participates in other forms of international cooperation. On 14 December 1955, Ceylon was admitted to membership in the UN. Sri Lanka is a member of ESCAP and all the nonregional specialized agencies, the Asian Development Bank, the Commonwealth of Nations, the Colombo Plan, the WTO, and G-77, among other intergovernmental organizations. It also signed the Law of the Sea treaty.

19 ECONOMY

Since 1980, the Sri Lankan economy, once dominated by agricultural, has experienced strong growth in its industrial and services sectors. While annual growth in agricultural output averaged only 2% between 1988 and 1998, industry expanded by 7.1% and services by 5.4%. Expansion of manufacturing (especially the fast-growing apparel industry), international trade-related services, and tourism accounted for much of the strong performance. As of 1998, the service sector commanded over 50% of GDP and industry has replaced agriculture as Sri Lanka's main source of export earnings. Economic growth is hampered by recurrent droughts, continuing hostilities in the 15-year civil war, high unemployment, and government overspending. Though per capita income in Sri Lanka remains low at $858, other social welfare indicators such as adult literacy, school enrollment, infant mortality and life expectancy compare very favorably with those of countries at much higher income levels.

From 1973 to 1977, the channeling of resources into social welfare programs, combined with frequent droughts and inflated world oil prices, helped to depress the economy and discourage business initiative. In 1977, the new UNP government accelerated economic growth by lifting most price controls, shifting government spending into capital investment, liberalizing foreign exchange and import restrictions, and eliminating some government monopolies to permit more business competition. The result of these policies was an annual increase in real GNP of 6% during 1978–81, compared with only 3% in 1971–77. However, the economic boom also catalyzed several years of high inflation through the mid-1980s.

In the latter half of the 1980s, the national economy faced several grave problems: escalating defense expenditures as a result of the civil insurgency, recurrent drought, stagnant government revenues and sharply depressed prices for the country's major export crops, tea and coconut-based goods. These conditions led to a resurgence of inflation, increasing unemployment, critical current account and balance of payment imbalances and stagnating economic growth. By 1989, unemployment stood at 18% while total growth in the GDP fell to 2% from 2.8% in 1988 and an average of 4.7% in 1980–85. Exports registered an increase of only 5% as compared with an average of 20% from 1984–88. Declining economic indicators spurred renewed stabilization and structural adjustment efforts by the government, which emphasized tightened monetary and fiscal policies and stimulating private sector investment through privatization.

In the 1990s the economy experienced a strong rebound as economic growth exceeded 5%. In 1996, the economy benefited from strong demand for tea from the CIS countries and improved rubber prices. Despite these encouraging trends, the civil war and a drought early in 1996 adversely affected the economy. Tea and rubber prices declined again in 1998. Inflation was up, exceeding

9%, and growth in the GDP was down to 4.7% by the end of 1998. The deficit soared to over 9% of GDP.

20INCOME

The US Central Intelligence Agency (CIA) reports that in 1998 Sri Lanka's gross domestic product (GDP) was estimated at $48.1 billion. The per capita GDP was estimated at $2,500. The annual growth rate of GDP was estimated at 4.7%. The average inflation rate in 1998 was 9.3%. The CIA defines GDP as the value of all final goods and services produced within a nation in a given year and computed on the basis of purchasing power parity (PPP) rather than value as measured on the basis of the rate of exchange. It was estimated that agriculture accounted for 18% of GDP, industry 31%, and services 51%.

The World Bank reports that for the same period per capita private consumption (in PPP terms) was $2,105. Private consumption includes expenditures of individuals, households, and non-governmental organizations. It was estimated that between 1990 and 1998 private consumption grew at an annual rate of 5.6%. Approximately 43% of household consumption was spent on food, 7% on fuel, 4% on health care, and 8% on education. The richest 10% of the population accounted for approximately 28% of household consumption and the poorest 10% approximately 3.5%.

21LABOR

In 1998, the economically active population totaled 6,693,000. The agricultural sector accounted for 35%; 22% worked in industry, and 39% were sales and service workers. The number of unemployed persons in 1998 was estimated at 701,000, or about 10.6% of the economically active population.

An employer is liable for compensation to workers hurt, disabled, or incurring occupational diseases while on the job but is not obligated to carry insurance. Sri Lanka has minimum wage, safety, health, and welfare laws and legislation dealing with women, young persons, and children in industry, but adequate staff to enforce the labor laws is lacking. In 1997, about 16,500 children younger than the minimum age of 14 were estimated to have been legally employed, with many thousands more employed in domestic service.

In 1999, 1,678 labor unions were registered. Union membership included over 70% of agricultural workers, totaling 900,000 members, including 650,000 women. During 1999, there were 128 strikes in the public sector. The largest trade union federations are the Ceylon Workers' Congress, the National Workers' Union, the Democratic Workers' Congress, and the Ceylon Federation of Labor. About 50–60% of the non-agricultural workforce was unionized in 1996.

Thousands of Sri Lankan workers are employed abroad, mostly in Saudi Arabia, Kuwait, UAE, Singapore, Hong Kong, Bahrain, Qatar, and Oman; many of them housemaids and nannies valued for their literacy and English language skills.

There is no national minimum wage, but there are minimum wages set in individual sectors and industries. The average such wage was $30 per month in industry, commerce, and the service sector, and $1.33 per day in agriculture as of 1999.

22AGRICULTURE

Agriculture, the mainstay of the economy, employs about 46% of the working population and contributes 21% to GDP. About 75% of those working in agriculture are engaged in the production of tea, rubber, and coconuts, the three crops that comprise nearly 60% of Sri Lanka's agricultural land. Tea production in 1998 was 280,000 tons; plantings were 190,000 hectares (469,000 acres). Rubber production was 96,000 tons, and coconut production totaled 1,999,000 tons.

Rice is the major staple crop, produced over much of the country. The major growing districts are Kurungala in the northwestern province, Ampara in the eastern province, Polonnaruwa and Anuradhapura in the north central province, and the Mahaweli area; together these areas account for 55% of production. The maha rice season crop (65% of production) is planted in the fall and harvested in the spring, while the yala rice crop (35%) is planted in the summer and harvested in the fall. Production of rice reached 2.7 million tons in 1998. Lesser crops include sugar, pepper, cinnamon, chilies, sesame, cardamom, tobacco, cashew nuts, betel leaves, coffee, and cocoa.

Under the Land Reform Law of 1972, all property holdings exceeding 20 hectares (50 acres), except for property controlled by publicly owned companies, were vested in the Land Reform Commission for redistribution; a total of 226,373 hectares (559,377 acres) were redistributed, including one-fifth of the land under tea. Under the Land Reform Amendment Bill of 11 October 1975, all publicly owned estates (including the major British-owned tea and rubber plantations) were nationalized. As of 1990, the Janatha Estate Development Boards and the Sri Lanka Plantation Corporations accounted for 60% of total tea production and 30% of the total area under rubber cultivation.

23ANIMAL HUSBANDRY

Sri Lanka's livestock population is comparatively small; in 1998 there were 1,599,000 head of cattle, 721,000 water buffalo, 519,000 goats, 76,000 hogs, 12,000 sheep, and 10 million chickens. Animals are not of high quality, partly as a consequence of religious considerations and primitive agricultural conditions. The natural pasturage lacks both nutritional value and palatability, and prospects for new pastures are not promising. In 1998, milk output was 216,000 tons from cattle and 72,000 tons from buffaloes, and 50,000 tons of eggs were produced.

24FISHING

Fishing produces less than the country's needs and yields a meager income to fishermen, most of whom use primitive boats and gear in the shallow waters surrounding the island. In 1997, the total fish catch was estimated at 247,000 tons, up from 165,397 tons in 1990. Exports of fish products were valued at nearly $75.4 million in 1997.

25FORESTRY

About 27.8% of the total land area consists of woodland. In 1997, 10,480,000 cu m of roundwood were cut. Forestry products included 5,000 cu m of sawn timber and 9,780,000 cu m of firewood for domestic use.

26MINING

Graphite, gemstone, and titanium minerals extraction are the primary operations of the mining industry in Sri Lanka. Graphite production amounted to 5,127 tons in 1997, and is controlled by the government. The island's gem industry is world famous. In the Ratnapura district there are considerable deposits of sapphire, ruby, chrysoberyl, beryl, topaz, spinel, garnet, zircon, tourmaline, quartz, and moonstone. A lapidary industry has been established for the international marketing of cut and polished precious and semiprecious gemstones. The estimated value of gemstone production in 1997 was $62.5 million. The beach sands contain large quantities of ilmenite, rutile, monazite, and zircon. Ilmenite and rutile (derived from titanium concentrate) production in 1997 amounted to 18,970 tons and 2,970 tons, respectively. Rare earth minerals of the cerium, yttrium, zirconium, niobium, tantalum, thorium, and uranium groups have been found; thorianite appears to be widely distributed. Large quantities of kaolin and apatite have also been found. There are large surface deposits of quartz sand. Limestone dating from the Miocene era is quarried from the Jaffna peninsula and used in the manufacture of cement. In the dry-zone coastal areas, salt is manufactured by solar evaporation of seawater.

27ENERGY AND POWER

The Sri Lanka Electricity Board, a state enterprise, supervises the generation and transmission of electric power in Sri Lanka. Installed capacity in 1998 was 1,555,000 kW, of which almost three-fourths was hydroelectric; power generation totaled 5,505 million kWh. The country's heavy dependence on hydro power creates shortfalls in times of drought, so the government plans to diversify the power sector, adding 2,500 MW of new capacity by 2012.

The Mahaweli hydroelectric project, originally begun in 1970, included the construction of four reservoirs and hydroelectric plants at Victoria, Kotmale, Randenigala, and Maduru Oya, all of which are now in place. The four hydroelectric stations have a combined capacity of 580,000 kW (with the Victoria station contributing 210,000 kW).

28INDUSTRY

Since 1977, the government's market-oriented economic policies have encouraged industrial growth in the private sector, particularly in textiles, wood products, rubber and plastics, food and beverages, and other consumer goods. While most small- and medium-owned enterprises are now privately owned, state ownership continues to predominate among the country's large corporations in basic industries such as oil refining, cement, chemicals, paper and plywood, fertilizers, and ceramics. Manufacturing accounts for about 17% of GDP about 44% of which is textiles, apparel, and leather products. The manufacturing sector grew by 6.3% in 1998, a good performance, but not as good as the 9.1% growth rate posted in 1997. The 1999 outlook, however was not as bright due to a decline in demand for a range of Sri Lank's exports.

The government is encouraging investment in industries that in which it believes Sri Lanka has a comparative advantage including: components for electronic assembling, ceramics and glassware, rubber-based industries, light and heavy engineering, and the manufacture of jewelry.

29SCIENCE AND TECHNOLOGY

With the launching in 1978 of a free-trade zone north of Colombo, Sri Lanka was able to establish such high-technology enterprises as the manufacture of integrated circuits and of control and relay panels. In 1982, two US electronics manufacturers contracted to build semiconductor assembly plants in the zone. The textile industry, located there, ranked nineteenth in 1985 as a supplier to the US. In 1987–97, 47 technicians and 191 scientists and engineers per 1 million population were engaged in research and development.

The Sri Lanka Association for the Advancement of Science, founded in 1960, is located in Colombo. Also in the city are the Ceylon Institute of Scientific and Industrial Research, founded in 1955; Natural Resources, Energy, and Science Authority of Sri Lanka (founded originally in 1968 as the National Science Council); Colombo Observatory, founded in 1907; and the National Academy of Sciences of Sri Lanka, founded in 1976; all in Colombo. The country also has research institutes devoted to coconuts, horticulture, medicine, rice, rubber, tea, and veterinary science. The Royal Botanic Gardens was founded in 1821 at Peradeniya, and a natural history museum was founded at Colombo in 1985. Sri Lanka has 13 universities and colleges offering courses in basic and applied sciences. In 1987–97, science and engineering students accounted for 34% of college and university enrollments.

30DOMESTIC TRADE

Most retail stores are small and unspecialized. Marketing and distribution are dominated by the strong and well-developed cooperative movement, which the government assists with loans, price guarantees, and supervision. Although government monopolies played a major role in the wholesale distribution of imported goods, as well as many domestic commodities during the 1970s and 1980s, liberalization policies since the late 1980s are decreasing direct state involvement in domestic trade. Prices are administered for a few staple commodities such as diesel, kerosene, electricity and flour.

The usual business hours are from 8:30 AM to 1 PM and 2 to 5 PM, Monday through Friday. Banks open from 9 AM to 1 PM on Monday and to 1:30 PM, Tuesday through Friday. Products are advertised in newspapers, trade journals, motion picture theaters, and on commercial radio. There are several advertising firms in Colombo, some of which have connections abroad.

31FOREIGN TRADE

Clothing and apparel is now the country's leading foreign exchange earner. Sri Lanka's traditional primary exports have been tea, natural rubber, and coconut products, especially desiccated coconut and coconut oil. However, the share of total export earnings accounted for by these three commodities declined steadily from 87% in 1972 to 48% in 1985 and 11.6% in 1995; tea decreased from its 58% share of total export value in 1972 to a low of 8.2% in 1995. Declining export shares for the country's agriculturally-based exports are due to adverse weather conditions in recent years as well as rapid growth in the export earnings of industrial products.

In 1998 garments accounted for 44% of Sri Lankan exports. Other commodity exports are tea (13%), diamonds and other precious gems (7.0%), and natural rubber and gums (2.3%). Sri Lanka produces a large portion of the world's tea exports (19%).

In 1994 Sri Lanka's imports were distributed among the following categories:

Consumer goods	7.0%
Food	14.1%
Fuels	6.2%
Industrial supplies	50.0%
Machinery	12.6%
Transportation	9.9%
Other	0.2%

Principal trading partners in 1998 (in millions of US dollars) were as follows:

COUNTRY	EXPORTS	IMPORTS	BALANCE
United States	1,688	209	1,479
United Kingdom	446	249	197
Germany	258	240	18
Japan	206	541	-335
Belgium	198	136	62
Korea	66	450	-384
India	46	630	-584
China (inc. Hong Kong)	45	725	-680
Singapore	44	577	-533
Malaysia	8	184	-176

32BALANCE OF PAYMENTS

Sri Lanka's balance-of-payments position is highly sensitive to price changes in the world market because it depends in large part upon a few export crops to pay for its imports. Since 1983, sharply rising defense expenditures, a decline in tourism caused by continuing civil violence, and slumping world tea and coconut prices have combined to exert pressure on the balance of payments. The deficit has also been partially offset by substantial foreign exchange earnings from tourism and from remittances by Sri Lankans working abroad. A 13% increase in export growth helped the current account deficit to decline from $393 million in 1997 to $288 million in 1998. The current account deficit has declined each year since 1994 when it stood at $860 million. Export growth in 1999, however, slowed considerably to 2% and earnings from tea exports had declined 40% due to the impact of the Russian economic crises in August 1998.

The US Central Intelligence Agency reports that in 1998 the purchasing power parity of Sri Lanka's exports was $4.5 billion while imports totaled $5.3 billion resulting in a trade balance of -$800 million.

The International Monetary Fund (IMF) reports that in 1998 Sri Lanka had exports of goods totaling $4,735 million and imports totaling $5,302 million. The services credit totaled $913 million and debit $1,359 million. The following table summarizes Sri Lanka's balance of payments as reported by the IMF for 1998 in millions of US dollars.

Current Account		-288
Balance on goods	-568	
Balance on services	-446	
Balance on income	-178	
Current transfers	903	
Capital Account		61
Financial Account		343
Direct investment abroad	...	
Direct investment in Sri Lanka	193	
Portfolio investment assets	89	
Portfolio investment liabilities	-112	
Other investment assets	73	
Other investment liabilities	100	
Net Errors and Omissions		109
Reserves and Related Items		-224

33BANKING AND SECURITIES

The Central Bank of Sri Lanka, established in 1949, began operations in 1950 with a capital of R15 million contributed by the government. The sole bank of issue, it administers and regulates the country's monetary and banking systems.

Although Sri Lanka has a fairly well diversified banking system, the two largest banks, the Bank of Ceylon and Peoples Bank, are state owned and operate inefficiently. They are considered to be inefficient, primarily owing to excessive government influence in their lending operations and overstaffing. The World Bank has identified the dominance of these two banks as a major constraint on the development of the financial sector. The simple solution, privatization, is not an option given the current political climate. Together, they accounted for two-thirds of commercial bank deposits in 1999.

In addition to the central bank and the two state owned banks, there are 7 private domestic commercial banks, 18 foreign banks, a national savings bank, 17 regional rural development banks, two large development finance institutions, a mortgage bank, and 10 merchant banks. US banks operating in Sri Lanka include Citibank, American Express, and Bankers Trust.

The Colombo's Brokers Association operates an organized stock market, whose transactions have grown significantly since the 1984 tea export boom increased liquidity in the economy. The Colombo Stock Exchange was established by the Association of Stock Brokers in 1987 and has established itself as one of the most efficient in the region. In 1998, there were 233 companies listed on the exchange with a combined market capitalization of $1.7 billion. The turnover ratio was 14.8%. The exchange was adversely affected by the pull out of foreign investors from the region after the nuclear tests in India and Pakistan. The market was also affected by the Asian economic crisis and the Russian financial crisis, suffering a 14% decline in 1998. The pessimism continued into 1999 as investors continued to pull money from the market.

34INSURANCE

Insurance was almost wholly a foreign enterprise until 1 January 1962, when the life insurance business was nationalized. The state-owned Insurance Corp. of Sri Lanka now has a monopoly on life insurance and all other insurance. In 1997, there were six insurance companies (two of which were state-owned), the National Savings Bank, and two pension funds.

35PUBLIC FINANCE

The US Central Intelligence Agency (CIA) estimates that in 1997 Sri Lanka's central government took in revenues of approximately $3 billion and had expenditures of $4.2 billion including capital expenditures of $1 billion. Overall, the government registered a deficit of approximately $1.2 billion. External debt totaled $8.55 billion.

The following table shows an itemized breakdown of government revenues and expenditures. The percentages were calculated from data reported by the International Monetary Fund. The dollar amounts (millions) are based on the CIA estimates provided above.

REVENUE AND GRANTS	100%	3,000
Tax revenue	80.9%	2,426
Non-tax revenue	15.1%	454
Capital revenue	0.0%	1
Grants	4.0%	119
EXPENDITURES	100%	4,200
General public services	8.4%	355
Defense	16.7%	703
Public order and safety	3.3%	140
Education	10.5%	442
Health	5.7%	239
Social security	12.8%	537
Housing and community amenities	2.2%	92
Economic affairs and services	16.2%	680
Other expenditures	2.5%	104
Interest payments	21.6%	908

The budget remained in deficit in 1998 reaching 9.2% of GDP, much higher than planned, primarily because of shortfalls in revenue and overruns on defense, wages, and pensions. Total government debt rose to $14 billion, approaching 90% of GDP with about half owed to foreign lenders. Interest payments on the mounting debt absorb 20% of total government expenditure and 28% of government revenue. The government expected the deficits to exceed 1999 projections as well.

36TAXATION

Individual income taxes are graduated, increasing from 10–35% of taxable income. At the beginning of 1996, the rate of corporate tax on resident and foreign companies was 35%, but substantial tax benefits, such as depreciation allowances and incentive deductions, were permitted. Tax holidays on profits were available for certain approved companies and for small or medium-sized companies and corporate bodies.

A turnover tax was in effect on imported articles of sale until April 1998 when it was replaced with a value-added tax called a goods and services tax (GST). The GST is applicable on most goods and services imported, produced, or sold locally. The GST has two rates: a standard 12.5% for most goods and services and zero rate for a limited number of essential goods and services like food items, petroleum products, public transport services, and health care. The new GST tax is the most important tax source for the government, although GST collections fell below targets in 1998.

Other taxes include a national security tax, an excise tax on over 250 items, and local property taxes.

[37]CUSTOMS AND DUTIES

Sri Lanka has a five-band import tariff schedule based on the Harmonized System of Classification. In 1999, the standard import tariff rates were zero, 5, 10, 30, and 35 percent. The tariff on automobiles is 30%. Diesel cars are subject to a further 60% excise duty. All imports of textile materials, yarn, and all related intermediate and capital goods required for the garment export industry are free of import duty as are a number of products critical to economic development like computers, medical and dental equipment, telecommunications equipment, and agricultural seeds and machinery. Within Sri Lanka's free-trade zone, imports of industrial and construction equipment, base metals, and coal and coke are duty-free. Export duties are levied on tea, rubber, and coconut products.

[38]FOREIGN INVESTMENT

The great agricultural enterprises, insurance companies, and banks were developed originally by foreign capital. In 1959, foreigners owned almost 36% of the country's rubber acreage and 6% of the tea plantations; 80% of the insurance business was written by foreign companies, and the banking business was largely a monopoly of British and Indian firms. After 1961, when nationalization became widespread, private investors were reluctant to place new funds in Sri Lanka. Consequently, during the 1960s, the country had to depend almost entirely on loans and short-term credits. During the 1970–77 period, foreign companies, principally Japanese, were more willing to collaborate with public sector enterprises.

With the change of direction in the government's economic policy since 1977, foreign investment flowed more freely into the private sector. The Greater Colombo Economic Commission (GCEC) and Foreign Investment Advisory Committee promoted outside investment in export-oriented and high-technology industries, largely through joint ventures in which majority equity is held by Sri Lankan companies. Exceptions to this policy were large luxury hotels and construction projects for the Mahaweli development program, in which foreign partners hold the major share. The GCEC's Investment Promotion Zone, the country's first free trade zone (established in 1978), had attracted 116 foreign companies by 1985; 96 firms operating in the zone, chiefly clothing manufacturers, employed 35,786 workers and made capital investments with a total value of R286 million during that year. Continued liberalization and deceleration of insurgency since 1989 have attracted greater foreign investment. The entire country is now an open investment zone, where 100% equity by foreign investors is possible. A national Board of Investment (BOI) is responsible for assisting entrepreneurs in meeting their basic business needs such as dealing with the appropriate government agencies and labor recruitment.

[39]ECONOMIC DEVELOPMENT

Since independence, successive governments have attempted ambitious economic development programs with mixed results. The nationalization in 1962 of three Western oil companies and in 1975 of large rubber and tea plantations was intended to end the nation's economic dependence and neocolonialism, and to create an egalitarian socialist society. The goals of the last five-year plan for 1972–76—to achieve an economic growth rate of 6% annually, to create new jobs, and thereby to ameliorate unemployment—were not met, in part because of drought and unexpected increases in the costs of crude oil, fertilizer, and other imports.

The UNP government elected in 1977 chose as the centerpiece of its development strategy the Mahaweli hydroelectric-irrigation-resettlement program, the largest development project ever undertaken in Sri Lanka. The project involved diverting the Mahaweli Ganga in order to irrigate 364,000 hectares (900,000 acres) and generate 2,037 million kwh of hydroelectricity annually from an installed capacity of 507 Mw. Launched in 1978, construction was largely completed by 1987, at a cost of about $2 billion. Even as the UNP government launched this massive capital program, it sought to encourage private investors, limit the scope of government monopolies, and reduce subsidies on consumer products. Foreign trade, investment, and tourism were all encouraged by the government authorities. In 1986, foreign aid rose 23% in real terms over 1985, largely to finance further massive hydroelectric projects.

While government development policies resulted in moderate growth during the late 1970s and early 1980s, the outbreak of civil war in 1983 led to a rapid rise in defense spending (from 1% of GDP in 1980 to over 4% in 1996), exacerbating structural weaknesses in the Sri Lankan economy. By 1989, rapidly declining economic growth and worsening fiscal and balance of payment problems reached crisis proportions, prompting renewed stabilization and adjustment efforts. Corrective policies involved stimulating savings through new banking regulations and other monetary-tightening measures, reduction of subsidies on wheat and fertilizers, government expenditure reductions, currency devaluation, privatization of many state enterprises, and other incentives for private investment. These measures resulted in greatly improved economic performance in the early 1990s, despite unfavorable weather and lingering insurgency. In 1996, as the market showed signs of weakening, the government reaffirmed its intention to pursue free-market policies as a way to strengthen the economy.

[40]SOCIAL DEVELOPMENT

Despite low per capita income, Sri Lankans have enjoyed a relatively high standard of living because of generous social welfare programs. Through a provident fund system, the government pays monthly allotments to the aged, sick, and disabled, to destitute widows, and to wives of imprisoned or disabled men. The program is financed by 8% employee contributions and 12% employer contributions. Old age benefits are paid as a lump sum grant equal to total contributions plus interest. Medical care is available free of charge in government hospitals and clinics. A 1995 law set up a system of family allowances, to be paid for by the government, for families earning less than 1,000 rupees per month.

To stimulate private efforts, the government makes grants to supplement the funds of volunteer agencies engaged in various welfare activities, particularly orphanages, homes for the aged, and institutions for the mentally and physically handicapped.

Although women have equal rights under law, their rights in family matters, including marriage, divorce, child custody, and inheritance, are often dictated by their ethnic or religious group. Recent legislative changes have strengthened the rights of women. Changes to the Penal code make the burden of proof more equitable in rape cases. New laws address sexual harassment in the workplace. However, discrimination against women in hiring, promotion and salary practices remains. In 1999 women made up about half the formal work force.

Sri Lanka's Tamil population, numbering 1 million, are not entitled to either Indian or Sri Lankan citizenship, and face systematic discrimination.

In 1999, human rights abuses were committed by both the government and Tamil separatist forces as part of ongoing hostilities between the two sides. These included poor prison conditions, torture, and arbitrary arrests, including mass arrests.

[41]HEALTH

The government provides medical service free or at a nominal cost to almost everyone, but its health program is hampered by a worsening shortage of trained personnel and hospital beds.

Medical standards, traditionally British, are considered excellent, but in recent years many Sri Lankan physicians and surgeons have moved their practices abroad—particularly to the US and UK, where remuneration is much higher. In 1990–97, there were 2.7 hospital beds per 1,000 people. There are a limited number of private hospitals and medical practitioners. Total health care expenditures in 1990–97 were 1.9% of GDP.

Malaria, smallpox, cholera, and plague have been virtually eliminated. Malnutrition, tuberculosis (3,405 cases in 1994), and the gastrointestinal group of infectious diseases are the chief medical problems. In 1993, there were 363,200 malaria cases. In 1991–95, 38% of children under 5 years of age were considered malnourished. In 1995, immunization rates for children up to one year old were tuberculosis (89%); diphtheria, pertussis, and tetanus (91%); polio (91%); and measles (88%). Safe water was accessible to 57% of the population in 1994–95.

The infant mortality rate in 1999 was 16.1 per 1,000 live births, while the maternal mortality rate was 30 per 100,000 live births for 1990–97. Birth control was used by 66% of married women in 1993. The birth rate was 18.1 per 1,000 people in 1999, and the general mortality rate was 6 per 1,000 inhabitants. Between 1984 and 1992, there were 32,000 civil war-related deaths. Other leading causes of death from 1990 statistics included communicable diseases and maternal/perinatal causes (232 per 100,000 people); noncommunicable diseases (459 per 100,000); and injuries (194 per 100,000). Average life expectancy in 1999 was 72.7 years. The HIV seroprevalence rate was 0.1 per 100 adults in 1997. There were only 58 cases in 1996.

42HOUSING

Rapid population increase, coupled with a lag in construction during and immediately following World War II, led to an acute housing shortage, high rents, high building costs, and many unsanitary and unfit houses in Sri Lanka's first decades after independence. According to estimates by the Ministry of Housing, 28,000–30,000 houses a year were built between 1970 and 1975, compared with 18,000–19,000 annually during the previous five-year period. Under the UNP government's urban development program, 184,860 public-sector housing units were built during the 1978–86 period.

The 1981 census showed a total of 2,813,844 housing units, of which 2,084,841 were rural, 511,810 urban, and 217,193 situated on agricultural estates. The average housing unit had 2.5 rooms and was occupied by 5.2 persons, or 2.1 persons per room. Although about 46% of urban units had electricity and 49% had running water, only 8.3% of rural houses were equipped with electricity and 5.1% supplied with piped-in water. About 51% of all housing units were semi-permanent, 42% were permanent, and 7% were improvised. Owners occupied 70%, 12% were occupied rent free, and 10% were rented.

43EDUCATION

For the year 2000, 8.4% of the adult population was estimated to be illiterate (males, 5.5%; females, 11.1%). All education from kindergarten up to and including university training is free. Education is compulsory for 10 years, except when schools are not within walking distance of the pupil's home.

The public educational system was consolidated in 1970 into five years of elementary, six years of lower secondary, and two years of higher secondary. In 1996, there were 9,554 primary schools, with 1,843,848 students and 66,339 teachers. Student-to-teacher ratio stood at 28 to one. In 1995, secondary schools had 2,314,054 students and 103,572 teachers. In the latter part of the 1990s, the estimated expenditure on education was 8.9% of the central government budget. Since 1986, the educational system has been separated into two systems based on language,

one in which Sinhalese is the medium of instruction and the other in which the medium is Tamil.

Beginning in 1978, Sri Lanka reorganized its higher education system; in 1986 there were nine universities: Colombo, Peradeniya, Moratuwa, Sri Jayawardhanapura, Kelaniya, Jaffna, Ruhuna, Open University, and Batticaloa. These universities operate as independent units under the University Grants Commission, which is funded by the Ministry of Education. Included in the consolidated university system are the former Vidyalankara University (established 1959), previously known as the Vidyalankara Pirivena (established 1875), a celebrated seat of learning for Oriental studies and Buddhist culture; the former Vidyadaya University (established 1959); and the former University of Ceylon (founded 1942). In 1995, universities and equivalent institutions had 2,636 teachers and 63,660 students.

44LIBRARIES AND MUSEUMS

The National Library in Colombo holds 206,300 volumes. The Public Library in Colombo is the largest public library in the country. Apart from the libraries in Anuradhapura, Jaffna, Kandy, and a few other towns, most public libraries have only small collections of books. The University of Peradeniya has holdings of 595,700 volumes, while the Colombo campus has 195,000. There are several special libraries in Colombo, including the National Museum Library, which contains 625,000 volumes (147,000 which are monographs) and has been a depository for Ceylonese and Sri Lankan publications since 1885.

The five national museums, at Colombo, Kandy, Ratnapura, and Galle, contain collections pertaining to paleontology, zoology, prehistory, archaeology, and ancient art. One of Asia's finest zoological collections, as well as the largest known collection of Sinhala palm-leaf manuscripts, is in the Colombo museum. Three national botanical gardens, located at three different elevations above sea level, represent Sri Lanka's three distinct zones of vegetation. There are several archeological, ethnographic, and folk museums in the country. The Dutch Period Museum, the Art Gallery of the Sri Lankan Society of Art, the Natural History Museum, and a university archaeological museum are all in Colombo.

45MEDIA

The central government owns and operates all telephone, telegraph, cable, and radio facilities, except in a few rural districts, which are served by private exchanges. In 1997 there were 352,681 telephones, more than half of which were in Colombo. In the same year, cellular subscribers numbered 114,888. Domestic telephone service is reportedly inadequate, while international service is good. The government operates both commercial and noncommercial radio broadcasting services in Sinhala, Tamil, and English and began television service in 1982. The Sri Lanka Broadcasting Corporation airs broadcasts on AM, FM, and shortwave. As of 1999, there were 12 AM and 5 FM radio stations and 21 television stations. In 1997 there were 210 radios, 91 television sets, and 6 mobile phones per 1,000 population.

As of 1999, Sri Lanka had more than 10 daily newspapers. The principal morning and evening dailies (with 1999 daily circulations) were the following:

	LANGUAGE	CIRCULATION
COLOMBO		
Dinamina (m)	Sinhala	140,000
Daily News (m)	English	85,000
Divaina (d) Sinhala		100,000
Virakesari (m)	Tamil	48,000

Sri Lanka also has more than 100 weekly and monthly publications.

The constitution provides for free speech and a free press; however, restrictions on national security grounds are said to be sometimes arbitrary and overly broad. In 1972, a five-member national Press Council with extensive powers over the press was established; since then varying degrees of censorship have been imposed with changing political conditions.

As of 1996, there were almost 20,000 personal computers. Online access is extremely limited, with less than 1 Internet host per 1,000 population in 1998.

46ORGANIZATIONS

Chambers of commerce include the National Chamber of Commerce of Sri Lanka, the Ceylon Chamber of Commerce, the Indian Chamber of Commerce, and the Moor Chamber of Commerce. There are numerous trade and industrial organizations.

47TOURISM, TRAVEL, AND RECREATION

International tourism has grown in Sri Lanka in response to the governments promotion of the industry. Europe is the leading generating region of tourists, accounting for over 60% of the 366,000 tourists in 1997. Tourism receipts were estimated at US$233 million that year. The country had 15,005 hotel rooms with 27,528 beds and a 49% occupancy rate.

The principal tourist attraction is the sacred city of Anuradhapura, home of the Seated Buddha, Buddhist temples, palaces, and the sacred bo tree, grown from a sapling of the tree under which the Buddha is said to have attained enlightenment. Other popular sites include the ancient cities of Polonnaruwa and Kandy, with its Dalada Maligawa temple, where a sacred tooth relic of the Buddha is preserved. The botanical gardens near Kandy and the Dehiwela Zoo at Colombo are also popular.

Sri Lanka's recreational facilities include the beach resorts of Bentota and Negombo, which, like Colombo, have modern hotels. Popular water sports are swimming, fishing, sailing, surfing, water skiing, and skin diving. The island has excellent facilities for golf, tennis, squash, soccer, rugby, and cricket.

Visitors need a valid passport and a visa, except for nationals of most Western European, ASEAN, and ANZUS countries, as well as Japan, who may stay for up to a month without a visa. Passengers traveling through infected areas must also possess valid certificates of vaccination against yellow fever.

According to 1999 UN estimates, the cost of staying in Colombo was $94 per day. Elsewhere in the country, travel expenses averaged $60 per day.

48FAMOUS SRI LANKANS

One of the great rulers of the Anuradhapura period was Dutugemunu (fl.100 BC), who is famous for having saved Ceylon and its religion from conquest by Indian invaders. Mahasen, a king in the 3d century AD, built many fine dagobas and other monuments that delight and amaze visiting art lovers. The classic period of Ceylonese art flourished under Kassapa, a king of the 5th century. The great figure of the Polonnaruwa period was Parakramabahu I (the Great, r.1153–86), who unified the government of Ceylon, built many magnificent structures, and organized the economy. The most famous political figure in modern Ceylon was Don Stephen Senanayake (1884–1952), leader of the independence movement and first prime minister of independent Ceylon. Solomon West Ridgway Dias Bandaranaike (1899–1959), prime minister from 1956 to 1959, is regarded as the founder of Ceylon as a socialist state. His widow, Sirimavo Bandaranaike (b.1916), was prime minister during 1960–65, 1970–77, and was appointed again in 1994. Her daughter, Chandrika Bandaranaike Kumaratunga (b.1946) was elected president in 1994. Junius Richard Jayewardene (1906–96), who helped usher in economic reforms and a free enterprise system, became Sri Lanka's first president in 1978 and served until 1982. Science-fiction writer Sir Arthur C. Clarke (b. England, 1917) is one of Sri Lanka's most famous expatriate residents. Born in Sri Lanka, Canadian author and poet Michael Ondaatje (b.1943) received the 1992 Booker McConnell Prize for his novel *The English Patient*.

49DEPENDENCIES

Sri Lanka has no territories or colonies.

50BIBLIOGRAPHY

Bruton, Henry J. *Sri Lanka and Malaysia*. New York: Oxford University Press, 1992.

De Silva, Chandra Richard. *Sri Lanka, a History*. New Delhi: Vikas, 1987.

Dissanayaka, T. D. S. A. *The Politics of Sri Lanka*. Colombo, Sri Lanka: Swastikha (Private) Ltd., 1994.

Fernando, Tissa, and Robert N. Kearney. *Sri Lanka: Profile of an Island Republic*. Boulder, Colo.: Westview, 1986.

Juppe, James. *Sri Lanka: Third World Democracy*. London: Cass, 1978.

Kanesalingam, V. *Economic Liberalisation in Sri Lanka*. Colombo, Sri Lanka: Friederich Ebert Stiftung, 1995.

Kemper, Steven. *The Presence of the Past: Chronicles, Politics, and Culture in Sinhala Life*. Ithaca: Cornell University Press, 1991.

Manor, James (ed.). *Sri Lanka in Change and Crisis*. New York: St. Martin's, 1984.

Peebles, Patrick. *Sri Lanka: A Handbook of Historical Statistics*. Boston: G. K. Hall, 1982.

Ross, Russell R. and Andrea Matles Savada (eds.). *Sri Lanka, a Country Study*. 2d ed. Washington, D.C.: Library of Congress, 1990.

Samaraweera, Vijaya. *Sri Lanka*. Santa Barbara, Calif.: Clio Press, 1987.

Spencer, Jonathan (ed.). *Sri Lanka: History and the Roots of Conflict*. New York: Routledge, 1990.

Sri Lanka: State of Human Rights, 1994. Colombo, Sri Lanka: Law & Society Trust, 1995.

Wilson, A. Jeyaratnam. *The Break-up of Sri Lanka: The Sinhalese-Tamil Conflict*. Honolulu: University of Hawaii Press, 1988.

SYRIA

Syrian Arab Republic

Al-Jumhuriyah al-'Arabiyah as-Suriyah

CAPITAL: Damascus (Dimashq).

FLAG: The national flag is a horizontal tricolor of red, white, and black stripes; in the white center stripe are two green five-pointed stars.

ANTHEM: *An-Nashid as-Suri (The Syrian National Anthem)* begins "Protectors of the nation, peace be upon you."

MONETARY UNIT: The Syrian pound (s£) is a paper currency of 100 piasters. There are coins of 25 and 50 piasters and 1 Syrian pound and notes of 1, 5, 10, 25, 50, 100, and 500 Syrian pounds. s£1 = $0.0217 ($1 = s£46.00) as of 31 March 2000.

WEIGHTS AND MEASURES: The metric system is the legal standard, but local units are widely used.

HOLIDAYS: New Year's Day, 1 January; Revolution Day, 8 March; Egypt's Revolution Day, 23 July; Union of Arab Republics Day, 1 September; National Day, 16 November. Muslim religious holidays include 'Id al-Fitr, 'Id al-'Adha', Milad an-Nabi, and Laylat al-Miraj. Christian religious holidays include Easter (Catholic); Easter (Orthodox); and Christmas, 25 December.

TIME: 2 PM = noon GMT.

¹LOCATION, SIZE, AND EXTENT

Situated in southwest Asia, at the eastern end of the Mediterranean Sea, Syria has an area of 185,180 sq km (71,498 sq mi). Comparatively, the area occupied by Syria is slightly larger than the state of North Dakota. Included in this total is the Golan Heights region (1,176 sq km/454 sq mi), which Israel captured in 1967 and annexed on 14 December 1981; the annexation was denounced by Syria and unanimously condemned by the UN Security Council. Syria extends 793 km (493 mi) ENE–WSW and 431 km (268 mi) SSE–NNW. It is bounded on the N by Turkey, on the E and SE by Iraq, on the S by Jordan, on the SW by Israel, and on the W by Lebanon and the Mediterranean Sea, with a total boundary length of 2,415 km (1,500 mi) following the 1949 armistice with Israel and of 2,446 km (1,520 mi) as of January 1988.

²TOPOGRAPHY

There are five main geographic zones: (1) the narrow coastal plain along the Mediterranean shore; (2) the hill and mountain regions, including the Ansariyah ('Alawite) Mountains in the northwest paralleling the coast, the eastern slopes of the Anti-Lebanon Mountains, and the Jabal Ad-Duruz in the southeast; (3) the cultivated area east of the Ansariyah and Anti-Lebanon ranges, which is widest in the north, discontinuous between Homs and Damascus; (4) the steppe and desert region, traversed by the Euphrates (Al-Furat) River; and (5) the Jazirah in the northeast, steppe country with low rolling hills.

The Anti-Lebanon Mountains, extending southward along the Lebanese border, serve as a catchment for the rainfall of central Syria. To the north of this range, the Ansariyah Mountains, which reach heights of over 1,500 m (5,000 ft), slope westward to the Mediterranean. The Orontes (Asi) River irrigates areas on the eastern side of the Ansariyah Mountains.

³CLIMATE

The climate varies from the Mediterranean type in the west to extremely arid desert conditions in the east. The coastal regions have hot summers and mild winters; in the mountains, summer heat is moderated according to elevation and the winters are much more severe.

The steppe and desert areas have extremely hot, arid summers and greatly varying winter temperatures ranging from 21°C (70°F) to below freezing. Average temperatures for Damascus range from about 21° to 43°C (70–109°F) in August and from about –4° to 16°C (25–61°F) in January. Rainfall averages about 75 cm (30 in) on the coast, around 125 cm (50 in) in some mountain areas, and less than 25 cm (10 in) in the eastern three-fifths of the country. In dry years, rainfall may be reduced by half.

⁴FLORA AND FAUNA

The coastal plain is highly cultivated, and the little wild growth found is mainly of the brushwood type, such as tamarisk. On the northern slopes of the Ansariyah range are remnants of pine forests, while oak and scrub oak grow in the less well-watered central portion. Terebinth is indigenous to the low hill country of the steppes, and wormwood grows on the plains. Some sections of the Jabal Ad-Duruz are covered with a dense maquis.

The wildlife of Syria includes types common to the eastern Mediterranean region, together with typical desert species. There is a diminishing number of bears in the mountains; antelope are found wherever grazing is available and human competition not too severe; there are also deer in some sections. Smaller animals include squirrel, wildcat, otter, and hare. In the desert, the viper, lizard, and chameleon are found in relatively large numbers. Native birds include flamingo and pelican, as well as various ducks, snipe, and other game birds.

[5]ENVIRONMENT

Much of Syria's natural vegetation has been depleted by farming, livestock grazing, and cutting of trees for firewood and construction. The thick forests that once covered western Syria have been drastically reduced; as a result, soil erosion and desertification are extensive. The salinity of the soil is also a problem, causing a loss of more than $300 million worth of agricultural products per year. Other environmental problems include pollution of coastal waters from oil spills and human wastes, and contamination of inland waterways by industrial wastes and sewage. Syria has 1.8 cubic miles of water. Eighty-three percent is used for farming and 10% for industrial activity. Thirty-two percent of the people living in rural areas do not have pure water. The pollution of the nation's water supply also leads to the spread of diseases. The nation's cities produce 1.3 million tons of solid waste per year. Environmental awareness has been a growing concern in the Arab world. The UN and Middle Eastern environmental organizations have sponsored Arab Environment Day to bring the focus of the nation's attention on environmental problems. The quantity of native wildlife has been so seriously depleted that in 1979 the government banned hunting for five years. In 1994, two of Syria's mammal species and 15 of its bird species were endangered. Eleven types of plants were also endangered. The Mediterranean monk seal is endangered, and the Anatolian leopard, cheetah, Asiatic wild ass, and Persian fallow deer are extinct.

[6]POPULATION

In 1994, Syria's population was 13,812,000, representing and annual growth rate since 1981 of 4%, one of the highest in the world. In mid-1996, the UNRWA estimated the population at 14,618,393, and the US Census Bureau estimated it at 15,609,000. Syria's 2000 population was estimated at 17,758,925. An estimated 3.0% of the population is 65 years of age or older. The projected population for the year 2005 is 20,530,000, assuming a crude birthrate of 32 per 1,000 population and a death rate of 5, resulting in a natural rate of change of 2.7% for the period 2000–2005. The population rate of change between 1995 and 2000 was 2.5%. The population density in 1998 was 83 per sq km (215 per sq mi), but most of it was concentrated in a small area; 70% of Syria's people live in Damascus and the six western provinces.

It was estimated that 55% of the population lived in urban areas in 2000, up from 47% in 1980. The capital city, Damascus, and its surrounding metropolitan area had a 2000 population of 2,335,000. The population of Aleppo (Halab), a northern trading and agricultural center, was an estimated 2,173,000. Other main cities are Homs (Hims), 481,000; Hamath (Hama); and Latakia (Al-Ladhiqqiyah). Syria's next census is scheduled to take place in 2004.

[7]MIGRATION

In the past there was sizable emigration by Syrians to Europe, Africa, and the Western Hemisphere, but emigration had virtually ceased by the late 1940s. Since World War I there has been substantial internal migration from the coastal mountains to the central plains and, in general, from rural areas to the towns. There is considerable migration across the borders with Lebanon and Jordan. About 150,000 Syrians working in Kuwait returned during 1990–91. As of October 1995, there were 300,000 Palestinian refugees in Syria. In 1997, the Syrian government accepted the UNHCR's protection mandate for all recognized refugees in the country. As of mid-1999, there were 7,210 registered refugees in Syria, including 3,950 urban refugees in Damascus and another 3,260 refugees living in El Hol Camp in Hassakeh Governorate. The net migration rate was zero in 1999.

[8]ETHNIC GROUPS

Racially, the Syrians are varied, and except where ethnic distinctions have found religious expression, racial types are generally intermixed. It is estimated that Arabs make up about 90.3% of the population. Other ethnic groups make up the remaining 9.7%, including Kurds, Armenians, and others.

[9]LANGUAGES

The official language and language of the majority is Arabic, but dialect variations are distinct from region to region and even from town to town. The written language, classical Arabic, based on the Koran (Qur'an), is the basis of the standard spoken form. Kurdish and Armenian are the principal minority languages. Aramaic, the language of Jesus, and Circassian are also widely understood. French and English are somewhat understood.

[10]RELIGIONS

Islam is the religion of the vast majority. Most of the Muslims are Sunnis (74%). Alawite, Druze, and other Muslim sects account for another 16% of the population. The Alawite constitute an important minority in Syria and hold a disproportionate share of political power; although they consider themselves Muslims, they combine their avowed creed with Christian rituals and esoteric cults. Also important are the Druzes (most of whom live in the Jabal Ad-Duruz), whose religion is an offshoot of Shi'a Islam. Orthodox Muslims, Alawites, and Druzes together constituted about 90% of the population in 1999. The Christian population—including Greek Orthodox, Armenian Catholic, Armenian Orthodox (Gregorian), Syrian Catholic, Syrian Orthodox, Maronite Christian, Protestant, and Nestorian—make up an estimated 10%. The small Jewish population is urban, living primarily in Damascus, Al Qamishli, and Aleppo.

Under the 1973 constitution, Islam is no longer declared to be the religion of the state, but the president of Syria must still be a Muslim, and Islamic law is a major source of legislation. Freedom of worship is guaranteed by the constitution. Armed opposition to the government by Muslim fundamentalists grouped in an Islamic Front took many lives during 1976–82. The movement collapsed following the government's suppression of a major uprising in Hamath in February 1982, an action in which upwards of 5,000 died.

[11]TRANSPORTATION

The Syrian national railway system consists of 1,998 km (1,241 mi) of standard gauge line: three sections are the Syrian section of the old Baghdad Railway; the main line from Damascus to Aleppo, with connections to Tartus, points in Lebanon, and the phosphate mines; and the railway linking Latakia, Aleppo, and Al-Qamishli, built with Soviet help and completed in 1981. There are also 315 km (196 mi) of narrow-gauge line—part of which is the pre–World War I Hejaz Railway—linking Damascus to Jordan and Lebanon. Syria is also connected by rail with Turkey (hence, with Europe) and Iraq.

The road system, though growing, remains inadequate in view of the demands imposed by increased economic activity. In 1997, Syria had 41,451 km (25,758 mi) of roads, of which only 9,575 km (5,950 mi) were paved, including 877 km (545 mi) of expressways. There are road connections between the major towns and with Iraq, Jordan, Lebanon, and Turkey.

Tartus and Latakia are the main ports. Jablah and Baniyas are minor ports. In 1998, the merchant fleet was comprised of 131 vessels with a capacity of 401,407 GRT. Also in 1998, Syria had 104 airports, of which 24 had paved runways. Damascus is a connecting point for a number of major airlines; the main passenger terminal of its international airport was completed in 1982. Another principal airport is Aleppo International at Aleppo. Syrian Arab Airlines provides service to Aleppo, Al-

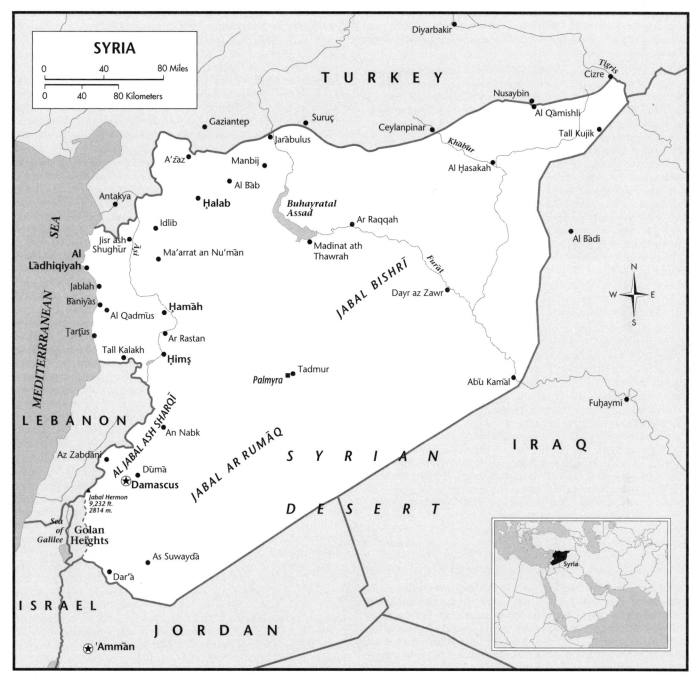

LOCATION: (1949): 32°30′ to 37°30′N; 35°50′ to 42°E. **BOUNDARY LENGTHS:** Turkey, 845 km (525 mi). Iraq, 596 km (370 mi). Jordan, 356 km (221 mi). Israel: 1949 armistice line, 76 km (47 mi); 1988 line, 80 km (50 mi). Lebanon, 359 km (223 mi). Mediterranean coastline, 183 km (114 mi). **TERRITORIAL SEA LIMIT:** 35 mi.

Qamishli, Latakia, and other airports; it also flies to other Arab countries and to Europe and Africa. In 1997, 1,235,000 passengers were carried on scheduled domestic and international flights.

¹²HISTORY

Archaeological excavations at Ebla, in northern Syria, have revealed that Syria was the center of a great Semitic empire extending from the Red Sea north to Turkey and east to Mesopotamia around 2500 BC. At that time, Damascus, traditionally the world's oldest continuously occupied city and certainly one of the world's oldest cities, was settled. Later, an

advanced civilization was developed along the Syrian and Lebanese coastlands under the Phoenicians (c.1600–c.800 BC), among whom trade, industry, and seafaring flourished. The wealth of the land attracted many conquerors, and Syria was invaded successively by Hittites, Egyptians, Assyrians, Persians, and others. In the 4th century BC, Syria fell to Alexander the Great, first in a long line of European conquerors. After the breakup of his empire, dominion over Syria was disputed by the Seleucid and Ptolemaic successor states, and Persians invaded when the opportunity arose; eventually the Seleucids gained control. In the 1st century BC, all of Syria, Lebanon, Palestine, and Transjordan was conquered by the Romans and organized as the province of Syria; these areas are termed "geographic" Syria. Christianity, particularly after its official recognition in the early 4th century AD by Constantine the Great, spread throughout the region.

In 637, Damascus fell to the Arabs. Most Syrians were converted to Islam, and Arabic gradually became the language of the area. Under the Umayyad caliphs, Damascus became the capital of the Islamic world and a base for Arab conquests. Under the 'Abbasids, the caliphate was centered at Baghdad, and Syria was reduced to provincial status. Thereafter, geographic Syria fell prey to a succession of invaders, including Byzantines and Crusaders from Western Europe. Some parts of Syria came under the sway of Seljuks and Ayyubids, a Kurdish dynasty. The latter was most prominent under its leader Saladin (Salah ad-Din). During the 13th century, Mongols frequently invaded Syria, and for 200 years parts of Syria were controlled by Mamluks, who ruled it from Egypt through local governors. In 1516, the Ottoman forces of Sultan Selim I defeated the Mamluks, and for the next four centuries, Syria was a province of the Ottoman Empire.

During World War I, Sharif Hussein (Husayn Ibn-'Ali) of Mecca threw in his lot with the Allies and revolted against Ottoman rule. After the war, with British forces in control, the formal entry of Allied troops into Damascus was made by Arab forces under Faisal (Faysal), Hussein's son, on 30 October 1918. Faisal and the Arab nationalists, whose number had been growing since 1912, opposed French aspirations to Syria and claimed independence under the terms of agreements between the British government and Hussein. In March 1920, Faisal was proclaimed king by a congress representing Syria, Lebanon, and Palestine. However, geographic Syria was divided into British and French mandates. In June, the French, who had been allotted a mandate for Syria and Lebanon by the Agreement of San Remo (April 1920), ejected Faisal and installed local administrations of their own choosing. Arab nationalists resented French rule; there was a major revolt from 1925 to 1927, and unrest persisted until the outbreak of World War II. In 1941, Free French and British forces wrested control of Syria from Vichy France. Two years later, under pressure from the UK and the US, the French permitted elections and the formation of a nationalist government. The UK and the US recognized Syria's independence in 1944, and the last French troops departed on 17 April 1946.

Two parties that had led the struggle for independence, the Nationalist Party and the People's Party, dominated Syrian political life in the immediate postwar period. However, the Palestine War of 1948–49, which resulted in the defeat of the Arab armies and the establishment of Israeli statehood, discredited the Syrian leadership. In December 1948, riots against the government were put down by the army, and several army factions struggled for more than a year to gain control of the Syrian state. Col. Adib Shishakli ruled Syria for most of the period from December 1949 to March 1954, when he was ousted by another army coup.

The years from 1954 to 1958 were marked by the growth of pan-Arab and left-of-center political forces at the expense of the traditional merchant-landowner class, which dominated the Nationalist and People's parties. Foremost among these forces was the Arab Socialist Ba'th Party, which saw in Gamal Abdel Nasser (Nasir), the president of Egypt, a kindred pan-Arabist. Military officers remained active in political affairs but were split into competing factions. Some elements of the Nationalist and People's parties sought to counter the left by seeking help from Iraq and other countries. In late 1957, influential military officers decided to seek unity with Egypt as a means of suppressing factionalism. Enthusiastically supported by the Ba'th and other pan-Arabists, they appealed to Cairo. Nasser agreed, and on 1 February 1958, Egypt and Syria proclaimed the union of Syria and Egypt as the United Arab Republic (UAR).

A monolithic single-party structure replaced the lively Syrian political tradition; decisions were made in Cairo; land reforms were introduced. Syrians chafed under Egyptian rule, and in September 1961, after a military coup, Syria seceded from the UAR. A period of political instability followed until, on 8 March 1963, power was seized by a group of leftist army officers calling themselves the National Council of the Revolutionary Command, and a radical socialist government dominated by the Ba'th Party was formed.

The period that followed was marked by internal struggles between the founders of the Ba'th Party and a younger generation of party militants, many in the military. That generation came to power in 1966 but split in succeeding years. In the June 1967 war between Israel, on one side, and Syria, Egypt, and Jordan on the other, Israel gained control of the Golan Heights. Gen. Hafez al-Assad (Hafiz al-Asad), a former chief of the Air Force and Defense Minister, became chief of state on 16 November 1970; he assumed the presidency, a reinstituted office, for the first of four seven-year terms beginning in March 1971, and a permanent constitution was ratified by popular referendum on 12 March 1973. On 6 October of that year, Syrian troops launched a full-scale attack against Israeli forces in the Golan Heights, as the Egyptians attacked in the Suez Canal area. After the UN cease-fire of 24 October, Israel remained in control of the Golan Heights, and Syria boycotted peace negotiations in Geneva. However, on 31 May 1974, Syria signed a US-mediated disengagement accord with Israel, restoring part of the Golan Heights to Syria and creating a buffer zone, manned by a UN peace-keeping force. The occupied sector of the Golan Heights was annexed by Israel in 1981; outside powers criticized and did not recognize the annexation.

In recent years, Syria has intervened militarily in neighboring Arab states to secure political ends. In September 1970, Syrian armored forces crossed the border into Jordan to support the Palestinians during the Jordanian civil war, but the Syrians were driven back by troops loyal to Jordan's King Hussein (Husayn) and by the threat of Israeli intervention. In 1976, Syrian troops entered Lebanon, nominally to enforce a cease-fire between Christian and Muslim forces but actually to help the Christian forces prevent a victory by leftist Muslims and Palestinians. Syria strongly opposed the Egyptian-Israeli peace treaty of 1979 and was one of the few Arab states to support Iran in its war against Iraq, with which Syria earlier had hoped to merge. Another merger plan, this one with Libya, was announced in September 1980, but the effort was stillborn. In October, Syria signed a 20-year friendship treaty with the USSR; subsequently Syria received large quantities of Soviet arms, including antiaircraft missiles, which it deployed in the Bekaa (Biqa') Valley in Lebanon. After Israel invaded southern Lebanon in June 1982, the Israelis knocked out the missile batteries, crippled Syria's Soviet-equipped air force, and trapped Syrian as well as Palestinian fighters in Beirut before allowing their evacuation. Having reequipped its army with Soviet weapons, Syria has maintained 25,000-30,000 troops in Lebanon ever since. In the continuing Lebanese civil war, Syria supported the Druze and Muslim militias against the Maronite Lebanese Forces.

Syria made repeated attempts to establish a cease-fire among Lebanon's factions. In 1989, it endorsed the Taif Accord for ending the conflict and, later, when Christian militia General Michel Aoun declared himself president of Lebanon and sought to expel the Syrian forces, assaulted his enclave with artillery and drove him out of the country. In 1991, Syria backed moves to disarm and disband the militias and signed a treaty with Beirut to put relations on a stable and peaceful basis. Under the Taif Accord, Syria was to have withdrawn its forces from Beirut and coastal areas by September 1992. The move was still pending in1999.

The authoritarian Assad regime has been condemned by outsiders for assisting terrorist and drug smuggling groups. Both charges have been played down since Syria joined the coalition of forces against Iraq in 1990 and agreed to participate in direct peace talks with Israel in 1991. The collapse of the Soviet Union removed Syria's most important external support, nullifying Assad's proclaimed strategy of refusing to negotiate with Israel until Syria had gained military parity.

Internally, the regime is resented for its denial of democracy and the concentration of power with members of Assad's minority religious sect, the Alawis. The most serious internal threat came from Islamic militants in the late 1970s and early 1980s. In 1982, Assad sent the army against their stronghold in Hama, devastating a section of the city and causing tens of thousands of casualties. There has been no serious threat to the regime since then and the Ba'th Party has continued to be used as a means of control throughout the country. In the 1990s, Assad took steps to liberalize economic controls and to permit some political freedoms. About 300 political prisoners were released in 1992 and Syrian Jews were again allowed to travel. Still, the country remains on the US State Department list of countries which support terrorism and US trade is severely restricted. In 1994 Syrian official met with representatives of Israel's Rabin-led government on the return of the Golan Heights—something Assad had wanted for decades. After Rabin's assassination, however, the talks were discontinued, and the stalemate between Syria and Israel continued. In 1997, US Secretary of State Madeleine Albright announced that she would visit Syria in an effort to get the stalled peace process back on track. Syria was officially guarded about the prospects for success as it remained deeply suspicious of Israel's right-wing Netenyahu government. In the same year, the Assad regime entered into negotiations with Iraq to open up its ports to the latter. Syria broke off diplomatic relations with Iraq after backing Iran in the 1980–99 war.

With the election of Labor leader Ehud Barak as prime minister of Israel in May 1999, new hope arose for improved relations with Israel, and a new round of peace talks between Syria and Israel was held in the US, near Washington, D.C., in January 2000. By the late 1990s, serious concerns had been raised about the health and mental status of Syria's president, who was reportedly having "mental lapses" and suspected to be suffering from some form of dementia, as well as other infirmities. Nevertheless, Assad was elected to a fifth seven-year term in 1999 in a nearly unanimous vote. Since the 1994 death in an automobile accident of Basel, the son whom the Syrian leader had been grooming to succeed him, another of Assad's sons, Bashir, had been given increased responsibilities. Assad died on 10 June 2000 of a heart attack; 34-year-old Bashir Assad was unanimously elected secretary-general by the Ba'th Party one week later. Parliament amended the constitution to lower the minimum age for a president from 40 to 34. In a July referendum, Bashir won overwhelming support to succeed his father, and he officially began a seven-year term as president on 17 July 2000.

13GOVERNMENT

After independence, Syria made several attempts at establishing a constitution. The constitution of 1950 was revived in amended form in 1962 and then abrogated. A provisional constitution adopted in April 1964 was suspended in 1966 and replaced to some extent by a continuing series of edicts. The fundamental law that thus emerged considered Syria a socialist republic forming part of the Arab homeland, required that the head of state be a Muslim, recognized Islamic law as a main source of legislation, ordained collective ownership of the means of production, but permitted some private ownership.

The constitution of 12 March 1973, embodying these principles and ratified by popular referendum, vests strong executive power in the president, who is nominated by the Ba'th Party and elected by popular vote to a seven-year term. The president, who appoints the cabinet (headed by a prime minister), also serves as commander-in-chief of the armed forces and as secretary-general of the Ba'th Party; three vice-presidents were named in March 1984, including President Assad's younger brother Rifaat, who was dismissed from this post in 1998. The unicameral People's Assembly has 250 members who are elected every four years, but who have no real power. Suffrage is universal, beginning at age 18. Syria has been under a state of emergency since 1963 (except for 1973-74).

Bashir Assad began a seven-year term as president in July 2000 following his father's death in June.

14POLITICAL PARTIES

The Arab Socialist Ba'th Party is Syria's dominant political institution. It has a countrywide organization and controls mass organizations for youth, students, women, and the like. Only the Ba'th may carry on political activity in the armed forces. It is far larger and more influential than the combined strength of its five partners in the National Progressive Front (NPF). This official political alignment, formed by President Assad in 1972, groups the Communist Party of Syria (SCP) and small leftist parties—the Syrian Arab Socialist Union (ASU), the Socialist Unionist Movement (ASUM), the Democratic Socialist Union Party (DSUP), and the Arab Socialist Party (ASP)—with the Ba'th. The Ba'th Party was founded in 1947 with goals of Arab liberation, Arab unity, and socialism. Ba'thists attained control of the government in 1963, but the party became divided into two factions, a wing of doctrinaire socialists and a more pragmatic wing. Assad, then minister of defense and a strong nationalist, seized power in a bloodless coup in November 1970 and purged the doctrinaire Ba'thists from the government. The Ba'thists have relied for public support on the minority Alawi sect, of which Assad is a member, and on the rural sector of the population generally. During his years as president, Assad appointed Ba'thist Alawis to influential positions in the government and in the military and security services. When Assad died on 10 June 2000 the Ba'th Party held a party congress—its first since 1985—and elected Bashir Assad secretary-general. Bashir Assad succeeded his father as president the next month.

Hafez Assad, the sole presidential candidate for over 20 years, won national plebiscites by 99% majorities on 12 March 1971, 8 February 1978, 13 March 1985, 2 December 1991, and 10 February 1999. His son, Bashir, won in July 2000 by a vote of 8.6 million to 22,000. In elections on 1 December 1998, the Ba'th won 135 seats; the ASU, 7; SCP, 8; ASUM, 7; ASP, 6; DSUP, 4; and independents, 83.

15LOCAL GOVERNMENT

Syria is divided into 13 provinces (muhafazat) and Damascus; every province has a governor (muhafiz) and council. Each province is in turn divided into districts (mantiqat), each headed by a qaimmaqam. Each district is further subdivided into subdistricts, each in the charge of a mudir. Governors are appointed by and are directly responsible to the authorities in Damascus.

16JUDICIAL SYSTEM

The Syrian legal system is based partly on French law and partly on Syrian statutes. Investigating magistrates determine whether a case should be sent to trial. Minor infringements are handled by Peace Courts, more serious cases go to courts of first instance. There are civil and criminal appeals courts, the highest being the Court of Cassation. Separate State Security Courts have jurisdiction over activities affecting the security of the government. In addition, Shari'ah courts apply Islamic law in cases involving personal status. The Druze and non-Muslim communities have their own religious courts.

A High Constitutional Court investigates and rules on petitions submitted by the president or one-fourth of the members of the People's Assembly challenging the constitutionality of laws or legislative decrees. This court has no jurisdiction to hear appeals for cases from the civil or criminal courts.

The constitution provides for an independent judiciary. The regular court system is independent; however, the state security courts are not completely independent from the executive.

There are no jury trials. The regular courts respect constitutional provisions safeguarding due process. The Supreme State Security Court tries political and national security cases. The Economic Security Court tries cases involving financial crimes. Both courts operate under the state of emergency rules overriding constitutional defendants' rights.

[17]ARMED FORCES

In 2000, the army had an estimated 215,000 regular troops (including conscripts) and 300,000 reserves, and included 7 armored divisions, 3 mechanized infantry divisions, a Republican Guard division, 4 independent infantry brigades, 3 SCUD missile brigades, 2 artillery brigades, 9 special forces battalions, and 1 border guard brigade. The army had more than 4,600 heavy and medium tanks and sophisticated antitank and antiaircraft weapons. The navy had 6,000 men and 4,000 reserves; naval vessels included 3 submarines, 2 frigates, 20 missile patrol craft, and 3 amphibious landing vessels. Naval aviation includes 24 armed helos. The air force had 40,000 men, 589 combat aircraft, and 72 armed helicopters. The air defense command numbered 55,000 with 25 air defense brigades and 2 SAM regiments. Paramilitary forces included a gendarmerie of 8,000 and a workers' militia with an estimated 100,000 members. In 1998, budgeted military expenditures totaled $2.7 billion or about 7.3% of the gross domestic product. The USSR, formerly Syria's principal weapons supplier, imported $2 billion-plus a year in armed forces supplies the 1980s. Syria has 22,000 troops in Lebanon and employs 150 Russian advisors. Some 1,029 UN observers of UNDOF work out of Damascus.

[18]INTERNATIONAL COOPERATION

Syria is a founding member of the UN, having joined on 24 October 1945, and belongs to ESCWA and all the nonregional specialized agencies except WIPO. It is a charter member of the Arab League, set up in 1945 to foster cooperation in foreign and domestic affairs. Syria also belongs to G-77 and OAPEC.

Between February 1958 and September 1961, Syria and Egypt were joined in the United Arab Republic. During that period, the UAR was technically joined with Yemen in the United Arab States, though with little practical effect. Another federation, established formally in April 1963 between Syria, Egypt, and Iraq, was never implemented; it was officially terminated in July 1963 after Nasserite loyalists attempted unsuccessfully to overthrow Syria's Ba'thist regime. On 1 January 1972, Syria formally became part of the Federation of Arab Republics, with Egypt and Libya; the federation also had little practical effect because of a deterioration in Egypt's relations with Syria and especially with Libya. In June 1974, Syria and Jordan established a joint commission to coordinate foreign and military policy. Subsequent efforts to establish unions with Iraq and Libya bore little fruit. Diplomatic relations between Syria and the US, which had been suspended after the 1967 Arab-Israeli war, were resumed on 16 June 1974, after US Secretary of State Henry Kissinger successfully mediated a Golan Heights disengagement agreement.

[19]ECONOMY

Despite recent economic reforms, Syria's economy continues to be dominated by the state with the government budget acting as the principle tool for managing the economy. The country's four banks are all owned by the government and interest rates are fixed by law. Syria's large public sector industrial firms are unproductive and unprofitable. Syria is traditionally an agricultural country; agriculture provided the livelihood of 40% of the work force and 26% of the GDP in 1999. Subsistence agriculture has given way in recent years to modern production and marketing methods. Wheat and barley constitute two-thirds of the cultivated area, but cotton is the main cash crop.

Development of the state-owned oil industry and exploitation of other mineral resources, notably phosphates, have helped to diversify Syrian industry, which was formerly concentrated in light manufacturing and textiles. Although Syria's oil production is small by Middle Eastern standards, oil accounted for 65% of Syria's exports in 1999.

Syria's economy has improved since 1990 due to a substantial increase in oil production, the recovery of the agricultural sector from drought, and economic reforms which boosted Syria's private sector. In addition, Syria received nearly $5 billion dollars in foreign aid as a "reward" for its participation in the coalition against Iraq during the Gulf War. Combined, these factors helped the economy register average annual growth rates of 5.3% from 1988 to 1998. Analysts, however, point to high government deficits, 20% inflation, and the slow pace of economic reform as potential threats to long term economic growth. Drought in 2000 threatened the economy further.

[20]INCOME

The US Central Intelligence Agency (CIA) reports that in 1998 Syria's gross domestic product (GDP) was estimated at $41.7 billion. The per capita GDP was estimated at $2,500. The annual growth rate of GDP was estimated at 2%. The average inflation rate in 1998 was 8.9%. The CIA defines GDP as the value of all final goods and services produced within a nation in a given year and computed on the basis of purchasing power parity (PPP) rather than value as measured on the basis of the rate of exchange. It was estimated that agriculture accounted for 26% of GDP, industry 21%, and services 53%.

Private consumption includes expenditures of individuals, households, and non-governmental organizations. It was estimated that between 1990 and 1998 private consumption grew at an annual rate of 2.3%.

[21]LABOR

The Syrian labor force is well educated and well trained in comparison with those of other Arab countries, but its size is small because about half the population is under 15 years of age and because many skilled workers are employed abroad in OPEC member nations. It has been estimated that 4,411,000 persons were employed in 1998. As of 1996, 40% worked in agriculture, 40% in services, and 20% in industry. The majority of employed women engage in agriculture, but small numbers of women have found employment in industry and in technical professions. There is a high level of underemployment, and unemployment was last officially reported at 6.8% in 1991. Many unskilled persons in agriculture and industry work only seasonally. The government is attempting to meet the demand for trained workers by establishing vocational schools.

The Labor Law of 1959 established the right of workers to form unions and empowered the government to regulate hours of work, vacations, sick leave, health and safety measures, and workers' compensation. However, unions must belong to the government's bureaucratic labor confederation. The confederation acts merely as a conduit to transfer directives from government decision makers to unions and workers. Thus there is not a meaningful right to strike or bargain collectively. The government also is authorized to arbitrate labor disputes. In 1996, about one-third of nonagricultural wage and salary earners belong to trade unions affiliated with the General Federation of Labor Unions. The statutory workweek is 36 hours. In 1999, the minimum wage was $42 per month in the public sector and $39 per month in the private sector.

22AGRICULTURE

About 6.1 million hectares (15.1 million acres) are arable, but the area actually cultivated is about 5.5 million hectares (13.6 million acres), or 30% of the total area. Since only one-third of cultivated land is irrigated, agriculture depends on rainfall, which is uncertain, and in lean years Syria becomes a net importer of wheat and barley; this strains the whole economy and hampers development. The government has two approaches to this problem: to increase the use of fertilizers in low rainfall areas and to add substantially to irrigated cultivation. The irrigated area was expected to be doubled through the Euphrates Dam project, which was completed in 1978. Lake Assad, formed by the dam, was planned eventually to provide irrigation for some 640,000 hectares (1,581,000 acres). Costs of land reclamation, technical difficulties due to gypsum in the soil, and low water, in part caused by Turkish damming upstream, have slowed progress. Total irrigated area had reached an estimated 1,168,000 hectares (2,886,000 acres) in 1997. The government has allocated an increasing share of its investments to irrigation, but full development of irrigation schemes is expected to take at least another 20 years. However, given the current water management policies, Syria could face a serious water shortage much sooner.

Traditionally, much of Syria's agricultural land was held by landowners in tracts of more than 100 hectares (250 acres); sharecropping was customary. This picture was greatly altered by the government's agrarian reform program, begun in 1958. The law, as modified in 1963, fixed the maximum holding of irrigated land at 15–50 hectares (37–124 acres) per person and that of nonirrigated land at 80 hectares (198 acres) per person. All expropriated land available for cultivation has been allotted to farmers.

The principal cash crop is cotton, but cotton's share of total export value declined from 33% in 1974 to 6% in 1997. Other cash crops are cereals, vegetables, fruit, and tobacco. Since the government suspended convertibility of the Syrian pound, grain and other agricultural products have been smuggled to Lebanon in exchange for goods not available through the state importing agencies.The following table lists production (in thousands of tons) for major agricultural commodities in 1996, 1997, and 1998:

	1996	1997	1998
Wheat	1,200	1,800	1,800
Barley	1,653	983	846
Corn, yellow	250	303	303
Tomatoes	409	407	468
Potatoes	439	266	553
Olives	648	403	763
Grapes	540	452	450
Apples	302	356	324
Oranges	373	236	438
Cotton lint	264	367	367
Sugar beets	974	1,126	1,323
Tobacco	18	17	19

23ANIMAL HUSBANDRY

Grazing land occupies 8.3 million hectares (20.5 million acres), or about 45% of Syria's total area. Stock raising contributes significantly to the Syrian economy. Between 1963 and 1981, livestock herds more than doubled in number, and since 1975 the

number of model farms, veterinary units, and livestock artificial insemination centers has increased considerably.

Sheep are the most important livestock animals in Syria, grazing on poorly developed wheat and barley fields and on the remains of crops such as wheat and corn. In 1998 there were an estimated 14 million sheep. Mutton production was an estimated 107,000 tons in 1998; sheep milk production, 515,000 tons. The price of mutton of the Awassi breed, which is in high demand in Syria, was about 35% higher than beef in 1995.

There were also 1,098,000 goats, 900,000 head of cattle, 7,000 camels, 2,000 buffaloes, and 20,000,000 chickens in 1998. Syria officially reported 275,000 turkeys, 55,000 geese, 46,000 ducks, and 1.5 million pigeons in 1994. Animals and animal products account for 40% of total agricultural output by value. Production of cow's milk in 1998 totaled 1,004,000 tons; cheese, 86,000 tons; butter and ghee, 14,000 tons; and eggs, 126,000 tons.

24FISHING

There is some fishing off the Mediterranean coast and from rivers and fish farms. The commercial catch was 7,721 tons in 1997, with common carp and tilapias from inland waters accounting for 20%.

25FORESTRY

Syria is almost entirely denuded of forests. Approximately 219,000 hectares (541,000 acres) were forestland in 1995, but only about 55,000 cu m of roundwood were produced in 1997. Most of the designated forestland consists either of wholly barren land or of rangeland with arboreous shrubs. The substantial forests are mainly on the northern slopes of the Ansariyah range, on the windward side of the Anti-Lebanon Mountains, and in the Latakia region.

26MINING

Syria's mineral resources are not extensive, but deposits of phosphate, iron, and petroleum have been exploited in recent years. The first phosphate plant began operating near Homs in 1971, and production of phosphate rock was 2,000,000 tons in 1996. Most of the phosphate is exported to Europe. Other mineral deposits include asphalt, salt, chromite, and marble, but only marble and salt are mined in commercial quantities. In 1996, output of salt totaled 112,000 tons; of marble, 18,000 cubic meters. The mineral industry is owned and controlled by the government.

27ENERGY AND POWER

Oil in commercial quantities was first discovered in the late 1950s. Production reached a record 10 million tons in 1976 and then declined to 9 million tons in 1984; since then, production has steadily increased to 14.5 million tons in 1988 and 31.7 million tons in 1995. In 1998, production was 546,000 barrels per day. In 1986, production of 2.5 million tons a year of low-sulphur crude from a new field, near Deir ez-Zor in eastern Syria, began, lessening Syrian dependence on external sources. By 1994, Syria was exporting 57% of its oil output. The proven reserves of Syria's five oil fields, all located in the northeastern part of the country, amounted to an estimated 2.5 billion barrels (400 million tons) of crude petroleum at the beginning of 2000. Oil output in recent years has reached a plateau, because older fields such as the Karatchuk (discovered in 1968) are reaching maturity. Production of oil is expected to steadily decline in upcoming years, and proven oil reserves are only expected to last until about 2010, while consumption increases as the population grows. As of 2000, however, it was estimated that only 36% of Syria's potential oil and gas deposits had been drilled. Oil remains crucial to Syria's economy, accounting for about 60% of export earnings in 1999. A 663-km (412-mi) pipeline linking the oil fields, the coast at Tartus, and the refinery at Homs was completed in 1968. The pipeline, carrying Iraqi oil across Syria to Lebanon, was closed by Syria in April 1982, showing Syrian support for Iran in the Iraqi-Iranian war. Syria also refused to support Iraq during the Persian Gulf War, for which it was "rewarded" with billions of dollars in foreign aid. In 1998, Syria and Iraq signed an agreement to reopen the pipeline, and it was reported ready for operation by March 2000.

All oil concessions were granted exclusively in 1964 to the General Petroleum Authority, a government agency that owns the Homs refinery. In 1972, the pipelines and facilities in Syria of the Iraq Petroleum Co. were nationalized; the same year, Syria joined OAPEC. During the early 1980s, the government-owned Syrian Petroleum Co. and three Syrian subsidiaries of US oil companies—Marathon, Shell, and Coastal States—were engaged in further oil exploration. Oil exploration has slowed in recent years; only four of the 14 companies present in Syria in 1991 remained there in 1999.

Syria's natural gas production, however, has increased ten-fold since the mid-1980s. Proven natural gas reserves were officially estimated at about 8.5 trillion cu ft (200 billion cu m) in early 2000. Production in 1998 totaled 208 billion cu ft (5.8 billion cu m). Syria's current energy strategy relies heavily on the substitution of natural gas for oil in power generation in order to free up as much oil as possible for export.

Prior to 1983, as much as 70% of the production of electricity was hydroelectric, primarily from the Euphrates River plant. Thermal production, primarily oil-fueled plants, supplied 57% of electricity production in 1998, while hydropower accounted for 43%. Total electricity production in 1998 was 17.5 billion kWh; installed capacity was 4,430,000 kW, up from 3,230,000 kW in 1988. The addition of electricity supply capacity has become a national priority; since 1993 several contracts have been awarded for new gas turbine power stations.

28 INDUSTRY

Syria has been renowned since ancient times for such handicrafts as Damascus brocade and Syrian soap. Some of these traditions endured even after 1933, when the first mechanized plant for spinning and weaving was set up in Aleppo. In 1965, the textile industry was nationalized and reorganized into 13 large state corporations. A series of nationalization measures after 1963 resulted in public control of most industry, but recent efforts have been made to stimulate the expansion of the private sector, as state-owned industries suffer from low productivity. In the 1970s, government policy began emphasizing domestic industrial production (coupled with high tariffs on imported consumer goods) of iron and steel, fertilizers, chemicals, and household appliances. In 1995, manufacturing and mining accounted for 14% of GDP.

Also important are the chemical and engineering industries, the food industry, and oil refining. The largest component of the chemical and engineering sector is the cement industry, which produced 6 million tons in 1995. Syria has three fertilizer plants, an iron-rolling mill at Homs, and factories producing furniture, refrigerators, paper, glass and plastic products, and television sets. Some 70,000 tons of crude steel were produced in 1995. Syrian refineries produced 61.7 million barrels of residual and distillate fuel oil in 1995, along with 9.8 million barrels of gasoline and 5 million barrels of naphtha.

29 SCIENCE AND TECHNOLOGY

Courses in basic and applied science are offered at Al-Baath University (founded in 1979 at Homs), the University of Aleppo (founded in 1960), the University of Damascus (founded in 1903), and Tishreen University (founded in 1971 at Lattakia). In 1987–97, science and engineering students accounted for 23% of college and university enrollments. Major scientific research institutions in Syria include the International Center for Agricultural Research in the Dry Areas (ICARDA), founded in 1977 at Aleppo and the Arab Center for the Study of Arid Zones and Dry Lands (ACSAD), founded in 1971 at Damascus. The country's advanced petrochemical technologies have been installed by foreign oil companies. In early 1987, an estimated 2,500 Soviet military technicians were stationed in Syria; civilian personnel also provided assistance in various fields.

30 DOMESTIC TRADE

Damascus and Aleppo are the principal commercial centers. Virtually all importers, exporters, and wholesalers have offices in one or both cities. The chief retail centers have general and specialized stores as well as large bazaars. Smaller bazaars and open markets are found in many Syrian towns and villages. Usual business hours are from 9 AM to 1 PM and from 3:30 PM to 7 PM. Friday is the weekly day of rest. Banking hours are Saturday–Thursday, 8 AM to 2 PM. An international fair is held every summer in Damascus. Advertising agencies use newspapers, magazines, moving picture theaters, signs on buses, and other media. In 1996, wholesale and retail trade contributed 27% to GDP.

The Syrian government cracked down on smuggling in May 1993. Most of the previously smuggled commodities can now be imported through official channels. Commodity smuggling from Lebanon, however, is still present and provides an "unofficial market" for imported products at the free market exchange rate reflective of world price levels.

31 FOREIGN TRADE

During the 1980s, Syria focused on increasing its trade with socialist nations. However, when the Soviet Union broke apart in 1991, Syria increased trade with European nations. In 1995, the EU countries took 57% of exports and supplied 33% of imports, while countries of the Middle East took 24.6% of exports and supplied 6.1% of imports. Principal trading partners in 1998 (in millions of US dollars) were as follows:

COUNTRY	EXPORTS	IMPORTS	BALANCE
Italy	626	254	372
France	508	213	295
Turkey	298	187	111
Lebanon	248	37	211
Saudi Arabia	235	91	144
Spain	143	61	82
Germany	52	276	-224
China (inc. Hong Kong)	26	141	-115
United States	16	186	-170
Ukraine	6	225	-219

Syria's main export commodities are crude petroleum (61%) and refined petroleum products (6.4%). Other exports include cotton (7.4%), garments (4.1%), vegetables (2.7%), and fruits and nuts (1.9%).

In 1995 Syria's imports were distributed among the following categories:

Consumer goods	4.7%
Food	14.0%
Fuels	1.1%
Industrial supplies	46.4%
Machinery	18.1%
Transportation	13.7%
Other	2.0%

32BALANCE OF PAYMENTS

Syria has had serious deficits in its trade balance since 1976, but import restrictions, foreign aid (especially from other Arab governments), and drawdown of foreign exchange holdings have enabled the government to cover the losses. Since the late 1980s, the government has been encouraging private sector trade. Private sector exports consequently skyrocketed from $79 million in 1987 to $517 million in 1990, thus reducing the trade deficit.

The US Central Intelligence Agency reports that in 1998 the purchasing power parity of Syria's exports was $4.2 billion while imports totaled $5.7 in 1997.

The International Monetary Fund (IMF) reports that in 1998 Syria had exports of goods totaling $3,135 million and imports totaling $3,307 million. The services credit totaled $1,795 million and debit $1,481 million. The following table summarizes Syria's balance of payments as reported by the IMF for 1998 in millions of US dollars.

Current Account		59
Balance on goods	-172	
Balance on services	314	
Balance on income	-606	
Current transfers	523	
Capital Account		20
Financial Account		437
Direct investment abroad	...	
Direct investment in Syria	80	
Portfolio investment assets	...	
Portfolio investment liabilities	...	
Other investment assets	-1,049	
Other investment liabilities	1,406	
Net Errors and Omissions		-115
Reserves and Related Items		-401

33BANKING AND SECURITIES

Syria's financial services sector is underdeveloped. Besides the Central Bank, there are five banks in the country, all of which are state-run. The Central Bank, founded in 1956, is the bank of issue for currency, the financial agent of the government, and the cashier for the treasury. The Agricultural Bank makes loans to farmers at low interest; the Industrial Bank (nationalized in 1961), the People's Credit Bank and the Real Estate Bank (both founded in 1966), and the Commercial Bank of Syria (formed in 1967 by a merger of five nationalized commercial banks) make loans in their defined sectors. Unused Syrian pounds cannot be sold back to the Commercial Bank and the private exchange of foreign currencies and Syrian pounds is a criminal act. These strict currency controls are the largest disincentives to investment and foreign trade. So decrepit is the country's financial services sector that most Syrian businessmen and foreigners use banks in either Lebanon or Cyprus. Foreign diplomats in Damascus, for instance, use accounts in the Chtaura, in Lebanon's Beqaa valley, around one hour by car from Damascus.

Private sector groups are calling for reforms such as private participation in banking, the creation of a stock exchange, and separation of the Central Bank of Syria from the government.

34INSURANCE

All insurance in Syria was nationalized in 1963 and is controlled by the government-owned General Insurance Organization of Syria (formerly the Syrian Insurance Co.). Motor vehicle insurance is compulsory.

35PUBLIC FINANCE

Although Syria was able to balance its budget in 1992, large military expenditures and continued subsidization of basic commodities and social services have produced deficits in subsequent years. The US Central Intelligence Agency estimates that, in 1998, government revenues totaled approximately $3.5 billion and expenditures $4.2 billion.

External debt totaled $22 billion. The majority of this amount (approximately $12 billion) is military debt owed to the former Soviet Union. It is questionable whether this debt will ever be repaid. Another $3 billion is owed to Western nations.

The following table shows an itemized breakdown of government revenue and expenditures. The percentages were calculated from data reported by the International Monetary Fund for the year 1998.

REVENUE AND GRANTS	100%
Tax revenue	67.5%
Non-tax revenue	32.0%
Grants	0.4%
EXPENDITURES	100%
General public services	3.8%
Defense	23.6%
Education	9.2%
Health	2.7%
Social security	2.7%
Housing and community amenities	1.7%
Recreation, cultural, and religious affairs	1.5%
Economic affairs and services	46.1%
Other expenditures	8.6%

36TAXATION

Relatively low salaries have kept the tax base narrow, and price controls have restricted the taxable profits from industry. There are taxes on income, production, expenditure, and consumption.

37CUSTOMS AND DUTIES

Goods imported into Syria are subject to customs duty and "unified" tax. Rates are progressive and, as of 1999, range from 1% to 250% depending on the government's view of the necessity for the products. Food and industrial raw materials carry low rates while luxury goods like automobiles have rates of 150–250%. The unified tax is surcharge on all imported goods and ranges from 6% to 35%. The tax helps to support the military, schools, and municipalities.

Syria is a member of the Arab Common Market, with Iraq, Jordan, Libya, Mauritania, and Yemen. Trade among these countries is free of customs duties (except for tobacco). There is a single-column tariff modified by trade and transit agreements with other Arab League states, under which member countries are granted preferential duties on some products and duty-free entry for others. Syria is a member of the Arab League Boycott of Israel.

38FOREIGN INVESTMENT

Although a government decree prohibits confiscation of foreign investments, there are no safeguards against nationalization of property. In addition, poor infrastructure, power outages, lack of financial services, and complex foreign exchange regulations, have all contributed to Syria's failure to attract significant amounts of foreign investment. In an attempt to correct the situation the government enacted reforms in 1991 designed to give substantial incentives to private business. Qualifying investors were granted tax holidays and duty-free privileges for the import of capital goods and inputs. These reforms succeeded in attracting new investment in the textiles, pharmaceuticals, food-processing, and other light industries. The primary investors have been from the Gulf states. In 1999 it was estimated that nearly 1,500 projects valued at $6.5 billion had been approved since the reforms of 1991.

Foreign firms with investments in oil exploration include Shell, Conoco, Elf, Mol, and Ina Nafta Plin. Other foreign investors include Mitsubishi, Samsung, Mobil, Nestle, and Prince Walid Bin Talal of Saudi Arabia.

³⁹ECONOMIC DEVELOPMENT

The transformation of Syria's economy began with the Agrarian Reform Law in 1958, which called for the expropriation of large tracts of land. During the union with Egypt, laws were passed for the nationalization of banks, insurance companies, and large industrial firms. After the Ba'th Party came to power in 1963, the socialist trend reasserted itself with greater force. A series of laws created a new banking system and instituted public ownership of all large industries. By the early 1970s, however, the government had relaxed many restrictions on trade, foreign investment, and private-sector activity, in an effort to attract private and foreign, especially Arab, contributions to Syria's economic growth.

Since 1961, a series of five-year plans has concentrated on developing the nation's infrastructure and increasing agricultural and industrial production. Investments reached 60% of the target under the first plan (1961–65); the second plan (1966–70) aimed to expand real GDP by 7.2% annually but achieved a yearly growth rate of only 4.7%. The third plan (1971–75) was disrupted by the 1973 Arab-Israeli war, but thanks to aid from other Arab states and large oil price increases, Syria experienced an economic boom with a high annual growth rate of 13%. The fourth plan (1976–80) was hampered by the high cost of Syria's military intervention in Lebanon and a cutoff of aid from Gulf states; economic growth varied widely, from –2.8% in 1977 to 9.2% in 1980.

Under the fifth plan (1981–85), development projects begun during the previous plan were to be continued or completed. Total investment was estimated at s£101 billion, of which 23% was to be provided by the private sector. Real GDP was to grow by 7.7% annually; actual growth rates ranged from 10.2% in 1981 to –3.6% in 1984, averaging 2.3% for the period.

Syria's sixth development plan (1986–90) emphasized increased productivity rather than new projects, with special emphasis on agriculture and agro-industries. Actual investment in agriculture accounted for 18.7% of total spending. The share of the industry and energy sector was at 19.7%, far below the planned 30.9%. Services received the highest share, with 53% of the total.

The seventh five-year plan (1991–95) proposed total investments of s£259 billion, more than double the amount spent under the previous plan. It aims at spending 81.7% of the total on the public sector and 18.3% on the mixed sector/private-sector cooperatives. Officials at the Supreme Planning Commission have stated that agriculture and irrigation continue to receive top priority, with self-sufficiency in cereal production a policy objective. Output in agriculture and manufacturing is planned to expand by 5.6% per annum.

During 1949–86, multilateral assistance to Syria totaled $822.7 million, of which 77% came through the IBRD. US loans and grants during the same period amounted to $581.9 million. Financial aid to Syria from Arab oil-producing states is not made public. Since 1982, Syria has received a million tons of oil annually from Iran, free of charge. Since Syria is in arrears on payments to the World Bank, disbursements were halted in 1988 and projects canceled. Syria has been in violation of the Brooke Amendment since 1985. The improvement in Syria's external payment position in 1989 as well as the resumption of aid flows to Syria in 1990 due to its participation in the coalition against Iraq helped to restore its ability to repay its debt.

⁴⁰SOCIAL DEVELOPMENT

The Ministry for Social and Labor Affairs was formed in 1956 to protect the interests of the working population, provide hygienic housing conditions for workers, and support philanthropic endeavors. A system of social insurance, introduced in 1959, provides old age pensions and disability and death benefits. The pension system is funded by 14% contributions from employers and 7% from employees. Retirement is set at age 60 with 180 months of contributions, or age 55 with 240 months. Survivors' pensions are paid to widows only; widowers are covered only if disabled. Employers also contribute 3% of payroll to fund workers' compensation providing temporary and permanent disability benefits, as well as medical and survivor benefits.

Although the government supports equal pay for equal work and encourages education for women, Islamic precepts govern many areas of women's lives, including marriage, divorce, child custody, and inheritance. Women are making slow gains in the workplace, however. In 1999, it was estimated that 6% of judges, 10% of lawyers, and 20% of university professors were women. In 1998, 10% of Parliamentarians (26 of 250) were women.

In the 1990s, the regime of President Hafez Assad was accused of widespread human rights violations. Amnesty International repeatedly charged that Syrian security forces detain thousands of political suspects without trial and subject prisoners to torture and in some cases to arbitrary execution. Public criticism of the Ba'th Party or of government officials is not permitted. Local human rights organizations are banned, although one international organization was allowed to conduct a limited fact-finding mission.

⁴¹HEALTH

Since World War II, malaria has been virtually eliminated with the aid of WHO, but intestinal and respiratory diseases associated with poor living conditions are still common, particularly in rural areas. In 1997, there were an estimated 75 cases of tuberculosis per 100,000 reported. In 1995, there were 185 cases of leprosy and 1,235 cases of measles reported; in 1993 there were 961 cases of malaria. In 1995, 88% of the population had access to safe water, with 71% having adequate sanitation.

The 1999 birth rate was 36.9 per 1,000 people, and about 36% of married women (ages 15 to 49) used contraception in 1993. In 1999, the infant mortality rate was 36.4 per 1,000 live births. In 1990–97, maternal mortality was 180 per 100,000 live births. The overall death rate was 5.4 per 1,000 people in 1999, and average life expectancy was 68 years for both men and women.

In 1947, Syria had only 37 hospitals, with a total of 1,834 beds, but by 1985, the number of hospitals had increased to 195, with 11,891 beds. In 1990–97, there were 1.1 hospital beds per 1,000 people. The government also maintains mobile hospital units, modern laboratories, X-ray centers, sanatoriums, and dispensaries. In 1991, there were 10,114 physicians, 3,362 dentists, 3,634 pharmacists, and 11,957 nurses. In 1990–97, there were 80 doctors per 100,000 people, with a nurse to doctor ratio of 1.2. The population per physician in 1993 was 1,159 and per nursing professional was 1,047.

Immunization rates for children up to one year old in 1995 were tuberculosis (100%); diphtheria, pertussis, and tetanus (100%); polio (100%); and measles (98%). In 1993, about 99% of the population had access to health care services. Total health care expenditures for 1990 were $283 million. Tobacco consumption rose from 3.3 in 1984–86 to 3.4 kg a year per adult in 1995. There were 36 cases of AIDS in 1996, with an HIV-1 seroprevalence rate of 0.0 per 100 adults in 1997.

⁴²HOUSING

The 1981–85 development plan allocated s£2.6 billion to construction projects, including housing. According to the latest available information for 1980-88, total housing units numbered 1,670,000 with 6.4 people per dwelling.

43EDUCATION

Elementary schooling is free and compulsory for six years. The adult illiteracy rates for the year 2000 were estimated at 25.6% (males, 11.7%; females, 39.6%). The school program starts with a primary course, after which the student may obtain an elementary-school certificate. In 1997 there were 2,690,205 primary-school pupils with 114,689 teachers in 10,783 schools. Student-to-teacher ratio stood at 23 to one. At the secondary level in the same year, there were 957,664 students and 64,661 teachers. Syria has four universities: the University of Damascus (founded in 1923); the University of Aleppo (1960); Tishrin University (Latakia, 1971); and Al-Ba'th University in Homs (1979). In 1995, all higher level institutions had a total of 4,733 teachers and 215,734 students.

44LIBRARIES AND MUSEUMS

The Assad National Library founded in 1984 in Damascus and an adjunct of the Arab Academy, has 214,500 volumes and is well known for rare books and manuscripts. There are three other national libraries, located in Aleppo, Homs, and Latakia. The library of the University of Damascus has 169,000 volumes. The Al Zohariah public library in Damascus has 100,000 volumes.

The most important museum is the National Museum in Damascus, founded in 1919. It contains ancient Oriental, Greek, Roman, Byzantine, and Islamic collections and houses the Directorate-General of Antiquities, established in 1947, which supervises excavations and conserves antiquities under the Antiquities Law. There are small museums in Aleppo, Hama, Homs, Palmyra, Tartos, and other cities.

45MEDIA

All communications facilities are owned and operated by the government, including postal service, telegraph, telephone, radio, and television. There were 550,000 main telephone lines in use in 1995. The Syrian Broadcasting Service transmits on medium wave and shortwave, and broadcasts in Arabic and 10 foreign languages. Syrian Arab TV has two stations. Altogether, there were 9 AM and 1 FM radio station in 1999, and 54 television stations. In 1997, Syria had 274 radios and 68 television sets in per 1,000 population.

Syrian newspapers are published by government ministries and popular organizations. Principal dailies in Arabic (with 1999 circulations) include Al-Ba'th, the party organ (75,000), Tishrin (75,000), and Al-Thawrah (75,000), all in Damascus.

Though the constitution provides for free expression of opinion in speech and writing, in practice the government is reported to restrict these rights significantly. Written criticism of the president, the president's family, the Ba'th party, the military, and the regime are not permitted.

As of 1996, there were some 1,400 personal computers in Syria.

46ORGANIZATIONS

Syria has chambers of commerce, industry, and agriculture. The most prominent organizations are the Arab Academy and the Arab Club, both in Damascus. The General Women's Federation was established in 1967 as one of several organizations through which the Ba'th Party has tried to mobilize popular energies and consolidate its control. Analogous groups include the General Union of Peasants, the General Federation of Trade Unions, the General Union of Students, and the Revolutionary Youth Organization. The cooperative movement is well developed.

47TOURISM, TRAVEL, AND RECREATION

Passports, visas, and smallpox vaccinations are required of visitors. In 1997 there were 2,332,000 tourists, mostly from neighboring Middle Eastern countries, and tourist expenditures totaled $1 billion. As of that year, Syria had 14,820 hotel rooms with 31,412 beds, and the hotel occupancy rate was 32%.

Syria has many famous tourist attractions, such as the Krak des Chevaliers, a Crusaders' castle; Ra's Shamrah, site of the ancient city of Ugarit; Ar-Rusafah, with its early Christian monuments and a Muslim palace; and the ancient town of Dura Europus (now As-Salihiyah). Palmyra, the capital of Queen Zenobia, is a fairly well preserved ruin of an Arabo-Hellenic city. The Umayyad Mosque, which incorporates parts of the Byzantine Cathedral of St. John the Baptist, in Damascus, is popular. Syria's mountains and Mediterranean beaches also attract visitors.

According to 1999 UN estimates, the cost of staying in Damascus was $145 per day. Daily expenses for travel in Aleppo were estimated at $125.

48FAMOUS SYRIANS

Among famous Syrians of an earlier period are Queen Zenobia of Palmyra (3d century AD), who led a series of military campaigns against the Romans in order to reopen trade routes; the philosopher Al-Farabi (Muhammad bin Muhammad bin Tarkhan abu Nasr al-Farabi, 872–950), considered by the Arab world as second only to Aristotle; the poet Al-Mutanabbi (Abu at-Tayyib Ahmad bin al-Husayn al-Mutanabbi, 915–65); the mystic-philosopher Shihab ad-Din as-Suhrawardi (d.1191); and the theologian-philosopher Taqi ad-Din Ahmad bin Taymiyah (1263–1328).

Of the Umayyad caliphs, Umar bin 'Abd-al-'Aziz (r.717–20) is still revered as a restorer of true Islam. In a later era, Nureddin (Nur ad-Din, 1118–74), ruler of Aleppo, annexed Damascus and brought Egypt under his control. By unifying Muslim forces against the Crusaders, he made possible the victories of the renowned Saladin (Salah ad-Din, 1138–93), sultan of both Syria and Egypt, whose tomb is in Damascus. Hafez al-Assad (Hafiz al-Asad, 1928–2000) ruled Syria from 1970–2000.

49DEPENDENCIES

Syria has no territories or colonies.

50BIBLIOGRAPHY

Ball, Warwick. Syria: A Historical and Architectural Guide. Essex, U.K.: Scorpion Publishers, 1994.

Batatu, Hanna. Syria's Peasantry, the Descendants of Its Lesser Rural Notables, and Their Politics. Princeton, N.J.: Princeton University Press, 1999.

Choueiri, Youssef M. (ed.). State and Society in Syria and Lebanon. Exeter: University of Exeter Press, 1993.

Collelo, Thomas (ed.). Syria: A Country Study. 3rd ed. Washington, D.C.: Library of Congress, 1988.

Commins, David Dean. Historical Dictionary of Syria. Lanham, Md.: Scarecrow, 1996.

Contemporary Syria: Liberalization Between Cold War and Cold Peace. Edited by Eberhard Kienle. London: British Academic Press, 1994.

Devlin, John F. Syria: Modern State in an Ancient Land. Boulder, Colo.: Westview, 1983.

Gaunson, A. B. The Anglo-French Clash in Lebanon and Syria, 1940–45. New York: St. Martin's, 1987.

Gelvin, James L. Divided Loyalties: Nationalism and Mass Politics in Syria at the Close of Empire. Berkeley: University of California Press, 1998.

Haddad, Robert M. Syrian Christians in a Muslim Society. Princeton, N.J.: Princeton University Press, 1970.

Hinnebusch, Raymond A. Authoritarian Power and State Formation in Ba'thist Syria: Army, Party, and Peasant. Boulder, Colo.: Westview Press, 1990.

History and Religion in Late Antique Syria. Edited by Han J. W. Drijvers. Aldershot, U.K.: Varorium, 1994.

Hopwood, Derek. *Syria 1945–1986: Politics and Society.* London: Unwin Hyman, 1988.

Khoury, Philip S. *Syria and the French Mandate: the Politics of Arab Nationalism 1920–1945.* Princeton University Press, 1987.

Klengel, Horst. *Syria, 3000 to 300 B.C.: A Handbook of Political History.* Berlin: Akademie Verlag, 1992.

Lesch, David W. *Syria and the United States: Eisenhower's Cold War in the Middle East.* Boulder, Colo.: Westview Press, 1992.

Maoz, Moshe. *Assad: The Sphinx of Damascus: A Political Biography.* New York: Weidenfeld & Nicholson, 1988.

Mardam Bey, Salma. *Syria's Quest for Independence.* Reading: Ithaca Press, 1994.

Perthes, Volker. *The Political Economy of Syria Under Asad.* London: I.B. Tauris, 1995.

Petran, Tabitha. *Syria.* New York: Praeger, 1972.

Pipes, Daniel. *Greater Syria: The History of an Ambition.* New York: Oxford University Press, 1990.

Quilliam, Neil. *Syria.* Santa Barbara, Calif.: Clio Press, 1999.

Roberts, David. *The Ba'th and the Creation of Modern Syria.* New York: St. Martin's, 1987.

Salibi, Kamal S. *Syria Under Islam: Empire on Trial.* New York: Caravan Books, 1977.

Seale, Patrick. *Assad of Syria: The Struggle for the Middle East.* Berkeley: University of California Press, 1989, 1988.

Seale, Patrick. *Struggle for Syria: A Study of Post-War Arab Politics, 1945–1958.* 2nd ed. New Haven, Conn.: Yale University Press, 1987.

Seccombe, Ian J. *Syria.* Santa Barbara, Calif.: Clio, 1987.

State and Society in Syria and Lebanon. Edited by Youssef M. Choueiri. New York: St. Martin's, 1994.

Tauber, Eliezer. *The Formation of Modern Syria and Iraq.* Ilford, U.K.: Frank Cass, 1994.

Waldner, David. *State Building and Late Development.* Ithaca, N.Y.: Cornell University Press, 1999.

TAIWAN

Republic of China
Chung Hwa Min Kuo

CAPITAL: T'aipei.

FLAG: The flag is red with a 12-pointed white sun on the blue upper left quadrant. The 12 points of the sun represent the 12 two-hour periods of the day in traditional Chinese horology and symbolize progress. The colors red, white, and blue represent the Three Principles of the people (San Min Chu I) of Sun Yat-sen, father of the Republic of China, and symbolize the spirit of liberty, fraternity, and equality.

ANTHEM: *Chung Hwa Min Kuo Kuo Ke (Chinese National Anthem).*

MONETARY UNIT: The new Taiwan dollar (NT$) is a paper currency of 100 cents. There are coins of 50 cents and 1, 5, and 10 dollars, and notes of 50, 100, 500, and 1,000 new Taiwan dollars. NT$1 = US$0.0325 (US$1 = NT$30.80) as of 31 March 2000.

WEIGHTS AND MEASURES: The metric system is employed in government and industrial statistics. Commonly used standards of weights and measures are the catty (1.1 lb or 0.4989 kg), the li (0.5 km or 0.31 mi), the ch'ih (0.33 m or 1.09 ft), and the chia (0.97 hectare or 2.39 acres).

HOLIDAYS: New Year's Day and the Founding of the Republic of China (1912), 1 January; Youth Day (formerly known as Martyrs' Day), 29 March; Tomb-Sweeping Day and Anniversary of the Death of Chiang Kai-shek, 5 April; Birthday of Confucius and Teachers' Day, 28 September; National Day (Double Tenth Day), 10 October; Taiwan Retrocession Day, 25 October; Chiang Kai-shek's Birthday, 31 October; Sun Yat-sen's Birthday, 12 November; Constitution Day, 25 December.

TIME: 8 PM = noon GMT.

¹LOCATION, SIZE, AND EXTENT

Taiwan, the seat of the Republic of China, lies in the western Pacific Ocean astride the Tropic of Cancer, less than 161 km (100 mi) from the southeast coast of mainland China, from which it is separated by the Taiwan (Formosa) Strait. To the NE, less than 129 km (80 mi) away, is the W end of the Japanese Ryukyu Islands; to the E is the Pacific Ocean; the Philippine island of Luzon lies 370 km (230 mi) to the S.

Besides the island proper, Taiwan comprises 21 small islands in the Taiwan group and 64 islands in the Penghu (Pescadores) group; the total area is 35,980 sq km (13,892 sq mi). Comparatively, the area occupied by Taiwan is slightly larger than the states of Maryland and Delaware combined. Leaf-shaped Taiwan island extends 394 km (245 mi) NNE–SSW and 144 km (89 mi) ESE–WNW; it has a coastline of 1,448 km (903 mi) and, with adjacent islands, an area of 35,873 sq km (13,851 sq mi). The Penghu group, lying 40 km (25 mi) west of Taiwan island, has a total area of 127 sq km (49 sq mi).

Also under the control of the Taiwan government are Quemoy (Chinmen) and Matsu, two island groups located strategically close to the mainland Chinese province of Fujian (Fukien). Quemoy is the biggest of a group of six islands, two of which are occupied by the People's Republic of China; it is situated in Xiamen (Amoy) Bay at 118°23′E and 24°27′N and has a total area of 176 sq km (68 sq mi). The Matsu group, consisting of Nankan (the largest), Peikan, Tungyin, and about 10 small islets, is located at 119°56′E and 26°9′N, 30.6 km (19 mi) off the mainland port city of Fuzhou; it has a total area of 28.8 sq km (11.1 sq mi).

²TOPOGRAPHY

Taiwan perches on the margin of the continental shelf. Along the west coast the sea is rather shallow, averaging 90 m (300 ft) and not exceeding 210 m (690 ft) at the deepest point; however, it deepens abruptly along the east coast, dropping to a depth of 4,000 m (13,000 ft) only 50 km (31 mi) offshore. The terrain is precipitous on the east coast, with practically no natural harbor except Suao Bay in the north. The west coast is marked by wide tidal flats. Kaohsiung, the southern port, is situated in a long lagoon called Haochiung Bay. The north coast with its many inlets provides Taiwan with its best harbor, Chilung (Keelung).

The eastern two-thirds of the island is composed of rugged foothill ranges and massive mountain chains. A low, flat coastal plain, extending from north to south, occupies the western third. Hsinkao Shan, with an elevation of 3,997 m (13,113 ft), is the highest peak on the island. Mild earthquake tremors are common.

All the rivers originate in the mountains in the central part of the island. They have short courses and rapid streams. The longest river, Choshui, draining westward, is only 183 km (114 mi) long. Only the Tanshui, which flows past T'aipei in the north, is navigable.

³CLIMATE

Taiwan enjoys an oceanic, subtropical monsoon climate. The warm and humid summer lasts from May until September, the mild winter from December until February. The average lowland temperature in January is 16°C (61°F) in the north and 20°C (68°F) in the south; the average July temperature is 28°C (82°F) in both the north and south. The growing season lasts throughout the year, except at elevations above 1,200 m (4,000 ft), where frost and snow occasionally occur.

The average rainfall is 257 cm (101 in), ranging from 127 cm (50 in) at the middle of the western coast to 635 cm (250 in) and more on exposed mountain slopes. Southwest monsoon winds blow from May through September and northeast monsoon winds from October to March. Only the extreme southwest has a distinct dry season. As a result of the tropical cyclonic storms that sweep out of the western Pacific, typhoons occur between June and October.

4FLORA AND FAUNA

The flora is closely related to that of southern China and the Philippines. Taiwan has almost 190 plant families, about 1,180 genera, and more than 3,800 species, of which indigenous members constitute about one-third of the total flora. Mangrove forest is found in tidal flats and coastal bays. From sea level to a height of 2,000 m (6,600 ft) is the zone of broad-leaved evergreen tropical and subtropical forest, where ficua, pandanus, palms, teak, bamboos, and camphors are commonly found. The mixed forest of broad-leaved deciduous trees and conifers occupies the next zone, extending from a height of 2,000 to 3,000 m (6,600–9,800 ft). Pines, cypresses, firs, and rhododendrons are grown in this region. Above this level is the zone of coniferous forests, composed mainly of firs, spruce, juniper, and hemlock.

The mammals so far discovered number more than 60 species, 45 of which appear to be indigenous to the island. The largest beast of prey is the Formosan black bear. Foxes, flying foxes, deer, wild boar, bats, squirrels, macaques, and pangolins are some of the mammals seen on the island. There are more than 330 species and subspecies of birds, of which 33 are common to the island, China, and the Philippines, and about 87 are peculiar forms. More than 65 species of reptiles and amphibians inhabit the island. There is an abundance of snakes, of which 13 species are poisonous. The insect life is rich and varied.

5ENVIRONMENT

The Environmental Protection Agency (EPA) has the main responsibility for environmental policy. Water pollution from raw sewage and industrial effluents is a significant problem in Taiwan. Outside the larger hotels and urban centers, the water is likely to be impure. Health problems like hepatitis result from waterborne contaminants. Water quality is regulated under provisions of the sanitary drinking water legislation of 1972 and the 1974 Water Pollution Control Act. Air pollution is another significant problem, complicated by a high pollen count. Solid waste disposal regulations and air quality standards were adopted in 1975. All factories are required to comply with established standards, the cost of installing antipollution devices being written off as a depreciable item over two years. Taiwan in 1978 adopted the safety procedures for nuclear facilities issued by the IAEA. In the mid-1980s, the government began tightening emission standards for automobiles and ordered many factories and power plants to install filters and dust collectors. The EPA announced plans in 1987 to install an island-wide pollution-monitoring system.

Wildlife management is the responsibility of the National Wildlife Protection Association of the Republic of China. The nation's marine life is threatened by the use of driftnets. Endangered or extinct species include the Formosan sika, Oriental white stork, and Lan Yü scops owl. Trade in endangered species has been reported.

6POPULATION

The population of Taiwan in 2000 was estimated at 22,319,222. An estimated 9.6% of the population is 65 years of age or older. The projected population for the year 2005 is 23,325,000, assuming a crude birthrate of 14 per 1,000 population and a death rate of 6, resulting in a natural rate of change of 0.8% for the period 2000–2005.

The population density, among the world's highest, was 665 per sq km (1,723 per sq mi) in 1996. T'aipei, the capital and principal city, had a metropolitan population of 2,880,000 in 2000, followed by Kaohsiung, with 1,534,000. Other large cities include T'aichung (794,960), T'ainan (694,930), and Panch'iao (543,982).

7MIGRATION

In 1963, the Nationalist government stated that since the completion of the Communist conquest of the mainland in 1949/50, a total of 146,772 Chinese refugees had come to Taiwan for resettlement. The number of refugees has varied from year to year. There may be as many as 100,000 illegal immigrants.

In 1986, the Taiwan government reported that there were 28,714,000 overseas Chinese (25,799,000 in Asia, 2,044,000 in the Americas, 584,000 in Europe, 214,000 in Oceania, and 73,000 in Africa), including those with dual nationality.

The net migration rate in 1999 was -0.02 migrants per 1,000 population.

8ETHNIC GROUPS

The term "Taiwanese" is often used when referring to those Chinese who are natives of the island as distinct from the 2 million "mainlanders" who migrated from China after the end of World War II. Most of the more than 20 million inhabitants of Taiwan are descendants of earlier immigrants from Fujian and Guangdong (Kwangtung) provinces in South China. They form several distinct groups. The Hakka are descendants of refugees and exiles from Guangdong who came to Taiwan before the 19th century; they are farmers and woodsmen who occupy the frontiers of settlement. The more numerous Fujians are descendants of peasants from Fujian who migrated to Taiwan in the 18th and 19th centuries; they form the bulk of the agricultural population.

The aboriginal population is primarily of Indonesian origin. They live mainly in central and eastern Taiwan. They are mainly divided into nine major tribes, with the Ami, Atayal, Paiwan, and Bunun accounting for about 88%; the balance is mainly distributed among the Puyuma, Rukai, Saisiyat, Tsou, and Yami. The language and customs of the aborigines suggest a close resemblance to the Malays.

In 1999, Taiwanese constituted 84% of the population; mainland Chinese 14%; and aborigine 2%.

9LANGUAGES

Most people on Taiwan now speak Mandarin Chinese (Peking dialect). It is the official language and is used in administration, jurisprudence, education, and, to a large extent, in commerce; it has come into increasingly common use during the last three decades. The Wade-Giles system of romanization, which has been replaced on the mainland by the pinyin system, is still used in Taiwan.

Native Taiwanese speak a variety of southern Chinese dialects, but mainly Southern FuKienese. This is the native tongue of about 70% of the population. It has also influenced the vocabulary of Mandarin spoken on Taiwan. There is also a sizable population of Hakka speakers. This dialect is mainly spoken in Kwantung Province on the mainland. As a result of 50 years of Japanese rule, most Taiwanese and aborigines over the age of 60 speak or understand Japanese. Tribal peoples speak dialects of the Malay-Polynesian family which have no written script.

10RELIGIONS

The Chinese are traditionally eclectic in their religious beliefs. The Taiwan folk religion is a fluid mixture of shamanism, ancestor worship, magic, ghosts and spirits, and aspects of animism. These commonly overlap with an individual's belief in Buddhism, Confucianism, Taoism, or other traditional Chinese religions. Natural phenomena have been deified, and ancestors, sages, virtuous women, and historical personalities have been given the status of gods. As of 1999, an estimated 93% of the population practiced some mixture of traditional Chinese folk religion overlapping with Buddhism, Confucianism, and Taoism.

The first Westerners to bring Christianity to Taiwan were the Dutch (1624). However, a great persecution of Christians took place when the island was lost to Cheng Ch'eng-kung in 1662. Christianity made another beginning in 1860, when a missionary from Scotland came to the island. The English Presbyterian Mission started its work in the southern part of Taiwan about 100 years ago. Since the end of World War II, more than 80 Protestant denominations have been established on the island, and the activities of Christian missions, many coming over from the mainland, have become widespread. As of 1999, Christians constituted 4.5% of the total population. Other religions made up the remaining 2%.

11 TRANSPORTATION

At last estimate, Taiwan had 4,600 km (2,900 mi) of railroad track. The main trunk line, now electrified, links the main cities of the populous west coast between Chilung and Kaohsiung. A second trunk line, the North Link between T'aipei and Hualien on the east coast, was completed in 1979. It connects with an eastern line between Hualien and T'aitung, which was modernized in the early 1980s. Construction of the 98-km (61 mi) South Link (between T'aitung and P'ingtung) has been completed. Forming the last link in the round-the-island rail system, the South Link opened on 6 December 1991, taking over 11 years and $770 million to complete. Construction of a US$6.5-billion rapid-transit system was just starting in T'aipei in 1989.

As of 1997, Taiwan had an estimated 19,634 km (12,201 mi) of highways, of which 17,171 km (10,670 mi) were paved, including 548 km (341 mi) of expressways. By 1995 there were 4,950,000 registered motor vehicles, 4,100,000 of which are passenger cars.

Taiwan has five international seaports, all of them extensively modernized in the 1970s. Kaohsiung in the southwest is by far the largest, handling about two-thirds of all imports and exports. Other major ports are Chilung, on the north coast; Hualien and Suao, both on the east coast; and T'aichung, on the west coast. As of 1998, Taiwan's merchant marine consisted of 180 vessels totaling 5,106,573 GRT.

Also in 1998, there were 39 airports, of which 36 had paved runways. There are two international airports. The main one, opened in 1979, is Chiang Kai-shek International Airport, at T'aoyüan, southwest of T'aipei; the other serves Kaohsiung. T'aipei Airport handles only domestic flights. Regular domestic flights also reach Hualien, T'aitung, Chiai, T'ainan, and several other cities. Principal air service is provided by China Air Lines, Taiwan's international airline, and other international carriers, and by Taiwan's leading domestic airline, Far Eastern Air Transport.

12 HISTORY

Although Taiwan can be seen on a clear day from the China mainland, ancient Chinese accounts contain few references to the island. The earliest inhabitants were Malayo-Polynesian aborigines. Historians have surmised from the brief information available in the early dynastic histories that Chinese emigration to Taiwan began as early as the T'ang dynasty (618–907). During the reign of Kublai Khan (1263–94), the first civil administration was established in the neighboring Pescadores. Taiwan itself, however, remained outside the jurisdiction of the Mongol Empire. During the Ming dynasty (1368–1644), Japanese pirates and Chinese outlaws and refugees wrested the coastal areas from the native aborigines. The Chinese settled in the southwest region, while the Japanese occupied the northern tip of the island.

LOCATION: 21°45′25″ to 25°56′39″N; 119°18′3″ to 124°34′30″E.
TERRITORIAL SEA LIMIT: 12 mi.

Significant Chinese settlement, by immigrants from Fujian and Guangdong, began in the 17th century.

In 1517, the Portuguese sighted the island and named it Ilha Formosa (Beautiful Island). The Dutch, who were disputing the monopoly of Far Eastern trade held by the Portuguese, captured the Pescadores in 1622 and used them as a base for harassing commerce between China, Japan, and the Philippines. Two years later, the Chinese offered the Dutch a treaty that gave them certain commercial privileges if they withdrew from the Pescadores and occupied instead a trading post on Taiwan. The Dutch complied by building Fort Zeelandia and Fort Providentia in the southwestern part of the island. The Spaniards, wishing to compete, seized the northern part of Chilung in 1626 and later extended their domain to nearby Tanshui. The Japanese, constrained by the policy of national seclusion adopted by the Tokugawa Shogunate, withdrew voluntarily in 1628. The Dutch captured the Spanish settlement in 1642 and, after putting down a Chinese uprising in 1656 with the aid of the aborigines, gained complete control of the island.

While the Dutch were consolidating their hold on Taiwan, the Ming dynasty on the China mainland was overthrown by the Manchus, who established the Qing (Ch'ing) dynasty (1644–1912). Remnants of the Ming forces, led by Zheng Chenggong (Cheng Ch'eng-kung Koxinga, 1624–62), son of a Chinese pirate and a Japanese mother, decided to establish an overseas base in Taiwan. They landed on the island in 1661 and ousted the Dutch in the following year. It was not until 1683 that the Manchus succeeded in wresting Taiwan from Zheng Chenggong's successors.

From 1683 to 1885, Taiwan was administered as a part of Fujian Province. During this period, Chinese colonization proceeded steadily, as the aborigines were either assimilated into the Chinese population or pushed back into the mountains. The imperial government, however, paid scant attention to the island administration. As a result, official corruption and inefficiency often provoked armed rebellions. In the latter part of the 19th century, the strategic importance of Taiwan for the defense of the South China coast was recognized by the authorities, particularly after the French bombardment and blockade of the island in 1884 during the Sino-French War over Annam. The local administration was reorganized, and the island was made into a separate province in 1885.

Upon the conclusion of the First Sino-Japanese War in 1895, Taiwan was ceded to Japan. Refusing to submit to Japanese rule, the islanders declared their independence and established a republic, although organized resistance against the Japanese lasted only a few months. Ineffective armed resistance, chiefly by aborigines, continued. Under the Japanese, the island's agricultural resources were developed rapidly to supply the needs of the home islands and the transportation infrastructure experienced modernization. A policy of Japanization of the Taiwan population was adopted and, by 1944, 71% of children attended primary school. During World War II, Japanese administrators began to orchestrate the island's industrialization in support of Japanese expansionism in south Asia.

In accordance with the Cairo Declaration of 1943 and the Potsdam Proclamation of 1945, Taiwan was restored to China in September 1945. The carpetbagging malpractices of the mainland Chinese officials, however, aroused the resentment of the local population. In February 1947, a police incident touched off a popular revolt, which was suppressed with bloodshed. In May, more troops were brought from the mainland and the Taiwanese leadership was systematically killed. Estimates of the dead range from 5,000 to 50,000. On 8 December 1949, as the Chinese Communists were sweeping the Nationalist armies off the mainland, the government of the Republic of China (ROC), led by Gen. Chiang Kai-shek (Jiang Jieshi), was officially transferred to Taiwan.

The Republic of China

With the removal of the ROC government to Taiwan, two million mainland Chinese came to the island where they instituted an authoritarian rule under martial law. Initially Chiang Kai-shek remained myopically focused on retaking the mainland, but as the stalemate continued, the government gradually shifted its attention to industrializing Taiwan. Strong government policies contributed to steady economic progress, first in agriculture and then in industry. In the 1950s, with US aid and advice, the ROC undertook a successful program of land redistribution. Japan

built an infrastructure; the Nationalists brought skills and capital; and the US poured in excess of two billion dollars in aid by 1968. Furthermore, Japanese investment and procurement boom during the Vietnam War in the 1960s further stimulated economic growth.

In 1951, Japan, signed the San Francisco Peace Treaty, thereby formally renouncing its claim to the island of Taiwan. In 1954, the ROC and the United States concluded a Mutual Defense Treaty and the US and Western nations supported Taiwan possession of a UN Security Council seat, while the Eastern bloc nations support PR China. Support for Taiwan's representation gradually eroded over the years, and on 25 November 1971 the General Assembly voted 75–36 (with 17 abstentions) to remove recognition from the ROC and recognize the PRC. In a significant policy reversal, the United States voted with the majority to seat the mainland government. Although maintaining full diplomatic ties with Taiwan, the US took the occasion of President Nixon's visit to China to acknowledge, in what became known as the Shanghai communiqué of February 1972, that "all Chinese on either side of the Taiwan Strait maintain there is but one China and that Taiwan is part of China. The United States government does not challenge that position."

By 1975, most nations shifted recognition from the ROC to the PRC. On 1 January 1979, the US formally recognized the PRC as the sole legal government of China and severed diplomatic ties with Taiwan. It also announced the unilateral termination of the 1954 US-ROC Mutual Defense Treaty, effective 1 January 1980, and withdrew its remaining military personnel. Nonetheless, the US continued to sell arms to Taiwan, and commercial and cultural contacts were unofficially maintained through the American Institute in Taiwan and the Coordination Council for North American Affairs. Taiwan successfully warded off worldwide political and economic isolation by maintaining a host of similar contacts with other countries.

When President Chiang Kai-shek died at age 87 on 5 April 1975, he was succeeded in office by former Vice-President Yen Chia-kan (Yan Jiagan). Leadership of the Nationalist Party (Kuomintang, Guomindang) and, hence, of the government passed to Chiang's elder son, Chiang Ching-kuo (Jiang Jingguo). The younger Chiang was elected to a six-year term as president in March 1978 and reelected in 1984. While control of the central government had remained in the hands of mainlanders in the first decades of the Nationalists' rule on Taiwan, Taiwanese Chinese increasingly won elections at local levels, and Chiang Ching-kuo instituted a policy of bringing more Taiwanese into the Nationalist Party. By the 1980s, economic development had produced a new middle class, and the passage of time, together with intermarriage between mainlanders and Taiwanese, had brought a new generation for which the distinction between mainlander and Taiwanese held diminished importance. These factors contributed to popular pressure for a more democratic government. In November 1986, 5,000–10,000 demonstrated in support of an exiled dissident, Hsu Hsin-liang (Xu Xinliang), when he was not allowed to return to Taiwan. Thousands protested the 38th anniversary of martial law in May 1987. And, in March 1990, more than 10,000 demonstrators demanded greater democracy and direct presidential elections. This was followed in the same month by a demonstration involving some 6,000 students.

In 1987 martial law was revoked and with that press restrictions were eased, citizens were allowed to visit relatives on the mainland, and opposition political parties formed. Then in January 1988, Chiang Ching-kuo died and was succeeded as president by the Vice-President, Lee Teng-hui (Li Denghui, 1923–). Lee, a protégé of Chiang Ching-kuo, was a native Taiwanese. In March 1990, the National Assembly reelected Lee as president for a six-year term. In July, he was also named Chairman of the Nationalist Party by the Party Congress.

In the early 1990s, as Taiwan increasingly opened its political system to greater democracy, the KMT's corrupt practices were revealed. However, after the 1992 legislative elections, the KMT emerged victorious as it still controlled most national media and opposition parties failed to mobilize voters. Vote-buying and other forms of fraud were also widespread. By the 1995 elections, however, the political environment changed because the KMT lost control of the media. Furthermore, the Control Yuan, the branch of government responsible for oversight, began to assert its independence by investigating KMT corruption. In local elections of 1994, for instance, state prosecutors convicted more than one third of 858 city and county representatives for vote-buying. Just prior to the 1995 national elections, it was revealed that the Minister of Justice had evidence of another extensive ring of vote-buying. The KMT took 54% of the vote (83 seats), its lowest majority ever and its major rival, the Democratic People's Party (DPP) obtained 54 seats and the Chinese New Party (CNP) captured 21 with 6 going to various independents. The constitution was also rewritten in 1995, calling for direct election of the president with the first election slated to be held in 1996.

Amid these democratic reforms, Taiwan faced a major international crisis in 1995 when President Lee was given a US visa to visit Cornell University, his alma mater. China objected vociferously and threatened military action against Taiwan. In a show of support for Taiwan and in opposition to PR China's launching of missile into Taiwan's territorial waters, the US dispatched a naval force to the region, only to further irritate PR China.

Prior to the presidential elections of March 1996, the formerly-united KMT began to splinter. Dissidents within the party and those who had previously left the KMT announced their intentions to run against Lee, who had been chosen by a party plenum in August 1995 as the official KMT candidate. Primary among these were Lin Yang-gang, a former Judicial Yuan president and current vice-chairman of the KMT, and Chien Li-an, president of the Control Yuan and former Minister of National Defense. Campaigning was intense, with scandals being revealed on all sides, but Lee received a resounding 54% compared to 21% for his nearest competitor.

President Lee was criticized by political opponents in 1997 as an increased wave of crime swept the island. In May 1997, more than 50,000 protestors gathered in the capital protesting the government's lack of action on issues of crime. Multiple members of the Executive Yuan resigned and Lee shuffled his cabinet. However, late in 1997, the KMT suffered severe losses in local and magistrate elections. The main opposition, the DPP, won 12 of the 23 constituency positions contested and led to the reorganization of the KMT following the resignation of the party's Secretary General. In 1998, the KMT recovered in the next set of elections but only to suffer a setback in summer elections that year. As the economy weakened from the Asian financial crisis, the government sought to deregulate the economy and decrease taxes. Relations with PR China again worsened as Taiwan prepared for presidential elections in 2000. On March 18, 2000, Chen Shui-bian, the DPP candidate and a former dissident leader imprisoned for his opposition to the KMT was elected president in a hotly contested race. He obtained 39.3% of the vote and Lien Chan (KMT) captured 23.1% while ex-KMT businessman James Soong ran as an independent and garnered 36.8%. Leading up to and following the election, the PRC warned the Taiwanese that the election of a pro-independence DPP candidate would lead to possible military action.

13GOVERNMENT

The government of the Republic of China in Taipei claims to be the central government of all of China. Its constitution was drafted by a constitutional convention at Nanjing (Nanking) on 15 November 1946; it was adopted on 25 December 1946 and promulgated by the national government on 1 January 1947. The government derives its powers from the National Assembly, which, according to the constitution, exercises political powers on behalf of the people. The first National Assembly, which was elected in November 1947, had 2,961 delegates, selected on the basis of regional and occupational representation. The Assembly has the power to elect and recall the president and the vice-president, amend the constitution, and approve constitutional amendments proposed by the legislative council (Legislative Yuan). The original delegates held their seats "indefinitely," until control of the mainland can be reestablished. Since 1969, the number of seats gradually increased with the addition of new seats for Taiwan. In April 1990, President Lee Teng-hui revoked the emergency decree of 1948 which had allowed the 1,947 deputies to remain in office and the "indefinite" deputies had to retire by December 1991.

The central government consists of the Office of the President, the National Assembly, and five governing branches (called "yuan"), namely the Executive Yuan, the Legislative Yuan, the Judicial Yuan, the Examination Yuan, and the Control Yuan.

The president is the head of state and of the Executive Yuan, which functions as a cabinet. His tenure of office is six years, with eligibility for a second term.Under the president, there are five government branches known as yuans (councils or departments): Legislative, Executive, Control, Examination, and Judicial. The Legislative Yuan, elected by popular vote, is the highest lawmaking body. As in the National Assembly, many members of the 1948 Legislative Yuan held their seats until 1991.

The Executive Yuan, comparable to the cabinet in other countries, is the highest administrative organ in the government. There are eight ministries, two commissions, and a number of subordinate organs under the Executive Yuan. The Premier—the President of the Executive Yuan—is appointed by the President of the republic, with the consent of the Legislative Yuan. The president is empowered to compel the premier to resign by refusing to sign decrees or orders presented by the latter for promulgation.

The Legislative Yuan is the highest organ of the State. It has a binding vote of no confidence which would lead to the dissolution of the Executive Yuan. Of its 225 members, 176 are chosen by universal suffrage and the remaining members are appointed through a system of proportional representation.

The Control Yuan, the highest supervisory organ, exercises censorial and audit powers over the government and may impeach officials. It also supervises the execution of the government budget.

The Examination Yuan is the equivalent of a civil service commission. It consists of two ministries. The Ministry of Examination appoints government personnel through competitive examination. The Ministry of Personnel registers, classifies, promotes, transfers, retires, and pensions. Its president, vice-president, and 19 commissioners are appointed by the president of the republic with the consent of the Control Yuan.

14POLITICAL PARTIES

The Chinese Nationalist Party, better known as the Kuomintang—KMT, is the dominant political party in Taiwan. The teachings of Sun Yat-sen (Sun Zhongshan), which stress nationalism, democracy, and people's livelihood, form the ideology of the party. After the fall of the mainland to the Communists in 1949, a reform committee was organized to chart a new program for the party. The other two main parties include the Democratic Progressive Party (DPP), with a pro-independence and liberal economic orientation, and the Chinese New Party, with a pan-Chinese and anticorruption message.

The KMT has a membership of 2.1 million members. Its organization is similar to that of the Chinese Communist Party.

The basic unit is the cell, which represents neighborhoods. The next levels include the district, county, and provincial congresses and committees. The highest levels include the National Congress and the Central Committee. The National Congress delegates serve four-year terms and is charged with the tasks of amending the party charter, determining the party platform and other important policies. It also elects the party chairman and the Central Committee members, and approves candidates nominated by the chairman to serve as vice chairmen and members of the Central Advisory Council. When the National Congress is in recess,   the supreme party organ is the Central Committee, which holds a plenary session every year.

The Central Standing Committee, which represents the Central Committee when that body is not in session, is the most influential organ in the KMT. It meets every Wednesday morning to deliberate and approve important policies for the party and the government, and to nominate people for important party and government positions, including ministers, vice ministers, and various commissioners.   The day-to-day affairs of the party are managed by the secretariat. All organization within the KMT are funded by profits from party-owned and operated business enterprises, ranging from newspapers and TV stations to electrical appliance companies and computer firms.

At the party's 14th National Congress held in August 1993, significant changes to the conduct of party affairs were made. It decided that the party chairman was to be elected by the National Congress through secret ballot. President Lee Teng-hui won 83 percent of the votes cast and was reelected chairman of the party. In addition, four vice-chairmen were added to the Central Committee after being nominated by the chairman and approved by the National Congress. It also decided that the chairman would appoint only ten to 15 of the 31 members of the Central Standing Committee, with the remaining members elected by the Central Committee. Finally, it decided to hold the National Congress every two years instead of four years.

Under martial law, from 1949 through 1986, the formation of new political parties was illegal, although there were two nominal, previously formed parties. Non-KMT candidates ran as independents or "Nonpartisans," with increasing success by the end of the 1970s. In September 1986, a group of "nonpartisans" formed a new opposition party, the Democratic Progressive Party (DPP), which had an orientation toward the Taiwanese population and advocated "self-determination." Although technically illegal, the DPP's candidates took 22% of the vote in the December 1986 elections, winning 12 out of 73 contested seats in the Legislative Yuan; the KMT won 59. The lifting of martial law in 1987 made the formation of new parties legal, although a new security law continued to restrict political activity. In the first fully competitive, democratic national elections, in December 1992, the KMT won 53% and the DPP 31% of the votes for the Legislative Yuan. Before the 1995 legislative elections, the KMT began to splinter and in 1994 the Chinese New Party (CNP) was formed by KMT defectors who favored strengthened ties with the mainland. In the 1995 balloting, however, the KMT was able to maintain its majority, winning 83 of the 164 seats in the Legislative Yuan. The DPP took 54, the CNP took 21 and six seats were won by independents. In the national assembly (334 seats) the KMT took 183, the DPP 99, the CNP 46, and six were won by others.

The Democratic Progressive Party, formed on September 28, 1986, now has approximately 200,000 members. The party's organizational structure closely resembles that of the Kuomintang. The DPP's National Congress elects 31 members to the Central Executive Committee and 11 members to the Central Advisory Committee. The Central Executive Committee in turn elects the 11 members of the Central Standing Committee. Its main leader is Taipei Mayor Chen Shui-bian. As a relatively new party with weaker organizational structure, the methods used for nominating the party's candidates for public offices changes quite frequently. At the party's sixth National Congress, held in April and May of 1994, a two-tier primary system was initiated under which ordinary members of the DPP vote for candidates in one primary election and party cadres vote in a second primary. The results of the two would then be combined, with equal weight given to both. At the second plenary meeting of the sixth National Congress held in March 1995, the nomination process for the presidential and gubernatorial candidates was modified to add open primaries for DPP members and nonmembers. It was further decided at the meeting that the party chairman would be elected directly by all members of the party starting in   1998. What most distinguishes the DPP from the two other major parties is its support of Taiwan independence, or the permanent political separation of Taiwan from the Chinese mainland. Although the DPP has incorporated Taiwan independence into its official platform, the urgency accorded to its realization is a source of factional   contention within the party. In more recent elections, the mainstream DPP leadership has tended to downplay the party's independence theme in an attempt to broaden voter support. Currently, there are on-going discussions to reform the DPP's party platform.

The Chinese New Party (NP) was formed in August 1993, shortly before the Kuomintang's 14th National Congress by a group of KMT reformers who broke away from the party in protest of the undemocratic practices of the KMT. Prominent leaders include the former Finance Minister Wang Chien-shien and former head of the Environmental Protection Administration Jaw Shau-kong. The NP adopted an anticorruption platform and championed social justice. The goal of the NP is to attract voters who are dissatisfied with the performance of the ruling KMT and opposed to the DPP's advocacy of Taiwan independence.

15 LOCAL GOVERNMENT

The Taiwan provincial government holds jurisdiction over the main island of Taiwan, 21 smaller islands in adjacent waters, and the 64 islands of the Penghu (Pescadores) group. The provincial capital is located at Taichung. The province is divided into 16 county (hsien) administrative areas and 3 municipalities under the direct jurisdiction of the provincial government. In addition, Taipei (since 1967) and Kaohsiung (since 1979) are self-governing "special" municipalities. Subdivisions of the county are the township (chen), the rural district or group of villages (hsiang), and the precinct. Quemoy and Matsu are administered by the military. At the local level and under the Taiwan Provincial Government, there are five cities—Keelung, Hsinchu, Taichung, Chiayi, and Tainan—and 16 counties, and under each county there are county municipalities.

The province is headed by a governor who is nominated by the President of the Executive Yuan and appointed by the President of the republic. Department heads and members of the Provincial Council are recommended by the governor for appointment by the Executive Yuan. The governor is the ex officio chairman of the appointed 21-member Provincial Council, the policy making body, and holds veto power over its resolutions. The provincial government can issue ordinances and regulations for the administration of the province as long as they do not conflict with laws of the central government. The mayors and city councils of Taipei and Kaohsiung are elected.

The Provincial Assembly, an elected body, meets for two yearly sessions of two months each. Nominally it possesses broad legislative powers; however, its prerogatives are circumscribed by a provision in its organic law that in the event of a disagreement between the provincial executive and the Assembly, the former may request a reconsideration. Should the Assembly uphold its original resolution, the provincial executive may submit the dispute to the Executive Yuan for final judgment. The Executive Yuan may dissolve the Provincial Assembly and order a new election if it holds that the Assembly is acting contrary to national policy.

At the end of 1996, the National Development Conference was convened to streamline local government operations. The county government is headed by an elected magistrate (hsien-chang) and the municipal government by a mayor (shih-chang). Each county or municipality has a representative body called the hsien, or municipal assembly. Further down are the councils and assemblies of townships and rural districts, each headed by a chief officer. All of these officials are elected by universal suffrage of citizens over age 20.

16JUDICIAL SYSTEM

The Judicial Yuan is Taiwan's highest judicial organ. It interprets the constitution and other laws and decrees, adjudicates administrative suits, and disciplines public functionaries. The president and vice-president of the Judicial Yuan are nominated and appointed by the president of the republic, with the consent of the Control Yuan. They, together with 16 grand justices, form the Council of Grand Justices, which is charged with the power and responsibility of interpreting the constitution, laws, and ordinances. The tenure of office of a grand justice is nine years. The judicial system is based on the principle of three trials in three grades of courts: district court, high court, and supreme court. The Supreme Court, the highest tribunal of the land, consists of a number of civil and criminal divisions, each of which is formed by a presiding judge and four associate judges. The judges are appointed for life.

In 1993 a separate Constitution Court was established. Staffed by the 16 grand justices of the Judicial Yuan, but with the Judicial Yuan excluded from the court, the new court is charged with resolving constitutional disputes, regulating the activities of political parties and accelerating the democratization process.

There is no right to trial by jury, but the right to a fair public trial is protected by law and respected in practice. Defendants are afforded a right to counsel and to a right to appeal to the High Court and the Supreme Court in cases in which the sentence exceeds three years. Those sentenced to three years or less may appeal only to the High Court. The Supreme Court automatically reviews all sentences to life imprisonment or death. There is also an administrative court.

The judicial system is based on civil law and Taiwan accepts compulsory jurisdiction of the International Court of Justice.

17ARMED FORCES

Two years' military service is compulsory for all male citizens. The armed forces totaled 376,000 in 2000, a decrease of 64,000 from 1986. The army had 240,000 members, the navy 68,000, the marines 30,000, and the air force 68,000. In addition, reserves totaled 1,657,500. The navy had 16 destroyers, 4 submarines, 21 frigates, and 104 patrol and coastal combatants; the air force had 598 combat aircraft. For the period 1985–91, US military sales to Taiwan totaled US$3 billion of $3.5 billion in imports. Taiwan uses US weapons of all kinds. It spent $7.44 billion on defense in 1998–99 or 2.8% of gross domestic product.

18INTERNATIONAL COOPERATION

The ROC, a charter member of the UN, became the first government to lose its recognition from that body following a General Assembly vote on 25 November 1971 to recognize the PRC as the sole legitimate representative of China. The ROC subsequently lost its membership in most UN bodies, as well as in several other international organizations—usually with its place taken by the PRC. As of 1999, the Asian Development Bank was one of the few major intergovernmental groups to which Taiwan still belonged; others included the ICC, IOC, and WCL. Taiwan has also applied for membership in the WTO.

As of September 1985, Taiwan had formal diplomatic ties with only 24 countries. The government claimed to have "substantive" trade relations with more than 140 countries and territories, however. Although trade with mainland China is officially forbidden, unofficial trade is substantial.

19ECONOMY

Under the Japanese, the island was developed as a major source of foodstuffs for Japan. Production of rice and sugar increased rapidly, but little effort was directed toward industrialization until after 1937. Immediately after World War II, a number of factors—including repatriation of Japanese technicians, dismantling of industrial plants, and lack of fertilizer for agriculture—caused a rapid deterioration of the economy, which was aggravated by the influx of refugees from the mainland. The situation improved after 1949 with the removal of the ROC government to Taiwan. The arrival of technical and experienced personnel and capital equipment from the mainland facilitated the island's economic rehabilitation. Currency and tax reforms stabilized the monetary situation. The supply of fertilizer from the US and a land reform program aided the revival of agricultural production.

Energetic government measures in the form of successive four-year plans, at first supplemented by US aid, resulted in substantial economic progress. In the first decade (1951–60), the stress was on agricultural development and the establishment of textile and other labor-intensive industries. From 1961 to 1970, the promotion of industrial products for export was emphasized. In 1963, Taiwan registered its first favorable trade balance. By 1965, the economy appeared stable enough to warrant the cessation of US economic aid programs. Medium and light industry led the expansion, with striking gains registered in electronics, household goods, and chemicals. The decade 1971–80 saw the development of such capital-intensive industries as steel, machinery, machine tools, and motor vehicle assembly. Such industries, based on imports of raw materials, were encouraged through massive government support for major infrastructural improvements in roads, railroads, ports, and electricity. During the 1980s, emphasis was placed on the development of high-technology industries. As a result, between 1981 and 1991, the share of high-technology industries in total manufactures increased from 20% to 29%, making Taiwan the 7th largest producer of computer hardware on the global market. The 1990s brought an influx of capital-rich investment, especially after 1996 when the first democratic elections were held. High-technology industries accounted for over 73% of total manufacturing, and 67% of exports in 1999.

Taiwan's GNP advanced at an average annual rate of 9% in real terms between 1952 and 1980. In contrast to Taiwan's industry-led economic growth of previous decades, since the late 1980s the country has undergone a shift towards a services-dominated economy. As of 1997, services made up almost 62% of the GDP, compared to less than 50% in the mid-1980s and 44% in the early 1960s. Taiwan has the world's third largest foreign exchange reserves and over $220 billion in two-way trade. Though still expanding in absolute terms, industry's share of the GDP declined from 52% in 1986 to 35% in 1997. Agriculture has continued to claim only a small share of the economy, making up less than 3% of the GDP in 1997. A lack of domestic resources hampers the development of agriculture and primary industries. An earthquake in September of 1999 caused major damages to Taiwanese lives and property, but reconstruction was expected to reach completion by at least 2000. Overall, the economy grew by 4.8% in 1998 and by 5% in 1999.

²⁰INCOME

The US Central Intelligence Agency (CIA) reports that in 1998 Taiwan's gross domestic product (GDP) was estimated at $362 billion. The per capita GDP was estimated at $16,500. The annual growth rate of GDP was estimated at 4.8%. The average inflation rate in 1998 was 2.1%. The CIA defines GDP as the value of all final goods and services produced within a nation in a given year and computed on the basis of purchasing power parity (PPP) rather than value as measured on the basis of the rate of exchange.

²¹LABOR

The civilian labor force in Taiwan was last estimated at 9.2 million in 1992. The share of persons employed in farming, forestry, and fishing has been declining steadily, while the share of the work force employed in mining, manufacturing, construction, and utilities has increased. As of 1997, about 10% of the labor force was engaged in agriculture, 62% in services, and 28% in industry and commerce.

Productivity has been improving. The law provides for an 8-hour day (which may be extended to 11 hours for men and 10 for women) and a six-day workweek; overtime is paid at 40–100% above the regular wage. Most large firms give allowances for transportation, meals, housing, and other benefits, which can increase base pay by 60–80%. A minimum of one week's vacation is provided after a year's employment, and there are 14 or 15 other paid holidays. Women are entitled to eight weeks of maternity leave at full pay and an extra paid holiday on Woman's Day (8 March). In 1999, the monthly minimum wage was $465.

Trade unions are weak and cannot be called unions in the real sense of the term, for the law does not provide for effective collective bargaining and also prohibits strikes, shutdowns, and walkouts in vital industries. The trade unions, organized under government supervision, tend to be used for carrying out government policies, but they carry on a considerable amount of welfare work. In 1999, there were 3,710 unions in Taiwan, with membership totaling 31% of all employed persons. The minimum age for employment is 15. Current occupational health and safety regulations provide only minimal protection and have a mixed record of enforcement.

²²AGRICULTURE

About 24% of the land was under cultivation in 1995. Although still important as both an export earner and a domestic food source, agriculture has fallen far from the preeminent position it long held in the Taiwan economy. From 1973 to 1987, the crop production growth rate increased on average only 0.1% per year. In 1998, agriculture accounted for 3.5% of GDP. Nearly 10.1% of the labor force was employed in agriculture. High production costs and low return have driven much of the agricultural work force away to industry. In 1997, there were some 780,000 farm households, down from 822,395 in 1993. Part-time farming households have accounted for over 80% of all farming households since 1980.

Rice, the principal food crop, is grown along the western plain and in the south. There were 364,000 ha (899,000 acres) of rice fields in 1997, when some 1.66 million tons of brown rice were produced. Taiwan's annual rice production exceeds demand; the island's per capita rice consumption has declined by over 50% since the mid-1970s due to changing diet preferences. Other food crops include sweet potatoes, bananas, peanuts, soybeans, and wheat. Sugar, pineapples, citrus fruits, crude tea, and asparagus are plantation-grown and are the principal cash and export crops. Small amounts of Taiwan's world-famous oolong tea, cotton, tobacco, jute, and sisal are also produced. A fast-rising industry, mushroom canning, led to the development of mushroom cultivation, a specialty crop well suited to Taiwan since it is labor-intensive and requires little space and small investment. Betel nuts have become Taiwan's second most valuable cash crop after rice. In 1997, 56,300 ha (139,000 acres) were planted in betel nuts, with a production of 156,000 tons. That year, exports of fresh flowers were valued at $350 million, going mostly to Japan, Hong Kong, and the US.

Generally, Taiwanese agriculture is characterized by high yields, irrigation, terracing, multiple cropping, intertillage, and extensive use of fertilizers. Farms are small, averaging 1.1 hectares (2.7 acres) of cultivable land per farm family. Mechanization, once confined largely to sugarcane and rice production, is increasing rapidly as a result of government subsidies and other incentives. Since there is an oversupply of rice, the government has encouraged farmers to grow soybeans, wheat, and corn, which are more profitable. The growing scarcity of land on Taiwan is causing serious disagreements over land resources between agricultural, industrial, and housing interests.

²³ANIMAL HUSBANDRY

Pastures in Taiwan occupy only 0.1% of the total land area. In 1997, livestock production was valued at over $3.2 billion, or 38.2% of Taiwan's gross agricultural production value. Hog production is Taiwan's most valuable farm product. In 1997, a major outbreak of hoof and mouth disease affected 6,147 hog farms. As a result, one-third of the hog population had to be destroyed, leaving an estimated hog inventory of 6.5 million in 1999. The government helped compensate pig farmers with $1.1 billion in low interest loans. Chickens and ducks are raised by most households.

²⁴FISHING

Production of fish products totaled 1.3 million tons in 1997 (20th in the world). Exports of seafood products totaled $1,781 million in 1997. In 1997, Taiwan accounted for 4.3% of the world's fresh, chilled and frozen fish exports, valued at $506.7 million, and 1.5% of the world's crustacean and mollusk exports, valued at $97.9 million. Squid, skipjack and yellowfin tuna, chub mackerel, shark, and milkfish are the main species of the marine catch. Deep-sea fishing, which was practically wiped out by World War II, has shown strong gains following heavy investments in vessels and harbors. In 1997, the value of aquacultural production was $949.8 million. Milkfish, tilapias, clams, oysters, and eels are the main species farmed.

²⁵FORESTRY

The total forest area was estimated at 2,102,312 ha (850,794 acres) in 1996. The roundwood harvest was estimated at 61,200 cu m in 1996, with timber production at 33,000 cu m (90% softwood). Domestic timber production only meets 1% of total demand; the value of wood imports totaled $2.2 billion in 1995. Taiwan's timber production has declined since the 1980s due to local labor shortages, intensifying environmental concerns, and logging restrictions. Principal timbers are oak, cedar, and hemlock. Taiwan is a major furniture exporter that relies heavily on imported wood products to support the industry.

²⁶MINING

Mining accounted for less than 1% of GDP in 1997. Coal, oil, and natural gas are the country's most valuable mine products. Dolomite, limestone, and marble are the most important nonfuel mineral commodities. Other minerals produced are small amounts of sulfur, pyrite, gold, silver, copper, manganese, mercury, petroleum, and natural gas. The western third of the island has adequate amounts of sand, gravel, and limestone for building purposes. The demand for mineral products has increased over the years, while local supplies are dwindling. Mineral production in 1997 included (in tons): dolomite,

198,000; limestone, 15,447,000; marble, 18,071,000; serpentine, 436,000; kaolin, 80,000; and salt, 62,484.

27ENERGY AND POWER

The island's installed power capacity reached 26,036,000 kW in 1998. Total electric power output reached 133,586 million kWh in 1998 (more than 60 times the 1,966 million kWh generated in 1955). As of 1998, Taiwan had six nuclear reactors at three plants with a combined installed capacity of 4,884 MW, and a fourth plant was slated to add another 5,000 MW by 2004. Primary energy requirements increased from about 33.3 million tons of oil (equivalent) in 1985 to about 66.1 million tons in 1995. Power is controlled by the Taiwan Power Co. (Taipower), a government-owned corporation, but some enterprises generate power for their own consumption. The principal sources for consumption in 1995 were oil (53.5%), coal (25.7%), nuclear energy (13.8%), natural gas (5.9%); and hydroelectricity (1.1%). In 1995, Taiwan consumed 850,000 barrels per day. Oil is imported from the Middle East, Indonesia, Brunei, and Venezuela. River basin development is being vigorously pushed for irrigation, flood control, and power generation. In addition, experiments during the late 1970s and 1980s concentrated on developing Taiwan's geothermal potential.

Coal production was 100,000 tons in 1997, down from 403,000 tons in 1991. The decline was due to government policies designed to close unsafe coal mines, high production costs, and reduced domestic reserves. The number of operating mines fell from 108 in 1985 to 41 at the start of 1995. Natural gas production amounted to 934 million cu m in 1997, while crude oil production was an estimated 4,000 barrels per day in 1998. Coal reserves at the end of 1996 amounted to 1.1 million tons; natural gas, 2.7 trillion cu ft (76 billion cu m).

28INDUSTRY

Under the Japanese, about 90% of the industrial enterprises were owned by the government or by Japanese corporations with government assistance. After the restoration of Taiwan to China in 1945, the ROC government took over these enterprises. Some were sold to private owners, and the rest were grouped under the management of 18 public corporations, operated either by the national government or by the provincial government, or by both. Added to the confiscated enemy properties were public enterprises evacuated from the mainland. As a result, government-operated enterprises came to dominate Taiwanese industry. Although the proportion accounted for by these enterprises in the production value of manufacturing industries has been falling in recent years in contrast to the private sector, it still accounts for a significant amount of value added. Beginning in 1992, Taiwan authorities have made efforts to reduce the size of the public sector. These efforts gained momentum in both 1998 and 1999 with privatization announcements that included the Chinese Petroleum Corp., Chunghwa Telecom Corp., and Taiwan Power Corp.

The average annual growth rate in manufacturing was 13% during 1953–62, 20% during 1963–72, 9.6% during 1973–85 and 5.9% for 1986–92, and 7% in 1997; the private sector outpaced the public sector during each of these periods. The number of workers in manufacturing rose from 362,000 in 1952 to 736,000 in 1967 and to almost 2.8 million in 1987. By 1992, however, this number declined to about 2.6 million as the rapidly expanding service sector absorbed more of the workforce. Industrial production for export has been encouraged by the establishment of free-trade export-processing zones (EPZs) in the Kaohsiung harbor area, at Nantze (near Kaohsiung), and at T'aichung. Since the late 1980s rising production costs and a 40% appreciation of the New Taiwan dollar have prompted many export-oriented companies to relocate their manufacturing

plants to mainland China and Southeast Asia. In particular; labor-intensive industries, such as toys, footwear, umbrellas, and garments, have relocated.

Production rose spectacularly after the end of World War II, especially between 1952 and the early 1980s. Slower economic growth since the mid-1980s and greater investment emphasis on heavy and high-technology industries as well as services has resulted in declining production figures for traditional manufactures such as cotton yarn and fertilizer. Television set production declined from 5.7 million in 1986 to 1.9 million units in 1994; caustic soda from 386,505 to 171,840 tons. Nevertheless, reflecting continued development of heavy and electronic industries, production increases continued to be registered for a number of key products. Cement production grew from 446,000 tons in 1952 to 14.8 million tons in 1986 and 22.5 million tons in 1995. Production of motor vehicles increased from 170,923 units in 1986 to 423,318 units in 1994; steel bars from 6.16 million to 18.82 million tons; synthetic fibers from 1.37 million to 2.51 million tons; polyvinyl chloride from 795,000 tons to 1.11 million tons; and ship building from 552,294 d.w.t. to 1.04 million d.w.t. Taiwan's computer manufacturing industry was the world's third largest in 1995. Nine of the top ten exporting firms in Taiwan in 1998 were electronic and computer manufacturing companies. Taiwan has become the world's leading supplier of computer peripherals, including motherboards, monitors, mice, interfaces, network cards, and graphic cards; and holds the largest market share of notebook computers and semiconductors.

29SCIENCE AND TECHNOLOGY

In the 1970s, Taiwan instituted its Science and Technology Development Program. Coordinated by the National Science Council, the program seeks to encourage the development of "knowledge-intensive" industries through grants for the training of scientific personnel, subsidies for recruitment of distinguished scientists from abroad, and grants to universities to promote scientific research. Specific goals of the program are to integrate and promote research in geothermal energy, battery-powered vehicles, electronics, cancer treatment, pharmaceuticals, nuclear safety, and the development of high-precision instrumentation and computers.

The Industrial Technology Research Institute is charged with the transfer of pertinent technologies developed to manufacturing and other industries. College students are encouraged to build careers in engineering and science. In 1979, the Science-Based Industrial Park was established at Hsinchu, near the National Tsinghua University, with the objective of encouraging computer manufacturing and other high-technology industries by offering loans, tax incentives, and low-cost housing and factory buildings. By 1990, over 60 companies had established R&D and joint production facilities there. These include computer, semiconductor, precision electronics and instrumentation, telecommunications, and biotechnology firms.

The highest institution for scientific research on Taiwan is the Academia Sinica (Chinese Academy of Sciences), founded in 1928 and now located in T'aipei. Its 18 associated institutes carry on research in mathematics, statistics, history and philology, economics, modern history, physics, botany, zoology, ethnology, chemistry, molecular biology, biological chemistry, biomedical sciences, atomic and molecular sciences, earth sciences, information science, nuclear energy, social sciences and philosophy, and American culture. An Atomic Energy Council, founded in 1955, promotes atomic research.

In T'aipei, the National Taiwan Science Education Center has a planetarium and various exhibits; the Taiwan Museum has exhibits on natural history, geology, and ethnography, and a spectroscopic dating laboratory for fossils. Taiwan has 23 universities and colleges that offer courses in basic and applied sciences.

30DOMESTIC TRADE

The marketing system is partly free and partly controlled. Salt, tobacco, alcoholic beverages, and certain commodities are produced and distributed by the government. Prices of basic living commodities are controlled. Retail sales in cities are handled by department stores, specialty shops, general stores, convenience stores, roadside stands, and peddlers. In 2000, Taiwan had over 1,000 supermarkets and 3,200 convenience stores. Since roadside stands and peddlers have little overhead and are satisfied with a small profit, their prices are generally lower than those of the large stores and shops, if the customer bargains. In recent years, wholesale discounters, hyper markets and franchises have become significant distribution channels for consumer goods, increasing the efficiency of the marketing system overall.

Chilung and T'aipei are the distribution centers for the northern end of the island, while Kaohsiung and T'ainan are the principal distribution centers for the southern area. Most registered import and export trading firms are located in T'aipei. Accounts are usually settled during festival periods, according to Chinese custom.

Local markets open about 7 AM and close at 6 PM or later. Business firms and stores are usually open from 9 AM to 5:30 PM, and in the morning on Saturdays, and some stores close as late as 10 PM. Most stores are open seven days a week. Banks are open six days a week: Monday–Friday, 9 AM to 3:30 PM, and Saturday, 9 AM to noon. As of 1st January 1998, government employees (excepting the police, health bureau, and customs) and most private companies take the second and fourth Saturday of the month off.

31FOREIGN TRADE

Foreign trade is of ultimate importance to the island economy. To fulfill both production and consumer needs, Taiwan must import large quantities of energy, industrial raw materials, food, and manufactured goods. With rising consumer wealth within Taiwan as well as tariff reductions and other liberalization measures by the government, imports have risen rapidly from $24 billion in 1986 to an estimated $122 billion in 2000.

The export pattern has changed significantly since the end of World War II. In 1952, industrial products represented only 10% of Taiwan's total exports and agricultural exports made up the rest; but by 1992, industrial exports (excluding processed agricultural products) had jumped to an overwhelming 95.7% share of the total. Exports increased from $8.2 billion in 1976 to an estimated $112 billion in 2000. However, the export growth rate has declined steeply in recent years, from 23% in 1986 to 13% in 1991 and 0.4% in 1992, due to recession in Taiwan's major markets and the movement of export-oriented manufacturing plants to China and Southeast Asia. Exports leveled off in 1997, and dropped by 9.4% in 1998, in part due to the financial crisis in all of Asia. The growth in services has overtaken that of industrial production.

Most of Taiwan's export commodities are electronic equipment and other small manufactured goods. The top ten exports are as follows:

	% OF COUNTRY TOTAL	% OF WORLD TOTAL
Transistors and valves	7.2	5.0
Office machine parts	6.8	8.3
Automatic data processing equipment	6.6	5.9
Telecoms equipment	3.7	3.6
Toys and sporting goods	2.9	10
Bicycles and motorcycles	2.8	18
Woven man-made fiber fabric	2.8	9.2
Articles of plastic	2.7	6.2
Base metal	2.4	7.1
Special textile fabric and products	2.3	14

The US remains Taiwan's single most important trade partner, although Japan has made major gains, becoming Taiwan's major supplier in the 1970s and 1980s. Over 18% of imports come from the US, while Taiwan exports more than 27% of goods to the US. Trade with mainland China via Hong Kong expanded rapidly during the late 1980s and early 1990s, resulting in a sharp increase in Taiwan's trade surplus with the latter country. Following cross-strait tension from 1995 onwards, Taiwan investors have limited their relations with mainland China, resulting in a 50% drop in investment during 1998. Exports to China fell by 13% in 1998.

32BALANCE OF PAYMENTS

There was a consistent trade surplus after the mid-1970s, which exceeded $10 billion after the mid-1980s through the mid-1990s. The US Central Intelligence Agency reports that in 1997 the purchasing power parity of Taiwan's exports was $122.1 billion while imports totaled $114.4 billion resulting in a trade balance of $7.7 billion. The 1998 current account surplus was $4.8 billion. Total foreign exchange reserves, the world's third largest after Japan and China, climbed to $95 billion. Total foreign debt was only $80 million in 1997.

33BANKING AND SECURITIES

Many banking institutions are either owned or controlled by the government. There were eleven public banks in 1998, with total assets of $261 billion, or 44%. The Bank of Taiwan (with 75 branches) used to issue currency notes, handle foreign exchange, act as the government's bank, and perform central banking functions in addition to its commercial banking activities; before reactivating the Central Bank of China (CBC) in T'aipei in 1961. The functions of the Central Bank include regulation of the money market, management of foreign exchange, issuance of currency, and service as fiscal agent for the government. The Bank of China is a foreign exchange bank with branch offices in major world capitals. The Bank of Communications is an industrial bank specializing in industrial, mining, and transportation financing. The Export-Import Bank of China, inaugurated 1 February 1979, assists in the financing of Taiwan's export trade. The Central Trust of China acts as a government trading agency and handles most of the procurements of government organizations. The Postal Savings System accepts savings deposits and makes domestic transfers at post offices.

At the end of 1998 there were 45 domestic commercial banks, six medium business banks, and 46 foreign banks. There were also 52 credit cooperatives, 287 farmers' credit unions, and 27 fishermen's credit unions. The government holds majority status in several of the most important banks, including the Bank of Taiwan, the Cooperative Bank of Taiwan, and the First Commercial Bank. The two largest private banks are the International Commercial Bank of China and the Overseas Chinese Commercial Banking Corp. By 1998, three large government-owned provincial banks were on their way towards privatization, and others were set to follow.

In 1990 the government announced the goal of establishing the island as a regional financial center. Its original target of 1996 was far too optimistic, and liberalization will have to be far more thoroughgoing than that to which the authorities are at present committed, but various steps are being taken towards this end. Restrictions on bringing in capital from abroad, limits on capital transfers both in and out of Taiwan by domestic firms and individuals, and the operations of foreign banks have been liberalized. On 18 February 1997, the Finance Ministry set up a 37-member financial reform task force, headed by the finance minister. This group spent ten months devising proposals in the following four areas: improving the overall efficiency of the banking system; development of capital and derivatives markets, and relaxation of the rules governing the kinds of business banks may conduct; improving market-regulating procedures such as credit evaluation systems, asset management, investor insurance, and insider trading rules; and strengthening banks' internal financial controls.

Taiwan's first private corporate bond issue was floated in 1958. The first stock exchange in Taiwan opened on 4 February 1962. Volume was low until liberalization measures opened the market to foreigners, and the Taiwan stock market surged in the early months of 1997, with the index smashing through the 8,000-point barrier for the first time since 5 March 1990. This milestone immediately prompted rumblings from the CBC that the market was overheated. Yet by May 1997, the market was flirting with the next resistance level, at 8,500 points. Authorities raised the limits to foreign ownership in companies listed on the TAIEX from 30% to 50% in 1999. Most limits on foreign ownership were ended in 2000, and the index was up by the 10,000 mark in that year.

34INSURANCE

Insurance in Taiwan is supervised by the Ministry of Finance and may be written only by a limited liability company or a cooperative association. Aside from group insurance operated by the government, life and annuity insurance are comparatively undeveloped in Taiwan. The Chinese tradition that the family should take care of its members in sickness and old age lowered demand in the past, but social change and rapid economic growth have modified this situation, especially in industrial areas. In 1986, the Taiwanese government agreed to allow US companies to compete equally for insurance business. In 1999, nine foreign nonlife insurers were authorized to run full branches in Taiwan.

35PUBLIC FINANCE

Central government revenues come mostly from taxation, customs and duties, and income from government monopolies on tobacco and wines; other revenues are derived from profits realized by government enterprises. Government accounts showed surpluses through the early 1980s.

Public authorities anticipated a growing fiscal deficit throughout the 1990s as Taiwan's six-year development plan required over $300 billion of investment in public infrastructural construction projects and in upgrading industries. In 1996, the government's deficit was equal to 4% of GDP. Growing demands for social welfare spending and increased defense spending (up 20% in 1996/97, the largest rise in over a decade) continued to put pressure on the budget. Outstanding debt reached 16% of GNP in 1998, up from 6% in 1991, and debt service payments consumed 15% of the central budget in 1999. The government was committed to balancing the budget by 2001. Austerity measures included controlling public sector consumption expenditures, limiting expansion of government expenditures, freezing government employment, limiting public employee pay raises, and encouraging private participation in major public projects. The government was also committed to reducing the public sector's role in the economy. National defense expenditures as a portion of the central budget dropped from over 40% in 1960 to 20% in 1999, and were set to fall to 15% in 2000.

The US Central Intelligence Agency (CIA) estimates that in 1998 Taiwan's central government took in revenues of approximately $40 billion and had expenditures of $55 billion. Overall, the government registered a deficit of approximately $15 billion.

36TAXATION

All taxes are collected by the local government and transferred to the relevant provincial or central government agency. Tax revenues reserved for the central government include the income tax, estate (inheritance) tax, gift tax, customs duty, stamp tax, commodity tax, securities transaction tax, and mine tax. The rates for income tax payment for individuals ranges from 6% to a top rate of 40%. Corporate income taxes range from 15% to 50%. A VAT was applied in April 1986, amounting to 5%. There are no social security or local income taxes in Taiwan.

37CUSTOMS AND DUTIES

Customs duties are important revenue earners and consist principally of import duties and tonnage dues; the former are levied on dutiable commodities, the latter on ships that call at Taiwan ports. The average rate was 8.2% in 1998. Duties range from 2% to 60%. The seven duty categories include rubber tires, cement, beverages, oil and gas, electrical appliances, glass, and automobiles. In 1998, Taiwan reduced tariffs on a wide range of items. Articles imported for military use, for relief, or for educational or research purposes are exempted from import duty. Duties on imported raw materials for business can be rebated. Some agricultural products are prohibited from importation, such as rice, sugar, chicken, some pork cuts, peanuts, and certain dairy products. Imports from Japan and mainland China are restricted due to balance of payments problems.

38FOREIGN INVESTMENT

Total foreign direct investment in Taiwan from 1952 to 1998 equaled $33 billion with about 25% of this amount invested in the electronics and information industries. Investment was particularly strong in nearly doubled from 1994 to 1995 due to a large number of investments electronic, chemical, and power generation projects. To attract foreign investment, and gain membership in the World Trade Organization, Taiwan has taken steps to liberalize its economy and improve its investment environment. Increasing effort is going into making Taiwan an "Asia-Pacific regional operations center" by pursuing cooperation agreements with foreign companies interested in locating regional headquarters there. The US is the largest foreign investor in Taiwan with approved investment projects totaling $8.3 billion or 25% of the total. Japan ranked second with investments of $8 billion. Total foreign investment approvals in 1998 equaled $5.3 billion. Taiwanese foreign investment in mainland China has almost halved since aggressions flared in 1996.

39ECONOMIC DEVELOPMENT

Since 1950, the government has adopted a series of economic plans to help guide and promote economic growth and industrialization. The first four-year economic development plan (1953–56) emphasized reconstruction and increased production of rice, fertilizers, and hydroelectric power; it resulted in an increase of 37% in GNP and 17% in income per capita. In the second four-year plan (1957–60), import substitution industries were encouraged. Industry and agriculture both registered significant gains; GNP increased by 31%, and national income per capita by 13%. The third four-year plan (1961–64) emphasized labor-intensive export industries, basic services, energy development, industries contributing to agricultural growth, and exploration and development of the island's limited natural resources. The results were a 42% increase in GNP and a 31% increase in per capita income. US loans and grants, totaling $2.2 billion, and foreign (mostly overseas Chinese) investment financed these early stages of development.

Following the curtailment of AID assistance in 1965, the fourth four-year plan (1965–68) was introduced, followed by the fifth four-year plan (1969–72); increases in GNP for these periods were 46% and 55%, respectively. By 1971, exports of manufactured goods had registered spectacular increases, and Taiwan's foreign trade pattern changed from one of chronic deficit to consistent trade surpluses. At this point, the government began to redirect its priorities from labor-intensive industries to the development of such capital-intensive sectors as shipbuilding, chemicals, and petrochemicals. The sixth four-year plan (1973–76), adversely affected by the worldwide recession, was terminated in 1975 after producing only an 19% increase in GNP. It was replaced by a six-year plan (1976–81) that focused on expansion of basic industries and completion of 10 major infrastructural projects, including rail electrification, construction of the North Link railroad, development of nuclear energy, and construction of the steel mill at Kaohsiung and of the new port of T'aichung.

In 1978, the six-year plan was revised, and 12 new infrastructural projects were added, including completion of the round-the-island railroad, construction of three cross-island highways, expansion of T'aichung Port's harbor, and expansion of steel and nuclear energy facilities. A subsequent four-year plan (1986–89), designed to supplement a longer-range 10-year plan (1980–89), had as a target average annual GNP increase of 6.5%. Among its goals were price stability, annual growth of 7.5% in the service sector, trade liberalization, encouragement of balanced regional development, and redirection of new industrial growth into such high-technology industries as computers, robotics, and bioengineering. In response to flagging export growth and a slowdown in private investment following a stock market collapse in 1990, the government devised a Six-Year Plan for 1991–97 aimed at economic revitalization. The final plan has targeted investment mainly in transportation, telecommunications, power generation and pollution control. A "Statute for Upgrading Industries" enacted in early 1991 continues the government's efforts to provide incentives for private investment in research and development and high-technology sectors of the economy. Economic development in the late 1990s focused on a continuing privatization of government enterprises, the opening of the Taiwan market to foreigners, and high investment in the technological sector.

40SOCIAL DEVELOPMENT

A social insurance system provides medical, disability, old age, survivor, and other benefits, with employers paying 4.6% of payroll and workers contributing 1.3% of earnings. Retirement is allowed at any age with 25 or more years of coverage. In 1995, a National Health Insurance program took effect. Under this program, workers can obtain medical care under private or public clinics, paid for by the National Health Insurance Bureau. Firms with five or more employers are required to fund a workers' compensation program, contributing up to 3% of payroll, depending on risk level of work. Unemployment benefits are funded by employers, employees, and the government.

All enterprises and labor organizations must also furnish welfare funds for workers and "welfare units," such as cafeterias, nurseries, clinics, and low-rent housing. Fishermen, farmers, and salt workers have their own welfare funds. Government programs include relief for mainland refugees, calamity-relief assistance, and direct assistance to children in needy families.

Most laws discriminating against women in regard to property, divorce, and child custody were only eliminated in the latter part of the 1990s. Among other measures, laws passed during this period allowed married women to retain their maiden names, gave them an equal voice in child custody disputes, and clarified their property rights. The law now provides for equitable distribution of conjugal property in divorce cases. In the workplace, women tend to receive lower salaries and less frequent promotion, and are often denied federally mandated maternity leave. Taiwanese women married to foreigners may not transmit their citizenship to their children.

Child abuse is a serious problem. In 1993 the Child Welfare Act was revised and now mandates that any citizen aware of child abuse or neglect must report it to the authorities.

Human rights are generally well respected, but some cases of police abuse continue to be reported.

41HEALTH

As a result of improved living conditions and mass vaccinations, significant progress has been made in controlling malaria, tuberculosis, venereal disease, leprosy, trachoma, typhoid, diphtheria, and encephalitis. In 1999, the death rate was estimated at 5 per 1,000 population. The infant mortality rate was 6 per 1,000 live births, and life expectancy was 77.5 years. At the end of 1985, Taiwan's public health facilities included 55 general hospitals and 888 health stations. In 1990, there were 22,300 doctors.

42HOUSING

The evacuation of more than 2 million persons from the mainland to an already densely populated island in 1949 made the provision of low-cost housing an early priority. By 1979, more than 150,000 units of public housing had been built. Since the 1970s, government housing programs have focused on the cities, with slum clearance and the construction of high-rise apartment dwellings for low-income groups the major priorities. Two new towns were constructed in the early 1980s, and a third was planned. The government set a target of 600,000 new housing units for the 1979–89 decade, but only 236,106 units were completed as of 1986. The total housing stock stood at 4,740,000 units in 1992. The number of people per dwelling was 4.3 as of 1988.

43EDUCATION

Taiwan enjoys one of the world's highest literacy rates because of its emphasis on education. In 1997 about 93% of people ages six or older were estimated to be literate. All children receive nine years of free and compulsory education provided at government expense, including six years in public primary school and three years in junior high. Salaries of the teaching staff are paid by local governments. While textbooks and tuition are free, children must buy their own notebooks and pencils. In 1968 the curriculum was revised with more emphasis on science, while maintaining the Chinese cultural tradition. In order to attend high school, students must pass an examination after junior high. After completing nine years of compulsory schooling, approximately 90.7% of students in the latter half of the 1990s continued their studies at a senior high or vocational school. Agriculture, engineering, commerce, maritime navigation, home economics, and nursing are some of the skills taught in vocational schools, which offer three-year programs.

As of 1997, Taiwan had over 100 institutions of higher education. More than 100,000 students take the joint college entrance exam each year. Approximately 61.9% of the candidates are admitted to a college or university. The government relaxed many restrictions which prevented students from studying abroad in the 1980s. Although Taiwan has a highly developed college curriculum, many students do travel abroad to study. Taiwanese college and graduate students are particularly interested in engineering, computer science, natural science, and business management. In the latter half of the 1990s, about 13,000 students annually pursued graduate study in the US.

44LIBRARIES AND MUSEUMS

The National Central Library in T'aipei holds more than 1,615,000 items, including a collection of rare Chinese books (180,000 volumes). The National Taiwan University in T'aipei has more than 1,500,000 volumes in collected holdings.

The major museums, all in T'aipei, are the National Palace Museum, National Museum of History, and the Taiwan Museum. The National Palace Museum houses one of the world's largest collections of Chinese art—the collection consists primarily of treasures brought from the mainland. The National Museum of History, founded in 1955, has more than 30,000 items in its collections of oracle bones and ritual vessels of the Shang and Chou dynasties, earthenware of the Sui and T'ang dynasties, stone engravings of the Han dynasty, and jade articles of the Chou dynasty. The Taiwan Museum has the most complete collection of natural history specimens in the country. The National Taiwan Science Education Center in T'aipei houses a planetarium and scientific exhibits.

45 MEDIA

Telecommunications services are owned by the government. By 1998 there were 11.5 telephone subscribers in Taiwan, as compared with 598,504 in 1974. Nearly all telephone service is automatic. The postal service is managed by the Directorate General of Posts under the Ministry of Communications.

Radio broadcasting stations in Taiwan are under the supervision of the Ministry of Communications. As of 1999 there were 158 AM and 48 FM radio stations and 29 television stations. The largest network is the Broadcasting Corp. of China, which operates three systems: an overseas service, known as the Voice of Free China; the mainland service, known as the Central Broadcasting Station, aimed at the Chinese mainland; and the domestic service. These stations broadcast in 14 languages and dialects. Television was introduced in 1962. In 1997 the number of television sets was estimated at 48 per 1,000 population, and the number of radios at 386.

The leading newspapers, their orientation, and estimated 1999 daily circulations are as follows:

	ORIENTATION	CIRCULATION
United Daily News (T'aipei)	Independent	1,300,000
China Daily News (T'aipei)	NA	100,000
China Times (T'aipei)	Independent	1,270,000
Central Daily News (T'aipei)	Official KMT	600,000
Independence Evening Post (T'aipei)	NA	340,700

The Central News Agency was established on the mainland by the KMT in 1924.

Though authorities generally respect constitutionally provided rights to free speech and free press, these rights are formally circumscribed by a law excluding the advocacy of communism or division of national territory. Controls over radio and television are said to be under a process of liberalization and privatization.

46 ORGANIZATIONS

The most influential private organizations are the occupational or trade associations. These include associations of farmers, fishermen, trade unions, business leaders, and professional persons. Organizations devoted to social welfare and relief work are sponsored by the government, by religious groups, and by civic clubs. The Taiwan Federation of Chambers of Commerce has branches in all the principal cities.

Cooperatives are an important adjunct to economic life, especially in the urban centers. In rural areas, agricultural cooperatives help the farmers transport and market special farm products such as fruits, tea, citronella oil, and handicrafts. Consumer cooperatives numbered 4,428 at the end of 1990, with 3,584,433 members. Cooperative farms, organized with the help of the government, operate either on a community basis, with the products distributed among the members, or on an individual basis, with the cooperative functioning as a purchasing, processing, and marketing agency.

Agricultural services and 4-H clubs in various parts of Taiwan provide training and social activities for boys and girls. Both the YMCA and YWCA are active in Taiwan, as is Little League baseball.

47 TOURISM, TRAVEL, AND RECREATION

In 1997, tourist arrivals totaled an estimated 2,372,000 of whom 65% were from East Asia and the Pacific. Tourism receipts totaled US$3.4 billion. Hotel construction has boomed as a result of government investment. In 1997 there were 19,402 rooms with a 64% occupancy rate. Visitors need a valid passport and tourist visa good for two weeks to 60 days.

T'aipei is the chief tourist attraction, with such popular sites as the seat of government in Presidential Square, Lungshan Temple, and the nearby National Palace Museum and famous Yangmingshan Park. Attractions outside the capital include Shihmen Dam recreation area, Lake Tzuhu, and the mausoleum of Chiang Kai-shek. The many temples and Dutch relics of T'ainan, Taiwan's oldest city, and Sun Moon Lake near T'aichung also attract numerous visitors. The national sports are baseball, soccer, and basketball.

48 FAMOUS TAIWANESE

Among the many Chinese scholars who have lived in Taiwan since 1949 are Hu Shih (1891–1962), philosopher and president of the Academia Sinica; Chiang Monlin (1886–1964), educator and chairman of the Joint Commission on Rural Reconstruction; Li Chi (1896–1979) and Tung Tso-pin (1895–1963), archaeologists, whose discoveries at the Anyang site laid the foundation for modern Chinese archaeology; and Tsiang Ting-fu (Ting-fu Fuller Tsiang, 1895–1965), historian and long-time delegate to the UN. Chang Ta-chien (1899–1983) is known for his painting of landscapes and figures and his copies of the famous Buddhist mural paintings of Tunhwang caves in Gansu Province. Lin Yutang (1895–1976), poet, philosopher, lexicographer, and historian, was one of China's foremost interpreters for Western cultures.

The outstanding political and military figure of Nationalist China and postwar Taiwan was Chiang Kai-shek (Chiang Chung-cheng, 1887–1975), who was responsible for sustaining the spirit of anticommunism in Taiwan. His son, Chiang Ching-kuo (1910–88), assumed leadership of the Taiwan government from Chiang Kai-shek's death to his own.

49 DEPENDENCIES

Taiwan has no territories or colonies.

50 BIBLIOGRAPHY

Ahern, Emily. The Anthropology of Taiwanese Society. Stanford, Calif.: Stanford University Press, 1981.

Copper, John F. Historical Dictionary of Taiwan (Republic of China). 2d ed. Lanham, Md.: Scarecrow Press, 2000.

Goddard, William G. Formosa: A Study in Chinese History. East Lansing: Michigan State University Press, 1966.

Hood, Steven J. The Kuomintang and the Democratization of Taiwan. Boulder, Colo.: Westview, 1997.

Hsiung, Ping-Chun. Living Rooms as Factories: Class, Gender, and the Satellite Factory System in Taiwan. Philadelphia, Pa.: Temple University Press, 1996.

Hsueh, Chi. The Foreign Factor: The Multinational Corporation's Contribution to the Economic Modernization of the Republic of China. Stanford, Calif.: Hoover Institution Press, 1990.

Kemenade, Willem van. (Diane Webb, trans.) China, Hong Kong, Taiwan, Inc.: The Dynamics to a New Empire. New York: Vintage Books, 1998.

Li, Kuo-ting. The Evolution of Policy Behind Taiwan's Development Success. New Haven: Yale University Press, 1988.

Lin, Zhiling and Thomas W. Robinson (eds.). The Chinese and their Future: Beijing, Taipei, and Hong Kong. Washington, D.C.: AEI Press, 1994.

Long, Simon. *Taiwan: China's Last Frontier.* New York: St. Martin's, 1990.

Marsh, Robert. *The Great Transformation: Social Change in Taipei, Taiwan Since the 1960s.* Armonk, N.Y.: M.E. Sharpe, 1996.

Metraux, Daniel Alfred. *Taiwan's Political and Economic Growth in the Late Twentieth Century.* Lewiston, N.Y.: E. Mellen Press, 1991.

Shepherd, John Robert. *Statecraft and Political Economy on the Taiwan Frontier, 1600–1800.* Stanford, Calif.: Stanford University Press, 1993.

Tien, Hung-mao. *The Great Transition: Political and Social Change in the Republic of China.* Stanford, Calif.: Hoover Institution Press, Stanford University, 1989.

Wang, Huei-Huang. *Technology, Economic Security, State, and the Political Economy of Economic Networks: a Historical and Comparative Research on the Evolution of Economic Networks in Taiwan and Japan.* Lanham, Md.: University Press of America, 1998.

Yu, Bin. *Dynamics and Dilemma: Mainland, Taiwan and Hong Kong in a Changing World.* New York: Nova Science Publishers, 1996.

TAJIKISTAN

Republic of Tajikistan
Respublica i Tojikistan

CAPITAL: Dushanbe.

FLAG: Three horizontal stripes of red (top), white, and green with a yellow crown and seven yellow, five-pointed stars in the center of the white stripe.

MONETARY UNIT: The Tajik ruble (TR) was introduced in May 1995. TR1=US$0.000595 (US$1=TR1680) as of 31 March 2000.

WEIGHTS AND MEASURES: The metric system is used.

HOLIDAYS: New Year's Day, 1 January; Navruz ("New Day"), 21 March; Independence Day, 9 September.

TIME: 6 PM = noon GMT.

¹LOCATION, SIZE, AND EXTENT

Tajikistan is located in southern Asia, between Uzbekistan and China. Comparatively, it is slightly smaller than the state of Wisconsin with a total area of 143,100 sq km (55,251 sq mi). Tajikistan's boundary length totals 3,651 km (2,269 mi).

Its capital city, Dushanbe, is located in the western part of the country.

²TOPOGRAPHY

The topography of Tajikistan features the Pamir and Altay mountains which dominate the landscape. The western Fergana Valley lies in the north with the Kafirnigan and Vakhsh valleys in the southwest. The major geographic feature in the south is the Panj River, which separates southern Tajikistan from northern Afghanistan. Six percent of Tajkistan's land is arable with approximately 5% under irrigation.

³CLIMATE

The climate is semiarid to polar in the Pamirs and Tien Sham mountains. The mean temperature in July is 30°C (86°F). The mean temperature in January is 0°C (32°F). Rainfall in the country averages 12.2 cm (4.8 in).

⁴FLORA AND FAUNA

Wildflowers can be found in the valleys of the mountains, Marco Polo sheep, yak, and snow leopards can be found in the mountains.

⁵ENVIRONMENT

Industrial emissions and excessive use of pesticides are leading causes of environmental damage in Tajikistan. Over the last 30 years, increased irrigation to support agricultural activity has resulted in harmful levels of soil salinity, which damage the soil and threaten its productivity.

The nation's water supply is threatened by pollution and inadequate sanitation facilities. Overutilization of the shrinking Aral Sea for irrigation purposes has caused it to become polluted. Eighty-five percent of Tajikistan's farm population does not have an indoor water supply. Only 0.6% of the country's total land area is protected; six of its mammal species and nine bird species are threatened. Threatened species include the argali, tiger, and snow leopard.

⁶POPULATION

The population of Tajikistan in 2000 was estimated at 6,194,373. An estimated 4.3% of the population is 65 years of age or older. The projected population for the year 2005 is 6,720,000, assuming a crude birthrate of 28 per 1,000 population and a death rate of 8, resulting in a natural rate of change of 2.0% for the period 2000–2005. The population rate of change between 1995 and 2000 was 1.9%. The population density in 1998 was 43 per sq km (111 per sq mi).

It was estimated that 33% of the population lived in urban areas in 2000, up from 34% in 1980. The capital city, Dushanbe, had a 2000 population of 664,000. Khojand (formerly Leninabad) had a population of about 163,000.

⁷MIGRATION

As a result of the civil war that began in 1991, more than 600,000 people were internally displaced, and 60,000 were forced into Northern Afghanistan by January 1993. Also between 1991 and 1995, 300,000 Russians, 30,000 Ukrainians, and 10,000 Belarusians all left Tajikistan. By April 1997, virtually all of the internally displaced people had returned to their homes. When the peace agreement was reached in June 1997, the UNHCR completed the repatriation of Tajik refugees from northern Afghanistan to Tajikistan. In 1998 the UNHCR started the voluntary repatriation of Tajik refugees from other countries. By 1999, some 20,000 refugees had returned to their places of origin. The net migration rate in 1999 was -5.34 migrants per 1,000 population.

⁸ETHNIC GROUPS

In 1999, Tajiks constituted 64.9% of the population and Uzbeks (who live in the northwest) 25%. The Russian population, declining because of emigration, comprised only 3.5%, down from 7.6% in 1989. Other varied ethnic groups made up the remaining 6.6%.

⁹LANGUAGES

Tajiki is an Indo-European language, related to Farsi and Pashto. In 1989, Tajiki became the sole official language of the country, displacing Russian and Uzbeki. Since 1995, Russian, which had retained its status as the language of international communication in government and business, has regained its previous

LOCATION: 15°0′N; 39°0′E. **BOUNDARY LENGTHS:** Total boundary lengths, 3,651 km (2,269 mi); Afghanistan, 1,206 km (749.4 mi); China, 414 km (257.3 mi); Kyrgyzstan, 870 km (541 mi); Uzbekistan, 1,161 km (721.4 mi).

status, albeit alongside Tajiki. Uzbeki is spoken in regions predominantly inhabited by Uzbeks.

The Tajiki language has no genders or cases, and its vocabulary is borrowed from Arabic, Uzbeki, and Russian. Since the 1940s, the Tajik alphabet has been a modified version of the Russian Cyrillic alphabet. Since the adoption of Tajiki as the national language, instruction of the Arabic-based Persian alphabet in schools has been encouraged, with teaching materials provided by Iran.

¹⁰RELIGIONS

An estimated 95% of citizens in 1999 considered themselves to be Muslims, but the degree of observance varies widely. About

3% of these are Ismailis, almost all residing in the remote Gorno-Badakhshan region. The rest of the Muslim population is Sunni. There are approximately 235,000 Christians, mostly ethnic Russians. The largest Christian group is Russian Orthodox; however, there are also Baptists, Roman Catholics, Seventh-Day Adventists, Korean Protestants, Lutherans, and Jehovah's Witnesses. Other religious minorities include Baha'is, Hare Krishnas, and Jews, each totaling less than 1% of the population.

¹¹TRANSPORTATION

Some 480 km (298 mi) of railroads are in common carrier service (not including industrial lines) in Tajikistan. A 258-km (160 mi)

line connects Dushanbe with Termez, Uzbekistan, and ultimately with the other rail systems of the former Soviet Union.

In 1996, there were some 13,700 km (8,513 mi) of roadways, of which 11,330 km (7,040 mi) were hard-surfaced. The major roads connect Khudzhand in the north to Kulyab in the south via Dushanbe. Only one main road services the eastern Gorno-Badakhshanskaya region, meandering from Khrough to Kyrgyzstan. Transportation in urban areas has suffered in recent years, primarily because supplies of gasoline from Russia have become unreliable. Roads connecting residential suburban areas with cities are not designed to handle large volumes of commuter traffic. Dushanbe has a system of electric trolleys and gas powered buses, but operation has been erratic due to a lack of spare parts and fuel.

Tajikistan had 59 airports at last estimate, of which 14 had paved runways. In 1997, the country's airlines carried 594,000 passengers on scheduled domestic and international flights.

12HISTORY

The territory of Tajikistan has been continuously inhabited since the early Stone Age. The first Central Asian states of Sogdia and Bactria in the first millennium BC, included portions of Tajikistan. The territory was Persian-controlled from the 6th century BC, until conquered by Alexander the Great in 329 BC. Much of Tajikistan was included in the Greco-Bactrian kingdom in 3rd century BC, and after displaced by the Tochari tribes who invaded Sogdia a century later. The Kushana kingdom was established in the first centuries of the Christian era, when a number of cities were established, and agriculture and commerce grew. In the 5th and 6th centuries, parts of Tajikistan were conquered by nomadic tribes, the Chionites and, later, the Ephthalites.

At the end of the 6th century the large Ephthalite empire was displaced by the Eastern Turkic Kaganate. Arabs conquered the area in the 8th century, introducing Islam. Later in the 9th century they were displaced by the Samanides, who encouraged the development of trade and of material culture. From the 10th to the 13th centuries a number of kingdoms succeeded one another in Central Asia; among the ones which included parts of Tajikistan were the Ghaznavids, the Karakhanids, the Ghorids, the Karakitai, and the Khwarazmites.

In 1219–1221 Genghiz Khan's troops conquered the entire area, destroying many cities. Tajikistan became part of the lands given to Genghiz Khan's son, Chagatai. In the 14th century Timur (Tamerlane) created a large empire, with its capital in Samarkand. In the 16th century Tajikistan was conquered by the Sheibanids, who had their capital in Bukhara. Portions of territory were included later in the Ashtarkhanid state and then in the Kokand Khanate, which emerged in the Fergana Valley in the mid 18th century Present-day Tajikistan was split between the Khanates of Bukhara and Kokand in the 18th and 19th centuries.

In 1863, Russia asserted a right to exercise dominance in Central Asia, and began the military conquest of the khanates. Bukhara and Samarkand were incorporated into Russia in 1868. Kokand was eliminated in 1876, and the border with Afghanistan was set by accord with England in 1895. At that point, part of Tajikistan was in the Emirate of Bukhara, part was in Turkestan. When the Tsar's draft call-up of 1916 was announced, rebellions broke out all over Central Asia, including in Tajikistan. These were suppressed, at great loss of life.

Northern Tajikistan was conquered by the Bolsheviks in 1918, who extended control to the rest of the country when Bukhara was captured, in 1920. Muslim guerrilla warfare termed the Basmachi Rebellion was finally suppressed in 1924. Tajikistan was established as an autonomous republic within the Uzbek Soviet Socialist Republic in 1924. The republic became a full Soviet Socialist Republic in 1929.

Border delineations in Central Asia were very arbitrary. For several hundred years educated Central Asians had used Persian and Turkic languages essentially equally, so that separation into Turkic-speaking Uzbeks and Persian-speaking Tajiks, as if to create separate nationalities, was primarily administrative. Bukhara and Samarkand, the major Tajik cities, were included in Uzbekistan, while Tajikistan was left only with smaller cities, and little arable land. People were forced to assume one nationality or another.

In the late Soviet period Tajikistan was the poorest and least developed of the republics. It comprised four separate areas, the elites of which competed for power. Traditionally power was held by people from Khojent, which is geographically and culturally closest to Uzbekistan's Fergana valley. They were contested by families and clans from Kulyab, south of Dushanbe. Poorest were people from the Gorno Badakhshan Autonomous Province, most of which is in the Pamir Mountains. The final area was Kurgan-Tyube, in the extreme south, where the influence of Islam was strong; public calls for establishing an Islamic state were heard there as early as 1976.

In 1985, Mikhail Gorbachev replaced longtime republic leader Rakhmon Nabiyev with Kakhar Makhkamov, whose control never penetrated to the most local levels. Riots in February 1990 exposed his weaknesses, and encouraged a proliferation of political parties and groups. When the August 1991 Soviet coup attempt came, Makhkamov was the only republic leader to welcome it. When the coup failed, Makhkamov was forced to resign, and Nabiyev returned to power.

The republic declared independence on 9 September 1991, and presidential elections were hotly contested 27 October 1991. Nabiyev used communist control of the media and cells in the workplace to influence the election. Despite this influence, his opponent Davlat Khudonazarov, a popular filmmaker, received more than 30% of the vote. Opposition to Nabiyev continued, however, resulting in massive demonstrations and the formation of a national guard by Nabiyev and militias by the oppositionists. In April 1992, demonstrators for and against Nabiyev took over two public squares in Dushanbe, about a mile apart. Clashes between the two caused several deaths, and tensions mounted. In May, the Russian garrison in Dushanbe stepped in to mediate tensions, brokering a compromise that called for Nabiyev to form a coalition government in which one-third of the ministerial posts would go to oppositionists. Nabiyev named his supporter, Akbarsho Iskandarov, the new legislative speaker to help form a coalition government, and brought token democrats and Islamists into the government, including Kazi-kolon Khojiakbar Turajonzoda, the senior Muslim cleric in the republic.

Civil disorder grew throughout summer 1992. In August 1992, Nabiyev was seized at gunpoint and forced to resign, and Iskandarov assumed control of the government. By this time full civil war had erupted, with thousands of casualties. In November, Iskandarov gave up his efforts to govern, and Uzbekistan and Russia joined in the efforts by hard-liners to drive the Iskandarov government and its supporters out of the country, mostly into neighboring Afghanistan. The rump Supreme Soviet, dominated by hard-liners, met in Khojand, and Imomaliy Rakhmonov became the leader. Rakhmonov, a Kulyabi, was a former collective farm chairman linked to a major hard-line warlord. Kulyabi and Khojenti hard-liners, assisted by Uzbekistan and Russia, launched a successful counteroffensive that by the end of 1992 had resulted in 20,000-40,000 casualties and up to 800,000 refugees or displaced persons, about 80,000 of whom fled to Afghanistan.

In 1993, the Commonwealth of Independent States (CIS) authorized "peacekeeping" in Tajikistan under the auspices of its Collective Peacekeeping Forces (CPF) treaty to protect what Russia terms "CIS borders." CPF consisted of Russia's 201st

Rifle Division, based in Tajikistan, and token Kazakh, Kyrgyz, and Uzbek troops (the Kyrgyz and Uzbek troops pulled out in 1998–99). Russian media reported in late 1999 that there were about 20,000 CPF, border, and other Russian troops in Tajikistan. The commander of the CPF troops in August 1999 stated that the role of his forces had largely shifted to the delivery of humanitarian cargos, clearing mines, and giving medical assistance. Nonetheless, plans to withdraw the CPF have not been announced, perhaps because in April 1999, Russia and Tajikistan signed a basing agreement for the 25-year presence of Russian troops.

After Tajik government and opposition emissaries agreed to a cease-fire in September 1994, the UNSC formally established a UN Mission of Observers in Tajikistan (UNMOT) in December 1994 with a mandate to monitor the cease-fire, later expanded to investigate cease-fire violations, monitor the demobilization of opposition fighters, assist ex-combatants to integrate into society, and offer advice for holding elections. The UN reported in late 1999 that UNMOT comprised 167 civilian staff and 37 military observers.

In November 1994, Rakhmanov held presidential elections in an attempt to legitimize his government. The main Tajik opposition groups boycotted this election and a constitutional referendum because they had no say in drawing up the draft constitution and would not be allowed to field their own candidates. Only one candidate besides Rakhmanov was permitted to run, Abdumalik Abdullojanov, a prominent politician in the northern Leninabad region and a former Tajik prime minister. Rakhmanov was elected president by a wide margin and his constitution was overwhelmingly approved. The Organization for Security and Cooperation in Europe (OSCE) declined to send monitors because it viewed the electoral process as not meeting its standards. Elections to a new 181-member legislature took place in February 1995. Four parties were allowed to compete, but restrictive nomination procedures ensured that about 40 percent of candidates ran unopposed. The election excluded virtually all opposition parties, and Western groups refused to monitor the "seriously flawed" vote.

In December 1996, the two sides agreed to set up a National Reconciliation Commission (NRC), an executive body composed equally of government and opposition emissaries. On June 27, 1997, Rakhmanov and United Tajik Opposition (UTO) leader Seyed Abdullo Nuri signed the *comprehensive peace agreement*, under which Rakhmanov remained president but 30% of ministerial posts were allocated to the opposition and Nuri headed the NRC.

As part of the peace process, in early September 1999, the Tajik legislature set presidential elections for November 6, 1999. Only after a popular referendum approved constitutional changes in late September, however, were the opposition Islamic Revival and Democratic parties legalized and allowed to gather 100,000 signatures to register nominees. Nominees complained that they did not have enough time to gather signatures and that Rakhmanov's appointees at the local level blocked signature-gathering. The Central Electoral Commission (CEC), controlled by Rakhmanov, then pronounced him the only candidate. This prompted the resignation of opposition members of the NRC and calls for an electoral boycott. To provide the gloss of a multi-candidate race, the CEC "registered" IRP nominee Davlat Usmon, though he refused to run. The CEC announced that 98% of 2.85 million Tajiks had turned out and 96.9% had voted for Rakhmanov, and only 2% for Usmon. Seeking to avert renewed civil war, Nuri agreed on November 5 to respect the outcome of the election and rejoin the NRC in return for pledges by Rakhmanov to allow fair legislative elections that were held in March 2000.

On 26 March 2000, Tajikistan disbanded its National Reconciliation Commission (NRC), created to implement 1997 peace accords ending the civil war. The accords set legislative elections held in March as the culmination of the peace process. Former rebel Seyed Abdullo Nuri, chairman of the NRC, called for quick settlement of remaining peace issues. The UN Security Council on March 21 praised the legislative elections and work of the NRC, and supported withdrawing UN observers in May 2000.

Although benchmarks of the peace process have been largely met, including the return of refugees, demilitarization of rebel forces, legalization of rebel parties, and the holding of presidential and legislative elections, stability in Tajikistan remains fragile. An unsuccessful insurrection in the Leninabad region of northern Tajikistan launched by notorious warlord Mahmud Khudoyberdiyev in November 1998 highlights concerns by some observers about secessionist tendencies in Leninabad region and about ethnic tensions between ethnic Tajiks and Uzbeks in Tajikistan.

13GOVERNMENT

The Tajik government has been in a state of flux as it has implemented the comprehensive peace settlement. President Rakhmanov retains extensive power and his supporters from the Kulyab region remain dominant in the government, though some high-level posts have been given to the opposition.

According to a Rakhmanov-designed constitution approved by referendum in November 1994, the Oliy Majlis (legislature) enacts laws, interprets the constitution, determines basic directions of domestic and foreign policy, sets dates for referenda and elections, and approves key ministerial and other appointments. The legislature also approves the state budget, determines tax policy, ratifies treaties, and approves a state of war or emergency as decreed by the president. The constitution also calls for creation of a presidium to "organize work," to be elected by the legislators and to be headed by the speaker. Laws are required to be passed by a two-thirds majority of the total number of deputies, and a presidential veto may be overridden by the same margin. The prime minister is appointed by the president. The Tajik legislature in June 1999 rubber-stamped constitutional changes proposed by Rakhmanov calling for a seven year presidential term, a two-house Supreme Assembly (legislature), and the legalization of religious parties. A popular referendum approved the changes on 26 September 1999.

An electoral law was approved with input from the opposition on 10 December 1999. The law calls for the upper legislative chamber, the National Assembly (representing regional interests), to consist of 33 members, and the lower chamber, the Assembly of Representatives, 63 members.

Elections to the lower legislative chamber were set for 27 February 2000 (and a runoff on 12 March). In all, 191 candidates contested 41 single mandate seats and 107 candidates on six party lists competed for 22 seats. Turnout was reported by the CEC at 93.23% of 2.87 million voters. In the party list voting, Rakhmanov's People's Democratic Party (PDP) won fifteen seats, the Communist Party won five seats, and the Islamic Renaissance Party won two seats. Twenty-seven single mandate seats were filled in the 1st round, and twelve in the 2nd. Most winners of these seats are PDP members. Over 107 U.N and OSCE observers monitored the race. They praised the "political pluralism" of the vote, since voters "were presented with a genuine and broad range of alternatives," but concluded that the electoral process must be improved "to meet the minimum democratic standards for equal, fair, free, secret, transparent, and accountable elections." They raised questions about freedom of the media, the independence of electoral commissions, the questionable de-registration of some candidates, apparently inflated turnout figures, and the transparency of vote tabulation. Thirty-three upper legislative chamber seats were filled on March 23 by indirect voting by local assemblies and the appointment of eight members by Rakhmanov. The UN Security Council on March 21 praised the legislative elections and work of the NRC, and supported withdrawing UN observers in May 2000.

14POLITICAL PARTIES

As part of the ongoing peace process, all parties had to undergo re-registration by March 1999. The parties registered at that time were the People's Democratic Party (PDP), Communist Party (TCP), the Party of Justice and Progress, Socialist Party, the Democratic Party ("Tehran platform"), Agrarian Party, and the Party of Justice and Accord. The main opposition parties were registered later. In late 1994, Rakhmanov orchestrated the creation of the PDP, and in April 1998 became its head. The TCP is headed by former Rakhmanov client Shodi Shabdolov. The TCP has fallen into Rakhmanov's disfavor, and some of its assets were nationalized in May 1998. A social democratic Party of Justice and Progress was formed by intellectuals and others in April 1998. The Democratic Party, founded in 1990, was banned in 1993. It split in 1994, with one new group forming the "Tehran platform." The remaining wing ("Almaty platform") was reregistered in December 1999. The main parties of the United Tajik Opposition (UTO) are the Democratic Party (Almaty platform) and the Islamic Rebirth Movement (primarily the Islamic Renaissance Party, IRP). The Society of Lali Badakhshan split from the UTO in 1999. The IRP was registered in September 1999. The IRP has traditionally drawn its strength from many unofficial (as opposed to state-sponsored) Islamic clerics.

15LOCAL GOVERNMENT

In the late Soviet era the republic was divided into three oblasts or regions and the Gorno Badakhshan Autonomous Region. The Tajik government has refused to recognize Gorno Badakhshan's demands for greater autonomy. The region surrounding the capital, Dushanbe, also was separately administered by the central government. A new region, Khatlon, was formed by Rakhmanov, comprising the former Qurghonteppa and Kulyab regions. Uzbekistan has some influence in the northern Leninabad (Khojenti) region, while Russian troops control the capital region and patrol the borders with Afghanistan and China. Regions, districts, and cities are governed by elected assemblies of people's deputies headed by a chairman. The chairman is appointed by the president, and the national legislature can dissolve local assemblies if it decides they are breaking the law.

16JUDICIAL SYSTEM

The judicial system from the Soviet period remains largely in place. There are courts at the city, district, regional, and national levels with a separate but parallel system of military courts. National level courts include the Supreme Court, the Constitutional Court, the Supreme Economic Court, and the Military Court. Regional and national level courts function in an appellate capacity to the lower courts.

The president appoints judges and the procurator general to five-year terms with confirmation by the legislature, and the president has the power to dismiss them. The court system suffers from a lack of trained judges and lawyers and from pressures applied by local political factions and the central government.

The law requires public trials except in cases involving national security or protection of minors. There is a right to appointed counsel in criminal cases. As in the Soviet period, the procurators are responsible for arrests, investigations, and prosecutions of defendants.

According to the U.S. State Department's *Country Reports on Human Rights Practices for 1999,* Tajikistan during most of the 1990s was an authoritarian state, where the government limited the right of citizens to change their government peacefully and freely. Tajik government security forces in 1999 were responsible for some killings and beatings of detainees, and also engaged in threats, extortion, looting, and other abuse of civilians. Prison conditions were life threatening, and the judicial system was subject to political and paramilitary pressure. Opposition forces were responsible for serious abuses of civilians, including killing, kidnaping, threats, and extortion. During 1999, several opposition parties were registered, but the November 1999 presidential election was not viewed by the OSCE as "free and fair." In December 1999, Rakhmanov issued a decree pledging to "contribute in every way possible to the exercise of freedom of speech, freedom of the press, and the right of access to the news media" as part of the comprehensive peace settlement.

17ARMED FORCES

There are an estimated 7,000–9,000 personnel in the armed forces. The army has about 7,000 with 40 main battle tanks. There are an estimated 1,200 paramilitary border guards. The defense budget for 1997 was $19.3 million or 1.8% of GDP. An opposition Islamic movement of 5,000 signed a peace agreement with the government in 1997 and was in the process of being integrated into the government forces.

18INTERNATIONAL COOPERATION

Tajikistan became a member of the UN on 2 March 1992. It also is a member of the OSCE, IMF, NACC, and the World Bank, and is applying for membership in other international organizations. It has observer status at the WTO. A member of the CIS, the country is recognized by the US and the EU countries. Western nations are especially concerned with the security of the country's uranium reserves. Tajikistan has especially close ties with Iran.

19ECONOMY

Tajikistan is the poorest of the post-Soviet republics. Agriculture, dominated by cotton production, is the largest of the country's economic sectors, providing 25% of GDP and 52% of total employment (with forestry). Industry is poorly developed, making up just 35% of total production and 17% of employment, and involving mainly electric power generation, aluminum production, and some labor intensive processing of local and imported raw materials. Imports provide virtually all of the country's manufactured consumer needs. Deposits of nonferrous metals are significant but underdeveloped.

Wracked by conflict between rival groups vying for control of the central government, Tajikistan has also been among the economies hardest hit by sociopolitical and economic instability following the dissolution of the USSR. Already in decline by the late 1980s, GDP shrunk by 0.6% in 1990 and 8.7% in 1991. Legislation adopted in 1992 aimed at laying the groundwork for the transition to a market economy and creating conditions favorable to badly needed foreign investment. Implementation of restructuring plans, however, was stunted by the outbreak of violent civil strife during the summer of 1992. The war severely weakened the economy and left Tajikistan dependent on Russia and Uzbekistan and on international humanitarian assistance for much of its basic subsistence needs. GDP declined by almost 17% in 1996 after posting a 12.4% decline in 1995. Thanks to a tight monetary policy, however, inflation fell from 635% in 1995 to below 5% in 1997.

A tentative peace agreement was signed in 1997. The transition from a command economy to a market driven one saw progress in 1996 and 1997 as the government proposed to speed up privatization efforts and enact fiscal, insurance, and banking reforms necessary to stabilize the economy and provide for economic growth. Inflation increased to over 46% in 1998 in the wake of the Russian financial crisis. GDP, however, grew at 5.3% for the same year.

[20]INCOME

The US Central Intelligence Agency (CIA) reports that in 1998 Tajikistan's gross domestic product (GDP) was estimated at $6 billion. The per capita GDP was estimated at $990. The annual growth rate of GDP was estimated at 5.3%. The average inflation rate in 1998 was 46%. The CIA defines GDP as the value of all final goods and services produced within a nation in a given year and computed on the basis of purchasing power parity (PPP) rather than value as measured on the basis of the rate of exchange. It was estimated that agriculture accounted for 25% of GDP, industry 35%, and services 40%.

The World Bank reports that for the same period per capita private consumption (in PPP terms) was $660. Private consumption includes expenditures of individuals, households, and nongovernmental organizations. Approximately 48% of household consumption was spent on food, 10% on fuel, 0% on health care, and 14% on education.

[21]LABOR

Total employment was reported at 1,143,000 in 1997, with 2.7% unemployment.

With the demise of the Soviet Union, there is no longer the mandate for a single labor union structure. As of 1996, the Confederation of Trade Unions remained the dominant labor organization (1.5 million members), even though it no longer is subordinate to the Communist Party. In April 1990, the independent Labor Union of Private Sector Enterprises and Organizations was formed and claimed 37,000 members in 1998.

Employment in Tajikistan may legally begin at age 16, or at age 15 with local trade union permission. Children from the age of 7 often help with harvests, but their work is considered "family assistance." The 40-hour work week is standard. A minimum wage is in place, although it does not provide a decent standard of living for the worker and family. An estimated 20% of industrial laborers worked in unhealthy or otherwise hazardous conditions, although many see this as greatly underreporting the number of persons working in substandard conditions. The minimum age for employment is 15 but many children work, especially in the agricultural sector.

[22]AGRICULTURE

Tajik agriculture relies extensively on irrigation. About 6% of the total area is cropland, although 23% is used for permanent pastures. A network of canals expands agriculture into semidesert areas. Agriculture accounted for 6% of GDP in 1998.

Cotton is the major commercial crop; three irrigated valleys (Vakhsh, Kofarnihon, and Zeravshan) are the sites of most production. As a result of chronic problems with machinery and the lack of spare parts, machine harvesting is declining. The 1998 cotton harvest was 154,000 tons, but less than 10,000 tons were picked by machine

Wheat is the staple grain and is grown mainly in the northern and southern plains. About one-third of the wheat crop is irrigated. In 1998, wheat production was 470,000 tons. Production has been declining in recent years because of lack of machinery and civil war. During the 1996/97 growing season, the government eliminated most of the state order for wheat, legalized contract farming, freed wheat prices, established commodity markets, and privatized 50,000 ha (124,000 acres) of land in order to encourage wheat production. Barley, potatoes, vegetables, and various fruits and melons are widely grown for domestic consumption.

Horticulture has been important since antiquity. Most orchards and vineyards are located in the northern valleys, where apricots, pears, plums, apples, cherries, pomegranates, figs, and nuts are grown.

[23]ANIMAL HUSBANDRY

Livestock herding is a major part of Tajikistan's economy. As of 1998, the livestock included 1,000,000 chickens, 1,600,000 sheep, 1,040,000 cattle, 618,000 goats, and 2,000 pigs. Meat production in 1998 included 20,000 tons of beef, 12,000 tons of mutton, and 2,000 tons of poultry. Livestock products in 1998 included cow's milk, 235,000 tons; goat's milk, 16,000 tons; cheese, 5,000 tons; wool (greasy), 2,000 tons; and honey, 1,000 tons.

[24]FISHING

Some fishing occurs in the upper Amu Darya River; the Kayrakkum Reservoir, and the Syrdar'ya River. The total catch was 285 tons in 1997, primarily carp.

[25]FORESTRY

Tajikistan's forests and woodlands occupied about 2.9% of the total land area in 1995. Forestry is of little commercial importance.

[26]MINING

Tajikistan's mineral wealth lies in the northwestern region. Metal resources include alunite, antimony, bauxite, bismuth, cadmium, copper, gold, iron, lead, manganese, mercury, molybdenum, nepheline syenite, nickel, rare metals, selenium, silver, strontium, tin, tungsten, and zinc. Nonmetallic resources include barite, boron, construction materials, dolomite, fluorospar, phosphates, precious and semiprecious stones, and salt. Mercury and antimony are mined at the Dzhidzhikrutskiy complex north of Dushanbe; arsenic, cadmium, tungsten, and lead-zinc north of the Zeravshan River; and uranium and graphite northeast of Khudzhand. Gold is mined southeast of Garm and in the Pamir Mountains. In 1996, production of primary aluminum fell to an estimated 198,300 tons. Gold production was 1.5 tons, with an increase to 3 tons planned for 1997. Mineral production totals for 1994 (in tons) included gypsum, 300,000; lead, 1,200; antimony, 1,000; mercury, 70; and bismuth, 12.

[27]ENERGY AND POWER

More than 95% of Tajikistan's electricity production is hydropower, provided by a series of dams and reservoirs on mountain rivers. Two major hydroelectric facilities on the Vakhsh River have attracted aluminum, chemical, and other energy-intensive industries oriented toward inexpensive energy. The Qayroqqum Dam on the Syrdar'ya River in the north (which forms a reservoir known as the "Tajik Sea") has a hydroelectric station which provides energy for the Fergana Valley in Uzbekistan. Further expansion of hydroelectric power was planned, especially around Khojand, with the potential of exporting energy to Pakistan. In 1998, total installed electrical capacity was 4,443,000 kW; production of electricity that year amounted to 13,270 million kWh.

Brown coal, though declining in production, is mined in the northeast and shipped by rail to Dushanbe; production totaled 122,000 tons in 1994. Natural gas is extracted from fields in the lower Kakhsh and elsewhere; reserves have been estimated at about 200 billion cu ft, but production has been minimal. Tajikistan also has small deposits of petroleum; production in 1998 amounted to about 3,000 barrels per day.

28INDUSTRY

A small number of state-owned enterprises dominate Tajikistan's industrial sector although the state's role in the sector is visibly declining with privatization. By early 1992, the state accounted for only 84% of asset ownership in the industrial sector, as compared to a high of 98% in the late 1980s. One of the largest enterprises in the country is an aluminum plant at Tursunzade, near the capital of Dushanabe, with a production potential of 500,000 tons annually. The smelter reportedly produced 230,000 tons of aluminum in 1995. Light industry includes mainly cotton cleaning, silk processing, textiles production, knitted goods, footwear, sewing, tanning, and carpet making. As of 1997, the government was in the process of privatizing Glavkhlopkoprom, the state organization that controls the ginning and partly the selling of cotton fiber. The food industry is the second-largest contributor to gross industrial output, processing domestically harvested fruit, wheat, tobacco, and other agricultural products. Aside from aluminum and other processed metals, the country's small intermediate and heavy industry subsectors produce engineering goods, hydroelectricity, power transformers, cables, and agricultural equipment.

29SCIENCE AND TECHNOLOGY

The Tajik Academy of Sciences, founded in 1951 at Dushanbe, has departments of physical-mathematical, chemical, and technical sciences; earth sciences; biological and medical sciences; and ten associated research institutes. Tajik State University has faculties of mechanics and mathematics, physics, chemistry, geology, and biology. Tajik Abu-Ali Ibn-Cina (Avicenna) State Medical Institute was founded in 1939. Tajik Agricultural Institute was founded in 1951. Tajik Technical University was founded in 1956. All four educational institutions are in Dushanbe. In 1987–97, science and engineering students accounted for 17% of college and university enrollments. In the same period, Tajikistan had 666 scientists per million population engaged in research and development.

30DOMESTIC TRADE

Although trade is still dominated by the state sector, transfer of much of the retail and wholesale trade sector into private ownership is targeted by the government. Two rounds of price liberalization lifted controls on most consumer and wholesale trade by early 1992, although subsidies and lowered ceilings have been applied to staple goods like flour, sugar, oil, bread, meat, and children's footwear. Trade on the black market has expanded significantly in the growing economic disarray since independence.

31FOREIGN TRADE

Aluminum, raw cotton, and textile products account for about 60% of Tajikistan's exports. Other exports include fruits and vegetable oils. Fuel, chemicals, intermediate industrial goods and equipment, manufactured consumer goods, textiles, and food are its principal import items. Principal trading partners in 1998 (in millions of US dollars) were as follows:

COUNTRY	EXPORTS	IMPORTS	BALANCE
Uzbekistan	308	199	109
Russia	54	83	-29
Italy	31	6	25
United States	30	13	17
Turkmenistan	8	39	-31
Kazakhstan	6	69	-63
Iran	4	53	-49
Germany	2	27	-25
Ukraine	1	84	-83
United Arab Emirates	n.a.	20	

32BALANCE OF PAYMENTS

Foreign income earnings depend highly upon cotton exports; since independence, the centrally planned economy has suffered from the effects of civil war, the severing of trade relations with other former Soviet republics, and a series of natural disasters. Short term, high interest debt accumulated in 1994–94 resulted in a national debt exceeding $780 million with debt service totaling $12 million in 1995. About $440 million of the total was owed to Russia, Uzbekistan, and Kazakhstan. Other major creditors included the US, Turkey, China, and India. External debt totaled $1 billion in 1997.

The US Central Intelligence Agency reports that in 1998 the purchasing power parity of Tajikistan's exports was $740 million while imports totaled $810 million resulting in a trade balance of -$70 million.

33BANKING AND SECURITIES

The National Bank of Tajikistan (NBT) is the country's bank charged with implementing a monetary policy and issuing currency. It was formally established as the central bank in 1991. Commercial and state banks include the Bank for Foreign Investment, three large banks formed from the former Soviet state bank, and three branches from the Russian Commercial Bank. The Law on Banks and Banking Activities, adopted in February 1991, allows banks to compete for resources freely (including the setting of deposit rates) and lifts specialization boundaries. However, competition is very limited. Under IMF pressure, the Tajik government is now seeking to introduce tighter regulation over the banking sector. There is no securities exchange.

34INSURANCE

No recent information is available.

35PUBLIC FINANCE

Revenues from domestic taxes and resources are limited. Expenditures are largely for grain, the supply of fuel and raw materials for industry, and to maintain the military. Despite proposals to liberalize the economy, the government continues to subsidize inefficient state enterprises. Only 11% of medium and large enterprises were privatized as of 1997.

36TAXATION

Tajikistan's maximum personal income tax rate is 40%; corporate taxes range from 25–60% with a standard rate of 30%. Also levied are a 20% VAT; a 10–90% excise tax; and a social security combination of 37% by employers and 1% by employees.

37CUSTOMS AND DUTIES

The government maintains a list of commodities and services subject to import licensing and quotas. Generally, imports are free of restrictions, including tariffs and quotas, with the exception of narcotics and firearms which are forbidden. Goods trades within the former Soviet Union are mostly free from import duties. There is a 28% value-added tax, and excise taxes are levied on some products.

38FOREIGN INVESTMENT

After independence, Tajikistan's government emphasized the promotion of foreign investment particularly to develop labor-intensive manufacturing industries. With ongoing civil unrest, however, few investments have flowed into the country and most foreign aid except that of Russia has been stalled. Difficulties also exist with currency convertibility, a prohibition on land ownership, and repatriation of profits and capital. In 1996 the government amended the foreign investments law to offer a two year exemption from taxes on profits to enterprises with investments of $100,000–500,000, and a four year exemption to enterprises with investments totaling $2–5 million. The peace agreement of 1997 did not bring in an immediate rush of foreign investment capital. Only $20 million was invested in that year.

39ECONOMIC DEVELOPMENT

Soviet development policy in Tajikistan prioritized the development of the country's agricultural and other primary resources, while capital goods and manufactured consumer goods were imported from elsewhere within the former USSR. Since the late 1970s, greater development of small food processing and consumer plants had been urged by local government officials in order to absorb more of the republic's rural labor force; however, these proposals found little favor with Soviet central planners. After independence, the government targeted the development of hydroelectric power production and a number of other industries (silk, fertilizer, fruit and vegetables, coal, nonferrous metals, and marble production), seen as particularly important for improving the country's export base.

In 1991, a "Program of Economic Stabilization and Transition to a Market Economy" was adopted by the newly independent government. In accordance with the program's principles, price liberalization, privatization measures, and fiscal reform were initiated in 1991 and 1992. The government's overthrow in the course of civil war in 1992, however, brought economic development to a virtual standstill and slowed the pace of economic reform. Renewed efforts during 1996–97 to move from a command economy to a market oriented one resulted in proposals to convert medium-sized and large state enterprises to joint-stock companies and to create securities market. Other proposals were aimed at turning land over to private farmers and at privatizing the cotton industry, which continues to dominate agricultural production. As of 1997, the private sector accounted for less than 30% of GDP.

40SOCIAL DEVELOPMENT

The government's social security systems have been threatened by civil war and economic turmoil. Refugees returning from Afghanistan after the war suffered from malnutrition and had high mortality rates in resettlement camps. Resettlement payments to refugee families had been promised by the government, but were not implemented in practice. Financial constraints have also led the government to fall behind in the payment of pensions.

There is no formal discrimination against women in employment, education, or housing. Women are increasingly working outside the home and are found in both the public and private sectors. Although under law they are supposed to receive the same pay for equal work as men, in practice this does not always occur. However, women in rural areas are less likely to receive a higher education or work outside the home, and were likely to marry early. Wife beating is a serious social problem, and appears to be particularly prevalent in rural areas. The number of women in government has declined since the Soviet era. In 1995, 5 female deputies were elected to the legislature.

Russian and Uzbek languages have not been granted official recognition, although radio and television transmission in these languages are permitted.

Political opposition groups are denied access to government-run radio and television. Opposition newspaper established in 1998, however, and were still publishing as of 1999. Serious human rights abuses continue to be committed by members of the security forces. Prison conditions are poor. Detention without charge is legal for up to 10 days. The government has not fulfilled its 1996 promise to appoint an ombudsman for human rights.

41HEALTH

In 1999, there was an infant mortality of 114.8 per 1,000 live births. The general mortality rate was 7.9 per 1,000 inhabitants. The total fertility rate of 5.7 in 1980 had decreased to 3.5 in 1999. The maternal mortality rate was 58 maternal deaths per 100,000 live births in 1990–97. Life expectancy was 64.3 years in 1999. In 1993, there was one doctor for every 424 people. Leading causes of death per 100,000 population in 1990 were communicable diseases and maternal/perinatal causes, 182; noncommunicable diseases, 558; and injuries, 53. In 1992, there were approximately 20,000 war-related deaths. Total health care expenditures in 1990 were $532 million.

The immunization rates for a child under one were as follows in 1990–96: tuberculosis (69%); diphtheria, pertussis, and tetanus (82%); polio (74%); and measles (97%).

The likelihood of dying after age 65 of heart disease in 1990–93 was 364 (men) and 378 (women) per 1,000 people. In 1991, there were 10,099 deaths due to cardiovascular disease in Tajikistan.

Diphtheria has spread widely throughout the former Soviet Union. In Tajikistan, reported diphtheria increased 180% from 680 cases in 1993 to 1,993 cases in 1994. Most cases were reported from the southern region of Kurgan Tyube which borders Afghanistan.

42HOUSING

In 1989, 13.8% of all privately owned urban housing had running water, 1.6% had sewer lines, 2.5% had central heating, and 82.5% had gas available. In 1990, Tajikistan had 9.3 sq m of housing space per capita and, as of 1 January 1991, 90,000 households (or 24.6%) were on waiting lists for urban housing.

43EDUCATION

The adult illiteracy rate was estimated at 0.8% for the year 2000 (males, 0.4%; females, 1.1%). Before the country came under Soviet control in 1920, there were no state-supported schools, only Islamic ones. Since then, many schools have been built. Education is free and compulsory between the ages of 7 and 17. Since 1989, there has been an increased emphasis on Tajik language, literature, and culture. In 1997 there were 638,674 primary students in 3,432 schools, with 27,172 teachers. Student-to-teacher ratio stood at 24 to one. In the same year, secondary schools enrolled 688,150 students and had 112,532 teachers. There are ten schools of higher education including the Universities of Dushanbe and Khudzhand. In 1995, all higher level institutions had a total of 108,203 pupils. In 1997, universities enrolled 76,613 students.

44LIBRARIES AND MUSEUMS

The Fardousi Tajik National Library in Dushanbe holds nearly 3 million volumes. The Republican Scientific and Technical Library of Tajikistan holds 4.7 million volumes, and the Tajik State University holds 1.03 million volumes. The Republican Historical, Regional and Fine Arts Museum is in Dushanbe. There are regional museums in Chodsent, Sorog, Isfara, Kulyab, Nurek, Pendzikent, and Ura Tyube.

45MEDIA

Telephone links to other former Soviet republics is by land line or microwave and to other countries through Moscow. As of 1991, there were 303,000 telephones. Tajik Radio broadcasts in Russian, Tajik, Persian, and Uzbek; Tajik Television, with four channels, broadcasts in Tajik, Russian, and Uzbek. Repeater television stations relay programs from Russia, Iran, and Turkey. Satellite earth stations receive Orbita and INTELSAT broadcasts. As of 1999 there was one state-owned radio station. In 1997, there were 281 televisions per 1,000 population.

According to 1990 statistics, 90% of Tajikistan's 74 newspapers were published in Tajik, and there were 48 periodicals. In 1999 there were two daily newspapers, *Turkmenskaya Iskra,* with a circulation of 62,946, and *Narodnaya Gazeta.* There are several publishing houses in Dushanbe, including educational, literary, and reference publishers.

Despite a 1991 law protecting already constitutionally provided free speech and press, the government is presently said to restrict these freedoms severely. Editors and journalists practice careful self-censorship, and supplies of newsprint, broadcasting facilities, and operating monies are controlled by the authorities.

Online access is extremely limited, with less than one Internet host per 1,000 population in 1998.

[46]ORGANIZATIONS

The Tajikistan Chamber of Commerce and the Tajikistan Industrial Association are important economic organizations. The most important mass movement in the country is the People's Front. The members of the Writers Union and intellectuals in the country formed the "Rascokbez" (Rebirth) Popular Front, an opposition movement opposed to the government of Tajikistan.

Tajikistan's Academy of Science coordinates and finances the scientific research of 19 affiliated natural sciences, social sciences, and humanity research institutions The country has one state-sponsored academic institution, the Tajik State University.

[47]TOURISM, TRAVEL, AND RECREATION

Civil strife has dampened Tajikistan's potential as a tourist site, already limited by the destruction of most ancient monuments and buildings by numerous earthquakes (500 in this century alone). Visas are required for entry into Tajikistan and are obtainable upon arrival or through Russian embassies abroad. There are daily flights from Moscow to the capital city of Dushanbe.

According to 1999 UN estimates, the cost of staying in Dushanbe was $187 per day. Elsewhere in the country, estimated travel costs averaged $75 per day.

[48]FAMOUS TAJIKISTANIS

Outstanding representatives of culture and literature in Tajikistan are the Tadzhik poet Rudaki (d. 941) and the scientist and poet Avicenna (Hussayn ibn 'Abd' Addallah ibn Sine, 980?–1037), born near Bukhara. Avicenna wrote an encyclopedia of science. Pre-Soviet Tajik cultural figures include the author Abdalrauf Fitrat, who wrote *Last Judgement,* and Sadridalin Aymi, author of the novels *Slaves* and *Dokhunala.*

[49]DEPENDENCIES

Tajikistan has no territories or colonies.

[50]BIBLIOGRAPHY

Atkin, Muriel. *The Subtlest Battle: Islam in Soviet Tajikistan.* Philadelphia: Foreign Policy Research Institute, 1989.

Rakowska-Harmstone, Teresa. *Russia and Nationalism in Central Asia: The Case of Tadzhikstan.* Baltimore: Johns Hopkins Press, 1970.

THAILAND

Kingdom of Thailand

Prates Thai

CAPITAL: Bangkok (Krung Thep).

FLAG: The national flag, adopted in 1917, consists of five horizontal stripes. The outermost are red; those adjacent are white; the blue center stripe is twice as high as each of the other four.

ANTHEM: There are three national anthems: *Pleng Sansen Phra Barami (Anthem Eulogizing His Majesty); Pleng Chard Thai (Thai National Anthem);* and *Pleng Maha Chati (Anthem of Great Victory),* an instrumental composition.

MONETARY UNIT: The baht (B) is divided into 100 satang. There are coins of 1, 5, 10, 25, and 50 satang and 1, 5, and 10 baht, and notes of 50 satang and 1, 5, 10, 20, 50, 60, 100, and 500 baht. B1 = $0.02632 ($1 = B37.99) as of 31 March 2000.

WEIGHTS AND MEASURES: The metric system is the legal standard, but some traditional units are also used.

HOLIDAYS: New Year's Day, 1 January; Chakkri Day, 6 April; Songkran Day, mid-April; Coronation Day, 5 May; Queen's Birthday, 12 August; Chulalongkorn Day, 23 October; King's Birthday, 5 December; Constitution Day, 10 December. Movable holidays include Makabuja Day, Plowing Festival, and Visakabuja Day.

TIME: 7 PM = noon GMT.

¹LOCATION, SIZE, AND EXTENT

Comprising an area of 514,000 sq km (198,456 sq mi) in Southeast Asia, Thailand (formerly known as Siam) extends almost two-thirds down the Malay Peninsula, with a length of 1,555 km (966 mi) N–S and a width of 790 km (491 mi) E–W. Comparatively, the area occupied by Thailand is slightly more than twice the size of the state of Wyoming. It is bordered on the NE and E by Laos, on the SE by Cambodia and the Gulf of Thailand (formerly the Gulf of Siam), on the S by Malaysia, on the SW by the Andaman Sea, and on the W and NW by Myanmar, with a total boundary length of 8,082 km (5,022 mi).

Thailand's capital city, Bangkok, is located on the Gulf of Thailand coast.

²TOPOGRAPHY

Thailand may be divided into five major physical regions: the central valley, the continental highlands of the north and northwest, the northeast, the southeast coast, and the peninsula. The heartland of the nation is the central valley, fronting the Gulf of Thailand and enclosed on three sides by hills and mountains. This valley, the alluvial plain of the Chao Phraya River and of its many tributaries and distributaries, is 365 km (227 mi) from north to south and has an average width of 160–240 km (100–150 mi). On this plain, and most especially on its flat deltaland bordering the Gulf, are found Thailand's main agricultural wealth and population centers.

The continental highlands lie north and west of the central valley. They include North Thailand, surrounded on three sides by Myanmar (Burma until June 1989) and Laos, which is a region of roughly parallel mountain ranges between which the Nan, Yom, Wang, Ping, and other rivers flow southward to join and create the Chao Phraya in the central valley. In the northernmost tip, drainage is northward to the Mekong River; on the western side, drainage runs westward to the Salween in Myanmar. Most of the people of North Thailand live in small intermontane plains and basins that are generally widenings in

the major river valleys. Doi Inthanon (2,576 m/8,451 ft) is the highest point in Thailand. Along the Myanmar border from North Thailand to the peninsula is a sparsely inhabited strip of rugged mountains, deep canyons, and restricted valleys. One of the few natural gaps through this wild mountain country is Three Pagodas Pass along the Thailand-Myanmar boundary, used by the Japanese during World War II for their "death railway" (now dismantled) between Thailand and Myanmar.

The northeast, much of it often called the Khorat, is a low, undulating platform roughly 120 to 210 m (400–700 ft) above sea level in the north and west, gradually declining to about 60 m (200 ft) in the southeast. Hill and mountain ranges and scarps separate the northeast from the central valley on the west and from Cambodia on the south; its northern and much of its eastern boundaries are marked by the Mekong River. Most of the northeast is drained by the Mun River and its major tributary, the Chi, which flow eastward into the Mekong. The northeast, in the rain shadow of the Indochina Cordillera, suffers from shortage of water and from generally thin and poor soils.

The small southeast coast region faces the Gulf of Thailand and is separated from the central valley and Cambodia by hills and mountains that rise in places to over 1,500 m (5,000 ft). This is a well-watered area, and the vegetation is, for the most part, lush and tropical. Most of the people live along the narrow coastal plain and the restricted river valleys that drain southward to the Gulf.

Peninsular Thailand extends almost 960 km (600 mi) from the central valley in the north to the boundary of Malaysia in the south and is anywhere from 16 to 217 km (10–135 mi) wide between the Gulf of Thailand on the east and the Andaman Sea (Indian Ocean) and Myanmar (Burma prior to June 1989) on the west. At the Isthmus of Kra, the Peninsula itself is only 24 km (15 mi) wide. A series of north-south ridges, roughly parallel, divide the Peninsula into distinct west and east coast sections. The west coastal plain is narrow—nonexistent in many places—and the coast itself is much indented and often very swampy. The east coastal plain is much wider, up to 32 km (20 mi) in sections, and the coast is smooth, with long beach stretches and few bays. Well-watered (especially the west coast), hot, and densely forested, the Peninsula, unlike most of Thailand, lies within the humid tropical forest zone.

³CLIMATE

Thailand has a tropical climate. For much of the country there are three distinct seasons: the hot season, from March through May; the rainy or wet monsoon, June to October; and the cool season, November through February. While continental Thailand receives most of its precipitation from June through October, rain occurs at all seasons in peninsular Thailand, the largest amount along the west coast from May to October, and along the east coast from October to January. For most of Thailand the temperature rarely falls below 13°c (55°F) or rises above 35°c (95°F), with most places averaging between 24°c and 30°c (75°F and 86°F). The annual rainfall ranges from 102 cm (40 in) in the northeast to over 380 cm (150 in) in the peninsula. Bangkok has an average annual temperature of 28°c (82°F); monthly mean temperatures range from a low of around 25°c (77°F) in December to a high of around 30°c (86°F) in May, and annual rainfall is about 150 cm (59 in).

⁴FLORA AND FAUNA

Many distinctive forms of plant and animal life are found. Forest-lands support hardwoods (notably teak), pine, bamboos, and betel and coconut palms; in the coastal lowlands, mangroves and rattan abound. Among the larger mammals are the bear, otter, and civet cat. Climbing animals include the gibbon and many species of monkeys. There are also sheep, goats, oxen, single-horned rhinoceroses, deer, tapirs, wild cattle, wild hogs, and snakes. About 1,000 varieties of birds are indigenous, and crocodiles, lizards, and turtles are numerous. Fish abound in the rivers and coastal waters.

⁵ENVIRONMENT

The Promotion and Enhancement of Environmental Quality Act of 1975 charges the National Environment Board with coordination of environmental protection programs in Thailand. The nation's water supply is at risk due to contamination by industry, farming activity, sewage, and salt water, especially in the Bangkok area. Thailand has 26.3 cu mi of water. Ninety percent is used for farming activities and 6% for industrial purposes. Thirty-three percent of the nation's city dwellers and 15% of the rural dwellers do not have pure drinking water. Thailand's cities produce 2.5 million tons of solid waste per year. Industry produces 2 million tons of toxic pollutants annually. Watershed regions, undergoing rapid deforestation as a result of increased cultivation of upland areas, have been targeted for protection in the fourth and fifth national plans; overexploitation and pollution of freshwater and marine fisheries have yet to be remedied. By the 1980s, Thailand had lost about 25% of its original mangrove area. Land use in urban areas is regulated by the City Planning Act of 1975, the Control of Construction of Buildings Act of 1936, and the 1960 Act for Cleanliness and Orderliness of the Country. Parts of Bangkok were reportedly sinking at a rate of 10 cm (4 in) a year because of depletion of the water table. Urban air and noise pollution was also severe, largely as a result of increasing automobile traffic. In 1992 Thailand was among 50 nations with the world's highest levels of industrial carbon dioxide emissions, which totaled 112.4 million metric tons, a per capita level of 2.02 metric tons.

Wildlife is partially protected under the Wild Animals Preservation and Protection Act of 1960, but species have been depleted through illegal hunting and trapping. In 1994, 26 of the nation's mammal species and 34 bird species were endangered. Sixty-eight types of plants were also endangered. Endangered or extinct species in Thailand include the pileated gibbon, tiger, Asian elephant, Malayan tapir, Sumatran rhinoceros, Fea's muntjac, Thailand brow-antlered deer, kouprey, green turtle, hawksbill turtle, olive ridley, leatherback, river terrapin, estuarine crocodile, Siamese crocodile, false gavial, and the Javan rhinoceros.

⁶POPULATION

The population of Thailand in 2000 was estimated at 61,163,833. An estimated 5.2% of the population is 65 years of age or older. The projected population for the year 2005 is 63,794,000 assuming a crude birthrate of 15 per 1,000 population and a death rate of 7 resulting in a natural rate of change of 0.8% for the period 2000–2005. The population rate of change between 1995 and 2000 was 0.8%. The population density in 1998 was 120 per sq km (311 per sq mi), but there are great regional variations in density.

Most Thais live in rural areas. It was estimated that only 22% of the population lived in urban areas in 2000, up from 17% in 1980. Bangkok is the single major urban area; the capital city, Bangkok, and its surrounding metropolitan area, had a 2000 population of 7,221,000. Outside of Bangkok, most major cities are provincial capitals, each generally centered in a changwat (province or county) with the same name as the city.

⁷MIGRATION

Immigration to Thailand, except for the Chinese, has traditionally been comparatively small. The decade of the 1920s was a period of large-scale Chinese immigration of 70,000 to 140,000 a year. Strict immigration regulations have all but stopped the legal flow of Chinese into the country, but during the Franco-Indochinese war some 45,000 Vietnamese refugees settled in Thailand. An immigration quota, introduced in 1947, now limits migration from any one country to 100 persons annually.

As of December 1992, the UN estimated that 63,600 refugees were living in Thailand; these represented part of the flood of over 4 million refugees who had left Cambodia, Laos, and Viet-Nam since the 1970s. Some 370,000 Cambodians on the Thai–Cambodian border were repatriated during 1992–93. The 36,000 Cambodian refugees who fled their country after the political and military events of 1997 were repatriated by April 1999, and three border camps were subsequently closed. In 1986, the Thai government began forcibly repatriating many refugees from Laos. As of May 1997, there were still 1,644 Laotians in Thailand. They were expected to repatriate at the end of June 1997; however, as of 1999 1,296 Lao still remained in the Ban Napho camp. On 20 July 1999, a meeting took place between UNHCR and the Thai and Laotian governments to discuss the return of 1,100 among the residual group, as well as alternative solutions for the remaining 196 who met refugee criteria. The last refugee camp for Vietnamese was closed in February 1997.

In June 1998, the Thai government formally requested increased UNHCR assistance for some 100,000 Karen and Karenni refugees living in 11 camps in Thailand along the Myanmar border. A comprehensive registration of the border population was completed through the joint efforts of the Thai government and UNHCR between March and May 1999. UNHCR is also working with the government to establish uniform criteria for accepting new arrivals from Myanmar, as it is unlikely that repatriation will be possible in the near future.

The net migration rate in 1999 was zero.

⁸ETHNIC GROUPS

Thailand contains more than 30 ethnic groups varying in history, language, religion, appearance, and patterns of livelihood. However, the Thai, akin to the Lao of Laos, the Shan of Myanmar (Burma prior to June 1989), and the Thai groupings of southern China, comprise about 75% of the total population of Thailand. The Thai may be divided into three major groups and three minor groups. Major groups are the Central Thai (Siamese) of the Central Valley; the Eastern Thai (Lao) of the Northeast (Khorat); the Northern Thai (Lao) of North Thailand; and the Southern Thain (Chao Pak Thai) of peninsular Thailand. Minor groups are the Phuthai of northeastern Khorat, the Shan of the far northwestern corner of northern Thailand, and the Lue in the northeastern section of northern Thailand. The several branches of Thai are united by a common language.

A major ethnic minority is the Chinese (about 14%), engaged in business and commerce throughout the country. Other varied ethnic groups account for the remaining 11% of the population. Malays (3–4%), in the southern peninsula near the border and, to a lesser extent, along the southeast coast; Khmers (1%), all along the Cambodian border from the Mekong to the Gulf of Thailand; and Vietnamese or Annamese, in the southern Khorat and on the southeast coast. Small numbers of residents from India, Europe, and the US live mainly in urban areas. Principal tribal groups, mainly hill peoples, include the Kui and Kaleung, in the northeast; the Mons, living mainly on the peninsula along the Burmese border; and the Karens, living along the northern Burmese border. There are, in addition, some 20 other minority groups, including the Akha, Musso, Meo, Kamuk, Tin, Lawa, and So; most of these peoples, primitive and small in number, live by shifting cultivation in rugged, isolated mountain or dense forest terrain.

9LANGUAGES

The Thai language, with northern, eastern, central (Bangkok or official Thai), and southern dialects, all distantly related to Chinese, prevails throughout the country. Thai, written in a distinctive alphabet, is thought to be part of the Sino-Tibetan language family, although links to Indian languages are also evident. The Thai dialects for the most part are mutually intelligible only with difficulty. Although the ethnic minorities (including the Malays) generally speak their own languages, Thai is widely understood. The Chinese population is largely bilingual. All official documents are in the central Thai language and script, although English, taught in many secondary schools and colleges, is also used in official and commercial circles.

10RELIGIONS

Hinayana Buddhism is the state religion of Thailand; only Buddhists are employed by the government, and the Thai monarch is legally required to be a Buddhist. Buddhism was the religion of an estimated 95% of the population in 1999. Although virtually all Thai are nominally Buddhists, the dominant form of religion in Thailand might be described as a spirit worship overlaid or mixed in varying degrees with Buddhist and Brahman beliefs imported from India. About 3.8% of the population, including the Malay ethnic minority, are Muslim. Among the other ethnic minorities, the Chinese practice a traditional mixture of Mahayana Buddhism, Taoism, Confucianism, and ancestor worship. Most Vietnamese are Mahayana Buddhists, and most Indians are Hindus (0.1% of the population). Christians have been active in Thailand since the 17th century and accounted for 0.5% of the population in 1999. Other varied religions make up the remaining 0.6%. There is a small Bahai community.

11TRANSPORTATION

Thailand's transportation system is not fully developed, but it is growing rapidly. Owned and operated by the government, the railways, consisting in 1996 of 4,623 km (2,872 mi) of track, radiate from Bangkok to Malaysia in the south, to the Cambodian border in the east, to Ubon Ratchathani and Nong Khai in the northeast, and to Chiang Mai in the north.

The highway system, significantly expanded during the 1960s and 1970s, serves many areas inaccessible to railway. In 1996 there were 64,600 km (40,142 mi) of roadway, including 62,985 km (39,139 mi) of paved road. Modern two-lane highways now connect Bangkok with the rest of the country. In 1995, registered motor vehicles totaled 5,000,000, including 1,350,000 passenger cars.

Waterways, both river and canal, are Thailand's most important means of inland transport; they carry much of the nation's bulk freight over a network of some 4,000 km (2,500 mi). The Chao Phraya River with its tributaries is the main traffic artery, and Bangkok is its focal point. The modern port of Bangkok at Klong Toey is the chief port for international shipping. Lying some 40 km (25 mi) inland from the sea, its harbor is navigable for vessels up to 10,000 tons, but constant dredging of the Chao Phraya is necessary. To relieve the congestion at Klong Toey, a new modern port was being developed at Sattahip, a former US naval base, and new seaports at Laem Chabang and Hap Ta Phut. Phuket Harbor in southern Thailand has been improved to accommodate 15,000-ton cargo ships. An extensive shipping service also exists along the Gulf of Thailand, and a small Thai merchant fleet plies between local and neighboring ports. In 1998 there were 293 oceangoing vessels of more than 1,000 gross tons in the Thai merchant fleet (up from only 80 in 1986), totaling 1,848,626 GRT.

Since the end of World War II, Bangkok has become an important center of international aviation. In 1998 there were 101 airports, of which 56 had paved runways. Principal airports include Bangkok International at Bangkok, Chiang Mai, Hat Yai at Haadyai, and Phuket International at Phuket. The government-owned Thai Airways International and Thai Airways Co. handle international and domestic air traffic, respectively. In 1997 scheduled airline traffic performed 30,827 million passenger-km (19,156 million passenger-mi) and 1,628 million ton-km (1,012 million ton-mi) of freight and carried 14,236,000 passengers.

12HISTORY

Archaeological excavations in the 1970s in Ban Chiang, northeastern Thailand yielded traces of a Bronze Age people, dating as far back as 3600 BC predating Bronze cultures in China and the Middle East. The technical achievements of the Ban Chiang society, as surmised from archaeological evidence, indicate the existence of a settled agrarian people with advanced knowledge of bronze and iron metallurgy. Moreover, the skills demonstrating in their pottery, housing, and printing of silk textiles reflect at least 2,000 years of prior development, a finding that challenges previous concepts of incipient civilization and technology, and Southeast Asia's role in it.

The Thai descended from the ancient Pamir plateau peoples, who are racially related to the Chinese, that migrated from southern China to mainland Southeast Asia. While in southern China, the Thai created the powerful Nan-Chao kingdom, but continued pressure from Chinese and Tibetans and the final destruction by Kublai Khan in 1253 forced the Thai southward across the mountain passes into Southeast Asia. After entering the valley of the Chao Phraya River, they defeated and dispersed the Khmer settlers, ancestors of the Cambodians, and established the Kingdom of Thailand.

By the mid-14th century, the Thai expanded and centralized their kingdom at the expense of the Lao, Burmese, and Cambodians. Although Thailand developed trading contacts with the Dutch and Portuguese and with the French and British in the 16th and 17th centuries respectively, it remained a feudal state with a powerful court of nobles. During the reigns of Mongkut (1851–

68) and his son Chulalongkorn (1868–1910), however, Thailand emerged from feudalism and entered the modern world. A cabinet of foreign advisers was formed; commercial treaties of friendship were signed with the British (1855) and with the US and France (1856); the power of nobles was curtailed, slavery abolished, and many court practices, such as prostration in the royal presence, were ended.

Despite the progressive policies of Mongkut and Chulalongkorn, the Thai government continued as an absolute monarchy. In 1932, however, a bloodless revolution of Westernized intellectuals led to a constitutional monarchy. Since that time, Thailand experienced multiple constitutions, changes of government, and military coups. With the government in a state of flux, political parties tended to cluster around strong personalities rather than political ideologies. At the start of World War II, Thailand, after annexing Burmese and Malayan territories, signed an alliance with Japan and declared war on the US and the UK. From 1932 through the 1940s, political life in Thailand centered around Pridi Banomyong and Marshal Phibul Songgram and thereafter around Marshal Sarit Thanarat, until his death in 1963. Sarit's handpicked heir, Marshal Thanom Kittikachorn, subsequently emerged as the country's political leader.

After the war, however, Thailand became an ally of the US through their common membership in the Southeast Asia Treaty Organization (SEATO), and various other bilateral treaties and agreements. In January 1965, China announced the formation of the Thailand Patriotic Front, whose purpose was "to strive for the national independence" of Thailand. A limited insurgency subsequently developed in the North and Northeast, growing in intensity in the late 1960s and early 1970s as the Southeast Asian conflict raged on Thailand's northern and northeastern borders. As a SEATO member, Thailand took a direct role in the Viet Nam war and supplied a small number of troops in support of the Republic of Vietnam (RVN). Furthermore, it granted US forces the use of air bases in Thailand for massive bombing sorties against the Democratic Republic of Vietnam and the Vietcong. US forces stationed in Thailand increased to as many as 25,000 by the end of 1972. With the termination of the direct US combat role in Vietnam in early 1973, the US began a gradual withdrawal of military personnel from Thailand. In March 1976, the Thai government ordered the US to close its remaining military installations in the country and to remove all but a few military aid personnel by July. The communist insurgency continued, with sporadic armed attacks on the government in remote northeastern border provinces.

Internally, Thailand weathered a series of political upheavals in the 1970s. In November 1971, Marshal Thanom, who had been reconfirmed as prime minister in the 1969 general elections, led a bloodless military coup that abrogated the constitution and imposed a state of martial law. In December 1972, an interim constitution that preserved military rule caused student and labor groups began agitating for a greater representation in Thai politics. By early October 1973, demonstrations erupted into riots, and on 14 October, Marshal Thanom resigned and quit the country. King Bhumibol Adulyadej stepped into the vacuum and named a national legislative assembly to draft a new constitution. On 7 October 1974, the new constitution—the tenth such document to be promulgated in Thailand since 1932—went into effect. On 26 January 1975, Thailand held its first truly open parliamentary elections since 1957. Some 42 parties competed in the balloting, which produced a coalition government under Seni Pramoj. In March 1975, Seni's government resigned following a no-confidence vote and a right-wing coalition government led by Kukrit Pramoj (Seni's brother) subsequently assumed control, but it too resigned in January 1976. Elections held in April restored Seni Pramoj to power as head of a four-party coalition, but when

LOCATION: 97° to 106°E; 6° to 21°N. **BOUNDARY LENGTHS:** Laos, 1,754 km (1,090 mi); Cambodia, 803 km (499 mi); Gulf of Thailand coastline, 1,875 km (1,165 mi); Malaysia, 576 km (358 mi); Andaman Sea coastline, 740 km (460 mi); Myanmar, 1,799 km (1,118 mi). **TERRITORIAL SEA LIMIT:** 12 mi.

civil disorder again erupted among students in Bangkok, he was overthrown by the military. The military-led government declared martial law, banned strikes and political parties, and enacted yet another constitution. Promulgation of a subsequent constitution in December 1978 paved the way for elections in 1979, 1983, and 1986. On 9 September 1985, the military swiftly diffused an abortive military coup within several hours. It was the 16th coup or attempt at a coup since 1932. Gen. Prem Tinsulanonda was appointed for a third term as Prime Minister following the 1986 elections.

Insurgents based in Laos and Cambodia contributed to the nation's political instability by launching guerrilla attacks on the country. Furthermore, an upsurge in the number of refugees from Laos and Cambodia contributed to a humanitarian crisis. In 1979, the government estimated the number of insurgents at 10,000. Following the Vietnamese victory in Cambodia in January 1979, thousands of insurgents took advantage of a government offer of amnesty and surrendered to Thai security forces while others were apprehended subsequently. By the beginning of 1986, fewer than 1,000 active Communist insurgents remained active, according to government estimates.

During 1985 and 1986, the Progress Party gained power when cabinet ministers were replaced. A parliamentary defeat over proposed vehicle tax legislation resulted in the dissolution of the House of Representatives. In July 1986 a general election for an enlarged house took place. Gen. Prem formed a coalition government and served as Prime Minister but opposition parties accused his government of corruption and mismanagement. Additional dissent arose over proposed copyright legislation aimed at controlling counterfeiting of Western products and intellectual property. In 1988 Gen. Prem dissolved summarily the House of Representatives and announced a general election. In the July 1988 election, the Chart Thai gained the largest number of seats. Although its leader, Gen. Chatichai Choonhavan, declared his unsuitability for Prime Minister, he was appointed nonetheless. Gen. Chatichai took an active role in foreign affairs and made bold initiatives to improve relations with Laos, Viet Nam, and Cambodia. His support declined as his preoccupation with foreign affairs was considered a detriment to his handling of domestic issues, especially regarding government response in the aftermath of a devastating typhoon in November 1989. In July 1990, accusations of corruption led to a motion of "no confidence" that failed to muster a majority in the House of Representatives. In December of that year, Gen. Chatichai resigned as Prime Minister, only to be reappointed the next day, enabling him to form a new coalition government.

On 23 February 1991, a bloodless military coup led by the National Peace Keeping Council (NPKC) ousted Chatichai's government alleging massive and systemic corruption. The NPKC declared martial law, abrogated the constitution, and dissolved the cabinet. An interim constitution approved by the king was published in March 1991. A former diplomat and business executive, Anand Panyarachun, was appointed Prime Minister. Despite public protest, a draft constitution presented in November was approved on 7 December 1991.

In March 1992, Gen. Suchinda became Prime Minister amid continued unrest. Two months later, Maj. Gen. Chamlong called for the resignation of Suchinda and an amendment to the constitution at a rally attended by 100,000 demonstrators. Chamlong pledged that he would fast to death, but gave the government a one-week grace period amended the constitution to prohibit the appointment of an unelected Prime Minister. When it appeared that the government might renege on this agreement, the peaceful demonstrations resumed. On 17 May 1992, about 150,000 demonstrators met at Sanam Luang parade grounds in central Bangkok. Leaders called for the demonstrators to walk toward Government House down Ratchadamnoen Avenue. With police considering the demonstrators' plan threatening and demonstrators looking for a confrontation, the venue for a violent clash existed. Demonstrators broke through roadblocks established up by the police and set fire to vehicles and a nearby police station. At 4 am on 18 May the demonstrators were counterattacked with armored vehicles and machine-guns. Government forces arrested Chamlong and killed over 100 demonstrators and detained several thousands. Four days of violence ended with intervention by the king. On 24 May, Suchinda resigned after political leaders guaranteed amnesty to military officers that participated in quelling the demonstrations. On 10 June, the National Assembly approved the constitutional amendments including the prohibition of unelected politicians from forming a cabinet. A general election followed on 13 September 1992, and Chuan Leekpai, leader of the winning Democratic Party, became Prime Minister.

Chuan's policies emphasized four goals: to eradicate corrupt practices, to reduce the powers of the appointed Senate, to decentralize government from Bangkok to the provinces, and to enhance rural development. Beginning in 1993 and into 1994, Chuan's government faced two "no confidence" motions in parliament, but the government emerged stronger after they failed. In 1994, Chamlong and Palang Dharma became more assertive in demands for constitutional reform, decentralization of state power, and progress in solving Bangkok's traffic problems, which are some of the worst in the world—some commutes reportedly taking up to six hours.

Ultimately corruption charges brought Chuan's governing coalition down. In late 1994, the New Aspirations Party (NAP), led by Chavalit Yongchaiyadh, left the ruling coalition over a planned electoral reform. In May 1995, prior to a vote of no confidence, Chuan dissolved parliament and called for new elections. Having served two years of a four-year term as Prime Minister, Chuan became Thailand's longest serving civilian leader in the modern era.

During the campaigning leading to the July 1995 elections, politicians spent 17 billion baht buying votes, a seemingly intractable problem. However, the otherwise fair balloting was won by the Chart Thai party, which took 92 (of 391) seats. The former PM, Chuan's Democrats secured 86; the NAP took 57; and Palang Dharma lost heavily, going from 47 to 23 seats. Chart Thai selected as its PM Banharn Silpa-archa. In appointing his cabinet, however, Banharn was immediately perceived as favoring the old corrupted elite, especially when he gave important ministerial posts to Montri Pongpanich and Chalerm Yubamroong, both of whom were well known for their ill-gotten wealth. Even the King, who is revered by Thai society, expressed dissatisfied with the caliber of the new ministers.

Not surprisingly, Banharn's government collapsed before the end of 1996 and elections took place on November 17, 1996. Chart Thai went from 96 seats to 39 as the NAP, led by coalition parties, and Minister of Defense Chavalit Yongchaiyudh, emerged victorious. They swept into power going from 57 seats to 125. Placing second in the balloting was the Democratic Party. Chavalit, one of Thailand's more respected politicians, vowed to appoint a cabinet of technocrats (he called them the "dream team") rather than cronies, and to rescue the Thai economy which had been faltering. Despite his pledge, however, 1997 was a disastrous year for the Thai economy. In mid-May, the stock market collapsed and speculative currency trading hammered the baht. The government intervened, but conditions deteriorated so badly that by July the government decided to float the baht, which had been pegged to the US dollar, causing a precipitous drop. In one day, the currency fell more than 17% against the dollar. The floating of the baht caused international headlines as neighboring Asian countries frantically scrambled to protect their own currencies. By September, 1997, the crisis had spread to Singapore, the Philippines, Malaysia, and Indonesia.

Failing to adjust to the crisis, the Minister of Finance Thanong resigned in October 1997 while students demanded the resignation of Chavalit. Despite a reshuffling of the cabinet in an attempt to placate Chart Pattana, Prime Minister Chavalit resigned on November 6. In November, Chuan Leepkai formed a coalition government that included his Democrat Party, Chart Thai, the SAP, Ekkaparb, the Seirtham Party, Palang Dharma, the Thai Party, and a majority of the Prachakorn Thai Party. Despite the perceived integrity of Chuan, the Thai baht continued to experience devaluation. The fragile government survived a no confidence vote in March 1998.

By May 1998, the Thai economy stabilized and began to recover slowly despite the swirling of allegations of corruption that led to the resignation of two ministers. The government accepted a significant International Monetary Fund bailout package and promised to deregulate the economy and adopt transparency. In March 1999, a major privatization bill passed the National Assembly, which allowed government enterprises to become corporate entities without legislative action. On 5 October 1998, Chuan reorganized the government and invited Chart Pattana into the government and extending the coalition's majority in the House of Representatives to 257. In April 1999, the leader of the NAP, Chavalit temporarily resigned as leader of the party in order to prepare for upcoming general elections.

In March 2000, the first ever Senate elections took place in accord with the 1997 constitution. The nonpartisan elections fielded 1,521 candidates who, by law, refrained from campaigning.

13 GOVERNMENT

Thailand has been a constitutional monarchy since 1932. The present king, Bhumibol Adulyadej, ascended to the monarchy in 1946 and became Rama IX on 5 May 1950. Until 1958, Thailand was governed under a constitution originally promulgated in December 1932. In October 1958, however, the constitution was suspended, and three months later the king proclaimed an interim basic law providing for a constituent assembly to draft a new constitution. Nine years in the making, a new constitution was promulgated in June 1968, and the first elections under it were held in 1969. The document was overturned In November 1971, Marshal Thanom Kittikachorn overturned the document despite being chosen by its rules.

A period of martial law under a National Executive Council ensued, with the military continuing in power through an interim constitution. A new constitution, promulgated in 1974, was suspended and replaced by martial law in 1976 when civil disorder ensued. The 1976 constitution was abrogated after an October 1977 coup and under an interim constitution, the king empowered a legislative assembly to draft a new governing document. This constitution, approved by the legislature on 18 December 1978, lifted the ban on political parties and eased some of the martial law provisions imposed in 1976.

On 23 February 1991, the National Peacekeeping Council (NPKC), led by the supreme commander of the Royal Thai Armed Forces, Gen. Sundhara Kongsompong, took over the administration of the country. On 9 December 1991, the NPKC promulgated a new constitution. It provided for a National Assembly comprised of elected representatives and an appointed Senate, and a cabinet headed by an appointed Prime Minister. This charter was sympathetic to the needs of the military and gave the junta power over the Senate. Protests that resulted in the deaths of pro-democracy demonstrators between 17–20 May 1992 quickly led to a constitutional amendment to provide for an elected Prime Minister and to curb some of the appointed Senate's power. This constitutional amendment was approved by the National Assembly on 10 June 1992 and required the Prime Minister to be a member of the House of Representatives. In addition, the revised constitution significantly cut back the powers of the Senate by ruling that the speaker of the lower House will be president of the Parliament (previously it was the speaker of the Senate). The Senate is also barred from initiating, or taking part in, "no-confidence" motions. The first elections under these reforms were held on 13 September 1992.

Efforts to amend the constitution again came before Parliament in April 1994, and the seven government-sponsored amendments were defeated. These amendments sought to reform Thailand's political structure by institutionalizing political parties and increase the role of the legislature. Prolonged debate and political indecision prevented the passage of these amendments until 27 September 1997, when the new Constitution passed with the King's endorsement. According to this constitution, the National Assembly would consist of 500 members, with 400 selected by respective constituencies and 100 seats allocated by proportional representation of all parties exceeding the 5% threshold of popular votes. In an attempt to stabilize the political situation and institutionalize parties, the new constitution requires representatives to resign their seat if they renounce or switch their party membership. The Senate, to consist of 200 nonpartisan members, requires all members to hold at least a baccalaureate.

14 POLITICAL PARTIES

Constitutional government in Thailand has been hindered by traditional public apathy, and political parties generally have been formed by military personalities rather than around political issues and programs. Military leader Phibul Songgram, who became Prime Minister in 1938, did not favor political parties. Phibul's immediate postwar successor, the pro-Japanese Pridi Banomyong, encouraged the growth of parties, but these were generally ineffective, primarily because of Thai inexperience with such institutions.

Upon Phibul and other military leaders' return to power in 1947, parties were banned. In a move designed to undercut a growing threat from other soldiers, Phibul reinstated political parties in 1955 in preparation of the elections for 1957. A new coup, led by Marshal Sarit Thanarat, deposed Phibul in 1957 and again banned political parties. Following the promulgation of a new constitution in June 1968, parties were again legalized and hotly contested the 1969 parliamentary elections. Prime Minister Thanom Kittikachorn's United Thai People's Party won a plurality (76) of the 219 seats in the House of Representatives, giving it a majority in partnership with 72 "independents" supported by Deputy Premier (and army chief) Praphas Charusathien. The Democrat Party, led by civilian politician Seni Pramoj, won 56 seats, becoming the chief opposition party. Following Marshal Thanom's 1971 coup, political activity again subsided in favor of the military. The collapse of military rule in October 1973 led to a resurgence of civilian political groups. In the parliamentary elections of 26 January 1975, 2,193 candidates from 42 political parties contested 269 seats in the House of Representatives. Voter apathy remained a problem, however, as only 47% of the electorate (33% in Bangkok) took part. The conservative Bangkok-based Democrat Party emerged with a meager plurality of 72 seats, thereby failing to secure a majority coalition. On 13 March, Kukrit Pramoj, leader of the Social Action Party (SAP), which held 18 seats, was elected Prime Minister in a controversial vote; he formed a ruling right-wing coalition with the Social Justice Party (45 seats), the Chat Thai (28 seats), and four smaller groups. The coalition collapsed in January 1975, and in new elections held on 4 April, Seni Pramoj gained the premiership.

In the wake of the 1976 coup, massive arrests were made of liberal and leftist political elements; political parties were banned, and martial law instituted. Political activity was restored and martial rule partially relaxed under the 1978 constitution. Subsequent elections, held on 22 April 1979, gave no party a clear majority. The SAP won a plurality of 82 seats, and the Thai Nation Party finished second with 38. Gen. Prem Tinsulanonda, who became Prime Minister in March 1980, formed a new coalition government after the April 1983 elections, in which the SAP emerged with a plurality of 92 seats. Several days after the elections, the Thai Nation Party, which had won 73 seats, subsumed the Siam Democratic Party, which controlled 18. In subsequent elections on 27 July 1986, the Bangkok-based Democrat Party improved its position greatly, winning 100 seats. The Thai Nation Party won 63, and the SAP, 51. These three parties, along with the small Rassadorn—or People's—Party which won 18 seats, formed a new coalition, but with Gen. Prem again as Prime Minister. The election campaign and balloting were marred by scattered incidents of violence.

In the bloodless military coup of 23 February 1991 by the National Peacekeeping Council (NPKC), Gen. Chatichai's government was turned out. The NPKC promulgated a provisional constitution, and after a brief period paved the way for a civilian interim government headed by Anand Panyarachun. A general election was held 22 March 1992, with 15 parties contesting 360 seats with 2,185 candidates. Persistent vote buying marred an election in which 59.2% of the electorate voted. Results were: Samakkhi Tham (79), Chart Thai (74), New Aspiration Party (72), DP (44), and Palang Dharma (41). A coalition government controlling 195 seats in the House of Representatives was comprised of Samakkhi Tham, Chart Thai, Pratchakorn Thai, the SAP and Rassadorn parties. Narong Wongman was proposed as Prime Minister until the US made allegations of Narong's involvement in illegal drug trafficking. In April 1992 Gen. Suchinda was named Prime Minister. His appointment as an unelected Prime Minister met with immediate protest. Agreement was reached to amend the Constitution to prevent an unelected Prime Minister, but an apparent change of mind by the government resulted in violent rioting. Suchinda resigned and constitutional amendments were approved by parliament on 10 June. The National Democratic Front, four parties that had opposed the military government, the DP, the New Aspiration Party, Palang Dharma, and Ekkaparb, formed an alliance to contest the elections called for in September 1992.

In the 13 September 1992 general election 12 parties contesting 360 seats in the House of Representatives. Voter turnout was 62.1%. Election results were: the DP (79), Chart Thai (77), Chart Pattana (60), New Aspiration Party (51), and SAP (22). The DP formed a coalition party with Palang Dharma (47 seats) and Ekkaparb (Solidarity) for control of 185 of the 360 seats. The SAP was invited to join the coalition. The leader of the DP, Chuan Leekpai, was named Prime Minister. Chaun served for two years—the longest continuous civilian rule in modern times—before scandal brought his government down in May 1995. Elections were held in July 1995 which were won by Chart Thai, taking 92 of the expanded body's 391 seats. Chuan's Democratic Party was next with 86 seats; the NAP took 57 and Phalang Dharma slipped from 47 to 23 seats. Banharn Silpa-archa was appointed Prime Minister, and was almost immediately assailed by the press—and even the King—for assembling a government of largely discredited cronies.

Banharn's coalition lasted barely 14 months and new elections were held in November 1996, the results of which were as follows: NAP, 125 seats; Democratic Party, 123; Chart Pattana, 52; Chart Thai, 39; SAP, 20; Prachakorn Thai Party, 18; Solidarity Party, 8; Seritham Party, 4; Muan Chan Party, 2; Phalang Dharma, 1; Thai Party, 1.

Constitutional changes, promulgated on 11 October 1997 will increase party discipline and loyalty. It requires representatives to resign their seat if they switch or renounce their party affiliations.

The current government consists of a coalition of the Democrat Party, Chart Thai, Solidarity Party, the Seritham Party, Chart Pattana, and 12 members of the Prachakorn Thai party. These twelve members were subsequently expelled from the Prachakorn Thai party.

15LOCAL GOVERNMENT

Thailand is divided into 76 administrative provinces (changwats), each under the control of an appointed governor responsible to the Ministry of the Interior. The Bangkok Metropolitan Administration has an elected governor and is divided into 24 districts. Numerous changes went into effect with the promulgation of the new constitution in 1997. Effectively immediately, all local administrators must now be elected directly by popular suffrage or by the approval of a local assembly. Furthermore, local government officials are prohibited from holding a permanent national position or receiving additional compensation from government related positions.

16JUDICIAL SYSTEM

The 1997 constitution provided for an independent judiciary and the guarantee of basic civil liberties. Courts of the first instance, juvenile courts, and magistrate's courts exist in Bangkok and in each of the provincial capitals. A court of appeal, sitting in Bangkok, hears cases for the entire kingdom. The Supreme Court, also in Bangkok, consists of at least three judges and decides only on points of law. Judges in Thailand are appointed (and removed) by the king. All appointments are subject to initial approval by a judicial commission. There is no trial by jury in Thailand.

The constitution also provided for establishment of a constitutional tribunal to adjudicate disputes among the courts. Military courts deal primarily with military justice, but have broader jurisdiction when martial law is in force. There is no appeal of decisions by military courts. Defendants in ordinary criminal courts are afforded a wide range of procedural due process protections. Although there is no right to counsel during the investigative phase of cases, detainees are afforded access to counsel during trial.

Islamic courts hear civil cases concerning members of the Muslim minority. The legal system is based on civil law with common law influence.

17ARMED FORCES

The armed forces are organized as 306,000 active duty personnel and 200,000 reservists. Males between the ages of 21 and 30 are liable for two years of active military duty and 23 years of various kinds of reserve status. The army, organized into 17 divisions and 33 smaller units, numbered 190,000 personnel in 2000. The air force, reorganized with US assistance, consisted of 43,000 personnel with 162 combat aircraft, plus transport, training, and helicopter rescue units. The navy had 73,000 personnel (including 20,000 marines) and was equipped with 14 frigates, 88 patrol and coastal combatants, and 32 other vessels. In addition, a volunteer defense corps of 50,000 was available for the maintenance of national security, along with other police forces for a total of 71,000 paramilitary troops. In 1997–98, Thailand spent $1.95 billion on defense, or 2.5% of gross domestic product.

18INTERNATIONAL COOPERATION

Thailand, a member of the UN since 16 December 1946, is the headquarters for ESCAP and belongs to all the nonregional specialized agencies. Bangkok has served as regional headquarters for several other UN agencies, and for the former Southeast Asia Treaty Organization (SEATO). Thailand is identified more closely than most Asian countries with the Western nations largely because of its alliance with the US. The country is a member of the Asian Development Bank, Asian and Pacific Council, ASEAN, the Association of Natural Rubber Producing Countries, G-77, and the International Tin Council. Thailand is a member of the WTO, and a signatory of the Law of the Sea.

Thailand is a participant in the Colombo Plan, and it receives economic aid from UN agencies for agricultural, industrial, and health projects. US assistance has been a vital factor in Thailand's economic development since World War II. Although never engaged in direct combat on Thai soil, the US has been Thailand's paramount military ally in recent decades, supplying funds, equipment, advisers, and large-scale training programs for personnel. On order of the Seni government, the US military presence in Thailand was almost completely withdrawn by mid-1976, although some US assistance, including military aid, continued.

Prior to the military and political upheavals of the 1970s, Kampuchea (known as Cambodia until 1976 and again from 1989), Laos, Thailand, and the RVN had been cooperating on the development of the lower Mekong Basin in terms of hydroelectric power, irrigation, navigation improvement, and flood control. As of the mid-1980s, however, the prospect for continued cooperation in the area appeared in doubt.

19ECONOMY

Thailand's economy has more than tripled since 1986, achieving approximately 9% real growth annually from 1989 to 1996, however the economy contracted in 1997 and 1998 due to the Asian financial crisis (at 1.3% and 9.4% respectively). The Thai government devalued the baht on July 2, 1997; the currency dropped by half during that year. The currency crisis, as well as financial mismanagement and high national debt brought the economy to a halt. The failed government bailout of financial institutions put the nation even further into debt.

Although agriculture still employs 54% of the labor force, in 1998 it only accounted for 12% of GDP, down from 16.7% in 1986. Rice remains the major crop, but other cash crops have become increasingly important. In addition to new crops introduced—corn and cassava (tapioca)—strong gains have been recorded in recent decades by rubber, cotton, sugarcane, and fruits and vegetables. Whereas agricultural growth has slowed, the industrial, commercial, and financial sectors have experienced dramatic growth rates which are expected to continue into the next century. The increasingly diversified manufacturing sector grew by an average of 9% during the 1990s and accounted for a third of GDP, up from 24% in 1987. Industrial production of computers and electronics, automobiles, garments and footwear, furniture and wood products, canned foods, gems and jewelry, toys and plastic products, is increasing rapidly. Tourism is also an important contributor to the economy and a major foreign exchange earner.

Economic growth, however, is threatened by shortages of skilled labor and infrastructure bottlenecks. It is estimated that only 20% of the workforce has more than a primary-school education. Thailand's economic boom is centered in Bangkok. As a result there is an increasing income gap between urban rich and rural poor, with almost 60% of population still working on farms. Labor migration has become a key fixture of the Thai economy. The uneven development between urban and rural areas leads to social problems that are the source of political instability. Efforts to promote industrial decentralization to areas outside of Bangkok are underway as overtaxed public works and diminishing water supplies cause concern.

Thailand also faces keen export competition from China, Indonesia, Viet Nam, Pakistan and Bangladesh, where cheap labor diminishes the competitiveness of Thailand's labor-intensive industries. In addition to a workforce ill equipped for a increas-

ingly industrialize economy, pollution, and clogged roads restrain competitiveness.

20INCOME

The US Central Intelligence Agency (CIA) reports that in 1998 Thailand's gross domestic product (GDP) was estimated at $369 billion. The per capita GDP was estimated at $6,100. The annual growth rate of GDP was estimated at -8.5%. The average inflation rate in 1998 was 4.3%. The CIA defines GDP as the value of all final goods and services produced within a nation in a given year and computed on the basis of purchasing power parity (PPP) rather than value as measured on the basis of the rate of exchange. It was estimated that agriculture accounted for 12% of GDP, industry 39%, and services 49%.

The World Bank reports that for the same period per capita private consumption (in PPP terms) was $2,050. Private consumption includes expenditures of individuals, households, and nongovernmental organizations. It was estimated that between 1990 and 1998 private consumption grew at an annual rate of 4.7%. Approximately 23% of household consumption was spent on food, 5% on fuel, 3% on health care, and 13% on education. The richest 10% of the population accounted for approximately 32% of household consumption and the poorest 10% approximately 2.8%.

21LABOR

The labor force in 1998 totaled some 33.35 million (compared with 21.7 million in 1981 and 15.1 million in 1967). Of the 32 million employed in the same year, about 50% were engaged in agriculture and related occupations, 20% in industry, and 30% in services. In 1994, unemployment amounted to 3.4% of the economically active population.

Because of persisting government opposition to unions, organized labor was not a major factor in Thai life prior to the 1970s. Labor legislation in 1969 delineated certain basic workers' rights, and unions were granted greater freedom to organize under the Labor Relations Act of 1975. The Thai Trade Union Congress is the largest labor federation. As of 1999, only 2% of the labor force (11% of industrial workers) was unionized. Minimum daily wage rates in 1999 ranged from $3.42 in Bangkok and the central valley provinces to $4.26 in the other regions. Legislation regulating hours and conditions of labor, workers' compensation, and welfare also exists. But these laws are weakly enforced. In one notorious example, 188 workers died in a fire at a toy factory in May 1994.

While forced labor is prohibited by the Thai constitution, there are reports that workers are physically prevented from leaving some sweatshops, especially ones which employ illegal immigrants from Laos, Cambodia, and Burma. These same sweatshops have also been accused of using physical coercion to meet production goals.

The minimum working age was raised to 15 in 1998, but this law has not traditionally been effectively enforced. As of 1999, it was estimated that there were between 850,000 to 1,480,000 children of the ages 6 to 14 working on family farms. Another 240,000 to 410,000 children were working in urban areas.

22AGRICULTURE

With some 20.4 million hectares (50.4 million acres) of farm land, of which about 10 million hectares (24.7 million acres) are under rice cultivation, Thailand continues to rely heavily on agriculture, although the country has suffered from declining export prices in recent years. Rice is the major crop grown; Thailand is the world's biggest rice exporter. Total exports of cereals in 1997 amounted to $1.2 billion, or 22.5% of all agricultural exports by value. Total rice production amounted to 23,240,000 tons in 1998. The government has embarked on large-scale irrigation projects and introduced higher-yielding varieties of rice in an effort to increase production.

Rubber, also a major export, is grown on the peninsula and, to a lesser extent, on the southeast coast. Total production in 1998 was 2,162,000 tons, the highest in the world and accounting for 28% of all production that year. Demand for natural rubber is growing along with the international concern about AIDS. Sugarcane production reached 50.6 million tons, while output of cassava (tapioca), traditionally important in Thailand, totaled 15.9 million tons. Thailand provides about 95% of the world's cassava exports. Much of the harvest is processed into chips and pellets and exported to the EU for fodder. Higher EU tariffs, however, have caused the Thai government to promote dairy, fruit, rubber, and cashew farming instead. Corn production, which has increased significantly in recent decades, reached 3.9 million tons in 1995. One third of annual corn production is consumed annually as fodder, with the remainder being exported to Europe and Japan. Kenaf, tobacco, cotton, and kapok are cultivated mainly for domestic use, but quantities of jute, cocoa, peanuts, soybeans, and medical plants are exported. Canned pineapple and fresh flowers, especially orchids, are important exports. The Thai government's official policy of encouraging mountain villagers to grow coffee, apples, strawberries, kidney beans, and other temperate crops instead of the lucrative opium poppy and marijuana has had some success; another aim of the project is to discourage deforestation through slash-and-burn cultivation. In 1987, King Bhumibol Adulyedej received a Magsaysay Award for International Understanding for his 20 years of effort in this area.

In the mid-1970s, farmers began to organize to express their discontent over the disparity between farm and nonfarm incomes. To improve farm conditions, the government legitimized squatters' rights to nearly 500,000 hectares (1,236,000 acres) of land classified as forest reserve and established credit and crop insurance programs for farmers. The government Marketing Organization for Farmers, founded in 1975, allows farmers to buy fertilizers, machinery, and equipment at the lowest possible prices and assists in crop marketing. It is also government policy to channel revenues from agricultural export taxes to a welfare fund called the Farmers Assistance Fund.

23ANIMAL HUSBANDRY
Cattle, used for plowing and harrowing, are important to rice farming, and most rural households have some cattle as well as hogs, chickens, and ducks. In 1998, Thailand had 7,000,000 head of cattle, 4,000,000 head of buffalo, 4,815,000 hogs, and 60,000 sheep. Other livestock included 165 million chickens and 22 million ducks. Elephants, important as draft animals in rural areas, are used to haul teak. Crocodiles, raised for their skins, are a specialty livestock product. Leading exports of animals and animal products in 1997 included (in millions of dollars): meat and meat products, $321; dairy products and eggs, $26.3; live animals, $825; and hides and skins, $0.9.

24FISHING
Fish is a major protein element in the Thai diet. Freshwater fish, abundantly found in rivers and canals, and marine fish (from the waters along the lengthy coastline) produced a catch of 3,488,104 tons in 1997 (9th in the world), as compared with 846,600 tons in 1967. Leading marine species in the 1997 harvest included (in tons): giant tiger prawn, 160,000; sardines, 132,200; anchovies, 115,300; Indian mackerels, 105,200; and threadfin breams, 67,200. Thailand exports cured fish to neighboring countries, and frozen shrimp and prawns mainly to Japan. In 1997, Thailand accounted for 4.6% of the world's exports of fish and fish products, valued at over $2,349 million. Aquacultural production in 1997 was valued at $1.78 billion. Giant tiger

prawn, tilapias, hybrid catfish, and green mussels accounted for most of the volume.

25FORESTRY
Thailand's forested area declined from 53% of the nation's land area in 1961 to only 26% by 1995, mainly as a result of the continued use of slash-and-burn practices by farmers. Of Thailand's 13.4 million ha (33.1 million acres) of forest, about 56% lies in the north, where teak and pine predominate. Rubber trees, planted mostly in the south, make up 10% of the forest area. The remainder consists of yang (keruing) plantations and rosewood, other species used as fuel, and smaller mangrove forests and conifers. Teak, once a major export, has declined in importance, largely because of government restrictions on cutting and past depletion of the forests through excessive harvesting and inadequate replanting. Yang, pradu, takien, krabak, and krabok are other traditional hardwoods that have suffered severe production declines. Thailand imposed a ban on logging government-owned timber in 1989. Lac, a resinous insect substance found on trees, has always had value for the Thai, but its derivatives—seedlac, sticklac, and shellac—have also found a ready international market. Other important forestry products include charcoal, gums and resins, and kapok fiber and seed.

In 1997 production of roundwood was estimated at 39.5 million cu m. Production of tropical hardwood products in 1997 included (in cubic meters): sawn wood, 322,000; wood pulp, 465,000; veneer, 156,000; and plywood, 156,000. Thailand is a negligible exporter of tropical logs and lumber. However, Thailand now exports primarily value-added wood products (mostly furniture, picture frames, utensils, and other items). Exports of wood products in 1997 totaled $1,541.6 million. Imports of logs, timber, and wood products in 1997 were valued at $570.6 million.

26MINING
Thailand is relatively poor in mineral reserves, except for tin and natural gas. Mining and quarrying in Thailand account for less than 1.5% of GDP and employed fewer than 30,000 workers. Tin ore is mined mainly on the southern peninsula; production in 1997 totaled 756 tons, most of it exported. Tin production has been steadily declining in the face of falling world prices and output curbs. Deposits of lignite were developed with US aid in the 1960s and have begun to show a good yield; 23,443,000 tons were produced in 1997. Iron ore is mined at Lop Buri for use in a small smelting plant; in 1997, total iron ore output was 43,840 tons. Other minerals exploited on a small scale include tungsten, lead, manganese, gold, silver, and many kinds of building stones. Rubies, sapphires, topaz, and zircon are also mined. The first commercial gypsum mine began operations in 1957; production in 1997 totaled 8,858,000 tons. Cement production in 1997 was 35,000,000 tons, up from 9,850,000 in 1987.

27ENERGY AND POWER
From 1975 to 1994, total installed generating capacity increased from 2,755,000 kW to 13,861,000 kW. In 1996, 61% of primary energy consumed was derived from oil, 20% from natural gas; 15% from coal; and the remainder from other sources. Distribution, however, is far from adequate, with only about 20% of the population having access to the system. The Metropolitan Electrical Authority serves Bangkok; the Provincial Electricity Authority provides service to the rest of the kingdom. Total national output in 1998 was 82,835 million kWh, up from 15,948 million kWh in 1981 and only 1,092 million kWh in 1964. Installed capacity in 1998 was 17.3 million kW.

Thailand is heavily dependent on imports of foreign oil. Proven and potential domestic deposits have been estimated at 296.2 million barrels in early 2000, but exploitation and development have been inhibited by declining oil prices. In 1998, crude oil production amounted to 75,000 barrels per day, mostly from the Sirikit oil field. Natural gas reserves were estimated at more than 12.5 trillion cu ft (354 billion cu m) in early 2000, and production has been aided by the exploitation of new fields in the Gulf of Thailand. Production in 1998 was put at 565 billion cu ft (15.9 billion cu m), almost double the 1995 amount. The privatization of the state-owned oil company, PTT, is scheduled for 2001. In 1999, the government introduced a new energy policy favoring increased use of natural gas.

28INDUSTRY

Seven government agencies supervise the Thai industrial sector. The Industrial Restructuring Committee was created in 1982 to coordinate the various agencies and to formulate policy proposals in line with economic development plans. The most important protective measure for the industrial sector were import tariffs. In the 1960s tariffs were low. During the 1970s tariffs increased, but at an uneven rate, some increased to above 90 percent. In conjunction with the Fifth Economic Development Plan the government in the 1980s attempted to form a more even tariff structure and to lower protectionism. Price control was another protective measure pervasive in the 1970s which was relaxed in the 1980s. In the 1990s trade liberalization continued.

Manufacturing grew at an average rate of 12% annually in the 1960s and 10% in the 1970s. Subsequently, falling commodity prices, rising interest rates, and reduced demand adversely affected manufacturing. Most industries still functioned on a modest scale, and Thailand continued to import most manufactured goods. However, growth in some areas has been impressive. From 1971 to 1985, production of food products nearly tripled, textiles grew over 500%, and transportation equipment showed even greater growth. In 1995, manufacturing accounted for about 29% of GDP.

As of 1995, Thailand's automotive industry was the fastest growing in the world in terms of expansion rates; the country is the second largest producer of motorcycles (1.3 million in 1994) and pickup trucks. Among the ASEAN nations, Thailand is the largest producer of petrochemicals, cement, and textiles. In 1995, Thailand's refineries produced 89.2 million barrels of refined petroleum products, including 51 million barrels of distillate and residual fuel oil, 19 million barrels of gasoline, and 12.5 million barrels of jet fuel. Cement production totaled 26.5 million tons in 1995. Other major industrial items produced include galvanized iron sheets, refined sugar, tires, and beer.

Since 1979, Thailand's manufacturing sector has increasingly diversified and made the largest contribution to the economy. The export-oriented component of the sector is dynamic and growing. In 1995, manufacturing output increased by 17%. The fastest growing manufacturing sectors in 1995 were as follows: cigarettes (up 81%), integrated circuits (36%), synthetic fibers (25%), commercial vehicles (23%), motorcycles (20%), and passenger cars (16%).

29SCIENCE AND TECHNOLOGY

The lack of skilled workers remains a drag on industrial development. Many students seek technical training overseas, and some receive postgraduate education in specialized technical subjects at the Asian Institute of Technology in Bangkok (founded in 1959 at Bangkok), which offers advanced degrees in agricultural engineering, human settlements, and computer applications. The institute also operates receiving equipment for LANDSAT transmissions that provide Southeast Asian countries with the aerial surveys vital to agricultural development, forest inventories, and city planning.

Scientific organizations include the Medical Association of Thailand (founded 1921); the Thailand Institute of Scientific and Technological Research (1963), the principle government research agency; and the Science Society of Thailand (1948), all headquartered in Bangkok. National science policy is the responsibility of the Ministry of Science, Technology and Energy. Research and development expenditures in 1987–97 totaled 0.13% of GNP; 103 scientists and engineers and 39 technicians per 1 million population were engaged in research and development.

In addition to the Asian Institution of Technology, 15 other universities offer courses in basic and applied sciences. In 1987–97, science and engineering students accounted for 18% of college and university enrollments. In 1998, high-tech exports were valued at $12.6 billion and accounted for 31% of manufactured exports.

30DOMESTIC TRADE

Bangkok, the port of entry and distribution point for the whole country, is the commercial center of Thailand; all foreign firms have their main offices there. Other commercially important cities are Chiang Mai (teak, rice, and textiles), Ubon Ratchathani (rice, jute, and leather), Phuket (tin), and Songkhla (rubber). Many essential commodities are grown and consumed by the producer, or distributed at the local level. Production for the domestic market has continued to increase led by high growth industries such as construction materials, foods and beverages, and electronic appliances. In the greater Bangkok metropolitan area, almost every kind of retail outlet is represented, including speciality shops and over 40 department stores. Thais spend an average of 23% (46% in Bangkok) of their food budget in restaurants. A large segment of retailing is Chinese controlled. In metropolitan areas, professional, personal, and technological services are available. Usual business hours are from 8:30 AM to 4:30 PM, Monday through Friday. Shops are open from 9 AM to 8 or 9 PM, and banks from 8:30 AM to 3:30 PM. Rather than shop in traditional "wet markets," a growing number of Thai consumers are utilizing western-style supermarkets. Newspaper, radio, television, and motion picture advertising is available. The annual Bangkok fair in December, originally conceived for entertainment, has developed into a trade fair.

31FOREIGN TRADE

Thailand supplies the world with a large proportion of its natural rubber, rice, and seafood exports. The top ten exports are as follows:

	% OF COUNTRY TOTAL	% OF WORLD TOTAL
Transistors and valves	5.1	1.8
Automatic data processing equipment	4.9	2.2
Shell fish	4.7	14
Natural rubber and gums	4.1	33
Office machines	3.9	2.4
Footwear	3.5	5.5
Rice	3.5	27
Preserved fish	3.0	18
Telecoms equipment	2.7	1.3
Articles of plastic	2.3	2.6

In 1997 Thailand's imports were distributed among the following categories:

Consumer goods	5.8%
Food	3.6%
Fuels	9.2%
Industrial supplies	32.4%
Machinery	39.3%
Transportation	7.9%
Other	1.8%

Principal trading partners in 1998 (in millions of US dollars) were as follows:

COUNTRY	EXPORTS	IMPORTS	BALANCE
United States	12,175	6,053	6,122
Japan	7,475	10,175	-2,700
Singapore	4,698	2,383	2,315
China (inc. Hong Kong)	4,554	2,587	1,967
Netherlands	2,181	446	1,735
United Kingdom	2,121	712	1,409
Malaysia	1,780	2,198	-418
Taiwan	1,743	2,240	-497
Germany	1,556	1,822	-266
Korea	626	1,496	-870

32 BALANCE OF PAYMENTS

In 1996, a weakening economy and a decline in export growth created a current account deficit that amounted to 8% of GDP. Simultaneously, high interest rates and a currency tied to the dollar attracted money to an economy without sufficient productive assets to support the inflow. The government was forced to pursue a high interest-rate policy to protect the currency. When the cost of doing so got too high, the government let the currency float against the dollar, which resulted in a 20% devaluation. By mid-1997, Thailand's short-term debt obligations had reached $23.4 billion, consuming three-quarters of its foreign reserve holdings. In August of 1997, Thailand agreed to an economic restructuring package with the IMF that included $10–20 billion in standby credits.

The International Monetary Fund (IMF) reports that in 1998 Thailand had exports of goods totaling $52,747 million and imports totaling $36,513 million. The services credit totaled $13,156 million and debit $11,998 million. The following table summarizes Thailand's balance of payments as reported by the IMF for 1998 in millions of US dollars.

Current Account		14,241
Balance on goods	16,234	
Balance on services	1,158	
Balance on income	-3,565	
Current transfers	415	
Capital Account		...
Financial Account		-14,455
Direct investment abroad	-130	
Direct investment in Thailand	6,941	
Portfolio investment assets	-202	
Portfolio investment liabilities	159	
Other investment assets	-3,824	
Other investment liabilities	-17,399	
Net Errors and Omissions		-3,007
Reserves and Related Items		3,222

33 BANKING AND SECURITIES

The central bank in the Bank of Thailand, established in 1942. It operates as an independent body under government supervision; its entire capital is owned by the government. The Bank issues notes, a function previously handled by the Ministry of Finance.

The financial sector is broad and diverse. In 1997 there were 37 commercial banks operating the Thailand, 16 domestic and 21 foreign owned. The top three Thai banks are Bangkok Bank, Krung Thai Bank, and Thai Farmers Bank. Many of Thailand's domestic banks are owned by a few wealthy Chinese families. Shareholdings in even the largest banks, led by Bangkok Bank and the Thai Farmers Bank, are structured to insure family control. US banks with full branches in Thailand include Citibank, Chase Manhattan Bank, and Bank of America.

In general, Thai banks have suffered management problems in recent years and are having difficulty in complying with capital-adequacy and other requirements set by the Bank for International Settlements (BIS). The baht currency crisis dealt a severe blow to the banking industry and has prompted a major restructuring of the banking industry. By mid-2000, nonperforming loans accounted for about a third of total lending, down from a peak of almost 48% mid-1999. Thai banks are being forced to accept big write-offs by selling non-performing loans for as little as 30% of the loan's face value.

The Thai domestic banking system has been criticized for failing to mobilize adequate domestic savings and for not offering adequate incentives to savers.

Thailand's first public stock exchange was opened in Bangkok on 30 April 1975 (the Securities Exchange of Thailand—SET). All of its 30 members were Thai-owned securities firms. The Ministry of Finance encourages companies to go public by reducing income tax for listed companies and also by according favorable tax treatment of dividends. It was not until the late 1980s that the market was taken seriously by the international and domestic financial communities. Because of the Asian financial crisis, the stock exchange lost its appeal as a source of corporate funds. In 1998, however, a four-year downward trend was reversed on news of a strengthened baht. The rally could not be sustained and by years end the SET index was down 4.5%, a substantial improvement over 1997s 55% decline. In all, the exchange lists 418 companies with a combined market capitalization of just under $35 billion. The turnover ratio is high at over 70%.

34 INSURANCE

There is a wide variety of insurance companies doing business in Thailand, including the American International Assurance Co., the Asian Reinsurance Corp., Assets Insurance Co., Bangkok Insurance Public Co., Commercial Union Assurance Co., Guardian Assurance Co., Indara Insurance Public Co., Navakij Insurance Public Co., Paiboon Insurance Co., Phatra Insurance Co., Safety Insurance Co., Samaggi Insurance Co., the Thai Insurance Public Co., the Viriyah Insurance Co., and Wilson Insurance Co.

35 PUBLIC FINANCE

The International Monetary Fund estimates that in 1998 Thailand's central government took in revenues of approximately $18.3 billion and had expenditures of $22.2 billion including capital expenditures of $7.5 billion. Overall, the government registered a deficit of approximately $3.9 billion. External debt totaled $96.7 billion. The following table shows an itemized breakdown of government revenues and expenditures in millions of US dollars. The percentages were calculated from data reported by the International Monetary Fund.

REVENUE AND GRANTS	100%	18,300
Tax revenue	88.2%	16,144
Non-tax revenue	11.1%	2,035
Capital revenue	0.1%	13
Grants	0.6%	108
EXPENDITURES	100%	22,200
General public services	4.7%	1,040
Defense	10.3%	2,295
Public order and safety	6.1%	1,359
Education	23.1%	5,134
Health	9.2%	2,035
Social security	4.1%	914
Housing and community amenities	4.8%	1,055
Recreation, cultural, and religious affairs	1.6%	350
Economic affairs and services	28.3%	6,293
Other expenditures	6.8%	1,500
Interest payments	1.0%	226

36TAXATION

Personal income tax rates are graduated from 5–37%. Business and individual citizens are also subject to a host of indirect taxes, including customs duties, sales tax, and excise taxes. Corporate income taxes on net profit in 1996 were levied at the flat rate of 30%. Stock dividends and capital gains are taxed as regular income.

All companies and individuals engaged in industry, commerce, or services are subject to a value-added tax (VAT). Effective August 1997, the highest rate of the VAT was increased from 7% to 10%. Remittances out of Thailand in the form of profits, income, or dividends are taxed at 25%. In addition, a municipal tax of 10% is levied on certain businesses. Reductions are available under the Investment Promotion Act. Import surcharges, designed to deter imports, were imposed in 1981 at rates between 5% and 30% on certain fibers, piston rings, palm oil, and telephones.

There are excise taxes on tobacco, petroleum products, alcoholic beverages and soft drinks, and other products. Automobiles are subject to a special tax based on engine size.

Thailand has double taxation treaties with 33 countries, including the United States, Canada, Australia, Belgium, Denmark, Finland, France, and Germany. The US treaty has been in force since January 1998.

37CUSTOMS AND DUTIES

Thailand's customs tariff is primarily for revenue, although in a limited fashion it protects local industry. No preferential treatment is afforded any country, and all goods are subject to the general rate. Only a few goods require import licenses, including some foods, materials, and industrial products. Products banned from import include aerosol mixtures of vinyl chloride monomers (for health reasons) and products constituting trademark infringement.

The Thai government began to reduce tariffs in 1994 although progress was impeded in 1997 due to a shortfall in government revenue. Still, duties that had ranged between 30–60% had been cut to between 1–45% with the total number of tariff bands reduced from 39 to 6. There is a zero rate for essential items like medical equipment and fertilizer. The rate is 30% for certain items designated as needing special protection, like fabrics, clothing, refrigerators, and air conditioners In addition to tariffs, some imports designated as luxury goods are subject to an excise tax.

Thailand is a member of the Association of Southeast Asian Nations (ASEAN) and the World Trade Organization (WTO). ASEAN members have established the ASEAN Free Trade Area (AFA) which aims to educe tariffs on most processed agricultural and industrial products traded among ASEAN countries to 0–5% by the year 2003. A proposal to link the economies of Australia and New Zealand to AFA is also under discussion.

38FOREIGN INVESTMENT

Growth of the Thai economy has been directly related to the flow of investments from abroad. In order to stimulate such investment, the government passed the Industrial Promotion Act (1962), which established the Board of Investment for Industry, renamed the Board of Investment (BOI) in 1972. The Alien Business Law of 1972 restricts the participation of non-Thai nationals in certain types of business activities, although proposals to reduce the number of businesses reserved for Thai nationals were under consideration in 1996. The BOI, the powers and responsibilities of which were broadened in 1977, grants the following benefits to promoted industries: guarantees against nationalization and competition from government industries; exemption from import duties and business tax on plant, machinery, spare parts, and raw materials; exemption from duty on exports; exemption from tax on corporate income for a specified period; and repatriation of capital and remittance of profits abroad. The BOI considers applications for promotional benefits to both Thai and foreign investors. Projects meeting any or all of the following criteria are eligible for investment incentives: significantly strengthen Thailand's balance-of-payments position, especially through production for export; support of the development of the country's resources; substantially increase employment; locate operations in the provinces; conserve energy or replace imported energy supplies; establish or develop industries which form the base for further stages of industrial development; or, projects considered necessary or important to the government.

In 1997 foreign direct investment in Thailand was just under $3 billion, up from $2.3 billion the year before. Of that amount, 19% was invested in real estate, down from 42% in 1995; 34% in industry; and 31% in trade. The Japanese were the largest investors with investments totaling just over $1 billion (about 35% of the total). Hong Kong accounted for 10%, the US for 19%, Singapore for 10%, and the UK for about 4%.

In 1997, Thai companies invested $555 million abroad, down from $789 million in 1996. About 20% of that amount ($110 million) went to the US and 19% ($107 million) to Singapore. Other countries favored by Thai investors include Vietnam ($49 million), Cambodia ($19 million), and Laos ($2.4 million), China ($36 million), Hong Kong ($9.6 million), and Malaysia ($4.4 million).

39ECONOMIC DEVELOPMENT

The Thai government, vulnerable in its financial dependence on a few primary commodities (rice, rubber, tin, and teak), has pursued a policy of economic diversification through industrial development and increased agricultural production. With the beginning of the first development plan in 1961, the government committed itself to the primacy of private enterprise and to a policy of fostering and assisting it. Thailand has also followed a policy of foreign trade and exchange liberalization. Foreign exchange control is nominal.

Thailand's first five-year plan, covering the period 1961–66, aimed to raise the standard of living by means of greater agricultural, industrial, and power production. In the second development plan (1967–71), emphasis was placed on agricultural development, highways, irrigation, education, and industrial development in the private sector. The third development plan (1972–76) placed special emphasis on improvements in the rural infrastructure, growth in the financial and commercial sectors, and further assistance to crop diversification and to import-substitution industries. The government also committed itself to a reduction in the role of state-owned enterprises. The first three plans did much to increase the standard of living and to bring new roads, irrigation schemes, and land reform to the prosperous Bangkok region. But these changes also increased the income gap between rural and urban Thailand and drew increasing numbers of migrants to the city in search of work. Accordingly, the fourth economic plan, covering the years 1977–81, emphasized decentralization of industry and economic growth from the capital region to the provinces. It also ended the policy of encouraging import-substitution industries and began the promotion of export-oriented industries able to benefit from the nation's low wage rates. Plans were made for the establishment of industrial estates under the direction of the Industrial Estate Authority of Thailand. The first estate, at Bangchan, 30 km (19 mi) from Bangkok, was fully occupied in 1980 by 51 companies, producing a range of industrial products, including automotive and electrical equipment, chemicals, and processed food. Another industrial estate, established in 1979 at Lard Krabang, also in the Bangkok vicinity, includes, in addition to a general industrial area, a duty-free export-processing zone open to manufacturers willing to establish high value-added and labor-intensive industries for export.

The fifth development plan, covering the years 1982–86, stressed reduction of rural poverty and social tensions and expansion of employment opportunities in the poorer regions. To this end, four investment promotion zones were established. After completion in 1981 of the natural gas pipeline from the Gulf of Thailand, investment priority was reassigned to the Eastern Seaboard Development Program. This ambitious program called for the creation of a new urban-industrial complex in the Rayong-Sattahip region that was expected to draw industries from the congested Bangkok area. Heavy industries were to be emphasized, with early construction of a natural gas separator and plants for the manufacture of soda ash, fertilizers, and petrochemicals. The sixth National Economic and Social Development Plan (1986–91) stressed continuing export promotion, streamlining of the public sector, and strict monetary and fiscal policies, with growth targeted at only about 5% yearly. Emphasis was placed on the less capital-intensive industries, and more emphasis was given to improved utilization of resources. The plan targeted private sector investment and initiatives. Privatization of state enterprises would proceed in clear-cut phases, and enterprises were required to seek their own revenue. Agricultural production was forecast to grow at 2.9% per year. The development of small-scale industry, particularly in rural areas, was emphasized. In 1993, the Eastern Seaboard Development Plan southeast of Bangkok—begun 10 years before as a US$4 billion investment—demonstrated results with the new port, Laem Chabang. This plan extends greater Bangkok, and the next phases include extending all main national arteries into four-lane highways and double-tracking the railway.

Themes for each region guided development. In the north, Chiang-mai, Lamphrun and Lampang, light and clean industries are encouraged, such as clothing, high-value electronics, and agro-industry. In the south, transport links and natural gas networks developed between the Andaman Sea and the Gulf of Thailand would attract heavy industry such as petrochemicals, and cross-border development with Malaysia would link with Penang's industrial sector. Development plans for the impoverished northeast included linking with Laos, Cambodia, and Viet Nam for processing raw materials from those countries, and for providing services involved with investment and manufacturing in those countries. The Board of Investment (BOI) encourages development with varying incentives for investors depending on zoned areas of the country. For instance, minimum wage rates in Zone 3 (73 provinces) are 20% below Zone 1 (greater Bangkok) and Zone 2 (provinces closest to Bangkok and eastern seaboard). Zone 3 investors would have eight-year tax holidays, with no requirement (such as in Zones 1 & 2) for export of all of their production. Cheap credit—6–7%—is available for rural areas, compared to 16% or more elsewhere. The T-BIRD—Thai Business Initiative Rural Development—is run by the Population and Community Development Association (PDA), one of Thailand's largest nongovernmental organizations. Schemes assisting villagers to remain on the land have been developed. Farmers are encouraged to raise more lucrative vegetable crops rather than drought-prone rice, pigs, dairy cows or chickens, and to form vegetable banks and/or rice pools. The dwindling of forest cover in Thailand impacts negatively on economic, as well as ecological, development, especially in rural areas. In the northeast, tourism and textile production is replacing the agriculture that had earlier replaced opium cultivation.

40 SOCIAL DEVELOPMENT

Since 1940, social welfare has been the responsibility of the government, and it is only in recent years that private organizations have actively engaged in social welfare programs. A 1990 law established a social security system which began paying disability and death benefits in 1991. Old age benefits (pensions) were introduced in 1998. In 1999, the pension system was funded by employers, employees, and the government; each source contributed an amount equal to 1% of the employee's wages. The social security law also provides for sickness and maternity benefits, which are provided to employees of firms with 10 or more workers. Employers are required to provide workers' compensation coverage, including temporary and permanent disability benefits, and medical and survivor benefits.

Women have equal legal rights in most areas, but inequities remain in domestic areas, including divorce and child support. In 1991, a Commission on Women's Affairs was established. The 1997 constitution protects women through the inclusion of six gender-related articles pertaining to equal rights. In addition, gender-equality clauses have been included in legislation setting up new government entities mandated by the constitution. A 1998 labor law made sexual harassment a crime. In 1999, women made up 44% of the work force.

Many women are trapped into prostitution through a system of debt bondage. Brothels provide a loan to parents of young women, and these women are required to work as prostitutes to pay off the loan. In many cases, this is done without the consent of the woman involved. Under the Penal Code, furthermore, prostitutes are considered criminals, but brothel owners and clients are not.

Many Thai minorities, including many of the hill tribe members, lack any type of documentation. As noncitizens, they are do not have full access to education and health care. They lack titles to their land, and may not vote in elections. The government has announced its intention to process and document these groups.

Human rights are generally well respected, but some abuses occur. Coerced confessions and the torture of suspects are occasionally reported. Overcrowding in prisons has resulted in poor conditions.

41 HEALTH

In the 1960s, the government, with UN and US assistance, extended free medical treatment, expanded health education activities in schools and rural areas, and built many hospitals. In the private sector, two-thirds of health care funding comes from employers and private households. A national social security scheme is underway, but private insurers are few. Owing largely to success in eradicating malaria and other tropical diseases, as well as to better sanitation and medical care, health conditions have steadily improved in Thailand. By 1995, 89% of the population had access to safe water, and 96% had adequate sanitation. Common diseases were malaria (115,220), tuberculosis (20,260), and leprosy (5,126) in 1995. From 1989–95, 13% of children under five years of age were considered malnourished. About 7% of births in 1993–96 were of low birthweight. In 1993, about 59% of the population had access to health care services. The 1990–95 immunization rates for a child under one were as follows: diptheria, pertussis, and tetanus (93%); polio (93%); measles (86%); and tuberculosis (98%). Health care facilities are concentrated in the Bangkok metropolitan area, where about 15% of the population is located. In 1989, there were 180 private hospitals and more than 11,000 private clinics. In 1990–97, there were a total of 1.7 beds per 1,000 people. Thai hospitals tend to be small in size.

In 1990–97, there were 20 doctors per 100,000 inhabitants, with a nurse to doctor ratio of 5.5. Thailand's birth rate was 16.5 per 1,000 people in 1999, and 74% of married women (ages 15 to 49) used contraception in 1993. In 1999, life expectancy was 69.2 years. Infant mortality was 29.5 per 1,000 live births, and maternal mortality was 16 per 100,000 live births in 1991–93. The general mortality rate was 7.2 per 1,000 people in 1999. Regional inequities in the distribution of health facilities and personnel persist, with Bangkok and other urban centers being much better supplied than rural areas. Total health care expenditures in 1990–97 were 3.9% of the gross domestic product.

The HIV seroprevalence rate was 2.2 per 100 adults in 1997. There were 22,135 AIDS cases reported in 1995, the most cases reported in all of Asia. The HIV-epidemic in Thailand is among the best-documented in the world, with over 780,000 living with HIV as of 1997. In brothel sex workers, the HIV infection rose from 3.5% in 1989 to 33% in late 1994.

Tobacco consumption has risen from 1.9 kg in 1984–86 to 2.0 kg a year per adult in 1995.

42HOUSING

Most families in Thailand live in dwellings that compare favorably with living facilities anywhere in Southeast Asia. The Thai government has stimulated housing and community development by means of a housing plan that provides government mortgages for building, renovation, or purchase of government land and houses. Under a self-help settlement scheme, the government sets up whole new communities, surveys sites, constructs roads and irrigation systems, and provides public utilities and medical care.

In 1973, to house Bangkok residents who had been living in makeshift shelters, the government formed the National Housing Authority (NHA), which undertook overall responsibility for coordination of public and private housing programs. By 1979, the NHA had completed 54,780 housing units. From 1979 to 1984, a total of 1,442,250 housing units were built in Thailand. In 1986, 86% of all living quarters were detached houses, 11% were row-houses, and 2% were single rooms. Owners occupied 84% of all dwellings, 8% were rented, 3% were occupied rent free, and 3% were occupied in exchange for a service. The total number of housing units in 1992 was 11,151,000.

43EDUCATION

The rate of adult illiteracy has been in decline. For the year 2000, adult illiteracy rates were estimated at 4.4% (males, 2.8%; females, 6.0%), a drop from an overall adult illiteracy rate of 6.2% in 1995. Compulsory education provisions, first introduced in 1921, call for universal school attendance starting at age seven through the fourth year of primary school or through age 15. In 1998 primary schools enrolled 5,927,902 students. Secondary schools in the same year enrolled 4,097,331 students. Both teacher training and technical and vocational training (especially in agriculture) have been stressed in recent development plans.

In 1998, about 1,522,142 students were enrolled in higher education programs. In Bangkok, Chulalongkorn University (founded 1917) is Thailand's most eminent university. Also in Bangkok are the University of Thammasart (founded 1933), specializing in social and political sciences, and Kasetsart University (founded 1943) specializing in agriculture. Newer universities established in provincial areas include Chiang Mai University (founded in 1964), Khon Kaen University (founded in the northeast in 1966), and Prince of Songkhla University (founded in 1968). King Mongkut's Institute of Technology was formed in 1971 through the amalgamation of three institutes, and eight colleges of education were combined into Sri Nakharin-wirot University in Bangkok in 1974. A correspondence school, the University of Ramkhamhaeng, opened in Bangkok in 1974 and the Sukhothai Thammathirat Open University began operations in 1978. In total there are 16 state universities in addition to 26 privately run colleges. There are also a large number of teacher training colleges.

44LIBRARIES AND MUSEUMS

The National Library (founded in 1905) contains about 1.2 million books and over 100,000 manuscripts. Other important libraries in Bangkok include the Asian Institute of Technology (200,000 volumes), Chulalongkorn University (264,700), the University of Thammasat (654,000), Kasetsart University (262,000), and Sri Nakharinwirot University (299,500). The Library of the Department of Science Services maintains a special collection of 450,000 volumes. Outside Bangkok, sizable collections are maintained at the University of Chiang Mai (190,000) and Khon Kaen University (270,000). The Economic and Social Commission for Asia and the Pacific holds 150,000 volumes.

The National Museum in Bangkok (founded in 1926) has an extensive collection of Thai artifacts, including sculptures, textiles, ceramics, jewels, coins, weapons, and masks. Many of Bangkok's temples and palaces contain excellent examples of Thai frescoes and sculptures. The Temple of the Emerald Buddha has a famous mural of the Ramayana, the Sanskrit epic, and the Marble Temple contains a fine collection of bronze and stone Buddhas.

Bangkok also houses the Bhirasi Institute of Modern Art, the Hill Tribes Museum, the Science Museum, and the Sood Sanquichien Prehistoric Museum and Laboratory. There are dozens of other provincial museums throughout the country.

45MEDIA

The Ministry of Communications is responsible for Thailand's public postal, telegraph, and telephone services. The postal service, employing both railway and air mail, operates from the central post office in Bangkok and covers the entire country. Telephone service now reaches the principal towns, with 2,184,900 main telephone lines in use in 1995 (compared with 98,000 in 1968), of which over 70% were in metropolitan areas. Thailand is a member of INTELSAT and maintains trans-Pacific and Indian Ocean satellite communications stations.

Ownership of broadcasting is both public and private. There are six government and military radio networks and Bangkok alone has five television stations. The first mainland Asian television station was established in Bangkok in 1955. As of 1999, there were 200 AM, 100 FM, and 5 television stations. In 1997 Thailand had 204 radios, 234 television sets, and 33 mobile phones per 1,000 population.

The first daily newspaper, the *Siam Daily Advertiser,* appeared more than a century ago. In 1995 there were 35 daily newspapers published in Bangkok, including eight in Chinese and four in English. The provinces have weekly and semiweekly publications, all in Thai, but no daily papers. Bangkok also has a variety of weekly and monthly periodicals, most appearing in Thai. Among Bangkok's leading daily newspapers (with language medium and estimated 1999 daily circulation) were:

	LANGUAGE	CIRCULATION
Thai Rath (m)	Thai	700,000
Daily News (m)	Thai	450,000
Ban Muang (m)	Thai	70,000
Matichon (m)	Thai	280,000
Sing Sian Yit Pao (m)	Chinese	80,000
Bangkok Post (m)	English	50,000
Srinakorn Daily News (m)	Chinese	80,000
Naew Na (d)	Thai	250,000
Phaya Crut (m)	Thai	100,000

Citizens are said to enjoy constitutionally provided freedom of speech and a free press. However, the law prohibits criticism of the royal family, threats to national security, and insults to Buddhism.

Online access is extremely limited, with fewer than 5 Internet hosts per 1,000 population in 1998.

46ORGANIZATIONS

Thailand has an extensive cooperative movement. Credit societies are the dominant type of cooperative; consumer cooperatives are the next largest, followed by agricultural marketing and processing cooperatives. Other kinds of cooperatives, mostly formed during and since the 1930s, include colonization and land improvement cooperatives.

Trade organizations under the Ministry of Economic Affairs include the Thai Chamber of Commerce, the Board of Trade, and several foreign trade associations. Cultural organizations include the Royal Institute (founded 1933); the Thai-Bhara Cultural Lodge (founded 1940), which sponsors studies in the fields of linguistics, philosophy, and religion; and the Siam Society (founded 1904), which issues studies on Thai art, literature, and science.

47TOURISM, TRAVEL, AND RECREATION

Tourism has become a vital industry in Thailand. In 1997, a total of $7 billion was spent in the country by 7,293,957 foreign visitors. That year there were 249,098 hotel rooms with a 47% occupancy rate. Most tourists visit Bangkok and its Buddhist temples (wats). All visitors must have passports; visitors from most countries may stay up to 15 days without a visa. Typhoid, tetanus, and gamma globulin immunizations are recommended, especially for travel in rural areas. Yellow fever inoculation is required of tourists arriving from an infected area.

Major sports include soccer and baseball. Thai bull, cock, and fish fighting are also popular (though illegal), along with Thai boxing, golf, badminton, and kite fighting.

The average daily cost of staying in Bangkok, according to 1999 UN estimates, was $135 per day. Elsewhere in Thailand, estimated travel costs range from $119 in Cha Am to $55 in Nakhon Ratchasima.

48FAMOUS THAI

Many ancient Thai kings enjoy legendary reputations. Rama Khamheng (the Great), a 13th-century monarch, is traditionally regarded as the inventor of the Thai alphabet; Rama Tibodi I in the 14th century promulgated the first-known Thai laws; Trailok instituted lasting governmental reforms in the 15th century; and Phya Tak in the 18th century rebuilt a war-defeated Thailand. Two great monarchs, Mongkut (r.1851–68) and his son Chula-longkorn (r.1868–1910), became famous for introducing Thailand to the modern world. They are, respectively, the king and his young successor in Margaret Landon's *Anna and the King of Siam*. Further progress toward modernization was accomplished in more recent times by three outstanding premiers: Phibul Songgram (1897–1964), Pridi Banomyong (1900–83), and Sarit Thanarat (1900–63). Prince Wan Waithayakon (1891–1976), foreign minister and Thailand's representative to the UN, played a major role in diplomacy for many years following World War II. Marshal Thanom Kittikachorn (b.1911) was leader of Thailand from 1963 until October 1973, when political protests compelled his resignation as prime minister. King Bhumibol Adulyadej (b.US, 1927) ascended the throne in 1946.

Prince Akat Damkoeng was the author in 1940 of the first modern novel written in Thailand, *Yellow Race, White Race*. Modern styles in painting and sculpture are reflected in the work of Chitr Buabusaya and Paitun Muangsomboon, and the traditional manner in the art of Apai Saratani and Vichitr Chaosanket.

49DEPENDENCIES

Thailand has no territories or colonies.

50BIBLIOGRAPHY

Benedict, Ruth. *Thai Culture and Behavior.* Ithaca, N.Y.: Cornell University Press, 1952.

Bowring, Sir John. *The Kingdom and People of Siam.* London: Parker, 1857.

Dixon, Chris J. *The Thai Economy: Uneven Development and Internationalisation.* New York: Routledge, 1999.

Ingram, James C. *Economic Change in Thailand, 1850–1970.* Stanford, Calif.: Stanford University Press, 1971.

Keyes, Charles F. *Thailand; Buddhist Kingdom as Modern Nation-State.* Boulder, Colo.: Westview Press, 1987.

Koeberle, Stefan and Johanna Witte. (eds.) *Building Thailand's Competitiveness: The Road to Economic Recovery.* Washington, D.C.: World Bank, 1998.

Kulick, Elliott. *Thailand's Turn: Profile of a New Dragon.* New York: St. Martin's, 1992.

LePoer, Barbara Leitch (ed.). *Thailand, A Country Study.* 6th ed. Washington, D.C.: Library of Congress, 1989.

Mulder, Niels. *Inside Thai Society: An Interpretation of Everyday Life.* 5th ed. Amsterdam: Pepin, 1996.

Mungkandi, Wiwat, and William Warren. *A Century and a Half of Thai-American Relations.* Bangkok: Chulalongkorn University Press, 1982.

Muscat, Robert J. *Thailand and the United States: Development, Security, and Foreign Aid.* New York: Columbia University Press, 1990.

——. *The Fifth Tiger: A Study of Thai Development Policy.* Helsinki: United Nations University Press, 1994.

Silcock, Thomas Henry. *Thailand: Social and Economic Studies in Development.* Durham, N.C.: Duke University Press, 1968.

Stowe, Judith A. *Siam becomes Thailand: A Story of Intrigue.* Honolulu: University of Hawaii Press, 1991.

Trerwiel, B. J. *A History of Modern Thailand, 1767–1942.* St. Lucia: Queensland University Press, 1983.

Wyatt, D. K. *Thailand.* New Haven, Conn.: Yale University Press, 1984.

Xuto, Somsakdi (ed.). *Government and Politics of Thailand.* New York: Oxford University Press, 1987.

TONGA

Kingdom of Tonga
Pule'anga Tonga

CAPITAL: Nuku'alofa, Tongatapu.

FLAG: The flag, adopted in 1862, is crimson with a cross of the same color mounted in a white canton.

ANTHEM: *Koe Fasi Oe Tu'i Oe Otu Tonga* (Tongan National Anthem) begins "'E 'Otua Mafimafi Ko homau 'Eiki Koe" ("O Almighty God above, Thou art our Lord and sure defense").

MONETARY UNIT: The Tongan pa'anga (T$) of 100 seniti is a paper currency at par with the Australian dollar. There are coins of 1, 2, 5, 10, 20, and 50 seniti, and 1 and 2 Tongan pa'angas, and notes of ½, 1, 2, 5, 10, 20, and 50 pa'angas. T$1 = US$0.6188 (US$1 = T$1.616) as of 31 March 2000.

WEIGHTS AND MEASURES: The metric system is the legal standard, but some imperial and local weights and measures are also employed.

HOLIDAYS: New Year's Day, 1 January; ANZAC Day, 25 April; Crown Prince's Birthday, 4 May; Independence Day, 4 June; King's Birthday, 4 July; Constitution Day, 4 November; Tupou I Day, 4 December; Christmas, 25–26 December. Movable religious holidays include Good Friday and Easter Monday.

TIME: 1 AM (the following day) = noon GMT.

¹LOCATION, SIZE, AND EXTENT

The Tonga archipelago, also known as the Friendly Islands, lies scattered east of Fiji in the South Pacific Ocean. Nuku'alofa, the capital, is about 690 km (430 mi) from Suva, Fiji, and about 1,770 km (1,100 mi) from Auckland, New Zealand. Consisting of 172 islands of various sizes, only 45 of which are inhabited, Tonga has a total area of 748 sq km (289 sq mi), including inland waters as well as Teleki Tokelau and Teleki Tonga (formerly the Minerva Reefs). Comparatively, the area occupied by Tonga is slightly more than four times the size of Washington, D.C. It extends 631 km (392 mi) NNE–SSW and 209 km (130 mi) ESE–WNW. Areas of the major islands are Tongatapu and 'Eua, 350 sq km (135 sq mi); Ha'apai, 119 sq km (46 sq mi); Vava'u, 143 sq km (55 sq mi); Niuatoputapu and Tafahi, 18 sq km (7 sq mi); and Niuafo'ou, 52 sq km (20 sq mi). The remaining islands have a combined area of 67 sq km (26 sq mi). Tonga's total coastline is about 419 km (260 mi).

²TOPOGRAPHY

The islands run roughly north–south in two parallel chains; the western islands are volcanic, and the eastern are coralline encircled by reefs. At 10,800 m (35,400 ft) deep, the Tonga Trench is one of the lowest parts of the ocean floor. The soil on the low-lying coral islands is porous, being a shallow layer of red volcanic ash, devoid of quartz, but containing broken-down limestone particles.

The volcanic islands range in height to a maximum of 1,033 m (3,389 ft) on Kao. Fonuafo'ou (formerly Falcon Island), about 65 km (40 mi) northwest of Nuku'alofa, is famous for its periodic submergences and reappearances, as a result of earthquakes and volcanic action. There are few lakes or streams. Tofua, Vava'u, Nomuka, and Niuafo'ou each have a lake, and there are creeks on 'Eua and one stream on Niuatoputapu. Other islands rely on wells and the storage of rainwater to maintain a water supply.

³CLIMATE

The climate of Tonga is basically subtropical. Because the islands are in the southeast trade wind area, the climate is cooler from May to November, when the temperature seldom rises above 27°C (81°F). The mean annual temperature is 23°C (73°F), ranging from an average daily minimum of 10°C (50°F) in winter to an average maximum of 32°C (90°F) in summer. Mean annual rainfall, most of which occurs from December to March during the hot season, is 178 cm (70 in) on Tongatapu, 188 cm (74 in) on Niuatoputapu, and 279 cm (110 in) on Vava'u. The mean relative humidity is 80%.

⁴FLORA AND FAUNA

Coconut palms, hibiscus, and other tropical trees, bushes, and flowers are abundant. Tonga is famous for its flying foxes.

⁵ENVIRONMENT

Agricultural activities in Tonga are exhausting the fertility of the soil. The forest area is declining because of land clearing, and attempts at reforestation have had limited success. Water pollution is also a significant problem due to salinization, sewage, and toxic chemicals from farming activities. The impurity of the water supply contributes to the spread of disease. The nation is also vulnerable to cyclones, flooding, earthquakes, and drought. The government has established a Water Master Plan to manage the nation's water resources for two decades. The National Development Plan is a more comprehensive attempt to address the nation's environmental concerns. There has been some damage to the nation's coral reefs from starfish and from coral and shell collectors. The Fiji banded iguana and the loggerhead, green sea, and hawksbill turtles are endangered. Overhunting threatens the native sea turtle populations.

⁶POPULATION

The population of Tonga in 2000 was estimated at 109,959. The projected population for the year 2005 is 114,000, assuming a crude birthrate of 23 per 1,000 population and a death rate of 6,

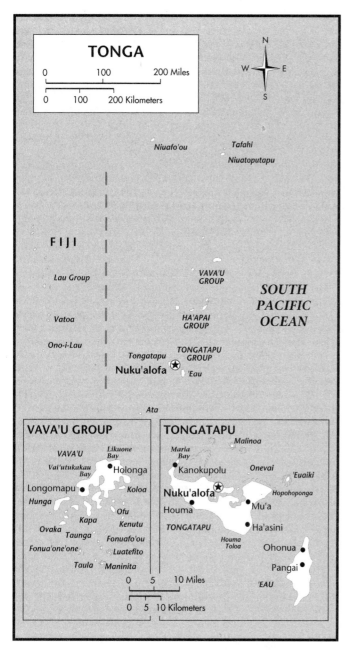

LOCATION: 15° to 23°30′s; 173° to 177°w. **TERRITORIAL SEA LIMIT:** 12 mi.

resulting in a natural rate of change of 1.7% for the period 2000–2005. The estimated population density in 1996 was 148.6 inhabitants per sq km (385 per sq mi).

It was estimated that 46% of the population lived in urban areas in 2000. Nuku'alofa, the capital and chief port, had a 2000 population of 40,000.

7MIGRATION

There is considerable movement toward the larger towns as population pressure on agricultural land increases. Some ethnic non-Tongans born on the islands migrate mainly to Fiji and New Zealand. Emigration by Tongan workers, both skilled and unskilled, has long been of concern to the government. In 1989 approximately 39,400 Tongans lived in the US, Australia, and New Zealand. There are expatriate Tongan communities in Brisbane and Sydney (Australia), Auckland (New Zealand), San Francisco (US), and on Hawaii. Persons wishing to reside in Tonga must obtain a government permit; permission is granted only to those taking up approved employment. Immigrant settlement is not encouraged because of the land shortage. The net migration rate in 1999 was -1.19 migrants per 1,000 population.

8ETHNIC GROUPS

The Tongans are a racially homogeneous Polynesian people. Less than 2% of the population is of European, part-European, Chinese, or non-Tongan Pacific island origin.

9LANGUAGES

Tongan, a Polynesian language not written down until the 19th century, is the language of the kingdom, but government publications are issued in both Tongan and English, and English is taught as a second language in the schools.

10RELIGIONS

Over 98% of Tongans are Christian. Free Wesleyan Methodists, headed by the Tongan monarch, Roman Catholics, and members of the Church of Jesus Christ of Latter-Day Saints each claim that 30–40% of all citizens are members of their faith. These three religious denominations make up at least 90% of the population. Seventh-Day Adventists, the Assembly of God, other Christian denominations, the Baha'i faith, Islam, and the Hindu faith are each represented in much smaller numbers.

11TRANSPORTATION

In 1996, Tonga had 680 km (423 mi) of roadways, of which 184 km (114 mi) were paved. There are no bridges in Tonga, but three islands in the Vava'u group are connected by two causeways. Tonga has no railways.

Nuku'alofa and Neiafu are the ports of entry for overseas vessels. In 1998, the merchant fleet consisted of 7 ships with a total of 17,754 GRT. Work on extending the port at Nuku'alofa began in 1985. The Pacific Forum Line and the Warner Pacific Line maintain scheduled service from Australia and New Zealand to Tonga via the Samoas and other islands, and cargo ships visit the group from time to time for shipments of copra. Internal sea connections are maintained by the Polynesia Triangle and by the Shipping Corp. of Polynesia.

In 1998 there were 6 airports, only 1 of which had a paved runway. Fua'Amotu International at Tongatapu is Tonga's principal airport. Air Pacific, Air New Zealand, Polynesian Airlines, and Hawaiian Air operate scheduled international flights from Fua'Amotu. The government-owned Friendly Island Airways has scheduled flights between Tongatapu, Ha'apai, 'Eua, Vava'u, and Niuatoputapu. In 1997, 49,000 passengers were carried on scheduled domestic and international airline flights.

12HISTORY

Since the Tongan language was not written down until the 19th century, the early history of Tonga (which means "south") is based on oral tradition. Hereditary absolute kings (Tu'i Tonga) date back to Ahoeitu in the 10th century. Around the 14th century, the twenty-third king, Kau'ulufonua, while retaining his sacred powers, divested himself of much of his executive authority, transferring it to his brother Ma'ungamotu'a, whom he thereafter called the Tu'i Ha'atakalaua. About the middle of the 17th century, the seventh temporal king, Fotofili, transferred the executive power to his brother Ngala, called the Tu'i Kanokupolu, and thereafter the powers gradually passed into the hands of the latter and his descendants. According to tradition, in the mid-19th century, upon the death of the then Tu'i Tonga, those powers were conferred upon the nineteenth Tu'i Kanokupolu, Taufa'ahu Tupou, founder of the present dynasty.

European chronicles disclose that the island of Niuatoputapu was discovered by the Dutch navigators Jan Schouten and Jacob le Maire in 1616. In 1643, Abel Tasman discovered Tongatapu, and from then until 1767, when Samuel Wallis anchored at Niuatoputapu, there was no contact with the outside world. Capt. James Cook visited the Tongatapu and Ha'apai groups in 1773 and again in 1777, and called Lifuka in the Ha'apai group the "friendly island" because of the gentle nature of its people—hence the archipelago received its nickname, the Friendly Islands. It was in the waters of the Ha'apai group that the famous mutiny on the British ship Bounty occurred in 1789. The first Wesleyan missionaries landed in Tonga in 1826.

The first half of the 19th century was a period of civil conflict in Tonga, as three lines of kings all sought dominance. They were finally checked during the reign of Taufa'ahu Tupou, who in 1831 took the name George. By conquest, George Tupou I (r.1845–93) gathered all power in his own hands and united the islands; he abolished the feudal system of land tenure and became a constitutional monarch in 1875. Meanwhile, by the middle of the century, most Tongans had become Christians, the great majority being Wesleyans, and the king himself was strongly influenced by the missionaries.

In the latter part of the century, there were religious and civil conflicts between the Wesleyan Mission Church and the newly established Free Wesleyan Church of Tonga. After the dismissal of the prime minister, the Rev. Shirley Waldemar Baker, in 1890, the new government allowed full freedom of worship. Ten years later, during the reign (1893–1918) of George II, a treaty of friendship was concluded between the UK and Tonga, and a protectorate was proclaimed. During World War II, Tongan soldiers under Allied command fought the Japanese in the Solomon Islands, and New Zealand and US forces were stationed on Tongatapu, which served as an important shipping point.

Two more treaties of friendship between the UK and Tonga were signed in 1958 and 1968, according to which Tonga remained under British protection, but with full freedom in internal affairs. On 4 June 1970, Tonga ceased being a British protectorate and became an independent member of the Commonwealth of Nations, with King Taufa'ahau Tupou IV—who had succeeded to the throne upon the death of his mother, Queen Salote Tupou (r.1918–65)—as head of state. The new status brought few immediate changes, apart from the fact that it added Tongan control of foreign affairs to self-rule in domestic matters.

In 1972, Tonga claimed the uninhabited Minerva Reefs (now Teleki Tokelau and Teleki Tonga), situated about 480 km (300 mi) southwest of Nuku'alofa, in order to prevent an Anglo-American corporation from founding an independent Republic of Minerva on the reefs in order to gain certain tax advantages. The nation in 1973 celebrated the bicentennial of Cook's first visit by inaugurating the new runway for jet aircraft at the main airport, near Nuku'alofa. The worst tropical storm in Tonga's history, Cyclone Isaac, devastated the islands in March 1982.

Many of the government's strongest critics gained seats in the 1987 legislative elections; the unprecedented turnover was thought to reflect changing attitudes toward traditional authority. However, the traditional leaders continued in charge of the government, with Prince Fatafehi Tu'ipelehake elected as Prime Minister. The island's dissident pro-democracy movement, led by Akilisi Pohive, won the February 1990 general election, but it remained a minority within the legislature. A government scandal over selling Tongan passports to Hong Kong Chinese led to popular support for the opposition. Baron Vaea replaced Prince Fatafehi Tu'ipelehake as Prime Minister August 1991. King Taufa'ahau Tupou IV organized the Christian Democratic Party in time for the 1993 election to provide greater coordination for his supporters and to weaken the democracy movement.

However, pressure from the pro-democracy forces continued in the February 1993 general election when the People's Democratic Movement won six of the nine seats open.

Parliamentary elections were held in March 1999, when about 51% of eligible voters cast ballots, the lowest voter turnout in the country's history. Five of the nine members elected were from the Human Rights and Democracy Movement (HRDM). King Taufa'ahu Tupou IV appointed his youngest son, 41-year-old Prince Lavaka Ata Ulukalala prime minister in January 2000. When the previous prime minister retired, observers speculated that the king's oldest son, Crown Prince Tupouto'a, would be named prime minister. It is likely that Tupouto'a was passed over for the post because of his stated opposition to preserving the king's right to make lifetime appointments. His younger brother, who became the country's fourth prime minister since 1950, has been outspoken in his criticism of the country's democracy movement.

13GOVERNMENT

Tonga is an independent kingdom. According to the constitution of 1875, as amended, the government is divided into three main branches: the sovereign, Privy Council, and cabinet; the Fale Alea (Legislative Assembly); and the judiciary. The King-in-Council is the chief executive body, and the cabinet, presided over by the appointed prime minister, makes executive decisions of lesser importance. Lawmaking power is vested in the 30-member Legislative Assembly, which consists of a speaker (appointed by the sovereign), the ten members of the Privy Council, 9 nobles elected to three-year terms by the 33 hereditary nobles of Tonga, and 9 representatives popularly elected to three-year terms. Sessions must be held at least once in every calendar year. Legislation passed by the Privy Council is subject to approval at the next meeting of the Legislative Assembly. Women voted for the first time in 1960, and the first woman was elected to the legislature in 1975. All literate citizens 21 years of age or older are eligible to vote.

14POLITICAL PARTIES

The Tonga People's Party (TPP), led by Viliami Fukofuka, and the pro-democracy Human Rights and Democracy Movements, led by Akilis Pohiva's were the principal political parties active in 2000.

15LOCAL GOVERNMENT

The islands are divided administratively into three districts: Vava'u in the north, Ha'apai in the center, and Tongatapu in the south. Ha'apai, Vava'u, and the outlying islands are administered by governors who are members of the Privy Council and are responsible to the prime minister. Minor officials perform statutory duties in the villages. Town and district officials have been popularly elected since 1965. They represent the central government in the villages; the district official has authority only over a group of villages.

Titles of nobility were first bestowed in 1875, and later in 1882, 1887, 1903, and 1923. With the hereditary titles were granted villages and lands.

16JUDICIAL SYSTEM

The Supreme Court exercises jurisdiction in major civil and criminal cases. Other cases, heard in the Magistrate's Court or the Land Court, may be appealed to the Supreme Court and then to the Court of Appeal, the appellate court of last resort. With the ratification of the 1968 friendship treaty, UK extraterritorial jurisdiction lapsed, and British and other foreign nations became fully subject to the jurisdiction of the Tongan courts. The judiciary is independent of the King and the executive branch, although Supreme Court justices are appointed by the king.

Criminal defendants are afforded the right to counsel and the right to a fair public trial is protected by law and honored in practice. The king may commute a death sentence. In addition, the court system consists of a court martial for the Tonga Defense Services, a court tribunal for the police force, and a court of review for the Inland Revenue Department.

[17]ARMED FORCES

The Tonga Defense Force was organized during World War II, became defunct in 1946 and was reactivated in 1952. It consists of a regular cadre and volunteers serving an initial training period, followed by attendance at annual training camps. Forces are organized into marines, royal guards, a navy, a police force, and a newly created air wing. The naval squadron consists of several fast patrol boats policing territorial waters.

[18]INTERNATIONAL COOPERATION

Tonga was admitted to the UN on 14 September 1999. It participates in ESCAP, FAO, ICAO, IFAD, IMF, ITU, UNESCO, UPU, and WHO. Tonga is also a member of the Asian Development Bank, Commonwealth of Nations, G-77, IBRD, and South Pacific Forum. It has also applied for WTO membership. Tongan representatives have attended and taken a leading part at South Pacific conferences. Since 1965, Tonga has received aid under the Australian South Pacific Technical Assistance Program. Tonga has only one diplomatic mission overseas, in the UK.

[19]ECONOMY

The economy is largely agricultural, depending principally on the export of copra and coconut products, bananas, and vanilla bean extract. In recent years, gourds (especially squash and pumpkins) have become a major export crop, providing almost half of total export earnings. Fishing (particularly snapper) has also grown in importance. There has been no development of mines, commercially exploitable forests, or large factories. The manufacturing sector remains small but is expanding. Tourism is the major source of foreign currency earnings, but the economy is still dependent on external aid. The sale of postage stamps and remittances from overseas workers are additional sources of revenue. By the late 1990s, economic growth slowed by approximately 3% annually.

[20]INCOME

The US Central Intelligence Agency (CIA) reports that in 1998 Tonga's gross domestic product (GDP) was estimated at $232 million. The per capita GDP was estimated at $2,100. The annual growth rate of GDP was estimated at -1.5%. The average inflation rate in 1998 was 3.6%. The CIA defines GDP as the value of all final goods and services produced within a nation in a given year and computed on the basis of purchasing power parity (PPP) rather than value as measured on the basis of the rate of exchange. It was estimated that agriculture accounted for 32% of GDP, industry 10%, and services 58%.

[21]LABOR

The total wage labor force in 1996 was 33,908. As of 1990, 36.5% were employed in agriculture, 14.4% in manufacturing, 22% in public administration and services, 8.1% in commerce, 5.7% in transportation and communication, 3.9% in construction, and 9.4% in other sectors. Many Tongans cultivate their own statutory holdings. The government has issued a labor code establishing a wage structure, a system of job classification, and provisions for workers' compensation. Holidays are prescribed by law. According to the constitution, it is not lawful to work, to play games, or to engage in trade on Sunday. Workers have the right, in theory, to form unions under the 1964 Trade Union Act, but as of 1999, none had been formed. Various

government agencies and public enterprises offer vocational training.

Child labor is not used in the wage sector and is virtually nonexistent throughout the economy. The workweek is limited to 40 hours. There is no minimum wage. Generally, labors laws are well-enforced on the main island of Tongatapu but are more inconsistently enforced on the outer islands.

[22]AGRICULTURE

About 69% of Tonga is agricultural land, including small amounts of permanent pasture. With increasing population pressure on the land, more land is being intensively cultivated and less is available for fallow. The use of fertilizers, high-protein strains of corn, and similar methods to improve the efficiency of land use has become increasingly necessary.

According to the constitution of 1875, all the land in the kingdom belongs to the crown and cannot be alienated. Much of it, however, consists of hereditary estates that were bestowed upon various chiefs, who lease the lands to farmers at a nominal annual rent. Since 1890, the crown has been responsible for the collection of rents and the granting of allotments.

On reaching the age of 16, every Tongan male taxpayer is entitled under the constitution to a tax allotment of 1 'api (3.34 ha/8.25 acres). These allotments are hereditary, pass from generation to generation in accordance with the law of succession, and may not be sold. A tenant may be ejected for nonpayment of rent or for failing to comply with the planting regulations, under which every Tongan holder of a tax allotment is legally required to plant 200 coconut trees, which he must keep free from weeds. In recent years, however, population increases have made it impossible to guarantee the 'api to all those entitled to one.

Principal subsistence crops are yams, taro, sweet potatoes, and manioc. Estimated production in 1998 included coconuts, 25,000 tons; sweet potatoes, 5,000 tons; cassava, 28,000 tons; oranges, 3,000 tons; and bananas, 1,000 tons. Vanilla beans have become an important cash crop, especially on Vava'u.

[23]ANIMAL HUSBANDRY

Beef cattle are generally kept for grazing in coconut plantations to keep the undergrowth in check and to provide additional income. Every householder has several hogs, which generally are not sold but are used for feasts. Sheep were brought into Tonga in 1954 but did not thrive, and in 1956 the entire flock was slaughtered. Livestock in 1998 included 81,000 hogs, 14,000 goats, 11,000 horses, and 9,000 head of cattle.

[24]FISHING

Fish are abundant in the coastal waters, but the fishing industry is relatively undeveloped, and the supply of fish is insufficient to meet local demand; thus, canned fish has been imported in recent years. Principal species caught are tuna and marlin. The fish catch was 2,739 tons in 1997; exports of fish products were valued at almost $1.57 million that year.

[25]FORESTRY

Forestland covers about 11% of Tonga's total area, mainly on 'Eua and Vava'u, but this diminishing resource has not been efficiently exploited, and much wood for construction must be imported. Roundwood production in 1997 was 5,000 cu m. There is a government sawmill on 'Eua. Charcoal is manufactured from logs and coconut shells.

[26]MINING

Tonga has few known mineral resources. A limited amount of crushed stone is produced at local quarries.

27 ENERGY AND POWER

All power is derived from thermal sources. Installed capacity in 1998 was about 7,000 kW; electricity production totaled 35 million kWh. Oil has been discovered through seepage into water wells, but test wells have been unproductive.

28 INDUSTRY

Encouragement of new industries was the goal of Tonga's five five-year plans (1966–2000). Industries include the manufacture of concrete blocks, metal products, woolen knitwear, leather goods, furniture, soft drinks, soap, sports equipment, yachts, and paint. At the government-backed Small Industry Centre, refrigerators, jewelry, bicycles, toys, furniture, wheelbarrows, miniexcavators, and other consumer goods are assembled for use locally and in neighboring countries. Long-established industries are coconut processing, sawmilling, and local handicrafts. Industry accounts for just 10% of GDP.

29 SCIENCE AND TECHNOLOGY

Hango Agricultural College, part of the Free Wesleyan Church Education System, offers diploma and certificate courses. Tonga Maritime Polytechnical Institute is located in Nuku'alofa.

30 DOMESTIC TRADE

Village stores carry a stock of flour, sugar, canned meats, textiles, hardware, soap, kerosene, tobacco, and matches; in the larger towns, these shops are managed by Tongans for European trading firms. Storekeepers act as agents for the Commodities Board and often extend credit to their customers until the end of the harvest. The board's produce division helps market bananas, melons, and pineapples. Development of cooperatives, which serve as savings-and-loan, produce-marketing, and handicraft-manufacturing organizations, has been actively pursued.

Usual banking hours are weekdays from 9:30 AM to 3:30 PM.

31 FOREIGN TRADE

Tonga suffers from chronic trade deficits. Vegetables, including squash, are Tonga's main export commodities (54%). Other exports include fish (15%), spices and vanilla (13%), and shell fish (3.8%).

In 1995 Tonga's imports were distributed among the following categories:

Consumer goods	13.8%
Food	25.0%
Fuels	12.3%
Industrial supplies	30.2%
Machinery	11.7%
Transportation	6.6%
Other	0.3%

Principal trading partners in 1998 (in millions of US dollars) were as follows:

COUNTRY	EXPORTS	IMPORTS	BALANCE
India	18	n.a.	
Japan	7	8	-1
United States	6	13	-7
Fiji	1	18	-17
Australia	1	10	-9
Samoa	1	n.a.	
United Kingdom	n.a.	2	
China (inc. Hong Kong)	n.a.	1	
New Zealand	n.a.	21	
Indonesia	n.a.	1	

32 BALANCE OF PAYMENTS

Since 1960, Tonga has had a growing trade deficit, offset by funds from the UK, New Zealand, Australia, and the Asian Development Bank (ADB). The US Central Intelligence Agency reports that in 1998 the purchasing power parity of Tonga's exports was $11.9 million while imports totaled $78.9 million resulting in a trade balance of -$67 million.

33 BANKING AND SECURITIES

The Bank of Tonga was formed in 1971, with the government holding 40% of the shares and 20% each held by the Bank of Hawaii, the Bank of New Zealand, and the Bank of New South Wales. The overseas banks provided staff and supervision for the Bank of Tonga, which offers all commercial services and has assumed responsibility for government savings, traders' current accounts, and foreign exchange dealings. The Tongan Development Bank (TDB) was founded in 1977.

Tonga's fiscal policy has traditionally been cautious, with taxation and expenditure measures balancing in the recurrent budget and the development budged being financed mainly through grants and soft loans. Legislation to set up a central bank was passed in late 1988 and the National Reserve Bank came into existence the following year. The Ministry of Finance, the Board of Currency Commissioners, the Board of Coinage Commissioners, and the island's only commercial bank, the Bank of Tonga, had until then jointly performed central bank functions. A second commercial bank, MBF Bank, was launched in late 1993.

Legislation has been passed to enable Tonga to become an international banking center. The legislation permits up to four foreign banks to establish operations in the capital.

Tonga has no stock issues or securities trading.

34 INSURANCE

Blue Shield (Oceania) Insurance covers life, health, travel, workers' compensation, total permanent disability, accident, and local consultation services. There were at least seven other major insurers doing business in Tonga in 1999.

35 PUBLIC FINANCE

About half of all public revenues accrued from customs duties on imported goods; the remainder came mainly from export duties, port fees, income taxes, and stamp revenues. Principal items of expenditure were public health, medical services, education, and agriculture.

The US Central Intelligence Agency (CIA) estimates that in 1997 Tonga's central government took in revenues of approximately $49 million and had expenditures of $120 million including capital expenditures of $75 million. Overall, the government registered a deficit of approximately $71 million. External debt totaled $65 million.

36 TAXATION

Income tax is levied at progressive rates. Businesses pay a flat rate of 15% on profits up to $100,000, and 30% thereafter. All male Tongans 16 years of age and older, except the aged and infirm, pay an annual head tax, the receipts of which are used to finance free education and medical benefits.

37 CUSTOMS AND DUTIES

Tonga has a single-column tariff based on the CCCN with custom duties ranging from 30–65% of the CIF. A 20% port and services tax is involved in the percentages. Tariffs are applied to most private sector imports, primarily for revenue purposes. Higher tariffs apply to cigarettes, alcoholic beverages, and petroleum, while public sector goods are exempt.

38 FOREIGN INVESTMENT

Although some non-Tongans have leased large plantations and residential and business sites, there is little private foreign investment. Government policy is that foreign investment is welcome, and that the government will arrange conditions for leasing of land, tax liberalization, and the issuance of import and export licenses. The bulk of Tonga's foreign reserves is invested in Australia.

[39] ECONOMIC DEVELOPMENT

Tonga's five-year plans (1966–2000) emphasized development of the islands' economic infrastructure, increasing agricultural production by revitalizing the copra and banana industries, improvements in telecommunications and transport, and expansion of tourism, industry, and exports. Through the nonprofit Commodities Board, the government has a trading monopoly in copra, bananas, melons, and other produce. In the 1990s, tourism revenues helped offset Tonga's large merchandise trade deficits, but substantial amounts of foreign aid continued to be required. From 1993–98, the economic growth was driven by a rise in exports of squash, increases in aid, and several large construction projects. As of 2000, the government was striving to reduce the budget deficit and support growth of the private sector.

[40] SOCIAL DEVELOPMENT

Every family is provided by law with sufficient land to support itself. There is no social welfare department; the medical and education departments and the missions provide what welfare services are available. The only pension scheme is one for civil servants.

Polynesian cultural traditions have kept most women in subservient roles, and few have risen to positions of leadership. Domestic violence is infrequent and is dealt with according to tribal law and custom. The government created a National Council of Women despite opposition from women's nongovernmental organizations who feared that its independence would be limited.

Human rights are generally well respected in Tonga. However, political dissent is suppressed.

[41] HEALTH

Tonga is free of malaria and most tropical diseases, but tuberculosis, filariasis, typhoid fever, dysentery, and various eye and skin diseases remain common health problems. Nevertheless, in comparison with many other Pacific islands, Tonga is a healthy country. Approximately 85% of children were vaccinated against measles in 1994. By 1969, a joint WHO-UNICEF project had considerably reduced the incidence of yaws. Other health projects deal with school sanitation, community water supplies, maternal and child health, and nursing education. The population has access to safe water and adequate sanitation.

Life expectancy in 1999 was 69.8 years. Infant mortality was 37.9 per 1,000 live births in 1999, and overall mortality was 6 deaths per 1,000 population. The fertility rate was 3.5 children per woman. Tongans receive free medical and dental treatment, but must pay for dentures. Non-Tongans are charged on a fixed scale. There is one government medical department hospital each in Tongatapu, Vava'u, Ha'apai, and Eau Island, with several dispensaries. The population per physician was 1,900 in 1996. There are 4 hospitals and 14 health care centers, with a total of 307 beds on the islands. In 1991, Tonga had 49 physicians; in 1989, 138 nurses and 30 mid-wives; and in 1988, 27 dentists. There were no cases of polio, malaria, or neonatal tetanus in 1994. Tuberculosis was seen in only 23 cases in 1994. Twelve AIDS cases were reported in 1999, with 8 resulting in death from the disease.

[42] HOUSING

Village houses usually have reed sides and a sloping roof thatched with sugarcane or coconut leaves; the posts are of ironwood, and braided cord takes the place of nails. More modern houses, especially in the towns, are built of wood, with roofs of corrugated iron. Unlike the village houses, they often contain more than one room and have verandas. In 1986 (the latest year for which there are statistics), the housing stock totaled 15,091 units, of which 60% were European-style wooden houses, 17% were European houses of bricks or cement, 8% were Tongan houses of wood with iron roofs, 7% were Tongan thatch houses, and 4% had wooden walls with thatch roofs.

Rainwater is stored in concrete cisterns. With the help of WHO, underground fresh water has been tapped to improve the water supply. The success of the plan has led to the extension of fresh water supplies to villages on all major islands.

Tongan taxpayers are entitled to an allotment of land from the governments. Each urban Tongan taxpayer receives an annual rent subsidy in lieu of this land allotment.

[43] EDUCATION

The first schools in Tonga were started by the Wesleyan Mission in 1828, even before the conversion to Christianity of the Tongans, and practically all primary education was controlled by the Mission until 1882 when the government took over the educational system. In 1906, various missionary organizations again were allowed to establish schools.

Primary education is compulsory for all Tongans. Adult literacy is estimated at higher than 90%. Mission schools, which follow a government syllabus, enroll about 8% of all primary pupils and 89% of students at postprimary level. No tuition is charged at government schools (except the high school), but small fees are charged at mission schools. In 1993 there were 16,792 pupils in Tonga's 115 primary schools, with 754 teachers and a student-to-teacher ratio of 22 to one. In the same year, secondary schools enrolled 16,750 students. Elementary instruction is given in the Tongan language; English is also taught. Selected Tongan students prepare for the New Zealand school certificate examination.

A teacher-training college, established in 1944, provides a two-year course. A government scholarship program provides the opportunity for Tongan students to pursue higher education abroad.

[44] LIBRARIES AND MUSEUMS

Since 1971, the Ministry of Education has operated a joint library service with the University of the South Pacific. Its library in Nuku'alofa has 9,000 volumes covering agriculture, small business management, adult education, and an important collection of Pacificana. The Ministry of Education library has 12,500 volumes. The Tonga College Museum's collection includes artifacts of Tonga's history. Notable monuments include the great trilithon known as the Ha'amanga and some 45 langis, great rectangular platforms of recessed tiers of coral limestone blocks that were erected as the tombs of medieval kings.

[45] MEDIA

The government's radiotelegraph station at Nuku'alofa has substations at Neiafu (Vava'u), Pangai, Ha'afeva and Nomuka (in the Ha'apai group), 'Eua, and Niuatoputapu. There is also a direct overseas telegraph service linking Nuku'alofa with Wellington, Suva, Apia, and Pago Pago. An internal radiotelephone service connects Nuku'alofa, 'Eua, Nomuka, Ha'afeva, and Vava'u, and a direct overseas radiotelephone service links Nuku'alofa to other Pacific island capitals. As of 1996, there were an estimated 3,500 telephones in use.

The Tonga Broadcasting Commission's Radio Tonga was established in 1961. It has two medium-wave transmitters of 10 kw each, and broadcasts about 75 hours a week in Tongan, English, Fijian, and Samoan; commercial advertising is accepted. As of 1999, there was 1 AM radio station and 1 television station. In 1997 Tonga had 600 radios and 18 television sets in use per 1,000 population.

The government publishes a weekly newspaper, the *Tonga Chronicle*, which has an average circulation (1999) of 7,000 copies in Tongan and English. There are also church newspapers issued by missions and a few private publications printed at regular intervals.

The constitution provides for free speech and a free press, although occasional infringements of press freedoms do occur. A 1999 US report on human right criticized the government for stifling freedoms of speech and the press. In non-government publications, opposition opinion appears regularly, usually without interference, but journalists were being targeted for prosecution in civil lawsuits by the minister of police.

46 ORGANIZATIONS

Every Tongan village has a community house where ceremonial cloth (tapa) is made by groups of women. The Tongan Women's Progressive Association, formed in 1956, conducts programs for the betterment of village conditions and holds classes in a variety of subjects. There are Boy Scout and Girl Guide groups, and meetings of Christian Endeavor societies and Bible classes are well attended. Extension of consumer cooperatives has been actively encouraged by the government.

47 TOURISM, TRAVEL, AND RECREATION

The tourist industry is a small but growing source of foreign exchange revenues. In 1997, there were 26,162 tourist arrivals, 8,470 from New Zealand, 4,812 from the United States, and 4,858 from Australia. Tourism receipts totaled $13 million. There were 695 rooms in hotels and other facilities in 1996.

Popular tourist sites are the royal palace and terraced tombs in Nuku'alofa. Most visitors enjoy a traditional evening feast of suckling pig, crayfish, chicken, and assorted accompaniments. Fishing, swimming, and sailing are popular, and rugby is a favorite spectator sport.

The minister of police grants prior-arrival visitors' permits up to a maximum of six months. Permits are not required from persons in direct transit, holders of Tongan passports, or foreign government officials traveling on official business. Vaccination against yellow fever is required.

In 1999 the UN estimated the cost of staying in Nuku'alofa at $85 per day. Staying in Vava'u costs $55–86 per day depending on the choice of hotel.

48 FAMOUS TONGANS

King George Tupou I (Taufa'ahu Tupou, 1797–1893) ruled for 48 years; during his reign, Tonga became a Christian nation, abolished serfdom, and acquired a constitution. His prime minister, Shirley Waldemar Baker (1831–1903), was a Wesleyan clergyman who, after being deposed in 1890, became an Episcopal minister and then returned to Tonga. The most famous Tongan of this century was Queen Salote Tupou (1900–1965), whose rule began in 1918. Her dynasty, the Tupou, is the third branch of the royal family and traces its descent back to Ahoeitu, the first Tu'i Tonga of whom there is record. Queen Salote's son, King Taufa'ahau Tupou IV (b.1918), succeeded to the throne in 1965 and was formally crowned in 1967.

49 DEPENDENCIES

Tonga has no territories or colonies.

50 BIBLIOGRAPHY

Bain, Kenneth. *The New Friendly Islanders: The Tonga of King Taufa'ahau Tupou IV.* London: Hodder & Stoughton, 1993.

Bott, Elizabeth. *Tongan Society at the Time of Captain Cook's Visit: Discussions with Her Majesty Queen Salote Tupou.* Honolulu: University of Hawaii Press, 1982.

Cook, James. *The Explorations of Captain James Cook in the Pacific, as Told by Selections of His Own Journals, 1768–1779.* New York: Heritage, 1958.

Ellem, Elizabeth W. *Queen Salote of Tonga: The Story of an Era 1900–1965.* Auckland, N.Z.: Auckland University Press, 1999.

Ferdon, Edwin N. *Early Tonga: As the Explorers Saw It, 1616–1810.* Tucson: University of Arizona Press, 1987.

Gailey, Christine Ward. *Kinship to Kingship: Gender Hierarchy and State Formation in the Tongan Islands.* Austin, Tex.: University of Texas Press, 1987.

Lawson, Stephanie. *Tradition Versus Democracy in the South Pacific: Fiji, Tonga, and Western Samoa.* New York: Cambridge University Press, 1996.

Marcus, George E. *The Nobility and the Chiefly Tradition in the Modern Kingdom of Tonga.* Honolulu: University of Hawaii Press, 1980.

Huntsman, Judith (ed.). *Tonga and Samoa: Images of Gender and Polity.* Christchurch, N.Z.: Macmillan Brown Centre for Pacific Studies, 1995.

Stanley, David. *Tonga-Samoa Handbook.* Emeryville, Calif.: Moon Publications, 1999.

TURKEY

Republic of Turkey
Türkiye Cumhuriyeti

CAPITAL: Ankara.

FLAG: The national flag consists of a white crescent (open toward the fly) and a white star on a red field.

ANTHEM: *Istiklâl Marşi (March of Independence).*

MONETARY UNIT: The Turkish lira (TL) is a paper currency of 100 kuruş. There are coins of 1, 5, 10, 20, 25, 50, and 100 liras, and notes of 5,000, 10,000, 20,000, 50,000, 100,000, 250,000, and 500,000 liras. TL1 = $0.000002 ($1 = TL572000.0) as of 31 March 2000.

WEIGHTS AND MEASURES: The metric system is the legal standard.

HOLIDAYS: New Year's Day, 1 January; National Sovereignty and Children's Day, 23 April; Spring Day, 1 May; Youth and Sports Day, 19 May; Victory Day, 30 August; Independence Day (Anniversary of the Republic), 29 October. Movable religious holidays include Şeker Bayrami (three days) and Kurban Bayrami (four days).

TIME: 3 PM = noon GMT.

¹LOCATION, SIZE, AND EXTENT

The Republic of Turkey consists of Asia Minor, or Anatolia (Anadolu); the small area of eastern Thrace (Trakya), or Turkey in Europe; and a few offshore islands in the Aegean Sea, with a total area of 780,580 sq km (301,384 sq mi), extending about 1,600 km (1,000 mi) SE–NW and 650 km (400 mi) NE–SW. Comparatively, the area occupied by Turkey is slightly larger than the state of Texas. Of the overall area, 97% is in Asia, and 3% in Europe. Turkey lies athwart the important Black Sea straits system—the Dardanelles, the Sea of Marmara, and the Bosporus. It is bordered on the N by the Black Sea, on the NE by Georgia and Armenia, on the E by Iran, on the SE by Iraq, on the S by Syria and the Mediterranean Sea, on the W by the Aegean Sea, and on the NW by Greece and Bulgaria, with a total boundary length of 9,827 km (6,106 mi). Turkey's capital city, Ankara, is located in the northwest part of the country.

²TOPOGRAPHY

Other than the low, rolling hills of Turkish Thrace, the fertile river valleys that open to the Aegean Sea, the warm plains of Antalya and Adana on the Mediterranean, and the narrow littoral along the Black Sea, the country is wrinkled by rugged mountain ranges that surround and intersect the high, semiarid Anatolian plateau. Average elevations range from 600 m (2,000 ft) above sea level in the west to over 1,800 m (6,000 ft) amid the wild eastern highlands. The highest point is Mount Ararat (Büyük Ağri Daği, 5,137 m/16,854 ft), which rises just within Turkey at the intersection of the Turkish, Armenian, and Iranian frontiers. There are over 100 peaks with elevations of 3,000 m (10,000 ft) or more. Other than the Tigris and Euphrates, which have their sources in eastern Anatolia, rivers are relatively small. Because the watersheds of these streams are semibarren slopes, the seasonal variations in flow are very great. The largest lake is Lake Van (3,713 sq km/1,434 sq mi); the other major lake is Lake Tuz (1,500 sq km/580 sq mi), whose water has a salinity level so high that it serves as a commercial source of salt. Turkey's 8,333 km (5,178 mi) of coastline provide few good natural harbors.

Most of Turkey lies within an earthquake zone, and recurrent tremors are recorded. On 29–30 March 1970, more than 1,000 earthquakes were felt in the Gediz region of western Turkey, killing 1,086 persons. A quake on 6 September 1975, 120 km (75 mi) west of Lake Van, resulted in at least 2,300 deaths, and another, on 24 November 1976, in the Van region, left an estimated 4,000 persons dead. On 30 October 1983, over 1,200 people were killed when a quake struck the Erzurum region, in the northeast. The record destructive earthquake, however, was that of 29 December 1939—near Erzincan—which killed 30,000 persons.

³CLIMATE

Turkey's southern coast enjoys a Mediterranean climate, and the Aegean coastal climate as far north as Izmir is much the same. The mean temperature range in these regions is 17–20°C (63–68°F), and the annual rainfall ranges from 71 to 109 cm (28–43 in). The northern Aegean-Marmara area is somewhat cooler, but also quite moist, the mean temperature range being 14–17°C (57–63°F) and annual rainfall between 56 and 71 cm (22 and 28 in). The Black Sea coast is also relatively mild (14–15°C/57–59°F) and very moist, with 71–249 cm (28–98 in) of rainfall. The central Anatolian plateau is noted for its hot, dry summers and cold winters: the average annual temperature is 8–12°C (46–54°F), and annual precipitation is 30–75 cm (12–30 in). With the exception of some warmer pockets in the valleys, the eastern third of Turkey is colder (4–9°C /39–48°F), and rainfall averages 41–51 cm (16–20 in). The little precipitation there is on the central plateau tends to be concentrated during the late fall and winter months.

⁴FLORA AND FAUNA

A wide variation of flora is found, semitropical to temperate, desert to alpine. In the mountains of southern, southwestern, and northern Turkey are extensive coniferous stands of commercial importance and some deciduous forest. Licorice, valonia oaks, and wild olive trees grow in the southwest. Principal varieties of wild animals are the fallow deer, red deer, roe deer, eastern mouflon, wild boar, hare, Turkish leopard, brown bear, red fox, gazelle, beech marten, pine marten, wildcat, lynx, otter, and badger. There is a large variety of birds, including the snow partridge, quail, great bustard, little bustard, widgeon, woodcock, snipe, and a variety of geese, ducks, pigeons, and rails. About 30 species of snakes are indigenous. Bees and silkworms are grown commercially.

⁵ENVIRONMENT

Environmental responsibilities are vested in the Under Secretariat for Environment and in the Ministry of Energy and Natural Resources. Among Turkey's principal environmental problems is air pollution in Ankara and other cities. The smog in Ankara grew worse after 1979, when the government banned oil heating systems in new buildings in order to reduce costly oil imports; the resultant increased burning of Turkish lignite, which is high in sulfur content, greatly increased the levels of sulfur dioxide and dust in the air. In 1983, the government reversed itself and banned the conversion of heating systems to coal. At the same time, it introduced an antipollution program designed to reduce air pollution levels by more than 50% within a year. In addition to heating restrictions, the plan called for strict traffic controls, the closing of the worst industrial polluters, a prohibition on the import of high-sulfur fuel oil, special emergency hospital wards for smog victims, and the building of green areas and parks in and around cities. In 1992, Turkey had the world's highest level of industrial carbon dioxide emission, which totaled 145.5 million metric tons, a per capita level of 2.49 metric tons. Turkey contributes 0.4% of the world's total gas emissions. A $220-million project to clean up the polluted water in the Golden Horn, an inlet of the Bosporus forming a harbor in Istanbul, was implemented in the 1980s. The nation's rivers are polluted with industrial chemicals. Among them, mercury has created a serious threat to the nation's water supply. As of 1995, 30% of rural dwellers lacked access to safe drinking water. Soil erosion affects both coastal and internal areas. The combination of water and wind eliminates 500 metric tons of soil each year.

In 1994, five of Turkey's mammal species and 18 of its bird species were endangered. Eighteen types of plants were threatened with extinction. Endangered or extinct species include the Anatolian leopard, Mediterranean monk seal, and hawksbill and green sea turtles.

⁶POPULATION

The population of Turkey in 2000 was estimated at 66,620,120. An estimated 5.3% of the population is 65 years of age or older. The projected population for the year 2005 is 71,663,000, assuming a crude birthrate of 19 per 1,000 population and a death rate of 5 resulting in a natural rate of change of 1.4% for the period 2000–2005. The population rate of change between 1995 and 2000 was 1.6%. The population density in 1998 was 82 per sq km (212 per sq mi).

It was estimated that 75% of the population lived in urban areas in 2000, up from 44% in 1980. Istanbul (formerly Constantinople), the largest city, had a 2000 metropolitan population of 9,413,000. The largest metropolitan areas after Istanbul were Ankara, the capital city, with a 2000 metropolitan population of 3,190,000; Izmir (formerly Smyrna), 2,399,000; Adana, 1,289,000; Bursa, 1,299,000; and Gaziantep, 926,000.

⁷MIGRATION

Much Turkish emigration has consisted of workers under contract for employment in EC countries. Germany alone had 1,779,600 Turks at the end of 1991. There are also large numbers of Turks in prosperous Muslim countries such as Sa'udi Arabia, the Gulf states, and Libya. In 1994, there were 14,000 Turkish Kurds in northern Iraq. The military conflict in southeastern

Turkey has internally displaced hundreds of thousands of persons; however, this problem has not been officially recognized by Turkey.

After the 1991 Gulf War, 500,000 Iraqi Kurds fled to Turkey. Most of these refugees have since repatriated or resettled in third countries. In 1992, 20,000 Bosnians came to Turkey, though all have left except for 4,000 as of March 1997. In 1999, nearly 18,000 Kosovar refugees sought asylum in Turkey, including 8,000 people evacuated from Macedonia; nearly all have since voluntarily repatriated. In addition to these mass arrivals, there are individual asylum seekers from Iran and Iraq. Non-European refugees are granted only temporary protection in Turkey, so nearly all must be resettled. In 1998, 1,629 refugees were resettled in the US, Canada, Australia, and the Nordic countries; approximately the same number was expected for 1999. The net migration rate was zero in 1999.

⁸ETHNIC GROUPS

About 80% of the population is Turkish. The major ethnic minority (by mother tongue), the Kurds, is estimated at 20%. Arabs, Turkmen, Circassians, Greeks, and others do account for a small percentage of the population. Hundreds of thousands of Armenians were either killed or forced to flee during and immediately following World War I; bitterness between Armenians and Turks continues to this day, and during the late 1970s and early 1980s, Armenian terrorists took the lives of more than two dozen Turkish diplomats. The Greek component in Turkey was reduced as a result of the 1919–22 hostilities with Greece, the 1923 Treaty of Lausanne (which provided for an exchange of population with Greece), and the post–World War II Cyprus controversy. The Kurds, some of whom were forcibly dispersed after an uprising in 1935, still tend to be concentrated in the southeastern provinces. The Arabs live in the south along the Syrian and Iraqi frontiers, and the Greeks, Armenians, and Jews live in Istanbul and, to a lesser extent, in Izmir. Separatist Kurdish groups are outlawed, and there is a heavy military presence in the nine provinces where a state of emergency has been in effect since 1987.

⁹LANGUAGES

Turkish, which belongs to the Ural-Altaic group, is the official language. In addition to the Roman alphabet, modern Turkish uses the letters ç, ğ, i (undotted), ö, ş, and ü, but no q, w, or x. With only minor exceptions, words are spelled phonetically. The language is agglutinative.

A 1928 language reform substituted the Roman alphabet for the Arabic script, which had been used by the Turks since their conversion to Islam. During the 1930s there was a state-sponsored effort to rid the language of Arabic and Persian words and grammatical constructions. Turkish grammatical rules are now applied for all words, regardless of origin, though many Persian and Arabic expressions persist. Traditionally, there was a great difference between vernacular Turkish and written Ottoman Turkish, the latter being heavily influenced by Arabic and Persian and almost unintelligible to the mass of Turks. This difference has been almost obliterated, though some regional differences in dialect, particularly in the villages, still make effective communication difficult.

Kurdish and Arabic are also spoken. Kurdish is a language of the Iranian group and is written in Arabic script in Turkey. Two of the three major dialects are spoken in Turkey.

¹⁰RELIGIONS

Religious freedom is provided for by the constitution. Although about 99.8% of the population is Muslim, there is no official state religion. Nonetheless, the state maintains urban mosques and other Muslim religious properties, licenses Muslim religious leaders, and provides Muslim religious education in the public

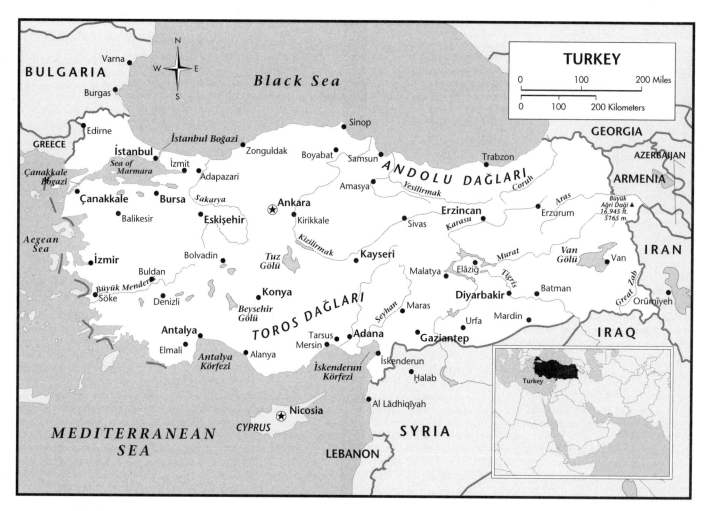

LOCATION: 25°40′ to 44°48′E; 35°51′ to 42°6′N. **BOUNDARY LENGTHS:** USSR, 610 km (379 mi); Iran, 454 km (282 mi); Iraq, 331 km (206 mi); Syria, 877 km (545 mi); Greece, 212 km (132 mi); Bulgaria, 269 km (167 mi); total coastline, 8,333 km (5,178 mi). **TERRITORIAL SEA LIMIT:** 6 mi, Aegean Sea; 12 mi, Mediterranean and Black seas.

schools. Proselytizing by either Muslim or non-Muslim is proscribed by law. Laws against the use of religion for political purposes are rigorously enforced. The vast majority of Turkish Muslims are Sunni, but there is a substantial Shi'a minority. Although at times suppressed by law, secret dervish orders have remained active in some areas.

In 1999, religious minorities included Christians and Jews, accounting for 0.2% of the population. The Greek Orthodox patriarch at Istanbul is considered first among equals of the seven patriarchs in the Eastern Orthodox churches. Turkey was a haven for Jewish refugees from Spain and Portugal in the late 15th and 16th centuries, and Jews have lived there in relative peace until recent years. On 6 September 1986, two armed men fired on worshippers in a synagogue in Istanbul, killing 22; various Arab groups claimed responsibility. On 8 July 1993, thirty-seven people died in connection with an attack by militant Muslim fundamentalists on a meeting of writers and intellectuals including supporters of the novelist Salman Rushdie.

11 TRANSPORTATION

Turkey's size and difficult terrain, together with limited economic resources, have proved great obstacles to the construction of transportation facilities. When the republic was founded in 1923 there were about 4,000 km (2,500 mi) of railway track and 7,400 km (4,600 mi) of motor roads in Anatolia and Thrace, all in disrepair. By 1996, 10,386 km (6,453 mi) of track connected

most of the important points in the country with Ankara, Istanbul, and the Black Sea and Mediterranean ports. The railways are owned and operated by the Turkish State Railways, a public corporation.

Animal transportation in most of the country has gradually given way to trucks and buses that use roads provided by extensive construction programs since World War II. In October 1973, the Bosporus Bridge in Istanbul was opened, facilitating the crossing of the Straits of the Bosporus by motorists; this six-lane steel suspension bridge had a main span of 1,074 m (3,524 ft). As of 1997, there were 382,397 km (237,621 mi) of roadways, of which 95,599 km (59,405 mi) were paved, including 1,560 km (969mi) of expressways.

The Turkish merchant fleet in 1998 consisted of 531 vessels of all types, totaling 5,913,171 GRT. The leading ports were Mersin, Istanbul, Izmir, Iskenderun, and Izmit.

Turkey had 117 airports in 1998, of which 81 had paved runways. Two international airports—Atatürk (Istanbul) and Esenboğa (Ankara)—are served by some 20 international air carriers. Other international airports include Antalya, Dalaman, and Adnan Menderes at Izmir. With minor exceptions, domestic air transportation is the monopoly of the semipublic Turkish Airways Corp. (Türk Hava Yollari), which connects most major centers within the country on a regular schedule and operates some international flights. In 1997, scheduled airline traffic amounted to 12,379 million passenger-km (7,692 million passenger-mi) and 255 million freight ton-km (158 million freight ton-mi) performed; 9,380,000 passengers were carried on scheduled domestic and international flights.

12HISTORY

In ancient times, Turkey was known as Asia Minor or Anatolia. Among the many inhabitants were the Hittites (c.1800–c.1200 BC), the first people to use iron; the Greeks, who, according to legend, destroyed Troy (or Ilium) about 1200 BC and who colonized the Aegean coast from about 1000 bc on; the Phrygians (c.1200–c.600 BC); the Lydians (c.700–546 BC), the first people to mint coins; the Persians (546–333 BC); and the Romans, beginning in the 2d century BC. Roman Emperor Constantine I (the Great) changed the name of the city of Byzantium to Constantinople (now Istanbul) and made it his capital in AD 330; a division between the Western and Eastern Roman Empires, with their respective capitals at Rome and Constantinople, became official in 395. Constantinople, seat of the Byzantine Empire, became the center of Eastern Orthodox Christianity, which officially separated from Roman Catholicism in 1054, when the pope and the patriarch of Constantinople excommunicated each other.

The Turks are a Ural-Altaic people who emerged from the plains between the Ural Mountains in Europe and the Altay Mountains in Asia. The forerunners of the inhabitants of present-day Turkey, known as the Seljuk Turks (named after the Turkish conqueror Seljuk, fl.10th century), defeated the Byzantines in the battle of Malazgirt (1071) and established themselves in Anatolia. They attained a highly developed Muslim culture in their great capital at Konya, in central Turkey. The Turkish conquest of Syria, including Palestine, led to the Crusades (1096–1270), a series of intermittent and inconclusive wars. Various Latin (Roman Catholic) and Greek (Eastern Orthodox) states were formed in parts of the Turkish Empire, but none lasted. The sack of the Christian city of Constantinople by Crusaders in 1204, followed by the establishment of the Latin Empire there (1204–61), shocked Europe and tended to discredit the Crusading movement.

Seljuk power was shattered when the Mongols, another Ural-Altaic people, swept across Asia Minor in 1243. As the Mongols withdrew, Turkish power revived and expanded under the Ottoman Turks, a group of frontier warriors whose first chief was Osman I (called Ottoman in the West, r.1300?–1326). In 1453, the Ottomans under Mehmet II (the Conqueror) occupied Constantinople and made it their capital. In 1516, they conquered Syria; in 1517, Egypt. In 1529, they were at the gates of Vienna, at which point the European expansion of Turkish power was stopped. The Turkish fleet was decisively defeated in a battle near Lepanto (now Navpaktos) in Greece in 1571. At its peak, generally identified with the reign of Sultan Süleyman I (the Magnificent, r.1520–66), the Ottoman Empire encompassed an estimated 28 million inhabitants of Asia Minor, much of the Arabian Peninsula, North Africa as far west as modern Algeria, the islands of the eastern Mediterranean, the Balkans, the Caucasus, and the Crimea. During the 17th, 18th, and 19th centuries, as a result of the rise of nationalism and encroachment by the European powers, it gradually shrank in size, the independence of the remainder being maintained only by shrewd balance-of-power diplomacy.

The process of modernization began with the Imperial Rescript of 1839, promulgated by Sultan Abdul Mejid (r.1839–61), and by a body of reforms known as the Tanzimat, which to some extent curbed the absolute powers of the sultan-caliph. (The Turkish sultans had added the title "caliph" following the conquest of Egypt in 1517.) The Illustrious Rescript of 1856 was largely dictated by Britain, France, and Austria as part of the negotiations leading to the settlement of the Crimean War (1853–56), a clash between the Russian and Ottoman Empires; it ensured equal rights for non-Muslims, provided for prison reform and the codification of Turkish law, and opened Turkey to European skills and capital. A constitution was introduced in 1876 by Sultan Abdul Hamid II (r.1876–1909) but was suspended in the following year. Thereafter, an absolute monarchy prevailed until the Young Turk revolution of 1908, at which time the constitution of 1876 was reinstated. In 1913, leaders of the Committee for Union and Progress (the organizational vehicle of the Young Turks) took effective control of the government under Sultan Mehmet V (r.1909–18). The principal leaders were Talat and Enver Paṣa, who, at the outbreak of World War I, threw what little remained of Ottoman strength behind the Central Powers, which had sided with Turkey in its fruitless attempt to retain its last major European possessions in the Balkan Wars of 1912–13. Although the Turks were unable to make any headway against British forces defending the Suez Canal, they did offer a heroic defense at Gallipoli (the Gelibolu Peninsula) and the Dardanelles, in a prolonged battle between Turkish and British-French forces that lasted from February 1915 to January 1916 and took the lives of about 100,000 soldiers on each side. In 1917, however, Turkish resistance collapsed, and the British pushed Turkey out of Syria, Palestine, Iraq, and Arabia. An armistice was concluded on 30 October 1918, and Enver Paṣa and his colleagues fled the country.

Before and during the war, Armenians sought to establish their independence and were brutally repressed by the Turks. Over a million people are said to have died being driven from their homes; many survived in exile.

On the basis of a series of earlier Allied agreements, the Ottoman Empire was to be stripped of all non-Turkish areas, and much of what remained—Asia Minor—was to be divided among the UK, France, Greece, and Italy. A substantial portion was actually occupied. In 1919, with Allied assistance, the Greeks invaded Anatolia through Izmir, but a Turkish nationalist resistance movement under the leadership of Mustafa Kemal (later called Atatürk), who had commanded a division at Gallipoli, finally defeated them in 1922. The sultan, being virtually captive in Istanbul, was disgraced in Turkish eyes by his identification with Allied policy. After much maneuvering, a rival nationalist government under Mustafa Kemal was established in Ankara and gained national and international recognition. On 1 November 1922, the sultanate was abolished by Mustafa Kemal's provisional government. The following year, the Ankara government negotiated the Treaty of Lausanne with the Allies, which recognized Turkish sovereignty over Asia Minor and a small area in Thrace. There was a massive exchange of Greek and Turkish populations. On 29 October 1923, a republic was proclaimed, with Ankara as its capital, and on 3 March 1924, the caliphate was abolished and all members of the dynasty banished.

During the next few years, a series of social, legal, and political reforms were accomplished that, taken collectively, became known as the Atatürk Reforms. They included the substitution of secular law for religious law, the writing of a republican constitution based on popular sovereignty, suppression of religious education in Turkish schools, introduction of a Roman alphabet to replace the Arabic script, and the legal upgrading of the position of women. With minor exceptions, political power resided in a single party, the Republican People's Party, and to a very substantial extent in Mustafa Kemal personally until his death in 1938. His chief of staff, Ismet Inönü (Paṣa), became president and established a two-party system of government with the formation of the opposition Democrat Party (DP) in 1946.

Although pro-Allied, Turkey remained neutral during most of World War II, but early in 1945 it declared war on the Axis and became a charter member of the UN. In 1947, the Truman Doctrine pledged US support to Turkey in the face of mounting

Soviet pressure. This move was followed by large-scale military and economic assistance from the US. Turkey thus became firmly committed to the Western alliances—NATO and the Central Treaty Organization, or CENTO (Baghdad Pact).

The DP came to power in 1950. Under Prime Minister Adnan Menderes, the government stressed rapid industrialization and economic expansion at the cost of individual liberties. Restrictive press laws were passed in 1954 and 1956, and by 1960 the Menderes government had curtailed judicial independence, university autonomy, and the rights of opposition parties. On 27 May 1960, after student demonstrations (joined by War College cadets and some army officers) were harshly suppressed, Prime Minister Menderes, President Celâl Bayar, and other government leaders were arrested by a newly formed Committee of National Unity. Gen. Cemal Gürsel became acting president and prime minister. Menderes was found guilty of violating the constitution and was hanged in 1961. A new constitution was popularly ratified in 1961, and elections were held in October. Gen. Gürsel was elected president by the New Grand National Assembly, and Inönü became prime minister of a coalition government.

The opposition Justice Party (JP) won 52.3% of the vote in the 1965 elections and formed a new government under Süleyman Demirel. Four years later, the JP was returned to power, and Prime Minister Demirel began a new four-year term. But Turkey's four top military commanders forced the resignation of Demirel's government in 1971 and called for a "strong and credible government" that would restore economic and political stability and suppress student disorders, which had steadily grown more frequent and more violent since 1968. Martial law had been imposed from June to September 1970, and a new "above party" government under Nihat Erim reimposed martial law in 11 provinces (including Ankara and Istanbul) from 1971 to 1973.

Political stability proved no easier to achieve: a succession of weak coalition governments, headed alternately by Demirel and Republican leader Bülent Ecevit, held office between 1973 and 1980. Ecevit's government was in power during the Greco-Turkish war on Cyprus in July–August 1974. Relations with Greece, strained by a dispute over mineral rights on the Aegean continental shelf, reached the breaking point on 15 July, when Cypriot President Makarios was overthrown in a Greek-led military coup. Fearing the island would be united with Greece, Turkish forces invaded on 20 July. A UN cease-fire came into effect two days later, but after peace talks at Geneva broke down, Turkish troops consolidated their hold over the northern third of the island by 16 August. As the result of this action, the US embargoed shipments of arms to Turkey until 1978; as of 1994, an estimated 25,000 or more Turkish troops remained on Cyprus to support the Turkish Republic of Northern Cyprus which only Turkey recognizes. In 1997, Turkish and Greek representative met with a UN mediator in an attempt to resolve the issue. No results were reported.

During the late 1970s, escalating acts of violence by political groups of the extreme left and right, coupled with economic decline, threatened the stability of Turkey's fragile democracy. By April 1980, 47,000 people had been arrested, and martial law had spread to 20 of Turkey's 67 provinces; at midyear, more than 5,000 persons had been killed (including former Prime Minister Nihat Erim), and the factional strife was claiming an average of 20 victims each day. With the legislature deadlocked, the military intervened in the political process for the third time in 20 years. A five-man military National Security Council (NSC), headed by Gen. Kenan Evren, took power in a bloodless coup on 12 September 1980. The NSC suspended the 1961 constitution, banned all political parties and activities, and arrested thousands of suspected terrorists. With the entire country under martial law, factional violence was drastically reduced. By April 1982, 40,000 alleged "political extremists" had been arrested; 23,000 had been

tried and convicted in martial law courts, some 6,000 of them for "ideological offenses." Under an NSC edict forbidding Turkey's former political leaders from speaking out on political matters, former Prime Minister Ecevit was twice arrested and imprisoned during 1981–82. In protest against the treatment of Ecevit, the EEC froze payment of $650 million in loans and grants previously pledged to Turkey.

In a national referendum on 7 November 1982, Turkish voters overwhelmingly approved a new constitution (prepared by a constituent assembly chosen by the NSC) under which Gen. Evren became president of the republic for a seven-year term; campaigning against ratification had been illegal under martial law. Parliamentary elections were held in November 1983, although martial law remained in effect. Following the elections, Turgut Özal, leader of the victorious Motherland Party, was installed as prime minister. Martial law was lifted in most provinces over the next two years, but emergency rule remained in effect; legislation was passed to broaden police powers, freedom of expression remained limited, and trials of alleged extremists continued. Human-rights groups complained of torture, suspicious deaths, overcrowding, and substandard conditions in Turkish jails; the government denied any improprieties. Özal's Motherland Party retained its parliamentary majority in November 1987 elections, and he was reelected for a second five-year term. In 1989, Özal was elected president. His Motherland Party continued in power but with declining popularity as shown in 1989 municipal elections. Özal's ambition was to tie Turkey closely to Europe but, despite improvements in Turkey's human rights record, its application for full membership in the European Union was deferred indefinitely. Özal also sought to give Turkey a leading role with the Turkic republics of former Soviet Central Asia. He continued Turkey's long-standing policy of quiet contacts with Israel while seeking better ties with the Arab states. During the Gulf War, he joined the embargo against Iraq, closed Iraq's oil pipelines, provided facilities for allied air raids and later supported protective measures for Iraqi Kurds. In compensation, Turkey received increased aid worth $300 million.

In October 1991 elections, the Motherland Party lost its parliamentary majority to the True Path and Social Democratic Party in coalition. True Path leader Demirel was named Prime Minister. He succeeded to the presidency in May 1993 following the death of Özal. Tansu Ciller, True Path chairperson, became Turkey's first female Prime Minister in July. In 1994, Ciller faced three major tasks: dealing with the problems of high inflation (about 70%) and unemployment as she continued Özal's free market policies of export-led growth (7–8%), reducing government regulations and privatization; pacifying the rebellious Kurdish areas of eastern Turkey where large numbers of troops have been tied down in a conflict that has taken thousands of lives and millions in treasure; and responding to the rising challenge to Turkey's secular nationalism from politically militant Islamic groups.

These problems continued, and in some cases escalated, and the Ciller government also faced scandals and a weakened resolve due to its fragile coalition majority.

Problems with Kurdish separatists, long-standing disagreements with Greece, and an unstable political environment plagued Turkey throughout 1995 and 1996.

The battle between the Turkish government and members of the Kurdistan Workers Party (PKK) that began in 1984 continued in late 1994 and the first half of 1995. The PKK sought the establishment of a separate Kurdish state. In fighting from 1984 until February 1995, more than 14,000 people had died.

The battle spilled beyond Turkey's borders on 20 March 1995, as 35,000 troops backed by tanks and jets pursued rebels into northern Iraq. In the biggest military operation in the history of the Turkish republic, the troops hunted for suspected PKK bases.

The PKK maintained the area was home only to Iraqi Kurds, not the PKK.

Turkey said it was targeting 2,400 guerrillas who had been mounting cross-border raids and that it would not pull out until a buffer zone or other plan was set up to keep the PKK from moving back into the area. Western leaders condemned the incursion, and the eventual Turkish pullout was seen as a reaction to that negative pressure.

Meanwhile, Turkey promised reforms to improve the lives of the 11 million Kurds living there. It said it would lift restrictions on broadcasts in Kurdish and allow Kurds to establish their own schools after the PKK was crushed.

The battle would continue until April 27, when Turkey declared that its mission to wipe out PKK base camps, arms depots, and supply routes in northern Iraq was a success. It said it would go back into Iraq if it again became necessary to strike at the rebels. Turkey said its next task would be to secure the border.

At the same time territorial conflicts with Greece erupted. On 1 June 1995, the Greek Parliament ratified the international Law of the Sea treaty, drawing protests from Turkish leaders who saw the move as an attempt by Greece to extend its territorial waters. Almost eight weeks later the two nations narrowly avoided confrontation over a cluster of uninhabited islands in the Aegean Sea. Though on January 31 Greek Prime Minister Constantine Simitis withdrew forces from the area, tensions remained high through April, when a Greek coast guard patrol boat fired on Turkish fishermen suspected of smuggling illegal migrants to the Greek islet of Strongili. Meanwhile in May tensions between Greek and Turkish soldiers on Cyprus escalated, culminating in the fatal shooting of a Greek soldier early in June.

The Kurdish and Greek issues were complicated by political instability within Turkey through the spring of 1996. On 20 September 1995, Prime Minister Tansu Ciller resigned when her coalition fell apart over budgetary matters. When Ciller lost a vote of confidence on October 15, her own party, the True Path, called for national elections December 24. Turkey's president Suleyman Demirel asked Ciller to form a new interim government, a coalition destroyed almost two months later by the triumph of the Islamic Welfare Party in the December elections. In an effort to block Islamic fundamentalists from gaining power, Ciller made overtures to her longtime rivals in the conservative Motherland Party. When negotiations failed, President Demirel in early January invited Islamic Welfare Party leader Necmettin Erbakan to form a government. This effort was unsuccessful, as was the early February attempt by Motherland Party head Mesut Yilmuz. The stalemate ended early in March when Ciller and Yilmuz agreed on a government that left the Islamic Welfare Party out. The following month, in retaliation, Islamic representatives in parliament successfully moved to investigate allegations of corruption against Ciller. As a result of infighting, the center-right coalition fell apart in early June, allowing Erbakan to become modern Turkey's first conservative Islamic prime minister. The instability, as well as Erbakan's anti-West, antisecular slogans, caused Turkey's economy to lapse and slowed foreign investment significantly.

Beginning in early 1997, Turkey's military leaders began to speak openly of their displeasure with the Islamist turn the country had taken under Erbakan's government—even intimating that if the government did not return to secular policies instituted by Ataturk nearly a century earlier, it would overthrow the government militarily. Erbakan had angered the military, which considers itself the defenders of the country's secularism, by proposing mandatory Islamic education and by making political overtures to Libya and Iran. Pressure from the military increased in late spring and early summer, and Turkey's neighbors in Europe and allies in the US also expressed concern over the direction the NATO member was taking. The crisis was resolved in July 1997, when the Welfare Party's coalition fell apart, and its leader, Erbakan, resigned his post. After the resignation, Mesut Yilmaz, leader of the Motherland Party, was asked by President Demirel to form a government. Erbakan, upon resigning, said he did so with the full intention of returning to office one day and predicted his ultra-conservative welfare party would win more than 21% in the next elections, then scheduled for 2000.

Mrs. Ciller came under heavy scrutiny again in early 1997 in a renewed round of allegations concerning her financial affairs. Opponents in Parliament and within her own party accused her and her husband of enriching themselves during her term as Prime Minister. The Parliamentary investigations came as Mrs. Ciller was defending herself against charges that her government and previous administrations condoned death squads. The scandal came to light in November 1996 after an automobile accident that killed a senior police official. Also in the car was a convicted drug smuggler wanted by Interpol and a high-ranking member of Parliament.

By November 1998, Yilmaz's government fell victim to another corruption scandal and Ecevit returned as interim prime minister. Within two months of returning to power, Ecevit scored a major victory for his government through the capture of Kurdish terrorist leader Abdulah Ocalan in Nairobi, Kenya. Ocalan had taken refuge in the Greek embassy in Nairobi and was apprehended while on the way to the airport (and an African country willing to provide him with asylum). Ocalan's capture brought relations with Greece to a new low as Ecevit accused Greece of being a state sponsor of terrorism.

In the wake of the terrorist leader's arrest, Ecevit called for early elections to be held in April 1999. The balloting resulted in a plurality for Ecevit's DSP (Democratic Left Party) which captured 136 of 550 seats (22.3% of the vote) in the parliament. The MHP came second with 129(18.1%), the Virtue Party (successor to the outlawed Welfare Party) dropped to 111 seats (15.5%), while the Motherland Party received 86 seats (13.3%). Ecevit formed a coalition with MHP and Motherland thus strengthening his position with the secularist military and isolating the Islamists.

Ecevit continued to make progress in foreign affairs throughout 1999 and into 2000. Relations in Greece saw marked improvement following a major earthquake that killed 20,000 Turkish citizens in August 1999. Greece was among the first nations to send aid—an act of humanitarian assistance warmly received by the Turkish government and public. When Greece suffered a smaller earthquake the following month, Turkey returned the favor. A dialogue on cooperation between the two countries in areas of mutual interest subsequently resulted in accords in the areas of trade and the fight against terrorism. Many international observers placed emphasis on the warm personal relationship between Turkish foreign minister Ismail Cem and his Greek counterpart George Papandreou. Finally, at the December 2000 EU summit in Helsinki, the EU member-states placed Turkey's name on the list of candidates for entry. Although most observers rule out Turkish membership for at least 10-15 years, the decision was a symbolic victory for Turkey as it symbolized the efforts of most Turks to identify with the West.

13 GOVERNMENT

The 1961 constitution vested legislative power in the Grand National Assembly, consisting of the House of Representatives, with a membership of 450 (elected for four-year terms), and the Senate of 165 members, of whom 150 were elected and 15 appointed by the president. The president of the republic—the head of state—was elected for a single seven-year term by a joint session of the National Assembly. The president was empowered to designate the prime minister from among the Assembly members; the prime minister in turn chose other cabinet ministers, who were responsible for general government policy.

The constitution ratified in November 1982, which replaced the 1961 document, declares Turkey to be a democratic and secular republic that respects the human rights of its citizens and remains loyal to the nationalistic principles of Atatürk. It vests executive powers in the president of the republic and the Council of Ministers. Legislative functions are delegated to the unicameral National Assembly, consisting of 400 members elected for five-year terms (the Senate was abolished). Under the constitution's "temporary articles," the five-person National Security Council (NSC) remained in power until the new parliament convened, at which time the NSC became a Presidential Council, to function for a period of six years before dissolving. These "temporary" provisions expressly forbade all former leaders of either the Justice or the Republican People's Party from participating in politics for 10 years; all former members of the previous parliament were forbidden to found political parties or to hold public office for five years. Proposals to change the voting age from 21 to 20 years and expand the National Assembly from 400 to 450 members were approved in May 1987. (By 1996, there were 500 seats.) A referendum in September 1987 approved a proposal to lift the 10-year ban on political participation by leaders of the Justice and Republican People's Parties and numerous other politicians.

Although the constitution guarantees individual freedoms, exceptions may be made in order to protect the republic and the public interest, or in times of war or other national emergency. The provision holding that an arrested person cannot be held for more than 48 hours without a court order may likewise be suspended in the case of martial law, war, or other emergency.

14POLITICAL PARTIES

The first significant nationwide party, the Republican People's Party (Cumhuriyet Halk Partisi—CHP), was organized by Mustafa Kemal in 1923. Strong, centralized authority and state economic planning marked its 27 years of power (1923–50). It deemphasized everything religious to the point of subordinating religious activity and organization to state control.

Not until 1946 did a second popular party, the Democrat Party (Demokrat Parti—DP), come into being. Initially formed by a small group of dissident CHP members of parliament, the DP demanded greater political and economic liberalism and specifically a relaxation of central controls. When they came to power in 1950, the Democrats put into effect their policies of economic expansion through rapid mechanization and free enterprise; they also emphasized rural development through liberal credit terms to farmers. These policies, aimed at broadening the base of the economy, helped to return the Democrats to power three times in succession. After 1954, however, the Democrat regime reinstituted many of the former controls and instituted others, notably over the press. The CHP condemned these moves as well as what it regarded as lack of economic planning and of adequate fiscal and commercial controls. Both the Democrats and the CHP supported a firmly pro-Western, anti-Communist foreign policy.

In the first elections of the Second Republic (October 1961), none of the four competing parties won a controlling majority in either chamber, and a coalition government was formed for the first time in 1962. The coalition, however, was short-lived, for the newly formed Justice Party (Adalet Partisi—AP) withdrew from the governing group of parties and became the chief political opposition. The AP, which became the main political force in the country after the 1965 elections, favored private enterprise (in this respect it can be considered the successor of the DP, which was banned in 1960). Organized originally by local Democrat leaders, the AP came to reflect the views of modernization-minded professionals as well as workers and villagers. In the

1965 elections, the AP won 53.8% of the seats in the House of Representatives and 61% of the Senate seats. The elections of October 1969 confirmed its legislative predominance.

In December 1970, dissident members of the AP created the Democratic Party (Demokratik Parti). Another new organization, the Republican Reliance Party (Cumhuriyetçi Güven Partisi—CGP), formed by dissident members of the CHP, put up its first candidates in the 1969 elections. The National Salvation Party (Milli Selâmet Partisi—MSP) was created in March 1973 for the purpose of preserving Islamic traditions and bringing about economic and social reforms. In the general elections of 14 October 1973, the CHP replaced the AP as the most popular party in Turkey, although it did not achieve a parliamentary majority, and the CHP and MSP formed a coalition government under Bülent Ecevit. After the Ecevit government fell in September 1974, more than six months passed before a new permanent government was formed by Süleyman Demirel. His minority Government of the Nationalist Front, which included representatives of the AP, CGP, MSP, and National Action Party (Milliyetçi Hareket Partisi), commanded 214 out of 450 National Assembly seats. After the CHP won 213 Assembly seats in the 1977 elections, Ecevit, having formed a minority cabinet, lost a parliamentary vote of confidence and had to resign. But his rival, Demirel, fared little better as prime minister, and his coalition government soon dissolved. Each served another brief stint as head of government prior to the 1980 military coup.

The new military government banned all political parties and, under the 1982 constitution, forbade the leaders of the AP and CHP from active participation in politics for 10 years. After the new constitution was approved, however, the government allowed the formation of new political groups. The first new party, the Nationalist Democracy Party, was formed in May 1983 by certain retired military officers, former government officials, and business leaders; it received support from the military but fared poorly in local and national elections and was disbanded three years later. Another new group, the rightist Great Turkey Party, was abolished by the government soon after its founding because of alleged close resemblances to the banned AP; the True Path Party (Dogru Yol Partisi—DYP) was established in its place but was not allowed to participate in the elections to the National Assembly on 6 November 1983. Also barred were the newly formed Welfare Party and the Social Democratic Party, and Demirel and other politicians were temporarily placed under military detention. The Populist Party, which the military was said to regard as a loyal opposition, and the Motherland Party (Anatavan Partisi—ANAP), formed by conservative business leaders and technocrats, did win approval to run. In the balloting, the ANAP won a majority in the National Assembly, with 212 out of 400 seats, and its leader, Turgut Özal, became prime minister on 13 December.

Subsequently, all parties were allowed to participate in local elections. In 1985, the Populist Party merged with the Social Democratic Party to form the Social Democratic Populist Party (Sosyal Demokrasi Halkçi Partisi—SDHP). The Free Democrat Party was formed in 1986 as a successor to the Nationalist Democracy Party. In September 1987, the 10-year ban on political participation by over 200 leaders of the AP and CHP was lifted after a referendum indicated approval by a bare majority of just over 50%. At the same time, Özal announced elections in November of that year and had a law passed requiring nomination of candidates by party leaders rather than by popular choice. After challenges from opposition groups, the Constitutional Court declared the new procedure illegal. In the November 1987 elections, Özal was reelected as prime minister, with 36.3% of the vote; the ANAP won 292 of the 450 seats in the National Assembly (although polling only 36% of the vote), the SDHP 99 seats, and the DYP 59 seats. A coalition of True

Path and Social Democrats defeated the Motherland Party in 1991. Outside the established political system are the Kurdistan Workers Party (PKK) and other smaller separatist parties which have been banned.

In 1993, Motherland Party leader Turgut Özal died while serving as president. He was succeeded by True Path leader Suleyman Demirel. In July of that year, Tansu Ciller, chairperson of True Path, became prime minister (Turkey's first female prime minister). Ciller headed a shaky coalition and in a budgetary debate in September 1995, her government collapsed. She lost a vote of confidence in October and new elections were held in December. The elections were won by the Welfare Party, which took 158 of 550 seats; although hardly a majority, this was 23 more seats than Ciller's True Path. Fearing an Islamic government, secularists scrambled to form a majority but failed, and in January 1996 President Demirel invited Welfare Party leader Erbakan to form a government.

The Erbakan government lasted barely a year and a half. While popular in rural areas, it faced strong opposition from the business elite—which tends to be pro-Western—and the military. Beginning in 1997, the military let it be known that if Erbakan did not uphold Turkey's secular traditions, it would overthrow the government and return it to secular parties. In July 1997 Erbakan resigned and Motherland Party leader Mesut Yilmaz was asked to form a government. Following allegations of corruption, the Yilmaz government fell in November 1998 and was replaced by an interim minority government headed by Ecevit pending early elections.

Another corruption scandal brought down the Yilmaz government in November 1998. Ecevit returned to head a minority government pending early elections in 1999. On 18 April 1999, Turkish voters gave Ecevit's DSP a plurality with 136 seats (22.3% percent of the vote. Ecevit went on to form a coalition government with the MHP and Motherland. In May 2000, President Demirel's long political career came to an end with the election of Ahmet Necdet Sezer as his successor.

15 LOCAL GOVERNMENT

The chief administrative official in each of Turkey's 79 provinces (vilayets or ils) is the provincial governor (vali), an appointee of the central government who is responsible to the Ministry of Internal Affairs. During the military takeover in 1980s, governors were made responsible to the military authorities, and provincial assemblies were suspended. In 10 southeastern provinces, a regional governor exercises authority under a state of emergency declared in 1987. For administrative purposes, provinces are subdivided into districts (kazas or ilces), which in turn are divided into communes (nahiyes or bucaks), comprising kasabas and villages. In municipalities and villages, locally elected mayors and councils perform government functions. Both levels of government have specified sources of income and prepare budgets for the allocation of such income, which are then subject to approval by the central government. Most public revenue, however, is collected by the Ministry of Finance in Ankara.

16 JUDICIAL SYSTEM

The judicial system was left substantially intact by the 1982 constitution, except for the addition of special state security courts to handle cases involving terrorism and state security. There are four branches of courts: civil, administrative, military, and constitutional.

Civil courts are specialized into five sections: civil, enforcement, criminal, commercial, and labor. The same judges may serve in various sections. Decisions of civil courts of original jurisdiction are appealable to a High Court of Appeals in Ankara. The High Court of Appeals also hears cases involving charges against members of the Cabinet and other high functionaries.

Administrative courts include courts of first instance, regional appellate courts, and a Council of State at the apex. The Council of State also renders advisory opinions on draft legislation.

The Military Courts have jurisdiction over military personnel and include courts of first instance and a Military Court of Appeals.

The Constitutional Court reviews the constitutionality of legislation at the time of passage both when requested by the required percentage of members of Parliament and in the context of review of constitutional issues which emerge during litigation.

The constitution guarantees the independence of the judiciary from the executive and provides for life tenure for judges. It also explicitly prohibits state authorities from issuing orders or recommendations concerning the exercise of judicial power. The High Council of Judges and Prosecutors selects judges and prosecutors for the higher courts and oversees those in lower courts. In practice, the courts act independently of the executive.

The constitution guarantees defendants the right to a public trial. The bar association is responsible for providing free counsel to indigent defendants. There is no jury system. All cases are decided by a judge or a panel of judges.

The European Court of Human Rights is the final arbiter in cases concerning human rights.

17 ARMED FORCES

The total armed forces strength in 2000 was 639,000 (including 528,000 conscripts), plus 378,700 reserves. The army had 525,000 men (462,000 conscripts) and included 14 armored brigades, 17 mechanized brigades, 9 infantry brigades, and 26 border defense battalions. An estimated 30,000 Turkish soldiers were stationed on Cyprus. The navy had 51,000 personnel including 3,100 marines and 34,500 conscripts; naval strength included 15 submarines, 21 frigates, 50 patrol and coastal combatants, 29 mine warfare vessels, and about 27 auxiliary ships. Naval aviation provides 29 ASW aircraft and armed helicopters. The air force had 63,000 personnel and 440 combat aircraft. Paramilitary forces totaled 202,200. The defense budget for 1997 was $6.7 billion or 4.3% of gross domestic product.

The principal challenge to Turkey is the guerrilla war run by the PPK party, the Kurdish resistance movement, thought to number 5,000, plus a support militia of 50,000.

18 INTERNATIONAL COOPERATION

Turkey is a charter member of the UN, having joined on 24 October 1945, and belongs to ECE and all the nonregional specialized agencies. In December 1964, Turkey became an associate member of the former EEC; Turkey applied in 1987 for membership in the EC, including full membership in the EEC, but the application was opposed by Greece (unanimous consent of all EEC members is required for admission). Turkey is also a member of the WTO and a member of the Council of Europe, NATO, and OECD. Because of the imposition of martial law in Turkey, the Council of Europe decided in 1981 not to seat Turkish delegates at its parliamentary sessions.

Relations with the US, Turkey's principal aid benefactor, were strained during the 1970s over the Cyprus issue. After the Turkish military forces, using US-supplied equipment, had occupied the northern third of the island, the US Congress in 1975 embargoed military shipments to Turkey in accordance with US law. In response, Turkey abrogated its 1969 defense cooperation agreement with the US and declared that it would take over US military installations in Turkey (except the NATO base at Adana). The US government then relaxed the arms embargo and finally ended it in 1978, after which Turkey lifted its ban on US military activities. Turkish-US relations improved markedly thereafter, and a new defense and economic cooperation agreement between the two countries was signed in 1980.

In 1986, the 1980 agreement was renewed, allowing the US to use some 15 Turkish military bases in exchange for continuing military and economic subsidies.

[19] ECONOMY

Turkey's once state-directed economy is a mix of modern industry and commerce and village agriculture and crafts. The trend towards urbanization, however, is clear as farmers and towns people are increasingly drawn to industrial cities like Istanbul, Denizli, and Bursa. Although the state continues to control half of the manufacturing sector and 60% of the financial sector, economic growth is being driven by the private sector led by an increasing number of foreign-oriented and highly competitive companies. Turkey also has a large black economy that some analysts estimate to be as large as 25–50% of the official economy. In 1996, the government's continued subsidies to state enterprises and its inability to tax the "unofficial" segment of the economy contributed to large budget deficits which most analysts identify as Turkey's primary impediment to sustained economic growth.

Since the end of World War II, the agricultural share of the economy has declined, while that of the industrial sector (including construction) has expanded. This shift in economic activity is in part the result of deliberate government policy. Mechanization of agriculture has produced a significant shift in population from farms to cities, necessitating substantial urban and industrial development and, hence, a high rate of investment. However, this heavy investment, plus an explosion of consumer demand, has also contributed to severe inflation and balance-of-payments problems.

During the late 1960s and early 1970s, Turkey enjoyed a high economic growth rate, averaging about 7% annually. This growth was financed largely by foreign borrowing, increased exports, and remittances from Turkish workers in Western Europe. As a result of the large increases in oil import costs during 1973-74, however, Turkey's economic growth declined in real terms during 1974–80, and the country suffered a severe financial crisis. Stabilization programs implemented in 1978 and 1979 under a standby agreement with the IMF proved inadequate, but in January 1980, as a condition of further IMF aid, Turkey imposed a more stringent economic reform program, involving currency devaluation, labor productivity improvements, and restructuring of the nation's inefficient state enterprises.

In response to the reforms, the GNP grew on average by 4.8% from 1980 to 1994, the highest rate of any OECD economy. In 1994, structural problems, including inflation rates of between 60–90% and budget deficits of between 6–12%, eventually took their toll, plunging the economy into its worst recession since WWII. Real GNP declined by 6% and the inflation rate exceeded 130%. The underlying strength of the economy, together with a government austerity program designed to reign-in spending, led to a turnaround in 1996, and in 1997 GNP grew by 8%. Despite the rebound, the structural problems remain, keeping the economy in a cyclical boom-bust growth pattern. In 1998, GDP growth was only 2.8%.

[20] INCOME

The US Central Intelligence Agency (CIA) reports that in 1998 Turkey's gross domestic product (GDP) was estimated at $425 billion. The per capita GDP was estimated at $6,600. The annual growth rate of GDP was estimated at 2.8%. The average inflation rate in 1998 was 70%. The CIA defines GDP as the value of all final goods and services produced within a nation in a given year and computed on the basis of purchasing power parity (PPP) rather than value as measured on the basis of the rate of

exchange. It was estimated that agriculture accounted for 14.4% of GDP, industry 28.7%, and services 56.9%.

The World Bank reports that for the same period per capita private consumption (in PPP terms) was $4,465. Private consumption includes expenditures of individuals, households, and non-governmental organizations. It was estimated that between 1990 and 1998 private consumption grew at an annual rate of 4.1%. Approximately 45% of household consumption was spent on food, 18% on fuel, 6% on health care, and 5% on education. The richest 10% of the population accounted for approximately 32% of household consumption and the poorest 10% approximately 2.3%.

[21] LABOR

Of the total civilian labor force of 23.4 million in 1998, 21,958,000 persons were employed. Of these, 46% worked in agriculture (including forestry and fishing). The unemployment rate was 6.6% in 1997, down from 8.2% in 1991.

A detailed labor code administered by the Ministry of Labor controls many aspects of labor-management relations. Turkey has a basic 45-hour workweek, with a maximum of 7.5 hours per day and Saturday a partial holiday. Overtime is limited, and must be paid for at a 50% premium. No overtime is permitted in night work, underground work, or in industries considered dangerous to health. Workers usually are entitled to one paid day off per week. Compulsory accident and occupational disease insurance has been in effect since 1946, and workers enjoy a variety of other social security coverages.

A 1946 law authorized the formation of labor unions and enabled them to engage in collective bargaining, and the right to strike was legally permitted in 1963, although general, solidarity, and wildcat strikes are explicitly prohibited. Employers' unions also exist, but members of one kind of union are prohibited from joining the other. There are four confederations, three public employees' unions, and 27 independent unions. As of 1999, slightly more than 13% of the total labor force was unionized. Union membership was largest in the textile industry, tobacco manufacturing, public utilities, transport and communications, and coal mining. After the 1960 overthrow of the Menderes government, trade unions pressed the government to act upon their demands for the right to strike, for collective labor contracts, and for various social benefits, which were provided for in law but had not been fully implemented. A new labor law enacted in 1967 broadened existing protection and coverage of nonagricultural workers.

The military government that took power in September 1980 immediately banned strikes and lockouts, suspended union activities, and prohibited employers from laying off workers without military authorization. After the prohibition was repealed in 1983, strikes in the subsequent years escalated (especially after 1987). In 1999, there were 34 strikes. The Turkish Confederation of Revolutionary Workers Unions (DISK), was closed down in 1980, and its leaders were arrested. In 1991, however, DISK was relegalized, and its $300 million in assets and property were returned in March 1992.

The minimum working age is 15, but in practice many children work out of economic necessity. It was estimated that one-third of Turkish workers were between the ages of 6–19.

The minimum wage was $199 per month in 1999.

[22] AGRICULTURE

About 29.2 million hectares (64.6 million acres), or 38% of Turkey's total land area, are considered arable; in any given year, about two-thirds of arable land is under crops, and one-third is fallow. Little uncultivated arable land remains. The average holding is not more than 4 or 5 hectares (10–12 acres). Dry grain farming—in which half the land must lie fallow each year—

offers little more than a subsistence standard of living. Almost half of the labor force is engaged in agriculture, which provided 18% of GDP in 1998. Large farms are concentrated mainly in the Konya, Adana, and Izmir regions. Agricultural methods still tend to be primitive, but modern machinery has been introduced. Much new land has been brought under cultivation since World War II, and the increased use of chemical fertilizers and expansion of irrigated lands have increased yields per acre overall. In 1997, about 14% of all arable land was irrigated. Nevertheless, crop yields are still extremely sensitive to variations in rainfall. In good crop years, Turkey exports cereals, but in drought years, it must import them.

About 90% of the cultivated area is devoted to cereals. Wheat is the principal crop, accounting for 63% of total grain production in 1998; 21,000,000 tons of wheat were grown in that year, followed by barley with 9,800,000 tons. Turkey also produced 20,000,000 tons of sugar beets and about 3,650,000 tons of grapes. Other agricultural products were grown in lesser but still important quantities in 1998: maize, 2,300,000 tons; sunflower seeds, 860,000 tons; cotton, 802,000 tons; and oranges, 830,000 tons.

Turkish tobacco is world famous for its lightness and mildness. Most of the crop is grown in the Aegean region, but the finest tobacco is grown around Samsun, on the Black Sea coast. Tobacco and tobacco products represented 17% of total agricultural exports in 1995 and 1.8% of all Turkish exports that same year. Some 262,000 tons of tobacco were produced in 1998. Most of the cotton crop is grown around Adana and Izmir. Other crops of commercial importance include olives (575,000 tons in 1998), tea (120,000 tons), fruits, nuts, and vegetable oil. Turkey usually leads the world in the production and export of hazelnuts (about 580,000 tons produced in 1998) and ranks after Iran and the US in pistachio nuts (40,000 tons).

The government stimulates production through crop subsidies, low taxation, price supports, easy farm credit, research and education programs, and the establishment of model farms. The government also controls the conditions under which farm products can move into world markets. For some products, such as grain, the government is the sole exporter. Turkey has recently begun exporting vegetables and fruits abroad, which has affected domestic market prices. Cotton and tobacco production levels are increasing as demands by the textile and cigarette industries have risen.

Turkey is one of seven countries authorized under the 1961 UN Convention on Narcotic Drugs to grow opium poppies for legitimate pharmaceutical purposes. In June 1971, after persistent US complaints that up to 80% of all opiates smuggled into the US were derived from Turkish poppies, the Turkish government banned poppy growing; however, after efforts to find substitute crops failed, the government decided to rescind the ban on 1 July 1974. Areas authorized for poppy cultivation were estimated at 37,500 hectares (92,700 acres) in 1983; 5,000 hectares (12,350 acres) of opium capsule were sown in 1985. Government steps to curtail illegal cultivation, refining, and export of opiates were reportedly successful; in fact, Turkey has been one of the few opium-growing countries to crack down hard on drug smuggling.

23 ANIMAL HUSBANDRY

Turkey is heavily overgrazed. Many animals are used for transport and draft purposes as well as to supply meat and dairy products. The principal animals of commercial importance are mohair goats and sheep. The sheep wool is used mainly for blankets and carpets, and Turkey is a leading producer of mohair. Nevertheless, animal husbandry is generally poorly developed despite the great number of animals. In 1998 there were 30.2 million sheep, 11.2 million head of cattle, 8.4 million goats, and 166 million chickens. Production of wool was estimated at

46,000 tons in 1998. Other livestock products included cow's milk, 8.9 million tons; poultry meat, 436,000 tons; and hen eggs, 756,000 tons. Turkish apiculture produced some 63,000 tons of honey in 1998, third in the world after China and the US.

24 FISHING

The total marine catch by Turkey's deep-sea fishermen was 422,502.1 tons in 1997, most of it anchovies and sardines caught as they migrate seasonally through the Bosporus. In addition, 77,760 tons of freshwater fish were caught. Fishing equipment and methods have been substantially upgraded in recent years. For most of the population, however, the sea is not an important source of food. Exports of fish and fish products amounted to $124.6 million in 1997.

25 FORESTRY

Forests, occupy 8,856,000 hectares (21,883,000 acres), or 11.5% of Turkey's total land area. State forests include almost all the forestland, while community or municipal forests and private forests are small. Care of state forests and all cutting therein are the responsibility of the Directorate-General of Forestry within the Ministry of Agriculture. The timber cut in 1997 yielded 18,050,000 cu m of roundwood, with 46% used as fuel wood. Production of sawn wood in 1997 was 4,268,000 cu m; wood pulp 382,000 tons; particleboard, 1,728,000 cu m, and paper and paperboard, 1,951,000 tons.

26 MINING

Turkey has a wide variety of known minerals, but its resources are only partially developed. Much of total mineral output is carried out by government-controlled organizations, principally the Coal Board and the Etibank, founded in 1935. The government is still a major player in most sectors of the Turkish minerals industry through various state-owned industrial corporations, banks, and shareholdings in a number of private companies. In recent years, the government has been encouraging mineral exports as well as domestic and foreign private mining investment. Turkey was the world's largest producer of boron in 1996, accounting for half the world's total production, and was a major producer of barite, celestite (strontium), emery, feldspar, limestone, magnesite, marble, perlite, and pumice. Other minerals actively exploited and marketed are copper, chromite, iron ore, sulfur, pyrite, manganese, mercury, lead, zinc, and meerschaum.

Production of chrome concentrate in 1996 was about 1.7 million tons. Iron ore output increased from 2,645,367 tons in 1987 to a reported 3,500,000 tons in 1996. Other minerals produced in 1996 (in thousands of tons) were lignite, 58,298; boron concentrates, 1,200; sulfur, 160; and strontium concentrates, 30. Eskişehir, in northwestern Anatolia, is the world center of meerschaum (sepiolite), and Turkey is famous for its meerschaum pipes. Production has fallen in recent years from the 1989 level of 10,350 kg to 500 kg in 1996.

The primary mineral sector's contribution to GDP is slightly more than 1%; however, value-added secondary mineral commodities, including petroleum products, add another 14% and account for some 70% of Turkey's manufacturing output. Exports of industrial minerals and derived chemicals in 1996 were $542 million. Ongoing privatization costs are expected to result in layoffs and the closure of inefficient operations.

27 ENERGY AND POWER

Turkey provides about 60% of its energy needs overall; but in recent years, it has had to import several times as much petroleum as it produced. The bituminous coal field at Zonguldak on the Black Sea coast produces excellent coking coal. In 1998, output of coal totaled 62.4 million tons (about 90% soft coal). In 1998, production of crude oil came to 65,000 barrels per day, while consumption totaled 632,000 barrels per day. Fuel imports in 1994 accounted for 35% of total imports, compared with 20.8% in 1990, 33.4% in 1985, and 48.4% in 1980. As of 1999, oil provided nearly half of Turkey's energy requirements, and about 90% of oil supplies were imported.

In 1996, Turkey had 1,735 km (1,078 mi) of crude oil and 2,315 km (1,439 mi) of petroleum products pipelines, along with 706 km (439 mi) of natural gas pipelines. Turkey's geographical location makes it a natural transshipment route between the major oil producing areas in the Middle East, Central Asia, and the Caucasus on the one hand, and consumer markets in Europe on the other. As of 1996, about 1.2 million barrels of oil per day were shipped via supertankers through the Bosporus, the narrow strait that connects the Black Sea to the Mediterranean Sea. Botas, a joint Turkish-Iraqi venture with its headquarters in Ankara, created a system of oil pipelines running from Iraq to Turkey, thus bypassing the Persian Gulf. The pipeline was shut down during the Gulf War, but in February 1996 Turkey and Iraq agreed to reopen the pipeline if Iraq and the UN could reach an agreement regarding the exchange of Iraqi oil for humanitarian aid. In 1998, it was reported that Iraq was smuggling up to 60,000 barrels per day of fuel and fuel products into Turkey.

Hydroelectric and thermal power plants in 1998 produced 106,711 million kWh of electricity (about 40% hydro) and had a net installed capacity of 21.9 million kW. In the 1960s, lignite and water increased in importance as sources of energy, while coal and diesel oil dropped, but from the 1970s into the early 1980s, the importance of oil increased relative to other sources. In the 1980s, lignite again came to play an increasing role. Privatization of state assets has been underway since 1986, and Turkey's electricity sector, which is over 90% state-owned, is a chief target of this effort. As of 1998, proposals to privatize state-owned refining assets were under discussion.

Between 1980 and 1994, Turkish electric power demand grew at an average annual rate of 9.1%, among the highest such rates in the world. As of 1996, the government planned to construct 24 lignite-fired units, 27 natural gas-fired units, 21 coal-fired units, 2 nuclear power plants, and 113 hydroelectric units. Geothermal power could supply up to an estimated 31.5 million kw of additional capacity, but little progress has been made on exploiting the potential.

28INDUSTRY

Overall industrial production, which had increased by annual rates of close to or over 10% from 1973 to 1977, fell sharply because of Turkey's financial crisis in 1978-79 and actually declined by 5% in 1979 and 1980. After the government's economic reform program slowed inflation and stabilized the lira, industrial production improved. Production rose 28% during 1985-87. State enterprises were restructured to reduce their government subsidies and to make them more productive and competitive with private firms. However, industry has continued to suffer from structural weaknesses and, in many firms, production facilities are obsolete. Production rose by an annual average of 4.5% during 1988-92.

The textile industry, the largest industrial unit in Turkey next to petroleum refineries, is centered in Izmir, Istanbul, Adana, and Kayseri. Major industrial complexes include the government-owned iron and steel mill at Karabuk and the Eregli iron and steel works. Other important Turkish enterprises are brick and tile, glass, leather, chemicals and pharmaceuticals, metalworking, cordage, flour milling, vegetable-oil extraction, fats and oils, paper products, printing and publishing, plastic products, and rubber processing. The sugar-beet industry ranks first among food-processing industries and produces more than domestic consumption requires. The automobile industry expanded rapidly

in the 1970s. Much of the production of machines, consumer goods, and tools takes place in hundreds of small machine shops and foundries, where little special-purpose machinery is used. Manufacturing output increased from $34.3 billion in 1994 to $44.7 billion in 1995 to $46.6 billion in 1996. Manufacturing accounted for 25.9% of GDP in 1996. Secondary mineral commodities, including refined petroleum products, steel, cement, glass, and certain chemicals account for over two-thirds of manufacturing output.

Industrial commodities produced in 1995 (in thousands of tons) included: coke, 3,030; crude steel, 12,100; pig iron and ferroalloys, 4,600; cement, 29,400; sugar, 1,472; and newsprint, 137. Consumer items such as home refrigerators, washing machines, sewing machines, and television receivers are also produced in Turkey. Motor vehicle production in 1995 totaled 282,440 (including 233,412 passenger cars); the leading manufacturers are Tofas and Oyak-Renault. Output of petroleum products in 1995 (in millions of barrels) included distillate and residual fuel oil, 105.8; gasoline, 29.5; naphtha, 10.8; jet fuel, 10.4; and liquefied petroleum gas, 8.5.

In 1998 industry accounted for 28.7% of GDP. Industrial production grew by 4.1%.

29SCIENCE AND TECHNOLOGY

Turkey's industrial economy has just begun to apply advanced technology to basic industries. The government body that coordinates scientific research is the Scientific and Technical Research Council of Turkey (founded 1963), in Ankara. The Mavmara Scientific and Industrial Research Institute (1972), in Istanbul, conducts research on basic and applied sciences, and industrial research. The Ankara Nuclear Research and Training Center (1967), attached to the Turkish Atomic Energy Authority, studies health physics, nuclear electronics, and plasma physics. The General Directorate of Mineral Research and Exploration (1935), also in Ankara, conducts the Geological Survey of Turkey and evaluates mineral resources.

The Turkish Natural History Museum was founded in 1968 at Ankara. Turkey has 29 universities that offer courses in basic and applied sciences. In 1987–97, science and engineering students accounted for 45% of college and university enrollments.

In 1987–97, total expenditures on research and development amounted to 0.5% of GNP; 291 scientists and engineers per 1 million population were engaged in research and development.

30DOMESTIC TRADE

Individual firms tend to be small and specialized. There is virtually no commercial activity in villages; the villager comes into the market town to buy and sell. Government-operated exchanges for cereals are located in municipalities. If the price of grain in the free market falls below the supermarket price, the government-operated exchanges purchase the grain and market it. In this manner, the government controls the price range of cereals.

Because of the scarcity of some commodities, the government controls the distribution of various essential goods, notably cement, coal, lignite, and steel. Under a 1954 law, municipal authorities enforce specified profit margins on designated commodities. These margins are established at four levels: importer or manufacturer, distributor, wholesaler, and retailer. Customarily, a Turkish wholesaler supplies credit to retailers who, in turn, often extend credit beyond their own means to consumers. Wholesalers' margins tend to be small because of low overhead and keen competition. Due to Turkey's high inflation rate, wholesalers usually try to maintain minimal stocks to reduce carrying costs.

In the early 1990s, Turkey's consumer market began to change, as its trade regime liberalized and broadcast media rapidly grew. Most commercial firms belong to chambers of commerce, which exist in all cities. Chambers of industry are increasingly important in larger manufacturing centers. The government sponsors an international trade fair every year at Izmir. Shops are normally open from 9 AM to 1 PM and from 2 to 7 PM, Monday through Saturday; smaller establishments tend to stay open later and not close for lunch. Banking hours are from 8:30 AM to noon and 1:30 to 5 PM Monday through Friday.

31FOREIGN TRADE

Turkey's trade balance has long been negative, but the deficit reached crisis proportions in 1974–75 and again in 1980-81, when import value was nearly double that of exports and the annual trade deficit approached $5 billion. In 1985, the government mandated the creation of four free trade and export processing zones aimed at expansion and diversification of exports. By 1990, the deficit had risen to over $9 billion and the ratio of exports to imports fell to 58%, compared to 81% in 1988. The gap narrowed slightly in 1991 and 1992, but widened in 1993. Exports have increased from $18.1 billion in 1994 to $21.6 billion in 1995 to $24.5 billion in 1996. Total imports in 1994 amounted to $23.3 billion, and rose to $35.7 billion in 1995 and $45 billion in 1996. Since 1994, strong domestic demand has caused imports to surge, along with the reduction of import duties that accompanied the introduction of the customs union in 1996. Imports in 1996 were up by 50% from 1993.

The garment and textile industry in Turkey makes the largest amount of commodity exports (27%). Other exports include iron and steel shapes and primary forms (8.7%), fruits and nuts (5.8%), and vegetables (2.3%).

In 1997 Turkey's imports were distributed among the following categories:

Consumer goods	6.9%
Food	3.7%
Fuels	10.2%
Industrial supplies	37.8%
Machinery	25.1%
Transportation	13.5%
Other	2.8%

Principal trading partners in 1998 (in millions of US dollars) were as follows:

COUNTRY	EXPORTS	IMPORTS	BALANCE
Germany	5,460	7,316	-1,856
United States	2,233	4,054	-1,821
United Kingdom	1,740	2,683	-943
Italy	1,557	4,235	-2,678
Russia	1,348	2,155	-807
France	1,307	3,034	-1,727
Netherlands	889	1,446	-557
Belgium-Luxembourg	670	1,203	-533
Spain	517	1,276	-759
Japan	113	2,046	-1,933

32BALANCE OF PAYMENTS

The US Central Intelligence Agency reports that in 1998 the purchasing power parity of Turkey's exports was $31 billion while imports totaled $47 billion resulting in a trade balance of -$16 billion.

The International Monetary Fund (IMF) reports that in 1998 Turkey had exports of goods totaling $31,220 million and imports totaling $45,552 million. The services credit totaled $23,321 million and debit $9,860 million. The following table summarizes Turkey's balance of payments as reported by the IMF for 1998 in millions of US dollars.

Current Account		1,871
Balance on goods	-14,332	
Balance on services	13,461	
Balance on income	-2,985	
Current transfers	5,727	
Capital Account		...
Financial Account		773
Direct investment abroad	-367	
Direct investment in Turkey	940	
Portfolio investment assets	-1,297	
Portfolio investment liabilities	-5,089	
Other investment assets	-1,464	
Other investment liabilities	8,050	
Net Errors and Omissions		-2,203
Reserves and Related Items		-441

33BANKING AND SECURITIES

The Central Bank of the Republic of Turkey was founded in 1930 as a privileged joint-stock company. It possesses the sole right of note issue and has the obligation of providing for the monetary requirements of the state agricultural and commercial enterprises by discounting the treasury-guaranteed bonds they issue. Money supply, as measured by M2, totaled TL2,514,023 billion at the close of 1995. In October 1996, foreign reserves, excluding gold, were $17,388 million. All foreign exchange transfers are handled exclusively by the Central Bank, which operates the clearing accounts under separate agreements with foreign countries. The bank has 25 domestic branches, plus a banknote printing plant and foreign branch offices in New York, London, Frankfurt, and Zürich.

As of 1998, Turkey had 72 banks. Banks supervised by the Central Bank play a declining role in the banking system. Around 34% of total bank assets are concentrated in four banks: the state-owned Agricultural Bank (Ziraat Bankasi), which is Turkey's biggest; the Housing Bank (Emlak Bankasi); and two private banks, Isbank and Akbank.

The major private banks are mostly linked to industrial conglomerates, such as the Cukurova Group, owning the Construction and Credit Bank (Yapi ve Kredi Bankasi), Pamukbank, and Interbank, and the Sabanci Group, which owns Akbank. Several Western commercial banks are also active, as are some Middle Eastern trading banks. There are also three so-called special finance houses, which have adopted Islamic banking practices. Many observers predict large-scale bank consolidation as Turkey continues liberalizing its economy.

The five big state banks suffer from serious structural problems. These include overstaffing, political interference, and non-performing loans to other state institutions, which are not recorded as such. Many small and medium-sized banks are also poorly run. Some of these were badly hit by the financial crash of early 1994, and three were forced to close. A widespread shakeout in the banking system is regarded as likely in the longer term.

Two of Turkey's most important banks, the Sümerbank and Etibank, are also state investment-holding companies. Another important state financial institution is the Agricultural Bank, which supplies credit to the farm population. The largest private commercial bank is the Business Bank. Another private bank, the Industrial Development Bank of Turkey, stimulates the growth of private industrial development and channels the flow of long-term debt capital into the private industrial sector for both short- and long-range development programs.

The first securities market in the Ottoman Empire was the Dersaadet Securities Exchange, established after the Crimean war in 1866. The Istanbul Stock Exchange opened in 1985 and the Istanbul Gold Exchange commenced operations ten years later.

Turkey's only securities exchange is located in Istanbul. Because of the shortage of foreign exchange, there are no transactions in foreign bonds and stocks. With few exceptions, trading is in government bonds. Virtually all securities issued by private enterprises are sold privately through personal arrangements between buyers and sellers. Still, the Istanbul Stock Exchange has developed impressively, if not erratically, in recent years.

34INSURANCE

Government regulations effective 1929 and subsequently amended require all insurance companies to reinsure 30% of each policy with the National Reinsurance Corp., a state organization; in 1954, life policies were exempted from this requirement. It is possible to secure insurance policies for flood damage, third-party liability, earthquake, commercial shipments, theft, fire, and accident, as well as life. Varied social security schemes are administered directly by the state.

The insurance market is officially regulated through the Ministry of Commerce.

35PUBLIC FINANCE

Beginning in 1983, the fiscal year was changed to start on 1 January instead of 1 March. The consolidated budget includes the general budget of the government (by ministry) and a number of annexed budgets, which pertain to semiautonomous state activities, such as universities. Additionally, each section is divided into operating and investment expenditures. The budget is invariably in deficit.

In early 1994, the budget deficit and high transfers to inefficient state enterprises led to an economic crisis with inflation peaking at 150%. The government replied with an austerity program that succeeded in reducing inflation but sent the economy into recession. The government's commitment to reform waned as the economy began to rebound in 1995. Expenditures again exceeded revenues, forcing the government to incur increasing amounts of expensive debt to fund current expenses and support state enterprises.

The US Central Intelligence Agency (CIA) estimates that in 1998 Turkey's central government took in revenues of approximately $44.4 billion and had expenditures of $58.5 billion including capital expenditures of $3.7 billion. Overall, the government registered a deficit of approximately $14.1 billion. External debt totaled $102 billion.

The following table shows an itemized breakdown of government revenues and expenditures. The percentages were calculated from data reported by the International Monetary Fund. The dollar amounts (millions) are based on the CIA estimates provided above.

REVENUE AND GRANTS	100%	44,400
Tax revenue	86.8%	38,540
Non-tax revenue	12.9%	5,719
Capital revenue	0.3%	130
Grants	0.0%	12
EXPENDITURES	100%	58,500
General public services	3.7%	2,144
Defense	8.9%	5,199
Public order and safety	5.0%	2,899
Education	11.2%	6,570
Health	4.1%	2,375
Social security	9.0%	5,287
Housing and community amenities	1.8%	1,048
Recreation, cultural, and religious affairs	1.3%	757
Economic affairs and services	14.4%	8,401
Other expenditures	14.3%	8,347
Interest payments	26.5%	15,474

36TAXATION

All persons domiciled in Turkey, whether of Turkish citizenship or otherwise, are subject to taxation on income. Certain categories of foreigners are taxed only on income earned in Turkey—specifically, foreign business representatives, consultants, scientists, government officials, press correspondents, and others who have come to Turkey with no intention of becoming permanent residents, regardless of their length of residence. Income tax rates are progressive, ranging up to 55%. The basic corporate tax is 25%; however, a withholding tax of 10% for public companies and 20% for private companies is levied. Furthermore, there is a surcharge of 10% assessed. Thus, the total effective corporate tax rate is 45–55%, A tax law of 1961 required farmers, not previously subject to income tax, to file a return.

Land and buildings are taxed on the basis of assessed value. Other levies include stamp taxes on documents, vouchers, shares, and securities; fees on legal, bank, and insurance transactions; output taxes; a petroleum production tax; a sales tax; service taxes; and inheritance and gift taxes. A European union-type value-added tax was introduced in 1992. As of 1996, the standard rate is 15%; however, rates vary from 1–40% depending on the product. Business establishments are subject to an old age insurance tax and an illness and disability tax, shared by employers and employees.

37CUSTOMS AND DUTIES

Turkish customs duties are assessed on an ad valorem basis only. Present customs classification conforms with standardized international nomenclature. Duty-free entry is provided for many types of imports. In 1996, Turkey aligned its tariffs with the EU's common external tariff system. Importers no longer need an import licence and import authorization from a bank. A government monopoly, TEKEL, controls alcohol and cigarette imports. Narcotics and weapons are strictly prohibited. Other charges include a value added tax (VAT) ranging from 0–23%, a 15% municipal tax, and a 10% stamp tax.

38FOREIGN INVESTMENT

Although Turkey has been the recipient of considerable foreign aid, its leaders have also recognized the need for private foreign investment. By 1970, foreign capital could operate in any field of economic activity open to Turkish private capital, and there was no limit on the percentage of foreign participation in equity capital. However, direct capital investment by foreign companies from 1960 to 1979 averaged no more than $20 million annually, very low by OECD standards. This changed dramatically in 1980 with new foreign investment policies that cut red tape to gain more rapid approval for investment applications; inflows of private capital increased to $97 million in 1980, $337 million in 1981, and $913 million in 1992. In 1997, foreign direct investment in Turkey totaled over $1 billion. A majority (56.8%) of this investment went into manufacturing, while 40.5% was in services, 1.6% in agriculture, and 1.1% in mining.

Total Turkish direct foreign investments abroad totaled over $1.4 billion in 1997. Just over $323 million (22.2% of the total) is invested in the UK, $297.7 million in Germany, $102.2 million in the Netherlands, and $86.2 million in Russia. Other destinations for Turkish investors include Azerbaijan, Luxembourg, Romania, and Kazakhstan.

39ECONOMIC DEVELOPMENT

Economic policy is formulated by the State Planning Organization. In June 1961, an integrated 15-year plan was announced, consisting of three five-year plans designed to achieve a 7% yearly increase in national income. In March 1963, the first five-year plan was inaugurated; this 1963–68 program to some extent fell short of its goals, but its average annual increase of 6.7% in GNP was still impressive. Two objectives of the second five-year plan (1968–72) were economic viability and social justice. The role of the public sector under this program was twofold: creation and expansion of the economic and social infrastructure and development of modern manufacturing industries. Economic policy, however, still sought the largest possible active role for private enterprise in the development of industries, and the government sought with limited success to encourage private activity through fiscal concessions, financial assistance, and state participation in mixed enterprises. The third five-year plan was inaugurated in 1973 with the objective of helping Turkey prepare for its future membership in the EC. The long-term goals were to increase the per capita GNP from $400 in 1972 to $1,500 by 1995, to reduce agriculture's share of the GDP to 12%, and to increase industry's share to 37%. One of the main aims of the third five-year plan, still largely unmet, was to increase the efficiency of the tax-collection service. In agriculture, the objectives were to increase food supplies for export and to feed a growing population through improved irrigation, technical advice to farmers, and the establishment of more cooperative farms.

All these efforts required large new investments and massive foreign loans which, coupled with the huge increases in the cost of oil imports after 1973, led to the financial crisis of 1977–78. Since 1980, Turkey has deliberately pursued a deflationary policy, allowing the international exchange rate of the lira to fluctuate on a daily basis from 1 May 1981. The government also delayed several ambitious development proposals, mainly because new foreign credits were not available. However, a number of smaller projects financed by the IBRD went forward. Meanwhile, the fourth (1979–83) and fifth (1985–90) five-year plans continued to stress industrial development, deflationary monetary policy, and export promotion. The creation of free trade zones, in the mid-1980s, was a major step in line with these policies.

Long-term economic programs adopted in 1991 and 1994 planned to reform social security and subsidy programs, implement tax reforms and improve tax administration, and restructure state enterprises, transferring certain inefficient ones to the private sector. By 1996, these plans had reduced the government's role in the economy, but huge budget deficits continued to plague the economy and further reforms are needed if Turkey is to solve its economic problems.

Turkey's geostrategic significance received a big boost in 1999 when its leaders, along with those of Azerbaijan, and Georgia agreed to the construction of an oil pipeline from the Caspian Sea port of Baku to the Turkish Mediterranean port of Ceyhan. Completion of the pipeline may come as soon as 2004.

Full membership in the European Union (EU) constitutes one of Turkey's chief aims. In December 1997 Turkey was effectively removed from the EU's list of candidates for entry. As a result, Turkey suspended its relations with the EU. However, the 1997 decision was reverse at the December 1999 EU summit in Helsinki as Turkey formally became a candidate for accession in the next round of EU enlargement. Turkey's chronic economic problems along with reservations about human rights preclude Turkish entry for at least a decade according to most observers. Nevertheless, Turkey's status as a candidate member provides clear goals for Turkish development.

40SOCIAL DEVELOPMENT

Since 1936, various forms of social security have been introduced, all of which are administered by the Social Insurance Institution and include industrial accident and disease, old age, sickness, disability, and maternity insurance. Pensions are financed by 9% contributions from employees, and 11% of payroll from employers. Employer contributions are higher for industries requiring arduous labor. To qualify for an old age pension, a worker must be at least 55 years old (50 for women) and must have worked at least 25 years in a qualified work place and made contributions on at least 5,000 days' wages. Employers also contribute an additional 1.5% to 7% to cover worker's injuries. In some localities, the social insurance organization operates its own hospitals and other facilities.

The social organization, Bağ-kur, pays monthly benefits to artisans, craftsmen, and other self-employed workers. Government workers are covered by the Government Employees Retirement Fund.

Turkey is a secular state and all citizens are proclaimed equal in the Constitution. The Civil Code explicitly bans sex-based privileges, yet proclaims the male as the legal head of the household. This grants the male the right to choose the place of residence, and most assets are held in the name of the husband. Women generally receive only one-fourth of the estate if widowed.

Women in urban areas are increasingly working outside the home. In 1999, women comprised nearly 50% of the workforce, and they can be found in most professional fields. However, they still hold fewer than 10% of managerial positions. In 1993 a woman became Turkey's Prime Minister. In 1999, however, only 23 women were voted into the 550 seat Parliament.

Reports of child abuse have increased in recent years. In 1995, the U.N. Convention on the Rights of the Child was ratified, but implementing legislation had yet to be passed.

The Constitution does not recognize the Kurds as a national, racial or ethnic minority. In 1991, however, the use of the Kurdish language was legalized for "nonpolitical communication." Nationalist Kurdish publications are subject to scrutiny and possible confiscation under the Anti-Terror Law.

The government is responsible for widespread human rights abuses, including beatings, torture, and killings by security forces. Freedom of speech and of the press are limited. A 1999 law suspended the sentences of journalists and other writers imprisoned for infractions involving freedom of expression, but only on condition that they not commit similar offenses within the next three years. Human rights organizations are subject to harassment and possible closure by the authorities.

41HEALTH

Free medical treatment, given at state hospitals or health centers, is provided by the state to any Turkish citizen who obtains a certificate of financial need from a local administrator. Public health care expenditures for 1990 were $4,281 million.

In 1992, there were 941 hospitals with 139,606 beds (2.4 per 1,000 people). Of this number, 616 were public, with 72,513 beds. In 1991, there was 1 doctor per 1,176 people; in 1994, there was one hospital bed per 403 people.

Malaria, cholera, and trachoma have been effectively controlled by large-scale public preventive measures. In 1996 there were 32 cases of tuberculosis per 100,000 people. In 1995, 91.7% of the population had access to safe water, and 94.4% had adequate sanitation. Immunization rates for children up to one year old in 1997 were tuberculosis (73%); diphtheria, pertussis, and tetanus (79%); polio (79%); and measles (76%). In 1995, there were 30,997 deaths of children under 5 from diarrheal disease. Malaria incidence has decreased from 47,156 in 1993 to 13,467 in 1995.

Turkey's 1999 birth rate was 21 per 1,000 people, and about 63% of married women (ages 15 to 49) used contraception in 1993. The total fertility rate in 1999 was 2.4 for every Turkish woman who lived through her childbearing years. Average life expectancy was 73 years in 1999.

Infant mortality was estimated at 36 per 1,000 live births in 1999; maternal mortality was 150 per 100,000 live births in

1991; and in 1999, general mortality was 5 per 1,000 people. Between 1984 and 1992, there were approximately 5,000 war-related deaths in the Kurd rebellion.

The HIV-1 seroprevalence rate was 0.0 per 100 adults in 1997. Only 194 AIDS cases were reported in 1996.

Smoking consumption in Turkey has increased from 2.0 kg a year per adult in 1984 to 2.2 kg in 1995.

42HOUSING

A traditional village house consists of sun-dried brick (adobe) or rough-hewn stone walls across which are laid timbers piled with brush and then topped with packed earth. The flat roof is often used for storage of feed grain. Floors are often bare earth covered with matting or lightweight carpets. Little furniture is used. Urban housing varies from houses similar to those in villages to modern, centrally heated apartment buildings. From 1981 through 1985, 305,890 new residential buildings containing 929,104 apartments were completed; virtually all these apartments had electricity, piped water, kitchens, and baths. As of 1985, 71% of all housing units were detached houses, 23% were apartments, 6% were squatters' houses, and under 1% were marginal dwellings. About 93% of all households were heated by stoves and 6% had central heating; 47% used coal for heating fuel and 43% used wood.

43EDUCATION

For the year 2000, adult illiteracy rates were estimated at 14.8% (males, 6.4%; females, 23.3%). Primary, secondary, and much of higher education is free. Education is compulsory for children ages 6 to 14 or until graduation from primary school (grade 5). However, owing to the inadequate number and distribution of schools and teachers, only about 56% of the children attend secondary school. Secondary schooling is for six years.

The regular school system consists of five-year primary schools, three-year junior high schools, and three-year high schools. Parallel to this system is a variety of technical, trade, and commercial schools. Among private schools in operation are a number of foreign schools and those maintained by ethnic or religious minorities. Among Turkey's 28 universities are the universities of Istanbul (founded 1453) and Ankara (founded 1946), the Technical University of Istanbul (founded 1773), and the Middle East Technical University at Ankara (founded 1957).

In 1997 there were 47,313 primary schools, with 6,389,060 students. Also in 1997, enrollment in all secondary-level schools was 4,760,892 students, with 218,829 teachers. The universities and other public higher institutions had 1,434,033 students and 50,313 faculty members that same year.

44LIBRARIES AND MUSEUMS

The National Library in Ankara had 960,000 volumes in 2000. There are two provincial branches of the library system as well: the Basset State Library in Istanbul with 500,000 volumes and the National Library of Izmir with 350,000 volumes. Major University collections include the Istanbul University and Documentation Center with 1.4 million volumes and one of the Middle East's finest rare book collections; the Middle East Technical University with 418,000 volumes, and the University of Ankara with 750,000 volumes.

The most famous museums and ancient buildings are located in Istanbul. The old seraglio, now Tip-top Museum, is perhaps the most famous; it houses a large collection of paintings, manuscripts, and historically important items. Nearby is the Ayasofya (Saint Sophia) Museum, the world-renowned Byzantine church. Next to it is the Blue Mosque, famous for the beauty of its interior and the grace of its dome. Also in Istanbul are the museums of archaeology and of the ancient Orient, housing one of the world's finest collections of Greek art, including the

sarcophagus of Alexander the Great. Additionally, the city is home to the Museum of Turkish written Art, the Istanbul Museum of Painting and Sculpture, and the Museum of Revolution. The Museum of Archaeology in Ankara contains the world's outstanding collection of Hittite works. Also in Ankara are Ataturk's Mausoleum and Museum, the Museum of Anatolian Civilizations, and the Museum of the Turkish Independence War and Turkish Republic. In Konya are located museums of Islamic art, one of which is housed in the mausoleum of Mevlana. Newer facilities include the decorative arts museums at the Beyler beyi and Dolmahbace palaces (both opened in Istanbul in 1984) and the Fire Brigade Museum in Fatib (1992). Along Turkey's Aegean coast are situated the ruins of Ephesus, Pergamum, Troy (Ilium), Halicarnassus, and other famous ancient cities. A zoological garden is located in Ankara.

45MEDIA

Postal, telephone, and telegraph service is owned and operated by a semi-independent government enterprise under the jurisdiction of the Ministry of Transport and Communications. Telephones in 1997 numbered about 17 million, with 1.5 million cellular subscribers. The state operated 15 AM and 94 FM radio stations as of 1995; in 1999 there were television broadcast stations. Turkey had 178 radios, television sets, and 26 mobile phones per 1,000 population in 1997.

In 1995, there were 399 daily newspapers in print (with a combined circulation of 4,000,000), many of which had small local circulations. The independent leftist *Istanbul daily Cumhuriyet* (1999 circulation 120,000) has been closed and reopened a number of times. Other leading Istanbul dailies (with 1999 circulation figures) are *Sabah* (722,950); *Hurriyet* (615,50); *Milliyet* (394,600), *Bugun* (179,180); and *Turkiye* (312,770).

Although the 1982 constitution guarantees freedom of expression, it also authorizes newspaper confiscations and closures in the cases of crimes against the unity, security, or republican principles of the state. After the 1980 coup, the military government, which had vested control of the press in the provincial martial law administrators, repeatedly closed down newspapers it claimed had published material damaging to the national interest. As of 1999, the government is still said to limit free expression significantly.

As of 1997, there were some 760,000 personal computers. Online access is extremely limited, with fewer than five Internet hosts per 1,000 population in 1998.

46ORGANIZATIONS

Professional organizations, charitable associations, student organizations, and athletic clubs are active in the major cities. There are several Masonic lodges and branches of the Rotary and Lions clubs. Women are active in a number of their own charitable organizations. Since World War II, international cultural associations have appeared, chief among them being Turkish-American, Turkish-French, Turkish-German, and Turkish-English.

Chambers of commerce and chambers of industry are semiofficial agencies for the control of import license and foreign exchange allocations.

47TOURISM, TRAVEL, AND RECREATION

Citizens of the US, Canada, Japan, and most Western European countries need a valid passport but no visa for stays of up to three months. Foreigners entering without a visa and remaining longer than three months must secure a residence permit from the police. No vaccinations or inoculations are required of visitors arriving directly from Europe or the US.

In 1997, 9,689,000 visitors (including same-day visitors) arrived in Turkey. Tourism receipts totaled $8.1 billion. There were 148,844 hotel rooms and 307,131 beds with a 55% occupancy rate that year.

In addition to the museums and monuments of Istanbul, places of interest include the Aegean ports of Izmir and Bodrun; the ancient cities of Troy (Ilium), Ephesus, Tarsus, Konya, Samsun, Erzurum, and Trabzon; Mt. Ararat, traditionally considered the landing place of Noah's Ark, the remains of which some expeditions have tried to find; the ski resort of Uludağ, 36 km (22 mi) south of Bursa; and the sea resort of Antalya, on the Mediterranean coast. Water sports, mountaineering, and football (soccer) are popular forms of recreation, as are such traditional Turkish sports as grease wrestling (yağli güreş), camel fighting (deve güreşi), and a horseback javelin competition (cirit oyonu) played mainly in eastern Turkey.

In 1999 the UN estimated the cost of traveling in Istanbul at $160 per day; the estimated daily cost of staying in Ankara was $116.

48FAMOUS TURKS

The most famous rulers before the coming of the Turks were Croesus (r.560–546 BC), a king of Lydia noted for his wealth and for the loss of his kingdom to the Persians; Constantine I (the Great; Flavius Valerius Aurelius Constantinus, b.Moesia, AD 280?–337), the first Roman emperor to accept Christianity and to use Constantinople as a capital; and Justinian I (the Great; Flavius Petrus Sabbatius Justinianus, b.Illyricum, 483–565), a Byzantine emperor whose collection of laws and legal principles has been the model for European law down to modern times. Outstanding political figures since the arrival of the Turks include Sultan Mehmet II (1429–81), conqueror of Constantinople in 1453; Sultan Süleyman I (the Magnificent, 1495–1566); the Barbarossa brothers, Aruj (1473?–1518) and Hayreddin Paşa (Khayr ad-Din, 1466?–1546), naval commanders, born in Mytilene, who established Turkish supremacy in the Mediterranean; Mehmet Köprülü Paşa (1583–1661), Mehmet IV's grand vizier and founder of a family line of outstanding grand viziers; Sultan Abdul Hamid II (1842–1918), a despotic ruler whose tyranny led to the formation of the Young Turk movement; Enver Paşa (1881–1922), Young Turk leader who was the ruler of Turkey during World War I; Mustafa Kemal Atatürk (1881–1938), World War I military commander, nationalist leader, and first president of the republic; Ismet Inönü (Paşa, 1884–1973), Atatürk's chief of staff and prime minister, who succeeded him as president (1938–50) and was the first prime minister of the Second Republic (1961–65); Celâl Bayar (1883–1986), who helped found the Democrat Party and was president (1950–60) until ousted by the military; and Adnan Menderes (1899–1961), prime minister (1950–60) until he was forced to resign and then executed.

Outstanding religious figures include Haci Bektaş Veli (1242–1337), founder of the Bektashi dervishes, and Mevlana (Celâleddin-i Rumi or Jalal al-Din Rumi, 1207–73), author of the epic Mesnevi (or Mathnavi) and founder of the Mevlevi dervishes.

Revered literary figures include the mystical poets Yunus Emre (1238?–1320?) and Süleyman Çelebi (d.1422), author of Mevlidi Sherif (Birth Song of the Prophet). Other significant poets of the imperial epoch are Ahmedi (1334–1413), Şeyhi (d.1429?); Fuzulî (1494–1555), renowned for his lyrical verses about platonic love; Ali Şir Nevâi (1441–1501); Nef'î (1582?–1636); Nabî (1642?–1712); Ahmet Nedim (1681–1730), perhaps Ottoman Turkey's greatest love poet; and Şeyh Galib (1757–98), the last great poet of the mystical and classical tradition. Renowned for his geographical and historical writings is Kâtip Çelebi (known in Europe as Haji Khalifa, 1609–57); the great traveler Evliya Çelebi

(1611–82) is noted for his books on travel and history. The greatest folk poet was the 17th-century minstrel Karacaoğlan.

Sinasi (1826–71), a dramatist, journalist, and essayist, was the first Turkish writer in the Western tradition. Other significant playwrights are Musaipzade Celal (1870–1959), Haldun Taner (1916–86), and Necati Cumali (b.1921). The poet Ziya Paşa (1825–80) was the outstanding literary figure of the reform period. Namik Kemal (Ahmed Kemal, 1840–88) and Mehmet Emin Yurdakul (1869–1944) dedicated their poetry to the achievement of political ideals. Four widely read novelists are Huseyin Rahmi Gurpinar (1864–1944), Ahmet Rasim (1864–1932), Halit Ziya Usakligil (1865–1945), and Mehmet Rauf (1871–1931). Omer Seyfettin (1884–1920) was a major short-story writer. Ziya Gökalp (1875–1924) was a noted poet and sociologist. Significant contemporary novelists include Halide Edib Adivar (1884–1966), Yakup Kadri Karaosmanoglu (1888–1974), Refik Halit Karay (1888–1974), Reşat Nuri Güntekin (1892–1957), Kemal Tahir Demir (1910–74), Orhan Kemal (1914–70), and Yasar Kemal Gokceli (b.1922). Two fine modern poets were Yahya Kemal Beyatli (1884–1958) and Nazim Hikmet Ran (1901–60). Two prominent journalists and political writers were Hüseyin Çahit Yalçin (1875–1957) and Ahmet Emin Yalman (1889–1973). Outstanding historians were Naima (1752–1815), Mehmet Fuat Köprülü (1890–1966), and Ahmet Zekî Velidî Toğan (1890–1970).

Other famous Turks include the architect Sinan (1490–1588), the miniaturist Abducelil Celebi Levni (d.1732), and the modern painter Bedri Rahmi Eyuboglu (1913–75). Famous contemporary composers include Ulvi Cemal Erkin (1906–72) and Ahmet Adnan Saygun (b.1907). The operatic soprano Suna Korad (b.1934) and bass-baritone Ayhan Baran (b.1929) have won renown in European musical circles.

49DEPENDENCIES

Turkey has no territories or colonies.

50BIBLIOGRAPHY

Ahmad, Feroz. The Turkish Experiment in Democracy, 1950–1975. London: Hurst, 1977.

———. The Making of Modern Turkey. New York: Routledge, 1993.

Berberoglu, B. Turkey in Crisis: From State Capitalism to Neocolonialism. Westport, Conn.: Hill, Lawrence, 1982.

Bianchi, Robert. Interest Groups and Political Development in Turkey. Princeton, N.J.: Princeton University Press, 1984.

Davison, Roderic H. Essays in Ottoman and Turkish History, 1774–1923: The Impact of the West. Austin: University of Texas Press, 1990.

Dodd, C. H. Democracy and Development in Turkey. Atlantic Highlands, N.J.: Humanities, 1979.

The Economy of Turkey Since Liberalization. Edited by V.N. Balasubramanyam and Subidey Togan. New York: St. Martin's, 1996.

Finkel, Andrew, and Nukhet Sirman (eds.) Turkish State, Turkish Society. New York: Routledge, 1990.

Hale, William. The Political and Economic Development of Modern Turkey. New York: St. Martin's, 1981.

———. Turkish Politics and the Military. New York: Routledge, 1994.

Heper, Metin, and Ahmet Evin (eds.). State, Democracy, and the Military: Turkey in the 1980s. New York: W. de Gruyter, 1988.

Heper, Metin, and Jacob M. Landau (eds.). Political Parties and Democracy in Turkey. New York: I.B. Tauris, 1991.

Heper, Metin. Historical Dictionary of Turkey. Metuchen, N.J.: Scarecrow, 1994.

Kasaba, Resat. *The Ottoman Empire and the World-economy: The Nineteenth Century.* Albany: State University of New York Press, 1988.

The Kurdish Nationalist Movement in the 1990s: Its Impact on Turkey and the Middle East. Edited by Robert Olson. Lexington, Ky.: University Press of Kentucky, 1996.

Palmer, Alan Warwick. *The Decline and Fall of the Ottoman Empire.* New York: M. Evans, 1993.

Persner, L. W. *Turkey's Political Crisis: Background, Perspectives, Prospects.* Washington, D.C.: Center for Strategic and International Studies, George Washington University Press, 1984.

Robinson, Richard D. *The First Turkish Republic.* Cambridge, Mass.: Harvard University Press, 1963.

Schick, Irvin C. and Ertugrul Ahmet Tonak (eds.). *Turkey in Transition: New Perspectives.* New York: Oxford University Press, 1987.

Shaker, Sallama. *State, Society, and Privatization in Turkey, 1979 – 1990.* Washington, D.C.: Woodrow Wilson Press Center, 1995.

Shaw, Stanford J., and Ezel Kural. *History of the Ottoman Empire and Modern Turkey.* 2 vols. Cambridge, England: Cambridge University Press, 1976.

Toprak, Binnez. *Islam and Political Development in Turkey.* Leiden: Brill, 1981.

Turkey: A Country Study. 5th ed. Edited by Helen Chapin Metz. Washington, D.C.: Department of the Army, 1996.

Weiker, Walter F. *The Modernization of Turkey from Atatürk to the Present Day.* New York: Holmes & Meier, 1981.

Zurcher, Erik Jan. *Turkey: A Modern History.* New York: I.B. Tauris, 1993.

TURKMENISTAN

Туркменистан
Turkmenistan

CAPITAL: Ashgabat (Ashkhabad).

FLAG: Green field with claret stripe of five carpet patterns; white crescent and five white stars symbolizing the five regions of Turkmenistan to the right of the stripe. Two crossed olive branches were added beneath the carpet patterns in 1997.

ANTHEM: *Independence Turkmenistan.*

MONETARY UNIT: Manat (MN), the unit of currency, was introduced by the government in November 1993. MN1 = US$0.00019 (US$1 = MN5250.0) as of 31 March 2000, but exchange rates are likely to fluctuate widely.

WEIGHTS AND MEASURES: The metric system is used.

HOLIDAYS: New Year's Day, 1 January; Flag Day, February 19; International Women's Day, 8 March; Novruz Bairam (first day of spring), 21 March; Victory Day, 9 May; Revival and Unity Day, 18 May; Independence Day, 27 October; Neutrality Day, 12 December.

TIME: 5 PM = noon GMT.

¹LOCATION, SIZE, AND EXTENT

Turkmenistan is located in southern Asia, bordering the Caspian Sea, between Iran and Uzbekistan. Comparatively, Turkmenistan is slightly larger than the state of California, with a total area of 488,100 sq km (188,456 sq mi). Turkmenistan shares boundaries with Kazakhstan and Uzbekistan on the N, Afghanistan on the SE, Iran on the SW, and the Caspian Sea on the W. Turkmenistan's boundary length totals 5,504 km (3,420 mi). Turkmenistan's capital city, Ashgabat (which means "city of love"), is located in the southwestern part of the country.

²TOPOGRAPHY

The topography features flat to rolling sandy desert with dunes to the Caspian Sea, which lies in the west. The Kara Kum desert occupies over 80% of Turkmenistan's total area. The desert is bounded by oases in the north that are watered by the Amu Darya, and by the Murgap, Tejen, and Atrek rivers in the south. The highest point in Turkmenistan is the Kougitangtau peak (3,137 m/11,293 ft), located along the eastern border near Uzbekistan. Only 3% of Turkmenistan's land is arable with approximately 2.5% under irrigation.

³CLIMATE

The climate is arid continental. In July the mean temperature is 28°C (82°F). The mean temperature in January is –4°C (25°F). It can become very hot in the Kara Kum desert, with daytime temperatures of 122°F not unusual. It does not rain much in Turkmenistan. Rainfall averages 25 cm (9.7 in) a year.

⁴FLORA AND FAUNA

The Kara Kum (Black Sea) desert covers most of the country, and there is little plant or animal life. Herders raise goats, camels, and sheep in the desert. Farmers use reservoirs for irrigation to grow crops not indigenous to the area.

⁵ENVIRONMENT

The most significant environmental problems in Turkmenistan include salinization of the soil and water pollution. The nation's water supply is threatened by chemical contaminants from farming activity. The problem is complicated by a lack of adequate sewage treatment facilities. A large share of the Amu Darya River's flow is diverted for irrigation, decreasing its contribution to the water supply from the Aral Sea. Water cycles have also affected the Garabogazol Aylagy, a lagoon-like appendage in the northwest that adjoins the Caspian Sea. It became fully enclosed because of a drop in the volume of the Caspian Sea, but is starting to rise again as the sea returns to previous levels. As of 1994, 2.3% of the country's total land area was protected. Eight mammal species, nine bird species, and one plant species are threatened. Threatened species include the cheetah, tiger and white-headed duck.

⁶POPULATION

The population of Turkmenistan in 2000 was estimated at 4,435,507. An estimated 4.2% of the population is 65 years of age or older. The projected population for the year 2005 is 4,791,000, assuming a crude birthrate of 25 per 1,000 population and a death rate of 9, resulting in a natural rate of change of 1.6% for the period 2000–2005. The population rate of change between 1995 and 2000 was 1.9%. The population density in 1998 was 10 per sq km (26 per sq mi).

It was estimated that 46% of the population lived in urban areas in 2000, up from 47% in 1980. The capital city, Ashgabat, had a 2000 population of 462,000. Other large cities include Chardzhou (164,000), Tashauz (114,000), Mary (94,000), and Nebit-Dag (89,000). Turkmenistan's next census is slated for January 2004.

⁷MIGRATION

Emigration to other former USSR republics exceeded immigration by 20,600 during 1979–90. More than 40,000 people fled from Tajikistan to Turkmenistan in 1992 to escape civil war. Repatriation of the Tajik refugees started in early 1998. As of September 1999, nearly 5,000 Tajik refugees had voluntarily repatriated. There were also some 13,000 Tajik refugees, mostly ethnic Turkmen, who expressed the desire to remain in Turkmenistan. Also in 1999, UNHCR was assisting a group of some 1,000 Afghan refugees to integrate locally. UNHCR also developed a contingency planning and emergency preparedness mechanism in order to handle potential future refugee influxes.

Between 1993 and 1995, 100,000 Russians left Turkmenistan. The net migration rate was -1.35 migrants per 1,000 population in 1999.

8ETHNIC GROUPS
There are over 100 distinct ethnic groups living in Turkmenistan. According to the 1995 census, 77% of the population consisted of ethnic Turkmens. That year, Uzbeks accounted for 9.2% of the population; Russians, 6.7%; Kazakhs, 2%; Ukrainians, 0.5%; and Armenians, Azeris, Tatars, and Beluji, 0.8%. Other groups present include Belarusans, Germans, Jews, Georgians, Moldovans, Uighurs, and Koreans. Like the Turkmens, the Uzbeks, Kazakhs, and Azeris are Turkic-speaking peoples.

9LANGUAGES
Turkmen, spoken by about 72% of the population, is mandatory in the schools. It is a Turkic language of the Oghuz group, related to Azeri, Turkish, and Uzbek. Prior to the Soviet era, Turkmens wrote their language using the Arabic script. In Turkmenistan, that script was changed to Latin and then Cyrillic before World War II. The government has begun to institute the Latin script again. The Turkmen language has been influenced by Persian and Arabic elements. In recent decades, many borrowed words from Russian also have been adopted. Russian remains in common use in government and business, and is spoken by 12% of the population. Uzbek is spoken by 9%; various other languages are spoken by 7%.

10RELIGIONS
There is no state religion, but about 88% of the population is Muslim, primarily Sunni, with strong elements of local shamanism and Sufi mysticism included in its practices. Religious congregations are required to register with the government; only registered religions can hold gatherings and proselytize. Although the constitution provides for religious freedom, the Law on Freedom of Conscience and Religious Organizations, which was amended in 1995 and again in 1996, also provides for significant government control of religion. For example, the government applies a 500-member standard on a local/regional basis. This restriction has caused problems for a number of minority religions, especially the Baha'i faith. Baha'is have been prevented from conducting services since 1997 and have been questioned by Interior Ministry authorities for holding private prayer meetings in their homes. They were permitted to gather in Ashgabat for a single day to celebrate the Nowruz (spring) holiday in March 1998 and again in 1999.

In January 1999, members of the Gregorian Armenian faith appealed to authorities to use a church pending their registration, but they have not yet received a reply. Jehovah's Witnesses filed an application for registration in January 1997 but remain unregistered, pending correction of mistakes in their application. Subsequent efforts to worship at meetings in their homes resulted in fines and seizures of religious materials.

Ethnic Turkmen (about 77% of the population), ethnic Uzbeks (9%), and ethnic Kazakhs (2%) are nominally Muslim. Ethnic Russians, who account for about 7% of the population, are largely members of the Russian Orthodox Church. The remaining 5% of the population is designated as other.

11TRANSPORTATION
Nebit-Dag, Ashgabat, Mary, and Chardzhou are connected by railroad to the nation's main port of Turkmenbashi on the Caspian Sea. Other lines include a railroad from Mary along the Murgab and Kushka rivers to Afghanistan and a line from Chardzhou along the Amu Dar'ya which nearly parallels Uzbekistan's border. Smaller rail spurs are located at Tashauz and Kerki. Rail lines were estimated at a total of 2,187 km (1,359 mi) in 1996.

Also in 1996, there were an estimated 24,000 km (14,914 mi) of roadways, of which 19,488 km (12,110 mi) were hard-surfaced. At last estimate, Turkmenistan had 64 airports, of which 22 had paved runways. In 1997, 1,093,000 passengers were carried on scheduled domestic and international airline flights.

12HISTORY
The territory of present-day Turkmenistan has been inhabited since the Stone Age, with evidence of agricultural communities as early as 6000 BC and of planned irrigation works from 3500 BC. The first states were Margiana and Parthia, from about 1000 BC. In 7th–6th centuries BC, Margiana was part of Bactria, while Parthia was part of the Median state. In the 6th–4th centuries BC the region was ruled by the Achaemenids, who were conquered by Alexander the Great at the end of the 4th century. In his wake there emerged a Parthian Empire which lasted until AD 224, when Persians of the Sassanid dynasty seized the territory. In the 5th century much of Turkmenistan was conquered by Ephthalites, who in turn were conquered in the 6th century by the Tiu-chue nomads, of Turkic origin. The Arab caliphate conquered Turkmenistan in 716, and began to introduce Islam. In the 10th century part of Turkmenistan was under Samanid control.

Oghuz Turks began to migrate into Turkmenistan in the 9th century. In 1040 the Seljuk clan took control of the territory, and held sway until the 13th century, when Turkmenistan was part of the Khwarazm-Shah state. The entire region was conquered by Mongols in 1219–1221, and Turkmenistan was split between the Golden Horde and the Chagatai Khanate, as well as the Hulaguid Khanate of Persia.

In the 1380s Turkmenistan became part of the empire of Timur (Tamerlane). By the 16th century part of the territory was ruled by the Khiva Khanate, part by Bukhara, and part by Persia. The course of the Amu Dar'ya river changed, and the Kara Kum desert claimed a great deal of once arable land.

Russia began to make commercial contacts with the Turkmens as early as the 16th century; by the 18th century almost all trade between Europe and Central Asia passed through Turkmenistan. Local tribes were used diplomatically by the Persians, Russians, and British as part of the Great Game of the 18th and 19th centuries. Beginning in 1865, Russia undertook direct annexation, which because of heavy resistance by the Turkmen tribesmen was not complete until the 1885, making Turkmen-istan the last portion of the Russian Empire to be conquered. The territory then was called the Transcaspian District.

Turkmen joined the uprising of 1916, when the Tsar attempted to draft Central Asians into work battalions, and remained in general rebellion throughout the period of the revolution and civil war. Muslim and nationalist opposition, whom the Russians called "basmachi," resisted the Bolsheviks until 1924, when the area was made part of the Trans-Caspian Republic. In 1925, the present-day territory became a Soviet Socialist Republic.

Throughout the Soviet period, Turkmenistan was the poorest and least assimilated of the republics. In 1985, longtime Communist Party boss M. Gapurov was fired by Mikhail Gorbachev, who picked Sapamurat Niyazov as new republic head. Niyazov has remained in power ever since. On October 27,

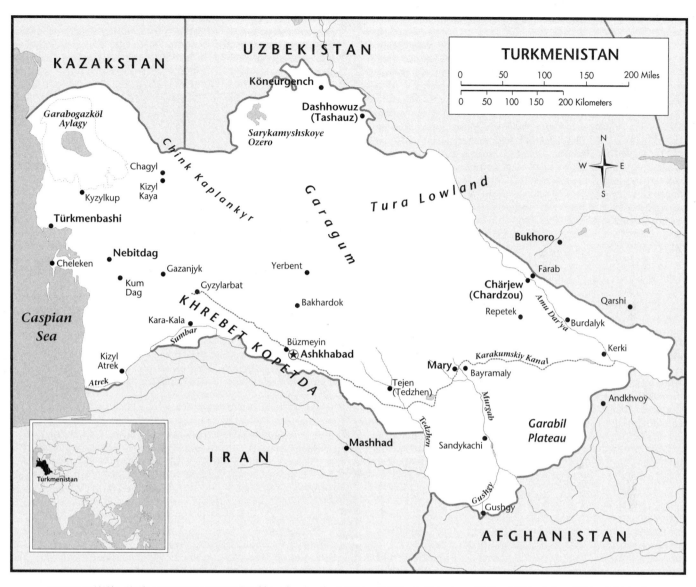

TURKMENISTAN

KAZAKSTAN

UZBEKISTAN

Köneürgench

Dashhowuz (Tashauz)

Garabogazköl Aylagy

Sarykamyshskoye Ozero

Chagyl

Kizyl Kaya

Kyzylkup

Türkmenbashi

Chink Kaplankyr

Garagum

Tura Lowland

Bukhoro

Farab

Chärjew (Chardzou)

Qarshi

Nebitdag

Cheleken

Gazanjyk

Yerbent

Kum Dag

Gyzylarbat

Bakhardok

Repetek

Burdalyk

KHREBET KOPETDA

Kara-Kala

Sumbar

Büzmeyin

✪ Ashkhabad

Amu Dar'ya

Kerki

Caspian Sea

Kizyl Atrek

Atrek

Mary

Karakumskiy Kanal

Bayramaly

Tejen (Tedzhen)

Andkhvoy

Murgab

Garabil Plateau

IRAN

Mashhad

Tedzhen

Sandykachi

Gushgy

Gushgy

AFGHANISTAN

Turkmenistan

LOCATION: 40°0′N; 60°0′E. BOUNDARY LENGTHS: Total boundary lengths, 3,736 km (2,322 mi); Afghanistan, 744 km (462.3 mi); Iran, 992 km (616.4 mi); Kazakhstan, 379 km (236 mi); Uzbekistan, 1,621 km (1007.3 mi).

1990, Niyazov received 98.3% of the popular vote in an uncontested election to the new post of president of Turkmenistan. Turkmenistan declared independence on 27 October 1991. After independence, Niyazov won another uncontested presidential election in June 1992 with 99.95% of the vote. In a referendum in January 1994, he received the support of 99.99% of the vote for extending his term until 2002. An elaborate cult of personality has grown up around Niyazov, who now prefers the title "Turkmenbashi," or "chief of all Turkmen." Niyazov is president, supreme commander of the armed forces, first secretary of the Democratic Party of Turkmenistan, head of the quasi-legislative Khalk Maslakhaty (People's Council), and chairman of the Cabinet of Ministers and the National Security Council. Changes to the Constitution were introduced in late December 1999 during a joint meeting of the Mejlis (legislature), the Khalk Maslakhaty, and Niyazov's National Revival Movement, to include naming Niyazov president for life.

Turkmenistan's "neutral" foreign policy is enshrined in its constitution. Niyazov has declared that Turkmenistan's "open door" or "permanent neutrality" policy precludes joining political or military alliances and entails good relations with the East and the West, though priority will be placed on relations with Central Asian and other Islamic states. Turkmenistan joined the Non-Aligned Movement in 1995, and the United Nations General Assembly in 1995 recognized Turkmenistan's status as a neutral state. Turkmenistan has pursued close ties with both Iran and Turkey. In addition to growing trade ties with Iran, Turkmenistan is also interested in cultural ties with the approximately one million Turkmen residing in Iran. Turkey is the largest foreign investor in Turkmenistan and has far surpassed Russia in trade turnover with Turkmenistan. Turkmenistan supports some of Russia's policies in the region while endeavoring, where possible, to resist, contravene, or reduce Russian influence. Russian military and border troops assisted Turkmenistan until it built up its own forces, and Russia's presence has been used to counter Uzbek policies in the region. In 1993, Russia and Turkmenistan agreed that Russian border guards would work with Turkmen border guards under Turkmen command at borders with Iran and Afghanistan. In 1999, Turkmenistan canceled this agreement, and the last of Russia's 1,000 border troops in Turkmenistan left in late 1999.

The new country has abundant resources that could bring in ample export earnings, ranging from oil, gas, electricity, coal, aluminum, and cotton to wool, grapes, and carpets. Turkmenistan's main natural gas export pipeline runs through Russia, which has closely controlled the volume, price, and destination. Seeking alternatives, Turkmenistan in December 1997 opened a 125-mile gas pipeline to connect with the Iranian pipeline system. On November 18, 1999, Turkmenistan, Azerbaijan, Georgia, and Turkey signed a declaration on a trans-Caspian and trans-Caucasus gas pipeline (expected to be completed in 2002 with an eventual capacity of sixteen billion meters per year), boosting chances for international financing for the pipeline. Turkmenistan has also explored building a pipeline through war-torn Afghanistan to Pakistan.

13GOVERNMENT

In May 1992, Turkmenistan became the first Central Asian republic to enact a post-independence constitution. It sets up a "secular democracy," and formally upholds the balance of powers between executive, legislative, and judicial branches, but in reality the republic is a presidential autocracy, under the control of President Niyazov. The executive branch of government is the responsibility of a prime minister and his cabinet, all of whom are appointed by the president. The republic's economy is centrally planned and controlled, as in Soviet times, giving the government wide powers. Niyazov issues edicts that have the force of law and appoints and removes judges and local officials. The constitution includes an impressive list of individual rights and safeguards (though not freedom of the press), but cautions that the exercise of rights must not violate national morality and public order, or damage national security. The new constitution creates a People's Council (Khalk Maslakhaty) with mixed executive and legislative powers, consisting of the president, ministers, the fifty legislators of the Supreme Council (Mejlis), sixty "people's representatives," and others. The people's representatives were elected by district in a virtually uncontested vote in December 1992. The Khalk Maslakhaty serves as a forum and rubber stamp for the president's policy initiatives. Resurrecting pre-Soviet customs, a Council of Elders, hand-picked by Niyazov, was also created to advise the president and choose presidential candidates. Oppositionists complained that both these bodies were designed to stifle dissent. A new Mejlis of 50 members was elected in December 1994. The candidates were all nominated by Niyazov, ran unopposed, and most were members of his DPT. The Mejlis routinely supports presidential decrees and has little legislative initiative.

The lack of democratization in Turkmenistan was accentuated during the April 11, 1998 election of sixty unpaid "people's representatives" to the Khalk Maslakhaty. Turnout was reported at 99.5%, though some of the candidates ran unchallenged and no real campaigning or political party contestation occurred.

Elections to the Turkmen 50-seat legislature (Mejlis) were held on December 12, 1999. Niyazov rejected a role for parties, stating that partisanship could lead to clan rivalries. Instead, he directed that nominating groups choose "professional" candidates, and they dutifully selected two candidates per constituency to run. There was no discussion of political issues or problems during the campaign. Prior to the race, Niyazov stepped up his repression of political and religious dissidents, and in late December pushed through a constitutional change naming Niyazov president for life. The OSCE refused to send monitors to oversee the elections, citing the government's control over the electoral process. Niyazov was formulating a *Rukhname*, a written guide to Turkmen national cultural and ethical personal behavior, which he planned to unveil in late 2000.

14POLITICAL PARTIES

The only legally registered party in the republic is the Democratic Party of Turkmenistan, which is what the Communist Party renamed itself in September 1991. Seeking to bring together most major cultural, religious, and public groups in a wider political bloc, in early 1994, Niyazov created a National Revival Movement, which he heads. Unregistered parties are tiny and have been severely repressed. Many of their leaders have been forced into exile or arrested. Most significant is the "Agzybirlik" (Unity) popular front. Banned in 1990, it mostly consists of Turkmen intellectuals and backs democratization and ties to Turkey. Opposition figure Avdy Kuliyev, former foreign minister, is in exile. Physician Pirkuli Tangrikuliyev announced that he wanted to create an opposition party and would run in the 1999 Mejlis election, but he was arrested and convicted of corruption. In late December 1999, a constitutional change was enacted naming Niyazov president for life.

15LOCAL GOVERNMENT

There are five large regional subdivisions, called velayets. Beneath these are shekhers, then etraps, then ovs. Velayets, shekhers, and etraps have executives called vekils who are appointed and dismissed by the president. In addition each administrative sub-unit has an elected assembly called a gengeshchi, the chairman of which is an archyn.

The clan system is said still to be very strong in Turkmenistan, and the velayets reflect distribution of the five major clans, whose totems are represented in the state flag.

16JUDICIAL SYSTEM

The court system remains substantially similar to that which existed in the Soviet era. There are 61 district and city courts, 6 provincial courts (including one for the capital city of Ashkhabad), and a Supreme Court. A Supreme Economic Court hears cases involving disputes between business enterprises and ministries. Military courts were abolished in 1997, and cases involved the armed forces are now tried in civilian courts. Decisions of lower courts are appealable to higher courts.

The constitution declares the establishment of an independent judiciary. In practice, the president's role in selecting and dismissing judges compromises judicial independence. The president appoints all judges for a term of five years, without legislative review, except for the chairman of the Supreme Court. Defendants in criminal cases are afforded a number of procedural due process rights, including the right to a public trial and the right to defense counsel. In practice, the government often denies these rights. There are few private lawyers. Defendants may petition the President for clemency. He has traditionally released large numbers of prisoners in periodically declared amnesties, though some political prisoners have appeared exempt from the amnesties.

According to most observers, Turkmenistan's humans rights record is extremely poor. The US State Department's *Country Reports on Human Rights Practices for 1999* states that the government severely restricts political and civil liberties. Arbitrary arrest, detention, unfair trials, and interference with citizens' privacy and correspondence are reported. Regime opponents are arrested on false charges and committed to psychiatric hospitals, peaceful demonstrations are forcibly dispersed, and security forces beat suspects, according to the State Department. The government severely restricts freedom of speech and completely controls and censors the media, forbidding the expression of criticism of the government. In signing the Helsinki Final Act in 1992, Niyazov stated that human rights are defined and limited by Turkmen national interests, namely, law and order and political stability. On September 14, 1999, he denied that there have been political prisoners in Turkmenistan during his rule. According to the State Department's *Annual Report on International Religious Freedom for 1999*, Turkmenistan severely represses religious minorities. On October 24, 1999, Niyazov reported that Turkmenistan in 1998–99 had confiscated tens of thousands of "illegally" imported religious books and expelled "dozens of foreign visitors... for attempting to turn our people against our sacred beliefs." Suppression has included Christian faiths and others.

17 ARMED FORCES

The total armed forces consist of 17,000–19,000 personnel; this includes both the army (14,000–16,000) and the air force (3,000). There are 570 main battle tanks and 89 combat aircraft. There are plans to form a navy in the future. The defense budget for 1998 was $88 million or 3% of GDP.

18 INTERNATIONAL COOPERATION

Turkmenistan was admitted to the UN on 2 March 1992, and is a member of the OSCE, ECO, IMF, and the World Bank. It is a member of the CIS, and is recognized by the US, EU countries, and many other nations of the world. It has observer status with the WTO. The US established formal diplomatic relations with Turkmenistan in February 1992.

19 ECONOMY

Turkmenistan boasts rich deposits of oil, gas, potassium, sulfur, and salts, which offer important potential sources of raw industrial inputs and high-value exports. Proven gas reserves in the country amount to 95 to 115 trillion cubic feet; proven oil reserves are 1.7 billion barrels. Despite this natural wealth, per capita GDP was less than half of the average Soviet republic in the late 1980s, and Turkmenistan's social welfare indicators are among the lowest in the former USSR. The economy is dominated by agriculture which generates 18% of GDP, accounts for 44% of employment (together with forestry), and supplies cotton both to other former Union republics and to the country's own industry. Industry contributes 50% to GDP and occupies 19% of the workforce.

Although the instability and trade disruptions following dissolution of the USSR have posed serious difficulties for Turkmenistan since 1990, its economy has been less severely affected than many of its post-Soviet counterparts. Contraction in output occurred mainly in industrial output while growth in the agricultural and transportation sectors—the latter particularly due to increased government investment—lessened the rate of decline in the overall economy.

Ultimate responsibility for economic policy setting lies with the Economic Committee in the Presidential Council. Turkmenistan has been among the more conservative of the post-Soviet republics in instituting a transition to a free market economy. Government plans envision a gradual reform over a 10 year period, in which the state will continue to play a directing role in the economy, albeit within a liberalized market environment. Currently, the country's farms and industrial enterprises produce largely on the basis of state orders, and the state-owned sector continues to employ 80% of the labor force. Initial moves toward price decontrol have been accompanied by a steady rise in retail and wholesale prices. After a 90% increase in 1991, retail prices surged by 800% in 1992 and have continued to increase since. Enlarged subsidies, increased wages and family allowances, and reinstatement of some price controls have been instituted by the government to cushion the effect of rising prices and offset the potential for social unrest, especially in light of developments in neighboring Tajikistan and other former Soviet republics. In November 1993, Turkmenistan dropped out of the ruble-based monetary union with other post-Soviet states and introduced its own currency, the manat. In 1994, Russia refused to allow the export of gas from Turkmenistan to markets paying in hard currency. Thus, major customers of Turkmenistan among the former Soviet republics began to accumulate large debts for gas deliveries, creating a small budget deficit in Turkmenistan for the first time. The economy remained depressed and inflation soared in 1995. Gas customers are still not able to pay for deliveries they receive from Turkmenistan, and the cotton crop was below average in 1995, extending the poor economic conditions into 1996. The Turkmen government estimated the inflation rate in 1996 to be 100%.

To resolve the weak economic conditions in its current gas markets, the Turkmenistan government has sought access to other export markets through Iran and Turkey. As of 1997, these new channels were years away from being viable. In 1996 and 1997, the government implemented a number of IMF-recommended economic reforms, including liberalization of foreign exchange and the maintenance of low fiscal deficits. State lands and industries began the process of privatization, and the energy sector was opened to foreigners. Despite these changes, GDP dropped by 11% in 1997 due to the Russian financial crisis and subsequently low energy exports; but GDP recovered by 5% in 1998. Inflation was recorded at 20% in 1998.

20 INCOME

The US Central Intelligence Agency (CIA) reports that in 1998 Turkmenistan's gross domestic product (GDP) was estimated at $7 billion. The per capita GDP was estimated at $1,630. The annual growth rate of GDP was estimated at 5%. The average inflation rate in 1998 was 20%. The CIA defines GDP as the value of all final goods and services produced within a nation in a given year and computed on the basis of purchasing power parity (PPP) rather than value as measured on the basis of the rate of exchange. It was estimated that agriculture accounted for 18% of GDP, industry 50%, and services 32%.

The World Bank reports that for the same period per capita private consumption (in PPP terms) was $1,120. Private consumption includes expenditures of individuals, households, and non-governmental organizations. Approximately 32% of household consumption was spent on food, 14% on fuel, 6% on health care, and 18% on education. The richest 10% of the population accounted for approximately 32% of household consumption and the poorest 10% approximately 2.6%.

21 LABOR

From 1985 to 1991, the size of the labor force grew by 2.7% per year. Of an estimated 2 million inhabitants of working age in 1998, agriculture engaged 44%; industry and construction 19%, and the remainder in other sectors.

As of 1999, there were no independent unions or attempts to register an independent trade union. The Federation of Trade Unions, now renamed the Colleagues Union, the government-associated organization of the Soviet era, is still present but divided along sectoral and regional differences. In 1999, the union claimed 1.3 million members.

Although Turkmen law does not protect the right to bargain collectively, strikes are allowed. State economic control is still prevalent, and little progress toward privatization has occurred. The standard legal workweek is 40 hours. Many industrial workers often labor in unsafe conditions, and agricultural workers especially are subjected to ecological health hazards. The minimum working age is 16 years except for in a few heavy industries where it is 18. Violations of the minimum working age do occasionally occur in rural areas, especially during the cotton harvesting season. There is no minimum wage. As of 2000, the average wage for public-sector employees was $77 per month.

[22]AGRICULTURE

About 30–35% of Turkmenistan is considered arable, but only 3.6% was under cultivation in 1997. Almost all the sown agricultural land is under irrigation. Yields are relatively low because of poor water usage, salinization, inefficient irrigation, and overdevelopment of cotton cultivation. In 1998, agriculture engaged 34% of the economically active population. Agriculture accounts for about 25% of GDP.

Cotton is the main crop, with production on the Mary and Tejen oases and along the Amu Dar'ya. Estimated cotton production for 1998 was 200,000 tons, up from 137,000 tons in 1996. Lack of machinery had caused significant portions of the cotton crop to go unharvested. Wheat also is cultivated to avoid dependency on unstable cotton export earnings. In 1998, estimated production was 600,000 tons. Citrus fruit, dates, figs, grapes, pomegranates, olives, and sugarcane are grown in irrigated groves and fields in the southwest. Sesame, pistachios, and oilseeds are other important export crops.

[23]ANIMAL HUSBANDRY

The inability to raise sufficient fodder impedes livestock development. The livestock population in 1998 included sheep, 5,400,000; cattle, 900,000; goats, 360,000; pigs, 35,000; asses, 26,000; horses, 16,000; and chickens, 3 million. Karakul sheep are raised for wool export; in 1998, 18,000 tons of greasy wool and 25,000 tons of sheep skins were produced. A private tannery in Mary processes about 100,000 sheepskins per year, selling its product to the state-run leathery factory.

Akhaltekin horses, raised at the Akhaltekin oasis, are a breed which dates date to the 3rd century. Bucephalus, the favorite horse of Alexander the Great, was Akhaltekin. In 1986, an Akhaltekin horse, Dancing Brave, was sold for $50 million. Akhaltekins have a large share of the racehorse breeding market worldwide, and are depicted on Turkmenistan's national emblem.

[24]FISHING

The Caspian Sea provides fishing resources; fishing is an important export activity. In 1997, the total catch was 8,828 tons, primarily Azov sea sprat.

[25]FORESTRY

About 8% of the land is forested. Arid conditions and the expansive Kara Kum desert inhibit the development of commercial forestry.

[26]MINING

Sulfur is mined at the Gaurdak complex in the east; Turkmenistan has the world's third-largest reserves of sulfur. An extensive mirabilite (sodium sulfate) site exists on the Gararbogazköl; ozocerite, iodine, and bromine are found on the Cheleken Peninsula; salt is mined north of Nebitdag. Other mineral deposits include potassium and polymetallic ores. In 1996, estimated production included (in tons): gypsum, 169,577; sodium sulfate, 30,820; sulfur (ground), 8,112; iodine, 255; ammonia nitrate, 137,181; gypsum, 169,577; and cement, 450,000.

[27]ENERGY AND POWER

Turkmenistan is essentially self-sufficient in energy resources, with natural gas by far the most plentiful resource. Proven reserves of natural gas in early 1999 amounted to 2.9 trillion cu m (101 trillion cu ft), or 2% of the world's total and the third largest in the world. Production in 1997 (excluding gas-flared or recycled) totaled 22.9 billion cu m (0.9 trillion cu ft). Natural gas is found primarily near Mary; these fields in south-central Turkmenistan account for 80% of annual production. Turkmenistan is a major exporter of natural gas to the former USSR, and is the only republic, besides Russia, to export to Europe. Several former Soviet republics now owe significant amounts of money to Turkmenistan; Ukraine, Georgia, Kazakhstan, Uzbekistan, and Azerbaijan combined owe about $1 billion. Turkmenistan is developing alternatives to Russia's pipeline network as part of its strategy to increase natural gas exports. About 49% of primary energy consumption was fueled by natural gas in 1998, with the remainder coming from oil. In 1998, Turkmenistan's total installed electrical capacity was 3,950,000 kW, and 8,745 million kWh were generated.

Oil is produced in small quantities in the west, on the Cheleken Peninsula, near Nebitdag and Kum Dag, and along the Caspian lowlands. In 1998, production amounted to about 131,000 barrels per day. Refining capabilities are limited and antiquated; both refineries are slated for modernization and expansion to help meet increased demand.

[28]INDUSTRY

After growing at an average rate of 2.3% during the 1980s, the industrial sector declined after the breakup of the Soviet Union. Industrial output declined by 15% in 1992, and fell 25% in 1994 after an increase in 1993. However, the rate of decline slowed to 7% by 1995. In 1996, over 90% of the value from industry came from state-owned enterprises. Industrial output for the first half of 1997 was down 35.2% from the same period in 1996, due to a halt in natural gas exports and a poor cotton harvest in 1996. Lack of export routes for natural gas continued to hurt industrial production in 1998, contributing only 1% to GDP in that year.

The textiles industry is dominated by large state-owned enterprises. Turkmen carpets are known worldwide for their quality, and represent a source of national pride for the people of Turkmenistan. Turkmen carpets have been known erroneously on Western markets by the label "Bukhara," which actually represented the Uzbekistan city where the carpets were sold. Turkmen carpets feature deep red wool, with stylized geometric patterns. Ornaments of Turkmen carpets are a component of the flag and national emblem of Turkmenistan.

Fuel-related production (mainly gas and oil) is the second-largest component of the industrial sector, accounting for about 22% of total sector output in value terms. The Turkmenbashi refinery has been the country's main oil processing center, with an annual capacity of 5 million tons. The new Chardzou refinery, completed in 1991, has a production capacity of 6 million tons and uses oil imported from Siberia. In 1998, production of refined petroleum totaled 6.3 million tons. In 1996, the output of oil refineries rose by 6%, making it possible to increase petrol production by 17.3% and diesel fuel production by 7.1%. Food processing (especially meat and dairy processing), construction materials, and electricity generation account for about 20% of total industrial output. Chemicals and machinery are other important manufacturing subsectors. In 1996, about half of all industrial enterprises cut output due to economic pressures caused by difficulties in the gas export market and a very poor cotton harvest. In 1998, these difficulties persisted.

[29]SCIENCE AND TECHNOLOGY

The Turkmen Academy of Sciences, headquartered in Ashkhabad, has 8 attached institutes concerned with natural sciences and technology. In addition, six independent institutes conduct medical research. In 1991, the Academy of Agricultural Sciences was established, and in 1992, the Academy of Medical Sciences was created, both in Ashkhabad. The Turkmen A.M. Gorkii State University, founded in 1950 at Ashkhabad, has faculties of physics, mathematics, and biology. Also in the same city are the Turkmen Agriculture Institute, the Turkmen Polytechnic Institute, and the Turkmen State Medical Institute (founded 1932).

30 DOMESTIC TRADE

Like the rest of the Turkmenistan economy, much of the country's retail and wholesale sector remain under the control of the central government. However, informal markets also operate in the country, at which a wide variety of consumer goods, including food, clothing and household wares, may be purchased. Transactions are conducted only in cash. The work week is from 9 AM to 6 PM, Monday to Friday, with an hour for lunch. Many government officials and businesses regularly work on Saturday.

31 FOREIGN TRADE

Like other Central Asian countries, Turkmenistan is highly trade dependent; 26% of domestic consumption derives directly from imports while exports are equivalent to about 22% of its annual production. While natural gas and processed cotton fiber are the country's most important export items, Turkmenistan is heavily dependent on imports for industrial equipment, industrial raw materials, and a number of basic food items such as grain, milk and dairy products, potatoes, and sugar. Food products accounted for 25% in 1995. Agricultural products accounted for about 20% of total exports in 1995. Exports of processed cotton, valued at $363 million, contributed 17% to total exports in 1994.

A disappointing cotton harvest in 1996 caused an 80% decline in cotton processing that year. Continuing difficulties with gas export payments resulted in a decrease in that sector as well.

Principal trading partners in 1998 (in millions of US dollars) were as follows:

COUNTRY	EXPORTS	IMPORTS	BALANCE
Iran	133	40	93
Italy	65	21	44
Tajikistan	49	15	34
Azerbaijan	47	22	25
Russia	39	103	-64
Turkey	38	105	-67
Kazakhstan	38	152	-114
Germany	27	95	-68
Uzbekistan	6	170	-164
Ukraine	1	133	-132

32 BALANCE OF PAYMENTS

The US Central Intelligence Agency reports that in 1997 the purchasing power parity of Turkmenistan's exports was $689 million while imports totaled $1.1 billion resulting in a trade balance of -$411 million.

The International Monetary Fund (IMF) reports that in 1997 Turkmenistan had exports of goods totaling $774 million and imports totaling $1,005 million. The services credit totaled $272 million and debit $675 million. The following table summarizes Turkmenistan's balance of payments for 1997 in millions of US dollars.

Current Account		-580
Balance on goods	-231	
Balance on services	-403	
Balance on income	85	
Current transfers	-31	
Capital Account		-9
Financial Account		1,060
Direct investment abroad	...	
Direct investment in Turkmenistan	108	
Portfolio investment assets	-5	
Portfolio investment liabilities	...	
Other investment assets	206	
Other investment liabilities	752	
Net Errors and Omissions		-73
Reserves and Related Items		-398

33 BANKING AND SECURITIES

The State Central Bank of Turkmenistan (SCBT) is charged with issuing currency and executing a monetary policy, and represents the top tier of a two-tiered banking system. Commercial banks are responsible for collection, settlement, and handling of assets for clients and other banks. The State Bank for Foreign Economic Activities has been established to provide hard currency credits for foreign economic activities.

The government has not released details of monetary policy since Turkmenistan left the ruble zone in November 1993. The currency reform involved a high degree of confiscation. Since then, the government is thought to have severely contracted the money supply in real terms as part of its bid to tackle inflation.

The banking decree of 20 February 1995 stated that: 75% of 1994 bank revenue was to be used for capital expenditure projects; banks were to lend to state-owned firms at an annual interest rate of 15%; and all excess bank profits were to be transferred to the state. Turkmenistan's banks are shackled with the usual problems of the former communist bloc. The Turkmen banks are poorly capitalized, have large loss-making portfolios to state-owned enterprises, and are burdened by an antiquated payments system which builds up arrears with ease.

Sberbank (the Savings Bank) ranks second behind the SCBT in significance, holding most household deposits, and is still state-owned. The local branch of Vneshekonombank has been incorporated as an independent foreign trade bank, and is also state-owned. Investbank is the industrial sector bank and Agroprombank the agricultural sector bank. Both are state-owned via stock distributed to state-owned enterprises. In 1994, there were ten further banks owned by state enterprises, two cooperative banks and two private banks.

34 INSURANCE

The Joint Stock Insurance Company "TIS" is operating direct insurance lines for aviation, cargo, fire, accident, and auto in Ashgabat.

35 PUBLIC FINANCE

Although still a centrally planned economy, Turkmenistan has slowly begun to decrease the size of the public sector's influence.

The US Central Intelligence Agency (CIA) estimates that in 1996 Turkmenistan's central government took in revenues of approximately $521 million and had expenditures of $548 million including capital expenditures of $83 million. Overall, the government registered a deficit of approximately $27 million. External debt totaled $2.14 billion.

36 TAXATION

Personal income taxes in Turkmenistan range from 10–40%; the maximum corporate rate is 45%, with a standard rate of 25%. Also levied are a value-added tax ranging from 16.67% to a standard rate of 20%, and a 6–15% withholding tax.

37 CUSTOMS AND DUTIES

Turkmenistan has a procedure for levying customs duties, export and import taxes and tariffs, and for the transit of goods, defined by the Customs Code of Turkmenistan. Certain imports from countries outside the rural area are prohibited or require a license. Turkmenistan is not a member of any free trade agreements and is not a member of the CIS customs union. It has signed trilateral agreements with Iran and Ukraine, Iran and Armenia, Iran and Bangladesh, Iran and the Philippines and is pursuing more such agreements. Turkmenistan has MFN status with the United States and Austria. Duties run from 10% to 100%, the average being 30%.

³⁸FOREIGN INVESTMENT

A law on foreign investment and other legislation regarding private entrepreneurship passed since 1991 now provide most of the conventional guarantees to foreign investors in Turkmenistan. However, until 1994, the purchase of property by foreign parties remained highly restricted. Reflecting some of this ambiguity, by 1992, only 23 joint ventures had been established, most of a relatively small scale and with negligible impact on foreign trade. Nevertheless, the country's political stability, rich natural resources, and increasingly liberal regulations are likely to make it a favored target for foreign investors in the near future. Significant inflows of foreign assistance have already allowed expansion of the petroleum industry to begin. Negotiations with foreign firms and several countries are underway for establishing a liquefied natural gas plant and the joint construction of a new gas pipeline to Europe that would bypass the need to transverse potentially unstable states of the former USSR.

In 1994, Turkmenistan's laws were modified to offer greater protection for property and rights of foreign investors and exemptions from duties and taxes for specific categories of investment; foreign investors registered in Turkmenistan, and enterprises importing and selling consumer goods there have been exempt from the value-added tax since March 1994. The Commodity and Raw Materials Exchange, created in 1994 to regulate all commercial transactions in Turkmenistan, registers individual trade contracts concluded by foreign companies and joint ventures, and charges a 0.2% commission. The State Agency for Foreign Investment (SAFI), established by presidential decree in 1996, monitors investments, reviews proposals and foreign currency credits, and may award priority status to projects favored by the government. There were no investment statistics reported by the government in 1998.

³⁹ECONOMIC DEVELOPMENT

Though still a largely agricultural and poorly developed economy, Turkmenistan's relatively well educated population and natural resources provide a promising basis for the growth of a diverse set of industries. Economic development is hampered by the outdated infrastructure that characterized Turkmenistan when it was still part of the Soviet Union. After gaining independence in 1991, the government began efforts to reduce the country's dependence on the export of raw materials and the import of finished and intermediate goods as well as basic foodstuffs. Initiated in time to help avoid some of the most severe economic dislocation being experienced in other post-Soviet republics, these efforts have included increasing wheat production and developing the country's oil and gas processing capacity, as well as investing in internal transportation facilities.

In addition to these changes, the government has also expressed commitment to a cautious reform agenda aimed at economic liberalization. The guiding principles of this program were detailed in a formal document in early 1991 calling for a series of legislative, fiscal, and monetary measures related to price controls, privatization, and industrial infrastructure development. More specific legislation and policies have followed, including new laws on privatization and foreign investment adopted in 1992, price decontrol measures taken the same year, adoption of a value-added tax and other tax reform, and measures taken to control the growth of money supply. Under the liberalized property regime, leasing arrangements have expanded in both the agricultural and industrial sectors. The leasing or purchase of individual enterprises by workers is favored by the current legislation, although land, water, and the oil and gas industries are excluded from the possibility of outright purchase by private individuals or companies. Despite liberalization only a handful of enterprises had been privatized by 1992 and four-fifths of the labor force remained employed in the state-owned sector. As of 1996, the government reported that 1,594 enterprises had been privatized; it also reported that over 90% of the value of goods produced by industry could be attributed to state-controlled enterprises. Most industrial enterprises continue to run on the basis of centrally planned state orders and resource allocations, although the government statistics report that the non-state share of retail trade had increased by 66%.

Following the government's expressed commitment to minimizing the negative impact of post-Soviet economic restructuring on the population, the terms for Turkmenistan's social safety net are more generous than many other former Soviet countries; allowances for large families, social security payments, as well as pensions have all been increased substantially since 1992, and as of 1993 all citizens receive free electricity and water. Potential fiscal imbalances resulting both from these increased expenditures and the end of transfers from the Soviet government have thus far been avoided by increased profit transfers from key enterprises, export duties, and a variety of smaller revenue sources. Twenty-nine percent of the 1992 budget expenditures was allocated to price-differential subsidies paid to retail agencies required to sell food and medicines below wholesale prices. Capital expenditures claimed a further 12% of total expenditures while combined social and cultural expenditures allocated to education, health care, and social security totalled about 30%. A five-year production and investment plan set out in 1992 proposed large investments in the development of infrastructure and the energy sector financed by the budget and large inflows of foreign investment. In line with the plan's long of food self-sufficiency and increased cotton processing, the budget for 1993 included financing for projects to expand grain production and cotton processing. Economic development was stymied by low natural gas exports in 1998.

⁴⁰SOCIAL DEVELOPMENT

Turkmenistan's current social security system was created in 1991, and provides old age, disability and survivor pensions to employed persons. A social pension is provided to those not eligible for employment-related pensions. Old age pensions are provided at age 62 for men who have 25 years of covered employment and at age 57 to women with 20 years of employment. The social security program is financed by 30% contributions from employers, and a voluntary contribution of 4% or more from employees. Unemployment benefits are provided for up to one year. Sickness and maternity benefits and workers' compensation were introduced in 1998. Maternity leave at full pay is provided for 112 days.

Under the constitution, women are protected from discrimination in employment, inheritance, marriage rights, and other areas. However, they are barred from working in some jobs deemed dangerous or ecologically unsafe. Women are also under-represented in management positions in most state economic enterprises. In 1995, the Deputy Chairman of the Parliament was a woman, as was the representative to the United Nations. As of 1999, 13 of 50 parliamentary seats were held by women.

Traditional attitudes and social pressure lead many women to work only in the home. Despite constitutional provisions, practicing Muslims often follow religious practices giving men precedence over women in property and inheritance matters.

Human rights violations reported in 1999 include arrest of political dissidents on false criminal charges and the mistreatment of prisoners. Freedom of religion is restricted by a law requiring that all officially recognized religions have at least 500 Turkmen citizens in any locality where they are practiced. Only the Russian Orthodox Church and the Sunni Muslim sect meet these requirements. There are no local human rights organizations, and it is unlikely that they would be tolerated.

41HEALTH

Health care expenditures for 1990 were $459 million. Average life expectancy was 61.1 years in 1999. In 1990–97, there were 3.2 doctors for every 1,000 people and 11.5 hospital beds. During 1994–95, safe water and sanitation was accessible to 85% and 60% of the population respectively. Immunization rates for children up to one year old in 1994 were tuberculosis, 97%; diphtheria, pertussis, and tetanus, 87%; polio, 94%; and measles, 90%. The infant mortality rate in 1999 was 73.1 per 1,000 live births; the maternal mortality rate in 1990–97 was 44 per 100,000 live births; and the general mortality rate was 8.7 per 1,000 people in 1999. Leading causes of death per 100,000 people in 1990 were communicable diseases and maternal/perinatal causes, 216; noncommunicable diseases, 737; and injuries, 68. There were 74 reported cases of tuberculosis per 100,000 people in 1997. In this former Soviet republic, mortality rates have increased significantly since the breakup. Cardiovascular disease deaths numbered at 13,638 in 1994. Only one case of AIDS was reported in 1995.

42HOUSING

In 1989, 27.3% of all privately owned urban housing had running water, 7.2% had sewer lines, 16% had central heating, and 1% had hot water. In 1990, Turkmenistan had 11.1 sq ft of housing space per capita and, as of 1 January 1991, 108,000 households (or 30.9%) were on waiting lists for urban housing.

43EDUCATION

The adult illiteracy rate was estimated at 0.3% in 1995 (males, 0.2%; females, 0.4%). Before the Soviet Union established control over the region in the 1920s, few schools, mainly Muslim, existed. Education is now state-funded and compulsory from the age of 7 to 17 (10 years). Upon completion of the eighth grade, students are tested and ten directed into technical, continuing, or discontinuing courses of study. The government reports 1,764 schools with enrollment of 850,000. In 1,400 of the schools, instruction is in the Turkmen language; in the remaining 364, Uzbek, Russian, Kazakh, and Karakalpak languages are used.

In 1990–91, all higher level institutions had 76,000 pupils enrolled. There are 14 institutions of higher learning, including one university at Ashgabat, the Turkmen State University (founded in 1950) with an enrollment of over 11,000 pupils. Turkmenistan also has 90 technical colleges.

44LIBRARIES AND MUSEUMS

The National Library of Turkmenistan in Ashgabat holds 5.5 million volumes and is the largest in the country. The Republican Scientific and Technical Library of Turkmenistan holds 900,000 volumes and the Turkmen Academy of Sciences, both in the capital, holds 2.1 million volumes. Turkmen University has the nation's largest library, holding 542,000 volumes. There are several fine museums in Ashgabat, including the National Museum of History and Ethnography, the State Museum of Fine Arts, and the Carpet Museum, as well as museums devoted to history and literature.

45MEDIA

In 1995, there were some 265,100 main telephone lines in use. Telephone links to other former Soviet republics and Iran are provided by land link or microwave and to other countries through Moscow. Turkmen Radio in Ashgabat broadcasts transmissions from Moscow, as does Turkmen Television, which also receives Turkish television broadcasts. As of 1999 there was 1 state-owned radio station and 3 television stations, and many programs were received from Russia and Turkey. Orbita and INTELSAT are received by satellite earth stations. In 1997, there were 96 radio sets and 175 television sets per 1,000 population. Turkmenistan has its own movie studio, Tukmenfilm.

There were two daily newspapers in 1995: *Turkmenistan* (circulation 73,170) and *Turmenskaya Iskra* (in Russian, 40,000). There are also a number of periodicals, mostly in Ashgabat.

The constitution provides for free expression, but in practice the government is said to severely limit press rights. The government owns and directly controls all radio, television, and print media, and is said to rarely allow criticism or opposition opinion in even the mildest forms.

Online access is extremely limited, with less than one Internet host per 1,000 population in 1998.

46ORGANIZATIONS

The economic affairs and other concerns of workers are handled by the Chamber of Committee and Industry and the Federation of Trade Unions of Turkmenistan, respectively. The most important mass movement in the country is the Communist Party. It controls all aspects of Turkmenistan's politics, society and culture. Its organizations of control are the Committee on National Security, Ministry of Internal Affairs, and various trade unions. The trade unions, all controlled by the state, serve to promote government production plans and policies.

47TOURISM, TRAVEL, AND RECREATION

In 1997 there were 332,425 tourists arriving in Turkmenistan spending $74 million. The largest country of origin was Iran, with 171,071 visitors. Tourism has been designated a priority area of economic development. Hotel rooms numbered 2,616 with 6,571 beds and an occupancy rate of 24%.

In 1999 the UN estimated the cost of staying in Ashgabat at $121 per day; elsewhere daily costs were approximately $84.

48FAMOUS TURKMENISTANIS

Saparmuryat A. Niyazov (b.1940) has been president of Turkmenistan since December 1991. Outstanding representatives of culture and literature of Turkmenistan include Abdulhekin Qulmukam Medoghli, a writer, researcher and political activist who was killed in 1937 during one of Stalin's purges, and the poet and thinker, Maktum Kuli, who first envisioned an independent Turkmenistan. The country has established the Makhtumkuli International Prize in his name and awarded it to President Niyazov.

49DEPENDENCIES

Turkmenistan has no territories or colonies.

50BIBLIOGRAPHY

Central Asia and the World: Kazakhstan, Uzbekistan, Tajikistan, Kyrgystan, and Turkmenistan. Edited by Michael Mandelbaum. New York: Council on Foreign Relations Press, 1994.

Dailey, Erika. *Human Rights in Turkmenistan.* New York: Helsinki Watch, 1993.

History of United Turkmenistan. Ankara: Turkish Association for Friendship with Turkmenistan, 1995.

International Monetary Fund. *Turkmenistan.* Washington, D.C.: International Monetary Fund, 1992.

Maslow, Jonathan Evan. *Sacred Horses: The Memoirs of a Turkmen Cowboy.* New York: Random House, 1994.

Republic of Turkmenistan: Short Analysis of Social and Political Situation. Moscow: Gorbachev Foundation, Dept. of Commercial Publications, 1992.

TUVALU

CAPITAL: Funafuti.

FLAG: The national flag has the Union Jack in the upper quarter nearest the hoist; nine yellow stars on a light blue field are arranged in the same pattern as Tuvalu's nine islands.

ANTHEM: *Tuvalu mo te Atua (Tuvalu for the Almighty).*

MONETARY UNIT: Both the Australian dollar (A$) and the Tuvaluan dollar (T$) of 100 cents are legal tender at par. There are coins of 1, 2, 5, 10, 20, and 50 Tuvaluan cents; 1 and 5 Tuvaluan dollars; and notes of 5, 10, 20, 50, and 100 Australian dollars. Almost all transactions are conducted in Australian dollars. A$1 = US$0.6203 (US$1 = A$1.612) as of 31 March 2000.

WEIGHTS AND MEASURES: The metric system is being introduced, but imperial measures are still commonly employed.

HOLIDAYS: New Year's Day, 1 January; National Children's Day, first Monday in August; Tuvalu Day, 1 October; Prince of Wales's Birthday, 14 November; Christmas Day, 25 December; Boxing Day, 26 December. Movable holidays include Commonwealth Day (March), and Queen's Official Birthday (June); movable religious holidays include Good Friday and Easter Monday.

TIME: Midnight = noon GMT.

¹LOCATION, SIZE, AND EXTENT

Tuvalu (formerly the Ellice Islands) comprises a cluster of nine islands, plus islets, located in the southwestern Pacific Ocean just south of the Equator. These remote atolls are situated about 1,050 km (650 mi) N of Suva, Fiji, and 4,000 km (2,500 mi) NE of Sydney, Australia. They lie in a 595-km-long (370-mi) chain extending over some 1,300,000 sq km (500,000 sq mi) of ocean and have a total land area of 26 sq km (10 sq mi). Comparatively, the area occupied by Tuvalu is about 0.1 times the size of Washington, D.C. Tuvalu has a coastline of 24 km (15 mi).

Tuvalu's capital city, Funafuti is located on the island of Funafuti.

²TOPOGRAPHY

Tuvalu consists entirely of low-lying coral atolls, none of which is more than 5 m (16 ft) above sea level; few of the atolls are more than 0.8 km (0.5 mi) wide. The islands are coral reefs on the outer arc of ridges formed by pressure from the Central Pacific against the ancient Australian landmass. On five islands, the reefs enclose sizable lagoons; the others are mere pinnacles rising abruptly from the ocean floor. Only two of the islands, Funafuti and Nukufetau, have natural harbors for oceangoing ships. There are no rivers on the islands.

³CLIMATE

Tuvalu has a tropical climate with little seasonal variation. The annual mean temperature of 30°C (86°F) is moderated by trade winds from the east. Rainfall averages over 355 cm (140 in), with most rain falling between November and February. Although the islands lie north of the main cyclone belt, Funafuti was devastated in 1894, 1972, and 1990.

⁴FLORA AND FAUNA

The surrounding sea is rich in flora and fauna, but land vegetation is limited to coconut palm, pandanus, and imported fruit trees. Pigs, fowl, and dogs, all of which were imported in the 19th century, flourish on the islands. The only indigenous mammal is the Polynesian rat. Birds include reef herons, terns, and noddies. There are 22 known species of butterfly and moth.

⁵ENVIRONMENT

Environmental dangers include uncontrolled spread of the crown of thorns starfish, which flourishes in deepened channels and is destructive to coral reefs; erosion of beachheads from the use of sand for building materials; and excessive clearance of forest undergrowth for firewood. About 40% of Funafuti is uninhabitable because the UK authorized the US to dig an airstrip out of the coral bed during World War II. Global warming and the related rise of sea levels are also a significant environmental concern for Tuvalu's residents. The encroachment of sea water also poses a threat of contamination to the nation's limited water supply, whose purity is already at risk due to untreated sewage and the by-products of the mining industry and farming. Natural hazards include earthquakes, cyclones, and volcanic activity. In 1986, the government approved the first phase of an EC-financed sea-wall system to protect the coast. Current fishing methods threaten Tuvalu's marine life. The green sea turtle and the leatherback turtle are endangered.

⁶POPULATION

The population of Tuvalu in 2000 was estimated at 10,730. An estimated 4.0% of the population is 65 years of age or older. The projected population for the year 2005 is 11,000, assuming a crude birthrate of 22 per 1,000 population and a death rate of 8, resulting in a natural rate of change of 1.4% for the period 2000–2005. Population density is high, with 390 residents per sq km (1,011 per sq mi) in 1996.

It was estimated that 52% of the population lived in urban areas in 2000. The most populated island is Funafuti, the capital, with a 2000 population of 4,000. Only about 15% of the population lives on Vaitupu, followed by Niutao (11%), Nanumea (11%), Nukufetau, Nanumanga, Nui, Nukulaelae, and Niulakita (formerly uninhabited).

7MIGRATION

During the 19th century, recruitment of Tuvaluans to work on plantations in other Pacific islands, Australia, and South America reduced the resident population from about 20,000 to 3,000; the islands have only recently recovered from the population loss. The net migration rate was zero in 1999.

8ETHNIC GROUPS

Apart from a few Europeans, the islanders are almost entirely Polynesian (96%) and have strong ties with the Samoans and Tokelauans. There is no evidence of pre-Polynesian settlement. Language and tradition indicate that the Tuvaluans were part of a Samoan-Tongan migration from the 14th through the 17th century.

9LANGUAGES

English and Tuvaluan, a Polynesian tongue related closely to Samoan, are the principal languages. A Gilbertese dialect is spoken on Nui.

10RELIGIONS

In 1865, a member of the London Missionary Society reached Tuvalu from Samoa, and Samoan pastors were sent to the islands. The Tuvaluans rapidly embraced the Christian faith, and today 97% of them are Protestants, members of the Church of Tuvalu, a congregationalist group. Seventh-Day Adventists account for 1.4% of the population; Baha'is for 1%; and others for 0.6%.

11TRANSPORTATION

Transportation is inadequate. Most roads are little more than tracks, although Funafuti has about 8 km (5 mi) of coral-impacted roads for use by the island's few cars and trucks. Funafuti and Nukufetau are the only seaports, used chiefly by freighters in the copra trade. Ships drawing up to 9 m (30 ft) can dock in Funafuti harbor at a deepwater wharf completed in 1980. In 1998, Tuvalu had a merchant fleet of 10 ships totaling 44,371 GRT. All the islands are served by Tuvalu's one inter-island ferry. Funafuti has one lone airport, a grass strip that cannot be used for jet aircraft.

12HISTORY

The islands were probably settled between the 14th and 17th centuries by Polynesians drifting west with prevailing winds from Samoa and other large islands. The first European to discover Tuvalu is thought to have been the Spanish navigator çlvaro de Menda–a de Neyra, who sighted Nui in 1568 and Niulakita in 1595. Further European contact was not made until the end of the 18th century. Between 1850 and 1875, the islands were raided by ships forcibly recruiting plantation workers for South America, Fiji, Hawaii, Tahiti, and Queensland. To help suppress such abuses, the Office of British High Commissioner for the Western Pacific was created in 1877.

In 1892, after ascertaining the inhabitants' wishes, the UK proclaimed the Ellice Islands (as Tuvalu was then known), together with the Gilberts, as a British protectorate. After further consultation, the protectorate became the Gilbert and Ellice Islands Colony in 1916. After the Gilberts were occupied by the Japanese in 1942, US forces occupied the Ellice group in 1943 and drove the Japanese out of the Gilberts. After the war, the ethnic differences between the Micronesians of the Gilberts and the Polynesians of the Ellice Islands led the Ellice Islanders to demand separation. In 1973, a British commissioner appointed to examine the situation recommended administrative separation of

the two island groups. The British government agreed, provided that the Ellice Islanders declared their wishes by referendum. The vote, held during August-September 1974 with UN observers in attendance, produced an overwhelming majority of 3,799Ñ293 for separation. Accordingly, on 1 October 1975, the Ellice Islands were established as the separate British colony of Tuvalu, and a ministerial system was instituted. Pursuant to a constitutional conference held at London in February 1978, Tuvalu became an independent member of the Commonwealth of Nations on 1 October 1979. Sir Fiatau Penitala Teo became Tuvalu's first governor-general, and Toaripi Lauti, chief minister at the time of independence, took office as Tuvalu's first prime minister. Following new elections in September 1981, Lauti was succeeded in office by Tomasi Puapua, who was reelected in September 1985. In March 1986, Tupua Leupena replaced Sir Fiatau Penitala Teo as governor-general. In a poll held that same year, Tuvaluans rejected the idea that Tuvalu should become a republic. As a result of the 1989 general election the Parliament elected Bikenibeu Paeniu as Prime Minister in September 1989. In the same election, Naama Latasi became the first woman to serve in Tuvalu's Parliament.

In the 1993 legislative elections Paeniu and Puapua, the man who he replaced as Prime Minister, each received six votes from the newly elected twelve-member parliament. A second round of votes were held in December that year, from which Puapua withdrew, and Kamuta Latasi was elected Prime Minister.

In 1994 Prime Minister Latasi spearheaded a movement to remove the British Union Jack from the country's flag as a symbolic gesture of independence. In 1995, after conservative French President Jacques Chirac announced his country's intention to conduct above-ground nuclear tests in the South Pacific, Tuvalu emerged as a regional leader in the highly vocal opposition.

In April 1997 the Union Jack was restored as part of Tuvalu's national flag by a vote of seven to five in the Parliament. Newly reelected Prime Minister Bikenibeau Paeniu restored the former flag design, which Latasi had changed without consideration of the views of Tuvalu's citizens. Tuvalu, Nauru, and Kiribati aligned with the Cook Islands and Niue to put pressure on Australian production of "greenhouse gases." These low-lying island nations are particularly vulnerable to future global warming. Already flooding in stormy weather, they pressed for a worldwide cut of 20% of 1990 emission levels by 2005. Australia rejected the proposal, citing 90,000 jobs would be lost if Australia was forced to reduce emissions.

In 1998 Tuvalu began selling internet addresses in its TV domain, i.e., all Tuvaluan internet addresses end with the letters "tv."

By April 1999 there was growing dissatisfaction with Prime Minister Paeniu's leadership. Paeniu was forced to give up his office after a no confidence vote of Parliament. On 27 April 1999 Ionatana Ionatana, former Minister of Education, was elected as Prime Minister by the twelve-member Parliament.

In August 1999 Tuvalu sought economic aid as it suffered through a severe drought. Australia, New Zealand, Japan and Britain promised assistance to ease the water shortage with desalination plants. Japan agreed to provide the plants; New Zealand would pay to transport them. Australia would provide technical assistance toward formulating water policies.

Reportedly, Tuvalu licensed its dot-TV domain for $50 million over ten years to an Internet incubator. In February 2000 Prime Minister Ionatana received the first installment of the licensing deal, $20 million, and invested it in trust funds. In the continuing dispute with Britain over Tuvaluan separation with the Gilberts (Kiribati), Ionatana suggested that Tuvalu become a republic.

[13]GOVERNMENT

Tuvalu is an independent constitutional monarchy. The head of state is the British monarch, whose representative on the islands is the governor-general, a Tuvaluan who has the power to convene and dissolve parliament (Manuella Tulaga since June 1994). There is a unicameral legislature, the House of Assembly, with twelve members elected to four-year terms by universal adult suffrage. Four islands (Funafuti, Nanumea, Niutao, and Vaitupu) elect two members each; the other islands elect one each. The cabinet is headed by the prime minister and has four ministers (all House members), plus the attorney-general.

[14]POLITICAL PARTIES

There are no political parties, and political life and elections are dominated by personalities. Small island constituencies with a few hundred kin-related electors judge the leaders by their service to the community.

[15]LOCAL GOVERNMENT

Local administration by elected island councils was established following the creation of the protectorate in 1892. Local governments were established on the eight inhabited islands by a 1966 ordinance that provided the framework for a policy aimed at financing local services at the island level. Funafuti's town council and the other seven island councils (Niulakita has none) each consist of six elected members, including a president.

[16]JUDICIAL SYSTEM

District magistrates were established with the protectorate in 1892, and a simple code of law based on mission legislation and traditional councils has been observed by native courts. Eight island courts were constituted in 1965 to deal with land disputes, among other local matters. In 1975 a High Court of Justice was set up to hear appeals from district courts. Appeals from the High Court may go to the Court of Appeals in Fiji and ultimately to the UK Privy Council in London.

The right to a fair public trial is respected in practice. Services of the public defender are available to all Tuvaluans free of charge. Defendants have the right to confront witnesses, present evidence, and to appeal. The judiciary is independent and free of governmental interference.

[17]ARMED FORCES

Tuvalu has no armed forces except for the local police, which includes a maritime surveillance unit. For defense the islands rely on Australian-trained volunteers from Fiji and Papua New Guinea.

[18]INTERNATIONAL COOPERATION

As a special member of the Commonwealth of Nations, Tuvalu is not represented at heads-of-government conferences. However, Tuvalu does cooperate with several Commonwealth regional bodies, particularly the South Pacific Forum, which it hosted in 1982. The country also belongs to UPU and has associate or special status at the IFRCS and Intelsat. It is a member of ESCAP, an applicant to the WTO, and a signatory of the Law of the Sea. In 1979, Tuvalu signed a treaty of friendship with the US, which in 1983 formally dropped its prior claim to four of the nine islands. Tuvalu opposes French nuclear testing in the South Pacific and signed the 1985 Rarotonga Agreement declaring the region a nuclear-weapons-free zone.

[19]ECONOMY

Prime Minister Toaripi Lauti noted at the time of independence (1979) that all Tuvalu has is sun and a portion of the Pacific. Economic life is simple, but there is no extreme poverty. Subsistence is based on intensive use of limited resources, namely

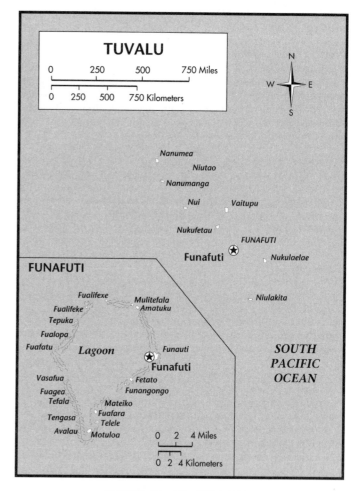

LOCATION: 5° to 11°s; 176° to 180°E.
TOTAL COASTLINE: 24 km (15 mi). **TERRITORIAL SEA LIMIT:** 12 mi.

coconuts and fish; copra is the only cash crop. The islands are too small and too remote for development of a tourist industry. The United Nations ranks Tuvalu among the least-developed countries. Tuvalu's GDP was estimated at $7.8 million for 1995, equivalent to $800 per capita (purchasing power parity). Inflation averaged 3.9% from 1985–93.

Recently, Tuvalu has garnered significant income from selling its the rights to internet addresses in its TV domain.

[20]INCOME

The US Central Intelligence Agency (CIA) reports that in 1995 Tuvalu's gross domestic product (GDP) was estimated at $7.8 million. The per capita GDP was estimated at $800. The annual growth rate of GDP was estimated at 8.7%. The CIA defines GDP as the value of all final goods and services produced within a nation in a given year and computed on the basis of purchasing power parity (PPP) rather than value as measured on the basis of the rate of exchange.

[21]LABOR

Most of the active labor force is engaged in subsistence agriculture, outside the cash economy. In Funafuti, the government-controlled philately bureau is the largest single employer, with a staff of several dozen workers. The nation's only trade union, the Tuvalu Seamen's Union, has about 600 members who work abroad on foreign merchant vessels. The nearly 1,000 public employees in Tuvalu were not unionized as of 1999. The minimum working age is 14 (15 for industrial employment). Generally children do not work outside of the traditional economy. The minimum age for shipboard employment is 18. As of 1999, the biweekly minimum wage was $81.25.

22AGRICULTURE

Although agriculture is the principal occupation, it contributes only 26% to the GDP. Agriculture is limited because of poor soil quality (sand and rock fragments), uncertain rains, and primitive catchment. Coconuts form the basis of both subsistence and cash cropping; the coconut yield in 1998 was about 2000 tons. Other food crops are pulaka (taro), pandanus fruit, bananas, and papayas.

23ANIMAL HUSBANDRY

The Agricultural Division, based on Vaitupu, has attempted to improve the quality and quantity of livestock to lessen the islands' dependency on imports. Pigs and fowl, which were imported in the 19th century, have been supplanted by goats and rabbits. In 1998, there were some 13,000 pigs on the islands. Honey is also produced.

24FISHING

Sea fishing, especially for tuna and turtle, is excellent. Although fishing is mainly a subsistence occupation, fish is sold in the capital, and bêche-de-mer is exported. The fish catch in 1997 was 400 tons, down from 1,460 tons in 1993. The average annual catch during 1994–97 was 440 tons. Japanese aid in 1982 provided a commercial fishing vessel for the islands. The Republic of Korea and Taiwan are both licensed to fish within the territorial waters of Tuvalu. In October 1986, Tuvalu, along with several other Pacific island nations, signed an agreement with the US giving US tuna boats the right to fish its offshore waters. The sale of fishing licenses annually contributes about a$80,000 to the government's revenues.

25FORESTRY

There is little useful timber on the islands.

26MINING

There is no commercial mining.

27ENERGY AND POWER

International aid by UNDP and the European Development Fund is helping to develop electrical power. Funafuti has a limited amount of electricity to operate its meteorological and broadcasting stations and for use by the hospital and hotel; very few private households have electrical service. Installed electrical capacity totaled 2,600 kW in 1990; electricity production that year amounted to 3 million kWh, or 330 kwh per capita. The Tuvalu Solar Electric Cooperative Society, formed in 1984, provides a limited supply of photovoltaic electricity.

28INDUSTRY

There is no industry apart from handicrafts, baking, and small-scale construction; the islands lack the population, capital, and resources to make commercial enterprises cost effective. In 1994, manufacturing contributed less than 2% to GDP.

29SCIENCE AND TECHNOLOGY

There is no advanced science and technology except for that imported under foreign aid programs.

30DOMESTIC TRADE

Cooperative societies dominate commercial life, controlling almost all retail outlets, the marketing of local handicrafts, and the supply of fish to the capital. Barter remains an important part of the subsistence economy. Offices are open from 7:30 AM to 4:15 PM, Monday to Thursday, and from 7:30 AM until 12:45 PM on Friday.

31FOREIGN TRADE

Copra, the main cash crop, took many years to recover from the 1972 hurricane and has been affected by fluctuating market prices (although there is a subsidy to producers). Other exports include handicrafts and postage stamps. Most food, fuel, and manufactured goods are imported. Merchandise exports were valued at A$347,000 in 1995, while imports amounted to A$10,327,000 that year. Tuvalu's principal trade partners are Fiji, Australia, and New Zealand.

32BALANCE OF PAYMENTS

The US Central Intelligence Agency reports that in 1989 the purchasing power parity of Tuvalu's exports was $.165 million while imports totaled $4.4 million resulting in a trade balance of -$4.235 million. In 1995, Tuvalu's trade deficit was A$9,980,000.

33BANKING AND SECURITIES

The Bank of Tuvalu was founded in Funafuti in 1980 and has branches on all the islands. The bank is jointly owned by the Tuvalu government (75%) and by Barclays Bank, which was responsible for its operation until mid-1985.

In 1995, the government bought Westpac's 40% shareholding in the National Bank of Tuvalu and now owns the bank outright. Westpac has managed the bank since it was established in 1980 and is expected to provide an advisory support service.

34INSURANCE

Insurance plays a minimal role in Tuvaluan life.

35PUBLIC FINANCE

The US Central Intelligence Agency (CIA) estimates that in 1989 Tuvalu's central government took in revenues of approximately $4.3 million and had expenditures of $4.3 million.

36TAXATION

Revenue is obtained principally by means of indirect taxation: stamp sales, the copra export tax, and fishing licenses. Income tax was levied on chargeable income on a sliding scale of 9–50% until 1983, when the rate was changed to a flat 30% of all individual income above A$1,800. A year later, the corporate rate was changed to 40%. Island councils also levy a head tax and a land tax based on territorial extent and soil fertility.

37CUSTOMS AND DUTIES

Since a single line tariff was implemented on 1 January 1975, trade preferences are no longer granted to imports from Commonwealth countries. Tariffs, applying mostly to private imports, are levied as a source of revenue. Most duties are ad valorem, with specific duties on alcoholic beverages, tobacco, certain chemicals, petroleum, cinematographic film, and some other goods.

38FOREIGN INVESTMENT

The cash economy is not sufficiently developed to attract substantial foreign investment. In 1981, the government established the Business Development Advisory Board to promote local and foreign investment in the Tuvalu economy; in 1993, the board became the Development Bank of Tuvalu. As of 1993, a new hotel was slated for construction on Funafuti by Taiwanese interests, and its airstrip was to be paved with aid from the EU.

[39]ECONOMIC DEVELOPMENT

Development aid, which rose rapidly during the 1960s, peaked at independence in 1979, when the UK undertook to provide £6 million. The Tuvalu Trust Fund was established in 1987 with A$27 million. The Fund receives contributions from Australia, New Zealand, the UK, Japan, Korea, and Tuvalu itself. The net income is paid to the Tuvalu government annually. As of 1994, the Fund amounted to A$36.8 million. Between 1990 and 1992, net total aid from Commonwealth countries and international agencies amounted to $8.2 million. Tuvalu hopes to increase its earnings by selling licenses for the use of its internet domain, TV.

[40]SOCIAL DEVELOPMENT

Tuvaluans cling strongly to their traditional way of life. Villages are organized on a communal rather than a clan basis and have a customary system of social welfare. Young men's clubs and women's committees are standard features of social life, concerning themselves with sailing, fishing, crafts, and child welfare.

Women generally play a subordinate role within the family and society at large. As of 1998, there were no women in parliament. Working women are primarily concentrated in the education and health sectors.

Human rights are well respected in Tuvalu. Serious crime is virtually nonexistent, and most prisoners are held for one night for offenses such as public drunkenness.

[41]HEALTH

There are no serious tropical diseases on the islands except for a dwindling number of leprosy and dysentery cases. In 1990, there were 1.8 hospital beds per 1,000 people. In 1992, there were 31 doctors per 100,000 people. The infant mortality rate was 25.5 per 1,000 live births in 1999. In the same year, the fertility rate was 3.1 per 1,000 population, and the overall mortality rate was 8.5 deaths per 1,000 population. A large portion of Tuvalu's population had access to safe water (100%) and sanitation (85%) in 1993. In 1995, the immunization rates for a child under one were as follows: diphtheria, pertussis, and tetanus (82%); polio (92%); measles (94%); and tuberculosis (88%). About 49% of children under one had been immunized for hepatitis B in 1995. The average life expectancy in 1999 was 64.1 years. Malaria was one of the most reported diseases in 1993, with 10,377 cases that year.

[42]HOUSING

Most islanders live in small villages and provide their own housing from local materials. After the 1972 hurricane, Funafuti was rebuilt with imported permanent materials, but there is still a critical housing shortage on Funafuti and Vaitupu. Government-built housing is largely limited to that provided for civil servants. In 1979, 46% of all dwellings had no sanitation facilities and only 10% had flush toilets; 44% received water from a communal tap and 30% drank well water.

[43]EDUCATION

All children receive free primary education from the age of 7. Education is compulsory for seven years. The Tuvaluan school system has seven years of primary and six years of secondary education. Secondary education is provided at Motufoua, a former church school on Vaitupu now jointly administered by the government. In 1994, 1,906 students were enrolled in 11 primary schools. In 1990, secondary schools had 345 students with 31 teachers. Tuvalu Marine School was opened in 1979 with Australian aid. In the same year, the University of the South Pacific (Fiji) established an extension center at Funafuti.

[44]LIBRARIES AND MUSEUMS

The first book published in Tuvalu was the Bible, in 1977. Apart from school facilities, the only library is the Parliamentary Library in Funafuti (600 volumes), which also houses the Archives.

[45]MEDIA

The government-owned Tuvalu Broadcasting Service, on Funafuti, transmits daily in Tuvaluan and also broadcasts news in English. In 1997 there were 373 radio receivers in use per 1,000 population. There is no commercial press, but *Tuvalu Echoes* (1999 circulation, 250) is published biweekly by the government. Other local publications are produced by the churches or the government. There is efficient inter-island communication. As of 1999, there were no television services. The government is reported to respect freedom of speech and of the press.

[46]ORGANIZATIONS

Apart from cooperative societies and local traditional bodies connected with island councils, there are few organizations. Organized youth groups include the Tuvalu Youth Fellowship and Pathfinder, and there are Girl Guide and Boy Scout troops on most islands. The Tuvalu Amateur Sports Association and the Pacific Red Cross are also notable.

[47]TOURISM, TRAVEL, AND RECREATION

Tuvalu's remoteness has discouraged tourism; the few visitors are on commercial or official business. In 1997, 1,000 tourists visited Tuvalu. That year there were 59 rooms in hotels and other facilities, and tourism receipts totaled US$300,000.

The UN estimated in 1999 that the daily cost of staying in Funafuti was $66; elsewhere costs were as low as $30 a day.

[48]FAMOUS TUVALUANS

Tuvalu's first prime minister was Toaripi Lauti (b. Papua New Guinea, 1928).

[49]DEPENDENCIES

Tuvalu has no territories or colonies.

[50]BIBLIOGRAPHY

Geddes, W. H., et al. *Atoll Economy: Social Change in Kiribati and Tuvalu.* Canberra: Australian National University Press, 1982.

MacDonald, Barrie. *Cinderellas of the Empire.* Canberra: Australian National University Press, 1982.

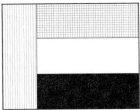

UNITED ARAB EMIRATES

United Arab Emirates

Al-Imarat al-'Arabiyah al-Muttahidah

CAPITAL: Abu Dhabi (Abu Zaby).

FLAG: The flag consists of a red vertical stripe at the hoist and three equal horizontal stripes of green, white, and black.

ANTHEM: The National Anthem is an instrumental piece without words.

MONETARY UNIT: The United Arab Emirates dirham (UD), introduced as the currency in May 1973, is divided into 100 fils. There are coins of 1, 5, 10, 25, and 50 fils and 1 and 5 dirham and notes of 5, 10, 50, 100, 200, 500, and 1,000 dirhams. UD1 = $0.2723 ($1 = UD3.673) as of 31 March 2000.

WEIGHTS AND MEASURES: The metric system and imperial and local measures are used.

HOLIDAYS: New Year's Day, 1 January; Accession of the Ruler of Abu Dhabi (Abu Dhabi only), 6 August; National Day, 2 December; Christmas, 25 December. Muslim religious holidays include Lailat al-Miraj, 'Id al-Fitr, 'Id al-'Adha', Hijra New Year, and Milad an-Nabi.

TIME: 4 PM = noon GMT.

¹LOCATION, SIZE, AND EXTENT

Comprising a total area of approximately 75,581 sq km (29,182 sq mi), including some 6,000 sq km (2,300 sq mi) of islands, the United Arab Emirates (UAE), in the eastern Arabian Peninsula, consists of seven states: Abu Dhabi, or Abu Zaby, with an approximate area of 67,350 sq km (26,000 sq mi); Dubai, or Dubayy, 3,900 sq km (1,500 sq mi); Sharjah, 2,600 sq km (1,000 sq mi); Ra's al-Khaimah, or Ra's al-Khaymah, 1,700 sq km (650 sq mi); Fujairah, or Al-Fujayrah, 1,150 sq km (450 sq mi); Umm al-Qaiwain, or Umm al-Qaywayn, 750 sq km (300 sq mi); and 'Ajman, 250 sq km (100 sq mi). Comparatively, the area occupied by UAE is slightly smaller than the state of Maine. Extending 544 km (338 mi) NE–SW and 361 km (224 mi) SE–NW, the UAE is bordered on the N by the Persian (or Arabian) Gulf, on the E by Oman, on the S and W by Sa'udi Arabia, and on the NW by Qatar, with a total boundary length of 2,185 km (1,358 mi). In the late 1970s, Sa'udi Arabia and Qatar reportedly reached a boundary agreement according to which a narrow corridor of land was ceded by Abu Dhabi, thus allowing Sa'udi Arabia access to the Gulf near the Khawr Duwayhin and eradicating the former Qatar-UAE frontier. However, through 1987, no documents attesting to the accord had been submitted to the UN. The remainder of the boundary with Sa'udi Arabia is not yet fully demarcated.

The UAE's capital city, Abu Dhabi, is located on the Persian Gulf.

²TOPOGRAPHY

The UAE consists mainly of sandy desert. It is bounded on the west by an immense sebkha, or salt flat, extending southward for nearly 112 km (70 mi). The eastern boundary runs northward over gravel plains and high dunes until it almost reaches the Hajar Mountains in the Ra's Musandam near Al-'Ayn. The flat coastal strip that makes up most of the UAE has an extensive area of sebkha subject to flooding. Some sand spits and mud flats tend to enlarge, and others enclose lagoons. A sandy desert with limestone outcroppings lies behind the coastal plain in a triangle

between the gravel plain and the mountains of the east and the sands of Sa'udi Arabia to the south. Far to the south, the oases of Al-Liwa' are aligned in an arc along the edge of dunes, which rise above 90 m (300 ft).

The main gravel plain extends inland and southward from the coast of Ra's al-Khaimah to Al-'Ayn and beyond. Behind Ra's al-Khaimah and separating Fujairah from the Persian Gulf is an area of mountains that rise over 900 m (3,000 ft) in height, with isolated cultivation. Finally, alluvial flats on the Gulf of Oman fill the bays between rocky spurs. South of Khor Fakkan (Sharjah), a continuous, well-watered fertile littoral strip known as the Batinah Coast runs between the mountains and the sea and continues into Oman. There are, in addition, many islands, most of which are owned by Abu Dhabi. These include Das, the site of oil operations, and Abu Musa, exploited for oil and red oxide.

³CLIMATE

The months between May and October are extremely hot, with shade temperatures of between 38° and 49°C (100–120°F) and high humidity near the coast. Winter temperatures can fall as low as 2°C (36°F) but average between 17° and 20°C (63–68°F). Normal annual rainfall is from 5 to 10 cm (2–4 in), with considerably more in the mountains; most rainfall occurs between November and February.

⁴FLORA AND FAUNA

Apart from cultivated plants, there are two categories of plant life in the UAE: the restricted salt-loving vegetation of the marshes and swamps, including the dwarf mangrove, and the desert plant community, which includes a wide range of flora that is most abundant after the fall of rain.

Animal and reptile life is similar to that of Bahrain, with the addition of the fox, wolf, jackal, wildcat, and lynx. Hedgehogs have been seen. More than 250 species of small birds have been reported in the UAE, along with many of the larger birds—kites, buzzards, eagles, falcons, owls, and harriers. Sea birds include a variety of gulls, terns, ospreys, waders, and flamingos. Popular

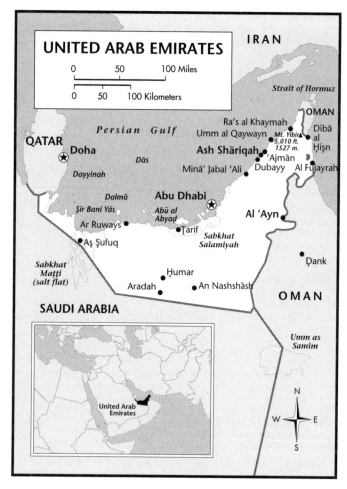

LOCATION: 51°3′ to 56°23′E; 22°30′ to 26°17′N. **BOUNDARY LENGTHS:** Persian Gulf coastline, 777 km (483 mi); Oman, 513 km (319 mi); Sa'udi Arabia, 586 km (364 mi); Qatar, 64 km (40 mi). **TERRITORIAL SEA LIMIT:** 3 mi, except Sharjah (12 mi).

game birds include the houbara (ruffed bustard), as well as species of ducks and geese.

5ENVIRONMENT

The clearing of natural vegetation, livestock overgrazing on rangelands, and extensive deforestation (in ancient times) have led to desertification. Overpumping of groundwater has brought a rise in soil salinity levels, and effluents from the oil industry have contributed to air pollution. In 1992, the UAE ranked among 50 countries with the world's highest levels of industrial carbon dioxide emissions, which totaled 70.6 million metric tons, a per capita level of 42.28 metric tons. The nation has 0.1 cubic miles of water. Eighty percent is used for farming activity and 9% is used for industrial purposes. The nation's cities produce 0.5 million tons of solid waste per year.

As of 1994, the nation did not have any of its land area protected by environmental legislation, but the government had begun to establish national parks to protect threatened flora and fauna. The Al-'Ayn zoological gardens contain some 280 species of wildlife, including the gazelle, which had been on the verge of extinction in the region. In 1994, four of the country's mammal species were endangered. Seven bird species were threatened with extinction. Endangered or extinct species in the UAE are the peregrine falcon, gray wolf, Arabian oryx, Arabian tahr, green sea turtle, and desert monitor.

6POPULATION

The population of United Arab Emirates in 2000 was estimated at 2,386,472. An estimated 2.0% of the population is 65 years of age or older. The projected population for the year 2005 is 2,611,000, assuming a crude birthrate of 21 per 1,000 population and a death rate of 4, resulting in a natural rate of change of 1.7% for the period 2000–2005. The population rate of change between 1995 and 2000 was 2.0%. The estimated population density was 36.7 per sq km (95 per sq mi) in 1996.

It was estimated that 86% of the population lived in urban areas in 2000. The capital city, Abu Dhabi, and its surrounding metropolitan area had a 2000 population of 928,000. Estimated populations of the other individual emirates were Dubai, 501,000; Sharjah, 314,000; Ra's al-Khaimah, 130,000; 'Ajman, 76,000; Fujairah, 63,000; and Umm al-Qaiwain, 27,000. The population of each emirate is concentrated largely in its capital. The towns of Abu Dhabi and Dubai are the most important urban centers; Abu Dhabi grew rapidly into a metropolitan area by attracting large numbers of internal and external migrants to its booming oil industry.

7MIGRATION

About 80% of the UAE's population originates from outside its borders. In the early 1980s, the government took steps to reduce the immigration rate by limiting the number of visas issued to foreign workers.

In September 1999, there were some 530 officially recognized refugees originating from Somalia, Uganda, Iraq, and Iran, as well as a number of Palestinians. The net migration rate was zero migrants per 1,000 population in 1999.

8ETHNIC GROUPS

South Asians accounted for 50% of the total population at last estimate. Emiris constituted 19%, while other Arabs and Iranians made up 23%. Other expatriates, including Westerners and East Asians, totaled 8%. Jordanians, Palestinians, Egyptians, Iraqis, and Bahrainis are employed throughout the bureaucracy, including the educational system.

9LANGUAGES

Arabic is the official and universal language. Persian, Hindi, and Urdu are minority languages. English is widely used in business. Farsi is spoken in Dubai.

10RELIGIONS

Virtually all UAE nationals and many immigrants are Muslims (96%). Most (85%) are Sunnis, and the remaining 16% are Shi'as. The government does not recognize all non-Muslim religions. In emirates that officially recognize and grant legal identity to non-Muslim groups, only a limited number of Christian groups are granted this recognition. While recognizing the difference between Roman Catholic, Eastern Orthodox, and Protestant Christianity, the authorities make no legal distinction between Christian groups, particularly Protestants. Non-Muslims, constituting approximately 4% of the population, are principally Christians and Hindus, but also include Buddhists, Parsis, Baha'is, and Sikhs.

11TRANSPORTATION

With most of the population concentrated in coastal towns and the Al-'Ayn oasis, road links between these centers have been given priority. There is now a paved coastal road linking Abu Dhabi, Dubai, Sharjah, 'Ajman, Umm al-Qaiwain, and R'as al-Khaimah. Roads linking the interior to the main towns have been constructed; of particular importance is the transpeninsular road from Fujairah through the Hajar Mountains. A six-lane, 209-km (130-mi) highway has been built between Abu Dhabi and Al-

'Ayn, and two bridges connect Abu Dhabi island with the mainland. Another highway links the UAE coastal network with the Trans-Arabian Highway at As-Silah on the Qatar border. In 1996 there were 4,835 km (3,004 mi) of paved highways. In 1995 there were 313,000 passenger cars and 72,824 commercial vehicles.

The UAE is well provided with port facilities. Dubai's Port Rashid, with its deep-water berths and warehouses, is one of the largest artificial harbors in the Middle East. Other ports are the Jabal 'Ali complex, also in Dubai, completed in 1980; Abu Dhabi's Port Zayid; Sharjah's Port Khalid; and the deepwater port at Ra's al-Khaimah. Sharjah constructed a new port at Khor Fakkan in the early 1980s; the Fujairah port became fully operational in 1983. In 1998, the merchant fleet consisted of 74 ships with a capacity totaling 1,093,795 GRT.

Also in 1998, there were 41 airports, of which 21 had paved runways. A new international airport in Abu Dhabi, on the mainland across from the island, opened in 1982. The other international airports in the UAE are in Dubai, Sharjah, and Ra's al-Khaimah. In July 1991, a "cargo village" opened at Dubai Airport, designed to handle 250,000 tons of cargo per year by 1997. The village operations can transfer cargo received at the port into air containers ready for airlift in three hours, and have the facilities to handle frozen and hazardous goods. In 1997, 4,720,000 passengers were carried on scheduled domestic and international airline flights.

12HISTORY

Although the Trucial Coast has for centuries been situated on one of the main trade routes between Asia and Europe, very little is known about the early history of the states that now make up the UAE. The northern states of the UAE, and in particular Ra's al-Khaimah, first came into historic prominence during the period of Portuguese occupation in the 16th and early 17th centuries, when Portugal used the territories as a base to fight a rear guard action against Persia. At that time and down to the mid-18th century, neighboring Oman played an integral role in the history of the maritime states.

Abu Dhabi island was settled by its present ruling family, Al-Nahyan, toward the end of the 18th century, and Dubai was founded by an offshoot of the same family in 1833. The late 18th and 19th centuries brought the division of the area between the Nahyan and the Qawasim, who ruled Ra's al-Khaimah and neighboring territories and whose clashes with British and Indian shipping led to British naval expeditions against what came to be known as the Pirate Coast. Treaties concluded in 1820 and 1835 established a formal relationship between the states of the southern Gulf and Britain that was to last until 1971. In 1853, the sheikhs agreed to a "perpetual maritime truce" to be enforced by the British navy. Under a treaty signed in 1892, the UK promised to protect the Trucial Coast from all aggression by sea and to lend its good offices in case of land attack. In 1955, the UK effectively intervened on the side of Abu Dhabi in the latter's dispute with Sa'udi Arabia over the Buraymi oasis, control of which is now shared by Abu Dhabi and Oman.

When, in 1968, the UK announced its intention to withdraw its forces from the area, a decision to establish a federation of Arab emirates—embracing the seven Trucial States, Bahrain, and Qatar—was agreed on in principle. However, it proved impossible to reconcile the differences among all the members, and in 1971, six Trucial States (excluding Ra's al-Khaimah) agreed on the establishment of the United Arab Emirates. The UAE was officially proclaimed a sovereign, independent nation on 2 December 1971, with Ra's al-Khaimah joining in early 1972.

Externally, the move to independence in 1971 placed the UAE in difficult straits with its two powerful neighbors, Sa'udi Arabia and Iran. Sa'udi Arabia asserted a territorial claim on a group of oases in the south of the UAE, and Iran laid claim to its offshore islands. In 1974, a border agreement on the Liwa' oases was signed with Sa'udi Arabia, but apparently has not been fully recognized by the rulers of either country. The dispute with Iran over the Abu Musa and Tumb Islands became tense when Iranian forces unilaterally asserted control over the UAE section of Abu Musa in 1992. In 1999, Iran still occupied the islands.

The UAE became a founding member in 1981 of the Gulf Cooperation Council (GCC), a political and economic alliance directed, at least implicitly, against Iran. During the Iran-Iraq war, the UAE gave aid to Iraq but also maintained diplomatic relations with Iran and sought to mediate the conflict.

In the Gulf War, forces from the UAE participated with allied troops and the government gave some $4.5 billion to the coalition war effort. Subsequently, the UAE has increasingly looked to the GCC, the US, and friendly Arab states for its security protection. The UAE's generosity with foreign aid to Arab states (over $15 billion through 1991) made it a significant player in the affairs of the region. In the years immediately after the war, the UAE accepted the stationing of US troops on its soil.

During the Yugoslav civil war, the UAE airlifted wounded Bosnian Muslim women and their families to Abu Dhabi, where they were given free medical treatment and housing, and financial support for one year. The country has also given heavily to Red Crescent relief organizations in Bosnia. Unlike its neighbors and partners in the GCC, Oman and Qatar, the UAE did not establish liaison offices in Israel—although it relaxed the Arab-wide boycott of Israel in the hope that lasting peace between the Palestinians and Israel would be forthcoming as a result of the Oslo Accords.

In 1991, the Bank of Commerce and Credit International (BCCI), which was based in the UAE and largely owned by the ruling family of Abu Dhabi, collapsed, causing repercussions all around the world. Accused of fraudulent dealings, the bank was officially liquidated in 1996, and the UAE cabinet resigned the following year. A sharp decline in oil prices in 1998 strongly affected the economy of the UAE, which recorded a drop of almost 6% in its GDP. At the end of 1999, the UAE celebrated the 25th anniversary of its founding, and the 30th anniversary of rule its president, Shaikh Zayid Bin Sultan Al Nuhayyan.

13GOVERNMENT

According to the provisional constitution of the UAE, promulgated on 2 December 1971, the executive branch of the UAE government consists of the Supreme Council of Rulers, headed by the president, and the Council of Ministers. The Council of Rulers, composed of the hereditary rulers of the seven emirates, has responsibility for formulation and supervision of all UAE policies, ratification of federal laws, and oversight of the union's budget. Sheikh Zayed bin Sultan al-Nahayyan, emir of Abu Dhabi, was elected president upon independence and has continuously been reelected to five-year terms ever since. The president is assisted by the Council of Ministers, or cabinet, headed by the prime minister. Sheikh Maktum ibn Rashid al-Maktoum, ruler of Dubai, has served as vice-president and prime minister since 1990, succeeding his father upon the latter's death. The member states are represented in the cabinet in numbers relative to their size and importance.

The Federal National Council, consisting of 40 delegates from the member emirates, appointed by their respective rulers for two-year terms, can question cabinet ministers and make recommendations to the Supreme National Council, but it has no legislative powers. The constitution stipulates the distribution of the 40 seats as follows: Abu Dhabi and Dubai, 8 each; Sharjah and Ra's al-Khaimah, 6 each; and 'Ajman, Umm al-Qaiwain, and Fujairah, 4 each. The Supreme National Council meets only occasionally.

After extending the 1971 interim constitution at five-years intervals for 25 years, the Supreme Council and the Federal National Council approved a measure removing the term "interim" in 1996, making the document a permanent constitution.

Most of the emirates are governed according to tribal traditions, including open meetings in which citizens express themselves directly to their rulers.

14POLITICAL PARTIES

No political parties exist in the UAE. Arab nationalist feeling has developed, however, and there is growing sentiment, particularly among urban youth, in favor of political liberalization and accelerated economic development. Several small clandestine groups with ties to radical Arab organizations or militant Islamic groups are believed to be active and are watched closely by the federation's security services.

15LOCAL GOVERNMENT

The major institutions of local government are the municipalities of Abu Dhabi town, Al-'Ayn, Dubai, Sharjah, Ra's al-Khaimah, Fujairah, 'Ajman, and Umm al-Qaiwain and a handful of traditional councils known as majalis and amiri diwans.

16JUDICIAL SYSTEM

Abu Dhabi, Dubai, and Sharjah have developed relatively sophisticated judicial systems based, as in other Gulf states, on a combination of Shari'ah law for civil matters, and contemporary legal codes. The 1971 constitution established a Supreme Court and an indeterminate number of courts of first instance. The Supreme Court consists of a president and a maximum of five judges, all of whom are appointed by presidential decree upon approval of the Supreme Council of Rulers. The Supreme Court president and member judges are deemed independent of the executive and legislative branches; once appointed, they cannot be removed. As of 1978 the lower courts were incorporated into a unified federal judiciary consisting of four tribunals.

Shari'ah courts in each emirate are subject to review in the Federal Supreme Court. There is no separate national security court system. Military tribunals try only military personnel and apply a system based on Western military judicial procedure.

Court systems in the Emirates of Dubai and Ra's-al-Khaimah function independently of the federal system. Each system has multiple levels of appeal and verdicts in capital cases are appealable to the president.

There are no jury trials. Under the Criminal Procedural Code, the accused has a right to counsel in capital cases and in those involving a possible penalty of life imprisonment. Due process rights are uniform under both the civil court and the Shari'ah court procedure.

17 ARMED FORCES

The armed forces of the UAE were placed under a unified command in 1976, and the forces of Abu Dhabi, Dubai, Ra's al-Khaimah, and Sharjah were merged. In 2000, the combined forces totaled 64,500 men, all volunteers. One-third are Asian contract soldiers. The army had 59,000 men, organized into 6 brigades. The navy was comprised of 1,500 men and 19 patrol and coastal combatants. The air force had 4,000 men, 99 combat aircraft, and 49 armed helicopters.

Many military personnel are expatriates from Oman, Jordan, and other countries. The UAE's military equipment is largely supplied by France, Germany, and the UK. Defense spending in 1999 was about $2.1 billion or 5% of gross domestic product. Morocco provides some 5,000 soldiers and police to the UAE.

18INTERNATIONAL COOPERATION

On 9 December 1971, shortly after achieving independence, the UAE became a member of the UN, and it now belongs to ESCWA and all the nonregional specialized agencies. The country is a member of G-77, GCC, the Islamic Conference, the Arab League, and OPEC. The UAE is a member of the WTO and signatory to the Law of the Sea.

19ECONOMY

The economy of the UAE centers primarily on oil and oil-based industries, but the share of this contribution to the GDP fell from 70% in 1980 to 22% in 1998. This is principally the result of falling oil prices, but also of growth in other sectors of the economy, such as manufacturing, finance and insurance, real estate, and government services. In Abu Dhabi, by far the wealthiest of the seven emirates, oil revenues are supplemented by income from a huge investment fund. Dubai joined the ranks of the oil producers only in 1971, and entrepôt trade continues to play a major role in its economy. In 1999, Abu Dhabi neared completion of a capacity expansion program that would increase capacity to 2.6 million barrels per day. Although 'Ajman has a small shipbuilding and ship repair yard and a recently established cement company, and Umm al-Qaiwain has a fish hatchery, a cement plant, and some small handicraft operations, these poorer emirates depend on federal aid—in effect, on revenue sharing by Abu Dhabi and Dubai. Oil production in Sharjah began in July 1974, and manufacturing and tourism there have been expanded. Ra's al-Khaimah has three large cement plants, pharmaceutical factory, a lime kiln, and the gulf's first explosives plant. Fujairah remains predominantly agricultural, but the emirate's government has also been developing an industrialization program, with emphasis on establishing mining-based industries.

In 1998, GDP equaled about $47 billion, down almost 6% from the previous year. GDP had grown at an annual rate of about 4.2% between 1988 and 1998. Petroleum extraction accounted for approximately 30% of GDP; wholesale and retail trade, 12%; government, 11%; business, 11%, and construction, 10%.

20INCOME

The US Central Intelligence Agency (CIA) reports that in 1998 the United Arab Emirates's gross domestic product (GDP) was estimated at $40 billion. The per capita GDP was estimated at $17,400. The annual growth rate of GDP was estimated at -5%. The average inflation rate in 1998 was 2.4%. The CIA defines GDP as the value of all final goods and services produced within a nation in a given year and computed on the basis of purchasing power parity (PPP) rather than value as measured on the basis of the rate of exchange. It was estimated that agriculture accounted for 3% of GDP, industry 52%, and services 45%.

21LABOR

In 1997, the total work force was estimated at about one million, but only a minority were UAE nationals, of whom women comprised 14%. Services accounts for 60% of employment, industry 32%, and agriculture 8%.

The UAE leans heavily on skilled labor, technology, and management abilities provided by foreigners. Non-UAE Arabs are employed at all economic levels, including the government bureaucracy and civil service. Manual labor is largely performed by Pakistanis and Iranians, while many Indians are to be found in clerical positions. Most domestic servants are women from Sri Lanka or the Philippines. There is a high proportion of Europeans at management levels. Until recently, the large influx of immigrants was insufficient to cope with labor needs. But with declining oil revenues in the mid-1980s, well-paying, skilled jobs were becoming harder to find in both the private and public sectors. The federal government and other state organizations began cutting back on employees. Many foreign workers were laid off and repatriated. A 1984 decree guarantees UAE nationals priority in hiring, in order to reduce dependence on expatriates.

Collective bargaining provisions do not exist, and strikes are strictly prohibited in the public sector. Rather, all labor contracts are reviewed by the Ministry of Labor to ensure that the pay will satisfy the employee's basic needs and secure a means of living.

There is no minimum wage. A standard work week of 8 hours per day, six days per week and minimum occupational health and safety requirements are not effectively enforced. Foreign workers are especially vulnerable to abuse. Widespread and credible reports indicate that foreign workers have had their passports confiscated, pay withheld, and are forced to work excessively long days far beyond the statutory maximum. Women working as domestic servants have also reported being sexually and physically abused.

Foreign workers have little redress for their grievances. UAE administrative bodies virtually never rule against a UAE employer, and UAE employers can prevent a foreign worker from switching to another employer.

[22] AGRICULTURE

Only about 81,000 hectares (200,000 acres) of land are cultivated. About 24% of cultivated land is used to grow vegetables, 30% fruit, 10% feed crops, and 36% for other uses. The most productive region is Ra's al-Khaimah, which receives underground water supplies from the nearby mountains of Oman and which enjoys the most plentiful rainfall. The main crops are tomatoes, melons, and dates.

The Digdagga Agricultural Trials Station in Ra's al-Khaimah is central to all agricultural research and training efforts in the UAE. Abu Dhabi has two large wheat farms at Al-'Ayn, and experimental farms at Rawaya and Mazaid (near Al-'Ayn) are designed to encourage local Bedouins to take up settled farming. The Abu Dhabi Arid Land Research Center on Sadiyat Island produces vegetables through special irrigation and hydroponic techniques. In 1998, UAE agriculture produced 581,000 tons of vegetables and 297,000 tons of fruit. Produce includes citrus, mangos, tomatoes, celery, potatoes, cucumbers, lettuce, melons, peppers, and fodder crops.

The Ministry of Agriculture and Fisheries reported a 48% increase in vegetable production between 1992 and 1995. Dates, traditionally grown on oases by nomads, are becoming less important because of vegetable and fruit production. In 1998, the UAE produced 250,000 tons of dates. The UAE currently satisfies about 60% of its domestic fruit and vegetable demand; bans on imports of certain vegetables and government incentives and subsidies are used to encourage domestic production. Roses and chrysanthemums are grown for export to Europe.

[23] ANIMAL HUSBANDRY

Livestock production has risen sharply in recent years. In 1998, the UAE had 1,000,000 goats, 385,000 sheep, 170,000 camels, and 76,000 head of cattle. Dairy farming is centered in Ra's al-Khaimah, with other dairy farms in Al Ain, Umm Al Quwain, Sharjah, and Dubai. The UAE produces about 90% of its dairy needs. Local poultry and egg production satisfy 27% and 40% of domestic demand, respectively. Five major producers account for 75% of the domestic chicken production. The poultry farm at Fujairah has the capacity to supply over 15% of domestic demand for broilers and eggs. Ra's al-Khaimah and Al Ain are other centers of poultry production. Production of poultry meat reached 30,000 tons in 1998, with imports of poultry meat (mainly from France, Denmark, the US, and Brazil). The UAE also re-exports poultry meat, mostly to Oman, former Soviet republics, and Iran.

[24] FISHING

Fishing is an important source of domestic food and fodder. From 1994 to 1996, per capita annual consumption of fish and shellfish in the UAE was 25.2 kg (55.4 lb) live weight equivalent, more than any other country in the Middle East. UAE coastal waters abound in fish and shellfish, and the country borders two high-potential fishing regions, the Persian Gulf and the Gulf of Oman. Many varieties of fish are caught, including rock cod, tuna, mackerel, sardines, anchovies, jack, marlin, red mullet, bream, and snapper. Over 70% of the catch typically is dried and processed into animal feed and fertilizer. The fish catch in 1997 was 114,358 tons, which supplied about 50% of local demand. Modern fishing techniques have been introduced with government assistance, and two new ports permitting the use of larger fishing boats were opened in 1981. The government also provides facilities for ship maintenance pro bono, as well as interest-free loans for the purchase of fishing boats and equipment. More than 3,000 fishing vessels annually operate in UAE waters. Umm Al Quwain is the site of a new 1,300 sq m marine farm which will research fish breeding. A fishmeal plant is in operation in Ra's al-Khaimah.

[25] FORESTRY

Natural woodland is scarce, apart from palm groves along the northern and eastern coasts. Forested areas covered only 60,000 hectares (148,000 acres), or about 0.7% of the total land area in 1995. The Forestry Department planted 80 million trees during 1980–95, at a cost of over $3 billion. Imports of forest products totaled $285.9 million in 1997.

[26] MINING

Apart from oil and natural gas, the minerals sector includes fertilizer production and production of construction materials, marble, and stone quarried from the Hajar Mountains. Copper and chromium have been found in Fujairah and Ra's al-Khaimah; in 1996, an estimated 56,000 tons of chromite ore were produced. Other production totals (in metric tons) were ammonia (nitrogen content) 365,000; urea, 250,000; and aluminum metal (primary ingot), 250,500.

[27] ENERGY AND POWER

The UAE, with crude oil production of 2,345,000 barrels per day in 1998 (up from 1,260,000 barrels per day in 1985), ranked as the third-largest producer in the Middle East (after Saudi Arabia and Iran). Total reserves of crude oil were estimated at the beginning of 1999 at 97.8 billion barrels, or about 10% of the world's total. Production is confined to Abu Dhabi, Dubai, Sharjah, and Ra's al-Khaimah, which together had an estimated maximum daily capacity of 2.6 million barrels in 1996. Abu Dhabi accounts for 94% of the total reserves, or about 92.2 billion barrels. Abu Dhabi's oil output comes almost exclusively from the onshore drilling activities of the Abu Dhabi Co. for Onshore Oil Operations (ADCO) and the offshore activities of Abu Dhabi Marine Operating Co. (ADMA-OPCO). Abu Dhabi has a 60% participation in the operations of both companies, which are managed by the government-owned Abu Dhabi National Oil Co. (ADNOC). The remaining 40% of ADCO's ownership is divided mainly among UK, US, and Dutch interests; the balance of ADMA-OPCO is owned by UK, French, and Japanese firms.

Offshore oil exploration by foreign companies has produced major new finds in recent years. Discovery of the offshore Butainah field in 1979 added about 1 billion barrels of oil to the UAE's proved reserves. That year, a US company, Amerada Hess, began producing crude oil at a rate of 15,000 barrels a day from the Arzanah offshore field. The Japan Oil Development Co. (JODCO), in partnership with ADNOC, began production at the offshore Umm ad-Dalkh field near Abu Dhabi in 1982. The two companies also agreed to develop three other small offshore areas, and both joined a French firm, CFP, to produce a projected 50,000 barrels of oil per day from the Upper Zakum field. The offshore Saleh field was found in 1983.

In 1981, Abu Dhabi and Dubai began to transfer up to half of their annual revenues from oil operations to the federation. The UAE's oil export receipts were $11 billion in 1999, down from $12.3 billion in 1985, and from $19.4 billion in 1980. Oil exports in 1995 accounted for 46% of total export revenue.

The UAE has two major refineries in Abu Dhabi, both operated by ADNOC, as well as two smaller facilities. In addition, there is a new $300 million condensate refinery in Dubai that began operations in 1999. Refined capacity was 287,800 barrels a day at the beginning of 1999. The UAE's proven natural gas reserves totaled about 6 trillion cu m (212 trillion cu ft); net production amounted to 37 billion cu m in 1998.

All electricity is thermally generated from oil or natural gas. Electric power production was 20,110 million kWh in 1998, when installed capacity was 5.5 million kW.

28 INDUSTRY

To diversify the economy, in the early 1990s the UAE introduced new industries, including aluminum, cement, pharmaceuticals, fabricated metals, processed foods, fertilizer, and explosives. Manufacturing as a percentage of GDP rose from 3.8% in 1980 to 7.7% in 1990 to 8.7% in 1995.

The Ar-Ruwais industrial complex in Abu Dhabi includes an oil refinery with a processing capacity of 120,000 barrels per day; a fertilizer factory, with a production capacity of 1,000 tons of ammonia and 1,500 tons of urea per day; and a gas liquefaction installation. Near Umm An-Nar, a large plant belonging to National Chlorine Industries produces salt, chlorine, caustic soda, and hydrochloric acid. In Dubai as of 2000, the industrial port complex at Jabal 'Ali was the largest manmade port in the world; it includes an aluminum smelter that produced 239,900 tons of ingots in 1995; the largest dry dock in the world, with a capacity of 1 million tons; and a free trade zone. Dubai's older industrial zone of Rashidiya is the site of some 40% of the emirate's processing industries. The other emirates have developed industries that produce construction-related materials such as cement, asphalt, and concrete blocks. Umm al-Qaiwain is planning to build a 120,000-ton-per-year aluminum smelter. In 1995, UAE refineries produced 69.3 million barrels of refined petroleum products, including 38.5 million barrels of residual and distillate fuel oil and 10.8 million barrels of gasoline.

According to the UAE's Ministry of Finance, there were 1,261 registered industrial establishments in 1995, with Sharjah accounting for 34.4%; Dubai, 33.1%; 'Ajman, 12.8%; Abu Dhabi, 11.9%; Ra's al-Khaimah, 4.3%; Umm al-Qaiwain, 2%; and Fujairah, 1.5%. The chemicals, petroleum, rubber, and plastics product industry had 259 registered establishments; metal products, machines, and engineering industry, 247; mining (excluding petroleum), 159; textiles, 157; food, beverages, and tobacco, 130; and other sectors, 309. Total investment in the industrial sector was UD14 billion in 1995, with 96,000 employees.

29 SCIENCE AND TECHNOLOGY

Advanced technology in the UAE has been imported mostly by foreign oil companies and is limited largely to heavy industry; nearly all of its technological specialists are foreigners. In the 1980s, the UAE took major steps to decrease its reliance on foreign scientists and technicians. The Ministry of Agriculture and Fisheries has a research center in Ra's al-Khaimah. United Arab Emirates University founded in 1976 at Al Ain, has faculties of sciences, engineering, agricultural sciences, medicine and health sciences. Ajman University College of Science and Technology was founded in 1988, Etisalat College of Engineering at Sharjah in 1989, and the The Higher Colleges of Technology at Abu Dhabi in 1988. In 1987–97, science and engineering students accounted for 24% of college and university enrollments.

30 DOMESTIC TRADE

Dubai remains the most important center of trade and commerce, although the commercial facilities of Abu Dhabi were slated for significant expansion in 2000. Barter methods still prevail outside the coastal towns, where specialized shops stocked with imported goods are common. Business hours tend to vary, although general hours of 8 AM to 1 PM and 4 to 7 PM are observed; most offices are closed Thursday afternoon, and Friday is the weekly holiday. Banks are open from 8 AM to noon, Saturday–Thursday.

31 FOREIGN TRADE

UAE's commodity exports were crude oil (45%), natural gas, reexports, dried fish, and dates as of 1997. Imports include machinery, vehicles, electrical equipment, aircraft, cosmetics, tobacco, steel, furniture, plastics, chemicals, and food products.

Principal trading partners in 1998 (in millions of US dollars) were as follows:

COUNTRY	EXPORTS	IMPORTS	BALANCE
Japan	7,583	3,150	4,433
Korea	1,930	1,647	283
India	1,638	1,789	-151
Singapore	957	1,127	-170
United Kingdom	842	2,845	-2,003
United States	644	2,607	-1,963
Germany	187	2,102	-1,915
China (inc. Hong Kong)	147	1,417	-1,270
France	107	1,352	-1,245
Italy	101	1,772	-1,671

32 BALANCE OF PAYMENTS

Oil and natural gas exports have allowed the UAE to sustain a trade surplus for many years, but changes in oil prices cause the surplus to fluctuate widely from year to year. The US Central Intelligence Agency reports that in 1997 the purchasing power parity of the United Arab Emirates's exports was $38 billion while imports totaled $29.7 billion resulting in a trade balance of $8.3 billion.

33 BANKING AND SECURITIES

The UAE Currency Board came into existence with its issuance of the UAE dirham in May 1973. In 1975–76, statutes came into force providing for the board's gradual transformation into a central bank, including powers to impose minimum liquidity ratios and other credit regulations. The board was replaced in 1980 by the UAE Central Bank, with enhanced authority to regulate the banking system. Capitalized at $81.7 million, the bank was granted additional capital of $2 billion from the government in 1982, which was to increase by 20% per year until a total deposit of $4 billion had been reached. The money supply, as measured by M2, was UD81.36 billion in 1995.

The oil boom of the 1980s brought with it the proliferation of commercial banks, making the UAE one of the most overbanked countries in the world. By 1987, strains were beginning to show and two banks collapsed. Bad loans were prevalent and some borrowers used the Islamic prohibition on riba (interest) as an excuse not to repay debts.

UAE banks were hit hard by the invasion of Kuwait in 1990, when partial withdrawals amounted to an estimated UD7 billion ($1.9 billion), or 7% of total deposits. In 1991, the Bank of Commerce and Credit International (BCCI), based in the UAE and owned in large part by the ruling family of Abu Dhabi, was accused of fraudulent dealings, and closed, damaging the credibility of the UAE banking system. However, because of improvements in the banking system, in 1999 the government cleared the way for establishment of an offshore banking center to be based in the free zone on Saadiyat Island, to enable UAE to compete with Bahrain. Also in 1999, the merger of two banks—National Bank of Dubai and Emirates Bank International—was announced.

As of 2000, the UAE was planning a stock exchange as part of the financial center on Saadiyat Island in Abu Dhabi.

34INSURANCE

Because of tightening federal regulations, the number of insurance companies declined from 126 in 1980 to 56 in 1987. The Federal Insurance Companies and Agents Law of 1984 requires all insurance companies established in the UAE to be public joint-stock companies, with equity wholly owned by UAE nationals. Companies already established in the country can obtain a concession from the local equity provision. Minimum capital must be UD10 million.

35PUBLIC FINANCE

A federal budget is prepared according to the UAE's development policy, while each emirate is responsible for municipal budgets and local projects. Conservative public expenditure policies have become more necessary as oil revenues have declined since 1983. Deficit spending is common. Abu Dhabi's oil income accounts for the bulk of federal revenues; under the constitution, each emirate contributes 50% of its net oil income to the federal budget.

The US Central Intelligence Agency (CIA) estimates that in 1998 the United Arab Emirates' central government took in revenues of approximately $5.4 billion and had expenditures of $5.8 billion including capital expenditures of $350 million. Overall, the government registered a deficit of approximately $400 million.

The following table shows an itemized breakdown of government revenues and expenditures. The percentages were calculated from data reported by the International Monetary Fund. The dollar amounts (millions) are based on the CIA estimates provided above.

REVENUE AND GRANTS	100%	5,400
Tax revenue	6.8%	365
Non-tax revenue	23.8%	1,284
Capital revenue	0.2%	12
Grants	69.2%	3,739
EXPENDITURES	100%	5,800
General public services	7.6%	439
Defense	31.5%	1,825
Public order and safety	14.0%	813
Education	17.7%	1,028
Health	7.6%	438
Social security	3.4%	198
Housing and community amenities	1.2%	71
Recreation, cultural, and religious affairs	1.5%	89
Economic affairs and services	5.8%	334
Other expenditures	9.7%	565

36TAXATION

Corporate taxes are paid only by oil companies (at rates that vary among emirates) and branches of foreign banks (at 20%). Municipal taxes are 5% on residential and 10% on commercial rents. A 5% tax is imposed on hotel services and entertainment. There is no personal income tax. As of 2000, companies engaged in business in the free zone on Saadiyat Island.

37CUSTOMS AND DUTIES

Dubai, the major area for foreign trade, is a free-trade zone and free port with no restrictions on imports or exports. The individual governments exert no control over imports, except for licensing. Customs duties are levied ad valorem; the rates differ among the emirates but are generally nominal (4% for most goods), except for a duty of 50% on alcoholic beverages (importation of which requires special permission). The duty on tobacco was increased from 80% to 100% in 2000. Duty-free imports include machinery, construction materials, foodstuffs, medicine, and printed matter. Food imports require a health certificate and meats require a certificate from a slaughterhouse that has been approved under Islamic law.

38FOREIGN INVESTMENT

All the emirates are eager to attract foreign investment. One obstacle to foreign investment may be the federal requirement that investments must be on a joint venture basis with the local partner owning at least 51% of the venture. The exception to this requirement is investment in the free trade zones where 100% foreign ownership is allowed. In 1995, the Jabal'Ali industrial free trade zone in Dubai had a total foreign investment of $3 billion. Middle Eastern countries had investments in 282 companies in the industrial zone; India, 124; and Japan, 27. Multinational companies operating in the Jabal'Ali industrial zone include the following: Samsung (ROK); Pioneer (Japan); General Motors, IBM, Mobil, and Toys "R" Us (US); and Ericsson (Sweden).

In 1996, UAE created the Abu Dhabi Free Zone Authority to regulate the development of Saadiyat Island, where there will be few restrictions on foreign companies. Companies opening offices there will be exempt from taxes, will be allowed to repatriate all profits and capital, to import labor; in addition, there will be no requirements to establish UAE partners. In 1999, the Emirates Global Capital Corporation was granted a 50-year contract to develop the 26 sq km (10 sq mi) zone, where a stock, commodities, and futures exchange was planned.

39ECONOMIC DEVELOPMENT

The federation used its vast oil wealth during the 1970s to transform the national economy through expansion of roads, ports, airports, communications facilities, electric power plants, and water desalination facilities, as well as construction of huge oil-processing complexes. With the completion of major infrastructural projects by the early 1980s, the focus of development shifted to diversifying the economy by establishing capital-intensive industries based on oil and gas resources.

The country's major industrial projects are the Jabal'Ali industrial zone in Dubai and the refinery complex at Ar-Ruwais in Abu Dhabi. Jabal 'Ali includes the Dubai Aluminum Co. smelter, a natural gas liquefaction plant, a cable factory, and a desalination plant that is one of the world's largest, with an output of about 25 million gallons of water daily. In mid-1995, 822 companies were operating in the Jabal 'Ali Free Zone.

In relation to GNP, the UAE is one of the world's major aid donors; the principal vehicle for bilateral aid has been the Abu Dhabi Fund for Arab Economic Development. The UAE makes regular annual payments to Syria, Jordan, Lebanon, and the PLO. Responding to Iraq's invasion of Kuwait in 1990, the UAE made significant financial contributions to assist the frontline states and to share the cost of the foreign military forces.

40SOCIAL DEVELOPMENT

There is no social security law in the UAE, but many welfare benefits are available to citizens, among them free hospital treatment and medical care and subsidies for education. Relief for any domestic catastrophe is provided from a disaster fund. If the father of a family is unable to work because of illness, disability, or old age, he receives help under the National Assistance Law; should he die or divorce his wife, the woman's future is secured. UAE nationals receive many government services, including health care, water, and electricity, free of charge.

Female employment is growing in government service and in occupations such as education and health. According to government statistics, women accounted for nearly 20% of the workforce in 1995. Women account for 65% of intermediate and secondary school teachers, 54% of health care workers, and nearly 40% of all government employees. They are also accepted for military service. As of 1997, there were no women in parliament. Women account for over 75% of the student body at the UAE University.

Women continue to suffer from official discrimination. Females may not leave the country without the permission of a male relative. Custody is given to mothers following divorce only in cases of children under seven. A married woman can work outside the home only with her husband's permission. Islamic precepts apply to family law, although some, such as polygamy for men, are not usually practiced.

Many domestic servants are foreigners who are sometimes subjected to mistreatment or abuse, and poor pay. If they leave their employers without fulfilling the terms of their contract, they may be barred from taken further employment.

The government restricts democratic freedoms and also limits freedoms of speech, assembly, association, press, and the right to a speedy trial.

41HEALTH

Health facilities have been expanded rapidly since independence. Modern hospitals have been built in Abu Dhabi, Dubai, and other towns. In 1991, there were 1,526 doctors and 2,800 nurses. In 1990–97, there were 0.8 doctors and 3.1 hospital beds per 1,000 population. Typhoid fever and tuberculosis are rare; malaria remains a problem, however. In 1995, 95% of the population had access to safe water, and 98% had adequate sanitation in 1994–1995. Only 2.5% of the GDP went to health expenditures during 1990–1997. In 1991–1993, 95% of the population had access to health care services.

Average life expectancy in 1999 was 75 years, and the infant mortality rate was 14.1 per 1,000 live births. General mortality was 3.1 per 1,000 people, and the country's 1999 birth rate was 18.8 per 1,000 people. Children up to one year old were immunized in 1994 against tuberculosis (98%); diphtheria, pertussis, and tetanus (90%); polio (90%); and measles (90%). Malaria incidence was 3,735 reported cases in 1993. The goiter prevalence was 40.4 per 100 school children in 1996. The HIV-1 seroprevalence rate in 1997 was 0.2 per 100 adults. The next year, there were only 8 cases of AIDS reported.

42HOUSING

The federal government is attempting to make modern low-cost homes available to poorer families, supplying them with amenities such as piped water, sewerage systems, and electricity. The Ministry of Housing constructed about 4,000 houses for free distribution to poor families between 1978 and 1981. In 1980, 33% of all housing units were flats, 30% were traditional Arabic dwellings, 9% were low-cost housing, 8% were shacks, and the remainder were sheds, caravans, single rooms, tents, and other facilities. About 85% had water closets and 26% had electricity, piped-in water, and access to a sewage system.

43EDUCATION

The educational system of the UAE has burgeoned since 1971. Education in the six northern emirates, formerly financed and administered by Kuwait, has been managed by the UAE Ministry

of Education since 1972. Education is compulsory for six years at the primary level, from age 6, and is free to all UAE citizens, as are school uniforms, books, equipment, and transportation. The system remains concentrated at the primary level. At the secondary level, children go through six years of education in two stages. In 1997, there were 259,509 pupils and 16,148 teachers at the primary level. Student-to-teacher ratio stood at 16 to one. In the same year, secondary schools had 180,764 pupils and approximately 11,000 teachers. In 1980, the government issued new regulations concerning private schools, which enrolled nearly 90,000 students in 1985; Arabic was made a compulsory subject, and segregation of classes by sex was required. United Arab Emirates University is at Al-'Ayn. In 1997, all higher level institutions had 16,213 students. Approximately 16.7% of the central government budget was allocated to education in the latter part of the 1990s. For the year 2000, adult illiteracy rates were estimated at 23.5% (males, 24.8%; females, 20.5%).

44LIBRARIES AND MUSEUMS

The Central Public Library has four branches and holds 100,000 volumes. The Higher Colleges of Technology (300,000 volumes), and the United Arab Emirates University (300,000 volumes) are in Abu Dhabi. The Al-Ain Museum (1971) is an archeological institution. There are local museums in Dubai, Fujairab, and Sharjah, which is also home to archaeological, historical, Islamic, and science museums.

45MEDIA

The communications system has been dramatically improved and expanded in recent years. Telecommunications operations in the emirates are all handled by ETISALAT. The Jabal 'Ali earth satellite station in Dubai maintains telephone and telegraph traffic, telex data transmission, and color television broadcasting; computer-controlled automatic telex systems have been installed in both Dubai and Abu Dhabi. In 1995, the UAE had 615,000 main telephone lines and some 7,000 telex lines. A color television network connects Abu Dhabi with Dubai and Sharjah. UAE Radio has broadcasting stations in four emirates; the first commercial station was opened in Abu Dhabi in 1980. As of 1999 there were 8 AM and 3 FM radio stations and 15 television stations. In 1997 the UAE had 354 radios, 294 television sets, and 132 mobile phones per 1,000 population.

Five Arabic-language dailies were published in 1999 in the UAE: Al-Ittihad (Federation, 1999 circulation 60,000), Al-Fajr (The Dawn, 20,700), and Al-Wahdah (Unity, 30,000 in 1995), in Abu Dhabi; Al-Bayan (32,650) in Dubai; and Al-Khalij (85,000) in Sharjah. There were three English-language dailies: the Gulf News (85,000) and Khaleej Times (48,000), published in Dubai, and the Emirates News (21,000), published in Abu Dhabi.

The Provisional Constitution provides for free expression; however, the government restricts expression in practice. All published materials must be licensed by the Ministry of Education, which governs content and allowable subjects. The media practice self-censorship on the subjects of government policy, the ruling families, national security, religion, and international relations.

As of 1996, there were some 90,000 personal computers and, in 1998, about 50 Internet hosts per 1,000 population.

46ORGANIZATIONS

There are chambers of commerce in the larger states. Various social and sporting clubs provide outlets for philanthropic work and recreation.

47TOURISM, TRAVEL, AND RECREATION

Except for Gulf nationals and citizens of the UK, most visitors must secure a visa in advance. Tourism is encouraged by all the emirates, whose varied scenery includes mountains, beaches, deserts and oases. Activities include visits to Bedouin markets, museums, zoos, and aquariums. Many large world-class hotels have opened in recent years. The emirates attract tourists from Western Europe during the winter, when the main attractions are the beaches and sunny climate. Tourists numbered 1,810,000 in 1998, with receipts totaling $540 million.

The cost of staying in Dubai, according to 1999 UN estimates, was $194 per day; estimated daily expenses for travel in Abu Dhabi was approximately $197.

[48]FAMOUS EMIRIANS

Sheikh Zayed bin Sultan an-Nahyan (b.1918) has been ruler of Abu Dhabi since 1966 and president of the UAE since 1971.

[49]DEPENDENCIES

The UAE has no territories or colonies.

[50]BIBLIOGRAPHY

Abu-Baker, Albadr S.S. *Political Economy of State Formation: The United Arab Emirates in Comparative Perspective.* N.p., 1996.

Abdullah, Muhammad Morsy. *The United Arab Emirates: A Modern History.* New York: Barnes & Noble, 1978.

Alkim, Hassan Hamdan. *The Foreign Policy of the United Arab Emirates.* London: Saqi, 1989.

American University. *Persian Gulf States: Country Studies.* 3d ed. Washington, D.C.: Government Printing Office, 1994.

Anthony, John Duke. *Arab States of the Lower Gulf: People, Politics, Petroleum.* Washington, D.C.: Middle East Institute, 1975.

Clements, Frank. *United Arab Emirates.* (rev. ed.) Santa Barbara, Calif.: Clio Press, 1998.

El Mallakh, Ragaei. *The Economic Development of the United Arab Emirates.* New York: St. Martin's, 1981.

Ghanem, Shihab M. A. *Industrialization in the United Arab Emirates.* Brookfield: Avebury, 1992.

Heard-Bey, Frauke. *From Trucial States to United Arab Emirates: A Society in Transition.* New York: Longman, 1982.

Henderson, Edward. *This Strange Eventful History: Memoirs of Earlier Days in the UAE and the Sultanate of Oman.* Dubai, U.A.E.: Motivate Publishing, 1993.

Oman and the United Arab Emirates. London: Lonely Planet, 2000.

Peck, Malcolm C. *The United Arab Emirates: A Venture in Unity.* Boulder, Colo.: Westview, 1986.

Stannard, Dorothy. (ed.) *Oman and the United Arab Emirates.* Singapore: APA Publications, 1998.

Taryam, Abdullah Omran. *The Establishment of the United Arab Emirates, 1950–85.* New York: Croom Helm, 1987.

Vine, Peter. *United Arab Emirates: Profile of a Country's Heritage and Modern Development.* London: Immel, 1992.

———. *United Arab Emirates in Focus.* London: Trident, 1999.

Zahlan, Rosemarie Said. *The Origins of the United Arab Emirates: A Political and Social History of the Trucial States.* New York: St. Martin's, 1978.

UNITED STATES
PACIFIC DEPENDENCIES

AMERICAN SAMOA

American Samoa, an unincorporated and unorganized insular US territory in the South Pacific Ocean, comprises that portion of the Samoan archipelago lying E of longitude 171°w. (The rest of the Samoan islands comprise the independent state of Western Samoa.) While the Samoan group as a whole has an area of 3,121 sq km (1,205 sq mi), American Samoa consists of only seven small islands (between 14° and 15°s and 168° and 171°w) with a total area (land and water) of 197 sq km (76 sq mi). Five of the islands are volcanic, with rugged peaks rising sharply, and two are coral atolls.

The climate is hot and rainy; normal temperatures range from 24°C (75°F) in August to 32°C (90°F) during December–February; mean annual rainfall is 330 cm (130 in), the rainy season lasting from December through March. Hurricanes are common. The native flora includes flourishing tree ferns, coconut, hardwoods, and rubber trees. There are few wild animals.

As of mid-1996, the estimated population was 59,556, an increase of 59% over the 1986 population estimate of 37,500. However, the total population has remained relatively constant for many years because of the substantial number of Samoans who migrate to the United States. The inhabitants, who are concentrated on the island of Tutuila, are almost pure Polynesian. English is the official language, but Samoan is also widely spoken. Most Samoans are Christians.

The capital of the territory, Pago Pago, on Tutuila, has one of the finest natural harbors in the South Pacific and is a duty-free port. Passenger liners call there on South Pacific tours, and passenger and cargo ships arrive regularly from Japan, New Zealand, Australia, and the US west coast. There are regular air and sea services between American Samoa and Western Samoa, and scheduled flights between Pago Pago and Honolulu.

American Samoa was settled by Melanesian migrants in the 1st millennium BC. The Samoan islands were visited in 1768 by the French explorer Louis-Antoine de Bougainville, who named them the Îles des Navigateurs as a tribute to the skill of their native boatmen. In 1889, the US, the UK, and Germany agreed to share control of the islands. The UK later withdrew its claim, and under the 1899 Treaty of Berlin, the US was internationally acknowledged to have rights extending over all the islands of the Samoan group lying east of 171°w, while Germany was acknowledged to have similar rights to the islands west of that meridian. The islands of American Samoa were officially ceded to the US by the various ruling chiefs in 1900 and 1904, and on 20 February 1929 the US Congress formally accepted sovereignty over the entire group. From 1900 to 1951, the territory was administered by the US Department of the Navy, and thereafter by the Department of the Interior. The basic law is the Constitution of 1966.

The executive branch of the government is headed by a governor who, along with the lieutenant governor, is elected by popular vote; before 1977, the two posts were appointed by the US government. Village, county, and district councils have full authority to regulate local affairs.

The legislature (Fono) is composed of the House of Representatives and the Senate. The 15 counties elect 18 matais (chiefs) to four-year terms in the senate, while the 20 house members are elected for two-year terms by popular vote within the counties. The secretary for Samoan affairs, who heads the Department of Local Government, is appointed by the governor. Under his administration are three district governors, the county chiefs, village mayors, and police officials. The judiciary, an independent branch of the government, functions through the high court and five district courts. Samoans living in the islands as of 17 April 1900 or born there since that date are nationals of the US. The territory sends one delegate to the US House of Representatives.

The economy is primarily agricultural. Small plantations occupy about one-third of the land area; 70% of the land is communally owned. The principal crops are bananas, breadfruit, taro, papayas, pineapples, sweet potatoes, tapioca, coffee, cocoa, and yams. Hogs and poultry are the principal livestock raised; dairy cattle are few. The principal cash crop is copra. More than half of the total labor force is employed by the federal and territorial government. The largest employers in the private sector, with more than 15% of the labor force, are two modern tuna canneries supplied with fish caught by Japanese, US, and Taiwanese fishing fleets. Between 80% and 90% of foreign trade is conducted with the US.

Samoans are entitled to free medical treatment, including hospital care. Besides district dispensaries, the government maintains a central hospital, a tuberculosis unit, and a leprosarium. US-trained staff physicians work with Samoan medical practitioners and nurses. The 170 bed LBJ Tropical Medical Center opened in 1986.

Education is a joint undertaking between the territorial government and the villages. School attendance is compulsory for all children from 6 through 18, and about 99% of the population 10 years of age and over is literate. The villages furnish the elementary-school buildings and living quarters for the teachers; the territorial government pays teachers' salaries and provides buildings and supplies for all but primary schools. Since 1964, educational television has served as the basic teaching tool in the school system. In 1995 total enrollment in elementary and secondary schools was 14,406. American Samoa Community College enrolled 1,249 in 1994/95.

Radiotelegraph circuits connect the territory with Hawaii, Fiji, and Western Samoa. Every village in American Samoa has telephone service.

GUAM

The largest and most populous of the Mariana Islands in the Western Pacific, Guam (13°28′N and 144°44′E) has an area, including land and water, of 540 sq km (208 sq mi) and is about 48 km (30 mi) long and from 6 to 12 km (4–7 mi) wide. The island is of volcanic origin; in the south, the terrain is mountainous, while the northern part is a plateau with shallow fertile soil. The central part of the island (where the capital, Agana, is located) is undulating country.

Guam lies in the typhoon belt of the Western Pacific and is occasionally subject to widespread storm damage. In May 1976, a typhoon with winds of 306 km/hr (190 mph) struck Guam, causing an estimated $300 million in damage and leaving 80% of the island's buildings in ruins. Guam has a tropical climate with little seasonal variation. Average temperature is 26°C (79°F); rainfall is substantial, reaching an annual average of more than 200 cm (80 in). Endangered species include the giant Micronesian kingfisher and Marianas crow.

The mid-1996 population, excluding transient US military and civilian personnel and their families, was estimated at 156,974, a growth of 36% over the 1986 estimate of 117,500. The increase was attributed largely to the higher birthrate and low mortality rate. The present-day Chamorro, who comprise about 47% of the permanent resident population, descend from the intermingling of the few surviving original Chamorro with the Spanish, Filipino, and Mexican settlers, plus later arrivals from the US, UK, Korea, China, and Japan. Filipinos (25%) are the largest ethnic minority. English is the official language, although Chamorro is taught in the primary schools. The predominant religion is Roman Catholicism.

The earliest known settlers on Guam were the original Chamorro, who migrated from the Malay Peninsula to the Pacific around 1500 BC. When Ferdinand Magellan landed on Guam in 1521, it is believed that as many as 100,000 Chamorro lived on the island; by 1741, their numbers had been reduced to 5,000—most of the population either had fled the island or been killed through disease or war with the Spanish. A Spanish fort was established in 1565, and from 1696 until 1898, Guam was under Spanish rule.

Under the Treaty of Paris that ended the Spanish-American War in 1898, the island was ceded to the US and placed under the jurisdiction of the Department of the Navy. During World War II, Guam was occupied by Japanese forces; the US recaptured the island in 1944 after 54 days of fighting. In 1950, the island's administration was transferred from the Navy to the US Department of the Interior. Under the 1950 Organic Act of Guam, passed by the US Congress, the island was established as an unincorporated territory of the US; Guamanians were granted US citizenship, and internal self-government was introduced.

The governor and lieutenant governor have been elected directly since 1970. A 21-member unicameral legislature elected for two years by adult suffrage is empowered to legislate on all local matters, including taxation and appropriations. The US Congress reserves the right to annul any law passed by the Guam legislature, but must do so within a year of the date it receives the text of any such law.

Judicial authority is vested in the district court of Guam, and appeals may be taken to the regular US courts of appeal and ultimately to the US Supreme Court. An island superior court and other specialized courts have jurisdiction over certain cases arising under the laws of Guam. The judge of the district court is appointed by the US president; the judges of the other courts are appointed by the governor. Guam's laws were codified in 1953.

Guam is one of the most important US military bases in the Pacific, and the island's economy has been profoundly affected by the large sums of money spent by the US defense establishment. During the late 1960s and early 1970s, when the US took the role of a major combatant in the Viet-Nam conflict, Guam served as a base for long-range US bombers on sorties over Indochina. In 1995/96, there were 4,508 active-duty US military personnel stationed on the island.

Prior to World War II, agriculture and animal husbandry were the primary activities. By 1947, most adults were wage earners employed by the US armed forces, although many continued to cultivate small plots to supplement their earnings. Since World War II, agriculture has generally contributed less than 1% of the GNP, partly because a considerable amount of arable land is taken up by military installations. Fruits and vegetables are grown and pigs and poultry are raised for local consumption, but most food is imported. Current fish catches are insufficient to meet local demand.

Tourism has become a major industry and sparked a boom in the construction industry in the mid-1980s. The number of visitors grew rapidly from 6,600 in 1967 to over 900,000 in 1992 and provided $600 million in revenues to the economy. The stagnation in the Japanese economy since the early 1990s has slowed the growth of Guam's tourism sector.

The Guam Rehabilitation Act of 1963 has funded the territory's capital improvement program. Further allocations in 1969 and 1977 provided over $120 million for additional capital improvements and development of the island's power installations. More than $200 million of federal funds were authorized for typhoon relief in 1977–78. Total expenditures by the government of Guam were $395 million in 1991; revenues were $525 million. Total grants from the US federal government in 1996/97 amounted to $134 million.

Guam had 1,955 business establishments (including 886 retail) in 1992, with sales of over $3 billion. Guam's foreign trade usually shows large deficits. The bulk of Guam's trade is with the US, Micronesia, and Japan.

US income tax laws are applicable in Guam; all internal revenue taxes derived by the US from Guam are paid into the territory's treasury. US customs duties, however, are not levied. Guam is a duty-free port. In its trade with the US mainland, Guam is required to use US shipping.

Typical tropical diseases are practically unknown today in Guam. Tuberculosis, long the principal killer, was brought under control by the mid-1950s. The Guam Memorial Hospital has a capacity of 147 beds. Village dispensaries serve both as public health units and first-aid stations. In addition, there are a number of physicians in private practice. Specialists from the US Naval Hospital in Guam, assisting on a part-time basis, have made possible a complete program of curative medicine.

School attendance is compulsory from the age of 6 through 16. In 1995/96, 33,502 pupils were enrolled in public elementary and secondary schools. The University of Guam and Guam Community College enrolled 6,449 students in 1994/95. There are 3 AM and 3 FM radio stations.

HOWLAND, BAKER, AND JARVIS ISLANDS

Howland Island (0°48′N and 176°38′W), Baker Island (0°14′N and 176°28′W), and Jarvis Island (0°23′S and 160°1′W) are three small coral islands, each about 2.6 sq km (1 sq mi) in area, belonging to the Line Islands group of the Central Pacific Ocean. All are administered directly from Washington as US unincorporated territories. Public entry is by special permit and generally restricted to scientists and educators. Howland was discovered in 1842 by US sailors, claimed by the US in 1857, and formally proclaimed a US territory in 1935–36. It was worked for guano by US and British companies until about 1890.

Baker, 64 km (40 mi) S of Howland, and Jarvis, 1,770 km (1,100 mi) E of Howland, also were claimed by the US in 1857, and their guano deposits were similarly worked by US and British enterprises. The UK annexed Jarvis in 1889. In 1935, the US sent colonists from Hawaii to all three islands, which were placed under the US Department of the Interior in 1936 and are administered as part of the National Wildlife Refuge system. Baker was captured by the Japanese in 1942 and recaptured by the US in 1944. The three islands lack fresh water and have no permanent inhabitants. They are visited annually by the US Coast Guard. A lighthouse on Howland Island is named in honor of the US aviatrix Amelia Earhart, who vanished en route to the island on a round-the-world flight in 1937.

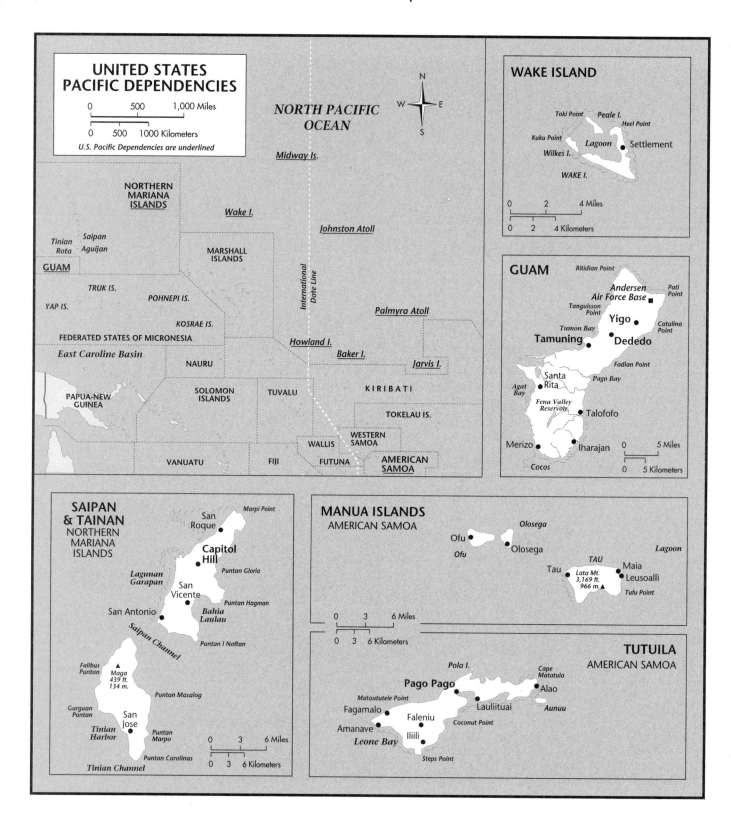

UNITED STATES PACIFIC DEPENDENCIES

0   500   1,000 Miles

0   500   1000 Kilometers

U.S. Pacific Dependencies are underlined

NORTH PACIFIC OCEAN

N W E S

Midway Is.

NORTHERN MARIANA ISLANDS

Wake I.

Johnston Atoll

Tinian *Saipan*
Rota *Aguijan*

GUAM

MARSHALL ISLANDS

International Date Line

TRUK IS.

POHNEPI IS.

YAP IS.

KOSRAE IS.

FEDERATED STATES OF MICRONESIA

East Caroline Basin

NAURU

Palmyra Atoll

Howland I.

Baker I.

Jarvis I.

PAPUA-NEW GUINEA

SOLOMON ISLANDS

TUVALU

KIRIBATI

TOKELAU IS.

WALLIS

WESTERN SAMOA

VANUATU

FIJI

FUTUNA

AMERICAN SAMOA

WAKE ISLAND

Toki Point *Peale I.*

Heel Point

Kuku Point

Lagoon Settlement

Wilkes I.

WAKE I.

0   2   4 Miles

0   2   4 Kilometers

GUAM

Ritidian Point

Andersen Air Force Base

Pati Point

Tanguisson Point

Tumon Bay

Yigo

Catalina Point

Tamuning **Dededo**

Fadian Point

Agat Bay

Santa Rita

Pago Bay

Fena Valley Reservoir

Talofofo

Merizo

Iharajan

Cocos

0   5 Miles

0   5 Kilometers

SAIPAN & TAINAN
NORTHERN MARIANA ISLANDS

Marpi Point

San Roque

Capitol Hill

Puntan Gloria

Lagunan Garapan

San Vicente

Puntan Hagman

San Antonio

Bahia Laulau

Saipan Channel

Puntan I Naftan

Falibus Puntan

▲ *Maga 439 ft. 134 m.*

Puntan Masalog

Gurguan Puntan

San Jose

Tinian Harbor

Puntan Marpo

Puntan Carolinas

Tinian Channel

0   3   6 Miles

0   3   6 Kilometers

MANUA ISLANDS
AMERICAN SAMOA

Olosega

Ofu

Olosega

Ofu

TAU

Lagoon

Tau

Lata Mt. 3,169 ft. 966 m. ▲

Maia

Leusoalli

Tufu Point

0   3   6 Miles

0   3   6 Kilometers

TUTUILA
AMERICAN SAMOA

Pola I.

Cape Matatula

Pago Pago

Alao

Mataututele Point

Lauliituai

Aunuu

Fagamalo

Faleniu

Coconut Point

Amanave

Iliili

Leone Bay

Steps Point

JOHNSTON ATOLL

Johnston Atoll, located in the North Pacific 1,151 km (715 mi) SW of Honolulu, consists of two islands, Johnston (16°44′N and 169°31′W) and Sand (16°45′N and 169°30′W), with a total land and water area of about 2.6 sq km (1 sq mi). The islands are enclosed by a semicircular reef. It was discovered by English sailors in 1807 and claimed by the US in 1858. For many years, it was worked for guano and was a bird reservation. Commissioned as a naval station in 1941, it remains an unincorporated US territory under the control of the US Department of the Air Force.

In recent years, it has been used primarily for the testing of nuclear weapons.

As of mid-1996 there were about 1,200 people living on the atoll. The atoll's population was composed entirely of government personnel and contractors. The atoll is equipped with an excellent satellite and radio telecommunications system.

MIDWAY

The Midway Islands (28°12'–17'N and 177°19'–26'W) consist of an atoll and two small islets, Eastern Island (177°20'W) and Sand Island (177°22'–24'W), 2,100 km (1,300 mi) WNW of Honolulu. Total land and water area is 5 sq km (2 sq mi). As of 1995, 453 military personnel lived on the base.

Discovered and claimed by the US in 1859 and formally annexed in 1867, Midway became a submarine cable station early in the 20th century and an airlines station in 1935. Made a US naval base in 1941, Midway was attacked by the Japanese in December 1941 and January 1942. In one of the great battles of World War II, a Japanese naval attack on 3–6 June 1942 was repelled by US warplanes. Midway is a US unincorporated territory; there is a closed naval station, and the islands are important nesting places for seabirds. In 1993, administrative control of Midway was transferred from the US Department of the Navy to the US Department of the Interior's Fish and Wildlife Service.

NORTHERN MARIANAS

The Northern Marianas, a US commonwealth in the Western Pacific Ocean, is comprised of the Mariana Islands excluding Guam (a separate political entity). Located between 12° and 21°N and 144° and 146°E, it consists of 16 volcanic islands with a total land area of about 475 sq km (183.5 sq mi). Only six of the islands are inhabited, and most of the people live on the three largest islands—Rota, 85 sq km (33 sq mi); Saipan, 122 sq km (47 sq mi); and Tinian, 101 sq km (39 sq mi).

The climate is tropical, with relatively little seasonal change; temperatures average 21–29°C (70–85°F), and relative humidity is generally high. Rainfall averages 216 cm (85 in) per year. The southern islands, which include Rota, Saipan, and Tinian, are generally lower and covered with moderately heavy tropical vegetation. The northern islands are more rugged, reaching a high point of 959 m (3,146 ft) on Agrihan, and are generally barren due to erosion and insufficient rainfall. Pagan and Agrihan have active volcanos, and typhoons are common from August to November. Insects are numerous and ocean birds and fauna are abundant. The Marianas mallard is a local endangered species.

The Northern Marianas had an estimated population of 52,284 in mid-1996. Three-fourths of the population is descended from the original Micronesian inhabitants, known as Chamorros. There are also many descendants of migrants from the Caroline Islands and smaller numbers of Filipino and Korean laborers and settlers from the US mainland. English is the official language and Chamorro and Carolinian are taught in school. However, only 14% of the population speaks English in the home. About 90% of the people are Roman Catholic.

It is believed that the Marianas were settled by migrants from the Philippines and Indonesia. Excavations on Saipan have yielded evidence of settlement around 1500 BC. The first European to reach the Marianas, in 1521, was Ferdinand Magellan. The islands were ruled by Spain until the Spanish defeat by the US in the Spanish-American War (1898). Guam was then ceded to the US and the rest of the Marianas were sold to Germany. When World War I broke out, Japan took over the Northern Marianas and other German-held islands in the Western Pacific. These islands (the Northern Marianas, Carolines, and Marshalls) were placed under Japanese administration as a League of Nations mandate on 17 December 1920.

Upon its withdrawal from the League in 1935, Japan began to fortify the islands, and in World War II they served as important military bases. Several of the islands were the scene of heavy fighting during the war. In the battle for control of Saipan in June 1944, some 23,000 Japanese and 3,500 US troops lost their lives in one day's fighting. As each island was occupied by US troops, it became subject to US authority in accordance with the international law of belligerent occupation. The US planes that dropped atomic bombs on Hiroshima and Nagasaki, bringing an end to the war, took off from Tinian.

On 18 July 1947, the Northern Mariana, Caroline, and Marshall islands formally became a UN trust territory under US administration. This Trust Territory of the Pacific Islands was administered by the US Department of the Navy until 1 July 1951, when administration was transferred to the Department of the Interior. From 1953 to 1962, the Northern Marianas, with the exception of Rota, were administered by the Department of the Navy.

The people of the Northern Marianas voted to become a US commonwealth by a majority of 78.8% in a plebiscite held on 17 June 1975. A covenant approved by the US Congress in March 1976 provided for the separation of the Northern Marianas from the Caroline and Marshall island groups, and for the Marianas' transition to a commonwealth status similar to that of Puerto Rico. The islands became internally self-governing in January 1978. On 3 November 1986, US President Ronald Reagan proclaimed the Northern Marianas a self-governing commonwealth; its people became US citizens. The termination of the trusteeship was approved by the UN Trusteeship Council in May 1986 and received the required approval from the UN Security Council. On 3 November 1986, the Constitution of the Commonwealth of the Northern Marianas Islands came into force.

A governor and a lieutenant governor are popularly elected for four-year terms. The legislature consists of 9 senators elected for four-year terms and 14 representatives elected for two-year terms. A district court handles matters involving federal law and a commonwealth court has jurisdiction over local matters.

The traditional economic activities were subsistence agriculture, livestock raising, and fishing, but much agricultural land was destroyed or damaged during World War II and agriculture has never resumed its prewar importance. Today, government employment and tourism are the mainstays of the economy. Tourism employs about 50% of the work force. The construction industry is also expanding, and there is some small-scale industry, chiefly handicrafts and food processing.

The Northern Marianas is heavily dependent on federal funds; the US government provided $228 million for capital developments, government operations, and special programs between 1986 and 1992. In 1996/97, federal grants to the Northern Marianas amounted to $31 million. The US also pays to lease property on Saipan, Tinian, and Farallon de Medinilla islands for defense purposes. The principal exports are garments, milk, and meat; imports include foods, petroleum, construction materials, and vehicles. US currency is the official medium of exchange.

Health care is primarily the responsibility of the commonwealth government and has improved substantially since 1978. Tuberculosis, once the major health problem, has been controlled. There is a hospital on Saipan and health centers on Tinian and Rota. The largest hospital in the commonwealth is a 74 bed, 110,000 square foot facility.

Education is free and compulsory for children between the ages of 8 and 14, and literacy is high. Enrollment in primary and secondary schools in 1995/96 totaled 10,634. Northern Marianas College had an enrollment of 1,253 in 1994/95. There are 2 AM, 1 FM, and 2 cable television stations.

PALMYRA ATOLL

Palmyra, an atoll in the Central Pacific Ocean, containing some 50 islets with a total area of some 10 sq km (4 sq mi), is situated about 1,600 km (1,000 mi) ssw of Honolulu at 5°52′N and 162°5′w. It was discovered in 1802 by the USS *Palmyra* and formally annexed by the US in 1912, and was under the jurisdiction of the city of Honolulu until 1959, when Hawaii became the 50th state of the US. It is now the responsibility of the US Department of the Interior. The atoll is privately owned by the Fullard-Leo family of Hawaii.

Kingman Reef, NW of Palmyra Atoll at 6°25′N and 162°23′N, was discovered by the US in 1874, annexed by the US in 1922, and became a naval reservation in 1934. Now abandoned, it is under the control of the US Department of the Navy. The reef only has an elevation of 1 m (3 ft) and is awash most of the time, making it hazardous for ships.

WAKE ISLAND

Wake Island, actually a coral atoll and three islets (Wake, Peale, and Wilkes) about 8 km (5 mi) long by 3.6 km (2.25 mi) wide, lies in the North Pacific 3,380 km (2,100 mi) w of Honolulu at 19°17′N and 166°35′E. The total land and water area is about 8 sq km (3 sq mi). Discovered by the British in 1796, Wake was long uninhabited.

In 1898, a US expeditionary force en route to Manila landed on the island. The US formally claimed Wake in 1899. It was made a US naval reservation in 1934, and became a civil aviation station in 1935. Captured by the Japanese on 23 December 1941, Wake was subsequently the target of several US air raids. It was surrendered by the Japanese in September 1945 and has thereafter remained a US unincorporated territory under the jurisdiction, since 1972, of the Department of the Air Force.

In 1995, 302 US military personnel and contractors inhabited Wake Island. The island is used for missile launches by the US Army's Space and Strategic Defense Command. It is a stopover and fueling station for civilian and military aircraft flying between Honolulu, Guam, and Japan.

UZBEKISTAN

Republic of Uzbekistan
Uzbekiston Respublikasi

CAPITAL: Tashkent (Toshkent).

FLAG: Horizontal bands of blue (top), white, and green separated by narrow red bands; white crescent moon and twelve stars on the blue band.

MONETARY UNIT: The som is the official currency, introduced when Uzbekistan left the ruble zone in November 1993. SOM1=$0.00520 ($1=SOM192.30) as of 31 March 2000.

WEIGHTS AND MEASURES: The metric system is used.

HOLIDAYS: Independence Day, 1 September.

TIME: 5 PM = noon GMT.

¹LOCATION, SIZE, AND EXTENT

Uzbekistan is located in central Asia bordering the Aral Sea, between Kazakhstan and Turkmenistan. Comparatively, it is slightly larger than the state of California, with a total area of 447,400 sq km (172,742 sq mi). Uzbekistan shares boundaries with Kazakhstan on the N, Kyrgyzstan and Tajikistan on the E, Afghanistan on the S, and Turkmenistan on the SW. Uzbekistan's boundary length totals 6,221 km (3,866 mi). Its capital city, Tashkent, is located in the eastern part of the country.

²TOPOGRAPHY

Uzbekistan consists of mostly flat to rolling sandy desert with dunes. The Fergana Valley lies in the east surrounded by mountainous Tajikistan and Kyrgyzstan. The Aral Sea lies in the northwest. There is semiarid grassland in the east. Ten percent of Uzbekistan's land is arable, most of which is under irrigation.

³CLIMATE

The climate is mid-latitude climatic desert. Temperatures in the desert can reach upwards of 32°C (90°F). In the capital city of Tashkent the mean temperature is 32°C (90°F) in the summer. In January the mean temperature is 3°C (37°F). Winter temperatures can fall below −23°C (−10°F) in some areas. There is very little rainfall in the country.

⁴FLORA AND FAUNA

Ecological damage has left much of the country devoid of animal life. The country, a member of the former Soviet Union, was part of Nikita Krushchev's 1954 "Virgin-Lands" plan. Khrushchev wanted Soviet farmers to grow cotton and grain on the steppes of Uzbekistan. At one point the country grew 70% of the Soviet Union's cotton. Unfortunately the farmers had to irrigate the crops to obtain meaningful results. Now the Amu Darya and Syr Darya rivers run dry in certain places. Half of the Aral Sea is now a dry lake bed, and the land is poisoned from the overuse of fertilizer.

⁵ENVIRONMENT

Uzbekistan's main environmental problems are soil salinity, land pollution, and water pollution. In 1992, Uzbekistan had the world's 27th highest level of carbon dioxide emissions, which totaled 123.5 million metric tons, a per capita level of 5.75 metric

tons. Chemicals used in farming, such as DDT, contribute to the pollution of the soil. Desertification is a continuing concern. The nation's forestlands are also threatened and continue to dwindle. Between 1983 and 1993, 42.% of Uzbekistan's forest and woodland area was lost.

The country's water supply also suffers from toxic chemical pollutants from industrial activity as well as fertilizers and pesticides. Uzbekistan has 1,051.9 cu mi of water. Sixty-five percent is used for farming and 29% is used for industrial purposes. The Aral Sea has been drying up and, as a result, pesticides and natural salts in its water have become increasingly concentrated. The nation's cities produce 45.8 million tons of solid waste per year.

As of 1994, only 0.5% of Uzbekistan's total land area was protected. In 1994, 20 of its mammal species were endangered, and 38 of its bird species were threatened with extinction. Threatened or rare species include the markhor, Central Asia cobra, and Asiatic wild dog.

⁶POPULATION

The population of Uzbekistan in 2000 was estimated at 24,422,518. An estimated 4.4% of the population is 65 years of age or older. The projected population for the year 2005 is 26,111,000, assuming a crude birthrate of 23 per 1,000 population and a death rate of 8, resulting in a natural rate of change of 1.5% for the period 2000–2005. The population rate of change between 1995 and 2000 was 1.9%. The population density in 1998 was 58 per sq km (150 per sq mi).

It was estimated that 42% of the population lived in urban areas in 2000, up from 41% in 1980. The capital city, Tashkent, and its surrounding metropolitan area, had a 2000 population of 2,495,000. Samarkand had a population of about 370,000.

⁷MIGRATION

Emigration to other former USSR republics exceeded immigration by 328,200 during 1979–90. In 1991, an estimated 400,000 Russians departed from Uzbekistan. As of 1996, 250,000 Crimean Tatars had left Central Asia for the Ukraine; most these Tatars were from Uzbekistan. In September 1999, there were an estimated 30,000 Tajik refugees and 8,000 Afghan refugees living in Uzbekistan; however, only 1,135 refugees and asylum seekers were registered with UNHCR. Up until 1999, refugees and asylum seekers were assigned no special status and were considered ordinary foreigners. However, in June 1999 the government completed a draft of the Migration Law, which passed the Cabinet of Ministers. The first reading of the draft Migration Law in Parliament was slated for sometime between December 1999 and March 2000. In August 1999, UNHCR handed over the list of registered refugees to the Ministry of Foreign Affairs; the government guaranteed that those on the list would not be detained or deported. The net migration rate was -2.44 migrants per 1,000 population in 1999.

⁸ETHNIC GROUPS

In 1996, 80% of the population was Uzbek. Russians constituted 5.5%; Tajiks made up 5%; Kazakhs accounted for 3%; Karakalpaks for 2.5%; Tatars 1.5%; and others 2.5%.

⁹LANGUAGES

Uzbek, the state language, was the most widely spoken non-Slavic tongue in the USSR. It is a Turkic language with six vowels—virtually identical to those of Tajik, which has surely influenced it—rather than the original eight or nine. In 1993, it was decided that the language would be written in the Roman alphabet rather than in the Cyrillic alphabet. In 1999, Uzbek was spoken by 74.3% of the population in Uzbekistan; Russian was spoken by 14.2%; Tajik by 4.4%; and other various languages by 7.1%.

¹⁰RELIGIONS

Freedom of religion is guaranteed under the constitution of 1992, adopted after independence, and there is a specific provision prohibiting the establishment of any state religion. Ethnic Uzbeks are primarily adherents of the Hanafi sect of Sunni Islam, but the Wahhabi sect has flourished as well in recent years. Muslims account for about 88% of the population; Eastern Orthodox Christians for 9%; and others for 3%. In 1999, Uzbekistan had a significant Jewish population of some 30,000, primarily in the cities of Tashkent, Bukhara, and Samarkand. Almost 70,000 Jews have emigrated to Israel or the US since independence. Other minority religions include small communities of Baptists, Roman Catholics, Lutherans, Seventh-Day Adventists, evangelical and Pentecostal Christians, Buddhists, Baha'is, and Hare Krishnas.

¹¹TRANSPORTATION

Uzbekistan has some 3,380 km (2,100 mi) of railroad track in common carrier service (not including industrial lines); separate lines serve eastern and western regions. In 1996, there were also 81,600 km (50,706 mi) of highways, of which 71,237 km (44,227 mi) are hard-surfaced. As a landlocked nation, there is no direct connection to the open sea; the Zeravshan River is the largest inland waterway. Uzbekistan had 3 airports in 1997, all with paved runways. In 1997, a total of 1,566,000 passengers were carried on scheduled domestic and international airline flights.

¹²HISTORY

Some parts of present-day Uzbekistan have been inhabited since the Paleolithic era. The first states in the region were Khwarazm, Bactria, Sogdiana, and the Parthian Empire, in the first millennium BC. The territory was consolidated under the Achaemenids in the 6th century BC, until it was conquered by Alexander the Great, 329–327 BC. The Greeks were displaced by the Tochari in the 3rd century BC. From the 1st century BC to the 4th century AD Uzbekistan was part of the Kushana Kingdom. This in turn was replaced by the Ephthalite state.

In the 6th century the area was part of the West Turkic Kaganate, a loose confederation of largely nomadic tribes. By the 8th century the region was conquered by the Arabs, who introduced Islam. The Ummayid dynasty was displaced by the Abbasids in 747–750. In the 9th century the Samanids took control of most of Central Asia, including Uzbekistan. Turkic tribes again began to push into the area from the east in the 10th century, eventually forming the Karakhanid state. A lesser part of that state, Khwarazm, grew more powerful in the 12th century and came to dominate most of Central Asia.

Genghiz Khan's Mongols invaded in 1219, conquering all of Central Asia by 1221. In 1224 Genghiz Khan's son Chagatai was made ruler of this area. As Chingisid influence waned, Timur (Tamerlane, 1336–1405) established an empire in Samarkand. Upon his death it split into Khorasan, ruled by his son Shah Rukh, and Maweranahr, ruled by his grandson, Ulgh Beg. Although Timur is now claimed as the father of the modern Uzbeks, more likely candidates are the Sheibanid, nomadic Uzbeks who fought to take the area in the early 16th century. They settled among the other populations and became farmers, making Bukhara their capital.

In the 16th century Khwarazm, Balkh, and Khiva separated from Bukhara, becoming separate principalities. Bukhara was conquered by Persia in 1740, but sovereignty was retaken soon after by the Mangyt dynasty, which ruled until 1920. In the early 19th century the Kokand Khanate grew powerful in the eastern part of present-day Uzbekistan.

Russia had begun trading with Bukhara, Khiva, and Kokand in the 18th century. Concern about British expansion in India and Afghanistan led eventually to Russian conquest, which began in the 1860s and ended in the 1880s, when Uzbekistan became part of Turkestan guberniia, with Bukhara and Khiva administered as separate emirates under Russian protection.

In 1916 Tsar Nicholas II issued a call for Central Asian males to be drafted into labor battalions. This sparked resistance throughout the region, including in Uzbekistan, which was violently repressed. During the conflict from 1917–1920, Uzbekistan was the site of competing attempts to create governments; the Bolsheviks announced a short-lived Turkestan Autonomous Republic, while a Muslim Congress also attempted an Autonomous Government of Turkestan. Red Army forces intervened savagely, but armed resistance continued as late as 1924, in the so-called Basmachi Rebellion.

The Uzbek Soviet Socialist Republic was created in 1925. In 1929, Tajikistan, which had been an administrative sub-unit, was elevated to full republic status, changing the boundaries. They were changed once again in 1936.

Under the leadership of long-time leader S. Rashidov, Uzbekistan was politically conservative during the 1970s and early 1980s. The republic was targeted for anti-corruption purges in the mid-1980s, when considerable fraud in the cotton industry was discovered. The leader as of 2000, Islam Karimov, was appointed by Moscow in 1989.

In March 1990, Karimov was elected to the newly created post of president by the Uzbek Supreme Soviet. Uzbekistan declared independence on 1 September 1991, in the aftermath of the abortive Moscow coup of 19–21 August. Karimov's presidency was reaffirmed in an election in December 1991. Since then, however, Karimov has been increasingly hostile to even the most basic tenets of democracy. True opposition parties were banned in 1992 and political reformers have been jailed or have fled the country. Parliamentary elections to the 250-seat Majlis were held on 24 December 1994 and 15 January 1995, with 231 seats going to Karimov's People's Democratic Party—the former Uzbek Communist Party. Following the elections, President Karimov held a referendum that extended his presidency until 2000.

Despite his anti-democratic leanings, Karimov received little criticism from the West or from Russia (which, in fact, supplies him with ample military backing) since he is seen as a buffer against the fundamentalist Muslim political and revolutionary movements in Central Asia—notably those in Afghanistan and in

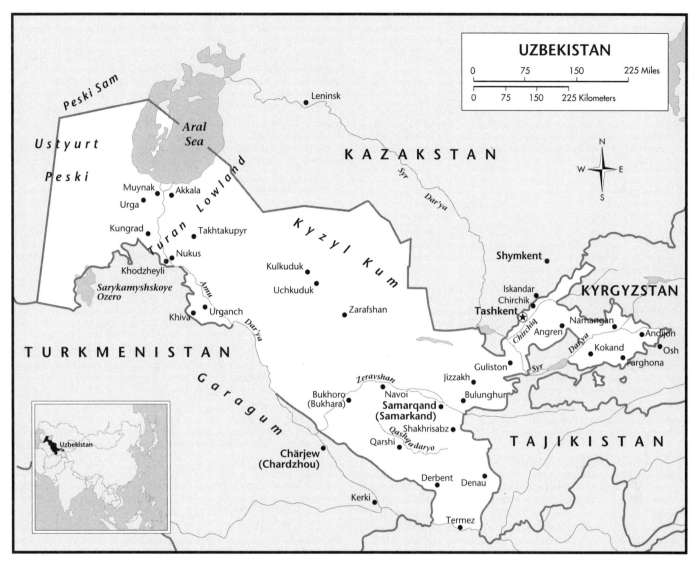

LOCATION: 41°0′N; 64°0′E. **BOUNDARY LENGTHS:** Total boundary lengths, 6,221 km (3,866 mi); Afghanistan, 137 km (85.1 mi); Kazakhstan, 2,203 km (1,369 miles); Kyrgyzstan, 1,099 km (683 mi); Tajikistan, 1,161 km (721.4 mi); Turkmenistan, 1,621 km (1,007.3 mi).

neighboring Tajikistan. In fact, Uzbekistan supplies arms to the secular factions in both countries' civil wars. Islamists in Uzbekistan have been less successful in fomenting revolt than in neighboring nations, but there is a sizeable movement, largely underground, in the Ferghana Valley in the country's eastern region.

13 GOVERNMENT

The state constitution adopted on 8 December 1992 mandates a civil democratic society. The executive branch consists of the president and his appointed prime minister and Cabinet of Ministers. The legislative branch consists of a unicameral Supreme Soviet of 150 seats. The judicial branch is appointed by the president, subject to legislative confirmation, for 5- and 10-year terms. The Supreme Assembly replaced the Soviet-era legislature and has 250 members. In 1992, President Islam Karimov banned opposition parties. The president is the head of state and has responsibility for the function of the other branches of government as well as for making sure the constitution is observed. He essentially rules by decree.

14 POLITICAL PARTIES

In the Soviet period, the only legal political party was the Communist Party. As Soviet control began to disintegrate in 1989–90, a number of mass-based "informal organizations" appeared which grew to be the equivalents of parties, although not all were legally registered. The largest, claiming as many as 100,000 members, was Birlik (Unity), founded by Abdurakhim Pulatov in 1989. Erk (Freedom) was founded in 1990 by M. Solih, who split away from Birlik; in 1991, Solih was a candidate for president, drawing approximately 12% of the vote. Another group, never legally registered, was the Islamic Renaissance Party.

After independence President Islam Karimov began to establish strong authoritarian control. Political opposition was forbidden. Opposition leaders have been beaten, jailed, and exiled. There were five registered parties as of 2000, but their platforms are essentially identical, and all parties with seats in parliament support the president. The People's Democratic Party (NDP) is the renamed Communist Party. Also registered were the Fatherland Progress Party (VTP) led by Vatan Tarrakiyeti; the Adolat (Justice) Social Democratic Party; the Democratic National Rebirth Party; and the Self-Sacrificers Party. Political pressure group, the Erk (Freedom) Democratic Party, reformed as a pro-Karimov party after repudiating founder, Muhamd Solih, who was forced into political exile. Another pressure group, the Birlik (Unity) Movement was officially banned in mid-1993, but continued to exist.

15LOCAL GOVERNMENT

The republic is divided into 12 oblasts, or provinces. There is also the autonomous Republic of Karakalpakstan, which has the right of legal secession, though is unlikely to exercise it. Administration is performed by locally elected councils, overseen by presidential appointees.

16JUDICIAL SYSTEM

The Soviet judiciary system, featuring trials by panels of three judges, still prevails. There are three levels of courts: district courts (people's courts) at the lowest level, regional courts, and the Supreme Court. District court decisions may be appealed through the higher levels. Under the constitution, the president appoints judges for 10-year terms.

Defendants have the right to an attorney and most trials are open to the public. In political cases, the judiciary may experience pressure from the government. A new criminal code is in place, eliminating the economic crimes punishable by death in the former Soviet code.

17ARMED FORCES

Uzbekistan has an army of 50,000 and an air force of 4,000, with 150 combat aircraft and 42 attack helicopters. In addition, it has about 17,000–19,000 internal security forces and a national guard of 1,000 organized into a single brigade. The defense budget for 1997 was $200 million or 1.4% of GDP.

18INTERNATIONAL COOPERATION

Uzbekistan was admitted to the UN on 2 March 1992. It is also a member of the OSCE, EBRD, FAO, IAEA, IMF, UNCTAD, and the World Bank. The country has signed the Nuclear Non-proliferation Treaty and is a member of the CIS. It has close ties with the US, Austria, South Korea, Malaysia, Indonesia, and Turkey. The US established formal ties with Uzbekistan in February 1992.

19ECONOMY

Although characterized by one of the lowest per capita incomes in the Central Asian and other post-Soviet republics, Uzbekistan's rich reserves of gold, oil, natural gas, coal, silver, and copper provide a promising endowment for future development. As a major source of cotton for the textile industry in the former USSR and the world's third largest cotton producer, Uzbekistan has a predominantly agricultural economy. Agriculture and agro-processing accounted for about half of GNP in 1996. In addition, much of the industrial production is linked to agriculture, including cotton harvesting equipment, textiles, and chemical fertilizers and pesticides. Only 12% of Uzbekistan's total cotton production and 60% of its silk cocoons were processed locally in the early 1990s, reflecting the country's principal role as supplier of raw material goods for downstream manufacturing elsewhere in the former USSR.

Uzbekistan has a centrally planned economic structure in which most production and employment remains in the state sector, and all health, education, social security, and welfare services are provided by the government. Measures taken toward establishing a greater market orientation within the economy have been more cautious than in many other post-Soviet countries. A differentiated process of price control liberalization was applied to the wholesale and retail sectors in 1991 in an attempt to avoid socially destabilizing surges in consumer prices. Nevertheless, inflation ran 790% in retail prices and 2,700% in wholesale prices in 1992; by the end of the year, real wage earnings had declined by 56%. The disruption of trading arrangements with former Soviet republics and the cessation of transfers from the Union's central government is evident in the erosion of other major economic indicators since 1990. In addition to a seriously deteriorating fiscal balance, estimated GDP shrank by 17% between 1991 and 1994. Following a breakdown in agreements over the conditions of a new ruble zone with Russia and other CIS countries, Uzbekistan adopted its own currency, the som, in late 1993.

When it became apparent that the slow pace of economic reform was not working, the government increased efforts to move from a command-driven to a market-oriented economy. Reforms included tighter monetary policies, cooperation with international financial institutions, increased privatization of state owned enterprises, and an improved environment for foreign investors. In response, the economy slowed its decline to 1% in 1996 and the inflation rate dropped to 35%, down from 1,300% in 1994. Additional reforms announced in 1996 aimed at increasing the private sector's share of GDP to 60%.

In 1999, the state continued to dominate the economy. GDP grew by 2.4% in 1997, and 3.4% in 1998, despite the Russian and Asian financial crises. Inflation was holding steady at 30%.

20INCOME

The US Central Intelligence Agency (CIA) reports that in 1998 Uzbekistan's gross domestic product (GDP) was estimated at $59.2 billion. The per capita GDP was estimated at $2,500. The annual growth rate of GDP was estimated at 1%. The average inflation rate in 1998 was 40%. The CIA defines GDP as the value of all final goods and services produced within a nation in a given year and computed on the basis of purchasing power parity (PPP) rather than value as measured on the basis of the rate of exchange. It was estimated that agriculture accounted for 31% of GDP, industry 27%, and services 42%.

The World Bank reports that for the same period per capita private consumption (in PPP terms) was $1,570. Private consumption includes expenditures of individuals, households, and non-governmental organizations. It was estimated that between 1990 and 1998 private consumption grew at an annual rate of 9.5%. Approximately 34% of household consumption was spent on food, 13% on fuel, 4% on health care, and 7% on education. The richest 10% of the population accounted for approximately 25% of household consumption and the poorest 10% approximately 3.1%.

21LABOR

The labor force was estimated at roughly ten million in 1998. As of 1995, agriculture and forestry engaged 44% of the labor force, services, 36%; and industry 20%.

The labor code adopted on 2 June 1992 recognizes the right for all workers to voluntarily create and join unions, which may in turn voluntarily associate territorially or sectorally and may choose their own international affiliations. Unions also were granted independence from government administrative and economic bodies (except where provided by law), and were encourage to develop their own charters, structure, and executive bodies.

The standard work week is 41 hours, and minimum wages are set by the Ministry of Finance in consultation with the Federation of Trade Unions. As of September 1999, the minimum wage was about $10.00 per month. Some factories have reduced work hours to avoid layoffs, and overtime pay is rarely given.

The minimum working age is 16, although 15-year-olds may work a shorter workday. The Labor Ministry has an inspection service to enforce compliance with this requirement. The Labor Ministry also inconsistently enforces occupational health and safely regulations, although many industrial plants continue to be hazardous, and most workers lack protective clothing and equipment.

22AGRICULTURE

Uzbekistan was the former Soviet Union's largest producer of fruits and vegetables. About 15% of the total area is crop land. In 1998, about 31% of GDP came from agriculture.

During the Soviet era, cotton was grown on almost half of all sown land. Cotton is grown in the crescent beginning in the Fergana Valley and extending south along the Tien Shan Mountains to Samarkand and Bokhara, and then west along the Amu Darya River. All cotton is flood irrigated. Plantings are generally in April, with the harvest coming in late August or early September. Fields are usually planted with alfalfa or corn every four or five years, but many fields are planted without rotation, leading to declining yields. Since independence, Uzbekistan has embarked on a policy to diversify agriculture and annual cotton lint production has declined to less than 1 million tons. Almost 40% of the gross value of agricultural production is derived from cotton; Uzbekistan was the world's fifth-largest producer of cotton lint in 1998 (after China, the US, India, and Pakistan), accounting for 5.3% of world supply, but cotton production declined severely in 1999, and worldwide prices dropped as well, causing serious strain in this important segment of the Uzbek economy.

Rice, wheat, barley, and corn are important grain crops. Rice is produced on 48 specialized state farms, and about 85% of the rice crop comes from the southwestern part of Karakalpakistan and the Khorezm region. In 1998, over 3.7 million tons of cereals were produced. Sesame, tobacco, onions, flax, and various fruits are also grown. Mulberry trees have been grown for silkworm breeding since the 4th century; some 2,000 tons of silk were produced in 1998.

23ANIMAL HUSBANDRY

Sheep are the main livestock product, with Karakyl sheep (noted for their black wool) raised in the Bukhara region. The livestock population in 1998 included 8 million sheep, 5.3 million head of cattle, 800,000 goats, 195,000 pigs, 26,000 donkeys, 150,000 horses, 26,000 camels, and about 12 million chickens. Meat production that year totaled 529,000 tons, of which 76% was beef, 15% was mutton, 3% was pork, and 6% was poultry. Wool (greasy) production in 1998 was estimated at 18,000 tons.

24FISHING

Fishing occurs mainly in the Fergana Valley. The Aral Sea in the north (the world's fourth-largest lake) is too saline and becoming more so, especially since its water surface area has decreased by 33% since 1960. The total catch in 1997 was 10,565 tons, primarily carp.

25FORESTRY

Forests and woodlands make up 22% of the total land area, mostly in the Fergana Valley and Zeravshan regions. Commercial forestry is not a significant part of the economy. Uzbekistan imported $5.8 million in forestry products during 1997.

26MINING

Besides natural gas, Uzbekistan possesses several mineral commodities. Uzbekistan was one of the world's leading producers of gold in 1996, which provided a significant source of foreign currency earnings. The nonferrous metals industry includes the mining of bismuth, cadmium, copper, lead, molybdenum, palladium, silver, tin, tungsten, and zinc. Metal production includes bismuth, cadmium, copper, gold, indium, molybdenum, rhenium, tungsten, silver, and zinc metals.

Uzbekistan also produces industrial minerals such as feldspar and fluorospar, along with a range of minerals for the construction industry.

Copper, lead-zinc, and molybdenum are mined at the Almalyk complex northeast of Tasken; gold at the Muruntau complex near Zarafshan; and fluorospar at the Toytepa complex, south of Tashkent. Production of fertilizers is an important part of the domestic chemical industry; the fertilizers are used for the production of cotton.

27ENERGY AND POWER

Uzbekistan is the eighth-largest producer of natural gas in the world. In 1999, production totaled 55.5 billion cu m (1,960 billion cu ft); proven reserves amounted to as much as 2.5 trillion cu m (74–88 trillion cu ft) at the start of 1998, located mainly in the western Qizilkum Desert.

Oil production in 1999 amounted to 213,000 barrels per day, mostly from the wells in the Fergana Valley. Since 1991, Uzbekistan has more than doubled its oil production and is now essentially self-sufficient in petroleum. Hydroelectric stations on the Syrdar'ya, Chirchiq, and Naryn rivers depend largely on Kyrgyzstan and Tajikistan for their power. In 1998, total installed electrical capacity was 11,751,000 kW, and production came to 43,470 million kWh in the same year. Brown coal deposits at the head of the Angren Valley, southeast of Tashkent, are used for local electricity generation. About 3.3 million tons of coal were produced in 1998.

28INDUSTRY

Growth of Uzbekistan's industrial production averaged 3.2% in the 1980s, although on a per capita basis, the republic's industrial output remained less than half that of the USSR average by the end of the decade. Most industry is based on the processing of local agricultural products. Soft goods (mainly cotton, wool, and silk fiber) and processed foods (including cottonseed oil, meat, dried fruit, wines, and tobacco) accounted for about 39% and 13% of industrial production respectively in 1990; their manufacture was concentrated in Tashkent and the Fergana Valley.

Uzbeklegprom, the state association for the production of light industry goods, produces about 90% of Uzbekistan's textiles. Production figures fell from 700 million sq m in 1993 to 650 million sq m in 1995, when total textile production was valued at $510 million. In the late 1990s, Uzbeklegprom sought to boost capacity with the assistance of several joint venture partners. Most textiles mills in Uzbekistan use outdated machinery with technology from the 1970s, and the investment cost of updating the entire industry was estimated at between $500 million and $1 billion.

Uzbekistan's machinery industry is the primary producer of machines and heavy equipment in Central Asia. Uzavtosanoat is the cornerstone of the country's automotive industry, and has developed joint ventures with Daimler-Benz (Germany) and Daewoo (ROK). The UzDaewoo-Avto plant in Andizhan began production in 1996 with the goal of 200,000 units annually by 2000. The aerospace industry centers around the Chkalov Tashkent Aircraft Production Co., a government-controlled enterprise that is one of the largest and most significant aircraft assembly plants in Central Asia.

Metal processing industries are clustered in the Olmaliq-Oharangan (Almalyk-Akhangaran) complex, southeast of Tashkent. Metal alloys, wire, rods and sheet and gas-based nitrogen are manufactured in Chirchiq, close to the Kazakhstan border in the northeast. Chemical fertilizers used mainly in cotton production are also produced in the Chirchiq.

[29]SCIENCE AND TECHNOLOGY

The Uzbek Academy of Sciences, headquartered in Tashkent, has departments of physical-mathematical sciences; mechanics; control processes; informatics; chemical-technological and earth sciences; and biological sciences. Uzbekistan has 45 research institutes conducting research in agriculture and veterinary sciences, technology, natural sciences, and medicine. Twenty-three colleges and universities offer scientific and technical training. In 1987–97, 1,763 scientists and engineers and 314 technicians per 1 million population were engaged in research and development.

[30]DOMESTIC TRADE

Although dominated by state-owned stores and distribution channels under the Soviet economy, retailing has seen a marked shift toward private business. Since 1992, thousands of small businesses have been privatized or leased to worker collectives, with the most progress in retail trade, consumer services, public catering, and local industry. Urban markets provide an important outlet for the sale of vegetables and other foodstuffs.

[31]FOREIGN TRADE

While supplying the former USSR with light industry goods (mainly cotton fiber), basic equipment related to agriculture and agricultural processing, and some oil, Uzbekistan has been highly dependent on the other former Soviet republics for critically needed grain, food, machinery, and other industrial inputs.

In 1998, exports included cotton, gold, natural gas, fertilizers, ferrous metals, textiles, food products, and automobiles. Imports included grain, machinery and parts, consumer durables, and foods.

Principal trading partners in 1998 (in millions of US dollars) were as follows:

COUNTRY	EXPORTS	IMPORTS	BALANCE
Russia	472	529	-57
Tajikistan	181	339	-158
Turkmenistan	155	7	148
Italy	148	74	74
Korea	129	422	-293
Germany	117	304	-187
France	88	152	-64
Kazakhstan	60	164	-104
United States	31	162	-131
Ukraine	27	153	-126

[32]BALANCE OF PAYMENTS

Uzbekistan was extremely reliant on cotton exports as a means of trade throughout its association with the former USSR, but earnings fluctuated widely from year to year depending on the performance of the agricultural sector. Exports of natural gas and petroleum generated much needed hard currency reserves within the next several years.

Uzbekistan received substantial financial support from the World Bank, IMF, and other multilateral lending institutions. Proceeds are used to finance the cotton industry, oil and gas development. to provide a social safety net, to maintain the water supply, and to further privatization efforts.

The US Central Intelligence Agency reports that in 1998 the purchasing power parity of Uzbekistan's exports was $3.8 billion while imports totaled $4.1 billion resulting in a trade balance of -$300 million.

[33]BANKING AND SECURITIES

After 1993, the banking system was headed by the National Bank of Uzbekistan (NBU), the former local branch of the Soviet Gosbank. The NBU attempted to increase its supervision over Uzbekistan's banks, the most important of which are state-owned. In 1997, the Central Bank of Uzbekistan (CBU) was in charge of the country's two-tier banking system, and had the responsibility of issuing soms, the country's currency unit, and regulating the commercial banks by setting reserve requirements and the discount rate. The other important state bank was the Uzbek National Bank of Foreign Economic Activities, which dealt exclusively with the foreign exchange rate.

Commercial banks in the country include the Uzbek Commercial Bank and the Uzbek Joint-Stock Innovation Bank. The country does not have a security market, but the trading of commodities is widely practiced in the country.

There were increasing hints from the government that the banking sector is in trouble. The first indicator of a banking crisis came with the sudden and unpublicized sacking in January 1997 of Ahmat Ibotov, the head of Promstroi Bank, the second-largest bank in Uzbekistan after the NBU. Then, on 26 February 1997, Mr. Karimov launched a scathing attack on the country's banks, accusing them of being corrupt and bureaucratic. The president also blamed the banks for maintaining excessively high interest rates. The CBU has also recently criticized the banks for poor credit risk evaluation and poor procedures over the issuing of bank guarantees.

In 1996, the authorities closed three banks, all supposedly for breaching lending limits set by the CBU. One of the main problems in the banking sector is over-concentration. The three largest banks, all of which are state-owned, control 86% of commercial banks' assets. The main culprit is the NBU, which accounts for 45% of assets.

[34]INSURANCE

Among the insurance companies doing business in Uzbekistan in 1997 were: GOSSTRAKH State Insurance Company of the Republic of Uzbekistan; JV, UMID Joint Stock Insurance Co.; MADAD Joint Stock Insurance Agency; and UZBEKINVEST National Insurance Co. of the Republic of Uzbekistan, which is government-owned.

[35]PUBLIC FINANCE

Uzbekistan's spiraling inflation as a member of the ruble zone necessitated the introduction of a transition currency after it left the ruble zone in November 1993. In 1994, the government undertook economic reforms, but privatization efforts have fallen short of expectations. Subsidies for basic consumer goods (except some food staples and energy products) and subsidized credit to industrial enterprises were substantially reduced during 1994 and 1995. In response, the budget deficit fell from a high of 16% of GDP in 1993 to 3.3% in 1995, but had escalated to nearly 7% by 1997. The external debt, $1.5 billion at the end of 1994, more than doubled to $3.3 billion by 1997. An enterprise profit tax, a value-added tax, and an excise tax on cotton supply the bulk of government revenues.

The US Central Intelligence Agency (CIA) estimates that in 1997 Uzbekistan's central government took in revenues of approximately $4.4 billion and had expenditures of $4.7 billion including capital expenditures of $1.1 billion. Overall, the government registered a deficit of approximately $300 million.

[36]TAXATION

The maximum personal income tax rate in Uzbekistan is 50%; corporate rates range from 10–60%, with a standard rate of 18%. Also levied is a 25% value-added tax.

[37]CUSTOMS AND DUTIES

Uzbekistan is a member of the Economic Cooperation Organization, together with Afghanistan, Azerbaijan, Kazakhstan, Kyrgyzstan, Tajikistan, Turkmenistan, Iran, Pakistan, and Turkey. Uzbekistan has also formed an economic union with

Kazakhstan and Kyrgyzstan. Imports are subject to customs duties at rates ranging from 1% to 4%.

38 FOREIGN INVESTMENT

While Uzbekistan's store of valuable natural resources is likely to provide a strong basis for covering the costs of long-term economic development, significant amounts of external funding will be needed to support its short-term development plans over the next decade. To stimulate foreign direct investment, legislation adopted in mid-1991 provides tax incentives and guarantees against expropriation, though falling short of securing the right to repatriate profits and third-party dispute arbitration. By the end of 1992, 450 joint ventures were registered in the country but only 135 were actually operating. The largest of these is with the US-based Newmont Mining Corp. Negotiations over further Western participation in the exploitation of a major oil field discovered in the Fergana Valley in early 1992 are currently underway. Fourteen bilateral agreements with China were signed in 1992.

In 1994, British-American Tobacco, one of the world's largest cigarette manufacturers, announced a $200 million deal to acquire 51% of state-owned Uztobacco. That same year, a Coca-Cola joint venture began operations in Uzbekistan. In August 1996, South Korea's Daewoo Group announced the planned investment of $2.5 billion in Uzbekistan to build telecommunications networks. Daewoo has invested $658 million to produce cars in Uzbekistan. In 2000 Uzbekistan and Israel announced plans to cooperate on the development of solar power technology.

In 1997, the International Monetary Fund, disappointed with Uzbekistan's rapid monetary growth, suspended the $180 million loan program. Many small- and medium-size Western businesses have begun freezing their investments or pulling out. Investors have complained that once the required bribes are paid and an investment is guaranteed, officials begin delaying, lengthening, and altering procedures so much that making a profit is often impossible. Despite the fact that the Uzbekistan economy appeared to be among the strongest in the late 1990s, government intervention in business deals were discouraging foreign companies from investing in the country.

39 ECONOMIC DEVELOPMENT

Under centralized Soviet economic planning, Uzbekistan's economic growth was fueled by expanded agricultural production, as extensive stretches of land were brought under irrigation particularly for cultivation of cotton. While highly critical of the former Soviet's government emphasis on promoting cotton monoculture in the republic, the country's new government has found that the country's economic fortunes are closely tied to cotton production, which has fallen steadily since the Soviet era.

Since independence the government has aimed at facilitating a greater market orientation in the economy, though the steps taken toward this goal have been smaller and slower-paced than in other parts of the former USSR. A series of basic laws and new policies have been adopted regarding property ownership, land, privatization, foreign investment, price controls, trade, taxes, and banking. In 1995 the government announced a Mass Privatization Program (MPP) with the objective of increasing the private sector's share of GDP form 40% to 60%. Although nearly 60,000 small businesses (96% of the total) and 14,000 farms (accounting for 11% of arable land) had been privatized by 1997, only 20% of Uzbekistan's medium and large-sized enterprises were in private hands. The new policy would transform 3,000 state enterprises into corporate entities with 51% controlling interest sold to the public and 30% to private investment funds.

For the immediate future, developing the country's oil and natural gas fields, bolstering cotton exports through productivity enhancement, and sustaining gold exports are likely to be key strategies for procuring some of the necessary financing to support economic development. In 1992, Uzbekistan signed an agreement with Russia transferring its share of the former Soviet Union's debt to the latter in exchange for relinquishing all claims on Soviet assets. One area of serious concern for the government is the increasing threat to public health and economic productivity posed by the environmental damage resulting from past development strategies. Addressing growing water shortages, severe river and lake pollution caused the heavy use of chemical inputs in agriculture, the desiccation of the Aral Sea due to massive irrigation, and high levels of both air and water pollution in the country's industrial centers are among the country's most pressing environmental management problems.

40 SOCIAL DEVELOPMENT

The current social security system was developed in 1994, and includes old age, disability and survivor's pensions, in addition to sickness, maternity, work injury, and unemployment benefits. Pensions are provides at age 60 for men and age 55 for women. The program is financed by a 32.5% contribution from employers and a 1% contribution by employees. Women are entitled to 126 days of maternity benefits plus three years unpaid maternity leave. Unemployment benefits are paid for entirely by employers. Benefits are paid for a maximum of 26 weeks. First-time job seekers are entitled to 50% of minimum wage for 13 weeks, 75% if they have dependents.

Although nominally equal under the law, women hold few high-level positions. As of 1999, 17 of 250 parliamentary seats were held by women. Traditional customs decree that women generally marry young and confine their activities to the home. As of 1997 women's enrollment in higher education was declining, and there was a reported increase in the incidence of suicide by self-immolation by women. In 1995, President Karimov created a deputy prime minister position responsible for advancing the role of women in all aspects of Uzbek society.

Human rights violations reported in 1999 include the mistreatment of detainees, especially in connection with the government crackdown following five terrorist bombings in Tashkent in February 1999. It is estimated that hundreds or even thousands of persons were arrested and remained in custody at the end of the year. Suspects may be held for three days without being charged. Some political prisoners are being held. The activities of human rights organizations are restricted.

41 HEALTH

The system of health care in Uzbekistan is comprehensive and services are provided mainly free of charge. Yet the overall efficacy of the Uzbek system appears to be low. The health sector is under unprecedented pressure to change its organization and financing. The withdrawal of enterprises and collective farms from the traditional role of financing the construction and recurrent communal services of local health facilities has created further budget pressures.

The infant mortality rate was 71.6 per 1,000 live births in 1999, and the general mortality rate was 7.7 per 1,000 people. The average life expectancy was 63.9 years in 1999. In 1994, 93% of children up to one year old were immunized against tuberculosis; 65% against diphtheria, pertussis, and tetanus; 79% against polio; and 71% against measles. Proper sanitation was available to only 18% of the population in 1995. Leading causes of death per 100,000 people in 1990 were communicable diseases and maternal/perinatal causes, 137; noncommunicable diseases, 601; and injuries, 65. There were 81 reported cases of tuberculosis per 100,000 people in 1997. In 1990–97, Uzbekistan had

3.2 doctors and 8.3 hospital beds per 1,000 people. Total public health care expenditures in 1990–97 were 3.3% of GDP.

The heart disease rates were well above the countries classified as "medium human development" by the World Health Organization. The likelihood of dying after age 65 of heart disease was 508 (male) and 538 (female) per 1,000 adults in 1990–93. At least 65,898 deaths were cardiovascular-disease-related in 1993.

42HOUSING

In 1989, 31.9% of all privately owned urban housing had running water, 11.3% had sewer lines, 21.1% had central heating, and 1.5% had hot water. In 1990, Uzbekistan had 12.1 sq m of housing space per capita and, as of 1 January 1991, 204,000 households (or 11.5%) were on waiting lists for urban housing.

43EDUCATION

The estimated adult illiteracy rate in 1995 was 0.3% (males, 0.2%; females, 0.4%). For centuries, Uzbekistan was a noted Muslim educational center. Muslim schools in the cities of Bukhara, Samarkand, Tashkent, and Khiva attracted students from other Muslim countries. In 1920, after the Soviet Union took control of the region, schools and mosques were closed down, and a secular state-funded educational system was established. The educational system is now being modified. In recent years, there has been an increased emphasis on Uzbek literature, culture, and history. Over 75% of the students are taught in the Uzbek language. In 1995, primary schools enrolled 1,905,693 students and employed 92,400 teachers. Student-to-teacher ratio stood at 21 to one. In the same year, secondary schools had 3,318,900 students and 340,200 teachers.

There are three universities in Uzbekistan: Tashkent State University; Nukus State University; and Samarkland Alisher Naroi State University. There are several other institutions offering specialized training. In 1992, all higher-level institutions had 24,787 teaching staff and enrolled 638,200 students.

44LIBRARIES AND MUSEUMS

The Alisher Navoi State Public Library of Uzbekistan in Tashkent holds 4.9 million volumes and is the largest library in the country. Also in the capital are the library of the Uzbek Academy of Sciences (1.5 million volumes), the Pedagogical Institute (808,000), Tashkent State University (2.46 million), and the Polytechnic Institute (756,000). Samarcand State University's library holds 1.6 million volumes, and the Pedagogical Institute Ulugbek in Fergana holds 295,000 volumes.

The State Art Museum, the Historical Museum, and the State Literary Museum are in Tashkent. The Museum of Culture and Art History is in Samarkand. There are local museums in Andizan, Buchara, Karsi, Namangan, and other cities.

45MEDIA

Telephone links to other former Soviet Republics are provided by land link or microwave and to other countries through Moscow. In 1998, there were 1.5 main telephone lines. Radio Tashkent, established in 1947, broadcasts in Uzbek, English, Urdu, Hindi, Farsi, Arabic, and Uighur. There is also a television station in Tashkent, and satellite earth stations receive Orbita and INTELSAT. As of 1999, there were 12 radio broadcast stations and 4 television stations. In 1997, there were 452 radio sets and 273 televisions in use per 1,000 population.

In 1995 there were 279 newspapers (12 dailies) and 93 periodicals, published in a variety of languages. The most widely read dailies include *Halk Suzi* (1999 circulation 52,000), *Pravda Vostoka* (35,000), and *Narodno Slovo* (21,000). Several different kinds of publishing houses are located in Tashkent.

Though the constitution provides for freedom of expression, the government is said to restrict those rights severely, controlling all information flow. A 1991 law prohibits offending the president.

As of 1991, there were 67 Internet hosts in Uzbekistan. Online access is extremely limited, with less than 1 Internet host per 1,000 population in 1998.

46ORGANIZATIONS

The Uzbekistan Chamber of Commerce and Industry promotes the country's exports in world markets. An umbrella organization, the Federation of Trade Unions of Uzbekistan, coordinates the activities of the country's trade unions. The Society for Human Rights is an important political association.

47TOURISM, TRAVEL, AND RECREATION

Uzbekistan tourist attractions include the Islamic cities of Samarkand, Bukhara, Khiva, and Kokand. Muslims from Pakistan, Iran, and the Middle East have been drawn to these sites with their palaces, mosques, madrasses (religious colleges), and pre-Islamic remains.

In an effort to increase tourism in recent years, several hotels have been built in the Uzbekistan, and historical monuments were reconstructed. In 1997 foreign visitors totaled 253,000.

According to 1999 UN estimates, the cost of staying in Tashkent ranged from $206–222 per day, depending upon the choice of accommodations. Elsewhere is Uzbekistan daily costs were estimated at $46.

48FAMOUS UZBEKISTANIS

Islam A. Karimov and Leonid Kuchma have been president and prime minister of Uzbekistan since October 1992, respectively. A famous 20th century writer is Abdullah Quaisi, who wrote the historical novels *Days Gone By* and the *Scorpion from the Pulpit*, published in the 1920s. Quaisi was killed in the 1930s during Stalin's purges. Ilyas Malayev (b.1936) is a popular poet and musician.

49DEPENDENCIES

Uzbekistan has no territories or colonies.

50BIBLIOGRAPHY

Craumer, Peter. *Rural and Agricultural Development in Uzbekistan*. London: Royal Institute of International Affairs, Russian and CIS Programme; distributed by the Brookings Institution, 1995.

Critchlow, James. *Nationalism in Uzbekistan: A Soviet Republic's Road to Sovereignty*. Boulder, Colo.: Westview Press, 1991.

Gippenreiter, Vadim Evgenevich. *Fabled Cities of Central Asia: Samarkand, Bukhara, Khiva*. New York: Abbeville Press, 1989.

Human Rights and Democratization in Uzbekistan and Turkmenistan. Washington, D.C.: Commission on Security and Cooperation in Europe, 2000.

Karimov, I. A. *Uzbekistan on the Threshold of the Twenty-first Century: Challenges to Stability and Progress*. New York: St. Martin's Press, 1998.

Malcomson, Scott L. *Borderlands—Nation and Empire*. Boston: Faber and Faber, 1994.

Mandelbaum, Micheal, ed. *Central Asia and the World: Kazakhstan, Uzbekistan, Tajikistan, Kyrgystan, and Turkmenistan*. New York: Council on Foreign Relations Press, 1994.

Melvin, Neil. *Uzbekistan: Transition to Authoritarianism on the Silk Road*. Amsterdam: Harwood Academic, 2000.

Nazarov, Bakhtiyar A. and Denis Sinor (eds.). *Essays on Uzbek History, Culture, and Language*. Bloomington, Ind.: Indiana University, 1993.

VANUATU

Republic of Vanuatu
République de Vanuatu
Ripablik blong Vanuatu

CAPITAL: Port-Vila.

FLAG: Red and green sections are divided horizontally by a gold stripe running within a black border and widening at the hoist into a black triangle on which is a pig's tusk enclosing two crossed yellow mele leaves.

ANTHEM: *Yumi, Yumi, Yumi (We, We, We).*

MONETARY UNIT: As of 1 January 1981, the vatu (VT) replaced at par value the New Hebridean franc as the national currency. There are coins of 100 vatu and notes of 100, 500, 1,000, and 5,000 vatu. VT1 = $0.008 (or $1 = VT131.80) as of 31 March 2000.

WEIGHTS AND MEASURES: The metric standard is used.

HOLIDAYS: New Year's Day, 1 January; May Day, 1 May; Independence Day, 30 July; Assumption, 15 August; Constitution Day, 5 October; National Unity Day, 29 November; Christmas Day, 25 December; Family Day, 26 December. Movable religious holidays include Good Friday, Easter Monday, and Ascension.

TIME: 11 PM = noon GMT.

¹LOCATION, SIZE, AND EXTENT

Vanuatu, formerly the Anglo-French Condominium of the New Hebrides, is an irregular Y-shaped chain of some 80 islands, with a total land area of about 14,760 sq km (5,699 sq mi) and a total coastline of 2,528 km (1,571 mi). Comparatively, the area occupied by Vanuatu is slightly larger than the state of Connecticut. Of the 70 inhabited islands, the largest is Espiritu Santo (3,947 sq km/1,524 sq mi); the island of Efate is the administrative center. The island chain is about 800 km (500 mi) long and lies about 1,000 km (600 mi) W of Fiji and 400 km (250 mi) NE of New Caledonia. Vanuatu and France both claim Matthew and Hunter islands, which lie between Vanuatu and New Caledonia; one of the islands has been occupied by French forces.

Vanuatu's capital city, Port-Vila, is located on the island of Efate.

²TOPOGRAPHY

The islands are of coral and volcanic origin; there are active volcanoes on several islands, including Ambrym, Lopevi, and Tanna. Most of the islands are forested and mountainous, with narrow coastal strips. The highest peak, Tabwemasana, on Espiritu Santo, rises 1,878 m (6,161 ft) above sea level. The islands are generally well watered.

³CLIMATE

The tropical oceanic climate is moderated by southeastern trade winds, which blow between the months of May and October. Winds are variable during the remainder of the year, and cyclones may occur. Average midday temperatures in Port-Vila range from 25°C (77°F) in winter to 29°C (84°F) in summer. Humidity averages about 74%, and rainfall on Efate is about 230 cm (90 in) a year.

⁴FLORA AND FAUNA

Despite its tropical forests, Vanuatu has a limited number of plant and animal species. There are no indigenous large mammals, poisonous snakes, or spiders. The 19 species of native reptiles include the flowerpot snake, found only on Efate. There are 11 species of bat (3 unique to Vanuatu) and 61 species of land and water birds. While the small Polynesian rat is thought to be indigenous, the large species arrived with Europeans, as did domesticated hogs, dogs, and cattle. (The wild pig and fowl appear to be indigenous.)

The region is rich in sea life, with more than 4,000 species of marine mollusks. Coneshell and stonefish carry poison fatal to humans. The giant East African snail arrived only in the 1970s but already has spread from the Port-Vila region to Luganville.

⁵ENVIRONMENT

Vanuatu's population growth has caused concern for the environment in several areas. Water pollution in urban areas is a problem due to inadequate sanitation systems. A majority of the country's population does not have access to a reliable supply of safe drinking water. The nation's logging industry threatens the forests and contributes to the problem of soil erosion. Forests currently cover 75% of the land area. The reefs on Vanuatu's coasts, which are the home of the country's marine life, are threatened by inappropriate fishing methods and siltation. In 1987, the government formed the National Advisory Committee on the Environment (NACE) to address the nation's developing environmental concerns. The estuarine crocodile and insular flying fox are threatened species.

⁶POPULATION

The population of Vanuatu in 2000 was estimated at 192,848. An estimated 3.8% of the population is 65 years of age or older. The projected population for the year 2005 is 212,000, assuming a crude birthrate of 25 per 1,000 population and a death rate of 7, resulting in a natural rate of change of 1.8% for the period 2000–2005.

The population is unevenly distributed, with the vast majority of Vanuatuans living in some 2,000 small villages. It was

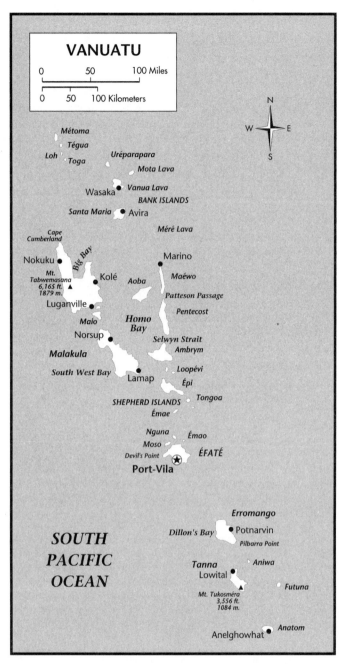

LOCATION: 13° to 21°s; 166° to 171°e. **TOTAL COASTLINE:** 2,528 km (1,571 mi).
TERRITORIAL SEA LIMIT: 12 mi.

estimated that only 20% of the population lived in urban areas in 2000. The most populous islands are Efate, Espiritu Santo, and Malekula. The capital city, Port-Vila, on Efate had a 2000 population of 23,000. Luganville on Espiritu Santo, the only other large town, had a population of 6,983.

7MIGRATION

Vanuatu's earliest known settlers probably migrated from the northwestern Pacific about 3,000 years ago. They were followed a thousand years later by migrants from the Solomon Islands. Tradition describes a series of subsequent incursions. In the 19th century, thousands of New Hebrides islanders were recruited as indentured laborers for plantation work in Australia, Fiji, New Caledonia, and Samoa. This migration gradually died down after the establishment of the Anglo-French Condominium, although voluntary emigration to New Caledonia continued until independence. In recent years, adverse economic conditions have encouraged emigration to Fiji, New Zealand, and the US. The net migration rate in 1999 was zero.

8ETHNIC GROUPS

Approximately 94% of the total population is of Melanesian origin. French constitute about 4% of the population. The remaining 2% is made up of Vietnamese, Chinese, and other Pacific Islanders.

9LANGUAGES

More than 100 languages and dialects are spoken in Vanuatu. Melanesian, the principal language, is related to Fijian and New Caledonian speech. Pidgin English, known as Bislama or Bichelama, is recognized by the constitution as the lingua franca, although English and French are also official languages. The national anthem is in Bislama, which is also used in parliamentary debate, with the proceedings reported in English and French as well. Children often speak as many as four languages, and every aspect of public life—including education, law, and the media—is complicated by language problems.

10RELIGIONS

About 80% of the population is considered to be Christian; other Vanuatuans follow indigenous traditional religions. The Anglican, Presbyterian, and Roman Catholic churches began missionary work in the New Hebrides during the 19th century. More recently, the Seventh-Day Adventists and other nontraditional Protestant groups have been active in mission work. Most mission schools have been handed over to the government, but the missions have continued to make important contributions to education and health. Since 1940, the John Frum cargo cult (a rejection of the white Christian's beliefs but not his goods) has flourished, mainly on Tanna and provides a remarkable example of religious development in a situation of cultural challenge and transition.

In 1995 the government passed a Religious Registration Act in response to concerns expressed by some established churches about the activities of new missionary groups, such as the Holiness Fellowship, Jehovah's Witnesses, and the Church of the Latter-Day Saints. It was repealed in 1997.

At last estimates, 36.7% of the population was Presbyterian; 15% was Anglican; another 15% was Catholic; 7.6% followed indigenous beliefs; 6.2% was Seventh-Day Adventist; 3.8% followed the Church of Christ; and 15.7% were designated as other.

11TRANSPORTATION

During World War II, Vanuatu became an important Allied base, and many roads and airstrips were built by the US forces. In 1996 there were 1,070 km (665 mi) of roads, of which 256 km (159 mi) were paved.

There were 32 small usable airfields serving all the main islands in 1998, of which 3 had paved runways. The chief airports are Bauerfield, on Efate, and Pekoa, on Espiritu Santo; both have been upgraded to handle jet aircraft. Air Vanuatu, the national airline operated by Ansett Airlines of Australia, maintains regular service to Australia; an internal airline, Air Melanesiae, links 22 airfields on various islands. Other external service is provided by Air Pacific, UTA, Polynesian Airlines, Solair, and Air Nauru. Port-Vila and Luganville are the chief seaports. In 1997, 75,000 passengers were carried on scheduled domestic and international flights. Small ships provide frequent interisland service. Vanuatu maintains a policy of open registry for merchant ships, allowing foreign shipowners to avoid the higher costs and regulations of registration under their own flags. As of 1998, there were 82 ships in the Vanuatuan merchant fleet, with a total capacity of 1,327,078 GRT.

12 HISTORY

Although the Portuguese navigator Pedro Fernandes de Queir established a short-lived settlement on Espiritu Santo in 1606, little more is known about the history of the New Hebrides until French and British explorers arrived in the late 18th century. Captain James Cook discovered, named, and charted most of the southern islands in 1774. The next century brought British and French missionaries, planters, and traders, and for many years the islanders suffered from the depredations of the recruiting ships and from other lawless acts by Europeans in the region.

By the Anglo-French Convention of 1887, a joint naval commission was established, with a resident commissioner to protect the lives and interests of the islanders. In 1906 following a London conference, the Anglo-French Condominium was established, largely to settle land claims and to end difficulties caused by lack of clear local jurisdiction. Indigenous political activity developed after World War II, with increasing native concern over land alienation and European dominance.

In 1975 a representative assembly replaced the nominated advisory council under which the New Hebrides had been governed; twenty-nine assembly members were elected by universal suffrage, nine members represented economic interests, and four members represented the traditional chiefs. In 1977 the National Party (Vanuaaku Pati), which held twenty-one of forty-two assembly seats, demanded independence and staged a boycott of the legislature; in response, at a conference in Paris, self-government was agreed on for 1978, to be followed by a 1980 referendum on independence. After considerable difficulty, a constitutional conference in 1979 finally agreed on an independence constitution. In the November 1979 elections for a newly constituted, fully elective assembly, the National Party, led by Father Walter Lini, obtained twenty-six of the thirty-nine seats.

In May 1980 however, a dissident francophone group, based on Espiritu Santo, attempted to break away and declared an independent government of Vemarana, under Jimmy Stevens and the Nagriamal Party. Attempts made during June to resolve the differences between the new central government and the rebels failed, and UK and French troops were sent to Luganville on 24 July. No shots were fired, but the soldiers remained until Vanuatu's formal declaration of independence on 30 July 1980. They were then replaced at the new government's request by forces from Papua New Guinea, who were assisted by the local police in putting down the rebellion.

Since independence, Vanuatu (Our Land Forever) has followed a nonaligned foreign policy. As of late 1987, it was the only South Pacific nation to have joined the nonaligned movement, and in January 1987 it signed a controversial fishing agreement with the USSR. In May 1987 Vanuatu announced a ban on all military ships and aircraft in a dispute over a proposed Libyan diplomatic mission. The dispute ended with the expulsion of two Libyan diplomats. Relations with the French government remained strained throughout much of the Lini government's rule, though they improved at the end of 1989 with the signing of the Matignon Accord relating to New Caledonia.

In December 1988 President George Ati Sokomanu attempted to dismiss the Lini government by ordering the dissolution of the country's Parliament. Sokomanu appointed Barak Sope as Prime Minister. Lini refused to surrender office and reconvened Parliament. Sope and several supporters were arrested and charged with inciting mutiny. Sope was sentenced to six years' imprisonment.

Fr. Lini lost a parliamentary vote of confidence in September 1991 and he was replaced by Donald Kalpokas. In December 1991 the francophone Union of Moderate Parties (UMP), led by Maxime Carlot Korman, won the largest bloc of seats and formed a coalition government with the National United Party (NUP), led by Lini. Strains between the coalition members led to Lini joining the opposition in August 1993, but Carlot Korman's government survived the defection.

Parliamentary elections were again held in 1995, with the UMP winning slightly more seats than the Vanuatu Party (VP), led by Donald Kalpokas. Rialuth Serge Vohor was prime minister from November 1995 until a no-confidence vote in Parliament forced his resignation on 7 February 1996. Maxime Carlot Korman was elected prime minister, forming a coalition, and Parliament appointed Kalpokas deputy prime minister. The coalition was considered to be weak, however. On 30 September 1996 Korman was ousted by a no-confidence motion. Vohor was reelected as prime minister. The Vohor government repealed the Ombudsman's Act, but President Jean Marie Leye refused to declare this piece of legislation as law. Leye, in the face of dissent and political crises, took action to dissolve parliament. The ruling coalition refused to step down, questioning the constitutional right of Leye to do this. The Court of Appeal ruled in January 1998 that Leye's actions were legal, thus opening the way for a new general election. In the election held 6 March 1998 the VP of Kalpokas improved its earlier performance, but could not claim a majority. Kalpokas rejoined forces with Fr. Lini and the NUP and coalesced with minority party legislators to gain a clear majority. Kalpokas was elected prime minister. Willie Jimmy was named deputy prime minister on 19 October 1998. Kalpokas resigned to avoid a no-confidence vote in late 1999, and Barak Sope of Melanesian Progressive Party (MPP) became prime minister.

At the South Pacific Forum in June 1999 Vanuatu supported a proposed Pacific Free Trade Area (FTA) that would initially include fourteen countries in the region. The South Pacific Forum set up the Pacific Kava Council to work at protecting the regional rights to kava and its uses. The kava plant's reputed relaxation properties had attracted the attention of producers of herbal medicines. The establishment of kava plantations in Central America threatened the Pacific Islands' production. Vanuatu joined with other small developing states (SIDS) through the United Nations SIDSnet, an Internet project linking over forty island nations worldwide to address issues like the economic hurdles of isolation and small markets. The United Nations Environment Program (UNEP) issued a report assessing the ecological and population threats faced by SIDS, Vanuatu included. The UN's Intergovernmental Panel on Climate Change announced its predictions on the consequences of global warming. Vanuatu was mentioned as already affected by inundation of low-lying areas and coastal regions by rising oceans.

13 GOVERNMENT

Under the independence constitution adopted in 1979 and effective in 1980, Vanuatu is an independent republic within the Commonwealth of Nations. The head of state is the president (Jean Marie Leye since 2 March 1994); the head of government is the prime minister (Donald Kalpokas since 6 March 1998). The unicameral legislature consists of fifty-two members (thirty-nine before 1987, and fifty before 1998) elected by universal adult suffrage to four-year terms. The cabinet is responsible to parliament, and the president is chosen by an electoral college for a five-year term. The electoral system includes a degree of proportional representation. A Council of Chiefs chosen by their peers in the chiefs' district councils advises the government on the protection of Vanuatuan languages and culture.

The People's Republic of China signed an accord with Vanuatu in December 1993 to finance 75% of a 3.6 million dollar hydroelectric dam on the northern island of Mallicolo. The Japanese government will help build a similar hydroelectric dam on the Sarakata River on the northern Vanuatu island of Santo.

14 POLITICAL PARTIES

The country has at least nine established political parties: the Union of Moderate Parties (UMP, Serge Vohor); the National United Party (NUP), led by Father Walter Lini until his death in February 1999); the Vanuatu Party (VP, Donald Kalpokas); Melanesian Progressive Party (MPP, Barak Sope); Friend Melanesian Party (FMP, Albert Ravutia); Tan Union (TU, Vincent Boulekone); and the Vanuatu Republic Party (Maxine Carlot Korman).

15 LOCAL GOVERNMENT

Vanuatu is divided into six provinces (Malampa, Penama, Sanma, Shefa, Tafea, Torba). There are municipal councils in Port-Vila and Luganville, and community councils elsewhere. Espiritu Santo and Tanna have special regional councils.

16 JUDICIAL SYSTEM

Despite the great difficulty in unifying laws based on the very different English and French traditions, Vanuatu has sought to establish a single system based on British criminal procedure and the French penal code. The constitution establishes a Supreme Court, with a chief justice and three other judges, as well as an appeals court. Village and island courts have jurisdiction over customary and other matters.

The judiciary is independent of the executive and free from military influence. The Constitution guarantees a range of procedural due process protections including the presumption of innocence, fair public trial, habeas corpus, and the prohibition against double jeopardy.

17 ARMED FORCES

The nation maintains close links with Papua New Guinea, where Vanuatuan cadets train for a mobile defense force under the auspices of the Australian Ministry of Defense, which also helps to train skilled manpower for national development tasks.

18 INTERNATIONAL COOPERATION

A member of the Commonwealth of Nations, Vanuatu joined the UN on 15 September 1981 and participates in FAO, IBRD, ICAO, IDA, IFC, IMF, UNCTAD, UNESCO, UPU, and WHO. It also belongs to the Asian Development Bank (which opened a regional office in Port-Vila in 1984), the French Community, G-77, and various regional Pacific bodies, and has applied for membership in the WTO. Vanuatu has taken an active role in Pacific affairs, campaigning for a nuclear-free zone and advocating independence for New Caledonia. Vanuatu has established diplomatic relations with a number of OECD countries, as well as China, Cuba, Vietnam, and Libya.

19 ECONOMY

Vanuatu has a mixed traditional and modern economy. Agriculture supports about 75% of the population, but the service industry is playing an increasingly important role in the economy. Services account for 65% of the GDP, while agriculture provides 21% and industry 14%. Tourism has been developed since the 1980s and, together with financial services, has become an important foreign exchange earner. The absence of personal and corporate income taxes have made Vanuatu an offshore financial center, and the government also earns fees from a "flag of convenience" shipping registry.

20 INCOME

The US Central Intelligence Agency (CIA) reports that in 1997 Vanuatu's gross domestic product (GDP) was estimated at $240 million. The per capita GDP was estimated at $1,300. The annual growth rate of GDP was estimated at -2.9%. The average inflation rate in 1997 was 4.3%. The CIA defines GDP as the value of all final goods and services produced within a nation in a given year and computed on the basis of purchasing power parity (PPP) rather than value as measured on the basis of the rate of exchange. It was estimated that agriculture accounted for 23% of GDP, industry 13%, and services 64%.

21 LABOR

About 80% of the people are engaged in peasant labor either for subsistence or producing such cash crops as copra. As of 1999, there were approximately 29,000 persons participating in the formal economy as wage earners. The employed wage-labor force is concentrated in Port-Vila and Luganville. For persons engaged in government enterprises, port work, construction, and certain other jobs, the terms of employment, wages, and union membership are set by legislation. The nation's first trade unions were formed in 1984. By 1992, there were seven trade unions; the largest two were the Oil and Gas Workers' Union and the Vanuatu Airline Workers' Union. However, a strike in 1994 staged by the Vanuat Public Servants Union resulted in the wholesale dismissal of hundreds of public servants. As a result, overall union membership has fallen from 4,000 in 1994 to less than 1,000 in 1999. The law prohibits children under 12 from working. Children between 12 and 18 may work under restricted hours and conditions. The Labor Department effectively enforces these laws. Since February 1995, the minimum wage has been raised to approximately $143 per month. The law mandates a 44-hour work week.

22 AGRICULTURE

About 10% of the land is cultivated. While most crops, including yams, taro, manioc, sweet potato, and breadfruit, are raised for local consumption, cash crops like copra, cocoa, and coffee have been increasingly important. Production of copra totaled 40,000 tons in 1998. Copra production was adversely affected by cyclones in 1985 and 1987.

In 1983, Vanuatu's first agricultural census was taken, with British assistance. A land alienation act passed in 1982 limits land ownership to indigenous owners and their descendants, but expatriates can lease land for up to 75 years.

23 ANIMAL HUSBANDRY

Hogs and fowl form part of the village economy. Vanuatu is ideal for cattle, and large numbers are raised on plantations; in 1998 there were an estimated 151,000 head of cattle, up from around 124,000 in 1990. The growing meat-packing industry produces frozen, chilled, and tinned beef; production of beef totaled about 4,000 tons (dressed carcass weight) in 1998, coming from 17,000 slaughtered head. The beef industry is centered on the island of Espiritu Santo, where the country's main abattoir is located. Beef is exported primarily to Japan, with a lesser amount going to New Caledonia.

24 FISHING

Although the South Pacific Fishing Co., a joint Vanuatuan government and Japanese venture, has facilities at Luganville that freeze and export both tuna and bonito to Japan and the US, the full fishery potential has not been realized. Fishing is currently focused on domestic consumption; exporting fish requires a government permit. Vanuatu's catch was 2,689 tons in 1997; exports totaled $1.3 million that year.

25FORESTRY

About 74% of the total land area is forest or bushland. Total roundwood production in 1997 was 63,000 cu m, with 38% burned as fuel. Sawnwood production totaled 7,000 cu m that year, and exports of forest products were valued at $2.1 million. The government approved the establishment of a large commercial forestry plantation on Espirito Santo in 1987.

26MINING

Vanuatu has few known minerals, although gold deposits have recently been discovered. A small manganese mine on Efate ceased exports in 1980.

27ENERGY AND POWER

Temporary generators established throughout the islands by the US during World War II have mostly deteriorated. Net installed capacity was about 11,000 kW in 1998, all of it conventional thermal; electricity production totaled 32 million kWh.

28INDUSTRY

The manufacturing sector is small: in 1996, it contributed about 13% to GDP. Industries include fish and food freezing, wood processing, and meat canning. Indigenous crafts include basketry, canoe building, and pottery. In 1990, National Breweries, a joint venture with Sweden, began producing Tusker beer and Pripps Lager. The annual industrial growth rate in 1993 was 3.4%.

29SCIENCE AND TECHNOLOGY

There is no advanced technology apart from overseas aid programs.

30DOMESTIC TRADE

A large part of the population still relies on barter. In Port-Vila, European businesses dominate commercial life; there are hotels, supermarkets, fashion shops, and patisseries, as well as recently established Australian steak houses and small Chinese restaurants. Some Vanuatuans have entered the cash economy in urban areas. The nation's numerous cooperative societies handle most of the distribution of goods on the islands. As part of a program to create regional trade centers, Japan donated $2.8 million in 1987 to build a wharf and commercial center on Malekula. Normal business hours in the capital are 7:30 to 11:30 AM and 1:30 to 4:30 PM, Monday–Friday. Banks in Vanuatu are open on weekdays from 8 to 11:30 AM and 1:30 to 3 PM.

31FOREIGN TRADE

In 1995, exports totaled VT3,173 million and imports amounted to VT10,480 million. Service receipts have helped offset the traditionally adverse trade balances. A commodities marketing board exports copra and cocoa, and cooperatives play a major role in foreign trade.

Most of Vanuatu's export commodities are foodstuffs, including fish (24%), oil seeds, (15%), meat (11%), shellfish (7.7%), cocoa (6.3%), vegetables (5.3%), fruit and nuts (2.1%); wood is also exported (8.6%).

Vanuatu's imports were distributed among the following categories:

Consumer goods	20.0%
Food	18.6%
Fuels	6.7%
Industrial supplies	21.3%
Machinery	19.7%
Transportation	11.0%
Other	2.6%

Principal trading partners in 1998 (in millions of US dollars) were as follows:

COUNTRY	EXPORTS	IMPORTS	BALANCE
Japan	22	14	8
Belgium	16	n.a.	
Germany	10	2	8
United States	5	44	-39
France	2	5	-3
Australia	n.a.	31	
Singapore	n.a.	10	
New Zealand	n.a.	7	
Fiji	n.a.	6	
China (inc. Hong Kong)	n.a.	4	

32BALANCE OF PAYMENTS

Continuing trade deficits have been offset by aid from the UK and France, but this assistance is being steadily reduced. The US Central Intelligence Agency reports that in 1996 the purchasing power parity of Vanuatu's exports was $30 million while imports totaled $97 million resulting in a trade balance of -$67 million.

The International Monetary Fund (IMF) reports that in 1998 Vanuatu had exports of goods totaling $34 million and imports totaling $76 million. The services credit totaled $116 million and debit $45 million. The following table summarizes Vanuatu's balance of payments as reported by the IMF for 1998 in millions of US dollars.

Current Account		5
Balance on goods	-42	
Balance on services	71	
Balance on income	-16	
Current transfers	-8	
Capital Account		-9
Financial Account		-1
Direct investment abroad	...	
Direct investment in Vanuatu	27	
Portfolio investment assets	-1	
Portfolio investment liabilities	...	
Other investment assets	6	
Other investment liabilities	-33	
Net Errors and Omissions		13
Reserves and Related Items		-8

33BANKING AND SECURITIES

Vanuatu's banking system includes a Central Bank, local retail banks, and a Development Bank that provides loans for agricultural projects, housing, and industrial development. The country's Financial Centre, a tax haven created by the British in 1971, is the third-largest source of government revenue. Favorable regulatory and tax structures have stimulated foreign interest in Vanuatu as an international financial center; more than 600 offshore companies and banks were registered in Port-Vila in 1985. Local banks require no minimum deposits for vatu accounts and a minimum of US$5,000, or the equivalent in major specified currencies, for foreign currency holdings. Vanuatu has no double taxation agreements with other countries, ensuring maximum confidentiality for international financial transactions. In late 1999, a number of foreign bank—including Deutsche Bank, Banker's Trust, and the Bank of New York—banned trading in US with Vanuatu because of suspected illegal activity being carried on through the Vanuatu financial center.

There is no stock exchange.

34INSURANCE

Insurance coverage is available through agents of overseas companies, mainly British and French.

35PUBLIC FINANCE

The US Central Intelligence Agency (CIA) estimates that in 1996 Vanuatu's central government took in revenues of approximately $94.4 million and had expenditures of $99.8 million including capital expenditures of $30.4 million. Overall, the government registered a deficit of approximately $5.4 million.

36TAXATION

Vanuatu has no income, corporation, or sales tax. Government revenues are derived from indirect taxes, which include stamp taxes, an excise tax on locally produced alcoholic beverages, a 10% hotel tax, and a rent tax.

37CUSTOMS AND DUTIES

Vanuatu imposes tariffs on both an ad valorem and specific basis. Tariff rates average 15–20%; however, rates for luxury goods could reach 200%. Printed matter is exempt. A 5% service tax is also charged on all imported goods. Export duties are levied on the country's primary products.

38FOREIGN INVESTMENT

The government encourages all forms of foreign investment, especially if there is joint local participation. There are no major foreign ownership restrictions, and duty exemptions are available on application to the Ministry of Finance. In late 1999 Vanuatu's Department of Trade announced that, to be considered, all foreign investment proposals must be accompanied by us$38,000. This action was taken because of the high number of project proposals approved that have not been implemented.

39ECONOMIC DEVELOPMENT

The British independence settlement provided grants of £23.4 million to Vanuatu, including £6.4 million in budgetary aid (with additional grants provided annually), £4 million for technical aid, and £13 million for development projects aimed at promoting national economic self-sufficiency. Projects under the five-year development plan for 1982–86 included harbor development, agricultural training, and road improvements. Aid for other infrastructural development is provided by Australia, New Zealand, the UN, and the EU. Government development projects emphasize local participation and preservation of Vanuatu's cultural heritage. In 1995, Vanuatu received us$45.8 million in aid from international sources.

40SOCIAL DEVELOPMENT

The majority of the people cling to traditional village life. The extended family system ensures that no islanders starve, while church missions and the social development section of the Education Ministry concentrate on rural development and youth activities. The government incorporates family planning into its overall maternal and child health program. A provident fund system established in 1987 provided lump-sum benefits for old age, disability, and death. Workers contributed 3% of earnings, and employers contribute 3% of payroll. Pensions were provided at the age of 55. There is no data available on the current status of this program.

Women are still largely confined to traditional cultural roles, and most marriages include a "bride-price" that encourages men to consider their wives as possessions. Women generally do not own land. Village chiefs usually act to reinforce the subordinate roles of women and are thus viewed as a primary obstacle to female advancement. There are no female leaders in Vanuatu's civic, business, or religious institutions. A disproportionate number of women lost their jobs due to cutbacks in government employment in 1999. In 1998, no members of Parliament were female.

Human rights are generally well respected in Vanuatu.

41HEALTH

Malaria is the most serious of the country's endemic diseases, which also include leprosy, tuberculosis, filariasis, and venereal diseases. Malaria was commonly reported (10,377 cases) in 1993, a decrease from 28,558 in 1990. In 1990, there were an estimated 200 cases of tuberculosis per 100,000 people reported. Safe water was available to 72% of Vanuatu's population during 1989–90.

Medical care is provided by 94 hospitals, health centers, and clinics administered by the Ministry of Health, assisted by WHO and a number of voluntary agencies. Local training schemes in basic community nursing are provided by Port-Vila hospitals, and local clinics train health and sanitation orderlies.

The country had 15 physicians in 1991. In 1999, the infant mortality rate was 59.6 per 1,000 live births. There were 500 deaths of children under 5 years old in 1990–95. Only 12% of married women were using contraception in 1989–90. The birth rate (28.5 per 1,000 people) far exceeded the general mortality rate (8.3 per 1,000) in 1999. The fertility rate in that year was 3.6 children per woman. Life expectancy was an average of 61.4 years in 1999. The immunization rates for children under one were as follows in 1994: diphtheria, pertussis, and tetanus (74%); polio (74%); measles (53%); and tuberculosis (86%).

42HOUSING

In urban areas only the emerging middle class can afford government-built housing. Other migrants to the towns buy plots of land and build cheap shacks of corrugated iron and waste materials, principally near Port-Vila and Luganville. The vast majority of villagers still build their own homes from local materials. The majority of dwellings are traditional Melanesian houses with earth or coral floors, no glass windows, and palm, bamboo, or cane walls and roofing. The most widely used exterior construction material was bush. In February 1987, a cyclone damaged 95% of the buildings in Port-Vila. In 1998, 87% of the population had access to safe drinking water.

43EDUCATION

The overall literacy rate is low (64% of the population), but literacy is relatively widespread among persons under 35 years of age. Primary education is available for almost all children except in a few remote tribal areas. Education is provided in either English or French. In 1992, there were 272 primary schools with 852 teachers and 26,267 students. Student-to-teacher ratio stood at 31 to one. General secondary schools had 220 teachers and 4,269 students in the same year. There were also 124 students in teacher training schools and 444 in vocational schools. Full secondary education is provided by the anglophone Malapoa College and the French Lycée at Port-Vila; limited secondary education is also available in five English postprimary schools and three French mission schools. For postsecondary education, especially medical and technical training, selected students go principally to Fiji, Australia, and New Zealand.

Government expenditure on education in 1995 amounted to 20% of the central government budget.

44LIBRARIES AND MUSEUMS

There is practically no secular reading matter in the country's many vernaculars. A cultural center at Port-Vila has a well stocked library of both French and English books and periodicals and houses fine collections of Melanesian art and artifacts, as well as a valuable stamp collection. The secondary schools also have libraries, and there is a small library in the parliament building. Efate has a small museum displaying South Pacific artifacts and current works of art. The Vanuatu Cultural Center and National Museum and a private fine arts museum are located in Port-Vila.

45MEDIA

The weekly government newspaper, *The Vanuatu Weekly,* appears in English, French, and Bislama. In 1999, it had a circulation of 2,500. Vanuatu is linked by telegraph and telex to Hong Kong; Paris; Noumea, New Caledonia; and Sydney, Australia. An earth satellite tracking station came into service in 1979. There were 4,100 telephones in 1995. Radio Vanuatu (founded 1966) broadcasts daily in English, French, and Bislama. As of 1999, there were 2 radio stations and 1 television station. In 1997 there were 254 radios and 10 television sets per 1,000 population.

The constitution provides for free speech and a free press; however, in practice these provisions are not always honored, threatening opposition groups and media representatives with revocations of licenses and permits. In 1999 Vanuatu's journalists were apprehensive of increasing attempts at government control of the media.

46ORGANIZATIONS

There are a great number of European organizations, but the cooperative movement has had the greatest local impact. Cooperative units have organized a training center in Port-Vila for such skills as accounting, management, law, and marketing. Cooperatives receive British aid and government support but remain firmly independent.

47TOURISM, TRAVEL, AND RECREATION

The number of tourist arrivals reached 52,085 in 1998, with over 32,000 from Australia alone. Tourist receipts totaled $46 million in 1997. That year there were 717 rooms in hotels and other establishments. Popular recreations include marine sightseeing, deep-sea fishing, sailing, and beachcombing for shells. According to 1999 UN estimates, the cost of staying in Port-Vila was approximately $172 per day. The daily cost of staying in Santos was $95, and Tanna Island was $69.

48FAMOUS VANUATUANS

Father Walter Hayde Lini (1943–99), ordained as an Anglican priest in 1970, served as prime minister in Vanuatu from 1980 to 1991.

49DEPENDENCIES

Vanuatu has no territories or colonies.

50BIBLIOGRAPHY

Douglas, Norman. *Vanuatu: A Guide.* Sydney: Pacific Publications, 1987.

Lini, Walter. *Beyond Pandemonium: From the New Hebrides to Vanuatu.* Wellington: Asia Pacific Books, 1981.

MacClancy, Jeremy. *To Kill a Bird with Two Stones: A Short History of Vanuatu.* Port-Vila: Vanuatu Cultural Center, 1981.

Geology and Offshore Resources of Pacific Island Arcs— Vanuatu Region. Houston, Tex.: Circum-Pacific Council for Energy and Mineral Resources, 1988.

Harrisson, Tom. *Living Among Cannibals.* New York: AMS Press, 1979.

Lindstrom, Lamont. *Knowledge and Power in a South Pacific Society.* Washington, D.C.: Smithsonian Institution Press, 1990.

Rodman, Margaret. *Masters of Tradition: Consequences of Customary Land Tenure in Longana, Vanuatu.* Vancouver: University of British Columbia Press, 1987.

Sturton, Mark. *Policy Modeling in the Small Island Economies of the South Pacific: The Case of Vanuatu.* Honolulu: East-West Center, 1989.

VIETNAM

Socialist Republic of Vietnam
Cong Hoa Xa Hoi Chu Nghia Viet Nam

CAPITAL: Hanoi.

FLAG: The flag is red with a five-pointed gold star in the center.

ANTHEM: *Tien Quan Ça (Forward, Soldiers!).*

MONETARY UNIT: The dong (D) is a paper currency of 10 hao and 100 xu. There are coins of 1, 2, and 5 xu, and notes of 5 xu, 1, 2, and 5 hao, and 1, 2, 5, and 10 dong. D1 = $0.000071 (or $1 = D14055.0) as of 31 March 2000.

WEIGHTS AND MEASURES: The metric system is the legal standard, but some traditional measures are still used.

HOLIDAYS: Liberation of Saigon, 30 April; May Day, 1 May; Independence Day, 2 September. Movable holidays include the Vietnamese New Year (Tet).

TIME: 7 PM = noon GMT.

¹LOCATION, SIZE, AND EXTENT

Situated on the eastern coast of mainland Southeast Asia, the Socialist Republic of Vietnam (SRV) has an area of 329,560 sq km (127,244 sq mi), extending 1,650 km (1,025 mi) N–S and 600 km (373 mi) E–W. Comparatively, the area occupied by Vietnam is slightly larger than the state of New Mexico. At its narrowest, Vietnam is only 50 km (31 mi) across. The nation is bordered on the N by China, on the E by the Gulf of Tonkin, on the E and S by the South China Sea, on the SW by the Gulf of Thailand, and on the W by Cambodia and Laos, with a total boundary length of 7,262 km (4,512 mi). Before unification, which was proclaimed on 3 July 1976, Vietnam was divided in two by the 17th parallel. To the south was the Republic of Vietnam (RVN), also known as South Vietnam; to the north, the Democratic Republic of Vietnam (DRV), also known as North Vietnam.

Vietnam, China, the Philippines, Brunei, Taiwan, and Malaysia claim all or part of the Spratly Islands and Paracel Islands, located in the South China Sea roughly 600 km (350 mi) east of Ho Chi Minh City and 400 km (250 mi) east of Da Nang, respectively. The Paracel Islands are known in Vietnamese as the Hoang Sa archipelago, and the Spratlys as the Truong Sa. Both archipelagoes are reportedly surrounded by rich undersea oil reserves, and are productive fishing grounds. China has occupied the Paracel Islands since 1974, when Chinese troops drove a South Vietnamese garrison from the western islands. Vietnam occupies six of the Spratlys, and has unsuccessfully engaged in negotiations with Malaysia and the Philippines over the remainder. Periodic clashes between Chinese and Vietnamese naval forces have taken place in the vicinity of both island groups.

Vietnam's capital city, Hanoi, is located in the northern part of the country.

²TOPOGRAPHY

Vietnam has been described as a carrying pole with a rice basket hanging from each end. The description is a fitting one, for a single mountain chain, the Annam Cordillera (in Vietnamese, Truong Son), extends along Vietnam's western border from north to south, connecting two "rice baskets," which are formed by the densely populated Red River Delta of the Tonkin region in the north and the rich Mekong River Delta in the south. Over two-thirds of the entire population of the country lives in the two low-lying delta regions, both of which are composed of rich alluvial soils brought down from the mountainous regions of southern China and mainland Southeast Asia. The remainder of the population lives along the narrow central coast, in the hilly regions of the Central Highlands north of Ho Chi Minh City (formerly Saigon), or in the mountains north and west of the Red River Delta. The highest mountain peak is Fan Si Pan (3,143 m/ 10,312 ft), near the northern border.

³CLIMATE

Vietnam is entirely located in the tropical belt lying between the equator and the Tropic of Cancer. While there are slight variations in temperature, depending on the season and the altitude, the primary seasonal changes are marked by variations in rainfall.

In the north, the rainy season extends from mid-April to mid-October; the city of Hanoi has a mean annual rainfall of 172 cm (68 in), and in the mountains, annual rainfall sometimes exceeds 406 cm (160 in). Daily temperatures fluctuate considerably in the Red River Delta region, particularly in the dry season, when the thermometer may drop as low as 5°C (41°F) in the region of Hanoi. During the rainy season, the average temperature in Hanoi is about 30°C (86°F).

The south is more tropical; temperatures in Ho Chi Minh City vary only between 18° and 33°C (64–91°F) throughout the year. Temperatures in the Central Highlands are somewhat cooler, ranging from a mean of about 17°C (63°F) in winter to 20°C (68°F) in summer. The rainy season extends from early May to November, with annual rainfall averaging about 200 cm (79 in) in lowland regions. The typhoon season lasts from July through November, with the most severe storms occurring along the central coast. Typhoons in this region frequently lead to serious crop damage and loss of life.

⁴FLORA AND FAUNA

The mountainous regions of Tonkin, as well as the Annam Cordillera, are characterized by tropical rain forest broken by large areas of monsoon forest. In the higher altitudes of the far northwest there are pine forests. Shifting cultivation has resulted in many sections of secondary forest. Tropical grasses are widespread, and there are mangrove forests fringing parts of the Red River Delta and in the Ca Mau peninsula, which juts into the Gulf of Thailand. Tropical evergreen forests predominate in the south, with extensive savanna in the southwest.

Deer and wild oxen are found in the more mountainous areas. There are many species of tropical birds and insects.

5ENVIRONMENT

During the Vietnam war, massive bombing raids and defoliation campaigns caused severe destruction of the natural foliage, especially in the Central Highlands in the south. In addition, dioxin, a toxic residue of the herbicide known as Agent Orange, had leached into water supplies.Over 50% of the nation's forests have been eliminated. UN sources estimate that Vietnam loses 160,000 to 200,000 hectares of forest land annually. The nation has 90.2 cu mi of water; 78% is used for farming activity and 9% is used for industrial purposes. As of 1995, 47% of urban dwellers and 68% of the rural population lacked access to safe drinking water. Salinization and alkalinization are a threat to the quality of the soil, as are excessive use of pesticides and fertilizers.

Environmental damage has also been caused by the slash-and-burn agriculture practiced by nomadic tribal peoples in the Central Highlands and in the mountainous regions in the north. The government is engaged in a program to introduce modern farming practices to these populations.

In 1994, 28 of Vietnam's mammal species and 34 bird species were endangered. Three-hundred and thirty-eight types of plants are also endangered. Endangered species include the tiger, elephant, Sumatran rhinoceros, Thailand brow-antlered deer, kouprey, river terrapin, Siamese crocodile (probably extinct), estuarine crocodile, Javan rhinoceros, and the pileated, crowned, and caped gibbons.

6POPULATION

Rapid population growth is a serious problem in Vietnam. According to the 1989 census, the total population was 64,411,668. In 1996, the population was estimated at 73,977,000. The annual growth rate averaged almost 2.2% during 1980–85, 2.15% during 1985–90, and 2.2% during 1990–95; the government attempted to reduce it to 1.7% through family planning measures, including late marriages and small families, in order to stabilize the population at 75 to 80 million by the end of the twentieth century. At the dawn of the twenty-first century, in 2000, Vietnam's population was estimated at 78,349,503. An estimated 4.8% of the population is 65 years of age or older. The projected population for the year 2005 is 83,442,000, assuming a crude birthrate of 19 per 1,000 population and a death rate of 6, resulting in a natural rate of change of 1.3% for the period 2000–2005. The population rate of change between 1995 and 2000 was 1.8%. The population density in 1998 was 238 per sq km (616 per sq mi).

It was estimated that 20% of the population lived in urban areas in 2000, up from 19% in 1980. The two largest urban areas in 2000 were Ho Chi Minh City (3,678,000) and the capital city, Hanoi (1,312,000).

7MIGRATION

The 1954 partition of Vietnam resulted in the exodus of over 820,000 refugees, the majority of them Catholics, from the northern part of the country. Most eventually settled with government assistance in the Central Highlands or on the outskirts of the capital city of Saigon (now Ho Chi Minh City). During the same period, about 80,000 Viet-Minh troops and their dependents moved from the south to the north.

The Vietnam war caused severe disruption of living patterns in both the north and the south. In the north, intensive US bombing of major industrial cities led to a dispersal of the population from urban areas, while a government-sponsored program resulted in the resettlement of nearly 1 million Vietnamese from crowded areas in the Delta to less densely populated regions in upland areas of the country. In the south, migration was primarily from the countryside to the cities, as millions of peasants fled their villages to escape the effects of the war or to seek employment in the affluent cities of Saigon and Da Nang. At the end of the war in 1975, nearly one-half of the population lived in urban areas, many in refugee camps on the edges of the major cities.

After seizing control of the south in 1975, the Hanoi regime announced a new program that called for the resettlement of over 10 million Vietnamese into uncrowded areas of the country by the end of the century. Many were to be moved from refugee camps in the south to New Economic Zones established in the Central Highlands or along the Cambodian border. Although the zones were unpopular because of poor living conditions, between the end of the war and 1981, nearly 1.5 million Vietnamese were resettled into new areas. The overall aim was to disperse the entire population into several hundred "agroindustrial districts" that would provide the basis for development of an advanced Socialist economy. Since 1981 another 2.1 million have been resettled.

In addition to this migration within the country, since the war there has been a substantial outflow of Vietnamese fleeing to other countries. About 150,000 were evacuated from the south in the final weeks of the war, many of them eventually settling in the United States. There were 593,213 people of Vietnamese ancestry in the US in 1990. In 1978, a new exodus began after the government nationalized all private trade and manufacturing in the country. During 1978-87, an estimated 1 million Vietnamese fled by sea to other countries in Southeast Asia, or overland to China. Many later resettled in Australia, France, the US, and other countries. From 1979 to 1984, 59,730 persons emigrated legally through the US Orderly Departure Program; this program was suspended by the Vietnamese government in 1986 but later resumed, with 57,000 emigrating to the US in 1993 alone. In 1984, the US started a program that offered asylum to Vietnamese political prisoners and all Asian-American children. This program was restarted in September 1987. Between 1975 and 1984, about 554,000 persons, known as the "boat people," emigrated illegally. In 1992, Vietnam signed agreements with the UK providing for the forcible repatriation of almost all the 55,700 "boat people" remaining in Hong Kong. The major refugee community was in China, which was harboring 285,500 Vietnamese of Chinese ancestry at the end of 1992.

As of May 1997, 3,000 Vietnamese remained in Hong Kong. By March 1999, some 110,000 non-refugee boat people had returned to Vietnam. In 1999, the net migration rate was -0.53 migrants per 1,000 population.

8ETHNIC GROUPS

About 85–90% of the population of the SRV is composed of ethnic Vietnamese. The racial origins of the Vietnamese are obscure, although many scholars believe they represent a mixture of Australoid peoples who lived in mainland Southeast Asia during the Stone Age with Mongoloid peoples who migrated into the area from southern China.

In addition to the ethnic Vietnamese, there are 53 other ethnic groups living in the SRV. Many, like the Tay, the Thai, the Nung, the Rhadé, and the Jarai, are nomadic tribal peoples living in the mountainous areas of the Central Highlands and along the Sino-Vietnamese border. The overseas Chinese (Hoa) are descendants of peoples who migrated into the area in recent centuries. The Cham and the Khmer are remnants of past civilizations that controlled the southern parts of the country.

and at least one-third of the vocabulary is derived from Chinese. Formerly, Vietnamese was written in Chinese characters, but under French rule a Romanized alphabet originally developed by Roman Catholic missionaries in the 17th century was adopted as the standard written form of the language. Most of the minority groups have their own spoken languages, and some have their own writing systems, but all children in the SRV today receive instruction in the national language. Other languages include Chinese, English, French, Khmer, and the tribal languages of Mon-Khmer and Malayo-Polynesian.

10 RELIGIONS

In 1998, the dominant religious belief was Buddhism. Many believers practice a mixture of Mahayana Buddhism, Taoism, and Confucianism, sometimes called Vietnam's "Triple Religion." It was under Chinese rule that these three major religions and philosophical systems entered the country. Three-fourths of the population are at least nominally Buddhist. Like many Asian peoples, the Vietnamese also practiced spirit worship, a form of religious belief that was particularly prevalent among the tribal peoples.

Christianity was first brought to Vietnam in the 17th century by Roman Catholic missionaries sponsored by the French, the Spanish, the Portuguese, or the papacy. Eventually, however, propagation of the Christian faith was forbidden by the imperial court, and Catholicism could only be practiced in secret. French priests were especially active in provoking the French decision to conquer Vietnam in the 19th century.

Under French rule, Christianity prospered, and when Vietnam restored its independence in 1954, there were more than 2 million Catholics in the country, a population that increased to between 6 and 7 million in 1998. Two millenarian religious sects, the Cao Dai and the Hoa Hao, also became popular among peasants and townspeople in the Mekong Delta. In 1998, the Cao Dai sect claimed 1.1 million adherents, and the Hoa Hao claimed 1.3 million.

Minority religions as of 1998 included various denominations of Protestant Christianity, Hindu, and Islam.

Since reunification in 1975, religious activities have been restricted, although freedom of religion is formally guaranteed in the 1980 constitution. The government granted permission in 1983 for church organizations to carry on activities that correspond to official policies, but it has cracked down on dissident elements that resist state control. In April 1999 the government issued a new decree on religion that prescribes the rights and responsibilities of religious believers. It states for the first time that no religious organization can reclaim lands or properties taken over by the State following the end of the 1954 war against French rule and the 1975 Communist victory in the south. The decree also states that persons formerly detained or imprisoned must obtain special permission from the authorities before resuming religious activities.

11 TRANSPORTATION

The war wreaked massive damage on Vietnam's transportation network, especially its railways, roads, and bridges. Further damage occurred during the Chinese invasion in 1979, after which direct rail and air connections with China were severed. The nation's truck fleet is ancient and seriously lacking in spare parts. Most goods move by small barges or sampans along the countless waterways. The length of inland navigable waterways totals about 17,702 km (11,000 mi), of which 29% is navigable year-round by vessels with less than a 1.8 m draft. Major ports such as Haiphong in the north and Da Nang in the south, are frequently clogged with goods because many of the stevedores— often overseas Chinese—have fled abroad. In 1998, Vietnam had a merchant fleet of 123 ships totaling 527,920 GRT.

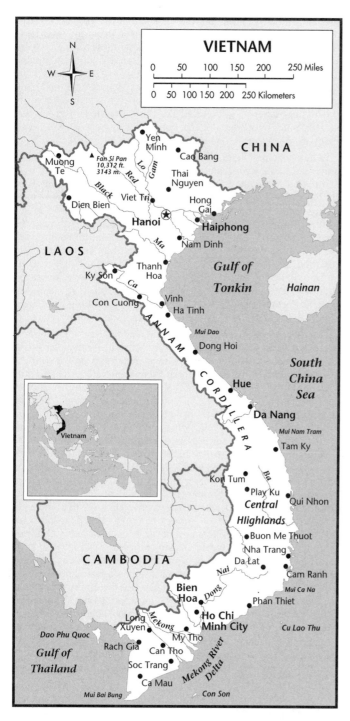

LOCATION: 102°10′ to 109°30′E; 8°30′ to 23°22′N. **BOUNDARY LENGTHS:** China, 1,281 km (796 mi); Cambodia, 982 km (610 mi); Laos, 1,555 km (966 mi). **COASTLINE:** 2,309 km (1,435 mi). **TERRITORIAL SEA LIMIT:** 12 mi.

Until recently, the largest ethnic minority in the country was the overseas Chinese, numbering more than 2 million. Many have fled the country for economic or political reasons in recent years, however; Chinese constituted 3% of the population in 1999. Other sizable minority groups are the Muong, the Tay, Meo, Khmer, Man, and Cham.

9 LANGUAGES

The official language of the SRV is Vietnamese (Quoc ngu). A tonal language, it bears similarities to Khmer, Thai, and Chinese,

Recognizing its importance to economic growth, the government is making a major effort to improve the transportation network. The railroads are to be expanded. There were 2,835 km (1,762 mi) of operable track in 1998; in addition, there were 224 km (139 mi) not restored to service after war damage. At last estimate there were 48 airports, 36 with permanent-surface runways. The nation's air fleet remains primitive, as the national airline (Hang Khong Vietnam) uses Soviet passenger liners built in the 1950s. In 1997, 2,527,000 passengers were carried on scheduled domestic and international flights. There were 93,300 km (57,977 mi) of roads in the country in 1996, but only 23,418 km (14,552 mi) were paved. There were an estimated 330,000 cars and 4 million motorcycles in 1995. The main route from Hanoi to Ho Chi Minh City badly needs improvement. In 1997, the government authorized the construction of a new north-south highway, the largest infrastructural project ever undertaken in Vietnam. The construction will take at least fifteen years, utilizing ten days of mandatory labor from almost every citizen between the ages of 18 and 45.

12HISTORY

During the first millennium BC, the Lac peoples, the ancestors of the modern-day Vietnamese, formed a Bronze Age civilization in the vicinity of the Red River Delta in northern Vietnam. The Lac were primarily rice farmers, although those living in mountain valleys occasionally practiced the slash-and-burn agriculture now prevalent among nomadic tribes in the Central Highlands and the mountainous regions in the north. In the 3d century BC, the Vietnamese kingdom of Van Lang was conquered by a Chinese military adventurer who incorporated the Red River Delta area into his own kingdom in southern China. A century later, Vietnam was integrated into the expanding Chinese empire. During 1,000 years of Chinese rule, Vietnamese society changed significantly as it was introduced to Chinese political and social institutions; Chinese architecture, art, and literature; and the Chinese written language. In AD 939, during a period of anarchy in China, Vietnamese rebels restored national independence.

During the next several hundred years, the Vietnamese Empire, then known as Dai Viet (Great Viet), gradually developed its own institutions and expanded steadily to the south. Under two great dynasties, the Ly (1009–1225) and the Tran (1225–1400), the Vietnamese fended off periodic attempts by China to resubjugate Vietnam, while gradually expanding southward at the expense of their southern neighbor, Champa. In the early 15th century, Chinese rule was briefly restored, but a national uprising led by Le Loi led to the expulsion of the Chinese and the formation of an independent Le Dynasty (1428–1788). Under the Le, expansion to the south continued, and the entire Mekong River Delta came under Vietnamese rule during the 17th century. But expansion brought problems, as a weakened Le court slipped into civil war between two princely families, the Trinh in the north and the Nguyen in the south.

The division of Vietnam into two separate political entities came at a time when European adventurers were beginning to expand their commercial and missionary activities into East and Southeast Asia. In 1771, a major peasant revolt led by the Tay Son brothers destroyed the Nguyen and the Trinh and briefly united the entire country under Emperor Nguyen Hue, ablest of the Tay Son. But a prince of the defeated Nguyen house enlisted the aid of a French Roman Catholic bishop and raised a military force that conquered the Tay Son and reunited the country under a new Nguyen Dynasty (1802–1945). When the founding emperor, Gia Long, died in 1820, his son Minh Mang refused to continue the commercial and missionary privileges granted by his predecessor to the French. In 1858, French forces attacked near Saigon and forced the defeated Vietnamese Empire to cede territory in the area to the French, which became the colony of Cochin China. In 1884, France completed its conquest of the country, establishing a protectorate over central and northern Vietnam (now renamed Annam and Tonkin). In 1895, the three sections of Vietnam were included with the protectorates of Laos and Cambodia into a French-ruled Indochinese Union.

The first Vietnamese attempts to resist French rule were ineffectual. Western-style nationalist movements began to form after World War I, and an Indochinese Communist Party, under the leadership of the veteran revolutionary Ho Chi Minh, was formed in 1930. After the collapse of France in World War II, Japan forced the French administration to accept a Japanese military occupation of Indochina. During the joint French-Japanese rule, Communist forces under the umbrella of the Viet-Minh Front began to organize for a national uprising at the end of the war. In March 1945, the Japanese, nearing defeat, disarmed the French and seized full administrative control over French Indochina. At the same time, the Japanese set up a puppet government, with Bao Dai, the figurehead emperor of Vietnam, as nominal ruler. Shortly after Japan surrendered to Allied forces in August 1945, Viet-Minh forces, led by the Indochinese Communist Party, launched the nationwide August Revolution to restore Vietnamese independence. On 2 September, President Ho Chi Minh declared the formation of an independent Democratic Republic of Vietnam (DRV) in Hanoi. Under the Potsdam agreements, Nationalist Chinese troops occupied all of Indochina north of the 16th parallel, while British troops occupied the remainder of the old Indochinese Union. Chinese commanders permitted the Viet-Minh to remain in political control of the north, but the British assisted the French to restore their authority in the south.

In March 1946, the French and the DRV signed a preliminary agreement (the Ho-Sainteny Agreement) recognizing Vietnam as a "free state" in the new French Union. The agreement also called for a plebiscite in Cochin China to permit the local population in that colony to determine their own future. During the summer of 1946, French and Vietnamese negotiators attempted without success to complete an agreement on the future of Vietnam. In September, Ho Chi Minh signed a modus vivendi calling for renewed talks early in 1947, but military clashes between Vietnamese and French troops in the DRV led to the outbreak of war in December 1946. The Franco–Viet-Minh war lasted nearly eight years, ending in July 1954 after a successful siege of the French garrison at Dien Bien Phu by Viet-Minh forces. According to the Geneva agreement signed on 21 July, Vietnam was temporarily partitioned along the 17th parallel, pending general elections to bring about national reunification. North of the parallel, the DRV began to build a Socialist society, while in the south, an anti-Communist government under the Roman Catholic politician Ngo Dinh Diem attempted with US aid to build a viable and independent state. In the summer of 1955, Prime Minister Diem refused to hold consultations with the DRV on elections called for by the Geneva accords. On 26 October, Diem proclaimed the Republic of Vietnam (RVN), with its capital at Saigon. In a referendum held three days earlier, Diem had defeated ex-Emperor Bao Dai, and in 1956, Diem became president of the RVN under a new constitution written with US support. With the Geneva accords thus abrogated, Vietnamese guerrillas, supported by the DRV, initiated low-level political and military activities to destabilize the Saigon regime. Their efforts were assisted by Diem's own shortcomings, as he brutally suppressed all political opposition and failed to take effective measures to bring to an end the unequal division of landholding in South Vietnam.

In December 1960, revolutionary forces in the south formed a National Liberation Front (NLF) to coordinate political activities against the Diem regime. Guerrilla activities by the People's Liberation Armed Forces (known in the US as the Viet-Cong) were stepped up, and Hanoi began to infiltrate trained cadres from the north to provide leadership to the revolutionary movement. Despite increasing economic and military assistance from the US, the Diem regime continued to decline, and in November 1963, Diem was overthrown by a military coup waged with the complicity of US President John F. Kennedy's administration, which had watched in dismay as Diem had alienated Buddhist elements by his open favoritism to fellow Roman Catholics. A Military Revolutionary Council, led by the popular southern general Duong Van (Big) Minh, was formed in Saigon. General Minh promised to continue efforts to defeat the insurgency movement in the south but was unable to reverse the growing political anarchy in Saigon. Early in 1964, he was replaced by another military junta. During the next 15 months, a number of governments succeeded each other, while the influence of the NLF, assisted by growing numbers of regular troops that were infiltrating from the north, steadily increased in the countryside. By early 1965, US intelligence was warning that without US intervention, South Vietnam could collapse within six months.

Beginning in February 1965, US President Lyndon Johnson took two major steps to reverse the situation in South Vietnam. American combat troops were introduced in growing numbers into the south, while a campaign of heavy bombing raids was launched on military and industrial targets in the north. In Saigon, the political situation stabilized with the seizure of power by a group of army officers led by Nguyen Van Thieu and Nguyen Cao Ky. Encouraged by the US, the new military regime drafted a constitution, and in elections held in September 1967, Gen. Thieu was elected president of the country. By 1967, US troop strength in South Vietnam had reached over 500,000, while US air strikes over DRV territory were averaging about 100 sorties a day. The Hanoi regime attempted to match the US escalation by increasing infiltration of North Vietnamese military units into the south, but under the sheer weight of US firepower, the revolution began to lose momentum, and morale was ebbing.

On 30 January 1968, in an effort to reverse the military decline on the battlefield and encourage the growing popular discontent with the war in the US, Hanoi launched the Tet Offensive, a massive effort to seize towns and villages throughout the south. The attempt to seize Saigon or force the collapse of the Saigon regime failed to achieve its objective, but the secondary aim of undermining support for the war in the US succeeded. President Johnson canceled plans to increase the US military commitment and agreed to pursue a political settlement. To bring about negotiations with Hanoi, a complete bombing halt was ordered on 1 November, just before the US presidential election that brought Richard M. Nixon to office as the new Republican president. President Nixon announced a policy of "Vietnamization," according to which US forces would be gradually withdrawn and the bulk of the fighting in the south would be taken over by RVN forces. On 30 April 1970, in order to destroy enemy sanctuaries beyond the South Vietnamese border, US and South Vietnamese forces invaded neutral Cambodia. The invasion backfired, however, stimulating the rise of revolutionary activities by the Hanoi-supported Cambodian Communist movement and arousing protests in the US that the war was being expanded. The withdrawal of US military forces continued, and in March 1972, the DRV attempted to test the capability of the South Vietnamese forces by launching a direct offensive across the 17th parallel. The "Easter Offensive" succeeded in capturing the provincial capital of Quang Tri, but further gains were prevented by the resumption of US bombing raids.

By this time, both sides were willing to compromise to bring the war to an end; on 26 October 1972, the DRV announced that the secret talks between US Secretary of State Henry Kissinger and its representative, Le Duc Tho, had produced a tentative agreement. Hanoi agreed to recognize the political authority of President Nguyen Van Thieu in Saigon, while the US agreed to complete the withdrawal of US forces without demanding the removal of existing North Vietnamese troops in the south. The negotiations briefly ran aground in late autumn, leading President Nixon to order an intensive bombing assault on the DRV, but the talks resumed in early January, and the Paris Agreement was formally signed on 27 January 1973.

The Paris Agreement and the withdrawal of US forces by no means signaled the end of the conflict. Clashes between revolutionary forces and South Vietnamese units continued in the south, while provisions for a political settlement quickly collapsed. In January 1975, North Vietnamese forces in the south launched a major military offensive in the Central Highlands. When South Vietnamese resistance in the area disintegrated, further attacks were launched farther to the north, and by late March the entire northern half of the country was in North Vietnamese hands. President Thieu resigned on 21 April, but his successor, Gen. Duong Van Minh, was unable to achieve a negotiated settlement. The capital of the RVN, Saigon, was occupied by North Vietnamese troops on 30 April. Thus ended a war in which some 2,000,000 Vietnamese and more than 56,000 Americans were killed and an estimated 4,000,000 people were injured. In the DRV, US bombing was estimated to have destroyed 70% of the industrial plant; in the RVN, more than 4 million were homeless. During the 1950–74 period, total US economic and military aid to Vietnam was $23.9 billion (including $16.1 billion in direct military aid), representing the largest bilateral assistance program in modern history. Chinese aid to the DRV (according to intelligence estimates) probably averaged over $200 million a year. No complete figures are available on the extent of Soviet assistance to the DRV, but some scholars estimate it at about $1 billion annually.

During the next 15 months, the DRV moved to complete national reunification of north and south. Nationwide elections for a new National Assembly were held on 25 April 1976. On 24 June, the first Assembly of the unified country met and proclaimed the establishment on 2 July of the Socialist Republic of Vietnam (SRV), with its capital remaining at Hanoi. In December, the Communist Party, known as the Vietnamese Workers' Party since 1951, was renamed the Vietnamese Communist Party. The NLF was dissolved into a nationwide Fatherland Front for the entire country. The nation's Communist leadership, with Le Duan the general secretary of the Communist Party and Pham Van Dong the prime minister, remained unchanged, while loyal members of the revolutionary movement in the south were given positions of prominence at the national level. Ton Duc Thang, figurehead president of the DRV after the death of Ho Chi Minh in 1969, remained in that position until his death in 1980.

Economic reconstruction and the building of a fully Socialist society proved more difficult than reunification. Nationalization of industry and collectivization of agriculture had been achieved in the north in the late 1950s, but the south proved more resistant to official efforts to end private enterprise after 1975. When the regime attempted to destroy the remnants of capitalism and private farming in the south in 1978, thousands fled, and the economy entered a period of severe crisis. Its problems were magnified by the outbreak of war with China. In December 1978, Vietnamese forces had invaded neighboring Kampuchea (known as Cambodia until 1976 and again from 1989) to overthrow the anti-Vietnamese government of the revolutionary Pol Pot. A pro-Vietnamese government was installed in early January 1979. China, which had been supporting Pol Pot to retain its own influence in Southeast Asia, mounted a punitive invasion of North Vietnam in February 1979. After a short but bitter battle that caused severe casualties on both sides, the Chinese forces withdrew across the border. China, however, continued to support guerrilla operations led by Pol Pot against the government in Kampuchea.

During the 1980s, the SRV attempted to recover from its economic crisis. Party leaders worked out a compromise permitting the survival of a small private sector while maintaining a program of gradual Socialist transformation. With the death of Le Duan in June 1986, a new leadership emerged under General Secretary Nguyen Van Linh at the Sixth National Party Congress. This leadership promised a new "openness" in political affairs and a policy of economic renovation (doi moi) to improve the livelihood of the population. A strong conservative coalition of party leaders seriously reduced Linh's effectiveness as they stressed the dangers of political liberalization and slowed the pace of economic reform. In March 1988 Prime Minister Pham Hung died, and Linh's choice of a conservative replacement, Do Muoi, was a clear concession to these groups.

Economic recovery continued to be difficult due to a serious lack of investment capital, resources, and technical skills. The SRV's internal problems were compounded by the continuing dispute with China. To protect itself from Chinese intimidation, Hanoi had formed a military alliance with the USSR and was deeply dependent upon Soviet economic assistance. The continuing civil war in Kampuchea also represented a steady drain on the SRV's slender resources and prevented foreign economic assistance, particularly from the US. In December 1988 the constitution was amended to remove derogatory references to the US, China, France and Japan, as an attempt to improve international relations. In August 1991 Do Muoi resigned as prime minister. His successor Vo Van Kiet favored free-market reforms. A new constitution was adopted by the National Assembly in April 1992. A general election took place in July 1992 and, for the first time, independent candidates were allowed to present themselves, but neither of the two deemed qualified were elected. On 23 September 1992, the National Assembly elected Lu Duc Anh as president and reelected Vo Van Kiet as prime minister.

In January 1989 the first direct talks between Vietnam and China since 1979 resulted in Vietnam's agreement to withdraw its troops from Cambodia by the end of September 1989 and China's agreement to end aid to the Khmer Rouge guerrillas once the Vietnamese withdrawal was achieved. Later, Vietnam insisted that the withdrawal was contingent on the end of all foreign military aid to factions opposing Cambodian Prime Minister Hun Sen. Hanoi hoped to use the September 1989 withdrawal of its troops from Cambodia as leverage for improved relations with the Association of Southeast Asian Nations (ASEAN), Japan, and the West. On 23 October 1991 a Cambodian peace agreement was signed, paving the way for Vietnam's eventual entry into ASEAN, which occurred in 1995.

During the 1990s, Vietnam stepped up its efforts to attract foreign capital from the West and regularize relations with the world financial system. At the same time, the country struggled with its intention not to descend too deeply into Western style consumerism, as demonstrated in 1996, when the government, while continuing to court foreign investment, banned consumer-goods advertising in foreign languages. That move angered Western investors and free-market Vietnamese, but marked the beginning of a countrywide attempt to purge society of overt Western decadence. Analysts attributed the drive to the aging hard-line leadership who looked at the doi moi reforms with intense skepticism.

After joining ASEAN in 1995, Vietnam began reframing its trade laws and began instituting legal reforms aimed at codifying its sometimes capricious statutory system. During 1995, a significant year in Vietnam's opening up to the world, the Communist Party held two meetings to discuss the establishment of a law-based civil society to replace the decades-old system of rule by fiat. In this spirit, the National Assembly passed a series of laws aligning the country with international standards on copyright protection—needed for World Trade Organization (WTO) membership—and other areas. An extensive document, called the Civil Code, was passed containing 834 articles ostensibly granting the Vietnamese people greater civil liberties. Other measures were decidedly investor-unfriendly, such as Prime Minister Kiet's decree that no more land would be turned over from rice production to industrial use. Subsequently, Vietnam's foreign investment rate slid from a peak of $8.6 billion in 1996, to just $1.4 billion in 1999.

In June 1996, the Communist Party held its Eighth Congress, its first full congress since 1991. Much was expected from the Congress in light of the country's ambiguous and, at times, conflicting moves toward openness and reform over the 12 years of doi moi. The Congress returned to power the aging leadership, granting additional five-year terms to General Secretary Do Muoi, President Le Duc Anh, and Prime Minister Vo Van Kiet. The Party issued decrees in favor of continued economic reform and international investment, but balked at the kind of market liberalization most internationalist investors perceive as necessary to the creation of a viable economy.

30 April, 2000 marked Vietnam's reunification after the long war between the Communists and the United States. Celebrations of the occasion, with military parades and a carnival atmosphere, were followed by the 6 May funeral of former Prime Minister Pham Van Dong. One of the original troika leading Vietnam during the struggle against France and the US, Dong (born in 1906) had been an influential, unswerving Communist conservative. It remains to be seen whether the inevitable winnowing of Vietnam's "gerontocracy" will result in significant liberalization.

Severe, violent unrest in the countryside during 1997 led to punishment of rural officials for corruption, and increased awareness of agricultural concerns. As much as 80% of Vietnam's population lives in farming communities. Expressions of rural discontent continued to emerge, even in the form of peasant anticorruption protests in the streets of Ho Chi Minh City. The Party hierarchy was somewhat reshuffled during 1997's central committee meetings. Tran Duc Luong was selected as the new president (the third most powerful rank in the troika including General Secretary and Prime Minister.) The ultimate hard-liner, Do Muoi, was succeeded as the Party's General Secretary by Gen. Le Kha Phieu. Muoi has remained a highly influential advisor to Phieu, and some observers feel that Muoi's constant pressure to hold the hard line have kept Phieu from coming into his own as a possibly more progressive leader. Almost the entire Party hierarchy is past what might be considered normal retirement age, but new, younger leaders, have been unable to rise to the top.

As aftereffects of the Asian economic crisis stunted the growth of Vietnam's economy, the country remained poor at the beginning of the 21st Century. In spite of strides in rice production, literacy and education, unemployment outpaces economic growth. Rural infrastructure languishes, and the urban gap between a rich elite and struggling masses is enormous. Socialist rhetoric and retrenchment failed to heal the divide, which also exists between North and South. Some effort has been made to recognize Party officials from the South, such as early 2000's appointment of Truong Tan Sang, who had been Ho Chi Minh City's Party head, to lead the Party's Economic Commission. The reformists within the Party have never been completely marginalized, only outmaneuvered by the old-time Marxists. Retired General Tran Do's open criticism of corruption and other failures of the system resulted in his expulsion from the Party in January 1999. Gen. Tran Do endured other forms of harassment, but it was not as severe as that meted out to other dissidents, due to his revered war veteran, communist faithful, status.

Issues of importance relevant to Vietnam's reintegration into the international system have included the status of Vietnamese refugees; border and troop withdrawal disputes with Cambodia, Thailand, and the People's Republic of China; conflicts over the Spratly and Paracel island groups in the South China Sea; conflicts with the US over the recovery of the remains of US soldiers missing-in-action (MIA); and Vietnamese cooperation in a diplomatic settlement in Cambodia. In October 1991 Vietnam agreed to accept the forced repatriation of Vietnamese refugees—known as boat people—who were designated economic migrants, not seekers of political asylum. The boat people were in camps around Asia from 1975– 1994. The "comprehensive plan of action" adopted by the UN High Commission for Refugees in 1989 reduced the number of boat people fleeing Vietnam. In 1994, the Commission decided that all those still living in camps were to be repatriated.

The Soviet economic assistance on which Vietnam had depended, withered away with the collapse of the USSR., although technical help from Russia remains important. With the loss of major Soviet aid, Vietnam's relations with the West began to warm considerably. In June 1992, Vietnam announced that all South Vietnamese officials had been released from reeducation camps, a US-mandated prerequisite for lifting its embargo against Vietnam. As a result, on 3 February 1994 President Bill Clinton lifted the US trade embargo against Vietnam. At the time Clinton lifted the embargo, there were still 2,238 US servicemen listed as missing. Vietnam agreed to cooperate with their recovery to the "fullest possible extent." Trade between the US and Vietnam has still been stymied by wrangling over agreements, including a stalemate in trade normalization talks in May 2000. Vietnam does not want to be perceived by China as overly friendly with the US, and the Party elite is very reluctant to embark on the economic overhaul that the US demands. This resistance to change mandated from outside has kept Vietnam from World Bank, International Monetary Fund, and World Trade Organization benefits, but has earned it some admiration among those who oppose those institutions' dominance. Vietnam's international economic relations often appear confused or confusing to observers, as the Party attempts to balance a certain level of openness with the strong will to preserve a socialist system that has become a rarity in the global economy.

Relations with Canada soured when Vietnam executed a Vietnamese-Canadian woman on heroin charges, in April 2000. The US Government (particularly members of Congress) remains critical of Vietnam's human rights policies, including arbitrary arrest and detention of citizens. In contradiction to assertions of commitment to the cause of human rights, authorities continue to severely limit freedom of speech, press, assembly and association, workers' rights, and rights of citizens to change their government. In 1995, for instance, nine Vietnamese were sentenced to 4–15 years in prison for attempting to convene a conference on democracy and human rights. Six members of a banned Buddhist group were sentenced to up to five years in prison for "sabotaging religious solidarity," and two longtime Communist Party members were sentenced to 12–15 months in jail for calling for political pluralism. Members of Vietnam's ethnic minorities such as the indigenous hill peoples have had difficulty protecting their land from logging and other encroachments. To celebrate the reunification anniversary in 2000, a large-scale amnesty of prisoners was held, which may have included political dissidents.

A May 2000 report, "Vietnam: Silencing of Dissent" by Human Rights Watch, detailed ways in which those expressing views counter to the Party line are subjected to "harassment and intimidation," although it noted that Vietnam has fewer actual political prisoners than in the past. The arrival of Internet access in Vietnam may begin to provide a means for free expression, although so far Internet content is government-monitored, and access is available only through Post Offices. Print and broadcast media remain firmly state-dominated.

The controversy between the People's Republic of China and the SRV over the control of the Spratly and Paracel archipelagoes in the South China Sea dates to the early part of this century. After the Vietnam War, when oil supplies became an issue, the dispute intensified, leading to numerous armed clashes between China and Vietnam. Vietnam, China, the Philippines, Brunei, Taiwan, and Malaysia claim all or part of the Spratly and Paracel archipelagoes. These competing claims have broad geopolitical implications regarding oil reserves, fishing rights, rights of passage for ships, prevention of nuclear dumping, and security in the region. In 1995, China occupied Mischief Reef, on an island in the area claimed by the Philippines and later that year China signed an agreement with a US oil exploration firm to drill for oil in waters claimed by Vietnam. As a member of ASEAN, Vietnam took its complaint to that body. In March 1997, a meeting of the ASEAN ambassadors was convened in Hanoi and the regional bloc emerged united in opposition to China's move against what they officially recognized as Vietnam's legal territory, marking the first time the ASEAN nations stood up in defiance of Beijing. The disputes over the islands remain unresolved at the beginning of the new century, although the main Spratlys tension of late has been between China and the Philippines.

13 GOVERNMENT

The Communist Party-controlled government of Vietnam has ruled under four state constitutions. The first was promulgated in 1946, the second in 1959, the third in 1980, and the fourth in 1992.

The 1946 constitution of the Democratic Republic of Vietnam (DRV), adopted shortly before the war with the French, was never fully implemented because of wartime conditions. On 1 January 1960, a new constitution was promulgated, instituting a largely presidential system to capitalize on Ho Chi Minh's considerable prestige. In the Republic of Vietnam (RVN), formerly South Vietnam, two constitutions were promulgated. The first, by the regime of Ngo Dinh Diem was introduced in 1956. The second was put forth when Nguyen Van Thieu was elected president in 1967. Like the DRV constitution, it created a modified presidential system, with a cabinet responsible to the legislative branch. Following the fall of the RVN in 1975, the north moved quickly toward national reunification. A nationwide National Assembly was elected in April 1976, and the Socialist Republic of Vietnam was proclaimed in early July. In December 1980, the SRV adopted a new constitution for the entire country. The new charter, more doctrinaire than its predecessors, described Vietnam as a "proletarian dictatorship" led by the Communist Party, and called for an early transition to full Socialist ownership. The highest state authority was the National Assembly. Members were elected for five-year terms by universal adult suffrage at age 18. The Assembly appointed the Council of Ministers (a cabinet of 33 ministers), the chairman of which ranked as premier. The Council of State (12 members in 1987) served as the collective presidency of Vietnam, elected by the National Assembly from among its own members and accountable to it.

In 1992 a new constitution was adopted by the National Assembly. Like the 1980 constitution it affirmed the central role of the Communist Party, stipulating that the party must be subject to the law. In support of a free-market economy, constitutional protection of foreign investment was guaranteed. However, land remained the property of the state, with individuals or enterprises entitled to the right to long-term leases that can be inherited or sold. The newly created position of president replaced the Council of State; the president has the right to appoint a prime minister subject to the approval of the National

Assembly. The National Assembly, with a maximum of 400 members, retained legislative power. Members are elected to five-year terms by universal adult suffrage.

14 POLITICAL PARTIES

The government of the SRV is a de facto one-party state ruled by the Vietnamese Communist Party (VCP). In theory, two other political parties, the Democratic Party and the Socialist Party, are granted legal existence. The Vietnamese Communist Party is the political successor to the Indochinese Communist Party, created in 1930 and formally dissolved in 1945. From 1945 until 1951, the party operated in clandestine fashion, until it emerged once more as the Vietnamese Workers' Party at the Second National Congress in 1951. The party assumed its current name in 1976, shortly after the unification of the country into the Socialist Republic of Vietnam.

The Communist Party is administered through an assembly of national delegates. National party conventions elect a Central Committee to guide party affairs between sessions of the national convention. The Central Committee in turn elects the Politburo, the highest policy making body, and a secretariat to direct day-to-day party operations.

The Democratic Party, founded in 1944, is composed chiefly of intellectuals, small entrepreneurs, and merchants. The Socialist Party, formed in 1946, represents the progressive intelligentsia. The programs of these two parties are generally indistinguishable from that of the Communist Party. An additional form of quasi-political organization in Vietnam is the United Front, composed of various functional, ethnic, and religious organizations under the umbrella of the Fatherland Front. The Fatherland Front is the linear successor of the Viet-Minh Front, formed in 1941 to provide the Communist Party with a broad organization to unify all elements in Vietnam against the French colonial regime. The Fatherland Front was formed in North Viet-Nam in 1955 as a device to mobilize the population to support the regime's goals. A similar organization, the National Liberation Front (NLF), was established in South Viet-Nam in 1960 by Nguyen Huu Tho to provide a political force in favor of national reunification. After the fall of the RVN in 1975, the NLF was merged into the Fatherland Front.

Under the RVN government, development of a political party system in the Western sense never passed the rudimentary stage. President Thieu, who headed the People's Alliance for Social Revolution, tried to consolidate anti-Communist political organizations in the RVN through a multiparty National Social Democratic Front, but formal political organizations were weak and plagued with religious and regional sectarianism. Wartime conditions and the lack of a national tradition of political pluralism were additional factors preventing the rise of a multiparty system. All such parties were abolished after the fall of Saigon in 1975.

In the SRV, elections for national and local office are controlled by the Communist Party and the state. In the July 1992 general elections 601 candidates contested 395 National Assembly seats. For the first time independent candidates—not Communist Party members or endorsed by organizations affiliated with the Party—were permitted to contest seats, although they did require Party approval in order to present themselves. Two candidates qualified, but neither was elected. In 1996, the Communist Party held its Eighth Congress, at which it was widely expected a new generation of leaders would be inaugurated; but, again the aging hard-line leaders were given another five-year term in office as the country struggled with the consequences of 12 years of economic reform and increased international openness. In 1998's national elections, the first three "self-nominated" candidates (not proposed by the Party or the Fatherland Front) managed to gain seats in the 450 member National Assembly. Women hold 26% of seats in the National Assembly as of May 2000, but have not yet risen to the top echelons of the Party.

15 LOCAL GOVERNMENT

Vietnam is divided into 50 provinces, 1 special zone (Vung Tau–Con Dao), and 3 municipalities (Hanoi, Haiphong, and Ho Chi Minh City), all administered by the national government. Districts, towns, and villages are governed by locally elected people's councils. Council candidates are screened by the party. Council members' responsibilities include upholding the Constitution and laws and overseeing local armed forces units. The councils in turn elect and oversee executive organs, called people's committees, to provide day-to-day administration. The entire system functions in a unitary fashion, with local organs of authority directly accountable to those at higher levels.

16 JUDICIAL SYSTEM

The judicial system of the SRV, as defined by the 1980 constitution, parallels that of the former DRV. The highest court in Vietnam is the Supreme People's Court, whose members are appointed for five-year terms by the National Assembly. In addition, there are local people's courts at each administrative level; military courts; and "special courts" established by the National Assembly in certain cases. Law enforcement is handled by the People's Organs of Control; the president, or procurator-general, of this body is appointed by the National Assembly.

Although the Constitution provides for the independence of judges and jurors, there is close control of the entire governmental system by the Vietnamese Communist Party (VCP) and a judicial selection process which favors appointment of jurists supportive of the VCP. Prison sentences are frequently imposed through administrative procedures without the protections of procedural due process or judicial review.

Trials are generally open to the public. Defendants have the right to be present at the trial, to have an attorney, and to cross-examine witnesses. The legal system is based on communist legal theory and French civil law. Rising crime, including violent robbery and extortion, in the cities, plus endemic corruption and smuggling, provide challenges for under-funded law enforcement agencies and the criminal justice system.

17 ARMED FORCES

Since reunification in 1975, Vietnam has emerged as one of the world's leading military powers. As of 2000, the People's Army of Vietnam was estimated at 484,000. Of that figure, the regular army had about 412,000 personnel, the air force 15,000, the air defense force 15,000, and the navy 42,000. Reserves numbered between 3–4 million. Military service is compulsory for two or three years; members of non-Vietnamese minority groups may have to serve two years.

Military expenditures were $650 million in 1997 or 9.3% of GDP. Military assistance from the then-Soviet Union reached $6 billion, 1987–91. Vietnam also has substantial quantities of US military hardware, including combat aircraft captured during the 1975 collapse of the RVN government. The naval base at Cam Ranh Bay, built by the US during the war, is now an air and naval base for Russia.

18 INTERNATIONAL COOPERATION

The SRV was admitted to UN membership on 20 September 1977. The nation belongs to ESCAP and all the nonregional specialized agencies; in mid-1983, however, Vietnam announced that it was indefinitely suspending its participation in the ILO. Vietnam is also a member of the Asian Development Bank and G-77, an applicant to the WTO, and a signatory to the Law of the Sea.

By 1982, the SRV had diplomatic relations with 112 countries. Relations with China have deteriorated since 1975, as Vietnam has moved to assert political dominance over the remainder of Indochina. The US lifted its trade embargo with Vietnam in February 1994, and on 11 July 1995, President Bill Clinton normalized diplomatic relations with the country. The first US embassy opened in Hanoi on 6 August 1995.

[19]ECONOMY

Wet-rice agriculture is the most important segment of the Vietnamese economy, and approximately one-quarter of the population was engaged in agriculture in 1998. The most diversified area in Southeast Asia in terms of mineral resources, Vietnam is well endowed with coal, tin, tungsten, gold, iron, manganese, chromium, and antimony. Foods, garments, shoes, machines, cement, chemical fertilizer, glass, tires, oil, coal, steel, and paper are the main industrial products. Most of the nation's mineral resources are located in the north, while the south is a major producer of rice and tropical agricultural products, such as rubber, coffee, and tea. The war took its heaviest economic toll on Vietnam's infrastructure, which even in the best of times was far from adequate to afford access to and mobilization of the country's agricultural and industrial resources. Further setbacks came in the late 1970s. According to official sources, in 1978 floods destroyed 3 million tons of rice, submerged over 1 million hectares (2.5 million acres) of cultivated land, and killed 20% of all cattle in the affected areas along the central coast. The termination of all Chinese aid in the same year, followed by the Chinese attack on the north in February–March 1979, dealt the economy further blows. Vietnam's economy had already been weakened by the military effort in Kampuchea (known as Cambodia until 1976 and again after 1989) and by the suspension of food aid from the EC, the UK, Australia, and New Zealand because of objections to Vietnam's refugee policies. Reportedly, the country came close to general famine in 1979.

In 1976, the regime announced a five-year plan, calling for rapid industrialization and Socialist transformation by the end of the decade. In 1979, faced with serious shortages of food and consumer goods, Vietnamese leaders approved a new program granting incentives for increased productivity and delaying the construction of farm collectives in the southern provinces. During the 1981–85 five-year plan, emphasis was placed on agriculture and the production of consumer goods. As a result, economic performance improved in the early 1980s, with the growth rate estimated at about 10% annually. Price inflation, however, became a major problem, averaging 700% in 1986–87.

The SRV's efforts at a transition from a state-controlled economy to a free-market-oriented economy have occurred in a political environment that rejects political pluralism. Motivated by a fear of being left behind economically, the government of Vietnam simultaneously fears the consequences of rapid development and accompanying social deterioration. It also does not want to abandon its socialist base, and fears any forces that promote increased democratization. Policy changes have been introduced incrementally. Still, the reforms have helped Vietnam's economy to grow at a rate of 9% a year during most of the 1990's and by almost 10% in 1996, but growth fell to about 5% in 1998 due to the Asian financial crisis. Growth in the industrial sector has been especially strong at 12% annually between 1988 and 1998. In Hanoi, the increased presence of a foreign community has spurred the availability of western-style restaurants and bars, hotel and airport renovation and upgrading, accessible public telephones, and advertising of consumer goods. On 3 February 1994 US President Bill Clinton lifted the thirty-year-old US trade embargo against Vietnam.

If Vietnam's economy is to experience sustained growth, massive improvements to transport and communications infra-structure, combined with industrial development and expansion of the export sector, are needed. Party leadership, moreover, is concerned about growing unemployment (estimated to be over 25% in 1995), the widening gap between rich and poor, bankruptcy, prostitution, and corruption. Several factors contributed to Vietnam's growing unemployment in the 1990s: natural increases in the population; monetary and other adjustments for hyperinflation, which intensified the unemployment problem by limiting growth in some sectors of the economy; the return of demobilized troops from Cambodia; repatriation of refugees; workers laid off from state enterprises; and returning guest workers. However, with capital investment, this labor force is a resource for growth in labor-intensive manufacturing, considering the low wage base in Vietnam, the good skill levels, and high motivation.

[20]INCOME

The US Central Intelligence Agency (CIA) reports that in 1998 Vietnam's gross domestic product (GDP) was estimated at $135 billion. The per capita GDP was estimated at $1,770. The annual growth rate of GDP was estimated at 4%. The average inflation rate in 1998 was 9%. The CIA defines GDP as the value of all final goods and services produced within a nation in a given year and computed on the basis of purchasing power parity (PPP) rather than value as measured on the basis of the rate of exchange. It was estimated that agriculture accounted for 28% of GDP, industry 30%, and services 42%.

The World Bank reports that for the same period per capita private consumption (in PPP terms) was $1,160. Private consumption includes expenditures of individuals, households, and nongovernmental organizations. It was estimated that between 1990 and 1998 private consumption grew at an annual rate of 10.2%. Approximately 49% of household consumption was spent on food, 15% on fuel, 4% on health care, and 18% on education. The richest 10% of the population accounted for approximately 30% of household consumption and the poorest 10% approximately 3.6%.

[21]LABOR

The total employed labor force in the SRV was estimated at about 40 million persons by 1998. In 1996, 71% worked in agriculture, about 10% in industry, and 19% in services. Open unemployment has recently become a problem and is further exacerbated by the army's planned demobilization of over 500,000 troops in the near future. However, a more prominent role given to private enterprise has the potential to leading to substantial job opportunity increases.

As of 1999, Vietnamese workers were not free to form or join independent unions. The government-controlled Trade Union Federation of Vietnam (VGCL) is the sole labor organization, and all workers automatically become members of the union of their workplace. In 1999, the VGCL had four million members throughout the country, including 95% of all public sector employees, 90% of workers in state-owned enterprises, and 70% of private sector workers.

Strikes are prohibited at enterprises that serve the public or are important to the national economy or defense. The Prime Minister decides what enterprises come under that definition. In 1999, there were about 60 strikes in all sectors. Unions also have the right to organize provided they seek approval from the VGCL. Most union activity has been directed against foreign-owned companies and, to a lesser extent, state-owned firms.

In 1999, the monthly minimum wage for foreign investment joint ventures was $45 in Ho Chi Minh City and Hanoi, and $40 elsewhere.

22AGRICULTURE

Nearly 68% of the labor force of the SRV derives its livelihood from agriculture; arable land in 1997 was 7,202,000 hectares (17,796,000 acres), of which 1,534,000 hectares (3,790,000 acres) were in permanent crops.

Only about 15% of the land in the north is arable, and 14% of it is already under intensive cultivation. Agriculture in the north is concentrated in the lowland areas of the Red River Delta and along the central coast to the south. The Mekong Delta, among the great rice-producing regions of the world, is the dominant agricultural region of the south. Excess grain from the area is shipped to the northern parts of the country. Annual food-grain production averaged 20 million tons in the early 1990s, reaching 30.7 million tons in 1998.

Rice, the main staple of the Vietnamese diet, occupies 94% of arable land. In the north, two and in some cases three crops a year are made possible through an extensive system of irrigation, utilizing upward of 4,000 km (2,500 mi) of dikes. Single-cropping remains the rule in the south, where heavy rains fall for six months of the year and virtually no rain at all during the other six months. The southern region's extensive network of canals is used mainly for transport and drainage, although some irrigational use was attempted under the RVN government. Rice production between 1975 and 1980 was adversely affected by bad weather and the regime's attempt to promote collectivization, but it began to rebound during the early 1980s. In 1980, 11.7 million tons of paddy rice were produced; output rose to 16.2 million tons in 1985 and to 19.2 million tons in 1990. Production totaled 29.1 million tons in 1998.

Other crops include corn, sorghum, cassava, sweet potatoes, beans, fruits, and vegetables. In 1998, estimated production (in thousands of tons) was sugarcane, 13,421; corn, 1,612; groundnuts in shell, 3887; and soybeans, 141. Rubber, formerly a major crop and a leading source of foreign exchange, was grown mostly on large plantations organized under the French colonial regime. As a result of the Vietnam war, practically all of the large plantations in the "redlands" area in the south were shut down, and damage to the trees was severe. In 1975, the SRV announced that rubber workers had resumed the extraction of latex from hundreds of thousands of rubber trees on plantations north and northwest of Ho Chi Minh City, most of which had lain fallow for years. Rubber production was given high priority by the Hanoi regime and increased from 40,000 tons in 1975 to an estimated 200,000 tons in 1998. Other industrial and export crops produced in Vietnam include coffee, tea, tobacco, pepper, and jute. In 1998, 392,000 tons of coffee, 47,000 tons of tea, 19,000 tons of jute, 32,000 tons of tobacco, and 53,000 tons of cashews were harvested.

Agriculture in the north has reached an advanced stage of collectivization. A land-reform program completed in 1956 distributed 810,000 hectares (2,002,000 acres) to 2,104,000 peasant families. The share of the Socialist sector in agricultural land increased from 1% in 1955 to 95% in 1975. By 1977, the north had 15,200 agricultural cooperatives and 105 state farms.

In the south, rapid collectivization began in 1978, when the regime announced a program to place the majority of southern farmers in low-level cooperative organizations by the end of the 1976–80 five-year plan. Popular resistance was extensive, however, and by 1981, less than 10% of the rural population was enrolled in full-scale collectives and a roughly equal number in low-level, semi-Socialist production solidarity teams and production collectives.

In an effort to make collectivization more palatable, the regime announced a "household contract" system, permitting members of cooperatives to lease collective land in return for an agreed proportion of total output. This system apparently encouraged many peasants to join cooperative organizations, and

the regime announced in mid-1986 that collectivization at the low level had been "basically completed" in the south, with 86.4% of the rural population enrolled in some form of collective organization.

23ANIMAL HUSBANDRY

The most important aspect of animal husbandry in the SRV remains the raising of draft animals, mainly water buffalo. Lack of feed, shelter, and technical guidance and an inability to control disease combine with the legacy of war damage to hinder the growth of this sector. Increasing the livestock is now a major priority of the Hanoi regime. The sizes of herds in 1998 (with 1975 figures in parentheses) was as follows: hogs, 18,132,000 (8,800,700); buffalo, 2,951,000 (2,193,000); and cattle 3,984,000 (1,485,000). Vietnam also had an estimated 514,000 goats, 120,000 horses, 126 million chickens, and 50 million ducks in 1998. Meat production totaled 1,654,000 tons in 1998, with pork accounting for 74%; poultry, 13%; buffalo meat, 12%; and others, 1%.

24FISHING

Fresh and dried fish and fish sauce (known as nuoc mam) are major ingredients of the Vietnamese diet, and fishing is an important occupation. Shrimp, lobster, and more than 50 commercial species of fish are found in Vietnamese waters. Ha Long Bay, the major fishing area of the north, is particularly rich in shrimp and crayfish. Fish also abound in Vietnam's rivers and canals.

The fishing industry was severely depleted after the Vietnam war, when many fishermen (often overseas Chinese) fled the country. The government has increased marine production into a major export industry. In 1997, ocean production was estimated at 1,107,500 tons, and inland production was estimated at 451,000 tons. Exports of fish products were valued at $607.4 million in 1997. Vietnamese aquacultural production that year was valued at $1.1 billion, primarily cyprinids and prawns.

25FORESTRY

In 1995, forests covered 28% of the total land area of Vietnam. Important forestry products include bamboo, resins, lacquer, quinine, turpentine, and pitch. Depletion of forests, however, has been serious, not only through US defoliation campaigns in the south during the war, but also because of the slash-and-burn techniques used by nomadic tribal groups in mountainous areas.

According to Western scientists who have visited the SRV in recent years, the damaged areas are recovering faster than anticipated, although reforestation has been slow and some regions are faced with sterility and erosion. Official policy currently emphasizes the replacement of natural forests with export crops such as cinnamon, aniseed, rubber, coffee, and bamboo. Roundwood production was estimated at 35,900,000 cu m in 1997, with 87% used as fuel wood.

26MINING

Vietnam has some important mineral resources, but the mining sector is still relatively small and undeveloped. The principal reserves, located mainly in the north, are anthracite coal, antimony, tin, chrome, apatite, phosphate, manganese, titanium, bauxite, copper, zinc, lead, nickel, graphite, mica, and some gold. Iron reserves are estimated at 520 million tons and apatite reserves at more than 1.7 billion tons. Coal production dominates the mining sector. The coal mines at Hong Gai, near Haiphong, are the most important in Southeast Asia. There is also a small coal-producing region in central Vietnam. Vietnam's movement toward a free market has resulted in increased international trade. Anthracite coal production in 1997 was 7.6 million tons. Metal production that year included zinc, 15,000 tons; tin, 4,700 tons; and gold, 10,000 kg. A new mining law governing licensing and exports was passed in 1996.

27 ENERGY AND POWER

Lack of energy is one of Vietnam's major obstacles to economic development. While coal output is substantial, most of it has been reserved for export. Until the late 1970s, the nation had no proved oil reserves, and hydroelectric power, while showing considerable potential, was poorly developed.

Since the end of the war, the regime has announced a number of major projects to provide the nation with sufficient energy resources. Several hydroelectric power stations are currently under construction, and some are already in operation. Hydropower accounted for 84% of the annual electrical output in 1996. Installed electric generating capacity in 1998 was 4.9 million kW, and 20,620 million kWh was generated.

In February 1975, the Mobil Oil Company, a US firm, struck oil off the southern coast, producing an initial outflow of 2,400 barrels per day. By mid-April, however, US oil firms—which had invested some $100 million in oil exploration in the RVN—had left the country. The SRV granted permission for several foreign companies to resume the search for oil, and in 1976 private concerns from the US, Japan, France, Canada, and the UK were quietly involved in negotiations to resume exploration. Offshore oil was also discovered by Soviet geologists working the Gulf of Tonkin. In the late 1970s, Western firms abandoned their explorations because of unpromising results, but the USSR continued its efforts and began to achieve promising results in late 1984. In September 1992, Vietnam demanded that China immediately withdraw all oil exploration ships from disputed waters in the Gulf of Tonkin. In April 1994, Mobil Corporation signed a production-sharing contract to explore for oil off the southern coast of Vietnam, becoming the first American company to drill in Vietnamese waters since 1975. As of 2000, about 30 foreign companies had been awarded contracts to operate in the waters off the southeastern coast. Vietnam estimated that it would need about $5 billion in foreign investment in its oil sector during 1996–2000 in order to fully develop its petroleum resources. Proven oil reserves as of 1 January 1999 totaled 600 million barrels; production in 1998 amounted to 246,000 barrels per day. In 1999, exports of petroleum accounted for about $2 billion, or 22% of total exports. Natural gas is believed to exist throughout much of northern Vietnam; proved reserves in 1999 were 193 billion cu m (6.8 trillion cu ft).

Control over the Spratly Islands remains a contentious issue between Vietnam, China, Taiwan, the Philippines, Brunei, and Malaysia. The reefs, many of which are partially submerged, lie atop an oil field containing an estimated 1–7 billion barrels of oil.

28 INDUSTRY

Most heavy and medium industry is concentrated in the north, including the state-owned coal, tin, chrome, and other mining enterprises; an engineering works at Hanoi; power stations; and modern tobacco, tea, and canning factories. The industrial sector in the south is characterized by light industry and consumer goods industry, including pharmaceuticals, textiles, and food processing, although there are some large utilities and cement works. Much of the industrial sector in the north was badly damaged by US bombing raids during the war. In the south, the private sector was permitted to continue in operation after 1975, but all industry and commerce above the family level was nationalized in March 1978. The results were disastrous, and the regime now permits the existence of a small private sector, mainly in the area of consumer goods and other light industry. The results have been generally favorable; industrial production in the 1980s increased at an average annual rate of 9.5%. During the 1990s, industrial production grew by about 12% per year. Industry accounted for 36% of GDP in 1998. Leading industrial sectors are food processing, garments, shoes, machine building, mining, cement, chemical fertilizers, glass, tires, oil, coal, steel, and paper.

The state-dominated industrial sector, which accounts for about 45% of the country's GDP, is still marked by inefficiency and low productivity and has retarded the growth of the private sector. This is due the low level of development, characterized by obsolete plants and machinery, shortages of capital, raw materials, energy and transport, and a command-style economic system. Many communist leaders believe that a reduction of the state sector would damage the party's legitimacy. As of 1997, state-owned cement, steel, sugar, and rice-exporting industries were in the process of being reorganized into monopoly cartels. Vietnam's assets include low wages, good skill levels, and a motivated work force.

Oil exports in 1997 totaled 9 million tons. Vietnam produces $18 billion cubic feet of gas per year. Both industries are controlled by the Vietnamese government (PETROVIETNAM). The government owns an estimated 6,000 state-owned enterprises (SOE's): the majority of non-agricultural enterprises. Most of these SOE's reflect the inefficiencies of parastatals, including debt, obsolete equipment and practices, and poor labor. In 1997, the government organized 2,000 SOE's into 88 conglomerates, accounting for 80% of the state sector and further monopolizing the industrial sector. Foreign investment, while welcome, is hard pressed to find opportunities outside of the Vietnam government's reach.

29 SCIENCE AND TECHNOLOGY

Science and technology have been one of the key weak spots in the Vietnamese economy and were targeted for significant growth during the second five-year plan (1976–80). Vietnam's leading learned societies are the Union of Scientific and Technical Associations (founded in 1983) and the General Association of Medicine (founded in 1955), both in Hanoi. The State Commission for Science and Technology supervises research at the universities and institutes attached to the Ministry of Higher Education; the Institute of Science organizes research at other institutions. All research institutes are attached to government ministries.

Courses in basic and applied sciences are offered at Cantho University (founded 1966), the Hanoi University of Technology (founded 1956), the University of Hanoi (refounded 1956), the University of Ho Chi Minh City (founded 1977), Ho Chi Minh City Pedagogical University of Technology (founded 1962), and various colleges. In 1996, the Hue College of Sciences (formerly the University of Hue) had 10 departments. Its library had 100,000 books with 50,000 titles.

In 1985, total expenditures on research and development amounted to 498 million dong; 20,000 scientists and engineers were engaged in research and development.

30 DOMESTIC TRADE

Since 1979, the government has permitted the existence of a private commercial sector, mainly in southern cities as Ho Chi Minh City and Da Nang. The number of state enterprises has fallen from 12,296 in 1989 to fewer than 6,000 in 1997, while the number of private businesses has grown to 19,000. Most private businesses are small shops and restaurants. The number of state companies has been reduced partially by mergers of smaller ones.

Two macroeconomic problems were severe in the late 1980s: hyperinflation and shortages of the major food crop, rice. The ambitious *doi moi* (renovation) program launched in 1989 had immediate results. Reforms included decentralizing economic decision-making and liberalizing prices. With increasing wealth and foreign demand the property market, construction throughout the country (but especially in Hanoi), and real estate sales and rentals in Hanoi and Ho Chi Minh City experienced a boom in the early 1990s. In 1991, private-enterprise and company laws were adopted by the National Assembly. It is estimated that private businesses account for 70% of domestic trade. Consumer items, durable, and non-durable goods, are available in greater abundance. The government has restricted the use of foreign imagery in outdoor advertising by placing limitations on foreign language, landscapes, and models.

Wholesalers in Vietnam consist of state-owned trading companies and private local wholesalers. Warehouses often have minimal facilities and equipment. The retail sector in Vietnam is undergoing rapid transformation, as new sales outlets and merchandising techniques have emerged. In the major urban areas, several Western-style mini-markets and privately-owned convenience stores have opened. Showrooms and service centers for electronics, appliances, and industrial goods offer wholesale and retail sales. In September 1996, the Saigon Superbowl opened in Ho Chi Minh City as Vietnam's first entertainment and retail center. Outside of the largest cities, retail outlets consist of family-operated market stalls or small street-front shops.

Business hours for government offices are usually Monday through Saturday between 7:30 AM and 4:30 PM, with a midday break sometime between 12:00 AM and 1:00 PM. Commercial offices are open from 8 AM to 5 PM; banks are open until 3 or 4 PM weekdays and until 11:30 AM on Saturdays. Shops and restaurants are open into the evenings and on Sundays.

31 FOREIGN TRADE

Beginning in 1980, emphasis was placed on the development of potential export commodities such as cash crops, marine products, and handicrafts, while imports were severely limited. To promote trade expansion with Japan, Singapore, and Hong Kong, several export-import firms were set up in Ho Chi Minh City under loose official supervision. The results were favorable but the experiment aroused distrust among communist party leaders, and the freewheeling enterprises were integrated into a single firm strictly supervised by the government.

The economic reforms of the late-1980s, including currency devaluation, adoption of a flexible exchange rate system, and lifting restrictions on foreign trade, contributed to the rapid growth in exports in the early 1990s. The US lifting of economic sanctions in 1994 pushed the volume of foreign trade even further upwards. Investments in Vietnam are contributing to the development and expansion of tourism. Vietnam joined the ASEAN Free Trade Area (AFTA) in 1995, committing itself to tariff reductions amongst member nations. Foreign trade in Vietnam, though, is still mostly restricted to a couple of state-owned agencies.

Import commodities include petroleum and steel products, motor vehicles and tractors, tires, foodstuffs, raw cotton, textiles, sugar, and grain. The most important export commodities for Vietnam are crude petroleum (21%), clothes (11%), and coffee (10%). Other exports include shell fish (9.7%), rice (8.2%), and shoes (8.1%). Principal trading partners in 1998 (in millions of US dollars) were as follows:

COUNTRY	EXPORTS	IMPORTS	BALANCE
Japan	1,589	1,467	122
Germany	809	395	414
United States	542	302	240
France	508	340	168
Australia	477	265	212
China (inc. Hong Kong)	410	1,687	-1,277
Singapore	385	1,666	-1,281
Taiwan	312	1,335	-1,023
Thailand	213	652	-439
Korea	167	1,498	-1,331

32 BALANCE OF PAYMENTS

Foreign investment is constricted by red tape and infrastructural problems. A more uniform and flexible exchange rate policy is expected to help increase exports. The merchandise trade deficit is partially offset by a surplus in the capital account which has benefited from an inflow of foreign money. This inflow, however, is making the Vietnamese currency overvalued (some argue by as much as 20–30%) and may be hurting exports by driving up the cost of goods. The 1998 financial crisis reflected the culmination of this overvaluation, which was remedied by 1999 with low import levels, and smaller investment figures.

The US Central Intelligence Agency reports that in 1998 the purchasing power parity of Vietnam's exports was $9.4 billion while imports totaled $11.4 billion resulting in a trade balance of -$2 billion.

33 BANKING AND SECURITIES

The State Bank of Vietnam, created in 1951, was the central bank of issue for the DRV, with numerous branches throughout the territory and an extensive agricultural and industrial loan service; in 1976, it became the central bank of the SRV. Foreign exchange is regulated by the Foreign Trade Bank. The Bank for Agricultural Development provides loans to the agricultural and fishing sectors.

Financial chaos became a constant threat during the final years of the RVN. The National Bank of Vietnam (NBV), established in 1954, was the sole authority for issuing notes, controlling credit, and supervising the formation of new banks and changes in banking establishments.

In early May 1975, shortly after the fall of Saigon, the new revolutionary regime announced the temporary closure of all banks in the south, although the RVN piaster continued to circulate as the only legal tender. Two months later, the National Bank of Vietnam was reopened under new management. Stringent regulations were announced to control inflation and limit currency accumulation. All private Vietnamese and foreign banks were closed in 1976. By then, the Hanoi regime had ordered a complete withdrawal from circulation of the RVN currency and its replacement by the dong, in use in the north.

Since the banking reorganization of July 1988, but particularly since 1992, Vietnam has moved to a diversified system in which state-owned joint-stock, joint-venture, and foreign banks provide services to a broader customer base. The first foreign representative bank office arrived in 1989. In 1992, foreign banks were granted permission to open full commercial branches. The government set up the Bank for the Poor in 1995, and gave it the task of lending to "the poor living in underprivileged areas." As of December 1998, in addition to four state-owned commercial banks, there were 52 joint-stock banks, 24 foreign bank branches, 4 joint-venture banks and 58 foreign banks with representative offices.

The state banks still dominate the system, state enterprises are still the main borrowers, and their lending is still predominantly short-term because of the skewed interest rate structure. These banks are the Bank of Foreign Trade (Vietcombank), the Vietnam Industrial and Commercial Bank (Incombank), the Vietnam Bank for Agriculture, and the Vietnam Bank for Investment and Development (BIDV).

Two banking decrees, issued in October 1990 and governing respectively commercial banks, credit cooperatives and other financial institutions, and the State Bank, aimed to regulate the financial system more strictly. Credit cooperatives had to be licensed by the State Bank rather than by local People's Committees. The first decree also gave the state commercial banks greater autonomy, and permitted them to compete with each other and to seek capital from sources other than the state. The second decree introduced new instruments through which the State Bank could control the banking sector, including open-market operations and varying reserve requirements and discount rates.

Despite these changes, the banking system is in poor health. Public confidence in the system remains low. Only 4% of all potential holders of accounts have actually opened one. There were only 10,000 bank accounts in the entire country in 1998. As of 1998, the Vietnam banking system had gained little international confidence. Loan fraud investigations and low loan liquidity have brought bank finances under scrutiny. In July of 2000, the Vietnam Stock Exchange opened its doors for the first time.

34INSURANCE

Before May 1975, life and property insurance coverage was available in the RVN from three small Vietnamese insurance companies and through local representatives of about 70 French, UK, and US insurance firms. By the end of 1975, all private insurance facilities had ceased to operate, and the Vietnam Insurance Co., established in the DRV in 1965, had become the nation's lone insurance firm. In 1981, the main types of insurance offered were motor vehicle, personal accident, hull and cargo, offshore exploration, aviation, and third-party risk.

In 1997, other insurance companies operating in Vietnam were Hochiminh Insurance Co., Nha Rong Joint-Stock Insurance Co., Petrolimex Joint Stock Insurance Co., Petrovietnam Insurance Co. (PVIC), Vietnam National Reinsurance Co., and the Yasuda Fire and Marine Insurance Co.

35PUBLIC FINANCE

The main sources of monetary revenue are income taxes, the sale of SOE's, and customs taxes. Annual deficits are financed by foreign aid. Monetary policy reforms enacted since 1988 helped end the hyperinflationary spiral of the 1980s. Aid from the former Soviet Union, formerly Vietnam's most prominent donor, was greatly reduced after the dissolution of the USSR in 1991. Foreign investment peaked in 1995 after the US declared an end to economic sanctions, but quickly receded thereafter. Implementation of a VAT in 2000 was expected to increase revenue.

The US Central Intelligence Agency (CIA) estimates that in 1996 Vietnam's central government took in revenues of approximately $5.6 billion and had expenditures of $6 billion including capital expenditures of $1.7 billion. Overall, the government registered a deficit of approximately $400 million. External debt totaled $22.4 billion.

The following table shows an itemized breakdown of government revenues and expenditures. The percentages were calculated from data reported by the International Monetary Fund. The dollar amounts (millions) are based on the CIA estimates provided above.

REVENUE AND GRANTS	100%	5,600
Tax revenue	84.4%	4,726
Non-tax revenue	12.1%	679
Capital revenue	0.7%	41
Grants	2.7%	153
EXPENDITURES	100%	6,000
General public services	6.4%	383
Education	13.5%	812
Health	3.9%	231
Social security	11.8%	708
Economic affairs and services	6.3%	379
Other expenditures	52.2%	3,130
Interest payments	3.3%	197

36TAXATION

Individual income is subject to a progressive tax ranging from 0% to 50%. In the industrial and commercial sector, taxes ranged from about 10% to 25% of actual profits. Indirect taxes include a turnover tax ranging up to 30% of gross receipts; a special sales tax on tobacco products, spirits, beer, and other items ranging from 15–100%; royalty taxes from 1–20% in most cases, and customs duties. A VAT is scheduled for implementation sometime after 2000.

37CUSTOMS AND DUTIES

All imports must be authorized by one of the state trading corporations. Customs duty is generally charged on imports and exports, with many exemptions and duty reductions available (including imports related to an aid program, and goods to be used for security, national defense, scientific, educational, training, or research purposes). The lowest rates apply to raw materials and capital equipment, while the highest rates apply to luxury goods (as high as 60%).

In 1994, the United States lifted its trade embargo on Vietnam and, in 1995, the two countries established formal relations.

38FOREIGN INVESTMENT

France was the dominant foreign investor in Indochina before World War II. Resident Chinese, however, played a major role in rice milling, retailing, and other activities (and continued to do so in the south through the early 1970s). Following the 1954 partition agreement, the French economic position in the DRV was completely liquidated, and the participation of private foreign investors in the DRV economy was prohibited. The RVN government encouraged the introduction of private capital. In March 1957, a presidential declaration provided guarantees against nationalization and expropriation without due compensation, temporary exemption from various taxes, and remittance of profits within existing regulations. Despite these efforts, because of wartime conditions, relatively little new private foreign investment was attracted to the country, apart from a few ventures by US and Japanese interests. In 1977, the SRV issued a new investment code in an effort to attract private foreign capital to help develop the country. However, because of stringent regulations and a climate of government suspicion of private enterprise, the 1977 code attracted little enthusiasm among potential investors. Only the USSR and France made sizable investments, although in recent years Japan has laid the foundation for future investment by bank loans. Beginning in 1984, the regime began to encourage the formation of joint ventures and announced that preparations were under way for a new foreign investment code.

In 1987 the National Assembly passed a liberalized investment law seeking to improve the overall investment climate and emphasize the development of export industries and services. The Vietnamese investment laws are much more liberal than those of other countries in Southeast Asia. The code permitted wholly owned foreign enterprises in Vietnam, levied low taxes on profits, allowed full repatriation of profits after taxes, and guaranteed foreign enterprises against government appropriation. The law also encouraged oil exploration. Factors hindering performance of foreign investors are bureaucracy, lack of management expertise, smuggling and corruption, and an underlying distrust and uncertainty on the part of officialdom.

In early 1994 the government announced three proposals intended to improve the investment environment and increase foreign trade: to expedite decisions for licensing on small investment projects; to eliminate the requirements for import-export licenses for certain unspecified commodities; and to prepare a list of industries that would be off limits to foreign investors. Another recent decision is to allow insurance companies and brokerages, and reinsurance between companies. The Foreign Investment Law was amended in 1996 to give more authority over investment licensing to local governments.

Foreign investment entered Vietnam at an average rate of $4 billion per year during the 1990s, however in 1999 this figure shrank to $1.4 billion, and the real amount for 1998 (in part due to the Asian financial crisis) was about 500 million. The government's goal was to realize $13–15 billion of implemented foreign capital by the year 2000. As of 1999, Singapore was the largest foreign investor with $5.9 billion of total investments approved by the Vietnam government between 1988 and 1999 (only $2 billion actualized). Other major investors included Taiwan, Hong Kong, Japan, South Korea, France, the British Virgin Islands, Russia, the US, and the UK. Their licensed capital came to a total of $22.4 billion, only $7.5 billion of which was actually spent.

39ECONOMIC DEVELOPMENT

With the defeat of the RVN forces in April 1975, Vietnam faced the task of restoring its infrastructure, damaged by the war, while working toward the goal of a technologically advanced society. Long-range planning centered on the second five-year plan (1976–80), which called for major emphasis on heavy industry and rapid agricultural growth. Due to factors including unfavorable weather, decreased foreign aid, and high military expenditures—combined with managerial inefficiency—the plan was a disaster. Industrial production grew by only 0.6% and agriculture by 1.9%. The third five-year plan (1981–85) was more modest in its objectives. Emphasis was placed on agricultural development and the promotion of consumer goods, with industrial development in the background. Socialist transformation remained a high priority, although a less rapid rate of change was expected than during the previous five years. Although the goals of the new plan were more realistic than those set for its predecessor, its success was limited. Growth figures in industry (9.5%) and agriculture (4.9%) improved significantly over the previous five years. Production remained spotty in key areas, however, and problems of mismanagement—primarily by the state sector—proliferated.

The fourth five-year plan (1986–90) continued the previous plan's emphasis on agricultural growth and expansion of exports and light industry. Efforts to promote Socialist transformation were to continue, but at a gradual pace and "by appropriate forms." Development aid continued to come primarily from the former USSR and other CMEA countries. In 1978, the SRV became fully integrated into the CMEA planning and development structure, and its five-year plans were coordinated with those of its CMEA partners. Planned Soviet outlays for the 1986–90 period totaled some $11–13 billion. This aid and trade waned with the decline of the USSR, with the full cutoff occurring in 1991. The SRV's new economic emphasis, *doi moi* (renovation) was instituted by Nguyen Van Linh following the Sixth National Party Congress (1986). His plan included policy and structural reforms for a market-based economic system: price decontrol (liberalized prices), currency devaluation, private sector expansion through decollectivization of agriculture (food production), legal recognition of private business, new foreign investment laws, autonomy of state enterprises, business accounting methods, devolution of government decision-making in industry to enterprise level, and limiting government participation to macroeconomic issues. Implementation of these policies was achieved with varied success.

Inflation policy and agricultural reform resulted in immediate increases in rice production. Vietnam changed from a net importer of rice to the third major rice exporter after Thailand and the US. Agriculture remains the most important economic sector, accounting for about one third of GDP and about 75% of the labor force. There were 12,000 government-owned companies employing 30% of Vietnam's labor force that held 75% of the country's assets, and monopolized 86% of bank credit in 1992. The privatization program met with resistance from conservative politicians, the companies, and from foreign investors. Conservatives feared that privatization undermined the economic basis of socialism, and foreign investors were wary of poor investments with meager legal underpinnings. Opposition from managers who would lose a "free hand," and employees whose jobs might be replaced by new equipment also arose. In 1994 the director and deputy director of the textile company that was the flagship for this privatization program were dismissed for alleged corruption. US President Bill Clinton's lifting of the 30-year-old trade embargo in 1994 opened the way for waiting American companies to do business in Vietnam. International assistance during the mid-1990s was from the World Bank for education and agricultural reforms, the Japan Overseas Economic Cooperation Fund for infrastructure programs, the UK for soft loans, technical training and refugee resettlement, and from the Asian Development Bank. A continuation of reforms promoting foreign investment and minimizing the state's role in the economy moved slowly in the late 1990s due to political corruption and inefficiencies. The Asian financial crisis negatively affected investor confidence in the region, severely reducing Vietnam's main focus of economic development as of late. A complete overhaul of the financial regulatory system is still necessary in order to stimulate the economy.

40SOCIAL DEVELOPMENT

The war hindered systematic provision of social services in both the DRV and the RVN. Social security legislation under the RVN included the workers' compensation provisions of the labor code of 1952, which required that some degree of medical care be given employees under contract. Also established by law in 1953 was an employer-financed family-allowance system, which covered about 15% of the population. In the DRV, social services had been provided to the extent that scarce resources permitted.

Since the end of the war in 1975, the SRV has been attempting to lay the foundations of an advanced Socialist society. However, attempts to improve social services were hampered by the poor performance of the economy. A social security scheme passed into law in 1995 provides old age, disability and surivivorship benefits, as well as worker's injury and medical insurance schemes. Coverage is compulsory for public employees and employees of companies with more than 10 workers. Pensions are funded by 5% of employee wages, 15% of employer payroll, and government contributions.

Women have full legal rights under law, but are subject to various forms of social discrimination. Few women are found in senior management or high level government positions, but business and the public sector nevertheless employ many women, and they are an important part of the economy. Women also generally receive lower wages than their male counterparts. As of 1997, 117 of 450 parliamentary seats were held by women.

The human rights record is poor, and there are continuing reports of arbitrary detention and the mistreatment of detainees during interrogation. However, restrictions on free speech and religion have been lessened slightly in recent years, as have restrictions on travel. Human rights organizations are not permitted to operate in Vietnam.

41HEALTH

Wars in Vietnam since 1946 have undermined much of the progress made by the DRV, RVN, and SRV in the health field. Especially severe was the damage to urban hospitals in the north. A 1976 WHO report indicated the dimensions of that destruction: 24 research institutes and specialized hospitals, 28 provincial hospitals, 94 district hospitals, and 533 community health centers, all destroyed mainly as the result of US bombing. The three decades of intermittent war also had a devastating effect on health conditions in the south. At the war's end in 1975, many endemic diseases were observed to be on the increase, in alarming contrast with trends among other affected countries in Southeast Asia. WHO reported in 1976 that malaria had been both widespread and increasing in the south in 1975. During 1965–74, 5,000 cases of bubonic plague were occurring annually, with a mortality rate of 5%. Saigon was said to have had a tuberculosis rate two to three times that in neighboring countries, while leprosy (involving an estimated 80,000–160,000 cases) was increasing. Commonly reported diseases in Vietnam were diarrheal disease (22,422 deaths in 1995); malaria (136,069 cases in 1993); and tuberculosis (35,813 in 1994). Venereal and paravenereal diseases were said to have afflicted 1 million persons in the south (about 5% of the total population) and, WHO claimed, 80% of RVN soldiers. Opiate addiction, it was said, affected about 500,000 persons. There is some evidence that HIV prevalence is spreading. In 1992–95, 324 of all intravenous drug users were said to be infected. The HIV-1 seroprevalence in 1997 was 0.2 per 100 adults. In 1996, 316 AIDS cases were reported. Tobacco consumption has increased from 1.0 kg a year per adult in 1984–86 to 1.1 kg in 1995.

Since reunification in 1975, some progress in health care has been made. Tuberculosis has been largely controlled (99 cases per 100,000 people reported in 1996), and the incidence of many contagious diseases has been reduced. In 1990–95, 38% of the population had access to safe water, and 21% had adequate sanitation. Immunization rates for children up to one year old in 1997 were tuberculosis (96%); diphtheria, pertussis, and tetanus (95%); polio (95%); and measles (96%).

The SRV reported life expectancy in 1999 to be 68 years, and infant mortality to be 35 per 1,000 live births. Maternal mortality was 200 per 100,000 live births in 1991–93, and overall mortality was 7 per 1,000 people in 1997.

In 1999 the birth rate was 21 per 1,000 people. An estimated 65% of married women (ages 15 to 49) were using contraception in 1994, and family planning services were provided to 2,157,000 people in 1992. Abortion is available on request. Vietnam's fertility rate in 1999 was 2.4, down nearly 2% from the previous 5-year period.

In 1991, the country had 275,560 physicians, 58,912 nurses, and 14,813 midwives. In 1992, there were 35 physicians per 100,000 people, with a nurse to doctor ratio of 4.9. In 1990, there were 3.3 hospital beds per 1,000 inhabitants. About 97% of the population had access to health care services in 1993, and the country spent $157 million on health care in 1990 or 5.2% of gross domestic product in 1990–95. Public health expenditures were 1% of GDP in 1993.

During the early 1980s, foreign visitors routinely reported observing severe cases of malnutrition and shortages of medical equipment and supplies. While conditions have probably improved as agricultural production has increased, most Vietnamese continue to live at the minimum level of subsistence. About 45% of all children under 5 were classified as malnourished in 1989–1995. In February of 1996, Vietnam was considering fortification of foods with iron and Vitamin A. In 1995, the Vietnamese government issued the National Plan of Action for Nutrition (1995–2000), which aimed to eliminate food insecurity, reduce undernutrition, and reduce micronutrient deficiencies.

42 HOUSING

Housing is a serious problem in the SRV, particularly in urban areas of the north where war damage caused problems of overcrowding, and lack of resources has hampered efforts to resolve the problem. By 1986, housing had become a critical problem in Hanoi, particularly in the central sections of the city, where per capita living space was reduced to four sq m. Large flats are gradually being erected in the suburbs to ease the problem. In the meantime, many families live in temporary quarters built directly on the sidewalk or attached to other buildings. Housing is less a problem in the countryside, where many farm families have begun to take advantage of a rising standard of living to build new houses of brick and stone. Similarly, in the south, housing is available to meet the requirements of the population because building construction had continued at a relatively high level during the war years. In 1989, the majority of housing units were semi-permanent (structures with brick walls and tile roofs lasting about 20 years).

43 EDUCATION

In the mid-1970s, literacy in the south was estimated at about 65%, while in the north a rate of 85% was claimed in 1975. By the year 2000, adult illiteracy rates for the reunified country were estimated at 6.7% (males, 4.3%; females, 9.0%). After 1975, the educational system in the south was restructured to conform to the Socialist guidelines that had been used in the DRV. The 12-year school cycle was reduced to 10 years, and the more than 20,000 teachers in the south were among those subjected to "reeducation." By 1976, some 1,400 tons of textbooks printed in the DRV had been shipped to the south, and the books used previously under the RVN were destroyed. In addition, more than 1,000 formerly private schools in the south were brought under state control. Today, education is free at all levels, and five years of primary education is compulsory.

In the mid-1980s, the educational system was rapidly expanding to cope with the nation's rising population. In 1998, primary schools had 324,431 teachers and 10,431,337 students, with a student-to-teacher ratio of 32 to one. In the same year, secondary schools had 226,491 teachers and 6,642,350 students. There are 90 colleges and three universities in the SRV. The major university is in Hanoi. In 1997, universities and equivalent institutions had 23,522 teachers and enrolled 509,300 students.

44 LIBRARIES AND MUSEUMS

The École Française d'Extrême-Orient maintained an extensive research library in Hanoi, which was transferred intact to the DRV. Now the National Library, it has about 1,200,000 volumes; the bulk of the present collection has been added since 1954 and includes a substantial number of Russian titles. The General Scientific Library in Ho Chi Minh City (formerly the National Library) maintains a collection of over 600,000 volumes. Many books in the south's library system were burned following the reunification, especially in the larger libraries at Ho Chi Minh City, Hué, and Da Nang. According to official sources, the number of libraries in the country has increased since 1975. Hanoi University Library holds 800,000 volumes and the Hanoi National Institute of Technology holds 700,000 volumes.

The collections of the Musée Louis-Finot, an archaeological and cultural museum established by the French in Hanoi, were transferred intact to the DRV. These collections, now part of the Historical Museum, contain artifacts and related material from archaeological discoveries in Thanh Hoa and Yen Bay, including a 2,500-year-old burial boat and an excellent array of bronze implements. Hanoi's National Art Gallery includes a folk-art collection and Vietnamese Bronze Age artifacts. Notable also is the Museum of the Revolution, grouping memorabilia of Vietnam's struggle for independence from the French since the early 1900s. The Army Museum, housed in the Hanoi Citadel, contains a collection of weapons and documents concerning the Indochina war. The Vietnamese Fine Arts Museum (1966) houses exhibits on the decorative and applied arts, and folk and modern art. The architecture of religious edifices and former Vietnamese imperial structures reflect the country's cultural heritage. The Ho Chi Minh City Museum, founded in 1977, has a section devoted to the revolution and another to ancient arts. The Ho Chi Minh Museum, also founded in 1977, studies his life and work.

45 MEDIA

Vietnam's postal, telegraph, and telephone services are under the Ministry of Communications. The country made significant progress in upgrading its telecommunications system in the 1990s: all provincial switchboards have been digitized and fiberoptic and microwave transmission systems have been extended from the major cities to the provinces. However Vietnam still lags behind its Southeast Asian neighbors. There were an estimated 800,000 telephones as of 1995.

Hanoi has a strong central broadcasting station, the Voice of Vietnam, boosted by local relay transmitters. Since 1975, almost the entire country has been blanketed by a wired loudspeaker system. Radio programs beamed abroad include broadcasts in Chinese, English, French, Japanese, Spanish, Thai, Bahasa Indonesia, Russian, Khmer, and Lao, and there are special broadcasts to mountain tribes. Television was introduced into the RVN in 1966, and an extensive service, reaching some 80% of the population, was in operation by the early 1970s. A pilot television station was inaugurated in the DRV in 1971. Many of the major cities now have television stations, all under the guidance of the Ministry of Information, which replaced the State Committee for Radio and Television in 1987. As of 1999, there were 228 FM radio stations. In 1997, Vietnam had 106 radios, 180 television sets, and 2 mobile phones per 1,000 population.

Most newspapers in the south were shut down by the PRG in 1975, but some papers that had been sympathetic to the NLF/DRV cause were allowed to continue publication. All press is strictly controlled by the Ministry of Culture and Information. Principal Vietnamese dailies (with their estimated 1999 circulations) are shown in the following table:

	AFFILIATION	CIRCULATION
HANOI		
Nhan Dan	Communist Party	200,000
Quan Doi Nhan Dan	Army	70,000
Hanoi Moi	Communist Party	35,000
HO CHI MINH CITY		
Giai Phong	Communist Party	100,000

46 ORGANIZATIONS

The principal mass organization is the Fatherland Front, which merged in January 1977 with the National Liberation Front and with the Vietnam Alliance of National, Democratic, and Peace Forces. The Fatherland Front draws up single slates of candidates in all elections and seeks to implement the political, economic, and social policies of the Communist Party. Other organizations that form part of the Fatherland Front are the Peasant Union, with some 5 million members; the Ho Chi Minh Communist Youth Union, with 4 million members; and the Vietnamese Women's Union, with 11.4 million members. Industrial and commercial enterprises are represented by the Chamber of Commerce of the SRV in Hanoi.

Many of the various types of organizations found in Western countries had existed in the RVN since the 1950s. Among them were the Boy Scouts and Girl Scouts, cooperatives, sports organizations, and various cultural, professional, and youth associations. Most of these bodies were disbanded after 1975.

47 TOURISM, TRAVEL, AND RECREATION

Vietnam possesses a number of historic and scenic areas of interest to tourists. In the north, the beauty of Ha Long Bay, with its countless grottoes and rock spits jutting vertically into the sea, is well known. Hanoi itself, with its historical monuments, its lakes and pagodas, and its extensive French colonial architecture, is extremely picturesque, but hotel facilities are both inadequate and expensive.

In 1986 and 1987, the government made plans to expand international and domestic airline service, double hotel capacity in the major cities, simplify the complicated visa restrictions, and grant shore leave passes to passengers on cruise ships stopping at Vietnamese ports. As a result of these measures, tourism grew rapidly. From 20,000 in 1986, tourist arrivals rose to 450,000 in 1992 and 1,715,637 in 1997. That year there were 56,000 hotel rooms with 106,421 beds and an occupancy rate of 43%. All visitors need visas and must register with the government within 48 hours of arrival.

According to 1999 UN estimates, the cost of staying in Ho Chi Minh City was $80 per day. Travel costs in Hanoi were estimated at $108 per day.

48 FAMOUS VIETNAMESE

Important figures in Vietnamese history include the sisters Trung Trac and Trung Nhi, national heroines who led a revolt (AD 40–43) against China when that nation was imperial master of Tonkin and North Annam; Ngo Quyen, who regained Vietnamese independence from China in 938; Tran Hung Dao, who defeated the forces of Kublai Khan in 1288; Emperor Le Loi, national hero and brilliant administrator, in whose reign the Vietnamese legal code was promulgated in 1407; Emperor Gia Long (d.1820), who reunified Vietnam in the early 19th century; and Le Van Duyet (1763–1832), a military leader who helped the emperor to unify the country.

Phan Boi Chau (1875–1940) was Vietnam's first modern nationalist and, like China's Sun Yat-sen, is claimed by Vietnamese Communists and nationalists alike as their spiritual leader. Ho Chi Minh ("The Enlightener"), born Nguyen That Thanh (1890–1969), was a man of many other pseudonyms. Ho Chi Minh was a founding member of the French Communist Party in 1920 and founded the Vietnamese Communist Party in 1930. Often referred to as "Uncle Ho," he was president of the DRV from 1945 until his death. Gen. Vo Nguyen Giap (1912–1975), a professor of history turned strategist, organized the first anti-French guerrilla groups in 1944, led the Viet-Minh in its eight-year struggle against France, and defeated the French at Dien Bien Phu; subsequently he served as minister of defense, commander in chief of the army, and vice-premier of the DRV. Truong Chinh ("Long March," 1906–1988), the DRV's foremost Communist thinker, was secretary-general of the Vietnamese Communist Party from 1940 until 1956, when he was purged from his post for having mismanaged the land reform; exonerated shortly thereafter, he was president of the Council of State (1981–87). Pham Von Dong (b.1906), a member of the nobility, joined the Vietnamese revolutionary movement at its inception and became minister of foreign affairs in 1954, premier of the DRV in 1955, and premier of the SRV in 1976; he resigned in 1987. Le Duan (1907–86), first secretary of the Communist Party, presided over Vietnam's reunification and the formation of the SRV. Le Duc Tho (1911–1990), a member of the Communist Party Politburo but with no post in the government, was the DRV's chief negotiator in talks that led to the 1973 Paris Peace Agreement; for his role, Le shared with US Secretary of State Henry Kissinger the 1973 Nobel Peace Prize.

Prominent political figures in the formation of the RVN included Bao Dai (Nguyen Vinh Thuy; b.France, 1913), who had served as nominal emperor of Annam under the Japanese and had attempted to form a unified national government after the war, and Ngo Dinh Diem (1901–63), who served as president of the RVN from its founding on 26 October 1955 until his overthrow and death in November 1963. Nguyen Cao Ky (b.1930), an RVN air force commander, took control of the government in the coup of June 1965. Gen. Nguyen Van Thieu (b.1923) was elected president of the RVN in the elections of September 1967 (with Ky as his vice-presidential running mate), an office he retained until the RVN's defeat in 1975. Both Thieu and Ky left the country in 1975, Thieu taking up residence in Taiwan and Ky in the US. The new leadership in the south, following the 1975 NLF victory, was headed by Pham Hung (1912–1988), chairman of the southern wing of the Communist Party since 1967; Huynh Thanh Phat (1913–1989), the PRG premier, who later became a member of the Council of State; and Nguyen Thi Binh (b.1927), the PRG's foreign affairs minister who had headed the NLF delegation at the Paris talks and who also became a Council of State Member. Pham Hung became premier of the SRV in 1987, and Vo Chi Cong (b.1913?) became president of the Council of State. Nguyen Van Linh (b.1913) became general secretary of the Communist Party in December 1986.

The 13th-century writer Nguyen Si Co is regarded as one of the first truly Vietnamese authors; he is best known for his collection titled *Chieu Quan Cong Ho.* Other leading literary figures are two 15th-century poets, Ho Huyen Qui and Nguyen Binh Khien; the latter's collection, *Bach Van Thi Tap,* is a classic of Vietnamese literature. Nguyen Du (1765–1820) wrote a famous novel in verse, *Kim Van Kieu.* Hoang Ngoc Phach, who wrote the romantic novel *To Tam* (1925), is credited with the introduction of Western literary standards into Vietnamese literature.

⁴⁹DEPENDENCIES
Vietnam has no territories or colonies.

⁵⁰BIBLIOGRAPHY

Beresford, Melanie. *National Unification and Economic Development in Vietnam.* New York: St. Martin's, 1989.

Buttinger, Joseph. *A Dragon Defiant: A Short History of Vietnam.* New York: Praeger, 1972.

Chanda, Nayan. *Brother Enemy: The War After the War.* San Diego: Harcourt Brace Jovanovich, 1986.

Cima, Ronald J. (ed.). *Vietnam: A Country Study.* Washington, D.C.: Library of Congress, 1989.

Duiker, William J. *Historical Dictionary of Vietnam.* Metuchen, N.J.: Scarecrow Press, 1989.

Fall, Bernard B. *The Two Viet-Nams: A Political and Military Analysis.* New York: Praeger, 1963.

———.*The Communist Road to Power in Vietnam.* 2d ed. Boulder, Colo.: Westview, 1996.

———,ed. *Ho Chi Minh on Revolution: Selected Writings, 1920–66.* New York: Praeger, 1967.

Fforde, Adam. *The Limits of National Liberation.* New York: Methuen, 1987.

Gardner, Lloyd C. *Approaching Vietnam: from World War II through Dienbienphu, 1941–1954.* New York: W.W. Norton, 1988.

Fall, Bernard B. (ed.) *Ho Chi Minh on Revolution: Selected Writings, 1920–66.* New York: Praeger, 1967.

Hoang, Van Chi. *From Colonialism to Communism: A Case History of North Vietnam.* New York: Praeger, 1964.

Hodgkin, Thomas L. *Vietnam: The Revolutionary Path.* New York: St. Martin's, 1980.

Karnow, Stanley. *Vietnam: A History.* New York: Viking, 1983.

Kolko, Gabriel. *Anatomy of a War: Vietnam, the United States, and the Modern Historical Experience.* New York: Pantheon, 1985.

Lewy, Guenter. *America in Vietnam.* New York: Oxford University Press, 1978.

Marr, David G., and Kristine Alilunas-Rodgers. *Vietnam.* Santa Barbara, Calif.: Clio Press, 1992.

Nguyen Khac Vien. *Contemporary Vietnam (1858–1980).* Hanoi: Red River, 1981.

Oberdorfer, Don. *Tet!* New York: Doubleday, 1971.

Olson, James Stuart. *Where the Domino Fell: America and Vietnam, 1945 to 1995.* 2d ed. New York: St. Martin's, 1996.

Pimlott, John. *Vietnam, the Decisive Battles.* New York: Macmillan, 1990.

Porter, Gareth. *Vietnam: the Politics of Bureaucratic Socialism.* Ithaca, N.Y.: Cornell University Press, 1993.

Shaplen, Robert. *Bitter Victory.* New York: Harper & Row, 1986.

Short, Anthony. *The Origins of the Vietnam War.* New York: Longman, 1989.

Terzani, Tiziano. *Giai Phong! The Fall and Liberation of Saigon.* New York: St. Martin's, 1976.

Truong Nhu Tang. *Vietcong Memoir.* San Diego: Harcourt Brace Jovanovich, 1986.

The United States and Vietnam from War to Peace: Papers from an Interdisciplinary Conference on Reconciliation. Edited by Robert M. Slabey. Jefferson, N.C.: McFarland & Co., 1996.

Williams, Michael C. *Vietnam at the Crossroads.* New York: Council on Foreign Relations Press, 1992.

Woodside, Alexander. *Community and Revolution in Modern Vietnam.* Boston: Houghton-Mifflin, 1976.

YEMEN

Republic of Yemen
Al-Jumhuriyah al-Yamaniyah

CAPITAL: Sana (Şan'ā).

FLAG: The national flag is a tricolor of red, white, and black horizontal stripes, with a green star on the white stripe.

ANTHEM: *Al-Watani (Peace to the Land).*

MONETARY UNIT: The Yemeni riyal (YR) is a paper currency of 100 fils. There are coins of 1, 5, 10, 25, and 50 fils and notes of 1, 5, 10, 20, 50, and 100 riyals. YR1 = $0.0062 (or $1 = YR161.00) as of 31 March 2000.

WEIGHTS AND MEASURES: The metric system is being introduced, but local measures remain in common use.

HOLIDAYS: Labor Day, 1 May; Day of National Unity, 22 May; Revolution Day, 26 September; National Day, 14 October; Independence Day, 30 November. Movable Muslim holidays include Laylat al-Miraj, 'Id al-Fitr, 'Id al-'Adha', Milad an-Nabi, and 1st of Muharram.

TIME: 3 PM = noon GMT.

¹LOCATION, SIZE, AND EXTENT

Yemen is located in the southern part of the Arabian Peninsula. It is slightly larger than twice the size of the state of Wyoming with a total area of 527,970 sq km (203,850 sq mi). Yemen shares boundaries with Sa'udi Arabia on the N, Oman on the E, Gulf of Aden on the S, and the Red Sea on the W, and has a total boundary length of 3,652 km (2,269 mi).

²TOPOGRAPHY

The topography of Yemen features a narrow coastal plain backed by flat-topped hills and rugged mountains. Dissected upland desert plains in the center of the country slope into the desert interior of the Arabian Peninsula. The highest known point is the summit of Jabal Hadhur, rising 3,760 m (12,336 ft) above the Red Sea coast. The western part of the country contains fertile soil in its highland plateaus which rise from about 1,200 to 3,000 m (4,000 to 10,000 ft). Approximately 6% of Yemen's land is arable. A system of wadis drain mountain slopes into the desert and into the Gulf of Aden.

³CLIMATE

Extreme humidity combines with high temperatures—as high as 54°C (129°F) in the shade—to produce a stiflingly hot climate. Winds blowing northwest in summer and southwest in winter bring little rain but cause severe sandstorms. During January and February, however, the temperature averages about 20°C (68°F). The climate of the highlands is generally considered the best in Arabia. Summers are temperate and winters are cool, with some frost. Temperatures vary from 22°C (72°F) in June, the hottest month, to 14°C (57°F) in January. Rainfall in the highlands ranges from 41 cm (16 in) at Sana to 81 cm (32 in) in the monsoon area of the extreme southwest. The average year-round temperature at Sana is 18°C (64°F).

⁴FLORA AND FAUNA

Vegetation is sparse along the coast, but in the highlands and wadis, it is plentiful. Acacia, date palm, and many fruit trees are common. Many varieties of grapes are cultivated. Custard apple, euphorbia, and spurge grow in abundance. Alpine roses, balsam, basil, wild elder, and Judas tree are among the flowers and herbs. Wild mammals include the baboon, gazelle, leopard, and mountain hare. Scorpions and millipedes are everywhere, but snakes are less common. Many varieties of birds are found, including the bustard, hawk, vulture, raven, parrot, hornbill, honeysucker, and weaver finch. More than 27,000 varieties of insects and over 600 specimens of flowering plants have been collected in Yemen.

⁵ENVIRONMENT

Yemen's main environmental problems have long been scarcity of water, soil erosion, and desertification. Water pollution is a problem due to contaminates from the oil industry, untreated sewage, and salinization The nation has 0.6 cubic miles of water with 93.4% used for farming activity and 2% for industrial purposes. Natural forests in mountainous areas have been destroyed by agricultural clearing and livestock overgrazing. The National Environmental Council, established in 1976, disseminates information on conservation. In response to the nation's environmental needs, the government of Yemen has created laws governing the use of the country's water supply. Law Number 42 (1991) protects water and marine life.

Endangered or extinct species include the northern bald ibis, the South Arabian leopard, and two species of turtle (green sea and hawksbill).

⁶POPULATION

The population of Yemen in 2000 was estimated at 17,521,085. An estimated 3.1% of the population is 65 years of age or older. The projected population for the year 2005 is 20,807,000, assuming a crude birthrate of 43 per 1,000 population and a death rate of 8, resulting in a natural rate of change of 3.5% for the period 2000–2005. The population rate of change between 1995 and 2000 was 3.7%. The population density in 1998 was 31 per sq km (80 per sq mi).

Most of the population is concentrated in the Tihama foothills and central highlands of the former YAR. Most of southern

Yemen is very sparsely populated. It was estimated that 38% of the population lived in urban areas in 2000, up from 20% in 1980. The capital city, Sanaa, had a 2000 population of 629,000. Other large cities include Taiz (2,206,000), Hodiedah (1,750,000), and Aden (562,000), the chief port and former capital of the PDRY. Yemen's next census was scheduled to take place in 2004.

7MIGRATION

There were 1,168,199 citizens of Yemen working abroad in 1986. Most were working in Sa'udi Arabia and other Gulf states. When Yemen took Iraq's side in the war that followed its 1990 annexation of Kuwait, Sa'udi Arabia effectively expelled an estimated 800,000–1,000,000 Yemeni workers by revoking their work privileges. These workers had been sending home some $3 billion a year in remittances.

Many people from the Wadi Hadramawt in southern Yemen have worked abroad in East Africa, India, and Indonesia for centuries. Following independence and the establishment of a leftist regime in the PDRY, more than 300,000 people fled to the north, including about 80,000 Yemenis from the YAR, and virtually all minority groups left the country. Subsequent political upheavals resulted in further emigration.

In 1992 more than 60,000 Yemenis returned from the Horn of Africa, chiefly because of turmoil in Somalia. In 1998 and 1999, Yemen experienced a significant influx of Somali asylum seekers, who fled their country for economic reasons. They were accommodated in a refugee camp in Al Ghahain, near Aden, supervised by the UN High Commissioner for Refugees (UNHCR). As of September 1999 the government had expressed its desire to move the camp to a new site about 140 km from Aden and was working with UNHCR to finalize a location. By the end of June 1999, UNHCR had helped 874 Somali refugees repatriate to safe areas in their homeland. In September 1999, there were approximately 57,000 Somali refugees, of whom 15,000 were being assisted by UNHCR. Other refugees were mainly from Eritrea, Ethiopia, and Middle Eastern countries.

The net migration rate in 1999 was zero.

8ETHNIC GROUPS

Since independence, the population has been almost entirely Arab. However, there are Afro-Arab concentrations in western coastal locations, South Asians in southern regions, and small European communities in major metropolitan areas. Many ethnologists contend that the purest "Arab" stock is to be found in the YAR. Classified as Joktanic Semites, the Yemenis claim descent from Himyar, great-grandson of Joktan, who, according to the book of Genesis, was descended from Shem, the son of Noah. Yemenis were prominent in the early armies of Islam and thus helped to Arabize much of the Middle East. The Tihama has been subjected to occupation and infiltration by many conquerors, and its people show significant admixtures of other racial types, including Negroid peoples. A small minority of Akhdam perform menial tasks throughout the country. The history of the Yemenite Jews predates by centuries the Islamic Hijra (AD 622). How they came to settle in the region has not been determined.

9LANGUAGES

Arabic, the national language, is spoken in a variety of dialects. In vocabulary and other features there is a considerable difference between the classical language used for writing and formal speaking and the spoken dialect used for ordinary discourse. Traces of the ancient South Arabian languages spoken prior to the coming of Muhammad appear in the dialects of the more remote districts of southern Yemen. Mahri, a rare and relatively

unstudied language of unknown origins, is spoken in the east. English is widely understood in the former PDRY.

10RELIGIONS

The Republic of Yemen is a Muslim country. Almost all of the inhabitants are Sunnis of the Shaf'i school, one of the four major schools of Islamic law. They reside chiefly in the coastal plains and the southwestern part of the country. Most of those remaining are Shi'as of the Zaydi sect, who live in the highlands. This sect, originating in the 9th century, takes its name from Zayd bin 'Ali (d.740), a descendant of Muhammad, and doctrinally is very close to Sunni Islam. In addition, there is a small minority of Isma'ilis, members of another Shi'a sect. Nearly all of the country's once sizable Jewish population has emigrated. There are no legal restrictions on the few hundred who remain, although there are traditional restrictions on places of residence and choice of employment. About 500 Jews live in the villages between Sana'a and Saada in northern Yemen. There are also small Christian and Hindu communities. In remote areas there is still evidence of shamanism, animism, and other indigenous forms of religion.

11TRANSPORTATION

Through the 1950s, the YAR's transportation system consisted of a few primitive mud tracks connecting the larger towns. Then, in 1961, technicians from China completed a 224-km (139-mi) road between Sana and Al-Hudaydah, the YAR's first asphalt highway. Seven years later, the US finished the 386-km (240-mi) highway linking Sana, Ta'izz, and Al-Mukha; the USSR completed a road from Ta'izz to Al-Hudaydah in 1969. Other paved roads extend from Sana to Ma'rib, from Sana to Sa'idah, from Ta'izz to At-Turba, from the Sana-Ta'izz highway to Al-Bayda, and from Ta'izz to Aden ('Adan) in the PDRY. By 1996, Yemen had about 64,725 km (40,220 mi) of roadway, of which only 5,243 km (3,258 mi) were paved. Passenger cars numbered only 227,800 in 1995, and there were 281,800 commercial vehicles.

Improvements to the main port of Al-Hudaydah have expanded berthing, storage, and handling facilities and increase cargo capacity to 1,750,000 tons annually. Other ports are Al-Mukha, Aden, and Salif, which have sheltered harbors and deepwater berths capable of taking 10,000-ton ships. In 1998, Yemen had a merchant fleet of 3 ships, totaling 12,059 GRT.

Progress in air transportation has been rapid in recent years. In 1998 there were 48 airports, 12 with paved runways. The principal airfield, capable of handling modern jet aircraft, is Ar-Rahba International Airport, north of Sana. There are smaller international airports at Al-Hudaydah, Ta'izz, and Aden. Yemen Airways (Alyemda), the national airline, operates services between Sana, Ta'izz, Al-Hudaydah, and Al-Bayda and also schedules flights to Egypt, Ethiopia, Kuwait, Sa'udi Arabia, and the UAE. The airline carried 707,000 passengers in 1997.

12HISTORY

Classical geographers divided Arabia into three regions: Arabia Petraea ("rocky"), Arabia Deserta ("deserted"), and Arabia Felix ("fortunate"). The last, the southwestern corner, included the territory now occupied by Yemen. The region was the site of a series of rich kingdoms that dominated world trade. The wealthy kingdom of Sheba (or Saba), with its capital at Ma'rib, is the best known of the South Arabian kingdoms. The prosperity of this kingdom (10th to 2d centuries BC) was based on the spice and incense trade. Competition from new trade routes undermined Sabaean prosperity and caused the kingdom to decline. From the 2d century BC to the 6th century AD, the Himyarite dynasty, of ethnic stock similar to that of the Sabaeans, ruled in Arabia Felix, and paganism gradually gave way to Christianity and Judaism.

The Himyarite hegemony was ended in 525 by invading Christian Ethiopians, whose rule lasted until 575, when they were

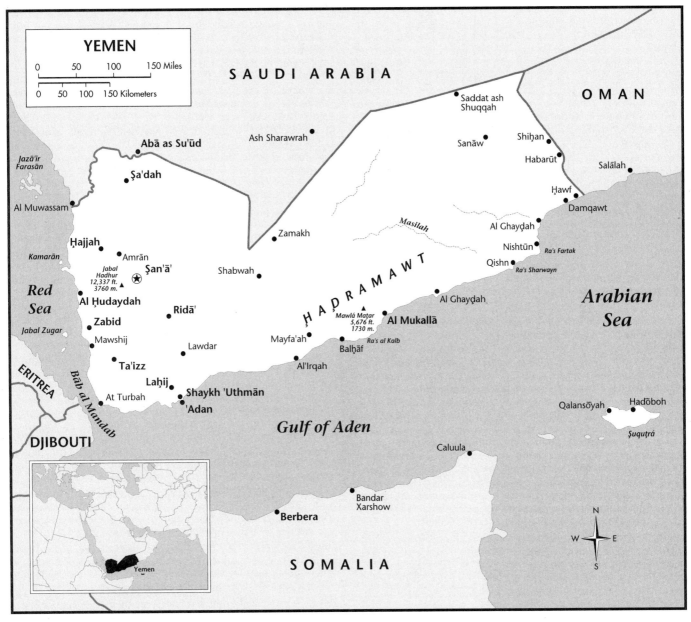

YEMEN

0   50   100   150 Miles

0   50   100   150 Kilometers

SAUDI ARABIA

OMAN

Saddat ash
Shuqqah

Abā as Su'ūd

Ash Sharawrah

Sanāw

Shiḥan

Jazā'ir
Farasān

Ṣa'dah

Habarūt

Salālah

Al Muwassam

Ḥawf

Damqawt

Zamakh

Al Ghayḍah

Ḥajjah

Nishtūn

Ra's Fartak

Kamarān

Amrān

Masīlah

Qishn

Ra's Sharwayn

Jabal
Hadhur
12,337 ft.
3760 m.

Ṣan'ā'

Shabwah

H A Ḍ R A M A W T

**Red
Sea**

Al Ḥudaydah

Ridā'

Al Ghayḍah

**Arabian
Sea**

Jabal Zugar

Zabid

Mawlā Maṭar
5,676 ft.
1730 m.

Al Mukallā

Mawshij

Lawdar

Mayfa'ah

Ra's al Kalb

Ta'izz

Balḥāf

Al'Irqah

ERITREA

Laḥij

Shaykh 'Uthmān

At Turbah

'Adan

Qalansōyah

Hadōboh

Bāb al Mandab

Gulf of Aden

Ṣuquṭrá

DJIBOUTI

Caluula

N
W   E
S

Bandar
Xarshow

Berbera

Yemen

S O M A L I A

LOCATION 12°41′ to 17°32′N; 42°32′ to 53°5′E. **BOUNDARY LENGTHS:** Oman, 288 km (179 mi); Sa'udi Arabia, 1,458 km (907 mi).

driven out by Persian invaders. Islam was accepted in the next century, and Yemen became the battleground of Muslim religious factions. The coastline (Tihama) was held by the Sunnis of the Shafi'i School, while the highlands were controlled by the Zaydis, a Shi'i sect.

In the 9th century, a Zaydi ruler, Yahya al-Hadi ila'l Haqq, founded a line of imams that survived until the second half of the 20th century. Nevertheless, Yemen's medieval history is a tangled chronicle of contesting local imams. The Fatimids of Egypt helped the Isma'ilis maintain dominance in the 11th century. Saladin (Salah ad-Din) annexed Yemen in 1173. The Rasulid dynasty (Kurdish and Turkish in origin) ruled Yemen, with Zabid as its capital, from about 1230 to the 15th century. In 1516, the Mamluks of Egypt annexed Yemen; but in the following year, the Mamluk governor surrendered to the Ottoman Turks, and Turkish armies subsequently overran the country. They were challenged by the Zaydi imam Qasim the Great (r.1597–1620)

and expelled from the interior around 1630. From then until the 19th century, the Ottomans retained control only of the coastal area, while the highlands generally were ruled by the Zaydi imams.

Early in the 19th century, Yemen was overrun by Wahhabis, but in 1818, Ibrahim Pasha, the son of Muhammad 'Ali of Egypt, drove them out of Yemen and reestablished Zaydi control. Egyptian troops occupied the main ports of Yemen until 1840, when they were withdrawn. The Zaydi imams recognized Ottoman suzerainty and paid a large annual subsidy to the Ottoman sultan. After 1840 the situation was anarchic, and law and order in any form was not reestablished until 1872, when the Ottomans again occupied Sana and consolidated their control. The northern mountains remained under the control of Zaydi imams from the Hamid ad-Din family. The Ottomans kept a large force in Yemen during World War I, but under the armistice terms evacuated it in 1918 and Yemen became independent.

In 1834 the British had occupied Aden as a coaling station on the route to India; the importance of the territory was substantially increased with the opening of the Suez Canal in 1869.

To protect its foothold in Aden the UK had signed a treaty of "protection and advice" with rulers of the tribes and states in the hinterland, leading to the adoption of the names Western Aden Protectorate (WAP) and Eastern Aden Protectorate (EAP). As long as northern Yemen remained at least nominally a part of the Ottoman Empire, relations on the frontier between the UK (in the WAP and EAP) and the Turks (in Yemen) were relatively peaceful.

During World War I the British supported the Idrisi tribe's attempt to establish itself in Yemen. In 1919 the UK occupied Al-Hudaydah, which came into Idrisi hands when the British withdrew in 1921. The Zaydis, now led by Imam Yahya ibn Muhammad Hamid ad-Din, who had become imam in 1891, waged an armed struggle against the Idrisis that ended when Imam Yahya seized Al-Hudaydah in 1925. The imam also sought to move into the states of the Western Aden Protectorate in an attempt to reestablish his suzerainty in these territories formerly held by the Yemenis. The Idrisis came under the protection of King Ibn Sa'ud, and in 1934, a war broke out between the Sa'udis and Yemenis. By the Treaty of Ta'if (May 1934), Yemen lost 'Asir to Sa'udi Arabia but won British and Sa'udi recognition of its independence. However, incursions by the imams against the UK protectorate in Aden continued until 1962.

In 1959 the UK formed the six WAP states into the Federation of Arab Emirates of the South, with others joining later. The inhabitants of Aden, who were more politically and economically advanced than those of the protectorates, opposed adherence to the federation. Nevertheless, Aden in 1963 was merged into the federation, which then became known as the Federation of South Arabia.

The dispute over the future form and direction of this new political entity, as well as over which other states would join it, resulted in several years of factional violence, as various political parties, labor organizations, and other groups struggled for political ascendancy. Finally, in 1967, the National Liberation Front (NLF) emerged as the strongest political group, and the UK agreed to negotiate with it concerning future independence. On 30 November 1967 all the states of the WAP and EAP were amalgamated, the last British soldiers withdrew, and the NLF declared the independence of the People's Republic of South Yemen. On 22 June 1969 the head of the NLF, Qahtan ash-Sha'bi, was deposed by a group of young leftists of the NLF. The new regime, headed by a five-man council, renamed the country the People's Democratic Republic of Yemen (PDRY), developed close ties with the USSR, and secured economic aid from it and China. A further political alignment occurred in 1971, when Salim Rubaya 'Ali became head of state and 'Abd al-Fattah Isma'il was named head of the party, in an uneasy rivalry. In 1978 Isma'il, the head of the Yemen Socialist Party (YSP), formerly the NLF, overthrew and executed President 'Ali and assumed the presidency. Isma'il resigned his position in 1980, ostensibly for reasons of health, and went into exile. 'Ali Nasir Muhammad al-Hasani, the prime minister, assumed the presidency.

Meanwhile, Yemen joined the League of Arab States in 1945, and in 1958, it formed a federation, the United Arab States, with the newly established United Arab Republic (UAR). In December 1961 however, the pro forma federal connection with Egypt was severed, and in September 1962 the government of Imam Muhammad al-Badr, only a few days old, was overthrown by revolutionary forces led by Brig. (later Marshal) 'Abdallah as-Sallal. He proclaimed himself president and commander-in-chief of the army and declared the establishment of the Yemen Arab Republic. Badr escaped to the northern regions of the YAR, where he organized a counterrevolutionary force.

A civil war between the royalists (defenders of the imamate) and the republican government broke out, and appeals by both sides for support brought about the active intervention of other Arab states. Sa'udi Arabia supported the royalist cause, and the UAR came to the assistance of the republic, dispatching up to 70,000 troops to the YAR; fighting was particularly bitter during the winter of 1963/64. Eventually the conflict subsided, as the Sa'udis curtailed their aid to the royalists and the Egyptians to the republicans. Sallal was deposed in November 1967 and replaced by a Republican Council. Talks between republican leaders and Sa'udi Arabia in March 1970 at Jiddah concluded with an agreement that ended the civil war and left the republicans in control.

In June 1974 'Abd ar-Rahman al-Iryani (who had been president since 1967) resigned, thrusting the country into a state of political confusion. By the end of the year Lt. Col. Ibrahim Muhammad al-Hamdi had emerged as president, heading a government with powers of centralized control that were progressively strengthened. Hamdi was assassinated by unknown assailants in October 1977. His successor, Col. Ahmad ibn Hussein al-Ghashmi, who formed a civilian government and established the Constituent People's Assembly, met a similar fate in June 1978, in a bomb blast in which PDRY involvement was suspected. Lt. Col. 'Ali 'Abdallah Saleh thereupon became president. In 1982, he inaugurated the General People's Congress as an instrument for popular political mobilization.

On 13 January 1986 PDRY President Muhammad attempted to eliminate his rivals within the YSP. A number of officials were killed, including Isma'il, and Muhammad was forced into exile, along with thousands of his followers. A civil war ensued during the following two weeks, in which about 4,200 died and the supporters of Muhammad were defeated. Haydar Abn Bakr al-'Attas, the prime minister, took over as acting president; Dr. Yasin Sa'id Nu'man was appointed prime minister, and 'Ali Salim al-Bayd was chosen as the new head of the YSP. President al-'Attas was officially elected in November 1986.

Since independence, the PDRY was embroiled in conflicts with all three of its neighbors. A separatist movement was supported in Oman; there were border skirmishes with Sa'udi forces in 1969 and 1973; and the PDRY fought a brief war with the YAR in February–March 1979. The war ended with a truce, mediated by the Arab League, and with an agreement in principle to seek unification of the two Yemens.

In late 1981 a constitution for the two Yemens was drafted. However, implementation was hampered by the continuing insurgency against President Saleh by the leftist National Democratic Front (NDF), which was based in, and reportedly aided by, the PDRY. Saleh was able to defeat the NDF militarily in 1982. Movement toward unification was maintained in repeated declarations and meetings through 1985, but no real progress was achieved. The January 1986 civil war in the PDRY set back relations between the two countries, particularly since 50,000 refugees fled the YAR, but both governments subsequently reaffirmed their commitment to unity.

In 1989 the leaders of the YAR and PDRY approved the 1981 draft constitution and their legislatures ratified it on 21 May 1990. The unified Republic of Yemen was proclaimed the following day. In the May 1990 election, 121 seats were won by the northern General People's Congress, sixty-two by Islaah (an Islamist and tribalist party), fifty-six by the southern Yemeni Socialist Party, forty-seven by independents, and fifteen by five other parties. On 22 May 1990 Ali Abdullah Saleh became the President of Yemen and Haidar Abu Bakr al-Attas the first Prime Minister, serving until 9 May 1994. A 30-month transition period was set for unifying the different political and economic systems. The army, police, and civil service were not integrated as planned, however. Meanwhile, the economy was hard hit by the consequences of Yemen's support for Iraq after the Kuwait invasion. It is estimated that Sa'udi Arabia expelled between 800,000 and 1 million Yemeni workers, thus depriving Yemen of some $3 billion in foreign exchange. In addition, the Sa'udis and Gulf states ended $2 billion in foreign aid. Unemployment in Yemen reached 30%.

Free and fair parliamentary elections were held in April 1992 with President Saleh's General People's Congress (GPC) barely missing a majority victory. A three-party coalition was formed but foundered in late 1993 when Vice President Ali al-Beidh of the Yemen Socialist Party boycotted meetings. Although the quarrel appeared to be patched up with an agreement in February 1994, fighting broke out in May of that year. In a few months, thousands of casualties had been suffered; tribes, clans, and militias were engaged in seeking their own selfish goals and the city of Aden was under siege. Some observers attributed the civil conflict to the recent discovery of massive oil reserves in the south and to Sa'udi Arabia's interest in weakening Yemen by promoting the breakup of the union. The future looked bleak, despite efforts of the UN and some Arab states to promote peace. Meanwhile, on 9 May 1994 Muhammed Said al Attar became acting Prime Minister until 6 October 1994 when Abdel Aziz Abdel Ghani took office.

Although bloody, the civil war was short-lived, with the north having subdued the rebellious south by July. Restoring civil order was difficult, especially in light of the dire economic straits faced by the country, which in 1995 had 70–90% inflation and a deficit of 17% of GDP. The IMF and World Bank stepped in after the war and instituted structural adjustment programs which brought inflation down below 10%, with further reduction to 6% expected in 1997 (for the non-oil sector).

In 1997 parliamentary elections were scheduled for May and it was expected that Saleh's GPC would retain its sizable majority. The international community expressed skepticism as to the fairness of the elections but, in the context of the Persian Gulf, they were expected to be reasonably fair. Notably, the YSP, representing the defeated south, announced that it would boycott the elections in protest of the GPC's collusion with Islaah, a tribal and Islamist party, to rig the elections. Saleh maintained the presidency and on 14 May 1997 Faraj Said Bin Ghanem became the new Prime Minister. On 29 April 1998 Bin Ghanem resigned and Abdel Karim al-Iriani became acting Prime Minister. In September 1999 President Ali Abdullah Saleh was reelected in Yemen's first direct presidential election. The YSP boycotted the election. Charges of fraud were made by the opposition with allegations of underage voting, multiple balloting, and unauthorized submission of ballots by absentee voters.

Yemen's history of kidnappings, over 100 Westerners in a half-dozen years, continued in 1998 through 2000. In the past the kidnappings were economically motivated, i.e., Yemeni tribesmen asking for money. However, the more recent ones appeared ideological --Muslims demanding the release of prisoners held by another Muslim group. Kidnappings damaged Yemen's economy by their impact on its tourist industry. Falling world oil prices also hit Yemen hard since oil accounts for over 80% of Yemen's exports. Yemen attempted to increase economic productivity with a campaign against qat (khat) chewing. Qat is a mild indigenous narcotic plant customarily chewed by some seventy-five percent of the Yemeni population. In August 1999 the Government led by President Salah, himself a qat user, launched a campaign to reduce qat usage by swearing off qat and encouraging others to follow his example. Anti-qat campaigns have been politically treacherous as former Prime Minister Mohsin al-Aini was ousted in 1972 after attempting to stamp out qat-chewing.

13 GOVERNMENT

The 1970 YAR constitution affirmed Islamic law as the basis of all legislation and established the unicameral Consultative Assembly as the supreme legislative body. The assembly was authorized to name the president and to appoint the ruling Executive Council. In the first national elections, held in 1971, voters selected 119 members of the Consultative Assembly; the forty remaining members were appointed by the president. This body was dissolved in 1974, and in 1978, it was replaced by the Constituent People's Assembly, with (as of 1987) ninety-nine members elected and sixty members appointed by the president for a two-year term.

In the General People's Congress (GPC), created in 1982, 700 of the 1,000 members were elected, with the other 300 appointed by the government. Between meetings (held every two years), the GPC's affairs were to be handled by a seventy-five-member standing committee. The president, elected by the Constituent People's Assembly for a five-year term, served as secretary-general of the GPC and commander-in-chief of the armed forces and appointed the prime minister and a ministerial council.

The 1970 constitution of the PDRY was ratified by the general command of the United Political Organization–National Front, which later became the Yemen Socialist Party (YSP). The Supreme People's Council, which had 111 members elected by universal suffrage at age eighteen, enacted laws; elected a Presidium and its chairman, who served as head of state; and chose the prime minister and the Council of Ministers. The YSP apparatus and the organs of government were closely intertwined.

The 1990 unity constitution established a political system based on free, multiparty elections. During the transitional period a presidential council was created with five members, three from the North and two from the South, to oversee executive operations. The council appointed a prime minister who picked a thirty-eight-member cabinet. A 301-member parliament was also formed, with 159 members chosen from the North, 111 from the South, and thirty-one at large.

Legislative elections were again held in 1993, with the GPC maintaining its majority (124 seats). Islaah won sixty-one seats and the YSP took fifty-five. Independent candidates won forty-seven and members of the country's dozens of other political/tribal parties took thirteen seats. Following the 1994 civil war, the GPC and Islaah formed a unity government. The next parliamentary elections were in April 1997. The GPC maintained its dominance taking 187 of 299 seats. The YSP, the only substantial opposition since the GPC and Islaah joined forces, boycotted the elections, which they said were being managed by the GPC leadership.

14 POLITICAL PARTIES

The National Liberation Front, which emerged in 1967 as the strongest faction in the disputes before South Yemen's independence, became the United Political Organization–National Front in 1970 and changed its name to the Yemeni Socialist Party (YSP) in 1978, when two smaller leftist parties were merged with it. This Marxist-Leninist organization, the PDRY's lone political party, was the only group to offer candidates in the 1986 legislative elections and survived to represent southern interests in the unified Yemen.

In pre-unification north Yemen, political parties in the Western sense played no role. Tribal allegiances were more important political factors. After unity, the northern leader, General Saleh, formed the General People's Congress (GPC) which became the country's largest party. The second largest bloc in the parliament is held by the Islaah Party (The Yemeni Congregation for Reform), a fusion of tribal and Islamic interests which opposed the unity constitution because it did not sufficiently adhere to Islamic principles. At least forty smaller parties have been active in the politics of unified Yemen, but the GPC, Islaah, and the YSP are the only ones of national significance. After the 1994 civil war, the GPC and Islaah formed a coalition government to establish civil order.

In the April 1997 legislative election the GPC won a landslide victory and no longer governed in coalition with Islaah. The YSP boycotted the April 1997 legislative election. In addition to these three main parties, as of 1997, the other parties active in the political arena that had fulfilled Yemen's legal procedures to practice political activities were the Peoples Nasserite Reformation Party, Liberation Front Party, Nasserite Democratic Party, League of the Sons of Yemen, Federation of Popular Forces, National Arab Socialist Baath Party, National Democratic Front, Al Haq Party, Yemen League Party, and the National Social Party. As of 1999, the active parties are GPC, Islaah, Yemeni Socialist Party (YSP), and Nasserite Unionist Party.

In September 1999 Yemen held the first direct presidential elections ever held on the Arabian peninsula. Longtime president Saleh captured 96.3% of the vote; Najeeb Qahtan al-Shaabi, his only opponent, won 3.7% of the vote. Led by the YSP a coalition of opposition groups boycotted this election.

15 LOCAL GOVERNMENT

The YAR was divided into eleven governorates (muhatazat), each headed by a governor. Each governorate contained a varying number of sectors (nawahi). Traditional divisions still extant included the uzlah, a group of villages (qura) of people who belong to the same tribe, headed by a sheikh; and the mahall, a group of houses administratively subordinate to a village. The central government retained ultimate authority over local officials, although certain administrative sanctions were granted to traditional local rulers.

In an effort to de-emphasize older loyalties and associations, the PDRY government created a highly centralized state and divided the country into six governorates, all closely controlled by the central authorities. Each had an appointed governor, and each was divided into districts, which were also administered by appointed officials.

The unified government established seventeen governorates, subdivided into districts. In the countryside, especially in the north and east, tribal authority is often stronger than formal government institutions.

16 JUDICIAL SYSTEM

Under a 1991 decree the separate judicial systems of the former YAR and the former PDRY have been unified at the Supreme Court level. The separate lower courts systems continue to function in their respective halves of the country. The judiciary, at the lower levels, is susceptible to pressure and influence from the executive branch. The court system consists of the Shari'a courts and the commercial courts.

The former YAR judicial system consisted of Shari'a law and courts for criminal and family law areas administered in each district by a hakim and commercial law and courts for business matters. In remote areas, tribal law was applied in tribal courts. The Shari'a courts applied Islamic law and litigants could appeal the decision of a hakim to another hakim, and from him take a final appeal to the Istinaf, the highest court of appeal, in Sana. Both sets of courts were considered generally fair and impartial. Former YAR state security courts were abolished with unification.

The former PDRY court system was organized in three tiers: magistrate or divisional courts, provincial courts, and military courts. Magistrate courts handled most criminal, juvenile, family, housing, agrarian, and other minor civil matters. Provincial

courts handled more serious criminal cases as well as inheritance cases, major civil claims and appeals form magistrates' courts. Shari'a courts applying Islamic law and tribal courts applying traditional law also existed alongside the modern court system.

Trials are public; however, the Shari'a courts and the commercial courts may conduct closed sessions for security or moral reasons.

17 ARMED FORCES

In 2000, the consolidated armed forces numbered 66,300, based on two years obligated service. The army of 61,000 has 35 brigades with Russian weapons, including 1,320 tanks and some 452 towed artillery pieces and missile launchers. The navy of 1,800 mans 13 patrol and coast combatants and 9 other ships. The air force, with 3,500 members, has 49 combat aircraft. The paramilitary has a national security force estimated at 50,000. Yemen spent $413.6 million for defense in 1999 or 7.6% of GDP.

18 INTERNATIONAL COOPERATION

Yemen joined the Arab League in 1945 and was admitted to UN membership on 30 September 1947; the republican government became Yemen's UN representative in December 1962. Yemen participates in the ESCWA and all the nonregional specialized UN agencies except IAEA. The country is also a member of G-77, a signatory to the Law of the Sea, and an applicant to the WTO.

Yemen is on good terms with both conservative and radical Arab states. Several thousand PLO fighters from Beirut were accepted in 1982. Military aid and advisers have been accepted from both the US and the former USSR.

19 ECONOMY

Traditionally an agricultural area, northern Yemen was self-sufficient in food and a net exporter of agricultural product until the Civil War in the 1960s and a prolonged drought in the early 1970s. In the late 1970s and early 1980s many farmers switched from labor intensive food crops to the more profitable cultivation of qat, a mild stimulant chewed by many Yemenis that has no significant export market. The economy of southern Yemen developed through foreign assistance (especially from the former USSR). The southern city of Aden, with its port and refinery, is the economic and commercial center of the country. The Yemeni economy depends on imports of wheat, flour and rice, and other foodstuffs. Trade deficits have been offset by remittances from Yemenis working abroad and by foreign aid.

Crude oil is now a significant sector of the economy, with exports accounting for over 80% of total exports. Following the unification of the country in 1990, responsibility for development of the oil sector fell to the state-owned general corporation for oil and mineral resources. Civil war in 1994 disturbed output. Yemen also has large reserves of natural gas. Oil output has been declining since 1995, and over 200 dry wells have been drilled, suggesting that the industry has passed its peak.

When Yemen aligned with Iraq during the Gulf War, Sa'udi Arabia and the Gulf states, Yemen's main aid donors and hosts to large numbers of Yemeni workers and their families, ended the Yemenis' privileged status. The economic impact of lost remittances was estimated at about $1 billion per year. After the Gulf crisis, Yemen was confronted with high unemployment, lost remittances, halving of US military aid, a sharp cutback in USAID programs, other canceled foreign assistance, and the cost of food imports and social services for the returnees totaling about $500 million.

Following the civil conflict in 1994, the government began a five-year program in 1995 that removed all controls on the exchange rate and cut the interest rate, as well as initialized trade policy reform, privatization, and the elimination of price controls. The reforms were favorably received by the World Bank and IMF, which agreed to provide aid. GDP grew at an average rate of 3.8% from 1988 to 1998; GDP was almost $5.7 billion (a 5.4% increase) in 1997. Approximately 80% of Yemen's debt to Russia was forgiven when Russia was admitted to the Paris Club in September 1997. A new liquefied natural gas drilling project promised exploitation of Yemen's 17 trillion cubic feet of gas reserves in subsequent years. GDP increased by only 1.8% in 1998.

20INCOME

The US Central Intelligence Agency (CIA) reports that in 1998 Yemen's gross domestic product (GDP) was estimated at $12.1 billion. The per capita GDP was estimated at $740. The annual growth rate of GDP was estimated at 1.8%. The average inflation rate in 1998 was 11%. The CIA defines GDP as the value of all final goods and services produced within a nation in a given year and computed on the basis of purchasing power parity (PPP) rather than value as measured on the basis of the rate of exchange. It was estimated that agriculture accounted for 16% of GDP, industry 46%, and services 38%.

The World Bank reports that for the same period per capita private consumption (in PPP terms) was $770. Private consumption includes expenditures of individuals, households, and non-governmental organizations. It was estimated that between 1990 and 1998 private consumption grew at an annual rate of 1.9%. Approximately 25% of household consumption was spent on food, 26% on fuel, 3% on health care, and 5% on education. The richest 10% of the population accounted for approximately 31% of household consumption and the poorest 10% approximately 2.3%.

21LABOR

In 1998, Yemen's work force was estimated at 5 million. According to 1992 estimates, 64% of the labor force is employed in agriculture and fishing, 25% in services, and 11% in commerce and industry.

United Yemen enacted a new labor code in 1995 (amended in 1997), which guaranteed the rights of unionization and collective bargaining. The Yemeni Confederation of Labor Unions, the country's only labor confederation, had 350,000 members in 15 unions in 1999.

There is no nationally fixed minimum wage. Although children under the age of 15 are prohibited from working, child labor is common, especially in rural regions. The labor code calls for a maximum 8-hour workday and a 40-hour work week.

22AGRICULTURE

The united Yemen, with its wide range of arable climatic zones, has the greatest potential for agricultural development of any nation on the Arabian Peninsula. Agriculture is an important part of the economy (accounting for 18% of GDP in 1998), despite the lack of arable land, scarcity of water, periodic droughts, and difficult terrain. Employment in the agricultural sector accounts for more than 52% of the workforce, but with only 2.9% of its land area arable, Yemen's potential for agricultural self-sufficiency is very remote. As of 1997, Yemen imported $1.17 billion in agricultural products, including $480 million in cereals.

Traditionally, Yemen was famous for its coffee, shipped from the port of Al-Mukha, from which the English word mocha derives. The main cash crop is qat, a mild stimulant chewed by many Yemenis on a daily basis, but not exported significantly because it is highly perishable. Industrial farming of fruits and vegetables, using modern irrigation techniques, provides a level of production to nearly satisfy domestic demand. As a high-cost producer, Yemen is not yet able to internationally compete in marketing its produce, especially since such exports are often blocked at the borders.

Agriculture output in 1998 (in 1,000 tons) included sorghum, 474; tomatoes, 231; wheat, 167; grapes, 155; bananas, 85; seed cotton, 24; sesame seed, 17; coffee, 11; and cotton, 5.

23ANIMAL HUSBANDRY

Animal husbandry is a key sector of the economy, and the export of hides and skins has long been an important source of foreign exchange. In 1998, the livestock population was estimated at 4,527,000 sheep, 4,089,000 goats, 1,130,000 head of cattle, 500,000 donkeys, and 180,000 camels.

Commercial production of poultry in Yemen began in the mid-1970s. Yemen produces about 95% of its annual consumption of eggs and is emerging as a significant producer of broilers (chicken meat). The brief civil conflict in 1994 hurt the industry by driving up the costs of imported feed and vaccines. About 56,000 tons of poultry were marketed by eight companies in 1998. About 26,000 tons of eggs were marketed in 1998.

24FISHING

Fishermen work along the Arabian Sea, Gulf of Aden, and Red Sea coasts. The annual fish catch in 1997 was about 115,654 tons. Principal species of that catch included Indian and Spanish mackerel, cuttlefish, lobster, and scavengers. Fish-processing plants are located at Al-Hudaydah and Al-Mukalla. Exports of fish and fish products were valued at $24 million in 1997. Pearl and coral diving have been practiced for centuries.

25FORESTRY

Forest and woodland coverage is negligible. Forests once covered Yemen, but overgrazing by goats and the systematic cutting of timber for fuel and construction have almost completely eliminated the forest cover, especially in the south. Roundwood production totaled 324,000 cu m in 1997, all of it used for fuel. Lumber imports amounted to $28.9 million in 1997.

26MINING

Until the discovery of petroleum, the mineral industry had been limited to the production of cement, dimension stone, gypsum, and salt. In 1996, production of cement amounted to 1,000,000 tons; dimension stone, 410,000 cubic meters; gypsum, 80,000 tons; and salt, 110,000 tons. The government of the new republic is focusing on creating conditions favorable to foreign investment, which could help develop the nation's mineral resources. The government has exclusive domain over the precious stone and hydrocarbon industries; mining legislation guarantees the rights of private property for all other commodities.

27ENERGY AND POWER

A number of companies have held oil concessions, but commercial deposits were not discovered until July 1984, when the US-based Hunt Oil Company struck oil in the eastern governorate of Ma'rib. As of 1999, Yemen had two aging refineries. The Aden facility had a capacity of 170,000 barrels per day before the 1994 civil war, and currently produces about 100,000 barrels per day. In February 1996, Iran agreed to help Yemen refurbish the refinery. The newer Ma'rib plant has a capacity of 10,000 barrels daily. Oil production is split between Canadian Occidental (which had been operating in North Yemen since 1987) in the Masillah block, US Hunt Oil in the Marib field, and three other operators. In early 1999, oil production amounted to 409,000 barrels per day. Proven oil reserves as of 1 January 2000 were 4 billion barrels. Exploration declined in 1994 due to civil war between the north and south but picked up again in 1997. The government set a production goal of 500,000 barrels per day by the end of 2000.

As of 1996, 26 foreign oil companies were active in Yemen. Most exploration occurs in the Ma'rib and Masillah fields, with some activity also in the eastern Hadhramaut an Hehara regions. Most new oil discoveries in recent years have been in southern Yemen.

With natural gas reserves estimated in early 2000 at 478 billion cu m (16.9 trillion cu ft), Yemen has potential as a gas producer. Most of the known reserves are concentrated in the Ma'rib-Jawf fields, operated by the Yemen Exploration and Production Company.

Total electricity production was 2,240 million kWh in 1998, over 90% of which was produced by public utilities. Net installed capacity in 1998 was 810,000 kW, entirely based on conventional thermal sources.

28INDUSTRY

In northern Yemen industry traditionally has been based on food processing, but this sub-sector has suffered from poor productivity of agriculture and reliance on imported raw materials. Building materials, textiles, leather wear, jewelry, and glass making are other industries in the north. The largest industry in southern Yemen is petroleum refining. Southern manufactures include clothing, processed food, metal products, soap, and perfumes. Industrial production accounts for 46% of GDP.

The refinery at Aden processed 60,000 barrels of petroleum per day in 1994 after sustaining damage in the civil war. Output reached 100,000 barrels per day by the start of 1995 with the repair of the main pumping station and two tapping units. That year, the refinery produced 26.5 million barrels of residual and distillate fuel oil, 10 million barrels of gasoline, and 3.5 million barrels of kerosene. A liquefied natural gas project (Yemen LNG), initiated in 1997, attracted a number of foreign partners.

New construction undertaken in the late 1990s bolstered Yemen's constructions materials industry.

29SCIENCE AND TECHNOLOGY

The University of Aden, founded in 1975 at Al-Mansoora, has faculties of science, arts, and education; agriculture; engineering; and medicine. Sana University, founded in 1970, has faculties of science, medicine and health sciences, engineering, and agriculture.

30DOMESTIC TRADE

At the center of most towns is a market place (sug), the lanes of which are lined with open-front booths where food and implements are displayed and sold. Some goods are bartered. Others sold for cash, usually after bargaining. The production of qat, a mild stimulant which many Yemenis chew, plays an important role in domestic trade. Relying on a highly sufficient internal distribution system, the production of qat would increase per capita GDP an estimated 15–20% were it included in the national income statistics. Corruption among civil servants is a common element of domestic commerce—soldiers at checkpoints confiscate money or qat, and businesses are often obliged to pay off local officials.

Customary business hours are from 8 AM—1 PM and from 4 PM—7 PM, Saturday–Thursday. Banks are open from 8 AM—12 PM (11:30AM on Thursdays).

31FOREIGN TRADE

Petroleum accounts for about 85% of the country's exports. Oil export revenues were estimated at $560 million in 1995 and $797 million in 1996. Other exports in recent years have included cotton, coffee, and dried and salted fish; imports included food and live animals, machinery and equipment, and manufactured goods.

In 1995 Yemen's imports were distributed among the following categories:

Consumer goods	10.3%
Food	24.1%
Fuels	7.8%
Industrial supplies	34.5%
Machinery	13.1%
Transportation	10.0%
Other	0.0%

Principal trading partners in 1998 (in millions of US dollars) were as follows:

COUNTRY	EXPORTS	IMPORTS	BALANCE
China (inc. Hong Kong)	375	75	300
Thailand	332	28	304
Korea	170	41	129
Singapore	88	69	19
Japan	55	75	-20
United States	41	125	-84
Saudi Arabia	33	254	-221
France	22	121	-99
United Arab Emirates	12	195	-183
United Kingdom	5	109	-104

32BALANCE OF PAYMENTS

Yemen's balance of payments was adversely affected in the early 1990s, as other nations sought to economically punish Yemen for its support of Iraq during the Persian Gulf War. In 1993, the current account deficit reached a peak of $1,217 million, foreign exchange reserves sank to just $144.6 million, and the trade deficit was $920 million. Transfers, consisting largely of remittances from Yemenis working in other Gulf states fell by 42% between 1990 and 1993.

The US Central Intelligence Agency reports that in 1998 the purchasing power parity of Yemen's exports was $1.6 billion while imports totaled $2.8 billion resulting in a trade balance of -$1.2 billion.

The International Monetary Fund (IMF) reports that in 1998 Yemen had exports of goods totaling $1,501 million and imports totaling $2,201 million. The services credit totaled $208 million and debit $570 million. The following table summarizes Yemen's balance of payments as reported by the IMF for 1998 in millions of US dollars.

Current Account		-228
Balance on goods	-701	
Balance on services	-362	
Balance on income	-422	
Current transfers	1,256	
Capital Account		...
Financial Account		-164
Direct investment abroad	...	
Direct investment in Yemen	-210	
Portfolio investment assets	...	
Portfolio investment liabilities	...	
Other investment assets	-119	
Other investment liabilities	164	
Net Errors and Omissions		-44
Reserves and Related Items		436

33BANKING AND SECURITIES

The republican government set up the Yemen Currency Board in 1964 with a capital of YR2 million; in 1971, the Currency Board was replaced by the Central Bank of Yemen. The state-owned Yemen Bank for Reconstruction and Development (YBRD), founded in 1962, finances development activities, and the International Bank of Yemen, organized in 1980, operates as a commercial bank. In the 1970s, the YBRD dominated the banking business, controlling some 70% of the loans outstanding in the YAR; during the same decade, a number of foreign commercial banks, including ones from Hong Kong, Iraq, Pakistan, the US, and the UK, opened offices in Sana.

Money supply has continued to grow rapidly. The economic recovery in 1995 and the partial liberalization of interest rates on bank deposits appear to have succeeded in encouraging the growth in savings as reflected in higher quasi-monetary holdings.

There is no stock exchange.

34INSURANCE

There were at least nine insurance firms in the Yemen in 1997. Much of the Yemen's insurance business is transacted abroad.

35PUBLIC FINANCE

Since unification, Yemen has run a budget deficit equivalent to 10–20% of GDP, financed primarily by bank credit. Yemen's decision to back Iraq in the Gulf War caused it to lose some $2 billion in development aid. The civil conflict in 1994 also exacerbated the need for external assistance and debt restructuring. The government estimated revenues would increase by 90% to YR301 billion in 1997, while expenditures would rise 72.5% to YR313 billion at that time. Increased oil revenues were expected to provide most of the increase in revenues.

The US Central Intelligence Agency (CIA) estimates that in 1998 Yemen's central government took in revenues of approximately $2.3 billion and had expenditures of $2.6 billion. Overall, the government registered a deficit of approximately $300 million. Total external debt was estimated at $4.9 billion.

The following table shows an itemized breakdown of government revenues and expenditures. The percentages were calculated from data reported by the International Monetary Fund. The dollar amounts (millions) are based on the CIA estimates provided above.

REVENUE AND GRANTS	100%	2,300
Tax revenue	38.6%	888
Non-tax revenue	59.4%	1,366
Capital revenue	0.5%	11
Grants	1.5%	34
EXPENDITURES	100%	2,600
General public services	22.0%	572
Defense	18.8%	488
Public order and safety	8.3%	216
Education	21.8%	567
Health	4.4%	114
Housing and community amenities	1.6%	42
Recreation, cultural, and religious affairs	2.8%	73
Economic affairs and services	11.5%	298
Interest payments	8.8%	229

36TAXATION

Personal income taxes are levied on wage workers and the self-employed. Taxes on business profits are graduated. Zakat (the religious charity tax) is state enforced. Taxes were increased substantially in the 1970s, with taxes on imports providing about 70% of total tax revenues. There are excise duties, road and vehicle taxes, port fees, a tax on rents, and telegraph fees. The state also derives income from the confiscated property of the imamate. The chronic budget deficits of the 1980s forced the government to place considerably more emphasis on the traditionally lax collection of taxes.

37CUSTOMS AND DUTIES

Import duties are generally levied at rates varying from 5% on essential goods to 50% on luxury items; medical and agricultural items are duty free, while tobacco is dutiable at 145%. Surcharges are added to these basic rates to cover defense expenditures, to finance schools and orphanages, and to assist the poor. Export duties are levied on a variety of products.

38FOREIGN INVESTMENT

Foreign investment is encouraged by the Yemeni government as is prospecting for more oil. Parliament has enacted a new investment law, but it has not yet been implemented. The law seeks to encourage joint ventures and especially to attract investments by expatriate Yemenis. Another new law authorizes free trade zones, the first planned for Aden. Oil companies, eager for a stake in one of the least explored tracts on the Arabian Peninsula, signed exploration and production agreements bringing signature bonuses and payments to the government of $436 million in 1991. In 1995, a consortium was established for the development of natural gas production. In addition to the government's 26% share, Total (France) had 36% equity; Hunt Oil (US), 14.6%; Exxon (US), 14.1%; and Yukong (ROK), 9.3%.

39ECONOMIC DEVELOPMENT

After unification in 1990, the new government assumed all debts incurred by former governments. Domestic political strains ultimately culminated in civil strife in 1994. As a result, the economy was further burdened with reconstruction costs.

The government launched a major reform program in 1995. The program included revenue mobilization through tax measures, depreciation of the customs valuation rate, the liberalization of cement prices, an increase of petroleum product prices by about 90%, and a 60% rise in electricity tariffs. The government's medium-term goal is to eliminate all subsidies by 1999–2001. Fiscal and monetary measures included the containment of primary non-development budget expenditures, partial reform of the exchange system (including currency depreciation), interest rate reform, and monetary management reforms. Furthermore, transportation and communication charges were deregulated, health and education fees were increased, and privatization programs were initiated. In 1996, 16 public enterprises were targeted for privatization. Laws prohibiting foreign investment in certain industrial sectors were abolished in 1996.

International aid has an ongoing role in the economy's development. In early 1996, the IMF agreed to provide a 15-month standby credit of $191 million, and the World Bank authorized the loan of $80 million to support the reform policies. The World Bank also decided to allocate government loans to Yemen worth $365 million during 1996–99. The EU also pledged grants worth $61.7 million in 1996/97, including $30 million in project finance. By the end of 1998, Yemen's external debt stood at $4.9 billion, equivalent to 40% of GDP.

40SOCIAL DEVELOPMENT

Families and tribes care for their sick, handicapped, unemployed, and widows and orphans. Those without family or tribal ties beg or have recourse to Islamic pious foundations (waqfs). The state operates orphanages and finances other welfare measures. Effective in 1988 a provident fund system provides old age, disability, survivor, and workers' compensation benefits. This program covers all employees, including Yemeni nationals working overseas. Workers contribute 6% of their wages, and employers pay 9% of payrolls. Old age benefits are paid as a one lump sum equivalent to 2.5% of earnings multiplied by the number of years worked. A health insurance program exists only for public employees. While the government has expanded its role in providing assistance, traditional means still predominate.

Women face considerable official and social discrimination. Polygamy is legal, and the practice of paying large dowries continues to be widespread. Women are required to obtain permission from a male member of the family in order to leave the house, and are rarely allowed to travel unaccompanied.

Women have limited access to education. Conservative estimates place the illiteracy rate for women at 76%, compared with 40–50% for men. Women in southern Yemen typically have a higher level of educational attainment than those in the north. Child marriage is common.

Women are permitted to vote, but social customs discourage most women from becoming politically active. In 1997, only 2 of 301 members of parliament were women.

Although reports of arbitrary arrest and detention continue, Yemen's human rights record has improved in some areas in recent years. The country's first direct presidential election was held in 1999. In the same year, three security officers were convicted of human rights abuses. International and domestic human rights organizations operate in Yemen.

41HEALTH

Only 1% of Yemen's gross domestic product went to public health expenditures in 1997. Malnutrition and the diseases associated with it are major health problems; 30% of children under five were malnourished in 1989–95. Malaria, typhus, tuberculosis, dysentery, whooping cough, measles, hepatitis, schistosomiasis, and typhoid fever are widespread, and sewage disposal of the most rudimentary type constitutes a general health hazard. In 1995, 74% of the urban population and 14% of the rural population had access to safe water. Only 40% of the urban population and 14% of the rural dwellers had adequate sanitation. In 1997, immunization rates for children up to one year old were tuberculosis (62%); diphtheria, pertussis, and tetanus (57%); polio (57%); and measles (51%). Civil conflict in July 1994 created a shortage of water, food, and medical supplies in Aden, exacerbating health problems.

Life expectancy in 1999 was estimated at 60 years; the infant mortality rate in 1999 was 70 per 1,000 live births. General mortality was 10 per 1,000 people in 1999.

Since the 1970s, many new hospitals and dispensaries have been established. In 1993, there was 1 hospital bed per 1,196 people. Medical personnel that year included 2,640 doctors, 120 dentists, and 6,480 nurses. In 1993, there was 1 doctor per 4,498 people.

There were only 22 AIDS cases in 1996. The HIV seroprevalence rate was 0.0 per 100 adults in 1997.

42HOUSING

Housing is inadequate; about one-fourth of urban housing units are huts, tents, or other makeshift structures. In the hot coastal region, most dwellings, except those of the ruling classes, are straw huts. In the highlands, the poorer people live in huts of stone or baked brick. Wealthier Yemenis live in large houses whose style is unique to southwestern Arabia: the lower part is generally built of sandstone, basalt, or granite, while the upper part, which may rise from two to eight stories, is usually of baked brick with windows outlined in decorative designs. Often a loggia topped with brass and open on all sides rises from the roof.

43EDUCATION

Early Yemeni education, with regard to medieval disciplines of law, religion, history and poetry, was sophisticated and, for a country of its type, remarkably widespread. Its people contributed nobly to medieval Islamic civilization. The Al-Azhar University of Cairo was well known for its education during the 10th and 11th centuries and it attracted students from nearby countries such as Ethiopia, Arabia, and Somalia. However, in the 19th and 20th centuries, there was slow progress in the field of education. Prior to the 1962 revolution, no proper educational system was in place. Civil war and internal political upheaval only worsened the situation.

In 1990, the literacy rate for the People's Democratic Republic of Yemen was 39.1% (males, 52.8%; females, 26.1%). The rate for the Yemen Arab Republic was 38.5% (males, 53.3%; females, 26.3%). In the unified Republic of Yemen, adult illiteracy rates for the year 2000 were estimated at 53.8% (males, 32.6%; females, 75.0%).

In 1997, primary schools enrolled 2,699,788 pupils and employed 90,478 teachers. Student-to-teacher ratio stood at 30 to one. At the secondary level in the same year, there were a total of 354,288 students.

There are two universities: Sana University (founded in 1970) and the University of Aden (established in 1975). Total university enrollment in 1997 reached 65,675. In addition, over 2,000 Yemenis are being educated at foreign universities.

44LIBRARIES AND MUSEUMS

Both the National and Miswal libraries are located in Aden. Each has a collection of 30,000 volumes. The Miswal Library also maintains another 9,000 volumes as a traveling library to serve citizens. The Library of the Great Mosque of Sana maintains a collection of 10,000 manuscripts. The British Council maintains two libraries: at Aden (3,000 volumes) and at Sana (10,4000 volumes).

The National Museum has branches in Aden and Sana. The Aden site focuses primarily on ancient, pre-Islamic civilizations. Aden is also home to the Crater Military Museum and the Crater Folk Museum. There are local museums in Taizz and Zafar.

45MEDIA

Since unification, efforts have been underway to upgrade the country's telecommunications infrastructure. Two-way radio links Yemen directly with Cairo and Rome. Telephone and telegraph facilities are available in major cities, and a modern dial telephone system has been installed in Sana, Ta'izz, and Al-Hudaydah. There were about 162,100 telephones in 1995. The government operates several radio stations and two television networks, one of them partly commercial. As of 1999, there were 4 AM and 1 FM station and 7 television broadcast stations. Yemen had 64 radios, 273 television sets, and 1 mobile phone per 1,000 population in 1997.

In the same year there were three daily newspapers: *Al-Thawrah* (circulation 110,000), published in Sana; *Al-Jumhuriyah* (100,000), in Ta'izz; and *Ar-Rabi Ashar Min Uktubar* (20,000), published in Aden.

The constitution restricts free expression. The relative freedom of the press established prior to the 1994 civil conflict has yet to be reestablished. The Ministry of Information owns or controls all media.

Online access is extremely limited, with less than one Internet host per 1,000 population in 1998.

46ORGANIZATIONS

The government has encouraged the formation of cooperatives, but private associations with political overtones are suspect. There are chambers of commerce in the major cities.

47TOURISM, TRAVEL, AND RECREATION

Tourists can visit historic and religious sites (such as the Ghumdau Palace and the Great Mosque in Sana) and exotic markets, and enjoy scenic areas including the Red Sea coast. Passports and visas are required by foreign visitors. Vaccination against yellow fever and cholera is recommended. In 1997, there were 81,000 tourist arrivals and receipts totaled $69 million. There were 8,109 hotel rooms with 16,700 beds and a 60% occupancy rate that year.

According to the 2000 United States government estimates, the cost of staying in Sanaa is approximately $146 per day. Elsewhere in the country, travel costs are less expensive.

[48]FAMOUS YEMENIS

Imam Yahya ibn Muhammad Hamid ad-Din (1869?–1948) ruled during the period when Yemen established its independence; he was assassinated during an uprising. 'Ali 'Abdallah Salih (b.1942) became president of the YAR in 1978, ending a period of upheaval in which his two immediate predecessors were assassinated. Field Marshal 'Abdallah as-Sallal (1920–94) was the first president of the YAR and held power from 1962 until a coup ousted him in 1967. 'Ali Nasir Muhammad al-Hasani (b.1940?) was prime minister of the PDYR in 1980 and president from 1980 to 1986. Haydar Abu Bakr al-'Attas (b.1939) was prime minister of the PDYR during 1985–86.

[49]DEPENDENCIES

Yemen has no territories or colonies.

[50]BIBLIOGRAPHY

Almadhagi, Ahmed Noman Kassim. *Yemen and the United States: A Study of Power and Super-State Relationship, 1962–1994.* London: I. B. Taurus Publishers, 1996.

American University. *The Yemens: Country Studies.* Washington, D.C.: Government Printing Office, 1986.

Bidwell, Robin. *The Two Yemens.* Boulder, Colo.: Westview, 1983.

Burrowes, Robert D. *Historical Dictionary of Yemen.* Lanham, Md.: Scarecrow, 1995.

Chaudhry, Kiren Aziz. *The Price of Wealth: Economies and Institutions in the Middle East.* Ithaca, N.Y.: Cornell University Press, 1997.

Crouch, Michael. *An Element of Luck: To South Arabia and Beyond.* New York: Radcliffe Press, 1993.

Dresch, Paul. *Tribes, Government, and History in Yemen.* New York: Oxford University Press, 1989.

Halliday, Fred. *Revolution and Foreign Policy: The Case of South Yemen, 1967–1987.* New York: Cambridge University Press, 1990.

Ismael, Tareq Y., and Jacqueline S. Ismael. *The People's Democratic Republic of Yemen: Politics, Economics and Society.* Boulder, Colo.: Lynne Rienner, 1986.

Kostiner, Joseph. *Yemen: The Tortuous Quest for Unity, 1990–1994.* London: Royal Institute of International Affairs, 1996.

Lackner, Helen. *P.D.R. Yemen: Outpost of Socialist Development in Arabia.* London: Ithaca Press, 1985.

Madaj, Abd al-Muhsin Madaj M. *The Yemen in Early Islam.* Atlantic Highlands, NJ: Ithaca Press, 1988.

Mundy, Martha. *Domestic Government: Kinship, Community and Polity in North Yemen.* London: I. B. Taurus, 1995.

Page, Stephen. *The Soviet Union and the Yemens: Influence in Asymmetrical Relationships.* New York: Praeger, 1985.

Pridham, B. R. (ed.). *Contemporary Yemen: Politics and Historical Background.* London: Croom Helm, 1984.

———. (ed.) *Economy, Society and Culture in Contemporary Yemen.* London: Croom Helm, 1985.

Stookey, Robert W. *South Yemen: A Marxist Republic in Arabia.* Boulder, Colo.: Westview, 1982.

Wenner, Manfred W. *The Yemen Arab Republic: Development and Change in an Ancient Land.* Boulder, Colo.: Westview Press, 1991.

The Yemeni War of 1994: Causes and Consequences. Edited by Jamal al-Suwaidi. London: Saqi Books, 1995.

INDEX TO COUNTRIES AND TERRITORIES

This alphabetical list includes countries and dependencies (colonies, protectorates, and other territories) described in the encyclopedia. Countries and territories described in their own articles are followed by the continental volume (printed in *italics*) in which each appears. Country articles are arranged alphabetically in each volume. For example, Argentina, which appears in *Americas*, is listed this way: Argentina—*Americas*. Dependencies are listed here with the title of the volume in which they are treated, followed by the name of the article in which they are dealt with. In a few cases, an alternative name for the same place is given in parentheses at the end of the entry. The name of the volume *Asia and Oceania* is abbreviated in this list to *Asia*.

Adélie Land—*Asia:* French Pacific Dependencies: French Southern and Antarctic Territories
Afars and the Issas, Territory of the—*Africa:* Djibouti
Afghanistan—*Asia*
Albania—*Europe*
Algeria—*Africa*
American Samoa—*Asia:* US Pacific Dependencies
Andaman Islands—*Asia:* India
Andorra—*Europe*
Angola—*Africa*
Anguilla—*Americas:* UK American Dependencies: Leeward Islands
Antarctica—*United Nations:* Polar Regions
Antigua and Barbuda—*Americas*
Arctic—*United Nations:* Polar Regions
Argentina—*Americas*
Armenia—*Europe*
Aruba—*Americas:* Netherlands American Dependencies: Aruba
Ashmore and Cartier Islands—*Asia:* Australia
Australia—*Asia*
Austria—*Europe*
Azerbaijan—*Asia*
Azores—*Europe:* Portugal

Bahamas—*Americas*
Bahrain—*Asia*
Bangladesh—*Asia*
Barbados—*Americas*
Basutoland—*Africa:* Lesotho
Bechuanaland—*Africa:* Botswana
Belarus—*Europe*
Belau—*Asia:* Palau
Belgium—*Europe*
Belize—*Americas*
Benin—*Africa*
Bermuda—*Americas:* UK American Dependencies
Bhutan—*Asia*
Bolivia—*Americas*
Bonin Islands—*Asia:* Japan (Ogasawara Islands)
Borneo, North—*Asia:* Malaysia
Bosnia and Herzegovina—*Europe*
Botswana—*Africa*
Bouvet Island—*Europe:* Norway
Brazil—*Americas*
British Antarctic Territory—*Americas:* UK American Dependencies

British Guiana—*Americas:* Guyana
British Honduras—*Americas:* Belize
British Indian Ocean Territory—*Africa:* UK African Dependencies
British Virgin Islands—*Americas:* UK American Dependencies
Brunei Darussalam—*Asia*
Bulgaria—*Europe*
Burkina Faso—*Africa*
Burma—*Asia:* Myanmar
Burundi—*Africa*

Caicos Islands—*Americas:* UK American Dependencies
Cambodia—*Asia*
Cameroon—*Africa*
Canada—*Americas*
Canary Islands—*Europe:* Spain
Cape Verde—*Africa*
Caroline Islands—*Asia:* Federated States of Micronesia; Palau
Carriacou—*Americas:* Grenada
Cayman Islands—*Americas:* UK American Dependencies
Central African Republic—*Africa*
Ceuta—*Europe:* Spain
Ceylon—*Asia:* Sri Lanka
Chad—*Africa*
Chile—*Americas*
Chilean Antarctic Territory—*Americas:* Chile
China—*Asia*
Christmas Island (Indian Ocean)—*Asia:* Australia
Christmas Island (Pacific Ocean)—*Asia:* Kiribati
Cocos Islands—*Americas:* Costa Rica
Cocos (Keeling) Islands—*Asia:* Australia
Colombia—*Americas*
Columbus, Archipelago of—*Americas:* Ecuador (Galapagos Islands)
Comoros—*Africa*
Congo—*Africa*
Congo, Democratic Republic of (former Zaire)—*Africa*
Cook Islands—*Asia:* New Zealand
Coral Sea Islands—*Asia:* Australia
Corn Islands—*Americas:* Nicaragua
Costa Rica—*Americas*
Côte d'Ivoire—*Africa*
Croatia—*Europe*
Cuba—*Americas*
Curaçao—*Americas:* Netherlands American Dependencies: Netherlands Antilles
Cyprus—*Asia*

ISBN 0-7876-0515-8

90000

Afghanistan

Australia

Azerbaijan

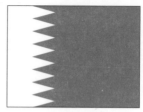

Bahrain

Bangladesh

Federated States
of Micronesia

Fiji

India

Indonesia

Iran

Kiribati

Korea, Democratic
People's Republic of

Korea, Republic of

Kuwait

Kyrgyzstan

Mongolia

Myanmar

Nauru

Nepal

New Zealand

Qatar

Sa'udi Arabia

Singapore

Solomon Islands

Sri Lanka

Turkey

Turkmenistan

Tuvalu

United Arab Emirates

Uzbekistan